ELEMENTS OF Literature

FIFTH COURSE

Literature of the United States *with* Literature of the Americas

ANNOTATED TEACHER'S EDITION

This is America,
This vast, confused beauty,
This staring, restless speed of loveliness . . .

— from "The Congressional Library" by Amy Lowell

HOLT, RINEHART AND WINSTON
Harcourt Brace & Company
Austin • New York • Orlando • Atlanta • San Francisco • Boston • Dallas • Toronto • London

CREDITS

Project Director: Kathleen Daniel
Executive Editor: Mescal Evler
Managing Editor: Robert R. Hoyt
Project Editor: Suzanne Thompson
Editorial Coordinator: Susan Lynch
Grade Level Editors: Cheryl Christian, Matthew H. Pangborn, Michael L. Smith
Editorial Staff: Joel Bourgeois, Sigman Byrd, Tracy Combs Duncan, Kate Ewing, Kathryn Rogers Johnson, Mary Malone, Michael Neibergall, Kate Unger
Editorial Support Staff: Roni Franki, Ruth A. Hooker, Kelly Keeley, Margaret Sanchez, Pat Stover
Editorial Permissions: Ann Farrar, Janet Harrington

Design, Photo Research, and Production: *Text Designer:* Ruth Riley; *Production and Manufacturing:* Beth Prevelige, *Senior Production Manager;* Simira Davis, *Production Assistant;* Michael Roche, *Manufacturing Coordinator; Electronic Files:* Preface, Inc.; *Cover Designer:* Caroline Abbott, Compendium Design, Inc.; *Cover Senior Art Director:* Pun Nio; *Design and Production Coordination:* Preface, Inc.; *Marketing Design:* Rebecca Bretz

Portions of this work were published in previous editions.

Acknowledgments appear on page 5, which is an extension of the copyright page.

Printed in the United States of America

ISBN 0-03-094928-9 4 5 6 041 00 99 98

Program Authors

Robert Anderson, John Malcolm Brinnin, and John Leggett established the literary framework of the Elements of Literature *program and developed instructional materials for the elements of drama, poetry, and fiction, respectively. Robert Probst established the pedagogical focus for the 1997 edition, and he developed and evaluated preselection and postselection material. Judith L. Irvin established the conceptual basis for the vocabulary and reading strands in the pupil's editions for grades 6–8 and in the teacher's editions for grades 6–12.*

Robert Probst is Professor of English Education at Georgia State University in Atlanta. For several years he was an English teacher—in both junior and senior high school—in Maryland and Supervisor of English for the Norfolk, Virginia, Public Schools. He is the author of *Response and Analysis: Teaching Literature in Junior and Senior High School.* He has also contributed chapters to such books as *Literature Instruction: A Focus on Student Response; Reader Response in the Classroom: Evoking and Interpreting Meaning in Literature; Handbook of Research on Teaching the English Language Arts; Transactions with Literature: A Fifty-Year Perspective;* and *For Louise M. Rosenblatt.* Dr. Probst has published articles in *English Journal, Journal of Reading, Educational Leadership, Revue des Langues Vivantes, The Clearing House,* and other publications. He is a member of the National Council of Teachers of English and has worked on the Council's Committee on Research, the Commission on Reading, and the Commission on Curriculum. Dr. Probst has also served on the Board of Directors of the Adolescent Literature Assembly. He is a colleague and faculty member of the Creative Education Foundation and a member of the National Conference on Language and Literacy.

Robert Anderson is a playwright, novelist, screenwriter, and teacher. His plays include *Tea and Sympathy; Silent Night, Lonely Night; You Know I Can't Hear You When the Water's Running;* and *I Never Sang for My Father.* His screenplays include *The Nun's Story* and *The Sand Pebbles.* Mr. Anderson has taught at The Writers' Workshop at the University of Iowa, the American Theater Wing Professional Training Program, and the Salzburg Seminar in American Studies. He is a past president of the Dramatists' Guild, vice president of the Authors' League of America, and a member of the Theater Hall of Fame. He lives in Connecticut and New York.

John Malcolm Brinnin, author of six volumes of poetry that have received many prizes and awards, is a member of the American Academy and Institute of Arts and Letters. He is also a critic of poetry and a biographer of poets and was for a number of years director of New York's famous Poetry Center. His teaching career, begun at Vassar College, included long terms at the University of Connecticut and Boston University, where he succeeded Robert Lowell as Professor of Creative Writing and Contemporary Letters. Mr. Brinnin has written *Dylan Thomas in America: An Intimate Journal* and *Sextet: T. S. Eliot & Truman Capote & Others.* His home is in Key West, Florida.

John Leggett is a novelist, a biographer, and a teacher. He went to The Writers' Workshop at the University of Iowa in the spring of 1969, expecting to work there for a single semester. In 1970, he assumed temporary charge of the program, and for the next seventeen years he was its director. Mr. Leggett's novels include *Wilder Stone, The Gloucester Branch, Who Took the Gold Away?, Gulliver House,* and *Making Believe.* He is also the author of the highly acclaimed biography *Ross and Tom: Two American Tragedies* and of the biography of William Saroyan called *A Daring Young Man.* A native New Yorker, Mr. Leggett now lives in California's Napa Valley.

Judith L. Irvin teaches courses in curriculum, middle school education, and educational leadership at Florida State University. Dr. Irvin is Chair of the Research Committee of the National Middle School Association and was the editor of *Research in Middle Level Education* for five years. She taught middle school for eight years before seeking her doctorate in Reading/Language Arts. Dr. Irvin writes a column, "What Research Says to the Middle Level Practitioner," for the *Middle School Journal.* Her many books include *Transforming Middle Level Education: Perspectives and Possibilities* and *Reading and the Middle School Student: Strategies to Enhance Literacy.*

Special Contributors

The special contributors wrote essays for the various collections of the text. Their essays are signed.

Gary Q. Arpin received his doctorate from the University of Virginia, where he taught for several years before taking a position with Western Illinois University at Macomb. He has written articles on John Berryman and other American poets, and has published a book, *John Berryman: A Reference Guide.* He currently is an editor at the *Reader's Digest* and lives in Katonah, New York.

Joseph Bruchac is a professional storyteller and author inspired by his American Indian heritage and the Adirondack region where he lives. His work has appeared in over 500 publications including the *American Poetry Review* and *National Geographic.* He has written over sixty books for adults and children—most recently *Long River* and *A Boy Called Slow.* His awards include the Cherokee Nation Prose Award, the Hope S. Dean Award for Notable Achievement in Children's Literature, and the Benjamin Franklin Award as "Person of the Year" by the Publisher's Marketing Association.

Thomas Hernacki is an educational writer specializing in modern and contemporary literature, particularly American poetry. A native of Chicago, he holds a master's degree in American Studies from New York University and a doctorate in English from Columbia University. His dissertation explores "the poetics of place" in the works of Wallace Stevens. In the 1970s he contributed to Northrop Frye's archetype-based literature series, *Uses of the Imagination.* Over the past two decades, Dr. Hernacki has directed the editorial development of numerous literature and composition textbooks for secondary schools.

Susan Allen Toth has written *Blooming: A Small-Town Girlhood,* about her childhood in Ames, Iowa, and a sequel, *Ivy Days: Making My Way Out East,* about her experiences at Smith College in Northampton, Massachusetts. She studied at the University of California at Berkeley and received her doctorate from the University of Minnesota. She currently teaches at Macalaster College in St. Paul, Minnesota. She contributes articles to many periodicals, including *Harper's, Redbook, McCall's,* and *The New York Times.*

Writers

The writers prepared instructional materials for the text under the supervision of Dr. Probst and the editorial staff.

Richard Cohen
Former Teacher
Novelist
Educational Writer and Editor
Madison, Wisconsin

Jan Freeman
Poet
Educational Writer and Editor
Williamsburg, Massachusetts

Phillis Goldenberg
Educational Writer and Editor
North Miami Beach, Florida

Lynn Hovland
Former Teacher
Educational Writer and Editor
Berkeley, California

Rose Sallberg Kam
Former Teacher
Educational Writer and Editor
Sacramento, California

Carroll Moulton
Former Teacher
Educational Writer and Editor
Southampton, New York

Susanna Nied
Former Teacher
Educational Writer and Editor
San Diego, California

Eileen Hillary Oshinsky
Educational Writer and Editor
Rhinebeck, New York

Mary Elizabeth Podhaizer
Former Teacher
Educational Writer and Editor
Colchester, Vermont

Gerry Tomlinson
Educational Writer and Editor
Lake Hopatcong, New Jersey

Joan Clark Tornow
Teacher
Austin, Texas

Sarah Wolbach
Educational Writer and Editor
Austin, Texas

Reviewers

The reviewers evaluated collections from the Annotated Teacher's Edition, *Fifth Course. For a list of the reviewers for the pupil's edition see p. vii of the* Pupil's Edition.

Lydia M. Aragón
Hillsboro High School
Hillsboro, OR

Jane C. Crawford
McCluer High School
St. Louis, MO

Kathleen Joyce
Southwest High School
Fort Worth, TX

Rosiland Lund
Glencoe High School
Hillsboro, OR

Lois Philpot
Penn-Trafford High School
Harrison City, PA

Brian Rowland
Plantation High School
Plantation, FL

Acknowledgments

For permission to reprint copyrighted material, grateful acknowledgment is made to the following sources:

African American Review, Indiana State University: From "The Blues Poetry of Langston Hughes" by Edward Waldron from *Negro American Literature Forum* (currently *African American Review*), vol. 5, no. 4 (1971). Copyright © 1971 by African American Review. ***Antioch Review, Inc.:*** From "Richard Wright's Blues" by Ralph Ellison from *Antioch Review,* vol. 5, no. 1, March 1945. Copyright 1945 by The Antioch Review, Inc. ***Arte Público Press:*** From "The Latin Deli: An Ars Poetica" by Judith Ortiz Cofer from *The Americas Review*, vol. 19, no. 1. Published by Arte Público Press-University of Houston, 1991. ***Atlantic Monthly Press:*** From "The Journey" from *New and Selected Poems* by Mary Oliver. Copyright © 1992 by Mary Oliver. ***Bantam Books, a division of Bantam Doubleday Dell Publishing Group, Inc.:*** From *The Souls of Black Folk* by W.E.B. DuBois. Copyright © 1969 by W.E.B. DuBois. ***Doubleday, a division of Bantam Doubleday Dell Publishing Group, Inc.:*** From interview with Garrett Hongo from *The Language of Life: A Festival of Poets* by Bill Moyers. Copyright © 1995 by Public Affairs Television, Inc., and David Grubin Productions, Inc. ***Rita Dove:*** From "The Satisfaction Coal Company" from *Selected Poems* by Rita Dove. Copyright © 1993 by Rita Dove. ***Farrar, Straus & Giroux, Inc.:*** From "The Social Function of Poetry" from *On Poetry and Poets* by T. S. Eliot. Copyright © 1957 by T. S. Eliot; copyright renewed © 1985 by Valerie Eliot. From "The Death of the Ball Turret Gunner" from *The Complete Poems* by Randall Jarrell. Copyright © 1969 by Mrs. Randall Jarrell. From footnote from "Writing Short Stories" from *Mystery and Manners: Occasional Prose* by Flannery O'Connor, edited by Sally and Robert Fitzgerald. Copyright © 1969 by the Estate of Mary Flannery O'Connor. ***GRM Associates, Inc., Agents for the Estate of Ida M. Cullen:*** From "Incident" and from "Tableau" from *Color* by Countee Cullen. Copyright © 1925 by Harper & Brothers; copyright renewed © 1953 by Ida M. Cullen. ***Paul Gitlin, Administrator of the Estate of Thomas Wolfe:*** From "His Father's Earth" from *The Web and the Rock* by Thomas Wolfe. Copyright 1937, 1938, 1939 by Maxwell Perkins as Executor; copyright renewed © 1967 by Paul Gitlin, C.T.A., Administrator of the Estate of Thomas Wolfe. ***Greenwood Publishing Group, Inc., Westport, CT 06881:*** From "Lorraine Hansberry" by Margaret Wilkerson from *Notable Women in the American Theatre: A Biographical Dictionary,* edited by A. M. Robinson, V. M. Roberts, and M. S. Barranger. Copyright © 1989 by Alice M. Robinson, Vera Mowry Roberts, and Milly S. Barranger. ***Grove/Atlantic, Inc.:*** From "Full Powers" from *A New Decade (Poems: 1958–1967)* by Pablo Neruda, translated by Alastair Reid. English translation copyright © 1969 by Alastair Reid. ***Harcourt Brace & Company:*** From "The Life You Save May Be Your Own" from *A Good Man Is Hard to Find* by Flannery O'Connor. Copyright © 1953, 1954, 1955 by Flannery O'Connor. From "Notes for a Preface" from *The Complete Poems of Carl Sandburg.* Copyright 1950 by Carl Sandburg; copyright renewed © 1978 by Margaret Sandburg, Helga Sandburg Crile, and Janet Sandburg. From "Acknowledgments" from *In Search of Our Mothers' Gardens: Womanist Prose* by Alice Walker. Copyright © 1974 by Alice Walker. From "The Beautiful Changes" from *The Beautiful Changes and Other Poems* by Richard Wilbur. Copyright 1947 and renewed © 1975 by Richard Wilbur. ***HarperCollins Publishers, Inc.:*** From "Mirror" from *Crossing the Water* by Sylvia Plath. Copyright © 1963 by Ted Hughes. Originally appeared in *The New Yorker.* ***Harvard University Press:*** From "Here follow Some Verses upon the Burning of Our House, July 10, 1666" from *The Works of Anne Bradstreet,* edited by Jeannine Hensley. Copyright © 1967 by the President and Fellows of Harvard College. Published by The Belknap Press of Harvard University Press, Cambridge, Mass. From "Life of an American Slave" from *The Narrative of the Life of Frederick Douglass.* Copyright © 1960 by the President and Fellows of Harvard College. ***Harvard University Press and the Trustees of Amherst College:*** From "Apparently with no surprise," from "Because I could not stop for Death," from "Heart! We will forget him!" from "I Heard a Fly buzz—when I died—" and from "I taste a liquor never brewed" from *The Poems of Emily Dickinson*, edited by Thomas H. Johnson. Copyright © 1951, 1955, 1979, 1983 by the President and Fellows of Harvard College. Published by The Belknap Press of Harvard University Press, Cambridge, Mass. ***Henry Holt and Company, Inc.:*** From "Design," from "Neither Out Far Nor In Deep," and from "Nothing Gold Can Stay" from *The Poetry of Robert Frost,* edited by Edward Connery Lathem. Copyright 1936 by Robert Frost; copyright © 1964 by Lesley Frost Ballantine; copyright © 1969 by Henry Holt and Co., Inc. ***Alfred A. Knopf, Inc.:*** From "The Weary Blues" from *Selected Poems* by Langston Hughes. Copyright 1926 by Alfred A. Knopf, Inc.; copyright renewed 1954 by Langston Hughes. From "Anecdote of the Jar" from *Collected Poems* by Wallace Stevens. Copyright 1923 and renewed 1951 by Wallace Stevens. ***Yusef Komunyakaa:*** From "Monsoon Season" from *Toys in a Field* by Yusef Komunyakaa. Copyright © 1986 by Yusef Komunyakaa. ***Julius Lester, c/o Claudia Menza Literary Agency:*** From "Afterword" by Julius Lester from *The Last Collected Plays: Les Blancs, The Drinking Gourd, What Use Are Flowers?* by Lorraine Hansberry, edited by Robert Nemiroff. Afterword copyright © 1972, 1983 by Julius Lester. ***The Modern Language Association of America:*** From "Chinese American Women Writers" by Amy Ling from *Redefining American Literary History,* edited by A. LaVonne Brown Ruoff and Jerry W. Ward, Jr. Copyright © 1990 by The Modern Language Association of America. ***William Morrow and Company, Inc.:*** From *Zen and the Art of Motorcycle Maintenance* by Robert M. Pirsig. Copyright © 1974 by Robert M. Pirsig. ***New Directions Publishing Corporation:*** From *Guadier-Brzeska: A Memoir* by Ezra Pound. Copyright © 1970 by Ezra Pound. From "Foreword" from *Selected Essays of William Carlos Williams.* Copyright 1931, 1936, 1938, 1939, 1940, 1942, 1944, 1946, 1948, 1949, 1951, 1954 by William Carlos Williams. ***The New York Times Company:*** From a review (of *Black Boy* by Richard Wright) by Orville Prescott from *The New York Times,* February 28, 1945, p. 21, as cited in *Richard Wright: The Critical Reception,* edited by John M. Reilly. Copyright © 1945 by The New York Times Company. From a review (of *A Raisin in the Sun* by Lorraine Hansberry) by Brooks Atkinson from *The New York Times,* March 12, 1959, as cited in *The New York Times Theater Reviews 1920–1970,* Vol. 6/1952–1959. Copyright © 1959 by The New York Times Company. ***The New Yorker:*** From "Hersey and History" by Roger Angell from *The New Yorker,* July 31, 1995. Copyright © 1995 by Roger Angell. ***W. W. Norton & Company, Inc.:*** From "An Introduction to *The Sound and the Fury*" by William Faulkner from *Mississippi Quarterly* 26, Summer 1973. Copyright © 1973 by Mrs. Jill Faulkner Summers, Executrix for the Estate of William Faulkner. From "Thomas Wolfe: You Can't Go Home Again (1940)" from *Now all we need is a Title: Famous Book Titles and How They Got That Way* by André Bernard. ***The Oakland Tribune/Alameda Newspaper Group:*** Quote by Amy Tan from "Biographic: In the Arts" from *Oakland Tribune,* November 26, 1989. Copyright © 1989 by Alameda Newspaper Group. ***Publishers Weekly, a division of Cahners Publishing Company:*** From "Raymond Carver" by Sybil Steinberg from *Publishers Weekly,* vol. 233, no. 21, May 27, 1988. Copyright © 1988 by Cahners Publishing Company. ***Putnam Publishing Group:*** From "Introduction" from *American Indian Prose and Poetry.* Copyright © 1962 by Margot Astrov. ***Random House, Inc.:*** From "Shine, Perishing Republic" from *Selected Poems* by Robinson Jeffers. Copyright © 1925 and renewed © 1953 by Robinson Jeffers. ***San Quentin News:*** From "San Francisco Group Leaves S.Q. Audience Waiting for Godot" from *San Quentin News,* November 28, 1957. Copyright © 1957 by San Quentin News. ***Scribner, a Division of Simon & Schuster:*** From *A Moveable Feast* by Ernest Hemingway. Copyright © 1964 by Mary Hemingway; copyright renewed © 1992 by John H. Hemingway, Patrick Hemingway, and Gregory Hemingway. ***Mark Shechner:*** From "Sad Music" by Mark Shechner, a review of *The Stories of Bernard Malamud,* from *The Partisan Review,* vol. 51, no. 3, 1984. Copyright © 1984 by Mark Shechner. ***Southern Illinois University:*** From "Flannery O'Connor: Backwoods Prophet in the Secular City" by Michael D. True from *PLL: Papers on Language and Literature,* Southern Illinois University, volume 5, no. 2, Spring 1969. Copyright © 1969 by the Board of Trustees, Southern Illinois University. ***The Texas Folklore Society:*** From song lyrics from "Follow the Drinking Gourd" by H. B. Parks from *Follow de Drinkin' Gou'd,* Publications of the Texas Folk-lore Society, No. VII, edited by J. Frank Dobie. Copyright 1928 by the Texas Folklore Society. ***University of Nebraska Press:*** From *Ancestral Voice: Conversations with N. Scott Momaday* by Charles L. Woodard. Copyright © 1989 by the University of Nebraska Press. ***University of South Carolina Press:*** From *Understanding Tim O'Brien* by Steven Kaplan. Copyright © 1995 by University of South Carolina. ***University Press of Mississippi:*** From *Conversations with John Updike,* edited by James Plath. Copyright © 1994 by the University Press of Mississippi. ***Viking Penguin, a division of Penguin Books USA Inc.:*** Quote by Willa Cather from *The Writer's Chapbook,* edited by George A. Plimpton. Copyright © 1989 by The Paris Review, Inc. From "Go Down Death—A Funeral Sermon" from *God's Trombones* by James Weldon Johnson. Copyright 1927 by The Viking Press, Inc.; copyright renewed © 1955 by Grace Nail Johnson.

Reference:

From "Cast, Crew, and Personnel" from *From Option to Opening: A Guide to Producing Plays Off-Broadway* by Donald C. Farber. Copyright © 1968, 1970, 1977 by Donald C. Farber. Published by Proscenium Publishers Inc., New York.

From "David Mamet" from *In Their Own Words: Contemporary American Playwrights* by David Savran. Copyright © 1988 by David Savran. Published by Theatre Communications Group, Inc.

Quote by T.S. Eliot from *The World Book Encyclopedia.* Copyright © 1985 by World Book Inc.

CONTENTS

TO THE *Teacher*

INTRODUCING ELEMENTS OF LITERATURE

Beginnings to 1800

COLLECTION *1*

VISIONS AND VOYAGES

COLLECTION 2

THE EXAMINED LIFE

COLLECTION 3

THE AMERICAN DREAM

American Romanticism
1800–1860

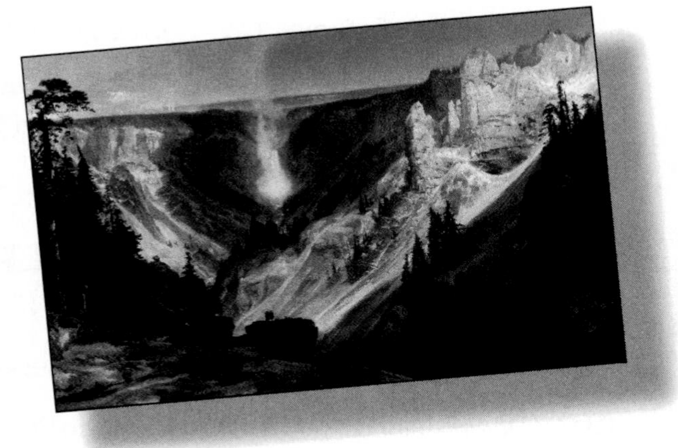

THE TRANSFORMING IMAGINATION
Collection Planning Guide **T150A–T150D**

The American Renaissance
A Literary Coming of Age
1840–1860

A New American Poetry
Whitman and Dickinson

COLLECTION 7 THE LARGE HEARTS OF HEROES

COLLECTION 8

TELL IT SLANT

The Rise of Realism

The Civil War and Postwar Period 1850–1900

SHACKLES

FROM INNOCENCE TO EXPERIENCE

The Moderns
1900–1950

COLLECTION 11 LOSS AND REDEMPTION

COLLECTION 12 THE DREAM AND THE REALITY

NO TIME FOR HEROES

SHADOWS OF THE PAST

I, TOO, SING AMERICA

MAKE IT NEW!

American Drama

REACHING FOR THE DREAM

Contemporary Literature 1950 to Present

THE WAGES OF WAR

DISCOVERIES AND AWAKENINGS

FROM GENERATION TO GENERATION

THE CREATED SELF

COLLECTION PLANNING GUIDE T1126A–T1126D

RESOURCE CENTER

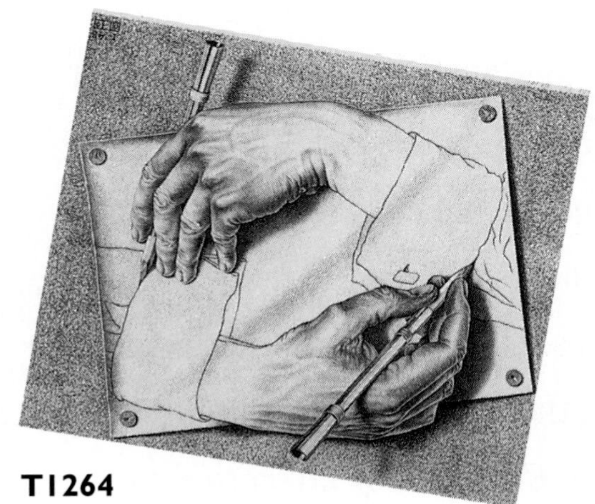

MAKING CONNECTIONS . . .

The ability to make connections is essential to living and learning. ***Elements of Literature*** makes the connections between **Literature and Life, Literature and Understanding, Literature and Writing, Literature and Language,** and **Literature Past and Present**.

One fundamental connection has always been at the heart of great literature—the empathetic link that enables a reader to participate fully in another's experience. Now, a new edition of ***Elements of Literature*** expands on this primary connection between reader and writer, helping students understand the intricate relationships that shape our literature and our lives. Using the world's greatest literature as a springboard, ***Elements of Literature*** takes students on a journey of discovery to explore the links that bind language and experience.

In this latest edition, the discovery of connections is enhanced by a new, more meaningful organization. The literature is grouped into Collections that help students explore universal themes, experience the treatment of themes in various genres, and understand the factors—both personal and historical—that influence a writer's choices.

Literature and Life Literature and Language Literature and Understanding Literature and Writing

Pupil's Edition Organization

Literary Collections

Literary Collections—each organized around a central theme characteristic of the historical period—form the instructional core of grades 11 and 12. Cross-references throughout each Collection refer students to related content in the *Resource Center.*

GRADE 11
Literature of the United States

Beginnings, to 1800
1. Visions and Voyages
2. The Examined Life
3. The American Dream

American Romanticism, 1800–1860
4. The Transforming Imagination

The American Renaissance: A Literary Coming of Age, 1840–1860
5. The Life Worth Living
6. The Realms of Darkness

A New American Poetry: Whitman and Dickinson
7. The Large Hearts of Heroes
8. Tell It Slant

The Rise of Realism: The Civil War and Postwar Period, 1850–1900
9. Shackles
10. From Innocence to Experience

The Moderns, 1900–1950
11. Loss and Redemption
12. The Dream and the Reality
13. No Time for Heroes
14. Shadows of the Past
15. I, Too, Sing America
16. Make it New!

American Drama
17. Reaching for the Dream

Contemporary Literature, 1950 to Present
18. The Wages of War
19. Discoveries and Awakenings
20. From Generation to Generation
21. The Created Self

GRADE 12
Literature of Britain

The Anglo-Saxons, 449–1066
1. Songs of Ancient Heroes

The Middle Ages, 1066–1485
2. The One Story Worth Telling

The Renaissance, 1485–1660
3. Love, Death, and Time
4. Under a Hand Accursed
5. The Power of the Word

The Restoration and the Eighteenth Century, 1660–1800
6. The Sting of Satire
7. An Appetite for Experience

The Romantic Period, 1798–1832
8. The Power of Imagination
9. The Quest for Beauty

The Victorian Period, 1832–1901
10. Love and Loss
11. The Paradox of Progress

The Twentieth Century
12. The Center Cannot Hold
13. The Transforming Imagination
14. Ourselves Among Others
15. Clashes of Culture

Resource Center

The *Resource Center* contains material for mini-lessons or for students to refer to independently. The handbooks include helpful information for improving writing, thinking, researching, and studying skills while ensuring concepts are accessible to a wide range of students. The *Resource Center* follows the literary Collections and contains the following sections:

- Handbook of Literary Terms
- Communications Handbook
- Language Handbook
- Glossary

Lesson Organization

At every level and in every lesson, ***Elements of Literature*** emphasizes making meaning—clarifying a personal response, shaping an interpretation, and moving beyond the text to make new connections.

> **"Meaning lies in that shared ground where the reader and the text meet—it isn't resident within the text, to be extracted like a nut from its shell."**
>
> —Robert Probst
> Author, ***Elements of Literature***

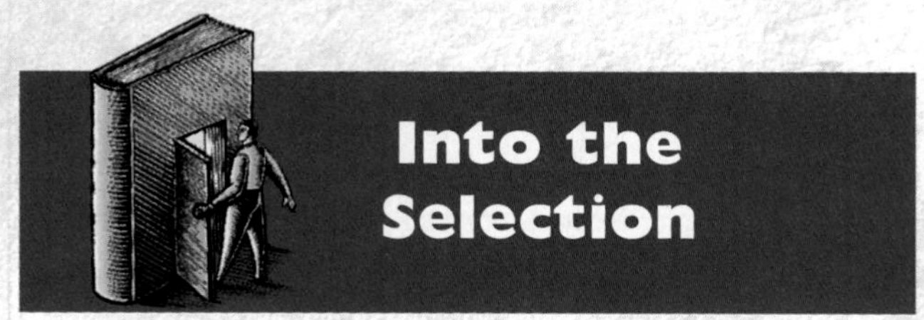

Author Biography

The **Author Biography** features provide background on the author, including quotations from the author about personal life experiences reflected in the selection. Each feature also explores the author's creative process and suggests other works by the author that may interest students.

Before You Read

Each **Before You Read** page helps students connect events or themes in the selection to their personal experiences and builds historical or literary background.

- **Reading Focus**
  These motivational features have students consider an issue, topic, or situation central to the selection. This early student involvement heightens awareness and makes reading purposeful.

- **Quickwrite**
  Brief writing prompts, often for independent activities, further develop the topic introduced in the *Reading Focus.* Students are asked to return to the *Quickwrite* after reading the selection to validate original impressions or record changes in opinions or feelings.

- **Elements of Literature**
  A key literary element is explained and defined in the context of the upcoming selection.

- **Background**
  Understanding the essential background of a particular selection enhances reading comprehension. *Background* describes historical or cultural contexts, defines key terms, explains critical concepts, or provides additional information about the author.

"We must try, first of all, to respect the nature of literary experience."

—Robert Probst

During the "Through" part of the lesson, students have firsthand experiences with the literature. They probe, challenge, and analyze their own and their classmates' responses and perceptions.

A Dialogue with the Text

This frequently occurring activity invites students to use their *Reader's Logs* to record perceptions, predictions, and feelings about the selection as they read.

Words to Own

Words to Own boxes encourage the acquisition of vocabulary by highlighting and defining target vocabulary words for prose selections.

Literature and . . .

These features enhance comprehension by providing additional background information or by making connections to other disciplines such as science, math, social studies, and art.

Connections

A number of selections are followed by a *Connections* feature: an additional work, often in a different genre, that makes a pertinent literary connection to the main selection. Newspaper articles, song lyrics, cartoons, poems, and essays appear as Connections, enabling students to compare and contrast different treatments of a theme and make relevant personal connections.

Making Meanings

Interesting, involving questions follow each selection, moving from personal response to high-level critical thinking.

- First Thoughts
- Reviewing the Text
- Shaping Interpretations
- Connecting with the Text
- Extending the Text
- Challenging the Text

"There are various ways of making meaning out of experience, and students should learn to exercise some responsibility in choosing."

—Robert Probst

Students extend their experiences and knowledge of literature, exploring their reactions through projects and activities.

Choices: Building Your Portfolio

Students follow their interests and develop new ones as they choose activities and projects for their portfolios.

- The *Writer's Notebook: Work in Progress* activities—found on each *Choices* page—help students explore and define topics for writing. These assignments guide students in basic skills that may be used later in the *Writer's Workshop* concluding each historical period.

Other portfolio activities include

• Speaking and Listening • Creative Writing •
• Critical Writing • Research • Art •
• Problem Solving • Cross-Curricular Connections •
• Performance • Cultural Connections •

Elements of Literature

In-depth features on key literary elements, from sonnet form and symbolism to plain style and kennings, reinforce newly encountered literary elements and place them in a broader context.

Language and Style

These activities focus on aspects of literary style and are used in conjunction with the study of the selection.

How to Own a Word

This feature teaches a specific strategy for vocabulary acquisition: semantic mapping, word analogies, and context clues, among others.

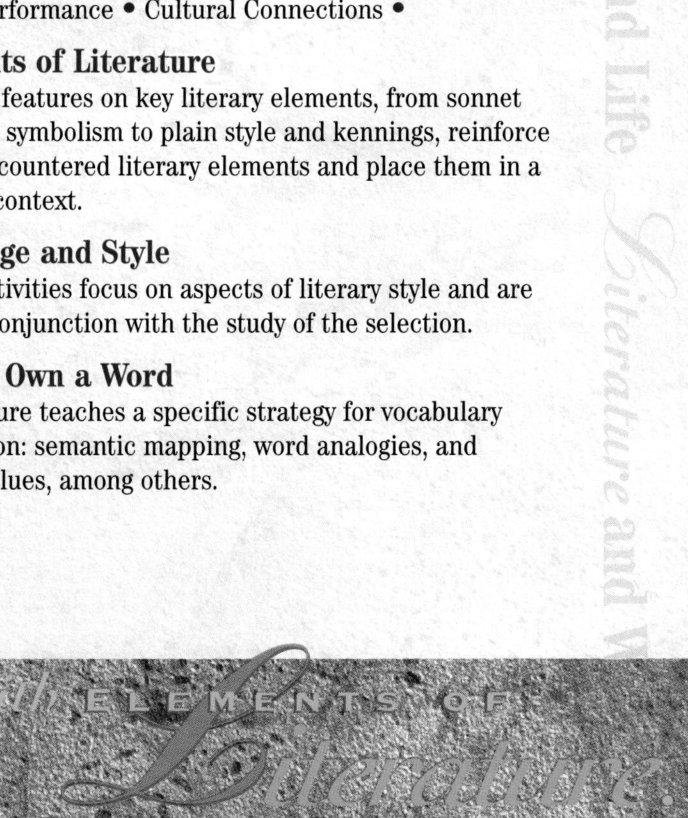

Literature and Life

Support for All Your Needs

Grades 11 and 12

Teaching Resources A and B

Two booklets per grade level provide Teaching Notes and blackline masters that support instruction in the *Pupil's Edition.*

- ***Teaching Notes*** introduce literary periods, provide selection summaries and objectives, and identify key literary elements. The notes also rate each selection's level of difficulty as easy, intermediate, or challenging for both vocabulary and concept. They frequently include additional historical/biographical material.
- ***Graphic Organizers for Active Reading*** are selection-based graphic organizer activities that aid students in one or all stages of the reading process.
- ***Language Link*** activity worksheets cover a complete scope and sequence of language skills, providing an independent strand of grammar, usage, and mechanics instruction.
- ***Words to Own*** are selection-based vocabulary activity worksheets that provide practice with and reinforcement of the *Words to Own* identified in the *Pupil's Edition.* Worksheets featuring additional vocabulary words are also provided for the collections containing a majority of poetry selections.
- ***Becoming a Strategic Reader*** worksheets for each literary period provide instruction and practice in reading strategies.
- ***Language Workshop*** worksheets reinforce, extend, and provide practice for the *Language Workshop* features in the *Pupil's Edition.*
- ***Cross-Curricular Activities*** are interdisciplinary, theme-based activities appropriate for team-teaching situations.

Language Development

Language Skills Worksheets offer a complete scope and sequence of language skills instruction and practice.

Assessment Options

Test Booklet

- *Selection Tests*
- *Collection Tests*
- *Literary Period Introduction Tests*
- *The American Language Tests (grade 11)*
- *The English Language Tests (grade 12)*
- *Literary Period Tests*
- *Standardized Test Preparation* worksheets

Integrated Performance Assessment, an independent, holistic assessment program, was developed in cooperation with the Center for Reading and Language Studies at Indiana University, Dr. Roger Farr, Director, and the HB Assessment Group. Each of four assessments consists of a Reading section that provides one or two authentic literary selections with a series of open-ended questions and a Writing section that elicits a specific form of writing.

The ***Portfolio Management System*** provides support for implementing portfolios in the classroom. It includes forms for self-, peer, and teacher assessment and blackline masters for developing and evaluating the following *Pupil's Edition* activities and projects.

- *Learning for Life* gives you a rubric for evaluating each *Learning for Life* assignment in the *Pupil's Edition.*
- *Writer's Workshop* offers a prewriting worksheet, a self-evaluation form, peer critique prompts and an evaluation rubric for each *Writer's Workshop* activity.
- *Choices: Building Your Portfolio* contains criteria for evaluating each activity that appears in this feature.

Test Generators—available for either Macintosh® or Windows®—enable you to revise, edit, or re-sort existing *Selection Tests* and *Standardized Test Preparation Items.*

Audiovisual Resources

Fine Art Transparencies, organized by Collection, help students make humanities connections with specific themes. Each transparency comes with two blackline masters—specific questions relate the art to a literary selection or to the Collection.

Instructional Transparencies include Literary Element, Reading Strategy, Vocabulary Strategy, and Revision Strategy transparencies.

Audiocassettes with Program Notes provide professional recordings of key selections and reflect a mix of genres, periods, and cultures.

Integrated Technology

Videodisc Programs for each level extend and enrich the literary content of the *Pupil's Edition.* Video segments linked to each Collection offer a variety of interesting connections, such as author biographies or interviews, historical background, cross-curricular content, or dramatic interpretations of literature.

Language Workshop Interactive Multimedia CD-ROM Software provides a comprehensive, interactive course of study in grammar, usage, and mechanics. Functions include automatic scoring of tests and exercises, prescriptions for individualized courses of study, and tracking of student grades. Available for Macintosh® or Windows®.

Writer's Workshop Interactive Multimedia CD-ROM Software provides support in eight challenging, standards-based writing assignments, giving students step-by-step guidance through the writing process. The program includes an on-line thesaurus, dictionary, spell-checker, language handbook, and bibliography-maker (MLA and APA styles). Available for Macintosh® and Windows®.

The ***Holistic Scoring Workshop*** is easy-to-use software that will introduce you to holistic scoring techniques. You'll practice scoring actual student papers and can compare the scores you would assign with those given by professional scorers.

The ***Staff Development Video Package*** gives you a comprehensive in-service and training program that provides an overview of ***Elements of Literature.*** A *User's Guide* is also included.

*L*ITERATURE—AN INVITATION TO A DIALOGUE

Dr. Robert Probst
Georgia State University

Surely, of all the arts, literature is most immediately implicated with life itself. The very medium through which the author shapes the text—language—is grounded in the shared lives of human beings. Language is the bloodstream of a common culture, a common history. Louise Rosenblatt

Literature and Life

Mathematicians, scientists, and engineers build bridges and send people to the moon, statisticians calculate our insurance premiums and life expectancy, and accountants figure our taxes and amortize our house payments, but the poets, dramatists, novelists, and story-writers have nonetheless remained at the center of life. They bind us together as a society and they define us as individuals within that society.

When we're very young we need stories almost as much as we need food and protection. They entertain us and help us sleep, but they also teach us how to get through the world. They tell us there are pots of gold waiting for us at the end of the rainbow, and they warn us about the trolls hiding under the bridges. They teach us about hope, fear, courage, and all the other elements of our lives. As we grow out of childhood, the great stories, poems, and plays of the world's literature encourage us to reflect on the issues that have intrigued men and women for centuries, inviting us into a continuing dialogue about human experience. When we're older, our own stories represent what we've done, capturing for us what we've made of our lives. Some we'll tell happily, some we'll tell with great pain, and some we may not tell at all, but they're all important because they are a way of making sense of our lives.

If literature is the ongoing dialogue about what it means to be human, then the language arts classroom is society's invitation to students to join that conversation. The texts we use represent the reflections of the world's cultures on the nature of human experience, and the writings we elicit from our students are their first efforts to join in that reflection. The classroom is the place for students to learn to read and reflect on visions of human possibilities offered them by the great literature and to begin to tell their own.

Literature offers an invitation to reflect, but it doesn't offer formulas to memorize or answers to write dutifully in notes so that later on, when life presents us with problems, we can pull out our tattered old notebooks and find our path sketched out for us. Literature is an invitation to a dialogue.

> *Literature offers us access to hidden experiences and perceptions.*

That, perhaps more than any other reason, is why it's so important that we teach literature and writing well. It's too easy to avoid the responsible thought demanded by the significant issues, too tempting to accept someone else's formulation of the truth. "Life imitates art," Richard Peck said in a speech in New Orleans in 1974, "especially bad art." By that he meant, I think, that we may too often give in to tempting laziness and allow our lives to be governed by visions of human possibilities that we take from film, television, or graffiti. The problem for teachers, of course, is to lead students not simply to absorb unthinkingly what art offers, but to reflect on it.

This textbook series tries to support teachers' efforts to lead students to think, to feel, and to take responsibility for themselves. It will have much in common with other textbooks. After all, we'd miss "The Raven" if he didn't land croaking on our window sill one morning just before homeroom, and twelfth grade wouldn't be the same without an evening or two around the hearth with Beowulf. But if this series has much in common with other textbooks, it will also have much that differs—new selections, perhaps by authors we haven't met before, exploring lives and circumstances that previously may not have been well represented in the pages of school texts. And similarly, there will be familiar approaches to teaching—perhaps specific activities—that we've all come to rely upon, but there will be other suggestions that emphasize aspects of literary experience, writing, and discussion that may not have been prominent in other books.

Principles of the Program

First among the principles of the program is that *the subject matter of the language arts classroom is human experience comprehended and expressed in language.* The classroom invites the student into the dialogue about the big issues of human experience. The content of literature is the content of our days and we think and feel about these issues before we enter the classroom and open the text.

When we do finally come to the text, it offers students an opportunity to begin to make sense of experience and to see it captured in the literature.

Implicit in this vision of the language arts is a second principle, *that learning in the English classroom is a creative act,* requiring students to make things with language. Reading literature is a process of engaging the text, weighing it against experience readers bring to it.

Similarly, writing isn't simply a matter of learning and applying the rules of grammar and usage or of memorizing the structure and strategies of narratives, descriptions, and arguments.

The third principle focuses on the encounter between student and content. It doesn't focus exclusively on the information and skills that have at times provided the framework for our instruction.

Nor, on the other hand, is teaching planned with thought *only* for the student's interests, needs, and desires, and thus organized around whatever concerns happen to predominate at the moment. It is, to borrow Rosenblatt's term, transactional.

For this series, *the integration of the several aspects of the English language arts program* is the fourth governing principle. Literature can't be taught effectively without work in composition. Writing, without the inspiration offered by good literature, remains shallow and undeveloped. Oral language has to be acquired in the context of groups working collaboratively. And so, these texts will suggest ways of interrelating instruction in literature, writing, and language.

Goals of the Program

We hope that in a curriculum planned to include these texts students would achieve several goals.

1. *They will learn about themselves, their assumptions and beliefs, through reading, discussing, and writing about literature and their own experience.*
2. *Students will learn about others, including those in their classrooms and communities, but also people of other cultures, other places, other times.*
3. *Students will learn how texts operate, how they shape our thinking and manipulate our emotions.*
4. *Students will learn how context shapes meaning.*
5. *Students will learn that there are many ways of dealing with experience, both literary and otherwise.*
6. *Students should learn the pleasures—aesthetic, intellectual, emotional, and social—of reading and writing, in the hope that these pleasures will capture them as readers and writers for the rest of their lives.*

Education doesn't—or shouldn't—end with the last diploma or degree received. We hope that our students will find some pleasure in learning so they'll continue to learn and think.

Working with the Series

You will find, as you work with selections in this textbook, that students have immediate responses to what they've read. That may be the place to start. The students' responses are very likely to lead you back to the issues you would have wanted to discuss anyway, and so the questions we've suggested might be addressed naturally during the flow of the discussion. Look for the potential in their reactions and their questions even before turning to the questions in the "First Thoughts" section. Then, the questions in the text can extend or expand the discussion.

The same might be said about the writing. The series has been designed so that experiences with literature, with writing, and with group processes will often be interconnected. We hope that the literature will inspire and shape the students' writing, that their writing will lead back to further reading, and that the discussions and group activities suggested will build a supportive community in which all this work can take place.

The objective in all of this is for students to be able to draw upon their literary heritage and their developing skill with written and spoken language so that, as humane and reasoning people, they may be responsibly engaged with the world around them. If the language arts class helps to achieve that goal, we should be well satisfied with our labors.

Dr. Robert Probst

Becoming a Strategic Reader

Dr. Judith Irvin
Florida State University

Most teachers think that during the elementary grades, students will learn to read and during the middle school years, most will master the process of reading. Unfortunately, many students begin their high school careers without important reading skills. Some may lack the conceptual understanding that most students have acquired developmentally in the lower grades, and this deficit has always kept them behind their peers in literacy abilities. Other students may be impeded by learning disabilities and so must learn alternate reading strategies in order to compensate for these disabilities.

Even though teachers may become frustrated with students who have difficulty reading at the high school level, they can help these students by building on their strengths, by concentrating on their comprehension, and by helping them to develop reading strategies such as skimming and scanning material and connecting texts with prior knowledge.

In the past, reading was viewed as a simple task of decoding words. Educators generally emphasized the strategies of sounding out words, recognizing words out of context by sight, and reproducing content by answering comprehension questions. Research has led to a new conceptualization of the reading process—that reading is a complex learning process. In this new view, readers construct meaning from a text, not simply by decoding words, but by using reading strategies that incorporate and expand their prior knowledge. Prior knowledge includes not only readers' knowledge of the definition of a word, but also their responses to the context of the word—the entire text. Careful reading of a text using strategies like those explained in the following material will allow readers to use their prior knowledge to create meaning and to extend their understanding of a text. As students become more involved in developing and reflecting on their reading and learning processes, meaning may now be defined as "something that is actively created rather than passively received" (Buehl, 1995, p. 8).

As will be explained, the process of constructing meaning is not linear, but recursive and interactive and helps to create a richer, more productive reading experience for the reader.

It is the interaction of what is in readers' minds with what is on the page . . . that helps them to comprehend what they read.

The Reader

Former models of reading focused on whether students had acquired specific skills. Recent models of reading allow that students come to a learning context with previous information about particular topics, with definite attitudes about reading, writing, and school in general, and with varying motivations for reading and learning. It is the interaction of what is in readers' minds with what is on the page within a particular context that helps them to comprehend what they read.

Schema Theory

It is impossible for readers to learn anything new without making connections to their prior knowledge or schemata. The schemata are like the components of an elaborate filing system inside every reader's head. If the reader's mind is the filing system, the schemata, then, are the ideas contained in the file folders within the system. For example, you probably have a schema for a computer, a mental picture of what a computer is and what it does. You probably also bring to that basic picture many other associations, ideas, and feelings. If you use computers regularly, your schema may include positive feelings about their limitless applications. If the computer revolution has left you yearning for the days of yellow note pads and typewriters, then you may have feelings of anxiety or frustration as you approach a computer manual. For teachers, it is important to remember that readers encountering new ideas must often be shown how the new material fits into their existing filing system.

The Text

The content, format, and organization of a text are factors that make a text easy or difficult for students to understand. If students' schemata tell them that a particular assignment will be difficult or unrelated to their personal experiences, they will probably be reluctant to read it and will most likely not make much meaning of it. The students know with one look that they will read and respond to a poem differently than they will to a chapter in a science book. A teacher should be prepared to exercise flexibility and sensitivity in presenting the text so as to encourage students to use their schemata to enhance their reading experiences.

The Context

Readers approach texts differently, and they also vary their reading according to their purposes. If they are reading for pleasure, students may skip over a difficult word or read an exciting passage more than once. But if they are reading a text for class, skipping a word might mean not understanding an important concept needed in class the next day. A reader's purpose for reading also dictates how attentive he or she is to details and how much effort will be put into remembering what is read. Similarly, when and where the reading is done affects the reading process. Readers will make less meaning from texts they read on the bus or with thoughts of a sick relative in the backs of their minds than they might make if they had a quiet space and clear thoughts.

Strategic Learning

Suppose that during a racquetball game you hit a straight shot down the right side of the court, and your opponent misses

Becoming a proficient reader and writer is a life-long process.

the ball. The point is yours. This well-placed shot may have been a lucky one, or it may have been the result of a strategy. Before you hit the ball, you may have noticed that your opponent was standing in the middle of the court, and you remembered that she is left-handed with a weak backhand. You hit the ball to exactly the right spot deliberately and strategically. The analogy of planning your shots in a game can be applied to learning.

Strategic learning involves analyzing the reading task, establishing a purpose for reading, and then selecting strategies for making meaning. A strategy is a conscious effort by the reader to attend to comprehension while reading. Weinstein explains that "learning strategies include any thoughts or behaviors that help us to acquire new information in such a way that the new information is integrated with our existing knowledge" (Weinstein, 1987, p. 590). Strategies occur before reading when readers activate prior knowledge by thinking and discussing the title and topic and by identifying a purpose for reading. They also occur during reading as readers use context to figure out unknown words and monitor their understanding, and beyond the reading when readers summarize or evaluate the main ideas of the text.

Metacognition

Reading is often referred to as a cognitive event. It is also a metacognitive event. Cognition refers to a person's using the knowledge and skills he or she possesses; metacognition refers to a person's awareness and understanding of that knowledge and conscious control over those skills. It is, essentially, thinking about one's way of thinking. Metacognition, then, is knowing how and when to use strategies to solve problems in understanding. It develops as a reader matures, usually during adolescence, but it can be taught and strengthened by explicit instruction and practice.

Becoming a proficient reader and writer is a life-long process. Accepting the premise that meaning is constructed in the mind of the learner implies that metacognitive abilities must be operational for learning to occur. The high school years are an ideal time to develop the metacognitive abilities that will serve them throughout life.

Strategic Reading in This Program

Good readers are strategic, and being strategic involves the metacognitive abilities to think, plan, and evaluate their understanding of a text. The following concepts, addressed in the Annotated Teacher's Edition and in Teaching Resources for *Elements of Literature,* help students to focus on their own reading strategies:

- activating schema (prior knowledge) and building background information
- predicting and confirming
- organizing information
- drawing conclusions
- making inferences
- text differences
- retelling/summarizing

Before students read, they are invited to use their prior knowledge by making predictions about the content of a selection, to establish a clear purpose for reading, and to think about reading strategies they might use as they read. During the reading process, students are guided to use context, to connect what they are reading with what they already know, and to continue to monitor and evaluate their comprehension. And, after completing their reading, students have opportunities to review their reading through peer discussion, class discussion, preparing entries in Reader's Logs, and using graphic organizers.

New research and practice in literacy learning reflects a more holistic view of understanding text. The *Elements of Literature* program provides students with opportunities to apply reading strategies to a variety of texts in a meaningful manner.

References

Buehl, D. *Classroom Strategies for Interactive Learning.* Schofield, WI: Wisconsin State Reading Association, 1995.

Weinstein, C. E. "Fostering Learning Autonomy Through the Use of Learning Strategies." *Journal of Reading* 30 (1987) 590–595.

Dr. Judith Irvin

What Is an Integrated Approach?

Dr. Karen Kutiper
Harris County Dept. of Education
Houston, Texas

An integrated language arts program focuses on the complementary nature of the literacy processes—reading, writing, listening, and speaking—rather than the teaching of each in isolation from the other. We are very much aware of the strong connections between reading and writing, and in the professional literature and at professional conferences we read and hear about ways to forge those connections. In reality those connections exist among all of the language arts—reading, writing, listening, and speaking. So rather than teaching the processes and their related skills separately, teachers weave them together in instructional contexts. Such an approach avoids the fragmentation of skills, takes advantage of the reciprocal relationship that exists among the literacy processes, and reflects the expanded use of literacy skills in the real world. Initial encounters with a wide range of quality texts often provide the starting points for these integrated classroom experiences.

How does an integrated approach help my students?
When supported by appropriate instruction, the interplay among the linguistic processes can produce greater competence in all areas. As youngsters have opportunities to respond to texts in writing, to share, to defend, and to refine those responses in dialogue with peers or with the teacher, they develop richer understandings of what they have read, leading to greater competence in reading and writing. When students have opportunities to respond both informally and formally to their own reading and writing and to the reading and writing of others, they increase their ability to communicate fluently and flexibly in any setting.

What is the teacher's role in the integrated classroom?
In these classrooms the teacher is a facilitator who guides and focuses the opportunities for response, who assesses student performance in order to plan appropriate supportive instruction, and who ensures that students are writing for a variety of audiences and purposes and reading widely from a range of texts, both literary and informative. Direct instruction in an integrated classroom takes many forms. Teachers become skilled at teaching mini-strategy lessons at the point of need—brief lessons on language conventions, reading of literature skills. These lessons emerge from a meaningful context for the students and provide real purpose for new learning. Whether a mini-lesson or a more elaborate one, teachers focus on structuring experiences that immerse students in language use and provide meaningful opportunities for reading, writing, listening, and speaking.

What are the key ingredients of the integrated classroom?
Obviously, a wide variety of quality and timely literature forms the foundation of the integrated classroom. The learners need opportunities to read extensively from teacher selected and self-selected materials. The organization of the classroom must facilitate occasions for the informal and formal written and oral responses that emerge from reading. At the heart of this classroom is a teacher who understands that quality instruction builds on students' backgrounds, who provides appropriate instructional scaffolding, and who offers students opportunities to participate in a wide range of literacy activities. Most importantly, this teacher acknowledges the active role students play in developing and refining their own literacy processes and involves them in meaningful and balanced learning experiences in which literacy skills and strategies are interwoven.

THE NEED FOR INCLUSION

Dr. Donna Kearns
UNIVERSITY OF CENTRAL OKLAHOMA

What Is Inclusion?

As the diverse threads of a garment bring beauty and durability to the fabric, so too do the children of today's diverse classrooms bring beauty and sensitivity to our schools and communities. Including all children in schools as we include a variety of threads in a special fabric allows for a fine weave. It becomes a closely knit cloth to provide strength for the community. Inclusion of children with disabilities and diverse needs in our classrooms represents a belief that a class can be made stronger by weaving those students into classrooms where true learning can take place through a variety of different techniques. These techniques are provided in classrooms where all students are included.

The term *inclusion* enjoys no one common definition among today's educators. However, most supporters of inclusion agree that it does provide for six basic principles that are important to the educational rights of all of America's children. Those principles include **zero reject, natural proportions, regular/special education collaboration, home school, age-appropriate,** and **ability awareness.**

The term **zero reject** refers to the fact that no students with disabilities are rejected from the regular education classrooms and schools in which they would participate if they did not have disabilities. We do not reject them in their real classroom placement on the basis of their disability, but rather we find techniques such as those presented in this book to assist them to experience success in the regular classroom in which every other child of their age is placed.

> *Including all children in schools as we include a variety of threads in a special fabric allows for a fine weave.*

When students with disabilities are placed in the regular education classroom at the rate consistent with the incidence of disabilities, there should be approximately no more than ten percent of students who have disabilities. This **natural proportion** element should ensure and reassure teachers that their classrooms will continue to be a mixture of students, the majority of whom have average or above average learning abilities—including some of those who may have disabilities.

Supporters of inclusion believe that students with disabilities are primarily the responsibility of the classroom teacher—just as every other student in that teacher's room is his or her responsibility. In addition, supporters carry a strong belief that supports must be provided by special education and related services personnel to enable teachers and students to experience success in the regular classroom. This textbook provides techniques for classroom teachers to use as well as some that may be used by those support personnel as they **collaborate** to provide services to students with disabilities who are included in the regular classroom. These support services are not provided in a corner of the room, but rather are intermingled within the same instructional area that is being used for all students in the lessons being presented. A collaborative effort enables the students and the teacher(s) to truly provide successful opportunities. A shared philosophy of inclusion and the rights of all children to learn from the teacher and from each other is essential for inclusion to work.

Children with disabilities have the right to attend the same school as their brothers and sisters as well as their neighborhood friends. The **home school** issue supports students' acceptance within their own community with little if any discrimination. By maintaining daily contact with the same people who live "next door," students with disabilities are viewed as peers and are respected. Classmates and peers begin to have a better awareness of

Schools cannot continue to meet the needs of all learners if we continue to educate the way we educated yesterday's students.

the abilities of students with disabilities—taking the focus off what they can't do and focusing instead on what they can do!

As students are placed in these general education classrooms, they are given **age-appropriate** placements. Students are not placed based on IQ or label, but rather on where their individual needs can best be met. When placement decisions are made, teachers and parents must work together to ensure that each student's needs are examined independently. Though some students may need to be placed in an educational program with their same-age peers, others may still enjoy opportunities that are considered by some as immature or not age-appropriate. It is important to keep in mind that age-appropriate is a term that differs from same-age.

Why Is Inclusion Important?

In the past, use of the word *inclusion* struck fear in the hearts of many educators. Fortunately, today, more and more educators understand that inclusion itself is not to be feared. It is a term that represents progress toward meeting the diverse needs of students in our changing population. Educational statistics have been presented in a variety of ways, but no matter how we examine the issue, we see that approximately one third of American children are at risk of school failure. Schools must change to meet the diverse needs of the students in our current population, not the students of even three to five years ago. Cultural groups in this country have changed dramatically over the past ten years. Schools cannot continue to meet the needs of all learners if we continue to educate the way we educated yesterday's students. Not only have cultures changed, but since 1987, one fourth of all preschool children have been living in poverty. Annually about 350,000 infants are born to mothers addicted to cocaine. These infants are entering the public school system in infant and early childhood programs. The "Leave It to Beaver" family exists in only a fraction of the population today. On any given night, approximately 50,000 to 200,000 children are homeless. These factors alone should tell us that we must change the way we educate today's students. These factors alone should tell us that all students need to be accepted and educated with their peers—those same peers who are a part of their community. Including all students in general education classrooms better ensures that all students have had equal opportunities to access the same educational programs and services and that their individual needs have been met—without labeling or discriminating in any manner.

How Can Teachers Use Inclusion Strategies to Help Students?

A strategy is a planned, deliberate activity used to acquire knowledge. It is generally understood that students with disabilities as well as others who are at risk of failure in school have few if any strategies to learn new information. Special educators have most often focused their educational techniques on teaching students strategies to learn new information. Unfortunately, students often misperceived what they were learning because the setting (the special education classroom) was a place they simply "went." It was not considered their classroom or home base. The content was not always developed around the techniques or strategies the teacher was teaching.

On the other hand, in the general education classroom, many students with disabilities and other special needs had little if any background of experience to draw from and often misperceived the content as it was presented. A merger of the content along with the strategies such as those presented in this text provides the student better information on *how* to learn the information as well as *what* to learn. We must remember that the purpose of education goes beyond learning content. Education is much more accurately described as learning how to learn. Students can enhance their learning by becoming aware of their own skills as they listen, read, write, and experience interactions in school situations. Teachers can promote this learning by assisting students in exploring how they learn while they are learning. Learning to use strategies effectively may encourage students to take responsibility for their learning and to affect positive self-perception as well as motivation. As educators, we must plan strategies to assist students in their learning process—not just in the presentation of the content. A critical element in assisting students in the learning process includes the use of instructional as well as cognitive strategies such as those presented in this text. We must teach students to become aware of their own strategies and to become good troubleshooters in the learning process. We do this by teaching strategies. It is believed that the use of flexible instructional strategies and the merger of content with cognitive strategies will assist all students to learn concepts presented in class—not just today, but for tomorrow and all the tomorrows to come.

ENGLISH LANGUAGE DEVELOPMENT

Dr. Stephen Krashen
UNIVERSITY OF SOUTHERN CALIFORNIA

The problem of helping the older limited-English-proficient student in a school without special programs, or with partial programs, cannot be totally solved. But the problem and the teacher's burden can be reduced. To see how this can be done, we will first briefly discuss the principles underlying ideal programs, describe an ideal program, and then see how this knowledge can be applied to the less-than-ideal situation.

The principles underlying successful programs for limited-English-proficient students are the same principles underlying successful foreign language programs and language arts programs for first-language and literacy development. There are a few fundamental hypotheses:

1. The Acquisition-Learning Hypothesis claims that we have two different ways of developing ability in language: Language *acquisition* is a subconscious process, that is, while it is happening, we do not know it is happening. In addition, once an aspect of language is acquired, we are not usually aware of it: The knowledge is stored subconsciously in our brains. A synonym for language acquisition is "picking up" a language.

Language *learning* is a conscious process, and the result of language learning is consciously stored in our brains. When we talk about "rules" and "grammar," we are usually talking about language learning.

2. The Monitor Hypothesis claims that our ability to use consciously learned language is severely limited. Conscious knowledge of language does not give us our fluency or play much of a role at all in language production or comprehension. It is acquisition, not learning, that is responsible for our ability to communicate. The only significant function of consciously learned knowledge is that it acts as a Monitor, or editor, operating on the output of the acquired system.

To clarify the role of conscious learning, I will first describe what happens in foreign language use. Assume you are trying to speak your intermediate Spanish (or French or German). The sentence you are about to speak pops into your mind. Then just before you produce it, just before you actually say it, you scan the sentence internally, you inspect it, think of the rules you learned in school, and you make corrections using these rules. (Or you blurt the sentence out, realize you made a mistake, and redo it.) This illustrates the use of the Monitor.

The Monitor is also used in the first language. We sometimes "monitor" when our acquired dialect differs from the "standard." I have to monitor, for example, if I want to get the *who/whom* distinction correct, or, in writing, when I need to distinguish *its* and *it's*. In both cases, I think about the rule.

The path to accuracy is not through better monitoring. It is not through developing an industrial-strength Monitor with detailed knowledge of rules and maintaining constant vigilance when we speak and write. The use of the Monitor, even for adults who are interested in the structure of language, is usually limited to the editing stage in writing, where it can make a small contribution. For children it hardly makes any contribution at all. The best way to increase accuracy is through acquisition, as we shall see later.

3. The Input Hypothesis is the central hypothesis in current language acquisition theory. It claims that we acquire language in only one way, when we understand what people tell us, and when we understand what we read. (I have called the "reading version" of the Input Hypothesis the "Reading Hypothesis.") We acquire language, in other words, when we understand messages, *what* is said or written, not *how* it is said or written. We use the term "comprehensible input" to refer to input that the acquirer understands.

Notice that the input hypothesis states that we acquire language from input (listening and reading), not output (speaking and writing). The ability to produce language, it is claimed, is a result of language acquisition, not a cause.

> *A synonym for language acquisition is "picking up" a language.*

More CI > More Language and Literacy Development

The research supporting the claim that more comprehensible input (CI) results in more language acquisition and literacy development is vast and consistent. This generalization holds in first language and second language, and in informal (outside the classroom) environments and formal (inside the classroom) environments. Studies show, for example, that those who get more comprehensible input outside the classroom acquire more. In addition, those who participate in free reading programs in school, such as sustained silent reading, make better gains in vocabulary and reading than those in traditional classes.

in order to help them establish a reading habit.

The above applications can be termed "direct" application of the principle of comprehensible input: Direct applications present comprehensible input in English. We can also help second language acquirers with methods and techniques that are indirect, but very powerful.

4. The Affective Filter Hypothesis claims that when language acquirers are in a high anxiety state, a block prevents the input from reaching the "language acquisition device." Thus, anxiety does not affect the process of language acquisition: It prevents input, even when it is comprehensible, from reaching those parts of the brain where language acquisition occurs.

Applications

We begin our discussion of application in the ideal case at the beginning level. Beginners, ideally, would participate in comprehensible-input-based methods such as Natural Approach and TPR for ESL. These methods attempt to fill the classroom time with interesting, comprehensible input, and do not require student production at early stages, nor are errors corrected.

At the intermediate level, limited-English-proficient students participate in sheltered-subject-matter classes, classes that consist only of intermediate-level ESL students and that teach subject matter in a comprehensible way. Research shows that students in these classes acquire a great deal of the second language and learn impressive amounts of subject matter at the same time (Krashen, 1991). They work because they provide a great deal of comprehensible input.

Intermediate students are encouraged to do a great deal of free voluntary reading. One interesting possibility is to combine sheltered-subject-matter teaching and free reading by teaching sheltered popular literature, a class designed to expose second language acquirers to a wide variety of interesting reading in the second language

Making English input more comprehensible using the first language

The first language can be used to supply background knowledge, knowledge of the world, and subject matter knowledge, which can help enormously in making English input more comprehensible.

Consider two limited-English-proficient students entering the fourth grade who are at approximately the same level in English. Child (1), who has been taught in her first language, has had an excellent background in math. Child (2) is very weak in math. In fourth grade, let us presume, math is taught only in English. Obviously child (1) will do much better in math than child (2). Child (1) will not only learn more math, she will also acquire more English, because she will get more comprehensible input. Child (2) will learn neither math nor English.

Developing literacy through the first language

A second indirect means of promoting English language development is the development of literacy through the first language. It is extremely efficient to develop literacy first in the child's first language. To see this, consider this three-step argument:

(1) We learn to read by reading. There is good evidence that we learn to read by understanding the message on the page, as argued by Smith (1988) and Goodman (1982).

(2) If we learn to read by reading, by making sense of what is on the page, it will be easier to learn to read a language we already understand.

(3) Once we can read, we can read. The ability to read transfers dramatically across languages, even if the writing systems are different. Thus, learning to read any language helps a person learn to read any other.

There is another sense in which literacy transfers across languages: the ability to use language to solve problems. This includes discovering new ideas as the writer moves from draft to draft. It also includes the ability to read selectively for information relevant to a problem one is trying to solve, the ability to use a library, etc. Clearly, once someone has developed this kind of competence in one language, it transfers to any other language: Once we are educated, we are educated.

> *The first language... can help enormously in making English input more comprehensible.*

Principles of successful programs

If the principles presented above are correct, they suggest that successful programs for limited-English-proficient students will have the following characteristics:

1. Comprehensible input in English, in the form of ESL and sheltered classes based on comprehensible input. This provides comprehensible input directly.

2. Subject matter teaching done in the first language, without translation. This indirect help provides background information that helps make the English children read and hear more comprehensible. (Methods that use the first language for concurrent translation are not effective in helping children acquire English [see e.g. Legaretta, 1979]; when a translation is available, the children do not attend to the input in the second language, and teachers do not have to try to make this input comprehensible.)

3. Literacy development in the first language, which transfers to the second language.

Evidence confirming the validity of these principles comes from studies showing that children who participate in programs that have these three characteristics do very well, at least as well as children in all-day English programs, and usually better (Krashen and Biber, 1988).

A fourth very desirable component is the continuation of the development of the primary language. There are good practical reasons (e.g. international business) and cognitive reasons (there is evidence that bilingualism may be beneficial for certain cognitive abilities), and a high level of competence in the first language contributes to a healthy sense of biculturalism, an avoidance of the state of "bicultural ambivalence," shame of the first culture and rejection of the second culture (Cummins, 1981).

Here is one way to set up a program that meets these characteristics. The plan presented here, sometimes referred to as the "Eastman" plan, has three components and several stages. In the beginning stage, all children, limited English proficient and native speakers of English, are mixed for art, music, and physical education. This makes sense for two reasons: It avoids segregation, and much of the English the children will hear will be comprehensible, thanks to the pictures in art and movement in PE. Also, at this stage, children receive high-quality comprehensible-input-based ESL classes and are taught all other subjects in the primary language, subjects that would be difficult to teach in English.

The intermediate-stage child is defined as the child who understands enough English to begin to learn some content through English. We begin with sheltered-subject-matter instruction in those subjects that, at this level, do not demand a great deal of abstract use of language, such as math and science. Subjects such as social studies and language arts remain in the first language.

At the advanced level, limited-English-proficient students join the mainstream, but not all at once: They enter one or two subjects at a time, beginning with math and science. When this occurs, social studies and language arts are taught as sheltered-subject-matter classes. Eventually, students do all subjects in the mainstream and continue first language development in language arts and social studies classes. These continuing first language classes are not all-day programs. Rather, they can take the place of (or supplement) foreign language study. Examine the possible progress of a limited-English-proficient student: She first has math in the primary language, then moves to sheltered math, and then finally to the mainstream. At every stage, instruction is comprehensible, and the sheltered class acts as a bridge from the first language class to the mainstream. This child will be at "grade level" in math when she enters the mainstream and will be familiar with the special kind of English used in math class.

Clearly, once someone has developed this kind of competence in one language, it transfers to any other language.

The Less-Than-Ideal Situation

In the less-than-ideal situation, it will not always be possible to supply everything that plans like the Eastman plan provide. We can, however, reduce the problem by attempting to ensure that the principles underlying such plans are satisfied.

A modified Eastman plan can be used in situations in which there are a number of limited-English-proficient children in one school, but they speak different first languages, and/or primary language instruction is not possible for other reasons (staffing, materials).

In these cases, two thirds of the plan can be carried out: the "mainstream" and "ESL/sheltered" components. This kind of program has the advantage of being comprehensible all day long, but it lacks the advantages of developing literacy in the first language and using the first language to supply subject matter knowledge. It will be better, however, than ESL "pull-out," simply putting the child in a class that is incomprehensible nearly all day long.

Quite often, however, even the modified Eastman plan is not possible. This occurs when there are a few limited English proficient children in the school and/or when coordination among teachers is not possible. In cases like this, the classroom teacher is faced with great diversity within one classroom.

Before discussing some solutions, some ways of reducing the burden, it needs to be pointed out that teachers today are facing a degree of diversity, of heterogeneity, that has never been seen before in the history of education. It is not usual to see a single class with native and fluent English speakers, students who speak no English at all (and who have a poor background in the primary language), and students who speak a wide variety of first languages. Traditional solutions will not work. Even if paraprofessionals are available, teachers must supervise them and wind up making two, three, or even four lesson plans every period. Bilingual teachers sometimes simply must translate to get through the period, an exhausting procedure that does not result in second language acquisition. And we wonder why teachers burn out so quickly! The real solution is to set up a plan similar to the Eastman plan, with team teaching. But let us consider the situation in which this is not possible. We will return to the principles underlying successful programs and see to what extent we can work toward them for our limited-English-proficient children.

The beginner

We can mimic the Eastman plan to some extent with the beginner. Of course, the art, music, and PE parts of the day will be

Table 1. The "Eastman" plan

stage	*mainstream*	*ESL/sheltered*	*first language*
beginning	art, music, PE	ESL	all core subjects
intermediate	art, music, PE	ESL, math, science	language arts, social studies
advanced	art, music, PE, development	ESL, social studies, language arts	continuing L1 math, science
mainstream	all subjects		continuing L1 development

the same regardless of whether the Eastman plan can be used or not; the children will be together for this part of the day. Comprehensible-input-based ESL can be of great help, even if it is done on a pull-out basis. The time to pull out the limited English speakers is the time of day when more proficient English speakers are doing the subject matter that requires the most abstract use of language and that will be the least comprehensible for the new second language acquirer: language arts and social studies.

When primary language instruction is not possible, there is still a great deal that can be done to get some of the positive effects of bilingual education.

When beginners in English are with the other children, we can make life easier on them and us and help their language acquisition by allowing a "silent period" and not forcing language production. When the children do begin to speak, we can help by not insisting on complete sentences and not correcting errors. If the teacher understands some of the child's first language, there is no reason not to utilize the natural approach procedure of allowing the child to respond in the first language. This will greatly facilitate communication.

Home use of the first language When primary language instruction is not possible, there is still a great deal that can be done to get some of the positive effects of bilingual education. First, we can encourage the use of the first language at home. Parents often ask if they should use more English at home, thinking that this will speed up English language development in their children. Unless the parent speaks English extremely well, switching to English has the danger of disturbing parent-child communication, which cripples both cognitive and emotional development. This view is confirmed by the research. Several studies show that when parents switch to exclusive use of the language of the country, school performance suffers (Cummins, 1981). We would much rather teach a child in kindergarten who does not speak English but who is well-adjusted and ready for school than a child who has picked up some English (from imperfect models) but who has not been communicating very well with his parents.

Helpers Another way we can make use of the first language without a full bilingual program is the judicious use of paraprofessionals and other helpers. If we have a helper who speaks the child's first language, we should use that helper to provide background knowledge and literacy in the child's first language. This help will usually be most effective in those subjects requiring the most use of abstract language: social studies and language arts.

Even when little help is available, it can be very valuable. Consider the case of a class with three Korean-speaking children who know little English. They are progressing fairly well in mathematics, because of their good background in their first language and because math does not require a high level of language ability in early grades. Assume we have a paraprofessional who speaks Korean and is available only one morning per week for one hour. My suggestion is that we inform the helper what will take place the following week in social studies. If it is the Civil War, the helper uses the one hour on Monday to provide the children with background information, in Korean, about the Civil War: who the combatants were, what the issues were, etc. This will make the history lessons much more comprehensible.

Classmates who speak the limited-English-proficient child's first language can help and sometimes do spontaneously. The first principle to follow is to allow this to occur. It is not a good policy to forbid the use of the first language in school: "English only" rules are not good for English. Peer help should be done the same way we do it in bilingual education programs: as a source of background information and academic knowledge in the first language, not as on-line translation.

There is also nothing wrong with an occasional translation in class: Teachers need not waste time in frustrating pantomime and paraphrase when the meaning of the word resists normal efforts and the teacher or another student knows the word in the child's first language. The problem is when the occasional translation becomes concurrent translation and there is no need to listen to the second language input.

Intermediates

One of the advantages of including sustained silent reading in the school day is that it automatically handles a great deal of heterogeneity. When children select what they want to read themselves, because they do not want to be bored or confused (Smith, 1994), they will select books that are interesting and comprehensible. There is very good evidence, in addition, that children do not simply choose the easiest possible books: Free reading is not always easy reading (Krashen, in press).

We should encourage children to read in their first language, as well as in English, during sustained silent reading. This procedure will help a great deal. First, it builds literacy in the primary language, and as we have argued

previously, literacy in the first language transfers to the second language. Second, reading is an excellent source of knowledge. Third, those who read a great deal in their first language probably will read a great deal in the second language.

When our limited-English-proficient students start doing free reading in English, they face a serious problem: the lack of books that are both comprehensible and interesting. Older students will find English books written for children their age too difficult and may find easier books less interesting. There is a solution: comic books. Many (but not all) comics are ideal for the second language acquirer.

There is nothing to fear from comic books. Research shows that children who read comics read as much, and sometimes more, than other children (Krashen, 1993; Ujiie and Krashen, in press). Comics provide a foundation that makes book reading much more comprehensible.

Light reading will not, in itself, produce the highest levels of competence. But it is an important bridge between basic conversational language and more advanced academic language. It is also very likely to be missing from the lives of language minority students, because of financial constraints and, in some cases, because of a view of light reading as unessential and "not serious." It is clear from the research, however, that light reading does not prevent heavier reading and that, in fact, it can act as a conduit to heavier reading.

Free reading is so powerful that it is likely that limited-English-proficient children in schools with a plentiful supply of interesting reading in the first language, plus a minimal bilingual program, will do better than children in a school with a "full" bilingual program but with few books in the first language. This is an easy way to get some of the advantages of bilingual education in cases where full programs are not possible.

What won't work

I have tried to illustrate some ways of helping limited-English proficient students. Let me now devote some time to discussing what won't help.

Create the need

Many people assume that we need to create situations in which children "need" to speak and communicate in English, assuming that language acquisition happens when we are forced to reproduce the language. This happens a great deal in "submersion" programs where no effort is made to make input comprehensible and no silent period is allowed.

But need alone is not enough—comprehensible input must be present. I cannot teach you to speak Russian simply by pointing a gun at your head and insisting you speak Russian. If, however, I speak to you in Russian in a way that is comprehensible, and make the message extremely interesting, you will acquire some Russian, whether you want to or not. Our focus should be on providing comprehensible input, not a highly stressed situation in which children do not understand what is going on.

> *We should encourage children to read in their first language, as well as in English, during sustained silent reading.*

Time pressure

Politicians commonly propose laws that proclaim that limited-English-proficient students be "at grade level" or transitioned out of bilingual programs in a certain amount of time, usually three years. This estimate is entirely arbitrary. How long a child takes is a matter of the literacy level he or she comes to school with, previous schooling, the print environment of the school, and the quality of the program.

Imposing time limits is based on the premise that LEP students will only acquire English if they are forced to, that they really don't want English. Actually, the opposite is true. LEP students typically have a strong drive for English. They don't need force and time constraints. They need a print-rich environment that provides them with comprehensible input.

Summary

We can utilize the principles underlying successful programs in dealing with cases in which full programs are not possible. Application of these principles in less than ideal situations will not make these situations ideal, but will improve life for both teachers and students. Unlike so many prescriptions given to teachers, the proposals presented here do not increase the teacher's burden. In fact, they reduce it.

Some proposals actually involve doing less:

- Not correcting oral or written errors made by language minority students;
- Not insisting on complete sentences when they speak in class;
- Encouraging free voluntary reading in both the first and second language.

There is no need to mark stacks of papers for grammatical errors, and teachers are given ten minutes (approximately) per day for pleasure reading!

References

Cummins, J. "The Role of Primary Language Development in Promoting Educational Success for Language Minority Students." *Schooling and Language Minority Students.* Sacramento, CA: California Department of Education, 1981. 3–49.

Goodman, K. *Language and Literacy.* London: Routledge and Kegan, 1982.

Krashen, S. "Is Free Reading Always Easy Reading?" *California English.* In Press.

___. *The Power of Reading.* Englewood, CO: Libraries Unlimited, 1993.

___."Sheltered Subject Matter Teaching" *Cross Currents* 18 (1991): 183–189.

Krashen, S., and D. Biber *On Course: Bilingual Education's Success in California.* Ontario, CA: California Association for Bilingual Education, 1988.

Lagarretta, D. "The Effects of Program Models on Language Acquisition by Spanish Speaking Children." *TESOL Quarterly* 8 (1979): 521-576.

Smith, F. *Understanding Reading.* 5th edition. Hillsdale, NJ: Erbaum, 1994.

Ujiie, J., and S. Krashen. "Comic Book Reading, Reading Enjoyment, and Pleasure Reading Among Middle Class and Chapter I Middle School Students." *Reading Improvement.* In Press.

Dr. Stephen Krashen

Poor Spelling?

Dr. Rebecca Bowers Sipe
ANCHORAGE SCHOOL DISTRICT,
DEPT. OF CURRICULUM AND INSTRUCTION
ANCHORAGE, ALASKA

Few curricular issues elicit as much concern or cause as much frustration as spelling. While spelling represents a small part of our curricular focus at the secondary level, students who repeatedly demonstrate poor spelling are subject to a host of criticisms.

In a print-intensive society such as ours, inability to spell may place an individual at risk: at risk of appearing uneducated or unconcerned; at risk of being labeled a poor writer and—potentially—at risk of becoming a poor thinker. Society makes few allowances for those who are poor spellers. As classroom teachers, it is imperative that we understand the dilemma confronting poor spellers and that we develop a repertoire of strategies to help struggling writers.

A Nation Obsessed

Despite Benjamin Franklin's suggestion that "an educated man should be able to spell any word at least six ways," today both schools and businesses maintain high expectations for spelling. With such high expectations, one might wonder how widespread spelling problems are in the United States. Dr. Thomas Kelly estimates that between 15 percent and 20 percent of the American population have significant difficulty with routine spelling. He calls these folks "closet bad spellers" (Kelly, 1992). Unfortunately, many poor spellers go through life assuming that their inability to spell condemns them to a lifetime of poor writing.

What does this mean for teachers of English? Certainly, writers need to be understood by readers. The presence of misspelled words in a final draft is a source of distraction and irritation. As teachers, we must help students gain control over spelling while we support them as emerging writers.

Spelling as a Writing Skill

Spelling is a writing skill and gains importance only when we write. Students deserve opportunities to explore the process of writing that works best for them. When students identify the process that works for them, they have a tool for life. Without this tool, each writing experience holds the potential for being a frustrating and mystifying ordeal.

While students need many opportunities to write for a variety of audiences and purposes in order to sense the differences in the requirements of each (Moffett, 1992), spelling gains importance in more formal modes. It is important for young writers to understand that final draft pieces represent them as writers. In such works correctness takes on significance.

Establishing Strategies

Providing poor spellers with appropriate resources is a must. Resources such as dictionaries, spelling checks, and personal spelling lists are valuable tools. Computers provide writers with ease in revision only dreamed of in years past; they allow poor spellers to concentrate on the total process of composing, not just on the spelling. In addition to resources, there are many instructional strategies available to help students who are poor spellers. These include word study, use of mnemonic devices, and multi-modality approaches. **At the primary level, phonics is a valuable tool for spelling.** Unfortunately, English is an eclectic language; as a student's written vocabulary becomes more sophisticated, phonics becomes a less reliable tool (Gentry, 1981). Poor spellers must go beyond phonics to overcome spelling difficulties.

Studying word families helps students to identify connections and patterns in language. When the word *honor* is studied, students may discuss *honorable, honoring, honored,* and *honorary.*

> *As teachers, we must help students gain control over spelling while we support them as emerging writers.*

From one word base, five new words are added to the written repertoire. Ideally, walls are covered with word webs so that students are literally surrounded with language.

Mnemonic devices often help students with the spelling of difficult words. I looked up the word *accommodate* every time I wrote it for most of my life until someone suggested that I had to remember to accommodate the twins. That's all it took. Now I remember to double both consonants every time. As children, many of us invented phrases to help us with the spelling of words such as arithmetic and geography. Teachers who encourage students to create pictures or jingles for confusing words make spelling less threatening and more fun.

For some learners, strategies must rely on tactile strengths. I have observed children tracing words in the palm of one hand with a finger from the other. These students rely on the feel of a word instead of on the visual image.

Different strategies will work for different learners, thus making a wide variety of instructional strategies necessary for use in the classroom. Tests or tasks that separate learners from the resources they need measure little and may actually hamper the student's progress as a writer.

Classroom Practice

What can we do in the classroom to encourage poor spellers?

- **Recognize that spelling is a writing skill and must be addressed as a part of the writing process.** Adult writers frequently use invented spelling in early drafts to hold the place of a word; young writers may find this a helpful strategy to use in rough drafts. Young writers need to understand that good writing often takes multiple revisions and that spelling really matters in the final draft.
- **Encourage students to maintain and use personal word lists and to analyze their errors**. Students should identify words they routinely use but have difficulty spelling. These words should become part of the student's core words for study. Since spelling is a developmental skill, not all students will be at the same place at the same time. It is important to recognize that spelling errors are not made at random. Helping students analyze the types of errors they make enables them to recognize their strengths and work on their weaknesses. Error analysis teaches proofreading skills by focusing attention on identification of words spelled correctly and analyzing the reasons why other words are misspelled (Shaughnessy, 1977). Much can be learned about the developmental level of students by studying the patterns of word invention they use. Students should be helped to understand that correct spelling speeds up the writing process. It enables the writer to get words down without having to worry about them. Weber and Henderson refer to this as automaticity, a critical level of development that frees the writer to concentrate on meaning instead of on spelling.
- **Concentrate on high-frequency words that are relevant to student writing.** Lists of such words are easily obtainable and form the basis of most current commercial programs. Dr. Earnest Horn developed one of the earliest lists around 1900. High-frequency words change little over time. As few as one thousand words constitute 90 percent of the words used in everyday writing; five thousand words account for 99.2 percent (Horn, 1926).
- **Make a distinction between vocabulary words and spelling words.** Vocabulary instruction is important, but vocabulary lists are an inappropriate substitute for spelling words. Students may be able to read and use a word long before they are able to spell it correctly.

Spelling skill has nothing to do with intelligence. Being a poor speller does not condemn one to being a **poor** writer any more than being a good speller guarantees that one will be a **good** writer. Nonetheless, students must understand that people will make judgments about them based on their writing. Knowing our needs and using appropriate strategies and resources will help students improve their spelling. Fortunately, there are numerous strategies available to learners.

References

Gentry, R. J. "Learning to Spell Developmentally." *The Reading Teacher* January 1981: 378–381.

Horn, E. "A Basic Writing Vocabulary." *University of Iowa Monographs in Education, First Series* April 1926: 4.

Kelly, T.F. "Spelling: Tyranny of the Irrelevant." *The Effective School Report* August 1992: 3.

Moffett, J., and B.J. Wagner. *Student-Centered Language Arts, K-12.* Portsmouth, MA: Boynton/Cook, 1992.

Shaughnessy, M. P. *Spelling: Errors and Expectations.* New York: Oxford University Press, 1979.

Weber, W. R., and E. H. Henderson. "A Computer-Based Program of Word Study: Effects on Reading and Writing." *Reading Psychology* 10 (1989): 157–171.

Dr. Rebecca Bowers Sipe

The Integration of Assessment and Instruction

> *What could more solidly assure that assessment reflects and measures instructional goals than to make it a part of instruction?*

Dr. Roger Farr
Indiana University

Assessment of student reading and writing has been important to educators and the public at large since the beginning of this century. Educators have needed some way to determine whether they are meeting their goals and objectives, and the public has wanted some means of making schools accountable for the considerable investment needed to maintain them. The development of large, standardized, very-short-answer tests has been one answer to these demands. They report normed scores that can be compared to a large national sample of students. Similar tests have been developed in most states as criterion-referenced measures that require a student to respond to an arbitrated number of particular educational objectives.

However, at the same time, emerging theory has persuasively described how language abilities actually develop, leading to new emphasis on teaching and measuring language performance as a process—not with the short-answer response typical of most tests used as accountability measures.

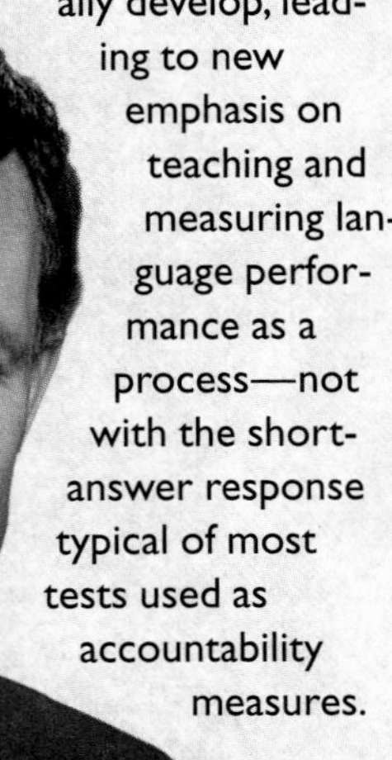

Writing tests have been around since 1915 and are now used in at least 35 states. There is new emphasis on writing on college entrance exams. Across all grades reading, writing, and thinking are being integrated in classroom instruction as a combined process.

Teachers have not defensively closed their ears to the critics' and general public's concern for accountability in the schools, however. They have been the primary constructors of city and state criterion-referenced measures attempting to measure and reflect the curricula they also helped structure. Through these tests, they have sought to raise their students' performances and scores on standardized tests and have analyzed the results for their implications for teaching.

Meanwhile, teachers have continued to use a variety of daily classroom assessments to inform their teaching. These include observation and a host of other informal techniques and assessments accompanying the texts they use. Teachers have tended to react to the increased instructional time that testing consumes by making their classroom assessment a valid learning experience for the student and an instructional opportunity. What could more solidly assure that assessment reflect and measure instructional goals than to make it a part of instruction?

This dynamic trend in school assessment goes far beyond merely using test results as indicators of what needs to be taught or retaught. It assesses student progress on an ongoing basis as youngsters use language to construct meaning by reading, writing, and thinking every day! The teacher assesses both by observing the process and by analyzing the product.

Often this effort involves having their students keep portfolios that include many types of writing. Much of this writing reacts to and applies information from different texts that the students have read. Frequently included, too, in student portfolios are one or more of a variety of journals. These portfolios are of two general types:

- The *working portfolio* contains all the drafts of a particular piece of writing and ideas for future writing and intentions for future reading. It has records (logs) of reading and writing and journal entries or brief descriptions, observations, or sketches that can be expanded or used in other ways. It is like an artist's studio full of works in progress and works finished.
- The *show portfolio* can be designed to serve numerous purposes: It can be a selection of pieces to demonstrate to parents and/or administrators how a student's language use is developing. It can introduce a student to a new teacher or school. It is like a show that an artist mounts from the works kept in his or her studio.

Teachers are learning that there is a host of ways that portfolios and publishing efforts can be analyzed to assess their students' progress as language users. Most of these projects involve rewriting and provide drafts leading to the more finished product, a set that reveals both language product and the process that leads to it.

Language-processing experiences can culminate in some sort of publishing to communicate with peers and other audiences. Classroom newsletters, creative writing magazines, and other publications develop audience awareness and a keen sense of purpose for writing. Frequently, these experiences involve the interaction of students reacting to and editing each other's work as on-going and interactive assessment. Since all this hinges on the belief that the best way to learn to read, write, and think is to do as much of it as possible, just noting the quantity and fluency of student production is highly revealing.

There are many other observations and analyses that teachers can make that systemize this kind of assessment to a degree that supports its use in reporting progress to parents and other educators. Almost all portfolios include logs of what students read. Teachers are now encouraged to set up opportunities for their students to keep such records. These include notes on their reaction to numerous texts, and writing/thinking efforts in which they apply the meaning they have constructed by reading. This basic language/thinking process often involves both synthesis of texts and critical reaction to them. More often than not, it promotes an appreciation of and critical reaction to literature as well as the use of good writing as a model and as the ignition to an original student effort.

Of course, good teachers have long used these kinds of activities. What is new, it appears, is the emphasis on integrating language/thinking processing and on assessing while instructing!

Publishers have come to a similar understanding about language use and assessment. They have developed interactive performance assessments that use text as prompts for student writing. These are usually presented with a prescribed writing task that identifies a believable audience and that is designed to seem highly valid to the student. Most often these prompts present several pieces of writing that may represent several genres. The student's thinking abilities are engaged by a task that calls for synthesis of and critical reaction to the texts in order to recommend some solution to an authentic problem.

In order to help the teacher analyze the student's performance on these interactive performance assessments, they are accompanied by a rubric that describes several ranks (or scores) for student responses for each of several key factors. For example, a student's response may be ranked from 3 (high) to 1 (low) on its indication (a) of how well the student has comprehended the text or texts, (b) of how well the student has written the response, and (c) of how well comprehension and writing have been integrated to accomplish the assigned task. Each rank for each factor may be described according to several subfactors: in writing, for example, the response may be ranked after considering organization, diction, and mechanics.

A second guide to scoring is even more helpful than the rubric. These assessments are given to a large and varied sample of students at the grade level for which each is created. Then a team of teachers or other specialists selects several sample or anchor papers to demonstrate each score of the ranking system for each factor. These are presented with analytical comments in a booklet with the rubric and are made available to teachers who use the assessment.

Most importantly, portfolios and performance assessment develop the habit of self-assessing so that students go through life interested in personal development as readers,writers, and thinkers.

Some teachers and groups of teachers are developing these integrated performance assessments on their own. Some of them use published assessments as their models. Although the process is not easy, teachers who have done it remark about how much the experience teaches them about their instructional values and goals.

The ranked results of performance assessments can be reported to parents, administrators, critics of education, and the public at large. The model or anchor papers and rubrics stand as a clear and revealing explication of what the ranks mean if those who would rely on them make the effort to understand the data being used. Thus, integrated performance assessment can serve to inform accountability interests along with scores from standardized and criterion-referenced assessment.

Most importantly, portfolios and performance assessment develop the habit of self-assessing so that students go through life interested in personal development as readers, writers, and thinkers. This awareness can occur only when the student believes that the goals and objectives against which progress is being measured are real, interesting, and empowering.

Portfolios do that in the extreme if the student is allowed to maintain an important degree of control over the collection. Equally important to the success of the portfolio in developing self-assessment is regular student-teacher conferencing to discuss the portfolio contents, analyze progress, and set new goals.

Integrated performance assessments can achieve this if they are built around interesting prompts and if the tasks seem valid. The results of these student efforts, which usually include drafts that can be analyzed for process, can be studied and discussed by the student and the teacher in conference; and their appropriateness for student self-analysis is emphasized when a student is encouraged to include the set in his or her portfolio.

While legislators and educators together struggle with attempts to create assessments that can report on educational progress and accountability, teachers have been demonstrating dynamic new emphases in integrating language and thinking processes while turning assessment into highly effective instruction.

Dr. Roger Farr

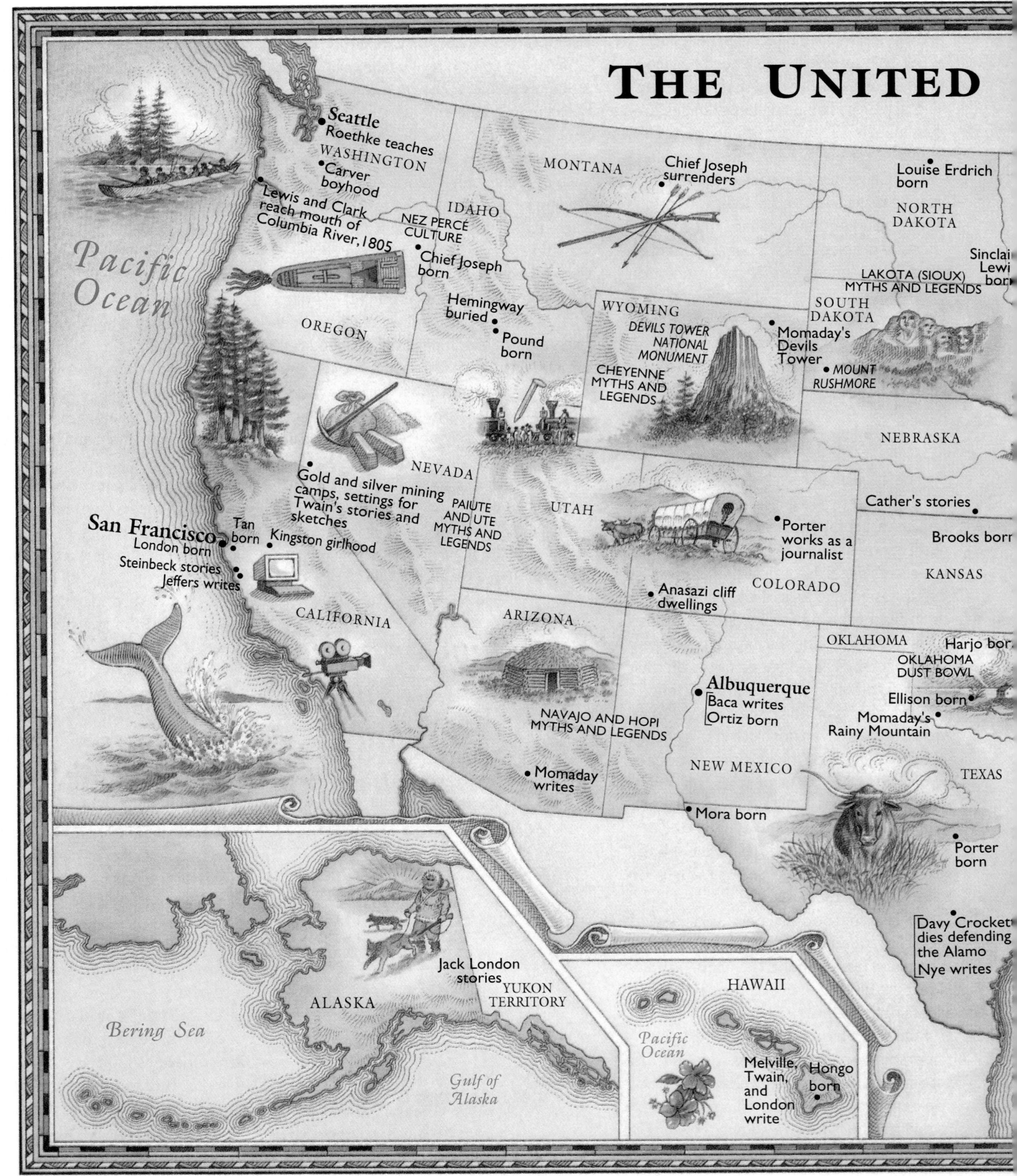

xxiv THE UNITED STATES

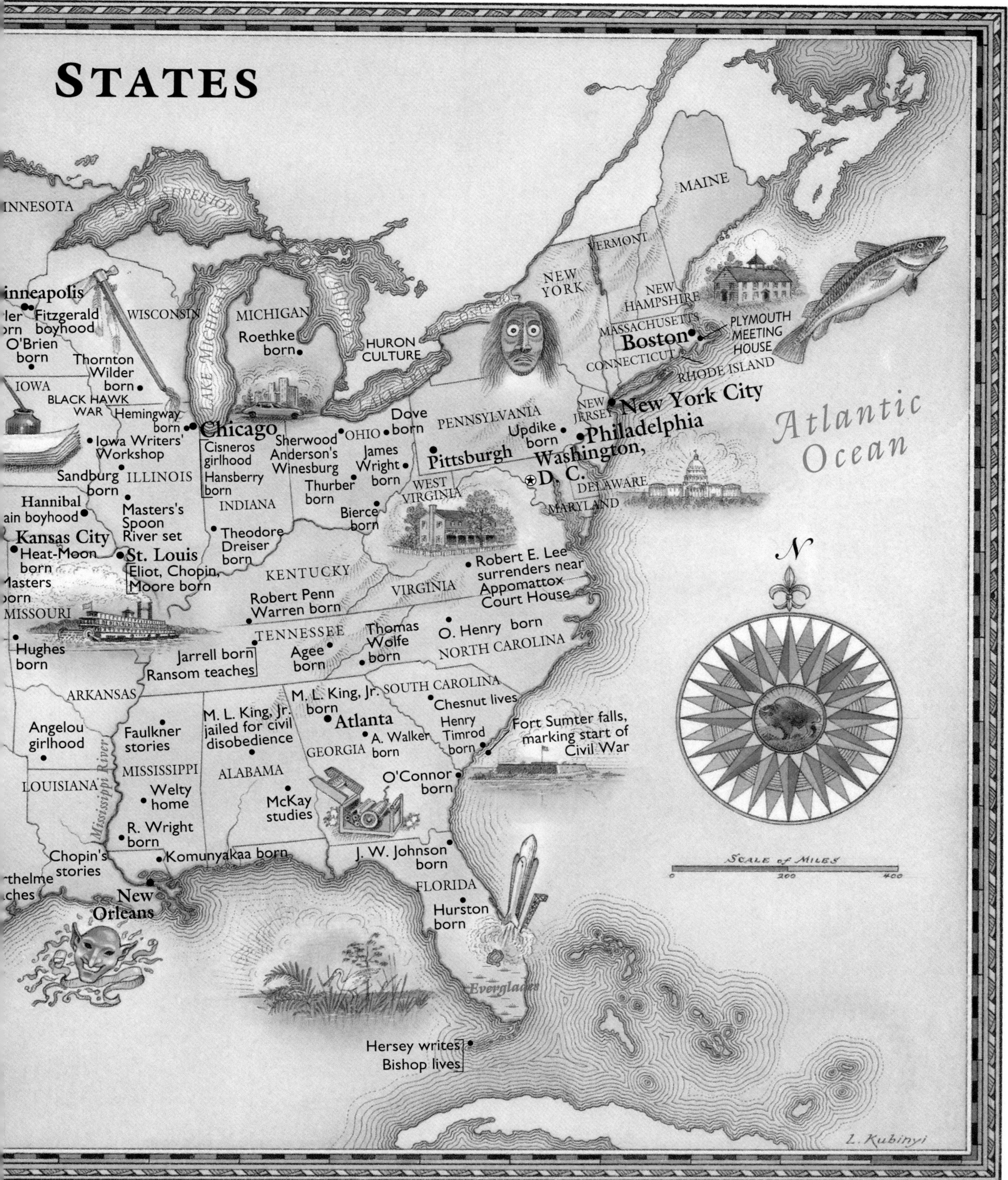

THE UNITED STATES xxv

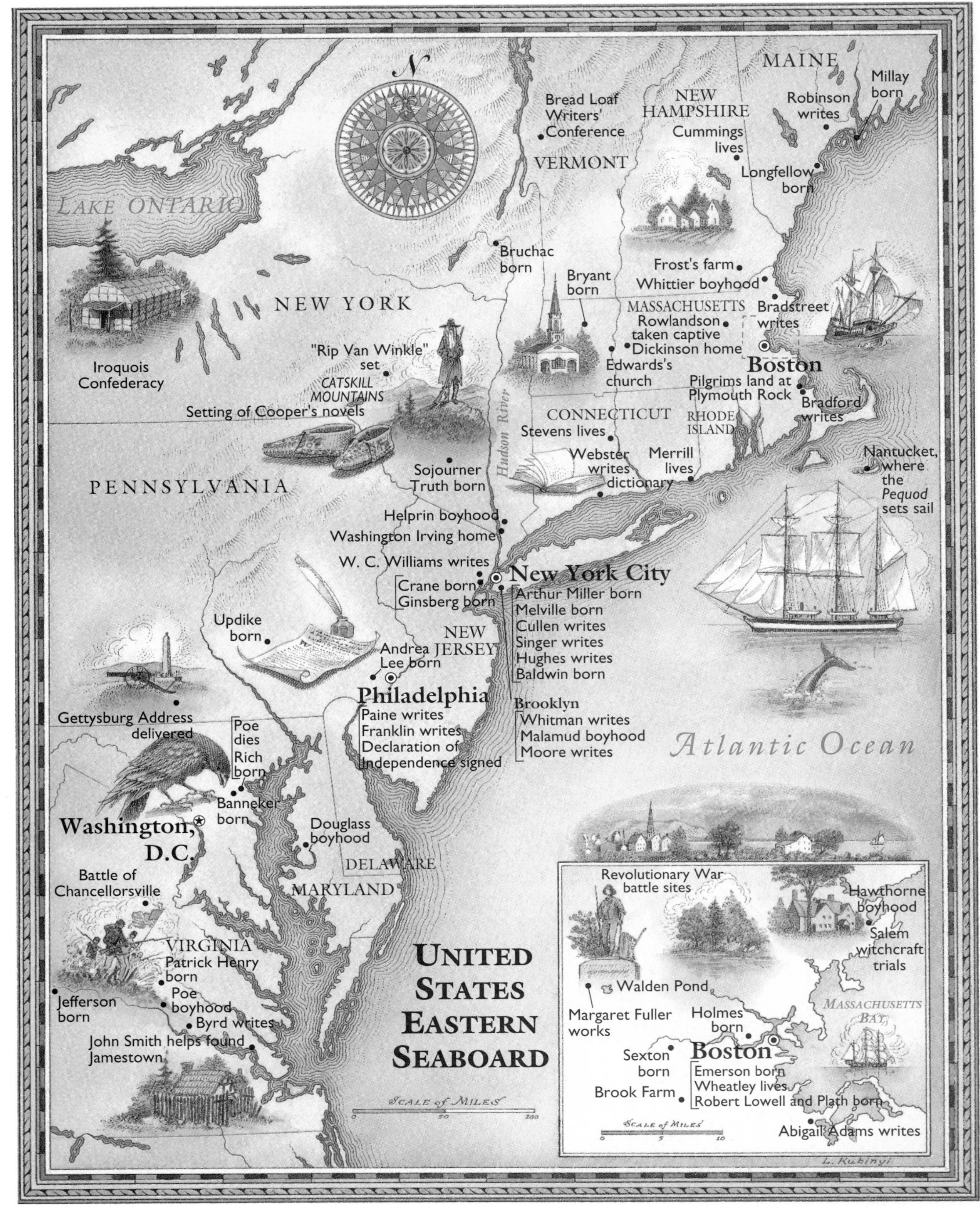

xxvi **UNITED STATES EASTERN SEABOARD**

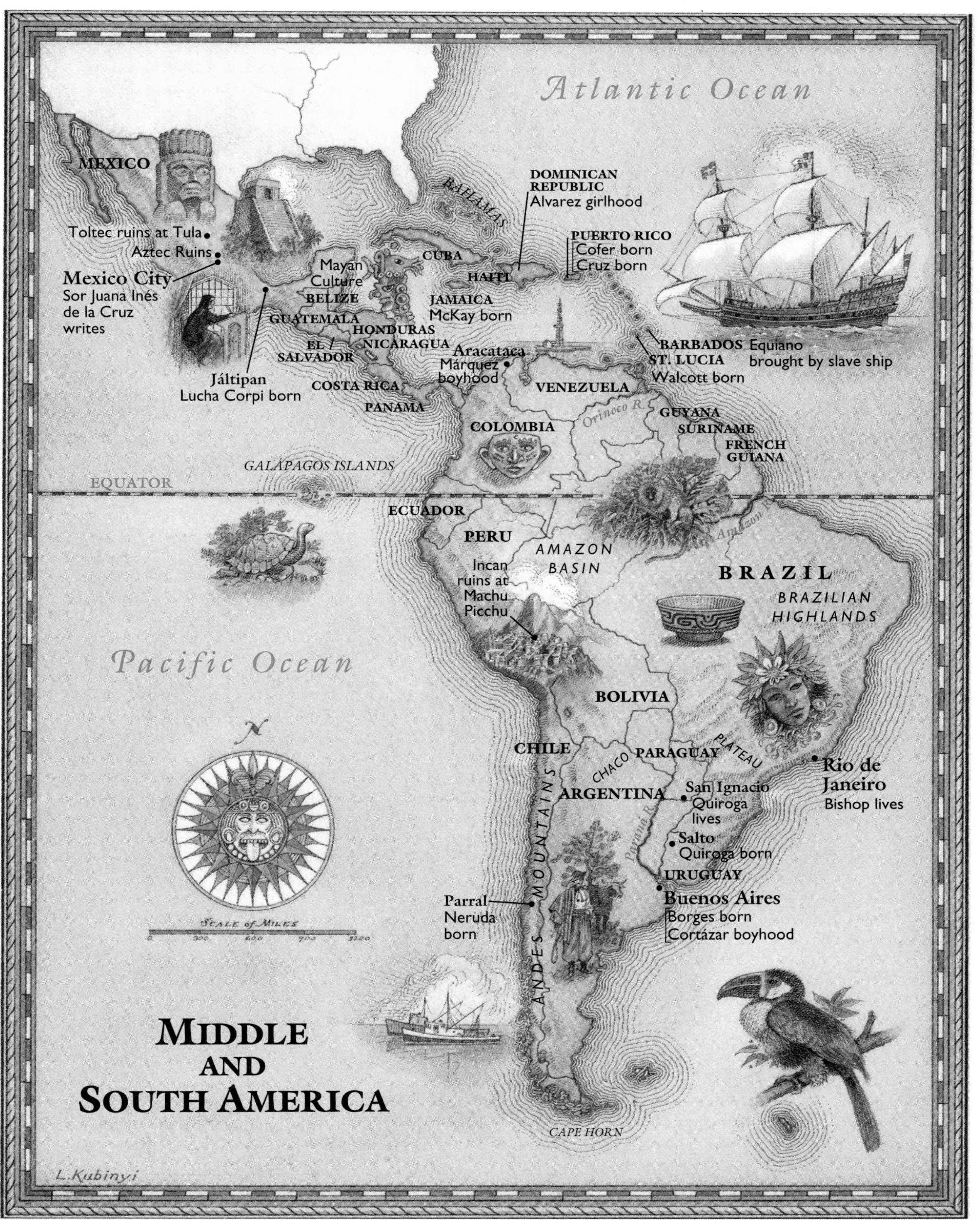

MIDDLE AND SOUTH AMERICA xxvii

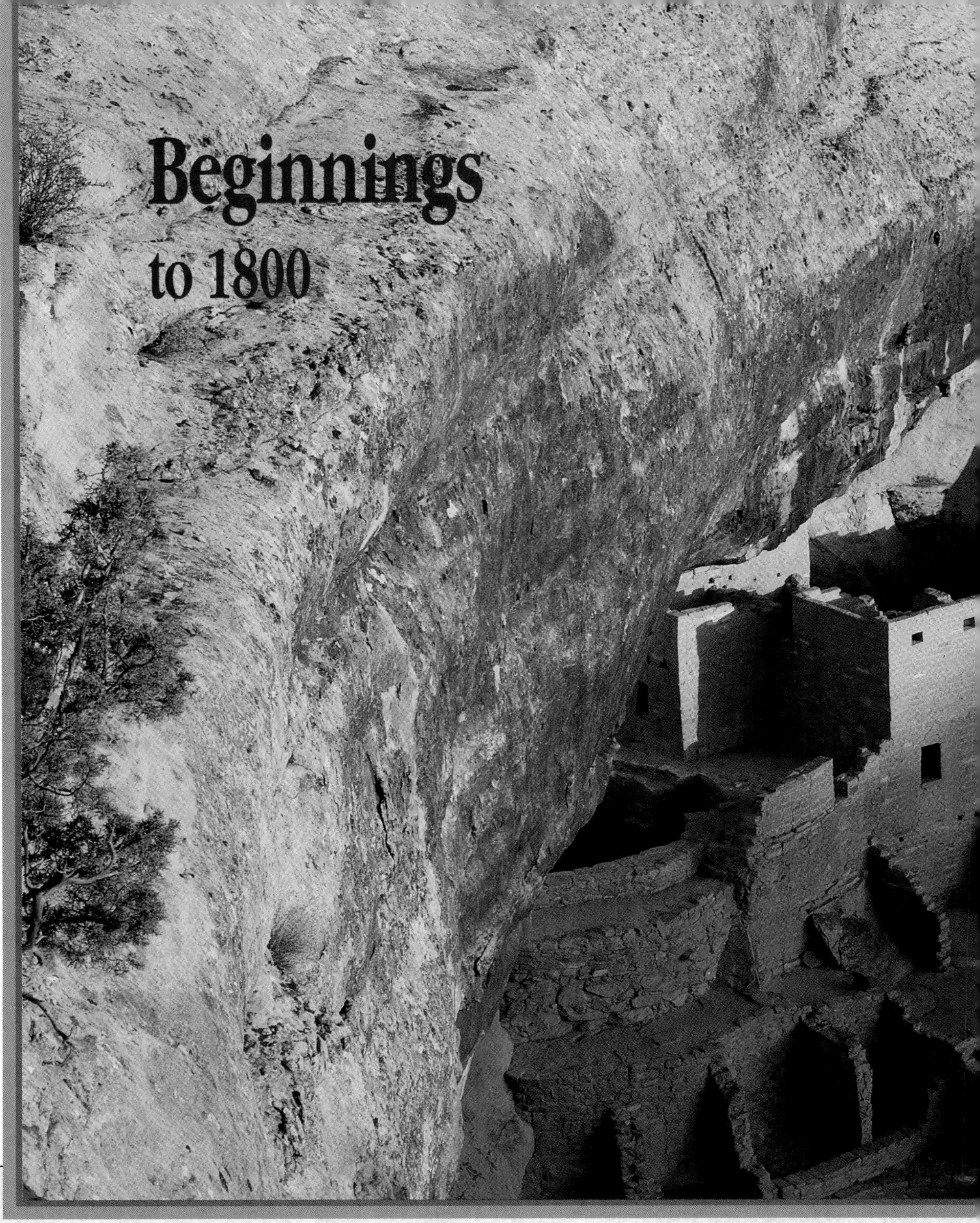

Beginnings
to 1800

***Elements of Literature:* Videodisc** Use the following bar codes to locate an exploration of the American dream interpreted in literature on the videodisc. For more information, see the Videodisc *Teacher's Manual.*

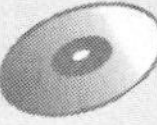

Videodisc Side A

	Part 1	Part 2
Begin Play English Track		
Begin Play Spanish Track		

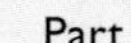

This ancient city was built about A.D. 1100 by a pueblo people known as Anasazi ("the old ones"). By 1300, three hundred years before the Pilgrims landed on Plymouth Rock, this beautiful city had been mysteriously abandoned.

Cliff Palace at Mesa Verde National Park, Colorado. © David Muench Photography.

1

ABOUT THE PHOTOGRAPH: EXPLORING THE SUBJECT

The Anasazi had been a nomadic people prior to settling down in Mesa Verde around A.D. 550. They became farmers, growing corn, beans, squash, and cotton. They also raised turkeys and hunted deer and mountain sheep with bow and arrow.

Cliff Palace, the largest cliff house in Mesa Verde National Park, was, at one time, home for 250 to 300 people. In addition to apartmentlike dwellings, Cliff Palace also had underground rooms, or kivas, where the Anasazi may have held religious ceremonies, conducted healing rites, or prayed for rain or good crops. They also served as gathering rooms and the Anasazi sometimes wove there. While it is not known why the Anasazi left their cliff dwellings, it is known that droughts and crop failures occurred in the region in the last quarter of the thirteenth century.

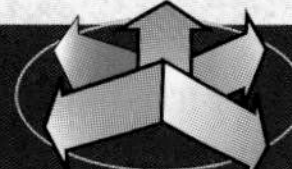

PROGRAM MANAGER

- **Summative Assessment** See **Literary Period Test: Beginnings, *Test Booklet,*** pp. 36–38, for a test on an additional text from the same historical era.
- **Application** For practice of a reading strategy for this unit, see **Becoming a Strategic Reader** worksheet, ***Teaching Resources A,*** pp. 5–6.
- **Performance Assessment** Use Assessment 1 in the ***Integrated Performance Assessment,*** Level F to evaluate reading and writing skills covered in collections 1–4. For help with evaluation, see ***Holistic Scoring Workshop*** software.

Responding to the Quotation

Encourage students to remember the phrase "city upon a hill," for it illustrates the Puritans' vision of their role in the Americas. The phrase comes from the Bible, Matthew 5:14–16, in Jesus' Sermon on the Mount, and its context is important: "You are the light of the world. A city built on a hill cannot be hid. No one after lighting a lamp puts it under the bushel basket, but on the lampstand, and it gives light to all in the house. In the same way, let your light shine before others so that they may see your good works and give glory to your Father in heaven."

What can you gather about the Puritans from Winthrop's quotation? [Possible responses: They feel they must set an example for others. They consider themselves a separate community from non-Puritans. They think that their behavior is very important and that there will be serious consequences if they do not live up to their professed beliefs.]

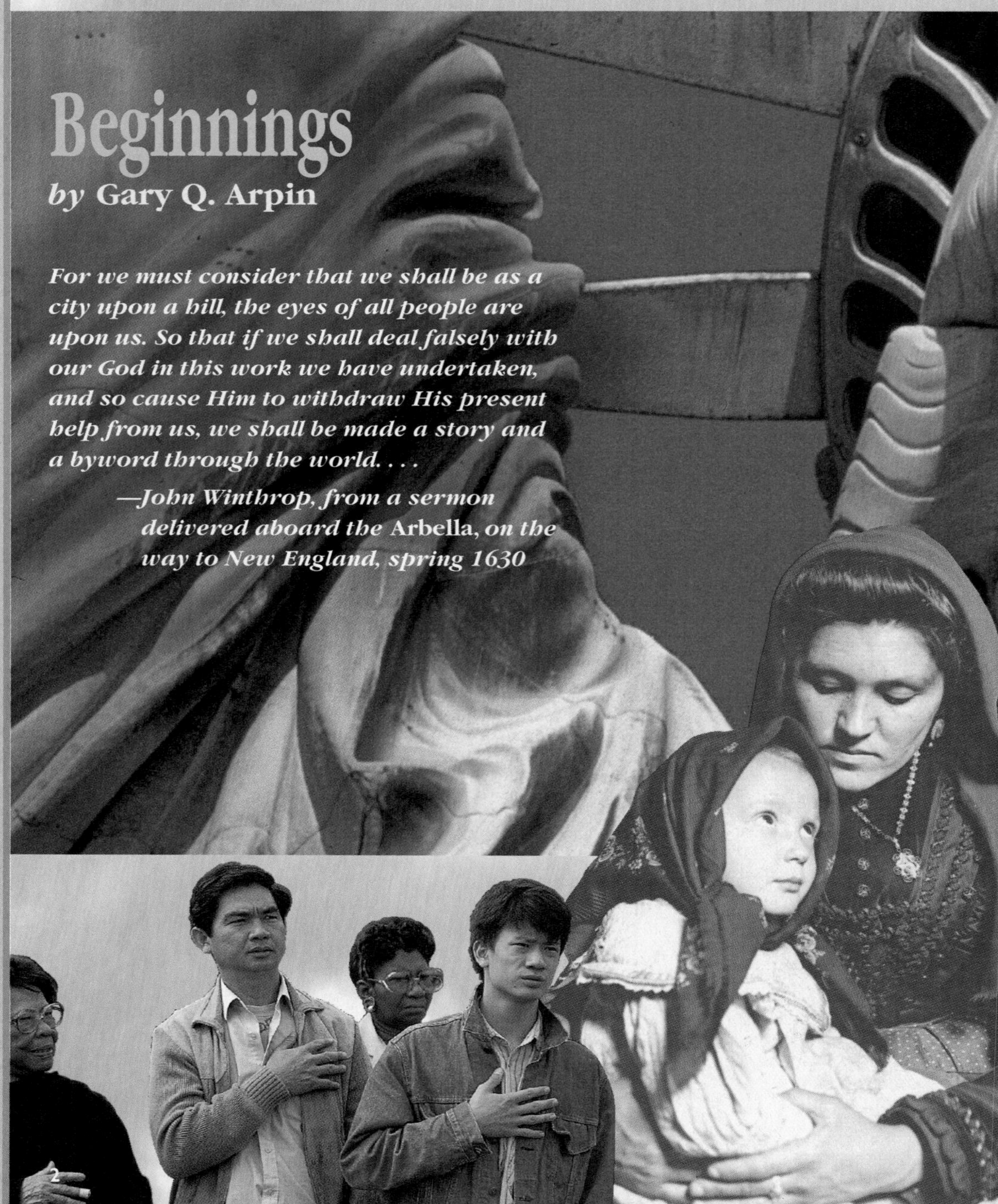

Beginnings

by Gary Q. Arpin

For we must consider that we shall be as a city upon a hill, the eyes of all people are upon us. So that if we shall deal falsely with our God in this work we have undertaken, and so cause Him to withdraw His present help from us, we shall be made a story and a byword through the world. . . .

—John Winthrop, from a sermon delivered aboard the* Arbella*, on the way to New England, spring 1630

2

The United States is a land of immigrants. The first people began entering North America on foot many thousands of years ago. Then came people in wooden sailing ships. Later, millions came against their will in the stifling holds of slave ships. Millions of others, lacking money for better accommodations, endured weeks of discomfort in cramped, uncomfortable steerage sections of ships. The latest immigrants probably are arriving by plane or even on flimsy rafts as you read these words. Most likely you, your relatives, or some of your classmates immigrated to this country.

The Granger Collection, New York.

RESPONDING TO THE PHOTOGRAPHS: VISUAL LITERACY

From these photographs, what conclusions can you draw about the people who immigrate to the United States? [Possible responses: Many people of different nationalities, races, and backgrounds migrate to the United States; or the photos show how hopeful some immigrants are about reaching the United States.] What do you think attracted the people in the photographs to the United States? [Possible responses: Personal liberty, economic opportunities, democracy, job and educational opportunities, a need for change.]

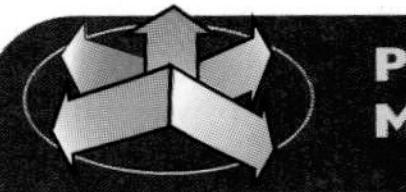

PROGRAM MANAGER

- **Planning Instruction** See Teaching Notes, *Teaching Resources A*, pp. 1–2, for additional teaching options about Beginnings.
- **Assessment** For assessment of the literary and historical events mentioned in the historical introduction, see Literary Period Introduction Test, *Test Booklet*, pp. 1–2.

Elements of Literature:
Videodisc Use the bar codes below to build background knowledge on the time period. For more information, see the Videodisc *Teacher's Manual.*

Videodisc Side A
Begin Play
English Track

Begin Play
Spanish Track

Time Line

• 1450–1615
In 1517, Martin Luther posted his Ninety-five Theses, a critique of the Roman Catholic Church. The invention of print helped spread Luther's ideas, contributing to the growth of the Reformation. The belief in salvation through faith and not through work overturned medieval beliefs and led to the rise of Protestant churches. In turn, the decreased influence of the Roman Catholic Church paved the way for separation of church and state.

• 1615–1699
Newton's principles revolutionized science and mathematics, and his ideas form the foundation of modern physics. His findings profoundly affect every aspect of science and engineering. Newton's discovery of these laws has made it possible for engineers and architects to design cars, trains, rockets, roller coasters, elevators, and high-rise buildings.

• 1730–1749
Montesquieu reclassified governments (traditionally classified as monarchy, aristocracy, and democracy) and based each on a principle: A republic is based on virtue; a monarchy on honor; and despotism on fear. He also classified powers as legislative, judicial, and executive, and he stated that these powers must be held by different individuals or groups and must act independently of each other. Montesquieu also wrote that climate influences the character of a society, but that this influence decreases as civilization progresses and laws, religion, and government hold more power.

Beginnings to 1800

Reverend Jonathan Edwards (1750-1755) by Joseph Badger. Oil on canvas.
Yale University Art Gallery, Bequest of Eugene Phelps Edwards (1938.74).

Literary Events

1450–1615

Spain's Miguel de Cervantes publishes his novel *Don Quixote*, in two parts, 1605, 1615

•

England's William Shakespeare writes *King Lear* and *Macbeth*, 1605–1606

1615–1699

Mary Rowlandson's captivity narrative is published, 1682

•

Anne Bradstreet's *The Tenth Muse Lately Sprung Up in America* is published in England, 1650

•

William Bradford writes *Of Plymouth Plantation*, 1630–1647

1700–1729

William Byrd writes *The History of the Dividing Line*, 1729

•

England's Jonathan Swift publishes the satiric novel *Gulliver's Travels*, 1726

•

England's Daniel Defoe publishes *Robinson Crusoe*, considered one of the first English novels, 1719

1730–1749

England's Henry Fielding publishes the novel *The History of Tom Jones*, 1749

•

Jonathan Edwards delivers his vivid sermon, "Sinners in the Hands of an Angry God," 1741

Cultural/Historical Events

1450–1615

Christopher Columbus lands on an island in the Bahamas, 1492

•

Songhai Empire in West Africa reaches peak, c. 1493–1528

•

Protestant Reformation starts in Germany, 1517

•

Aztec Empire falls to Spanish army, 1521

•

Cabeza de Vaca lands in Florida, 1528

•

Settlement founded at Jamestown, Virginia, 1607

1615–1699

Mayflower Pilgrims land at Plymouth, 1620

•

Great Migration of Puritans to New England begins, c. 1630

•

Mughal emperor Shah Jahan builds Taj Mahal, in northern India, 1632–1638

•

Metacomet's war on Massachusetts Colonies begins, 1675

•

England's Isaac Newton explains laws of motion and gravity in *Principia Mathematica*, 1687

•

Slavery exists in all English colonies in North America, 1690

•

Twenty people executed in witch trials in Salem, Massachusetts, 1692

1700–1729

About 251,000 European settlers live in what is now the United States, 1700

•

Smallpox epidemic hits Boston, 1721

•

German composer Johann Sebastian Bach completes the oratorio *St. Matthew Passion*, 1729

1730–1749

The Great Awakening is touched off by a traveling English preacher, 1740–1745

•

George Frideric Handel's *Messiah* is first performed, in Dublin, Ireland, 1742

•

France's Charles de Montesquieu publishes *The Spirit of Laws*, a study of government later reflected in the U.S. Constitution, 1748

Arresting a witch in the streets of Salem.
The Granger Collection, New York.

USING THE TIME LINE

Have students group themselves according to fields they are interested in, such as science, government, religion, philosophy, fine arts, and music. Have the groups generate a list of significant events in their field of specialization between 1450 and 1800 that are not listed on the time line. Have them discuss among themselves the impact of each event. Depending on the amount of time you have, they could generate this list from information they already have, or they could conduct research. For example, students interested in science and technology can contribute the invention of reusable type and a press that could make repeated impressions by Johannes Gutenberg in the 1440s and 1450s; invention of reusable type and the press sped up the process of duplicating the written word and allowed more people access to print. Transfer the dates listed in the pupil's edition onto kraft paper, and hang the time line on the wall. Ask the groups to add their dates and events to the kraft paper and to explain to the class the significance of the events.

Benjamin Franklin's sister-in-law Anne Franklin becomes first woman to edit a newspaper in America, 1762

•

England's Samuel Johnson publishes his monumental *Dictionary of the English Language,* 1755

•

John Woolman publishes two antislavery essays, 1754, 1762

Thomas Paine publishes *Common Sense,* 1776

•

Patrick Henry demands liberty from British rule, at the Virginia Convention, 1775

•

Phillis Wheatley publishes *Poems on Various Subjects, Religious and Moral,* 1773

•

Benjamin Franklin begins to write his *Autobiography,* 1771

The Federalist, a series of essays by Alexander Hamilton, James Madison, and John Jay, urges voters to approve the U.S. Constitution, 1787–1788

•

Thomas Jefferson publishes *Notes on the State of Virginia,* 1784–1785

•

France's Michel-Guillaume Jean de Crèvecoeur publishes *Letters from an American Farmer,* 1782

Phillis Wheatley.
The Granger Collection, New York.

England's Samuel Taylor Coleridge publishes *The Rime of the Ancient Mariner,* a long Romantic poem, 1798

1750–1769

Benjamin Franklin's experiments with a kite and a key prove that lightning is a manifestation of electricity, 1752

•

French and Indian War officially ends as British gain control of most French North American territory, 1763

•

American colonists hold Stamp Act Congress to protest a direct British tax, 1765; British repeal tax, 1766

1770–1779

Boston Tea Party occurs in Boston Harbor, 1773

•

First shots of American Revolution fired at Lexington and Concord, Massachusetts, April 19, 1775

•

Second Continental Congress adopts Declaration of Independence, July 4, 1776

Boston Tea Party.
Culver Pictures.

1780–1789

U.S. governed under Articles of Confederation, 1781–1788

•

American Revolutionary War ends as British surrender at Yorktown, Virginia, October 1781

•

Austrian composer Wolfgang Amadeus Mozart finishes the opera *Don Giovanni,* 1787

•

George Washington inaugurated as first president under U.S. Constitution, 1789

•

French Revolution begins, 1789

1790–1800

First census in America sets population at about 3.9 million, 1790

•

New York Stock Exchange organized, 1792

•

Invention of cotton gin leads to increase in slave labor, 1793

•

English physician Edward Jenner develops smallpox vaccine, 1796

•

Napoleon Bonaparte becomes dictator of France, 1799

•

Library of Congress established, 1800

•

Washington, D.C., named capital of U.S., 1800

Stamp from Stamp Act, 1765.
Courtesy of The New-York Historical Society.

•1750–1769

Woolman was a Quaker leader who worked as a tailor. He was quite successful in business, but he renounced it, feeling it involved him too much in the material concerns of the world and took him away from spiritual matters. Woolman developed his hatred for slavery at an early age: during his apprenticeship when he was asked to write a bill of sale for a slave, and while working in the South he witnessed slavery firsthand. Woolman even refused to buy products, such as sugar and dyes, produced through slave labor. Later in life he also worked for American Indian rights.

A. Exploring the Historical Period

American Indians are descendants of the Paleo-Indians. Students should be aware that Native Americans are called by various names, including American Indians, and should be referred to as nations, tribes, or societies, depending on the wishes of the group. Advise students to refer to each American Indian group as that group wishes itself called.

B. Exploring the Culture

At the time the Europeans first arrived, the Pequots lived in what is now known as Connecticut, and spoke an Algonquian language. Friction between the Pequots and the settlers led to open fighting called the Pequot War (1636–1637). After their defeat, some Pequots separated into small bands and left the area; others were killed; and many were sold into slavery. Those who surrendered were scattered among other American Indian groups. Use of Pequot place names was abolished, and the Pequot name itself was forbidden. Despite these setbacks, the Pequots and their culture survive.

C. Critical Reading: Speculating

? How might the goals of the Spanish explorers as described here have affected their writing? [Possible answers: They may have resorted to exaggeration or lies. Or they might have accentuated the positive and omitted or downplayed the negative.]

The First Migration: Ice Age Travelers

Black Coat, a Cherokee chief (1836) by George Catlin. Oil on canvas.

The Granger Collection, New York.

Archaeological evidence tells us that anywhere from twenty to over forty thousand years ago, Ice Age hunters traveling with dogs crossed the Bering land bridge (now submerged under the Bering Strait) from Siberia to what is now Alaska. Slowly, these people and their descendants migrated south. Over the centuries, other migrants followed that route across the strait (some adventurers possibly used other means to reach the shores of North America). By the 1490s, when the great wave of European exploration of the (A) Americas started, numerous groups of American Indians were scattered across the continent. Societies populating what is now the United States and Canada were relatively small; most were made up of only a few thousand people. (By contrast, societies in present-day Mexico and Central America were much larger; the Aztec Empire of Mexico, for instance, included several million people.)

> Columbus did not discover a new world; he established contact between two worlds, both already old.
>
> —J. H. Parry, *The Spanish Seaborne Empire* (1966)

What's important to remember is that there were people here when the Europeans arrived in the fifteenth century; descendants of those people are still here, and their traditions remain. In 1994, for example, the Pequots, whom the English met when they arrived in what (B) is now Connecticut, Rhode Island, and Massachusetts, donated ten million dollars to the new National Museum of the American Indian in Washington, D.C., to promote and save native cultures.

People first migrated to North America from twenty to over forty thousand years ago. When the first Europeans arrived in the fifteenth century, American Indians were living in diverse societies spread across the continent.

The Europeans Arrive: The Explorers

The first written observations of life in this vast continent were recorded in Spanish and French by the European explorers of the fifteenth and sixteenth centuries. These writings open a window to a tumultuous time when the so-called New World was the heady focus of the dreams and desires of an entire era. Christopher Columbus (1451–1506), Francisco Vásquez de Coronado (1510–1554), and many others described the Americas in a flurry of eagerly read letters, journals, and books. (C) Hoping to fund further expeditions, the explorers emphasized the Americas' abundant resources, the peacefulness and hospitality of the inhabitants, and the promise of the unlimited wealth to be gained from fantastic treasuries of gold.

Eskimo comb.

Breton Littlehales/ National Geographic Image Collection.

Turtle and *Flamingo* (1585–1587) by John White. Watercolor.

Copyright British Museum, London. Courtesy of Lee Boltin.

OPTIONS FOR TEACHING

STRATEGIES FOR INCLUSION

Less Proficient Readers Have students begin by reading only the summaries of each section of the introduction. Make sure they can define *American Indians, Puritans, rationalism, deism,* and *self-made*. Have them read the quotations on pp. 7, 8, and 14 that refer to American Indians or Puritans. Then, ask them to read the introduction.

Auditory Begin by reading the quotations to students. To set a purpose for reading, have them use this information to predict what kinds of information and topics will be covered in the introduction. Then, have students read each section of the introduction. Afterward, they may review their predictions for accuracy.

Visual Have students use the time line to find one or more events that they already know about, and have them talk in pairs about the events they identify. As students read each section of the introduction, they should refer to the time line, locating on the line the dates and events of each section.

New York Power Authority. © 1997 T. H. Benton and R. P. Benton Testamentary Trusts/Licensed by VAGA, New York.

Jacques Cartier's Discovery of the St. Lawrence River (1957) by Thomas H. Benton. Tempera on canvas (7′ × 6′).

In 1528, only thirty-six years after Columbus first sighted that flickering fire on the beach of San Salvador, a Spaniard named Alvar Núñez Cabeza de Vaca (c. 1490–1557) landed with an expedition (he was its treasurer) on the west coast of what is now Florida. Cabeza de Vaca and others left the ship and marched inland. They did not return. Their fleet waited an entire year for them, then departed for Mexico, giving up the explorers for dead. Lost in the Texas Gulf area, Cabeza de Vaca and his companions wandered for the next eight years in search of other Europeans who would help them to get home. Cabeza de Vaca's narrative of his journeys through what is now Texas is a gripping adventure story. It is also **D**

> Europeans did not find a wilderness here; rather, however involuntarily, they made one. Jamestown, Plymouth, Salem, Boston, Providence, New Amsterdam, Philadelphia—all grew upon sites previously occupied by Indian communities. So did Quebec and Montreal and Detroit and Chicago. The so-called settlement of America was a resettlement, a reoccupation of a land made waste by the diseases and demoralization introduced by the newcomers.
>
> —Francis Jennings, *The Invasion of America* (1975)

RESPONDING TO THE ART: VISUAL LITERACY

How would you characterize the reception of the Europeans by the people in this painting? [Possible responses: He seems to be welcome and is greeted by some of the area's inhabitants; or some of the inhabitants seem suspicious of Cartier or surprised at his arrival.] **How does the artist call attention to Cartier and his crew?** [Possible responses: Cartier is in the center of the painting, looking down from the top of a hill; or the flag waves behind him, and everyone is looking at him.]

D. Humanities Connection
The publication of these reports led to the explorations of Marcos de Niza, Francisco Coronado, and Hernando de Soto.

INTEGRATING THE LANGUAGE ARTS

Strategic Reading Have students apply information they have read about the Puritans to complete the following chart. Ask them to determine what each group at the top of the chart would say about each issue located on the side of the chart. Have students in groups of three share their charts and defend their responses.

	Members of Church of England	Puritans	Rationalists
Business			
Government			
Religious beliefs			
Education			
Health			

A. Responding to the Quotation

In Cuba, de Las Casas had firsthand contact with the Spanish rule in the Americas. He was an *encomendero,* a colonist with the right to have natives work for him in virtual slavery. He became a Dominican priest in 1512 and apparently rethought his role, for he gave up his *encomienda.* Given de Las Casas' experience, how might you evaluate his statement? [Possible responses: His words are persuasive, because he has seen how the system works. Or he focuses on the pain that he has seen, because that is what stands out from his experience.]

B. Language Note: Vocabulary

Gripe refers to sharp intestinal pains.

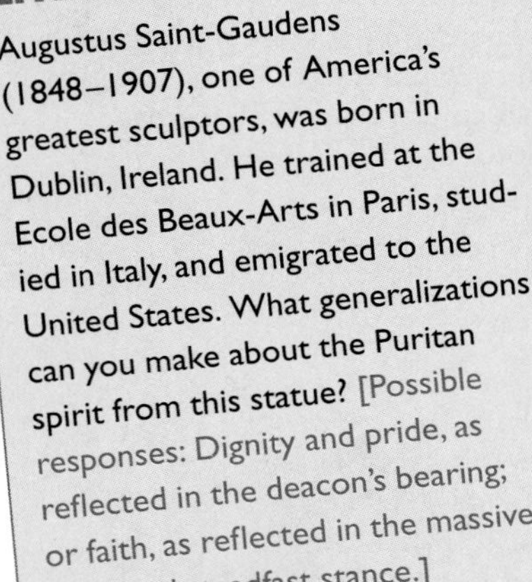

RESPONDING TO THE ART: VISUAL LITERACY

Augustus Saint-Gaudens (1848–1907), one of America's greatest sculptors, was born in Dublin, Ireland. He trained at the Ecole des Beaux-Arts in Paris, studied in Italy, and emigrated to the United States. What generalizations can you make about the Puritan spirit from this statue? [Possible responses: Dignity and pride, as reflected in the deacon's bearing; or faith, as reflected in the massive Bible and steadfast stance.]

a firsthand account of the habits of some of the indigenous people in what is now the United States: what they ate (very little), how they housed themselves, and what their religious beliefs were. De Vaca also provides the first account of some animals and plants that the Europeans had never known existed.

Cabeza de Vaca and his shipmates were alternately captives or companions of the various Native American peoples they encountered on their long trek. Here is part of de Vaca's account of the expedition's experiences with a tribal group in the Gulf Coast area, struggling to survive a famine.

> A The reason why the [Europeans] have killed and destroyed such infinite numbers of souls is solely because they have made gold their ultimate aim, seeking to load themselves with riches in the shortest time. . . . These lands, being so happy and so rich, and the people so humble, so patient, and so easily subjugated, they have . . . taken no more account of them . . . than—I will not say of animals, for would to God they had considered and treated them as animals—but as even less than the dung in the streets.
>
> —Bartolomé de Las Casas, *Very Brief Account of the Destruction of the Indies* (1542)

> Their support is principally roots, of two or three kinds, and they look for them over the face of all the country. The B food is poor and gripes the persons who eat it. The roots require roasting two days: Many are very bitter, and withal difficult to be dug. They are sought the distance of two or three leagues, and so great is the want these people experience, that they cannot get through the year without them. Occasionally they kill deer, and at times take fish; but the quantity is so small and the famine so great, that they eat spiders and the eggs of ants, worms, lizards, salamanders, snakes, and vipers that kill whom they strike; and they eat earth and wood, and all that there is, the dung of deer, and other things that I omit to mention; and I honestly believe that were there stones in that land they would eat them. They save the bones of the fishes they consume, of snakes and other animals, that they may afterward beat them together and eat the powder.
>
> —Cabeza de Vaca

The first Europeans to visit the Americas were the explorers. Their enthusiastic accounts of the beauty and wealth of the Americas led to increased expeditions to what Renaissance Europeans saw as the New World.

OPTIONS FOR TEACHING

CROSSING THE CURRICULUM

Science/Health Have students choose a topic related to smallpox and research it. They may be interested in looking at sources that document the responses to Mather's proposed inoculation campaign; Lady Mary Wortley Montagu's introduction of inoculation in Great Britain; the Turkish physician whose work served as a source for Mather; Edward Jenner, who later developed the cowpox vaccine; or the incidence of smallpox in the late twentieth century. Have students create displays of their topic, including pictures as well as a written paper. Invite students to examine each other's displays and to read each other's work.

Art Have each student locate an artwork or a handicraft that shows the distinctive character of a particular American Indian group (they may use a photograph or a drawing). Have students share their findings, discussing the cultural aspects represented. Use students' findings to discuss the diversity of cultures among American Indians.

The Puritan Legacy

Interesting and valuable as the explorers' writings are, they are not central to the development of the American literary tradition in the way the writings of the Puritans of New England are. In many respects, the American character has been shaped by the moral, ethical, and religious convictions of the Puritans.

The first and most famous group of these English Puritans landed, in 1620, on the tip of Cape Cod, just before Christmas. They were followed, ten years later, by seven hundred more Puritan settlers. By 1640, as many as twenty thousand English Puritans had sailed to what they called New England.

Although the real commerce of the Puritans was with heaven, they were competent in the business of the world as well: The founding of a new society in North America was a business venture as well as a spiritual one. For the Puritans, the everyday world and the spiritual world were closely intertwined. C

(Left) Page from *The Day of Doom* by Michael Wigglesworth.

Seal on meeting notice.

Who Were These Puritans?

Puritan is a broad term, referring to a number of Protestant groups that, beginning about 1560, sought to "purify" the Church of England, which since the time of Henry VIII (who reigned from 1509 to 1547) had been virtually inseparable from the country's government. D Like other Protestant reformers on the European continent, English Puritans wished to return to the simpler forms of worship and church organization described in the New Testament. For them, religion was first of all a personal, inner experience. They did not believe that the clergy or the government should or could act as an intermediary between the individual and God. E

Many Puritans suffered persecution in England. Some were put in jail and whipped, their noses slit and their ears lopped off. Some fled England for Holland. But fearing that in Holland they would lose their identity as English Protestants, a small group led by William Bradford (page 26) and others set sail in 1620 for what was advertised as the New World. There they hoped to build a new society patterned after God's word.

The Puritans were single-minded visionaries convinced of the rightness of their beliefs, but they were also practical and businesslike. They felt that Christian worship and church organization should be simplified in order to more closely resemble Biblical models. Many Puritans were persecuted for their beliefs and fled England for Holland and, ultimately, for North America.

The Puritan Deacon Samuel Chapin (1899) by Augustus Saint-Gaudens. Bronze model.
James Graham & Sons, Inc., New York.

C. Exploring the Historical Period
Journeys to set up colonies in what is now New England were financed by businessmen who looked forward to receiving repayment in goods. The two joint stock companies that King James I licensed to organize settlements in Virginia were the Plymouth Company and the London Company. The Pilgrims' trip to North America was financed by a group of about seventy men known as the Adventurers, who invested various amounts of money in the enterprise.

D. Expansion
Separation of church and state is a basic principle of American society. Such separation was not the practice in England before King Henry VIII's break with the pope. Afterward, the link between the Church of England and the state was weaker than that between the Roman Catholic Church and the state, but the bond still existed. How would the Puritans have viewed separation of church and state? [Possible answer: Because of their views on the individual's relationship with God and their dislike for the Church of England, most of them did not want a national church in the Americas. But they did believe that government had to follow the law of God.]

E. Exploring the Culture
The Puritans used only practices, ceremonies, and adornments that they believed to be documented in the Bible. They wanted to do away with clerical vestments, stained-glass windows, and the use of incense.

CROSSING THE CURRICULUM

Social Studies *You may want to obtain permission from parents or guardians and from the parties students will contact before they begin work on this activity.* Ask each student to locate one or two people who came to the United States from another country and to interview them about their reasons for immigrating. As students present their findings to the class, ask two volunteers to create a chart on poster board, showing the variety of reasons. Have students discuss whether reasons for coming to the United States have changed much over time. Such a chart might look like the following.

Date of Arrival	Reasons for Coming

A. Critical Reading: Speculating

? What do you think might explain these symptoms? [Possible answers: The girls were playacting. Or the girls had come to believe themselves possessed, and so convulsions and hallucinations were brought about by hysteria.]

B. Critical Reading: Finding Cause and Effect

Explain Tituba's actions and their results. [Possible answer: She was coerced into confessing and giving information that implicated others.] Tituba was imprisoned rather than condemned to death. Have students compare the various fates she might have faced with the one she did experience, being sold by the colony.

C. Responding to the Quotation

? How does this quotation reflect Puritan thinking? [The Puritans believed Adam and Eve sinned and that, as a consequence, we are all sinners.]

D. Exploring the Culture

Puritans believed in predestination—that is, that God had chosen the souls that would be saved prior to their birth, and that therefore, people were saved by grace, rather than by their own acts.

A CLOSER LOOK

THE SALEM WITCHCRAFT TRIALS

The Trial for Witchcraft of George Jacobs, August 5, 1692 (1855) by T. H. Matteson. Oil on canvas.

Courtesy Peabody Essex Museum, Salem, Massachusetts. Photograph by Mark Sexton.

During the cold, dreary winter of 1691–1692, the daughter and the niece of Samuel Parris, a minister in Salem Village, Massachusetts, began to dabble in magic. By February the two girls started having fits. Lesions appeared on their skin, and it seemed as though they were being choked by invisible hands. A doctor diagnosed the girls as being the victims of malicious witchcraft. (A)

Urged to name those responsible for bewitching them, the girls accused Sarah Good and Sarah Osborne, two unpopular women from the village, and Tituba, a slave whom Samuel Parris had brought back from Barbados. During the subsequent trial, the girls writhed and moaned and behaved as though they were being choked. Based on this "evidence," Sarah Good was condemned. In an attempt to save her own life, Tituba confessed to being a witch. She claimed that there was a coven of witches in Massachusetts and testified that she had seen several names written in blood in the Devil's book. The witch hunt had begun. (B)

(C) In Adam's Fall
We sinned all.

—*The New England Primer* (c. 1683)

Puritan Beliefs: Sinners All?

For a people who were so convinced they were right, the Puritans had to grapple with complex uncertainties. At the center of Puritan theology was an uneasy mixture of certainty and doubt. The certainty was that because of Adam and Eve's sin of disobedience, most of humanity would be damned for all eternity. But the Puritans were also certain that God in his mercy had sent his son Jesus Christ to earth to save particular people. (D)

The doubt centered on whether a particular individual was one of the saved (the "elect") or one of the damned (the "unregenerate"). How did you know if you were saved or damned?

As it turns out, you did not know. A theology that was so clear-cut in its division of the world between saints and sinners was fuzzy when it came to determining which were which. There were two principal indications of the state of your soul, neither of them completely certain. You were saved by the grace of God, and you could *feel* this grace arriving, in an intensely emotional fashion. The inner arrival of God's grace was demonstrated by your outward

Warrant for the arrest of Ann Pudeator (1692).
Courtesy Peabody Essex Museum, Salem, Massachusetts.

OPTIONS FOR TEACHING

ASSESSMENT TOOLS

Check Test: Multiple Choice

1. Puritans believed that they could be saved by (a) prayer (b) good deeds (c) God's grace [c]
2. Puritans saw the hand of God in (a) American Indian ceremonies (b) stained-glass windows (c) everyday events [c]
3. Cotton Mather proposed combating the smallpox epidemic by (a) rounding up witches (b) inoculation (c) continuous prayer [b]
4. Deists believed that people were (a) inherently sinful (b) inherently good (c) not responsible for their actions [b]
5. Most of the literature written in America during the Age of Reason consisted of (a) political tracts (b) epic poetry (c) religious tracts [a]

Informal Assessment Review students' schemata together with them by asking them to describe new learning acquired through this selection. Ask them to refer to their chart from the Strategic Reading activity on p. T7. Note whether they distinguish between prior knowledge and acquired knowledge as well as whether they have retained important information from the selection. Make a brief note on the discussion for future reference.

Zealous ministers like Cotton Mather argued that the epidemic of witchcraft proved beyond a doubt that New England was a holy place, since the Devil was so interested in it. Mather and others demanded that all witches be rooted out and severely punished. Hundreds of people from Salem and other eastern Massachusetts towns came forward to testify that they were victims of witchcraft.

Before long the prisons were overcrowded, and a special court was established in Salem Village. Within the next ten months, about 150 people in this small community were accused of witchcraft. Neighbors, especially those with long-standing quarrels, turned on each other. Between June and September, nineteen people were hanged, and one man, Giles Corey, who had refused to plead either innocent or guilty, was crushed to death under a pile of stones.

What really happened at Salem? Many historians believe that Salem experienced a mass hysteria, a sort of shared delusion. Still others have suggested that a more restrictive form of government recently imposed on the Massachusetts Bay Colony, in addition to new economic pressures in the Colony's towns, may have led to bitterness, aggression, and outright paranoia. Perhaps the strict society of Puritan New England finally erupted under the strain of its repression. A recent theory proposes that fear of unusual or powerful "nonconformists"—particularly women—may have led to an attempt to constrain (E) their behavior. Statistics show that the majority of the "witches" were unmarried women between the ages of forty and sixty: eccentric and independent loners with abrasive personalities. Some of them may have been "cunning folk," that is, midwives or people with unusual healing abilities and knowledge of herbal remedies. But perhaps most significantly, they were often women who could (F) potentially come into their fathers' inheritances and become independent property owners—something the patriarchal Puritans would have seen as a threat to male power. We may never (G) know exactly why events in Salem occurred as they did, but the question continues to fascinate students of human behavior.

behavior. After receiving grace, you were "reborn" as a member of the community of saints, and you behaved like a saint. People hoping to be among the saved examined their inner lives closely for signs of grace, and they tried to live exemplary lives. So American Puritans came to value self-reliance, industriousness, temperance, and simplicity. These were, coincidentally, the ideal qualities needed to carve out a new society in a strange land.

God's altar needs not our polishing.
—*The Bay Psalm Book* (1640)

Puritans believed that Adam and Eve's sin had damned most people for all eternity. They also believed that Jesus Christ had been sent to earth to save particular people, known as the "elect." It was difficult to know for certain if one was saved or damned, so the Puritans tried to behave in as exemplary a manner as possible.

Puritan Politics: Government by Contract

In the Puritan view, a covenant, or contract, existed between God and humanity. This spiritual covenant was a useful model for worldly social organization as well: Puritans believed that people should enter freely into agreements concerning their government. On the *Mayflower,* for example,

E. Cultural Connections
You may want to point out similarities to McCarthyism in this atmosphere of widespread accusations and implications. During the Cold War of the 1950s, fear of communism reached a zenith. Initially, Senator Joseph R. McCarthy, a Wisconsin Republican, charged that communists dominated the State Department. Thousands of individuals were accused of communist associations, often with little or no evidence. As in the case of neighbors in Salem trying to settle feuds, the accusations may have come from anger or fear unrelated to the charges.

F. Critical Reading: Speculating
In 1696, a judge repented; then twelve of the jurors repented. Eventually, Ann Putnam, one of the chief accusers, apologized. In 1711, the state reimbursed heirs of most of the victims in amounts up to 150 pounds sterling. Seven victims, who had no family come forward to demand pardon, remain guilty on the records. What do you think the false accusers could have done to make amends? [Possible answers: No amends could be made; or large sums of money would help account for property seized and loss of income.]

G. Critical Reading: Evaluating an Interpretation
Have students summarize the theories that attempt to explain what happened to the girls in Salem. [Possible answers: Salem experienced mass hysteria. Restrictive government and economic pressures led to aggression within the community. The town feared nonconformists.] Have students evaluate the theories in class discussion.

RESPONDING TO THE ILLUSTRATION: EXPLORING THE SUBJECT

Because paper was scarce and expensive, hornbooks were invented to protect the paper on which children's lessons were printed. A hornbook, shown here spanning these two pages, consisted of a sheet of paper with a simple lesson pasted to a flat board with a handle. The lesson printed on the hornbook paper usually included the alphabet, a benediction, the Lord's Prayer, and Roman numerals. Covering the whole board was a thin, flat, transparent sheet of horn that protected the paper. The hornbook could be attached to a child's belt or worn around the neck.

A. Exploring the Historical Period

There had been witch hunts before those in Salem, notably in western Europe in the 1500s and 1600s. But in the winter of 1692 in Salem, a concentrated series of over two hundred accusations led to at least fifty-nine trials and thirty-one convictions.

The Granger Collection, New York.

Pilgrims Signing the Compact Aboard the Mayflower, *November 11, 1620* (19th century). Colored mezzotint.

the Puritans composed and signed the Mayflower Compact, outlining how they would be governed once they landed. In this use of a contractual agreement, they prepared the ground for American constitutional democracy.

On the other hand, because the Puritans believed the saintly "elect" should exert great influence on government, their political views tended to be undemocratic. There was little room for compromise. The witchcraft hysteria in Salem, Massachusetts, in 1692 (pages 10–11), resulted in part from fear that the community's moral foundation was threatened, and therefore its political cohesion was also in danger.

Characteristics of Puritan Writing

- The Bible provided a model for Puritan writing: a conception of each individual life as a journey to salvation. Puritans saw direct connections between Biblical events and their own lives.
- Puritans used writing to explore their inner and outer lives for signs of the workings of God.
- Diaries and histories were the most common forms of expression in Puritan society, because they directly expressed the workings of God.
- Puritans favored a plain style, similar to that of the Geneva Bible. They stressed clarity of expression and avoided complicated figures of speech.

The Bible in America

The Puritans read the Bible as the story of the creation, fall, wanderings, and rescue of the human race. Within this long and complex narrative, each Puritan could see connections to events in his or her own life or to events in the life of the community. Each Puritan was trained to see life as a pilgrimage, or journey, to salvation. Each Puritan learned to read his or her life the way a literary critic reads a book.

The Puritans believed that the Bible was the literal word of God. Reading the Bible was

ABCDE HIJKL OPQR VUW abcde klmnc tvuw A·E

a necessity for all Puritans, as was the ability to understand theological debates. For these reasons, the Puritans placed great emphasis on education. Thus, Harvard College, originally intended to train Puritan ministers for the rapidly expanding Colony, was founded in 1636, only sixteen years after the first Pilgrims had landed. And, just three years later, the first printing press in the American Colonies was set up. B

Their beliefs required the Puritans to keep a close watch on both the inner and outer events of their lives. This central aspect of the Puritan mind greatly affected their writings. Diaries and histories were important forms of Puritan literature, because they were records of the workings of God. C

Puritan belief in a spiritual compact between God and humanity paved the way for American constitutional democracy. The Puritans emphasized education so that people could read and understand the Bible and follow religious debates. Diaries and histories were important forms of Puritan literature.

Title page of the *Bay Psalm Book* (1640).

The Granger Collection, New York.

The Age of Reason: Tinkerers and Experimenters

By the end of the seventeenth century, new ideas that had been fermenting in Europe began to present a challenge to the unshakable faith of the Puritans.

The Age of Reason, or the Enlightenment, began in Europe with the philosophers and scientists of the seventeenth and eighteenth centuries who called themselves rationalists. **Rationalism** is the belief that human beings can arrive at truth by using reason, rather than by relying on the authority of the past, on religious faith, or on intuition. D

The Puritans saw God as actively and mysteriously involved in the workings of the universe; the rationalists saw God differently. The great English rationalist Sir Isaac Newton (1642–1727), who devised the laws of gravity and motion, compared God to a clockmaker. Having created the perfect mechanism of this universe, God then left his creation to run on its own, like a clock. The rationalists believed that God's special gift to humanity was reason—the ability to think in an ordered, logical manner. This gift of reason enabled people to discover both scientific and spiritual truth. Everyone, then, had the capacity to regulate and improve his or her own life. E

While the theoretical background for the Age of Reason took shape in Europe, a home-grown practicality and interest in scientific tinkering or experimenting already thrived in the American Colonies. From the earliest Colonial days, Americans had to be generalists and tinkerers; they had to make do with what they had, and they had to achieve results.

Sir Isaac Newton, President of the Royal Society (1802). Engraving, after a painting by Vanderbank.

The Granger Collection, New York.

Hornbook for children.

Rare Book Department, Free Library of Philadelphia.

B. Critical Reading: Speculating

? How might Puritan beliefs have helped increase the availability of basic education? [Possible answer: Education would be necessary for all classes of people and for women as well as men if everyone were expected to read the Bible.]

C. Literary Connections

The Puritan diaries include such works as the *Journal* of John Winthrop, the *Diary* of Samuel Sewall, and *The Journal of Madame Knight;* the histories include *Of Plymouth Plantation* by William Bradford and Cotton Mather's book *Magnalia Christi Americana.*

D. Humanities Connection

Some scholars date the beginnings of the Enlightenment to 1662, when the British scientific academy known as the Royal Society was founded under the patronage of King Charles II.

E. Exploring the Culture

The view that God created a well-ordered universe, controlled by immutable laws and operating without divine intervention, is the central belief of deism. This belief in a world without divine intervention clashes directly with the belief of many Christians in revelation, divine providence, and final judgment. Deists generally offered naturalistic explanations for miracles in the Bible and allegorical interpretations for Biblical prophecies. Proponents saw deism as a way of reconciling religion and the new science, which seemed to undermine many traditional Christian beliefs.

A. Expansion
Mather's Puritan beliefs did not necessarily conflict with his scientific interests. Daniel J. Boorstin comments that "The Puritan emphasis on sin thus seemed to reinforce the empirical emphasis of American science." According to Mather, sin caused diseases and illness.

B. Expansion
Smallpox had first come to the Americas in the sixteenth century when Europeans who were immune to the disease unwittingly infected Native Americans such as the Aztecs.

The Smallpox Plague

A The unlikely hero of America's first foray into scientific exploration was the strict Puritan minister Cotton Mather (1663–1728), who was interested in natural science and medicine.

In April 1721, a ship from the West Indies docked in Boston Harbor. This was not unusual, for trade with the West Indies was one of the foundations of New England economic life. This B ship was different, though. For in addition to its cargo of sugar and molasses, this ship carried smallpox.

In the seventeenth and eighteenth centuries, smallpox was one of the scourges of life, as the AIDS virus is today. The disease spread rapidly, disfigured its victims, and was often fatal. The outbreak in Boston in 1721 was a major public-health problem. What was to be done?

Horrible outbreaks of smallpox had ravaged Native Americans ever since the white settlers first landed. Smallpox had been unknown in North America, and the native people had no immunity to the virus. Nearly a century before Boston's smallpox outbreak, Bradford described the horrors of the disease:

For want of bedding and linen and other helps . . . they fall into a lamentable condition as they lie on their hard mats, the pox breaking and mattering and running one into another, their skin cleaving by reason thereof to the mats they lie on. When they turn them, a whole side will flay off at once as it were, and they will be all of a gore blood, most fearful to behold. And then being very sore, what with cold and other distempers, they die like rotten sheep.

—William Bradford

Paul Revere's house, Boston.

At the time of the smallpox epidemic, Cotton Mather was working on what would be the first scholarly essay on medicine written in America. In his opening sentences he reveals his Puritan perspective: "Let us look upon sin as the cause of sickness." His religious point of view did not, however, prevent Mather from seeking cures for specific diseases. He had heard of a method for dealing with smallpox devised by a Turkish physician. The method seemed illogical, but it apparently worked. It was called inoculation. In June 1721, as the smallpox epidemic spread throughout Boston, Mather began a public campaign for inoculation.

Boston's medical community was violently opposed to such an experiment, especially one borrowed from the Muslims. The debate was vigorous, raging all the summer and into the fall. Controversy developed into violence: In November, Mather's house was bombed.

Despite such fierce opposition, Mather succeeded in inoculating nearly three hundred people. By the time the epidemic was over, in March of the following year, only six of these had died. Of the almost six thousand other people who contracted the disease (nearly half of Boston's population),

Cotton Mather (1727) by Peter Pelham. Mezzotint.

The Granger Collection, New York.

(Left) Paul Revere statue, Boston.
(Right) Old State House, Boston.

BEGINNINGS 15

RESPONDING TO THE ART: VISUAL LITERACY

Where do you think the action in the background illustration is taking place? [Possible responses: A rural area or a small town in America.] What do you think the people in the illustration do for a living? [Possible responses: Farm, raise horses; perhaps some are teachers or preachers.] Does this resemble the Puritan New England that you had imagined? Why or why not? [Possible responses: Yes, because it is simple, austere, quiet, and untainted; or no, I expected such an illustration to focus on church life.]

A. Literary Connections
Benjamin Franklin wrote in his *Autobiography* about a later outbreak of smallpox: "In 1736 I lost one of my sons, a fine boy of four years old, by the smallpox, taken in the common way. I long regretted bitterly, and still regret that I had not given it to him by inoculation. This I mention for the sake of parents who omit that operation, on the supposition that they should never forgive themselves if a child died under it; my example showing that the regret may be the same either way, and that, therefore, the safer should be chosen."

B. Reader's Response: Extending the Text
? Do the two points discussed in this and the following paragraph, contradictory qualities and a practical approach to social and scientific research, characterize American life today? [Sample responses: Yes, because while we are worried about air pollution, we still drive more than necessary. No, because we invent to make a task easier or to make a profit, not because we have to for survival.]

C. Critical Reading: Predicting
? What prediction does Crèvecoeur make about America's future? Has that prediction come true? [Possible answer: He says that America's diversity will bring about new attitudes, a new way of life, and a new race of people. Answers concerning whether this has occurred will vary. Encourage students to explain their opinions about the accuracy of this prediction.]

D. Expansion
Prominent deists included men such as Benjamin Franklin, Thomas Jefferson, and Thomas Paine.

(A) about eight hundred and fifty had died. The evidence, according to Mather's figures, was clear: Whether or not inoculation made much sense to scientists, it worked.

(B) The smallpox controversy illustrates two interesting points about American life in the early eighteenth century. First, it shows that contradictory qualities of the American character often existed side by side. Puritan thinking was not limited to a rigid and narrow interpretation of the Bible; a devout Puritan like Mather could also be a practical scientist.

Mather's experiment also reveals that a practical approach to social change and scientific research was necessary in America. The frontier farmer with little access to tools shared a problem with the scientist who had few books and a whole new world of plants and animals to catalog. American thought had to be thought in action: an urge to improve the public welfare by being willing to experiment, to try things out, no matter what the authorities might say.

(C) What then is . . . this new man? . . . He is an American, who, leaving behind him all his ancient prejudices and manners, receives new ones from the new mode of life he has embraced, the new government he obeys, and the new rank he holds. . . . [In America] individuals of all nations are melted into a new race of men, whose labors . . . will one day cause great changes in the world.

—Michel-Guillaume Jean de Crèvecoeur, *Letters from an American Farmer* (1782)

Deism: Are People Basically Good?

Like the Puritans, the rationalists discovered God through the medium of the natural world, but in a different way. Rationalists thought it unlikely that God would choose to reveal himself only at particular times to particular people. It seemed much more reasonable to believe that God had made it possible for *all* people at *all* times to discover natural laws through their God-given power of reason.

(D) This outlook, called **deism** (dē′iz′əm), was shared by many eighteenth-century thinkers, including many founders of the American nation. American deists came from different religious backgrounds. But the deists avoided supporting specific religious groups. They sought, instead, the principles that united all religions.

Deists believed that the universe was orderly and good. In contrast to the Puritans, deists stressed humanity's goodness. They believed in the perfectibility of every individual through the use of reason. God's objective, in the deist view, was the happiness of his creatures. Therefore, the best form of worship was to do good for others. There already existed in America an impulse to improve people's lives, as Cotton Mather's struggle to save Boston from small-

Thomas Jefferson (1805) by Rembrandt Peale. Oil on canvas. Accession number 1867.306.
Collection of The New-York Historical Society.

The Battle of Bunker Hill (detail) (1776) by Winthrop Chandler (1747–1790). United States. Oil on canvas (34½″ × 53⅝″).
Museum of Fine Arts, Boston/Gift of Mr. and Mrs. Gardner Richardson (1982.281).

pox illustrates. Deism elevated this impulse to one of the nation's highest goals. To this day, social welfare is still a political priority and still the subject of fierce debate.

The American struggle for independence was justified largely by appeals to rationalist principles. The Declaration of Independence bases its arguments on rationalist assumptions about the relations between people, God, and natural law.

In contrast to Puritans, deists believed that God was available to all people all of the time. Deists believed that people were inherently good, that every individual had the gift of reason and with that gift could perfect himself or herself and society.

> Reason and free inquiry . . . are the natural enemies of error, and of error only.
>
> —Thomas Jefferson, *Notes on the State of Virginia* (1785)

RESPONDING TO THE ART: EXPLORING THE SUBJECT

After the battles of Lexington and Concord, more than fifteen thousand troops assembled near Boston to halt the five thousand British soldiers stationed there. The colonists worked to fortify Bunker Hill and Breed's Hill. Although they were soon discovered, they endured a cannonade from British men-of-war in the harbor and from a battery across the river. Even after the British landed on the hill and led a second and third attack, British casualties outnumbered American casualties one thousand to four hundred, thus bolstering Colonial confidence and encouraging the revolutionary cause.

A. Reader's Response: Connecting with the Text

? What contemporary autobiographies do you know by self-made Americans? [Sample responses: Sam Walton's *Sam Walton, Made in America: My Story;* or Lee Iacocca's *Iacocca: An Autobiography.*]

Quickwrite

Before students begin, make sure they are clear on the difference between rationalists and deists. Have them work in small groups to brainstorm attributes that characterize Puritan and rationalist beliefs. Ask them to look for behaviors and attitudes that reflect these attributes today. Newspapers and news magazines may help students who need concrete examples.

Self-Made Americans

Most of the literature written in the American Colonies during the Age of Reason was, understandably, rooted in reality. This was an age of pamphlets, since most literature was intended to serve practical or political ends. Following the Revolutionary War (1775–1783), the problems of organizing and governing the new nation were of the highest importance.

E Pluribus Unum. Woodcarving.

Shelburne Museum, Shelburne, Vermont. Photograph by Ken Burris.

The unquestioned masterpiece of the American Age of Reason is Benjamin Franklin's *Autobiography* (page 86). Franklin used the autobiographical narrative, a form common in Puritan writing, and took out its religious justification. Written in clear, witty prose, this account of the development of the self-made American provided the model for a story that would be told again and again. In the twentieth century, it appears in F. Scott Fitzgerald's novel (A) *The Great Gatsby* (1925), as well as in the countless biographies and autobiographies of self-made men and women on the best-seller lists today.

The masterpiece of the Revolutionary era is Franklin's* Autobiography. *Franklin took the Puritan impulse toward self-examination and molded it into the classic American rags-to-riches story—the triumph of the self-made person.

Benjamin Franklin.

Drawing by David Levine. Reprinted with permission from *The New York Review of Books.* Copyright © 1967 NYREV, Inc.

The Rationalist Worldview

- People arrive at truth by using reason rather than by relying on the authority of the past, on religion, or on nonrational mental processes like intuition.
- God created the universe but does not interfere in its workings.
- The world operates according to God's rules, and through the use of reason we can discover those rules.
- People are basically good and perfectible.
- Since God wants people to be happy, they worship God best by helping other people.
- Human history is marked by progress toward a more perfect existence.

Quickwrite

Legacies of the Puritans and Rationalists

Puritan beliefs and the beliefs of the rationalists—do you see evidence of these worldviews around you today? Think especially of arguments about government, social welfare, and self-improvement. Write down a few of your observations. Are Puritanism and rationalism alive and well in American public life today? Give some examples.

Collection 1 VISIONS AND VOYAGES

Theme: The Beginnings of the United States

Those who converged in what is now the United States were diverse groups of Native Americans, Europeans, and Africans. The clash of cultures and the denial of human rights were a part of the settlement of North America, as was the quest for religious freedom and economic growth.

Thematic Focus

The selections in Collection 1 illustrate the diverse values, experiences, and beliefs of the early settlers.

- **Literature of the Americas: The Sky Tree/ The Earth Only/ The House Made of Dawn** *from* **The Night Chant/ Coyote Finishes His Work** Native American spirituality is revealed in a creation myth, a personal song, a ceremonial chant, and a trickster tale.
- *from* **Of Plymouth Plantation** Pilgrims voyage to and settle in New England in their quest for religious freedom.
- *from* **A Narrative of the Captivity** The selection is an account of a capture by Native Americans, as experienced by a Puritan woman.
- *from* **The History of the Dividing Line** Byrd criticizes his predecessors and outlines the religious beliefs of a Native American.
- *from* **The Interesting Narrative of the Life of Olaudah Equiano** An African recounts how he became a slave and was forced to come to the United States.

Literary Focus

Literary Element	Selection / Feature
The Plain Style/Archaisms	**Of Plymouth Plantation**
Allusion	**A Narrative of the Captivity**
Satire	**The History of the Dividing Line**
Autobiography	**The Interesting Narrative of the Life of Olaudah Equiano**

Writing Focus

The following flow chart shows how the writing assignment for each selection relates to and builds toward the culminating writing assignment presented in the Writer's Workshop at the end of the unit.

Selection	Work-in-Progress Assignment
Of Plymouth Plantation	Compile a list of personal setbacks p. 36
A Narrative of the Captivity	Freewrite about changing perceptions p. 47
The History of the Dividing Line	List vivid phrases p. 55
The Interesting Narrative of the Life of Olaudah Equiano	Make notes on restriction of rights p. 66
Writer's Workshop	Write an autobiographical incident pp. 130–133

Collection Planner

PUPIL'S EDITION

SELECTION/ FEATURE	Literary Elements / Active Reading	Writing	Speaking and Listening	Language and Vocabulary
Literature of the Americas: The Sky Tree as told by Joseph Bruchac (p. 22) **The Earth Only** Used-As-A-Shield (p. 23) from **The House Made of Dawn** from **The Night Chant** trans. by Washington Matthews (p. 23) **Coyote Finishes His Work** retold by Barry Lopez (p. 24)	• Reader's Log p. 21		• Finding Common Ground: Discuss/ Research/Report p. 25	
from **Of Plymouth Plantation** William Bradford (pp. 26–37)	• Reader's Log p. 27 • Plain Style p. 35 • Archaisms p. 37	• The Plain Style: Rewrite sentences p. 35 • Critical Writing: Write contrast essay p. 36	• Speaking and Listening: Represent Pilgrims and American Indians in panel discussion p. 36	• How to Own a Word: When a Dictionary Can Help p. 37
from **A Narrative of the Captivity** Mary Rowlandson (pp. 38–47)	• Reader's Log p. 39 • Allusion p. 39	• Critical Writing: Explain Biblical allusions p. 47 • Creative Writing: Write journal entry from another point of view p. 47		
from **The History of the Dividing Line** William Byrd (pp. 49–55)	• Reader's Log p. 50 • Satire p. 50	• Critical Writing: Write comparison/contrast essay p. 55 • Creative Writing: Write Puritan journal entry p. 55		
from **The Interesting Narrative of the Life of Olaudah Equiano** Olaudah Equiano (pp. 56–66)	• Reader's Log p. 57 • Autobiography p. 57	• Critical Writing: Write comparison/contrast essay p. 66 • Creative Writing/Art: Create children's book p. 66		

Collection Resources

Teaching Resources A	Audiovisual Resources Binder	Test Booklet
Cross-Curricular Activity p. 24	Fine Art Transparency 1.1	Collection 1 Test pp. 11–14

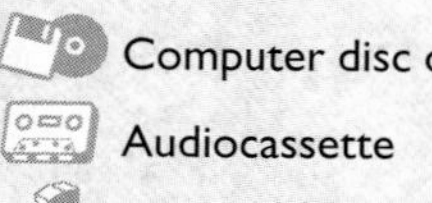
Computer disc or CD-ROM

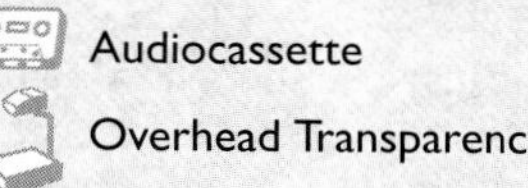
Audiocassette

Overhead Transparency

PROGRAM RESOURCES

Electronic Media	Teaching Resources with Organizer: Teaching Resources A	Teaching Resources with Organizer: Other Resources	Audiovisual Resources Binder
	• Teaching Notes p. 2		• Selected Reading Audiocassette 1, Side A
• Language Workshop: Nouns • Test Generator	• Teaching Notes pp. 2–3 • Reading Organizer p. 7 • Language Link pp. 8–9 • Words to Own pp. 10–11	• Test Booklet: Selection Test pp. 3–4 • Language and Writing Skills Worksheets pp. 11–12 • Portfolio Management System pp. 48–49, 67	• Elements of Literature Transparency 1.2 • How to Own a Word Transparency 1.3
• Language Workshop: Pronouns • Test Generator	• Teaching Notes p. 3 • Reading Organizer p. 12 • Language Link pp. 13–14 • Words to Own p. 15	• Test Booklet: Selection Test pp. 5–6 • Language and Writing Skills Worksheets pp. 13–14 • Portfolio Management System pp. 39, 68	• Selected Reading Audiocassette 1, Side A
• Language Workshop: Verbs • Test Generator	• Teaching Notes pp. 3–4 • Reading Organizer p. 16 • Language Link pp. 17–18 • Words to Own p. 19	• Test Booklet: Selection Test pp. 7–8 • Language and Writing Skills Worksheets pp. 16–17 • Portfolio Management System pp. 53, 69	
• Language Workshop: Adjectives, Adverbs • Test Generator	• Teaching Notes p. 4 • Reading Organizer p. 20 • Language Link pp. 21–22 • Words to Own p. 23	• Test Booklet: Selection Test pp. 9–10 • Language and Writing Skills Worksheets pp. 15, 18 • Portfolio Management System pp. 54–55, 70	• Selected Reading Audiocassette 1, Side A

Proofreading Warm-ups

You may use the following exercises to help students practice their proofreading skills. Copy a set of incorrect sentences onto the chalkboard, and have students find and correct the spelling, punctuation, usage, and mechanical errors in each sentence.
Ask students to share and discuss their responses.

	Sentences with Errors	Sentences Corrected	Skills Covered
1	**a.** the puritans beleived that the bible was the literal word of god **b.** diarys and historys was important forms of puritan literature	**a.** The Puritans believed that the Bible was the literal word of God. **b.** Diaries and histories were important forms of Puritan literature.	Capitalization, Spelling, Subject-verb agreement, End marks
2	**a.** Cotton Mathers experimental Smallpox innoculation's was successful **b.** many lifes were saved public welfare improved	**a.** Cotton Mather's experimental smallpox inoculations were successful. **b.** Many lives were saved; public welfare improved.	Apostrophe usage, Capitalization, Subject-Verb agreement, Spelling, Semicolon usage, End marks
3	**a.** the american indian worldview is not that of a strait line but of a circle **b.** in thier worldview the universe is not dominated by human beans	**a.** The American Indian worldview is not that of a straight line, but of a circle. **b.** In their worldview the universe is not dominated by human beings.	Capitalization, Spelling, Comma usage, End marks
4	**a.** have you read William Bradfords account of the plymouth settlement **b.** alot of the pilgrim's faced severe hardships on board the mayflower	**a.** Have you read William Bradford's account of the Plymouth settlement? **b.** A lot of the Pilgrims faced severe hardships on board the <u>Mayflower.</u>	Capitalization, Apostrophe usage, Spelling, Underline ship names, End marks
5	**a.** like the pilgrims the vietnamese boat people came to America in search of a better life for theirselfs **b.** me and Kim done a report of the boat people for are project	**a.** Like the Pilgrims, the Vietnamese boat people came to America in search of a better life for themselves. **b.** Kim and I did a report on the boat people for our project.	Capitalization, Comma usage, Pronoun error, Verb error, Spelling, End marks
6	**a.** Mary Rowlandsons narrative about her capture by native americans are full of biblical quotations **b.** i find captivity narrative's to be fascinating reading proclaimed Jack	**a.** Mary Rowlandson's narrative about her capture by Native Americans is full of Biblical quotations. **b.** "I find captivity narratives to be fascinating reading," proclaimed Jack.	Apostrophe usage, Capitalization, Subject-verb agreement, Quotation marks, Comma usage, End marks
7	**a.** during the seventeenth-century the public eagerly devoured account's of captures by american indians **b.** some accounts mixed Truth with Fiction	**a.** During the seventeenth century, the public eagerly devoured accounts of captures by American Indians. **b.** Some accounts mixed truth with fiction.	Capitalization, Hyphen usage, Comma usage, Apostrophe usage, End marks
8	**a.** in addition to the Puritans of New England there was the Southern planters also known as the Cavaliers **b.** as a group the Cavaliers background and social views were quiet diffrent from the puritans.	**a.** In addition to the Puritans of New England, there were the Southern planters, also known as the Cavaliers. **b.** As a group, the Cavaliers' background and social views were quite different from the Puritans'.	Capitalization, Comma usage, Subject-verb agreement, Apostrophe usage, Spelling, End marks
9	**a.** unlike the plain writing style of the Puritan's Byrds writing uses satire **b.** in The History of the Dividing Line Byrd discuses Native American religious beliefs	**a.** Unlike the plain writing style of the Puritans, Byrd's writing uses satire. **b.** In <u>The History of the Dividing Line,</u> Byrd discusses Native American religious beliefs.	Capitalization, Apostrophe usage, Comma usage, Underline titles, Spelling, End marks
10	**a.** Olaudah Equiano was the 1st African Writer to reach a large audience of American Reader's **b.** Equianos writting is a powerfull account of being kidnapped as a child and sold	**a.** Olaudah Equiano was the first African writer to reach a large audience of American readers. **b.** Equiano's writing is a powerful account of being kidnapped as a child and sold.	Write out abbreviations, Capitalization, Apostrophe usage, Spelling, End marks

Collection 1

VISIONS AND VOYAGES

Native American Literatures
Bradford
Rowlandson
Byrd
Equiano

The Journey

One day you finally knew
what you had to do, and began,
though the voices around you
kept shouting
their bad advice—
though the whole house
began to tremble
and you felt the old tug
at your ankles.
"Mend my life!"
each voice cried.
But you didn't stop.
You knew what you had to do,
though the wind pried
with its stiff fingers
at the very foundations—
though their melancholy
was terrible.
It was already late
enough, and a wild night,
and the road full of fallen
branches and stones.
But little by little,
as you left their voices behind,
the stars began to burn
through the sheets of clouds,
and there was a new voice,
which you slowly
recognized as your own,
that kept you company
as you strode deeper and deeper
into the world,
determined to do
the only thing you could do—
determined to save
the only life you could save.

—Mary Oliver (1935–)

"The Journey"

? How does this poem capture the spirit or vision of the voyagers and settlers you read about in the historical introduction? [Possible responses: The Puritans tried to stay within the British community but realized what they had to do—they had to leave. Those who condemned people for witchcraft in Salem eventually realized the error they had made and they confessed their wrongdoing. A new nation was born.]

PORTFOLIO ASSESSMENT

Parent/Guardian Involvement For forms that will help a parent or guardian review and respond to a student's portfolio, see the ***Portfolio Management System,*** pp. 62–63.

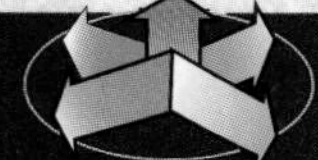

PROGRAM MANAGER

- **Integrated Assessment** For a summative assessment of the literature and language skills taught in this collection, see **Collection 1 Test, *Test Booklet,*** pp. 11–14.
- **Instructional Support** See **Fine Art Transparency** 1.1. Review teacher's notes for transparencies in the ***Audiovisual Resources Binder*** for suggestions on how to tie the transparencies to specific reading selections.
- **Extending Collection Theme** See **Cross-Curricular Activity: Visions and Voyages, *Teaching Resources A,*** p. 24 for activities in other disciplines and for evaluation criteria.

PLANNING GUIDE

Into the Selections

Through the Selections

Beyond the Selections

RESPONDING TO THE PHOTOGRAPH: VISUAL LITERACY

What does the costume for this dance tell you about its place in the Comanche culture? [Possible responses: The costume is a decorative and elaborate work of art; it represents Comanche handicraft and skill, but it is used for a dance that resembles a battle.]

LITERATURE OF THE AMERICAS

NORTH AMERICA

The Sun Still Rises in the Same Sky: Native American Literatures

by Joseph Bruchac

Background

Few peoples have been as appreciated and, at the same time, as misrepresented as the many different cultures today called "American Indian" or "Native American." Images of "Indians" are central to mainstream America, from Longfellow's misnamed epic poem *The Song of Hiawatha* (which actually tells the story of the Chippewa hero Manabozho, not the Iroquois Hiawatha) to the "cowboys and Indians" tradition of movies about the Old West. Yet it's only recently that the authentic literary voices of Native Americans have received serious attention. Native American literature has been a living oral tradition, but it was never treated with the same respect as European, or Western, literature. But Western literature itself has its roots firmly planted in the oral tradition—such ancient classics as the *Odyssey* and *Beowulf,* long before they were written down, were stories kept alive by word of mouth. The vast body of American Indian oral literatures, encompassing dozens of epic narratives and countless thousands of stories, poems, songs, oratory, and chants, was not even recognized by Western scholars until the late 1800s. Until then, it was assumed that Native Americans had no literature.

Part of the problem scholars had in recognizing the rich traditions of American Indian literature was translating the texts from hundreds of different languages—a task often best done by Native Americans themselves. Over the decades, various American Indian writers—N. Scott Momaday, Louise Erdrich, Simon J. Ortiz, and Leslie Marmon Silko, among others—have revitalized Native American literature by combining their fluency in English with a deep understanding of their own languages and traditions.

We can make some important generalizations about American Indian oral traditions. First of all, Native American cultures use stories to teach moral lessons and convey practical information about the natural world. A story from the Abenaki people of Maine, for example, tells how Gluskabe catches all of the game animals. He is then told by

PROGRAM MANAGER

- **Planning Instruction** See Teaching Notes, *Teaching Resources A,* p. 2, for a summary and objectives for these selections.
- **Audiotaped Readings** To help less proficient readers or auditory learners through the lesson, use the Selected Reading, Audiocassette 1, Side A, in the *Audiovisual Resources Binder.*

his grandmother to return the animals to the woods. They will die if they are kept in his bag, she tells him, and if they do die, there will be no game left for the people to come. In this one brief tale, important, life-sustaining lessons about greed, the wisdom of elders, and game management are conveyed in an entertaining and engaging way.

American Indian literatures also reflect a view of the natural world that is more inclusive than the one typically seen in Western literature. The Native American universe is not dominated by human beings. Animals and humans are often interchangeable in myths and folk tales. Origin myths may even feature animals or birds as the instruments of creation.

All American Indian cultures also show a keen awareness of the power of metaphor. Words are as powerful and alive as the human breath that carries them. Songs and chants can make things happen—call game animals, bring rain, cure the sick, or destroy an enemy. For Native Americans, speech, or oratory—often relying on striking similes drawn from nature—is a highly developed and respected literary form.

Passed on from generation to generation, oral traditions preserve historical continuity. But these traditions are also, like the Native American peoples themselves, tenacious, dynamic, and responsive to change. The American Indian worldview is not that of a progressive straight line, but of an endless circle. This cyclical nature of existence is reflected both in the natural world itself, with its changing seasons and cycles of birth, death, and rebirth, and in Native American ceremonies repeated year after year. Each summer, for example, the Lakota people have their Sun Dance. In pre-Columbian times, they went to the Sun Dance on foot; after the coming of the Spanish, they rode horses to the annual event. Today, the Lakota arrive by automobile. While a European eye might see the technology of transport as the important point of this anecdote, to a Lakota the issue of changing transportation is unimportant. It is, after all, only a different way of getting to the same place. The sun still rises in the same sky.

Quickwrite

Before you read these examples of Native American literature, make a KWL chart like the one below. Fill out the first two columns—what you already know about Native American literature and culture and what you'd like to learn about it. Leave the third column blank for now.

K What I Know	W What I Want to Know	L What I Learned

Into the Selections

Background

- Despite the inattention to Native American literature before the late 1800s, American Indians did publish. The first history by an American Indian was published in 1827, the first autobiography in 1829, and the first book of poetry in 1868; also, the Library of Aboriginal Literature was founded in 1885 to preserve classics of the oral tradition.
- The Lakota are one of the three divisions of the Dakota, or Sioux. The Lakota, or Teton, in turn have seven main divisions. Originally, the Sun Dance was performed to give thanks to the Supreme Being, represented by the sun, and to ask the Supreme Being to provide for their needs in the coming year. Today, for one division of the Lakota, the Oglala, the dance symbolizes both their unity and their separateness from all other peoples.

Quickwrite

To help students start to organize information, tell them that they could include points from the introduction to Native American Literatures in the What I Know column.

A. Expansion
One type of Native American myth about the world is the earth diver myth, common among northeast American Indian cultures. In these myths, the earth is covered by water in the beginning and one or more creatures—usually an otter, muskrat, beaver, or loon—dive down into the watery depths to bring up a piece of earth. That clump is then placed on the back of a great turtle—which is why many Native American peoples refer to North America as Turtle Island.

B. Reader's Response: First Thoughts
? Why do you think the woman is named Ancient Woman? [Sample responses: The name may signify her age or the wisdom that comes with age.]

C. Reader's Response: Connecting with the Text
Eating from a tree of fruit is also important in the story of creation in Genesis in the Bible. Why do you think a tree filled with fruit might be important in both stories? [Sample responses: Fruit is a symbol of life and abundance. Or it is readily available and may be eaten with little or no tending or preparation.]

D. Literary Element: Symbol
? What does the rooting of the tree symbolize? [Possible answer: The tree will grow anew, and life will not end.]

The Sky Tree

A In the beginning, Earth was covered with water. In Sky Land, there were people living as they do now on Earth. In the middle of that land was the great Sky Tree. All of the food which the people in that Sky Land ate came from the great tree.

The old chief of that land lived with his wife, whose name was Aataentsic,[1] meaning "Ancient Woman," in their long house near the great tree. B It came to be that the old chief became sick, and nothing could cure him. He grew weaker and weaker until it seemed he would die. Then a dream came to him, and he called Aataentsic to him.

"I have dreamed," he said, "and in my dream I saw how I can be healed. I must be given the fruit which grows at the very top of Sky Tree. C You must cut it down and bring that fruit to me."

Aataentsic took her husband's stone ax and went to the great tree. As soon as she struck it, it split in half and toppled over. As it fell, a hole opened in Sky Land, and the tree fell through the hole. Aataentsic returned to the place where the old chief waited.

"My husband," she said, "when I cut the tree, it split in half and then fell through a great hole. Without the tree, there can be no life. I must follow it."

Then, leaving her husband, she went back to the hole in Sky Land and threw herself after the great tree.

As Aataentsic fell, Turtle looked up and saw her. Immediately Turtle called together all the water animals and told them what she had seen.

"What should be done?" Turtle said.

Beaver answered her. "You are the one who saw this happen. Tell us what to do."

"All of you must dive down," Turtle said. "Bring up soil from the bottom, and place it on my back."

Immediately all of the water animals began to dive down and bring up soil. Beaver, Mink, Muskrat, and Otter each brought up pawfuls of wet soil and placed the soil on Turtle's back until they had made an island of great size. When they were through, Aataentsic settled down D gently on the new Earth, and the pieces of the great tree fell beside her and took root.

—*from* the Huron–Eastern Woodland tradition, *as told by* Joseph Bruchac

Navajo sand painter at Hubbell Trading Post, Ganado, Arizona.
Jerry Jacka Photography.

1. Aataentsic (ä'tä·ent'sik).

OPTIONS FOR TEACHING

STRATEGIES FOR INCLUSION

Less Proficient Readers Before students begin to read, call attention to the references to *Hiawatha, Beowulf,* and the *Odyssey* in the first paragraph of the introduction. Locate and show illustrations from those texts. Have available some books by the writers mentioned in the second paragraph, so that they are not just names to students.

Auditory Have students locate American Indian music that could be played as a backdrop to the oral reading of the selections. Have them play their selections and explain why they chose the selections to accompany the oral pieces.

INTEGRATING THE LANGUAGE ARTS

Strategic Reading To encourage students to make predictions during the reading of a story, such as "The Sky Tree" on p. 22, read the title aloud to them, and ask what they think the story will be about. Then, read the first paragraph aloud, and ask them to determine whether their prediction is supported. Ask them to expand on that first prediction or to revise it. Continue until all the paragraphs have been read.

The Earth Only (E)

Wica'hcala kin	The old men
heya'pelo'	say
maka' kin	the earth
lece'la	only
tehan yunke'lo	endures
eha' pelo'	You spoke
ehan'kecon	truly
wica' yaka pelo'	You are right.

—*composed by* Used-As-A-Shield (Teton Sioux), *translated in* 1918

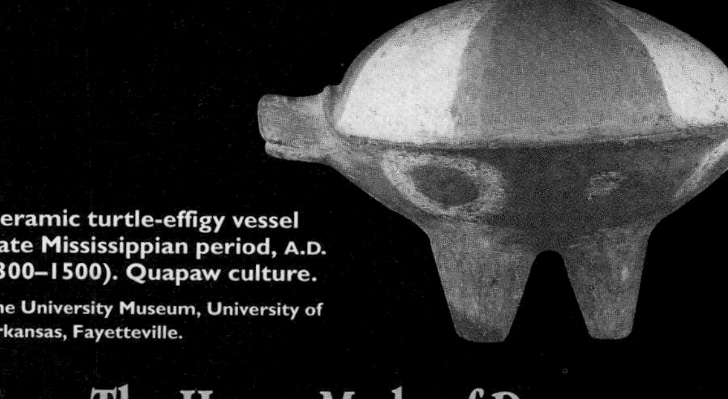

Ceramic turtle-effigy vessel (late Mississippian period, A.D. 1300–1500). Quapaw culture.

The University Museum, University of Arkansas, Fayetteville.

from The House Made of Dawn
from The Night Chant (F)

In Tsegihi,
In the house made of dawn,
In the house made of evening twilight,
In the house made of dark cloud,
In the house made of male rain,
In the house made of dark mist,
In the house made of female rain,
In the house made of pollen,
In the house made of grasshoppers,
Where the dark mist curtains the doorway,
The path to which is on the rainbow,
Where the zigzag lightning stands on top,
Where the he-rain stands high on top,
Oh, male divinity!
With your moccasins of dark cloud, come to us. . . .

I have made your sacrifice.
I have prepared a smoke for you.
My feet restore for me.
My limbs restore for me.
My body restore for me.
My mind restore for me.
My voice restore for me. . . .

Happily I recover.
Happily my interior grows cool.
Happily my limbs regain their power.
Happily my head becomes cool.
Happily I hear again.
Happily I walk.
Impervious to pain, I walk.
Feeling light within, I walk.
With lively feelings, I walk. . . .

—*from* the Navajo tradition, *translated by* Washington Matthews

Storyteller figurine by Helen Cordero. Pottery. Cochiti Pueblo, New Mexico.

Courtesy of The Heard Museum, Phoenix, Arizona/Jerry Jacka Photography.

E. Exploring the Culture
The making of personal songs is an important tradition among many American Indian people. Rather than being part of an anonymous oral tradition, these songs are credited to individuals. They may impart some philosophical insight about life, express emotion, or relate to the person's attempt to obtain spiritual power.

A poet, Orpingalik, quoted in "The Netsilik Eskimo," defines *songs* as follows: "Songs are thoughts, sung out with the breath when people are moved by great forces and ordinary speech no longer suffices. Man is moved just like the ice floe sailing here and there out in the current. His thoughts are driven by a flowing force when he feels joy, when he feels sorrow. Thoughts can wash over him like a flood, making his blood come in gasps and his heart throb. Something like an abatement in the weather will keep him thawed up, and then it will happen that we, who always think we are small, will feel still smaller. And we will fear to use words. But it will happen that the words we need will come of themselves. When the words we want to use shoot up by themselves—we get a new song."

F. Exploring the Culture
The Night Chant is part of a Dine (Navajo) ceremony incorporating sand painting, singing, and the gathering of a large number of people to lend support to the person who is ill. Among the Dine, health is regarded as natural. Sickness is a result of imbalance. The Night Chant ceremony restores balance to the person who is ill. The Dine word *hozhoni,* translated here as "happily," has a meaning that combines the concepts of beauty, peace, harmony, and happiness.

CROSSING THE CURRICULUM

Health Divide the class into small groups to research healing practices and ceremonies such as the Night Chant. Assign or let each group choose a topic, such as prayers, songs, and particular ceremonies that use song and chant.

Fine Arts Have four students retell each of the Native American selections orally so they may have a sense of how these stories were originally heard. Students need not memorize word for word, but they should learn their selections well enough to retain their stylistic flavor and important details.

Social Sciences Encourage students to determine what groups of American Indians have lived, or continue to live, in the students' local area. Have them locate additional myths that have been written down, and start an audiotape library for the class. Students may collect tapes of stories from the oral tradition that have been recorded and make tapes of ancient stories as told by members of a local American Indian group. *You may want to obtain permission from parents or guardians and from the parties students will contact before they begin work on this activity.* ☞

A. Critical Reading: Analyzing Character

? How would you characterize Coyote? [Possible answers: He is protective, creative, generous, imaginative, wise, and talented.]

B. Reader's Response: First Thoughts

? What do you think of Coyote? [Sample responses: He seems like a god. It is hard to imagine someone who does all that Coyote does also making mistakes and being foolish. Or he seems more human to me than godlike, because he makes mistakes. Or he seems like a leader or hero.]

C. Expansion

The trickster, one of the favorite characters in Native American stories, often takes the form of an animal. Tricksters live (and sometimes die) by their wits. To be sure, tricksters are not always admirable. They represent a mythology and a set of religious beliefs carried forward from the past into the present. The trickster figure represents the dual nature of human beings, and for that reason trickster tales usually present their protagonists as complex characters, mixing humor and seriousness, earthiness and spirituality.

D. Expansion

The Nez Percé lived on the lower Snake River in central Idaho and in Oregon and Washington. Today, about fifteen hundred Nez Percé live in Idaho on a reservation, but most live in the general United States population.

Coyote Finishes His Work

From the very beginning, Coyote was traveling around all over the earth. He did many wonderful things when he went along. He killed the monsters and the evil spirits **A** that preyed on the people. He made the Indians, and put them out in tribes all over the world because Old Man Above wanted the earth to be inhabited all over, not just in one or two places.

He gave all the people different names and taught them different languages. This is why Indians live all over the country now and speak in different ways.

He taught the people how to eat and how to hunt the buffalo and catch eagles. He taught them what roots to eat and how to make a good lodge and what to wear. He **B** taught them how to dance. Sometimes he made mistakes, and even though he was wise and powerful, he did many foolish things. But that was his way.

C Coyote liked to play tricks. He thought about himself all the time, and told everyone he was a great warrior, but he was not. Sometimes he would go too far with some trick and get someone killed. Other times, he would have a trick played on himself by someone else. He got killed this way so many times that Fox and the birds got tired of bringing him back to life. Another way he got in trouble was trying to do what someone else did. This is how he came to be called Imitator.

Coyote was ugly too. The girls did not like him. But he was smart. He could change himself around and trick the women. Coyote got the girls when he wanted.

One time, Coyote had done everything he could think of and was traveling from one place to another place, looking for other things that needed to be done. Old Man saw him going along and said to himself, "Coyote has now done almost everything he is capable of doing. His work is almost done. It is time to bring him back to the place where he started."

So Great Spirit came down and traveled in the shape of an old man. He met Coyote. Coyote said, "I am Coyote. Who are you?"

Old Man said, "I am Chief of the earth. It was I who sent you to set the world right."

"No," Coyote said, "you never sent me. I don't know you. If you are the Chief, take that lake over there and move it to the side of that mountain."

"No. If you are Coyote, let me see you do it."

Coyote did it.

"Now, move it back."

Coyote tried, but he could not do it. He thought this was strange. He tried again, but he could not do it.

Chief moved the lake back.

Coyote said, "Now I know you are the Chief."

Old Man said, "Your work is finished, Coyote. You have traveled far and done much good. Now you will go to where I have prepared a home for you."

Then Coyote disappeared. Now no one knows where he is anymore.

Old Man got ready to leave, too. He said to the Indians, "I will send messages to the earth by the spirits of the people who reach me but whose time to die has not yet come. They will carry messages to you from time to time. When their spirits come back into their bodies, they will revive and tell you their experiences.

"Coyote and myself, we will not be seen again until Earthwoman is very old. Then we shall return to earth, for it will require a change by that time. Coyote will come along first, and when you see him you will know I am coming. When I come along, all the spirits of the dead will be with me. There will be no more Other Side Camp. All the people will live together. Earthmother will go back to her first shape and live as a mother among her children. Then things will be made right."

Now they are waiting for Coyote.

D —*from* the Nez Percé tradition, *retold by* Barry Lopez

OPTIONS FOR TEACHING

PROFESSIONAL NOTES

Thematic Connections: "Visions and Voyages" Generalizing from these American Indian works, have students describe some characteristics of the Native American vision. They may include community orientation, respect for the world, humor, spirituality, and connectedness. Discuss with students what they may gain from an understanding of Native American traditions. They may touch on such issues as history and intercultural differences and similarities.

Critical Comment: Native American Voices Scholars attest to the stereotypes and misrepresentations of American Indian cultures in mainstream culture in the United States and suggest remedies for the harm done: "Until recently . . . the popular concept of Indian literature was shaped not by the Indian and not even by his translator but by the white American writer or moviemaker. . . . There is no better way to correct the misrepresentations that have ingrained themselves in our folklore than to listen to the genuine voices of the Indian peoples. Since their poems are really songs meant to be chanted or sung as part of various rituals, it is indeed the voices of the Indians, ancient and authentic, despite the drawbacks of translation, that we hear when we read them."

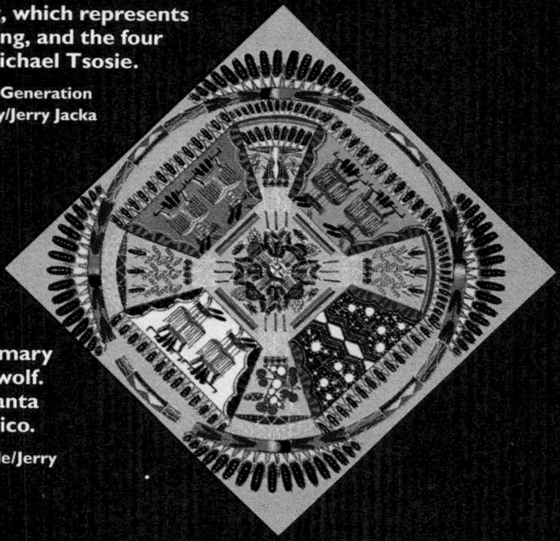

Sand painting, which represents storm, lightning, and the four seasons, by Michael Tsosie.

Courtesy of Fifth Generation Trading Company/Jerry Jacka Photography.

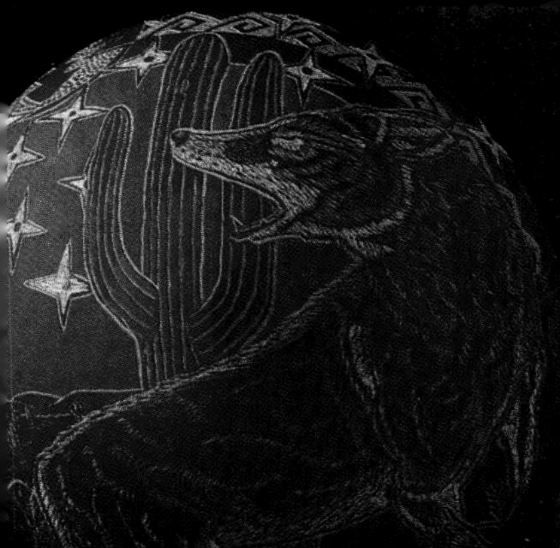

Coyote Crooner by Rosemary "Apple Blossom" Lonewolf. Pottery (3½″ × 4½″). Santa Clara Pueblo, New Mexico.

Courtesy Gallery 10, Scottsdale/Jerry Jacka Photography.

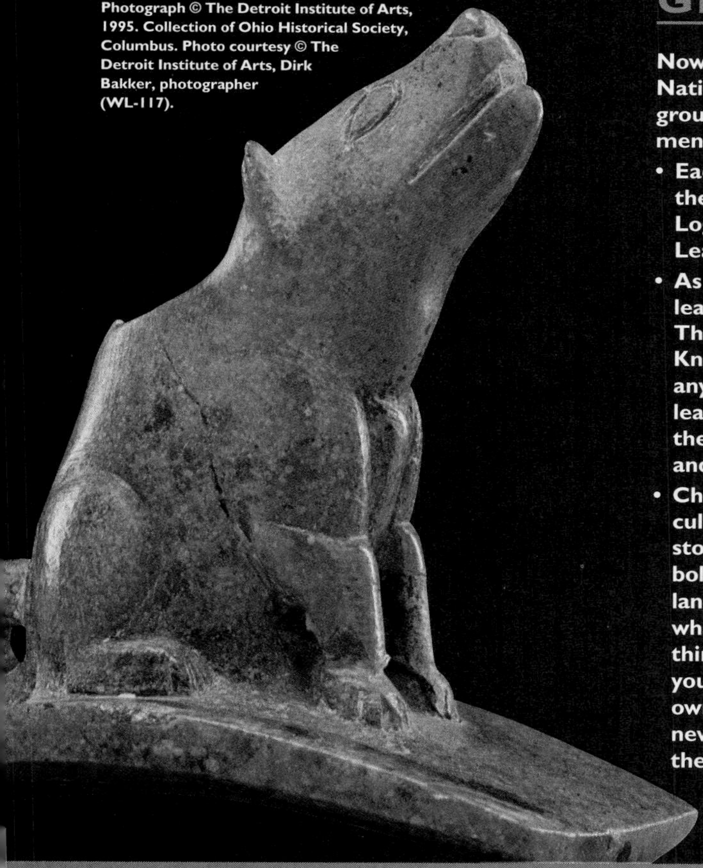

Coyote-Effigy Platform Pipe (Middle Woodland period, 200 B.C.–A.D. 100). Pipestone; Temper mound (6.4″ × 7″). Scioto County, Ohio. Ohio Hopewell culture.

Photograph © The Detroit Institute of Arts, 1995. Collection of Ohio Historical Society, Columbus. Photo courtesy © The Detroit Institute of Arts, Dirk Bakker, photographer (WL-117).

FINDING COMMON GROUND

Now that you've read these examples of Native American literature, meet in small groups to share your questions, comments, and discoveries.

- **Each person in the group should review the KWL chart in his or her Reader's Log and fill in the third column, "What I Learned."**
- **As a group, discuss what members learned from reading these selections. Then go back to the "What I Want to Know" column, and decide if there are any other topics you'd like to discuss and learn more about. Be sure someone in the group records the suggested topics and any group responses.**
- **Choose some aspect of Native American culture you'd like to learn more about: storytelling, ceremonies, healing, symbols, dances, myths, historical figures, language, art, environmental issues, or whatever else you like. Choose something that grabs your interest, and, by yourself or with a partner, develop your own avenue of exploration. Share your newfound knowledge with the rest of the class.**

Finding Common Ground

Suggest to students that the way they present their material needs as much thought as the way they research the subject. To complement the oral tradition represented in these selections, ask students to find an engaging way to orally present their findings. For example, for a report on storytelling, students could actually tell some stories. For a report on ceremonies, students could locate pictures or video clips to show to the class.

Technology Tip

Much Native American literature can be found on the Internet. Ask your students to do key word searches on the World Wide Web to find samples. *You may want to preview any Internet activity that you suggest to students. Because these resources are sometimes public forums, their content can be unpredictable.*

ASSESSMENT TOOLS

Check Test: Completion

1. Although some of them have been published, most Native American stories, songs, and tales are in the _____ tradition. [oral]
2. Native Americans use stories to _____. [teach a lesson and convey practical information]
3. In Native American origin myths _____ can be creators. [birds or animals]
4. Coyote disappeared _____. [because his work was finished]
5. Native Americans do not see the world in a linear fashion, where events happen one after the other; they see life as _____. [an endless circle]

Self-Reflection After students have completed this section, ask them to reflect on the state of their knowledge about Native Americans. Encourage them to use their KWL charts to compare with a partner how their views and ideas have changed and grown during the reading of these American Indian selections.

ABOUT THE AUTHOR

Bradford may seem an unlikely candidate for a spy, but during his tenure as governor, he was instrumental in exposing two troublemakers who were trying to undermine the colony. John Oldham and John Lyford came to the Plymouth community in 1623 and 1624, respectively. Soon they were joined in plots to sow discontent among the colonists and were sending letters to England that attacked the leaders of the colony. After intercepting the letters, Bradford copied them, and the men were brought to trial and confronted with the evidence. Bradford reports that while Lyford was struck speechless, Oldham became enraged because the governors had intercepted and opened his letters. Both conspirators were exiled from the colony.

William Bradford

(1590–1657)

William Bradford's life displayed a mixture of the commonplace and the extraordinary that was characteristic of the Puritan experience. Bradford was the son of a prosperous farmer in Yorkshire, England. He received no higher education but instead was taught the practical arts of farming. Despite his lack of formal training (or perhaps because of it), Bradford was to become a successful, longstanding Colonial governor in America, dealing out justice and settling disputes.

Growing up in England, Bradford took a radical step when he was twelve years old. Inspired by his reading of the Bible and by the sermons of a Puritan minister, Bradford began attending the meetings of a small group of Nonconformists, despite the vehement objections of his family and friends. It was illegal for Nonconformists to worship publicly, so the group met furtively in a private house in the nearby town of Scrooby. In 1606, when the group organized as a separate Congregational church, Bradford joined them. In 1608, under increasing pressure of persecution and fearful that they would be imprisoned, the Scrooby group crossed the North Sea to Holland. In 1620, after twelve years in Holland, the group was aided by London profiteers and merchants, who lent them a ship and crew as an investment. In September the Nonconformists sailed for America in order to found a community where they would be free to worship and live according to their beliefs.

For Bradford the hardships of the long ocean voyage did not end with the landing at Plymouth. In December, while the *Mayflower* was anchored in Provincetown Harbor, Bradford and other men took a small boat ashore to scout for a place to land and build shelter. When they returned, Bradford learned that his young wife had fallen or jumped from the ship. Perhaps Dorothy Bradford was in despair when land was finally sighted and she did not see the hoped-for green hills of an earthly paradise. Beyond the ship lay only the bleak sand dunes of Cape Cod. That bitter winter, half the settlers were to die of cold, disease, and malnutrition.

Page from *Of Plimoth Plantation* by William Bradford.

Courtesy of the State Library of Massachusetts.

The following year, Bradford was elected governor of the plantation. "If he had not been a person of more than ordinary piety, wisdom, and courage," the Puritan preacher Cotton Mather later recorded, Bradford would "have sunk" under the difficulties of governing such a shaky settlement. Bradford proved to be an exemplary leader, and he went on to be elected governor of the Colony no fewer than thirty times.

As the Plymouth Colony prospered and grew, it also gradually disintegrated as a religious community, despite Bradford's efforts to hold it together. The ideal of the "city on the hill," the Pilgrims' dream of an ideal society founded on religious principles, gradually gave way to the realities of life in the new land. Bradford's record of this grand experiment ends in disappointment. When more fertile areas for settlement were found and when Boston became a more convenient port to England, Plymouth lost much of its population. "Thus was this poor church left," Bradford wrote in 1644, "like an ancient mother grown old and forsaken of her children. . . . Thus, she that had made many rich became herself poor."

WORDS TO OWN

The following vocabulary words are defined in the Words to Own at the bottom of the pupil's page.

profane p. 29	sundry p. 30
haughty p. 29	relent p. 32
execrations p. 29	discourse p. 32
reproved p. 29	confederates p. 33
consultation p. 30	comprised p. 33

PORTFOLIO ASSESSMENT

Portfolio Assessment For help with self- and teacher assessment of reading skills, see the ***Portfolio Management System,*** pp. 48–49.

Before You Read
from Of Plymouth Plantation

Reading Focus
Journey to Salvation

Every age has at least one figure or heroic type that seems to embody its ideals and aspirations. The Puritans who came to America identified so powerfully with one figure that they called themselves by that name: "Pilgrim." A pilgrim is someone who makes a pilgrimage, or a journey to a holy place. But for the Puritans, the word *pilgrimage* took on a wider meaning—it was a journey to salvation.

For the Pilgrims, the outward journey of their lives and the specific voyage to America were also inner, spiritual journeys. "A Christian is sailing through this world unto his heavenly country," the poet Anne Bradstreet (page 68) wrote some years after sailing across the Atlantic to America. "We must, therefore, be here as strangers and pilgrims, that we may plainly declare that we seek a city above."

A Dialogue with the Text

READER'S LOG

As you read Bradford's history, write down the particular hardships that the Pilgrims encounter on their journey to America and during their first winter in New England. How do they respond to and deal with these hardships? Note, also, the points at which Bradford refers to God's role in the events of the voyage.

Elements of Literature
The Plain Style

In their style of writing, as well as in their style of worship, the Puritans favored the plain, the unornamented, and the simple. Even though Puritan writings seem difficult to read to us today, in their own day the style the Puritans wrote in was considered simple and direct. This **plain style** emphasized simple sentences and the use of everyday words from common speech, and it steered clear of elaborate **figures of speech** and **imagery.**

The **plain style** is a way of writing that stresses simplicity and clarity of expression.

For more on the Plain Style, see page 35 and the Handbook of Literary Terms.

Background
In 1630, Bradford began to write this account of the Plymouth settlement, and he continued to write an annual account until 1647. Unlike many other early Colonial histories, it was not composed for immediate publication or to attract more colonists, but was intended to inspire future generations to carry on the Pilgrims' ideals. The first nine chapters of Bradford's history were copied into the Plymouth church records, but the entire manuscript was lost when British troops plundered the church during the Revolutionary War. Almost a century later, Governor Bradford's vellum-bound volume was discovered in the library of the bishop of London. *Of Plymouth Plantation* was first published in 1856 by the Massachusetts Historical Society. The manuscript was finally returned to the United States in 1897, and it can be seen today in the Boston State House.

Quick Planning Guide

Into the Selection

Through the Selection

Beyond the Selection

Program Manager

- **Planning Instruction** See **Teaching Notes, *Teaching Resources A,*** pp. 2–3, for objectives, a summary, and literary elements.
- **Instructional Support** Before beginning the instructional lesson, see **Graphic Organizer for Active Reading, *Teaching Resources A,*** p. 7, for a Through the Selection activity.
- **Instructional Support** See **Fine Art Transparency** 1.1. Review teacher's notes for transparencies in the ***Audiovisual Resources Binder.***
- **Assessment** See **Selection Test, *Test Booklet,*** pp. 3–4.
- **Language Link** For instruction and practice in nouns, see **Language Link, *Teaching Resources A,*** pp. 8–9, and ***Language and Writing Skills Worksheets,*** pp. 11–12.
- **Reinforcement** Use the **Words to Own** worksheet in ***Teaching Resources A,*** pp. 10–11.

Into the Selection

Using **Before You Read** p. 27

Reading Focus

Ask students to identify a heroic ideal for immigrants today. Have them discuss the various possibilities. Then, introduce the pilgrim as a heroic figure to the Puritans who came to the American continent; finally, have students read the Reading Focus.

Background

Before its loss, the manuscript for *Of Plymouth Plantation* had been passed by inheritance as well as borrowed by several readers, including Increase Mather and his son, Cotton Mather. Reverend Thomas Prince used it for research and kept it in his library in Boston's Old South Church until the Revolution. Evidently someone on the British side took the manuscript when the British occupied the church during the war, and British writers' use of it revealed its presence there to Americans. In 1897, it was returned to Massachusetts.

from Of Plymouth Plantation

William Bradford

But that which was most sad and lamentable was, that in two or three months' time half of their company died . . .

Options for Teaching

Strategies for Inclusion

Less Proficient Readers Students may have particular trouble with pronouns in this selection. Although Bradford was a Pilgrim, he writes about the Pilgrims in the third person. A review of third person pronouns may help. Students may work in pairs, using common sense and agreement clues to come to consensus on pronoun meaning for a passage.

Spatial Students may benefit by having a time line on which to record events. Encourage students to decide whether a horizontal or a vertical form will work better to help them recall the order of events. Remind students to give equal time periods equal spacing on their time lines.

Auditory For better comprehension, pair students, and have them take turns reading the selection aloud and following along in the book. As they read, have them pause occasionally, allowing the student who has read along silently to give the other a brief summary of the passage just read.

Special Needs To help students who have trouble identifying main ideas and sequence, have them create Storyboards depicting ten incidents from the story, in sequence, with a caption for each illustration. Students with speech or hearing disabilities may prefer this activity over an oral presentation, because it allows them to demonstrate understanding without having to speak.

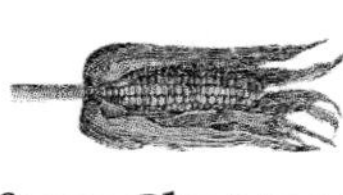

from Chapter 9

Of their Voyage, and how they Passed the Sea; and of their Safe Arrival at Cape Cod

September 6 [1620]. These troubles[1] being blown over, and now all being compact together in one ship, they put to sea again with a prosperous wind, which continued divers[2] days together, which was some encouragement unto them; yet, according to the usual manner, many were afflicted with seasickness. **A** And I may not omit here a special work of God's providence. There was a proud and very profane young man, one of the seamen, of a lusty,[3] able body, which made him the more haughty; he would always be condemning the poor people in their sickness and cursing them daily with grievous execrations; and did not let to tell them that he hoped to help to cast half of them overboard before they came to their journey's end, and to make merry with what they had; and if he were by any gently reproved, he would curse and swear most bitterly. But it pleased God before they came half seas over, to smite this young man with a grievous disease, of which he died in a desperate manner, and so was himself the first that was thrown overboard. Thus his curses light on his own head, and it was an astonishment to all his fellows for they noted it to be the just hand of God upon him. **B**

1. **troubles:** the return of the *Speedwell* to England and the transfer of her passengers to the *Mayflower.*
2. **divers** (dī′vərz): many.
3. **lusty:** energetic; robust.

Words to Own

profane (prō·fān′) *adj.:* irreverent.
haughty (hôt′ē) *adj.:* proud; disdainful of something or someone.
execrations (ek′si·krā′shənz) *n.:* angry words; curses.
reproved (ri·pro͞ovd′) *v.:* reprimanded.

Ear of corn (1535), pages 29, 31, 32, 33.
The Granger Collection, New York.

Landing of the Pilgrims at Plymouth (1803) by Michel Felice Corné. Oil on canvas.

Courtesy of the Pilgrim Society, Plymouth, Massachusetts.

Through the Selection

A. Literary Element: Point of View
Bradford uses the third-person plural to refer to the Pilgrims in general. Even when speaking particularly of himself as an individual Pilgrim, he uses the third-person masculine.

B. Literary Element: Plain Style
The Puritans believed that the will of God directs and guides the universe. This belief is demonstrated in the moral anecdotes Bradford includes in his autobiography. What spiritual lesson does this anecdote teach? [Possible answers: Those who flaunt the will of God will be punished. Pride goes before a fall.]

Integrating the Language Arts

Strategic Reading Before students read, have them preview Bradford's selection, using the three steps of previewing.

- Skim the title, trying to determine meaning from it.
- Study and try to interpret the pictures or illustrations included with the selection.
- Skim the subheads (usually in boldface or italics) to get a sense of the structure and to find out the main ideas in the different sections.

Explain to students that these steps can also be used after reading to review a selection.

Language and Style To help students understand Bradford's style, challenge them to take the structure of the first sentence in his second paragraph and to use it to create their own sentence. Have them begin by substituting another *–ed* action verb for the word *enjoyed.* Students might change nouns, verbs, adverbs, and adjectives to create a sentence that is probably unlike anything they have ever written before. [Possible response: After they had hiked gentle slopes and trails for a week, they were endangered many times by rockslides, and their food was seriously depleted by many bears, and their crumbling morale made very low. Also, one of the tent poles in the rucksack was bent and unusable, which put them in some concern that the tent would not be able to last the night.]

A. Critical Reading: Drawing Conclusions
The Pilgrims' response to the problem with the main beam shows that they are practical as well as pious. Why would practicality be vital to the Pilgrims' success? [Possible answer: Once they reach North America, the Pilgrims expect to be self-sufficient, providing for their own shelter, food, and medical care.]

B. Exploring the Historical Period
Perceptive readers will notice that Cape Cod was named before the Pilgrims landed. In 1614, Captain John Smith had mapped the North American coast from Maine to Cape Cod. Colonial place names were taken from natural features (Cape Cod Bay was full of codfish), from Anglicized American Indian names (Massachusetts, named for its location close to a large hill), or from English place names or royal-family names (Plymouth; Cape Ann). Students may enjoy tracing the origins of other Colonial place names.

C. Exploring the Historical Period
The Pilgrims expected to settle in Virginia within the grant area of the London Company, but they landed too far north, outside the area controlled by the company. Uncertain of their status because they had no legal government, they created the Mayflower Compact while still aboard ship, the first agreement by a Colonial group in North America to govern itself. This document established majority rule by the male church members among the colonists. The original of this document is missing, but we know its wording because Bradford quotes it in *Of Plymouth Plantation.*

After they had enjoyed fair winds and weather for a season, they were encountered many times with crosswinds and met with many fierce storms with which the ship was shroudly[4] shaken, and her upper works made very leaky; and one of the main beams in the midships was bowed and cracked, which put them in some fear that the ship could not be able to perform the voyage. So some of the chief of the company, perceiving the mariners to fear the sufficiency of the ship as appeared by their mutterings, they entered into serious consultation with the master and other officers of the ship, to consider in time of the danger, and rather to return than to cast themselves into a desperate and inevitable peril. And truly there was great distraction and difference of opinion amongst the mariners themselves; fain[5] would they do what could be done for their wages' sake (being now near half the seas over) and on the other hand they were loath[6] to hazard their lives too desperately. But in examining of all opinions, the master and others affirmed they knew the ship to be strong and firm underwater; and for the buckling of the main beam, there was a great iron screw the passengers brought out of Holland, which would raise the beam into his place; the which being done, the carpenter and master affirmed that with a post put under it, set firm in the lower deck and otherways bound, he would make it sufficient. And as for the decks and upper works, they would caulk them as well as they could, and though with the working of the ship they would not long keep staunch,[7] yet there would otherwise be no great danger, if they did not overpress her with sails. So they committed themselves to the will of God and resolved to proceed.

In sundry of these storms the winds were so fierce and the seas so high, as they could not bear a knot of sail, but were forced to hull[8] for divers days together. And in one of them, as they thus lay at hull in a mighty storm, a lusty young man called John Howland, coming upon some occasion above the gratings was, with a seele[9] of the ship, thrown into sea; but it pleased God that he caught hold of the topsail halyards[10] which hung overboard and ran out at length. Yet he held his hold (though he was sundry fathoms underwater) till he was hauled up by the same rope to the brim of the water, and then with a boathook and other means got into the ship again and his life saved. And though he was something ill with it, yet he lived many years after and became a profitable member both in church and commonwealth. In all this voyage there died but one of the passengers, which was William Butten, a youth, servant to Samuel Fuller, when they drew near the coast.

But to omit other things (that I may be brief) after long beating at sea they fell with that land which is called Cape Cod;[11] the which being made and certainly known to be it, they were not a little joyful. After some deliberation had amongst themselves and with the master of the ship, they tacked about and resolved to stand for the southward (the wind and weather being fair) to find some place about Hudson's River[12] for their habitation. But after they had sailed that course about half the day, they fell amongst dangerous shoals and roaring breakers, and they were so far entangled therewith as they conceived themselves in great danger; and the wind shrinking upon them withal, they resolved to bear up again for the Cape and thought themselves happy to get out of those dangers before night overtook them, as by God's good providence they did. And the next day they got into the Cape Harbor[13] where they rid in safety. . . .

Being thus arrived in a good harbor, and brought safe to land, they fell upon their knees and blessed the God of Heaven who had brought them over the vast and furious ocean, and

4. **shroudly** (shro͞od′lē): shrewdly, used here in its archaic sense of "wickedly."
5. **fain** (fān): archaic for "gladly."
6. **loath** (lōth): reluctant.
7. **staunch** (stônch): watertight.
8. **hull:** to float without using the sails.
9. **seele:** sudden lurch to one side.

10. **halyards** (hal′yərdz): ropes for raising a sail.
11. **Cape Cod:** They sighted Cape Cod at daybreak on November 9, 1620.
12. **Hudson's River:** They were trying for Manhattan Island. Henry Hudson had made his voyage in 1609 and had claimed the area for the Dutch, but the English did not recognize the Dutch claim.
13. **Cape Harbor:** now called Provincetown Harbor. The sea voyage from England had taken sixty-five days.

WORDS TO OWN
consultation (kän′səl·tā′shən) *n.:* meeting to discuss or plan.
sundry (sun′drē) *adj.:* some.

OPTIONS FOR TEACHING

COOPERATIVE LEARNING

Review To review the material, ask students to work in groups and to assume the perspective of American Indians who secretly observed the Pilgrims and recorded their doings in a journal. This activity will encourage both a chronological review of events and a shift in perspectives that may help students gain insight into the Pilgrims' beliefs. Let students assume that the American Indians were able to observe or overhear reports about everything Bradford recorded. Have two or three students in each group generate ideas and one student record them. Then, the whole group may revise the work and present it to the class.

CLASSROOM MANAGEMENT

Social Sciences Grouping For works such as this one that relates to United States history, make sure that students who have taken a course in United States social studies are grouped with students who have not. Students familiar with history will be able to share prior knowledge and insights with others.

Peer Pairing Pair advanced students with less proficient readers to figure out pronoun references in the Strategies for Inclusion feature on p. T28. Encourage advanced students to model several examples of how they figured out the references, explain the strategies they used, and support their peers who try to apply these strategies themselves.

delivered them from all the perils and miseries thereof, again to set their feet on the firm and stable earth, their proper element. . . .

But here I cannot but stay and make a pause, and stand half amazed at this poor people's present condition; and so I think will the reader, too, when he well considers the same. Being thus passed the vast ocean, and a sea of troubles before **D** in their preparation (as may be remembered by that which went before), they had now no friends to welcome them nor inns to entertain or refresh their weather-beaten bodies; no houses or much less towns to repair to, to seek for succor.[14] It is recorded in Scripture[15] as a mercy to the Apostle and his shipwrecked company, that the barbarians showed them no small kindness in refreshing **E** them, but these savage barbarians, when they met with them (as after will appear) were readier to fill their sides full of arrows than otherwise. And for the season it was winter, and they that know the winters of that country know them to be sharp and violent, and subject to cruel and fierce storms, dangerous to travel to known places, much more to search an unknown coast. Besides, what could they see but a hideous and desolate wilderness, full of wild beasts and wild men—and what multitudes there might be of them they knew not. Neither could they, as it were, go up to the top of Pisgah[16] to view from this wilderness a more goodly country to feed their hopes; for which way soever they turned their eyes (save upward to the heavens) they could have little solace **F** or content in respect of any outward objects. For summer being done, all things stand upon them with a weather-beaten face, and the whole country, full of woods and thickets, represented a wild and savage hue. If they looked behind them, there was the mighty ocean which they had passed and was now as a main bar and gulf to separate them from all the civil parts of the world. . . .

What could now sustain them but the Spirit of God and His grace? May not and ought not the children of these fathers rightly say: "Our fathers were Englishmen which came over this great ocean, and were ready to perish in this wilderness; but they cried unto the Lord, and He heard their voice and looked on their adversity,"[17] etc.? "Let them therefore praise the Lord, because He is good: And His mercies endure forever." "Yea, let them which have been redeemed of the Lord, show how He hath delivered them from the hand of the oppressor. When they wandered in the desert wilderness out of the way, and found no city to dwell in, both hungry and thirsty, their soul was overwhelmed in them. Let them confess before the Lord His lovingkindness and His wonderful works before the sons of men."[18]

from Chapter 11

The Starving Time

[1620–1621] But that which was most sad and lamentable was, that in two or three months' time half of their company died, especially in January and February, being the depth of winter, and wanting houses and other comforts; being infected with the scurvy and other diseases which **G** this long voyage and their inaccommodate condition had brought upon them. So as there died sometimes two or three of a day in the foresaid time, that of 100 and odd persons, scarce fifty remained. And of these, in the time of most distress, there was but six or seven sound persons who to their great commendations, be it spoken, spared no pains night nor day, but with abundance of toil and hazard of their own health, fetched them wood, made them fires, dressed them meat, made their beds, washed their loathsome clothes, clothed and unclothed them. In a word, did all the homely and necessary offices for them which dainty and queasy stomachs cannot endure to hear named; and all this willingly and cheerfully, without any grudging in the least, showing herein their true love unto their friends and brethren; a rare example and worthy to be remembered. Two of these seven were Mr. William Brewster, their

14. **succor** (suk′ər): aid.
15. **Scripture:** In the Acts of the Apostles (Chapter 28), Paul tells how the shipwrecked Christians were helped by the "barbarous people" of Malta.
16. **Pisgah** (piz′gə): mountain from which Moses first viewed the Promised Land.
17. **they cried . . . their adversity:** paraphrase of Deuteronomy 26:7.
18. **Let them . . . the sons of men:** paraphrase of Psalm 107.

D. Humanities Connection
This reference to "a sea of troubles" echoes William Shakespeare's *Hamlet.* In the famous soliloquy, "To be or not to be," Hamlet asks "Whether 'tis nobler in the mind to suffer / The slings and arrows of outrageous fortune, / Or to take arms against a sea of troubles. . . ." Do you think that Bradford is more likely to have acquired the phrase from Shakespeare or to have coined it himself? [He probably got it, consciously or not, from Shakespeare. *Hamlet* was produced in London in 1600–1601, and by the time Bradford wrote his history, the play was widely known.]

E. Literary Element: Point of View
Although Bradford was on the *Mayflower* himself, he writes about these events in the third person. Why do you think he writes in this way? [Possible answers: Perhaps he does not want the text to seem like a personal narrative. Perhaps he is emphasizing the community over the individual.]

F. Reader's Response: First Thoughts
Consider the reasons for this voyage and the prospects the Pilgrims faced. How would you have felt? [Sample responses: Sad, for the journey was long and the future bleak; or determined to meet the challenge of the wilderness.]

G. Exploring the Historical Period
Other colonists experienced similar trouble. John White left the Roanoke Colony in 1587 because he saw they were going to run out of supplies, and the colony disappeared before he could return. The Jamestown Colony endured a "starving time" in 1609–1610 when nine out of ten settlers died.

CROSSING THE CURRICULUM

Social Sciences Students may compare and contrast other stories of Colonial settlements to Bradford's. They could read portions of or read about John Smith's *A True Relation of Such Occurrences and Accidents of Noate as Hath Hapned in Virginia* and *The Generall Historie of Virginia, New-England, and the Summer Isles.* They could also read Edward Wingfield's *A Discourse of Virginia,* Thomas Morton's *New English Canaan,* John Winthrop's journals, Roger Williams's *A Key into the Language of America,* or letters collected in John Demos's *Remarkable Providences, 1600–1760.* Students should set up a panel discussion with each person impersonating a settler and talking about various experiences.

Science The Master's unwillingness to share the beer may not have stemmed from pure greed—it is possible that he was concerned about the quality of the drinking water that he and his men would have on the return voyage. Ask students to research any problems with supplying fresh water to the *Mayflower.* After groups present their findings, ask students to revisit their interpretation of the dispute over beer.

Home Economics Encourage students to find out how Puritan beliefs were apparent in the colonists' clothing and furniture. Have them report to the class, using visual materials to support their findings.

A. Humanities Connection
Henry Wadsworth Longfellow (p. 175) took Myles (or Miles) Standish as the subject for his fictionalized account of the colony at Plymouth, *The Courtship of Miles Standish.* Still, the poem presents a paradoxical character that mirrors the paradoxical portrait painted in this passage—the military leader who does not belong to the community but who is a gentle and tireless nurse to community members in need.

B. Critical Reading: Making Inferences
? Why do you think the Master changes his mind? [Perhaps seeing members of his company beginning to sicken and die brings home to him the suffering that those on shore are enduring.]

C. Literary Element: Plain Style
In this paragraph, a moral anecdote written in clear, straightforward language compares the Pilgrims' compassionate nature to that of the sailors.

D. Expansion
In an earlier part of Bradford's narrative not included in this selection, he tells how the Pilgrims had several times taken corn and beans from the American Indians' stores without permission, although he says they planned to and did repay them some six months later. This, as well as the fact that the Pilgrims settled in a land that was already occupied, suggests that Bradford's interpretation of the situation may not be the only one possible.

(A) reverend Elder, and Myles Standish,[19] their Captain and military commander, unto whom myself and many others were much beholden in our low and sick condition. And yet the Lord so upheld these persons as in this general calamity they were not at all infected either with sickness or lameness. And what I have said of these I may say of many others who died in this general visitation, and others yet living; that whilst they had health, yea, or any strength continuing, they were not wanting to any that had need of them. And I doubt not but their recompense is with the Lord.

But I may not here pass by another remarkable passage not to be forgotten. As this calamity fell among the passengers that were to be left here to plant, and were hasted ashore and made to drink water that the seamen might have the more beer, and one[20] in his sickness desiring but a small can of beer, it was answered that if he were their own father he should have none. The disease began to fall amongst them also, so as almost half of their company died before they went away, and many of their officers and lustiest men, as the boatswain, gunner, three quartermasters, the cook and others. (B) At which the Master was something strucken and sent to the sick ashore and told the Governor he should send for beer for them that had need of it, though he drunk water homeward bound.

(C) But now amongst his company there was far another kind of carriage in this misery than amongst the passengers. For they that before had been boon companions in drinking and jollity in the time of their health and welfare, began now to desert one another in this calamity, saying they would not hazard their lives for them, they should be infected by coming to help them in their cabins; and so, after they came to lie by it, would do little or nothing for them but, "if they died, let them die." But such of the passengers as were yet aboard showed them what mercy they could, which made some of their hearts relent, as the boatswain (and some others) who was a proud young man and would often curse and scoff at the passengers. But when he grew weak, they had compassion on him and helped him; then he confessed he did not deserve it at their hands, he had abused them in word and deed. "Oh!" (saith he) "you, I now see, show your love like Christians indeed one to another, but we let one another lie and die like dogs." Another lay cursing his wife, saying if it had not been for her he had never come this unlucky voyage, and anon cursing his fellows, saying he had done this and that for some of them; he had spent so much and so much amongst them, and they were now weary of him and did not help him, having need. Another gave his companion all he had, if he died, to help him in his weakness; he went and got a little spice and made him a mess of meat once or twice. And because he died not so soon as he expected, he went amongst his fellows and swore the rogue would cozen[21] him, he would see him choked before he made him any more meat; and yet the poor fellow died before morning.

Indian Relations

(D) All this while the Indians came skulking about them, and would sometimes show themselves aloof off, but when any approached near them, they would run away; and once they stole away their tools where they had been at work and were gone to dinner. But about the 16th of March, a certain Indian came boldly amongst them and spoke to them in broken English, which they could well understand but marveled at it. At length they understood by discourse with him, that he was not of these parts, but belonged to the eastern parts where some English ships came to fish, with whom he was acquainted and could name sundry of them by their names, amongst whom he had got his language. He became profitable to them in acquainting them with many things concerning the state of the country in the east parts where he lived, which was afterward profitable unto them; as also of the people here, of their names, number

19. **Myles Standish** (c. 1584–1656): a soldier who had been hired to handle the colonists' military affairs. Not a member of the Puritan congregation, he still became a most steadfast ally.
20. **one:** Bradford himself.

21. **cozen** (kuz′ən): cheat.

WORDS TO OWN
relent (ri·lent′) *v.:* soften.
discourse (dis′kôrs′) *n.:* conversation.

OPTIONS FOR TEACHING

PROBLEM SOLVING/CRITICAL THINKING

Strangers The Pilgrims are suspicious and wary of strangers. Ask students to review as a class what they have been taught about how to deal with strangers. How can they reconcile personal safety issues with issues of bias? Have them work together to form a plan, and then have them model techniques for dealing with strangers.

Independence The Pilgrims set off to be independent and self-sufficient in a situation that was more than they could have handled alone. As students start thinking about going away to college or looking for work and living in a different place, they may have some of the same concerns about independence and dependence. After students voice their concerns, provide an opportunity for them to talk with recent graduates who have begun college or taken a job. Allow students to list questions in advance so they will be prepared.

PROFESSIONAL NOTES

Thematic Connections: "Visions and Voyages" Discuss how the Pilgrims' vision became a reality. [Students should mention factors such as the settlers' own endurance and loyalty, the generosity and knowledge of the American Indians, and the agricultural possibilities of the North American coast.]

and strength, of their situation and distance from this place, and who was chief amongst them. His name was Samoset.[22] He told them also of another Indian whose name was Squanto,[23] a native of this place, who had been in England and could speak better English than himself.

Being, after some time of entertainment and gifts dismissed, a while after he came again, and five more with him, and they brought again all the tools that were stolen away before, and made way for the coming of their great Sachem, called Massasoit.[24] Who, about four or five days after, came with the chief of his friends and other attendance, with the aforesaid Squanto. With whom, after friendly entertainment and some gifts given him, they made a peace with him (which hath now continued this 24 years)[25] in these terms:

1. That neither he nor any of his should injure or do hurt to any of their people.
2. That if any of his did hurt to any of theirs, he should send the offender, that they might punish him.
3. That if anything were taken away from any of theirs, he should cause it to be restored; and they should do the like to his.
4. If any did unjustly war against him, they would aid him; if any did war against them, he should aid them.
5. He should send to his neighbors confederates to certify them of this, that they might not wrong them, but might be likewise comprised in the conditions of peace.
6. That when their men came to them, they should leave their bows and arrows behind them.

E

After these things he returned to his place called Sowams, some 40 miles from this place, but Squanto continued with them and was their interpreter and was a special instrument sent of God for their good beyond their expectation. He directed them how to set their corn, where to take fish, and to procure other commodities, and was also their pilot to bring them to unknown places for their profit, and never left them till he died. He was a native of this place, and scarce any left alive besides himself. He was carried away with divers others by one Hunt, a master of a ship, who thought to sell them for slaves in Spain. But he got away for England and was entertained by a merchant in London, and employed to Newfoundland and other parts, and lastly brought hither into these parts by one Mr. Dermer, a gentleman employed by Sir Ferdinando Gorges and others for discovery and other designs in these parts. . . .

F

First Thanksgiving

They began now to gather in the small harvest they had, and to fit up their houses and dwellings against winter, being all well recovered in health and strength and had all things in good plenty. For as some were thus employed in affairs abroad, others were exercised in fishing, about cod and bass and other fish, of which they took good store, of which every family had their portion. All the summer there was no want; and now began to come in store of fowl, as winter approached, of which this place did abound when they came first (but afterward decreased by degrees). And besides waterfowl there was great store of wild turkeys, of which they took many, besides venison, etc. Besides they had about a peck of meal a week to a person, or now since harvest, Indian corn to that proportion. Which made many afterward write so largely of their plenty here to their friends in England, which were not feigned but true reports.[26]

G

22. Samoset (sam′ə·set′) (1590?–1655): a Pemaquid from Maine.
23. Squanto (skwän′tō) (1585?–1622): one of the few survivors of the Patuxets, an Algonquian people. He later joined Massasoit's Wampanoags.
24. Massasoit (mas′ə·soit′) (c. 1580–1661): sachem (chief) of the Wampanoags, who lived in the area which became Rhode Island and southern Massachusetts.
25. With whom . . . this 24 years: The treaty was kept faithfully until the reign of Massasoit's younger son, Metacomet (1639?–1676), also known to the colonists as King Philip. (See Mary Rowlandson's narrative on page 40.)
26. Which made . . . true reports: Although the specific day of the Plymouth colonists' first Thanksgiving is not known, it occurred in the fall of 1621. For three days, Massasoit and almost a hundred of his men joined the Pilgrims, feasting and playing games.

WORDS TO OWN
confederates (kən·fed′ər·its) *n.:* allies; persons who share a common purpose.
comprised (kəm·prīzd′) *v.:* included.

E. Reader's Response: Extending the Text
Point out that in clauses 1 through 4, the third-person plural pronouns refer to the Pilgrims while the third-person singular masculine pronouns refer to Massasoit. In clause 5, the first *them* refers to the American Indians and the second to the Pilgrims. In clause 6, *their* and *they* refer to the American Indians, and *them* refers to the Pilgrims. What do you think of these terms? [Sample responses: Clauses 1, 2, 5, and 6 protect the Pilgrims but not the American Indians. Only clauses 3 and 4 are fair and equal. The Pilgrims are trying to protect themselves.]

F. Exploring the Culture
Through Squanto, the Pilgrims learned the agricultural, geographical, and economic practices of the American Indians. Squanto guided them in hunting, fishing, and using alewives (a type of herring) to fertilize corn, pumpkins, and beans.

G. Expansion
This passage depicts the community when there was common ownership and sharing among the Pilgrims. But by 1623, this joint ownership had ended and individual ownership became the rule. For the Puritans, worldly prosperity was a sign of God's having placed them among the elect, so they worked extra hard. By 1648, the Pilgrims had finished paying off their debts to the merchants who had financed their trip, had developed a profitable trade in corn and cattle with the Massachusetts Bay Colony, and were trading furs. Perhaps these changes gave rise to the claim by some that Puritan industry fostered the rise of capitalism.

ASSESSMENT TOOLS

Peer Assessment When student groups are presenting, have the audience evaluate their performance by making notes in a chart like the following. Develop the criteria you would like for them to evaluate, or use the following.

Criteria	Comments
Content	
Support	
Organization	
Tone	

Check Test: Questions and Answers
1. The sailor who condemns the sick Pilgrims ends up _____. [dying]
2. The majority of the Pilgrims stayed on the *Mayflower* while a few left to _____. [search for a suitable place to make a settlement]
3. During the starving time, the Pilgrims and the sailors each lost _____. [half their populations]
4. The Pilgrims and Massasoit met to make a _____. [treaty]
5. By the first Thanksgiving in 1621, the food supply was _____. [varied and well established]

A. Exploring the Historical Period

The United States and the former South Vietnam fought together in the Vietnam War (1957–1975) to prevent the Communists of North Vietnam from taking over South Vietnam. After long years of fighting, the United States agreed to withdraw under a cease-fire agreement. However, fighting continued after the withdrawal, and gradually South Vietnam abandoned outposts it could no longer protect. The Communists began their offensive in 1974 and the capital of South Vietnam fell in 1975. During the war thousands of Vietnamese were killed, wounded, or made homeless, and the country was heavily bombed. Many South Vietnamese sought asylum in the United States.

B. Reader's Response: First Thoughts

? How might you have reacted to Van Dinh's disappearance had you been a family member? [Sample responses: Great sadness at not having her with them, anxiety over not knowing whether she was alive, determination to try to contact United States immigration officials, or frustration at not being able to find out anything about her.]

C. Critical Reading: Analyzing Character

? What admirable qualities does this family have? [Possible answers: They are able to take misfortune and begin anew. They work hard. They contribute to society.]

Connections A NEWS FEATURE

An American Story

ANTHONY LEWIS

A Fifteen years ago this Thanksgiving weekend, a ten-year-old Vietnamese boy named Viet Dinh arrived in this country as a refugee. He was with his mother, four sisters, and a brother. They had two hundred dollars, which they spent on used winter coats.

They were boat people. They had left Vietnam on a small fishing boat, which lost its engine in a storm. They drifted for days until they made it to Malaysia—swimming in at night to avoid patrol boats that had fired at them. After months in a refugee camp, they were cleared for admission to the United States and flown to Portland, Oregon.

Two members of the family were left behind in Vietnam: Viet Dinh's father, Phong Dinh, and his older sister Van Dinh, who was twenty then. She stayed behind to help their father.

Phong Dinh had been a city councilman in Vung Tau during the Saigon regime. When the Communists took over in 1975, he was sent to a reeducation camp. He escaped from the camp on June 12, 1978, and was on the run when his wife and six children left.

Over the next five years, Phong Dinh tried unsuccessfully twenty-five times to get out of Vietnam by boat. He paid boatmen who never turned up or who were arrested. Finally, in 1983, he made it to the Philippines, and then to the United States.

That left the oldest child, Van Dinh. She had helped her father pay the boatmen. But it was six years before she managed to leave herself: on a boat that reached Hong Kong in August 1989.

B The family here knew that she had left Vietnam because they got a message to that effect. But for a year they did not know she was in a Hong Kong refugee camp; indeed, they did not know whether she had landed anywhere or had gone down at sea, as many boat people had.

Van Dinh was kept in the locked Hong Kong camp for three years, waiting for clearance as a refugee. With her was her five-year-old son, Quan, who had a congenital heart condition. That made her desperate to reach the United States, but for years she could not even get an interview with those in charge of the refugee process in Hong Kong.

At the end of 1991, Viet Dinh, then twenty-three years old, sent me an essay he had written about his sister Van's plight in Hong Kong. I forwarded it to the *New York Times* Op-Ed page, and the editors published it in January 1992.

Last month I had another letter from Viet Dinh. It had good news about his sister. After his Op-Ed piece was published, other papers picked up the story. The Hong Kong authorities, feeling the pressure, finally interviewed Van Dinh—and found that she was entitled to refugee status. In September 1992, she made it to Portland. The family was reunited after fifteen years.

There is more to tell about the Dinh family, as I learned when I interviewed Viet. His parents are running a small grocery in Salem, Oregon. A sister, Anh, helps them. Another sister, Thu, is an accountant. Kathleen and Leanne are C computer programmers. Viet's one brother, Bao, is an architect.

The child with the heart condition, Van's son Quan, has been treated in Portland. He is doing fine.

Van herself, after fourteen months in the United States, is

Patrick Barvie/Gamma Liaison.

Vietnamese boat people rescued by the cargo ship *Medecins du Monde*.

studying at a community college in Salem and working as an assembler in an electronics plant. "After she gets her English and cultural skills together," Viet said, "I think she'd like to open a business."

It is an American story, and one that I wish members of Congress and their constituents who are fulminating these days about "the immigrant threat" would think about. The Dinh family is doing exactly what immigrants on the Lower East Side and so many other places did in past years: struggling for themselves and making this country better.

There is no other country that has taken in so many people from so many places and cultures, and gained so much in the process. To turn away from that tradition now would do the United States great damage.

One more thing about Viet Dinh. His recent letter ended: "I graduated from the Harvard Law School in June and am now a law clerk for Judge Laurence H. Silberman of the U.S. Court of Appeals in Washington. Next year I clerk for Justice Sandra Day O'Connor at the Supreme Court."

—*from The New York Times*, November 26, 1993

34 BEGINNINGS

CONNECTING WITH *OF PLYMOUTH PLANTATION*

Although they are written in different centuries, Bradford's narrative and "An American Story" are both about immigrants coming to the United States. Ask students to note similarities and differences between the immigrant experiences of 1620 and 1978. To help students organize and analyze information, draw a chart like the following on the chalkboard. Ask students to describe the Dinhs' experience, and as they do so, write the responses in the Dinh column. Then, discuss with students whether the Dinhs' experiences would also describe the Puritans' experience. Ask students what similarities the groups shared and what differences arose. Note the students' remarks in the appropriate columns.

Dinh	Puritan	
	Similarities	Differences

Making Meanings

First Thoughts

Reviewing the Text

With several students, compile a chronology of the main incidents in Bradford's history.

1. What qualities or beliefs of the Puritans do you think enabled them to deal with the hardships they encountered on their voyage and during their first year? (Be sure to review the text and the notes you made in your Reader's Log.)

Shaping Interpretations

2. At what points in his history does Bradford give inner, spiritual significance to outward events?
3. Consider the treaty drawn up with Massasoit (Chapter 11), and explain whether or not you feel its terms were equally favorable to both parties. What seems to be Bradford's attitude toward the Wampanoag?
4. One event that Bradford does not describe is the death of his wife, who either fell or jumped overboard in Provincetown Harbor. What reasons can you propose for his having omitted it? How would his history have been different if he had included this tragedy?

Extending the Text

5. In what ways might the Pilgrims' experiences be relevant to contemporary pioneers or refugees? In your response, take into account the experiences of the Dinh family in "An American Story" (Connections, page 34).

Elements of Literature

The Plain Style

At the beginning of his history, Bradford says he will try to unfold his story "in a plain style, with singular regard unto the simple truth in all things." He means that he will not imitate the ornate "high style" that was in fashion in England at the time—a style that used classical **allusions,** Latin quotations, and elaborate **figures of speech,** as in this 1629 example from the poet and Anglican clergyman John Donne:

> First, for the incomprehensibleness of God, the understanding of man hath a limited, a determined latitude; it is an intelligence able to move that sphere which it is fixed to, but could not move a greater: I can comprehend *naturam naturatam,* created nature, but for that *natura naturans,* God himself, the understanding of man cannot comprehend.

In a sense, Bradford's stylistic preference reflected the division between the Puritans and the Anglicans in matters of worship. A plain writing style was in keeping with the Puritans' preference for plainness in all other things, especially in church ritual. They thought that a "plain style" was much more effective than an elevated or "high style" in revealing God's truth. The **plain style** imitated the style of the Bible the Puritans used: the Geneva Bible, published in 1560. (Other English Protestants of the time used the elegant King James translation, published in 1611.) Simple sentences, everyday language, and direct, unembellished statements—without such figures of speech as **similes** and **metaphors**—were the chief characteristics of the plain style.

Bradford's style may seem far from "plain" to a modern reader because it abounds in Biblical quotations and allusions. Also, his syntax and vocabulary are now **archaic,** or no longer in common use.

1. Identify and write down three of Bradford's sentences that contain elements of the plain style.
2. Recast the sentences into plain, modern prose. In doing this, how has the "Biblical" sound been affected?

who need to be contained. Clauses 1, 2, 5, and 6 protect only the Pilgrims; only clauses 3 and 4 are fair and equal. Bradford seems hesitant to trust the Wampanoag despite the fact that they returned tools they had taken.

4. Possible answer: In his attempt to keep the narrative objective, he may have chosen not to treat his wife's death any more fully than that of any other settler. The history would have become a more personal account and lost some of its representative feeling.

Extending the Text

5. **(Evaluation)** Possible response: Both may have fears about coming to a place they do not know. Contemporary refugees have to adjust to a society that is already well established and may have to learn to speak a different language. The Pilgrims' dealings with the American Indians were also complicated by their speaking different languages, although they spoke through an interpreter.

Elements of Literature

Answers

1. Answers will vary. Before having students begin the exercise, go over the first sentence from the chapter on the starving time on p. 31. It fits the plain style in that the language is everyday and its statements unembellished. It has no similes or metaphors. Bradford also uses words that mean roughly the same thing, *sad* and *lamentable*.
2. A recasting of the first sentence from the chapter on the starving time on p. 31 might read: It was sad that in the winter half the group died of various illnesses brought on by the trip over and lack of housing.

Making Meanings

First Thoughts

1. Possible responses: Courage, perseverance, and endurance; or belief in the rightness of their cause and in God.

Reviewing the Text

Passengers from *Speedwell* and *Mayflower* consolidated; cursing sailor dies; main beam cracks and is repaired; rescue of John Howland; landing at Cape Cod; the starving time; Samoset and Squanto arrive; peace treaty with Massasoit; first Thanksgiving.

Shaping Interpretations

2. The death of the profane seaman; the rescue of John Howland; the safe completion of the journey; the continued health of those who serve the sick during the starving time; Squanto's arrival.
3. Possible answer: The terms are clearly weighted in favor of the Pilgrims, and the Wampanoag are considered the aggressors

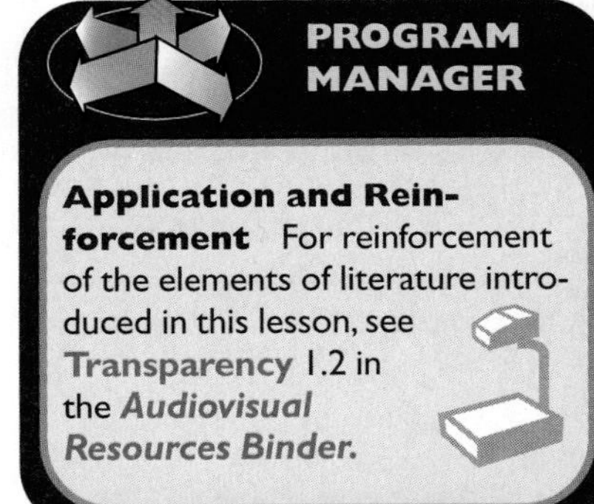

Application and Reinforcement For reinforcement of the elements of literature introduced in this lesson, see **Transparency 1.2** in the ***Audiovisual Resources Binder.***

Choices: Building Your Portfolio

1. **Writer's Notebook** *Remind students to choose a situation they would not mind sharing with others.* Also, remind them to save their work. They may use it as prewriting for the Writer's Workshop on p. 130.
2. **Critical Writing** The contrasts may become very apparent to students if they construct a Venn diagram, labeling one circle "Bradford's account" and the other "Smith's account," and noting similarities and differences on the diagram. You may wish to use the Transparency 5: Venn diagram in the Transparency Package.

Bradford's account | Smith's account

3. TECHNOLOGY **Speaking and Listening** Ask your students to present their conclusions in the form of United Nations resolutions. Invite your school's Model UN sponsor to discuss how conflicts today are resolved in the United Nations. Videotape their work. Have students play the tape, pause after each viewpoint is presented, and evaulate the viewpoint. Students should continue in this fashion until the tape is finished.

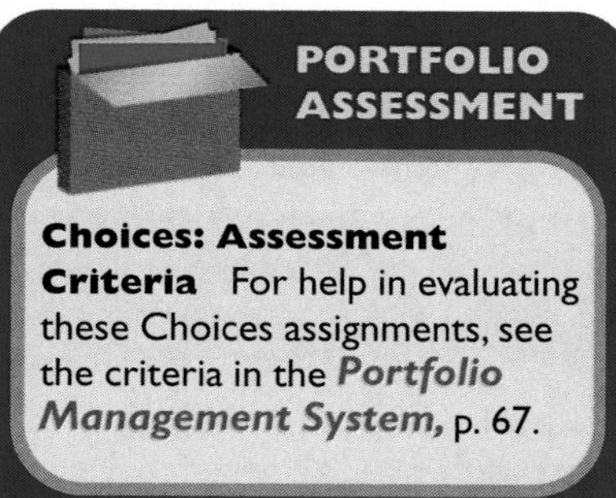

PORTFOLIO ASSESSMENT

Choices: Assessment Criteria For help in evaluating these Choices assignments, see the criteria in the ***Portfolio Management System,*** p. 67.

CHOICES: Building Your Portfolio

Writer's Notebook

1. Collecting Ideas for an Autobiographical Incident

WORK IN PROGRESS

According to one of Murphy's Laws, if anything can go wrong, it will. Most of us learn the hard way that when we try to do something—take a trip, for example, or reach a particular goal—the best-laid plans can often go awry. Make a list of challenges, setbacks, or hardships you've overcome on your "life's journey." Keep your notes for possible use in the Writer's Workshop on page 130.

Critical Writing

2. Come to America!

Captain John Smith (c. 1580–1631) led the first permanent English settlement in America at Jamestown, Virginia, in 1607. He hoped to establish another colony in New England, and in order to attract settlers, he wrote a pamphlet. In the following excerpt, Smith, somewhat like a contemporary travel agent, attempts to persuade people to join him in the new land. Write a brief essay in which you contrast Smith's rosy promises with Bradford's actual experiences in Colonial America. Contrast the **purposes** of the two writers and their intended **audiences.**

> Here nature and liberty afford us that freely which in England we want, or it costs us dearly. What pleasure can be more than (being tired with any occasion ashore) in planting vines, fruits, or herbs, in contriving their own grounds to the pleasure of their own minds, their fields, gardens, orchards, buildings, ships, and other works, etc.; to re-create themselves before their own doors, in their own boats upon the sea, where man, woman, and child, with a small hook and line, by angling may take divers sorts of excellent fish at their pleasures? And is it not pretty sport to pull up twopence, sixpence, and twelvepence as fast as you can haul and veer a line? He is a very bad fisher [who] cannot kill in one day with his hook and line one, two, or three hundred cods, which dressed and dried, if they be sold there for ten shillings the hundred [pounds], though in England they will give more than twenty, may not both the servant, the master, and merchant be well content with this gain? If a man work but three days in seven, he may get more than he can spend, unless he will be excessive. . . .
>
> For hunting, also, the woods, lakes, and rivers afford not only chase sufficient for any that delight in that kind of toil or pleasure, but such beasts to hunt that besides the delicacy of their bodies for food, their skins are so rich as may well recompense thy daily labor with a captain's pay.
>
> —John Smith, *from* "A Description of New England," 1616

Speaking and Listening

3. When Cultures Clash

As a class, divide into two groups, one representing the Pilgrims and the other the American Indians. Each of the two groups should further divide into smaller groups to discuss problems, conflicts, and grievances that have arisen, or may arise in the future, between the two cultures. Afterward, each small group should choose a person to represent the group's viewpoint in a panel discussion. Start with a brief statement by each panelist, followed by questions from all class members.

STRATEGIES FOR INCLUSION

Visual For activity #1, have students track the challenges, setbacks, hardships, and progress in their "journey" on a time line. Then, have them highlight their setbacks in red and their advancements in green.

Learners Having Difficulty Students may feel more comfortable with activity #3 if their opening statement is written with the help of their group. Have students predict some of the questions that might be asked so that the group can help panelists prepare to answer them.

HOW TO OWN A WORD

When a Dictionary Can Help

English speakers from long ago used words that we no longer use or that have changed meaning over time. These obsolete words are called **archaisms.** No matter how carefully we read, we cannot always discover the meanings of archaic words by using clues in the text. We need outside help—a dictionary.

Most of the time, when you want to look up a word you don't know, a collegiate or abridged dictionary will be all you need. But when you are reading a work of early American literature, you may need to use an unabridged dictionary, such as *Webster's Third New International Dictionary,* unabridged, or the *Oxford English Dictionary* (called the *OED* for short). These dictionaries give complete lists of definitions.

In Bradford's history, Bradford describes the fate of "a *proud* and very profane young man" (page 29). You might be surprised to see all the possible meanings of *proud.* Here's what the unabridged *Webster's* has to say, in part, about the word:

> **proud** \ˈpraud\ *adj* -ER/-EST [ME, fr. OE *prūd, prūt,* *prob.* fr. OF *prod, prud, prut, prou* good, capable, brave, fr. LL *prode* advantageous, advantage, fr. L *prodesse* to be useful, be beneficial, fr. *prod-* (var. of *pro-* before, forward) + *esse* to be—more at PRO-, IS] **1 :** feeling or showing pride: as **a :** having or displaying inordinate self-esteem <goaded the ~ baronage—J. R. Green> <his cold and ~ nature—A. Conan Doyle> **b :** highly satisfied or pleased : deeply gratified: ELATED, EXULTANT <~to have such men—Sherwood Anderson> <a ~ boy . . . he has made something with his own hands—*Better Homes & Gardens*>—often used with *of* <~ of his success> <a record to be ~ of> **c** *chiefly Midland* : GLAD, DELIGHTED <we'd be ~ to have you stay for supper> **d :** marked by a proper or becoming self-respect <too ~ to fight—Woodrow Wilson> <brought a ~ . . . efficiency to everything she did—Fred Majdalany> **2 a :** marked by stateliness or magnificence : SPLENDID <~ princes and humble peasants—Vicki Baum> <~ old castles—E. O. Hauser> **b :** giving reason or occasion for pride : GLORIOUS <a ~ heritage> <our *~est* feat—Joyce Cary> <his *~est* moment—Paul Pickrel> **3 :** marked by great vitality or power: VIGOROUS–EXUBERANT: as **a** *of an animal* : full of spirit : METTLESOME <a ~ steed> **b** *of a body of water* : overflowing its banks : SWOLLEN <the ~ stream> **c** *of granulation tissue* : growing exuberantly <~ growth in an old wound>

Because you encounter archaisms so infrequently, you'll probably want to keep a careful record of these words in a vocabulary notebook so that you can review them. You may want to make a chart like the following.

Word ______________________	
Word's etymology	
Meaning in this context	
Is meaning still in use?	
Is word still in use?	
Other common meanings	
Does the word imply a value judgment? If so, what evidence supports it?	
Dictionary (or dictionaries) used	

Try It Out

Use an unabridged dictionary to help you determine the meanings of the following underlined words from Bradford's history.

1. "These troubles being blown over, and now all being <u>compact</u> together in one ship . . ." (page 29)
2. ". . . and on the other hand they were loath to <u>hazard</u> their lives too desperately." (page 30)
3. ". . .they had now . . . no houses or much less towns to <u>repair</u> to, to seek for succor." (page 31)

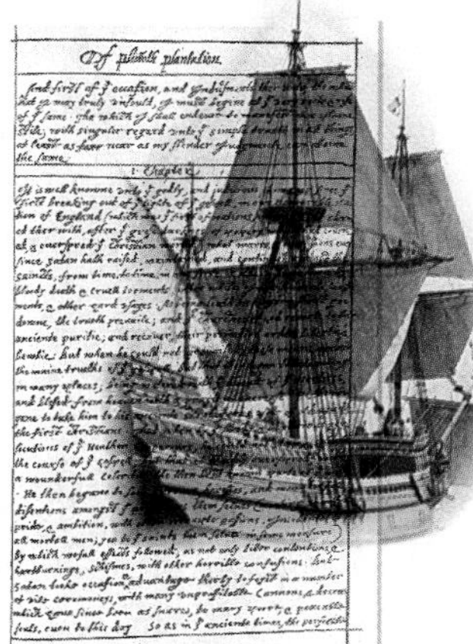

Of Plimoth Plantation by William Bradford. *Mayflower II,* a re-creation of the *Mayflower.*
Ms. courtesy of the State Library of Massachusetts. Mayflower photo courtesy of Plimoth Plantation.

How to Own a Word

Mini-Lesson: When a Dictionary Can Help

Begin by advising students that Puritan writers used an English similar to that used by Shakespeare and in the King James Bible, but that Puritans did not write as eloquently or in as complicated a style as those who translated the Bible. Consequently, Puritan writings can appear more modern than those of Shakespeare or the Biblical translators. The words the Puritans used may seem familiar to us, but they may have meant something different to them.

Try It Out: Answers

1. *compact,* meaning "packed closely together."
2. *hazard,* meaning "to endanger."
3. *repair,* meaning "to go to a place."

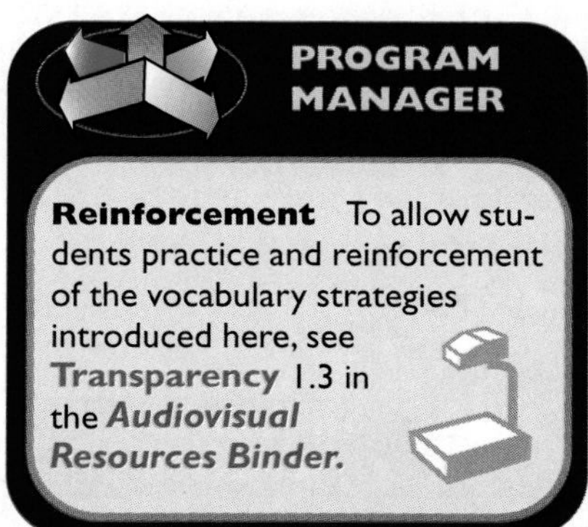

CROSSING THE CURRICULUM

Science/Mathematics Encourage students to use vocabulary notebooks or note cards to record words that correspond to a specific scientific field or historical period, or for names of geometric figures, theorems, postulates, and formulas. They may want to keep separate notebook sections for different fields or periods, use different colored note cards, or file cards separately in a file box. Have students work in groups to discuss the categories that would be helpful in their entries.

STRATEGIES FOR INCLUSION

Kinesthetic Rather than having a vocabulary notebook, some students may prefer to use note cards, which they can manipulate, divide into stacks of known and unknown, and format for their own ease. Encourage students to use the medium that works best for them.

QUICK PLANNING GUIDE

Into the Selection

Through the Selection

Beyond the Selection

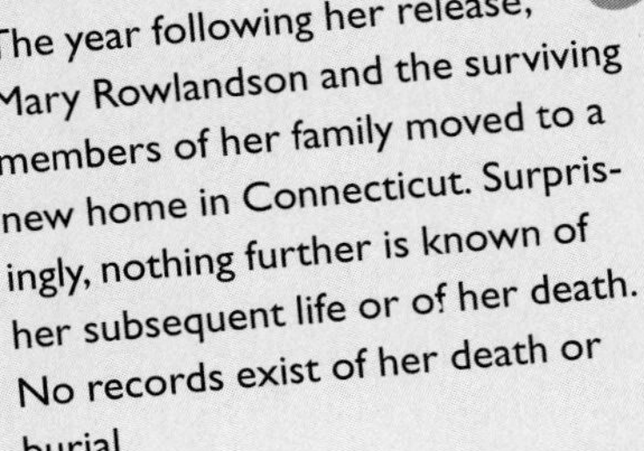

ABOUT THE AUTHOR

The year following her release, Mary Rowlandson and the surviving members of her family moved to a new home in Connecticut. Surprisingly, nothing further is known of her subsequent life or of her death. No records exist of her death or burial.

Mary Rowlandson

(c. 1636–c. 1678)

A

NARRATIVE

OF THE

CAPTIVITY, SUFFERINGS AND REMOVES

OF

Mrs. *Mary Rowlandson*,

Who was taken Prisoner by the INDIANS with several others, and treated in the most barbarous and cruel Manner by those vile Savages: With many other remarkable Events during her TRAVELS.

Written by her own Hand, for her private Use, and now made public at the earnest Desire of some Friends, and for the benefit of the afflicted.

BOSTON:

Printed and Sold at John [illegible]'s Printing Office, [illegible] to the *Three Doves* in Marlborough Street.

Courtesy of American Antiquarian Society.

From June 1675 to August 1676, the Wampanoag chief, Metacomet, called King Philip by the colonists, carried out a series of bloody raids on Colonial settlements in what is now called King Philip's War. The Puritans viewed the war as a sign of God's punishment for the sins of their young people (who had taken to dancing and wearing their hair long), but a conflict between colonists and American Indians was probably inevitable. It was the natural result of growing encroachments by the settlers on American Indian land. The native people of New England had been forced into ever more restricted areas, and, although they had sold the land, they rejected conditions stipulating that they could no longer hunt on it. To them, "selling" meant selling the right to share the land with the buyers, not selling its exclusive ownership.

Matters came to a head when Metacomet's former assistant, who had given information to the colonists, was killed by his own people. His killers were tried and hanged by the Puritans. This was too much for Metacomet to bear, and two weeks later the most severe war in the history of New England began. Its tragic result was the virtual extinction of the indigenous way of life in the region. Among the war's victims was Mary Rowlandson, the wife of the Congregational minister of Lancaster, a frontier town of about fifty families that was located thirty miles west of Boston. On a February morning, she and her three children were carried away by a Wampanoag raiding party that wanted to trade hostages for money. After eleven weeks and five days of captivity, Rowlandson's ransom was paid. She was to survive for only two more years.

Rowlandson's captors, it is important to realize, were only slightly better off than their prisoners. Virtually without food, they were chased from camp to camp by Colonial soldiers. Their captives, they thought, were the only currency with which to buy supplies and food. In a graphic passage, Rowlandson describes the lengths to which the Wampanoag were driven by their hunger, eating horses, dogs, frogs, skunks, rattlesnakes, and even tree bark. "They would pick up old bones," she wrote, "and cut them to pieces at the joints, and if they were full of worms and maggots, they would scald them over the fire to make the vermin come out, and then boil them, and drink up the liquor. . . . They would eat horse's guts, and ears, and all sorts of wild birds which they could catch. . . . I can but stand in admiration," she concluded, "to see the wonderful power of God in providing for such a vast number of our enemies in the wilderness, where there was nothing to be seen."

Rowlandson's narrative not only presents a terrifying and moving tale of frontier life but also provides insight into how the Puritans viewed their lives with a characteristic double vision. For Rowlandson, as for other Puritans, events had both a physical and a spiritual significance. She did not want merely to record her horrifying experience; she wished to demonstrate how it revealed God's purpose. The full title of her narrative illustrates this intention: *The Sovereignty and Goodness of God, Together with the Faithfulness of His Promises Displayed: Being a Narrative of the Captivity and Restoration of Mrs. Mary Rowlandson.*

WORDS TO OWN

The following vocabulary words are defined in the Words to Own at the bottom of the pupil's page.

Before You Read

from A Narrative of the Captivity

Reading Focus

Survival Skills

Who hasn't listened with rapt attention to stories of people enduring life-threatening circumstances—a flood, a plane crash on a snowy mountain, an earthquake, a wartime siege, or captivity as a hostage or prisoner of war? Perhaps our fascination with such stories comes from wondering how we would survive if we were put to the same test—instead of just sitting in safe surroundings reading about it.

A Dialogue with the Text

As you read, list the points at which Mary Rowlandson links her sufferings with the sufferings of people in the Bible. Note, also, how she feels about her captors. How does she interpret the events of her captivity in terms of her faith in God?

Portrait of Ninigret II, Chief of the Niantic Indians (c. 1681). Anonymous. American. Oil on canvas ($33\frac{1}{8}'' \times 30\frac{1}{8}''$).

Museum of Art, Rhode Island School of Design. Gift of Mr. Robert Winthrop (48.246).

Elements of Literature

Allusions

The Puritans regarded Biblical captivity narratives, such as the enslavement of Moses and the Israelites by the Egyptians, as allegories representing the Christians' liberation from sin through the intervention of God's grace. Rowlandson views her experiences as a repetition of the same Biblical pattern and uses **allusions** to reflect her own situation. Through apt quotations from the Bible, Rowlandson places her experiences in the context of the ancient Biblical captivities.

An **allusion** is a reference to someone or something that is known from history, literature, religion, politics, sports, science, or some other branch of culture.

For more on Allusion, see the Handbook of Literary Terms.

Background

King Philip's War began fifty-five years after the Pilgrims landed in Plymouth. By 1675, there were about forty thousand settlers and about twenty thousand American Indians in New England. During the attack on Lancaster by the Wampanoag, the town was virtually destroyed: Twenty people were killed, and twenty-four, including Mary Rowlandson, were taken captive.

Into the Selection

Using Before You Read p. 39

Reading Focus

Have students discuss what local, state, or national stories of survival have been recently in the news. Ask them to talk about what characteristics the survivors have in common.

Elements of Literature

Make sure students can differentiate between an allusion, which is usually unacknowledged, and a quotation. Have them identify the clues that would differentiate the two. [Quotations would have quotation marks and possibly partial or full attribution. Sometimes editors add references to allusions, but this added information would be found in brackets, footnotes, or endnotes.]

Background

In order to understand the extent of the damage to the town of Lancaster, students should know that besides the twenty dead, there were others shot, stabbed, or hatcheted and that a number of the houses were burned.

Portfolio Assessment

Portfolio Assessment

For help with self- and teacher assessment of reading skills, see the ***Portfolio Management System***, p. 39.

Program Manager

- **Planning Instruction** See **Teaching Notes, *Teaching Resources A***, p. 3, for objectives, a summary, literary elements, and additional information.
- **Instructional Support** Before beginning the instructional lesson, see **Graphic Organizer for Active Reading, *Teaching Resources A***, p. 12, for a Through the Selection activity.
- **Audiotaped Readings** To help auditory learners, use the **Selected Reading, Audiocassette 1, Side A**, in the ***Audiovisual Resources Binder***.
- **Assessment** See **Selection Test, *Test Booklet***, pp. 5–6.
- **Language Link** For a review of pronouns, see **Language Link, *Teaching Resources A***, pp. 13–14, and ***Language and Writing Skills Worksheets***, pp. 13–14.
- **Reinforcement** Use the **Words to Own** worksheet in ***Teaching Resources A***, p. 15.

Through the Selection

A. Reader's Response: First Thoughts
Record your response to this portion of text. [Sample responses: I feel sorry for Rowlandson; or Rowlandson must have been terrified for her child.]

from A Narrative of the Captivity

Mary Rowlandson

The Move to an Indian Village on the Ware River, Near Braintree (February 12–27)

The morning being come, they prepared to go on their way. One of the Indians got up upon a horse, and they set me up behind him, with my poor sick babe in my lap. A very wearisome and tedious day I had of it; what with my own wound, and my child's being so exceeding sick, and in a lamentable condition with her wound. It may be easily judged what a poor feeble condition we were in, there being not the least crumb of refreshing that came within either of our mouths from Wednesday night to Saturday night, except only a little cold water. This day in the afternoon, about an hour by sun, we came to the place where they intended, *viz.*[1] an Indian town, called Wenimesset, norward of Quabaug. . . . I sat much alone with a poor wounded child in my lap, which moaned night and day, having nothing to revive the body, or cheer the spirits of her, but instead of that, sometimes one Indian would come and tell me one hour, that your master will knock your child in the head, and then a second, and then a third, your master will quickly knock your child in the head.

A

1. **viz.:** Latin for "namely."

WORDS TO OWN

wearisome (wir′i·səm) *adj.:* fatiguing; exhausting.
tedious (tē′dē·əs) *adj.:* tiring; dreary.
lamentable (lam′ən·tə·bəl) *adj.:* regrettable; distressing.

King Philip's sash, ornamented with glass beads (late 1600s). Wampanoag.

Peabody Museum, Harvard University. Photo by Hillel Burger.

OPTIONS FOR TEACHING

STRATEGIES FOR INCLUSION

Advanced To focus on Mary Rowlandson's change of attitude toward American Indians, have students research a larger portion or the whole of Mary Rowlandson's account. They could report to their classmates on the sections of text not included in their textbook. This activity might allow for fuller class participation.

English Language Development To help students evaluate their reading, have them draw pictures of three difficulties Mary Rowlandson has in captivity. Have students describe the examples they chose, telling how Rowlandson finds comfort during her captivity. Ask students to explain which is more helpful to her: her belief in God or the assistance of kind people in the Wampanoag.

Visual To help students recall the material, have them work in pairs to take notes by making an illustration or graphic organizer for every one or two paragraphs of the selection.

Interpersonal Group students and encourage them (1) to discuss Mary Rowlandson's strategies for dealing with her sufferings and (2) to compare them to strategies they have used during hard times. *Remind students to choose a situation they would not mind sharing with others.*

This was the comfort I had from them, miserable comforters are ye all, as he said.[2] Thus nine days I sat upon my knees, with my babe in my lap, till my flesh was raw again; my child being even ready to depart this sorrowful world, they bade me carry it out to another wigwam (I suppose because they would not be troubled with such spectacles) whither I went with a very heavy heart, and down I sat with the picture of death in my lap. About two hours in the night, my sweet babe like a lamb departed this life, on February 18, 1675. It being about six years and five months old. It was nine days from the first wounding, in this miserable condition, without any refreshing of one nature or another, except a little cold water. I cannot but take notice, how at another time I could not bear to be in the room where any dead person was, but now the case is changed; I must and could lie down by my dead babe, side by side all the night after. I have thought since of the wonderful goodness of God to me, in preserving me in the use of my reason and senses, in that distressed time, that I did not use wicked and violent means to end my own miserable life. In the morning, when they understood that my child was dead they sent for me home to my master's wigwam: (by my master in this writing, must be understood Quanopin, who was a Sagamore,[3] and married King Philip's[4] wife's sister; not that he first took me, but I was sold to him by another Narragansett Indian, who took me when first I came out of the garrison). I went to take up my dead child in my arms to carry it with me, but they bid me let it alone: There was no resisting, but go I must and leave it. When I had been at my (B) master's wigwam, I took the first opportunity I could get, to go look after my dead child: When I came I asked them what they had done with it. Then they told me it was upon the hill: Then they went and showed me where it was, where I saw the ground was newly digged, and there they told me they had buried it: There I left that child in the wilderness, and must commit it, and myself also in this wilderness condition, to him who is above all. (C) God having taken away this dear child, I went to see my daughter Mary, who was at this same Indian town, at a wigwam not very far off, though we had little liberty or opportunity to see one another. She was about ten years old, and taken from the door at first by a Praying Ind.[5] and afterward (D) sold for a gun. When I came in sight, she would fall aweeping; at which they were provoked, and would not let me come near her, but bade me be gone; which was a heart-cutting word to me. I had one child dead, another in the wilderness, I knew not where, the third they would not let me come near to: "Me (as he said) have ye bereaved of my Children, Joseph is not, and Simeon is not, and ye will take Benjamin also, all these things are against me."[6] I could not sit still in this condition, but kept walking from one place to another. And as I was going along, my heart was (E) even overwhelmed with the thoughts of my condition, and that I should have children, and a nation which I knew not ruled over them. Whereupon I earnestly entreated the Lord, that He would consider my low estate, and show me a token for good, and if it were His blessed will, some sign and hope of some relief. And indeed quickly the Lord answered, in some measure, my poor prayers: For as I was going up and down mourning and lamenting my condition, my son came to me, and asked me how I did; I had not seen him before, since the destruction of the

2. **he said:** The Biblical allusion is to Job 16:2. In the passage cited, Job addresses those who try to console him in his afflictions. God had severely tested Job's faith by causing Job to lose his children and his money, and to break out in boils all over his body.
3. **Sagamore** (sag′ə·môr′): a secondary chief in the hierarchy of several Native American peoples.
4. **King Philip's:** Metacomet (1639?–1676), son of Massasoit (c. 1580–1661) and chief of the Wampanoag from 1661 to 1676, was called King Philip by the colonists. In 1675, Metacomet led the Wampanoag and other American Indians in an attempt to end settlements in New England. The colonists retaliated, and both sides sustained heavy losses of life in the resulting massacres, which came to be known as King Philip's War. Mary Rowlandson's captivity was part of this conflict. (See William Bradford's narrative *Of Plymouth Plantation*, page 28.)
5. **Praying Ind.:** Native Americans who converted to Christianity were known as "praying Indians." The Colonial assemblies allowed these converts to live in self-governing towns.
6. **Me . . . against me:** Rowlandson quotes Jacob's lament in Genesis 42:36. Jacob had only his youngest son, Benjamin, at home.

Words to Own

entreated (en·trēt′ed) *v.:* asked sincerely; prayed to.

B. Literary Element: Allusion
Rowlandson identifies her suffering with that of Job in the Bible, whom God made to suffer to test his fidelity, despite his obedience to God. Job 16:11–12 reads "God hath delivered me over to the ungodly, and turned me over into the hands of the wicked. I was at ease, but he hath broken me asunder: he hath also taken me by my neck, and shaken me to pieces, and set me up for his mark." But like Job, she cannot believe that God is unjust.

C. Literary Element: Allusion
Rowlandson uses the term *wilderness* in the literal sense to refer to her barren surroundings. In the figurative sense, she borrows a metaphor from the Bible for a spiritual wasteland or desert sojourn during which a soul feels as if it is separate from God, although God still watches over it.

D. Expansion
While this particular "Praying Indian" was untrustworthy—he took Rowlandson's daughter away from her—many stayed loyal to the settlers and remained firm in their new faith. On the other hand, some Native Americans who converted to Christianity were cruelly mistreated by the colonists during the war for fear that they might revert to their "savage ways."

E. Exploring the Culture
Rowlandson's use of Biblical quotations shows that she continually finds her own life mirroring episodes in the Bible. This connection gives meaning to her experience and suffering.

STRATEGIES FOR INCLUSION

Special Needs Students who have trouble maintaining attention may gain a better understanding of the use of allusions by drawing from their own experiences. To personalize Rowlandson's style for them, work with students to create a chart in which they match their own experiences with passages from the Bible or another sacred work that reflect a variety of emotions. For each passage, have students first identify the emotion expressed and then record an incident from their own lives reflecting that same emotion. *Remind students to choose a situation they would not mind sharing with others.* Have students in groups of three talk about their findings. They should use a chart like the following.

Bible Passage	Emotion Expressed	Personal Experience
["The morning stars together, and all the sons of God shouted for joy." Job 38:7]	[Joy, happiness]	[A time when student felt great joy]

☞

LITERATURE AND HISTORY

To help students understand how settlers' actions provoked American Indian aggression, ask students in groups of three to research various American Indian groups, such as the Iroquois, Abenaki, Mohawks, Hurons, Penobscots, Cherokees, Shawnees, and Comanches, that took captives or were in contact with captives. Students should explore why these groups took such action. Have groups elect one student representative to sit on a panel that will relate the groups' findings to the rest of the class.

A. Critical Reading: Speculating

? Why do you think Rowlandson's captors permit her to have and to read a Bible? [Possible answer: The Native Americans give her a Bible because they do not want her upset and they know having a Bible will comfort her.]

LITERATURE AND HISTORY

Captivity Narratives

Mary Rowlandson's *A Narrative of the Captivity* was one of the most widely read prose works of the seventeenth century. It was especially popular in England, where people were eager for lurid tales of native inhabitants in the Americas. Rowlandson's story went through at least thirty editions, and it inspired a mass of imitations that were often partially faked or purely fictional. These "captivity" stories became one of the most widely produced forms of entertainment in America, but they had a tragic side effect: They contributed to the further deterioration of relations between American Indians and colonists.

Between the seventeenth and nineteenth centuries, as settlers moved westward and occupied American Indian lands, tensions between the two groups increased. American Indians, in retaliation for various injustices, raided settlements and took captives to ransom, to enslave, or to sell to the French or even to other native peoples. These captives didn't necessarily suffer grim fates: Some captives actually chose to remain with their captors and were adopted by them; a few married American Indians and never expressed any desire to return to their original homes. Many of those who escaped or were ransomed recorded their experiences when they returned home. Eventually, thousands of captivity tales—of varying quality and accuracy—sprouted up all over the country. Scarcely any first editions of these books remain, as they were literally read and re-read to shreds by an eager public.

From Providence to propaganda. Because early captivity narratives were almost all told from the limited first-person point of view, they didn't provide much context for settlers' actions that may have provoked American Indian aggression. Typically, seventeenth-century captivity narratives begin with a brief description of a raid and the rounding up of hostages; they then focus on the gritty details of the day-to-day struggle for survival. The captives in these early narratives generally accept their condition as a

town, and I knew not where he was, till I was informed by himself, that he was amongst a smaller parcel of Indians, whose place was about six miles off; with tears in his eyes, he asked me whether his sister Sarah was dead; and told me he had seen his sister Mary; and prayed me, that I would not be troubled in reference to himself. . . . (A) I cannot but take notice of the wonderful mercy of God to me in those afflictions, in sending me a Bible. One of the Indians that came from Medfield fight, had brought some plunder, came to me, and asked me, if I would have a Bible, he had got one in his basket. I was glad of it, and asked him, whether he thought the Indians would let me read. He answered, yes: So I took the Bible, and in that melancholy time, it came into my mind to read first the 28th chapter of Deuteronomy,[7] which I did, and when I had read it, my dark heart wrought on this manner, that there was no mercy for me, that the blessings were gone, and the curses come in their room, and that I had lost my opportunity. But the Lord helped me still to go on reading till I came to Chapter 30 the seven first

7. **28th chapter of Deuteronomy:** In Deuteronomy 28, Moses warns that God will bless those who obey Him and curse those who do not.

WORDS TO OWN

plunder (plun′dər) *n.:* goods seized, especially during wartime.

melancholy (mel′ən·käl′ē) *adj.:* sad; sorrowful.

OPTIONS FOR TEACHING

INTEGRATING THE LANGUAGE ARTS

Strategic Reading To help students make predictions and compare them with actual outcomes, ask them to write predictions about the selection in the first column of a chart like the following. While they are reading, they should record any changes in their predictions. After studying the selection, they should re-read their predictions and complete the third column. Encourage volunteers to read their entries.

Predictions	Changes in Predictions	Actual Outcomes
[The child will die.]	[They may take the child from her.]	[They allow her to keep the child and it dies.]

Speaking and Listening If possible, obtain a complete copy of Mary Rowlandson's narrative. Ask students to choose a passage and to prepare a dramatic reading. Students should pay attention to the basic elements of speech performance. This activity will give them practice in oral interpretation and enlarge their understanding of the historical circumstance.

Language and Vocabulary Have students list geographical locations mentioned in the text. Ask what they notice about these names and what the implications are. They should recognize that most of the names are from American Indian languages and that this fact indicates their long-term habitation of this area and, by extension, their claim to the land.

punishment sent by God to test their faith, and any relief from their suffering is always evidence of Divine Providence, not sympathy from their captors. But by the eighteenth century, continuing animosity between settlers and American Indians, aggravated by the French and Indian War, led to a different kind of captivity narrative, one that was an undisguised expression of hatred toward Native Americans. No longer were captivity narratives instructive tales of physical and spiritual survival in the wilderness; now they were inflammatory propaganda, smugly asserting the superiority of Europeans.

Sensationalism and stereotypes. By the early nineteenth century, propaganda had turned into pure sensationalism. Journalists and authors of lurid fiction, gifted at manipulating the fantasies and prejudices of the reading public, revised the original narratives. They pulled out all the stops, using melodramatic plot devices and long passages of grisly detail. The public eagerly read these "penny dreadfuls" (the popular term for cheap magazines with tales of horror and crime), shuddering with mixed fascination and horror at fictional tales of American Indian atrocities and the suffering of innocent captives. The tawdriness of these publications didn't go unnoticed by more educated readers. Many actual nineteenth-century captives were reluctant to publish their stories, afraid that, by association with sleazy popular magazines, their experiences would not be taken seriously.

Some historians have argued that captivity narratives, by advancing the stereotype of the "savage Indian," made it easier for settlers to justify occupation of American Indian lands. By the late nineteenth century, with the "Indian threat" a thing of the past, captivity narratives gradually became less popular. But, unfortunately, stereotypes of the "bad" Indian and the "virtuous" European settler remained in the popular imagination well into the twentieth century, appearing in countless Western novels, Hollywood movies, and television programs.

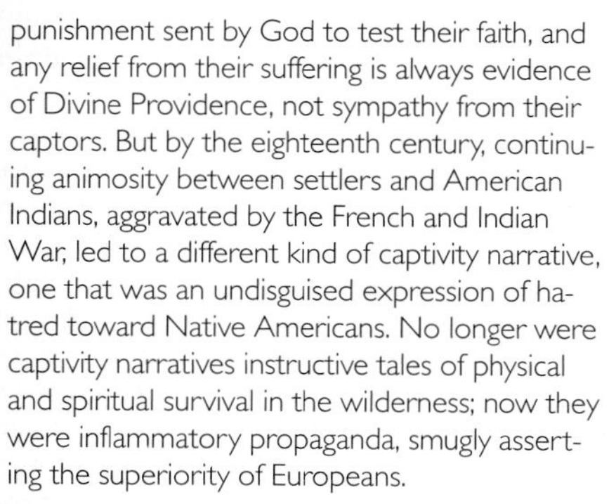

verses, where I found, there was mercy promised again, if we would return to Him by repentance; and though we were scattered from one end of the earth to the other, yet the Lord would gather us together, and turn all those curses upon our enemies. I do not desire to live to forget this Scripture, and what comfort it was to me. . . . **B**

The Fifth Remove

The occasion (as I thought) of their moving at this time, was, the English Army, it being near and following them: For they went, as if they had gone for their lives, for some considerable way, and then they made a stop, and chose some of their stoutest men, and sent them back to hold the English Army in play while the rest escaped: And then, like Jehu,[8] they marched on furiously, with their old, and with their young: Some carried their old decrepit mothers, some carried one, and some another. Four of them carried a great Indian upon a bier; but going through a thick wood with him, they were hindered, and could make no

8. **Jehu** (jē′hoo′): ninth century B.C. Israelite king. Jehu was said to be a "furious driver" (2 Kings 9:20), and Rowlandson's allusion here is to the speed and fury with which her captors moved away from the English Army.

Words to Own

decrepit (dē·krep′it) *adj.:* run down; worn out by age or use.

B. Reader's Response: Shaping Interpretations

? What is Rowlandson's purpose in writing the narrative? [Sample responses: She feels the need to justify for the public her relationship with the American Indians. She wants to show how God has seen her through trials.]

CROSSING THE CURRICULUM

Home Economics Mary Rowlandson's skill at sewing changed her status in the American Indian community. Students might study clothing from the 1670s to determine what Rowlandson would have had to do in order to produce the garments she made. Students could make and display garments, or illustrate the steps in their construction, and present research findings to the class.

Health Mary Rowlandson went for days without food and with very little water. Students who enjoy hiking and other sports that include journeys into the wilderness should find out about the bare necessities for survival. Students should present their information to the class, using speeches, charts, and illustrations, as though they are preparing the class in a wilderness survival course.

A. Critical Reading: Speculating

? When does Rowlandson write her narrative? [Possible responses: She does not write this as a day-to-day journal but may have recorded her recollections shortly after the time the events take place. Most captivity narratives were written soon after the captives returned from the wilderness.]

B. Critical Reading: Expressing an Opinion

? After favoring Rowlandson by giving her a light load, her captor refuses to give her a spoonful of meal when Rowlandson feels faint. How do you explain this paradoxical behavior? [Possible answers: There is a difference between granting a hidden favor—a lightened load that no one else need suspect—and an overt sign of favor before the rest of the community. Rowlandson's captor does not want to spoil her, does not think it is really necessary, or is too concerned with the coming river crossing to give Rowlandson her full attention.]

C. Critical Reading: Making Inferences

When Rowlandson wants to comfort herself, she turns to her Bible with its promises of God's love. The American Indians try to comfort her by giving her food. Why do you think they do this? [Possible answers: Since food is life sustaining, it would give Rowlandson proof that they did not mean to kill her. Or since food is so scarce, it is a tangible proof of friendship. Food is the only thing they have that holds any value for Rowlandson.]

haste; whereupon they took him upon their backs, and carried him, one at a time, till they came to Bacquaug River. Upon a Friday, a little after noon we came to this river. When all the company was come up, and were gathered together, I thought to count the number of them, but they were so many, and being somewhat in motion, it was beyond my skill. In this travel, because of my wound, I was somewhat favored in my load; I carried only my knitting work and two quarts of parched meal: Being very faint I asked my mistress to give me one spoonful of the meal, but she would not give me a taste. They quickly fell to cutting dry trees, to make rafts to carry them over the river: and soon my turn came to go over: By the advantage of some brush which they had laid upon the raft to sit upon, I did not wet my foot (which many of themselves at the other end were mid-leg deep) which cannot but be acknowledged as a favor of God to my weakened body, it being a very cold time. I was not before acquainted with such kind of doings or dangers. "When thou passeth through the waters I will be with thee, and through the Rivers they shall not overflow thee," Isaiah, 43:2. A certain number of us got over the river that night, but it was the night after the Sabbath before all the company was got over. On the Saturday they boiled an old horse's leg which they had got, and so we drank of the broth, as soon as they thought it was ready, and when it was almost gone, they filled it up again.

The first week of my being among them, I hardly ate anything; the second week, I found my stomach grow very faint for want of something; and yet it was very hard to get down their filthy trash: but the third week, though I could think how formerly my stomach would turn against this or that, and I could starve and die before I could eat such things, yet they were sweet and savory to my taste. . . .

The Sixth Remove

We traveled on till night; and in the morning, we must go over the river to Philip's crew. When I was in the canoe, I could not but be amazed at the numerous crew of pagans that were on the bank on the other side. When I came ashore, they gathered all about me, I sitting alone in the midst: I observed they asked one another questions, and laughed, and rejoiced over their gains and victories. Then my heart began to fail: And I fell aweeping which was the first time to my remembrance, that I wept before them. Although I had met with so much affliction, and my heart was many times ready to break, yet could I not shed one tear in their sight: but rather had been all this while in a maze, and like one astonished: But now I may say as, Psalm 137:1, "By the rivers of Babylon, there we sat down: yea, we wept when we remembered Zion." There one of them asked me, why I wept, I could hardly tell what to say: Yet I answered, they would kill me: "No," said he, "none will hurt you." Then came one of them and gave me two spoonfuls of meal to comfort me, and another gave me half a pint of peas; which was more worth than many bushels at another time. Then I went to see King Philip, he bade me come in and sit down, and asked me whether I would smoke it (a usual compliment nowadays amongst saints and sinners) but this no way suited me. For though I had formerly used tobacco, yet I had left it ever since I was first taken. It seems to be a bait, the devil lays to make men lose their precious time: I remember with shame, how formerly, when I had taken two or three pipes, I was presently ready for another, such a bewitching thing it is: But I thank God, He has now given me power over it; surely there are many who may be better employed than to lie sucking a stinking tobacco pipe.

Now the Indians gather their forces to go against North Hampton: Overnight one went about yelling and hooting to give notice of the design. Whereupon they fell to boiling of groundnuts, and parching of corn (as many as had it) for their provision: And in the morning away they went. During my abode in this place, Philip spoke to me to make a shirt for his boy, which I did, for which he gave me a shilling: I offered the money to my master, but he bade me keep it: And with it I bought a piece of horseflesh. Afterward he

WORDS TO OWN

savory (sā′vər·ē) *adj.:* appetizing; agreeable.
affliction (ə·flik′shən) *n.:* pain; hardship.
bewitching (bē·wich′iŋ) *adj.:* enticing; irresistible.

OPTIONS FOR TEACHING

CLASSROOM MANAGEMENT

Focus Take advantage of the dramatic nature of the selections in this Collection to engage students whose unfamiliarity with the language and history of the period is causing them some frustration. Use cooperative learning and reading aloud to move quickly through a first reading, and focus more on discussion and projects instead of unfamiliar or archaic expressions.

Managing the Reader's Response Classroom Discussion at first should focus on the students' responses, and initially, teachers should avoid shaping students' responses with their own questions. To encourage open-ended discussion, ask "What did you think?" or "Any thoughts or feelings?" Students will come to understand that you are trying to open up the discussion.

Wampum belt. Iroquois.

Peabody Essex Museum, Salem, Massachusetts/Peabody Museum Collections. Photo by Mark Sexton.

asked me to make a cap for his boy, for which he invited me to dinner. I went, and he gave me a pancake, about as big as two fingers; it was made of parched wheat, beaten, and fried in bear's grease, but I thought I never tasted pleasanter meat in my life. There was a squaw who spoke to me to make a shirt for her *sannup*,[9] for which she gave me a piece of bear. Another asked me to knit a pair of stockings, for which she gave me a quart of peas: I boiled my peas and bear together, and invited my master and mistress to dinner, but the proud gossip, because I served them both in one dish, would eat nothing, except one bit that he gave her upon the point of his knife. . . .

The Move to the Ashuelot Valley, New Hampshire

But instead of going either to Albany or homeward, we must go five miles up the river, and then go over it. Here we abode[10] awhile. Here lived a sorry Indian, who spoke to me to make him a shirt. When I had done it, he would pay me nothing. But he living by the riverside, where I often went to fetch water, I would often be putting of him in mind, and calling for my pay: At last he told me if I would make another shirt, for a papoose not yet born, he would give me a knife, which he did when I had done it. I carried the knife in, and my master asked me to give it him, and I was not a little glad that I had anything that they would accept of, and be pleased with. When we were at this place, my master's maid came home, she had been gone three weeks into the Narragansett country, to fetch corn, where they had stored up some in the ground: She brought home about a peck and half of corn. This was about the time that their great captain, Naananto,[11] was killed in the Narragansett country. My son being now about a mile from me, I asked liberty to go and see him, they bade me go, and away I went: but quickly lost myself, traveling over hills and through swamps, and could not find the way to him. And I cannot but admire at the wonderful power and goodness of God to me, in that, though I was gone from home, and met with all sorts of Indians, and those I had no knowledge of, and there being no Christian soul near me; yet not one of them offered the least imaginable miscarriage to me. I turned homeward again, and met with my master, he showed me the way to my son. . . .

But I was fain to go and look after something to satisfy my hunger, and going among the wigwams, I went into one, and there found a squaw who showed herself very kind to me, and gave me a piece of bear. I put it into my pocket, and came home, but could not find an opportunity to broil it, for fear they would get it from me, and there it lay all that day and night in my stinking pocket. In the morning I went to the same squaw, who had a kettle of groundnuts boiling; I asked her to let me boil my piece of bear in her kettle, which she did, and gave me some groundnuts to eat with it: And I cannot but think how pleasant it was to me. I have sometime seen bear baked very handsomely among the English, and some like it, but the thoughts that it was bear, made me tremble: But now that was savory to me that one would think was enough to turn the stomach of a brute creature.

One bitter cold day, I could find no room to sit down before the fire: I went out, and could not tell what to do, but I went in to another wigwam, where they were also sitting round the fire, but the squaw laid a skin for me, and bid me sit down, and gave me some groundnuts, and bade me come again: and told me they would buy me, if they were able, and yet these were strangers to me that I never saw before. . . .

9. ***sannup*** (san′up): husband.
10. **abode** (ə·bōd′): stayed.

11. **Naananto:** Naananto, or Canonchet (d. April 3, 1676), was a Narragansett leader who was the driving force behind the American Indians' wish to exterminate the New England colonists that resulted in King Philip's War. After his death, the conflict soon ended.

D. Language Note: Structure
Paragraphs by Bradford, Byrd, and Rowlandson do not always cover a single topic. Rather, loosely connected or coincidentally linked subjects are often grouped together.

E. Critical Reading: Drawing Conclusions
? How would you characterize Rowlandson's changing relationship with her captors? [Possible answers: The relationship becomes one of economics, not just dependency. She becomes less like a slave and more like an indentured servant, although she is not treated exactly like either one of these.]

F. Reader's Response: Challenging the Text
? Why do you think Rowlandson makes a point that the Native Americans do not harm her? [Sample responses: She is particularly vulnerable, being alone and lost. They can harm her but do not. She may be reluctant to condemn them categorically.] How objective do you believe Rowlandson's narrative to be? [Sample responses: She judges them harshly. Or she may understand them better than she did before she was captured. Or although she writes of her struggle, she does state that she was not mistreated by the American Indians.]

G. Cultural Connections
? Slave owners throughout history and across cultures treat their slaves differently. Rowlandson's record shows this, as does Equiano's (see pp. 57–65). How does this woman treat Rowlandson differently than do other American Indians? [Possible response: The woman lays a skin for her, feeds her, and invites her to come again, giving signs of respect.]

ASSESSMENT TOOLS

Ongoing Assessment Archaic language in this Collection may make comprehension and class discussion difficult for some students. Assess student participation based on the more easily addressed Reader's Response questions. Begin discussion by using the Reader's Response questions only. This strategy might help engage students who have difficulty with the language and style of the selection, giving them an opportunity to contribute to class discussion.

Check Test: True-False

1. After her capture Rowlandson is not allowed to see any of her children except Sarah. [False]
2. One of Rowlandson's captors, who has stolen a Bible, gives it to Rowlandson. [True]
3. Despite the constant traveling and the cold weather, the Native Americans have enough dried fruit and meat with them so that food is not a problem. [False]
4. Rowlandson smokes a pipe with King Philip (Metacomet), because it is an American Indian custom and she hopes not to offend him. [False]
5. Rowlandson interprets her captivity as God's test of her faith. [True]

Making Meanings

First Thoughts

1. Possible responses: Her strong belief in God; having a Bible; seeing her other son and daughter.

Reviewing the Text

a. Possible responses: Some American Indians treat her well, for they lighten her load and give her a Bible. Others treat her less well—they threaten to kill her wounded child or will not let her see her daughter Mary.

b. She makes articles of clothing for her captors. She gets used to food that at first disgusted her.

c. The captors at one point refuse her a spoonful of meal; they boil an old horse's leg; not everyone has parched corn; the maid has to go to Narragansett to fetch corn.

d. Possible answer: Her ability to resist committing suicide; getting a Bible; her son's unexpected arrival.

Shaping Interpretations

2. Possible responses: She thinks some are kinder and more generous than others and some are positively cruel, but I do not see any change in her attitude. She still separates herself from them: They are heathen; she is Christian. Or her attitude changes, because she writes that no one did her harm.

3. Possible response: She alludes to the story of Job and his "miserable comforters" when he suffered affliction, and the wanderings of the Hebrews in the wilderness. These stories parallel her loss and wandering. One of her children dies. Symbolically, only the spiritual, as seen in her relationship with God, can comfort. She literally moves where her captors move, but she is also tested spiritually, and seeks God in her wandering.

4. Possible responses: It has a plot with good versus evil; it tells of a culture and situation that is exotic to those in England; it has a lot of suspense; it is true; it is spiritually uplifting.

It is one-sided in that it does not tell any of what the colonists had done to the American Indians, and it presents the view of a captive who had herself not injured the American Indians, thereby making them appear especially cruel.

MAKING MEANINGS

First Thoughts

1. Review the notes you made in your Reader's Log. What do you think helped Mary Rowlandson survive?

Reviewing the Text

a. What does Rowlandson tell us about how she was treated by her captors?

b. What jobs does Rowlandson do to earn her food? How does her attitude toward food change while she is a captive?

c. Find the details that reveal that Rowlandson's captors themselves are desperate to find food.

d. Identify at least three occasions during her captivity in which Rowlandson is able to see Divine Providence at work.

Shaping Interpretations

2. What conflicting attitudes, if any, does Rowlandson reveal toward her captors? Do you think her attitude toward her captors changes as the narrative progresses? Explain.

3. The Puritans' habit of seeing specific meaning in their experiences helped them find significance in even very minor events. Describe at least two **allusions** to Biblical stories that Rowlandson makes during her captivity. In what specific ways does each of these Biblical stories resemble Rowlandson's?

4. Rowlandson's narrative was enormously popular in England. What reasons can you propose for its popularity? What aspects of Rowlandson's journal might have promoted stereotyped and hostile views toward American Indians?

5. In his classic work of psychology, *Man's Search for Meaning,* Dr. Viktor Frankl, a survivor of the Nazi concentration camps of World War II, tells how the best chance for survival in the camps was not physical endurance or general health but an internal sense that the experience, no matter how horrifying, had some ultimate meaning for the prisoner. Those who had strong religious faith, committed political views, or even just a strong love of family were far more likely to survive, both physically and mentally. In your view, what was Mary Rowlandson's ultimate source of meaning?

Challenging the Text

6. Despite her efforts to be accurate, Rowlandson's journal is full of **subjective reporting.** Instead of using neutral language (words with neither positive nor negative **connotations**), subjective reporting relies on "emotionally loaded" words—words with strongly positive or negative connotations. Select any extract from Rowlandson's journal, and find the emotionally loaded words or phrases that reveal her attitude toward her captors. What words or phrases does Rowlandson use that a detached, objective historian would *not* use?

Three American Indian baskets and a string of wampum.

Baskets: Peabody Museum, Harvard University, Cambridge, Massachusetts. Photo by Hillel Burger. Wampum: Peabody Essex Museum, Salem, Massachusetts/Peabody Museum Collections. Photo by Mark Sexton.

5. Possible response: Mary Rowlandson may have believed that her trials were meant to strengthen her soul and prepare her for heaven.

Challenging the Text

6. (Evaluation) Possible responses: Rowlandson, quoting Job 16:2, calls the American Indians "miserable comforters" (p. 41). She refers to their food as "filthy trash" (p. 44).

Choices: Building Your Portfolio

Writer's Notebook

1. Collecting Ideas for an Autobiographical Incident

You've probably had the experience of changing your perception of someone or something. A negative viewpoint can soften over time and become more positive. But the reverse is also true: A good opinion or feeling can go sour. Write down your recollections of an instance in your life when your perception or opinion of something or someone changed as a result of a specific incident. Save your notes for possible use in the Writer's Workshop on page 130.

Critical Writing

2. Psalm of Suffering

On page 44, Mary Rowlandson makes an **allusion** to Psalm 137, which is a well-known "captivity" psalm. It was composed when the Israelites were held captive in Babylon by King Nebuchadnezzar. Read Psalm 137 below, and in a brief essay explain why Rowlandson thought of this psalm at a certain point in her sufferings. What parallel would she see between her experience and that of the psalmist? In her mind, what would "Babylon" be?

Creative Writing

3. The Other Side of the Story

Write a journal entry from the point of view of a Wampanoag. Explain the position of your people, giving your reasons for the attack on the settlement and an explanation for the desperate conditions you have been enduring. Use history texts or encyclopedias as your sources. (You will find information under "King Philip's War" and "Metacomet.")

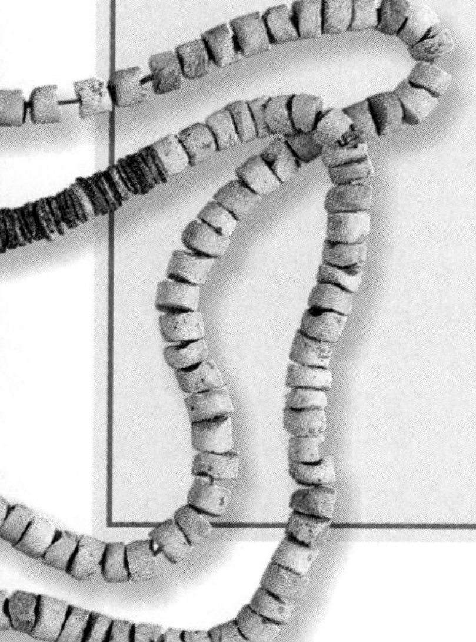

By the rivers of Babylon, there we sat down, yea, we wept, when we remembered Zion.

We hanged our harps upon the willows in the midst thereof.

For there they that carried us away captive required of us a song; and they that wasted us required of us mirth, saying, Sing us one of the songs of Zion.

How shall we sing the Lord's song in a strange land?

If I forget thee, O Jerusalem, let my right hand forget her cunning.

If I do not remember thee, let my tongue cleave to the roof of my mouth; if I prefer not Jerusalem above my chief joy.

Remember, O Lord, the children of Edom in the day of Jerusalem; who said, Raze it, raze it, even to the foundation thereof.

O daughter of Babylon, who art to be destroyed; happy shall he be, that rewardeth thee as thou hast served us.

Happy shall he be, that taketh and dasheth thy little ones against the stones.

—Psalm 137

Choices: Building Your Portfolio

1. **Writer's Notebook** *Remind students to choose a topic they would not mind sharing with others.* Also, remind students to save their work. They may use it as prewriting for the Writer's Workshop on p. 130. Before students begin, ask the class to brainstorm categories of change and to jot their ideas on the chalkboard. Possibilities include gaining maturity, moving, or falling in love.
2. **Critical Writing** Students who are not familiar with Biblical history should be provided with background: Israel was the home of believers in one God and was situated amid idol-worshipping groups, among them the Babylonians.
3. **Creative Writing** Have students begin by writing specific questions they want to answer during the research process. Ask them to leave a space after each question to provide room for answers. As they conduct their research, have students make notes by placing answers next to their questions. Students can use these notes when they write their journal entries.

Choices: Assessment Criteria For help in evaluating these Choices assignments, see the criteria in the *Portfolio Management System*, p. 68.

STRATEGIES FOR INCLUSION

Advanced For activity #1, students may want to immediately work some of their jottings into a longer narrative, anecdote, or poem while they have the feeling of the incident captured.

Learners Having Difficulty Group students with different writing abilities, and have them collaborate on the research and journal entry for activity #3. Learners experiencing difficulty could be responsible for items such as note cards and the bibliography or source list.

A. Exploring the Historical Period
The Cavaliers were royalists, aristocratic supporters of King Charles I during the English Civil Wars of 1642-1651.

B. Humanities Connection
It was typical for planters to send their sons to be educated in England. The writing of Byrd, for example, reflects his English roots and education: His early work is considered very like that of the English Restoration and his later pieces resemble literary works popular in the reigns of Queen Anne and the early Hanover kings.

C. Humanities Connection
Robert Beverley (1673–1722), Byrd's brother-in-law, had a style and an outlook different from those of the Southerners described here. He was neither an Anglophile nor an aristocrat, but a Virginia farmer. He wrote *History of Virginia* in 1703 to correct the errors being perpetuated about English colonies in the Americas.

The Southern Planters

A In addition to the Puritan tradition of New England, there was another literary tradition in the American Colonies. This literature came from the Southern planters, also known as the Cavaliers, a group of people whose background and social views varied considerably from those of the Puritans.

There were many possible reasons for the differences. One factor may have been climate. The Southern climate was kind; it was warm and mild, and the land was enormously fertile. The Northern climate was harsher; springs and summers were brief, and winters were long and cold. Even the land in New England was hard. Its outcroppings of granite and bedrock broke plows and made farming difficult.

But economic and religious factors were even more important. The landholdings in New England were small for the most part; many colonists were small farmers or tradespeople who lived in villages and owned very little land. But the Southern planter was an aristocrat, the virtual ruler of a huge territory that was maintained by plentiful slave labor (though slavery was common in New England in those days, too).

Opposing Worldviews

Most Southerners belonged to the Church of England. In general, they were much more interested in the outside world—literature, music, art, politics, and the world of nature—than they were in the scrupulous examination of their own souls. Where the Puritan feared that the world's beauties were lures and sources of temptation, the Southerner saw the world as something to be conquered and enjoyed.

B The Southern planters shared the worldview of the English Renaissance, with its emphasis on classical literature and scientific inquiry. Thus, when the Southerners wrote about life in America, they were apt to write about it in traditional ways. Even a work as original as *The Sotweed Factor* (1708), Ebenezer Cooke's humorous tale of a tobacco merchant, was written in the bouncy couplets popular for satire in England.

A Renaissance Man

C In many ways, William Byrd is a representative figure for the Southern writers of the Colonial period. He was truly a Renaissance man. He translated Greek and Latin works, composed original poetry (mostly satiric verse), and wrote about mathematics and medicine. Writing a generation before Thomas Jefferson (page 114), Byrd displayed the same intellectual curiosity that his fellow Virginian would so strongly exemplify later.

Byrd described the pleasures of the Southern planter's life: "I have a large family of my own, and my doors are open to everybody, yet I have no bills to pay. . . . I live in a kind of independence of everyone but Providence. . . . I must take care to keep all my people to their duty. . . . But then 'tis an amusement in this silent country."

William Byrd

(1674–1744)

It is worth remembering that Jamestown, Virginia, was named for James I, the king who vowed to harry the Puritans out of England. Virginia itself was named for Elizabeth I, the "Virgin Queen." These place names—and many others in the South—remind us of an important difference between Virginia and the Colonies of New England. New England was settled largely by those in conflict with British intellectual, theological, and social life; Virginia was settled by those in harmony with that life. By and large, the fervent, short-haired puritanical Roundheads went to New England; the aristocratic, long-haired, worldly Cavaliers went to Virginia.

William Byrd (1704) by the Studio of Sir Godfrey Kneller. Oil on canvas.

Colonial Williamsburg Foundation, Williamsburg, Virginia (D583.1087).

William Byrd was a thorough Cavalier—worldly, sophisticated, and gentlemanly. Byrd was born in Virginia, the son of a wealthy landowner and merchant, but he was educated in England, where he spent half his life. In London, he acquired a passion for the theater, which the Puritans had once outlawed as immoral. Byrd had many scientific interests: He was even a member of the Royal Society, that pillar of the British scientific establishment.

Byrd alternated between living in England and living in Virginia. He preferred London, with its elegant homes, witty conversation, and gambling tables. During his visits to Westover, his 26,000-acre home in Virginia, he tried to keep alive both his social and intellectual life. Westover's gardens are still renowned, and its library of almost 4,000 volumes was rivaled in Byrd's time only by Cotton Mather's library in New England.

Byrd had little in common with the New Englanders. He kept a diary, as many Puritans did. But the Puritans' diaries are primarily records of spiritual examination. Byrd's diary records the pleasures and practical concerns of a man of the world. Dinners, flirtations with women, literature, and natural science were of greater interest to him than matters of the spirit. In London in 1719, for example, he recorded a typical day:

> May 28. I rose about 7 o'clock and read a chapter in Hebrew and some Greek. I neglected my prayers, but had milk for breakfast. The weather was still warm and clear and very dry, the wind north. About eleven came Annie Wilkinson but I would not speak with her. I was disappointed in the [absence] of Mrs. B—s who wrote me word she would come and breakfast with me, so I read some English and ate some bread and butter because I was to dine late and about 3 o'clock went to dine with Sir Wilfred Lawson and ate some mutton. After dinner we talked a little and about 6 o'clock went to Kensington in Sir Wilfred's coach where there was a ball in the gardens and several ladies and among the rest Miss Perry whom I stuck most to and she complained I squeezed her hand. Here I stayed until 1 o'clock and then came home and neglected my prayers.

In 1728, Byrd joined a survey expedition of the disputed boundary line between Virginia and North Carolina. *The History of the Dividing Line* is far more than a simple record of that expedition. Witty and elegantly written, it is filled with philosophical observations and barbed comments on American Colonial life.

ABOUT THE AUTHOR

William Byrd was a man who liked to keep secrets. *The History of the Dividing Line* is only one of the histories that Byrd wrote about the survey of the disputed boundary: The other was his private journal, written first, and often referred to as the *Secret History*. The *Secret History* was a personal journal where he recorded private thoughts at the time, applied unflattering nicknames to some members of the expedition, and revealed information that would have caused a scandal had it become generally known. Byrd used the *Secret History* to write *The History of the Dividing Line*, a formal account intended for publication.

QUICK PLANNING GUIDE

Into the Selection

Through the Selection

Beyond the Selection

BEFORE YOU READ

FROM THE HISTORY OF THE DIVIDING LINE

Reading Focus

The Observer's Eye

Byrd's *History of the Dividing Line* is a record of personal experience, written while Byrd was helping out on a survey expedition. Byrd must have realized the value of his experience, understanding that a journey of any kind is an opportunity to observe and learn. By paying close attention—by seeing clearly, not merely looking—any traveler can learn about people, places, and practices that are different from those with which he or she is familiar.

A Dialogue with the Text

In the first extract from the *History,* Byrd ironically describes the "modish frenzy" of early travelers to America, a fashionable craze that he compares to a "distemper" or illness. As you read each section of Byrd's journal, pay attention to Byrd's **tone.** Jot down any words, phrases, or expressions that make Byrd seem very "modern"—and funny.

Elements of Literature

Satire

The ironic, barbed approach Byrd takes in his *History* is in sharp contrast to the straightforward style of a Puritan such as William Bradford (page 26). Like many British writers of his time, Byrd excels at **satire,** the use of ridicule to expose the shortcomings of things he observes.

> **Satire** is a type of writing that ridicules the shortcomings of people or institutions, usually in an attempt to bring about some change.
>
> *For more on Satire, see the Handbook of Literary Terms.*

Background

William Byrd began his *History* in 1728. By then, more than a century had passed since the first English settlers reached Virginia. Byrd's journal was found among his personal papers after his death and wasn't published until 1841.

from The History of the Dividing Line

William Byrd

Early Virginia Colonies

As it happened some ages before to be the fashion to saunter to the Holy Land and go upon other Quixote adventures,[1] so it was now grown the humor to take a trip to America. The Spaniards had lately discovered rich mines in their part of the West Indies, which made their maritime neighbors eager to do so too. (A) This modish frenzy, being still more inflamed by the charming account given of Virginia by the first adventurers, made many fond of removing to such a Paradise.

Happy was he, and still happier she, that could

1. **Quixote** (kē·hōt′ē) **adventures:** foolish adventures, like those taken by the mad hero of Miguel de Cervantes's novel *The Ingenious Gentleman Don Quixote de la Mancha.*

WORDS TO OWN

The following vocabulary words are defined in the Words to Own at the bottom of the pupil's page.

procure p. 51	prudent p. 52
allay p. 51	populous p. 53
eminent p. 51	squeamish p. 53
reprobates p. 51	propagated p. 53
disdained p. 52	venerable p. 54

PORTFOLIO ASSESSMENT

Portfolio Assessment For help with self- and teacher assessment of reading skills, see the *Portfolio Management System,* p. 53.

get themselves transported, fondly expecting their coarsest utensils in that happy place would be of massy[2] silver.

This made it easy for the Company to procure as many volunteers as they wanted for their new colony, but, like most other undertakers who have no assistance from the public, they starved the design by too much frugality; for, unwilling to launch out at first into too much expense, they shipped off but few people at a time, and those but scantily provided. The adventurers were, besides, idle and extravagant and expected they might live without work in so plentiful a country.

B These wretches were set ashore not far from Roanoke Inlet, but by some fatal disagreement or laziness were either starved or cut to pieces by the Indians.

Several repeated misadventures of this kind did for some time allay the itch of sailing to this new world, but the distemper broke out again about the year 1606. Then it happened that the Earl of Southampton and several other persons eminent for their quality and estates were invited into the Company, who applied themselves once more to people the then almost abandoned colony. For this purpose they embarked about an hundred men, most of them reprobates of good families and related to some of the Company who were men of quality and fortune.

The ships that carried them made a shift to find a more direct way to Virginia and ventured

2. **massy:** weighty.

WORDS TO OWN

procure (prō·kyoor′) *v.:* to gain; obtain; acquire.
allay (a·lā′) *v.:* lessen; relieve.
eminent (em′ə·nənt) *adj.:* well known for excellence; important; outstanding.
reprobates (rep′rə·bāts′) *n. pl.:* people without any sense of duty or decency.

The Plantation (c. 1825). Unknown American artist. Oil on wood (19⅛″ × 29½″).

The Metropolitan Museum of Art, Gift of Edgar William and Bernice Chrysler Garbisch, 1963 (63.201.3).

WILLIAM BYRD 51

Into the Selection

Using **BEFORE YOU READ** p. 50

Reading Focus

Ask students to write twenty observational notes on a place they have been a few times, such as a restaurant, a large room, or a field, and to bring these notes to class. Divide the class into groups of four to talk about the places and the kinds of observations they made. Afterward, have the class as a whole discuss whether they know that place better after having written and discussed their notes.

Through the Selection

A. Humanities Connection

Byrd is referring to accounts such as that of John Smith in his *A True Relation of Such Occurrences and Accidents of Noate as Hath Hapned in Virginia* and *A Description of New England.* The latter functioned as advertising for the Colonies and was not entirely truthful. For example, Smith writes that people in Virginia can easily have what costs a great deal in England.

B. Expansion

Although some false clues have been discovered, what happened to the colonists at Roanoke is not known. Another theory is that the colonists may have gone to live with a friendly American Indian nation.

PROGRAM MANAGER

- **Planning Instruction** See Teaching Notes, *Teaching Resources A,* pp. 3–4, for objectives, a summary, and literary elements for this selection.
- **Instructional Support** Before beginning the instructional lesson, see Graphic Organizer for Active Reading, *Teaching Resources A,* p. 16, for Into the Selection and Through the Selection activities.
- **Assessment** See Selection Test, *Test Booklet,* pp. 7–8.
- **Language Link** For instruction and practice in verbs, see Language Link, *Teaching Resources A,* pp. 17–18, and *Language and Writing Skills Worksheets,* pp. 16–17.
- **Reinforcement** Use the Words to Own worksheet in *Teaching Resources A,* p. 19.

A. Literary Element: Style
Compare this paragraph to a paragraph in *Of Plymouth Plantation.* Which seems more modern? Why? [Students may identify shorter sentence length, less convoluted syntax, fewer run-ons and fragments, colloquial word choice, lively rhythm, relatively simple style, and simpler punctuation as stylistic elements that make Byrd's text seem more modern.]

B. Critical Reading: Metacognition
? What can you do to comprehend and recall the details in this paragraph? [Possible answers: I could slow down my reading, break the paragraph and the sentences into parts, make notes, and repeat information in a sentence to myself after I have read it.]

C. Literary Element: Satire
? How would you describe Byrd's tone? [Satirical.] What does he suggest about the colonists' priorities? [They are more interested in leisure than in religion.]

D. Reader's Response: Shaping Interpretations
? How would you characterize Byrd based on his comments here? [Sample responses: He seems practical and community-minded; or he has more interest in the prosperity of the colony than in personal fulfillment.]

(A) through the capes into the Bay of Chesapeake. The same night they came to an anchor at the mouth of Powhatan, the same as James River, where they built a small fort at a place called Point Comfort.

(B) This settlement stood its ground from that time forward, in spite of all the blunders and disagreement of the first adventurers and the many calamities that befell the colony afterward. The six gentlemen who were first named of the Company by the Crown and who were empowered to choose an annual president from among themselves were always engaged in factions and quarrels, while the rest detested work more than famine. At this rate the colony must have come to nothing had it not been for the vigilance and bravery of Captain Smith,[3] who struck a terror into all the Indians round about. This gentleman took some pains to persuade the men to plant Indian corn, but they looked upon all labor as a curse. They chose rather to depend upon the musty provisions that were sent from England; and when they failed they were forced to take more pains to seek for wild fruits in the woods than they would have taken in tilling the ground. Besides, this exposed them to be knocked in the head by the Indians and gave them fluxes[4] into the bargain, which thinned the plantation very much. To supply this mortality, they were reinforced the year following with a greater number of people, amongst which were fewer gentlemen and more laborers, who, however, took care not to kill themselves with work. These found the first adventurers in a very starving condition but relieved their wants with the fresh supply (C) they brought with them. From Kecoughtan[5] they extended themselves as far as Jamestown, where, like true Englishmen, they built a church that cost no more than fifty pounds and a tavern that cost five hundred.

3. **Captain Smith:** John Smith (c. 1580–1631) helped found Jamestown, Virginia, the first permanent English settlement in America.
4. **fluxes** (fluks′iz): dysentery; severe diarrhea.
5. **Kecoughtan** (kē′kō′tan): present-day site of Hampton, Virginia.

As the Colony grew, violence frequently erupted between the settlers and the American Indians. Byrd offers his solution to the conflicts between the two cultures.

Intermarriage

They had now made peace with the Indians, but there was one thing wanting to make that peace lasting. The natives could by no means persuade themselves that the English were heartily their friends so long as they disdained to intermarry (D) with them. And, in earnest, had the English consulted their own security and the good of the colony, had they intended either to civilize or convert these gentiles,[6] they would have brought their stomachs to embrace this prudent alliance.

The Indians are generally tall and well proportioned, which may make full amends for the darkness of their complexions. Add to this that they are healthy and strong, with constitutions untainted by lewdness and not enfeebled by luxury. Besides, morals and all considered, I cannot think the Indians were much greater heathens than the first adventurers, who, had they been good Christians, would have had the charity to take this only method of converting the natives to Christianity. For, after all that can

6. **gentiles** (jen′tīlz′): here, nonbelievers. Historically, among Christians, *gentile* meant a pagan or nonbeliever. (*Gentile* comes from a Latin word meaning "foreigner.") The term is more commonly used by Jews to refer to those who are not Jewish.

WORDS TO OWN

disdained (dis·dānd′) *v.:* refused; disapproved, scorned.
prudent (pro͞od′'nt) *adj.:* well thought out; cautious.

OPTIONS FOR TEACHING

STRATEGIES FOR INCLUSION

Logical-Mathematical Encourage students to focus on Byrd's comparison of English–Native American relations with French–Native American relations and to record Byrd's evaluation of each. Supply a graphic organizer like the following that may be filled out for each relationship, modifying it to fit the selection.

	Fact 1:
	Fact 2:
	Fact 3:
Evaluation:	

Less Proficient Readers To help students process information in long sentences and paragraphs, ask them to work in pairs and to summarize each paragraph in a sentence stating the main idea.

Visual To help them identify the groups and places that Byrd discusses (the Holy Land, West Indies, Virginia, Roanoke Inlet, Southampton, Bay of Chesapeake, James River, Point Comfort, and Kecoughtan), provide a large map on which students may locate and mark the location of each place mentioned in the selection.

be said, a sprightly lover is the most prevailing[7] missionary that can be sent amongst these or any other infidels.

Besides, the poor Indians would have had less reason to complain that the English took away their land if they had received it by way of a portion with their daughters. Had such affinities been contracted in the beginning, how much bloodshed had been prevented and how populous would the country have been, and, consequently, how considerable! Nor would the shade of the skin have been any reproach at this day, for if a Moor may be washed white in three generations, surely an Indian might have been blanched in two.

The French, for their parts, have not been so squeamish in Canada, who upon trial find abundance of attraction in the Indians. Their late grand monarch thought it not below even the dignity of a Frenchman to become one flesh with this people and therefore ordered 100 livres[8] for any of his subjects, man or woman, that would intermarry with a native.

By this piece of policy we find the French interest very much strengthened amongst the savages and their religion, such as it is, propagated just as far as their love. And I heartily wish this well-concerted scheme don't hereafter give the French an advantage over His Majesty's good subjects on the northern continent of America.

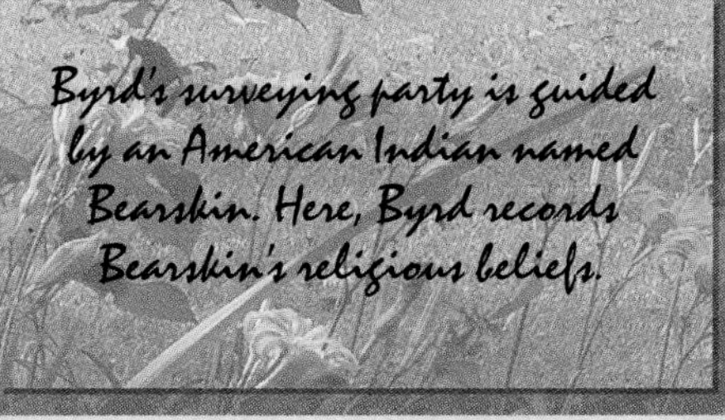

Byrd's surveying party is guided by an American Indian named Bearskin. Here, Byrd records Bearskin's religious beliefs.

7. **prevailing** (prē·vāl′iŋ): convincing.
8. **livres** (lē′vərz): former French monetary unit worth about a pound of silver each.

The Native Religion

In the evening we examined our friend Bearskin concerning the religion of his country, and he explained it to us without any of that reserve to which his nation is subject. He told us he believed there was one supreme god, who had several subaltern[9] deities under him. And that this master god made the world a long time ago. That he told the sun, the moon, and stars their business in the beginning, which they, with good looking-after, have faithfully performed ever since. That the same power that made all things at first has taken care to keep them in the same method and motion ever since. He believed that God had formed many worlds before he formed this, but that those worlds either grew old and ruinous or were destroyed for the dishonesty of the inhabitants. That God is very just and very good, ever well pleased with those men who possess those godlike qualities. That he takes good people into his safe protection, makes them very rich, fills their bellies plentifully, preserves them from sickness and from being surprised or overcome by their enemies. But all such as tell lies and cheat those they have dealings with he never fails to punish with sickness, poverty, and hunger and, after all that, suffers them to be knocked on the head and scalped by those that fight against them.

He believed that after death both good and bad people are conducted by a strong guard into a great road, in which departed souls travel together for some time till at a certain distance this road forks into two paths, the one extremely level and the other stony and mountainous. Here the good are parted from the bad

9. **subaltern** (səb·ôl′tərn): subordinate; of inferior rank or position.

Words to Own

populous (päp′yo͞o·ləs) *adj.:* crowded with people.
squeamish (skwēm′ish) *adj.:* easily offended.
propagated (präp′ə·gāt′id) *v.:* transmitted or spread.

E. Critical Reading: Identifying Main Ideas

? What are Byrd's two important points in this and the previous paragraph? [First, the English disdained to intermarry with the American Indians; second, the behavior differences between the American Indians and the English do not warrant the superiority the English felt because they were "good Christians."]

F. Expansion

In fact, Wahunsonacock, Pocahontas's father and the leader of the Powhatans, makes a similar point in his appeal for truce during the winter of 1609–1610, when he asks why the colonists take by force what they can have by love and by asking in friendship.

G. Critical Reading: Analyzing Viewpoints

Compare and contrast the views in this paragraph with the Puritan views presented by Bradford. [Possible answer: The Puritans seem to believe that even good people will suffer trials for their spiritual growth. Bearskin's view seems to be that bad fortune comes only to bad people. Bearskin does not subscribe to the notion of grace that the Puritans do: The choice of behaving well or poorly seems to be a matter of free will, not of divine predestination.]

INTEGRATING THE LANGUAGE ARTS

Writing: Diary Entry Although *The History of the Dividing Line* is a journal, it does not deal only with daily affairs. To help students better identify with Byrd and broaden their range of topics, have them write their own journals. Ask students to make a list of the topics Byrd covers (such as history, economics, and other cultures) and to use it to create a diary entry of their own that focuses on a topic that Byrd writes about. Students may assume a persona of Byrd's time or write from their own contemporary point of view.

Strategic Reading To help students focus on their reading, have them work in pairs to read the text in the three separate portions designated by the headings. Both students should read a section of text silently and then write questions concerning content, connections to other reading, or ideas about expansion. Then, the first student asks the second student the questions noted. The second student answers, and the two work together to summarize their learning. The roles are reversed for each section of text. Model this process before having students do it.

Grammar Byrd places an adjectival phrase after a noun: "mat richly woven" and "place above mentioned" (p. 54). Ask students to rephrase these descriptions. Ask them where we generally place adjectives in modern English. [Before the noun.]

A. Reader's Response: Shaping Interpretations

? How would you characterize Bearskin's description of the afterlife? [Sample responses: It is very much like an ideal of earthly life with no work, sickness, aging, or death. Or it is filled with pleasures.]

B. Humanities Connection

In this paragraph, Byrd uses three classical Greek mythological allusions to explain Bearskin's views: The Furies, Medusa, and the Harpies. This may be interpreted in at least two different levels: (1) Byrd is trying to understand what Bearskin says in terms of what is familiar to him; (2) there are fundamental similarities, not only in beliefs, but also in basic images and symbols among the various religions.

C. Language Note: Diction

Use of the word *mere* suggests Byrd's condescension to and sense of superiority over Bearskin. However, Byrd does try to find similarities between Bearskin's religion and his own idea of what religion should be.

by a flash of lightning, the first being hurried away to the right, the other to the left. The right-hand road leads to a charming, warm country, where the spring is everlasting and every month is May; and as the year is always in its youth, so are the people, and particularly the women are bright as stars and never scold. That in this happy climate there are deer, turkeys, elks, and buffaloes innumerable, perpetually fat and gentle, while the trees are (A) loaded with delicious fruit quite throughout the four seasons. That the soil brings forth corn spontaneously, without the curse of labor, and so very wholesome that none who have the happiness to eat of it are ever sick, grow old, or die. Near the entrance into this blessed land sits a venerable old man on a mat richly woven, who examines strictly all that are brought before him, and if they have behaved well, the guards are ordered to open the crystal gate and let them enter into the land of delight.

The left-hand path is very rugged and uneven, leading to a dark and barren country where it is always winter. The ground is the whole year round covered with snow, and nothing is to be seen upon the trees but icicles. All the people are hungry yet have not a morsel of anything to eat except a bitter kind of potato, that gives them the dry gripes[10] and fills their whole body with loathsome ulcers that stink and are insupportably painful. Here all the women are old and ugly, having claws like a panther with which they fly upon the men that slight their passion. For it seems these haggard old furies[11] are intolerably fond and expect a vast deal of cherishing. They talk much and exceedingly shrill, giving exquisite pain to the drum of the (B) ear, which in that place of the torment is so tender that every sharp note wounds it to the quick. At the end of this path sits a dreadful old woman on a monstrous toadstool, whose head is covered with rattlesnakes instead of tresses, with glaring white eyes that strike a terror unspeakable into all that behold her. This hag pronounces sentence of woe upon all the miserable wretches that hold up their hands at her tribunal. After this they are delivered over to huge turkey buzzards, like harpies,[12] that fly away with them to the place above mentioned. Here, after they have been tormented a certain number of years according to their several degrees of guilt, they are again driven back into this world to try if they will mend their manners and merit a place the next time in the regions of bliss.

This was the substance of Bearskin's religion and was as much to the purpose as could be expected from a mere state of nature, without (C) one glimpse of revelation or philosophy. It contained, however, the three great articles of natural religion: the belief of a god, the moral distinction between good and evil, and the expectation of rewards and punishments in another world.

10. **dry gripes:** stomach cramps.
11. **furies** (fyoor′ēz): violent, vengeful women. In Greek and Roman mythology, the Furies are fierce avenging spirits.
12. **harpies** (här′pēz): evil mythological creatures with women's heads and birds' wings and legs.

Words to Own

venerable (ven′ər·ə·bəl) *adj.:* respected; esteemed for age or distinguished character.

OPTIONS FOR TEACHING

ASSESSMENT TOOLS

Ongoing Assessment When asking several students to read aloud, take brief notes on their pronunciation, enunciation, pauses, emphasis, pitch, and tone. If you find problems shared by several students, teach a mini-lesson on the topic. Repeat this observation periodically to chart progress.

Check Test: Multiple Choice

1. Byrd pictures the earliest Virginia settlers as (a) pious (b) lazy (c) timid (d) enterprising [b]
2. Byrd says the colonists at Roanoke (a) moved West (b) returned to England or migrated to Canada (c) starved or were killed by Native Americans (d) intermarried with Native Americans [c]
3. Intermarriage between the English colonists and the Native Americans, according to Byrd, would serve to (a) ensure a lasting peace (b) disgrace Captain Smith (c) promote trade (d) enrage the Puritans [a]
4. Bearskin believes in (a) predestination (b) an angry god (c) many equal gods (d) a group of gods with one master [d]
5. Byrd praises Bearskin's religion for three things, including (a) distinguishing between good and evil (b) a portrait of the harpies (c) a belief in many gods (d) an analysis of guilt and redemption [a]

MAKING MEANINGS

First Thoughts

1. Did you find Byrd more or less interesting than the other Colonial writers you've read? What passages did you write in your Reader's Log because they struck you as funny or "modern"?

Reviewing the Text

a. What reasons does Byrd suggest for the failure of the first Virginia settlements?

b. Explain Byrd's point of view about the first colonists and their expectations of life in North America.

c. Why does Byrd favor intermarriage with American Indians?

d. What, according to Byrd, are the three basic religious beliefs of Bearskin, the American Indian guide?

Shaping Interpretations

2. What examples of **satire** did you find in Byrd's account of the early settlers of Virginia? Based on this scathing portrait, what personal qualities do you think Byrd admired?
3. Why might Byrd's observations on the first settlements in Virginia be less reliable than Bradford's on the Plymouth Colony (page 28)?
4. According to his description of Bearskin's religious beliefs, what "articles," or elements, of religion does Byrd consider most important? How closely do his views agree with those expressed by Mary Rowlandson (page 40)?

Extending the Text

5. What issues, events, or attitudes in American society today would be good topics for satire?

CHOICES: Building Your Portfolio

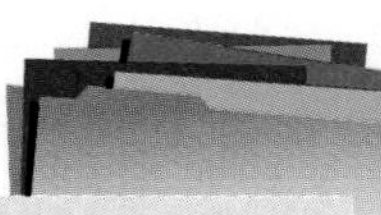

Writer's Notebook

1. Collecting Ideas for an Autobiographical Incident

WORK IN PROGRESS

Byrd's keen perceptions and mastery of the language resulted in phrases such as this: ". . . their coarsest utensils . . . would be of massy silver" (page 51). Make a list of phrases that describe vividly an experience you have had that was significant in some way. Keep your notes; you may find them useful in the Writer's Workshop on page 130.

Critical Writing

2. Different as Night and Day

In a brief essay, compare and contrast the excerpts from Byrd's *History* with William Bradford's account of the Puritan landing at Plymouth (pages 28–33). Consider specifically how the two accounts differ in purpose, tone, and style.

Creative Writing

3. Puritans and Planters

Imagine that you are a Puritan who has just returned from a visit to Jamestown. In a journal entry, describe the Southern planters, their approach to life, their physical appearance, and their interests, contrasting them with members of your own Puritan society.

Making Meanings

First Thoughts

1. Possible response: He was more interesting because his tone was not preachy, and he has a sense of humor. The first section about the immigrants' quest pokes fun at the first adventurers and their greed.

Reviewing the Text

a. People had unrealistic expectations, and were idle and extravagant; the Company did not provide adequate provisions; settlers were poorly chosen; settlers disagreed with the American Indians.

b. Byrd says that many settlers were encouraged to travel to Virginia by false accounts of explorers and adventurers and that they expected to become wealthy without working.

c. It would create a lasting peace between them.

d. Belief in a supreme god who made the world; belief in a heavenly afterlife for good people; and belief in a hell-like afterlife for bad people, who are tormented by buzzards. Then, they are sent back into the world to have a chance to improve their behavior.

Shaping Interpretations

2. Examples of satire: The settlers expecting "massy silver"; the comparison of cost of the Jamestown church and the tavern; the English concerns about the American Indians' complexions. Byrd admires people who have realistic expectations, cooperate, and are industrious.
3. Byrd's desire to be funny might outweigh his desire to be accurate; being more distant from his subject in space and time, he does not have sources of information as good as Bradford's.
4. Possible responses: Byrd considers important the belief in a god, the moral distinction between good and evil, and the anticipation of reward or punishment in an afterlife. Whereas Rowlandson shows the Puritan tendency to regard even the most mundane event as evidence of God's will, Byrd is more worldly and practical. Students may agree, however, that Byrd's essential religious beliefs do not differ greatly from those of Rowlandson.

Extending the Text

5. **(Synthesis)** Possible responses: The government, certain political leaders, or dieting.

Choices: Building Your Portfolio

1. **Writer's Notebook** *Remind students to choose a situation they would not mind sharing with others.* Also, remind them to save their work. They may use it as prewriting for the Writer's Workshop on p. 130.

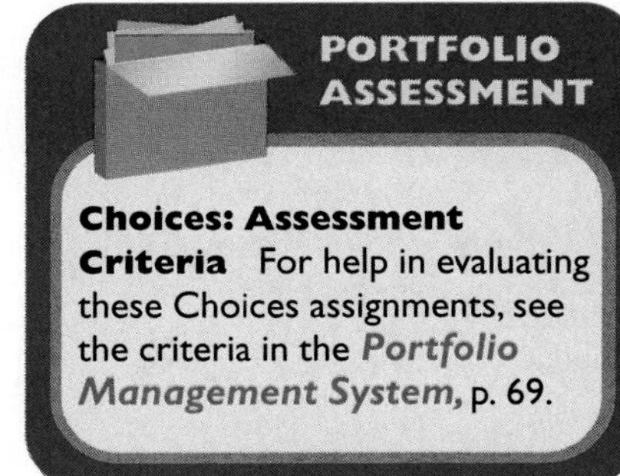

Choices: Assessment Criteria For help in evaluating these Choices assignments, see the criteria in the ***Portfolio Management System,*** p. 69.

QUICK PLANNING GUIDE

Into the Selection

Author Biography p. 56
Before You Read p. 57
- **Reading Focus: Scaffolding** Students discover extent of slave trade.
- **Quickwrite: Set a Purpose** Chart prior knowledge, desired learning, and actual learning in Reader's Log
- **Elements of Literature: Autobiography**

Through the Selection

from The Interesting Narrative of the Life of Olaudah Equiano pp. 57–65
Words to Own pp. 58–64
Student to Student p. 65
"Africa"
Making Meanings p. 66

Beyond the Selection

Choices: Building Your Portfolio p. 66
- **Writer's Notebook:** Collect ideas for an autobiographical incident
- **Critical Writing:** Compare and contrast immigration experiences in essay
- **Creative Writing/Art:** Prepare a nonfiction children's book

WRITERS ON WRITING

Equiano begins his autobiography with an analysis of the difficulties of the genre: "People generally think those memoirs only worthy to be read or remembered which abound in great or striking events; those in short, which, in a high degree excite either admiration or pity: all others they consign to contempt and oblivion. . . . I offer here the history of neither a saint, a hero, nor a tyrant."

Olaudah Equiano
(c. 1745–1797)

Olaudah Equiano (ō·lo͞o′dä ek′wē·än′o) was the first African writer to reach a sizable audience of American readers. A member of the Ibo people, Equiano was born in a part of West Africa that is now Nigeria. When he was only eleven years old, Equiano, along with his sister, was kidnapped from his home by African raiders involved in the slave trade. Over a period of six or seven months, during which he and his sister were separated, the slave traders took Equiano to a series of way stations. When he reached the coast, Equiano was put aboard one of the infamous slave ships bound for Barbados, an island in the West Indies, in the Caribbean. Slave labor was in demand to work on the sugar plantations in the Caribbean. In his narrative, Equiano vividly describes this cruel and horrifying part of the slave route, which was known as "the Middle Passage."

After a short stay in Barbados, Equiano was sold to a British military officer, who gave him the name Gustavus Vassa—ironically, the name of a Swedish freedom fighter. Equiano served with this officer during the Seven Years' War between England and France and gained great skill as a seaman. In time, a Quaker merchant from Philadelphia purchased Equiano. From his own profitable business ventures while managing his master's business, Equiano saved enough money to purchase his freedom in 1766, after having been enslaved for almost ten years. He was twenty-one years old.

After buying his freedom, Equiano worked as a sailor and led an exciting and adventurous life, sailing on exploratory expeditions to the Arctic and Central America. He finally settled in England, where he made his living as a free servant, a musician, and a barber. He also became active in the antislavery movement. In 1781, the captain of the *Zong,* which was transporting more than four hundred Africans to Jamaica, threw overboard a third of the shackled captives in order to collect the insurance. In 1783, Equiano was instrumental in bringing this atrocity to the attention of the public and the British naval authorities. When the abolition of the slave trade became a hotly debated issue in the English Parliament, Equiano actively campaigned against slavery, writing letters to officials and newspapers and visiting abolitionist leaders.

Olaudah Equiano (18th century English School) in the style of Sir Joshua Reynolds by an unknown artist. Oil on canvas.

Royal Albert Memorial Museum, Exeter City Museums and Art Gallery, Exeter, England.

Equiano's autobiography, published in England in 1789, was titled *The Interesting Narrative of the Life of Olaudah Equiano, or Gustavus Vassa, the African.* Reprinted in New York in 1791, the book—considered the first great black autobiography—proved popular with readers in the United States as well as abroad. The author's account of the horrors he suffered struck a responsive chord with northern abolitionists, but by then Equiano had settled in London. In 1792, he married an Englishwoman, Susanna Cullen.

Though Equiano traveled widely, he never returned to the United States. Nor did he ever again see his native Africa, to which he dreamed of returning. He defined himself, to the end of his life, simply as "the African."

WORDS TO OWN

The following vocabulary words are defined in the Words to Own at the bottom of the pupil's page.

assailant p. 58	countenances p. 61
distraction p. 59	dejection p. 61
alleviate p. 60	copious p. 63
interspersed p. 60	improvident p. 63
commodious p. 60	moderate p. 64

PORTFOLIO ASSESSMENT

Portfolio Assessment For help with teacher assessment of reading skills, see the ***Portfolio Management System,*** pp. 54–55.

Before You Read

from The Interesting Narrative of the Life of Olaudah Equiano

Reading Focus

Against Their Will

The first Africans in the Americas were unwilling immigrants who arrived on slave ships before 1600. Between the seventeenth and nineteenth centuries, about ten million people were captured in Africa and enslaved, shipped to North and South America and the islands of the West Indies. People were literally seized from their homes and sold as commodities, with no thought for their human rights.

Quickwrite

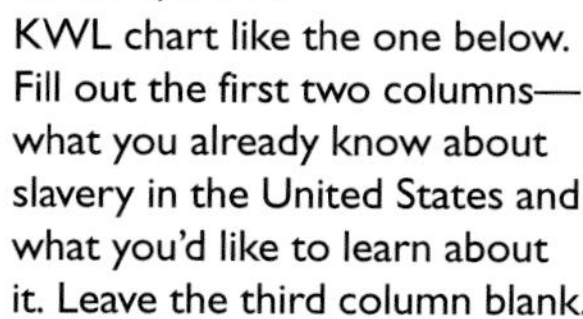

Before you read Equiano's account, make a KWL chart like the one below. Fill out the first two columns—what you already know about slavery in the United States and what you'd like to learn about it. Leave the third column blank.

K What I Know	W What I Want to Know	L What I Learned

Elements of Literature

Autobiography

Equiano's **autobiography** is one of the first slave narratives to be published. Many accounts of the horrors of slavery were firsthand accounts used by abolitionists in the nineteenth century to fuel the crusade against slavery.

An **autobiography** is a firsthand account of a writer's own life.

For more on Autobiography, see the Handbook of Literary Terms.

from The Interesting Narrative of the Life of Olaudah Equiano

Olaudah Equiano

Kidnapped

My father, besides many slaves, had a numerous family of which seven lived to grow up, including myself and a sister (A) who was the only daughter. As I was the youngest of the sons I became, of course, the greatest favorite with my mother and was always with her; and she used to take particular pains to form my mind. I was trained up from my earliest years in the art of war, my daily exercise was shooting and throwing javelins, and my mother adorned me with emblems after the manner of our greatest warriors. In this way I grew up till I was turned the age of 11, when an end was put to my happiness in the following manner. Generally when the grown people in the neighborhood were gone far in the

Using Before You Read p. 57

Reading Focus

Ask students to jot down how the captured Africans might have felt seeing strange people, leaving their homeland and people, and facing an uncertain future. Have them share their ideas in small groups.

Elements of Literature

Marion Wilson Starling tells us that from the estimated 60,000 slaves who escaped to freedom, 6006 wrote or told their stories to interviewers between 1703 and 1944. In all history, this stands as the largest collection of testimony from a people coming out of slavery.

A. Reader's Response: First Thoughts

? Initially, what do you think the narrator's attitude toward slavery will be? [Sample responses: Because his family owned slaves, he might take it for granted. He might approve of it. Or he may see trouble with it.]

Program Manager

- **Planning Instruction** See Teaching Notes, *Teaching Resources A,* p. 4, for objectives, a summary, literary elements, and additional historical information for this selection.
- **Instructional Support** See Graphic Organizer for Active Reading, *Teaching Resources A,* p. 20, for Into the Selection and Through the Selection activities.
- **Audiotaped Readings** To help auditory learners, use the Selected Reading, Audiocassette 1, Side A, in the *Audiovisual Resources Binder.*
- **Assessment** See Selection Test, *Test Booklet,* pp. 9–10.
- **Language Link** For a review of adjectives and adverbs, see Language Link, *Teaching Resources A,* pp. 21–22, and *Language and Writing Skills Worksheets,* pp. 15,18.
- **Reinforcement** Use the Words to Own worksheet in *Teaching Resources A,* p. 23.

A. Exploring the Culture
Kidnapping people in order to enslave them seems to be a way of life in Africa at this time. The business of kidnapping people for work did not happen in Africa alone. In seventeenth-century England, men, women, and children were kidnapped and sent to America to work as servants.

B. Reader's Response: Connecting with the Text
? How is the kidnapping of Equiano similar to and different from the kidnapping of Mary Rowlandson?
[Sample responses: The colonists and American Indians are at war when Rowlandson is kidnapped, while here the kidnappers seem to be professional slavers. Rowlandson is given no food for days, but she is neither gagged nor tied, while Equiano is unable to take any food and is both gagged and tied.]

fields to labor, the children assembled together in some of the neighbors' premises to play, and commonly some of us used to get up a tree to look for (A) any assailant or kidnapper that might come upon us, for they sometimes took those opportunities of our parents' absence to attack and carry off as many as they could seize. One day, as I was watching at the top of a tree in our yard, I saw one of those people come into the yard of our next neighbor but one to kidnap, there being many stout young people in it. Immediately on this I gave the alarm of the rogue and he was surrounded by the stoutest of them, who entangled him with cords so that he could not escape till some of the grown people came and secured him.

But alas! ere long it was my fate to be thus attacked and to be carried off when none of the grown people were nigh. One day, when all our people were gone out to their works as usual and only I and my dear sister were left to mind the house, two men and a woman got over our walls, and in a moment seized us both, and without giving us time to cry out or make resistance they stopped our mouths and ran off with us into the nearest wood. Here they tied our hands and continued to carry us as far as they could till night came on, when we reached a small house where (B) the robbers halted for refreshment and spent the night. We were then unbound but were unable to take any food, and being quite overpowered by fatigue and grief, our only relief was some sleep, which allayed our misfortune for a short time. The next morning we left the house and continued traveling all the day. For a long time we had kept to the woods, but at last we came into a road which I believed I knew. I had now some hopes of being delivered, for we had advanced but a little way before I discovered some people at a distance,

Words to Own
assailant (ə·sāl′ənt) *n.:* attacker.

Slave Deck of the Albanoz (1843–1847) by Lt. Francis Meynell. Watercolor on paper.
National Maritime Museum, Greenwich, England.

OPTIONS FOR TEACHING

STRATEGIES FOR INCLUSION

Kinesthetic Have students act out scenes from Equiano's narrative to aid comprehension and recall. Encourage them to choose scenes that are both dramatic and visually impressive.

Musical The dramatic events that Equiano relates lend themselves well to musical accompaniment. Encourage students either to choose music that they feel conveys the mood or to compose and record their own music. Students should specify which section of text they are accompanying.

English Language Development Point out that English was not Equiano's first language. He heard it first when he was eleven or twelve—and yet this autobiography is written in a fluent and powerfully effective prose style. Use this example of second-language acquisition to encourage readers who are having difficulty with this Collection.

Linguistic Students may prefer to write an outline or summary to help them keep track of occurrences in the text, rather than the more visually oriented graphic organizer suggested in Strategic Reading on p. T59. Allow students to record information in the way that best suits their individual learning styles.

on which I began to cry out for assistance: But my cries had no other effect than to make them tie me faster and stop my mouth, and then they put me into a large sack. They also stopped my sister's mouth and tied her hands, and in this manner we proceeded till we were out of the sight of these people.

When we went to rest the following night they offered us some victuals, but we refused it, and the only comfort we had was in being in one another's arms all that night and bathing each other with our tears. But alas! we were soon deprived of even the small comfort of weeping together. The next day proved a day of greater sorrow than I had yet experienced, for my sister and I were then separated while we lay clasped in each other's arms. It was in vain that we besought them not to part us; she was torn from me and immediately carried away, while I was left in a state of distraction not to be described. I cried and grieved continually, and for several days I did not eat anything but what they forced into my mouth. At length, after many days' traveling, during which I had often changed masters, I got into the hands of a chieftain in a very pleasant country. This man had two wives and some children, and they all used me extremely well and did all they could to comfort me, particularly the first wife, who was something like my mother. Although I was a great many days' journey from my father's house, yet these people spoke exactly the same language with us. This first master of mine, as I may call him, was a smith, and my principal employment was working his bellows, which were the same kind as I had seen in my vicinity. They were in some respects not unlike the stoves here in gentlemen's kitchens, and were (C) covered over with leather; and in the middle of that leather a stick was fixed, and a person stood up and worked it in the same manner as is done to pump water out of a cask with a hand pump. I believe it was gold he worked, for it was of a lovely bright yellow color and was worn by the women on their wrists and ankles. . . .

Soon after this my master's only daughter and child by his first wife sickened and died, which affected him so much that for some time he was almost frantic, and really would have killed himself had he not been watched and prevented. However, in a small time afterward he recovered and I was again sold. I was now carried to the left of the sun's rising, through many different countries and a number of large woods. The people I was sold to used to carry me very often when I was tired either on their shoulders or on their backs. (D) I saw many convenient well-built sheds along the roads at proper distances, to accommodate the merchants and travelers who lay in those buildings along with their wives, who often accompany them; and they always go well armed.

From the time I left my own nation I always found somebody that understood me till I came to the seacoast. The languages of different nations did not totally differ, nor were they so copious as those of the Europeans, particularly the English. (E) They were therefore easily learned, and while I was journeying thus through Africa I acquired two or three different tongues. In this manner I had been traveling for a considerable time, when one evening, to my great surprise, whom should I see brought to the house where I was but my dear sister! As soon as she saw me she gave a loud shriek and ran into my arms—I was quite overpowered: Neither of us could speak, but for a considerable time clung to each other in mutual embraces, unable to do anything but weep. Our meeting affected all who saw us, and indeed I must acknowledge, in honor of those sable destroyers of human rights, that I never met with any ill-treatment or saw any offered to their slaves except tying them, when necessary, to keep them from running away.

When these people knew we were brother and sister they indulged us to be together, and the man to whom I supposed we belonged lay with us, he in the middle while she and I held one another by the hands across his breast all night; and thus for a while we forgot our misfortunes in the joy of being together: But even this small comfort was soon to have an end, for scarcely had the fatal morning appeared when she was again torn from me forever! I was now more miserable, if possible, than before. The small relief which her presence gave me from pain was gone, and the wretchedness of my situation was redoubled by my anxiety after her fate and my apprehensions

Words to Own

distraction (di·strak′shən) *n.:* mental disturbance or distress.

C. Critical Reading: Drawing Conclusions

? When he says "here," where does Equiano mean? [Students should realize that he does not mean Africa but is referring to where he is as he writes the autobiography. They may guess the United States, but he moved to England in 1777, and his autobiography was published in 1789.]

D. Reader's Response: First Thoughts

? Why do you think they carry him? [Sample responses: To keep him in good health so that he could be sold at a better price; or because the slave owners liked him.]

E. Cultural Connections

Call attention to this passage, and point out that in Africa, as on other continents, different peoples speak different, but in some cases related, languages.

INTEGRATING THE LANGUAGE ARTS

Writing: Rewrite To help students see the difference distance makes on looking back on one's history, ask them to rewrite a portion of Equiano's history as they think an eleven- or twelve-year-old might write it. Tell them to pay attention to diction and sentence structure and to consider carefully the point of view in terms of knowledge, experience, and expectations.

Strategic Reading To help students relate what they know to what they learn, assign dates to a time line similar to the following example. Before studying the Equiano selection, ask the class to record historical events above the time line. Students should contribute historical facts from other reading in this class and social science classes. As students continue reading, they will add newly acquired information below the time line.

TIME LINE — EVENTS YOU ALREADY KNOW

(event) (date)	(event) (date)	(event) (date)	Emancipation Proclamation 1863
(date) (event)	(date) (event)	(date) (event)	

EVENTS YOU LEARN ABOUT

A. Critical Reading: Drawing Conclusions

? How would you characterize the treatment Equiano receives here? [Possible answer: He is treated as a guest according to customs that are familiar to him.]

B. Literary Element: Irony

Irony occurs when there is a discrepancy between appearance and reality. Explain the irony of Equiano's situation as he describes it here. [Possible answer: It appears that he is being treated as a guest or member of the family, so much so that he forgets his situation and his sufferings. Suddenly, with no warning he is sold.]

C. Reader's Response: Connecting with the Text

At this low point Equiano talks only about the changes in his feelings. How does this differ from how Bradford and Rowlandson record dealing with low points? [Sample responses: They both record how religion supports them in difficult times, how it makes their sufferings bearable and gives meaning to the events in their lives. Neither Bradford nor Rowlandson contrasts low points with high points.]

D. Literary Element: Irony

Encourage students to find the irony in Equiano's view of the slave traders, especially in comparison with the way the white slavers view their cargo. [Possible answer: Each views the other with suspicion largely on the basis of physical appearance. The whites' appearance and insolent treatment of him make Equiano think they are devils, in contrast to the African slavers, whom he finds fairly humane.]

lest her sufferings should be greater than mine, when I could not be with her to alleviate them. . . .

I did not long remain after my sister. I was again sold and carried through a number of places till, after traveling a considerable time, I came to a town called Tinmah in the most beautiful country I had yet seen in Africa. It was extremely rich, and there were many rivulets which flowed through it and supplied a large pond in the center of town, where the people washed. Here I first saw and tasted coconuts, which I thought superior to any nuts I had ever tasted before; and the trees, which were loaded, were also interspersed amongst the houses, which had commodious shades adjoining and were in the same manner as ours, the insides being neatly plastered and whitewashed. Here I also saw and tasted for the first time sugar cane. Their money consisted of little white shells the size of the fingernail. I was sold here for 172 of them by a merchant who lived and brought me there. I had been about two or three days at his house when a wealthy widow, a neighbor of his, came there one evening, and brought with her an only son, a young gentleman about my own age and size. Here they saw me; and, having taken a fancy to me, I was bought of the merchant, and went home with them. Her house and premises were situated close to one of those rivulets I have mentioned, and were the finest I ever saw in Africa: They were very extensive, and she had a number of slaves to attend her. The next day I was washed and perfumed, and when mealtime came I was led into the presence of my mistress, and ate and drank before her with her son. This filled me with astonishment; and I could scarce help expressing my surprise that the young gentleman should suffer me, who was bound, to eat with him who was free; and not only so, but that he would not at any time either eat or drink till I had taken first, because I was the eldest, which was agreeable to our custom. Indeed everything here, and all their treatment of me, made me forget that I was a slave. The language of these people resembled ours so nearly that we understood each other perfectly. They had also the very same customs as we. There were likewise slaves daily to attend us, while my young master and I with other boys sported with our darts and bows and arrows, as I had been used to do at home. In this resemblance to my former happy state I passed about two months; and I now began to think I was to be adopted into the family, and was beginning to be reconciled to my situation, and to forget by degrees my misfortunes, when all at once the delusion vanished; for without the least previous knowledge, one morning early, while my dear master and companion was still asleep, I was wakened out of my reverie to fresh sorrow, and hurried away even amongst the uncircumcised.

Thus at the very moment I dreamed of the greatest happiness, I found myself most miserable; and it seemed as if fortune wished to give me this taste of joy only to render the reverse more poignant. The change I now experienced was as painful as it was sudden and unexpected. It was a change indeed from a state of bliss to a scene which is inexpressible by me, as it discovered to me an element I had never before beheld and till then had no idea of, and wherein such instances of hardship and cruelty continually occurred as I can never reflect on but with horror. . . .

The Slave Ship

The first object which saluted[1] my eyes when I arrived on the coast was the sea, and a slave ship which was then riding at anchor and waiting for its cargo. These filled me with astonishment, which was soon converted into terror when I was carried on board. I was immediately handled and tossed up to see if I were sound by some of the crew, and I was now persuaded that I had gotten into a world of bad spirits and that they were going to kill me. Their complexions too differing so much from ours, their long hair and the language they spoke (which was very different from any I had ever heard) united to confirm me in this belief. Indeed such were the horrors of my views and fears at the moment that, if ten thousand worlds had been my own, I would have freely parted with them all to have exchanged my condition with that of the meanest[2] slave in my own

1. saluted: met.
2. meanest: lowest.

WORDS TO OWN

alleviate (ə·lē′vē·āt′) *v.:* to relieve; reduce.
interspersed (in′tər·spʉrsd′) *v.:* placed at intervals.
commodious (kə·mō′dē·əs) *adj.:* spacious.

OPTIONS FOR TEACHING

COOPERATIVE LEARNING

Grouping Take learning styles into consideration when forming groups for a dramatic reading of this selection. For a full reading production, have auditory and linguistic learners generate sound effects and dialogue, visual learners create props and backdrops, and kinesthetic learners arrange and direct the blocking of the reading.

Students Who Study Latin Students who have studied Latin may have an advantage in learning the vocabulary words. Pair these students with students who have not had Latin so they may work on vocabulary words prior to beginning the selection.

country. When I looked round the ship too and saw a large furnace or copper boiling and a multitude of black people of every description chained together, every one of their countenances expressing dejection and sorrow, I no longer doubted of my fate; and quite overpowered with horror and anguish, I fell motionless on the deck and fainted. When I recovered a little I found some black people about me, who I believed were some of those who had brought me on board and had been receiving their pay; they talked to me in order to cheer me, but all in vain. I asked them if we were not to be eaten by those white men with horrible looks, red faces, and loose hair. They told me I was not, and one of the crew brought me a small portion of spirituous liquor in a wineglass, but being afraid of him I would not take it out of his hand. One of the blacks therefore took it from him and gave it to me, and I took a little down my palate, which instead of reviving me, as they thought it would, threw me into the greatest consternation at the strange feeling it

WORDS TO OWN

countenances (koun′tə·nəns·əz) *n. pl.:* faces.

dejection (dē·jek′shən) *n.:* discouragement.

A galley manned by slaves.

The Bettmann Archive.

CLASSROOM MANAGEMENT

Block Scheduling Devote a portion of each department or team meeting to discussion of the block. Communicate with colleagues about the problems, issues, successes, failures, concerns, and advantages of the longer class period. Making this a regular feature of meetings will help reduce teacher anxiety as well as provide additional ideas and support.

CROSSING THE CURRICULUM

Social Sciences Not all whites remained insensitive to the human misery on slave ships. John Newton (1725–1807), composer of "Amazing Grace," was a servant in Africa, the manager of a slave "factory," and later the captain of a slaver. He wrote that any dishonesty he found in the Africans was a direct result of their contact with Europeans. He later regretted his participation in the slave trade, and wrote the pamphlet *Thoughts upon the African Slave Trade* to promote the abolition of slavery. Students should research his shipboard logs, his journals, and the pamphlet and should report their findings to the class in a multimedia presentation that combines music, illustrations or artwork, and a narrative of Newton's thoughts on slavery.

A. Critical Reading: Making Inferences

? What is the worst aspect of Equiano's suffering? [His ignorance of what to expect fuels his imagination. He imagines "horrors of every kind" that are far worse than what will actually happen to him.]

B. Critical Reading: Speculating

? Why is Equiano beaten for not eating while on the ship? [Possible answer: On the ship Equiano is cargo—part of the crew's profit. If he does not eat and grows weak and dies as a result, they will lose some of their expected gain. The crew forces him to eat so that he can be sold at the end of the voyage.]

C. Reader's Response: Connecting with the Text

? How is Equiano's characterization of how the whites treat each other similar to Bradford's description of the *Mayflower* sailors' behavior? [Sample responses: Equiano and Bradford both describe a hostile attitude untempered by kindness or mercy; or they have little regard for human life.]

D. Exploring the Historical Period

Most ship captains ruled their crews with absolute authority, and sailors had no recourse against their orders and judgments. This sailor is probably punished for some infraction.

E. Expansion

Students may be surprised at some of the things Equiano imagines about his captors—that they are evil spirits, that they have no country beyond the boat, that they make the ship move by magic spells, and so forth. This is partly explained by the fact that he is only about eleven when he arrives at the coast and is taken aboard the slave ship.

produced, having never tasted such any liquor before. Soon after this the blacks who brought me on board went off, and left me abandoned to despair.

A I now saw myself deprived of all chance of returning to my native country or even the least glimpse of hope of gaining the shore, which I now considered as friendly; and I even wished for my former slavery in preference to my present situation, which was filled with horrors of every kind, still heightened by my ignorance of what I was to undergo. I was not long suffered to indulge my grief; I was soon put down under the decks, and there I received such a salutation in my nostrils as I had never experienced in my life: **B** So that with the loathsomeness of the stench and crying together, I became so sick and low that I was not able to eat, nor had I the least desire to taste anything. I now wished for the last friend, death, to relieve me; but soon, to my grief, two of the white men offered me eatables, and on my refusing to eat, one of them held me fast by the hands and laid me across, I think, the windlass,[3] and tied my feet while the other flogged me severely. I had never experienced anything of this kind before, and although, not being used to the water, I naturally feared that element the first time I saw it, yet nevertheless could I have got over the nettings I would have jumped over the side, but I could not; and besides, the crew used to watch us very closely who were not chained down to the decks, lest we should leap into the water: And I have seen some of these poor African prisoners most severely cut for attempting to do so, and hourly whipped for not eating. This indeed was often the case with myself. In a little time after, amongst the poor chained men I found some of my own nation, which in a small degree gave ease to my mind. I inquired of these what was to be done with us; they gave me to understand we were to be carried to these white people's country to work for them. I then was a little revived, and thought if it were no worse than working, my situation was not so desperate: But **C** still I feared I should be put to death, the white people looked and acted, as I thought, in so savage a manner; for I had never seen among my people such instances of brutal cruelty, and this not only shown toward us blacks but also to some of the whites themselves. **D** One white man in particular I saw, when we were permitted to be on deck, flogged so unmercifully with a large rope near the foremast that he died in consequence of it; and they tossed him over the side as they would have done a brute. This made me fear these people the more, and I expected nothing less than to be treated in the same manner. I could not help expressing my fears and apprehensions to some of **E** my countrymen: I asked them if these people had no country but lived in this hollow place (the ship): They told me they did not, but came from a distant one. "Then," said I, "how comes it in all our country we never heard of them?" They told me because they lived so very far off. I then asked where were their women? Had they any like themselves? I was told they had: "And why," said I, "do we not see them?" They answered, because they were left behind. I asked how the vessel could go? They told me they could not tell, but that there were cloths put upon the masts by the help of the ropes I saw, and then the vessel went on; and the white men had some spell or magic they put in the water when they liked in order to stop the vessel. I was exceedingly amazed at this account and really thought they were spirits. I

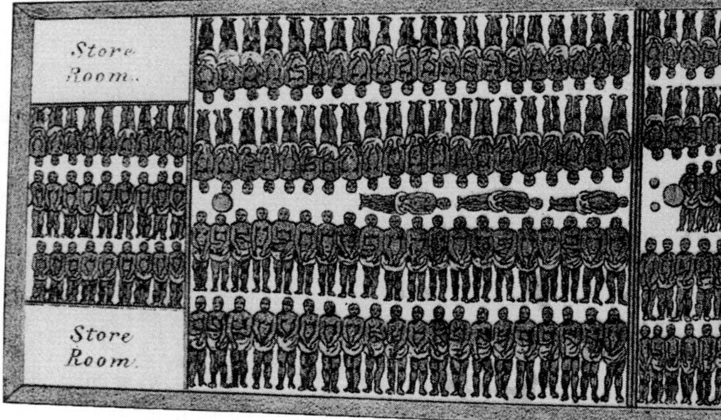

Drawing showing people squeezed together on the lower deck of a slave ship.

3. **windlass** (wind'ləs): device used to raise and lower heavy objects, like a ship's anchor.

OPTIONS FOR TEACHING

CROSSING THE CURRICULUM

History Equiano indirectly compares slavery in Africa to his enslavement by white traders. Have students discuss the differences Equiano describes. Students should then research the history of slavery in Africa and in the United States, the various reasons for its existence at different points in time, and how the practice changed and grew over the years. Students should create a display of their findings, including drawings or pictures with explanatory captions and a time line.

Geography Equiano travels to several places in Africa. Students should select and study a West African people, kingdom, province, or empire in existence at the time, researching its cultural practices and beliefs, its history, and its political and economic history. Students should present a travelogue of their findings about the African group they have chosen, accompanied by illustrations of artifacts and the landscape.

therefore wished much to be from amongst them for I expected they would sacrifice me: But my wishes were vain, for we were so quartered that it was impossible for any of us to make our escape.

While we stayed on the coast I was mostly on deck, and one day, to my great astonishment, I saw one of these vessels coming in with the sails up. As soon as the whites saw it they gave a great shout, at which we were amazed; and the more so as the vessel appeared larger by approaching nearer. At last she came to an anchor in my sight, and when the anchor was let go I and my countrymen who saw it were lost in astonishment to observe the vessel stop, and were now convinced it was done by magic. Soon after this the other ship got her boats out, and they came on board of us, and the people of both ships seemed very glad to see each other. Several of the strangers also shook hands with us black people, and made motions with their hands, signifying I suppose we were to go to their country; but we did not understand them. At last, when the ship we were in had got in all her cargo, they made ready with many fearful noises, and we were all put under deck so that we could not see how they managed the vessel.

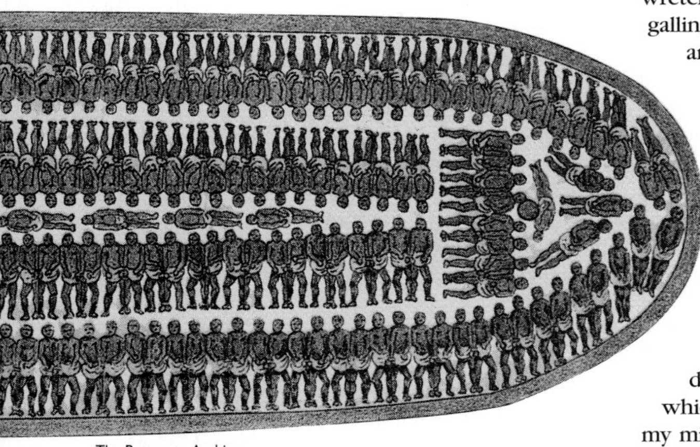

The Bettmann Archive.

But this disappointment was the least of my sorrow. The stench of the hold[4] while we were on the coast was so intolerably loathsome that it was dangerous to remain there for any time, and some of us had been permitted to stay on the deck for the fresh air; but now that the whole ship's cargo were confined together it became absolutely pestilential. The closeness of the place and the heat of the climate, added to the number in the ship, which was so crowded that each had scarcely room to turn himself, almost suffocated us. This produced copious perspirations, so that the air soon became unfit for respiration from a variety of loathsome smells, and brought on a sickness among the slaves, of which many died, thus falling victims to the improvident avarice, as I may call it, of their purchasers. This wretched situation was again aggravated by the galling of the chains, now become insupportable, and the filth of the necessary tubs,[5] into which the children often fell and were almost suffocated. The shrieks of the women and the groans of the dying rendered the whole a scene of horror almost inconceivable. Happily perhaps for myself I was soon reduced so low here that it was thought necessary to keep me almost always on deck, and from my extreme youth I was not put in fetters. In this situation I expected every hour to share the fate of my companions, some of whom were almost daily brought upon deck at the point of death, which I began to hope would soon put an end to my miseries. Often did I think many of the inhabitants of the deep much more happy than myself. I envied them the freedom they enjoyed, and as often wished I could change my condition for theirs. Every circumstance I met with served only to render my state more painful, and heighten my apprehensions and my opinion of the cruelty of the whites. One day they had taken a number of fishes, and when they had killed and satisfied themselves with as many as they thought fit, to our astonishment who were on the deck, rather than give any of them to us to eat as we expected, they tossed the remaining fish into the sea again, although we

4. **hold:** enclosed area below a ship's deck, where cargo is usually stored.

5. **necessary tubs:** toilets.

Words to Own

copious (kō'pē·əs) *adj.:* great amounts of.
improvident (im·präv'ə·dənt) *adj.:* careless; not providing for the future.

F. Critical Reading: Metacognition

Ask students what questions they have at this point. [Possible answers: How will they survive? How many will die? How does Equiano survive?] As they continue to read, have them note answers to their questions or new questions they may have. Students should explain the reasoning behind their questions and answers.

G. Critical Reading: Making Inferences

? What does Equiano mean when he refers to the slavers' "improvident avarice"? [Possible answer: If the slavers were less greedy, they would put fewer slaves on a ship, improving sanitation and health conditions. This way more people would arrive in the Americas alive, and the slavers would earn more money.]

H. Critical Reading: Speculating

Here the sailors refuse to feed the slaves despite their entreaties, while earlier Equiano is beaten for not eating. How do you make sense of the two incidents? [Possible answer: Earlier, the slaves may have been forced to eat as a matter of policy to keep them healthy and thus more valuable. The later incident may just be an individual example of cruelty.]

PROBLEM SOLVING/CRITICAL THINKING

Dealing with Prejudice Equiano is very free in talking about his prejudices, and his autobiography is an attempt to persuade others to reflect on and change their own biases. Ask students to create a group presentation inspired by the Equiano passage, dealing with prejudice. This project requires that students target a specific kind of prejudice, identify it fully, consider factors that may have created it, brainstorm ways to address it, and make recommendations about putting their best ideas into action. The presentation could be a multimedia presentation or an oral report. In their presentation, groups should identify the prejudice and its ramifications, and recommend ways to address the prejudice. *Remind students to choose a situation they would not mind sharing with others.* You may wish to choose topics for students to discuss, Try to group students heterogeneously, but also be sure to take into account the sensitivity and maturity level of individual students. ☞

A. Reader's Response: First Thoughts

? How do you explain the actions of the slaves and the sailors? [Sample responses: The slaves are acting out of despair, having given up hope. The sailors, seeing some of their valuable cargo destroyed, flog the rescued slaves as a lesson to other would-be jumpers.]

B. Expansion

Despite the horrors of his kidnapping and voyage, Equiano still retains his curiosity and interest in the world around him.

C. Expansion

Customarily, two triangles of trade during this time are recognized: one connecting New England, England, and the West Indies; the second connecting New England, the West Indies, and Africa. The second triangle—which carried sugar and molasses to New England, rum to Africa, and slaves to the West Indies—is traditionally called the triangle trade. However, *From Slavery to Freedom* by John Hope Franklin and Alfred A. Moss, Jr., shows a more complicated pattern of trade routes not easily simplified into triangles.

begged and prayed for some as well as we could, but in vain; and some of my countrymen, being pressed by hunger, took an opportunity when they thought no one saw them of trying to get a little privately; but they were discovered, and the attempt procured them some very severe floggings.

One day, when we had a smooth sea and moderate wind, two of my wearied countrymen who were chained together (I was near them at the time), preferring death to such a life of misery, somehow made through the nettings and jumped into the sea: Immediately another quite dejected fellow, who on account of his illness was suffered to be out of irons, also followed their example; and I believe many more would very soon have done the same if they had not been prevented by the ship's crew, who were instantly alarmed. Those of us that were the most active were in a moment put down under the deck, and there was such a noise and confusion amongst the people of the ship as I never heard before, to stop her and get the boat out to go after the slaves. However two of the wretches were drowned, but they got the other and afterward flogged him unmercifully for thus attempting to prefer death to slavery. In this manner we continued to undergo more hardships than I can now relate, hardships which are inseparable from this accursed trade. Many a time we were near suffocation from the want of fresh air, which we were often without for whole days together. This and the stench of the necessary tubs carried off many.

During our passage I first saw flying fishes, which surprised me very much: They used frequently to fly across the ship and many of them fell on the deck. I also now first saw the use of the quadrant; I had often with astonishment seen the mariners make observations with it, and I could not think what it meant. They at last took notice of my surprise, and one of them, willing to increase it as well as to gratify my curiosity, made me one day look through it. The clouds appeared to me to be land, which disappeared as they passed along. This heightened my wonder, and I was now more persuaded than ever that I was in another world and that everything about me was magic. At last we came in sight of the island of Barbados, at which the whites on board gave a great shout and made many signs of joy to us. We did not know what to think of this, but as the vessel drew nearer we plainly saw the harbor and other ships of different kinds and sizes, and we soon anchored amongst them off Bridgetown. Many merchants and planters now came on board, though it was in the evening. They put us in separate parcels and examined us attentively. They also made us jump, and pointed to the land, signifying we were to go there. We thought by this we should be eaten by these ugly men, as they appeared to us; and when soon after we were all put down under the deck again, there was much dread and trembling among us, and nothing but bitter cries to be heard all the night from these apprehensions, insomuch that at last the white people got some old slaves from the land to pacify us. They told us we were not to be eaten but to work, and were soon to go on land where we should see many of our countrypeople. This report eased us much; and sure enough soon after we were landed there came to us Africans of all languages.

We were conducted immediately to the merchant's yard, where we were all pent up together like so many sheep in a fold without regard to sex or age. As every object was new to me everything I saw filled me with surprise. What struck me first was that the houses were built with stories, and in every other respect different from those in Africa: But I was still more astonished on seeing people on horseback. I did not know what this could mean, and indeed I thought these people were full of nothing but magical arts. While I was in this astonishment one of my fellow prisoners spoke to a countryman of his about the horses, who said they were the same kind they had in their country. I understood them though they were from a distant part of Africa, and I thought it odd I had not seen any horses there; but afterward when I came to converse with different Africans I found they had many horses amongst them, and much larger than those I then saw.

We were not many days in the merchant's custody before we were sold after their usual manner, which is this: On a signal given, (as the beat of a drum) the buyers rush at once into the yard where the slaves are confined, and make choice of that parcel they like best. The noise and clamor with which this is attended and the eagerness visible in the countenances of the buyers serve not a little to

WORDS TO OWN

moderate (mäd′ər·it) *adj.:* gentle.

OPTIONS FOR TEACHING

PROFESSIONAL NOTES

Cultural Diversity This selection provides a rich opportunity for all students to reach a better understanding of human perspectives during the era of slavery. Some students may find themselves identifying strongly with the anger and suffering of those enslaved. Other students may grapple with feelings of blame and guilt regarding the actions and attitudes of slaveholders. Allow all students time to write down thoughts in their private journals and the opportunity to express their feelings in class.

Thematic Connections: "Visions and Voyages" Ask students to consider how Equiano's point of view is affected by his capture and voyage. As students suggest answers, focus discussion on the fact that Equiano, in the natural course of things, may have grown up to be a slaveholder like his father, but through his own suffering came to be repelled by slavery.

increase the apprehensions of the terrified Africans, who may well be supposed to consider them as the ministers of that destruction to which they think themselves devoted. In this manner, without scruple, are relations and friends separated, most of them never to see each other again. I remember in the vessel in which I was brought over, in the men's apartment there were several brothers who, in the sale, were sold in different lots; and it was very moving on this occasion to see and hear their cries at parting. O, ye nominal Christians! might not an African ask you, Learned you this from your God who says unto you, Do unto all men as you would men should do unto you? Is it not enough that we are torn from our country and friends to toil for your luxury and lust of gain? Must every tender feeling be likewise sacrificed to your avarice? Are the dearest friends and relations, now rendered more dear by their separation from their kindred, still to be parted from each other and thus prevented from cheering the gloom of slavery with the small comfort of being together and mingling their sufferings and sorrows? Why are parents to lose their children, brothers their sisters, or husbands their wives? Surely this is a new refinement in cruelty which, while it has no advantage to atone for it, thus aggravates distress and adds fresh horrors even to the wretchedness of slavery.

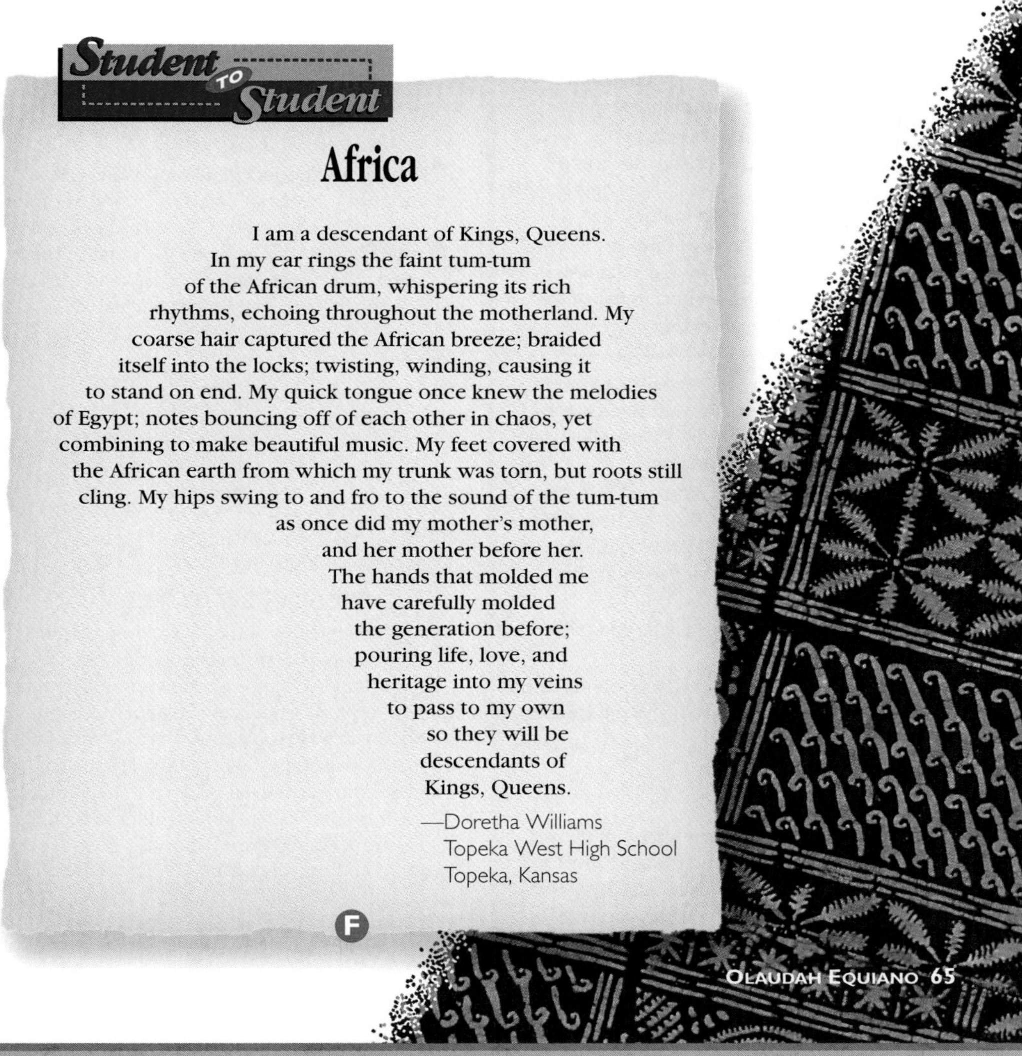

Student to Student

Africa

I am a descendant of Kings, Queens.
In my ear rings the faint tum-tum
of the African drum, whispering its rich
rhythms, echoing throughout the motherland. My
coarse hair captured the African breeze; braided
itself into the locks; twisting, winding, causing it
to stand on end. My quick tongue once knew the melodies
of Egypt; notes bouncing off of each other in chaos, yet
combining to make beautiful music. My feet covered with
the African earth from which my trunk was torn, but roots still
cling. My hips swing to and fro to the sound of the tum-tum
as once did my mother's mother,
and her mother before her.
The hands that molded me
have carefully molded
the generation before;
pouring life, love, and
heritage into my veins
to pass to my own
so they will be
descendants of
Kings, Queens.

—Doretha Williams
Topeka West High School
Topeka, Kansas

D. Reader's Response: Connecting with the Text

? What similarities do you find between this criticism of the slavers made by Equiano and the criticisms of the English colonists made by Byrd? [Sample responses: They each accuse the group they analyze of treating those of other races unequally; or they make social appeals based on religion.]

E. Literary Element: Autobiography

Equiano writes not just for his own recollection or to record his experiences for posterity but to raise people's consciousness about the horrors to which slaves are routinely subjected. How does this section reveal his purpose? [Possible answer: The address to "ye nominal Christians" followed by a series of questions asked of them shows his persuasive intent to change the opinions of Christian whites reading his narrative.]

F. Reader's Response: Shaping Interpretations

? What vision does the speaker have of her heritage? How does she celebrate that heritage? [Sample responses: She envisions her ancestors as proud, regal, and noble; or she builds upon her heritage and envisions a bright future for her own children. She celebrates it in her references to royal lineage, to music and song, and to her foremothers, as well as in her molding the poem into the shape of the African continent.]

ASSESSMENT TOOLS

Peer Assessment Have students work in pairs to examine each other's processes for creating the writing assignment on p. T59. They should ask the following questions.

- Did you use a real-life model of an eleven-year-old's language? If not, how did you choose a language style?
- Did you read your work aloud to check the diction and style?
- Did you use a peer or other editor to help you make revisions?

Check Test: Fill-in-the-Blank

1. Equiano and _____ are kidnapped when he is eleven. [his sister]
2. Equiano is frightened as much by the crew's _____ as by their language and behavior. [appearance]
3. The first things Equiano sees when he reaches the coast are the sea and _____. [a slave ship]
4. For refusing to eat, Equiano is _____. [flogged]
5. Two slaves _____ rather than continue life on the ship. [jump overboard]

Making Meanings

First Thoughts

1. Possible responses: the man and woman seizing the children, and Equiano and his sister being separated. Students may respond that they learned Africans themselves had slaves and that the quarters on the slave ships were inhumanely crowded.

Reviewing the Text

a. Owners tend to treat him well, and on one occasion so well that he forgets he is a slave.
b. They are parted several days after being kidnapped and after he meets her on the road north to Timnah.
c. Possible responses: He has never seen a white person. They speak to him in an unusual language.
d. By not eating or by attempting to jump over the side.
e. Because he is sick and frail.

Shaping Interpretations

2. The pampered son of a slaveholder, he was being raised to be a warrior. Possible responses: Coming from a family of slaveholders makes him seem less a victim; or no child should have to suffer like that.
3. Possible responses: They probably want to see if he is fit for sea travel and for sale. Perhaps they would have kept him off the ship, as not worth their while to transport.
4. He probably gives it as an example of the sailors' brutality. They treat each other as brutally as they treat the Africans, but he has never seen such cruelty in his homeland.
5. Possible response: While the crew's main goal is to sell its "cargo" for the best market price, it does not consistently make decisions to further this end and sometimes acts as though its main goal is cruelty. The crew denies the Africans food and packs them in too tightly. Conditions are unsanitary.

Extending the Text

6. **(Synthesis)** Possible response: Human beings are capable of great evil and easily corrupted, especially when profit can be gained and there is no concerted effort to stop them or punish them for their activity. Current events: the behavior of terrorists, members of gangs or cults.

Making Meanings

First Thoughts

1. What **images** from Equiano's account are most memorable or horrifying to you? Fill out the third column in the KWL chart you made in your Reader's Log, and share at least five things you have learned about the slave trade by reading this excerpt.

Reviewing the Text

a. How is Equiano treated by his captors and owners while he is still enslaved in West Africa?
b. Under what circumstances is Equiano twice parted from his sister?
c. Why does Equiano think that some of his captors on board the ship are spirits?
d. How do some Africans on board the ship try to escape life in bondage?
e. Why does the ship's crew keep Equiano on deck most of the time?

Shaping Interpretations

2. What was Equiano's life like before he was taken captive? How does his description of his life influence your reading of his enslavement?
3. Equiano is "handled and tossed up" by some of the crew as soon as he is taken on board the ship. Why? What do you think would have happened to him if the crew had found him unsatisfactory?
4. Why does Equiano include the flogging of a crew member in his account?
5. How would you describe the basic contradiction between the crew's main goal and the treatment of its captives?

Extending the Text

6. How do you account for the depth of human cruelty described in this **autobiography?** What current events reveal a similar capacity for brutishness and cruelty in human nature?

Choices: Building Your Portfolio

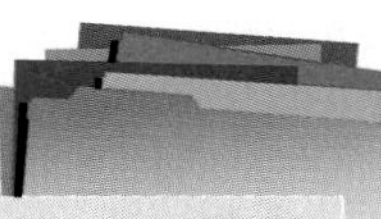

Writer's Notebook

1. Collecting Ideas for an Autobiographical Incident

Work in Progress

Write down your memories of an incident in your life when you felt that one of your rights was being restricted or otherwise jeopardized. What kind of action, if any, were you able to take to protect that right? What did you learn about yourself as a result of the incident? Keep your notes for possible use in the Writer's Workshop on page 130.

Critical Writing

2. Immigration Experiences

Equiano's experience of immigrating to the Americas was quite different from that of the Pilgrims. In a brief essay, compare and contrast Equiano's experience with that of the Pilgrims. You might want to use a Venn diagram like the following to generate ideas:

Equiano	Both	Pilgrims
came against his will	difficult journey	came freely

Creative Writing / Art

3. Teach Your Children Well

Create a picture book for children that will teach them about some aspect of African American heritage—perhaps something that you've just learned from Equiano's account. Research your topic, and write up your findings in clear, easy-to-read language for children. You might even want to write in poetic form, as the student writer on page 65 did. Illustrate your children's book.

Beyond the Selection

Choices: Building Your Portfolio

1. **Writer's Notebook** *Remind students to choose a situation they would not mind sharing with others.* Also, remind students to save their work. They may use it as prewriting for the Writer's Workshop on p. 130.

Portfolio Assessment

Choices: Assessment Criteria For help in evaluating these Choices assignments, see the criteria in the *Portfolio Management System,* p. 70.

THE EXAMINED LIFE

Theme: **Looking Inward**

In the sixteenth, seventeenth, and eighteenth centuries, people in North America expressed a desire for spiritual and moral balance. They looked inward as well as outward to others for guidance and direction. Their spiritual quests took many routes: from private poems, journals, and prayers to fiery sermons admonishing sinners to be "reborn."

Thematic Focus

Each selection in Collection 2 is representative of the spiritual and intellectual beliefs of the early colonists.

- **Here Follow Some Verses Upon the Burning of Our House, July 10, 1666** The speaker of this poem accepts her loss with Puritan stoicism.
- **Huswifery** Using an elaborate conceit, the speaker prays to be transformed into a being worthy of glorifying God.
- *from* **Sinners in the Hands of an Angry God** This evangelical sermon is Jonathan Edwards's famous attempt to persuade his congregation to become "born again."
- *from* **The Autobiography** This excerpt describes the author's journey from Boston to Philadelphia and his efforts to improve himself.

Literary Focus

Literary Element	Selection / Feature
Inversion	**Here Follow Some Verses Upon the Burning of Our House, July 10, 1666**
The Conceit	**Huswifery**
Figures of Speech	**Sinners in the Hands of an Angry God**

Writing Focus

The following flow chart shows how the writing assignment for each selection relates to and builds toward the culminating writing assignment presented in the Writer's Workshop at the end of the unit.

Selection	Work-in-Progress Assignment
Here Follow Some Verses Upon the Burning of Our House, July 10, 1666	Freewrite about testing by challenges p. 71
Huswifery	List incidents that helped define your identity p. 74
Sinners in the Hands of an Angry God	Freewrite about fear and anxiety as motivators p. 83
The Autobiography	Freewrite about your most valuable character trait p. 98
Writer's Workshop	Write an autobiographical incident pp. 130–133

Collection 2 THE EXAMINED LIFE

Collection Planner

SELECTION/ FEATURE	PUPIL'S EDITION			
	Literary Elements / Active Reading	Writing	Speaking and Listening	Language and Vocabulary
Here Follow Some Verses Upon the Burning of Our House, July 10, 1666 Anne Bradstreet (pp. 68–71)	• Reader's Log p. 69 • Inversion p. 69	• Critical Writing: Write essay on Bradstreet's attitude p. 71 • Speaking and Listening: Write noninverted version of Bradstreet's poem p. 71	• Speaking and Listening: Present noninverted version of Bradstreet's poem p. 71	
Huswifery Edward Taylor (pp. 72–74)	• Reader's Log p. 73 • The Conceit p. 74	• Critical Writing: Compare extended metaphors p. 74 • Elements of Literature: Write conceit p. 74		
Literature of the Americas: World, in Hounding Me . . . Sor Juana Inés de la Cruz (pp. 75–76)	• Reader's Log p. 76		• Finding Common Ground: Hold "salon" discussion p. 76	
from **Sinners in the Hands of an Angry God** Jonathan Edwards (pp. 77–83) Primary Sources: Two Journals (p. 82)	• Reader's Log p. 78 • Figures of Speech p. 78	• Critical Writing: Write comparison essay p. 83 • Creative Writing: Write script p. 83	• Panel Discussion: Compare sermons of yesterday and today p. 83	
from **The Autobiography** Benjamin Franklin (pp. 84–98) Spotlight On: Sayings of Poor Richard (p. 95) **Connections:** from **All I Really Need to Know I Learned in Kindergarten** Robert Fulghum (p. 96)	• Reader's Log p. 85	• Critical Writing: Write comparison/contrast essay p. 98 • Critical Writing: Write brief report p. 98 • Crossing the Curriculum: Science: Write report, comic strip, documentary script, or children's story p. 98 • Critical Writing: Write book proposal p. 98 • Creative Writing: Create almanac p. 98 • Research/Art: Create aphorisms booklet p. 98	• Crossing the Curriculum: Science: Present oral report p. 98	

Collection Resources

Teaching Resources A	Audiovisual Resources Binder	Test Booklet
Cross-Curricular Activity pp. 42	Fine Art Transparency 2.1	Collection 2 Test pp. 21–24

 Computer disk or CD-ROM

 Audiocassette

 Overhead Transparency

PROGRAM RESOURCES

Electronic Media	Teaching Resources with Organizer: Teaching Resources A	Teaching Resources with Organizer: Other Resources	Audiovisual Resources Binder
• Language Workshop: Prepositions, Conjunctions, and Interjections • Test Generator	• Teaching Notes p. 25 • Reading Organizer p. 28 • Language Link pp. 29–30	• Test Booklet: Selection Test pp. 15–16 • Language and Writing Skills Worksheets pp. 19–20 • Portfolio Management System pp. 39, 71	• Selected Reading Audiocassette 1, Side A • Elements of Literature Transparency 2.2
• Test Generator	• Teaching Notes pp. 25–26 • Reading Organizer p. 31	• Test Booklet: Selection Test pp. 15–16 • Portfolio Management System pp. 48–49, 72	
	• Teaching Notes p.26		• Selected Reading Audiocassette 1, Side A
• Language Workshop: Subjects of sentences, Simple predicates, and Complements • Test Generator	• Teaching Notes p. 26 • Reading Organizer p. 32 • Language Link pp. 33–34 • Words to Own p. 35	• Test Booklet: Selection Test pp. 17–18 • Language and Writing Skills Worksheets pp. 86, 88–89 • Portfolio Management System pp. 54–55, 73	• Elements of Literature Transparency 2.3
• Language Workshop: Compound subjects and Compound verbs • Test Generator	• Teaching Notes p. 27 • Reading Organizer p. 36 • Language Link pp. 37–38, 40–41 • Words to Own p. 39	• Test Booklet: Selection Test pp. 19–20 • Language and Writing Skills Worksheets p. 87 • Portfolio Management System pp. 53, 74–75	

Proofreading Warm-ups

You may use the following exercises to help students practice their proofreading skills. Copy a set of incorrect sentences onto the chalkboard, and have students find and correct the spelling, punctuation, usage, and mechanical errors in each sentence. Ask students to share and discuss their responses.

	Sentences with Errors	Sentences Corrected	Skills Covered
1	**a.** Bradstreet like many other writer's were influenced by Shakespeare **b.** when a phrase are taken out of normal word order it is called a inversion	**a.** Bradstreet, like many other writers, was influenced by Shakespeare. **b.** When a phrase is taken out of normal word order, it is called an inversion.	Comma usage, Apostrophe usage, Subject-verb agreement, Capitalization, Standard usage, End marks
2	**a.** alot of old poems like Bradstreet's used inversion to accomodate the demand's of meter or ryhme **b.** Shakespeare is another writter who used inversions, Romeo and Juliet have many examples	**a.** A lot of old poems like Bradstreet's used inversion to accomodate the demands of meter or rhyme. **b.** Shakespeare is another writer who used inversions; Romeo and Juliet has many examples.	Capitalization, Standard usage, Apostrophe usage, Spelling, Semicolon usage, Italicize (underline) play titles, Subject-verb agreement, End marks
3	**a.** Taylors poem Huswifery uses a conceit **b.** on a first reading I had a hard time understanding the extended metaphor of makeing clothe and experiencing Gods grace	**a.** Taylor's poem "Huswifery" uses a conceit. **b.** On a first reading, I had a hard time understanding the extended metaphor comparing making cloth to experiencing God's grace.	Apostrophe usage, Quotation marks for poem titles, Capitalization, Comma usage, Spelling, End marks
4	**a.** Sor Juana Inés de la Cruz was a brillaint Catholic Nun who wrote poems plays songs and essays **b.** she rote at about the same time as the puritan poets' Bradstreet and Taylor	**a.** Sor Juana Inés de la Cruz was a brilliant Catholic nun who wrote poems, plays, songs, and essays. **b.** She wrote at about the same time as the Puritan poets Bradstreet and Taylor.	Spelling, Capitalization, Comma usage, Apostrophe usage, End marks
5	**a.** Jonathan Edwards helped to bring about the religious revival known as the great awakening **b.** Edwards lived in Stockbridge Massachusetts for eight years he then moved to NJ	**a.** Jonathan Edwards helped to bring about the religious revival known as the Great Awakening. **b.** Edwards lived in Stockbridge, Massachusetts, for eight years; he then moved to New Jersey.	Capitalization, Comma usage, Semicolon usage, Write out abbreviation, End marks
6	**a.** although Edwards was a fire and brimstone preacher he shared characteristics with secular thinkers to **b.** Edwards believed in reason and learning the value of independant intellect and the power of the human will	**a.** Although Edwards was a fire-and-brimstone preacher, he shared characteristics with secular thinkers, too. **b.** Edwards believed in reason and learning, the value of independent intellect, and the power of the human will.	Capitalization, Hyphen usage, Comma usage, Spelling, End marks
7	**a.** Benjamin Frannklin is a intresting historical figure to study declared Pat **b.** he was devoted to self improvement she continued	**a.** "Benjamin Franklin is an interesting historical figure to study," declared Pat. **b.** "He was devoted to self-improvement," she continued.	Quotation marks, Spelling, Comma usage, Capitalization, Hyphen usage, End marks
8	**a.** at fourty one Franklin had made enough $ to retire from business **b.** after retiring he helped draft the declaration of independance in 1776	**a.** At forty-one, Franklin had made enough money to retire from business. **b.** After retiring, he helped draft the Declaration of Independence in 1776.	Capitalization, Spelling, Hyphen usage, Comma usage, Write out abbreviation, End marks
9	**a.** Franklins "The Autobiography" contains a account of his plan for self improvement **b.** Franklins biggest publishing sucess was Poor Richard's Almanack	**a.** Franklin's The Autobiography contains an account of his plan for self-improvement. **b.** Franklin's biggest publishing success was Poor Richard's Almanack.	Apostrophe usage, Italicize (underline) book titles, Standard usage, Hyphen usage, Spelling, End marks
10	**a.** Benjamin Banneker, was an african american, who published Almanacs **b.** he urged Thomas Jefferson to abolish slavery	**a.** Benjamin Banneker was an African American who published almanacs. **b.** He urged Thomas Jefferson to abolish slavery.	Comma usage, Capitalization, End marks

Collection 2 THE EXAMINED LIFE

Bradstreet
Taylor
Cruz
Edwards
Franklin

All my life I had been looking for something, and everywhere I turned someone tried to tell me what it was. I accepted their answers too, though they were often in contradiction and even self-contradictory. I was naïve. I was looking for myself and asking everyone except myself questions which I, and only I, could answer. It took me a long time and much painful boomeranging of my expectations to achieve a realization everyone else appears to have been born with: That I am nobody but myself.

—Ralph Ellison, *from Invisible Man*

Responding to the Quotation
Ellison writes that he has searched for meaning and identity in a variety of places, but ultimately has had to look inside himself for answers. Ask students whether people can find themselves only by looking inward. [Possible responses: Ellison is correct; people can find out who they are only by looking inside themselves. Or people can also find out who they are by listening to others and learning from the experiences of others.] What might Ellison's statement reveal about the Collection to follow? [Possible responses: The speakers in the Collection may be raising questions about life and examining their lives to find the answers. Or the speakers in the selections may be experiencing crises and trying to discover where to turn.]

PORTFOLIO ASSESSMENT

Parent/Guardian Involvement For forms that will help a parent or guardian review and respond to a student's portfolio, see *Portfolio Management System*, pp. 62–63.

PROGRAM MANAGER

- **Integrated Assessment** For a summative assessment of the literature and language skills taught in this collection, see Collection 2 Test, *Test Booklet*, pp. 21–24.
- **Instructional Support** See Fine Art Transparency 2.1. Review teacher's notes for transparencies in the *Audiovisual Resources Binder* for suggestions on how to tie the transparencies to specific reading selections.

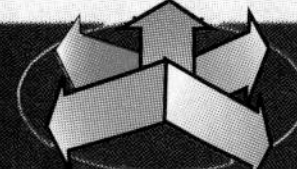

- **Extending Collection Theme** See Cross-Curricular Activity: The Examined Life, *Teaching Resources A*, p. 42, for activities in other disciplines and for evaluation criteria.

QUICK PLANNING GUIDE

Into the Poem

Author Biography p. 68

Before You Read p. 69

- **Reading Focus:** Students consider ways that people deal with things that go wrong.
- **A Dialogue with the Text: Set a Purpose** Respond in Reader's Log to poet's questions
- **Elements of Literature: Inversion**

Through the Poem

"Here Follow Some Verses upon the Burning of Our House, July 10, 1666" pp. 69–70

Making Meanings p. 71

Beyond the Poem

Choices: Building Your Portfolio p. 71

- **Writer's Notebook:** Collect ideas for an autobiographical incident
- **Critical Writing:** Write an essay analyzing the poem
- **Speaking and Listening:** Write "noninverted" version of the poem

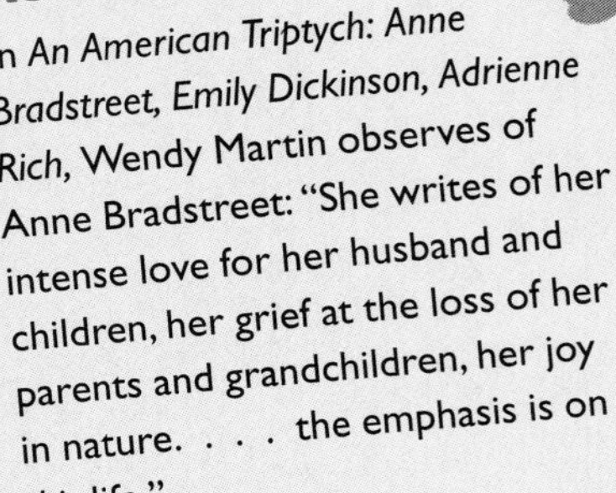

ABOUT THE AUTHOR

In *An American Triptych: Anne Bradstreet, Emily Dickinson, Adrienne Rich,* Wendy Martin observes of Anne Bradstreet: "She writes of her intense love for her husband and children, her grief at the loss of her parents and grandchildren, her joy in nature. . . . the emphasis is on *this* life."

Anne Bradstreet

(1612–1672)

Anne Bradstreet (1948) by Harry Grylls. Stained glass (10' × 18').

Reproduced by kind permission of the vicar and church wardens of St. Botolph's Church, Boston, England.

Who could have guessed that the writer who would begin the history of American poetry would be an immigrant, teenage bride? This fact seems less far-fetched when we know something about the life of the young woman who came from England to America when the Colonies were no more than a few villages precariously perched between the ocean and the wilderness.

Shakespeare was still alive when Anne Bradstreet was born, and like many budding poets, she found in Shakespeare, and in other great English poets, sources of inspiration and technique that would one day run like threads of gold through the fabric of her own work. However, what most determined the course of Anne Bradstreet's life was not a poetic influence but a religious one.

Anne Bradstreet was born into a family of Puritans. She accepted their reformist views as naturally as most children accept the religious teachings of a parent. When she was about sixteen, she married a well-educated and zealous young Puritan by the name of Simon Bradstreet. Two years later, in 1630, Simon, Anne, and Anne's father journeyed across the Atlantic to the part of New England around Salem that would become known as the Massachusetts Bay Colony. There her father and then her husband rose to prominence, each serving as governor of the colony, while Anne kept house first in Cambridge, then Ipswich, and finally in Andover. She raised four boys and four girls and, without seeking an audience or publication, found time to write poems.

Bradstreet's poems might never have come to light had it not been for John Woodbridge, her brother-in-law and a minister in Andover. In 1648, he went to England and, in 1650, without consulting the author herself, published Bradstreet's poems in London under the title *The Tenth Muse Lately Sprung Up in America . . . By a Gentlewoman in those Parts.*

In one stroke, an obscure wife and mother from the meadows of New England was placed among the nine Muses of art and learning sacred to the ancient Greeks. In itself, this was embarrassing enough. But in the middle of the seventeenth century, the real arrogance was that a woman would aspire to a place among the august company of established male poets. *The Tenth Muse* fared better with critics and the public than Anne expected (later, even the learned Puritan minister Cotton Mather praised her work), and she felt encouraged to write for the rest of her life.

Today, Anne Bradstreet is remembered not for her elaborate earlier poems that focus on public events, but for a few simple, personal lyrics about such things as the birth of children, the death of grandchildren, her love for her husband, her son's departure for England, and her own illnesses and adversities. In a letter to her children just before she died, she wrote: "Among all my experiences of God's gracious dealings with me I have constantly observed this, that He hath never suffered me long to sit loose from Him, but by one affliction or other hath made me look home, and search what was amiss."

PORTFOLIO ASSESSMENT

Portfolio Assessment For help with self- and teacher assessment of reading skills, see the ***Portfolio Management System,*** p. 39.

Before You Read

Here Follow Some Verses upon the Burning of Our House, July 10, 1666

Reading Focus

Tests of Strength

How we deal with losses in life is perhaps the greatest test of our inner strength. Some losses are so enormous that they shake us to our core and challenge our very sense of self. Response to such a loss is the topic of this poem: It portrays an internal debate, a kind of dialogue between self and soul.

A Dialogue with the Text

READER'S LOG

As you read, note the points at which the speaker questions her own thoughts and emotions. What answers does she give to these questions? What conclusions does she reach? Also, write your own responses: How do you think a person could cope with the destruction of a home?

Elements of Literature

Inversion

This poem is filled with **inversions**. In an inversion, the words of a sentence or phrase are wrenched out of normal English word order: "In silent night when rest I took," instead of "In silent night when I took rest." In English poetry written in earlier centuries, poets used inversion frequently to accommodate the demands of **meter** or **rhyme**.

Here Follow Some Verses upon the Burning of Our House, July 10, 1666

Anne Bradstreet

In silent night when rest I took
For sorrow near I did not look
I wakened was with thund'ring noise
And piteous shrieks of dreadful voice.
That fearful sound of "Fire!" and "Fire!" **A**
Let no man know is my desire.
I, starting up, the light did spy,
And to my God my heart did cry
To strengthen me in my distress
And not to leave me succorless.°
Then, coming out, beheld a space
The flame consume my dwelling place.
And when I could no longer look,
I blest His name that gave and took,°
That laid my goods now in the dust.
Yea, so it was, and so 'twas just.
It was His own, it was not mine,
Far be it that I should repine;
He might of all justly bereft

10. succorless (suk′ər·lis): without aid or assistance; helpless.
14. that gave and took: allusion to Job 1:21, "The Lord gave, and the Lord hath taken away; blessed be the name of the Lord."

Into the Poem

Using Before You Read p. 69

A Dialogue with the Text

Demonstrate on the chalkboard the following chart students could use to examine these questions.

Speaker Questions Self
[Why is my house burning?]

Speaker's Answers
[Calls God for help]

Speaker's Conclusions
[Blesses God's name; it is his will]

Reader's Responses
[She copes through her remarkable courage and faith in God.]

Through the Poem

A. Literary Element: Alliteration

? What alliteration is used in this line? What effect does the line have? [The *f* sound in *fearful, fire,* and *fire.* Possible answer: The line powerfully conveys the fearful feeling of waking up to find the house on fire.]

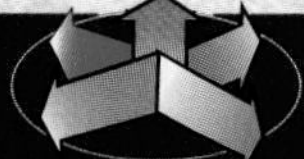

Program Manager

- **Planning Instruction** See Teaching Notes, *Teaching Resources A,* p. 25, for objectives, a summary, literary elements, and additional information.
- **Instructional Support** See Graphic Organizer for Active Reading, *Teaching Resources A,* p. 28, for an Into the Poem activity.
- **Audiotaped Readings** To help auditory learners, use the Selected Reading, Audiocassette 1, Side A, in the *Audiovisual Resources Binder.*

- **Application** For reinforcement of the elements of literature, see Transparency 2.2 in the *Audiovisual Resources Binder.*
- **Assessment** See Selection Test, *Test Booklet,* pp. 15–16.
- **Language Link** For practice in prepositions, conjunctions, and interjections, see Language Link, *Teaching Resources A,* pp. 29–30, and *Language and Writing Skills Worksheets,* pp. 19–20.

A. Reader's Response: Connecting with the Text

? How would the loss of a home now compare with its loss in 1666? [Sample responses: The loss was greater then because things such as furniture and books are more easily replaced now; or the loss of personal history would probably be equally devastating.]

B. Language Note: Repetition

? What repetition do you note and what is its effect? [The words *no* and *nor.* Students may suggest that the repetition stresses the piling up of losses.]

C. Literary Element: Allusion

The phrase *all's vanity* in l. 36 comes from a Biblical source. What is the allusion? ["Vanity of vanities! All is vanity." Ecclesiastes 1:2; these words also appear in 12:8.]

D. Literary Element: Metaphor

Point out the powerful metaphor of "dunghill mists," combining the earthy image of warm dung on cold ground covered by mist, and the image of misted, impaired judgment that would cause Bradstreet to fail to see things in correct Puritan perspective.

E. Literary Element: Inversion

? What inversion do you note in l. 53? [The object of the infinitive *to love* precedes the imperative *let me.*] What is the effect of this inversion? [By putting *world* before *no longer let me love,* Bradstreet emphasizes that she is not to love the world, but to love God and heaven.]

But yet sufficient for us left.
When by the ruins oft I past
My sorrowing eyes aside did cast,
And here and there the places spy
Where oft I sat and long did lie:
Here stood that trunk, and there that chest,
There lay that store I counted best.
A My pleasant things in ashes lie,
And them behold no more shall I.
B Under thy roof no guest shall sit,
Nor at thy table eat a bit.
No pleasant tale shall e'er be told,
Nor things recounted done of old.
No candle e'er shall shine in thee,
Nor bridegroom's voice e'er heard shall be.
In silence ever shall thou lie,
C Adieu, Adieu,° all's vanity.
Then straight I 'gin my heart to chide,
And did thy wealth on earth abide?
Didst fix thy hope on mold'ring dust?
The arm of flesh didst make thy trust?
D Raise up thy thoughts above the sky
That dunghill mists away may fly.
Thou hast an house on high erect,
Framed by that mighty Architect,
With glory richly furnished,
Stands permanent though this be fled.
It's purchased and paid for too
By Him who hath enough to do.
A price so vast as is unknown
Yet by His gift is made thine own;
There's wealth enough, I need no more,
Farewell, my pelf,° farewell my store.
E The world no longer let me love,
My hope and treasure lies above.

36. Adieu (à·dyö′): French for "goodbye."

52. pelf: wealth or worldly goods. Sometimes used as a term of contempt.

Museum of Fine Arts, Boston, Gift of Samuel Bradstreet (19.602).

Embroidered chair seat cover (1725–1750) by the Bradstreet family. American, New England, Boston area. Colored wool embroidered on cotton and linen twill (44 cm × 54 cm).

OPTIONS FOR TEACHING

STRATEGIES FOR INCLUSION

Learners Having Difficulty Go through the poem line by line, paraphrasing each line—especially those with inversions—into language that all students can understand. Students will also need some help in translating archaic contractions (*e'er, 'gin*) and words (*repine, bereft*). Make sure students know that *Adieu*, l.36, is French for "goodbye."

English Language Development Read aloud ll. 25–36. Bring in a box to symbolize the trunk holding Anne Bradstreet's treasures. Ask each student to draw a picture of one item Bradstreet lost and to place the drawing inside the box. Then, ask a student to take out an illustration, and have the class discuss why this item symbolizes a "vanity" in Bradstreet's life and not the true value of her life. Have individuals take out other illustrations, and have the class discuss them until all illustrations have been considered.

Auditory Have students scan the poem for meaning, and then read it aloud so that they can hear the iambic tetrameter pattern Bradstreet followed so carefully. Challenge students to find the two places in which the *–ed* word ending must be pronounced as a separate syllable for the lines to scan. [ll. 45 and 47.] Have students try to read the poem without turning it into a simple singsong. Having them copy her words in running prose rather than in poetic lines may help them with the rhythm.

MAKING MEANINGS

First Thoughts

1. Sometimes "bad things" happen to "good people." Do you think any good can come from adversity? Explain.

Shaping Interpretations

2. What are some of the specific losses that Bradstreet dwells on in the first half of the poem?
3. Bradstreet speaks of another "house" in an **extended metaphor** at the end of the poem. What is this house, who is its architect, and how is it more perfect than the house she has lost? (For more information about extended metaphor, see page 188.)
4. *Pelf*—a word designating riches or worldly goods—is usually used only when the riches or goods are considered to be slightly tainted, ill-gotten, or stolen. Why do you suppose Bradstreet uses such a bitter word in line 52 to describe her own cherished treasures?

Extending the Text

5. A popular slogan reads "Whoever dies with the most toys wins." Clearly, Bradstreet doesn't agree. What are your thoughts on that slogan?

Challenging the Text

6. Some readers have felt that, by so lovingly enumerating her losses, Bradstreet is "crying out to heaven" in a way that unconsciously reveals more attachment to her earthly possessions than she would admit to. On the other hand, what Bradstreet does *not* reveal in this poem is significant: Hundreds of books, as well as her papers and all her unpublished poems, were also lost in the fire. Referring to your Reader's Log notes, explain whether or not, by the end of the poem, you are convinced that the speaker means what she says.

Cradle of Peregrine White, first English child born in New England.

Courtesy of the Pilgrim Society, Plymouth, Massachusetts.

CHOICES: Building Your Portfolio

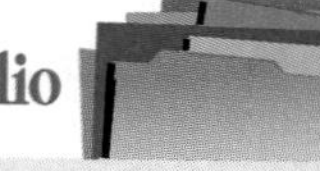

Writer's Notebook

1. Collecting Ideas for an Autobiographical Incident

WORK IN PROGRESS

Write a few sentences about a time in your own life that seemed to you like a "baptism of fire"—a time when you were tested by challenges, such as peer pressure. Keep your notes for possible use in the Writer's Workshop on page 130.

Critical Writing

2. Trials and Tribulations

In the Book of Job in the Bible, Job endures great misery, yet he is still able to say, "The Lord gave, and the Lord hath taken away; blessed be the name of the Lord" (Job 1:21). Bradstreet expresses a similar attitude in her poem; twice she checks herself from mourning over the loss of her beloved possessions. The first instance is in lines 14–20; the second begins with line 37. In a brief essay, discuss Bradstreet's attitude toward earthly suffering and the providence of God.

Speaking and Listening

3. A Noninverted Version

Look for **inversions** in Bradstreet's poem, and rewrite the lines so that the words appear in normal order. (The second line, for example, would normally be written, "I did not look near for sorrow.") Prepare a "noninverted" version of Bradstreet's poem, and read it to the class. What happens to the beat, or **rhythm,** of the poem?

Making Meanings

First Thoughts

1. Possible response: One good thing that could come from adversity is that a person might become stronger from having experienced misfortune.

Shaping Interpretations

2. The loss of her home, places where she used to sit and lie, a trunk, a chest, and the loss of future pleasant hours in the house with guests and new family members.
3. The house is heaven, whose architect is God (l. 44). It is more perfect than the poet's earthly home because it is richly furnished with glory. It has also been paid for with a price "so vast as is unknown" (l. 49), probably a reference to the suffering and death of Christ.
4. She has come to regard her earthly treasures as insignificant—even bad—compared with the treasure of immortal life.

Extending the Text

5. **(Evaluation)** Some students may find the saying ironic while others may think it a motto to live by.

Challenging the Text

6. **(Evaluation)** Answers will vary. Within the context of the poem there is little reason to doubt Bradstreet's sincerity or religious beliefs. Her human impulse to lament misfortune seems, on the textual evidence, to have been conquered by her faith.

Choices: Building Your Portfolio

1. **Writer's Notebook** *Remind students to choose a situation they would not mind sharing with others.* Remind students to save their work. They may use it as prewriting for Writer's Workshop on p. 130. Suggest that students begin by brainstorming a general class list of possible crises.

STRATEGIES FOR INCLUSION

Visual Have students organize their ideas for activity #2 by using a chart like the following:

	Attitude toward suffering	Attitude toward God
ll. 14–20		
ll. 37–54		

PORTFOLIO ASSESSMENT

Choices: Assessment Criteria For help in evaluating these Choices assignments, see the criteria in the ***Portfolio Management System,*** p. 71.

QUICK PLANNING GUIDE

Into the Poem

Author Biography p. 72
Before You Read p. 73
- **Reading Focus:** Students learn Puritan belief that self-identity was shaped by God.
- **A Dialogue with the Text: Set a Purpose** Compare in Reader's Log two different things
- **Background: Scaffolding** The term *huswifery*

Through the Poem

"Huswifery" p. 73
Making Meanings p. 74
Elements of Literature p. 74

Beyond the Poem

Choices: Building Your Portfolio p. 74
- **Writer's Notebook:** Collect ideas for an autobiographical incident
- **Critical Writing:** Write an essay that compares and evaluates metaphors

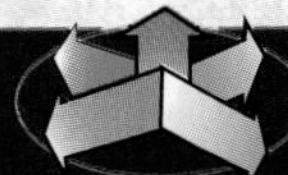

ABOUT THE AUTHOR

While it is not known how Taylor met his first wife, Elizabeth Fitch, two of his letters to her survive, both of which contain poetry. One is a complicated, rhymed acrostic that pledges her his love; the other is a longer poem with some humor but also some instruction in the duties of marriage. It seems that Fitch, too, wrote poetry, and sent it to Taylor. Together they had eight children, five of whom died before the death of Taylor's wife in 1689.

Edward Taylor

(1642?–1729)

To Puritans, the universe of God's Creation was sublime and magnificent. But to Edward Taylor, the universe could also be—*a bowling alley,* with God the bowler and the sun his bowling ball. This is the kind of imaginative surprise that made Taylor unique among American Puritan writers.

The publication in 1939 of *The Poetical Works of Edward Taylor* was the third important instance in American literature when buried poetic treasure was discovered. The first discovery occurred when Anne Bradstreet's brother-in-law carried her "private" poems to England and had them printed without her consent. The second occurred in 1890, when the heirs of Emily Dickinson (page 372) ignored her wishes and published the poems she had saved carefully in little packets that were to be destroyed after her death.

Michael Cornish.

Headstone on Reverend Silas Bigelow's grave in Paxton, Massachusetts (1769). Carved by William Young.

Of these discoveries, the case of Edward Taylor is perhaps the most remarkable. Taylor wrote an enormous amount of poetry, but he allowed only a portion of one poem to be published during his lifetime. For many years, his brilliant poems moldered in the archives of Yale Library, to which Taylor's grandson had donated them. Then, once again, a body of work that an author had expected to remain unpublished came to light—in this case, with such compelling force as to cause the history of early poetry in America to be rewritten.

Edward Taylor was born in Leicestershire, England, near the town of Coventry. Like Anne Bradstreet, he was raised in a family that held dissenting views about many of the practices of the Church of England. Taylor lost a teaching position in England because he refused to take an oath—required by the royal Act of Uniformity—that conflicted with his religious beliefs. Feeling more and more uncomfortable in the religious climate of his country, where the Act of Uniformity was contributing to the persecution of Puritans, he determined to seek the freedom that other Nonconformists had found in Colonial America. In 1668, Taylor sailed for Boston.

Friends had equipped Taylor with letters of introduction to some of the established Colonial leaders, among them the great Puritan minister Increase Mather (1639–1723). Impressed with the young man's credentials and charmed by his personality, Mather and other influential people eased Taylor's way into Harvard College.

After training for the ministry, Taylor accepted a call in 1671 to become pastor of a church in Westfield, Massachusetts. Taylor stayed in Westfield for the rest of his life. During his fifty-eight years in this frontier town, he faithfully tended the spiritual needs of his flock. Taylor himself increased the flock by fourteen members—he had eight children by his first wife and six by his second. By the time he died in 1729, Taylor had outlived a number of his children.

After Taylor's death, only one book of poetry was found in his personal library—Anne Bradstreet's *The Tenth Muse Lately Sprung Up in America.* Like Bradstreet, Taylor could have had little notion that his poems, which he had scrupulously put away, would outlive him with a radiance bright enough to penetrate the darkness of two centuries of obscurity.

PROGRAM MANAGER

- **Planning Instruction** See **Teaching Notes, *Teaching Resources A,*** pp. 25–26, for objectives, a summary, and literary elements for this selection.
- **Instructional Support** Before beginning the instructional lesson, see **Graphic Organizer for Active Reading, *Teaching Resources A,*** p. 31, for a Through the Poem activity.
- **Assessment** See **Selection Test, *Test Booklet,*** pp. 15–16.

Before You Read
Huswifery

Reading Focus
By the Grace of God

Today many people believe that individual identity is shaped by numerous factors, such as family, friends, education, geography, and personal beliefs. The Puritans believed that each aspect of their identity was shaped by God, and that all their emotions, thoughts, desires, and behavior should be directed toward God's service and glorification. The Puritans endlessly examined their lives for evidence of God's grace.

A Dialogue with the Text

READER'S LOG

This poem contains a complex, extended comparison between two very different things—making cloth and experiencing God's grace. As you read the poem, keep a double-entry journal. In one column, list the implements and materials used in spinning cloth. In the second column next to each item, list the spiritual experience that Taylor compares to the act of spinning.

Background

Huswifery (huz'wif'ər·ē) is an archaic spelling of *housewifery,* which means "the care and management of a household." It suggests the whole range of domestic responsibilities, as well as the qualities of thrift and orderliness. A *housewife* (huz'if) also came to be the name for a small sewing kit.

Huswifery

Edward Taylor

Make me, O Lord, thy Spinning Wheel complete.
  Thy Holy Word my Distaff° make for me. **A**
Make mine Affections thy Swift Flyers neat
  And make my Soul thy holy Spool to be.
  My Conversation make to be thy Reel
  And reel the yarn thereon spun of thy Wheel.

Make me thy Loom then, knit therein this Twine:
  And make thy Holy Spirit, Lord, wind quills:°
Then weave the Web thyself. The yarn is fine.
  Thine Ordinances° make my Fulling Mills.°
  Then dye the same in Heavenly Colors Choice,
  All pinked° with Varnished° Flowers of Paradise.

Then clothe therewith mine Understanding, Will,
  Affections, Judgment, Conscience, Memory,
My Words, and Actions, that their shine may fill
  My ways with glory and thee glorify.
  Then mine apparel shall display before ye
  That I am Clothed in Holy robes for glory.

2. distaff (dis'taf'): On spinning wheels, the distaff is a stick around which fibers are wound before they are spun into thread. Flyers help govern the rate of spinning. The finished thread is wound upon a reel, or spool.

8. quills: a loom's spools or bobbins, on which thread is wound before weaving.

10. ordinances: religious rules and laws. **fulling mills:** Fulling, or milling, is the term used for the processing of raw wool cloth through a combination of washing, heating, and compressing. The cloth is processed in fulling mills to preshrink and treat the individual fibers, thereby enhancing its appearance in finished fabrics.

12. pinked: decorated. **varnished:** embellished.

Into the Poem

Using **Before You Read** p. 73

Reading Focus

Ask students to examine their own beliefs about what shapes the identity of people today. To help students clarify their thinking, have them complete a chart like the following.

Identity Element	Shaping Factors
Emotions	
Thoughts	
Desires	
Behavior	

A. Literary Element: Inversion
Like Bradstreet, Taylor uses inversion to work out his meter (iambic pentameter) and rhyme scheme (*ababcc*). Ask students to find examples of inverted word order and to express these lines in normal order. [Other inversions occur in ll. 5 and 10.]

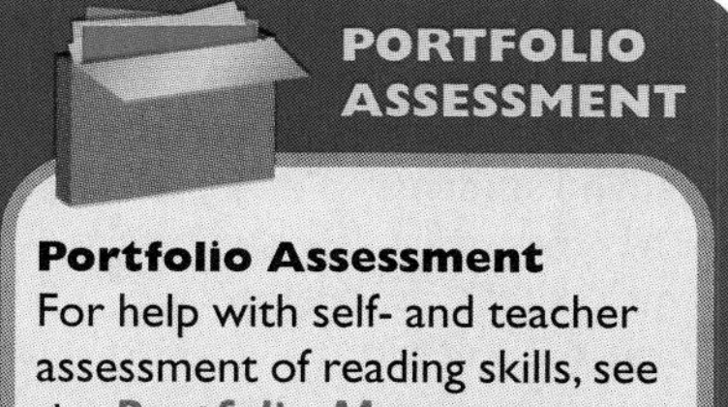

PORTFOLIO ASSESSMENT

Portfolio Assessment
For help with self- and teacher assessment of reading skills, see the ***Portfolio Management System,*** pp. 48–49.

Options for Teaching

Strategies for Inclusion

English Language Development Discuss the relationships among the words *spinning wheel, yarn, loom, weave, cloth,* and *garment,* and explain how these words illustrate a movement toward Edward Taylor's goal of spiritual growth. Have students write down their own personal goals. Ask them to create a written metaphor or to draw a picture that illustrates their movement toward their goals. *Remind students to choose goals they would not mind sharing with others.*

Integrating the Language Arts

Strategic Reading After students have first read the poem silently, read it aloud to them. Have them write two questions about the poem, which may be "If . . .," "How would . . .," "Why . . .," or "What does . . . mean?" questions. Ask each student to pick one question and to respond to it in writing as best as he or she can. Ask students to meet in groups of four and to share their questions. The group should answer each question cooperatively.

Making Meanings

First Thoughts

1. Possible responses: Emotionally, because of the religious content, or intellectually, because of the extended metaphor. Or I feel distant from the poem as I am not familiar with spinning wheels.

Shaping Interpretations

2. A spinning wheel; an instrument of God.
3. Students should list specific parts of the spinning wheel and how the speaker applies them to his life. For example, students may say that in l. 2 the speaker asks that the Bible be like the distaff, the central core on which he, like the fibers, is bound.
4. The speaker is intimate with God. If the speaker centers his life on God, he will be complete and fulfilled.
5. The speaker comes to stand before God at judgment; the garment woven by his holy life has prepared him for heaven.
6. The speaker aspires to making the most of what God gives him.

Choices: Building Your Portfolio

1. **Writer's Notebook** *Remind students to choose a situation they would not mind sharing with others.* Also remind students to save their work. They may use it as prewriting for the Writer's Workshop on p. 130.
2. **Critical Writing** Suggest that, as prewriting, students complete a two-column chart like the following with notes about similarities in the two selections. Encourage students to form their own opinions about the effectiveness of the metaphors and to meet in small groups to discuss their conclusions.

Taylor	Jackson
[Uses physical object: spinning wheel]	[Uses physical object: blanket]

Making Meanings

First Thoughts

1. Did you respond emotionally or intellectually to Taylor's extended comparison? Did you feel involved with the poem or distant from it? Why?

Shaping Interpretations

2. The poet states his main **metaphor** in the first line. What does he ask the Lord to make him?
3. Using your Reader's Log entries to help you review the poem, describe the specific ways that Taylor extends this central **metaphor.**
4. Describe the relationship between this speaker and God. What does the speaker say will make him a complete and fulfilled person?
5. What transformation does the poet describe in the last two lines?
6. *Huswifery* can mean "thrift," or making the most of what one has. Who is practicing the art of huswifery in this poem?

Elements of Literature

The Conceit

In poetry, the term **conceit** refers to a startling **extended metaphor** or other **figure of speech** that makes a surprising, even shocking, connection between two different things. The connection may be witty, strange, exaggerated, or cleverly elaborate. When Emily Dickinson (page 372) compared the setting sun to a housewife sweeping up the sky with multicolored brooms and carelessly dropping shreds behind her, she created more than a metaphor: She created a conceit.

Conceits, then, are startling figures of speech that are extended as far as the poet wants to take them. They are exercises of imagination, devices for making us see sometimes profound connections between vastly different things in the world.

Make up an original conceit. Begin by thinking of ordinary comparisons. Then try to match one half of a comparison with something no one is likely to have thought of before. Begin your conceit with this format: ______ is like ______.

Choices: Building Your Portfolio

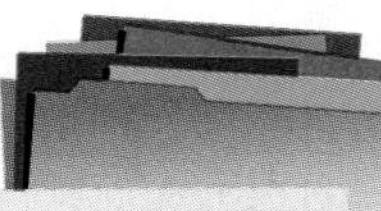

Writer's Notebook

1. Collecting Ideas for an Autobiographical Incident

Write down two or three incidents in your own life that helped define your identity. Keep your notes for possible use in the Writer's Workshop on page 130.

WORK IN PROGRESS

Critical Writing

2. Spinning Metaphors

In the excerpt below from the Reverend Jesse Jackson's speech to the Democratic Convention in 1988, Jackson develops an interesting **extended metaphor.** Although Jackson and Taylor are comparing different things, look for similarities in their metaphors. In a brief essay, examine these questions: Does each speaker conclude the metaphor with a kind of transformation? How is each metaphor visual—what does each help you see? In general, how effective do you find each extended metaphor to be?

> America's not a blanket, woven from one thread, one color, one cloth. When I was a child growing up in Greenville, South Carolina, and Grandmother could not afford a blanket, she didn't complain, and we did not freeze. Instead she took pieces of old cloth—patches, wool, silk, gabardine, crockersack on the patches—barely good enough to wipe off your shoes with.
>
> But they didn't stay that way very long. With sturdy hands and a strong cord, she sewed them together into a quilt, a thing of beauty and power and culture.
>
> Now . . . we must build such a quilt.
>
> —Jesse Jackson

Choices: Assessment Criteria For help in evaluating these Choices assignments, see the criteria in the ***Portfolio Management System,*** p. 72.

STRATEGIES FOR INCLUSION

TECHNOLOGY

Spatial To help students understand the visual nature of figurative language referred to in activity #2, ask them to create a multimedia illustration of the metaphors of Taylor's poem and Jackson's speech using drawing software, imported clip art, video and audio clips, and presentation software. For example, a visual representation of Jackson's speech might include a map of the United States covered with patchwork or a quilt made of various cultural images or languages combined with a reading of the excerpt.

Sor Juana Inés de la Cruz

(1648–1695)

Juana Ramírez de Asbaje was born in a village located between two volcanoes southeast of Mexico City. A solitary child with unusual intellectual curiosity, Juana learned to read and write by the age of six or seven. At age six, she heard of the university in Mexico City and pleaded with her mother to send her there dressed like a man. Her request denied, she threw herself into reading and study in her grandfather's library—a world of books and learning that, in the seventeenth century, was still a man's world. As a child she continued to learn Latin after taking only twenty lessons. She was a harsh taskmaster, cutting off her hair if she failed to learn her Latin grammar according to the schedule she had set for herself. "It didn't seem right to me," she wrote, "that a head so naked of knowledge should be dressed up with hair." She also stopped eating cheese, one of her favorite foods, because she had heard that it dulled the mind.

At sixteen, Juana was presented at the court of the Spanish viceroy in Mexico City, where she charmed everyone with her wit, beauty, and brilliance. She served as a lady-in-waiting for four years, then abruptly decided to enter a convent at the age of twenty, taking the name Sor (Sister) Juana Inés de la Cruz. For the next twenty-five years, she lived in a small apartment where she studied and wrote, amassing a huge library of about four thousand volumes and collecting musical and scientific instruments. She also proved to be a shrewd businesswoman, accruing a fortune, making investments, and serving as the convent's bookkeeper and archivist.

Courtesy of Schalkwijk/Art Resource, New York.

Sor Juana Inés de la Cruz (1750) by Miguel Cabrera (1695–1768). Oil on canvas.

Sor Juana's superiors in the Catholic Church continually criticized her for her intellectual pursuits and justifications of secular learning. Most controversial was her long autobiographical letter to a Catholic bishop, in which she defended the rights of women to be educated and intellectually independent—even to undertake public careers. For reasons that are unclear, Sor Juana suddenly abandoned her studies and sold her library, giving the money to the poor and devoting herself exclusively to her religious duties. She wrote nothing during the last two years of her life. In 1695, while nursing her sisters who had been stricken with the plague, Sor Juana became ill and died.

RESPONDING TO THE ART: VISUAL LITERACY

Given what you have read about Sor Juana Inés de la Cruz, do you think that this painting depicts her accurately? Why or why not? [Possible responses: Yes, because it features her doing what she was known for (reading and writing); or yes, it places her in appropriate surroundings (her library).] If you knew nothing about her, what could you infer about her life style and personality from the painting? [Possible responses: She is a nun; she is quiet, intense, serious and studious; she spends her time reading and studying.]

PROGRAM MANAGER

- **Planning Instruction** See **Teaching Notes, *Teaching Resources A,*** p. 26, for a summary and objectives for this selection.
- **Audiotaped Readings** To help less proficient readers or auditory learners through the lesson, use the **Selected Reading, Audiocassette 1, Side A,** in the ***Audiovisual Resources Binder.***

A Dialogue with the Text

Have students make a chart like the following before they read to clarify the elements they will analyze. Before they read Sor Juana's poem, ask them to fill in theme, style, and imagery beside Bradstreet and Taylor to review their ideas.

	Theme	Style	Imagery
Bradstreet			
Taylor			
Sor Juana			

A. Language Note: Parts of Speech

? How does the translation play with parts of speech in ll. 3–4? [The word *stock* is used first as a verb and then as a noun.]

B. Reader's Response: Shaping Interpretations

? What do you think the speaker is saying here? [Sample responses: Time takes away beauty, or beauty cannot be trusted.] Do you agree with the speaker? [Sample responses: Time does take away beauty—we age and die. Or time does not take away beauty because beauty can be found within.]

C. Literary Element: Rhyme Scheme

If possible, have someone read the poem in Spanish. Have students study the Spanish poem and its translation for rhyme scheme. [The Spanish version is *abba abba cdc dcd;* the translation is *abba cddc efg egf.*] How do you account for the difference? [The translator is faithful to the spirit of the rhyme scheme even though it is altered. Students may see how difficult it is to translate a poem.]

Finding Common Ground

Have each student write down topics to discuss before the groups meet. When students meet as a group, ask them to share all the topics each group member wrote down. Invite them to begin their discussion with the topic that most students in the group mentioned they feel is most important.

Before You Read

World, in Hounding Me . . .

Background

At about the same time the Puritan poets Anne Bradstreet and Edward Taylor were in New England writing poems in praise of God, the brilliant Catholic nun Sor Juana Inés de la Cruz was writing poems, plays, songs, and essays in a convent in New Spain (in present-day Mexico). The contemporary Mexican poet Octavio Paz (1914–   ) considers Sor Juana's poems to be among "the most elegant and refined in Spanish. Few poets in our language equal her, and those who surpass her can be counted on the fingers of one hand." In her own time, Sor Juana was called "the tenth muse from Mexico," and her visitors spent evenings in an atmosphere similar to one of Europe's most cultivated salons, discussing ideas and reciting poems over biscuits, fruit, and cups of chocolate.

A Dialogue with the Text

As you read the following poem by Sor Juana, write down your thoughts, feelings, and questions.

- What similarities or differences do you notice between this poem and those you have read by Bradstreet and Taylor with regard to **theme, style,** or **imagery**?
- What is your overall reaction to the poem?

World, in Hounding Me . . .

Sor Juana Inés de la Cruz

translated from the Spanish by **Alan S. Trueblood**

World, in hounding me, what do you gain?
How can it harm you if I choose, astutely,
rather to stock my mind with things of beauty,
than waste its stock on every beauty's claim?
Costliness and wealth bring me no pleasure;
the only happiness I care to find
derives from setting treasure in my mind,
and not from mind that's set on winning treasure.
I prize no comeliness.° All fair things pay
to time, the victor, their appointed fee
and treasure cheats even the practiced eye.
Mine is the better and the truer way:
to leave the vanities of life aside,
not throw my life away on vanity.

9. **comeliness:** beauty.

En perseguirme, mundo . . .

Sor Juana Inés de la Cruz

En perseguirme, mundo, ¿qué interesas?
¿En qué te ofendo, cuando sólo intento
poner bellezas en mi entendimiento
y no mi entendimiento en las bellezas?
Yo no estimo tesoros ni riquezas;
y así, siempre me causa más contento
poner riquezas en mi pensamiento
que no mi pensamiento en las riquezas.
Y no estimo hermosura que, vencida,
es despojo civil de las edades,
ni riqueza me agrada fementida,
teniendo por mejor, en mis verdades,
consumir vanidades de la vida
que consumir la vida en vanidades.

Finding Common Ground

Using the notes you wrote in your Reader's Log, meet in small groups to hold your own "salon" in which you discuss your questions about and responses to this poem.

- Each person in the group should share his or her notes.
- As a group, agree on the topics you want to talk about that are suggested by this poem: how you feel about Sor Juana's message, how the poem is similar to or different from the poetry of the Puritan writers you have read, or whatever else you want to discuss.

Connecting with "The Examined Life"

The poem favors the life of the mind and spirit over a life of material beauty. It reveals the results of careful examination and deliberate choice. The speaker has presented both sides of the question and her own choice. Place students in small groups and have them discuss Sor Juana's poem. Ask them what the speaker examines and values, and in what ways these examinations and values compare to those of the other selections in the Collection.

Assessment Tools

Observation Assessment As students conduct their group discussions, appoint one person from each group to provide a written observation. This could include notations about time on task, participation of each member, and the group's focus on chosen topics. In addition to narrative comments, the observer could rate the group's performance on a six-point scale, with six being strong in all areas and one being weak in all areas.

Jonathan Edwards

(1703–1758)

Despite his fire-and-brimstone imagery, Jonathan Edwards was not merely a stern, zealous preacher. He was a brilliant, thoughtful, and complicated man. Science, reason, and observation of the physical world confirmed Edwards's deeply spiritual vision of a universe filled with the presence of God.

Edwards's abilities were recognized early. Groomed to succeed his grandfather as pastor of the Congregational Church in Northampton, Massachusetts, Edwards entered Yale when he was only thirteen. When his grandfather died in 1729, Edwards mounted the pulpit and quickly established himself as a strong-willed and charismatic pastor.

Edwards's formidable presence and vivid sermons helped to bring about the religious revival known as the Great Awakening. This revival began in Northampton in the 1730s and during the next fifteen years spread throughout the eastern seaboard. The Great Awakening was marked by waves of conversions that were so intensely emotional as to amount at times to mass hysteria.

The Great Awakening began at a time when enthusiasm for the old Puritan religion was declining. To offset the losses in their congregations, churches had been accepting growing numbers of "unregenerate" Christians—people who accepted church doctrine and lived upright lives but who had not confessed to being born again in God's grace, and so were not considered to be saved.

Edwards became known for his extremism as a pastor. In his sermons he didn't hesitate to accuse prominent church members, by name, of relapsing into sin. Edwards's strictness eventually proved to be too much for his congregation, and in 1750 he was dismissed from his prestigious position as pastor of Northampton. After rejecting a number of pastorships offered to him, Edwards relocated to the raw and remote Mohican community of Stockbridge,

Yale University Art Gallery, Bequest of Eugene Phelps Edwards (1938.74).

Reverend Jonathan Edwards (1750–1755) by Joseph Badger (1708–1765). Oil on canvas (28½″ × 22″).

Massachusetts. After eight years of missionary work in virtual exile, shared with his wife Sarah Pierrepont, Edwards was named president of the College of New Jersey (later called Princeton University). Three months after assuming this position, he died of a smallpox inoculation—a modern medical procedure that, ironically, had been promoted by the fierce Puritan minister Cotton Mather.

Intellectually, Edwards straddled two ages: the modern, secular world exemplified by such men as Benjamin Franklin (page 84), and the religious world of his zealous Puritan ancestors. He believed (like Franklin) in reason and learning, the value of independent intellect, and the power of the human will. On the other hand, he believed (like Mather) in the lowliness of human beings in relation to God's majesty and the ultimate futility of merely human efforts to achieve salvation. Edwards, as "the last Puritan," stood between Puritan America and modern America. Tragically, he fit into neither world.

ABOUT THE AUTHOR

Not only was Edwards a prolific writer, but he also fathered eleven children. His letters paint him as an affectionate and thoughtful father and husband. He measured the height of Mt. Tom with his son Timmy. In Boston he helped his daughters earn pin money by selling the fans they made. He referred to his marriage to Sarah as an "uncommon union." They were a striking couple, tall and regal in demeanor: he reserved, she at ease. She took care of the household and charmed their guests; he would often spend thirteen hours a day in his study. He frequently wrote on anything at hand—invitations, invoices, slips of paper. She must have delighted to see him return home from a summer ride, paper slips of his jottings pinned all over his coat.

QUICK PLANNING GUIDE

Into the Selection

Author Biography p. 77
Before You Read p. 78

- **Reading Focus: Scaffolding** Students consider how fear motivates people.
- **A Dialogue with the Text: Set a Purpose** List vivid or frightening phrases or details in Reader's Log
- **Background:** A famous sermon
- **Elements of Literature: Figures of Speech**

Through the Selection

"Sinners in the Hands of an Angry God" pp. 79–81
Words to Own pp. 79–81
Primary Sources p. 82
Making Meanings p. 83

Beyond the Selection

Choices: Building Your Portfolio p. 83

- **Writer's Notebook:** Collect ideas for an autobiographical incident
- **Critical Writing:** Compare texts in an essay
- **Speaking and Listening:** Compare today's sermons to Edwards's sermon in a panel discussion
- **Creative Writing:** Create a script

BEFORE YOU READ

FROM SINNERS IN THE HANDS OF AN ANGRY GOD

Reading Focus

The Great Motivator

Ralph Waldo Emerson (page 216) wrote that "Fear is an instructor of great sagacity and the herald of all revolutions." Many people would agree that fear is one of the most powerful motivators of human behavior. Fear of injury makes us buckle our seat belts. Fear of failure makes some of us study or work harder. Edwards and other pastors used harsh warnings in their sermons to make "sinners" understand the precariousness of their situation by actually *feeling* the fear and horror of their sinful state.

A Dialogue with the Text

As you read Edwards's sermon, note in your Reader's Log the phrases or details that you find particularly vivid or frightening. Make special note of the three central **figures of speech** in paragraphs 4–7.

Background

This is Edwards's most famous sermon, which he delivered on a visit to the congregation at Enfield, Connecticut, in 1741. The "natural men" he is trying to awaken and persuade are those people in the congregation who have not been "born again," meaning they have not accepted Christ as their savior. Edwards's methods in the sermon were influenced by the work of the English philosopher John Locke (1632–1704). Locke believed that everything we know comes from experience, and he emphasized that understanding and feeling were two distinct kinds of knowledge. (To Edwards, the difference between these two kinds of knowledge was like the difference between reading the word *fire* and actually being burned.) Although Edwards read this sermon in his usual straightforward, unemotional manner, it had such a powerful effect on the congregation that several times he had to ask his shrieking and swooning audience for quiet.

Elements of Literature

Figures of Speech

Figures of speech describe one thing in terms of another, very different thing. Although Edwards's belief in eternal damnation is literal, he uses figures of speech to compare God's wrath to ordinary, everyday things that his listeners could relate to and understand.

> **Figures of speech** are words or phrases that compare one thing to another, unlike thing.
>
> *For more on Figures of Speech, see the Handbook of Literary Terms.*

The Progress of Sin (detail) (1744) by Benjamin Keach. Woodcut.

Sinclair Hamilton Collection. Graphic Arts Collections. Visual Materials Division. Department of Rare Books and Special Collections. Princeton University Libraries.

78 BEGINNINGS

WORDS TO OWN

The following vocabulary words are defined in the Words to Own at the bottom of the pupil's page.

provoked p. 79	omnipotent p. 80
appease p. 79	abhors p. 81
constitution p. 80	abominable p. 81
contrivance p. 80	ascribed p. 81
inconceivable p. 80	induce p. 81

PORTFOLIO ASSESSMENT

Portfolio Assessment For help with teacher assessment of reading skills, see the *Portfolio Management System,* pp. 54–55.

from Sinners in the Hands of an Angry God

Jonathan Edwards

So that, thus it is that natural men are held in the hand of God, over the pit of hell; they have deserved the fiery pit, and are already sentenced to it; and God is dreadfully provoked, His anger is as great toward them as to those that are actually suffering the executions of the fierceness of His wrath in hell, and they have done nothing in the least to appease or abate that anger, neither is God in the least bound by any promise to hold them up one moment: The devil is waiting for them, hell is gaping for them, the flames gather and flash about them, and would fain lay hold on them, and swallow them up; the fire pent up in their own hearts is struggling to break out: And they have no interest in any Mediator, there are no means within reach that can be any security to them. A

WORDS TO OWN

provoked (prō·vōkt′) *adj.:* enraged; angered.

appease (ə·pēz′) *v.:* to calm; satisfy.

Into the Selection

Using BEFORE YOU READ p. 78

A Dialogue with the Text

Suggest that after students make their lists, they devise a way of evaluating their details. They could rank them according to their effectiveness, or they could evaluate each independently on a scoring system they devise. Or use Transparency 10: Evaluation Chart in the Transparency Package. Then, have students share in pairs why they made the choices they did.

Through the Selection

A. Literary Element: Parallelism

Point out to students that some of the power of Edwards's sermon derives from his use of parallel constructions: "The devil is waiting for them, hell is gaping for them, the flames gather and flash about them."

PROGRAM MANAGER

- **Planning Instruction** See Teaching Notes, *Teaching Resources A,* p. 26, for objectives, a summary, literary elements, and additional information.
- **Instructional Support** See Graphic Organizer for Active Reading, *Teaching Resources A,* p. 32, for a Through the Selection activity.
- **Application and Reinforcement** For reinforcement of the elements of literature introduced in this lesson, see Transparency 2.3 in the *Audiovisual Resources Binder.*
- **Assessment** See Selection Test, *Test Booklet,* pp. 17–18.
- **Language Link** For practice in subjects, predicates, and complements, see Language Link, *Teaching Resources A,* pp. 33–34, and *Language and Writing Skills Worksheets,* pp. 86, 88–91.
- **Reinforcement** Use the Words to Own worksheet in *Teaching Resources A,* p. 35.

A. Critical Reading: Identifying Main Ideas

? What does Edwards hope his sermon will accomplish? [He wants to bring about the conversion of unconverted people in the congregation.]

B. Literary Element: Figure of Speech

? What is the meaning of the metaphor Edwards uses here? [People who depend on their own way of life, rather than on God, to keep them from hell are like people expecting thin air to hold them in suspension.]

C. Literary Element: Figure of Speech

The "wrath of God" extended metaphor begins with a straightforward simile. What is the simile? ["The wrath of God is like great waters that are dammed for the present. . . ."]

D. Literary Element: Figure of Speech

? What are the three extended metaphors in this and the next two paragraphs? [Dammed waters = wrath of God; bow and arrow = God's wrath/justice; spider = human being ("you") over pit of hell.] Remind students that figures of speech can occur *within* figures of speech. The entire paragraph beginning with "The wrath of God," for example, is an extended metaphor, an elaborate comparison between dammed waters and the wrath of God.

In short, they have no refuge, nothing to take hold of; all that preserves them every moment is the mere arbitrary will, and uncovenanted, unobliged forbearance of an incensed God.

A The use of this awful subject may be for awakening unconverted persons in this congregation. This that you have heard is the case of every one of you that are out of Christ. That world of misery, that lake of burning brimstone, is extended abroad under you. There is the dreadful pit of the glowing flames of the wrath of God; there is hell's wide gaping mouth open; and you have nothing to stand upon, nor anything to take hold of; there is nothing between you and hell but the air; it is only the power and mere pleasure of God that holds you up.

You probably are not sensible of this; you find you are kept out of hell, but do not see the hand of God in it; but look at other things, as the good state of your bodily constitution, your care of your own life, and the means you use for your own preservation. **B** But indeed these things are nothing; if God should withdraw His hand, they would avail no more to keep you from falling, than the thin air to hold up a person that is suspended in it.

Your wickedness makes you as it were heavy as lead, and to tend downward with great weight and pressure toward hell; and if God should let you go, you would immediately sink and swiftly descend and plunge into the bottomless gulf, and your healthy constitution, and your own care and prudence, and best contrivance, and all your righteousness, would have no more influence to uphold you and keep you out of hell, than a spider's web would have to stop a fallen rock. . . .

C The wrath of God is like great waters that are dammed for the present; they **D** increase more and more, and rise higher and higher, till an outlet is given; and the longer the stream is stopped, the more rapid and mighty is its course, when once it is let loose. It is true, that judgment against your evil works has not been executed hitherto; the floods of God's vengeance have been withheld; but your guilt in the meantime is constantly increasing, and you are every day treasuring up more wrath; the waters are constantly rising, and waxing more and more mighty; and there is nothing but the mere pleasure of God that holds the waters back, that are unwilling to be stopped, and press hard to go forward. If God should only withdraw His hand from the floodgate, it would immediately fly open, and the fiery floods of the fierceness and wrath of God, would rush forth with inconceivable fury, and would come upon you with omnipotent power; and if your strength were ten thousand times greater than it is, yea, ten thousand times greater than the strength of the stoutest, sturdiest devil in hell, it would be nothing to withstand or endure it.

The bow of God's wrath is bent, and the arrow made ready on the string, and justice bends the arrow at your heart, and strains the bow, and it is nothing but the mere pleasure of God, and that of an angry God, without any promise or obligation at all, that keeps

Words to Own

constitution (kän′stə·to͞o′shən) *n.:* physical condition.
contrivance (kən·trī′vəns) *n.:* scheme; plan.
inconceivable (in′kən·sēv′ə·bəl) *adj.:* unimaginable; beyond understanding.
omnipotent (äm·nip′ə·tənt) *adj.:* all-powerful.

OPTIONS FOR TEACHING

STRATEGIES FOR INCLUSION

Learners Having Difficulty Edwards's sermon should be presented orally and dramatically in all classes by a student or a person from outside the class who is an accomplished speaker. Students having a difficult time reading the sermon can gain a general impression of its style, content, and tone from hearing it read aloud.

Advanced Since Edwards's fire-and-brimstone sermon is based on the Bible, have students compare and contrast the content and style of the passages on wrath and hellfire from the New Testament with the sermon. For example, students could read and study Luke 3:1–9 (John the Baptist's preaching about the wrath of God) and Revelation 6:8–17 (the breaking of the fifth through seventh seals when the day of wrath has come).

English Language Development To help students grasp the main idea and the tone of Edwards's piece, have them recopy the introductory statement, rewriting the first paragraph into simple sentences. Ask them to highlight one phrase that illustrates God's anger toward humanity and to discuss what words give the phrase such intense emotion.

the arrow one moment from being made drunk with your blood. Thus all you that never passed under a great change of heart, by the mighty power of the Spirit of God upon your souls; all you that were never born again, and made new creatures, and raised from being dead in sin, to a state of new, and before altogether unexperienced light and life, are in the hands of an angry God. However you may have reformed your life in many things, and may have had religious affections,[1] and may keep up a form of religion in your families and closets,[2] and in the house of God, it is nothing but His mere pleasure that keeps you from being this moment swallowed up in everlasting destruction. However unconvinced you may now be of the truth of what you hear, by and by you will be fully convinced of it. Those that are gone from being in the like circumstances with you, see that it was so with them; for destruction came suddenly upon most of them; when they expected nothing of it, and while they were saying, peace and safety: Now they see, that those things on which they depended for peace and safety, were nothing but thin air and empty shadows.

The God that holds you over the pit of hell, much as one holds a spider, or some loathsome insect over the fire, abhors you, and is dreadfully provoked: His wrath toward you burns like fire; He looks upon you as worthy of nothing else but to be cast into the fire; He is of purer eyes than to bear to have you in His sight; you are ten thousand times more abominable in His eyes than the most hateful venomous serpent is in ours. You have offended Him infinitely more than ever a stubborn rebel did his prince; and yet it is nothing but His hand that holds you from falling into the fire every moment. It is to be ascribed to nothing else, that you did not go to hell the last night; that you was suffered to awake again in this world, after you closed your eyes to sleep. And there is no other reason to be given, why you have not dropped into hell since you arose in the morning, but that God's hand has held you up. There is no other reason to be given why you have not gone to hell, since you have sat here in the house of God, provoking His pure eyes by your sinful wicked manner of attending His solemn worship. Yea, there is nothing else that is to be given as a reason why you do not this very moment drop down into hell. **E**

F O sinner! Consider the fearful danger you are in: It is a great furnace of wrath, a wide and bottomless pit, full of the fire of wrath, that you are held over in the hand of that God, whose wrath is provoked and incensed as much against you, as against many of the damned in hell. You hang by a slender thread, with the flames of divine wrath flashing about it, and ready every moment to singe it, and burn it asunder; and you have no interest in any Mediator, and nothing to lay hold of to save yourself, nothing to keep off the flames of wrath, nothing of your own, nothing that you ever have done, nothing that you can do, to induce God to spare you one moment. . . . **G**

1. **affections:** feelings.
2. **closets:** rooms for prayer and meditation.

WORDS TO OWN

abhors (ab·hôrz′) *v.:* scorns; hates.
abominable (ə·bäm′ə·nə·bəl) *adj:* disgusting; loathsome.
ascribed (ə·skribd′) *v.:* attributed to a certain cause.
induce (in·do͞os′) *v.:* to persuade; force; cause.

E. Reader's Response: First Thoughts

? What is your opinion of Edwards at this point in his sermon?
[Sample responses: He is too judgmental; or he is right about sin; or his analogy of God holding sinners over the open flame as one would a spider is frightening.]

F. Language Note: Apostrophe
Tell students that in an apostrophe, the speaker usually addresses an absent person or personified thing. The word *O* often appears in an apostrophe: "O liberty!" "O times! O customs!" Ask students if Edwards is merely addressing his audience when he says "O sinner!" or if he is using an apostrophe. [Edwards is addressing an unspecified person in his audience. Thus his "O sinner!" should probably be regarded as a direct address.]

G. Language Note: Repetition
Ask students to identify the use of repetition in this passage. ["nothing to lay hold of to save yourself, nothing to keep off the flames of wrath, nothing of your own, nothing that you ever have done, nothing that you can do."] Ask students what is the effect of this repetition. [Possible answers: It emphasizes Edwards's belief that people cannot be saved by their actions alone. Edwards uses this emphasis to persuade his audience to convert.]

INTEGRATING THE LANGUAGE ARTS

Strategic Reading Ask students to determine how successful Edwards is in persuading his audience to convert. Have them use the following chart to summarize and evaluate the major points Edwards makes in each paragraph. After students have completed the reading and the chart, have them talk in groups of three about whether Edwards succeeds in his mission.

	Points	Evaluation
First paragraph	[God determines the fate of individuals.]	[Edwards uses frightening imagery of devils and of fire in people's hearts.]
Second paragraph		

CROSSING THE CURRICULUM

Social Sciences Have students research the Great Awakening to discover the origins of the movement, its progress, and the effects of the movement. Have students take on the persona of someone from that time period, tracing the history of the movement in three diary entries. These entries could be posted in the class or read as a reader's theater presentation to the class.

Primary Sources

After reading his journal entry, students may find that they have a better understanding of Edwards, who wrote with such tenderness about his future bride and found the sweetness of God in nature.

Students may note that in the journal, the word *sweetness* is often used to describe God, quite a change from the terrifying God of the sermon. Also distinct from the sermon, the words *meekness, grace, gentleness,* and *love* are used.

PRIMARY Sources | **TWO JOURNALS**

When Jonathan Edwards was twenty years old, he wrote a journal entry describing thirteen-year-old Sarah Pierrepont of New Haven. Edwards idealized Sarah and viewed her as a source of great spiritual strength. He wrote this tribute before he had even seen her. They were married four years later. In the second entry, from his unfinished autobiography, Edwards records a spiritual experience.

Sarah Pierrepont

They say there is a young lady in [New Haven] who is beloved of that Great Being who made and rules the world, and that there are certain seasons in which this Great Being, in some way or another invisible, comes to her and fills her mind with exceeding sweet delight, and that she hardly cares for anything, except to meditate on Him—that she expects after a while to be received up where He is, to be raised up out of the world and caught up into heaven; being assured that He loves her too well to let her remain at a distance from Him always. There she is to dwell with Him, and to be ravished with His love and delight forever. Therefore, if you present all the world before her, with the richest of its treasures, she disregards it and cares not for it, and is unmindful of any pain or affliction. She has a strange sweetness in her mind, and singular purity in her affections; is most just and conscientious in all her conduct; and you could not persuade her to do anything wrong or sinful, if you would give her all the world, lest she should offend this Great Being. She is of a wonderful sweetness, calmness, and universal benevolence of mind; especially after this Great God had manifested Himself to her mind. She will sometimes go about from place to place, singing sweetly; and seems to be always full of joy and pleasure; and no one knows for what. She loves to be alone, walking in the fields and groves, and seems to have someone invisible always conversing with her.

—Jonathan Edwards

My Sense of Divine Things

. . . And as I was walking there, and looking up on the sky and clouds, there came into my mind so sweet a sense of the glorious *majesty* and *grace* of God, that I know not how to express. I seemed to see them both in a sweet conjunction; majesty and meekness joined together; it was a sweet, and gentle, and holy majesty; and also a majestic meekness; an awful sweetness; a high, and great, and holy gentleness.

After this my sense of divine things gradually increased, and became more and more lively, and had more of that inward sweetness. The appearance of everything was altered; there seemed to be, as it were, a calm, sweet cast, or appearance of divine glory, in almost everything. God's excellency, his wisdom, his purity, and love, seemed to appear in everything; in the sun, and moon, and stars; in the clouds and blue sky; in the grass, flowers, trees; in the water, and all nature; which used greatly to fix my mind. I often used to sit and view the moon for continuance; and in the day spent much time in viewing the clouds and sky, to behold the sweet glory of God in these things; in the meantime, singing forth, with a low voice, my contemplations of the Creator and Redeemer. And scarce anything, among all the works of nature, was so sweet to me as thunder and lightning; formerly, nothing had been so terrible to me. Before, I used to be uncommonly terrified with thunder, and to be struck with terror when I saw a thunderstorm rising; but now, on the contrary, it rejoiced me. I felt God, so to speak, at the first appearance of a thunderstorm; and used to take the opportunity, at such times, to fix myself in order to view the clouds and see the lightning's play, and hear the majestic and awful voice of God's thunder, which oftentimes was exceedingly entertaining, leading me to sweet contemplations of my great and glorious God.

—Jonathan Edwards

STRATEGIES FOR INCLUSION

Learners Having Difficulty After students have read the Edwards excerpts, ask them to write what they understand. Ask them to identify words or phrases that are confusing and to write questions they have about the work. They should then read the work a second time, keeping in mind their ideas, confusing words and phrases, and questions. After they have read a second time, have them write what new ideas they have, what they still find confusing, and any new answers or questions.

Musical Have students set the second journal entry to music or sounds. Then, have them set "Sinners in the Hands of an Angry God" to music. Ask them to share the music with the class and to tell how the music fits each piece, how they made their decisions, and how the musical pieces resemble or differ from each other in representing Edwards's work.

Making Meanings

First Thoughts

1. If you had been a member of the congregation listening to Edwards's sermon, what do you think your reaction would have been?

Reviewing the Text

Identify the three famous **figures of speech** that Edwards develops in paragraphs 4–7 of the sermon. What things is he comparing in each one? How does Edwards extend each figure of speech?

Shaping Interpretations

2. What references in the sermon might be interpreted as **allusions** to divine mercy?
3. Edwards is directing his sermon to what he calls "natural men," those members of his congregation who have not been "reborn." Review your Reader's Log notes. What **images** in the first four paragraphs do you think helped Edwards's listeners to *feel* the peril of their unregenerate condition?
4. Edwards strikes fear into the hearts of his listeners in order to persuade them to act to avoid everlasting torment. Which specific **metaphors** or **similes** in the sermon do you think were probably the most persuasive?

Challenging the Text

5. If you had a chance to respond to Edwards, what would you say?

Choices: Building Your Portfolio

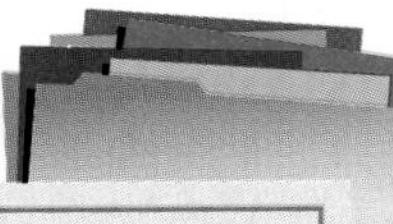

Writer's Notebook

1. Collecting Ideas for an Autobiographical Incident

The world champion boxer Sugar Ray Leonard once wrote of his success, "What helped me develop my quickness was fear. I think the rougher the opponent, the quicker I am." Freewrite about an incident in your own life when fear or anxiety motivated you to take action, make a change, or try harder at something. Save your notes for possible use in the Writer's Workshop on page 130.

Critical Writing

2. The Other Edwards

In a brief essay, compare the ideas about God that Edwards expresses in his sermon with those he expresses in Primary Sources (page 82). How do you explain the apparent differences between the "two" Edwardses?

Speaking and Listening

3. Fire and Fervor

Today's evangelistic religious leaders are the successors to Jonathan Edwards and other revivalist preachers of the Great Awakening. With four or five other students, form a panel to discuss the following questions in class: (a) Are "fire-and-brimstone" sermons still effective today, or are other methods used to motivate congregations? (b) What aspects of Edwards's sermon would be effective today? (c) Would modern telecommunications enhance or detract from Edwards's sermon?

Creative Writing

4. What the Parishioners Said

You and your family have just returned to your home in Enfield after listening to Pastor Edwards's sermon. Write a script of a conversation between the members of your family, including the reactions of both adults and children.

Mrs. Jonathan Edwards (1750–1755) by Joseph Badger (1708–1765). Oil on canvas ($30\frac{3}{8}$" × $25\frac{1}{2}$").

Yale University Art Gallery, Bequest of Eugene Phelps Edwards (1938.75).

Making Meanings

First Thoughts

1. Possible responses: Fear or outrage.

Reviewing the Text

The images of the dammed water, the bow and arrow, and the spider all relate to the wrath of God. Like waters temporarily blocked by a dam, God's anger is ready to burst forth. His wrath will bend like a bow to send the arrow of retribution into a sinner's heart. His wrath holds humanity like a spider over the fire of the pit of hell.

Edwards extends all three metaphors with powerful rhetoric. He speaks of rising waters and of God's hand on the floodgate. He tells of the mounting tension on the bow, which will inevitably lead to God's letting loose the arrow of vengeance on sinful humans. He extends the figure of the spider when he says to the congregation, "You are ten thousand times more abominable in His eyes, than the most hateful, venomous serpent is in ours."

Shaping Interpretations

2. God's hand holding his listeners up and keeping them out of hell, at least for the moment.
3. The "fiery pit" of hell in the first paragraph, its "gaping mouth" in the second, humans falling through thin air in the third. In the fourth, he compares human weakness to the heaviness of lead, which will draw them down to hell just as surely as a heavy rock will smash a spider's web.
4. Answers will vary. Students will probably make their choices from the images in response #3.

Challenging the Text

5. **(Synthesis)** Responses will vary. Students may respond with their own religious views.

Choices: Building Your Portfolio

1. **Writer's Notebook** *Remind students to write on situations they would not mind sharing with others.* Remind students to save their work. They may use it as prewriting for the Writer's Workshop on p. 130.
3. **Speaking and Listening** To help panelists prepare, play audiotapes of modern evangelists. While the tapes are playing, have students listen for and jot down ways in which these speakers deliver their messages. Prompt them to listen for such vocal features as pauses, rising pitch, tremors, and stress.

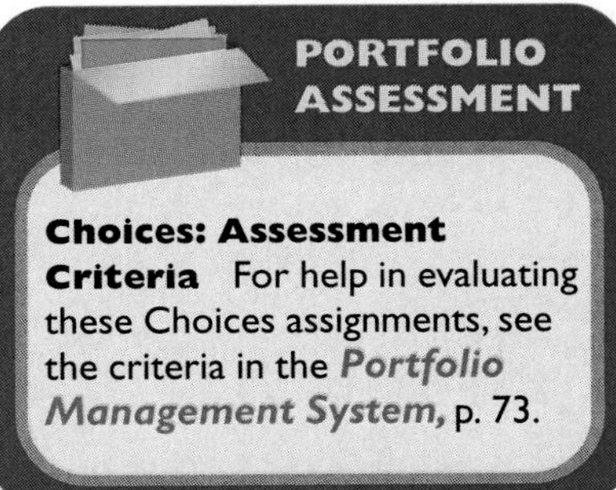

Choices: Assessment Criteria For help in evaluating these Choices assignments, see the criteria in the *Portfolio Management System*, p. 73.

QUICK PLANNING GUIDE

Into the Selection

Author Biography pp. 84–85
Before You Read p. 85

- **Reading Focus: Prior Knowledge** Students analyze American success stories.
- **Quickwrite:** Chart success in Reader's Log
- **Background:** Apprenticeship

Through the Selection

from The Autobiography pp. 86–94
Words to Own pp. 86–94
Literature and Science pp. 90–91
Spotlight On p. 95
Connections: An Essay
from All I Really Need to Know I Learned in Kindergarten **p. 96**
Making Meanings p. 97

Beyond the Selection

Choices: Building Your Portfolio p. 98

- **Writer's Notebook:** Collect ideas for autobiographical incident
- **Critical Writing:** Compare two writers in an essay
- **Critical Writing:** Track virtues in a brief report
- **Crossing the Curriculum: Science:** Research scientific work
- **Critical Writing:** Write a proposal
- **Creative Writing:** Create an almanac
- **Research/Art:** Publish aphorisms

Benjamin Franklin

(1706–1790)

Few people have been so energetically devoted to improvement—both self-improvement and the improvement of society—as Benjamin Franklin. Franklin's many accomplishments can only be summarized. One of seventeen children, he rose from poverty to eminence even though he had to leave school early in order to work. By the time he was twenty-four, he was a prosperous merchant, owner of a successful print shop, and publisher of *The Pennsylvania Gazette*. He helped found the Academy of Philadelphia (which became the University of Pennsylvania), the American Philosophical Society, and the first public library in America. He promoted numerous municipal projects in Philadelphia: paved streets, sewer lines, improved street lighting, and a fire brigade. He was a scientist and an important inventor: His research, especially on electricity, resulted in his election to England's Royal Society. In addition, he invented an open heating stove (called a Franklin stove), bifocal eyeglasses, a type of harmonica, and a rocking chair that could swat flies. Like Thomas Jefferson (page 114), Franklin was a tinkerer, constantly looking for ways to make things work a little better or more efficiently.

Benjamin Franklin (1777) by Jean-Baptiste Greuze. Oil on canvas (28⅝″ × 22⅝″).

Scientist, Socialite, and "Snake"

At forty-one, Franklin had made enough money to retire from business. He hoped to devote the rest of his life to study and scientific research, but this was not to be. Franklin possessed uncommon talents as a diplomat and negotiator, and for the rest of his life he used these skills in the service of his state and his country. Franklin lived in London in the 1750s and '60s, representing the interests of Pennsylvania as an agent of the Pennsylvania Assembly. A decade later he was back in London lobbying for the Colonies in their dispute with Britain, hoping to bring about a reconciliation that would prevent war. Franklin's wit and charm made him enormously popular in London for many years; he once said that he was invited out to dinner there six nights a week. But by 1774, when he was sixty-eight, the stress between Britain and the Colonies had become too great for even this shrewd diplomat to control. The King's Privy Council publicly attacked him for his policies; the British press called him an "old snake." Franklin finally relinquished his hopes for peace and sailed for America in 1775.

When Franklin arrived home, he was greeted with news that the first battles of the Revolutionary War had been fought at Lexington and Concord, Massachusetts. The "shot heard round the world" had been fired. After helping to draft the Declaration of Independence in 1776, Franklin left for Paris to negotiate the treaty that brought the French into the war on America's side. When Franklin landed in France, Lord Stormont, the British ambassador, caustically remarked: "I look upon him as a dangerous engine, and am very sorry that some English frigate did not meet with him by the way."

The Jack of All Trades

In Paris, Franklin was even more popular than he had once been in England. Playing the role of the

WORDS TO OWN

The following vocabulary words are defined in the Words to Own at the bottom of the pupil's page.

assert p. 86	arduous p. 92
arbitrary p. 86	rectitude p. 92
indiscreet p. 86	facilitate p. 93
abate p. 88	subsequent p. 94
itinerant p. 89	eradicate p. 94

sophisticated but homespun American, Franklin described himself as "an old man, with gray hair appearing under a marten fur cap, among the powdered heads of Paris." When the Revolution was over, he helped negotiate the peace, and he was a member of the Constitutional Convention in 1787. His death three years later was cause for international mourning.

Franklin's practicality, like the success story of his life, is typically American, but it has not been universally admired throughout the nation's history. The American novelist Herman Melville (page 311) gave this picture of Franklin: "Jack of all trades, master of each and mastered by none—the type and genius of his land. Franklin was everything but a poet." Franklin did lack a poet's depth of imagination and emotion, but his literary talents and accomplishments were substantial. He was especially gifted as a wit, as the lightly ironic tone of his *Autobiography* testifies.

Franklin's talents were so great that he could have left his mark on many areas of intellectual accomplishment. As the biographer Carl Van Doren wrote of him, "Mind and will, talent and art, strength and ease, wit and grace met in him as if nature had been lavish and happy when he was shaped."

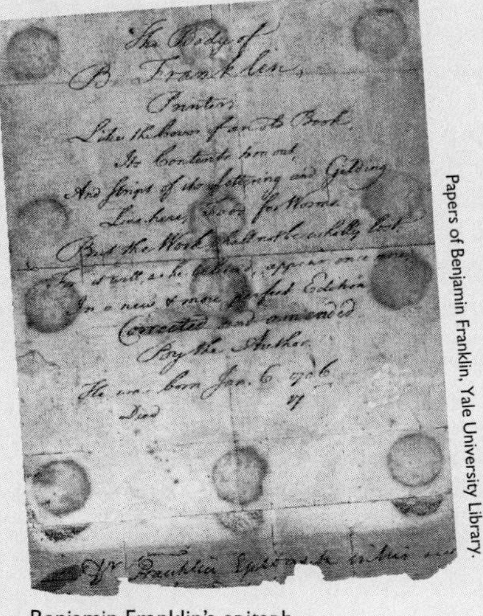
The Body of
B. Franklin,
Printer;
Like the Cover of an old Book,
Its Contents torn out,
And stript of its Lettering and Gilding,
Lies here, Food for Worms.
But the Work shall not be wholly lost,
For it will, as he believ'd, appear once more,
In a new & more perfect Edition,
Corrected and amended
By the Author.
He was born Jan. 6. 1706.
Died 17

Papers of Benjamin Franklin, Yale University Library.

Benjamin Franklin's epitaph.

Before You Read
from The Autobiography

Reading Focus
The Road to Success

"Rags-to-riches" is the Cinderella-like success story at the core of American life and culture. The famous 1941 movie *Citizen Kane* chronicles just such a success story—the meteoric rise of a person from humble beginnings to fame and renown. Rags-to-riches is the story of many old-time Hollywood movie stars and producers (such as Charlie Chaplin) and of this country's early business and industrial giants (such as Andrew Carnegie), many of whom were immigrants from other lands. It is still the story of many people today, from well-known athletes, performers, and other celebrities to unsung people you might even know yourself.

Quickwrite
READER'S LOG

Using a chart like the one below, make a list of qualities that you think are necessary for success. Can these qualities be acquired, or do people have to be born with them? Do you think that the same basic qualities are required to be successful at anything?

A Successful Person		
IS decisive	HAS goals	DOES planning

Background
Franklin began his *Autobiography* when he was sixty-five and continued it intermittently for years, although he never finished it and it was not published during his lifetime. When Franklin was a teenager, he was apprenticed to his older brother James, who printed a Boston newspaper. As an apprentice, Franklin felt he was treated harshly, and disputes arose between the brothers. This selection begins with Franklin's escape from a second, secret "indenture," or contract of service, that his brother had forced him to sign.

Using **Before You Read** p. 85

Reading Focus
Have students brainstorm a list you put on the chalkboard of self-made people from all walks of life. Suggest Sam Walton and Oprah Winfrey as examples. After the list has been completed, ask students to discuss how each individual is successful.

Background
Explain briefly how the system of apprenticeship worked in the eighteenth century. A youth signed a contract, called an *indenture,* obligating the youth to work for someone skilled in a craft or trade for room and board for a given number of years. In return, the apprentice gained skill in the craft or trade. Those who completed the apprenticeship were free to sell their labor.

Portfolio Assessment
For help with self- and teacher assessment of reading skills, see the ***Portfolio Management System,*** p. 53.

Program Manager

- **Planning Instruction** See Teaching Notes, *Teaching Resources A,* p. 27, for objectives, a summary, literary elements, and additional information.
- **Instructional Support** See Graphic Organizer for Active Reading, *Teaching Resources A,* p. 36, for an Into the Selection activity.
- **Instructional Support** See Fine Art Transparency 2.1. Review teacher's notes in the ***Audiovisual Resources Binder***.
- **Assessment** See Selection Test, *Test Booklet,* pp. 19–20.
- **Language Link** For practice in identifying and using compound subjects and verbs, see Language Link, *Teaching Resources A,* pp. 37–38, and *Language and Writing Skills Worksheets,* p. 87. For practice in revision, see Language Link, *Teaching Resources A,* pp. 40–41.
- **Reinforcement** Use the Words to Own worksheet in *Teaching Resources A,* p. 39.

A. Expansion

Franklin often drew figures of speech from printing, reflecting his long experience with that trade. His use of *errata* ("errors in print") to refer to mistakes in life is an example. Franklin uses a similar figure of speech in his epitaph, written in 1728: "The body of Benjamin Franklin, Printer (like the cover of an old book, its contents torn out and stripped of its lettering and gilding), lies here food for worms; but the work shall not be lost, for it will . . . appear once more in a new and more elegant edition, revised and corrected by the Author."

B. Critical Reading: Drawing Conclusions

? What possible character flaws or negative traits has Franklin revealed in these two paragraphs? How might they contribute to his decision to leave Boston? [He suggests he may be "too saucy and provoking," "a little obnoxious," and "pointed at with horror by good people as an infidel or atheist." Students may suggest that he is leaving to make a fresh start where his reputation is not tarnished.]

from The Autobiography

Benjamin Franklin

Leaving Boston

At length, a fresh difference arising between my brother and me, I took upon me to assert my freedom, presuming that he would not venture to produce the new indentures. It was not fair in me to take this advantage, and this I therefore **A** reckon one of the first errata[1] of my life; but the unfairness of it weighed little with me, when under the impressions of resentment for the blows his passion too often urged him to bestow upon me, though he was otherwise not an ill-natured man: Perhaps I was too saucy and provoking.

Benjamin Franklin. Drawing by David Levine. Reprinted with permission from *The New York Review of Books*. Copyright © 1973 NYREV, Inc.

When he found I would leave him, he took care to prevent my getting employment in any other printing house of the town, by going round and speaking to every master, who accordingly refused to give me work. **B** I then thought of going to New York, as the nearest place where there was a printer; and I was rather inclined to leave Boston when I reflected that I had already made myself a little obnoxious to the governing party, and, from the arbitrary proceedings of the Assembly in my brother's case, it was likely I might, if I stayed, soon bring myself into scrapes; and farther, that my indiscreet disputations about religion began to make me pointed at with horror by good people as an infidel or atheist. I determined on the point, but my father now siding with my brother, I was sensible that, if I attempted to go openly, means would be used to prevent me. My friend Collins, therefore, undertook to manage a little for me. He agreed with the captain of a New York sloop for my passage, under the notion of my being a young acquaintance of his, that had got a naughty girl with child, whose friends would compel me to marry her, and therefore I could not appear or come away publicly. So I sold some of my books to raise a little money, was taken on board privately, and as we had a fair wind, in three days I found myself in New York, near 300 miles from home, a boy of but 17, without the least recommendation to, or knowledge of any person in the place, and with very little money in my pocket.

I wished to live without committing any fault at any time.

1. **errata** (er·rät′ə): Latin for "errors"; a printer's term.

WORDS TO OWN

assert (ə·surt′) *v.:* to declare; claim.
arbitrary (är′bə·trer′ē) *adj.:* based on whims or individual preferences.
indiscreet (in′di·skrēt′) *adj.:* careless in speech or action.

OPTIONS FOR TEACHING

STRATEGIES FOR INCLUSION

Kinesthetic/Auditory To help students identify with the difficulties Franklin experienced when he moved to a new community, have students work in pairs to create and enact for the class the dialogue that might have occurred between the hungry young Franklin and the baker.

Intrapersonal Have students imitate Franklin's example by trying to follow two of his resolutions. Ask students to track their progress once a week for a month. Then, based on what they have learned, ask them to write both a letter as though they were asking an advice columnist for help and the corresponding response as though they were the columnist.

Logical-Mathematical Have students examine Franklin's system for recording his progress in attaining virtues. They should develop an alternative method such as a rating scale or an improved chart to analyze and record data. Have them present their new system to the class.

Philadelphia Museum of Art: Mr. and Mrs. Wharton Sinkler Collection (P198423).

Benjamin Franklin Drawing Electricity from the Sky (c. 1805) by Benjamin West (1738–1820). Oil on paper on canvas (13¼″ × 10″).

RESPONDING TO THE ART: ABOUT THE ARTIST

Like Franklin, Benjamin West was also a Quaker. Born in 1738 in Pennsylvania, West moved to Philadelphia and then to New York, where he painted portraits. He moved to London in 1763, established himself as a history painter, and received George III's patronage. West freed history painting from antiquated conventions by depicting people from modern history in modern dress.

WRITERS ON WRITING

Franklin believed that imitation of good models was an effective way of learning to write. In *The Autobiography,* he describes how he learned from imitating *The Spectator* papers of the British writers Joseph Addison and Richard Steele: "I thought the writing excellent, and wished, if possible, to imitate it. With this view, I took some of the papers, and making short hints of the sentiment in each sentence, laid them by a few days, and then without looking at the book, tried to complete the papers again. . . . Then I compared my *Spectator* with the original, discovered some of my faults, and corrected them."

STRATEGIES FOR INCLUSION

Special Needs To help students tie Franklin's lofty ideals to their own experience, have them work in mixed-ability groups to compile their own "words to live by." Imitating the Connections essay from *All I Need to Know I Learned in Kindergarten* on p. 96 would probably provide incentive for this assignment. Students should begin by filling in the sentence "All I need to know I learned ______." Then, they should create a chart describing a familiar object, person, or place in the left column. In the right, they should make up a maxim indicating what they learned from each characteristic. Each group should share its chart with the other groups in a whole-class read around. Such a chart might look like the following:

All I needed to know I learned from my car.

Description	Maxim (Rule of Conduct)
has transmission	Sometimes you have to shift gears.
has brakes	Know when it's time to stop.
has horn	Signal when you're in trouble.
needs gas	Eat, drink, and sleep enough to keep yourself running.

A. Language Note: Style
Point out Franklin's condensed writing style by asking students to list the events described in this passage of less than one hundred words. [Storm at sea; ripped sails; landing on Long Island; man falls overboard, is rescued by his hair, asks Franklin to dry a book for him, and sleeps.]

Metacognition What vivid details help readers see the scenes described? [Students may point out specific words including rotten sails, drunken Dutchman, sinking, shock pate, ducking, sobered.]

B. Literary Element: Dialogue
Although the combining of dialogue with narrative was not common before John Bunyan's day (1628–1688), the practice was by no means unknown. Miguel de Cervantes (1547–1616) and François Rabelais (1494?–1553) mixed narration and dialogue to good effect. Another example, which it appears Franklin did not think of in this connection, is the Bible, in which dialogue and narration are often combined.

My inclinations for the sea were by this time worn out, or I might now have gratified them. But, having a trade, and supposing myself a pretty good workman, I offered my service to the printer in the place, old Mr. William Bradford,[2] who had been the first printer in Pennsylvania, but removed from thence upon the quarrel of George Keith. He could give me no employment, having little to do, and help enough already; but says he, "My son at Philadelphia has lately lost his principal hand,[3] Aquila Rose, by death; if you go thither, I believe he may employ you." Philadelphia was 100 miles further; I set out, however, in a boat for Amboy,[4] leaving my chest and things to follow me round by sea.

In crossing the bay, we met with a squall that tore our rotten sails to pieces, prevented our getting into the Kill,[5] and drove us upon Long Island. In our way, a drunken Dutchman, who was a passenger too, fell overboard; when he was sinking, I reached through the water to his shock pate,[6] and drew him up, so that we got him in again. His ducking sobered him a little, and he went to sleep, taking first out of his pocket a book, which he desired I would dry for him. It proved to be my old favorite author, Bunyan's *Pilgrim's Progress*,[7] in Dutch, finely printed on good paper, with copper cuts,[8] a dress better than I had ever seen it wear in its own language. I have since found that it has been translated into most of the languages of Europe, and suppose it has been more generally read than any other book, except perhaps the Bible. Honest John was the first that I know of who mixed narration and dialogue; a method of writing very engaging to the reader, who in the most interesting parts finds himself, as it were, brought into the company and present at the discourse. . . .

When we drew near the island, we found it was at a place where there could be no landing, there being a great surf on the stony beach. So we dropped anchor, and swung round toward the shore. Some people came down to the water edge and hallooed to us, as we did to them; but the wind was so high, and the surf so loud, that we could not hear so as to understand each other. There were canoes on the shore, and we made signs, and hallooed that they should fetch us; but they either did not understand us, or thought it impracticable, so they went away, and night coming on, we had no remedy but to wait till the wind should abate; and, in the meantime, the boatman and I concluded to sleep, if we could; and so crowded into the scuttle,[9] with the Dutchman, who was still wet, and the spray beating over the head of our boat, leaked through to us, so that we were soon almost as wet as he. In this manner we lay all night, with very little rest; but, the wind abating the next day, we made a shift to reach Amboy before night, having been thirty hours on the water, without victuals,[10] or any drink but a bottle of filthy rum, and the water we sailed on being salt.

2. **William Bradford:** one of the first American printers; not to be confused with *Of Plymouth Plantation* author William Bradford (page 26). Bradford (1663–1752) set up the first printing presses in Philadelphia (1685) and New York (1693).
3. **principal hand:** best employee.
4. **Amboy:** Perth Amboy, New Jersey.
5. **Kill:** channel (from the Dutch *kil*). Based on the explorations of Henry Hudson in 1609, the Dutch claimed land in the Middle Colonies and gave Dutch names to some of its geographic features.
6. **shock pate** (pāt): shaggy head.
7. ***Pilgrim's Progress*:** religious allegory by the Puritan writer John Bunyan (1628–1688), first published in 1678. It tells how the hero, Christian, makes his journey to salvation. Notice that Franklin admires the book for literary and historical, rather than religious, reasons.
8. **copper cuts:** engravings.
9. **scuttle:** covered opening in hull or deck of a ship.
10. **victuals** (vit′'lz): food; often incorrectly spelled "vittles."

WORDS TO OWN
abate (ə·bāt′) *v.:* lessen.

OPTIONS FOR TEACHING

INTEGRATING THE LANGUAGE ARTS

Writing: Paragraph Have students in groups create an extended paragraph supporting the following statement: Franklin's *Autobiography* reflects Puritan influences. Have them consider plain style, hard work, and self-improvement.

Strategic Reading Have students work in pairs to make inferences based on their reading of how Franklin achieved success. Students should read three or four paragraphs and record their inferences on a chart such as the following. Ask students to support their inferences with information from the text. Once they have finished reading, ask them to note the actual outcome and to compare it with their inferences. Groups should share their charts with the class. Finally, help students identify the metacognitive processes used while they were making inferences.

Inference	[Franklin will have trouble with others.]
Textual Support	[He says he has been obnoxious to people in government.]
Outcome	[He gets out of town with the help of a friend.]
Evaluation of Thought Process	[I revised my thinking, based on reading about his friendship with Collins.]

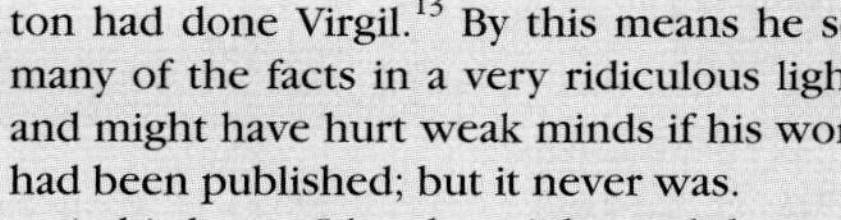

In the evening I found myself very feverish, and went in to bed; but, having read somewhere that cold water drank plentifully was good for a fever, I followed the prescription, sweat plentiful most of the night, my fever left me, and in the morning, crossing the ferry, I proceeded on my journey on foot, having fifty miles to Burlington,[11] where I was told I should find boats that would carry me the rest of the way to Philadelphia. **C**

It rained very hard all the day; I was thoroughly soaked, and by noon a good deal tired; so I stopped at a poor inn, where I stayed all night, beginning now to wish that I had never left home. I cut so miserable a figure, too, that I found, by the questions asked me, I was suspected to be some runaway servant, and in danger of being taken up on that suspicion. However, I proceeded the next day, and got in the evening to an **D**

Speak not but what may benefit others or yourself; avoid trifling conversation.

Drawing by David Levine. Reprinted with permission from *The New York Review of Books.* Copyright © 1973 NYREV, Inc.

inn, within eight or ten miles of Burlington, kept by one Dr. Brown. He entered into conversation with me while I took some refreshment, and, finding I had read a little, became very sociable and friendly. Our acquaintance continued as long as he lived. He had been, I imagine, an itinerant doctor, for there was no town in England, or country in Europe, of which he could not give a very particular account. He had some letters,[12] and was ingenious, but much of an unbeliever, and wickedly undertook, some years after, to travesty the Bible in doggerel verse, as Cotton had done Virgil.[13] By this means he set many of the facts in a very ridiculous light, and might have hurt weak minds if his work had been published; but it never was.

At his house I lay that night, and the next morning reached Burlington, but had the mortification to find that the regular boats were gone a little before my coming, and no other expected to go before Tuesday, this being Saturday; wherefore I returned to an old woman in the town, of whom I had bought gingerbread to eat on the water, and asked her advice. She invited me to lodge at her house till a passage by water should offer; and being tired with my foot traveling, I accepted the invitation. She understanding I was a printer, would have had me stay at that town and follow my business, being ignorant of the stock necessary to begin with. **E** She was very hospitable, gave me a dinner of oxcheek with great goodwill, accepting only of a pot of ale in return; and I thought myself fixed till Tuesday should come. However, walking in the evening by the side of the river, a boat came by, which I found was going toward Philadelphia, with several people in her. They took me in, and, as there was no wind, we rowed all the way; and about midnight, not having yet seen the city, some of the company were confident we must have passed it, and would row no farther; the others knew not where we were; so we put toward the shore, got into a creek, landed near an old fence, with the rails of which we made a fire, the night being cold, in October, and

11. **Burlington:** Burlington, New Jersey; about eighteen miles from Philadelphia.
12. **letters:** education.

13. **doggerel . . . Virgil:** Doggerel is irregularly constructed comical verse, often used for satirical purposes. In 1664, Charles Cotton (1630–1687) published a doggerel version, or a parody, of the *Aeneid*, an epic poem by the Roman poet Virgil (70–19 B.C.).

WORDS TO OWN
itinerant (ī·tin′ər·ənt) *adj.:* traveling.

C. Reader's Response: First Thoughts

? How would you describe Franklin's character at this point?
[Sample responses: He is brave, hearty, humorous, resourceful, or foolhardy.]

D. Exploring the Historical Period

Students may not understand why a runaway servant would be likely to be "taken up"—that is, arrested. Explain that many servants were bondsmen and bondswomen—indentured to their employers for passage to the colony or for debt. Servants who tried to escape from this condition of near slavery could be forcibly returned to their employers.

E. Expansion

You may need to explain that by "the stock necessary to begin with," Franklin means the press, type, and other apparatus needed to equip a print shop.

CLASSROOM MANAGEMENT

Block Scheduling Ask students to complete their Quickwrite at the beginning of class (five to ten minutes). Then, have them snake read the selection aloud (fifteen to twenty minutes). Next, show a video to reinforce the selection (twenty to twenty-five minutes). After a class discussion of the selection, have student pairs write their answers to Making Meanings (twenty to twenty-five minutes). Conclude the block by having volunteers share their answers with the class (ten to fifteen minutes).

Teacher's Reflection To evaluate your interactions with students, you may find it helpful to audiotape a class discussion. You can use the following criteria for evaluation: uses reflective responses to help students clarify and examine their ideas; gives students time to think; communicates respect for students and their ideas. Evaluate your results, set specific goals for improvement, and continually reassess achievements and establish new goals.

Managing the Reader's Response Classroom As students read the story, have them write down questions they might have. Have students use these questions during class sessions for clarification and discussion. ☞

LITERATURE AND SCIENCE

Ask students to discuss which of Banneker's many accomplishments seems most remarkable. Have students research other inventors of the time. Students may consider Thomas Jefferson or Robert Fulton. Ask students to make displays of these inventors' accomplishments, and hold a science and technology fair where students can visit and examine each display.

A. Critical Reading: Analyzing Character

? Why might a person with little money be generous? Do you agree with Franklin's analysis? What might be some other reasons? [Answers will vary. Students will likely agree with him. They may suggest moral and ethical reasons a person might be generous.]

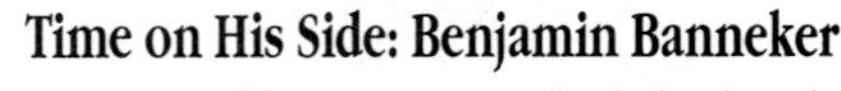

LITERATURE AND SCIENCE

Time on His Side: Benjamin Banneker

Poor Richard's Almanack (page 95) was a best-seller in its time, but Benjamin Franklin is not the only important figure in the history of the American almanac. Between 1792 and 1797, six remarkable almanacs were published by Benjamin Banneker (1731–1806), a Maryland farmer, astronomer, mathematician, and the only African American ever to have calculated almanacs. Banneker's almanacs, published in twenty-eight editions, were among the most successful almanacs of his era.

Self-taught scientist . . . Benjamin Banneker was the son of free African Americans. His grandmother was an Englishwoman, and his grandfather, who claimed to be an African prince, had the name Bannke or Bannaka. His grandmother taught him to read and write, and for a while he attended a one-room, interracial school where, recalled an African American classmate, "all his delight was to dive into his books." Banneker was mostly self-taught, and throughout his life he acquired considerable computational skill. For enjoyment he devised mathematical puzzles, some of them in verse. At twenty-two, using only a borrowed pocket watch and a picture of a clock as models, Banneker built a functioning wooden clock, each gear carved by hand, which struck the hours for over fifty years. Later in life, Banneker fell in love with the stars, and, in 1788, he calculated a solar eclipse using nothing but books as a guide.

there we remained till daylight. Then one of the company knew the place to be Cooper's Creek, a little above Philadelphia, which we saw as soon as we got out of the creek, and arrived there about eight or nine o'clock on the Sunday morning, and landed at the Market Street wharf.

Arrival in Philadelphia

I have been the more particular in this description of my journey, and shall be so of my first entry into that city, that you may in your mind compare such unlikely beginnings with the figure I have since made there. I was in my working dress, my best clothes being to come round by sea. I was dirty from my journey; my pockets were stuffed out with shirts and stockings, and I knew no soul nor where to look for lodging. I was fatigued with traveling, rowing, and want of rest, I was very hungry; and my whole stock of cash consisted of a Dutch dollar, and about a shilling in copper. **A** The latter I gave the people of the boat for my passage, who at first refused it, on account of my rowing; but I insisted on their taking it. A man being sometimes more generous when he has but a little money than when he has plenty, perhaps through fear of being thought to have but little.

Then I walked up the street, gazing about till near the market house I met a boy with bread. I had made many a meal on bread, and, inquiring where he got it, I went immediately to the baker's he directed me to, in Second Street, and asked for biscuit, intending such as we had in Boston; but they, it seems, were not made in Philadelphia. Then I asked for a three-penny loaf, and was told

OPTIONS FOR TEACHING

COOPERATIVE LEARNING

Generating Discussion Questions Have students work in small groups to write six questions that require higher-order thinking skills for oral discussion about *The Autobiography.* Suggest that the questions ask for the following skills: examining significant ideas, drawing conclusions about Franklin and success based on data from the text, and relating the reading to personal experience. Have groups exchange their lists of questions to use for discussion.

CROSSING THE CURRICULUM

Social Sciences Have students work in groups to research the process of printing in the 1700s. Students may be surprised to discover the labor required to produce one page of print. Have students create a bulletin-board display of the printing process of Franklin's time.

Banneker published his almanacs to advance not only the cause of science, but also the cause of African Americans. In 1791, Banneker sent a manuscript copy of his first almanac to Secretary of State Thomas Jefferson, along with a famous letter in which he urges Jefferson to recognize the equality of all people and calls for the abolition of slavery. Jefferson in turn sent the almanac to the Academy of Sciences in Paris, the foremost body of scientific learning in France. Thus, Banneker achieved transatlantic fame through his almanacs, as Franklin did through his writings and diplomatic career.

Benjamin Banneker, from one of his almanacs, c. 1795, by an unknown artist. Woodcut.

Maryland Historical Society.

. . . and star-gazing sage. Banneker was described by those who knew him as having the thoughtful demeanor of a sage as he leaned on the long staff that he always carried with him. Toward the end of his life, living alone in a small log house on his farm, Banneker continued to watch the stars, putter in his garden, study bees and locusts, play the violin and flute, and record his observations in a journal that became a unique record of an eighteenth-century almanac maker's method. His lifelong preoccupation with the measurement of time assured him a prominent place in the early history of science in America. Appropriately, the wooden clock Banneker had constructed kept excellent time until two days after his death: As Banneker's body was being lowered into his grave, his house a few yards away caught fire, destroying the clock he had made more than fifty years before.

they had none such. So not considering or knowing the difference of money, and the greater cheapness nor the names of his bread, I bade him give me three-penny worth of any sort. He gave me, accordingly, three great puffy rolls. I was surprised at the quantity, but took it, and, **B** having no room in my pockets, walked off with a roll under each arm, and eating the other. Thus I went up Market Street as far as Fourth Street, passing by the door of Mr. Read, my future wife's father; when she, standing at the door, saw me, and thought I made, as I certainly did, a most awkward, ridiculous appearance. Then I turned and went down Chestnut Street and part of Walnut Street, eating my roll all the way, and, coming round, found myself again at Market Street wharf, near the boat I came in, to which I went for a draft of the river water; and, being filled with one of my rolls, gave the other two to a woman and her child that came down the river in the boat with us, and were waiting to go farther.

Thus refreshed, I walked again up the street, which by this time had many clean-dressed people in it, who were all walking the same way. I joined them, and thereby was led into the great meetinghouse of the

Tolerate no uncleanliness in body, clothes, or habitation.

Drawing by David Levine. Reprinted with permission from *The New York Review of Books.* Copyright © 1973 NYREV, Inc.

B. Reader's Response: Shaping Interpretations

? What is surprising about Franklin's visit to the bakery? [Sample responses: It is as if he is in a foreign country, though he has only traveled from Boston to Philadelphia. Or there is no common currency, and it appears that the value of money (three pennies) differs. Or the names of breads and cookies are not the same.]

Technology Tip

TECHNOLOGY Much information on Benjamin Franklin can be found on the Internet. For example, the Benjamin Franklin Web site at **http://sln.fi.edu/franklin/rotten.html** includes a video file of the film *Glimpses of the Man.* The complete text of Franklin's autobiography is available via Gopher at **wiretap.spies.com/00/Library/Classic/franklin.txt**. *You may want to preview any Internet activity that you suggest to students. Because these resources are sometimes public forums, their content can be unpredictable.*

PROBLEM SOLVING/CRITICAL THINKING

Words to Live By To develop strong moral habits on his own, Franklin wrote a list of thirteen virtues to live by. After discussing the meaning of each, have students list and discuss the four most important virtues for teenagers today to live by.

PROFESSIONAL NOTES

Cultural Diversity Students may work in small groups to discuss the values Franklin extols. Have students compare Franklin's values with virtues and values of various cultures with which they might be familiar.

RESPONDING TO THE ART: EXPLORING THE SUBJECT
Explain to students that this scene was engraved about ten years after Franklin's death and therefore looks quite different from the way it did in 1729 when the young Franklin landed at the Market Street Wharf, a few blocks east of this long street (that is, to the right of the scene). George Washington, Franklin, Betsy Ross, and many other notables of the Revolutionary era worshipped at Christ Church, the steeple of which is visible in this engraving.

A. Exploring the Culture
Explain that a Quaker meeting for worship has no predetermined form or ritual. Any member may speak out in prayer or praise. Or the entire congregation may sit silently in prayer or contemplation. It was during such a period of silent communion that the exhausted Benjamin Franklin fell asleep in the meeting house.

B. Expansion
In introducing Franklin's scheme for attaining moral perfection, inform students that during his two years in London, Franklin had led a rather free and easy life. It was to correct the follies of this period of his life that Franklin undertook this program of self-improvement.

Quakers near the market. I sat down among them, and, after looking round awhile and hearing nothing said, being very drowsy through labor and want of rest the preceding **A** night, I fell fast asleep, and continued so till the meeting broke up, when one was kind enough to rouse me. This was, therefore, the first house I was in, or slept in, in Philadelphia. . . .

Arriving at Moral Perfection

It was about this time I conceived the bold **B** and arduous project of arriving at moral perfection. I wished to live without committing any fault at any time; I would conquer all that either natural inclination, custom, or company might lead me into. As I knew, or thought I knew, what was right and wrong, I did not see why I might not always do the one and avoid the other. But I soon found I had undertaken a task of more difficulty than I had imagined. While my care was employed in guarding against one fault, I was often surprised by another; habit took the advantage of inattention; inclination was sometimes too strong for reason. I concluded, at length, that the mere speculative conviction that it was our interest to be completely virtuous, was not sufficient to prevent our slipping; and that the contrary habits must be broken, and good ones acquired and established, before we can have any dependence on a steady, uniform rectitude of conduct. For this purpose I therefore contrived the following method.

WORDS TO OWN
arduous (är′jo͞o·əs) *adj.:* difficult.
rectitude (rek′tə·to͞od′) *n.:* correctness.

Second Street, North from Market Street, with Christ Church, Philadelphia (1799) by W. Birch & Son. Colored line engraving.

The Granger Collection, New York.

OPTIONS FOR TEACHING

ASSESSMENT TOOLS

Check Test: Questions and Answers

1. When he realized Franklin was quitting, what did his brother do? [Made it impossible for Franklin to get further printing work in Boston.]
2. What lie did Franklin use to get secret passage to New York? [He claimed he had gotten a girl pregnant and would have to marry her if he did not flee.]
3. How did he save the drunk man? [He pulled him out of the water by his hair.]
4. Why did Franklin not stay in New York? [He could not get work in printing.]
5. Where did Franklin first take rest in Philadelphia? [At a Quaker meeting.]

Peer Assessment Have students evaluate the questions written by student groups in the Cooperative Learning activity on p. T90. Have them write their comments in a chart like the following.

Criteria	Comments
Examines significant ideas	
Requires textual support	
Makes personal connections	

In the various enumerations of the moral virtues I had met with in my reading, I found the catalog more or less numerous, as different writers included more or fewer ideas under the same name. Temperance, for example, was by some confined to eating and drinking, while by others it was extended to mean the moderating every other pleasure, appetite, inclination, or passion, bodily or mental, even to our avarice and ambition. I proposed to myself, for the sake of clearness, to use rather more names, with fewer ideas annexed to each, than a few names with more ideas; and I included under thirteen names of virtues all that at that time occurred to me as necessary or desirable, and annexed to each a short precept, which fully expressed the extent I gave to its meaning.

These names of virtues, with their precepts, were:

1. *Temperance. Eat not to dullness; drink not to elevation.*
2. *Silence. Speak not but what may benefit others or yourself; avoid trifling conversation.*
3. *Order. Let all your things have their places; let each part of your business have its time.*
4. *Resolution. Resolve to perform what you ought; perform without fail what you resolve.*
5. *Frugality. Make no expense but to do good to others or yourself; i.e., waste nothing.*
6. *Industry. Lose no time; be always employed in something useful; cut off all unnecessary actions.*
7. *Sincerity. Use no hurtful deceit; think innocently and justly, and, if you speak, speak accordingly.*
8. *Justice. Wrong none by doing injuries, or omitting the benefits that are your duty.*
9. *Moderation. Avoid extremes; forbear resenting injuries so much as you think they deserve.*
10. *Cleanliness. Tolerate no uncleanliness in body, clothes, or habitation.*
11. *Tranquility. Be not disturbed at trifles, or at accidents common or unavoidable.*
12. *Chastity. Rarely use venery*[14] *but for health or offspring, never to dullness, weakness, or the injury of your own or another's peace or reputation.*
13. *Humility. Imitate Jesus and Socrates.*[15] C

My intention being to acquire the *habitude* of all these virtues, I judged it would be well not to distract my attention by attempting the whole at once, but to fix it on one of them at a time; and, when I should be master of that, then to proceed to another, and so on, till I should have gone through the thirteen; and, as the previous acquisition of some might facilitate the acquisition of certain others, I arranged them with that view, as they stand above. D *Temperance* first, as it tends to procure that coolness and clearness of head, which is so necessary where constant vigilance was to be kept up, and guard maintained against the unremitting attraction of ancient habits, and the force of perpetual temptations. This being acquired and established, *silence* would be more easy; and my desire being to gain knowledge at the same time that I improved in virtue, and considering that in conversation it was obtained rather by the use of the ears than of the tongue, and therefore wishing to break a habit I was getting into of prattling, punning, and joking, which only made me acceptable to trifling company, I gave *silence*

14. venery (ven'ər·ē): sex.
15. Socrates (säk'rə·tēz') (470–399 B.C.): Greek philosopher. He is said to have lived a simple, virtuous life.

WORDS TO OWN
facilitate (fə·sil'ə·tāt') *v.:* simplify.

C. Literary Element: Irony

? Can you find any irony in Franklin's virtue number thirteen? [Possible answer: A humble man might be presumptuous in thinking he could "imitate Jesus and Socrates."]

D. Critical Reading: Making Inferences

? What do you learn about Franklin from his plan for moral development? [He is very diligent and orderly, attempts to control emotional behavior with reason, and is organized and logical.]

A. Expansion

Pythagoras attracted a number of disciples who followed rigorous ascetic practices intended to perfect the soul. Franklin's reference to Pythagoras's advice relates to the daily effort to perfect these virtues. Pythagoras's moral teaching contained many specific rules, some of which may have seemed arbitrary or ambiguous to the disciples. Questioning followers were answered with the famous reply *autos epha,* meaning "He (himself) has said it." The Latin words *ipse dixit,* translated from the Greek, have come to refer to any arbitrary or dogmatic statement.

B. Reader's Response: Connecting with the Text

? Who in our culture today might be considered similar to Franklin? What are their similarities and differences? [Sample responses: Self-help writers, evangelists, psychologists, or theologians. They attempt to help people learn to conduct virtuous lives, or they help people examine life.]

the second place. This and the next, *order,* I expected would allow me more time for attending to my project and my studies. *Resolution,* once become habitual, would keep me firm in my endeavors to obtain all the subsequent virtues; *frugality* and *industry* freeing me from my remaining debt, and producing affluence and independence, would make more easy the practice of *sincerity* and *justice,* etc., etc. Conceiving then, that, agreeably **A** to the advice of Pythagoras[16] in his Golden Verses, daily examination would be necessary, I contrived the following method for conducting that examination.

I made a little book, in which I allotted a page for each of the virtues. I ruled each page with red ink, so as to have seven columns, one for each day of the week, marking each column with a letter for the day. I crossed these columns with thirteen red lines, marking the beginning of each line with the first letter of one of the virtues, on which line, and in its proper column, I might mark, by a little black spot, every fault I found upon examination to have been committed respecting that virtue upon that day.

I determined to give a week's strict attention to each of the virtues successively. Thus, in the first week, my great guard was to avoid every[17] the least offense against *temperance,* leaving the other virtues to their ordinary chance, only marking every evening the faults of the day. Thus, if in the first week I could keep my first line, marked T, clear of spots, I supposed the habit of that virtue so much strengthened, and its opposite weakened, that I might venture extending my attention to include the next, and for the following week keep both lines clear of spots. Proceeding thus to the last, I could go through a course complete in thirteen weeks, and four courses in a year. And like him who, having a garden to weed, does not attempt to eradicate all the bad herbs at

Form of the Pages

Temperance							
Eat not to dullness. Drink not to elevation.							
	S	*M*	*T*	*W*	*T*	*F*	*S*
T							
S							
O							
R							
F							
I							
S							
J							
M							
Cl							
T							
Ch							
H							

once, which would exceed his reach and his strength, but works on one of the beds at a time, and, having accomplished the first, proceeds to a second, so I should have, I hoped, **B** the encouraging pleasure of seeing on my pages the progress I made in virtue, by clearing successively my lines of their spots, till in the end, by a number of courses, I should be happy in viewing a clean book, after a thirteen weeks' daily examination. . . .

16. **Pythagoras** (pi·thag′ə·rəs): Greek philosopher and mathematician of the sixth century B.C.
17. **every:** archaic for "even."

Words to Own

subsequent (sub′si·kwənt) *adj.:* following.
eradicate (i·rad′i·kāt′) *v.:* to eliminate.

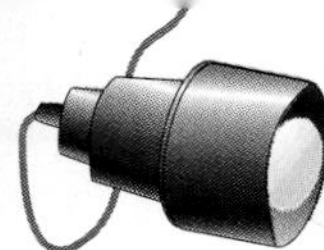

SPOTLIGHT ON

Sayings of Poor Richard

Panel from an engraving for Benjamin Franklin's *Poor Richard Illustrated* (c. 1800).

The Granger Collection, New York.

Poor Richard's Almanack was Franklin's biggest publishing success, and it continued to appear for over twenty-five years. Every house had an almanac. Almanacs calculated the tides and the phases of the moon, claimed to forecast the weather for the next year, and even provided astrological advice for those who believed in it. Many almanacs also supplied recipes, jokes, and **aphorisms.** "Poor Richard" was an imaginary astrologer, who had a critical wife named Bridget. One year Bridget wrote the maxims, to answer those her husband had written the year before on female idleness. Once, Bridget included better weather forecasts so that women would know the good days for drying their clothes. (A)

Franklin took Poor Richard's wit and wisdom where he found it—from old sayings in other languages, from other writers, and from popular adages. He never hesitated to rework the texts to suit his own purposes. For example, for the 1758 almanac, Franklin skimmed all his previous editions to compose a single speech on economy. This speech, called "The Way to Wealth," has become one of the best known of Franklin's works. It has been mistakenly believed to be representative of Poor Richard's wisdom. Poor Richard often called for prudence and thrift, but he just as often favored extravagance.

1. Love your neighbor; yet don't pull down your hedge.
2. If a man empties his purse into his head, no man can take it away from him. An investment in knowledge always pays the best interest.
3. Three may keep a secret if two of them are dead.
4. Tart words make no friends; a spoonful of honey will catch more flies than a gallon of vinegar.
5. Glass, china, and reputation are easily cracked and never well mended.
6. Fish and visitors smell in three days.
7. He that lieth down with dogs shall rise up with fleas.
8. One today is worth two tomorrows.
9. A truly great man will neither trample on a worm nor sneak to an emperor.
10. A little neglect may breed mischief; for want of a nail the shoe was lost; for want of a shoe the horse was lost; for want of a horse the rider was lost; for want of the rider the battle was lost.
11. If you would know the value of money, go and try to borrow some; he that goes a-borrowing goes a-sorrowing.
12. He that composes himself is wiser than he that composes books.
13. He that is of the opinion that money will do everything may well be suspected of doing everything for money.
14. If a man could have half his wishes, he would double his troubles.
15. 'Tis hard for an empty bag to stand upright.
16. A small leak will sink a great ship.
17. A plowman on his legs is higher than a gentleman on his knees.
18. Keep your eyes wide open before marriage, half shut afterward.
19. Nothing brings more pain than too much pleasure; nothing more bondage than too much liberty.

(B) (C)

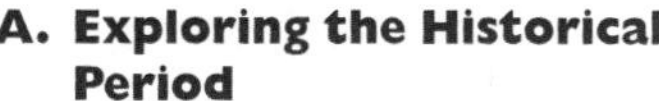

A. Exploring the Historical Period

To give students an idea of the personality Franklin originally created for Richard Saunders, read part of the preface to the first *Poor Richard's Almanack* in 1733.

> COURTEOUS READER,
> . . . The plain truth of the matter is, I am excessive poor, and my wife, good woman, is, I tell her, excessive proud; she cannot bear, she says, to sit spinning in her shift of tow, while I do nothing but gaze at the stars; and has threatened more than once to burn all my books and rattling-traps, (as she calls my instruments,) if I do not make some profitable use of them for the good of my family.

B. Reader's Response: Connecting with the Text

? What kind of person might you become if you lived by all these maxims? Consider your personal virtue, yourself in relation to others, and yourself in relation to material goods. [Sample responses: Maybe I would be wealthy or at least have more money. Or trying to live by of all of these maxims would drive me crazy.]

C. Critical Reading: Analyzing the Aphorisms

? Do you think Poor Richard would agree or disagree with the following statements? (a) Even close friends need some privacy from each other. [Agree] (b) Live for tomorrow. [Disagree] (c) May all your wishes come true. [Disagree] (d) There is dignity in hard work. [Agree] (e) Beauty is in the eye of the beholder. [Agree] (f) A mind is a terrible thing to waste. [Agree]

STRATEGIES FOR INCLUSION

Special Needs To give students who have difficulty speaking an opportunity to demonstrate their comprehension of the selection without having to make an oral presentation, have them create road signs depicting one or more of Poor Richard's sayings. Discuss and, if possible, bring in samples of road signs such as Stop, Yield, or Do Not Enter. For example, students could illustrate maxim #7 with a triangular sign, similar to a Yield sign, on which is pictured a pillow beside a sleeping dog, with a man standing near scratching at a multitude of tiny but visible fleas all over his body. Ask students to display their signs to the class and to talk about how they arrived at making their signs.

INTEGRATING THE LANGUAGE ARTS

Language and Style To clear up for students any confusion caused by the parallel structure of many maxims, explain the structure of one or two of the maxims. For instance, maxim #12 uses the word *composes* in its two clauses. To some students, the meanings—composing oneself and composing or writing a book—will be clear. Other students may need help in understanding that *composes* is a metaphor for developing one's life as carefully as one would write a book. *Compose* in the first part of the sentence also has a second meaning: "to make oneself calm."

A. Critical Reading: Finding Main Ideas

? What is Fulghum's main point? [Possible answer: That although life seems complex, basic values need not be complicated.]

B. Reader's Response: Challenging the Text

? Which of these maxims do you agree with? disagree with? [Sample responses: Not hitting people sounds good; violence starts wars. Or not everyone needs a nap every afternoon.]

Connections

AN ESSAY

Behind Ben Franklin's project for achieving moral perfection lies what seems to be a common human impulse—the need to simplify life, to get at the root of what's fundamental to us. In 1986, Robert Fulghum (fo͝ol'jum) published some thoughts of his own about how to live a full and happy life, in a best-selling book called *All I Really Need to Know I Learned in Kindergarten.*

from All I Really Need to Know I Learned in Kindergarten

Robert Fulghum

Each spring, for many years, I have set myself the task of writing a personal statement of belief: a Credo. When I was younger, the statement ran for many pages, trying to cover every base, with no loose ends. It sounded like a Supreme Court brief, as if words could resolve all conflicts about the meaning of existence.

The Credo has grown shorter in recent years—sometimes cynical, sometimes comical, sometimes bland—but I keep working at it. Recently I set out to get the statement of personal belief down to one page in simple terms, fully understanding the naïve idealism that implied. . . .

(A) I realized then that I already know most of what's necessary to live a meaningful life—that it isn't all that complicated. *I know it.* And have known it for a long, long time. Living it—well, that's another matter, yes? Here's my Credo:

All I really need to know about how to live and what to do and how to be I learned in kindergarten. Wisdom was not at the top of the graduate-school mountain, but there in the sandpile at Sunday School. These are the things I learned:

Share everything.
Play fair.
Don't hit people.
Put things back where you found them.
Clean up your own mess.
Don't take things that aren't yours.
Say you're sorry when you hurt somebody.
Wash your hands before you eat.
Flush.
Warm cookies and cold milk are good for you.
Live a balanced life—learn some and think some and draw and paint and sing and dance and play and work every day some.
(B) Take a nap every afternoon.
When you go out into the world, watch out for traffic, hold hands, and stick together.
Be aware of wonder. Remember the little seed in the Styrofoam cup: The roots go down and the plant goes up and nobody really knows how or why, but we are all like that.
Goldfish and hamsters and white mice and even the little seed in the Styrofoam cup—they all die. So do we.
And then remember the Dick-and-Jane books and the first word you learned—the biggest word of all—LOOK.

. . . Think what a better world it would be if we all—the whole world—had cookies and milk about three o'clock every afternoon and then lay down with our blankies for a nap. Or if all governments had as a basic policy to always put things back where they found them and to clean up their own mess.

And it is still true, no matter how old you are—when you go out into the world, it is best to hold hands and stick together.

CONNECTING WITH *THE AUTOBIOGRAPHY* AND *POOR RICHARD'S ALMANACK*

In *The Autobiography* Franklin reveals his attempt to achieve moral perfection and delineates the virtues he worked to acquire. In *Poor Richard's Almanack* Franklin condenses the wisdom he has attained over the years, while in *All I Really Need to Know I Learned in Kindergarten* Fulghum returns to the sagacity of his childhood. Both Franklin and Fulghum look inside themselves and examine not just their own lives, but life in general. Ask students to share the wisdom they have received from their elders and to reflect on what they themselves learned in kindergarten. Students could also reflect on more immediate experiences and share what they have learned about life in the past year. *Remind students to chose situations they would not mind sharing with others.* Ask them to note what differences and similarities they see between the wisdom that people acquire with age and the knowledge that children have. Invite students to add to this wealth of knowledge by examining what lessons Bradstreet, Taylor, and Edwards would contribute.

Making Meanings

First Thoughts

1. If you had to name one character trait that you think made Franklin a success, what would it be? Review the chart you made in your Reader's Log to help you decide.

Reviewing the Text

a. Why did Franklin decide to leave Boston secretly? How did he raise money for the journey from Boston to New York?
b. Today the trip from Boston to Philadelphia on a comfortable train takes five hours. Trace the stages of Franklin's journey to Philadelphia.
c. What was Franklin's condition in life when he arrived in Philadelphia?
d. What virtue does Franklin place first on his list for achieving moral perfection? Why?

Shaping Interpretations

2. Franklin examines his actions and motives, discussing them at length throughout the *Autobiography.* Yet many of his personality traits are revealed through his actions, not through direct statements. What does the difficult journey from Boston to Philadelphia reveal about the **character** of young Franklin?
3. What does Franklin's project for moral perfection reveal about his views of human nature and his attitudes toward education? Do you agree or disagree with his views?
4. Franklin ends his list of virtues with "humility." Did you find evidence of pride—the opposite of humility—in his history? If so, where?
5. Which virtue on Franklin's list do you think is most important? least important? Why?

Connecting with the Text

6. Franklin resolves to acquire certain virtues through which he believes he will improve himself. Think of one of your own past resolutions, perhaps one you made on a New Year's Eve. Were you able to keep it? Do you think making a resolution, as Franklin did, is a productive way of improving oneself? Explain.

Extending the Text

7. Compare Robert Fulghum's list of things learned in kindergarten (Connections, page 96) to Franklin's list of virtues and their precepts. Which list, in general, do you think would apply more broadly to people today? In general, how does Franklin's scheme for arriving at moral perfection compare with self-help books available today?

Challenging the Text

8. Reactions to Franklin's *Autobiography* have sometimes been negative. Read the following comment by Mark Twain. Based on Twain's **tone,** how does Twain feel about Franklin? Do you agree or disagree with Twain's assessment? Why?

> [Franklin had] a malevolence which is without parallel in history; he would work all day and then sit up nights and let on to be studying algebra by the light of a smoldering fire, so that all the boys might have to do that also, or else have Benjamin Franklin thrown upon them. Not satisfied with these proceedings, he had a fashion of living wholly on bread and water, and studying astronomy at mealtime—a thing which has brought affliction to millions of boys since, whose fathers had read Franklin's pernicious biography.
>
> —Mark Twain

9. As we read any **autobiography,** we have to ask ourselves if the writer is creating a character called "Myself," the same way that a novelist creates a fictional character. Has Franklin, the great inventor, invented an idealized version of himself in his autobiography? In other words, is he trying to make himself look good? Or do you think he is presenting himself just as he really was, warts and all? Explain and justify your opinion.

Making Meanings

First Thoughts

1. Possible responses: Intelligence or sense of humor.

Reviewing the Text

a. He feels that his brother and father will prevent him from departing if he tries to leave openly. He sells some of his books.
b. He sets out from Boston for New York in a boat and arrives three days later. He travels to Philadelphia by way of Amboy in a ship, whose sails are torn in a squall. The ship is driven toward Long Island. The water is too rough for them to land, so the passengers wait in the boat all night. They reach Amboy in thirty hours. Continuing to Philadelphia, he takes a ferry in the morning and then proceeds on foot. At noon he stops at an inn. The next morning he proceeds on foot and reaches an inn eight to ten miles from Burlington. The following morning he reaches Burlington and that evening boards a boat that he helps row to Philadelphia, arriving the next morning.
c. He wears dirty work clothes, their pockets bulging with shirts and stockings; he is tired and hungry and has only a little money.
d. Temperance; it guards against succumbing to old habits and temptations.

Shaping Interpretations

2. Possible responses: Franklin's saving the man during the storm reveals that he is quick-thinking; his curing himself of a fever reveals that he attends to his reading and is practical and self-reliant; his speed in locating lodgings when he misses the boat to Philadelphia reveals that he is resourceful and personable.
3. He believes that human beings are capable of improving themselves. Franklin believes education should be methodically organized and planned. Students may agree or disagree.
4. Some students will agree that Franklin is disarmingly direct and that he does not hesitate to criticize his own feelings when he feels he deserves such criticism.
5. Possible responses: Justice is most important because injustice is wrongdoing. Humility is least; you cannot get ahead without talking about your good points. Students may agree or disagree but should support their views.

Connecting with the Text

6. Students will probably agree that resolutions are a productive way of improving oneself.

Extending the Text

7. **(Evaluation)** Possible responses: Fulghum's list is more in keeping with today's emphasis on virtue in social relationships over personal virtue. The lists have in common a concern for orderliness and justice.

Challenging the Text

8. **(Analysis** and **Evaluation)** Some will say Twain's ironic tone suggests he admires Franklin, for Twain imposes a playful purpose for Franklin's actions: making others look bad. Others will say Twain dislikes Franklin, for generations of fathers have made their sons work hard and eat poorly so that they may grow up to be like Franklin.
9. **(Evaluation)** Some will say that Franklin idealizes himself when he writes of his attempts to achieve moral excellence. Others will say that he reveals his warts when he writes of the humorous picture he makes after leaving the bakery.

Choices: Building Your Portfolio

1. **Writer's Notebook** Remind students to save their work. They may use it as prewriting for the Writer's Workshop on p. 130. Have students first think of an achievement they are proud of, and then the most important character trait that enabled them to achieve that success.
2. **Critical Writing** Demonstrate for students how to set up their comparison in a chart.

	Edwards	Franklin
Goals		
Reasons		
Means		

3. **Critical Writing** Ask students to devise their own criteria for evaluating their progress. Have them include the criteria in their report.
4. **Crossing the Curriculum: Science** Suggest students first decide the genre they will use. Let that choice guide their research as they consider purpose and audience.
5. **Critical Writing** Advise students that a proposal is a plan presented for consideration that will be accepted or rejected. Give students suggestions for appropriate formats. Also, discuss audience and tone, so that students will consciously decide what types of appeals to use in their writing.
6. **Creative Writing** Students may want to develop a persona for their almanac, as Franklin did for his. If so, encourage them to use their imaginations to invent one or two characters who give a central tone and theme to the almanac.
7. **Research/Art** Suggest that students consider as additional sources for content the sayings and injunctions of family members and other people they know.

CHOICES: Building Your Portfolio

Writer's Notebook

1. Collecting Ideas for an Autobiographical Incident

WORK IN PROGRESS

A favorite question of job interviewers and college admissions officers is "What do you regard as your greatest strength?" Identify the character trait in yourself that you consider the most important or most valuable, and freewrite about an incident that demonstrated this trait in action. Did this aspect of your personality contribute to your success at something? Keep your notes for possible use in the Writer's Workshop on page 130.

Critical Writing

2. Puritan Heirs

Re-read the selection from Jonathan Edwards (page 77), and write a brief essay in which you compare and contrast the Puritan preacher with Ben Franklin. Consider the following when writing your essay: (a) each man's goals in life; (b) his reasons for having these goals; and (c) the means by which he achieves his goals. Be sure to cite at least one way in which these two Americans, both heirs of the Puritan tradition, are alike.

Critical Writing

3. Virtually Virtuous

Develop your own list of virtues and accompanying precepts. (You don't need as many as Franklin outlined, but you should have at least seven.) Then create your own "book of virtues," patterned after Franklin's own (page 94). For one week, keep daily track of your "progress in virtue." (Unlike Franklin, you'll be keeping track of all the virtues simultaneously, not successively.) At the end of a week, write a brief report on how well the "book of virtues" worked for you. What did you learn? Is this a habit you'd like to continue?

Crossing the Curriculum: Science

4. Scientific Minds

Research either Benjamin Franklin's or Benjamin Banneker's (page 90) contributions to science and invention. What were their greatest accomplishments? What was the most surprising discovery each man made? Present your findings about either man's scientific interests, methods, and discoveries in one of the following forms: a written or oral report; a comic strip; a script for a documentary; or a story for children.

Critical Writing

5. Yes, But Will It Sell?

Write a proposal to the editor in chief of a publishing company, persuading him or her that Franklin's *Autobiography* should be published in a special new edition and marketed as a self-help book. Using quotes from the *Autobiography*, give specific reasons why people today can still learn from Franklin.

Creative Writing

6. Almanac Attack

As a class, create an almanac that covers a one-month period. Include forecasts, special school and community events, and your own original maxims, jokes, and recipes.

Research / Art

7. Words from the Wise

Research **aphorisms** from Franklin and other sources (you might find some on bumper stickers and T-shirts) that you think would be especially helpful to high school students, and collect them in the form of a small booklet called "Words to Live By." You may use calligraphy, illustrations, or computer graphics to decorate your booklet.

Drawing by David Levine. Reprinted with permission from *The New York Review of Books*. Copyright © 1973 NYREV, Inc.

Justice Resolution Tranquility Frugality Order Cleanliness

PORTFOLIO ASSESSMENT

Choices: Assessment Criteria For help in evaluating these Choices assignments, see the criteria in the ***Portfolio Management System,*** pp. 74–75.

STRATEGIES FOR INCLUSION

Linguistic Students may benefit from using a tape recorder to prepare themselves for writing in any of these activities. Students may talk about the task they are attempting to complete, develop ideas, organize thoughts, try alternate ways of writing a sentence or paragraph, or deal with writing problems. Using a tape recorder will help them reflect on their own problem-solving processes.

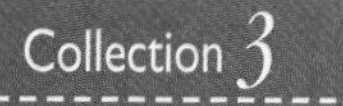

THE AMERICAN DREAM

Theme: **Words of Action**

The words of the writers who helped shape an emerging nation are the words that still define the American dream: liberty, equality, and justice.

Thematic Focus

The selections in Collection 3 illustrate how words define dreams.

- **Speech to the Virginia Convention** Patrick Henry urges his fellow representatives to rise and fight for liberty.
- *from* **The Crisis, No. 1** Thomas Paine exhorts his audience to battle the tyranny and injustice of British rule.
- *from* **The Autobiography: The Declaration of Independence** Thomas Jefferson describes the changes that Congress made to the original draft of the Declaration.

Literary Focus

Literary Element	Selection / Feature
Persuasion	**Speech to the Virginia Convention**
Style	**The Crisis, No. 1**
Parallelism	**The Autobiography: The Declaration of Independence**

Writing Focus

The following flow chart shows how the writing assignment for each selection relates to and builds toward the culminating writing assignment presented in the Writer's Workshop at the end of the unit.

Selection	Work-in-Progress Assignment
Speech to the Virginia Convention	Write about a turning point in life for an autobiographical incident p. 105
The Crisis, No. 1	Describe a team effort made for a common cause for an autobiographical incident p. 112
The Autobiography: The Declaration of Independence	Freewrite about the benefits and burdens of freedom for an autobiographical incident p. 125
Writer's Workshop	Write an autobiographical incident pp. 130–133

Collection 3 **THE AMERICAN DREAM**

Collection Planner

SELECTION / FEATURE	PUPIL'S EDITION			
	Literary Elements / Active Reading	Writing	Speaking and Listening	Language and Vocabulary
Speech to the Virginia Convention Patrick Henry (pp. 100–105)	• Reader's Log p. 101 • Persuasion p. 101	• Critical Writing: Write comparison-contrast essay p. 105	• Speaking and Listening: Deliver updated speech p. 105	
from **The Crisis, No. 1** Thomas Paine (pp. 106–112) Spotlight On: Phillis Wheatley (p. 113)	• Reader's Log p. 107 • Style p. 107	• Critical Writing: Write evaluative essay p. 112 • Creative Writing: Express feelings about Paine's words p. 112		
from **The Autobiography: The Declaration of Independence** Thomas Jefferson (pp. 114–125) Primary Sources: A Letter from Jefferson to His Daughter (p. 124)	• Reader's Log p. 115 • Parallelism p. 115	• Critical Writing: Respond to a letter p. 125	• Speaking and Listening: Conduct panel discussion p. 125	
The American Language "Revolutionary" English Gary Q. Arpin (pp. 127–129)				• Try It Out: Research word histories p. 129
Writer's Workshop: Autobiographical Incident (pp. 130–133)		• Writing process: Autobiographical incident pp. 130–133	• Evaluating and Revising: Discuss drafts in small groups p. 133	
Language Workshop: Coordinating Conjunctions (p. 134)				• Language Handbook: Combining by coordinating ideas p. 1238 • Coordinating conjunctions p. 134
Learning for Life: The Immigrant Experience (p. 135)		• Write multimedia script p. 135	• Present play p. 135	

Collection Resources

Teaching Resources A	Audiovisual Resources Binder	Test Booklet
Cross-Curricular Activity p. 58	Fine Art Transparency 3.1	Collection 3 Test pp. 33–35

 Computer disk or CD-ROM

 Audiocassette

Overhead Transparency

PROGRAM RESOURCES

Electronic Media	Teaching Resources with Organizer		Audiovisual Resources Binder
	Teaching Resources A	Other Resources	
• Language Workshop: Gerunds and gerund phrases • Test Generator	• Teaching Notes p. 43 • Reading Organizer p. 46 • Language Link pp. 47–48 • Words to Own p. 49	• Test Booklet: Selection Test pp. 25–26 • Language and Writing Skills Worksheets p. 74 • Portfolio Management System pp. 39, 76	• Selected Reading, Audiocassette 1, Side A • Elements of Literature Transparency 3.2
• Test Generator	• Teaching Notes p. 44 • Reading Organizer p. 50 • Words to Own p. 51	• Test Booklet: Selection Test pp. 27–28 • Portfolio Management System pp. 48–49, 77	• Selected Reading, Audiocassette 1, Side A
• Language Workshop: Infinitives and infinitive phrases • Test Generator	• Teaching Notes p. 45 • Reading Organizer p. 52 • Language Link pp. 53–54 • Words to Own p. 55	• Test Booklet: Selection Test pp. 29–30 • Language and Writing Skills Worksheets p. 75 • Portfolio Management System pp. 54–55, 78	
• Test Generator	• Teaching Notes p. 45	• Test Booklet: Selection Test pp. 31–32	
• Writer's Workshop 2: Autobiographical Incident		• Portfolio Management System pp. 79–81	• Revision Transparencies 3.3–3.4
• Language Workshop: Connective words and phrases	• Language Workshop pp. 56–57		
		• Portfolio Management System p. 82	

Proofreading Warm-ups

You may use the following exercises to help students practice their proofreading skills. Copy a set of incorrect sentences onto the chalkboard, and have students find and correct the spelling, punctuation, usage, and mechanical errors in each sentence. Ask students to share and discuss their responses.

	Sentences with Errors	Sentences Corrected	Skills Covered
1	**a.** the shot heard round the world is a famous line from Concord hymn **b.** its a poem about the Battle that marked the begining of the revolutionary war	**a.** "The shot heard round the world" is a famous line from "Concord Hymn." **b.** It's a poem about the battle that marked the beginning of the Revolutionary War.	Quotation marks, Capitalization, Apostrophe usage, Spelling, End marks
2	**a.** with the stamp act the British parliament levied taxes on all newspapers **b.** after he had gave a speach against the stamp act Henry was a figure in Virginia Politics	**a.** With the Stamp Act, the British Parliament levied taxes on all newspapers. **b.** After he gave a speech against the Stamp Act, Henry was a figure in Virginia politics.	Capitalization, Comma usage, Verb errors, Spelling, End marks
3	**a.** on march 23 1775 Henry delivered his speech to the Virginia House of Burgesses **b.** the house had met to deside how to respond to the british	**a.** On March 23, 1775, Henry delivered his speech to the Virginia House of Burgesses. **b.** The House had met to decide how to respond to the British.	Capitalization, Comma usage, Spelling, End marks
4	**a.** persuasion, a form of speaking or wrighting that aims to move to action **b.** Patrick Henrys speach defended his Resolution to take up arms against Britian	**a.** Persuasion is a form of speaking or writing that aims to move to action. **b.** Patrick Henry's speech defended his resolution to take up arms against Britain.	Capitalization, Comma usage/Sentence fragments, Spelling, Apostrophe usage, End marks
5	**a.** are most persuasive writter Paine lived in England for the first thirty seven years' of his life **b.** in january 1776 Paine published a pamphlet titled Common Sense	**a.** Our most persuasive writer, Paine, lived in England for the first thirty-seven years of his life. **b.** In January 1776, Paine published a pamphlet titled <u>Common Sense</u>.	Capitalization, Spelling, Comma usage, Hyphen usage, Apostrophe usage, Underline pamphlet titles, End marks
6	**a.** Thomas Paines Common Sense denounced King Geo. III **b.** he also wrote a series' of 16-pamphlets called the American Crisis	**a.** Thomas Paine's <u>Common Sense</u> denounced King George III. **b.** He also wrote a series of sixteen pamphlets called <u>The American Crisis</u>.	Apostrophe usage, Underline pamphlet titles, Write out abbreviations, Hyphen usage, Write out numerals, Capitalization, End marks
7	**a.** Phillis Wheatley, published her 1st poem when she was bearly thirteen **b.** alot of people including George Washington praised Wheatleys work	**a.** Phillis Wheatley published her first poem when she was barely thirteen. **b.** A lot of people, including George Washington, praised Wheatley's work.	Comma usage, Write out numerals, Spelling, Nonstandard usage, Apostrophe usage, End marks
8	**a.** Thomas Jefferson the brillaint 3rd President of the United States **b.** during the revolution Congress choose him to help draft the Declaration	**a.** Thomas Jefferson was the brilliant third president of the United States. **b.** During the Revolution, Congress chose him to help draft the Declaration.	Sentence fragment, Spelling, Write out numerals, Capitalization, End marks
9	**a.** did you no that 4 other writers worked with Jefferson on the Declaration asked Ms Harden **b.** Jefferson shows the deletions and insertions congress made to this famous Document she continued	**a.** "Did you know that four other writers worked with Jefferson on the Declaration?" asked Ms. Harden. **b.** "Jefferson shows the deletions and insertions Congress made to this famous document," she continued.	Quotation marks, Capitalization, Spelling, Write out numerals, Period with abbreviations, End marks
10	**a.** the advise in Jefferson's letter to his daughter remind's me of Benjamin Franklins self improvement program **b.** jefferson exhorts his daughter to develope the habit's of industry and activity	**a.** The advice in Jefferson's letter to his daughter reminds me of Benjamin Franklin's self-improvement program. **b.** Jefferson exhorts his daughter to develop the habits of industry and activity.	Capitalization, Spelling, Apostrophe usage, Hyphen usage, End marks

Collection 3 THE AMERICAN DREAM

Henry
Paine
Wheatley
Jefferson

Concord Hymn

By the rude bridge that arched the flood,
Their flag to April's breeze unfurled,
Here once the embattled farmers stood
And fired the shot heard round the world.

The foe long since in silence slept;
Alike the conqueror silent sleeps;
And Time the ruined bridge has swept
Down the dark stream which seaward creeps.

On this green bank, by this soft stream,
We set today a votive stone;
That memory may their deed redeem,
When, like our sires, our sons are gone.

Spirit, that made those heroes dare
To die, and leave their children free,
Bid Time and Nature gently spare
The shaft we raise to them and thee.

—Ralph Waldo Emerson (1803–1882)

"Concord Hymn"

? What role do deeds and heroes from the past play in your feelings about your civic duties, freedom, and the American dream? [Answers will vary. Let students freewrite in their Reader's Logs until their responses form. Invite students to create their own "Hymn" like Emerson's and allow volunteers to share theirs with the class.]

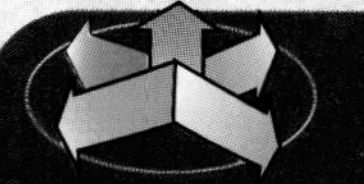

PROGRAM MANAGER

- **Integrated Assessment** For a summative assessment of the literature and language skills taught in this collection, see **Collection 3 Test, *Test Booklet,*** pp. 33–35.
- **Instructional Support** See **Fine Art Transparencies** 3.1. Review teacher's notes for transparencies in the ***Audiovisual Resources Binder*** for suggestions on how to tie the transparencies to specific reading selections.
- **Extending Collection Theme** See **Cross-Curricular Activity: The American Dream, *Teaching Resources A,*** p. 58, for activities in other disciplines and for evaluation criteria.

PORTFOLIO ASSESSMENT

Parent/Guardian Involvement For forms that will help a parent or guardian review and respond to a student's portfolio, see the ***Portfolio Management System,*** pp. 62–63.

QUICK PLANNING GUIDE

Into the Selection

Author Biography p. 100

Before You Read p. 101

- **Reading Focus:** Students note words that define the American dream.
- **A Dialogue with the Text:** Chart appeals to reason and emotion in Reader's Log
- **Elements of Literature: Persuasion**
- **Background: Scaffolding** Students imagine Henry's speech.

Through the Selection

"Speech to the Virginia Convention" pp. 102–104

Words to Own pp. 102–104

Making Meanings p. 105

Beyond the Selection

Choices: Building Your Portfolio p. 105

- **Writer's Notebook:** Write about decisive event
- **Critical Writing:** Compare and contrast Patrick Henry's and Jonathan Edwards's speeches
- **Speaking and Listening:** Recast speech with contemporary issues

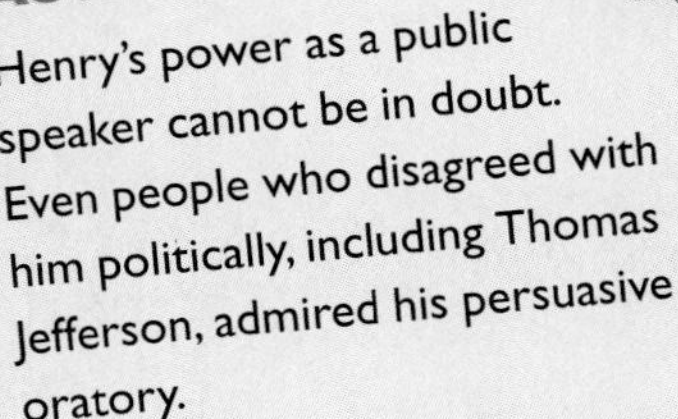

ABOUT THE AUTHOR

Henry's power as a public speaker cannot be in doubt. Even people who disagreed with him politically, including Thomas Jefferson, admired his persuasive oratory.

Patrick Henry

(1736–1799)

One fiery act can catapult someone from obscurity to fame. That is what happened to Patrick Henry, a young representative who stood up in the Virginia House of Burgesses one day in 1765. He delivered a dynamic, thundering speech against the hated Stamp Act, with which the British Parliament instituted taxes on all newspapers and public documents. For the ten years following his declaration of resistance, Henry—a tall, lank, somber-looking man who favored the kind of clothing a preacher might wear—was recognized as one of the most persuasive figures in Virginia politics.

Henry had not always been so successful. Born in a frontier region of Virginia, he was raised in a cultured but modest environment. During his youth the country was undergoing the religious revival known as the Great Awakening, and young Patrick often accompanied his mother to hear the sermons of the traveling preachers. Later, as a young man, he made several unsuccessful stabs at farming and merchant life before discovering his love of oratory and his true calling: the law.

In 1765, the twenty-nine-year-old lawyer was chosen to represent his region in the Virginia House of Burgesses. Henry's speech against the Stamp Act was the first of the two most famous speeches in American Colonial history. The second, his famous "liberty or death" speech, came ten years later in 1775 as the Colonies were nearing the breaking point with England. Following the Boston Tea Party in December 1773, the British had closed the port of Boston and inaugurated other harsh measures referred to by the colonists as the "Intolerable Acts." When the First Continental Congress protested these acts, the British Crown relieved the Colonies of taxation on a number of conditions. One condition was that the colonists fully support British rule and contribute toward the maintenance of British troops in America, whose numbers were increasing greatly. On March 20, 1775, the Virginia House of Burgesses held a convention in St. John's Episcopal Church in Richmond to decide how to respond to the growing British military threat. George Washington and Thomas Jefferson (page 114) were both present.

Patrick Henry (1820–1830). Anonymous. Oil on canvas. Shelburne Museum, Shelburne, Vermont. Photograph by Ken Burris.

On March 23, after several speeches in favor of compromise with the British, Patrick Henry rose to defend his resolution to take up arms. Later, a clergyman who was present recalled that during Henry's speech he felt "sick with excitement." As the speech reached its climax, Henry is said to have grabbed an ivory letter opener and plunged it toward his chest at the final word *death.*

Henry persuaded the delegation. The Virginia Convention voted to arm its people against England. On April 19, 1775, the Battle of Lexington, Massachusetts, ignited the Revolutionary War.

WORDS TO OWN

The following vocabulary words are defined in the Words to Own at the bottom of the pupil's page.

solace p. 102	spurned p. 104
insidious p. 102	inviolate p. 104
martial p. 104	adversary p. 104
supplication p. 104	vigilant p. 104
avert p. 104	inevitable p. 104

PORTFOLIO ASSESSMENT

Portfolio Assessment For help with self-assessment of reading skills, see the *Portfolio Management System,* p. 39.

Before You Read

Speech to the Virginia Convention

Reading Focus

Words into Actions

Words—acts of both thought and feeling—shape us; they are tools of self-making. We know now how much blood and suffering resulted from Henry's words "Give me liberty or give me death!" and what pride his impassioned cry continues to generate years after it was spoken. The "American dream," as we loosely call our aspirations toward freedom, self-reliance, and self-creation, is defined in large part by the words of the men and women who helped to shape America in its early years.

A Dialogue with the Text

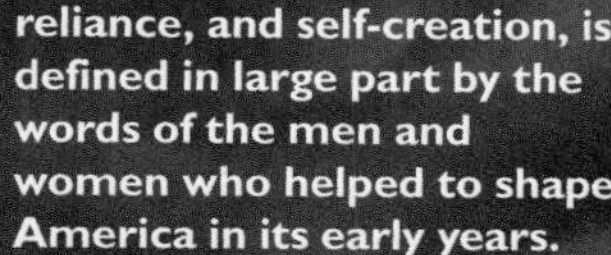

In a double-column chart, keep track of the two methods of Henry's appeal—reason and emotion. In one column, write down his reasons for wanting war, and in the other column write down his emotional appeals. How does Henry seize his listeners' feelings as he advances his arguments? Note which appeals have the strongest effect on you.

Elements of Literature

Persuasion

Persuasion is a form of speaking or writing that aims to move an audience to take a specific action. A good persuasive speaker or writer uses both head and heart—reasons and feelings, or logic and emotion—to win over an audience. To be successful at persuading an audience, a writer or speaker must provide reasons to support a particular opinion or course of action. In the final analysis, though, audiences are often won over not only by the force of the speaker's arguments but also by the power of his or her personality.

Persuasion is a form of discourse that uses reason and emotional appeals to convince another person to think or act in a certain way.

For more on Persuasion, see the Handbook of Literary Terms.

Background

The historian Garry Wills described Patrick Henry in this way: ". . . he had the actor's trick, in his oratory, of lifting his whole body up toward climaxes, along with his voice, as if he *could* add cubits by wanting to. . . . No one who beheld him incandescent with a Cause ever forgot the experience. . . ."

Although Henry's speech is one of the most famous in all American oratory, no manuscript of it exists. Henry's biographer, William Wirt, pieced together the traditionally accepted text forty years after it was delivered, using notes of people who were present at the speech. Thomas Jefferson (page 114) himself, who heard the original oration, read Wirt's text and suggested no changes. As you read Henry's speech, try to envision the physical surroundings of its delivery: an eighteenth-century church in Richmond, Virginia, on an early spring day. Try, also, to imagine how Henry delivered his speech.

Into the Selection

Using Before You Read p. 101

Reading Focus

Ask students to discuss what the "American dream" means to them. Note their responses on the chalkboard.

A Dialogue with the Text

Have students use a graphic organizer like the one below to keep track of Henry's appeals as they read:

Appeals

To Reason	To Emotion
[• truth • past conduct of British]	[• patriotic • urgency and danger • God]

Background

Have volunteers read from the speech, using the techniques described by Gary Wills. Then, have students discuss delivery techniques used by the volunteer speakers. Do students find any similarities to Henry?

Program Manager

- **Planning Instruction** See **Teaching Notes, *Teaching Resources A,*** p. 43, for more information for this selection.
- **Instructional Support** See **Graphic Organizer for Active Reading, *Teaching Resources A,*** p. 46, for a Through the Selection activity.
- **Audiotaped Readings** To help auditory learners, use the **Selected Reading, Audiocassette 1, Side A,** in the ***Audiovisual Resources Binder.***
- **Assessment** See **Selection Test, *Test Booklet,*** pp. 25–26.
- **Language Link** To review gerunds and gerund phrases, see **Language Link, *Teaching Resources A,*** pp. 47–48, and ***Language and Writing Skills Worksheets,*** p. 74.
- **Reinforcement** Use the **Words to Own** worksheet in ***Teaching Resources A,*** p. 49.

Through the Selection

A. Exploring the Historical Period
This speech was made in support of Henry's resolution calling for the formation of a local militia. Previous speakers had opposed the measure, arguing that it would provoke England to harsh actions. Although his listeners were moved by his speech, many minds remained unchanged; his resolution passed by a margin of only five votes.

B. Language Note: Fallacy
? What is the fallacy Henry uses in this statement? [He points out only two choices: freedom or slavery.]

C. Literary Element: Metaphor
? What metaphor does Henry use here? [Experience that guides him is likened to a lamp.]

D. Reader's Response: First Thoughts
? What is the effect of the series of questions and answers in this passage? [Sample responses: Questions and answers are helpful in holding the attention of an audience; or they create suspense.]

Speech to the Virginia Convention

Patrick Henry

Mr. President: No man thinks more highly than I do of the patriotism, as well as abilities, of the very worthy gentlemen who have just addressed the House. But different men often see the same subject in different lights; and, therefore, I hope that it will not be thought disrespectful to those gentlemen, if, entertaining as I do, opinions of a character very opposite to theirs, I shall speak forth my sentiments freely and without reserve. This is no time for ceremony. The question before the House is one of awful moment[1] to this country. For my own part I consider it as nothing less than a question of freedom or slavery; and in proportion to the magnitude of the subject ought to be the freedom of the debate. It is only in this way that we can hope to arrive at truth, and fulfill the great responsibility which we hold to God and our country. Should I keep back my opinions at such a time, through fear of giving offense, I should consider myself as guilty of treason toward my country, and of an act of disloyalty toward the majesty of heaven, which I revere above all earthly kings.

Mr. President, it is natural to man to indulge in the illusions of hope. We are apt to shut our eyes against a painful truth, and listen to the song of that siren, till she transforms us into beasts.[2] Is this the part of wise men, engaged in a great and arduous struggle for liberty? Are we disposed to be of the number of those who, having eyes, see not, and having ears, hear not, the things which so nearly concern their temporal salvation? For my part, whatever anguish of spirit it may cost, I am willing to know the whole truth; to know the worst and to provide for it.

I have but one lamp by which my feet are guided; and that is the lamp of experience. I know of no way of judging of the future but by the past. And judging by the past, I wish to know what there has been in the conduct of the British ministry for the last ten years, to justify those hopes with which gentlemen have been pleased to solace themselves and the House? Is it that insidious smile with which our petition[3] has been lately received? Trust it not, sir; it will prove a snare to your feet. Suffer not yourselves to be betrayed with a kiss. Ask yourselves how this gracious reception of our petition comports[4] with these warlike preparations which cover our waters and darken our land. Are fleets and armies necessary to a work of love and reconciliation? Have we shown ourselves so unwilling to be reconciled, that force must be called in to win back our love? Let us not deceive ourselves, sir. These are the implements of war and subjugation; the last arguments to which kings resort.

1. **awful moment:** great importance.
2. **listen . . . beasts:** In Greek mythology, the sirens are sea-maidens whose seductive singing lures men to wreck their boats on coastal rocks. In the *Odyssey*, an epic by the Greek poet Homer (c. eighth century B.C.), Circe, an enchanter, transforms Odysseus' men into swine after they arrive at her island home. Henry's allusion combines these two stories.
3. **our petition:** The First Continental Congress had recently protested against new tax laws. King George III had withdrawn the laws conditionally, but the colonists were unwilling to accept his conditions.
4. **comports:** agrees.

Words to Own
solace (säl′is) *v.:* to comfort.
insidious (in·sid′ē·əs) *adj.:* sly; sneaky.

OPTIONS FOR TEACHING

STRATEGIES FOR INCLUSION

Auditory Play the recording of Henry's speech, (Audiocassette 1, Side A, in the *Audiovisual Resources Binder*) to give students an idea of the tone, rhythm, and passion with which the speech was likely given. You may also want to play a recording of a modern speech by John F. Kennedy, Martin Luther King, Jr., or Franklin Delano Roosevelt. Have the class discuss their favorite speeches and reasons for preferring one over the other. Draw a cluster diagram of the speeches on the chalkboard, and make sure students record the clusters in their notebooks to use later for prewriting a speech.

INTEGRATING THE LANGUAGE ARTS

Strategic Reading Most students will have heard of Patrick Henry. Before they read the speech, ask them to predict what Henry will urge the Virginia Convention to do. To help students make predictions to compare with the actual speech, ask them to write predictions in the first column of a chart like the one below. After they have studied the speech, ask them to return to their predictions and to complete the second column. Encourage volunteers to read their entries.

My Prediction	Actual Outcome

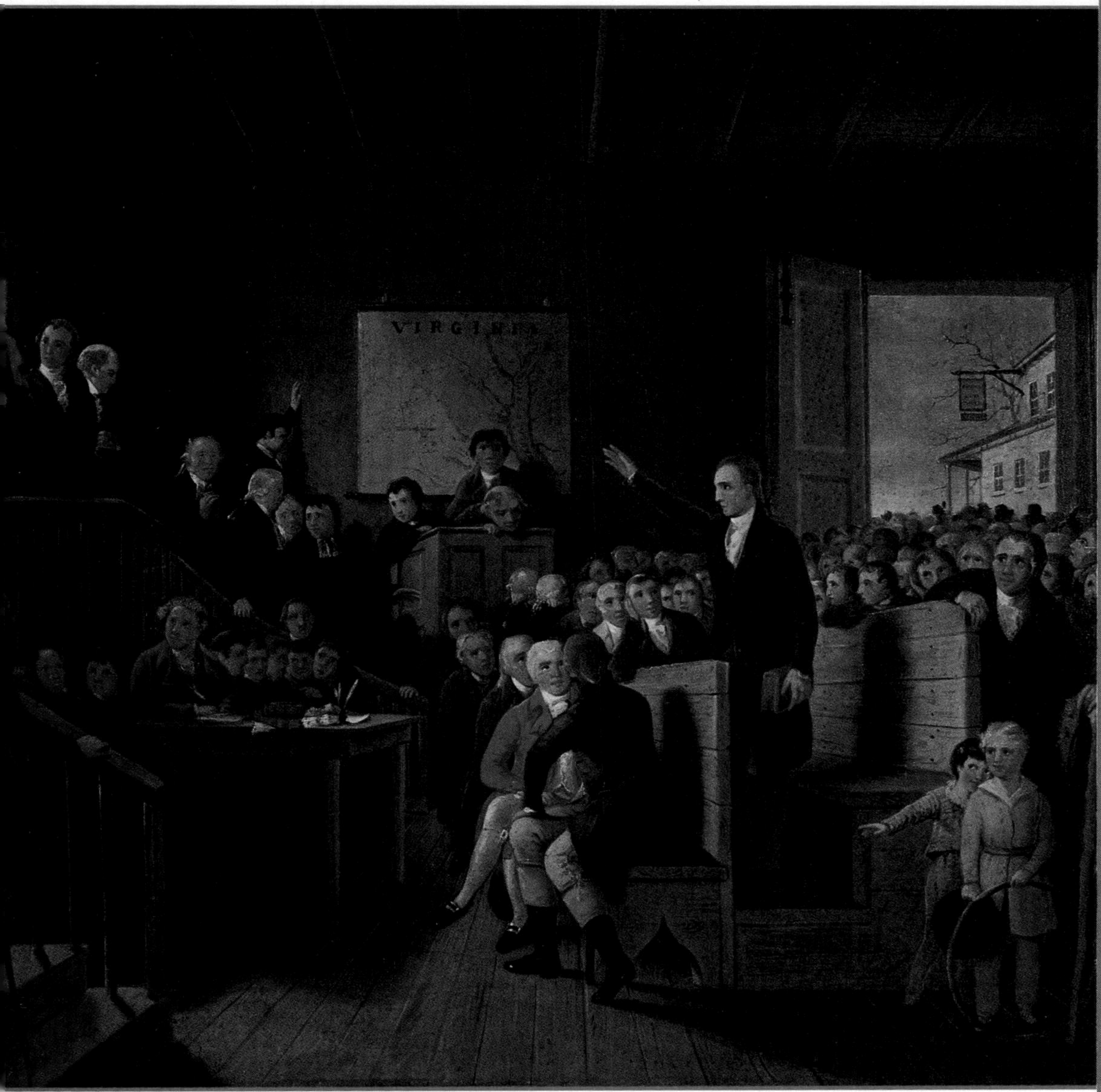

Patrick Henry Arguing the Parson's Cause (c. 1830), attributed to George Cooke. Oil on canvas.

Virginia Historical Society, Richmond, Virginia.

Technology Tip

The Discovery Channel, The Learning Channel, and the Public Broadcasting System have many documentary programs on the historical period of the American Revolution. Contact your local cable representative or television station for information on when such programs air. The Discovery Channel also maintains a World Wide Web site at **http ://www.discovery.com**. *You may want to preview any Internet activity before suggesting it to students. Because these resources are sometimes public forums, their content can be unpredictable.*

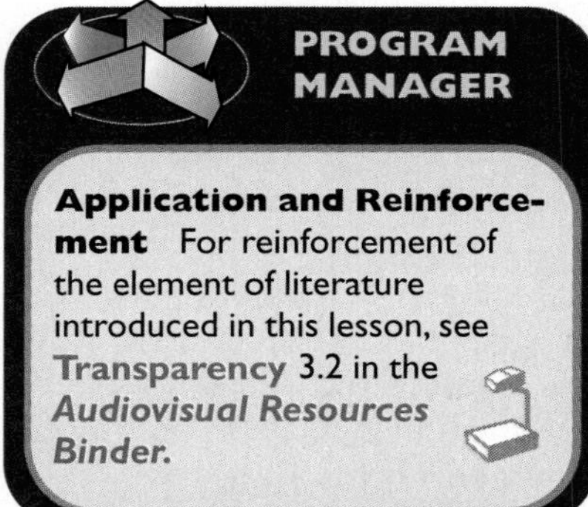

CROSSING THE CURRICULUM

Speech and Drama Have students work in small groups divided into two teams to debate the topic proposed in Henry's speech as if they were members of the Virginia Convention. Have the whole class vote on what course of action to take (if any).

Mathematics Have students work in pairs to research and create a bar graph on a poster showing (1) how much money the Virginia Convention allotted to arming its people, (2) what this amount equals in today's dollars, (3) the amount of Virginia's contributions to the maintenance of British troops in the United States, and (4) a comparison of Virginia's economy (net worth and growth) before and after the Revolution. Discuss whether the Revolutionary War was cost-effective.

ASSESSMENT TOOLS

Check Test: True-False

1. Patrick Henry may have been influenced by the sermons of Jonathan Edwards. [True]
2. Henry says that it would be disastrous to know the whole truth. [False]
3. At the time of the speech, the First Continental Congress had already assembled. [True]
4. Henry says that the only recourse for the colonists is to arm themselves. [True]
5. Henry assumes there will be four million colonists fighting against the British. [False]

A. Language Note: Style
Explain that a periodic sentence is one in which the main clause or some other essential grammatical element is postponed until the very end. Tell students that this device is often used in formal speeches. Have students recast this sentence, putting the main clause ("we must fight") first to compare the effect.

B. Literary Element: Persuasion
? Why is Henry's conclusion persuasive? [Possible answers: Henry shows that he is willing to risk his own death, not just the deaths of others. He implies that life is not worth living without freedom, so risking death in the cause of freedom is risking nothing.]

Making Meanings p. 105

First Thoughts

1. Responses will vary. Students will probably suggest that the most famous lines are the most powerful.

Reviewing the Text

The main idea is that if colonists do not act immediately to protect their freedoms, they will lose them completely.

Shaping Interpretations

2. Henry compares the British threat to a coming storm. He compares the fight of the Colonists against the British to the wars of the ancient Israelites.
3. The series of questions occurs near the middle of the paragraph.

   It is rhetorically more effective to let the audience members draw their own conclusions. Provided that they answer the questions in a certain way, Henry will be able to count on their support, since their answers are their *own* opinions.

Extending the Text

4. **(Synthesis) a.** Henry's point is that illusory hopes are like the sirens and the beautiful Circe in Homer's *Odyssey,* who were attractive on the surface but destructive in reality. Henry urges his listeners not to surrender their freedom in exchange for false hopes of peace. Students will probably agree that this allusion, like Henry's others, might have equal relevance to some situations today.

   b. The allusion to the Bible is a graceful, but pointed, way for Henry to remind his listeners that they must not be like the heedless people whom the prophet upbraided in ancient Israel.

   c. The allusion is to the disloyal apostle Judas. Henry warns his listeners not to heed the apparently mild British reaction to the Colonists' petition against the new taxation laws.

I ask gentlemen, sir, what means this martial array, if its purpose be not to force us to submission? Can gentlemen assign any other possible motives for it? Has Great Britain any enemy, in this quarter of the world, to call for all this accumulation of navies and armies? No, sir, she has none. They are meant for us; they can be meant for no other. They are sent over to bind and rivet upon us those chains which the British ministry have been so long forging. And what have we to oppose to them? Shall we try argument? Sir, we have been trying that for the last ten years. Have we anything new to offer on the subject? Nothing. We have held the subject up in every light of which it is capable; but it has been all in vain. Shall we resort to entreaty and humble supplication? What terms shall we find which have not been already exhausted? Let us not, I beseech you, sir, deceive ourselves longer. Sir, we have done everything that could be done, to avert the storm which is now coming on. We have petitioned; we have remonstrated; we have supplicated; we have prostrated ourselves before the throne, and have implored its interposition[5] to arrest the tyrannical hands of the ministry and Parliament. Our petitions have been slighted; our remonstrances have produced additional violence and insult; our supplications have been disregarded; and we have been spurned, with contempt, from the foot of the throne. In vain, after these things, may we indulge the fond[6] hope of peace and reconciliation. There is no longer any room for hope. If we wish to be free—if we mean to preserve inviolate those inestimable privileges for which we have been so long contending—if we mean not basely to abandon the noble struggle in which we have been so long engaged, and which we have pledged ourselves never to abandon until the glorious object of our contest shall be obtained, we must fight! I repeat it, sir, we must fight! An appeal to arms and to the God of Hosts is all that is left us!

They tell us, sir, that we are weak; unable to cope with so formidable an adversary. But when shall we be stronger? Will it be the next week, or the next year? Will it be when we are totally disarmed, and when a British guard shall be stationed in every house? Shall we gather strength by irresolution and inaction? Shall we acquire the means of effectual resistance, by lying supinely on our backs, and hugging the delusive phantom of hope, until our enemies shall have bound us hand and foot? Sir, we are not weak, if we make a proper use of the means which the God of nature hath placed in our power. Three millions of people, armed in the holy cause of liberty, and in such a country as that which we possess, are invincible by any force which our enemy can send against us. Besides, sir, we shall not fight our battles alone. There is a just God who presides over the destinies of nations; and who will raise up friends to fight our battles for us. The battle, sir, is not to the strong alone; it is to the vigilant, the active, the brave. Besides, sir, we have no election.[7] If we were base enough to desire it, it is now too late to retire from the contest. There is no retreat, but in submission and slavery! Our chains are forged! Their clanking may be heard on the plains of Boston! The war is inevitable—and let it come! I repeat it, sir, let it come!

It is in vain, sir, to extenuate the matter. Gentlemen may cry peace, peace—but there is no peace. The war is actually begun! The next gale that sweeps from the north will bring to our ears the clash of resounding arms! Our brethren are already in the field! Why stand we here idle? What is it that gentlemen wish? What would they have? Is life so dear, or peace so sweet, as to be purchased at the price of chains and slavery? Forbid it, Almighty God! I know not what course others may take; but as for me, give me liberty, or give me death!

5. **interposition:** intervention; stepping in to try to solve the problem.
6. **fond:** foolishly optimistic.
7. **election:** choice.

WORDS TO OWN
martial (mär′shəl) *adj.:* warlike.
supplication (sup′lə·kā′shən) *n.:* earnest plea.
avert (ə·vʉrt′) *v.:* to prevent; turn away.
spurned (spʉrnd) *v.:* rejected.
inviolate (in·vī′ə·lit) *adj.:* uncorrupted.
adversary (ad′vər·ser′ē) *n.:* opponent.
vigilant (vij′ə·lənt) *adj.* used as *n.:* watchful.
inevitable (in·ev′i·tə·bəl) *adj.:* not avoidable.

MAKING MEANINGS

First Thoughts

Reviewing the Text
What is the **main idea** of Henry's speech?

1. Review your Reader's Log notes. How did Henry's speech affect you? Were you more affected by his appeals to reason or his appeals to emotion?

Shaping Interpretations

2. In paragraph four, what **metaphors** does Henry use to describe the coming war?
3. Henry makes use of the **rhetorical question**—a question that is asked for effect. Rhetorical questions, which are often used in **persuasion,** presume the audience agrees with the speaker on the answers, and so no answer is expected or required. Find a series of rhetorical questions in the fifth paragraph of this speech. Why do you think Henry uses this device, rather than straightforward statements of fact, to make his points? How does this technique make his speech more persuasive?

Extending the Text

4. Because Henry's audience knew the Bible, as well as classical mythology, the orator knew he could count on certain **allusions** to have emotional effects. Look up the classical or Biblical passages Henry alludes to in each of the following statements from his speech. How would each allusion relate to the conflict in Virginia in 1775? Could any of them relate to life today? Explain.
   a. "We are apt to . . . listen to the song of that siren, till she transforms us into beasts." (*Odyssey,* Books 10 and 12)
   b. "Are we disposed to be of the number of those who, having eyes, see not, and having ears, hear not the things which so nearly concern their temporal salvation?" (Ezekiel 12:2)
   c. "Suffer not yourselves to be betrayed with a kiss." (Luke 22:47–48)

CHOICES: Building Your Portfolio

Writer's Notebook

1. Collecting Ideas for an Autobiographical Incident

WORK IN PROGRESS

Write about an action you took or a particular time in your life that seems like a turning point—a decisive period that helped define the person you are today. Save your notes for possible use in the Writer's Workshop on page 130.

Critical Writing

2. Politician and Preacher

Compare and contrast Henry's speech with Jonathan Edwards's sermon "Sinners in the Hands of an Angry God" (page 79). Consider the specific ways in which the speeches are alike and how they are different. Use the following chart to help organize your material.

	Edwards	Henry
Speaker's purpose and audience		
Main idea		
Appeals to reason and emotion		
Use of rhetorical questions and other literary devices		
Overall effectiveness		

Speaking and Listening

3. A Call to Action

Recast part or all of Henry's speech to pertain to some issue today that calls for action—poverty, drugs, crime, or military intervention to help a country struggling for human rights. Deliver the recast speech to the class.

Choices: Building Your Portfolio

1. **Writer's Notebook** Remind students to save their work. They may use it as prewriting for the Writer's Workshop on pp. 130–133. Have the class brainstorm a list of turning points in the lives of people they know or have heard or read about.
2. **Critical Writing** Allow students to work in pairs to complete the chart, each student being responsible for reviewing one speech, but both completing a chart combining the material.
3. **Speaking and Listening** Have students work in small groups on this assignment. In order to ensure variety, have each group select a different issue.

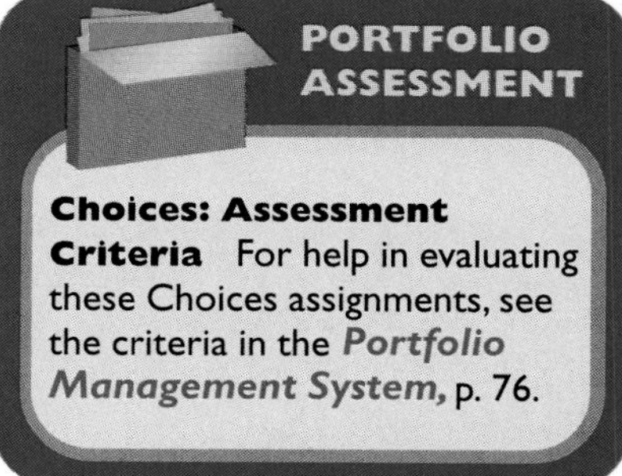

Choices: Assessment Criteria For help in evaluating these Choices assignments, see the criteria in the ***Portfolio Management System,*** p. 76.

STRATEGIES FOR INCLUSION

Visual For activity #1, have students label the three areas of a graph like the one following to generate details and analyze the cause and effect relationship between actions or events and personal change.

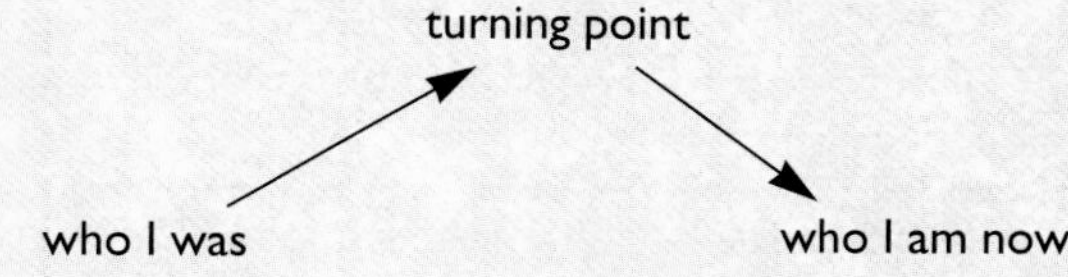

English Language Development To help students draw upon the language skills they possess but may lack confidence in, use a tape recorder for activity #3. Students can compose their recast speeches orally and record, listen to, edit, and practice their speeches before delivering them to the class.

ABOUT THE AUTHOR

Paine's attempt to organize his fellow tax collectors to demand higher wages was regarded as revolutionary in the England of 1774. Although his part in this agitation cost him his job, it proved fortunate in the long run. It was while lobbying for his fellow excise men that Paine met and impressed Benjamin Franklin, who provided letters of reference which enabled Paine to make a start as a journalist in America.

Thomas Paine

(1737–1809)

The most persuasive writer of the American Revolution came from an unlikely background. Thomas Paine, the poorly educated son of a corset maker, was born in England and spent his first thirty-seven years drifting through occupations—corset maker, grocer, tobacconist, schoolteacher, tax collector. In 1774, Paine was dismissed from his job as a tax collector for attempting to organize the employees in a demand for higher wages (an unusual activity in those days). Like many others at that time and since, he came to America to make a new start.

Thomas Paine (1806–1807) by John Wesley Jarvis. Oil on canvas.

National Gallery of Art, Washington, D.C., Gift of Marion B. Maurice.

With a letter of introduction from Benjamin Franklin (page 84), whom he had met in London, Paine went to Philadelphia, where he worked as a journalist. In the conflict between England and the Colonies, he quickly identified with the underdog. In January 1776, he published the most important written work in support of American independence: *Common Sense,* a forty-seven-page pamphlet that denounced King George III as a "royal brute" and asserted that a continent should not remain tied to an island. The pamphlet sold a half million copies—in a country whose total population was roughly two and a quarter million.

After the Revolution, Paine lived peacefully in New York and New Jersey until 1787, when he returned to Europe. There he became involved once more in radical revolutionary politics, supporting the French Revolution. In 1791, he composed *The Rights of Man,* a reply to the English statesman Edmund Burke's condemnation of the French revolt. *The Rights of Man* was an impassioned defense of republican government and a call to the English people to overthrow their king. Although he was not living in England at the time, Paine was tried for treason there and banned from the country. Safe in France from English law, he was briefly celebrated as a hero of the French Revolution but was soon imprisoned in France for being a citizen of an enemy nation (England). James Monroe, the American minister to France at the time, gained his release in 1794 by insisting that Paine was an American citizen.

Paine's final notable work, *The Age of Reason,* was published in two parts, the first in 1794 and the second in 1796. Expounding the principles of deism (page 16), the book was controversial in America. Americans did not fully understand the book and thought Paine was an atheist—that he did not believe in God. When Paine returned to America in 1802, he was a virtual outcast, scorned as a dangerous radical and nonbeliever. He was stripped of his right to vote, had no money, and was continually harassed. When he died in New York in 1809, he was denied burial in consecrated ground. His body was buried on his farm in New Rochelle.

Even in death, though, Thomas Paine was not allowed to rest. In 1819, an English sympathizer dug up Paine's body and removed it and the coffin to England, intending to erect a memorial to the author of *The Rights of Man.* But no monument was ever built. The last record of Paine's remains shows that the coffin and the bones were acquired by a furniture dealer in England in 1844.

WORDS TO OWN

The following vocabulary words are defined in the Words to Own at the bottom of the pupil's page.

tyranny p. 108	relinquished p. 108
consolation p. 108	pretense p. 108
celestial p. 108	dominion p. 109
impious p. 108	eloquence p. 110
ravage p. 108	perseverance p. 111

PORTFOLIO ASSESSMENT

Portfolio Assessment For help with self-assessment of reading skills, see the ***Portfolio Management System,*** pp. 48–49.

Joe Viesti/Viesti Associates.

Reenactment of a redcoat musket firing, Trenton, New Jersey.

Before You Read

from The Crisis, No. 1

Reading Focus

A Common Cause

At various times in life, we have to put aside personal feelings and make sacrifices for a common cause or team effort. The early American colonists had to put their commitment to a common cause to a real test, for much was being asked of them. At the time Thomas Paine wrote *The Crisis, No. 1,* the colonists had to make a crucial decision: Should they kneel as English subjects, or stand as Americans? As Benjamin Franklin (page 84) said, "We must all hang together, or assuredly we shall all hang separately."

Quickwrite

The first sentence of this essay is justly famous and could be applied to other crucial times in human history. Write down other occasions you can think of that have tried "men's [and women's] souls." (Think of civil rights issues, environmental struggles, women's rights, and other emotionally charged issues.) What values were at stake? What were the positions of the opposing groups?

Elements of Literature

Style

A writer's **style** is determined by sentence length, **diction**, and use of **figurative language** and **imagery.** Thomas Paine uses a combination of styles: Direct, common speech is mixed with heightened, impassioned expressions sharpened by dramatic rhetorical techniques. Paine says that he speaks "in language as plain as A, B, C," yet he also includes such lofty declarations as "What we obtain too cheap, we esteem too lightly; 'tis dearness only that gives everything its value."

Style is the distinctive way in which a writer uses language.

For more on Style, see the Handbook of Literary Terms.

Background

In 1776, Paine joined the Continental army as it retreated across New Jersey to Philadelphia. During the journey he began writing a series of sixteen pamphlets called *The American Crisis,* commenting on the war and urging Americans not to give up the fight. The first of these pamphlets was read to Washington's troops in December 1776, a few days before the army recrossed the Delaware River to attack the British-held city of Trenton, New Jersey.

QUICK PLANNING GUIDE

Into the Selection

Author Biography p. 106

Before You Read p. 107

- **Reading Focus:** Students read about the sacrifices of the American colonists.
- **Quickwrite: Prior Knowledge** Write in Reader's Logs about crucial times in history
- **Elements of Literature: Style**
- **Background: Scaffolding** Encounter the important role Paine's pamphlets played in the American Revolution.

Through the Selection

from "The Crisis, No. 1" pp. 108–111

Words to Own pp. 108–111

Making Meanings p. 112

Spotlight On p. 113

Beyond the Selection

Choices: Building Your Portfolio p. 112

- **Writer's Notebook:** Describe team effort
- **Critical Writing:** Write a reply to the author
- **Creative Writing:** Imagine how listeners might have felt

PROGRAM MANAGER

- **Planning Instruction** See Teaching Notes, *Teaching Resources A,* p. 44, for objectives, a summary, literary elements, and additional historical information for this selection.
- **Instructional Support** Before beginning the instructional lesson, see Graphic Organizer for Active Reading, *Teaching Resources A,* p. 50, for a Through the Selection activity.
- **Assessment** See Selection Test, *Test Booklet,* pp. 27–28.
- **Reinforcement** Use the Words to Own worksheet in *Teaching Resources A,* p. 51.

Into the Selection

Using **BEFORE YOU READ** p. 107

Reading Focus

Encourage students to examine the position in which the colonists were placed. What arguments can they see for the colonists remaining loyal to the British Crown? What arguments can they see for the colonists who wanted independence?

Elements of Literature

Paine uses both common and elevated speech in his writing. Discuss style in clothing, relating it to levels of speech formality. We have plain clothes, jeans and T-shirts, and plain prose. We also have tuxedos and evening gowns and elevated, formal language.

Through the Selection

A. Language Note: Vocabulary
Explain that *dearness* here is the opposite of *cheapness;* it means "difficulty of obtaining."

from The Crisis, No. 1

Thomas Paine

These are the times that try men's souls. The summer soldier and the sunshine patriot will, in this crisis, shrink from the service of his country; but he that stands it NOW, deserves the love and thanks of man and woman. Tyranny, like hell, is not easily conquered; yet we have this consolation with us, that the harder the conflict, the more glorious the triumph. What we obtain too (A) cheap, we esteem too lightly; 'tis dearness only that gives everything its value. Heaven knows how to put a proper price upon its goods; and it would be strange indeed, if so celestial an article as FREEDOM should not be highly rated. Britain, with an army to enforce her tyranny, has declared that she has a right (*not only to* TAX) but "to BIND *us in* ALL CASES WHATSOEVER,"[1] and if being *bound in that manner,* is not slavery, then is there not such a thing as slavery upon earth. Even the expression is impious, for so unlimited a power can belong only to God.

Whether the independence of the continent was declared too soon, or delayed too long, I will not now enter into as an argument; my own simple opinion is, that had it been eight months earlier, it would have been much better. We did not make a proper use of last winter, neither could we, while we were in a dependent state. However, the fault, if it were one, was all our own; we have none to blame but ourselves. But no great deal is lost yet; all that Howe[2] has been doing for this month past, is rather a ravage than a conquest, which the spirit of the Jerseys[3] a year ago would have quickly repulsed, and which time and a little resolution will soon recover.

I have as little superstition in me as any man living, but my secret opinion has ever been, and still is, that God Almighty will not give up a people to military destruction, or leave them unsupportedly to perish, who have so earnestly and so repeatedly sought to avoid the calamities of war, by every decent method which wisdom could invent. Neither have I so much of the infidel in me, as to suppose that he has relinquished the government of the world, and given us up to the care of devils; and as I do not, I cannot see on what grounds the king of Britain can look up to heaven for help against us: A common murderer, a highwayman,[4] or a housebreaker, has as good a pretense as he. . . .

I once felt all that kind of anger, which a man ought to feel, against the mean[5] principles that are held by the Tories:[6] A noted one, who kept a tavern at Amboy,[7] was standing at his door, with as pretty a child in his hand, about eight or nine years old, as I ever saw, and after speaking his mind as freely as he thought was prudent, finished with this unfatherly expression, *"Well! Give me peace in my day."* Not a man lives on the continent but fully believes that a separation must sometime or other

1. **to bind . . . whatsoever:** In response to Colonial protests over the Stamp Act (which taxed all commercial and legal documents in the Colonies), Parliament repealed the act on March 17, 1766. On the same day, it passed the Declaratory Act, which stated that Parliament had the right "to make laws . . . to bind the colonies and people of America . . . in all cases whatsoever."
2. **Howe:** Sir William Howe (1729–1814), commander in chief (1775–1778) of the British forces in America during the Revolution.
3. **Jerseys:** New Jersey was at this time divided into East Jersey and West Jersey.
4. **highwayman:** thief who patrols the roads frequented by travelers, with the intent of stealing their valuables.
5. **mean:** low.
6. **Tories:** those who supported British rule in the American Colonies.
7. **Amboy:** Perth Amboy, New Jersey.

WORDS TO OWN

tyranny (tir'ə·nē) *n.:* oppression.
consolation (kän'sə·lā'shən) *n.:* comfort.
celestial (sə·les'chəl) *adj.:* divine; perfect.
impious (im'pē·əs) *adj.:* irreverent.
ravage (rav'ij) *n.:* act of violent destruction.
relinquished (ri·liŋ'kwisht) *v.:* given up.
pretense (prē·tens') *n.:* false claim.

OPTIONS FOR TEACHING

STRATEGIES FOR INCLUSION

Learners Having Difficulty If students become confused by Paine's argument, suggest they divide the pamphlet into four parts to help them organize their thoughts: (1) the emotional appeal; (2) justification of the military retreat; (3) criticism of Tories and appeal to sympathizers; and (4) faith that the Revolution will succeed. Ask students to note where each part begins and ends.

INTEGRATING THE LANGUAGE ARTS

Grammar Point out some of Paine's very short sentences that sound like aphorisms, or wise sayings. Not a word is wasted in these sentences. Sometimes Paine connects two such bare-boned sentences with a semicolon to create a compound sentence. Ask students to find examples of Paine's bare-boned compound sentences and then to write three compound sentences of their own about Paine's ideas.

Strategic Reading To help students analyze structure, ask them to record Paine's main ideas, details, and transitions, using a graphic organizer like the following one.

Main ideas	Details	Transitions

finally take place, and a generous parent should have said, *"If there must be trouble let it be in my day, that my child may have peace"*; and this single reflection, well applied, is sufficient to awaken every man to duty. Not a place upon earth might be so happy as America. Her situation is remote from all the wrangling world, and she has nothing to do but to trade with them. A man can distinguish himself between temper and principle, and I am as confident, as I am that God governs the world, that America will never be happy till she gets clear of foreign dominion. Wars, without ceasing, will break out till that period arrives, and the continent must in the end be conqueror; for though the flame of liberty may sometimes cease to shine, the coal can never expire.

America did not, nor does not want[8] force; but she wanted a proper application of that force. Wisdom is not the purchase of a day, and it is no wonder that we should err at the first setting off. From an excess of tenderness, we were unwilling to raise an army, and trusted our cause to the temporary defense of a well-meaning militia. A summer's experience has now taught us better; yet with those troops, while they were collected, we were able to set bounds to the progress of the enemy, and—thank God!—they are again assembling. I always consider militia as the best troops in the world for a sudden exertion, but they will not do for a long campaign. Howe, it is probable, will make an attempt on this city;[9] should he fail on this side the Delaware, he is ruined: If he succeeds, our cause is not ruined. He stakes all on his side against a part on ours; admitting he succeeds, the consequence will be, that armies from both ends of the continent will march to assist their suffering friends in the middle

8. **want:** lack.

9. **this city:** Philadelphia.

WORDS TO OWN

dominion (də·min′yən) *n.:* rule.

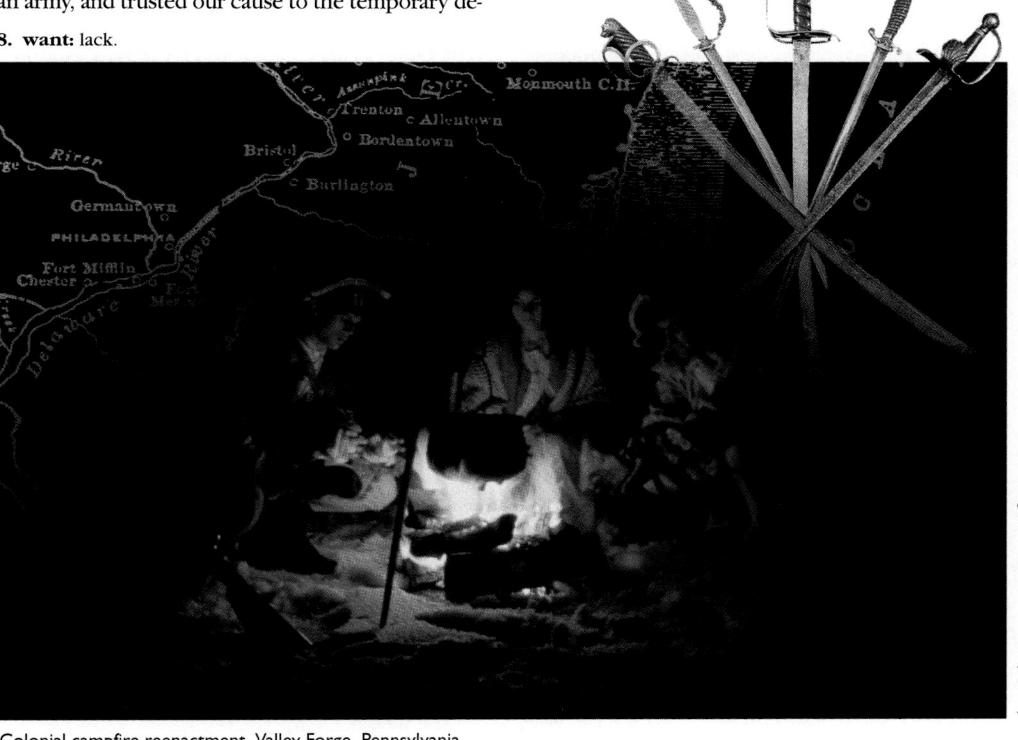

Colonial campfire reenactment, Valley Forge, Pennsylvania.

The Granger Collection, New York (swords).

B. Critical Reading: Analyzing Argument
Point out that Paine cleverly makes a harmless statement by the Tory tavern keeper sound cowardly and selfish. It was, after all, quite understandable for him to wish for peace. Moreover, as a Tory, the tavern keeper did not accept the inevitability of revolution and was therefore not asking that trouble be postponed for a later generation. This trick shows how ably Paine fashions an argument out of the slightest materials.

C. Language Note: Vocabulary
Explain that by *militia* Paine means an army of citizens quickly raised to meet a temporary emergency. An army, by contrast, is better trained, better equipped, and more suitable for a long campaign.

CLASSROOM MANAGEMENT

Managing the Reader's Response Classroom

- To encourage everyone in the class to participate in brainstorming sessions, create a noncritical environment. Insist that no idea be ridiculed or laughed down, since even the silliest idea can spark the formation of a truly workable and brilliant concept.
- A high energy level produces the most frequent and useful contributions from students. Letting your interest show, quickly clustering or writing the ideas on the chalkboard, and making your own rapid additions all help fan the creative flame.
- Call on students who rarely offer suggestions in brainstorming sessions. Moving quickly from one to the other, giving no time for reflection, will usually get these students participating before they know it.

A. Literary Element: Style
Paine's frequent use of Biblical allusions implies that God is on the side of the Colonists. The allusion here implies that to be good Christians, the audience must follow Paine's advice.

B. Critical Reading: Making Inferences

? What appeal is Paine making here? In what ways is it familiar? [He appeals to fear. Politicians sometimes evoke the image of a person's house under attack by evildoers in order to elicit fear and make the listener receptive to a proposed solution.]

states; for he cannot go everywhere; it is impossible. I consider Howe the greatest enemy the Tories have; he is bringing a war into their country, which, had it not been for him and partly for themselves, they had been clear of. Should he now be expelled, I wish with all the devotion of a *Christian,* that the names of Whig[10] and Tory may never more be mentioned; but should the Tories give him encouragement to come, or assistance if **A** he come, I as sincerely wish that our next year's arms may expel them from the continent, and that congress appropriate their possessions to the relief of those who have suffered in well doing. A single successful battle next year will settle the whole. America could carry on a two years' war by the confiscation of the property of disaffected[11] persons; and be made happy by their expulsion. Say not that this is revenge, call it rather the soft resentment of a suffering people, who, having no object in view but the *good* of *all,* have staked their *own all* upon a seemingly doubtful event. Yet it is folly to argue against determined hardness; eloquence may strike the ear, and the language of sorrow draw forth the tear of compassion, but nothing can reach the heart that is steeled with prejudice.

Quitting this class of men, I turn with the warm ardor of a friend to those who have nobly stood, and are yet determined to stand the matter out: I call not upon a few, but upon all; not on *this* state or *that* state, but on *every* state; up and help us; lay your shoulders to the wheel; better have too much force than too little, when so great an object is at stake. Let it be told to the future world, that in the depth of winter, when nothing but hope and virtue could survive, that the city and the country, alarmed at one common danger, came forth to meet and to repulse it. Say not that thousands are gone, turn out your tens of thousands;[12] throw not the burden of the day upon Providence, but *"show your faith by your works,"*[13] that God may bless

Sentry and cannon reenactment, Valley Forge, Pennsylvania.

you. It matters not where you live, or what rank of life you hold, the evil or the blessing will reach you all. The far and the near, the home counties and the back, the rich and the poor, will suffer or rejoice alike. The heart that feels not now, is dead: The blood of his children will curse his cowardice, who shrinks back at a time when a little might have saved the whole, and made *them* happy. (I love the man that can smile at trouble; that can gather strength from distress; and grow brave by reflection.) 'Tis the business of little minds to shrink; but he whose heart is firm, and whose conscience approves his conduct, will pursue his principles unto death. My own line of reasoning is to myself as straight and clear as a ray of light. Not all the treasures of the world, so far as I believe, could have induced me to support an offensive war, for I think it murder; but if a thief breaks into my house, burns and destroys my property, and kills or **B** threatens to kill me, or those that are in it, and to *"bind me in all cases whatsoever,"* to his absolute will, am I to suffer it? What signifies it to me, whether he who does it is a king or a common man; my countryman, or not my countryman; whether it be done by an individual villain or an army of them? If we reason to the root of things we shall find no difference; neither can any just

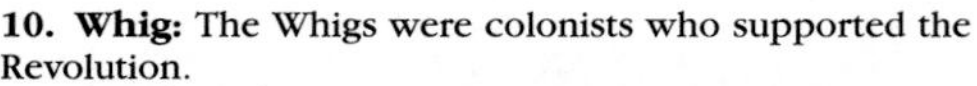

10. **Whig:** The Whigs were colonists who supported the Revolution.
11. **disaffected:** disloyal, especially toward the government.
12. **thousands:** "Saul hath slain his thousands, and David his ten thousands" (1 Samuel 18:7).
13. **show . . . works:** "Show me thy faith without thy works, and I will show thee my faith by my works" (James 2:18).

WORDS TO OWN

eloquence (el'ə·kwəns) *n.:* well-articulated, persuasive speech.

OPTIONS FOR TEACHING

CROSSING THE CURRICULUM

History Ask students to work in groups to research and write newspaper reports on Washington's early unsuccessful campaign around New York City in the late summer of 1776, the Battle of White Plains, and the retreat to Pennsylvania, which Paine briefly alludes to in "The Crisis, No. 1."

PROFESSIONAL NOTES

Thematic Connections: "The American Dream" Work with the class to discuss reasons why this selection is included in a collection with the theme "The American Dream." [Possible answer: It clearly and passionately expresses reasons the Colonies should fight for freedom.]

cause be assigned why we should punish in the one case and pardon in the other. Let them call me rebel, and welcome, I feel no concern from it; but I should suffer the misery of devils, were I to make a whore of my soul by swearing allegiance to one whose character is that of a sottish,[14] stupid, stubborn, worthless, brutish man. I conceive likewise a horrid idea in receiving mercy from a being, who at the last day shall be shrieking to the rocks and mountains to cover him, and fleeing with terror from the orphan, the widow, and the slain of America.

There are cases which cannot be overdone by language, and this is one. There are persons too who see not the full extent of the evil which threatens them; they solace themselves with hopes that the enemy, if he succeeds, will be merciful. Is this the madness of folly, to expect mercy from those who have refused to do justice; and even mercy, where conquest is the object, is only a trick of war; the cunning of the fox is as murderous as the violence of the wolf; and we ought to guard equally against both. Howe's first object is partly by threats and partly by promises, to terrify or seduce the people to deliver up their arms and to receive mercy. The ministry recommended the same plan to Gage,[15] and this is what the Tories call making their peace, *"a peace which passeth all understanding,"*[16] *indeed!* A peace which would be the immediate forerunner of a worse ruin than any we have yet thought of. Ye men of Pennsylvania, do reason upon these things! Were the back counties to give up their arms, they would fall an easy prey to the Indians, who are all armed; this perhaps is what some Tories would not be sorry for. Were the home counties to deliver up their arms, they would be exposed to the resentment of the back counties, (C) who would then have it in their power to chastise their defection at pleasure. And were any one state to give up its arms, *that* state must be garrisoned by Howe's army of Britains and Hessians[17] to preserve it from the anger of the rest. Mutual fear is the principal link in the chain of mutual love, and woe be to that state that breaks the compact. Howe is mercifully inviting you to barbarous destruction, and men must be either rogues or fools that will not see it. I dwell not upon the powers of imagination; I bring reason to your ears; and in language as plain as A, B, C, hold up truth to your eyes.

I thank God that I fear not. I see no real cause for fear. I know our situation well and can see the way out of it. While our army was collected, Howe dared not risk a battle, and it is no credit to him that he decamped from the White Plains, and waited a mean opportunity to ravage the defenseless Jerseys;[18] but it is great credit to us, that, with a handful of men, we sustained an orderly retreat for near an hundred miles, brought off our ammunition, all our field pieces, the greatest part of our stores, and had four rivers to pass. None can say that our retreat was precipitate,[19] for we were near three weeks in performing it, that the country[20] might have time to come in. Twice we marched back to meet the enemy, and remained out till dark. The sign of fear was not seen in our camp, and had not some of the cowardly and disaffected inhabitants spread false (D) alarms through the country, the Jerseys had never been ravaged. Once more we are again collected and collecting, our new army at both ends of the continent is recruiting fast, and we shall be able to open the next campaign with sixty thousand men, well armed and clothed. This is our situation, and who will may know it. By perseverance and fortitude we have the prospect of a glorious issue; by cowardice and submission, the sad choice of a variety of evils—a ravaged country—a depopulated city—habitations without safety, and slavery without hope—our homes turned into barracks and bawdy-houses for Hessians, and a future race to provide for, whose fathers we shall doubt of. Look on this picture and weep over it! And if there yet remains one thoughtless wretch who believes it not, let him suffer it unlamented.

14. sottish (sät'ish): stupid or foolish from too much drinking.
15. Gage: General Thomas Gage (1721–1787), head of the British forces in America (1763–1775) before General Howe.
16. a peace . . . understanding: ironic echo of Paul's epistle to the Philippians (4:7).
17. Hessians (hesh'ənz): German troops, mostly from the region of Hesse, hired to fight on the British side.
18. White Plains . . . Jerseys: Howe had defeated Washington at White Plains, New York, in 1776 but had failed to press his advantage.
19. precipitate (prē·sip'ə·tit): sudden; unexpected.
20. country: the local people. Paine uses the term to refer to local volunteers.

Words to Own

perseverance (pur'sə·vir'əns) *n.*: persistence.

C. Literary Element: Parallel Structure

? What examples of parallelism has Paine used here? [The three sentences beginning with *Were*.]

D. Critical Reading: Making Generalizations

? Based on the evidence in this paragraph as well as those preceding, how would you characterize Paine? [Reflective, courageous, just, optimistic, and eloquent.]

INTEGRATING THE LANGUAGE ARTS

Writing: Story Newspaper Have students working in groups prepare a newspaper edition reporting the publication of Paine's pamphlet. Students should prepare a news report with headline, a picture, and an editorial. They should add reports about incidents they imagine taking place at the same time. Each student should be responsible for a separate feature.

ASSESSMENT TOOLS

Check Test: True-False

1. Paine believes that the Colonies should have acted against Britain eight months before they did. [True]
2. Paine compares the king to a murderer and a thief. [True]
3. Paine describes the retreat to the Delaware as disorganized but courageous. [False]
4. Paine believes American isolation from Europe would create necessary hardship after gaining independence. [False]
5. Paine believes only those should fight who have nothing or no one to lose. [False]

Making Meanings

First Thoughts

1. Possible responses: The first and third paragraphs. In addition, the eleventh and final paragraphs.

Reviewing the Text

a. The British king is evil and unjust and has usurped God's unlimited power; heaven rates freedom highly; God will not give the colonists up to devils.

b. Allegiance to the king, based on selfish fear, merely defers a conflict that is inevitable. Also, loving parents will sacrifice now for their children's later benefit.

c. Fears of enslavement, a ravaged countryside, depopulated cities, unsafe houses, and houses of ill repute.

d. The Colonies must fight against Britain. Supporting details: Statement that God sides with the just, reminder that the British will be brutal if they win.

Shaping Interpretations

2. A *summer soldier* will not fight in the winter, when fighting is arduous. Similarly, a *sunshine patriot* is not a patriot when times are rough.
3. Self-interest in mutual protection may be the most compelling reason for standing united.
4. It is as just to rebel against England, which has trespassed on the colonists' rights, as it is to turn on a thief who trespasses on one's own property. An opponent might say that England is not a thief.

Extending the Text

5. **(Evaluation)** Responses will vary. Students may say that people today would respond to Paine's arguments and style, but not as srongly as Paine's readers did.

Choices: Building Your Portfolio

1. **Writer's Notebook** Remind students to save their work. They may use it as prewriting for the Writer's Workshop on pp. 130–133.

Making Meanings

First Thoughts

1. Which passages in this excerpt were especially stirring?

Reviewing the Text

a. What reasons does Paine give for his confidence that God will help the Americans and not the British?

b. Explain Paine's point in telling the **anecdote** about the Tory tavern keeper and his child.

c. What powerful emotional appeal does Paine make in the conclusion of his essay?

d. What is Paine's **main idea**? What are some of his chief supporting details?

Shaping Interpretations

2. The pamphlet opens with two famous **images** (page 108). What kinds of people does Paine identify with summer and sunshine? Why are these images appropriate?
3. Explain the meaning of Paine's **metaphor** "Mutual fear is the principal link in the chain of mutual love" (page 111). Do you agree or disagree with this idea, and why?
4. An **analogy** is a comparison between two things that are alike in certain respects. Analogies are used often in **argument** and **persuasion** to demonstrate the logic of one idea by showing how it is similar to another, accepted idea. Analogies can be tricky, though, because few ideas or situations are completely alike in all aspects. What analogy does Paine draw when he talks about the thief (page 108)? What point is he making, and how might an opponent answer?

Extending the Text

5. Could any of Paine's arguments be applied to contemporary political situations? (Review the Quickwrite you wrote in your Reader's Log for ideas.) How do you think people today would respond to Paine's arguments and his writing **style**?

Choices: Building Your Portfolio

Writer's Notebook

1. Collecting Ideas for an Autobiographical Incident

WORK IN PROGRESS

Have you ever joined with others in a team effort for a common cause? Briefly describe the experience: What was the purpose of banding together? Did taking part in group action involve personal sacrifices on your part? Save your notes for possible use in the Writer's Workshop on page 130.

Critical Writing

2. A Paine Prescription

"Not a place upon earth might be so happy as America. Her situation is remote from all the wrangling world, and she has nothing to do but to trade with them. . . . I am . . . confident . . . that America will never be happy till she gets clear of foreign dominion" (page 109). In a brief essay, evaluate these words from Paine's pamphlet. Considering the world as it is today, how would you reply to Paine?

Creative Writing

3. Crisis Zone

Imagine you are one of the volunteers who listened to this pamphlet being read a few days before Christmas, in 1776, just before you were to cross the frozen Delaware River and attack General Howe and his troops in Trenton. In a paragraph, poem, or song lyrics, express how you felt while the pamphlet was being read, and describe the responses of the people around you.

Sir William Howe (1729–1814), British commander-in-chief in America during Revolutionary War.

The Granger Collection, New York.

PORTFOLIO ASSESSMENT

Choices: Assessment Criteria For help in evaluating these Choices assignments, see the criteria in the ***Portfolio Management System***, p. 77.

STRATEGIES FOR INCLUSION

Interpersonal/Musical For activity #3, have students reenact the reaction of Colonial troops to the pamphlet. They should imagine themselves sitting around a campfire like the one illustrated on p. 109 after hearing Paine's pamphlet read. Or, let students perform or play library recordings of American Revolutionary fife and drum music while someone reads a selection of Paine's text.

SPOTLIGHT ON

Phillis Wheatley: A Revolutionary Woman

Phillis Wheatley (1773). Frontispiece of *Poems* by Phillis Wheatley. Engraving.

The Granger Collection, New York.

All the odds were stacked against her—she was an enslaved African, young, and female. But Phillis Wheatley (c. 1753–1784) published her first poem when she was barely thirteen, and by the time she was twenty years old she had developed a reputation as a poet whose work was praised by George Washington and Thomas Jefferson (page 114). (A)

When Phillis Wheatley was about seven or eight years old, she, like Olaudah Equiano (page 56), was stolen from her home in West Africa. She arrived in America on board a slave ship in 1761. At first, of course, she spoke no English. But she was purchased by the Wheatley family of Boston to assist Mrs. Susanna Wheatley and was treated kindly. Pleased to find this young woman intelligent and eager to learn, the Wheatleys provided her with an excellent education, equal to that of any free person in Boston at the time.

Susanna Wheatley arranged the London publication of a volume of Phillis's poems in 1773; the book received generally encouraging reviews, and it was read widely in England, France, and the American Colonies. Around this time, Phillis was given her freedom, though she chose to remain with the Wheatleys. When they died, she married John Peters, a freeman, in 1778.

Wheatley's poems imitate the style popular in the poetry of her time: She uses a Latinate vocabulary, inversions, and elevated diction. (B) The following stanza is from her poem to the earl of Dartmouth, who had just been appointed secretary of state in charge of the American Colonies (1772). Dartmouth, she hopes, will be open to the colonists' grievances.

***from* To the Right Honorable William, Earl of Dartmouth, His Majesty's Principal Secretary of State for North America, etc.**

Should you, my lord, while you peruse my song,
Wonder from whence my love of *Freedom* sprung, (C)
Whence flow these wishes for the common good,
By feeling hearts alone best understood,
I, young in life, by seeming cruel fate
Was snatch'd from *Afric's* fancy'd happy seat:
What pangs excruciating must molest,
What sorrows labor in my parent's breast? (D)
Steel'd was that soul and by no misery mov'd
That from a father seiz'd his babe belov'd:
Such, such my case. And can I then but pray
Others may never feel tyrannic sway?

—Phillis Wheatley

Wheatley's life ended on a tragic note. Her married life was filled with personal, financial, and familial hardships. Wheatley bore three children, but none of them survived. When she herself was sick and poor, the same society that lavished attention on her as a kind of "sideshow attraction"—an enslaved woman who could write lofty poetry—abandoned her to a position of powerlessness and anonymity. She died in her early thirties, destitute and grieving, without having published another book of poems. Since her death, however, her poems have been reprinted and, in the twentieth century, have again attracted lavish attention. Today Phillis Wheatley is praised as a true pioneer—the first African American poet in North America.

A. Cultural Connections
Phillis Wheatley was born in the area of what is now Senegal or Ghana. One source for her estimated age is the loss of her baby teeth.

B. Literary Element: Style
You may want to have students compare Wheatley's style with that of Anne Bradstreet. [Both imitate popular English poetry.]

C. Reader's Response: First Thoughts
? Where do you think Wheatley's love of freedom comes from? [Sample responses: From the fact that she was captured and enslaved as a child; or, because of her experiences, she prays that other people might not be subjected to tyranny.] Have students quickwrite how they would have responded to Wheatley's plea.

D. Literary Element: Diction
? How would you explain the power of these two lines? [Wheatley focuses on her parent's pain rather than on her own horror at being a young child stolen from home and sold into slavery.]

PROGRAM MANAGER

Audiotaped Readings To help less proficient readers or auditory learners through the lesson, use the **Selected Reading, Audiocassette 1, Side A,** in the ***Audiovisual Resources Binder.***

OPTIONS FOR TEACHING

INTEGRATING THE LANGUAGE ARTS

Strategic Reading To make the poem more accessible, have students:

- Read the poem three times; aloud is best.
- Write a response to the poem.
- Write the most important line.
- Share response and line with a group.
- Discuss the differences in the group instead of the similarities. Remind students not to insist they are correct.
- Listen to the group's ideas and write a response.

STRATEGIES FOR INCLUSION

English Language Delevopment To help students understand the poem, have them:

- Copy the poem, skipping a space between each line.
- Mark unknown words and confusing phrases with colored markers.
- Read the poem aloud in groups of three.
- Share the marked parts. Help each other figure out the unclear parts.
- Write a response to the poem, and share it with other groups.

QUICK PLANNING GUIDE

Into the Selection

Author Biography p. 114

Before You Read p. 115

- **Reading Focus: Set a Purpose** Students consider responsibilities of freedom.
- **Quickwrite: Prior Knowledge** List benefits and responsibilities of freedom in Reader's Log
- **Elements of Literature: Parallelism**
- **Background:** Students consider Congress's changes to the Declaration.

Through the Selection

from The Autobiography: The Declaration of Independence pp. 116–123

Words to Own pp. 117–123

Literature and Politics pp. 120–121

Primary Sources p. 124

Making Meanings p. 125

Beyond the Selection

Choices: Building Your Portfolio p. 125

- **Writer's Notebook:** Freewrite about benefits and burdens of freedom
- **Critical Writing:** Respond to a letter
- **Speaking and Listening:** Discuss what the Declaration means by *equal*

ABOUT THE AUTHOR

Much of Jefferson's correspondence encourages activity: "Never put off till tomorrow what you can do to-day." Also, "Nothing is troublesome that we do willingly." Like Franklin, Jefferson encourages humility, "Pride costs us more than hunger, thirst and cold."

Thomas Jefferson

(1743–1826)

At a White House dinner in 1962 honoring forty-nine Nobel Prize winners, President John F. Kennedy hailed his guests as "the most extraordinary collection of talent, of human knowledge, that has ever been gathered together at the White House, with the possible exception of when Thomas Jefferson dined alone." President Kennedy was exaggerating only slightly.

Thomas Jefferson, the brilliant and versatile third president of the United States, was an accomplished statesman, architect, botanist, paleontologist, linguist, and musician. He displayed the range of interests that we associate with the eighteenth-century mind at its best.

Jefferson was born in the red-clay country of what is now Albemarle County, Virginia. Jefferson's father, a surveyor and magistrate, died when Thomas was fourteen, but he had provided his son with an excellent classical education and a 5,000-acre estate. After attending the College of William and Mary, Jefferson became a lawyer, a member of the Virginia House of Burgesses, and a spokesperson for the rights of personal liberty and religious freedom. In 1774, he wrote a pamphlet called *A Summary View of the Rights of British America,* a call for the rejection of parliamentary authority. This pamphlet established his reputation, and two years later, Congress chose him to help draft the Declaration of Independence.

During the Revolution, Jefferson served for a time as governor of Virginia. When the British invaded Virginia, he retired to Monticello, the home he had designed, and devoted himself to his family and to scientific research. During this time he also composed most of his *Notes on the State of Virginia.* Shortly after Jefferson's beloved wife Martha died in 1782, he returned to public life, in part as an escape from his private grief. He served as minister to France, secretary of state, vice president, and president from 1801–1809.

A determined opponent of federal power, Jefferson embodied the principles of what would come to be called Jeffersonian democracy. He believed in the rights of individuals and states to govern themselves as much as possible. Politically and personally, he strove to keep power vested in the agrarian backbone of the country. He also expanded the country enormously in 1803: The Louisiana Purchase doubled the size of the United States, adding land that would later be divided into part or all of fifteen states. And as for Jefferson's presidential style, he avoided public displays and wore simple clothes: A president, he thought, should neither act nor look like a king. At state dinners, he eliminated seating by rank.

After his presidency, Jefferson retired once again to Monticello. He devoted his energy to establishing the University of Virginia, planning its courses of study and designing many of its buildings. In 1826, both Jefferson (at eighty-three) and the former president John Adams (at ninety) became gravely ill. Both hoped to live to see the fiftieth anniversary of the independence they had done so much to ensure. Jefferson died on the morning of July 4, several hours before Adams, whose last words were "Thomas Jefferson still survives."

Thomas Jefferson (1791) by Charles Willson Peale. Oil on canvas.

Independence National Historical Park, Philadelphia, Pennsylvania.

WORDS TO OWN

The following vocabulary words are defined in the Words to Own at the bottom of the pupil's page.

censures p. 117	abdicated p. 121
transient p. 118	confiscation p. 122
constrains p. 118	magnanimity p. 122
expunge p. 118	renounce p. 123
candid p. 118	acquiesce p. 123

Before You Read

from The Autobiography: The Declaration of Independence

Reading Focus

The Burden of Freedom

Without a doubt, the cornerstone of the "American dream" is the ideal of freedom. The words of the Declaration of Independence are a ringing affirmation of freedom. Yet Jefferson knew well that freedom's twin is responsibility—every kind of liberty we enjoy has to be balanced by an equal amount of personal responsibility.

Quickwrite

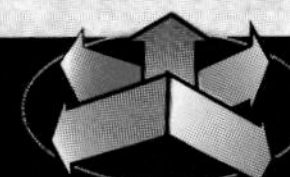

Write the word *freedom* at the top of a page. Beneath it, draw a set of scales in balance. On one side of the scales, write all the benefits of freedom you can think of. On the other side of the scales, write the costs of such freedom—the responsibilities or sacrifices that these benefits demand from us.

Elements of Literature

Parallelism

Parallelism is the repeated use of sentences, clauses, or phrases with identical or similar structures. For example, when Jefferson cites the truths that are "self-evident," he begins each clause with *that.* He also begins a long series of paragraphs with the words "He has. . . ." Jefferson's use of parallelism emphasizes his view that all the truths he presents are of equal importance. The parallel structure also creates a stately **rhythm** or cadence in the Declaration. Listen for this cadence as you read passages aloud.

> **Parallelism** or parallel structure is the repetition of grammatically similar words, phrases, clauses, or sentences to emphasize a point or stir the emotions of a reader or listener.
>
> *For more on Parallelism, see the Handbook of Literary Terms.*

Background

Four other writers worked with Jefferson on the draft of the Declaration that was submitted to Congress: John Adams of Massachusetts, Roger Sherman of Connecticut, Robert Livingston of New York, and Benjamin Franklin of Pennsylvania (page 84). Few changes were made by these other writers, but Congress insisted on several major alterations. Jefferson was upset by what he called "mutilations" of his document.

In this excerpt from his *Autobiography,* Jefferson offers a fascinating glimpse of how the most celebrated document in American history was put together. The underlined passages in the Declaration show the parts omitted by Congress. The words added by Congress appear in the margins. Think about why Congress may have made the changes it did to the original draft.

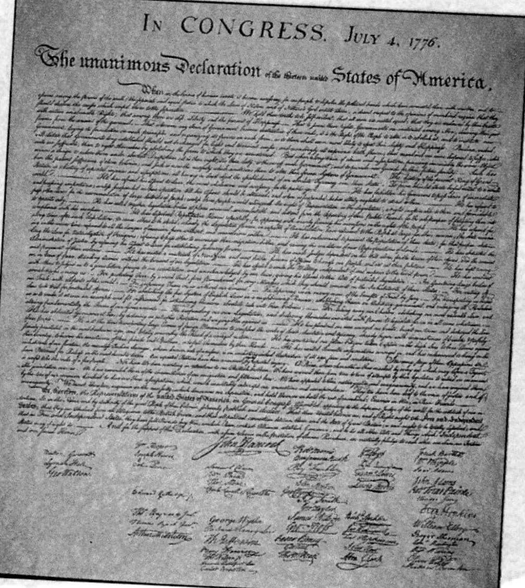

Declaration of Independence.

National Archives.

Using **Before You Read** p. 115

Reading Focus

Have students discuss what they see as their personal responsibilities in a democracy that guarantees freedom. You may want them to consider what role education plays.

Quickwrite

Invite students to note these freedoms and responsibilities in their Reader's Logs. Ask students if the freedoms are worth the cost of the responsibilities.

Elements of Literature

To help students hear the cadences of **parallelism,** have one student read aloud the repeated phrases, while the others take turns reading the new words in each clause. This will enable everyone to hear the repeated tones of the parallel words and the varying tones of the new words.

Background

Point out to students that a committee was appointed to draft the Declaration. The members asked Jefferson to write the first draft, which he did in about two weeks. Then, other committee members worked with him on minor revisions to the draft.

Program Manager

- **Planning Instruction** See Teaching Notes, *Teaching Resources A,* p. 45, for objectives, a summary, literary elements, and additional historical and biographical information for this selection.
- **Instructional Support** Before beginning the instructional lesson, see Graphic Organizer for Active Reading, *Teaching Resources A,* p. 52, for a Through the Selection activity.
- **Assessment** See Selection Test, *Test Booklet,* pp. 29–30.
- **Language Link** For instruction and practice of infinitives and infinitive phrases, see Language Link, *Teaching Resources A,* pp. 53–54, and *Language and Writing Skills Worksheets,* p. 75.
- **Reinforcement** Use the Words to Own worksheet in *Teaching Resources A,* p. 55.

PORTFOLIO ASSESSMENT

Portfolio Assessment
For help with teacher assessment of reading skills, see the ***Portfolio Management System***, pp. 54–55.

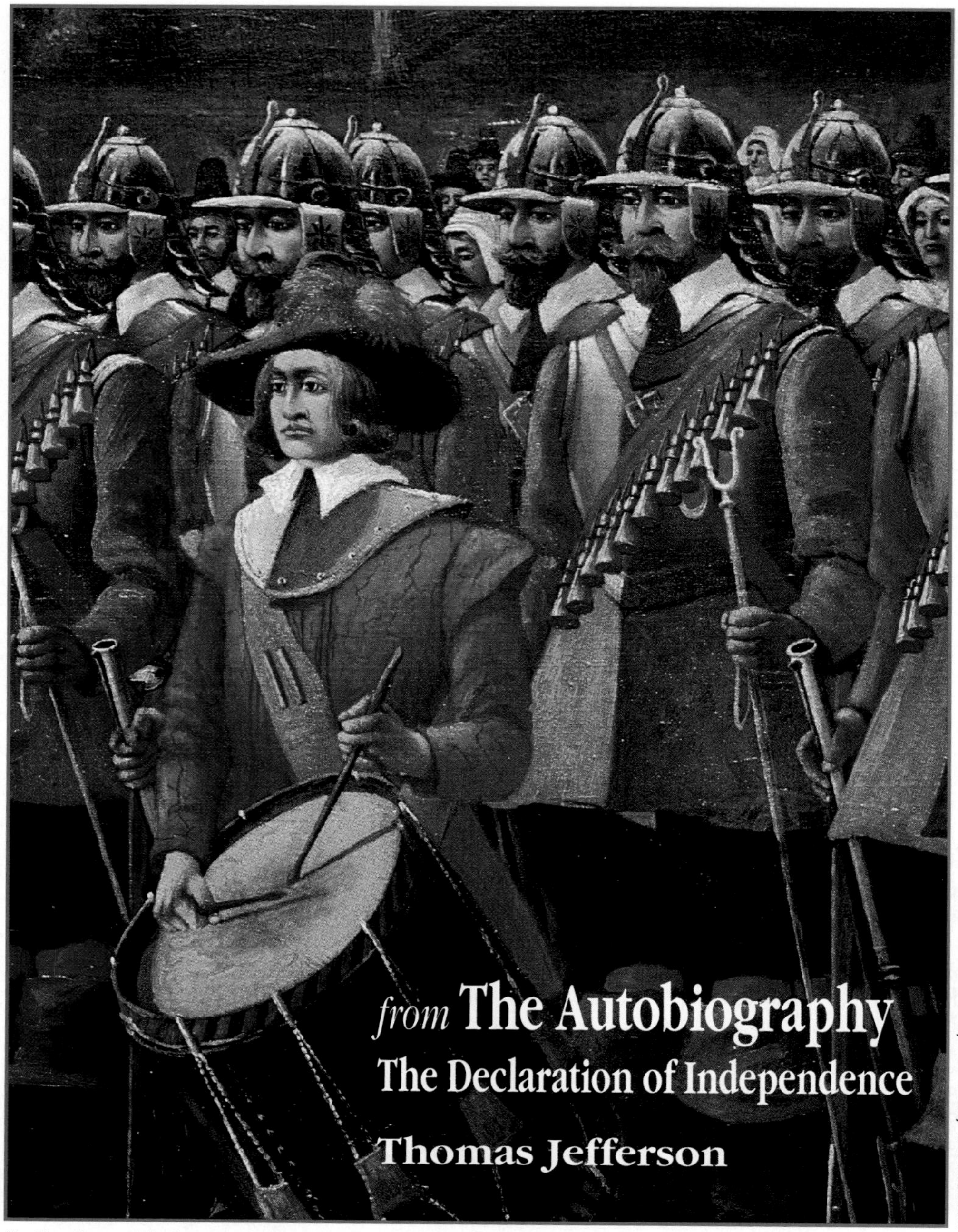

from The Autobiography
The Declaration of Independence
Thomas Jefferson

Courtesy Richard Pasley/Viesti Associates.

The First Muster of the Ancient and Honorable Artillery Company (detail) (1902) by F. Russell Bates. Oil on canvas (48" x 30"). Ancient and Honorable Artillery Company, Faneuil Hall, Boston.

OPTIONS FOR TEACHING

STRATEGIES FOR INCLUSION

Visual Students might enjoy watching a video of *1776*, a musical by Peter Stone and Sherman Edwards about the writing of the Declaration of Independence. Have students compare Jefferson in the movie with the real-life Jefferson as revealed in his writings.

Advanced Have students work in pairs to argue against excluding the material that was deleted from the Declaration. Refer students to the opening passage from *The Autobiography*, which presents Jefferson's explanation of the deletions. Students should take turns presenting arguments in favor of keeping the material.

Kinesthetic Bring in a facsimile of the Declaration for students to examine. Then, have students enact the signing of the Declaration of Independence by having each student come up and sign his or her name as the Declaration is read aloud by different readers.

Congress proceeded the same day to consider the Declaration of Independence, which had been reported and lain on the table the Friday preceding, and on Monday referred to a committee of the whole. The pusillanimous[1] idea that we had friends in England worth keeping terms with, still haunted the minds of many. For this reason, those passages which conveyed censures on the people of England were struck out, lest they should give them offense. The clause too, reprobating the enslaving the inhabitants of Africa, was struck out in complaisance to South Carolina and Georgia, who had never attempted to restrain the importation of slaves, and who, on the contrary, still wished to continue it. Our northern brethren also, I believe, felt a little tender under those censures; for though their people had very few slaves themselves, yet they had been pretty considerable carriers of them to others. The debates, having taken up the greater parts of the 2d, 3d, and 4th days of July, were, on the evening of the last, closed; the Declaration was reported by the committee, agreed to by the House, and signed by every member present, except Mr. Dickinson.[2] As the sentiments of men are known not only by what they receive, but what they reject also, I will state the form of the Declaration as originally reported. The parts struck out by Congress shall be distinguished by a black line drawn under them; and those inserted by them shall be placed in the margin, or in a concurrent column. A

1. **pusillanimous** (pyo͞o'si·lan'ə·məs): cowardly; lacking courage.

2. **Mr. Dickinson:** John Dickinson (1732–1808), one of Pennsylvania's representatives to the Second Continental Congress, led the conservative opposition to the Declaration and refused to sign the document.

WORDS TO OWN

censures (sen'shərz) *n. pl.:* strong, disapproving criticisms.

A Declaration by the Representatives of the United States of America, in General Congress Assembled

When, in the course of human events, it becomes necessary for one people to dissolve the political bands which have connected them with another, and to assume among the powers of the earth the separate and equal station to which the laws of nature and of nature's God entitle them, a decent respect to the opinions of mankind requires that they should declare the causes which impel them to the separation. B

We hold these truths to be self-evident: that all men are created equal; that they are endowed by their creator with inherent and inalienable rights;[3] that among these are life, liberty, and the pursuit of happiness; that to secure these rights, governments are instituted among men, deriving their just powers from the consent of the governed; that whenever any form of government becomes destructive of these ends, it is the right of the people to alter or to abolish it, and to institute new government, laying its foundation on such principles, and organizing its powers in such form, as to them shall seem most likely to effect their safety and happiness. Prudence, indeed, will dictate that governments long established should not be

certain

3. **inalienable** (in·āl'yən·ə·bəl) **rights:** rights that cannot be taken away.

Thomas Jefferson (date and artist unknown). Fragment of white marble.
Maryland Historical Society.

A. Exploring the Historical Period

In *Letters from a Farmer in Pennsylvania,* John Dickinson (1732–1808) had objected to British laws he considered not only unfair but also illegal; however, he favored economic pressures and conciliation. He refused to sign the Declaration and was later an author of the Articles of Confederation and a defender of the U.S. Constitution.

B. Cultural Connections

The Declaration of Independence was a source of strength and inspiration to the French during their Revolution. It continues to inspire people seeking liberty and justice. The Declaration makes clear that revolution is not a frivolous act, but must be enacted only in extreme conditions.

INTEGRATING THE LANGUAGE ARTS

Strategic Reading Ask students to record on a K-W-L chart what they already know and what they want to know about the Declaration of Independence. When they have finished reading the document, have them complete the third column.

Already Know	Want to Know	Have Learned

Language and Vocabulary Have student groups study Jefferson's language. Groups should evaluate five sentences using these questions: How does the structure vary from standard expression today? What words are unusual in this context? Is the idea clearly conveyed? Why might Jefferson have chosen this form of expression? Groups should report back to the class with a poster-sized chart illustrating their findings.

A. Reader's Response: Challenging the Text

? What effect do the indicated changes have on the Declaration? [Sample responses: The changes make the statement weaker; or, the changes make it less offensive.] In your opinion, why were the changes made? [Possibly as a political compromise with the delegates who did not want a complete break with the British people.]

B. Expansion

The repeated pronoun *He* on this page refers to "the present king of Great Britain" (George III) in the second paragraph of the Declaration.

changed for light and transient causes; and accordingly all experience hath shown that mankind are more disposed to suffer while evils are sufferable, than to right themselves by abolishing the forms to which they are accustomed. But when a long train of abuses and usurpations,[4] begun at a distinguished[5] period and pursuing invariably the same object, evinces a design to reduce them under absolute despotism, it is their right, it is their duty to throw off such government, and to provide new guards for their future security. Such has been the patient sufferance of these colonies; and such is now the necessity which constrains them to expunge their former systems of government. The history of the present king of Great Britain is a history of unremitting injuries and usurpations, among which appears no solitary fact to contradict the uniform tenor of the rest, but all have in direct object the establishment of an absolute tyranny over these states. To prove this, let facts be submitted to a candid world for the truth of which we pledge a faith yet unsullied by falsehood.

alter

repeated

all having

He has refused his assent to laws the most wholesome and necessary for the public good.

He has forbidden his governors to pass laws of immediate and pressing importance, unless suspended in their operation till his assent should be obtained; and, when so suspended, he has utterly neglected to attend to them.

He has refused to pass other laws for the accommodation of large districts of people, unless those people would relinquish the right of representation in the legislature, a right inestimable to them, and formidable to tyrants only.[6]

He has called together legislative bodies at places unusual, uncomfortable, and distant from the depository of their public records, for the sole purpose of fatiguing them into compliance with his measures.

He has dissolved representative houses repeatedly and continually for opposing with manly firmness his invasions on the rights of the people.

He has refused for a long time after such dissolutions to cause others to be elected, whereby the legislative powers, incapable of annihilation, have returned to the people at large for their exercise, the state remaining, in the meantime, exposed to all the dangers of invasion from without and convulsions within.

4. **usurpations** (yo͞o′zər·pā′shənz): acts of unlawful or forceful seizure of property, power, rights, and the like.
5. **distinguished** (di·stiŋ′gwisht): clearly defined.
6. **formidable . . . only:** causing fear only to tyrants.

WORDS TO OWN

transient (tran′shənt) *adj.:* temporary; passing.
constrains (kən·strānz′) *v.:* forces.
expunge (ek·spunj′) *v.:* to erase; remove.
candid (kan′did) *adj.:* unbiased; fair.

OPTIONS FOR TEACHING

COOPERATIVE LEARNING

Comparing Documents Have students work in groups of four to research the Declaration of the Rights of Man and of the Citizen, the Bill of Rights of the French Constitution. An article including all or most of the text may be found in major encyclopedias. Ask students to compare the principles set forth in the document with those contained in the Declaration of Independence. Groups may find it helpful to split into two subgroups; one to find and research the French document, and the other to summarize it. Have groups present ideas for comparison on charts to accompany their oral presentations.

CLASSROOM MANAGEMENT

Managing the Reader's Response Classroom Encourage students to express their ideas and to do more advanced thinking. In teaching students to think critically, focus attention on each necessary skill separately. Using the following questions may be helpful.

- How did you arrive at your response?
- Can you find evidence in the text that supports your view?
- Can you add anything to what has been said?

He has endeavored to prevent the population of these states; for that purpose obstructing the laws for naturalization of foreigners, refusing to pass others to encourage their migrations hither, and raising the conditions of new appropriations of lands.

He has suffered the administration of justice totally to cease in some of these states refusing his assent to laws for establishing judiciary powers. obstructed / by

He has made our judges dependent on his will alone for the tenure of their offices, and the amount and payment of their salaries.

He has erected a multitude of new offices, by a self-assumed power and sent hither swarms of new officers to harass our people and eat out their substance. C

He has kept among us in times of peace standing armies and ships of war without the consent of our legislatures.

He has affected to render the military independent of, and superior to, the civil power.

He has combined with others[7] to subject us to a jurisdiction foreign to our constitutions and unacknowledged by our laws, giving

7. **others:** members of British Parliament and their supporters and agents.

Yale University Art Gallery, Trumbull Collection.

The Declaration of Independence, July 4, 1776 (1787–1820) by John Trumbull. Oil on canvas.

C. Literary Element: Diction

? What loaded words does Jefferson use here? [*Swarms, harass, eat out their substance.*] Why might he have used them? [Possible answer: Jefferson is apparently furious at the treatment of the colonists by many English officers.]

Technology Tip

TECHNOLOGY Ask your students to explore the issues set forth in the Declaration of Independence. A good place to begin is The Freedom Forum, a Web site devoted to promoting freedom of the press and free speech. The URL is **http://www.nando.net/prof/freedom/1994/freedom.html**. *You may want to preview any Internet activity. Because these resources are sometimes public forums, their content can be unpredictable.*

CROSSING THE CURRICULUM

History Have students research the life of Thomas Jefferson to find two facts or anecdotes about him—one that makes him seem believable and human, and one that adds to his mystique as a person of extraordinary accomplishments. Have students share their findings with the class in the form of a dramatic monologue.

Architecture Have pairs of students research Jefferson's work in architecture. Suggest that they bring to class pictures of Monticello, the University of Virginia buildings he designed, or the classical models he drew on. You might create a bulletin board display of the pictures.

Government Jefferson had an excellent classical education and believed that educated voters would make good choices. Have students explore their own ideas about voting and education in small groups and then draw up a curriculum for the education of an ideal electorate. ☞

LITERATURE AND POLITICS

Ask students to look on the back of a quarter and examine the eagle pictured there. Have students discuss their own interpretations of the Constitution's debt to the Iroquois.

A. Critical Reading: Expressing an Opinion

? Of the many wrongs cataloged in the paragraph, which do you find to be the most offensive? [Possible answers: Sending many armed troops, cutting off trade, or suspending Colonial legislatures.]

LITERATURE AND POLITICS

Legacy of Peace and Unity: The Iroquois Constitution

Before Revolutionary patriots put pen to paper to draft the U.S. Constitution in 1787, Colonial leaders such as Thomas Jefferson and Benjamin Franklin studied examples of government from Greek and Roman times, examples from the Bible, and an example flourishing closer to home: the Iroquois Confederacy.

The Iroquois Confederacy, also known as the League of Five Nations, was a union of the Senecas, Cayugas, Onondagas, Oneidas, and Mohawks (the Tuscaroras joined later). Around 1500, so the legend goes, a Mohawk visionary named Dekanawidah convinced the nations to unite in order to establish peace and to protect "life, property and liberty." Thanks to the constitution they created, called the Law of the Great Peace, the confederacy became a formidable power; by 1750, it numbered about fifteen thousand people, and Iroquois hunters and warriors ranged over one million square miles.

The oldest living constitution. The Iroquois Constitution, which still governs the Iroquois today, is regarded as the world's oldest living constitution. It gives member tribes equal voice in the nation's affairs, spells out a system of checks and balances, and guarantees political and religious freedom. Most amazing by European standards, the Iroquois Constitution grants extensive political power to women, who hold the right to nominate and impeach chiefs. The constitution specifies that "Women shall be considered the progenitors of the Nation. They shall own the land and the soil. Men and women shall follow the status of the mother."

The Iroquois Confederacy had what Jefferson and Franklin were searching for: a constitution infused with basic principles of democracy and federalism. Franklin

his assent to their acts of pretended legislation for quartering large bodies of armed troops among us; for protecting them by a mock trial from punishment for any murders which they should commit on the inhabitants of these states; for cutting off our trade with all parts of the world; for imposing taxes on us without our consent; for depriving us [ ] of the benefits of trial by jury; for transporting us beyond seas to be tried for pretended offenses; for abolishing the free system of English laws in a neighboring province,[8] establishing therein an arbitrary government, and enlarging its boundaries, so as to render it at once an example and fit instrument for introducing the same absolute rule into these states; for taking away our charters, abolishing our most valuable laws, and altering fundamentally the forms of our governments; for suspending our own legislatures, and declaring themselves invested with power to legislate for us in all cases whatsoever.

in many cases

colonies

8. **neighboring province:** Quebec in Canada.

OPTIONS FOR TEACHING

PROFESSIONAL NOTES

Cultural Diversity Ask students to work in small groups to do research on voters' rights in other countries. Challenge them to find one country that has long had universal suffrage, one that recently acquired it, and one that does not have it. Ask students to explore the educational systems in the three countries to see if they can draw any conclusions about the connections between education and voters' rights. Have groups create a collage representing the rights of voters in the countries.

Thematic Connections: "The American Dream" Allow students to explore these questions: How necessary is freedom to the American dream? Who was free in Jefferson's time? Who could vote? What might account for the problems in this system? How can change be both great and still not enough? Have students quickwrite in their Reader's Logs responses to the questions.

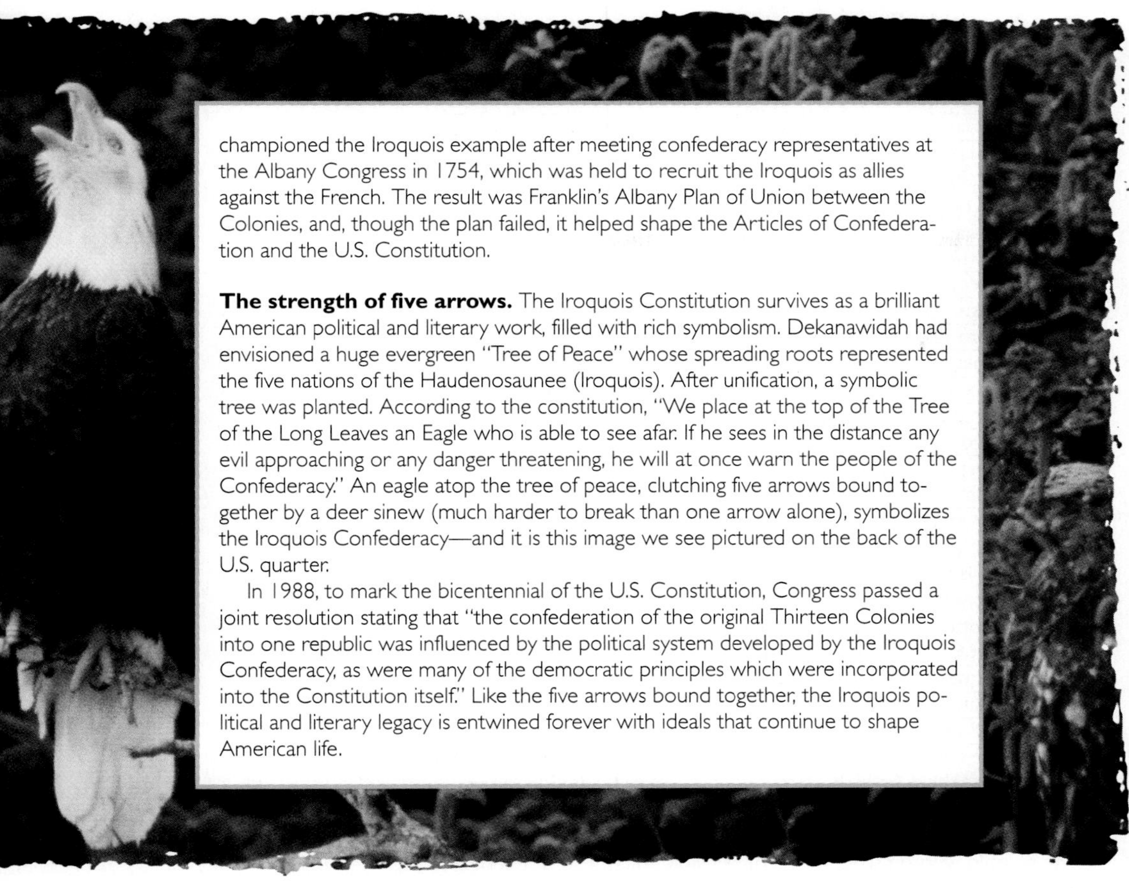

championed the Iroquois example after meeting confederacy representatives at the Albany Congress in 1754, which was held to recruit the Iroquois as allies against the French. The result was Franklin's Albany Plan of Union between the Colonies, and, though the plan failed, it helped shape the Articles of Confederation and the U.S. Constitution.

The strength of five arrows. The Iroquois Constitution survives as a brilliant American political and literary work, filled with rich symbolism. Dekanawidah had envisioned a huge evergreen "Tree of Peace" whose spreading roots represented the five nations of the Haudenosaunee (Iroquois). After unification, a symbolic tree was planted. According to the constitution, "We place at the top of the Tree of the Long Leaves an Eagle who is able to see afar. If he sees in the distance any evil approaching or any danger threatening, he will at once warn the people of the Confederacy." An eagle atop the tree of peace, clutching five arrows bound together by a deer sinew (much harder to break than one arrow alone), symbolizes the Iroquois Confederacy—and it is this image we see pictured on the back of the U.S. quarter.

In 1988, to mark the bicentennial of the U.S. Constitution, Congress passed a joint resolution stating that "the confederation of the original Thirteen Colonies into one republic was influenced by the political system developed by the Iroquois Confederacy, as were many of the democratic principles which were incorporated into the Constitution itself." Like the five arrows bound together, the Iroquois political and literary legacy is entwined forever with ideals that continue to shape American life.

He has abdicated government here withdrawing his governors, and declaring us out of his allegiance and protection.

by declaring us out of his protection, and waging war against us. (B)

He has plundered our seas, ravaged our coasts, burnt our towns, and destroyed the lives of our people.

He is at this time transporting large armies of foreign mercenaries to complete the works of death, desolation, and tyranny already begun with circumstances of cruelty and perfidy [ ] unworthy the head of a civilized nation.

scarcely paralleled in the most barbarous ages, and totally (C)

He has constrained our fellow citizens taken captive on the high seas, to bear arms against their country, to become the executioners of their friends and brethren, or to fall themselves by their hands.

He has [ ] endeavored to bring on the inhabitants of our frontiers, the merciless Indian savages, whose known rule of warfare is

excited domestic insurrection among us, and has

WORDS TO OWN

abdicated (ab′di·kāt′id) *v.:* given up responsibility for.

B. Critical Reading: Analyzing Tone

? What effect does the addition by Congress have on the Declaration? [Adding these words increases the severity of the charges made against George III.]

C. Literary Element: Parallelism

? How many paragraphs in the final draft of the Declaration begin with "He has" or "He is"? [Eighteen.] What do these paragraphs have in common? [Each is a charge against the king of England.]

COOPERATIVE LEARNING

Graphic Organizer Have students work in groups of four to create a graphic organizer that expresses the main ideas of the Declaration. You might suggest a flow chart or a cluster or ladder diagram. Students may find it helpful to take notes on the ideas, decide on an appropriate graphic organizer, and then collect and display the information. Show how to graph one idea in a chart or diagram on the chalkboard.

Sharing Cooperative Learning Results Following a cooperative learning activity, have each group present its work to the class. Have all group members stand for the presentation, even if the group has designated a speaker to show the group's visual work. As a conclusion, ask other group members for further contributions.

A. Critical Reading: Making Inferences
It is well known that Thomas Jefferson owned slaves. Nevertheless, based on the material omitted by Congress, what does his opinion of slavery seem to be? [Possible answer: He thinks it is a violation of the right of liberty, and he blames King George for the trouble between the European colonists and the African slaves.]

B. Language Note: Grammar
This sentence in the final draft is elegant, complex, and clear. Ask students to point out the subjects and verbs of the four clauses and to indicate how each clause functions in the sentence. [The subject and verb of the main clause are *prince* and *is*. One subordinate clause modifies *prince*. Its subject and verb are *character* and *is marked*. Another subordinate clause modifies *act*. Its subject and verb are *which* and *may define*. Yet another subordinate clause modifies *people*. Its subject and verb are *who* and *mean to be*.]

an undistinguished destruction of all ages, sexes, and conditions of existence.

He has incited treasonable insurrections of our fellow citizens, with the allurements of forfeiture and confiscation of our property.

(A) He has waged cruel war against human nature itself, violating its most sacred rights of life and liberty in the persons of a distant people who never offended him, captivating and carrying them into slavery in another hemisphere, or to incur miserable death in their transportation thither. This piratical warfare, the opprobrium[9] of INFIDEL powers, is the warfare of the CHRISTIAN king of Great Britain. Determined to keep open a market where MEN should be bought and sold, he has prostituted his negative[10] for suppressing every legislative attempt to prohibit or to restrain this execrable commerce. And that this assemblage of horrors might want no fact of distinguished die,[11] he is now exciting those very people to rise in arms among us, and to purchase that liberty of which he has deprived them, by murdering the people on whom he also obtruded them: thus paying off former crimes committed against the LIBERTIES of one people, with crimes which he urges them to commit against the LIVES of another.

In every stage of these oppressions we have petitioned for redress in the most humble terms: Our repeated petitions have been answered only by repeated injuries.

(B) A prince whose character is thus marked by every act which may define a tyrant is unfit to be the ruler of a [ ] people who mean to be free. Future ages will scarcely believe that the hardiness of one man adventured, within the short compass of twelve years only, to lay a foundation so broad and so undisguised for tyranny over a people fostered and fixed in principles of freedom. — free

Nor have we been wanting in attentions to our British brethren. We have warned them from time to time of attempts by their legislature to extend a jurisdiction over these our states. We have reminded them of the circumstances of our emigration and settlement here, no one of which could warrant so strange a pretension: that these were effected at the expense of our own blood and treasure, unassisted by the wealth or the strength of Great Britain: that in constituting indeed our several forms of government, we had adopted one common king, thereby laying a foundation for perpetual league and amity with them: but that submission to their parliament was no part of our constitution, nor ever in idea, if history may be credited: And, we [ ] appealed to their native justice and magnanimity as well as to the ties of our — an unwarrantable / us — have — and we have conjured[12] them by

9. **opprobrium** (ə·prō′brē·əm): shameful conduct.
10. **negative:** veto.
11. **fact of distinguished die:** clear stamp or mark of distinction. Jefferson is being sarcastic here.
12. **conjured** (kən·jo͞ord′): solemnly called upon.

Words to Own
confiscation (kän′fis·kā′shən) *n.:* seizure of property by authority.
magnanimity (mag′nə·nim′ə·tē) *n.:* nobility of spirit.

(Background) The Great Seal of the United States, original version; present seal reverse.
The Bettmann Archive.

Options for Teaching

Assessment Tools

Check Test: True-False
1. The Declaration of Independence explains the necessity and right of the Colonies to declare independence. [True]
2. Jefferson did not care that Congress deleted passages of his draft. [False]
3. The Declaration blames the king of England, rather than the British people, for the state of war. [True]
4. Jefferson's draft of the Declaration states that the king has waged war on human nature. [True]
5. The Declaration states that the Colonies had declared allegiance to the king, not to the jurisprudence of British Parliament. [True]

Ongoing Assessment Have students complete the following self-assessment statements after participating in group activities.
1. My contribution to the group was ______.
2. What I liked best about my group's work was ______.
3. One thing the group could have done better was ______.

common kindred to disavow these usurpations which were likely to interrupt our connection and correspondence. They too have been deaf to the voice of justice and of consanguinity,[13] and when occasions have been given them, by the regular course of their laws, of removing from their councils the disturbers of our harmony, they have, by their free election, re-established them in power. At this very time too, they are permitting their chief magistrate to send over not only soldiers of our common blood, but Scotch and foreign mercenaries to invade and destroy us. These facts have given the last stab to agonizing affection, and manly spirit bids us to renounce forever these unfeeling brethren. We must endeavor to forget our former love for them, and hold them as we hold the rest of mankind, enemies in war, in peace friends. We might have been a free and a great people together; but a communication of grandeur and of freedom, it seems, is below their dignity. Be it so, since they will have it. The road to happiness and to glory is open to us too. We will tread it apart from them and acquiesce in the necessity which denounces[14] our eternal separation [ ]!

would inevitably

We must therefore

and hold them as we hold the rest of mankind, enemies in war, in peace friends.

We, therefore, the representatives of the United States of America in General Congress assembled, [ ] do in the name, and by the authority of the good people of these states reject and renounce all allegiance and subjection to the kings of Great Britain and all others who may hereafter claim by, through or under them; we utterly dissolve all political connection which may heretofore have subsisted between us and the people or parliament of Great Britain: And finally we do assert and declare these colonies to be free and independent states, and that as free and independent states, they have full power to levy war, conclude peace, contract alliances, establish commerce, and to do all other acts and things which independent states may of right do.

appealing to the supreme judge of the world for the rectitude of our intentions,

colonies, solemnly publish and declare, that these united colonies are, and of right ought to be free and independent states; that they are absolved from all allegiance to the British crown, and that all political connection between them and the state of Great Britain is, and ought to be, totally dissolved;

And for the support of this declaration, [ ] we mutually pledge to each other our lives, our fortunes, and our sacred honor.

with a firm reliance on the protection of divine providence,

The Declaration thus signed on the 4th, on paper, was engrossed on parchment, and signed again on the 2d of August.

13. **consanguinity** (kän'saŋ·gwin'ə·tē): kinship; family relationship.
14. **denounces** (dē·nouns'iz): archaic for "announces, proclaims."

WORDS TO OWN
renounce (ri·nouns') *v.*: to give up.
acquiesce (ak'wē·es') *v.*: agree or accept quietly.

Syng silver used at the signing of the Declaration of Independence, Independence Hall, Philadelphia, Pennsylvania.
Joe Viesti/Viesti Associates.

C. Reader's Response: Shaping Interpretations
? What does the deleted passage mean? Why might it have been deleted? [Sample responses: Jefferson denounces the mercenaries in the British forces sent to the Colonies; or, he would have chosen peaceful coexistence, but these wrongs make that impossible. It might have been considered unnecessary since the points are covered in the remaining sentences.]

D. Literary Element: Style
? How many sentences compose the next-to-last paragraph of the final draft? How would you describe the style? [One sentence. It is elegant, involved, complex, elevated, and sophisticated.]

E. Expansion
Explain that the parchment copy of the Declaration was badly damaged in an 1823 attempt to make a copperplate facsimile and is now barely legible in parts. That copy of the Declaration is now on display in the National Archives Building in Washington, D.C.

Primary Sources

In the next to last paragraph, Jefferson refers to his many losses—the death of his wife, discredit resulting from the invasion of British forces in Virginia during his term as governor (1779–1781), and the childhood deaths of three of his children.

Making Meanings p. 125

First Thoughts

1. The passage beginning "We hold these truths to be self-evident . . ." because it is well known and embodies the democratic spirit.

Reviewing the Text

a. A "decent respect" for the opinions of others required them to explain the reasons for such drastic action.

b. "All men are created equal" and have "inalienable rights" that include "life, liberty, and the pursuit of happiness."

c. The refusal to assent to necessary laws; the harassment of legislative bodies; the dissolution of representative bodies; preventing the states from being settled and populated; the coercion of judges; the maintenance of standing armies in the Colonies; the plunder of coasts and destruction of towns; the coercion of citizens taken prisoner on the high seas; and inciting American Indians to war against the colonists.

d. Jefferson refers to the deletion of the clause accusing the king of perpetuating the slave trade.

Shaping Interpretations

2. The omission objecting to submission to the English Parliament; the change to "would inevitably" from "were likely to" destroy the colonists' connection with the English people; the deletion of "renounce forever these unfeeling brethren"; and the omission of the people of Great Britain in the last paragraph. Most citizens of the new country still felt close personal ties to England—many had relatives there.

3. Stylistic changes include "inherent and" to "certain"; the deletion of "begun at a distinguished period"; "among which appears . . . have" to "all having"; the deletion of "and continually." Political changes include "expunge" to "alter"; "in many cases"; the deletion of the reference to slavery; "a people who mean to be free" to "a free people."

4. The paragraph beginning "He has combined with others . . ." contains a number of clauses beginning with the word *for* plus a present participle ("for protecting," "for imposing"). The repetition creates a feeling of mounting offenses and contributes to a regular, almost poetic rhythm. The last lines, "our lives, our fortunes, and our sacred honor," repeat the word *our* in structurally balanced phrases. This parallelism adds emphasis to the personal commitment of the passage and a rhythm that builds to a powerful conclusion.

PRIMARY Sources  A LETTER

A Letter from Jefferson to His Daughter

In 1784, Jefferson was sent to Paris to work out the treaty ending the Revolutionary War. Jefferson stayed in France for five years. His daughter Patsy was in a Catholic convent school in Paris when Jefferson wrote this letter from the south of France. The wrist Jefferson complains of in the letter had been injured a few months earlier.

Aix-en-Provence, March 28, 1787

I was happy, my dear Patsy, to receive, on my arrival here, your letter informing me of your health and occupations. I have not written to you sooner because I have been almost constantly on the road. My journey hitherto has been a very pleasing one. It was undertaken with the hope that the mineral waters of this place might restore strength to my wrist. Other considerations also concurred. Instruction, amusement, and abstraction from business, of which I had too much at Paris. I am glad to learn that you are employed in things new and good in your music and drawing. You know what have been my fears for some time past; that you do not employ yourself so closely as I could wish. You have promised me a more assiduous attention, and I have great confidence in what you promise. It is your future happiness which interests me, and nothing can contribute more to it (moral rectitude always excepted) than the contracting a habit of industry and activity. Of all the cankers of human happiness, none corrodes it with so silent, yet so baneful a tooth, as indolence. . . . It is while we are young that the habit of industry is formed. If not then, it never is afterward. The fortune of our lives therefore depends on employing well the short period of youth. If at any moment, my dear, you catch yourself in idleness, start from it as you would from the precipice of a gulf. You are not, however, to consider yourself as unemployed while taking exercise. That is necessary for your health, and health is the first of all objects. For this reason if you leave your dancing master for the summer, you must increase your other exercise. I do not like your saying that you are unable to read the ancient print of your Livy,[1] but with the aid of your master. We are always equal to what we undertake with resolution. A little degree of this will enable you to decipher your Livy. If you always lean on your master, you will never be able to proceed without him. It is a part of the American character to consider nothing as desperate; to surmount every difficulty by resolution and contrivance. In Europe there are shops for every want. Its inhabitants therefore have no idea that their wants can be furnished otherwise. Remote from all other aid, we are obliged to invent and to execute; to find means within ourselves, and not to lean on others. Consider therefore the conquering your Livy as an exercise in the habit of surmounting difficulties, a habit which will be necessary to you in the country where you are to live, and without which you will be thought a very helpless animal, and less esteemed. . . .

You ask me to write you long letters. I will do it, my dear, on condition you will read them from time to time, and practice what they will inculcate. Their precepts will be dictated by experience, by a perfect knowledge of the situation in which you will be placed, and by the fondest love for you. This it is which makes me wish to see you more qualified than common. My expectations from you are high: yet not higher than you may attain. Industry and resolution are all that are wanting. Nobody in this world can make me so happy, or so miserable, as you. Retirement from public life will ere long become necessary for me. To your sister and yourself I look to render the evening of my life serene and contented. Its morning has been clouded by loss after loss till I have nothing left but you. I do not doubt either your affection or dispositions. But great exertions are necessary, and you have little time left to make them. Be industrious then, my dear child. Think nothing unsurmountable by resolution and application, and you will be all that I wish you to be. . . .

Continue to love me with all the warmth with which you are beloved by, my dear Patsy, yours affectionately,

TH: JEFFERSON

1. **Livy:** Roman historian (59 B.C.–A.D. 17).

MAKING MEANINGS

First Thoughts

1. What word, phrase, or **image** struck you as most important? Why?

> **Reviewing the Text**
>
> a. Explain why the Continental Congress wanted to publish its reasons for separating itself from Britain.
>
> b. The word *self-evident* refers to the truths that are accessible to our common sense. List the truths that Jefferson cites in particular.
>
> c. List the offenses charged to the king of England.
>
> d. Identify the specific clause struck out by Congress that Jefferson refers to in his opening paragraph. What does it accuse the king of doing?

Shaping Interpretations

2. What changes show a desire not to make an absolute break with the English people? Why do you think it would be important that the new nation maintain its "consanguinity," or close kinship, with the English people?
3. Which changes seem to have been adopted primarily for stylistic reasons, such as clarity or greater impact, and which for political reasons?
4. Find at least two passages in the Declaration that use **parallelism.** What is the effect of the parallel structure on the *idea* of the passage?

CHOICES: Building Your Portfolio

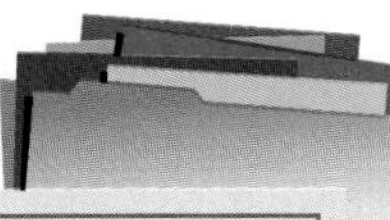

Writer's Notebook

1. Collecting Ideas for an Autobiographical Incident

Americans are fond of saying, "It's a free country." But freedom has its costs. After reviewing your Reader's Log, freewrite about an experience you've had when you realized that freedom can bring both benefits and burdens, gains and losses. Keep your notes; you may use them later in the Writer's Workshop on page 130.

Critical Writing

2. I Am Woman

On March 31, 1776, Abigail Adams (1744–1818) wrote to her husband John Adams, who was on the committee preparing the Declaration of Independence. In a brief essay, respond to this excerpt from her letter.

> ... in the new Code of Laws which I suppose it will be necessary for you to make, I desire you would remember the ladies, and be more generous and favorable to them than your ancestors. Do not put such unlimited power into the hands of the husbands. Remember all men would be tyrants if they could. If particular care and attention is not paid to the ladies, we are determined to foment a rebellion, and will not hold ourselves bound by any laws in which we have no voice, or representation.
>
> —Abigail Adams

Speaking and Listening

3. Equal Signs

In "Harrison Bergeron," a famous short story by Kurt Vonnegut, Jr. (1922–), Vonnegut imagines a future America in which "everybody was finally equal": "Nobody was smarter than anybody else. Nobody was better-looking than anybody else. Nobody was stronger or quicker than anybody else." In a panel discussion, explore what you and your classmates think the framers of the Declaration meant by the word *equal.*

Choices: Building Your Portfolio

1. **Writer's Notebook** Remind students to save their work. They may use it as prewriting for the Writer's Workshop on pp. 130–133.
2. **Critical Writing** Suggest that students select a persona to use for this writing activity. When they respond, who is the speaker? Is it the students themselves, writing from across the centuries? Is it Abigail Adams's husband, John Adams, and if so, does he tell her he will look out for the rights of women? Is the response from someone else of her era, and if so, does this person share her concerns?
3. **Speaking and Listening** Encourage the panel moderator to ask for clarification, elaboration, and explanation. You may want panels to have recorders who keep track of the main ideas and look for similarities and differences in opinions.

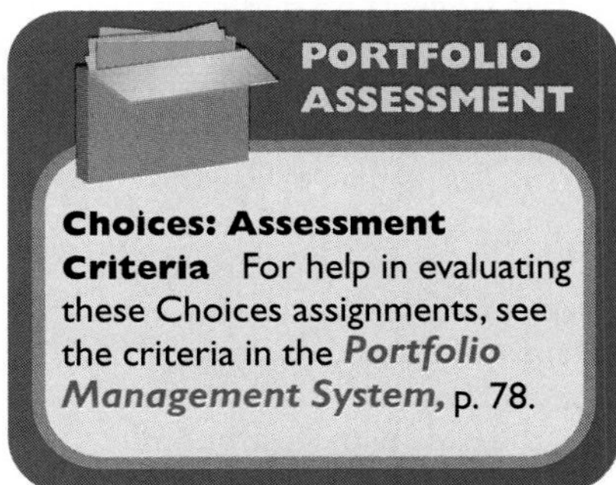

Choices: Assessment Criteria For help in evaluating these Choices assignments, see the criteria in the ***Portfolio Management System,*** p. 78.

STRATEGIES FOR INCLUSION

Visual

- For activity #1, have students work in small groups to brainstorm the many kinds of freedoms we have in the United States.
- Next, have groups brainstorm a responsibility or cost that accompanies each freedom.
- Groups should use a graphic organizer like the one here to show the relationships between freedoms and responsibilities.

Freedom	Responsibility
speech	cannot libel, slander, shout "fire" in theater

Interpersonal For activity #2, have students work in pairs to discuss the letter by Abigail Adams before responding to it. What threat does she make in her letter, and what does this indicate about her character? How does she follow the example of her husband and his peers?

Read On

Portfolio Assessment Options

The following projects can help you evaluate and assess your students' reading accomplishments outside of class. Videotapes or audiotapes of completed projects may be included in students' portfolios.

- **Illustrate a Reading** Encourage students to become more sensitive to sounds, rhythms, moods, and feelings displayed in prose and poetry by having them illustrate in a drawing or a painting their interpretation of the reading they have done. Students may also include audiocassettes of sounds to complement their illustrations.
- **Review on a Card** Have students review on an index card the book they have read. They should also include the title of the book, the author, the topic, and a brief synopsis. The card should be turned in and filed by topic. The file box may then be used as a resource for students who are looking for books to read about particular topics.
- **Research a Related Topic** Have students research a particular topic that the book addresses. For Arthur Miller's play, students could research the witchcraft trials; for Nathaniel Hawthorne's book, students could research the consequences of breaking a law—civil or church—in Puritan times. The students' findings should be presented informally to the class with illustrations.
- **Tell the Story** Have students work in groups of five or six for storytelling. Students should sit in a circle. Each student becomes one of the characters from the book he or she has read. Students tell the story from that character's point of view. All students get a turn to tell their stories.

Coming to America

"It was 1906. I was six years old and we were on a train with some other immigrants. . . . When people on the train spoke to me in Russian, I said, 'Speak only English. I'm an Americanka now.'" Thus recalls Sonia Walinsky, just one of dozens of immigrants—both common people and well-known individuals—whose testimonials Joan Morrison and Charlotte Fox Zabusky gathered in *American Mosaic* (E. P. Dutton), a collection of vivid remembrances by immigrants from many lands.

For a Captive Audience

In 1704, as part of the fighting during the War of the Spanish Succession, or Queen Anne's War, a French and American Indian raiding party captured a family of British Puritans in Deerfield, Massachusetts. Though the rest of the family was released, young Eunice Williams remained with the Mohawks, refusing to return home even when she could. The prize-winning historian John Demos tells Eunice's gripping story in *The Unredeemed Captive* (Alfred A. Knopf).

Profoundly Puritan

A *crucible* is a great trial or test of endurance. *The Crucible* is the twentieth-century playwright Arthur Miller's masterful work about some of the most famous trials in American history, the 1692 witchcraft trials in Salem, Massachusetts. Several film versions of the play also exist.

Also set in Puritan times, *The Scarlet Letter* by Nathaniel Hawthorne is a brief but powerful tale dealing with sin and its consequences. It touches on many of the major conflicts in literature—emotion vs. reason, love vs. hate, the individual vs. society. The book has inspired several film adaptations.

Another Passage

In 1830, African American Rutherford Calhoun, newly freed from slavery, stows away on a ship without realizing it is bound for Africa and the slave trade. His trip is chronicled in Charles Johnson's National Book Award–winning novel *Middle Passage* (Atheneum), another view of the experience of slavery.

Revolutionary Tales

What was it like to be there when "the shot heard round the world" was fired? In *April Morning* (Crown), Howard Fast describes the first battle of the Revolution from the viewpoint of young Adam Cooper of the Lexington militia. For another view of the time, try Fast's historical novel, *Citizen Tom Paine* (Grove Press), the story of the famous patriot from his early days in poverty to his last days in infamy.

FOR FURTHER EXPLORATION

Fiction

Black Boy by Richard Wright
The Jungle by Upton Sinclair
My Antonia by Willa Cather
Texas by James Michener
Barrio Boy by Ernesto Galarza

Nonfiction

A Government of Our Own: The Making of the Confederacy by William C. Davis

Song

Songs of Gold Mountain by Marlon K. Hom

The American Language

"Revolutionary" English

by Gary Q. Arpin

As American English began to develop in the years following the settlement of North America by Europeans, differences between British and American usage became more and more apparent. British travelers noticed that Americans spoke with a nasality that was disagreeable to their British ears. The visitors also noticed what they thought of as corruptions of the language: Words were being used in "barbarous" ways, and brand-new words were being coined at an alarming rate. (A)

Effects of Physical Separation

The simple fact of physical separation caused some of the differences between British and American English. Differences in pronunciation, for example, became marked as the accents of speakers on both sides of the ocean gradually changed. Such differences are apparent even today; for example, British speakers omit the vowel before the second *r* in words like *secretary* and *laboratory*, but most Americans pronounce all the syllables in such words.

Physical separation also resulted in differences in usage. In the Colonies, for example, and especially in New England, it was common to hear someone speak of throwing a *rock*. In Britain, however, *rock* continued to refer only to a massive stone, such as Plymouth Rock. Throwing a rock would have seemed as odd to a British person as tossing a boulder would be to an American.

Sometimes the meaning or usage of a word would change in England while Americans retained its older meaning. The American usage of *guess* to mean "suppose" is an example of this. In the eighteenth and nineteenth centuries, "I guess" in this sense sounded odd to British visitors, who would have said, "I suppose." But these visitors were unaware that "I guess" had been common in England until the eighteenth century. (It even appears in the writings of Chaucer and Shakespeare.) The British also criticized Americans for saying *fall* instead of *autumn,* apparently unaware that *fall* had been used in England until around 1750.

Ugly Americanisms

The word *Americanism* came into use to describe a word or expression that originated in the United States or that was peculiar to the States. The word was first used in print in 1781 by the Reverend John Witherspoon, a Scottish clergyman who had come to this country in 1768 to become president of the College of New Jersey (now Princeton University). Witherspoon traveled a good deal and recorded words and phrases that were peculiar to the United States. (B) Many of these words are so common today that it's hard to imagine a time when they might have been considered unusual. Among the Americanisms recorded by Witherspoon were *to notify,* meaning "to inform"; *mad,* in the sense of "angry"; *chunks,* to describe big pieces of wood; *spell,* meaning "a period of time" (as in "a spell of bad weather"); *once in a while,* meaning "occasionally"; and *tote,* meaning "to carry."

Some critics considered English to be a complete language that had evolved through the centuries to a state of perfection in the eighteenth century. Any change was horrendous to them, especially any change brought about by people thought to be unrefined. As one writer put it around 1800, "A language, arrived at its zenith, requires no introduction of new words." (C)

Some years later, the same point was made by a British purist in response to a question posed by the American language

A. Cultural Connections
Thomas Jefferson once said that "new circumstances . . . call for new words, new phrases, and the transfer of old words to new objects."

B. Critical Reading: Finding Details
? In what three fundamental ways do British and American English differ? [Pronunciation, usage, and vocabulary.]

C. Reader's Response: Connecting with the Text
? What things in this decade do you think will have a lasting effect on the English language? [Sample responses: The space program, biotechnology, home videos, computers, foreign relations, or new immigrants.]

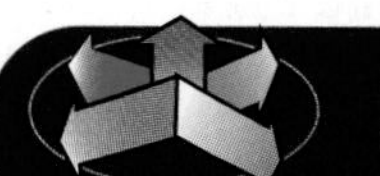

PROGRAM MANAGER

- **Planning Instruction** See Teaching Notes, *Teaching Resources A,* p. 45, for objectives.
- **Assessment** See The American Language, *Test Booklet,* pp. 31–32.

OPTIONS FOR TEACHING

STRATEGIES FOR INCLUSION

Visual/Auditory Show students a British movie such as *Howards End* or *The Remains of the Day.* Have students identify specific phrases, pronunciations, vocabulary, or grammar that they find difficult to understand. Use these examples to discuss how American and British English have diverged.

Art Ask students to create and illustrate political cartoons from their reading of *The American Language*. Students may work individually or with partners. Bring to class examples of political cartoons to share and model.

Interpersonal Have students work in groups of three to discuss *The American Language*. Have each student tell the other two about some unusual word usage that he or she has heard from another language or another part of the country. ☞

A. Reader's Response: Extending the Text

? Can literature be used as an authority for usage if American speech keeps changing? [Sample responses: Even though speech keeps changing, literature can represent accepted usage; or speech is too dynamic and evolving to ever be set in stone in literature.]

B. Critical Reading: Finding Details

? Why did people think that there was little authority supporting the constant changes in American usage of the English language? [America was a new country, and there was little distinctly American literature at that time.]

C. Reader's Response: Challenging the Text

? Are there differences in American English today? [Sample responses: Yes, the differences in dialect and vocabulary found across the United States denote various regional influences and backgrounds; or no, there are no significant differences.]

expert Noah Webster (page 195). Webster had asked, "If a word becomes universally current in America . . . why should it not take its station in the language?" The British purist, a certain Captain Basil Hall, replied, "Because there are words enough already."

> If, as many people thought, literature was an authority for usage, then there was little authority supporting American usage.

Reinforcing the purist's position was the fact that until the early nineteenth century, there was little distinctly *American* literature. There was not much demonstration of the *power* of the American idiom, and little indication that American speech could lead to anything of lasting worth. If, as many people thought, literature was an authority for usage, then there was little authority supporting American usage.

Many people on both sides of the question expected, or feared, that the two forms of English would eventually grow separate until the two groups would no longer understand each other. They predicted that Americans, completely cut off from their past, would have to read the works of Shakespeare and Milton in translation.

"What Language Should Americans Speak?"

The conflict between purists and advocates of change was especially heated in America in the eighteenth and nineteenth centuries. On the American side, the rejection of English authority in language was for some an aspect of America's rejection of English political authority. In 1788, a march in New York supporting the ratification of the U.S. Constitution contained a language contingent. This group carried a scroll advocating the use of something called "Federal English." A Federal English would establish the independence of American English and, at the same time, preserve the purity of the language in its new home.

The most radical political position on language argued for the establishment in America of a completely new language. At various times French, Greek, and Hebrew were suggested as alternatives. Each had as its principal virtue, apparently, the fact that it was not English. Nor was it Spanish, the other main Colonial language, or one of the many Native American languages. (Though words like *raccoon* from Virginia Algonquian and *totem* from Ojibwa have been with us since the eighteenth century, English was only minimally influenced by the languages of American Indians, largely because political dominance was held by English-speaking settlers.)

Democratic Language

Some proponents of American English pointed to the humble, democratic character of the language as its greatest virtue: Class distinctions were not marked by accents in America, as they were in Britain, and geographical differences in speech were not nearly as important.

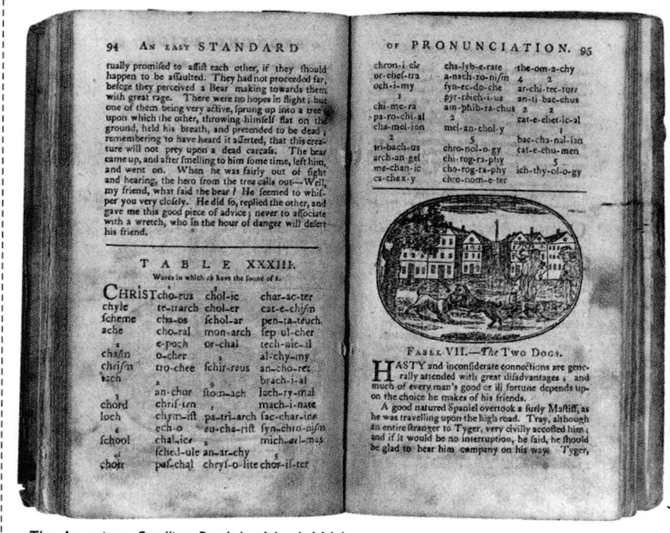
94 AN EASY STANDARD

tually promiſed to aſſiſt each other, if they ſhould happen to be aſſaulted. They had not proceeded far, before they perceived a Bear making towards them with great rage. There were no hopes in flight; but one of them being very active, ſprung up into a tree; upon which the other, throwing himſelf flat on the ground, held his breath, and pretended to be dead; remembering to have heard it aſſerted, that this creature will not prey upon a dead carcaſs. The bear came up, and after ſmelling to him ſome time, left him, and went on. When he was fairly out of ſight and hearing, the hero from the tree calls out—Well, my friend, what ſaid the bear? He ſeemed to whiſper you very cloſely. He did ſo, replied the other, and gave me this good piece of advice; never to aſſociate with a wretch, who in the hour of danger will deſert his friend.

TABLE XXXIII.

Words in which *ch* have the ſound of *k*.

CHRIST cho-rus chol-ic char-ac-ter
chyle te-trarch chol-er cat-e-chiſm
ſcheme cha-os ſchol-ar pen-ta-teuch
ache cho-ral mon-arch ſep-ul-cher
e-poch or-chal tech-nic-al
chaſm o-cher al-chy-my
chriſm tro-chee ſchir-rous an-cho-ret
tach brach-i-al
an-chor ſtom-ach lach-ry-mal
chord chriſ-ten mach-i-nate
loch chym-iſt pa-tri-arch ſac-char-ine
ech-o eu-cha-riſt ſyn-chro-niſm
ſchool chal-ice mich-ael-mas
ſched-ule an-ar-chy
choir paſ-chal chryſ-o-lite chor-iſ-ter

OF PRONUNCIATION. 95

chron-i-cle cha-lyb-e-rate the-om-a-chy
or-cheſ-tra a-nach-ro-niſm
och-i-my ſyn-ec-do-che ar-chi-tec-ture
pyr-rhich-i-us an-ti-bac-chus
chi-me-ra am-phib-ra-chus
pa-ro-chi-al cat-e-chet-ic-al
cha-mel-ion mel-an-chol-y
bac-cha-nal-ian
tri-bach-us chro-nol-o-gy cat-e-chu-men
arch-an-gel chi-rog-ra-phy
me-chan-ic cho-rog-ra-phy ich-thy-ol-o-gy
ca-chex-y chro-nom-e-ter

FABLE VII.—*The* TWO DOGS.

HASTY and inconſiderate connections are generally attended with great diſadvantages; and much of every man's good or ill fortune depends upon the choice he makes of his friends.

A good natured Spaniel overtook a ſurly Maſtiff, as he was travelling upon the high road. Tray, although an entire ſtranger to Tyger, very civilly accoſted him; and if it would be no interruption, he ſaid, he ſhould be glad to bear him company on his way. Tyger,

The American Spelling Book by Noah Webster.

New York Public Library.

OPTIONS FOR TEACHING

INTEGRATING THE LANGUAGE ARTS

Strategic Reading The Directed Reading-Thinking Activity lets students set their own purposes for reading, and tests and evaluates their ideas through observation and organization of available data. Students should write their responses:

1. Answer the following two questions after reading the title and looking at the pictures and other graphics.
   a. What do you think the reading selection is about?
   b. Why do you think so?
2. Read until you can tell if your guess about the reading was correct.
   a. Were you right or wrong?
   b. How do you know?
3. Before you continue reading, answer these questions:
   a. What do you think will happen next?
   b. Why?
4. Read until you can tell what happened next.
   a. Were you right or wrong?
   b. How do you know?

Remind students that subtitles should be restated as a question and serve as the purpose for reading the section they introduce.

Because of this, an American would (in theory, at least) be immediately understood and accepted wherever he or she went in the country, which was not the case in England. Of course, there were still some regional differences in language. One writer's observation that "America has no dialects" was surely overstated.

John Adams (1735–1826) argued for the establishment of an American academy that would try to govern the usage of English in America and protect it against whatever changes might originate in England in the future. Having established its democratic purpose and its independence from the British, American English would thereafter remain stable or at least change only in approved ways.

Language Resists Rules

Language changes primarily according to the way it is used, not the way authorities say it should be used. Thomas Jefferson (page 114), perhaps the best American linguist of the Revolutionary period, took the most reasonable view. Speaking of the foundations of an American academy, he wrote:

> If, like the French Academicians, it were proposed to *fix* our language, it would be fortunate that the step was not taken in the days of our Saxon ancestors, whose vocabulary would ill express the science of this day.

Thus, Jefferson found himself at odds with both British and American purists. And he was right. The move for an academy finally died, and the American language continued to develop in its own unpredictable and exuberant ways.

Try It Out

1. Eighteenth-century British purists complained about the ways Americans adapted words to suit life in the Colonies. Their criticism was based on an assumption that words should develop historically from their roots, not in response to need and usage. Explain how the histories of the following words, all in common English usage, puncture the purists' argument. A good dictionary will give you the information you need.

clue	precocious
companion	steward
daughter	town
expedite	

2. Look up the following items in an American dictionary that includes British pronunciations (such as *Webster's New World Dictionary*) or in a British dictionary (like the *Oxford English Dictionary*). How is each pronounced in Great Britain? in the United States?

ate	schedule
been	lieutenant
clerk	the letter z

3. The following expressions are all Americanisms—they originated in America or have a usage peculiar to American speech. What do the words reveal about features and customs that were uniquely American? What other Americanisms can you add to the list?

cold snap	potpie
dude	ranch
everglade	salt lick
Indian summer	snowshoe

4. In France and in Quebec province in Canada, official or semiofficial organizations try to regulate the usage of language. Such organizations decide on proper spelling and whether a foreign word should be accepted into the language, among other things. Should such an organization oversee American English as John Adams suggested? Together with four or five other students, discuss this issue. The discussion should (1) begin by stating why the question is of interest to Americans; (2) present some reasons why an American-language regulatory commission would be a good idea; (3) offer some reasons why language regulation would *not* be a good idea; and (4) conclude by stating whether such an organization to regulate American English should or should not be established.

D. Cultural Connections

The idea that language changes according to the way it is used is a controversial one among many language scholars. For example, while the word *author* is used by many Americans today as a verb as well as a noun, language purists continue to resist accepting these changes; others like the use of *host* as a verb, or *they* as a referent for everyone.

Try It Out: Answers

1. The histories of these words prove that the British themselves had long since adapted their words in response to need and usage, often drawing on other languages for needed words.
2. ate: (et) in England
   been: (bēn) in England
   clerk: (klärk) in England
   schedule: (shed′yo͞o l) in England
   lieutenant: (lef ten′ ənt) in England
   the letter z: (zed) in England
3. Answers regarding what the words reveal about features and customs peculiar to American life will vary. Responses may include distinctly American elements of climate, diet, geography, topography, agriculture, and development of the economy.
4. In order to have an organized discussion, encourage each group to begin by brainstorming and then to respond to each area of discussion.

ASSESSMENT TOOLS

Check Test: Questions and Answers

1. In what three fundamental ways do British and American English differ? [Pronunciation, usage, and vocabulary.]
2. What was a cause for differences between British and American English? [Physical separation.]
3. What is an *Americanism?* [A word or expression that originated in or that was peculiar to the United States.]
4. What was the purists' view in regard to American English? [They objected to changes originating in America.]
5. What was Thomas Jefferson's view regarding the English language? [He thought that the language should change with the times.]

QUICK PLANNING GUIDE

Motivation

Bring several autobiographical books, magazine articles or newspaper stories to class and ask students to discuss ways in which they are similar to and different from the autobiographical writings of Bradstreet and Franklin. Point out that each work is in some way a self-examination. Explain to students that their assignment will be to write about an autobiographical incident in a way that examines some aspect of their selves.

PROGRAM MANAGER

Computer Guided Instruction For a related autobiographical incident assignment that students may use as additional instruction, see *Writer's Workshop 2.*

BUILDING YOUR PORTFOLIO

Writer's Workshop

Technology HELP

See Writer's Workshop 2 CD-ROM. *Assignment: Autobiographical Incident.*

ASSIGNMENT
Write a narrative about a significant incident in your life that helped you to learn more about yourself.

AIM
To express yourself; to inform.

AUDIENCE
Your classmates, family, or general readers.

NARRATIVE WRITING

AUTOBIOGRAPHICAL INCIDENT

The ancient Greeks followed an important maxim: "Know thyself." The Greek philosopher Plato went even further and said, "The life which is unexamined is not worth living." Many of the early American writers you have studied in these collections struggled to make sense of themselves and their experiences. From the Puritan tendency to examine oneself for signs of salvation to Benjamin Franklin's inventory of methods for attaining moral perfection to the latest biographies, memoirs, and self-help books on the best-seller lists, self-examination has been an important feature of the American character. You can do a little of your own self-examination by writing about an **autobiographical incident:** an event from your life that taught you something, that contributed to your self-knowledge.

Prewriting

WORK IN PROGRESS

1. **Choosing an incident.** An incident is a specific occurrence—usually one that takes place over a short period of time, from a few minutes to a few days. The incident you choose to narrate might be a moment of crisis or danger, but it might just as likely be a quiet, seemingly ordinary event or encounter that nevertheless had significance for you. If you've kept your Writer's Notebook notes from these collections, you may already have some ideas for an autobiographical incident you want to recount.

   If you still haven't decided what to write about, it might help to draw a "road map" of your life, starting at birth and extending to the present. As you extend the line, jot down significant events that come to mind. At points where you think the course of your life changed in an important way, draw a turn in the road. Look over your road map, and select the topic that draws your interest the most and isn't too private to comfortably share with others.

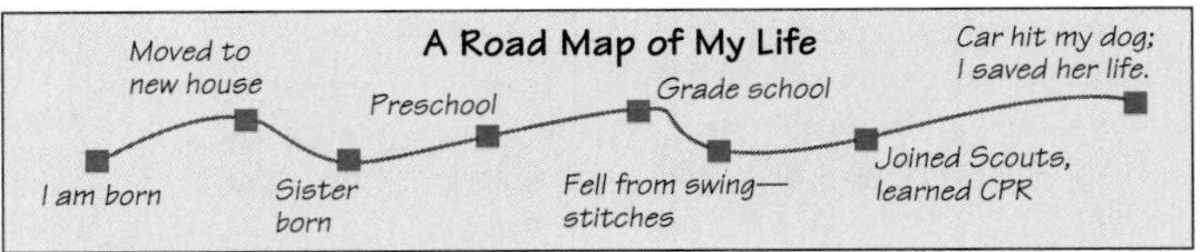

2. **Freewriting to remember details.** To recall specific details about your incident, freewrite your memories of it. Pay special attention to

PORTFOLIO ASSESSMENT

- **Generating Ideas** To help students in prewriting, use the heuristic in the ***Portfolio Management System,*** p. 79.
- **Assessment Rubric** For a rubric that can be used to assess students' progress in writing, see the ***Portfolio Management System,*** p. 81.

details that involve the senses: What smells, sounds, sights, tastes, and textures characterized your experience? If you have difficulty recalling details of the incident, here are some memory-prompting techniques you can try:

- **Visualizing.** Close your eyes and see the scene in your mind. Jot down images as they occur to you.
- **Visiting.** If you can, go back to the location where the event took place. Note details, and give your memories time to emerge.
- **Interviewing.** Talk to people who were involved—family members, friends, neighbors, and teachers. Ask how they remember the incident.
- **Using memory "souvenirs."** Find objects and other artifacts you associate with the incident—a photo, a scarf, a song, even a perfume scent—and focus on the memories they bring back.

The list you generate can give you a menu of materials from which to choose. Select the details that ring true and that will give the reader a vivid picture of the incident you are relating.

3. **Discovering your meaning.** Most likely, the meaning of your incident will emerge in the process of writing. You might, however, want to write a brief, private statement of what the incident meant to you. Or, you may want to discuss it with a friend or relative. These steps can help you focus your ideas when you're shaping your initial draft.

Drafting

1. **Establishing the context.** Your readers may need some background, or context, in order to understand how and why the incident is significant in your life. Select necessary details about people, places, relationships, and prior events that put the incident in context. Be careful, however, not to bog down your narrative with background information that's irrelevant.
2. **Conveying a tone.** Depending on the incident, its effects, and your own personality, your attitude toward the subject might be lighthearted, satirical, nostalgic, angry, rueful, or solemn. This attitude will come across to readers as the **tone** of your narrative. As you write, and as you re-read your first draft, make sure that the tone you are using is deliberately chosen and is the one you wish to communicate to your readers.
3. **Ordering events.** Most narratives move forward chronologically, from the first event in a sequence to the last. To give yourself a basic framework for your narrative during this initial draft stage, try following the pattern of organization shown on page 132. In revision stages, you can experiment

Strategies for Elaboration

Here are some effective ways to open an autobiographical incident.

1. **Start with intriguing dialogue:** "Any particular reason there's a fish in the bathtub?" Janine asked me nonchalantly.
2. **Hint at things to come:** A box of old, musty books changed my life.
3. **Turn up the atmosphere and suspense:** I had always suspected that the old house next door was haunted. After what happened to me there on my thirteenth birthday, I was certain of it.
4. **Join events in progress:** This was it—my first vocal solo with the choir. So I opened my mouth and—squeaked.

Teaching the Lesson

Remind students that the purposes of writing about an autobiographical incident are to share a personal insight with others, to express themselves, and to provide information.

This lesson includes instruction for each stage of the writing process. Guide students by modeling each stage with your own writing.

Prewriting

Remind students to choose an incident they would not mind sharing with others. Tell students that they may write about anything from simple moments that taught them something to events that changed their lives.

Drafting

Ask students to focus on how the incident started. Ask students to write at least one alternate opening, using one of the Strategies for Elaboration on p. 131.

OPTIONS FOR TEACHING

STRATEGIES FOR INCLUSION

Advanced To give students experience with writing their autobiographical incident in a different genre, have them write a poem—such as a ballad, or a narrative or lyric poem—about the same incident. Students may wish to read English ballads, or Longfellow's "The Cross of Snow" on p. 178 or Frost's "The Death of the Hired Man" on p. 569, to get a sense of the narrative power of different types of poems.

Visual Ask students to proofread a partner's autobiographical incident and to circle any coordinating conjunctions. Students should then read their partner's paper a second time and underline in another color any sentences that could be connected to make the writing more coherent. This exercise will help prepare students for the Language Workshop on p. 134.

Evaluating and Revising

Ask students to use the Evaluation Criteria for an Autobiographical Incident on p.133 when reviewing each other's papers. Remind students to read their sentences carefully and to use connective words whenever appropriate. For help with coordinating conjunctions, refer students to the Language Workshop on p. 134.

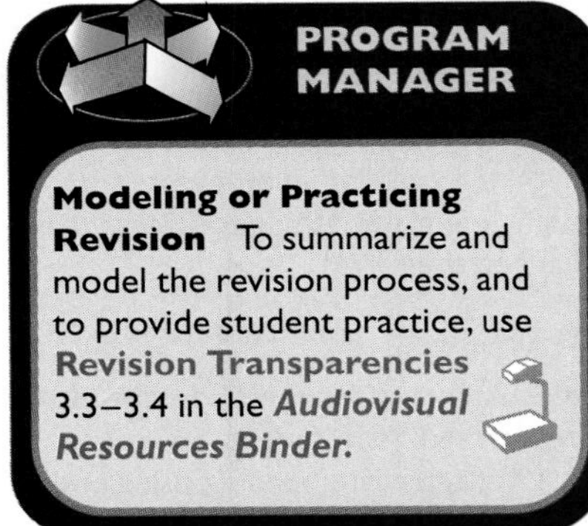

Modeling or Practicing Revision To summarize and model the revision process, and to provide student practice, use **Revision Transparencies** 3.3–3.4 in the ***Audiovisual Resources Binder.***

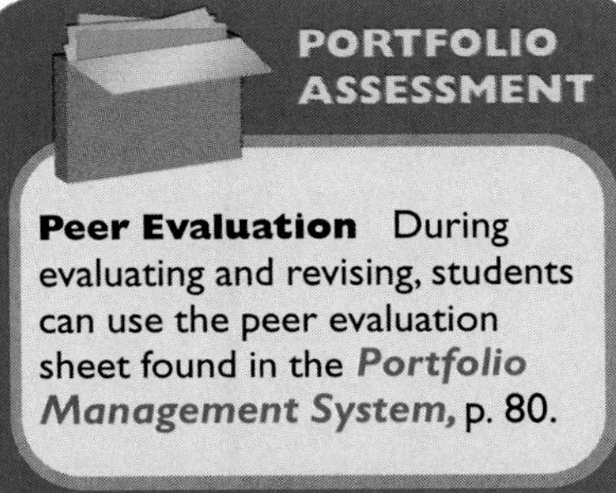

Peer Evaluation During evaluating and revising, students can use the peer evaluation sheet found in the ***Portfolio Management System,*** p. 80.

Try It Out: Answers

Students' frameworks will vary. Make sure that each framework includes an introduction, a chronological list of events, and a conclusion.

Try It Out

Fill out the following to generate a framework for your essay.

Introduction (attention-getting opening)

____

____

Order of events

1. ________________
2. ________________
3. ________________

Conclusion (statement of the significance of the event)

____

____

with the order, perhaps beginning with the climax of the action and then using flashbacks to show what led up to the central incident. Some writers even begin with a reflection on the meaning of the experience.

4. **Using narrative devices.** Your autobiographical incident essay can benefit from the use of these narrative devices—the stock in trade of autobiographical as well as fiction writers.
   - **Be specific: Show, don't simply tell.** Use specific names of people, places, and objects. Instead of "dog," write "Bobbi, my black Labrador retriever." Record specific actions such as gestures, movements, body language: "My heart pumped as wildly as my arms and legs as I ran from the front porch to the horrible scene in the middle of the street." Use all the types of sensory images, not just visual ones: Describe sounds, smells, tastes, and physical sensations.
   - **Use dramatic techniques.** Use flashbacks or foreshadowing if they increase suspense and help your pacing. Play on the element of surprise by withholding some important information from your readers until the crucial moment. Add tension and suspense: Treat your key scene like the climax of a movie, slowing your pace in order to "zoom in" on the pivotal moment of your incident. Use the verbal equivalent of such cinematic techniques as long shots and close-ups.
   - **Use realistic dialogue.** Record as accurately as you can what you and others said. Dialogue can effectively reveal character and move the events of your narrative forward.
5. **Writing a satisfying conclusion.** Your conclusion may simply reveal the final outcome of events or consist of a few reflective comments. Or, it may be the place where you make clear how the incident you reported was significant for you. For example, your clearheaded response to an incident in which your dog was run over by a car might have been a central event in the development of your self-confidence. You'll want to share the feelings you remember as you recall the incident as well as the insights you gained from it.

Model: A Conclusion

All through my childhood I had felt a bit uncertain of myself. An overweight kid, I was hopeless at most sports, and although I was a pretty good student, I had always agonized over tests and homework. Anything new, even if it was something as simple as learning a new craft at camp or going to a party where I didn't know many people, always filled me with dread. What if I wasn't good enough? What if I failed? Those feelings of inadequacy were never quite as strong after the incident with my dog Bobbi when I was eleven. I had kept my head during a crisis and saved my dog's life. I knew that I was a capable, competent kid—that a lot of my friends probably wouldn't have done as well in a similar situation. My love for my dog had made me brave, and my moment of bravery made me believe in myself to a degree I never had before. It was a good feeling.

OPTIONS FOR TEACHING — INTEGRATING THE LANGUAGE ARTS

Strategic Reading When students are satisfied with the content of their first drafts, they should re-read the drafts to look for ways to make them more clear and precise. Students should read the drafts three times, each time focusing on one of the following steps:

1. Scan the writing, looking for simple errors.
2. Read the writing, focusing on content.
3. Read the writing again, focusing on usage, mechanics, and grammatical errors.

Language and Style Ask students to have partners read their autobiographical incidents and point out language and style changes that might be made. The partner and writer should discuss specific improvements such as adding more sensory details or dialogue, while the writer takes notes.

Evaluating and Revising

1. **Peer review.** With a small group of students, read and discuss one another's autobiographical narratives. Some good focal points for discussion are these:
   - Did the writer describe the experience in sufficient detail? Was there anything more you felt you needed or wanted to know?
   - Were any details out of place or unnecessary?
   - What areas could the writer most improve on? Does the narrative need more sensory details, better pacing, more dialogue, a different and more effective organization?
   - How effective was the writer in getting you to care about the incident and the effect it had on his or her life? Did the writing seem honest and personal? Was the tone appropriate to the content?
   - Did the narrative come to a satisfying conclusion? Could you understand why the incident was significant for the writer?
2. **Self-evaluation.** After you've listened to your peers' comments, reread your paper while considering which comments you agree with. You are the author and the ultimate judge of what changes will make your piece more effective.

   Look over the Evaluation Criteria, and see if your essay contains everything on the list. Identify three areas for improvement in your essay, and make appropriate revisions.

Proofreading

After improving your paper's content, style, and structure as much as you can, polish it to correct any errors in grammar, spelling, or mechanics.

Publishing

Consider reading your autobiographical narrative aloud to the class, or exchange papers with another student to read silently. You might prepare a clean copy of your essay for publication in a class book of autobiographical narratives. You could also make a cassette recording of your essay for others to listen to.

Reflecting on Your Writing

Now, consider this writing experience as an autobiographical incident in itself. Think and write about what you have learned. Use the sentence starters below as springboards for reflection. Remember to date your work for your portfolio.

1. The method that I found most helpful for recalling the details of the incident was . . . .
2. The most rewarding part of writing this essay was . . . . The part that was most challenging was . . . .
3. Some things I think I do well in my writing are . . . . Some areas for improvement are . . . .
4. If I were to write another autobiographical incident in the future, I would do . . . differently because . . . .

Evaluation Criteria

A good autobiographical incident

1. *focuses on a single incident*
2. *includes enough background information for the reader to understand what happened*
3. *presents events in a logical, coherent order*
4. *includes sensory details and describes specific actions to bring the incident to life*
5. *makes the personal significance of the incident clear through either implication or direct statement*

Language Handbook HELP

Quotation marks: page 1246.

Reteaching

If students are having difficulty writing, provide them with a simple graphic organizer and ask them to use it to record depictions of symbols, images, and physical objects they remember from their incidents. Then, have students write short capsule explanations of the significance of each of the items in the graphic organizer. Ask students to write detailed descriptions for a few of the more important capsule explanations. Then, help them work their detailed descriptions into paragraphs for use in their papers.

Closure

Ask students to describe the similarities and differences between their autobiographical incidents and the autobiographical works they have read in books, magazines, or newspapers.

Portfolio

Reflecting on Your Writing

- Remind students that it is important to maintain a written record of their reflections because it will help them to remember which activities or procedures enabled them to write most effectively.
- Have students include their responses to the Reflecting on Your Writing questions in their portfolios, attached to their autobiographical incidents.

COOPERATIVE LEARNING

Book Making Have students work in groups of five to create books containing their autobiographical incidents. Students should read the incidents written by group members and organize them by topic or by other criteria. Students should select a group leader, an illustrator for the book cover, a typist or word processor, a bookbinder, and a spokesperson. Have students show their books to the class, talk about how they put them together, and read a few passages from each essay.

ASSESSMENT TOOLS

Self-Assessment Ask students to evaluate their essays using the following scale and list of criteria.

1=Needs work 2=Adequate 3=Superior

____ Focuses on a single event
____ Includes enough background information for the reader to understand what happened
____ Presents events in a logical, coherent order
____ Includes sensory details and describes specific actions to bring the incident to life
____ Makes the personal significance of the incident clear through either implication or direct statement

Language Workshop

Connecting to Students' Writing

As a proofreading exercise, have students select a piece of writing from their portfolios. Ask them to use the graphic organizer below to add connective words to the sentences in each paragraph where connectors are needed in order to provide coherence and logic to their writing. Tell students that they do not need to use connective words to connect all sentences.

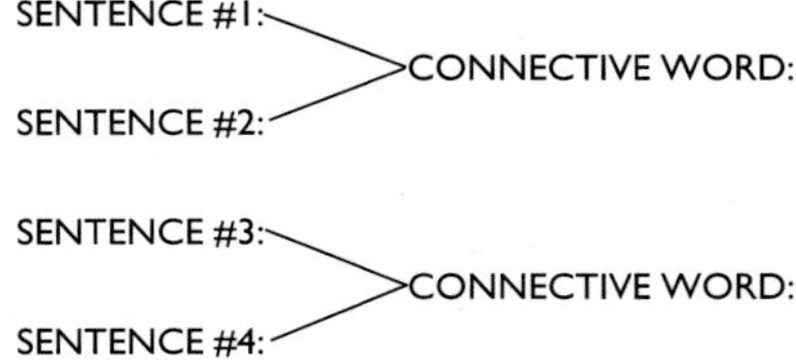

Try It Out: Answers

1. Franklin wished to achieve moral perfection, so he devised a book in which he could record his transgressions and his progress.
2. It is not easy to achieve moral perfection, but one can still try.

PROGRAM MANAGER

- **Extra Practice and Guided Instruction** For more instruction and practice on coordinating conjunctions, see Language Workshop in *Teaching Resources A*, pp. 56–57.
- **Extra Practice or Guided Instruction** See *Language Workshop:* Connective words and phrases for more practice or guided instruction in connective words.

Technology HELP

See Language Workshop CD-ROM. *Key word entry: connective words and phrases.*

Language Handbook HELP

Combining by coordinating ideas: page1238.

Linking It Up: Coordinating Conjunctions

Here's one way to describe Benjamin Franklin's plight when he first arrived in Philadelphia:

> Benjamin Franklin was practically penniless when he arrived in Philadelphia. He was able to buy some bread.

Here's a better way to express the same information:

> Benjamin Franklin was practically penniless when he arrived in Philadelphia, *yet* he was able to buy some bread.

In the second sentence, the writer combined two related thoughts into a single sentence by using a connective word—in this case, the **coordinating conjunction** *yet.* Separating two thoughts into two sentences is not incorrect; there are times when short, simple sentences sound best. However, using **coordinating conjunctions** to combine two thoughts into one sentence can result in more graceful wording.

Some Connective Words and What They Indicate

Conjunction	Indicates
and	similarity, addition
but	opposition, contrast
yet	opposition, contrast
or	choice
nor	negation
so	cause and effect, result
for	explanation

All the words in the chart above function as coordinating conjunctions, but some can also function as other parts of speech. For example, *for* is a preposition in this sentence: "We went to the store *for* apples." However, the word *for* is a conjunction in this sentence: "We went to a store downtown, *for* the store on our block was closed." To combine two related sentences into a single sentence, you will need to select an appropriate conjunction.

Try It Out

Combine each pair of sentences into one sentence, using the most appropriate conjunction from the chart. Make necessary revisions so that the resulting sentence reads smoothly.

1. Franklin wished to achieve moral perfection. He devised a book in which he could record his transgressions and his progress.
2. It is not easy to achieve moral perfection. One can still try.

Writer's Workshop Follow-Up: Revising

Re-read the autobiographical narrative you wrote for the Writer's Workshop (page 130). Are there any short, choppy sentences that could be combined? Where appropriate, use conjunctions to combine sentences and make your writing flow more gracefully.

✔ QUICK CHECK: Coordinating Conjunctions

Combine the following sentences using coordinating conjunctions.

[1] William Brewster and Myles Standish tended the sick during the starving time. They were not infected with either sickness or lameness. [William Brewster and Myles Standish tended the sick during the starving time, yet they were not infected with either sickness or lameness.]

[2] Anne Bradstreet did not seek an audience or publication for her writing. She did not seek notoriety. [Anne Bradstreet did not seek an audience or publication for her writing, nor did she seek notoriety.]

[3] Franklin did lack a poet's depth. His literary talents were substantial. [Franklin did lack a poet's depth, but his literary talents were substantial.]

[4] Thomas Jefferson was president of the United States. He wanted to be remembered for authoring the Declaration of Independence. [Thomas Jefferson was president of the United States, but he wanted to be remembered for authoring the Declaration of Independence.]

CREATIVE PROBLEM SOLVING

LEARNING FOR LIFE

The Immigrant Experience

Problem

The three collections you've studied thus far tell the stories of some of the earliest immigrants to America. The experiences of each early immigrant group were unique.

Project

Use library and community resources to research the experiences of one or more immigrant groups, past or present.

Preparation

Form a small research team. Agree on responsibilities for each team member. Decide which aspect, or aspects, of the immigrant experience each member will focus on.

Procedure

1. Research the experiences of one or more of the following groups on their journeys to America:
   - Africans brought to the United States to be enslaved
   - Irish who immigrated as a result of the potato famine in the 1840s
   - Jews who fled persecution in eastern Europe, Russia, and Nazi Germany
   - Cubans who fled from Fidel Castro's Communist revolution
   - Vietnamese who came after the Vietnam War ended in 1975
   - other groups currently immigrating to the United States in large numbers from Mexico, the Philippines, Russia, the Dominican Republic, China, India, and Poland, as well as people from the Caribbean, Middle East, Latin America, Southeast Asia, and other parts of the world
2. Supplement library research by interviewing people in your own community who are recent immigrants or who remember stories about grandparents, parents, or other relatives who immigrated to the United States.
3. Keep a record of all your sources. Evaluate and organize your information. Then prepare your presentation. You may want to focus on the following topics for the group or groups you are researching:
   - how the circumstances of the immigration affected the subsequent adjustment of the group in the United States
   - particular obstacles encountered in this country
   - important achievements and accomplishments
   - contributions to U.S. society
   - noteworthy individuals

Presentation

Present your research in one of the following formats (or another format that your teacher approves):

1. **Original Play**
   Write and present a play in which your team presents the story of an immigrant group or groups in the United States. Use props, costumes, food, music, and other audio and visual support to enliven your portrayal.
2. **Time Line**
   As a class, collaborate on a wall-sized time line that includes names and numbers of immigrant groups, dates of significant events in the history of U.S. immigration, quotations, illustrations and photographs, and other data you want to include.
3. **Multimedia Presentation**
   Write a script based on your findings, and read it to the class, supplementing it with audio and visual supports: recorded music, photos, slides, overhead transparencies, posters, video or audio interviews, and props (clothing, food, art objects).

No matter which format you choose, consider sharing your presentation with an audience outside the class: school, library, newspaper, TV station, or a cultural or ethnic club or association.

Processing

What did you learn about the immigrant experience by doing this project? For your portfolio, write your reflections on this statement: "Every American is descended from immigrants."

Learning for Life

Technology Tip

TECHNOLOGY Give students various hardware and software options for preparing and presenting multimedia research reports. If students use a multimedia computer system, their finished reports might include the printed text of the report, illustrations or photographs, and any recorded oral commentary that they wish to make. Then, they may store their reports on the computer after they present them. If a multimedia system is not available, students may produce reports by using separate components, such as a computer with presentation software, or color slides and an audio recorder. As students conduct research for their projects, encourage them to collect ideas for photographs and illustrations. Or, if possible, attach a camera to a multimedia computer and allow students to digitize and store their own photographs or short videos.

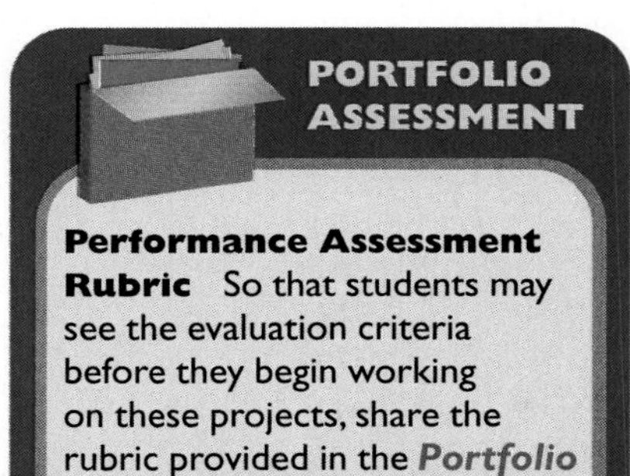

Performance Assessment Rubric So that students may see the evaluation criteria before they begin working on these projects, share the rubric provided in the ***Portfolio Management System,*** p. 82.

DEVELOPING WORKPLACE COMPETENCIES

Preparation	Procedure	Presentation
Makes decisions Works on teams Demonstrates individual responsibility	Acquires data Evaluates data	Thinks creatively Exhibits self-esteem Selects equipment Communicates ideas and information

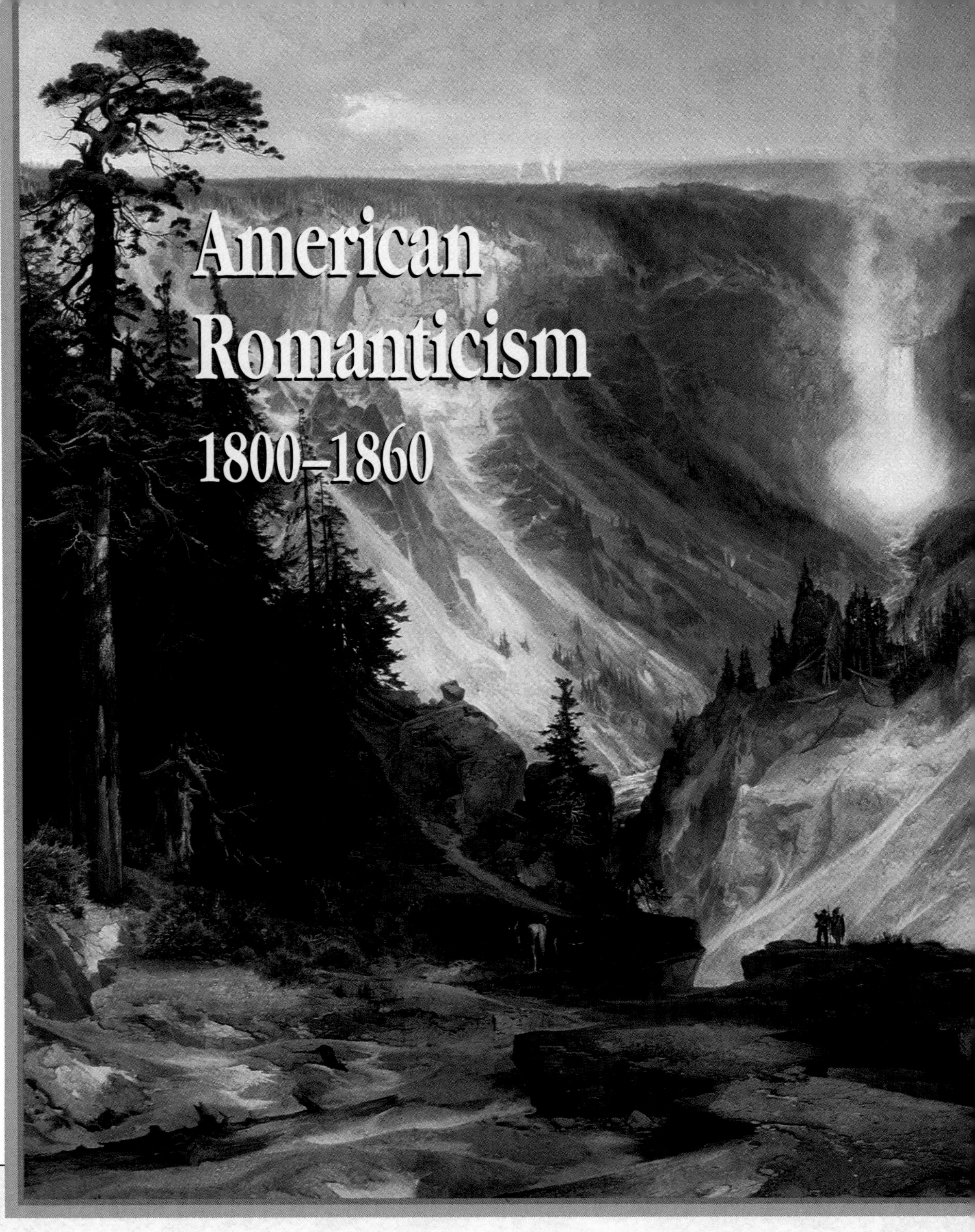
American
Romanticism
1800–1860

The Grand Canyon of the Yellowstone (1872) by Thomas Moran (1837–1926). Oil on canvas (84″ × 144 1/4″).
Loaned by the U.S. Department of the Interior. Office of the Secretary. National Museum of American Art, Washington, D.C./Art Resource.

RESPONDING TO THE ART: ABOUT THE ARTWORK

Thomas Moran was born in England in 1837 and immigrated to the United States in 1844. Moran was a member of the second generation of the Hudson River school, a group of landscape painters who were united by a Romantic approach to rendering the spirit of the American landscape. This spirit is captured in Moran's *The Grand Canyon of the Yellowstone*, a grand portrait of perhaps the best-known natural landscape of the American West. In what ways is the landscape "romantic"? [Possible responses: It is intense; it appeals to the emotions rather than to the intellect.]

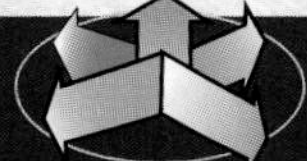

PROGRAM MANAGER

- **Summative Assessment** See **Literary Period Test: American Romanticism, *Test Booklet,*** pp. 54–56, for a test on an additional text from the same historical era.
- **Application** For practice of a reading strategy for this unit, see **Becoming a Stategic Reader** worksheet, ***Teaching Resources A,*** pp. 64–65.

Responding to the Quotation

? In what ways today do we look to the past to understand the present? [Possible responses: We look at past wars and why they happened, to try to avoid the same mistakes and to think of better solutions. We see what we could have done better and try to improve what we are doing today. We want to do things differently from the people who went before us.]

American Romanticism

by Gary Q. Arpin

The essence of romanticism is the ability to wonder and to reflect. In searching the meaning of the known, the human spirit reaches for the unknown; in trying to understand the present, it looks to the past and to the future.

—Robert E. Spiller (American critic)

Philadelphia from Belmont (West Park).
Culver Pictures.

A. Literary Connections

Charles Brockden Brown was one of the first professional writers in America. Trained as a lawyer in Philadelphia, he moved to New York to pursue his literary career. He wrote his best Gothic novels in a two-year period, after which he gave up full-time writing and entered business. He was admired and appreciated by some of the best writers of his day, but ultimately his work lacks the depth and consistency to be considered lasting literary art.

Huntingdon County, Pennsylvania. Raystown Lake.

© H. Mark Weidman.

The Pattern of the Journey

The journey—there is probably no pattern so common in all of narrative literature, from the Bible, to the Greek epic the *Odyssey,* to modern films like *The Wizard of Oz* and *Forrest Gump*. Very early in his *Autobiography* (page 86), Benjamin Franklin describes in great detail an important American journey: a personal quest in which he leaves his home in Boston and travels to Philadelphia. The significance of Franklin's journey is clear: It is a declaration of independence, a move away from the constraints of his family and toward a city where he might prosper. It is, in other words, a quest for opportunity. Without stretching the metaphor too greatly, we can see in Franklin's journey an expression of both his personal goals and the goals of eighteenth-century America: a reaching out for independence, prosperity, commerce, and urbane civilization.

> The long-distance journey is part of our history, both real and fictional: Lewis and Clark, the pioneers in their Conestogas, the Joads in their overloaded jalopy. Something about the nation—its breadth, its variety, its vastness—beckons the adventurer, the eccentric, the fame seeker. Balloonists, glider pilots, joggers, and bladers. People on pogo sticks and unicycles.
>
> —*New York Times* April 24, 1995

Franklin wrote about his journey to Philadelphia in 1771. In 1799, the American writer Charles Brockden Brown described a very different journey to Philadelphia in his Romantic novel *Arthur Mervyn.* In this tale a young farmboy hero leaves his home in the country for Philadelphia. Instead of finding a place of promise where he can make his dreams come true, however, the boy is plunged into a plague-ridden urban world of decay, corruption, and evil. The Philadelphia of this novel is no city of promise; it is an industrial hell that devours all hope and ambition.

The journeys described in Franklin's *Autobiography* and Brown's *Arthur Mervyn* make clear the differences between

Elements of Literature:
Videodisc Use the bar codes below to build background knowledge on the time period. For more information, see the Videodisc *Teacher's Manual.*

Videodisc Side B

Begin Play English Track

Begin Play Spanish Track

PROGRAM MANAGER

- **Planning Instruction** See Teaching Notes, *Teaching Resources A,* p. 59, for additional teaching options about American Romanticism.
- **Assessment** For assessment of the literary and historical events mentioned in the historical introduction, see Literary Period Introduction Test, *Test Booklet,* pp. 39–40.

Time Line

• 1790–1809

The publication of *Lyrical Ballads* is generally considered the beginning of Romantic poetry in England. Wordsworth's preface to the second edition (1800) outlines the poetic principles he and Coleridge subscribed to. This preface emphasizes the role of emotion in poetry and urges poets to draw inspiration from the everyday life and speech of ordinary people.

• 1810–1819

Francis Scott Key wrote "The Star Spangled Banner" as a poem, and it was later set to the music of "To Anacreon in Heaven" by the English composer John Stafford Smith. The song officially became the national anthem by an act of Congress in 1931.

• 1820–1829

In addition to his dictionaries, Noah Webster published a grammar book and a speller that sold sixty million copies and that distinguished American spelling from British. Webster also edited important political journals and campaigned for a strong federal government.

• 1830–1839

De Tocqueville was sent to the United States by the French government in 1831 to study the American penitentiary system, but he ultimately wrote the earliest analysis of American democracy. Besides studying government and administration, he evaluated social conditions—including American literature, which he found lacking.

American Romanticism 1800–1860

Literary Events

1790–1809

William Wordsworth and Samuel Taylor Coleridge publish *Lyrical Ballads,* a landmark of English Romanticism, 1798

•

England's Mary Wollstonecraft publishes *A Vindication of the Rights of Woman,* 1792

1810–1819

James Fenimore Cooper.
The Granger Collection, New York.

William Cullen Bryant publishes "Thanatopsis," 1817

1820–1829

Noah Webster publishes a landmark dictionary of American English, 1828

•

James Fenimore Cooper publishes *The Pioneers*, 1823

•

Washington Irving publishes *The Sketch Book of Geoffrey Crayon, Gent.*, 1820

1830–1839

France's Alexis de Tocqueville publishes *Democracy in America,* a noted study of U.S. political and social institutions, 1835

•

John Greenleaf Whittier publishes *Justice and Expediency,* in which he calls for the abolition of slavery, 1833

•

Oliver Wendell Holmes publishes "Old Ironsides," 1830

Cultural/Historical Events

1790–1809

First ten amendments, Bill of Rights, added to U.S. Constitution, 1791

•

Eli Whitney's improved cotton gin increases U.S. cotton cultivation and expands demand for slave labor, 1794

Smithsonian Institution.

•

U.S. population is 5.3 million, 1800

•

Washington, D.C., becomes U.S. capital, 1800

•

President Thomas Jefferson negotiates Louisiana Purchase from France, more than doubling U.S. territory, 1803

1810–1819

Miguel Hidalgo y Costilla launches the Mexican war of independence from Spain, 1810

•

British burn much of Washington, D.C., in War of 1812, 1814

•

Francis Scott Key writes "The Star-Spangled Banner" commemorating the War of 1812, 1814

•

Napoleon I of France is defeated at Waterloo and subsequently exiled, 1815

•

Simón Bolívar, South American independence leader, becomes Greater Colombia's first president, 1819

1820–1829

Missouri admitted as a slave state, Maine as a free state, in Missouri Compromise, 1820–1821

•

Liberia founded on west coast of Africa as a settlement for freed U.S. slaves, 1822

•

Peru assures its independence by defeating Spain at Ayacucho, 1824

•

Erie Canal opens, connecting Great Lakes and Atlantic Ocean, 1825

•

Thomas Jefferson and John Adams die on same day, July 4, 1826

1830–1839

Underground Railroad, a secret system for helping fugitive slaves reach safety, is organized, c. 1830

•

Thomas Cole completes *The Oxbow,* an early Hudson River School Romantic landscape painting, 1836

•

Queen Victoria of England is crowned, 1837

Smithsonian Institution.

Portrait of Queen Victoria (1877). Windsor Workshop. Tapestry.
Victoria & Albert Museum, London/Art Resource.

USING THE TIME LINE

Assign two events from the lower half of the time line to pairs of students, and give the pairs three minutes to write down as much information as they know about the events. In some cases, students may not know much about the events they are assigned, but suggest that they might infer significance based on what they learned from reading the introductory material. For example, in 1803 Thomas Jefferson negotiated the Louisiana Purchase. Students can infer that this addition increased the international stature of the United States, promoted national identity, removed the threat of French takeover, and gave the country access to more natural resources. Ask students to read their explanations to the class. You might have other students check for further information in an encyclopedia.

Margaret Fuller publishes *Woman in the Nineteenth Century,* the first full-length study of women's position in American society, 1845

•

Edgar Allan Poe publishes *The Raven and Other Poems,* 1845

•

Ralph Waldo Emerson publishes his first collection, *Essays,* including "Self-Reliance" and "The Over-Soul," 1841

Margaret Fuller.
The Granger Collection, New York.

James Russell Lowell publishes *The Biglow Papers,* satirical poems opposing the Mexican War and written in a Yankee dialect, 1848

Emily Dickinson begins to copy her poems into bound booklets, 1858

•

Henry David Thoreau publishes *Walden,* 1854

•

Herman Melville publishes *Moby-Dick; or, The Whale,* 1851

•

Nathaniel Hawthorne publishes *The Scarlet Letter,* 1850

Henry Wadsworth *Longfellow* (1871) by Theodore Wust. Watercolor on ivory.

National Portrait Gallery, Smithsonian Institution, Washington, D.C./Art Resource.

Henry Wadsworth Longfellow publishes *The Courtship of Miles Standish,* 1858

•

Walt Whitman publishes the first edition of his book of poems, *Leaves of Grass,* 1855

1840–1849

1850–1859

U.S. population is 17.1 million, 1840

•

Brook Farm undertakes experiment in cooperative living, 1841–1847

•

By Treaty of Nanking, China cedes Hong Kong to Great Britain and opens five ports to foreign trade, 1842

•

First baseball game under rules resembling the modern sport played at Hoboken, N.J.; the New York Club defeats the Knickerbockers 23 to 1, 1846

•

U.S. annexes Texas, Mexico, 1845; leads to war with Mexico, 1846–1848

Famine in Ireland due to potato crop failure causes increased emigration from Ireland to U.S., 1846

•

Lucretia Mott and Elizabeth Cady Stanton organize first women's rights convention in the U.S. at Seneca Falls, N.Y., 1848

•

California gold rush begins as thousands of gold miners travel to Sacramento area, 1849

The Granger Collection, New York.

Oberlin College established as one of first coeducational colleges in the U.S., 1850

•

The New York Times founded, 1851

•

Modern Republican Party organized to oppose the extension of slavery, 1854

•

After Indian revolt against British East India Company rule, British government takes over administration of India, 1858

Commodore Matthew Perry opens two Japanese ports to U.S. trade, 1854

•

U.S. Supreme Court's *Dred Scott* decision antagonizes antislavery forces, 1857

•

Library of Congress.

Abraham Lincoln and Stephen A. Douglas stage a noted series of seven debates as candidates for the Illinois seat in the U.S. Senate, 1858

• **1840–1849**

In *Woman in the Nineteenth Century* Margaret Fuller argues for equal opportunity for women and for the abolition of stereotyped gender roles. She points out the injustice of extending the vote to African Americans while restricting similar rights for women. She advocates giving women a rigorous education. Freeing women from societal restrictions, she argues, will promote harmony and growth for all.

A. Exploring the Historical Period
The journey to the town became a popular American theme for literary realists of the 1890s and early twentieth century, perhaps partly in response to immigration and industrialization. Dreiser and Crane (see pp. 484–485) were among the first great American storytellers of the city.

B. Expansion
Rip's desire to escape responsibility and hard work is in direct contrast to Franklin's strong commitment to the work ethic of his Puritan ancestors. This contrast is another difference between the approaches to life of the Romantics (Rip) and the Rationalists (Franklin).

A CLOSER LOOK

Courtesy Schweitzer Gallery, New York.

Broadway at Spring Street (1855) by Hyppolite Sebron (1801–1879). Oil on canvas (29¼″ × 42½″).

THE CITY, GRIM AND GRAY

In the first half of the nineteenth century, the largest American cities were Boston, Philadelphia, Baltimore, Charleston, and, largest of all, New York. The Romantic writers represented in this collection would have been very familiar with New York; some of them, like Washington Irving and William Cullen Bryant, even lived there. What was life like in the largest American city of the early 1800s?

Between 1820 and 1840, the population of New York more than doubled, from 124,000 to 312,000 people. In the 1830s, the first official tenements were built—buildings where a bathtub might be shared with four hundred families, where eight or more people might live in a single room without furniture, and where tenants might be ragpickers who kept their smelly stashes inside their homes. The soundtrack to the squalor and dinginess of life in one of these buildings might be provided by the bloodcurdling screeches of chickens being slaughtered indoors for the night's meal.

The city streets were fouled with droppings from the main source of transportation: horses. When a horse was injured in a collision or had collapsed from malnutrition or overwork, it was left to die on the curbside. Its body might remain on the street for days or weeks at a time. Given

A the views of the rationalists and those of the Romantics. To Franklin and other rationalists, the city was a place to find success and self-realization. To the Romantic writers who came after Franklin, though, the city, far from being the seat of civilization, was often a place of moral ambiguity and, worse, of corruption and death.

The characteristic Romantic journey is to the countryside, which Romantics associated with independence, moral clarity, and healthful living. Sometimes, though, as in the works of Gothic-influenced writers like Edgar Allan Poe (page 260), the Romantic journey was a voyage to the B country of the imagination. But whatever the destination of the Romantic journey, it was a flight both *from* something and *to* something. In fact, America's first truly popular professional writer is today known principally for an immortal story about an escape from civilization and responsibility. The writer was Washington Irving, and the escape was made by Rip Van Winkle (page 154).

American Romanticism can best be described as a journey away from the corruption of civilization and the limits of rational thought and toward the integrity of nature and the freedom of the imagination.

OPTIONS FOR TEACHING

STRATEGIES FOR INCLUSION

Less Proficient Readers To help students learn strategies for assimilating information they read, ask the class to outline the first section of the introduction ("The Pattern of the Journey"). Emphasize that the first sentence in a paragraph often contains the main idea and can be used for a major heading, while critical details usually follow. Elicit suggestions from several students, and record their outline on the chalkboard. Go over the outline with the class, suggesting where information can be deleted and where other information can be added.

Visual To help students get a mental picture of Gothic forms, show them a photograph of a Gothic structure, such as Notre Dame in Paris. A French teacher on campus may have a full-color poster to lend the class. Point out that the enormous size of such buildings and the detail of their decoration appealed to the sense of the unusual that the Romantics valued.

such conditions, it's no surprise that disease was rampant. In Manhattan in the summer of 1832, one third of the city's population—those who could afford to leave—left the city to escape a cholera epidemic that killed an average of one hundred people a day. **C**

There were 20,000 homeless children on the streets of New York. Some worked in sweatshops, some sold toothpicks or newspapers, others turned to petty crime. If they lived to be twenty, they were lucky; disease, accidents, exposure, violence, and starvation took most of them long before that time.

Crime and violence were no strangers to the city. Waterfront gangs often included "pirates" who would kill for next to nothing. On the infamous Cherry Street, 15,000 sailors were robbed in a single year. Throughout the city, buildings sometimes burned to the ground while various competing fire companies fought with each other over who had the right to put out the fire. There were even riots on the streets: In 1834, men opposed to the abolition of slavery burned down homes, churches, and a school, trying to destroy free African Americans and their supporters.

There was one bright spot in the picture of squalor and degradation, though: talk in the 1840s of constructing a huge and expensive city park, to be built for "health and recreation." It was the poet William Cullen Bryant's idea—a dream of bringing a taste of the blessed countryside to a city wracked with poverty, illness, and crime. But New Yorkers would have to wait until after the Civil War for their oasis: Central Park would not become a completed reality until 1876. **D**

Culver Pictures.

A tenement-house alley gang.

The Romantic Sensibility: Celebrating the Imagination

In general, **Romanticism** is the name given to those schools of thought that value feeling and intuition over reason. The first rumblings of Romanticism were felt in Germany in the second half of the eighteenth century. Romanticism had a strong influence on literature, music, and painting in Europe and England well into the nineteenth century. But Romanticism came relatively late to America and, as you will see in this collection and in the collections that follow, it took different forms. **E**

Romanticism, especially in Europe, developed in part as a reaction against **rationalism.** In the sooty wake of the Industrial Revolution, with its squalid cities and wretched working conditions, people had come to realize the limits of reason. The Romantics came to believe that the imagination was able to apprehend truths that the rational mind could not reach. These truths were usually accompanied by powerful emotion and associated with natural, unspoiled beauty. To the Romantic sensibility the imagination, spontaneity, individual feelings, and wild nature were of greater value than reason, logic, planning, and cultivation. The Romantics did not flatly reject

> The question of common sense is always "What is it good for?"—a question which would abolish the rose and be answered triumphantly by the cabbage.
>
> —James Russell Lowell

C. Exploring the Historical Period
The cholera epidemic was part of a much larger outbreak of the disease throughout the United States and, indeed, all over the world. Cholera is a bacterial disease of the digestive system that causes diarrhea, vomiting, dehydration, and severe muscle cramps, and that sometimes ends in death with kidney failure or heart attack. People contract this disease by consuming contaminated food or water.

D. Expansion
The park was designed by Frederick Law Olmsted and Calvert Vaux to turn an area of swamps, dumps, quarries, and pigsties into a place of tranquillity and beauty in the heart of one of the busiest cities in the world. In addition to trees and rolling lawns, the park includes a zoo, a skating rink, a medieval castle, a world-class art museum, theaters, and much more.

E. Exploring the Culture
Jean Jacques Rousseau is generally considered the father of Romanticism, although German writers such as Schiller and Goethe gave the movement its real impetus. In England the great Romantic writers were Wordsworth, Coleridge, Byron, Shelley, Keats, and Scott; and in France the chief Romantic writers were Victor Hugo, George Sand, Alexander Dumas (the elder), and Stendhal. Romantic composers included Beethoven, Berlioz, the Schuberts, and Mendelssohn; and Romantic painters included Delacroix, Ingres, Corot, and Millet.

STRATEGIES FOR INCLUSION

Special Needs Help students assimilate the characteristics of American Romanticism by offering them a mnemonic device. Go over each of the terms in the device, making sure students understand their meaning and can explain their connection to the introduction.

Examples
<u>5 i's of Romanticism:</u>
i ntuition
i magination
i nnocence
i nspiration from supernatural and from nature
i nner experience

☞

A. Reader's Response: First Thoughts
Both of these Romantic strategies for seeking beauty are based on the premise that the industrial world does not offer beauty to the beholder. Is this premise valid today? [Sample responses: Yes, factories and industrial sites are ugly. Or no, cities have their own charm and offer a different variety of beauty.]

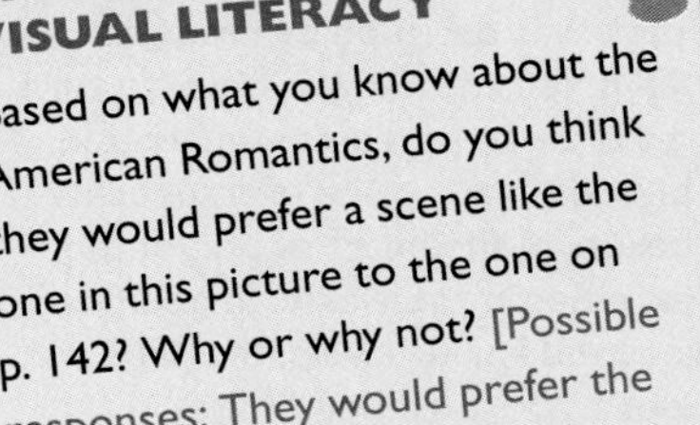

RESPONDING TO THE ILLUSTRATION: VISUAL LITERACY

Based on what you know about the American Romantics, do you think they would prefer a scene like the one in this picture to the one on p. 142? Why or why not? [Possible responses: They would prefer the one on this page because it reflects the Romantics' attraction to beauty and the natural world; it is more pastoral and contemplative.]

logical thought as invalid for all purposes. But for the purpose of art, they placed a new premium on intuitive, "felt" experience.

To the Romantic mind, poetry was the highest and most sublime embodiment of the imagination. Romantic artists often contrasted poetry with science, which they saw as destroying the very truth it claimed to seek. Edgar Allan Poe, for example, called science a "vulture" with wings of "dull realities," preying on the hearts of poets.

Romanticism, originally a European movement, emphasized feeling and intuition over reason, sought wisdom in natural beauty, and valued poetry above all other works of the imagination.

Characteristics of American Romanticism

- Values feeling and intuition over reason
- Places faith in inner experience and the power of the imagination
- Shuns the artificiality of civilization and seeks unspoiled nature
- Prefers youthful innocence to educated sophistication
- Champions individual freedom and the worth of the individual
- Contemplates nature's beauty as a path to spiritual and moral development
- Looks backward to the wisdom of the past and distrusts progress
- Finds beauty and truth in exotic locales, the supernatural realm, and the inner world of the imagination
- Sees poetry as the highest expression of the imagination
- Finds inspiration in myth, legend, and folk culture

Romantic Escapism: From Dull Realities to Higher Realms

A The Romantics wanted to rise above "dull realities" to a realm of higher truth. They did this in two principal ways. First, the Romantics searched for exotic settings in the more "natural" past or in a world far removed from the grimy and noisy industrial age. Sometimes they found this world in the supernatural realm, or in old legends and folklore. Second, the Romantics tried to contemplate the natural world until dull reality fell away to reveal underlying beauty and truth.

We can most easily see the first Romantic

F Street, Washington, D.C. (1821) by Baroness Hyde de Neuville (c. 1749–1849). Watercolor and pencil ($7^1/_2'' \times 9^7/_8''$).

Courtesy of the New-York Historical Society.

OPTIONS FOR TEACHING

INTEGRATING THE LANGUAGE ARTS

Strategic Reading Because the introduction discusses literary times and philosophies new to students, you might engage them in Reciprocal Teaching activities. Assign students different sections of the introduction and ask them to write two test questions about their individual sections. After students have finished reading all of the introduction and have written questions on their sections, have them turn to a partner who was an "expert" on another section. Ask students to quiz each other on their sections. Have students change partners until all students have been asked questions and given answers for all the sections in the introduction.

The Metropolitan Museum of Art, Reisinger Fund, 1926 (26.90).

Island of the Dead (1880) by Arnold Böcklin (1827–1901). Oil on wood (29″ × 48″).

approach in the development of the Gothic novel, with its wild, haunted landscapes, supernatural events, and mysterious medieval castles. The Gothic, with its roots in French, German, and English literature, seemed an unlikely transplant to the new nation of America, where there were seemingly no places old enough to have accumulated a contingent of ghosts or to reek of the decay of ages. But even writers in America, notably Edgar Allan Poe, were attracted to the exotic, otherworldly trappings of the Gothic. In America, particularly in the works of Poe, the Gothic took a turn toward the psychological exploration of the human mind. B

The second Romantic approach, the contemplation of the natural world, is evident in many lyric poems. In a typical Romantic poem, the speaker sees a commonplace object or event. A flower found by a stream or a waterfowl flying overhead brings the speaker to some important, deeply felt insight, which is then recorded in the poem. This contemplative process is similar to the way the Puritans drew moral lessons from nature. The difference is one of emphasis and goal. The Puritans' lessons were defined by their religion. In nature they found the God they knew from the Bible. The Romantics, on the other hand, found a far less clearly defined divinity in nature. Their contemplation of the natural world led to a more generalized emotional and intellectual awakening. C

> They who dream by day are cognizant of many things which escape those who dream only by night.
>
> —Edgar Allan Poe

American Romanticism took two roads on the journey to understanding higher truths. One road led to the exploration of the past and of exotic, even supernatural, realms; the other road led to the contemplation of the natural world.

B. Humanities Connection
Used in reference to literature in the eighteenth century, the term *Gothic* meant "barbaric." To the nineteenth-century Romantics, the term came to be synonymous with "medieval" and associated with anything that is primitive, natural, free, and unfettered by the constraints of reason.

C. Humanities Connection
The direct contemplation of nature as a source of spiritual knowledge and inspiration became a cardinal point in the doctrines of Ralph Waldo Emerson and other Transcendentalists (see pp. 210–213 and 216–225).

CROSSING THE CURRICULUM

Art Invite students to locate prints and photos of artwork by members of the Hudson River School of painting, such as Thomas Cole, Albert Bierstadt, and Frederick E. Church, and to bring the examples to class for display. Interested students might also report on photography by some members of the school. Add available photographs to the class display. Ask students to discuss the ways artwork and literature from the Romantic era are similar in content or style.

History Have students find out about the westward expansion that occurred in North America in the first half of the nineteenth century. Ask students to concentrate on a single region, such as the South or the Midwest, and to make maps showing how the country grew. Have students report their findings to the class.

A. Literary Connections
Cooper wrote another novel in 1823, *The Pilot,* which has the distinction of being the first American sea story. In addition to *The Pioneers,* the Leatherstocking tales include *The Last of the Mohicans, The Prairie, The Pathfinder,* and *The Deerslayer.*

B. Expansion
In *The Pioneers* Natty Bumppo is imprisoned for shooting a deer out of season, and this action indicates that his frontier ethics are at odds with the artificial laws of the town. Eventually, he flees the town for the Western wilderness. Natty Bumppo's nickname Leatherstocking comes from the deerskin leggings he wears. Bumppo remains an uncorrupted "natural" man throughout the series, embracing the moral code of American Indians, who respect nature and try to live in harmony with it.

The American Novel and the Wilderness Experience

During the Romantic period, the big question about American literature was: Would American writers continue to imitate the English and European models, or would they finally develop a distinctive literature of their own? While the Romantic poets of the period were still staying close to traditional forms, American novelists were discovering that the subject matter available to them was very different from the subjects available to European writers. America provided a sense of limitless frontiers that Europe, so long settled, simply did not possess. Thus, the development of the American novel coincided with westward expansion, with the growth of a nationalist spirit, and with the rapid spread of cities. All these factors tended to reinforce the idealization of frontier life. A "geography of the imagination" developed, in which town, country, and frontier would play a powerful role in American life and literature—as they continue to do today.

> You steal Englishmen's books and think Englishmen's thoughts,
> With their salt on her tail your wild eagle is caught;
> Your literature suits its each whisper and motion
> To what will be thought of it over the ocean.
>
> —James Russell Lowell, *from A Fable for Critics*

We can see how the novel developed in America by looking at the early career of James Fenimore Cooper (1789–1851). Cooper's first novel, *Precaution* (1820), describes life in an English country vicarage. His second novel, *The Spy* (1821), was influenced by the romances of the Scottish novelist Sir Walter Scott, though it is set during the American Revolution. It was in his third novel, *The Pioneers* (1823), that Cooper finally broke free of European constraints. In this novel, Cooper explored uniquely American settings and characters: frontier communities, American Indians, backwoodsmen, and the wilderness of western New York and Pennsylvania. Most of all, he created the first American heroic figure: Natty Bumppo (also known variously as Hawkeye, Deerslayer, and Leatherstocking), a heroic, virtuous, skillful frontiersman whose simple morality, love of nature, distrust of town life, and almost superhuman resourcefulness mark him as a true Romantic hero. It was this character who appeared in the rest of the Leatherstocking tales—a highly popular series of sequels that Cooper wrote over the next eighteen years.

The Deerslayer OR THE FIRST WAR-PATH BY JAMES FENIMORE COOPER with pictures by N. C. Wyeth NEW YORK CHARLES SCRIBNER'S SONS

Title page of *The Deerslayer* (1925) illustrated by N. C. Wyeth (1882–1945).

American novelists looked to westward expansion and the development of the frontier for inspiration, creating subject matter that broke with European tradition.

OPTIONS FOR TEACHING

CLASSROOM MANAGEMENT

Block Scheduling Teaching for a longer period of time can be successfully organized with the help of a small spiral notebook. After each class, take a few minutes to record the basics of each lesson. Include information regarding absentees, assigned homework, missing homework assignments, problems, solutions, or any other pertinent information. Keeping a notebook will enable the teacher to stay on track when students are not in class every day.

PROFESSIONAL NOTES

TECHNOLOGY

Technology Tip To help you prepare for this Collection, browse the Electronics Archives for Teaching the American Literatures on the World Wide Web at **http://www.georgetown.edu/tamlit/tamlit-home.html**.

The Deerslayer (detail) (1925) illustrated by N. C. Wyeth (1882–1945).

A New Kind of Hero

Most Europeans had an image of the American as unsophisticated and uncivilized. This was a stereotype that Ben Franklin, when he lived in France, took great pains to demonstrate was unfair and untrue. But Cooper and other Romantic novelists who followed him took no such pains. Instead, by creating such heroes as Natty Bumppo, they turned the insult on its head. Virtue, they implied, was in American innocence, not in European sophistication. Eternal truths were waiting to be discovered not in dusty libraries or crowded cities or glittering court life, but in the American wilderness that was unknown and unavailable to Europeans.

It has been a matter of marvel to my European readers, that a man from the wilds of America should express himself in tolerable English. I was looked upon as something new and strange in American literature. . . .

—Washington Irving

RESPONDING TO THE ILLUSTRATION: EXPLORING THE SUBJECT

How does the man in the illustration exemplify the "new" hero of America? [Possible responses: He appears to be a frontiersman; he is in a natural environment and not a city.] What does the picture say about the man's relationship with nature? Use details from the picture to support your answer. [Possible responses: He seems to be a part of nature because his posture is victorious and strong; he is dressed for the wilderness.]

Technology Tip

Ask your students to create their own version of the American hero using a computer paintbrush program.

ASSESSMENT TOOLS

Check Test: Questions and Answers

1. Romantic literature is often about a journey from ___ to ___. [the city, nature]
2. America's first truly popular professional writer was ___. [Washington Irving]
3. Romanticism prefers feeling to ___. [reason]
4. The typical Romantic hero is ___ and ___. [young, innocent, nature-loving, adventurous]
5. The Fireside Poets were so called because ___. [their poems were read aloud at family firesides]

Self-Reflection After students have read the Collection introduction, have them ask themselves the following questions:

1. How often do I notice nature?
   Often Occasionally Seldom
2. Of what value is nature to me?
   Great Moderate Little
3. How much effort am I willing to give to help preserve nature?
   Great effort Some effort Little effort

RESPONDING TO THE PHOTOGRAPHS: IDEAS FOR WRITING

Have students imagine that they are screenwriters for both of the movies that these stills represent. Ask them to invent a scenario for each still and to include a few lines or a brief soliloquy that the heroes of each film would speak. Have them record their responses in their Reader's Logs or share them with the class.

Cooper's Natty Bumppo is a triumph of American innocence and an example of one of the most important outgrowths of the early American novel: the American Romantic hero. Here at last was a new kind of heroic figure, one quite different from the hero of the Age of Reason. The rationalist hero—exemplified by a real-life figure such as Ben Franklin—was worldly, educated, sophisticated, and bent on making a place for himself in civilization. The typical hero of American Romantic fiction, on the other hand, was youthful, innocent, intuitive, and close to nature. He was also, by today's standards, hopelessly uneasy with women, who were usually seen (by male writers, at least) to represent civilization and the impulse to "domesticate."

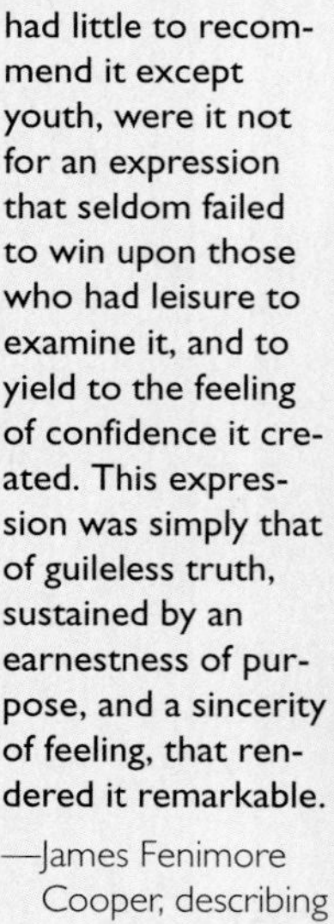

His face would have had little to recommend it except youth, were it not for an expression that seldom failed to win upon those who had leisure to examine it, and to yield to the feeling of confidence it created. This expression was simply that of guileless truth, sustained by an earnestness of purpose, and a sincerity of feeling, that rendered it remarkable.

—James Fenimore Cooper, describing Natty Bumppo, *from The Deerslayer*

20th Century Fox (Courtesy Kobal).

Daniel Day-Lewis as Natty Bumppo in the movie *The Last of the Mohicans* (1992).

Harrison Ford in the movie *Raiders of the Lost Ark* (1981).

Photofest.

Today, Americans still create Romantic heroes; the twentieth-century descendants of Natty Bumppo are all around us. They can be found in the guise of dozens of pop culture heroes: the Lone Ranger, Superman, Luke Skywalker, Indiana Jones, and any number of Western, detective, and fantasy heroes.

The American Romantic hero possesses qualities of youthfulness, innocence, intuitiveness, and closeness to the natural world that set him solidly apart from the hero of the Age of Reason.

Characteristics of the American Romantic Hero

- Is young, or possesses youthful qualities
- Is innocent and pure of purpose
- Has a sense of honor based not on society's rules but on some higher principle
- Has a knowledge of people and of life based on deep, intuitive understanding, not on formal learning
- Loves nature and avoids town life
- Quests for some higher truth in the natural world

American Romantic Poetry: Read at Every Fireside

The American Romantic novelists looked for new subject matter and innovative themes, but the opposite tendency appears in the works of the Romantic poets represented in this collection. Like Franklin, these Romantic poets wanted to prove that Americans were not unsophisticated hicks, and they attempted to prove this by working solidly within European literary traditions rather than by crafting a different and unique American voice. Even when they constructed poems with American settings and subject matter, the American Romantic poets used typically English themes, meter, and imagery. In a sense, they wrote in a style that a cultivated person from England who had recently immigrated to America might be expected to use. (A)

In many respects the American poets in this collection looked backward—over their shoulders, as it were—at established European literary models. Their poetry was limited by this slavish devotion to tradition and by their own allegiance to standard meter and diction, which resulted in poems with skillful but predictable "dum-de-dum" rhythms. Yet, for generations, many of their poems were staples of home and school reading.

In fact, the Fireside Poets, as the Boston group of Henry Wadsworth Longfellow (page 175), John Greenleaf Whittier (page 181), Oliver Wendell Holmes (page 187), and James Russell Lowell (1819–1891) was called, were, in their own time and for many decades afterward, the most popular poets America had ever produced. In many ways their popularity has never been matched. They were called "Fireside Poets" because their poems were so often read aloud at the fireside as family entertainment. They were also sometimes called "Schoolroom Poets" because their poems were, for many years, memorized and recited in American classrooms. (B)

Although the Fireside Poets' attempts to create a new American literature relied too reverently on the literature of the past, we should not view them only as backward-looking traditionalists. Certainly, they were not

A. Expansion
Even though the poets of this period were imitative of their English colleagues, their work still represented something new and refreshing that had not been seen in North America before. The Puritans and others before the Romantics wrote relatively little poetry, and the poetry they did write was that of a much older tradition. By attempting to deal with the North American landscape and North American social conditions, the Romantic poets established a new foundation for later poets.

B. Expansion
The Fireside Poets published their works in everything from inexpensive paperback editions to expensive illustrated editions, with prices to suit every income. Their poetry had mass appeal, but it also demanded thought and attention from the reader. These poets used many allusions to mythology, history, and the Bible, and their long, convoluted sentences were challenging. Consequently, many modern readers find the Fireside Poets difficult to read.

RESPONDING TO THE ILLUSTRATION: VISUAL LITERACY

Ask students how they think the Fireside Poets would respond to the illustration when writing a poem about it. Which details would they concentrate on? [Possible responses: The landscape, American Indian people and culture.] Some students may wish to compose an extemporaneous poem or story in the tradition of the Fireside Poets.

Quickwrite

Remind students to give reasons to support their choice of the kind of person they would be. In addressing the last question, students might find it useful to develop lists of traits in the form of a chart like the one that follows.

Rationalist Traits	Romantic Traits

The Granger Collection, New York.

***Hiawatha's Wedding* (1858) by Currier & Ives. Colored lithograph.**

great innovators. Their choice of subject matter—love, patriotism, nature, family, God, and religion—was, for the most part, comforting rather than challenging to their audience. Their poetry could be preachy and didactic, their symbolism could be heavy and obvious, and they often wrote in a "pretty" or pleasing style that took the edge off their messages. However, Whittier, for one, wrote powerful antislavery poems, and all of the Fireside Poets furthered the evolution of American poetry by introducing uniquely American subject matter in their choices of topics: American folk themes, descriptions of the American landscape, abolitionist issues, American Indian culture, and celebrations of American people, places, and events.

Limited by their essential literary conservatism, the Fireside Poets were unable to recognize the poetry of the future, which was being written right under their noses. Whittier's response in 1855 to reading the first volume of a certain poet's work was to throw the book into the fire. Ralph Waldo Emerson's response was much more farsighted. "I greet you," Emerson wrote to this maverick new poet, Walt Whitman, "at the beginning of a great career."

The Fireside Poets, immensely popular in their time, created some poems of lasting merit, but their essential literary conservatism prevented them from being truly innovative. The first uniquely American poetry was yet to be created.

A German woman, with a strong accent, called to talk with [Longfellow] about "The Building of the Ship," which she was planning to read in public, and which she called "The Lunch of the Sheep." As he was standing at the front door one August morning, a woman in black came up to him and inquired whether this was the house in which Longfellow had been born; when he explained that it was not, she went on to ask, "Did he die here?"

—Newton Arvin, *from Longfellow: His Life and Work*

Quickwrite

Rationalist or Romantic?

If you had to classify yourself as either a rationalist or a Romantic, which would you be? Would you be a practical, ambitious, worldly Benjamin Franklin or an intuitive, close-to-nature Romantic? Which traits—of either school of thought—do you truly value and think you would like to encourage in your own life? Freewrite an exploration of your thoughts on this issue.

THE TRANSFORMING IMAGINATION

Theme: Inspiration and Understanding

American Romanticism emphasized feeling and intuition over reason. Common features included looking to the past as well as to nature for guidance and wisdom. The exotic and the supernatural were also embraced in this imaginative inner journey of transformation in the search for and understanding of a higher truth.

Thematic Focus

Each selection in Collection 4 illustrates one of the common features of American Romanticism.

- **Rip Van Winkle** A harassed husband finds himself and his village changed after a twenty-year enchanted slumber.
- **Thanatopsis** Nature teaches us to embrace our destiny with death as part of the cosmic life cycle.
- **The Ropewalk** The poet spins visions of sunshine and shadow as he watches factory workers toil.
- **The Cross of Snow** The speaker compares his grief to an unchanging feature on a mountainside.
- *from* **Snow-Bound: A Winter Idyll** The poet describes a fabulous world with exotic imagery as he and his family look upon a snow-covered farmyard.
- **The Chambered Nautilus** A seashell sheds its past to embrace a more expansive present, giving heavenly inspiration to an observer.
- **Old Ironsides** A historic ship is valued for its accomplishments.

Literary Focus

Literary Element	Selection / Feature
Setting	**Rip Van Winkle**
Sonnet	**The Cross of Snow**
Idyll; Allusions	**Snow-Bound: A Winter Idyll**
Extended Metaphor; Apostrophe	**The Chambered Nautilus**

Writing Focus

The following flowchart shows how the writing assignment for each selection relates to and builds toward the culminating writing assignment presented in the Writer's Workshop at the end of the Collection.

Selection	Work-in-Progress Assignment
Rip Van Winkle	Freewrite about a setting for an observational essay p. 167
Thanatopsis	Freewrite a description for an observational essay p. 174
The Ropewalk **The Cross of Snow**	Freewrite observations for an observational essay p. 180
Snow-Bound: A Winter Idyll	Describe an event for an observational essay p. 186
The Chambered Nautilus **Old Ironsides**	Freewrite a description for an observational essay p. 193
Writer's Workshop	Write an observational essay pp. 198–201

Collection Planner

SELECTION/ FEATURE	PUPIL'S EDITION			
	Literary Elements / Active Reading	Writing	Speaking and Listening	Language and Vocabulary
Rip Van Winkle Washington Irving (pp. 152–168)	• Reader's Log p. 153 • Setting p. 153 • Motifs p. 162	• Critical Writing: Write essay p. 167 • Critical Writing: Write essay p. 167 • Creative Writing: Create epilogue p. 167 • Creative Writing: Write article p. 167 • Creative Writing/Art: Compile profile p. 167		• Language and Style: Inflated Language p. 166 • How to Own a Word: Context Clues p. 168
Thanatopsis William Cullen Bryant (pp. 169–174) **Connections: Sea Canes** Derek Walcott (p. 173)	• Reader's Log: p. 170	• Critical Writing/Creative Writing: Write letter p. 174		• Language and Style: Inversions and Sentence Rhythm p. 174
The Ropewalk; The Cross of Snow Henry Wadsworth Longfellow (pp. 175–180)	• Reader's Log pp. 176, 178 • Sonnet p. 180	• Critical Writing: Write essay p. 180		
from **Snow-Bound: A Winter Idyll** John Greenleaf Whittier (pp. 181–186)	• Reader's Log p. 182 • Idyll p. 182 • Allusions p.186	• Critical Writing: Write essay p. 186	• Speaking and Listening/ Critical Thinking: Discuss antislavery poems p. 186	• Language and Style: Whittier's Allusions p. 186
The Chambered Nautilus; Old Ironsides Oliver Wendell Holmes (pp.187–193) **Student to Student** (p.192)	• Reader's Log pp. 188, 190 • Extended Metaphor p. 188 • Apostrophe p. 188	• Critical Writing: Write essay p. 193 • Technical Writing: Write objective description p. 193 • Creative Writing/Research/ Art: Write and illustrate short story p. 193 • Creative Writing: Write meditation p. 193		
American Language: American Romanticism (pp. 195-197)				• Try It Out p. 197
Writer's Workshop: Observational Essay (pp. 198–201)		• Writing process: Observational Essay pp. 198–201		
Language Workshop: Inserting Modifiers (p. 202)				• Inserting modifiers p. 202
Learning for Life: Environmental Concerns (p. 203)		• Write proposal p. 203 • Make posters, brochures, and fliers p. 203	• Interview environmentalists p. 203	

Collection Resources

Teaching Resources A	Audiovisual Resources Binder	Test Booklet
Cross-Curricular Activity p. 79	Fine Art Transparency 4.1	Collection 4 Test pp. 51–53

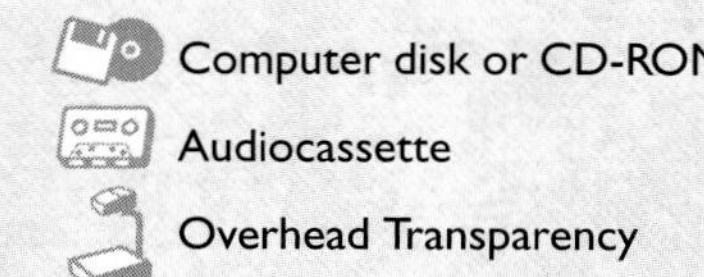

PROGRAM RESOURCES

Electronic Media	Teaching Resources with Organizer: Teaching Resources A	Teaching Resources with Organizer: Other Resources	Audiovisual Resources Binder
• Language Workshop: Prepositional phrases • Test Generator	• Teaching Notes pp. 59–60 • Reading Organizer p. 66 • Language Link pp. 67–68 • Words to Own p. 69	• Test Booklet: Selection Test pp. 41–42 • Language and Writing Skills Worksheets p. 19 • Portfolio Management System pp. 39, 83–84	• Elements of Literature Transparency 4.2 • How to Own a Word Transparency 4.3
• Test Generator	• Teaching Notes p. 61 • Reading Organizer p. 70 • Words to Own pp. 75–76	• Test Booklet: Selection Test p. 43 • Portfolio Management System pp. 48–49, 85	
• Test Generator	• Teaching Notes pp. 61–62 • Reading Organizer pp. 71–72 • Words to Own pp. 75–76	• Test Booklet: Selection Test pp. 44–45 • Portfolio Management System pp. 53, 86	• Selected Reading Audiocassette 1, Side A
• Test Generator	• Teaching Notes p. 62 • Reading Organizer p. 73 • Words to Own pp. 75–76	• Test Booklet: Selection Test p. 46 • Portfolio Management System pp. 53, 87	
• Test Generator	• Teaching Notes pp. 62–63 • Reading Organizer p. 74 • Words to Own pp. 75–76	• Test Booklet: Selection Test pp. 47–48 • Portfolio Management System pp. 54–55, 88–89	
	• Teaching Notes p. 63	• Test Booklet: The American Language pp. 49–50	
• Writer's Workshop: Observational Writing		• Portfolio Management System pp. 90–92	• Revision Transparencies 4.4–4.5
• Language Workshop: Inserting modifiers	• Language Workshop: Combining sentences pp. 77–78	• Language and Writing Skills Worksheets p. 111	
		• Portfolio Management System p. 93	

Proofreading Warm-ups

You may use the following exercises to help students practice their proofreading skills. Copy a set of incorrect sentences onto the chalkboard, and have students find and correct the spelling, punctuation, usage, and mechanical errors in each sentence. Ask students to share and discuss their responses.

	Sentences with Errors	Sentences Corrected	Skills Covered
1	**a.** if you would of looked at the timeline then you would know that Wordsworth and Coleridge published Lyrical Ballads in 1798. **b.** we dont read storys like that no more	**a.** If you had looked at the time line, then you would know that Wordsworth and Coleridge published Lyrical Ballads in 1798. **b.** We don't read stories like that anymore.	Capitalization, Nonstandard usage, Comma usage, Underline titles, Apostrophes, Spelling, Double negatives, End marks
2	**a.** to be poor in New York city in the nineteenth century would be hard **b.** do you concider yourself to be more of a practicle person then a dreamer Sharon asked	**a.** To be poor in New York City in the nineteenth century would be hard. **b.** "Do you consider yourself to be more of a practical person than a dreamer?" Sharon asked.	Capitalization, Quotation marks, Spelling, End marks
3	**a.** one characteristic of the american Romantic heroe is a sense of honer based on some higher principal **b.** do you think Indiana Jones exploits are to unbeleivable	**a.** One characteristic of the American Romantic hero is a sense of honor based on some higher principle. **b.** Do you think Indiana Jones's exploits are too unbelievable?	Capitalization, Spelling, Apostrophes, End marks
4	**a.** some of washington Irvings storys were based on german folktales **b.** i think that if more husband's did there share of the household work there would be more domestic harmony	**a.** Some of Washington Irving's stories were based on German folk tales. **b.** I think that if more husbands did their share of the household work, there would be more domestic harmony.	Capitalization, Apostrophes, Spelling, Homonyms, Comma usage, End marks
5	**a.** was Rip Van Winkle a ne'er do well or was he just a good natured man who enjoyed not doing to much **b.** alot of people have saw the movie Back To The Future	**a.** Was Rip Van Winkle a ne'er-do-well, or was he just a good-natured man who enjoyed not doing too much? **b.** A lot of people have seen the movie Back to the Future.	Capitalization, Hyphens, Comma usage, Homonyms, Spelling, Verb tenses, Underline titles, End marks
6	**a.** william Cullen Bryant was only sixteen-years-old when he wrote thanatopsis **b.** I couldnt of wrote a poem like that when I was sixteen my dad said	**a.** William Cullen Bryant was only sixteen years old when he wrote "Thanatopsis." **b.** "I couldn't have written a poem like that when I was sixteen," my dad said.	Capitalization, Hyphens, Quotation marks, Apostrophes, Standard usage, Verb error, End marks
7	**a.** henry wadsworth longfellow was a nineteenth century poet who was born in Portland Maine on the atlantic coast **b.** the poem the cross of snow is a petrarchan sonnet	**a.** Henry Wadsworth Longfellow was a nineteenth-century poet who was born in Portland, Maine, on the Atlantic coast. **b.** The poem "The Cross of Snow" is a Petrarchan sonnet.	Capitalization, Hyphens, Comma usage, Quotation marks, End marks
8	**a.** whittier composed a popular poem that was a idle a nostalgic description of a pleasant rural homey scene **b.** whittiers poem has several illusions to architecture literature and history	**a.** Whittier composed a popular poem that was an idyll, a nostalgic description of a pleasant, rural, homey scene. **b.** Whittier's poem has several allusions to architecture, literature, and history.	Capitalization, Standard usage, Spelling, Comma usage, Apostrophes, End marks
9	**a.** the Chambered Nautilus by Oliver Wendell Holmes uses an apostrophe **b.** holmes poem Old Ironsides was written about the american warship the USS constitution	**a.** "The Chambered Nautilus," by Oliver Wendell Holmes, uses an apostrophe. **b.** Holmes's poem "Old Ironsides" was written about the American warship the USS Constitution.	Capitalization, Quotation marks, Comma usage, Standard usage, Apostrophes, Underline ship names, End marks
10	**a.** the fireside poets was grate writer's **b.** there poems show alot of imagination	**a.** The Fireside Poets were great writers. **b.** Their poems show a lot of imagination.	Capitalization, Subject-verb agreement, Spelling, Apostrophes, Homonyms, Standard usage, End marks

THE TRANSFORMING IMAGINATION

Collection 4

Irving
Bryant
Longfellow
Whittier
Holmes

A Blessing

Just off the highway to Rochester, Minnesota,
Twilight bounds softly forth on the grass,
And the eyes of those two Indian ponies
Darken with kindness.
They have come gladly out of the willows
To welcome my friend and me.
We step over the barbed wire into the pasture
Where they have been grazing all day, alone.
They ripple tensely, they can hardly contain their happiness
That we have come.
They bow shyly as wet swans. They love each other.
There is no loneliness like theirs.
At home once more,
They begin munching the young tufts of spring in the darkness.
I would like to hold the slenderer one in my arms,
For she has walked over to me
And nuzzled my left hand.
She is black and white,
Her mane falls wild on her forehead,
And the light breeze moves me to caress her long ear
That is delicate as the skin over a girl's wrist.
Suddenly I realize
That if I stepped out of my body I would break
Into blossom.

—James Wright (1927–1980)

"A Blessing"

? In what ways is Wright's imagination transformed? [Possible responses: He has an inner, spiritual experience with the ponies. He responds to nature personally. He transforms his experience into a poem.]

PORTFOLIO ASSESSMENT

Parent/Guardian Involvement For forms that will help a parent or guardian review and respond to a student's portfolio, see *Portfolio Management System,* pp. 62–63.

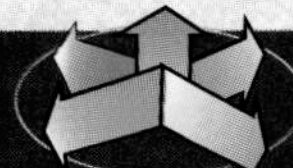

PROGRAM MANAGER

- **Integrated Assessment** For a summative assessment of the literature and language skills taught in this collection, see Collection 4 Test, *Test Booklet,* pp. 51–53.
- **Instructional Support** See Fine Art Transparency 4.1. Review teacher's notes for transparencies in the *Audiovisual Resources Binder* for suggestions on how to tie the transparencies to specific reading selections.
- **Extending Collection Theme** See Cross-Curricular Activity: The Transforming Imagination, *Teaching Resources A,* p. 79, for activities in other disciplines and for evaluation criteria.

QUICK PLANNING GUIDE

Into the Story

Through the Story

Beyond the Story

Washington Irving

(1783–1859)

Many people in Europe and England felt that America would never develop a literary voice of its own. But then came Washington Irving, the youngest and not-too-well-educated son of a pious hardware importer and his amiable wife. Irving, who was from New York City, had a genius for inventing comic fictional narrators. (In fact, he did not sign his real name to his work until he was over fifty.) The first of these narrators Irving called Jonathan Oldstyle, Gent.—a caricature of those British writers who could not accept the simple values of the new nation.

Irving's second invented narrator was called Diedrich Knickerbocker. Irving pretended that Knickerbocker was the author of a book called *A History of New York, from the Beginning of the World to the End of the Dutch Dynasty.* The mysterious Knickerbocker is supposed to have left the manuscript to his landlord in payment of back rent. This fake and comical history, in which the entire American past is ridiculed, established Washington Irving as the foremost New York satirist.

All this time Irving was enjoying the literary societies that were popular then in New York. His interest in law, which he practiced halfheartedly, was lukewarm. In 1815, he was sent off by his father to Liverpool, England, to look after the failing overseas branch of the family business. Irving found the business beyond repair, but he loved the British literary scene and stayed abroad for seventeen years. He was particularly attracted to the works of the Romantic novelist Sir Walter Scott (1771–1832), who gave Irving advice that was to make his reputation. Scott told the younger writer to read the German Romantics and find inspiration in folklore and legends.

Now Irving made the decision he had previously lacked the courage to make. He decided against putting further energy into business and its "sordid, dusty, soul-killing way of life." He would now give himself entirely to writing. In 1817, Irving began to write the first drafts of stories based on German folk tales. These were narrated by yet another of Irving's comic voices, Geoffrey Crayon, and the stories were collected under the title *The Sketch Book* (1819–1820). This book carried Irving to the summit of international success.

Historic Hudson Valley, Tarrytown, New York.

Washington Irving (1809) by John Wesley Jarvis (1780–1840). Oil on wood panel (33″ × 26″).

Something about Irving's comic narrators touched a responsive chord in the American public. Even though Irving borrowed openly from a European past, he brought to his material a droll new voice, as inflated as a preacher's or politician's at one moment, self-mocking the next. It was a voice the new nation recognized as its own.

Irving gave his country its first international literary celebrity. This was a role Irving enjoyed exploiting to the fullest. He had always loved parties and people and praise. Now he had access to the literary circles of the world. It was a remarkable achievement for the unpromising child of a middle-class American family.

Irving never again wrote anything that matched the success of the two great comic tales in *The Sketch Book.* Today we remember Irving for Rip Van Winkle who slept through the American Revolution, and the Headless Horseman who plagued the lovelorn Yankee schoolteacher Ichabod Crane in the dreamy glen of Sleepy Hollow, in New York's lush Hudson Valley.

WORDS TO OWN

The following vocabulary words are defined in the Words to Own at the bottom of the pupil's page.

scrupulous p. 154
obsequious p. 155
malleable p. 155
amiable p. 155
vehemently p. 157
placid p. 157
reiterated p. 159
torpor p. 165
fidelity p. 165
conscientious p. 165

PORTFOLIO ASSESSMENT

Portfolio Assessment For help with self- and teacher assessment of reading skills, see the ***Portfolio Management System,*** p. 39.

Before You Read
Rip Van Winkle

Reading Focus
Brave New World

It's human nature to wonder about the future. As we go through life we "grow" into the future gradually, changing just as people, places, and events change around us. We might not even notice the changes that are occurring in us and around us every day. But what if, instead of growing older along with the rest of the world, you were placed in suspended animation for twenty years and then awakened? Because you would have been "asleep" for all that time, you would not have aged or changed in any way. The world, however, would be very different.

Quickwrite

Write some impressions of what you think the world will be like in twenty years. What do you think will change in the world? How would your life, specifically, be affected by the passage of twenty years?

Elements of Literature
Setting

Misty mountaintops, a mysterious forest, an old-fashioned village, a distant era—these are some details of **setting** that Irving uses in "Rip Van Winkle." Like many Romantic writers, Irving was fascinated by times past and by wild, natural landscapes. In this story it is setting that effects a magical change in the hero and sets the **plot** in motion.

Setting is the physical, geographical, and historical environment in which a story takes place.

For more on Setting, see the Handbook of Literary Terms.

Background
Even for its first readers in 1819, "Rip Van Winkle" was a story about times past. The story begins just before the Revolutionary War, which started in 1775—before Irving was even born. Irving draws on the history of the America he knew during his childhood, when George Washington was everyone's hero and the Democrats and Federalists were the young nation's two political parties.

Into the Story

Using **Before You Read** p. 153

Reading Focus
Ask students to make predictions about big changes that might occur if they were in suspended animation for the next twenty years. They may use the following chart to organize their thoughts.

Areas of Change	Present	Future
Housing		
Transportation		
Communication		
Technology		
Entertainment		
Other areas		

Quickwrite
Have students draw from ideas they generate in the Reading Focus activity to write their Reader's Log entries. They might comment on all of the areas in the chart or concentrate on one area that particularly interests them.

Program Manager

- **Planning Instruction** See *Teaching Notes, Teaching Resources A,* pp. 59–60, for objectives, a summary, major literary elements, and additional historical and biographical information.
- **Instructional Support** See *Graphic Organizer for Active Reading, Teaching Resources A,* p. 66, for an Into the Story activity.
- **Application and Reinforcement** For reinforcement of the elements of literature introduced in this lesson, see *Transparency* 4.2 in the *Audio-visual Resources Binder.*
- **Assessment** See *Selection Test, Test Booklet,* pp. 41–42.
- **Language Link** For instruction in prepositional phrases, see *Language Link, Teaching Resources A,* pp. 67–68, and *Language and Writing Skills Worksheets,* p. 19.
- **Reinforcement** Use the Words to Own worksheet in *Teaching Resources A,* p. 69.

A. Literary Element: Plot
The italicized opening of the story is a frame device, written in a different voice from that of the main narrator. You might ask students to skim this opening and to begin closer reading with the text that is not italicized.

B. Critical Reading: Making Connections
? What does the phrase in quotation marks mean? [People are no longer angry about the errors in Knickerbocker's work; they are just sorry he made them.]

Rip Van Winkle

A Posthumous Writing of Diedrich Knickerbocker

Washington Irving

A *The following tale was found among the papers of the late Diedrich Knickerbocker, an old gentleman of New York, who was very curious in the Dutch history of the province, and the manners of the descendants from its primitive settlers. His historical researches, however, did not lie so much among books, as among men; for the former are lamentably scanty on his favorite topics; whereas he found the old burghers,[1] and still more, their wives, rich in that legendary lore so invaluable to true history. Whenever, therefore, he happened upon a genuine Dutch family, snugly shut up in its low roofed farmhouse, under a spreading sycamore, he looked upon it as a little clasped volume of black letter,[2] and studied it with the zeal of a bookworm.*

The result of all these researches was a history of the province, during the reign of the Dutch governors, which he published some years since. There have been various opinions as to the literary character of his work and, to tell the truth, it is not a whit better than it should be. Its chief merit is its scrupulous accuracy, which indeed was a little questioned on its first appearance, but has since been completely established; and it is now admitted into all historical collections as a book of unquestionable authority.

The old gentleman died shortly after the publication of his work, and now that he is dead and gone, it cannot do much harm to his memory to say that his time might have been much better employed in weightier labors. He, however, was apt to ride his hobby his own way; and though it did now and then kick up the dust a little in the eyes of his neighbors, and grieve the spirit of some friends for whom he felt the truest deference and affection; yet his errors and follies B *are remembered "more in sorrow than in anger," and it begins to be suspected that he never intended to injure or offend. But however his memory may be appreciated by critics, it is still held dear by many folk whose good opinion is well worth having; particularly by certain biscuit bakers, who have gone so far as to imprint his likeness on their New Year cakes, and have thus given him a chance for immortality, almost equal to being stamped on a Waterloo[3] medal, or a Queen Anne's farthing.[4]*

1. **burghers:** citizens.
2. **black letter:** ornamental printing type; now called Old English or Gothic.
3. **Waterloo:** Belgian town where the British and their allies finally defeated Napoleon I, emperor of France, on June 18, 1815.
4. **farthing:** former British coin worth about one fourth of a penny.

Words to Own
scrupulous (skro͞o′pyə·ləs) *adj.*: careful; painstaking.

Options for Teaching

Strategies for Inclusion

English Language Development To help students establish setting, use a map of the eastern United States to locate New York, the Hudson River Valley, and the Catskill Mountains. Using descriptions from the first two paragraphs, discuss the geography of the Appalachian area. Share available photographs.

Special Needs New or unusual vocabulary is easily remembered by students when they illustrate the vocabulary words, as below. Display posters in the classroom, or place words on index cards to be used for individual study.

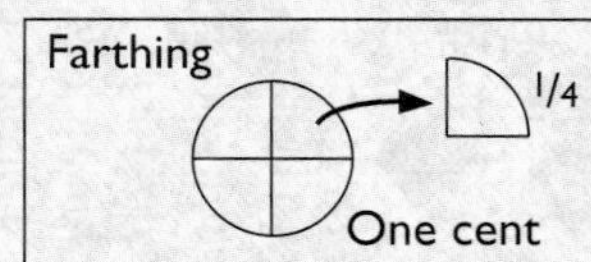

Musical Ask students to think about filming the story of Rip Van Winkle and to choose the scene they find most appealing. Have them make up a tune or rhythm that is appropriate for accompanying the scene, and have them explain to the class why they made this choice. The class can then discuss how musical accompaniment sets the tone and mood for filmed scenes.

Whoever has made a voyage up the Hudson must remember the Kaatskill[5] Mountains. They are a dismembered branch of the great Appalachian family, and are seen away to the west of the river swelling up to noble height and lording it over the surrounding country. Every change of season, every change of weather, indeed every hour of the day, produces some change in the magical hues and shapes of these mountains, and they are regarded by all the good wives far and near as perfect barometers. When the weather is fair and settled they are clothed in blue and purple, and print their bold outlines on the clear evening sky; but sometimes, when the rest of the landscape is cloudless, they will gather a hood of gray vapors about their summits, which, in the last rays of the setting sun, will glow and light up like a crown of glory.

At the foot of these fairy mountains the voyager may have descried the light smoke curling up from a village, whose shingle roofs gleam among the trees, just where the blue tints of the upland melt away into the fresh green of the nearer landscape. It is a little village of great antiquity, having been founded by some of the Dutch colonists in the early times of the province, just about the beginning of the government of the good Peter Stuyvesant,[6] (may he rest in peace!) and there were some of the houses of the original settlers standing within a few years; built of small yellow bricks brought from Holland, having latticed windows and gable fronts, surmounted with weathercocks.

In that same village, and in one of these very houses (which to tell the precise truth was sadly timeworn and weather-beaten) there lived many years since, while the country was yet a province of Great Britain, a simple good-natured fellow of the name of Rip Van Winkle. He was a descendant of the Van Winkles who figured so gallantly in the chivalrous days of Peter Stuyvesant, and accompanied him to the siege of Fort Christina.[7] He inherited, however, but little of the martial character of his ancestors. I have observed that he was a simple good-natured man; he was moreover a kind neighbor, and an obedient, henpecked husband. Indeed to the latter circumstance might be owing that meekness of spirit which gained him such universal popularity; for those men are most apt to be obsequious and conciliating abroad, who are under the discipline of shrews at home. Their tempers doubtless are rendered pliant and malleable in the fiery furnace of domestic tribulation, and a curtain lecture[8] is worth all the sermons in the world for teaching the virtues of patience and long-suffering. A termagant[9] wife may therefore in some respects be considered a tolerable blessing—and if so, Rip Van Winkle was thrice blessed.

Certain it is that he was a great favorite among all the good wives of the village, who as usual with the amiable sex, took his part in all family squabbles, and never failed, whenever they talked those matters over in their evening gossippings, to lay all the blame on Dame[10] Van Winkle. The

RIP VAN WINKLE

Title page of *Rip Van Winkle* (1921) by N. C. Wyeth (1882–1945). Lithograph.

5. **Kaatskill:** original Dutch spelling of *Catskill*.
6. **Peter Stuyvesant** (stī′və·sənt): last Dutch governor of New Netherland (1646–1664), the Dutch colony in America. Irving is being ironic here. Stuyvesant was unpopular with the Dutch colonists, who considered him intolerant and harsh.

7. **Fort Christina:** Delaware's first permanent settlement; founded by Swedish colonists on the Delaware River and captured by Stuyvesant from the Swedes in 1655. Present-day site of Wilmington, Delaware.
8. **curtain lecture:** scolding delivered by a wife to her husband, from behind the curtains of an old-fashioned bed.
9. **termagant** (tʉr′mə·gənt): abusive; scolding.
10. **Dame:** title formerly used for the woman in charge of a household.

WORDS TO OWN

obsequious (əb·sē′kwē·əs) *adj.*: obedient; submissive.
malleable (mal′ē·ə·bəl) *adj.*: capable of being shaped.
amiable (ā′mē·ə·bəl) *adj.*: agreeable; likable.

C. Critical Reading: Predicting

? What might the early, detailed description of the mountains suggest about their eventual role in the story? [Somehow the distant mountains will be significant.]

Metacognition Ask students which specific details convinced them of the mountains' significance.

D. Literary Element: Setting

To help students accept the long descriptive paragraphs at the beginning of the story as a literary convention of Irving's day, have different students read each paragraph aloud. Ask students to imagine the story as a movie introduction, with each paragraph zooming in closer than the one before it: first an establishing shot of the Catskill (Kaatskill) Mountains, then a view of the village, then a close-up of the Van Winkle house, and finally a steady focus on Rip himself.

E. Reader's Response: First Thoughts

? What attitude does the narrator seem to have toward Rip? [Sample responses: He seems to be chuckling about Rip's nature and habits; the narrator is poking fun; or he likes Rip's friendliness.]

INTEGRATING THE LANGUAGE ARTS

Strategic Reading Have students read to the point where Rip first awakens. Ask students who are not already familiar with the story to predict what will happen. Have students familiar with the plot suggest a conclusion they think is equally logical. Without distinguishing between predictions and suggestions, write responses on the chalkboard. After students have read the story, ask them to evaluate each response in terms of what information the story provided when they made predictions or suggestions.

Speaking and Listening Have pairs of students select a passage from Irving's story to divide and read aloud to one another. Ask students to practice individually first, considering where they will pause for suspense, raise or lower their voices, or slow down for emphasis. As partners read to each other, have the listener note three specific lines that were read with special effectiveness. Finally, invite volunteers to read to the class while listeners note readers' tactics to make reading effective.

Writing: Dialogue Ask students to work in pairs to compose a dialogue for the men who spend their time sitting in the shade in front of Nicholaus Vedder's inn. Remind students to use quotation marks and to change paragraphs for each new speaker. Some students might enjoy presenting their dialogues to the class. ☞

A. Literary Element: Character

? How is Rip unlike the typical American frontier hero? [He is not deliberately seeking to explore or do anything new, and he is not animated by a spirit of either adventure or labor. If anything, he is helpless and passive.]

B. Critical Reading: Making Inferences

? Why does Rip say nothing in response to his wife? [He knows she is right, so he has nothing to say to defend himself.]

children of the village too would shout with joy whenever he approached. He assisted at their sports, made their playthings, taught them to fly kites and shoot marbles, and told them long stories of ghosts, witches, and Indians. Whenever he went dodging about the village he was surrounded by a troop of them hanging on his skirts, clambering on his back and playing a thousand tricks on him with impunity; and not a dog would bark at him throughout the neighborhood.

The great error in Rip's composition was an insuperable aversion to all kinds of profitable labor. It could not be from the want of assiduity[11] or perseverance; for he would sit on a wet rock, with a rod as long and heavy as a Tartar's lance,[12] and fish all day without a murmur, even though he should not be encouraged by a single nibble. He would carry a fowling piece[13] on his shoulder for hours together, trudging through woods, and swamps and up hill and down dale, to shoot a few squirrels or wild pigeons; he would never refuse to assist a neighbor even in the roughest toil, and was a foremost man at all country frolics for husking Indian corn, or building stone fences; the women of the village too used to employ him to run their errands and to do such little odd jobs as their less obliging husbands would not do for them—in a word Rip was ready to attend to anybody's business but his own; but as to doing family duty, and keeping his farm in order, he found it impossible.

In fact he declared it was of no use to work on his farm; it was the most pestilent little piece of ground in the whole country; everything about it went wrong and would go wrong in spite of him. His fences were continually falling to pieces; his cow would either go astray or get among the cabbages; weeds were sure to grow quicker in his fields than anywhere else; the rain always made a point of setting in just as he had some outdoor work to do. So that though his patrimonial estate had dwindled away under his management, acre by acre until there was little more left than a mere patch of Indian corn and potatoes, yet it was the worst-conditioned farm in the neighborhood.

His children too were as ragged and wild as if they belonged to nobody. His son Rip, an urchin begotten in his own likeness, promised to inherit the habits with the old clothes of his father. He was generally seen trooping like a colt at his mother's heels, equipped in a pair of his father's castoff galligaskins,[14] which he had much ado to hold up with one hand, as a fine lady does her train in bad weather.

Rip Van Winkle, however, was one of those happy mortals of foolish, well-oiled dispositions, who take the world easy, eat white bread or brown, whichever can be got with least thought or trouble, and would rather starve on a penny (A) than work for a pound. If left to himself, he would have whistled life away in perfect contentment, but his wife kept continually dinning in his ears about his idleness, his carelessness, and the ruin (B) he was bringing on his family. Morning, noon, and night, her tongue was incessantly going, and everything he said or did was sure to produce a torrent of household eloquence. Rip had but one way of replying to all lectures of the kind, and that by frequent use had grown into a habit. He shrugged his shoulders, shook his head, cast up his eyes, but said nothing. This, however, always provoked a fresh volley from his wife, so that he was fain to draw off his forces and take to the outside of the house—the only side which in truth belongs to a henpecked husband.

Rip's sole domestic adherent was his dog Wolf who was as much henpecked as his master, for Dame Van Winkle regarded them as companions in idleness, and even looked upon Wolf with an evil eye as the cause of his master's going so often astray. True it is, in all points of spirit befitting an honorable dog, he was as courageous an animal as ever scoured the woods—but what courage can withstand the ever-during and all-besetting[15] terrors of a woman's tongue? The moment Wolf entered the house his crest fell, his tail drooped to the ground or curled between his legs, he sneaked about with a gallows air,[16] casting many a

11. **assiduity** (as′ə·dyo͞o′ə·tē): close and continuous application of effort.
12. **Tartar's lance:** Tartars, more correctly called Tatars, are a Turkic-speaking people of Europe and Asia. They invaded China and eastern Europe in the thirteenth century. Each Tatar cavalryman carried a battle-ax, a sword, and a twelve-foot lance.
13. **fowling piece:** shotgun used in hunting wild birds.
14. **galligaskins** (gal′i·gas′kinz): loose, baggy pants.
15. **ever-during and all-besetting:** everlasting and continually attacking.
16. **with a gallows air:** like someone condemned to be hanged.

OPTIONS FOR TEACHING

COOPERATIVE LEARNING

Brainstorming New Adventures Have students work in small groups to brainstorm ideas for adventures Rip might have had before his long sleep in the mountains. Ask each group to come up with two adventures that are plausible for a person of Rip's character and personality. Encourage students to choose one of their two adventures to illustrate as a comic strip. Let one member of each group share the group's efforts with the class.

Selecting and Analyzing Humorous Sentences Let students work in small groups to select through consensus the one sentence from the story that they find most humorous. Ask each group to analyze the chosen sentence in terms of the inflated language in the sentence, and to share the selection with the class. Artistically inclined students might provide an illustration.

sidelong glance at Dame Van Winkle, and at the least flourish of a broomstick or ladle he would fly to the door with yelping precipitation.[17]

Times grew worse and worse with Rip Van Winkle as years of matrimony rolled on; a tart temper never mellows with age, and a sharp tongue is the only edged tool that grows keener with constant use. For a long while he used to console himself when driven from home, by frequenting a kind of perpetual club of the sages, philosophers, and other idle personages of the village which held its sessions on a bench before a small inn, designated by a rubicund portrait of his majesty George the Third. Here they used to sit in the shade, through a long lazy summer's day, talking listlessly over village gossip, or telling endless sleepy stories about nothing. But it would have been worth any statesman's money to have heard the profound discussions that sometimes took place, when by chance an old newspaper fell into their hands from some passing traveler. How solemnly they would listen to the contents as drawled out by Derrick Van Bummel the schoolmaster, a dapper, learned little man, who was not to be daunted by the most gigantic word in the dictionary; and how sagely they would deliberate upon public events some months after they had taken place.

The opinions of this junto[18] were completely controlled by Nicholaus Vedder, a patriarch of the village, and landlord of the inn, at the door of which he took his seat from morning till night, just moving sufficiently to avoid the sun and keep in the shade of a large tree; so that the neighbors could tell the hour by his movements as accurately as by a sundial. It is true he was rarely heard to speak, but smoked his pipe incessantly. His adherents, however (for every great man has his adherents), perfectly understood him and knew how to gather his opinions. When anything that was read or related displeased him, he was observed to smoke his pipe vehemently, and to send forth short, frequent, and angry puffs; but when pleased he would inhale the smoke slowly and tranquilly and emit it in light and placid clouds, and sometimes taking the pipe from his mouth and letting the fragrant vapor curl about his nose, would gravely nod his head in token of perfect approbation.

From even this stronghold the unlucky Rip was at length routed by his termagant wife who would suddenly break in upon the tranquility of the assemblage and call the members all to naught; nor was that august personage Nicholaus Vedder himself sacred from the daring tongue of this terrible virago,[19] who charged him outright with encouraging her husband in habits of idleness.

Poor Rip was at last reduced almost to despair; and his only alternative to escape from the labor of the farm and the clamor of his wife, was to take gun in hand and stroll away into the woods. Here he would sometimes seat himself at the foot of a tree and share the contents of his wallet[20] with Wolf, with whom he sympathized as a fellow sufferer in persecution. "Poor Wolf," he would say, "thy mistress leads thee a dog's life of it, but never mind my lad, whilst I live thou shalt never want a friend to stand by thee!" Wolf would wag his tail, look wistfully in his master's face, and if dogs can feel pity I verily believe he reciprocated the sentiment with all his heart.

In a long ramble of the kind on a fine autumnal day, Rip had unconsciously scrambled to one of the highest parts of the Kaatskill Mountains. He was after his favorite sport of squirrel shooting and the still solitudes had echoed and reechoed with the reports of his gun. Panting and fatigued he threw himself, late in the afternoon, on a green knoll, covered with mountain herbage, that crowned the brow of a precipice. From an opening between the trees he could overlook all the lower country for many a mile of rich woodland. He saw at a distance the lordly Hudson, far, far below him, moving on its silent but majestic course, with the reflection of a purple cloud, or the sail of a lagging bark[21] here and there sleeping on its glassy bosom, and at last losing itself in the blue highlands.

17. **precipitation:** haste; suddenness.
18. **junto** (jun′tō): council; group with a common purpose.
19. **virago** (vi·rā′gō): quarrelsome, scolding woman.
20. **wallet:** knapsack.
21. **lagging bark:** slow-moving boat.

WORDS TO OWN

vehemently (vē′ə·mənt·lē) *adv.*: emphatically.
placid (plas′id) *adj.*: calm; quiet.

C. Literary Element: Stereotype

? How would you describe Irving's portrayal of marriage in this story?
[It is stereotyped, with the nagging wife and the henpecked husband.]

D. Reader's Response: Shaping Interpretations

? Why does Vedder not talk?
[Sample responses: Talking takes more energy than he wants to expend; or he thinks his opinions are superior to those of his neighbors, and he does not wish to waste words on them.]

CLASSROOM MANAGEMENT

Selecting Reporters One quick way to select reporters for group work is to have the oldest or youngest member of each group give the report. Other possibilities include: the person whose birthday comes earliest in the year, the person whose name falls last in the alphabet, and the person whose birthday falls nearest the first day within a month.

Setting Time Limits You might find it useful to set specific time limits for distinct stages of cooperative learning activities. For example, in the Cooperative Learning activity on p. T156 in which students select a humorous sentence, you could set a limit of five minutes for the groups to come to consensus on their sentences. Time limits should be flexible if students are obviously working but are unable to meet the deadline.

Managing the Reader's Response Classroom During discussions, have students address each other by name when they respond to each other's statements to foster cooperation and self-esteem.

A. Critical Reading: Speculating

? According to the way Irving has characterized Rip's wife so far, how might she act when he returns home? [Possible answer: She might shout, shoo him out of the house, throw pans, or otherwise express her anger.]

B. Critical Reading: Finding Details

? What clues indicate that this character is magical and not an ordinary person? [He is small, bearded, and wears old-fashioned and oddly decorated clothes. In short, he resembles the trolls, gnomes, elves, and leprechauns who populate European folk and fairy tales.]

Courtesy of the Shelburne Museum, Shelburne, Vermont. Photograph by Ken Burris.

Rip Chased from Home by His Wife (detail) (1880) by Albertus Del Orient Browere (1814–1887). Oil on canvas (36″ × 50″).

On the other side he looked down into a deep mountain glen, wild, lonely, and shagged, the bottom filled with fragments from the impending cliffs and scarcely lighted by the reflected rays of the setting sun. For some time Rip lay musing on this scene, evening was gradually advancing, the mountains began to throw their long blue shadows over the valleys, he saw that it would be dark, long before he could reach the village, and he heaved a heavy sigh when he thought of encountering the terrors of Dame Van Winkle. **A**

As he was about to descend he heard a voice from a distance hallooing "Rip Van Winkle! Rip Van Winkle!" He looked around, but could see nothing but a crow winging its solitary flight across the mountain. He thought his fancy must have deceived him and turned again to descend, when he heard the same cry ring through the still evening air: "Rip Van Winkle! Rip Van Winkle!"—at the same time Wolf bristled up his back and giving a low growl, skulked to his master's side, looking fearfully down into the glen. Rip now felt a vague apprehension stealing over him; he looked anxiously in the same direction and perceived a strange figure slowly toiling up the rocks and bending under the weight of something he carried on his back. He was surprised to see any human being in this lonely and unfrequented place, but supposing it to be someone of the neighborhood in need of his assistance he hastened down to yield it.

On nearer approach he was still more surprised at the singularity of the stranger's appearance. He was a short, square-built old fellow, with thick bushy hair and a grizzled beard. His dress was of the antique Dutch fashion, a cloth jerkin[22] strapped round the waist, several pair of breeches, the outer one of ample volume decorated with rows of buttons down the sides and bunches at the knees. He bore on his shoulder a stout keg that seemed full of liquor, and made signs for Rip to approach and assist him with the load. **B** Though rather shy and distrustful of this new acquaintance Rip complied with his usual alacrity, and mutually relieving each other they clambered up a narrow gully apparently the dry

22. **jerkin** (jur′kin): sleeveless jacket.

OPTIONS FOR TEACHING

CROSSING THE CURRICULUM

Art Ask some students to draw or paint pictures of Rip before his long sleep and others to produce pictures of Rip after he wakes up. Have volunteers pair these pictures for display in the classroom.

Science Rip's long sleep is obviously an exaggeration, but some scientists study sleep and sleep disorders to help people who have sleep-related problems. Invite students to arrange a panel discussion or poster display on sleep or dream research. If your community has a sleep-disorder clinic, consider inviting a guest speaker to discuss the work of the clinic with the class.

Health/Math Ask students to conduct a survey of other students about the amount of sleep they get in each twenty-four-hour period. A small group of students can work together to produce a questionnaire for members of the class to administer to five or six other classes. They should also have each student keep a daily log for one week of the amount of sleep he or she gets. Have students graph the results of their survey. The school newspaper might be interested in publishing the results of students' investigation.

bed of a mountain torrent. As they ascended, Rip every now and then heard long rolling peals like distant thunder, that seemed to issue out of a deep ravine or rather cleft between lofty rocks, toward which their rugged path conducted. He paused for an instant, but supposing it to be the muttering of one of those transient thundershowers which often take place in mountain heights, he proceeded. Passing through the ravine they came to a hollow like a small amphitheater, surrounded by perpendicular precipices, over the brinks of which impending trees shot their branches, so that you only caught glimpses of the azure sky and the bright evening cloud. During the whole time Rip and his companion had labored on in silence, for though the former marveled greatly what could be the object of carrying a keg of liquor up this wild mountain, yet there was something strange and incomprehensible about the unknown, that inspired awe and checked familiarity.

On entering the amphitheater new objects of wonder presented themselves. On a level spot in the center was a company of odd-looking personages playing at ninepins.[23] They were dressed in a quaint, outlandish fashion—some wore short doublets,[24] others jerkins with long knives in their belts and most of them had enormous breeches of similar style with that of the guide's. Their visages too were peculiar. One had a large head, broad face, and small piggish eyes. The face of another seemed to consist entirely of nose, and was surmounted by a white sugarloaf hat, set off with a little red cock's tail. They all had beards of various shapes and colors. There was one who seemed to be the commander. He was a stout old gentleman, with a weather-beaten countenance. He wore a laced doublet, broad belt and hanger,[25] high-crowned hat and feather, red stockings, and high-heeled shoes with roses[26] in them. The whole group reminded Rip of the figures in an old Flemish painting, in the parlor of Dominie Van Schaick the village parson, and which had been brought over from Holland at the time of the settlement.

What seemed particularly odd to Rip was, that though these folks were evidently amusing themselves, yet they maintained the gravest faces, the most mysterious silence, and were, withal, the most melancholy party of pleasure he had ever witnessed. Nothing interrupted the stillness of the scene, but the noise of the balls, which, whenever they were rolled, echoed along the mountains like rumbling peals of thunder.

As Rip and his companion approached them they suddenly desisted from their play and stared at him with such fixed statuelike gaze, and such strange uncouth, lackluster countenances, that his heart turned within him, and his knees smote together. His companion now emptied the contents of the keg into large flagons[27] and made signs to him to wait upon the company. He obeyed with fear and trembling; they quaffed the liquor in profound silence and then returned to their game.

By degrees Rip's awe and apprehension subsided. He even ventured, when no eye was fixed upon him, to taste the beverage, which he found had much of the flavor of excellent Hollands.[28] He was naturally a thirsty soul and was soon tempted to repeat the draft. One taste provoked another, and he reiterated his visits to the flagon so often that at length his senses were overpowered, his eyes swam in his head—his head gradually declined and he fell into a deep sleep.

On awaking he found himself on the green knoll from whence he had first seen the old man of the glen. He rubbed his eyes—it was a bright, sunny morning. The birds were hopping and twittering among the bushes, and the eagle was wheeling aloft and breasting the pure mountain breeze. "Surely," thought Rip, "I have not slept here all night." He recalled the occurrences before he fell asleep. The strange man with a keg of liquor—the mountain ravine—the wild retreat among the rocks—the woebegone party at ninepins—the flagon—"ah! that flagon! that wicked flagon!" thought Rip—"what excuse shall I make to Dame Van Winkle?"

He looked round for his gun, but in place of the clean well-oiled fowling piece he found an old

23. **ninepins:** a bowling game.
24. **doublets:** closefitting jackets.
25. **hanger:** short, curved sword hung from the belt.
26. **roses:** ornaments shaped like roses; often called rosettes.

27. **flagons:** bottlelike containers for liquids.
28. **Hollands:** Dutch gin.

WORDS TO OWN
reiterated (rē·it′ə·rāt′id) *v.:* repeated.

C. Literary Element: Symbolism

? What does the thunder suggest? [Literally, the thunder suggests an impending storm. Symbolically, it suggests that something bad is about to happen.]

D. Literary Element: Description

? How do the extended descriptions of the little men, the amphitheater, and the ninepins game contribute to the atmosphere of the story? [They help make a fantasy environment seem real, and they help draw the reader in.]

E. Critical Reading: Drawing Conclusions

? In plain language, what appears to make Rip fall asleep? [Rip has too much Dutch gin to drink and passes out.]

PROFESSIONAL NOTES

Cultural Diversity Dame Van Winkle seems to dominate Rip and their family. Form heterogeneous student groups to discuss how family members relate to one another in various cultural traditions. Ask students to suggest how these relationships might be most accurately described across a broad culture, rather than in an individual experience. Some topics that groups might explore include how household chores are divided up, which adult handles family finances, who has the final word in rules for the children to follow, and how major decisions are made within families. Students may have varying impressions of their own and other cultures. Allow students to discuss differences in their observations.

Thematic Connections: "The Transforming Imagination" "Rip Van Winkle" exemplifies the theme of the transforming imagination in American Romanticism. The story itself is inspired by folk culture and relies on the supernatural, a significant departure from past writing in the United States. Rip himself is transformed by his experience, for when he leaves town he is regarded as lazy but kind, and when he returns, he is welcomed as something of a celebrity. Irving seems to value Rip's youthful innocence and kindness towards others over the sophistication and worldliness revered by past generations. ☞

A. Literary Element: Suspense

? How does Irving create suspense? [Possible answer: The vivid descriptions of specific changes make the reader wonder how long Rip will be confused and what his final response will be.]

B. Critical Reading: Finding Details

? What clues let us know a great deal of time has passed? [The rust on the gun, the stiffness in Rip's joints, the changes in fashion, the unfamiliarity of faces, and the length of Rip's beard.]

firelock[29] lying by him, the barrel encrusted with rust; the lock falling off and the stock[30] worm-eaten. He now suspected that the grave roysters of the mountain had put a trick upon him, and having dosed him with liquor, had robbed him of his gun. Wolf too had disappeared, but he might have strayed away after a squirrel or partridge. He whistled after him and shouted his name—but all in vain; the echoes repeated his whistle and shout, but no dog was to be seen.

He determined to revisit the scene of the last evening's gambol, and if he met with any of the party, to demand his dog and gun. As he arose to walk he found himself stiff in the joints and wanting in his usual activity. "These mountain beds do not agree with me," thought Rip, "and if this frolic should lay me up with a fit of the rheumatism, I shall have a blessed time with Dame Van Winkle." With some difficulty he got down into the glen; he found the gully up which he and his companion had ascended the preceding evening, but to his astonishment a mountain stream was now foaming down it; leaping from rock to rock, and filling the glen with babbling murmurs. He, however, made shift to scramble up its sides working his toilsome way through thickets of birch, sassafras, and witch hazel, and sometimes tripped up or entangled by the wild grapevines that twisted their coils and tendrils from tree to tree, and spread a kind of network in his path.

At length he reached to where the ravine had opened through the cliffs, to the amphitheater—but no traces of such opening remained. The rocks presented a high impenetrable wall over which the torrent came tumbling in a sheet of feathery foam, and fell into a broad deep basin black from the shadows of the surrounding forest. Here then poor Rip was brought to a stand. He again called and whistled after his dog—he was only answered by the cawing of a flock of idle crows, sporting high in air about a dry tree that overhung a sunny precipice; and who, secure in their elevation seemed to look down and scoff at the poor man's perplexities.

What was to be done? The morning was passing away and Rip felt famished for want of his breakfast. He grieved to give up his dog and gun; he dreaded to meet his wife; but it would not do to starve among the mountains. He shook his head, shouldered the rusty firelock, and with a heart full of trouble and anxiety, turned his steps homeward.

As he approached the village he met a number of people, but none whom he knew, which somewhat surprised him, for he had thought himself acquainted with everyone in the country round. Their dress too was of a different fashion from that to which he was accustomed. They all stared at him with equal marks of surprise, and whenever they cast their eyes upon him, invariably stroked their chins. The constant recurrence of this gesture induced Rip involuntarily to do the same, when to his astonishment he found his beard had grown a foot long!

He had now entered the skirts of the village. A troop of strange children ran at his heels, hooting after him and pointing at his gray beard. The dogs too, not one of which he recognized for an old acquaintance, barked at him as he passed. The very village was altered—it was larger and more populous. There were rows of houses which he had never seen before, and those which had been his familiar haunts had disappeared. Strange names were over the doors—strange faces at the windows—everything was strange. His mind now misgave him; he began to doubt whether both he and the world around him were not bewitched. Surely this was his native village which he had left but the day before. There stood the Kaatskill Mountains—there ran the silver Hudson at a distance—there was every hill and dale precisely as it had always been—Rip was sorely perplexed—"That flagon last night," thought he, "has addled my poor head sadly!"

It was with some difficulty that he found the way to his own house, which he approached with silent awe, expecting every moment to hear the

29. **firelock:** early type of gun.
30. **stock:** wooden handle attached to metal gun barrel.

OPTIONS FOR TEACHING

PROBLEM SOLVING/CRITICAL THINKING

Truth or Fabrication Irving uses conventional literary devices to make a tale of fantastic proportions appear believable [biographical information on a gentleman interested in history, a subtitle, a note on a note]. As they read, have students list instances where Crayon attempts to convince the reader of the truth of the tale he reports. After they finish reading, ask students how readers can determine the truth of the tale. Ask them to discuss what strategies they use to determine whether what they hear from others, what they see on television, and what they read in newspapers, magazines, and books is truthful. Have students write down strategies the class decides are effective.

Solutions to Confrontations Ask students to work in small groups to brainstorm answers to the following question: How could Rip have avoided confrontations with his wife? After each group has generated at least five possible solutions, make a master list for the class to discuss. After the discussion, ask students to individually rank the three solutions they think are most workable and to compile a rank-order list for the whole class.

Courtesy of the Shelburne Museum, Shelburne, Vermont. Photograph by Ken Burris.

Rip Van Winkle Asleep (detail) (1880) by Albertus Del Orient Browere (1814–1887). Oil on canvas.

shrill voice of Dame Van Winkle. He found the house gone to decay—the roof fallen in, the windows shattered, and the doors off the hinges. A half-starved dog that looked like Wolf was skulking about it. Rip called him by name but the cur snarled, showed his teeth, and passed on. This was an unkind cut indeed—"My very dog," sighed poor Rip, "has forgotten me!"

He entered the house, which, to tell the truth, Dame Van Winkle had always kept in neat order. It was empty, forlorn, and apparently abandoned. This desolateness overcame all his connubial[31] fears—he called loudly for his wife and children—the lonely chambers rung for a moment with his voice, and then all again was silence. **C**

He now hurried forth and hastened to his old resort, the village inn—but it too was gone. A large, rickety wooden building stood in its place, with great gaping windows, some of them broken, and mended with old hats and petticoats, and over the door was printed "The Union Hotel, by Jonathan Doolittle." Instead of the great tree, that used to shelter the quiet little Dutch inn of yore, there now was reared a tall naked pole with something on top that looked like a red nightcap,[32] and from it was fluttering a flag on which was a singular assemblage of stars and stripes—all this was strange and incomprehensible. He recognized on the sign, however, the ruby face of King George under which he had smoked so many a peaceful pipe, but even this was singularly metamorphosed.[33] The red coat was changed for one of blue and buff; a sword was held in the hand instead of a scepter; the head was decorated with a cocked hat, and underneath was printed in large characters[34] GENERAL WASHINGTON. **D**

There was as usual a crowd of folk about the door; but none that Rip recollected. The very character of people seemed changed. There was a busy, bustling disputatious tone about it, instead of the accustomed phlegm and drowsy tranquility.

31. **connubial** (kə·no͞o′bē·əl): related to marriage.

32. **red nightcap:** "liberty cap"; worn as a symbol of independence during the French and American Revolutions.

33. **metamorphosed** (met′ə·môr′fōzd′): transformed.

34. **characters:** letters.

C. Reader's Response: First Thoughts

? How would you feel if you woke up in a world you no longer knew and which no longer knew you? [Sample responses: Panicked, confused, frightened, curious.]

D. Critical Reading: Metacognition

? At what point in the passage did you become convinced the American Revolution had taken place while Rip slept? [Possible answers: When Rip sees the stars and stripes; or when Rip sees that a picture of George Washington has replaced the picture of King George.]

ASSESSMENT TOOLS

Check Test: Questions and Answers

1. Rip Van Winkle is a young man in the _____ century. [eighteenth]
2. His region of New York state had originally been settled by the _____. [Dutch]
3. The little men play a bowling game called _____. [ninepins]
4. When Rip returns from sleep, the colonies have become _____. [independent]
5. As an old man, Rip lives with his _____. [daughter]

Self-Assessment: Reading As students interact with the story, have them use the following scale to rate their reading performances.

1. As I read the story, I used the footnotes and the glossary to find the meanings of unfamiliar words.
   Frequently Occasionally Seldom
2. I re-read sections of the story that were not clear to me the first time I read them.
   Frequently Occasionally Seldom
3. After reading portions of the story, I mentally reviewed the events in order.
   Frequently Occasionally Seldom

A. Literary Element: Satire
Irving satirizes the politicians of his day and may be implying that the narrow partisanship of the people has led them to forget generosity.

LITERATURE AND FOLKLORE

Have students collaborate on a short story conclusion. Ask students to write the conclusion from the point when the protagonist awakens in a time frame different from the original setting. Students might generate their own ideas or use one of the following prompts: Sleeping Beauty awakens in modern times or in the age of cave dwellers; Han Solo, of the *Star Wars* movies, is released from frozen sleep only to discover he is on Earth in the eighteenth century; a student studying for a final exam awakens in the remote past or the distant future. Give student groups enough class time to formulate ideas and generate a first draft. Have groups share their results. Students should keep these first draft ideas in their portfolios. Invite interested students to polish their story endings or to write a complete narrative.

He looked in vain for the sage Nicholaus Vedder with his broad face, double chin, and fair long pipe, uttering clouds of tobacco smoke instead of idle speeches. Or Van Bummel the schoolmaster doling forth the contents of an ancient newspaper. **A** In place of these a lean bilious-looking fellow with his pockets full of handbills, was haranguing vehemently about rights of citizens—elections—members of Congress—liberty—Bunker's hill—heroes of Seventy-six—and other

LITERATURE AND FOLKLORE

Enchanted Slumbers

Like *Gulliver's Travels* and *Alice's Adventures in Wonderland,* "Rip Van Winkle" has had a lasting appeal for both children and adults. Part of its popularity may be traced to age-old folk tale elements that appear in the story. (Irving based the story on a German legend.)

Some of the common narrative elements, or **motifs,** that "Rip Van Winkle" shares with folk tales from around the world include mysterious supernatural beings, a sleep-inducing potion, and a perilous journey. To most readers, though, the most memorable motif in "Rip Van Winkle" is Rip's twenty-year sleep. Dozens of myths, folk tales, and legends feature the enchanted slumber as a story element—most people are familiar with "Sleeping Beauty," for example, if only from the Disney film. In many of these tales, the hero enters a cave or another hidden place and falls into a magic sleep that may last for centuries. Often, tales about enchanted sleepers are associated with popular beliefs about legendary characters: King Arthur, Quetzalcoatl, Merlin, Charlemagne, and William Tell are all associated with "sleeper" legends. According to some legends—the most famous is the tale of Britain's King Arthur—the slumbering hero will awaken from the long sleep when the people's need for help is greatest, perhaps far in the future.

So haunting and appealing is the concept of the "enchanted slumber" that it keeps appearing in our popular arts. Horror movies and comic books have happily repeated the by-now-familiar scene of a vampire, mummy, or other undead creature rising from a casket or tomb after centuries of confinement. In many contemporary stories, though, the long sleep is made possible through technology, as in Woody Allen's film *Sleeper,* the fantasy film *Forever Young,* and numerous science fiction stories and films about people who are purposely or accidentally frozen and revived in the future. Such stories, like the myths and folk tales that preceded them, touch on two compelling human fantasies: the wish to see what the world of the future will look like, and the desire to cheat death by outlasting our normal life span.

words which were a perfect Babylonish jargon[35] to the bewildered Van Winkle.

The appearance of Rip with his long grizzled beard, his rusty fowling piece, his uncouth dress, and an army of women and children at his heels soon attracted the attention of the tavern politicians. They crowded around him eyeing him from head to foot, with great curiosity. The orator bustled up to him, and drawing him partly aside, inquired "on which side he voted?"—Rip stared in vacant stupidity. Another short but busy little fellow, pulled him by the arm and rising on tiptoe, inquired in his ear "whether he was Federal or Democrat?"[36]—Rip was equally at a loss to comprehend the question—when a knowing, self-important old gentleman, in a sharp cocked hat, made his way through the crowd, putting them to the right and left with his elbows as he passed, and planting himself before Van Winkle, with one arm akimbo, the other resting on his cane, his keen eyes and sharp hat penetrating as it were into his very soul, demanded in an austere tone—"what brought him to the election with a gun on his shoulder and a mob at his heels, and whether he meant to breed a riot in the village?"—"Alas gentlemen," cried Rip, somewhat dismayed, "I am a poor quiet man, a native of the place, and a loyal subject of the King—God bless him!"

Here a general shout burst from the bystanders—"A Tory![37] a Tory! a spy! a Refugee![38] hustle him! away with him!"—It was with great difficulty that the self-important man in the cocked hat restored order; and having assumed a tenfold austerity of brow demanded again of the unknown culprit, what he came there for and whom he was seeking. The poor man humbly assured him that he meant no harm; but merely came there in search of some of his neighbors, who used to keep about the tavern.

"—Well—who are they?—name them."

Rip bethought himself a moment and inquired, "Where's Nicholaus Vedder?"

There was a silence for a little while, when an old man replied, in a thin, piping voice, "Nicholaus Vedder? Why he is dead and gone these eighteen years! There was a wooden tombstone in the churchyard that used to tell all about him, but that's rotted and gone too."

"Where's Brom Dutcher?"

"Oh he went off to the army in the beginning of the war; some say he was killed at the storming of Stoney Point—others say he was drowned in a squall at the foot of Antony's Nose[39]—I don't know—he never came back again."

"Where's Van Bummel the schoolmaster?"

"He went off to the wars too—was a great militia general, and is now in Congress."

Rip's heart died away at hearing of these sad changes in his home and friends, and finding himself thus alone in the world—every answer puzzled him too by treating of such enormous lapses of time and of matters which he could not understand—war—Congress, Stoney Point—he had no courage to ask after any more friends, but cried out in despair, "Does nobody here know Rip Van Winkle?" (B)

"Oh. Rip Van Winkle?" exclaimed two or three—"oh to be sure!—that's Rip Van Winkle—yonder—leaning against the tree."

Rip looked and beheld a precise counterpart of himself, as he went up the mountain: apparently as lazy and certainly as ragged! The poor fellow was now completely confounded. He doubted his own identity, and whether he was himself or another man. In the midst of his bewilderment the man in the cocked hat demanded who he was—what was his name? (C)

"God knows," exclaimed he, at his wit's end, "I'm not myself.—I'm somebody else—that's me yonder—no—that's somebody else got into my shoes—I was myself last night; but I fell asleep on the mountain—and they've changed my gun—and everything's changed—and I'm changed—and I can't tell what's my name, or who I am!"

35. Babylonish jargon: confusing language. According to Genesis 11:1–9, when the people of the earth tried to build a tower high enough to reach heaven, God caused the people to speak many different languages. Because they could no longer communicate, they abandoned the project, which is now known as the Tower of Babel.
36. Federal or Democrat: American political parties after the Revolution. Federals favored a strong centralized government; Democrats favored states' rights.
37. Tory: one who supported British rule in the American Colonies.
38. Refugee: member of a group of British sympathizers, especially in New York State, who attacked supporters of the American cause, during the Revolutionary period.

39. Antony's Nose: mountain near West Point in New York.

B. Reader's Response: Shaping Interpretations

? How does Rip feel about not recognizing anyone in the altered setting? [Sample responses: Confused; more frustrated than terrified, at first.]

C. Expansion

The undercurrent of this seemingly comic tale is revealed by Rip's frightening confrontation with a son who has usurped him. The narrator says that Rip was no longer sure of his own identity. Beneath the charm of the telling, we see a man at the end of his tether, alone, frightened, grief-stricken. The multiplicity of layers in the story is surely one reason it retains a grip on the imagination.

A. Critical Reading: Analyzing Character

? Why does Rip take comfort in the news of his wife's death? [He is relieved to be free of her. He might also be comforted that he was not the only person capable of making her angry.]

Metacognition How did you arrive at your conclusion? [Possible answers: Rip had feared facing his wife, and now he will not have to. These facts lead to the conclusion that he is relieved to be free of her. The fact that she died in a fit of anger at a peddler proves she could lose her temper with strangers and family members alike.]

B. Literary Element: Tone

? How does the tone change at this point? [It becomes less tense and dramatic, more genial and folkloric, through the switch from dialogue to leisurely narration.]

C. Critical Reading: Analyzing Tone

? What words and phrases help restore the genial tone? [Words such as *snug* and *cheery* serve this purpose.]

The bystanders began now to look at each other, nod, wink significantly, and tap their fingers against their foreheads. There was a whisper also about securing the gun, and keeping the old fellow from doing mischief—at the very suggestion of which, the self-important man in the cocked hat retired with some precipitation. At this critical moment a fresh likely looking woman pressed through the throng to get a peep at the gray-bearded man. She had a chubby child in her arms, which frightened at his looks began to cry. "Hush Rip," cried she, "hush you little fool, the old man won't hurt you." The name of the child, the air of the mother, the tone of her voice all awakened a train of recollections in his mind. "What is your name my good woman?" asked he.

"Judith Gardenier."

"And your father's name?"

"Ah, poor man, Rip Van Winkle was his name, but it's twenty years since he went away from home with his gun and never has been heard of since—his dog came home without him—but whether he shot himself, or was carried away by the Indians nobody can tell. I was then but a little girl."

Rip had but one question more to ask, but he put it with a faltering voice—

"Where's your mother?"—

Oh she too had died but a short time since—she broke a blood vessel in a fit of passion at a New England peddler.—

(A) There was a drop of comfort at least in this intelligence. The honest man could contain himself no longer—he caught his daughter and her child in his arms.—"I am your father!" cried he—"Young Rip Van Winkle once—old Rip Van Winkle now!—does nobody know poor Rip Van Winkle!"

All stood amazed, until an old woman tottering out from among the crowd put her hand to her brow and peering under it in his face for a moment exclaimed—"Sure enough!—it is Rip Van Winkle—it is himself—welcome home again old neighbor—why, where have you been these twenty long years?"

(B) Rip's story was soon told, for the whole twenty years had been to him but as one night. The neighbors stared when they heard it; some were seen to wink at each other and put their tongues in their cheeks, and the self-important man in the cocked hat, who when the alarm was over had returned to the field, screwed down the corners of his mouth and shook his head—upon which there was a general shaking of the head throughout the assemblage.

It was determined, however, to take the opinion of old Peter Vanderdonk, who was seen slowly advancing up the road. He was a descendant of the historian of that name, who wrote one of the earliest accounts of the province. Peter was the most ancient inhabitant of the village and well versed in all the wonderful events and traditions of the neighborhood. He recollected Rip at once, and corroborated his story in the most satisfactory manner. He assured the company that it was a fact handed down from his ancestor the historian, that the Kaatskill Mountains had always been haunted by strange beings. That it was affirmed that the great Hendrick Hudson,[40] the first discoverer of the river and country, kept a kind of vigil there every twenty years, with his crew of the *Half Moon*—being permitted in this way to revisit the scenes of his enterprise and keep a guardian eye upon the river and the great city called by his name.[41] That his father had once seen them in their old Dutch dresses playing at ninepins in a hollow of the mountain; and that he himself had heard one summer afternoon the sound of their balls, like distant peals of thunder.

(C) To make a long story short—the company broke up, and returned to the more important concerns of the election. Rip's daughter took him home to live with her; she had a snug well-furnished house, and a stout cheery farmer for a husband whom Rip recollected for one of the

40. Hendrick Hudson: Henry Hudson (?–1611), an English navigator hired by the Dutch, explored the river later named for him, in his ship, the *Half Moon*. Hudson's explorations were the basis for early Dutch claims in North America.

41. great . . . name: Hudson, New York.

urchins that used to climb upon his back. As to Rip's son and heir, who was the ditto of himself seen leaning against the tree; he was employed to work on the farm; but evinced an hereditary disposition to attend to anything else but his business.

Rip now resumed his old walks and habits; he soon found many of his former cronies, though all rather the worse for the wear and tear of time; and preferred making friends among the rising generation, with whom he soon grew into great favor. Having nothing to do at home, and being arrived at that happy age when a man can be idle, with impunity, he took his place once more on the bench at the inn door and was reverenced as one of the patriarchs of the village and a chronicle of the old times "before the war." It was some time before he could get into the regular track of gossip, or could be made to comprehend the strange events that had taken place during his torpor. How that there had been a revolutionary war—that the country had thrown off the yoke of Old England and that instead of being a subject of his majesty George the Third, he was now a free citizen of the United States. Rip in fact was no politician; the changes of states and empires made but little impression on him; but there was one species of despotism under which he had long groaned and that was petticoat government. Happily that was at an end—he had got his neck out of the yoke of matrimony, and could go in and out whenever he pleased without dreading the tyranny of Dame Van Winkle. Whenever her name was mentioned, however, he shook his head, shrugged his shoulders, and cast up his eyes; which might pass either for an expression of resignation to his fate or joy at his deliverance.

He used to tell his story to every stranger that arrived at Mr. Doolittle's Hotel. He was observed at first to vary on some points, every time he told it, which was doubtless owing to his having so recently awaked. It at last settled down precisely to the tale I have related and not a man, woman, or child in the neighborhood but knew it by heart. Some always pretended to doubt the reality of it, and insisted that Rip had been out of his head, and that this was one point on which he always remained flighty. The old Dutch inhabitants, however, almost universally gave it full credit—Even to this day they never hear a thunderstorm of a summer afternoon about the Kaatskill, but they say Hendrick Hudson and his crew are at their game of ninepins; and it is a common wish of all henpecked husbands in the neighborhood, when life hangs heavy on their hands, that they might have a quieting draft out of Rip Van Winkle's flagon.

Note

The foregoing tale one would suspect had been suggested to Mr. Knickerbocker by a little German superstition about the emperor Frederick *der Rothbart* and the Kypphauser Mountain;[42] the subjoined note, however, which he had appended to the tale, shows that it is an absolute fact, narrated with his usual fidelity.—

"The story of Rip Van Winkle may seem incredible to many, but nevertheless I give it my full belief, for I know the vicinity of our old Dutch settlements to have been very subject to marvelous events and appearances. Indeed I have heard many stranger stories than this, in the villages along the Hudson; all of which were too well authenticated to admit of a doubt. I have even talked with Rip Van Winkle myself, who when last I saw him was a very venerable old man and so perfectly rational and consistent on every other point, that I think no conscientious person could refuse to take this into the bargain—nay I have seen a certificate on the subject taken before a country justice and signed with a cross in the justice's own handwriting. The story therefore is beyond the possibility of doubt.

D. K."

42. **emperor . . . Mountain:** Frederick I, emperor of the Holy Roman Empire (1155–1190); also called der Rothbart (German for "red beard"). Although he died near the Mediterranean during the Crusades, according to folk legend he sleeps on Kypphauser (now called Kyffhauser) Mountain in Germany.

Words to Own

torpor (tôr′pər) *n.:* inactive period.
fidelity (fə·del′ə·tē) *n.:* accuracy.
conscientious (kän′shē·en′shəs) *adj.:* careful and honest.

D. Language Note: Inflated Language

? What is the effect of the inflated language in this phrase? [It adds to the comic tone.]

E. Reader's Response: Shaping Interpretations

? Is Rip a different person for having had his experiences in the mountains? [Sample responses: Not really, since Rip immediately reverts to his old ways without any apparent change in his personality. Or Rip is happier because he can make new friends.]

F. Expansion

The "Note" returns the story to the frame device, a technique which reasserts the tale's authenticity. Irving satirizes these notes.

Making Meanings

First Thoughts

1. Possible response: Rip escapes from his scolding wife.

Reviewing the Text

Before	After
Wife scolds Rip meets stranger Rip goes to mountain with stranger Rip drinks	Rip returns to village Rip finds daughter Rip's wife has died Woman recognizes him Rip tells story to townspeople and to visitors

Shaping Interpretations

2. The supposedly reliable Crayon relays a supposedly substantiated Knickerbocker account. The tone is lightly ironic.
3. Descriptions of the group on the mountain and references to New York's Dutch past. His early description of the mountains reflects his love of nature.
4. The frame device, and descriptions of Rip, the interactions between Rip and his wife, Rip's son, the "junto," Rip's behavior on the mountain, and Rip's awakening to the changes in the town. Irving pokes fun at folklorists, the Van Winkles, the townspeople, and politicians.
5. The theme is escape from the cares and problems of life. Most students will probably find the theme relevant and will point to escapist entertainment as an example of how many people attempt escape today.

Connecting with the Text

6. Responses will vary. Some students may say that the challenging writing style makes it harder to appreciate the humor.

Extending the Text

7. **(Synthesis)** Franklin sought involvement in public affairs and was committed to hard work. Rip flees even family involvement and is lazy. The contemporary entrepreneur is a Franklin type, while a loafing do-nothing is the Rip type.

Challenging the Text

8. **(Evaluation)** Responses will vary. Discuss old and current TV shows. *The Taming of the Shrew* is an example from classical literature, and "The Secret Life of Walter Mitty" (pp. 625–628) is a modern literary example. Although Irving was not promoting a loafing bachelor lifestyle, he seems to sympathize with Rip and to criticize Dame Van Winkle.

Language and Style

Answers

1. In paragraphs three through seven, most of the sentences contain inflated language. Students can choose from these or from others throughout the story.
2. Answers will vary. Students should render the statements in plain English sentences that have the same literal meaning as the original.
3. Answers will vary. Some students may say the inflated language made the reading more difficult. Encourage them to persevere with challenging material by pointing out that the more they read, the easier comprehension becomes. Let students know that you realize the material requires special effort, which is why you are working with them.

MAKING MEANINGS

First Thoughts

1. In what ways is this a classic story of wish fulfillment?

Reviewing the Text

Make a before-and-after chart of what happened in the story before Rip's sleep and what happened after he woke up.

Shaping Interpretations

2. In his introductory note, the narrator (who is Geoffrey Crayon) explains that the manuscript of "Rip Van Winkle" was written by Diedrich Knickerbocker, the narrator of Irving's earlier *History of New York*. How does Irving use his two narrators—Geoffrey Crayon and Diedrich Knickerbocker—to defend the tale's credibility? How would you describe Irving's **tone** in these introductory passages?
3. What details in "Rip Van Winkle" do you think reveal a Romantic fascination with the past and nature? Find some descriptions of the **setting** that you think reflect a Romantic's point of view.
4. Irving was a Romantic, but he was also a satirist. What elements of this story—including the narrator's commentaries—are **satirical**? Who or what are Irving's targets?
5. How would you state the **theme** of this story? Do you think the theme is still relevant to readers in the late twentieth century? Explain.

Connecting with the Text

6. Above all, "Rip Van Winkle" is regarded as a comic tale. Do you, as a late twentieth-century reader, find the story humorous, or do you think it's too outdated to be funny to us today? Explain your response.

Extending the Text

7. How does the fictional **character** of Rip Van Winkle contrast with the historical character of Benjamin Franklin, the self-made man (page 84)? Where do you still see both character types in American life today?

Challenging the Text

8. Dame Van Winkle and Rip are **stereotyped characters** that have been found in literature throughout the ages—the nagging wife and the henpecked husband. Can you identify these character types in current literature and in popular movies and TV shows? What is your response to Irving's characterization of Dame Van Winkle? Was Irving (who remained a bachelor and hated the business life) biased in favor of the ne'er-do-well Rip?

LANGUAGE AND STYLE

Irving's Inflated Language

A critic once said that Irving's humor was "literary slapstick," full of "hyperbole, grotesque caricature," and "flagrant puns." One of the hallmarks of Irving's humor is his use of **inflated,** or exaggerated, language to describe commonplace things. For example, rather than simply saying that Rip is "lazy," or that he "hates work," Irving states that Rip has "an insuperable aversion to all kinds of profitable labor."

1. Find at least two other comically inflated descriptions of Rip's family life.
2. How could each inflated description be phrased in plain English?
3. How did this element of Irving's **style** affect your reading of the story?

Washington Irving.

Drawing by David Levine. Reprinted with permission from *The New York Review of Books*. Copyright ©1976 NYREV, Inc.

Choices: Building Your Portfolio

Writer's Notebook

1. Collecting Ideas for an Observational Essay

Think of a familiar **setting** that has particular meaning to you—whether it's a seacoast, a park, the basketball court where you play, or your school cafeteria—and freewrite a description of that place to make a reader "see" it clearly. Focus on the details that a Romantic writer would notice: colors, weather, atmosphere, textures, and so on. To generate **images,** try using a cluster of words and images like the one below. Keep your notes; you may find them helpful later for the Writer's Workshop (page 198).

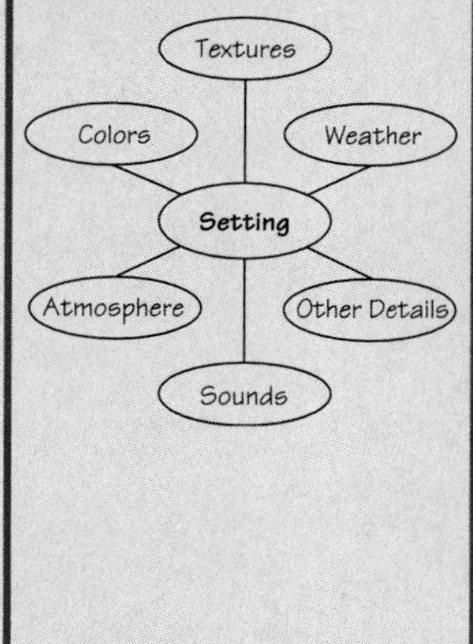

Critical Writing

2. Parallel Awakenings

Rip's awakening has been seen by many critics as a parallel to the awakening of the new American nation. In a short essay, cite the specific story details that support the idea that Rip's emancipation from his wife is like America's emancipation from the dominance of Great Britain. In your essay, discuss the ideas of independence and maturity.

Critical Writing

3. The Battle of the Sexes

This story reflects a **conflict** that has been used by hundreds of other writers of comedy, before and after Irving. The conflict might be described as the battle of the sexes. In a brief essay, tell how Irving's story reflects this conflict; name other comedies (in books, on TV, and in the movies) that use the same conflict; and explain your own response to its continued use and popularity.

Photofest.

ABC's TV show *Home Improvement* with Patricia Richardson (left) and Tim Allen.

Creative Writing

4. Dame Van Winkle Has Her Say

Write an epilogue to this story called "Dame Van Winkle." Describe her response to Rip's disappearance. Was she also emancipated? Will you have Dame Van Winkle tell her own story or let Diedrich Knickerbocker continue?

Creative Writing

5. Back to the Future

Go back to the Quickwrite you wrote in your Reader's Log (page 153), and use it as a springboard for a brief article taken from a newspaper twenty years from today. Your article can be about a current event of the time; it can also be an editorial or even an advice column.

Creative Writing / Art

6. Missing Person

You're a private investigator trying to discover the whereabouts of the missing Rip Van Winkle. First, compile a profile or dossier on Rip: a list of his character traits, a list of possible motives he may have had for wanting to escape, and brief interviews with people who knew him. Include a "missing person" portrait of Rip.

Beyond the Story

Choices: Building Your Portfolio

1. **Writer's Notebook** Remind students to save their work. They may use it as prewriting for the Writer's Workshop on p. 198.
2. **Critical Writing** Have small groups brainstorm the major events of the American Revolutionary period before they begin trying to find parallels in the story. A graphic organizer such as the following one might help students organize the connections they make.

Story's events		
Parallels to history		

3. **Critical Writing** Many situation comedies are based on the battle of the sexes. Ask students who are having difficulty getting started to reflect on one sitcom and to apply their insights to the story.
4. **Creative Writing** As a prewriting activity, allow students to work in pairs to conduct an interview, with one student taking the part of Dame Van Winkle and the other taking the part of an interviewer.
5. **Creative Writing** Have students study sample newspaper articles, editorials, and advice columns before they begin.
6. **Creative Writing/Art** Have students begin by sharing ideas about what a missing person dossier pulled from a detective's file might look like.

STRATEGIES FOR INCLUSION

Auditory As students work on activity #1, you might allow pairs of students to work together. Suggest that one student tell the other what setting he or she plans to describe. Have the partner ask questions that help to elicit details. The first student can jot down the words as they come to mind. Have students take turns.

Linguistic Encourage students creating Dame Van Winkle's speech for activity #4 to mentally enact the scene in which she sets forth her side of the story. After students have envisioned her reaction, encourage them to write down the details they imagined and to review their notes as they write her epilogue to the story.

PORTFOLIO ASSESSMENT

Choices: Assessment Criteria For help in evaluating these Choices assignments, see the criteria in the ***Portfolio Management System,*** pp. 83–84.

How To Own A Word

Mini-Lesson: Context Clues

Divide the class into several groups, and ask each group to locate five sentences, each containing a vocabulary word they are not familiar with. Have student groups determine which parts of the surrounding sentence for each word can be considered context clues according to the seven types illustrated in How to Own a Word. Ask groups to draw conclusions about the meanings of the words they have chosen and to have a checker in the group verify meanings in a dictionary. Finally, ask groups to share their findings and to discuss which types of context clues seem to appear most often in Irving's work.

PROGRAM MANAGER

Reinforcement To allow students practice and reinforcement of the vocabulary strategy introduced in this collection, see **Transparency** 4.3 in the ***Audiovisual Resources Binder***.

How to Own a Word

Context Clues: Using Clues in the Text to Discover Word Meanings

Using **context clues**—clues to meaning that are in the text—is the best way to figure out the meaning of a word without interrupting yourself to check the dictionary. A word's context includes the words and sentences that surround it. But context clues can be hard to spot because they aren't labeled. It's up to you to discover the relevant material if it's there. Washington Irving's "Rip Van Winkle" provides examples of seven kinds of context clues (there are more) that you will commonly encounter in your reading.

1. Example

". . . they ***quaffed*** the liquor in profound silence. . . ." (page 159)

Liquor is an example of something you can *quaff.* You can figure out that *quaff* means "to drink."

2. Restatement

"He even ventured . . . to taste the beverage . . . and was soon tempted to repeat the ***draft.***" (page 159)

"Repeat the *draft*" seems to restate "taste the beverage," so *draft* means "drinking."

3. Summary

". . . he was observed to smoke his pipe ***vehemently,*** and to send forth short, frequent, and angry puffs. . . ." (page 157)

The clause after the comma summarizes his "vehement" smoking: *Vehement* apparently means "with strong feeling" or "emphatically."

4. Contrast

". . . he was rarely heard to speak, but smoked his pipe ***incessantly.***" (page 157)

The conjunction *but* sets up an opposition—it helps you know that *incessantly* is the opposite of "rarely." *Incessantly* means "without stopping."

5. Items in a Series

"They were dressed in a ***quaint,*** outlandish fashion. . . ." (page 159)

The comma between *quaint* and *outlandish* lets you know they may be close in meaning. In this case they are synonyms for *strange.*

6. Coordinating Conjunction

"He was surprised to see any human being in this lonely and ***unfrequented*** place. . . ." (page 158)

The conjunction *and* gives you a clue that two words may be close in meaning. *Lonely* provides a clue to the meaning of *unfrequented.*

7. Cause and Effect

". . . Rip felt ***famished*** for want of his breakfast." (page 160)

"For want of" indicates that being *famished* is a result of not having eaten breakfast. *Famished* means "extremely hungry."

Try It Out

A word map like the one below can help you use context clues to figure out words or phrases you may not know. It can also help you to make further associations to the new word that will enable you to "own" the word—to make it an active part of your vocabulary.

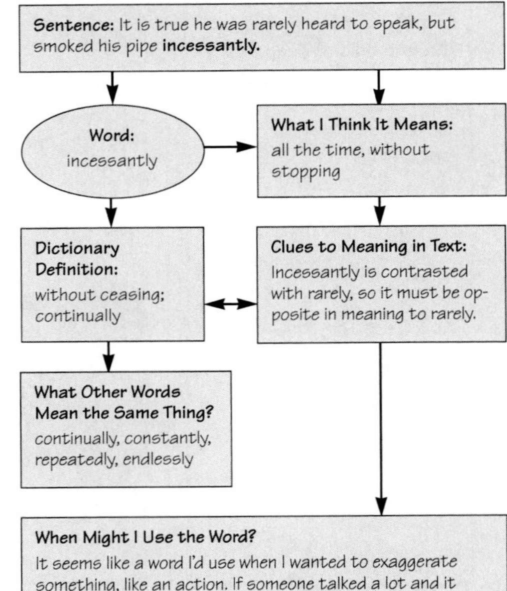

OPTIONS FOR TEACHING

STRATEGIES FOR INCLUSION

Auditory Let students choose a working partner. Have one student read aloud a sentence from "Rip Van Winkle" or another selection that contains an unfamiliar word and a context clue. The other student can then determine the meaning of the unfamiliar word and explain how he or she arrived at its meaning. Students can alternate reading the sentences and giving the answers.

Spatial On strips of heavy paper, write out examples of sentences that employ the various context clues described in How to Own a Word. Next, write out the names of the context clues on separate strips of heavy paper, and, on the back, color-code the two sets of strips with felt-tip markers. Let students practice matching the example sentences with the types of context clues. Students can check their accuracy by checking the color coding on the back of each example and clue to see if they match.

Visual Prepare a handout with a set of sentences that contain the context clues described in How to Own a Word. Ask students to draw a line under the unfamiliar word and to draw a circle or rectangle around the context clue that the sentence contains. Then, ask them to write a simple definition based on the context clue for the unfamiliar word. Have a volunteer check dictionary definitions for any word that remains unclear.

William Cullen Bryant

(1794–1878)

Poetry is a lonely occupation, but not a solitary one. Poets of any consequence rarely write in isolation from the influence of their predecessors or from the influence of other poets of their own time. When William Cullen Bryant was still an adolescent, he read a book of poems that would change his life: *Lyrical Ballads,* published in 1798 by his great English contemporaries William Wordsworth and Samuel Taylor Coleridge. This volume of poetry and theory focused the expression and much of the philosophy of the Romantic era. The book was a powerful source of inspiration for poets who wanted to replace conventional poetic diction with the common speech of their own time. Bryant was one of these poets—the first mature American Romantic, the country boy who translated the messages of English Romanticism into his native tongue.

William Cullen Bryant (1833) by James Frothingham (1786–1864). American. Oil on canvas (21″ × 17½″).

Courtesy Museum of Fine Arts, Boston. Gift of Maxim Karolik for the M. & M. Karolik Collection of American Paintings, 1815–1865 (62.271).

Two other important factors supported the influence of English Romanticism on Bryant's poetry. One factor was Bryant's own growing attraction to the philosophy of deism (page 16), which held that divinity could be found in nature. The other factor was the geography of his surroundings, which placed Bryant in immediate contact with everything that supported this philosophy.

By the time of Bryant's birth, western Massachusetts was no longer a Colonial frontier, but a widely settled countryside. Over the next hundred years and more, its farms, steepled towns, and mountain forests would be the homes of many poets. These writers would find in their surroundings metaphors to express their sense of correspondence between human life and the life of nature. After Bryant, the same New England seasons would turn for Herman Melville and Emily Dickinson, and later for Robert Frost and Richard Wilbur. All these poets were intimate with the shadows and whispers of the Berkshires and the adjacent Green Mountains. All would make their own small plot of ground part of the permanent landscape of American poetry.

Bryant was born in Cummington, Massachusetts. His father was a physician, and his mother came from a family of clergy. Bryant's literary gifts were evident from an early age: By the age of nine he was already writing poetry and had earned a reputation as a prodigy.

Bryant was tutored for a career as a lawyer, but with the publication of "Thanatopsis" his literary future was assured. In his late twenties he moved to New York City and for many years played the triple role of editor, critic, and poet.

Bryant became not only a famous literary figure, but also an influential voice in religion and politics. An outspoken liberal, Bryant supported social reform, free speech, and the growing movement for the abolition of slavery. He was also one of the founders of the Republican Party, which, in his lifetime, would produce one of America's great presidents, Abraham Lincoln. When Bryant died at the age of eighty-three, he was a millionaire and so widely honored at home and abroad that he had become a kind of national monument, the widely acknowledged "father of American poetry."

Today Bryant's poems are not read as the spiritual counsels they were meant to be; instead, they are read as period pieces that authentically reflect their time. Yet even when Bryant's poems seem more like moral fables than free expressions of the imagination, they ring with an air of piety and sincerity no one can doubt.

ABOUT THE AUTHOR

Although Bryant is today best known as a poet, he spent nearly fifty years as editor in chief and part owner of the New York *Evening Post.* In this capacity he had enormous influence as a liberal Democrat in support of Andrew Jackson. So strong were his pro-Jackson beliefs that he once horsewhipped, on Broadway in New York City, the editor of another publication for his insulting remarks about Jackson. Bryant left the Democratic Party temporarily over the issue of slavery, to which he was ardently opposed.

QUICK PLANNING GUIDE

Into the Poem

Through the Poem

Beyond the Poem

Munson-Williams-Proctor Institute Museum of Art, Utica, New York.

Fawn's Leap, Catskill, New York (detail) (1868) by John W. Hill (1812–1879). Oil on canvas (30″ × 38″).

Before You Read

Thanatopsis

Reading Focus

The Endless Cycle

Romantic poets looked to nature for lessons—lessons that we too can see all around us. One of the ever-present lessons of nature is the organic cycle of birth, growth, death, and rebirth. What are some of the ways that nature reminds us of this endless cycle of life, death, and rebirth? Do you find this aspect of nature disturbing or comforting? Explain.

A Dialogue with the Text

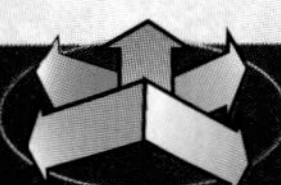

As you read the poem, you may wish to keep a double-entry journal. In one column, record any passage from the poem that particularly interests you. (It may remind you of something in your own experience, or strike you as especially interesting, or it may be something you disagree with or don't quite understand.) In the other column, jot down your response to the passage. Pay special attention to Nature's "lesson" starting with line 17 and ending with line 72.

Background

Bryant composed the first version of this poem when he was only sixteen, during solitary rambles in the woods. In the poem, he draws moral lessons from nature, which was typical of the popular poetry of his time. *Thanatopsis* is a word Bryant coined by joining two Greek words, *thanatos* (death) and *opsis* (seeing). The word is defined by the poem: a way of looking at death and a way of thinking about it.

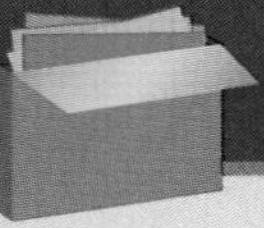

PORTFOLIO ASSESSMENT

Portfolio Assessment

For help with self- and teacher assessment of reading skills, see the *Portfolio Management System,* pp. 48–49.

PROGRAM MANAGER

- **Planning Instruction** See Teaching Notes, *Teaching Resources A,* p. 61, for objectives and literary elements for this selection.
- **Instructional Support** Before beginning the instructional lesson, see Graphic Organizer for Active Reading, *Teaching Resources A,* p. 70, for an Into the Poem activity.
- **Assessment** See Selection Test, *Test Booklet,* p. 43.
- **Reinforcement** Use the Words to Own worksheet in *Teaching Resources A,* pp. 75–76.

Thanatopsis A

William Cullen Bryant

To him who in the love of Nature holds
Communion with her visible forms, she speaks
A various language; for his gayer hours
She has a voice of gladness, and a smile
And eloquence of beauty, and she glides
Into his darker musings, with a mild
And healing sympathy, that steals away
Their sharpness, ere° he is aware. When thoughts
Of the last bitter hour come like a blight
Over thy spirit, and sad images
Of the stern agony, and shroud, and pall,°
And breathless darkness, and the narrow house,°
Make thee to shudder, and grow sick at heart;—
Go forth, under the open sky, and list°
To Nature's teachings, while from all around—
Earth and her waters, and the depths of air—
Comes a still voice.—
Yet° a few days, and thee
The all-beholding sun shall see no more
In all his course; nor yet in the cold ground,
Where thy pale form was laid, with many tears,
Nor in the embrace of ocean, shall exist
Thy image. Earth, that nourished thee, shall claim
Thy growth, to be resolved to earth again,
And, lost each human trace, surrendering up
Thine individual being, shalt thou go
To mix forever with the elements,
To be a brother to the insensible rock
And to the sluggish clod, which the rude swain°
Turns with his share,° and treads upon. The oak
Shall send his roots abroad, and pierce thy mold.

Yet not to thine eternal resting place
Shalt thou retire alone, nor couldst thou wish
Couch more magnificent. Thou shalt lie down
With patriarchs of the infant world—with kings,
The powerful of the earth—the wise, the good,
Fair forms, and hoary seers° of ages past,
All in one mighty sepulcher.° The hills
Rock-ribbed and ancient as the sun,—the vales
Stretching in pensive quietness between;
The venerable woods—rivers that move
In majesty, and the complaining brooks
That make the meadows green; and, poured round all,
Old Ocean's gray and melancholy waste,—

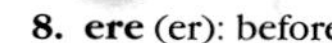
8. ere (er): before.

11. pall (pôl): coffin cover.
12. narrow house: grave.

14. list: listen.

17. Yet . . . : Here, the voice of Nature begins to speak.

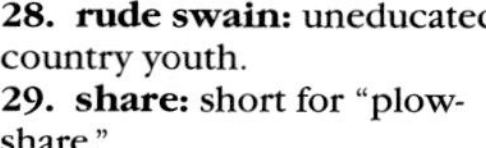
28. rude swain: uneducated country youth.
29. share: short for "plowshare."

36. hoary seers: white-haired prophets.
37. sepulcher (sep′əl·kər): burial place.

Using **BEFORE YOU READ** p. 170

Reading Focus

To help students visualize the cycles, ask them to complete the following chart. If possible, play Vivaldi's *The Four Seasons* while students complete the chart.

Season	Events in Nature	Events in Life
Spring	[Budding flowers]	[Birth]
Summer		
Autumn		
Winter		

A. Critical Reading: Speculating
? What if Bryant had titled his poem "Looking at Death"? What would readers gain? What would they lose? [Possible answers: The English title would make the subject of the poem clear to everyone. However, the Greek title lends a sense of learnedness and seriousness of purpose that the English title does not convey.]

OPTIONS FOR TEACHING

STRATEGIES FOR INCLUSION

Kinesthetic To help students identify imagery, have them construct poster-board pies. Ask student pairs to cut a circle with a twelve-inch diameter from poster board and to divide the circle into eight pie slices of equal size. On each slice write a phrase from the poem that contains an image. Half the images should deal with death as sleep, and half with death as a return to the chain of nature. Have students write "Sleep" on four spring-loaded clothespins and "Nature" on four others. Ask students to trade circles with another pair, and have them identify the type of imagery on each slice by pinning the appropriate clothespin to the circle. Students can color-code the backs of the slices and the clothespins.

Special Needs To help students relate to the poem, have small groups share passages from Reader's Logs to create a visual presentation for three passages. Students could draw, make collages, or shoot videos. Each group should present its work to the class, explaining how it fits the poem. As the poem is read aloud to the class, visuals should be presented in the order that passages appear in the poem, thus helping with comprehension and sequence.

A. Critical Reading: Making Inferences

? Why does the speaker single out this possibility to consider? [Many people fear dying alone and being forgotten when they are dead.]

B. Reader's Response: First Thoughts

? Is it consoling to think that everyone must die? [Sample responses: Yes, because it makes you realize you can't avoid death, so you may as well learn to accept it; or no, because people do not like to die.]

C. Humanities Connection

Some have approached death with stoical, noble acceptance, which derives from the behavior of Socrates in the face of death in Plato's dialogue *Phaedo,* and from the urgings of Marcus Aurelius's *The Meditations of Marcus Aurelius.* Others reject an attitude of resignation, as in Dylan Thomas's "Do Not Go Gentle into That Good Night."

D. Reader's Response: Challenging the Text

When "Thanatopsis" was first published in *The North American Review* in 1817, it did not contain the first seventeen lines or the last fifteen lines in the present version of the poem. These were added for Bryant's book *Poems,* published in 1821. Would the poem be better without the last fifteen and one-half lines? Explain your answer. [Sample responses: Yes, because these lines merely repeat the ideas already expressed. Or no, because these lines emphasize the optimism of the ending.]

Are but the solemn decorations all
Of the great tomb of man. The golden sun,
The planets, all the infinite host of heaven,
Are shining on the sad abodes of death,
Through the still lapse of ages. All that tread
The globe are but a handful to the tribes
That slumber in its bosom.—Take the wings
Of morning,° pierce the Barcan wilderness,°
Or lose thyself in the continuous woods
Where rolls the Oregon,° and hears no sound,
Save his own dashings—yet the dead are there:
And millions in those solitudes, since first
The flight of years began, have laid them down
In their last sleep—the dead reign there alone.
So shalt thou rest, and what if thou withdraw
In silence from the living, and no friend
Take note of thy departure? All that breathe
Will share thy destiny. The gay will laugh
When thou art gone, the solemn brood of care
Plod on, and each one as before will chase
His favorite phantom; yet all these shall leave
Their mirth and their employments, and shall come
And make their bed with thee. As the long train
Of ages glides away, the sons of men,
The youth in life's fresh spring, and he who goes
In the full strength of years, matron and maid,
The speechless babe, and the gray-headed man—
Shall one by one be gathered to thy side,
By those, who in their turn shall follow them.

So° live, that when thy summons comes to join
The innumerable caravan, which moves
To that mysterious realm, where each shall take
His chamber in the silent halls of death,
Thou go not, like the quarry slave at night,
Scourged to his dungeon, but, sustained and soothed
By an unfaltering trust, approach thy grave,
Like one who wraps the drapery of his couch
About him, and lies down to pleasant dreams.

51. Take . . . morning: allusion to Psalm 139:9: "If I take the wings of the morning . . ." **Barcan wilderness:** desert near Barca (now al-Marj), Libya, in North Africa.

53. Oregon: early name for the Columbia River, which flows between Washington and Oregon.

73. So . . . : The speaker's voice resumes here.

OPTIONS FOR TEACHING

INTEGRATING THE LANGUAGE ARTS

Strategic Reading Help students monitor their own reading process by demonstrating how you read a difficult selection. Read aloud the first few lines of the poem. Talk about the image it gives you, recall related information, relate it to prior knowledge, point out a confusing phrase or word, or show how you adjust your thinking as you read. Then, have student pairs take turns reading through the rest of the poem together. Each student should read aloud a few lines, pause, and talk to the other student, using the monitoring strategies you have demonstrated.

CROSSING THE CURRICULUM

Social Studies Ask students to research and report to the class on attitudes toward death in various cultures. Have students organize their information in the following chart:

Culture	Attitude

Art Ask students to find pictures that remind them of some of the nature scenes mentioned in the poem. Have students bring the pictures to class and explain why they chose the pictures they selected.

Connections: A Poem

Derek Walcott, who was born in 1930 on the island of St. Lucia in the Caribbean, won the 1992 Nobel Prize in literature. In "Sea Canes," Walcott, like Bryant, reflects on nature as he tries to come to his own understanding of loss and death. "Sea Canes" refers to wild canes—tall, slender, bamboo-like plants that grow near water.

Sea Canes

Derek Walcott

Half my friends are dead.
I will make you new ones, said earth.
No, give me them back, as they were, instead,
with faults and all. I cried.

Tonight I can snatch their talk
from the faint surf's drone
through the canes, but I cannot walk

on the moonlit leaves of ocean
down that white road alone,
or float with the dreaming motion

of owls leaving earth's load.
O earth, the number of friends you keep
exceeds those left to be loved.

The sea canes by the cliff flash green and silver;
they were the seraph lances of my faith,
but out of what is lost grows something
stronger

that has the rational radiance of stone,
enduring moonlight, further than despair,
strong as the wind, that through dividing canes

brings those we love before us, as they were,
with faults and all, not nobler, just there.

A. Literary Element: Personification

? What is the effect of personifying the earth? [Possible answers: The earth becomes friendly and caring. Or it makes the speaker's loss even sadder as even the earth tries to comfort him.]

B. Critical Reading: Drawing Conclusions

? What might the speaker feel? [Possible answers: The speaker wants those friends and loved ones to come back. The speaker is lonely and is having trouble coping with the loss of loved ones. The speaker can remember experiences shared with those who have died, but he or she is still depressed.]

C. Reader's Response: Shaping Interpretations

? What is it that grows stronger out of loss? [Sample responses: The memories the speaker has of those who have died; or the intensity of the love felt for those who have died.]

ASSESSMENT TOOLS

Check Test: True-False

1. According to the speaker, nature can help you to confront death. [True]
2. The still voice says we will keep our individuality after death. [False]
3. The speaker says kings and the reader shall be as one after death. [True]
4. The speaker compares the earth to a large grave. [True]
5. The speaker indicates that nothing can lessen the pain of death. [False]

CONNECTING WITH "THANATOPSIS"

Although Bryant's poem "Thanatopsis" and Walcott's "Sea Canes" are both about death, "Thanatopsis" focuses on those who are concerned about their own death, and "Sea Canes," on those who mourn the deaths of loved ones. Have students discuss what the speakers of these two poems would say to each other. Then, ask pairs of students to write the script for a radio call-in show, with the speaker of "Sea Canes" calling in for advice from the speaker of "Thanatopsis."

Making Meanings

First Thoughts

1. Responses will vary. Some may be struck by the idea of nature speaking to them.

Shaping Interpretations

2. In ll. 17–30, those who die become part of nature's rebirth. It is a comfort because it emphasizes the unity of all the living and dead.
3. From stern finality to consolation. We will not be alone in death; our resting place will be magnificent; and we will lie down with the great of past generations.
4. The speaker advises readers to live life so that they will be able to accept death. Some will find the advice useful and consoling; others will find it difficult to accept.
5. "Unfaltering trust" (l. 79), "pleasant dreams" (l. 81), lying down with the good (ll. 33–35), and the image of sleep support the interpretation of a traditional afterlife. Resolving to earth again (l. 23), "surrendering up/Thine individual being" (ll. 24–25), and "mix[ing] forever with the elements" (l. 26) support the interpretation of an afterlife where people rejoin the chain of nature.
6. Some will say it is about death because it tries to explain death as a natural part of the cycle of life; others will say it is about life because in nature, death leads to rebirth.

Connecting with the Text

7. Most will say a more mature writer because of elevated vocabulary, complicated sentence structure, and sophisticated ideas.

Challenging the Text

8. **(Synthesis)** Responses will vary. The question of how to deal with death is as important today as it was in Bryant's time.

Making Meanings

First Thoughts

1. What thoughts or feelings expressed in "Thanatopsis" strike you as especially important or puzzling or controversial? Be sure to check your Reader's Log entries.

Shaping Interpretations

2. How does this poem reveal the Romantic conviction that the universe, far from operating like a machine, is really a living organism that undergoes constant cyclical changes? How is this "organic" view of the universe comforting to the speaker?
3. In line 31, what shift in the **tone** of the poem occurs? What comfort is offered in this section of the poem?
4. At the conclusion of the speech of the "still voice" (line 72), the speaker's voice resumes for the concluding section, or summing up. In your own words, state the main thrust of his advice. Do you find his advice wise and consoling, or disturbing? Or do you have some other reaction? Explain.
5. Some readers think this poem expresses a traditional notion of an afterlife in heaven, while others find in it a very untraditional view of an afterlife in which people rejoin the great chain of Nature instead of ascending to a heavenly realm. Which **images** in the poem support each of these interpretations?
6. Is this poem about death or about life? Explain.

Connecting with the Text

7. Bryant began writing "Thanatopsis" when he was sixteen years old. Does the poem seem to you to be the work of a teenager? Why or why not?

Challenging the Text

8. Many readers today read a poem like "Thanatopsis" simply as a period piece that only has historical interest, yet Bryant's intention was that his poem be taken seriously as spiritual counsel. In what ways does Bryant's poem still speak to us today, if at all?

Language and Style

Inversions and Sentence Rhythm

Bryant manipulates language to create **rhythm** and other **sound effects.** He often uses **inversion**—a reversal of the usual English word order. For example, "Yet not to thine eternal resting place / Shalt thou retire alone" is an inversion of "Yet thou shalt not retire alone to thine eternal resting place."

1. Find three examples of inversion in the first thirty lines of "Thanatopsis."
2. Revise each example to conform to usual English word order. How do your revisions change the rhythm and affect the clarity of the lines?

Choices: Building Your Portfolio

Writer's Notebook

1. Collecting Ideas for an Observational Essay

Freewrite a brief but detailed description of something familiar in your everyday surroundings that has meaning for you: a favorite recreational area, a season of the year, or a weather condition. Keep your notes; you may find them helpful in the Writer's Workshop on page 198.

Critical Writing / Creative Writing

2. A Puritan Writes to a Romantic

How might Anne Bradstreet (page 68) or Jonathan Edwards (page 77) have reacted to Bryant's meditation on death? Write a letter from Bradstreet or Edwards to Bryant that conveys Puritan reactions to the poem.

Art

3. Picture This

You have been commissioned to provide illustrations for two poems: Bryant's "Thanatopsis" and Walcott's "Sea Canes" (page 173). Create an image for each poem that communicates each poet's individual insights.

Language and Style

Answers

1. "While from all around—/ . . . Comes a still voice" (ll. 15–17), "and thee/The all-beholding sun shall see no more" (ll. 17–18), and "shall exist/Thy image" (ll. 21–22).
2. "A still voice comes from all around"; "the all-beholding sun shall see thee no more"; "thy image shall exist." Answers will vary.

Beyond the Poem

Choices: Building Your Portfolio

1. **Writer's Notebook** Remind students to save their work. They may use it as prewriting for the Writer's Workshop on p. 198.

PORTFOLIO ASSESSMENT

Choices: Assessment Criteria For help in evaluating these Choices assignments, see the criteria in the ***Portfolio Management System,*** p. 85.

Henry Wadsworth Longfellow

(1807–1882)

National Portrait Gallery, Smithsonian Institution, Washington, D.C./Art Resource.

Henry Wadsworth Longfellow (1871) by Theodore Wust (1860–1901). Watercolor on ivory (3½″ × 2¾″).

Longfellow was and still is the most popular poet America has ever produced. With the possible exception of Robert Frost (page 558), no twentieth-century poet has ever reached "household name" status, let alone achieved the kind of recognition suggested by the word *popular*.

Longfellow's immense popularity was based largely on his appeal to an audience hungry for sermons and lessons. That audience wanted assurances that their cherished values would prevail over the new forces of history—such as industrialization—that were threatening to destroy them. In themselves, the values Longfellow endorsed were positive forces in the making of the American character. But his tendency to leave these values unexamined led to poetry that often offered easy comfort at the expense of illumination.

Born in Portland, Maine, Longfellow was never far from the rocks and splashing waves of the Atlantic Coast, or from the cultural and religious influences of the well-to-do families who lived "north of Boston." Longfellow's early interest in foreign languages and literature led him naturally to an academic career. After attending Portland Academy, he continued his education at nearby Bowdoin College (where Nathaniel Hawthorne was one of his classmates), and then pursued three additional years of study in France, Spain, Italy, and Germany. When he returned, he joined the Bowdoin faculty, married, and began to write a series of prose sketches drawn from his experiences abroad.

During a second European trip in 1835, Longfellow's young wife died of a miscarriage. When he returned to America, still dealing with a "sorrow and a grief that almost killed," the young widower became a professor of French and Spanish at Harvard; seven years later he married Frances Appleton, whom he had met in Europe after his first wife's death. He settled into eighteen years of happily married life, living in the Cambridge mansion Craigie House (a gift from his new father-in-law), fathering six children, and producing some of his most celebrated poetry, much of it based on American legends: *Evangeline* (1847) and *The Song of Hiawatha* (1855).

By 1854, Longfellow had resigned from Harvard and devoted himself to writing full time. But seven years later a second tragedy struck: His wife Frances died in a fiery accident at home, when a lighted match or hot sealing wax she was using on a letter ignited her summer dress. Longfellow tried to save her, smothering the flames with a rug, and was badly burned himself.

Longfellow now devoted himself to his work with a religious and literary zeal. By the end of his long and productive life, he had become for Americans the symbolic figure of The Poet: wise, gray-bearded, haloed with goodness, and living in a world of still-untold romance. He was given honorary degrees by Cambridge and Oxford Universities in England and was received by Queen Victoria. Two years after his death, Longfellow's marble image was unveiled in the Poets' Corner in Westminster Abbey. He was the first American to be so honored.

ABOUT THE AUTHOR

Longfellow's family roots grow deep into the soil of New England. His mother was descended from the Pilgrims who settled Plymouth Colony in Massachusetts, and his maternal grandfather was a general in the Revolutionary War. His father, whose ancestors settled in Massachusetts in 1680, was a prominent state legislator and member of the U.S. Congress.

Longfellow entered Bowdoin College as a sophomore when he was sixteen years old. In addition to Nathaniel Hawthorne, his classmates at Bowdoin included the future president Franklin Pierce. After he graduated at eighteen, Longfellow was offered the first professorship of foreign languages at Bowdoin.

QUICK PLANNING GUIDE

Into the Poem

Author Biography p. 175
Before You Read: "The Ropewalk" **p. 176,** "The Cross of Snow" **p. 178**

Through the Poem

"The Ropewalk" p. 177
"The Cross of Snow" p. 178
Making Meanings p. 179
Elements of Literature p. 180
The Sonnet

Beyond the Poem

Choices: Building Your Portfolio p. 180
- **Writer's Notebook:** Collect ideas for an observational essay
- **Critical Writing:** Compare past and present in a brief essay
- **Art:** Create contrasting posters

PORTFOLIO ASSESSMENT

Portfolio Assessment
For help with self- and teacher assessment of reading skills, see the *Portfolio Management System,* p. 53.

BEFORE YOU READ
THE ROPEWALK

Reading Focus

Sunshine and Shadow
The Romantic poets—perhaps Longfellow in particular—were keenly aware of the play of opposites in life. They knew that something beautiful might be created at the expense of great pain and suffering, and that a seemingly negative experience could lead to unexpected joy. In nineteenth-century popular literature, this idea of a balance of opposites was sometimes referred to as "sunshine and shadow." "Sunshine"—positive feelings and experiences—cannot exist without "shadow"—the inevitable negative experiences in a human life.

Quickwrite

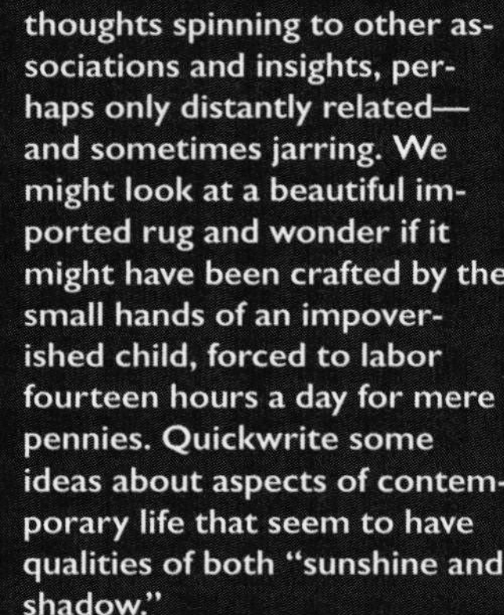

Sometimes we see something that sends our thoughts spinning to other associations and insights, perhaps only distantly related—and sometimes jarring. We might look at a beautiful imported rug and wonder if it might have been crafted by the small hands of an impoverished child, forced to labor fourteen hours a day for mere pennies. Quickwrite some ideas about aspects of contemporary life that seem to have qualities of both "sunshine and shadow."

Background

A ropewalk was a rope factory—a long, narrow building along which workers hurried, laying out strands to be spun into rope. Such rope factories were once common in New England; they would have been a familiar sight to someone who lived in the nineteenth century. Like all industries at that time, they often employed as laborers young children from poor families. In Longfellow's time thoughtful people were becoming increasingly aware of the dehumanizing effects of factory work.

Stark remnants of these factories can still be seen today in states like Connecticut and Massachusetts.

Interior of a Ropewalk (1830) by Charles Bird King (1785–1862). Oil on canvas (39" × 54¼").

Bayly Art Museum of the University of Virginia, Charlottesville, Virginia.

PROGRAM MANAGER

- **Planning Instruction** See **Teaching Notes, *Teaching Resources A,*** pp. 61–62.
- **Instructional Support** See **Graphic Organizer for Active Reading, *Teaching Resources A,*** p. 71 for a Through the Poem activity and p. 72 for an Into the Poem activity.
- **Audiotaped Readings** To help auditory learners, use the **Selected Reading, Audiocassette 1, Side A,** of "The Cross of Snow" in the ***Audiovisual Resources Binder.***
- **Assessment** See **Selection Test, *Test Booklet,*** pp. 44–45.
- **Instructional Support** To help students broaden understanding, see **Transparency** 4.1 located in the ***Audiovisual Resources Binder.***
- **Reinforcement** Use the **Words to Own** worksheet in ***Teaching Resources A,*** pp. 75–76.

The Ropewalk

Henry Wadsworth Longfellow

In that building, long and low,
With its windows all a-row,
  Like the portholes of a hulk,°
Human spiders spin and spin,
Backward down their threads so thin
  Dropping, each a hempen° bulk.

At the end, an open door;
Squares of sunshine on the floor
  Light the long and dusky lane;
And the whirring of a wheel,
Dull and drowsy, makes me feel
  All its spokes are in my brain.

As the spinners to the end
Downward go and reascend,
  Gleam the long threads in the sun;
While within this brain of mine
Cobwebs brighter and more fine A
  By the busy wheel are spun.

Two fair maidens in a swing,
Like white doves upon the wing,
  First before my vision pass;
Laughing, as their gentle hands
Closely clasp the twisted strands,
  At their shadow on the grass.

Then a booth of mountebanks,°
With its smell of tan° and planks,
  And a girl poised high in air
On a cord, in spangled dress,
With a faded loveliness,
  And a weary look of care.

Then a homestead among farms,
And a woman with bare arms
  Drawing water from a well;
As the bucket mounts apace,
With it mounts her own fair face, B
  As at some magician's spell.

Then an old man in a tower,
Ringing loud the noontide hour,
  While the rope coils round and round
Like a serpent at his feet,
And again, in swift retreat,
  Nearly lifts him from the ground.

Then within a prison yard,
Faces fixed, and stern, and hard,
  Laughter and indecent mirth;
Ah! it is the gallows tree!°
Breath of Christian charity,
  Blow, and sweep it from the earth!

Then a schoolboy, with his kite
Gleaming in a sky of light,
  And an eager, upward look;
Steeds pursued through lane and field;
Fowlers° with their snares concealed;
  And an angler° by a brook.

Ships rejoicing in the breeze,
Wrecks that float o'er unknown seas,
  Anchors dragged through faithless sand;
Sea fog drifting overhead,
And, with lessening line and lead,°
  Sailors feeling for the land.

All these scenes do I behold,
These, and many left untold,
  In that building long and low;
While the wheel goes round and round,
With a drowsy, dreamy sound,
  And the spinners backward go.

3. hulk: ship.
6. hempen: made of hemp, a fibrous plant used to make rope.
25. mountebanks (mount′ə·baŋks′): people who attracted audiences with jokes and stories, then sold them worthless goods or otherwise tricked victims out of their money.
26. tan: tannin, a chemical used in the process of turning animal hides into finished leather.
46. gallows tree: post and crossbar on which criminals were once executed by hanging.
53. fowlers: hunters of wild birds.
54. angler: one who fishes with hook and line.
59. line and lead: weighted rope tossed over the side of a boat to measure water depth.

Using **BEFORE YOU READ** p. 176

Background

To spin rope, the ropemaker put straightened hemp around his or her waist and attached a few strands to the spinning wheel. The ropemaker then walked backward, feeding fiber into the wheel. Turned by another worker, the spinning wheel twisted the fibers together. Ropewalks had to be in long buildings to give the ropemaker room to walk back far enough to make a long strand of rope.

A. Critical Reading: Making Inferences

? What is the Romantic element in these lines? [The assertion of the superiority of the poet's imagination to real life. The cobwebs are described as being finer than those in the literal scene, so they represent an improved viewpoint.]

B. Literary Element: Figure of Speech

? How does the woman's face appear to move with the bucket? [The woman's face is reflected in the water in the bucket as she looks down at it in the well. As the bucket moves upward, her reflected face moves also.]

STRATEGIES FOR INCLUSION

Special Needs To help students understand similes, ask them to read a copy of the poem and to highlight the phrases that begin with *like* or *as*. Then, have students draw an arrow to the object or creature the phrase describes, as in the example from lines 2–3:

With its windows all a-row
  Like the portholes of a hulk,

To check for understanding, have students write similes describing themselves, an object, and a feeling. Ask volunteers to put examples of their work on the chalkboard.

INTEGRATING THE LANGUAGE ARTS

Strategic Reading After they read the poem, have students write questions in their Reader's Logs that they would like to ask the speaker. Then, have them write the answers the questions might receive. Ask student pairs to share their questions and answers.

Speaking and Listening Ask a group of students to prepare a dramatic reading of "The Ropewalk." Some of the poem can be read by a narrator (perhaps a chorus), and some of the stanzas can be read by individual characters. You might let the group practice their reading using a tape recorder, so they can hear the differences in each practice reading.

Using Before You Read p. 178

Quickwrite

If students have difficulty thinking of images from nature, lead the entire class in a discussion of the following possibilities: deep shade, a dried creek bed, a barren field, and a dark cloud. Let students choose one of these, or an image they think of themselves, as a basis for their freewriting activity.

A. Reader's Response: First Thoughts

? What image is suggested by the halo of light around Mrs. Longfellow's head in her portrait? [Sample responses: She seems to have a spotlight on her; or it makes the reader think about a picture of a saint.]

B. Literary Element: Symbolism

? What does the cross symbolize? [Possible answer: Each person must carry his or her figurative cross through life (that is, endure hardships), just as Jesus carried his cross to his crucifixion. The cross is the grief the poet still feels for his wife's death.]

Before You Read
The Cross of Snow

Reading Focus

A Meaningful Image

Romantic poets often used aspects of nature to mirror or express emotions that might be too painful or personal to express directly. In this poem the poet has taken a dramatic sight from nature and transformed it through words into a powerful **image** that conveys several layers of intensely personal meaning.

Quickwrite

READER'S LOG

Of all human emotions, grief is one of the most difficult to express adequately. Think of an image from nature that could be used to describe a feeling of great grief. Set up your comparison like a **metaphor:** "Grief is ________." Then explore in writing some of the ways grief is like this image you have chosen.

Background

"I shall win this lady, or I shall die," Longfellow had written of Fanny Appleton, his second wife, who kept him waiting seven years before she agreed to marry him. Longfellow wrote this poem eighteen years after Fanny died in a fire. Three years later, Longfellow died without having shown it to anyone. Discovered among his papers, it was published four years later and immediately became one of his most famous poems. With a large audience waiting to read everything he wrote, why did Longfellow put this lyric aside?

Mount of the Holy Cross–Colorado (1873) by William Henry Jackson. Tinted photograph. Historical Society of Colorado.

The Cross of Snow

Henry Wadsworth Longfellow

In the long, sleepless watches of the night,
 A gentle face—the face of one long dead—
 Looks at me from the wall, where round its head
 The night lamp casts a halo of pale light.
Here in this room she died; and soul more white
 Never through martyrdom of fire was led
 To its repose; nor can in books be read
 The legend of a life more benedight.°
There is a mountain in the distant West
 That, sun-defying, in its deep ravines
 Displays a cross of snow upon its side.
Such is the cross I wear upon my breast
 These eighteen years, through all the changing scenes
 And seasons, changeless since the day she died.

8. **benedight** (ben′ə·dīt′) *adj.*: archaic for "blessed."

Options for Teaching

Strategies for Inclusion

Intrapersonal Ask students to choose a group of lines from the poem that they personally find effective and to record and paraphrase them in the following chart. Next, have students briefly describe an association they make with the lines, perhaps a connection to a loss if the lines are from the octave or an association with nature if the selected lines come from the sestet. Ask students to suggest a title for a poem they might write based on their associations. Encourage them to write a poem or to provide an illustration.

Selected lines:
Paraphrase:
Associations:
Poem title:

Integrating the Language Arts

Strategic Reading As students re-read "The Cross of Snow," have them pause to consider the main idea in the first eight lines. Ask students to write a sentence expressing the main idea and to exchange their idea informally with a neighbor. Have students suggest one-sentence summaries for the main idea in the last six lines, as well. Then, ask several volunteers to read their two summary sentences to the class. Finally, discuss differences in student perception and expression.

MAKING MEANINGS

The Ropewalk

First Thoughts

1. Which scenes or **images** from the poem remain most vivid in your mind or had the strongest effect on you? Did any images remind you of aspects of contemporary life you jotted down in your Reader's Log Quickwrite? Explain.

Shaping Interpretations

2. By the end of stanza 3, the poet has presented a series of **images** of the factory and of the spinners at work. Describe what the workers are doing. What are the "cobwebs" mentioned at the end of this stanza?
3. New England factories of the nineteenth century often were unpleasant places with working conditions that would be regarded as intolerable today. What **simile** in stanza 1 does Longfellow use to describe the factory? What is the implication of the **metaphor** comparing the factory workers to spiders?
4. Describe the changes of **tone** as the speaker imagines scene after scene. What opposing aspects of human life—"sunshine and shadow"—is the speaker holding "in balance"? How do you think he feels about the "human spiders"?

Challenging the Text

5. Do you think that this poem paints a persuasive picture of the disturbing, dehumanizing effects of factory work in the nineteenth century, or is it a sanitized, Romantic view of industrialization? Or is it, perhaps, a little of both? Explain.

The Cross of Snow

First Thoughts

1. How did you respond to the strong personal emotion expressed in the poem? Were any of Longfellow's **images** of grief similar to the **metaphor** you explored in your Reader's Log Quickwrite? Explain.

Shaping Interpretations

2. The phrase "martyrdom of fire" in line 6 might confuse readers who did not know that Longfellow's wife had died in a fire. What is Longfellow suggesting about his wife's character when he uses such a powerful word to describe her death?
3. The phrase "watches of the night" usually refers to the rounds made by a watchman as he guards a house or a neighborhood. At certain hours the watch would call "All is well." What are Longfellow's figurative "watches of the night" (line 1)?
4. Explain how the phrase "sun-defying" (line 10) suggests conditions of weather and geology that might actually produce a permanent cross of snow on the side of a mountain. How does the poet relate the idea of a "sun-defying" formation of snow to his own feelings?
5. In everyday speech a cross, in the sense of a burden, is something to *bear* or *shoulder*. But Longfellow says that his is "the cross I wear upon my breast" (line 12). Why do you think he uses that phrase instead of referring to it as a cross he bears?

Extending the Text

6. What do you think about public expressions of personal grief? (Remember that Longfellow did not show "The Cross of Snow" to anyone during his lifetime.) How does the mass media—TV, radio, magazines, newspapers—affect our views of what's private and what's not? (Think of examples from news programs, talk shows, magazines, and documentaries.)

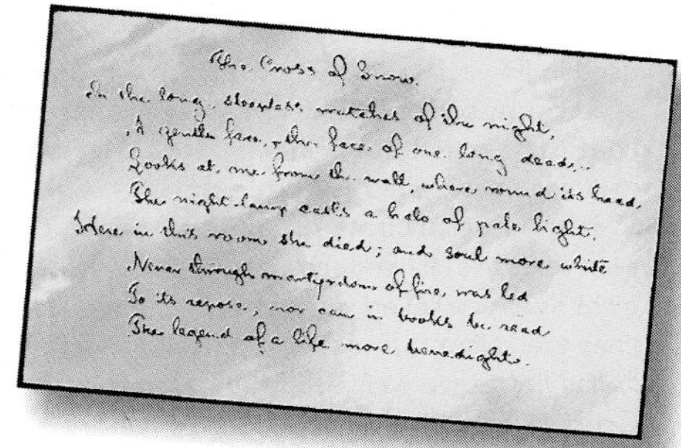

The Cross of Snow.
In the long, sleepless watches of the night,
A gentle face, the face of one long dead,
Looks at me from the wall, where round its head
The night-lamp casts a halo of pale light.
Here in this room she died; and soul more white
Never through martyrdom of fire was led
To its repose, nor can in books be read
The legend of a life more benedight.

Portion of the original manuscript of "The Cross of Snow" by Henry Wadsworth Longfellow.

Making Meanings "The Ropewalk"

First Thoughts

1. Possible responses: The image of human spiders spinning a web of rope. Work on an assembly line today may be similar to working on a ropewalk.

Shaping Interpretations

2. The spinners climb up and down as they operate the machines that spin out the lengths of rope. The "cobwebs" are the images spun in the speaker's imagination.
3. He compares the factory to a large ship, with windows in a row like portholes. The metaphor implies that the work has dehumanized these people by turning them into mere unthinking spiders.
4. The shifts in tone may be described as follows: playful and lighthearted in stanza 4; hectic and tense in stanza 5; homely and peaceful in stanza 6; dramatic and tense in stanza 7; dark and bitter in stanza 8; a sudden shift to a lighthearted tone in stanza 9; rapid shifts in tone from light to dark to hopeful in stanza 10. Stanza 10 opens with a lighthearted scene of ships "rejoicing" in the breeze, then shifts to a grim picture of aimlessly floating wrecks, and of anchors losing their grip in the sand; the stanza closes with a hopeful tone, with sailors using rope leads to determine that they are approaching land. The shifts in tone in these stanzas suggest that the human condition is varied; great joy and great misery either exist at the same time or follow each other swiftly in succession. The speaker seems to sympathize with the plight of the human spiders.

Challenging the Text

5. **(Evaluation)** Responses will vary. Many students will probably feel that the poem presents a sanitized, Romantic view of industrialization.

"The Cross of Snow"

First Thoughts

1. Possible responses: The strong emotion expressed in the poem is appropriate for the loss of a wife.

Shaping Interpretations

2. In the Christian tradition, martyrdom is usually associated with saints who die for their faith. He emphasizes his wife's purity and spirituality.
3. These are the times when, unable to sleep, the poet broods on the past and mourns his wife.
4. The literal sense is "untouched, or impenetrable, by sunlight." High altitudes and deep crags might result in a permanent cross of snow on a mountainside. The poet's grief is too deep to be melted by any ray of happiness, just as the cross of snow in the deep crags cannot be melted by the rays of the sun.
5. The poet wears his "cross"—his grief—upon his breast because it is in his heart.

Extending the Text

6. **(Evaluation)** Sample response: Sometimes it helps people deal with grief if they tell others how they feel.

Elements of Literature

Mini-Lesson: The Sonnet

In most Italian sonnets, like "The Cross of Snow," the poet states a problem, describes a conflict, or asks a question in the octave. In the sestet the poet offers a solution, a comment, or a resolution. Ask students to re-read the first eight lines of "The Cross of Snow." What problem or conflict do these lines contain? [The poet's sleepless nights and the memories he has of his dead wife.] In the sestet, what new comment does the poet make about his ordeal? [The changeless cross of snow has become a symbol of the grief he feels over his wife's death.] Students should also note that the rhyme scheme of the poem is *abba abba cde cde.*

Beyond the Poem

Choices: Building Your Portfolio

1. **Writer's Notebook** Remind students to save their work. They may use it as prewriting for the Writer's Workshop on p. 198.
2. **Critical Writing** Help students generate examples for their essays. Brainstorm with them a list of modern-day jobs that involve assembly-line production techniques or repetitious tasks.
3. **Art** Discuss nineteenth-century working conditions with the class before they begin. Point out that restrictions we now take for granted, such as the forty-hour work week, the legal minimum wage, and restrictions on child labor, did not exist in the 1800s.

PORTFOLIO ASSESSMENT

Choices: Assessment Criteria For help in evaluating these Choices assignments, see the criteria in the ***Portfolio Management System,*** p. 86.

ELEMENTS OF LITERATURE

The Sonnet

"The Cross of Snow" is a **sonnet**—a rhymed fourteen-line poem, usually written in **iambic pentameter.** "Iambic pentameter" means that each line is composed of five iambs. An **iamb** is a pair of syllables in which an unstressed syllable is followed by a stressed syllable (˘′).

The sonnet is one of the oldest and most enduring poetic forms in world literature. Two of its early masters were the Italian poet Petrarch (1304–1374) and the English playwright William Shakespeare (1564–1616). In later periods the sonnet was taken up by other writers such as John Milton, William Wordsworth, John Keats, Elizabeth Barrett Browning, Edna St. Vincent Millay, John Berryman, E. E. Cummings, and Robert Lowell.

Two principal forms of the sonnet have been used in English. In the **Elizabethan,** or **Shakespearean,** sonnet, there are three groups of four lines each, called **quatrains,** followed by two final rhyming lines, called a **couplet.**

In the **Petrarchan,** or **Italian,** sonnet, the fourteen lines are divided into two groups: The first eight lines are called the **octave,** and the last six lines are called the **sestet.** Longfellow, who knew Italian literature well, used the Italian form for "The Cross of Snow."

What is the subject stated in the octave in "The Cross of Snow"? What comment is made on the subject in the sestet? What is the **rhyme scheme**?

What Is a Sonnet?

1. A sonnet has fourteen lines arranged in a specific pattern. It uses a set rhyme scheme.
2. The rhyme scheme in a Petrarchan, or Italian, sonnet is *abba, abba, cde, cde.*
3. The rhyme scheme in a Shakespearean sonnet is *abab, cdcd, efef, gg.*
4. The first part of a sonnet usually introduces a subject. The last group of lines makes a comment on the subject. When you read a sonnet, look for the subject and the comment on the subject.

CHOICES: Building Your Portfolio

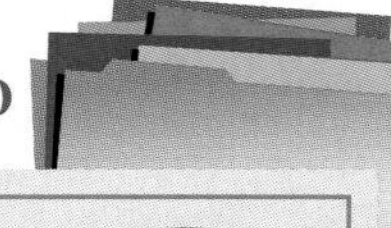

Writer's Notebook

1. Collecting Ideas for an Observational Essay

Perhaps you once celebrated a basketball game victory with classmates, only to feel a bit saddened when you saw an injured member of the defeated team being comforted by a friend. Freewrite some of your observations of "sunshine and shadow" aspects of a scene, object, process, or event. Save your notes; you may use them later in the Writer's Workshop on page 198.

Critical Writing

2. The More Things Change, the More They Stay the Same

In a brief essay, discuss how the sentiments Longfellow expresses in "The Ropewalk" might still be relevant today. Is factory work today any less dehumanizing than it was in the nineteenth century? What would a modern-day Longfellow have to say about some of today's high-tech jobs?

Art

3. What You Don't See . . .

The owners of Longfellow's rope factory want you to create a poster advertising their factory. You have a strong social conscience, though, and decide to make two posters: one that shows what the rope factory owners *want* people to see, and another that shows the reality. Draw, paint, or make a collage of your two versions of the rope factory, based on **imagery** in Longfellow's poem.

STRATEGIES FOR INCLUSION

Kinesthetic To help students understand iambic rhythm discussed in Elements of Literature, write a number of exemplary phrases on the chalkboard. [Examples: The students write, a poet thinks, the summer heat, and so on.] As students read the phrases in chorus, ask them to tap on their desks on the stressed syllables. Ask them to read a line aloud in chorus and to tap out the rhythm as they read.

John Greenleaf Whittier

(1807–1892)

John Greenleaf Whittier sent five dollars and this advice to a young man who had asked for help with his schooling: "I am sorry for the circumstance of thy condition for I have known what it is to be without money, and to live by hard labor. But, as to education, use thy leisure in educating thyself. Read and study a little every day, and before thee art twenty years of age, thee will find that a school is not needed."

Unlike the other Fireside Poets—Longfellow, Holmes, and Lowell—who were raised in privilege and enjoyed a distinguished education, Whittier was born into a poor Quaker family and had little formal schooling. Whittier started to write poetry when he was about fourteen years old, after his schoolmaster lent him a book by the popular Scottish poet Robert Burns (1759–1796), who had revived the Scottish literary heritage and written memorably of rural life.

At nineteen Whittier met the man whose influence would change the course of his life: the abolitionist William Lloyd Garrison (1805–1879). Garrison, then the editor of the local newspaper, had published a poem by the unknown young poet, and out of curiosity he journeyed out to the family farm to meet Whittier. He urged Whittier's father to give his son more schooling. "Poetry will not give him *bread,*" was the father's terse reply.

With Garrison's help, the young Whittier found work in Boston as a newspaper editor. He soon immersed himself in current affairs, working side by side with Garrison, one of the most influential leaders in the antislavery movement. Whittier believed, as Garrison did, that slavery was not only unconstitutional, but also a sin against humanity—a conviction supported by his Quaker beliefs. At twenty-five Whittier paid for the publication of his own pamphlet, *Justice and Expediency* (1833), in which he called for an immediate end to slavery. As a result of his stand against slavery, Whittier faced stone-throwing mobs, and magazines refused to print his poems.

Courtesy Trustees of the Whittier Homestead, Haverhill, Massachusetts.

John Greenleaf Whittier (1833) by Robert Peckham (1785–1877). Oil on canvas (27″ × 21½″).

In 1835, Whittier was elected to the Massachusetts state legislature. For the next quarter century, until the outbreak of the Civil War, Whittier worked tirelessly for the abolition of slavery. He contributed poems and articles to the *National Era,* which he also edited from 1847 to 1860. (It was this weekly newspaper that published Harriet Beecher Stowe's powerful antislavery novel, *Uncle Tom's Cabin,* in installments during 1851–1852.)

After the Civil War, Whittier retired to Amesbury, Massachusetts, where he wrote *Snow-Bound* (1866), a long poem of 759 lines that many critics consider his masterpiece. The poem made Whittier famous and, for the first time, financially comfortable.

Until he was well into his eighties, Whittier continued to publish poetry on homey incidents from rural life, episodes from Colonial history, and the humanitarian ideals of justice, religious faith, and tolerance. As much as his poetry, Whittier's humane convictions and moral example left a permanent mark on his era.

ABOUT THE AUTHOR

During the first part of his lifetime, Whittier devoted most of his energy to the abolition of slavery. Whittier never married, choosing instead to help support his family.

The household he writes about consists of his mother and father, a brother, two sisters, an unmarried aunt, an unmarried uncle, and the district schoolmaster who boards with the family. All of these people would have been together when the snow made it difficult for them to go outdoors.

QUICK PLANNING GUIDE

Into the Poem

Author Biography p. 181
Before You Read p. 182

- **Reading Focus: Scaffolding** Students discover people uniting in hardship.
- **Quickwrite: Prior Knowledge** Freewrite in Reader's Log about a situation that produced a sense of unity
- **Background:** Information about nineteenth-century farm life

Through the Poem

from Snow-Bound: A Winter Idyll pp. 182–185
Making Meanings p. 186
Language and Style p. 186

Beyond the Poem

Choices: Building Your Portfolio p. 186

- **Writer's Notebook:** Collect ideas for an observational essay
- **Critical Writing:** Evaluate a best-seller in an essay
- **Speaking and Listening/Critical Thinking:** Read and discuss Whittier's abolitionist poems

PORTFOLIO ASSESSMENT

Portfolio Assessment
For help with self- and teacher assessment of reading skills, see the *Portfolio Management System,* p. 53.

BEFORE YOU READ
FROM SNOW-BOUND: A WINTER IDYLL

Reading Focus

United We Stand
Sometimes hard times hold a blessing in disguise—they can draw us closer to other people. A warm bond of intimacy can develop even between total strangers who find themselves stranded, in trouble, or sharing unexpected pressures and hardships.

Quickwrite

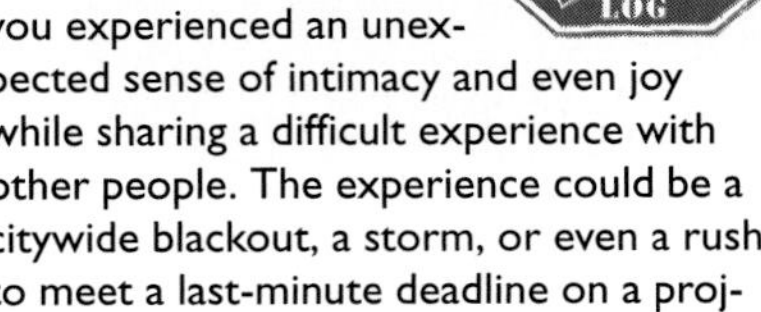

Write about a time when you experienced an unexpected sense of intimacy and even joy while sharing a difficult experience with other people. The experience could be a citywide blackout, a storm, or even a rush to meet a last-minute deadline on a project. What do you remember about the experience?

Background

An **idyll** is a nostalgic work describing a pleasant rural scene or homey setting. In *Snow-Bound* Whittier looks back fondly on the life he spent as a boy in the farmhouse in Haverhill, Massachusetts, where his family had lived since 1688. Whittier remembers what we would call "an extended family," a gathering under one roof of eight or nine related people of varying ages, along with the male boarder who taught school nearby. Imprisoned by the storm, these people had to live for days without news of the outside world. Their rooms were dimly lighted by candles or perhaps by oil lamps. Their food, stored in crocks, barrels, and briny vats, was kept in the cellar. Water came from a pump in the kitchen or a well in the yard. The bathroom as we know it today did not exist. For heat and cooking they burned wood. Life, in a word, was hard. But, like many people, Whittier found in his past a kind of benediction.

from Snow-Bound: A Winter Idyll

John Greenleaf Whittier

To the memory of the household it describes, this poem is dedicated by the author

The sun that brief December day
Rose cheerless over hills of gray,
And, darkly circled, gave at noon
A sadder light than waning moon.
Slow tracing down the thickening sky
Its mute and ominous prophecy,
A portent seeming less than threat,
It sank from sight before it set.
A chill no coat, however stout,
Of homespun stuff could quite shut out,
A hard, dull bitterness of cold,
That checked, mid-vein, the circling race
Of lifeblood in the sharpened face,
The coming of the snowstorm told.
The wind blew east; we heard the roar
Of Ocean on his wintry shore,
And felt the strong pulse throbbing there
Beat with low rhythm our inland air.

Meanwhile we did our nightly chores,—
Brought in the wood from out of doors,
Littered° the stalls, and from the mows°
Raked down the herd's-grass for the cows:
Heard the horse whinnying for his corn;
And, sharply clashing horn on horn,
Impatient down the stanchion° rows
The cattle shake their walnut bows;°
While, peering from his early perch
Upon the scaffold's pole° of birch,
The cock his crested helmet bent
And down his querulous challenge sent.

21. littered: scattered straw for beds. **mows:** haylofts where feed is stored.
25. stanchion (stan′chən): device placed around a cow's neck to keep the cow in its stall.
26. walnut bows: wooden yokes for harnessing cattle.
28. scaffold's pole: pole in the loft of a barn.

PROGRAM MANAGER

- **Planning Instruction** See Teaching Notes, *Teaching Resources A,* p. 62, for objectives and literary elements for this poem.
- **Instructional Support** Before beginning the instructional lesson, see Graphic Organizer for Active Reading, *Teaching Resources A,* p. 73, for an Into the Poem activity.
- **Assessment** See Selection Test, *Test Booklet,* p. 46.
- **Reinforcement** Use the Words to Own worksheet in *Teaching Resources A,* pp. 75–76.

The Cotters Saturday Night (detail) (c. 1815) by Eunice Pinney (1770–1849). Pen and watercolor on paper.

Board of Trustees, National Gallery of Art, Washington, D.C. Gift of Edgar William and Bernice Chrysler Garbisch.

Unwarmed by any sunset light
The gray day darkened into night,
A night made hoary° with the swarm
And whirl-dance of the blinding storm,
As zigzag, wavering to and fro,
Crossed and recrossed the wingëd snow:
And ere the early bedtime came
The white drift piled the window frame,
And through the glass the clothesline posts
Looked in like tall and sheeted ghosts.

So all night long the storm roared on:
The morning broke without a sun;
In tiny spherule° traced with lines
Of Nature's geometric signs,
In starry flake, and pellicle,°
All day the hoary meteor fell;
And, when the second morning shone,
We looked upon a world unknown,
On nothing we could call our own.
Around the glistening wonder bent
The blue walls of the firmament,
No cloud above, no earth below,—
A universe of sky and snow!
The old familiar sights of ours
Took marvelous shapes; strange domes and
towers
Rose up where sty or corncrib stood,
Or garden wall, or belt of wood;
A smooth white mound the brush pile
showed,
A fenceless drift what once was road;
The bridle post an old man sat
With loose-flung coat and high cocked hat;
The well curb° had a Chinese roof;
And even the long sweep,° high aloof,
In its slant splendor, seemed to tell
Of Pisa's leaning miracle.°

33. **hoary** (hôr′ē): white, as with age or frost.
43. **spherule** (sfer′o͞ol): sphere.
45. **pellicle** (pel′i·kəl): thin film. Whittier is describing different kinds of falling snow.

62. **well curb:** frame over a well.
63. **sweep:** long pole with a bucket attached, used for getting water from a well.
65. **Pisa's leaning miracle:** Leaning Tower of Pisa in Italy. Whittier refers to it as a miracle because it looks as if it should fall over.

OPTIONS FOR TEACHING

STRATEGIES FOR INCLUSION

Musical Ask students to find music that would be appropriate to set the mood for the various sections of the poem. You might consider having students play recordings of the music they find as the poem is read aloud in class. Have them explain their choices after the reading.

Spatial Ask students to arrange classroom furniture and imagine it as though it were the furniture in the living room of the farmhouse. If it is impractical to move classroom furniture, ask students to sketch a floor plan of the room, showing the location of the various items mentioned in the poem.

Using **BEFORE YOU READ** p. 182

Reading Focus

Students can use a simple chart like the one following to help organize their ideas.

Hardships	Ways People Support Others

A. Reader's Response: First Thoughts

? How would your expectations of this poem change if the title were "Blizzard" or "Shut In"? [Sample responses: Both of the alternative titles suggest harsh and dangerous situations, while *Snow-Bound* suggests neither harshness nor danger. Or "shut in" implies that they cannot get out.]

B. Literary Elements: Rhythm and Rhyme

Whittier uses rhymed couplets in iambic tetrameter. If students read the poem aloud, have them emphasize a more natural, conversational style. Point out that much of the difficulty they may experience in reading the poem arises from the demands of the rhyme and meter.

C. Literary Element: Imagery

Line 48 is a key line, marking a change from realistic description to magical imaginings.

D. Critical Reading: Making Inferences

? What effect does the snowfall have on the area surrounding the house? [It conceals familiar objects and converts them into strange shapes.]

A. Reader's Response: Challenging the Text

Lines 66–73 return the description to the realistic level, but after the children make the tunnel, they are once again free to indulge their fantasies, up to l. 92. How do you think the boy's narrative would have resembled or differed from this poem, written when he was an older man looking back at his childhood? [Sample responses: He may have focused on the fantastic and ignored the realistic. Or he would not have commented on the experience as he does in ll. 68–69.]

B. Critical Reading: Drawing Conclusions

? Why do the animals react the way they do? [They are hungry and glad to see the boys because now they will be fed.]

C. Literary Element: Personification

? Why does the poet describe the brook as a person? [To make the point that the family considers it a friend.]

Technology Tip

TECHNOLOGY Have your students share their response to "Snow-Bound" by discussing it via e-mail with other students who have read the poem.

(A)
A prompt, decisive man, no breath
Our father wasted: "Boys, a path!"
Well pleased, (for when did farmer boy
Count such a summons less than joy?)
Our buskins° on our feet we drew;
With mittened hands, and caps drawn low,
To guard our necks and ears from snow,
We cut the solid whiteness through.
And, where the drift was deepest, made
A tunnel walled and overlaid
With dazzling crystal: We had read
Of rare Aladdin's° wondrous cave,
And to our own his name we gave,
With many a wish the luck were ours
To test his lamp's supernal powers.
We reached the barn with merry din,
And roused the prisoned brutes within.
(B)
The old horse thrust his long head out,
And grave with wonder gazed about;
The cock his lusty greeting said,
And forth his speckled harem led;
The oxen lashed their tails, and hooked,
And mild reproach of hunger looked;
The hornëd patriarch of the sheep,
Like Egypt's Amun° roused from sleep,
Shook his sage head with gesture mute,
And emphasized with stamp of foot.

All day the gusty north wind bore
The loosening drift its breath before;
Low circling round its southern zone,
The sun through dazzling snow mist shone.
No church bell lent its Christian tone
To the savage air, no social smoke
Curled over woods of snow-hung oak.
A solitude made more intense
By dreary-voicëd elements,
The shrieking of the mindless wind,
The moaning tree boughs swaying blind,
And on the glass the unmeaning beat
Of ghostly fingertips of sleet.
Beyond the circle of our hearth
No welcome sound of toil or mirth

70. buskins (bus′kinz): calf- or knee-high leather boots.
77. Aladdin's: Aladdin is a young man in *The Arabian Nights* who finds a treasure in a cave.
90. Amun: god of ancient Egypt (also spelled Amon or Ammon). He is sometimes represented as a human with a ram's head.

Winter in the Country: A Cold Morning (1862) by George Henry Durrie (1820–1863). Oil on canvas (26″ × 36″).

Unbound the spell, and testified
Of human life and thought outside.
(C)
We minded° that the sharpest ear
The buried brooklet could not hear,
The music of whose liquid lip
Had been to us companionship,
And, in our lonely life, had grown
To have an almost human tone.

As night drew on, and, from the crest
Of wooded knolls that ridged the west,
The sun, a snow-blown traveler, sank
From sight beneath the smothering bank,

110. minded: realized.

OPTIONS FOR TEACHING

STRATEGIES FOR INCLUSION

English Language Development Using only selected details, write one or two sentences to summarize each of the poem's nine stanzas. Pair students or place them in small groups, and have them use the sentences you composed to create a scroll with nine frames. Have wooden dowels or cardboard tubes, paper, and tape ready. For the frames, have students illustrate the images created in each of the stanzas, using one page per stanza. Allow them to tape pages together in sequence, attach each end to a dowel or tube, roll it up, and present it to their classmates, describing each frame.

INTEGRATING THE LANGUAGE ARTS

Strategic Reading Some students may have trouble with the inverted phrasing Whittier uses throughout the poem. Pull out three or four sentences that are particularly difficult, and go over these with students before they begin reading the poem on their own.

Vocabulary Several words in the poem are now archaic. Ask students to find some of these words. Write a master list of them on the chalkboard as they call out the words to you. Have student pairs choose a word from the master list, consult a dictionary for the word's meaning, and create a poster to illustrate the word. Display the posters in the classroom for students to refer to when discussing the poem.

Courtesy of the Shelburne Museum, Shelburne, Vermont. Photograph by Ken Burris.

We piled, with care, our nightly stack
Of wood against the chimney back,—
The oaken log, green, huge, and thick,
And on its top the stout backstick;
The knotty forestick laid apart,
And filled between with curious art
The ragged brush; then, hovering near,
We watched the first red blaze appear,
Heard the sharp crackle, caught the gleam
On whitewashed wall and sagging beam,
Until the old, rude-furnished room
Burst, flowerlike, into rosy bloom;
While radiant with a mimic flame
Outside the sparkling drift became, D
And through the bare-boughed lilac tree
Our own warm hearth seemed blazing free.
The crane and pendent trammels° showed,
The Turks' heads° on the andirons° glowed;
While childish fancy, prompt to tell
The meaning of the miracle,
Whispered the old rhyme: *"Under the tree,*
When fire outdoors burns merrily,
There the witches are making tea."

The moon above the eastern wood
Shone at its full; the hill range stood
Transfigured in the silver flood,
Its blown snows flashing cold and keen,
Dead white, save where some sharp ravine
Took shadow, or the somber green
Of hemlocks turned to pitchy black
Against the whiteness at their back.
For such a world and such a night
Most fitting that unwarming light,
Which only seemed where'er it fell E
To make the coldness visible.

Shut in from all the world without,
We sat the clean-winged° hearth about,
Content to let the north wind roar
In baffled rage at pane and door,
While the red logs before us beat
The frost line back with tropic heat;
And ever, when a louder blast
Shook beam and rafter as it passed,
The merrier up its roaring draft
The great throat of the chimney laughed;
The house dog on his paws outspread
Laid to the fire his drowsy head,
The cat's dark silhouette on the wall
A couchant° tiger's seemed to fall;
And, for the winter fireside meet,
Between the andirons' straddling feet,
The mug of cider simmered slow,
The apples sputtered in a row,
And, close at hand, the basket stood
With nuts from brown October's wood.

136. crane . . . trammels: swinging arm (crane) attached to the fireplace, with iron hooks (trammels) from which cooking pots are hung.
137. Turks' heads: ornamental shapes resembling turbans. **andirons:** metal supports used to hold wood in a fireplace.
156. clean-winged: Turkey wings were used to brush ashes from the hearth.
168. couchant (kou′chənt): reclining.

RESPONDING TO THE ILLUSTRATION: VISUAL LITERACY

What elements of this illustration convey the mood or atmosphere of this poem? [Possible responses: The snow and the bare trees convey coldness. The buildings suggest a sense of warmth and family inside the house, for they are farm buildings and a home, and they are placed close together in the illustration. It seems peaceful and quiet, for there is little activity in the illustration.] Compare and contrast your descriptions with those of your classmates.

D. Critical Reading: Analyzing the Imagery

? How does the snowdrift outside become sparkling? [It reflects the firelight that comes through a window.]

E. Reader's Response: Shaping Interpretations

? What effect does the image of visible coldness create? [Sample responses: It intensifies the coldness by making it perceptible to more than one sense. Or it helps the reader imagine the snow.]

CROSSING THE CURRICULUM

Science Ask students to find out the meteorological principles that govern the formation of snow and to report to the class as though they were meteorologists forecasting weather on the nightly news. Some students might also find out the average snowfall in Massachusetts and in your local area, and report these facts as well.

Architecture Ask students to draw an aerial map of the farm described in the poem. They should include the location and relative size of the farmhouse, the barn, and any other buildings they imagine the farm would include. They can also include topographical features such as the brook and the woods.

ASSESSMENT TOOLS

Check Test: Fill-in-the-Blank

1. The family make their living by ______. [farming]
2. The father has his sons cut a ______ in the snow. [path]
3. The sharpest ear cannot hear the ______ outside. [brook]
4. The children have read of ______ cave. [Aladdin's]
5. At night the family ______. [sits by the fire]

Making Meanings

First Thoughts

1. Possible responses: A world completely white with a crisp, blue sky. People huddled around a fireplace telling stories.

Shaping Interpretations

2. Images include: "The sun . . . / Rose cheerless over hills of gray" (ll. 1–2); "darkly circled, gave at noon/ A sadder light" (ll. 3–4); "the roar/Of ocean on his wintry shore" (ll. 15–16); "the strong pulse" of the "inland air" (ll. 17–18).
3. Possible answers: The reference to Chinese roof (l. 62) and the allusion to the Leaning Tower of Pisa (ll. 63–65).
4. They wish they could use Aladdin's lamp to grant wishes. The other details include the rhyme mentioning witches in ll. 140–142, the chimney seeming to laugh in l. 164, and the cat's shadow appearing to be a tiger's in l. 168.

Connecting with the Text

5. Possible responses: depressed and bored, or happy and excited.

Language and Style

Answers

1. Architecture: Scaffold's pole in the barn (l. 28); Chinese roof on the well curb (l. 62); and the Leaning Tower of Pisa (l. 65).
2. Literature: Aladdin (ll. 77–80) is a character in *The Arabian Nights,* a collection of ancient folk tales.
3. History: Amun (line 90) is an Egyptian god. These allusions reveal that Whittier assumes his reader has extensive knowledge of the ancient and medieval worlds.

Possible answer: Whittier may have had a broad education that included a study of many different subjects and cultures.

MAKING MEANINGS

First Thoughts

1. What did you see as you read this part of *Snow-Bound?* Discuss your impressions with other class members.

Shaping Interpretations

2. The first eighteen lines of the poem create a **mood** of foreboding and expectation. List the **images** that help build this sense that something is about to happen.
3. The poet emphasizes the fabulous nature of the snowbound world. What specific **imagery** helps us see his farmyard as if it's an exotic sight from another world?
4. Another reference to folklore and the fabulous occurs in the lines describing the crystal cave. In line 80, what do the boys wish they could do? What other details in the poem connect the fabulous or the imaginary with the snowbound farmhouse?

Connecting with the Text

5. A few days spent locked up with family or friends would have some effect on your mood. How do you think you would feel if you were snowbound or otherwise confined with other people? Refer to your Reader's Log Quickwrite for ideas.

LANGUAGE AND STYLE

Whittier's Allusions

Snow-Bound was an enormously popular poem, and until a few decades ago, parts of it could be recited by almost every schoolchild in America. However, the poem is not necessarily "easy"; what makes it difficult for some readers are its many **allusions**—references to people and events from history, literature, the arts, or other branches of culture.

Go over the poem and find allusions to (1) architecture, (2) literature, and (3) history. What do these allusions tell you about the kind of education Whittier assumed his readers would have?

CHOICES: Building Your Portfolio

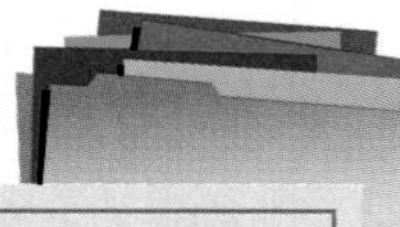

Writer's Notebook

1. Collecting Ideas for an Observational Essay

Recall an event that stands out in your memory: enjoying a good time with friends or family, waiting out a storm or flood, or discovering something that gave you great satisfaction. (The Quickwrite you wrote in your Reader's Log might provide you with an idea.) Write a brief description of the event, using a "reporter's eye" to create **images** that will help readers see the scene as you experienced it. Keep your notes; you may find them useful in the Writer's Workshop on page 198.

Critical Writing

2. The Pull of the Past

When *Snow-Bound* was published, it was an immediate best-seller, and it continued to be reprinted well into the twentieth century. By then, the kind of life it pictures had all but vanished. In one paragraph or more, explain how you would account for the continuing appeal of this poem. Include in your analysis any similar appeals to the romantic past that you find in today's movies, TV shows, books, or popular songs.

Speaking and Listening / Critical Thinking

3. End Slavery!

In his own time Whittier considered himself an abolitionist first and a poet second. Find several of Whittier's antislavery poems—"The Hunters of Men" or "The Farewell," for example—and read them aloud to the class. Then, as a class, discuss the effectiveness of these poems as antislavery messages.

Beyond the Poem

Choices: Building Your Portfolio

1. **Writer's Notebook** Remind students to save their work. They may use it as prewriting for the Writer's Workshop on p. 198.

PORTFOLIO ASSESSMENT

Choices: Assessment Criteria For help in evaluating these Choices assignments, see the criteria in the *Portfolio Management System,* p. 87.

Oliver Wendell Holmes

(1809–1894)

"Everybody wants to have a hand in a great discovery," Oliver Wendell Holmes wrote in 1846, when, for the first time, an American surgeon used gas to make a patient unconscious during surgery. Holmes, a physician himself, suggested the word *anesthesia* (without feeling), and the name stuck.

A descendant of Anne Bradstreet (page 68), Holmes was born into an already distinguished family in Cambridge, Massachusetts, and he graduated from Harvard College—just a short distance from home. Before turning to medicine, Holmes had studied law, a subject he found "cold and cheerless." He was a twenty-one-year-old law student when the United States government's plan to destroy the warship USS *Constitution* inspired him to write "Old Ironsides," a poem that aroused public sentiment to save the ship and made him famous.

In spite of this early taste of literary glory, Holmes became a physician—a profession he chose because he felt it could teach him about humanity. He was twenty-seven when he published his first book of poetry and, almost at the same time, was awarded a medical degree from Harvard. Combining poetry and medicine did not seem unusual to Dr. Holmes, who was said to hear poetic meter in the rhythm of the human heart.

One of the founders of the *Atlantic Monthly* magazine in 1857 (he also named it), Holmes gained a national reputation from a series of chatty, urbane, and sometimes irreverently witty essays that were eventually collected under the title *The Autocrat of the Breakfast Table* (1858). The leading character, recognizable to most readers as Holmes himself, presided over the lively table talk at an imaginary Boston boardinghouse.

Holmes's poetry is, for the most part, light and even comic. It comments on the social and intellectual shortcomings of his contemporaries, particularly those who aspired to higher forms of verse than he himself dared to write.

Courtesy Boston Athenaeum (UR22.1936).

Oliver Wendell Holmes (1858) by Thomas Hicks (1823–1890). Oil on canvas (53.4 cm × 43.1 cm).

But, on the evidence of his serious poems, such as "The Chambered Nautilus," Holmes had earned the right to judge, not from an envious spirit but in the confidence of an equal talent.

Today, Holmes is perhaps remembered more as a phenomenon—an aristocrat with the common touch, an artist with a passion for science—than as a poet. The famous wit that made his books best-sellers in their day has long become outdated, but the benign figure of Oliver Wendell Holmes remains. It is impossible to forget the gentleness and humor of a man who, beginning his practice as a young physician, hung out a sign saying GRATEFUL FOR SMALL FEVERS.

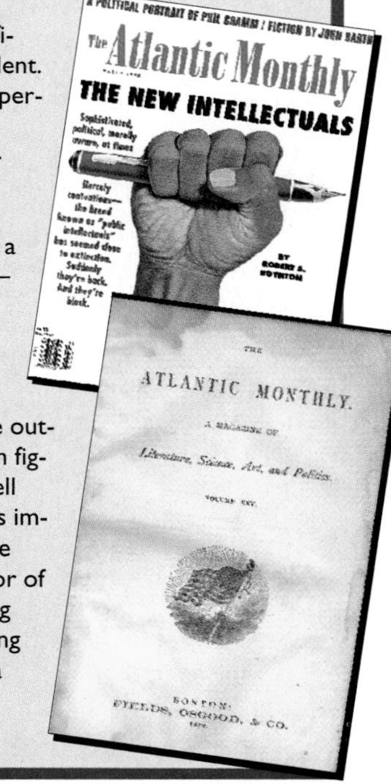

ABOUT THE AUTHOR

Holmes exercised his literary talent and considerable wit at Harvard. He wrote clever secretary's reports for the Hasty Pudding Club, adding to them poems and puns about the proceedings. In February 1830, Holmes's poems began appearing anonymously in Harvard publications. Although his poetry was well received, he maintained his anonymity. Five months later he signed with only an *H*. Despite the success of several poems and of "Old Ironsides," published in September 1830, he did not sign all three of his initials to a poem until March 1831, and he did not sign his name until 1833.

QUICK PLANNING GUIDE

Into the Poem

Author Biography p. 187

Before You Read: "The Chambered Nautilus" **p. 188** "Old Ironsides" **p. 190**

Through the Poem

"The Chambered Nautilus" p. 189

"Old Ironsides" p. 190

Student to Student p. 192

"The Sea"

Making Meanings pp. 192–193

Beyond the Poem

Choices: Building Your Portfolio p. 193

- **Writer's Notebook:** Collecting ideas for an observational essay
- **Critical Writing:** Paraphrase and evaluate poem's message in an essay
- **Crossing the Curriculum: Technical Writing:** Research and write a scientific description
- **Creative Writing/Research/Art** Write and illustrate a short story for children
- **Creative Writing:** Write a meditation

PORTFOLIO ASSESSMENT

Portfolio Assessment
For help with teacher assessment of reading skills, see the ***Portfolio Management System,*** pp. 54–55.

BEFORE YOU READ
THE CHAMBERED NAUTILUS

Reading Focus

Things Change
Throughout our lives we outgrow old things and move on to new ones: clothes, attitudes, interests, jobs, types of entertainment—even friendships. As we learn more about ourselves and the world, we're often challenged to widen our perspectives and stretch ourselves—and the process isn't always comfortable.

A Dialogue with the Text

As you read the poem, keep notes in your Reader's Log tracking your responses to the text. Include any questions you may have about the poem.

Elements of Literature

Extended Metaphor
A **metaphor** is a figure of speech that makes a comparison between one thing and another very different thing. Sometimes writers extend a metaphor—that is, they take it as far it can logically be developed. An **extended metaphor** may continue for several lines, or it may be developed throughout an entire work.

> An **extended metaphor** is a figure of speech developed throughout several lines or an entire work.
>
> *For more on Metaphor, see the Handbook of Literary Terms.*

Background

A nautilus is a sea creature that lives in a shell, one of those mollusks that grow year by year from the size of a tiny bead to the size of a pumpkin. In Holmes's own description the nautilus shell is composed of a "series of enlarging compartments successively dwelt in by the animal that inhabits the shell, which is built in a widening spiral." The word *nautilus* comes from the Greek word for "sailor," reminding us that the Greeks thought this shell could actually move on the surface of the water, using a membrane as its sail. The nautilus is not only one of the most beautiful objects in nature; it is also one of the most fragile life-containing vessels.

The first three stanzas of this poem are a meditation upon the life and death of the nautilus. In the next-to-last stanza, the poet begins an **apostrophe** (a direct address to an object or to someone who is not present). The visual description here is like the scene in Shakespeare's *Hamlet* (Act V), in which a gravedigger unearths the skull of a man Hamlet knew. Hamlet holds the skull up to the light and speaks words about life and destiny that the skull evokes for him. We might picture the speaker in "The Chambered Nautilus" holding the shell before him and speaking.

PROGRAM MANAGER

- **Planning Instruction** See **Teaching Notes, *Teaching Resources A,*** pp. 62–63, for objectives, literary elements, and additional biographical information for these poems.
- **Instructional Support** Before beginning the instructional lesson, see **Graphic Organizer for Active Reading, *Teaching Resources A,*** p. 74, for an Into the Poem activity.
- **Assessment** See **Selection Test, *Test Booklet,*** pp. 47–48.
- **Reinforcement** Use the **Words to Own** worksheet in ***Teaching Resources A,*** pp. 75–76.

The Chambered Nautilus

Oliver Wendell Holmes

This is the ship of pearl, which, poets feign,°
Sails the unshadowed main,—
The venturous bark that flings
On the sweet summer wind its purpled wings
In gulfs enchanted, where the siren° sings,
And coral reefs lie bare,
Where the cold sea maids° rise to sun their streaming hair.

Its webs of living gauze no more unfurl;
Wrecked is the ship of pearl!
And every chambered cell,
Where its dim dreaming life was wont to dwell,
As the frail tenant shaped his growing shell,
Before thee lies revealed,—
Its irised° ceiling rent,° its sunless crypt unsealed! **A**

Year after year beheld the silent toil
That spread his lustrous coil;
Still, as the spiral grew,
He left the past year's dwelling for the new,
Stole with soft step its shining archway through,
Built up its idle door,
Stretched in his last-found home, and knew the old no more.

Thanks for the heavenly message brought by thee,
Child of the wandering sea,
Cast from her lap, forlorn!
From thy dead lips a clearer note is born
Than ever Triton blew from wreathèd horn!°
While on mine ear it rings,
Through the deep caves of thought I hear a voice that sings:—

Build thee more stately mansions, O my soul,
As the swift seasons roll!
Leave thy low-vaulted past!
Let each new temple, nobler than the last,
Shut thee from heaven with a dome more vast,
Till thou at length art free,
Leaving thine outgrown shell by life's unresting sea! **B**

1. feign (fān): archaic for "imagine."

5. siren (sī′rən): in Greek mythology, one of a group of sea maidens whose seductive singing lures sailors to wreck their ships on coastal rocks.
7. sea maids: mermaids or sea nymphs.

14. irised (ī′risd): iridescent; rainbowlike. Iris is the Greek goddess of the rainbow. **rent:** torn.

26. than . . . wreathèd (rē*th*′id) **horn:** echoes a line from "The World Is Too Much with Us," a sonnet by English poet William Wordsworth (1770–1850): "Or hear old Triton blow his wreathèd horn." In Greek mythology, Triton is a sea god, often represented as blowing a trumpet made from a conch shell. *Wreathèd* means "coiled" or "spiral-shaped."

Into the Poem

Using **BEFORE YOU READ** p. 188

Background

The nautilus's chambers are connected to one another by a tube. The animal is able to force gases into the chambers through the tube, making the whole shell act as a float. When the animal wants to go into deep water, it absorbs the gases from the chambers, and when it wants to rise to the surface, it fills the chambers with gases to help it float upward.

Through the Poem

A. Critical Reading: Making Inferences

? In the phrase "dim dreaming life," is Holmes also commenting on human life? What evidence in the poem supports your answer? [The metaphor of the nautilus as a "tenant" in l. 12 suggests that Holmes is drawing parallels between the nautilus and humanity.]

B. Literary Element: Extended Metaphor

? What two things are compared in the extended metaphor? [The human soul is compared to the nautilus, and the growth of the nautilus is compared to the growth of the soul.]

OPTIONS FOR TEACHING

STRATEGIES FOR INCLUSION

Logical-Mathematical Students can apply the golden ratio, which will relate the shape of the shell to a series of nested rectangles. Have them draw rectangle *ABDC*, form square *EBDF* inside the rectangle, form square *AEHG* inside the new rectangle, and continue the process until they have formed five nested rectangles. Have them use a compass to make quarter-circles in each square. The resulting spiral will give them the growth pattern of the nautilus.

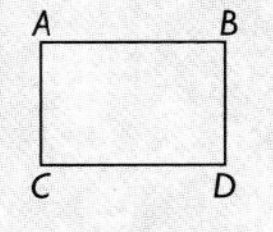

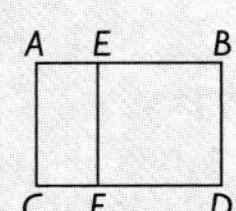

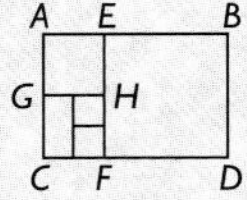

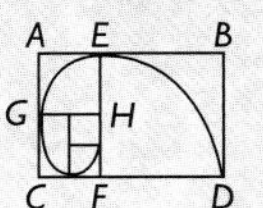

Visual Students may profit from seeing a picture of a nautilus shell, especially a cross-sectional depiction. Ask them to study the picture and to explain to the class how the chambers are related to one another and how they can tell where one chamber ends and another one begins.

Using Before You Read p. 190

Reading Focus

Ask students to think of ways in which words have had a powerful effect. Have them fill in the empty circles in a cluster diagram like the one that follows with specific examples of each item.

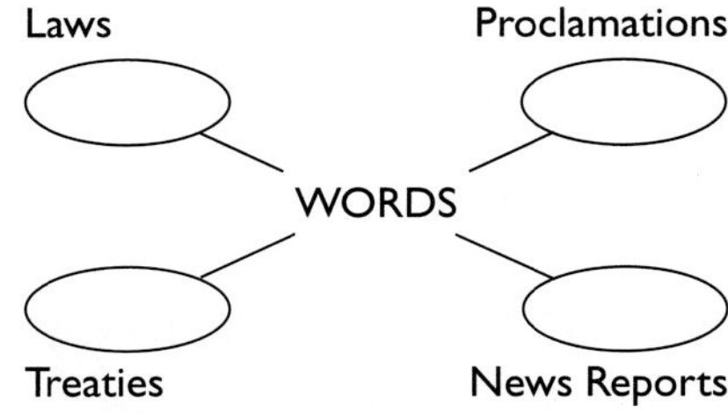

A. Literary Element: Irony

? Why is the opening line ironic? [It appears that Holmes wants the ship destroyed, but he really wants the opposite.]

Metacognition How did you decide the line is ironic? [Possible answer: The background information given with the poem tells readers the purpose. Since the first line appears to contradict this purpose, it can only be ironic.]

B. Literary Element: Metaphor

? How does the ship resemble a meteor? [It strikes quickly.] How realistic do you think this metaphor is? [Answers will vary, but most students will probably find it unrealistic. You can remind them that a sailing ship was probably the fastest means of transportation in 1830.]

C. Reader's Response: Shaping Interpretations

? What qualities of the eagle make it a fitting metaphor? [Sample responses: The eagle is the bird that rules the skies because of its swiftness, strength, and ability to strike targets. The eagle is also symbolic of the United States, under whose flag the ship sailed.]

Before You Read
Old Ironsides

Reading Focus

Word Power

As the old saying tells us, "The pen is mightier than the sword." Words can be powerful tools for resolving conflicts, righting wrongs, or otherwise influencing human actions and emotions. Words can preserve or destroy, praise or protest. They can change the world. The words in this poem saved an American legacy: a historic ship.

Quickwrite

Think of some historical object or place in your own state, city, town, or neighborhood that is being threatened with destruction—or could be one day. Jot down as many reasons as you can think of for why this piece of history should be preserved.

Background

In 1830, the forty-four-gun American warship USS *Constitution,* which had defeated the British warship *Guerrière* in the War of 1812, was scheduled to be scrapped. Holmes sent this poem to the Boston *Daily Advertiser* in protest. The poem aroused public sentiment and saved the ship, which you can still visit in Boston Harbor today.

Old Ironsides

Oliver Wendell Holmes

(A) Ay, tear her tattered ensign° down!
Long has it waved on high,
And many an eye has danced to see
That banner in the sky;
Beneath it rung the battle shout,
And burst the cannon's roar—
(B) The meteor of the ocean air
Shall sweep the clouds no more.

Her deck, once red with heroes' blood,
Where knelt the vanquished foe,
When winds were hurrying o'er the flood,
And waves were white below,
No more shall feel the victor's tread,
Or know the conquered knee—
The harpies° of the shore shall pluck
(C) The eagle of the sea!

Oh, better that her shattered hulk
Should sink beneath the wave;
Her thunders shook the mighty deep,
And there should be her grave;
Nail to the mast her holy flag,
Set every threadbare sail,
And give her to the god of storms,
The lightning and the gale!

1. ensign (en′sīn′): a flag, especially one flown from a ship.

15. harpies (här′pēz): in Greek mythology, creatures with the head and body of a woman, and the wings, claws, legs, and tail of a bird. The harpies came to symbolize cruel, grasping people who prey on helpless victims.

Richard Pasley/Stock Boston.

Options for Teaching
Integrating the Language Arts

Strategic Reading Students may find it easier to read "Old Ironsides" if they divide the poem into sentences. Have students write the poem as though it were prose, treating the semicolons as periods and the dashes as colons. Then, have them read and paraphrase each sentence individually until they have grasped the sense of the lines.

Speaking and Listening Ask students to prepare and deliver an oral reading of "Old Ironsides" that emphasizes the verbal irony the poem contains. They can practice their readings several times using a tape recorder. While students are replaying their own voices, have them listen for appropriate pauses, voice intonation, and the slowing down of their speech to indicate key points. Then, have them present their reading to the class.

RESPONDING TO THE PHOTOGRAPH: EXPLORING THE SUBJECT

The USS *Constitution,* built between 1794 and 1797, was launched on October 21, 1797. The *Constitution* gained a reputation as an undefeatable ship after surviving battles with the Barbary powers in 1803 and 1804. During a battle against the English warship *Guerrière,* a sailor supposedly saw shot from the British guns bouncing off the *Constitution's* sides, and thus the ship came to be known as *Old Ironsides. Old Ironsides* was commissioned into active service in 1931 and returned to the Boston Naval Shipyard in 1934.

USS *Constitution* in Boston Harbor.

CROSSING THE CURRICULUM

Architecture Ask students to look up information about the design and construction of the USS *Constitution.* Have them display the designs to the class as though they were presenting their design to a client for approval. Have them use a model of the ship, if one is available.

Social Sciences Take students to a local history museum and show them what artifacts have been preserved in your community. Alternatively, invite a member of the local historic society to speak to students about buildings, ships, or vehicles that have been restored and how they are significant. Have students discuss how local artifacts and people's feelings about them relate to the poem.

CLASSROOM MANAGEMENT

Collecting Resources Several items in Making Meanings and Choices ask students to write about saving historic places or objects in your locale. It might be helpful to ask your school librarian to put together a cart of books and other media that deal with local and state places of historical interest. Students may consult these sources in the classroom as they work on the activities.

Making Meanings "The Chambered Nautilus"

First Thoughts

1. Possible responses: I saw a structure like a spiral staircase. I had trouble with the "irised ceiling rent."

Reviewing the Text

a. The nautilus is compared to a "ship of pearl" sailing on the ocean.
b. the "main" (l. 2), or open sea, "gulfs enchanted" (l. 5), and "coral reefs" (l. 6).
c. The nautilus has been "wrecked" (l. 9)—taken from the sea and split open.
d. The speaker is grateful for the nautilus' message, to grow physically, spiritually, mentally, and emotionally.

Shaping Interpretations

2. "Silent toil/That spread his lustrous coil" (ll. 15–16); "the spiral grew" (l. 17); "left the past year's dwelling for the new" (l. 18); moved through "its shining archway" (l. 19); "Built up its idle door" (l. 20).
3. The creature building its nautilus shell is a metaphor for the human soul striving toward heaven. The "stately mansions," or nautilus chambers, represent the spiritual achievements of the soul; the "low-vaulted past," or previous chamber, represents the earlier, less spiritual state of the soul; "each new temple," or chamber, represents each step of the soul toward heaven; the "outgrown shell" is a suggestion of the body discarded by the soul in death; the "unresting sea" represents life.

Extending the Text

4. **(Evaluation)** Possible responses: It has endured because it is relatively easy to read and has an important message. It will endure because of its intrinsic beauty. Or it will not endure because people are not as interested in reading poetry as they once were.

Challenging the Text

5. **(Evaluation)** Possible response: Both are optimistic. "Thanatopsis" may seem more pessimistic since its subject is death, but it focuses on death as unity with nature.

The Sea

Shells and pebbles roll in
the mist of gentle waves.
A mother cries, a daughter
mourns.
The ship went down in the
storm.
Timber is tossed by the
mountains of the violent sea,
which churns against the cliffs.
The captain's cry, the
shipmate's tears.
As the angry waves scatter
their hope like sea spray
against the wind.

—Elizabeth Enloe
Shades Valley Resource
Learning Center
Birmingham, Alabama

MAKING MEANINGS

The Chambered Nautilus

First Thoughts

1. What did you see as you read the poem? What did you have a difficult time visualizing? Look back over your Reader's Log entries, and discuss passages you had questions about.

Reviewing the Text

a. What **metaphor** describes the nautilus in line 1?
b. What **images** in the first stanza help you picture where the nautilus first sailed?
c. According to the second stanza, what has happened to the nautilus?
d. Why does the speaker thank the nautilus in the fourth stanza?

Shaping Interpretations

2. Stanza 3 describes the ways the nautilus grows. The poet uses a **metaphor** comparing the nautilus to a person who changes homes. What details describe how this happens year after year?
3. Step by step, describe the **extended metaphor.** What are the "stately mansions" (line 29), the "low-vaulted past" (line 31), "each new temple" (line 32), the "outgrown shell" (line 35), and the "unresting sea" (line 35)?

Extending the Text

4. "The Chambered Nautilus" is one of the most enduring poems in American literature. (Abraham Lincoln is said to have known it by heart.) Why do you think this poem has endured? Do you think it will still be read one hundred years from now? Be sure to give your reasons.

Challenging the Text

5. Did you find this poem more optimistic than Bryant's "Thanatopsis" (page 171)? Why or why not?

Old Ironsides

First Thoughts

1. Do you think that historical relics like *Old Ironsides* should be preserved? If, very soon, *Old Ironsides* were found to be in danger of sinking at its dock in Boston, do you think most Americans would let it go? Give reasons why or why not.

Shaping Interpretations

2. In simple terms, what message does the first stanza present? What is **ironic** about the way Holmes states his message?
3. When a ship is broken up in the dockyards, it is said to be *scrapped*—that is, stripped of everything valuable or reusable. Is Holmes comparing

192 AMERICAN ROMANTICISM

"Old Ironsides"

First Thoughts

1. Possible responses: Yes, it is important for us to remember what people did for the country in the past. Most would want to keep it as it is a symbol of victory.

Shaping Interpretations

2. *Old Ironsides* has too noble a history, and too much patriotic meaning, to be scrapped. Holmes emphasizes the irony of the first two lines by evoking the ship's former glory.
3. Holmes is suggesting that those who are responsible for arranging that the ship be scrapped, and who will profit from it, are the vulturelike harpies.
4. Answers will vary. Students may suggest that the ship symbolizes the nation's heroic past, threatened by progress and modern ways.
5. It appealed to the emotions, especially patriotism, of its readers. Words and phrases like "heroes' blood" (l. 9) and "vanquished foe" (l. 10) appeal to Americans' patriotism.

the directors of the scrapping business to harpies in stanza 2, or is his scorn directed at someone else? Explain.

4. What do you think the poet wants the ship to **symbolize**?
5. Why do you think this poem was successful in getting the public to save the ship? Point out specific words and phrases that you found particularly persuasive.

Extending the Text

6. Think about specific issues in today's world that have inspired public movements for preservation. Do you think a poem like "Old Ironsides" would be able to sway public opinion today? Why or why not?

Extending the Text

6. **(Evaluation)** Possible response: Poems may not be able to sway public opinion today, for the public may not believe poetry is as important as it thought it was in the eighteenth century. However, a song could probably sway public opinion today.

CHOICES: Building Your Portfolio

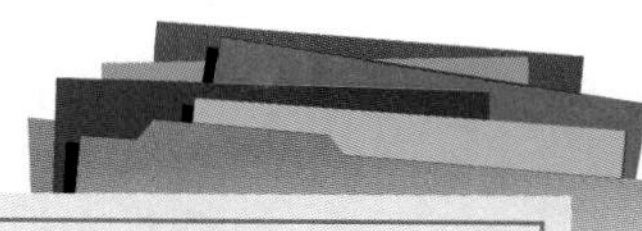

Writer's Notebook

1. Collecting Ideas for an Observational Essay

Think of something you value that is facing destruction or is in danger of fading from existence. Freewrite a description of this place, thing, or aspect of life. (You might further develop the Quickwrite you did before you read "Old Ironsides.") Provide specific details about what you think your subject represents and what beauty or meaning will be lost forever if it vanishes. Save your notes for the Writer's Workshop on page 198.

WORK IN PROGRESS

Critical Writing

2. A Heavenly Message

In a brief essay, discuss the message of Holmes's poem "The Chambered Nautilus." First, discuss in what part of the poem the "heavenly message" of the shell is revealed. Then **paraphrase** this message—that is, state in your own words what the "voice that sings" says to the speaker. Finally, discuss whether you feel the poet has been successful in developing and leading up to the poem's message. Does the message seem tacked on to give the poem a moral, or is it a natural outgrowth of the poem? How can you relate the message of the poem to your own life?

Crossing the Curriculum: Technical Writing

3. A Scientific Stance

How would Holmes the scientist have described the chambered nautilus? Gather scientific data about the nautilus from other sources, and write an objective, accurate, scientific description of the creature. Include specific data on its vital statistics. What questions might a scientist ask of the nautilus? Present your findings in class. Include a scientific illustration, if you wish.

Creative Writing / Research / Art

4. The Story of a Ship

Research the history of the USS *Constitution,* from its days as a warship to its current use as a tourist attraction in Boston Harbor. Write a short story for children in which you describe the ship and tell its life story. Provide your own colorful illustrations, and give your story a title.

Creative Writing

5. A Meditation

We might imagine that Holmes was inspired to write "The Chambered Nautilus" while he was looking at the beautiful nautilus shell. The student poem on page 192 might have been written while the writer was looking at or thinking about the sea. Write a meditation of your own, imitating one of these poems. Focus on some object or scene that brings memories, lessons, events, or stories to mind. Open with a line that tells what you are looking at.

Choices: Building Your Portfolio

2. **Critical Writing** Students might benefit from small-group discussion of this assignment before they begin working on it on their own. Ask students to spend five minutes on each of the three directives about the message of the poem. Remind them that they should take notes on the ideas of others in their groups, so they can incorporate these into their own essays.
3. **Crossing the Curriculum: Technical Writing** If students have difficulty getting started, prompt them with some of the following questions:
   - What shape does it have?
   - What other organisms does it resemble? In what ways? How does it differ from them?
   - Where does it live?
   - How does it grow?
   - What can you gather about its way of life from examining it?

Choices: Assessment Criteria For help in evaluating these Choices assignments, see the criteria in the ***Portfolio Management System,*** pp. 88–89.

OPTIONS FOR TEACHING

STRATEGIES FOR INCLUSION

Kinesthetic Students might find it helpful in completing activity #2 above to have the assignment written out on separate index cards that correspond with the parts of the assignment. Students may also write their ideas for each part of the assignment on index cards, so they can spread them out and see the relationship of ideas to one another.

Learners Having Difficulty Have students work in pairs to collaborate on activity #3. Ask one student to read aloud half of the information they have found, while the other takes notes. Then, have them switch roles. The note taker should stop the reader whenever necessary to establish the important points.

Read On

Portfolio Assessment Options

The following projects can help you evaluate and assess your students' reading accomplishments outside class. Videotapes or audiotapes of completed projects may be included in students' portfolios.

- **Draw a Storyboard** Have students draw a Storyboard leading to and including the climax of a book or a folk tale. Students should illustrate in any medium at least five frames in their Storyboards. Have students explain their choices of medium and the ways in which they represented the scenes. Display their artwork.
- **Research a Related Topic** Have students each research an interesting topic related to one of the books mentioned. For Phelps's book, students could find additional folk tales of a particular country. Students could research life in nineteenth-century New York City to verify the accuracy of Finney's book. For Davis's book, students could research factory life in American cities during the nineteenth century. Ask students to present their findings to the class and to show maps, illustrations, or photographs of their subjects.
- **Create a Pantomime** Have students work in groups to create a pantomime for a series of related scenes from a novel or story. Have one student work as a director to guide students through their acting as they practice, introduce the scenes to the class, and afterward explain the decisions students made in producing the pantomime.

Women of Wonder

If "Rip Van Winkle" whetted your appetite for folk tales, consider *The Maid of the North* (Holt, Rinehart and Winston) by Ethel Johnston Phelps. The author collects and retells a variety of traditional folk tales with one thing in common—the heroes are all enterprising females! The twenty-one tales come from many parts of the world, including Africa, Japan, Scandinavia, and North America.

Past, Present, and Future

"If Albert Einstein is right once again . . . then hard as it may be to comprehend, the summer of 1894 *still exists*." Modern-day magazine photographer Si Morley proves Einstein's theory when he travels back to nineteenth-century New York City in Jack Finney's best-selling science fiction classic *Time and Again* (Simon and Schuster). Further time-travel adventures appear in Finney's recent sequel, *From Time to Time* (Simon and Schuster).

In That Building, Long and Low

What was life like for an American factory worker in the early nineteenth century? Rebecca Harding Davis paints a grim but vivid picture in *Life in the Iron Mills* (The Feminist Press). Originally serialized in *Atlantic Monthly* in 1861, Davis's highly readable but long-forgotten classic was recently discovered by author Tillie Olsen, who writes the introduction.

By the Seashore

"One never knows what chance treasures these easy unconscious rollers may toss up, on the smooth white sand of the conscious mind; what perfectly rounded stone, what rare shell from the ocean floor." In her acclaimed book *Gift from the Sea* (Random House), Anne Morrow Lindbergh describes a seaside vacation in which the shells she discovers on the beach prompt valuable inner discoveries about life.

The Rockets' Red Glare

If you liked Oliver Wendell Holmes's "Old Ironsides," then answers to questions like these might really interest you: Why was the Battle of New Orleans fought after the War of 1812 was officially over? Which battle scenes inspired "The Star-Spangled Banner"? Popular historian Walter Lord answers these and other questions in *The Dawn's Early Light* (W. W. Norton), a lively account of the conflict known in its day as the Second War of Independence.

FOR FURTHER EXPLORATION

Short Story
"The Legend of Sleepy Hollow" by Washington Irving

Poetry
"To a Waterfowl" by William Cullen Bryant
"Inscription for the Entrance to a Wood" by William Cullen Bryant
"Annabel Lee" by Edgar Allan Poe

Nonfiction
Yankee from Olympus by Catherine Bowen
The Lives of a Cell: Notes of a Biology Watcher by Lewis Thomas

Movies
Somewhere in Time
Ladyhawke
Far and Away

The American Language

"Noah's Ark": Webster's Dictionary *by Gary Q. Arpin*

By the nineteenth century, many Americans felt the need for some kind of authority to govern matters of usage. In England, the ultimate linguistic authority was royal—the King's English. In America, matters were very different.

In a relatively stable social structure, people of a particular class will speak the way their friends and associates speak, and matters of right and wrong speech patterns won't even be raised. In societies where social structure is fluid, though—as it was and still is in America—the matter becomes more complex.

In eighteenth-century England, for instance, the rigid social structure began to give as the middle class grew. People of humble origins had started to become successful in business. These newly well-to-do sent their children to recently founded schools that, among other things, taught the language habits of the aristocracy the middle class wanted to imitate. Written grammars dictating English usage became popular, and schoolmasters began to take over authority in matters of English language usage. (A) *A New Guide to the English Tongue* (1740) by Thomas Dilworth was a popular grammar book in England.

In America the teaching of English arose for similar reasons. Before the Revolution it would have been difficult to find an "English School" in the Colonies—that is, a school that taught English grammar rather than Latin grammar. After the Revolution, though, regular instruction in English grammar became common in the public schools. However, the only available textbooks came from England. This was clearly an awkward situation for a new nation that wanted to establish linguistic independence and justify its use of language to carping British critics.

An American Spelling Book

Enter Noah Webster (1758–1843), a schoolmaster from Connecticut. Webster was looking for a way to finance his legal education, and he was also passionately dedicated to the cause of American English. (B) To help advance these two causes, Webster published a spelling book in 1783, when he was twenty-five. Even though it was based in important respects on English models—Dilworth's grammar and Samuel Johnson's great *Dictionary of the English Language* (1755)—the spelling book turned out to be a major force in the drive for American linguistic independence. Over the generations, *The American Spelling Book* (also known as the "Blue-Backed Speller") was issued in numerous editions, and more than sixty million copies were sold.

Webster prepared his speller and his later textbooks for a purpose:

> . . . to reform the abuses and corruption which . . . tincture the conversation of the polite part of Americans . . . and especially to render the pronunciation . . . accurate and uniform by demolishing those obvious distinctions of provincial dialects.

Webster reasoned that accurate and uniform American spelling would lead to uniform American speech, and that uniformity in speech would "reconcile the people of America to each other." (C)

Consistency in Spelling

The whole idea of consistency in spelling was fairly new in Webster's time and was directly related to the increasing use of the printing press. (D) Until the 1700s, people followed rather

A. Expansion
The existence of written grammars of a language, along with dictionaries and a body of literary works, is a major indicator that a language has a standard form. English achieved this status by the 1770s in England and by the mid-1800s in the United States. French had all three indicators by the end of the 1600s.

B. Expansion
Noah Webster (1758–1843) had an extremely varied and busy career. He fought beside his father in the Revolution, owned and edited a daily newspaper in New York City, wrote influential pamphlets in favor of ratification of the Constitution (and on subjects from banking to epidemiology), worked for the enactment of copyright laws, wrote and published a revised version of the Bible, served in the General Assembly of Connecticut and the General Court of Massachusetts—among other activities.

C. Critical Reading: Finding Cause and Effect
? What attitude might have caused Webster to be dedicated to the cause of American English? [Possible answer: Webster may have wanted cultural, as well as political, independence from England, and a distinctive language was one way to achieve this.]

D. Expansion
While the idea of consistency was fairly new, Webster was not the first person to try to reform English spelling. As early as 1568, entrepreneur Sir Thomas Smythe called for consistency in spelling. In 1768, Benjamin Franklin made up a new alphabet, eliminating some letters and adding others, in an attempt to bring about consistent spelling. His attempt did not succeed.

PROGRAM MANAGER

- **Planning Instruction** See Teaching Notes, *Teaching Resources A,* p. 63, for objectives for this feature.
- **Assessment** See The American Language, *Test Booklet,* pp. 49–50.

A. Critical Reading: Expressing an Opinion

? Given the pronunciations of words like *music* and *public*, did Webster really improve the spelling of those words by eliminating the *k*? [Possible answer: No. The last sound of both words is /k/. The letter *c* is sometimes pronounced /k/ and sometimes /s/ (as in *certain*), but *c* seems not to have a sound of its own. Webster probably would have improved spelling more by spelling the words *musik* and *publik*.]

B. Cultural Connections

Some people believe *women* should be spelled *womyn* to eliminate the dependence on men that they believe the traditional spelling implies. Should language, especially spelling, be as political as this controversy suggests it is? [Responses will vary. Some students may be unaware of the political controversy surrounding certain aspects of language and may find the issue trivial. This may be a good opportunity to discuss the role of language in shaping attitudes.]

C. Expansion

Webster seems to reflect a descriptivist attitude toward language in this quotation, which means that he feels he should describe the language as he sees it rather than make value judgments about its worth. When he tells people how words should be spelled, Webster reflects prescriptivist attitudes, which means that he feels correct language usage should be prescribed by some authority. Since the middle of the twentieth century, most linguists have regarded the two approaches as complementary.

flexible rules of spelling. In fact, some letters of the alphabet were not completely fixed: *i, j, y, u, v,* and *w* were not yet distinct letters. Sometimes a word would be written with an e at the end and sometimes not. Thus, *join* might be written *ioyn* or *joyne* or *ioyne*. The word *the* was frequently written *ye*, the *y* in this case being a form of an obsolete Middle English letter that stood for the sound *th*.

Early editions of Webster's American speller were quite conservative—that is, most of the spellings were consistent with Samuel Johnson's English spellings. A The main exception was Webster's omission of *k* in words ending in *–ck*. Where Dr. Johnson's dictionary had *publick* and *musick*, Webster's speller had *public* and *music*. By 1789, though, Webster offered more radical ideas regarding spelling, and they aroused a great deal of mocking resistance, even in his own country.

Webster's first principle was the "omission of all superfluous or silent letters"—such as the k in *musick* and all silent vowels and consonants. *Bread, give, friend, programme, travelled,* and *built* thus became *bred, giv, frend, program, traveled,* and *bilt.*

Webster's second principle was to regularize spelling and sound. For example, *grieve* and *mean* contain the same vowel sounds spelled differently. Webster used ee for both as well as anywhere that sound occurred—*greev* and *meen,* and also *pleez* and *bleet.* Similarly, *laugh* and *draught* became *laf* and *draft, plough* became *plow,* and B *women* became *wimmin.*

Webster gradually yielded to public pressure and modified his more radical spellings. Still, virtually all of the present differences between British and American spelling were advocated by Webster.

Webster's First Dictionary (1806)

Readers were no doubt very surprised when they came across words spelled *tung, fether, soop,* and *definit* in Webster's first dictionary, *A Compendious Dictionary of the English Language,* published in 1806.

> Many of Webster's spelling reforms and odd pronouncements make him appear to be a crackpot, and there is no question that there was something of the crackpot about him.

Many of Webster's recommended pronunciations must have been surprising as well. Webster disliked fashionable and urban people and manners almost as much as he disliked British ways. He hated any pronunciation that smacked of being affected or too fashionable. Webster rejected the *yu* sound in words such as *lecture, nature, figure,* and *tenure* as affectations. He recommended that they be pronounced *lecter, nater, figger,* and *tenor.*

Webster laid down stern rules regarding spelling and pronunciation, but he was often willing to bow to the practice of common people in matters of grammar and usage. The single thread running through these two contradictory attitudes was Webster's democratic desire for a common, regular American language.

Many of Webster's spelling reforms and odd pronouncements make him appear to be a crackpot, and there is no question that there was something of the crackpot about him. He had a degree from Yale, but as a linguist he was self-taught. Like many self-taught people, he had odd gaps in his learning. As a result, his etymologies, or word histories, were frequently incorrect.

Webster's American Dictionary (1828)

Even though his enthusiasms and spotty knowledge led him astray, Webster was no fool, and he was enormously energetic. His 1806 dictionary defined 37,000 words and indicated their pronunciation. The 1828 *American Dictionary of the English Language* was an incredible accomplishment for one person. It defined 70,000 words and provided etymologies as well as pronunciations. More than 12,000 definitions were published for the first time. Webster was the first lexicographer to include Americanisms such as *lot* ("a piece of land"), *to spell* ("to relieve someone at work"), and *clever* C ("good-natured"). "Such local terms exist," Webster had written some years before, "in spite of lexicographers and critics. Is this *my* fault? And if local

OPTIONS FOR TEACHING

STRATEGIES FOR INCLUSION

Spatial To help students understand the progression toward standardization of the American language, draw the following time line on the chalkboard. Ask students to draw their own time lines and to place on them the specific dates and events mentioned in "Noah's Ark." In addition, have students draw on the time line pictures that represent the events noted. Such a time line might look like the following:

pre-1700s — contemporary times

flexible rules of spelling — Webster's *New World Dictionary*

Less Proficient Readers To prepare students for reading the assignment, point out the unusual words in the sections "Consistency in Spelling" and "Webster's First Dictionary" on pp. 195–196. Have them point to the words as you read over them. Have students repeat words after you say them.

Advanced Have students continue Webster's work by writing proposals to change the spelling of words to agree with their sounds. Have them each write a business letter that states the reason that a certain spelling should be changed and includes a list of words that can be treated in the same fashion.

terms exist, why not explain them? . . . How are such words to be understood without the aid of a dictionary?"

The *American Dictionary* also included the new American meanings of older English words and settled for all time the changes in word endings that distinguish American from modern British usage: *–er* for *–re* (*center* rather than *centre*); *–or* for *–our* (*favor* rather than *favour*); *–c* for *–ck* (*music* rather than *musick*); *–ck* for *–que* (*check* rather than *cheque*); *–ize* for *–ise* (*legalize* rather than *legalise*); and *–ler* for *–ller* (*traveler* rather than *traveller*). We say *skedule* rather than *shedule* because Webster thought the pronunciation of *schedule* should follow the example of *school*.

Webster's Legacy

English purists shuddered to learn of Webster's determination to include American words and usages, and one critic suggested that the resulting volume of "foul and unclean" things be dubbed "Noah's Ark."

But Webster's pronouncements, even when they had little sound linguistic reasoning behind them, settled the uncertainties about authority in American English. Generations of Americans decided on the correctness of a word or a usage or a spelling by "looking it up in Webster's," and every household had to have a copy of Webster's dictionary next to the Bible.

By 1828, Webster's views of the development of American English had moderated, though his patriotism had not diminished. "The body of the language is the same as in England," he wrote in the Preface to the *American Dictionary*, "and it is desirable to perpetuate that sameness." In the same Preface, though, he pointed proudly at the burgeoning American literature as a source of richness and at the growth of the language as a source of pride.

Over the years many of Noah Webster's etymologies have been corrected, and spelling has been regularized further. Old words have taken on new meanings, and thousands of new words have been added to American English. Yet Webster was a central figure in the evolution of American English, and his name continues to signify excellence in dictionaries. Two of the United States' biggest sellers, *Webster's New World Dictionary* and *Merriam-Webster's Collegiate Dictionary,* still proudly display his name in their titles. Webster would have been pleased to have seen the fruits of his labors.

Try It Out

1. Consider this sentence written by Webster in his reformed spelling. "Every possible reezon that could ever be offered for altering the spelling of wurds, stil exists in full force; and if a gradual reform should not be made in our language, it wil proov that we are less under the influence of reezon than our ancestors." What inconsistencies do you see in Webster's reformed spelling?

D

Find a brief prose passage of your choice and write it in your own simplified—but consistent—spelling. Accompany your passage with a brief explanation of the rules of your reformed spelling.

2. Make a list of words that are spelled in similar ways but are pronounced differently (such as *tough* and *bough*). Then make a list of pairs of words that are spelled differently but have similar pronunciations (such as *dead* and *bed*). How would a consistent spelling rule help, for example, students for whom English is a second language? Would there be any drawbacks to consistent spelling?
3. Nonstandard forms of simplified spellings have flourished in product names ("Tastee Treetz"); road signs ("Thruway North"); and even pop music groups ("Boyz II Men"). List five other examples of nonstandard spellings from your everyday experience. Then try inventing five original product or business names that use nonstandard spellings.

D. Critical Reading: Making Connections

? What advantages has the continuation of a common language between Great Britain and the United States produced for people in both countries? [Answers will vary. Most answers will focus on the fact that the common language has enabled people to share ideas and many aspects of culture more easily.]

Metacognition How did you arrive at your answer? [Possible answer: People can share with friends when they can communicate with them directly. Common language enables whole countries to share with one another.]

Try It Out: Possible Answers

1. The elimination of unsounded double consonants (stil and wil, but full remains) and of silent letters (proov, but possible and influence remain). Webster gradually yielded to publik pressur and modified his mor radikal spellings. Changed *c* for *k* and eliminated silent *e*.
2. Responses will vary. Words spelled similarly but pronounced differently include *tomb* and *comb* and *touch* and *couch.* Words that are spelled differently but have similar pronunciations include *tough* and *gruff* and *tight* and *bite.* Most students will probably feel that consistent spelling rules would help students for whom English is a second language and that there are no drawbacks to consistent spelling except, perhaps, in personal names that are spelled inconsistently to emphasize individuality.
3. Possible responses: The Beatles and names that include "lite" or "E-Z."

INTEGRATING THE LANGUAGE ARTS

Strategic Reading To help summarize the main ideas in the selection, ask students to fill out the first two columns of the following chart as they read the material. Then, during class discussion, have them add information to the third column.

The American Language		
Section Title	Main Ideas	Class Notes
[Introduction]	[Grammars became popular]	[Written grammar in England by 1770s]

ASSESSMENT TOOLS

Check Test: Fill-in-the-Blank

1. The English middle class felt that words should be used the way __________ used them. [the aristocracy]
2. Webster felt that uniform American spelling and speech would __________. [bring Americans together]
3. The new idea of consistency in spelling was directly related to the increasing use of the __________. [printing press]
4. The two books of Webster's that had the biggest influence on American language were a __________ and a __________. [spelling book/dictionary]
5. Webster had rules about spelling and pronunciation, but he would bow to the usage of __________. [common people]

QUICK PLANNING GUIDE

Observational Essay

Motivation

Bring to class an item that is unusual and that students are not likely to be familiar with. The item may be a seashell, an antique, a figurine, a strange tool, or another item. Tell students to observe the object carefully. Pass the item around the classroom. After everyone has seen the object, ask students each to write down one detail they observed about it. Make a list on the chalkboard of the details students observed. Have the class come to consensus about which details are concrete and specific and which are vague. Point out that the writing assignment they are about to work on will require details that are both concrete and specific.

BUILDING YOUR PORTFOLIO

Writer's Workshop

Technology HELP

See Writer's Workshop 2 CD-ROM. *Assignment: Observational Writing.*

ASSIGNMENT
Write a vivid description of a person, place, object, animal, or event you've observed.

AIM
To inform; to express a point of view.

AUDIENCE
Your teacher, other students, and general readers.

Try It Out
One way to hone your observational skills is to quickly list ten things you have observed today—anything from another student to a car you admired. Choose one of the ten things from your list, and make a cluster of every detail you remember about it: colors, actions, textures, and anything else you observed.

DESCRIPTIVE WRITING

OBSERVATIONAL ESSAY

The role of the observer—the spectator on the sidelines—can be a rewarding one if you're truly paying attention to your experiences. The Romantic writers in this collection used clearsighted observation of the world around them as the starting point for many of the selections you've read. Whittier's observations of a storm and its aftermath led him to write a lovingly detailed description of a household imprisoned by snowdrifts in *Snow-Bound;* Holmes's observations of a nautilus shell led him to reflect on the soul's journey through life. Observational writing enables you, in the role of an objective observer, to share your perceptions of interesting people, places, events, and objects that you've had firsthand experience with.

Prewriting

WORK IN PROGRESS

1. **Choosing a significant subject.** There are so many possible subjects that it can be hard to settle on one. Should you write about what it's like to be a spectator at your school's basketball games? How about your observations of the neighbor's dog, which you secretly suspect is a canine genius? Could you describe the person you see at the bus stop every weekday, who in spite of limited means has a real flair for dressing in stylish, creative ways? Here's a simple principle for choosing: *Write about something that's meaningful and important to you.*

   If you've kept your notes from your Writer's Notebook in this collection, you might have a head start in choosing a subject. If you're still stumped for a topic, search your memory and quickwrite a list of persons, places, objects, animals, and events, as quickly as they enter your mind. Then read over your list, and circle one or two entries that grab your interest.

2. **Creating a context and gathering details.** In observational writing, you'll have to supply your readers with a **context** for your subject. *Where* is it? *When* is it? *Why* is it important?

   Let's say you want to describe your favorite place in your home: the kitchen. Once you've said "kitchen," you've defined a subject, but your job has just begun. The cornerstone of observational writing is **description,** and description consists largely of **sensory details.**

   To find sensory details, take some time to vividly imagine your subject. Probably, visual details will be the first ones you think of, but try to go beyond them to details involving the other senses: hearing, touch, taste,

PROGRAM MANAGER

Computer Guided Instruction For a related observational writing assignment that students may use as additional instruction, see *Writer's Workshop 2.*

PORTFOLIO ASSESSMENT

- **Generating Ideas** To help students in prewriting, use the heuristic in the *Portfolio Management System,* p. 90.
- **Assessment Rubric** For a rubric that can be used to assess students' progress in writing, see the *Portfolio Management System,* p. 92.

smell. (How did the kitchen smell on your mother's birthday when your uncle added a sprig of *epazote* to the big pot of beans he was stirring on the gas stove?) Sometimes you'll even want to go beyond sensory details to details of action, background, and history that fill out the context of your description. (Do you have fond memories of doing your homework on the kitchen table that's been in your family for generations?)

A list, or even a cluster, is a handy tool for assembling details for observational writing. It's a good idea to generate more details than you know you can use—as you write, you'll probably find yourself adjusting your focus, throwing out some details and bringing in new ones. Which of your details contribute to the overall impression you're trying to create? Which are unnecessary and even detract from your dominant impression?

Model

The Family Kitchen

fading blue wallpaper and white cabinets with paint peeling off
old, black iron stove with gas flame
Grandpa's big hands carefully holding flour-coated tortillas
an egg splattered on the floor, bright yellow against dark brown linoleum
smell of freshly made tortillas
caldo de pollo scenting the air

Peanuts reprinted by permission of United Feature Syndicate, Inc.

Drafting

1. **Organizing your description.** There are three commonly used ways to organize an observational essay:
   - **Spatial order.** For descriptions of places—and sometimes even of people and objects—it often makes sense to organize your essay

Strategies for Elaboration

1. **Use narrative devices.** Use **anecdotes**—brief stories that illustrate a point—and **dialogue** to bring a richer experience to your readers.
2. **Find the right angles.** Think like a movie director. Vary your focus. Describe your subject from a variety of angles: medium shots to close-ups, distance shots to pan—or moving—shots.
3. **Be specific.** Use specific, concrete, sensory language. Don't say "bicycle"; say "ruby-red, 15-speed mountain bike."
4. **Use figurative language.** Richly visual metaphors and similes will catch your readers' attention and help them to imagine more vividly what you're describing.

Teaching the Lesson

Ask a volunteer to read the assignment aloud. Make sure students understand the purpose of their writing—to describe someone or something so that the subject comes alive for readers.

This lesson includes instruction for each stage of the writing process. Guide students through the process by modeling each step of the process with your own writing.

Prewriting

Once students have selected a significant subject to write about, suggest they gather and organize sensory details, using a chart like the following. Remind students that the subject they choose may not evoke all five senses. After students have completed the chart, ask them to highlight the details in the chart that contribute to the overall impression they are trying to create.

Sense	Details
Sight	
Hearing	
Smell	
Touch	
Taste	

Try It Out

Brainstorm with students as a class possible subjects they have observed. To help them get started, suggest such items as bus seats, an old sweater, breakfast, a stranger on the street, a school corridor, or a flower bed. To help students develop a cluster of sensory details, use Transparency 3: Cluster Diagram, or, as an alternative, use Transparency 7: Sensory Details Chart in the Transparency Package.

OPTIONS FOR TEACHING

STRATEGIES FOR INCLUSION

Spatial If students are describing a place that is convenient to visit, you might recommend that they go there and take notes on what they see. Encourage them to organize their notes using a chart like the one in Prewriting on p. T199.

Auditory Help students visualize the details of the person, place, or object they are going to describe by having them talk through a description with another student. One student can relate his or her description while the other jots down notes about what the first student describes. These notes can form the basis of a list of sensory details that can be incorporated into each student's essay.

Visual As students evaluate their writing in preparation for revision, have them mark sensory details in their essays, using different highlighter colors for different senses. Suggest that they also underline transitional elements and circle verbs. Later, they can decide if the highlighted, underlined, and circled items need revision.

Drafting

If students have trouble beginning their essays, encourage them to focus on what they want to accomplish in their writing.

- Encourage them to finish the following statement: "I want to show ______." [Example: I want to show that my exotic garden constantly blooms.]
- Encourage students to rewrite the "I want to show" statements as thesis statements for their essays by leaving off the first part of the statements. [Example: My exotic garden constantly blooms.]

Evaluating and Revising

- Students should use the checklists under Peer Review and in Evaluation Criteria to evaluate their own and others' essays.
- Have students keep a list of how many concrete, sensory details they find as they read the essays. This list might lead students to add or delete details.

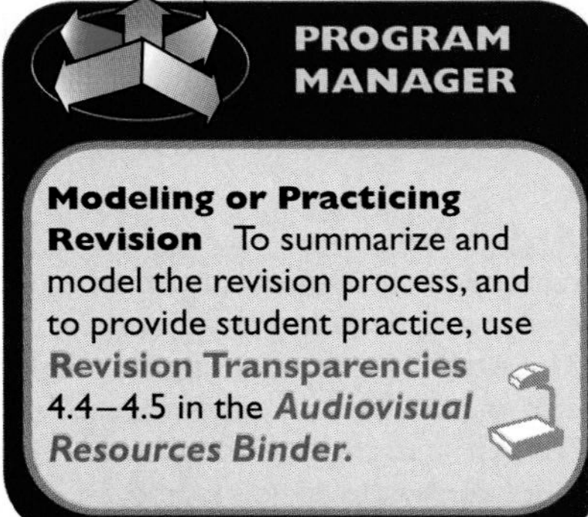

PROGRAM MANAGER

Modeling or Practicing Revision To summarize and model the revision process, and to provide student practice, use **Revision Transparencies** 4.4–4.5 in the ***Audiovisual Resources Binder.***

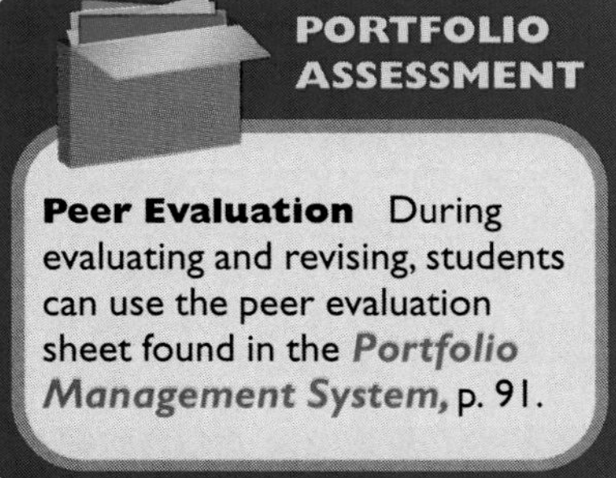

PORTFOLIO ASSESSMENT

Peer Evaluation During evaluating and revising, students can use the peer evaluation sheet found in the ***Portfolio Management System,*** p. 91.

according to the visual properties of the subject you're describing. If you're describing a room, you might start from the front and work your way to the back, or from back to front. If you're describing a geographical location, you might start from the left and move to the right, or vice versa. If you're describing an object, you might move clockwise or counterclockwise, or from top to bottom. The important thing is that you help the reader to see a complete picture, yet still focus on the most important details.

- **Order of importance.** In descriptions of people and objects, it often helps to emphasize the most important details by putting them either at the beginning or at the end of the essay. This pattern of organization is like adjusting a camera to focus on some details while letting others recede into the background. Order of importance also helps to convey your feelings about a subject, since the details you focus on reveal your interests and attitudes.
- **Chronological order.** When you're describing an event, such as a family meal, backstage frenzy the first night of your high school play, or a rap group's performance, you'll probably have the most success arranging details in the order in which they occurred. (You might include flashbacks to fill in necessary information.) Describing how you first encountered the subject, what happened next, and how you think of it now is also a form of chronological order.

Language Handbook HELP

Tenses and their uses: pages 1224 - 1225.

2. **Grabbing them from the beginning.** As you begin your description, think of yourself as a movie director. With your "camera," single out one unusual detail, and focus on it in your first paragraph. Compare your subject to something else: You might include an original **metaphor** or **simile** or other figure of speech that throws new light on the subject. You might try using a unique point of view. (For example, how did your kitchen look to you when you were a small child? How do you think you'll look back on your neighborhood when you're eighty years old?) You might build in some comparisons by describing a place when no people are present and when it's full of people. You could even open with an anecdote, or brief story.
3. **Creating a dominant impression.** Whether you're observing the sea, the stars, a mudslide, or a mosquito, the subject is interacting with *you* in some way, having an effect on your particular values and interests. You'll describe your subject from an angle that shows your unique viewpoint. Often, a single theme, or dominant impression, will come through in your description, but it doesn't have to be stated explicitly. You don't have to say, for instance, "Sitting in my family's kitchen makes me feel comfortable and secure." The dominant impression will come across in your word choice, tone, choice of details, and the progress of the description from point to point.
4. **Ending memorably.** An observational essay doesn't necessarily need a summary or restatement of its contents, but neither should it just sputter to a close. You might end with an anecdote or with a memorable image that sums up your dominant impression.

OPTIONS FOR TEACHING

INTEGRATING THE LANGUAGE ARTS

Grammar Review passive voice. During revision, tell students to rewrite passive voice sentences in the active voice.

Language and Style Have students eliminate wordiness. Ask them to go through their drafts and to draw boxes around all the adjectives. Then, have each replace multiple adjectives in a series with a single adjective or specific noun.

COOPERATIVE LEARNING

Group Revision Strategies Each student should read his or her paper aloud to the others in the group. As they listen, the other group members should make notes about words, phrases, or sentences that do not sound quite right. After the reader has finished, the other group members should share their notes and explain where they thought they heard problems. This activity can supplement peer reading and responding.

Evaluating and Revising

1. **Peer review.** Give a copy of your essay to another student, or read it aloud, and ask him or her to be your critic. Ask the following questions:
   - Did my descriptions help you see the subject in detail? Could I add anything that would help you visualize the subject more clearly?
   - Does the essay move from point to point smoothly? Is the pattern of organization appropriate to the subject, or would another kind of organization have worked better?
   - Do you think I created a dominant impression? Does the essay help you to understand how I feel about the subject? If it doesn't, how could I more effectively convey my feelings?
   - What do you wish my essay included that it doesn't?
2. **Self-evaluation.** Re-read your essay, and read or listen to your peer's comments. It's up to you to decide which of your reader's suggestions and which of your own second thoughts are convincing enough to lead to revisions. Underline passages that you agree need some more work.

Proofreading

Make a clean copy of your essay, and review it for errors in mechanics, spelling, grammar, and usage.

Publishing

Share a copy of your essay with friends and relatives, especially those who were involved in some way with the subject of your description. If you described a person, place, or event associated with your school, submit your essay to the school newspaper or literary magazine. If you described something or someone in your community, do some research to see if there's a place you can get your work published, such as a community newspaper or an organization's newsletter. When you share your essay, you might want to illustrate it with a picture of your subject.

Reflecting on Your Writing

Write a brief reflection on your observational writing experience. (Put the date on your essay and your reflection.) Use these sentence starters as prompts for your reflection.

1. The prewriting strategy that worked best for me was . . . .
2. I chose . . . as my pattern of organization because . . . .
3. As I wrote, some things I discovered were . . . .
4. Describing my feelings about my subject was . . . .
5. The next time I write an observational essay, I'll . . . .

Revision STRATEGIES

Have you included so many details that your essay moves at a snail's pace? so few that a reader can't visualize what you're describing? The revision stage is the place to reshape your descriptions to just the right length and focus.

Evaluation Criteria

A good observational essay
1. *clearly identifies its subject*
2. *locates the subject in the context of a specific time and place*
3. *selects and organizes descriptive details so that the reader can clearly visualize the subject*
4. *uses language, structure, and point of view to create a dominant impression and a meaningful, individual perspective on the subject*

Proofreading

Remind students that careful proofreading is a sign of respect for their readers and that it encourages others to take their writing seriously.

Closure

- Ask student volunteers to review orally the process of writing an observational essay. Write the steps on the chalkboard as they are mentioned.
- Have several student volunteers read their papers to the class.

Enrichment

Science Connection

Scientists are professional observers who write extended observational essays. Ask students to choose an observable object, such as a shell, an animal, or a plant. Ask them to consult an essay on a similar subject in a science textbook or magazine and then to write an observational essay on the topic they chose. For example, students could model their extended observational essay about a ferret on an article about gophers.

Portfolio

Reflecting on Your Writing

- Encourage students to reflect on each stage of the writing process.
- Have students attach their reflections to their observational essays and place all of this material in their portfolios.

PROFESSIONAL NOTES

Timesaver Save time in class by participating in one of the small groups during evaluation and revision. Give each member of the group a copy of a member's draft. Work through it orally, demonstrating how students should handle each other's papers and providing incidental instruction on grammar, usage, and mechanics as problems arise in the paper.

ASSESSMENT TOOLS

Peer Assessment Students can use the following criteria to assess their own work and the work of others.

Low					High
1	2	3	4	5	6

___ Is the subject clearly identified?

___ Does the writer create a context for the subject?

___ Does the organization of the descriptive details help the reader visualize the subject?

___ Does the essay use language, structure, and point of view to establish a meaningful perspective?

Language Workshop

Connecting to Students' Writing

Ask students each to select a piece of writing from their portfolios and to work through it, circling repeated words in any short, choppy sentences they find. Have them underline base sentences. Then, have them combine sentences by inserting modifiers into each base sentence. Encourage students to follow the Guidelines for Inserting Modifiers in Sentences. Ask students to work individually or in pairs on this assignment.

Try It Out: Possible Answers

1. The children of the village shouted with joy and expectancy whenever Rip Van Winkle approached.
2. Rip's daughter took him to her snug, well-furnished home.

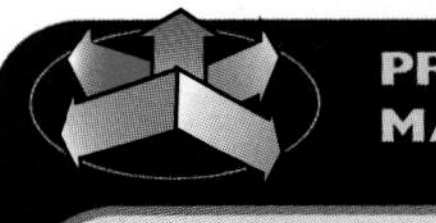

PROGRAM MANAGER

- **Extra Practice and Guided Instruction** For more instruction and practice on inserting modifiers, see **Language Workshop** in ***Teaching Resources A,*** pp. 77–78.
- **Extra Practice or Guided Instruction** See ***Language Workshop:* Inserting Modifiers** for more practice or guided instruction in inserting modifiers.

Language Workshop

Technology HELP

See Language Workshop CD-ROM. *Key word entry: inserting modifiers.*

Language Handbook HELP

Using modifiers: pages 1227–1228.

Try It Out

Turn each of the following sentence pairs into a single sentence by inserting modifiers from the second sentence into the base sentence.

1. The children of the village shouted whenever Rip Van Winkle approached. They shouted with joy and expectancy.
2. Rip's daughter took him to her home. Her home was snug and well furnished.

Smoothing It Out: Inserting Modifiers

Imagine that Washington Irving had described Rip Van Winkle in this way:

> Rip Van Winkle was a simple fellow. He was also good-natured and helpful.

The description above is passable, but it's choppy and bland. (Try reading it aloud to see why.) Here is a more vivid and readable description:

> Rip Van Winkle was a simple, good-natured, helpful fellow.

The following provides information about where Rip Van Winkle lived. But, once again, the sentences are short and choppy:

> Rip Van Winkle lived at the foot of the Kaatskill Mountains. He lived in a small house. It was timeworn and weather-beaten.

If the information were combined into one sentence, it would read much more smoothly:

> Rip Van Winkle lived in a small, timeworn, weather-beaten house at the foot of the Kaatskill Mountains.

Guidelines for Inserting Modifiers in Sentences

1. If your description is made up of several short, choppy sentences, look for the one that is your **base sentence**—the sentence that expresses the central idea. In the first example above, "Rip Van Winkle was a simple fellow" is the base sentence.
2. Look for modifiers in the other descriptive sentences. A modifier may be an adjective, adverb, prepositional phrase, or some other word or phrase that helps describe a word.
3. Insert modifiers from the other sentences into the base sentence. Where necessary, change the word order and punctuation. For example, you might need to change a period to a comma.
4. When you transfer a modifier from one sentence to another, make sure it modifies the same word it used to.

Writer's Workshop Follow-Up: Revising

Re-read the observational essay you wrote for the Writer's Workshop (page 198). Does it contain any bland or choppy sentences that you could combine by using modifiers? Don't be overly eager to combine sentences; sometimes a short, unembellished sentence is exactly right for your purposes.

✓ QUICK CHECK: Inserting Modifiers

Turn the following sentence groups into single sentences by inserting modifiers.

[1] Rip heard thunder. The thunder rolls were long. The thunder seemed distant. [Rip heard long, distant rolls of thunder.]

[2] The people inside the house huddled. Outside the snow fell. The people sat close to the fire. The fire glowed brightly. [The people inside the house huddled close to the brightly glowing fire while the snow fell outside.]

[3] The face watched him from the wall. She had a gentle face. She had died eighteen years ago. She had been his wife. [The gentle face of his wife, who had died eighteen years ago, watched him from the wall.]

[4] The ship had fought many a battle. Its tattered flag waved over the deck. The flag waved proudly. [The tattered flag waved proudly over the deck of the ship that had fought many a battle.]

CREATIVE PROBLEM SOLVING

LEARNING FOR LIFE

Environmental Concerns

Problem

American Romantic writers shared the belief that human beings can learn lessons from nature and that human activities should be conducted in harmony with the natural world. What are we doing today to ensure a better harmony with nature? What more can we do?

Project

Increase public consciousness of some aspect of environmentalism. Explore specific ways that you, your family, your school, or your community can move toward a lifestyle that is in greater harmony with nature.

Preparation

1. Brainstorm with other students to identify various environmental groups in your community, and arrange to interview representatives from several of these groups. Include as possible interviewees city planners, soil conservationists, organic farmers, wildlife biologists, and any other workers who deal with environmental issues.
2. Contact environmental organizations, and request brochures, mission statements, essays, and articles. Organizations to contact include the Sierra Club, National Audubon Society, Environmental Defense Fund, World Wildlife Fund, and the U.S. Environmental Protection Agency.
3. Research some aspect of the history of the environmental movement. Look up information on key figures, such as John Muir, John James Audubon, and Rachel Carson. Also consider writers and artists who have made the environment a central topic in their works.

Procedure

1. If you are interviewing individuals, prepare a list of questions beforehand, but think of these questions as only a general guide. The person, or persons, being interviewed may introduce some interesting angle or a different topic.
2. Examine and evaluate your research, narrowing it down to a manageable topic that truly interests you.
3. If you are researching the history of the environmental movement, go beyond the library to other sources of information: city parks, environmental organizations, museums, and galleries.

Presentation

Present your information in one of the following formats (or in another format that your teacher approves):

1. **An Ecologically Sound Business**
   Write up a proposal for a business that would be environment-friendly. Include with your proposal a statement of your business philosophy, as well as a scrapbook that includes published materials (articles, brochures) that lend credibility to your idea for a business. You may also include quotations from environmental groups, transcripts of your interviews with people who work with the environment, and any visuals (artwork, photographs, diagrams, graphs) that support your proposal.
2. **An Advertising Campaign**
   With one or more other students, plan and develop an advertising campaign to make your school and community more environmentally aware. Make posters, design and create brochures and fliers, and come up with catchy slogans and logos that will get your message across.
3. **Video Documentary**
   Film a short video documentary on some aspect of the environmental movement. Show the video documentary to your class.

Processing

What did you learn about contemporary environmentalism by doing this project? What are some beliefs and policies you discovered that you agree with? Are there any ideas you disagree with? Write a reflection for your portfolio.

Learning for Life

Technology Tip

TECHNOLOGY

As a part of their advertising campaign, suggest that students create thirty- or sixty-second television commercials or public information spots, using a video recorder. Encourage students to incorporate their logo designs and slogans, as well as background music for soundtracks. Before students prepare their projects, invite a representative from a community television station to speak with them. Professional news reporters, photographers, or advertising counselors may be willing to assist students with their advertising campaigns by offering advice or providing demonstrations. In lieu of professional advice, students may tape and study a variety of television commercials that focus on public service topics.

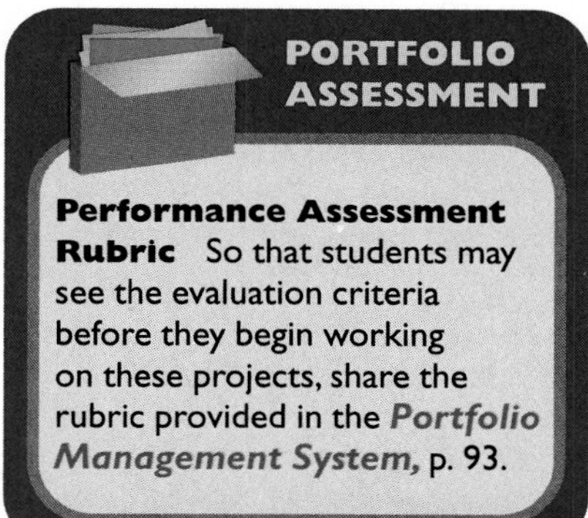

PORTFOLIO ASSESSMENT

Performance Assessment Rubric So that students may see the evaluation criteria before they begin working on these projects, share the rubric provided in the *Portfolio Management System*, p. 93.

DEVELOPING WORKPLACE COMPETENCIES

Preparation	Procedure	Presentation
Makes decisions Works well with people from diverse backgrounds Acquires data	Processes information Thinks creatively Evaluates data	Communicates ideas and information Applies technology to specific tasks

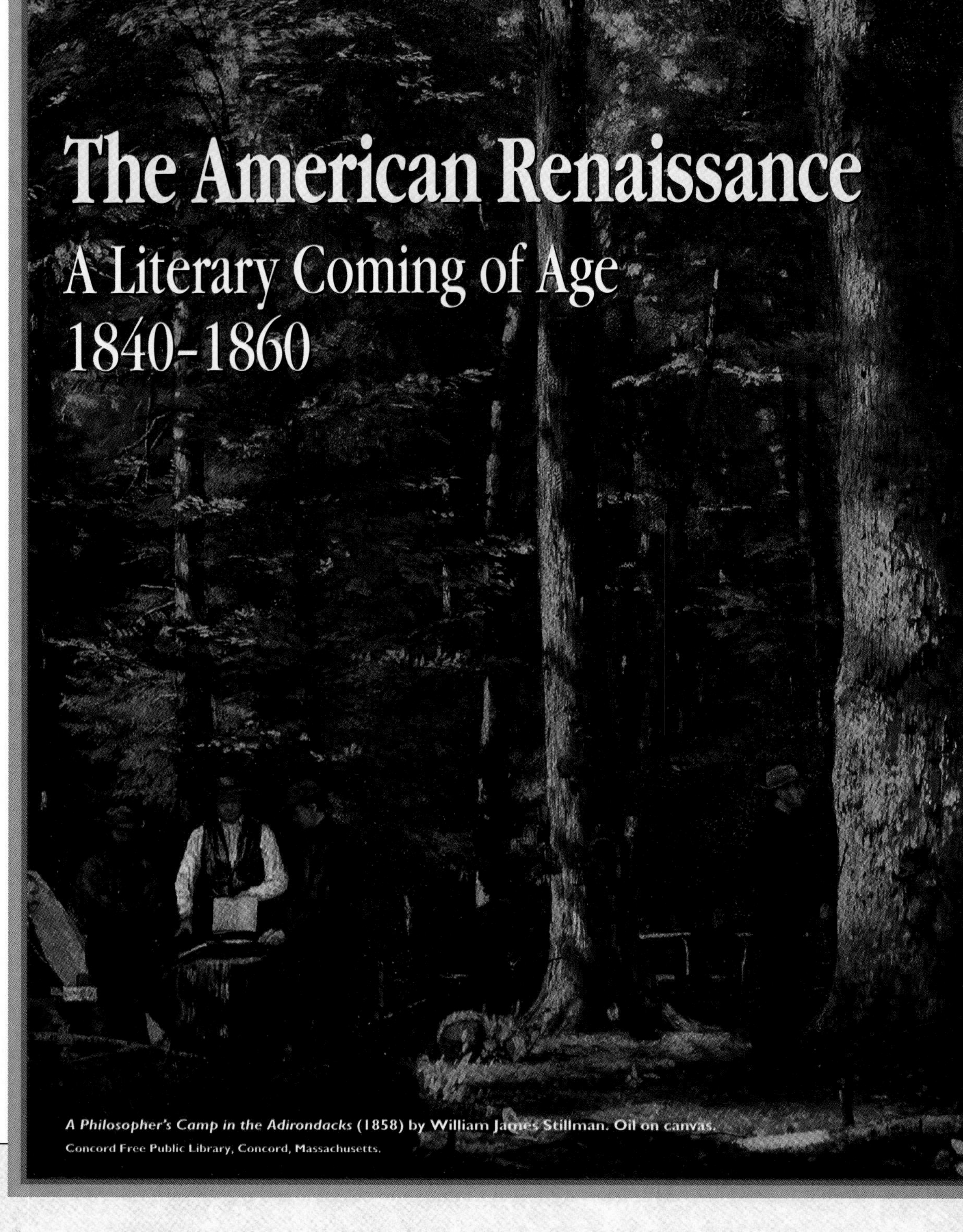

A Philosopher's Camp in the Adirondacks (1858) by William James Stillman. Oil on canvas.
Concord Free Public Library, Concord, Massachusetts.

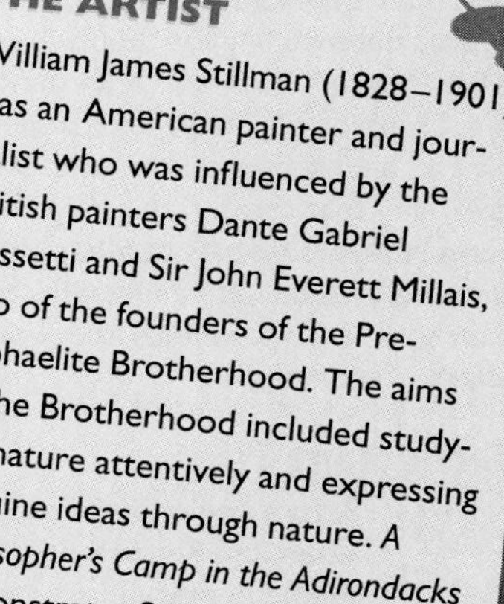

RESPONDING TO THE ART: ABOUT THE ARTIST

William James Stillman (1828–1901) was an American painter and journalist who was influenced by the British painters Dante Gabriel Rossetti and Sir John Everett Millais, two of the founders of the Pre-Raphaelite Brotherhood. The aims of the Brotherhood included studying nature attentively and expressing genuine ideas through nature. *A Philosopher's Camp in the Adirondacks* demonstrates Stillman's appreciation of the outdoors and reflects an attempt to show an ideal relationship between people and nature.

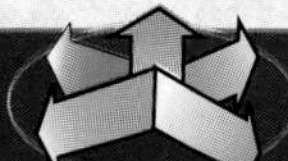

PROGRAM MANAGER

- **Summative Assessment** See **Literary Period Test: The American Renaissance,** ***Test Booklet,*** pp. 84–86, for a test on an additional text from the same historical era.
- **Application** For practice of a reading strategy for this unit, see **Becoming a Strategic Reader** worksheet, ***Teaching Resources A,*** pp. 87–88.
- **Performance Assessment** Use **Assessment 2** in the ***Integrated Performance Assessment, Level F*** to evaluate reading and writing skills covered in collections 5–8.

Responding to the Quotation

Emerson speaks of Americans coming into their own as a nation and of individuals determining for themselves what they will think and how they will live. Emerson also believes that all people can be inspired alike by the divine creativity that created the universe. Have students discuss to what extent they feel free to determine what will happen to them and what they will be able to accomplish.

Technology Tip

TECHNOLOGY Before beginning "The American Renaissance," find supplementary historical documents at the American Studies Web site. The URL is **http: //pantheon.cis.yale.edu/~davidp /amstud. html**. *You may want to preview any Internet activity that you suggest to students. Because these resources are sometimes public forums, their content may be unpredictable.*

Museum of Fine Arts, Boston, M. and M. Karolik Collection.

Girls' Evening School (c. 1840). American. Anonymous. Pencil and watercolor (13½″ × 18⅛″).

The American Renaissance

A Literary Coming of Age *by* Gary Q. Arpin

Literature the Americans have none . . . . In the four quarters of the globe, who reads an American book?

—Sydney Smith, English critic, 1818

We have listened too long to the courtly muses of Europe. . . . The mind of this country, taught to aim at low objects, eats upon itself. . . . We will walk on our own feet; we will work with our own hands; we will speak our own minds. . . . A nation of men will for the first time exist, because each believes himself inspired by the Divine Soul which also inspires all men.

—Ralph Waldo Emerson
from "The American Scholar," 1837

PROGRAM MANAGER

- **Planning Instruction** See Teaching Notes, *Teaching Resources A*, pp. 81–82, for additional teaching options about the American Renaissance.
- **Assessment** For assessment of the literary and historical events mentioned in the historical introduction, see Literary Period Introduction Test, *Test Booklet*, pp. 57–58.

***Elements of Literature:* Videodisc** Use the bar codes below to build background knowledge on the time period. For more information, see the Videodisc *Teacher's Manual.*

Videodisc Side B

Begin play
English Track

Begin play
Spanish Track

A remarkable party took place on August 5, 1850, in Stockbridge, Massachusetts. Among those attending were a Boston publisher and two of his authors, Oliver Wendell Holmes (page 187) and Nathaniel Hawthorne (page 296), and a New York editor and two of *his* authors, Cornelius Mathews and Herman Melville (page 311). The party began in the morning with a climb in the Berkshire Mountains. The group was in good humor—in part, perhaps, because of a champagne picnic lunch. During the climb, Melville leaned out over the steep cliffs to demonstrate how sailors took in sail. Hawthorne, usually very restrained, loosened up enough to look wildly about for the great carbuncle (a deep-red gem), the subject of a tale, based on a local legend, that he had written many years before. Ⓐ Ⓑ

The hike in the Berkshires was followed in the evening by a long dinner. The table conversation turned to American literature. In response to a statement made by Holmes praising English writers, Melville vigorously defended American writers.

Would there ever be an American writer as great as England's William Shakespeare? This question started a heated discussion, with Melville again firmly supporting the American side. Hawthorne found himself agreeing with Melville, whom he had never met before.

> It is that blackness in Hawthorne that . . . fixes and fascinates me. Ⓒ
>
> —Herman Melville

By the mid–nineteenth century, learned people still debated whether America would ever produce great writing. At a celebrated gathering in 1850, Nathaniel Hawthorne and Herman Melville firmly agreed that it would.

Bandbox.

Cooper-Hewitt National Design Museum, Smithsonian Institution/Art Resource.

THE ATLANTIC MONTHLY.

A MAGAZINE OF LITERATURE, ART, AND POLITICS.

VOL. I.—NOVEMBER, 1857.—NO. I.

DOUGLAS JERROLD.

A. Expansion

Periodicals flourished at this time. The Transcendentalist *The Dial* began publication in 1840; *Harper's Magazine* was founded in 1850; and *The New York Times* first rolled off the press in 1851.

B. Expansion

In Hawthorne's story "The Great Carbuncle," eight people search for a fabled garnet of great splendor. One dies in the search, another is blinded by the garnet, and yet another is impoverished. A husband and wife reject the jewel, which "would have dimmed all earthly things" and live happily the rest of their lives.

C. Responding to the Quotation

? In what ways can a person be fixed and fascinated by a Hawthorne-like darkness? [Possible responses: The power of evil can be frightening; or someone can be interested in the psychology of the mind.]

OPTIONS FOR TEACHING

STRATEGIES FOR INCLUSION

Intrapersonal Have students read A Closer Look on pp. 210–211. Ask them to form small groups and talk about how life is different today. Have them discuss what they would be doing if they had lived during the American Renaissance. Then, have groups tell the class what they discussed.

Spatial To help students remember and grasp the ideas of Transcendentalism, have them draw pictures or symbols for each of the five key points in A Transcendentalist's View of the World on p. 212. Then, ask students to form groups of four and pair off within each group. One pair will show a picture, and the other pair will identify which point of Transcendentalist thought is portrayed. Have pairs alternate showing and identifying.

Musical Have students set to music the sections "The Transcendentalists" on pp. 210–211; "Emerson and Transcendentalism" on p. 212; and "Melville, Hawthorne, and Poe" on pp. 213–214. They should vary their music selections for each author mentioned. Have students explain their choices.

RESPONDING TO THE ILLUSTRATION: RELATED EXPRESSION SKILLS

Ask students to write what they think is the story behind Hester's knock at the door or to find music that fits the mood of the engraving.

A. Humanities Connection
Melville found the cannibalistic Typee tribe kinder and more humane than many self-professed Christians of the time. Before agreeing to publish *Typee,* his publishers censored passages that attacked Western civilization. His novel bears some relationship to "Of Cannibals," the 1580 French essay by Michel de Montaigne, who wrote about the humanity of cannibalistic "savages."

B. Expansion
Melville saw the darkness of his times, denouncing slavery and exposing the abuses by the powerful. Hawthorne denounced the overzealousness of some Puritans during the Salem witch trials.

Hawthorne and Melville: Opposites Attract

It seemed highly unlikely that these two writers would become friends. Herman Melville was an ex-sailor with little **A** formal education. He had lived in the South Seas and had written a remarkable first novel, *Typee* (1846), about his adventures. At the time of the party, Melville was hard at work on his fifth novel, which, it appeared, would be very long.

> Think of it. To go down to posterity as a "man who lived among the cannibals."
>
> —Herman Melville, writing about himself to Hawthorne

Nathaniel Hawthorne, who was fifteen years older than Melville, was well educated, reserved, and a bit of a loner. He had written many short stories and had recently published *The Scarlet Letter* (1850), a novel about sin and hypocrisy in Puritan New England.

Despite their different backgrounds, a friendship sprang up between the two writers. "I met Melville the other day," Hawthorne wrote to a friend, "and liked him so much that I have asked him to spend a few days with me before leaving these parts." This was the beginning of an association that came at a critical point in Melville's life, when he was hard at work on his masterpiece, *Moby-Dick.* After the meeting, Melville sat down and read Hawthorne's works—and was exposed for the first time to what he called the "power of blackness" in Hawthorne's writing.

Puritan children averting their eyes from Hester Prynne. From *The Scarlet Letter* by Nathaniel Hawthorne. Lithograph after a painting by George H. Boughton.

The Granger Collection, New York.

B ***Nathaniel Hawthorne and Herman Melville discovered a common bond: They both saw a dark side to human existence, and they sought to record this aspect of human nature in their works.***

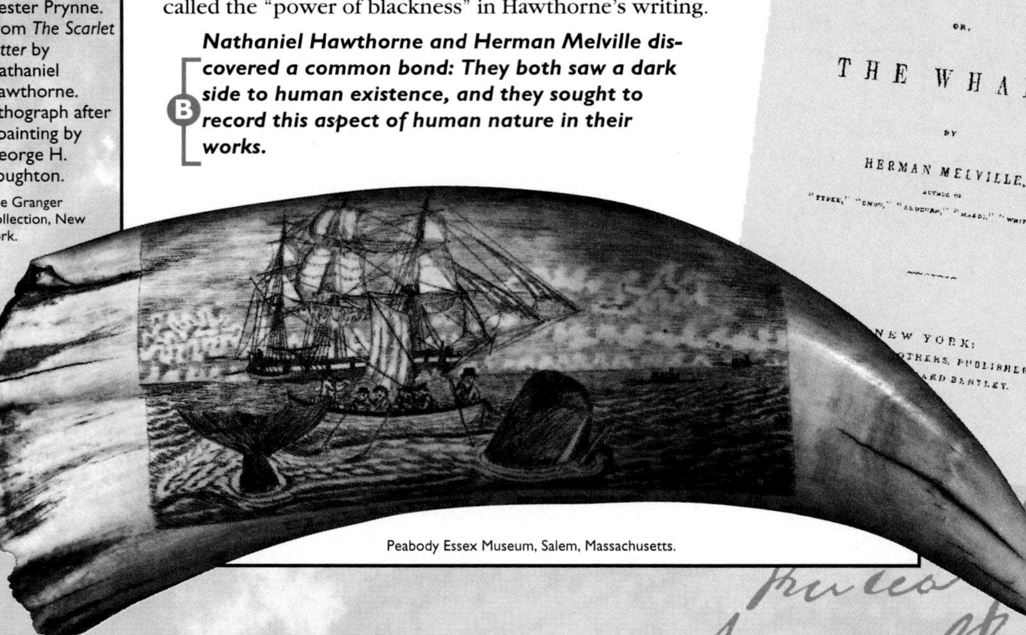

Peabody Essex Museum, Salem, Massachusetts.

OPTIONS FOR TEACHING

INTEGRATING THE LANGUAGE ARTS

Strategic Reading To help students master the ideas of the Transcendentalists, have them follow the Cornell style of taking notes as they read. Have them divide their papers into three columns. The middle column is for note taking, the left for key words arising from the notes, and the right for summary points of the page.

Key Words	Notes	Summary
[Go beyond]	[Matters of ultimate reality, God the universe, the self—transcend, or go beyond mere human experience]	[Transcend experience]

Speaking and Listening Remind students that when they speak, eye contact with their listener(s) indicates interest and respect. Have students practice eye contact when they discuss the introduction or give presentations on it.

Vocabulary Have students study the terms *romance, romantic,* and *Romanticism* so they understand the distinctions in the ways the terms can be used. Ask them to look up the terms in the Handbook of Literary Terms and in dictionaries. Have them record the definitions in their Reader's Logs.

First Flowering: A Declaration of Literary Independence

The immediate result of Melville's meeting with Hawthorne was a magazine essay in which Melville passionately defended American literature. Stating that England was in many ways "alien to us," Melville urged American readers to "prize and cherish" their own writers. In a burst of literary patriotism, Melville claimed that, in Hawthorne, America was very close to producing its own Shakespeare.

Melville's horn blowing for American writing coincided with a vital period in American literature. It was a time when the American landscape and American culture would finally find their place in a literature distinct from European models. Writers were aware of this, and they sometimes used the word *renaissance* (ren′ə·säns′), meaning "rebirth," to describe this extraordinary explosion of American literary genius. When Americans referred to themselves as living in a renaissance, they were comparing their times to the European Renaissance, a period of extraordinary cultural vitality that lasted from about the fourteenth to the sixteenth century. A better term, however, for what happened in the still-raw America of the mid-1800s might be "coming of age." From 1849 to 1855, American writers produced a remarkable body of work, enough masterpieces for a national literature.

> Nothing is at last sacred but the integrity of your own mind.
>
> —Ralph Waldo Emerson

In the mid–nineteenth century, writers such as Nathaniel Hawthorne, Ralph Waldo Emerson, Henry David Thoreau, and Herman Melville produced some of the early masterpieces of American literature.

Intellectual and Social Life in New England

This burst of American literature can be traced in large measure to the intellectual and social ferment in New England. New England had long been known for its interest in self-improvement and intellectual inquiry. This interest found expression in the Lyceum (lī·sē′əm) movement, begun in 1826 in Millbury, Massachusetts. Lyceum organizations, soon established in many communities, had a number of goals, including educating adults, training teachers, establishing museums, and instituting social reforms. A typical part of a Lyceum program was a course of lectures in winter. These became immensely popular in New England and the Midwest. One of the most popular speakers was Ralph Waldo Emerson (page 216).

This was a time of social improvement in other ways too. New England was a center of many reform movements. Horace Mann dedicated

Lyceum Lecture by James Pollard Espy at Clinton Hall (1841) by an unknown artist. Pen and ink.

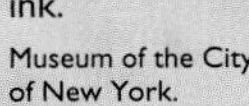

Museum of the City of New York.

C. Expansion

Melville was noted for wild mood swings, alternating between grandiose exuberance and melancholic dejection. His essay on Hawthorne was the fruit of the former—as were many of his finest creative passages. His claim that Hawthorne was close to being an American Shakespeare would have seemed exaggerated to most people even then, given Hawthorne's much more limited range.

D. Responding to the Quotation

? What historical figures followed their moral principles rather than society's customs? [Possible responses: Martin Luther King, Jr., Mohandas Gandhi, Cesar Chavez.] What might have happened had these people not kept their integrity? [Possible responses: Civil rights might not have been won; India might have remained under British rule; farm workers might not have organized against exploitation.]

E. Humanities Connection

The European Renaissance, a great revival of classical learning, began in Italy in the 1300s, spread north to Germany and Holland, and reached England by Shakespeare's time.

F. Humanities Connection

America experienced another rebirth: From the 1920s Harlem Renaissance of African Americans in New York sprang great creative genius.

G. Exploring the Culture

Josiah Holbrook founded the Lyceum movement in 1826. By 1835, fifteen states had lyceums; by 1860, more than three thousand lyceums existed. People went to lyceum halls much as they go to movies today. They heard lectures about famous people, remote geographic locations, and the latest discoveries in science.

COOPERATIVE LEARNING

Team Teaching Have students number off from one to seven until each student has a number. Then, have them form seven groups. Assign each group a section of the introduction to teach to the rest of the class. When making assignments, combine the first section with A Closer Look, and also combine the last two sections ("Emerson's Optimistic Outlook" and "Melville, Hawthorne, and Poe"). Ways to teach the lesson may vary. Some ways of teaching include conducting a class discussion, presenting a theatrical piece, or involving students in an activity.

American Renaissance Board Game Form groups that contain students with various learning styles, including one visual, one kinesthetic, and one interpersonal learner. Have each group design a board game for the American Renaissance. The game could be based on the trivia of American Renaissance facts, personalities, and events, and could use categories such as Dark Romantics, Transcendentalists, and Intellectual and Social Life. Students may add to and refine their games as they read the selections by the authors in the unit. Once the games are completed, have groups play each other's games.

A. Expansion

Fuller was well educated by her father. She associated with the Transcendentalists, wrote reviews and collections of essays, edited *The Dial* for two years, and toured extensively. Fuller believed women had been educated to be ornaments and not to think. Between 1839 and 1844, she held "Conversations" on topics ranging from poetry to ethics to draw out women and enable them to realize their potential. Fuller's conversations were so popular that she was eventually pressed to admit men.

Willard, educator and promoter of grade school and higher education for women, was the principal of a girls' academy and later established her own girls' boarding school, Troy Female Seminary. In 1860, Peabody opened the first English-language kindergarten in the United States, after the German model.

B. Exploring the Culture

The early 1800s saw a shift from agriculture to industry, from rural to urban life. Factories replaced the call for the skill of the artisan, and armies of Irish and German immigrants were hired at low wages to run machines. Several writers, including Lydia Child and Rebecca Harding Davis as well as Melville and Margaret Fuller, addressed the worsening plight of the factory workers.

A CLOSER LOOK

THAT WAS THEN...

What would your life be like if you lived in the 1840s?

For one thing, it probably would be shorter. On average, you could expect to live only about forty years. A quarter of your friends would die relatively young, many of them victims of tuberculosis, the nineteenth-century plague.

Your world would be far less crowded than it is now. In 1840, there were about 17 million people living in the United States. (In contrast, by 1995 there were about 260 million Americans.) Some 3 million of them were of African heritage, and of those, only about half a million were not enslaved.

Back of the State House in Philadelphia by William Birch.
Library of Congress.

himself to improving public education; Dorothea Dix sought to relieve the horrible conditions in institutions for the mentally ill; William Lloyd Garrison and other abolitionists struggled to put an end to slavery; feminists like Elizabeth Peabody, Margaret Fuller, and Emma Willard campaigned to increase women's rights. (A)

(B) Social causes, both reasonable and crackpot, abounded during this time. Numerous utopian (yo͞o·tō′pē·ən) projects—plans for creating a more perfect society—were developed. In 1840, Emerson wryly remarked that every man who could read had plans in his pocket for a new community. Emerson was speaking from personal experience, for he was a member of one of the most influential of these utopian groups.

Ralph Waldo Emerson was a primary force behind the flowering of American culture. He helped inspire numerous reform movements that aimed to improve public education, end slavery, elevate the status of women, and generally smooth the edges off the rough social conditions of the time. Various utopian groups drew up comprehensive plans for a better society.

The Transcendentalists: True Reality Is Spiritual

Emerson's utopian group quickly became known as "The Transcendental Club." The term *transcendental* comes from the eighteenth-century

OPTIONS FOR TEACHING

CLASSROOM MANAGEMENT

Block Scheduling Encourage students, especially those new to block scheduling, to discuss their impressions of the longer class periods. They may have concerns that can be addressed quickly. This discussion can accomplish two things: It can allow a short break between activities, and student feedback can be utilized when planning additional lessons.

Speaking and Listening To enable students to orally present to the class their Crossing the Curriculum: Social Sciences research findings on p. T211, have one student in the group introduce and state the topic. A second student can discuss the group's findings, using chronological order, and a third student, who may be more reticent to speak, can conclude by summing up the major points of their study.

Managing the Reader's Response Classroom If students' comments seem to be made without support from the material, urge them to return to the text to explain how they reached their conclusions. Guide them in adjusting their conclusions if no support can be found.

Cities were rapidly expanding in the 1840s. The five largest were Boston, New York City, Philadelphia, Baltimore, and Charleston. Visitors to New York were stunned by the filth there. There was no citywide garbage collection, and pigs moved freely about the streets.

Chances are you'd live in the country, though, in a house heated by wood or coal fires and lit by oil lamps. Your father most likely would be a farmer, and your mother probably would concentrate on taking care of the home but would help out with the farm. You would probably have several brothers or sisters. If you went to school (many young people didn't), you'd likely [C] walk to a one-room schoolhouse. There, side-by-side with students of varying ages, you'd be taught reading, writing, arithmetic, and proper behavior. It's possible you'd already be married at your age. Both rich and poor married quite young—as early as thirteen or fourteen in the South.

What would you do for fun? In rural areas, you'd probably go dancing on weekend nights or attend cornhusking contests or quilting bees. You might start learning about a new pastime called baseball—the first game closely resembling the modern sport took place in 1846. You might read for entertainment. But wherever you lived, your main form of entertainment would probably be visiting friends and neighbors.

Who would be your heroes? Probably not athletes or entertainers. The main heroes were politicians, especially those with military backgrounds. Just about everyone's favorite hero was George Washington.

German philosopher Immanuel Kant. The word refers to the idea that in determining the ultimate reality of God, the universe, the self, and other important matters, one must transcend, or go beyond, everyday human experience in the physical world. Intuition is an important tool for discovering truth.

For Emerson, **Transcendentalism** was not a new philosophy but "the very oldest of thoughts cast into the mold of these new times." That "oldest of thoughts" was Idealism, which had already been articulated by the Greek philosopher Plato in the fourth century B.C. Idealists said that true reality involved ideas rather than the world as perceived by the senses. Idealists sought the permanent reality that underlay physical appearances. The Americans who called themselves Transcendentalists were idealists, but in a broader, more practical sense. Like many Americans today, they believed in human perfectibility, and they worked to achieve this goal.

> To recall these village lyceums, these rude country halls, evening meetings in odd churches, barns, schools, and banquet rooms, tents spread in preparation for the idyllic summer's opening of the college year . . . is to imagine a time when people still looked to literary men for guidance. . . . Emerson made a thousand appearances, crossed the Mississippi on ice in dead winter to deliver a lecture in Iowa, was bumped, jostled, frozen in wagons, carriages, flatboats, steamboats, trains (where he felt so solitary that he vowed he would go over to any man reading a book and hug him).
>
> —Alfred Kazin, *from An American Procession*

C. Expansion
By the 1860s, some twenty years later, most regions except for the South had publicly funded primary education. The rate of school attendance exploded.

CROSSING THE CURRICULUM

Social Sciences Have students form groups of two or three. Ask each group to choose, research, and report on a different topic mentioned in the period introduction. Examples include: Horace Mann and education, Dorothea Dix's work for mental hospitals, the women's rights movement, whaling, baseball, and the utopian projects. The groups should report their findings to the class.

Health Have student pairs look up information on the effects of tuberculosis and poor sanitation on the population at the time of the American Renaissance. Students may also want to study tuberculosis in today's society and research how the problems of sanitation have been addressed. Students should graph the number of cases of tuberculosis then and now or illustrate differences in sanitation and display their graphs and artwork in the classroom.

Fine Arts Ask students to locate pieces or illustrations of folk art of the period, to show them to the class, and to talk about how the folk art is indicative of the times. Other students may wish to locate Currier and Ives prints and to explain how they capture the spirit of the times. ☞

A. Humanities Connection
The Transcendentalist's view that everything in the world is a reflection of the Divine Soul is derived from the Hindu idea of *atman,* which means that each individual soul is made of the same stuff as the universal World-Soul.

B. Humanities Connection
Remind students of Edwards's sermon "Sinners in the Hands of an Angry God" on pp. 79–81 and his journals on p. 82, Rowlandson's account of captivity on pp. 40–45, and Taylor's poetry on p. 73.

A Transcendentalist's View of the World

- A Everything in the world, including human beings, is a reflection of the Divine Soul.
- The physical facts of the natural world are a doorway to the spiritual or ideal world.
- People can use their intuition to behold God's spirit revealed in nature or in their own souls.
- Self-reliance and individualism must outweigh external authority and blind conformity to custom and tradition.
- Spontaneous feelings and intuition are superior to deliberate intellectualism and rationality.

Emerson and Transcendentalism: The American Roots

Though Emerson was skeptical of many of the Transcendentalists' ideas and projects, he was the most influential and best-known member of the group, largely because of his lectures and books. His writing and that of his friend Henry David Thoreau (page 230) clearly and forcefully expressed Transcendental ideas. As developed by Emerson, Transcendentalism grafted ideas from Europe and Asia onto a homegrown American philosophical stem. Its American roots included Puritan thought, the beliefs of the eighteenth-century religious revivalist Jonathan Edwards (page 77), and the Romantic tradition exemplified by William Cullen Bryant (page 169).

> I was simmering, simmering, simmering; Emerson brought me to a boil.
>
> —Walt Whitman

B The Puritans believed that God revealed himself to people through the Bible and through the physical world. William Bradford (page 26), for example, saw the death of an abusive sailor on the *Mayflower* as the direct action of God in the human world. Anne Bradstreet (page 68) saw evidence of God in the grandeur of nature. Jonathan Edwards found God's wisdom, purity, and love in the sun, moon, and stars—in fact, in all of nature. This native mysticism—also typical of **Romanticism**—reappears in Emerson's thought. "Every natural fact," Emerson wrote, "is a symbol of some spiritual fact."

Transcendentalism was based partly on the philosophy of Idealism, which dated back to ancient Greece. It was based also on the ideas of American thinkers ranging from the Puritans to the nineteenth-century Romantics. Transcendentalists viewed nature as a doorway to a mystical world holding important truths.

Ralph Waldo Emerson. Drawing by David Levine. Reprinted with permission from *The New York Review of Books.* Copyright ©1968 NYREV, Inc.

Emerson's Optimistic Outlook

Emerson's mystical view of the world sprang not from logic but from intuition. Intuition is our capacity to know things spontaneously and immediately through our emotions rather than through our reasoning abilities. Intuitive thought—the

OPTIONS FOR TEACHING

PROBLEM SOLVING/CRITICAL THINKING

Addressing Pains The Dark Romantics acknowledged the existence of pain and evil in human life. Have students discuss pains and evils that existed during the early to mid-1800s. Suggest they refer to the section "Intellectual and Social Life in New England" on pp. 209–210, and A Closer Look on pp. 210–211, and consult their findings from Crossing the Curriculum: Social Sciences and Health on p. T211. Ask them to discuss pains and evils present in society today and to find ways to address or cope with them. Help them organize their information by placing the following chart on the chalkboard or on an overhead projector and filling in or asking a student scribe to fill in the major points discussed.

Source	Pain/Evil	Coping
That Was Then . . .	[death of loved ones from tuberculosis]	[They accepted that life was short.]
Crossing the Curriculum: Social Studies	[deficiency of women's education]	[Margaret Fuller's "Conversations"]
Group Discussion About Today	[the threat of contracting AIDS]	[education—knowing how it is contracted]

> I unsettle all things. No facts are to me sacred; none are profane; I simply experiment, an endless seeker, with no Past at my back.
>
> —Ralph Waldo Emerson

kind Emerson believed in—contrasts with the rational thinking of someone like Benjamin Franklin (page 84). Franklin did not gaze on nature and feel the presence of a Divine Soul; Franklin looked at nature and saw something to be examined scientifically and used to help humanity. C

An intense feeling of optimism was one product of Emerson's belief that we can find God directly in nature. God is good, and God works through nature, Emerson believed. Therefore, even the natural events that seem most tragic—disease, death, disaster—can be explained on a spiritual level. Death is simply a part of the cycle of life. We are capable of evil because we are separated from a direct, intuitive knowledge of God, according to Emerson. But if we simply trust ourselves—that is, trust in the power each of us has to know God directly—then we will realize that each of us is also part of the Divine Soul, the source of all good. D

> "What do you think of the world to come?" an admirer asked the philosopher.
>
> "One world at a time," Thoreau replied.

Emerson's sense of optimism and hope appealed to audiences who lived in a period of economic downturns, regional strife, and conflict over slavery. Your condition today, Emerson seemed to tell his readers and listeners, may seem dull and disheartening, but it need not be. If you discover the God within you, he suggested, your lives will partake of the grandeur of the universe.

Emerson believed in the power of intuition, our ability to learn directly without conscious use of reasoning. He emphasized the importance of each individual, and his outlook was optimistic.

Old Manse in Concord, where first Emerson and then Hawthorne lived.
Steve Solum/ Bruce Coleman, Inc.

Melville, Hawthorne, and Poe: A Challenge to the Transcendentalists

Emerson's idealism was exciting for his audiences, but not all the writers and thinkers of the time agreed with Transcendentalist thought. "To one who has weathered Cape Horn as a common sailor," Herman Melville wrote of Emerson's ideas, "what stuff all this is." E

Some people think of Nathaniel Hawthorne, Herman Melville, and Edgar Allan Poe (page 260) as anti-Transcendentalists, because their view of the world seems so profoundly opposed to the optimistic view of Emerson and his followers. But these Dark Romantics, as they are

C. Humanities Connection
Franklin's view exemplifies deism, the idea that the universe was rationally designed by a divinity who endowed humanity with reason but who does not interfere with the minute workings of the universe.

D. Humanities Connection
Here is one of the origins of the positive thinking and self-realization trends of the twentieth century. Emerson's influence runs deep: "Trust Yourself" is the title of a 1985 song by Bob Dylan.

E. Exploring the Historical Period
While Emerson was speaking of lofty ideals in New England, the California gold rush began in 1848.

PROFESSIONAL NOTES

Cultural Diversity Both Emerson and Melville call for a time when American writers would be recognized on their own merits. Discuss with students what it takes for writers and creative individuals in various cultures to be recognized by their own communities and by the world.

Thematic Connections: "A Literary Coming of Age" Ask students in what ways American writers had begun to establish their own identities, as discussed in the introduction on p. 207 and in "First Flowering: A Declaration of Literary Independence" on p. 209.

A. Humanities Connection
Students have many opportunities to discuss symbolism in this unit. The symbolism of specific works is discussed in Elements of Literature on p. 280, and Making Meanings questions on p. 288 (Poe, "The Raven"), p. 308 (Hawthorne, "The Minister's Black Veil"), and on pp. 320 and 328 (Melville, *Moby-Dick*).

Quickwrite

Ask students to refer to A Transcendentalist's View of the World on p. 212 and to draw up a list of characteristics of the Dark Romantics before responding in their Reader's Logs.

> That blue-eyed darling Nathaniel knew disagreeable things in his inner soul. He was careful to send them out in disguise.
> —D. H. Lawrence, on Hawthorne

known, had much in common with the Transcendentalists. Both groups valued intuition over logic and reason. Both groups, like the Puritans before them, saw signs and symbols in human events—as Anne Bradstreet found spiritual significance in the fire that destroyed her house (page 69). (Not surprisingly, **A** the Dark Romantics used the literary technique of **symbolism** to great effect in their works.)

> . . . in certain moods, no man can weigh this world without throwing in something, somehow like Original Sin, to strike the uneven balance.
> —Herman Melville

The Dark Romantics didn't disagree with Emerson's belief that spiritual facts lie behind the appearances of nature; they disagreed with the premise that those facts are necessarily good, or harmless. Emerson, they felt, had taken the ecstatic, mystical elements of Puritan thought and ignored its dark side—its emphasis on Original Sin, its sense of the innate depravity of human beings, and its Calvinistic notions of predestination. The Dark Romantics came along to redress the balance. Their view of existence developed from both the mystical and the melancholy aspects of Puritan thought. In their works, they explored the conflict between good and evil, the psychological effects of guilt and sin, and even madness and derangement in the human psyche. Behind the pasteboard masks of social respectability, the Dark Romantics saw the blankness and the horror of evil. From this imaginative, unflinching vision they shaped a uniquely American literature.

Portrait of Edgar Allan Poe (1985) by Rick McCollum. Oil on linen board with oil pencil.

Courtesy Rick McCollum.

The works of writers such as Hawthorne, Melville, and Poe acknowledged the existence of sin, pain, and evil in human life and formed a counterpoint to the optimism of the Transcendentalists.

READER'S LOG

Quickwrite

How Do You See Yourself?

Do you agree with the Transcendentalists' optimistic views of human perfectibility? Or are you more like the Dark Romantics, believing that the world has a dark, irrational side that can't be ignored? Write down your own opinions about the ideas of the Transcendentalists and the Dark Romantics. How do you see yourself in relation to them?

OPTIONS FOR TEACHING

ASSESSMENT TOOLS

Check Test: Multiple Choice

1. The opposites that attracted were (a) Hawthorne and Poe (b) Emerson and Hawthorne (c) Emerson and Melville (d) Hawthorne and Melville [d]
2. The Lyceum movement refers to (a) the emergence of high schools (b) the formation of a writers' union (c) an organization that promoted lectures and museums (d) a movement for medical reform [c]
3. Transcendentalists believed that (a) nature reveals spiritual facts (b) the dark side of the human mind must be acknowledged (c) both a and b (d) neither a nor b [a]
4. The American roots for Transcendentalism can be found in (a) Franklin (b) Edwards (c) Byrd (d) Jefferson [b]
5. Melville, Poe, and Hawthorne disagreed with the Transcendentalists about (a) nature (b) optimism (c) logic (d) intuition [b]

Peer Assessment When student groups are presenting reports, have the audience evaluate their performances. Develop the criteria you would like them to use to evaluate the groups, or use the following chart:

Criteria	Comments
Content	
Support	
Organization	

THE LIFE WORTH LIVING

Theme: The Transcendent Individual

The philosophy of transcendentalism influenced many writers of the mid–nineteenth century. These writers espoused intuition, self-reliance, individualism, and a love of nature as ways to behold the universal spirit.

Thematic Focus

The following selections in Collection 5 stress reliance on one's own thinking.

- *from* **Nature** Emerson encourages readers to look to nature to find themselves.
- *from* **Self-Reliance** Emerson urges people to trust their inner voices.
- *from* **Walden, or Life in the Woods** Thoreau moves to the woods to ponder what is necessary to live a meaningful life.
- *from* **Resistance to Civil Government** Thoreau explains civil disobedience as a means of social protest.

Literary Focus

Literary Element	Selection / Feature
Imagery	**Nature**
Figure of Speech	**Self-Reliance**
Point of View	**Walden, or Life in the Woods**
Paradox	**Resistance to Civil Government**

Writing Focus

The following flow chart shows how the writing assignment for each selection relates to and builds toward the culminating writing assignment presented in the Writer's Workshop at the end of the unit.

Selection	Work-in-Progress Assignment
Nature and **Self-Reliance**	Brainstorm list of controversial issues p. 229
Walden, or Life in the Woods	Write several questions for controversial issues p. 247
Resistance to Civil Government	Write ideas defining controversial issue p. 258
Writer's Workshop	Write persuasive essay pp. 331–337

Collection Planner

PUPIL'S EDITION

SELECTION / FEATURE	Literary Elements / Active Reading	Writing	Speaking and Listening	Language and Vocabulary
from **Nature** from **Self-Reliance** Ralph Waldo Emerson (pp. 216–229) Spotlight On: Emerson's Aphorisms (p. 222) Primary Sources: Hawthorne Talks About Emerson (p. 223) **Student to Student** (p. 227)	• Reader's Log pp. 218, 224 • Imagery p. 218 • Figure of Speech pp. 224, 228	• Critical Writing/Creative Writing: Write response p. 229 • Critical Writing: Explain paradoxical statements p. 229 • Critical Writing: Write extended definition p. 229 • Crossing the Curriculum: Social Studies: Write description p. 229	• Speaking and Listening: Discuss modern aphorisms in small group p. 229 • Crossing the Curriculum: Social Studies: Plan utopia with partner(s) p. 229	• Language and Style: Emerson's Figures of Speech Interpret/Explain figures of speech p. 228
from **Walden, or Life in the Woods** Henry David Thoreau (pp. 230–247) **Connections:** from **Heaven Is Under Our Feet** Don Henley (p. 245)	• Reader's Log p. 232 • Point of View p. 232	• Critical Writing: Write essay p. 247 • Critical Writing: Apply quotation to *Walden* p. 247 • Creative Writing: Write from Thoreau's point of view p. 247 • Creative Writing: Write journal entry p. 247 • Creative Writing/ Performance: Write journal entry p. 247 • Crossing the Curriculum: Science: Research nature topic p. 247	• Creative Writing/ Performance: Impersonate journal writer for class p. 247 • Crossing the Curriculum: Science: Share nature research with class p. 247	• Language and Style: Thoreau's Metaphors: Express in own words p. 246
from **Resistance to Civil Government** Henry David Thoreau (pp. 248–258) Primary Sources: "A Healthy and Wholesome Man to Know" (p. 255) **Connections:** from **Letter from Birmingham City Jail** Martin Luther King, Jr. (p. 256)	• Reader's Log p. 248 • Paradox p. 248	• Critical Writing: Write essay using emotional appeals p. 258 • Critical Writing: Write comparison/contrast essay p. 258 • Creative Writing/Drama: Write one-scene play p. 258 • Crossing the Curriculum: Social Studies: Write report on nonviolent resistance p. 258	• Creative Writing/ Drama: Perform one-scene play p. 258 • Crossing the Curriculum: Social Studies: Present report p. 258	• Language and Style: Precise Meanings of Words: Discuss differences and modern meanings p. 257

Collection Resources

Teaching Resources A	Audiovisual Resources Binder	Test Booklet
Cross-Curricular Activity p. 102	Fine Art Transparency 5.1	Collection 5 Test pp. 67–70

Computer disk or CD-ROM

Audiocassette

Overhead Transparency

PROGRAM RESOURCES

Electronic Media	Teaching Resources with Organizer: Teaching Resources A	Teaching Resources with Organizer: Other Resources	Audiovisual Resources Binder
• Language Workshop: Appositives and Appositive phrases • Test Generator	• Teaching Notes pp. 83–84 • Reading Organizer pp. 89, 93 • Language Link pp. 90–91 • Words to Own pp. 92, 94	• Test Booklet: Selection Test pp. 59–60, 61–62 • Language and Writing Skills Worksheets p. 54 • Portfolio Management System pp. 39, 94–95	• Selected Reading Audiocassette 1, Side B • Elements of Literature Transparency 5.2
• Language Workshop: Common Usage Problems 1 • Test Generator	• Teaching Notes pp. 84–85 • Reading Organizer p. 95 • Language Link pp. 96–97 • Words to Own pp. 98–99	• Test Booklet: Selection Test pp. 63–64 • Language and Writing Skills Worksheets pp. 1–3 • Portfolio Management System pp. 53, 96–97	• Selected Reading Audiocassette 1, Side B
• Test Generator	• Teaching Notes p. 86 • Reading Organizer p. 100 • Words to Own p. 101	• Test Booklet: Selection Test pp. 65–66 • Portfolio Management System pp. 54–55, 98–99	

Proofreading Warm-ups

You may use the following exercises to help students practice their proofreading skills. Copy a set of incorrect sentences onto the chalkboard, and have students find and correct the spelling, punctuation, usage, and mechanical errors in each sentence. Ask students to share and discuss their responses.

	Sentences with Errors	Sentences Corrected	Skills Covered
1	**a.** in the mid 19th century people still debated whether America would ever produce grate writing **b.** some of the early masterpieces of american literature was written then	**a.** In the mid-nineteenth century, people still debated whether America would ever produce great writing. **b.** Some of the early masterpieces of American literature were written then.	Capitalization, Hyphen usage, Spelling out numbers, Comma usage, Spelling, Subject-verb agreement, End marks
2	**a.** during the mid nineteenth Century there was intellectual ferment **b.** various utopian groups were responces to this ferment	**a.** During the mid-nineteenth century, there was intellectual ferment. **b.** Various utopian groups were responses to this ferment.	Capitalization, Hyphen usage, Comma usage, Spelling, End marks
3	**a.** emersons utopian group became known as "the transcendental club" **b.** the word transcendental comes from the german philosopher Kant	**a.** Emerson's utopian group became known as "The Transcendental Club." **b.** The word <u>transcendental</u> comes from the German philosopher Kant.	Capitalization, Apostrophe usage, Underline words used as words, End marks
4	**a.** the word transcendental refers to the idea that one must go beyond everyday experiance **b.** Transcendentalists were idealists they beleived in human perfectibility	**a.** The word <u>transcendental</u> refers to the idea that one must go beyond everyday experience. **b.** Transcendentalists were idealists; they believed in human perfectibility.	Capitalization, Underline words used as words, Spelling, Semicolon usage, End marks
5	**a.** on a trip to europe Emerson met the english romantic poet's William Wordsworth and Samuel Taylor Coleridge **b.** Emerson settled in Concord and married Lydia Jackson	**a.** On a trip to Europe, Emerson met the English Romantic poets William Wordsworth and Samuel Taylor Coleridge. **b.** Emerson settled in Concord and married Lydia Jackson.	Capitalization, Comma usage, Apostrophe usage, End marks
6	**a.** emerson to supplement a meager income begun to give public lecture's **b.** he demanded that american scholars free theirselves from the past	**a.** Emerson, to supplement a meager income, began to give public lectures. **b.** He demanded that American scholars free themselves from the past.	Capitalization, Comma usage, Verb tense, Apostrophe usage, Standard usage, End marks
7	**a.** in his book Nature Emerson uses imagery to show the reader seen's of nature that he loves **b.** Emersons image of a "transparent eyeball," is a famous passage	**a.** In his book <u>Nature</u>, Emerson uses imagery to show the reader scenes of nature that he loves. **b.** Emerson's image of a "transparent eyeball" is a famous passage.	Capitalization, Underline book titles, Comma usage, Spelling, Apostrophe usage, End marks
8	**a.** imagine building a house for $28.12 exclaimed Mrs Hebert **b.** thats what Thoreau did; when he built his house at Walden Pond she explained	**a.** "Imagine building a house for $28.12!" exclaimed Mrs. Hebert. **b.** "That's what Thoreau did when he built his house at Walden Pond," she explained.	Quotation marks, Capitalization, Exclamation point usage, Period for abbreviations, Apostrophe usage, Semi-colon usage, Comma usage, End marks
9	**a.** the movie Dead Poets Society quotes Thoreaus work Walden **b.** Walden also inspired Don Henley to found the Walden Woods Project to protect the area from real-estate dev.	**a.** The movie <u>Dead Poets Society</u> quotes Thoreau's work <u>Walden</u>. **b.** <u>Walden</u> also inspired Don Henley to found the Walden Woods Project to protect the area from real-estate development.	Capitalization, Underline movie titles, Apostrophe usage, Underline book titles, Write out abbreviations, End marks
10	**a.** thoreaus essay Resistance to Civil Gov't. has inspired many people to use civil disobedience as a means of political protest **b.** kings famous Letter explains the diffrence between just and unjust laws	**a.** Thoreau's essay "Resistance to Civil Government" has inspired many people to use civil disobedience as a means of political protest. **b.** King's famous letter explains the difference between just and unjust laws.	Capitalization, Apostrophe usage, Quotation marks, Write out abbreviations, Spelling, End marks

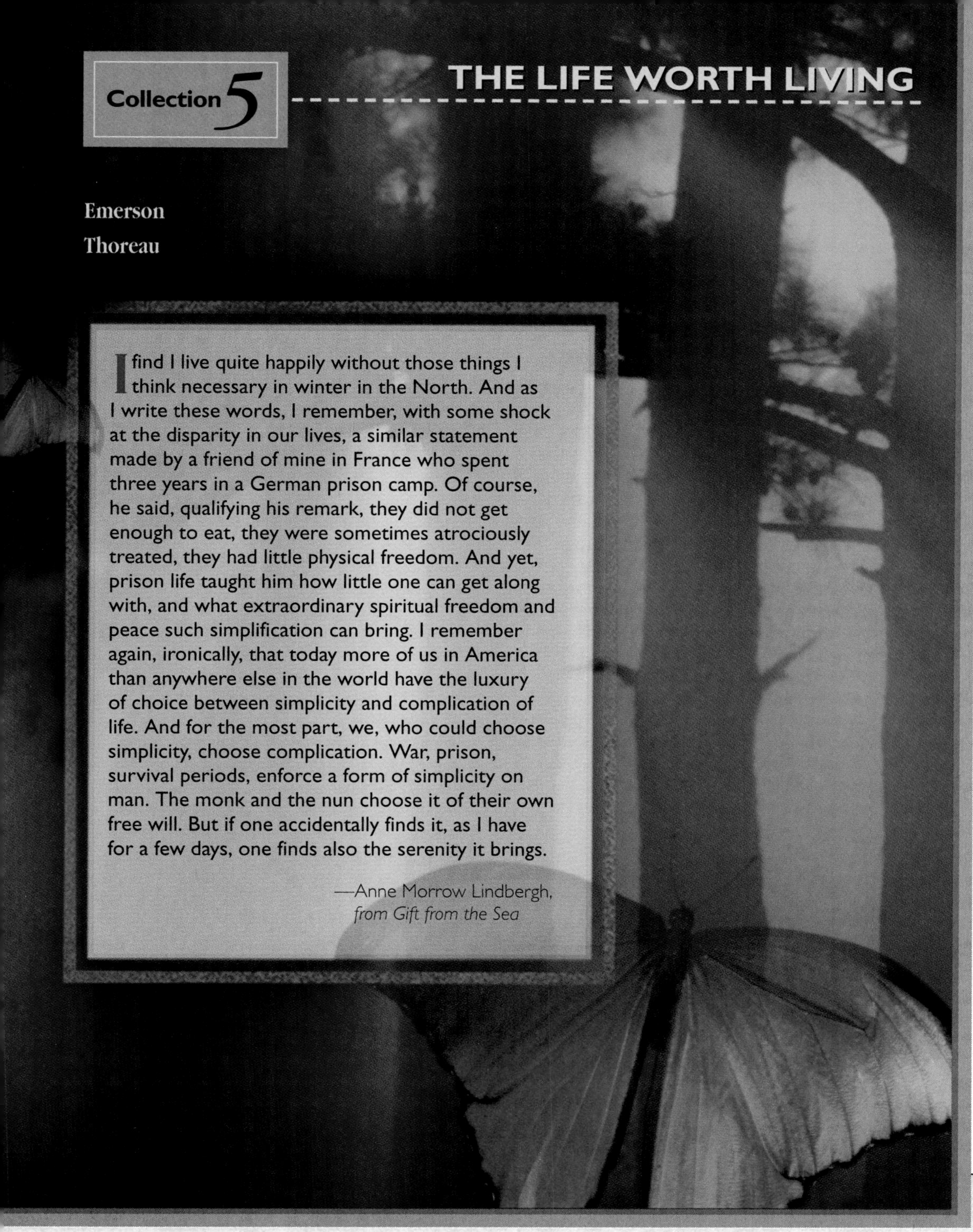

Collection 5

THE LIFE WORTH LIVING

Emerson

Thoreau

I find I live quite happily without those things I think necessary in winter in the North. And as I write these words, I remember, with some shock at the disparity in our lives, a similar statement made by a friend of mine in France who spent three years in a German prison camp. Of course, he said, qualifying his remark, they did not get enough to eat, they were sometimes atrociously treated, they had little physical freedom. And yet, prison life taught him how little one can get along with, and what extraordinary spiritual freedom and peace such simplification can bring. I remember again, ironically, that today more of us in America than anywhere else in the world have the luxury of choice between simplicity and complication of life. And for the most part, we, who could choose simplicity, choose complication. War, prison, survival periods, enforce a form of simplicity on man. The monk and the nun choose it of their own free will. But if one accidentally finds it, as I have for a few days, one finds also the serenity it brings.

—Anne Morrow Lindbergh,
from Gift from the Sea

Responding to the Quotation

? In what ways does the material world complicate lives? [Possible responses: People have to spend time taking care of possessions. They are obsessed with buying more things. They forget what is important—spending time with people, enjoying nature, or just having time to think.] Judging from this quotation, what do you think the Collection will be about? [Possible responses: Doing without, simplifying, war or prison, periods of survival.]

Parent/Guardian Involvement For forms that will help a parent or guardian review and respond to a student's portfolio, see ***Portfolio Management System,*** pp. 62–63.

PROGRAM MANAGER

- **Integrated Assessment** For a summative assessment of the literature and language skills taught in this collection, see **Collection 5 Test, *Test Booklet,*** pp. 67–70.
- **Instructional Support** See **Fine Art Transparency** 5.1. Review teacher's notes for transparencies in the ***Audiovisual Resources Binder*** for suggestions on how to tie the transparency to specific reading selections.
- **Extending Collection Theme** See **Cross-Curricular Activity: The Life Worth Living, *Teaching Resources A,*** p. 102, for activities in other disciplines and for evaluation criteria.

Ralph Waldo Emerson

(1803–1882)

Shortly before the poet Walt Whitman died, he honored a man whose ideas had influenced him profoundly throughout his own long and controversial career. "America in the future," he wrote, "in her long train of poets and writers, while knowing more vehement and luxurious ones, will, I think, acknowledge nothing nearer [than] this man, the actual beginner of the whole procession."

"This man" was Ralph Waldo Emerson. Emerson expressed, better than anyone before him, the advantages of a young land—its freedom from the old, corrupt, and dying thought and customs of Europe; its access to higher laws directly through nature rather than indirectly through books and the teachings of the past; its energy; and its opportunity to reform the world.

Emerson was one of those rare writers who appealed both to intellectuals and to the general public. His influence on the popular mind—thanks to the thousands of lectures he gave throughout the United States—was strong. Although Emerson had something of a reputation for being hard to understand, his lectures were usually quite accessible. "I had heard of him as full of transcendentalisms, myths, and oracular gibberish," Herman Melville wrote a friend after hearing Emerson lecture. "To my surprise, I found him quite intelligible." Melville added wryly, "To say truth, they told me that that night he was unusually plain."

Despite his great influence, it is difficult even to classify what kind of writer Emerson was. *Essayist* is too limited, and *philosopher* is too broad. The best term, perhaps, is *poet*—a poet whose best work was not always in verse.

"I am born a poet," Emerson wrote to his fiancée, Lydia Jackson, in 1835, "of a low class without doubt, yet a poet. That is my nature and vocation. My singing, be sure, is very 'husky,' and is for the most part in prose. Still am I a poet in the sense of a perceiver and dear lover of the harmonies that are in the soul and in matter. . . ."

The Pennsylvania Academy of the Fine Arts, Philadelphia. Gift of Horace Howard Furness (1899.8).

Ralph Waldo Emerson (c. 1867) by William Henry Furness, Jr. (1828–1867). Oil on canvas (45¾″ × 36$^{3}/_{16}$″).

The Burden of Expectation

Emerson was born in Boston in 1803 to a family that was cultured but poor. When he was only eight years old, his father, a Unitarian minister, died of tuberculosis. His mother, left with six growing children to care for, opened a boardinghouse.

The father's place in the lives of the Emerson children was taken by their aunt. Mary Moody Emerson was a strict Calvinist who emphasized self-sacrifice and whose enormous energy drove the Emerson boys to achievement. "She had the misfortune," Emerson later wrote, "of spinning with a greater velocity than any of the other tops."

Every step of Emerson's life had been laid out for him from an early age. He was to go to Harvard and become a minister like his father and the seven generations of Emersons before him. Emerson uncomfortably obeyed. His life was a series of attempts to establish his own identity against this background of expectation.

Young Rebel

Emerson entered Harvard at fourteen. He was an indifferent student, although he read widely in philosophy and theology. Upon graduation, Emerson took a job at a school run by his uncle and prepared himself, with many doubts, for the Unitarian ministry. In 1829, at the age of twenty-five, he accepted a post at Boston's Second Church; that same year, he married Ellen Tucker, a beautiful but fragile seventeen-year-old already in the early stages of tuberculosis. Seventeen months later, Ellen died.

Emerson's grief coincided with a growing disbelief in some of the central doctrines of his religion. In June 1832, he shocked his congregation by resigning the ministry and setting off on an extended tour of Europe. There he met and conversed with the Romantic poets William Wordsworth and Samuel Taylor Coleridge, as well as other influential writers.

Emerson's New Pulpit

Returning to the United States in late 1833, Emerson settled in Concord, Massachusetts, and soon married Lydia Jackson. He began to supplement his meager income by giving lectures and found in that occupation "a new pulpit," as he once wrote. Emerson's view was distinctively American in that he denied the importance of the past: "Let us unfetter ourselves of our historical associations and find a pure standard in the idea of man."

The last phrase points to Emerson's focus on humanity. Individual men and women were part of this "idea of man" in the same way that individual souls were part of a larger entity, which Emerson later called the "Over-Soul." The idea of nature also corresponded to the idea of man—both were part of a universal whole in which people could see their souls reflected.

Over the years, Emerson's influence grew. In 1837, he excited the student audience at Harvard with the lecture now known as "The American Scholar." In the speech, Emerson demanded that American scholars free themselves from the shackles of the past. "Our day of dependence," he declared, "our long apprenticeship to the learning of other lands, draws to a close."

A year later, Emerson was invited back to Harvard to speak to a group of divinity students. His speech, "The Divinity School Address," called for a rejection of institutional religion in favor of a personal relation with God. Religious truth, Emerson said, was "an intuition. It cannot be received at second hand." The lecture so outraged Harvard authorities (who heard in it a denial of the divinity of Christ) that three decades passed before Emerson was allowed to speak there again.

Twilight of an Idol

With the author's growing fame, Concord increasingly became a destination for truth-seeking young people who looked to Emerson as their guru. The young responded to Emerson's predictions that they were on the verge of a new age; intellectuals responded to his philosophical ideas about the relations among humanity, nature, and God; and society as a whole responded to his optimism.

That optimism was dealt a severe blow in 1842 when Emerson's son Waldo died of scarlet fever at the age of five. By nature a rather reserved man, Emerson had found in Waldo someone to whom he could show his love spontaneously. At the child's death, he shrank into an emotional shell from which he never emerged. "How can I hope for a friend," he wrote in his journal, "who have never been one?"

In later years, Emerson suffered from a severe loss of memory and had difficulty recalling the most ordinary words. This affliction resulted in his increasing public silence, and when he did appear in public, he read from notes. Near the end of his life, agreeing to such a performance, he remarked, "A queer occasion it will be—a lecturer who has no idea of what he is lecturing about, and an audience who don't know what he *can* mean."

In the autumn of 1881, Walt Whitman paid Emerson a visit of respect and was asked to dinner. Whitman wrote that Emerson "though a listener and apparently an alert one, remained silent through the whole talk and discussion. A lady friend [Louisa May Alcott] quietly took a seat next to him, to give special attention. A good color in his face, eyes clear, with the well-known expression of sweetness, and the old clear-peering aspect quite the same." Six months later, Emerson was dead.

ABOUT THE AUTHOR

Emerson's comfort in his life must have been his journal. Although he was not the best of students, he spent a good deal of time writing and reading when other youths were playing, hunting, or dancing. He was not clear about what profession he wished to pursue, but he daydreamed about becoming a painter. He taught school, unhappily, for three years but was good to his students and continued writing in his journal and reading challenging books. Although not an academic scholar, he was a far-sighted thinker of a different ilk. In one of his entries he even foresaw inventions to come: the phonograph and the radio.

QUICK PLANNING GUIDE

Into the Selections

Through the Selections

Beyond the Selections

Choices: Building Your Portfolio p. 229
- **Writer's Notebook:** Collect ideas for a controversial issue
- **Critical Writing/Creative Writing:** Respond in an essay, parable or poem to Emerson's aphorisms
- **Critical Writing:** Explain the meanings of paradoxes in *Nature*
- **Critical Writing:** Write an extended definition of a human quality
- **Speaking and Listening:** Create and discuss modern aphorisms
- **Crossing the Curriculum: Social Studies:** Plan a community on a map and write a description

BEFORE YOU READ

FROM NATURE

By permission of the Houghton Library, Harvard University, Cambridge, Massachusetts.

Caricature of Emerson by Christopher Pearce Cranch from *Illustrations of the New Philosophy.*

Reading Focus

Nature Nurtures

Exhilarated by nature's beauty and tranquility, Emerson felt he was in tune with his better self, in harmony with eternal things. If today we commune with nature in order to find ourselves, we may be taking up Emerson's search for "an original relation to the universe."

A Dialogue with the Text

As you read this excerpt from *Nature,* keep a double-entry journal. In one column, write down any sentences or passages that strike you, because you either agree or disagree with them or have questions about them. In the other column, write your responses to each sentence or passage.

Elements of Literature

Imagery

Emerson the poet helps out Emerson the philosopher in this essay, *showing* us scenes of nature that he loves rather than just *telling* us about his feelings in general. As you read, look for the **imagery**—descriptive language that appeals to one or more of the five senses—that Emerson uses.

> **Imagery** is the use of language to evoke a picture or concrete sensation of a person, thing, place, or an experience.
>
> *For more on Imagery, see the Handbook of Literary Terms.*

Background

In his introduction to the book *Nature,* from which the following chapter is taken, Emerson offers a clue to the underlying purpose of his work when he encourages his contemporaries to look directly at nature:

"Our age is retrospective. It builds the sepulchers of the fathers. It writes biographies, histories, and criticism. The foregoing generations beheld God and nature face to face; we, through their eyes. Why should we not also enjoy an original relation to the universe? Why should we not have a poetry and philosophy of insight and not of tradition, and a religion by revelation to us, and not the history of theirs?"

WORDS TO OWN

The following vocabulary words are defined in the Words to Own at the bottom of the pupil's page.

perpetual p. 219	integrate p. 220
sublime p. 219	slough p. 221
admonishing p. 219	perennial p. 221
manifold p. 220	blithe p. 221
indubitably p. 220	occult p. 221

PORTFOLIO ASSESSMENT

Portfolio Assessment For help with self-assessment of reading skills, see the *Portfolio Management System,* p. 39.

National Museum of American Art/Smithsonian Institution/Art Resource: Gift of Thomas M. Evans and Museum Purchase through the Smithsonian Collections Acquisition Program.

Dover Plains, Dutchess County, New York (1848) by Asher Brown Durand. Oil on canvas (42 ½″ × 60 ½″).

from Nature

Ralph Waldo Emerson

To go into solitude, a man needs to retire as much from his chamber[1] as from society. I am not solitary while I read and write, though nobody is with me. But if a man would be alone, let him look at the stars. The rays that come from those heavenly worlds, will separate between him and vulgar things. One might think the atmosphere was made transparent with this design, to give man, in the heavenly bodies, the perpetual presence of the sublime. Seen in the streets of cities, how great they are! If the stars should appear one night in a thousand years, how would men believe and adore; and preserve for many generations the remembrance of the city of God which had been shown! But every night come out these envoys of beauty, and light the universe with their admonishing smile. (A)

1. **chamber:** room.

WORDS TO OWN

perpetual (pər·pech′o͞o·əl) *adj.:* constant; unchanging.
sublime (sə·blīm′) *adj.* used as *n.:* that which inspires awe.
admonishing (ad·män′ish·iŋ) *v.* used as *adj.:* mildly warning.

Using BEFORE YOU READ p. 218

Reading Focus

Suggest students think of a time when they were alone in a natural setting. Places could include the mountains, an ocean, or a wooded area. Ask the class to talk about their experiences and about whether it is possible to have "an original relation to the universe" in the twentieth century.

Elements of Literature

Ask students to look for **imagery** of stars, the sky, and the woods and to note these images in their double-entry journals. They should indicate what senses the images appeal to and what feelings Emerson wishes to express.

A. Critical Reading: Identifying Main Ideas

Ask students to paraphrase the first paragraph. [Essentially, Emerson is merely saying that the stars are sublime.] The sentence "If the stars should appear one night in a thousand years . . ." was used by Isaac Asimov as the premise for the classic science-fiction story "Nightfall."

PROGRAM MANAGER

- **Planning Instruction** See Teaching Notes, *Teaching Resources A,* pp. 83–84, for objectives, a summary, literary elements, and information.
- **Instructional Support** See Graphic Organizer for Active Reading, *Teaching Resources A,* p. 89, for a Through the Selection activity.
- **Application and Reinforcement** For reinforcement of the elements of literature introduced in this lesson, see Transparency 5.2 in the *Audiovisual Resources Binder.*
- **Assessment** See Selection Test, *Test Booklet,* pp. 59–60.
- **Language Link** For practice in using appositives and appositive phrases, see Language Link, *Teaching Resources A,* pp. 90–91, and *Language and Writing Skills Worksheets,* p. 76.
- **Reinforcement** Use the Words to Own worksheet in *Teaching Resources A,* p. 92.

A. Reader's Response: First Thoughts

? Why does Emerson conclude that few adults can see nature? [Sample responses: Most adults cannot see nature because they have lost their innocence. Only by holding on to the spirit of infancy can someone truly see nature.]

B. Reader's Response: Challenging the Text

? Do you agree or disagree with Emerson's claim that children have a deeper wisdom than adults? Why or why not? [Sample responses: Yes, children's ability to see things has not yet been clouded by what they will learn as they grow older. Or no, adults sometimes overlook nature, but when they take the time, they see more because of their experience.]

C. Reader's Response: Challenging the Text

? Do you agree with Emerson's portrayal of nature as always benign? Why or why not? [Sample responses: Emerson overlooks hurricanes and snowstorms. This oversight may reflect his comfortable lifestyle or his view that nature can do no wrong. Or Emerson may not be thinking about radical changes in nature.]

D. Literary Element: Imagery

? To what senses do Emerson's images appeal? [Touch—the sun's warmth, crossing the snow. Sight—snow puddles, twilight.]

The stars awaken a certain reverence, because though always present, they are always inaccessible; but all natural objects make a kindred impression, when the mind is open to their influence. Nature never wears a mean appearance. Neither does the wisest man extort all her secret, and lose his curiosity by finding out all her perfection. Nature never became a toy to a wise spirit. The flowers, the animals, the mountains, reflected all the wisdom of his best hour, as much as they had delighted the simplicity of his childhood.

When we speak of nature in this manner, we have a distinct but most poetical sense in the mind. We mean the integrity of impression made by manifold natural objects. It is this which distinguishes the stick of timber of the woodcutter, from the tree of the poet. The charming landscape which I saw this morning, is indubitably made up of some twenty or thirty farms. Miller owns this field, Locke that, and Manning the woodland beyond. But none of them owns the landscape. There is a property in the horizon which no man has but he whose eye can integrate all the parts, that is, the poet. This is the best part of these men's farms, yet to this their warranty deeds[2] give no title.

To speak truly, few adult persons can see nature. Most persons do not see the sun. At least they have a very superficial seeing. The sun illuminates only the eye of the man, but shines into the eye and the heart of the child. (A) The lover of nature is he whose inward and outward senses are still truly adjusted to each other; who has retained the spirit (B) of infancy even into the era of manhood. His intercourse with heaven and earth, becomes part of his daily food. In the presence of nature, a wild delight runs through the man, in spite of real sorrows. Nature says—he is my creature, and maugre[3] all his impertinent griefs, he shall be glad with me. (C) Not the sun or the summer alone, but every hour and season yields its tribute of delight; for every hour and change corresponds to and authorizes a different state of the mind, from breathless noon to grimmest midnight. Nature is a setting that fits equally well a (D) comic or a mourning piece. In good health, the air is a cordial[4] of incredible virtue. Crossing a bare common, in snow puddles, at twilight, under a clouded sky, without having in my thoughts any occurrence of special good fortune, I have enjoyed a perfect exhilaration. Almost I fear to think how glad I am. In the woods too, a man casts off his years,

2. **warranty deeds:** legal documents showing ownership of property.
3. **maugre** (mô′gər): archaic for "in spite of" or "despite."
4. **cordial** (kôr′jəl): a liquor that stimulates the heart.

WORDS TO OWN

manifold (man′ə·fōld′) *adj.:* many different.
indubitably (in·do͞o′bi·tə·blē) *adv.:* without a doubt.
integrate (in′tə·grāt′) *v.:* unify.

OPTIONS FOR TEACHING

STRATEGIES FOR INCLUSION

English Language Development Before they read, have students discuss the following questions: How do you feel when you look at the stars? What other aspects of nature might elicit similar emotions? After they read, and after you have gone over Emerson's main points, have them compare their prereading responses with Emerson's ideas.

Special Needs To help students understand the meaning of **paradox,** have each student make up a paradox from his or her own life. Examples:

- surrounded by water but not a drop to drink
- lots of money but cannot buy love
- with a group, but lonely

Writing their own paradoxes will help students comprehend Emerson's paradoxes and the selection itself. Have them keep a list of paradoxes as they study both Emerson and Thoreau.

INTEGRATING THE LANGUAGE ARTS

Strategic Reading Have students make a chart with two columns. After they read the first sentence of the selection, have students write in column one their predictions of what Emerson will say about nature. In column two they will write what he actually says.

My Prediction	Actual Outcome
[He won't be alone in nature.]	[He is part of the Universal Being.]

as the snake his slough, and at what period soever of life, is always a child. In the woods, is perpetual youth. Within these plantations of God, a decorum and sanctity reign, a perennial festival is dressed, and the guest sees not how he should tire of them in a thousand years. In the woods, we return to reason and faith. There I feel that nothing can befall me in life—no disgrace, no calamity, (leaving me my eyes,) which nature cannot repair. Standing on the bare ground—my head bathed by the blithe air, and uplifted into infinite space—all mean egotism vanishes. I become a transparent eyeball. I am nothing. I see all. The currents of the Universal Being circulate through me; I am part or particle of God. The name of the nearest friend sounds then foreign and accidental. To be brothers, to be acquaintances—master or servant, is then a trifle and a disturbance. I am the lover of uncontained and immortal beauty. In the wilderness, I find something more dear and connate[5] than in streets or villages. In the tranquil landscape, and especially in the distant line of the horizon, man beholds somewhat[6] as beautiful as his own nature. **E**

The greatest delight which the fields and woods minister, is the suggestion of an occult relation between man and the vegetable. I am not alone and unacknowledged. They nod to me and I to them. The waving of the boughs in the storm, is new to me and old. It takes me by surprise, and yet is not unknown. Its effect is like that of a higher thought or a better emotion coming over me, when I deemed I was thinking justly or doing right. **F**

Yet it is certain that the power to produce this delight, does not reside in nature, but in man, or in a harmony of both. It is necessary to use these pleasures with great temperance. For, nature is not always tricked[7] in holiday attire, but the same scene which yesterday breathed perfume and glittered as for the frolic of the nymphs, is overspread with melancholy today. Nature always wears the colors of the spirit. To a man laboring under calamity, the heat of his own fire hath sadness in it. Then, there is a kind of contempt of the landscape felt by him who has just lost by death a dear friend. The sky is less grand as it shuts down over less worth in the population. **G**

5. **connate:** inborn.
6. **somewhat:** something.
7. **tricked:** dressed up.

Words to Own

slough (sluf) *n.:* outer layer of a snake's skin, which is shed periodically.
perennial (pər·en′ē·əl) *adj.:* recurring yearly.
blithe (blīth) *adj.:* carefree.
occult (ə·kult′) *adj.:* hidden.

E. Reader's Response: Shaping Interpretations

? Do you find it contradictory that in the same breath Emerson says, "all mean egotism vanishes," and "I see all. The currents of the Universal Being circulate through me"? [Sample responses: There is no contradiction. He means that he has become part of something far greater than himself. Or it is contradictory, because he has the Universal Being circulate through himself. That is egoism.]

F. Literary Element: Personification

? In what ways does Emerson personify nature? [Nature has an "occult" or hidden relationship with people. It nods, waves, and takes by surprise.] What is the effect of this personification? [Possible answer: Interaction with nature on a personal level promotes a higher level of thought and emotion.]

G. Critical Reading: Metacognition

? How did you get the meaning of the last paragraph? [Possible answers: I went back over each sentence after I read the whole paragraph. I tried to find examples in my own life to compare to what Emerson was saying.]

Crossing the Curriculum

Fine Arts Have students locate pieces of art illustrating the various ways artists see one element of nature, such as fields or woods. Have them present the artwork and describe how the artists respond to nature.

Science Emerson refers to many aspects of the natural world: the stars, the sun, changing seasons, air, clouds, woods, fields, and changes in weather. Have students pick one aspect and study it. Students should not only conduct research on it but also observe it in nature and record their thoughts and discoveries in a daily log for one week. Ask students to share their findings in class.

Assessment Tools

Check Test: True-False

1. Emerson writes that people look at the stars each night with the same wonder they would if the stars appeared only once in a thousand years. [False]
2. Emerson feels most adults do not delight in nature as much as children do. [True]
3. According to Emerson, most people see nature only superficially. [True]
4. Emerson believes that in nature there is perpetual age. [False]
5. Emerson asserts we will see that there is a hidden relationship between ourselves and the natural world. [True]

A. Exploring the Historical Period
Following the War of 1812, the country began to expand, adding new states. A whole generation had now been born in the United States.

B. Reader's Response: Extending the Text
? If Emerson were alive today, do you think he would still believe this aphorism? Why? [Sample responses: Yes, people who have any kind of weapon still have the potential to be dangerous. No, people are learning not to put out each other's eyes.]

C. Literary Element: Simile
? Why are similes well suited for aphorisms? [The use of similes help writers take a big idea and explain it in a few words.]

Technology Tip

Ask students how we might also say "Computers are the best of things, well used; abused, among the worst." Ask them whether the same could be said of television.

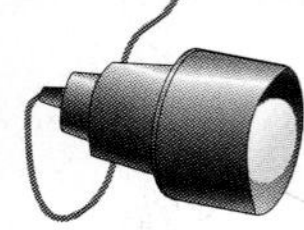

SPOTLIGHT ON

Emerson's Aphorisms

A Study Table (1882) by William Harnett. Oil on canvas ($39\frac{7}{8}'' \times 51\frac{3}{8}''$).

Munson-Williams-Proctor Institute Museum of Art, Utica, New York.

Studded throughout Emerson's work are quotable, memorable sayings on broad topics such as poetry, religion, and the nature of humankind. These are **aphorisms**—short statements that express wise or clever observations about life. (Aphorisms are also called "maxims" or "adages.") Try paraphrasing Emerson's aphorisms in your own words: You'll see how much meaning the writer has packed into a few words. That, of course, is what makes an aphorism memorable.

Many of Emerson's aphorisms originated in the journal he began keeping when he was a junior in college; by the end of his life, it filled many volumes.

(A) I confess I am a little cynical on some topics, and when a whole nation is roaring Patriotism at the top of its voice, I am fain[1] to explore the cleanness of its hands and purity of its heart. I have generally found the gravest and most useful citizens are not the easiest provoked to swell the noise, though they may be punctual at the polls.

—*Journals*, 1824

(B) Don't trust children with edge tools. Don't trust man, great God, with more power than he has, until he has learned to use that little better. What a hell should we make of the world if we could do what we would! Put a button on the foil[2] till the young fencers have learned not to put each other's eyes out.

—*Journals*, 1832

The maker of a sentence, like the other artist, launches out into the infinite and builds a road into Chaos and old Night, and is followed by those who hear him with something of wild, creative delight.

—*Journals*, 1834

(C) Poetry must be as new as foam and as old as the rock.

—*Journals*, 1844

1. **fain:** obliged.

2. **foil:** sword.

The invariable mark of wisdom is to see the miraculous in the common.

—*Nature*

A man is a god in ruins.

—*Nature*

Nothing can bring you peace but yourself. Nothing can bring you peace but the triumph of principles.

—"Self-Reliance"

Prayer as a means to effect a private end is meanness and theft. It supposes dualism and not a unity in nature and consciousness. As soon as the man is at one with God, he will not beg. He will then see prayer in all action.

—"Self-Reliance"

This time, like all times, is a very good one, if we but know what to do with it.

—"The American Scholar"

Books are the best of things, well used; abused, among the worst.

—"The American Scholar"

Public and private avarice make the air we breathe thick and fat.

—"The American Scholar"

OPTIONS FOR TEACHING

STRATEGIES FOR INCLUSION

Intrapersonal Have students read the aphorisms to determine which ones ring true according to their own experiences. Ask them to write the aphorisms in their Reader's Logs and to explain their choices. Ask them to turn their responses in to you.

Special Needs Place each of Emerson's aphorisms on a small strip of paper. Have pairs of students choose one to present to the class—showing its meaning either through a dramatic, visual, or oral presentation.

INTEGRATING THE LANGUAGE ARTS

Strategic Reading Have students work in groups of three to determine what Emerson implies about people in his aphorisms. Have students use the following chart to identify what he says and what he implies.

Says	Implies
[The whole nation is talking about patriotism.]	[Truly patriotic people show their patriotism by voting, not by boasting or talking.]

Language and Style Have students make a list of similes and metaphors about people, their class, poetry, and books. Discuss any similarities and differences between their comparisons and Emerson's.

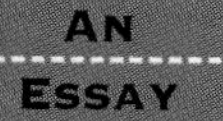

Primary Sources | An Essay

Hawthorne Talks About Emerson

Emerson, who thought of sin as merely a child's case of measles on the world, and Nathaniel Hawthorne, who plumbed the nature of evil, could never talk together. For a time, Hawthorne lived at Brook Farm, a self-governing, experimental community of Transcendentalists, founded by the minister George Ripley. But he left after a few months, finding the high-minded discussions stifling. Hawthorne then lived for a time in a house called the Old Manse in Concord, the same house where Emerson had written his first book, *Nature*. Here, in a passage from his essay called "The Old Manse," Hawthorne talks about Emerson and the "hobgoblins" who came to Concord seeking answers to the riddle of the world.

These hobgoblins of flesh and blood were attracted thither by the widespreading influence of a great original thinker, who had his earthly abode at the opposite extremity of our village. His mind acted upon other minds of a certain constitution with wonderful magnetism, and drew many men upon long pilgrimages to speak with him face to face. Young visionaries—to whom just so much of insight had been imparted as to make life all a labyrinth[1] around them—came to seek the clue that should guide them out of their self-involved bewilderment. Gray-headed theorists—whose systems, at first air, had finally imprisoned them in an iron framework—traveled painfully to his door, not to ask deliverance, but to invite the free spirit into their own thralldom.[2] People that had lighted on a new thought, or a thought that they fancied new, came to Emerson, as the finder of a glittering gem hastens to a lapidary,[3] to ascertain its quality and value. Uncertain, troubled, earnest wanderers through the midnight of the moral world beheld his intellectual fire as a beacon burning on a hilltop, and, climbing the difficult ascent, looked forth into the surrounding obscurity more hopefully than hitherto. The light revealed objects unseen before—mountains, gleaming lakes, glimpses of a creation among the chaos; but also, as was unavoidable, it attracted bats and owls and the whole host of night birds, which flapped their dusky wings against the gazer's eyes, and sometimes were mistaken for fowls of angelic feather. Such delusions always hover nigh whenever a beacon-fire of truth is kindled.

For myself, there had been epochs of my life when I, too, might have asked of this prophet the master word that should solve me the riddle of the universe; but now, being happy, I felt as if there were no question to be put, and therefore admired Emerson as a poet of deep beauty and austere tenderness, but sought nothing from him as a philosopher. It was good, nevertheless, to meet him in the wood paths, or sometimes in our avenue, with that pure, intellectual gleam diffused about his presence like the garment of a shining one; and he so quiet, so simple, so without pretension, encountering each man alive as if expecting to receive more than he could impart. And, in truth, the heart of many an ordinary man had, perchance, inscriptions which he could not read. But it was impossible to dwell in his vicinity without inhaling more or less the mountain atmosphere of his lofty thought, which, in the brains of some people, wrought a singular giddiness—new truth being as heady as new wine. Never was a poor little country village infested with such a variety of queer, strangely dressed, oddly behaved mortals, most of whom took upon themselves to be important agents of the world's destiny, yet were simply bores of a very intense water. . . .

—Nathaniel Hawthorne,
from "The Old Manse"

1. **labyrinth:** maze.
2. **thralldom:** servitude.
3. **lapidary:** gem dealer.

Primary Sources

Hawthorne was happy because he had recently married Sophia Peabody. They were both extremely retiring by nature, so the courtship was a rather awkward one, but they were both ecstatic about the results. Referring to the accidental nature of their courtship, Hawthorne etched Sophia's words on a windowpane in the Manse with her ring: "Man's accidents are God's purposes"—in itself an aphorism worthy of Emerson.

STRATEGIES FOR INCLUSION

Less Proficient Readers To help students see the differences between Emerson and his visitors that Hawthorne points out, have them list in a chart like the following the characteristics of those who came to visit Emerson and of Emerson himself.

Visitors	Emerson
[Doubtful, anxious]	[Quiet, simple]

Linguistic Before they read "Hawthorne Talks About Emerson," have students write an account of a time when they sought advice from another person. *Remind students to choose a situation they would not mind sharing with others.* Ask volunteers to read their accounts to the class. After they read their accounts and "Hawthorne Talks About Emerson," ask students to share how their accounts are similar to or different from Hawthorne's.

Into the Selection

Using Before You Read p. 224

Reading Focus

Remind students that in order to live on what was considered a wild continent, Americans emphasized individual survival. Strong faith in oneself and a creed of self-reliance assisted people during hard times. Ask students to list reasons the new country needed such a creed.

PROGRAM MANAGER

- **Planning Instruction** See Teaching Notes, *Teaching Resources A,* p. 84, for objectives, a summary, literary elements, and additional information for this selection.
- **Instructional Support** See Graphic Organizer for Active Reading, *Teaching Resources A,* p. 93, for a Through the Selection activity.
- **Audiotaped Readings** To help learners through the lesson, use the Selected Reading, Audiocassette 1, Side B in the *Audiovisual Resources Binder.*
- **Instructional Support** See Fine Art Transparency 5.1. Review teacher's notes for transparencies in the *Audiovisual Resources Binder* for teaching suggestions.
- **Assessment** See Selection Test, *Test Booklet,* pp. 61–62.
- **Reinforcement** Use the Words to Own worksheet in *Teaching Resources A,* p. 94.

Before You Read

FROM **SELF-RELIANCE**

Reading Focus

Rugged Individualism

For Americans in the early years of the country's history, belonging to a bold, young nation was a tremendous source of group pride. Perhaps the greatest source of that pride was the high value the group placed on individual liberty. In 1841, Emerson responded to this creed of individualism in the culture around him and nourished it with his essay "Self-Reliance."

Quickwrite

READER'S LOG

Write down the associations you make with the word *self-reliance:* definitions, examples, and synonyms. How does self-reliance differ from selfishness or self-centeredness?

Elements of Literature

Figures of Speech

Emerson makes many of his points through a series of **figures of speech** that compare abstract ideas with ordinary things or events, such as "Society is a joint-stock company."

A **figure of speech** is a word or phrase that describes one thing in terms of another and is not meant to be taken literally.

For more on Figures of Speech, see page 78 and the Handbook of Literary Terms.

Long Island Farmer Husking Corn (1833–1834) by William Sidney Mount. Oil on canvas mounted on panel ($20\frac{7}{8}'' \times 16\frac{7}{8}''$).

The Museums at Stony Brook, Stony Brook, New York, Gift of Mr. & Mrs. Ward Melville.

from Self-Reliance

Ralph Waldo Emerson

WORDS TO OWN

The following vocabulary words are defined in the Words to Own at the bottom of the pupil's page.

conviction p. 225	transcendent p. 225
proportionate p. 225	benefactors p. 225
imparted p. 225	conspiracy p. 225
manifest p. 225	aversion p. 225
predominating p. 225	integrity p. 225

There is a time in every man's education . . . when he arrives at the conviction that envy is ignorance; that imitation is suicide; that he must take himself for better, for worse, as his portion; that though the wide universe is full of good, no kernel of nourishing corn can come to him but through his toil bestowed on that plot of ground which is given to him to till. The power which resides in him is new in nature, and none but he knows what that is which he can do, nor does he know until he has tried. Not for nothing one face, one character, one fact makes much impression on him, and another none. This sculpture in the memory is not without preestablished harmony. **(A)** The eye was placed where one ray should fall, that it might testify of that particular ray. We but half express ourselves, and are ashamed of that **(B)** divine idea which each of us represents. It may be safely trusted as proportionate and of good issues, so it be faithfully imparted, but God will not have his work made manifest by cowards. A man is relieved and gay when he has put his heart into his work and done his best; but what he has said or done otherwise, shall give him no peace. It is a deliverance which does not deliver. In the attempt his genius deserts him; no muse befriends; no invention, no hope.

Trust thyself: Every heart vibrates to that iron string. Accept the place the divine Providence has **(C)** found for you; the society of your contemporaries, the connection of events. Great men have always done so and confided themselves childlike to the genius of their age, betraying their perception that the absolutely trustworthy was seated at their heart, working through their hands, predominating in all their being. And we are now men, and must accept in the highest mind the same transcendent destiny; and not minors and invalids in a protected corner, not cowards fleeing before a revolution, but guides, redeemers, and benefactors, obeying the Almighty effort, and advancing on Chaos and the Dark. . . .

These are the voices which we hear in solitude, but they grow faint and inaudible as we enter into the world. Society everywhere is in conspiracy against the manhood of every one of its members. Society is a joint-stock company in which the members agree for the better securing of his bread to each shareholder, to surrender the liberty and culture of the eater. The virtue in most request is conformity. Self-reliance is its aversion. It loves not realities and creators, but names and customs.

Whoso would be a man must be a nonconformist. He who would gather immortal palms[1] must not be hindered by the name of goodness, but must explore if it be goodness. Nothing is at last sacred but the integrity of your own mind. Absolve you to yourself, and you shall have the suffrage of the world. . . .

A foolish consistency is the hobgoblin of little minds, adored by little statesmen and philosophers and divines. With consistency a great soul has simply nothing to do. He may as well concern himself with his shadow on the wall. Speak what you think now in hard words, and tomorrow speak what tomorrow thinks in hard words again, though it contradict everything you said today—"Ah, so you shall be sure to be misunderstood"—Is it so bad then to be misunderstood? Pythagoras was misunderstood, and Socrates, and Jesus, and Luther, and Copernicus, and Galileo, and Newton,[2] and every pure and wise spirit that ever took flesh. To be great is to be misunderstood. . . .

1. **he who . . . immortal palms:** he who would win fame. In ancient times, palm leaves were carried as a symbol of victory or triumph.
2. **Pythagoras . . . Newton:** people whose contributions to scientific, philosophical, and religious thought were ignored or suppressed during their lifetimes.

Words to Own

conviction (kən·vik′shən) *n.:* belief.
proportionate (prō·pôr′shən·it) *adj.:* having a correct relationship between parts; balanced.
imparted (im·pärt′əd) *v.:* revealed.
manifest (man′ə·fest′) *adj.:* plain; clear.
predominating (prē·däm′ə·nāt′iŋ) *v.* used as *adj.:* having influence.
transcendent (tran·sen′dənt) *adj.:* excelling; surpassing.
benefactors (ben′ə·fak′tərz) *n. pl.:* people who help others.
conspiracy (kən·spir′ə·sē) *n.:* secret plot with a harmful or illegal purpose.
aversion (ə·vur′zhən) *n.:* intense dislike.
integrity (in·teg′rə·tē) *n.:* sound moral principles; honesty.

Through the Selection

A. Literary Element: Figures of Speech

? What does Emerson mean by "this sculpture in the memory"? [Possible answers: He seems to be saying that some people, events, or facts seem familiar when you first meet them, almost as if the people or facts were known or the event had already happened. Or people we encounter may remind us of other people we already know.]

B. Critical Reading: Expressing an Opinion

? Do you agree that people only half express themselves? Why or why not? [Possible answers: Yes, people are too afraid to express themselves fully because of what society might think. Or no, people express themselves fully; in some cases their expression disturbs the rights of others.]

C. Reader's Response: Challenging the Text

Emerson implies that greatness comes not so much through striving as through acceptance of one's fate. Do you agree? Why or why not? [Sample responses: No, greatness means fame, not just doing one's best. Or yes, there is greatness in doing something well, even if it is cleaning the house.]

Options for Teaching

Integrating the Language Arts

Strategic Reading To better equip students with an understanding of "Self-Reliance," have them make a three-column chart as shown. Students should fill in the columns with textual information and notes from classroom discussion.

Self-Reliance

Emerson's Beliefs	Text References	Class Discussion
[Good comes only to those who work.]	["though the wide universe . . ."]	[Feel self-esteem when working]

Cooperative Learning

Misunderstood People Divide the class into seven groups, and have each group research one of the seven people listed in the last paragraph of the selection on p. 225. Each student in the group should research a different accomplishment or age range in the person's life. Have each group explain to the class why they think Emerson chose these seven to illustrate his phrase: "To be great is to be misunderstood." One student could be elected by each group to act as spokesperson, or different group members could report on what they discovered individually.

LITERATURE AND SOCIETY

Place students in groups of four. Have each group choose and conduct research on one of the utopian societies mentioned in "Onward to Utopia." Have each group come to a consensus on whether such a society could exist today. Ask groups to report their findings to the class and to explain whether the utopia could succeed.

Technology Tip

Invite a history teacher to your classroom to discuss the social events of Emerson's day, especially utopian reform. Have the class discuss how the history of the period relates to the excerpt from "Self-Reliance." Videotape the conversation for use with other classes.

Literature and Society

Onward to Utopia

For thousands of years people have tried to create utopias—communities that reflect a particular philosophy of how to live. The word *utopia,* based on a Greek word meaning both "no place" and "good place," originated during the Renaissance. From Pythagoras and Plato in ancient Greece to Thomas More in sixteenth-century England to the commune experiments of the 1960s, men and women have experimented with utopian communities.

Emerson was in the thick of 1830s utopian reform. The utopian group that met in each other's homes starting in 1836 became known as "The Transcendental Club" and included a wide range of members and beliefs. Besides Emerson, there was George Ripley, founder of Brook Farm in Massachusetts, a self-governing experimental community that survived for six years and was home briefly to Nathaniel Hawthorne. There was Bronson Alcott, a radical educator who co-founded the community Fruitlands and was the father of Louisa May Alcott (author of *Little Women*). And there was Margaret Fuller, an influential feminist and critic, who edited the Transcendentalist publication *The Dial.*

Why did utopian communities flourish in the United States during the mid–nineteenth century? For one thing, it was a time of great uncertainty and change as citizens struggled with slavery, the oppression of women, the genocide of American Indians, and the dehumanizing effects of industrialization. Rebelling against the status quo, utopian communities tried to create prosperous and harmonious environments. Many were religious communities founded on ideals of nonviolence and communal ownership, and some were transplants from Europe: The Shaker communities, founded by Ann Lee, got their start in England about 1772. In many utopian communities, African Americans and women could find more equality than in society at large. In fact, many utopian societies were founded by women.

Community members often had to abide by rules that were, to put it mildly, extreme. At Fruitlands, the short-lived vegetarian community established by Bronson Alcott, residents were permitted to eat only vegetables that grew up toward heaven—no root vegetables such as carrots and potatoes were allowed! They also did not take milk from cows or wool from sheep, nor would they use animals to pull plows.

Most utopian ventures failed within a few years; as the Transcendentalists of Brook Farm discovered, innovative thinkers aren't necessarily willing or successful farmers. But several utopian communities did endure for decades, and some—the Shakers, the Oneida Community, and the Amana Church Society—not only still exist but also are widely known for products they produce, from furniture to flatware. In all, more than 100,000 Americans participated in utopian communities in the nineteenth century, hoping to enjoy healthy, productive, and harmonious lives.

OPTIONS FOR TEACHING

PROBLEM SOLVING/ CRITICAL THINKING

Minority Views Have groups of four discuss the importance of the minority view in a civilized society and how it can inform the majority's opinion. Groups should consider past or current minority views. For example, the need of the minority to have more equal access to education led to the movement for school desegregation. In turn, this helped the majority see the need for providing equal opportunity for all. Have the groups brainstorm ideas. Ask the groups to report their findings to the class.

ASSESSMENT TOOLS

Check Test: True-False

1. Emerson believes envy of others is "ignorance." [True]
2. Emerson feels we must trust ourselves and accept the place providence has found for us. [True]
3. According to Emerson, to be great is to be understood by those around you. [False]
4. Emerson says we should speak in "hard words" even if we contradict ourselves. [True]
5. According to Emerson, we should listen to our intuition before the wisdom of sages from our past. [True]

Imagination

A personal response to Ralph Waldo Emerson's essay, "Self-Reliance"

Imagine a flower growing in a garden. Create the surroundings—perhaps a brook or a tree, possibly a butterfly nearby. Picture the tranquility of the scene. Now color the sky and the grasses. (A) What color will your flower be? Red? White? Yellow? Did you choose that color because it was that of a flower you had seen somewhere in nature or in a painting? Did you color your flower according to accepted values—a red rose, a yellow daffodil, a white lily—laid down years ago by other artists or nature itself? Now close your eyes for a moment and visualize a brilliant purple rose in your garden. What do you think? Is that flower wrong? Many people would think a purple rose silly, the product of an ignorant child, perhaps. They would tell you that roses can't possibly be purple—everybody knows that! And yet, who can say that an idea is wrong? A purple rose. Think: If the world accepted only "normal" visions, nothing new would ever be created. No one would dare stray from the "luster of the firmaments laid down by bards and sages." There would be no imagination, no fantasy, no chimerical creatures.

Imagine a great arch, soaring into the heavens—a "firmament," if you will, of "bards and sages." People of long ago built this arch, strengthening it with their ideas, extending the graceful curve until it once again touched the ground. They cherished their arch and nurtured it with fancy and imagination. The keystone proclaimed in scripted letters: "Imagine! From a gleam in the darkness can a new world be created!" The arch shone in the sunlight, ethereal and majestic. Then, the imagination stopped—people condemned fanciful inventions and the people who imagined them. People closed their minds, determined to preserve the old way of thinking as the only correct way. Relinquishing their creativity, they discarded their visions in favor of "normality," the way things "should be." Slowly, the arch crumbled. (B) With no imagination to sustain its graceful form, it grew weaker and weaker, eventually vanishing altogether. As it faded into people's memories, their universe, too, shrank quietly, until they realized that they had nothing left; every object had its "normal" shape, size, and color.

And so they sit, clutching their red roses, amidst the remains of their imagination. (C)

—Shelby Pearl, James Madison High School, Vienna, Virginia

A. Literary Element: Style

? In what ways does Pearl draw readers into the essay? [Through the use of the imperative, calling upon the imagination, and the use of imagery.]

B. Reader's Response: First Thoughts

? Why do you think people cling to older ways of thinking? [Sample responses: They fear something new and different because they may not be able to change. Or they may wield power through the older ways and may not wish to give up that power.]

C. Critical Reading: Expressing an Opinion

? At what stage are people today imagining the arch or allowing it to fade into memory? [Possible answers: It is fading because people are still afraid of anything new. Or the arch is being rebuilt as people are looking for new ways to solve old problems.]

CONNECTING WITH "SELF-RELIANCE"

Shelby Pearl takes the artistic process and applies it to self-reliant thought. She reveres the imagination, the power that lives in humankind, according to Emerson. Have students discuss what other processes would be inhibited if people did not use their imagination. Emerson notes that society will not progress if people conform to outmoded thought. Pearl shows, through an extended metaphor, what happens to a society that conforms. Ask students to discuss what can happen to society when people sit in the ruins of their imagination, when they fail to rely on the integrity of their own minds.

Making Meanings from Nature

First Thoughts

1. Possible responses: It is possible to have a mystical relationship with nature. Many people today go on retreats and spend a lot of time in healthful solitude. People can be close to nature on trips to parks, on a bike ride, or sitting outside.

Reviewing the Text

Possible response: "To go into solitude, a man needs to retire as much from his chamber as from society." If you are going to be really alone, do not just leave your family and home; leave people and the material world.

Shaping Interpretations

2. Possible response: People might be awestruck by the sight. They would believe in and adore God, and they would preserve for many generations the memory of the stars as showing the "city of God." People do not spend enough time admiring nature's beauty.
3. Emerson means "the integrity of impression made by manifold natural objects." He refers to an imaginative sense of looking at nature directly, in all its beauty and wholeness. Emerson says that while a woodcutter will see a stack of timber, a poet will see a tree; while an ordinary person will see a collection of farms, the poet will see them as an entire landscape, bounded by the horizon.
4. He becomes "part or particle of God" when his own ego vanishes. Then he becomes the transparent eyeball, seeing all. The Universal Being circulates through him. God is spirit; therefore, only by becoming spirit-like or "transparent" and transcending the physical world can one really see nature.
5. God is found in the perfect harmony between people and nature.

Connecting with the Text

6. Possible responses: Children take joy in nature and do not try to control it. Or as people grow older, their lives become clouded with the drive for material goods, and they lose direct contact with nature.

MAKING MEANINGS

from **Nature**

First Thoughts

1. Look back over your Reader's Log entries, and discuss passages that struck you. Do you think it's possible for people today to achieve the kind of mystical relationship with nature that Emerson describes? Why or why not?

Reviewing the Text

What three or four sentences from the essay do you think express Emerson's most crucial points? Rewrite each sentence in your own words.

Shaping Interpretations

2. How would our attitude toward the stars change if they appeared only once every thousand years? What point is Emerson making about nature with this attention-getting example?
3. What do you think Emerson means by a "poetical sense" of looking at nature? What **images** illustrate the distinction between nature used for practical benefits and nature viewed in this poetic way?
4. Emerson's **image** of a "transparent eyeball" in the fourth paragraph is one of the most famous passages in all of his works. How is this image a description of a visionary experience of God?
5. Describe the relation presented, starting in the fourth paragraph, between people, nature, and God. According to Emerson, is God to be found only in nature, only in people, or in some elements they share?

Connecting with the Text

6. "To speak truly," Emerson says, "few adult persons can see nature." Emerson sees children as having the advantage over adults when it comes to having a direct experience of nature. Do you agree with Emerson? What do people seem to lose as they grow older?

from **Self-Reliance**

First Thoughts

1. Re-read the associations you made with self-reliance in your Reader's Log. How does your definition compare with Emerson's reflections?

Reviewing the Text

a. According to the second paragraph, what is the destiny of every human being?
b. What is the opposite of self-reliance?

Shaping Interpretations

2. What do you think Emerson means by "that divine idea which each of us represents" (paragraph 1)?
3. What does Emerson think of people who call for consistency in thought and action and who fear being misunderstood?

Connecting with the Text

4. Do you think there's too little, too much, or just the right amount of emphasis on individualism in our society today? What might Emerson have thought about our focus on the individual?
5. If this essay were to be delivered as a political address during a presidential campaign today, how do you think people would respond?

LANGUAGE AND STYLE

Emerson's Figures of Speech

In "Self-Reliance," Emerson makes many of his points through a series of **figures of speech**—comparisons between two things that are basically unlike each other.

1. What does Emerson compare with these ordinary things and events: planting corn, an iron string, a joint-stock company, a shadow on the wall? Interpret each figure of speech.
2. Explain what Emerson means by the famous **metaphor** that opens the final paragraph. What exactly does he mean by the following terms: a "hobgoblin," a "little mind," a "foolish consistency"? What do you think Emerson would consider a "wise" consistency?

from "Self-Reliance"

First Thoughts

1. Possible responses: Emerson's definition reaches much further. His trusting yourself is similar to my listening to yourself.

Reviewing the Text

a. Every person must accept the place that providence has accorded.
b. The opposite of self-reliance is conformity—bowing to the pressures of society.

Shaping Interpretations

2. The potential in each of us for expression and fulfillment.
3. He calls them old and urges us to ignore them, even though they may misunderstand.

Connecting with the Text

4. Possible responses: There is too much emphasis on the individual; we have lost the ability to consider the needs of each other and of society at large. Or there is not enough emphasis on the individual; we are giving up too many

CHOICES: Building Your Portfolio

Writer's Notebook

1. Collecting Ideas for a Controversial Issue

Brainstorm a list of controversial issues that people debate and disagree about. Write down as many topics as you can possibly think of—don't censor yourself. Keep your notes; you may use them later in the Writer's Workshop on page 331.

WORK IN PROGRESS

Critical Writing / Creative Writing

2. Wisdom in a Nutshell

On page 227, you'll find a student response to this statement from another portion of Emerson's "Self-Reliance": "A man should learn to detect and watch that gleam of light which flashes across his mind from within, more than the luster of the firmament of bards and sages." Write your own response in the form of an essay, **fable,** or poem (about one page long) to one of the following statements from Emerson:

a. "Envy is ignorance."
b. "Trust thyself: Every heart vibrates to that iron string."
c. "To be great is to be misunderstood."
d. "A foolish consistency is the hobgoblin of little minds."

Critical Writing

3. Positively Paradoxical

Emerson was fond of using **paradox,** the linking of seemingly contradictory elements (as in the line from *Romeo and Juliet:* "Parting is such sweet sorrow"). Read the following sentences from *Nature,* and write a brief explanation of the meaning of each paradox. End your explanation with an expression of each statement in your own words.

a. "I am not solitary while I read and write, though nobody is with me."
b. "But every night come out these envoys of beauty, and light the universe with their admonishing smile."
c. "Most persons do not see the sun."
d. "Almost I fear to think how glad I am."

Critical Writing

4. A Definitive Definition

"Self-Reliance" is one long definition. But Emerson's definition of self-reliance is fuller, more thought-provoking, more poetic, more personal, and less exact than a dictionary definition. Write a one- or two-paragraph **extended definition** of a human quality that you feel is valuable or important. Like Emerson, you might want to begin with a hook, an attention-grabbing introduction.

Speaking and Listening

5. Sage Sayings

With a small group of classmates, brainstorm a list of modern **aphorisms:** lines from popular songs or political speeches, things you've read, things you've heard in conversation, things you yourself have said or thought—even sayings from bumper stickers or T-shirts. Have one member of the group write down the sayings. As a group, interpret and briefly discuss each entry. What do these sayings tell you about the values of modern society? Compare and contrast them with Emerson's values.

Crossing the Curriculum: Social Studies

6. Inventing Utopia

With one or more partners, make a plan for a community based on the ideals you've found in Emerson. Give the community a name, and decide on a geographical setting for it. What kind of government would the community have? What would be its economic base? What would be the attractions of life in this community? What would the population be? What problems would the community face? Finally, draw a map of your fictional community, and write a description of its goals.

individual rights. Emerson might appreciate our focus if it leads to self-reliance; if it leads to selfishness, he would not approve.

5. Possible responses: People would approve. Or some people would be frightened by potential changes.

Language and Style

Answers

1. Planting corn nourishes people because they create and nurture something of their own. The iron string is compared to trust and to an individual's attachment to providence, society, and events. Everyone is part of the Universal Being. Society is compared to the joint-stock company because the company is made up of many members and cannot exist with only one member. Members receive profits according to the dictates of society and their conformity to those dictates. Society promotes dependence, not self-reliance. A shadow on the wall represents emptiness.
2. Consistency of thought does not allow for progress or change. A hobgoblin is a frightening creature; a little mind is not open to new thought; and a foolish consistency maintains the status quo at the expense of progress. A wise consistency would be to consider new and multiple sides of an issue or thought.

Choices: Building Your Portfolio

1. **Writer's Notebook** Remind students to save their work. They may use it as prewriting for the Writer's Workshop on p. 331. To help students get started listing ideas, have them bring in and look at the front page and editorial pages of a newspaper.
2. **Critical Writing/Creative Writing** Suggest that students find examples to illustrate the statement they choose: the work of great men and women who have been self-reliant, events in the lives of people they know, or hypothetical situations.
3. **Critical Writing** To help students understand the context of each **paradox** and explain its meaning, have them re-read the paragraph from which it was taken.
4. **Critical Writing** Have students brainstorm a list of abstract qualities, such as love, peace, envy, and community. Ask them to choose one and create **similes** comparing the quality to something concrete.
5. **Speaking and Listening** Have one student in each group monitor the discussion and watch the time.
6. **Crossing the Curriculum: Social Studies** Ask each student in the partnership to be responsible for a particular concern, such as food, health, education, security, or housing.

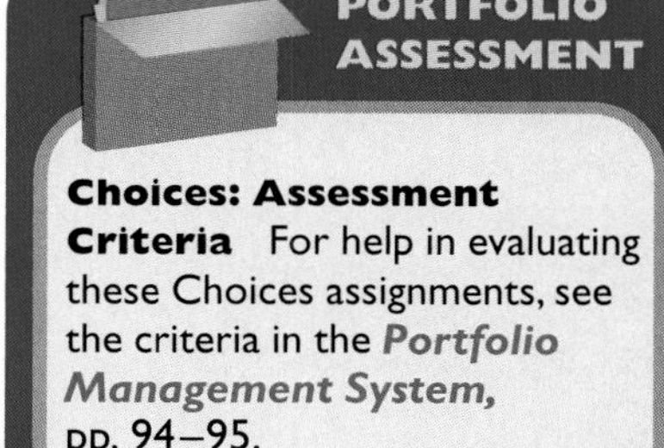

Choices: Assessment Criteria For help in evaluating these Choices assignments, see the criteria in the ***Portfolio Management System,*** pp. 94–95.

Henry David Thoreau

(1817–1862)

On July 4, 1845 (the date was deliberately chosen), a young man ended a three-year stay at the house of a friend and moved to a cabin on the shores of Walden Pond in Massachusetts. He was almost twenty-eight years old and, to all appearances, a failure. He had lasted only two weeks as a schoolteacher (he refused to whip a child, then a mandatory form of punishment); his public lectures had been uninspiring; the woman to whom he had proposed marriage had turned him down; and he had little interest in the family business. Despite his impressive Harvard education, he had not realized his literary ambitions.

If ever a person looked like a self-*un*made man, a man who had squandered the advantages of intelligence, education, and the friendship of brilliant and successful people, it was Henry David Thoreau. On top of all his other problems, Thoreau was difficult to get along with. Three days before Thoreau went to Walden, the writer Nathaniel Hawthorne (page 296) wrote to a New York publisher that Thoreau was "tedious, tiresome, and intolerable. And yet," Hawthorne added, "he has great qualities of intellect and character."

Even his closest friends had doubts about Thoreau. "He seemed born for great enterprise and for command," Emerson said years later at Thoreau's funeral, "and I so much regret the loss of his rare powers of action, that I cannot help counting it a fault in him that he had no ambition. Wanting this, instead of engineering for all America, he was the captain of a huckleberry party."

National Portrait Gallery/Smithsonian Institution/Art Resource.

Henry David Thoreau (1856) by Benjamin D. Maxham. Photograph.

What Emerson failed to see, and what Thoreau knew (or hoped) all along, was that by leading a berry-picking party on a jaunt in the woods he could "engineer for all America" in the most profound way. This paradox is at the center of Thoreau's life and work.

The Student Who Wouldn't Wear Black

Thoreau was born in Concord, Massachusetts, in 1817. His father was a moderately successful manufacturer of pencils. His mother took in boarders, among them the sister of Emerson's wife, thus establishing the relationship between the two families. As a boy, Thoreau tramped the woods and fields around Concord, often with a fishing rod and seldom with a gun. No one knew Concord as well as he did.

Thoreau entered Harvard in 1833 and graduated four years later without any literary distinction. Independent and eccentric even then, he attended chapel in a green coat, "because," he wrote, "the rules required black." He never ranked higher than the middle of his class, but he was extremely well read. At Harvard, mostly on his own, he became thoroughly familiar with English literature and with the German philosophers who provided many of the underpinnings of Transcendentalism.

After returning to Concord and teaching school, Thoreau went to New York in 1843, but he pined for his hometown. After six months of struggling, he gave up and returned to Concord. A friend proposed that Henry and he sail to Europe and work their way across the Continent, but Henry turned him down. He appeared to be floundering, but in fact he knew what he was doing; Thoreau's voyage would be inward, and it would depart from Walden Pond, where Emerson had offered him the use of some land.

Walden: Life in Its Essence

The experiment at Walden Pond was an attempt to rediscover the grandeur and heroism of a simple life led close to nature. The fact that Thoreau's cabin was only two miles from town—that he had really only set himself up in the suburbs of Concord, to which he commuted almost daily—was not really the point. Walden offered a focus for his contemplative urge. "I wish to meet the facts of life," he wrote in his journal, "the vital facts, which are the phenomena or actuality the gods meant to show us . . . and so I came down here."

This private confrontation was to Thoreau's mind the truly heroic enterprise of his time. "I am glad to remember tonight as I sit by my door," he wrote on the evening of July 7, "that I too am at least a remote descendant of that heroic race of men of whom there is a tradition. I too sit here on the shore of my Ithaca, a fellow wanderer and survivor of Ulysses."

When he looked toward town, Thoreau saw his fellow citizens so caught up in making a living that they had become one-dimensional. "The mass of men," as one of the most famous sentences in *Walden* puts it, "lead lives of quiet desperation." He hoped to wake them up and show them that the heroic enterprise of confronting the "vital facts of life" lay literally in their own back yards.

Walden—one of the most well-known works ever produced in America—owes much of its artistic success to Thoreau's blending of style and content. He looked to nature, rather than to the stylists of the past, for a model. To Thoreau, a style that imitated nature would speak fundamental spiritual truths. Thoreau wished to build sentences "which lie like boulders on the page, up and down or across; which contain the seed of other sentences, not mere repetition, but creation; which a man might sell his grounds and castles to build."

Thoreau the Protester

It was while he was at Walden that Thoreau's other famous act took place. As a protest against the Mexican War, which he and many others saw as an attempt to extend American slaveholding territory, Thoreau refused to pay his poll tax, and spent a night in jail as a result. While at Walden, and again in 1851 (after the Fugitive Slave Act had been passed), Thoreau helped fugitives escaping slavery make their way to Canada. In 1859, he was one of the first defenders of John Brown, the radical abolitionist who staged a famous raid on the Federal arsenal at Harpers Ferry in Virginia.

Thoreau remained at Walden for a little more than two years. In 1847, he left the cabin and moved back into the Emersons' house, in exchange for a few hours a day of odd jobs and gardening. During the next few years, he worked on *Walden* (which was published in 1854) and essays such as "Resistance to Civil Government." The latter, delivered as a lecture in 1848 and published as an essay in 1849, had little immediate influence, but few essays have had such an overwhelming, long-term effect on human history. It was especially important in helping to inspire the passive resistance used by Mohandas K. Gandhi in India and, later, by Martin Luther King, Jr., in the United States.

Thoreau moved back into his parents' house in 1848 and lived there the rest of his life. He supported himself by making pencils, taking odd jobs—he was an excellent carpenter, mason, and gardener—and doing survey work on the land around Concord. He became a kind of local recordkeeper, a fount of knowledge about the amount of rainfall and snowfall and the first days of frost. He could predict to the day when each wildflower in the area would bloom.

In 1860, Thoreau caught a cold, and it soon became clear that beneath the cold lay incurable tuberculosis. He faced his coming death with great calm. The town constable, Sam Staples (who had jailed Thoreau for refusing to pay his poll tax), told Emerson that he "never saw a man dying with so much pleasure and peace."

"Henry, have you made your peace with God?" his aunt is said to have asked him toward the end. "Why, Aunt," he replied, "I didn't know we had ever quarreled."

ABOUT THE AUTHOR

Thoreau's life appeared to be a series of failed attempts at beginning new enterprises. Before journeying to Walden, he and his brother John opened a private school in 1839 that lasted only two years. The two brothers, however, instituted a new educational practice—field trips for nature study, a commonplace idea in today's schools. Although not noted during his lifetime as a major contributor to American letters, in 1960 Thoreau gained admission to the Hall of Fame for great Americans. The admiration of his work by Mohandas Gandhi and Martin Luther King, Jr., helped call attention to his contribution to American literature.

QUICK PLANNING GUIDE

Into the Selection

Author Biography pp. 230–231

Before You Read p. 232

- **Reading Focus: Scaffolding** Students ask questions about fulfillment.
- **A Dialogue with the Text: Set a Purpose** Write in Reader's Log expectations of life in the woods and evaluate Thoreau
- **Elements of Literature: Point of View**
- **Background:** Inquiring about the meaning of life

Through the Selection

from Walden pp. 233–244

Words to Own pp. 233–244

Connections: An Essay p. 245

from "Heaven Is Under Our Feet"

Making Meanings p. 246

Language and Style p. 246

Beyond the Selection

Choices: Building Your Portfolio p. 247

- **Writer's Notebook:** Collect ideas for a controversial issue
- **Critical Writing:** Write about Romanticism and *Walden* in a brief essay
- **Critical Writing:** Write an essay about wisdom in small things
- **Creative Writing:** Write a paragraph from Thoreau's point of view about modern life
- **Creative Writing:** Record in journal thoughts on a particular day
- **Creative Writing/Performance:** Write a journal entry on Walden Pond from Puritan or rationalist perspective
- **Crossing the Curriculum: Science:** Research aspect of nature for an oral report

BEFORE YOU READ

FROM WALDEN, OR LIFE IN THE WOODS

Reading Focus

What's Necessary

Thoreau went to Walden Pond to find out what was necessary in life and what could be done without. He discovered that the key to making his life more fulfilling was to make it simpler.

Few people go off to the woods for a couple of years to find out how they really want to live. Every thinking person, however, stops at times to ask, "How do I really want to live? What do I need in order to feel fulfilled—and what am I doing now that's unnecessary?" Thoreau can be an inspiration for anyone who asks these questions.

A Dialogue with the Text

READER'S LOG

Imagine that you are planning to move to a cabin in the woods near Walden Pond for the next two years. Your life there will be simple; there won't be any conveniences. You will have an occasional visitor and will be able to walk into a town two miles away; aside from that, your life will offer little more in excitement than a battle between ants, and little more in company than the visit of a bird.

In your Reader's Log, write down your expectations about your experience: what you hope to learn, how you think you'll cope, what your goals are. Then, as you read the excerpt from *Walden,* write responses to Thoreau's observations in your log. Note, for example, if you strongly agree or disagree with Thoreau's view of an event, or if you think you would have responded differently.

Elements of Literature

Point of View

In the second paragraph of this excerpt, Thoreau justifies using the **first-person point of view** to narrate his experiences at Walden Pond. "[I]t is, after all, always the first person that is speaking," he writes. Think about what Thoreau might mean. As you read, look for passages in which you think the use of the first person makes a difference.

In the **first-person point of view,** the narrative is told by a particular person who uses personal pronouns such as *I* and *we* to describe experiences.

For more on Point of View, see the Handbook of Literary Terms.

Background

A temporary move to a site near a large pond in Concord, Massachusetts, resulted in a work of literature that was to become an American classic. Thoreau moved to Walden because he wanted to find out what life is. That is a question people still ask; it is something people the world over have always asked, when they have had the leisure to think about it.

WORDS TO OWN

The following vocabulary words are defined in the Words to Own at the bottom of the pupil's page.

pertinent p. 233	effete p. 239
encumbrance p. 234	incessantly p. 240
impervious p. 235	derision p. 243
temporal p. 236	tumultuous p. 243
superfluous p. 237	ethereal p. 244

PORTFOLIO ASSESSMENT

Portfolio Assessment For help with self- and teacher assessment of reading skills, see the ***Portfolio Management System,*** p. 53.

from Walden, or Life in the Woods

Henry David Thoreau

I DO NOT PROPOSE TO WRITE AN ODE TO DEJECTION, BUT TO BRAG AS LUSTILY AS CHANTICLEER[1] IN THE MORNING, STANDING ON HIS ROOST, IF ONLY TO WAKE MY NEIGHBORS UP. (A)

1. **chanticleer:** a rooster; from the name of the rooster in the folk epic "Reynard the Fox" and in Geoffrey Chaucer's "Nun's Priest's Tale."

Site of Thoreau's cabin at Walden Pond.
Library of Congress.

from Economy

When I wrote the following pages, or rather the bulk of them, I lived alone, in the woods, a mile from any neighbor, in a house which I had built myself, on the shore of Walden Pond, in Concord, Massachusetts, and earned my living by the labor of my hands only. I lived there two years and two months. At present I am a sojourner in civilized life again.

I should not obtrude my affairs so much on the notice of my readers if very particular inquiries had not been made by my townsmen concerning my mode of life, which some would call impertinent, though they do not appear to me at all impertinent, but, considering the circumstances, very natural and pertinent. Some have asked what I got to eat; if I did not feel lonesome; if I was not afraid; and the like. Others have been curious to learn what portion of my income I devoted to charitable purposes; and some, who have large families, how many poor children I maintained. I will therefore ask those of my readers who feel no particular interest in me to pardon me if I undertake to answer some of these questions in this book. In most books, the *I*, or first person, is omitted; in this it will be retained; that, in respect to egotism, is the main difference. We commonly do not remember that it is, after all, always the first person that is speaking. I should not talk so much about myself if there were anybody else whom I knew as well. Unfortunately, I am confined to this theme by the narrowness of my experience. (B) Moreover, I, on my side, require of every writer, first or last, a simple and sincere account of his own life, and not merely what he has heard of

WORDS TO OWN

pertinent (pʉr′tə·nənt) *adj.:* to the point; applying to the situation.

Using **BEFORE YOU READ** p. 232

Reading Focus

Have students make three specific wishes that if fulfilled, would make their lives complete. Remind them that everyone probably has the same goal in mind: to lead a happy, healthful, and purposeful life. However, while everyone's basic needs are similar, people take different routes toward fulfilling those needs. Suggest how life can be more satisfying when a person has less, and point out the **irony** inherent in the statement "Less is more."

A. Reader's Response: First Thoughts

? What do you see in Thoreau's prologue? [Sample responses: He uses metaphor to emphasize his point. Or it is ironic that few people heard him speak, but millions talk about what he did.]

B. Literary Element: Point of View

? How would this paragraph be different if it were not written in **first person**? [Possible answers: It would not be as personal. It would lose some of its humor.]

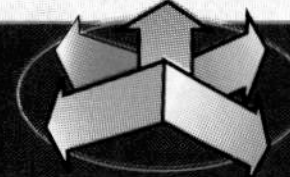

PROGRAM MANAGER

- **Planning Instruction** See Teaching Notes, *Teaching Resources A,* pp. 84–85, for objectives, a summary, literary elements, and information.
- **Instructional Support** See Graphic Organizer for Active Reading, *Teaching Resources A,* p. 95, for an Into the Selection activity.
- **Audiotaped Readings** To help students through the lesson, use the Selected Reading, Audiocassette 1, Side B, in the *Audiovisual Resources Binder.*
- **Instructional Support** See Fine Art Transparency 5.1. Review teacher's notes in the *Audiovisual Resources Binder.*
- **Assessment** See Selection Test, *Test Booklet,* pp. 63–64.
- **Language Link** For practice in correcting usage problems see Language Link, *Teaching Resources A,* pp. 96–97, and *Language and Writing Skills Worksheets,* pp. 1–3.
- **Reinforcement** Use the Words to Own worksheet in *Teaching Resources A,* pp. 98–99.

A. Reader's Response: Challenging the Text

? Do you agree that the foremost requirement of a writer is "a simple and sincere account of his own life"? Why or why not? [Sample responses: It would seem to limit one's reading. Even if all autobiographies were sincere, it would still be useful to have biographies. Or a simple account would seem more truthful.]

B. Reader's Response: Shaping Interpretations

? What does Thoreau's style of humor say to you about him? [Sample responses: It reflects his practical nature; even his joke has a basis in factual reporting. Or his humor is rather morbid.]

C. Critical Reading: Finding Details

? How does Thoreau build his cellar? [He digs it into the side of a hill, six feet square by seven feet deep. The sides are left standing and are not walled up with brick or stone.]

other men's lives; some such account as he would send to his kindred from a distant land; for if he has lived sincerely, it must have been in a distant land to me. Perhaps these pages are more particularly addressed to poor students. As for the rest of my readers, they will accept such portions as apply to them. I trust that none will stretch the seams in putting on the coat, for it may do good service to him whom it fits. . . .

By the middle of April, for I made no haste in my work, but rather made the most of it, my house was framed and ready for the raising. I had already bought the shanty of James Collins, an Irishman who worked on the Fitchburg Railroad, for boards. James Collins's shanty was considered an uncommonly fine one. When I called to see it he was not at home. I walked about the outside, at first unobserved from within, the window was so deep and high. It was of small dimensions, with a peaked cottage roof, and not much else to be seen, the dirt being raised five feet all around as if it were a compost heap. The roof was the soundest part, though a good deal warped and made brittle by the sun. Doorsill there was none, but a perennial passage for the hens under the door board. Mrs. C. came to the door and asked me to view it from the inside. The hens were driven in by my approach. It was dark, and had a dirt floor for the most part, dank, clammy, and aguish,[2] only here a board and there a board which would not bear removal. She lighted a lamp to show me the inside of the roof and the walls, and also that the board floor extended under the bed, warning me not to step into the cellar, a sort of dust hole two feet deep. In her own words, they were "good boards overhead, good boards all around, and a good window"—of two whole squares originally, only the cat had passed out that way lately. There was a stove, a bed, and a place to sit, an infant in the house where it was born, a silk parasol, gilt-framed looking glass, and a patent new coffee mill nailed to an oak sapling, all told. The bargain was soon concluded, for James had in the meanwhile returned. I to pay four dollars and twenty-five cents tonight, he to vacate at five tomorrow morning, selling to nobody else meanwhile: I to take possession at six. It were well, he said, to be there early, and anticipate certain indistinct but wholly unjust claims on the score of ground rent and fuel. This he assured me was the only encumbrance. At six I passed him and his family on the road. One large bundle held their all—bed, coffee mill, looking glass, hens—all but the cat; she took to the woods and became a wild cat, and, as I learned afterward, trod in a trap set for woodchucks, and so became a dead cat at last.

I took down this dwelling the same morning, drawing the nails, and removed it to the pond side by small cartloads, spreading the boards on the grass there to bleach and warp back again in the sun. One early thrush gave me a note or two as I drove along the woodland path. I was informed treacherously by a young Patrick that neighbor Seeley, an Irishman, in the intervals of the carting, transferred the still tolerable, straight, and drivable nails, staples, and spikes to his pocket, and then stood when I came back to pass the time of day, and look freshly up, unconcerned, with spring thoughts, at the devastation; there being a dearth of work, as he said. He was there to represent spectatordom, and help make this seemingly insignificant event one with the removal of the gods of Troy.[3]

I dug my cellar in the side of a hill sloping to the south, where a woodchuck had formerly dug his burrow, down through sumac and blackberry roots, and the lowest stain of vegetation, six feet square by seven deep, to a fine sand where potatoes would not freeze in any winter. The sides were left shelving, and not stoned; but the sun having never shone on them, the sand still keeps its place. It was but two hours' work. I took particular pleasure in this breaking of ground, for in almost all latitudes men dig into the earth for an equable temperature. Under the most splendid house in the city is still to be found the cellar where they store their roots as of old, and long after the superstructure has disappeared posterity

2. **aguish** (ā′gyo͞o·ish): likely to cause ague, or fever and chills.

3. **the gods of Troy:** In Virgil's (70–19 B.C.) *Aeneid,* the conquering Greeks carry off the images of the Trojan gods after the fall of Troy.

WORDS TO OWN

encumbrance (en·kum′brəns) *n.:* burden; hindrance.

OPTIONS FOR TEACHING

STRATEGIES FOR INCLUSION

Spatial Help students see how Thoreau simplified his living space. Using chalk or tape, have students lay out on the classroom floor the size of Thoreau's house. They can also determine where the chimney, closet, windows, and trapdoors may have been best placed.

Less Proficient Readers As students read each section, have them jot down questions they have about the reading and ideas they have found. At the end of each section, have students ask you their questions. Then, ask them to state the main idea of each section.

Intrapersonal In a one-minute reflection period after each section, ask students to think about the ideas Thoreau presents and to connect them to their own lives. After the reflection, ask volunteers to share their thoughts.

remark its dent in the earth. The house is still but a sort of porch at the entrance of a burrow.

At length, in the beginning of May, with the help of some of my acquaintances, rather to improve so good an occasion for neighborliness than from any necessity, I set up the frame of my house. No man was ever more honored in the character of his raisers[4] than I. They are destined, I trust, to assist at the raising of loftier structures one day. I began to occupy my house on the 4th of July, as soon as it was boarded and roofed, for the boards were carefully featheredged and lapped,[5] so that it was perfectly impervious to rain, but before boarding I laid the foundation of a chimney at one end, bringing two cartloads of stones up the hill from the pond in my arms. I built the chimney after my hoeing in the fall, before a fire became necessary for warmth, doing my cooking in the meanwhile out of doors on the

4. raisers: Thoreau's helpers included the Transcendentalist writers Ralph Waldo Emerson (1803–1882), Bronson Alcott (1799–1888), and William Ellery Channing (1780–1842), hence the reference in the next sentence to raising loftier structures one day.

5. featheredged and lapped: The edges were cut at an angle and overlapped.

Words to Own

impervious (im·pur'vē·əs) *adj.*: resistant; impenetrable.

Walden Revisited (c. 1936) by N. C. Wyeth. Tempera on panel.
Brandywine River Museum, Chadds Ford, Pennsylvania; Estate of Carolyn Wyeth.

D. Critical Reading: Speculating

? What might Thoreau have had in mind when he decided to occupy his house on July 4? [Possible answer: He might have wanted to make a statement about his declaration of independence from the civilized world where he felt imprisoned.]

Responding to the Art: Visual Literacy

Have students look closely at Wyeth's rendering of Thoreau and his surroundings. Ask them to discuss what kind of person they think Thoreau seems to be from this painting. [Possible responses: Interesting, thoughtful, likable, sociable, lonely.] Have them observe how Wyeth's use of light and shade helps to create a link between Thoreau and the landscape, and an aura around both.

STRATEGIES FOR INCLUSION

English Language Development Before students read, have them work in pairs to list things and activities they could eliminate from their lives in order to simplify it. Ask them what would happen and how they would feel as they eliminated each item on their list. Have them discuss the advantages and disadvantages of a simpler way of life, both for the individual and for society as a whole. Have students keep their lists in mind as they read *Walden.*

Special Needs To help students sequence events, have them read the passage and list the steps in building Thoreau's house and farm as though they were writing in their own diaries or workman's notebooks. For students who need visual cues, illustrate each step in the process on an overhead transparency so they can see the progress from preconstruction to project completion.

A. Reader's Response: Shaping Interpretations

? How does Thoreau feel about people's building their own houses? [Sample responses: He says that there is no more simple or natural occupation. He feels that building a home is a job for the person who plans to live in the house and should not be relegated to a hired builder because it is a personal and important event.]

B. Language Note: Commas

? What is the effect of the use of commas as Thoreau describes his house? [The use of commas in the description gives a feeling of the precision and step-by-step process Thoreau uses as he constructs his house. It also shows his pattern of thinking.]

C. Reader's Response: Extending the Text

? What does Thoreau's recording of minute details of his expenditures say to readers today? How does it relate to the way people build their homes in the 1990s? [Sample responses: Thoreau became very emotionally attached to his home in a different way in the nineteenth century because he did the measuring, sawing, nailing, and hammering himself. Today, it is difficult for a single person to build his or her own home. Permits, special licenses, and town ordinances inhibit people from constructing their own homes. Today, people's emotional attachment to their homes is of a different order than Thoreau's.]

ground, early in the morning: which mode I still think is in some respects more convenient and agreeable than the usual one. When it stormed before my bread was baked, I fixed a few boards over the fire, and sat under them to watch my loaf, and passed some pleasant hours in that way. In those days, when my hands were much employed, I read but little, but the least scraps of paper which lay on the ground, my holder, or tablecloth, afforded me as much entertainment, in fact answered the same purpose as the *Iliad*.[6]

(A) It would be worth the while to build still more deliberately than I did, considering, for instance, what foundation a door, a window, a cellar, a garret, have in the nature of man, and perchance never raising any superstructure until we found a better reason for it than our temporal necessities even. There is some of the same fitness in a man's building his own house that there is in a bird's building its own nest. Who knows but if men constructed their dwellings with their own hands, and provided food for themselves and families simply and honestly enough, the poetic faculty would be universally developed, as birds universally sing when they are so engaged? But alas! we do like cowbirds and cuckoos, which lay their eggs in nests which other birds have built, and cheer no traveler with their chattering and unmusical notes. Shall we forever resign the pleasure of construction to the carpenter? What does architecture amount to in the experience of the mass of men? I never in all my walks came across a man engaged in so simple and natural an occupation as building his house. . . .

Before winter I built a chimney, and shingled the sides of my house, which were already impervious to rain, with imperfect and sappy shingles made of the first slice of the log, whose edges I was obliged to straighten with a plane.

(B) I have thus a tight shingled and plastered house, ten feet wide by fifteen long, and eight-foot posts, with a garret and a closet, a large window on each side, two trapdoors, one door at the end, and a brick fireplace opposite. The exact cost of my house, paying the usual price for such materials as I used, but not counting the work, all of which was done by myself, was as follows; and I give the details because very few are able to tell exactly what their houses cost, and fewer still, if any, the separate cost of the various materials which compose them—

(C)

Boards,	*$ 8 03 ½*	*mostly shanty boards*
Refuse shingles for roof and sides,	*4 00*	
Laths,	*1 25*	
Two secondhand windows with glass,	*2 43*	
One thousand old brick,	*4 00*	
Two casks of lime,	*2 40*	*That was high*
Hair,	*0 31*	*More than I needed*
Mantle-tree iron,	*0 15*	
Nails,	*3 90*	
Hinges and screws,	*0 14*	
Latch,	*0 10*	
Chalk,	*0 01*	
Transportation,	*1 40*	*I carried a good part on my back*
In all,	*$28 12 ½*	

. . . Before I finished my house, wishing to earn ten or twelve dollars by some honest and agreeable method, in order to meet my unusual expenses, I planted about two acres and a half of light and sandy soil near it chiefly with beans, but

6. **the *Iliad*:** Homer's epic about the Greek siege of Troy.

WORDS TO OWN

temporal (tem′pə·rəl) *adj.:* worldly.

OPTIONS FOR TEACHING

INTEGRATING THE LANGUAGE ARTS

Strategic Reading Have students in small groups discuss and write down what they already know about solitude. Then, have them think about why Thoreau would want to live alone. Ask them to write down what they want to know. Once they have read the selection, have them write what they have discovered about Thoreau and about living in solitude. Student groups should complete the following chart as they work.

Know	Want to Know	Have Learned
[It is lonely.]	[How to avoid the loneliness.]	

Writing: Narrative Paragraph To help students incorporate a variety of styles into their expository writing, have them review how Thoreau uses **narrative** in "Brute Neighbors" on pp. 240–243 to illustrate a point. Ask them to consider an event that taught them something about life and to write a narrative paragraph that illustrates what they have learned. *Remind students to choose a situation they would not mind sharing with others.*

also a small part with potatoes, corn, peas, and turnips. The whole lot contains eleven acres, mostly growing up to pines and hickories, and was sold the preceding season for eight dollars and eight cents an acre. One farmer said that it was "good for nothing but to raise cheeping squirrels on." I put no manure whatever on this land, not being the owner, but merely a squatter, and not expecting to cultivate so much again, and I did not quite hoe it all once. I got out several cords of stumps in plowing, which supplied me with fuel for a long time, and left small circles of virgin mold, easily distinguishable through the summer by the greater luxuriance of the beans there. The dead and for the most part unmerchantable wood behind my house, and the driftwood from the pond, have supplied the remainder of my fuel. I was obliged to hire a team and a man for the plowing, though I held the plow myself. My farm outgoes for the first season were, for implements, seed, work, etc., $14.72 ½. The seed corn was given me. This never costs anything to speak of, unless you plant more than enough. I got twelve bushels of beans, and eighteen bushels of potatoes, beside some peas and sweet corn. The yellow corn and turnips were too late to come to anything. My whole income from the farm was

	$23 44,
Deducting the outgoes,	14 72 ½
There are left,	$ 8 71 ½

beside produce consumed and on hand at the time this estimate was made of the value of $4.50—the amount on hand much more than balancing a little grass which I did not raise. All things considered, that is, considering the importance of a man's soul and of today, notwithstanding the short time occupied by my experiment, nay, partly even because of its transient character, I believe that that was doing better than any farmer in Concord did that year. . . . (D)

from Where I Lived, and What I Lived For

. . . I went to the woods because I wished to live deliberately, to front only the essential facts of life, and see if I could not learn what it had to teach, and not, when I came to die, discover that I had not lived. I did not wish to live what was not life, (E) living is so dear; nor did I wish to practice resignation, unless it was quite necessary. I wanted to live deep and suck out all the marrow of life, to live so sturdily and Spartan-like[7] as to put to rout all that was not life, to cut a broad swath and shave close, to drive life into a corner, and reduce it to its lowest terms, and, if it proved to be mean, (F) why then to get the whole and genuine meanness of it, and publish its meanness to the world; or if it were sublime, to know it by experience, and be able to give a true account of it in my next excursion. For most men, it appears to me, are in a strange uncertainty about it, whether it is of the devil or of God, and have *somewhat hastily* concluded that it is the chief end of man here to "glorify God and enjoy him forever."[8]

Still we live meanly, like ants; though the fable tells us that we were long ago changed into men; like pygmies we fight with cranes;[9] it is error upon error, and clout upon clout, and our best virtue has for its occasion a superfluous and evitable wretchedness. Our life is frittered away by detail. An honest man has hardly need to count more than his ten fingers, or in extreme cases he may add his ten toes, and lump the rest. Simplicity, simplicity, simplicity! I say, let your affairs be as two or three, and not a hundred or a thousand; instead of a million count half a dozen, and keep your accounts on your thumbnail. In the midst of this chopping sea of civilized life, such are the (G)

7. Spartan-like: like the Spartans, the hardy, frugal, and highly disciplined citizens of the ancient Greek city-state Sparta.

8. glorify . . . forever: answer to catechism question, "What is the chief end of man?"

9. the fable . . . cranes: In a Greek fable, Zeus changes ants into men. In the *Iliad,* Homer compares the Trojans to cranes fighting with pygmies.

Words to Own

superfluous (sə·pʉr′flo͞o·əs) *adj.:* unnecessary.

D. Critical Reading: Drawing Conclusions

? Why does Thoreau believe that he did better with his small profit than any other farmer in Concord? [Because the experiment was good for his soul.]

E. Reader's Response: Shaping Interpretations

? What is Thoreau searching for that he cannot find in civilized society? [Sample responses: He wants to live close to nature and to get away from the unnecessary things that clutter his life. Or he may feel that civilized society does not allow him to follow his conscience.]

F. Critical Reading: Finding Cause and Effect

? Why does Thoreau wish to retreat into solitude for two years? [Isolation will help him clear his mind and delve inward, which he believes is the source of enlightenment.] Remind students that Emerson says, "To go into solitude, a man needs to retire as much from his chamber as from society" on p. 219. Thoreau follows the precepts set down by Emerson.

G. Language Note: Style

? What aspects of Thoreau's writing help chart a new style? [Thoreau's repetition of certain words adds emphasis: "Simplicity, simplicity, simplicity!" and "Simplify, simplify." Also, his use of words like *fritter* and phrases like *lump the rest* makes his writing accessible to everyone, not just a select audience.]

COOPERATIVE LEARNING

Learning from Thoreau and Nature Have students make their own journals. Spend a class period outside, and have students write what they see, hear, and think. Students should return to their Cooperative Learning groups and share what they discovered.

CLASSROOM MANAGEMENT

Student Choice Allowing individual students to choose an activity ensures their involvement in learning and helps them make decisions. This is particularly true for intrapersonal learners. For example, have students choose which of the Crossing the Curriculum assignments on p. T238 they prefer to do.

A. Literary Element: Metaphor

? What comparisons does Thoreau make in this passage? [He compares the railroad to a rider. He also compares the sleepers, or railroad ties, to people.] What is the effect of this passage? [The comparison places more emphasis on Thoreau's meaning: that people are being controlled by what they create instead of controlling their creations and that workers have suffered greatly in building the railroad. The comparison is more striking when implied indirectly through metaphor than when stated directly.]

clouds and storms and quicksands and thousand-and-one items to be allowed for, that a man has to live, if he would not founder and go to the bottom and not make his port at all, by dead reckoning, and he must be a great calculator indeed who succeeds. Simplify, simplify. Instead of three meals a day, if it be necessary eat but one; instead of a hundred dishes, five; and reduce other things in proportion. Our life is like a German Confederacy,[10] made up of petty states with its boundary forever fluctuating, so that even a German cannot tell you how it is bounded at any moment. The nation itself, with all its so-called internal improvements, which, by the way are all external and superficial, is just such an unwieldy and overgrown establishment, cluttered with furniture and tripped up by its own traps, ruined by luxury and heedless expense, by want of calculation and a worthy aim, as the million households in the land; and the only cure for it, as for them, is in a rigid economy, a stern and more than Spartan simplicity of life and elevation of purpose. It lives too fast. Men think that it is essential that the *Nation* have commerce, and export ice, and talk through a telegraph, and ride thirty miles an hour, without a doubt, whether *they* do or not; but whether we should live like baboons or like men, is a little uncertain. If we do not get out sleepers,[11] and forge rails, and devote days and nights to the work, but go to tinkering upon our *lives* to improve *them,* who will build railroads? And if railroads are not built, how shall we get to heaven in season? But if we stay at home and mind our business, who will want railroads? We do not ride on the railroad; it rides upon us. Did you ever think what those sleepers are that underlie the railroad? Each one is a man, an Irishman, or a Yankee man. The rails are laid on them, and they are covered with sand, and the cars run smoothly over them. They are sound sleepers, I assure you. And every few years a new lot is laid down and run over; so that, if some have the pleasure of riding on a rail, others have the misfortune to be ridden upon. And when they run over a man that is walking in his sleep, a super-

10. German Confederacy: At the time Thoreau was writing, Germany was not yet a unified nation.

11. sleepers: British usage for "railroad ties"; so called because they lie flat.

Courtesy Winterthur Museum, Winterthur, Delaware.

Quaker Ladies (1956) by Andrew Wyeth. Watercolor and drypoint.

OPTIONS FOR TEACHING

CROSSING THE CURRICULUM

Architecture Have students design a hut that would adequately shelter them in a particular location in their region. Remind them to consider the demands of the climate, the characteristics of the site, and the materials native to their region. Students should create a blueprint and describe how the hut is to be constructed to meet the demands and limitations of the area. Display their blueprints in the classroom.

Industrial Arts Have students evaluate Thoreau's carpentry skills. Ask them to assess the precision of his measurement and how he uses tools. Have students draft a report as though they were construction supervisors.

Science Have students research the production of beans. Students should learn about different varieties of beans, how they are cultivated, and to which diseases and weeds beans are most susceptible. As a culmination of their research, students should plant, tend, and harvest their own bean crop.

numerary[12] sleeper in the wrong position, and wake him up, they suddenly stop the cars, and make a hue and cry about it, as if this were an exception. I am glad to know that it takes a gang of men for every five miles to keep the sleepers down and level in their beds as it is, for this is a sign that they may sometime get up again. . . .

from Solitude

. . . Some of my pleasantest hours were during the long rainstorms in the spring or fall, which confined me to the house for the afternoon as well as the forenoon, soothed by their ceaseless roar and pelting; when an early twilight ushered in a long evening in which many thoughts had time to take root and unfold themselves. In those driving northeast rains which tried the village houses so, when the maids stood ready with mop and pail in front entries to keep the deluge out, I sat behind (B) my door in my little house, which was all entry, and thoroughly enjoyed its protection. In one heavy thundershower the lightning struck a large pitch pine across the pond, making a very conspicuous and perfectly regular spiral groove from top to bottom, an inch or more deep, and four or five inches wide, as you would groove a walking stick. I passed it again the other day, and was struck with awe on looking up and beholding that mark, now more distinct than ever, where a terrific and resistless bolt came down out of the harmless sky eight years ago. Men frequently say to me, "I should think you would feel lonesome down there, and want to be nearer to folks, rainy and snowy days and nights especially." I am tempted to reply to such—This whole earth which we inhabit is but a point in space. How far (C) apart, think you, dwell the two most distant inhabitants of yonder star, the breadth of whose disk cannot be appreciated by our instruments? Why should I feel lonely? Is not our planet in the Milky Way? This which you put seems to me not to be the most important question. What sort of space is that which separates a man from his fellows and makes him solitary? I have found that no exertion of the legs can bring two minds much nearer to one another. What do we want most to dwell near to? Not to many men surely, the depot, the post office, the barroom, the meetinghouse, the schoolhouse, the grocery, Beacon Hill, or the Five Points, where men most congregate, but to the perennial source of our life, whence in all our experience we have found that to issue, as the willow stands near the water and sends out its roots in that direction. This will vary with different natures, but this is the place where a wise man will dig his cellar. . . .

12. **supernumerary** (sōō′pər·nōō′mə·rər′ē): additional; unnecessary.

from The Bean Field

Meanwhile my beans, the length of whose rows, added together, was seven miles already planted, were impatient to be hoed, for the earliest had grown considerably before the latest were in the ground; indeed they were not easily to be put off. What was the meaning of this so steady and self-respecting, this small Herculean labor, I knew not. I came to love my rows, my beans, though so many more than I wanted. They attached me to the earth, and so I got strength like Antaeus.[13] But why should I raise them? Only Heaven knows. This was my curious labor all summer—to make this portion of the earth's surface, which had yielded only cinquefoil, blackberries, johnswort, and the like, before, sweet wild fruits and pleasant flowers, produce instead this pulse.[14] What shall I learn of beans or beans of me? I cherish them, I hoe them, early and late I have an eye to them; and this is my day's work. It is a fine broad leaf to look on. My auxiliaries are the dews and rains which water this dry soil, and what fertility is in the soil itself, which for the most part is lean and effete. My enemies are worms, cool days, and most of all woodchucks. The last have nibbled for me a quarter of an acre clean. But what right had I to oust johnswort and the rest, and break up their ancient herb garden? Soon, however, the

13. **Antaeus** (an·tē′əs): in Greek mythology, the giant who draws strength from the earth, his mother.
14. **pulse:** beans, peas, and other edible seeds of plants having pods.

WORDS TO OWN

effete (e·fēt′) *adj.:* sterile; unproductive.

B. Reader's Response: Extending the Text

? What larger significance can you draw from Thoreau's description of the thunderstorm? [Sample responses: It shows the power of nature, which is everywhere. Or the thunderstorm shows how fragile people's existence is.]

C. Reader's Response: Challenging the Text

? Do you agree with Thoreau that people spend too much time avoiding solitude? Do people today spend too much time in front of television and videos? Do they seek virtual reality when all they have to do is look at a sunset? [Sample responses: People who avoid solitude are afraid to be alone. Or people spend more time in front of the television and less time talking with each other face to face. Or television keeps people who are confined to their homes company.]

PROBLEM SOLVING/CRITICAL THINKING

Economizing Have students look up *economy* and discuss Thoreau's use of the word. Ask students to examine their own lives and to write a journal entry on how they could economize. Have students meet in groups of four to discuss their findings. Students could extend the activity by analyzing in small groups how their community could economize.

PROFESSIONAL NOTES

Thematic Connections: "The Life Worth Living" Have students discuss how Thoreau's image of marching to the beat of a different drummer complements Emerson's description of the nonconformist. Ask them how Thoreau lives out the life Emerson writes about in "Self-Reliance."

A. Expansion

"I was determined to know beans" is a witticism aimed at the common saying "He doesn't know beans." Thoreau may have been responding to his Concord neighbors, who thought of him as an eccentric crank.

B. Humanities Connection

In this section, Thoreau again draws a **comparison** between the labors of ordinary people and the acts of Greek heroes, making ordinary labor also seem heroic.

C. Exploring the Historical Period

Thoreau writes a **narrative** of a war between ants. His description parallels human warfare, as he calls the ant battle an "internecine" war. This label also applies to the struggle going on in the country regarding slavery. What important internecine historical event was about to occur? [The Civil War.]

remaining beans will be too tough for them, and go forward to meet new foes. . . .

It was a singular experience that long acquaintance which I cultivated with beans, what with planting, and hoeing, and harvesting, and threshing, and picking over and selling them—the last was the hardest of all—I might add eating, for I did taste. I was determined to know beans. When they were growing, I used to hoe from five o'clock in the morning till noon, and commonly spent the rest of the day about other affairs. Consider the intimate and curious acquaintance one makes with various kinds of weeds—it will bear some iteration in the account, for there was no little iteration in the labor—disturbing their delicate organizations so ruthlessly, and making such invidious distinctions with his hoe, leveling whole ranks of one species, and sedulously cultivating another. That's Roman wormwood—that's pigweed—that's sorrel—that's pipergrass—have at him, chop him up, turn his roots upward to the sun, don't let him have a fiber in the shade, if you do he'll turn himself t'other side up and be as green as a leek in two days. A long war, not with cranes, but with weeds, those Trojans who had sun and rain and dews on their side. Daily the beans saw me come to their rescue armed with a hoe, and thin the ranks of their enemies, filling up the trenches with weedy dead. Many a lusty crest-waving Hector,[15] that towered a whole foot above his crowding comrades, fell before my weapon and rolled in the dust. . . .

from Brute Neighbors

. . . One day when I went out to my woodpile, or rather my pile of stumps, I observed two large ants, the one red, the other much larger, nearly half an inch long, and black, fiercely contending with one another. Having once got hold they never let go, but struggled and wrestled and rolled on the chips incessantly. Looking farther, I was surprised to find that the chips were covered with such combatants, that it was not a *duellum,* but a *bellum,*[16] a war between two races of ants, the red always pitted against the black, and frequently two red ones to one black. The legions of these Myrmidons[17] covered all the hills and vales in my wood yard, and the ground was already strewn with the dead and dying, both red and black. It was the only battle which I have ever witnessed, the only battlefield I ever trod while the battle was raging; internecine[18] war; the red republicans on the one hand, and the black imperialists on the other. On every side they were engaged in deadly combat, yet without any noise that I could hear, and human soldiers never fought so resolutely. I watched a couple that were fast locked in each other's embraces, in a little sunny valley amid the chips, now at noonday prepared to fight till the sun went down, or life went out. The smaller red champion had fastened himself like a vise to his adversary's front, and through all the tumblings on that field never for an instant ceased to gnaw at one of his feelers near the root, having already caused the other to go by the board; while the stronger black one dashed him from side to side, and, as I saw on looking nearer, had already divested him of several of his members. They fought with more pertinacity than bulldogs. Neither manifested the least disposition to retreat. It was evident that their battle cry was "Conquer or die." In the meanwhile there came along a single red ant on the hillside of this valley, evidently full of excitement, who either had dispatched his foe, or had not yet taken part in the battle; probably the latter, for he had lost none of his limbs; whose mother had charged him to return with his shield or upon it.[19] Or perchance he was some Achilles, who had nourished his wrath apart, and had now come to avenge or rescue his Patroclus.[20] He saw this unequal com-

15. **Hector:** In the *Iliad,* Hector is the Trojan prince killed by the Greek hero Achilles.
16. **not a *duellum,* but a *bellum:*** not a duel, but a war.
17. **Myrmidons:** Achilles' soldiers in the *Iliad. Myrmex* is Greek for "ant."
18. **internecine** (in'tər·nē'sin): harmful to both sides of the group.
19. **return . . . upon it:** echoes the traditional charge of Spartan mothers to their warrior sons: return victorious or dead.
20. **Achilles . . . Patroclus:** In the *Iliad,* Achilles withdraws from the battle at Troy but rejoins the fight after his friend Patroclus is killed.

WORDS TO OWN

incessantly (in·ses'ənt·lē) *adv.:* without stopping.

OPTIONS FOR TEACHING

ASSESSMENT TOOLS

Check Test: True-False

1. Thoreau gathers the material and builds the house without help from neighbors. [False]
2. Thoreau hoped to earn some money from his crops; however, he just breaks even after deducting planting and seed costs. [False]
3. A laughing loon easily outwits Thoreau as he chases the bird around Walden Pond in a small boat. [True]
4. Thoreau says he left Walden Pond because he had other lives to lead and did not want to fall into a worn routine. [True]
5. Thoreau tells his readers they should all live as he did, for only by living away from society and with nature are people able to know their possibilities. [False]

Informal Assessment: Reading In order to evaluate how students are reading strategically, use the following scale:

Never		Sometimes		Always
1	2	3	4	5

___ Activates prior knowledge before reading the selection
___ Generates a list of what he or she wants to know
___ Uses that information to interact with the text

bat from afar—for the blacks were nearly twice the size of the red—he drew near with rapid pace till he stood on his guard within half an inch of the combatants; then, watching his opportunity, he sprang upon the black warrior, and commenced his operations near the root of his right foreleg, leaving the foe to select among his own members; and so there were three united for life, as if a new kind of attraction had been invented which put all other locks and cements to shame. I should not have wondered by this time to find that they had their respective musical bands stationed on some eminent chip, and playing their national airs the while, to excite the slow and cheer the dying combatants. I was myself excited somewhat even as if they had been men. The more you think of it, the less the difference. And certainly there is not the fight recorded in Concord history, at least, if in the history of America, that will bear a moment's comparison with this, whether for the numbers engaged in it, or for the patriotism and heroism displayed. For numbers and for carnage it was an Austerlitz or Dresden.[21] Concord Fight! Two killed on the patriots' side, and Luther Blanchard wounded! Why here every ant was a Buttrick—"Fire! for God's sake fire!"—and thousands shared the fate of Davis and Hosmer.[22] There was not one hireling there. I have no doubt that it was a principle they fought for, as much as our ancestors, and not to avoid a threepenny tax on their tea; and the results of this battle will be as important and memorable to those whom it concerns as those of the Battle of Bunker Hill, at least. (D)

I took up the chip on which the three I have particularly described were struggling, carried it into my house, and placed it under a tumbler on my windowsill, in order to see the issue. Holding a microscope to the first-mentioned red ant, I saw that, though he was assiduously gnawing at the near foreleg of his enemy, having severed his remaining feeler, his own breast was all torn away, exposing what vitals he had there to the jaws of the black warrior, whose breastplate was apparently too thick for him to pierce; and the dark carbuncles of the sufferer's eyes shone with ferocity such as war only could excite. They struggled half an hour longer under the tumbler, and when I looked again the black soldier had severed the heads of his foes from their bodies, and the still living heads were hanging on either side of him like ghastly trophies at his saddlebow, still apparently as firmly fastened as ever, and he was endeavoring with feeble struggles, being without feelers and with only the remnant of a leg, and I know not how many other wounds, to divest himself of them; which at length, after half an hour more, he accomplished. I raised the glass, and he went off over the windowsill in that crippled state. Whether he finally survived that combat, and spent the remainder of his days in some Hôtel des Invalides,[23] I do not know; but I thought that his industry would not be worth much thereafter. I never learned which party was victorious, nor the cause of the war; but I felt for the rest of that day as if I had had my feelings excited and harrowed by witnessing the struggle, the ferocity and carnage, of a human battle before my door. . . .

In the fall the loon (*Colymbus glacialis*) came, as usual, to molt and bathe in the pond, making the woods ring with his wild laughter before I had risen. At rumor of his arrival all the Mill-dam sportsmen are on the alert, in gigs and on foot, two by two and three by three, with patent rifles and conical balls and spyglasses. They come rustling through the woods like autumn leaves, at least ten men to one loon. (E) Some station themselves on this side of the pond, some on that, for the poor bird cannot be omnipresent; if he dive here he must come up there. But now the kind October wind rises, rustling the leaves and rippling the surface of the water, so that no loon can be heard or seen, though his foes sweep the pond with spyglasses, and make the woods resound with their discharges. The waves generously rise and dash angrily, taking sides with all waterfowl, and our sportsmen must beat a retreat to town and shop and unfinished jobs. But they were too often successful. When I went to get a pail of

21. Austerlitz or Dresden: major battles of the Napoleonic Wars.

22. Luther . . . Hosmer: All these men fought at the Battle of Concord, the first battle of the Revolutionary War. Major John Buttrick led the minutemen who defeated the British. Isaac Davis and David Hosmer were the two colonists killed.

23. Hôtel des Invalides: Home for Disabled Soldiers, a veterans' hospital in Paris, France. The body of Napoleon I (1769–1821) is buried there.

D. Language Note: Analogy

? Does Thoreau's battle of the ants parallel the battle of Concord? Why or why not? [Possible answers: No, to compare the two minimizes the war for independence. Yes, such a parallel is Thoreau's way of saying that all of life's struggles are equally important and are relative.]

E. Literary Element: Setting

? How does the setting of Walden contrast with the story of the hunters and the loon? [The setting of Walden is tranquil and peaceful. The loon is a natural inhabitant, and the hunters—ten men to one loon—are intruders who disturb the peace.]

A. Critical Reading: Finding Details

? How does Thoreau's use of minute details involve the reader?

[His use of details seems to give the reader insight into his pattern of thought, to bring the reader into the story, and to coincide with his philosophical reason for going to Walden—to live life to its fullest.]

B. Expansion

This paragraph, which contains Thoreau's description of the loon, is a relatively digressive piece of nature writing, in contrast to his more compact, aphoristic philosophical passages. But the loon passage in its entirety can be read as a philosophical **metaphor** on the relationship between people and nature or between people and the underlying realities of existence.

water early in the morning I frequently saw this stately bird sailing out of my cove within a few rods.[24] If I endeavored to overtake him in a boat, in order to see how he would maneuver, he would dive and be completely lost, so that I did not discover him again, sometimes, till the latter part of the day. But I was more than a match for him on the surface. He commonly went off in a rain.

As I was paddling along the north shore one very calm October afternoon, for such days especially they settle onto the lakes, like the milkweed down, having looked in vain over the pond for a loon, suddenly one, sailing out from the shore toward the middle a few rods in front of me, set up his wild laugh and betrayed himself. I pursued with a paddle and he dived, but when he came up I was nearer than before. He dived again, but I miscalculated the direction he would take, and we were fifty rods apart when he came to the surface this time, for I had helped to widen the interval; and again he laughed long and loud, and with more reason than before. He maneuvered so cunningly that I could not get within half a dozen rods of him. Each time, when he came to the surface, turning his head this way and that, he coolly surveyed the water and the land, and apparently chose his course so that he might come up where there was the widest expanse of water and at the greatest distance from the boat. It was surprising how quickly he made up his mind and put his resolve into execution. He led me at once to the widest part of the pond, and could not be driven from it. While he was thinking one thing in his brain, I was endeavoring to divine his thought in mine. It was a pretty game, played on the smooth surface of the pond, a man against a loon. Suddenly your adversary's checker disappears beneath the board, and the problem is to place yours nearest to where his will appear again. Sometimes he would come up unexpectedly on the opposite side of me, having apparently passed directly under the boat. So long-winded was he

24. **rods:** One rod measures 16½ feet.

Common Loon (1833) by John James Audubon. Watercolor, graphite, gouache, pastel.

Collection of the New-York Historical Society.

and so unwearyable, that when he had swum farthest he would immediately plunge again, nevertheless; and then no wit could divine where in the deep pond, beneath the smooth surface, he might be speeding his way like a fish, for he had time and ability to visit the bottom of the pond in its deepest part. It is said that loons have been caught in the New York lakes eighty feet beneath the surface, with hooks set for trout—though Walden is deeper than that. How surprised must the fishes be to see this ungainly visitor from another sphere speeding his way amid their schools! Yet he appeared to know his course as surely underwater as on the surface, and swam much faster there. Once or twice I saw a ripple where he approached the surface, just put his head out to reconnoiter, and instantly dived again. I found that it was as well for me to rest on my oars and wait his reappearing as to endeavor to calculate where he would rise; for again and again, when I was straining my eyes over the surface one way, I would suddenly be startled by his unearthly laugh behind me. But why, after displaying so much cunning, did he invariably betray himself the moment he came up by that loud laugh? Did not his white breast enough betray him? He was indeed a silly loon, I thought. I could commonly hear the plash of the water when he came up, and so also detected him. But after an hour he seemed as fresh as ever, dived as willingly, and swam yet farther than at first. It was surprising to see how serenely he sailed off with unruffled breast when he came to the surface, doing all the work with his webbed feet beneath. His usual note was this demoniac laughter, yet somewhat like that of a waterfowl; but occasionally, when he had balked me most successfully and come up a long way off, he uttered a long-drawn unearthly howl, probably more like that of a wolf than any bird; as when a beast puts his muzzle to the ground and deliberately howls. This was his looning—perhaps the wildest sound that is ever heard here, making the woods ring far and wide. I concluded that he laughed in derision of my efforts confident of his own resources. Though the sky was by this time overcast, the pond was so smooth that I could see where he broke the surface when I did not hear him. His white breast, the stillness of the air, and the smoothness of the water were all against him. At length, having come up fifty rods off, he uttered one of those prolonged howls, as if calling on the god of loons to aid him, and immediately there came a wind from the east and rippled the surface, and filled the whole air with misty rain, and I was impressed as if it were the prayer of the loon answered, and his god was angry with me; and so I left him disappearing far away on the tumultuous surface. . . .

from Conclusion

. . . I left the woods for as good a reason as I went there. Perhaps it seemed to me that I had several more lives to live, and could not spare any more time for that one. It is remarkable how easily and insensibly we fall into a particular route, and make a beaten track for ourselves. I had not lived there a week before my feet wore a path from my door to the pond side; and though it is five or six years since I trod it, it is still quite distinct. It is true, I fear, that others may have fallen into it, and so helped to keep it open. The surface of the earth is soft and impressible by the feet of men; and so with the paths which the mind travels. How worn and dusty, then, must be the highways of the world, how deep the ruts of tradition and conformity! I did not wish to take a cabin passage, but rather to go before the mast and on the deck of the world, for there I could best see the moonlight amid the mountains. I do not wish to go below now.

I learned this, at least, by my experiment: That if one advances confidently in the direction of his dreams, and endeavors to live the life which he has imagined, he will meet with a success unexpected in common hours. He will put some things behind, will pass an invisible boundary; new, universal, and more liberal laws will begin to establish themselves around and within him; or the old laws be expanded, and interpreted in his favor in a more liberal sense, and he will live with the license of a higher order of beings. In proportion as he simplifies his life, the laws of the

Words to Own

derision (di·rizh′ən) *n.:* ridicule; contempt.
tumultuous (to͞o·mul′cho͞o·əs) *adj.:* stormy; turbulent.

C. Exploring the Historical Period

In contrast to the natural setting of the loon, the United States was in the midst of the Industrial Revolution. A short distance away, the city of Lowell, Massachusetts, patterned itself after the industrial cities of England. It strove to be different, however, by creating a different kind of work force in which workers would stay only a brief time in the city and take advantage of its cultural offerings. Though many advances came about during this period, the Industrial Revolution also gave rise to tales of the squalor and woe of factory life. The discourse on the loon contrasts with a historical period in which the new nation was flexing its industrial and inventive muscle. People sought control over nature. Such efforts by people to control nature, for many writers, were at odds with what they believed was the natural order of things.

D. Literary Connections

? Whom does Thoreau echo here? [He echoes Emerson in "Self-Reliance." Like Emerson, Thoreau wrote about the need for self-reliance and the drawbacks of mindless conformity. If a small path that led to his house could be worn in such a short period of time, imagine, he says, how worn the highways must be and, therefore, the "ruts of tradition and conformity."]

A. Critical Reading: Identifying Main Ideas

? How does Thoreau denounce what some are saying about the new nation? [Thoreau believes people must be allowed to chart their own course. He suggests people tend to their own affairs and be who they were meant to be.]

B. Exploring the Historical Period

? What events going on at this time in American history make Thoreau say that some people hear "a different drummer" and should be allowed to "step to the music [each] hears"? [First, the issue of slavery was dividing the country. Second, the Mexican War outraged many Americans who believed the United States provoked the war in order to expand its territory. Third, the notion of manifest destiny was beginning to grip the population. This theory stated that the new nation had a God-given right to expand its territory, although it meant destruction of Native American cultures.]

C. Language Note: Style

? What effect does Thoreau's question have? [Possible answer: It elevates his point. The hatching of a small insect that was dormant for decades mirrors the hatching of ideas in the human mind once the mind has been released from its "well-seasoned tomb."]

D. Expansion

The last four sentences are ringing and apocalyptic. Ask students to paraphrase them in order to discuss their meaning. [The mere passing of time will not help us grasp the significance of our lives. We can understand only if we seek to understand. There is always more to learn.]

universe will appear less complex, and solitude will not be solitude, nor poverty poverty, nor weakness weakness. If you have built castles in the air, your work need not be lost; that is where they should be. Now put the foundations under them. . . .

(A) Some are dinning in our ears that we Americans, and moderns generally, are intellectual dwarfs compared with the ancients, or even the Elizabethan men. But what is that to the purpose? A living dog is better than a dead lion.[25] Shall a man go and hang himself because he belongs to the race of pygmies, and not be the biggest pygmy that he can? Let everyone mind his own business, and endeavor to be what he was made.

(B) Why should we be in such desperate haste to succeed and in such desperate enterprises? If a man does not keep pace with his companions, perhaps it is because he hears a different drummer. Let him step to the music which he hears, however measured or far away. It is not important that he should mature as soon as an apple tree or an oak. Shall he turn his spring into summer? If the condition of things which we were made for is not yet, what were any reality which we can substitute? We will not be shipwrecked on a vain reality. Shall we with pains erect a heaven of blue glass over ourselves, though when it is done we shall be sure to gaze still at the true ethereal heaven far above, as if the former were not? . . .

The life in us is like the water in the river. It may rise this year higher than man has ever known it, and flood the parched uplands; even this may be the eventful year, which will drown out all our muskrats. It was not always dry land where we dwell. I see far inland the banks which the stream anciently washed, before science began to record its freshets. Everyone has heard the story which has gone the rounds of New England, of a strong and beautiful bug which came out of the dry leaf of an old table of apple-tree wood, which had stood in a farmer's kitchen for sixty years, first in Connecticut, and afterward in Massachusetts—from an egg deposited in the living tree many years earlier still, as appeared by counting the annual layers beyond it; which was heard gnawing out for several weeks, hatched perchance by the heat of an urn. (C) Who does not feel his faith in a resurrection and immortality strengthened by hearing of this? Who knows what beautiful and winged life, whose egg has been buried for ages under many concentric layers of woodenness in the dead dry life of society, deposited at first in the alburnum[26] of the green and living tree, which has been gradually converted into the semblance of its well-seasoned tomb—heard perchance gnawing out now for years by the astonished family of man, as they sat round the festive board—may unexpectedly come forth from amidst society's most trivial and handselled[27] furniture, to enjoy its perfect summer life at last!

I do not say that John or Jonathan[28] will realize all this; but such is the character of that morrow which mere lapse of time can never make to dawn. (D) The light which puts out our eyes is darkness to us. Only that day dawns to which we are awake. There is more day to dawn. The sun is but a morning star.

25. **A living dog . . . lion:** Ecclesiastes 9:4.

26. **alburnum:** sapwood; soft wood between the inner bark and the hard core of a tree.

27. **handselled:** given as a mere token of good wishes; therefore, of no great value in itself.

28. **John or Jonathan:** John Bull and Brother Jonathan were traditional personifications of England and the United States respectively.

WORDS TO OWN

ethereal (ē·thir′ē·əl) *adj.:* not earthly; spiritual.

A Journal Page (1845) by Henry David Thoreau. Pen and ink.
The Pierpont Morgan Library, New York.

Connections — An Essay

In 1990, the musician Don Henley of the rock group the Eagles founded the Walden Woods Project to protect a part of Walden Woods under threat of real-estate development. Here Henley talks about how Thoreau and Emerson contributed to his "spiritual awakening" and his commitment to the preservation of Walden Woods.

from Heaven Is Under Our Feet

Don Henley

I honestly don't remember when I was first introduced to the works of Henry David Thoreau or by whom. It may have been my venerable high school English teacher, Margaret Lovelace, or it may have been one of my university professors. I was lucky enough to have a few exceptional ones and that is sometimes all a kid needs—just one or two really good teachers can make all the difference in the world. It can inspire and change a life. . . .

Thoreau's writing struck me like a thunderbolt. Like all great literature, it articulated something that I knew intuitively, but could not quite bring into focus for myself. I loved Emerson, too, and his essay, "Self-Reliance," was instrumental in giving me the courage to become a songwriter. The works of both men were part of a spiritual awakening in which I rediscovered my hometown and the beauty of the surrounding landscape, and, through that, some evidence of a "Higher Power," or God, if you like. This epiphany brought great comfort and relief. . . .

. . . [T]here has been a great deal of curiosity, speculation, and, in some quarters, skepticism bordering on cynicism, as to how and why I came to be involved in the movement to preserve the stomping grounds of Henry David Thoreau and his friend and mentor, Ralph Waldo Emerson. What, in other words, is California rock and roll trash doing meddling around in something as seemingly esoteric and high-minded as literature (pronounced "LIT-tra-chure"), philosophy, and history—the American Transcendentalist Movement and all its ascetic practitioners. Seems perfectly natural to me. American Literature, like the air we breathe, belongs—or should belong—to everybody. . . . The great halls of learning may keep Thoreau's literature and principles alive, but they will be of little help in fortifying the well from whence they sprang.

. . . Unfortunately, the focus of preservation efforts has come to rest on the pond and its immediate surroundings. That is all well and good, except that there remain approximately two thousand six hundred acres that are inside the historic boundaries of Walden Woods and deserve protection as well. Thoreau did not live *in* Walden Pond; he lived beside it. The man did not walk on water, he walked several miles a day through the woods, and his musings and writings therein figure at least as prominently in his literature as Walden Pond does. In other words, the width and breadth of his inspiration, the scope of his legacy is not limited to one sixty-two-acre pond, and it is absurd to think so. Walden Woods is not a pristine, grand tract of wilderness, but it is still, for the most part, exceedingly beautiful and inspiring. It is, for all intents and purposes, the cradle of the American environmental movement and should be preserved for its intrinsic, symbolic value or, as Ed Schofield, Thoreau Society president, so succinctly put it, "When Walden goes, all the issues radiating out from Walden go, too. If the prime place can be disposed of, how much easier to dispose of the issues it represents." Otherwise, we might just as well turn all our national parks, our monuments to freedom and independence, into theme parks and shopping malls.

A. Expansion

Henley's essay is one of several included in *Heaven Is Under Our Feet,* a collection of essays written by writers, entertainers, politicians, and environmentalists to help support the Walden Woods Project. Henley has raised over nine million dollars for the project.

B. Critical Reading: Identifying Main Ideas

? What is Henley's main argument? [That Walden Woods itself should be preserved, not just the pond, for it is the entire environment that Thoreau wrote about, not just the small piece of land on which the house was situated. To lose the woods would be to fail to see Thoreau's point about the importance of nature.]

C. Reader's Response: Extending the Text

? What issues stem from Walden? [Sample responses: Taking care of the environment, the importance of observation in daily life, working with natural resources, or relying on one's own self.]

Technology Tip

After your students read the essay, they may want to explore *The Electronic Drummer,* the hypertext newsletter produced by the Thoreau Institute, found at **http://www.teleport.com/~rot**. *The Electronic Drummer* explores contemporary environmental issues. *You may want to preview any Internet activity that you suggest to students. Because these resources are sometimes public forums, their content can be unpredictable.*

CONNECTING WITH *WALDEN*

Henley protests the potential land development of Walden Woods and works to see that the woods be preserved. With the help of Emerson and Thoreau, Henley has discovered for himself the kind of life worth living. He has learned from Emerson to rely on himself, to listen to his own conscience, and to broaden his thinking and not be tempted to conform to more narrow-minded thinking in society. This enables him to speak out against what he sees as an injustice, the development of Walden Woods. Henley has also learned from Thoreau. He has come into an appreciation of his own hometown and its beauty and acquired the courage to march to the tune of the drummer he hears. Ask students to discuss, in detail, what Henley may have derived from Thoreau's *Walden,* and invite them to share what they themselves have learned from Thoreau's work.

Making Meanings

First Thoughts

1. Possible responses: Thoreau is wordy, but his ideas are sound. Given the continuing fight for civil rights, his message is still valid today. Or getting close to nature is not important today.

Reviewing the Text

a. Many people have asked Thoreau about his experiment at Walden.
b. He went to the woods to live simply and to confront only the essential elements of life.
c. He says that Earth is a point in space, a part of the Milky Way, and suggests he cannot possibly be lonely in a natural setting.
d. He takes great pleasure in being closely connected to the earth.

Shaping Interpretations

2. Possible response: People should strive to cut out the nonessential aspects of their lives so they can concentrate on important aspects.
3. Possible responses: Thoreau is skeptical about technological progress. Progress takes away from nature. Or no, technological advances improve and simplify people's lives.
4. Possible response: In order to enjoy the role of nature in their lives, people must take the trouble to observe nature carefully.
5. Possible response: Those who work at fulfillment may achieve it.

Connecting with the Text

6. Students may say their goals differed from Thoreau's. Some may say they have gained a healthier respect for nature.

Extending the Text

7. **(Evaluation)** Possible responses: *Walden* has influenced those who wish to preserve nature and who argue for caution when people alter the landscape. Walden Woods should be preserved. Or it is enough to preserve the pond.

Challenging the Text

8. **(Evaluation)** Possible responses: Thoreau is not talking in the extreme. He may, in fact, be telling people to slow down and consider those things in life that are basic: family, individual liberty, human understanding, and survival. Or I agree with Stegner; Thoreau abandoned any contact with society when he went to Walden.

Language and Style

Answers

1. Possible answer: Thoreau asks those not totally appreciative of his lifestyle and his writing not to change his meaning to fit their particular philosophy, because it may help those who are suited to it.
2. Possible answer: Thoreau wanted to live a rich life and to learn as much from it as he possibly could.
3. Possible answer: If people do not follow the crowd, they may have different ideals and goals. Let them live according to their own ways, even if those ways are different from others'.

MAKING MEANINGS

First Thoughts

1. What do you think of Thoreau — as a writer and as a personality? Is his message still valid, or do you find it dated and irrelevant?

Reviewing the Text

a. According to the second paragraph in "Economy," why has Thoreau decided to write about his life?
b. How does Thoreau answer the questions implied in the title "Where I Lived, and What I Lived For"?
c. What arguments does Thoreau present in "Solitude" to demonstrate that he is not lonely in his isolated situation?
d. What satisfactions does Thoreau find in the labor of raising beans in "The Bean Field"?

Shaping Interpretations

2. What does Thoreau mean when he says, "Simplify, simplify" (page 238)? Do you think he has a valid point here? Explain.
3. How would you summarize Thoreau's ideas on technological progress, judging from what he says about railroads and other inventions of his era? Do you agree with him? Why or why not?
4. What do you think Thoreau means in his final paragraph by the words "Only that day dawns to which we are awake"?
5. What do you think is the lesson of the **fable** of the apple-tree wood table at the conclusion of *Walden?*

Connecting with the Text

6. Re-read the Reader's Log entry you made as you read this selection. How do the views you expressed compare and contrast with those of Thoreau? Have you changed your views at all since reading the excerpt? Explain your answer.

Extending the Text

7. In Connections on page 245, the rock star Don Henley declares that Walden Woods is the "cradle of the American environmental movement and should be preserved for its intrinsic, symbolic value." In what ways do you think Thoreau's *Walden* has influenced the entire environmental movement in the United States? Do you agree with Henley that Walden Woods should be preserved because it has symbolic value to our society? Explain.

Challenging the Text

8. The Pulitzer Prize–winning author Wallace Stegner (1909–1993), who admired much of Thoreau's thought, once made this observation about Thoreau's message in *Walden:* "At times he sounds perilously like his spiritual descendants of the 1960s, who trusted no one over thirty and believed that they existed outside of, and were exempt from, the society they were protesting." Do you agree or disagree with Stegner's statement? Support or refute it with examples from *Walden.*

LANGUAGE AND STYLE

Thoreau's Metaphors

Thoreau's **metaphors** are highly visual. Though they're clever and original, they aren't far-fetched. Thoreau takes his comparisons from nature and from other things he and his audience are familiar with, such as clothes and sailing.

Express each of the following metaphors from Thoreau in your own words:

1. "As for the rest of my readers, they will accept such portions as apply to them. I trust that none will stretch the seams in putting on the coat, for it may do good service to him whom it fits." (page 234)
2. "I wanted to live deep and suck out all the marrow of life. . . ." (page 237)
3. "If a man does not keep pace with his companions, perhaps it is because he hears a different drummer. Let him step to the music which he hears, however measured or far away." (page 244)

Choices: Building Your Portfolio

Writer's Notebook

1. Collecting Ideas for a Controversial Issue

In the Writer's Notebook on page 229, you brainstormed a list of ideas for a controversial issue. By now you might have added to your list—especially after reading Thoreau. Review your topics. Underneath each topic, write three to five questions that you would like to explore. For example, if one of your topics is preserving wilderness areas, you might pose the question "Should wilderness areas be preserved at the cost of new housing?" Save your notes for possible use in the Writer's Workshop on page 331.

Critical Writing

2. Isn't It Romantic?

In a brief essay, identify evidence of the Romantic point of view that you see in *Walden*—the emphasis on intuition, the power of nature, and human emotion. Is Thoreau a Romantic, in your opinion? In what ways is he *not* a Romantic?

Critical Writing

3. Words from the Wise

"The invariable mark of wisdom," Emerson wrote, "is to find the miraculous in the common." Using Emerson's statement as your topic sentence, choose a scene from *Walden,* and in a brief essay discuss how Thoreau finds "the miraculous in the common."

Creative Writing

4. Thoreau Speaks Out

Thoreau would undoubtedly have strong, and probably controversial, opinions on many aspects of present-day technology and society. Write a paragraph or two expressing Thoreau's opinion on a fact of modern life. Use the **first-person point of view.** Try to find support in *Walden* for the position you (as Thoreau) present.

Creative Writing

5. Simple Gifts

Walden does not record monumental events; it describes the ordinary events that most people would let pass unnoticed. Do the same for a day in your life. Take a few minutes at intervals throughout the day to write down your impressions of what is going on around you. At the end of the day, record in a journal what you saw, what you heard, and what you thought. Did anything remind you of Thoreau's experiences? Did anything convey a lesson or seem to hold a message?

Creative Writing / Performance

6. Different Strokes

Suppose that a Puritan like Mary Rowlandson (page 38) or a rationalist like Benjamin Franklin (page 84) had done the "Walden experiment." Write a journal entry from the point of view of the Puritan or rationalist of your choice, recording your experience of solitude at Walden Pond. What lessons or morals do you draw from your experience? How is your perspective different from Thoreau's? Read your journal entry aloud to the class, impersonating your journal writer.

Crossing the Curriculum: Science

7. Walden, Naturally

Thoreau is remembered not only as a philosophical writer but as a keen observer of nature. Choose an aspect of nature that Thoreau mentions—an ant war, a loon, a bean field, or something less obvious—and do some research in the school or local library. Find at least three facts about the subject that go beyond the information Thoreau provides. Report your findings to the class.

Beyond the Selection

Choices: Building Your Portfolio

1. **Writer's Notebook** Remind students to save their work. They may use it as prewriting for the Writer's Workshop on p. 331.
2. **Critical Writing** Ask students to discuss three pieces of evidence from the text that prove their point.
3. **Critical Writing** Suggest students address in their essays the three key words in Emerson's statement: *wisdom, miraculous,* and *common.*
4. **Creative Writing** To help students find support in *Walden* for their position, suggest they consult their Reader's Log entries from the second part of A Dialogue with the Text exercise on p. 232.
5. **Creative Writing** To prepare for writing the longer journal entry, have students brainstorm a list of things that they did from the time they woke up until they arrived at school. Then, have them write a paragraph on what they learned from one event that day. Afterward, have them write ways they could expand their entry by writing a description of the event or adding sensory details or dialogue.
6. **Creative Writing/Performance** Ask students to review material from the historical introduction on pp. 9–18 before they begin writing.
7. **Crossing the Curriculum: Science** Students may wish to consult science teachers and practicing scientists for more information.

STRATEGIES FOR INCLUSION

Visual Have students think about a present-day technological issue for activity #4 by using a cluster such as the following. You may wish to demonstrate the process by using Transparency 3: Cluster Diagram in the Transparency Package. Students may write their questions out to the side or below an issue. They may wish to choose the issue with the most questions or most significant questions.

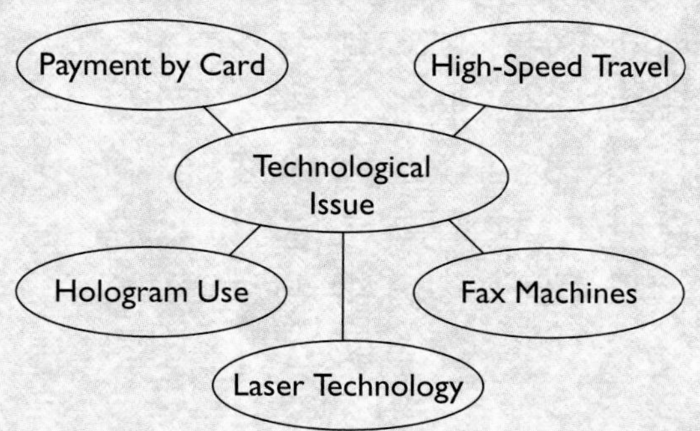

PORTFOLIO ASSESSMENT

Choices: Assessment Criteria For help in evaluating these Choices assignments, see the criteria in the ***Portfolio Management System,*** pp. 96–97.

QUICK PLANNING GUIDE

Into the Selection

Before You Read p. 248

- **Reading Focus: Set a Purpose** Students evaluate Thoreau's position.
- **Quickwrite: Prior Knowledge** Respond to civil disobedience in Reader's Log
- **Elements of Literature: Paradox**
- **Background:** Thoreau's night in jail

Through the Selection

from "Resistance to Civil Government" pp. 249–254
Words to Own pp. 249–251
Primary Sources p. 255
Connections: A Letter p. 256
from "Letter from Birmingham City Jail"
Making Meanings p. 257
Language and Style p. 257

Beyond the Selection

Choices: Building Your Portfolio p. 258

- **Writer's Notebook:** Write ideas for a controversial issue
- **Critical Writing:** Support or oppose Thoreau in a brief essay
- **Critical Writing:** Write a brief essay to compare and contrast Thoreau's ideas and the Declaration of Independence
- **Creative Writing/Drama:** Write and stage a one-scene play
- **Crossing the Curriculum: Social Studies:** Prepare and present a brief research report on history of non-violent civil disobedience

BEFORE YOU READ
FROM RESISTANCE TO CIVIL GOVERNMENT

Reading Focus
Civil Disobedience

The idea of civil disobedience is probably familiar to you if you know anything about the U.S. civil rights struggles of the 1960s or the struggle of Mohandas K. ("Mahatma") Gandhi's followers for the independence of India in the first half of the twentieth century. Both movements took inspiration from the essay that follows.

Some readers have concluded that this essay shows that Thoreau merely wanted to withdraw from life and all its hard questions. Others see Thoreau's action as the logical outcome of his convictions. Decide for yourself if Thoreau's position is justified.

Gandhi during the last months of his life in Birla House, New Delhi, India. Photograph.
Henri Cartier-Bresson/Magnum.

Quickwrite
READER'S LOG

Under what circumstances, if any, would you be willing to go to jail for a moral or political principle? Write a brief description of the principle and of your feelings about it—or explain why you wouldn't be willing to commit civil disobedience under any circumstances.

Elements of Literature
Paradox

A **paradox** is a statement that expresses the complexity of life by showing how opposing ideas can be both contradictory and true, as in Emily Dickinson's famous line "Tell all the Truth but tell it slant—" (page 386). Paradox was one of Thoreau's favorite literary devices. The idea that a contradiction can contain a truth is in itself paradoxical—and truthful.

> A **paradox** is a statement that seems to contradict itself, but that reveals a truth.
>
> *For more on Paradox, see the Handbook of Literary Terms.*

Background
In July 1846, Thoreau's stay at Walden Pond was interrupted by a night in jail. Thoreau was arrested because he refused to pay a tax to the state—primarily because he was opposed to the government's support of slavery. The Concord police offered to pay the tax for Thoreau, but he refused that also. He was forced, therefore, to spend the night in jail, and he might have spent more time there, except that someone, probably his aunt, paid the tax for him. This night in jail inspired the essay known as "Resistance to Civil Government" or "Civil Disobedience."

WORDS TO OWN

The following vocabulary words are defined in the Words to Own at the bottom of the pupil's page.

expedient p. 249	insurrection p. 250
perverted p. 249	penitent p. 250
posterity p. 250	effectual p. 251
alacrity p. 250	obstruction p. 251
inherent p. 250	impetuous p. 251

PORTFOLIO ASSESSMENT

Portfolio Assessment For help with teacher assessment of reading skills, see the ***Portfolio Management System,*** pp. 54–55.

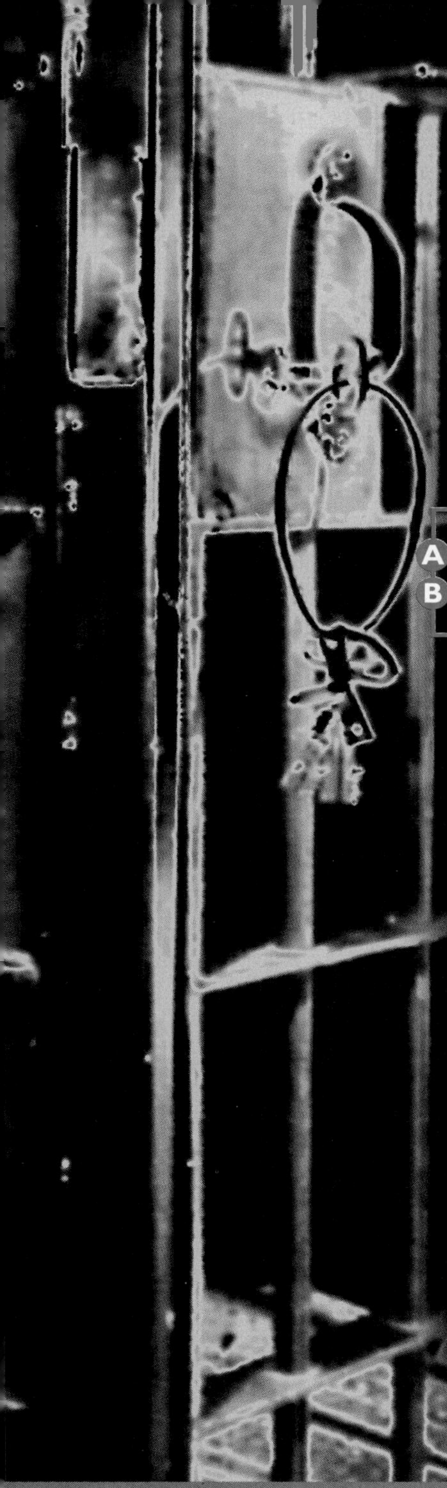

from Resistance to Civil Government

Henry David Thoreau

A B I heartily accept the motto—"That government is best which governs least";[1] and I should like to see it acted up to more rapidly and systematically. Carried out, it finally amounts to this, which also I believe—"That government is best which governs not at all"; and when men are prepared for it, that will be the kind of government which they will have. Government is at best but an expedient; but most governments are usually, and all governments are sometimes, inexpedient. The objections which have been brought against a standing army, and they are many and weighty, and deserve to prevail, may also at last be brought against a standing government. The standing army is only an arm of the standing government. The government itself, which is only the mode which the people have chosen to execute their will, is equally liable to be abused and perverted before the people can act through it. Witness the present Mexican war, the work of comparatively a few individuals using the standing government as their tool; for, in the outset, the people would not have consented to this measure.[2]

1. **That . . . least:** This statement, attributed to Thomas Jefferson, was the motto of the New York *Democratic Review,* which had published two of Thoreau's essays.
2. **this measure:** On May 9, 1846, President James K. Polk (1795–1849) received word that Mexico had attacked United States troops. He then asked Congress to declare war, which they did on May 13. Some Americans, including Thoreau, thought the war was unjustified. Because Thoreau would not support the war with his taxes, he went to jail.

WORDS TO OWN

expedient (ek·spē′dē·ənt) *n.:* convenience; means to an end.
perverted (pər·vurt′id) *v.:* misdirected; corrupted.

Using **BEFORE YOU READ** p. 248

Elements of Literature

Write a list of contradictions on the chalkboard. Examples include "less is more" and "You have to spend money to make money." Have students think of situations where these statements might be true.

A. Literary Element: Paradox

? This passage begins with a paradox. The statement seems both contradictory and true. How can a government govern not at all? [Possible answers: It would not interfere in day to day activities. Or it would exist only to ease matters, such as establishing a common currency in a country.]

B. Reader's Response: First Thoughts

? Would Thoreau's assertion "That government is best which governs not at all" work in a complex society? [Sample responses: Although many might say this is true, few would give up those parts of the government that are personally useful to them. Or in a complex society, values are not shared, so people need a strong government.]

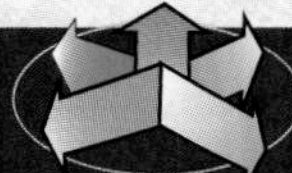

PROGRAM MANAGER

- **Planning Instruction** See Teaching Notes, *Teaching Resources A,* p. 86, for objectives, a summary, literary elements, and additional historical and biographical information for this selection.
- **Instructional Support** Before beginning the instructional lesson, see Graphic Organizer for Active Reading, *Teaching Resources A,* p. 100, for a Through the Selection activity.
- **Assessment** See Selection Test, *Test Booklet,* pp. 65–66.
- **Reinforcement** Use the Words to Own worksheet in *Teaching Resources A,* p. 101.

A. Reader's Response: Extending the Text

? How can a balance be created between the will of the majority and the rights of the minority? What would happen if people did what they thought was right? [Sample responses: An increased representation of the minority in government would help balance interests. The country would be at odds if all people did what they thought best.]

B. Critical Reading: Making Connections

Thoreau makes a distinction: People do not have to oppose wrongdoing actively, but they can refuse to be a part of it. How does this fit in with other principles Thoreau advocates in *Walden*? [Possible answers: He felt people should work out their own beliefs without interference. Or if people follow the direction of their dreams, they will be successful. It is important for people to "step to the music" they hear.]

C. Exploring the Historical Period

Thoreau spoke out loudly against the Mexican War, as he felt it was an attempt to extend the United States' slaveholding property.

This American government—what is it but a tradition, though a recent one, endeavoring to transmit itself unimpaired to posterity, but each instant losing some of its integrity? It has not the vitality and force of a single living man; for a single man can bend it to his will. It is a sort of wooden gun to the people themselves; and, if ever they should use it in earnest as a real one against each other, it will surely split. But it is not the less necessary for this; for the people must have some complicated machinery or other, and hear its din, to satisfy that idea of government which they have. Governments show thus how successfully men can be imposed on, even impose on themselves, for their own advantage. It is excellent, we must all allow; yet this government never of itself furthered any enterprise, but by the alacrity with which it got out of its way. *It* does not keep the country free. *It* does not settle the West. *It* does not educate. The character inherent in the American people has done all that has been accomplished; and it would have done somewhat more, if the government had not sometimes got in its way. For government is an expedient by which men would fain[3] succeed in letting one another alone; and, as has been said, when it is most expedient, the governed are most let alone by it. Trade and commerce, if they were not made of India rubber, would never manage to bounce over the obstacles which legislators are continually putting in their way; and, if one were to judge these men wholly by the effects of their actions, and not partly by their intentions, they would deserve to be classed and punished with those mischievous persons who put obstructions on the railroads.

But, to speak practically and as a citizen, unlike those who call themselves no-government men, I ask for, not at once no government, but *at once* a better government. Let every man make known what kind of government would command his respect, and that will be one step toward obtaining it.

After all, the practical reason why, when the power is once in the hands of the people, a majority are permitted, and for a long period continue, to rule, is not because they are most likely to be in the right, nor because this seems fairest to the minority, but because they are physically the strongest. But a government in which the majority rule in all cases cannot be based on justice, even as far as men understand it. Can there not be a government in which majorities do not virtually decide right and wrong, but conscience?—in which majorities decide only those questions to which the rule of expediency is applicable? Must the citizen ever for a moment, or in the least degree, resign his conscience to the legislator? Why has every man a conscience, then? I think that we **A** should be men first, and subjects afterward. It is not desirable to cultivate a respect for the law, so much as for the right. The only obligation which I have a right to assume, is to do at any time what I think right. . . .

B It is not a man's duty, as a matter of course, to devote himself to the eradication of any, even the most enormous wrong; he may still properly have other concerns to engage him; but it is his duty, at least, to wash his hands of it, and, if he gives it no thought longer, not to give it practically his support. If I devote myself to other pursuits and contemplations, I must first see, at least, that I do not pursue them sitting upon another man's shoulders. I must get off him first, that he may pursue his contemplations too. See what gross inconsistency is tolerated. **C** I have heard some of my townsmen say, "I should like to have them order me out to help put down an insurrection of the slaves, or to march to Mexico—see if I would go"; and yet these very men have each, directly by their allegiance, and so indirectly, at least, by their money, furnished a substitute. The soldier is applauded who refuses to serve in an unjust war by those who do not refuse to sustain the unjust government which makes the war; is applauded by those whose own act and authority he disregards and sets at nought; as if the State were penitent to that degree that it hired one to scourge it while it sinned, but not to that degree that it left off sinning for a moment. Thus, under the name of order

3. **fain:** archaic for "gladly" or "willingly."

WORDS TO OWN

posterity (päs·ter′ə·tē) *n.:* generations to come.
alacrity (ə·lak′rə·tē) *n.:* promptness in responding; eagerness.
inherent (in·hir′ənt) *adj.:* inborn.
insurrection (in′sə·rek′shən) *n.:* rebellion; revolt.
penitent (pen′i·tənt) *adj.:* sorry for doing wrong.

OPTIONS FOR TEACHING

STRATEGIES FOR INCLUSION

Auditory Read aloud passages or have students listen to recordings of Thoreau's essay. Have them explain in their journals why this treatise lends itself to being read aloud. [Thoreau narrates stories that have **conflict.** His description of the jail has lyrical qualities.]

Special Needs Have students look through newspapers and magazines and select articles that cover civil disobedience. Have them list the government's position as well as the opposition's position. Ask students to evaluate each position and decide whether the disobedience is justifiable. Helping students relate current issues to Thoreau's essay will promote understanding of his point of view.

Logical-Mathematical Ask students to use the following chart to track Thoreau's reasoning and to test his ideas. Students should see if they can discover other ways for Thoreau to address the issue or find analogies to Thoreau's problem by asking on what other issues people could take a similar stand.

Problem	Analogies	Other Issues
[Jailed for objection to war]	[Martin Luther King, Jr., jailed for civil rights protest]	[Desegregation] [The draft]

and civil government, we are all made at last to pay homage to and support our own meanness. After the first blush of sin, comes its indifference and from immoral it becomes, as it were, *unmoral*, and not quite unnecessary to that life which we have made. . . .

I meet this American government, or its representative the State government, directly, and face to face, once a year, no more, in the person of its tax-gatherer; this is the only mode in which a man situated as I am necessarily meets it; and it then says distinctly, Recognize me; and the simplest, the most effectual, and, in the present posture of affairs, the indispensablest mode of treating with it on this head, of expressing your little satisfaction with and love for it, is to deny it then. My civil neighbor, the tax-gatherer, is the very man I have to deal with—for it is, after all, with men and not with parchment that I quarrel—and he has voluntarily chosen to be an agent of the government. How shall he ever know well what he is and does as an officer of the government, or as a man, until he is obliged to consider whether he shall treat me, his neighbor, for whom he has respect, as a neighbor and well-disposed man, or as a maniac and disturber of the peace, and see if he can get over this obstruction to his neighborliness without a ruder and more impetuous thought or speech corresponding with his action? I know this well, that if one thousand, if one hundred, if ten men whom I could name—if ten *honest* men only—aye, if *one* HONEST man, in this State of Massachusetts, *ceasing to hold slaves,* were actually to withdraw from this copartnership, and be locked up in the county jail therefor, it would be the abolition of slavery in America. For it matters not how small the beginning may seem to be: What is once well done is done forever. . . .

I have paid no poll tax[4] for six years. I was put into a jail once on this account, for one night; and, as I stood considering the walls of solid stone, two or three feet thick, the door of wood and iron, a foot thick, and the iron grating which strained the light, I could not help being struck with the foolishness of that institution which treated me as if I were mere flesh and blood and bones, to be locked up. I wondered that it should have concluded at length that this was the best use it could put me to, and had never thought to avail itself of my services in some way. I saw that, if there was a wall of stone between me and my townsmen, there was a still more difficult one to climb or break through, before they could get to be as free as I was. I did not for a moment feel confined, and the walls seemed a great waste of stone and mortar. I felt as if I alone of all my townsmen had paid my tax. They plainly did not know how to treat me, but behaved like persons who are underbred. In every threat and in every compliment there was a blunder; for they thought that my chief desire was to stand the other side of that stone wall. I could not but smile to see how industriously they locked the door on my meditations, which followed them out again without let or hindrance, and *they* were really all that was dangerous. As they could not reach me, they had resolved to punish my body; just as boys, if they cannot come at some person against whom they have a spite, will abuse his dog. I saw that the State was half-witted, that it was timid as a lone woman with her silver spoons, and that it did not know its friends from its foes, and I lost all my remaining respect for it, and pitied it. . . .

They plainly did not know how to treat me, but behaved like persons who are underbred.

The night in prison was novel and interesting enough. The prisoners in their shirt sleeves were enjoying a chat and the evening air in the doorway, when I entered. But the jailer said, "Come, boys, it is time to lock up"; and so they dispersed, and I heard the sound of their steps returning into the hollow apartments. My roommate was

4. **poll tax:** fee some states and localities required from each citizen as a qualification for voting. It is now considered unconstitutional in the United States to charge such a tax.

WORDS TO OWN

effectual (e·fek′cho͞o·əl) *adj.:* productive; efficient.
obstruction (əb·struk′shən) *n.:* blockage; hindrance.
impetuous (im·pech′o͞o·əs) *adj.:* impulsive.

D. Critical Reading: Drawing Conclusions

? What does the tax gatherer represent to Thoreau? [The government.]

E. Expansion

The idea that a single righteous person, or a small group of such persons, can redeem a whole society has strong Biblical echoes—see Genesis 18.

F. Critical Reading: Making Connections

? What point is Thoreau trying to make about the lone woman with silver spoons? [Such a person would be so worried about losing her possessions that she would not be able to tell whom she could trust. Thoreau is trying to make a similar point about government.]

G. Humanities Connection

? How is Thoreau's stay in jail similar to the experiences of Mohandas Gandhi and Martin Luther King, Jr.? [All three were jailed for political protest of laws they considered unjust.]

INTEGRATING THE LANGUAGE ARTS

Writing: Script Have students in pairs write a script of a scene between Thoreau and Sam Staples, the tax gatherer and constable who arrests him. The scene should reveal the difficulties both people experience—Staples's following the dictates of the state and Thoreau's following his own principles.

Strategic Reading Point out that Thoreau repeats the word *government* in four paragraph openings. Have students create a cluster to illustrate Thoreau's main points about government in each of these paragraphs. Use the following cluster to begin.

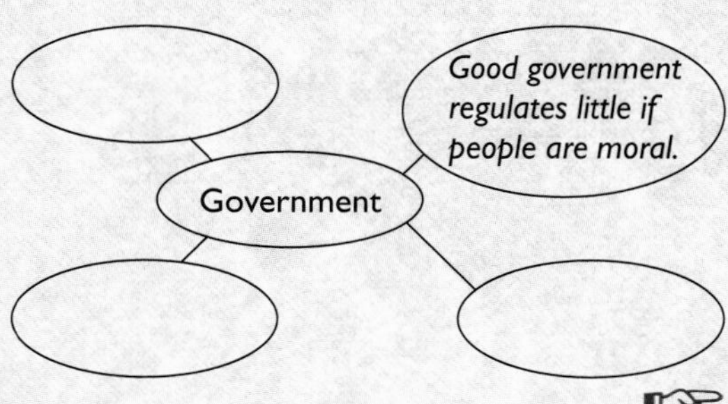

RESPONDING TO THE ART: ABOUT THE ARTIST

Horace Pippin (1888–1946) was a self-taught African American artist from Westchester, Pennsylvania, who began painting at the age of forty-two. He is known for the emotional depth of his work, which he achieved through a sophisticated use of form, color, and detail.

John Brown Going to His Hanging (1942) by Horace Pippin. Oil on canvas (24 1/8" × 30 1/4").

OPTIONS FOR TEACHING

COOPERATIVE LEARNING

Oral Choral Reading Have students with varying reading proficiency meet in groups of three. Have them share possible ways they might read aloud a passage from the text and where they should place emphasis in their reading. Have students make a tape of their passage, reading in unison. Students should play their tapes for the class and state how they arrived at their decision to read the passage the way they did.

CROSSING THE CURRICULUM

Social Sciences Have students research similar instances of civil resistance, such as the Boston Tea Party, Europeans hiding Jews during World War II, or the Civil Rights movement. Students should create newspaper stories describing the events they research.

Music Have students bring in music that could provide a backdrop for Thoreau's treatise. Have them determine whether the text lends itself to patriotic rhythms, marching bands, or drums.

The Pennsylvania Academy of the Fine Arts, Philadelphia, John Lambert Fund (1943.11).

introduced to me by the jailer, as "a first-rate fellow and a clever man." When the door was locked, he showed me where to hang my hat, and how he managed matters there. The rooms were whitewashed once a month; and this one, at least, was the whitest, most simply furnished, and probably the neatest apartment in the town. He naturally wanted to know where I came from, and what brought me there; and, when I had told him, I asked him in my turn how he came there, presuming him to be an honest man, of course; and, as the world goes, I believe he was. "Why," said he, "they accuse me of burning a barn; but I never did it." As near as I could discover, he had probably gone to bed in a barn when drunk, and smoked his pipe there; and so a barn was burnt. He had the reputation of being a clever man, had been there some three months waiting for his trial to come on, and would have to wait as much longer; but he was quite domesticated and contented, since he got his board for nothing, and thought that he was well treated.

He occupied one window, and I the other; and I saw, that, if one stayed there long, his principal business would be to look out the window. I had soon read all the tracts that were left there, and examined where former prisoners had broken out, and where a grate had been sawed off, and heard the history of the various occupants of that room; for I found that even here there was a history and a gossip which never circulated beyond the walls of the jail. Probably this is the only house in the town where verses are composed, which are afterward printed in a circular form, but not published. I was shown quite a long list of verses which were composed by some young men who had been detected in an attempt to escape, who avenged themselves by singing them.

I pumped my fellow prisoner as dry as I could, for fear I should never see him again; but at length he showed me which was my bed, and left me to blow out the lamp.

It was like traveling into a far country, such as I had never expected to behold, to lie there for one night. It seemed to me that I never had heard the town-clock strike before, nor the evening sounds of the village; for we slept with the windows open, which were inside the grating. It was to see my native village in the light of the middle ages, and our Concord was turned into a Rhine stream, and visions of knights and castles passed before me. They were the voices of old burghers that I heard in the streets. I was an involuntary spectator and auditor of whatever was done and said in the kitchen of the adjacent village inn—a wholly new and rare experience to me. It was a closer view of my native town. I was fairly inside of it. I never had seen its institutions before. This is one of its peculiar institutions; for it is a shire town.[5] I began to comprehend what its inhabitants were about. **(A)**

5. **shire town:** town where a court sits, like a county seat.

A. Humanities Connection
Thoreau is saying that this one night in jail has changed his way of seeing. Compare and contrast this to the experience of Rip Van Winkle on pp. 154–165. [Rip endured profound physical changes during his much longer separation from his townspeople, but at the end Rip fit in comfortably with them. Thoreau suffers no physical changes, learns a lot about the attitudes of the townspeople, and does not fit comfortably with them.]

PROBLEM SOLVING/CRITICAL THINKING

Determining Injustice Have students identify when a practice is unjust. Using a Venn diagram, such as Transparency 5 in the Transparency Package, ask students to identify what made each practice unjust and to determine what these unjust practices have in common. Add circles to the diagram as students add practices. Have them generalize and define what makes a practice unjust.

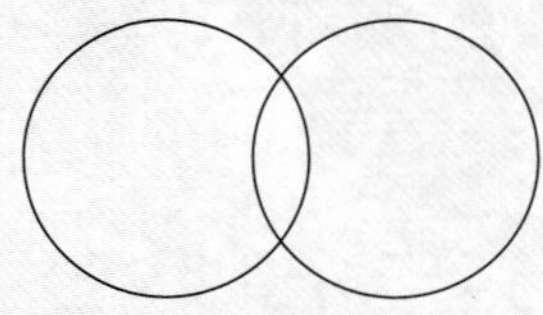

PROFESSIONAL NOTES

Cultural Diversity Have students identify and discuss instances of civil resistance in varying cultures in the United States and around the world. Have students talk about the goals of those who resist, their experiences, and the progress they have made.

A. Critical Reading: Making Inferences

? What does Thoreau imply when he says someone "interfered" in his release from prison? [Possible answer: He might have preferred to remain in jail just to prove his point.]

B. Literary Element: Irony

The last sentence of this paragraph is ironic. What does their lack of awareness of the jail say about Thoreau's neighbors? [It suggests both their indifference and hypocrisy.]

C. Critical Reading: Making Inferences

? Why might the members of the huckleberry party be "impatient to put themselves under [his] conduct"? [Possible answer: Thoreau's actions were based on moral rectitude. There is, therefore, a high degree of respect for him. Ultimately, the members of the party know they cannot live by the strict moral code Thoreau lives by.]

Metacognition How did you derive your answer? [Possible answer: The author biography on pp. 230–231 talks about Emerson's reaction to the huckleberry party. Thoreau writes that the townspeople talk of not going to fight in Mexico yet pay taxes that support the fighting.]

D. Expansion

This last paragraph is the central exposition of Thoreau's political ideas in this essay. It might be read aloud. Two sentences worth special attention and discussion are the ones beginning "The progress from an absolute to a limited monarchy . . ." and "There will never be a really free and enlightened State. . . ."

In the morning, our breakfasts were put through the hole in the door, in small oblong-square tin pans, made to fit, and holding a pint of chocolate, with brown bread, and an iron spoon. When they called for the vessels again, I was green enough to return what bread I had left; but my comrade seized it, and said that I should lay that up for lunch or dinner. Soon after, he was let out to work at haying in a neighboring field, whither he went every day, and would not be back till noon; so he bade me good day, saying that he doubted if he should see me again.

(A) When I came out of prison—for someone interfered, and paid the tax—I did not perceive that great changes had taken place on the common, such as he observed who went in a youth, and emerged a tottering and gray-headed man; and yet a change had to my eyes come over the scene—the town, and State, and country—greater than any that mere time could effect. I saw yet more distinctly the State in which I lived. I saw to what extent the people among whom I lived could be trusted as good neighbors and friends; that their friendship was for summer weather only; that they did not greatly purpose to do right; that they were a distinct race from me by their prejudices and superstitions, as the Chinamen and Malays are; that, in their sacrifices to humanity, they ran no risks, not even to their property; that, after all, they were not so noble but they treated the thief as he had treated them, and hoped, by a certain outward observance and a few prayers, and by walking in a particular straight though useless path from time to time, to save their souls. (B) This may be to judge my neighbors harshly; for I believe that most of them are not aware that they have such an institution as the jail in their village.

I please myself with imagining a State at last which can afford to be just to all men, and to treat the individual with respect as a neighbor...

It was formerly the custom in our village, when a poor debtor came out of jail, for his acquaintances to salute him, looking through their fingers, which were crossed to represent the grating of a jail window, "How do ye do?" My neighbors did not thus salute me, but first looked at me, and then at one another, as if I had returned from a long journey. I was put into jail as I was going to the shoemaker's to get a shoe which was mended. (C) When I was let out the next morning, I proceeded to finish my errand, and, having put on my mended shoe, joined a huckleberry party, who were impatient to put themselves under my conduct; and in half an hour—for the horse was soon tackled[6]—was in the midst of a huckleberry field, on one of our highest hills, two miles off; and then the State was nowhere to be seen.

This is the whole history of "My Prisons." . . .

(D) The authority of government, even such as I am willing to submit to—for I will cheerfully obey those who know and can do better than I, and in many things even those who neither know nor can do so well—is still an impure one: To be strictly just, it must have the sanction and consent of the governed. It can have no pure right over my person and property but what I concede to it. The progress from an absolute to a limited monarchy, from a limited monarchy to a democracy, is a progress toward a true respect for the individual. Is a democracy, such as we know it, the last improvement possible in government? Is it not possible to take a step further toward recognizing and organizing the rights of man? There will never be a really free and enlightened State, until the State comes to recognize the individual as a higher and independent power, from which all its own power and authority are derived, and treats him accordingly. I please myself with imagining a State at last which can afford to be just to all men, and to treat the individual with respect as a neighbor; which even would not think it inconsistent with its own repose, if a few were to live aloof from it, not meddling with it, nor embraced by it, who fulfilled all the duties of neighbors and fellow men. A State which bore this kind of fruit, and suffered it to drop off as fast as it ripened, would prepare the way for a still more perfect and glorious State, which also I have imagined, but not yet anywhere seen.

6. **tackled:** harnessed.

OPTIONS FOR TEACHING

ASSESSMENT TOOLS

Check Test: True-False

1. Thoreau believes people would lead better lives if there were stronger state governments. [False]
2. Thoreau says people need government for directing the tasks of educating, settling territories, and keeping the country free. [False]
3. Thoreau feels that jail is a ridiculous institution that locks up his body but not his mind. [True]
4. Thoreau feels that he gets a closer view of his town and understands its people better because of his night in jail. [True]
5. According to Thoreau, the ideal state is one in which individuals are free to be themselves even if they wish to live away from the society of others. [True]

Ongoing Assessment To assess students' oral strategies in reading in the Cooperative Learning activity on p. T252, evaluate students by using the following scale:

Seldom		Sometimes		Always
1	2	3	4	5

Did students have trouble with the passage when reading aloud? _____

Did students use their voices with appropriate emphasis on certain phrases and words? _____

Did students use intonation and vary rhythm? _____

PRIMARY **Sources** | TWO JOURNALS

"A Healthy and Wholesome Man to Know"

On August 31, 1842, the young Thoreau had dinner with Nathaniel Hawthorne (page 296). In his notebooks, Hawthorne gave this description of his guest (whose name he spells "Thorow").

Henry David Thoreau in his traveling outfit, at age 37 (c. 1854). Sketch.

The Bettmann Archive.

Mr. Thorow dined with us yesterday. He is a singular character—a young man with much of wild original nature still remaining in him; and so far as he is sophisticated, it is in a way and method of his own. He is as ugly as sin, long-nosed, queer-mouthed, and with uncouth and somewhat rustic, although courteous manners, corresponding very well with such an exterior. But his ugliness is of an honest and agreeable fashion, and becomes him much better than beauty. He was educated, I believe, at Cambridge, and formerly kept school in this town; but for two or three years back, he has repudiated all regular modes of getting a living, and seems inclined to lead a sort of Indian life. . . . He has been for some time an inmate of Mr. Emerson's family; and, in requital, he labors in the garden, and performs such other offices as may suit him—being entertained by Mr. Emerson for the sake of what true manhood there is in him. Mr. Thorow is a keen and delicate observer of nature—a genuine observer, which, I suspect, is almost as rare a character as even an original poet; and Nature, in return for his love, seems to adopt him as her especial child, and shows him secrets which few others are allowed to witness. He is familiar with beast, fish, fowl, and reptile, and has strange stories to tell of adventures, and friendly passages with these lower brethren of mortality. . . . With all this he has more than a tincture of literature—a deep and true taste for poetry, especially the elder poets. . . . On the whole, I find him a healthy and wholesome man to know.

—Nathaniel Hawthorne

• • • • •

Hawthorne's daughter described a skating trio on the Concord River: Emerson, Thoreau, and Hawthorne are on the ice. (In ancient Greece, a *dithyramb* was a wild, emotional hymn. In Greek and Roman myth, Bacchus is the god of wine and merrymaking.)

One afternoon, Mr. Emerson and Mr. Thoreau went with him [Hawthorne] down the river. Henry Thoreau is an experienced skater, and was figuring dithyrambic dances and Bacchic leaps on the ice—very remarkable, but very ugly, methought. Next him followed Mr. Hawthorne who, wrapped in his cloak, moved like a self-impelled Greek statue, stately and grave. Mr. Emerson closed the line, evidently too weary to hold himself erect, pitching headforemost, half lying on the air.

—Rose Hawthorne Lathrop

Primary Sources

After the dinner party mentioned here, Hawthorne and Thoreau went to a nearby river and Thoreau demonstrated his skill at paddling. For seven dollars Hawthorne bought *The Musketaquid,* the canoe Thoreau greatly valued. He had built it with his brother John, whose death in January 1842 had left him empty. He and his brother had canoed in it in 1839 on a trip that convinced Thoreau he was a poet and not a schoolmaster.

Hawthorne later wrote to a friend that Thoreau "despises the world, and all that it has to offer, and like other humorists, is an intolerable bore . . . I shall cause it to be known to him that you sat up till two o'clock reading his book; and he will pretend that it is of no consequence, but will never forget it . . . he is not an agreeable person, and in his presence one feels ashamed of having any money, or a house to live in, or so much as two coats to wear, or having written a book that the public will read—his own mode of life being so unsparing a criticism on all other modes, such as the world approves."

STRATEGIES FOR INCLUSION

Auditory Some students might grasp the meaning of Hawthorne's lengthy sentences by hearing them read aloud. Have students take turns reading orally, sentence by sentence. After each sentence, invite students to comment on Hawthorne's description of Thoreau; also, ask whether the sentences become easier to understand after hearing them read.

Visual Hawthorne provides a physical description of Thoreau in the excerpt; Lathrop describes Thoreau in action. To help students synthesize this information, have them create an artistic portrait of Thoreau or of the trio skating. Students should scan the text for details and use these to create a sketch that could serve as an illustration for Thoreau's work.

A. Expansion
King was held for eight days. He spent his first twenty-four hours in jail in solitary confinement and was not allowed to see his lawyers. While King was in jail, eight Alabama priests, rabbis, and ministers wrote a plea published in newspapers asking that the African American community withdraw any support from civil rights demonstrations. King wrote his letter on whatever paper he could find: in the margin of a newspaper that contained the clergymen's plea, on scraps of writing paper, and on a pad supplied by his attorneys.

B. Critical Reading: Drawing Conclusions
? Under what other circumstances could a law be unjust? [Possible answer: A law that harms the minority even though the minority can exercise the right to vote.]

C. Critical Reading: Identifying Main Ideas
? What two definitions apply to the *law* in this sentence? [In the first instance, King refers to actual laws enacted by government bodies. In the second instance, he refers to law as a principle, that is, as the embodiment of justice.]

Connections — A Letter

A The Reverend Dr. Martin Luther King, Jr., was a leader of the U.S. civil rights movement in the 1960s. He wrote this open letter on April 16, 1963, while serving a sentence for participating in a civil rights demonstration.

from Letter from Birmingham City Jail

Martin Luther King, Jr.

You express a great deal of anxiety over our willingness to break laws. This is certainly a legitimate concern. Since we so diligently urge people to obey the Supreme Court's decision of 1954 outlawing segregation in the public schools, it is rather strange and paradoxical to find us consciously breaking laws. One may well ask, "How can you advocate breaking some laws and obeying others?" The answer is found in the fact that there are two types of laws: there are *just* and there are *unjust* laws. I would agree with Saint Augustine that "An unjust law is no law at all."

Now what is the difference between the two? How does one determine when a law is just or unjust? A just law is a man-made code that squares with the moral law or the law of God. An unjust law is a code that is out of harmony with the moral law. . . .

B An unjust law is a code inflicted upon a minority which that minority had no part in enacting or creating because they did not have the unhampered right to vote. Who can say that the legislature of Alabama which set up the segregation laws was democratically elected? Throughout the state of Alabama all types of conniving methods are used to prevent Negroes from becoming registered voters and there are some counties without a single Negro registered to vote despite the fact that the Negro constitutes a majority of the population. Can any law set up in such a state be considered democratically structured?

These are just a few examples of unjust and just laws. There are some instances when a law is just on its face and unjust in its application. For instance, I was arrested Friday on a charge of parading without a permit. Now there is nothing wrong with an ordinance which requires a permit for a parade, but when the ordinance is used to preserve segregation and to deny citizens the First Amendment privilege of peaceful assembly and peaceful protest, then it becomes unjust.

I hope you can see the distinction I am trying to point out. In no sense do I advocate evading or defying the law as the rabid segregationist would do. This would lead to anarchy. One who breaks an unjust law must do it *openly, lovingly* (not hatefully as the white mothers did in New Orleans when they were seen on television screaming, "nigger, nigger, nigger"), and with a willingness to accept the penalty. C I submit that an individual who breaks a law that conscience tells him is unjust, and willingly accepts the penalty by staying in jail to arouse the conscience of the community over its injustice, is in reality expressing the very highest respect for law.

Martin Luther King, Jr., being arrested.
Charles Moore/Black Star.

CONNECTING WITH "RESISTANCE TO CIVIL GOVERNMENT"

King, as does Thoreau, defines an unjust law as one that violates universal moral principles and inhibits rights such as life, liberty, and the pursuit of happiness that Jefferson wrote of in the Declaration of Independence. Both King and Thoreau spent time in jail because they acted on their beliefs: Thoreau consciously disobeying a law; King breaking one while working to have another law removed. Both speak of their experiences in writing, one in an essay, the other in a letter. Ask students to talk about their reactions to Thoreau's essay and King's letter and to evaluate the effectiveness of each.

MAKING MEANINGS

First Thoughts

1. Would you have spent the night in jail as Thoreau did? Explain.

> **Reviewing the Text**
>
> a. Explain what Thoreau thinks is wrong with majority rule. What does he say is the only obligation he has a right to assume?
>
> b. What does Thoreau predict about slavery in America?
>
> c. Explain why Thoreau was put in jail. What were his feelings about the government when he was in jail?
>
> d. At the end of the essay, what qualities does Thoreau envision in an ideal "perfect and glorious State"?

Shaping Interpretations

2. Explain the truth in each of these **paradoxes.**
   a. "I saw that, if there was a wall of stone between me and my townsmen, there was a still more difficult one to climb or break through, before they could get to be as free as I was." (page 251)
   b. "I felt as if I alone of all my townsmen had paid my tax." (page 251)
3. How are Thoreau's perceptions of his fellow citizens changed by his night in jail?
4. What idea is Thoreau stressing in telling us about getting his shoe fixed and leading the huckleberry party on the day he was released?
5. From what you know about American Romanticism (pages 138–150), would you say that Thoreau's assumptions and points in this essay are fundamentally Romantic? Explain.
6. What influences of Emerson's thought can you find in "Resistance to Civil Government"?

Connecting with the Text

7. Review the notes you made in your Reader's Log about civil disobedience. Which of Thoreau's arguments did you find convincing, and which did you disagree with? Could there be civil order if each person always followed his or her own conscience? Explain.

Extending the Text

8. Comment on how Thoreau's main points in this essay relate to the points Martin Luther King, Jr., makes in Connections (page 256). How do Thoreau's and Dr. King's views relate to American life today?

Challenging the Text

9. Imagine that someone has made the following observation: "When Thoreau let someone pay the tax for him, he betrayed his own principles. He became just like the people he criticized, who opposed the Mexican War but supported it with their tax money. If he had wanted to make a truly courageous and effective protest, he should have insisted on staying in jail." Do you agree with this statement? Why or why not?

LANGUAGE AND STYLE

Precise Meanings of Words

1. "After the first blush of sin," writes Thoreau on page 251, "comes its indifference and from immoral it becomes, as it were, *un*moral . . ."
   a. The word *indifference* can mean "neutrality" or "apathy." What is the difference between the two meanings? Which meaning does the word have here?
   b. How is *unmoral* different from *immoral*?
2. Thoreau was arrested because he did not pay "poll tax."
   a. The word *poll* comes from a Middle English word for "top of the head." Usage has added other meanings, including the sense of "individual" ("one head"). What do you think a "poll tax" is?
   b. What do the words *poll, pollster,* and *poll booth* mean today? How are they related to the sense of "head"?

Making Meanings

First Thoughts

1. Possible responses: Yes, if I believe in the cause. Or I would not risk going to jail.

Reviewing the Text

a. He says government based on majority rule cannot be based on justice, since the majority will harm the minority. He feels his only obligation is to do what he thinks is right.

b. If only one honest man were to fight against slavery by going to jail in protest, it would lead to the abolition of slavery in America.

c. He refused to pay his poll tax. He feels it foolish and timid. He loses respect for it and pities it.

d. Thoreau says that an ideal state will "recognize the individual as a higher and independent power" from which all the state's authority will be derived. The state will be just to all people and will allow those who wish to live apart from it to do so without retribution.

Shaping interpretations

2. a. Thoreau means that the townspeople are imprisoned by conformity.
   b. By following his own conscience, he has figuratively paid his tax—that is, he has rendered a service to the state and to his fellow townspeople.
3. He feels that their friendship is "for summer weather only." He feels they are narrowminded.
4. Being jailed did not disrupt his life or his enjoyment of nature.
5. Responses will vary, but most will see his assumptions as Romantic. Romantic ideas include Thoreau's stress on the integrity of the individual and on conscience as a higher imperative than the rules of the state, his vision of Concord as a medieval town, and his concluding description of an ideal government.
6. Emerson's faith in the power of the individual to shape his or her own destiny and his emphasis on the value of integrity and self-reliance.

Connecting with the Text

7. Possible responses: People should try to solve problems, not just protest them. Yes, if each person followed his or her conscience. Or no, people's perceptions of what is right and wrong differ.

Extending the Text

8. **(Evaluation)** Possible responses: Peaceful protest tends to be tolerated today. People would probably be fined if they failed to pay taxes.

Challenging the Text

9. **(Evaluation)** Possible responses: He made his point. He did not need to stay. Or he should have stayed, for by leaving, he weakened the position of those opposed to the war.

Language and Style

Answers

1. a. *Neutrality* implies not deciding on a position; *apathy* implies not caring about taking a position. Thoreau means apathy here.
   b. *Unmoral* signifies that which has no inherent morality and is neither moral or immoral; *immoral* signifies that which is corrupt according to social standards.
2. a. Possible answer: A tax on an individual for voting rights.
   b. *Poll* means the casting of votes; *pollster* refers to one who takes surveys; a *poll booth* is where one goes to vote. They all have to do with individual votes and counting.

Beyond the Selection

Choices: Building Your Portfolio

1. **Writer's Notebook** Remind students to save their work. They may use it as prewriting for the Writer's Workshop on p. 331. Allow students to make lists of points or to write their ideas in statements as they see fit.
2. **Critical Writing** Remind students that it will help the reader if they state their positions in the introduction to their essays.
3. **Critical Writing** Remind students that organization is important when contrasting. To help them with organization, have them complete the following chart.

Source	Similar	Different
Declaration		
Thoreau		

4. **Creative Writing/Drama** Students may want to read their writing aloud during the drafting process to hear how the words sound.
5. **Crossing the Curriculum: Social Studies** Ask students to focus on the person's beliefs and actions relating to nonviolent resistance and to stay away from distracting biographical details.

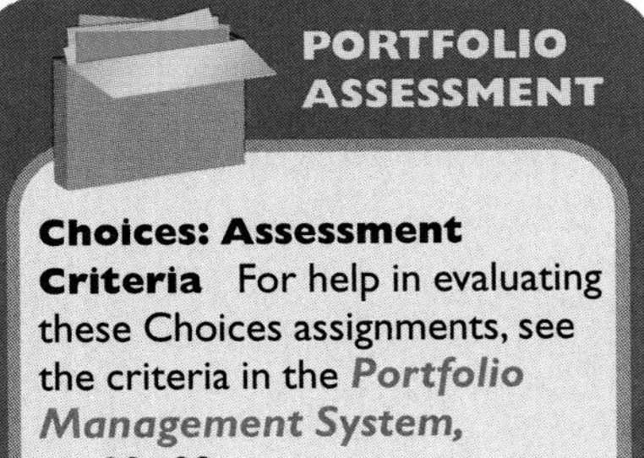

PORTFOLIO ASSESSMENT

Choices: Assessment Criteria For help in evaluating these Choices assignments, see the criteria in the *Portfolio Management System,* pp. 98–99.

CHOICES: Building Your Portfolio

Writer's Notebook

1. Collecting Ideas for a Controversial Issue

If you have already brainstormed a list of possible topics for an essay about a controversial issue and written questions about them, it's time to focus on the issue you want to write about, determine your position on it, and define it so that it can be argued effectively. At the top of a page, write your issue. Then write your ideas defining the issue and clarifying your position on it. Save your notes for possible use in the Writer's Workshop on page 331.

Critical Writing

2. Taking a Stand

Write a brief essay either in support of or in opposition to this statement from "Resistance to Civil Government": "That government is best which governs not at all." Include at least two emotional appeals in your essay.

Critical Writing

3. Declarations of Independence

In a brief essay, compare and contrast Thoreau's ideas in his essay with the ideas in the Declaration of Independence (page 117). Cite specific passages from both documents to support your views.

Creative Writing/ Drama

4. Thoreau's Night in Jail

Write and perform a one-scene play called "Thoreau's Night in Jail." Keep all the action within the setting of the Concord jail. In addition to Thoreau, you may want to use his jailer and his fellow prisoner as characters; feel free to add other characters, either real or fictional.

Crossing the Curriculum: Social Studies

5. Resisters All

Prepare and present a brief research report on some aspect of the history of nonviolent resistance or civil disobedience. You might focus on an event or movement, or report on a figure like Mohandas K. Gandhi, Martin Luther King, Jr., Cesar Chavez, Leo Tolstoy, Rosa Parks, Lech Walesa, Daw Aung San Suu Kyi, or Nelson Mandela.

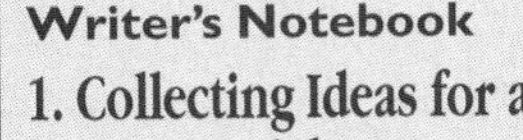

Nelson Mandela.

AP/Wide World Photos.

STRATEGIES FOR INCLUSION

Learners Having Difficulty To prepare for activity #3, have student groups of three read passages from the Declaration of Independence and "Resistance to Civil Government." Ask one student to read aloud the Declaration while the other two write down important ideas. Have another student read from "Resistance to Civil Government" while the other two listen for ideas similar to or different from those in the Declaration and write them down.

Visual To further their research in activity #5, students may wish to view videotapes of political speeches and appearances of the person they are studying. Students may also view documentaries on the lives and accomplishments of these leaders.

THE REALMS OF DARKNESS

Theme: **Into the Depths of Darkness**
The group of writers known as the Dark Romantics use symbolism to explore the dark side of the human mind. In their search for an understanding of the human psyche, they plumb inner depths, examining the irrational, guilt-ridden, obsessive side of humanity.

Thematic Focus

Each selection explores the darker side of human nature.

- **The Fall of the House of Usher** The gloomy, oppressive world of Roderick Usher and his sister Madeline is symbolized by the house that engulfs them.
- **The Raven** Mourning the loss of a love, the speaker of this narrative poem succumbs to despair and hopelessness.
- **House Taken Over** A brother and sister's dependence on each other is symbolized by the bizarre loss of their ancestral home.
- **The Minister's Black Veil** The minister's black veil symbolizes the secret, hidden guilt that lies in every human heart.
- *from* **Moby-Dick** One man's obsessive, revengeful nature is revealed in his pursuit of the great white whale.

Literary Focus

Literary Element	Selection / Feature
Atmosphere/Symbols/Connotations	**The Fall of the House of Usher**
Sound Effects: Rhythm/Rhyme/ Alliteration/Refrain/Onomatopoeia	**The Raven**
Symbols/Archaisms	**The Minister's Black Veil**
Characterization	**Moby-Dick**

Writing Focus

The following flow chart shows how the writing assignment for each selection relates to and builds toward the culminating writing assignment presented in the Writer's Workshop at the end of the unit.

Selection	Work-in-Progress Assignment
The Fall of the House of Usher	List several emotional appeals using words with strong connotative meanings p. 281
The Raven	Write three details or examples supporting your position on a controversial issue p. 289
The Minister's Black Veil	Find topics for a persuasive essay p. 309
Moby-Dick	Take notes for a persuasive essay p. 329
Writer's Workshop	Write persuasive essay pp. 331–337

Collection 6 **THE REALMS OF DARKNESS**

Collection Planner

PUPIL'S EDITION

SELECTION / FEATURE	Literary Elements / Active Reading	Writing	Speaking and Listening	Language and Vocabulary
The Fall of the House of Usher Edgar Allan Poe (pp. 260–281) **Connections: The Fall of the House of Usher** Reed Whittemore (p. 279)	• Reader's Log p. 262 • Atmosphere p. 262 • Symbols p. 280 • Connotations p. 281	• Critical Writing: Write interpretative essay p. 281 • Creative Writing: Retell story in another genre p. 281	• Music: Choose or compose background music for story/Play for class p. 281	• Language and Style: List words with gloomy connotations/Rewrite opening sentences of story p. 281
The Raven Edgar Allan Poe (pp. 282–289) Primary Sources: Poe's Process: Writing "The Raven" (p. 287)	• Reader's Log p. 282 • Sound effects: Rhythm, Rhyme, Alliteration p. 282 • Sound effects: Internal rhyme, Refrain, Rhyme scheme, Alliteration, Onomatopoeia p. 288	• Critical Writing: Write response p. 289 • Creative Writing/ Performance: Write humorous parody p. 289 • Art: Make collage and write explanation p. 289	• Creative Writing/ Performance: Perform parody for class p. 289	
House Taken Over Julio Cortázar (pp. 290–295)	• Reader's Log p. 290		• Finding Common Ground: Discuss story p. 295	
The Minister's Black Veil Nathaniel Hawthorne (pp. 296–310)	• Reader's Log p. 298 • Symbols p. 298 • Archaisms p. 308	• Critical Writing: Write essay on writers p. 309 • Critical Writing: Write comparison essay p. 309 • Creative Writing: Write sketch p. 309 • Creative Writing/Performance: Write and perform script p. 309 • Critical Writing: Write response essay p. 309	• Critical Thinking/ Speaking and Listening: Discuss Hawthorne and Poe in small group; share ideas with class p. 309 • Creative Writing/ Performance: Write and perform condensed version of story for class p. 309	• Language and Style: Rewrite archaisms in modern English p. 308 • How to Own a Word: Etymologies p. 310 • Try It Out: Research etymologies p. 310
from **Moby-Dick** Herman Melville (pp. 311–329)	• Reader's Log p. 313 • Characterization p. 313	• Critical Writing: Write essay on symbol p. 329 • Critical Thinking/Speaking and Listening: Prepare analysis chart p. 329 • Critical Writing: Write comparison essay p. 329 • Creative Writing: Write as Ahab p. 329 • Crossing the Curriculum: Science: Write report on whales/whaling p. 329	• Critical Thinking/ Speaking and Listening: Discuss analysis of Captain Ahab p. 329 • Crossing the Curriculum: Science: Present report on whales/whaling p. 329	
Writer's Workshop: Controversial Issue (pp. 331–337)		• Writing process: Persuasive essay pp. 331–337		
Language Workshop: Parallel Structure (p. 338)				• Language Handbook: Using parallel structure pp. 1235–1236 • Parallel Structure p. 338
Learning for Life: A Model of Self-Reliance (p. 339)		• Write encyclopedia entry p. 339 • Write short story p. 339 • Prepare brochure p. 339		

Collection Resources

Teaching Resources A	Audiovisual Resources Binder	Test Booklet
Cross-Curricular Activity p. 122	Fine Art Transparency 6.1	Collection 6 Test pp. 81–83

 Computer disk or CD-ROM
 Audiocassette
 Overhead Transparency

PROGRAM RESOURCES

Electronic Media	Teaching Resources with Organizer: Teaching Resources A	Teaching Resources with Organizer: Other Resources	Audiovisual Resources Binder
• Language Workshop: Participles and Participial phrases • Test Generator	• Teaching Notes pp. 103–105 • Reading Organizer p. 109 • Language Link pp. 110–111 • Words to Own p. 112	• Test Booklet: Selection Test pp. 71–72 • Language and Writing Skills Worksheets p. 73 • Portfolio Management System pp. 39, 100–101	• Elements of Literature Transparency 6.2
• Test Generator	• Teaching Notes p. 105 • Reading Organizer p. 113	• Test Booklet: Selection Test pp. 73–74 • Portfolio Management System pp. 53, 102	• Elements of Literature Transparency 6.3 • Selected Reading, Audiocassette 1, Side B
	• Teaching Notes p. 106		
• Language Workshop: Usage • Test Generator	• Teaching Notes pp. 106–107 • Reading Organizer p. 114 • Language Link pp. 115–116 • Words to Own p. 117	• Test Booklet: Selection Test pp. 75–76 • Language and Writing Skills Worksheets pp. 4–7 • Portfolio Management System pp. 54–55, 103–104	• Elements of Literature Transparency 6.4 • How to Own a Word Transparency 6.5
• Test Generator	• Teaching Notes pp. 107–108 • Reading Organizer p. 118 • Words to Own p. 119	• Test Booklet: Selection Test pp. 77–78, 79–80 • Portfolio Management System pp. 48–49, 105–106	
• Writer's Workshop 2: Controversial Issue		• Portfolio Management System pp. 107–109	• Revision Transparencies 6.6–6.7
• Language Workshop: Parallel Structure	• Language Workshop: Achieving Parallel Structure pp. 120–121		
		• Portfolio Management System p. 110	

Proofreading Warm-ups

You may use the following exercises to help students practice their proofreading skills. Copy a set of incorrect sentences onto the chalkboard, and have students find and correct the spelling, punctuation, usage, and mechanical errors in each sentence. Ask students to share and discuss their responses.

	Sentences with Errors	Sentences Corrected	Skills Covered
1	**a.** “did you know that Edgar Allan Poes works has been translated into many languages? asked Ms. Gonzalez. **b.** “some popular writers including Stephen King point to Poe as thier literary forefather” she added	**a.** “Did you know that Edgar Allan Poe’s works have been translated into many languages?” asked Ms. Gonzalez. **b.** “Some popular writers, including Stephen King, point to Poe as their literary forefather,” she added.	Capitalization, Apostrophe usage, Subject-verb agreement, Quotation marks, Comma usage, Spelling, End marks
2	**a.** poe uses alot of gothic details to create a spooky atmosphere in The Fall of the House of Usher **b.** strange sound’s and a person burried alive is some of these details	**a.** Poe uses a lot of Gothic details to create a spooky atmosphere in “The Fall of the House of Usher.” **b.** Strange sounds and a person buried alive are some of these details.	Capitalization, Spelling, Quotation marks for short story titles, Apostrophe usage, Subject-verb agreement, End marks
3	**a.** poes poem The Raven was popular when it was 1st published in 1845 **b.** altho Poe became a household name with this poem it didnt make him rich	**a.** Poe’s poem “The Raven” was popular when it was first published in 1845. **b.** Although Poe became a household name with this poem, it didn’t make him rich.	Capitalization, Apostrophe usage, Quotation marks for poem titles, Write out abbreviation, Spelling, Comma usage, End marks
4	**a.** one of Nathaniel Hawthornes ancestors was a judge who played a minor role in sentencing people to death during the Salem whitch trails **b.** hawthorne’s father a sea captain died during a voyage, and left his wife with 3 infants to raise	**a.** One of Nathaniel Hawthorne’s ancestors was a judge who played a minor role in sentencing people to death during the Salem witch trials. **b.** Hawthorne’s father, a sea captain, died during a voyage and left his wife with three infants to raise.	Capitalization, Apostrophe usage, Spelling, Comma usage, Write out numerals, End marks
5	**a.** like the other Dark Romantic’s Hawthorne used symbolism **b.** the story The Minister’s Black Veil is set in Puritan times it uses the black veil as a symbol	**a.** Like the other Dark Romantics, Hawthorne used symbolism. **b.** The story “The Minister’s Black Veil” is set in Puritan times; it uses the black veil as a symbol.	Capitalization, Apostrophe usage, Comma usage, Quotation marks for short story title, Semicolon usage, End marks
6	**a.** a archaism is old fashioned, language that is no longer in common use **b.** the word waggery is an example from “The Minister’s black veil”.	**a.** An archaism is old-fashioned language that is no longer in common use. **b.** The word waggery is an example from “The Minister’s Black Veil.”	Capitalization, Standard usage, Hyphen usage, Comma usage, Underline words used as words, Quotation marks (Order of punctuation), End marks
7	**a.** one can learn by consulting a dictionery to find out a words etymology **b.** a etymology the history of a word’s origin’s and development	**a.** One can learn by consulting a dictionary to find out a word’s etymology. **b.** An etymology is the history of a word’s origins and development.	Capitalization, Spelling, Apostrophe usage, Standard usage, Fragment, End marks
8	**a.** herman melville author of Moby-Dick was a sailor for 5 years **b.** upon his return Melville wrote several semiautobiographical Sea Tales’	**a.** Herman Melville, author of Moby-Dick, was a sailor for five years. **b.** Upon his return, Melville wrote several semiautobiographical sea tales.	Capitalization, Comma usage, Underline book title, Write out numeral, Apostrophe usage, End marks
9	**a.** call me Ishmael, is the famous opening line to Melville’s novel Moby-Dick **b.** in this novel Melville created the larger than life character captain Ahab.	**a.** “Call me Ishmael” is the famous opening line to Melville’s novel Moby-Dick. **b.** In this novel, Melville created the larger-than-life character Captain Ahab.	Quotation marks, Capitalization, Comma usage, Underline book title, Hyphen usage, End marks
10	**a.** captian Ahabs monomaniacal goal, is to kill Moby-Dick **b.** its more than likely that animal welfare groups would not approve of his goal	**a.** Captain Ahab’s monomaniacal goal is to kill Moby-Dick. **b.** It’s more than likely that animal welfare groups would not approve of his goal.	Capitalization, Spelling, Apostrophe usage, Comma usage, Usage, End marks

THE REALMS OF DARKNESS

Poe

Cortázar

Hawthorne

Melville

If you cannot bear the silence and the darkness, do not go there; if you dislike black night and yawning chasms, never make them your profession. If you fear the sound of water hurrying through crevices toward unknown and mysterious destinations, do not consider it. Seek out the sunshine. It is a simple prescription. Avoid the darkness.

It is a simple prescription, but you will not follow it. You will turn immediately to the darkness. You will be drawn to it by cords of fear and of longing. You will imagine that you are tired of the sunlight; the waters that unnerve you will tug in the ancient recesses of your mind; the midnight will seem restful—you will end by going down.

—Loren Eiseley,
from The Night Country

The Granger Collection, New York.

Responding to the Quotation

? What does this passage from *The Night Country* tell you about the selections you are about to read? [Possible responses: They are filled with fear, suspense, and darkness which will draw the reader like a magnet. Or they will explore the darkness mentioned in the period introduction.]

RESPONDING TO THE ART: VISUAL LITERACY

This is a portrait of Edgar Allan Poe (see pp. 260–261 for a biography) who is known for his suspenseful and eerie short stories. Ask students what they would surmise about his character from his appearance. [Possible responses: Perhaps he was an intense, intimidating man. He seems serious, pensive, and mysterious.]

PORTFOLIO ASSESSMENT

Parent/Guardian Involvement For forms that will help a parent or guardian review and respond to a student's portfolio, see ***Portfolio Management System,*** pp. 62–63.

PROGRAM MANAGER

- **Integrated Assessment** For a summative assessment of the literature and language skills taught in this collection, see **Collection 6 Test, *Test Booklet,*** pp. 81–83.
- **Instructional Support** See **Fine Art Transparency** 6.1. Review teacher's notes for transparencies in the ***Audiovisual Resources Binder*** for suggestions on how to tie the transparencies to specific reading selections.
- **Extending Collection Theme** See **Cross-Curricular Activity: The Realms of Darkness, *Teaching Resources A,*** p. 122, for an activity in other disciplines and for evaluation criteria.

WRITERS ON WRITING

Poe wrote that a skillful literary artist fashions a tale to achieve "a certain unique or single *effect*. . . . In the whole composition there should be no word written, of which the tendency, direct or indirect, is not to the one pre-established design."

Technology Tip

Students may find more information about Edgar Allan Poe on the World Wide Web at **http://138.232.92.2/sg/poe/poe. html**. *You may want to preview any Internet activity that you suggest to students. Because these resources are sometimes public forums, their content can be unpredictable.*

Edgar Allan Poe

(1809–1849)

The Bettmann Archive.

Edgar Allan Poe.

"The want of parental affection," wrote Poe, "has been the heaviest of my trials." Edgar Poe was, indeed, most unfortunate in his parents. His father, David Poe, was a mediocre traveling actor who drank heavily. His mother, Elizabeth Arnold, was a talented actress who was deserted by her husband when Edgar was still a baby. She died on tour in Richmond, Virginia, leaving Edgar virtually an orphan before his third birthday.

The boy was taken in by John and Frances Allan, a charitable and childless couple in Richmond. John Allan, an ambitious and self-righteous merchant, became Edgar's guardian (and the source of the writer's middle name). He provided generously for Edgar's early education, but he never formally adopted the boy.

Although Frances Allan was kind to Edgar, the boy grew up feeling both the lack of a natural father and the disapproval of his foster father. John Allan made no secret of his disappointment in Edgar—in his idleness, in his indifference to business life, and in his literary ambitions. Surely Allan's criticism added to Edgar's growing moodiness.

Breaking Away

At seventeen, Edgar entered the University of Virginia. He did well in his studies but was resentful of the meager allowance Allan gave him. When he tried to earn extra money by gambling, he went deep into debt. On discovering this, Allan refused to help his foster son and instead withdrew him from college.

After an especially bitter quarrel with Allan, Poe ran off to Boston to make his own way in the world. There, in 1827, he published a small volume of poems, *Tamerlane*. The book did not attract much attention, and Poe could find no other work. In despair, he joined the army. He was promoted to the rank of sergeant major, but he disliked the enlisted man's life and appealed to Allan for help. At the request of his wife, who was dying, Allan interceded for Edgar (for the last time) and agreed to help him enter the U.S. Military Academy at West Point.

While waiting to get into the Academy, Poe published a second book of poems, *El Aaraaf*, in 1829 and received his first real recognition as a writer. The next year, while at West Point, Poe learned that Allan (now a widower) had remarried and that the woman was young enough to have children. Since this appeared to end all hope of becoming Allan's heir, Poe had himself dismissed from West Point.

Exploring the Darkness and the Depths

Poe moved in with an aunt, Maria Poe Clemm, in Baltimore, Maryland. In 1835, he married her thirteen-year-old daughter, Virginia. The difference in their ages and Virginia's poor health resulted in a very odd marriage. But need and a strong sense of family drew the three housemates together.

Poe supported his family by working as an editor at various magazines. He wrote when he could find the time, completing his only full-length novel, *The Narrative of Arthur Gordon Pym*, several years after his marriage. But it was his short stories that had the greatest effect on other writers.

In "The Gold Bug," and in the tales built around that intuitive sleuth C. Auguste Dupin,

"The Purloined Letter" and "The Murders in the Rue Morgue," Poe laid the foundations for the modern detective story. In fact, he inspired Sir Arthur Conan Doyle to create Sherlock Holmes. And in tales such as "The Tell-Tale Heart," "The Cask of Amontillado," and "Hop-Frog," Poe inspired the Russian novelist Feodor Dostoevski (1821–1881) to explore the criminal mind.

Poe was a master of the psychological thriller. His tales of the ghastly and the grotesque are peopled with distraught narrators, deranged heroes, and doomed heroines. Yet his purpose in creating such characters was not to present readers with convincing likenesses of human beings—nor merely to shock and frighten. Instead, Poe wanted to take us behind the curtain that separates the everyday from the incredible. He wanted to leave behind the sunlit, tangible, rational world and discover the unsettling truth that lies in the dark, irrational depths of the human mind.

Small Triumphs and Great Tragedy

Poe produced a considerable body of work in spite of humiliating poverty and a serious drinking problem. The slightest amount of alcohol made him senseless; yet he drank to escape a reality he found agonizing. Publication of his poem "The Raven" in 1845 brought him some fame at last, but financial security still eluded him.

When Virginia died of tuberculosis in 1847, Poe and "Muddy" (Virginia's mother) were left alone. Poe grew more unstable and contracted illnesses, including a brain lesion that would leave him little time to live. But he pursued romance relentlessly, always looking for someone to "adopt" him. In 1849, during a visit to Virginia to a woman he hoped to marry, Poe disappeared. A week later, he was found in a Baltimore tavern—drunk and delirious, his clothing torn and wet from a raging storm. He regained enough consciousness to pray "Lord help my poor soul" before he died four days later. It was a tragic yet strangely appropriate end to the tortured life of a man obsessed by images of the human soul facing the terrors of loss and death.

Literature and Popular Culture

Poe the Pop Icon

Can you guess what Edgar Allan Poe has in common with Elvis Presley, Marilyn Monroe, the Beatles, and the cast of *Star Trek*? Like all of the above, Poe is a legend of popular culture. Consider these facts:

- Poe's works have been translated into virtually every language.
- Such popular writers as Stephen King and Ray Bradbury point to Poe as their literary forefather.
- The Mystery Writers of America annually honors great achievements in mystery writing with the "Edgar"—the equivalent of an Oscar or an Emmy.
- Poe has been immortalized in the popular arts, on everything from posters, buttons, and coffee mugs to bumper stickers and T-shirts.
- Poe has been "ushered" into twentieth-century pop culture through dozens of film adaptations, including *The Masque of the Red Death, The Black Cat, The Tomb of Ligeia,* and *The Pit and the Pendulum.*

Keep your eye out for Poe. He may be closer than you think.

Vincent Price in *The Masque of the Red Death.*

Movie Still Archives.

LITERATURE AND POPULAR CULTURE

Poe might be surprised to learn he is a legendary figure. Have students discuss how Poe might have handled such great fame and financial success if it had happened during his lifetime (see the author biography on pp. 260–261). Ask students if they think it would have made him happy and how it might have changed him.

Ask students to discuss other legendary figures of popular culture—writers, rock stars, movie legends, and so on. Invite students to consider how fame affected the person, why fame is so difficult to deal with, and whether it is possible to be both successful and happy.

QUICK PLANNING GUIDE

Into the Story

Author Biography **pp. 260–261**
Literature and Popular Culture **p. 261**
Before You Read **p. 262**

- **Reading Focus:** Students consider why we read frightening stories.
- **Quickwrite: Prior Knowledge** Freewrite in Reader's Log about images associated with horror
- **Elements of Literature: Atmosphere**

Through the Story

"The Fall of the House of Usher" pp. 263–279
Words to Own **pp. 264–278**
Literature and Popular Culture **p. 276**
Connections: A Poem **p. 279**
"The Fall of the House of Usher"
Making Meanings **p. 280**
Elements of Literature **p. 280**

- Conventional symbols
- Personal symbols
- Guidelines for finding symbols

Language and Style **p. 281**

Beyond the Story

Choices: Building Your Portfolio **p. 281**

- **Writer's Notebook:** Collect ideas for a controversial issue
- **Critical Writing:** Defend interpretation in a brief essay
- **Creative Writing:** Rewrite story in another genre
- **Music:** Find and play music to accompany story
- **Art:** Draw the house of Usher

Before You Read
The Fall of the House of Usher

Reading Focus
The Furnishings of Our Nightmares

Why do we watch movies like *Dracula, Psycho,* and *Jurassic Park?* Why do we make best-sellers of books by authors such as Stephen King and Dean Koontz?

In everyday life, we all feel fright from time to time: We tremble, sweat, get tense. Maybe those responses are designed to send us flying from danger to a less threatening place. Perhaps it's the need to periodically rehearse those feelings in a safe place that sends us to those scary movies and terrifying tales.

Quickwrite

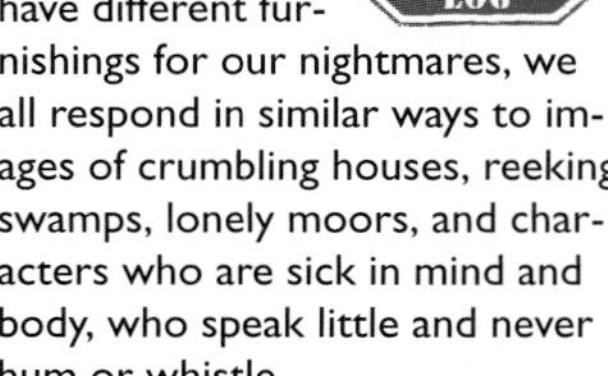

Although we each have different furnishings for our nightmares, we all respond in similar ways to images of crumbling houses, reeking swamps, lonely moors, and characters who are sick in mind and body, who speak little and never hum or whistle.

Freewrite for a few minutes about the images and ideas that you associate with horror stories. What books have you read or what movies have you seen that are truly horrifying? What, in your opinion, are the qualities of an effective horror story?

Elements of Literature
Atmosphere

A rotting mansion, mysterious illnesses, strange sounds at night, a person buried alive: Poe uses all of these Gothic details—and more (a list of them would stretch to the bottom of the page)—to create a single effect, a mood or **atmosphere,** of dread and menace. Notice how Poe begins to build his mood in the very first paragraph of this story, with its hissing *s* sounds and powerful sensory images. It's a good paragraph to read aloud—listen to its sounds and feel its effects. Which words and phrases in this opening paragraph make you aware that the narrator is leaving one region and entering another, uncertain one?

Atmosphere is the mood or feeling created in a piece of writing.

For more on Atmosphere, see the Handbook of Literary Terms.

Illustration by Wilfred Satty for "The Fall of the House of Usher."

WORDS TO OWN

The following vocabulary words are defined in the Words to Own at the bottom of the pupil's

pervaded p. 264	vivacious p. 267	similitude p. 274
sojourn p. 264	pallid p. 267	demeanor p. 275
equivocal p. 266	inordinate p. 267	obstinate p. 276
discernible p. 266	insipid p. 268	prodigious p. 277
specious p. 266	palpable p. 269	potency p. 278
scrutinizing p. 266	stupor p. 269	emaciated p. 278
profuse p. 267	morbid p. 271	

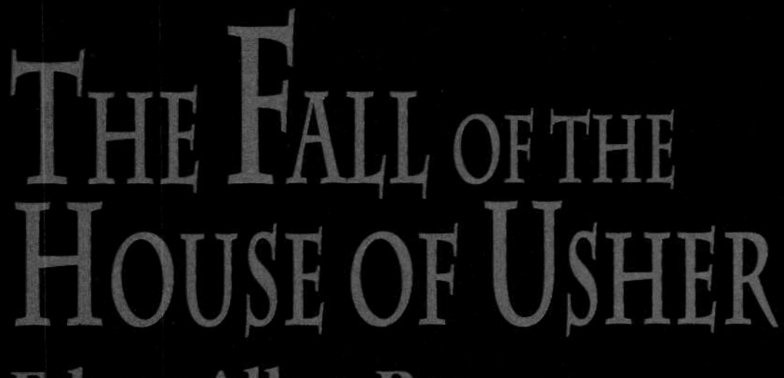

THE FALL OF THE HOUSE OF USHER

Edgar Allan Poe

Into the Story

Using BEFORE YOU READ p. 262

Reading Focus

Have students work in groups of three or four to discuss a frightening movie or book they have all seen or read. Ask them to describe their reactions to the movie or book in a chart like the following. Students should include three or four particularly memorable scenes.

Book or Movie Title		
Memorable Scene	What Happened	How I Felt

Quickwrite

Students may want to think about the movie or book they discussed in the Reading Focus activity. Remind them to write the first thoughts that come to mind.

PORTFOLIO ASSESSMENT

Portfolio Assessment
For help with self- and teacher assessment of reading skills, see the *Portfolio Management System,* p. 39.

PROGRAM MANAGER

- **Planning Instruction** See Teaching Notes, *Teaching Resources A,* pp. 103–105, for objectives, a summary, literary elements, and information.
- **Instructional Support** See Graphic Organizer for Active Reading, *Teaching Resources A,* p. 109, for a Through the Story activity.
- **Instructional Support** See Fine Art Transparency 6.1 and Instructional Transparency 6.2. Review teacher's notes in the *Audiovisual Resources Binder* for teaching suggestions.
- **Assessment** See Selection Test, *Test Booklet,* pp. 71–72.
- **Language Link** For practice in participles and participial phrases, see Language Link, *Teaching Resources A,* pp. 110–111, and *Language and Writing Skills Worksheets,* p. 73.
- **Reinforcement** Use the Words to Own worksheet in *Teaching Resources A,* p. 112.

A. Literary Elements: Alliteration and Atmosphere

Ask students to identify the alliteration in the first line. [The *d's* of *during, dull, dark,* and *day.*] What effect does it create? [A mood of death and depression.]

B. Literary Element: Personification

? How does Poe characterize the house? [It has eyes for windows, yet its vacant expression implies a lack of caring or thought.]

Answer to Boxed Question

He feels "a sense of insufferable gloom." He senses that something is terribly wrong, but he is not sure what it is.

C. Reader's Response: First Thoughts

? How would you feel about visiting the House of Usher? [Possible responses: Uneasy; after approaching the house, I do not think I would want to go any further. Or I may not like the way the house looked, but I think I would go in because I would be concerned for my friend.]

Son cœur est un luth suspendu;
Sitôt qu'on le touche il résonne.[1]

—*De Béranger*

During the whole of a dull, dark, and soundless day in the autumn of the year, when the clouds hung oppressively low in the heavens, I had been passing alone, on horseback, through a singularly dreary tract of country; and at length found myself, as the shades of the evening drew on, within view of the melancholy House of Usher. I know not how it was—but, with the first glimpse of the building, a sense of insufferable gloom pervaded my spirit. I say insufferable; for the feeling was unrelieved by any of that half-pleasurable, because poetic, sentiment, with which the mind usually receives even the sternest natural images of the desolate or terrible. I looked upon the scene before me—upon the mere[2] house, and the simple landscape features of the domain—upon the bleak walls—upon the vacant eyelike windows—upon a few rank sedges[3]—and upon a few white trunks of decayed trees—with an utter depression of soul which I can compare to no earthly sensation more properly than to the afterdream of the reveler upon opium—the bitter lapse into everyday life—the hideous dropping off of the veil. There was an iciness, a sinking, a sickening of the heart—an unredeemed dreariness of thought which no goading of the imagination could torture into aught[4] of the sublime. What was it—I paused to think—what was it that so unnerved me in the contemplation of the House of Usher? It was a mystery all insoluble; nor could I grapple with the shadowy fancies that crowded upon me as I pondered. I was forced to fall back upon the unsatisfactory conclusion, that while, beyond doubt, there *are* combinations of very simple natural objects which have the power of thus affecting us, still the analysis of this power lies among considerations beyond our depth. It was possible, I reflected, that a mere different arrangement of the particulars of the scene, of the details of the picture, would be sufficient to modify, or perhaps to annihilate its capacity for sorrowful impression; and, acting upon this idea, I reined my horse to the precipitous brink of a black and lurid tarn[5] that lay in unruffled luster by the dwelling, and gazed down—but with a shudder even more thrilling than before—upon the remodeled and inverted images of the gray sedge, and the ghastly tree stems, and the vacant and eyelike windows.

> The narrator is riding on horseback to the home of his childhood friend, Roderick Usher, whom he has not seen in many years.
>
> ? *What are the narrator's first impressions as he draws near to the house of Usher?*

Nevertheless, in this mansion of gloom I now proposed to myself a sojourn of some weeks. Its proprietor, Roderick Usher, had been one of my boon companions in boyhood; but many years had elapsed since our last meeting. A letter, however, had lately reached me in a distant part of the country—a letter from him—which, in its wildly importunate nature, had admitted of no other than a personal reply. The MS.[6] gave evidence of nervous agitation. The writer spoke of acute bodily illness—of a mental disorder which oppressed him—and of an earnest desire to see me, as his best, and indeed his only personal friend, with a view of attempting, by the cheerfulness of my society, some alleviation of his malady. It was the manner in which all this, and much more, was said—it was the apparent *heart* that went with his request—which allowed me no room for hesitation; and I accordingly obeyed forthwith what I still considered a very singular summons.

Although, as boys, we had been even intimate associates, yet I really knew little of my friend. His reserve had been always excessive and habitual. I

1. ***Son cœur . . . il résonne:*** "His heart is a suspended lute; / Whenever one touches it, it resounds." From "Le Refus" ("The Refusal") by Pierre-Jean de Béranger (1780–1857).
2. **mere** (mir): lake.
3. **sedges:** grasslike plants that grow in watery ground.
4. **aught:** anything.
5. **tarn:** small but deep mountain lake. Its waters are dark from the decomposition of vegetation and because there is no circulation.
6. **MS.:** abbreviation for "manuscript."

WORDS TO OWN

pervaded (pər·vād'id) *v.:* spread throughout.
sojourn (sō'jurn) *n.:* short stay.

OPTIONS FOR TEACHING

STRATEGIES FOR INCLUSION

Special Needs Since the vocabulary in "The Fall of the House of Usher" may be very difficult for some students, have them draw pictures to help them remember the meanings of difficult words. Place these images around the room or on bulletin boards as visual cues so students can refer to them as they read, discuss, and write about this story.

Auditory Appoint certain students to provide sound effects as you or a student reads aloud the section of the story in which the narrator reads the *Mad Trist,* beginning on p. 276 with "I had arrived at that well-known portion . . . " and ending with "Completely unnerved, I leaped to my feet . . . " on p. 277. Ask them to create the sounds of the cracks, rattling, storm, grating, screams, and metallic ringing as the text is read.

By permission of the Houghton Library, Harvard University, Cambridge, Massachusetts.

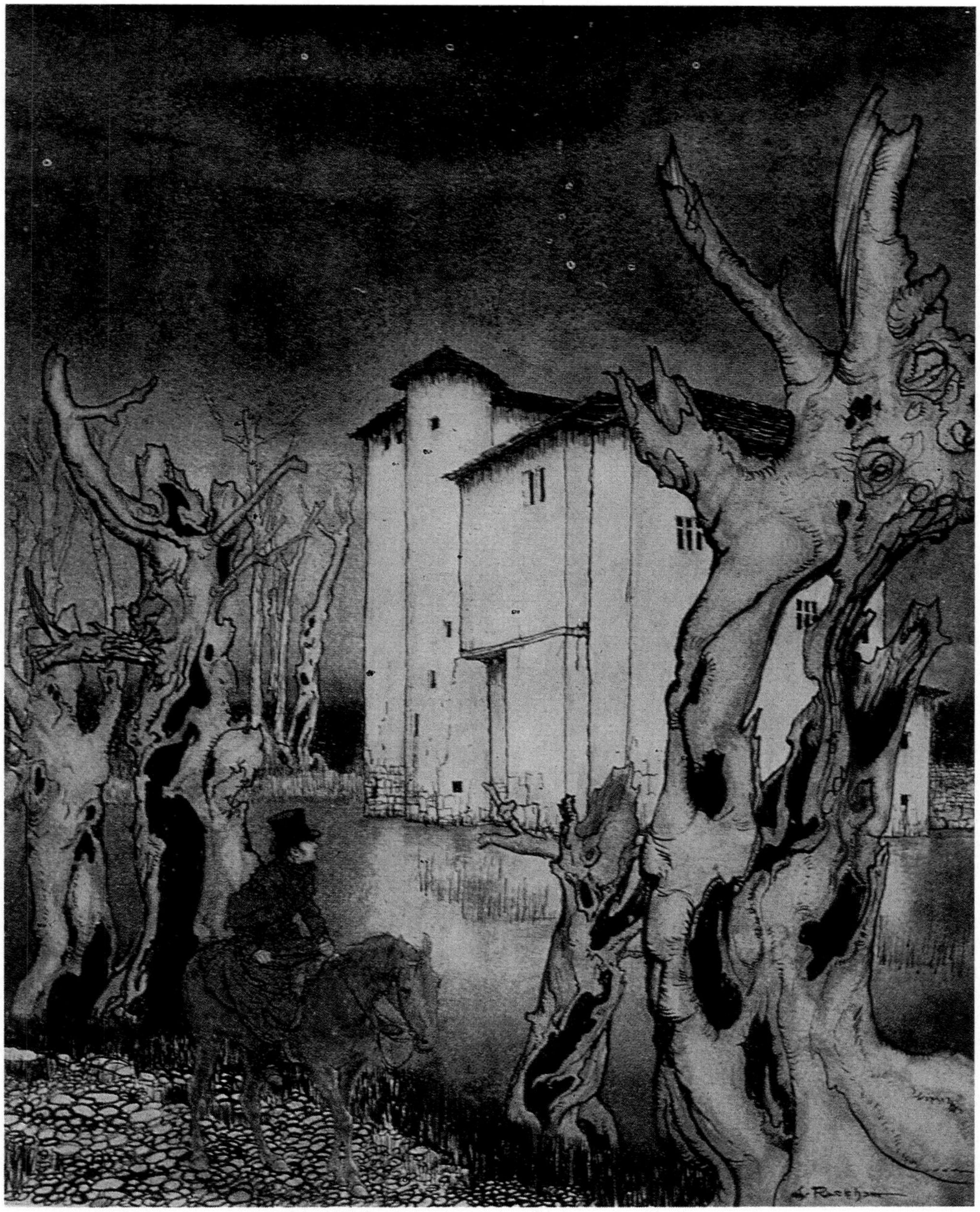

Illustration by Arthur Rackham for "The Fall of the House of Usher."

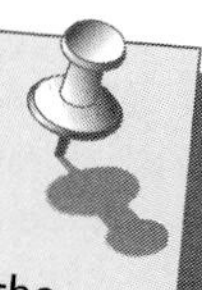

RESPONDING TO THE ART: VISUAL LITERACY

Arthur Rackham was one of the greatest illustrators of the Victorian age. He specialized in illustrating fairy tales. Ask students to turn back to this picture when reading the description of the house on p. 266, in the second full paragraph. Has Rackham done Poe's words justice? Explain. Has he transcribed the description exactly? Explain. [Possible responses: Rackham captures the gloomy mood through the dead trees. Or the house differs from Poe's description, for there is no fissure zigzagging from the roof of the building.]

STRATEGIES FOR INCLUSION

Visual To help students respond to the story, have them create a movie poster for a proposed film version of "The Fall of the House of Usher." Ask them to study movie posters—old and new—before they begin designing. They should include on their posters the title and any additional information that they think would draw a crowd to see the movie.

Kinesthetic To enable students to express their interpretations of Madeline and Roderick Usher near the end of the story, ask students to act out the scene in which Madeline comes to the door, the narrator leaps to his feet, Madeline falls on Roderick, Roderick dies, and the narrator flees. Have several groups of students portray the actions. Then, students discuss and compare the presentations.

A. Critical Reading: Summarizing

? What does the phrase "the entire family lay in the direct line of descent" mean? [That each generation of Ushers had only one son to carry on the family name.]

B. Critical Reading: Making Inferences

? What does Poe accomplish by blurring the boundaries between the family and its house? [Possible answer: He identifies them with each other so that the house can be a symbol for the family.]

Answer to Boxed Question

The tangled fungi covering the house; the inconsistency between the house's overall soundness and the crumbling of individual stones; a fissure from the roof down the wall to the lake.

C. Literary Element: Foreshadowing

? What might this description of the house foretell? [The family may crumble.]

D. Language Note: Vocabulary

Explain the term *Gothic*. [A type of medieval architecture using arches and spires; also writings about terror, wonder, and mystery, usually set in a remote and desolate place.]

Technology Tip

Ask your students to create a Gothic screen saver. Typical motifs include eerie mansions and creaky sounds. Examples may be found on commercial screen saver software.

was aware, however, that his very ancient family had been noted, time out of mind, for a peculiar sensibility of temperament, displaying itself, through long ages, in many works of exalted art, and manifested, of late, in repeated deeds of munificent yet unobtrusive charity, as well as in a passionate devotion to the intricacies, perhaps even more than to the orthodox and easily recognizable beauties, of musical science. I had learned, too, the very remarkable fact, that the stem of the Usher race, all time-honored as it was, had put (A) forth, at no period, any enduring branch; in other words, that the entire family lay in the direct line of descent, and had always, with very trifling and very temporary variation, so lain. It was this deficiency, I considered, while running over in thought the perfect keeping of the character of the premises with the accredited character of the people, and while speculating upon the possible influence which the one, in the long lapse of centuries, might have exercised upon the other—it was this deficiency, perhaps, of collateral issue,[7] and the consequent undeviating transmission, from sire to son, of the patrimony with the name, which had, at length, so identified the two as to (B) merge the original title of the estate in the quaint and equivocal appellation of the "House of Usher"—an appellation which seemed to include, in the minds of the peasantry who used it, both the family and the family mansion.

I have said that the sole effect of my somewhat childish experiment—that of looking down within the tarn—had been to deepen the first singular impression. There can be no doubt that the consciousness of the rapid increase of my superstition—for why should I not so term it?—served mainly to accelerate the increase itself. Such, I have long known, is the paradoxical law of all sentiments having terror as a basis. And it might have been for this reason only, that, when I again uplifted my eyes to the house itself, from its image in the pool, there grew in my mind a strange fancy—a fancy so ridiculous, indeed, that I but mention it to show the vivid force of the sensations which oppressed me. I had so worked upon my imagination as really to believe that about the whole mansion and domain there hung an atmosphere peculiar to themselves and their immediate vicinity—an atmosphere which had no affinity with the air of heaven, but which had reeked up from the decayed trees, and the gray wall and the silent tarn—a pestilent and mystic vapor, dull, sluggish, faintly discernible, and leaden-hued.

The mansion's reflection in the water is eerie, almost dreamlike.

Shaking off from my spirit what *must* have been a dream, I scanned more narrowly the real aspect of the building. Its principal feature seemed to be that of an excessive antiquity. The discoloration of ages had been great. Minute fungi overspread the whole exterior, hanging in a fine tangled webwork from the eaves. Yet all this was apart from any extraordinary dilapidation. No portion of the masonry had fallen; and there appeared to be a wild inconsistency between its still perfect adaptation of parts, and the crumbling condition of the individual stones. In this there was much that reminded me of the specious totality (C) of old woodwork which has rotted for long years in some neglected vault, with no disturbance from the breath of the external air. Beyond this indication of extensive decay, however, the fabric gave little token of instability. Perhaps the eye of a scrutinizing observer might have discovered a barely perceptible fissure, which, extending from the roof of the building in front, made its way down the wall in a zigzag direction, until it became lost in the sullen waters of the tarn.

? *What details in this description of the house seem most significant?*

Noticing these things, I rode over a short causeway to the house. A servant-in-waiting took my (D) horse, and I entered the Gothic archway of the

7. **collateral issue:** relatives, such as cousins, who share the same ancestors but who are not in a direct line of descent.

Words to Own

equivocal (ē·kwiv′ə·kəl) *adj.:* having more than one meaning.

discernible (di·sʉrn′ə·bəl) *adj.:* noticeable.

specious (spē′shəs) *adj.:* seemingly sound, but not really so.

scrutinizing (skro͞ot′′n·īz′iŋ) *v.* used as *adj.:* carefully observant.

OPTIONS FOR TEACHING

INTEGRATING THE LANGUAGE ARTS

Strategic Reading Encourage students to work through the literal meaning of the story by reading in pairs. Be sure that each pair includes at least one fluent reader. Ask pairs to read the text aloud, first one student, then the other, freely expressing any thoughts about content, any problems they encounter and how to resolve them, any connections to real-life characters or situations, and interpretations or judgments they are making.

Speaking and Listening Divide the class into four small groups. Have them choose a section of the text that contains descriptive narrative, such as the opening paragraphs on pp. 264–268, or a section that is laced with urgency or emotional dialogue, such as the paragraph that begins "'Not hear it?'" (p. 278). Groups should create a Reader's Theater presentation of the chosen passage. Review elements of speech such as pitch, tone, articulation, accent, and pace. Ask them to assign roles; provide sound effects and music; plan lighting, props, and costumes; rehearse their scene; and finally present it to the class.

hall.[8] A valet, of stealthy step, thence conducted me, in silence, through many dark and intricate passages in my progress to the *studio* of his master. Much that I encountered on the way contributed, I know not how, to heighten the vague sentiments of which I have already spoken. While the objects around me—while the carvings of the ceilings, the somber tapestries of the walls, the ebon blackness of the floors, and the phantasmagoric[9] armorial trophies which rattled as I strode, were but matters to which, or to such as which, I had been accustomed from my infancy—while I hesitated not to acknowledge how familiar was all this—I still wondered to find how unfamiliar were the fancies which ordinary images were stirring up. On one of the staircases, I met the physician of the family. His countenance, I thought, wore a mingled expression of low cunning and perplexity. He accosted me with trepidation and passed on. The valet now threw open a door and ushered me into the presence of his master.

The room in which I found myself was very large and lofty. The windows were long, narrow, and pointed, and at so vast a distance from the black oaken floor as to be altogether inaccessible from within. Feeble gleams of encrimsoned light made their way through the trellised panes, and served to render sufficiently distinct the more prominent objects around; the eye, however, struggled in vain to reach the remoter angles of the chamber, or the recesses of the vaulted and fretted[10] ceiling. Dark draperies hung upon the walls. The general furniture was profuse, comfortless, antique, and tattered. Many books and musical instruments lay scattered about, but failed to give any vitality to the scene. I felt that I breathed an atmosphere of sorrow. An air of stern, deep, and irredeemable gloom hung over and pervaded all.

Upon my entrance, Usher arose from a sofa on which he had been lying at full length, and greeted me with a vivacious warmth which had much in it, I at first thought, of an overdone cor-

8. **Gothic . . . hall:** The hallway looked like a Gothic arch—high, pointed, and elaborately carved.
9. **phantasmagoric** (fan·taz′mə·gôr′ik): images appearing to change rapidly, like the events in a dream.
10. **fretted:** carved in an ornamental architectural design.

diality—of the constrained effort of the *ennuyé*[11] man of the world. A glance, however, at his countenance, convinced me of his perfect sincerity. We sat down; and for some moments, while he spoke not, I gazed upon him with a feeling half of pity, half of awe. Surely, man had never before so terribly altered, in so brief a period, as had Roderick Usher! It was with difficulty that I could bring myself to admit the identity of the wan being before me with the companion of my early boyhood. Yet the character of his face had been at all times remarkable. A cadaverousness[12] of complexion; an eye large, liquid, and luminous beyond comparison; lips somewhat thin and very pallid, but of a surpassingly beautiful curve; a nose of a delicate Hebrew model, but with a breadth of nostril unusual in similar formations; a finely molded chin, speaking, in its want of prominence, of a want of moral energy; hair of a more than weblike softness and tenuity;[13] these features, with an inordinate expansion above the regions of the temple, made up altogether a countenance not (E)

11. **ennuyé** (än·nwē·ā′): French for "bored" or "jaded."
12. **cadaverousness:** paleness or gauntness, as a corpse.
13. **tenuity:** fineness; lack of substance.

Words to Own

profuse (prō·fyōōs′) *adj.:* abundant.
vivacious (vī·vā′shəs) *adj.:* cheerful; lively.
pallid (pal′id) *adj.:* pale.
inordinate (in·ôr′də·nit) *adj.:* excessive.

E. Literary Element: Character
In this paragraph, Poe relies on descriptions rather than dramatization—on telling us rather than showing us what Roderick Usher is like. How effective is this telling? How could Usher's characterization have been made more vivid? [Possible answers: The extended description seems effective; it might be more vivid if the speaker had quoted some of Usher's words.]

INTEGRATING THE LANGUAGE ARTS

Mechanics Read aloud to students some of the sentences containing a large number of dashes, such as in the paragraph that begins "He admitted, however, . . ." on p. 269, while they listen carefully. Have students determine why Poe uses dashes and what mood or feeling the sentences suggest. [The dashes indicate an abrupt break in thought or speech and make the narrator sound nervous, agitated, and high-strung.] Ask students to rewrite three such sentences in a calmer tone. When they remove the dashes, students may omit some words or break long sentences into shorter ones. Ask them what effect the changed sentences have on the telling of the story.

Writing: Radio Script Have students meet in groups of three and adapt "The Fall of the House of Usher" to a fifteen-minute radio presentation. Ask them to write the script and to include directions for sound effects and background music that re-create the story's mood. If time permits, ask groups to record their adaptations and play them for the class or to perform their adaptations live, as though they were in a recording studio.

Answer to Boxed Question

"Cadaverousness of complexion; an eye large, liquid, and luminous . . . ; lips somewhat thin and very pallid . . . ; a nose of a delicate Hebrew model . . . ; a finely molded chin . . . ; hair of a more than weblike softness . . . "; "nervous agitation"; "alternately vivacious and sullen."

A. Critical Reading: Speculating

Ask students to note the inconsistencies of Usher's behavior. [Nervousness and attempts to overcome it; liveliness and sullenness; indecision and energy.] What might account for his wildly swinging moods and differing actions? [Possible answer: manic depression]

B. Expansion

Research indicates that a predisposition to certain mental illnesses such as clinical depression and schizophrenia is almost certainly inherited.

easily to be forgotten. And now in the mere exaggeration of the prevailing character of these features, and of the expression they were wont to convey, lay so much of change that I doubted to whom I spoke. The now ghastly pallor of the skin, and the now miraculous luster of the eye, above all things startled and even awed me. The silken hair, too, had been suffered to grow all unheeded, and as, in its wild gossamer texture, it floated rather than fell about the face, I could not, even with effort, connect its arabesque[14] expression with any idea of simple humanity.

> The narrator is shocked by how much Roderick Usher has changed over the years.
>
> ? *What details in the description of Roderick Usher give you a vivid picture of his physical appearance and mannerisms?*

A In the manner of my friend I was at once struck with an incoherence—an inconsistency; and I soon found this to arise from a series of feeble and futile struggles to overcome an habitual trepidancy—an excessive nervous agitation. For something of this nature I had indeed been prepared, no less by his letter, than by reminiscences of certain boyish traits, and by conclusions deduced from his peculiar physical conformation and temperament. His action was alternately vivacious and sullen. His voice varied rapidly from a tremulous indecision (when the animal spirits seemed utterly in abeyance) to that species of energetic concision—that abrupt, weighty, unhurried, and hollow-sounding enunciation—that leaden, self-balanced and perfectly modulated guttural utterance, which may be observed in the lost drunkard, or the irreclaimable eater of opium, during the periods of his most intense excitement.

It was thus that he spoke of the object of my visit, of his earnest desire to see me, and of the solace he expected me to afford him. B He entered, at some length, into what he conceived to be the nature of his malady. It was, he said, a constitutional and a family evil, and one for which he despaired to find a remedy—a mere nervous affection,[15] he immediately added, which would undoubtedly soon pass. It displayed itself in a host of unnatural sensations. Some of these, as he detailed them, interested and bewildered me; although, perhaps, the terms, and the general manner of the narration had their weight. He suffered much from a morbid acuteness of the senses; the most insipid food was alone endurable; he could wear only garments of certain texture; the odors of all flowers were oppressive; his eyes were tortured by even a faint light; and there were but peculiar sounds, and these from stringed instruments, which did not inspire him with horror.

To an anomalous[16] species of terror I found him a bounden slave. "I shall perish," said he, "I *must* perish in this deplorable folly. Thus, thus, and not otherwise, shall I be lost. I dread the events of the future, not in themselves, but in their results. I shudder at the thought of any, even the most trivial, incident, which may operate upon this

Illustration by Wilfred Satty for "The Fall of the House of Usher."

The New York Public Library, Picture Collection.

14. **arabesque:** strangely mixed; fantastic.
15. **affection:** ailment; disorder.

16. **anomalous:** abnormal.

WORDS TO OWN
insipid (in·sip′id) *adj.:* bland; without flavor.

OPTIONS FOR TEACHING

COOPERATIVE LEARNING

Calming Power of Fine Arts
Painting, playing an instrument, and reading soothe Roderick's nerves. Divide the class into an art group, a music group, and a literature group. Tell each group to locate pieces of art, music, or literature that the narrator might have used to successfully calm or soothe Roderick's nerves. During their searches, the groups may wish to consult a teacher in their respective fine arts field. Once the groups have located their works, they should prepare to show, play, or read them and to explain their calming effect. The groups should also provide class members with a list of all the works they found.

intolerable agitation of soul. I have, indeed, no abhorrence of danger, except in its absolute effect—in terror. In this unnerved—in this pitiable condition—I feel that the period will sooner or later arrive when I must abandon life and reason together, in some struggle with the grim phantasm, FEAR."

I learned, moreover, at intervals, and through broken and equivocal hints, another singular feature of his mental condition. He was enchained by certain superstitious impressions in regard to the dwelling which he tenanted, and whence, for many years, he had never ventured forth—in regard to an influence whose supposititious[17] force was conveyed in terms too shadowy here to be restated—an influence which some peculiarities in the mere form and substance of his family mansion, had, by dint of long sufferance, he said, obtained over his spirit—an effect which the *physique* of the gray walls and turrets, and of the dim tarn into which they all looked down, had, at length, brought about upon the *morale* of his existence.

Usher reveals that he suffers from a nervous disorder that heightens all his senses.

? *What other "singular feature" of Usher's mental condition does the narrator learn?*

He admitted, however, although with hesitation, that much of the peculiar gloom which thus afflicted him could be traced to a more natural and far more palpable origin—to the severe and long-continued illness—indeed to the evidently approaching dissolution—of a tenderly beloved sister—his sole companion for long years—his last and only relative on earth. "Her decease," he said, with a bitterness which I can never forget, "would leave him (him the hopeless and the frail) the last of the ancient race of the Ushers." While he spoke, the lady Madeline (for so was she called) passed slowly through a remote portion of the apartment, and, without having noticed my presence, disappeared. I regarded her with an utter astonishment not unmingled with dread—and yet I found it impossible to account for such feelings. A sensation of stupor oppressed me, as my eyes followed her retreating steps. When a door, at length, closed upon her, my glance sought instinctively and eagerly the countenance of the brother—but he had buried his face in his hands, and I could only perceive that a far more than ordinary wanness had overspread the emaciated fingers through which trickled many passionate tears.

The disease of the lady Madeline had long baffled the skill of her physicians. A settled apathy, a gradual wasting away of the person, and frequent although transient affections of a partially cataleptical[18] character, were the unusual diagnosis. Hitherto she had steadily borne up against the pressure of her malady, and had not betaken herself finally to bed; but, on the closing in of the evening of my arrival at the house, she succumbed (as her brother told me at night with inexpressible agitation) to the prostrating power of the destroyer; and I learned that the glimpse I had obtained of her person would thus probably be the last I should obtain—that the lady, at least while living, would be seen by me no more.

Usher, who has not left his mansion in years, discloses a natural reason for his gloom: the strange illness of his sister Madeline.

For several days ensuing, her name was unmentioned by either Usher or myself: And during this period I was busied in earnest endeavors to alleviate the melancholy of my friend. We painted and read together; or I listened, as if in a dream, to the wild improvisations of his speaking guitar. And thus, as a closer and still closer intimacy admitted me more unreservedly into the recesses of his spirit, the more bitterly did I perceive the futility of all attempt at cheering a mind from which dark-

17. **supposititious** (sə·päz′ə·tish′əs): supposed; assumed; hypothetical.

18. **cataleptical** (kat′ə·lep′tik·əl): Catalepsy is an emotional condition, associated with disorders such as epilepsy and schizophrenia, which may cause the victim to lose sensation and the ability to move the limbs, or even the entire body. In a cataleptic attack, Madeline could be as stiff as a corpse.

Words to Own

palpable (pal′pə·bəl) *adj.:* obvious; perceivable.
stupor (sto͞o′pər) *n.:* state of mental dullness; loss of the senses.

Answer to Boxed Question

Usher feels overpowered by the house itself. It governs his mood. He has not left the house for many years.

C. Critical Reading: Finding Cause and Effect

? What might be the reasons for Usher's behavior as indicated in this paragraph and the one before it? [Possible answers: His senses are acute; the house itself has depressed him; he is deathly afraid of fear itself; his sister is dying.]

D. Expansion

Here Poe may be describing a form of schizophrenia sometimes called catatonia, in which the patient may alternate between states of agitation and states of stupor.

Classroom Management

Grouping When a cooperative learning activity calls for a presentation, reassure students who are not comfortable speaking in front of the class by placing them in groups with students who do feel comfortable. Have those less comfortable students take notes or present visual aids on the first three or four occasions that a group meets and presents. To encourage them to speak after these initial presentations, assign an activity in which all group members must speak, however briefly, in front of the class. Allow the quieter students to consult notes as they speak.

Block Scheduling After reading the story, pair students. To maintain motivation, for ten to fifteen minutes, ask them to write five to ten questions and answers regarding the story. Collect all of the papers and ask the class the student-generated questions for twenty to twenty-five minutes. Close the block with students' creating a Reader's Response: Extending the Text question and then ask students to pose their questions and to invite volunteers to share their responses.

RESPONDING TO THE ART: VISUAL LITERACY

The painting seems to follow Poe's precept that the most powerful subject for a work of art is the death of a beautiful young woman; it shows that in the nineteenth century, Poe was not alone in this idea. How would you describe the mood of this painting? [Dark and heavy] Other than the fact that the painting is of a dead woman, why do you suppose this painting was chosen to illustrate the story? [The rooms, the darkness, and the heavy drapery seem consistent with the description of the House of Usher.]

The Last Sleep (c. 1858) by George Cochran Lambdin (1830–1896). American. Oil on canvas.
North Carolina Museum of Art, Raleigh, Gift of Peter A. Vogt.

ness, as if an inherent positive quality, poured forth upon all objects of the moral and physical universe, in one unceasing radiation of gloom.

I shall ever bear about me a memory of the many solemn hours I thus spent alone with the master of the House of Usher. Yet I should fail in any attempt to convey an idea of the exact character of the studies, or of the occupations, in which he involved me, or led me the way. An excited and highly distempered ideality[19] threw a sulfureous[20] luster over all. His long improvised dirges will ring forever in my ears. Among other things, I hold painfully in mind a certain singular perversion and amplification of the wild air of the last waltz of Von Weber.[21] From the paintings over which his elaborate fancy brooded, and which grew, touch by touch, into vaguenesses at which I shuddered the more thrillingly, because I shuddered knowing not why—from these paintings (vivid as their images now are before me) I would in vain endeavor to educe more than a small portion

19. **distempered ideality:** mental derangement.
20. **sulfureous** (sul·fyo͞or′ē·əs): hellish; infernal. Poe's description probably comes from the yellowish color of sulfur, which is associated with the fires of hell.

21. **Von Weber:** Carl Maria von Weber (1786–1826), German Romantic composer.

OPTIONS FOR TEACHING

CROSSING THE CURRICULUM

Health Have students form a medical board to examine Usher's symptoms and determine a diagnosis and prognosis for his ailment. Have individual students consult medical references and psychologists to formulate their diagnoses and prognoses. *You may want to obtain permission from parents or guardians and from the parties students will contact before they begin working on this activity.* Students should also recommend a treatment plan, if appropriate. Ask the medical board to meet as a panel in front of the class to discuss their findings and come to a consensus about Usher's case.

Music Usher plays a guitar and accompanies himself in singing the ballad called "The Haunted Palace." Have students compose or locate music for the ballad. Tell them they may put the words to a familiar tune rather than inventing a whole new one. Ask student volunteers who play an instrument to play the ballad for the class.

Fine Art Usher paints in an abstract style years before the technique was popularized in reality. Ask students to bring pictures of abstract paintings to class and to talk about them and the painters. Once the class views the paintings, ask students to talk about why that style or those particular paintings suit Roderick Usher.

which should lie within the compass of merely written words. By the utter simplicity, by the nakedness of his designs, he arrested and overawed attention. If ever mortal painted an idea, that mortal was Roderick Usher. For me at least—in the circumstances then surrounding me—there arose out of the pure abstractions which the hypochondriac contrived to throw upon his canvas, an intensity of intolerable awe, no shadow of which felt I ever yet in the contemplation of the certainly glowing yet too concrete reveries of Fuseli.[22]

The narrator tries to cheer up Usher by painting with him and listening to songs on his guitar. He is awed by Usher's musical and artistic creations.

One of the phantasmagoric conceptions of my friend, partaking not so rigidly of the spirit of abstraction, may be shadowed forth, although feebly, in words. A small picture presented the interior of an immensely long and rectangular vault or tunnel, with low walls, smooth, white, and without interruption or device. Certain accessory points of the design served well to convey the idea that this excavation lay at an exceeding depth below the surface of the earth. No outlet was observed in any portion of its vast extent, and no torch, or other artificial source of light was discernible; yet a flood of intense rays rolled throughout, and bathed the whole in a ghastly and inappropriate splendor.

I have just spoken of that morbid condition of the auditory nerve which rendered all music intolerable to the sufferer with the exception of certain effects of stringed instruments. It was, perhaps, the narrow limits to which he thus confined himself upon the guitar, which gave birth, in great measure, to the fantastic character of his performances. But the fervid *facility* of his *impromptus*[23] could not be so accounted for. They must have been, and were, in the notes, as well as in the words of his wild fantasias (for he not unfrequently accompanied himself with rhymed verbal improvisations), the result of that intense mental collectedness and concentration to which I have previously alluded as observable only in particular moments of the highest artificial excitement. The words of one of these rhapsodies I have easily remembered. I was, perhaps, the more forcibly impressed with it, as he gave it, because, in the under or mystic current of its meaning, I fancied that I perceived, and for the first time, a full consciousness on the part of Usher, of the tottering of his lofty reason upon her throne. The verses, which were entitled "The Haunted Palace," ran very nearly, if not accurately, thus:

What are some of the characteristics of the works of art and musical compositions that Roderick produces? As you read the lyric "The Haunted Palace," ask yourself what it reveals about Roderick's frame of mind.

I

In the greenest of our valleys,
By good angels tenanted,
Once a fair and stately palace—
Radiant palace—reared its head.
In the monarch Thought's dominion—
It stood there!
Never seraph[24] spread a pinion[25]
Over fabric half so fair.

II

Banners yellow, glorious, golden,
On its roof did float and flow;
(This—all this—was in the olden
Time long ago)
And every gentle air that dallied,
In that sweet day,
Along the ramparts plumed and pallid,
A winged odor went away.

22. **Fuseli:** Johann Heinrich Fuseli (1742–1825), Swiss painter who lived in England and illustrated the epics of Milton and the tragedies of Shakespeare. He often painted scenes of horror and the supernatural.
23. **impromptus** (im·prämp′to͞oz′): spontaneous performances.

24. **seraph:** angel.
25. **pinion** (pin′yən): wing.

WORDS TO OWN
morbid (môr′bid) *adj.:* diseased; unhealthy.

A. Expansion
Note Poe's anticipation of abstract painting, more than half a century before it appeared on canvas.

Answer to Boxed Question
His paintings were abstract, and one of them showed the inside of a rectangular tunnel, a comparison to a tomb. His music was loud, disturbing, and filled with fantastic ideas. "The Haunted Palace" talks about a human mind haunted by "evil things." All of Usher's artistic efforts displayed a tortured sensibility and a disordered mind.

B. Literary Element: Allegory
Remind students of the way in which Poe identifies the family and the house of Usher. The personification of the house in this poem strengthens the parallel between it and Usher himself. The poem may be read as an allegory of Usher's loss of reason and the fall of his house and family.

PROBLEM SOLVING/CRITICAL THINKING

Creating Atmosphere Have students chart how Poe creates **atmosphere** in "The Fall of the House of Usher." Students should consider how such elements as **descriptions, onomatopoeia, sensory images,** and **figurative language** create an atmosphere of dread and menace. Ask students to complete a chart like the following, citing a textual reference and indicating the technique Poe used. As students continue reading from this Collection, ask them to complete similar charts for each selection. After they have finished reading the selections and completing their charts, have them discuss how the atmosphere in each selection differs from that in the others and how effective each writer is in creating atmosphere.

Textual Reference	Technique
["Vacant and eyelike windows" of the house.]	[Personification.]

Answer to Boxed Question
The phrase "House of Usher" has come to designate both the family and the family mansion; Usher believes the gray stones of the house and all that is around it have consciousness and embody the fate of the Usher family. The appearance of the house, both inside and out, has a striking resemblance to Usher's physical and mental condition.

III

Wanderers in that happy valley
    Through two luminous windows saw
Spirits moving musically
    To a lute's well-tunéd law,
Round about a throne, where sitting
    (Porphyrogene!)[26]
In state his glory well befitting,
    The ruler of the realm was seen.

IV

And all with pearl and ruby glowing
    Was the fair palace door,
Through which came flowing, flowing, flowing,
    And sparkling evermore,
A troop of Echoes whose sweet duty
    Was but to sing,
In voices of surpassing beauty,
    The wit and wisdom of their king.

V

But evil things, in robes of sorrow,
    Assailed the monarch's high estate;
(Ah, let us mourn, for never morrow
    Shall dawn upon him, desolate!)
And, round about his home, the glory
    That blushed and bloomed
Is but a dim-remembered story
    Of the old time entombed.

VI

And travelers now within that valley,
    Through the red-litten[27] windows, see
Vast forms that move fantastically
    To a discordant melody;
While, like a rapid ghastly river,
    Through the pale door,
A hideous throng rush out forever,
    And laugh—but smile no more.

I well remember that suggestions arising from this ballad led us into a train of thought wherein there became manifest an opinion of Usher's which I mention not so much on account of its novelty, (for other men have thought thus,) as on account of the pertinacity with which he maintained it. This opinion, in its general form, was that of the sentience[28] of all vegetable things. But, in his disordered fancy, the idea had assumed a more daring character, and trespassed, under certain conditions, upon the kingdom of inorganization.[29] I lack words to express the full extent, or the earnest *abandon* of his persuasion. The belief, however, was connected (as I have previously hinted) with the gray stones of the home of his forefathers. The conditions of the sentience had been here, he imagined, fulfilled in the method of collocation of these stones—in the order of their arrangement, as well as in that of the many *fungi* which overspread them, and of the decayed trees which stood around—above all, in the long undisturbed endurance of this arrangement, and in its reduplication in the still waters of the tarn. Its evidence—the evidence of the sentience—was to be seen, he said, (and I here started as he spoke,) in the gradual yet certain condensation of an atmosphere of their own about the waters and the walls. The result was discoverable, he added, in that silent, yet importunate and terrible influence which for centuries had molded the destinies of his family, and which made *him* what I now saw him—what he was. Such opinions need no comment, and I will make none.

> Usher expresses his belief that not only all living things but also all nonliving things are sentient, or conscious.
>
> ? *What specific details in the story thus far suggest that Usher's belief is reflected by his surroundings?*

Our books—the books which, for years, had formed no small portion of the mental existence of the invalid—were, as might be supposed, in strict keeping with this character of phantasm. We pored together over such works as the *Ververt et Chartreuse* of Gresset; the *Belphegor* of

26. **porphyrogene** (pôr·fir′ə·jēn′): Poe coined this word from "porphyry," a purple dye reserved for royalty, to mean "one born to the purple," or "one of royal blood."
27. **red-litten:** red-lighted; Poe coined this archaic-sounding term.

28. **sentience** (sen′shəns): consciousness.
29. **kingdom of inorganization:** world of inorganic objects.

OPTIONS FOR TEACHING

PROFESSIONAL NOTES

Thematic Connections: "The Realms of Darkness" The words *terror* and *beauty* are used on p. 275 to describe the storm. Ask students to discuss why these very different words are appropriate for the mood of this story and the theme of the Collection.

Technology Tip The House of Usher is a Web site featuring information about Edgar Allan Poe and electronic texts of his work. The URL is **http:/infoweb.magi.com/~forrest/index.html**. *You may want to preview any Internet activity that you suggest to students. Because these resources are sometimes public forums, their content can be unpredictable.*

Machiavelli; the *Heaven and Hell* of Swedenborg; *The Subterranean Voyage of Nicholas Klimm* by Holberg; the Chiromancy of Robert Flud, of Jean D'Indaginé, and of De la Chambre; the Journey into the Blue Distance of Tieck; and *The City of the Sun*[30] of Campanella. One favorite volume was a small octavo edition of the *Directorium Inquisitorum,* by the Dominican Eymeric de Gironne; and there were passages in Pomponius Mela, about the old African Satyrs and Ægipans, over which Usher would sit dreaming for hours. His chief delight, however, was found in the perusal of an exceedingly rare and curious book in quarto Gothic—the manual of a forgotten church—the *Vigiliae Mortuorum secundum Chorum Ecclesiae Maguntinae.*[31]

30. ***Ververt et Chartreuse . . . City of the Sun:*** Works listed include books on mysticism, magic, and horror. Many of them foreshadow what is to happen to Madeline Usher and illuminate Roderick Usher's state of mind.
31. ***Vigiliae Mortuorum:*** Latin for "vigil of the dead."

I could not help thinking of the wild ritual of this work, and of its probable influence upon the (A) hypochondriac, when, one evening, having informed me abruptly that the lady Madeline was no more, he stated his intention of preserving her corpse for a fortnight (previously to its final interment), in one of the numerous vaults within the main walls of the building. The worldly reason, however, assigned for this singular proceeding, was one which I did not feel at liberty to dispute. The brother had been led to his resolution (so he told me) by consideration of the unusual character of the malady of the deceased, of certain obtrusive and eager inquiries on the part of her medical men, and of the remote and exposed situation of the burial ground of the family. I will not deny that when I called to mind the sinister countenance of the person whom I met upon the staircase,[32] on the day of my arrival at the house, I had no desire to oppose what I regarded as at best but a harmless, and by no means an unnatural, precaution.[33]

Usher suddenly announces that his sister Madeline has died. Before her final burial, Usher plans to inter Madeline temporarily in a vault within the house, to prevent her body from being stolen for dissection.

At the request of Usher, I personally aided him in the arrangements for the temporary entombment. The body having been encoffined, we two alone bore it to its rest. The vault in which we placed it (and which had been so long unopened that our torches, half smothered in its oppressive atmosphere, gave us little opportunity for investigation) was small, damp, and entirely without means of admission for light; lying, at great depth, immediately beneath that portion of the building in which was my own sleeping apartment. It had been used, apparently, in remote feudal times, for the worst purposes of a dungeon-keep,[34] and, in later days, as a place of deposit for powder, or

32. **person . . . staircase:** the doctor.
33. **precaution:** Usher wishes to be sure his sister's body will not be dissected by doctors. At the time, bodies were sometimes stolen and sold to medical students for dissection and study.
34. **dungeon-keep:** underground prison.

A. Literary Element: Plot
Point out to students that, after a long digression, the plot resumes with the words, ". . . one evening."

ASSESSMENT TOOLS

Peer Assessment To help groups enjoy and critique their Reader's Theater productions on p. T266, have students videotape the various productions. View the videos in class, and have performing students make comments about areas of concern, such as their script, reading, staging, and technical production; then, open the floor to comments from other students. Have each group complete the following group self-evaluation:

1. We did our best work in (script writing, technical production, acting, directing) because ________.
2. We could have improved ________ by doing ________.
3. We would have liked to have done ________, because ________.

Check Test: Questions and Answers

1. How does the narrator know Usher? [They were childhood friends.]
2. How does the narrator try to calm Roderick on the night of the storm? [By reading to him.]
3. What two coincidental sounds occur on the night of the storm? [A cracking or ripping sound; an unusual screaming or grating sound.]
4. Where do Roderick and the narrator first see Madeline after she breaks out of her coffin? [She is standing outside the door.]
5. What happens to the mansion as the narrator flees from it? [It collapses.]

A. Humanities Connection
In describing brother and sister, Poe seems to be using the theme of the doppelgänger, or mysterious double, who follows and frightens the protagonist. He also uses this theme in "William Wilson." Dostoevski used it in his novella *The Double*.

Answer to Boxed Question
The tomb is a small, dark, damp dungeon; the floor and entryway are covered in copper. The heavy iron door makes a grating noise as it is opened. The narrator notices a strong resemblance between the brother and sister; she appears to be in a state of suspended animation, for there is still color in her skin and a smile lingers on her face.

B. Critical Reading: Expressing an Opinion
? What differences do you note in Usher's behavior in this paragraph and why has he changed? [Possible answer: While he was inconsistent in behavior before and was at least warm at times, now he seems to be near death and acting out of terror. He is mired in grief over the loss of his twin.]

C. Reader's Response: First Thoughts
? How do you think you would have felt by this time if you were in the narrator's place? [Sample responses: Afraid, anxious, or impatient to get away.]

some other highly combustible substance, as a portion of its floor, and the whole interior of a long archway through which we reached it, were carefully sheathed with copper. The door, of massive iron, had been, also, similarly protected. Its immense weight caused an unusually sharp grating sound, as it moved upon its hinges.

Having deposited our mournful burden upon tressels within this region of horror, we partially turned aside the yet unscrewed lid of the coffin, and looked upon the face of the tenant. A striking similitude between the brother and sister now first arrested my attention; and Usher, divining, perhaps, my thoughts, murmured out some few words from which I learned that the deceased and himself had been twins, and that sympathies of a scarcely intelligible nature had always existed between them. Our glances, however, rested not long upon the dead—for we could not regard her unawed. The disease which had thus entombed the lady in the maturity of youth, had left, as usual in all maladies of a strictly cataleptical character, the mockery of a faint blush upon the bosom and the face, and that suspiciously lingering smile upon the lip which is so terrible in death. We replaced and screwed down the lid, and, having secured the door of iron, made our way, with toil, into the scarcely less gloomy apartments of the upper portion of the house.

? *Describe Madeline's temporary tomb. What does the narrator notice about Madeline's appearance and condition after looking at her corpse?*

And now, some days of bitter grief having elapsed, an observable change came over the features of the mental disorder of my friend. His ordinary manner had vanished. His ordinary occupations were neglected or forgotten. He roamed from chamber to chamber with hurried, unequal, and objectless step. The pallor of his countenance had assumed, if possible, a more ghastly hue—but the luminousness of his eye had utterly gone out. The once occasional huskiness of his tone was heard no more; and a tremulous quaver, as if of extreme terror, habitually characterized his utterance. There were times, indeed, when I thought his unceasingly agitated mind was laboring with some oppressive secret, to divulge which he struggled for the necessary courage. At times, again, I was obliged to resolve all into the mere inexplicable vagaries[35] of madness, for I beheld him gazing upon vacancy for long hours, in an attitude of the profoundest attention, as if listening to some imaginary sound. It was no wonder that his condition terrified—that it infected me. I felt creeping upon me, by slow yet certain degrees, the wild influences of his own fantastic yet impressive superstitions.

It was, especially, upon retiring to bed late in the night of the seventh or eighth day after the placing of the lady Madeline within the dungeon, that I experienced the full power of such feelings. Sleep came not near my couch—while the hours waned and waned away. I struggled to reason off the nervousness which had dominion over me. I endeavored to believe that much, if not all of what I felt, was due to the bewildering influence of the gloomy furniture of the room—of the dark and tattered draperies, which, tortured into motion by the breath of a rising tempest, swayed fitfully to and fro upon the walls, and rustled uneasily about the decorations of the bed. But my efforts were fruitless. An irrepressible tremor gradually pervaded my frame; and, at length, there sat upon my very heart an incubus[36] of utterly causeless alarm. Shaking this off with a gasp and a struggle, I uplifted myself upon the pillows, and, peering earnestly within the intense darkness of the chamber, harkened—I know not why, except that an instinctive spirit prompted me—to certain

35. **vagaries** (vā′gər·ēz): whims.
36. **incubus** (in′kyo͞o·bəs): nightmare. In medieval times, it was believed that nightmares were caused by demons (incubi) who tormented sleeping persons.

WORDS TO OWN
similitude (sə·mil′ə·to͞od′) *n.:* likeness.

A week after Madeline's death, an agitated Usher wanders through the house. The narrator, unable to sleep, is overcome by the atmosphere of dread around him.

? *Describe the emotional states of the narrator and Roderick. In what ways are their reactions similar?*

low and indefinite sounds which came, through the pauses of the storm, at long intervals, I knew not whence. Overpowered by an intense sentiment of horror, unaccountable yet unendurable, I threw on my clothes with haste (for I felt that I should sleep no more during the night), and endeavored to arouse myself from the pitiable condition into which I had fallen, by pacing rapidly to and fro through the apartment.

I had taken but few turns in this manner, when a light step on an adjoining staircase arrested my attention. I presently recognized it as that of Usher. In an instant afterward he rapped, with a gentle touch, at my door, and entered, bearing a lamp. His countenance was, as usual, cadaverously wan—but, moreover, there was a species of mad hilarity in his eyes—an evidently restrained *hysteria* in his whole demeanor. His air appalled me—but anything was preferable to the solitude which I had so long endured, and I even welcomed his presence as a relief.

"And you have not seen it?" he said abruptly, after having stared about him for some moments in silence—"you have not then seen it?—but, stay! you shall." Thus speaking, and having carefully shaded his lamp, he hurried to one of the casements, and threw it freely open to the storm.

The impetuous fury of the entering gust nearly lifted us from our feet. It was, indeed, a tempestuous yet sternly beautiful night, and one wildly singular in its terror and its beauty. A whirlwind had apparently collected its force in our vicinity; for there were frequent and violent alterations in the direction of the wind; and the exceeding density of the clouds (which hung so low as to press upon the turrets of the house) did not prevent our perceiving the lifelike velocity with which they flew careering from all points against each other, without passing away into the distance. I say that even their exceeding density did not prevent our perceiving this—yet we had no glimpse of the moon or stars—nor was there any flashing forth of the lightning. But the under surfaces of the huge masses of agitated vapor, as well as all terrestrial objects immediately around us, were glowing in the unnatural light of a faintly luminous and distinctly visible gaseous exhalation which hung about and enshrouded the mansion. **D**

On a night when neither can sleep, a crazed Usher knocks on the narrator's door and throws open the window. It is a stormy night, and a bizarre glow illuminates everything outside.

"You must not—you shall not behold this!" said I, shudderingly, to Usher, as I led him, with a gentle violence, from the window to a seat. "These appearances, which bewilder you, are merely electrical phenomena not uncommon—or it may be that they have their ghastly origin in the rank miasma of the tarn.[37] Let us close this casement—the air is chilling and dangerous to your frame. Here is one of your favorite romances. I will read, and you shall listen;—and so we will pass away this terrible night together."

The antique volume which I had taken up was the *Mad Trist* of Sir Launcelot Canning;[38] but I had called it a favorite of Usher's more in sad jest than in earnest; for, in truth, there is little in its uncouth and unimaginative prolixity[39] which could have had interest for the lofty and spiritual ideality of my friend. **E** It was, however, the only book immediately at hand; and I indulged a vague hope that the excitement which now agitated the hypochondriac, might find relief (for the history of mental disorder is full of similar anomalies) even in the extremeness of the folly which I should read. Could I have judged, indeed, by the

37. **rank miasma** (mī·az′mə) . . . **tarn:** The decomposing matter of the tarn could have given rise to swamp gas or electrical discharges, resulting in frightening optical illusions.

38. ***Mad Trist* of Sir Launcelot Canning:** a book invented by Poe for this story.

39. **prolixity** (prō·lik′sə·tē): wordiness.

WORDS TO OWN

demeanor (di·mēn′ər) *n.:* behavior; conduct.

Answer to Boxed Question

Both are seized by feelings of hysteria and horror. The narrator has begun to fall prey to Usher's delusions and madness.

D. Humanities Connection

The luminous gas is an important **atmospheric** effect. It and the whirlwind exemplify the idea that the external environment mirrors human emotions.

E. Literary Element: Plot

The thematically appropriate story within a story is a typically Gothic touch. Why might Poe include a long passage from a made-up book at this point? [One of the devices Poe uses to build suspense is stopping the action of the story. Inserting this scene has this effect, with the added benefit that the words he is quietly reading to Roderick are suddenly echoed in reality.]

LITERATURE AND POPULAR CULTURE

Have students research and write a report on some of the most famous women Gothic writers, such as the Brontë sisters or Mary Shelley. Ask them to include information about the historical context of the writing. Have them research what may have led these authors to write Gothic stories and whether they led tragic lives, as Poe did, or just had fertile imaginations.

Answer to Boxed Question
He suggests that Usher should listen to him read a romantic novel.

LITERATURE AND POPULAR CULTURE

Women of the Gothic Tradition

What is Gothic? The word *Gothic* comes from an architectural style of the late Middle Ages in Europe. People later used the term *Gothic* to describe a kind of romantic, scary novel that sprang up in Germany in the late 1700s and early 1800s. These eerie Gothic novels summoned up the mysterious atmosphere suggested by all those old castles and cathedrals, whose dank dungeons and secret passageways might have witnessed any number of sinister or even supernatural events.

Real page-turners. One of the earliest and most successful Gothic novels in English was written by a woman. Ann Radcliffe's *The Mysteries of Udolpho* (1794) was only the first of many Gothics penned by women, who took up writing Gothic novels as a way to make a living. The public eagerly devoured these sensational stories, which sold the way Stephen King best-sellers do today. Gothic novels so saturated the popular culture of the time that, in 1818, the English writer Jane Austen wrote *Northanger Abbey,* a novel that parodies the Gothic. By the nineteenth century, several novels of high literary merit by women writers fell solidly within the Gothic framework: Mary Shelley's *Frankenstein, or the Modern Prometheus,* Charlotte Brontë's *Jane Eyre,* and Emily Brontë's *Wuthering Heights.* In our time, women writers such as Shirley Jackson, Daphne du Maurier, Barbara Michaels, and others have kept the Gothic tradition alive and well.

? *What does the narrator do to distract Usher?*

wild overstrained air of vivacity with which he harkened, or apparently harkened, to the words of the tale, I might well have congratulated myself upon the success of my design.

I had arrived at that well-known portion of the story where Ethelred, the hero of the *Trist,* having sought in vain for peaceable admission into the dwelling of the hermit, proceeds to make good an entrance by force. Here, it will be remembered, the words of the narrative run thus:

"And Ethelred, who was by nature of a doughty[40] heart, and who was now mighty withal, on account of the powerfulness of the wine which he had drunken, waited no longer to hold parley with the hermit, who, in sooth, was of an obstinate and maliceful turn, but, feeling the rain upon his shoulders, and fearing the rising of the tempest, uplifted his mace outright, and, with

40. **doughty** (dout'ē): courageous.

WORDS TO OWN
obstinate (äb'stə·nət) *adj.:* stubborn.

blows, made quickly room in the plankings of the door for his gauntleted hand; and now pulling therewith sturdily, he so cracked, and ripped, and tore all asunder, that the noise of the dry and hollow-sounding wood alarumed and reverberated throughout the forest."

At the termination of this sentence I started, and for a moment, paused; for it appeared to me (although I at once concluded that my excited fancy had deceived me)—it appeared to me that, from some very remote portion of the mansion, there came, indistinctly, to my ears, what might have been, in its exact similarity of character, the echo (but a stifled and dull one certainly) of the very cracking and ripping sound which Sir Launcelot had so particularly described. It was, beyond doubt, the coincidence alone which had arrested my attention; for, amid the rattling of the sashes of the casements, and the ordinary commingled noises of the still increasing storm, the sound, in itself, had nothing, surely, which should have interested or disturbed me. I continued the story:

The narrator continues reading aloud from the book about a medieval knight.

"But the good champion Ethelred, now entering within the door, was sore enraged and amazed to perceive no signal of the maliceful hermit; but, in the stead thereof, a dragon of a scaly and prodigious demeanor, and of a fiery tongue, which sate in guard before a palace of gold, with a floor of silver; and upon the wall there hung a shield of shining brass with this legend enwritten—

Who entereth herein, a conqueror hath bin;
Who slayeth the dragon, the shield he shall win;

And Ethelred uplifted his mace, and struck upon the head of the dragon, which fell before him, and gave up his pesty breath, with a shriek so horrid and harsh, and withal so piercing, that Ethelred had fain to close his ears with his hands against the dreadful noise of it, the like whereof was never before heard."

Here again I paused abruptly, and now with a feeling of wild amazement—for there could be no doubt whatever that, in this instance, I did actually hear (although from what direction it proceeded I found it impossible to say) a low and apparently distant, but harsh, protracted, and most unusual screaming or grating sound—the exact counterpart of what my fancy had already conjured up for the dragon's unnatural shriek as described by the romancer. (A)

Oppressed, as I certainly was, upon the occurrence of this second and most extraordinary coincidence, by a thousand conflicting sensations, in which wonder and extreme terror were predominant, I still retained sufficient presence of mind to avoid exciting, by any observation, the sensitive nervousness of my companion. I was by no means certain that he had noticed the sounds in question; although, assuredly, a strange alteration had, during the last few minutes, taken place in his demeanor. From a position fronting my own, he had gradually brought round his chair, so as to sit with his face to the door of the chamber; and thus I could but partially perceive his features, although I saw that his lips trembled as if he were murmuring inaudibly. His head had dropped upon his breast—yet I knew that he was not asleep, from the wide and rigid opening of the eye as I caught a glance of it in profile. The motion of his body, too, was at variance with this idea—for he rocked from side to side with a gentle yet constant and uniform sway. Having rapidly taken notice of all this, I resumed the narrative of Sir Launcelot, which thus proceeded:

"And now, the champion, having escaped from the terrible fury of the dragon, bethinking himself of the brazen shield, and of the breaking up of the enchantment which was upon it, removed the carcass from out of the way before him, and approached valorously over the silver pavement of the castle to where the shield was upon the wall; which in sooth tarried not for his full coming, but fell down at his feet upon the silver floor, with a mighty great and terrible ringing sound."

No sooner had these syllables passed my lips, than—as if a shield of brass had indeed, at the moment, fallen heavily upon a floor of silver—I became aware of a distinct, hollow, metallic, and clangorous, yet apparently muffled reverberation. Completely unnerved, I leaped to my feet; but the measured rocking movement of Usher was

Words to Own
prodigious (prō·dij′əs) *adj.:* of great size and power.

A. Language Note: Repetition

? What is the effect of the repetition of *grating,* which was first used when they placed Madeline in the tomb on p. 274? What other word adds to this effect? [It heightens the tension of the story. The tension is intensified by the addition of the word *screaming.*]

Answer to Boxed Question
He begins hearing the same noises in the mansion that he has been reading about in the book. The atmosphere is one of high tension and suspense.

A. Expansion
Premature burial was one of Poe's favorite themes, appearing as well in "The Cask of Amontillado" and "The Premature Burial." Usher's climactic mad speech echoes the narrator's in "The Tell-Tale Heart."

Answer to Boxed Question
That his sister was buried alive; "And now—tonight—Ethelred—ha! ha!—the breaking of the hermit's door, and the death cry of the dragon, and the clangor of the shield!—say, rather, the rending of her coffin, and the grating of the iron hinges of her prison, and her struggles within the coppered archway of the vault!"

> ? *What coincidences unnerve the narrator during his reading of the book? How would you describe the atmosphere of the story at this point?*

undisturbed. I rushed to the chair in which he sat. His eyes were bent fixedly before him, and throughout his whole countenance there reigned a stony rigidity. But, as I placed my hand upon his shoulder, there came a strong shudder over his whole person; a sickly smile quivered about his lips; and I saw that he spoke in a low, hurried, and gibbering murmur, as if unconscious of my presence. Bending closely over him, I at length drank in the hideous import of his words.

"Not hear it?—yes, I hear it, and *have* heard it. Long—long—long—many minutes, many hours, many days, have I heard it—yet I dared not—oh, pity me, miserable wretch that I am!—I dared not—I *dared* not speak! *We have put her living in the tomb!* Said I not that my senses were acute? I *now* tell you that I heard her first feeble movements in the hollow coffin. I heard them—many, many days ago—yet I dared not—*I dared not speak!* And now—tonight—Ethelred—ha! ha!—the breaking of the hermit's door, and the death cry of the dragon, and the clangor of the shield!—say, rather, the rending of her coffin, and the grating of the iron hinges of her prison, and her struggles within the coppered archway of the vault! Oh whither shall I fly? Will she not be here anon? Is she not hurrying to upbraid me for my haste? Have I not heard her footstep on the stair? Do I not distinguish that heavy and horrible beating of her heart? *Madman!*"—here he sprang furiously to his feet, and shrieked out his syllables, as if in the effort he were giving up his soul—*"Madman! I tell you that she now stands without the door!"*

> Hearing the noises in the house, Usher has become increasingly distraught.
>
> ? *What horrible conjecture has Usher not dared to express until now? Locate the sentence that explains the exact connection between the three noises in the story of Ethelred and the three noises in the house of Usher.*

As if in the superhuman energy of his utterance there had been found the potency of a spell—the huge antique panels to which the speaker pointed, threw slowly back, upon the instant, their ponderous and ebony jaws. It was the work of the rushing gust—but then without those doors there *did* stand the lofty and enshrouded figure of the lady Madeline of Usher. There was blood upon her white robes, and the evidence of some bitter struggle upon every portion of her emaciated frame. For a moment she remained trembling and reeling to and fro upon the threshold—then, with a low moaning cry, fell heavily inward upon the person of her brother, and in her violent and now final death agonies, bore him to the floor a corpse, and a victim to the terrors he had anticipated.

> The wind blows open the door, revealing a new terror in the hallway outside.

From that chamber, and from that mansion, I fled aghast. The storm was still abroad in all its wrath as I found myself crossing the old cause-

WORDS TO OWN

potency (pōt'n·sē) *n.:* strength; power.
emaciated (ē·mā'shē·āt'id) *v.* used as *adj.:* unusually thin.

way. Suddenly there shot along the path a wild light, and I turned to see whence a gleam so unusual could have issued; for the vast house and its shadows were alone behind me. The radiance was that of the full, setting, and blood-red moon, which now shone vividly through that once barely discernible fissure, of which I have before spoken as extending from the roof of the building, in a zigzag direction, to the base. While I gazed, this fissure rapidly widened—there came a fierce breath of the whirlwind—the entire orb of the satellite burst at once upon my sight—my brain reeled as I saw the mighty walls rushing asunder—there was a long tumultuous shouting sound like the voice of a thousand waters—and the deep and dank tarn at my feet closed sullenly and silently over the fragments of the *"House of Usher."*

> **?** *What happens to Roderick Usher? to the house of Usher? to the narrator? What image are you left with at the end of the story?*

Connections

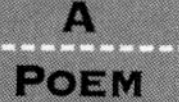

A POEM

The Fall of the House of Usher

Reed Whittemore

It was a big boxy wreck of a house
Owned by a classmate of mine named Rod Usher,
Who lived in the thing with his twin sister.
He was a louse and she was a souse.

While I was visiting them one wet summer, she died.
We buried her,
Or rather we stuck her in a back room for a bit, meaning to bury her
When the graveyard dried.

But the weather got wetter.
One night we were both waked by a twister,
Plus a screeching and howling outside that turned out to be sister
Up and dying again, making it hard for Rod to forget her.
He didn't. He and she died in a heap, and I left quick,
Which was lucky since the house fell in right after,
Like a ton of brick.

Answer to Boxed Question
Usher dies of shock and fright when his sister, now dying, falls on him; the narrator flees the house as it collapses into the tarn. Students may say they are left with an image of the red moon hovering over the dark waters of the tarn, where a few ripples indicate where the house sank.

B. Reader's Response: Connecting with the Text

? What movies or stories resemble this story? [Sample responses: Stephen King's *The Shining,* Anne Rivers Siddons's *The House Next Door,* Ray Bradbury's "April 2005—Usher II" in *The Martian Chronicles,* and Shirley Jackson's *The Haunting of Hill House.*]

C. Critical Reading: Expressing an Opinion

Explain which version you prefer. [Possible answers: The story, because it is more detailed and frightening. The poem, because the story was hard to believe and the poem makes fun of it. Or they are both different. The Poe story is well-written and effective; the poem resembles an inside joke, and you have to know the story to fully appreciate the poem. It also provides some comic relief and advises readers not to take the Poe story too seriously.]

CONNECTING WITH POE'S "THE FALL OF THE HOUSE OF USHER"

Whittemore satirizes Poe's story in a parody that uses the same title. Parodies achieve their effects by humorously oversimplifying or exaggerating certain features of the original work. Ask students to discuss what specific features of Poe's work Whittemore simplifies or exaggerates. Invite them to share other features that make the poem comic. [Plot line, the description of the house, and the language are greatly simplified. The storm is turned into a tornado. The rhyme scheme and the rhythm make the poem comic. Line 7 acts as a humorous qualifier for ll. 5 and 6. The short sentence in l. 13 adds comic emphasis.]

Making Meanings

First Thoughts

1. Possible responses: Poe was successful; it seems that something terrible will happen, but readers do not know what.

Reviewing the Text

Narrator arrives at House of Usher; Roderick Usher and his sister, Madeline, are in a state of depression and physical decline; narrator is unable to relieve Usher; Madeline apparently dies; narrator and Usher place her in a dungeon vault; Madeline reappears days later, falls dead upon her brother, and he dies of shock; narrator flees from house; house collapses and sinks into lake.

Shaping Interpretations

2. They reveal a tortured sensibility and a disordered mind.
3. Possible response: Roderick and Madeline were two closely related sides of the same personality.
4. He tries to understand and sympathize with Usher's malady. He takes part with Roderick in artistic pursuits. Conveying Madeline's body to the vault unnerves him. Finally, the narrator admits, "I felt creeping upon me, by slow yet certain degrees, the wild influences of his own fantastic yet impressive superstitions." Responses will vary, but students may indicate it makes them doubt the accuracy or truth of the events taking place.
5. Possible responses: They were simply descendants of a family with a long history of mental and physical illnesses. Or Madeline is epileptic and Roderick suffers from paranoia. Roderick's volatile state and Madeline's catatonia.
6. Possible responses: A ghost, for the narrator says he is beginning to be influenced by the fantastic, too. They screwed down the lid of the coffin and a living person could not get out. Or a real person; she has a physical presence for she falls on her brother.
7. Possible responses. Usher's disordered imagination eventually shuts out the outside world. Usher's world collapses because it loses connection with the other aspects of reality. Fantasy replaces reality and results in destruction and madness. The fall of the house might symbolize the final collapse of Usher and his family. Poe's symbolism may suggest that if undisciplined aesthetic impulses are given free reign, the result may be that the mind will crack and disintegrate into insanity or death.

Challenging the Text

8. **(Evaluation)** Possible response: The details make sense. Roderick need not have mentioned his twin to his childhood friend. Or the details did not make sense. How could Madeline have gotten out of the coffin after they had screwed down the lid?

Making Meanings

First Thoughts

1. Review your Reader's Log notes about the qualities of an effective horror story. How successful was Poe's use of Gothic devices in creating an **atmosphere** of dread?

Reviewing the Text

Imagine that you are telling a friend about the story. List the main events in chronological order.

Shaping Interpretations

2. What do Roderick's artistic efforts—his guitar solo, his painting, and his poem "The Haunted Palace"—reveal about his state of mind?
3. Why do you think Poe made Roderick and Madeline *twins*—not just brother and sister?
4. The story is presented from the **point of view** of a typical Poe narrator—a character who claims to provide an objective view, but whose rationality becomes suspect during the course of the tale. What evidence can you find that the narrator's state of mind may be approaching Roderick's? How does this uncertainty about the narrator's objectivity affect your response to the story's events?
5. What do you suppose was basically wrong with the Ushers? What evidence do you find to support this view?
6. What do you think is happening at the end of the story, when Madeline Usher appears? (Is she a hallucination, a ghost, or a real person who has been buried alive?) Support your response with evidence from the story.
7. Poe said that the poem "The Haunted Palace" is meant to suggest a disordered brain. How might the whole story be read as an allegory of a journey into the human mind? (An **allegory** is a story or poem that can be read on one level for its literal meaning and on a second level for its symbolic meaning.) What could the final *fall* of the house represent?

Challenging the Text

8. Do any details in this story fail to make sense to you? For example, how could the narrator not have known his old friend had a *twin*? Discuss your challenges with other readers.

Elements of Literature

Poe's Symbols

What do these symbols mean to you?

   π

The images above are sometimes called conventional or public symbols. This means that they are well known, at least in a particular culture, and that their meaning is agreed upon.

Writers and artists often create their own unique **symbols.** In this story, for example, Poe has Roderick mention his strange theory of the "sentience," or consciousness, of the mansion's stones. It could be that Poe is suggesting a relationship between the house and Roderick's mind. As we think about this, we might decide that the decaying house symbolizes Roderick's decaying sanity.

With a small group, make a list of details from Poe's story that might be symbolic. Next to each item, write your guess as to what it symbolizes.

Guidelines for Recognizing Symbols

1. **A symbol is a concrete object, person, place, or action that operates on at least two levels: It functions as itself, and it stands for a wider meaning.**
2. **Symbols are often visual.**
3. **The symbol is identified with something that is very different from it, yet the two things share a similar quality.**
4. **The writer gives the symbol a great deal of emphasis.**
5. **The symbol usually has something to do with the story's theme.**

Language and Style

Poe's Connotations

All words have particular **denotations,** or specific dictionary definitions. Some words also have **connotations**—associations and emotional overtones that people have come to attach to them. For example, the word *puzzling* suggests that something is mildly confusing or confounding. The word *bewildering* goes a step further, suggesting that something is so puzzling as to be hopelessly confusing.

Words that have especially strong positive or negative connotations are called **loaded** or **suggestive words.** Poe felt that a story's mood, or **atmosphere,** was of paramount importance, so it's no surprise that he often used suggestive words to manipulate our emotional responses.

1. Re-read the famous first paragraph of Poe's story. Which words suggest decay, sterility, finality, and emptiness? List them.
2. Rewrite the first few sentences of the first paragraph. Change the time of day, the time of year, and the weather conditions to paint a cheerful or cozy picture of the house of Usher. How does your choice of words change the atmosphere of the paragraph?

Choices: Building Your Portfolio

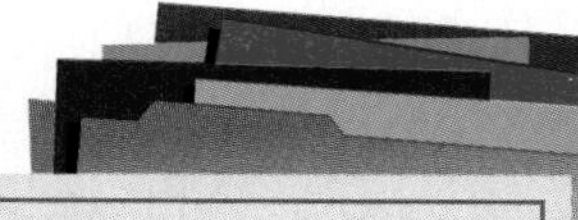

Writer's Notebook

1. Collecting Ideas for a Controversial Issue

Using the topic you explored earlier (page 258), or another controversial topic of your choice, write down two or three emotional appeals. Use words with strong **connotative** meanings to persuade readers to accept your position on the issue. Save your notes for possible use in the Writer's Workshop on page 331.

Critical Writing

2. What's It All About?

Select one of these interpretations of "The Fall of the House of Usher"—or develop a position of your own—and defend it in a brief essay.

- The story is symbolic. The house represents the diseased, dying Usher family.
- The narrator is insane. The entire story is a projection of his mind.
- Roderick and Madeline represent two sides of the same mind: the conscious and the unconscious.
- The story is an **allegory** about an artist who is drawn on a journey through the dark side of the human mind.

Creative Writing

3. Changing Genres

Tell the story of the house of Usher in another genre: a poem, a newspaper article, a magazine interview, a script, a picture book, a comic strip—even a drawing or song. For inspiration, see Reed Whittemore's poem "The Fall of the House of Usher" (page 279).

Music

4. Setting Poe to Music

Search for music—classical, jazz, contemporary instrumental, rock, movie soundtracks—that to you evokes the **atmosphere** and events of Usher. Play the music you have selected for the class, and explain why you chose it. If you are a musician, try composing instrumental music or a song.

Art

5. Going Gothic

What does the house of Usher *look* like? Draw, paint, or even build your vision of this ghastly Gothic structure.

Language and Style

Answers

1. *dull, dark, soundless, autumn, oppressively, dreary, evening, melancholy, insufferable gloom, unrelieved, desolate, terrible, bleak, vacant, rank, decayed, depression, hideous, iciness, sinking, sickening, unredeemed dreariness, unnerved, insoluble, shadowy fancies, annihilate, sorrowful, precipitous brink, black and lurid tarn, unruffled luster, gray sedge, ghastly tree stems, vacant and eyelike windows*
2. Possible answer: "During the morning of a bright, sunshiny day filled with bird song in the spring of the year, when the white clouds floated benignly high in the heavens, I had been passing alone, on horseback, through an unusually picturesque tract of country; and at length found myself, as noon approached, within view of the joyous House of Usher." The rewritten sentence changes the mood from negative to positive.

Choices: Building Your Portfolio

1. **Writer's Notebook** Remind students to save their work. They may use it as prewriting for the Writer's Workshop on p. 331.
4. **Music** To extend the activity, ask students to digitize the music and to add video clips or photo files to create a multimedia presentation.

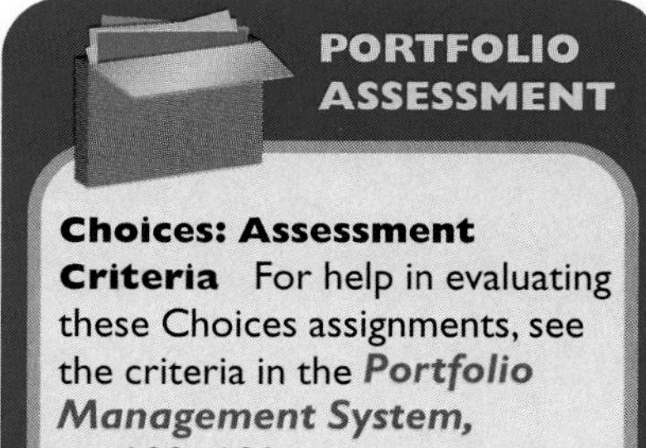

Choices: Assessment Criteria For help in evaluating these Choices assignments, see the criteria in the ***Portfolio Management System,*** pp. 100–101.

Elements of Literature

Mini-Lesson: Symbols

Ask students to identify each of the symbols shown on p. 280 and to describe what each of the symbols means to them. Remind students that they are surrounded by symbols. Have students work in groups of three to come up with a list of public symbols that they see every day. Ask the groups to design personal symbols that might represent them. Have groups share their findings and their symbols with the class.

Answers

Examples include:

- the vacant, eyelike windows of the house, symbolizing Roderick's feeling of loss
- the gloomy, decaying house, symbolizing the condition of the family
- Roderick's picture of a vault or tunnel, its tomblike appearance symbolizing the condition of Roderick's mind
- the frequent and violent alterations in the direction of the wind, symbolizing changes in Roderick's mood

QUICK PLANNING GUIDE

Into the Poem

Before You Read p. 282

- **Reading Focus: Scaffolding** Students explore an aspect of the dark side of human nature.
- **A Dialogue with the Text: Set a Purpose** Record musical or clever lines in Reader's Log
- **Elements of Literature: Sound Effects**
- **Background** "The Raven" was a hit

Through the Poem

"The Raven" pp. 282–286

Primary Sources p. 287

Making Meanings p. 288

Elements of Literature p. 288

- Internal rhyme
- Alliteration
- Onomatopoeia

Beyond the Poem

Choices: Building Your Portfolio p. 289

- **Writer's Notebook:** Write down vivid examples and details to use for a controversial essay
- **Critical Writing:** Explain in a paragraph the meaning of a statement by Poe
- **Creative Writing/Performance:** Write a parody of "The Raven"
- **Art:** Create a collage of Poe

BEFORE YOU READ

THE RAVEN

Reading Focus

Exploring the Dark Side

"The Raven" has the sound of a lyric, but, actually, it is a narrative poem with a plot that leads the reader from curiosity to horror. The poem explores one aspect of the dark side of human nature: what Poe himself called "that species of despair which delights in self-torture." In the current jargon of psychology, the narrator "projects" onto the bird whatever his own wild imagination dredges up.

A Dialogue with the Text

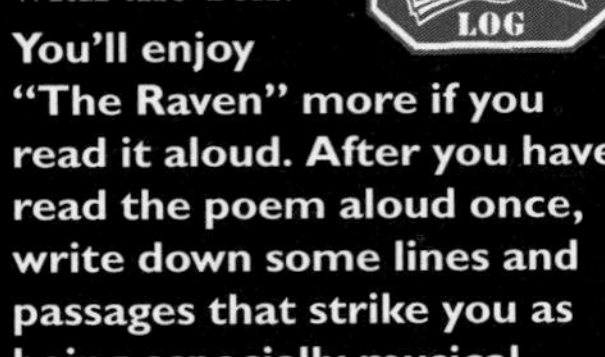

You'll enjoy "The Raven" more if you read it aloud. After you have read the poem aloud once, write down some lines and passages that strike you as being especially musical, clever, or memorable.

Elements of Literature

Sound Effects

One of the reasons "The Raven" became so popular was that it was "catchy" the way a song can be. Like many songs, the poem uses evocative rhythms, clever rhymes, alliteration, and other sound effects. These elements make the poem cry out for oral interpretation. (For more on Sound Effects, see page 288 and the Handbook of Literary Terms.)

Background

It may be hard to imagine today, but when Poe's "The Raven" was first published in 1845, it was a hit—a popular success with the same kind of impact that the Beatles' first single had in 1962. It seemed as though everyone read "The Raven," recited it, and talked about it. Poe became a household name with this poem, but it didn't make him rich; he received only about ten dollars for it.

The Raven

Edgar Allan Poe

A

Once upon a midnight dreary, while I pondered, weak and weary,
Over many a quaint and curious volume of forgotten lore—
While I nodded, nearly napping, suddenly there came a tapping,
As of someone gently rapping, rapping at my chamber door—
" 'Tis some visitor," I muttered, "tapping at my chamber door—
Only this and nothing more."

B

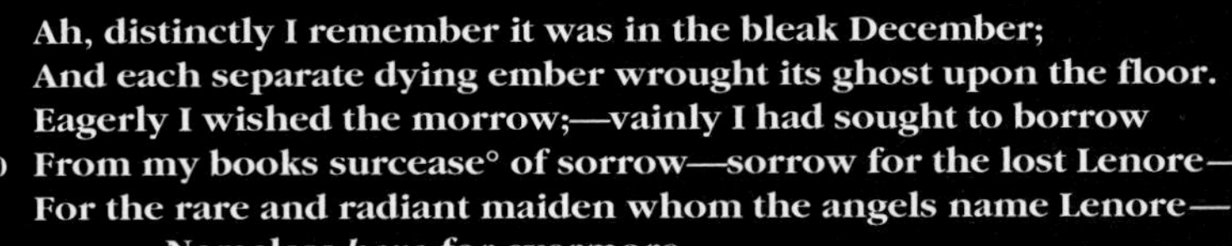

Ah, distinctly I remember it was in the bleak December;
And each separate dying ember wrought its ghost upon the floor.
Eagerly I wished the morrow;—vainly I had sought to borrow
From my books surcease° of sorrow—sorrow for the lost Lenore—
For the rare and radiant maiden whom the angels name Lenore—
Nameless *here* for evermore.

10. surcease: an end.

PROGRAM MANAGER

- **Planning Instruction** See Teaching Notes, *Teaching Resources A,* p. 105, for objectives, a summary, literary elements, and additional historical information.
- **Instructional Support** Before beginning the instructional lesson, see Graphic Organizer for Active Reading, *Teaching Resources A,* p. 113, for a Through the Story activity.
- **Application and Reinforcement** For reinforcement of the elements of literature introduced in this lesson, see Transparency 6.3 in the *Audiovisual Resources Binder.*
- **Audiotaped Readings** To help readers through the lesson, use the Selected Reading, Audiocassette 1, Side B, in the *Audiovisual Resources Binder.*
- **Assessment** See Selection Test, *Test Booklet,* pp. 73–74.

And the silken, sad, uncertain rustling of each purple curtain **C**
Thrilled me—filled me with fantastic terrors never felt before;
So that now, to still the beating of my heart, I stood repeating
" 'Tis some visitor entreating entrance at my chamber door—
Some late visitor entreating entrance at my chamber door;—
This it is and nothing more."

Presently my soul grew stronger; hesitating then no longer,
"Sir," said I, "or Madam, truly your forgiveness I implore;
But the fact is I was napping, and so gently you came rapping,
And so faintly you came tapping, tapping at my chamber door,
That I scarce was sure I heard you"—here I opened wide the door;——
Darkness there and nothing more.

Deep into that darkness peering, long I stood there wondering, fearing,
Doubting, dreaming dreams no mortal ever dared to dream before;
But the silence was unbroken, and the stillness gave no token, **D**
And the only word there spoken was the whispered word, "Lenore?"
This I whispered, and an echo murmured back the word, "Lenore!"
Merely this and nothing more.

Back into the chamber turning, all my soul within me burning,
Soon again I heard a tapping somewhat louder than before.
"Surely," said I, "surely that is something at my window lattice;
Let me see, then, what thereat is, and this mystery explore—
Let my heart be still a moment and this mystery explore;—
'Tis the wind and nothing more!"

Open here I flung the shutter, when, with many a flirt and flutter,
In there stepped a stately Raven of the saintly days of yore;°
Not the least obeisance° made he; not a minute stopped or stayed he;
But, with mien of lord or lady, perched above my chamber door—
Perched upon a bust of Pallas° just above my chamber door—
Perched, and sat, and nothing more.

Then this ebony bird beguiling my sad fancy into smiling,
By the grave and stern decorum of the countenance it wore,
"Though thy crest be shorn and shaven, thou," I said, "art sure no craven,
Ghastly grim and ancient Raven wandering from the Nightly shore—
Tell me what thy lordly name is on the Night's Plutonian shore!"°
Quoth the Raven "Nevermore."

38. Raven . . . of yore: "Of yore" is an obsolete way of saying "of time long past." Poe's allusion is to 1 Kings 17:1–6, which tells of the prophet Elijah being fed by ravens in the wilderness.
39. obeisance (ō·bā′səns): gesture of respect or subservience.
41. Pallas: Pallas Athena, the Greek goddess of wisdom.
47. Plutonian shore: Pluto is the Greek god of the underworld—the land of darkness—called Hades (hā′dēz′). Hades is separated from the world of the living by several rivers, hence the mention of a shore.

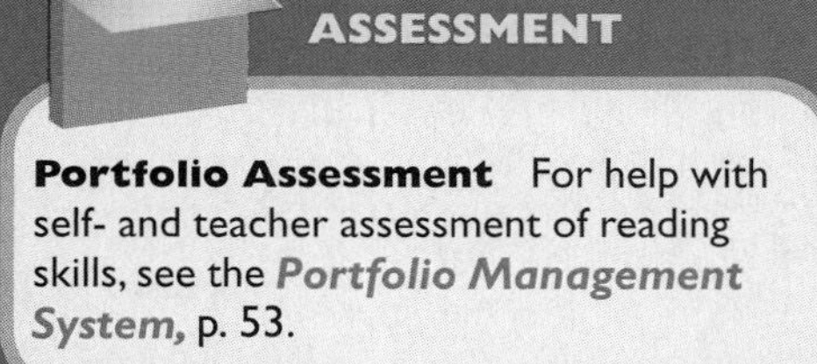

PORTFOLIO ASSESSMENT

Portfolio Assessment For help with self- and teacher assessment of reading skills, see the ***Portfolio Management System,*** p. 53.

Into the Poem

Using BEFORE YOU READ p. 282

A Dialogue with the Text

Ask students to read their lines and passages aloud to a partner and to explain the cleverness and musicality of the lines.

Through the Poem

A. Literary Element: Rhyme
Have students identify the rhyme scheme of the poem. *[abcbbb]* Be sure that they notice that every stanza uses one rhyming sound throughout the poem. Discuss the difficulty of this accomplishment.

B. Literary Element: Setting
? What details of the opening two stanzas create an atmosphere of mystery or foreboding? [Dreary midnight, strange books, in December, ghostlike shadows.]

C. Literary Element: Alliteration
? What alliteration is in the first line of the stanza? [Repetition of *s* sounds in "silken," "sad," and "uncertain rustling."] How does the alliteration add to the suspense? [The hissing of the *s* sounds sinister.]

D. Reader's Response: First Thoughts
? What reactions do you have to the speaker? [Sample responses: He seems uneasy, because the tapping could be a stranger. Or he seems extremely lonely and perhaps a bit mad.]

A. Literary Connections
Poe makes the point that good things in life do not last. Compare this to Robert Frost's "Nothing Gold Can Stay" on p. 562.

B. Critical Reading: Finding Details

? How does the narrator rationalize his fears? [He tells himself that "nevermore" is the only word the raven learned from a previous, unhappy master.]

C. Literary Element: Sound Effects

? What sound effects does Poe use here? [Possible answers: Alliteration—the repeated *g* sounds, in a terse string of adjectives; onomatopoeia—the curtains rustle.] What is the effect of these sound effects? [They build tension.]

D. Reader's Response: Shaping Interpretations

? Why does the speaker repeat phrases? [Sample responses: The velvet cushion reminds him of his loss of Lenore, and he is obsessed with that loss; or he is going mad, so he repeats himself.]

Much I marveled this ungainly fowl to hear discourse so plainly,
Though its answer little meaning—little relevancy bore;
For we cannot help agreeing that no living human being
Ever yet was blessed with seeing bird above his chamber door—
Bird or beast upon the sculptured bust above his chamber door,
With such name as "Nevermore."

But the Raven, sitting lonely on the placid bust, spoke only
That one word, as if his soul in that one word he did outpour.
Nothing farther then he uttered—not a feather then he fluttered—
Till I scarcely more than muttered "Other friends have flown before—
On the morrow *he* will leave me, as my Hopes have flown before."
Then the bird said "Nevermore."

Startled at the stillness broken by reply so aptly spoken,
"Doubtless," said I, "what it utters is its only stock and store
Caught from some unhappy master whom unmerciful Disaster
Followed fast and followed faster till his songs one burden bore—
Till the dirges of his Hope that melancholy burden bore
Of 'Never—nevermore.' "

But the Raven still beguiling my sad fancy into smiling,
Straight I wheeled a cushioned seat in front of bird, and bust and door;
Then, upon the velvet sinking, I betook myself to linking
Fancy unto fancy, thinking what this ominous bird of yore—
What this grim, ungainly, ghastly, gaunt, and ominous bird of yore
Meant in croaking "Nevermore."

This I sat engaged in guessing, but no syllable expressing
To the fowl whose fiery eyes now burned into my bosom's core;
This and more I sat divining, with my head at ease reclining
On the cushion's velvet lining that the lamplight gloated o'er,
But whose velvet-violet lining with the lamplight gloating o'er,
She shall press, ah, nevermore!

OPTIONS FOR TEACHING

STRATEGIES FOR INCLUSION

Kinesthetic To involve students in the poem, have them draw or sketch the narrator in his study and the Raven perched on the bust of Pallas.

Learners Having Difficulty The **rhythm** and **rhyme** of the poem sometimes make it easy for the narrative to get lost. Suggest that students read the poem twice. The first time they should read it for the story. The second time they should concentrate on the poetic effects.

English Language Development Read the first stanza of the poem aloud, and have students read it after you. Continue reading each stanza, having students repeat after you until all stanzas are read. Then, pair each student with a more proficient reader and assign several stanzas to each pair. Have them practice reading the selection responsively, the first student reading l. 1 and the second reading l. 2, and so on, until they can read with the natural rhythms of the poem. Have them practice for a few minutes each day for several days. Then, have each pair read their stanzas in front of the class.

285

RESPONDING TO THE ILLUSTRATION: ABOUT THE ARTWORK

The illustrator used a scratchboard to draw this menacing raven. A scratchboard is a glossy, chalk-covered cardboard which is covered with ink. Drawings are made on the scratchboard by scratching through the ink to the white surface. Although this technique lends itself easily to simple line drawings or designs, very complex, realistic drawings, like this raven that resembles Poe's black bird, can be created with scratchboard as well.

INTEGRATING THE LANGUAGE ARTS

Strategic Reading The day before teaching the poem, assign each stanza to a different student, and tell students they will read aloud the following day. Allow them time in class to practice. Encourage them to read as expressively and fluently as they can. In addition, encourage them to ask you how to pronounce unfamiliar words.

Vocabulary In the poem are many examples of words that were archaic even in Poe's time, yet Poe deliberately chose to include them. Ask students to find examples of these terms in the poem and to list a modern equivalent. [Answers include "thy"—your, "hath"—has, "methought"—it seemed to me.] Ask students to consider what the older terms add to the poem that more modern terms cannot provide.

Language and Style Ask several students to listen for the words "nevermore," "Lenore," and "Quoth the raven" while the poem is being read. Have them count the instances of each word or phrase. [These appear eleven, eight, and five times, respectively.] After the reading, have students report their findings, and discuss with the class the effectiveness of the repetition.

A. Language Note: Dashes

? What is the effect of Poe's use of dashes? [The resulting short, broken phrases show the speaker's increasing frenzy and nervous agitation.]

B. Expansion

This "nevermore" cruelly dashes the speaker's fondest hope: that he will meet Lenore again in the afterlife.

C. Literary Element: Imagery

Have students note the emotional power of "Take thy beak from out my heart."

D. Critical Reading: Analyzing Repetition

? What effect does the repetition of "still is sitting" have? [It adds emotional force by emphasizing the unending presence of the raven.]

E. Reader's Response: Challenging the Text

? How did this poem make you feel? Were you able to take it seriously? [Sample responses: I felt the nervousness of the speaker, and it made *me* nervous. I took it seriously. Or I did not feel much. The rhythm and rhyme got in the way of the meaning.]

Then, methought, the air grew denser, perfumed from an unseen censer
Swung by seraphim° whose footfalls tinkled on the tufted floor.
"Wretch," I cried, "thy God hath lent thee—by these angels he hath sent thee
Respite—respite and nepenthe° from thy memories of Lenore;
Quaff, oh quaff this kind nepenthe and forget this lost Lenore!"
Quoth the Raven "Nevermore."

"Prophet!" said I, "thing of evil!—prophet still, if bird or devil!—
Whether Tempter sent, or whether tempest tossed thee here ashore,
Desolate yet all undaunted, on this desert land enchanted—
On this home by Horror haunted—tell me truly, I implore—
Is there—*is* there balm in Gilead?°—tell me—tell me, I implore!"
Quoth the Raven "Nevermore."

"Prophet!" said I, "thing of evil!—prophet still, if bird or devil!
By that Heaven that bends above us—by that God we both adore—
Tell this soul with sorrow laden if, within the distant Aidenn,°
It shall clasp a sainted maiden whom the angels name Lenore—
Clasp a rare and radiant maiden whom the angels name Lenore."
Quoth the Raven "Nevermore."

"Be that word our sign of parting, bird or fiend!" I shrieked, upstarting—
"Get thee back into the tempest and the Night's Plutonian shore!
Leave no black plume as a token of that lie thy soul hath spoken!
Leave my loneliness unbroken!—quit the bust above my door!
Take thy beak from out my heart, and take thy form from off my door!"
Quoth the Raven "Nevermore."

And the Raven, never flitting, still is sitting, *still* is sitting
On the pallid bust of Pallas just above my chamber door;
And his eyes have all the seeming of a demon's that is dreaming,
And the lamplight o'er him streaming throws his shadow on the floor;
And my soul from out that shadow that lies floating on the floor
Shall be lifted—nevermore!

80. seraphim: the highest of the nine ranks of angels; often pictured as having three sets of wings.
82. nepenthe (nē·pen′thē): a sleeping potion that people once believed would relieve pain and sorrow. Eventually it came to stand for anything that brought such relief.
89. Is . . . Gilead: literally, "Is there any relief from my sorrow?" Poe paraphrases a line from Jeremiah 8:22: "Is there no balm in Gilead?" Gilead was a region in ancient Palestine known for its healing herbs, such as balm. Balm has come to mean any healing ointment.
93. Aidenn: Arabic for "Eden" or "Heaven."

OPTIONS FOR TEACHING

CROSSING THE CURRICULUM

Fine Art The Raven alights on a bust of Pallas. Ask students to locate photographs of busts of Pallas Athena, the Greek goddess of wisdom. Ask them to show their findings to the class and to explain how the Raven's perching on the bust contributes to the mood of the poem.

Science Have students conduct research on ravens. Ask them to consider how they live, what they eat, where they roost, what kinds of nests they build, and what parts of the world they inhabit. Ask students to create a display for other students to view and to include in it a brief paragraph explaining why the raven is an appropriate bird for Poe's poem.

COOPERATIVE LEARNING

Lenore's Death Have students meet in groups of four or five. Allow them to work together for ten or fifteen minutes to come up with a plausible story about what happened to Lenore. Ask them to develop a time line of events and to make a list of details. Have groups tell their stories to the class.

PRIMARY **Sources** AN ESSAY

Poe's Process: Writing "The Raven"

Several years after the hugely successful publication of "The Raven," Poe wrote an essay describing how he composed the poem. He described the writing of the poem as though he were solving a mathematical puzzle. Here are the first stages of Poe's writing process:

1. He decided he wanted to write a poem with a melancholy effect.
2. Then he decided that the melancholy would be reinforced by the refrain "Nevermore" (he liked its sound) and that a raven would utter the refrain. (Before he settled on a raven, though, he considered an owl and even a parrot.)
3. Finally, he decided his subject would be what he thought was the most melancholy subject in the world: a lover's mourning for a beautiful woman who has died.

Now Poe was ready to write. The first stanza he wrote, he claimed, was the climactic one, lines 85–90. From there he set about choosing his details: the interior space in which the lover, who is a student, and the Raven are brought together; the tapping that introduces the Raven; the fact that the night is stormy rather than calm; and the action of the Raven alighting on the bust of Pallas.

Then Poe goes on to describe his writing process:

> . . . The raven addressed, answers with its customary word, "Nevermore"—a word which finds immediate echo in the melancholy heart of the student, who, giving utterance aloud to certain thoughts suggested by the occasion, is again startled by the fowl's repetition of "Nevermore." The student now guesses the state of the case, but is impelled, as I have before explained, by the human thirst for self-torture, and in part by superstition, to propound such queries to the bird as will bring him, the lover, the most of the luxury of sorrow, through the anticipated answer "Nevermore.". . .
>
> It will be observed that the words "from out my heart," involve the first metaphorical expression in the poem. They, with the answer, "Nevermore," dispose the mind to seek a moral in all that has been previously narrated. The reader begins now to regard the Raven as emblematical [symbolic]—but it is not until the very last line of the very last stanza, that the intention of making him emblematical of *Mournful and never ending Remembrance* is permitted distinctly to be seen. . . .
>
> —Edgar Allan Poe

Illustration by Wilfred Satty for "The Fall of the House of Usher."

Primary Sources

After students have read Poe's explanation of his own writing process, ask them to discuss the explanation, considering whether they think most writers begin with an idea or with an inspiration. Ask students how they themselves begin writing.

STRATEGIES FOR INCLUSION

Visual To help students understand how Poe first developed the poem, provide students with a copy of it. Ask them to cut it apart by stanzas and then to categorize the stanzas as Poe claims he wrote the poem. (The climax, setting of the room, tapping, details of the night, and Raven's alighting on the bust.)

CROSSING THE CURRICULUM

Music Have students work in groups of three or four to discuss the mood Poe worked to create in "The Raven." Ask them to choose or compose music that Poe might choose to be played in the background when his poetry is being read. Ask students to play the music as they read portions of "The Raven" aloud. Have the class vote on which music they think best sets the mood.

Making Meanings

First Thoughts

1. Possible responses: It was just a figment of his imagination. He was physically and mentally exhausted. Or the raven was real and encountering it after losing Lenore pushed the speaker over the edge and into madness.

Shaping Interpretations

2. The atmosphere is mysterious and ominous. The narrator describes the time of the events as "bleak December." The dying embers in the fireplace produce "ghosts upon the floor." The curtains rustle sadly, and the narrator feels "fantastic terrors."
3. The bird has become a demonic force for the narrator; its prophecy that he may never forget his sorrow makes it seem to the narrator as if the raven has wounded his heart.
4. Although the poem starts somberly, the first appearance of the Raven evokes a kind of amusement in the speaker (stanzas 7–9); he even jokes about the Raven's name being "Nevermore." The speaker's mood becomes more reflective in stanzas 10–13; he wonders what misfortune can have befallen the Raven's master. It is only in stanza 14 that the speaker realizes the visit of the Raven may be intended as a message for him. In stanzas 15 and 16, he asks the Raven whether his sorrow will end, knowing the answer "Nevermore" will increase his sorrow. In stanza 18, he says the Raven has remained on the bust of Pallas to this day, his eyes resembling those of a demon. He also tells us that his own soul is in the shadow of the Raven and will never be lifted up again. The exaggerated nature of both claims perhaps suggests that the speaker has gone mad.
5. Students should refer to the poem's rhyme scheme and meter and to Poe's use of internal rhyme, alliteration, and onomatopoeia.
6. The Raven's presence is an unending reminder of the speaker's loss and sorrow.
7. Students may say it symbolizes death, the pain of loss, or despair. A chicken would be too humorous; a hawk would be too vicious; a sparrow too small; a dove or nightingale too gentle. The raven set the mood Poe wanted.

MAKING MEANINGS

First Thoughts

1. Do you think there really *was* a raven in the speaker's chambers? Why or why not? What is your explanation for what happened on that "midnight dreary" in the speaker's room?

Shaping Interpretations

2. How would you describe the **atmosphere** created by the setting? Which **images** in the beginning of the poem create this atmosphere?
3. In line 101, what do you think the speaker might mean when he begs the bird, "Take thy beak from out my heart"?
4. The speaker's **tone** changes as the Raven gradually turns from a comic figure into a demonic figure. Trace these changes in tone. Is there evidence in the last stanza that the speaker goes mad? Explain.
5. How did the poem's **sound effects** affect your response to the poem? Go back to the text and your Reader's Log, and cite passages that you'd especially like to read aloud to the class.
6. By the end of the poem, what do you think it means that the Raven "*still* is sitting" in the speaker's chamber?
7. Many readers take the Raven as a **symbol**—it functions as a real raven in the poem, but it also has a broader, figurative meaning. What, in your opinion, does the Raven symbolize? Why do you suppose Poe chose a raven to carry this meaning rather than a chicken, hawk, sparrow, or other bird? (For more on symbols, see page 280.)

Connecting with the Text

8. What do you make of the speaker of this poem? Freewrite some thoughts that you imagine might be running through his head during or after the events of the poem. Then get together with a small group of other students, and take turns being the speaker, who has been put on the "hot seat" to answer questions. Remember to answer the other students' questions as though you were the speaker of the poem.

Extending the Text

9. Can the loss of a loved one really cause a person to go mad with despair, as this poem seems to suggest? Discuss any other stories you know of in which a person is driven to despair by the loss of someone he or she loves.

Challenging the Text

10. Suppose someone said to you that "The Raven" is not worth reading because it's unbelievable. How would you answer this challenge?

ELEMENTS OF LITERATURE

Poe's Sound Effects

"The Raven" is a virtuoso performance in the use of **internal rhyme**—rhyme that occurs within the lines, or repetition of an end rhyme within a line. "Dreary" and "weary" in line 1 prepare us for a pattern of internal rhyming sounds. "Napping," "tapping," and "rapping" in lines 3 and 4 make us expect more. Some of Poe's rhymes are ingenious. Not many writers, for example, would think of rhyming "window lattice" with "what thereat is" (lines 33–34).

Another skillful use of repetition occurs with the **refrain** "Nevermore"; it is also an important element in the **rhyme scheme** of the poem. Poe keeps the sound of the word echoing in our ears through repetition combined with changes in tone.

Throughout the poem, Poe uses the technique of **alliteration** (the repetition of a consonant sound) to create **onomatopoeia**—the use of words with sounds that actually echo their sense. A good example of alliteration is in line 71, where the hard *g* is repeated four times, almost resulting in a tongue twister: "this *g*rim, un*g*ainly, *g*hastly, *g*aunt, and ominous bird of yore."

1. Locate the internal rhymes in lines 79–84 and 91–96. What other internal rhymes can you find?
2. What other word are you reminded of when you hear the refrain "Nevermore"? How does this echo affect you?
3. Where in lines 13–18 and 37–42 is alliteration used to create onomatopoeia?

Connecting with the Text

8. Students should base their thoughts on evidence in the poem and demonstrate the change in the speaker's tone as the story progresses.

Extending the Text

9. **(Synthesis)** Some students will agree; others will think it cannot happen. Examples of other works include *Romeo and Juliet* and "The Highwayman."

Challenging the Text

10. **(Evaluation)** Possible responses: The fantastic and romantic drama of the poem makes it intriguing and fun to read. Or the poem is an outstanding example of the creative use of poetic devices.

CHOICES: Building Your Portfolio

Writer's Notebook

1. Collecting Ideas for a Controversial Issue

In the Writer's Workshop on page 331, you'll write about a controversial issue. You can use vivid images and even a repeated refrain—as Poe does in "The Raven"—to make your arguments more persuasive. Review your Writer's Notebook entries for topics, or choose a controversial issue you know something about. Write down at least three details supporting your position. Try to arouse your readers' feelings and persuade them to agree with you. Can you think of an effective refrain? Keep your notes for possible use in the Workshop.

WORK IN PROGRESS

Critical Writing

2. What's His Problem?

In Primary Sources (page 287), Poe explains that the speaker in "The Raven" is impelled "by the human thirst for self-torture." In a paragraph, explain what you think this statement means, and tell whether or not you think the speaker in the poem exhibits this compulsion.

Creative Writing / Performance

3. A Poe-etic Parody

One of the best measures of a popular success is the number of times it has been parodied. "The Raven" has surely been one of the world's most successful poems, for it has been parodied countless times. In Poe's day, parodies with such titles as "The Craven," "The Turkey," and "The Mammoth Squash" abounded. One parodist used the poem as an inspiration for a political lampoon:

> Once upon an evening dreary, the Council pondered weak and weary,
> Over many a long petition which was voted down a bore.

Try your own hand at parody by writing at least two stanzas of a humorous version of "The Raven" that imitates Poe's **rhyme scheme** and use of **sound effects.** (See Elements of Literature on page 288.) You may want to change the name Lenore to another name that has many possible rhymes. Perform your humorous poem for the class.

Art

4. A Portrait of Poe

Make a collage "portrait" of Edgar Allan Poe by putting together different visual items—colors, images, and even textures—that, to you, suggest Poe and his works. You might want to refer to Poe's typical settings and characters, as well as to his thematic concerns and actual events in his life. When you have completed your collage, write a "Note from the Artist" explaining what each element in the collage stands for.

"One more time."

Elements of Literature

Mini-Lesson: Poe's Sound Effects

Have one student read aloud the first paragraph on **internal rhyme.** Ask students to write a line using internal rhyme and to share it with the class. Have another student read the second paragraph and stanzas 15 and 16 from the poem. Ask students to discuss the effect of the **rhyme scheme** in these two stanzas. Finally, have a third student read the paragraph on **alliteration,** and have students compose two phrases that use alliteration and then share them with the class.

Answers

1. **Internal rhymes** can be found in stanzas 14 and 16 in ll. 79, 81–83, 91, and 93–95. Internal rhymes occur in the first line of each stanza and in the third and fourth lines of each stanza. In stanza 1, the rhyme in the first line is carried into the second, and in stanzas 1, 3, and 13—as in stanzas 14 and 16—the rhyme in the third and fourth lines is carried into the fifth line by repetition of the rhyming word in the fourth. Last, an internal rhyme occurs in the first words of l. 14.
2. We are reminded of "Lenore." Students may say the echo leaves them with a feeling of finality or hopelessness.
3. In ll. 13–18, **onomatopoeia** is created by the alliteration "silken, sad, uncertain rustling of each purple curtain." In ll. 37–42, it is created in "Open here I *f*lung the shutter, when, with many a *f*lirt and *f*lutter."

Choices: Building Your Portfolio

1. **Writer's Notebook** Remind students to save their work. They may use it as prewriting for the Writer's Workshop on p. 331.

PROGRAM MANAGER

Application and Reinforcement
For reinforcement of the elements of literature introduced in this lesson on p. 288, see **Transparency** 6.3 in the ***Audiovisual Resources Binder.***

PORTFOLIO ASSESSMENT

Choices: Assessment Criteria For help in evaluating these Choices assignments, see the criteria in the ***Portfolio Management System,*** p. 102.

Technology Tip

For students who speak Spanish, biographical information on Julio Cortázar is available on the World Wide Web at **http://lenti.med.umn.edu/~ernesto/Cortazar/Cortazar.html**. This site also includes the text in Spanish of selected stories by Cortázar as well as a list of some of his works. *You may want to preview any Internet activity that you suggest to students. Because these resources are sometimes public forums, their content can be unpredictable.*

Background

Based on what they already know about Poe's writing, ask students how they think the brother and sister will react to what is happening in "House Taken Over."

A Dialogue with the Text

Suggest that students use a three-column chart for taking notes. In the left column, students should write the questions; they should then jot down their notes in the middle column. The third column should be used for taking notes during the Finding Common Ground discussion on p. 295.

Questions	Notes	Discussion
What humdrum routines mark the daily life of the narrator and his sister?		

PROGRAM MANAGER

Planning Instruction See Teaching Notes, *Teaching Resources A,* p. 106, for objectives and a summary for this selection.

LITERATURE OF THE AMERICAS
ARGENTINA

Julio Cortázar
(1914–1984)

Julio Cortázar was born in Brussels, Belgium, to Argentine parents. The family returned to Argentina when Cortázar was six, and he was educated there. As an adult, he first supported his writing career by teaching high school and university courses, then by managing a publishing association, and finally by working as a translator. A change in Argentina's political regime caused him to move to France in 1951. In Paris, he worked as a translator for the United Nations. He eventually became a French citizen, but he retained his Argentine citizenship, and he always thought of himself as both South American and European.

Because Cortázar believed that sober, objective reality masks a hidden dimension of the fantastic, he used his stories to awaken readers to that dimension. Like nightmares that begin with ordinary scenes that are distorted into something bizarre, his stories move seamlessly from reality to fantasy. As the critic Alexander Coleman observed, "Cortázar's stories start in a disarmingly conversational way, with plenty of local touches. . . . But something always seems to go awry just when we least expect it."

One of Cortázar's short stories was the basis for Michelangelo Antonioni's classic film *Blow Up* (1966).

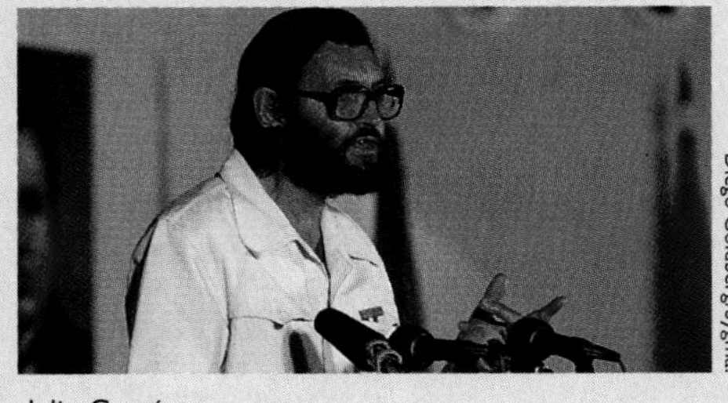

Diego Goldberg/Sygma.

Julio Cortázar.

BEFORE YOU READ

Background

Julio Cortázar once explained the effects of first reading Edgar Allan Poe at the age of nine: "I stole the book . . . because my mother didn't want me to read it; she thought I was too young and she was right. The book scared me and I was ill for three months, because I believed in it."

Cortázar's fascination with Poe continued into his adult life. As a translator, he rendered four books of Poe into Spanish. As a writer, he echoed Poe in producing novels and stories in which nightmare intrudes into ordinary reality.

Cortázar's link with Poe is especially noticeable in "House Taken Over." As in Poe's "The Fall of the House of Usher," a house is occupied by the last members of a family line. In Cortázar's house, a brother and a sister experience a gradual, mysterious takeover of their ancestral home. They accept the takeover calmly . . . or do they?

A Dialogue with the Text

As you read "House Taken Over," write down notes in response to these questions:

- What humdrum routines mark the daily life of the narrator and his sister?
- At what point do you begin to think there is something strange about their house?
- How does the behavior of the brother and sister during sleep differ from their behavior during waking hours?
- What does this difference in behavior tell you about their real feelings—or fears?
- Who—or what—do you think the narrator and his sister mean by "they"?
- How is this story similar to and different from Poe's "The Fall of the House of Usher"?

OPTIONS FOR TEACHING

STRATEGIES FOR INCLUSION

Visual Ask students to draw a floor plan of the house and indicate where the narrator and his sister live at various stages in the story.

Auditory If possible, lower the lights to provide a more suspenseful atmosphere, and have students sit in a circle on the floor when they come into the room. Tell them that you will begin reading "House Taken Over" aloud and that when you stop reading they can choose whether they want you to continue reading or to read silently to themselves. Have students follow in their textbooks. Stop on p. 293 at "But it's the house I want to talk about, the house and Irene, I'm not very important." Those who wish to read silently may return to their desks. Continue reading the story to those who stay.

House Taken Over

Julio Cortázar

translated from the Spanish *by* **Paul Blackburn**

We liked the house because, apart from its being old and spacious (in a day when old houses go down for a profitable auction of their construction materials), it kept the memories of great-grandparents, our paternal grandfather, our parents, and the whole of childhood. **A**

Irene and I got used to staying in the house by ourselves, which was crazy, eight people could have lived in that place and not have gotten in each other's way. We rose at seven in the morning and got the cleaning done, and about eleven I left Irene to finish off whatever rooms and went to the kitchen. We lunched at noon precisely; then there was nothing left to do but a few dirty plates. It was pleasant to take lunch and commune with the great hollow, silent house, and it was enough for us just to keep it clean. We ended up thinking, at times, that that was what had kept us from marrying. Irene turned down two suitors for no particular reason, and María Esther went and died on me before we could manage to get engaged. We were easing into our forties with the unvoiced concept that the quiet, simple marriage of sister and brother was the indispensable end to a line established in this house by our grandparents. We would die here someday, obscure and distant cousins would inherit the place, have it torn down, sell the bricks, and get rich on the building plot; or more justly and better yet, we would topple it ourselves before it was too late. **B**

A. Reader's Response: First Thoughts

? Do you think people today feel this way about the houses in which they live? [Sample responses: No, because very few people live in old family houses today; or yes, some people get so attached to their houses that they find it hard to move even when they have to.]

B. Critical Reading: Predicting

? What will happen to the brother and sister and to the house? [Possible answers: They will die together in the house. Or the house will crumble and they will escape.]

INTEGRATING THE LANGUAGE ARTS

Writing: Epilogue Have pairs of students work together to write an epilogue to the story. What becomes of the brother and sister? What happens to the house? Do the brother and sister change as a result of their experience? Have the pairs agree on **plot** between themselves. They should decide who will write which parts, spend time writing, and then read each other's work, merge the parts, and revise.

CLASSROOM MANAGEMENT

Managing the Reader's Response Classroom Before conducting a class discussion, have students discuss three or four specific questions in small groups for ten or fifteen minutes. Provide each group with one page listing the questions, or write the questions on the chalkboard. Ask groups to be sure each person has a chance to talk. When the students hold a discussion as a class, they will have had a chance to think about the questions and more students will be inclined to participate. ☞

RESPONDING TO THE ART: ABOUT THE ARTWORK

Attempting to express the subconscious through various media in literature and the visual arts, such poets as André Breton and Paul Eluard and artists such as Salvador Dali, Giorgio De Chirico, and René Magritte, *surrealists,* drew insight from the imagery found in dreams and hallucinations. The patterns, textures, and color combinations of a painting indicate the path to the subconscious of the artist. Magritte (1898–1967), a Belgian surrealist, painted in a realistic but unsettling style, juxtaposing unrelated images or opposite qualities within the same work. For instance, in *The Empire of Light,* a streetlight shines in front of a house in broad daylight, the qualities of light of both night and day present.

The Empire of Light **(1954) by René Magritte. Oil on canvas (146 cm × 114 cm).**

Royal Museum of Fine Arts, Brussels, Belgium. Courtesy Art Resource. © 1995 C. Herscovici, Brussels/Artists Rights Society (ARS), New York.

OPTIONS FOR TEACHING

ASSESSMENT TOOLS

Check Test: Questions and Answers

1. How do the narrator and his sister spend their days? [They clean the house; she knits; he reads and goes to bookstores.]
2. What is the first indication of trouble in the house? [The narrator hears noises in the library or dining room.]
3. What do the brother and sister miss most about the rooms they can no longer go into? [The personal items they have left in the rooms.]
4. How does the narrator fill his time after he has lost his books? [Working on his father's stamp collection.]
5. What does the narrator do with the house key when he and his sister flee? [He tosses it down a sewer.]

Irene never bothered anyone. Once the morning housework was finished, she spent the rest of the day on the sofa in her bedroom, knitting. I couldn't tell you why she knitted so much; I think women knit when they discover that it's a fat excuse to do nothing at all. **A** But Irene was not like that, she always knitted necessities, sweaters for winter, socks for me, handy morning robes and bedjackets for herself. Sometimes she would do a jacket, then unravel it the next moment because there was something that didn't please her; it was pleasant to see a pile of tangled wool in her knitting basket fighting a losing battle for a few hours to retain its shape. Saturdays I went downtown to buy wool; Irene had faith in my good taste, was pleased with the colors and never a skein[1] had to be returned. **B** I took advantage of these trips to make the rounds of the bookstores, uselessly asking if they had anything new in French literature. Nothing worthwhile had arrived in Argentina since 1939.

But it's the house I want to talk about, the house and Irene, I'm not very important. **C** I wonder what Irene would have done without her knitting. One can reread a book, but once a pullover is finished you can't do it over again, it's some kind of disgrace. One day I found that the drawer at the bottom of the chiffonier, replete with mothballs, was filled with shawls, white, green, lilac. Stacked amid a great smell of camphor[2]—it was like a shop; I didn't have the nerve to ask her what she planned to do with them. We didn't have to earn our living, there was plenty coming in from the farms each month, even piling up. But Irene was only interested in the knitting and showed a wonderful dexterity, and for me the hours slipped away watching her, her hands like silver sea urchins, needles flashing, and one or two knitting baskets on the floor, the balls of yarn jumping about. It was lovely.

How not to remember the layout of that house. The dining room, a living room with tapestries, the library, and three large bedrooms in the section most recessed, the one that faced toward Rodríguez Peña.[3] Only a corridor with its massive oak door separated that part from the front wing, where there was a bath, the kitchen, our bedrooms, and the hall. One entered the house through a vestibule[4] with enameled tiles, and a wrought-iron grated door opened onto the living room. You had to come in through the vestibule and open the gate to go into the living room; the doors to our bedrooms were on either side of this, and opposite it was the corridor leading to the back section; going down the passage, one swung open the oak door beyond which was the other part of the house; or just before the door, one could turn to the left and go down a narrower passageway which led to the kitchen and the bath. When the door was open, you became aware of the size of the house; when it was closed, you had the impression of an apartment, like the ones they build today, with barely enough room to move around in. Irene and I always lived in this part of the house and hardly ever went beyond the oak door except to do the cleaning. Incredible how much dust collected on the furniture. It may be Buenos Aires is a clean city, but she owes it to her population and nothing else. There's too much dust in the air, the slightest breeze and it's back on the marble console tops and in the diamond patterns of the tooled-leather desk set. It's a lot of work to get it off with a feather duster; the motes rise and hang in the air, and settle again a minute later on the pianos and the furniture. **D**

I'll always have a clear memory of it because it happened so simply and without fuss. Irene was knitting in her bedroom, it was eight at night, and I suddenly decided to put the water up for *maté*.[5] I went down the corridor as far as the oak door, which was ajar, then turned into the hall toward the kitchen, when I heard something in the library or the dining room. The sound came through muted

1. **skein** (skān): coiled length of thread or yarn.
2. **camphor:** chemical used as an insect repellent.
3. **Rodríguez Peña:** street in Buenos Aires, Argentina.
4. **vestibule:** small entrance hall.
5. **maté** (mä′tā′): tealike beverage made from dried leaves of a South American evergreen tree.

A. Literary Element: Symbol

? What might knitting symbolize? [Possible answers: The passage of time; the monotony of their routines.]

B. Critical Reading: Drawing Conclusions

? Why does Irene not shop for knitting wool herself? [Possible answers: She does not like to mingle with people and is afraid to leave the house; she likes to involve her brother in what she does.]

C. Language Note: Sentence Structure

? What is the effect of this run-on sentence? [Possible answers: It places emphasis on the phrase "I'm not very important"; it makes the narrator seem insistent.]

D. Literary Element: Analogy

? How is the dust connected with the narrator and Irene? [They are much like the dust: They can be active for a time but always settle back into their routines.]

CONNECTING WITH "THE REALMS OF DARKNESS"

Gothic fiction is a style of writing characterized by the use of desolate or remote settings and macabre, mysterious, or violent incidents. As Cortázar found out early in his life, Poe is one of the great Gothic writers. Ask students to list Gothic elements in "House Taken Over" in a chart like the following, and to compare them with those they have found in the Poe selections. Have them state how these elements reflect the realms of darkness.

Element	Poe	Cortázar

A. Critical Reading: Drawing Conclusions
Something has been happening in the house that the reader did not know about. What is it? How do the narrator and his sister react? [Possible answers: The house has been taken over by some mysterious element. Both the narrator and his sister try to continue their lives as though nothing is happening.]

B. Literary Element: Irony
? What is the irony of this statement? [It is ironic that they feel leaving their bedrooms is a bother, because they do not do much anyway.]

C. Reader's Response: Shaping Interpretations
? What do these lines reveal about the characters? [Sample responses: They have coped with their loss; they have stopped worrying about what is on the other side of the door; or they have no purpose in life.]

(A) and indistinct, a chair being knocked over onto the carpet or the muffled buzzing of a conversation. At the same time or a second later, I heard it at the end of the passage which led from those two rooms toward the door. I hurled myself against the door before it was too late and shut it, leaned on it with the weight of my body; luckily, the key was on our side; moreover, I ran the great bolt into place, just to be safe.

I went down to the kitchen, heated the kettle, and when I got back with the tray of *maté,* I told Irene:

"I had to shut the door to the passage. They've taken over the back part."

She let her knitting fall and looked at me with her tired, serious eyes.

"You're sure?"

I nodded.

"In that case," she said, picking up her needles again, "we'll have to live on this side."

I sipped at the *maté* very carefully, but she took her time starting her work again. I remember it was a gray vest she was knitting. I liked that vest.

The first few days were painful, since we'd both left so many things in the part that had been taken over. My collection of French literature, for example, was still in the library. Irene had left several folios of stationery and a pair of slippers that she used a lot in the winter. I missed my briar pipe, and Irene, I think, regretted the loss of an ancient bottle of Hesperidin.[6] It happened repeatedly (but only in the first few days) that we would close some drawer or cabinet and look at one another sadly.

"It's not here."

One thing more among the many lost on the other side of the house.

But there were advantages, too. The cleaning was so much simplified that, even when we got up late, nine-thirty for instance, by eleven we were sitting around with our arms folded. Irene got into the habit of coming to the kitchen with me to help get lunch. We thought about it and decided on this: while I prepared the lunch, Irene would cook up dishes that could be eaten cold in the evening. (B) We were happy with the arrangement because it was always such a bother to have to leave our bedrooms in the evening and start to cook. Now we made do with the table in Irene's room and platters of cold supper.

Since it left her more time for knitting, Irene was content. I was a little lost without my books, but so as not to inflict myself on my sister, I set about reordering papa's stamp collection; that killed some time. We amused ourselves sufficiently, each with his own thing, almost always getting together in Irene's bedroom, which was the more comfortable. Every once in a while, Irene might say:

"Look at this pattern I just figured out, doesn't it look like clover?"

After a bit it was I, pushing a small square of paper in front of her so that she could see the excellence of some stamp or another from Eupen-et-Malmédy.[7] (C) We were fine, and little by little we stopped thinking. You can live without thinking.

(Whenever Irene talked in her sleep, I woke up immediately and stayed awake. I never could get used to this voice from a statue or a parrot, a voice that came out of the dreams, not from a throat. Irene said that in my sleep I flailed about enormously and shook the blankets off. We had the living room between us, but at night you could hear everything in the house. We heard each other breathing, coughing, could even feel each other reaching for the light switch when, as happened frequently, neither of us could fall asleep.

Aside from our nocturnal rumblings, everything was quiet in the house. During the day there were the household sounds, the metallic click of knitting needles, the rustle of stamp-album pages turning. The oak door was massive, I think I said that. In the kitchen or

6. **Hesperidin** (hes·per′i·din): liquid made from the rind of citrus fruits and used for various medicinal purposes.

7. **Eupen-et-Malmédy** (ə·pen′ā·mäl′mā·dē′): district in eastern Belgium.

the bath, which adjoined the part that was taken over, we managed to talk loudly, or Irene sang lullabies. In a kitchen there's always too much noise, the plates and glasses, for there to be interruptions from other sounds. We seldom allowed ourselves silence there, but when we went back to our rooms or to the living room, then the house grew quiet, half-lit, we ended by stepping around more slowly so as not to disturb one another. I think it was because of this that I woke up irremedially and at once when Irene began to talk in her sleep.) D

Except for the consequences, it's nearly a matter of repeating the same scene over again. I was thirsty that night, and before we went to sleep, I told Irene that I was going to the kitchen for a glass of water. From the door of the bedroom (she was knitting) I heard the noise in the kitchen; if not the kitchen, then the bath, the passage off at that angle dulled the sound. Irene noticed how brusquely I had paused, and came up beside me without a word. We stood listening to the noises, growing more and more sure that they were on our side of the oak door, if not the kitchen then the bath, or in the hall itself at the turn, almost next to us.

We didn't wait to look at one another. I took Irene's arm and forced her to run with me to the wrought-iron door, not waiting to look back. You could hear the noises, still muffled but louder, just behind us. I slammed the grating and we stopped in the vestibule. Now there was nothing to be heard.

"They've taken over our section," Irene said. The knitting had reeled off from her hands and the yarn ran back toward the door and disappeared under it. When she saw that the balls of yarn were on the other side, she dropped the knitting without looking at it. E

"Did you have time to bring anything?" I asked hopelessly.

"No, nothing."

We had what we had on. I remembered fifteen thousand pesos in the wardrobe in my bedroom. Too late now.

I still had my wristwatch on and saw that it was 11 P.M. I took Irene around the waist (I think she was crying) and that was how we went into the street. Before we left, I felt terrible; I locked the front door up tight and tossed the key down the sewer. It wouldn't do to have some poor devil decide to go in and rob the house, at that hour and with the house taken over. F

Finding Common Ground

When you have finished writing your notes on the story, meet in a small group to discuss your observations. Have one member of the group record conclusions the group agrees upon.

- Take turns sharing what you wrote in your Reader's Logs.
- Focus especially on the huge omission left by Cortázar—the identity of "they." What conclusion does the group reach about who "they" are? What evidence supports this conclusion?
- After you have compared and contrasted Cortázar's story with Poe's "The Fall of the House of Usher," think about the main point of Cortázar's story. Is the main point of "House Taken Over" the end of a family line, or something else? What evidence supports your conclusions?
- Reconvene as a class, and listen to reports from all of the groups. Has class discussion changed your initial interpretation of the story?

D. Critical Reading: Finding Details

? What is their behavior like at night? [They try not to disturb each other. Irene talks in her sleep. The narrator tosses in his sleep or wakes up.]

E. Reader's Response: Shaping Interpretations

? Who or what are "they"? [Sample responses: Evil creatures of some kind; or it is only their imagination—nothing is there, and they have gone mad from doing nothing.]

F. Reader's Response: Challenging the Text

? Do you think the ending to this story is appropriate? Why or why not? [Sample responses: The fantastic implications of the ending fit the story; or it is difficult to interpret the author's meaning.]

Finding Common Ground

Have students appoint a monitor to make sure everyone has a turn to speak. Each student in the group should describe the identity of "they." The monitor should also ask students to provide specific evidence from the text and to indicate the page on which the evidence is found so students can follow arguments. Once everyone has had a turn, students should talk together to evaluate the ideas. Students should then discuss the main point of Cortázar's story in a similar fashion.

QUICK PLANNING GUIDE

Into the Story

Through the Story

Beyond the Story

Nathaniel Hawthorne (1840) by Charles Osgood. Oil on canvas.

Peabody Essex Museum, Salem, Massachusetts. Photo by Mark Sexton (121.459).

Nathaniel Hawthorne

(1804–1864)

Nathaniel Hawthorne was an unusually handsome man, with a loving and beloved wife. By midlife he had earned recognition as a writer and won the admiration of his contemporaries. Nevertheless, he became increasingly dissatisfied, remote, and disappointing to his friends. It was as if his dark insights into the human heart had cast gloom into his own. His fiction, which has survived the changing tastes of many generations and is more admired today than when it was written, is fueled by an awareness of the guilt that accompanies a Puritan conscience. This shadow of guilt appears to have darkened Hawthorne's life.

The source of darkness is thought to lie in Hawthorne's illustrious ancestors. William Hathorne, a serious soldier and judge, came to the Massachusetts Colony in 1630. Hawthorne describes him in the preamble to *The Scarlet Letter* as the "bearded, sable-cloaked, and steeple-crowned progenitor." William Hathorne's son, John, was also a judge. During the Salem witch trials of 1692, he played a minor role in sentencing nineteen of the accused to death.

By 1804, however, the year of Hawthorne's birth in Salem, the family had lost its wealth and renown. His own father, a sea captain, died during a voyage and left his grief-stricken wife with three young children to raise and few resources beyond the charity of relatives.

Prisoner of the Dismal Chamber

Hawthorne (who added the *w* to the family name to ensure a broad *a* in its pronunciation) attended schools in Salem and college at Bowdoin in Maine. Here, by his own judgment, he was an idle student, "rather choosing to nurse my own fancies than to dig into Greek roots." He chewed tobacco, played cards, drank wine at the taverns, and avoided intellectual company in favor of pleasure. After graduation, Hawthorne wrote to his sister Elizabeth, "I shall never make a distinguished figure in the world, and all I hope or wish is to plod along with the multitude." There is good reason to believe that this was an ironic statement, concealing an ambition that burned intensely.

Returning to Salem, Hawthorne set himself up in what he called the "dismal chamber," a room on the third floor of the family house. He kept himself a virtual prisoner there for the next twelve years, until he had learned the craft of fiction. In 1837, Hawthorne emerged to publish a collection of stories, *Twice-Told Tales*. They offered a vision of the human heart as a lurking place for the secrets of past sins. The book won Hawthorne just enough success to encourage further work.

Over the next few years Hawthorne courted and became engaged to Sophia Peabody, and he briefly joined the utopian experiment in communal living at Brook Farm. Neither the shoveling of manure nor the endless, lofty discussions of the Transcendentalists appealed to him. After their marriage in 1842, the Hawthornes

WORDS TO OWN

The following vocabulary words are defined in the Words to Own at the bottom of the pupil's page.

semblance p. 300	obscurity p. 305
iniquity p. 301	pensively p. 305
ostentatious p. 301	antipathy p. 305
sagacious p. 301	plausibility p. 305
portend p. 303	resolute p. 307

PORTFOLIO ASSESSMENT

Portfolio Assessment For help with teacher assessment of reading skills, see the ***Portfolio Management System,*** pp. 54–55.

moved into the Old Manse in Concord, where Emerson had lived before them. Hawthorne often walked with Thoreau and Emerson, but neither creativity nor warm friendship resulted.

A Novel with No "Cheering Light"

Making only the barest living from his stories, Hawthorne had to accept a political appointment as surveyor to the Salem customhouse in 1846. The job freed him from financial worry, but he hated the work. In 1849, he lost the job. Despite this loss and the simultaneous death of his mother, he somehow found the energies for his masterwork, *The Scarlet Letter.* It was, he said, "positively a hell-fired story, into which I found it almost impossible to throw any cheering light."

The novel is set in Puritan Boston during the mid–seventeenth century. The title refers to a cloth letter *A* that the narrator finds in a customhouse, along with documents outlining the tragic story of Hester Prynne, who bore an illegitimate child. Refusing to name the baby's father, she was sentenced to wear the scarlet *A* (for adultery) on her breast. The tale is one of sin and redemption, and the tragic consequences of hypocrisy and concealed guilt.

The novel's publication in 1850 brought Hawthorne wide acclaim, some money, and the admiration and friendship of Herman Melville. Another great novel, *The House of the Seven Gables,* appeared the following year.

Out of Harmony with His Times

In 1853, President Franklin Pierce—Hawthorne's old friend from his days at Bowdoin—offered Hawthorne the post of United States consul at Liverpool. Hawthorne and his family lived in Europe for seven years. As an expatriate, however, he found his creativity dwindling, and he had become inexplicably dejected. Even his return to America in 1860 was oddly cheerless. After his years abroad, he was disenchanted with both the Europe where he had been and the America from which he now felt estranged. His old friend Pierce, for whom he had written a campaign biography in 1852, had been defeated for reelection. Abraham Lincoln was in the White House, and with the onset of the Civil War, Hawthorne felt out of harmony with his times.

Back in Concord, Hawthorne found himself unable to complete the several fiction projects he had promised his publisher. His health declined. On the night of May 18, 1864, while on a trip with Pierce, Hawthorne died in a New Hampshire hotel room.

Emerson felt that Hawthorne, no longer able to endure his solitude, "died of it." Emerson also noted in his journal, after attending Hawthorne's funeral, that he was sorry he hadn't known Hawthorne better. And he recorded this sadly ironic anecdote: "One day, when I found him on the top of his hill, in the woods, he paced back the path to his house, and said, *'This path is the only remembrance of me that will remain.'* "

The Granger Collection, New York.

ABOUT THE AUTHOR

Hawthorne may have in some way resembled Mr. Hooper of "The Minister's Black Veil." He wore black and wrapped himself in a large cloak, which, on occasion, obscured his face and gave him a mysterious appearance. Hawthorne may indeed resemble his other guarded characters the Reverend Arthur Dimmesdale of *The Scarlet Letter,* and Goodman Brown of "Young Goodman Brown," who hide their secrets beneath figurative, if not literal, veils.

PROGRAM MANAGER

- **Planning Instruction** See Teaching Notes, *Teaching Resources A,* pp. 106–107, for objectives, a summary, literary elements, and additional information.
- **Instructional Support** See Graphic Organizer for Active Reading, *Teaching Resources A,* p. 114, for a Through the Story activity.
- **Application and Reinforcement** For reinforcement of the element of literature, see Transparency 6.4 in the *Audiovisual Resources Binder.*
- **Assessment** See Selection Test, *Test Booklet,* pp. 75–76.
- **Language Link** For instruction in usage, see Language Link, *Teaching Resources A,* pp. 115–116, and *Language and Writing Skills Worksheets,* pp. 4–7.
- **Reinforcement** Use the Words to Own worksheet in *Teaching Resources A,* p. 117.

Into the Story

Using Before You Read p. 298

A Dialogue with the Text

Have students keep their notes. After they have read the story, have them look back at their notes to see if they agree with their initial predictions.

Background

Hawthorne's opinion of his Puritan ancestors' attitudes was a common one. Although the Puritans were plain, ordinary citizens, they came to be regarded as gloomy fanatics. It was humorously commented that they disapproved of bear baiting, not because the bear suffered but because spectators enjoyed the event.

Before You Read

The Minister's Black Veil

Reading Focus

Secret Sin

The narrator of this story remarks that the "saddest of all prisons" is a person's "own heart." Hawthorne expertly imagined the sometimes fantastic ways in which people suffer guilt for secret sins they have committed in the past. He shows us that guilty secrets serve to isolate people from the world and from their relationships with others.

A Dialogue with the Text

READER'S LOG

When you come to Goodman Gray's line "Our parson has gone mad!" (page 300), stop and write down three possible reasons why the minister has draped his face with the black material ordinarily used by mourners.

Elements of Literature

Symbol

A **symbol** is something that has meaning in itself but also stands for something more than itself. Hawthorne—indeed, all the Dark Romantics—used symbolism as a technical strategy in his writing. As the title suggests, Hawthorne's central symbol in this story is a "horrible black veil," a "dismal shade" that separates its wearer from the world.

As you read, be aware of the ways this symbol directs your thoughts to the story's central **theme**.

> A **symbol** is a person, place, thing, or event that has meaning in itself and also stands for something more than itself.
>
> *For more on Symbol, see page 280 and the Handbook of Literary Terms.*

Background

This story, like much of Hawthorne's best work, is set in the times of his Puritan ancestors, an era he viewed as "characterized by . . . gloom and piety."

Hawthorne added the following note to the story: "Another clergyman in New England, Mr. Joseph Moody, of York, Maine, who died about eighty years since, made himself remarkable by the same eccentricity that is here related of the Reverend Mr. Hooper. In this case, however, the symbol had a different import. In early life he had accidentally killed a beloved friend; and from that day till the hour of his own death, he hid his face from men."

Illustration by Elenore Plaisted Abbott for "The Minister's Black Veil" from the 1900 edition of *Twice-Told Tales*.
Houghton Mifflin Company.

Options for Teaching

Strategies for Inclusion

Auditory Have students read aloud the scene between Elizabeth and Mr. Hooper on pp. 304–305; choose a student to read the narrator's part as well. Encourage the readers to convey Elizabeth's passion and Mr. Hooper's resistance.

Kinesthetic Have students act out the scene between Elizabeth and Mr. Hooper silently. Have these students prepare for the scene by re-reading it in the story and noting the gestures Elizabeth uses. Ask volunteers to "ad lib," or improvise, these gestures and others they deem appropriate for the two characters in this scene.

English Language Development To help students understand Mr. Hooper's veil and people's reactions to it, show photos of people wearing veils. Discuss who usually wears veils and why they do. Ask students how it would feel to wear a veil or how they feel when they see someone wearing a veil. After they read, have them point out how Mr. Hooper's veil is similar to or different from other people's veils. Ask them to find different points in the story where Hawthorne describes the townspeople's reactions to the veil. Have students compare these fictional reactions with their own feelings.

“He has changed himself into something awful, only by hiding his face.”

The Minister's Black Veil

A Parable

Ⓐ

Nathaniel Hawthorne

The sexton[1] stood in the porch of Milford meetinghouse, pulling lustily at the bell rope. The old people of the village came stooping along the street. Children, with bright faces, tripped merrily beside their parents, or mimicked a graver gait, in the conscious dignity of their Sunday clothes. Spruce bachelors looked sidelong at the pretty maidens, and fancied that the Sabbath sunshine made them prettier than on weekdays. When the throng had mostly streamed into the porch, the sexton began to toll the bell, keeping his eye on the Reverend Mr. Hooper's door. The first glimpse of the clergyman's figure was the signal for the bell to cease its summons.

1. **sexton:** church officer or employee whose duties may include maintenance, ringing the bells, and digging graves.

A. Literary Element: Parable
Parables are short stories that often come from religious scriptures and teach a moral; often, their meaning is ambiguous and elusive rather than clear-cut. Ask students why they think Hawthorne might have called his story a parable. [Possible answers: It contains a moral. Its meaning is ambiguous. It shows Hawthorne's concern with sin and atonement. He might have been trying to address the strong Puritan tradition in Massachusetts.]

RESPONDING TO THE ILLUSTRATION: VISUAL LITERACY

In this illustration, Mr. Hooper seems to be walking with his head bowed. Why? [Possible responses: He is probably weighed down with the sin his veil symbolizes. Or, he is concerned over his parishioners' lack of understanding about the veil.] How are the other figures in the illustration behaving? Is their behavior consistent with details in the selection? [The little girl seems frightened of Mr. Hooper. The women seem to be trying to figure him out. Their behavior is consistent with the details of the selection.]

INTEGRATING THE LANGUAGE ARTS

Strategic Reading To help students understand the importance of sequence, have them work in groups to chart on a time line the order of events in the story. When groups finish their sequences, ask them to compare lists and to discuss the effectiveness of the sequence.

[Mr. Hooper approaches the meeting house.]

first event — second event

Grammar Consider the conversation between Elizabeth and Mr. Hooper on pp. 304–305. Have student pairs identify the crucial adverbs as well as the verbs they modify [“smile glimmered faintly,” “earnestly inquired,” “merely replied,” “said . . . mournfully,” “cried . . . passionately,” “slowly departed”]. After they have found the adverbs, have them read the sentences without the adverbs. Ask the pairs to write comments about the enhanced meaning the adverbs give to the sentences. Ask the pairs to rewrite the dialogue using different adverbs and to write how this changes the meaning. Ask each pair to meet with another pair and share their findings. ☞

A. Literary Element: Symbol

? What might the black veil symbolize? [Possible answers: Evil, death and mourning, or despair.]

B. Reader's Response: First Thoughts

? Why might Mr. Hooper have put on the black veil? [Sample responses: He has sinned and feels guilty. Or he has committed adultery as the Reverend Dimmesdale did in *The Scarlet Letter.* Or his face is disfigured.] Is it important to know why he wears the veil? [Sample responses: No, it is his personal business, not ours. Or yes, it would give us more knowledge about his character if we knew why he wears it.]

C. Reader's Response: Shaping Interpretations

Ask students to respond to the question. [Sample responses: He has done something wrong and is hiding from God as Adam did. Or he does not want to face the church members because he has done something wrong or disapproved of them.]

"But what has good Parson Hooper got upon his face?" cried the sexton in astonishment.

All within hearing immediately turned about, and beheld the semblance of Mr. Hooper, pacing slowly his meditative way toward the meetinghouse. With one accord they started, expressing more wonder than if some strange minister were coming to dust the cushions of Mr. Hooper's pulpit.

"Are you sure it is our parson?" inquired Goodman[2] Gray of the sexton.

"Of a certainty it is good Mr. Hooper," replied the sexton. "He was to have exchanged pulpits with Parson Shute of Westbury; but Parson Shute sent to excuse himself yesterday, being to preach a funeral sermon."

The cause of so much amazement may appear sufficiently slight. Mr. Hooper, a gentlemanly person of about thirty, though still a bachelor, was dressed with due clerical neatness, as if a careful wife had starched his band, and brushed the weekly dust from his Sunday's garb. There was but one thing remarkable in his appearance. (A) Swathed about his forehead, and hanging down over his face, so low as to be shaken by his breath, Mr. Hooper had on a black veil. On a nearer view, it seemed to consist of two folds of crape,[3] which entirely concealed his features, except the mouth and chin, but probably did not intercept his sight, farther than to give a darkened aspect to all living and inanimate things. With this gloomy shade before him, good Mr. Hooper walked onward, at a slow and quiet pace, stooping somewhat and looking on the ground, as is customary with abstracted men, yet nodding kindly to those of his parishioners who still waited on the meetinghouse steps. But so wonder-struck were they, that his greeting hardly met with a return.

"I can't really feel as if good Mr. Hooper's face was behind that piece of crape," said the sexton.

"I don't like it," muttered an old woman, as she hobbled into the meetinghouse. "He has changed himself into something awful, only by hiding his face."

(B) "Our parson has gone mad!" cried Goodman Gray, following him across the threshold.

A rumor of some unaccountable phenomenon had preceded Mr. Hooper into the meetinghouse, and set all the congregation astir. Few could refrain from twisting their heads toward the door; many stood upright, and turned directly about; while several little boys clambered upon the seats, and came down again with a terrible racket. There was a general bustle, a rustling of the women's gowns and shuffling of the men's feet, greatly at variance with that hushed repose which should attend the entrance of the minister. But Mr. Hooper appeared not to notice the perturbation of his people. He entered with an almost noiseless step, bent his head mildly to the pews on each side, and bowed as he passed his oldest parishioner, a white-haired great-grandsire, who occupied an armchair in the center of the aisle. It was strange to observe, how slowly this venerable man became conscious of something singular in the appearance of his pastor. He seemed not fully to partake of the prevailing wonder, till Mr. Hooper had ascended the stairs, and showed himself in the pulpit, face to face with his congregation, except for the black veil. That mysterious emblem was never once withdrawn. It shook with his measured breath as he gave out the psalm; it threw its obscurity between him and the holy page, as he read the Scriptures; and while he prayed, the veil lay heavily on his uplifted countenance. (C) Did he seek to hide it from the dread Being whom he was addressing?

Such was the effect of this simple piece of crape, that more than one woman of delicate nerves was forced to leave the meetinghouse. Yet perhaps the pale-faced congregation was almost as fearful a sight to the minister, as his black veil to them.

Mr. Hooper had the reputation of a good preacher, but not an energetic one: He strove to win his people heavenward, by mild persuasive influences, rather than to drive them thither, by the thunders of the Word. The sermon which he now delivered, was marked by the same characteristics of style and manner, as the general series of his pulpit oratory. But there was something, either in the sentiment of the discourse itself, or in

2. **Goodman:** form of polite address similar to *mister.*
3. **crape:** kind of black cloth worn as a sign of mourning; from the French word *crêpe.*

WORDS TO OWN

semblance (sem′bləns): *n.:* outward appearance.

OPTIONS FOR TEACHING

CLASSROOM MANAGEMENT

Managing the Reader's Response Classroom

When posing questions for discussion, allow plenty of time for students to consider each question and formulate a response. Have students call for a clarification of the question if they need further information. Allowing all students time to think promotes their comfort in speaking to large groups and gives time for everyone to formulate an answer.

the imagination of the auditors, which made it greatly the most powerful effort that they had ever heard from their pastor's lips. It was tinged, rather more darkly than usual, with the gentle gloom of Mr. Hooper's temperament. The subject had reference to secret sin, and those sad mysteries which we hide from our nearest and dearest, and would fain conceal from our own consciousness, even forgetting that the Omniscient[4] can detect them. A subtle power was breathed into his words. Each member of the congregation, the most innocent girl, and the man of hardened breast, felt as if the preacher had crept upon them, behind his awful veil, and discovered their hoarded iniquity of deed or thought. Many spread their clasped hands on their bosoms. There was nothing terrible in what Mr. Hooper said; at least, no violence; and yet, with every tremor of his melancholy voice, the hearers quaked. An unsought pathos came hand in hand with awe. So sensible were the audience of some unwonted attribute in their minister, that they longed for a breath of wind to blow aside the veil, almost believing that a stranger's visage would be discovered, though the form, gesture, and voice were those of Mr. Hooper.

At the close of the services, the people hurried out with indecorous confusion, eager to communicate their pent-up amazement, and conscious of lighter spirits, the moment they lost sight of the black veil. Some gathered in little circles, huddled closely together, with their mouths all whispering in the center; some went homeward alone, wrapped in silent meditation; some talked loudly, and profaned the Sabbath day with ostentatious laughter. A few shook their sagacious heads, intimating that they could penetrate the mystery; while one or two affirmed that there was no mystery at all, but only that Mr. Hooper's eyes were so weakened by the midnight lamp, as to require a shade. After a brief interval, forth came good Mr. Hooper also, in the rear of his flock. Turning his veiled face from one group to another, he paid due reverence to the hoary heads, saluted the middle-aged with kind dignity, as their friend and spiritual guide, greeted the young with mingled authority and love, and laid his hands on the little children's heads to bless them. Such was always his custom on the Sabbath day. Strange and bewildered looks repaid him for his courtesy. None, as on former occasions, aspired to the honor of walking by their pastor's side. Old Squire Saunders, doubtless by an accidental lapse of memory, neglected to invite Mr. Hooper to his table, where the good clergyman had been wont to bless the food, almost every Sunday since his settlement. He returned, therefore, to the parsonage, and, at the moment of closing the door, was observed to look back upon the people, all of whom had their eyes fixed upon the minister. A sad smile gleamed faintly from beneath the black veil, and flickered about his mouth, glimmering as he disappeared.

"How strange," said a lady, "that a simple black veil, such as any woman might wear on her bonnet, should become such a terrible thing on Mr. Hooper's face!"

"Something must surely be amiss with Mr. Hooper's intellects," observed her husband, the physician of the village. "But the strangest part of the affair is the effect of this vagary, even on a sober-minded man like myself. The black veil, though it covers only our pastor's face, throws its influence over his whole person, and makes him ghostlike from head to foot. Do you not feel it so?"

"Truly do I," replied the lady; "and I would not be alone with him for the world. I wonder he is not afraid to be alone with himself!"

"Men sometimes are so," said her husband.

The afternoon service was attended with similar circumstances. At its conclusion, the bell tolled for the funeral of a young lady. The relatives and friends were assembled in the house, and the more distant acquaintances stood about the door, speaking of the good qualities of the deceased, when their talk was interrupted by the appearance of Mr. Hooper, still covered with his black veil. It was now an appropriate emblem. The clergyman stepped into the room where the corpse was laid, and bent over the coffin, to take a last farewell of his deceased parishioner. As he stooped, the veil hung straight down from his forehead, so that, if her eyelids had not been

4. **the Omniscient:** the all-knowing God.

Words to Own

iniquity (i·nik'wi·tē): *n.:* wickedness.
ostentatious (äs'tən·tā'shəs) *adj.:* conspicuous.
sagacious (sə·gā'shəs) *adj.:* wise; keenly perceptive.

D. Critical Reading: Drawing Conclusions

? What does Hawthorne mean by "secret sin"? [Possible answer: A sin someone has committed that no one else knows about.]

E. Critical Reading: Analyzing Details

? What are the different reactions to the veil from the people of Mr. Hooper's parish? [Some do not like it. Most stare. Others gather in little whispering circles. Some go home alone. Some talk and laugh loudly. A few pretend to know the mystery.] Why do they act the way they do? [Possible answer: They try to cope with the situation in a way that makes them feel more comfortable, be it to think alone or pretend to know everything or act in some other fashion.]

F. Expansion

Note that Mr. Hooper is not changing his life or manners in any way except to wear the veil. This makes it a kind of controlled scientific experiment in which only one variable is altered. Hawthorne had a fascination for the experimental process, as revealed in another of his stories, "Rappaccini's Daughter," and his novel about experimental living in a utopian lifestyle at Brook Farm, *The Blithedale Romance*.

COOPERATIVE LEARNING

"Off or On?" Have students conduct a mock trial. Instruct students to take a sheet of blank paper, draw a vertical line down the center, and label one side "On" and the other side "Off." Tell them to list reasons for Mr. Hooper to remove the veil ("off") or to keep it ("on"). At the end of the brainstorming session, divide the class into three approximately equal groups as follows: (1) those who had more reasons for removing the veil ("off"), (2) those who had more reasons for keeping the veil ("on"), and (3) those who had almost an equal number of reasons in each column (jury). Tell students they will conduct a mock trial to decide the fate of Mr. Hooper's veil. Give the groups time to discuss and prepare their strongest arguments. Allow them to organize by appointing a leading lawyer, assistants, and a recording secretary. The jury should not observe the preparations of the "off" and "on" groups. The teacher serves as judge. At the conclusion of the trial, allow the jury to be alone for deliberations. Then, have them announce their verdict. A spokesperson can explain the reasons for their verdict. ☞

A. Reader's Response: Connecting with the Text
In this paragraph, Hawthorne inserts macabre effects: the death of a young woman and a suggestion of the supernatural when the corpse appears to shudder. At this point, how would you compare Hawthorne's writing with Poe's? [Sample responses: Poe's style seems more intense, his word choice more affected, his sentences longer, or his events more dramatic than Hawthorne's.]

RESPONDING TO THE ART: ABOUT THE ARTWORK

The various attitudes of the congregation are portrayed in Julius Gari Melchers's (1860–1932) *The Sermon.* While some look to the front of the church in awe, presumably at the minister, others drift off or stare dreamily in other directions. One of the central figures is a stern, self-righteous woman who appears to be more interested in the attentiveness, or lack thereof, of a fellow churchgoer. The subject of this painting, a sermon at the Dutch Reformed Church, was inspired by the everyday lives of peasants in the Dutch town of Egmond-aan-Zee where Melcher established himself in 1884.

The Sermon (1886) by Julius Gari Melchers. Oil on canvas.

National Museum of American Art, Bequest of Henry Ward Ranger through The National Academy of Design. Courtesy Art Resource.

closed forever, the dead maiden might have seen his face. Could Mr. Hooper be fearful of her glance, that he so hastily caught back the black veil? A person, who watched the interview between the dead and living, scrupled[5] not to affirm, that, at the instant when the clergyman's features were disclosed, the corpse had slightly shuddered, rustling the shroud and muslin cap, though the countenance retained the composure of death. A superstitious old woman was the only witness of this prodigy.[6] From the coffin, Mr. Hooper passed into the chamber of the mourners, and thence to the head of the staircase, to make the funeral prayer. It was a tender and heart-dissolving prayer, full of sorrow, yet so imbued with celestial hopes, that the music of a heavenly harp, swept by the fingers of the dead, seemed faintly to be heard among the saddest accents of the minister. The people trembled, though they but darkly understood him, when he prayed that they, and himself, and all of mortal race, might be ready, as he trusted this young maiden had been, for the dreadful hour that should snatch the veil from their faces. The bearers went heavily forth,

5. **scrupled:** hesitated.
6. **prodigy:** extraordinary act that foretells the future.

OPTIONS FOR TEACHING

CROSSING THE CURRICULUM

Social Sciences To give students experience with what it might be like to be Mr. Hooper or to be a member of his community, have those who have access to a sewing machine sew a veil according to the descriptions in the story. Ask them to wear their veils during class one day. Have students record in their logs their reactions to wearing or to seeing the veil. The following day, have student volunteers share their reactions with the class.

Art Have groups of students produce design renderings for a film version of "The Minister's Black Veil." Each student should choose a different aspect of production to illustrate. One student should render designs for the costumes and submit swatches of fabrics to be used in each costume. Another should illustrate or build models of the various sets. A third should draw storyboards for the action and placement of the characters in each scene. Have students present their work to the class and describe the decisions they made. Arrange to exhibit their work in a school display case.

and the mourners followed, saddening all the street, with the dead before them, and Mr. Hooper in his black veil behind.

"Why do you look back?" said one in the procession to his partner.

"I had a fancy," replied she, "that the minister and the maiden's spirit were walking hand in hand."

"And so had I, at the same moment," said the other.

That night, the handsomest couple in Milford village were to be joined in wedlock. Though reckoned a melancholy man, Mr. Hooper had a placid cheerfulness for such occasions, which often excited a sympathetic smile, where livelier merriment would have been thrown away. There was no quality of his disposition which made him more beloved than this. The company at the wedding awaited his arrival with impatience, trusting that the strange awe, which had gathered over him throughout the day, would now be dispelled. But such was not the result. When Mr. Hooper came, the first thing that their eyes rested on was the same horrible black veil, which had added deeper gloom to the funeral, and could portend nothing but evil to the wedding. Such was its immediate effect on the guests, that a cloud seemed to have rolled duskily from beneath the black crape, and dimmed the light of the candles. The bridal pair stood up before the minister. But the bride's cold fingers quivered in the tremulous hand of the bridegroom, and her deathlike paleness caused a whisper, that the maiden who had been buried a few hours before, was come from her grave to be married. If ever another wedding were so dismal, it was that famous one, where they tolled the wedding knell.[7] After performing the ceremony, Mr. Hooper raised a glass of wine to his lips, wishing happiness to the new-married couple, in a strain of mild pleasantry that ought to have brightened the features of the guests, like a cheerful gleam from the hearth. At that instant, catching a glimpse of his figure in the looking glass, the black veil involved his own spirit in the horror with which it overwhelmed all others. His frame shuddered—his lips grew white—he spilt the untasted wine upon the carpet—and rushed forth into the darkness. For the Earth, too, had on her Black Veil.

The next day, the whole village of Milford talked of little else than Parson Hooper's black veil. That, and the mystery concealed behind it, supplied a topic for discussion between acquaintances meeting in the street, and good women gossiping at their open windows. It was the first item of news that the tavern keeper told to his guests. The children babbled of it on their way to school. One imitative little imp covered his face with an old black handkerchief, thereby so affrighting his playmates, that the panic seized himself, and he well nigh lost his wits by his own waggery.[8]

It was remarkable, that, of all the busybodies and impertinent people in the parish, not one ventured to put the plain question to Mr. Hooper, wherefore he did this thing. Hitherto, whenever there appeared the slightest call for such interference, he had never lacked advisers, nor shown himself averse to be guided by their judgment. If he erred at all, it was by so painful a degree of self-distrust, that even the mildest censure would lead him to consider an indifferent action as a crime. Yet, though so well acquainted with this amiable weakness, no individual among his parishioners chose to make the black veil a subject of friendly remonstrance. There was a feeling of dread, neither plainly confessed nor carefully concealed, which caused each to shift the responsibility upon another, till at length it was found expedient to send a deputation of the church, in order to deal with Mr. Hooper about the mystery, before it should grow into a scandal. Never did an embassy so ill discharge its duties. The minister received them with friendly courtesy, but became silent, after they were seated, leaving to his visitors the whole burden of introducing their important business. The topic, it might be supposed, was obvious enough. There was the black veil, swathed round Mr. Hooper's forehead, and concealing every feature above his placid mouth, on which, at times, they could perceive the glimmering of a melancholy smile. But that piece of crape, to their

7. **If . . . wedding knell:** reference to Hawthorne's story "The Wedding Knell." A knell is the ringing of a bell.

8. **waggery:** joke.

Words to Own
portend (pôr·tend') *v.:* signify.

B. Literary Element: Dialogue

? What effect does the dialogue have on the pace of the story? [It quickens the pace. Hawthorne keeps the narrative moving with a series of contrasts, alternating dramatic dialogue-based scenes with longer narrative passages.]

C. Reader's Response: Shaping Interpretations

The narrator explains why no one simply asked Mr. Hooper his reasons for putting on the veil. Is the narrator's explanation convincing? [Sample responses: Yes, because they all seem distant from him because he is a minister. Or no, surely there are people close to him who would ask him why he wears the veil.]

PROBLEM SOLVING/CRITICAL THINKING

Decisions and Complications Mr. Hooper makes a decision that he feels is morally responsible, but it is unpopular with the townspeople. Have students discuss the difficulties people experience when following their consciences, making unpopular decisions, and encountering misunderstanding and negative reactions. Ask students to consider whether Mr. Hooper could have handled his situation differently and what people who make difficult decisions can do to gain acceptance or understanding. ☞

A. Critical Reading: Predicting

? Who might this be? [Possible answers: His mother, his sister, his girlfriend, his housekeeper.]

Her eyes were fixed insensibly on the black veil, when, like a sudden twilight in the air, its terrors fell around her.

imagination, seemed to hang down before his heart, the symbol of a fearful secret between him and them. Were the veil but cast aside, they might speak freely of it, but not till then. Thus they sat a considerable time, speechless, confused, and shrinking uneasily from Mr. Hooper's eye, which they felt to be fixed upon them with an invisible glance. Finally, the deputies returned abashed to their constituents, pronouncing the matter too weighty to be handled, except by a council of the churches, if, indeed, it might not require a general synod.[9]

A But there was one person in the village, unappalled by the awe with which the black veil had impressed all beside herself. When the deputies returned without an explanation, or even venturing to demand one, she, with the calm energy of her character, determined to chase away the strange cloud that appeared to be settling round Mr. Hooper, every moment more darkly than before. As his plighted[10] wife, it should be her privilege to know what the black veil concealed. At the minister's first visit, therefore, she entered upon the subject, with a direct simplicity, which made the task easier both for him and her. After he had seated himself, she fixed her eyes steadfastly upon the veil, but could discern nothing of the dreadful gloom that had so overawed the multitude: It was but a double fold of crape, hanging down from his forehead to his mouth, and slightly stirring with his breath.

"No," said she aloud, and smiling, "there is nothing terrible in this piece of crape, except that it hides a face which I am always glad to look upon. Come, good sir, let the sun shine from behind the cloud. First lay aside your black veil: Then tell me why you put it on."

Mr. Hooper's smile glimmered faintly.

"There is an hour to come," said he, "when all of us shall cast aside our veils. Take it not amiss, beloved friend, if I wear this piece of crape till then."

"Your words are a mystery too," returned the young lady. "Take away the veil from them, at least."

"Elizabeth, I will," said he, "so far as my vow may suffer me. Know, then, this veil is a type and a symbol, and I am bound to wear it ever, both in light and darkness, in solitude and before the gaze of multitudes, and as with strangers, so with my familiar friends. No mortal eye will see it withdrawn. This dismal shade must separate me from the world: Even you, Elizabeth, can never come behind it!"

"What grievous affliction hath befallen you," she earnestly inquired, "that you should thus darken your eyes forever?"

"If it be a sign of mourning," replied Mr. Hooper, "I, perhaps, like most other mortals, have sorrows dark enough to be typified by a black veil."

"But what if the world will not believe that it is the type of an innocent sorrow?" urged Elizabeth. "Beloved and respected as you are, there may be whispers, that you hide your face under the consciousness of secret sin. For the sake of your holy office, do away this scandal!"

The color rose into her cheeks, as she intimated the nature of the rumors that were already

9. **synod** (sin'əd): governing body of a group of churches.
10. **plighted:** promised.

OPTIONS FOR TEACHING

PROFESSIONAL NOTES

Thematic Connections: "The Realms of Darkness" Ask students to consider the Poe selections that have already been studied in this Collection ("The Fall of the House of Usher," on pp. 263–279 and "The Raven," on pp. 282–286). Ask them to use a chart like the following one to compare these selections to "The Minister's Black Veil" and to note what features the selections have in common. [A death, a secret, a troubled person, some element of the supernatural or the unexplainable.]

Feature	Selection	Support
[A death]	["The Fall of the House of Usher"] ["The Minister's Black Veil"]	[Madeline and Roderick Usher die.] [The dead maiden.]

abroad in the village. But Mr. Hooper's mildness did not forsake him. He even smiled again—that same sad smile, which always appeared like a faint glimmering of light, proceeding from the obscurity beneath the veil.

"If I hide my face for sorrow, there is cause enough," he merely replied; "and if I cover it for secret sin, what mortal might not do the same?"

And with this gentle, but unconquerable obstinacy, did he resist all her entreaties. At length Elizabeth sat silent. For a few moments she appeared lost in thought, considering, probably, what new methods might be tried, to withdraw her lover from so dark a fantasy, which, if it had no other meaning, was perhaps a symptom of mental disease. Though of a firmer character than his own, the tears rolled down her cheeks. But, in an instant, as it were, a new feeling took the place of sorrow: Her eyes were fixed insensibly on the black veil, when, like a sudden twilight in the air, its terrors fell around her. She arose, and stood trembling before him.

"And do you feel it then at last?" said he mournfully.

She made no reply, but covered her eyes with her hand, and turned to leave the room. He rushed forward and caught her arm.

"Have patience with me, Elizabeth!" cried he passionately. "Do not desert me, though this veil must be between us here on earth. Be mine, and hereafter there shall be no veil over my face, no darkness between our souls! It is but a mortal veil—it is not for eternity! Oh! you know not how lonely I am, and how frightened to be alone behind my black veil. Do not leave me in this miserable obscurity forever!" **B**

"Lift the veil but once, and look me in the face," said she.

"Never! It cannot be!" replied Mr. Hooper.

"Then, farewell!" said Elizabeth.

She withdrew her arm from his grasp, and slowly departed, pausing at the door, to give one long, shuddering gaze, that seemed almost to penetrate the mystery of the black veil. But, even amid his grief, Mr. Hooper smiled to think that only a material emblem had separated him from happiness, though the horrors which it shadowed forth, must be drawn darkly between the fondest of lovers.

From that time no attempts were made to remove Mr. Hooper's black veil, or, by a direct appeal, to discover the secret which it was supposed to hide. By persons who claimed a superiority to popular prejudice, it was reckoned merely an eccentric whim, such as often mingles with the sober actions of men otherwise rational, and tinges them all with its own semblance of insanity. But with the multitude, good Mr. Hooper was irreparably a bugbear.[11] He could not walk the streets with any peace of mind, so conscious was he that the gentle and timid would turn aside to avoid him, and that others would make it a point of hardihood to throw themselves in his way. The impertinence of the latter class compelled him to give up his customary walk, at sunset, to the burial ground; for when he leaned pensively over the gate, there would always be faces behind the gravestones, peeping at his black veil. A fable went the rounds, that the stare of the dead people drove him thence. **C** It grieved him, to the very depth of his kind heart, to observe how the children fled from his approach, breaking up their merriest sports, while his melancholy figure was yet afar off. Their instinctive dread caused him to feel, more strongly than aught else, that a preternatural[12] horror was interwoven with the threads of the black crape. In truth, his own antipathy to the veil was known to be so great, that he never willingly passed before a mirror, nor stooped to drink at a still fountain, lest, in its peaceful bosom, he should be affrighted by himself. This was what gave plausibility to the whispers, that Mr. Hooper's conscience tortured him for some great crime, too horrible to be entirely concealed, or otherwise than so obscurely intimated. Thus, from beneath the black veil, there rolled a cloud into the sunshine, an ambiguity of sin or sorrow, which enveloped the poor minister, so that love or sympathy could never reach him. It **D**

11. **bugbear:** source of irrational fears.
12. **preternatural:** abnormal; supernatural.

WORDS TO OWN

obscurity (əb·skyo͝or′ə·tē) *n.:* something hidden or concealed.
pensively (pen′siv·lē) *adv.:* thinking deeply or seriously.
antipathy (an·tip′ə·thē) *n.:* strong dislike.
plausibility (plô′zə·bil′i·tē) *n.:* believability.

B. Reader's Response: First Thoughts

? How would you feel if you were Elizabeth? [Sample responses: Curious, anxious, stunned, rejected.] How would you feel if you were Mr. Hooper? [Sample responses: Torn between removing the veil and leaving it on, saddened, lonely, frightened.]

C. Expansion

Note that even before putting on the veil, Mr. Hooper had been melancholy—his customary form of recreation had been walking to the cemetery.

D. Readers Response: Shaping Interpretations

? What reasons have the parishioners given thus far for Mr. Hooper's wearing the veil? [Sample responses: His eyes are weak. Something must be wrong with his intellect. He acts upon an eccentric whim. His conscience tortures him. Ghosts and fiends consort with him.] Which are believable? [Sample responses: He acts upon an eccentric whim. His conscience tortures him.]

ASSESSMENT TOOLS

Check Test: True-False

1. The veil makes Mr. Hooper a more effective minister. [True]
2. Mr. Hooper himself is horrified to see what he looks like with the black veil over his face. [True]
3. No one besides his fiancée ever bothers to ask Mr. Hooper why he wears the veil. [True]
4. Governor Belcher, who has asked that Mr. Hooper give the election-day sermon, withdraws the offer when Mr. Hooper refuses to remove the veil. [False]
5. Mr. Hooper momentarily withdraws the veil just before his death. [False]

Peer Assessment Have students use the following criteria to evaluate their group in the Cooperative Learning activity on p. T301.

1=Strong 2=Good 3=Fair
4=Needs improvement 5=Weak

a. ___ Everyone in the group was serious about the assigned task.
b. ___ Everyone respected the opinions of each member of the group.
c. ___ Everyone contributed to the group effort.

A. Literary Element: Irony
Note that Mr. Hooper's strange behavior leads the people to revere him and need him all the more as their minister. The consciousness of sin brings one closer to God. Why do people revere him? [Possible answers: They see the veil as penance, and his supposed conviction of sin inspires them. They are in awe of behavior that they cannot understand.]

B. Literary Element: Metaphor
? What is the effect of this metaphor? [Possible answers: It makes Mr. Hooper's pain more severe. It shows that he is isolated from the world.]

was said, that ghost and fiend consorted with him there. With self-shudderings and outward terrors, he walked continually in its shadow, groping darkly within his own soul, or gazing through a medium that saddened the whole world. Even the lawless wind, it was believed, respected his dreadful secret, and never blew aside the veil. But still good Mr. Hooper sadly smiled, at the pale visages of the worldly throng as he passed by.

Among all its bad influences, the black veil had the one desirable effect, of making its wearer a very efficient clergyman. By the aid of his mysterious emblem—for there was no other apparent cause—he became a man of awful power, over souls that were in agony for sin. His converts always regarded him with a dread peculiar to themselves, affirming, though but figuratively, that, before he brought them to celestial light, they had been with him behind the black veil. Its gloom, indeed, enabled him to sympathize with all dark affections. Dying sinners cried aloud for Mr. Hooper, and would not yield their breath till he appeared; though ever, as he stooped to whisper consolation, they shuddered at the veiled face so near their own. Such were the terrors of the black veil, even when Death had bared his visage! Strangers came long distances to attend service at his church, with the mere idle purpose of gazing at his figure, because it was forbidden them to behold his face. But many were made to quake ere they departed! Once, during Governor Belcher's[13] administration, Mr. Hooper was appointed to preach the election sermon. Covered with his black veil, he stood before the chief magistrate, the council, and the representatives, and wrought so deep an impression, that the legislative measures of that year, were characterized by all the gloom and piety of our earliest ancestral sway.

In this manner Mr. Hooper spent a long life, irreproachable in outward act, yet shrouded in dismal suspicions; kind and loving, though unloved, and dimly feared; a man apart from men, shunned in their health and joy, but ever summoned to their aid in mortal anguish. As years wore on, shedding their snows above his sable veil, he acquired a name throughout the New England churches, and they called him Father Hooper. Nearly all his parishioners, who were of mature age when he was settled, had been borne away by many a funeral: He had one congregation in the church, and a more crowded one in the churchyard; and having wrought so late into the evening, and done his work so well, it was now good Father Hooper's turn to rest.

Several persons were visible by the shaded candlelight, in the death chamber of the old clergyman. Natural connections he had none. But there was the decorously grave, though unmoved physician, seeking only to mitigate the last pangs of the patient whom he could not save. There were the deacons, and other eminently pious members of his church. There, also, was the Reverend Mr. Clark, of Westbury, a young and zealous divine, who had ridden in haste to pray by the bedside of the expiring minister. There was the nurse, no hired handmaiden of death, but one whose calm affection had endured thus long, in secrecy, in solitude, amid the chill of age, and would not perish, even at the dying hour. Who, but Elizabeth! And there lay the hoary head of good Father Hooper upon the death-pillow, with the black veil still swathed about his brow and reaching down over his face, so that each more difficult gasp of his faint breath caused it to stir. All through life that piece of crape had hung between him and the world: It had separated him from cheerful brotherhood and woman's love, and kept him in that saddest of all prisons, his own heart; and still it lay upon his face, as if to deepen the gloom of his darksome chamber, and shade him from the sunshine of eternity.

For some time previous, his mind had been confused, wavering doubtfully between the past and the present, and hovering forward, as it were, at intervals, into the indistinctness of the world to come. There had been feverish turns, which tossed him from side to side, and wore away what little strength he had. But in his most convulsive struggles, and in the wildest vagaries of his intellect, when no other thought retained its sober influence, he still showed an awful solicitude lest the black veil should slip aside. Even if his bewildered soul could have forgotten, there was a faithful woman at his pillow, who, with averted eyes, would have covered that aged face, which she had last beheld in the comeliness of manhood. At

13. **Governor Belcher's:** Jonathan Belcher (1682–1757) was governor of the Massachusetts Bay Colony from 1730 to 1741.

. . . there he sat, shivering with the arms of death around him, while the black veil hung down . . .

length the death-stricken old man lay quietly in the torpor of mental and bodily exhaustion, with an imperceptible pulse, and breath that grew fainter and fainter, except when a long, deep, and irregular inspiration seemed to prelude the flight of his spirit.

The minister of Westbury approached the bedside.

"Venerable Father Hooper," said he, "the moment of your release is at hand. Are you ready for the lifting of the veil, that shuts in time from eternity?" C

Father Hooper at first replied merely by a feeble motion of his head; then, apprehensive, perhaps, that his meaning might be doubtful, he exerted himself to speak.

"Yea," said he, in faint accents, "my soul hath a patient weariness until that veil be lifted."

"And is it fitting," resumed the Reverend Mr. Clark, "that a man so given to prayer, of such a blameless example, holy in deed and thought, so far as mortal judgment may pronounce; is it fitting that a father in the church should leave a shadow on his memory, that may seem to blacken a life so pure? I pray you, my venerable brother, let not this thing be! Suffer us to be gladdened by your triumphant aspect, as you go to your reward. Before the veil of eternity be lifted, let me cast aside this black veil from your face!"

And thus speaking, the Reverend Mr. Clark bent forward to reveal the mystery of so many years. But, exerting a sudden energy, that made all the beholders stand aghast, Father Hooper snatched both his hands from beneath the bedclothes, and pressed them strongly on the black veil, resolute to struggle, if the minister of Westbury would contend with a dying man.

"Never!" cried the veiled clergyman. "On earth, never!"

"Dark old man!" exclaimed the affrighted minister, "with what horrible crime upon your soul are you now passing to the judgment?"

Father Hooper's breath heaved; it rattled in his throat; but, with a mighty effort, grasping forward with his hands, he caught hold of life, and held it back till he should speak. He even raised himself in bed; and there he sat, shivering with the arms of death around him, while the black veil hung down, awful, at that last moment, in the gathered terrors of a lifetime. And yet the faint, sad smile, so often there, now seemed to glimmer from its obscurity, and linger on Father Hooper's lips.

"Why do you tremble at me alone?" cried he, turning his veiled face round the circle of pale spectators. "Tremble also at each other! Have men avoided me, and women shown no pity, and children screamed and fled, only for my black veil? What, but the mystery which it obscurely typifies, has made this piece of crape so awful? When the friend shows his inmost heart to his friend; the lover to his best-beloved; when man does not vainly shrink from the eye of his Creator, loathsomely treasuring up the secret of his sin; then deem me a monster, for the symbol beneath which I have lived, and die! I look around me, and, lo! on every visage a Black Veil!" D

While his auditors shrank from one another, in mutual affright, Father Hooper fell back upon his pillow, a veiled corpse, with a faint smile lingering on the lips. Still veiled, they laid him in his coffin, and a veiled corpse they bore him to the grave. The grass of many years has sprung up and withered on that grave, the burial-stone is moss-grown, and good Mr. Hooper's face is dust; but awful is still the thought, that it moldered beneath the Black Veil! E F

Words to Own

resolute (rez′ə·lo͞ot′) *adj.:* determined.

C. Language Note: Ambiguity

? What does the minister of Westbury mean by "the lifting of the veil"? [The passing from life into death, but he also means the literal lifting of the veil.]

D. Critical Reading: Drawing Conclusions

? Why does Mr. Hooper state that he wears the veil? [He wears the veil as a symbol of all those who try to hide their sins from each other and from God.]

E. Readers' Response: Challenging the Text

? Is this a good conclusion to the story? [Sample responses: No, because Mr. Hooper has lived as an example all his life, and he needs a moment when he does not have to be the example. Or yes, for if Mr. Hooper were to remove the veil, it would undermine his feelings about how people hide their sins. Hawthorne's story would lose its point.]

F. Critical Reading: Expressing an Opinion

? Did you change your theory of why the minister wears the black veil? [Possible answers: Yes, at first I focused on trying to figure out what his sin was. Or no, I still think something may have happened between him and the young woman who died.]

Metacognition What factors affected your answer? [Possible answers: Reading Hooper's statements at the end of the story changed my mind. Or I have found people tend to hide specific sins.]

Making Meanings

First Thoughts

1. Possible responses: I would feel uncomfortable; I would think the person is trying to hide something. I would try to respect the person's wishes.

Reviewing the Text

a. The congregation is shocked.
b. Hooper is neat, gentle, and kind. The congregation seems to have been well disposed toward him.
c. At the funeral, the people tremble and are deeply moved by his prayer. At the wedding, the guests regard the veil as an ominous portent that spreads a shadow over a happy occasion.
d. He says that the veil is a symbol of universal secret sin and that he is bound to wear it forever. Elizabeth says that the world may not believe that the veil is the sign of an innocent sorrow. She warns Hooper that people will gossip about him, whispering that he has been involved in some scandal, and that his ministry may be compromised. She then appeals to their love and asks him to cast aside the veil once for her sake.

Shaping Interpretations

2. Elizabeth is the one person in the village who is not at first appalled by Hooper's veil. She dares to do what all the other villagers have been afraid to do: She asks Hooper with a direct simplicity why he wears the veil. Up to this point, Elizabeth seems loving, caring, and full of common sense. But in the course of her interview with Hooper, Elizabeth's attitude changes. When Hooper resists her entreaties, Elizabeth becomes sorrowful and then terrified. Hawthorne never directly explains her change of attitude, and students may have various opinions for its cause, such as she feels convicted of sin or she realizes their relationship is over.
3. Probably the torment of a guilty conscience, or simply the awareness of one's own sinfulness, confines a person in his or her own melancholy. Some may say that knowledge of one's own sin can torment; others may say that people can live at ease with the knowledge. Students will probably think that everyone in the story harbors knowledge of their sins.
4. Some students may agree that the narrator's tone is emotional. Words that contribute to the tone include "black," "concealed his features," "darkened aspect," "gloomy shade," "lay heavily," "horrible," "portend nothing but evil," "cloud . . . rolled duskily," and "dimmed the light of the candles." They darken the tone and atmosphere.
5. Hooper seems to assert that all those around him are secret sinners who deny the fact of their evil to themselves, to others, and to God. Some may say the veil represents knowledge of the evil in the world or Hooper's mourning of people's denial of their evil.
6. Although the veil continually inspires fear, Hawthorne emphasizes that its one desirable effect is to make Hooper an even better clergyman than before.
7. Students may agree that the moral lesson is that perhaps we are all secret sinners who fail to acknowledge our guilt. It is a parable in that it has a moral lesson, is short, can be ambiguous, and has a religious theme.

MAKING MEANINGS

First Thoughts

1. How would you react to someone who voluntarily goes through life with his or her face hidden?

Reviewing the Text

a. How does the congregation respond to their first sight of Mr. Hooper's black veil?
b. Briefly describe Hooper's **character** as revealed in the story's opening paragraphs. What does the congregation's attitude toward him seem to have been up to this point?
c. In a single afternoon, Hooper presides at both a funeral and a wedding. How do people react to the presence of the veil at each event?
d. What explanation does Hooper give to Elizabeth, his fiancée, of why he wears the veil? What arguments against wearing the veil does she make?

Shaping Interpretations

2. Trace the progression of Elizabeth's response to the veil. How do you explain her changing attitudes?
3. Explain the narrator's remark on page 306 about the human heart being the "saddest of all prisons." Do you agree or disagree? Do you think this observation refers only to Hooper, or is it true of everyone in the story?
4. Would you describe the narrator's **tone** as neutral or emotional? (Think particularly of the words the narrator uses in referring to the veil.) Make a list of specific connotative words and phrases that contribute to the story's tone. How do the words the narrator uses affect the story's tone and **atmosphere**?
5. On his deathbed, Hooper says, "I look around me, and, lo! on every visage a Black Veil!" Explain that statement; then review the notes you made in your Reader's Log. In what ways is Hooper's veil a **symbol**? What do you think it symbolizes?
6. Does Hooper's veil have any positive effects during his long life? Explain.
7. Hawthorne added the subtitle "A Parable" to this story, indicating the importance moral themes had for him. A **parable** is a short, simple story from which a moral or religious lesson can be drawn. Unlike many of the world's parables, which come from religious scriptures such as the Bible, this story is a literary parable with meanings that may be ambiguous and elusive rather than clear-cut. What would you say is the moral lesson of this story—its **theme,** or main idea? In what sense *is* it a parable?
8. Why do you think the villagers bury Hooper without removing the veil?

Connecting with the Text

9. Almost all people, at some point in life, have done things that made them feel guilty and that they have concealed from others. What do you think is useful and beneficial about having a sense of guilt, and what is harmful about it? In what ways can guilt isolate people, and in what ways can it bring people together?

LANGUAGE AND STYLE

Hawthorne's Archaisms

Hawthorne's story, though symbolic and ambiguous in meaning, is told in a plain, accessible style. If modern readers have trouble with Hawthorne, it is with his **archaic** or old-fashioned language (see page 37). **Context clues** (page 168) should help you figure out any language that is strange. Which word or words in each of the following passages from the story are rarely used today? How would you rephrase each passage in a modern idiom? Are any of these words used today in different senses?

1. "So sensible were the audience of some unwonted attribute in their minister. . . ." (page 301)
2. "A superstitious old woman was the only witness of this prodigy." (page 302)
3. ". . . he well nigh lost his wits by his own waggery." (page 303)
4. ". . . having wrought so late into the evening. . . ." (page 306)

Choices: Building Your Portfolio

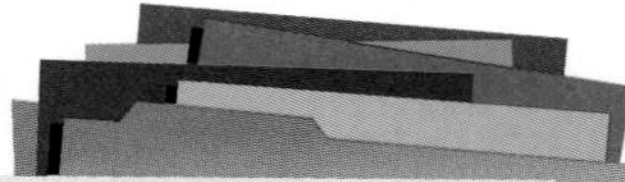

Writer's Notebook

1. Collecting Ideas for a Controversial Issue

You can find topics for persuasive essays in the literature you read. For example, you might find a specific passage in Hawthorne's famous story that you would like to support or argue with. Or, you might find an issue here that people disagree on—perhaps something on the nature of guilt or the psychological effects of isolation. Or, you might want to take a controversial stand on interpreting this story. Take notes on possible topics, jot down details to support your position, and save your work for possible use in the Writer's Workshop on page 331.

Critical Writing

2. Natural Differences

In *Nature,* on page 221, Emerson says that we are "part or particle of God," and that in the beauties of nature we can behold something "as beautiful as [our] own nature." In a brief essay, explain how Emerson's views of human nature compare or contrast with Hawthorne's. Cite specific passages from both writers to support what you say. Do you agree with either writer? Why or why not?

Critical Writing

3. The Puritan Influence

In a brief essay, compare and contrast the attitudes revealed in Hawthorne's story to attitudes held by Puritans such as Jonathan Edwards (see Edwards's sermon "Sinners in the Hands of an Angry God" on page 79). Consider especially attitudes toward sin, guilt, and the conditions necessary for salvation. How do you think Hawthorne felt about the tenets of Puritanism?

Creative Writing

4. Behind the Veil

Write a brief autobiographical sketch of Mr. Hooper, using his **first-person point of view.** Using clues from the text, and your own imagination, have Hooper explain the significance of the veil and how he first thought of wearing it. Let him describe how he feels wearing it all the time.

Critical Thinking/ Speaking and Listening

5. Rating the Prose

In a group of three or more students, discuss similarities and differences between Hawthorne and Poe, based on your reading of their works. Compare and contrast their literary styles, their choices of subject matter, their **themes,** and their use of **symbolism.** Discuss which author's work you prefer and why. Present your group's "verdict" to the rest of the class.

Creative Writing/ Performance

6. Unveiling the Story

With one or more partners, write a condensed version of the story, to be spoken aloud. You'll need to create some dialogue on the basis of narrated scenes. The major characters will be Hooper, Elizabeth, and the narrator, who will summarize events and describe characters. Perform your reader's theater for the class.

Critical Writing

7. A Crime of Dark Dye

Edgar Allan Poe said that Hooper wore the veil because ". . . a crime of dark dye (having reference to the 'young lady') has been committed. . . ." What do you think Poe is referring to? Does this interpretation make sense to you, or do you think it is too literal? (Think about whether the story would have been more effective had Hawthorne revealed why Hooper wears the veil.) Write a brief essay expressing your views.

Language and Style

Answers

1. *unwonted.* The audience was unaccustomed to seeing in their minister. . . . Today it means "not common" or "rare."
2. *prodigy.* A superstitious woman was the only witness of this ominous event. Today it refers to "a child genius."
3. *well nigh* and *waggery.* He almost lost his wits joking. Both have the same meaning today, even though they are not commonly used.
4. *wrought.* Having spoken so late. . . . Today it means "to be formed."

Choices: Building Your Portfolio

1. **Writer's Notebook** Remind students to save their work. They may use it as prewriting for the Writer's Workshop on p. 331.
2. **Critical Writing** Suggest that students use a prewriting chart or a sheet of paper divided into columns headed "Emerson" and "Hawthorne" to organize and gather details. Divide the class into small groups of varying abilities to work on their charts together.
4. **Creative Writing** Before students begin writing, have them work in pairs to review the text and work out their ideas. For students who need help getting started, suggest that they begin their sketch by writing, "I remember thinking about how I could get my point across to the congregation."

8. Possible responses: They may do so out of fear or respect, or because they agree with Hooper that all people try to hide their sin.

Connecting with the Text

9. Possible responses: Guilt helps us try to do right. It keeps us from committing further wrongs. Guilt may, however, drive us to despair. Guilt can isolate people by making them feel bad about themselves or by making them feel that they are different from everyone else. Guilt can also spur people to confess, thereby sharing their weaknesses with others who understand and have weaknesses, too.

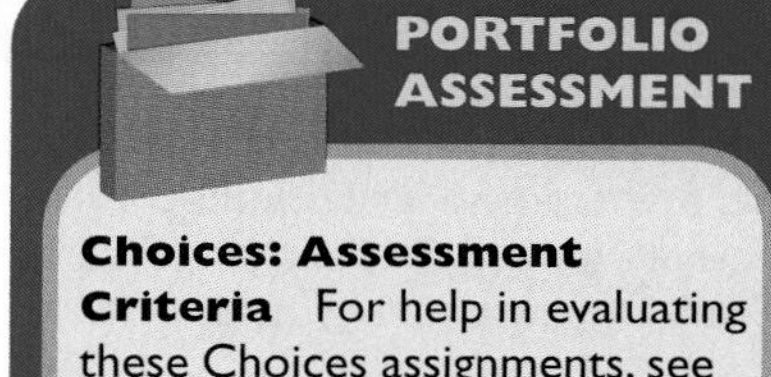

PORTFOLIO ASSESSMENT

Choices: Assessment Criteria For help in evaluating these Choices assignments, see the criteria in the ***Portfolio Management System,*** pp. 103–104.

How to Own a Word

Mini-Lesson: Etymologies

Choose one of the words from the text and work through the recording process with students. Then, have students work in pairs to complete their own charts. To encourage students to use their new words, ask students to record in their notebooks the contexts in which they use the words in conversation over the next week.

Try It Out: Answers

superstitious; from Latin *superstitio,* "excessive fear of the gods"; meaning "any belief, based on ignorance, that is inconsistent with known laws of science."
ambiguity; from Latin *ambigere,* "to wander"; meaning "having two possible meanings."
prelude; from Latin *praeludere,* "to play beforehand"; meaning "anything serving as the introduction to an event or performance."
vagaries; from Latin *vagari,* "to wander"; meaning "an odd or whimsical idea."
portend; from Latin *portendere,* "to stretch"; meaning "to be an omen."
iniquity; from Latin *iniquus,* "unequal"; meaning "wickedness."
All information for the above answers is taken from *Webster's New World Dictionary Third College Edition.*

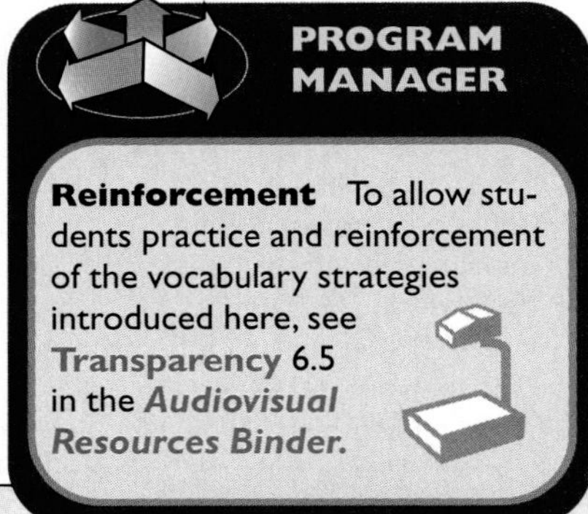

PROGRAM MANAGER

Reinforcement To allow students practice and reinforcement of the vocabulary strategies introduced here, see **Transparency** 6.5 in the ***Audiovisual Resources Binder.***

How to Own a Word

Etymologies—Tracing the Origins of Words

While some languages have few imported words, English is a language full of borrowings. Many English words come originally from Latin by way of Germanic languages or Old English. Other words have Greek, French, Native American, or Spanish origins. And this is just the tip of the iceberg.

Since Latin words make up such a large part of our language, learning the meaning of an English word that comes from Latin may help you understand the meanings of other English words derived from Latin. Such words are considered members of the same word family. You can learn about word families by consulting a dictionary to discover a word's **etymology**—the history of its origins and development.

Hanging Tales on Words

Learning the etymology of a word can help you to quickly recognize related words. It can also help you to remember a new word by giving you interesting and perhaps surprising information. For example, the noun *volcano* is derived from *Vulcan,* the Roman god of fire and forges. If you can use a word's etymology to "hang a tale" on a word—that is, associate an interesting fact or anecdote with it—you're more likely to remember the word.

The Granger Collection, New York.

Vulcan making a new armor for Achilles.

Here are some words that come from Latin. All of them appear in Hawthorne's story. See if the etymologies help you to remember and use these words.

averted from *a–,* from + *vertere,* to turn
Meaning: turned away from; kept from happening

celestial from *caelestis,* heaven
Meaning: of the heavens

discern from *dis–,* apart + *cernere,* to separate
Meaning: to separate (a thing) mentally from another or others; recognize as separate or different

obscurity from *obscurus,* covered over
Meaning: the condition of being unclear or indistinct, or not easily understood

placid from *placidus,* to please
Meaning: undisturbed; tranquil; calm; quiet

preclude from *pre–,* before + *claudere,* to close
Meaning: to make impossible, especially in advance; shut out; prevent

sagacious from *sagax,* wise; foreseeing
Meaning: having or showing keen perception or discernment and sound judgment

Did you notice that a word related to *discern—discernment*—was used in the definition of *sagacious?* That's another link you could use to help you remember the meaning.

Try It Out

When you find an unfamiliar word, looking it up in a dictionary and recording its etymology along with its meaning can both help you remember it *and* make it a permanent part of your vocabulary. Try using a chart like the one below to record etymologies for the following words from Hawthorne and any other new words you want to own and use.

superstitious (page 302)
ambiguity (page 305)
prelude (page 307)
vagaries (page 306)
portend (page 303)
iniquity (page 301)

Word	
Etymology	
Meanings	
Where Found	

STRATEGIES FOR INCLUSION

Spatial/Visual Have students create a visual representation that will help them remember both the meaning and the etymology of each vocabulary word. Students should draw their image, then list the word, meaning, and etymology below the image.

CROSSING THE CURRICULUM

Geography Ask students to list street names, car types, advertising slogans, or other words found in their neighborhoods that may have a Latin etymology. You may want to have students work in teams to see which group can come up with the most words. Students should present their words, along with their etymologies, to the class.

Herman Melville

(1819–1891)

It is the central irony of Herman Melville's career that his triumphant achievement, now widely recognized as one of the greatest American novels, was almost wholly ignored while its author was alive. Melville's contemporaries—so absorbed with success; so eager to discover it, bestow it, reward it, celebrate it—passed by *Moby-Dick* without the barest recognition.

As a result, Melville spent the last third of his life in poverty and despair, thinking himself a failure. His disappointment was even more painful because he had known easy, early success with his adventure stories. With ambitious, serious work, he met only failure and humiliation.

It is a further irony that Melville became resigned to the contempt of the world; that in spite of the painfulness of the world's judgment, he deliberately decided in the world's favor. In a remark that was to be echoed by the twentieth-century novelist William Faulkner, Melville once remarked that "failure is the true test of greatness."

Herman Melville (1870) by Joseph Eaton. Oil on canvas.
By permission of the Houghton Library, Harvard University, Cambridge, Massachusetts (H585).

A Whale Ship Was His College

Herman Melville was born into a distinguished family—wealthy Boston merchants on his father's side, early New York landowners on his mother's, Revolutionary War heroes on both. But his father went bankrupt in 1830, suffered an emotional breakdown, and died when Melville was twelve. Melville's mother, an austere, God-fearing woman, moved with her eight children from New York City to Albany. Under the pressures of poverty, she became even more remote from her children.

The teenage Melville clerked in his brother's hat store and in his uncle's bank, taught school in Pittsfield, Massachusetts, and tried writing articles and stories. However, faced with a grim life in his family's house, he took to the sea in 1839 as cabin boy on a merchant ship.

A whaling expedition to the South Seas followed in 1841. A year and a half later, Melville jumped ship at the Marquesas Islands and stumbled upon the valley of the Typees, who were reputed to be cannibals but turned out to be gentle and hospitable. After a month, Melville signed on to an Australian ship, which he deserted in a semimutiny at Papeete. He roamed the islands of Tahiti and Moorea, working in the fields and studying island life, before joining a whaler to Honolulu, and then enlisting as a seaman on a U.S. Navy frigate. When his ship docked at Boston in October 1844, a career's worth of seagoing adventure had ended. Ishmael, the young narrator of *Moby-Dick,* surely voices Melville's own sentiments when he says, "A whale ship was my Yale College and my Harvard."

The Road to Success

In less than two years, Melville produced a book of slightly fictionalized travel memoirs, *Typee,* that became an immediate success. With the publication of four other semiautobiographical sea tales between 1847 and 1850, Melville became one of the most popular authors of the

ABOUT THE AUTHOR

The author's father, Allan Melvill, had failed in business and had declared bankruptcy when Herman was eleven. Herman's mother then changed the spelling of his family name from Melvill to Melville to dissociate the family from her husband's failure. Interestingly, Hawthorne (Hathorne) had also changed the spelling of his family name.

Technology Tip

Information on Herman Melville can be found at **http://www.melville.org**. The Web site includes links to information on whaling, sailing, and more. *You may want to preview any Internet activity that you suggest to students. Because these resources are sometimes public forums, their content can be unpredictable.*

QUICK PLANNING GUIDE

Into the Story

Author Biography pp. 311–312

Before You Read p. 313

- **Reading Focus: Set a Purpose** Students compare the mystery of the whale to the mystery of human existence.
- **A Dialogue with the Text:** Describe in Reader's Log Ahab's thoughts and feelings.
- **Elements of Literature: Characterization**
- **Background** *Moby-Dick* rediscovered

Through the Story

from Moby-Dick pp. 313–327

Words to Own pp. 315–318, 322–327

Making Meanings pp. 320, 328

Beyond the Story

Choices: Building Your Portfolio p. 329

- **Writer's Notebook:** Collect ideas for a controversial issue
- **Critical Writing:** Explain Moby-Dick as a symbol in an essay
- **Critical Thinking/Speaking and Listening:** Analyze Ahab in a discussion
- **Critical Writing:** Compare monologue to Transcendentalist ideas in an essay
- **Creative Writing:** Write Ahab's thoughts in two or three paragraphs
- **Crossing the Curriculum: Science:** Research whales for an oral report

day. He was now married to the former Elizabeth Shaw, daughter of an old family friend. In the course of their long and often troubled marriage, she bore four children and was never more loyal and devoted than at times of crisis.

In the fall of 1850, Melville bought a farm near Pittsfield, Massachusetts. Nathaniel Hawthorne, who lived in nearby Lenox, responded to Melville's admiration, and they saw much of each other. Hawthorne's example encouraged Melville, who was writing a book that would both exploit his whaling experience and, on a far more ambitious plane, seek the ultimate truth of human existence. That truth, and the mystery of whether it is benign or evil in nature, is embodied in Moby-Dick, the great white whale that gives the book its title and central symbol.

Melville found the perfect narrator for his whale story in a young character named Ishmael, who has a keen eye and a questioning voice. Moreover, Melville saw his other main character clearly: Captain Ahab, standing on the *Pequod's* quarter-deck with his peg leg, his heart full of brooding vengeance. In Ahab, Melville created an obsessed, tragic, larger-than-life figure with few equals in American literature.

When he finished *Moby-Dick* in July 1851, Melville sensed that he had taken a great risk and won. He dedicated his great novel to Hawthorne and wrote him, "I have written a wicked book, and feel spotless as the lamb."

To Risk All—and Lose

Yet for all Melville's bright expectations, *Moby-Dick* was a failure. Critics and readers alike were either puzzled or indifferent, and Melville finally had to admit that his literary career had foundered. He wrote Hawthorne:

> The calm, the coolness, the silent grass-growing mood in which a man *ought* always to compose—that, I fear, can seldom be mine. Dollars damn me; and the malicious Devil is forever grinning in upon me, holding the door ajar. My dear Sir, a presentiment [feeling of fear about the future] is on me—I shall at last be worn out and perish. . . . What I feel most moved to write, that is banned—it will not pay. Yet, altogether, write the *other* way I cannot. So the product is a final hash, and all my books are botches.

Melville was in debt, unable to meet the needs of his family, and in ill health. However, he continued to hope for a change in his fortunes. In the next six years, he published three poorly received novels.

In 1856, Melville scraped together enough money for a trip to Europe and the Middle East. He returned home with his emotions restored, but his literary and financial fortunes still low.

In 1866, Melville found a job, much as Hawthorne had, with the customhouse. But if the work gave him the financial security he yearned for, the "grass-growing" peace of mind was still denied him. A different kind of tragedy hit the following year when his son Malcolm took to his room and killed himself with a pistol.

True to the Dreams of Youth

Although Melville never stopped writing during this dark period, almost none of his work found a publisher, and he was obliged to bring it out in private editions of only a few copies. To end this period in Melville's life, there was further tragedy. In 1886, his son Stanwix, always an unstable wanderer, died in San Francisco.

At about the same time, Elizabeth, Melville's wife, came into a small inheritance which allowed her husband to retire from the customhouse and begin work on a book that would become another masterpiece. This was *Billy Budd.* When Melville died on September 28, 1891, the novella lay unwanted in his desk drawer. In 1924, thirty-three years later, it was published and acclaimed. Near the desk where Melville had composed it, a note was found. It read, "Keep true to the dreams of thy youth."

WORDS TO OWN

The following vocabulary words are defined in the Words to Own at the bottom of the pupil's page.

rejoinder p. 315	ferocity p.322
imprecations p. 317	apparition p. 323
inscrutable p. 317	ubiquitous p. 323
tacit p. 318	erudite p. 323
volition p. 318	incapacitated p. 327

PORTFOLIO ASSESSMENT

Portfolio Assessment For help with self- and teacher assessment of reading skills, see the ***Portfolio Management System,*** pp. 48–49.

Before You Read

from **Moby-Dick**

Reading Focus

The Meaning of a White Whale

Moby-Dick is both a thrilling sea story about men who hunt whales in wooden boats and a search for the truth of human existence. The mystery of whether existence is benign, indifferent, or evil is embodied in Moby-Dick, the great white whale.

A Dialogue with the Text

Ahab's purpose—and obsession—in *Moby-Dick* is to hunt down the white whale. As you read, take notes on what Ahab feels and thinks about Moby-Dick.

Elements of Literature

Characterization

To create the larger-than-life **characterization** of Captain Ahab, Melville uses all the tools at a writer's command: He tells us directly (through the narrator, Ishmael) what Ahab is like, he describes Ahab's appearance and clothing, he lets us overhear Ahab speaking and thinking, he shows Ahab in action, and he shows us how other characters feel about and behave toward Ahab.

Characterization is the process by which a writer reveals a character's personality.

For more on Characterization, see the Handbook of Literary Terms.

Background

In 1853, barely two years after the publication of *Moby-Dick*, a fire at the publisher's destroyed most of the copies of the book, as well as the printer's plates. This greatly decreased the chances for readers of that era to read and evaluate the book. Melville was not rediscovered by critics until the 1920s.

from Moby-Dick

Herman Melville

Two chapters from Melville's great novel will give you only a taste of its characters, setting, plot, and themes. The novel opens with the famous line, "Call me Ishmael." The narrator who adopts this pseudonym is a moody young New Yorker who takes to sea to escape the "damp, drizzly November in my soul." First traveling to the Massachusetts seaport of New Bedford, he shares a room with a South Sea Islander named Queequeg. Becoming friends, the two go to the island of Nantucket, where they sign on for a three-year voyage on the whaling ship Pequod, *under the command of the mysterious Captain Ahab. While still ashore, Ishmael receives warnings of disaster; but he ships out anyway, and the* Pequod, *weirdly decorated with whale bones, sets sail on an icy Christmas Day. The officers and crew are an assortment of men from all over the world: South Pacific islanders, Massachusetts Gay-Head Indians, inhabitants of the Isle of Man off the coast of Ireland, and more. The harpooners are Queequeg, Tashtego, and Daggoo; the first, second, and third mates are Starbuck, Stubb, and Flask, respectively.*

Shortly before the chapter "The Quarter-Deck," Stubb and Ahab have quarreled violently, and an ominous dream has suggested to Stubb that he beware of his captain's anger. In this chapter, Ahab calls the men to assemble on the deck, where he will reveal the true nature of his quest.

Illustration by Rockwell Kent from *Moby-Dick*.
Columbia University Libraries, Rare Books and Manuscripts.

Using Before You Read p. 313

Reading Focus

Place students in small groups, and ask them to think of everything they know about whales. Have them list words and phrases that describe both physical and symbolic characteristics of the whale. Based on their lists, have them predict what they think will happen to the men and the whales and whether existence for each will be benign, indifferent, or evil.

Elements of Literature

Ask students to keep a character profile journal. As they read, students should use the following chart to list details of Ahab's character.

Methods of Characterization	Ahab
Narrator tells directly about Ahab	[Ahab walked deck after breakfast.]
Appearance	
Ahab's speaking	
Ahab's thoughts	
Ahab's actions	
How other characters feel about Ahab	

Program Manager

- **Planning Instruction** See **Teaching Notes, *Teaching Resources A,*** pp. 107–108, for objectives, a summary, literary elements, and additional historical and biographical information for this selection.
- **Instructional Support** Before beginning the instructional lesson, see **Graphic Organizer for Active Reading, *Teaching Resources A,*** p. 118, for a Through the Story activity.
- **Assessment** See **Selection Test, *Test Booklet,*** pp. 77–78, 79–80.
- **Reinforcement** Use the **Words to Own** worksheet in ***Teaching Resources,*** p. 119.

Into the Story

A. Expansion
As the stage direction, *"Enter Ahab: Then all"* shows, this scene is dramatized almost as if it were a play. It also shows Melville's debt to Shakespeare.

B. Literary Elements: Simile
? What effect does comparing the dents Ahab's ivory leg makes in the planks to "geological stones" have? [It magnifies Ahab's effect on his environment and continues to emphasize the symbolic nature of events.]

C. Reader's Response: First Thoughts
? What might be the "chick" in Ahab that pecks to get out? [Sample responses: The chick might be angry at someone; or it might be a secret motive Ahab is trying to keep inside.]

The Quarter-Deck

A *(Enter Ahab: Then all.)*

It was not a great while after the affair of the pipe,[1] that one morning shortly after breakfast, Ahab, as was his wont, ascended the cabin gangway to the deck. There most sea captains usually walk at that hour, as country gentlemen, after the same meal, take a few turns in the garden.

B Soon his steady, ivory stride was heard, as to and fro he paced his old rounds, upon planks so familiar to his tread, that they were all over dented, like geological stones, with the peculiar mark of his walk. Did you fixedly gaze, too, upon that ribbed and dented brow; there also, you would see still stranger footprints—the footprints of his one unsleeping, ever-pacing thought.

But on the occasion in question, those dents looked deeper, even as his nervous step that morning left a deeper mark. And, so full of his thought was Ahab, that at every uniform turn that he made, now at the mainmast and now at the binnacle,[2] you could almost see that thought turn in him as he turned, and pace in him as he paced; so completely possessing him, indeed, that it all but seemed the inward mold of every outer movement.

C "D'ye mark him, Flask?" whispered Stubb; "the chick that's in him pecks the shell. 'Twill soon be out."

The hours wore on—Ahab now shut up within

1. **affair of the pipe:** Ahab had thrown his pipe overboard one evening when he realized that he had no business with "this thing that is meant for sereneness."

2. **binnacle:** upright stand holding the ship's compass.

OPTIONS FOR TEACHING

STRATEGIES FOR INCLUSION

Visual To help motivate students to read the selections and comprehend the power of whales, show pictures or slides of whales, or let them go to the library, bring back illustrated books on whales, and show these to the class.

Musical To help set the tone for *Moby-Dick,* locate tapes of ocean waves and sounds (foghorns and storms) and of classical music, such as Debussy's *La Mer.* Play the tape as an introduction or background to the reading of the selection.

English Language Development Have pairs of students write a few sentences in outline form, listing the main events or ideas in each chapter. Then, place each student pair with a more proficient reader, and have them work together to add more details to the outline.

Kinesthetic Allow students the opportunity to dramatize the great "communion scene" with Ahab offering the chalices of wine (the harpoon sockets) to the men as testimony to their commitment. Encourage students to use props and costumes.

his cabin; anon, pacing the deck, with the same intense bigotry of purpose in his aspect.

It drew near the close of day. Suddenly he came to a halt by the bulwarks,[3] and inserting his bone leg into the auger hole there, and with one hand grasping a shroud, he ordered Starbuck to send everybody aft.

"Sir!" said the mate, astonished at an order seldom or never given on shipboard except in some extraordinary case.

"Send everybody aft," repeated Ahab. "Mastheads, there! Come down!"

When the entire ship's company were assembled, and with curious and not wholly unapprehensive faces were eyeing him, for he looked not unlike the weather horizon when a storm is coming up, Ahab, after rapidly glancing over the bulwarks, and then darting his eyes among the crew, started from his standpoint; and as though not a soul were nigh him resumed his heavy turns upon the deck. With bent head and half-slouched hat he continued to pace; unmindful of the wondering whispering among the men; till Stubb cautiously whispered to Flask, that Ahab must have summoned them there for the purpose of witnessing a pedestrian feat. But this did not last long. Vehemently pausing, he cried—

"What do ye do when ye see a whale, men?"

"Sing out for him!" was the impulsive rejoinder from a score of clubbed[4] voices.

3. **bulwarks** (bul′wərks): above-deck part of a ship's side.

4. **clubbed:** united.

Words to Own

rejoinder (ri·join′dər) *n.:* answer.

INTEGRATING THE LANGUAGE ARTS

Strategic Reading Have students make predictions about the selection before they begin reading. As they read, students should revise and add to their predictions. When they have finished, students can make confirmations of their predictions. Emphasize to students that their confirmations should evaluate the thought processes that went into their predictions. They may use a graphic organizer like the following.

Pre-reading Predictions	Reading Predictions	Confirmations

Speaking and Listening Review with the class the definition of **simile.** [A comparison of two unlike things, using *like* or *as*.] Then, have a fluent reader read the passage on p. 316 which begins "'Moby-Dick?' shouted Ahab." Instruct the rest of the class to listen carefully for as many similes as they can recognize. They must remember the simile and cannot write it down. Have the reader stop after "Moby-Dick—Moby-Dick!" on p. 316. Ask students to repeat the similes they remember, and tell why they remember them.

A. Critical Reading: Finding Details

? What features of the white whale make him look particularly sinister? ["wrinkled brow," "crooked jaw," "three holes punctured in his starboard fluke."]

B. Literary Element: Characterization

? What can you infer about these three crew members from their names? [Possible answers: They are from some far-off islands or exotic maritime countries. Ahab has assembled an unusual collection of sailors for his unusual quest.]

C. Critical Reading: Drawing Conclusions

? How do these three react to Ahab's description of the white whale? [They are interested and surprised. They might remember something unusual about this whale.]

"Good!" cried Ahab, with a wild approval in his tones; observing the hearty animation into which his unexpected question had so magnetically thrown them.

"And what do ye next, men?"

"Lower away, and after him!"

"And what tune is it ye pull to, men?"

"A dead whale or a stove[5] boat!"

More and more strangely and fiercely glad and approving grew the countenance of the old man at every shout; while the mariners began to gaze curiously at each other, as if marveling how it was that they themselves became so excited at such seemingly purposeless questions.

But, they were all eagerness again, as Ahab, now half-revolving in his pivot hole, with one hand reaching high up a shroud, and tightly, almost convulsively grasping it, addressed them thus—

"All ye mastheaders have before now heard me give orders about a white whale. Look ye! d'ye see this Spanish ounce of gold?"—holding up a broad bright coin to the sun—"it is a sixteen-dollar piece, men. D'ye see it? Mr. Starbuck, hand me yon top-maul."[6]

While the mate was getting the hammer, Ahab, without speaking, was slowly rubbing the gold piece against the skirts of his jacket, as if to heighten its luster, and without using any words was meanwhile lowly humming to himself, producing a sound so strangely muffled and inarticulate that it seemed the mechanical humming of the wheels of his vitality in him.

Receiving the top-maul from Starbuck, he advanced toward the mainmast with the hammer uplifted in one hand, exhibiting the gold with the other, and with a high raised voice exclaiming: "Whosoever of ye raises me a white-headed whale with a wrinkled brow and a crooked jaw; whosoever of ye raises me that white-headed whale, (A) with three holes punctured in his starboard fluke[7]—look ye, whosoever of ye raises me that same white whale, he shall have this gold ounce, my boys!"

"Huzza! huzza!" cried the seamen, as with swinging tarpaulins they hailed the act of nailing the gold to the mast.

"It's a white whale, I say," resumed Ahab, as he threw down the top-maul; "a white whale. Skin your eyes for him, men; look sharp for white water; if ye see but a bubble, sing out."

(B) All this while Tashtego, Daggoo, and Queequeg had looked on with even more intense interest and surprise than the rest, and at the mention of (C) the wrinkled brow and crooked jaw they had started as if each was separately touched by some specific recollection.

"Captain Ahab," said Tashtego, "that white whale must be the same that some call Moby-Dick."

"Moby-Dick?" shouted Ahab. "Do ye know the white whale then, Tash?"

"Does he fantail[8] a little curious, sir, before he goes down?" said the Gay-Header deliberately.

"And has he a curious spout, too," said Daggoo, "very bushy, even for a parmacety,[9] and mighty quick, Captain Ahab?"

"And he have one, two, tree—oh! good many iron in him hide, too, Captain," cried Queequeg disjointedly, "all twiske-tee be-twisk, like him—him——" faltering hard for a word, and screwing his hand round and round as though uncorking a bottle—"like him—him——"

"Corkscrew!" cried Ahab, "aye, Queequeg, the harpoons lie all twisted and wrenched in him; aye, Daggoo, his spout is a big one, like a whole shock of wheat, and white as a pile of our Nantucket wool after the great annual sheepshearing; aye, Tashtego, and he fantails like a split jib in a squall. Death and devils! men, it is Moby-Dick ye have seen—Moby-Dick—Moby-Dick!"

"Captain Ahab," said Starbuck, who, with Stubb and Flask, had thus far been eyeing his superior with increasing surprise, but at last seemed struck with a thought which somewhat explained all the wonder. "Captain Ahab, I have heard of Moby-Dick—but it was not Moby-Dick that took off thy leg?"

"Who told thee that?" cried Ahab; then pausing, "Aye, Starbuck; aye, my hearties all round; it was Moby-Dick that dismasted me; Moby-Dick that brought me to this dead stump I stand on now. Aye, Aye," he shouted, with a terrific, loud, animal

5. **stove:** with a hole smashed in it.
6. **top-maul:** heavy wooden hammer.
7. **starboard fluke:** right-hand side of the whale's tail.
8. **fantail:** spread the tail like a fan.
9. **parmacety** (pär′mə·sed′ē): slang for "spermaceti" (a sperm whale).

OPTIONS FOR TEACHING

COOPERATIVE LEARNING

Studying Character Assign students to eight groups, and assign each group a different character—Ahab, Stubb, Flask, Starbuck, Ishmael, Tashtego, Daggoo, and Queequeg—to investigate. Have the groups write down every description, comment, and quotation attributed to their assigned character and build a personality profile from this information. One student may gather descriptions and comments; another may write down the quotations. Once they have finished with the data gathering, have each group collaboratively write a biographical sketch. Ask students to appoint a spokesperson to read their report to the class. After each group has read its report, ask the other groups to orally evaluate the accuracy or appropriateness of the sketch.

CLASSROOM MANAGEMENT

Saving Time If you need to save time in having students complete the questions in the Making Meanings feature, assign students only one item to work on, making sure each item is covered by someone. Have students report on their answers to the whole class, and encourage other students to take notes on these reports. If the class is large, assign the same item to more than one student.

sob, like that of a heart-stricken moose; "Aye, aye! it was that accursed white whale that razeed[10] me; made a poor pegging lubber[11] of me for ever and a day!" Then tossing both arms, with measureless imprecations he shouted out: "Aye, aye! and I'll chase him round Good Hope and round the Horn, and round the Norway Maelstrom, and round perdition's flames before I give him up. And this is what ye have shipped for, men! to chase that white whale on both sides of land, and over all sides of earth, till he spouts black blood and rolls fin out. What say ye, men, will ye splice[12] hands on it, now? I think ye do look brave."

"Aye, aye!" shouted the harpooners and seamen, running closer to the excited old man: "a sharp eye for the White Whale; a sharp lance for Moby-Dick!"

"God bless ye," he seemed to half sob and half shout. "God bless ye, men. Steward! Go draw the great measure of grog.[13] But what's this long face about, Mr. Starbuck; wilt thou not chase the White Whale? Art not game for Moby-Dick?"

"I am game for his crooked jaw, and for the jaws of Death too, Captain Ahab, if it fairly comes in the way of the business we follow; but I came here to hunt whales, not my commander's vengeance. How many barrels will thy vengeance yield thee even if thou gettest it, Captain Ahab? It will not fetch thee much in our Nantucket market."

"Nantucket market! Hoot! But come closer, Starbuck; thou requirest a little lower layer. If money's to be the measurer, man, and the accountants have computed their great countinghouse the globe, by girdling it with guineas, one to every three parts of an inch; then, let me tell thee, that my vengeance will fetch a great premium *here*!"

"He smites his chest," whispered Stubb, "what's that for? Methinks it rings most vast, but hollow."

"Vengeance on a dumb brute!" cried Starbuck, "that simply smote thee from blindest instinct! Madness! To be enraged with a dumb thing, Captain Ahab, seems blasphemous."

"Hark ye yet again—the little lower layer. All visible objects, man, are but as pasteboard masks. But in each event—in the living act, the undoubted deed—there, some unknown but still reasoning thing puts forth the moldings of its features from behind the unreasoning mask. If man will strike, strike through the mask! How can the prisoner reach outside except by thrusting through the wall? To me, the White Whale is that wall, shoved near to me. Sometimes I think there's naught beyond. But 'tis enough. He tasks me; he heaps me; I see in him outrageous strength, with an inscrutable malice sinewing it. That inscrutable thing is chiefly what I hate; and be the White Whale agent, or be the White Whale principal, I will wreak that hate upon him. Talk not to me of blasphemy, man; I'd strike the sun if it insulted me. For could the sun do that, then could I do the other; since there is ever a sort of fair play herein, jealousy presiding over all creations. But not my master, man, is even that fair play. Who's over me? Truth hath no confines. Take off thine eye! More intolerable than fiends' glarings is a doltish stare! So, so; thou reddenest and palest; my heat has melted thee to anger-glow. But look ye, Starbuck, what is said in heat, that thing unsays itself. There are men from whom warm words are small indignity. I meant not to incense thee. Let it go. Look! see yonder Turkish cheeks of spotted tawn—living, breathing pictures painted by the sun. The pagan leopards—the unrecking and unworshipping things, that live; and seek, and give no reasons for the torrid life they feel! The crew, man, the crew! Are they not one and all with Ahab, in this matter of the whale? See Stubb! he laughs! See yonder Chilean! he snorts to think of it. Stand up amid the general hurricane, thy one tossed sapling cannot, Starbuck! And what is it? Reckon it. 'Tis but to help strike a fin; no wondrous feat for Starbuck. What is it more? From this one poor hunt, then, the best lance out of all Nantucket, surely he will not hang back, when every foremast-hand has clutched a whetstone? Ah! constrainings seize thee; I see! the billow lifts thee! Speak, but speak!—Aye, aye! thy silence, then, *that* voices thee. (*Aside*) Something shot from my dilated nostrils, he has inhaled it in his lungs.

10. razeed (rā·zēd′): to *razee* is to make a wooden warship lower by removing the upper deck.
11. lubber: big, slow, clumsy person.
12. splice: join.
13. grog: watered-down liquor drunk by sailors.

Words to Own

imprecations (im′pri·kā′shənz) *n. pl.:* curses.
inscrutable (in·skro͞ot′ə·bəl) *adj.:* mysterious.

D. Critical Reading: Analyzing Character

? What is Ahab's response to Starbuck's query about whether Moby-Dick took off Ahab's leg? [He acknowledges in a frenzied manner that it was Moby-Dick.] What does the manner of his response suggest about Ahab? [That he is fixated on taking revenge for losing his leg.]

E. Exploring the Culture

In Melville's day, whales were hunted for their whale oil, a valuable product taken from the blubber (fat) of the whale. This oil was used for fuel in lanterns, perfumes, soap, food, and other products. A large whale, according to Melville himself, could provide up to a hundred barrels of oil, an amount equaling ten tons. In 1851, the year *Moby-Dick* appeared, more than seven hundred whaling ships were searching the seven seas for large whales.

F. Reader's Response: Extending the Text

This passage is one of Ahab's great soliloquies. Its vision of the world as masks and its exhortation "Strike through the mask!" are the pinnacles of Melville's negative transcendentalism. Is the metaphor of the masks applicable to life as you know it? Explain. [Sample responses: Yes, people still have little meaning in their lives unless something motivates them. Or no, most people find meaning in all sorts of things.] How can we live according to the directive "Strike through the mask"? [Sample responses: People can strike through the mask, if they have one, by pursuing their dreams or by getting rid of anything that holds them back from doing what they would like to do.]

CROSSING THE CURRICULUM

Art Have students paint or sketch either a whaling scene, complete with harpoon boats and whales, or Captain Ahab, peg-legged on deck. Have students hang their artwork around the room, and invite students to view and discuss it.

History In connection with *Moby-Dick,* ask students to find out about whaling in the nineteenth century. Students should research the importance of whale oil to industry, the ships and equipment used to whale hunt, and the way whalers lived at sea. Have students write diary entries of a whaler over a week's time.

PROBLEM SOLVING/CRITICAL THINKING

Starbuck's Dilemma Although Starbuck realizes that Ahab is mad, he seems to feel powerless about dissuading his captain from pursuing the whale; he has tried reasoning with Ahab. Have student groups analyze Starbuck's position and determine what he could do to prevent Ahab from chasing Moby-Dick. Ask each group to propose at least two options. Make sure that they consider the consequences of these options. Have each group choose their best option and present it to the class. After all groups have presented, hold a class discussion. Then, have students vote on the best solution.

A. Expansion
Here begins the communion scene with its powerful allusion to a religious sacrament, the celebration of the Last Supper.

Starbuck now is mine; cannot oppose me now, without rebellion."

"God keep me!—keep us all!" murmured Starbuck lowly.

But in his joy at the enchanted, tacit acquiescence of the mate, Ahab did not hear his foreboding invocation; nor yet the low laugh from the hold; nor yet the presaging vibrations of the winds in the cordage; nor yet the hollow flap of the sails against the masts, as for a moment their hearts sank in. For again Starbuck's downcast eyes lighted up with the stubbornness of life; the subterranean laugh died away; the winds blew on; the sails filled out; the ship heaved and rolled as before. Ah, ye admonitions and warnings! Why stay ye not when ye come? But rather are ye predictions than warnings, ye shadows! Yet not so much predictions from without, as verifications of the foregoing things within. For with little external to constrain us, the innermost necessities in our being, these still drive us on.

"The measure! the measure!" cried Ahab.

Receiving the brimming pewter, and turning to the harpooneers, he ordered them to produce their weapons. Then ranging them before him near the capstan,[14] with their harpoons in their hands, while his three mates stood at his side with their lances, and the rest of the ship's company formed a circle round the group; he stood for an instant searchingly eyeing every man of his crew. But those wild eyes met his, as the bloodshot eyes of the prairie wolves meet the eye of their leader, ere he rushes on at their head in the trail of the bison; but, alas! only to fall into the hidden snare of the Indian.

"Drink and pass!" he cried, handing the heavy charged flagon to the nearest seaman. "The crew alone now drink. Round with it, round! Short drafts—long swallows, men; 'tis hot as Satan's hoof. So, so; it goes round excellently. It spiralizes in ye; forks out at the serpent-snapping eye. Well done; almost drained. That way it went, this way it comes. Hand it me—here's a hollow! Men, ye seem the years; so brimming life is gulped and gone. Steward, refill!

"Attend now, my braves. I have mustered ye all round this capstan; and ye, mates, flank me with your lances; and ye, harpooneers, stand there with your irons; and ye, stout mariners, ring me in, that I may in some sort revive a noble custom of my fisherman fathers before me. O men, you will yet see that—— Ha! boy, come back? bad pennies come not sooner. Hand it me. Why, now, this pewter had run brimming again, wert not thou St. Vitus's imp[15]—away, thou ague!

"Advance, ye mates! Cross your lances full before me. Well done! Let me touch the axis." So saying, with extended arm, he grasped the three level, radiating lances at their crossed center; while so doing, suddenly and nervously twitched them; meanwhile, glancing intently from Starbuck to Stubb, from Stubb to Flask. It seemed as though, by some nameless, interior volition, he would fain have shocked into them the same fiery emotion accumulated within the Leyden jar[16] of his own magnetic life. The three mates quailed before his strong, sustained, and mystic aspect. Stubb and Flask looked sideways from him; the honest eye of Starbuck fell downright.

"In vain!" cried Ahab; "but, maybe, 'tis well. For did ye three but once take the full-forced shock, then mine own electric thing, *that* had perhaps expired from out me. Perchance, too, it would have dropped ye dead. Perchance ye need it not. Down lances! And now, ye mates, I do appoint ye three cupbearers to my three pagan kinsmen there—yon three most honorable gentlemen and noblemen, my valiant harpooneers. Disdain the task? What, when the great Pope washes the feet of beggars, using his tiara for ewer?[17] Oh, my sweet cardinals! your own condescension, *that* shall bend ye to it. I do not order ye; ye will it. Cut

14. **capstan:** similar to a winch; a large cylinder, usually on a ship's deck, around which cables are wound to lift heavy objects such as anchors and weights.

15. **St. Vitus's imp:** Saint Vitus is the patron saint of people ill with chorea, a nervous disorder characterized by irregular, jerking movements. An imp is a mischievous child or young demon. Ahab is complaining that the steward's clumsiness caused the pitcher of grog to be spilled.
16. **Leyden jar:** device for storing electrical charges.
17. **tiara for ewer:** literally, "crown for a pitcher"; a reference to the practice of the pope washing the feet of the poor on Holy Thursday, in imitation of Jesus' washing the feet of his disciples.

WORDS TO OWN
tacit (tas′it) *adj.:* implied but not expressed openly.
volition (vō·lish′ən) *n.:* will.

OPTIONS FOR TEACHING

PROFESSIONAL NOTES

Thematic Connections: "The Realms of Darkness" Ahab is a madman. Have the students compare and contrast his behavior with that of the three other characters from the unit: Roderick Usher, the narrator of "The Raven," and Mr. Hooper. Ask them to focus on the similarities of each character's behavior and then consider why they all belong in the unit entitled "The Realms of Darkness." Have students complete a chart like the following.

Similarities
Usher
Narrator "The Raven"
Mr. Hooper
Ahab
Realms of Darkness

Peabody Essex Museum, Salem, Massachusetts (M16265).

Sailors—Companion to the Tailors (mid–19th century). Unsigned, attributed to John Cranch. Oil on wood panel.

RESPONDING TO THE ART: IDEAS FOR WRITING

The sailors depicted in this painting could well have been on the *Pequod.* Ask students to consider what might have been taking place during this scene and to write a journal entry from the perspective of one of these men.

ASSESSMENT TOOLS

Observation Assessment: Reading As students read aloud, as in the Integrating the Language Arts activities on p. T315, use the following points to observe and assess their reading performance. Rate them on a scale of 1 to 5, with 5 being the highest.

1. Recognizes each word.
   Never — Half the Time — Always
   1 2 3 4 5
2. Reads fluently in phrases or sentences.
   Never — Half the Time — Always
   1 2 3 4 5
3. Reads with expression.
   Never — Half the Time — Always
   1 2 3 4 5

Check Test: True-False

"The Quarter-Deck"

1. Captain Ahab calls every single member of the ship's crew to assemble for his commands. [True]
2. Ahab offers an extra week's wages for any sailor who spots the white whale. [False]
3. The three harpooners are asked to take a drink as an oath to their dedication to kill the white whale. [True]
4. The narrator's name is Ishmael. [True]
5. Moby-Dick had a deformed lower jaw that made him look malicious. [True]

Making Meanings

First Thoughts

1. Possible responses: obsessed, romantic, insane. Ahab scares me, or Ahab intrigues me.

Reviewing the Text

a. To assemble so that he can address them. He wants to sharpen the crew's eagerness to chase and kill the great white whale.

b. According to Ahab, Moby-Dick has a white head, a wrinkled brow, and a crooked jaw. He has three holes punctured in his starboard (right) fluke. He fantails curiously, and many harpoons are twisted in him.

c. He orders them to tilt their harpoons upward, so that liquor can be poured into the sockets. He then orders them to drink and swear to the death of Moby-Dick.

d. At the paragraph that begins with "But in his joy at the enchanted, tacit acquiescence of the mate . . ." The premonitions of the low laugh in the hold and the vibrations of the winds in the cordage, and the comparison of the Leyden jar.

Shaping Interpretations

2. Starbuck says that Ahab's thirst for vengeance on a dumb brute seems blasphemous. Starbuck's misgivings suggest that he has a balanced sense of the order of the universe and that he foresees that Ahab's unnatural quest for vengeance will lead to disaster.
3. Starbuck is probably afraid of Ahab.
4. One paraphrase may be: People, objects, and events are lifeless, irrational, and static until the energy of an action or deed gives them meaning. Ahab implies that one can find meaning only through action or deed.
5. He sees in the whale "outrageous strength" and "inscrutable malice," and he feels personally the destruction it has wreaked on him. He hates the enigmatic quality of the whale above all, and he vows that he will bring the beast and its hatred under control.
6. Ahab's comparison of himself to the pope and of the mates to the cardinals. Melville's allusion to washing "the feet of beggars" refers to a traditional ceremony on Holy Thursday, when the pope, imitating Christ and as a sign of humility, washes the feet of twelve people. Students may suggest that

your seizings and draw the poles, ye harpooneers!"

Silently obeying the order, the three harpooneers now stood with the detached iron part of their harpoons, some three feet long, held, barbs up, before him.

"Stab me not with that keen steel! Cant[18] them; cant them over! know ye not the goblet end? Turn up the socket! So, so; now, ye cupbearers, advance. The irons! take them; hold them while I fill!" Forthwith, slowly going from one officer to the other, he brimmed the harpoon sockets with the fiery waters from the pewter.

"Now, three to three, ye stand. Commend the murderous chalices! Bestow them, ye who are now made parties to this indissoluble league. Ha! Starbuck! but the deed is done! Yon ratifying sun now waits to sit upon it. Drink, ye harpooneers! drink and swear, ye men that man the deathful whaleboat's bow—Death to Moby-Dick! God hunt us all, if we do not hunt Moby-Dick to his death!" The long, barbed steel goblets were lifted; and to cries and maledictions[19] against the White Whale, the spirits were simultaneously quaffed down with a hiss. Starbuck paled, and turned, and shivered. Once more, and finally, the replenished pewter went the rounds among the frantic crew; when, waving his free hand to them, they all dispersed; and Ahab retired within his cabin.

18. **cant:** overturn or tilt.

19. **maledictions** (mal'ə·dik'shənz): curses.

MAKING MEANINGS

First Thoughts

1. What words would you use to describe Captain Ahab? Do you pity him, fear him, or do you have another reaction?

Reviewing the Text

a. After his obsessive pacing of the deck, what command does Ahab issue to the crew? Why does Ahab meet with his crew?

b. What do you learn about Moby-Dick's appearance from Ahab's dialogue with his crew?

c. Toward the end of the chapter, what does Ahab order the mates to do with their lances?

d. Where does the narrative shift from Ishmael's **point of view** to an **omniscient** point of view? What details in this chapter could only be known by an omniscient narrator?

Shaping Interpretations

2. What are Starbuck's misgivings about Ahab's pursuit of the great white whale? What does this tell us about Starbuck's **character**?
3. Why do you think Starbuck gives in to Ahab?
4. Explain the idea Ahab expresses in his famous **metaphor** comparing visible objects to "pasteboard masks" (page 317). What do you think he means when he says "strike through the mask"?
5. Review the notes you made in your Reader's Log. What **symbolic** meaning might the white whale have for Ahab? (Recall Ahab's comment that the white whale "is that wall. . . . Sometimes I think there's naught beyond.")
6. What details in the drinking scene suggest a **parody** or mockery of a religious ritual? What might the scene signify about Ahab's quest?
7. What do you learn about Ahab's **character** when he says "Talk not to me of blasphemy, man; I'd strike the sun if it insulted me" (page 317)? What did he say prior to this that sounded like blasphemy—that is, mockery of God?
8. Identify the details in this chapter that **foreshadow** disaster and destruction for the *Pequod* and its crew. What do you think will happen next?

Extending the Text

9. Who are Ahab and Ishmael in the Bible? Look up Ahab's story in I Kings 16:29–22:40 and Ishmael's story in Genesis 21:9–21. Why do you think Melville chose these names for his captain and narrator?

the details of the scene signify that Ahab's quest is somehow blasphemous.

7. The statement suggests Ahab's qualities of pride, determination, and ferocity. In his prior statement, he said that he would "wreak . . . hate" upon the "inscrutable thing"—suggesting that he regards the power of the whale (and maybe the inscrutable power of God) as hateful and worthy of attack.
8. Possible response: The premonitions on p. 318 (the "low laugh from the hold" and the "presaging vibrations of the winds in the cordage"), and Melville's apostrophe beginning "Ah, ye admonitions and warnings!" The whale will destroy Ahab, the ship, and every member of the crew but Ishmael.

Extending the Text

9. **(Synthesis)** The Bible describes Ahab, king of Israel, as a man who did evil, and reinstated the worship of idols. The prophet Elijah threatens his destruction. Melville may have chosen this name for its connotation of evil and godlessness. The son of Abraham and Hagar, the maid of Abraham's wife, Ishmael is an outcast. The name is symbolic of a displaced person or wanderer.

Following the ritual on the quarter-deck, in which Ahab fills the harpoon-tips with liquor and reveals the object of his chase, we hear three characters privately reflect on their journey's goal. Ahab recognizes himself as a driven man; Starbuck reflects on what he sees as the captain's insanity; and Stubb fatalistically resigns himself to whatever destiny may bring. That night a squall threatens to strike the ship, and the crew become tense. At last we are about to meet the object of Ahab's obsession—the white whale, Moby-Dick.

from Moby-Dick

I, Ishmael, was one of that crew; my shouts had gone up with the rest; my oath had been welded with theirs; and stronger I shouted, and more did I hammer and clinch my oath, because of the dread in my soul. A wild, mystical, sympathetical feeling was in me; Ahab's quenchless feud seemed mine. With greedy ears I learned the history of that murderous monster against whom I and all the others had taken our oaths of violence and revenge. A

For some time past, though at intervals only, the unaccompanied, secluded White Whale had haunted those uncivilized seas mostly frequented by the sperm whale fishermen. But not all of them knew of his existence; only a few of them, comparatively, had knowingly seen him; while the number who as yet had actually and knowingly given battle to him, was small indeed. For, owing to the large number of whale-cruisers; the disorderly way they were sprinkled over the entire watery circumference, many of them adventurously pushing their quest along solitary latitudes, so as seldom or never for a whole twelvemonth or more on a stretch, to encounter a single news-telling sail of any sort; the inordinate length of each separate voyage; the irregularity of the times of sailing from home; all these, with other circumstances, direct and indirect, long obstructed the spread through the whole worldwide whaling fleet of the special individualizing tidings concerning Moby-Dick. It was hardly to be doubted, that several vessels reported to have encountered, at such or such a time, or on such or such a meridian, a sperm whale of uncommon magnitude and malignity,[1] which whale, after doing great mischief to his assailants, had completely escaped them; to some minds it was not an unfair presumption, I say, that the whale in question must have been no other than Moby-Dick. Yet as of late

1. **malignity** (mə·lig′nə·tē): intense ill will.

A. Literary Element: Foreshadowing

? In Ishmael's opening statement, what indications are there that disaster looms? [Ishmael mentions the "dread in my soul," a "wild, mystical, sympathetical feeling," "Ahab's quenchless feud," "murderous monster," and "greedy ears."]

OPTIONS FOR TEACHING

STRATEGIES FOR INCLUSION

Less Proficient Readers In this passage, readers learn what people say about Moby-Dick. Some of what people say is based in truth; a good deal of what they say is based on rumor or superstition. Have students complete a chart like the following to distinguish between what may be true of Moby-Dick and what may be exaggeration. On one side of the chart, have students list probable truths; on the other, rumors and folklore. Ask students to write the source of each listing beside it.

Truth	Rumor
[The whale took Ahab's leg.]	[Moby-Dick is immortal.]
[Ahab's testimony.]	[Superstitions of whalers.]

Visual Have students refer to descriptions of Moby-Dick and draw or paint two pictures of him. Ask students to use quotations from the text as captions for their work.

Advanced/Auditory Have pairs of advanced students record audiotapes for auditory students to use while reading *Moby-Dick*. Ask the advanced students to practice reading before they record and to use sound effects to heighten listener interest. ☞

A. Exploring the Historical Period

The destructive power of whales was not exaggerated by Melville. Thomas Heffernan's book, *Stove by a Whale: Owen Chase and the Essex,* tells of a November 20, 1820, incident in which an eighty-five-foot sperm whale attacked and sank the whaling ship *Essex* in the middle of the Pacific Ocean. A survivor, Owen Chase, wrote a sixty-three-page account of the frightful ramming by the whale. Chase and several other witnesses survived for three months on a smaller whaleboat until they were rescued off the coast of Chile. Another article, "Mocha Dick,"appeared in 1839. In it, J. N. Reynolds describes a ferocious white whale, sporting nineteen harpoons, that had caused the death of thirty men by ramming several ships. Melville acknowledged reading both of these accounts.

B. Literary Element: Tone

Compare Melville's use of the supernatural with that of Hawthorne and Poe. Does Melville intend for the reader to believe it? Do Hawthorne and Poe? [Possible answer: Melville uses the supernatural in a symbolic way to emphasize the conflict between good and evil. Hawthorne is more concerned with the psychological effect of sin. Poe's Gothic tales are not to be taken literally.]

C. Reader's Response: First Thoughts

? What kind of courage would it take to row a small harpoon boat close to such a mammal and to have only a sharp spear, or harpoon, to throw at it? [Sample responses: More courage than I have. Or the sailors must be crazy or really need or want the money badly.]

the sperm whale fishery had been marked by various and not unfrequent instances of great ferocity, cunning, and malice in the monster attacked; therefore it was, that those who by accident ignorantly gave battle to Moby-Dick; such hunters, perhaps, for the most part, were content to ascribe the peculiar terror he bred, more, as it were, to the perils of the sperm whale fishery at large, than to the individual cause. In that way, mostly, the disastrous encounter between Ahab and the whale had hitherto been popularly regarded.

And as for those who, previously hearing of the White Whale, by chance caught sight of him; in the beginning of the thing they had every one of them, almost, as boldly and fearlessly lowered for him, as for any other whale of that species. But at length, such calamities did ensue in these assaults—not restricted to sprained wrists and ankles, broken limbs, or devouring amputations—but fatal to the last degree of fatality; those repeated disastrous repulses, all accumulating and piling their terrors upon Moby-Dick; those things had gone far to shake the fortitude of many brave hunters, to whom the story of the White Whale had eventually come.

Nor did wild rumors of all sorts fail to exaggerate, and still the more horrify the true histories of these deadly encounters. For not only do fabulous rumors naturally grow out of the very body of all surprising terrible events—as the smitten tree gives birth to its fungi; but, in maritime life, far more than in that of terra firma, wild rumors abound, wherever there is any adequate reality for them to cling to. And as the sea surpasses the land in this matter, so the whale-fishery surpasses every other sort of maritime life, in the wonderfulness and fearfulness of the rumors which sometimes circulate there. For not only are whalemen as a body unexempt from that ignorance and superstitiousness hereditary to all sailors; but of all sailors, they are by all odds the most directly brought into contact with whatever is appallingly astonishing in the sea; face to face they not only eye its greatest marvels, but, hand to jaw, give battle to them. Alone, in such remotest waters, that though you sailed a thousand miles, and passed a thousand shores, you would not come to any chiseled hearthstone, or aught hospitable beneath that part of the sun; in such latitudes and longitudes, pursuing too such a calling as he does, the whaleman is wrapped by influences all tending to make his fancy pregnant with many a mighty birth.

No wonder, then, that ever gathering volume from the mere transit over the wildest watery spaces, the outblown rumors of the White Whale did in the end incorporate with themselves all manner of morbid hints, and half-formed fetal suggestions of supernatural agencies, which eventually invested Moby-Dick with new terrors unborrowed from anything that visibly appears. So that in many cases such a panic did he finally strike, that few who by those rumors, at least, had heard of the White Whale, few of those hunters were willing to encounter the perils of his jaw.

But there were still other and more vital practical influences at work. Not even at the present day has the original prestige of the sperm whale, as fearfully distinguished from all other species of the leviathan,[2] died out of the minds of the whalemen as a body. There are those this day among them, who, though intelligent and courageous enough in offering battle to the Greenland or right whale, would perhaps, either from professional inexperience, or incompetency, or timidity, decline a contest with the sperm whale; at any rate, there are plenty of whalemen, especially among those whaling nations not sailing under the American flag, who have never hostilely encountered the sperm whale, but whose sole knowledge of the leviathan is restricted to the ignoble monster primitively pursued in the North; seated on their hatches, these men will hearken with a childish fireside interest and awe, to the wild, strange tales of Southern whaling. Nor is the preeminent tremendousness of the great sperm whale anywhere more feelingly comprehended, than on board of those prows which stem him. . . .

So that overawed by the rumors and portents concerning him, not a few of the fishermen recalled, in reference to Moby-Dick, the earlier days of the sperm whale fishery, when it was

2. **leviathan** (lə·vī′ə·thən): huge sea monster.

WORDS TO OWN

ferocity (fə·räs′ə·tē) *n.:* fierce cruelty.

OPTIONS FOR TEACHING

INTEGRATING THE LANGUAGE ARTS

Strategic Reading Divide the class into mixed-ability pairs for an Echo Reading. Have the more confident reader read the story aloud while the less proficient reader follows along in the textbook and repeats.

Writing: Found Poem Ask students to review the selection and to choose eight words or phrases that best represent Moby-Dick, Ahab, or the chapter itself. Then, ask them to meet in groups of three and to narrow their choices to four words or phrases. Then, ask each group to read one word or phrase, without pausing between groups. Continue in this fashion until all words or phrases have been read. The groups will have composed a Found Poem.

Old Lighthouse Museum, Stonington, Connecticut.

Painted sternboard from the ship *Mary and Susan*.

oftentimes hard to induce long-practiced right whalemen to embark in the perils of this new and daring warfare; such men protesting that although other leviathans might be hopefully pursued, yet to chase and point lance at such an apparition as the sperm whale was not for mortal man. That to attempt it, would be inevitably to be torn into a quick eternity. On this head, there are some remarkable documents that may be consulted.

D Nevertheless, some there were, who even in the face of these things were ready to give chase to Moby-Dick; and a still greater number who, chancing only to hear of him distantly and vaguely, without the specific details of any certain calamity, and without superstitious accompaniments, were sufficiently hardy not to flee from the battle it offered.

One of the wild suggestings referred to, as at last coming to be linked with the White Whale in the minds of the superstitiously inclined, was the unearthly conceit that Moby-Dick was ubiquitous; that he had actually been encountered in opposite latitudes at one and the same instant of time.

Nor, credulous as such minds must have been, was this conceit altogether without some faint show of superstitious probability. For as the secrets of the currents in the seas have never yet been divulged, even to the most erudite research; so the hidden ways of the sperm whale when beneath the surface remain, in great part, unaccountable to his pursuers; and from time to time have originated the most curious and contradictory speculations regarding them, especially concerning the mystic modes whereby, after sounding to a great depth, he transports himself with such vast swiftness to the most widely distant points.

It is a thing well known to both American and English whale-ships, and as well a thing placed upon authoritative record years ago by Scoresby, that some whales have been captured far north in

Words to Own

apparition (ap′ə·rish′ən) *n.*: unexpected sight or ghostlike figure that appears suddenly.

ubiquitous (yo͞o·bik′wə·təs) *adj.*: everywhere at the same time.

erudite (er′yo͞o·dīt′) *adj.*: scholarly; well informed.

D. Reader's Response: Shaping Interpretations

? Given the horrible stories that are known about Moby-Dick, why do you suppose the men are willing to continue the search? [Sample responses: They have been worked into a frenzy by Ahab. Or they have their reputations as whalers to consider. Or they are afraid of Ahab.]

Cooperative Learning

Read All About It Have student groups create two newspaper articles of the whale tales mentioned in Ishmael's account. Ask them to write their articles in the spirit of Melville's time and to include illustrations. The articles could be front-page stories, editorials, feature stories, or lengthy obituaries. Ask two students in each group to be writers and the others to be managing editor, illustrator, researcher, and newsstand manager. The newsstand manager will be responsible for "selling" the papers to the class by calling out headlines and reading the articles.

Classroom Management

Setting Limits Set appropriate time limits for class presentations. For many students, three to five minutes is a good deal of time for a short presentation. With group work, be clear that students must accomplish their goals within a given time period, and monitor them so that they do not waste time. Depending on the emphasis you give an assignment or on the size of your class, you might want to allow more or less time for preparation and presentation.

RESPONDING TO THE ART: EXPLORING THE SUBJECT

Whaling ships carried small open boats that the whalers could maneuver close enough to a whale to harpoon it. When the whale became exhausted, they killed it with sharp lances. Onboard ship, whalers removed blubber from the whale and extracted oil from the blubber by cooking it in large iron pots. By 1850, many voyages could last as long as four or five years, with cargo ships carrying the oil to shore periodically so the whaling ship could continue hunting.

the Pacific, in whose bodies have been found the barbs of harpoons darted in the Greenland seas. Nor is it to be gainsaid, that in some of these instances it has been declared that the interval of time between the two assaults could not have exceeded very many days. Hence, by inference, it has been believed by some whalemen, that the Nor'west Passage,[3] so long a problem to man, was never a problem to the whale. . . .

Forced into familiarity, then, with such prodigies as these; and knowing that after repeated, intrepid assaults, the White Whale had escaped alive; it cannot be much matter of surprise that some whalemen should go still further in their superstitions; declaring Moby-Dick not only ubiquitous, but immortal (for immortality is but ubiquity in time); that though groves of spears should be planted in his flanks, he would still swim away unharmed; or if indeed he should ever be made to spout thick blood, such a sight would be but a ghastly deception; for again in unensanguined[4] billows hundreds of leagues away, his unsullied jet would once more be seen.

But even stripped of these supernatural surmisings, there was enough in the earthly make and incontestable character of the monster to strike the imagination with unwonted power. For, it was not so much his uncommon bulk that so much distinguished him from other sperm whales, but, as was elsewhere thrown out—a peculiar snow-white wrinkled forehead, and a high, pyramidical white hump. These were his prominent features; the tokens whereby, even in the limitless, uncharted seas, he revealed his identity, at a long distance, to those who knew him.

The rest of his body was so streaked, and spotted, and marbled with the same shrouded hue, that, in the end, he had gained his distinctive appellation of the White Whale; a name, indeed, literally justified by his vivid aspect, when seen gliding at high noon through a dark blue sea, leaving a milky-way wake of creamy foam, all spangled with golden gleamings.

Nor was it his unwonted magnitude, nor his remarkable hue, nor yet his deformed lower jaw, that so much invested the whale with natural terror, as that unexampled, intelligent malignity which, according to specific accounts, he had over and over again evinced in his assaults. More than all, his treacherous retreats struck more of dismay than perhaps aught else. For, when swimming before his exulting pursuers, with every apparent symptom of alarm, he had several times

A Whaling Scene (mid–19th century). Unsigned. Oil on canvas.

3. **Nor'west Passage:** nonexistent river, allegedly through Canada, that sailors believed connected the Atlantic and Pacific Oceans.
4. **unensanguined** (un·en·saŋ′gwind): unbloodied.

OPTIONS FOR TEACHING

CROSSING THE CURRICULUM

Social Sciences Have students research the construction of whaling ships, including the number and purposes of the decks on board, where and how the crew lived, the kinds of wood used, and the floor plan of the decks. Ask students to either build a model or illustrate the ship and the layout of the decks. Have them share their findings with the class. Display their work.

Science Ishmael distinguishes between right whalers and sperm whalers. If possible, invite a cetologist or oceanographer to class to discuss the differences between whales, especially right and sperm whales. If such experts are not available, have students research the differences and report to the class why right whalers would be reluctant to hunt sperm whales.

Health Have students research monomania and its history. They may want to consult psychologists as well as to read books and articles on the disorder. *You may want to obtain permission from parents or guardians and from the parties students will contact before they begin work on this activity.* Ask students to role-play a psychiatrist and to talk about the disorder, Ahab's behavior, and recommendations for treatment.

Peabody Essex Museum, Salem, Massachusetts. Photo by Mark Sexton (M17109).

been known to turn round suddenly, and, bearing down upon them, either stave[5] their boats to splinters, or drive them back in consternation to their ship.

Already several fatalities had attended his chase. But though similar disasters, however little bruited[6] ashore, were by no means unusual in the fishery; yet, in most instances, such seemed the White Whale's infernal aforethought of ferocity, that every dismembering or death that he caused, was not wholly regarded as having been inflicted by an unintelligent agent. **A**

Judge, then, to what pitches of inflamed, distracted fury the minds of his more desperate hunters were impelled, when amid the chips of chewed boats, and the sinking limbs of torn comrades, they swam out of the white curds of the whale's direful wrath into the serene, exasperating sunlight, that smiled on, as if at a birth or a bridal.

His three boats stove around him, and oars and men both whirling in the eddies, one captain, seizing the line-knife from his broken prow, had dashed at the whale, as an Arkansas duelist at his foe, blindly seeking with a six-inch blade to reach the fathom-deep life of the whale. That captain was Ahab. And then it was, that suddenly sweeping his sickle-shaped lower jaw beneath him, Moby-Dick had reaped away Ahab's leg, as a mower a blade of grass in the field. No turbaned Turk, no hired Venetian or Malay, could have smote him with more seeming malice. Small reason was there to doubt, then, that ever since that almost fatal encounter, Ahab had cherished a wild vindictiveness against the whale, all the more fell for that in his frantic morbidness he at last came to identify with him, not only all his bodily woes, but all his intellectual and spiritual exasperations. **B** The White Whale swam before him as the monomaniac incarnation of all those malicious agencies which some deep men feel eating in them, till they are left living on with half a heart and half a lung. That intangible malignity which has been from the beginning; to whose dominion even the modern Christians ascribe one-half of the worlds; which the ancient Ophites of the East reverenced in their statue devil—Ahab did not fall down and worship it like them; but deliriously transferring its idea to the abhorred White Whale, he pitted himself, all mutilated, against it. All that most maddens and torments; all that stirs up the lees of things; all truth with malice in it; all that cracks the sinews and cakes the brain; all the subtle

5. **stave:** smash.

6. **bruited** (brōōt′id): reported; rumored.

A. Exploring the Culture

Note the prejudice of the day. Whales were considered unintelligent and malign, whereas today we believe them to be the opposite.

B. Critical Reading: Analyzing Character

Moby-Dick and Captain Ahab may be equal foes in the sense that they are evenly and appropriately matched to do battle. To make the contest even more fitting, each foe hates the other with complete dedication. What motivates the whale to attack? ["That intangible malignity which has been [in it] from the beginning."] Why does Ahab seek revenge? [Moby Dick had sliced off his leg like a mower cuts "a blade of grass in the field."] Are they equal foes? [Possible answers: Yes, either may vanquish the other. No, the whale seems to have a greater advantage because of its size.]

PROBLEM SOLVING/CRITICAL THINKING

Rumor Has a Thousand Tongues Ishmael relates two accounts that place Moby-Dick in opposite latitudes at the same time. Ask students what the characters in *Moby-Dick* should have done when faced with conflicting accounts. Ask students how the characters could have ascertained the truth—or falsity—of divergent claims. Then, have students discuss how the high school senior should respond in the following hypothetical situation.

One high school senior is considering applying to a local university. A student at the university claims that he knows people who had low SAT scores but were admitted. Another student who attends the university states that she does not know of anyone who got into the school with an SAT score below 1250 and that the university students all have grade-point averages of at least 3.0. ☞

A. Reader's Response: Connecting with the Text

? What other characters in stories, books, movies, or television shows exhibit symptoms of monomania? [Sample responses: The narrator of Poe's "The Tell-Tale Heart," Dr. Frankenstein, Captain Nemo from Jules Verne's *Twenty Thousand Leagues Under the Sea,* and Khan from *Star Trek II: The Wrath of Khan.*]

demonisms of life and thought; all evil, to crazy Ahab, were visibly personified, and made practically assailable in Moby-Dick. He piled upon the whale's white hump the sum of all the general rage and hate felt by his whole race from Adam down; and then, as if his chest had been a mortar, he burst his hot heart's shell upon it.

A It is not probable that this monomania in him took its instant rise at the precise time of his bodily dismemberment. Then, in darting at the monster, knife in hand, he had but given loose to a sudden, passionate, corporal animosity; and when he received the stroke that tore him, he probably but felt the agonizing bodily laceration, but nothing more. Yet, when by this collision forced to turn toward home, and for long months of days and weeks, Ahab and anguish lay stretched together in one hammock, rounding in midwinter that dreary, howling Patagonian Cape; then it was, that his torn body and gashed soul bled into one another; and so interfusing, made him mad. That it was only then, on the homeward voyage, after the encounter, that the final monomania seized him, seems all but certain from the fact that, at intervals during the passage, he was a raving lunatic; and, though unlimbed of a leg, yet such vital strength yet lurked in his Egyptian chest, and was moreover intensified by his delirium, that his mates were forced to lace him fast, even there, as he sailed, raving in his hammock. In a straitjacket, he swung to the mad rockings of the gales. And, when running into more sufferable latitudes, the ship, with mild stunsails spread, floated across the tranquil tropics, and, to all appearances, the old man's delirium seemed left behind him with the Cape Horn swells, and he came forth from his dark den into the blessed light and air; even then, when he bore that firm, collected front, however pale, and issued his calm orders once again; and his mates thanked God the direful madness was now gone; even then, Ahab, in his hidden self, raved on. Human madness is oftentimes a cunning and most feline thing. When you think it fled, it may have but become transfigured into some still subtler form. Ahab's full lunacy subsided not, but deepeningly contracted; like the unabated Hudson, when that noble Northman flows narrowly, but unfathomably through the Highland gorge. But, as in his narrow-flowing monomania, not one jot of Ahab's broad madness had been left behind;

OPTIONS FOR TEACHING

PROFESSIONAL NOTES

Critical Comment: Characters' Changing Behavior An editor of Melville's shorter works, Warner Berthoff, writes: "Some of the liveliest sequences in Melville's fiction occur when characters normally at ease with themselves and their attitude to life (like the fine old lawyer of 'Bartleby') are overborne by some strange new phenomenon of behavior and carried quite out of themselves by sudden excitement." Have students discuss which characters are swept away by excitement in *Moby-Dick* and to what degree they are "overborne."

so in that broad madness, not one jot of his great natural intellect had perished. That before living agent, now became the living instrument. If such a furious trope[7] may stand, his special lunacy stormed his general sanity, and carried it, and turned all its concentrated cannon upon its own mad mark; so that far from having lost his strength, Ahab, to that one end, did now possess a thousandfold more potency than ever he had sanely brought to bear upon any one reasonable object. . . .

Now, in his heart, Ahab had some glimpse of this, namely: all my means are sane, my motive and my object mad. Yet without power to kill, or change, or shun the fact, he likewise knew that to mankind he did long dissemble; in some sort, did still. But that thing of his dissembling was only subject to his perceptibility, not to his will determinate. Nevertheless, so well did he succeed in that dissembling, that when with ivory leg he stepped ashore at last, no Nantucketer thought him otherwise than but naturally grieved, and that to the quick, with the terrible casualty which had overtaken him. **B**

The report of his undeniable delirium at sea was likewise popularly ascribed to a kindred cause. And so too, all the added moodiness which always afterward, to the very day of sailing in the *Pequod* on the present voyage, sat brooding on his brow. Nor is it so very unlikely, that far from distrusting his fitness for another whaling voyage, on account of such dark symptoms, the calculating people of that prudent isle were inclined to harbor the conceit, that for those very reasons he was all the better qualified and set on edge, for a pursuit so full of rage and wildness as the bloody hunt of whales. Gnawed within and scorched without, with the unfixed, unrelenting fangs of some incurable idea; such an one, could he be found, would seem the very man to dart his iron and lift his lance against the most appalling of all brutes. Or, if for any reason thought to be corporeally incapacitated for that, yet such an one would seem superlatively competent to cheer and howl on his underlings to the attack. But be all this as it may, certain it is, that with the mad secret of his unabated rage bolted up and keyed in him, Ahab had purposely sailed upon the present voyage with the one only and all-engrossing object of hunting the White Whale. Had any one of his old acquaintances on shore but half dreamed of what was lurking in him then, how soon would their aghast and righteous souls have wrenched the ship from such a fiendish man! They were bent on profitable cruises, the profit to be counted down in dollars from the mint. He was intent on an audacious, immitigable, and supernatural revenge.

Here, then, was this gray-headed, ungodly old man, chasing with curses a Job's whale[8] round the world, at the head of a crew, too, chiefly made up of mongrel renegades, and castaways, and cannibals—morally enfeebled, also, by the incompetence of mere unaided virtue or right-mindedness in Starbuck, the invulnerable jollity of indifference and recklessness in Stubb, and the pervading mediocrity in Flask. Such a crew, so officered, seemed specially picked and packed by some infernal fatality to help him to his monomaniac revenge. How it was that they so aboundingly responded to the old man's ire—by what evil magic their souls were possessed, that at times his hate seemed almost theirs; the White Whale as much their insufferable foe as his; how all this came to be—what the White Whale was to them, or how to their unconscious understandings, also, in some dim, unsuspected way, he might have seemed the gliding great demon of the seas of life—all this to explain, would be to dive deeper than Ishmael can go. The subterranean miner that works in us all, how can one tell whither leads his shaft by the ever shifting, muffled sound of his pick? Who does not feel the irresistible arm drag? **C** What skiff in tow of a seventy-four[9] can stand still? For one, I gave myself up to the abandonment of the time and the place; but while yet all a-rush to encounter the whale, could see naught in that brute but the deadliest ill.

7. **trope** (trōp): figure of speech.

8. **Job's whale:** curse or affliction. In the Bible, Job was visited with grievous afflictions as a test of his faith in God.

9. **skiff . . . seventy-four:** small boat being pulled by a larger one.

WORDS TO OWN

incapacitated (in'kə·pas'ə·tāt'id) *adj.:* disabled.

B. Reader's Response: Challenging the Text

Note that the first-person narrator, Ishmael, shows us the inner thoughts of another character, Ahab. This is technically a violation of sound creative writing principles. There is no confrontation scene between Ishmael and Ahab in *Moby-Dick,* yet it was important to show us something of Ahab's inner life, so Melville resorted to this method. Does the method work? Would you recommend it to other writers? Explain. [Sample responses: No, the switching back and forth is too confusing and does not seem realistic. Or yes, there is no other way to show the hate Ahab has. If that is the only way to show it, then other writers should use the same technique.]

C. Reader's Response: Shaping Interpretations

? What does Ishmael mean by "the subterranean miner that works in us all"? [Sample responses: Forces of evil, our unconscious, or our fate.]

ASSESSMENT TOOLS

Observation Assessment: Reading As students write and discuss their responses to the chapter, use the following points to assess their performance.

1=Rarely 2=Sometimes 3=Often

_____1. Makes personal connections

_____2. Attends to lengthy nar

Check Test: True-False

"Moby-Dick"

1. Ishmael's excitement about hunting for Moby-Dick is unclouded by dread. [False]
2. The white color is not the only distinctive feature of Moby-Dick. [True]
3. When the whale takes his leg, Ahab loses all will to live. [False]
4. The people of Nantucket know Ahab as a demented man. [False]
5. Ishmael believes that nothing good can come of the search for Moby-Dick. [True]

Making Meanings

First Thoughts

1. Possible responses: "The subterranean miner that works in us all," because it is a frightening thought; or "Human madness is oftentimes a cunning and most feline thing," because the statement reminds me of Poe's work.

Reviewing the Text

Possible responses: "Nevertheless, some there were, who even in the face of these things were ready to give chanse to Moby-Dick." Ahab "was a raving lunatic." "Here, then, was a gray-headed, ungodily old man, chasing with curses a Job's whale round the world." These statements characterize some of the sailors and Ahab.

Shaping Interpretations

2. According to Ishmael, Ahab became monomaniacal sometime after his encounter with Moby-Dick, during the long months of his recuperation. After the attack, Ahab pretends to have recovered from his madness. Ahab's rational demeanor convinces the people of Nantucket that he is fit to be captain of another whaling voyage.
3. They suggest that he is ubiquitous, or present everywhere, and that he is immortal. The effect builds up suspense and horror.
4. The narrator's attitude seems ambiguous. On the one hand, he says he is "all a-rush to encounter the whale." On the other hand, he calls Ahab an "ungodly old man" and refers to the crew as a collection of "mongrel renegades, and castaways, and cannibals." He feels that the whale itself represents the "deadliest ill." Ishmael underscores the idea of fate, referring to the "infernal fatality" of this particular crew turning up to help the captain in his "monomaniac revenge."
5. Melville refers several times to the diversity of races, outlooks, and backgrounds among the members of the ship's crew, and several references in the last paragraph of the chapter convey a generalized picture of the *Pequod's* voyage, so that it may be regarded as symbolic of humanity's voyage as a whole. Ishmael refers to Ahab chasing a Job's whale "round the world." And in wondering about his mixed feelings, he uses the arresting image of "The subterranean miner that works in us all"—doubt and fear are compared to the sounds of a miner's pick deep below the surface of our conscious minds.

Extending the Text

6. **(Synthesis)** Possible response: In the physical description of Moby-Dick, Melville pictures the whale "seen gliding at high noon through a dark blue sea, leaving a milky-way wake of creamy foam, all spangled with golden gleamings." These contradictory qualities appear in volcanoes, storms, fires, and predators.

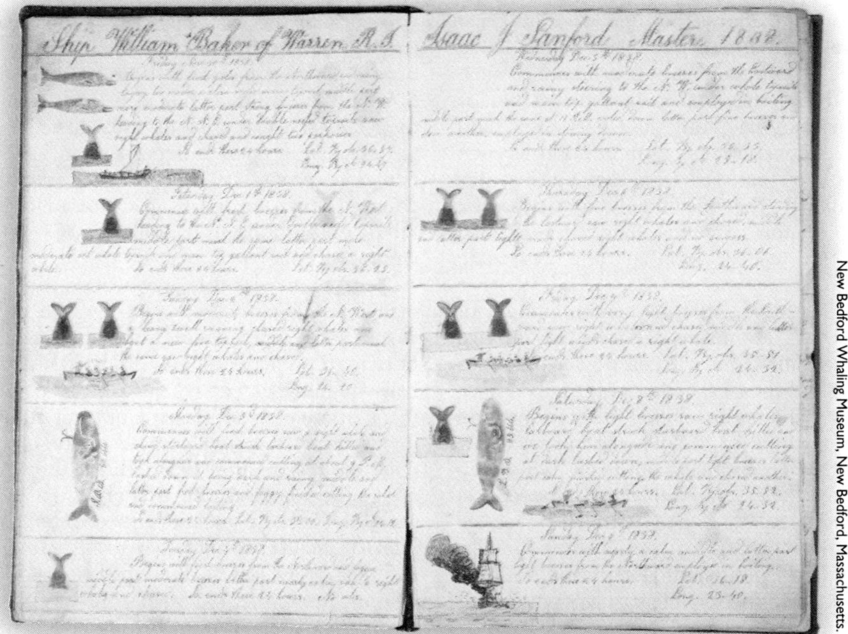
Ship William Baker of Warren R. I. Isaac J Sanford Master

New Bedford Whaling Museum, New Bedford, Massachusetts.

Page from whaling logbook.

MAKING MEANINGS

First Thoughts

1. What idea or statement in this chapter did you respond to most strongly? Explain.

> **Reviewing the Text**
>
> With a partner or two, write down all the passages in this chapter that you think are especially significant.

Shaping Interpretations

2. According to Ishmael, how did Ahab become monomaniacal, or obsessed with one idea? After Moby-Dick's attack, how is Ahab's rational behavior deceptive—but how does it also help him toward his goal?
3. What supernatural qualities do the sailors attribute to Moby-Dick? What is the effect of turning Moby-Dick into a mythical monster?
4. The final paragraph draws a picture of the *Pequod's* crew as they travel the world's oceans on Ahab's quest. What is the narrator's attitude here toward the ship's captain, the crew, and the quest?
5. In what sense can the ship and its company be seen as a microcosm—a world in miniature—and as a **symbol** for the "ship" of humanity?

Extending the Text

6. What **images** used to describe Moby-Dick in this chapter suggest beauty as well as horror? Can you think of any other instances (from life or literature) where these two qualities are combined in one person or event or thing?

Choices: Building Your Portfolio

Writer's Notebook

1. Collecting Ideas for a Controversial Issue

Melville's novel is full of ideas that you could use as the focus of a persuasive essay. For example, take notes on the passages you recorded with your partner (page 328): Would any of these give you a topic for an essay? How does the passage connect to life today, in your opinion? What do you think the passage means? Do you disagree with the passage? Save your notes for the Writer's Workshop on page 331.

WORK IN PROGRESS

Critical Writing

2. Who Knows, Exactly?

The British novelist and poet D. H. Lawrence wrote this about *Moby-Dick*:

> A hunt. The last great hunt.
> For what?
> For Moby-Dick, the huge white sperm whale: who is old, hoary, monstrous, and swims alone; who is unspeakably terrible in his wrath, having so often been attacked; and snow-white.
> Of course he is a symbol.
> Of what?
> I doubt that even Melville knew exactly. That's the best of it.
> —D. H. Lawrence

In a brief essay, explain what you think Moby-Dick **symbolizes**—insofar as you can tell from what you've read. Cite passages to support your interpretation.

Critical Thinking / Speaking and Listening

3. Analyzing Ahab

In a discussion, analyze the **character** of Captain Ahab. To prepare your analysis, gather your data in a chart like the following:

What we know about Ahab:	
From his speech	
From his actions	
From his appearance	
From his thoughts	

Critical Writing

4. Transcendentally Speaking

Write a brief essay comparing Ahab's **monologue** in "The Quarter-Deck" (beginning on page 317 with "Hark ye yet again . . .") to Transcendentalist ideas. In what ways does the speech reflect Transcendentalist thought, and in what ways does it reject it? (For a review of Transcendentalist ideas, see pages 210–212.) In your essay, you might want to include quotations from Emerson or Thoreau.

Creative Writing

5. The Voice of Ahab

We hear the events of *Moby-Dick* from Ishmael's **point of view.** Now let Captain Ahab speak. In two or three paragraphs, write his thoughts on the night after the ritual on the quarter-deck. What does Ahab want? What does he fear? How does he feel about the crew?

Crossing the Curriculum: Science

6. Where Are the Whales?

Prepare a brief oral report to your class on some aspect of whales or whaling that interests you: for example, what the major types of whales are, how the whale population has changed since the 1850s, what whaling activities continue today, and what efforts have been made to preserve whales from extinction. Accompany your report with visual supports such as graphs, maps, or photographs.

Choices: Building Your Portfolio

1. **Writer's Notebook** Remind students to save their work. They may use it as prewriting for the Writer's Workshop on p. 331.
2. **Critical Writing** Read aloud D. H. Lawrence's comments about *Moby-Dick,* and discuss the symbolism students see in the great white whale.
3. **Critical Thinking/Speaking and Listening** Have students conduct their discussions in groups of varying abilities. Suggest that groups begin their discussions by assigning these specific roles to group members: facilitator, questioner, clarifier.
4. **Critical Writing** Before students begin writing, suggest that they work in pairs to organize their ideas by noting differences and similarities between Ahab's monologue and Transcendentalist ideas on a Venn diagram such as the one on Transparency 5 in the Transparency Package.
5. **Creative Writing** Before students begin writing, have them work in pairs to review their Reader's Logs and the questions in Making Meanings for "The Quarter-Deck" chapter.
6. **Crossing the Curriculum: Science** Some students may prefer to work in small groups, with each person responsible for presenting a specific aspect of the report.

PORTFOLIO ASSESSMENT

Choices: Assessment Criteria For help in evaluating these Choices assignments, see the criteria in the ***Portfolio Management System,*** pp. 105–106.

STRATEGIES FOR INCLUSION

Auditory Some students may benefit by orally presenting their conclusions in activity #1. Remind students that in writing a strong conclusion, they might sum up their most important ideas, repeat their strongest arguments, or give a call to action—something they want their audience to do. Have students work in pairs to try out their conclusions with each other.

Visual For activity #6, show the class a documentary on whales or whaling. Point out how the documentary presents factual information. Suggest that students include this information in their reports. Invite them to use visual aids, such as pictures or charts, in their presentations.

Read On

Portfolio Assessment Options

The following projects can help you evaluate and assess your students' reading accomplishments outside of class. The completed projects, including videotapes, may be kept as part of the students' portfolios.

- **Plan a Movie** Students can work on a proposal for a movie to be made from one of the Shirley Jackson stories or one of the stories of fantastic literature. The proposal can be in the form of a looseleaf or bound notebook and can contain photographs, pictures, sketches, and an outline. In preparing their proposals, students might consider the following questions: Which Hollywood actors will have the main roles? What will the main set look like? What will the movie's title be? What music will be played during opening and closing credits? What lighting and special effects will be necessary? Will the entire story be used?
- **Create an Editorial Comic Strip** Students can develop an editorial comic strip based on one of the nonfiction selections. Suggest that students first come up with a one- or two-sentence summary of the author's main idea and then think of an effective way to illustrate this concept in a short series of panels.
- **Videotape an Interview** Students who have read the same book might enjoy playing the roles of interviewer and interviewee. One student can dress as a TV news reporter and prepare a list of questions. The other student can use props and dress that is appropriate to the interviewee and prepare answers to the questions. After students feel confident with their presentation, a third student can videotape their encounter.

Time Is But a Stream

In *The Survival of the Bark Canoe* (Farrar, Straus & Giroux), John McPhee explores the New England wilderness on a no-frills paddling trip in a handmade birch-bark canoe, much as Henry David Thoreau once did. Thoreau's own journey is chronicled in *A Week on the Concord and Merrimack Rivers* (Ticknor and Fields).

Civil Disobedience

In the struggle for India's independence, Mohandas K. (Mahatma) Gandhi successfully put Thoreau's ideas on nonviolent resistance into action to effect change. Gandhi's successes helped inspire Martin Luther King, Jr., in the United States. Find out more about Gandhi's achievements in *An Autobiography: The Story of My Experiments with Truth* (Greenleaf Books) and in the award-winning film *Gandhi* (1982), directed by Richard Attenborough and featuring Ben Kingsley in the title role.

More Unwholesome Houses

Shirley Jackson's eerie fiction often focuses on houses that are not quite . . . normal. In *We Have Always Lived in the Castle* (Viking Press), two odd sisters live in the strangest house in town. In *The Haunting of Hill House* (Viking Penguin), a group of psychics tries to discover if Hill House really *is* haunted. The latter book was adapted into a classic horror film, *The Haunting* (1963), directed by Robert Wise and starring Julie Harris.

A Smorgasbord of Scares

The critic Alberto Manguel defines "fantastic literature"—including horror, fantasy, and magic realism—as "the impossible seeping into the possible." *Black Water* and *Black Water 2* (Clarkson N. Potter), edited by Manguel, are anthologies of short "fantastic literature" by an international list of authors including Edgar Allan Poe, Nathaniel Hawthorne, Julio Cortázar, Ursula K. Le Guin, and Ryunosuke Akutagawa.

Save the Whales

As a result of all that nineteenth-century whaling, whales are endangered in our own century. The Canadian environmentalist Farley Mowat pleads for the preservation of these intelligent creatures in *A Whale for the Killing* (Little, Brown), his real-life account of a tormented whale trapped in a Newfoundland tide pool.

FOR FURTHER EXPLORATION

Novels
An American Childhood by Annie Dillard
Night by Elie Wiesel

Poetry
"To a Skylark" by Percy Bysshe Shelley
Poems of Edgar Allan Poe selected by Dwight Macdonald
"What I Expected" by Stephen Spender

Nonfiction
Bare Bones edited by Tim Underwood and Chuck Miller

Movies
Dracula (1931)
Frankenstein (1931)
A River Runs Through It

BUILDING YOUR PORTFOLIO

Writer's Workshop

PERSUASIVE WRITING

Controversial Issue

In "Resistance to Civil Government," Thoreau tries to persuade people to look at government in a new way—a way that certainly not everyone would agree with. Disagreement is the essence of controversy, and a controversial issue is one that reasonable people can argue convincingly from both sides. Many current local, national, and world events qualify as controversial issues, since people may take sides on them. When you take up a controversial issue in writing, your primary goals are to communicate your views on the issue and to persuade your readers to take your position seriously—even to change their minds. To achieve these goals, you will draw on an arsenal of persuasive techniques to present and defend your point of view.

Prewriting

1. **Finding out what you care about.** If you've kept any of the Writer's Notebook activities from these collections, you might already have ideas for a controversial issue you'd like to write about. If not, one way to generate ideas for an issue worth writing about is to list topics. On a piece of paper, draw a vertical line down the center. In the left-hand column, brainstorm a list of controversial topics. Your possible topics could relate to your town, your city, your state, or the nation, or they might be suggested by subjects you've been studying in school. (Controversy can even stem from a literary work: Did Madeline Usher really come back from the dead? Was there really a raven in the young scholar's room?) In the right-hand column, write ideas for possible issues connected with these topics. List the ideas in question form. For example, your list might include the topic "drinking among young people." A question suggested by this topic might be, "Should the drinking age be raised to twenty-three?" If you want to explore a controversial literary issue, your list could include relevant quotations from a story or poem you want to work with. Think of issues that have not only captured your intellectual interest, but also stirred your emotions.

   Another way to discover current controversial issues is to read the editorial page in your local newspaper and to closely watch television news programs. Should your city have a teen curfew? Should your state require helmets for bicycle riders? Should the federal government set aside land to protect an endangered species? In each case, the issue is a matter of dispute about which reasonable people disagree.

Technology HELP

See Writer's Workshop 2 CD-ROM. *Assignment: Controversial Issue.*

Assignment
Write an essay in which you take a stand on a controversial issue that you feel strongly about.

Aim
To shape your audience's feelings and related opinions; to persuade them to take your position seriously; to urge an audience to take an action or change a stance on an issue.

Audience
Individuals or a group interested in your issue; your teacher; your classmates.

QUICK PLANNING GUIDE

Controversial Issue

PROGRAM MANAGER

Computer Guided Instruction For a related assignment on controversial issues that students may use as additional instruction, see *Writer's Workshop 2.*

PORTFOLIO ASSESSMENT

- **Generating Ideas** To help students in prewriting, use the heuristic in the *Portfolio Management System,* p. 107.
- **Assessment Rubric** For a rubric that can be used to assess students' progress in writing, see the *Portfolio Management System,* p. 109.

Motivation

Bring in editorial pages from regional newspapers to give students some ideas about controversial issues. You also might provide samples of editorials and letters to the editor in national news, sports, or humanities magazines so that students see a broader range of possible issues. Students should select a topic that will be interesting to their intended audience.

- Which issues are intended for specific interest groups?
- Which issues is the general population apt to be interested in?
- Which issues are likely to spark an interest among students?

Teaching the Lesson

- This lesson includes an excerpt from Thoreau's "Resistance to Civil Government" as a model for the use of connotative language.
- This lesson includes instruction for each stage of the writing process. Guide students by modeling each stage with your own writing, or work with students as a class to construct a class model.

Try It Out: Possible Answers

1. teenage curfews
2. freedom of speech
3. the minimum wage
4. homelessness

Try It Out

Find a possible topic for a controversial issue essay by completing one or more of these sentences:

1. There really ought to be a law against _____.
2. One right I think is in jeopardy today is _____.
3. If I could change anything about life in the United States today, I'd change _____.
4. I really think people need to get together and do something about _____.

Strategies for Elaboration: Finding a Topic

- Read the Letters to the Editor sections in your school and local newspapers.
- Watch local and national news programs on television.
- Discuss current controversial issues with family and friends.
- Go over your Reader's Log and other class notes to find a controversial literary issue you might want to argue.
- Consider both sides of the issues that interest you, and develop a point of view for each issue.

2. **Selecting and defining one issue.** Put an asterisk next to the topics about which you have the strongest feelings and have the most to say. Share these preferred topics with one or two classmates, explaining your positions on these topics. (Listen to the ideas of your peers, too, to help them clarify their thinking.) Talking about your topics will help you to decide which one interests you the most. Use these questions to help you make a final decision:
   - Is the issue important to you?
   - Can the issue be argued, and can the arguments be supported with evidence? (For example, whether living in the city is better than living in the country is a matter of personal preference; it can't be supported with evidence.)
   - Is there an audience that is interested in this topic and that you would like to convince?
3. **Trying out a position statement.** Write a brief, direct statement of where you stand on the issue. This is your **position statement,** or **proposition**—the thesis statement of your persuasive essay. For example, if your question is "Should there be a teen curfew to curtail juvenile crime?" then your position statement might read, "The most effective way to cut down on juvenile crime in our city is to implement a teen curfew." Your position statement might be one, two, or three sentences long. In many cases, the position statement indicates one or two broad, fundamental reasons for the writer's position.
4. **Setting up a pro-con table.** It's important that you understand and anticipate all the arguments and counterarguments that your issue gives rise to. Make a two-column chart labeled "Pro" on the left-hand side and "Con" on the right-hand side. In the Pro column, jot down all the reasons you can think of for the "in favor" side of the issue; in the Con column, list all the reasons you can think of for the "against" side. (See page 333 for an example.)
5. **Listing arguments and counterarguments.** Using your pro-con table as a basis, write a more extensive list of possible arguments to support your side and a list of possible counterarguments, or **rebuttals,** for the other view. Once again, share your prewriting with a group of classmates. They might provide reasons that you have overlooked, and they can comment upon the validity of the arguments you have thought of.

OPTIONS FOR TEACHING

STRATEGIES FOR INCLUSION

Auditory To help students evaluate their essays before they revise them, suggest that they record their drafts on audiotape or have partners record them. Then, they may listen to their work, stopping the tape at places that do not flow well or that need strengthening. After students have made some written revisions, they may again record their essays to hear how they sound.

Logical-Mathematical Encourage students to use an informal poll as part of the evidence supporting their positions. For example, if students are writing in favor of the mandatory use of seatbelts, they could poll their classmates to see how many agree. If they are writing in favor of exempting certain students from final exams, they could devise a questionnaire to find out the conditions students would propose.

Advanced Students might want to take this assignment one step further by planning complete advertising campaigns to get their positions across. They need to determine what kind of media exposure would be most effective, how they would present their positions, and who would represent them. They should display or present their campaigns by hanging visuals in the classroom or hall or by playing audiotapes or videotapes to their classmates.

What happens if, as you collect arguments for and against the issue, you come across an opposing argument that you can't refute? In fairness, you can't just ignore such an argument; you must acknowledge it and affirm its validity. This is called **conceding a point.** It's not a weakness to give the opposing side a nod; in fact, it's a sign of strength that shows you have thoroughly considered all sides and are being fair.

Model

Topic: Should there be a citywide teen curfew?

Pro	Con
controls gang violence	prohibits legitimate activities
minimizes auto accidents	requires expanded police force
reduces underage drinking	further overloads justice system with people who may have broken no other law
minimizes vandalism	takes away liberties from those not involved in criminal activities

6. **Searching for evidence.** You should do some research to find objective, reliable, intellectual support for your position. This may include library research to find irrefutable facts—statistics, examples, and anecdotes. It may also include interviews with people who, as authorities on the issue, can offer expert opinions. Brainstorm a list of possible research sources you can consult for evidence in support of your issue. Then begin your search.

Communications Handbook HELP

Taking notes and documenting sources: pages 1210–1213.

Drafting

1. **Your credibility is at stake.** To be truly effective, your essay will have to be well reasoned, with plenty of support that no one could argue with—examples, expert opinions, quotations, statistics—any kind of evidence that makes a good case for your position. You may want to emphasize logic. Or you may want to appeal more to your readers' emotions. Regardless of the approach you choose, you must argue your position forcefully and deal convincingly with arguments against your stance.
2. **Crafting an effective introduction.** In persuasive writing, it's important to make your readers care about the issue from the outset. Get them to realize that the issue affects them—even if they're on the other side. Begin with an attention-getting anecdote or example, a surprising statistic, or a single memorable sentence or rhetorical question. (A rhetorical question is a question asked to make people think; it is not a "real" question that actually requires an answer. See page 105.) Then, clearly identify the issue, and state your position on it.
3. **Organizing your work.** There are three major ways to organize a controversial issue essay:
   - **Order of importance.** You can develop your argument according to order of importance, beginning with either the most important or the least important reason for supporting your position. If, for example, you

Prewriting

If students have difficulty thinking of controversial issues that interest them, suggest some of the following topics.

- raising the age at which one can get a driver's license
- switching to year-round schools
- having all-night prom lock-ins
- raising the number of credits needed for graduation
- tying driver's licenses to passing grades
- requiring community service for graduation

As students make their lists, remind them that for a topic to be controversial it must have two defensible sides. For example, someone could argue for or against a ban on smoking in a restaurant. However, a person could not argue that smoking is good for one's physical health.

Drafting

Students might find the following chart helpful in organizing their essays.

Position Statement:
Supporting Evidence
1. ____________________
2. ____________________
3. ____________________
Counterargument: ____________________
Rebuttal: ____________________
Restatement of Thesis: ____________________

INTEGRATING THE LANGUAGE ARTS

Language and Style Using words that influence an audience is important when writing about a controversial subject. To give students more practice in recognizing connotation, have them list synonyms for the words *eat* and *odor.* Divide the synonyms into three groups: positive connotation, neutral connotation, and negative connotation, as on the following chart. Then, have students go back to their own writing and circle words whose connotations do not strengthen their position. Have student pairs propose better terms for each other's papers.

	Eat	Odor
Positive Connotation	[dine]	[fragrance]
Neutral Connotation	[consume]	[smell]
Negative Connotation	[gulp]	[stench]

begin with the most important reason, then you would move methodically through your other reasons, ending with the least important. It's often more effective to save the heaviest ammunition for last, leading from the least to the most important reason.

- **Chronological order.** The order in which events occur in time is chronological order. Presenting your reasons in this order is especially helpful in making cause-and-effect relationships clear.
- **Logical order.** In logical order, you present your opponents' positions or arguments and then present your refutations of them through comparison and contrast. You may present all the objections first, followed by all your rebuttals; or you may move back and forth from each objection to its respective rebuttal.

4. **Using logical appeals.** Rather than merely listing abstract arguments to support your position, make your arguments concrete. Whenever possible, use your library research to add documented facts, anecdotes, quotations, and expert opinions. Provide real-life examples of the causes and effects of the position you are arguing for or against. An extended example, or case study, can sometimes be sustained throughout most of an essay or even be used as an organizational device. Well-reasoned hypothetical examples, or scenarios, can sometimes be used for support as well, especially if you make the scenario believable. All of these are **logical appeals**—appeals that are made to the audience's reason. Logical appeals include both reasons and evidence, and they make your arguments more appealing to the audience because they engender trust. They also make it harder for the other side to challenge you and for your audience to reject your reasoning. But watch out for *overgeneralizations* (broad statements that lack sufficient supporting detail), *oversimplification* (concentrating on only one or a few aspects of a complex issue), and other lapses in logic. Proof that your thinking is sloppy and lacks objectivity can diminish your audience's trust in you.

Communications Handbook HELP

Preparing for the debate (Logical Fallacies): pages 1215–1216.

5. **Appealing to emotions.** The power of persuasive writing resides not just in logical argument, but also in emotional appeals. To develop emotional appeals, think about the evidence you've collected that will speak to your readers' hearts more than to their minds: Examples, vivid details, anecdotes, and personal experiences can all be used effectively in appealing to people's emotions. One emotional appeal for teen curfews might focus on the fear older people feel when they encounter a group of teenagers on the street after dark.
6. **The power of loaded words.** You are using emotional appeals when you take advantage of the power of **connotative language.** Every word has a **denotative meaning**—its dictionary definition—as well as its **connotative meaning**—the feelings or attitudes the word suggests. Words like *integrity, honor,* and *steadfastness* have positive associations, or connotations, and if you used them in describing a political candidate, you would be giving him or her excellent "press." But words like *rigidity, self-interest,* and *stubbornness* have some negative connotations, and your candidate would come off looking less desirable if you used those words in connection with

OPTIONS FOR TEACHING

INTEGRATING THE LANGUAGE ARTS

Usage Have students check their writing for sentences that have parallel ideas. Remind students to link ideas in a sentence by placing them in the same grammatical form. Refer them to the Language Workshop on p. 338. Have students check their work to see if they can improve balance in their sentences by using parallel structure.

Strategic Reading Have students read their rough drafts aloud to themselves. When they stumble over a phrase or have to re-read a sentence, they should mark that place in their essays. Then, they can go back and see whether that section needs revision. If a student has difficulty understanding his or her own meaning, other readers are likely to have difficulty also. Have them revise where needed.

COOPERATIVE LEARNING

Informal Debate Have an even-numbered small group of students work together on a controversial issue. Half of the students should take one position and the other half should take the opposing stand. Each student should prepare part of the argument supporting the position. Students also must anticipate the counterarguments. Each side should present its position to the class. Then, have each side give a two-minute rebuttal.

him or her. Connotative words are "loaded" words that pack a punch. Used sparingly and carefully, they will cause readers to become not only intellectually involved, but emotionally involved as well. Consider the following example from Thoreau's "Resistance to Civil Government."

Model

> I saw that, if there was a *wall of stone* between me and my townsmen, there was a still more *difficult* one to climb or *break through*, before they could get to be as free as I was. I did not for a moment feel *confined*, and the walls seemed a great waste of *stone and mortar*. I felt as if I alone of all my townsmen had paid my tax. They plainly did not know how to treat me, but behaved like persons who are *underbred*. In every *threat* and in every compliment there was a *blunder;* for they thought that my chief desire was to stand the other side of that *stone wall*.
>
> —Henry David Thoreau

The italicized words and phrases have strong connotative meanings. In choosing these particular words, Thoreau is able to evoke an emotional response that extends beyond the literal meaning of the passage. His feelings about the restrictive nature of government come through loud and clear.

7. **Audience.** When writing about a controversial issue, it's crucial to consider your audience's response, since affecting their opinions is your primary goal. Think about how much your audience already knows about your issue, and provide background information accordingly. Also, think about whether they are likely to agree or disagree with your position. If they are inclined to disagree, put yourself in their shoes: What counterarguments will be the most compelling? What points might you have to concede? Be sure you present your rebuttals as effectively as you can.
8. **Tone.** Regardless of subject or audience, the tone of a controversial issue essay should be committed, confident, and sincere. How formal it is depends on your subject and audience. A letter to the editor, for example, might be direct and personal and might contain contractions, colloquial language, and humor. On the other hand, a class essay exploring a controversial issue in literature is likely to be more formal and serious.
9. **Closing your essay.** The conclusion of your essay should leave the audience feeling that an issue has been adequately and fairly explored. You might repeat your position statement at the end but in different words than those used at the beginning. Or, you might make a strong statement about what might happen if the course of action you recommend is not followed. In this case, your final sentence might briefly describe the positive outcome that you think would result if your course of action is taken. Some writers use their conclusions to encourage opposing sides to work together in new ways. Others end with a call to action aimed solely at their supporters. The

Strategies for Elaboration

Here's how you might use connotative language if your issue were the pros and cons of a teenage curfew. If you were in favor of a curfew, you might select words and phrases with strong negative connotations, such as "danger," "the dead of night," "gunfire," "treacherous roads," and "out of control." (Later, in your closing, you might choose words or phrases with strong positive connotations, such as "safe," "family time," "together," and so forth.)

CROSSING THE CURRICULUM

Social Sciences People whose names appear in history books often took positions or made decisions that sparked controversy. It often takes years before others can judge the importance or value of these actions. Have students pretend that they are one of the people who took a stand—such as President Franklin Roosevelt declaring war on Japan, President Harry S. Truman dropping atomic bombs on Hiroshima and Nagasaki, Cesar Chavez calling for grape and lettuce boycotts in California, or Rosa Parks refusing to give up her seat on a segregated bus. Ask students to research the person's position and to write an explanation that person might give for taking his or her stand. They should write as though the event has just happened.

Fine Arts The use of tax revenue to finance projects in the humanities has become a controversial issue. Students who are studying drama, music, dance, or art might want to research and address this issue. Remind them that they will need counterarguments for people who feel that the humanities have no practical value. Invite them to send a letter or editorial to the local newspaper for possible publication.

Evaluating and Revising

- In self-evaluation and for peer review, students may use the Evaluation Criteria for a good controversial issue essay. Remind students to be alert for the appropriate use of connotative language.
- To check for adequate development of supporting details in their essays, students may use highlighters of different colors to mark each item of evidence.
- Students should check for a smooth rhythm. If they find their sentences are not balanced, they should correct any lapses in parallelism. Refer them to the Language Workshop on p. 338. This workshop contains strategies for achieving parallel structure.

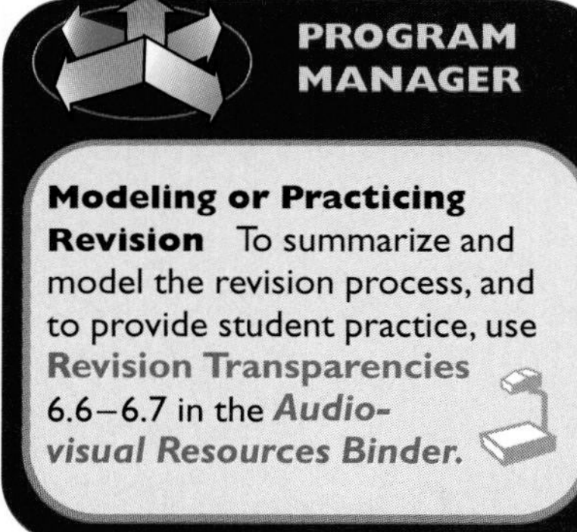

PROGRAM MANAGER

Modeling or Practicing Revision To summarize and model the revision process, and to provide student practice, use **Revision Transparencies** 6.6–6.7 in the ***Audio-visual Resources Binder.***

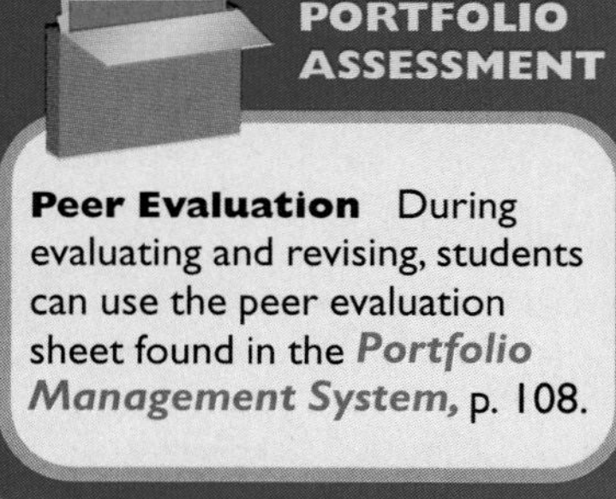

PORTFOLIO ASSESSMENT

Peer Evaluation During evaluating and revising, students can use the peer evaluation sheet found in the ***Portfolio Management System,*** p. 108.

Proofreading and Publishing

- Remind students that a carefully proofread essay will help readers take their ideas seriously.
- Give the address of the local newspaper to students who are interested in presenting their essays to the general public.

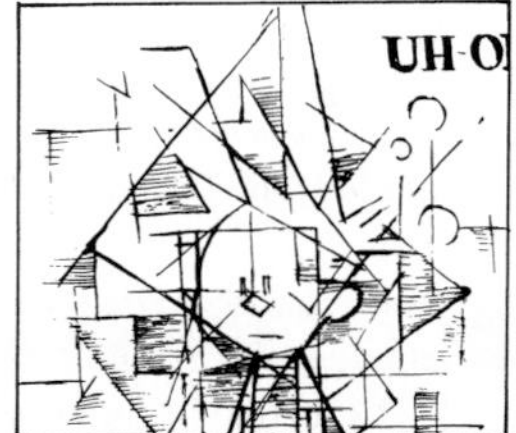

kind of ending you choose will depend on your own imagination as well as on the issue itself and the real-world consequences you are advocating. In your conclusion, you must be clear about what outcome you want to achieve as a result of your essay.

Evaluating and Revising

1. **Peer review.** Exchange essays with a classmate. As you read each other's essays, consider the following questions:
   - Is the issue well defined and interesting to you?
   - Is the writer's position clearly stated at the beginning of the essay?
   - Does the writer use both logical and emotional appeals effectively?
   - Which reasons are most persuasive? least persuasive? Which should be developed further?
   - Is the order in which reasons are presented effective? If not, what changes should the writer make?
   - Is the evidence relevant and credible?
   - Does the writer convincingly rebut arguments to his or her position? Does he or she gracefully concede points?
   - Could you tell what outcome the writer desires?
   - Does the writer seem to have considered the intended audience?

Revision STRATEGIES

Review your essay or speech for unclear writing. Make abstract ideas concrete. Use straightforward diction and clear syntax. If any sentences are convoluted, rewrite them.

OPTIONS FOR TEACHING

PROFESSIONAL NOTES

Another Approach In explaining their positions, students sometimes begin sentences with the phrases *There is* or *There are*. Suggest during the proofreading stage that students re-read their essays, circle any use of these two phrases, and see if they can discover a more active way to begin the sentence.

Timesaver Students may do part of the assignment at home. The prewriting and revising stages might best be done in the classroom so that students may ask for help if they need it.

2. **Self-evaluation.** When writing an essay about a controversial issue, you must assume that your essay will be read by people who tend to disagree with you as well as by people who tend to agree with you. It is important not to insult those who may disagree. You should respectfully acknowledge the opposing point of view while still attempting to persuade opponents to come over to your side. While you want to use strong, connotative language, you must avoid annoying the people whose opinions you wish to influence. Pay especially close attention to the response you get from peers or others who read your draft and who disagree with your position. They can provide you with especially useful feedback as to the persuasive power of your essay. If you can win their respect with your arguments, then you may be able to influence their opinions, too. Have you listened to constructive criticism with an open mind?

   Underline passages that seemed to make your readers or listeners puzzled, impatient, or bored, and revise them so that they are stronger, both in terms of logic and language. Varying your sentence structure can also help you retain your readers' interest. However, don't assume that disagreement on your audience's part means ineffectiveness on your part. People can disagree with even the most powerful persuasive writing. Be true to your position throughout your essay.

Language Handbook HELP

Combining sentences for variety: page 1238.

Proofreading

Keep in mind that your purpose in writing a controversial issue essay is to influence an audience's opinions. Errors of mechanics, grammar, or usage may cast doubt on your credibility and will certainly give ammunition to those who oppose your position. Proofread your essay carefully, and make any corrections necessary. Prepare a clean copy, and proofread it again to make sure all errors have been corrected.

Publishing

After all your hard work, you should consider sending this essay to your community or school newspaper as a letter to the editor. Seeing your work in print can be very satisfying. You could also present your essay to a local group that is concerned about the issue you've addressed. In class, distribute your essay, mount it on a bulletin board, or publish it in a class collection.

Reflecting on Your Writing

Respond to these questions in your portfolio.

1. Did you have strong feelings about a current issue in your school, community, or country? What did you learn about yourself?
2. What did you find most challenging about writing a controversial issue essay?
3. Did you find it informative to read early drafts written by other students? Explain.
4. Did you discover ways to use logical and/or emotional appeals to make your writing especially persuasive? Which appeals were most successful?
5. What did you find most difficult about this experience? What was easiest?

Evaluation Criteria

A good controversial issue essay

1. *clearly defines the issue and the writer's stand on it*
2. *includes a strong and credible position statement (thesis)*
3. *develops a position clearly, using both logical and emotional appeals in convincing and well-developed arguments*
4. *includes and answers important counterarguments, showing consideration of the audience's point of view*
5. *is organized logically*
6. *has a conclusion that shows that the writer is clear about the outcome he or she desires*

ASSESSMENT TOOLS

Self-Evaluation Have students use the following scale and statements to assess their progress before they begin to write their final drafts.

A=Agree
D=Disagree
N=Needs improvement

_____ I have clearly defined the issue and stated my position.

_____ I have included a strong and credible position statement.

_____ I have developed my position using logical and emotional appeals in well-developed arguments.

_____ I have anticipated counterarguments.

_____ I have logically organized my paper.

_____ I have a strong conclusion.

Reteaching

Students sometimes have trouble taking a firm stand or providing strong evidence to support their positions. Work with these students in a small group. After you have checked that their topics are appropriate, have them each make a cluster diagram such as the one following, with the position in the middle and the reasons and evidence in surrounding circles. Have the group discuss each person's diagram.

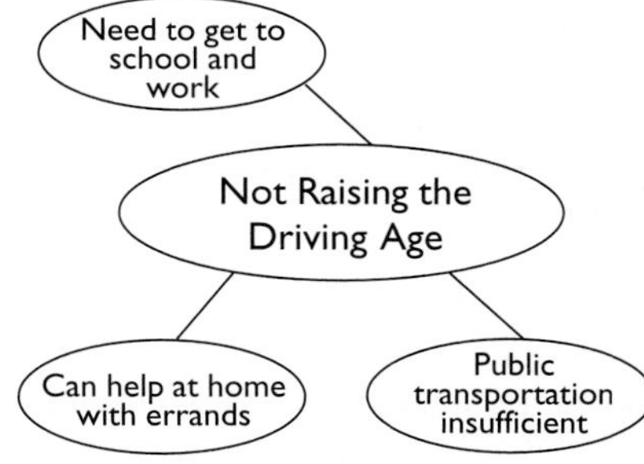

Closure

Have students discuss what makes a persuasive essay successful and what helps the reader understand or even agree with a particular position. Ask them what they have learned from this assignment and what they would like to improve in their own writing.

Extension

Have the class design an advertising campaign to promote a position on a social or political issue. Have students form groups of four, and ask each group to develop either a brochure, a sixty-second television advertisement, or a thirty-second radio spot to inform people about the issue and to convince them to take action. Then, have the class present the campaign to the school or to the community.

Portfolio

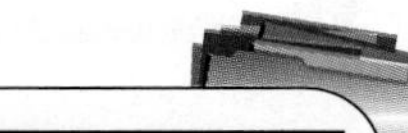

Reflecting on Your Writing

- Encourage students to consider whether they feel more strongly about their positions after they have written about the issues.
- Ask students to answer the questions and to attach the answers to their essays.

Language Workshop

Connecting to Students' Writing

As a proofreading exercise, ask students to return to their writing and to identify sentences where ideas should be linked. Have them underline the words that express each idea. Ask them to check whether the same grammatical form is used to state each idea.

For example:
Melville wrote about Ishmael's voyage on the *Pequod* and the obsession Ahab had with a whale.
Revised:
Melville wrote about Ishmael's voyage on the *Pequod* and Ahab's obsession with a whale.

Try It Out: Answers

1. To Emerson, it was important that people be nonconformists, be true to themselves, and listen to their intuition.
2. Thoreau's writing style involves the use of paradox, imagery, and figures of speech.
3. Many students find it easier to read Thoreau's *Walden* than Emerson's work.

PROGRAM MANAGER

- **Extra Practice and Guided Instruction** For more instruction and practice of using parallel structure, see ***Language Workshop*** in ***Teaching Resources A,*** pp. 120–121.
- **Extra Practice or Guided Instruction** See ***Language Workshop: Parallel Structure*** for more practice or guided instruction in parallel structure.

Technology HELP

See Language Workshop CD-ROM. *Key word entry: parallel structure.*

Language Handbook HELP

Using parallel structure: pages 1235–1236.

Try It Out

Rewrite the following sentences, making them parallel in structure.

1. To Emerson, it was important that people be nonconformists, true to themselves, and listen to their intuition.
2. Thoreau's writing style involves the use of paradox, imagery, and he also used many figures of speech.
3. Many students find it easier to read Thoreau's *Walden* than reading anything by Emerson.

Keeping It in Balance: Parallel Structure

When you link ideas within a sentence, be aware of balance in your writing. You can make your writing smoother and more balanced by using **parallel structure,** placing equivalent ideas in the same grammatical form.

In the following sentence, the boldface structures are *not* parallel:

> The professor said that **to read Emerson** is more useful than **watching television.**

"To read" is an infinitive form, but "watching" is a gerund. You can make the structures parallel by changing the sentence so that both forms are equivalent, as in the following example:

> The professor said that **reading Emerson** is more useful than **watching television.** [gerunds in both cases]

The key to parallel structure is balance: You use the same grammatical form to express equal, or parallel, ideas. If you use a gerund to express one idea, pair it with another gerund to express the ideas to which it is linked. Pair an infinitive with an infinitive, a clause with a clause, a noun with a noun, and so on.

Here are some situations when you would want to be certain that your sentences have parallel structure.

1. Use parallel structure when you link coordinate ideas.

   Emerson believed **that people must be true to their unique capabilities** and **that they must practice self-reliance.** [noun clause paired with noun clause]

2. Use parallel structure to compare or contrast ideas.

   Emerson's **lectures** were often more accessible than his **essays.** [noun contrasted with a noun]

3. Use parallel structure to link ideas when you are using **correlative conjunctions**—pairs of conjunctions such as *both . . . and, either . . . or, neither . . . nor,* or *not only . . . but also.*

   Emerson was *not only* **a great lecturer** *but also* **a gifted poet**.

Writer's Workshop Follow-Up: Revising

Parallel structures are important in persuasive writing because a smoothly repetitive rhythm stirs the reader's emotions and creates a tone of authority. Re-read the persuasive essay you wrote on a controversial issue for the Writer's Workshop (page 331), and correct any lapses in parallelism.

✔ QUICK CHECK: Parallel Structure

Use parallel structure to link ideas in these sentences.

[1] *Walden* was a book about Thoreau's philosophy and it helped expand his reputation.
[*Walden* revealed Thoreau's philosophy and helped expand his reputation.]

[2] Some people prefer Emerson's poetry to reading his prose.
[Some people prefer Emerson's poetry to his prose.]

[3] In Hawthorne's "The Minister's Black Veil," the minister does not remove the veil, and he and Elizabeth do not get married. [In Hawthorne's "The Minister's Black Veil," the minister neither removes the veil nor marries Elizabeth.]

[4] Poe wrote fiction, and he was also a poet.
[Poe wrote not only fiction but also poetry.]

CREATIVE PROBLEM SOLVING

LEARNING FOR LIFE

A Model of Self-Reliance

Problem

Emerson's self-reliant individual is a nonconformist who finds his or her strength and fulfillment in solitude and in being true to his or her unique nature. "Nothing is at last sacred but the integrity of your own mind," Emerson tells us. In *Walden,* Thoreau makes a similar observation: "If a man does not keep pace with his companions, perhaps it is because he hears a different drummer." Who is the self-reliant individual? What can we learn from the person who "hears a different drummer"?

Project

Research a living or dead person who you think fulfills Emerson's ideal of the self-reliant individual—someone who stands apart from the multitude and exemplifies traits of integrity, nonconformity, and uniqueness. Demonstrate how that person can be a role model for us all.

Preparation

1. Re-read the excerpt from Emerson's essay "Self-Reliance," and make notes on what qualities he identifies as being central to the self-reliant individual. If you disagree with any of his points, make note of your disagreements. Add any qualities that you think are necessary for a self-reliant person to possess.
2. You may already have some ideas about people, living or dead, who strike you as being models of self-reliance. If you don't have any ideas, brainstorm with your teacher, family, or classmates. Look through magazines, newspapers, encyclopedias, and books for ideas. Perhaps someone you know personally fits your definition of a self-reliant person.

Procedure

1. List the criteria you've come up with for a truly self-reliant person. Your criteria may be based solely on Emerson's ideas, or you may introduce some of your own criteria.
2. Research and take notes on the person you have chosen as an example of a self-reliant person. If the person is someone in your community or someone you know well, tape-record an interview with him or her.

Presentation

Present what you have learned in one of the following formats (or another format your teacher approves):

1. **Encyclopedia Entry**
   Write an encyclopedia entry about the person. Instead of simply presenting a detailed narrative of the events of the person's life, focus on his or her accomplishments and philosophy. Demonstrate how this person is, or was, truly self-reliant. Include photos, illustrations, or original artwork.
2. **Short Story**
   Write a short story about the self-reliant person you researched. Describe the person's daily life, thoughts and feelings, and the reactions of others to his or her individuality and accomplishments. Publish your story for the class or school.
3. **School for Self-Reliance**
   Prepare a brochure advertising a private school founded by the person you researched. The school should be dedicated to building self-reliant individuals, and it should emphasize the virtues and knowledge that the founder considers most helpful in life. Include a statement of the school's philosophy and an outline of the course of study—what subjects will be taught, what extracurricular activities will be encouraged, how classes will be run, and so on. Illustrate your brochure.

Processing

What did you learn about Emerson's principles of self-reliance by completing this project? Is it really possible to live a self-reliant life? Is it desirable to be a nonconformist? Are there any drawbacks to being self-reliant? Write your reflections for your portfolio.

Learning for Life

Technology Tip

TECHNOLOGY After they have written encyclopedia entries, ask students to compile and publish their entries using computer software. Suggest that they illustrate their entries with scanned sketches or with clip art. Students may wish to collect, alphabetize, and merge their entries into a series based on accomplishments, or they may organize entries in class volumes or sets. When publishing, students may want to copy their work onto diskettes for future reference. If possible, consider having students compile encyclopedia entries from all classes to be put on one CD-ROM volume. Have them donate a copy of their work to the school library.

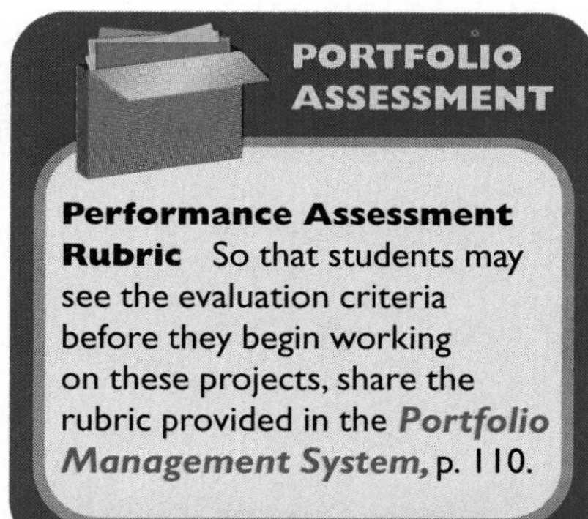

Performance Assessment Rubric So that students may see the evaluation criteria before they begin working on these projects, share the rubric provided in the ***Portfolio Management System,*** p. 110.

DEVELOPING WORKPLACE COMPETENCIES		
Preparation	**Procedure**	**Presentation**
Processes information Uses resources well Makes decisions	Processes information Acquires data	Communicates ideas and information Exhibits self-esteem Teaches others

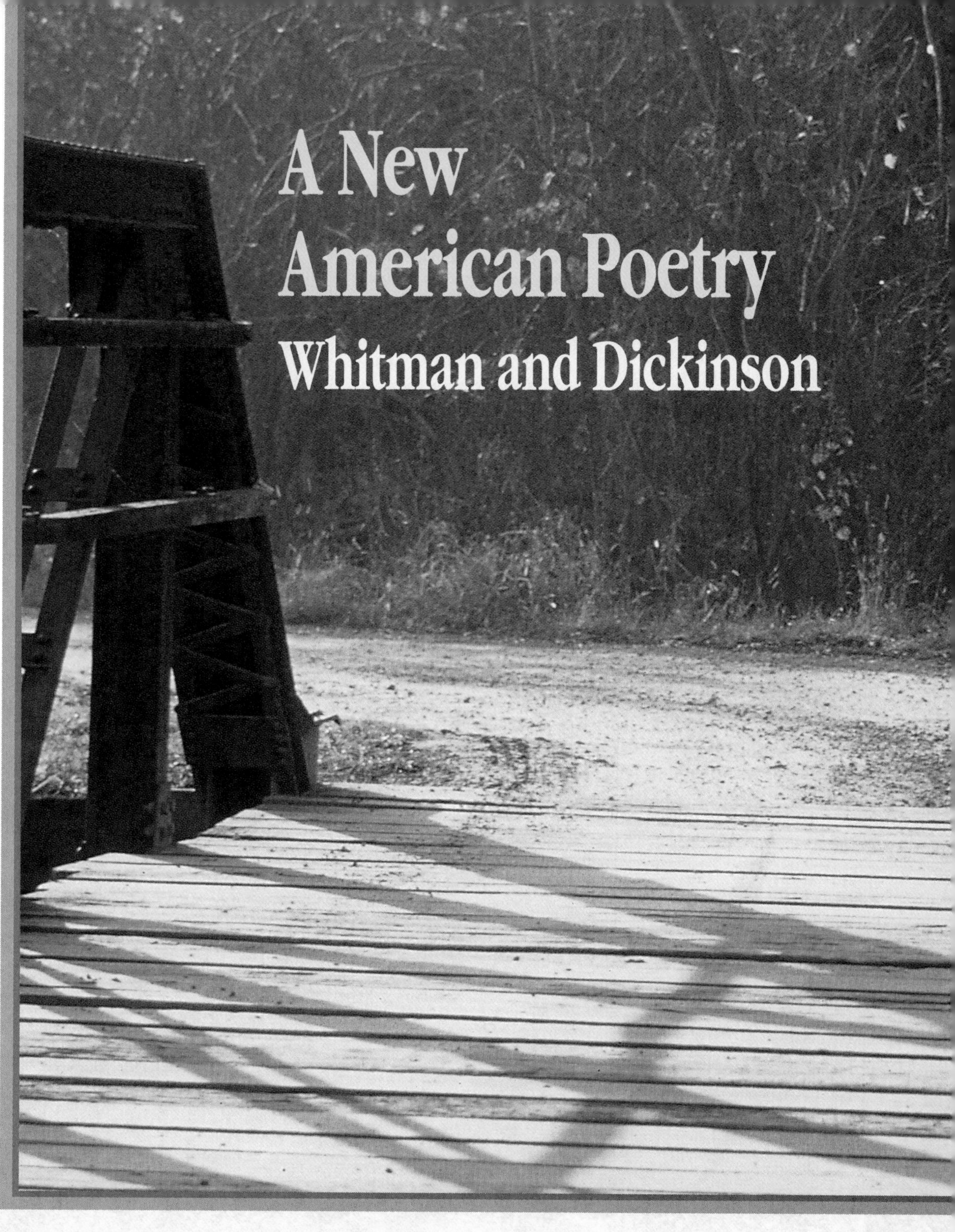
A New
American Poetry
Whitman and Dickinson

RESPONDING TO THE ART: VISUAL LITERACY

What might the solitary figure in this opening illustration suggest about the two writers in the collections that follow? [Possible response: The figure may suggest that the two writers worked in isolation from others; or it may suggest that the works of the two writers stood apart from the works of other writers of the period.]

341

PROGRAM MANAGER

- **Summative Assessment** See **Literary Period Test: New American Poetry,** ***Test Booklet,*** pp. 95–98, for a test on an additional text from the same historical era.
- **Application** For practice of a reading strategy for this unit, see **Becoming a Strategic Reader** worksheet, ***Teaching Resources A,*** pp. 128–129.

Responding to the Quotations

? What is Whitman suggesting about himself? [Possible response: He thinks of himself as one with nature and the earth.] What feelings do the lines by Emily Dickinson suggest? [Possible answer: Isolation, loneliness, bitterness, unhappiness]

A. Expansion

The line by Walt Whitman is from "Song of Myself" #52, p. 359. The lines by Emily Dickinson are the beginning of her poem #441. Read the entire poem to the class, and ask students whether their opinions of the first two lines change.

A New American Poetry

Whitman and Dickinson

by **John Malcolm Brinnin**

If you want me again look for me under your boot-soles.
—Walt Whitman

A

This is my letter to the World
That never wrote to me—
—Emily Dickinson

The two greatest American poets of the nineteenth century were so different from one another, both as artists and as personalities, that only a nation as varied in character as the United States could possibly contain them.

Walt Whitman worked with bold strokes on a broad canvas; Emily Dickinson worked with the delicacy of a miniaturist. Whitman was sociable and gregarious, a traveler; Dickinson was private and shy, content to remain in one secluded spot through all of her lifetime.

While both poets were close observers of people and of life's daily activities, the emphasis they gave to what impressed them was so distinct as to make them opposites. Whitman was the public spokesman of the masses and the prophet of progress. "I hear America singing," he said, and he joined his eloquent voice to that chorus. Dickinson was the obscure homebody, peering through the curtains of her house in a country village, who found in nature metaphors for the spirit and recorded them with no thought of an audience. Whitman expected that his celebration of universal brotherhood and the bright destiny of democracy would

OPTIONS FOR TEACHING

STRATEGIES FOR INCLUSION

Advanced Have students research aspects of the historical backdrop for the poetry of Whitman and Dickinson, such as the Civil War; the role of women in the late nineteenth century; and women writers of the time, such as Rebecca Harding Davis, Louisa May Alcott, Sarah Orne Jewett, and Kate Chopin (p. 435). Groups or individuals should report this information to the entire class using handouts.

Less Proficient Readers To help students predict main ideas, point out that the title and subtitle of a piece of writing usually indicate the main ideas expressed. Ask students to speculate on the meaning of the titles "A New American Poetry," "Two Seams in the Fabric," and "Models for Future Poets." Then, have the class discuss the introduction, focusing on these three ideas.

be carried like a message into the future. Dickinson expected nothing but oblivion for the poetry that was her "letter to the World."

Whitman and Dickinson were true innovators who expressed themselves in poetic voices that broke with the established literary traditions of their time.

Walt Whitman.

Drawing by David Levine. Reprinted with permission from *The New York Review of Books.* Copyright © 1970 NYREV, Inc.

Two Seams in the Fabric

Whitman's career might be regarded as another American success story—the story of an amiable young man who drifted into his thirties, working at one job after another, never "finding himself" until, at his own expense, he boldly published *Leaves of Grass* (1855). The book made him famous around the world. Dickinson's career as a poet began after her death. It is one of those ironies of history in which a writer dies unknown, only to have fame thrust upon her by succeeding generations. B

> A great poem is for ages and ages in common and for all degrees and complexions and all departments and sects and for a woman as much as a man and a man as much as a woman. A great poem is no finish to a man or a woman but rather a beginning.
>
> —Walt Whitman, *Leaves of Grass*

Emily Dickinson's bed.

B. Exploring the Historical Period

Other events during 1850–1855 in American literature include the appearance of Hawthorne's *The Scarlet Letter,* Melville's *Moby-Dick,* and Thoreau's *Walden.* During the same period, the Sioux ceded a vast area of land to the U.S. government, Senator Charles Sumner emerged as a leader in the fight against slavery, Florence Nightingale departed for Turkey to treat British soldiers fighting the Crimean War, and Commodore Matthew C. Perry opened trade with Japan.

PROGRAM MANAGER

- **Planning Instruction** See **Teaching Notes, *Teaching Resources A,*** pp. 123–124, for additional teaching options about A New American Poetry.
- **Assessment** For assessment of the literary and historical events mentioned in the historical introduction, see **Literary Period Introduction Test, *Test Booklet,*** pp. 87–88.

STRATEGIES FOR INCLUSION

Special Needs Poets in the deaf community compose and perform poetry in American Sign Language. If possible, contact an expert on the deaf community in your area to find out if there are any local poets who compose in American Sign Language. If so, invite them to perform their poetry for the entire class.

English Language Development Refer students to Whitman's quotation about the proof of a poet on p. 344. To demonstrate to students that a word can have both a concrete and an abstract meaning, pose these questions to the class: What are common objects that absorb? [Sponge; towel; cloth.] How can a country absorb people? [A country absorbs people when they become part of that nation.]

Elements of Literature:* Videodisc** To build background knowledge on the time period, use the following bar codes to locate appropriate material on the videodisc. For more information, see the Videodisc ***Teacher's Manual.

Videodisc Side A

Begin Play, English Track

Begin Play, Spanish Track

Whitman and Dickinson represent two distinct seams in the fabric of American poetry, one slightly uneven and the other carefully measured and stitched tight. Whitman was as extravagant with words as he was careless with repetition and self-contradiction. Aiming for the large, overall impression, he filled his pages with long lists as he strained to catalog everything in sight. His technique is based on **cadence**—the long, easy sweep of sound that echoes the Bible and the speeches of orators and preachers. This cadence is the basis for his **free verse:** poetry without rhyme or meter.

> The proof of a poet is that his country absorbs him as affectionately as he has absorbed it.
>
> — Walt Whitman, *Leaves of Grass*

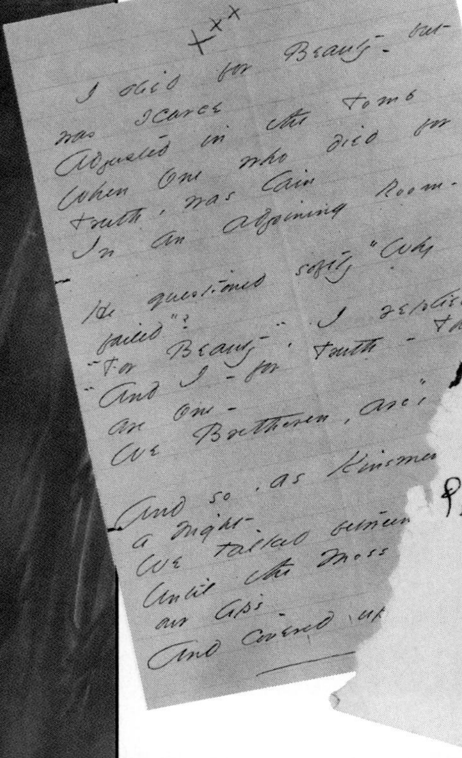

Manuscript for "I died for Beauty" by Emily Dickinson.

By permission of the Houghton Library, Harvard University, Cambridge, Massachusetts.

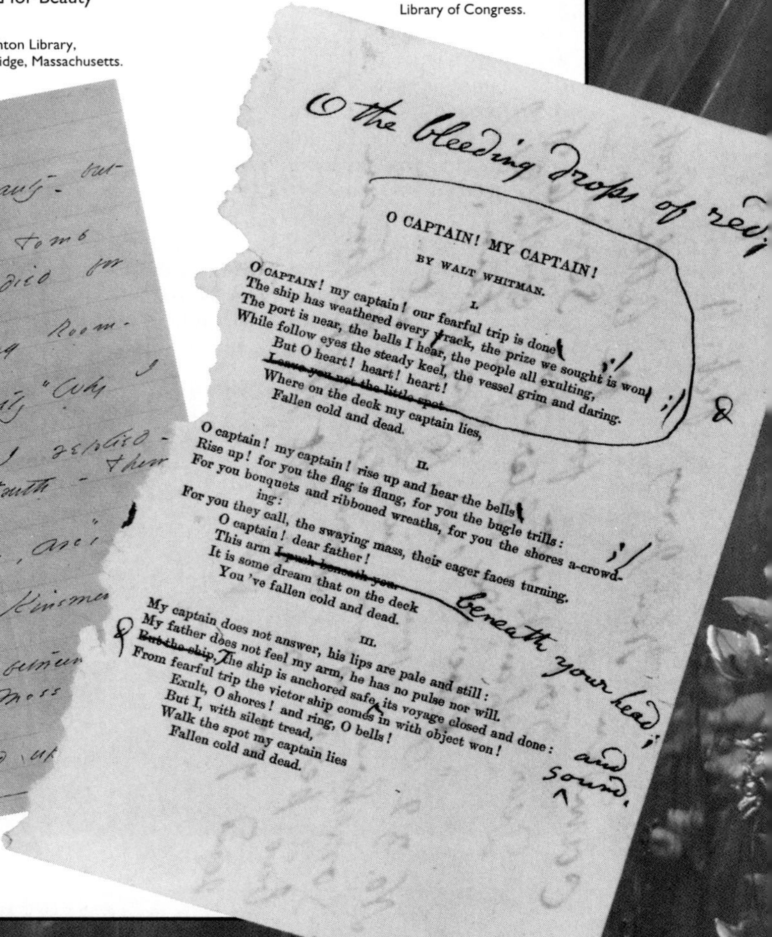

Revisions made by Walt Whitman to his poem "O Captain! My Captain!"

Library of Congress.

OPTIONS FOR TEACHING

CROSSING THE CURRICULUM

Art Invite students to research the art of the time period and to bring in pictures to class that demonstrate nineteenth century artistic views. They can probably find pictures of home life as well as Civil War and industrial reform subjects. Have students discuss whether these pictures are like the word pictures in Whitman's poetry.

Social Sciences Ask students to research and report orally to the class or to create a poster on the great reform movements of the nineteenth century. Whitman reflected the mood of the times in his concern for and interest in common people.

Geography Use a map of the United States to point out the vastness of Whitman's travels. Ask students to discuss what role travel and varied experience play in the development of a poet.

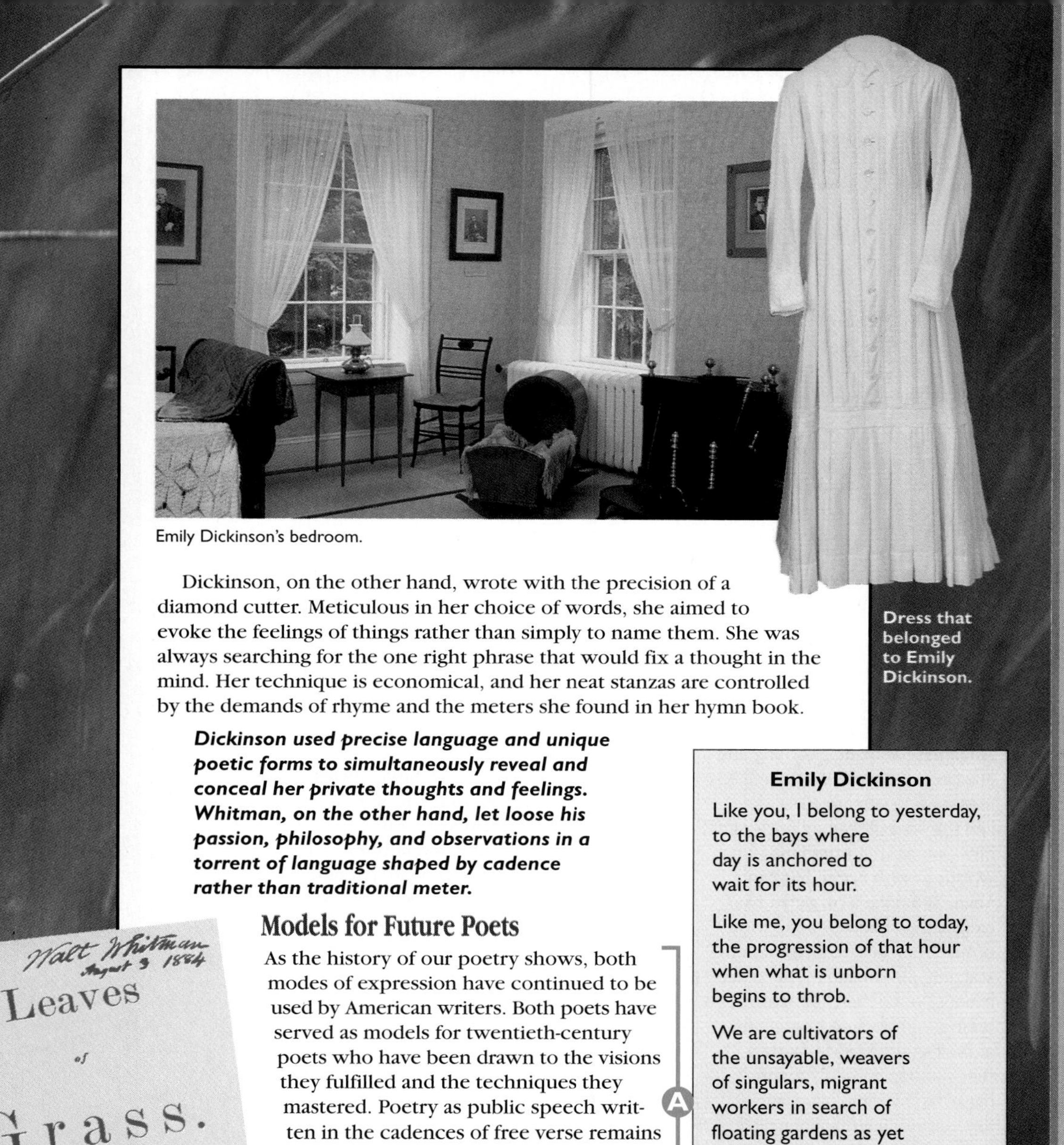

Emily Dickinson's bedroom.

Dress that belonged to Emily Dickinson.

Dickinson, on the other hand, wrote with the precision of a diamond cutter. Meticulous in her choice of words, she aimed to evoke the feelings of things rather than simply to name them. She was always searching for the one right phrase that would fix a thought in the mind. Her technique is economical, and her neat stanzas are controlled by the demands of rhyme and the meters she found in her hymn book.

Dickinson used precise language and unique poetic forms to simultaneously reveal and conceal her private thoughts and feelings. Whitman, on the other hand, let loose his passion, philosophy, and observations in a torrent of language shaped by cadence rather than traditional meter.

Models for Future Poets

As the history of our poetry shows, both modes of expression have continued to be used by American writers. Both poets have served as models for twentieth-century poets who have been drawn to the visions they fulfilled and the techniques they mastered. Poetry as public speech written in the cadences of free verse remains a part of our literature; poetry as private observation, carefully crafted in rhyme and meter, still attracts young writers who tend to regard poems as experiences rather than as statements. (A)

Emily Dickinson

Like you, I belong to yesterday,
to the bays where
day is anchored to
wait for its hour.

Like me, you belong to today,
the progression of that hour
when what is unborn
begins to throb.

We are cultivators of
the unsayable, weavers
of singulars, migrant
workers in search of
floating gardens as yet
unsown, as yet unharvested.

—Lucha Corpi,
translated from the Spanish by
Catherine Rodríguez-Nieto

A. Reader's Response: First Thoughts

? Which poet, so far, better fits your image of a poet? Explain your answer. [Sample responses: Whitman fits my image of a free-spirited adventurous type; or Dickinson fits my image of the reclusive, dreamy poet.]

ASSESSMENT TOOLS

Check Test: Short Answers

1. Who is described as "spokesman of the masses and the prophet of progress"? [Whitman.]
2. Who apparently attempted to catalog the entire range of American life? [Whitman.]
3. Who is remembered as having lived a hidden, obscure life? [Dickinson.]
4. Who wrote in the broad cadences of free verse? [Whitman.]
5. Who is praised for meticulously crafted verses of "gemlike artistry"? [Dickinson.]

Quickwrite

Tell students that, even if they do not feel a strong identification with either poet, they can still write their responses to the poems, noting details, language, themes, and tones that they find interesting or have questions about.

Walt Whitman's birthplace.

Courtesy of the Walt Whitman Birthplace Association.

The coequal importance of the two poetic methods has never been more clearly affirmed than in the following words by Ezra Pound (page 773). Pound speaks for himself here as a poet more attuned to the abbreviations of Dickinson than to the expansiveness of Whitman. Nevertheless, he offers in this poem a benediction that represents the feeling of every poet who has envied the gemlike artistry of Dickinson and the all-embracing power of Whitman:

A Pact

I make a pact with you, Walt Whitman—
I have detested you long enough.
I come to you as a grown child
Who has had a pig-headed father;
I am old enough now to make friends.
It was you that broke the new wood,
Now is a time for carving.
We have one sap and one root—
Let there be commerce between us.

—Ezra Pound

A Damascus blade gleaming and glancing in the sun was her wit. Her swift poetic rapture was like the long glistening note of a bird one hears in the June woods at high noon, but can never see. Like a magician she caught the shadowy apparitions of her brain and tossed them in startling picturesqueness to her friends, who, charmed with their simplicity and homeliness as well as profundity, fretted that she had so easily made palpable the tantalizing fancies forever eluding their bungling, fettered grasp.

—*from* Susan Dickinson's obituary for Emily Dickinson, published in the *Springfield Republican,* May 18, 1886

Quickwrite

Whitman was a very public poet; Dickinson, a private one. Yet both have had a lasting influence on American poets who have followed them. Write your thoughts and feelings about poetry. What do you think is the value of poetry? What roles can poets and poetry serve in contemporary life?

OPTIONS FOR TEACHING

ASSESSMENT TOOLS

Observation Assessment You may want to give students a daily grade for each positive contribution to class discussion. If students are informed about this procedure ahead of time, they will be encouraged to prepare. The grading system might include the following:

- 100 = logical comment backed up with specific support from the text
- 85 = logical comment with general explanation
- 75 = comment somewhat lacking in logic but nevertheless demonstrating some familiarity with the text

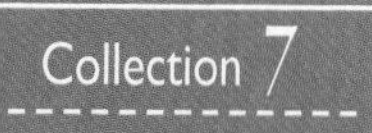

THE LARGE HEARTS OF HEROES

Theme: An Everyday Epic

Walt Whitman ushered in an American epic when he published and expanded *Leaves of Grass*. Breaking with tradition, he wrote songs celebrating the joys and richness of everyday life. He abandoned meter in favor of free verse and wrote about topics that were previously considered unsuitable. In doing so, he created a distinctly American voice with which to celebrate American heroes.

Thematic Focus

Each selection in Collection Seven illustrates a poetic voice that broke with the established literary traditions of the time.

- **I Hear America Singing** The harmony of diverse occupations is celebrated in this poem.
- **Song of Myself, 10** Different scenes from the American experience are juxtaposed in this poem.
- **Song of Myself, 33** Whitman empathizes with some unlikely heroes.
- **Song of Myself, 52** Whitman touches on the main themes present in *Song of Myself*
- **A Sight in Camp in the Daybreak Gray and Dim** Whitman describes his impressions while viewing the remains of Civil War casualties.
- **Plenos Poderes/Full Powers** Poet Pablo Neruda echoes Whitman.

Literary Focus

Literary Element	Selection / Feature
Catalog	**I Hear America Singing**
Free Verse; Alliteration; Assonance; Imagery; Onomatopoeia; Parallel structure; Cadence	**Song of Myself, 10**
Coda	**Song of Myself, 52**
Images	**Plenos Poderes/Full Powers**

Writing Focus

The following flow chart shows how the writing assignment for the selections relates to and builds toward the writing assignment presented in the Writer's Workshop at the end of the unit.

Selection	Work-in-Progress Assignment
Poems of Walt Whitman	List past incidents and recall thoughts for a reflective essay p. 365
Writer's Workshop	Write a reflective essay pp. 401–403

Collection 7 **THE LARGE HEARTS OF HEROES**

Collection Planner

PUPIL'S EDITION

SELECTION / FEATURE	Literary Elements / Active Reading	Writing	Speaking and Listening	Language and Vocabulary
I Hear America Singing, Song of Myself, 10, Song of Myself, 33, Song of Myself, 52, A Sight in Camp in the Daybreak Gray and Dim Walt Whitman (pp. 348–366) **Connections: Who Understands Me but Me** Jimmy Santiago Baca (pp. 360–361) Primary Sources: from Specimen Days (pp. 363–364)	• Reader's Logs pp. 351, 353, 356, 359, 362 • Catalog p. 351 • Free verse p. 355 • Alliteration p. 355 • Assonance p. 355 • Imagery p. 355 • Onomatopoeia p. 355 • Parallel structure p. 355 • Cadence p. 355 • Coda p. 359	• Critical Writing: Write comparative essay p. 365 • Creative Writing/ Speaking and Listening: Write poem and give reading p. 365 • Critical Writing: Write essay about nature pp. 365–366 • Critical Writing/Speaking and Listening: Write speech p. 366 • Music: Compose music p. 366 • Art: Create book cover p. 366 • Crossing the Curriculum: History: Make photo-graphic chart p. 366	• Creative Writing/ Speaking and Listening: Poetry reading p. 365 • Creative Writing/ Speaking and Listening: Present Speech p. 366	
Literature of the Americas: Full Powers Pablo Neruda (pp. 367–370)	• Reader's Log p. 368		• Finding Common Ground: Share comments from Reader's Logs p. 370	

Collection Resources

Teaching Resources A	Audiovisual Resources Binder	Test Booklet
Cross-Curricular Activity p. 139	Fine Art Transparency 7.1	Selection Test pp. 89–90

 Computer disk or CD-ROM

 Audiocassette

 Overhead Transparency

PROGRAM RESOURCES

Electronic Media	Teaching Resources with Organizer: Teaching Resources A	Teaching Resources with Organizer: Other Resources	Audiovisual Resources Binder
• Test Generator • Language Workshop: Clauses	• Teaching Notes pp. 123–127 • Reading Organizers pp. 130–134 • Language Link pp. 135–136 • Words to Own pp. 137–138	• Test Booklet: Selection Test pp. 89–90 • Language and Writing Skills Worksheets p. 79 • Portfolio Management System pp. 53, 111–113	• Selected Readings Audiocassette 1 Side B • Elements of Literature Transparency 7.2
	• Teaching Notes p. 127		

COLLECTION PLANNER

Proofreading Warm-ups

You may use the following exercises to help students practice their proofreading skills. Copy a set of incorrect sentences on to the chalkboard and have students find and correct the spelling, punctuation, usage, and mechanical errors in each sentence. Ask students to share and discuss their responses.

	Sentences with Errors	**Sentences Corrected**	**Skills Covered**
1	**a.** after reading leafs of grass emerson wrote whitman the most important letter of his career **b.** without asking emersons permission whitman had the letter printed	**a.** After reading Leaves of Grass, Emerson wrote Whitman the most important letter of Whitman's career. **b.** Without asking Emerson's permission, Whitman had the letter printed.	Capitalization, Underlining titles, Comma usage, Unclear pronouns, Apostrophes, End marks
2	**a.** whitman was borne on a farm near huntington long island **b.** in 1824 the family moved to brooklyn where whitmans father was an unsucesful builder	**a.** Whitman was born on a farm near Huntington, Long Island. **b.** In 1824, the family moved to Brooklyn, where Whitman's father was an unsuccessful builder.	Capitalization, Spelling, Comma usage, Apostrophes, End marks
3	**a.** at 11 whitman learnt printing a trade he would be asociated with as a printer journalist and editor **b.** a couple of years later when he was 17 he was teaching school on long island	**a.** At age eleven, he learned printing, a trade with which he would be associated as a printer, journalist, and editor. **b.** When he was seventeen, he taught school on Long Island.	Capitalization, Spelling out numbers, Comma usage, Spelling, Misplaced modifiers, Verb tenses, End marks
4	**a.** in eighteen hundred thirty eight and thirty nine he edited a newspaper that still exists today called the long islander **b.** he wrote short stories and poems for magasines and edited newspapers	**a.** In 1838–1839, he edited a newspaper, The Long Islander, which still exists today. **b.** He wrote short stories and poems for magazines, and he edited newspapers.	Capitalization, Spelling out numbers, Comma usage, Usage, Underlining titles, Spelling, End marks
5	**a.** as a contributer to the new orleans crescent he made a trip to the south **b.** 14 years later whitman went to the battlefront in virginia to find his brother who had been wounded	**a.** As a contributor to the New Orleans Crescent, he made a trip to the South. **b.** Fourteen years later, Whitman went to the battlefront in Virginia to find his brother, who had been wounded.	Capitalization, Spelling, Comma usage, Underlining titles, End marks
6	**a.** payed for and in part typeset by whitman himself leaves of grass was published in 1855 **b.** launched his career as a poet	**a.** Paid for and, in part, typeset by Whitman himself, Leaves of Grass was published in 1855. **b.** Leaves of Grass launched his career as a poet.	Capitalization, Comma usage, Underlining titles, Sentence fragments, End marks
7	**a.** whitman volunteered to nurse federale and confederite soldiers in military hospitals in washington D C **b.** in drum-taps whitman printed poems based on his war time experiences	**a.** Whitman volunteered to nurse Federal and Confederate soldiers in military hospitals in Washington, D. C. **b.** In Drum-Taps, Whitman printed poems based on his wartime experiences.	Capitalization, Comma usage, Spelling, Underlining titles, End marks
8	**a.** when lilacs last in the dooryard bloom'd and O captain! my captain! commerate the death of lincoln. **b.** whitman suffered a stroke when he remained in washington until 1873	**a.** "When Lilacs Last in the Dooryard Bloom'd" and "O Captain! My Captain!" commemorate the death of Lincoln. **b.** Whitman remained in Washington until 1873, when he suffered a stroke.	Capitalization, Quotation marks, Comma usage, Spelling, End marks
9	**a.** after moving to camden new jersey he remained there until his death **b.** later leaves of grass brought whitman world-wide fame he welcomed writers from around the globe to his home	**a.** After moving to Camden, New Jersey, he remained there until his death. **b.** Later, Leaves of Grass brought Whitman worldwide fame; he welcomed writers from around the globe to his home.	Capitalization, Comma usage, Semicolon usage, Underlining titles, End marks
10	**a.** he records his autobiographical notes in a journal called specimen days **b.** whitman is buried in a tomb in harleigh cemetary which he designed himself	**a.** He recorded his autobiographical notes in a journal called Specimen Days. **b.** Whitman is buried in Harleigh Cemetery in a tomb that he designed himself.	Capitalization, Verb tenses, Underlining titles, Misplaced modifiers, Spelling, End marks

Collection 7 THE LARGE HEARTS OF HEROES

Whitman
Neruda

from Song of Myself

1.

I celebrate myself, and sing myself,
And what I assume you shall assume,
For every atom belonging to me as good belongs to you.

I loaf and invite my soul,
I lean and loaf at my ease observing a spear of summer grass.

My tongue, every atom of my blood, form'd from this soil, this air,
Born here of parents born here from parents the same, and their
    parents the same,
I, now thirty-seven years old in perfect health begin,
Hoping to cease not till death.

Creeds and schools in abeyance,
Retiring back a while sufficed at what they are, but never forgotten,
I harbor for good or bad, I permit to speak at every hazard,
Nature without check with original energy.

—Walt Whitman, *from Leaves of Grass*

from "Song of Myself"

? What does the philosophical notion of the poem reveal about the poet's heroic heart? [That, to him, everyone is part of the whole of nature, and the poet and reader are somehow one; or that Whitman celebrates the heroic spirit of every individual.]

PROGRAM MANAGER

- **Audiotaped Readings** To help less proficient readers or auditory learners through the lesson, use the **Selected Readings, Audiocassette 1, Side B,** in the ***Audiovisual Resources Binder.***
- **Integrated Assessment** For a summative assessment of the literature and language skills taught in this collection, see **Selection Test, *Test Booklet,*** pp. 89–90.
- **Instructional Support** See **Fine Art Transparency** 7.1. Review teacher's notes for transparencies in the ***Audiovisual Resources Binder*** for suggestions on how to tie the transparencies to specific reading selections.
- **Extending Collection Theme** See **Cross-Curricular Activity: The Large Hearts of Heroes, *Teaching Resources A,*** p. 139, for an activity in another discipline and for evaluation criteria.

PORTFOLIO ASSESSMENT

Parent/Guardian Involvement For forms that will help a parent or guardian review and respond to a student's portfolio, see the ***Portfolio Management System***, pp. 62–63.

WRITERS ON WRITING

"Be simple and clear" were the first words that Walt Whitman wrote in one of his notebooks. He felt that to be a poet was to be himself, to express himself frankly, fully, and clearly. It meant that his poetry was addressed to all people, regardless of their status; everyone was invited to understand him.

Technology Tip

Much of Whitman's work may be found as part of Project Bartleby, a World Wide Web library of electronic texts and hypertexts maintained by Columbia University at **http://www.cc.columbia.edu/acis/bartleby/whitman**.

Walt Whitman

(1819–1892)

Less than a hundred years after the United States was founded, the new nation found its voice in a poet who spoke to all the world. His name was Walt Whitman, and he struck a note in literature that was as forthright, as original, and as deeply charged with democracy's energies as the land that produced him.

Student of the World

Whitman was born on May 31, 1819, to parents of Dutch and English descent. They kept a farm in West Hills, Long Island, in what is today the town of Huntington. His father's ancestors had come from England only twenty years after the landing of the *Mayflower* and had settled in Connecticut. On his mother's side, his ancestors were among the early immigrants from Holland who settled on Manhattan Island and along the Hudson River. Whitman and his seven brothers and sisters were able to assume their essential American-ness with an uncommon confidence. They knew their American grandparents, and they grew up in circumstances that allowed them both the communal experience of country life and the experience of Brooklyn, a new city on its way to becoming a metropolis.

Here young Walter went to school until he was eleven. He then worked as an office clerk and printer's assistant, and for a time he taught school. On weekends spent along the beaches and in the woods of Long Island, Whitman read Sir Walter Scott, the Bible, Shakespeare, Homer, Dante, and ancient Hindu poetry. He never became a scholar; he never went to college.

Before Whitman was twenty, his feeling for the written word and his fascination with the boomtown atmosphere of Brooklyn led him into journalism. After ten years of this, he took a kind of working vacation—a difficult overland trip by train, horse-drawn coach, and riverboat to New Orleans. There he put his journalistic talent to work for the *Crescent* and his own talent for observation to work for himself. After a few months, he returned to New York by way of the Great Lakes and a side trip to Niagara Falls. By this time Whitman had added to his limited sense of America the experience of a wilderness surrendering its vastness to civilization. He also had become acquainted with the entirely alien culture that French Catholic New Orleans represented to him.

Back in Brooklyn, Whitman accepted an offer to become editor of the *Brooklyn Freeman*. For the next six or seven years, he supplemented his income as a part-time carpenter and building contractor. All this while, he was keeping notebooks and quietly putting together the sprawling collection of poems that would transform his life and change the course of American literature.

The Making of a Masterpiece

In 1855, Whitman published his collection at his own expense under the title *Leaves of Grass*. Since the book was too boldly new and strange to win the attention of reviewers or readers who had fixed ideas about poetry, its publication went all but unnoticed. To stir up interest in the book, he sent samples to people whose endorsement he thought might be useful. One of these samples reached Ralph Waldo Emerson, who at once wrote to Whitman the most important letter Whitman would ever receive:

> Concord, Massachusetts, 21 July, 1855
>
> Dear Sir—I am not blind to the worth of the wonderful gift of *Leaves of Grass*. I find it the most extraordinary piece of wit and wisdom that America has yet contributed. I am very happy in reading it, as great power makes us happy. It meets the demand I am always making of what seemed the sterile and stingy Nature, as if too much handiwork, or too much lymph in the temperament, were making our Western wits fat and mean.
>
> I give you joy of your free and brave thought. I have great joy in it. I find incomparable things said incomparably well, as they must be. I find the courage of treatment

which so delights us, and which large perception only can inspire.

I greet you at the beginning of a great career, which yet must have had a long foreground somewhere, for such a start. I rubbed my eyes a little, to see if this sunbeam were no illusion; but the solid sense of the book is a sober certainty. It has the best merits, namely, of fortifying and encouraging.

I did not know until I last night saw the book advertised in a newspaper that I could trust the name as real and available for a post-office. I wish to see my benefactor, and have felt much like striking my tasks and visiting New York to pay you my respects.

R. W. Emerson

The "long foreground" of which Emerson wrote had not been the careful, confident period of preparation to which many poets devote themselves before they are ready to publish. Instead, it had been a precarious existence. Journalism had kept Whitman going financially, but not even the editorials he wrote for the *Brooklyn Eagle* had brought him distinction. On the surface, at least, his "long foreground" of preparation had been a mixture of hack work and jack-of-all-trades ingenuity.

By the time he was ready to declare himself a poet and to publish the first version of his book, Walt Whitman was unique. *Leaves of Grass* is a masterpiece that Whitman was to expand and revise through many editions. Its process of growth did not end until the ninth, "deathbed" edition was published in 1891, thirty-six years after its first appearance. It is a spiritual autobiography that tells the story of an enchanted observer who says who he is at every opportunity and claims what he loves by naming it. "Camerado," he wrote, "this is no book / Who touches this touches a man."

In the Crowd, but Not of It

The figure we know today as Walt Whitman was conceived and created by the poet himself. Whitman endorsed his "image" and sold it to the public with a promoter's skill worthy of P. T. Barnum, the great show manager of the nineteenth century. At first glance that figure is a bundle of contradictions. Whitman seems to have had the theatrical flair of a con artist and the selfless dignity of a saint; the sensibility of an artist and the carefree spirit of a hobo; the blustery egotism of a braggart and the demure shyness of a shrinking violet. On second glance these contradictions disappear: Walt Whitman was everything he seemed to be. The figure he so carefully crafted and put on display was not a surrogate, but the man himself.

Walt Whitman.

Courtesy of Ohio Wesleyan University, Bayley-Whitman Collection, Delaware, Ohio.

ABOUT THE AUTHOR

When Whitman was seventeen, he rejoined his family on Long Island and began five years of intermittent teaching at country and small-town schools. He started a newspaper of his own in 1838 and worked briefly on another newspaper. Whitman was an innovative teacher, but the farm families he boarded with considered him lazy. Instead of helping with chores, he preferred taking part in debates, writing poems and articles about teaching, or studying.

QUICK PLANNING GUIDE

Into the Poems

Through the Poems

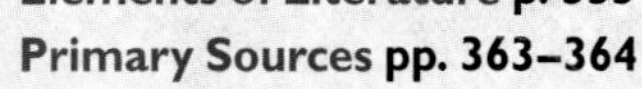

Beyond the Poems

- **Writer's Notebook:** Collect ideas for a reflective essay
- **Critical Writing:** Contrast Whitman with the Fireside Poets in an essay
- **Creative Writing/Speaking and Listening:** Write a free-verse poem
- **Critical Writing:** Contrast Whitman with Taylor and Emerson
- **Critical Writing:** Compare Whitman's poetic and prose styles
- **Critical Writing/Speaking and Listening:** Present a speech
- **Music:** Play a musical tribute
- **Art:** Design a book cover
- **Crossing the Curriculum: History:** Create a museum display

"One would see him afar off," wrote the great naturalist John Burroughs, "in the crowd but not of it—a large, slow-moving figure, clad in gray, with broad-brimmed hat and gray beard—or, quite as frequently, on the front platform of the street horse-cars with the driver. . . . Whitman was of large mold in every way, and of bold, far-reaching schemes, and is very sure to fare better at the hands of large men than of small. The first and last impression which his personal presence always made upon one was of a nature wonderfully gentle, tender, and benignant. . . . I was impressed by the fine grain and clean, fresh quality of the man. . . . He always had the look of a man who had just taken a bath."

If there is a side of Whitman that today we would associate with "image building," or self-promotion, there is nothing in his poetry to suggest that it was anything but the product of the kind of genius that permanently changes the history of art. He modified standard, "King's English" diction and abandoned traditional rhyme schemes and formal meters in favor of the rhythms and speech patterns of free verse.

Everything Under the Sun

The result was poetry that could sing and speak of everything under the sun. Its sweep was easy and its range was broad. Suddenly, poetry was no longer a matter of organized word structures that neatly clicked shut at the last line; instead, it was a series of open-ended units of rhythm that flowed one into the other and demanded to be read in their totality.

"Whitman throws his chunky language at the reader," writes the critic Paul Zweig. "He cajoles and thunders; he chants, celebrates, chuckles, and caresses. He spills from his capacious American soul every dreg of un-Englishness, every street sound thumbing its nose at traditional subject matter and tone. Here is Samson pulling the house of literature down around his ears, yet singing in the ruins."

Walt Whitman had invented a way of writing poetry that perfectly accommodated his way of seeing. His form is loose enough to allow for long lists and catalogs abundant in detail; it is also flexible enough to include delicate moments of lyricism as well as stretches of blustering oratory. This form served Whitman as observer and prophet—as a private man tending the wounded in the hospital wards of the Civil War, and as the public man who gave voice to the grief of a nation in his great elegy for the slain Abraham Lincoln, "When Lilacs Last in the Dooryard Bloom'd." Most important, Whitman's technique was the instrument by which the message of one man in a particular time became, for all time, the message of America.

An American Epic

When Whitman died in 1892, he had fulfilled a great personal intention. He had enlarged the possibilities of American poetry to include the lyricism of simple speech and the grand design of the epic.

How is *Leaves of Grass* like an epic? Who is its hero? What is its action? The hero is the poet, and he is a hero not of the ancient past but of the future. As in all epics, the action takes the form of a journey. In *Leaves of Grass,* the journey is the one the speaker takes as he becomes a poet:

> I am the poet of the Body and I am the poet of
>   the Soul . . .
> I am the poet of the woman the same as the
>   man . . .
> I am not the poet of goodness only, I do not
>   decline to be the poet of wickedness
>   also. . . .

By the end of his epic journey, which even takes him down into the depths of a kind of hell, the poet has also been transformed. The "I" has become identified with every element in the universe and has been reborn as something divine. The poet has become the saving force that Whitman believed was the true role of the American poet.

Nothing quite like it had ever been done in America before.

Before You Read

I Hear America Singing

Reading Focus

Work of Their Own

This famous lyric appears in *Leaves of Grass* and serves to introduce one of the poet's major themes: America's cultural diversity. In this poem, Whitman celebrates work through the "varied carols" of men and women who take pride in their occupations.

Quickwrite

Why do you think a poet who celebrates American culture would focus on work songs rather than on love songs or some other kind of song? Write down the sorts of jobs you would expect to be celebrated in a truly American epic written today.

Elements of Literature

Catalog

One of the most obvious characteristics of Whitman's poetry is his frequent use of **catalogs**—long lists of related things, people, or events. Keep an eye out for catalogs in this poem and others by Whitman.

Into the Poem

Using Before You Read p. 351

Reading Focus

Ask students to think of the kinds of working sounds Whitman might hear today. Have them make a list of occupations and sounds.

Quickwrite

Review the definition of an **epic:** a long, narrative poem about heroes. Then, have students discuss whether work can be considered heroic and whether it is suitable to celebrate in poetry.

Portfolio Assessment

Portfolio Assessment

For help with self- and teacher assessment of reading skills, see the *Portfolio Management System,* p. 53.

Program Manager

- **Planning Instruction** See Teaching Notes, *Teaching Resources A,* pp. 125–127, for objectives, summaries, literary elements, and additional historical and biographical information for these selections.
- **Instructional Support** Before beginning the instructional lesson, see Graphic Organizer for Active Reading, *Teaching Resources A,* pp. 130–134, for Beyond the Poems activities.
- **Assessment** See Selection Test, *Test Booklet,* pp. 89–90.
- **Language Link** For instruction and practice in identifying and using clauses, see Language Link, *Teaching Resources A,* pp. 135–136, and *Language and Writing Skills Worksheets,* pp. 79–84.
- **Reinforcement** Use the Words to Own worksheet in *Teaching Resources A,* pp. 137–138.

A. Literary Element: Catalog
Point out that this list of occupations and descriptions is an example of one of Whitman's many catalogs.

Making Meanings

First Thoughts

1. Perhaps the poem is really about the diversity of the American people and their abilities.

Shaping Interpretations

2. It may be a romantic vision, for the workers do not have the control over their lives that is implied. Or students may feel there is a joy to be found in work.

Extending the Text

3. **(Synthesis)** Whitman might write about the office and the assembly-line worker, the fast-food employee, and the transportation-industry worker. Or students may feel that because modern lives are more stressful, Whitman might hear more complaining than singing. Whether people find joy in work may depend more on the individual than the occupation.

I Hear America Singing

Walt Whitman

I hear America singing, the varied carols I hear,
Those of mechanics, each one singing his as it should be blithe and strong,
The carpenter singing his as he measures his plank or beam,
The mason singing his as he makes ready for work, or leaves off work,
The boatman singing what belongs to him in his boat, the deckhand singing on the steamboat deck,
The shoemaker singing as he sits on his bench, the hatter singing as he stands,
The wood-cutter's song, the plowboy's on his way in the morning, or at noon intermission or at sundown,
The delicious singing of the mother, or of the young wife at work, or of the girl sewing or washing,
Each singing what belongs to him or her and to none else,
The day what belongs to the day—at night the party of young fellows, robust, friendly,
Singing with open mouths their strong melodious songs.

Construction of the Dam (1937) by William Gropper. Mural study, Department of the Interior, National Park Service.

National Museum of American Art, Washington, D.C./Courtesy Art Resource.

Making Meanings

First Thoughts

1. Perhaps what Whitman has in mind here are not the actual work songs associated with various trades, but something more subtle. What would you say this poem is really about?

Shaping Interpretations

2. A feeling of acceptance, even of contentment, runs throughout the sounds of these many voices. Considering the long hours and small pay of laborers in the nineteenth century, would you say Whitman is romanticizing or idealizing their lot? Or would you say the songs he hears are expressions of independence and joy in life? Support your response with specific references to the poem.

Extending the Text

3. Imagine what kinds of singing Whitman might hear if he were alive today. In what ways might these "songs" be different from those he heard in his own time? In what ways would they be the same as what he heard? Review the notes you made in your Reader's Log for ideas.

Options for Teaching

Integrating the Language Arts

Strategic Reading After students have read the poem, have them analyze the attitudes of each worker based on the images that Whitman creates and how they relate to the poem's theme. Students should list the attributes and textual support. At the end of their lists, students should write statements summarizing what Whitman is saying about work.

Usage To encourage variety in the use of prepositional and participial phrases, point out the sentence structure of the first stanza of the poem on pp. 353–354, which differs from those in the rest of the poem. The simple subject and predicate are "I hunt," accompanied by a series of descriptive phrases. Ask students to write some sentences modeled after Whitman's.

Before You Read
from Song of Myself, 10

Reading Focus
The Poet as Director
Here the speaker both observes and participates in the diversity of American experience. Whitman carefully juxtaposes different scenes and emotions in these movielike glimpses into the broad American scene. The speaker presents himself as though he were not only the cinematographer who shoots the pictures but also the director behind each scene who arranges just what each frame will look like.

A Dialogue with the Text

Pay attention to the arrangement of details and images in this poem. As you read, briefly summarize the scene that is presented in each stanza, and write down your feelings about each "frame" as it is presented.

from Song of Myself
Walt Whitman

10.

Alone far in the wilds and mountains I hunt,
Wandering amazed at my own lightness and glee,
In the late afternoon choosing a safe spot to pass the night,
Kindling a fire and broiling the fresh-kill'd game,
Falling asleep on the gather'd leaves with my dog and gun by my side.

The Yankee clipper is under her sky-sails,° she cuts the sparkle and scud,°
My eyes settle the land, I bend at her prow or shout joyously from the deck.

The boatmen and clam-diggers arose early and stopt for me,
I tuck'd my trowser-ends in my boots and went and had a good time;
You should have been with us that day round the chowder-kettle. **A**

I saw the marriage of the trapper in the open air in the far west, the bride was a red girl,
Her father and his friends sat near cross-legged and dumbly smoking, they had moccasins to their feet and large thick blankets hanging from their shoulders,
On a bank lounged the trapper, he was drest mostly in skins, his luxuriant beard and curls protected his neck, he held his bride by the hand,
She had long eyelashes, her head was bare, her coarse straight locks descended upon her voluptuous limbs and reach'd to her feet.

6. **sky-sails:** small sails atop a square-rigged mast. **scud:** windblown sea spray or foam.

Into the Poem

Using **Before You Read** p. 353

Reading Focus
To help students understand how important the selection of details is to the poet or director, ask the class to brainstorm details of such school events as a football game or a fair. List the details on the chalkboard; then, ask them which details should be left in and which should be omitted in a poem or movie.

Through the Poem

A. Literary Element: Imagery
? What images are evoked by the two brief scenes described here?
[Possible answers: In the first scene the poet sees himself alone on a ship looking toward land. The second scene evokes the image of him sharing a meal with a group of people.]

PROGRAM MANAGER

Audiotaped Readings To help less proficient readers or auditory learners through the lesson, use the **Selected Readings, Audiocassette 1, Side B,** in the ***Audiovisual Resources Binder.***

CROSSING THE CURRICULUM

Social Sciences Ask students to research some of the occupations people had during Whitman's lifetime and to create a poster showing occupations that no longer seem to play important roles in society today or have disappeared altogether.

CLASSROOM MANAGEMENT

Managing the Reader's Response Classroom
Because students are often called on to form a response rather quickly, try preparing a set of Reader's Response questions that students may review before they read a selection. Ask them to look for answers as they read, to record their immediate reactions in their Reader's Logs, and to make alterations as they read further, before they share orally with the class. ☞

A. Critical Reading: Summarizing

Ask students to describe the speaker. [Possible answer: The speaker is a humanitarian who has dared to shelter and help a runaway.]

Making Meanings

First Thoughts

1. Students may refer to their Reader's Logs for responses to this question. Have students identify specific details from the text in their answers.

Shaping Interpretations

2. (1) Hunting in the wilds—contentment; (2) Sailing a Yankee Clipper—joy; (3) Clamming on a beach—happiness; (4) Far west marriage—curiosity; (5) At home—compassion.
3. In the first three scenes, the speaker is joyous. In the fourth scene, the speaker becomes more focused and serious. In the last scene, the plight of the runaway slave moves the speaker deeply. The changing tone has a sobering effect.
4. The sequence of participles in l. 4–5 and the verbs connected by "and" in ll. 18–22. The cadence creates feelings of passing time, and the stacking of details paints a complete picture.
5. The stanza shows that the speaker is sensitive, caring, compassionate, and trusting.

Connecting with the Text

6. Make sure students support their responses with details from the poem and from their own experiences.

The runaway slave came to my house and stopt outside,
I heard his motions crackling the twigs of the woodpile,
Through the swung half-door of the kitchen I saw him limpsy° and weak,
And went where he sat on a log and led him in and assured him,
And brought water and fill'd a tub for his sweated body and bruis'd feet,
And gave him a room that enter'd from my own, and gave him some coarse clean
 clothes,
And remember perfectly well his revolving eyes and his awkwardness,
And remember putting plasters on the galls° of his neck and ankles;
He stayed with me a week before he was recuperated and pass'd north,
I had him sit next me at table, my fire-lock lean'd in the corner.

17. limpsy: limp; exhausted.
22. galls: sores.

Lost on the Prairie (1837) by Alfred Jacob Miller. Watercolor on paper (9¼″ × 13½″).
Stark Museum of Art, Orange, Texas.

Making Meanings

First Thoughts

1. What **images** of sight, touch, and sound in this poem are most vivid to you?

Shaping Interpretations

2. In the five stanzas of this poem, the speaker observes and participates in five American scenes. Go back to your Reader's Log, and identify the scene in each stanza. Describe the feeling that the scene suggests.
3. Whitman changes the **tone** of this poem when he describes the fourth and fifth scenes. Identify the tone of the first three scenes. What is the tone of the last two scenes? What effect do you think the poet hoped to create by changing the tone?
4. When you read the poem aloud, what repetitions of sentence patterns help create a **cadence**—a rhythmic rise and fall of your voice as the lines are spoken aloud? What feelings does the cadence create?
5. In the last scene, the "runaway slave" is one of thousands who entrusted their lives to those who would help them escape. What do you think the stanza—especially the last line—shows about the speaker's character?

Connecting with the Text

6. If you could drop yourself into one particular American setting today, which would you choose? Explain your response.

Elements of Literature

Free Verse

Today we are so used to poetry written in free verse that we take it for granted. But in Whitman's time, Americans preferred poetry that was like the poetry being written in England; they expected a poem to show the very strictest concern for **meter** and **rhyme.** Thus, Whitman's sprawling lines were revolutionary, as was his daring use of American slang, foreign words, and words he occasionally made up to suit his purpose.

Free verse is poetry that is written without concern for regular rhyme schemes and meter. But free verse is not really free at all. Whitman abandoned meter and regular rhyme schemes, but he made full use of these other literary elements:

- **Alliteration:** the repetition of similar consonant sounds
- **Assonance:** the repetition of similar vowel sounds
- **Imagery:** the use of language to evoke visual pictures, as well as sensations of smell, hearing, taste, and touch
- **Onomatopoeia:** the use of words whose sounds echo their meaning (such as *buzz*)
- **Parallel structure:** the repetition of the same or similar words, phrases, clauses, or sentences

When you read Whitman's lines aloud, you hear **cadence,** the run of words that rise and fall in emphasis when he has a particular point to make and measures his lines to emphasize it. As you can see from Whitman's poems, cadence does not depend on any strict count of stressed syllables.

Poets who, like Whitman, choose to write in cadence have nothing but their own sense of balance and proportion to tell them when a line should end and when it should continue. They must rely completely on their own sense of spacing and timing, and on their own feelings about what sounds right to them.

In the twentieth century, many poets have accepted the challenge of writing in free verse, trusting their own sense of balance and measure. A poem written in regular meter might be compared to a metronome, which keeps a predictable, mechanical beat. Free verse, on the other hand, might be compared to the style of a jazz drummer, who varies the beat throughout a performance.

To best hear Whitman's cadences, you should read his poems aloud. In the collection opener, "Song of Myself," Number 1 (page 347), you should hear no fewer than thirty-three occurrences of the same consonant sound. What sound do you hear? What other examples of **repetition** help create the **rhythms** and music in Whitman's supposedly "free" verse?

Elements of Literature

Mini-Lesson: Free Verse

After going over the definitions of **alliteration, assonance, imagery, onomatopoeia,** and **parallel structure** in the text, divide the class into groups of four to make lists of examples of each literary element. They should find examples in popular songs and in poetry they have read. Then, each student should write at least one example of each element. Groups should share their lists with the class. If possible, put at least one advanced student in each group.

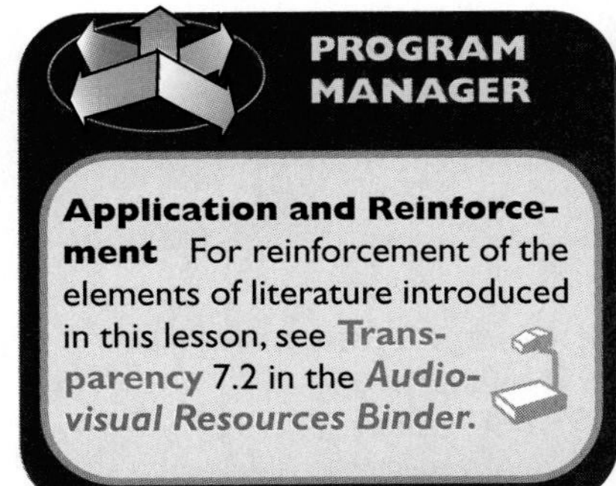

Program Manager

Application and Reinforcement For reinforcement of the elements of literature introduced in this lesson, see Transparency 7.2 in the *Audiovisual Resources Binder.*

Strategies for Inclusion

Learners Having Difficulty When discussing the Elements of Literature feature above, you may want to identify one poetic element at a time, gradually encouraging students to work independently. For example, the whole class could find examples of **alliteration;** then, pairs of students might find other examples; finally, students could find additional examples alone. Follow the same procedure with **assonance, imagery, onomatopoeia,** and **parallel structure.**

Kinesthetic The reading of strongly rhythmical poetry such as Whitman's can be directed much as a piece of music is conducted. Let students work in groups to conduct the oral reading of a poem, including physical movements like bending, rising on toes, and swaying arms. Each group will need to annotate the poem, indicating rises, falls, and movements; then they should practice responding to the conductor before presenting a choral reading to the class.

Using Before You Read p. 356

Reading Focus

Have students expand their thinking by listing unsung or unlikely heroes, such as people who are selfless and receive no recognition, and who are unexpectedly kind. Ask students if and how they identify with these types of heroes.

A. Reader's Response: First Thoughts

? Is the skipper a hero? [Sample responses: Yes, he recognizes the danger of the wrecked ship, does not give in during the storm, is faithful day and night, and saves the drifting ship; or no, he is just doing his job.]

B. Critical Reading: Finding Details

? Who are the martyrs that the poet mentions so far in the poem? [A condemned witch and an escaping slave.]

Before You Read

from Song of Myself, 33

Reading Focus

All These I Am

Much of Whitman's work is distinguished by his attempt to erase the line between observer and object. The poet does this in order to—imaginatively speaking—*become* the thing or person he is talking about. Whitman is capable not only of sympathy, but also of *empathy*—the ability to share in another's thoughts or feelings. This excerpt from the thirty-third section of "Song of Myself" includes one of Whitman's most famous lines: "I am the man, I suffer'd, I was there." Through empathy, Whitman explores the greatness of heart that characterizes some unlikely heroes.

A Dialogue with the Text

READER'S LOG

Throughout "Song of Myself," Whitman honors individuals whose hardships and courageous acts make them true heroes. As you read, write down words and phrases that reveal Whitman's ability to feel empathy for those quite different from himself.

from Song of Myself

Walt Whitman

from 33.

I understand the large hearts of heroes,
The courage of present times and all times,
How the skipper saw the crowded and rudderless wreck of
  the steam-ship, and Death chasing it up and down the
  storm,
How he knuckled tight and gave not back an inch, and was
  faithful of days and faithful of nights,
And chalk'd in large letters on a board, *Be of good cheer, we
  will not desert you;*
How he follow'd with them and tack'd with them three days
  and would not give it up,
How he saved the drifting company at last,
How the lank loose-gown'd women look'd when boated from
  the side of their prepared graves,
How the silent old-faced infants and the lifted sick, and the
  sharp-lipp'd unshaved men;
All this I swallow, it tastes good, I like it well, it becomes mine,
I am the man, I suffer'd, I was there.°

The disdain and calmness of martyrs,
The mother of old, condemn'd for a witch, burnt with dry
  wood, her children gazing on,
The hounded slave that flags in the race, leans by the fence,
  blowing, cover'd with sweat,
The twinges that sting like needles his legs and neck, the
  murderous buckshot and the bullets,
All these I feel or am.

1–11. I understand . . . I was there: This stanza was inspired by an actual incident that occurred in 1853. According to reports in the New York *Weekly Tribune* of January 21, 1854, the ship *San Francisco* sailed from New York City on December 22, 1853, destined for South America. A violent storm hit the ship several hundred miles out of port, washing many passengers overboard. The captain of another ship helped rescue the survivors. A copy of the newspaper story was found among Whitman's papers after his death.

Options for Teaching

Strategies for Inclusion

Learners Having Difficulty Have students work in small groups to discuss a confusing or interesting aspect of the poem above. Each group should put its question in the middle of a sheet of paper and build a web around the question by answering it in several possible ways. Groups may then compare their webs and develop a combined web that represents that group's understanding of the poem.

Linguistic Ask students to develop "Song of Myself" #33 into a Reader's Theater performance and to present it to the class. Divide the class into groups of four, and ask them to divide the poem into four parts for this activity. The groups should perform each of the parts as a separate scene.

The Brooklyn Museum, Gift of Miss Gwendolyn O.L. Conkling (40.59.1).

A Ride for Liberty—The Fugitive Slaves (c. 1862) by Eastman Johnson. Oil on board (22″ × 26¼″).

I am the hounded slave, I wince at the bite of the dogs,
Hell and despair are upon me, crack and again crack the marksmen,
I clutch the rails of the fence, my gore dribs,° thinn'd with the ooze of my skin,
I fall on the weeds and stones,
The riders spur their unwilling horses, haul close,
Taunt my dizzy ears and beat me violently over the head with whip-stocks.

Agonies are one of my changes of garments,
I do not ask the wounded person how he feels, I myself become the wounded person,
My hurts turn livid upon me as I lean on a cane and observe.

I am the mash'd fireman with breast-bone broken,
Tumbling walls buried me in their debris,
Heat and smoke I inspired,° I heard the yelling shouts of my comrades,
I heard the distant click of their picks and shovels,
They have clear'd the beams away, they tenderly lift me forth.

19. dribs: dribbles.

28. inspired: breathed in.

C. Critical Reading: Making Inferences

? What evidence is there in these lines of the poet's empathy? [Possible answers: The poet says that he wears the agonies of others. He becomes the wounded person and thus feels the agony firsthand.]

D. Critical Reading: Analyzing Details

? What happens to the fireman? [Possible answers: He is injured while fighting a fire; or the walls of a burning building collapse on him, breaking his breast bone.]

INTEGRATING THE LANGUAGE ARTS

Strategic Reading To explore Whitman's line breaks and line lengths, have students work in groups to use Interrupted Reading. One person reads aloud while others follow along. When another student notices a definite break in the line, he or she breaks in and reads aloud, and the other reader stops and follows along with the group.

English Language Development/Art Have students list all the nouns and verbs in the poem that are unfamiliar to them. Work with them to help them understand these unfamiliar words by giving them definitions or showing them pictures. Then, ask students to develop simple statement about the poem using the nouns and verbs.

CLASSROOM MANAGEMENT

Block Scheduling Block schedules generally provide more time for one-on-one conferences with students before, during, and after class. Plan for this time, and encourage students to make use of it to approach you with the same questions or problems they otherwise might have waited until lunchtime or after school to discuss.

A. Literary Element: Rhythm Point out to students that the rhythm in these lines enhances the scene of the attack on the fort. For example, the repetition of the word *again* emphasizes the constant bombardment. The shorter lines resemble the bursts of cannon fire, and the alliterative sounds of the letter *r* help to create the images of the sounds of drums and artillery.

Making Meanings

First Thoughts

1. Possible answers: I was surprised by the diversity of the heroes; I think the burning of the woman accused of witchcraft was the most moving, because she was burned with "her children gazing on."

Shaping Interpretations

2. The ship's captain; a condemned woman; runaway slaves; a firefighter; an artillerist in war. Students should give examples of details that appeal to the senses.
3. The speaker makes restatements in ll. 16–17, 26, 36, 37–38, and 42. The reader gradually comes to feel Whitman's complete empathy with these heroes.
4. The tone is empathetic, admiring, and compassionate. The speaker admires and cares for heroes.
5. Short lines are usually the most emphatic and thus most important. See ll. 11, 16, and 38. Often they are meant to be spoken more slowly.
6. Whitman's concept of heroism centers around people of action, people who face up to challenges—a ship's captain, a firefighter, a slave, or an artillerist.

Connecting with the Text

7. The use of the first-person pronoun causes many readers to identify with the people in the poem.

Extending the Text

8. **(Synthesis)** Possible responses: Martin Luther King, Jr., and Rosa Parks, because they took a stand for what they believed in.

I lie in the night air in my red shirt, the pervading hush is for
 my sake,
Painless after all I lie exhausted but not so unhappy,
White and beautiful are the faces around me, the heads are
 bared of their fire-caps,
The kneeling crowd fades with the light of the torches.

Distant and dead resuscitate,
They show as the dial or move as the hands of me, I am the
 clock myself.

I am an old artillerist, I tell of my fort's bombardment,
I am there again.

Again the long roll of the drummers,
Again the attacking cannon, mortars,
Again to my listening ears the cannon responsive.

I take part, I see and hear the whole,
The cries, curses, roar, the plaudits for well-aim'd shots,
The ambulanza° slowly passing trailing its red drip,
Workmen searching after damages, making indispensable
 repairs,
The fall of grenades through the rent roof, the fan-shaped
 explosion,
The whizz of limbs, heads, stone, wood, iron, high in the air.

Again gurgles the mouth of my dying general, he furiously
 waves with his hand,
He gasps through the clot *Mind not me—mind—the
 entrenchments.*

44. **ambulanza** (am·boo͞·lant′sa): Italian for "ambulance."

Making Meanings

First Thoughts

1. How did you respond to Whitman's **catalog** of heroic individuals? Which details packed the strongest emotional punch?

Shaping Interpretations

2. Look back at your Reader's Log notes. With which heroes does Whitman empathize? What **images** of sight and sound help us feel we also are there?
3. At what moments does the speaker restate the point that "I am the man, I suffer'd, I was there"? What is the effect of these restatements?
4. How would you describe the speaker's **tone**? What are his feelings for these heroes?
5. Notice the way Whitman alternates between groups of very long lines and groups of very short lines. What is the reason for each short line? How would you use your voice in reading each short line aloud?
6. What do the heroes Whitman describes suggest about the poet's concept of heroism?

Connecting with the Text

7. Whitman empathizes with people by using the pronoun *I*. How does his use of the **first-person point of view** affect you as you read this poem?

Extending the Text

8. If you could add a contemporary hero to this poem, whom would you choose, and why?

OPTIONS FOR TEACHING

PROFESSIONAL NOTES

Cultural Diversity Discuss with students the qualities or actions that make everyday people heroic. Have students compose short lists of heroic acts, real or fictional, that they know from stories they have heard or read. Students may compare their lists with those of others in the class and discuss if different cultures have different ideas of heroism. Encourage students to be open-minded and receptive to others' ideas.

Before You Read
from Song of Myself, 52

Reading Focus
Symphony of Themes
In this final song, Whitman restates some of the **themes** that have run throughout "Song of Myself." The poet weaves these themes in and out of this final verse like a composer filling a song with familiar refrains. Since the most insistently present element throughout "Song of Myself" is the mind and spirit of the speaker himself, this passage is highly personal. True to his nature, Whitman mocks his own egotism. But, true to his confidence in himself, he also proclaims his importance—and his inescapability.

A Dialogue with the Text

The final section of "Song of Myself" is a coda—a summing up and restatement of the entire poem's themes. As you read this concluding section of the poem, write down your observations about how particular lines and phrases echo themes and concepts you've already encountered in the Whitman poems you've read.

from Song of Myself
Walt Whitman

52.

The spotted hawk swoops by and accuses me, he complains of my gab and my loitering.

I too am not a bit tamed, I too am untranslatable,
I sound my barbaric yawp over the roofs of the world.

The last scud° of day holds back for me,
It flings my likeness after the rest and true as any on the shadow'd wilds,
It coaxes me to the vapor and the dusk.

I depart as air, I shake my white locks at the runaway sun,
I effuse° my flesh in eddies, and drift it in lacy jags.

I bequeath myself to the dirt to grow from the grass I love,
If you want me again look for me under your boot-soles.

You will hardly know who I am or what I mean,
But I shall be good health to you nevertheless,
And filter and fiber your blood.

Failing to fetch me at first keep encouraged,
Missing me one place search another,
I stop somewhere waiting for you.

4. **scud:** windblown mist and low clouds.
8. **effuse:** spread out.

Into the Poem

Using Before You Read p. 359

Reading Focus
Ask students to review what Whitman has written in other poems about the mind and spirit of the speaker. Have them list specific phrases or lines in which the speaker expresses himself. Put these references on the overhead projector or on the chalkboard for students to refer to as they read "Song of Myself" #52.

Through the Poem

A. Literary Element: Metaphor
The poet identifies with the hawk and extends the hawk comparison throughout the poem. Have students discuss which lines evoke the soaring freedom sought by both the hawk and the poet. [Possible answers: ll. 7, 8 "depart as air," "eddies," "drift it in lacy jags."]

B. Critical Reading: Analyzing Details
? What evidence is there in these lines that Whitman considers himself a poet for all people? [Possible answers: He uses images such as dirt, grass, boot-soles, and blood to describe his nearness to the people. His stopping and waiting indicates his accessibility.]

Options for Teaching
Integrating the Language Arts

Writing: Poem Just as the hawk becomes a **metaphor** for the speaker's spirit in poem #52, students can find metaphors for their own lives. After students have brainstormed possible metaphors or symbols, have them write about their spirits, ideas, desires, or philosophies in a poem, using a metaphor or personal symbol as the central motif. *Remind students to choose a situation they would not mind sharing with others.*

Program Manager

Audiotaped Readings To help less proficient readers or auditory learners through the lesson, use the **Selected Readings, Audiocassette 1, Side B,** in the ***Audiovisual Resources Binder.***

A. Reader's Response: First Thoughts

? Does the speaker in the poem really live without water, treetops, sunshine, or tears? [Sample responses: No, the poem exaggerates to make a point; or it is possible that the speaker has lived without some of those things considered necessary to life; to some degree he or she has experienced deprivation.]

B. Literary Element: Parallel Structure

The repetition of words and phrases—*they* do that, so *I* do this—structures much of the poem and provides unity and **cadence** to this free verse poem. It also contrasts with and thereby emphasizes the importance of the "I" that begins each line in ll. 17–21.

C. Critical Reading: Expressing an Opinion

? In what sense can the speaker's experience be called beautiful? [Possible answer: Even though the speaker has suffered, the experience is beautiful because of the personal triumph of the spirit over circumstance.]

PROGRAM MANAGER

Audiotaped Readings To help less proficient readers or auditory learners through the lesson, use the **Selected Reading, Audiocassette 1, Side B,** in the ***Audiovisual Resources Binder.***

Connections

A POEM

Michael O'Shaughnessy/Red Crane Books.

Jimmy Santiago Baca.

Who Understands Me but Me

Jimmy Santiago Baca

They turn the water off, so I live without water,
they build walls higher, so I live without treetops,
they paint the windows black, so I live without sunshine,
they lock my cage, so I live without going anywhere,
they take each last tear I have, I live without tears,
they take my heart and rip it open, I live without heart,
they take my life and crush it, so I live without a future,
they say I am beastly and fiendish, so I have no friends,
they stop up each hope, so I have no passage out of hell,
they give me pain, so I live with pain,
they give me hate, so I live with my hate,
they have changed me, and I am not the same man,
they give me no shower, so I live with my smell,
they separate me from my brothers, so I live without brothers,
who understands me when I say this is beautiful?
who understands me when I say I have found other freedoms?

I cannot fly or make something appear in my hand,
I cannot make the heavens open or the earth tremble,
I can live with myself, and I am amazed at myself, my love, my beauty,
I am taken by my failures, astounded by my fears,
I am stubborn and childish,
in the midst of this wreckage of life they incurred,

CONNECTING WITH WHITMAN'S POETRY

After reading the Whitman poems in this Collection, students should be able to understand the heroism inherent in Jimmy Santiago Baca's poem as the speaker struggles with poverty and isolation. Have students model the structure of "Who Understands Me but Me" by following the *They* ____, *so I* ____, format, substituting heroic actions from their experiences or from local news or newspapers. Remind students to search for simple or subtle acts of heroism rather than famous ones. Hold a poetry reading honoring these brave deeds. Invite other classes, the entire school, or members of the community, and, if possible, the local heroes to attend the reading.

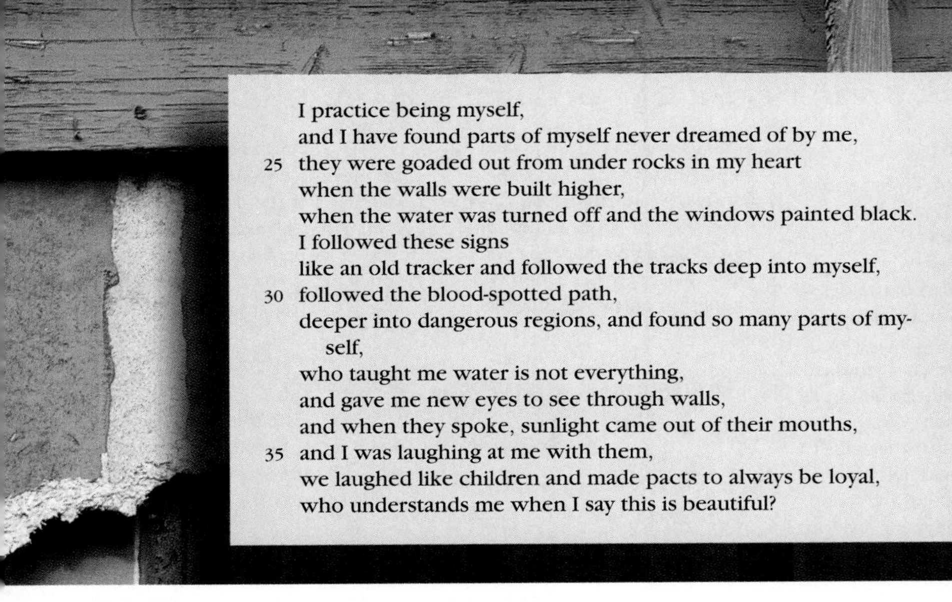

I practice being myself,
and I have found parts of myself never dreamed of by me,
they were goaded out from under rocks in my heart
when the walls were built higher,
when the water was turned off and the windows painted black.
I followed these signs
like an old tracker and followed the tracks deep into myself,
followed the blood-spotted path,
deeper into dangerous regions, and found so many parts of my-
self,
who taught me water is not everything,
and gave me new eyes to see through walls,
and when they spoke, sunlight came out of their mouths,
and I was laughing at me with them,
we laughed like children and made pacts to always be loyal,
who understands me when I say this is beautiful?

MAKING MEANINGS

First Thoughts

1. What, in your own words, is the speaker's parting message in Whitman's poem? What feelings did this message bring out in you?

Shaping Interpretations

2. How does Whitman show his connection to the natural world in this poem? For example, what qualities does he say he shares with the spotted hawk? Support your answer with lines or **images** from the poem.

3. What verb tense does Whitman use in this poem and other selections from "Song of Myself"? How would the effect have been different if the speaker had spoken in a different tense?

4. What might Whitman mean by line 10: "If you want me again look for me under your boot-soles"?

5. The first line of "Song of Myself" is "I celebrate myself, and sing myself"; the last line is "I stop somewhere waiting for you." Taking into account all that you have learned of the poet's character and the range of his poetry, tell what you think the last words of poem Number 52 reveal about Whitman's overall purpose in writing "Song of Myself." Go back to your Reader's Log for ideas.

Connecting with the Text

6. Suppose you had to select a line or word from Whitman's works to characterize him. Which line(s) or word(s) from these excerpts from "Song of Myself" would you select, and why?

Extending the Text

7. What connections do you see between Baca's poem on page 360 and Whitman's poems? Consider each poet's style and his message.

8. You've already studied some of the American poets who preceded Whitman—Poe (page 260), Longfellow (page 175), Bryant (page 169), and other Romantics. Based on what you know about the work of these earlier poets, what do you think Whitman means when he describes his own poetry as his "barbaric yawp" (line 3)?

Challenging the Text

9. Some readers of this poem have further taken the meaning of "barbaric yawp" to refer to the way Great Britain and Europe might have viewed the "American experiment" of democracy. What do you think?

ASSESSMENT TOOLS

Self-Reflection Ask students to do a self-reflection assessment based on their study of Walt Whitman and his poetry. Have students respond to the following questions: (1) How would I describe Whitman's poetry in specific terms? (2) What did I learn from studying Whitman's poetry? (3) What did I learn about myself from this study? (4) What challenges or problems did I encounter? (5) In what ways might I pursue further study of Whitman, his poetry, or his world? Ask students to share their answers in small groups.

Making Meanings

First Thoughts

1. Responses will vary. Responses should touch on the interconnectedness of all people and the natural world. Students' feelings may range from exhilaration to confusion.

Shaping Interpretations

2. He says in ll. 2–3 that he is not tamed, that he is untranslatable, and that he, like the hawk, makes a wild sound.

3. Present tense. The poem would lose its immediacy and intensity if Whitman used the past tense.

4. He intends his poetry to be as accessible as the earth to the average person. The great life force, of which he is part, is as close as the earth and as easy to tap into.

5. The connection of the first and last words of the poem, *I* and *you,* illustrates Whitman's sense of connectedness to others and to the reader.

Connecting with the Text

6. Possible responses include l. 42 from #33: "I take part, I see and hear the whole"; others may vary.

Extending the Text

7. (Synthesis) Both poets celebrate the endurance of the human spirit.

8. (Evaluation) Whitman wrote in a wild, free style and abandoned the rhyme and rhythm conventions of earlier poetry. His is the first American poetry that did not imitate European poetic forms. All people can identify with Whitman's love of freedom.

Challenging the Text

9. (Evaluation) Encourage students to support their answers with specific facts. One possible reference might be l. 10 in "Song of Myself" #1. Here, he throws off the teachings and rules of the past to find a poetry that can carry his message.

Into the Poem

Using **BEFORE YOU READ** p. 362

Reading Focus

Have the class discuss whether the experience of suffering is necessary for someone to develop compassion.

Through the Poem

A. Literary Element: Setting
Point out to students that "gray and dim" refers to the daybreak. The phrase is a form of pathetic fallacy, reflecting the dismal sight of the wounded men. As a reference to the wounded men themselves, the phrase parallels the way the speaker first sees the men, covered with "gray and heavy blanket."

B. Critical Reading: Finding Details
Ask students to note the ages of the wounded men and to determine what effect the poet achieves by describing these soldiers side by side. [Possible answer: Whitman makes the men symbolically represent all soldiers by presenting an older man, a boy, and a young man.]

C. Literary Element: Symbol
Ask students to note Whitman's reference to Christ, who suffered and asked people to love one another and live in harmony. Whitman mentions him here as a symbol of the suffering during the Civil War.

BEFORE YOU READ

A SIGHT IN CAMP IN THE DAYBREAK GRAY AND DIM

Reading Focus

The Suffering of Thousands
In December 1862, Whitman traveled to Virginia to care for his brother George, who was wounded at the first battle of Fredericksburg. Though he discovered that George's injuries were minor, Whitman witnessed the terrible suffering of hundreds of other young men. Whitman volunteered to assist the staffs of several medical field units and hospitals. Comforting and feeding the injured and dying, bringing them treats, dressing their wounds, reading to them, and writing letters home to their families, Whitman helped to care for close to a hundred thousand soldiers by the end of the war. His experiences brought a wider dimension of tragedy into his poetry.

A Dialogue with the Text

READER'S LOG

When Whitman was visiting his wounded brother in Virginia, he took these notes:

"*Sight at daybreak*—in camp in front of the hospital tent on a stretcher (three dead men lying), each with a blanket spread over him—I lift up one and look at the young man's face, calm and yellow—'tis strange!

(Young man: I think this face of yours the face of my dead Christ!)"

As you read the following poem, write down the **images** that Whitman has drawn from his wartime notes.

Wounded Drummer Boy (c. 1862–1865) by William Morris Hunt (1824–1879). American. Oil on canvas (14″ × 19¼″).

Museum of Fine Arts, Boston/Gift from the Isaac Fenno Collection (18.393).

A Sight in Camp in the Daybreak Gray and Dim

Walt Whitman

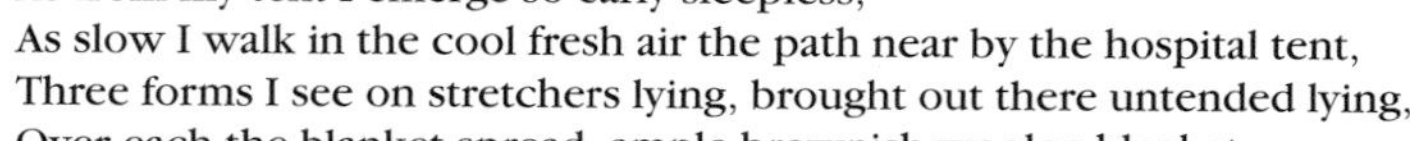

A sight in camp in the daybreak gray and dim,
As from my tent I emerge so early sleepless,
As slow I walk in the cool fresh air the path near by the hospital tent,
A Three forms I see on stretchers lying, brought out there untended lying,
Over each the blanket spread, ample brownish woolen blanket,
Gray and heavy blanket, folding, covering all.

Curious I halt and silent stand,
Then with light fingers I from the face of the nearest the first just lift the blanket;
Who are you elderly man so gaunt and grim, with well-gray'd hair, and flesh all sunken about the eyes?
Who are you my dear comrade?

B Then to the second I step—and who are you my child and darling?
Who are you sweet boy with cheeks yet blooming?

Then to the third—a face nor child nor old, very calm, as of beautiful yellow-white ivory;
Young man I think I know you—I think this face is the face of the Christ himself,
C Dead and divine and brother of all, and here again he lies.

OPTIONS FOR TEACHING

STRATEGIES FOR INCLUSION

Advanced Ask student pairs to describe the views of war conveyed in episodes of a current television series about war. Using support from these series, each pair should write a comparison and contrast essay that compares a contemporary outlook on war with Whitman's outlook.

English Language Development To help students connect **themes** from nineteenth-century poetry to modern events, remind them that during the American Civil War, 1861 to 1865, families were divided by geography and by philosophical beliefs. Discuss with students that the **image** of the last soldier's body is a reminder that everyone is equal in war.

PRIMARY **Sources** A JOURNAL

from Specimen Days

The following extracts are from Whitman's "memoranda book," which he called *Specimen Days.*

The Inauguration

March 4, 1865—The President[1] very quietly rode down to the Capitol in his own carriage, by himself, on a sharp trot, about noon, either because he wished to be on hand to sign bills, or to get rid of marching in line with the absurd procession, the muslin temple of liberty, and pasteboard monitor. I saw him on his return, at three o'clock, after the performance was over. He was in his plain two-horse barouche,[2] and looked very much worn and tired; the lines, indeed, of vast responsibilities, intricate questions, and demands of life and death, cut deeper than ever upon his dark brown face; yet all the old goodness, tenderness, sadness, and canny shrewdness, underneath the furrows. (I never see that man without feeling that he is one to become personally attached to, for his combination of purest, heartiest tenderness, and native western form of manliness.) By his side sat his little boy, of ten years. There were no soldiers, only a lot of civilians on horseback, with huge yellow scarves over their shoulders, riding around the carriage. (At the inauguration four years ago, he rode down and back again surrounded by a dense mass of armed cavalrymen eight deep, with drawn sabers; and there were sharpshooters stationed at every corner on the route.) I ought to make mention of the closing levee[3] of Saturday night last. Never before was such a compact jam in front of the White House—all the grounds filled, and away out to the spacious sidewalks. I was there, as I took a notion to go—was in the rush inside with the crowd—surged along the passageways, the Blue and other rooms, and through the great East Room. Crowds of country people, some very funny. Fine music from the Marine band, off in a side place. I saw Mr. Lincoln, dressed all in black, with white kid gloves and a claw-hammer coat, receiving, as in duty bound, shaking hands, looking very disconsolate, and as if he would give anything to be somewhere else.

1. **The President:** Abraham Lincoln. He would be assassinated in April, just a month after Whitman wrote this.
2. **barouche** (bə·ro͞osh′): four-wheeled, horse-drawn carriage.
3. **levee:** reception.

The Real War Will Never Get in the Books

And so goodbye to the war. I know not how it may have been, or may be, to others—to me the main interest I found (and still, on recollection, find) in the rank and file of the armies, both sides, and in those specimens amid the hospitals, and even the dead on the field. To me the points illustrating the latent personal character and eligibilities of these States, in the two or three millions of American young and middle-aged men, North and South, embodied in those armies—and especially the one-third or one-fourth of their number, stricken by wounds or disease at some time in the course of the contest—were of more significance even than the political interests involved. (As so much of a race depends on how it faces death, and how it stands personal anguish and sickness. As, in the glints of emotions under emergencies, and the indirect traits and asides in Plutarch, we get far profounder clues to the antique world than all its more formal history.)

Future years will never know the seething hell and the black infernal background of countless minor scenes and interiors, (not the

Primary Sources

Whitman was perhaps premature in his judgment about war writers. Stephen Crane was able to write convincingly about the Civil War even though he was not born until 1871 and lacked the firsthand contact with the war that Whitman had. Have students compare Whitman's descriptions of the Civil War with Crane's descriptions in "A Mystery of Heroism" on pp. 486–492 in Collection 10. Then, ask students to compare "The Inauguration" to Lincoln's Gettysburg Address on p. 479 in Collection 10.

STRATEGIES FOR INCLUSION

Less Proficient Readers Let students work in pairs to list the facts given above about Lincoln and about the war. Then, ask students to decide why these particular details were reported by Whitman. [He shows the loneliness and sadness of Lincoln, the pain and cruelty and suffering of the war.]

Advanced Encourage students to study these extracts at a higher level and to note Whitman's use of rhetorical methods to make his points. Some strategies include the frequent use of dashes to insert further comment; the long sentences of the reasoning man, trying for thoughtful analysis; and the connotative language, such as referring to bodies with the term *carcasses.*

Auditory The conversational **tone** of Whitman's writing in *Specimen Days* lends itself to oral reading. Assign good readers one paragraph each to prepare a reading for the entire class. Stop at the end of each paragraph for the listeners to summarize what has been said and to make comments. ☞

Making Meanings

First Thoughts

1. Responses will vary. Students may feel sympathy, sadness, or loss.

Shaping Interpretations

2. Whitman develops the setting by using images from his notes—three dead men with blankets spread over them, lifting a blanket to see a young man's face, and the daybreak "gray and dim."
3. The dead man was young and had sacrificed his life in an effort directed toward peace and unity. Whitman may be using the trio symbolically to evoke the Christian notion of the Father, Son, and Holy Spirit.
4. The tone is somber. The speaker is sleepless and walks slowly as he spies the forms lying on stretchers. At the end, he evokes the memory of Christ's Crucifixion.
5. There is a fundamental theme of camaraderie in the poem. Whitman's point is that the Civil War has ruthlessly violated the bonds between people.

Extending the Text

6. **(Evaluation)** Images include the camp (ll. 1–3), the three bodies from a distance (ll. 4–6), lifting the blanket from the first man's face (ll. 8–10), looking at the face of the second figure (ll. 11–12), and looking at the face of the third man (ll. 13–15).
7. **(Evaluation)** Responses should indicate the images the student identifies in Whitman as well as examples of that same image in one or more of the suggested media productions.

official surface courteousness of the generals, not the few great battles) of the Secession war; and it is best they should not—the real war will never get in the books. In the mushy influences of current times, too, the fervid atmosphere and typical events of those years are in danger of being totally forgotten. I have at night watched by the side of a sick man in the hospital, one who could not live many hours. I have seen his eyes flash and burn as he raised himself and recurred to the cruelties on his surrendered brother, and mutilations of the corpse afterward. (See, in the preceding pages, the incident at Upperville—the seventeen killed as in the description, were left there on the ground. After they dropped dead, no one touched them—all were made sure of, however. The carcasses were left for the citizens to bury or not, as they chose.)

Such was the war. It was not a quadrille[4] in a ballroom. Its interior history will not only never be written—its practicality, minutiae of deeds and passions, will never be even suggested. The actual soldier of 1862–1865, North and South, with all his ways, his incredible dauntlessness, habits, practices, tastes, language, his fierce friendship, his appetite, rankness, his superb strength and animality, lawless gait, and a hundred unnamed lights and shades of camp, I say, will never be written—perhaps must not and should not be.

The preceding notes may furnish a few stray glimpses into that life, and into those lurid interiors, never to be fully conveyed to the future. The hospital part of the drama from 1861 to 1865, deserves indeed to be recorded. Of that many-threaded drama, with its sudden and strange surprises, its confounding of prophecies, its moments of despair, the dread of foreign interference, the interminable campaigns, the bloody battles, the mighty and cumbrous and green armies, the drafts and bounties—the immense money expenditure, like a heavy-pouring constant rain—with, over the whole land, the last three years of the struggle, an unending, universal mourning wail of women, parents, orphans—the marrow of the tragedy concentrated in those Army Hospitals—(it seemed sometimes as if the whole interest of the land, North and South, was one vast central hospital, and all the rest of the affair but flanges)—those forming the untold and unwritten history of the war—infinitely greater (like life's) than the few scraps and distortions that are ever told or written. Think how much, and of importance, will be—how much, civic and military, has already been—buried in the grave, in eternal darkness.

—Walt Whitman

4. **quadrille** (kwə·dril'): French dance for four couples.

Making Meanings

First Thoughts

1. What was your emotional response to "A Sight in Camp"? What specific words or **images** affected your response the most?

Shaping Interpretations

2. Look back at the notes you took in your Reader's Log. How did Whitman develop the **setting** from the notes that inspired the poem?
3. Why, given the circumstances of the Civil War, might the poet have seen the face of Christ on one of the dead soldiers? What might be the significance of the fact that the "forms" are a trio?
4. In Whitman's poems, we seem to be overhearing a man's conversation with himself. How would you describe the **tone** of this poem? What main elements support your description?
5. The point of the poem is never openly stated. What do you think is the **message** behind the poem?

Options for Teaching

Crossing the Curriculum

Social Sciences Help students to connect their learning in other classes with their study of Whitman by brainstorming all that they have learned in U.S. history about Abraham Lincoln and the Civil War. Then, ask whether Whitman's comments have added to their understanding of both topics.

Music Ask students to choose songs or ballads written about the Civil War to accompany oral readings of Whiman's writings. Ask them to explain why they chose the songs that they did.

Extending the Text

6. One of Whitman's biographers, Paul Zweig, says that Whitman had a genius for the single line, "the verbal snapshot." Do you agree with this observation? Which **images** in this poem make particularly unusual and evocative "verbal snapshots"?

7. Think of movies or television series you have seen set during the Civil War. Based on what you know about the Civil War, which media depictions strike you as best capturing the "real war" that Whitman describes in *Specimen Days* (page 363)?

CHOICES: Building Your Portfolio

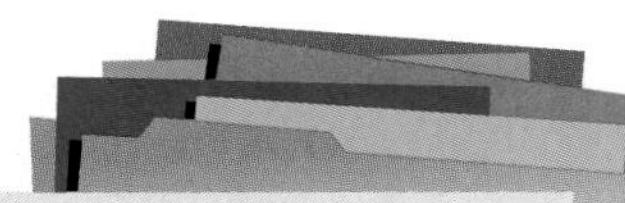

Writer's Notebook

1. Collecting Ideas for a Reflective Essay

Make two columns in your Writer's Notebook. In the first column, list some experiences you've had, large or small, recently or long ago. In the second column, write down some ideas that each incident makes you think about. For example, perhaps you once saw some young children playing war games and found yourself wondering if conflict is an inevitable part of the human condition. Save your notes for possible use in the Writer's Workshop on page 401.

Critical Writing

2. Rebel with a Cause

In a brief essay, contrast Whitman's subject matter and **style** with those of one of the Fireside Poets (pages 175–193). In your essay, respond to the following statement by Whitman:

"For grounds for *Leaves of Grass,* as a poem, I abandoned conventional themes, which do not appear in it: none of the stock ornamentation or choice plots of love or war, or high, exceptional personages of Old World song . . . no legend, or myth, or romance, nor euphemism, nor rhyme."

Creative Writing / Speaking and Listening

3. In the Whitman Tradition

Write a free-verse poem in the style of Walt Whitman, using one of the poems in this collection as a model. (You could even begin your poem with one of Whitman's openers, such as "I hear America singing" or "I celebrate myself.") Before you start, make notes on the following to help you decide on subject matter:

- How would Whitman celebrate diversity today?
- Who would be his overlooked heroes?
- What landscapes would he cherish?
- With whom would he empathize?
- What "songs," or lives, would he pay tribute to?

In **free verse** (page 355), you are not restricted to the use of rhymes and regular meters, but you will want to use **imagery** and **sound effects** (alliteration, repetition, parallel structure), as well as one or more of Whitman's techniques: catalogs, rolling cadences, and modulations of voice that result in a specific tone.

When you finish your poem, organize a class poetry reading. As you and other students read your poems aloud, identify the images and tone that seem the most like those Whitman used.

Critical Writing

4. Reading Nature

You have seen that it was a habit of the Puritans to "read" nature for signs of divinity. You have also seen how the Transcendentalists "read" nature.

Beyond the Poems

Choices: Building Your Portfolio

1. **Writer's Notebook** Remind students to save their work. They may use it as prewriting for the Writer's Workshop on p. 401.
2. **Critical Writing** Invite students to make cluster diagrams of both subject matter and style for Whitman and the Fireside Poets before they write their contrast essay.
3. **Creative Writing/Speaking and Listening** Encourage students to make lists of items to be included in their poems. Have them share these lists in small groups. After the poems are written, let the students read them aloud to each other in pairs; the listeners should give feedback by pointing out similarities to Whitman's poems.
4. **Critical Writing** Ask students to organize their thinking by using a three-column chart. Have students list for their essays at least three examples of how each writer "read" nature.

Bradford	Emerson	Whitman
[North American wilderness not a Pisgah, from where Moses viewed the Promised Land. (p. 31)]	[The Universal Being circulates through people who are close to nature (p. 221).]	

STRATEGIES FOR INCLUSION

Special Needs In order to help students better understand Whitman's statement and complete the activity more easily, divide the class into mixed-ability groups with four members per group for activity #2. Have them discuss what they think Whitman means by the quotation, and ask them to find examples from *Leaves of Grass* to support their opinions before they write their essays.

Learners Having Difficulty Students who are uneasy about their skills may feel more comfortable working in pairs or in small groups for activity #3. Each group can work together and turn in one project. With this procedure, it will be important to establish specific tasks (such as discussion leader, writer, and reviser) although all students are responsible for helping to create a successful project.

5. **Critical Writing** Have students add a third column to their charts titled Examples/Quotations. Ask them to list specific examples and quotations from Whitman's prose and poetry that highlight the differences and similarities in tone, democratic feelings, lists and catalogs, and vigorous language.
6. **Critical Writing/Speaking and Listening** Divide the class according to the modern writer students chose. Have pairs within each group take the roles of Whitman and the contemporary writer and to improvise a literary dialogue between them. Then, each pair should exchange roles. After the role-playing and before they write their speeches, have students take notes on what transpired.
7. **Music** Some students may want to work in groups that include writers as well as musicians to create a spoken-word performance with musical accompaniment.
8. **Art** Let students choose whether to work alone or in pairs for this project. Have them create a cluster diagram to help them gather ideas before they begin the book cover.
9. **Crossing the Curriculum: History** Have students work in groups of four or five for this activity. Assign different aspects of the war to each group so that displays are not duplicated.

In a brief essay, compare and contrast Whitman's "reading" of nature with that of the Puritan Edward Taylor (page 72) and the Transcendentalist Ralph Waldo Emerson (page 216).

Critical Writing

5. You Can't Take the Poetry Out of the Prose

Read the sample of Whitman's prose writing in Primary Sources on page 363. In a brief essay, compare Whitman's prose **style** with that of his poems. Before you write, collect your data in a chart like the following:

	Prose	Poetry
Tone		
Democratic feelings		
Use of lists and catalogs		
Use of vigorous language		

Critical Writing / Speaking and Listening

6. Whitman Lives On

Many great poets around the world have been inspired by the **style, themes,** and **tone** of Walt Whitman's poetry. Read Baca's poem "Who Understands Me but Me" on page 360 or Pablo Neruda's poem "Full Powers" on page 369. Then, imagining that you are Whitman, write a three-paragraph speech in which you discuss your response to the poem your literary descendant has written. How would Whitman react to the message of Baca or Neruda? Would he be pleased to recognize his influence and encourage similarities between his poems and those of his poetic descendant? Present your speech to the class.

Music

7. Musical Whitman

Music, singing, melody—Whitman's poetry is full of references to music and sound. Find a recording of vocal or instrumental music that expresses the spirit of Walt Whitman's poetry, and play it for the class. Or, if you wish, compose and play your own musical tribute to Whitman.

Art

8. Design a Book Cover

In the first edition of *Leaves of Grass,* Whitman selected a green, pebbled cloth for the cover of his book. He stamped the title *Leaves of Grass* in gold paint, using simple letters with roots descending from the letters and leaves shooting up above them. The book was the size of a piece of typewriter paper, about eight by eleven and a quarter inches.

Design a new cover for Whitman's *Leaves of Grass.* Try to reflect the feeling or content of the poems in your design, but also reflect your personal response to Whitman's poetry. Hold an art show, and display your cover design with the designs of other students.

Crossing the Curriculum: History

9. Eyewitnesses

At your school or local library, find a book of pictures by a Civil War photographer (page 414). Make a chart comparing photographic depictions of soldiers with Whitman's poetic depiction in "A Sight in Camp in the Daybreak Gray and Dim." Set up a museum display using reproductions of Civil War photographs accompanied by captions written in Whitmanesque style.

Maria Stenzel/National Geographic Image Collection, Courtesy Walt Whitman House, Camden, New Jersey.

PORTFOLIO ASSESSMENT

Choices: Assessment Criteria For help in evaluating these Choices assignments, see the criteria in the ***Portfolio Management System,*** pp. 111–113.

STRATEGIES FOR INCLUSION

Auditory Ask students to read Whitman's writings aloud for activity #5. This may help them to identify the differences in tone and language more easily.

Sygma.

Pablo Neruda.

Pablo Neruda

(1904–1973)

Pablo Neruda was born and educated in Chile. Neruda wrote that he went out "hunting poems" as a child, and he received his first acclaim as a poet at the age of sixteen when he won first prize in a poetry competition. By the age of twenty he was already regarded as a young poet with great promise. In addition to enjoying an enormously full and diverse life as a writer, Neruda served as a diplomat and a member of the Chilean Senate for several years. He also lived in exile from his homeland when the Chilean right-wing government outlawed his socialistic political party and terminated his senatorial position. Before resettling on Isla Negra, in Chile, in 1953, Neruda lived in many countries around the world, including Burma (now called Myanmar), Italy, Spain, France, Mexico, Russia, and China. In 1971, he was awarded the Nobel Prize in literature. Known for his diverse range of poetic styles and voices, Neruda is celebrated for his humanism, his call for peace and equality, and his love and respect for the natural elements of the world. His poems are questions, riddles, political shouts, observations, homages, and introspective movements toward truth. Like Whitman, he has influenced and inspired many of the great poets of the twentieth century.

ABOUT THE AUTHOR

Once, while playing near his home as a child, Neruda spotted another child's hand reaching through a space in a fence to offer him a toy lamb. Neruda ran to his house and then hurried back with a pine cone—"half-open, balsamic, sweet-smelling"—and put it through the space toward the unknown child on the opposite side. When asked why he wrote poetry, Neruda would sometimes talk about this experience from his childhood. "Poetry is like bread," Neruda wrote, "and it must be shared by everyone, the men of letters and the peasants, by everyone in our vast, incredible, extraordinary family of man."

CONNECTING WITH WHITMAN'S POETRY

Like Walt Whitman, Pablo Neruda uses images from nature in his poetry. Ask students to make a cluster diagram like the following to compare Neruda's images from nature in "Full Powers" with Whitman's images from nature in the excerpt from "Song of Myself" on p. 359.

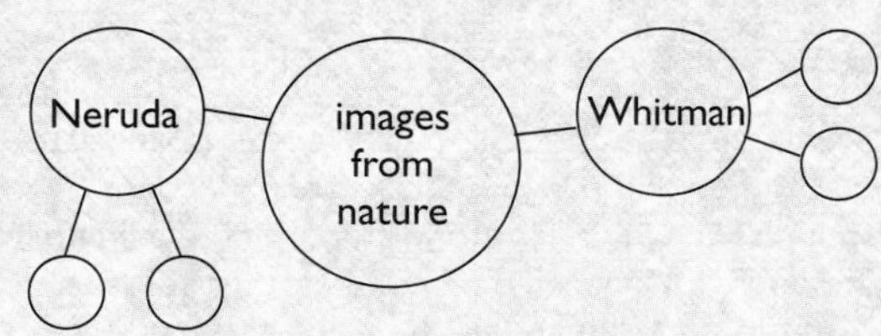

Background

Whitman, in "Song of Myself" #52, bequeaths himself to the dirt in order to filter the blood of others; Neruda expresses a related sentiment in the closing line of his long poem, *The Heights of Macchu Picchu.* The two poets also share an elemental love of the earth and humanity.

A Dialogue with the Text

Have students use a graph like the one below to record these observations. They should divide the paper into two columns, one for main ideas and quotations and one for comments on those ideas.

Ideas & Quotations	Comments

PROGRAM MANAGER

Planning Instruction See **Teaching Notes, *Teaching Resources A,*** p. 127, for objectives and a summary for this selection.

Before You Read

Full Powers

Background

Like many great writers the world over, the Chilean poet Pablo Neruda was deeply inspired by Walt Whitman's *Leaves of Grass.* In fact, this Nobel laureate declared that Whitman was his most important literary influence. Neruda made the following remarks to a New York City audience a year before his death:

"I was barely fifteen when I discovered Walt Whitman, my primary creditor. I stand here among you today still owing this marvelous debt that has helped me live.

"To renegotiate this debt is to begin by making it public, by proclaiming myself the humble servant of the poet who measured the earth with long, slow strides, pausing everywhere to love and to examine, to learn, to teach, and to admire. . . . Clearly, he feared neither morality nor immorality, nor did he attempt to define the boundaries between pure and impure poetry. He is the first absolute poet, and it was his intention not only to sing but to impart his vast vision of the relationships of men and of nations. In this sense, his obvious nationalism is part of an organic universality. He considers himself indebted to happiness and sorrow, to advanced cultures and primitive societies.

"Greatness has many faces, but I, a poet who writes in Spanish, learned more from Walt Whitman than from Cervantes [Spain's premier Renaissance novelist, poet, and playwright]. In Whitman's poetry the ignorant are never humbled, and the human condition is never derided.

"We are still living in a Whitmanesque epoch. . . . The bard complained of the all-powerful European influence that continued to dominate the literature of his time. In fact, it was he, Walt Whitman, in the persona of a specific geography, who for the first time in history brought honor to an American name."

A Dialogue with the Text

In many ways, Whitman and Neruda are two poets cut from the same cloth. As you read Neruda's poem, write down **images** and feelings that remind you of parts of "Song of Myself." Be especially aware of lines that seem to actually refer to Whitman's poetry.

OPTIONS FOR TEACHING

INTEGRATING THE LANGUAGE ARTS

Strategic Reading To help students appreciate the sounds of the two languages and to connect sound to meaning, have one student read a line of the poem in Spanish, then have another student read the same line in English, going back and forth until the poem has been read in both languages, one line at a time. Then, have another student read the Spanish poem in full, followed by the English translation in full. Ask students to discuss what feelings and associations were raised by the readings.

Plenos Poderes

Pablo Neruda

A puro sol escribo, a plena calle,
a pleno mar, en donde puedo canto,
sólo la noche errante me detiene
pero en su interrupción recojo espacio,
recojo sombra para mucho tiempo.

El trigo negro de la noche crece
mientras mis ojos miden la pradera
y así de sol a sol hago las llaves:
busco en la oscuridad las cerraduras
y voy abriendo al mar las puertas rotas
hasta llenar armarios con espuma.

Y no me canso de ir y de volver,
no me para la muerte con su piedra,
no me canso de ser y de no ser.

A veces me pregunto si de donde
si de padre o de madre o cordillera
heredé los deberes minerales,

los hilos de un océano encendido
y sé que sigo y sigo porque sigo
y canto porque canto y porque canto.

Full Powers

Pablo Neruda

translated from the Spanish by
Ben Belitt and Alastair Reid

I write in the clear sun, in the teeming street, **A**
at full sea-tide, in a place where I can sing; **B**
only the wayward night inhibits me,
but, interrupted by it, I recover space,
I gather shadows to last me a long time. **C**

The black crop of the night is growing
while my eyes meanwhile take measure of the meadows.
So, from one sun to the next, I forge the keys.
In the darkness, I look for the locks **D**
and keep on opening broken doors to the sea,
for it to fill the wardrobes with its foam.

And I do not weary of going and returning.
Death, in its stone aspect, does not halt me.
I am weary neither of being nor of non-being.

Sometimes I puzzle over origins—
was it from my father, my mother, or the mountains
that I inherited debts to minerality,

the fine threads spreading from a sea on fire?
And I know that I keep on going for the going's sake,
and I sing because I sing and because I sing.

A. Literary Element: Point of View

? From what point of view is this poem written? [First-person point of view.]

B. Reader's Response: Connecting with the Text

? Which Whitman poem in this Collection refers to poetry as "singing"? [Sample responses: "I Hear America Singing" on p. 352; or, "Song of Myself" on pp. 347, 353, 356, 359.]

C. Critical Reading: Analyzing Lyric Poems

? How are Neruda's and Whitman's poems similar? How are they different? [Possible answers: Students may hear a similar songlike cadence. However, they may also note that Whitman's singing is a joyous celebration of workers, while Neruda's song is a dark search for the self that connects life and death.]

D. Critical Reading: Finding Details

? Which words or phrases indicate a search for the self or understanding? [Possible answers: Keys, locks, opening broken doors.]

CLASSROOM MANAGEMENT

Combining Experiences In order to get the maximum input for their Reader's Logs, have students make individual lists before working in groups; then, each student will have something to contribute to the discussion.

Assigning Tasks So that each group works productively, assign roles or ask students to volunteer for tasks so that each group member has a responsibility: discussion leader (makes sure everybody gets to contribute), note taker (records suggestions by all groups members), timer (makes sure the group stays on task and follows a schedule), and exhibit designer (prepares exhibit for presentation to the class).

A. Reader's Response: Extending the Text

? What might the symbol of the sea mean? [Sample responses: The sea may represent death surrounding him; or, the sea is life-affirming, since it gives a view to the living.]

Finding Common Ground

To make sure that each student has an opportunity to participate in the group discussion, instruct groups to select leaders and note takers. The leader's job is to call on one student at a time to read his or her notes and observations. The note taker records the key images for the entire group to organize and present to the rest of the class in an oral report or on a poster.

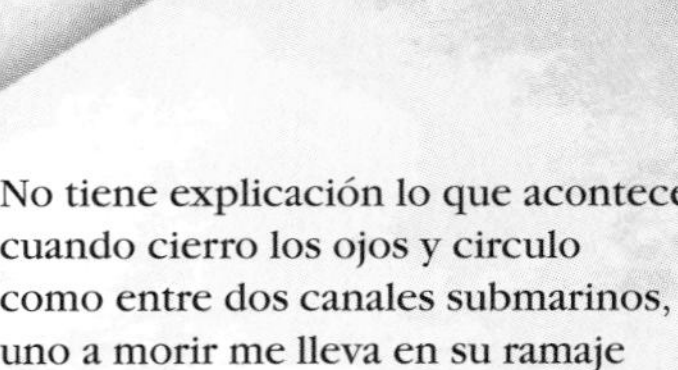

No tiene explicación lo que acontece
cuando cierro los ojos y circulo
como entre dos canales submarinos,
uno a morir me lleva en su ramaje
y el otro canta para que yo cante.

Así pues de no ser estoy compuesto
y como el mar asalta el arrecife
con cápsulas saladas de blancura
y retrata le piedra con la ola,
así lo que en la muerte me rodea
abre en mí la ventana de la vida
y en pleno paroxismo estoy durmiendo.
A plena luz camino por la sombra.

There is no way of explaining what does happen
when I close my eyes and waver
as between two lost channels under water.
One lifts me in its branches toward my dying,
and the other sings in order that I may sing.

And so I am made up of a non-being,
and, as the sea goes battering at a reef
in wave on wave of salty white-tops
and drags back stones in its retreating wash,
so what there is in death surrounding me
opens in me a window out to living,
and, in the spasm of being, I go on sleeping.
In the full light of day, I walk in the shade.

Finding Common Ground

Now that you've read Neruda's poem, meet in a small group, and share the comments you recorded in your Reader's Logs.

Read your notes aloud, and discuss each other's observations and thoughts.

- Identify the **images** and feelings that different members of your group jotted down.
- Discuss the elements in the poem that seem to refer directly to Whitman's "Song of Myself."
- List the qualities that Whitman and Neruda seem to share. For instance, how do they view themselves in relation to others? How do they view the natural world in relation to the world of people and industry?
- Share your observations and thoughts with the rest of the class.

Options for Teaching

Assessment Tools

Self-Reflection Ask students to review their Reader's Logs while they think and write about the spirit of their own lives. They can refer to Neruda, Whitman, or both in expressing their thoughts.

Ongoing Assessment Ask students periodically to review and summarize any entries about Whitman's or Neruda's poetry they have made in their Reader's Logs. Allow students a few minutes of class time to write and to submit their summaries. Invite students to repeat the activity at the end of the Collection and to compare their responses: Have their opinions changed? Explain. How have their critical reading skills improved?

TELL IT SLANT

Theme:

Theme: Dazzling Gradually
Emily Dickinson's poetry is challenging in its simplicity. Able to see the universal in the particular, Dickinson uses slant rhyme, metaphor, paradox, irony, and unconventional punctuation to express profound truths with commonplace themes.

Thematic Focus

A key feature of Dickinson's poetry is her succinct, idiosyncratic expression of thought.

- **Heart! We will forget him!** An attempt to forget a lover reveals the conflict between a thinking mind and a feeling heart.
- **If you were coming in the Fall** Time imagery and figures of speech illustrate the yearning one feels with unfulfilled love.
- **The Soul selects her own Society** The wise soul knows the best course to follow when it chooses certain things or people above others.
- **Some keep the Sabbath going to Church** The speaker observes that there is more than one way to keep the Sabbath and get to heaven.
- **I taste a liquor never brewed** A metaphor of inebriation describes a joyous, reckless zest for life.
- **Much Madness is divinest Sense** The paradox of truly independent thinking is explored.
- **Apparently with no surprise** Life and death calmly play out a drama.
- **Tell all the Truth but tell it slant** Truth is best told obliquely.
- **Success is counted sweetest** Detachment is needed to truly comprehend success.
- **Because I could not stop for Death** The poet imaginatively captures the experience of death in an extended metaphor.
- **I heard a Fly buzz—when I died** The moment of death is described, paradoxically, with sensory detail.
- **I died for Beauty—but was scarce** Truth and beauty are one even in death.

Literary Focus

Literary Element	Selection / Feature
Slant rhyme	**Dickinson poems**

Writing Focus

The following flow chart shows how the writing assignment for each selection relates to and builds toward the culminating writing assignment presented in the Writer's Workshop at the end of the unit.

Selection	Work-in-Progress Assignment
Dickinson poems	Freewrite about a topic to explore p. 396
Writer's Workshop	Write a reflective essay pp. 401–403

Collection 8 **TELL IT SLANT**

Collection Planner

SELECTION/ FEATURE	PUPIL'S EDITION			
	Literary Elements / Active Reading	Writing	Speaking and Listening	Language and Vocabulary
Heart! We will forget him! **If you were coming in the Fall** **The Soul selects her own Society** **Some keep the Sabbath going to Church** **I taste a liquor never brewed** **Much Madness is divinest Sense** **Apparently with no surprise** **Tell all the Truth but tell it slant** **Success is counted sweetest** **Because I could not stop for Death** **I heard a Fly buzz— when I died** **I died for Beauty— but was scarce** Emily Dickinson (pp. 372–396) Primary Sources: An Edited Poem (p. 377) **Student to Student** (p. 380) **Connections: Emily Dickinson's Homestead** Anne Bernays (p. 389) Primary Sources: Higginson's Account of Dickinson (p. 394)	• Reader's Log pp. 374, 376, 378, 381, 382, 383, 385, 386, 388, 391, 392, 393 • Elements of Literature: Slant Rhyme p. 380	• Critical Writing: Write essay comparing one of Dickinson's poems with a work from another poet p. 396 • Creative Writing: Write poem using one of Dickinson's themes and several of her techniques p. 396 • Critical Writing/Music: Analyze Dickinson's use of traditional hymn meter in her poetry p. 396	• Critical Writing/ Music: Sing Dickinson poem to the tune of "O God, Our Help in Ages Past" p. 396 • Performance/ Research: Prepare and perform dramatic monologue in Dickinson's voice p. 396	
The American Language: A Period of Vocabulary Growth Gary Q. Arpin (pp. 398–400)				• Try It Out p. 400
Writer's Workshop: Reflective Essay (pp. 401–403)		• Writing Process: Reflective essay pp. 401–403		
Language Workshop: Varying Sentence Beginnings (p. 404)				• Language Handbook: Revising for variety p. 1237 • Varying Sentence Beginnings p. 404
Learning for Life (p. 405)		• Write brochure p. 405	• Conduct mock interviews p. 405	

Collection Resources

Teaching Resources A	Audiovisual Resources Binder	Test Booklet
Cross-Curricular Activity p. 165	Fine Art Transparency 8.1	Selection Test pp. 91–92

Computer disk or CD-ROM
Audiocassette
Overhead Transparency

PROGRAM RESOURCES

Electronic Media	Teaching Resources with Organizer: Teaching Resources A	Teaching Resources with Organizer: Other Resources	Audiovisual Resources Binder
• Test Generator	• Teaching Notes pp. 141–146 • Reading Organizers pp. 148–156, 158–160 • Language Link p. 157 • Words to Own pp. 161–162	• Test Booklet: Selection Test pp. 91–92 • Portfolio Management System pp. 39, 114–115	• Elements of Literature Transparency 8.2 • Selected Readings, Audiocassette 1, Side B
• Test Generator	• Teaching Notes p. 147	• Test Booklet: The American Language pp. 93–94	
		• Portfolio Management System pp. 116–118	• Revision Transparencies 8.3–8.4
• Language Workshop: Sentence beginnings	• Language Workshop pp. 163–164		
		• Portfolio Management System p. 119	

Proofreading Warm-ups

You can use the following exercises to help students practice their proofreading skills. Copy a set of incorrect sentences on the chalkboard and have students find and correct the spelling, punctuation, usage, and mechanical errors in each sentence. Ask students to share and discuss their responses.

	Sentences with Errors	Sentences Corrected	Skills Covered
1	**a.** emily dickinson, was born into a well to do new England family **b.** when she was old enough Emily was sent too a Boarding School	**a.** Emily Dickinson was born into a well-to-do New England family. **b.** When she was old enough, Emily was sent to a boarding school.	Capitalization, Comma usage, Hyphen usage, Spelling, End Marks
2	**a.** dickinson sent a few of her poems' to the Editor of the Atlantic Monthly **b.** the editor Thomas Wentworth Higginson encouraged her work	**a.** Dickinson sent a few of her poems to the editor of the Atlantic Monthly. **b.** The editor, Thomas Wentworth Higginson, encouraged her work.	Capitalization, Apostrophe usage, Underline magazine title, Comma usage, End marks
3	**a.** slant rhyme is a close but not exact rhyming sound, its also called off rhyme or half rhyme **b.** Word pears like society/majority and nerve/love is examples of slant rhyme.	**a.** Slant rhyme is a close, but not exact, rhyming sound; it's also called off rhyme or half rhyme. **b.** Word pairs like society/majority and nerve/love are examples of slant rhyme.	Capitalization, Comma usage, Semicolon usage, Apostrophe usage, Spelling, Subject-Verb agreement, End marks
4	**a.** the theme of heart! we will forget him! is unrequited love **b.** in the 2nd stanza lines 2 and 4 are an example of slant rhyme	**a.** The theme of "Heart! We will forget him!" is unrequited love. **b.** In the second stanza, lines two and four are an example of slant rhyme.	Capitalization, Quotation marks for poem titles, Comma usage, Write out abbreviations/numerals, End marks
5	**a.** witch of Dickinson's poems do you like best asked Mr. Roche **b.** I think Id chose Tell all the Truth but tell it slant" said Sarah	**a.** "Which of Dickinson's poems do you like best?" asked Mr. Roche. **b.** "I think I'd choose 'Tell all the Truth but tell it slant,'" said Sarah.	Quotation marks (double and single), Capitalization, Spelling, Apostrophe usage, Verb error, End marks
6	**a.** the poem Much Madness is divinest Sense reminds me of Thoreau's line about marching to the beat of a different drummer said Mr. Crumpton **b.** the poem explore's how threatening idependant thinking can be to the group mentality	**a.** "The poem 'Much Madness is divinest Sense' reminds me of Thoreau's line about marching to the beat of a different drummer," said Mr. Crumpton. **b.** The poem explores how threatening independent thinking can be to the group mentality.	Quotation marks (double and single), Capitalization, Comma usage, Apostrophe usage, Spelling, End marks
7	**a.** the poem Some keep the Sabbath going to Church was the 5th of 7 poems published in Dickinson's life-time **b.** although Dickinson rejected her families religion she was a spiritual person	**a.** The poem "Some keep the Sabbath going to Church" was the fifth of seven poems published in Dickinson's lifetime. **b.** Although Dickinson rejected her family's religion, she was a spiritual person.	Capitalization, Quotation marks for poem titles, Write out abbreviations/numerals, Hyphen usage, Spelling, Apostrophe usage, Comma usage, End marks
8	**a.** emily dickinsons home in Amherst Massachusetts is open to the public **b.** can we gets extra credit for visiting it inquired Tom hopefuly	**a.** Emily Dickinson's home in Amherst, Massachusetts, is open to the public. **b.** "Can we get extra credit for visiting it?" inquired Tom hopefully.	Capitalization, Apostrophe usage, Comma usage, Verb error, Spelling, End marks
9	**a.** american english enjoyed growth in the Nineteenth Century **b.** backwoods english spoken by people who lived west of the allegheny mountains contributed colorfull expressions	**a.** American English enjoyed growth in the nineteenth century. **b.** Backwoods English, spoken by people who lived west of the Allegheny Mountains, contributed colorful expressions.	Capitalization, Nonstandard usage, Comma usage, Spelling, End marks
10	**a.** writers begun to use vernacular which is a regions common spoken language during the 19th century **b.** mark twain used vernacular in the adventures of huckleberry finn	**a.** Writers began to use vernacular, which is a region's common spoken language, during the nineteenth century. **b.** Mark Twain used vernacular in The Adventures of Huckleberry Finn.	Capitalization, Verb error, Comma usage, Apostrophe usage, Write out abbreviation/numerals, Underline book titles, End marks

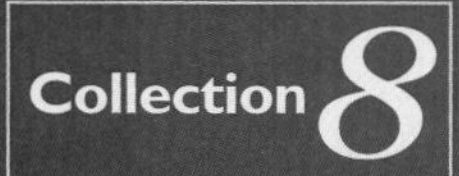

Emily Dickinson

We think of her hidden in a white dress
among the folded linens and sachets
of well-kept cupboards, or just out of sight
sending jellies and notes with no address
to all the wondering Amherst neighbors.
Eccentric as New England weather
the stiff wind of her mind, stinging or gentle,
blew two half-imagined lovers off.
Yet legend won't explain the sheer sanity
of vision, the serious mischief
of language, the economy of pain.

—Linda Pastan (1932–   )

"Emily Dickinson"

? Which two aspects of Dickinson does Pastan contrast in this poem? What does this poem suggest to you about the relationship between Dickinson's poetry and her legend? [Possible responses: Pastan contrasts the legend of Dickinson's eccentric personal life with the sanity, mischief, and economy of her poetry. Pastan suggests that there is nothing in the legend to account for the genius in Dickinson's work.]

PORTFOLIO ASSESSMENT

Parent/Guardian Involvement For forms that will help a parent or guardian review and respond to a student's portfolio, see the ***Portfolio Management System,*** pp. 62–63.

PROGRAM MANAGER

- **Integrated Assessment** For a summative assessment of the literature and language skills taught in this collection, see **Selection Test, *Test Booklet,*** pp. 91–92.
- **Instructional Support** See **Fine Art Transparency** 8.1. Review teacher's notes for transparencies in the ***Audiovisual Resources Binder*** for suggestions on how to tie the transparencies to specific reading selections.
- **Extending Collection Theme** See **Cross-Curricular Activity: Tell It Slant, *Teaching Resources A,*** p. 165 for an activity in another discipline and for evaluation criteria.

QUICK PLANNING GUIDE

Into the Poems

Through the Poems

Beyond the Poems

- **Writer's Notebook:** Freewrite reflective notes
- **Critical Writing:** Write an essay comparing one of Dickinson's poems to the work of another poet
- **Creative Writing:** Write a poem
- **Critical Writing/Music:** Write analysis of hymn meter
- **Performance/Research:** Present a dramatic monologue
- **Art:** Create a poetry booklet

Emily Dickinson

(1830–1886)

A brief outline of Emily Dickinson's life reads like the plot of a story destined to become a legend. Once upon a time there was born to a religious and well-to-do New England family a daughter, whom they named Emily. As a child, she was lively, well behaved, and obedient; she took pleasure in the busy household of which she was a part and in the seasonal games, parties, and outings of a village snowy cold in winter and brilliantly green and flowering in the summer.

At home she learned to cook and sew. When she was old enough, she was sent to a school where strict rules did not keep Emily and the other girls from displaying their high spirits as they enjoyed the entertainments of boarding school life. Emily took part in these, but not always with as much enthusiasm as she might have. As she said many years later, something sad and reserved in her nature made her "a mourner among the children."

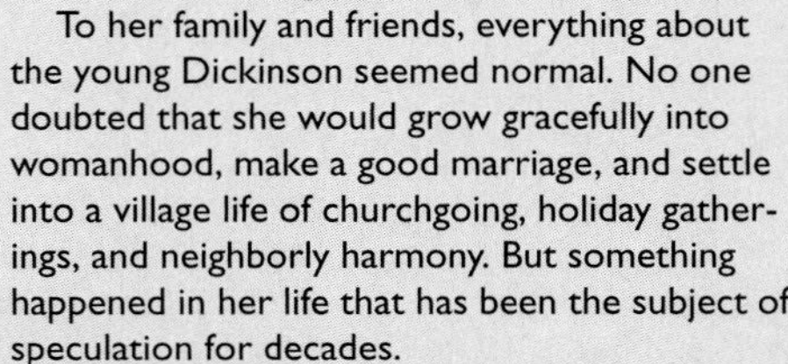

Culver Pictures.

To her family and friends, everything about the young Dickinson seemed normal. No one doubted that she would grow gracefully into womanhood, make a good marriage, and settle into a village life of churchgoing, holiday gatherings, and neighborly harmony. But something happened in her life that has been the subject of speculation for decades.

When Dickinson was twenty-four years old, her father, who had become a U.S. congressman, took her with him to Washington, D.C., and then on to Philadelphia. The journey seems to have marked the start of a turning point in her life. Her father may have taken her with him because she had fallen in love with someone she could never marry. This person might have been a married lawyer, older than Emily, a man who would die that year of tuberculosis.

Whatever happened, it seems likely that in the course of the journey, Emily fell in love with someone else: Charles Wadsworth, who was also married and who was pastor of the Arch Street Presbyterian Church in Philadelphia. Letters to Wadsworth show that Dickinson saw him as a "muse," someone who could inspire her, someone she could love passionately in her imagination.

But, in 1862, Wadsworth took up a new assignment in San Francisco. His leaving seems to have caused a great crisis in Dickinson's life: "I sing," she wrote around this time, "as the boy does by the burying ground, because I am afraid."

The Recluse of Amherst

The young woman quietly and abruptly withdrew from all social life except that involving her immediate family. Within a few years, dressed always in white—like the bride she would never become—she had gone into a state of seclusion. Her only activities were household tasks and the writing of poems that she either kept to herself or sent out as valentines, birthday greetings, or notes to go with the gift of a cherry pie or a batch of cookies.

Around the time that Wadsworth was preparing to move to California, Dickinson sent a few of her poems to Thomas Wentworth Higginson (page 394). As editor of the *Atlantic Monthly,* Higginson had been encouraging the work of younger poets. Higginson never became a substitute for Wadsworth, but he did serve as a kindly, distant "teacher" and "mentor." Eventually, Dickinson gave up hope of ever finding a wider audience than her few friends and relatives. About 1861, she wrote "I'm Nobody! Who are you? / Are you—Nobody—too?"

During her lifetime, Emily Dickinson published no more than a handful of her typically

PORTFOLIO ASSESSMENT

Portfolio Assessment For help with self-assessment of reading skills, see the *Portfolio Management System,* p. 39.

brief poems. She seemed to lack all concern for an audience, and she went so far as to instruct her family to destroy any poems she might leave behind after her death. Still, she saw to it that bundles of handwritten poems were carefully wrapped and put away in places where, after her death, friendly, appreciative, and, finally, astonished eyes would find them. The poems were assembled and edited by different family members and friends; they were then published in installments so frequent that readers began to wonder when they would ever end.

Then, in 1955, a collection called *The Poems of Emily Dickinson* was finally made available. This was the devoted work of Thomas H. Johnson, a scholar who, unlike Dickinson's earlier editors, refrained from making "presentable" entities of poems whose punctuation, rhyme schemes, syntax, and word choice were frequently baffling. Instead, he attempted to remain faithful to the original manuscript.

As a result of Johnson's research, whole generations of readers who had grown up on Dickinson poems were faced with new versions of those poems, versions that sometimes rescued Dickinson's originals from the tamperings of her first editors. And sometimes these originals made emphases which, in the interest of "smoothness," those editors had overlooked. Yet, at other times, comparisons also revealed that Dickinson's first editors had often served her well—in spirit, if not always in the way demanded by scholarship.

Here is an example of how one stanza was changed by the original editors. Johnson's version is first:

We passed the School, where Children strove
At Recess—in the Ring—
We passed the Fields of Gazing Grain—
We passed the Setting Sun—

And this is how the early editor changed it:

We passed the school where children played
Their lessons scarcely done;
We passed the fields of gazing grain,
We passed the setting sun.

The Secret of Genius

When Dickinson died at the age of fifty-five, hardly anyone knew that the strange, shy woman in their midst was a poet whose sharp and delicate voice would echo for generations to come. Some eighty years after her death, when the quarrels among her relatives who had inherited her manuscripts had died down and all her poems were finally published, she was recognized as one of the greatest poets America, and perhaps the world, had produced.

The self-imposed restrictions of Dickinson's actual life were more than matched by her ability to see the universal in the particular, and vice versa. She perceived the relationship between a drop of dew and a flood, between a desert and a grain of sand. These perceptions helped her make metaphors that embraced experiences far beyond the limited compass of Amherst village life.

Yet, no matter how far her imagination ranged, Dickinson never denied those experiences their truth as aspects of a cycle of existence important in itself. When an Amherst neighbor's barn caught fire and lit up the sky, it was a real barn at the edge of a real pasture, and its loss became a matter of local anguish. But these local actualities did not prevent Dickinson from regarding the incident as a reminder of ultimate doom, of the Biblical prophecies of destruction of the earth by fire.

Behind the now famous legend of Emily Dickinson, and the plays and novels that have romanticized and sentimentalized her life, is a woman whose genius made its own rules, followed its own commands, and found its own fulfillment. Emily Dickinson's life as a recluse may have been richer, more varied, and—in the satisfactions that come with the exercise of natural talent—even happier than the lives of those around her. In the prospect of history, we can see that the untold secret of Emily Dickinson's emotional life is secondary to the great secret of her genius, the secret that destiny would not let her keep.

WRITERS ON WRITING

In a letter to Thomas Wentworth Higginson, Dickinson described her standards for judging poetry: "If I read a book and it makes my whole body so cold no fire can ever warm me, I know that is poetry. If I feel physically as if the top of my head were taken off, I know that is poetry. These are the only ways I know it."

Technology Tip

Much of Emily Dickinson's work can be found as part of Project Bartleby, a hypertext library of electronic texts maintained by Columbia University. The URL for Dickinson's poetry is **http://www.cc.columbia.edu/acis/bartleby/dickinson**. *You may want to preview any Internet activity that you suggest to students. Because these resources are sometimes public forums, their content can be unpredictable.*

PROGRAM MANAGER

- **Planning Instruction** See **Teaching Notes, *Teaching Resources A,*** pp. 141–146, for objectives, a summary, literary elements, and additional information.
- **Instructional Support** See **Graphic Organizer for Active Reading, *Teaching Resources A,*** pp. 148–156, 158–160, for Into the Poem or Through the Poem activities.
- **Audiotaped Readings** To help readers through the lesson, use the **Selected Readings, Audiocassette 1, Side B,** in the ***Audiovisual Resources Binder.***
- **Assessment** See **Selection Test, *Test Booklet,*** pp. 91–92.
- **Language Link** For instruction and practice in revision, see **Language Link, *Teaching Resources A,*** p. 157 and ***Language and Writing Skills Worksheets,*** pp. 9–10, 127–128, 140–142.
- **Reinforcement** Use the **Words to Own** worksheet in ***Teaching Resources A,*** pp. 161–162.

Using **BEFORE YOU READ** p. 374

Reading Focus

Remind students that personal conflict can result when the thinking mind and the feeling heart do not agree. Have students create a diagram like the one following that shows a conflict between the heart and mind. The conflict need not be dramatic; it could be an everyday problem, such as whether to buy a new camera or to save money for college.

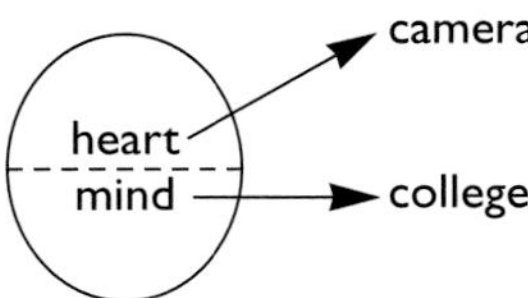

Quickwrite

To help students think of examples, ask them to consider decisions that might be made in their community, such as whether to use vacant land for a parking lot or a playground. Ask them whether people's opinions about the decisions might be influenced more by arguments based on intellect or arguments based on feelings.

BEFORE YOU READ
HEART! WE WILL FORGET HIM!

Reading Focus

The Head and the Heart

Here we have Dickinson's version of the old story of unrequited love—or of love that is impossible because of the circumstances of the lovers. The substance of this poem is conflict—between will and emotion, between the thinking mind and the feeling heart.

Quickwrite

READER'S LOG

Are most people persuaded more by the promptings of intellect or of feeling? In your Reader's Log, write examples that support your opinion.

Heart! We will forget him!

Emily Dickinson

A
Heart! We will forget him!
You and I—tonight!
You may forget the warmth he gave—
I will forget the light!

B
When you have done, pray tell me
That I may straight begin!
Haste! lest while you're lagging
I remember him!

Original manuscript of Emily Dickinson's "I keep my pledge" and "Heart! We will forget him!"

OPTIONS FOR TEACHING

STRATEGIES FOR INCLUSION

Less Proficient Readers Before students read "Heart! We will forget him!", write the words *forget* and *remember* on the chalkboard. Briefly discuss a few of the common ways the words are used, and then ask students to look for them in the poem as they read. After students finish reading, ask them to write a one-sentence explanation of the poem using *forget* and *remember.*

Musical Have students bring in contemporary songs that deal with trying to recover from a broken heart. Students may compare the contemporary lyrics, **rhythm,** and **rhyme** with Dickinson's.

English Language Development To evaluate reading comprehension after students have finished "Heart! We will forget him!", ask them to complete the following sentences in writing: *The speaker tells her heart she will ______. She may want to forget because ______.* Collect their work, and then provide discussion skills practice by asking students to explain orally to partners which specific words or statements in the poem influenced their responses.

Munson-Williams-Proctor Institute Museum of Art, Utica, New York. 4444.

Memories (1885–1886) by William M. Chase. Oil on canvas (50½″ × 37″).

A. Literary Element: Apostrophe

The poem uses apostrophe—a type of personification that is a direct address to an absent or dead person or to something abstract or inanimate. Ask students to identify what the speaker addresses. [Possible answer: The speaker addresses her heart.]

B. Reader's Response: Challenging the Text

? How well does Dickinson's punctuation help to convey her ideas? [Sample responses: It works well and provides the right emphasis and rhythm to convey her feelings; or Dickinson uses too many exclamation marks, which take away from the parts of the poem that need more emphasis.]

INTEGRATING THE LANGUAGE ARTS

Strategic Reading Have student pairs read one of the poems aloud to each other. One student should read the first stanza to the other student, who then paraphrases what was just read. Students then exchange roles as reader and paraphraser. Together they should decide what the poem means and then write their interpretation down. Finally, discuss the poem as a class and ask the class as a whole to come to a consensus about the meaning of the poem.

Writing: Poem Have students create their own poems using **apostrophe.** Students may use the form of "Heart! We will forget him!" and merely replace selected words and phrases, or they may create their own completely original poems. Suggest the following example:

Waves! We will beat them all!
You and I—tomorrow!
You will throw my surfboard high—
I will win the laurel.

Into the Poem

Using BEFORE YOU READ p. 376

Reading Focus

Read aloud a few of the early poems of John Donne or a few works from other metaphysical poets. Choose poems that contain especially far-fetched or fantastic images or comparisons, and works in which the poet takes something ordinary and attempts to give it profound significance.

Through the Poem

A. Reader's Response: First Thoughts

? Do you think the images and comparisons in these stanzas are too far-fetched or fantastic to work well? Why or why not? [Sample responses: No, the image of the speaker winding the months up like a ball of yarn works very well; or no, it's still hard to picture someone brushing a whole summer away.]

B. Critical Reading: Making Generalizations

Have students state the **theme** of the poem. [Possible answer: Some people are prepared to wait forever for the perfect love as long as they believe their love will arrive at the promised time.]

BEFORE YOU READ
IF YOU WERE COMING IN THE FALL

Reading Focus

From the Ordinary, the Extraordinary

Poetry becomes metaphysical when its **imagery** and **figures of speech** are intellectual and sometimes far-fetched and fantastic. In metaphysical poetry, ordinary things are often seen in relation to the universal. Private emotions, such as unfulfilled love, take on the importance of great and profound events. See if you think this poem meets these requirements.

Quickwrite

Think of a story, movie, or song that deals with the hope of romantic fulfillment—a hope so profound that it can be maintained almost forever. Jot down some notes on this question: Why do you think this topic interests so many people?

Pastoral Scene by George Inness (1825–1894). Oil on canvas (51 cm × 76 cm).
R. C. Love Gallery, Chicago. Courtesy Rosenthal Art Slides, Worcester, Massachusetts.

If you were coming in the Fall

Emily Dickinson

If you were coming in the Fall,
I'd brush the Summer by
With half a smile, and half a spurn,
As Housewives do, a Fly.

If I could see you in a year,
I'd wind the months in balls—
And put them each in separate Drawers,
For fear the numbers fuse—

If only Centuries, delayed,
I'd count them on my Hand,
Subtracting, till my fingers dropped
Into Van Dieman's Land,°

If certain, when this life was out—
That yours and mine, should be
I'd toss it yonder, like a Rind,
And take Eternity—

But, now, uncertain of the length
Of this, that is between,
It goads me, like the Goblin Bee—
That will not state—its sting.

12. **Van Dieman's** (dē′mənz) **Land:** former name of Tasmania, an island that is a state of Australia.

OPTIONS FOR TEACHING

COOPERATIVE LEARNING

Question-and-Answer Pairs

Allow students to work in pairs to answer the Making Meanings questions on p. 379. Inform them that they will be graded not only on the accuracy of their answers, but also on the degree of collaboration they show in arriving at them. Ask students to read the questions first and to reach agreement on what each question asks. Then, ask students to write answers that include support or excerpts from the poems. Students should then exchange papers and review their partners' work. After they are certain they understand their partners' responses, ask them to work with their partners to write a new response that combines information from both of their answers. Ask students to submit their original individual responses along with the collaborative answers they created, and compare the responses to calculate a grade for the cooperative effort they show, along with the grade students would receive for the correctness of their answers.

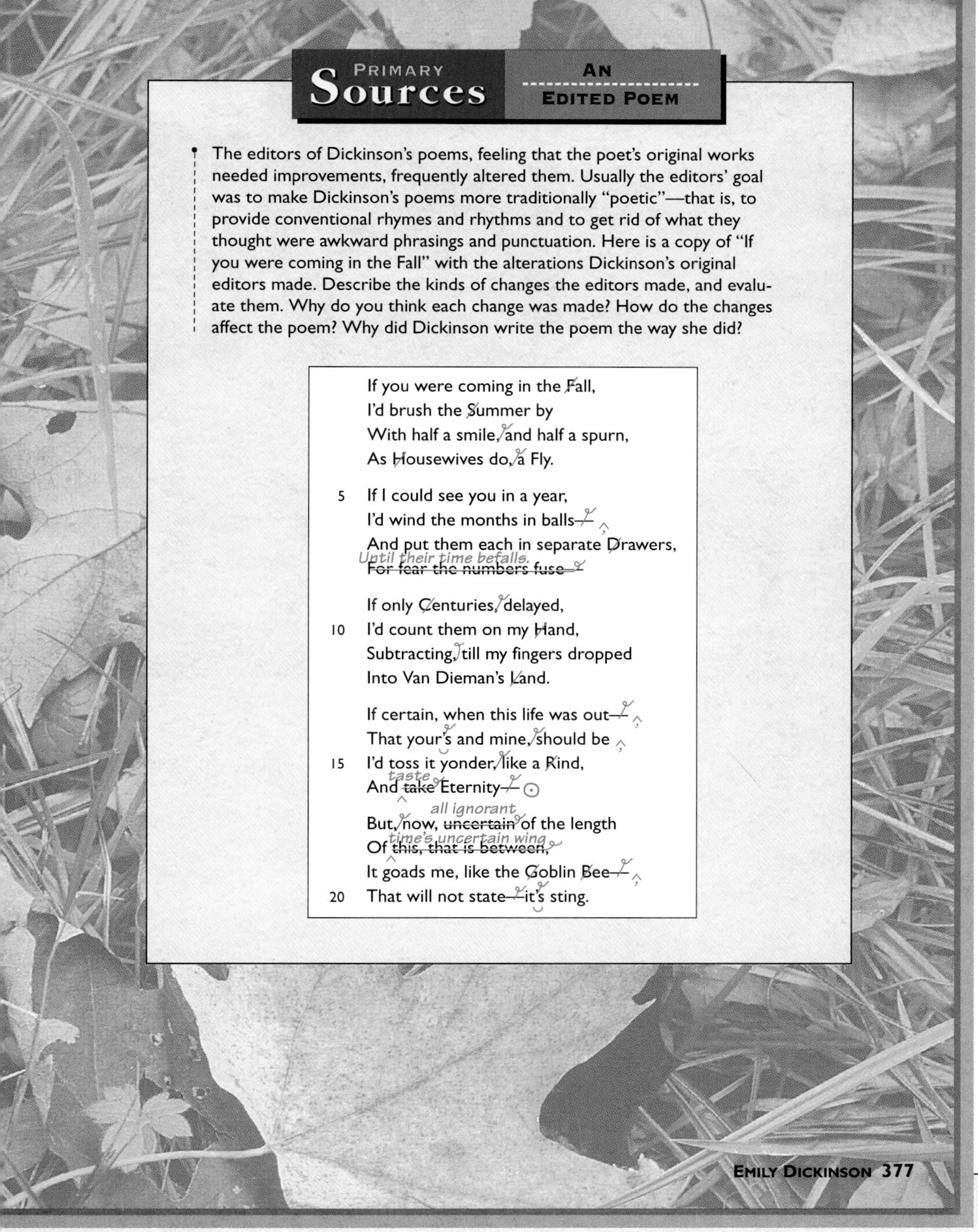

PRIMARY **Sources** AN EDITED POEM

The editors of Dickinson's poems, feeling that the poet's original works needed improvements, frequently altered them. Usually the editors' goal was to make Dickinson's poems more traditionally "poetic"—that is, to provide conventional rhymes and rhythms and to get rid of what they thought were awkward phrasings and punctuation. Here is a copy of "If you were coming in the Fall" with the alterations Dickinson's original editors made. Describe the kinds of changes the editors made, and evaluate them. Why do you think each change was made? How do the changes affect the poem? Why did Dickinson write the poem the way she did?

If you were coming in the Fall,
I'd brush the Summer by
With half a smile, and half a spurn,
As Housewives do, a Fly.

If I could see you in a year,
I'd wind the months in balls—
And put them each in separate Drawers,
Until their time befalls.
~~For fear the numbers fuse—~~

If only Centuries, delayed,
I'd count them on my Hand,
Subtracting, till my fingers dropped
Into Van Dieman's Land.

If certain, when this life was out—
That your's and mine, should be
I'd toss it yonder, like a Rind,
And ~~take~~ *taste* Eternity—

But, now, ~~uncertain~~ *all ignorant* of the length
Of ~~this, that is between,~~ *time's uncertain wing,*
It goads me, like the Goblin Bee—
That will not state—it's sting.

Primary Sources

Dickinson's early editors mistook originality for error, and her poems did not appear as she wrote them until the 1950s. Dickinson's frequent use of dashes, capitalization, and elliptical phrasing were unconventional in her time, and the reasons behind many of her stylistic choices remain somewhat obscure.

CLASSROOM MANAGEMENT

Managing the Reader's Response Classroom Before the class begins a new selection, try to draw students into the reading by conducting a class discussion that builds on students' prior knowledge of a subject, theme, or other element they will encounter in the selection. The topic of the discussion will need to be varied depending on the prior knowledge of students in each class, but any truly interactive discussion will help to orient students and give them a purpose for reading.

Block Scheduling Students may sometimes finish a lesson or classroom activity more quickly than you anticipate. To prevent being left with a large amount of class time and no planned activity to fill it, prepare instructions and student materials for a set of activities that may be adapted to various types of stories or poems. The activities should be open-ended and based on students' choices of favorite ideas, images, scenes, or other elements from the selection they are studying.

Using **BEFORE YOU READ** p. 378

Reading Focus

Ask students to list three qualities they consider when choosing friends. Use a Venn diagram to show students how one's friends may be reflections of oneself or of an ideal self.

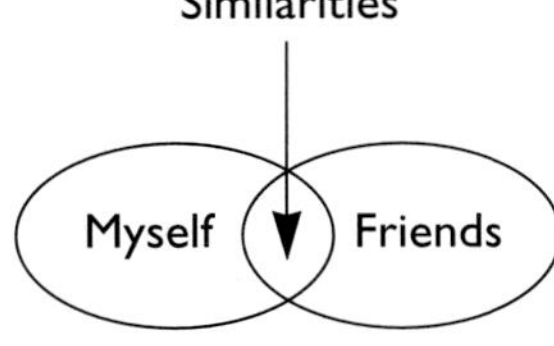

A. Reader's Response: Connecting with the Text

? How does your attitude about choosing your own society compare with Dickinson's ? [Sample responses: It is difficult today to be so picky because society is so diverse and complex. Or Dickinson's view about shutting out the world sounds appealing.]

BEFORE YOU READ

THE SOUL SELECTS HER OWN SOCIETY

Reading Focus

Choices of the Soul

This poem is about choices and the mysterious instinct that leads each one of us to prefer certain things and cherish certain people above all others. In Dickinson's view, this instinct has less to do with the discriminations of the mind than with the yearnings of that spiritual part of us that some call the soul.

Quickwrite

How do you think most people select their friends, with their minds (thoughts) or with their souls (feelings)? Write your responses to this question in your Reader's Log.

Woman with Parasol—Turned to Left (1886) by Claude Monet. Oil on canvas.

Musée d'Orsay, Paris. Courtesy Giraudon/Art Resource.

The Soul selects her own Society

Emily Dickinson

The Soul selects her own Society—
Then—shuts the Door—
To her divine Majority—
Present no more—

Unmoved—she notes the Chariots—pausing—
At her low Gate—
Unmoved—an Emperor be kneeling
Upon her Mat—

I've known her—from an ample nation—
Choose One—
Then—close the Valves of her attention—
Like Stone—

OPTIONS FOR TEACHING

ASSESSMENT TOOLS

Informal Assessment Use journals to evaluate how students think they are doing in class. Take a few minutes of class time to have students respond in writing to prompts such as the ones below.

- I think that in this class I have really improved at _______ because _______.
- I think that I am not doing as well at _______ because _______.
- My favorite activity in this class is _______ because _______.

At the end of class, collect the journals and read the entries without making comments. Use the responses to make adjustments for individual problems or to create mini-lessons for the whole class.

Making Meanings

Heart! We will forget him!

First Thoughts

1. Review your Quickwrite notes. Whom do you identify with in this poem—the head or the heart? Why?

Shaping Interpretations

2. Why do you think the heart is asked to take the lead in this situation?
3. What do you think the speaker means by "warmth" and "light"?
4. Exclamation points punctuate this little poem, as if the speaker were saying, "Hurry up! We must get this over with!" Why do you suppose the speaker is in such a hurry?
5. What **tone** do you hear in this poem?

Connecting with the Text

6. If you wanted to forget someone, would you first try to forget the "warmth" or "light" of that person? Explain.

If you were coming in the Fall

First Thoughts

1. Look over your Quickwrite notes. Do you think the hopes expressed in the poem are fairly common, or far-fetched? Explain.

Shaping Interpretations

2. How would you describe the speaker's situation? How does she feel about it?
3. What two things are being compared in the **simile** in the first stanza?
4. In the second stanza, what domestic articles are the months compared to? Why does the speaker put them in separate drawers?
5. Van Dieman's Land has come to mean places on the globe farthest away from us. Given this information, how would you paraphrase the third stanza?
6. How would you describe the speaker's **tone** in the first four stanzas? How does it change in the fifth stanza, where her exaggerations disappear? What goads her, or pushes and prods her, against her will?
7. In folklore, a goblin is a tormenting creature. What do you think Dickinson is suggesting when she says that the bee is a goblin and will not "state" its sting?

Challenging the Text

8. What changes, if any, would you suggest in capitalization and punctuation in this poem? Why?

The Soul selects her own Society

First Thoughts

1. What advantages and disadvantages may lie in a selection as strict as this soul makes? After reviewing your Quickwrite notes, explain whether you think most people make choices like this.

Shaping Interpretations

2. *Majority* has at least two meanings: "having reached full legal age" (or "having come into one's own") and "the greater part of something." It could also mean "superiority" (an obsolete usage). What do you think it means in this poem? What kind of person does the adjective "divine" suggest?
3. Do you think the phrase "Valves of her attention" is derived from organic things (valves of a clamshell) or mechanical ones (valves of a faucet)? What do you picture happening here?
4. Dickinson's early editors changed the word *valves* to *lids.* How does this change the **metaphor**? How does it change what you *see*?
5. Look at the **meter** of lines 10 and 12. How does their rhythmical pattern differ from the corresponding lines in the first and second stanzas? What is the effect of this difference?

Challenging the Text

6. Dickinson did not give her poems titles. Her editors called this poem "Exclusion." In what ways does this title apply? In what ways is it limiting?

Making Meanings
"Heart! . . ."

First Thoughts

1. Some students will identify with the head, while others will identify with the heart.

Shaping Interpretations

2. Perhaps the speaker feels it will be harder for the heart than for the mind to forget; therefore, the heart is asked to take the lead.
3. *Warmth* may mean love; *light* may mean intelligence.
4. The speaker is afraid that she will weaken in her resolution to forget her loved one.
5. Regret, determination, or impatience.

Connecting with the Text

6. Possible response: It would be easier to forget a person's "light" first because that seems more fleeting.

"If you were . . ."

First Thoughts

1. It is likely that many people would feel as strongly as the speaker.

Shaping Interpretations

2. The speaker's situation is unbearable, and it troubles her.
3. The speaker compares waiting all summer to brushing off a fly.
4. Balls of yarn that are separated so they will not become entangled.
5. I would count the centuries on my fingers until I reached the farthest place on the earth.
6. The tone in the first four stanzas is wistful and longing. Then the tone changes to one of resignation, is vaguely melancholic, and in the final two lines, even bitter. Her own uncertainty about the length of her wait goads her.
7. A goblin suggests trickery. Therefore, it will not openly state its trick. In this case, the trick is the doubt that she is left to endure.

Challenging the Text

8. **(Evaluation)** Students will probably suggest a variety of punctuation and capitalization changes to make the poems easier to read and understand.

"The Soul . . ."

First Thoughts

1. A disadvantage is that the soul might isolate itself. An advantage is that the soul might be pure.

Shaping Interpretations

2. It may mean maturity. *Divine* suggests a god.
3. Perhaps valves of a heart or of a musical instrument.
4. The word *lids* metaphorically suggests that the soul has eyes.
5. Lines 10 and 12 are reduced from four to two syllables. It slows down the rhythm.

Challenging the Text

6. **(Synthesis)** The title "Exclusion" gives the impression of a select group and of a limited ability to derive knowledge from a varied world. It limits by confining the poem's meaning to a social one.

Elements of Literature

Possible Answers

1. One exact rhyme: *door/more.* The other five rhymes are slant. The reader probably expects to hear a more exact rhyme in each case.
2. The slant rhyme in "Success is counted sweetest" of *today/Victory* suggests the hollowness and irony in achieving fame by dying for a lost cause.

A. Language Note: Punctuation Point out how the use of dashes in this stanza clearly shows that this poem is modelled on Dickinson's style.

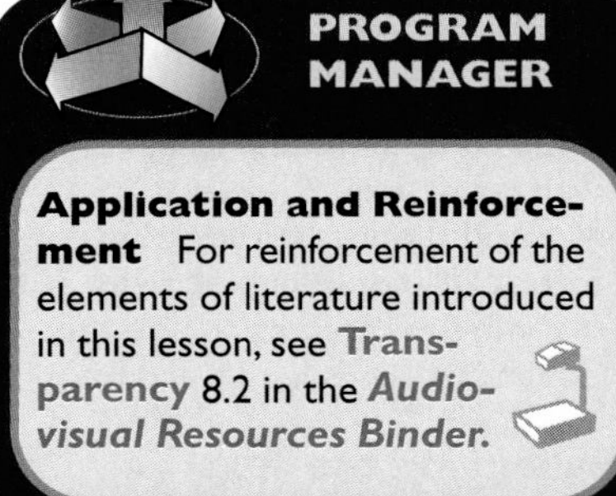

PROGRAM MANAGER

Application and Reinforcement For reinforcement of the elements of literature introduced in this lesson, see **Transparency** 8.2 in the ***Audiovisual Resources Binder.***

ELEMENTS OF LITERATURE

Slant Rhyme

Not long ago, **exact rhyme**—two or more words whose syllables share identical sounds, as in the words *free* and *bee*—was part of every poet's craft. Today it is still the most familiar aspect of sound in poetry. But rhyme has, over the years, fallen out of favor with many poets. One reason is that these poets feel almost all the exact rhymes in English have been used over and over again. Another reason is that imposed rhymes can act as a constraint and can limit expression. Some poets, as a solution, have abandoned rhyme altogether. Other poets, like Dickinson, use slant rhyme.

Slant rhyme is a close, but not exact, rhyming sound. (It is also called **off rhyme, half rhyme,** or **approximate rhyme.**) Word pairs like *society/majority* or *nerve/love* are examples of slant rhymes—"not quite, but almost" rhyming sounds. Part of the shock value of Dickinson's poems comes from her use of slant rhyme. Slant rhyme makes many readers uncomfortable—in the way that a sharp or flat note on a piano would disturb a listener who wasn't expecting it.

Slant rhyme is a subtle use of sound. It is often used to force our attention onto particular words. For example, the last word in "The Soul selects her own Society," *stone,* stands out because it doesn't match exactly in sound with the word *one.* Why is it important that the word *stone* be emphasized? To hear and understand the difference, imagine that Dickinson had ended her poem with the words, "And be done."

First printing of *Poems* by Emily Dickinson.

Amherst College Library, Amherst, Massachusetts.

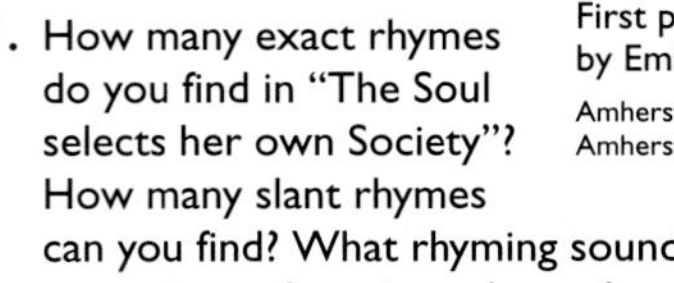

1. How many exact rhymes do you find in "The Soul selects her own Society"? How many slant rhymes can you find? What rhyming sounds were you expecting to hear in each case?
2. Look through Dickinson's other poems for slant rhymes. Read them aloud, and see if you can identify the purpose and effect of each rhyme.

Student TO Student

The Mirror Girl—stares back at me

(In the Style of Emily Dickinson)

The Mirror Girl—stares back at me—
With a Look that knows too much—
And a Skin that's never felt the Burn
Of a soft—caressing—Touch

She speaks with Lips that smile—and laugh—
But never have been—kissed—
And cries with careful—Countenance—
That never has been missed

The Mirror Girl is cold and crystal—
Hard enough to feel—
But who is to say, on the other Side,
She's not the One who's real?

The Mirror Girl is a stoic Thing—
That does not pain or ache—
But while I suffer and endure—
The Mirror Girl merely—breaks

—Brigid Spackman
James E. Taylor Senior High School
Katy, Texas

First appeared in *Merlyn's Pen: The National Magazines of Student Writing*

CONNECTING WITH DICKINSON'S POETRY

To help students identify those elements of Dickinson's poetry that the student author modelled in "The Mirror Girl—stares back at me," read the poem aloud slowly. Then, put the poem on an overhead transparency and circle the elements as students note them. [Capitals, dashes, syntax.] Ask students how the student poem is different from Dickinson's. [Ideas, exact rhyme.] Invite students to create their own poems modelled on one of Dickinson's. Ask them to try to incorporate slant rhyme. Have volunteers read their poems aloud, and ask the class to identify elements they think are typical of Dickinson's poetry.

Before You Read
Some keep the Sabbath going to Church

Reading Focus

Transcendence

Although she rejected the teachings of her family's Congregationalist church, Dickinson was a deeply spiritual poet who constantly reflected on the divine. The fifth of seven poems published in her lifetime appeared on March 12, 1864. It was titled "My Sabbath," and unlike this version, it used the word "going" instead of "getting" in line 11. Later called "A Service of Song," it was included in a collection published in 1890, after Dickinson's death.

Quickwrite

Does a church—or any place of worship—have to be a human-built construction made expressly for worship, or can there be a broader understanding of what a church is? Record your thoughts in your Reader's Log.

Collection of The New-York Historical Society.

Bobolink (1822) by John J. Audubon. Watercolor, graphite, pastel, gouache, selective glazing.

Some keep the Sabbath going to Church

Emily Dickinson

Some keep the Sabbath going to Church—
I keep it, staying at Home—
With a Bobolink for a Chorister°—
And an Orchard, for a Dome— **A**

Some keep the Sabbath in Surplice°—
I just wear my Wings—
And instead of tolling the Bell, for Church,
Our little Sexton°—sings.

God preaches, a noted Clergyman—
And the sermon is never long,
So instead of getting to Heaven, at last—
I'm going, all along. **B**

3. **chorister:** choir member.
5. **surplice** (sur′plis): loose white vestment worn by clergy or choir members on top of longer robes.
8. **sexton:** church officer or employee whose various duties may include maintenance and ringing the bells.

Into the Poem

Using **Before You Read** p. 381

Quickwrite

To help students get started, have them create a cluster of places that inspired a sense of wonder or awe in them.

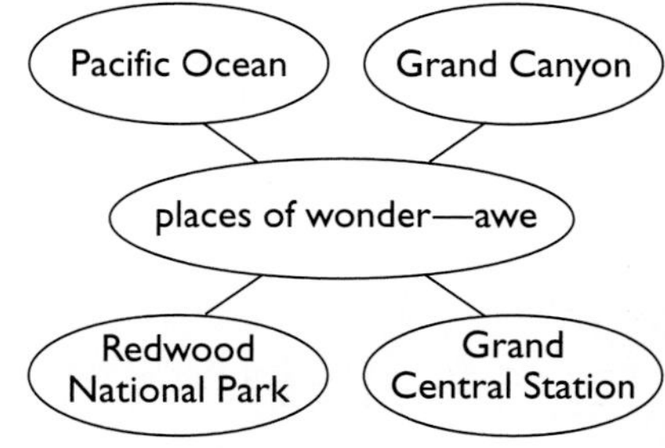

A. Reader's Response: First Thoughts

? What images come to mind when you read the first stanza? [Sample responses: Dickinson's church is a garden in an orchard; or the songbirds form a choir.]

B. Literary Element: Tone

Point out that Dickinson uses a playful tone to convey a serious theme.

Options for Teaching

Strategies for Inclusion

Special Needs Students who have difficulty responding to the concentrated imagery in poetry often benefit from prereading activities based on images from the poems they will be reading. Before students read "Some keep the Sabbath going to Church," display or distribute to the class photos of a church, a songbird, and an orchard. Then, divide the class into mixed-ability pairs. Give students ten minutes to brainstorm ideas for an original poem in which a church, a songbird, and an orchard are important images. Then, ask students to jot down short descriptions of their poem ideas. Call on students to read their descriptions aloud. After students have finished reading the poem, ask them to compare it to their original poem ideas. ☞

Using **BEFORE YOU READ** p. 382

Reading Focus

Work with the class to create a list on the chalkboard of words that might be used to describe the state of mind of an artist struck by inspiration. [Possible responses: *Enchanted, enraptured, dizzy, delirious, feverish.*] Keep the list on the chalkboard as the poem is read aloud in class. Point out that Dickinson uses the word *transport* in other poems to describe the same state of mind.

A. Expansion
During the 1860s, Dickinson suffered from an eye disorder that caused periods of blurred vision or near blindness. During this crisis, Dickinson produced poetry prolifically, including this poem.

B. Critical Reading: Finding Cause and Effect
? What is the effect of the speaker's intoxicating communion with nature? [Possible answer: She feels that she could live forever in these surroundings.]

BEFORE YOU READ

I TASTE A LIQUOR NEVER BREWED

Reading Focus

Intoxicating Inspiration

Some critics believe that Dickinson is making fun of Emerson (page 216) in the following poem. Like Emerson's poem "Bacchus," this poem compares a poet's feeling of inspiration to the feeling of intoxication some get when drinking liquor. However, in contrast to Emerson's serious tone and reference to Greek mythology, Dickinson presents a humorous view of bees and butterflies, seraphs and saints.

Quickwrite

READER'S LOG

Record some of your own remembrances of what it feels like to be inspired, or describe some of the qualities you associate with inspiration.

Passion Flowers and Hummingbirds (c. 1865) by Martin Johnson Heade. Oil on canvas (15¼″ × 21½″).

Gift of Mrs. Maxim Karolik for the M. and M. Karolik Collection of American Paintings, 1815–1865. Courtesy of Museum of Fine Arts, Boston.

A I taste a liquor never brewed

Emily Dickinson

I taste a liquor never brewed—
From Tankards scooped in Pearl—
Not all the Vats upon the Rhine°
Yield such an Alcohol!

Inebriate° of Air—am I—
And Debauchee° of Dew—
Reeling—thro endless summer days—
From inns of Molten Blue—

When "Landlords" turn the drunken Bee
Out of the Foxglove's° door—
When Butterflies—renounce their "drams"—
I shall but drink the more!

Till Seraphs° swing their snowy Hats—
And Saints—to windows run—
To see the little Tippler°
Leaning against the—Sun—

3. Rhine: an allusion to the Rhine River in Germany, an area that is noted for fine wines and beers.
5. inebriate: intoxicated.
6. debauchee (deb′ô·shē′): person who indulges in pleasures.
10. foxglove's: A foxglove is a kind of plant with cuplike flowers.
13. seraphs: angels of the highest order.
15. tippler: drinker.

OPTIONS FOR TEACHING

CROSSING THE CURRICULUM

Geography Point out that Dickinson refers in her poetry to seasons, to plants and animals, and to natural features she saw near her home in Amherst. In "If you were coming in the Fall" (p. 376), "I taste a liquor never brewed" (p. 382), "Apparently with no surprise" (p. 385), "Success is counted sweetest" (p. 388), "Because I could not stop for Death" (p. 391), and "I heard a Fly buzz—when I died" (p. 392), Dickinson mentions flies, bees, a songbird (bobolink), dew, a flower (foxglove), butterflies, the sun, frost, nectar, fields of grain, and a storm. To help familiarize students with the natural world that inspired Dickinson, ask them to do research to find maps, drawings, paintings, or other resources that illustrate the geography, climate, and plant and animal life of the Connecticut River Valley, in which Amherst lies. Encourage students to make use of multimedia resources; a good electronic encyclopedia may contain an illustration of a foxglove flower, and perhaps even a recording of a bobolink's song. Create a "Dickinson's World" display in a section of the classroom to showcase the results of students' research.

Before You Read
Much Madness is divinest Sense

Reading Focus
The Solace of Solitude

Since her death, Dickinson has often been portrayed as the mad recluse of Amherst. In fact, Dickinson lived as many other great poets (and quite a few "ordinary" people) have lived —deliberately choosing solitude for contemplation, reading, and writing.

Quickwrite
READER'S LOG

Write down what you think the unusual title of this poem means.

Much Madness is divinest Sense
Emily Dickinson

Much Madness is divinest Sense—
To a discerning Eye—
Much Sense—the starkest Madness—
'Tis the Majority
In this, as All, prevail—
Assent—and you are sane—
Demur—you're straightway dangerous—
And handled with a Chain—

A

Garden at Emily Dickinson's house.

Into the Poem

Using **BEFORE YOU READ** p. 383

Reading Focus
Read aloud the "Solitude" excerpt from Thoreau's *Walden* on p. 239. Ask the class what Thoreau and Dickinson gained by choosing solitude. Then, ask students to name a few positive things anyone might experience during a period of contemplative isolation. [Possible responses: Realizations, insights, creative breakthroughs, a sense of peace or wonder.]

Through the Poem

A. Critical Reading: Making Inferences
Ask students what the poet seems to say about madness and sanity in these lines. [Possible answers: Those people who go against the majority are often thought of as mad and are shunned. To the poet, madness means divine inspiration, which she sees as a higher sense.]

PROBLEM SOLVING/CRITICAL THINKING

Rejecting Conformity After students have read "Some keep the Sabbath going to Church" on p. 381 and "Much Madness is divinest Sense" on p. 383, point out that each poem may be read as both an acceptance of solitude and a rejection of narrow community standards. Ask students if Dickinson's personal isolation may have also distanced her from possible sympathetic peers who might have understood her and her ideas. Have students work in groups to discuss alternatives (other than creative solitude) that would have allowed Dickinson to interact more with the outside world without conforming or sacrificing her personal identity.

PROFESSIONAL NOTES

Thematic Connections: "Tell It Slant" Ask students what truths are expressed in "Much Madness is divinest Sense" on p. 383. [Possible responses: Opinions some people consider crazy are often profoundly wise; opinions some consider thoughtful are often completely insane; dissenting opinions are considered dangerous or unsound by the majority.] Ask students why Dickinson may have chosen to express her truths in verse instead of in prose. [Possible response: Verse adds a poetic slant that makes the ideas seem more concentrated and profound. The same ideas, written out as prose statements, might sound strident or preachy.]

Making Meanings "Some keep . . ."

First Thoughts

1. Possible response: Dickinson's poem broadened my understanding of what a church can be.

Shaping Interpretations

2. She communes with nature. If she kept the Sabbath as others do, she might not have the same mystical experience.
3. Her relationship to nature is a mystical one. The metaphors are wings, an orchard as a church dome, and birds as a choir.
4. Possible response: By living in a natural setting, she is perpetually in a religious state of mind.

Extending the Text

5. **(Analysis)** People who prefer solitude might share Dickinson's view. Those who see God revealed in nature may also. Those who maintain a more orthodox view might disagree with her.

Challenging the Text

6. **(Evaluation)** Students may suggest titles that have a link to nature, because of the imagery of the first stanza, or titles that make a personal statement about religious choice.

"I taste a liquor . . ."

First Thoughts

1. Nature inspires her. Some students may have felt what the speaker feels.

Shaping Interpretations

2. The beauty of nature. She finds it too inspiring to stop.
3. The tone is giddy and somewhat exaggerated. The mention of "little Tippler" adds a humorous note.
4. The poet notes that she will work harder as those around her are less inspired—she will "drink the more." She is determined.

Extending the Text

5. **(Synthesis)** Responses will vary. The poem could also pertain to human enjoyment of nature.

MAKING MEANINGS

Some keep the Sabbath going to Church

First Thoughts

1. Review your Quickwrite notes. What is your response to the speaker's "Church"?

Shaping Interpretations

2. In what ways does the speaker keep the Sabbath? How might keeping the Sabbath as others do affect her worship?
3. What is the speaker's relationship to nature? How is this revealed in the **metaphors** she chooses?
4. What do you think the speaker means in the last line when she says "I'm going, all along"?

Extending the Text

5. What kinds of people might share Dickinson's preference? Who would disagree with her way of keeping the Sabbath?

Challenging the Text

6. Which title do you feel best suits the poem: "My Sabbath," "A Service of Song," or "Some keep the Sabbath going to Church"? Or do you have a better title? Explain your answer.

I taste a liquor never brewed

First Thoughts

1. What inspires the speaker? Review your Quickwrite notes, and explain whether you have ever felt what this speaker is feeling.

Shaping Interpretations

2. What is the speaker drinking in the poem? Why doesn't she want to stop?
3. How would you describe the **tone** of the poem? What details in the poem create this effect?
4. What change does the poet note in the third stanza? What feelings does the change bring about in the speaker?

Extending the Text

5. Many readers see this poem, at least in part, as a description of the inspiration that drives artists to create. What other human activities or emotions could it pertain to?

Much Madness is divinest Sense

First Thoughts

1. What kinds of people might take this poem as a personal "anthem"? Does anything in this poem reflect ideas you have had about yourself?

Shaping Interpretations

2. What is the meaning of the **paradox,** or apparent contradiction, in the first three lines? How does it affect the poem's meaning?
3. What do you think is the poem's **theme**? What does the speaker think about the individual's proper relationship to society?
4. Dickinson liked to use dashes—a mark of punctuation her first editors usually removed. How do dashes help emphasize certain ideas in this poem?
5. What would you say is Dickinson's **tone** in this poem? What similarities do you notice to other poems in this collection?

Extending the Text

6. The public has often said of creative and independent thinkers that they are "crazy." Name at least three writers, artists, inventors, or other creative types who are or have been considered "mad." In what ways is their "madness" really a kind of "sense," at least in terms of their work? (Did you mention these ideas in your Quickwrite?)

"Much Madness . . ."

First Thoughts

1. Possible response: Creative people and independent thinkers. *Remind students to choose ideas about themselves that they would not mind sharing.*

Shaping Interpretations

2. The paradox is that the madder you are, the more you might make sense of the world; the dividing line between madness and genius may be a fine one. It creates an ironic tone.
3. Possible responses: The majority opinion may not always be correct. If you disagree with the majority, you may be persecuted.
4. The dashes force phrasing and end-of-line pauses that sculpt the poet's meaning.
5. The poem's ominous tone makes it most similar to "The Soul selects her own Society."

Extending the Text

6. **(Synthesis)** Examples will vary. Creative madness is a kind of sense because it leads to uncommon insights.

Before You Read
Apparently with No Surprise

Reading Focus

Metaphor Metamorphosis
Dickinson had only to look out her window to see the ordinary—and extraordinary—powers of nature at work. In using **metaphors** built on images of birds, flies, and flowers, her deceptively innocent observations reveal deep and sometimes disturbing ideas.

Quickwrite

Do you think nature is essentially benign, or threatening and hostile? Create a double-column chart in which you write evidence of nature's benevolence in one column and evidence of nature's destructiveness in the other.

Jim Zipp/Photo Researchers.

Apparently with no surprise

Emily Dickinson

Apparently with no surprise
To any happy Flower
The Frost beheads it at its play—
In accidental power—
The blonde Assassin passes on—
The Sun proceeds unmoved
To measure off another Day **(A)**
For an Approving God.

Using **BEFORE YOU READ** p. 385

Quickwrite

To help students get started, chart a few examples on the chalkboard using the following diagram.

Benign	Hostile
[Nature gives food, water, beauty. It provides materials for housing, clothes, art.]	[Nature also destroys with flood, storm, disease.]

A. Literary Element: Tone
Dickinson's nature poems often seem to be humorous puzzles in which the reader must search for a subject. However, in the final lines of these poems, the tone often changes from playful to ominous.

Options for Teaching

Strategies for Inclusion

Kinesthetic Point out the strong sense of movement Dickinson creates in "Apparently with no surprise" on p. 385. Have students find the action verbs in the poem and ask them to visualize or pantomime the motions they describe as you read the poem aloud. After the class has become familiar with the movements, ask students to describe them in their own words. [Possible responses: The first motion is sharp and final; the second motion is even and continuous—like a smoothly moving second hand on a clock.]

Interpersonal Ask students to copy a phrase from a poem in this Collection onto an index card. Then, give students five minutes to share and discuss their choices with other students. Ask students to copy onto their cards one phrase from at least three other students, along with their reasons for choosing their phrases. After five minutes, begin to call on students to read their phrases aloud, along with one phrase they collected from another student. Ask them to describe the other students' reasons for their phrase selections.

Using **Before You Read** p. 386

Reading Focus

Discuss with the class how Dickinson might have used her work to deal with questions about her own identity, painful feelings of grief and loss, and concerns about her anonymity as a poet.

A. Literary Element: Metaphor Dickinson uses the metaphor of truth as a dazzling light. Ask students to paraphrase these lines to make the comparison clear. [Possible answer: Truth must enlighten gradually or it may overwhelm.]

B. Reader's Response: Extending the Text

? To what kinds of truths must people be led gradually? [Sample responses: People sometimes have to be led gradually to accept truths that contradict their previous assumptions.]

Before You Read
Tell All the Truth but Tell It Slant

Reading Focus

Forms of Truth

Dickinson's famous line "Tell all the Truth but tell it slant" may reveal her method of survival as well as the essence of her own poetry.

Quickwrite

READER'S LOG

What do you think it would mean to tell the truth "slant"? Write some examples of the truth "told slant."

Tell all the Truth but tell it slant

Emily Dickinson

Tell all the Truth but tell it slant—
Success in Circuit° lies
Too bright for our infirm Delight
The Truth's superb surprise
A **As Lightning to the Children eased**
With explanation kind
The Truth must dazzle gradually
B **Or every man be blind—**

2. circuit: an indirect path.

Options for Teaching

Integrating the Language Arts

Strategic Reading Divide the class into small groups, and then read aloud "Success is counted sweetest" on p. 388. Have students discuss the meaning of the poem while one student takes notes. Then, have a representative report to the class what each group discovered in the poem. Lead a class discussion on the poem that builds on the ideas of each group.

Crossing the Curriculum

Science Have students conduct independent research on the problems scientists have had in historically presenting new theories, especially controversial ones, to the public. Ask students to decide, based on this research, which approaches work best when confronting society with new scientific ideas.

Yale University Art Gallery, Bequest of Stephen Clark, B.A. 1903.

Rooms by the Sea (1951) by Edward Hopper. Oil on canvas.

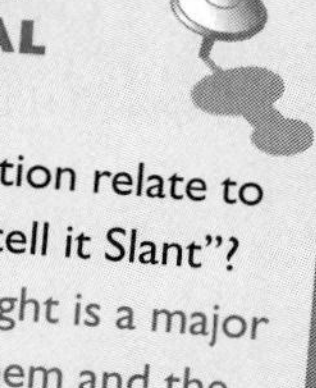

RESPONDING TO THE ART: VISUAL LITERACY

How does this illustration relate to "Tell all the Truth but tell it Slant"? [Possible responses: Light is a major element in both the poem and the painting; the slant of the light in the painting is like the slant of truth in the poem.]

CLASSROOM MANAGEMENT

Managing the Reader's Response Classroom
Students working in Reader's Response-based cooperative groups may be more productive if you implement a few of the following suggestions.

- Model any speaking and listening activity in front of the class before students attempt the activity in their groups.
- Quietly observe each group just long enough to make sure the group is on task, then move on and briefly observe a different group.
- Try to avoid commenting on group procedures while students are working. Instead, after groups have finished, give students suggestions for improvement that they can use during the next collaborative assignment.
- Whenever possible, avoid giving direct answers to queries from groups. Instead, respond with questions that encourage students to turn to the other members of their groups for answers and assistance.

Using **BEFORE YOU READ** p. 388

Background

Remind students how carefully Dickinson prepared and saved her poems in small, hand-sewn packets. Ask them to consider whether she might have been anticipating posthumous publication instead of publication during her lifetime.

A. Reader's Response: First Thoughts

? Do you agree with Dickinson that those who never succeed appreciate success the most? [Sample response: Yes, people who work hard to be successful value success more as a goal.]

B. Literary Element: Symbol

Dickinson uses military imagery symbolically to convey an image of success in terms of victory and defeat.

BEFORE YOU READ

SUCCESS IS COUNTED SWEETEST

Reading Focus

The Taste of Fame

In 1862, Dickinson sent this poem along with three others to Thomas Wentworth Higginson, editor of the *Atlantic Monthly,* to ask his advice about the quality of her poems. It is one of several poems that show Dickinson's feelings about success and her struggles with the world.

Quickwrite

READER'S LOG

Write down some of your own thoughts about success. Is success only in the eye of the beholder? Can success contain the seeds of failure?

Background

Literary scholars debate Dickinson's disinterest in publishing and recognition. This poem, included in *A Masque of Poets,* is one of the poems that Dickinson did publish during her lifetime. Ironically, many readers thought it was written by Ralph Waldo Emerson (page 216).

Taps (c. 1907–1909) by Gilbert Gaul. Oil on canvas (32¾″ × 43″).

Collection of the Birmingham Museum of Art, Birmingham, Alabama; Gift of John Meyer.

Success is counted sweetest

Emily Dickinson

Success is counted sweetest
By those who ne'er succeed.
To comprehend a nectar°
Requires sorest° need.

Not one of all the purple Host°
Who took the Flag today
Can tell the definition
So clear of Victory

As he defeated—dying—
On whose forbidden ear
The distant strains of triumph
Burst agonized and clear!

3. nectar: a name for the drink of the Greek and Roman gods; also, a term applied to any delicious beverage.
4. sorest: deepest; most extreme.
5. host: army; multitude.

OPTIONS FOR TEACHING

ASSESSMENT TOOLS

Peer Assessment: Oral Reading The following scale and criteria might be used by a reader's peers after they hear him or her read aloud a poem from this Collection. Ask peer reviewers to give specific examples of what they liked and suggestions on how the reader might improve. The peer evaluations should be shared with the reader in a private conference with the instructor, and goals should be set and suggestions for improvement made at that time.

Key: 1=Needs work 2=Fair 3=Superior

Student Name: ____________________

_____ Loudness (1–3)
_____ Clarity (1–3)
_____ Smoothness (1–3)
_____ Emphasis (1–3)
_____ Pronunciation (1–3)
_____ Total (5-15)

I liked the reading because ____________.
I think the reader could improve by ________.

A MAGAZINE ARTICLE

The following excerpts describe a visit to the Dickinson house—called the Homestead—in Amherst, Massachusetts. (See photo on page 383.)

Emily Dickinson's Homestead

The place today is decidedly light, airy, underfurnished. Even so, Emily Dickinson's singular presence is felt almost from the moment you step inside the front door and your guide begins to talk about "Emily" as if the two of them had recently had a tête-à-tête about fresh flowers or what sort of cake to bake for Sunday dinner. . . .

At the Homestead, as in a good many other "restored" writers' houses, most of the furniture, curtains, toys, saucepans, and God-knows-what-else have been gathered together decades after its owners have removed to a far less stressful existence. Very little of the actual stuff is there; most of it has been gathered by buying or begging from folks who happen to own pieces that fit the particular decorating bill. While the outside walls are intact, the domestic apparatus inside them is only an approximation of what was there when the famous writer lived in its midst. Yet we go out of our way to visit these temples to the Word, if only for a whiff of the Great One who once prowled the premises seeking the mot juste[1] or staring out the window, waiting for a nudge from the muse. . . .

Emily's bedroom contains the few things that almost certainly belonged to her: a Franklin stove, a sleigh bed adorned with a paisley shawl I was dying to touch but was not quick enough. The family cradle is here, too, an odd touch in a spinster's room. In the middle of the room, one of her dresses (it looks like a size eight) is draped on a headless dummy inside a Plexiglas case. The display destroys the illusion that she might return from her beloved garden at any moment. But the dress is irresistible—made of heavy white cotton with twelve nickel-sized buttons down the front, long sleeves, a custom-ordered patch pocket (to tuck scraps of paper into), and the trim look of a head nurse's uniform. On the windowsill is a basket with a cord attached to it, which she filled with cookies she baked and then lowered out the window to nephews and nieces.

We were told by our guide . . . that Emily was "lucky in a way—she never had to go out to work" and that she was "witty and funny." Pointing to pictures of three men in Emily's life, [the guide] said that the poet "only liked intellectual men. My pick [for Emily's true love] is Bowles," meaning Samuel Bowles, editor of the *Springfield Daily Republican,* who may have been the "Master" to whom Emily addressed a series of letters. Bowles was married. Personally, I think Emily tended to pick her men for their unavailability—what she didn't need was a husband.

—Anne Bernays, *from* "A Poet's Safe Haven in Amherst," *The New York Times Magazine,* October 1, 1989

1. **mot juste** (mō zhüst′): French for "right word."

A. Reader's Response: First Thoughts

? What do you think Emily Dickinson's "singular presence" was like? [Sample responses: Since she was so eccentric and reclusive, she might have seemed spooky; or she might have seemed intellectual, just like her writing.]

B. Expansion

The Dickinson home is an imposing two-story structure sitting behind a metal fence and a tall row of hemlock. Huge trees border the front sidewalk. Gardens flank the sides and rear; these areas, plus an orchard and a field, comprised much of Dickinson's world.

C. Critical Reading: Evaluating and Interpretation

? Do you agree that Dickinson was lucky because she never had to go out to work? [Possible answers: She was lucky not to have to work so that she could instead focus on poetry; or, a whole world of experience was denied her because she did not go out to work.]

CONNECTING WITH DICKINSON'S POETRY

Ask students which poems in this Collection might connect with the image of Dickinson's life that Bernays provides in this piece. [Possible responses: "Heart! We will forget him!" on p. 374, "The Soul selects her own Society" on p. 378.] Then, have students re-read Linda Pastan's "Emily Dickinson" on p. 371. Remind students that Pastan's poem is about the gap between Dickinson's legend and the brilliance of her poetry.

Call on students to give their opinions about the degree to which the available biographical information on Dickinson should be used to help to explain her work. Finally, ask students what unanswered questions about Dickinson's life are raised by her poetry, especially by the poems in this Collection.

Making Meanings "Apparently . . ."

First Thoughts

1. Responses will vary. Nature seems to have no regard for the death of a flower.

Shaping Interpretations

2. The frost.
3. The flower is a laughing, happy child. The frost is called an assassin, and the sun is uncaring.
4. The pun plays on the double meaning of *unmoved:* the primary sense is "unfeeling"; the word also means "stationary."
5. God approves. The speaker may feel sympathy.

Extending the Text

6. **(Analysis)** Emerson focuses on the majesty of nature; the speaker here focuses on the uncaring power of nature.

"Tell all the Truth . . ."

First Thoughts

1. Slant is a poetic angle on a truth; lying is a distortion of the truth.

Shaping Interpretations

2. Going around the truth. "The Truth's superb surprise" is too bright.
3. Children's fears of lightning are eased when it is explained to them kindly.
4. The surprise of direct truth is too shocking. *Dazzle:* "enlighten." *Blind:* "uncomprehending."
5. The metaphor is that truth is an intensely bright light.

Challenging the Text

6. **(Synthesis)** Responses will vary. Because poetry tries to tell its truths with metaphor, symbol, and implication, this lyric is a reference to the way all poetry works.

"Success . . ."

First Thoughts

1. Possible response: The defeated.

Shaping Interpretations

2. The first kind is abstract—the desire for success. The second is concrete—the extreme need or thirst for nectar. In both cases, the idea of need is present.
3. The "purple host" is a multitude of wounded soldiers.
4. The ear will never respond to the sounds of triumph directed toward it.
5. The image of a dying warrior suggests that she was sending a message that no one would hear.

Connecting with the Text

6. Responses will vary. Images from an athletic competition might be appropriate.

Extending the Text

7. **(Synthesis)** It seems common and logical. Responses to the second question will vary.

MAKING MEANINGS

Apparently with no surprise

First Thoughts

1. What is the message of this poem? Do you feel it is shocking, reassuring, or something else?

Shaping Interpretations

2. Who is the "blonde Assassin"?
3. How are the flower, the frost, and the sun **personified** in this poem? What kind of person does each seem to be?
4. A **pun** is a play on words based on multiple meanings of a single word or words that sound alike but mean different things. What pun is in line 6? How would you explain it?
5. According to the speaker, how does God feel about the flower's beheading? How do you think the speaker feels?

Extending the Text

6. How does the speaker's attitude toward nature differ from Emerson's attitude in the excerpt from his essay *Nature* (page 219)? Is either point of view supported by the chart you made in your Reader's Log? Explain.

Tell all the Truth but tell it slant

First Thoughts

1. Look back over your Quickwrite notes. How would you define the word *slant* as it is used in line 1? Is telling something "slant" different from lying?

Shaping Interpretations

2. What is "Circuit"? What is "too bright for our infirm Delight" (line 3)?
3. Lines 5 and 6 provide an example to illustrate the poet's point about truth. As is typical of Dickinson's technique, she omits several words in these lines. How would you rephrase the lines to make a full sentence?
4. According to the last two lines, why must the truth be told "slant"? How would you define *dazzle* and *blind* here?
5. What **metaphor** is implied in line 7? What is "Truth" being compared with?

Challenging the Text

6. Do you agree with the poet's message? In what way can this lyric be seen as a reference to the way all poetry "works"?

Success is counted sweetest

First Thoughts

1. Who do *you* think is likely to count success sweetest?

Shaping Interpretations

2. Two kinds of desire are balanced in the first stanza. How would you define them? What is their relationship to each other?
3. Purple is a color associated with blood shed in battle. What is the "purple Host" in line 5?
4. Why is the ear "forbidden" in line 10?
5. What **image** does Dickinson use as a concrete illustration of success? What does this illustration suggest about the way she thought of her own struggles with the world?

Connecting with the Text

6. "Victory" is considered in military terms here. Can you think of similar circumstances—in your own life, in the news, in books, in movies, or in television shows—in which the situation in this poem, and its conclusion, might be repeated?

Extending the Text

7. Review your Quickwrite notes. Do you think the feeling expressed in the poem is common? Does it relate to your life in any way? Explain.

Before You Read
Because I could not stop for Death

Reading Focus
Drawn by Death

Like many other **metaphors** in Dickinson's poetry, the one in this poem imaginatively captures the most awesome and inevitable of human experiences—death—and does so with playfulness and wit. The literal elements of the metaphor are simple: Dying is compared to an unexpected ride in a horse-drawn carriage. But these are just about the only simple elements in a poem that depends for its effect on **irony,** on gradual comprehension, and on a blithe **tone** that is much at odds with the subject of the story being told.

A Dialogue with the Text

While Dickinson leads her readers along her journey in this poem, she uses time in an interesting and unusual way. As you read, describe what is happening in each stanza, and note when the events occur.

Because I could not stop for Death
Emily Dickinson

Because I could not stop for Death— **A**
He kindly stopped for me—
The Carriage held but just Ourselves—
And Immortality.

We slowly drove—He knew no haste
And I had put away
My labor and my leisure too,
For His Civility—

We passed the School, where Children strove
At Recess—in the Ring—
We passed the Fields of Gazing Grain—
We passed the Setting Sun—

Or rather—He passed Us—
The Dews drew quivering and chill—
For only Gossamer,° my Gown—
My Tippet—only Tulle°—

We paused before a House that seemed **B**
A Swelling of the Ground—
The Roof was scarcely visible—
The Cornice°—in the Ground—

Since then—'tis Centuries—and yet
Feels shorter than the Day
I first surmised the Horses Heads
Were toward Eternity—

15. gossamer: thin, soft material.
16. tippet . . . tulle: Her shawl, or tippet, was made only of fine netting, or tulle.
20. cornice: architectural term for a projecting, horizontal molding at the top of a building.

Into the Poem

Using **Before You Read** p. 391

A Dialogue with the Text
Remind students that their Reader's Logs are for their own use as a record of their experience and understanding of each work they read. Their entries for this selection may have questions and personal reactions to words, images, ideas, or other elements of the poem, along with any descriptions of what is happening in each stanza.

A. Reader's Response: First Thoughts

? Why could the speaker not "stop for Death"? [Sample responses: She might be too busy; or, she might be too attached to earthly life.]

B. Literary Element: Metaphor

The grave is compared to a house, a word that has comforting connotations. The low roof and the repetition of the word *ground* emphasize that this is a final resting place within the earth.

Options for Teaching
Strategies for Inclusion

Advanced Ask students to independently locate and read Carl Sandburg's short poem "Cool Tombs." Have students write a brief explication of the poem along with a paragraph or two in which they compare and contrast it with Dickinson's "I died for Beauty—but was scarce" on p. 393. Ask students to pay special attention to the **atmosphere, tone,** and **diction** of each poem.

English Language Development Point out the verb *be* in ll. 8 and 10 of "I heard a Fly buzz—when I died" on p. 392. Remind students that these are ungrammatical uses of the verb, and ask what form of the verb would be correct in each line. [*Was,* in both lines.] Ask students why Dickinson may have chosen this unconventional use for *be.* [Possible answers: For the long e sound; for the pun on the word *bee.*] ☞

Using **BEFORE YOU READ** p. 392

Reading Focus

Point out that a variety of poems have been written about death—some dark and ominous, some light and frivolous. Ask students what they think might be an appropriate mood or atmosphere for a poem about death, and ask them to explain why.

A. Reader's Response: First Thoughts

? Based on the first line, what kind of poem do you think this will be? [Sample responses: A poem about a near-death experience; or, a cautionary poem.] After students have read the poem, ask them if their predictions were correct.

B. Literary Element: Atmosphere

? What word would you use to describe the atmosphere created in this poem, especially in this final stanza and in the opening stanza? [Possible answers: Heavy, dull, lazy, lethargic, still, quiet, calm, placid, peaceful.]

Metacognition Ask students to describe the elements in the poem that led them to their conclusions about its atmosphere. [Possible answer: Dickinson repeats the word *stillness* and seems to be describing a room that is quiet except for the buzzing of a fly and the sounds of breathing. The gentle, rolling **meter** and long vowel sounds also contribute to the lethargic feel of the poem.]

BEFORE YOU READ
I HEARD A FLY BUZZ—WHEN I DIED

Reading Focus

Death Be Not Proud

This poem begins with such boldness and continues with such quick shifts of attention that we may not stop to think about what we are hearing—a voice from the dead.

Quickwrite

READER'S LOG

Write down what you would expect someone to sense at the time of death—that ultimate moment when we cannot "see to see."

I heard a Fly buzz—when I died

Emily Dickinson

A I heard a Fly buzz—when I died—
The Stillness in the Room
Was like the Stillness in the Air—
Between the Heaves of Storm—

The Eyes around—had wrung them dry—
And Breaths were gathering firm
For that last Onset—when the King
Be witnessed—in the Room—

I willed my Keepsakes—Signed away
What portion of me be
Assignable—and then it was
There interposed a Fly—

B With Blue—uncertain stumbling Buzz—
Between the light—and me—
And then the Windows failed—and then
I could not see to see—

Wind from the Sea (1947) by Andrew Wyeth. Tempera (18½″ × 27½″).

Mead Art Museum, Amherst College, Gift of Charles and Janet Morgan.

OPTIONS FOR TEACHING

INTEGRATING THE LANGUAGE ARTS

Strategic Reading To help students clearly understand how **imagery** helps clarify the meaning of a poem, use the collaborative technique of Jigsaw Reading, which allows each student to become an expert. Divide the class into home groups; assign each person in each group a stanza in a poem. Then, reassemble into expert groups (those students with the same stanza) to determine exactly what the stanza says, the role of imagery, and the best way to explain these ideas to home groups. Experts then return to their home groups, share content learned in expert groups, and teach their home groups about their stanza. The home groups should now examine how each stanza contributes to the poem as a whole.

Before You Read

I died for Beauty—but was scarce

Reading Focus

Beauty and Truth

The following lines, which conclude John Keats's "Ode on a Grecian Urn," are among the most famous lines in English poetry:

> "Beauty is truth, truth beauty"—that is all
> Ye know on earth, and all ye need to know.

Emily Dickinson knew these lines, and in this poem she presents her own version of the theme suggested by Keats.

Quickwrite

Beauty and Truth are two concepts that have been defined and debated for centuries. Write your own definitions of Beauty and Truth.

Michael Cornish.

I died for Beauty—but was scarce

Emily Dickinson

I died for Beauty—but was scarce (A)
Adjusted in the Tomb
When One who died for Truth, was lain
In an adjoining Room—

He questioned softly "Why I failed"?
"For Beauty," I replied—
"And I—for Truth—Themself are One—
We Bretheren, are," He said— (B)

And so, as Kinsmen, met a Night—
We talked between the Rooms—
Until the Moss had reached our lips—
And covered up—our names—

Into the Poem

Using **Before You Read** p. 393

Reading Focus

Show students photographs of a few famous sculptures such as Michelangelo's *David* or Rodin's *The Thinker,* and discuss how truthfully each artist tried to capture the beauty of the human form.

A. Reader's Response: Shaping Interpretations

? What kinds of people might describe themselves as having died for beauty? [Sample responses: A person who died from a broken heart; a person who died trying to bring more life or beauty into the world.]

B. Expansion

Keats's famous "Ode on a Grecian Urn" (1819) describes the perfection and timelessness of art as contrasted with the living, changing world. The contrast is suggested by the eternally frozen figures on an imaginary Greek urn with a pastoral theme. The ode ends with the two lines to which Dickinson alludes—the urn's response to the speaker of the poem.

Professional Notes

Cultural Diversity After students have read "Because I could not stop for Death" on p. 391, "I heard a Fly buzz—when I died" on p. 392, and "I died for Beauty—but was scarce" on p. 393, read aloud Federico García Lorca's "Gacela of the Dark Death" ("Gacela de la muerte oscura") and ask students how the attitude toward death Lorca offers in the poem differs from the attitude Dickinson expresses in her poems.

Thematic Connections: "Tell It Slant" Ask students how "Because I could not stop for Death" on p. 391 might be seen as an illustration of Dickinson's sentiment that the truth should be told with a slant. [Possible response: Most poems that try to express a truth about death are dark and ominous; the slant Dickinson takes is to offer a different perspective on death by describing it in a detached, casual voice.]

Primary Sources

Point out the similarities between some of the sentiments Dickinson expresses in this letter to Higginson and some of the sentiments she expresses in her poetry. In particular, point out Dickinson's comment about her "terror" in the fourth paragraph of the letter, her comment about immortality in the fifth paragraph, and her comments about her companions in the sixth paragraph. Also, point out that the playful **tone** of the comments is also echoed in some of her poetry.

PRIMARY **Sources** | A MAGAZINE ARTICLE

Higginson's Account of Dickinson

In 1862, Emily Dickinson sent the critic Thomas Wentworth Higginson a letter and four poems, asking for critical help. Dickinson saw him as a mentor, and they corresponded for several years. Four years after Dickinson's death, Higginson assisted Mabel Loomis Todd in editing Dickinson's poems. The following year, Higginson wrote an article in the *Atlantic Monthly* about his experiences with Emily Dickinson.

I remember to have ventured on some criticism which she afterwards called "surgery," and on some questions, part of which she evaded, as will be seen, with a naive skill such as the most experienced and worldly coquette might envy. Her second letter (received April 26, 1862) was as follows:

> Mr. Higginson,—Your kindness claimed earlier gratitude, but I was ill, and write today from my pillow.
>
> Thank you for the surgery; it was not so painful as I supposed. I bring you others, as you ask. . . .
>
> You asked how old I was? I made no verse, but one or two, until this winter, sir.
>
> I had a terror since September, I could tell to none; and so I sing, as the boy does of the burying ground, because I am afraid.
>
> You inquire my books. For poets, I have Keats, and Mr. and Mrs. Browning. For prose, Mr. Ruskin, Sir Thomas Browne, and the Revelations. I went to school, but in your manner of the phrase had no education. When a little girl, I had a friend who taught me Immortality; but venturing too near, himself, he never returned. Soon after my tutor died, and for several years my lexicon was my only companion. Then I found one more, but he was not contented I be his scholar, so he left the land.
>
> You ask of my companions. Hills, sir, and the sundown, and a dog large as myself, that my father bought me. They are better than beings because they know, but do not tell; and the noise in the pool at noon excels my piano.
>
> I have a brother and sister; my mother does not care for thought, and father, too busy with his briefs to notice what we do. He buys me many books, but begs me not to read them, because he fears they joggle the mind. They are religious, except me. . . .
>
> But I fear my story fatigues you. I would like to learn. Could you tell me how to grow, or is it unconveyed, like melody or witchcraft?
>
> You speak of Mr. Whitman. I never read his book, but was told that it was disgraceful. . . .

. . . I must soon have written to ask her for her picture, that I might form some impression of my enigmatical correspondent. To this came the following reply, in July 1862:

> Could you believe me without? I had no portrait, now, but am small, like the wren; and my hair is bold, like the chestnut bur; and my eyes, like the sherry in the glass, that the guest leaves. Would this do just as well?
>
> It often alarms father. He says death might occur, and he has molds [photographs] of all the rest, but has no mold of me. . . .

—Thomas Wentworth Higginson, *from* "Emily Dickinson's Letters"

OPTIONS FOR TEACHING

STRATEGIES FOR INCLUSION

Intrapersonal Ask students to suppose that they are poets or artists who have been asked to write letters describing themselves to their creative mentors. Suggest that, like Dickinson, they try to convey some sense of their creative work through their self-descriptions, and ask them to write down four or five sentences that might appear in their letters.

Auditory To give students a greater sense of the playful tone Dickinson used in her correspondence with Higginson, read the excerpts from her letter aloud in a voice appropriate to the sentiments she expresses. After students have listened, ask them what reasons Dickinson may have had for choosing this particular tone to address Higginson.

MAKING MEANINGS

Because I could not stop for Death

First Thoughts

1. If you were going to **personify** Death, would Death be like the person described in this poem? Why or why not?

Shaping Interpretations

2. Can you paraphrase the first two lines in a way that emphasizes their **irony**? What word in line 2 tells you that the tone is ironic?
3. In stanza 2, *civility* means "politeness." How does this kind of behavior on the part of Death and the speaker extend the **irony** of the first stanza?
4. What three things do the riders pass in stanza 3? What is significant about the fact that the sun passes the carriage in stanza 4, and the nature of the change in temperature? Look back over your Reader's Log notes to decide.
5. Stanza 5 is a riddle in itself. What is the nearly buried house?
6. Do you think the concluding stanza introduces a **tone** of terror, because the speaker has suddenly realized she will ride on forever, conscious of being dead? Or is the poem really an expression of trust and even triumph? Explain your response.

Challenging the Text

7. The critic Alfred Kazin said of the last stanza of this poem: "What that famous Eternity is, we cannot say." Do you agree with Kazin? What do *you* think Dickinson meant by the "Eternity" the horses were going toward?

I heard a Fly buzz—when I died

First Thoughts

1. Do you find this poem grotesque, moving, humorous, or something else? Look back over your Quickwrite notes, and explain whether or not you were surprised by the poem's conclusion.

Shaping Interpretations

2. According to the second and third stanzas, how had the speaker and those around her prepared for death?
3. What are the dying person and those around her expecting to find in the room? What appears instead, and why is this **ironic**?
4. In line 4, Dickinson used the word "Heaves" to refer to the behavior of storms. Why is "Heaves" an appropriate word to describe what is happening in the poem?
5. How does the poet use pauses and specific words in lines 12 and 13 to make the appearance of the fly dramatic and lively?
6. In the third stanza, what portion of the speaker is "assignable"? What portion, by implication, is *not* assignable?
7. Who is the "King" (line 7)? What does the phrase "the Windows failed" (line 15) mean?
8. What **tone** do you hear in this poem? What feeling do you think the poet expresses by inserting the fly into this deathbed scene?

I died for Beauty—but was scarce

First Thoughts

1. What thoughts and feelings would you say are expressed in this poem? Are they similar to or different from those you recorded in your Quickwrite notes? Explain.

Shaping Interpretations

2. What is the situation described in the first stanza? What do the two speakers have in common that allows one of them to claim they are "Bretheren"—that is, brothers?
3. In the third stanza the "Moss" is real, but it is also a **metaphor.** What do you think it represents? What is significant in the fact that it covers up the speakers' names?
4. **Slant rhyme** makes the last word stand out. Do you think this is an important word? Why or why not?
5. What do you think Dickinson's **message** is? Would you say it is optimistic or pessimistic?

Making Meanings "Because . . ."

First Thoughts

1. Responses will vary. However, students may note that death is often personified in much more hideous, frightful terms.

Shaping Interpretations

2. "Because I was too busy to think about Death, he came upon me when I least expected it." The ironic word is *kindly*.
3. The notion of Death being civil—a trait not commonly associated with death—extends the irony of the word *kindly* in the first stanza.
4. They pass a school, fields of grain, and a sunset. The sun's passing brings nightfall, dark, and cold.
5. The house is the speaker's tomb.
6. The poem seems to express trust and triumph rather than terror.

Challenging the Text

7. **(Evaluation)** Eternity may mean permanent death or everlasting life.

"I heard . . ."

First Thoughts

1. Responses will vary. Students may see humor in the irony of the situation. Instead of seeing a profound image, the speaker merely hears a fly.

Shaping Interpretations

2. They prepared for death by crying until their tears dried up, firming up their breath, and making a will.
3. They are expecting death; ironically, the fly interrupts the expectation of a solemn, religious death.
4. *Heaves* suggests the last gasps of life.
5. The pause in l. 13 sets a staccato rhythm that adds to the description of the fly. *Interposed* in l. 12 is unexpected and formal. In l. 13, "uncertain stumbling Buzz" uses alliteration, assonance, and onomatopoeia.
6. The portion that is assignable is her material goods. The unassignable portion is her spirit.
7. The King might be God or even Death. The windows failing is probably the light fading, the speaker's eyes clouding, or the darkness of death.
8. For some the tone might be bizarrely comic, for others grotesquely cold.

"I died . . ."

First Thoughts

1. Possible response: Those who supported goodness—truth and beauty—during their lives will meet together in death for mutual comfort. Or those who support truth and beauty end in oblivion instead of eternity.

Shaping Interpretations

2. One speaker is in the tomb when another is brought in. They are brothers because they both died for beauty and truth.
3. The moss metaphorically suggests a passage of time that results in oblivion.
4. The sound of the last word, *names,* clashes with *rooms*. The word *names* is important, because a name is a part of a person's identity.
5. Students might say that Dickinson's message is inherent in the irony expressed; beauty is elusive; death overtakes us all.

Choices: Building Your Portfolio

1. **Writer's Notebook** Remind students to save their work. They may use it as prewriting for the Writer's Workshop on p. 401.
2. **Critical Writing** Have students freewrite the definitions of the elements before writing their essays.
3. **Creative Writing** Students may find it helpful to look at other forms of poetry such as concrete poetry, sonnets, blank verse, and haiku. Have students try these forms as they use Dickinson's themes to create poems of their own.
4. **Critical Writing/Music** Ask students to consider in their essays how Dickinson avoids the monotony of traditional hymnal meter while adhering to the form.
5. **Performance/Research** Remind students that researching biographies about Dickinson might provide insight about her views. Suggest that one student in the group serve as director, another create the props, and a third perform the monologue.
6. **Art** Invite other classes to a book-signing party where students may present their handiwork, read their poems, and make gifts of their books.

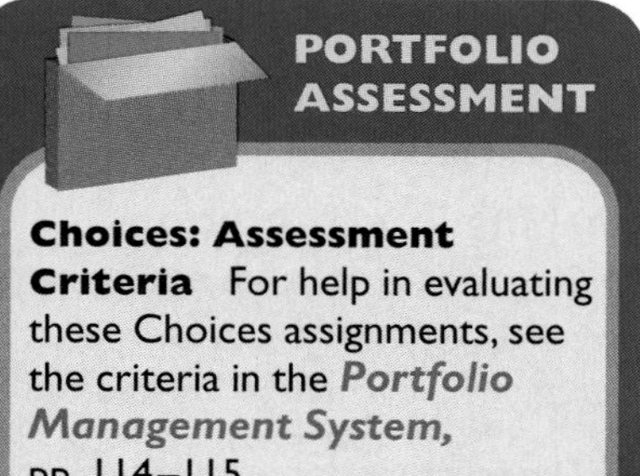

Choices: Assessment Criteria For help in evaluating these Choices assignments, see the criteria in the ***Portfolio Management System,*** pp. 114–115.

CHOICES: Building Your Portfolio

Writer's Notebook

1. Collecting Ideas for a Reflective Essay

WORK IN PROGRESS

Choose one of the topics you jotted down in the chart you made (page 365), or choose a new subject based on Dickinson's poems that you would like to explore. Perhaps you'd like to reflect on a passage from one of her poems. Freewrite your thoughts on whatever topic you select. Don't censor your thoughts—the point of the freewrite is to help you discover what you think about the topic. Save your notes for the Writer's Workshop on page 401.

Critical Writing

2. The Soul Selects Its Own Poetry

In a brief essay, compare and contrast one of Emily Dickinson's poems with "Huswifery" by Edward Taylor (page 73), "Upon the Burning of Our House" by Anne Bradstreet (page 69), "World, in Hounding Me" by Sor Juana Inés de la Cruz (page 76), or "Thanatopsis" by William Cullen Bryant (page 171). In your essay, consider such elements as **subject matter, theme, tone,** and **figures of speech.**

Creative Writing

3. The Dickinson Way

Write a poem that treats one of the themes that engaged Emily Dickinson: love and loss, the spiritual life, death and immortality, nature, or the power of the imagination. You might even use one of Dickinson's lines as your opener. Experiment with **metaphors, similes,** and **slant rhymes.** Try out Dickinson's style of punctuation and capitalization, or invent your own unique style. For inspiration, read the student poem on page 380.

Critical Writing / Music

4. Hymn to Her

Dickinson let the strict **meters** she found in her hymnbook provide the basic beat for her poems, but the variations she introduced gave her poems subtlety and prevented monotony. In a brief essay, analyze at least two of her poems to show how she uses this traditional hymn meter:

8 syllables in line 1
8 syllables in line 3

6 syllables in line 2
6 syllables in line 4

Then show how she also uses a short hymn meter of 6, 6, 8, and 6 syllables. To see how closely some of the poems conform to a hymn meter, you might try singing "If you were coming in the Fall" to the tune of "O God, Our Help in Ages Past."

Performance / Research

5. Dickinson Onstage

With a partner or a small group, prepare a script for a performance called "An Evening with Emily Dickinson." In the script, let Dickinson tell about her life, her views of poetry and language, and her feelings about nature, faith, and eternity. Include in your performance readings of selected poems. Present your performance for the class.

Art

6. Cover to Cover

Dickinson sewed the final copies of her poems into the form of small booklets. To make your own small book, fold four pages of white paper in half. Select poems you would like to reproduce—either your own, Dickinson's, or some of your favorite poems by different poets. On the first page, design a book cover including a title. Then, copy one poem onto each of the remaining pages. Try to make your penmanship or calligraphy suggest feelings conveyed in the poems. Finally, sew your book along the fold.

OPTIONS FOR TEACHING

STRATEGIES FOR INCLUSION

Visual Before students begin activity #5, show the class a portion of Hal Holbrook's *Mark Twain Tonight,* or a portion of another video recording of an actor or actress performing a dramatic monologue in the character of a famous writer or artist. Ask students to take notes on elements of the performance they would like to incorporate into their own presentations.

Auditory Before students begin activity #4, play the audio recording of "Oh God, Our Help in Ages Past" (on Audiocassette 1, Side B, in the *Audiovisual Resources Binder*) to give the class a sense of the special qualities of the meter that Dickinson used as a basis for so much of her poetry. Ask students to consider what Dickinson may have admired about the form.

Song of Himself

Around the turn of the twelfth century, the Persian scientist Omar Khayyám produced several well-known works in mathematics and astronomy, as well as a series of quatrains, or four-line poems, for which he is now even more famous. The brilliant 1850s English translation by Edward FitzGerald of *The Rubáiyát of Omar Khayyám* made Khayyám the rage of the Victorian era. This powerful expression of the Persian poet's personal vision and philosophy of life has remained in print for over a century.

Legacy in Latin America

Who's the most popular U.S. poet in Latin America? The answer is probably Walt Whitman. One of his greatest admirers was the Cuban poet José Martí, who introduced Whitman's work to Spanish-speaking audiences at the turn of the century. Whitman's influence on Martí's own verse is evident in *José Martí: Major Poems* (Holmes and Meier), a bilingual edition with English translation by Elinor Randall, edited by Philip Foner.

Beholder of Mysteries

"I am no scientist," Annie Dillard says of herself. "I am a wanderer with a background in theology and a penchant for quirky facts." In *Pilgrim at Tinker Creek* (Harper and Row), Dillard draws on her experiences in an isolated Virginia valley to create a memorable reflection on life, death, and the mysteries of nature.

The Country Way

Maxine Kumin has always drawn from nature in producing her vivid poetry. *In Deep* (Viking) is the Pulitzer Prize–winning poet's collection of essays on country living. Of special interest is the last essay, "A Sense of Place," which examines nature's role in inspiring the poetic imagination.

Before and After Dickinson

Did you know that the world's first known poet was a woman? Her name was Enheduanna, and she was born around 2300 B.C. She was the daughter of a king and served as a Sumerian moon priestess. She is just one of many women poets whose works appear in *A Book of Women Poets from Antiquity to Now* (Schocken Books), a collection edited by Aliki and Willis Barnstone.

Read On

Portfolio Assessment Options

The following projects can help you evaluate and assess your students' reading accomplishments outside of class. The completed projects, including audiotapes, may be kept as part of the students' portfolios. If students are doing oral presentations and want them included in their portfolios, have someone videotape or tape-record the presentations.

- **Create a Collage** Each of the writers has a vision of the world. Have students create a collage with words and pictures that reflect how their author perceives the world.
- **Record an Advertisement** Radio advertisements have to rely on the power of words, the voice of the commentator, and sound effects to create a commercial that captures listeners' attention. Have students work alone or with a partner to create a radio commercial for the book they have read. Remind students that the commercial has to contain specific details from the book.
- **Research a Time** Poets are products of their times. Students may conduct research about the time and place in which the poet lived. For example, they may find out about the twelfth-century Persia of Omar Khayyám, the ancient Sumer of Enheduanna, or the late nineteenth century Cuba of José Martí. Students may use the information to write comments for the dust jacket of the book they read.
- **Hold a Reading** Have students choose a poem or a prose excerpt that is particularly meaningful to them. Ask them to practice saying the piece with appropriate expression. Then, hold a reading in class. Students may read their selections and answer questions from listeners.

FOR FURTHER EXPLORATION

Nonfiction

Conversations with Walt Whitman by Sadakichi Hartmann
Selected Letters of Walt Whitman edited by Edwin H. Miller
Emily Dickinson's Letters edited by Theodora Van Wagenen Ward
Emily Dickinson: Woman Poet by Paula Bennet

Poetry

"Woman" by Alice Walker
"One Perfect Rose" by Dorothy Parker

Films

Beautiful Dreamers
Dead Poets Society

A. Expansion
Westerners favored other colorful, polysyllabic words as well. Ask students if they know the meanings of these words: *discombobulate* (confuse), *hornswoggle* (swindle), *squablification* (quarreling), *lollapalooza* (extraordinary person or thing), and *absquatulate* (go away, skedaddle).

B. Exploring the Historical Period
A number of frontier expressions still in existence derive from the game of poker, the French origins of which were quickly forgotten as its popularity spread: *you bet, call one's bluff, square deal, poker face, up the ante, throw in one's hand, ace up one's sleeve,* and *stacked deck.* Trade in beaver pelts contributed *eager beaver* and *work like a beaver.* The gold rush contributed *bonanza, diggings, El Dorado, pan out, stake a claim,* and *strike it rich.*

- **Planning Instruction** See Teaching Notes, *Teaching Resources A,* p. 147 for objectives.
- **Assessment** See The American Language, *Test Booklet,* pp. 93–94.

The American Language

A Period of Vocabulary Growth

by Gary Q. Arpin

Languages are always changing and growing, adding new words and expressions and shading the meaning of terms that already exist. American English enjoyed a remarkable period of growth in the first half of the nineteenth century as a variety of sources contributed to its expanding vocabulary.

Backwoods English

The word *backwoods* was first recorded in 1709. Some sixty-five years later, the word *backwoodsman* appeared. John Pickering, a linguist in the nineteenth century, wrote that the word was applied "by the people of the commercial towns in the United States, to those who inhabit the territory westward of the Allegheny Mountains." Backwoodsmen themselves used more colorful terms. They called themselves *ring-tailed roarers* or *mollagausaugers* (courageous men). The exploits of the backwoodsmen during the War of 1812 made them famous, and when Davy Crockett came to Washington, D.C., in 1827 as a congressman from Tennessee, people stared at him in the street. The following year, another backwoodsman, Andrew Jackson, was elected president.

Backwoods English teems with exaggeration and exuberant bragging—language equal to the awesome task of surviving on a new frontier. Crockett almanacs, collections of speeches by Davy Crockett that were popular from the 1830s to the 1850s, brought this backwoods language into Eastern homes. Here's an example:

> Hosses, I am with you! and while the stars of Uncle Sam, and the stripes of his country wave triumphantly in the breeze, whar, whar, whar is the craven, low-lived, chicken-bred, toad-hoppin', red-mounted, bristle-headed mother's son of ye who will not raise the beacon light of triumph, smouse the citadel of the aggressor, and squeeze ahead for Liberty and Glory! Whoop! h-u-rah, hosses, come along—Crockett's with you—show us the enemy!

Courtesy American Antiquarian Society.
Woodcut from *Davy Crockett Almanac* (1835).

Most backwoods slang had a short life, though some words and phrases have survived. Phrases like *fly off the handle, pull up stakes, a knock-down-drag-out fight, up a tree,* and *doing a land-office business* all date from this period.

The American Vernacular in Literature

The first half of the nineteenth century resounded with calls to establish an independent national literature describing the American landscape and dealing with American manners and interests, and by midcentury American literature was in full flower. To describe American phenomena, writers began to turn to the **vernacular**—the common spoken language of a region. The Crockett almanacs were a kind of subliterature, but by the 1870s, Mark Twain (page 450) was recording the language of the American West in substantial books like *Adventures of Huckleberry Finn, Roughing It,* and *Life on the Mississippi.*

Walt Whitman (page 348) also used American vernacular to create literature of a high order. In *Leaves of Grass,* he proclaims the virtues of American English:

OPTIONS FOR TEACHING

STRATEGIES FOR INCLUSION

Linguistic Have students work in pairs to produce a dictionary of Americanisms. One student may make line drawings or cartoon illustrations while the other student writes the dictionary entries.

> The English language befriends the grand American expression. . . . It is the powerful language of resistance—it is the dialect of common sense. It is the speech of the proud and melancholy races and of all who aspire. It is the chosen tongue to express growth, faith, self-esteem, freedom, justice, equality, friendliness, amplitude, prudence, decision, and courage. It is the medium that shall well nigh express the inexpressible.

Whitman frequently tapped American vernacular in his verse. For instance, he quite pointedly employed an Americanism (*to loaf*) in the first lines of "Song of Myself" (page 347):

> I loaf and invite my soul,
> I lean and loaf . . . observing a spear of summer grass.

In *Two Years Before the Mast* (1840), Richard Henry Dana, Jr., called *loafer* "the newly invented Yankee word." Four years later, in *Martin Chuzzlewit,* part of which is set in America, the British novelist Charles Dickens put *loaf* in quotation marks to show that it was a peculiarly American term. Whitman's use of the verb *loaf* eleven years later proclaimed his Americanness just as surely as if he had called himself a ring-tailed roarer.

The Language of the Stump: Political Coinage

> Whitman's use of the verb *loaf* proclaimed his Americanness just as surely as if he had called himself a ring-tailed roarer.

The American vernacular did not appear only in literature. It was also spoken on the political platform, or "stump." (Candidates for office would stand on tree stumps to deliver their speeches.) Here is part of a speech by a candidate for office in Oregon in 1858:

> Fellow-citizens, you might as well try to dry up the Atlantic Ocean with a broomstraw, or draw this 'ere stump from under my feet with a harnessed gadfly, as to convince me that I ain't gwine to be elected this heat [race]. My opponent don't stand a chance; not a sniff. Why, he ain't as intellectual as a common sized shad. . . . If thar's anybody this side of whar the sun begins to blister the yea'th [heath] that can wallop me, let him show himself—I'm ready. Boys, I go in for the American Eagle, claws, stars, stripes, and all; and may I bust my everlastin' buttonholes ef I don't knock down, drag out, and gouge everybody as denies me!

This so-called stump style is long gone, but many phrases coined by politicians of the period are still used. For instance, the word *gerrymander* was coined in 1812 after Massachusetts Governor Elbridge Gerry reorganized the state election districts in order to maintain control of the state senate. One of the resulting districts was absurdly long and serpentine. The artist Gilbert Stuart saw a map of the districts in the office of a local newspaper editor. Noting its resemblance to a salamander, Stuart gave the district a head, wings, and claws. The editor proclaimed it a "gerrymander," and thus the word was born.

The Saint Louis Art Museum. Lent by The People of Missouri.

Stump Speaker (1853–1854). Drawing from *Stump Speaking* by George Caleb Bingham. Brush, black ink, and wash over pencil (11½″ × 9½″).

The Language of the Press

Newspapers began to flourish in America in the late 1830s, thanks to improved printing methods that made penny newspapers profitable. Papers tried to attract readers with colorful language. One of the ways they did this was to invent whimsical abbreviations. The most famous Americanism of

C. Expansion
According to etymologists, *loafer,* meaning "a lazy person," is an Americanism first recorded in 1830. It probably is derived from the German *Landläufer,* meaning "vagabond." The verb *loaf* seems to have been formed from the noun *loafer,* rather than the other way around.

D. Cultural Connections
Another political phrase that comes from this period is *slush fund. Slush* referred to the surplus fat from a ship's galley. When the ship was in port, the slush was sold and the money was put into a fund to purchase luxuries for the crew. Later, *slush fund* took on its present meaning of money used for corrupt political purposes.

INTEGRATING THE LANGUAGE ARTS

Strategic Reading Have students work in pairs to use the strategy of Reciprocal Teaching; students read a portion of the text, and one student asks the other questions about its content or underlying ideas. Caution students not to dwell on marginal details but to focus on the main ideas. The students change roles, with the second student now asking the first student questions. After reading each portion of the text, students should take turns summarizing what they have learned.

A. Expansion

Once the Chisolm Trail had been established by Jesse Chisolm in 1866, cow- and ranch-related terms also flooded the language: *cowboy, cowhand, cowpuncher, cowpoke, bronco buster, wrangler, range rider, cattle baron.* Frontier settlers dealing with American Indians and Spanish-speaking Mexicans contributed enduring pidgin phrases such as *no can do* and *long time no see.*

Try It Out: Possible Answers

1. A sample answer for each suffix is given. *Mythology* from the Latin *mythologia*; *hucksterism* from the Middle English *hokestere* and the Greek *ismos; weatherize* from the Middle English *weder* and the Greek *izein*; *devilish* from the Middle English *devel* and the Greek *iskos*.
2. Use the noun *soundbite* as an example.
3. Ask students to submit photocopies of their sources for loanwords.

them all—*OK*—originated as a witty abbreviation. *OK* was first used to mean "oll korrect" (a deliberate misspelling of "all correct") in a Boston newspaper in 1839. *OK* might never have survived as an expression had the New York Democratic Club not dubbed itself "The OK Club" during the 1840 presidential election. The Democrats intended *OK* to stand for "Old Kinderhook," a nickname for their candidate, President Martin Van Buren, a native of the town of Kinderhook, New York. Their opponents, however, claimed that *OK* stood for "oll korrect" and that the expression had been coined by former president Andrew Jackson, who had misspelled "all correct." (This was to remind voters that Van Buren was Jackson's personal choice as successor and to make fun of Jackson's limited education.) "OK!" became a Democratic rallying cry during that boisterous election year and remained in widespread popular use.

The Influence of Immigrants

The late 1840s saw a tremendous increase in the number of immigrants to the United States. In 1845, about 100,000 immigrants arrived; by 1854, the number had grown to 500,000. A large number of immigrants during the mid–nineteenth century were Germans, many of whom sought haven from political disorder. The German influence on American English was strong, especially in words for food (*sauerkraut, frankfurter, hamburger, noodle*). German also gave us *kindergarten* (children's garden); *bum* (probably from *bummler,* meaning "loafer"); *dumb,* in the sense of "stupid" (from *dumm*); and *fresh,* meaning "saucy" or "impertinent" (from *frech,* "impudent").

However, the greatest source of **loanwords**—words borrowed from other languages—in the nineteenth century was Spanish. As Americans moved westward into territory originally settled by the Spanish, they came upon a host of items that are still known by their Spanish names. *Mustang, lasso, ranch, fiesta, plaza, bronco, canyon,* and *patio* are just a few commonly used English words of Spanish origin.

Try It Out

1. Americans frequently change nouns into verbs or adjectives, and verbs into nouns or adjectives, often through the addition of a suffix. The first suffix popularly used in the United States to make new nouns was *–ery. Printery* was coined in 1638. Other common suffixes used to change a word's function are *–logy, –ism, –ize,* and *–ish.* Make a list of five words that have been formed by the addition of each of these suffixes. What information is given in the dictionary about each word's origin?
2. Nearly every occupation coins its own special vocabulary, which may then find its way into general usage. Compile a brief dictionary of the special vocabulary of people in a business or industry you are familiar with (stockbrokers, doctors, lawyers, politicians, advertisers, news reporters, weather forecasters, restaurant workers, computer programmers, athletes, musicians, and so on). Explain the meaning of each word or phrase, and, if you can, explain its derivation. Which of these words or phrases have been picked up and used by people outside the occupation? How many have been added to American English in the last twenty years or less? (Think of terms like *compact disc, virtual reality,* and *fax.*)
3. With a partner or small group, make a "Loanword Lexicon"—a dictionary of words used in American English that were originally borrowed from other languages. You might try making a dictionary of loanwords from a particular language—Spanish or Japanese, for example—or a dictionary of specialized words (names of animals, foods, or inventions, for example) that are actually loanwords.

OPTIONS FOR TEACHING

ASSESSMENT TOOLS

Check Test: True-False

1. Backwoods English is formal and precise. [False]
2. Davy Crockett is a fictitious figure from the days of the frontier. [False]
3. The common spoken language of a region is called the vernacular. [True]
4. *OK* began as a shortened form for *okay.* [False]
5. The word *kindergarten* means "children's garden" in German. [True]

EXPOSITORY WRITING

REFLECTIVE ESSAY

Walt Whitman and Emily Dickinson shared their reflections about life by writing about them in verse. Deep and honest reflection isn't just the domain of poetry, however. In the prose form called the reflective essay, writers can arrive at broad truths about life by exploring just about anything under the sun.

A reflective essay usually originates in a specific incident, observation, quotation, or abstract concept, called the *occasion*. The occasion causes the writer to make connections to more general, even universal, truths about existence. Reflections can be humorous or deeply philosophical; they can be written simply for oneself or with a broad audience in mind. They can be prompted by large-scale dramatic events like war and by small, seemingly insignificant incidents like reading a story to a small child.

Prewriting

1. **Springboards for reflection.** A poem you've read, remembered moments or objects from your past, social trends you've observed, a witty quotation you've found—any of these can be occasions for reflection. You could even reflect on an abstract quality, such as creativity or integrity. Perhaps one of your Writer's Notebook assignments from collections 7 and 8 has inspired you with an idea.

   If you are starting from scratch and need to find a suitable subject, try making a two-column list of incidents and observations you recall from the past week. Briefly describe each incident or observation—the occasion—in the left column, and in the right column, make a note about the significance of each experience—your reflections on it.

WORK IN PROGRESS

Model

Incident or Observation	Thoughts / Reflections
bumped into curb during driver's ed	*Mistakes are part of learning.*
finally got the courage to mend quarrel with Danielle	*Most anger is momentary and pointless.*
couldn't fall asleep for hours last night —but got an idea for a poem while lying awake	*Creativity is mysterious and can come at odd times.*
looked at my seashell collection, which I hadn't touched in months	*What makes people collect things?*

Technology HELP

See Writer's Workshop 2 CD-ROM. *Assignment: Reflective Essay.*

ASSIGNMENT
Write an essay in which you begin with a specific occasion (an incident, observation, abstract concept, or quotation) and explore your thoughts and reflections about it, arriving at a general truth about life.

AIM
To inform; to express yourself.

AUDIENCE
Your teacher, classmates, and general readers.

QUICK PLANNING GUIDE

WW **Reflective Essay**

Motivation

Ask students to think about a time when they were in a new or unfamiliar situation—for example, beginning classes at a new school, trying out for a sports team, or performing in front of an audience. Have students reflect on the experience and then freewrite about it for three minutes. Invite volunteers to share their writing.

Teaching the Lesson

Remind students that a reflective essay is a personal kind of writing that allows a reader to share in or understand the writer's feelings about an incident.

This lesson includes suggestions for each stage of the writing process. If you have done any reflective writing, you might share it with students.

PROGRAM MANAGER

Computer Guided Instruction For a related reflective essay assignment that students may use as additional instruction, see *Writer's Workshop 2.*

PORTFOLIO ASSESSMENT

- **Generating Ideas** To help students in prewriting, use the heuristic in the *Portfolio Management System,* p. 116.
- **Assessment Rubric** For a rubric that can be used to assess students' progress in writing, see the *Portfolio Management System,* p. 118.

Prewriting

Remind students that their reflective essays do not have to be about momentous occasions in their lives. Point out that although they may write about such events, often the best reflective essays are about seemingly commonplace incidents.

Drafting

Explain that a reflective essay is more interesting if the writer uses language that shows rather than tells. Give students two or three statements that tell; then ask students for suggestions to change them into statements that show.

Evaluating and Revising

- Remind students to use the Evaluation Criteria on p. 403.
- If students have difficulty varying sentence beginnings, refer them to the Language Workshop on p. 404.

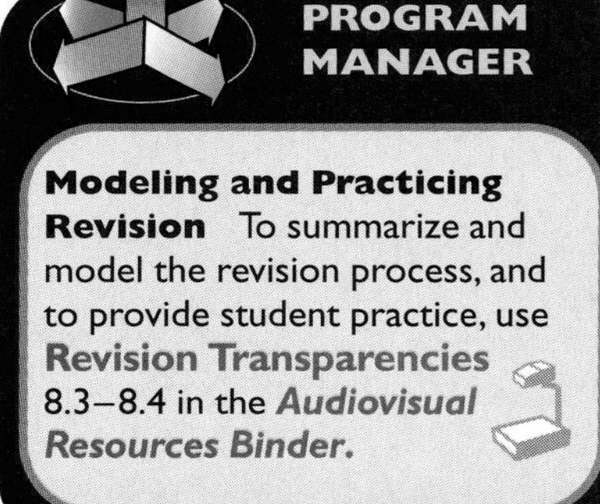

PROGRAM MANAGER

Modeling and Practicing Revision To summarize and model the revision process, and to provide student practice, use **Revision Transparencies** 8.3–8.4 in the ***Audiovisual Resources Binder.***

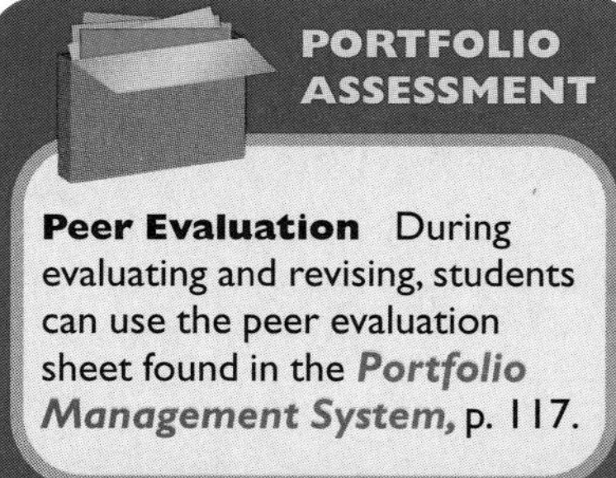

PORTFOLIO ASSESSMENT

Peer Evaluation During evaluating and revising, students can use the peer evaluation sheet found in the ***Portfolio Management System,*** p. 117.

Try It Out

Freewrite about an incident from your own experience that illustrates the general truth behind each quotation.

1. "The reward of a thing well done is to have done it."
—Ralph Waldo Emerson
2. "Nothing is so much to be feared as fear."
—Henry David Thoreau
3. "When in doubt tell the truth."
—Mark Twain

Strategies for Elaboration

The reflective essay can use many of the same narrative techniques as fiction.

- **Pacing.** Vary your pacing. Try using flashbacks occasionally, not just straightforward chronological order.
- **Dialogue.** Recording what you or others said will make an incident seem more real.
- **Description.** Show, don't tell. Use vivid sensory details to bring your writing to life.

2. **Food for thought.** If a topic intrigues you, then it will probably have a similar effect on your readers. Freewrite for five or ten minutes on the occasion you have chosen. Write down every thought that comes to you, without concern for logic or consistency. Recall the sensory details of the experience, too.
3. **But what do you really want to say?** Re-read your freewriting, and identify your emotions and opinions about the occasion. Sum them up in a single, general statement that your readers can apply to their own experience: "The worst thing about staying angry with someone isn't so much what it does to them; it's what it does to you" or "Creativity is still a mystery to us—the best creative ideas often come when you think you're doing nothing at all." This generalization will be your central idea, or thesis.

Drafting

1. **Inviting the reader inside.** The opening of your essay should be an invitation to your reader, a way of grabbing their interest. Avoid the common trap of stating your subject directly, of beginning in a preachy, moralizing style: "Letting anger get the better of you is never worth it." A better way is to approach your subject indirectly. You might quote something a classic essayist said on the subject and then connect it to your own experience. You might open with an attention-grabbing question or an allusion or analogy that your audience recognizes. There are as many ways to begin as there are writers.
2. **Organizing your thoughts.** Most reflective essays move from the specific to the general, or weave in and out between the two. There's no one right way to organize a reflective essay, but here are some possible choices:
   - You can start with the specific occasion and move in and out of it, letting each detail of the experience in turn suggest thoughts and reflections relating to the general truth you're leading up to.
   - You can relate an occasion—an incident, perhaps, or a larger event in the world—in its entirety and then move to a reflection on the particular details of your subject that cause you to reflect on a general truth about the human condition.
   - You can present several related incidents or occasions that shed light on the general truth you're exploring.
   - You can start with a quotation or an incident that illustrates a general, abstract concept—the need for creativity in everyday life, for example—and relate some personal experiences that show how the general concept is played out in your own and other people's lives.
3. **Ending with insight.** Just as you opened your reflective essay with a punch, you should end it in a memorable way. The best reflective essays leave the reader with an "Aha!" feeling. Some essays end with direct philosophical statements, answering the questions they have raised. Others are indirect, implying rather than stating their conclusions directly. A description, a question, a well-expressed insight, or a personal anecdote can make a satisfying conclusion for your essay.

OPTIONS FOR TEACHING

STRATEGIES FOR INCLUSION

Visual To help students develop their ideas, ask them to expand the two-column model by making a cluster of their feelings.

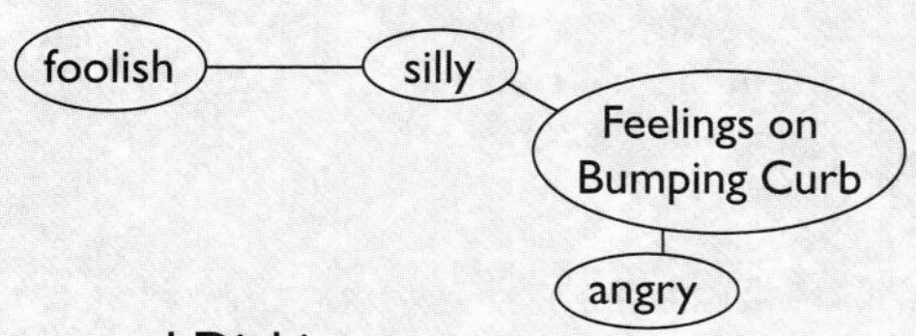

Musical Students who are musically inclined might write their essay about a piece of music that is meaningful to them. For maximum effect, students should listen to the music as they are planning and writing. If possible, have them include a recording of the musical work when they hand in their essay.

Evaluating and Revising

1. **Peer review.** Exchange papers with one or more other students. As a peer reader, use the following questions to critique a reflective essay.
   - Did the essay begin in an intriguing way? Did it make me want to read more? How could the opening be improved?
   - Was the essay organized in a way that made sense to me and enabled me to follow the writer's train of thought?
   - Could I "hear" the writer's style and personality coming out in his or her unique voice?
   - Did the flow of reflections culminate in a true insight? Can I put into words the generalization the writer made?
2. **Self-evaluation.** Try reading your essay aloud to see whether the tone you want comes across in your words. Are you specific and concrete enough? Could another person read your work and easily trace the path between your occasion and your final insight? Underline passages that you think need more work.

Proofreading

Correct any errors in spelling, grammar, usage, or mechanics. Be especially aware of how well you captured your unique voice. If your writing sounds stilted, see if you can make it sound more natural by adding sentence variety.

Publishing

If you wish, submit a copy of your reflective essay to your school newspaper or literary magazine, or distribute copies to family and friends. If your essay would be appropriate for a local publication, such as a church bulletin or a particular organization's newsletter, send your essay to the editor with a query letter. You could also take the creative process a step further and use your reflective essay as source material for an original poem or other creative work.

Reflecting on Your Writing

Put the date on your essay, and put the essay in your portfolio, along with a brief written reflection. To help focus your thoughts on your reflective essay, use the following sentence starters:

1. One thing I learned by reflecting on this occasion was . . . .
2. The next time I write a reflective essay, I will try the following techniques: . . . .
3. If I could rewrite the essay, I would omit . . . and include . . . .
4. I think I was particularly successful in . . . . I could improve my performance by . . . .

Communications Handbook HELP

Taking notes and documenting sources: pages 1210–1213.

Language Handbook HELP

Revising for variety: page 1237.

Evaluation Criteria

A good reflective essay

1. *presents in detail a specific occasion: an incident, observation, quotation, or abstract concept*
2. *generalizes from a concrete occasion to a broader, abstract truth*
3. *is organized effectively so that it clearly traces the path from an occasion to a deeply felt insight*
4. *truthfully expresses the personality and insights of the writer through a personal voice and a consistent style*
5. *concludes with a general insight about life that is expressed either implicitly or explicitly*

Reteaching

After students have chosen a topic, ask them to write a one or two sentence statement of what they hope their readers will understand about the significance of the event. When they have completed a draft, they should ask a partner to explain the significance of the incident. Then, students should compare their partners' remarks with their own original statements.

Closure

Ask students to explain the similarities and differences between a reflective essay and a lyric poem.

Portfolio

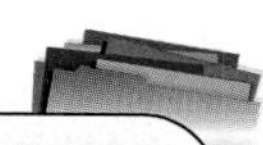

Reflecting on Your Writing

- Ask students to describe what readers could learn about them.
- Ask students to answer the Reflecting on your Writing questions on p. 403 and to attach them to their reflective essays.

ASSESSMENT SCALE

Self-Assessment Ask students to evaluate their reflective essays using the following scale and list of criteria.

1=Needs work 2=Adequate 3=Superior

____ Presents in detail a specific occasion: an incident, observation, quotation, or abstract concept

____ Generalizes from a concrete occasion to a broader, abstract truth

____ Is organized effectively so that it clearly traces the path from an occasion to a deeply felt insight

____ Truthfully expresses the personality and insights of the writer through a personal voice and a consistent style

____ Concludes with a general insight about life that is expressed either implicitly or explicitly

Language Workshop

Connecting to Students' Writing

Have students take another look at their reflective essays, or if they prefer, have them choose another piece of writing from their portfolios. Ask students to underline those sentences in their essays that begin with a subject. Then, have them try to begin several of the sentences in different ways to make their writing flow more smoothly.

Try It Out: Possible Answers

1. Although Walt Whitman never went to college, he did read widely.
2. Remarkably rich in her inner life, Emily Dickinson was a reclusive person.
3. Although Whitman's poems are long, they are, in the opinion of many academics, as laboriously crafted as Dickinson's short poems.
4. To attempt to rank Dickinson and Whitman in order of greatness is beside the point.

- **Extra Practice and Guided Instruction** For more instruction and practice on sentence beginnings, see ***Language Workshop*** in ***Teaching Resources A***, pp. 163–164.
- **Extra Practice or Guided Instruction** See ***Language Workshop: Sentence beginnings*** for more practice or guided instruction in punctuation.

Technology HELP

See Language Workshop CD-ROM. *Key word entry: sentences—beginnings.*

Language Handbook HELP

Revising for variety: page 1237.

Variety Is the Spice: Varying Sentence Beginnings

The basic, no-frills English sentence begins with a subject that is closely followed by a verb: *Emily Dickinson wrote poems.* But if every sentence followed that same pattern, readers would be unbearably bored. By using a variety of sentence beginnings, you can improve your style and hold your readers' interest. To vary sentences, you can use introductory words, phrases, or clauses.

1. Start a sentence with a modifier or modifiers.
   Private and *reclusive,* Emily Dickinson rarely tried to publish her poetry.
2. Start a sentence with a transitional word or phrase.
   However, Dickinson's choice of subjects was bold and adventurous.
3. Start a sentence with a prepositional phrase.
   Throughout his writing career, Walt Whitman publicized himself frequently and enthusiastically.
4. Start a sentence with a verbal phrase.
   To understand a poem, read it at least twice.
5. Start a sentence with a dependent clause.
   After they died, Whitman and Dickinson took their places among the greatest nineteenth-century poets.

Try It Out

With a partner, revise each of the following sentences by altering their beginnings, using the strategy indicated in parentheses.

1. Walt Whitman never went to college, but he read widely. (transition)
2. Emily Dickinson was a reclusive person whose inner life was remarkably rich. (modifier)
3. Whitman's long poems are, in the opinion of many academics, as laboriously crafted as Dickinson's short poems. (dependent clause)
4. It is beside the point to attempt to rank Dickinson and Whitman in order of greatness. (verbal phrase)

Writer's Workshop Follow-Up: Revising

Re-read the reflective essay you wrote for the Writer's Workshop (page 401). Do too many of your sentences begin the same way? If so, revise them using strategies you've learned in this lesson. Remember to reword sentences for clarity, being careful to place phrase modifiers close to the words they modify. Don't feel that every sentence has to begin with a phrase or clause, however; sometimes a simple sentence will give you exactly the tone and emphasis you need.

✔ QUICK CHECK: Varying Sentence Beginnings

Revise these sentences by varying their beginnings. Use any strategy you prefer.

[1] Dickinson became well known after her death. [After her death, Dickinson became well known.]
[2] Whitman aimed for an overall impression by the use of long lists. [Using long lists, Whitman aimed for an overall impression.]
[3] Whitman, sociable and gregarious, liked to travel. [Sociable and gregarious, Whitman liked to travel.]
[4] Dickinson was a private person who did not expect to publish her poems. [Since Dickinson was a private person, she did not expect to publish her poems.]

CREATIVE PROBLEM SOLVING

LEARNING FOR LIFE

The Changing World of Work

Problem

In "I Hear America Singing," Walt Whitman presents a catalog of occupations that would have been familiar in his time. Since Whitman's time, however, the world of work has changed drastically, and it continues to change at a rapid rate. How will the world of work change for the average American in the next decade?

Project

Research one career field to discover how it may change over the next decade, what skills a person will need in order to work in that field, and what new occupations may emerge in that field.

Preparation

1. Decide what aspect of the broad topic *occupations* you'll focus on. Choose a field that you think you might be interested in pursuing one day. If you're interested in health care, for instance, you might want to research developing trends in health-care careers.
2. Use the *5W-How?* questions (*Who? What? When? Where? Why? How?*) to help you find the information you need. *How* will health care change? *Who* will be most affected by the changes? *When* are changes likely to occur?
3. Brainstorm a list of possible resources for your research.

Procedure

1. Start by getting an overview of your chosen occupation by consulting the government publications the *Dictionary of Occupational Titles* and the *Occupational Outlook Handbook.*
2. Cast your net wide for research information, but be sure you're using reliable and current sources.
   - Consult up-to-date government publications and professional articles.
   - Contact trade and professional organizations, and request publications from them.
   - Check with special-interest newsgroups on the Internet.
   - Consult local college or university career services offices.
   - Interview someone currently working in the field you're interested in.
3. Analyze your findings. Can you make some educated guesses about how the occupation you have researched will change in the next decade or so? How can people interested in that occupation prepare themselves for it?

Presentation

To present your findings, use one of the following formats (or another that your teacher approves):

1. **Radio Spot**
   Tape-record for possible broadcast a radio program in which you share your findings about coming changes in the occupation you researched. Advise people who want to follow that career path about what they might have to do in order to keep pace with these changes.
2. **Brochure**
   Create a brochure that could be used by a student career services office or a vocational-technical center ten years from now. The brochure should give specific information about education, training, and job skills necessary for the career you have researched. Make your brochure look as professional as possible; use desktop publishing, if you can, and provide illustrations.
3. **A Mock Interview**
   With another student, write and act out a scenario in which a person ten years from now is interviewing for a job in the field you researched. The dialogue of the interview should reveal what tasks and responsibilities the job will entail, what kind of education and skills are necessary, and what kind of career path the person being interviewed can expect.

Processing

What challenges await the American worker, and how do you think you and other students can better prepare yourselves for the future world of work? Write a reflection for your portfolio.

Learning for Life

Technology Tip

TECHNOLOGY Students may create an electronic brochure using a computer as an information station in the classroom. The electronic brochure might contain interactive question-and-answer segments, illustrations, and a brief quiz. Invite a school guidance counselor to talk with students about the changes in career possibilities that are anticipated for the next ten years. To complete the assignment, students should compare the anticipated possibilities with existing careers to create training, education, and skill guidelines. When the brochure is completed, set up the information station in the classroom and encourage students to use it for their own college and career planning.

Performance Assessment Rubric So that students may see the evaluation criteria before they begin working on these projects, share the rubric provided in the ***Portfolio Management System,*** p. 119.

DEVELOPING WORKPLACE COMPETENCIES

Preparation	Procedure	Presentation
Makes decisions Reasons Uses resources	Acquires data Applies technology to specific tasks Processes information	Communicates ideas and information Thinks creatively Works on teams

ABOUT THE ART: EXPLORING THE HISTORICAL PERIOD

The painting depicts Fort Sumter in the harbor of Charleston, South Carolina, after the first decisive battle of the Civil War. Because South Carolina had seceded from the Union, the fort, a federal stronghold, was in a precarious position in March 1861. When President Lincoln commanded that the fort be sent supplies, Confederate General P. G. T. Beauregard responded by ordering the evacuation of the fort. When federal troops refused, Confederate forces fired on the fort on April 12, 1861, for thirty-four hours, until the federal troops surrendered. The conflict over Fort Sumter led to the five-year war between the states.

The Rise of Realism

The Civil War and Postwar Period

1850–1900

Evening Gun, Fort Sumter (1864) by John Gadsby Chapman, from a sketch made by his son, Conrad Wise Chapman. Oil on board.
Museum of the Confederacy Collection, Richmond, Virginia.

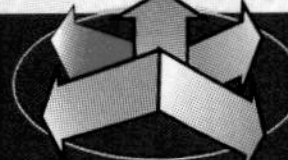

PROGRAM MANAGER

- **Summative Assessment** See **Literary Period Test: The Rise of Realism, *Test Booklet,*** pp. 122–126, for a test on an additional text from the same historical era.
- **Application** For practice of a reading strategy for this unit, see **Becoming a Strategic Reader** worksheet, ***Teaching Resources A,*** pp. 170–171.
- **Performance Assessment** Use **Assessment 3** in the, ***Integrated Performance Assessment, Level F,*** to evaluate reading and writing skills covered in collections 9–16.

For help with evaluation, see ***Holistic Scoring Workshop*** software.

Responding to the Quotation

The quotation is from Crane's *War is Kind* (1899), a collection of epigrammatic free verse anticipating some strands of twentieth-century poetry. What does the quotation imply about the speaker's philosophy of life? [Possible responses: People are insignificant when compared to the universe. Or people think they are important, but find out they are not as important as they think they are.]

Technology Tip

Before beginning the period introduction, show students the electronic resources available from the United States Civil War Center at Louisiana State University. The Center's Web site includes links to photographs, recordings, and letters pertaining to the Civil War. The URL is **http://www.cwc.lsu.edu/civlink.htm**. *You may want to preview any Internet activity that you suggest to students. Because these resources are sometimes public forums, their content can be unpredictable.*

The Rise of Realism

The Civil War and Postwar Period

by **Gary Q. Arpin**

Photograph by Mathew Brady.
The Bettmann Archive.

A man said to the universe:
"Sir, I exist!"
"However," replied the universe,
"The fact has not created in me
A sense of obligation."

—Stephen Crane

Archive Photos.

A scene from the Civil War by an unknown artist.

On the evening of April 12, 1861, Walt Whitman attended the opera at the Academy of Music in Manhattan. After the opera, he was walking down Broadway toward Brooklyn when, as he later wrote, "I heard in the distance the loud cries of the newsboys, who came presently tearing and yelling up the street, rushing from side to side even more furiously than usual. I bought an extra and crossed to the Metropolitan Hotel . . . where the great lamps were still brightly blazing, and, with a crowd of others, who gathered impromptu, read the news, which was evidently authentic."

The news that Whitman and the others read so avidly was of the Confederate attack on Fort Sumter, the opening shots of the Civil War. Thus solemnly

War is at best barbarism. . . . Its glory is all moonshine. . . . War is hell.
—Union General William Tecumseh Sherman

Quilt by Varina Davis.
The Museum of the Confederacy, Richmond, Virginia. Photograph by Katherine Wetzel.

RESPONDING TO THE ART: VISUAL LITERACY

How does the art on these two pages characterize the soldiers? [Possible responses: The soldiers look serious. In the painting the man on the horse looks as though he is about to deliver a message; his horse looks tired. The man at the campfire looks as though either the coffee is not very good or he does not have enough. In the Brady photograph, the wounded soldier looks pained. He may be refusing the water offered him by the well-dressed soldier. They all look as though they are tired of war.]

PROGRAM MANAGER

- **Planning Instruction** See Teaching Notes, *Teaching Resources A,* p. 167, for additional teaching options about the Rise of Realism.
- **Assessment** For assessment of the literary and historical events mentioned in the historical introduction, see Literary Period Introduction Test, *Test Booklet,* pp. 99–100.

Elements of Literature:
Videodisc Use the bar codes below to access information on the time period. For more information, see Videodisc *Teacher's Manual.*

Videodisc Side B

Begin Play
English Track

Begin Play
Spanish Track

Time Line

• **1850–1859**
Sojourner Truth was born a slave, named Isabella, in New York State, but was freed in 1827 when the state abolished slavery. In 1843, she changed her name to Sojourner Truth, to suggest "itinerant preacher," and left her home to preach religion, feminism, and abolition. A powerful orator, she occasionally shared the platform with Frederick Douglass. In her best-known speech, "Ain't I a Woman," delivered in 1851 at a women's rights convention (see quotation on p. 417), Truth argued effectively against those who protest that women cannot have the same rights as men since Jesus Christ was a man. She asked, "Where did your Christ come from? From God and a woman! Man had nothing to do with him." She argued that if Eve was strong enough to "turn the world upside down all alone," then women together should be able to turn it right side up again. One account reports that during an 1858 speech, Truth was heckled by men claiming she was too forceful to be a woman; in response, Truth bared her breasts, and turned shame back on her persecutors.

• **1850–1859**
Harriet Jacobs (1813–1897), born into slavery in North Carolina, was sexually harrassed by her owner's father, Dr. James Norcom. To stop him, Jacobs began a relationship with a young white lawyer named Sawyer, by whom she had two children. Jacobs went into hiding in 1835 to escape Norcom, and spent almost seven years in a crawl space in her grandmother's house. Sawyer was able to buy their children. Jacobs escaped to the North in 1842, and was later pursued by Norcom after the passage of the Fugitive Slave Act. She was eventually freed. Her narrative, *Incidents in the Life of a Slave Girl,* describes her life in bondage.

The Civil War and Postwar Period 1850–1900

LITERARY EVENTS

Sojourner Truth (1864) by an unidentified photographer.
National Portrait Gallery, Smithsonian Institution, Washington, D.C.

Sojourner Truth, abolitionist and women's rights advocate, dictates *Narrative of Sojourner Truth,* c. 1850

France's Gustave Flaubert publishes a classic realistic novel, *Madame Bovary,* 1856

•

Herman Melville publishes *The Piazza Tales,* short stories including "Bartleby the Scrivener," 1856

•

Harriet Beecher Stowe publishes an influential novel about slavery, *Uncle Tom's Cabin,* 1851–1852

Harriet Beecher Stowe (c. 1852). Daguerreotype.
The Granger Collection, New York.

Bret Harte publishes the short story "The Outcasts of Poker Flat," 1869

Russian author Leo Tolstoy completes his panoramic novel *War and Peace,* 1869

•

Louisa May Alcott publishes a popular novel about growing up, *Little Women,* 1868–1869

Louisa May Alcott. Oil over a photograph.
The Granger Collection, New York.

1850–1859 | **1860–1869**

CULTURAL/HISTORICAL EVENTS

Fugitive Slave Act imposes stiff penalties on anyone helping a person escape enslavement, 1850

•

Susan B. Anthony and Elizabeth Cady Stanton become co-leaders of U.S. women's rights movement, early 1850s

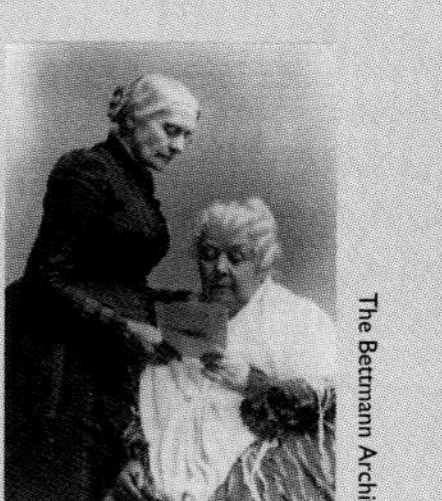
Susan B. Anthony and Elizabeth Cady Stanton.
The Bettmann Archive.

The Sepoy Rebellion, a large-scale uprising against British rule in India, ends, 1858

•

England's Charles Darwin explains his groundbreaking theory of evolution in *Origin of Species,* 1859

Julia Ward Howe by John Elliott (c. 1910) and William H. Cotton (c. 1925). Oil on canvas.
National Portrait Gallery, Gift of Mrs. John Elliott 1933. Courtesy Art Resource.

First shots of Civil War fired, April 1861

•

Confederate troops defeat Union forces at Bull Run in Virginia, in the first major battle of the Civil War, July 1861

•

Julia Ward Howe publishes the song "The Battle Hymn of the Republic," 1862

•

President Abraham Lincoln delivers the Gettysburg Address at the dedication of a Civil War cemetery, November 1863

•

Confederate surrender at Appomattox Court House in Virginia ends Civil War, April 1865

President Lincoln is assassinated in Ford's Theater, Washington, D.C., April 14, 1865

•

The Thirteenth Amendment to the U.S. Constitution, outlawing slavery, is ratified, 1865

•

U.S. purchases Alaska from Russia, 1867

•

Restoration of Meiji emperor opens a period of modernization in Japan, 1867

Abraham Lincoln (1863). Photograph by Alexander Gardner.
Library of Congress.

USING THE TIME LINE

To broaden students' understanding of what was taking place in the world, have students work in groups of three to research more thoroughly an event on the time line. For example, one group could research the women's rights movement of the early 1850s, another Rockefeller's founding of the Standard Oil Company, and another Freud's publication of *The Interpretation of Dreams.* Have groups report their information to the class. After groups have presented their findings, ask students to discuss how they think this information might have influenced the writers who are mentioned in the period introduction.

Henry James.
Archive Photos.

William Dean Howells.
The Granger Collection, New York.

1870–1879

Henry James publishes the novel *Daisy Miller,* a study of European and American manners, 1878

Mark Twain publishes the popular novel *The Adventures of Tom Sawyer* and begins work on a famous sequel, *Adventures of Huckleberry Finn,* 1876

John D. Rockefeller founds the Standard Oil Company of Ohio, 1870

Sioux soldiers defeat U.S. forces under Gen. George A. Custer, on the Little Bighorn, in Dakota Territory, 1876

Alexander Graham Bell patents the first telephone, 1876

Thomas Edison patents the first phonograph, 1878

1880–1889

William Dean Howells publishes the realistic novel *The Rise of Silas Lapham,* 1885

José Martí, Cuban writer and independence leader, publishes his poetry collection *Ismaelillo,* 1882

Russian novelist Fyodor Dostoyevsky publishes *The Brothers Karamazov,* 1879–1880

Clara Barton organizes the American Red Cross, 1881

Booker T. Washington founds Tuskegee Institute, 1881

Statue of Liberty is dedicated, 1886

1890–1900

Stephen Crane publishes *The Red Badge of Courage,* about a soldier's response to the Civil War, 1895

Kate Chopin publishes *Bayou Folk,* short stories about life in Louisiana, 1894

Russia's Anton Chekhov writes the realistic drama *Uncle Vanya,* 1899

African American writer Paul Laurence Dunbar publishes his poetry collection *Lyrics of Lowly Life,* 1896

Sarah Orne Jewett publishes *The Country of the Pointed Firs,* about life in a Maine seaport, 1896

James Naismith invents game of basketball, at Springfield, Massachusetts, 1891

Naturalist John Muir publishes *The Mountains of California,* 1894

German physicist Wilhelm Roentgen discovers X-rays, 1895

Athens, Greece, is the site of the first modern Olympic Games, 1896

U.S. annexes Hawaii and wins Spanish-American War (gaining Puerto Rico, Guam, and the Philippines), 1898

U.S. population is about 76 million, 1900

Austrian physician Sigmund Freud advances the field of psychiatry by publishing *The Interpretation of Dreams,* 1900

Crazy Horse and Sitting Bull Mounted Before Their Warriors at the Little Bighorn, 25 June 1876 by Amos Bad Heart Bull. Pictograph.

The Granger Collection, New York.

- **1870–1879**
A number of battles in the Little Bighorn Campaign preceded and followed Custer's defeat, many fought over land rights. When Custer disobeyed the plan of attack, the Sioux were able to kill him and all his men. The Sioux surrendered later in the year after a period of sustained fighting. The battle marked the last major victory for the Sioux and the beginning of the end of major fighting in the West between the Native Americans and the United States.

- **1880–1889**
Booker T. Washington's approach toward improving the quality of life for African Americans after the war sparked debate. He believed their interests were best served through vocational education, not through participation in politics. Critics disagreed with his emphasis on vocational skills at the expense of academic skills, and with his de-emphasis on political activity. However, Washington was influential in securing funding for institutions. At the time of Washington's death, Tuskegee had some fifteen hundred students and an endowment of two million dollars.

- **1890–1900**
Muir became a naturalist after he nearly lost an eye while working on mechanical inventions. He was instrumental in establishing Sequoia and Yosemite National Parks in California, in designating thirteen national forests, and in influencing Theodore Roosevelt's conservation program.

A. Reader's Response: First Thoughts
Emerson had warned that war would be inevitable if slavery were not abolished. From your studies, do you also consider slavery the key issue of the war?
[Sample responses: Slavery was the key issue of the Civil War; or the war had to happen in order to unite the North and the South and so eliminate any future thoughts of secession by any territory]

B. Expansion
As both sides were relatively untrained and disorganized, some historians think the war could have ended with this battle. Early in the battle the Union nearly broke the left flank of the Confederate line. Had it done so, the Confederates may have lost the battle and the war at that time. Late in the battle, the Union retreated. Had the Confederates pursued them, they might have captured Washington. But the war was to be long and horrible, as those who came to the battle to picnic and watch what they thought would be a quick victory soon learned.

C. Cultural Connections
Whitman is important to American literature as a writer of realism because he had the courage to write exactly what he saw and felt. The dialects that he used were familiar to the American people and consequently made his writing that much more real.

Young Soldier: Separate Study of a Soldier Giving Water to a Wounded Companion (1861) by Winslow Homer (1836–1910). Oil, gouache, black crayon on canvas (36 cm × 17.5 cm).

Cooper-Hewitt, National Design Museum, Smithsonian Institution; Gift of Charles Savage Homer, Jr/Courtesy Art Resource.

began, for one of the few American poets or novelists who would witness it firsthand, the greatest cataclysm in United States history.

Responses to the War: Idealism . . .

In Concord, Massachusetts, home of Ralph Waldo Emerson, Henry David Thoreau, Nathaniel Hawthorne, and many other intellectual leaders of the nation, army volunteers met in 1861 at the bridge that Emerson had immortalized in "Concord Hymn" (page 99), his famous poem about the beginning of the American Revolution. Emerson had for decades warned that this day would come if slavery were not abolished. Now that the day had arrived, he was filled with patriotic fervor. He watched the Concord volunteers march to Boston, and he visited a navy yard, declaring that "sometimes gunpowder smells good." **A**

Emerson had great respect for the Southern will to fight, however, and he suspected, quite rightly, that the war would not be over in a few months as some people had predicted. When the Concord volunteers returned a few months later from the First Battle of Bull Run (July 1861), defeated and disillusioned, many of them unwilling to reenlist, Emerson maintained his conviction that the war must be pursued. **B**

Still, Northern disillusionment after the early defeat at Bull Run was strong. With a keen eye for the sad details, Whitman recorded the sense of gloomy defeat in Washington in late July when Northern troops returned from the disaster of Bull Run: **C**

> The defeated troops commenced pouring into Washington over the Long Bridge at daylight on Monday, 22nd—day drizzling all through with rain. The Saturday and Sunday of the battle

> The war with its defeats and uncertainties is immensely better than what we lately called the integrity of the Republic, as amputation is better than cancer.
>
> —Ralph Waldo Emerson

OPTIONS FOR TEACHING

STRATEGIES FOR INCLUSION

Auditory After reading the period introduction about the rise of realism, have students work in groups of three. Each group member will tell what he or she remembers from their reading. If students cannot remember, they can ask for prompts from their group members. If a student relates something incorrect, the other group members must provide the correct information. Using this strategy enables the students to review what they have read and to hear it in different ways.

Kinesthetic Have students create a graphic or pictorial representation depicting what they have read in the period introduction. Ask students to use the subheadings, the authors' names, or the years that events took place to organize information. Suggest that students draw word maps, charts, time lines, tree diagrams, or pictures to represent information. This strategy enables students to view the ideas presented in their reading.

(20th, 21st) had been parched and hot to an extreme—the dust, the grime and smoke, in layers, sweated in followed by other layers again sweated in, absorbed by those excited souls—their clothes all saturated with the clay-powder filling the air—stirred up everywhere on the dry roads and trodden fields by the regiments, swarming wagons, artillery, etc.—all the men with this coating of murk and sweat and rain, now recoiling back, pouring over the Long Bridge—a horrible march of twenty miles, returning to Washington baffled, humiliated, panic-struck. Where are the vaunts, and the proud boasts with which you went forth? Where are your banners, and your bands of music, and your ropes to bring back your prisoners? Well, there isn't a band playing—and there isn't a flag but clings ashamed and lank to its staff.

—Walt Whitman

Civil War ambulance.
Culver Pictures.

> Future years will never know the seething hell and the black infernal background of the countless minor scenes and interiors . . . and it is best they should not—the real war will never get in the books.
>
> —Walt Whitman

A patient in Armory Square Hospital, Washington, D.C., during the Civil War. Photograph (detail).

Courtesy of The New-York Historical Society, New York.

Late in 1862, Whitman traveled to Virginia to find his brother George, who had been wounded in battle. After George was nursed back to health, Whitman remained in Washington off and on, working part time and serving as a volunteer hospital visitor, comforting the wounded and writing to their loved ones. The condition of the wounded was appalling. Many of the injured had to remain on the battlefield for two or three days until the camp hospitals had room for them. Antiseptics were primitive, as were operating-room techniques. Anesthesia was virtually unknown. A major wound meant amputation or even death.

Whitman estimated that in three years as a camp hospital volunteer, he visited tens of thousands of wounded men. "I am the man," he had written in "Song of Myself," "I suffer'd, I was there," and now he *was* there, in the real heart of

D. Cultural Connections
Many women also volunteered as nurses and worked side by side with the men. Dorothea Dix, who was in charge of all the female Union nurses—some three thousand women—was demanding and extremely strict. "Dragon Dix" would only allow women to be nurses if they were over thirty years of age, wore plain black or brown dresses, and were not interested in the attentions of the male patients. With her no-nonsense attitude, Dix did improve the conditions for the patients. In the South, Sally Tompkins worked with six others to nurse 1,333 wounded men in Richmond. Their record was unparalleled in the nation, for only seventy-three of these men died. Tompkins became the only recognized female officer in the Confederacy.

E. Reader's Response: First Thoughts

? Why do you think hospital conditions were so poor? [Sample responses: There was a lack of qualified or experienced medical personnel. Or the medical workers did not have the equipment and supplies to handle the large number of casualties. Or the transportation of the day could not get large amounts of what was needed to places in a short amount of time.]

INTEGRATING THE LANGUAGE ARTS

Strategic Reading Guided Reading is a strategy that helps students recall information and organize the facts from their reading. Assign students a purpose for reading, such as relating the historical events to the literature or characterizing each literary movement. Then, have students read the material. Ask them what they recall, and list this information on the chalkboard or on an overhead transparency. Have them read the introduction a second time to see if any important information has been left out. Add any additional information the students recall to the list already begun. To help the students organize the information, draw a graphic organizer such as a blank outline or cluster diagram on the chalkboard or transparency. Guide students to suggest categories and then to state what information belongs in each category. Fill in the organizer as the class works through the procedure together. ☞

A. Reader's Response: First Thoughts

What do you think Whitman saw in the patients that he cared for that gave him such optimism? [Sample responses: The men were loyal to their side. The men on each side developed a strong bond. The men were optimistic about winning the war and had hope for the future. Or the men had great courage in the face of death.]

B. Literary Connections

Melville's *Battle-Pieces* (1866) contains seventy-two elegiac Civil War poems. Compare the poems with those of Whitman in *Drum-Taps and Sequel* (1865–1866).

Technology Tip

Civil War era photographs are available from the National Archives via Gopher at **gopher.nara.gov:70/11/inform/dc/audvis/still/civwar** or via the World Wide Web at **http://gopher.nara.gov:70/11/inform/dc/audvis/still/civwar.html**. *You may want to preview any Internet activity that you suggest to students. Because these resources are sometimes public forums, their content can be unpredictable.*

A CLOSER LOOK

Eyes of an Era

Television's close-up coverage of modern warfare has made the thick of battle a common sight on the nightly news. But during the American Civil War, photographs were the closest thing to newscasts. By the latter part of the 1800s, technical advances began to allow for truly mobile photographers. As a result, the Civil War became the first war to be fully documented in pictures. Cameras went on the march, up in observation balloons, and to sea on battleships. More than three hundred civilian photographers covered the Union's Army of the Potomac alone. But newspapers could not yet reproduce photos, so photographers did brisk business selling "war views" and portraits of soldiers directly to the public.

Cameras of the time could not capture motion; charging troops and thrusting bayonets came out as hazy blurs. But cameras richly recorded the preparations and the aftermath of war. After battles, photographers roamed the killing fields, shooting pictures while wearing handkerchiefs across their faces to block the stench of death. They captured the war's still lifes—fields and forests filled with dead soldiers, blasted cities and landscapes, and scenes taken inside prisons, hospitals, and camps.

Many of the pioneering Civil War photojournalists were probably motivated more by profit than by a sense of history. The most famous of these war photographers was Mathew Brady (c. 1823–1896). Brady was among the first photographers to think of moving mini-darkrooms into combat areas; usually, these darkrooms were customized delivery wagons, which soldiers nicknamed "what-is-it" wagons. Though Brady helped inspire Civil War photography with his views of the First Battle of Bull Run in 1861, more often he employed courageous photographers, such as Alexander Gardner and Timothy O'Sullivan, to take their cameras onto the battlefields. Brady helped guarantee the war's rich visual record, but

America. In his poems, he had presented a panoramic vision of America; now America passed through the hospital tents in the form of wounded men from every state in the Union and the Confederacy. Nevertheless, out of the horror that he (A) viewed, Whitman was able to derive an optimistic vision of the American character, of "the actual soldier of 1862–65 . . . with all his ways, his incredible dauntlessness, habits, practices, tastes, language, his fierce friendship, his appetite, rankness, his superb strength—and a hundred unnamed lights and shades."

. . . and Disillusionment

The war that strengthened Whitman's optimism served at the same time to justify Herman Melville's pessimism. Melville's poems about the war, collected in (B) *Battle-Pieces and Aspects of the War* (1866), were often dark and foreboding. Of the elation following the firing on Fort Sumter, Melville wrote:

Woman freed from slavery learning to read. Leib Image Archives, York, Pennsylvania.

414 THE RISE OF REALISM: THE CIVIL WAR AND POSTWAR PERIOD

OPTIONS FOR TEACHING

CROSSING THE CURRICULUM

Music Divide the class into small groups and assign them an author who is mentioned in the period introduction. Have students research the music that was popular during the time the author was writing. If possible, have students get a recording of one or two pieces of music to play in class. Have a class discussion about the music, why it was popular, and how it may have affected the author and the literature of the time.

Social Sciences Ask students to research various aspects of society during and immediately after the Civil War in both the North and South. Students could be divided into groups and assigned such topics as clothing, food, housing, or entertainment. Have students present their information to the class. Have a class discussion about the differences between the North and the South.

Fine Arts Have students locate photographs that Mathew Brady took of people and events of the Civil War. Ask them to create a museum display of the photographs, complete with captions they write for each one. Have students lead their classmates through an art tour of Brady's work.

it was the skill and heroism of Gardner, O'Sullivan, and nameless others that actually produced the legacy of Civil War pictures.

Gardner came closer than anyone else to capturing an actual battle scene when he set his camera on a ridge overlooking the Battle of Antietam in Maryland in 1862. Gardner's genius at film processing and composition helped raise photographic coverage of the war to the level of art. He recognized that "verbal representations" of the war "may or may not have the merit of accuracy; but photographic presentments of them will be accepted by posterity with an undoubting faith."

O'Sullivan was one of the bravest and most brilliant of Brady's assistants. When bridge builders whom O'Sullivan was photographing were targeted by enemy sharpshooters, he calmly continued taking pictures while men screamed and fell. One of O'Sullivan's post-battle pictures shows corpses littering the quiet Gettysburg Cemetery; a sign hanging by the cemetery gatepost proclaims, with grim irony, that there is a five-dollar fine for discharging a firearm within cemetery limits.

Photographers fought heavy equipment, stray bullets, rain, mud, insects, foliage, wandering livestock, and frozen hands. Processing photographs in the field was complicated and messy: Many pictures were ruined when they were washed in streams where debris could stick to the gummy image.

Though about a million photos were taken, the photographic record of the war is incomplete. Neither Brady, Gardner, nor O'Sullivan arrived in time to capture the surrender at Appomattox in 1865. And lack of supplies made Confederate field photography virtually nonexistent after 1861.

Sadly, most Civil War photographers and their work fell into obscurity after the war. Hundreds of glass negatives were sold to gardeners for greenhouse windows, and, decades later, many of the glass plates ended up as eyepieces in gas masks worn by soldiers in World War I.

O, the rising of the People
    Came with the springing of the grass,
They rebounded from dejection
    After Easter came to pass.
And the young were all elation
    Hearing Sumter's cannon roar. . . .
But the elders with foreboding
    Mourned the days forever o'er,
And recalled the forest proverb,
    The Iroquois' old saw:
Grief to every graybeard
    When young Indians lead the war.

—Herman Melville

C

Artist sketching the battlefield of Gettysburg, July, 1863. Photograph by T. H. O'Sullivan.
Library of Congress.

Melville was fascinated by the war, but he never wrote a novel about it. The poems in *Battle-Pieces,* based on newspaper accounts of the battles as well as visits to battlefields, record the heroism and futility of the fighting on both sides and demonstrate respect for Southern soldiers as well as Northern troops. But in some of the best poems, there is a sense of human nature being stripped bare, revealing not the heroism and strength that Whitman found, but, rather, humanity's basic evil.

C. Critical Reading: Drawing Conclusions

? What are the different attitudes of Whitman and Melville toward the soldiers? [Possible answer: Whitman saw the courage and patriotism of soldiers he encountered, and Melville saw the naiveté and recklessness of young soldiers.]

COOPERATIVE LEARNING

Regionalism Divide the class into groups of five. Explain to them that they are going to write a skit and present it to the class. The skit must be written in the style of a regionalist. Students should depict the region they live in. It will be important that each group choose a leader, discuss their region, approach the writing through a regionalist's perspective, and choose someone to research and write a brief report on the area. The students will then choose who will write the skit and who will perform it. Remind students that regionalists often ridiculed an area and viewed it from the outside.

Honor Civilian Heroes Have students work in groups of five to plan a formal presentation to honor civilian heroes of the Civil War, such as Walt Whitman. You might suggest heroes such as Clara Barton, a nurse; Mathew Brady and Alexander Gardner, photographers; or Belle Boyd, a Confederate spy. Students will have to research the people they choose to honor. They may also wish to devise an award appropriate for each hero. Each group should decide who will act as host, who will play the parts of the heroes, who will write the introductions and acceptance speeches, and who will be responsible for props and costumes.

A. Expansion
Irving died before the war began, spending time abroad and working on his five-volume *Life of Washington* before he died. Longfellow was busy raising children after his wife died in 1861. Holmes was professor of anatomy and physiology, and later dean of the Harvard Medical School. Although Bryant was editor of the *New York Evening Post* and supported the Free Soil movement, in his poetry he kept a distance from the war; his poem "Civil War" denounces the war's carnage but avoids taking sides. Whittier used his talent to write pamphlets and articles against slavery.

B. Expansion
Henry Adams became a professor of history and editor of the *North American Review.* He studied the medieval world and women's social position in early civilizations. He wrote two novels that sympathized with women and their lack of social and political power. In *The Education of Henry Adams,* which won him a posthumous Pulitzer Prize, Adams traces the shift in the world from an emphasis on following custom to an emphasis on following a multiplicity of directions and possibilities. He also wrote about the increasing emphasis on technology as a driving force.

C. Expansion
Stephen Crane had absolutely no battle experience himself. He was able to write about the realities of the Civil War from his impressions of stories told by Civil War veterans and of photographs taken during the Civil War.

The American Civil War (1861–1865) resulted in terrible bloodshed as the national government sought to preserve the Union by ending the secession of Southern states. Despite his firsthand experience of the aftermath of battle, Walt Whitman retained an optimistic view of the American character. But the horrors of war merely reinforced the pessimism of Herman Melville.

The War in Literature

There was enough atrocity and heroism in the war to feed the views of both Melville and Whitman. What is odd, though, is that Melville's *Battle-Pieces* (which was ignored until the twentieth century) and Whitman's *Drum-Taps* (1865) and *Specimen Days and Collect* (1882) comprise the bulk of the war's immediate legacy of poetry and fiction. Although there were many works of historical interest—soldiers' letters and diaries, as well as journalistic writings—works of literary significance were rare, prompting the question: Why did an event of such magnitude result in such a scant literary output?

> With malice toward none; with charity for all; with firmness in the right, as God gives us to see the right, let us strive on to finish the work we are in; to bind up the nation's wounds; to care for him who shall have borne the battle, and for his widow, and his orphan—to do all which may achieve and cherish a just and lasting peace, among ourselves, and with all nations.
>
> —President Abraham Lincoln, Second Inaugural Address, March 4, 1865

Modern readers think that one byproduct of a war is a literary account of it, largely in the form of novels and poems by people who participated in the war. Modern writers like Ernest Hemingway went to war intending to return with the material for novels. This was not the case with the Civil War. Few major American writers saw the Civil War firsthand. Emerson was in Concord during most of the war, "knitting socks and mittens for soldiers," as he wrote to **A** his son, and "writing patriotic lectures." Thoreau, who had been a fervent abolitionist, died in 1862, and Hawthorne died two years later. Emily Dickinson remained in Amherst, Massachusetts, but the country's grief with the war seems to have informed her poetry. Of the younger generation of writers, William Dean Howells, Henry **B** James, and Henry Adams were abroad. Perhaps most important, though, traditional literary forms of the time were inadequate to express the horrifying details of the Civil War. The literary form most appropriate for handling such strong material—the realistic novel—had not yet been fully developed in the United States. Thus, the great novel of the war, **C** *The Red Badge of Courage,* had to wait to be written by a man who was not born until six years after the war had ended: Stephen Crane.

Detail from original manuscript of Stephen Crane's *The Red Badge of Courage.* University of Virginia Library.

OPTIONS FOR TEACHING

CLASSROOM MANAGEMENT

Group Learning When students are working in small groups it is important that they know what the goals of the group are and how much time is being allotted for the activity. It may be helpful to prepare a handout for each student and review the handout before beginning the activity. The handout might include

- a list of roles for each person in the group
- a list of the procedures involved in completing the activity
- time allotments for each part of the activity

Individual Processing For cooperative learning to be successful, it is important that each student assess his or her participation in the group. Ask students to use the following criteria to analyze their cooperative learning experience:

1. How would you characterize the discussion and the interaction between you and other group members?
2. How did you use your time?
3. What did you gain from group work?

Comments ______________________

Sojourner Truth's visit with Abraham Lincoln at the White House, October 29, 1864. Painting by an unknown artist.

Very little important poetry and fiction issued directly from the Civil War, largely because few major American writers experienced the war firsthand. Direct accounts of the war found their way into other types of literature, however, including poignant letters and diaries. The "real war" would not find a place in American fiction until the development of the realistic novel.

The Rise of Realism

One of the most enduring subjects for prose fiction has always been the exploits of larger-than-life heroes. Born of the chivalric romance, the **romantic novel** presents readers with lives lived idealistically—beyond the level of everyday life. The heroes and heroines of the novels of James Fenimore Cooper, for example, engage in romantic adventures

> Look at me! Look at my arm! I have plowed and planted, and gathered into barns, and no man could head me! And ain't I a woman? I could work as much and eat as much as a man—when I could get it—and bear the lash as well! And ain't I a woman? I have borne thirteen children, and seen most sold off to slavery, and when I cried out with my mother's grief, none but Jesus heard me! And ain't I a woman?
>
> —Sojourner Truth

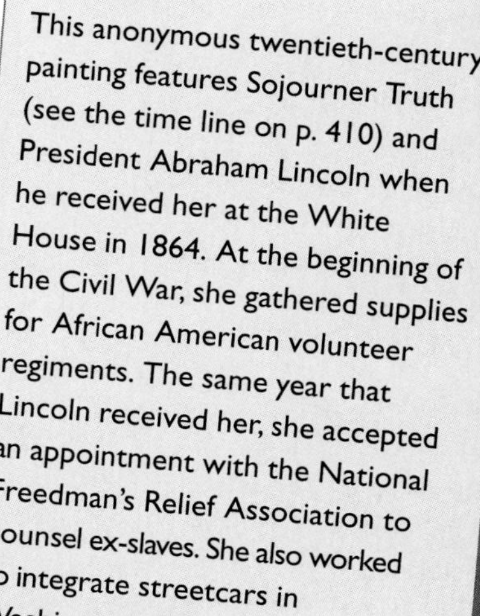

RESPONDING TO THE ART: EXPLORING THE SUBJECT

This anonymous twentieth-century painting features Sojourner Truth (see the time line on p. 410) and President Abraham Lincoln when he received her at the White House in 1864. At the beginning of the Civil War, she gathered supplies for African American volunteer regiments. The same year that Lincoln received her, she accepted an appointment with the National Freedman's Relief Association to counsel ex-slaves. She also worked to integrate streetcars in Washington, D.C.

PROBLEM SOLVING/CRITICAL THINKING

Goal Setting It takes courage for writers to deviate from the norm, as did the first writers of realism in America. These writers often had a social agenda or goal. Have students discuss what might have been one of the writer's thought process about the consequences of his or her writing. Then, have students think of something they have been wanting to do or change that involves courage. Have students use a graphic like the following to organize their thoughts.

What to do or change:
↓
Research (knowledge)
Support (people)
↓
Ways to accomplish goal

RESPONDING TO THE PHOTOGRAPH: VISUAL LITERACY

Have students discuss how they think a realist might view this photograph. Ask them what is happening in the photograph and how they think it might influence or inspire a realist author. What details of the photograph might the realist choose to depict and how? [Possible responses: An accurate and detailed description of the children and the way they are dressed, the alley in which they are standing and how it reflects their living conditions.] What kind of social issues are evident in the photograph that might be addressed in realist literature? [Possible responses: Poverty, inadequate sanitation, neglect.]

A. Reader's Response: Extending the Text

? If you were reading a book written by a twentieth-century realist, what might you be reading about? [Sample responses: Discrimination, civil rights, homeless people, or the national debt.]

filled with courageous acts, daring chases, and exciting escapes. Cooper's Leatherstocking, or Hawkeye, like his modern-day heirs James Bond and Indiana Jones, has uncommon abilities that enable him to survive and prevail. His adventures are a far cry from the ordinary lives led by most of Cooper's readers. Such exciting exploits have always been a staple of prose fiction—and, before that, of epic poetry.

In America, the great fiction writers of the mid-nineteenth century, Edgar Allan Poe, Nathaniel Hawthorne, and Herman Melville, shared an aversion to simple realism. These writers used romance not simply to entertain readers, but to reveal truths that would be hidden in a realistic story that limited itself to what actually could happen.

A After the Civil War, however, a new generation of writers came of age. They were known as **realists,** writers who aimed at a "very minute fidelity" to the common course of ordinary life. Their subjects were drawn from the slums of the rapidly growing cities, from the factories that were rapidly replacing farmlands, and from the lives of far from idealized characters: poor factory workers, corrupt politicians, even prostitutes.

Children in Mullen's Alley, off Cherry Street, New York City (c. 1888). Photograph by Jacob Riis.

The Granger Collection, New York.

OPTIONS FOR TEACHING

PROFESSIONAL NOTES

Cultural Diversity After the Civil War, dime novels became very popular, especially among the young people. Dime novels were low-priced paperbound stories—Wild west adventure stories, detective thrillers, science fiction stories, and tales about superheroes.

Cultural Diversity Have students work in small groups to explore the differences between the way of living in the North and in the South immediately after the Civil War. Ask each group to consider a different aspect, such as the growth of cities in the North, the type of work prevalent in each region, and living conditions in the various states. Have students report their findings to the class.

TECHNOLOGY **Technology Tip** Students may discuss what they learn with others interested in the Civil War by logging in to the Usenet newsgroup **alt.war.civil.usa**. *You may want to preview any Internet activity that you suggest to students. Because these resources are sometimes public forums, their content can be unpredictable.*

Realism Takes Root in Europe

Realism was well entrenched in Europe by the time it began to flower in the United States. It developed in the work of such writers as Daniel Defoe, George Eliot, Anthony Trollope, Honoré de Balzac, Stendhal, Gustave Flaubert, and Leo Tolstoy. **B** These writers tried to represent faithfully the environment and the manners of everyday life: the way ordinary people lived and dressed, and what they thought and felt and talked about.

> The only reason for the existence of a novel is that it does attempt to represent life.
>
> —Henry James

> Language grows out of life, out of its needs and experiences. . . . Good work in language presupposes and depends on a real knowledge of things.
>
> —Annie Sullivan

But realism was not simply concerned with recording wallpaper patterns, hairstyles, or the subjects of conversations. It sought also to explain *why* ordinary people behave the way they do. Realistic novelists often relied on the emerging sciences of human and animal behavior—biology, psychology, and sociology—as well as on their own insights and observations.

The literary movement known as realism dominated American fiction from the late nineteenth century to the middle of the twentieth. Realists sought to accurately portray real life, without filtering it through personal feelings, romanticism, or idealism.

American Regionalism: Brush Strokes of Local Color

In America, realism had its roots in **regionalism,** literature that emphasizes a specific geographic setting and that makes use of the speech and manners of the people who live in that region. Sarah Orne Jewett, Kate Chopin, Harriet Beecher Stowe, Bret Harte, and Charles W. Chesnutt are noted early regionalists who recorded the peculiarities of speech and temperament in their parts of a rapidly expanding nation. **C** (Regionalism flourished again in the 1920s and 1930s, especially in the South, and is still today an important aspect of American literature.)

While regional writers strove to be realistic in their depiction of speech patterns and manners, they were often unrealistic—even sentimental—in their depiction of character and social environment. For example, the Southern writer Thomas Nelson Page, who wrote popular post–Civil War novels about the South before the war, stressed the romantic "moonlight and magnolia" environment at the expense of the realities of a social world that relied on slavery. Realism as a literary movement in the United States went far beyond regionalism in its concern for accuracy in portraying social conditions and human motivation.

Original edition of Mark Twain's *Adventures of Huckleberry Finn* (1885). The Granger Collection, New York.

B. Expansion

Defoe's *The Life and Strange Surprising Adventures of Robinson Crusoe of York, Mariner* (1719) is generally lauded as the first English novel and details how a shipwrecked sailor survives on a tropical island. During the Victorian era, Eliot's *The Mill on the Floss* (1860) and Trollope's *The Warden* (1855) showed great psychological insight. Balzac's (1799–1850) *The Human Comedy* was a lifelong work—a series of novels about a group of characters from which he constantly drew. Balzac is credited with helping to create the genre of the novel by providing his fiction with a sequence of events, strong characters, and effective dialogue. In *The Red and the Black* (1830), Stendhal reveals his belief that people are motivated only by self-interest. Flaubert's *Madame Bovary* (1857) is the psychological study of a woman bored with small-town life. Tolstoy's *War and Peace* (1865–1869) is a complex interweaving of a large cast of characters and a commentary on the war that affects their lives.

C. Expansion

Jewett lived and wrote in Maine and focused on the relationships between women in a rural setting. Bret Harte was one of the first shapers of the myth of the American West. While Harte was graphic in his description of violence, his characters romanticized the West. Beneath hardened exteriors, they were always gentlemen or ladies—gamblers with hearts of gold, gentle farmers driven to use guns, and dance-hall women motivated by compassion. One of Chesnutt's characters, the former slave Uncle Julius, tells "conjure tales" that seem to sentimentalize antebellum plantation life but actually provide an ironic commentary on those who romanticize it.

ASSESSMENT TOOLS

Self-Reflection Give students an opportunity to evaluate their efforts. Have students answer the following questions after reading the period introduction. Students should turn in their answers for your review. Use the answers as a springboard for individual discussion with students.

Always Usually Sometimes Never

___**1.** I pay attention when we are reading orally in class.

___**2.** I concentrate on my work.

___**3.** I listen when other students are asking questions or during a discussion.

___**4.** I ask questions.

___**5.** I make effective use of my time.

☞

RESPONDING TO THE ART: ABOUT THE ARTIST

Famous for his depiction of the American West, Frederic Remington (1861–1909) was not only a painter but also a sculptor and magazine illustrator. A native of New York, Remington had little formal training in art. At Yale, he dropped an art course to pursue athletics. His art career dates from a trip from Montana to Texas in 1880. A sketch from this trip was accepted by *Harper's Weekly* in 1882. Remington's work often has a strong narrative element that captures both the characters and action of the vanishing West.

Coming and Going of the Pony Express (1900) by Frederic Remington. Oil on canvas (26″ × 39″).

The Thomas Gilcrease Institute of American History and Art, Tulsa, Oklahoma.

> All modern American literature comes from one book by Mark Twain called *Huckleberry Finn.*
>
> —Ernest Hemingway

Mark Twain is the best-known example of a regional writer whose realism far surpassed local bounds. Although he first established his reputation as a regional humorist, Twain evolved into a writer whose comic view of society became increasingly satiric. His best novel, *Adventures of Huckleberry Finn* (1884), describes the moral growth of a comic character in an environment that is at the same time physically beautiful and morally repugnant. *Huckleberry Finn* combines a biting picture of some of the injustices inherent in pre–Civil War life with a lyrical portrait of the American landscape.

American realism had its roots in regionalism, literature that focuses on a relatively small geographical area and attempts to accurately reproduce the speech and manners of that region.

OPTIONS FOR TEACHING

ASSESSMENT TOOLS

Check Test: Questions and Answers

1. What kind of novel presents lives lived on an idealistic plane? [Romantic.]
2. What kind of novel reproduces daily life, probes motivation, and examines social issues? [Realistic.]
3. Who liked to put a straightforward American into the complex society of a European drawing room? [Henry James.]
4. Who wrote novels, such as *The Octopus,* dealing with the impact of social forces on individuals? [Frank Norris.]
5. What school of thought views human behavior as determined by biological and environmental forces? [Naturalism.]

Realism and Naturalism: A Lens on Everyday Life

The most active proponent of realism in American fiction was William Dean Howells, editor of the influential magazine *The Atlantic Monthly.* In both his fiction and his critical writings, Howells insisted that realism should deal with the lives of ordinary people, be faithful to the development of character even at the expense of action, and discuss the social questions perplexing Americans. Howells's "smiling realism" portrayed an America where people may act foolishly but where their good qualities eventually win out. "Ah! poor Real Life, which I love," Howells wrote in one of his many essays, "can I make others share the delight I find in thy foolish and insipid face?" For Howells, life *was,* even at its worst, merely "foolish and insipid," and this proved to be his greatest limitation as a novelist.

Other realistic novelists viewed life as a much rougher clash of contrary forces. The Californian Frank Norris, for example, agreed with Howells that the proper subject for fiction was the ordinary person, but he found Howells's fiction too strait-laced and narrow. It was, Norris said, "as respectable as a church and proper as a deacon." Norris was an earthier writer, interested in the impact of large social forces on individuals. His best-known novel, *The Octopus* (1901), is about the struggles between wheat farmers and the railroad monopoly in California. Norris was not the first to use the novel to examine social institutions with the aim of reforming them; Harriet Beecher Stowe's novel *Uncle Tom's Cabin* (1852) had been published before the Civil War and, according to Lincoln (and many historians), played a large part in helping to cause the war. But *Uncle Tom's Cabin* was more melodrama than realistic fiction.

Norris is generally considered to be a **naturalist.** Following the lead of the French novelist Emile Zola, naturalists relied heavily on the growing scientific disciplines of psychology and sociology. (A) In their fiction, they attempted to dissect human behavior with as much objectivity as a scientist would dissect a frog or a cadaver. For naturalists, human behavior was determined by forces beyond the individual's power, especially by biology and environment. The naturalists tended to look at human life as a grim losing battle. Their characters often had only limited choices and motivations. In the eyes of some naturalist writers, human beings were totally subject to the natural laws of the universe; like animals, they lived crudely, by instinct, unable to control their own destinies.

Advertisement for Harriet Beecher Stowe's *Uncle Tom's Cabin* (1852).

Culver Pictures.

A. Expansion

Zola wrote a series of twenty novels and titled it *Rougon-Macquart: The Natural and Social History of a Family Under the Second Empire.* He believed heredity determined human nature and that few people could escape a dark fate if they descended from a weak or evil family member. According to Zola, these adverse qualities could be eliminated only through education and medicine.

Technology Tip

TECHNOLOGY

Invite a history teacher to discuss the daily lives of Americans in the mid–nineteenth century. Videotape the discussion for use with other classes.

A. Critical Reading: Identifying Main Ideas

? What is the major focus of Jamesian realism? [Psychological motivation.]

B. Reader's Response: Connecting with the Text

? What is the difference between Crane's use of psychology and that of James? [Sample responses: Crane focuses on people's responses to dangerous or life-threatening situations; James on people's inner thoughts and motivations in social settings. Or Crane sets his stories on the battlefield, James in the drawing room.]

A Dialogue with the Text

READER'S LOG

After students have responded in their Reader's Logs, have them share their charts in groups of three. Then, invite them to make any additions they would like to the What I Want to Know column.

Psychological Fiction: Inside the Human Mind

A On the other hand, the New York–born Henry James, considered America's greatest writer of the **psychological novel,** concentrated principally on fine distinctions in character motivation. James was a realist, but no realist could be further from the blunt, naturalistic view that people were driven by animal-like instincts. In his finely tuned studies of human motivation, James opened the inner mind to the techniques of fiction. He was mainly interested in complex social and psychological situations. Many of his novels, including *Daisy Miller* (1878) and *The Portrait of a Lady* (1881), take place in Europe, because James considered European society to be both more complex and more sinister than American society. He frequently contrasts innocent, eager Americans with sophisticated, more reserved Europeans. In a typically "Jamesian" fiction, a straightforward American confronts the complexities of European society and either defeats or is defeated by them.

> [Crane's] importance lies not only in those few works of his which completely come off, like "The Open Boat," but in his constantly seeking the primitive facts, the forbidden places, the dangerous people.
>
> —Alfred Kazin

Stephen Crane was as profound a psychologist as James, but his principal interest was the human character at moments of stress. For James, the proper setting for an examination of human behavior under pressure was the drawing room; for Crane, it was the battlefield, the streets of a slum, or a lifeboat lost at sea. Although Crane is sometimes referred to as a naturalist, he is probably best thought of as an **ironist;** he was the first of many modern American writers—later including Ernest Hemingway and Kurt Vonnegut, Jr.—to juxtapose human pretensions with the indifference of the universe. B Of all the nineteenth-century realists, only Crane could describe a stabbing death (in his story "The Blue Hotel") in this coolly cynical manner: "[The blade] shot forward, and a human body, this citadel of virtue, wisdom, power, was pierced as easily as if it had been a melon." It would take this sensibility to get the "real war" in the books at last.

Realism in American literature branched out in several directions, from the "smiling realism" of William Dean Howells to the gritty naturalism of Frank Norris, and from the psychological realism of Henry James to the ironic stance of Stephen Crane.

A Dialogue with the Text

READER'S LOG

Think about what you already know (from history classes, reading, films, and other sources) about such topics as the Civil War, slavery, Reconstruction, the expansion and settlement of the frontier, and the rise of cities and industry after the Civil War. Make a KWL chart (see page 431 for an example) in which you write down your knowledge about this period of American history and literature and what you want to know about it. Keep your chart, and fill out what you have learned as you read the two collections that follow.

SHACKLES

Theme: Rattling the Chains of Oppression

Realism took hold among American writers in the mid–nineteenth century, soon after the end of the Civil War. Focusing on the feelings and thoughts of ordinary people, realists depicted people's politically and psychologically oppressive environments; these writers, dedicated to accurately portraying life, did not turn from such issues as slavery, poverty, and other forms of injustice encountered by the characters they drew.

Thematic Focus

The protagonists of the selections in Collection 9 confront oppression or experience relief.

- **The Battle with Mr. Covey** The enslaved young Frederick Douglass fights his master and discovers that no one can "own" him but himself.
- **A Pair of Silk Stockings** Frugal Mrs. Sommers goes on a shopping spree that restores both her dignity and her identity for one glorious day.

Literary Focus

Literary Element	Selection / Feature
Character/Metaphor	**The Battle with Mr. Covey**
Character/Symbolism/Conflict	**A Pair of Silk Stockings**

Writing Focus

The following chart shows how the writing assignment for each selection relates to and builds toward the culminating assignment presented in the Writer's Workshop at the end of the unit.

Selection	Work-in-Progress Assignment
The Battle with Mr. Covey	Make a KWL chart to select a topic for a report of information p. 431
A Pair of Silk Stockings	Brainstorm topics and methods of presentation for a report of information p. 445
Writer's Workshop	Write a report of information pp. 515–519

Collection 9 **SHACKLES**

Collection Planner

SELECTION / FEATURE	PUPIL'S EDITION: Literary Elements / Active Reading	Writing	Speaking and Listening	Language and Vocabulary
The Battle with Mr. Covey Frederick Douglass (pp. 424–434) Spotlight On: Spirituals and "Code" Songs (pp. 432–434)	• Reader's Log p. 425	• Critical Writing: Write essay p. 431 • Creative Writing: Write letter or journal entry from Douglass's point of view p. 431 • Crossing the Curriculum/History: Research biographies of freedom fighters p. 431	• Crossing the Curriculum/History: Present panel discussion p. 431	• Language and Style: Douglass's Metaphors p. 431
A Pair of Silk Stockings Kate Chopin (pp. 435–448) **Connections: Now and Then, America** Pat Mora (p. 444) Spotlight On: Native American Oratory (pp. 446–448)	• Reader's Log p. 436	• Critical Writing: Write comparative essay p. 445 • Creative Writing: Write continuation of story p. 445		

Collection Resources

Teaching Resources A	Audiovisual Resources Binder	Test Booklet
Cross-Curricular Activity p. 178	Fine Art Transparency 9.1	Collection 9 Test pp. 105–108

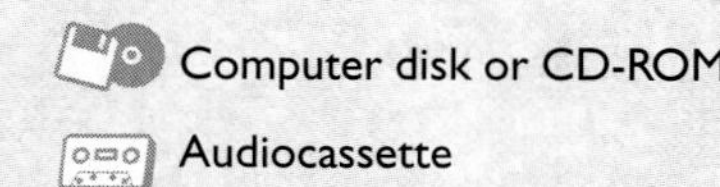

PROGRAM RESOURCES

Electronic Media	Teaching Resources with Organizer		Audiovisual Resources Binder
	Teaching Resources A	Other Resources	
• Language Workshop: Noun clauses • Test Generator	• Teaching Notes p. 168 • Reading Organizer p. 172 • Language Link pp. 173–174 • Words to Own p. 175	• Test Booklet: Selection Test pp. 101–102 • Language and Writing Skills Worksheets p. 81 • Portfolio Management System pp. 39, 120	• Selected Reading Audiocassette 2, Side A
• Test Generator	• Teaching Notes p. 169 • Reading Organizer p. 176 • Words to Own p. 177	• Test Booklet: Selection Test pp. 103–104 • Portfolio Management System pp. 53, 121	• Selected Readings Audiocassette 2, Side A • Selected Reading Audiocassette 2, Side A

Proofreading Warm-ups

You may use the following exercises to help students practice their proofreading skills. Copy a set of incorrect sentences onto the chalkboard, and have students find and correct the spelling, punctuation, usage, and mechanical errors in each sentence. Ask students to share and discuss their responses.

	Sentences with Errors	Sentences Corrected	Skills Covered
1	**a.** few magor writers did experience the civil war 1861–1865 first-hand **b.** herman melville based the poems in Battle-Pieces And Aspects Of The War partly on newspaper acounts.	**a.** Few major writers experienced the Civil War (1861–1865) firsthand. **b.** Herman Melville based the poems in Battle-Pieces and Aspects of the War partly on newspaper accounts.	Capitalization, Spelling, Verb tense error, Parentheses, Underline book titles, End marks
2	**a.** melville who authurred the great novel Moby-Dick saw evil in humanity. **b.** Walt Whitman best known for his collection Leaves of Grass, veiwed human nature optimistic	**a.** Melville, who authored the great novel Moby-Dick, saw evil in humanity. **b.** Walt Whitman, best known for his collection Leaves of Grass, viewed human nature optimistically.	Capitalization, Comma usage, Spelling, Underline book titles, Adverbs, End marks
3	**a.** romantic novels present larger than life characters in aventurous situtions **b.** realism attemts to depict every day life and people accurate	**a.** Romantic novels present larger-than-life characters in adventurous situations. **b.** Realism attempts to depict everyday life and people accurately.	Capitalization, Hyphens, Spelling, Usage, Adverbs, End marks
4	**a.** the french novelist emile zola a naturalist disected human behavior as tho he was a scientist **b.** both realists and naturalists focuss on storys about ordinery people	**a.** The French novelist Emile Zola, a naturalist, dissected human behavior as though he were a scientist. **b.** Both realists and naturalists focus on stories about ordinary people.	Capitalization, Comma usage, Spelling, Verb tense error, End marks
5	**a.** not only were slaves owned said james in utter amazement "but they could also be rented **b.** mr covey had striked and abused his slave yet mr. thomas defended him	**a.** "Not only were slaves owned," said James in utter amazement, "but they could also be rented!" **b.** Mr. Covey had struck and abused his slave, yet Mr. Thomas defended Mr. Covey.	Capitalization, Quotation marks, Comma usage, Past participles, Ambiguous modifier, End marks
6	**a.** reading Douglass's account Minh said he would of ran away then and there **b.** can your attitudes change another persons behavior	**a.** Reading Douglass's account, Minh said he would have run away then and there. **b.** Can your attitudes change another person's behavior?	Capitalization, Comma usage, Standard usage, Apostrophes (possessive), End marks
7	**a.** once he excaped Frederick Douglass became a fevent abolitionist, fighting from slaverey **b.** in the long run education is a more affective weapon then guns	**a.** Once he escaped, Frederick Douglass became a fervent abolitionist, fighting against slavery. **b.** In the long run, education is a more effective weapon than guns.	Capitalization, Spelling, Comma usage, Preposition error, Usage, End marks
8	**a.** 19th century victorians condemmed Chopins novel as imoral **b.** the womens rihts movement isn't hardly new in the united states	**a.** Nineteenth-century Victorians condemned Chopin's novel as immoral. **b.** The women's rights movement is hardly new in the United States. [*or* is not new]	Capitalization, Spelling out numbers, Hyphens, Spelling, Apostrophes (possessive), Double negative, End marks
9	**a.** one week ago mrs. sommers will find the perfect gift for herself **b.** if i realized what time it was i would of hurried	**a.** One week ago, Mrs. Sommers found the perfect gift for herself. **b.** If I had realized what time it was, I would have hurried.	Capitalization, Comma usage, Verb tense consistency, Standard usage, End marks
10	**a.** each of the officil commitees need to raise $500 **b.** every member of the mens' chior must sing their best tonite	**a.** Each of the official committees needs to raise five hundred dollars. **b.** Every member of the men's choir must sing his best tonight.	Capitalization, Agreement, Spelling, Spelling out numbers, Apostrophe error (possessive), End marks, Pronoun agreement (number)

Collection 9 SHACKLES

Douglass
Spirituals and "Code" Songs
Chopin
American Indian Oratory

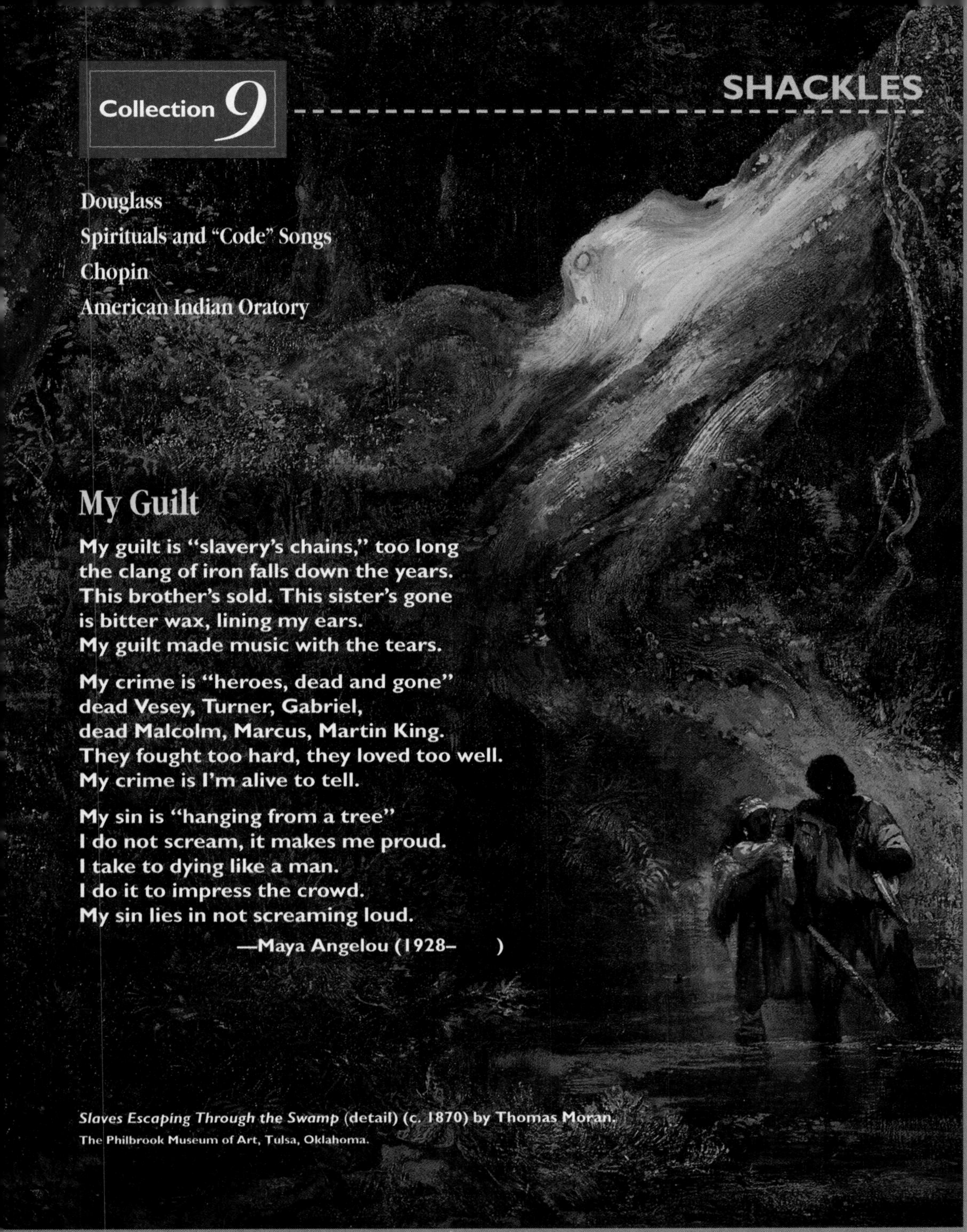

My Guilt

My guilt is "slavery's chains," too long
the clang of iron falls down the years.
This brother's sold. This sister's gone
is bitter wax, lining my ears.
My guilt made music with the tears.

My crime is "heroes, dead and gone"
dead Vesey, Turner, Gabriel,
dead Malcolm, Marcus, Martin King.
They fought too hard, they loved too well.
My crime is I'm alive to tell.

My sin is "hanging from a tree"
I do not scream, it makes me proud.
I take to dying like a man.
I do it to impress the crowd.
My sin lies in not screaming loud.

—Maya Angelou (1928–)

Slaves Escaping Through the Swamp (detail) (c. 1870) by Thomas Moran.
The Philbrook Museum of Art, Tulsa, Oklahoma.

"My Guilt"

? Why do you think "My Guilt" is representative of what you will be reading in this Collection? [Possible answer: "My Guilt" is about having experienced persecution and not complaining loudly enough so that something is done about it. The writer feels the shackles placed on her by society, and she feels badly about accepting them. It seems that the Collection will be about the bondage of human beings, the pain they feel, and the anguish of not being able to end the bondage and the suffering.]

PORTFOLIO ASSESSMENT

Parent/Guardian Involvement For forms that will help a parent or guardian review and respond to a student's portfolio, see the ***Portfolio Management System,*** pp. 62–63.

PROGRAM MANAGER

- **Integrated Assessment** For a summative assessment of the literature and language skills taught in this collection, see **Collection 9 Test, *Test Booklet,*** pp. 105–108.
- **Instructional Support** See **Fine Art Transparency 9.1.** Review teacher's notes for transparencies in the ***Audiovisual Resources Binder*** for suggestions on how to tie the transparencies to the reading selection.
- **Extending Collection Theme** See **Cross-Curricular Activity: Shackles, *Teaching Resources A,*** p. 178 for activities in other disciplines and for evaluation criteria.

QUICK PLANNING GUIDE

Into the Selection

Author Biography p. 424

Before You Read p. 425

- **Reading Focus: Scaffolding** Students learn of Douglass's fight for dignity.
- **A Dialogue with the Text: Set a Purpose** Predict in Reader's Log the outcome of events
- **Background:** Douglass's life as a slave

Through the Selection

"The Battle with Mr. Covey" pp. 426–430

Words to Own pp. 426–430

Making Meanings p. 430

Language and Style p. 431

Beyond the Selection

Choices: Building Your Portfolio p. 431

- **Writer's Notebook:** Collect ideas for an informative report
- **Critical Writing:** Relate Douglass to Emerson in a brief essay
- **Creative Writing:** Write a letter or journal entry as Douglass responding to another writer
- **Crossing the Curriculum: History** Present the life of a freedom fighter in a panel discussion

Spotlight On pp. 432–434

Frederick Douglass

(1818?–1895)

Chester County Historical Society, West Chester, Pennsylvania.

Frederick Douglass was born into slavery in Talbot County, on the Eastern Shore of Maryland, and was separated from his mother soon after his birth. "The practice of separating children from their mothers," wrote Douglass years later, "and hiring the latter out at distances too great to admit of their meeting, except at long intervals, is a marked feature of the cruelty and barbarity of the slave system. But it is in harmony with the grand aim of slavery, which, always and everywhere, is to reduce man to a level with the brute. It is a successful method of obliterating from the mind and heart of the slave all just ideas of the sacredness of *the family*. . . ."

Since records were not kept of the birth of children born into slavery, Douglass was never sure of his exact age: "Genealogical trees do not flourish among slaves," he was to remark ironically later. Although Douglass received no formal education, he did teach himself to read with the help, at first, of members of the household he served. Later, these same people became furious when they saw Douglass reading a book or a newspaper; education, they decided, was incompatible with being enslaved.

When Douglass was about twenty-one, he satisfied his hunger for freedom by escaping to Massachusetts, where he married and soon started to make public speeches in support of the abolitionist cause. He changed his last name from Bailey to Douglass, after the hero of the romantic novel *The Lady of the Lake* by Sir Walter Scott.

In 1845, Douglass went to England, largely because of the danger he faced as a fugitive, especially after the publication that same year of his autobiography, *The Narrative of the Life of Frederick Douglass, an American Slave*. In England, he mobilized antislavery sentiment and became independent when British friends collected around $700 to purchase his freedom.

When he returned to the United States in 1847, Douglass founded a newspaper, the *North Star*. (The name was chosen because escapees used this star as a guide north.) In his newspaper, Douglass championed the abolition of slavery. In 1855, he published a revised version of his life's story, titled *My Bondage and My Freedom*. These "escape" narratives, like earlier "captivity" stories (page 40), were enormously popular, and Douglass's were widely read and most influential in the abolitionist cause.

When the Civil War began, Douglass worked ardently for the Underground Railroad, the secret network of abolitionists and their sympathizers that helped many people held in slavery escape to the North. He also energetically helped to recruit African American soldiers for the Union armies.

Continuing to write and lecture after the war, Douglass argued that the surest way to rehabilitate his tragically scarred people was through education. In 1881, he published yet another version of his autobiography, titled *The Life and Times of Frederick Douglass*. Today, Douglass is revered for the courage with which he insistently proclaimed his profoundly humane values, and admired for the quiet eloquence of his writing style.

424

WORDS TO OWN

The following vocabulary words are defined in the Words to Own at the bottom of the pupil's page.

intimated p. 426	singular p. 429
comply p. 426	attributed p. 429
interpose p. 428	curry p. 429
solemnity p. 429	expiring p. 430
render p. 429	afforded p. 430

PORTFOLIO ASSESSMENT

Portfolio Assessment For help with self- and teacher assessment of reading skills, see the ***Portfolio Management System***, p. 39.

BEFORE YOU READ
THE BATTLE WITH MR. COVEY

Reading Focus
Fighting Back
While he was still enslaved, Frederick Douglass fought against society's shackles to assert his human rights and defend his dignity against a brutal, dehumanizing institution. His courageous action became a remarkable turning point in his life.

A Dialogue with the Text

As you read, fill out an event-prediction-outcome chart like the one below. Each time Douglass acts to assert his human rights, write down your prediction—or fear—about what might happen to him as a result. As you continue reading, write down what actually happens. Do any of the outcomes surprise you?

Event in Story	Prediction About Outcome	Actual Outcome

Background
Douglass has been compared with Benjamin Franklin (page 84), another self-made man who struggled against tremendous odds to achieve distinction at a critical time in his nation's history. But Douglass's story, of course, is different from Franklin's. Franklin was never enslaved. He was never "owned" by another human being and considered to be of no more significance than a piece of personal property.

In the following selection from *The Narrative of the Life of Frederick Douglass*, Douglass provides a graphic account of a critical incident that occurred when he was sixteen years old. Earlier in his narrative, he explained to his readers "how a man was made a slave"; now he sets out to explain "how a slave was made a man." At the time, Douglass was owned by a man named Thomas who had rented Douglass for a year to a man named Covey.

Into the Selection

Using BEFORE YOU READ p. 425

A Dialogue with the Text
Before students begin reading the excerpt, ask them to recall what they know about slavery from various sources. After reading the selection and completing the event-prediction-outcome chart, ask students to talk as a class about what clues led them to accurately predict an outcome.

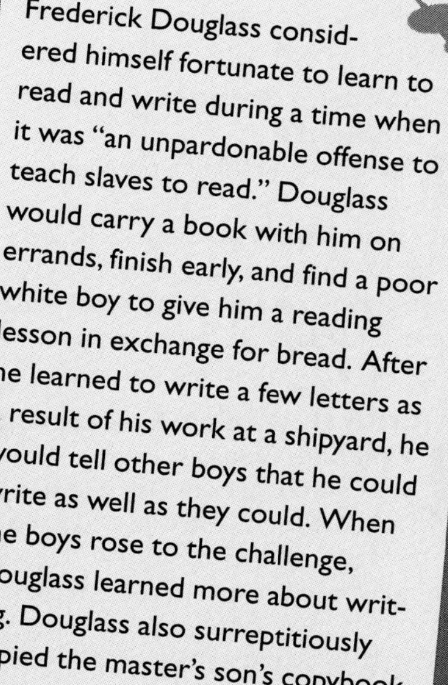

ABOUT THE AUTHOR
Frederick Douglass considered himself fortunate to learn to read and write during a time when it was "an unpardonable offense to teach slaves to read." Douglass would carry a book with him on errands, finish early, and find a poor white boy to give him a reading lesson in exchange for bread. After he learned to write a few letters as a result of his work at a shipyard, he would tell other boys that he could write as well as they could. When the boys rose to the challenge, Douglass learned more about writing. Douglass also surreptitiously copied the master's son's copybook.

PROGRAM MANAGER

- **Planning Instruction** See Teaching Notes, *Teaching Resources A,* p. 168, for objectives, a summary, literary elements, and additional information.
- **Instructional Support** See Graphic Organizer for Active Reading, *Teaching Resources A,* p. 172, for a Through the Selection activity.
- **Audiotaped Readings** To help readers through the lesson, use the Selected Reading, Audiocassette 2, Side A, in the *Audiovisual Resources Binder.*
- **Instructional Support** See Fine Art Transparency 9.1. Review teacher's notes for transparencies in the *Audiovisual Resources Binder* for teaching suggestions.
- **Assessment** See Selection Test, *Test Booklet,* pp. 101–102.
- **Language Link** For instruction and practice in identifying and using noun clauses, see Language Link, *Teaching Resources A,* pp. 173–174, and *Language and Writing Skills Worksheets,* p. 81.
- **Reinforcement** Use the Words to Own worksheet in *Teaching Resources A,* p. 175.

A. Critical Reading: Identifying Main Ideas

? What does Douglass suggest about the importance of Covey to this part of the narrative? [Events involving himself and Mr. Covey will be the focus of this section.] What does Douglass suggest about the importance of Covey to the overall course of his life? [One or more of those events have come to be, in retrospect, a turning point for Douglass.]

Metacognition What kinds of events will you look for to support this main idea? [Possible answers: Events in which he triumphs over Covey; or events in which he asserts himself to Covey and regains his dignity.]

B. Reader's Response: First Thoughts

? How do you think a person could be "made a slave"? [Sample responses: By being beaten, belittled, or treated worse than animals.] What do you think a person would feel under these conditions? [Sample responses: Anger, guilt, helplessness, sadness.]

C. Critical Reading: Speculating

? Why does Douglass decide to walk seven miles in his condition? [Possible answer: He felt he had been mistreated one time too often.] Do you think it will help him to complain? [Possible answers: Yes, the beatings may stop. Even if they do not, he will have tried to do something about his condition. Or no, he will use a lot of physical and emotional energy and nothing may come of it.]

The Battle with Mr. Covey

Frederick Douglass

A I have already intimated that my condition was much worse, during the first six months of my stay at Mr. Covey's, than in the last six. The circumstances leading to the change in Mr. Covey's course toward me form an epoch in my humble history. B You have seen how a man was made a slave; you shall see how a slave was made a man. On one of the hottest days of the month of August, 1833, Bill Smith, William Hughes, a slave named Eli, and myself, were engaged in fanning wheat.[1] Hughes was clearing the fanned wheat from before the fan, Eli was turning, Smith was feeding, and I was carrying wheat to the fan. The work was simple, requiring strength rather than intellect; yet, to one entirely unused to such work, it came very hard.

About three o'clock of that day, I broke down; my strength failed me; I was seized with a violent aching of the head, attended with extreme dizziness; I trembled in every limb. Finding what was coming, I nerved myself up, feeling it would never do to stop work. I stood as long as I could stagger to the hopper with grain. When I could stand no longer, I fell, and felt as if held down by an immense weight. The fan of course stopped; everyone had his own work to do; and no one could do the work of the other, and have his own go on at the same time.

Mr. Covey was at the house, about one hundred yards from the treading yard where we were fanning. On hearing the fan stop, he left immediately, and came to the spot where we were. He hastily inquired what the matter was. Bill answered that I was sick, and there was no one to bring wheat to the fan. I had by this time crawled away under the side of the post-and-rail fence by which the yard was enclosed, hoping to find relief by getting out of the sun. He then asked where I was. He was told by one of the hands.

He came to the spot, and, after looking at me awhile, asked me what was the matter. I told him as well as I could, for I scarce had strength to speak. He then gave me a savage kick in the side, and told me to get up. I tried to do so, but fell back in the attempt. He gave me another kick, and again told me to rise. I again tried, and succeeded in gaining my feet; but, stooping to get the tub with which I was feeding the fan, I again staggered and fell. While down in this situation, Mr. Covey took up the hickory slat with which Hughes had been striking off the half-bushel measure, and with it gave me a heavy blow upon the head, making a large wound, and the blood ran freely; and with this again told me to get up. I made no effort to comply, having now made up my mind to let him do his worst. In a short time after receiving this blow, my head grew better. Mr. Covey had now left me to my fate.

C At this moment I resolved, for the first time, to go to my master, enter a complaint, and ask his protection. In order to [do] this, I must that afternoon walk seven miles; and this, under the circumstances, was truly a severe undertaking. I was exceedingly feeble; made so as much by the kicks and blows which I received, as by the severe fit of sickness to which I had been subjected. I, however, watched my chance, while Covey was looking in an opposite direction, and started for St. Michael's. I succeeded in getting a considerable distance on my way to the woods, when Covey discovered me, and called after me to come back, threatening what he would do if I did not come. I disregarded both his calls and his threats, and made my way to the woods as fast as my feeble state would allow; and thinking I might be overhauled by him if I kept the road, I walked through the woods, keeping far enough from the road to

1. **fanning wheat:** separating the good, usable grain from the useless stalks and husks.

Words to Own

intimated (in′tə·māt′əd) *v.:* stated indirectly; hinted.
comply (kəm·plī′) *v.:* to obey a command; agree to a request.

Frederick Douglass Series No. 10 (1938–1939) by Jacob Lawrence. Casein tempera on gessoed hardboard (17 ⅞″ × 12″).
Hampton University Museum, Hampton, Virginia.

OPTIONS FOR TEACHING

STRATEGIES FOR INCLUSION

Musical Remind students that Douglass became famous for his oratory as well as for his writing. Then, have students look for and comment upon phrases or passages in the narrative that would appeal to the "ear" of the reader. Such devices include rhythm (for example, "I stood as long as I could stagger to the hopper with grain"), pitch and volume (as in the passage in which Covey repeatedly kicks Douglass), and pauses (as in "You have seen how a man was made a slave; you shall see how a slave was made a man"). Students may wish to expand on this activity by preparing and presenting an oral interpretation.

Intrapersonal The teenage Douglass of this narrative is an independent thinker. Encourage students who have displayed a preference for making their own decisions and taking the initiative to share their insights into the narrator's character; in particular, ask them how Douglass might have kept his independent spirit alive even in the midst of such an oppressive society.

English Language Development To help prepare students for the story and to provide oral practice, have students follow in their textbooks as you read the first seven lines of the selection. Ask students to work in groups to predict what will happen and to discuss how a slave might be made a man and why Douglass's last six months with Covey might be better than his first six.

RESPONDING TO THE ART: ABOUT THE ARTIST

This painting of the fight between Frederick Douglass and his master, Mr. Covey, as described in Douglass's autobiography, is one of a series devoted to Douglass by American artist Jacob Lawrence (born 1917). One of the first African American artists to be accepted in the established art world, Lawrence painted works concerning the history and experience of African Americans in the United States. Other works include three series devoted to Harriet Tubman, Harlem, and war. This painting from the Douglass series exemplifies primitive elements of Lawrence's style.

INTEGRATING THE LANGUAGE ARTS

Strategic Reading Students who struggle with some of the fine points of the narrative can still respond to its powerful images and vivid episodes. To help them do so, consider a Random Reading. As students work through the narrative, have them note in their Reader's Logs anything that creates a strong mental image or anything that otherwise moves them. Invite them to read their notes aloud when they are ready to share. Allow more than one student to share the same passage.

Writing: Letters Ask students how they think Douglass would respond to Equiano's book (pp. 57–65) and how Equiano might respond in turn. Have them prepare the letters the two might have written to each other.

Speaking and Listening During the Great Depression, one federal work project sent oral historians throughout the country to collect the stories of former slaves. Invite students to recreate an interview between such a historian and a former slave who had heard the adult Douglass speak about his past or had heard about "The Battle with Mr. Covey" from parents or grandparents who had known the teenage Douglass. Ahead of time, have the rest of the class prepare questions; then, have the students giving the recreation work together on the responses, using Douglass's narrative for details.

A. Literary Element: Character

? What traits of character are shown by Douglass in this journey to his master? [Possible answers: Determination, perseverance, courage, stoicism.]

B. Language Note: Word Usage

The statement that he "should have" bled to death may cause confusion, for it is a usage rarely employed today. This use of *should* will occur again in the narrative, and students need to be sensitive to its meaning. Make sure students understand that Douglass is not expressing a wish that he had bled to death but amazement that something so probable did not, in fact, happen.

C. Reader's Response: Extending the Text

? What might motivate someone to side with a person who is so obviously an oppressor? [Sample responses: Feeling mistrust toward the accuser; being governed by economic considerations rather than by sympathy; needing to rationalize the system; needing to assert authority.]

Frederick Douglass Series No. 9 (1938–1939) by Jacob Lawrence. Casein tempera on gessoed hardboard (12″ × 17⅞″).

Hampton University Museum, Hampton, Virginia.

A avoid detection, and near enough to prevent losing my way.

I had not gone far before my little strength again failed me. I could go no farther. I fell down, and lay for a considerable time. The blood was yet B oozing from the wound on my head. For a time I thought I should bleed to death; and think now that I should have done so, but that the blood so matted my hair as to stop the wound. After lying there about three quarters of an hour, I nerved myself up again, and started on my way, through bogs and briers, barefooted and bareheaded, tearing my feet sometimes at nearly every step; and after a journey of about seven miles, occupying some five hours to perform it, I arrived at master's store. I then presented an appearance enough to affect any but a heart of iron. From the crown of my head to my feet, I was covered with blood. My hair was all clotted with dust and blood; my shirt was stiff with blood. My legs and feet were torn in sundry places with briers and thorns, and were also covered with blood. I suppose I looked like a man who had escaped a den of wild beasts, and barely escaped them.

In this state I appeared before my master, humbly entreating him to interpose his authority for my protection. I told him all the circumstances as well as I could, and it seemed, as I spoke, at times to affect him. He would then walk the floor, and seek to justify Covey by saying he expected I C deserved it. He asked me what I wanted. I told him, to let me get a new home; that as sure as I lived with Mr. Covey again, I should live with but to die with him; that Covey would surely kill me; he was in a fair way for it. Master Thomas ridiculed the idea that there was any danger of Mr. Covey's killing me, and said that he knew Mr. Covey; that he was a good man, and that he could not think of taking me from him; that, should he do so, he would lose the whole year's wages; that I belonged to Mr. Covey for one year, and that I must go back to him, come what might; and that I must not trouble him with any more stories, or that he would himself *get hold of me.* After threatening me thus, he gave me a very large dose of salts, telling me that I might remain in St. Michael's that night (it being quite late), but that I must be off back to Mr. Covey's early in the morning; and that if I did not, he would *get hold of me,* which meant that he would whip me.

I remained all night, and, according to his orders, I started off to Covey's in the morning (Saturday morning), wearied in body and broken in spirit. I got no supper that night, or breakfast that morning. I reached Covey's about nine o'clock; and just as I was getting over the fence that divided Mrs. Kemp's fields from ours, out ran Covey

WORDS TO OWN

interpose (in′tər·pōz′) *v.*: to put forth in order to intervene.

OPTIONS FOR TEACHING

CLASSROOM MANAGEMENT

Budgeting Time If time constraints make it difficult to read "The Battle with Mr. Covey" entirely in class, take students through the paragraph that ends, "Mr. Covey had now left me to my fate" (p. 426). Offer the following questions to guide students as they complete the reading independently.

- How will Douglass regain his strength?
- Will people around him try to help him, or will they feel that he is in the wrong?
- Can Mr. Covey change? If so, what might make him reconsider the way he treats slaves?

Managing the Reader's Response Classroom When assigning a selection, place students in one of three groups, one which is responsible for presenting an interpretation of the selection, a second for asking questions of the first, and a third for evaluating both the content of the presentation and the interaction of the two groups. After students have read the assignment, allow the presenting group time to prepare their interpretation and the questioning group time to develop questions to ask of the presenters. On the day of the presentation, allow the first group to present their interpretation, then invite the second group to ask questions. Finally, have the third group evaluate the session.

with his cowskin, to give me another whipping. Before he could reach me, I succeeded in getting to the cornfield; and as the corn was very high, it afforded me the means of hiding. He seemed very angry, and searched for me a long time. My behavior was altogether unaccountable. He finally gave up the chase, thinking, I suppose, that I must come home for something to eat; he would give himself no further trouble in looking for me. I spent that day mostly in the woods, having the alternative before me—to go home and be whipped to death, or stay in the woods and be starved to death. **D**

That night, I fell in with Sandy Jenkins, a slave with whom I was somewhat acquainted. Sandy had a free wife who lived about four miles from Mr. Covey's; and it being Saturday, he was on his way to see her. I told him my circumstances, and he very kindly invited me to go home with him. I went home with him, and talked this whole matter over, and got his advice as to what course it was best for me to pursue. I found Sandy an old advisor.[2] He told me, with great solemnity, I must go back to Covey; but that before I went, I must go with him into another part of the woods, where there was a certain *root,* which, if I would take some of it with me, carrying it *always on my right side,* would render it impossible for Mr. Covey, or any other white man, to whip me. He said he had carried it for years; and since he had done so, he had never received a blow, and never expected to while he carried it. I at first rejected the idea, that the simple carrying of a root in my pocket would have any such effect as he had said, and was not disposed to take it; but Sandy impressed the necessity with much earnestness, telling me it could do no harm, if it did no good. To please him, I at length took the root, and, according to his direction, carried it upon my right side. This was Sunday morning. **E**

I immediately started for home; and upon entering the yard gate, out came Mr. Covey on his way to meeting. He spoke to me very kindly, made me drive the pigs from a lot near by, and passed on toward the church. Now, this singular conduct of Mr. Covey really made me begin to think that there was something in the *root* which Sandy had given me; and had it been on any other day than Sunday, I could have attributed the conduct to no other cause than the influence of that root; and as it was, I was half inclined to think the *root* to be something more than I at first had taken it to be. All went well till Monday morning. On this morning, the virtue of the *root* was fully tested.

Long before daylight, I was called to go and rub, curry, and feed the horses. I obeyed, and was glad to obey. But while thus engaged, while in the act of throwing down some blades from the loft, Mr. Covey entered the stable with a long rope; and just as I was half out of the loft, he caught hold of my legs, and was about tying me. As soon as I found what he was up to, I gave a sudden spring, and as I did so, he holding to my legs, I was brought sprawling on the stable floor. Mr. Covey seemed now to think he had me, and could do what he pleased; but at this moment—from whence came the spirit I don't know—I resolved to fight; and, suiting my action to the resolution, I seized Covey hard by the throat; and as I did so, I rose. He held on to me, and I to him. My resistance was so entirely unexpected, that Covey seemed taken all aback. He trembled like a leaf. This gave me assurance, and I held him uneasy, causing the blood to run where I touched him with the ends of my fingers. Mr. Covey soon called out to Hughes for help. Hughes came, and, while Covey held me, attempted to tie my right hand. While he was in the act of doing so, I watched my chance, and gave him a heavy kick close under the ribs. This kick fairly sickened Hughes, so that he left me in the hands of Mr. Covey.

This kick had the effect of not only weakening Hughes, but Covey also. When he saw Hughes bending over with pain, his courage quailed.[3] He asked me if I meant to persist in my resistance. I told him I did, come what might; that he had used me like a brute for six months, and that I was determined to be used so no longer. With that, he

2. **an old advisor:** someone who can offer good advice.

3. **quailed:** faltered.

WORDS TO OWN

solemnity (sə·lem′nə·tē) *n.:* seriousness.
render (ren′dər) *v.:* make.
singular (siŋ′gyə·lər) *adj.:* remarkable.
attributed (ə·trib′yo͞ot·id) *v.:* believed to result from.
curry (kʉr′ē) *v.:* to groom.

D. Critical Reading: Evaluating an Interpretation

? Do you agree that these are the only two options available to Douglass? Explain. [Possible answer: These may seem the only options at the moment, but there must be other things that Douglass can do—run away, for example, or return and try to make Covey believe that he has learned his lesson.]

E. Cultural Connections

The root that Jenkins recommends is a *talisman*—an object believed to bring good luck and to ward off evil. An interest in talismans continues today in various cultures. In the United States today, for example, the small bear fetish used by some Native Americans has become a popular jewelry item, Michael Jordan wears his Carolina blue shorts every game for confidence, and most students have seen or even owned such "good-luck charms" as four-leaf clovers.

CROSSING THE CURRICULUM

Architecture Ask an interested team of students to give a presentation about plantation housing. The presentations should include visuals (such as three-dimensional models of the plantation or slides of different homes, in different styles, including a large overview of a real or imaginary plantation) and might address questions such as the following:

- Did "house" slaves' accommodations differ from those of "field" slaves?
- How were slaves' quarters built?
- How many people might live in a single slave dwelling?
- Where were slaves' quarters located in relation to the master's house?
- Is there any record of what any slaves said about the differences in housing for masters and slaves?

Geography Have students use a map of the United States (from that era, if possible) to trace a possible escape route from a point of their choice in the South to a point of freedom in the North. Which route could be traveled most quickly? Which held the greatest challenges? Which might be used by an adult traveling alone—or by adults with children? Work with students to display the finished projects. Tell students that Douglass escaped from Baltimore. They may wish to figure out the route he took.

Making Meanings

First Thoughts

1. Possible responses: Douglass's fight with Covey or Douglass's decision to let Covey do his worst.

Reviewing the Text

a. He decides to go to his master, enter a complaint, and ask for his protection. Thomas advises Douglass to go back to Covey.
b. He is angry and searches for Douglass.
c. Sandy Jenkins tells Douglass about a root that he should always carry on his right side so that he will never be beaten by a white man again. He gets the courage to return to Covey's.
d. Douglass's battle with Covey and his decision to fight back. This decision revives his sense of manhood and his desire to be free.

Shaping Interpretations

2. According to Douglass, his own fighting spirit is more powerful.
3. Douglass relates with humor how he rejects the idea that the root would protect him and how earnestly Jenkins presses him to take it. He also recounts with wry humor how Mr. Covey's apparently gentle behavior on Sunday almost convinces him that the root has supernatural powers.
4. Douglass is honest, hard-working, cooperative, obedient, courageous, proud, defiant, determined.
5. Covey is cruel, merciless, mean and cowardly. He is a violent bully. Like many bullies, he is cowed when faced with firm resistance.
6. By "a slave in form," Douglass means his outer, legal designation as a slave. By saying that he was no longer a "slave in fact," he refers to the pride and independence of his inner spirit.

Extending the Text

7. **(Synthesis)** Possible responses: It is true that freedom from bondage is gratifying. It may not be true in that freedom obtained through force may not be as satisfying as freedom gained from slave owners realizing the immorality of slavery. When people in charge refuse to acknowledge injustice, victims must think of ways to help themselves. Or violent oppression may well in turn lead to violence.

strove to drag me to a stick that was lying just out of the stable door. He meant to knock me down. But just as he was leaning over to get the stick, I seized him with both hands by his collar, and brought him by a sudden snatch to the ground. By this time, Bill came. Covey called upon him for assistance. Bill wanted to know what he could do. Covey said, "Take hold of him, take hold of him!" Bill said his master hired him out to work, and not to help to whip me; so he left Covey and myself to fight our own battle out. We were at it for nearly two hours. Covey at length let me go, puffing and blowing at a great rate, saying that if I had not resisted, he would not have whipped me half so much. The truth was, that he had not whipped me at all. I considered him as getting entirely the worst end of the bargain; for he had drawn no blood from me, but I had from him. The whole six months afterward, that I spent with Mr. Covey, he never laid the weight of his finger upon me in anger. He would occasionally say, he didn't want to get hold of me again. "No," thought I, "you need not; for you will come off worse than you did before."

This battle with Mr. Covey was the turning point in my career as a slave. It rekindled the few expiring embers of freedom, and revived within me a sense of my own manhood. It recalled the departed self-confidence, and inspired me again with a determination to be free. The gratification afforded by the triumph was a full compensation for whatever else might follow, even death itself. He only can understand the deep satisfaction which I experienced, who has himself repelled by force the bloody arm of slavery. I felt as I never felt before. It was a glorious resurrection, from the tomb of slavery, to the heaven of freedom. My long-crushed spirit rose, cowardice departed, bold defiance took its place; and I now resolved that, however long I might remain a slave in form, the day had passed forever when I could be a slave in fact.

Words to Own

expiring (ek·spīr′iŋ) *v.* used as *adj.:* dying.
afforded (ə·fôrd′əd) *v.* used as *adj.:* given; provided.

Making Meanings

First Thoughts

1. Review the chart you made in your Reader's Log. Which details, events, or aspects of Douglass's account surprised you?

Reviewing the Text

a. What action does Douglass take after Covey strikes him? What does Thomas advise Douglass to do?
b. What is Covey's reaction when Douglass returns from his visit to Thomas?
c. Explain how Sandy Jenkins helps Douglass.
d. Describe what Douglass calls the turning point in his life as a slave.

Shaping Interpretations

2. The root that Sandy Jenkins gives to Douglass is a *talisman,* an object believed to possess supernatural powers. What does Douglass discover is even more powerful than the root?
3. What elements of humor do you find in the part of the story involving Sandy Jenkins? Explain.
4. Based on this account, how would you **characterize** the young Frederick Douglass?
5. What does the entire incident reveal about Covey's **character**?
6. At the end of the selection, Douglass distinguishes between being "a slave in form" and "a slave in fact." Explain the meaning of this distinction.

Extending the Text

7. "He only can understand the deep satisfaction which I experienced, who has himself repelled by force the bloody arm of slavery" (page 430). In what ways is Douglass's statement true? In what ways might it not be true? Discuss how Douglass's feelings might apply to the problems of racism today.

OPTIONS FOR TEACHING

ASSESSMENT TOOLS

Check Test: Questions and Answers

1. How old was Douglass when these events took place? [He was about sixteen years old.]
2. Why does Covey beat him? [Covey may think that Douglass is feigning illness as an act of rebellion.]
3. How does Master Thomas respond when Douglass comes to him for help? [He refuses to take Douglass back before the rental period is over; he suggests that the beating was Douglass's own fault.]
4. Who is Sandy Jenkins, and how does he help Douglass? [Jenkins, a fellow slave, gives Douglass a root to carry in his pocket, promising that it will keep him from being whipped.]
5. What happens on the Monday after Douglass's return? [Douglass is attacked by Covey. Douglass fights back, and after a two-hour brawl, Covey lets him go.]

LANGUAGE AND STYLE

Douglass's Metaphors

At the end of the selection, Douglass uses **metaphors** that suggest resurrection and rebirth.

1. Explain the comparison implied in this line: "It [the battle] rekindled the few expiring embers of freedom." How are these **images** related to the idea of rebirth?
2. What is Douglass implicitly comparing slavery with when he refers to "the bloody arm of slavery"?
3. Find the passage that specifically compares Douglass's experience to a rebirth. In this comparison, what is being compared with what?

CHOICES: Building Your Portfolio

Writer's Notebook

1. Collecting Ideas for an Informative Report

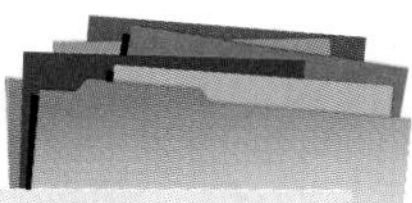

Douglass's narrative is a rich source of information, perspectives, and imagery on topics such as slavery, human rights, self-esteem, racism, and freedom. In a KWL chart like the one below, explore a topic suggested by Douglass's narrative that you would be interested in gathering more information about. Save your notes for possible use in the Writer's Workshop on page 515.

K What I Know	W What I Want to Know	L What I Learned

Critical Writing

2. Emerson Applied

Re-read Emerson's essay "Self-Reliance" (page 224). Then, write a brief essay in which you (a) explain which of Emerson's ideas relate to Douglass's experience, and (b) identify any of Emerson's ideas that seem to be contradicted by Douglass's narrative.

Creative Writing

3. Responding to Other Voices

You have already read the work of other writers who have championed principles of freedom, such as Bradford, Jefferson, Paine, Franklin, Emerson, Thoreau, and Whitman. Write a letter or a journal entry in which Douglass responds to one of these writers, expressing his views of their writings, beliefs, actions, or achievements.

Crossing the Curriculum: History

4. Freedom Fighters

With two other students, research the lives of three people who have opposed racial discrimination in the twentieth century. Among the people you might consider are the South African leaders Nelson Mandela, Stephen Biko, or Desmond Tutu; the Burmese freedom fighter Daw Aung San Suu Kyi; the American civil rights leaders Malcolm X or Martin Luther King, Jr.; the protesters against internment of Japanese Americans in the United States during World War II; Raoul Wallenberg or Oskar Schindler, who saved Jewish lives during the Nazi Holocaust in Europe. Present a panel discussion in which each student summarizes the life and career of a freedom fighter and explains how that person helped advance the cause of human rights.

Desmond Tutu.
UPI/Bettmann.

Language and Style

Answers

1. A fading hope for freedom is compared to the embers of a dying fire; the battle is compared to a spark or puff of air that rekindles the fire. Any new fire offers warmth and light—a source of rebirth. Fire is also central to the image of the phoenix, said to die on a pyre and be reborn again from the ashes. Fire is also a symbol of intensity.
2. The word *arm* personifies slavery as a cruel taskmaster who inflicts death, wounds, or pain (the word *bloody*) and as the society that condones such oppression.
3. "It was a glorious resurrection, from the tomb of slavery, to the heaven of freedom" (p. 430). Slavery is compared to death and confinement; freedom is compared to resurrection and release.

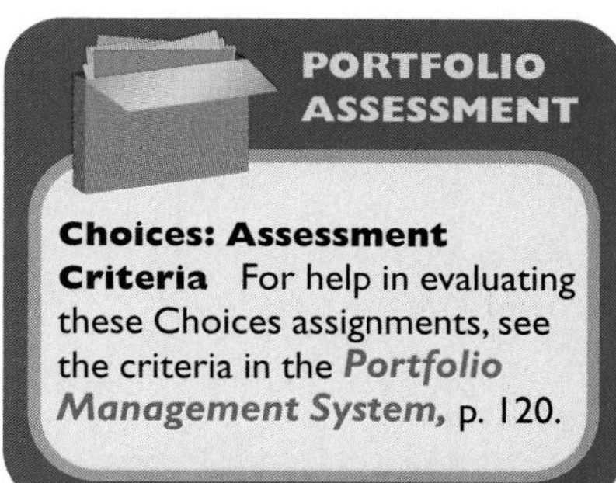

Choices: Assessment Criteria For help in evaluating these Choices assignments, see the criteria in the ***Portfolio Management System,*** p. 120.

STRATEGIES FOR INCLUSION

Learners Having Difficulty When students are taking notes for their essay in activity #2, have them use the following guidelines:

- Use cards of the same size (4" x 6" cards are recommended.)
- Fill out a bibliography card for each source. Ask them to number each card.
- Place one main idea or quotation on each card. Have them list page numbers on which they found the material as well as the bibliography card number of their source.
- Use abbreviations and phrases.
- Leave space at the bottom of each card for notes on how and where they might use the information.
- Place a descriptive heading at the top of each card that highlights the main idea of each note.

Note cards can be put on a table or desktop and can be moved around when students are organizing their information.

Auditory Have students work in groups of three to prepare for the panel discussion in activity #4. Each student should read his or her summary into a cassette recorder. Ask all three group members to listen to each recording and to critique it for content as well as delivery. Ask students to revise their summaries accordingly.

A. Critical Reading: Making Inferences

? Why do you think a "silent slave" would be disliked? [Possible answers: A noisy slave could be found easily; a silent slave would be harder to trace. A lack of noise would create suspicion about what the slave actually was doing—perhaps not only avoiding work but even planning to escape.]

B. Exploring the Historical Period

Frederick Douglass explains that *allowance day* was "the two days at the end of each month, when the slaves from the different farms came to get their monthly allowance of meal and meat. These were gala days for the slaves, and there was much rivalry among them as to *who* should be elected to go up to the great house farm for the allowance, and, indeed, to attend to any business at this, (for them,) the capital."

SPOTLIGHT ON

Spirituals and "Code" Songs

National Portrait Gallery, Smithsonian Institution. Courtesy Art Resource.

Frederick Douglass (detail) (c. 1844), attributed to Elisha Hammond. Oil on canvas (27½″ × 22½″).

The moving and intensely emotional songs known as "spirituals" came out of the oral tradition among Africans held in slavery in the South before the time of the Civil War. Spirituals, like other kinds of folk literature and music, were composed by anonymous artists and passed on by word of mouth. Conveyed orally, they were inevitably altered and refined, so that many different versions of a particular spiritual might exist. Some spirituals may have been based on African melodies and rhythms.

In this passage from *My Bondage and My Freedom,* Frederick Douglass writes eloquently about songs of slavery—called "sorrow songs" by the later African American writer W.E.B. Du Bois.

Slaves are generally expected to sing as well as to work. A silent slave is not liked by masters or overseers. (A) *"Make a noise, make a noise,"* and *"bear a band"* are the words usually addressed to the slaves when there is silence amongst them. This may account for the almost constant singing heard in the southern states. . . . On (B) allowance day, those who visited the great house farm were peculiarly excited and noisy. While on their way, they would make the dense old woods, for miles around, reverberate with their wild notes. These were not always merry because they were wild. On the contrary, they were mostly of a plaintive cast, and told a tale of grief and sorrow. In the most boisterous outbursts of rapturous sentiment, there was ever a tinge of deep melancholy. I have never heard any songs like those anywhere since I left slavery, except when in Ireland. There I heard the same *wailing notes,* and was much affected by them. It was during the famine of 1845–1846. In all the songs of the slaves, there was ever some expression in praise of the great house farm; something which would flatter the pride of

OPTIONS FOR TEACHING

STRATEGIES FOR INCLUSION

Auditory Play recordings of "Go Down, Moses" and "Follow the Drinking Gourd." Among the recordings of "Go Down, Moses" is one by Paul Robeson, found on *The Power and the Glory* (Columbia CK47337; CD and audiocassette). One recording of "Follow the Drinking Gourd" appears on *The Weavers at Carnegie Hall* (Vanguard 73101; CD and audiocassette) Ask students to write about the feelings that are evoked while listening to these songs.

Musical Students who enjoy singing may want to find sheet music for some spirituals and sing them for the class.

Visual In order for students to "decode" a "code" song and to fully understand the double meanings, have them draw a chart like the following. They should paraphrase the songs' literal meaning under one column and their "code" meanings under another.

Song	Literal Meaning	Code Meaning
"Follow the drinking gourd"	[When the sun rises and the first quail calls.]	[That will be time to leave.]

the owner, and, possibly, draw a favorable glance from him.

. . . I cannot better express my sense of them now, than ten years ago, when, in sketching my life, I thus spoke of this feature of my plantation experience:

. . . The hearing of those wild notes always depressed my spirits, and filled my heart with ineffable sadness. The mere recurrence, even now, afflicts my spirit, and while I am writing these lines, my tears are falling. To those songs I trace my first glimmering conceptions of the dehumanizing character of slavery. I can never get rid of that conception. Those songs still follow me, to deepen my hatred of slavery, and quicken my sympathies for my brethren in bonds. If any one wishes to be impressed with a sense of the soul-killing power of slavery, let him go to Colonel Lloyd's plantation, and, on allowance day, place himself in the deep, pine woods, and there let him, in silence, thoughtfully analyze the sounds that shall pass through the chambers of his soul, and if he is not thus impressed, it will only be because "there is no flesh in his obdurate heart."

—Frederick Douglass

Harriet Tubman and the Freedom Train (1989) by Barbara Olsen. Gouache, collage (22½″ × 30″).

Spirituals were concerned above all with issues of freedom: spiritual freedom in the form of salvation and literal freedom from the shackles of slavery. Many people during the time of slavery were called "Moses" by those looking for a deliverer to loose their chains. Harriet Tubman, for example, used "Moses" as her code name in her work with the Underground Railroad. A Methodist minister named Francis Asbury was also known as "Moses," and according to some scholars, the spiritual "Go Down, Moses" really is a plea for Asbury's help. Ultimately, of course, the name Moses refers to the man who, according to the Book of Exodus in the Bible, delivered the ancient Israelites from slavery in Egypt. C

Some of the songs were "code songs" or "signal songs"—that is, details in the songs provided runaways with directions, times, and meeting places for their escape. For example, the drinking gourd in "Follow the Drinking Gourd" is the Big Dipper constellation; two stars in the bowl of the Big Dipper point to the North Star. A drinking gourd is actually the shell of a vegetable related to the squash or melon, dried and hollowed out for drinking.

RESPONDING TO THE ART: ABOUT THE ARTWORK

The figures in this collage were painted with gouache, watercolor that is made opaque by adding a filler such as gum. The layers applied are thick compared to watercolors and their colors become lighter and more opaque as they dry, but the technique allows for bright colors and great detail as found in this collage. The term *gouache* comes from an Italian word, *guazzo,* meaning "water color," derived from the Latin *aquatio,* meaning "watering."

C. Expansion

Some scholars believe that this spiritual also had its use as a "code" song, announcing that Tubman would be coming to an area.

Technology Tip

Students who wish to learn more about spirituals can access the Gospel and Spiritual Music page, a division of the Southern Folklife Collection Web site, located at **http://ils.unc.edu/liz/gospel.html**. *You may want to preview any Internet activity that you suggest to students. Because these resources are sometimes public forums, their content can be unpredictable.*

Morgan Freeman reads the story of the Drinking Gourd for Rabbit Ears Radio, distributed by Public Radio International. Rabbit Ears Radio also produces videotapes and CDs. Contact your local public radio station for information.

CROSSING THE CURRICULUM

Music Have students imagine that your community, as it exists today, is a place from which people want to escape. Have students work in groups to create one of the following:

- A "code" song that uses local landmarks to trace a path to freedom. (In this case, have students sketch a map before they create song details.)
- A spiritual based upon another story of deliverance as found in the Bible. Assign students who are familiar with biblical references among the groups or have them serve as "floating" consultants.

Art Have students paint a mural depicting the sorrow that was evident in the slaves' songs. If it meets administrative approval, have them paint it on a wall outside the classroom. Otherwise, have them paint it on kraft paper that can be displayed outside the classroom.

Social Sciences Have students locate and "decode" other "code" songs that were sung by the slaves. Have them share their findings with the class. [Harriet Tubman used "Wade in the Water" to tell her "passengers" how to throw off bloodhounds. Nat Turner sang "Steal Away" to call people together. "Good News, Member" let people know that a runaway slave had reached freedom.]

RESPONDING TO THE ART: EXPLORING THE SUBJECT

Some scholars believe the painting may depict a wedding. Jumping over a broomstick, or other stick, was often part of the marriage ceremony for enslaved African Americans. Other scholars have suggested that the painting may illustrate a dance similar to those performed by the Yoruba of northern and southwestern Nigeria.

A. Expansion

If students are not familiar with the events upon which this song is based, encourage them to read Exodus 3–12. The following details are most directly relevant: The Hebrews are in bondage to the Pharaoh. Moses announces to the Pharaoh (Ramses II probably reigned at that time) that God has commanded that the Hebrews be allowed to leave Egypt. At Ramses' first refusal, Moses' staff is turned into a serpent, and the waters of the Nile are turned blood red. When Ramses remains adamant, Egypt is cursed with plagues of frogs, gnats, and flies. Next, the Egyptian animals suffer from an epidemic, and a plague of boils descends on both people and animals, followed by fierce lightning and hail storms, an invasion of locusts, and daylight darkness. Ramses agrees to free the Hebrews, however, only when the firstborn sons of the Egyptians, including that of Ramses, are smitten.

B. Literary Element: Symbol

? Whom does Israel represent? [The slaves.] What does Egypt represent? [Possible answers: The South; anywhere that oppression exists.] Who are Pharaoh and Moses? [Possible answers: *Pharaoh* is a code name for slaveowners or politicians who refuse to abolish slavery. *Moses* is a code name for a hoped-for leader who returns for the slaves.]

The Old Plantation (c. 1795) by an unknown artist (South Carolina). Watercolor on laid paper ($11\frac{11}{16}'' \times 17\frac{7}{8}''$).
Abby Aldrich Rockefeller Folk Art Center, Williamsburg, Virginia.

(A) Go Down, Moses

Go down, Moses,
Way down in Egypt land
Tell old Pharaoh
To let my people go.

When Israel was in Egypt land
Let my people go
Oppressed so hard they could not stand
Let my people go.

(B) Go down, Moses,
Way down in Egypt land
Tell old Pharaoh,
"Let my people go."

"Thus saith the Lord," bold Moses said,
"Let my people go;
If not I'll smite your firstborn dead
Let my people go."

Go down, Moses,
Way down in Egypt land,
Tell old Pharaoh,
"Let my people go!"

Follow the Drinking Gourd

When the sun comes back and the first quail calls,
Follow the drinking gourd,
For the old man is a-waiting for to carry you to freedom
If you follow the drinking gourd.

[Refrain]
Follow the drinking gourd,
Follow the drinking gourd,
For the old man is a-waiting for to carry you to freedom
If you follow the drinking gourd.

The river bank will make a very good road,
The dead trees show you the way,
Left foot, peg foot traveling on
Follow the drinking gourd. [Refrain]

The river ends between two hills,
Follow the drinking gourd.
There's another river on the other side,
Following the drinking gourd. [Refrain]

Where the little river meets the great big river,
Follow the drinking gourd.
The old man is a-waiting for to carry you to freedom,
If you follow the drinking gourd. [Refrain]

OPTIONS FOR TEACHING

PROFESSIONAL NOTES

Critical Comment: Sorrow Songs The African American scholar and activist W.E.B. Du Bois (1868–1963) referred to spirituals as "Sorrow Songs." However, he spoke of something besides "sorrow" as their predominant feature: "Through all of the Sorrow Songs there breathes a hope—a faith in the ultimate justice of things. The minor cadences of despair change often to triumph and calm confidence. Sometimes it is faith in life, sometimes a faith in death, sometimes assurance of boundless justice in some fair world beyond. But whichever it is, the meaning is always clear: that sometime, somewhere, men will judge men by their souls and not by their skins." Du Bois also described these songs "not simply as the sole American music, but as the most beautiful expression of human experience born on this side of the seas. . . . the singular spiritual heritage of the nation and the greatest gift of the Negro people."

Kate Chopin

(1851–1904)

The Missouri Historical Society, St. Louis, Missouri.

Kate Chopin's work went unrecognized, and was even scorned, during her lifetime. Along with many other literary pioneers, Chopin never lived to see her work vindicated.

Kate Chopin was born Katherine O'Flaherty in St. Louis, Missouri, to an Irish immigrant father and a mother descended from French Creole aristocrats. (Creoles are people of French or Spanish descent who are born in the states bordering the Gulf of Mexico but who retain their European culture.) Kate's prosperous parents encouraged her early interest in music and reading; her mother invited such a flurry of stimulating visitors to their house that Kate sometimes escaped to the attic to read. She was given lessons in French and piano for a time by her worldly great-grandmother, who stirred the child's imagination with vivid tales of old St. Louis. Kate became a witty and popular young woman with a notably independent turn of mind.

At nineteen, Kate married Oscar Chopin, a French Creole from New Orleans, and they enjoyed a long European honeymoon, visiting art galleries and attending operas. The Chopins settled in Louisiana and reared a family of six children, but, when Kate was thirty-two, Oscar died suddenly from swamp fever. Kate returned to St. Louis, and it was then that she began to write. She published a poem when she was thirty-eight, followed by some short stories. In 1890, she published her first novel.

Chopin's short stories concern the life of French Creoles in Louisiana. Published in national magazines and collected in two volumes called *Bayou Folk* (1894) and *A Night in Acadie* (1897), the stories were praised for their accurate portrayal of the French Creole strand in American culture. Chopin's theme, however, was a much more controversial matter: the repression of women in Victorian America.

This theme was presented most dramatically in her novel *The Awakening* (1899). The novel portrays a dissatisfied New Orleans wife who breaks from the confines of her marriage and, in her quest for freedom, flagrantly defies the Victorian ideals of motherhood and domesticity. The novel was greeted with hostility by American critics, who condemned it as sordid and vulgar. Victorians, who looked to literature for moral lessons, saw only an immoral lesson in *The Awakening*. The novel was removed from circulation in St. Louis libraries, some of Chopin's friends shunned her, and the local arts club denied her membership. Chopin was disheartened enough by this rejection to allow her writing to languish, and she produced little more before her death in 1904. After her death, her work fell into obscurity, and often copies of her books couldn't even be obtained.

The Awakening and many of Chopin's other works were rediscovered decades after her death. With the help of discerning critics and the women's movement of the 1960s and 1970s, Kate Chopin is now recognized as a novelist of skill and perception, whose work appeared half a century before its time.

ABOUT THE AUTHOR

By several accounts, Chopin was happy in her own marriage. Oscar Chopin valued her intellect, spontaneity, and individuality and allowed her latitude to do as she pleased. She could make him laugh with her storytelling and impressions of his relatives. Although the Chopins entertained a good deal, they invariably preferred each other's company to that of those around them. Chopin came from a wealthy family and her husband had done well as a cotton broker. The business failed, however, and when he died, Chopin had to raise six children on limited finances. She may well have felt something of what Mrs. Sommers feels in "A Pair of Silk Stockings."

QUICK PLANNING GUIDE

Into the Story

Author Biography p. 435

Before You Read p. 436

- **Reading Focus: Prior Knowledge** Students discuss escape from routine.
- **A Dialogue with the Text: Set a Purpose** Predict in Reader's Log how Mrs. Sommers will spend money and guess her feelings
- **Background:** Invention of nylon as well as the effects of inflation

Through the Story

"A Pair of Silk Stockings" pp. 437–443

Words to Own pp. 437–443

Literature and History pp. 440–441

Primary Sources p. 443

Connections: A Poem p. 444
"Now and Then, America"

Making Meanings p. 445

Beyond the Story

Choices: Building Your Portfolio p. 445

- **Writer's Notebook:** Collect ideas for an informative report
- **Critical Writing:** Compare and contrast two writers in essay
- **Creative Writing:** Write story of character's future life

Spotlight On pp. 446–448

BEFORE YOU READ

A PAIR OF SILK STOCKINGS

Reading Focus

Escaping the Humdrum

From time to time, everyone feels trapped by the humdrum duties of daily life. All of us—probably even rock stars and world travelers—fantasize about escape from routines that come to feel boring or confining. For a nineteenth-century woman of limited means trying to satisfy the needs of her family, even a brief reprieve from the demands of domestic life could be a life-changing bid for freedom and a temporary escape from society's shackles.

A Dialogue with the Text

Read the story's first two paragraphs, and then stop. Write down your predictions about what Mrs. Sommers will do with her unexpected gift of money—a sum equivalent to a generous weekly salary in the 1890s. Then, at the end of the story, write your guess as to what Mrs. Sommers is feeling.

Background

As you read, be aware that nylon had not yet been invented in the 1890s; most women wore long, thick, cotton stockings. Silk stockings ranked as pure luxury. Also, as you'll see in this story, fifteen dollars in the 1890s could buy far more than two tickets to the movies.

The Cup of Tea (1879) by Mary Cassatt (1844–1926). Oil on canvas (36⅜″ × 25¾″).

The Metropolitan Museum of Art, New York. From the Collection of James Stillman. Gift of Dr. Ernest G. Stillman, 1922 (22.16.17).

WORDS TO OWN

The following vocabulary words are defined in the Words to Own at the bottom of the pupil's page.

judicious p. 437
appreciable p. 437
veritable p. 437
acute p. 438
laborious p. 440
reveling p. 440
fastidious p. 440
preposterous p. 441
gaudy p. 442
poignant p. 443

PORTFOLIO ASSESSMENT

Portfolio Assessment For help with self- and teacher assessment of reading skills, see the *Portfolio Management System,* p. 53.

A Pair of Silk Stockings

Kate Chopin

Little Mrs. Sommers one day found herself the unexpected possessor of fifteen dollars. It seemed to her a very large amount of money, and the way in which it stuffed and bulged her worn old *porte-monnaie*[1] gave her a feeling of importance such as she had not enjoyed for years.

The question of investment was one that occupied her greatly. For a day or two she walked about apparently in a dreamy state, but really absorbed in speculation and calculation. She did not wish to act hastily, to do anything she might afterward regret. **A** But it was during the still hours of the night when she lay awake revolving plans in her mind that she seemed to see her way clearly toward a proper and judicious use of the money.

1. ***porte-monnaie*** (pôrt·mô·ne′): French for "purse."

A dollar or two should be added to the price usually paid for Janie's shoes, which would ensure their lasting an appreciable time longer than they usually did. She would buy so-and-so many yards of percale[2] for new shirtwaists for the boys and Janie and Mag. She had intended to make the old ones do by skillful patching. **B** Mag should have another gown. She had seen some beautiful patterns, veritable bargains in the shop windows. And still there would be left enough for new stockings—two pairs apiece—and what darning that would save for a while!

2. **percale:** finely woven cotton cloth.

WORDS TO OWN

judicious (jo͞o·dish′əs) *adj.:* cautious; wise.
appreciable (ə·prē′shə·bəl) *adj.:* measurable.
veritable (ver′i·tə·bəl) *adj.:* genuine; true.

Using **BEFORE YOU READ** p. 436

Reading Focus

Ask students to list the routines in their lives that seem boring or confining. Then, have students work with a partner to talk about what makes these routines boring. Have students share their ideas with the class.

A. Reader's Response: First Thoughts

? What might Mrs. Sommers do that she "might afterward regret"?

[Sample responses: Spend money on something foolish. Or get in trouble with her husband for spending the money.]

B. Critical Reading: Making Inferences

? What do these thoughts reveal about Mrs. Sommers' life?

[Possible answers: Money is a constant worry. Mrs. Sommers often must compromise on clothes for the children. She spends a great deal of time mending and patching what she does buy.]

PROGRAM MANAGER

- **Planning Instruction** See Teaching Notes, *Teaching Resources A,* p. 169, for objectives, a summary, literary elements, and additional historical and biographical information for this selection.
- **Instructional Support** Before beginning the instructional lesson, see Graphic Organizer for Active Reading, *Teaching Resources A,* p. 176, for a Through the Selection activity.
- **Audiotaped Readings** To help less proficient readers or auditory learners through the lesson, use the Selected Reading, Audiocassette 2, Side A, in the *Audiovisual Resources Binder.*

- **Assessment** See Selection Test, *Test Booklet,* pp. 103–104.
- **Reinforcement** Use the Words to Own worksheet in *Teaching Resources A,* p. 177

A. Critical Reading: Analyzing Character

? What kind of person might have this sort of "vision"? [Possible answers: A mother who worries about providing for her children; or a person who thinks of others first.]

B. Reader's Response: Connecting with the Text

? What does "tomorrow never comes" mean? [Sample responses: Mrs. Sommers deals with just one day at a time. Or if the future is a "monster," tomorrow could be something she does not want to happen.] How does Mrs. Sommers's image of her future compare with your own? [Sample responses: I count pennies now; I hope I will not have to later. Or times are better now; more money is available. Or I intend to get a good job.]

C. Critical Reading: Finding Details

? What sentence signals that Mrs. Sommers may be about to change her behavior? [The sentence "But that day she was a little faint and tired."]

D. Language Note: Sensory Words

? How does Chopin's word choice make these stockings seem attractive, even seductive? [She uses words that evoke the sense of sight—*sheeny, glisten*—and the sense of touch—*silk, soft, glide*. The words *glisten* and *glide* also appeal to the ear, even if the image does not. The word *diamond* conveys richness.]

(A) She would get caps for the boys and sailor hats for the girls. The vision of her little brood looking fresh and dainty and new for once in their lives excited her and made her restless and wakeful with anticipation.

The neighbors sometimes talked of certain "better days" that little Mrs. Sommers had known before she had ever thought of being Mrs. Sommers. She herself indulged in no such morbid retrospection.[3] She had no time—no second of time to devote to the past. The needs of the present absorbed her every faculty. (B) A vision of the future like some dim, gaunt monster sometimes appalled her, but luckily tomorrow never comes.

(C) Mrs. Sommers was one who knew the value of bargains; who could stand for hours making her way inch by inch toward the desired object that was selling below cost. She could elbow her way if need be; she had learned to clutch a piece of goods and hold it and stick to it with persistence and determination till her turn came to be served, no matter when it came.

But that day she was a little faint and tired. She had swallowed a light luncheon—no! when she came to think of it, between getting the children fed and the place righted, and preparing herself for the shopping bout, she had actually forgotten to eat any luncheon at all!

She sat herself upon a revolving stool before a counter that was comparatively deserted, trying to gather strength and courage to charge through an eager multitude that was besieging breastworks[4] of shirting and figured lawn. An all-gone limp feeling had come over her and she rested her hand aimlessly upon the counter. She wore no gloves. By degrees she grew aware that her hand had encountered something very soothing, very pleasant to touch. She looked down to see that her hand lay upon a pile of silk stockings. A placard nearby announced that they had been reduced in price from two dollars and fifty cents to one dollar and ninety-eight cents; and a young girl who stood behind the counter asked her if she wished to examine their line of silk hosiery. (D) She smiled, just as if she had been asked to inspect a tiara of diamonds with the ultimate view of purchasing it. But she went on feeling the soft, sheeny luxurious things—with both hands now, holding them up to see them glisten, and to feel them glide serpentlike through her fingers.

Two hectic blotches came suddenly into her pale cheeks. She looked up at the girl.

"Do you think there are any eights-and-a-half among these?"

There were any number of eights-and-a-half. In fact, there were more of that size than any other. Here was a light blue pair; there were some lavender, some all black, and various shades of tan and gray. Mrs. Sommers selected a black pair and looked at them very long and closely. She pretended to be examining their texture, which the clerk assured her was excellent.

"A dollar and ninety-eight cents," she mused aloud. "Well, I'll take this pair." She handed the girl a five-dollar bill and waited for her change and for her parcel. What a very small parcel it was! It seemed lost in the depths of her shabby old shopping bag.

Mrs. Sommers after that did not move in the direction of the bargain counter. She took the elevator, which carried her to an upper floor into the region of the ladies' waiting rooms. Here, in a retired corner, she exchanged her cotton stockings for the new silk ones which she had just bought. She was not going through any acute mental process or reasoning with herself, nor was she

3. **morbid retrospection:** brooding on unpleasant things in the past.
4. **breastworks:** low walls put up as barricades. The bolts of shirting material and fine patterned cotton, or "figured lawn," are compared to barricades being stormed by shoppers.

WORDS TO OWN

acute (ə·kyo͞ot′) *adj.:* keen; sharp.

OPTIONS FOR TEACHING

STRATEGIES FOR INCLUSION

Linguistic "A Pair of Silk Stockings" contains several words and phrases that are foreign or that evoke the culture of the 1890s. Encourage students who demonstrate a sensitivity to word choice to comment (after doing a little outside research, if necessary) on such words as *portemonnaie, shirtwaists, figured lawn,* and *crème-frappé.*

Visual Help students imagine a world that was starting to look like today's society but that still differed in a variety of ways. Bring in some pictures of cities in the 1890s (perhaps from a library picture file or from a history textbook) and discuss them before having students read independently. If applicable, display—perhaps with the help of a local historical society—some pictures of your community as it appeared in the 1890s; students will enjoy looking for buildings that still exist and commenting on how parts of town have changed.

Special Needs Use the Whip-Around-Pass strategy when discussing students' Reader's Responses on pp. T437, 438, and 443 or Making Meanings: First Thoughts on p. 445. This strategy involves asking each student in turn to address the subject or to say, "I pass." It serves to increase the number of students who participate as well as to give them practice in responsible self-management. This activity will especially benefit students who have motivational problems as well as those students who are reluctant to join in class discussion.

The Fitting (1891) by Mary Cassatt (1844–1926).
Color print with drypoint, softground, and aquatint (14¾″ × 10⅛″).

Chester Dale Collection, The National Gallery of Art, Washington, D.C.

RESPONDING TO THE ART: VISUAL LITERACY

Have students discuss how they think this painting is an appropriate illustration for "A Pair of Silk Stockings." [Possible response: It shows a woman having a dress fitted, which is not unlike Mrs. Sommers purchasing shoes and stockings.] **What might a pair of silk stockings mean to people of different classes in this time period?** [Possible response: Because they were probably expensive, someone from the upper class might take them for granted, while someone with less money might see them as a luxury.]

INTEGRATING THE LANGUAGE ARTS

Strategic Reading Have students team up with partners to work through Chopin's story using a Think-Aloud approach, in which partners freely question each other and otherwise encourage the other's comments as they read. Afterward, ask students to write brief evaluations of this activity. They should note insights gained through the exchange and give an overall rating of the format's effectiveness.

Writing: Prequel Invite pairs or groups of students to write a prequel to "A Pair of Silk Stockings," expanding on the "better days" that Mrs. Sommers once enjoyed and showing what happened to change her life. A panel of student judges might choose two stories to read to the class, or all of the stories might be displayed for students to read.

Speaking and Listening One of this story's most notable characteristics is the richness of its descriptions. Invite students to read aloud favorite passages, trying to use their voices to set each scene. To extend this activity, have a group of interested students present "A Pair of Silk Stockings" as a radio drama, complete with sound effects and background music.

LITERATURE AND HISTORY

Have students read "Elegant Discomfort." Ask them what fashions are popular today for each gender and for different age groups. Have them discuss what discomforts we suffer for fashion and the reasons for doing so. Invite them to talk about how people are judged by their clothing.

A. Critical Reading: Finding Cause and Effect

? Why is Mrs. Sommers behaving so unusually? [Possible answers: She is exhausted from years of penny-pinching worry and is taking a holiday from her real life. Or she is not able to think straight because she has gone so long without food.]

B. Critical Reading: Analyzing Character

? As you read this paragraph, how are your impressions of Mrs. Sommers starting to change? Do you like her more now, or less? [Possible answers: She seemed like a household drudge before; now she is showing more life. I like her better because I prefer people who go after what they want. Or she seems a little more snobbish, which makes me like her less.]

Literature and History

Elegant Discomfort

In the 1890s, clothing was layered, hot, heavy, and expensive. Rows of buttons fastened everything from men's pants to women's long gloves. Styles followed those of London and Paris. City shops carried, at a range of prices, everything from boots to ribbons, but women's dresses were still custom-made. By today's standards, people did not own much clothing, and they often had old garments remodeled instead of buying expensive new ones. The natural fabrics—wool, silk, cotton—could be spoiled by the harsh soaps of the day, so clothes were brushed more often than they were cleaned. Men and women alike used perfumes and scents to conceal odor.

Stepping out in style. A well-turned-out man in the 1890s wore a derby hat and a lined suit. His shirt had a long tail and a detachable collar. His coat was buttoned so high that it sometimes concealed his cravat (tie)—the one item declaring his personal taste. His underclothes might be knitted from wool. For outerwear, he might own an Inverness cape (a loose overcoat with an arm-length cape) or an Ulster (a long, belted coat). Men generally kept their hair trimmed above the collar, and many wore full moustaches or neat beards.

The fashionable woman of the time wore a large, brimmed hat and a full-length suit or dress. For clerical work or the new crazes of tennis and bicycling,

striving to explain to her satisfaction the motive of her action. She was not thinking at all. (A) She seemed for the time to be taking a rest from that laborious and fatiguing function and to have abandoned herself to some mechanical impulse that directed her actions and freed her of responsibility.

How good was the touch of the raw silk to her flesh! She felt like lying back in the cushioned chair and reveling for a while in the luxury of it. She did for a little while. Then she replaced her shoes, rolled the cotton stockings together, and thrust them into her bag. After doing this she crossed straight over to the shoe department and took her seat to be fitted.

(B) She was fastidious. The clerk could not make her out; he could not reconcile her shoes with her stockings, and she was not too easily pleased. She held back her skirts and turned her feet one way and her head another way as she glanced down at the polished, pointed-tipped boots. Her foot and ankle looked very pretty. She could not realize that they belonged to her and were a part of herself. She wanted an excellent and stylish fit, she

WORDS TO OWN

laborious (lə·bôr′ē·əs) *adj.:* difficult; involving much hard work.
reveling (rev′əl·iŋ) *v.:* taking pleasure.
fastidious (fas·tid′ē·əs) *adj.:* difficult to please; critical.

OPTIONS FOR TEACHING

CLASSROOM MANAGEMENT

Cooperative Learning If you present the Social Sciences activity on p. T441, you might give students the option of working through it in Jigsaw fashion. In this cooperative-learning technique, students as a class agree on the topics on which each group will report, and each group chooses a member to become an "expert" on that topic. "Experts" work together on research; then each "expert" returns to his or her group to share the information gained. If you make this a Jigsaw activity, encourage students to evaluate the format's effectiveness.

Volume Control If students engage in Think-Aloud reading (see the Strategic Reading suggestion, p. T439), classroom noise might become a problem. Arrange for a silent signal (such as flashing the classroom lights twice) if noise levels need to drop.

Block Scheduling To help stay organized if you are on a block schedule, fill in only the dates classes actually meet on class rosters and record grades only on the days classes meet. This may help avoid confusion later regarding what dates students were in class and what assignments were given.

C. Expansion

A kid glove is made of kidskin, leather from the skin of a young goat. The expression "to handle with kid gloves" means to treat someone or something tactfully and considerately.

D. Critical Reading: Speculating

? What can you gather about her past? [Possible answers: She came from a family that had money. Or she and her husband had more money to spend before they had children.]

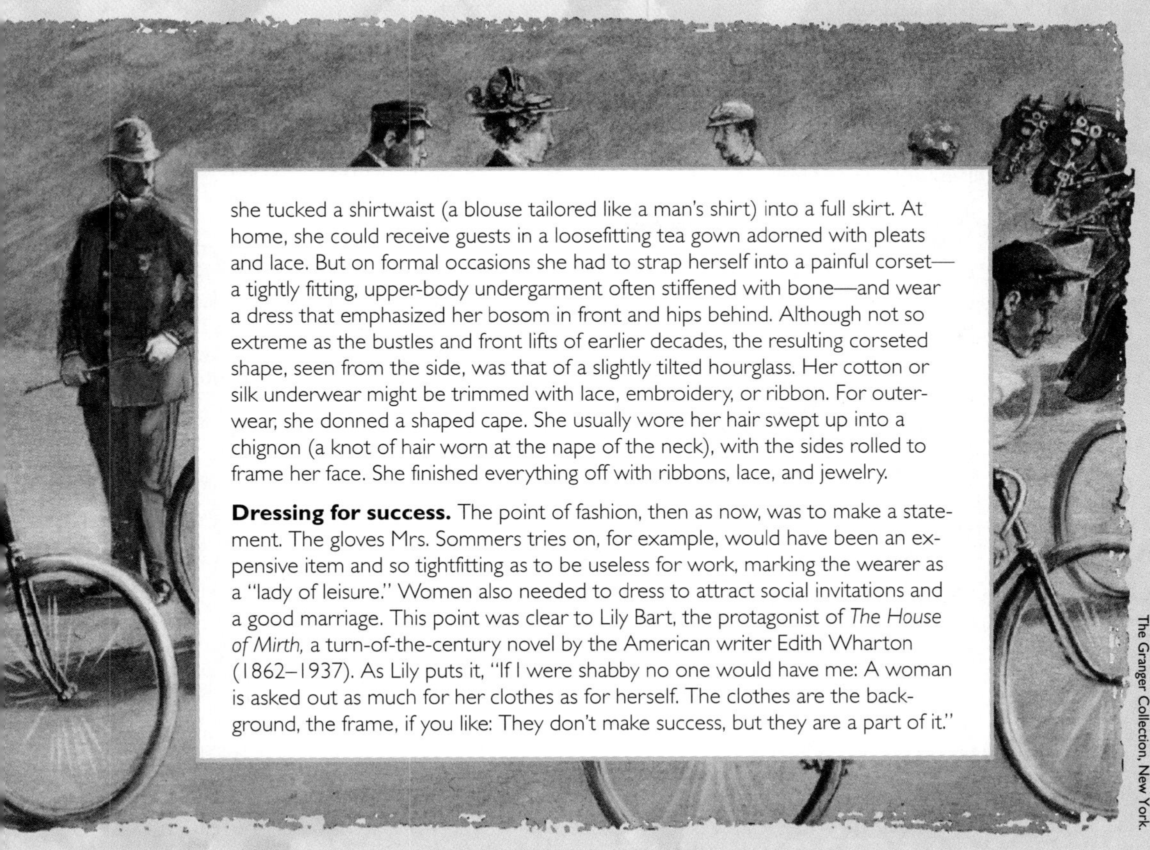

she tucked a shirtwaist (a blouse tailored like a man's shirt) into a full skirt. At home, she could receive guests in a loosefitting tea gown adorned with pleats and lace. But on formal occasions she had to strap herself into a painful corset—a tightly fitting, upper-body undergarment often stiffened with bone—and wear a dress that emphasized her bosom in front and hips behind. Although not so extreme as the bustles and front lifts of earlier decades, the resulting corseted shape, seen from the side, was that of a slightly tilted hourglass. Her cotton or silk underwear might be trimmed with lace, embroidery, or ribbon. For outerwear, she donned a shaped cape. She usually wore her hair swept up into a chignon (a knot of hair worn at the nape of the neck), with the sides rolled to frame her face. She finished everything off with ribbons, lace, and jewelry.

Dressing for success. The point of fashion, then as now, was to make a statement. The gloves Mrs. Sommers tries on, for example, would have been an expensive item and so tightfitting as to be useless for work, marking the wearer as a "lady of leisure." Women also needed to dress to attract social invitations and a good marriage. This point was clear to Lily Bart, the protagonist of *The House of Mirth,* a turn-of-the-century novel by the American writer Edith Wharton (1862–1937). As Lily puts it, "If I were shabby no one would have me: A woman is asked out as much for her clothes as for herself. The clothes are the background, the frame, if you like: They don't make success, but they are a part of it."

The Granger Collection, New York.

told the young fellow who served her, and she did not mind the difference of a dollar or two more in the price so long as she got what she desired.

It was a long time since Mrs. Sommers had been fitted with gloves. On rare occasions when she had bought a pair they were always "bargains," so cheap that it would have been preposterous and unreasonable to have expected them to be fitted to the hand.

Now she rested her elbow on the cushion of the glove counter, and a pretty, pleasant young creature, delicate and deft of touch, drew a long-wristed "kid" over Mrs. Sommers's hand. **C** She smoothed it down over the wrist and buttoned it neatly, and both lost themselves for a second or two in admiring contemplation of the little symmetrical gloved hand. But there were other places where money might be spent.

There were books and magazines piled up in the window of a stall a few paces down the street. Mrs. Sommers bought two high-priced magazines such as she had been accustomed to read in the days when she had been accustomed to other pleasant things. **D** She carried them without wrapping. As well as she could she lifted her skirts at the crossings. Her stockings and boots and well-fitting gloves had worked marvels in her bearing—had given her

Words to Own

preposterous (prē·päs′tər·əs) *adj.:* ridiculous.

CROSSING THE CURRICULUM

Mathematics Fifteen dollars does not seem to be "a very large amount of money" today; invite students to discover specifically what it was worth in the 1890s. Have students study newspapers and magazines of the era (if available on microfilm) as well as history books. Challenge them to find out and report on

- what a restaurant meal, a pair of kid gloves, and other items mentioned in the story probably would have cost at that time
- how long a person (in particular, a woman) of that era might have to work to earn that much money and at what various occupations
- what Mrs. Sommers's spending spree might cost in today's dollars

Social Sciences Have interested students research and report to the class on various aspects of urban life in the 1890s. Students might form committees and collaborate to present facts on politics, employment (for men, women, and children), leisure pursuits (including sports), technology (including inventions), immigration, fashion, popular culture, or another subject that interests them. Encourage students to think of original ways to present their information—perhaps through skits, radio or TV talk shows, or rap songs.

A. Literary Element: Symbolism

? What do Mrs. Sommers's purchases mean to her? [Possible answers: They give her pleasure in themselves and perhaps symbolize an earlier, "better" life. Or they represent self-esteem and freedom.]

Trade card of a glove manufacturer (c. 1890).

A a feeling of assurance, a sense of belonging to the well-dressed multitude.

She was very hungry. Another time she would have stilled the cravings for food until reaching her own home, where she would have brewed herself a cup of tea and taken a snack of anything that was available. But the impulse that was guiding her would not suffer her to entertain any such thought.

There was a restaurant at the corner. She had never entered its doors; from the outside she had sometimes caught glimpses of spotless damask and shining crystal, and soft-stepping waiters serving people of fashion.

When she entered, her appearance created no surprise, no consternation, as she had half feared it might. She seated herself at a small table alone, and an attentive waiter at once approached to take her order. She did not want a profusion; she craved a nice and tasty bite—a half dozen bluepoints,[5] a plump chop with cress, a something sweet—a crème-frappé,[6] for instance; a glass of Rhine wine, and after all a small cup of black coffee.

While waiting to be served she removed her gloves very leisurely and laid them beside her. Then she picked up a magazine and glanced through it, cutting the pages with a blunt edge of her knife.[7] It was all very agreeable. The damask was even more spotless than it had seemed through the window, and the crystal more sparkling. There were quiet ladies and gentlemen, who did not notice her, lunching at the small tables like her own. A soft, pleasing strain of music could be heard, and a gentle breeze was blowing through the window. She tasted a bite, and she read a word or two, and she sipped the amber wine and wiggled her toes in the silk stockings. The price of it made no difference. She counted the money out to the waiter and left an extra coin on his tray, whereupon he bowed before her as before a princess of royal blood.

There was still money in her purse, and her next temptation presented itself in the shape of a matinée poster.

It was a little later when she entered the theater, the play had begun, and the house seemed to her to be packed. But there were vacant seats here and there, and into one of them she was ushered, between brilliantly dressed women who had gone there to kill time and eat candy and display their gaudy attire. There were many others who were there solely for the play and acting. It is safe to say there was

5. **bluepoints:** small oysters.
6. **crème-frappé** (krem·fra·pā'): dessert similar to ice cream.
7. **cutting . . . knife:** At one time, magazines and books were often sold with folded, untrimmed pages. These outer edges had to be cut apart before one could read them.

WORDS TO OWN

gaudy (gôd'ē) *adj.:* cheap; showy.

OPTIONS FOR TEACHING

ASSESSMENT TOOLS

Peer Assessment After students have read "A Pair of Silk Stockings," ask them to share their first thoughts about it with partners. Have each student use the following statements to rate his or her partner's comments.

1=Definitely 2=Probably 3=Doubtful

___ Understands the facts and basic meaning of the story

___ Relates the story to the "Shackles" theme of the Collection

___ Offers insights about theme, characterization, and other story elements

___ Makes personal connections

Check Test: Questions and Answers

1. Initially, how does Mrs. Sommers plan to spend the money that she has received? [To buy or make clothes for her children.]
2. How does she come to make the first use of the money for herself? [She buys a pair of silk stockings.]
3. According to the narrator, how do Mrs. Sommers's purchases make her feel? [They give her "a feeling of assurance."]
4. What uses of the money would be considered "entertainment"? [Magazines, lunch in a fancy restaurant, and a matinee.]
5. How does Mrs. Sommers feel as she returns home? [She has a deep, poignant longing not to return to her difficult "real" life.]

no one present who bore quite the attitude which Mrs. Sommers did to her surroundings. She gathered in the whole—stage and players and people in one wide impression, and absorbed it and enjoyed it. She laughed at the comedy and wept—she and the gaudy woman next to her wept over the tragedy. And they talked a little together over it. And the gaudy woman wiped her eyes and sniffled on a tiny square of filmy, perfumed lace and passed little Mrs. Sommers her box of candy. B

The play was over, the music ceased, the crowd filed out. It was like a dream ended. People scattered in all directions. Mrs. Sommers went to the corner and waited for the cable car.

A man with keen eyes, who sat opposite her, seemed to like the study of her small, pale face. It puzzled him to decipher what he saw there. In truth, he saw nothing—unless he were wizard enough to detect a poignant wish, a powerful longing that the cable car would never stop anywhere, but go on and on with her forever. C

Words to Own

poignant (poin′yənt) *adj.:* emotionally moving.

Primary Sources | **A Biography**

Vogue Stories

Kate Chopin had trouble selling her stories. *Vogue* magazine, whose readership consisted mainly of young women from wealthy families, published much of her work.

The title of Chopin's last *Vogue* story of the 1890s, "A Pair of Silk Stockings," suggests a tale for the rich—but it is really a message to *Vogue* readers about how the other half lives. Its central character, a struggling mother who once had "certain better days," must now scrimp to buy necessities for her children. But when Mrs. Sommers suddenly finds herself with fifteen dollars, she yields to temptation and spends all the money on herself: silk stockings, new boots, kid gloves, a tasty lunch, and a matinée. On the streetcar home, she feels "a poignant wish, a powerful longing that the cable car would never stop anywhere, but go on and on with her forever."

Mrs. Sommers was the kind of woman that *Vogue* readers might pass by on the street without noticing—but by the late 1890s, living frugally in St. Louis, Kate Chopin had seen the effects of poverty and urban strife on women. *Vogue,* unlike other magazines, did not expect her to write for "the young person" about domesticity and womanly self-sacrifice. *Vogue* allowed her to describe what she had seen, honestly and fearlessly.

Vogue moved with her; other magazines refused.

—Emily Toth, *from Kate Chopin*

The Bettmann Archive.

B. Exploring the Culture
According to Chopin, Mrs. Sommers attended a play that combined elements of comedy and tragedy. In the 1890s, this may well have meant a play about American life (as opposed to prior generations' preference for European plays). That does not necessarily mean, however, that it was a play about "real" life; rather, comedies that exaggerated aspects of urban life were quite fashionable. Also popular at this time were melodramas, sometimes featuring an honest young woman who must fend off a city slicker. These plays often had vivid special effects—snowstorms, fires, and the like—and cost from ten to thirty cents per ticket.

C. Reader's Response: Challenging the Text
? Do you think that it was wise of Chopin to introduce a new character at the very end of the story? Explain. [Sample responses: It was wise, for the man is a valuable addition in that he offers a different perspective, enabling us to see Mrs. Sommers as strangers see her. Or Chopin did well, for the man's view of Mrs. Sommers suggests that every person has a "story" that others do not know anything about. Or it was not wise, for readers wonder what might happen between the two of them.]

Primary Sources

Have several students do some research to find out which magazines still encourage new writers to send manuscripts and which rely primarily on material sent by literary agents. Students can consult professional guides such as *The Writer's Market, The Writer's Handbook,* and *Literary Market Place.* Encourage students to discuss their findings.

STRATEGIES FOR INCLUSION

Visual Bring in a copy or facsimile of a 1890s *Vogue* magazine to give students an idea of what it published and of the culture in which the story was set.

Interpersonal Ask students to speculate on and discuss what motives Kate Chopin might have had in writing her story and publishing it in *Vogue* magazine.

CROSSING THE CURRICULUM

Art Have students illustrate "A Pair of Silk Stockings" for *Vogue* magazine. Have them research the illustrations of the period, and ask them to illustrate the story in the same style. Display their work.

Mathematics *Vogue* magazine was sold primarily to young, wealthy women. Have students find out what the cost of the magazine was in the 1890s and what the cost would be of a comparable magazine today. Also, have students determine the price *Vogue* paid for a short story in the 1890s and what a magazine might pay today. Keeping inflation in mind, have them determine whether the increase in price today over what *Vogue* paid in the 1890s is in keeping with the increase in the cost of living.

A. Reader's Response: First Thoughts

? How do you respond to the speaker's question? [Sample responses: I agree with the speaker: I do not want to rot. Or she paints a dismal picture of the graveyard, but that is how many look.]

B. Reader's Response: Shaping Interpretations

? How do you interpret this line? [Sample responses: The speaker feels restricted by life in the United States; or the speaker wants to do something different with her life and does not want to do what others do.]

C. Literary Element: Contrast

? How does this "in" contrast with those that have come before? [Possible answer: The previous ones have been repetitive and emphasized confinement; this one contrasts and focuses on the speaker's being accepted for the person she is.]

D. Critical Reading: Making Inferences

? How does the speaker view death? [Possible answers: Death is part of the cycle of life. The speaker wants to be commemorated by life after she dies and not by plastic flowers.]

PROGRAM MANAGER

Audiotaped Readings To help less proficient readers or auditory learners through the lesson, use the **Selected Reading, Audiocassette 2, Side A,** in the ***Audiovisual Resources Binder.***

Connections A POEM

Now and Then, America

Pat Mora

Who wants to rot
beneath dry, winter grass
in a numbered grave
in a numbered row
in a section labeled Eternal Peace
with neighbors plagued
by limp, plastic roses
springing from their toes?
Grant me a little life now and then, America.

Who wants to rot
as she marches through life
in a pinstriped suit
neck chained in a soft, silk bow
in step, in style, insane.
Let me in
to boardrooms wearing hot
colors, my hair long and free,
maybe speaking Spanish.
Risk my difference, my surprises.
Grant me a little life, America.

And when I die, plant *zempasúchitl,*
flowers of the dead, and at my head
plant organ cactus, green fleshy
fingers sprouting, like in Oaxaca.
Let desert creatures hide
in the orange blooms.
Let birds nest in the cactus stems.
Let me go knowing life
flower and song
will continue right above my bones.

Pat Mora.
Arte Publico Press.

CONNECTING WITH "A PAIR OF SILK STOCKINGS"

Have students discuss the ways in which both Mrs. Sommers in "A Pair of Silk Stockings" and the speaker in "Now and Then, America" may feel shackled or chained. Ask them to identify what each wants for their lives. Students could use a cluster like the following to help them organize their thoughts.

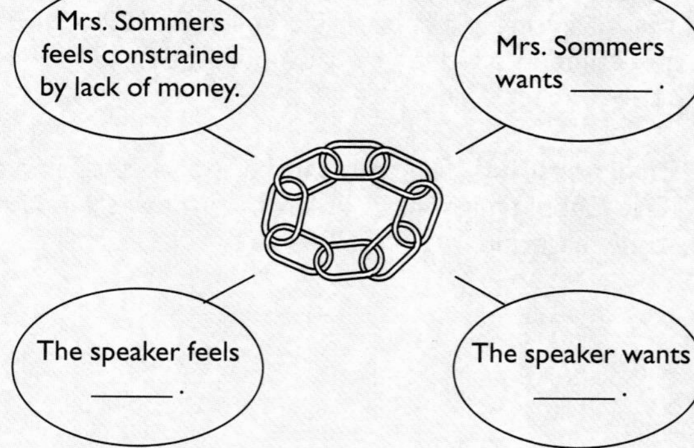

Making Meanings

First Thoughts

Reviewing the Text

a. List the uses Mrs. Sommers plans to make of the fifteen dollars.

b. List the items on which Mrs. Sommers actually spends the money.

1. What is Mrs. Sommers feeling as we leave her on the streetcar? Look back at your Reader's Log notes. When her afternoon has ended and she must return to her family, how do you think Mrs. Sommers will feel?

Shaping Interpretations

2. The author describes her as "little Mrs. Sommers," and we learn that she has four children, lacks the time to recall "better days," and regards the future as a "dim, gaunt monster." No mention is made of her husband or source of income. How would you describe the **character** of Mrs. Sommers? How do you feel about what she does with the fifteen dollars?
3. What details about Mrs. Sommers's earlier life might help explain the motivation for her shopping spree?
4. When Mrs. Sommers first feels the silk stockings, they "glide serpentlike" through her fingers. What does a serpent often **symbolize** in Western culture? Explain whether or not you think Chopin's use of the word here is significant.

Extending the Text

5. This story is over a hundred years old. Do you think it is an old-fashioned story that could not happen today, or is the story still relevant? Could you see Mrs. Sommers in a TV sitcom? Could her conflict also be experienced by a man?

Challenging the Text

6. A feminist critic might say that this story is about a woman who strikes out to gain personal freedom and identity. A Marxist critic might say it is about the class struggle. The critic Barbara C. Ewell writes, "The power of money to enhance self-esteem and confidence is the core of this poignant tale." Which critic, if any, do you agree with? Why?

Choices: Building Your Portfolio

Writer's Notebook

1. Collecting Ideas for an Informative Report

WORK IN PROGRESS

Brainstorm a list of topics suggested by Chopin's story that you would be interested in reporting on, such as women's issues, the evolution of clothing, or city life in the 1890s. For each topic, list some effective ways to present the information that you might gather for your report: interviews, descriptions, drawings, and tables or charts. Save your notes for possible use in the Writer's Workshop on page 515.

Critical Writing

2. Breaking Bonds

Both Chopin and Pat Mora (Connections, page 444) write about escape, freedom, identity, and individuality. In a brief essay, compare and contrast the two writers' attitudes toward these **themes.** What kinds of images do they each use to convey their messages?

Creative Writing

3. The Untold Story

At the end of the story, Mrs. Sommers wishes the cable car could "go on and on" without ever stopping. What do you think the rest of Mrs. Sommers's life will be like? (Do you think she ever purchased more silk stockings in those gorgeous colors she failed to buy the first time?) Write one or more paragraphs telling the rest of Mrs. Sommers's story. Try to keep your version consistent with the character created in the story.

Making Meanings

First Thoughts

1. Possible responses: Mrs. Sommers does not want to go home. Mrs. Sommers will feel she has been selfish or that has wasted money.

Reviewing the Text

a. At first Mrs. Sommers intends to buy shoes, fabric and a pattern for clothes, stockings, caps, and hats—all for her children.

b. She buys herself silk stockings, shoes, gloves, and magazines. She eats in a fine restaurant and attends a play.

Shaping Interpretations

2. Possible responses: She is a thoughtful woman. She has selfishly indulged herself at the expense of her children. Or she well deserves a day off and a bit of self-indulgence.
3. Mrs. Sommers apparently was better off before her marriage. She did not have to scrimp and compromise to make purchases. Her behavior in the shoe store suggests she used to be very particular about style and fit, with price no object. There were "pleasant things" in those days, including high-priced magazines.
4. A serpent often symbolizes sin, temptation, or evil. The word *serpentlike* is appropriate because the luxurious stockings tempt Mrs. Sommers away from her selfless intention to buy clothing for her children and into a day of self-indulgent spending.

Extending the Text

5. **(Synthesis)** Possible responses: It is not old-fashioned, for people still want to escape their situations today. Or it is old-fashioned, because people today do not go into ecstasy over a pair of silk stockings. She would not appear in a sitcom because her story is too sad; it is not funny. Men could act on the same impulse; they need escape at times, too.

Challenging the Text

6. **(Evaluation)** Student opinions will vary. Ask them to defend their views with details from the story. Those who defend the feminist view might note that Mrs. Sommers struggles for freedom from overwhelming, never-ending burdens. Those who defend the Marxist view might say her poverty is a condition of her class resulting from the oppression of capitalism. Those who defend Ewell's view might say money enables Mrs. Sommers to have a moment of relief.

Choices: Building Your Portfolio

1. **Writer's Notebook** Remind students to save their work. They may use it as prewriting for the Writer's Workshop on p. 515.

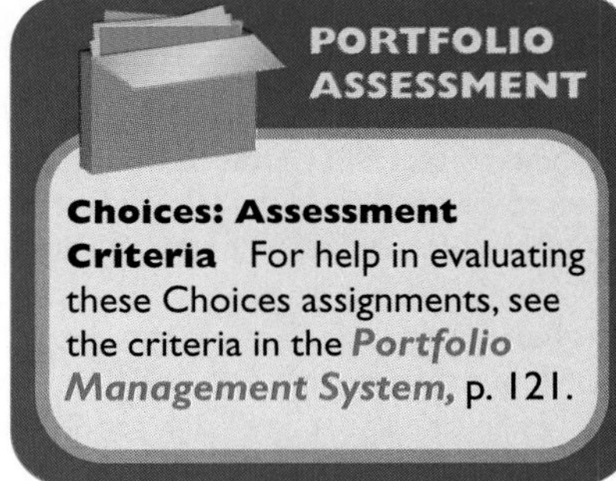

A. Exploring the Historical Period
Black Hawk was both a famous orator and a skilled warrior. He participated in war parties at the age of fifteen, and he trained to become a medicine man. During the War of 1812, he aided the British; afterward, he continued to urge his band of Sauks to fight against the white Americans who were uprooting their lives. After his capture, Black Hawk was sent to see several cities along the East Coast, and he became convinced that the whites were too powerful and numerous to defeat. He died in a Native American village along the Des Moines River in 1838.

B. Critical Reading: Expressing an Opinion
Black Hawk's speech is persuasive in intent. Why, then, do you think he spends so much time on description? [Possible answer: He wants to paint a rich picture to remind his listeners of all that was good in their lives and to reinforce the sense of loss; it is that sense of loss that will drive his persuasive intent.]

C. Literary Element: Figures of Speech
? How does Black Hawk use **personification** and **metaphor** here? [He speaks of the Sauks' glory as if it had run away; he compares their former standing to that of a bear and their present standing to that of a rabbit.] What overall image does he seem to be conveying to his listeners? [The image of a spiritually impoverished people.]

SPOTLIGHT ON

American Indian Oratory

In the nineteenth century, American Indians felt keenly the shackles placed on them by the United States government. As the westward migration of European settlers increased, due in part to the California gold rush (1849) and the Civil War (1861–1865), Native Americans were forced to defend their land; more than two hundred fierce battles were fought between 1869 and 1878 alone.

For centuries, most American Indians have relied on spoken language for diplomacy, decision making, and preservation of their history and culture. In Native American cultures, spoken language mystically links the natural and spiritual worlds and has the power to shape and control events. Thus, American Indians have often chosen their leaders in part for their eloquence. Important speeches are even memorized exactly as spoken and passed on orally to future generations.

Faced with the destruction of their traditional way of life, Native Americans hoped that eloquent words might succeed where other weapons had failed. Their hopes were misplaced.

A

Black Hawk

Black Hawk (1767–1838) was born in what today is Illinois. He was leader of the Sauks—a group of Algonquian peoples native to the present states of Michigan, Wisconsin, and Illinois. A proven warrior since his teens, Black Hawk earned renown for personal bravery and for spellbinding oratory that roused his listeners to action. Although he was eventually captured, Black Hawk spent much of his life battling against the spread of European settlement. In the following excerpt from the speech he made in April 1832, Black Hawk inspires his people to defend their land.

"For More Than a Hundred Winters Our Nation Was a Powerful, Happy, and United People"

Headmen, Chiefs, Braves, and Warriors of the Sauks: For more than a hundred winters our nation was a powerful, happy, and united people. B The Great Spirit gave to us a territory, seven hundred miles in length, along the Mississippi, reaching from Prairie du Chien[1] to the mouth of the Illinois River. This vast territory was composed of some of the finest and best land for the home and use of the Indian ever found in this country. The woods and prairies teemed with buffalo, moose, elk, bear, and deer, with other game suitable to our enjoyment, while its lakes, rivers, creeks, and ponds were alive with the very best kinds of fish, for our food. The islands in the Mississippi were our gardens, where the Great Spirit caused berries, plums, and other fruits to grow in great abundance, while the soil, when cultivated, produced corn, beans, pumpkins, and squash of the finest quality and largest quantities. Our children were never known to cry of hunger, and no stranger, red or white, was permitted to enter our lodges without finding food and rest. Our nation was respected by all who came in contact with it, for we had the ability as well as the courage to defend and maintain our rights of territory, person, and property against the world. Then, indeed, was it an honor to be called a Sauk, for that name was a passport to our people traveling in other C territories and among other nations. But an evil day befell us when we became a divided nation, and with that division our glory deserted us, leaving us with the hearts and heels of the rabbit in place of the courage and strength of the bear.

All this was brought about by the long guns, who now claim all our territory east of the

1. **Prairie du Chien:** trading town at the junction of the Wisconsin and Mississippi Rivers; now a city in Wisconsin.

OPTIONS FOR TEACHING

STRATEGIES FOR INCLUSION

Special Needs Cooperative learning is a good way to foster participation and to teach acceptance of differing ability levels. After students listen to or read each speech, have them work in groups to express, in complete sentences, the main idea and tone of each speech.

English Language Development Memorization and recitation are excellent practice for pronunciation. Divide the class into two groups and assign one speech to each group. Have each student read the entire speech and memorize an assigned portion of it for homework. Then, let each group perform their speech in unison for the other group in class.

COOPERATIVE LEARNING

Native American Research Have students work in groups of five. Ask them to research one of the Native American groups mentioned here—Sauks or Nez Percé. Groups will need to assign topics to each member. The group will also need to assign someone to be responsible for graphics and pictures. Have each group present its completed research findings to the class. Then, ask the class to talk about the similarities and differences between the Native American groups.

Black Hawk and Five Other Saukie Prisoners (1861–1869) by George Catlin. Oil on paperboard mounted on heavier paperboard (18⅝″ × 24¹⁵⁄₁₆″).

National Gallery of Art, Washington, D.C. Paul Mellon Collection. Photo by Bob Grove.

Black Hawk, Prominent Sauk Chief (1832) by George Catlin. Oil on canvas (29″ × 24″).

National Museum of American Art, Washington, D.C. Gift of Mrs. Joseph Harrison, Jr. Courtesy Art Resource.

Mississippi, including Saukenuk,[2] our ancient village, where all of us were born, raised, lived, hunted, fished, and loved, and near which are our corn lands, which have yielded abundant harvests for a hundred winters, and where sleep the bones of our sacred dead, and around which cluster our fondest recollections of heroism and noble deeds of charity done by our fathers, who were Sauks, not only in name, but in courage and action. I thank the Great Spirit for making me a Sauk, and the son of a great Sauk chief, and a lineal descendant of Nanamakee, the founder of our nation.

The Great Spirit is the friend and protector of the Sauks, and has accompanied me as your War Chief upon the warpath against our enemies, and has given me skill to direct and you the courage to achieve a hundred victories over our enemies upon the warpath. . . . The Great Spirit created this country for the use and benefit of his red children, and placed them in full possession of it, and we were happy and contented. Why did he send the palefaces across the great ocean to take it from us? When they landed on our territory they were received as long-absent brothers whom the Great Spirit had returned to us. Food and rest were freely given them by our fathers, who treated them all the more kindly on account of their weak and helpless condition. Had our fathers the desire, they could have crushed the intruders out of existence with the same ease we kill the bloodsucking mosquitoes. Little did our fathers then think they were taking to their bosoms, and warming them to life, a lot of torpid, half-frozen, and starving vipers, which in a few winters would fix their deadly fangs upon the very bosoms that had nursed and cared for them when they needed help.

—Black Hawk

2. **Saukenuk:** a village of the Sauk (a Native American people) that is located where the Rock River joins the Mississippi; present-day site of Rock Island, Illinois.

D. Reader's Response: First Thoughts

? Of all these details relating to the Sauks' past location, which one do you think Black Hawk considers most important? [Sample responses: The "heroism and noble deeds" of his listeners' ancestors who lived there. Or the ancestors themselves.]

Metacognition How did you derive your answer? [Possible answer: The detail comes last, as if it were the end of a sequence arranged in order of importance. Or he talks about people at the beginning and at the end of this passage.]

E. Literary Element: Metaphor

? How are the "palefaces" like "torpid, half-frozen, and starving vipers"? [When European settlers first came, they needed the Native Americans' help to survive. The Native Americans gave that help, only to be overpowered when the whites grew strong.]

PROGRAM MANAGER

Audiotaped Readings To help readers through the lesson, use the **Selected Reading, Audiocassette 2, Side B,** in the ***Audiovisual Resources Binder.***

CROSSING THE CURRICULUM

Art Have students create a collage depicting their responses to the experiences of the Native Americans described in the speeches.

Geography On a large map of the United States, have students label the areas where particular Native American groups lived originally, and where they traveled or were relocated.

Health In light of Black Hawk's remarks, have students analyze the eating habits of the Sauks or other Native American groups of the time. Ask students to determine how specific changes in diet may have affected their health.

Social Sciences The speakers in this feature are among the best known of all Native American leaders. Some information about each speaker appears in the text and in the Exploring the Historical Period notes; but encourage students (working individually or in small groups) to research each speaker's life in greater detail and report to the class. Encourage students to include information about the speeches; in particular, ask them to note whether each speech was a high or low point in the speaker's life and how the speech either ended a series of events or set new events into motion. Students also might include information about how each leader is viewed by Native Americans today.

A. Exploring the Historical Period

Chief Joseph was admired in his own time both by his people and by whites. In the history of the displacement of Native Americans, he is remembered as a figure of poignant heroism.

In 1863, the group of Nez Percé led by Chief Joseph's father refused to sign a treaty that would send them to a reservation. In 1871, the old chief, now dying, urged his son, "You must stop your ears whenever you are asked to sign a treaty selling your home. . . . This country holds your father's body. Never sell the bones of your father and your mother." After their 1877 flight, only 431 people out of some 700 remained in the refugee band, most of them women and children. On October 5, Chief Joseph gave this speech of surrender to General Oliver O. Howard and Colonel Nelson A. Miles.

B. Literary Element: Repetition

? What repeated word conveys Chief Joseph's grief over what has happened to his people? [Dead.] How do the phrasing and the sentence structure further underscore the idea? [Many of the sentences are phrased in the same way, in the passive voice, forming a catalog of those who have died.]

C. Reader's Response: Shaping Interpretations

? After he had fought so valiantly, why do you think Chief Joseph gave up all hope? [Sample responses: He saw his people suffering and he knew that he and his people could not go back to the way life had been. Or he knew there was no way he could fight and win.]

(A) Chief Joseph

Born in what is now Oregon, Chief Joseph (c.1840–1904) has become a symbol of the heroic fighting spirit of his people, the Nez Percé. In battles during 1877, he fought thirteen different U.S. military commands, defeating almost all of them. He then conducted a masterful, one thousand-mile retreat toward Canada through the mountainous country of the Pacific Northwest. His caravan, which included women and children, made it to within forty miles of the border before exhaustion and near starvation forced them to surrender after eleven weeks of flight. Chief Joseph delivered the following speech upon his surrender to the U.S. Army in October 1877. He spent the rest of his life on a reservation in the present-day state of Washington.

"I Will Fight No More Forever"

Tell General Howard[1] I know his heart. What he told me before, I have in my heart. I am tired of fighting. Our chiefs are killed. Looking Glass[2] is dead. Toohoolhoolzote[3] is dead. The old men are all dead. It is the young men who say yes and no. He who led on the young men is dead. (B) It is cold and we have no blankets. The little children are freezing to death. My people, some of them, have run away to the hills and have no blankets, no food; no one knows where they are—perhaps freezing to death. I want to have time to look for my children and see how many I can find. Maybe I shall find them among the dead. Hear me, my chiefs. I am tired; my heart is sick and sad. From where the sun now stands I will fight no more forever. (C)

—Chief Joseph

1. **General Howard:** Oliver Otis Howard (1830–1909), Civil War general and founder of Howard University in Washington, D.C. (1867). Howard was the military commander who presented the Nez Percé with an ultimatum to give up their land in Idaho and move to a reservation.
2. **Looking Glass** (c. 1823–1877): ally of Chief Joseph. Looking Glass was killed in battle on the day this speech was given.
3. **Toohoolhoolzote** (c. 1810–1877): Nez Percé shaman and chief who argued against giving up Nez Percé lands.

OPTIONS FOR TEACHING

ASSESSMENT TOOLS

Peer Assessment To encourage students to become effective members of a cooperative group as in the Cooperative Learning activity on p. T446, have them assess their participation by writing down comments on how well they did on each of the following:

1. Contributing to the discussion
2. Encouraging others to speak
3. Evaluating the group's comments

Check Test: Questions and Answers

1. How does Black Hawk claim the Sauks were regarded by others? [They were respected for their courage and ability to defend their land, and for their hospitality to strangers.]
2. How does Black Hawk want his listeners to respond to the wrongs against them? [He wants them to go to war.]
3. What changes does Black Hawk observe in his people? [They have become a divided nation.]
4. What became of Chief Joseph and his people? [They retreated toward Canada, surrendered, and retired to a reservation in the state of Washington.]
5. Why does Chief Joseph desire to "fight no more forever"? [He is tired of fighting; his people are dead, dying, or lost without provisions; he wants to find as many in his family as are still alive.]

FROM INNOCENCE TO EXPERIENCE

Theme: **The Inner and Outer Self**

American Realism relied on the emerging sciences of human and animal behavior; to this new knowledge, writers added their own observations of living in a country that had finally come of age, severely tested by a war that pitted region against region. From this experience grew the literary movement known as Regionalism, which emphasized people's peculiarities of manner, attitude, and speech pattern in a particular geographic setting.

Thematic Focus

The protagonists of the selections in Collection 10 experience conflicts involving self-knowledge and the external world.

- *from* **Life on the Mississippi** The river, once known and understood scientifically, is no longer a source of mystery and wonder.
- **An Occurrence at Owl Creek Bridge** Here are the thoughts and images in Peyton Farquhar's mind moments before he is hanged.
- **A Mystery of Heroism** Private Collins darts across a battlefield on a dare, an act that may be no more foolish or heroic than war itself.
- **To Build a Fire** Lacking practical knowledge and experience—or animal instincts—a man tries to survive in the barren Yukon.

Literary Focus

Literary Element	Selection / Feature
Extended Metaphor	**Life on the Mississippi**
Point of View	**An Occurrence at Owl Creek Bridge**
Situational Irony	**A Mystery of Heroism**
Naturalism	**To Build a Fire**

Writing Focus

The following chart shows how the writing assignment for each selection relates to and builds toward the culminating writing assignment presented in the Writer's Workshop at the end of the unit.

Selection	Work-in-Progress Assignment
Life on the Mississippi	Freewrite about a place for a report of information p. 464
An Occurrence at Owl Creek Bridge	List research sources for a report of information p. 474
A Mystery of Heroism	Conduct an attitudinal survey for a report of information p. 494
To Build a Fire	Freewrite about ways to approach audiences for a report of information p. 510
Writer's Workshop	Write an informative report pp. 515-519

Collection 10 **FROM INNOCENCE TO EXPERIENCE**

Collection Planner

SELECTION/ FEATURE	PUPIL'S EDITION			
	Literary Elements / Active Reading	Writing	Speaking and Listening	Language and Vocabulary
from **Life on the Mississippi** Mark Twain (pp. 450–465) Spotlight On: Mark Twain's Humor (p. 465)	• Reader's Log p. 452 • Extended Metaphor p. 452	• Critical Writing: Write essay p. 464 • Creative Writing: Write description p. 464 • Art/Research: Write paragraphs p. 464 • Creative Writing/ Research/Art: Write magazine story p. 464	• Speaking and Listening: Perform oral reading p. 464	• Language and Style: Twain's Humor p. 463
An Occurrence at Owl Creek Bridge Ambrose Bierce (pp. 466–483) Spotlight On: Voices from the Civil War (pp. 476–483)	• Reader's Log p. 467 • Point of View p. 467	• Critical Writing: Write memorandum for adaptation p. 474 • Creative Writing: Write narrative exploring character's thoughts p. 474		• How to Own a Word: Affixes p. 475
A Mystery of Heroism Stephen Crane (pp. 484–494) **Student to Student** (p. 493)	• Reader's Log p. 485 • Situational Irony p. 485	• Critical Writing: Write summary p. 494 • Creative Writing: Write poem or short prose piece p. 494		
To Build a Fire Jack London (pp. 495–510) **Connections: Cold Kills** Paul G. Gill, Jr., M.D. (p. 508)	• Reader's Log p. 496 • Naturalism p. 496	• Critical Writing: Write essay p. 510 • Creative Writing/ Role-Playing: Create dialogue p. 510 • Crossing the Curriculum: Science: Create survival manual p. 510 • Creative Writing: Write story p. 510	• Creative Writing/ Role-Playing: Role-play dialogue p. 510 • Performance: Present tape-recorded oral reading p. 510 • Performance: Make a recording p. 510	
The American Language American Dialects Gary Q. Arpin (pp. 512–514)	• American Dialects pp. 512–514			• Try It Out: Explore dialect p. 514
Writer's Workshop: Informative Report (pp. 515–519)		• Writing process: Write informative report pp. 515–519		
Language Workshop: Adverb and Adjective Clauses (p. 520)				• Try It Out: Combine sentences using clauses p. 520
Learning for Life: Monitoring the Media (p. 521)		• Research the media p. 521	• Panel discussion p. 521	

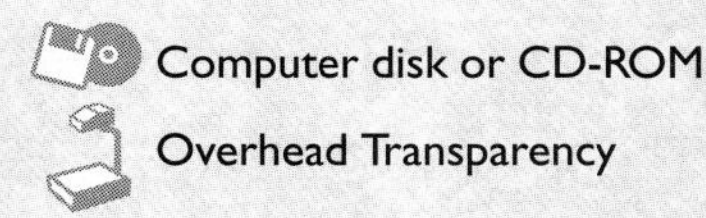

Collection Resources

Teaching Resources A	Audiovisual Resources Binder	Test Booklet
Cross-Curricular Activity p. 201	Fine Art Transparency 10.1	Collection 10 Test pp. 119–121

PROGRAM RESOURCES

Electronic Media	Teaching Resources with Organizer		Audiovisual Resources Binder
	Teaching Resources A	Other Resources	
• Language Workshop: Adjective clauses • Test Generator	• Teaching Notes p. 179 • Reading Organizer p. 182 • Language Link pp. 183–184 • Words to Own pp. 185–186	• Test Booklet: Selection Test pp. 109–110 • Language and Writing Skills Worksheets p. 80 • Portfolio Management System p. 39, pp. 122–123	• Elements of Literature Transparency 10.2
• Language Workshop: Misplaced modifiers • Test Generator	• Teaching Notes p. 180 • Reading Organizer p. 187 • Language Link pp. 188–189 • Words to Own p. 190	• Test Booklet: Selection Test pp. 111–112 • Language and Writing Skills Worksheets pp. 66–67 • Portfolio Management System p. 39, p. 124	• Elements of Literature Transparency 10.4 • How to Own a Word Transparency 10.5
• Language Workshop: Adverb clauses • Test Generator	• Teaching Notes pp. 180–181 • Reading Organizer p. 191 • Language Link pp. 192–193 • Words to Own p. 194	• Test Booklet: Selection Test pp. 113–114 • Language and Writing Skills Worksheets p. 82 • Portfolio Management System pp. 48–49, p. 125	
• Language Workshop: Works cited list • Test Generator	• Teaching Notes p. 181 • Reading Organizer p. 195 • Language Link pp. 196–197 • Words to Own p. 198	• Test Booklet: Selection Test pp. 115–116 • Language and Writing Skills Worksheets pp. 204–208 • Portfolio Management System pp. 54–55, pp. 126–127	• Elements of Literature Transparency 10.3
• Test Generator		• Test Booklet: The American Language pp. 117–118	
• Writer's Workshop 2: Informative Report		• Portfolio Management System pp. 128–130	• Revision Transparencies 10.6–10.7
• Language Workshop: Clauses	• Combining Sentences with Adverb and Adjective Clauses pp. 199–200	• Language and Writing Skills Worksheets pp. 79–84	
		• Portfolio Management System p. 131	

Proofreading Warm-ups

You may use the following exercises to help students practice their proofreading skills. Copy a set of incorrect sentences onto the chalkboard, and have students find and correct the spelling, punctuation, usage, and mechanical errors in each sentence. Ask students to share and discuss their responses.

	Sentences with Errors	Sentences Corrected	Skills Covered
1	**a.** mark twains father Twains real name was Samuel Langhorne Clemens was an unpractical bisnussman **b.** look it up in the index a detailed listing of a books contents at the back of this volumne	**a.** Mark Twain's father (Twain's real name was Samuel Langhorne Clemens) was an impractical businessman. **b.** Look it up in the index (a detailed listing of a book's contents) at the back of this volume.	Capitalization, Apostrophes (possessives), Parentheses, Usage, Spelling, End marks
2	**a.** its ironical that some people think of Twain one of the countrys formost satirist as a childrens authur **b.** some authers adopt pen names or psydonyms to protect his privacy	**a.** It's ironic that some people think of Twain, one of the country's foremost satirists, as a children's author. **b.** Some authors adopt pen names, or pseudonyms, to protect their privacy.	Capitalization, Apostrophes (contractions), Usage, Comma usage, Apostrophes (possessives), Spelling, Agreement, End marks
3	**a.** their's was a tough assinement our's was more easy **b.** hims' brothers and mine inlisted in the Army last tuseday	**a.** Theirs was a tough assignment; ours was easier. **b.** His brothers and mine enlisted in the army last Tuesday.	Capitalization, Pronouns (possessive), Spelling, Semicolon usage, Comparative modifiers, End marks
4	**a.** at about the age of 16 writer stephen Crane all ready had a job **b.** born after the civil war had ended Crane wrote The Red Badge Of Courage, a great novel about that era	**a.** At about the age of sixteen, writer Stephen Crane already had a job. **b.** Born after the Civil War had ended, Crane wrote <u>The Red Badge of Courage</u>, a great novel about that era.	Capitalization, Spelling out numbers, Comma usage, Usage, Underlining book titles, End marks
5	**a.** alright the captain growled who woke me up **b.** mom says its alright to stay out later on week-ends	**a.** "All right," the captain growled. "Who woke me up?" **b.** Mom says it's all right to stay out later on weekends.	Quotation marks, Capitalization, Punctuating dialogue, Apostrophe (contraction), Usage, Hyphen errors, End marks
6	**a.** rosa wasn't barely interested in the civil war untill she seen the TV series by Ken Burns **b.** gerald reveiwed the movie for his schools newspaper along time ago	**a.** Rosa was barely interested in the Civil War until she saw the TV series by Ken Burns. **b.** Gerald reviewed the movie for his school's newspaper a long time ago.	Capitalization, Double negative, Spelling, Past tense, Apostrophe (possessive), Usage, End marks
7	**a.** jack and his friends food was eaten by a bear while camping at Yellowstone national park **b.** they didnt listin careful enough to the locale experts advise	**a.** Jack and his friend's food was eaten by a bear while they were camping at Yellowstone National Park. **b.** They didn't listen carefully enough to the local expert's advice.	Capitalization, Apostrophes (compound possessives), Ambiguous modifiers, Apostrophes (contractions), Spelling, Adverbs, End marks
8	**a.** everywheres the man looked the lanscape was white, pure, white **b.** jack London was a proliffic writer of exiting, adventure storyes	**a.** Everywhere the man looked, the landscape was white, pure white. **b.** Jack London was a prolific writer of exciting adventure stories.	Capitalization, Nonstandard usage, Comma usage, Spelling, Plural nouns, End marks
9	**a.** whenever you backpack in the wildeness you should have taken a partener a long **b.** when is the last time shana went to oakland CA	**a.** Whenever you backpack in the wilderness, you should take a partner along. **b.** When was the last time Shana went to Oakland, California?	Capitalization, Spelling, Comma usage, Verb tense consistency, Usage, Spelling out abbreviations, End marks
10	**a.** naturalistic writers don't try and prettyfy reality **b.** just between you and i, which selection do you like better of all	**a.** Naturalistic writers don't try to prettify reality. **b.** Just between you and me, which selection do you like best of all?	Capitalization, Nonstandard usage, Spelling, Pronouns (objects of prepositions), Superlative modifiers, End marks

Collection 10

FROM INNOCENCE TO EXPERIENCE

Twain
Bierce
Voices from the Civil War
Crane
London

Shiloh

A Requiem

(April, 1862)

Skimming lightly, wheeling still,
   The swallows fly low
Over the field in clouded days,
   The forest-field of Shiloh—
Over the field where April rain
Solaced the parched ones stretched in pain
Through the pause of night
That followed the Sunday fight
   Around the church of Shiloh—
The church so lone, the log-built one,
That echoed to many a parting groan
      And natural prayer
   Of dying foemen mingled there—
Foemen at morn, but friends at eve—
   Fame or country least their care:
(What like a bullet can undeceive!)
   But now they lie low,
While over them the swallows skim,
   And all is hushed at Shiloh.

—Herman Melville (1819–1891)

Shiloh National Battlefield, Tennessee.

"Shiloh"
The poem shows a loss of innocence, as well as a loss of life. According to the poet, what is gained by the experience of the battle? [Possible responses: Soldiers and witnesses may come to reflect on their common humanity or to appreciate the solace and beauty of nature. The experience also teaches that the romantic ideals of fame and patriotism can be deceiving.]

PORTFOLIO ASSESSMENT

Parent/Guardian Involvement For forms that will help a parent or guardian review and respond to a student's portfolio, see the ***Portfolio Management System,*** pp. 62–63.

PROGRAM MANAGER

- **Integrated Assessment** See Collection 10 Test, *Test Booklet,* pp. 119–121.
- **Reinforcement** To allow students practice in using affixes, see Transparency 10.5 in the ***Audiovisual Resources Binder.***
- **Instructional Support** See Fine Art Transparency 10.1. Review teacher's notes for transparencies in the ***Audiovisual Resources Binder*** for suggestions on how to tie the transparencies to specific reading selections.
- **Extending Collection Theme** See Cross-Curricular Activity: From Innocence to Experience, ***Teaching Resources A,*** p. 201, for an activity in other disciplines and for evaluation criteria.

WRITERS ON WRITING

Twain's approach to storytelling was based on ideas from the American oral storytelling tradition. He says, "I do not claim that I can tell a story as it ought to be told. I only claim to know how a story ought to be told, for I have been almost daily in the company of the most expert story-tellers for many years. . . . The humorous story is told gravely; the teller does his best to conceal the fact that he even dimly suspects that there is anything funny about it."

Mark Twain

(1835–1910)

Mark Twain is the most celebrated humorist in American history. His ability to make us laugh has contributed to the singular popularity of his books, not just in Twain's own time but in following generations. Since humor is by nature very difficult to translate from language to language, it is even more surprising to find that Twain's appeal has traveled throughout the world.

The great humorist is also, ironically, our great realist. Behind the backwoods humor—especially in his novel *Adventures of Huckleberry Finn*—is a revelation of the illusions that exist in American life. Huck's journey on a raft with the escaped slave Jim is not a "hymn to boyhood." It is a dramatization of the grim realities of a slaveholding society.

Although Twain became remarkably successful, his later life was shadowed by disappointment and tragedy, and as he grew older he turned into a bitter man. He once told his friend William Dean Howells, the influential novelist and editor of *The Atlantic Monthly,* "Everyone is a moon and has a dark side which he never shows to anybody."

"Mark Twain!"

Twain was born Samuel Langhorne Clemens in the backwoods of Missouri. His father, John Clemens, a bright, ambitious, but impractical Virginian, had married Jane Lampton, a witty, dynamic woman who was also a great beauty. When John's store failed in 1839, he moved his hopes and his family to Hannibal, Missouri—the Mississippi River town that Sam, writing as Mark Twain, would later fashion into the setting of the most renowned boyhood in American literature, that of Tom Sawyer.

Sam's own carefree boyhood ended at twelve when his father died. Helping to support his mother and sister, he went to work setting type and editing copy for the newspaper started by his older brother Orion. At eighteen, Sam set out on his own. Over the next fifteen years, he worked as a printer in various towns from Missouri to the East Coast. Smitten by a love for the magical steamboats that plied the Mississippi, he even apprenticed himself for a time to the greatest of the steamboat pilots, Horace Bixby. From Bixby, Sam Clemens learned the bends and shallows of the great river from Minnesota to the Louisiana delta. It was the leadsman's cry of "Mark twain!"—announcing a water depth of two fathoms (twelve feet)—that provided him with his celebrated pen name.

A Gold Mine of Humor

For a short time during the Civil War, Twain was a soldier with a company of Confederate irregulars. (He said he learned more about retreating than fighting.) But he soon abandoned the military life for that of a gold prospector in Nevada. While he found little gold there, he did discover the rich mine of storytelling within himself. With his Missouri drawl and relaxed manner, Twain captivated audiences. His secret lay in his deft use of a faintly pompous platform

PORTFOLIO ASSESSMENT

Portfolio Assessment For help with self-assessment of reading skills, see the *Portfolio Management System,* p. 39.

manner: In pretending not to recognize the coarseness or absurdity of his material, Twain's deadpan attitude added to his material's hilarity.

Twain soon turned his comic voice to prose, working as a journalist between 1862 and 1871. In 1865, he achieved wide recognition as a humorist with the publication of his hilarious version of an old tall tale, "The Celebrated Jumping Frog of Calaveras County." Four years later, Twain's dispatches from a Mediterranean tour were published as a book titled *The Innocents Abroad.* This satirical travelogue poked fun at the traditional American pilgrimage to the monuments of European civilization. Over five thousand copies were sold in the first month, and more than thirty-one thousand within the year. Twain launched a prosperous literary career that was the prize of his expansive times.

An American Masterpiece

At thirty-five, with a raffish, barroom air about him, Twain was a dubious candidate for marriage, but he courted Olivia Langdon, the daughter of an affluent family from Elmira, New York. She was a delicate, proper woman, but Twain overcame all resistance, and, in 1870, Livy's father gave the couple his consent and a lavish wedding. Twain embarked on a marriage of unceasing devotion.

In 1871, Twain moved to Hartford, Connecticut, where he built an enormous home that is still visited today by thousands of tourists. The next year he published *Roughing It,* which drew on his experiences as a tenderfoot in the West. Then William Dean Howells invited Twain to do a series for *The Atlantic Monthly* about his days as a riverboat pilot. Those reminiscences eventually were expanded into the book *Life on the Mississippi* (1883).

By the mid-1870s, Twain was also at work on *The Adventures of Tom Sawyer.* This celebration of boyhood absorbed him but presented difficulties of voice and point of view. Twain could not be sure if he was writing a book for children or for adults. Nevertheless, in writing the book, he made an imaginative return to the Hannibal of his childhood and succeeded in transforming it into a compelling myth. The book was well received when it was published in 1876.

In *Adventures of Huckleberry Finn* (1884), Twain found the voice he had been seeking. Through Huck's natural, slangy, first-person narration, Twain forged a new relation between expression and content, causing a revolution in American literature. As Ernest Hemingway (page 650), speaking through a fictional character, later put it, "All modern American literature comes from one book by Mark Twain called *Huckleberry Finn.*" T. S. Eliot (page 661), a fellow Missourian, added that Twain's was "a new way of writing . . . a literary language based on American colloquial speech."

Loss and Legacy

Twain was never able to duplicate the success of *Huckleberry Finn,* but he continued to produce popular books, including *A Connecticut Yankee in King Arthur's Court* (1889) and *Pudd'nhead Wilson* (1894). Twain's later years were marked by financial and professional disappointment as well as personal tragedy. His fascination with business and getting ahead financially, so typical of the young nation and its new middle class, led him to invest heavily and disastrously in the Paige typesetting machine. The economic panic of 1893 bankrupted him.

Then illness overtook the close-knit Clemens family. Suzy, Twain's eldest daughter, died of meningitis in 1896. His wife, a permanent invalid during her last years, died in 1904. In a final blow, Jean, his youngest daughter, died in an epileptic seizure in 1909. "Possibly," said Twain after Jean's death, "I know now what the soldier feels when a bullet crashes through his heart." Four months later, he, too, was dead.

As loss followed loss, and as the whole country seemed to lose its vitality and become more complex, Twain had turned into an obsessive, embittered old man. In his final years, the subject matter of his work was his own disillusionment on a grand scale; the great comic writer appeared to be at war not only with the human race, but also with the God who had created it.

QUICK PLANNING GUIDE

Into the Selection

Author Biography pp. 450–451

Before You Read p. 452

- **Reading Focus:** Students consider the difference between expectations and reality.
- **Quickwrite** Write about developing a skill or an ability in Reader's Log
- **Elements of Literature: Extended Metaphor**
- **Background: Scaffolding** The appeal of steamboats

Through the Selection

from **Life on the Mississippi pp. 453–462**

Words to Own pp. 453–462

Literature and Folklore pp. 458–459

Making Meanings p. 463

Language and Style p. 463

Beyond the Selection

Choices: Building Your Portfolio p. 464

- **Writer's Notebook:** Collect ideas for a report
- **Critical Writing:** Write an essay on humor
- **Creative Writing:** Compare and contrast two views
- **Speaking and Listening:** Read orally from Twain's work
- **Art/Research:** Choose pictures that capture Twain's Mississippi and explain each in a paragraph
- **Creative Writing/Research/Art:** Write and illustrate a magazine feature on steamboats

Spotlight On p. 465

WORDS TO OWN

The following vocabulary words are defined in the Words to Own at the bottom of the pupil's page.

inanimate p. 453	benevolence p. 455
complacency p. 453	misgivings p. 460
subside p. 454	blandly p. 460
interminable p. 454	void p. 461
serenely p. 455	somber p. 462

Into the Selection

Using Before You Read p. 452

Reading Focus

Ask students why the expectations do not match the reality described. Encourage them to think about experiences when their expectations were not met.

Quickwrite

Encourage students who have trouble identifying a topic to think small. Have they learned: How to burp a baby? How to make an omelet? The manual alphabet? The words to a favorite song?

Elements of Literature

Ask students to recall any extended metaphors used for comic effect in folk tales or fairy tales.

Background

Record the jobs that were most appealing to students when they were younger. Have students tally up the jobs and find the most popular career. Then, survey the class again to find out what jobs are most appealing to them now. Have them compare the two lists. What do they notice?

Before You Read

from Life on the Mississippi

Reading Focus

Losing Its Luster

Sometimes, gaining something we've looked forward to isn't half as pleasurable as the anticipation of getting it. The person whose biggest wish is to be a movie actor might imagine all the glamorous trappings of that profession, but the reality of being an actor has more to do with hard work, discipline, and daily repetition than it does with adulation and fame. Experience brings its own rewards, but it can also make things seem too ordinary and familiar—lacking mystery and magic.

Quickwrite

Think about something you wished for—a skill or ability, or perhaps an honor or award—and then successfully gained. Were you in any way disappointed after achieving your goal? Write a few sentences describing how you felt after your wish came true.

Elements of Literature

Extended Metaphor

An **extended metaphor** is a **figure of speech** that makes a comparison between two unlike things and extends the comparison as far as the writer wants to take it. Much of Twain's humor comes from the surprise of two very unlike things joined to create an extended—and hilarious—comic metaphor.

An **extended metaphor** is a figure of speech that makes a comparison between two unlike things and extends the comparison as far as the writer wants to take it.

For more on Extended Metaphor, see page 188 and the Handbook of Literary Terms.

Background

As a youth, Twain was so fascinated by riverboats that he persuaded Horace Bixby, the locally famous pilot of the *Paul Jones,* to teach him how to navigate the river between New Orleans and St. Louis (a distance of about seven hundred miles) for five hundred dollars. Twain was not alone in his dream; every boy along the Mississippi, black or white, yearned to work on a steamboat. It didn't matter whether the job was clerk, engineer, mate, or pilot; life on the river meant adventure. "Once a day a cheap, gaudy packet [boat] arrived upward from St. Louis," Twain wrote, "and another downward from Keokuk. Before these events, the day was glorious with expectancy; after them, the day was a dead and empty thing."

Twain did succeed in becoming a steamboat pilot. These two chapters from *Life on the Mississippi* describe a time when he was still an apprentice, or "cub," pilot being trained by Horace Bixby.

Champions of the Mississippi by Currier & Ives. Lithograph.
Museum of the City of New York. Scala/Art Resource.

Program Manager

- **Planning Instruction** See Teaching Notes, *Teaching Resources A,* p. 179, for additional information for this selection.
- **Instructional Support** See Graphic Organizer for Active Reading, *Teaching Resources A,* p. 182, for a Through the Story activity.
- **Assessment** See Selection Test, *Test Booklet,* pp. 109–110.
- **Language Link** See Language Link, *Teaching Resources A,* pp. 183–184, and *Language and Writing Skills Worksheets,* p. 80.
- **Reinforcement** Use the Words to Own worksheet in *Teaching Resources A,* pp. 185–186.
- **Reinforcement** See Transparency 10.2 in the *Audiovisual Resources Binder.*

from Life on the Mississippi

Mark Twain

Perplexing Lessons

At the end of what seemed a tedious while, I had managed to pack my head full of islands, towns, bars, "points," and bends;[1] and a curiously inanimate mass of lumber it was, too. However, inasmuch as I could shut my eyes and reel off a good long string of these names without leaving out more than ten miles of river in every fifty, I began to feel that I could take a boat down to New Orleans if I could make her skip those little gaps. But of course my complacency could hardly get start enough to lift my nose a trifle into the air,

1. **islands . . . bends:** geographic features used in river navigation. Each numbered point was a landmark on a curve or bend in the river.

Words to Own

inanimate (in·an′ə·mit) *adj.:* lifeless.
complacency (kəm·plā′sən·sē) *n.:* self-satisfaction.

Through the Selection

A. Critical Reading: Metacognition

In an earlier section, Twain tells about recording this material: "I had a notebook that fairly bristled with the names of towns, 'points,' bars, islands, bends, reaches, etc., but the information was to be found only in the notebook—none of it was in my head." Now, at the beginning of this section, it is in his head.

If you needed to have material of this nature "in your head," how would you go about learning it? [Answers will vary. Some students may point out that the strategy of simply memorizing the list will not be effective in the long run, because a pilot must recognize these elements on the river, not just know the names.]

B. Critical Reading: Analyzing Character

? How would you characterize the speaker? [Possible answers: He does not realize the difficulty and skill involved, nor the level of detail needed to carry out the vocation he has chosen to pursue; or he is an innocent.]

Options for Teaching

Strategies for Inclusion

Less Proficient Readers Introducing the analogy of learning to drive a car may help students grasp some of the ideas about the "feel" of the river in the selection. Remind students of the "shape" of familiar roads, such as those in their neighborhoods.

Auditory Students may benefit from hearing the selection read aloud. For some students, oral reading will help them identify the humor in the piece, which they might not recognize in written form.

English Language Development Students need some background knowledge to appreciate this piece. They should have the opportunity to see a picture of a steamboat and a view of the Mississippi River that emphasizes the difficulty of steering a boat there. Students who have not driven may benefit from the school's driving simulator or from a comparison to a video game.

A. Cultural Connections
Students should be aware of the types of jobs that include apprenticeship as part of their training (the trades, for example) and should recognize that this is an age-old teaching strategy for passing on certain types of knowledge—hands-on practice. Refer students to Ben Franklin's experiences as an apprentice, and encourage them to compare and contrast Franklin's experience with Twain's.

B. Literary Element: Point of View
Twain is telling the story from the point of view of his younger self and, at the same time, making fun of himself. How does he do this here? [With a deadpan reference using an incongruous juxtaposition of unexpected elements—grandmother and protoplasm—and through implied seriousness that leads to a foolish answer.]

C. Literary Element: Extended Metaphor
Twain uses the technique of extended metaphor to humorous effect. Here, his comparison of his volatile chief to gunpowder is given power and depth by showing how the comparison is true in great detail.

D. Reader's Response: Shaping Interpretations
? What does Bixby mean when he says the shape of the river is different in the daytime? [Sample responses: He means that the shape seems different by day when he can see the riverbank; or the river's shape changes from day to night.]

E. Critical Reading: Summarizing
? Which sense will fail you in every one of the situations Bixby mentions? [Sight.]

(A) before Mr. Bixby would think of something to fetch it down again. One day he turned on me suddenly with this settler[2]—

"What is the shape of Walnut Bend?"

(B) He might as well have asked me my grandmother's opinion of protoplasm.[3] I reflected respectfully, and then said I didn't know it had any particular shape. My gunpowdery chief went off with a bang, of course, and then went on loading and firing until he was out of adjectives.

(C) I had learned long ago that he only carried just so many rounds of ammunition, and was sure to subside into a very placable and even remorseful old smoothbore[4] as soon as they were all gone. That word "old" is merely affectionate; he was not more than thirty-four. I waited. By and by he said—

(D) "My boy, you've got to know the *shape* of the river perfectly. It is all there is left to steer by on a very dark night. Everything else is blotted out and gone. But mind you, it hasn't the same shape in the night that it has in the daytime."

"How on earth am I ever going to learn it, then?"

"How do you follow a hall at home in the dark? Because you know the shape of it. You can't see it."

"Do you mean to say that I've got to know all the million trifling variations of shape in the banks of this interminable river as well as I know the shape of the front hall at home?"

"On my honor, you've got to know them *better* than any man ever did know the shapes of the halls in his own house."

"I wish I was dead!"

"Now I don't want to discourage you, but"—

"Well, pile it on me; I might as well have it now as another time."

(E) "You see, this has got to be learned; there isn't any getting around it. A clear starlight night throws such heavy shadows that if you didn't know the shape of a shore perfectly you would claw away from every bunch of timber, because you would take the black shadow of it for a solid cape;[5] and you see you would be getting scared to death every fifteen minutes by the watch.[6] You would be fifty yards from shore all the time when you ought to be within fifty feet of it. You can't see a snag[7] in one of those shadows, but you know exactly where it is, and the shape of the river tells you when you are coming to it. Then there's your pitch-dark night; the river is a very different shape on a pitch-dark night from what it is on a starlight night. All shores seem to be straight lines, then, and mighty dim ones, too; and you'd *run* them for straight lines only you know better. You boldly drive your boat right into what seems to be a solid, straight wall (you knowing very well that in reality there is a curve there), and that wall falls back and makes way for you. Then there's your gray mist. You take a night when there's one of these grisly, drizzly, gray mists, and then there isn't *any* particular shape to a shore. A gray mist would tangle the head of the oldest man that ever lived. Well, then, different kinds of *moonlight* change the shape of the river in different ways. You see"—

> *"Have I got to learn the shape of the river according to all these five hundred thousand different ways? If I tried to carry all that cargo in my head it would make me stoop-shouldered."*

"Oh, don't say anymore, please! Have I got to learn the shape of the river according to all these five hundred thousand different ways? If I tried to carry all that cargo in my head it would make me stoop-shouldered."

"*No!* you only learn *the* shape of the river; and you learn it with such absolute certainty that you can always steer by the shape that's *in your head,* and never mind the one that's before your eyes."

2. **settler:** colloquial for "something [such as Bixby's question] that does a person in."
3. **protoplasm:** living matter basic to all plant and animal cells.
4. **smoothbore:** gun with no grooves inside its barrel.
5. **cape:** land projecting into water.
6. **by the watch:** The workday on a steamboat was divided into three 4-hour periods, or watches, every twelve hours: two watches for work and one off-watch for rest.
7. **snag:** tree trunk dangerous to navigation because it is partly or completely underwater.

WORDS TO OWN
subside (səb·sīd') *v.:* to settle down.
interminable (in·tʉr'mi·nə·bəl) *adj.:* endless.

OPTIONS FOR TEACHING

CLASSROOM MANAGEMENT

Block Scheduling In order to maintain student enthusiasm during a longer class period, plan to vary activities every twenty to twenty-five minutes. Combine different activities, such as short lecture, pair share, small-group discussion, and activities that involve some student movement. These varied activities are important to keep students focused during the longer time span.

Grouping When you create homogeneous groups, consider the skills, knowledge, and abilities that will be at a premium for the particular task to be performed. It is not just advanced students who round out a group. For example, students who have knowledge of rivers and piloting would have valuable information to share with their classmates. Students who know detailed sports statistics or who have memorized pieces on their musical instruments may have insights for others when it comes to the problem-solving exercise on p. T456.

COOPERATIVE LEARNING

Character Sociograms Have students work in groups of three or four to create Character Sociograms—graphics with symbols and words that show the relationships between characters. Challenge students to include all the characters they have read about in the story so far and to be creative in the kind of symbols they produce to show how each character relates to the others.

"Very well, I'll try it; but after I have learned it can I depend on it? Will it keep the same form and not go fooling around?"

Before Mr. Bixby could answer, Mr. W—— came in to take the watch, and he said—

"Bixby, you'll have to look out for President's Island and all that country clear away up above the Old Hen and Chickens. The banks are caving and the shape of the shores changing like everything. Why, you wouldn't know the point above 40.[8] You can go up inside the old sycamore snag,[9] now."

So that question was answered. Here were leagues[10] of shore changing shape. My spirits were down in the mud again. Two things seemed pretty apparent to me. One was, that in order to be a pilot a man had got to learn more than any one man ought to be allowed to know; and the (F) other was, that he must learn it all over again in a different way every twenty-four hours.

That night we had the watch until twelve. Now it was an ancient river custom for the two pilots to chat a bit when the watch changed. While the relieving pilot put on his gloves and lit his cigar, his partner, the retiring pilot, would say something like this—

"I judge the upper bar is making down a little at Hale's Point; had quarter twain with the lower lead and mark twain[11] with the other."

"Yes, I thought it was making down a little, last trip. Meet any boats?"

"Met one abreast the head of 21,[12] but she was away over hugging the bar, and I couldn't make her out entirely. I took her for the 'Sunny South'—hadn't any skylights forward of the chimneys."

And so on. And as the relieving pilot took the wheel his partner[13] would mention that we were in such and such a bend, and say we were abreast of such and such a man's woodyard or plantation. This was courtesy; I supposed it was *necessity.* But Mr. W—— came on watch full twelve minutes late on this particular night—a tremendous breach of etiquette; in fact, it is the unpardonable sin among pilots. So Mr. Bixby gave him no greeting whatever, but simply surrendered the wheel and marched out of the pilothouse without a word. I was appalled; it was a villainous night for blackness, we were in a particularly wide and blind part of the river, where there was no shape or substance to anything, and it seemed incredi- (G) ble that Mr. Bixby should have left that poor fellow to kill the boat trying to find out where he was. But I resolved that I would stand by him anyway. He should find that he was not wholly friendless. So I stood around, and waited to be asked where we were. But Mr. W—— plunged on serenely through the solid firmament of black cats that stood for an atmosphere, and never opened his mouth. Here is a proud devil, thought I; here is a limb of Satan that would rather send us all to destruction than put himself under obligations to me, because I am not yet one of the salt of the earth and privileged to snub captains and lord it over everything dead and alive in a steamboat. I presently climbed up on the bench; I did not think it was safe to go to sleep while this lunatic was on watch.

However, I must have gone to sleep in the course of time, because the next thing I was aware of was the fact that day was breaking, Mr. W—— gone, and Mr. Bixby at the wheel again. So it was four o'clock and all well—but me; I felt like a skinful of dry bones and all of them trying to ache at once.

Mr. Bixby asked me what I had stayed up there for. I confessed that it was to do Mr. W—— a benevolence—tell him where he was. It took five minutes for the entire preposterousness of the thing to filter into Mr. Bixby's system, and then I judge it filled him nearly up to the chin; because he paid me a compliment—and not much of a one either. He said—

8. point above 40: numbered navigational point on the river beyond the landmark numbered 40.
9. inside . . . snag: It may not be necessary but still can do no harm to explain that "inside" means between the snag and the shore. [Twain's note]
10. leagues: One league equals about 3 miles.
11. quarter . . . mark twain: Two fathoms. Quarter twain is 2¼ fathoms, [or] 13½ feet. Mark three is three fathoms. [Twain's note] These measures of water depth are calculated by using a lead weight attached to a rope. One fathom, or "mark one," equals 6 feet. Two fathoms, or "mark twain," equals 12 feet.
12. abreast . . . 21: beside landmark, or point, 21.
13. partner: "Partner" is technical for "the other pilot." [Twain's note]

Words to Own

serenely (sə·rēn′lē) *adv.:* calmly.
benevolence (bə·nev′ə·ləns) *n.:* kindness.

F. Exploring the Historical Period
A pilot's responsibilities were great. The steamboat was an essential element in increasing transportation to and from the interior of the country. Steamboats regularly transported goods up and down the Mississippi River by 1817. The development of steamboats, railroads, and canal transportation made national marketing possible.

G. Critical Reading: Drawing Conclusions
? How does the narrator interpret Bixby's failure to speak? [He thinks it is a dangerous omission due to Mr. W——'s inexcusably late appearance on watch, and he expects the boats to crash because Mr. W—— won't know where he is.]

Integrating the Language Arts

Language and Vocabulary The extended metaphor can be used for other purposes besides humor. Have students read Shakespeare's Sonnet XVIII; the first line is, "Shall I compare thee to a summer's day?" Or have students review Dickinson's "Because I could not stop for Death—" (p.391). Work with students to analyze the effect of the extended metaphor. Encourage students to look for other examples of extended metaphors in their reading.

Strategic Reading To organize information about the skills and techniques needed for good piloting, have students record these elements in a cluster diagram such as the one shown. Students can make the diagrams as they read the selection and use their organizers to review the story.

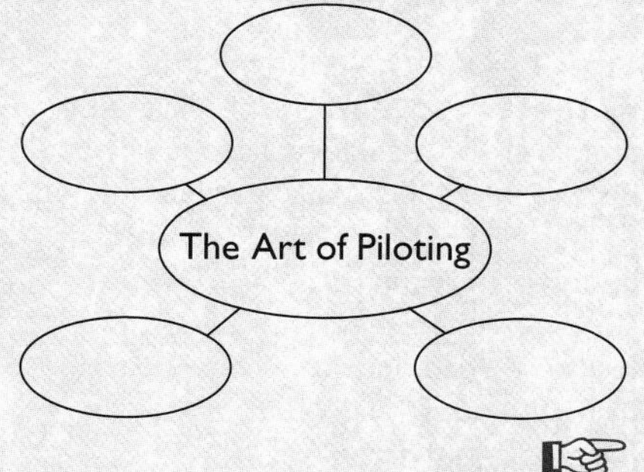

☞

A. Humanities Connection
Even realist literature had boundaries beyond which it would not go. So as not to disturb sensitive readers, letters in the word *damnation!* were omitted.

B. Literary Element: Understatement
Here, Twain uses understatement to create humor. He focuses on the relatively trivial matter of the damage to the window sash, purposely ignoring the injuries that he would have received if he had been "slammed . . . through the window." This shift of emphasis makes the brutality bearable for the reader, while calling attention to the incredible mistake that Twain almost committed.

C. Critical Reading: Comparing and Contrasting
Contrast Twain's and Bixby's strategies for studying the features on the river. [Twain is looking for fixed points. Bixby steers by looking at changes.]

"Well, taking you by and large, you do seem to be more different kinds of an ass than any creature I ever saw before. What did you suppose he wanted to know for?"

I said I thought it might be a convenience to him.

A "Convenience! D-nation! Didn't I tell you that a man's got to know the river in the night the same as he'd know his own front hall?"

"Well, I can follow the front hall in the dark if I know it *is* the front hall; but suppose you set me down in the middle of it in the dark and not tell me which hall it is; how am *I* to know?"

"Well, you've *got* to, on the river!"

"All right. Then I'm glad I never said anything to Mr. W——"

"I should say so. Why, he'd have slammed you through the window and utterly ruined a hundred dollars' worth of window sash[14] and stuff."

B I was glad this damage had been saved, for it would have made me unpopular with the owners. They always hated anybody who had the name of being careless, and injuring things.

I went to work now to learn the shape of the river; and of all the eluding and ungraspable objects that ever I tried to get mind or hands on, that was the chief. I would fasten my eyes upon a sharp, wooded point that projected far into the river some miles ahead of me, and go to laboriously photographing its shape upon my brain; and just as I was beginning to succeed to my satisfaction, we would draw up toward it and the exasperating thing would begin to melt away and fold back into the bank! If there had been a conspicuous dead tree standing upon the very point of the cape, I would find that tree inconspicuously merged into the general forest, and occupying the middle of a straight shore, when I got abreast of it! No prominent hill would stick to its shape long enough for me to make up my mind what its form really was, but it was as dissolving and changeful as if it had been a mountain of butter in the hottest corner of the tropics. Nothing ever had the same shape when I was coming downstream that it had borne when I went up. I mentioned these little difficulties to Mr. Bixby. He said—

C "That's the very main virtue of the thing. If the shapes didn't change every three seconds they wouldn't be of any use. Take this place where we are now, for instance. As long as that hill over yonder is only one hill, I can boom right along the way I'm going; but the moment it splits at the top and forms a V, I know I've got to scratch to starboard[15] in a hurry, or I'll bang this boat's brains out against a rock; and then the moment one of the prongs of the V swings behind the other, I've got to waltz to larboard[16] again, or I'll have a misunderstanding with a snag that would snatch the keelson[17] out of this steamboat as neatly as if it were a sliver in your hand. If that hill didn't change its shape on bad nights there would be an awful steamboat graveyard around here inside of a year."

It was plain that I had got to learn the shape of the river in all the different ways that could be thought of—upside down, wrong end first, inside out, fore-and-aft, and "thort-ships"[18]—and then know what to do on gray nights when it hadn't any shape at all. So I set about it. In the course of time I began to get the best of this knotty lesson, and my self-complacency moved to the front once more. Mr. Bixby was all fixed, and ready to start it to the rear again. He opened on me after this fashion—

"How much water did we have in the middle crossing at Hole-in-the-Wall, trip before last?"

I considered this an outrage. I said—

"Every trip, down and up, the leadsmen[19] are singing through that tangled place for three quarters of an hour on a stretch. How do you reckon I can remember such a mess as that?"

"My boy, you've got to remember it. You've got to remember the exact spot and the exact marks the boat lay in when we had the shoalest[20] water, in every one of the five hundred shoal places between St. Louis and New Orleans; and you mustn't get the shoal soundings and marks[21] of

14. **window sash:** frame that holds window glass.

15. **scratch to starboard:** move quickly to the right side of the boat.
16. **larboard:** the left side of the boat.
17. **keelson:** wood or metal beams fastened along a boat's keel to strengthen it. The keel is the timber along the boat's bottom that supports the frame.
18. **fore-and-aft, and "thort-ships":** end to end and shore to shore.
19. **leadsmen:** workers who use a lead line to measure the water's depth.
20. **shoalest:** most shallow.
21. **soundings and marks:** measurements of water depth.

INTEGRATING THE LANGUAGE ARTS

Writing: Poem Ask students to write a short poem with an extended metaphor on a subject that they can discuss in detail. Possible topics are a person, a sport, or a pet. Have the class brainstorm techniques for moving forward when the metaphor seems to lead to a dead end. For example, try using the question "What if?" to prompt creativity.

PROBLEM SOLVING/ CRITICAL THINKING

Memorizing To help students understand how Twain memorized the shape of the river, have students work in groups of four to discuss techniques for dealing with remembering large amounts of information in detail. Students should share techniques and strategies, discussing how they might vary their strategies for different kinds of tasks.

PROFESSIONAL NOTES

Thematic Connections: "From Innocence to Experience" Have students discuss how the last two paragraphs of the selection are a clear indication that young Twain has passed from innocence to experience.

one trip mixed up with the shoal soundings and marks of another, either, for they're not often twice alike. You must keep them separate."

When I came to myself again, I said—

"When I get so that I can do that, I'll be able to raise the dead, and then I won't have to pilot a steamboat to make a living. I want to retire from this business. I want a slush-bucket and a brush; I'm only fit for a roustabout.[22] I haven't got brains enough to be a pilot; and if I had I wouldn't have strength enough to carry them around, unless I went on crutches." **D**

"Now drop that! When I say I'll learn[23] a man the river, I mean it. And you can depend on it, I'll learn him or kill him."

Continued Perplexities

There was no use in arguing with a person like this. I promptly put such a strain on my memory that by and by even the shoal water and the countless crossing marks[24] began to stay with me. But the result was just the same. I never could more than get one knotty thing learned before another presented itself. Now I had often seen pilots gazing at the water and pretending to read it as if it were a book; but it was a book that told me nothing. **E** A time came at last, however, when Mr. Bixby seemed to think me far enough advanced to bear a lesson on water-reading. So he began—

"Do you see that long slanting line on the face of the water? Now, that's a reef. Moreover, it's a bluff reef.[25] There is a solid sandbar under it that is nearly as straight up and down as the side of a house. There is plenty of water close up to it, but mighty little on top of it. If you were to hit it you would knock the boat's brains out. Do you see where the line fringes out at the upper end and begins to fade away?"

22. roustabout: deckhand; laborer on a boat.
23. learn: "Teach" is not in the river vocabulary. [Twain's note]

24. crossing marks: points on the river where a boat could cross safely.
25. bluff reef: hidden sandbar with a high, steep front. Its position is indicated by lines or ripples on the water.

The pilothouse of *The Great Republic.*

The Bettmann Archive.

D. Critical Reading: Drawing Conclusions

? What is Twain's point? [It is so difficult a task that to accomplish it would take a miracle—that is, divine intervention.]

E. Cultural Connections

Different cultures value different kinds of intelligence. Twain shows in his comparison of watching the river and reading a book that he values linguistic intelligence and uses it as the measure and reference point for his experience.

CROSSING THE CURRICULUM

Art Have students identify a work of art in which something is created by analysis (as described in Pirsig's comment on p. T462). Give students an opportunity to share their discoveries with classmates and explain the rationale for their choices.

Social Studies Have students work in small groups to explore various aspects of steamboats: their invention, their importance in the development of transportation to the interior of the country, and their role in the life of the Midwestern states. Have all the groups put together a joint presentation.

PROFESSIONAL NOTES

TECHNOLOGY

Technology Tip Students may learn more about Twain by accessing the Web site Mark Twain Resources on the World Wide Web at **http://web.syr.edu/~fjzwick/twainwww.html**. *You may want to preview any Internet activity that you suggest to students. Because these resources are sometimes public forums, their content can be unpredictable.*

LITERATURE AND FOLKLORE

Have students research other items of folklore about the Mississippi River. Students can use encyclopedias, books about the Mississippi, or folklore anthologies or journals as their sources. Each student can present orally one item to the class. Then, discuss with students why they think there are so many stories told about the river. They can review their reasons after reading the description of the river's beauty that closes the selection.

A. Literary Element: Personification

Here, Twain talks about the boat as if it were a person. What effect does this have? [Possible answers: It makes the boat a character and shows how its individual quirks and tendencies seem to give it personality. It also emphasizes how important handling the boat's peculiar ways are to making the trip safe. Until now, the pilot's expert knowledge of the shape of the river has received most of the attention.]

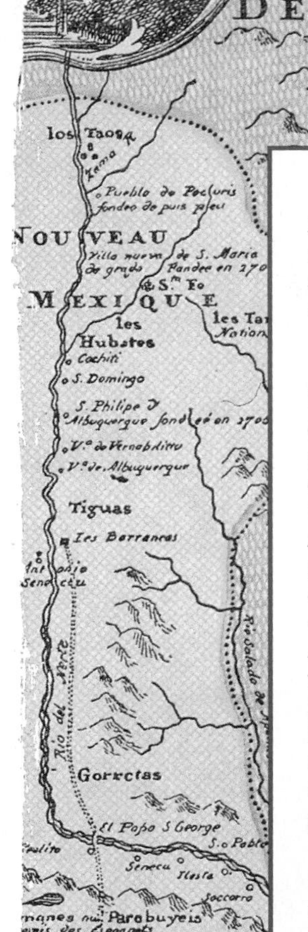

LITERATURE AND FOLKLORE

The Lure and Lore of the Mississippi

It was a monstrous big river down there—sometimes a mile and a half wide; we run nights, and laid up and hid daytimes. . . . we slid into the river and had a swim, so as to freshen up and cool off; then we set down on the sandy bottom where the water was about knee deep, and watched the daylight come.

—Mark Twain, *Adventures of Huckleberry Finn*

In the folklore of the Mississippi (Algonquian for "big river"), the river has many contradictory aspects: It is god, devil, giver of prosperity, destroyer of life and property, even trickster-hero. (The river is seen as a trickster because, when its course periodically changes, its changing configurations sometimes alter state lines, actually "moving" plantations and farms from one state to another.) The African American folklorist Ruth Bass once described the river's power and unpredictability: "Ole Miss' was lying mighty peaceful and tenderlike now, but she could be high-handed when she took a notion." That unpredictability has given rise to hundreds of superstitions and folk sayings. According to one African American folk belief, the river's evil spirit becomes angry and drowns anyone who dares swim across. Mississippi navigators claim the river never lets go of a person who falls in the water with clothes on. A Louisiana saying has it that it's bad luck to throw an animal into the river. On the other hand, according to some folk beliefs, if a person washes his or her face in the Mississippi, bad luck can change to good luck.

Sea monsters and other scares. Tales and legends associated with the "big river" run a vast course as long as the river itself. On the bluffs along the Mississippi, Native Americans made rock carvings, or petroglyphs, to depict supernatural beings they saw around them. Members of the Illinois people told Father Hennepin, a seventeenth-century explorer, that on the bluffs near present-day Minneapolis were "some Tritons and other Sea Monsters painted

"Yes, sir."

"Well, that is a low place; that is the head of the reef. You can climb over there, and not hurt anything. Cross over, now, and follow along close under the reef—easy water there—not much current."

I followed the reef along till I approached the fringed end. Then Mr. Bixby said—

A "Now get ready. Wait till I give the word. She won't want to mount the reef: a boat hates shoal water. Stand by—wait—*wait*—keep her well in hand. *Now* cramp her down![26] Snatch her![27] Snatch her!"

He seized the other side of the wheel and helped to spin it around until it was hard down, and then we held it so. The boat resisted, and refused to answer for a while, and next she came surging to starboard, mounted the reef, and sent a

26. **cramp her down:** turn the wheel sharply.
27. **Snatch her:** Act quickly.

OPTIONS FOR TEACHING

ASSESSMENT TOOLS

Check Test: Questions and Answers

1. Why does a pilot need to know the shape of the river? [It's what she or he steers by.]
2. When Mr. W —— came on watch, Twain was afraid that _____. [Mr. W —— didn't know where he was on the river.]
3. According to Mr. Bixby, the changing shape of the landscape _____. [Helps guide the pilot in knowing what to expect.]
4. Bixby gave Twain the wheel and promised to be back before the next point, but instead he _____. [Hid and watched Twain to see how he would handle it.]
5. Twain gained knowledge of the river, but for him it lost its _____. [Romance and beauty.]

which the boldest Men durst not look upon, there being some Enchantment in their face." Farther south, near Alton, Illinois, inmates of the state prison who were quarrying rock in the 1850s came upon the traces of two huge bird petroglyphs. Their origin, according to a tradition of the Illinois people, involves a gigantic bird that preyed on humans long before the white settlers came. After whole villages were destroyed, a chief offered himself to the bird as armed warriors lay in ambush. The Great Spirit, in admiration of the chief's cunning and bravery, allowed the chief to live, and the murderous bird died with a "wild, fearful scream." In memory of the event, the bird's image was engraved on the bluff.

The haunted river. The Mississippi also has its share of ghost stories. One Chippewa legend from Minnesota tells of a white panther that spoke the people's language and served as their prophet. A young warrior killed the panther and brought upon himself the curse of roaming forever, "a starving and undying skeleton." When the moon has a red cast or the sky is purple, legends say, the ghost of the warrior can be seen wandering the banks of the river. Another story, this one from Creole folklore, warns that zombies haunt a number of Louisiana bayous. On a shoal called Devil Flats, a zombie who carries his own dismembered head under his arm takes care on his evening walks to turn the head so that its eyes can take in the tranquil twilight scene.

On somewhat more scientific footing are the mysterious reports from Devil's Punch Bowl, near Natchez, Mississippi. The Bowl is a several-acre pit in a river bluff; it may have been caused by a prehistoric meteorite. Ship captains report that when their ship approaches the spot, their compass needles go wild and sometimes spin around completely. Some people theorize that this happens because of the iron sunk into the earth by the meteorite. But Devil's Punch Bowl is also said to have been a meeting place for pirates who preyed upon river traffic, and a hiding place for their stolen loot. Thus, the more romantic explanation for the erratic behavior of compasses is that it is caused by the huge pots of gold and silver coins buried by the pirates.

The Mississippi may or may not guard lost treasure, but it most certainly has riches in legend and lore.

The Granger Collection, New York.

Engraved map of Mississippi region and the Louisiana province (1687).

long, angry ridge of water foaming away from her bows.[28]

"Now watch her; watch her like a cat, or she'll get away from you. When she fights strong and the tiller slips a little, in a jerky, greasy sort of way, let up on her a trifle; it is the way she tells you at night that the water is too shoal; but keep edging her up, little by little, toward the point. You are well up on the bar, now; there is a bar under every point, because the water that comes down around it forms an eddy and allows the sediment to sink. Do you see those fine lines on the face of the water that branch out like the ribs of a fan? Well, those are little reefs; you want to just miss the ends of them, but run them pretty close. Now look out—look out! Don't you crowd that slick, greasy-looking place; there ain't nine feet there; she won't stand it. She begins to smell it; look

28. **bows:** front part of a boat.

B. Reader's Response: First Thoughts

? Do you understand Bixby's explanation of when to "let up on her a trifle"? [Sample responses: Yes, he means to release the wheel a little when the boat resists; or no, it is confusing.]

ASSESSMENT TOOLS

Ongoing Assessment Ask students to rate their own overall performance within their groups. Each student also should indicate areas that need improvement. These student self-assessments may be used along with your own observations in pupil-teacher conferences.

My Contribution to My Group

Good ☐ Fair ☐ Poor ☐

Ways I Could Improve

____

____

____

A. Critical Reading: Evaluating an Interpretation

? Is it reasonable to consider Twain's view of piloting a romantic one? [It is reasonable because rationality is not important in his conception of piloting; the romantic essence lies in the performance, not in studying, knowledge, and skill.]

sharp, I tell you! Oh blazes, there you go! Stop the starboard wheel! Quick! Ship up to back! Set her back!"[29]

The engine bells jingled and the engines answered promptly, shooting white columns of steam far aloft out of the 'scape pipes, but it was too late. The boat had "smelt"[30] the bar in good earnest; the foamy ridges that radiated from her bows suddenly disappeared, a great dead swell[31] came rolling forward and swept ahead of her, she careened far over to larboard, and went tearing away toward the other shore as if she were about scared to death. We were a good mile from where we ought to have been, when we finally got the upper hand of her again.

The engine bells jingled and the engines answered promptly, shooting white columns of steam far aloft out of the 'scape pipes, but it was too late.

During the afternoon watch the next day, Mr. Bixby asked me if I knew how to run the next few miles. I said—

"Go inside the first snag above the point, outside the next one, start out from the lower end of Higgins's woodyard, make a square crossing[32] and"—

"That's all right. I'll be back before you close up on the next point."

But he wasn't. He was still below when I rounded it and entered upon a piece of river which I had some misgivings about. I did not know that he was hiding behind a chimney to see how I would perform. I went gaily along, getting prouder and prouder, for he had never left the boat in my sole charge such a length of time before. I even got to "setting" her and letting the wheel go, entirely, while I vaingloriously turned my back and inspected the stern marks[33] and hummed a tune, a sort of easy indifference which I had prodigiously admired in Bixby and other great pilots. Once I inspected rather long, and when I faced to the front again my heart flew into my mouth so suddenly that if I hadn't clapped my teeth together I should have lost it. One of those frightful bluff reefs was stretching its deadly length right across our bows! My head was gone in a moment; I did not know which end I stood on; I gasped and could not get my breath; I spun the wheel down with such rapidity that it wove itself together like a spider's web; the boat answered and turned square away from the reef, but the reef followed her! I fled, and still it followed still it kept—right across my bows! I never looked to see where I was going, I only fled. The awful crash was imminent—why didn't that villain come! If I committed the crime of ringing a bell, I might get thrown overboard. But better that than kill the boat. So in blind desperation I started such a rattling "shivaree"[34] down below as never had astounded an engineer in this world before, I fancy. Amidst the frenzy of the bells the engines began to back and fill in a furious way, and my reason forsook its throne—we were about to crash into the woods on the other side of the river. Just then Mr. Bixby stepped calmly into view on the hurricane deck.[35] My soul went out to him in gratitude. My distress vanished; I would have felt safe on the brink of Niagara, with Mr. Bixby on the hurricane deck. He blandly and sweetly took his toothpick out of his mouth between his fingers, as if it were a cigar—we were just in the act of climbing an overhanging big tree, and the passengers were scudding astern[36] like rats—and lifted up these commands to me ever so gently—

"Stop the starboard. Stop the larboard. Set her back on both."[37]

29. **Ship . . . back:** Put it in reverse.
30. **smelt:** dialect for "smelled." That is, the boat recognized water too shallow for safety.
31. **great dead swell:** huge wave.
32. **make a square crossing:** go directly between crossing marks.
33. **stern marks:** landmarks already passed and thus astern of, or behind, the boat.
34. **shivaree** (shiv′ə·rē′): noisy celebration.
35. **hurricane deck:** topmost deck of a steamboat.
36. **scudding astern:** running to the back of the boat.
37. **Stop . . . both:** Halt the forward motion of the boat by stopping both the right and left paddle wheels, and put both wheels in reverse.

Words to Own

misgivings (mis′giv′iŋz) *n. pl.:* doubts; worries.
blandly (bland′lē) *adv.:* mildly.

The boat hesitated, halted, pressed her nose among the boughs a critical instant, then reluctantly began to back away.

"Stop the larboard. Come ahead on it. Stop the starboard. Come ahead on it. Point her for the bar."

I sailed away as serenely as a summer's morning. Mr. Bixby came in and said, with mock simplicity—

"When you have a hail,[38] my boy, you ought to tap the big bell three times before you land, so that the engineers can get ready."

I blushed under the sarcasm, and said I hadn't had any hail.

"Ah! Then it was for wood, I suppose. The officer of the watch will tell you when he wants to wood up."

B

I went on consuming, and said I wasn't after wood.

"Indeed? Why, what could you want over here in the bend, then? Did you ever know of a boat following a bend upstream at this stage of the river?"

"No, sir—and *I* wasn't trying to follow it. I was getting away from a bluff reef."

"No, it wasn't a bluff reef; there isn't one within three miles of where you were."

"But I saw it. It was as bluff as that one yonder."

"Just about. Run over it!"

"Do you give it as an order?"

"Yes. Run over it."

"If I don't, I wish I may die."

"All right; I am taking the responsibility."

I was just as anxious to kill the boat, now, as I had been to save her before. I impressed my orders upon my memory, to be used at the inquest,[39] and made a straight break for the reef. As it disappeared under our bows I held my breath; but we slid over it like oil.

"Now don't you see the difference? It wasn't anything but a *wind* reef. The wind does that."

"So I see. But it is exactly like a bluff reef. How am I ever going to tell them apart?"

"I can't tell you. It is an instinct. By and by you will just naturally *know* one from the other, but you never will be able to explain why or how you know them apart."

C

It turned out to be true. The face of the water, in time, became a wonderful book—a book that was a dead language to the uneducated passenger, but which told its mind to me without reserve, delivering its most cherished secrets as clearly as if it uttered them with a voice. And it was not a book to be read once and thrown aside, for it had a new story to tell every day. Throughout the long twelve hundred miles there was never a page that was void of interest, never one that you could leave unread without loss, never one that you would want to skip, thinking you could find higher enjoyment in some other thing. There never was so wonderful a book written by man; never one whose interest was so absorbing, so unflagging, so sparklingly renewed with every reperusal. The passenger who could not read it was charmed with a peculiar sort of faint dimple on its surface (on the rare occasions when he did not overlook it altogether); but to the pilot that was an *italicized* passage; indeed, it was more than that, it was a legend[40] of the largest capitals, with a string of shouting exclamation points at the end of it; for it meant that a wreck or a rock was buried there that could tear the life out of the strongest vessel that ever floated. It is the faintest and simplest expression the water ever makes, and the most hideous to a pilot's eye. In truth, the passenger who could not read this book saw nothing but all manner of pretty pictures in it, painted by the sun and shaded by the clouds, whereas to the trained eye these were not pictures at all, but the grimmest and most dead earnest of reading matter.

D

The face of the water, in time, became a wonderful book—a book that was a dead language to the uneducated passenger. . . .

Now when I had mastered the language of this water and had come to know every trifling feature that bordered the great river as familiarly as I

38. **hail:** call to land.
39. **inquest:** inquiry by a jury or panel investigating a crime.

40. **legend:** inscription.

WORDS TO OWN
void (void) *adj.:* empty.

B. Literary Element: Irony

? What causes the humor in this ironic situation? [Bixby pretends to misunderstand Twain's motives in ringing the bell and suggests all kinds of reasons that he knows are not the real ones. Each time, Twain must explain himself and grows more and more embarrassed.]

C. Reader's Response: Connecting with the Text

? What kinds of things do you know by instinct? Give some examples. [Sample responses: How to drive, play sports, or understand people's motivations or character.]

D. Critical Reading: Finding Details

? Upon what details does Twain base the comparison of understanding the face of the water to reading a book? [Answers should include the following: The water, like a book in a dead language, is not understood by the uninitiated; it has a new story to tell every day; it is interesting through and through; re-reading is invaluable; it has italicized passages.]

A. Literary Connections

In his book *Zen and the Art of Motorcycle Maintenance,* Robert Pirsig extends Twain's idea. "When analytic thought, the knife, is applied to experience, something is always killed in the process. . . . Mark Twain's experience comes to mind, in which, after he had mastered the analytic knowledge needed to pilot the Mississippi River, he discovered the river had lost its beauty. Something *is* always killed. But what is less noticed in the arts—something is always created too. And instead of just dwelling on what is killed it's important also to see what's created and to see the process as a kind of death-birth continuity that is neither good nor bad, but just *is*."

B. Critical Reading: Drawing Conclusions

? What romantic illusions has Twain been stripped of by this point? [His ideas of the romantic life of pilots and their nonchalant approach to their work.]

C. Reader's Response: Extending the Text

Twain and Pirsig extend the experience of piloting to consider the act of analysis and its effects on the analyzer. What do you think is the larger significance of their discoveries? [Sample responses: Overanalyzing can lead to a loss of appreciation; or losing romance and beauty is necessary in order to gain knowledge.]

The Bettmann Archive.

knew the letters of the alphabet, I had made a valuable acquisition. But I had lost something, too. I had lost something which could never be restored to me while I lived. All the grace, the beauty, the poetry had gone out of the majestic river! I still keep in mind a certain wonderful sunset which I witnessed when steamboating was new to me. A broad expanse of the river was turned to blood; in the middle distance the red hue brightened into gold, through which a solitary log came floating, black and conspicuous; in one place a long, slanting mark lay sparkling upon the water; in another the surface was broken by boiling, tumbling rings, that were as many-tinted as an opal; where the ruddy flush was faintest, was a smooth spot that was covered with graceful circles and radiating lines, ever so delicately traced; the shore on our left was densely wooded, and the somber shadow that fell from this forest was broken in one place by a long, ruffled trail that shone like silver; and high above the forest wall a clean-stemmed dead tree waved a single leafy bough that glowed like a flame in the unobstructed splendor that was flowing from the sun. There were graceful curves, reflected images, woody heights, soft distances; and over the whole scene, far and near, the dissolving lights drifted steadily, enriching it, every passing moment, with new marvels of coloring.

I stood like one bewitched. I drank it in, in a speechless rapture. The world was new to me, and I had never seen anything like this at home. But as I have said, a day came when I began to cease from noting the glories and the charms which the moon and the sun and the twilight wrought upon the river's face; another day came when I ceased altogether to note them. Then, if that sunset scene had been repeated, I should have looked upon it without rapture, and should have commented upon it, inwardly, after this fashion: This sun means that we are going to have wind tomorrow; that floating log means that the river is rising, small thanks to it; that slanting mark on the water refers to a bluff reef which is going to kill somebody's steamboat one of these nights, if it keeps on stretching out like that; those tumbling "boils" show a dissolving bar and a changing channel there; the lines and circles in the slick water over yonder are a warning that that troublesome place is shoaling up dangerously; that silver streak in the shadow of the forest is the "break" from a new snag,[41] and he has located himself in the very best place he could have found to fish for steamboats; that tall dead tree, with a single living branch, is not going to last long, and then how is a body ever going to get through this blind place at night without the friendly old landmark?

No, the romance and the beauty were all gone from the river. All the value any feature of it had for me now was the amount of usefulness it could furnish toward compassing the safe piloting of a steamboat. Since those days, I have pitied doctors from my heart. What does the lovely flush in a beauty's cheek mean to a doctor but a "break" that ripples above some deadly disease? Are not all her visible charms sown thick with what are to him the signs and symbols of hidden decay? Does he ever see her beauty at all, or doesn't he simply view her professionally, and comment upon her unwholesome condition all to himself? And doesn't he sometimes wonder whether he has gained most or lost most by learning his trade?

41. **"break" . . . snag:** ripple or line in the water indicating a newly fallen tree.

Words to Own

somber (säm′bər) *adj.:* gloomy; dark.

Making Meanings

First Thoughts

1. He describes the river becoming a source of factual information for him, not a thing to be enjoyed in and of itself; yet, not everyone loses enjoyment of something because it is well known—for some, familiarity leads to greater joy. Students may or may not have had similar experiences.

Reviewing the Text

a. ". . . All the million trifling variations of shape in the banks of this interminable river."

b. He mistakes a wind reef for a bluff reef and, in trying to avoid it, almost runs the boat into the bank.

c. The river looks different under different conditions of light and weather; the shape of the shore changes; the shape of the shore looks different as you draw abreast of features that you had seen from a distance; things look different going upstream than they do going downstream.

d. He says the "grace, the beauty, the poetry" and the "romance and the beauty were all gone from the river."

MAKING MEANINGS

First Thoughts

1. Twain ruefully reports that "the romance and the beauty were all gone from the river." Do you think he is describing a common human reaction? Describe an example of this kind of experience. (Look back over the notes you made in your Reader's Log.)

Reviewing the Text

a. What huge body of information is Twain told he must learn as well as he knows a hall in his own home?

b. What happens the night Twain believes he is left at the wheel alone?

c. Explain the factors that make "learning the river" a great challenge.

d. What does Twain say he has lost when he finally learns the language of the river?

Shaping Interpretations

2. In "Perplexing Lessons," what does Bixby mean when he says that Twain must learn the shape of the river?

3. In the chapter titled "Continued Perplexities," an **extended metaphor** compares the river with a book that "had a new story to tell every day" (page 461). Find three specific comparisons Twain makes between reading a book and "reading" the river.

4. Twain says that "All the grace, the beauty, the poetry had gone out of the majestic river!" (page 462). In what sense is he describing a loss of "innocence" that comes about as a result of increased experience?

Connecting with the Text

5. Think about the episode in which Bixby lets Twain get into trouble before giving him quiet guidance. On the basis of your own experience with a variety of teachers, do you rate Bixby as a good teacher or a poor one? Give the reasons for your answer.

Challenging the Text

6. Twain first wrote about his Mississippi experiences for *The Atlantic Monthly,* a magazine edited by William Dean Howells. Howells said of Twain's first installment, "It almost made the water in our ice pitcher muddy as I read it." Does Twain bring the river to life as vividly as Howells implies, or does Howells praise Twain's descriptive abilities too much? Support your response with examples from the text.

LANGUAGE AND STYLE

Twain's Humor

Humor is hard to explain, but we do know that comic devices are often used in humorous writings, and when they are used by a genius like Twain, they can make us laugh.

- **Hyperbole:** outrageous exaggeration made for effect: ". . . when I faced to the front again my heart flew into my mouth so suddenly that if I hadn't clapped my teeth together I should have lost it" (page 460).
- **Comic metaphors:** comparisons between two unlike things that create colorful, hilarious images. Twain's metaphors often involve incongruity—two seemingly mismatched or even opposite images, events, or elements are unexpectedly joined: "My gunpowdery chief went off with a bang . . . and then went on loading and firing until he was out of adjectives" (page 454). Many of Twain's funniest comparisons are **extended metaphors.**
- **Understatement:** saying less than what is meant, usually for ironic purposes: "I was glad this damage had been saved, for it would have made me unpopular with the owners" (page 456).

1. Review the excerpt, and locate at least one example of each of the three comic devices listed above. Read aloud the places where Twain uses each of these techniques.

2. Which of these humorous techniques is used most frequently in this excerpt from *Life on the Mississippi*? Overall, how would you describe Twain's humor?

Shaping Interpretations

2. Bixby means that he must know the river's features so well that he should not have to stop to think about them, but just react instinctively.

3. (1) Just as books are understood only by the educated, the "face of the water" was understood only by those educated in its language. (2) If you failed to read a "page of the river," you would be the loser, just as if you skipped pages in a well-written book. (3) Like a good book, the river never had a page that was devoid of interest.

4. In learning to "read" the river in order to ensure safe passage for the steamboat, he has lost the ability to view the river as an aesthetic object.

Connecting with the Text

5. Since Twain does learn the intricate and complicated job of navigating the river and says of Bixby's advice, "It turned out to be true," Bixby could be called a good teacher.

Challenging the Text

6. **(Evaluation)** Possible response: Twain is a great naturalistic writer: His deadpan way of telling humorous incidents (for example, Twain's "benevolence" toward Mr. W——) and the level and type of detail (the conversation between pilots as they trade duty) do bring the river to life in a special way.

Language and Style

Possible Answers

1. **Hyperbole**—referring to Mr. W—— as a "proud devil . . . a limb of Satan" (p. 455).
Comic metaphor—felt like a "skinful of dry bones . . . trying to ache at once" (p. 455).
Understatement—"little difficulties" he mentions to Bixby (p. 456).

2. Some students will say hyperbole, some understatement. Both are used frequently. Students may describe Twain's humor as dry and, for the most part, understated.

✔ QUICK CHECK: Humorous Devices

Identify each passage below as an example of hyperbole, comic metaphor, or understatement.

[1] When I took the slipper away from my neighbor's Chihuahua, Sunshine, it was as if a cloud had passed over the dog's face. What I thought was a smile was actually a flash of lightning, and then I could hear from the back of its throat the thunder rolling in to threaten the region around my ankles with a hail of gnashing little teeth. [comic metaphor]

[2] Juan didn't like Mondays, but he had been surprisingly happy until he broke his leg. [understatement]

[3] On our trip we saw mosquitoes as big as vultures and saw vultures as big as 747's. The bears, however, were bear-sized: somewhere between a refrigerator and a small moving van. [hyperbole]

[4] I saw a film so frightening that my hair stood on end within the first minute and continued to partially block the view of the people behind me until the theater lights finally came back on. [hyperbole]

Choices: Building Your Portfolio

1. **Writer's Notebook** Remind students to save their work. They may use it as prewriting for the Writer's Workshop on p. 515.
2. **Critical Writing** For activity #2, encourage students to choose at least two comedians to compare Twain with. Have them create cluster diagrams of each comic's techniques.
3. **Creative Writing** Encourage students to choose a situation, event, or topic that will reveal interesting, important, or striking contrasts. *Tell students that they do not have to share anything they would feel uncomfortable discussing with others.*
4. **Speaking and Listening** Obtain Twain's essay "How to Tell a Story" and read it to students to help them understand Twain's ideas about how humor should be read.
5. **Art/Research** Suggest that students make notes to help them keep Twain's descriptions in mind. They might make a list, a cluster diagram, or a small sketch to refer to while researching.
6. **Creative Writing/Research/Art** Have students watch *Show Boat* so that they have a frame of reference for their article before proceeding with their research. Remind students that focusing on one question will guide their research and lead to a more detailed, in-depth article.

CHOICES: Building Your Portfolio

Writer's Notebook

1. Collecting Ideas for an Informative Report

WORK IN PROGRESS

Think of a place you would like to write a report about—perhaps a place in your neighborhood or town that is special to you, or a place that is threatened, such as a landmark in danger of being demolished. List some ideas of how you might approach your topic. You could focus your report on a question about the place, or how it has changed over time, or why it has meaning for you and others. Also, make some notes of ideas for drawings or maps you could use in an informative report. Save your notes for possible use in the Writer's Workshop on page 515.

Critical Writing

2. Comic Relief

Twain's use of humorous devices is one of the strongest characteristics of his work. With reference to both *Life on the Mississippi* and Spotlight On Mark Twain's Humor (page 465), explore in a brief essay how Twain's use of humor is like or unlike the use of humor by today's humorists and comedians. How do contemporary comics appeal to their particular audiences? Would Twain hold up today as a stand-up comic or a humorous writer? Explain.

Creative Writing

3. Double Vision

The last three paragraphs of this excerpt from *Life on the Mississippi* examine two very different ways of looking at the river. Try writing your own descriptive piece in which you compare and contrast two different views of something:

- your feelings before and after taking a particular action
- how you see some aspect of your life now and how you saw it in the past
- how a favorite place of yours looks in the daytime and at night

Speaking and Listening

4. A Real Character

Alone or with a partner, rehearse an oral reading of Twain's writing—either from the excerpts in this text or from another book. To prepare for your reading, you might want to watch the video *Mark Twain Gives an Interview,* with the actor Hal Holbrook portraying Mark Twain. You might also want to use simple props—a hat or an object representing a pilot's wheel—to help keep you in character. Perform your reading for the class.

Art / Research

5. Big River

Locate paintings, drawings, or engravings of the Mississippi River. Select three to five works that in your opinion best capture the Mississippi that Twain portrays in this excerpt. For each work, write a brief paragraph explaining why you chose it, and cite appropriate descriptions from Twain. Set up a display for your class, mounting your explanatory paragraph next to a photocopy or reproduction of each visual you've selected.

Creative Writing / Research / Art

6. It Just Keeps Rollin' Along

The editor of a travel magazine has asked you to write an article about the traditions and history of the Mississippi steamboat. Research the answers to such questions as these: When was the peak of the steamboat era? Did certain boats, captains, or pilots become famous? Where are the old steamboats now? How accurate are depictions like the musical *Show Boat* (available on video) in portraying the realities of the steamboat era? Write up your findings as a magazine story; include pictures for your article.

PORTFOLIO ASSESSMENT

Choices: Assessment Criteria For help in evaluating these Choices assignments, see the criteria in the ***Portfolio Management System,*** pp. 122–123.

STRATEGIES FOR INCLUSION

Spatial For activity #1, encourage students to consider a presentation that would move across, through, or around a place. Perhaps they could start at the outside and move in, or at the inside and move outward. Have them make a map to show their spatial presentation.

Visual To help students grasp the concept in activity #3 of different perspectives, show them Vincent van Gogh's paintings when he was in varying states of mental health or Monet's pictures of the Japanese bridge in his garden before his eyesight got bad, when he was nearly blind, and after the operation that restored his sight.

Learners Having Difficulty To help students with activity #4, provide cue cards or a prompter. Give them only one or two "Speaking Tips" to focus on at a time, such as using a performance voice and making eye contact with the audience.

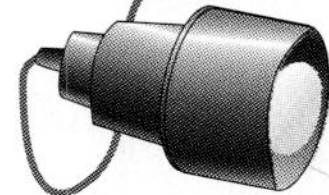

SPOTLIGHT ON

Mark Twain's Humor

During his lifetime, Mark Twain was better known as a lecturer than as a novelist, and he found considerable financial reward on the lecture circuit. Eyewitnesses reported that Twain had a genius for deadpan delivery, deliberately drawing out his remarks—and ending them with a perturbed expression. The **anecdotes** and maxims he delivered on stage would later be published in book form and sold by subscription in elaborate, illustrated volumes. A

Twain's maxims have taken on the force of **proverbs,** a phenomenon securing his position as a pioneer of American humor. Here is a sampling of his many and varied one-liners.

Caricature of Mark Twain by Keppler. Lithograph.
The Bettmann Archive.

It's better to keep your mouth shut and appear stupid than to open it and remove all doubt.

By trying, we can easily learn to endure adversity. Another man's, I mean.

If the man doesn't believe as we do, we say he is a crank, and that settles it. I mean, it does nowadays, because now we can't burn him. B

There are many humorous things in the world; among them, the white man's notion that he is less savage than the other savages.

There are several good protections against temptations, but the surest is cowardice.

If you pick up a starving dog and make him prosperous, he will not bite you. This is the principal difference between a dog and a man. C

Few things are harder to put up with than the annoyance of a good example.

When I was a boy of fourteen, my father was so ignorant I could hardly stand to have the old man around. But when I got to be twenty-one, I was astonished at how much he had learned in seven years.

It takes your enemy and your friend, working together, to hurt you to the heart; the one to slander you and the other to get the news to you.

Nothing so needs reforming as other people's habits.

A sin takes on new and real terrors when there seems a chance that it is going to be found out.

Behold, the fool saith, "Put not all thine eggs in the one basket"—which is but a manner of saying, "Scatter your money and your attention"; but the wise man saith, "Put all your eggs in the one basket and—*watch that basket.*"

A. Expansion

A reviewer from the New York *Tribune,* reviewing a lecture given by Twain in 1867, wrote: "No other lecturer, of course excepting Artemus Ward, has so thoroughly succeeded in exciting the mirthful curiosity, and compelling the laughter of his hearers. Mark Twain's delivery is deliberate and measured to the last degree. He lounges comfortably around his platform, seldom referring to notes, and seeks to establish a sort of button-hole relationship with his audience. . . . [H]is style is his own and needs to be seen to be understood."

B. Critical Reading: Analyzing Humor

? What techniques does Twain use in each maxim to create humor? [Possible answers: creating assumptions and then creating irony, caustic wit, surprising responses, saying things others probably feel but do not have the courage to say.]

C. Reader's Response: Shaping Interpretations

? Is this quotation funny? Reexamine all of Twain's quotations to see which you think are funny and which are not. [Sample responses: They are all funny; or some are "too true," "too caustic," or "too cruel" to be funny.]

STRATEGIES FOR INCLUSION

Auditory Students will benefit from hearing the one-liners read aloud, as they were first delivered by Twain in his lectures. Read the proverbs aloud, or have a perceptive reader and speaker declaim them. Discuss with students the tone of the proverbs.

INTEGRATING THE LANGUAGE ARTS

Strategic Reading Have students read the first two paragraphs only, focusing on cues that will determine how the remainder of the text should be read. Students should be able to glean that the quotations were meant to be read aloud in the course of a performance before a live audience.

ASSESSMENT TOOLS

Informal Assessment Assess students' performances of the material as they complete the exercises. Use the following measurement scale.
High=Delivers the material with appropriate intonation, gestures, and pauses that add humor to the delivery.
Medium=Several items from the above description are missing or weak.
Low=The piece is read, not performed. Pauses are not used.

QUICK PLANNING GUIDE

Into the Story

Author Biography p. 466

Before You Read p. 467

- **Reading Focus:** Students consider the power of imagination.
- **A Dialogue with the Text: Prior Knowledge** Write observations in Reader's Log
- **Elements of Literature: Point of View**
- **Background: Scaffolding** The landscape of the story

Through the Story

"An Occurrence at Owl Creek Bridge" pp. 468–473

Words to Own pp. 468–473

Making Meanings p. 474

Beyond the Story

Choices: Building Your Portfolio p. 474

- **Writer's Notebook:** Gather notes for a report of information
- **Critical Writing:** Plan a movie adaptation
- **Creative Writing:** Imitate Bierce's stream-of-consciousness technique in a creative piece

How to Own a Word p. 475

Spotlight On pp. 476–483

Ambrose Bierce

(1842–1914?)

Ambrose Bierce by J.H.E. Partington (1843–1899). Oil on canvas.

The Huntington Library, San Marino, California.

Ambrose Bierce infused his writing with an attitude of scorn for all the sentimental illusions human beings cling to. His dark vision of life centers on warfare and the cruel joke it plays on humanity. This bleak vision assures Bierce's place in our literary history.

Bierce was born in 1842, the tenth of thirteen children in the family of an eccentric and unsuccessful farmer named Marcus Aurelius Bierce. The Bierces lived in a log cabin in Meigs County, Ohio. Bierce was educated primarily through exploring his father's small library.

At nineteen, Bierce joined the Ninth Indiana Volunteers and saw action at the bloody Civil War battles of Shiloh and Chickamauga. He was also part of General Sherman's march to the sea in 1864. Bierce was once severely wounded and was cited for bravery no fewer than fifteen times.

At the war's end, Bierce reenlisted, but several years in the peacetime army left him discouraged about his prospects. He left the army and joined his brother Albert to work at the United States Mint in San Francisco. He began to contribute caustically witty, short pieces to the city's weeklies.

A growing reputation as a muckraking reporter brought Bierce the editorship of the San Francisco *News Letter* and the acquaintance of the literary community, including Mark Twain (page 450). When the financier Collis P. Huntington, head of the Southern Pacific Railroad, asked Bierce's price for silence on the railroad's tax fraud case, Bierce is said to have replied: "My price is about seventy-five million dollars, to be handed to the Treasurer of the United States." Bierce's disillusionment with the deceit and greed of his times continued to spur his pen and earned him the nickname "Bitter Bierce."

Bierce married in 1871 and moved to England, where he spent the next four years editing and contributing to humor magazines and making his first attempts at fiction. On his return to San Francisco in 1876, he wrote a regular column. This was the most active and fruitful time of Bierce's life. He became the witty scholar and literary dictator of the West Coast, but he never achieved wide recognition for his stories.

The Devil's Dictionary, first published in 1906 as *The Cynic's Word Book,* was more successful. In his dictionary, Bierce offered a collection of definitions filled with irony and sardonic humor. He defined war as a "by-product of the arts of peace," and peace as "a period of cheating between two periods of fighting." A cynic was a person who "sees things as they are, not as they ought to be. Hence the custom among the Scythians of plucking out a cynic's eyes to improve his vision."

In 1913, when Bierce was lonely and weary of his life, he asked his few friends to "forgive him in not perishing where he was." He set off for Mexico to report on, or join in, its revolution. "Goodbye," he wrote. "If you hear of my being stood up against a Mexican stone wall and shot to rags please know that I think it a pretty good way to depart this life. It beats old age, disease, or falling down the cellar stairs." No further word was ever heard from him.

WRITERS ON WRITING

Mark Twain delighted in colloquial speech; Ambrose Bierce shunned informal language. Have students compare Bierce's and Twain's language and comment on the following quotation from Bierce: "Slang is the speech of him who robs the literary garbage cans on their way to the dump."

WORDS TO OWN

The following vocabulary words are defined in the Words to Own at the bottom of the pupil's page.

sentinel p. 468	pivotal p. 471
deference p. 469	appalling p. 472
chafed p. 469	gyration p. 472
perilous p. 470	abrasion p. 472
oscillation p. 471	malign p. 473

BEFORE YOU READ
AN OCCURRENCE AT OWL CREEK BRIDGE

Reading Focus
All in the Mind
Can we ever really understand the complexities of the human mind? What's real? What's imaginary? When someone we love is long overdue, we can conjure up the details of disaster in a few seconds and make ourselves sick with worry. On the other hand, we can lift ourselves out of a blue mood by focusing on an event we can look forward to. Imagine, then, the extremes to which the human imagination might go in a time of severe, even life-threatening, stress. If a person were threatened with imminent death, what kinds of thoughts might pass through his or her mind? Would the mind provide a calming refuge or intensify the fear and horror?

A Dialogue with the Text

As you journey with Bierce's hero, pause three or four times to write down your own feelings, thoughts, or observations. What developments make you afraid for the hero? When do you feel relieved or even happy for him? What doubts, questions, or other reactions arise in your mind at other times?

Elements of Literature
Point of View
In the different sections of Bierce's story, watch for these variations in **point of view: (1) omniscient,** in which the narrator seems to know everything about all characters or events; (2) **objective,** in which the narrator reports without comment, much as a camera would record a scene; and (3) **third-person limited,** in which the narrator zooms in on the thoughts and feelings of a single character.

Point of view is the vantage point from which a writer tells the story.

For more on Point of View, see the Handbook of Literary Terms.

Background
The belief that life will prove gratifying and will reward our virtues is so strong that it has become a main current in storytelling. But this romantic notion has its inevitable counterpart in realism and naturalism—fiction that conforms to the truth as it is experienced rather than as we would like it to be.

Bierce's no-punches-pulled story is set in the deep South during the Civil War (1861–1865). He invites us to sympathize with the hero, a Southerner who has tried to help the Confederate cause, and he portrays the Union side as brutal and treacherous. Yet the horrors of war may serve only as an external setting for the landscape that *really* interests the writer. That landscape is the inside of the mind of a man condemned to death.

Into the Story

Using **BEFORE YOU READ** p. 467

Reading Focus
Ask students if they have ever visualized something so completely that it seemed real. Then, read the first three sentences of the Reading Focus text. Ask students about other times when people might visualize in an especially vivid way. Then, read the last two sentences and have the class discuss them.

Background
Invite the class to brainstorm stories from their reading or from movies that depict life as it really is or life as people would like it to be. Cluster the stories according to type on the chalkboard, and discuss the relative merits of the different approaches.

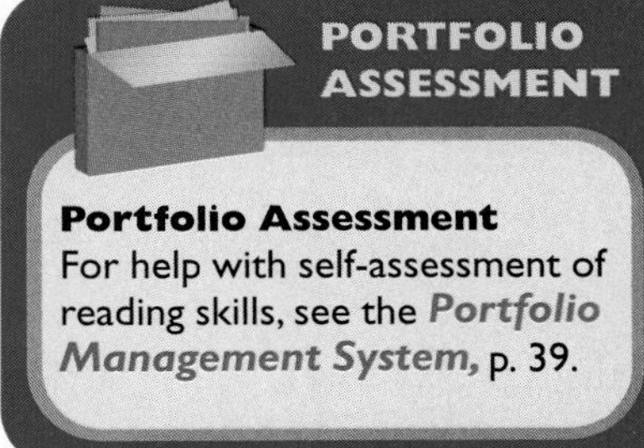

Portfolio Assessment
For help with self-assessment of reading skills, see the ***Portfolio Management System,*** p. 39.

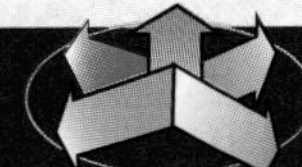

PROGRAM MANAGER

- **Planning Instruction** See Teaching Notes, *Teaching Resources A,* p. 180, for additional information for this selection.
- **Instructional Support** See Graphic Organizer for Active Reading, *Teaching Resources A,* p. 187, for a Through the Story activity.
- **Assessment** See Selection Test, *Test Booklet,* pp. 111–112.
- **Language Link** See Language Link, *Teaching Resources A,* pp. 188–189, and *Language and Writing Skills Worksheets,* p. 67.
- **Reinforcement** Use the Words to Own worksheet in *Teaching Resources A,* p. 190.
- **Reinforcement** See Transparency 10.4 in the *Audiovisual Resources Binder.*

Through the Story

A. Critical Reading: Analyzing Narration

? How would you describe the narrator's relationship to the action? [Possible answer: The narrator seems objective and removed.]

B. Critical Reading: Summarizing

? What is the situation at the beginning of the story? [A man is about to be hanged from a railroad bridge by soldiers in the Federal (Union) army. The setting is northern Alabama, sometime during the Civil War.]

C. Literary Element: Personification

? What effect does Bierce achieve by personifying death? [Possible answer: He emphasizes the necessity of showing respect when death is present.]

An Occurrence at Owl Creek Bridge

Ambrose Bierce

I

A man stood upon a railroad bridge in northern Alabama, looking down into the swift water twenty feet below. The man's hands were behind his back, the wrists bound with a cord. A rope closely encircled his neck. It was attached to a stout cross-timber above his head, and the slack fell to the level of his knees. Some loose boards laid upon the sleepers[1] supporting the metals of the railway supplied a footing for him and his executioners—two private soldiers of the Federal army, directed by a sergeant who in civil life may have been a deputy sheriff. At a short remove upon the same temporary platform was an officer in the uniform of his rank, armed. He was a captain. A sentinel at each end of the bridge stood with his rifle in the position known as "support," that is to say, vertical in front of the left shoulder, the hammer resting on the forearm thrown straight across the chest—a formal and unnatural position, enforcing an erect carriage of the body. It did not appear to be the duty of these two men to know what was occurring at the center of the bridge; they merely blockaded the two ends of the foot planking that traversed it.

Beyond one of the sentinels nobody was in sight; the railroad ran straight away into a forest for a hundred yards, then, curving, was lost to view. Doubtless there was an outpost farther along. The other bank of the stream was open ground —a gentle acclivity[2] topped with a stockade of vertical tree trunks, loopholed for rifles, with a single embrasure through which protruded the muzzle of a brass cannon commanding the bridge. Midway of the slope between bridge and fort were the spectators—a single company of infantry in line, at "parade rest," the butts of the rifles on the ground, the barrels inclining slightly backward against the right shoulder, the hands crossed upon the stock. A lieutenant stood at the right of the line, the point of his sword upon the ground, his left hand resting upon his right. Excepting the group of four at the center of the bridge, not a man moved. The company faced the bridge, staring stonily, motionless. The sentinels, facing the banks of the stream, might have been statues to adorn the bridge. The captain stood with folded arms, silent, observing the work of his subordinates, but making no sign. Death is a dignitary who when he comes announced is to be received with formal manifestations of respect,

1. **sleepers:** railroad ties.
2. **acclivity:** uphill slope.

WORDS TO OWN

sentinel (sen′ti·nəl) *n.:* guard; sentry.

OPTIONS FOR TEACHING

STRATEGIES FOR INCLUSION

Visual/Spatial As students read the text, ask them to focus on the kinds of camera shots they would use if they were filming a movie of the story. Students can think of the relationship of camera techniques to the narrative techniques. Have students dramatize in a storyboard of five panels a scene of their own choice.

English Language Development The sequence of events in this story is complex and may be particularly hard for students to follow. Elicit the events in the order that they appear in the story and write them on the board. Then, divide the class into small groups and have them put the events in chronological order. Check their work.

Learners Having Difficulty Students may benefit from reading the story with a partner. Partners can pause after each section of the story to summarize for each other the events in that section. Partners can read the story aloud, trading off the role of reader after each paragraph.

even by those most familiar with him. In the code of military etiquette, silence and fixity are forms of deference.

The man who was engaged in being hanged was apparently about thirty-five years of age. He was a civilian, if one might judge from his habit, which was that of a planter. His features were good—a straight nose, firm mouth, broad forehead, from which his long, dark hair was combed straight back, falling behind his ears to the collar of his well-fitting frock coat. He wore a moustache and pointed beard, but no whiskers; his eyes were large and dark gray, and had a kindly expression which one would hardly have expected in one whose neck was in the hemp. Evidently this was no vulgar assassin. The liberal military code makes provision for hanging many kinds of persons, and gentlemen are not excluded.

The preparations being complete, the two private soldiers stepped aside and each drew away the plank upon which he had been standing. The sergeant turned to the captain, saluted, and placed himself immediately behind that officer, who in turn moved apart one pace. These movements left the condemned man and the sergeant standing on the two ends of the same plank, which spanned three of the crossties of the bridge. The end upon which the civilian stood almost, but not quite, reached a fourth. This plank had been held in place by the weight of the captain; it was now held by that of the sergeant. At a signal from the former, the latter would step aside, the plank would tilt and the condemned man go down between two ties. The arrangement commended itself to his judgment as simple and effective. His face had not been covered nor his eyes bandaged. He looked a moment at his "unsteadfast footing," then let his gaze wander to the swirling water of the stream racing madly beneath his feet. A piece of dancing driftwood caught his attention, and his eyes followed it down the current. How slowly it appeared to move! What a sluggish stream!

He closed his eyes in order to fix his last thoughts upon his wife and children. The water, touched to gold by the early sun, the brooding mists under the banks at some distance down the stream, the fort, the soldiers, the piece of drift—all had distracted him. And now he became conscious of a new disturbance. Striking through the thought of his dear ones was a sound which he could neither ignore nor understand, a sharp, distinct, metallic percussion like the stroke of a blacksmith's hammer upon the anvil; it had the same ringing quality. He wondered what it was, and whether immeasurably distant or nearby—it seemed both. Its recurrence was regular, but as slow as the tolling of a death knell. He awaited each stroke with impatience and—he knew not why—apprehension. The intervals of silence grew progressively longer; the delays became maddening. With their greater infrequency the sounds increased in strength and sharpness. They hurt his ear like the thrust of a knife; he feared he would shriek. What he heard was the ticking of his watch.

He unclosed his eyes and saw again the water below him. "If I could free my hands," he thought, "I might throw off the noose and spring into the stream. By diving I could evade the bullets and, swimming vigorously, reach the bank, take to the woods, and get away home. My home, thank God, is as yet outside their lines; my wife and little ones are still beyond the invader's farthest advance."

As these thoughts, which have here to be set down in words, were flashed into the doomed man's brain rather than evolved from it, the captain nodded to the sergeant. The sergeant stepped aside.

II

Peyton Farquhar was a well-to-do planter, of an old and highly respected Alabama family. Being a slave owner and, like other slave owners, a politician, he was naturally an original secessionist and ardently devoted to the Southern cause. Circumstances of an imperious nature, which it is unnecessary to relate here, had prevented him from taking service with the gallant army that had fought the disastrous campaigns ending with the fall of Corinth,[3] and he chafed under the inglorious

3. **Corinth:** Union forces under General William S. Rosecrans (1819–1898) took Corinth, Mississippi, on October 4, 1862.

Words to Own

deference (def′ər·əns) *n.:* respect.
chafed (chāft) *v.:* became impatient.

D. Literary Element: Diction

? What effect does the phrase "engaged in being hanged" have on you? [Possible answers: It sounds like a minor occupational activity, like a man writing a letter; or it is an understatement that emphasizes the cruelty of the act.]

E. Reader's Response: First Thoughts

? What is your reaction to this description? [Sample responses: I wonder why a man of this description is being hanged; or I feel sympathy for him.]

F. Literary Element: Point of View

? How does the point of view change? [The narration suddenly shifts to reflect the condemned man's thought.]

G. Critical Reading: Analyzing Description

? How does the description in this paragraph differ from that in the first two paragraphs? What does the change signify? [Possible answers: It is more lyrical. Students may think it reflects a romantic sensibility.]

H. Literary Element: Impressionism

? How do time and sound change in this paragraph? What effect does this create? [Possible answer: Time seems to be slowed down while sound seems to be amplified. It seems to convey the man's mental state.]

STRATEGIES FOR INCLUSION

Logical-Mathematical Some students may have difficulty understanding Farquhar's motivation and basic outlook on life. Pair these students with romantic, idealistic students who may be able to explain the protagonist's outlook, and together they can create a poster graphing Farquhar's motives.

Special Needs Many students may find it difficult to understand the sequence of events in this story, particularly since some of the events that lead to the protagonist's death are implied rather than explicitly stated. After students have read the story, give them strips of paper on which are written the following events and have students work to put the strips in logical order: protagonist's death, disguised Confederate soldier gives information about bridge, protagonist imagines escaping, protagonist is captured, protagonist attempts to burn bridge.

INTEGRATING THE LANGUAGE ARTS

Strategic Reading After students have read the selection, review it as a class, working with students to distinguish between fantasy and reality. Ask them to identify the beginning and end of the fantasy and to describe its characteristic elements. Consider using Transparency 5: Venn Diagram in the Transparency Package. ☞

A. Critical Reading: Drawing Conclusions

? Why is this dictum villainous? [Possible answers: It leads Farquhar on his mission of espionage. Its practice by the Federal scout tempts Farquhar to his destruction.]

B. Reader's Response: First Thoughts

? What impression do you get of the Farquhars from this paragraph? [Sample responses: They are gracious aristocrats who find sitting on a rustic bench and bringing water to a soldier very romantic; or they are naive.]

C. Critical Reading: Making Inferences

? How do these two paragraphs, plus Farquhar's earlier conversation with the soldier in Confederate uniform, explain how Farquhar comes to be standing on the Owl Creek bridge with a rope around his neck? What information is left out? [Possible answers: A disguised Union scout tempts him to sabotage the position held by the Union. One thing that is left out is why Farquhar is singled out. Is he a leader among the planters? Does the Union simply want to make an example of someone?]

restraint, longing for the release of his energies, the larger life of the soldier, the opportunity for distinction. That opportunity, he felt, would come, as it comes to all in wartime. Meanwhile he did what he could. No service was too humble for him to perform in aid of the South, no adventure too perilous for him to undertake if consistent with the character of a civilian who was at heart a soldier, and who in good faith and without too much qualification assented to at least a part of the frankly villainous dictum that all is fair in love and war. (A)

One evening while Farquhar and his wife were sitting on a rustic bench near the entrance to his grounds, a gray-clad soldier rode up to the gate and asked for a drink of water. Mrs. Farquhar was only too happy to serve him with her own white hands. While she was fetching the water, her husband approached the dusty horseman and inquired eagerly for news from the front. (B)

"The Yanks are repairing the railroads," said the man, "and are getting ready for another advance. They have reached the Owl Creek bridge, put it in order, and built a stockade on the north bank. The commandant has issued an order, which is posted everywhere, declaring that any civilian caught interfering with the railroad, its bridges, tunnels, or trains will be summarily hanged. I saw the order."

"How far is it to the Owl Creek bridge?" Farquhar asked.

"About thirty miles."

"Is there no force on this side the creek?"

"Only a picket post half a mile out, on the railroad, and a single sentinel at this end of the bridge."

"Suppose a man—a civilian and student of hanging—should elude the picket post and perhaps get the better of the sentinel," said Farquhar, smiling, "what could he accomplish?"

The soldier reflected. "I was there a month ago," he replied. "I observed that the flood of last winter had lodged a great quantity of driftwood against the wooden pier at this end of the bridge. It is now dry and would burn like tow."

(C) The lady had now brought the water, which the soldier drank. He thanked her ceremoniously, bowed to her husband, and rode away. An hour later, after nightfall, he repassed the plantation, going northward in the direction from which he had come. He was a Federal scout.

III

As Peyton Farquhar fell straight downward through the bridge, he lost consciousness and was as one already dead. From this state he was awakened—ages later, it seemed to him—by the pain of a sharp pressure upon his throat, followed by a sense of suffocation. Keen, poignant agonies seemed to shoot from his neck downward through every fiber of his body and limbs. These pains appeared to flash along well-defined lines of ramification and to beat with an inconceivably rapid periodicity. They seemed like streams of pulsating fire heating him to an intolerable temperature. As to his head, he was conscious of nothing but a feeling of fullness—of congestion. These sensations were unaccompanied by thought. The intellectual part of his nature was already effaced; he had power only to feel, and feeling was torment. He was conscious of motion. Encompassed in a luminous cloud, of which he was now merely the fiery heart, without material

WORDS TO OWN

perilous (per'ə·ləs) *adj.*: dangerous.

OPTIONS FOR TEACHING

INTEGRATING THE LANGUAGE ARTS

Writing: Found Poem Have students review the story to find lines for a found poem. Students should include two or three Words to Own in their poems. Before students choose the lines for their poems, they should decide what elements of Peyton Farquhar's experience they want to focus on—for example, his emotions, his actions, or his peculiar point of view. Students can illustrate and display their poems.

Speaking and Listening Have students imagine that the Federal scout and Farquhar meet just before Farquhar is hanged. What might they say to each other? Have pairs of students volunteer to improvise a dialogue between the two.

Language and Vocabulary Ask students to look for examples of consonance in the selection and to identify the effect(s) of its use. [Some students may think it heightens the reader's sensibility to parallel Farquhar's heightened sensibility.]

substance, he swung through unthinkable arcs of oscillation, like a vast pendulum. Then all at once, with terrible suddenness, the light about him shot upward with the noise of a loud plash; a frightful roaring was in his ears, and all was cold and dark. The power of thought was restored; he knew that the rope had broken and he had fallen into the stream. There was no additional strangulation; the noose about his neck was already suffocating him and kept the water from his lungs. To die of hanging at the bottom of a river!—the idea seemed to him ludicrous. He opened his eyes in the darkness and saw above him a gleam of light, but how distant, how inaccessible! He was still sinking, for the light became fainter and fainter until it was a mere glimmer. Then it began to grow and brighten, and he knew that he was rising toward the surface—knew it with reluctance, for he was now very comfortable. "To be hanged and drowned," he thought, "that is not so bad; but I do not wish to be shot. No; I will not be shot; that is not fair." D

He was not conscious of an effort, but a sharp pain in his wrist apprised him that he was trying to free his hands. He gave the struggle his attention, as an idler might observe the feat of a juggler, without interest in the outcome. What splendid effort!—what magnificent, what superhuman strength! Ah, that was a fine endeavor! Bravo! The cord fell away; his arms parted and floated upward, the hands dimly seen on each side in the growing light. He watched them with a new interest as first one and then the other pounced upon the noose at his neck. They tore it away and thrust it fiercely aside, its undulations resembling those of a water snake. "Put it back, put it back!" He thought he shouted these words to his hands, for the undoing of the noose had been succeeded by the direst pang that he had yet experienced. His neck ached horribly; his brain was on fire; his heart, which had been fluttering faintly, gave a great leap, trying to force itself out at his mouth. His whole body was racked and wrenched with an insupportable anguish! But his disobedient hands gave no heed to the command. They beat the water vigorously with quick, downward strokes, forcing him to the surface. He felt his head emerge; his eyes were blinded by the sunlight; his chest expanded convulsively, and with a supreme and crowning agony his lungs engulfed a great draft of air, which instantly he expelled in a shriek! E

He was now in full possession of his physical senses. They were, indeed, preternaturally keen and alert. Something in the awful disturbance of his organic system had so exalted and refined them that they made record of things never before perceived. He felt the ripples upon his face and heard their separate sounds as they struck. He looked at the forest on the bank of the stream, saw the individual trees, the leaves, and the veining of each leaf—saw the very insects upon them: the locusts, the brilliant-bodied flies, the gray spiders stretching their webs from twig to twig. He noted the prismatic colors in all the dewdrops upon a million blades of grass. The humming of the gnats that danced above the eddies of the stream, the beating of the dragonflies' wings, the strokes of the water spiders' legs, like oars which had lifted their boat—all these made audible music. A fish slid along beneath his eyes, and he heard the rush of its body parting the water. F

He had come to the surface facing down the stream; in a moment the visible world seemed to wheel slowly round, himself the pivotal point, and he saw the bridge, the fort, the soldiers upon the bridge, the captain, the sergeant, the two privates, his executioners. They were in silhouette against the blue sky. They shouted and gesticulated, pointing at him. The captain had drawn his pistol, but did not fire; the others were unarmed. Their movements were grotesque and horrible, their forms gigantic.

Suddenly he heard a sharp report and something struck the water smartly within a few inches of his head, spattering his face with spray. He heard a second report, and saw one of the sentinels with his rifle at his shoulder, a light cloud of blue smoke rising from the muzzle. The man in the water saw the eye of the man on the bridge gazing into his own through the sights of the rifle. He observed that it was a gray eye and remembered having read that gray eyes were keenest, G

Words to Own

oscillation (äs′ə·lā′shən) *n.:* regular back-and-forth movement.

pivotal (piv′ə·təl) *adj.:* central; acting as a point around which other things turn.

D. Reader's Response: Connecting with the Text

? What do you think of this attitude? [Sample responses: Being shot, too, would be unfair on top of being tricked and hanged; or it is hard to know what to make of it.]

E. Reader's Response: Shaping Interpretations

? What does the cord falling away and the arms floating up indicate? [Sample responses: Farquhar's perception is altered; he is out of his mind; or something magical is happening.]

F. Critical Reading: Finding Details

? How has Farquhar's vision changed? [Possible answer: Now he not only sees lyrical details of nature, but also sees them in more detail; or the tiniest things affect his senses in a deep, rich way.]

G. Critical Reading: Speculating

? Is it possible that he can see the shooter's eye? [Possible answer: It is unlikely that after observing the soldiers in silhouette he is able to see them clearly enough to distinguish eye color.]

Crossing the Curriculum

Social Studies Some students might be interested in researching the role of spies during the Civil War. Ask students to research a spy and to report orally to the class, using visual aids (photographs or overhead transparencies) if available. Challenge students to research a woman spy if they wish.

Industrial Arts Work with the industrial arts teacher, if desired, and divide the class into small task groups to research and build models of railroad bridges. Each group should be responsible for one specific aspect, such as finding bridge photos, bringing materials, or actual construction. Models should show an understanding of the construction techniques used during the nineteenth century.

Art Students may want to compare Farquhar's intense perceptions after his escape to paintings and drawings by impressionists. Works by American impressionists Mary Cassatt and James Whistler would be good choices for students to research. Have students show examples of the works to the class.

A. Reader's Response: Shaping Interpretations

? How do you explain Farquhar's ability to elude all the shots he compares to the noise of the crashing water at Niagara Falls? [Sample responses: It is unlikely and hints of unreality; or he is able to dodge effectively because he is in the water.]

B. Exploring the Historical Period

Reliable repeating rifles were first available in 1860, but the U.S. Army standard weapon during the Civil War was the Springfield service rifle that had to be reloaded after every shot. This explains the use of the ramrods.

C. Critical Reading: Analyzing Character

? How does a naive civilian know every move the military will make in attempting to recapture him? [Possible answers: He had visited camps, so maybe he has more familiarity than it seemed at first; or perhaps this is not really happening—maybe it is a dream or his imagination.]

D. Critical Reading: Speculating

? Why is he so enthralled with the sand? [Possible answer: Because he has finally reached dry land and is grateful.]

and that all famous marksmen had them. Nevertheless, this one had missed.

A counterswirl had caught Farquhar and turned him half round; he was again looking into the forest on the bank opposite the fort. The sound of a clear, high voice in monotonous singsong now rang out behind him and came across the water with a distinctness that pierced and subdued all other sounds, even the beating of the ripples in his ears. Although no soldier, he had frequented camps enough to know the dread significance of that deliberate, drawling, aspirated chant; the lieutenant on shore was taking a part in the morning's work. How coldly and pitilessly—with what an even, calm intonation, presaging, and enforcing tranquility in the men—with what accurately measured intervals fell those cruel words:

"Attention, company! . . . Shoulder arms! . . . Ready! . . . Aim! . . . Fire!"

Farquhar dived—dived as deeply as he could. (A) The water roared in his ears like the voice of Niagara, yet he heard the dulled thunder of the volley and, rising again toward the surface, met shining bits of metal, singularly flattened, oscillating slowly downward. Some of them touched him on the face and hands, then fell away, continuing their descent. One lodged between his collar and neck; it was uncomfortably warm and he snatched it out.

As he rose to the surface, gasping for breath, he saw that he had been a long time underwater; he was perceptibly farther downstream—nearer to safety. (B) The soldiers had almost finished reloading; the metal ramrods flashed all at once in the sunshine as they were drawn from the barrels, turned in the air, and thrust into their sockets. The two sentinels fired again, independently and ineffectually.

The hunted man saw all this over his shoulder; he was now swimming vigorously with the current. His brain was as energetic as his arms and legs; he thought with the rapidity of lightning.

"The officer," he reasoned, "will not make that martinet's[4] error a second time. It is as easy to dodge a volley as a single shot. He has probably already given the command to fire at will. God help me, I cannot dodge them all!"

4. **martinet's:** A martinet is a disciplinarian of military rigidity.

An <u>appalling</u> plash within two yards of him was followed by a loud, rushing sound, *diminuendo,*[5] which seemed to travel back through the air to the fort and died in an explosion which stirred the very river to its deeps! A rising sheet of water curved over him, fell down upon him, blinded him, strangled him! The cannon had taken a hand in the game. As he shook his head free from the commotion of the smitten water, he heard the deflected shot humming through the air ahead, and in an instant it was cracking and smashing the branches in the forest beyond.

(C) "They will not do that again," he thought; "the next time they will use a charge of grape.[6] I must keep my eye upon the gun; the smoke will apprise me—the report arrives too late; it lags behind the missile. That is a good gun."

Suddenly he felt himself whirled round and round—spinning like a top. The water, the banks, the forests, the now distant bridge, fort and men—all were commingled and blurred. Objects were represented by their colors only; circular horizontal streaks of color—that was all he saw. He had been caught in a vortex and was being whirled on with a velocity of advance and <u>gyration</u> that made him giddy and sick. In a few moments he was flung upon the gravel at the foot of the left bank of the stream—the southern bank—and behind a projecting point which concealed him from his enemies. The sudden arrest of his motion, the <u>abrasion</u> of one of his hands on the gravel, restored him, and he wept with delight. (D) He dug his fingers into the sand, threw it over himself in handfuls, and audibly blessed it. It looked like diamonds, rubies, emeralds; he could think of nothing beautiful which it did not resemble. The trees upon the bank were giant garden plants; he noted a definite order in their arrangement, inhaled the fragrance of their blooms. A strange, roseate light shone through the spaces

5. ***diminuendo*** (də·min′yo͞o·en′dō): decreasing in loudness.

6. **charge of grape:** cannon charge of small iron balls, called grapeshot.

WORDS TO OWN

appalling (ə·pôl′iŋ) *adj.:* dismaying.
gyration (jī·rā′shən) *n.:* circular movement; whirling.
abrasion (ə·brā′zhən) *n.:* scrape.

OPTIONS FOR TEACHING

COOPERATIVE LEARNING

Grouping For the industrial arts project, one strategy of grouping students is to consider the task as having four important parts: creating or finding a design, creating a blueprint, reading the plans while others build, and the actual construction. Thus there are roles for students with kinesthetic, spatial, visual, interpersonal, logical-mathematical, and auditory intelligences. Try to create a good mix in each group.

CLASSROOM MANAGEMENT

Block Scheduling Read a story aloud to the class (twenty to twenty-five minutes). To maintain interest during the longer class period, have students work with partners to complete a crossword puzzle using Words to Own (twenty to twenty-five minutes). Next, ask students to study the Words to Own with their partners (fifteen to twenty minutes). Give a vocabulary quiz (fifteen to twenty minutes). Using this schedule during the longer class period is particularly helpful for students who may have difficulty studying on their own. It also immediately assesses student mastery of Words to Own.

among their trunks, and the wind made in their branches the music of aeolian harps.[7] He had no wish to perfect his escape—was content to remain in that enchanting spot until retaken.

A whiz and rattle of grapeshot among the branches high above his head roused him from his dream. The baffled cannoneer had fired him a random farewell. He sprang to his feet, rushed up the sloping bank, and plunged into the forest.

All that day he traveled, laying his course by the rounding sun. The forest seemed interminable; nowhere did he discover a break in it, not even a woodsman's road. He had not known that he lived in so wild a region. There was something uncanny in the revelation. E

By nightfall he was fatigued, footsore, famishing. The thought of his wife and children urged him on. At last he found a road which led him in what he knew to be the right direction. It was as wide and straight as a city street, yet it seemed untraveled. No fields bordered it, no dwelling anywhere. Not so much as the barking of a dog suggested human habitation. The black bodies of the trees formed a straight wall on both sides, terminating on the horizon in a point, like a diagram in a lesson in perspective. Overhead, as he looked up through this rift in the wood, shone great golden stars looking unfamiliar and grouped in strange constellations. He was sure they were arranged in some order which had a secret and malign significance. The wood on either side was full of singular noises, among which—once, twice, and again—he distinctly heard whispers in an unknown tongue. F

His neck was in pain and lifting his hand to it he found it horribly swollen. He knew that it had a circle of black where the rope had bruised it. His eyes felt congested; he could no longer close them. His tongue was swollen with thirst; he relieved its fever by thrusting it forward from between his teeth into the cold air. How softly the turf had carpeted the untraveled avenue—he could no longer feel the roadway beneath his feet!

Doubtless, despite his suffering, he had fallen asleep while walking, for now he sees another scene—perhaps he has merely recovered from a delirium. He stands at the gate of his own home. All is as he left it, and all bright and beautiful in the morning sunshine. He must have traveled the entire night. As he pushes open the gate and passes up the wide white walk, he sees a flutter of female garments; his wife, looking fresh and cool and sweet, steps down from the veranda to meet him. At the bottom of the steps she stands waiting, with a smile of ineffable joy, an attitude of matchless grace and dignity. Ah, how beautiful she is! He springs forward with extended arms. As he is about to clasp her he feels a stunning blow upon the back of the neck; a blinding white light blazes all about him with a sound like the shock of a cannon—then all is darkness and silence! G

Peyton Farquhar was dead; his body, with a broken neck, swung gently from side to side beneath the timbers of the Owl Creek bridge. H

WORDS TO OWN

malign (mə·līn′) *adj.:* harmful; evil.

7. **aeolian harps:** stringed instruments that are played by the wind. Aeolus is the god of the winds in Greek mythology.

E. Critical Reading: Drawing Conclusions

? What do you think this means? [Possible answers: He is disoriented after his frightening experiences, and he is lost; or the scene described is not really happening. Some students may interpret this as a foreshadowing of his death.]

F. Critical Reading: Speculating

? Why is a landscape that should be familiar unfamiliar? [Possible answers: He is disoriented; the Union army has done things that have changed the landscape, such as taking prisoners or tearing down the buildings that used to be along the road; or the scene is happening only in his imagination.]

G. Critical Reading: Drawing Conclusions

? What happened? [He is dead.]

H. Literary Element: Theme

? How is the theme of illusion versus reality played out in this work? [Possible answers: Farquhar's romantic illusions about war are ended by his capture and death. The illusion of Farquhar's romantic escape from death ends with the conclusion of the story.]

PROBLEM SOLVING/ CRITICAL THINKING

Evaluating Advice Farquhar's death can be attributed to his taking advice he should not have taken. Ask students to consider how to decide whether to take someone's advice. Have them work in small groups to generate a list of criteria. Then, have a class meeting in which groups compare and consolidate their lists. Possible criteria include, for example, the authority, experience, expertise, and motivation of the advisor.

ASSESSMENT TOOLS

Check Test: True-False

1. Farquhar is a Confederate captain who has been captured in a sabotage attempt. [False]
2. Farquhar has been condemned to death by firing squad. [False]
3. Farquhar was entrapped by a Union scout into sabotaging a bridge. [True]
4. In the middle part of the story, Bierce uses flashback to explain why Farquhar is being executed. [True]

Self-Reflection: Reading Encourage students to reflect on their thought processes as they read the selection for the first time by taking brief notes as they read. When did they suspect that something was not right with Farquhar's escape? What clues led them to feel uncomfortable with the narration? Encourage them to continue these metacognitive reflections after their initial reading.

Making Meanings

First Thoughts

1. Possible responses: I was shocked to find out that he had not escaped but was instead dying. Or I knew all along that it was a fantasy.

Reviewing the Text

a. He is about to be hanged.
b. A Union spy comes to Farquhar's house and tells him that Union soldiers have been working on the Owl Creek bridge and will hang any civilian who interferes with their travel. Farquhar makes plans to burn the bridge.
c. A few seconds.
d. He imagines that the rope breaks, that he eludes the soldiers, and that he makes his way home to his wife.

Shaping Interpretations

2. Third-person limited. It is appropriate because it reveals the workings of Farquhar's imagination.
3. Responses will vary. Farquhar's gentlemanly bearing and the Union soldier's trick may prejudice readers toward Farquhar and the Confederate side. Some students may think the story is primarily about the violence people commit against each other.
4. Possible responses: He manipulates my feelings by encouraging the false hope that Farquhar has escaped. But he prepares me for the surprise ending with words and phrases that indicate that the escape is a fantasy.

Extending the Text

5. **(Synthesis)** Possible responses: The story shows that the terror of death heightens sense perceptions and distorts time and distance. The story also shows that the condemned may fantasize about a second chance. Students may refer to out-of-body or near-death experiences reported in newspapers to judge the believability of Bierce's presentation.

Challenging the Text

6. **(Evaluation)** Possible responses: I thought it was a mean trick, but a meaningful one both for Farquhar and the reader: It presents a cynical view of the universe, in which trust is always misplaced and hope is a sham. I think it was just a technical exercise for Bierce and has no profound meaning.

MAKING MEANINGS

First Thoughts

1. Did you feel that the outcome of this story was credible and powerful, or did you feel cheated by the surprise ending? What kind of ending had you been led to anticipate? Explain your response.

Reviewing the Text

a. State the situation Peyton Farquhar faces in Part I.
b. Part II of the story is a flashback. List its events in chronological order.
c. How much time actually elapses between the opening and closing lines of Part III?
d. Summarize in one sentence what Farquhar imagines in Part III.

Shaping Interpretations

2. The third part of the story, which occurs within the few seconds before Farquhar dies, is presumably a fantasy. What **point of view** does the writer use here? Why is this point of view particularly appropriate?
3. Do you think Bierce tries to enlist your sympathies toward either the Union or the Confederate side? Or does the story seem to be focused on a more general **theme** about the nature of the war? Cite evidence from the story.
4. Review the notes you made in your Reader's Log. How did Bierce manipulate your feelings? How did he prepare you for the ending?

Extending the Text

5. What does this story reveal about the psychology of a person in a life-or-death situation? On the basis of personal experience or of true-life stories you know about, do you find this psychology believable or far-fetched? Explain.

Challenging the Text

6. The critics Cleanth Brooks and Robert Penn Warren have said that Bierce's story depends too much on a quirk of human psychology and is thus a mere "case study" that does not reveal anything important about human nature, as good fiction does. Do you agree? Why or why not?

CHOICES: Building Your Portfolio

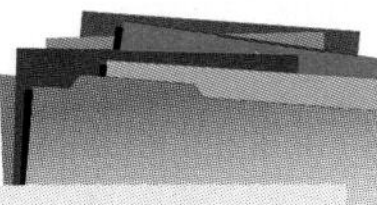

Writer's Notebook

1. Collecting Ideas for an Informative Report

WORK IN PROGRESS

Make some notes about interesting topics this story suggests (perhaps the use of spies during the Civil War or current psychological theories of stress). Then, write down a list of possible sources of information you could consult for your research: library resources, community sources (local museums or historical societies), and so on. Save your notes for possible use in the Writer's Workshop on page 515.

Critical Writing

2. In the Director's Chair

Write a memorandum to a film producer outlining your plans for adapting this story into a movie. Point out scenes where you would use each of the following techniques: (a) close-up shot; (b) panoramic shot; (c) moving-camera shot; (d) quick cut to new scene; (e) fast motion; (f) slow motion; (g) fuzzy image; (h) sound effects. Include any other information that will persuade the producer to make the film.

Creative Writing

3. Imitation of Bierce

Write a brief narrative in which you explore the inner workings of the mind of a character subjected to a moment of intense pressure or an extraordinary crisis. Try to imitate Bierce by shifting your narrative between external reality and internal fancy.

PORTFOLIO ASSESSMENT

Choices: Assesment Criteria For help in evaluating these Choices assignments, see the criteria in the ***Portfolio Management System,*** p. 124.

STRATEGIES FOR INCLUSION

Visual/Auditory For activity #2, let students work in pairs to create a soundtrack and storyboard to accompany their memorandum. Students can make a brief list of music that reflects the mood of the story. Their storyboards should consist of no more than ten sketches in a series of panels. Have the pairs use their work to deliver a "pitch" to the class.

Affixes: The Long and Short of It

Prefixes and suffixes are examples of **affixes,** word parts attached to the beginning or end of a base word or root to make a new word. Knowing some frequently used affixes can help you quickly unlock the meanings of words that at first glance seem long and inaccessible.

In fact, *inaccessible* is a good word to start with. Ambrose Bierce uses it in "An Occurrence at Owl Creek Bridge": "He opened his eyes in the darkness and saw above him a gleam of light, but how distant, how inaccessible!" (page 471). Context tells you that *inaccessible* has a similar meaning to *distant.* But that doesn't quite get you to a full understanding of the word's meaning. To do that, try using affix analysis.

There are many prefixes and suffixes in English, but some are more commonly used than others. **Prefixes** are added to the beginning of a **base word** or **root** and always change its meaning. Some prefixes adjust their spelling so that the resulting word will be easier to say.

Prefixes	Meanings	Examples
co–, col–, com–	with, together	coexist, collide, compare
con–, cor–	with, together	convene, correspond
de–	away, from, off	defect, desert
dis–	away, off, opposing	dismount, dissent
em–, en–	cause to be, put into	empower, enrobe
ex–, e–, ef–	away from, out, up	excise, emigrate efface
in–, im–, il–, ir–	not	incapable, impious, illegal, irregular
pro–	forward, in place of, favoring	proceed, pronoun, pro-American
re–	back, again	recede, recur
un–	not, reverse of	untrue, unfold

Suffixes are added to the end of a base word or root. **Inflectional suffixes,** like *-ed* and *-ing,* usually just change the tense, person, or number of a word (generally a verb). **Derivational suffixes,** like the ones listed below, change the entire meaning of a root or base word.

Suffixes	Meanings	Examples
–able, –ible	able, likely	capable, flexible
–al	doer, pertaining to	rival, autumnal
–ant, –ent	actor, showing	servant, superintendent
–ate	having, characteristic of	collegiate
–ence	act, condition, fact	patience, evidence
–er, –or	doer	baker, director
–ic	dealing with, caused by, showing	classic, choleric, workaholic
–ion, –tion	action, result, state	union, fusion, selection
–ive	belonging or tending to	detective, native
–ous	marked by, given to	religious, furious
–y	quality, action	jealousy, inquiry

The chart below shows one way that you can use affixes to analyze the meaning of a word.

Word	Prefix	Base/ Root	Suffix(es)	Meaning of Word
inaccessible	in– *meaning:* not	access *meaning:* to obtain	–ible *meaning:* able	not able to be obtained

Try It Out

Use the information about affixes to make your own chart showing the meanings of these words from "An Occurrence at Owl Creek Bridge."

1. inglorious
2. roseate
3. infrequency
4. commandant
5. manifestations
6. recurrence
7. deflected
8. disobedient
9. encircled
10. exalted

1. **Writer's Notebook** Remind students to save their work. They may use it as prewriting for the Writer's Workshop on p. 515.

How to Own a Word

Mini-Lesson: Affixes

Have a volunteer read the first two paragraphs aloud. Ask, "What context clue tells you that *inaccessible* has a meaning similar to *distant?*" [Parallel construction.] Have a volunteer read the next two paragraphs. Invite students to say words with the prefix adjusted and without: *enbarrass, embarrass; enploy, employ.* Have students decide which suffixes are inflectional and which are derivational.

Try It Out: Possible Answers

Word	Prefix	Base/ Root	Suffixes	Meaning of Word
inglorious	in- *meaning:* not	glory *meaning:* renown	-ous *meaning:* marked by	marked by lack of renown
roseate		rose *meaning:* a flower	-ate *meaning:* having a characteristic of	having a characteristic of a rose
infrequency	in- *meaning:* not	frequent *meaning:* often	-y *meaning:* quality	not occurring often
commandant	com- *meaning:* with	mand *meaning:* order, entrust	-ant *meaning:* actor	actor entrusted with orders
manifestations		manifest *meaning:* evident	-ations *meaning:* result, state	results of being evident
recurrence	re- *meaning:* again	curr *meaning:* to run	-ence *meaning:* condition	condition of happening again
deflected	de- *meaning:* away	flected *meaning:* bended		bended away
disobedient	dis- *meaning:* opposing	obedi *meaning:* obey	-ent *meaning:* showing	showing a refusal to obey
encircled	en- *meaning:* cause to be	circled *meaning:* surrounded		caused to be surrounded
exalted	ex- *meaning:* out, away	alted *meaning:* placed high		placed high and away

STRATEGIES FOR INCLUSION

English Language Development Students whose primary language is not English encounter many new word parts as well as new vocabulary words in the right column of the chart. They will benefit by having a chance to compare the prefixes and suffixes most commonly used in English with those in their primary language. They can see if prefixes and suffixes are used for similar or different purposes and become accustomed to the role affixes play in the English language.

A. Exploring the Historical Period

Many people believed that this would be a quick conflict. In fact, the Civil War lasted four years and claimed some 618,000 lives, an average of 423 per day—more Americans than were killed in all of America's other wars combined.

SPOTLIGHT ON

Voices from the Civil War

There are few literary records of the Civil War, but there are many personal testimonies in the form of letters, diaries, and memoirs. Some of these were written by well-known figures, but most were the work of ordinary people caught up in the most extraordinary and painful events of America's history. The following excerpts provide a brief history of the war in the voices of those who experienced it, including an Indiana farm boy, President Lincoln, Frederick Douglass, a Southern gentlewoman, and a Union soldier who witnessed the surrender of General Robert E. Lee.

The Granger Collection, New York (cannon).

It is often said that any civil war is a war of brother against brother, but we must think a moment to realize what this meant in nineteenth-century America. The United States at the time was a mobile society, and many families, especially in the border states, had friends and relatives in both the North and the South. For such families, the Civil War was a profoundly personal conflict.

A In April 1861, several months after seven Southern states had formally seceded from the Union, Confederate forces demanded the surrender of the Union garrison on Fort Sumter, located on an island in the harbor of Charleston, South Carolina. At dawn on the twelfth of April, fighting began. Here is the response of Theodore Upson, a teenage farm boy in Indiana, to the news of the attack on Fort Sumter.

Theodore Upson

APRIL 1861

Father and I were husking out some corn. We could not finish before it wintered up. When William Cory came across the field (he had been down after the mail) he was excited and said, "Jonathan, the Rebs have fired upon and taken Fort Sumter." Father got white and couldn't say a word.

William said, "The president will soon fix them. He has called for 75,000 men and is going to blockade their ports, and just as soon as those fellows find out that the North means business, they will get down off their high horse."

Father said little. We did not finish the corn and drove to the barn. Father left me to unload and put out the team and went to the house. After I had finished I went in to dinner. Mother said, "What is the matter with Father?" He had gone right upstairs. I told her what we had heard. She went to him. After a while they came down. Father looked ten years older. We sat down to the table. Grandma wanted to know what was the trouble. Father told her and she began to cry. "Oh, my poor children in the South! Now they will suffer! God knows how they will suffer! I knew it would come! Jonathan, I told you it would come!"

"They can come here and stay," said Father.

"No, they will not do that. There is their home. There they will stay. Oh, to think that I should have lived to see the day when brother should rise against brother. . . ."

Mother had a letter from the Hales. Charlie and his father are in their [that is, the Confederate] army and Dayton wanted to go but was too young. I wonder if I were in our army and they should meet me would they shoot me. I suppose they would.

—*from The Blue and the Gray: The Story of the Civil War as Told by Participants, edited by* Henry Steele Commager

OPTIONS FOR TEACHING

STRATEGIES FOR INCLUSION

Auditory/Kinesthetic Have students work in groups to create a tableau of some of the figures whose voices are represented here. Each figure should "come to life" and speak part of his or her selection. As students perform their tableaux, encourage them to give their characters an appropriate accent. If you can find recordings of an Indiana accent and a Southern accent, they will help students create a more authentic performance.

English Language Development Some students may not be acquainted with U.S. history. Before reading the passages, elicit from students what they know about the Civil War already. Fill in the gaps in their knowledge, making sure they know when it took place and why it was fought. Make sure they know essential vocabulary such as *Abolitionist, Confederate,* and *Union.*

Intrapersonal Have students characterize in a short descriptive paragraph each person whose voice is represented here. Students' characterizations should draw from evidence in the text.

Walt Whitman (page 348) was too old to fight in the Civil War, but he did volunteer his services as a nurse in army hospitals. The following is an excerpt from his description of the wounded after the Battle of Chancellorsville, one of the bloodiest in the war, and one that Stephen Crane depicts in *The Red Badge of Courage.*

Walt Whitman

Then the camps of the wounded—O heavens, what scene is this?—is this indeed *humanity*—these butchers' shambles? There are several of them. There they lie, in the largest, in an open space in the woods, from 200 to 300 poor fellows—the groans and screams—the odor of blood, mixed with the fresh scent of the night, the grass, the trees—that slaughterhouse! O well is it their mothers, their sisters cannot see them—cannot conceive, and never conceived, these things. One man is shot by a shell, both in the arm and leg—both are amputated—there lie the rejected members. Some have their legs blown off—some bullets through the breast—some indescribably horrid wounds in the face or head, all mutilated, sickening, torn, gouged out—some in the abdomen—some mere boys—many rebels, badly hurt—they take their regular turns with the rest, just the same as any—the surgeons use them just the same. Such is the camp of the wounded—such a fragment, a reflection afar off of the bloody scene—while over all the clear, large moon comes out at times softly, quietly shining.

—Walt Whitman, *from Specimen Days*

In July 1861, Major Ballou wrote to his wife, Sarah, in Rhode Island. One week after he wrote this letter, Major Ballou was killed in the First Battle of Bull Run, Virginia.

Major Sullivan Ballou

. . . I know I have but few claims upon Divine Providence, but something whispers to me—perhaps it is the wafted prayer of my little Edgar, that I shall return to my loved ones unharmed. If I do not, my dear Sarah, never forget how much I love you, nor that when my last breath escapes me on the battlefield, it will whisper your name.

Forgive my many faults, and the many pains I have caused you. How thoughtless, how foolish I have sometimes been! How gladly would I wash out with my tears every little spot upon your happiness. . . .

But, O Sarah! If the dead can come back to this earth and flit unseen around those they love, I shall be always with you in the brightest day and the darkest night . . . *always, always,* and when the soft breeze fans your cheek, it shall be my breath, or the cool air your throbbing temple, it shall be my spirit passing by. Sarah, do not mourn me dead: Think I am gone and wait for me, for we shall meet again. . . .

(Below) Unidentified women, photographed around 1850.

Wounded soldiers (1864). Library of Congress.

The Granger Collection, New York.

The Granger Collection, New York.

B. Expansion
Whitman's career as a nurse began after he visited his younger brother who had been wounded at Antietam. During the war, Whitman estimated that he made more than six hundred visits to hospitals and camps and ministered to one hundred thousand sick and wounded soldiers, Union and Confederate. He nursed the injured, read to them, and distributed small gifts. He also played the game Twenty Questions and declaimed his poetry to amuse the wounded. Whitman's prose account of his experiences, *Memoranda During the War,* was privately published many years later and in 1882 was combined with other prose writings in a book called *Specimen Days*. Whitman's experiences convinced him of the horrors of war. In 1863, he wrote, "My opinion is *to stop the war now.*"

C. Expansion
The reading of this letter was one of the more poignant moments in Ken Burns's 1990 PBS documentary *The Civil War.*

STRATEGIES FOR INCLUSION

Learners Having Difficulty Many students will benefit from an approach that engages as many of their senses as possible. During your study of this Collection, bring to class pictures of scenes from the Civil War. In addition, ask students to interview their parents and other relatives to find out if any of their ancestors fought in or were affected by the Civil War. Students can then share any interesting stories with the class.

INTEGRATING THE LANGUAGE ARTS

Strategic Reading Work with students to identify the genre of each piece, and have them note in their Reader's Logs how genre shapes style.

Language and Vocabulary Ask students to find distinguishing features in the language and vocabulary of the various selections. They may notice childlike language, rhetorically sophisticated language, or emotional language. Have students keep a list of the different kinds of voices.

A. Critical Reading: Making Inferences

? How do you think Hunter would feel the next day or the day after, when he went into battle against these same Yankees? [Possible answer: He probably would have conflicting feelings.]

Alexander Hunter was a college boy who joined the Seventeenth Virginia Regiment at the outbreak of the war. His book, *Johnny Reb and Billy Yank,* provides a lively look at life in the Confederate Army. Here he describes a meeting between Union and Confederate soldiers.

Alexander Hunter

Johnny Reb and Billy Yank

It was in the latter part of August [1863]; orders were given to be prepared to go on [guard duty] early in the morning; and until a late hour the men were busy cooking rations and cleaning equipment.

Before the mists had been chased by the rising sun, the company in close column of fours marched down the road. Men and animals were in perfect condition, brimful of mettle and in buoyant spirits.

The route lay along the banks of the river; upon the winding course of which, after several hours riding, the regiment reached its destination and relieved the various [guards]. A sergeant and squad of men were left at each post . . . to watch the enemy on the other side of the Rappahannock. . . .

The Rappahannock, which was at this place about two hundred yards wide, flowing slowly oceanward, its bosom reflecting the roseate-hued morn, was as lovely a body of water as the sun ever shone upon. The sound of the gentle ripple of its waves upon the sand was broken by a faint "halloo" which came from the other side.

"Johnny Reb; I say, J-o-h-n-n-y R-e-b, don't shoot!"

Joe Reid shouted back, "All right!"

"What command are you?"

The spoken words floated clear and distinct across the water, "The Black Horse Cavalry. Who are you?"

"The Second Michigan Cavalry."

"Come to the bank," said our spokesman, "and show yourselves; we won't fire."

"On your honor, Johnny Reb?"

"On our honor, Billy Yank."

In a second a large squad of blue-coats across the way advanced to the water's brink. The Southerners did the same; then the former put the query.

"Have you any tobacco?"

"Plenty of it," went out our reply.

"Any sugar and coffee?" they questioned.

"Not a taste nor a smell."

"Let's trade," was shouted with eagerness.

"Very well," was the reply, ". . . meet us here this evening."

"All right," they answered; then added, "Say, Johnny, want some newspapers?"

"Y-e-s!"

"Then look out, we are going to send you some."

"How are you going to do it?"

"Wait and see. . . ."

Eagerly he watched. . . . Presently he shouted:

"Here they come!" and then in a tone of intense admiration, "I'll be doggoned if these Yanks are not the smartest people in the world."

On the other side were several miniature boats and ships—such as schoolboys delight in—with sails set; the gentle breeze impelled the little crafts across the river, each freighted with a couple of newspapers. . . .

Drawing lots, Joe Boteler, who found luck against him, started to town, with a muttered curse, to buy tobacco. . . .

Joe returned in the evening with a box of plug tobacco about a foot square; but how to get it across was the question. The miniature boats could not carry it, and we shouted over to the Yanks that we had about twenty pounds of cut plug, and asked them what we must do? They hallooed back to let one of us swim across, and declared that it was perfectly safe. . . . I volunteered. Having lived on the banks of the Potomac most of my life, I was necessarily a swimmer. . . .

As I approached the shore the news of my coming reached camp, and nearly all the Second Michigan were lined up along the bank.

I felt a little queer, but had perfect faith in their promise and kept on without missing a stroke. . . . The blue-coats crowded around me and gave me a hearty welcome, . . . and heaped the craft with offerings of sugar, coffee, lemons, and even candy.

A Bidding my friends the enemy good-bye, I swam back with the precious cargo, and we had a feast that night.

—Alexander Hunter, *from Johnny Reb and Billy Yank*

INTEGRATING THE LANGUAGE ARTS

Speaking and Listening Read aloud a passage from "Voices of the Civil War" to model the way one pauses, emphasizes certain words, and raises or lowers the pitch of the voice to help listeners comprehend. Let students pick their own short passages and practice in pairs to read aloud with proper emphasis and pitch; then, have students present their passages to the class. Encourage students in the audience to comment on which techniques help listeners understand a passage.

ASSESSMENT TOOLS

Check Test: Multiple Choice

1. Upson's story mainly shows how the war (a) delayed harvest (b) divided families (c) disrupted the mail [b]
2. Whitman emphasizes the suffering of (a) the wounded (b) entire families (c) animals [a]
3. According to Lincoln, the cemetery at Gettysburg is consecrated by (a) his presence (b) Congress (c) those who fought there [c]
4. Douglass wanted African Americans to (a) join the Union army (b) unmask slavery (c) criticize the country's mistakes [a]
5. Flint's description of the surrender at Appomattox concentrates on (a) the fine impression Traveler created (b) General Grant's uncouth dress (c) General Lee's demeanor in defeat [c]

Pennsylvania Historical and Museum Commission.

The Battle of Gettysburg (detail) (1863) by John Frederick Rothermel. Oil on canvas.

On July 7, 1863, a few days after the Battle of Gettysburg, Lincoln noted in an informal address how important this battle had been, but concluded that he was "not prepared to make [a speech] worthy of the occasion." B

Several months later, in November of that year, Lincoln in fact delivered a speech on this theme, perhaps the most memorable of his career, at the dedication of the cemetery in Gettysburg. C

Abraham Lincoln

The Gettysburg Address

Fourscore and seven years ago our fathers brought forth on this continent a new nation, conceived in Liberty, and dedicated to the proposition that all men are created equal.

Now we are engaged in a great civil war, testing whether that nation, or any nation so conceived and so dedicated, can long endure. We are met on a great battlefield of that war. We have come to dedicate a portion of that field as a final resting place for those who here gave their lives that that nation might live. It is altogether fitting and proper that we should do this.

But, in a larger sense, we cannot dedicate—we cannot consecrate—we cannot hallow—this ground. The brave men, living and dead, who struggled here, have consecrated it far above our poor power to add or detract. The world will little note nor long remember what we say here, but it can never forget what they did here. It is for us the living, rather, to be dedicated here to the unfinished work which they who fought here have thus far so nobly advanced. It is rather for us to be here dedicated to the great task remaining before us—that from these honored dead we take increased devotion to that cause for which they gave the last full measure of devotion—that we here highly resolve that these dead shall not have died in vain—that this nation, under God, shall have a new birth of freedom—and that government of the people, by the people, for the people, shall not perish from the earth.

—Abraham Lincoln
November 19, 1863

RESPONDING TO THE ART

"Death of Reynolds" is only a section of the colossal painting of the Battle of Gettysburg commissioned by the Pennsylvania legislature. Rothermel (1817–1895), the artist, was highly regarded in his day. Ask students to share their reactions to the scene depicted in the painting.

B. Exploring the Historical Period

The Battle of Gettysburg, July 1–3, 1863, was the war's greatest single battle and the major turning point. The Confederate Army was taking a heavy toll, but could not quite smash the Army of the Potomac. Then Major General George Pickett led a force of fifteen thousand against the main body of Union troops. The assault did not succeed, and the Confederate Army—now one third smaller—retreated. In all, the toll at Gettysburg was 5,660 dead, 27,000 wounded, and 10,500 missing.

C. Expansion

The featured speaker at the gathering at Gettysburg on November 19, 1863, was Edward Everett, former governor of Massachusetts, and he spoke for nearly two hours. Lincoln followed with his 269-word speech, which lasted under two minutes. Lincoln was disappointed with his speech, but Everett praised him, writing to him: "I should be glad if I could flatter myself that I came as near to the central idea of the occasion, in two hours, as you did in two minutes."

PROFESSIONAL NOTES

TECHNOLOGY

Technology Tip To find more voices on the Civil War, access the Web site of the United States Civil War Center at **http://www.cwc.lsu.edu/civlink.html**. The page includes links to letters, diaries, and other related documents. *Since addresses on the Internet sometimes serve as a public forum, content may be unpredictable. You may want to check the address before having students access it.*

A. Critical Reading: Expressing an Opinion

? Were the soldiers right to insist on full pay? [Possible answer: Most students probably will agree that they were.]

B. Cultural Connections

Women on both sides made heroic contributions during the Civil War. Clara Barton (1821–1912), the "Angel of the Battlefield," ministered to the wounded even without official authorization. She eventually was appointed superintendent of nurses with the Army of the James. After the war, Barton gathered records on missing Union soldiers and was able to identify many thousands of them, particularly victims of the notorious Andersonville Prison in Georgia. In 1881, Barton founded the American branch of the International Association of the Red Cross.

Susie King Taylor was born in slavery near Savannah, Georgia, in 1848. In April 1862, when she was fourteen, her uncle took her and his own seven children behind the Union lines. Taylor found work as a launderer for an African American troop, and soon found herself doing emergency work tending the wounded.

In 1902, Taylor wrote down her memory of her experiences with an African American regiment at Camp Saxton in Georgia.

Sgt. Baldwin of Company G, Fifty-sixth U.S. Colored Infantry (1863). Tintype.

The Granger Collection, New York.

Susie King Taylor

The first colored troops did not receive any pay for eighteen months, and the men had to depend wholly on what they received from the commissary established by General Saxton. A great many of these men had large families, and as they had no money to give them, their wives were obliged to support themselves and children by washing for the officers of the gunboats and the soldiers, and making cakes and pies which they sold to the boys in camp. Finally, in 1863, the government decided to give them half pay, but the men would not accept this. They wanted "full pay" or nothing. They preferred rather to give their services to the state, which they did until 1864, when the government granted them full pay, with all the back pay due. . . . **A**

About four o'clock, July 2, the charge [into battle] was made. . . . [The first] one [of the wounded] brought in was Samuel Anderson of our company. . . . Then others of our boys, some with their legs off, arm gone, foot off, and wounds of all kinds imaginable. They had to wade through creeks and marshes, as they were discovered by the enemy and shelled very badly. A number of the men were lost. . . .

B My work now began. I gave my assistance to try to alleviate their sufferings. I asked the doctor at the hospital what I could get for them to eat. They wanted soup, but that I could not get; but I had a few cans of condensed milk and some turtle eggs, so I thought I would try to make some custard. I had doubts as to my success, for cooking with turtle eggs was something new to me; but the adage has it, "Nothing ventured, nothing done," so I made a venture and the result was a very delicious custard. This I carried to the men, who enjoyed it very much.

—Susie King Taylor, *from Reminiscences of My Life in Camp*

Harriet Tubman Series No. 29 (1939–1940) by Jacob Lawrence. Casein tempera on gessoed hardboard ($17\frac{7}{8}'' \times 12''$).

Hampton University Museum, Hampton, Virginia.

The most famous African American spokesperson during the Civil War was Frederick Douglass (page 424). Douglass used all of his eloquence and passionate oratory to persuade African Americans in the North to enlist in the Union Army. Eventually, a number of all-black volunteer regiments were formed and trained. (The 1989 film *Glory* reenacts the tragic exploits of one such regiment.) About 180,000 African Americans enlisted, including two of Douglass's sons. The following call to action first appeared in Douglass's own newspaper in March 1863.

C

Frederick Douglass

When first the rebel cannon shattered the walls of Sumter and drove away its starving garrison, I predicted that the war then and there inaugurated would not be fought out entirely by white men. Every month's experience during these dreary years has confirmed that opinion. A war undertaken and brazenly carried on for the perpetual enslavement of colored men, calls logically and loudly for colored men to help suppress it. Only a moderate share of sagacity was needed to see that the arm of the slave was the best defense against the arm of the slaveholder. Hence with every reverse to the national arms, with every exulting shout of victory raised by the slaveholding rebels, I have implored the imperiled nation to unchain against her foes, her powerful black hand. Slowly and reluctantly that appeal is beginning to be heeded. Stop not now to complain that it was not heeded sooner. It may or it may not have been best that it should not. This is not the time to discuss that question. Leave it to the future. When the war is over, the country is saved, peace is established, and the black man's rights are secured, as they will be, history with an impartial hand will dispose of that and sundry other questions. Action! Action! not criticism, is the plain duty of this hour. Words are now useful only as they stimulate to blows. The office of speech now is only to point out when, where, and how to strike to the best advantage. There is no time to delay. The tide is at its flood that leads on to fortune. From East to West, from North to South, the sky is written all over, "Now or never." Liberty won by white men would lose half its luster. "Who would be free themselves must strike the blow." "Better even die free, than to live slaves." This is the sentiment of every brave colored man amongst us.

D

—*from The Life and Times of Frederick Douglass*

The following is just a small sample of memorable quotations from Frederick Douglass's speeches and writings.

We are *Americans,* speaking the same language, adopting the same customs, holding the same general opinions . . . and shall rise and fall with Americans.

Once let the black man get upon his person the brass letters "U.S."; let him get an eagle on his button, and a musket on his shoulder, and bullets in his pocket, and there is no power on the earth or under the earth which can deny that he has earned the right of citizenship in the United States.

The day dawns; the morning star is bright upon the horizon! The iron gate of our prison stands half open. One gallant rush from the North will fling it wide open, while four millions of our brothers and sisters shall march out into liberty. The chance is now given you to end in a day the bondage of centuries, and to rise in one bound from social degradation to the plane of common equality with all other varieties of men.

—*from The Life and Times of Frederick Douglass*

The Granger Collection, New York.

Unidentified Union Army soldier with his wife, around 1865.

C. Expansion

One black regiment was organized in Boston, then a center of abolitionist activity. The story of the 54th, the division to which Douglass's two sons belonged, is told in the PBS documentary "The Massachusetts 54th Colored Infantry" (part of *The American Experience* series).

D. Exploring the Historical Period

Because of Northern racism, Lincoln was not persuaded to send such a regiment into combat until after he issued the Emancipation Proclamation in 1863. Until then, most African American soldiers performed noncombat roles. Even in the South, African Americans did noncombat duty until March 1865, when they were authorized to serve in the Confederate army—but shortly thereafter the war ended.

A. Literary Connections
Chesnut alludes to II Samuel 12, where King David's child by Bathsheba falls ill. David weeps and prays, but after the child dies, "David arose from the earth, and washed, and anointed himself, and changed his apparel . . . he came to his own house; and they set bread before him, and he did eat" (v. 20). Asked why he cried before the child died and not after, David replies (v. 22–23), "While the child was yet alive, I fasted and wept; for I said, Who can tell whether God will be gracious to me, that the child may live? But now he is dead, wherefore should I fast? Can I bring him back again?"

Have students apply this story to Mary Chesnut's situation. [Like David, she feels that prayer is no longer of use; it is time for life to go on.]

B. Exploring the Historical Period
Jefferson Davis (1808–1889) served as a U.S. senator and as secretary of war under President Franklin Pierce. Elected president of the Confederacy in 1861, he exhibited able executive leadership and was at least partly responsible for the South's powerful showing against the more numerous Northern forces. He often clashed with Southern governors, however, as they defended their own states' rights. Davis was captured in Georgia in April 1865, imprisoned for two years, and indicted for treason, but never tried.

C. Expansion
William Tecumseh Sherman's march through Georgia began with the fall of Atlanta in September 1864. Atlanta's mills, munitions factories, and railroad connections made it vital to the South, so Sherman ordered Atlanta evacuated and burned.

Mary Boykin Chesnut was the wife of James Chesnut, ex-senator from South Carolina and aide to Jefferson Davis, president of the Confederacy. During the course of the war, Mary Chesnut traveled from city to city in the South as the capital of the Confederacy changed. She kept up with the latest war news through her husband and their wide circle of knowledgeable and influential friends. Mary Chesnut was sophisticated, witty, and sensitive. Her diaries present an invaluable firsthand view of the war.

In April 1861, Mary Chesnut had been in Charleston, South Carolina, when the attack on Fort Sumter took place, beginning the Civil War. As she had been present at the beginning of the war, Mary Chesnut was also present at its end. In Columbia, South Carolina, she received the news, increasingly depressing, from the field.

Mary Boykin Chesnut (1856) by Samuel Osgood (1801–1885). Oil on canvas adhered to masonite (48″ × 30″).

National Portrait Gallery, Smithsonian Institution; on loan from Serena Williams Miles Van Rensselaer. Courtesy Art Resource.

Mary Chesnut

SEPTEMBER 1, 1864

The battle is raging at Atlanta, our fate hanging in the balance.

SEPTEMBER 2, 1864

A Atlanta is gone. Well that agony is over. Like David, when the child was dead, I will get up from my knees, will wash my face and comb my hair. There is no hope, but we will try to have no fear. . . .

SEPTEMBER 21, 1864

B The president [of the Confederacy] has gone West. He has sent for Mr. Chesnut.

I went with Mrs. Rhett to hear Dr. Palmer [a minister]. I did not know before how utterly hopeless was our situation. This man is so eloquent; it was hard to listen and not give way. Despair was his word, and martyrdom. He offered us nothing more in this world than the martyr's crown. He is not for slavery, he says; he is for freedom, the freedom to govern our own country as we see fit. He is against foreign interference in our state matters. That is what Mr. Palmer went to war for, it appears. Every day shows that slavery is doomed the world over. For that he thanked God. He spoke of this time of our agony; and then came the cry: "Help us, Oh God! Vain is the help of man." So we came away shaken to the depths. . . .

The end has come, no doubt of the fact. . . . We are going **C** to be wiped off the face of the earth. Now what is there to prevent Sherman taking General Lee in the rear. We have but two armies, and Sherman is between them now.

SEPTEMBER 29, 1864

These stories of our defeats in the Valley fall like blows upon a dead body. Since Atlanta, I have felt as if all were dead within me, forever. Captain Ogden of General Chesnut's staff dined here today. Had ever a Brigadier with little or no brigade so magnificent a staff? The reserves, as somebody said, are gathered by robbing the cradle and the grave of men too old and boys too young. . . .

OCTOBER 30, 1864

Every man is being hurried to the front. Today Mr. Chesnut met a poor creature coming from the surgeon's with a radiant face and a certificate. "General, see! I am exempt from service; one leg utterly useless, the other not warranted to last three months."

—Mary Chesnut, *from A Diary from Dixie*

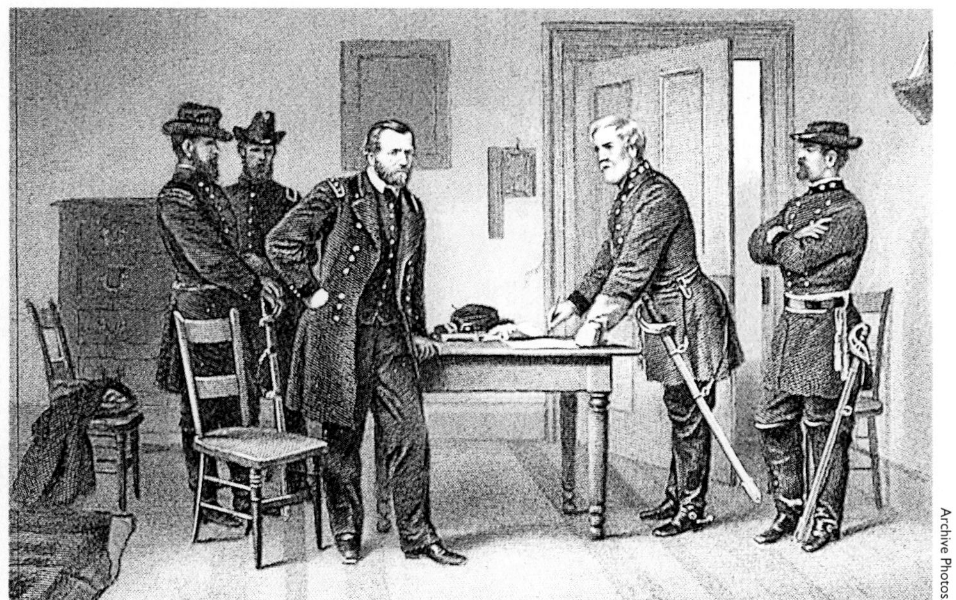

Archive Photos.

Surrender of General Lee.

On April 9, 1865, Lee surrendered to Grant at Appomattox Court House. Seth Flint, a Union soldier who witnessed the event, described the scene. D

Seth M. Flint

I Saw Lee Surrender

Grant looked like an old and battered campaigner as he rode into the yard. His blue blouse was unbuttoned and underneath could be seen his undershirt. He was unlike Lee.

What a brave pair of thoroughbreds Lee and Traveler were. That horse would have attracted attention anywhere. General Lee's uniform was immaculate and he presented a superb martial figure. But it was the face beneath the gray felt hat that made the deepest impression on me. I have been trying to find a single word that describes it and I have concluded that "benign" is the adjective I'm after, because it means *kindly* and *gracious.* There was something else about him that aroused my deep pity that so great a warrior should be acknowledging defeat. . . .

Four o'clock—the door opened. Out came General Lee, his soldierly figure erect, even in defeat. We stiffened and gave him a salute, and the man in gray courteously returned it. At the moment his soul must have been heavy with sorrow—the years of desperate struggle fruitless—and yet he could return the salute of some Yankee troopers. E

After the departure of General Lee, we quickly learned the happy news of the surrender and it spread like wildfire through the army. That night was one of the happiest I have ever known.

When I sounded taps, the sweetest of all bugle calls, the notes had scarcely died away when from the distance—it must have come from General Lee's headquarters—came, silvery clear, the same call. The boys on the other side welcomed peace. Soldiers don't carry hatred.

—Seth M. Flint, *from* "I Saw Lee Surrender"

D. Exploring the Historical Period

Robert E. Lee (1807–1870) was offered command of the Union army, but he chose to stay with the Confederacy when his home state of Virginia seceded in 1861. He became commander of the Confederate army in May 1862 and made a number of daring and successful raids northward. After Gettysburg, however, he gradually fell back until he was forced to surrender at Appomattox. He was indicted for treason, but never tried.

Like Lee, Ulysses S. Grant (1822–1885) was a West Point graduate, and both had served in the Mexican War. Grant was not made commander of the Union forces until March 1864. He at once planned to confront the enemy aggressively at every point so that the Confederate armies could not support each other. He himself led the main campaign against Lee, and their two armies engaged in a number of terrible battles before the surrender at Appomattox. In 1868, Grant was elected eighteenth president of the United States; he was reelected in 1872.

E. Expansion

A few months later, Lee would write: "The war being at an end . . . I believe it to be the duty of every one to unite in the restoration of the country, and the establishment of peace and harmony."

QUICK PLANNING GUIDE

Into the Story

Author Biography: pp. 484–485
Before You Read p. 485
- **Reading Focus: Prior Knowledge** Students consider heroism.
- **Quickwrite** Contrast foolishness with heroism.
- **Elements of Literature: Situational Irony**
- **Background: Scaffolding** Learn of battle conditions in the Civil War

Through the Story

"A Mystery of Heroism" pp. 487–492
Words to Own pp. 487–492
Student to Student p. 493
"What About Glory"
Making Meanings p. 493

Beyond the Story

Choices: Building Your Portfolio p. 494
- **Writer's Notebook:** Survey attitudes toward war for a report of information
- **Critical Writing:** Summarize Crane's attitude toward war in an essay
- **Creative Writing:** Write a poem or prose piece

Stephen Crane

(1871–1900)

UPI/Bettmann.

Stephen Crane was the youngest of the fourteen children of a Methodist minister and his devout wife. Although frail as a child, Stephen grew up in upstate New York with a yearning to become a baseball star. He put in a year first at Lafayette College and then at Syracuse University (where he was captain of the baseball team) before he decided to try earning a living as a writer.

When Crane was about sixteen years old, he went to work for his brother Townley's news agency in Asbury Park, New Jersey. Later, struggling to make a living as a reporter in New York City, Crane was drawn to the city's underside. What he called his "artistic education" on the Bowery (Skid Row) kept him hungry and often ill.

Crane lived at the Art Students' League on East Twenty-third Street, writing his first significant fiction based on his explorations of the city's slums and saloons. This was *Maggie: A Girl of the Streets* (1893), a somber, somewhat shocking novel, whose plot involved brutality, alcoholism, prostitution, and suicide.

Maggie revealed Crane as a pioneer of **naturalism**—a literary movement that dissected human instincts and behavior and examined the social environment that "conditioned" people to turn out as they did. The novel was impossibly grim for popular magazines, and Crane borrowed $700 to have it printed. The copies of the little yellow paperback lay piled in his rented room for want of readers.

Crane's apparent failure with *Maggie* was followed by a triumph—a short novel titled *The Red Badge of Courage* (1895). Using an impressionistic technique, Crane filtered the events of the novel through the eyes of Henry Fleming, a young soldier at the Civil War battle of Chancellorsville. (In fiction, **impressionism** is a technique whereby the writer gives us not objective reality, but one character's impression of that reality.) As William Dean Howells observed, Crane's genius seemed to "spring to life fully armed" with this book. Crane had been born after the Civil War, but he had read about it and had seen Mathew Brady's famous battlefield photographs (page 414). "I have never been in a battle, of course," wrote Crane later, "and I believe that I got my sense of the rage of conflict on the football field. The psychology is the same. The opposing team is an enemy tribe."

The Red Badge of Courage made Crane into a celebrity, a national expert on war, and he spent the rest of his short life writing about it for the newspapers. In fact, he became the prototype of the adventurous correspondent who not only writes about sensational events but also lives a sensational life, delighting in shocking conservative readers.

One of the fascinating elements of Crane's life was the degree to which he interwove his fiction and his real-life experiences. It was as if he had invented a war in his novels and then

PROGRAM MANAGER

- **Planning Instruction** See Teaching Notes, *Teaching Resources A,* pp. 180–181, for objectives, a summary, literary elements, and additional biographical information for this selection.
- **Instructional Support** Before beginning the instructional lesson, see Graphic Organizer for Active Reading, *Teaching Resources A,* p.191, for a Through the Story activity.
- **Assessment** See Selection Test, *Test Booklet,* pp. 113–114.
- **Language Link** For instruction and practice in identifying and using adverb clauses, see Language Link, *Teaching Resources A,* pp. 192–193, and *Language and Writing Skills Worksheets,* p. 82.
- **Reinforcement** Use the Words to Own worksheet in *Teaching Resources A,* p. 194.

had to pursue the brush fires of his own times in order to confirm what he had written. Nor was experience wasted on him. When he sailed from Florida in late 1896 to cover a gunrunning operation to Cuba, he was shipwrecked off the Florida coast and endured a fifty-hour struggle against the sea. The result was his superb story "The Open Boat" (1898).

Before this ill-fated journey, Crane had stopped off at the Hotel de Dream in Jacksonville, Florida, and had taken up with the hostess, Cora Taylor. She soon decided that she would stay with him and become the first female war correspondent. This oddly matched couple later went off to Greece to cover a war. They settled eventually in England, renting a huge, dilapidated, medieval house in Sussex.

All of these adventures were taking their toll on Crane's always delicate health. Still, he continued to travel and write, desperate now to pay for Cora's extravagant domestic life. In 1899, he produced his second volume of poems, *War Is Kind* (page 494). But tuberculosis was sapping his strength. Crane died in June 1900, at a sanitarium in the Black Forest of Germany. He was only twenty-eight years old.

Detail from original manuscript page:
The Red Badge of Courage by Stephen Crane.
University of Virginia Library.

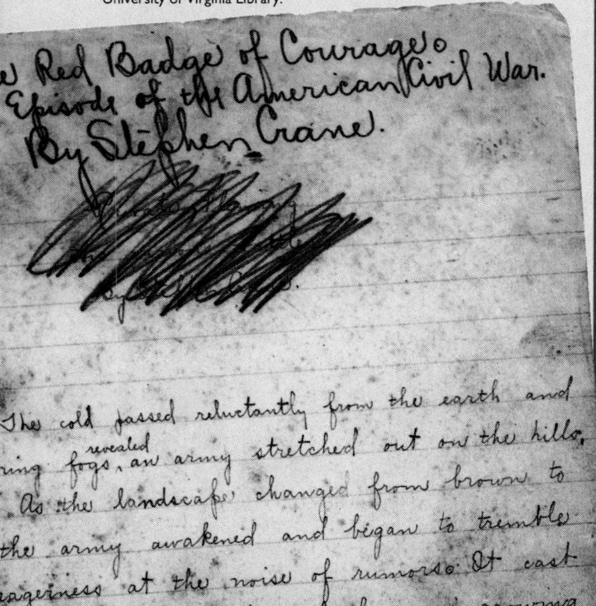
Red Badge of Courage.
Episode of the American Civil War.
By Stephen Crane.

The cold passed reluctantly from the earth and
retiring fogs, an army stretched out on the hills,
As the landscape changed from brown to
the army awakened and began to tremble
eagerness at the noise of rumors. It cast

Before You Read
A Mystery of Heroism

Reading Focus

Fool or Hero?
What is heroism? Is it exceptional courage? fearlessness? If a person ignores normal human fear and risks his or her life for something others regard as trivial, is it an act of heroism or a deed of utmost foolishness?

Quickwrite

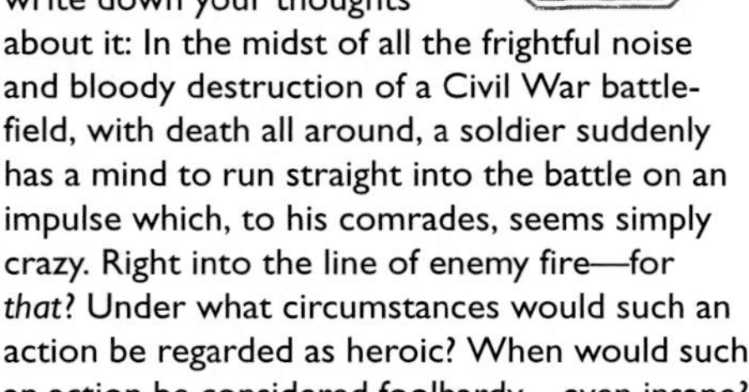

Imagine this scene, and then write down your thoughts about it: In the midst of all the frightful noise and bloody destruction of a Civil War battlefield, with death all around, a soldier suddenly has a mind to run straight into the battle on an impulse which, to his comrades, seems simply crazy. Right into the line of enemy fire—for *that*? Under what circumstances would such an action be regarded as heroic? When would such an action be considered foolhardy—even insane?

Elements of Literature

Situational Irony
Situational irony occurs when what actually happens differs from what one expects will happen. Such an irony is at the heart of this story.

> **Situational irony** takes place when there is a discrepancy between what is expected to happen and what actually happens.
>
> *For more on Irony, see the Handbook of Literary Terms.*

Background

Firsthand accounts of Civil War battles speak of the stifling smoke and crashing noise of battle. Often, one soldier would escape death and another would die by the merest chance. Dazed by battle, soldiers could find it difficult later on to explain the reasons for their actions.

Into the Story

Using Before You Read p. 485

Reading Focus

Have students work in small groups to define *heroism.* Encourage them to work until they come to a consensus. Give each group a chance to share their ideas and then discuss any differences in their definitions.

Quickwrite

After students have read the text, ask them to begin by making up two rationales—one that they would consider a good reason for dashing into battle and one that would be foolhardy. Have them write about each rationale and explain why they evaluate them as they do.

Background

Ask students to identify what kinds of situations and experiences might contribute to the disorientation that soldiers may feel.

About the Author

Although Crane was never in battle, his family had strong feelings about war. During the American Revolutionary War, his great uncle, who had joined the Continental Army at age seventeen, was captured by the Hessians and shot for refusing to reveal information. It is also said that Crane's father, a Methodist minister, was one of the first clerics to urge forgiveness after the Civil War ended.

Portfolio Assessment

Portfolio Assessment For help with self-assessment of reading skills, see the ***Portfolio Management System,*** pp. 48–49.

Words to Own

The following vocabulary words are defined in the Words to Own at the bottom of the pupil's page.

conflagration p. 487	gesticulating p. 490
stolidity p. 488	provisional p. 490
obliterated p. 488	retraction p. 490
prostrate p. 489	indolent p. 491
ominous p. 489	blanched p. 492

RESPONDING TO THE ART: VISUAL LITERACY

In what way is contemporary warfare different from the kind of battle depicted in this scene? [Possible responses: Contemporary weapons include machine guns and tanks. Swords and cannon are still used in this scene. The soldiers in the painting stand and fire cannon instead of moving around quickly with lighter-weight weapons.] Do you think that one is more violent than the other? Why or why not? [Possible responses: Will vary. Some students may suggest that newer weapons are more capable of destroying more lives, while others might think that war is just as violent either way.]

The Hornet's Nest (1895) by Thomas Corwin Lindsay. Oil on canvas.
Courtesy Cincinnati Historical Society.

OPTIONS FOR TEACHING

STRATEGIES FOR INCLUSION

Less Proficient Readers Students who have trouble with the alternations between description and dialogue will benefit from having the plot portions read to them separately. To help them follow the story line, have students create a Storyboard with drawings of the main actions.

Special Needs For students who would benefit from a sharper focus, have the reading begin on page 489, "There was a quarrel in A Company," thus omitting much of the description so that students may focus on the story of Collins.

Auditory/Visual A dramatic reading may help students imagine the action of this selection. Read the selection yourself, or ask another adult to read it. Have students draw their impressions as they hear the story.

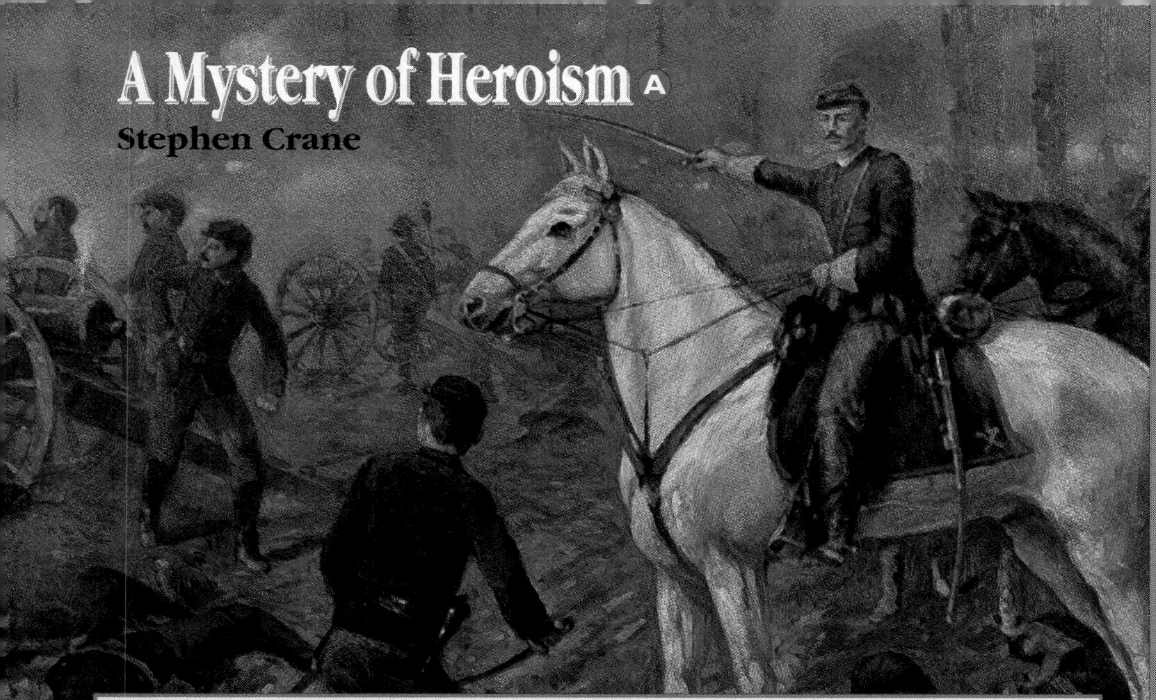

A Mystery of Heroism A

Stephen Crane

The dark uniforms of the men were so coated with dust from the incessant wrestling of the two armies that the regiment almost seemed a part of the clay bank which shielded them from the shells. On the top of the hill a battery[1] was arguing in tremendous roars with some other guns, and to the eye of the infantry, the artillerymen, the guns, the caissons,[2] the horses, were distinctly outlined upon the blue sky. When a piece was fired, a red streak as round as a log flashed low in the heavens, like a monstrous bolt of lightning. The men of the battery wore white duck trousers, which somehow emphasized their legs, and when they ran and crowded in little groups at the bidding of the shouting officers, it was more impressive than usual to the infantry.

1. **battery:** set of heavy guns.
2. **caissons** (kā′sənz): ammunition wagons.

Fred Collins of A Company was saying: "Thunder, I wisht I had a drink. Ain't there any water round here?" Then somebody yelled: "There goes th' bugler!" B

As the eyes of half of the regiment swept in one machine-like movement, there was an instant's picture of a horse in a great convulsive leap of a death wound and a rider leaning back with a crooked arm and spread fingers before his face. On the ground was the crimson terror of an exploding shell, with fibers of flame that seemed like lances. A glittering bugle swung clear of the rider's back as fell headlong the horse and the man. In the air was an odor as from a conflagration.

Words to Own
conflagration (kän′flə·grā′shən) *n.:* huge fire.

A. Expansion
This story, like *The Red Badge of Courage,* was written before Crane had experienced war firsthand. He had interviewed Civil War veterans, but they told him only dry facts and statistics. They seemed unable to recall—or at least to articulate—their thoughts and feelings about war. Crane drew upon his own imagination to fill in those thoughts and feelings. He succeeded so well that many veterans wrote to ask Crane what regiment he had served in, and others were convinced that they had served with him. Ask students whether Stephen Crane's lack of real war experience is important to their interpretation of the story.

B. Reader's Response: First Thoughts
? How is this paragraph different from the preceding one? [Sample responses: It doesn't seem to go with the paragraph that precedes it; there is a switch from description to dialogue; or the wish for a drink is ironic in the same paragraph with the bugler's death.]

STRATEGIES FOR INCLUSION

English Language Development To help students develop their oral skills and prepare them for the story, put them in pairs or groups of three and have them tell their partners about something dangerous they have done. Tell them to explain why they put themselves in danger and whether they think they were brave or foolish for doing what they did. *Tell students that they do not have to discuss anything they would feel uncomfortable sharing with other students.*

Learners Having Difficulty Students who have difficulty reading will benefit from prereading activities that focus their attention and motivate them by helping them to relate reading material to their own lives. Before students read, share with them your own personal heroes and ask them to do the same. What are the characteristics or actions that make these people heroic? Have students read with the purpose of deciding whether they consider Collins a hero.

INTEGRATING THE LANGUAGE ARTS

Strategic Reading Have student pairs carefully read and map the story, noting switches from description to narration and plot points. Point out that the narrative sections get longer and finally blend with and encompass the description. ☞

A. Critical Reading: Summarizing

? What has suffered damage in the battle? What has endured so far? [The house, fence, and well house are severely damaged. The "fair little meadow" is apparently untouched.]

B. Reader's Response: Challenging the Text

? Why do you think Crane included this detail? [Sample responses: This is a way for two soldiers to deal with the stress of the battlefield; or it presents an ironic contrast—the philosophizing soldiers arguing in the midst of infantry volleys.]

C. Expansion

The "swing" team are horses harnessed to swing guns from one direction to another. What do the actions of the men and animals suggest? [Both the men and the animals are terrified.]

D. Critical Reading: Drawing Conclusions

? Why does the officer smile? [The officer smiles to encourage the other men despite his pain and possibly to distract them from the grim thoughts that the sight of his wounded arm brings up.]

E. Literary Element: Figure of Speech

? What figure of speech is used to describe the destruction of the meadow? Is this effective? Why? [Personification: meadow's suffering, massacre of grass; simile: exploded shells like "an imprecation in the face of a maiden." Making the meadow seem human makes its destruction more poignant.]

The Bettmann Archive.

Union soldier.

Sometimes they of the infantry looked down at a fair little meadow which spread at their feet. Its long, green grass was rippling gently in a breeze. Beyond it was the gray form of a house half torn to pieces by shells and by the busy axes of soldiers who had pursued firewood. The line of an old fence was now dimly marked by long weeds and by an occasional post. A shell had blown the well house to fragments. Little lines of gray smoke ribboning upward from some embers indicated the place where had stood the barn. **A**

From beyond a curtain of green woods there came the sound of some stupendous scuffle as if two animals of the size of islands were fighting. At a distance there were occasional appearances of swift-moving men, horses, batteries, flags, and, with the crashing of infantry, volleys were heard, often, wild and frenzied cheers. In the midst of it all, Smith and Ferguson, two privates of A Company, were engaged in a heated discussion, which involved the greatest questions of the national existence. **B**

The battery on the hill presently engaged in a frightful duel. The white legs of the gunners scampered this way and that way and the officers redoubled their shouts. The guns, with their demeanors of stolidity and courage, were typical of something infinitely self-possessed in this clamor of death that swirled around the hill.

One of a "swing" team was suddenly smitten quivering to the ground and his maddened brethren dragged his torn body in their struggle to escape from this turmoil and danger. A young soldier astride one of the leaders swore and fumed in his saddle and furiously jerked at the bridle. An officer screamed out an order so violently that his voice broke and ended the sentence in a falsetto[3] shriek. **C**

The leading company of the infantry regiment was somewhat exposed and the colonel ordered it moved more fully under the shelter of the hill. There was the clank of steel against steel.

A lieutenant of the battery rode down and passed them, holding his right arm carefully in his left hand. And it was as if this arm was not at all a part of him, but belonged to another man. His sober and reflective charger went slowly. The officer's face was grimy and perspiring and his uniform was tousled as if he had been in direct grapple with an enemy. He smiled grimly when the men stared at him. He turned his horse toward the meadow. **D**

Collins of A Company said: "I wisht I had a drink. I bet there's water in that there ol' well yonder!"

"Yes; but how you goin' to git it?"

For the little meadow which intervened was now suffering a terrible onslaught of shells. Its green and beautiful calm had vanished utterly. Brown earth was being flung in monstrous handfuls. And there was a massacre of the young blades of grass. They were being torn, burned, obliterated. Some curious fortune of the battle had made this gentle little meadow the object of the red hate of the shells and each one as it exploded seemed like an imprecation[4] in the face of a maiden. **E**

The wounded officer who was riding across this expanse said to himself: "Why, they couldn't

3. **falsetto:** artificially high voice.
4. **imprecation:** curse.

Words to Own

stolidity (stə·lid′ə·tē) *n.:* showing no emotion.
obliterated (ə·blit′ər·āt′əd) *v.:* destroyed.

OPTIONS FOR TEACHING

STRATEGIES FOR INCLUSION

Speaking and Listening Have students read the dialogue in groups, particularly the exchange between Collins, the captain, and the colonel, and the exchange before Collins walks into the field. Remind them to consider characterization as they decide how to read the part.

Writing: Personal Letter Have students write a personal letter from Collins to his family that describes his thoughts, emotions, and experiences. Encourage students to assume the persona of Collins in their writing and to take into consideration Collins's audience. What would they write home if they were Collins? Ask for volunteers to read their letters aloud.

PROBLEM SOLVING/ CRITICAL THINKING

Dares How can people turn down a dare and save face? Divide the class into small groups. Have students discuss dares—the one presented here, and others from literature, movies, or real life. Encourage them to use a graphic organizer like the one following to formulate an approach to dares, including a script of what they might say and a list of whom they can go to for support. Then, have each group perform a dramatic reading of their script for the class.

shoot any harder if the whole army was massed here!"

A shell struck the gray ruins of the house and as, after the roar, the shattered wall fell in fragments, there was a noise which resembled the flapping of shutters during a wild gale of winter. Indeed the infantry paused in the shelter of the bank, appeared as men standing upon a shore contemplating a madness of the sea. The angel of calamity had under its glance the battery upon the hill. Fewer white-legged men labored about the guns. A shell had smitten one of the pieces, and after the flare, the smoke, the dust, the wrath of this blow was gone, it was possible to see white legs stretched horizontally upon the ground. And at that interval to the rear, where it is the business of battery horses to stand with their noses to the fight awaiting the command to drag their guns out of the destruction or into it or wheresoever these incomprehensible humans demanded with whip and spur—in this line of passive and dumb spectators, whose fluttering hearts yet would not let them forget the iron laws of man's control of them—in this rank of brute soldiers there had been relentless and hideous carnage. From the ruck[5] of bleeding and prostrate horses, the men of the infantry could see one animal raising its stricken body with its forelegs and turning its nose with mystic and profound eloquence toward the sky.

. . . there was a noise which resembled the flapping of shutters during a wild gale of winter.

Some comrades joked Collins about his thirst. "Well, if yeh want a drink so bad, why don't yeh go git it?"

"Well, I will in a minnet if yeh don't shut up."

A lieutenant of artillery floundered his horse straight down the hill with as great concern as if it were level ground. As he galloped past the colonel of the infantry, he threw up his hand in swift salute. "We've got to get out of that," he roared angrily. He was a black-bearded officer, and his eyes, which resembled beads, sparkled like those of an insane man. His jumping horse sped along the column of infantry.

The fat major standing carelessly with his sword held horizontally behind him and with his legs far apart, looked after the receding horseman and laughed. "He wants to get back with orders pretty quick or there'll be no batt'ry left," he observed.

The wise young captain of the second company hazarded[6] to the lieutenant colonel that the enemy's infantry would probably soon attack the hill, and the lieutenant colonel snubbed him.

A private in one of the rear companies looked out over the meadow and then turned to a companion and said: "Look there, Jim." It was the wounded officer from the battery, who some time before had started to ride across the meadow, supporting his right arm carefully with his left hand. This man had encountered a shell apparently at a time when no one perceived him and he could now be seen lying face downward with a stirruped foot stretched across the body of his dead horse. A leg of the charger extended slantingly upward precisely as stiff as a stake. Around this motionless pair the shells still howled.

There was a quarrel in A Company. Collins was shaking his fist in the faces of some laughing comrades. "Dern yeh! I ain't afraid t' go. If yeh say much, I will go!"

"Of course, yeh will! Yeh'll run through that there medder, won't yeh?"

Collins said, in a terrible voice: "You see, now!" At this ominous threat his comrades broke into renewed jeers.

Collins gave them a dark scowl and went to find his captain. The latter was conversing with the colonel of the regiment.

"Captain," said Collins, saluting and standing at attention. In those days all trousers bagged at the knees. "Captain, I want t' git permission to go git some water from that there well over yonder!"

The colonel and the captain swung about simultaneously and stared across the meadow.

5. **ruck:** mass; crowd.

6. **hazarded:** risked saying.

Words to Own

prostrate (präs′trāt′) *adj.:* lying flat on the ground.
ominous (äm′ə·nəs) *adj.:* sinister; foreboding.

F. Literary Element: Symbolism
? Why does Crane describe the devastation of the gray house? [Crane symbolically portrays the destruction of normal daily life; the color gray may suggest that he is referring particularly to the destruction of the Confederacy and the devastation of the South.]

G. Literary Element: Point of View
? How does the point of view switch in this passage? [Suddenly, the horses' perspective of human beings is presented.]

H. Language Note: Dialect
Note that *medder* is *meadow.* Why does Crane use dialect with Collins and the other soldiers but not with the officers? [It shows the soldiers as ordinary, uneducated men and emphasizes the social distance between the officers and the rank-and-file soldiers.]

I. Critical Reading: Predicting
? What do you think will happen? [Possible answers: Once Collins asks permission and it is granted, he must follow through; or he will change his mind when it comes time to set out.]

PROBLEM SOLVING/CRITICAL THINKING

Dare	My Lines	Support
[hop a moving train]	["Do I look like I want my legs flattened?"]	[older sibling]

☞

A. Critical Reading: Drawing Conclusions

? Why did the colonel call Collins a lad? [Possible answer: The colonel is protective of his soldier and tries to persuade him to give up the idea. His concern leads him to use an affectionate rather than a military term of address.]

B. Reader's Response: Shaping Interpretations

? Can you tell whether Collins wants to go? [Sample responses: He does not want to go; or he has mixed feelings. He wants to go to save face, but he does not want to because it is dangerous.]

C. Critical Reading: Making Inferences

? What makes Collins go? [Resentment toward his companions is one factor. After Collins talks to the colonel and the captain, he receives what could be seen as an order from the colonel that is hard to refuse.]

D. Literary Element: Situational Irony

? What is ironic about Collins's insistence on going to the well? [He does not really want to go; he feels forced into it by his comrades, who are amazed by his foolhardiness.]

E. Reader's Response: Connecting with the Text

? What happens in Collins's mind that is similar to what happens in Farquhar's mind in "An Occurrence at Owl Creek Bridge"? [Sample response: Both Collins and Farquhar have a heightened sense of their surroundings, and both experience a change in their time perception.]

The captain laughed. "You must be pretty thirsty, Collins?"

"Yes, sir; I am."

"Well—ah," said the captain. After a moment he asked: "Can't you wait?"

"No, sir."

(A) The colonel was watching Collins's face. "Look here, my lad," he said, in a pious sort of a voice. "Look here, my lad." Collins was not a lad. "Don't you think that's taking pretty big risks for a little drink of water?"

"I dunno," said Collins, uncomfortably. Some of the resentment toward his companions, which perhaps had forced him into this affair, was beginning to fade. "I dunno wether 'tis."

The colonel and the captain contemplated him for a time.

"Well," said the captain finally.

"Well," said the colonel, "if you want to go, why go."

Collins saluted. "Much obliged t' yeh."

As he moved away the colonel called after him. "Take some of the other boys' canteens with you an' hurry back now."

"Yes, sir. I will."

(B) The colonel and the captain looked at each other then, for it had suddenly occurred that they could not for the life of them tell whether Collins wanted to go or whether he did not.

They turned to regard Collins and as they perceived him surrounded by gesticulating comrades the colonel said: "Well, by thunder! I guess he's going."

Collins appeared as a man dreaming. In the midst of the questions, the advice, the warnings, all the excited talk of his company mates, he maintained a curious silence.

They were very busy in preparing him for his ordeal. When they inspected him carefully it was somewhat like the examination that grooms give a horse before a race; and they were amazed, staggered by the whole affair. Their astonishment found vent in strange repetitions.

(C) "Are yeh sure a-goin'?" they demanded again and again.

"Certainly I am," cried Collins, at last furiously.

He strode sullenly away from them. He was swinging five or six canteens by their cords. It seemed that his cap would not remain firmly on his head, and often he reached and pulled it down over his brow.

There was a general movement in the compact column. The long animal-like thing moved slightly. Its four hundred eyes were turned upon the figure of Collins.

"Well, sir, if that ain't th' derndest thing. I never thought Fred Collins had the blood in him for that kind of business."

"What's he goin' to do, anyhow?"

"He's goin' to that well there after water."

"We ain't dyin' of thirst, are we? That's foolishness."

"Well, somebody put him up to it an' he's doin' it."

(D) "Say, he must be a desperate cuss."

When Collins faced the meadow and walked away from the regiment, he was vaguely conscious that a chasm, the deep valley of all prides, was suddenly between him and his comrades. It was provisional, but the provision was that he return as a victor. He had blindly been led by quaint emotions and laid himself under an obligation to walk squarely up to the face of death.

But he was not sure that he wished to make a retraction even if he could do so without shame. As a matter of truth he was sure of very little. He was mainly surprised.

(E) It seemed to him supernaturally strange that he had allowed his mind to maneuver his body into such a situation. He understood that it might be called dramatically great.

However, he had no full appreciation of anything excepting that he was actually conscious of being dazed. He could feel his dulled mind groping after the form and color of this incident.

Too, he wondered why he did not feel some keen agony of fear cutting his sense like a knife. He wondered at this because human expression had said loudly for centuries that men should feel

Words to Own

gesticulating (jes·tik'yo͞o·lāt'iŋ) *v.* used as *adj.*: gesturing, especially with the hands and arms, while speaking.

provisional (prō·vizh'ə·nəl) *adj.*: temporary; for the time being.

retraction (ri·trak'shən) *n.*: withdrawal.

OPTIONS FOR TEACHING

CLASSROOM MANAGEMENT

Reading Aloud To involve all students in the process of reading the text aloud, use groups for in-class readings, assigning parts to each student to make sure that everybody gets several chances to read. Each group may simultaneously read aloud the assigned section of text. On the chalkboard, list stopping points where the group should pause and summarize what has occurred in the passage.

Managing the Reader's Response Classroom Create a comfort zone for students by encouraging and praising individuals for their responses. To ensure that their reactions are based on the story, encourage students to return to the text to support their reasoning.

CROSSING THE CURRICULUM

Geography Have students identify any Civil War monuments in your state. If it has none, have them identify a state that does, research the battles that took place at these sites, and create a map of the battles to show their importance in the war.

afraid of certain things and that all men who did not feel this fear were phenomena, heroes.

He was then a hero. He suffered that disappointment which we would all have if we discovered that we were ourselves capable of those deeds which we most admire in history and legend. This, then, was a hero. After all, heroes were not much.

No, it could not be true. He was not a hero. Heroes had no shames in their lives and, as for him, he remembered borrowing fifteen dollars from a friend and promising to pay it back the next day, and then avoiding that friend for ten months. When at home his mother had aroused him for the early labor of his life on the farm, it had often been his fashion to be irritable, childish, diabolical, and his mother had died since he had come to the war.

Charge of VMI Cadets at New Market (1914) by Benjamin West Clinedinst. Oil on canvas (18″ × 23″).

Virginia Military Institute, Lexington, Virginia.

He saw that in this matter of the well, the canteens, the shells, he was an intruder in the land of fine deeds. **F**

He was now about thirty paces from his comrades. The regiment had just turned its many faces toward him.

From the forest of terrific noises there suddenly emerged a little uneven line of men. They fired fiercely and rapidly at distant foliage on which appeared little puffs of white smoke. The spatter of skirmish firing was added to the thunder of the guns on the hill. The little line of men ran forward. A color sergeant fell flat with his flag as if he had slipped on ice. There was hoarse cheering from this distant field.

G Collins suddenly felt that two demon fingers were pressed into his ears. He could see nothing but flying arrows, flaming red. He lurched from the shock of this explosion, but he made a mad rush for the house, which he viewed as a man submerged to the neck in a boiling surf might view the shore. In the air, little pieces of shell howled and the earthquake explosions drove him insane with the menace of their roar. As he ran the canteens knocked together with a rhythmical tinkling.

As he neared the house, each detail of the scene became vivid to him. He was aware of some bricks of the vanished chimney lying on the sod. There was a door which hung by one hinge.

Rifle bullets called forth by the insistent skirmishers came from the far-off bank of foliage. They mingled with the shells and the pieces of shells until the air was torn in all directions by hootings, yells, howls. The sky was full of fiends who directed all their wild rage at his head.

When he came to the well he flung himself face downward and peered into its darkness. There were furtive silver glintings some feet from the surface. He grabbed one of the canteens and, unfastening its cap, swung it down by the cord. The water flowed slowly in with an indolent gurgle.

And now as he lay with his face turned away he was suddenly smitten with the terror. It came upon his heart like the grasp of claws. All the power faded from his muscles. For an instant he was no more than a dead man.

The canteen filled with a maddening slowness in the manner of all bottles. Presently he recovered his strength and addressed a screaming oath

WORDS TO OWN

indolent (in′də·lənt) *adj.:* lazy.

F. Reader's Response: Challenging the Text

? Is Collins an intruder in the land of fine deeds? [Sample responses: No, he has tried his best; or yes, his deed is foolish and not noble.]

G. Critical Reading: Analyzing Tone

? How does the narrative tone change in the last sentence? [It changes from impressionistic and gruesome to a fairly plain statement of fact.]

CROSSING THE CURRICULUM

Architecture Just as the gray house was destroyed in this story, many important and interesting works of architecture have been destroyed in wars. Have students choose a war and find out about the destruction of architectural landmarks and any rebuilding efforts that may have followed. Have them build or draw models that show these works of architecture.

Social Studies Have students research the tactics involved in a Civil War battle. Have students mark maps to show the tactical moves to illustrate their oral reports to the class. An expert from a local military base might be a valuable source of information.

Art Ask students to find pictures of a Civil War battle scene that they think represents the mood or spirit of Crane's story. Give students the opportunity to share their discoveries and discuss the reasons for their choices in small groups. Have students create a bulletin board with the Civil War art.

A. Critical Reading: Making Inferences

? Why did he bother to draw a bucket of water? [Possible answer: His motivation now is to accomplish what he set out to do. It seems unlikely that he is conscious of his own thirst anymore.]

B. Expansion

The angel of death is generally considered to be a spiritual being that brings death. Given this, what is a "practical angel of death"? [A material thing that could actually cause death, such as cannonballs or bullets.]

C. Critical Reading: Expressing an Opinion

? Why did Collins go back? [Possible answers: His humanity overcame his fear; having been scared so long, another minute didn't seem to matter; or he couldn't live with himself if he didn't go back.]

to it. He leaned over until it seemed as if he intended to try to push water into it with his hands. His eyes as he gazed down into the well shone like two pieces of metal and in their expression was a great appeal and a great curse. The stupid water derided him.

There was the blaring thunder of a shell. Crimson light shone through the swift-boiling smoke and made a pink reflection on part of the wall of the well. Collins jerked out his arm and canteen with the same motion that a man would use in withdrawing his head from a furnace.

He scrambled erect and glared and hesitated. On the ground near him lay the old well bucket, with a length of rusty chain. He lowered it swiftly into the well. The bucket struck the water and then turning lazily over, sank. When, with hand reaching tremblingly over hand, he hauled it out, it knocked often against the walls of the well and spilled some of its contents.

In running with a filled bucket, a man can adopt but one kind of gait. So through this terrible field over which screamed practical angels of death Collins ran in the manner of a farmer chased out of a dairy by a bull.

His face went staring white with anticipation—anticipation of a blow that would whirl him around and down. He would fall as he had seen other men fall, the life knocked out of them so suddenly that their knees were no more quick to touch the ground than their heads. He saw the long blue line of the regiment, but his comrades were standing looking at him from the edge of an impossible star. He was aware of some deep wheel ruts and hoof prints in the sod beneath his feet.

The artillery officer who had fallen in this meadow had been making groans in the teeth of the tempest of sound. These futile cries, wrenched from him by his agony, were heard only by shells, bullets. When wild-eyed Collins came running, this officer raised himself. His face contorted and blanched from pain, he was about to utter some great beseeching cry. But suddenly his face straightened and he called: "Say, young man, give me a drink of water, will you?"

Collins had no room amid his emotions for surprise. He was mad from the threats of destruction.

"I can't," he screamed, and in this reply was a full description of his quaking apprehension. His cap was gone and his hair was riotous. His clothes made it appear that he had been dragged over the ground by the heels. He ran on.

The officer's head sank down and one elbow crooked. His foot in its brass-bound stirrup still stretched over the body of his horse and the other leg was under the steed.

But Collins turned. He came dashing back. His face had now turned gray and in his eyes was all terror. "Here it is! Here it is!"

The officer was as a man gone in drink. His arm bended like a twig. His head drooped as if his neck was of willow. He was sinking to the ground, to lie face downward.

Collins grabbed him by the shoulder. "Here it is. Here's your drink. Turn over! Turn over, man, for God's sake!"

With Collins hauling at his shoulder, the officer twisted his body and fell with his face turned toward that region where lived the unspeakable noises of the swirling missiles. There was the faintest shadow of a smile on his lips as he looked at Collins. He gave a sigh, a little primitive breath like that from a child.

Collins tried to hold the bucket steadily, but his shaking hands caused the water to splash all over the face of the dying man. Then he jerked it away and ran on.

The regiment gave him a welcoming roar. The grimed faces were wrinkled in laughter.

His captain waved the bucket away. "Give it to the men!"

The two genial, skylarking young lieutenants were the first to gain possession of it. They played over it in their fashion.

When one tried to drink, the other teasingly knocked his elbow. "Don't, Billie! You'll make me spill it," said the one. The other laughed.

Suddenly there was an oath, the thud of wood on the ground, and a swift murmur of astonishment from the ranks. The two lieutenants glared at each other. The bucket lay on the ground empty.

Words to Own

blanched (blancht) *v.* used as *adj.*: drained of color.

Making Meanings

First Thoughts

1. Students should support their responses with details from the story and their own experiences. If they decide he is a fool, they should provide evidence of his lack of judgment; if they decide he is a hero, they should cite examples or indications of his bravery.

Reviewing the Text

a. He is hit by a shell; later he asks Collins for water.
b. He is disappointed because he is ordinary, and if he is heroic, then heroes are not much.
c. He runs away, but then he brings him a drink.
d. None.

Options for Teaching

Assessment Tools

Check Test: Multiple Choice

1. The occasion of the story is (a) a dress parade (b) a furious battle (c) a military retreat [b]
2. As they wait, the infantry witnesses (a) an artillery exchange (b) a tank attack (c) an aircraft attack [a]
3. Collins ventures into the bombardment in order to (a) save a wounded comrade (b) spy on the enemy (c) get some water [c]
4. The wounded officer asks Collins to (a) drag him to shelter (b) give him some of the water (c) call for help [b]
5. At the end, (a) the bucket lies on the ground, empty (b) the lieutenants drink all the water and toss the bucket away (c) Collins drinks the water himself [a]

What About Glory

Ask the child,
Who, without an answer,
Asks her brother,
"What is he like?"

Ask the brother,
Who, missing the memory,
Asks his mother,
"When will he be back?"

And ask the mother
Who, without a husband,
Asks herself, "Why'd
He have to be a hero?"

—Pindar VanArman
Gonzaga College High School
Washington, D.C.

MAKING MEANINGS

First Thoughts

1. What was your first reaction to the story? Did you consider Collins a hero or a fool? Why? Review your Reader's Log Quick-write to help you decide.

Shaping Interpretations

2. There is a good deal of "rank" in this story—several lieutenants, a captain, a major, a colonel, and a lieutenant colonel. But Collins is a private. Discuss whether or not you think his lowly rank is significant in any way.
3. When Crane "paints" the battle scene in colorful language, he draws our attention to the legs of certain men who are wearing white duck (linen) trousers. Why do you think Crane emphasizes the **image** of the men's white legs? What does the white contrast with?
4. In modern war, it has been said, machines resemble humans, and humans resemble machines. Find two or three examples from this story showing that Crane believes war **personifies** machines and dehumanizes people. What do you think of this idea about the dehumanizing effects of war and the glorification of its machines?
5. What **situational irony** occurs at the end of the story as a result of Collins's action?

Reviewing the Text

a. What happens to the lieutenant who holds his wounded right arm carefully in his left hand?
b. Why is Collins disappointed when it occurs to him that he could be called a hero?
c. What does the maddened Collins do when the wounded lieutenant asks him for water?
d. How much of the water in the bucket does Collins get to drink?

Connecting with the Text

6. What do you think is Collins's **motive** for his daring act? Simple thirst? The reactions of his comrades? Some other force within him? In what sense might the "mystery" in the title of the story refer to Collins's motivation?

Challenging the Text

7. The ending of the story is **ambiguous**—that is, it is open to more than one interpretation. Do you think the lieutenants spilled the water, or was the bucket empty by the time Collins got back? Does the empty bucket mean something? Explain how you interpreted the final lines of the story, and comment on whether or not you think this is a good ending.

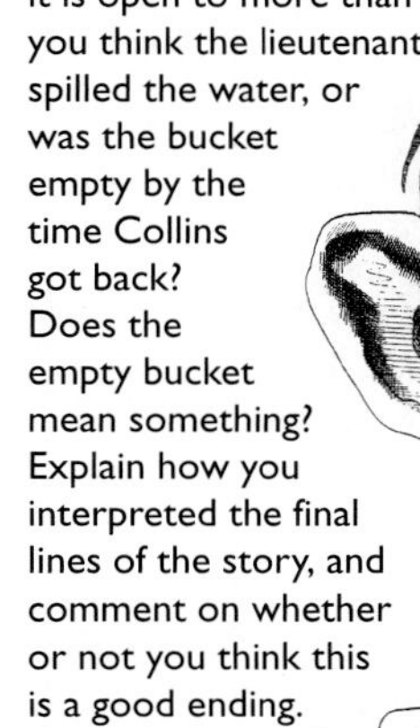

Stephen Crane.

Drawing by David Levine. Reprinted with permission from *The New York Review of Books.* Copyright © 1968 NYREV, Inc.

CONNECTING WITH "A MYSTERY OF HEROISM"

Ask students to discuss how this poem relates to the theme of the story. [Possible answers: It questions the value and definition of bravery, it asks what makes a hero, and it examines the effects of a hero's actions on others.]

A. Language Note: Repetition

What is the effect of the repetition in the poem? [Possible answers: The repetition adds urgency to the poem's search for answers; it reflects the characters' incessant worry; it reiterates the main idea.]

B. Reader's Response: Shaping Interpretations

What do you know about the character referred to as "he"? [Sample responses: He is a father and husband whose duty has kept him away from home for a long time. He is probably a soldier off fighting a war while his family waits for his return.]

Shaping Interpretations

2. Collins's low rank makes him representative of ordinary people. It also makes his rejection of his own heroism more poignant.
3. White is associated with innocence and purity and is therefore ironic on the battlefield. The color contrasts dramatically with the red of exploding shells and the blood and gore of the wounded and dying.
4. The artillery argues with the other guns; the guns are "stolid" and "courageous." The soldiers' eyes sweep in a "machine-like movement." Most students will agree that war dehumanizes.
5. After Collins's fearful journey, no one gets any water.

Connecting with the Text

6. Students may suggest that thirst combined with his comrades' taunts moved him to action. Perhaps a mysterious force provided him with an opportunity to learn something about himself.

Challenging the Text

7. **(Synthesis)** Some students will think the lieutenants spilled the water; some will say Collins spilled it running back; but others will have different interpretations. The empty bucket seems to represent the futility of human action. Answers will vary on whether the ending is good or not. Make sure students give examples from the text to support their answers.

Choices: Building Your Portfolio

1. **Writer's Notebook** Remind students to save their work. They may use it as prewriting for the Writer's Workshop on p. 515.
2. **Critical Writing** Ask students to compare the speaker's attitude in the poem to the narrator's attitude in the story. Before they begin writing, encourage students to make a list of points on which they will base their summary.
3. **Creative Writing** Consider using Transparency 3: Cluster Diagram in the Transparency Package for student use to brainstorm and cluster all the ideas that Crane's work suggests to them. Encourage students to let their imaginations roam freely and touch upon any and all subjects that occur to them. Then, they will have more choices to select from before writing their poems or prose pieces.

CHOICES: Building Your Portfolio

Writer's Notebook

1. Collecting Ideas for an Informative Report

WORK IN PROGRESS

One approach to researching a topic might involve surveying people about their attitudes. To gather information about current attitudes toward war, you could distribute copies of Crane's "A Mystery of Heroism" or "War Is Kind" to ten people, together with a questionnaire that explores their feelings about war. Write up a summary of the responses you get, and keep your notes for possible use in the Writer's Workshop on page 515.

Critical Writing

2. The Outrage of War

Write a brief essay in which you summarize Stephen Crane's attitudes toward war, based on your reading of "A Mystery of Heroism" and the Crane poem, "War Is Kind," on this page. In your essay, respond to these questions: (a) Is anyone in the story or the poem a hero in the sense of being willing to risk his life for a high moral principle? (b) Does any scene in the poem remind you of a scene in the story? (c) Do you find **irony** in Crane's attitudes toward war? (d) Does Crane really show you that war is kind?

Creative Writing

3. War Is . . .

Write a poem or a short prose piece about one of the subjects or **themes** suggested by Crane's works. For inspiration, see the Student to Student poem "What About Glory" on page 493.

War Is Kind

Do not weep, maiden, for war is kind.
Because your lover threw wild hands toward the sky
And the affrighted steed ran on alone,
Do not weep.
War is kind.

Hoarse, booming drums of the regiment,
Little souls who thirst for fight,
These men were born to drill and die.
The unexplained glory flies above them,
Great is the Battle-God, great, and his Kingdom—
A field where a thousand corpses lie.

Do not weep, babe, for war is kind.
Because your father tumbled in the yellow trenches,
Raged at his breast, gulped and died,
Do not weep.
War is kind.

Swift blazing flag of the regiment,
Eagle with crest of red and gold,
These men were born to drill and die.
Point for them the virtue of slaughter,
Make plain to them the excellence of killing
And a field where a thousand corpses lie.

Mother whose heart hung humble as a button
On the bright splendid shroud of your son,
Do not weep.
War is kind.

—Stephen Crane, 1896

STRATEGIES FOR INCLUSION

Special Needs Portfolio choices should be adapted in ways that allow students to actively participate at their own levels and to meet individual goals. For example, for activity #3, a student who has difficulty writing could express ideas about war via a drawing, collage, or musical composition, and students with hearing impairments could create a poem in American Sign Language.

Visual For activity #2, encourage students to draw, paint, or build a visual representation that compares attitudes toward war.

Musical For activity #3, students may be able to make their presentations more powerful by adding musical accompaniment to their poems or prose pieces.

PORTFOLIO ASSESSMENT

Choices: Assessment Criteria For help in evaluating these Choices assignments, see the criteria in the ***Portfolio Management System,*** p. 125.

Jack London

(1876–1916)

In his teens and twenties, Jack London adventured on sea and ice. Then, in the sixteen remaining years of his life, he turned out nearly fifty volumes of essays and fiction. Known during his lifetime as a passionate socialist, London is remembered today not for his political convictions, but for his exciting, fast-paced adventure stories. Even his harshest critic, Ambrose Bierce (page 466), called London's novel *The Sea Wolf* a "rattling good story."

London was born into a poor family in San Francisco. As a boy, he was largely uncared for by his parents. He delivered newspapers, worked on an ice wagon, set up pins in a bowling alley, and worked in a cannery. "Almost the first thing I realized were responsibilities," he says. "I worked hard from my eighth year." He graduated from grammar school in Oakland, across the bay from San Francisco.

Meanwhile, London read everything he could find in the public library, especially stories of real-life adventure. In his teens, he plunged into danger. "I joined the oyster pirates in the bay; shipped as sailor on a schooner; took a turn at salmon fishing; shipped before the mast and sailed for the Japanese coast on a seal-hunting expedition. After sealing for seven months I came back to California, and took odd jobs. . . ."

London was still in his teens when he settled in Oakland again. He began to write, selling a few pieces to local papers. After attending high school for one year, he managed to pass the entrance exams for the University of California at Berkeley by cramming on his own. The combination of work, school, and writing proved to be too much, however, and he quit halfway through his freshman year. He submerged himself in writing for the next three months. But he earned practically nothing, so in 1897 he took off to prospect for gold in the Klondike—part of the Yukon Territory in northwestern Canada.

London became sick and had to leave the Klondike in less than a year, but the experience

The Bettmann Archive.

convinced him that life is a struggle in which the strong survive and the weak do not. London's short stories and novels dramatize his belief that "civilized" beings are either destroyed or re-created in savage environments.

London's first major success was a story collection, *The Son of the Wolf* (1900). Readers were thrilled by the shocking brutality of his stories, then hooked by the action and adventure. His most famous short story, "To Build a Fire" (1908), focuses on survival. His most famous novel, *The Call of the Wild* (1903), celebrates the escape to freedom of a sled dog named Buck.

London became a millionaire from his writings, and success greatly altered his life. In 1900, he married and had two daughters, but his wife sued him for divorce in 1905. He remarried and established his home at Glen Ellen in Sonoma County, north of San Francisco. There he intended to create a magnificent ranch estate, but he lost interest when Wolf House, his nearly completed mansion, burned down in 1913. London, for years an alcoholic, suffered in his later years from kidney disease and depression. One evening in November 1916, when the physical pain finally became unendurable, London took a lethal dose of narcotics and lapsed into a coma. He died the next evening; he was forty years old.

ABOUT THE AUTHOR

Jack London is one of the most widely translated American authors. He explored many different styles in his writing, and his works range from an account of the life of the homeless and poor in London, England in *The People of the Abyss* (1903) to the autobiographical novel *Martin Eden* (1909). London was a fervent socialist, but he was also influenced heavily by the German philosopher Friedrich Nietzsche's idea of a "superman" who by force of will rises above the masses. He is still known best for his adventure tales.

PROGRAM MANAGER

- **Planning Instruction** See **Teaching Notes, *Teaching Resources A,*** p. 181, for objectives, a summary, and literary elements for this selection.
- **Instructional Support** See **Graphic Organizer for Active Reading, *Teaching Resources A,*** p. 195, for a Through the Story activity.
- **Assessment** See **Selection Test, *Test Booklet,*** pp. 115–116.
- **Language Link** See **Language Link, *Teaching Resources A,*** pp. 196–197, and ***Language and Writing Skills Worksheets,*** pp. 205–208.
- **Reinforcement** Use the **Words to Own** worksheet in ***Teaching Resources A,*** p. 198.
- **Reinforcement** See **Transparency** 10.3 in the ***Audiovisual Resources Binder.***

QUICK PLANNING GUIDE

Into the Story

Through the Story

Beyond the Story

Before You Read
To Build a Fire

Reading Focus
Cold, Cruel World

"To Build a Fire" must be the coldest story ever written. It is also one of the most effective examples of a conflict between a human being and the elements of nature. London draws on his own experience of prospecting for gold in the Yukon—a bleak, nearly sunless region of northwestern Canada—to give authenticity to the story.

But this is ultimately far more than a "person versus nature" story. It is a grimly realistic tale about a man who is "quick and alert in the things of life, but only in the things, and not in the significances"—an "innocent" who is not prepared for a cruel and unforgiving environment.

You may want to dress warmly as you read.

To Build

Day had broken cold and gray, exceedingly cold and g

A Dialogue with the Text

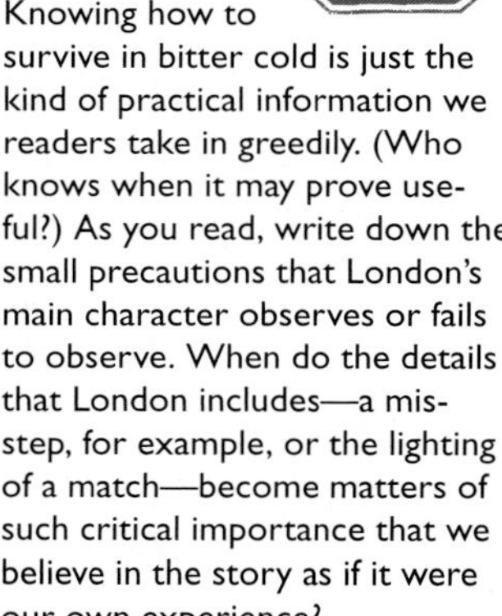

Knowing how to survive in bitter cold is just the kind of practical information we readers take in greedily. (Who knows when it may prove useful?) As you read, write down the small precautions that London's main character observes or fails to observe. When do the details that London includes—a misstep, for example, or the lighting of a match—become matters of such critical importance that we believe in the story as if it were our own experience?

Elements of Literature
Naturalism

The naturalists were a group of nineteenth-century writers who went beyond realism in an attempt to portray life exactly as it is. Naturalist writers, influenced by the scientist Charles Darwin's (1809–1882) theories of natural selection and survival of the fittest, believed human behavior to be determined by heredity and environment. Relying on new theories in sociology and psychology, the naturalists dissected human behavior with detachment and objectivity, like scientists dissecting laboratory specimens. **Naturalism** presents human beings as subject to natural forces beyond their control. This idea is at the center of "To Build a Fire."

Naturalism was a nineteenth-century literary movement that claimed to portray life exactly as it is, with detachment and objectivity.

For more on Naturalism, see page 421 and the Handbook of Literary Terms.

PORTFOLIO ASSESSMENT

Portfolio Assessment
For help with teacher assessment of reading skills, see the ***Portfolio Management System,*** pp. 54–55.

WORDS TO OWN

The following vocabulary words are defined in the Words to Own at bottom of the pupil's page.

intangible p. 497	extremities p. 502
undulations p. 497	recoiled p. 502
protruding p. 498	imperceptible p. 503
solidity p. 499	excruciating p. 504
imperative p. 502	ensued p. 504

Day had broken cold and gray, exceedingly cold and gray, when the man turned aside from the main Yukon trail and climbed the high earth bank, where a dim and little-traveled trail led eastward through the fat spruce timberland. It was a steep bank, and he paused for breath at the top, excusing the act to himself by looking at his watch. It was nine o'clock. There was no sun or hint of sun, though there was not a cloud in the sky. It was a clear day, and yet there seemed an intangible pall over the face of things, a subtle gloom that made the day dark, and that was due to the absence of sun. This fact did not worry the man. He was used to the lack of sun. It had been days since he had seen the sun, and he knew that a few more days must pass before that cheerful orb, due south, would just peep above the skyline and dip immediately from view.

The man flung a look back along the way he had come. The Yukon lay a mile wide and hidden under three feet of ice. On top of this ice were as many feet of snow. It was all pure white, rolling in gentle undulations where the ice jams of the freeze-up had formed. North and south, as far as his eye could see, it was unbroken white, save for a dark hairline that curved and twisted from around the spruce-covered island to the south, and that curved and twisted away into the north, where it disappeared behind another spruce-covered island.

Words to Own

intangible (in·tan′jə·bəl) *adj.:* difficult to define; vague.

undulations (un′dyo͞o·lā′shənz) *n. pl.:* wavelike motions.

Using **Before You Read** p. 496

Reading Focus

Ask students to recall stories in which specific knowledge of a cruel environment is of great importance. [Students may mention mystery or science fiction stories, for example.] Ask them to explain how the environment figured in the **plots** of the stories they mentioned. Then, have them think about why such knowledge might be so critical.

A. Reader's Response: First Thoughts

? Why do you think the protagonist does not have a name? [Sample responses: It makes him a representative of all people; without experience and knowledge, anyone could find himself or herself in a dangerous, new environment; or the author proposes that people are insignificant in the greater scheme of things or that this particular man is insignificant.]

B. Critical Reading: Making Inferences

? What does this sentence reveal about the man's character? [Possible answers: He will not admit weakness; or he easily tricks himself into viewing himself in the best possible light.]

OPTIONS FOR TEACHING

STRATEGIES FOR INCLUSION

Advanced Have students analyze how the description of the environment affects the mood of the story. If possible, have them compare it to a wintry landscape in a work of literature with a very different mood.

English Language Development Help students with the pronunciations of proper nouns and foreign words in the first three paragraphs (Yukon, Chilkoot, and *cheechako*), or read the first three paragraphs aloud to prevent early frustration.

Interpersonal The role of older people in society varies from culture to culture, making it an interesting topic of discussion for students. In "To Build a Fire," a young man ignores the advice of an older man with disastrous results. Have students work in groups to come up with a list of five things older people know more about and five things younger people know more about. Have them share their lists.

A. Reader's Response: Connecting with the Text

? What impression would a **setting** like this have on you? Have you ever seen a setting that seemed this inhospitable to humans? [Sample responses: The setting is disturbing and frightening; or it is challenging and exciting. It reminds me of other wilderness areas, a large unfamiliar city, or an outer space setting from science fiction.]

B. Critical Reading: Analyzing Character

? What problems could this outlook lead to? [Possible answers: Recognizing danger too late; taking unreasonable risks.]

C. Critical Reading: Analyzing Character

? What does the verb *plunged* indicate about the man's character? [It shows his impetuousness and his lack of forethought.]

D. Literary Element: Irony

? What is ironic about this statement? [The man is so out of touch with nature that he is surprised when a temperature of more than fifty degrees below zero makes him feel cold.]

E. Critical Reading: Comparing and Contrasting

In a chart like the one below, have students compare and contrast the man and the dog as revealed in this paragraph :

Dog	Man
[native to area] [newcomer] [sensitive to nature's warning] [not named]	[part of nature] [intruder] [ignores warning] [not named]

This dark hairline was the trail—the main trail—that led south five hundred miles to the Chilkoot Pass, Dyea, and salt water; and that led north seventy miles to Dawson, and still on to the north a thousand miles to Nulato, and finally to St. Michael on the Bering Sea, a thousand miles and half a thousand more.

(A) But all this—the mysterious, far-reaching hairline trail, the absence of sun from the sky, the tremendous cold, and the strangeness and weirdness of it all—made no impression on the man. It was not because he was long used to it. He was a newcomer in the land, a *cheechako,*[1] and this was his first winter. The trouble with him was that he (B) was without imagination. He was quick and alert in the things of life, but only in the things, and not in the significances. Fifty degrees below zero meant eighty-odd degrees of frost. Such fact impressed him as being cold and uncomfortable, and that was all. It did not lead him to meditate upon his frailty as a creature of temperature, and upon man's frailty in general, able only to live within certain narrow limits of heat and cold, and from there on it did not lead him to the conjectural[2] field of immortality and man's place in the universe. Fifty degrees below zero stood for a bite of frost that hurt and that must be guarded against by the use of mittens, earflaps, warm moccasins, and thick socks. Fifty degrees below zero was to him just precisely fifty degrees below zero. That there should be anything more to it than that was a thought that never entered his head.

As he turned to go on, he spat speculatively. There was a sharp, explosive crackle that startled him. He spat again. And again, in the air, before it could fall to the snow, the spittle crackled. He knew that at fifty below, spittle crackled on the snow, but this spittle had crackled in the air. Undoubtedly it was colder than fifty below—how much colder he did not know. But the temperature did not matter. He was bound for the old claim on the left fork of Henderson Creek, where the boys were already. They had come over across the divide from the Indian Creek country, while he had come the roundabout way to take a look at the possibilities of getting out logs in the spring from the islands in the Yukon. He would be into camp by six o'clock; a bit after dark, it was true, but the boys would be there, a fire would be going, and a hot supper would be ready. As for lunch, he pressed his hand against the protruding bundle under his jacket. It was also under his shirt, wrapped up in a handkerchief and lying against the naked skin. It was the only way to keep the biscuits from freezing. He smiled agreeably to himself as he thought of those biscuits, each cut open and sopped in bacon grease, and each enclosing a generous slice of fried bacon.

(C) He plunged in among the big spruce trees. The trail was faint. A foot of snow had fallen since the last sled had passed over, and he was glad he was without a sled, traveling light. In fact, he carried nothing but the lunch wrapped in the handker- (D) chief. He was surprised, however, at the cold. It certainly was cold, he concluded, as he rubbed his numb nose and cheekbones with his mittened hand. He was a warm-whiskered man, but the hair on his face did not protect the high cheekbones and the eager nose that thrust itself aggressively into the frosty air.

(E) At the man's heels trotted a dog, a big native husky, the proper wolf dog, gray-coated and without any visible or temperamental difference from its brother, the wild wolf. The animal was depressed by the tremendous cold. It knew that it was no time for traveling. Its instinct told it a truer tale than was told to the man by the man's judgment. In reality, it was not merely colder than fifty below zero; it was colder than sixty below, than seventy below. It was seventy-five below zero. Since the freezing point is thirty-two above zero, it meant that one hundred and seven degrees of frost obtained. The dog did not know anything about thermometers. Possibly in its brain there was no sharp consciousness of a condition of very cold such as was in the man's brain. But the brute had its instinct. It experienced a vague but menacing apprehension that subdued it and made it slink along at the man's heels, and that made it question eagerly every unwonted[3] movement of

1. ***cheechako*** (chē·chä′kō): Chinook jargon for "newcomer" or "tenderfoot."
2. **conjectural:** based on guesswork or uncertain evidence.
3. **unwonted:** unusual.

WORDS TO OWN

protruding (prō·tro͞od′iŋ) *v.* used as *adj.:* sticking out.

OPTIONS FOR TEACHING

STRATEGIES FOR INCLUSION

Less Proficient Readers Help students think of problems one might encounter in the wilderness by asking them to recall novels, movies, or television programs in which survival is an important theme or the main focus. Have them brainstorm the types of dangerous situations people encounter in the wild and the kinds of strategies that help them survive.

Special Needs Many students will enjoy the story if they get the support they need to make it through. Because they may be tired after the large amount of reading they have done for this unit, have students read this last story in pairs, with students taking turns reading aloud to one another. Mention that if they have difficulty while reading, they might ask their partners for help. Giving few directions for the paired reading will allow for maximum self-direction. If students ask how long each student should read, you might suggest that students do not have to read exactly the same amount and that they each read for the amount of time that feels comfortable and fair to each partner. After they have finished reading, encourage students to discuss their responses to the story. Pairs might also answer the Making Meanings questions together.

the man, as if expecting him to go into camp or to seek shelter somewhere and build a fire. The dog had learned fire, and it wanted fire, or else to burrow under the snow and cuddle its warmth away from the air.

The frozen moisture of its breathing had settled on its fur in a fine powder of frost, and especially were its jowls, muzzle, and eyelashes whitened by its crystaled breath. The man's red beard and moustache were likewise frosted, but more solidly, the deposit taking the form of ice and increasing with every warm, moist breath he exhaled. Also, the man was chewing tobacco, and the muzzle of ice held his lips so rigidly that he was unable to clear his chin when he expelled the juice. The result was that a crystal beard of the color and solidity of amber was increasing its length on his chin. If he fell down it would shatter itself, like glass, into brittle fragments. But he did not mind the appendage. It was the penalty all tobacco chewers paid in that country, and he had been out before in two cold snaps. They had not been so cold as this, he knew, but by the spirit thermometer[4] at Sixty Mile he knew they had been registered at fifty below and at fifty-five.

He held on through the level stretch of woods for several miles, crossed a wide flat, and dropped down a bank to the frozen bed of a small stream. This was Henderson Creek, and he knew he was ten miles from the forks. He looked at his watch. It was ten o'clock. He was making four miles an hour, and he calculated that he would arrive at the forks at half past twelve. He decided to celebrate that event by eating his lunch there.

The dog dropped in again at his heels, with a tail drooping discouragement, as the man swung **F** along the creek bed. The furrow of the old sled trail was plainly visible, but a dozen inches of snow covered the marks of the last runners. In a month no man had come up or down that silent creek. The man held steadily on. He was not much given to thinking, and just then particularly, he had nothing to think about save that he would eat lunch at the forks and that at six o'clock he would be in camp with the boys. There was nobody to talk to; and, had there been, speech **G** would have been impossible because of the ice muzzle on his mouth. So he continued monotonously to chew tobacco and to increase the length of his amber beard.

Once in a while the thought reiterated itself **H** that it was very cold and that he had never experienced such cold. As he walked along he rubbed his cheekbones and nose with the back of his mittened hand. He did this automatically, now and again changing hands. But rub as he would, the instant he stopped his cheekbones went numb, and the following instant the end of his nose went numb. He was sure to frost his cheeks; he knew that, and experienced a pang of regret that he had not devised a nose strap of the sort Bud wore in the cold snaps. Such a strap passed across the cheeks, as well, and saved them. But it didn't matter much, after all. What were frosted cheeks? A **I** bit painful, that was all; they were never serious.

Empty as the man's mind was of thought, he was keenly observant, and he noticed the changes in the creek, the curves and bends and timber jams, and always he sharply noted where he placed his feet. Once, coming around a bend, he shied abruptly, like a startled horse, curved away **J** from the place where he had been walking, and retreated several paces back along the trail. The creek, he knew, was frozen clear to the bottom—no creek could contain water in that arctic winter—but he knew also that there were springs that bubbled out from the hillsides and ran along under the snow and on top of the ice of the creek. He knew that the coldest snaps never froze these springs, and he knew likewise their danger. They were traps. They hid pools of water under the snow that might be three inches deep, or three feet. Sometimes a skin of ice half an inch thick covered them, and in turn was covered by the snow. Sometimes there were alternate layers of water and ice skin, so that when one broke through he kept on breaking through for a while, sometimes wetting himself to the waist.

That was why he had shied in such panic. He **K** had felt the give under his feet and heard the crackle of a snow-hidden ice skin. And to get his feet wet in such a temperature meant trouble and

4. **spirit thermometer:** alcohol thermometer. In places where the temperature often drops below the freezing point of mercury, alcohol is used in thermometers.

WORDS TO OWN

solidity (sə·lid′ə·tē) *n.:* firmness; solidness.

F. Critical Reading: Making Inferences

? What does the sharp contrast between the man's and the dog's moods mean? [Possible answers: There is no bond or connection between the man and the animal, such as you would expect between a person and his or her pet.]

G. Literary Element: Symbol

? What does the impossibility of speech symbolize? [Possible answers: The dangerous situation he is in; the loss of function—he may lose other important functions as the coldness sets in.]

H. Critical Reading: Predicting

? What do you think this repetition of the fact that it is cold means? [Possible answer: The man does not react differently, no matter how many times he repeats it to himself. It may mean that his inaction will put him in grave danger.]

I. Literary Element: Foreshadowing

? What does his reaction to frostbite on his cheeks suggest? [Possible answers: He continues to underestimate forces of nature; or he thinks he is immune to them.]

J. Literary Element: Simile

? How does London convey the man's sense of instinct? [When the man shows good sense, he is compared to an animal.]

K. Critical Reading: Comparing and Contrasting

? How is this reaction to nature different from his earlier reactions? [Possible answer: This is the first reaction that is sensible. He recognizes danger and tries to avoid it.]

INTEGRATING THE LANGUAGE ARTS

Strategic Reading To help students read effectively, have pairs read together, stopping every two pages in the story to discuss the text. Tell students they may express reactions, pose problems, ask their partner's opinion, and consider what elements they like or dislike about the story.

Writing: Poem Ask students to work in pairs to write a poem in which a person or people come into **conflict** with nature. They may base the poem on "To Build a Fire" or an idea of their own. Have them decide how the conflict will be resolved before they begin. Encourage them to use a strong description of the **setting,** as London does, to set the mood of the piece.

Language and Style A protagonist without a name can make a strong statement for a writer. Have students find other works with unnamed main characters. Students can share their findings. ☞

A. Reader's Response: Connecting with the Text

? Is it fair to make the dog take the risk? [Sample responses: No, it is cruel and selfish; or yes, a human's life is more valuable than an animal's.]

danger. At the very least it meant delay, for he would be forced to stop and build a fire, and under its protection to bare his feet while he dried his socks and moccasins. He stood and studied the creek bed and its banks, and decided that the flow of water came from the right. He reflected awhile, rubbing his nose and cheeks, then skirted to the left, stepping gingerly and testing the footing for each step. Once clear of the danger, he took a fresh chew of tobacco and swung along at his four-mile gait.

In the course of the next two hours he came upon several similar traps. Usually the snow above the hidden pools had a sunken, candied appearance that advertised the danger. Once again, however, he had a close call; and once, suspecting danger, he compelled the dog to go on in front. The dog did not want to go. It hung back until the man shoved it forward, and then it went quickly across the white, unbroken surface. Suddenly it broke through, floundered to one side, and got away to firmer footing. It had wet its forefeet and legs, and almost immediately the water that clung to it turned to ice. It made quick efforts to lick the ice off its legs, then dropped down in the snow and began to bite out the ice that had formed between the toes. This was a matter of instinct. To permit the ice to remain would mean sore feet. It did not know this. It merely obeyed the mysterious prompting that arose from the deep crypts[5] of

5. **crypts:** hidden recesses.

INTEGRATING THE LANGUAGE ARTS

Strategic Reading As a postreading activity, have students make a cause-and-effect chart showing all the contributing factors that lead to the man's death. Then, discuss whether there is one main cause for the man's death or whether a number of contributing factors are responsible for his death.

CLASSROOM MANAGEMENT

Block Scheduling To help maintain student attention during the longer class time, make and play a tape of this story for the class to hear (twenty to twenty-five minutes). After a general discussion, have students work with partners to create an illustration based on some aspect of the story. Then, have students share and explain their illustrations (twenty-five to thirty minutes). Conclude with students completing Making Meanings or allow time for students to make Reader's Log notes (twenty to twenty-five minutes).

Cooperative Learning As students work together in groups, encourage them to practice the following techniques:

- openness to trying others' suggestions
- consolidating ideas rather than choosing one over another, when possible
- maintaining awareness of their own strengths and weaknesses
- listening until other people are done talking

its being. But the man knew, having achieved a judgment on the subject, and he removed the mitten from his right hand and helped tear out the ice particles. He did not expose his fingers more than a minute, and was astonished at the swift numbness that smote[6] them. It certainly was cold. He pulled on the mitten hastily, and beat the hand savagely across his chest. B

At twelve o'clock the day was at its brightest. Yet the sun was too far south on its winter journey to clear the horizon. The bulge of the earth intervened between it and Henderson Creek, where the man walked under a clear sky at noon and cast no shadow. At half past twelve, to the minute, he arrived at the forks of the creek. He was pleased at the speed he had made. If he kept it up, he would certainly be with the boys by six. He unbuttoned his jacket and shirt and drew forth his lunch. The action consumed no more than a quarter of a minute, yet in that brief moment the numbness laid hold of the exposed fingers. He did not put the mitten on, but instead struck the fingers a dozen sharp smashes against his leg. Then he sat down on a snow-covered log to eat. The sting that followed upon the striking of his fingers against his leg ceased so quickly that he was startled. He had had no chance to take a bite of biscuit. He struck the fingers repeatedly and returned them to the mitten, baring the other hand for the purpose of eating. He tried to take a mouthful, but the ice muzzle prevented. He had forgotten to build a fire and thaw out. He chuckled at his foolishness, and as he chuckled he noted the numbness creeping into the exposed fingers. Also, he noted that the stinging which had first come to his toes when he sat down was already passing away. He wondered whether the toes were warm or numb. He moved them inside the moccasins and decided that they were numb. C

He pulled the mitten on hurriedly and stood up. He was a bit frightened. He stamped up and down until the stinging returned into the feet. It certainly was cold, was his thought. That man from Sulfur Creek had spoken the truth when telling how cold it sometimes got in the country. And he had laughed at him at the time! That showed one must not be too sure of things. There was no mistake about it, it *was* cold. He strode up and down, stamping his feet and threshing his arms, until reassured by the returning warmth. D Then he got out matches and proceeded to make a fire. From the undergrowth, where high water of the previous spring had lodged a supply of seasoned twigs, he got his firewood. Working carefully from a small beginning, he soon had a roaring fire, over which he thawed the ice from his face and in the protection of which he ate his biscuits. For the moment the cold of space was outwitted. E The dog took satisfaction in the fire, stretching out close enough for warmth and far enough away to escape being singed.

When the man had finished, he filled his pipe and took his comfortable time over a smoke. Then he pulled on his mittens, settled the earflaps of his cap firmly about his ears, and took the creek trail up the left fork. The dog was disappointed and yearned back toward the fire. This man did not know cold. Possibly all the generations of his ancestry had been ignorant of cold, of real cold, of cold one hundred and seven degrees below freezing point. But the dog knew; all its ancestry knew, and it had inherited the knowledge. And it knew that it was not good to walk abroad in such fearful cold. It was the time to lie snug in a hole in the snow and wait for a curtain of cloud to be drawn across the face of outer space whence this cold came. On the other hand, there was no keen intimacy between the dog and the man. The one was the toil slave of the other, and the only caresses it had ever received were the caresses of the whiplash and of harsh and menacing throat sounds that threatened the whiplash. So the dog made no effort to communicate its apprehension to the man. It was not concerned in the welfare of the man; it was for its own sake that it yearned back toward the fire. But the man whistled, and spoke to it with the sound of whiplashes, and the dog swung in at the man's heels and followed after.

The man took a chew of tobacco and proceeded to start a new amber beard. Also, his moist breath quickly powdered with white his moustache, eyebrows, and lashes. There did not seem to be so many springs on the left fork of the Henderson, and for half an hour the man saw no signs of any. And then it happened. At a place where there were no signs, where the soft, unbroken snow seemed to advertise solidity beneath, the

6. **smote:** powerfully struck; past tense of *smite.*

B. Language Note: Diction

? Why do you think London used the word *savagely* here? [Possible answer: It suggests a lack of thought coupled with desperation that characterizes the man at this moment.]

C. Critical Reading: Finding Details

? What danger signs do you see here? [Possible answers: His forgetting to build a fire shows incredible inattention to the situation; his laughter at his own foolishness continues the cavalier attitude he has had from the start; the numbness of his fingers and stinging of his toes less than halfway through his journey is a bad sign.]

D. Critical Reading: Metacognition

? What do you think now of your earlier prediction of the story's outcome, given more evidence? [Students may revise their predictions, depending on what they originally predicted and how well they have been able to follow London's clues.]

E. Critical Reading: Finding Details

? What strategies help him defeat the cold for the moment? [He has brought matches with him; he locates a good supply of wood; he is careful; he starts small and builds slowly.]

CLASSROOM MANAGEMENT

Marking a Text Encourage students to experiment with ways of marking the text of this story to identify patterns and find meaning. Provide self-stick notes for this exercise, if possible. Afterward, have students work in groups to compare their techniques and findings. Have a class discussion during which you put a portion of the text on the overhead projector and show how you might mark it. Then, encourage students to add their own observations. You may want to give students additional opportunities to mark texts in later readings.

CROSSING THE CURRICULUM

Geography/Mathematics Have students study weather information to discover what areas of Earth have temperatures cold enough to be dangerous to people. Then, ask students to figure out what percentage of the land this includes and to make a map or chart to illustrate their findings.

Health Have students find out the latest information on frostbite—what it does and the best ways to prevent and treat it. Have students prepare pamphlets to share with the school community. Even if your area does not experience cold weather, many people encounter climate changes on vacation—frostbite can occur even on summer hikes in the mountains.

A. Critical Reading: Analyzing Character

? What does the man blame for his getting wet? Is this appropriate? [Possible answer: He blames his luck. Students may think that since he has failed to take the proper precautions on this trip, it would be more appropriate to blame himself.]

B. Language Note: Description

? Why do you think the level of detail changes here? [As the actions become more crucial, the level of detail increases.]

C. Literary Element: Tone

? How does the tone change here? [There is an increase in the intensity and suspense.]

D. Critical Reading: Drawing Conclusions

? What is the effect of repeating that he is safe? [Possible answer: It implies that he is not safe—it is another of his mistaken, cavalier notions.]

E. Critical Reading: Comparing and Contrasting

? What does the old-timer's seriousness imply? What does the man's reaction suggest? [Possible answers: The old-timer knows the danger of the climate. He passes on the collective wisdom of years of experience. The man thinks that he is beyond this wisdom and that he is self-sufficient.]

F. Reader's Response: Shaping Interpretations

? How do you interpret this latest statement about the feeling in the man's hands? [Sample responses: It is not just his hands now but his nervous system that is affected; or he is like a marionette with the wires cut.]

man broke through. It was not deep. He wet himself halfway to the knees before he floundered out to the firm crust.

(A) He was angry, and cursed his luck aloud. He had hoped to get into camp with the boys at six o'clock, and this would delay him an hour, for he would have to build a fire and dry out his footgear. This was imperative at that low temperature—he knew that much; and he turned aside to the bank, which he climbed. On top, tangled in the underbrush about the trunks of several small spruce trees, was a high-water deposit of dry firewood—sticks and twigs, principally, but also larger portions of seasoned branches and fine, dry, last year's grasses. He threw down several large pieces on top of the snow. (B) This served for a foundation and prevented the young flame from drowning itself in the snow it otherwise would melt. The flame he got by touching a match to a small shred of birch bark that he took from his pocket. This burned even more readily than paper. Placing it on the foundation, he fed the young flame with wisps of dry grass and with the tiniest dry twigs.

He worked slowly and carefully, keenly aware of his danger. Gradually, as the flame grew stronger, he increased the size of the twigs with which he fed it. He squatted in the snow, pulling the twigs out from their entanglement in the brush and feeding directly to the flame. He knew there must be no failure. (C) When it is seventy-five below zero, a man must not fail in his first attempt to build a fire—that is, if his feet are wet. If his feet are dry, and he fails, he can run along the trail for a half a mile and restore his circulation. But the circulation of wet and freezing feet cannot be restored by running when it is seventy-five below. No matter how fast he runs, the wet feet will freeze the harder.

All this the man knew. The old-timer on Sulfur Creek had told him about it the previous fall, and now he was appreciating the advice. Already all sensation had gone out of his feet. To build the fire, he had been forced to remove his mittens, and the fingers had quickly gone numb. His pace of four miles an hour had kept his heart pumping blood to the surface of his body and to all the extremities. But the instant he stopped, the action of the pump eased down. The cold of space smote the unprotected tip of the planet, and he, being on that unprotected tip, received the full force of the blow. The blood of his body recoiled before it. The blood was alive, like the dog, and like the dog it wanted to hide away and cover itself up from the fearful cold. So long as he walked four miles an hour, he pumped that blood, willy-nilly, to the surface; but now it ebbed away and sank down into the recesses of his body. The extremities were the first to feel its absence. His wet feet froze the faster, and his exposed fingers numbed the faster, though they had not yet begun to freeze. Nose and cheeks were already freezing, while the skin of all his body chilled as it lost its blood.

(D) But he was safe. Toes and nose and cheeks would be only touched by the frost, for the fire was beginning to burn with strength. He was feeding it twigs the size of his finger. In another minute he would be able to feed it with branches the size of his wrist, and then he could remove his wet footgear, and, while it dried, he could keep his naked feet warm by the fire, rubbing them at first, of course, with snow. The fire was a success. He was safe. He remembered the advice of the old-timer on Sulfur Creek, and smiled. The old-timer had been very serious in laying down the law that no man must travel alone in the Klondike after fifty below. (E) Well, here he was; he had had the accident; he was alone; and he had saved himself. Those old-timers were rather womanish, some of them, he thought. All a man had to do was to keep his head and he was all right. Any man who was a man could travel alone. But it was surprising, the rapidity with which his cheeks and nose were freezing. And he had not thought his fingers could go lifeless in so short a time. Lifeless they were, for he could scarcely make them move together to grip a twig, and they seemed remote from his body and from him. When he touched a twig, he had to look and see whether or not he (F) had hold of it. The wires were pretty well down between him and his finger ends.

All of which counted for little. There was the fire, snapping and crackling and promising life

Words to Own

imperative (im·per′ə·tiv) *adj.:* absolutely necessary; compulsory.

extremities (ek·strem′ə·tēz) *n. pl.:* limbs of the body, especially hands and feet.

recoiled (ri′koil′d) *v.:* shrank away; drew back.

OPTIONS FOR TEACHING

PROFESSIONAL NOTES

Thematic Connections: "From Innocence to Experience" The man did not have a chance to profit from his experience, beyond realizing that the old-timer was right and that the man had caused his own death. Ask students how they have profited from reading about the man's experience.

Cultural Diversity The man challenged his society's notions about safety and risk-taking. Discuss with students what kinds of risks they find acceptable and what kinds of risks they reject. Then, encourage them to consider various cultures' standards for what is appropriate in risk-taking behaviors.

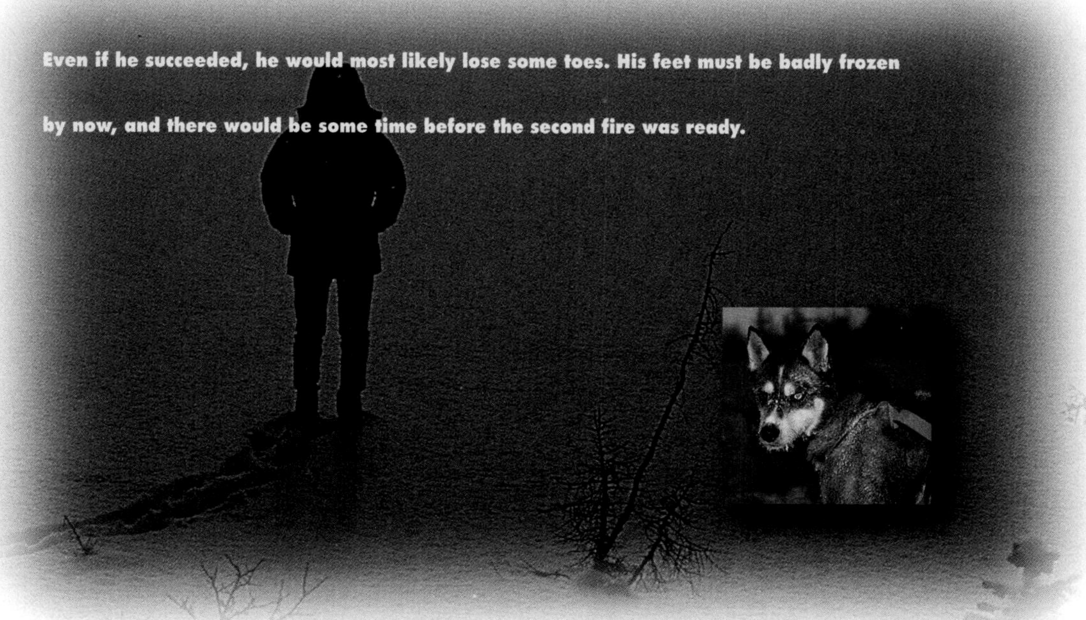

with every dancing flame. He started to untie his moccasins. They were coated with ice; the thick German socks were like sheaths of iron halfway to the knees; and the moccasin strings were like rods of steel all twisted and knotted as by some conflagration. For a moment he tugged with his numb fingers, then, realizing the folly of it, he **G** drew his sheath knife.

But before he could cut the strings it happened. It was his own fault, or, rather, his mistake. He should not have built the fire under the spruce tree. He should have built it in the open. But it had been easier to pull the twigs from the bush and drop them directly on the fire. Now the tree under which he had done this carried a weight of snow on its boughs. No wind had blown for weeks, and each bough was fully freighted. Each time he had pulled a twig he had communicated a slight agitation to the tree—an imperceptible agitation, so far as he was concerned, but an agitation sufficient to bring about the disaster. High up in the tree one bough capsized its load of snow. This fell on the boughs beneath, capsizing them. This process continued, spreading out and involving the whole tree. It grew like an avalanche, and it descended without warning upon the man and the fire, and the fire was blotted out! Where it had burned was a mantle of fresh and disordered snow.

The man was shocked. It was as though he had **H** just heard his own sentence of death. For a moment he sat and stared at the spot where the fire had been. Then he grew very calm. Perhaps the old-timer on Sulfur Creek was right. If he had only had a trail mate, he would have been in no danger **I** now. The trail mate could have built the fire. Well, it was up to him to build the fire over again, and this second time there must be no failure. Even if he succeeded, he would most likely lose some toes. His feet must be badly frozen by now, and there would be some time before the second fire was ready.

Such were his thoughts, but he did not sit and think them. He was busy all the time they were passing through his mind. He made a new foundation for a fire, this time in the open, where no treacherous tree could blot it out. Next he

Words to Own

imperceptible (im′pər·sep′tə·bəl) *adj.:* not easily perceived.

G. Critical Reading: Drawing Conclusions

? What folly does the man recognize here? [He realizes the folly of trying to use his numb fingers.]

H. Literary Element: Foreshadowing

? What might this statement foreshadow? [The man's death.]

I. Critical Reading: Drawing Conclusions

? What is the man doing? [He is regretting not listening to the old-timer, but it is too late.]

ASSESSMENT TOOLS

Check Test: True-False

1. The man's trouble is that he lacks imagination. [True]
2. The man is walking without a buddy in a temperature of more than fifty below zero. [True]
3. The man builds a fire as soon as he stops for lunch. [False]
4. The dog warns the man when they come near the springs. [False]
5. The man is safe at the end because the boys from camp will find him. [False]

A. Critical Reading: Comparing and Contrasting

? How is this fire-building sequence similar to and different from the earlier one? [He lacks control of the materials this time, but the methodicalness and the forethought in gathering materials are the same.]

B. Critical Reading: Speculating

? Why can he not feel the bark? [Possible answer: His fingers—tissue and bone—are completely frozen and have no feeling.]

C. Critical Reading: Drawing Conclusions

? Why is this development important? [Possible answer: It has introduced a new factor—panic—which might significantly affect the man's ability to act calmly and rationally.]

D. Critical Reading: Making Inferences

? How is the man's attitude toward the dog changing? [Possible answer: His attitude is changing from disinterest to envy of a creature that is not suffering.]

E. Critical Reading: Finding Sequence

? How has the description of his fingers changed now? [His fingers have gone from being numb, to lifeless, to unwired, to dead. This does not bode well for the man's survival.]

gathered dry grasses and tiny twigs from the high-water flotsam.[7] He could not bring his fingers together to pull them out, but he was able to gather them by the handful. In this way he got many rotten twigs and bits of green moss that were undesirable, but it was the best he could do. (A) He worked methodically, even collecting an armful of the larger branches to be used later when the fire gathered strength. And all the while the dog sat and watched him, a certain yearning wistfulness in its eyes, for it looked upon him as the fire provider, and the fire was slow in coming.

(B) When all was ready, the man reached in his pocket for a second piece of birch bark. He knew the bark was there, and, though he could not feel it with his fingers, he could hear its crisp rustling as he fumbled for it. Try as he would, he could not clutch hold of it. And all the time, in his consciousness, was the knowledge that each instant (C) his feet were freezing. This thought tended to put him in a panic, but he fought against it and kept calm. He pulled on his mittens with his teeth, and threshed his arms back and forth, beating his hands with all his might against his sides. He did this sitting down, and he stood up to do it; and all the while the dog sat in the snow, its wolf brush of a tail curled around warmly over its forefeet, its sharp wolf ears pricked forward intently as it (D) watched the man. And the man, as he beat and threshed with his arms and hands, felt a great surge of envy as he regarded the creature that was warm and secure in its natural covering.

After a time he was aware of the first faraway signals of sensation in his beaten fingers. The faint tingling grew stronger till it evolved into a stinging ache that was excruciating, but which the man hailed with satisfaction. He stripped the mitten from his right hand and fetched forth the birch bark. The exposed fingers were quickly going numb again. Next he brought out his bunch of sulfur matches. But the tremendous cold had already driven the life out of his fingers. In his effort to separate one match from the others, the whole bunch fell in the snow. He tried to pick it out of (E) the snow, but failed. The dead fingers could neither touch nor clutch. He was very careful. He drove the thought of his freezing feet, and nose, and cheeks, out of his mind, devoting his whole soul to the matches. He watched, using the sense of vision in place of that of touch, and when he saw his fingers on each side of the bunch, he closed them—that is, he willed to close them, for the wires were down, and the fingers did not obey. He pulled the mitten on the right hand, and beat it fiercely against his knee. Then, with both mittened hands, he scooped the bunch of matches, along with much snow, into his lap. Yet he was no better off.

After some manipulation he managed to get the bunch between the heels of his mittened hands. In this fashion he carried it to his mouth. The ice crackled and snapped when by a violent effort he opened his mouth. He drew the lower jaw in, curled the upper lip out of the way, and scraped the bunch with his upper teeth in order to separate a match. He succeeded in getting one, which he dropped on his lap. He was no better off. He could not pick it up. Then he devised a way. He picked it up in his teeth and scratched it on his leg. Twenty times he scratched before he succeeded in lighting it. As it flamed he held it with his teeth to the birch bark. But the burning brimstone went up his nostrils and into his lungs, causing him to cough spasmodically. The match fell into the snow and went out.

The old-timer on Sulfur Creek was right, he thought in the moment of controlled despair that ensued: After fifty below, a man should travel with a partner. He beat his hands, but failed in exciting any sensation. Suddenly he bared both hands, removing the mittens with his teeth. He caught the whole bunch between the heels of his hands. His arm muscles, not being frozen, enabled him to press the hand heels tightly against the matches. Then he scratched the bunch along his leg. It flared into flame, seventy sulfur matches at once! There was no wind to blow them out. He kept his head to one side to escape the strangling fumes, and held the blazing bunch to the birch bark. As he so held it, he became aware of sensation in his hand. His flesh was burning. He could smell it.

7. **high-water flotsam:** branches and debris washed ashore by a stream or river during the warm months when the water is high.

Words to Own

excruciating (eks·kro͞o′shē·āt′iŋ) *adj.:* extreme; intense.

ensued (en·so͞od′) *v.:* resulted.

OPTIONS FOR TEACHING

ASSESSMENT TOOLS

Self-Reflection: Reading Literature Answer each of the following items, rating your performance (1) rarely, (2) sometimes, or (3) always.

_____ **1.** I ask myself why characters act the way they do as I am reading.

_____ **2.** I try to predict what characters will do next as I am reading.

_____ **3.** I note words and ideas that interest or puzzle me as I am reading.

_____ **4.** I jot down ideas for discussion or writing as I am reading.

_____ **5.** I try to notice symbols as I am reading.

Deep down below the surface he could feel it. The sensation developed into pain that grew acute. And still he endured it, holding the flame of matches clumsily to the bark that would not light readily because his own burning hands were in the way, absorbing most of the flame.

At last, when he could endure no more, he jerked his hands apart. The blazing matches fell sizzling into the snow, but the birch bark was alight. He began laying dry grass and the tiniest twigs on the flame. He could not pick and choose, for he had to lift the fuel between the heels of his hands. Small pieces of rotten wood and green moss clung to the twigs, and he bit them off as well as he could with his teeth. He cherished the flame carefully and awkwardly. It meant life, and it must not perish. The withdrawal of blood from the surface of his body now made him begin to shiver, and he grew more awkward. A large piece of green moss fell squarely on the little fire. He tried to poke it out with his fingers, but his shivering frame made him poke too far, and he disrupted the nucleus of the little fire, the burning grasses and tiny twigs separating and scattering. He tried to poke them together again, but in spite of the tenseness of the effort, his shivering got away with him, and the twigs were hopelessly scattered. Each twig gushed a puff of smoke and went out. The fire provider had failed. As he looked apathetically about him, his eyes chanced on the dog, sitting across the ruins of the fire from him, in the snow, making restless, hunching movements, slightly lifting one forefoot and then the other, shifting its weight back and forth on them with wistful eagerness.

The sight of the dog put a wild idea into his head. He remembered the tale of the man, caught in a blizzard, who killed a steer and crawled inside the carcass, and so was saved. He would kill the dog and bury his hands in the warm body until the numbness went out of them. Then he could build another fire. He spoke to the dog, calling it to him; but in his voice was a strange note of fear that frightened the animal, who had never known the man to speak in such a way before. Something was the matter, and its suspicious nature sensed danger—it knew not what danger, but somewhere, somehow, in its brain arose an apprehension of the man. It flattened its ears down at the sound of the man's voice, and its restless, hunching movements and the liftings and shiftings of its forefeet became more pronounced; but it would not come to the man. He got on his hands and knees and crawled toward the dog. This unusual posture again excited suspicion, and the animal sidled mincingly away.

The man sat up in the snow for a moment and struggled for calmness. Then he pulled on his mittens, by means of his teeth, and got up on his feet. He glanced down at first in order to assure himself that he was really standing up, for the absence of sensation in his feet left him unrelated to the earth. His erect position in itself started to drive the webs of suspicion from the dog's mind; and when he spoke peremptorily,[8] with the sound of whiplashes in his voice, the dog rendered its customary allegiance and came to him. As it came within reaching distance, the man lost his control. His arms flashed out to the dog, and he experienced genuine surprise when he discovered that his hands could not clutch, that there was neither bend nor feeling in the fingers. He had forgotten for the moment that they were frozen and that they were freezing more and more. All this happened quickly, and before the animal could get away, he encircled its body with his arms. He sat down in the snow, and in this fashion held the dog, while it snarled and whined and struggled.

But it was all he could do, hold its body encircled in his arms and sit there. He realized that he could not kill the dog. There was no way to do it. With his helpless hands he could neither draw nor hold his sheath knife nor throttle the animal. He released it, and it plunged wildly away, its tail between its legs and still snarling. It halted forty feet away and surveyed him curiously, with ears sharply pricked forward. The man looked down at his hands in order to locate them, and found them hanging on the ends of his arms. It struck him as curious that one should have to use his eyes in order to find out where his hands were. He began threshing his arms back and forth, beating the mittened hands against his sides. He did this for five minutes, violently, and his heart pumped enough blood up to the surface to put a stop to his shivering. But no sensation was aroused in his hands. He had an impression that they hung like weights on

8. **peremptorily** (pər·emp′tə·ri·lē): in a commanding way.

F. Language Note: Style

? What effect does the narrator's matter-of-factness have about the man's hands burning? [Possible answers: It makes readers care less about the man; it shows how unimportant this man's fate is to the world; or it makes the man's suffering more poignant and horrific.]

G. Literary Element: Theme

The theme of being out of touch with nature reaches a new height as the man destroys the fire that could save him.

H. Literary Element: Naturalism

? How is the story not a romantic one? [Possible answers: In a romantic tale, the man would have survived despite everything. Here, it seems he is doomed to failure. This is not a world for romantics but a world in which a person must use every bit of skill to survive.]

I. Reader's Response: Extending the Text

? How would you compare the value of the dog's instinct to the man's judgment? [Sample responses: The dog's instinct is better than the man's ideas and thoughts; or the dog's instinct is more valuable, since it survives easily, while the man struggles for his life.]

J. Literary Element: Theme

In the beginning of the story, the narration implies that the man is unrelated to the earth and nature. Now it has become true in a more profound way.

K. Critical Reading: Making Inferences

? What is the dog responding to? [Possible answers: Power; habit; fear.]

L. Critical Reading: Summarizing

? What has the man lost? [The power to put his will into action, even to save his life.]

A. Reader's Response: Shaping Interpretations
This is the first time the man fears that he might die. When did you first think he might die? [Sample responses: In the beginning when he sets out alone; or when he gets his feet wet.]

B. Critical Reading: Drawing Conclusions
? Why is he angry? [His thinking is no longer rational. He feels outsmarted and cheated by nature. He is jealous of the dog's warmth.]

C. Reader's Response: Shaping Interpretations
? What is happening to him? [Sample responses: His detachment from his body (because it is frozen) has become so great that he is moving into the realm of fantasy, having an out-of-body experience; he is dreaming; or he is denying the reality of his situation.]

the ends of his arms, but when he tried to run the impression down, he could not find it.

A A certain fear of death, dull and oppressive, came to him. This fear quickly became poignant as he realized that it was no longer a mere matter of freezing his fingers and toes, or of losing his hands and feet, but that it was a matter of life and death, with the chances against him. This threw him into a panic, and he turned and ran up the creek bed along the old, dim trail. The dog joined in behind and kept up with him. He ran blindly, without intention, in fear such as he had never known in his life. Slowly, as he plowed and floundered through the snow, he began to see things again—the banks of the creek, the old timber jams, the leafless aspens, and the sky. The running made him feel better. He did not shiver. Maybe, if he ran on, his feet would thaw out; and, anyway, if he ran far enough, he would reach the camp and the boys. Without doubt he would lose some fingers and toes and some of his face; but the boys would take care of him, and save the rest of him when he got there. And, at the same time, there was another thought in his mind that said he would never get to the camp and the boys; that it was too many miles away, that the freezing had too great a start on him, and that he would soon be stiff and dead. This thought he kept in the background and refused to consider. Sometimes it pushed itself forward and demanded to be heard, but he thrust it back and strove to think of other things.

It struck him as curious that he could run at all on feet so frozen that he could not feel them when they struck the earth and took the weight of his body. He seemed to himself to skim along above the surface, and to have no connection with the earth. Somewhere he had once seen a winged Mercury,[9] and he wondered if Mercury felt as he felt when skimming over the earth.

His theory of running until he reached camp and the boys had one flaw in it: He lacked the endurance. Several times he stumbled, and finally he tottered, crumpled up, and fell. When he tried to rise, he failed. He must sit and rest, he decided, and next time he would merely walk and keep on going. As he sat and regained his breath, he noted that he was feeling quite warm and comfortable. He was not shivering, and it even seemed that a warm glow had come to his chest and trunk. And yet, when he touched his nose or cheeks, there was no sensation. Running would not thaw them out. Nor would it thaw out his hands and feet. Then the thought came to him that the frozen portions of his body must be extending. He tried to keep this thought down, to forget it, to think of something else; he was aware of the panicky feeling that it caused, and he was afraid of the panic. But the thought asserted itself, and persisted, until it produced a vision of his body totally frozen. This was too much, and he made another wild run along the trail. Once he slowed down to a walk, but the thought of the freezing extending itself made him run again.

And all the time the dog ran with him, at his heels. When he fell down a second time, it curled its tail over its forefeet and sat in front of him, facing him, curiously eager and intent. B The warmth and security of the animal angered him, and he cursed it till it flattened down its ears appeasingly. This time the shivering came more quickly upon the man. He was losing in this battle with the frost. It was creeping into his body from all sides. The thought of it drove him on, but he ran no more than a hundred feet when he staggered and pitched headlong. It was his last panic. When he had recovered his breath and control, he sat up and entertained in his mind the conception of meeting death with dignity. However, the conception did not come to him in such terms. His idea of it was that he had been making a fool of himself, running around like a chicken with its head cut off—such was the simile that occurred to him. Well, he was bound to freeze anyway, and he might as well take it decently. With this newfound peace of mind came the first glimmerings of drowsiness. A good idea, he thought, to sleep off to death. It was like taking an anesthetic. Freezing was not so bad as people thought. There were lots worse ways to die.

He pictured the boys finding his body next day. C Suddenly he found himself with them, coming along the trail and looking for himself. And, still with them, he came around a turn in the trail and found himself lying in the snow. He did not belong with himself anymore, for even then he was out of himself, standing with the boys and looking

9. **Mercury:** messenger of the gods in Roman mythology. He wears winged sandals and a winged hat.

. . . he came around a turn in the trail and found himself lying in the snow. He did not belong with himself anymore, for even then he was out of himself, standing with the boys and looking at himself in the snow.

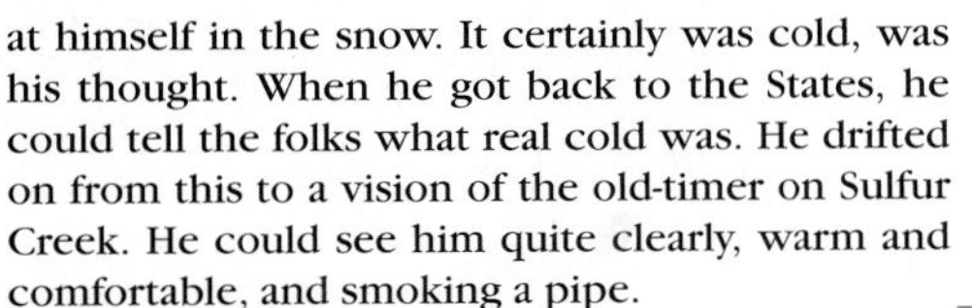

at himself in the snow. It certainly was cold, was his thought. When he got back to the States, he could tell the folks what real cold was. He drifted on from this to a vision of the old-timer on Sulfur Creek. He could see him quite clearly, warm and comfortable, and smoking a pipe.

"You were right, old hoss; you were right," the man mumbled to the old-timer of Sulfur Creek. D

Then the man drowsed off into what seemed to him the most comfortable and satisfying sleep he had ever known. The dog sat facing him and waiting. The brief day drew to a close in a long, slow twilight. There were no signs of a fire to be made, and, besides, never in the dog's experience had it E known a man to sit like that in the snow and make no fire. As the twilight drew on, its eager yearning for the fire mastered it, and with a great lifting and shifting of forefeet, it whined softly, then flattened its ears down in anticipation of being chidden[10] by the man. But the man remained silent. Later, the dog whined loudly. And still later it crept close to the man and caught the scent of death. This made the animal bristle and back away. A little longer it delayed, howling under the stars that leaped and danced and shone brightly in the cold sky. Then it turned and trotted up the trail in the direction of the camp it knew, where were the other food providers and fire providers.

10. **chidden:** scolded; past participle of *chide.*

D. Literary Element: Irony
The man's admission that the old-timer was right comes too late to save his life. What message do you think London is conveying? [Possible answers: The indifference of the natural world to humans; the unfitness of humans in the race for survival on the planet; the lack of any force of good in the world; an attack on romanticism.]

E. Critical Reading: Making Inferences
? What does the dog rely on to make a decision? [It relies on the expectation that the man will provide fire, the custom of how men behave, the instinctual desire for the fire's warmth, and the smell of death.]

A. Critical Reading: Analyzing Purpose

? What effect is the article intended to have upon the reader? [Possible answer: The matter-of-fact reporting of the process is probably designed to inform or frighten.]

B. Reader's Response: Extending the Text

? Will the information here inspire any changes in your behavior? [Sample responses: Yes, I will dress carefully and be careful in cold weather; or no, I never go out in extreme cold anyway.]

Connections A MAGAZINE ARTICLE

Cold Kills: Hypothermia

A Here's what happens when you develop frostbite. After sitting out in the cold for a few hours, you develop hypothermia. The blood vessels in your skin and extremities clamp down in order to minimize further heat loss. Standing on ice or cold ground draws the warmth out of your feet, and the skin and subcutaneous tissues of your toes freeze. Chilled arterioles beneath the frozen tissue constrict, and blood flow through the capillaries slows as the blood becomes thick and syrupy. Clots form and block the capillary bed, thus depriving the tissues of oxygen and nutrients. Blood running into the limb is then diverted away from the capillary beds by shunts that cyclically open and close, allowing waves of warm blood to surge into the hands and feet at intervals. When your core temperature drops further, these shunts remain open, and the tissues begin to freeze. The feet, hands, ears, and nose are most vulnerable to frostbite because they are more likely to be exposed to the cold, they are distant from the warm core, and their large surface-to-volume ratio causes them to cool rapidly.

Frostnip is the mildest form of cold injury. It causes stinging pain, then numbness and a small white patch on the cheeks, nose, or ears. Immediate rewarming is the treatment.

B Frostnip that is ignored progresses to superficial frostbite involving the skin and the subcutaneous tissues. The skin remains bloodless, pale and cold to the touch, but the tissue beneath the surface remains soft and pliable. A day or so after the injury, large blisters develop. After a few more days, the blisters heal and a hard, dry eschar forms. This is a thick, black scar that separates from the underlying tissue in a few weeks and is replaced by new skin.

Deep frostbite is freezing of the superficial as well as deep structures, including nerve, muscle, tendon, and even bone. The affected part is hard as wood, purple or red in color, cool to the touch, and has no feeling. In contrast to superficial frostbite, in which the injured part is sensitive, warm, and pink after rewarming, the part remains cold and blue after thawing. Small blood blisters may form after one to three weeks, and the part may remain swollen for months. Eventually, it mummifies and falls off.

—Paul G. Gill, Jr., M.D., *from* "Winning the Cold War," *Outdoor Life*, February 1993

CONNECTING WITH "TO BUILD A FIRE"

Ask students to work in pairs to explain how this article relates to the story. Each pair should share its results with the class. [The article expands upon the information in the story by giving scientific facts about the effects of extreme cold on the human body.]

MAKING MEANINGS

First Thoughts

1. How did you feel about the way the story ended? Did you predict this kind of ending? Explain.

> **Reviewing the Text**
>
> Outline the **plot** of the story. Start by identifying the man's mission. Explain what causes the man to build two different fires, and what happens to each fire. Describe what happens to the man and to the dog by the end of the story.

Shaping Interpretations

2. Several times in the story, the man recalls the old-timer from Sulfur Creek. What key advice did the old-timer give him? Why do you think the man did not follow his advice?
3. Early in the story, London writes, "The animal was depressed by the tremendous cold. It knew that it was no time for traveling" (page 498). This passage alerts you to possible trouble ahead. Locate four other passages that **foreshadow** later events. Explain the link between each passage and the later event.
4. London does not merely tell you that it is extremely cold. He gives details that make you *feel* the cold. For example, he notes the "sharp, explosive crackle" when the man spits into the frigid air. Review the notes you made in your Reader's Log, and list five other details from the story that make the cold real to you.
5. In the story, a man who thinks is contrasted with a dog who reacts by instinct. How do the man and the dog differ in the ways they approach the great cold? What point do you think London is making?
6. Re-read the definition of **naturalism** that precedes this selection (page 496). How does this story reflect key naturalist beliefs? How do you feel about this philosophy's view of human beings?

Connecting with the Text

7. The central character is not particularly likable. He's described as "without imagination," he ignores the advice of his elders, and he has no love for dogs. Would you have enjoyed the story more—or less—if the man were portrayed in a more sympathetic light? (For instance, suppose that he were a more humble man who loved animals.) Give specific reasons to support your opinion.

Challenging the Text

8. London wrote another, more commercially acceptable ending for an earlier version of "To Build a Fire." In the first version, the man survives, returns to camp, and learns an important lesson: Never travel alone. Do you think this ending improves the story or weakens it? Explain your opinion.

Making Meanings

First Thoughts

1. Some students will not like the ending; others will say it was predictable due to the tone and setting. Be sure students give examples from the text to support their answers.

Reviewing the Text

Possible response: A man sets out toward an old claim with a dog, ignoring advice to travel with a partner in weather colder than fifty below. He builds a fire so he can thaw out when he eats lunch. He must build another fire after he falls into a spring and wets his legs and feet. A load of snow from a spruce tree falls on the second fire and puts it out. Try as he might, he is unable to build another fire because his hands are too frozen to move.

As he realizes that he will freeze to death, he decides to sleep rather than fight anymore. The dog finally senses that the man is dead and heads off toward the camp.

Shaping Interpretations

2. The old-timer advised him not to travel alone in extremely cold weather. The man is stubborn and thoughtless.
3. The third, fourth, fifth, and sixth paragraphs particularly foreshadow fatal results due to the man's inexperience, his underestimation of the cold, his relative helplessness on his own, and his dangerous carelessness.
4. (1) "muzzle of ice" (2) "the instant he stopped his cheekbones went numb" (3) "The creek . . . was frozen clear to the bottom" (4) "his moist breath quickly powdered with white his mustache, eyebrows, and lashes." (5) "the moccasin strings were like rods of steel"
5. The dog is sensitive to nature's signs and reacts emotionally to the danger by becoming depressed, while the man ignores the warnings and smiles at the "supposed" danger. The dog tries to follow its instinct, while the man fails to apply his rationality or imagination to the situation. London's point is that animal instinct is superior to human intellect.
6. The story shows a man subject to natural forces beyond his control. Students may agree that humans are subject to nature in some ways, but humans can also overcome nature—through force, technology, or ingenuity—in other ways.

Connecting with the Text

7. Students may say that they would have felt more sympathy if the man had been more likable.

Challenging the Text

8. **(Evaluation)** Responses will vary. Make sure students support their opinions with examples from the text and from their own experience. Students may say that the ending of the first version weakens the drama and danger of the story, and that it would not have as powerful a message because the man did not have to pay a price for his foolishness.

Choices: Building Your Portfolio

1. **Writer's Notebook** Remind students to save their work. They may use it as prewriting for the Writer's Workshop on p. 515.
2. **Critical Writing** Students may identify both the external conflict between the man and the cold and the internal conflict between the man and his body. Have students work with partners to brainstorm about the conflicts.
3. **Creative Writing/Role-Playing** Before students write, encourage them to decide how much stage direction (if any) they will give to their role-players. Will they simply write the words to be spoken? Will they include adverbs telling how the words will be spoken? Will they add any other commentary? Which approach will make the work most interesting?
5. **Performance** Help students check sources for sound effects recordings. If none are available, have students create their own sound effects, or bring in examples of sound effects from soundtracks or other recorded material.
6. **Creative Writing** Remind students that writing the ending first and then writing the plot points that lead up to the ending is one way to set up a suspenseful ending without giving it away.

Choices: Building Your Portfolio

Writer's Notebook

1. Collecting Ideas for an Informative Report

WORK IN PROGRESS

When you write an informative report, you will want to adjust your writing to suit your audience. For practice, think of a topic this story made you want to learn more about (for example, Jack London's life, the effects of cold on humans, the geography of the Yukon, or the naturalist literary movement). Imagine three different audiences for your report (for example, third-graders, a wilderness-exploration group, or a group of parents in your neighborhood). Make some notes about how you would tailor your approach and tone for each audience. Save your notes for possible use in the Writer's Workshop on page 515.

Critical Writing

2. Opposing Forces

"To Build a Fire" contains both **internal** and **external conflict.** Identify what you consider the most important conflict of the story. In a brief essay, identify the opposing forces in this conflict. Use passages from the text to support your choice of this conflict as central to the story. Which force in the story wins?

Creative Writing / Role-Playing

3. Setting Out

Imagine that it's just before the story "To Build a Fire" begins. The man in the story is saying goodbye to his partners as he prepares to start out alone on the Yukon trail. Create a **dialogue** that occurs between the man and two of his partners. Then, with two classmates, role-play the dialogue for the class.

Crossing the Curriculum: Science

4. Survival Manual

You've been hired by a wilderness adventure company to create a "survival manual" for a group of people who will be traveling by foot in Yukon Territory during the winter, when the ground is covered by several feet of snow. Based on what you have learned from London's story, as well as information you've gained from reading about hypothermia in Connections (page 508), work with a partner to make a list of the equipment and supplies these trekkers must assemble before they start out. After each item, write a sentence or two explaining its importance. To accompany the list of supplies, create a list of safety precautions and "what to do if's" (what to do if you get frostbite, etc.). Illustrate your survival manual, if you wish.

Performance

5. Special Sound FX

Consider how different sounds—or lack of all sound at some points—could enhance the drama if this story were performed on audiocassette. With three or four other students, plan a recording of the story. First, break the story into small scenes. For each scene, list the **sound effects** you would use to heighten the tension. Be sure to include short, specific sounds, such as the matches that fall "sizzling into the snow." Also, select background music for various parts of the story. (Consider all kinds of music, from classical to rock to rap.) Finally, practice reading the story aloud, and record your reading together with sound effects and music. Play your recording for the class.

Creative Writing

6. Against All Odds

Write a survival story of your own, in which a character's life is threatened by a hostile environment: a weather condition, an isolated place, a terrain that poses difficulties. Like "To Build a Fire," your story should be built on realistic details that create suspense and a "you are there" feeling. Build to a strong climax, and try to keep from giving away your ending.

PORTFOLIO ASSESSMENT

Choices: Assessment Criteria For help in evaluating these Choices assignments, see the criteria in the ***Portfolio Management System,*** pp. 126–127.

STRATEGIES FOR INCLUSION

English Language Development The specialized vocabulary needed for activity #4 may cause difficulties for some students. Provide them with a list of equipment, and have them work in pairs to select nine items from the list and one item not on the list. Before they write the assignment for homework, have them explain their choices to another pair of students.

Advanced For activity #4, ask students to research the harsh conditions of the Arctic. Encourage students to bring information to class about techniques that people use to ensure survival under harsh winter conditions.

Follow the Drinking Gourd

Henry Brown nailed himself into a box and had it shipped to Philadelphia. Harriet Tubman risked her own life many times to lead fugitives north and out of slavery. They are just two of the many daring "passengers" and "conductors" whose firsthand accounts describe the flight from slavery to freedom in *The Underground Railroad* (Prentice Hall), edited by Charles L. Blockson.

Where the Buffalo Roamed

What was the westward expansion like from the American Indian point of view? Dee Brown's *Bury My Heart at Wounded Knee* (Holt, Rinehart and Winston) is a powerful, well-documented American Indian history of the West.

The Great American Novel

Ernest Hemingway wrote, "All modern American literature comes from one book by Mark Twain called *Huckleberry Finn*." Widely regarded as Twain's masterpiece, *Adventures of Huckleberry Finn* is a wise and funny novel about a young boy coming of age on the Mississippi River. Several film adaptations are also available on video, and the novel has been adapted as a Tony award-winning Broadway musical, *Big River.*

The War Between the States

Though Stephen Crane never fought in the Civil War, he carefully researched it for *The Red Badge of Courage,* his famous novel about a young Union soldier. On video are both *The Red Badge of Courage* and Stephen Crane's *Three Miraculous Soldiers,* based on Crane's ironic story of a young girl's encounters with both Union and Confederate soldiers. For a nonfiction account of the war, consider *The Civil War: An Illustrated History* (Alfred A. Knopf), by Geoffrey C. Ward, et al., the companion volume to the popular PBS TV series, which is also available on video.

The Frozen North

If "To Build a Fire" piqued your interest in cold and desolate places, try *Arctic Dreams* (Scribner's), Barry Lopez's exciting account of a real-life journey through northern climes. For more outdoor adventure from Jack London, try *The Call of the Wild* and *White Fang*—two "dog stories" of undisputed literary merit, both of which are available as film adaptations.

Read On

Portfolio Assessment Options

The following projects can help you evaluate and assess your students' reading accomplishments outside of class. Videotapes or audiotapes of completed projects may be included in students' portfolios.

- **Create a Folder Game** Have students work in groups of three to create a folder game that relates to the plot of the book they have read as well as to the characters in the book. (All three students need to have read the same book.) When other students in the class play the game, they should have a clear understanding of what the book is about. Group members must decide on directions for the game, invent rules, include game pieces, and design the game folder.
- **Design a Movie Poster** Have students design a poster to promote the movie of the book they have just read. The poster should include the main characters in the book as well as the title and author's name. Students could even cast famous actors and actresses in the parts if they choose. Tell students to be sure that the poster depicts a scene from the book and is persuasive enough to cause others to want to see the movie.
- **Write a Children's Book** Have students tell a story about the book they have read in the form of a children's book. Have them include pictures on each page, an attractive cover, and a new title appropriate for children. Be sure to tell students to use simple vocabulary and language that young children will understand.

FOR FURTHER EXPLORATION

Fiction

All Quiet on the Western Front by Erich Maria Remarque
Invisible Man by Ralph Ellison
The Assistant by Bernard Malamud
My Ántonia by Willa Cather
Billy Budd, Sailor by Herman Melville

Short Stories

"The Open Boat" by Stephen Crane
"In Another Country" by Ernest Hemingway
"Flight" by John Steinbeck
"The Lucid Eye in Silver Town" by John Updike

Poetry

"Douglass" by Paul Lawrence Dunbar
"Life's Tragedy" by Paul Lawrence Dunbar
"Slavery, a Poem" by Hanna More
Songs of Innocence by William Blake
Songs of Experience by William Blake

Films and Videos

Dances with Wolves
Little Big Man
Indian Summer
The Civil War

A. Cultural Connections
Cooper felt that the main reason for so little variation between the various dialects was due to the large number of immigrants arriving in America from Europe.

B. Reader's Response: First Thoughts
? Who do you think was right—Cooper or Twain? [Sample responses: I agree with Cooper because the immigrants at that time were from Europe. I agree with Twain because Twain was a realist and he wrote what he heard.]

C. Reader's Response: First Thoughts
? Do you think that regional distinctions could detract from the nation being unified? [Sample responses: It would because the immigrants would want to retain their heritages and cultures. No, because the people came to America knowing that this was a new country and that everyone would have to work together in order to become a respected nation.]

D. Reader's Response: Extending the Text
? If you had to describe the inhabitants of a region of America today, would dialect be a part of your description, as it was Twain's? [Sample responses: I would include the dialect because it tells so much about the people—where they are from, their generation, what type of work they have been involved in (blue-collar work or white-collar work)—and also because there are probably more dialects in America today because of continued immigration.]

The American Language

American Dialects

by Gary Q. Arpin

(A) James Fenimore Cooper, writing for a British audience in 1828, boasted about the absence of American dialects: "In America, while there are provincial or state peculiarities in tone, and even in the pronunciation and use of certain words, there is no patois [dialect]. An American may distinguish between the Georgian and the New England man, but you cannot." Americans, Cooper claimed, were too active and mobile for dialects to establish themselves—a point with which many other observers agreed.

Yet, a little over fifty years later, another American writer claimed to be using no less than seven dialects from a fairly small region in a single novel, *Adventures of Huckleberry Finn.* "In this book," Mark Twain wrote in an explanatory note, "a number of dialects are used, to wit: the Missouri Negro dialect; the extremest form of the backwoods South-Western dialect; the ordinary 'Pike-County' dialect; and four modified varieties of this last."

Unity or Variety?

Quite a bit had changed in America in that fifty years, but not enough to create a wholesale explosion of dialects where none had existed before. Even if Twain was exaggerating about his "four modified varieties" of the "'Pike-County' dialect," *Huckleberry Finn* depends for part of its effect on its use of (B) dialect. Who was right about American dialects—Cooper or Twain?

Cooper was looking at an America that he was contrasting with England—a young, unified, mobile, democratic country, in which differences, if there were any, were kept within the family. Moreover, Cooper saw the country evolving toward even greater unity.

Twain, on the other hand, was looking very closely at a particular region of America and at distinctions of ethnicity, education, upbringing, and geography, all of which had small but significant effects on speech. He was also looking at a country whose recent Civil War had underscored the disunity of its people.

The views of Cooper and Twain toward American dialects represent two ways of looking at America and American speech. The Cooper view saw America as a unified nation marked principally by its distinctness from England. Twain saw the nation in terms of regional distinctions.

The Cooper view was shared by people like Noah Webster. Webster's dream was to stamp out local dialects and further unify the country (see page 195). He stated his attitude in this comparison between American and British language: "We are less infected with various dialects, the remains of the different conquerors of the English nation, than the inhabitants of (C) England." A dialect in Webster's view was a weakness, an infection to be cured by education and spelling reform.

(D) But Twain and other regional writers saw the local speech as one of the best ways of describing the inhabitants of a region. Dialect stories and poems, in fact, were very popular in the late nineteenth and early

"There wuz Maw and me, surrounded by screamin' Frenchmen, our Michelin-book lost and our faithful Cook's tour-guide nowhar in sight! . . ."

Fisher/Punch/Rothco.

OPTIONS FOR TEACHING

STRATEGIES FOR INCLUSION

Learners Having Difficulty Some students see little need to adapt their language styles to fit a particular situation. Ask for three volunteers to role-play in front of the class. Prepare a script for a person who is conducting a job interview and a script for the first person who is being interviewed. Prepare the second script for the person who sees no need to adapt his or her language style. After this interview, do not make any comments. Have the second person come to be interviewed. Prepare this script for a person who does adapt his or her language style for the situation. When both interviews have been completed, discuss reasons why the second person interviewed would get the job over the first person interviewed and the importance of being able to adapt language styles.

Advanced Have students conduct a survey of dialects on television. Students could look at a TV program guide to analyze which programs use predominantly standard English and which programs feature speakers with regional or ethnic dialects. Ask students to categorize the shows and to draw conclusions about the kinds of programs in which dialect is found and the areas where it is unacceptable.

twentieth centuries. They were usually comic, and much of their humor derived from funny pronunciations and peculiar local words. At the same time, these stories and poems in regional dialect illustrated the wisdom of the common person.

A New Englander called Hosea Biglow was a famous "common-sense" character created by James Russell Lowell in his First Series of *The Biglow Papers,* a collection of dialect poems. In the following excerpt, Hosea's New England speech patterns are shown, as he addresses recruiting officers for the Mexican War—a conflict which Hosea, in his common sense, strongly disapproves of.

> Ez fer war, I call it murder—
> There you hev it plain an' flat;
> I don't want to go no furder
> Than my Testyment fer that;
> God hez sed so plump an' fairly,
> It's ez long ez it is broad,
> An' you've gut to git up airly
> Ef you want to take in God.

What Is a Dialect?

In his novel about the Great Depression of the 1930s, *The Grapes of Wrath,* John Steinbeck records a conversation between migrant workers from different parts of the country. Here, the Joads, from Oklahoma, meet Ivy Wilson, from Kansas:

> "We're Joads," said Pa. "We come from right near Sallisaw."
>
> "Well, we're proud to meet you folks," said Ivy Wilson. "Sairy, these is Joads."
>
> "I knowed you wasn't Oklahomy folks. You talk queer kinda—that ain't no blame, you understan'."
>
> "Ever'body says words different," said Ivy. "Arkansas folks says 'em different, and Oklahomy folks says 'em different. And we seen a lady from Massachusetts, an' she said 'em differentest of all. Couldn't hardly make out what she was sayin'."

What makes these Americans so different in speech is, of course, what linguists call dialect. A **dialect** can be defined as the characteristic language habits of a particular speech community. A speech community can be looked at in a very broad sense (as "American" versus "British"), or it can be subdivided almost endlessly. In fact, since no two people speak in exactly the same way, we might even say that each person speaks in his or her own dialect. (Linguists even have a term—*idiolect*—for the speech peculiar to one individual at one specific period of his or her life.) Though there are differences in the way the Joads, the Wilsons, and the puzzling lady from Massachusetts speak, they all are still clearly "American."

E

> Since no two people speak in exactly the same way, we might even say that each person speaks in his or her own dialect.

Dialects are distinguished from standard English and from each other in three principal ways:

F

1. In pronunciation: Pa Joad says "Oklahomy" and drops the final "d" in *understand.* ("Kinda" for *kind of* is a form of rapid speech, not dialect.)
2. In vocabulary: Pa Joad uses an expression typical of his region when he says they come from "right near" Sallisaw.
3. In grammar: Pa says "knowed" instead of *knew,* "you wasn't" instead of *you weren't,* and "that ain't no blame."

The grammar of a language is its most profound element—like the skeleton of an animal. Grammar is likely to be changed only superficially in a dialect. There can be an English dialect in which a person can say "Them was good peaches," but not one in which a person can say "Peaches good was them." When fundamental grammar rules are violated, the language becomes incoherent. Differences in vocabulary between dialects are more common, and most common are differences in pronunciation.

The main factors contributing to the formation of American dialects have been (1) settlement patterns—who settled in a region, where they came from, and how long they stayed there; (2) distance from a major cultural center; (3) influence of new immigrants; and (4) migration patterns.

G

English speakers settled first in the East, and the greatest profusion of dialects still exists

E. Reader's Response: Extending the Text

? What is characteristic of the dialect in your community? [Sample responses will include specific words and pronunciations, expressions, phrases, or a particular accent that is common in the community.]

F. Critical Reading: Finding Details

? In what three ways are dialects distinguished from standard English? [Grammar, vocabulary, pronunciation]

G. Critical Reading: Expressing an Opinion

? Do you think immigrants wanted to retain their dialects? [Possible answers: No, because they came to America to start over. Yes, because many people from one country settled in the same area and maintained their dialect for as long as possible. Examples of this are areas in New York City, such as Chinatown and Little Italy.]

INTEGRATING THE LANGUAGE ARTS

Strategic Reading When students are reading to learn new information, it is necessary for them to read at a slower rate in order to comprehend the material. It is also necessary for students to ask questions about the material. The PQ3R reading strategy enables students to be prepared to read (P), to ask questions (Q), and to read, recite, and review (3R). In order to be prepared to read, students must look over the reading and read any subtitles, words in bold print, or captions under pictures or graphs. Students are accessing their background knowledge about the subject when they are preparing to read. When students question, they can turn the subtitles into questions or write down questions that they might have. Questioning gives students a reason to read. The students then read and recite. To recite, students recall everything that they can remember about the reading. After finishing all of the reading, students review all of the important information.

A. Reader's Response: First Thoughts

? How do you think that class is evident from a dialect? [Sample responses: The upper classes had more education so they used standard vocabulary and grammar.]

Try It Out: Answers

1. Answers will vary. Students will respond according to the way they speak, depending on what region they are from.
2. African American, New York City, 1980s.
   In pronunciation: The narrator says "axin," "talkin," and "bout."
   In vocabulary: The narrator uses an expression typical of her region when she says "run a hand over."
   In grammar: The narrator says "you all" instead of *all of you,* and "run a hand" instead of *ran a hand.*
   Kentucky, 1970s.
   In pronunciation: Edda says "law."
   In vocabulary: Clausie says "while" for *awhile,* and she says "neither" for *either.*
   In grammar: Clausie says "y'all" instead of *all of you* and "them Russians" instead of *the Russians.*

Assessment See **The American Language, *Test Booklet*,** p. 117-118.

there. As settlers moved westward, they mixed dialects in the new communities in the West, and their original dialects became less and less evident.

Three Major Dialect Regions

Scholars have divided eastern American speech into three basic types of English: Northern, Midland, and Southern. Within these three general classifications, there are large and small areas with their own linguistic peculiarities. Western states, in general, have blended these dialects, since their English-speaking settlers originally came from all three areas.

As a rule, regional differences in vocabulary and pronunciation are the easiest to pinpoint. If you take a *pail of swill* out to feed the hogs, you're probably a Northern farmer. If you take out a *bucket of slops,* you're probably from the South. If you pronounce *greasy* to rhyme with *we see,* you're probably from the North. If you pronounce it to rhyme with *easy,* you're probably from the Midland or South. Speakers in the Midland usually sound the *r* in words like *barn* and *horse,* while older speakers in the Northern and Southern regions tend to eliminate it. Bostonians, as we know, "pahk the cah." Southerners say something like "pawk the caw." Bostonians sometimes add an *r* to the end of a word, as President John F. Kennedy did when he spoke of "Cuber" rather than "Cuba." Midlanders usually make no distinction between the pronunciations of *horse* and *hoarse* and *mourning* and *morning.* Older Northerners and Southerners usually say something like "hawss" and "hohse," respectively, and "mawnin' " and "mohnin'." Southerners pronounce the *u* sound in words like *duty* and *news* as "you": "dyuty" and "nyews." Most Northern and Midland speakers say "dooty" and "nooz."

(A) In literature, the accurate portrayal of regional speech is an excellent way of creating both an individual character and a member of a class. The South, with its rich oral culture, is the region where dialect has been most effectively used in literature, in the works of such writers as William Faulkner (page 713), Flannery O'Connor (page 672), and Bobbie Ann Mason. All of these writers—and more—have made it clear that speech patterns are an essential aspect of both our character and our environment.

Try It Out

1. The objects or activities named by the words in each group below are all the same, but people in different regions of the country give them different names. Which word do you use? Do all of your classmates agree?
   a. *couch, sofa, davenport,* or *divan?*
   b. *faucet, spigot,* or *tap?*
   c. *spider, skillet,* or *frying pan?*
   d. *stand in line* or *stand on line?*

   Draw up a list of five words that you think are used only in your region. Then swap lists with two other students. Do you all agree that the words are regional dialect?
2. For each of the following passages, list examples of dialect in (1) vocabulary, (2) pronunciation, and (3) grammar.

African American, New York City, 1980s

"I'm axin you all a simple question. You keep talkin bout what's proper for a woman my age. How old am I anyhow?" And Joe Lee slams his eyes shut and squinches up his face to figure. And Task run a hand over his ear and stare into his glass like the ice cubes goin calculate for him. And Elo just starin at the top of my head like she goin rip the wig off any minute now.

—Toni Cade Bambara, *from* "My Man Bovanne"

Kentucky, 1970s

"Law, I wouldn't want to be cremated the way some of them are doing now," says Edda. "To save space."

"Me neither," says Clausie with a whoop. "Did y'all see one of them Russians on television while back? At his funeral there was this horse and buggy pulling the body, and instead of a casket there was this little-bitty vase propped up there. It was real odd looking."

—Bobbie Ann Mason, *from* "The Rookers"

PROFESSIONAL NOTES

Technology Tip The American Dialect Society maintains a Web page at **http://www.msstate.edu/Archives/ADS**. *You may want to preview any Internet activities that you suggest to students. Because these resources are sometimes public forums, their content can be unpredictable.*

ASSESSMENT TOOLS

Check Test: Questions and Answers

1. Twain saw America in terms of regional distinctions. [True]
2. A *dialect* is the characteristic language habits of a particular speech community. [True]
3. An *idiolect* is the speech of one individual for his or her life. [False]
4. No two people speak in exactly the same way. [True]
5. There are four basic types of English in eastern American speech. [False]

EXPOSITORY WRITING

INFORMATIVE REPORT

Informative writing is the kind of writing you'll do most often during your school career and, in most cases, during your working life. A vast amount of the writing you encounter every day—the textbook you hold in your hands, the liner notes for a CD recording, or the articles in your local newspaper—serves to inform you of something. Your goal as the writer of an informative report—also known as a report of information or a research paper—is to collect, organize, synthesize, and present facts in order to expand your readers' knowledge of a topic.

Prewriting

1. **Find a topic.** Whether the choice of a topic is up to you, or whether you're required to focus on a narrow topic within a general subject area, begin by brainstorming a list of topics you are interested in. Write a brief list of potential subjects. If you kept any of your Writer's Notebook jottings from Collections 9 and 10, you may already have some potential subjects and notes on those subjects. Highlight a couple of the strongest possibilities, and decide which one most appeals to you and might be most interesting to readers. Any of these historical topics could in turn suggest contemporary topics that interest you: an aspect of current African American music, groups who stage reenactments of Civil War battles, or contemporary war-story writers, such as Tim O'Brien.

2. **Narrow your topic, and freewrite about it.** In most cases, the first topic you come up with will be too broad to effectively handle in a research report. Your next step, then, will be to narrow the focus of the broad topic you're considering—to go from "the Civil War," for example, to the more specific topic "women's roles during the Civil War."

   Once you have narrowed your topic, freewrite on what you already know about it, and generate questions that you will want to find answers to.

3. **Be sure you have a topic that can be researched.** The questions you decide to explore should be ones for which answers exist in research sources that you can obtain. For any topic you choose, you should be able to find five or six good sources that are readily available to you through the library or other research resources.

Technology HELP

See Writer's Workshop 2 CD-ROM. *Assignment: Informative Report.*

ASSIGNMENT
Write a research report on a factual topic readers would be interested in learning more about.

AIM
To inform.

AUDIENCE
Your teacher and classmates, or other people interested in your topic.

Try It Out
With a partner or small group, review the introduction to "The Rise of Realism: The Civil War and Postwar Period" (pages 408–422). Then, brainstorm a list of possible subjects mentioned in the introduction that you think would make interesting topics to write about.

QUICK PLANNING GUIDE

Informative Report

Motivation

Bring to class several examples of informative writing. Examples can include newspaper articles, inserts from utilities bills, liner notes from a CD or cassette, a yearly report from a financial institution, or an article about how a movie was made. Ask students to discuss the similarities they find in the examples.

Try It Out: Possible Answers

Walt Whitman's Views of Civil War
Bret Harte and Early American Regionalism
The Role of *Uncle Tom's Cabin* in Causing the Civil War

PROGRAM MANAGER

- **Computer Guided Instruction** For a related assignment that students may use as additional instruction, see ***Writer's Workshop 2.***
- **Reinforcement** See **Transparencies** 10.6–10.7 in the ***Audiovisual Resources Binder.***

PORTFOLIO ASSESSMENT

- **Generating Ideas** To help students in prewriting, see the ***Portfolio Management System,*** p. 128.
- **Portfolio Assessment** For a rubric that can be used to assess students' progress in writing, see the ***Portfolio Management System,*** p. 130.

Teaching the Lesson

- Write the word *inform* on the chalkboard. Have students brainstorm about the word. Write all their responses on the chalkboard, and discuss ways in which people might be informed. Ask one or two students to summarize the discussion.
- Be sure students understand that the purpose of writing a report of information is to expand the reader's knowledge of a topic.

This lesson includes instruction for each stage of the writing process. Guide students by modeling each stage with your own writing.

Prewriting

When writing a report of information, there are many steps to complete before the actual writing of a first draft. Students may use the form below to remain organized and on schedule:

Topic: **Areas to Focus on:** **1.** **2.** **3.**
Rough Thesis Statement:
Research (checklist): ___ Encyclopedias ___ Almanacs and yearbooks ___ Atlas ___ Biographical references ___ Vertical file ___ Indexes ___ Card catalog ___ *Readers' Guide to Periodical Literature* ___ Other: (Record all source information and any facts and ideas relevant to your report.)
Organize Your Material (checklist): ___ Take notes ___ Brainstorm ___ Use a diagram or chart ___ Make an outline ___ Other:

Strategies for Elaboration

Decide which of your sources are most useful by applying the four *Rs*:

1. How **relevant** to your topic is the information in the source?
2. How **reliable** are facts found in the source?
3. How **recent** is the source?
4. How **representative** is the source concerning the different sides of the issues it reports?

Guidelines for Researching

- Start with a list of major topics or questions you need to look up.
- Write down definitions of key terms your research turns up. Depending on your audience's level of knowledge, you may need to define some or all of these terms in your report.
- When making a note of a quotation, be sure to copy the exact words to ensure the accuracy of your writing. Also, keep a precise record of the source so that you can look it up again.

4. **Anticipate audience needs.** Before you start to write, it's important to think about the audience you'll be writing for. To anticipate your audience's needs, ask yourself the following questions:
   - What will my readers probably already know about the topic?
   - What will they need to know in order to understand the topic?
   - What will they be curious about? What will they be most interested in?
5. **Research your topic.** Though general reference books are often the first step in researching an informative paper, specialized reference books, such as biographical dictionaries and subject encyclopedias, are even more valuable once you begin digging into your topic. Check the card or on-line catalog of a library, the *Readers' Guide to Periodical Literature,* the indexes to major newspapers, and the library's vertical file. Also, look elsewhere for sources of information: Depending on your subject, you might contact government offices, museums, historical societies, newspapers, and even living experts.

   Throughout your research, you should be aware of striking a balance between primary and secondary sources. A **primary source** is original, firsthand information, such as a letter, a journal entry, an autobiography, or a historical document. A **secondary source** is information about, or derived from, primary sources: critical writings, reviews, encyclopedia entries, biographies, and so on. If primary sources are available, make use of them; secondary sources are usually plentiful, but try not to use them exclusively. Be sure to evaluate all sources carefully for accuracy and balance. Take notes from both primary and secondary sources on index cards, or use some other method that you have found helpful.
6. **Examine your approach.** The nature of your subject, your sources, and your attitudes go into shaping your approach, or angle. Some informative reports are concerned with presenting the newest findings about a subject. Others explore the development of the subject over time or its importance in a larger context. A report may show the causes and effects of a phenomenon, or compare and contrast it to a related phenomenon.
7. **State a controlling idea.** Re-read your notes, and summarize the **controlling idea,** or **thesis,** of your research report in a brief statement. In informative writing, the controlling idea is an objective statement of the main concern of the report; it defines the boundaries of the subject. Here are some examples of controlling ideas.
   - Harriet Beecher Stowe, though initially not an abolitionist herself, furthered the abolitionist cause and helped pave the way to the Civil War through her book *Uncle Tom's Cabin.*
   - The gambler with a heart of gold, the gentle farmer driven to a gunfight to defend his family, the tough-but-tender dance-hall girl—all of these familiar, stereotypical western characters owe their existence to one writer, Bret Harte.
8. **Organize.** Present your information in a logical sequence. You can create a framework for organizing an informative report using one of the following methods:
   - chronological order (usually, from earliest to latest)

OPTIONS FOR TEACHING

STRATEGIES FOR INCLUSION

Visual Students may be unfamiliar with some of the resources that are available for their research. Arrange with the school librarian a time when you can take your class to have the librarian point out the encyclopedias, atlases, *Readers' Guide to Periodical Literature,* card catalog, vertical file, and other resources. Students might make a map showing where the resources are found in the library.

Learners Having Difficulty Students who have not written an informative report before may feel overwhelmed. Meet with these students individually to set up a plan whereby you can check the progress of their research. You can check each numbered step in the writing process. When the work is broken down into smaller parts, students may feel more confident about accomplishing an assignment.

Advanced Allow students who have access to a computer to use the Internet as a research tool. Ask students to report their success or lack of success in obtaining useful information and to offer any suggestions to other students about using the Internet. You might also point out to students that a public library or area university library may have its card catalog linked to the Internet.

- order of importance (from most to least important, or least to most important)
- block comparison and contrast (Examine a series of aspects of one subject, then the same aspects, in the same order, for a second subject.)
- point-by-point comparison and contrast (Examine one aspect for the first subject, and then the same aspect for the second subject, and so on.)

9. **Outline.** List the major aspects of your topic as main headings, in an order that reflects your approach to the subject. Your preliminary outline may change during the course of drafting and revising. For now, you might make separate piles of index cards—or computer files—to represent your major headings. Within each pile or file, cluster information into subheadings. Look for holes in your outline—headings that haven't been fully explored, relevant questions that haven't been answered. Do additional research to fill in the holes.

Drafting

1. **Begin forcefully.** The introductory paragraph of an informative report has two purposes: to define the subject and to get the reader interested. Try to accomplish both purposes in one stroke by defining your subject in a memorable, engaging way. You might begin with a surprising fact or statistic that has a bearing on your thesis; a quotation from an expert on your subject; or a question that balances different views of the subject. Describing a scene or narrating an anecdote can also be effective ways to open your report.
2. **Develop your points.** Follow your outline, checking off each item as you cover it to make sure you don't omit any essential information. As you draft, though, you may find yourself reworking your outline to match your increased understanding of what is truly important about the subject, what can be left out, and where each subtopic naturally falls into place.
3. **Define terms.** Define the terms your intended audience probably hasn't encountered before; leave undefined the terms they probably already understand. If you were writing an article on Civil War weaponry for a general audience, you would probably define *Gatling gun* and *Arkansas toothpick.* In an article for Civil War buffs, though, you could give specialized information about those weapons without first having to explain what they are.
4. **Support your points.** Back up generalizations with specific examples and, if space permits, anecdotes. Flesh out the subject with details. Try to use concrete words rather than abstract ones to ease the reader's understanding of new concepts. Use facts and figures to demonstrate the validity of your statements, and provide necessary background information.
5. **Use quotations as seasoning.** The exact words of expert sources can add interest and authority to an informative report, but you should avoid overusing direct quotations. In general, use quotations when they are memorable or when the wording of the statement makes a difference. Otherwise, summarize or paraphrase—but be sure to use your own

Language Handbook HELP

Using quotation marks: page 1246.

Drafting

Work with the class to transfer prewriting material to their reports. Remind students that their report should begin with an introduction that attracts the reader's attention immediately. They may use an unusual fact or interesting short anecdote. This introduction should also include the purpose or controlling idea of the report in a thesis statement.

COOPERATIVE LEARNING

Interview To offer students insights into the art of interviewing, have them each locate a magazine interview with a well-known person. Ask students to summarize the interview and then to work with a partner to explore how quotations from the interview can be incorporated into a report. Ask each student to write two examples of useful quotations. Volunteers can share their work with the class.

INTEGRATING THE LANGUAGE ARTS

Strategic Reading Students may be reading this Writer's Workshop in spurts—reading a little, working on their own writing, and then returning to the feature. As they read, have them track their progress by using a Metacognitive Journal. In one column of the journals, students should note how key points from the feature apply to their own writing; in the other column, they should jot down notes about how they are growing as writers.

Speaking and Listening Before students begin work on their reports, pair students together to work as update partners. At least twice a week, set aside time for the partners to meet and to give each other an update, or progress report, on their research. This will enable students to ask each other questions, to offer suggestions, and to share information and ideas.

Evaluating and Revising

- Encourage students to do both a peer review and a self-evaluation of their drafts. Invite them to comment about the insights gained from each method of review.
- Discuss the Evaluation Criteria on page 519. Encourage students to turn each criterion into a question and to apply the questions to their drafts.

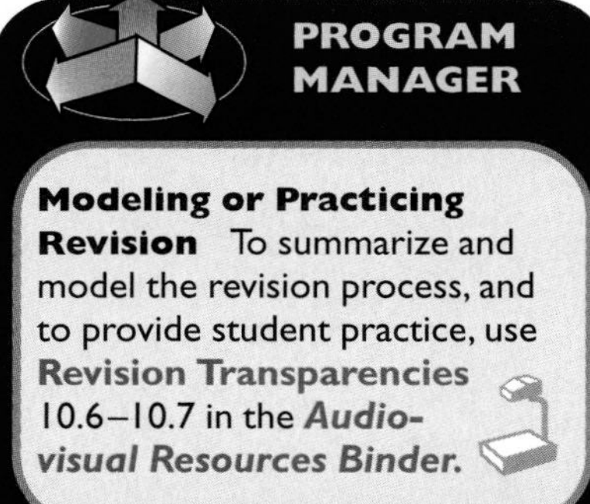

PROGRAM MANAGER

Modeling or Practicing Revision To summarize and model the revision process, and to provide student practice, use **Revision Transparencies** 10.6–10.7 in the ***Audio-visual Resources Binder.***

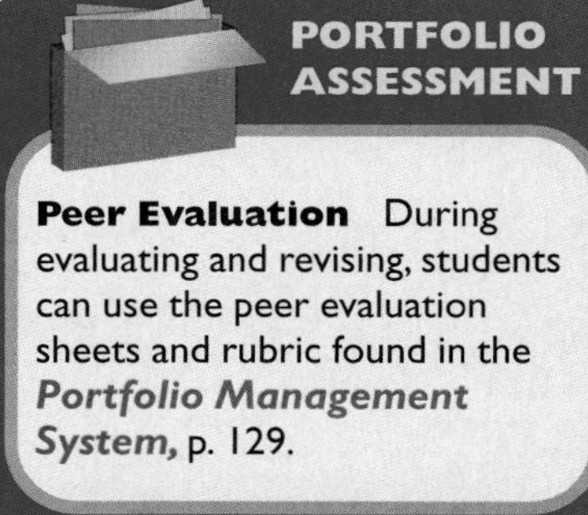

PORTFOLIO ASSESSMENT

Peer Evaluation During evaluating and revising, students can use the peer evaluation sheets and rubric found in the ***Portfolio Management System,*** p. 129.

Proofreading

Remind students that proofreading is an opportunity to polish their work by correcting any errors in spelling, capitalization, punctuation and usage.

Publishing

- Encourage students to choose one of the publishing formats described on page 519. If students express an interest in other formats, have them clear their ideas with you before publishing their work.
- If possible, arrange for a publishing option that draws in readers from other classes, from students' families, and from the community.

Documenting Sources: Parenthetical Citations and Works Cited

One crucial aspect of writing an informative report is deciding which information you must document. Use these guidelines to help determine whether you need to document a piece of information.

- In general, don't document information that appears in several reference works. For example, the main facts of Frederick Douglass's life, such as birth and death dates, need no documentation because they are readily available in standard references.
- Document unusual, little known facts, or facts and statistics your readers might question.
- Document the source of each direct quotation and paraphrase.
- Document theories or opinions that are not your own.
- Document any data from surveys, experiments, or research studies.

When you do document, you'll credit sources in two places—in parenthetical citations and in the Works Cited list at the end of your essay.

Parenthetical citations occur within the body of your essay. They are references that appear in parentheses after quoted or paraphrased material from a particular source. In many cases, all that you'll need in a parenthetical citation is the author's last name and a page number. For example, here's what a parenthetical citation might look like in a report on slave narratives:

> According to one critic, Equiano's story became "the prototype for the nineteenth-century slave narrative" (Gates xiv).

Your parenthetical citation tells the reader that you have picked up your quotation from a critical work by Gates that they will find documented in full in your Works Cited list at the end of your paper. (Note that the citation is placed before the final punctuation mark of the sentence, phrase, or clause you're documenting.)

Here's how your Works Cited entry for the same source will look:

> Gates, Henry Louis, Jr., ed. The Classic Slave Narratives. New York: New American Library, 1987.

The list of Works Cited contains all the works cited in your essay, with full bibliographic information that will enable readers to locate the sources you used. For more complete information on documenting sources in a research report, be sure to consult the latest edition of the *MLA Handbook for Writers of Research Papers.*

Communications Handbook HELP

Taking notes and documenting sources: pages 1210–1213.

wording and sentence structure, and to credit your source. Otherwise, you'll be guilty of plagiarism, the theft of another writer's original words or ideas.

6. **Establish an authoritative stance.** Your tone and point of view should consistently make your audience feel that you know what you are writing about. Depending on your intended audience, your report may be

CROSSING THE CURRICULUM

Mathematics Point out to students that it helps the reader to have a visual interpretation of statistics in such a form as a chart or graph. Have students create visual interpretations of their statistics to include with their reports. Students could draw their graphs, or they could use graphics on a computer to create visual interpretations.

CLASSROOM MANAGEMENT

Small-Group Brainstorming It is important for all students to feel as though they can express themselves in class. When students are brainstorming in small groups, review the following behavior tips with them:

1. All ideas are accepted.
2. Encourage everyone to participate.
3. Criticism is not part of brainstorming.
4. Work toward many intelligent responses.

either formal or somewhat informal in its level of language. Most informative reports written as class assignments are relatively formal; they are serious and objective in tone and use the third-person point of view.

7. **Wrap it up neatly.** The ending of an informative report usually repeats the main point, or points, in a different way. It might also put the subject in a larger context or suggest topics for further exploration.

Evaluating and Revising

1. **Peer review.** Exchange papers with a partner, and ask questions such as the following:
   - How and where could the report be made more interesting?
   - Were the transitions from point to point smooth?
   - What additional information would make this a stronger report?
   - What, if anything, in the report is irrelevant to the subject and audience?
   - What did you learn, and what else would you like to have learned from this report?
2. **Self-evaluation.** Read your report as if you were an outsider trying to learn about the subject. In evaluating your peers' comments, pay special attention to ones that indicate places in the report where more factual support is needed or where the organization of points seems jumbled. Revise with your audience in mind, improving readability as well as content and organization.

Proofreading

Correct all mechanical errors, being especially careful to see that all facts and statistics are accurately transcribed, all names correctly spelled, and all quotations properly punctuated and in the exact words of the original source.

Publishing

If your report was written for a class assignment, handing it in and showing it to classmates will be its primary form of publication. Other forms of publication might grow out of your subject matter: Look for a special-interest magazine or a local publication interested in what you are writing about.

Reflecting on Your Writing

Date the report. Then, write a brief reflection on this writing experience, considering questions such as these:

1. What did I learn about my subject matter?
2. How effectively did I utilize research sources?
3. How could I have better tailored my report to my specific audience?
4. Do I find informative writing easier, or harder, than more personal types of writing? Why?
5. How do I expect to be able to use informative writing skills in the future?

Revision STRATEGIES

Clear transitions smoothly guide your reader from subtopic to subtopic, from idea to idea. If you are dealing with the development of a subject over time, transitions such as first, then, next, last, *and* finally *will be important. When linking examples, appropriate transitions include* also *and* and. *For discussions of cause and effect, transitions such as* therefore, thus, so, *and* because *come into play. So do transitions that show exceptions, such as* but, however, though, although, yet, rather, instead, *and* nevertheless.

Evaluation Criteria

A good informative report

1. *sets forth its subject clearly*
2. *has an identifiable controlling idea, or thesis, which directs the writer's approach*
3. *tailors the tone and level of language to the intended audience*
4. *presents facts objectively, avoiding expressions of personal opinion*
5. *supports its points adequately, using a variety of strategies*
6. *is organized in a way that supports the writer's purpose and is suitable to the subject*
7. *conveys an attitude, or stance, that is authoritative and consistent*

Reteaching

When researching, students often take notes that have nothing to do with their specific topic. Before students do any research, have them write down questions to be answered by the research. In this way, they will have a direction for their research before they begin.

Closure

Ask students to explain what is important about report writing. Have them list different types of report writing that they discovered when doing their research.

Extension

Ask students each to exchange reports with a partner and to write a summary of the partner's report. The summary should only be one paragraph long.

Enrichment

Social Studies Connection

Have students research reports that were written during the Civil War and post–Civil War period. Ask them to bring the results of their research to class. Discuss the differences between reports written then and reports written recently.

Portfolio

Reflecting on Your Writing

Tell students to keep a written record of their reflections on their writing in order to be able to review them before future writing activities. They may use the notes to determine which procedures enable them to write best.

ASSESSMENT TOOLS

Self-Reflection Encourage students to assess their writing as they work through the writing process. Have them use the following criteria for self-assessment.

4=Always 3=Often 2=Sometimes 1=Never

1. ____ sets forth its subject clearly
2. ____ has an identifiable thesis that directs the writer's approach
3. ____ uses a tone and level of language appropriate to the intended audience
4. ____ presents facts objectively, avoiding expressions of personal opinion
5. ____ supports its points
6. ____ is well organized
7. ____ conveys a consistent, authoritative stance

Language Workshop

Connecting to Students' Writing

As a proofreading exercise, have students each choose a piece of writing from their portfolios. Ask them to read through their papers, noting sentences that could be joined by using either an adverb clause or an adjective clause. Have students revise their papers by using adverb and adjective clauses. Then, have them each work with a partner to proofread each other's paper for correct usage of these clauses.

Try It Out: Possible Answers

1. Mark Twain's humor became caustic when he was in his old age. (adverb clause)
2. The hero of "To Build a Fire" fears dying from hypothermia because he is lost and alone in the snow. (adverb clause)
3. Kate Chopin's fiction, which shows women struggling against obstacles to their freedom, has been rediscovered in recent years. (adjective clause)
4. Although code songs often contained directions for enslaved people escaping to freedom, they were often sung in the presence of slaveholders. (adverb clause)
5. Ambrose Bierce was nicknamed "Bitter Bierce" because he was disillusioned by the greed and deceit of humanity. (adverb clause)

Language Workshop

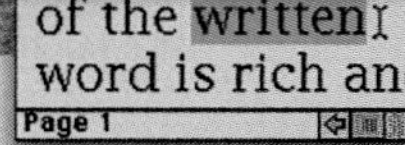

Technology HELP

See Language Workshop CD-ROM. *Key word entry: adverb clauses* or *adjective clauses.*

Language Handbook HELP

The subordinate clause: pages 1231–1232.

Appropriate Additions: Adverb and Adjective Clauses

You can give your writing flavor, variety, and a smooth flow by using adjective and adverb clauses in your sentences. An **adjective clause** is a clause that modifies a noun or pronoun. Adjective clauses begin with the pronouns *who, whom, whose, which,* or *that.* An **adverb clause** is a clause that modifies a verb, an adjective, or another adverb. Adverb clauses begin with subordinating conjunctions such as *after, although, because, before, if, since, unless, until, when,* and *while.*

Use adverb and adjective clauses to combine two simple sentences into a single complex sentence.

EXAMPLE Sojourner Truth wrote passionately for the abolition of slavery. Her first name means "visitor."

Joined by adjective clause:

Sojourner Truth, **whose first name means "visitor,"** wrote passionately for the abolition of slavery.

(**Note:** If an adjective clause is not essential to the meaning of a sentence, it is a **nonrestrictive clause** and needs to be set off from the rest of the sentence with a comma or commas, as in the example above. If the clause is essential to the meaning of the sentence, it is a **restrictive clause,** and no commas are necessary.)

EXAMPLE Frederick Douglass fought with a slaveholder. Douglass was still enslaved then.

Joined by adverb clause:

While Frederick Douglass was still enslaved, he fought with a slaveholder.

(**Note:** When you place an adverb clause at the beginning of a sentence, separate it from the independent clause with a comma, as in the example above.)

Try It Out

Combine each pair of sentences by using either an adjective clause or an adverb clause. State which kind of clause you have used.

1. Mark Twain's humor became caustic. It happened in his old age.
2. The hero of "To Build a Fire" is lost and alone in the snow. He fears dying from hypothermia.
3. Kate Chopin's fiction has been rediscovered in recent years. Her fiction shows women struggling against obstacles to their freedom.
4. Code songs often contained directions for enslaved people escaping to freedom. These songs were often sung in the presence of slaveholders.
5. Ambrose Bierce was nicknamed "Bitter Bierce." He was disillusioned by the greed and deceit of humanity.

Writer's Workshop Follow-Up: Revising

Look again at the informative report you wrote for the Writer's Workshop on page 515. Where can you improve your style by using adverb and adjective clauses to combine two simple sentences into a single complex sentence?

QUICK CHECK: Adverb and Adjective Clauses

In each sentence, underline the clause. Then, identify the clause as either *adjective* or *adverb*.

[1] Because he had researched the Civil War, Crane was able to write *The Red Badge of Courage.* [Adverb clause]
[2] Everyone listened while our teacher read *Moby-Dick* by Herman Melville. [Adverb clause]
[3] Some of us have read *Leaves of Grass,* which was written by Walt Whitman. [Adjective clause]
[4] I have read nearly every book that Kate Chopin has written. [Adjective clause]
[5] The writer was an American whom everyone admired. [Adjective clause]

CREATIVE PROBLEM SOLVING

LEARNING FOR LIFE

Monitoring the Media

Problem

Painters and sketch artists had recorded earlier wars visually, but the supposedly objective eye of the camera lens made the Civil War and its aftermath more immediate and horribly real to people than earlier conflicts had been. How do the different news media today (television, newspapers, magazines) affect the messages we receive and the assumptions we make about events of consequence taking place in our world?

Project

Compare and contrast television and print media coverage of an important current event in order to evaluate the power of the media to shape perceptions.

Preparation

1. As a group, choose a current event to monitor: a war or other political situation, a disaster, or an ongoing social problem, such as gang violence or the war against drugs. The event should be one that has been in the news for a while and that will probably have a high profile for a time.
2. Further divide the group into two halves, one to monitor television coverage of the event and one to monitor print coverage (newspapers, magazines).

Procedure

1. Monitor your medium for coverage of the current event. Keep notes about such aspects as
   - how frequently the event or situation is reported
   - how prominently the event is featured in the coverage
   - the types of coverage that are most common (reports, interviews, news analyses, newsmagazine segments, lengthy articles, editorials, polls, and so on)
2. You may want to address these questions:
   - Does the coverage seem to take sides, or is it neutral?
   - How does the medium use photographs or film footage?
   - How does *seeing* something on the news differ from *reading* about it?
3. Make notes about how your perceptions of the current event are shaped by the medium's coverage. What are the particular strengths and weaknesses of the medium you have monitored? Are there differences in coverage even among TV networks or among the same types of newspapers and magazines?

Presentation

Present your findings about media coverage in one of the following formats (or another that your teacher approves):

1. **Panel Discussion**
   As a group, conduct a panel discussion on differences in media coverage. Address issues you have focused on during your monitoring. Also, evaluate each medium's strengths and shortcomings, and recommend how coverage could be improved.
2. **The Medium Is the Message**
   Create a *Consumer Reports*–style bulletin rating the media you monitored. Summarize characteristics that set each particular news medium apart from others—strengths and weaknesses in reporting, tendencies toward bias, the influence of personalities on news coverage, and so on.
3. **Interview with a Newscaster or Journalist**
   Arrange an in-class interview with a local television news reporter, a writer or editor for a local newspaper or magazine, or a freelance journalist. Prepare beforehand a list of questions on the subject of media coverage. Ask the interviewee to share his or her perceptions of news coverage.

Processing

What did you learn about the power of media to shape perceptions? How can you be more aware of possible media bias? Write a reflection for your portfolio.

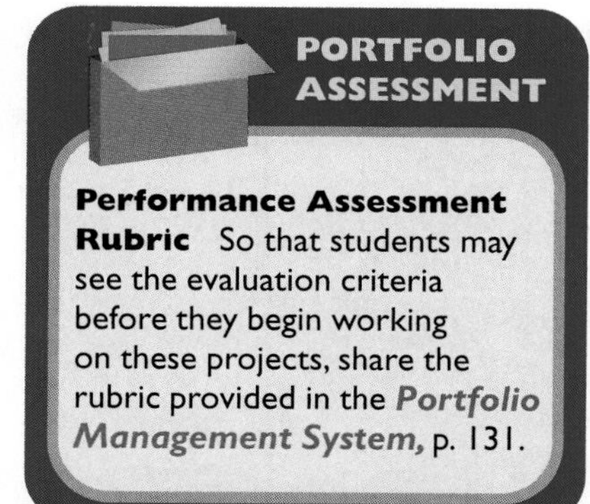

Performance Assessment Rubric So that students may see the evaluation criteria before they begin working on these projects, share the rubric provided in the ***Portfolio Management System,*** p. 131.

Technology Tip

If possible, organize the panel discussion so that students can use the school's electronic resources. Using the school resource center, tape students' panel discussion on media coverage in two or three segments. Offer the taped discussion for viewing by other classrooms. If classrooms are networked with television monitors and a central video recorder, several classrooms may view the discussion simultaneously. To involve the student audience, invite interested students throughout the school to write editorials about the discussion topic and to list questions for the panelists. Ask panelists to read and answer audience questions and to respond to the editorials during their discussion sessions. Students may also expand their discussion on the differences in media by comparing the written comments on the topic to audience involvement with the videotaped presentation.

DEVELOPING WORKPLACE COMPETENCIES

Preparation	Procedure	Presentation
Acquires data Organizes and maintains files for data Applies technology to specific tasks Exhibits sociability	Evaluates data Interprets information Processes information Makes decisions Uses self-management skills Reasons Thinks creatively	Demonstrates individual responsibility Works on teams Uses resources well Teaches others Communicates ideas and information

RESPONDING TO THE ART: ABOUT THE ARTIST

John Sloan (1871–1951) is known for painting highly realistic scenes inspired by everyday events. He helped form The Eight, a group of New York artists dedicated to realistic representation of contemporary life. Critics eventually called them the Ashcan School. The group was involved in organizing the 1913 Armory Show, which introduced controversial modern art to the United States.

The Moderns

1900–1950

Men travel faster now, but I do not know if they go to better things.

—Willa Cather, Death Comes for the Archbishop

Sixth Avenue Elevated at Third Street (1928) by John Sloan. Oil on canvas (30″ × 40″).

Responding to the Quotation

? How does this quotation characterize modern life? [Possible responses: While society appears to be advancing in modern times, it may, in fact, be falling behind. Technology enables people to do more and do it more quickly. However, it is what people do with the technology that determines whether a society advances and improves the welfare of all of its members. Or if people in modern times do not have worthy goals, their lives may not amount to much.]

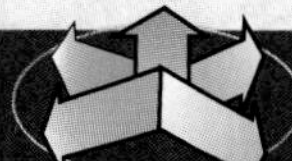

PROGRAM MANAGER

- **Summative Assessment** See Literary Period Test: The Moderns, *Test Booklet,* pp. 195–198, for a test on an additional text from the same historical era.
- **Application** For practice of a reading strategy for this unit, see Becoming a Strategic Reader worksheet, *Teaching Resources B,* pp. 11–12.

Responding to the Quotation

? What does Sherwood Anderson mean when he says he had a world, but it slipped away from him? [Possible responses: He lost friends and loved ones in the war and they had made up an important part of his world; or the war caused him to re-evaluate his values and assumptions about how he should live his life.]

A. Expansion

While the statistics are imprecise, the sheer number of people involved in World War I is sufficient to warrant the name the Great War. Some sixty-five million military people were mobilized by all of the warring nations, and estimates of the number of soldiers and sailors killed range from eight to ten million, including approximately 115,000 Americans. In addition, between six and seven million civilians lost their lives, and roughly twenty-one million people were wounded. These numbers are staggering, but they do not tell the full story because many of the people killed in the war were men and women of genius who would have served as the leaders of the future.

In addition to the carnage of the war itself, a massive pandemic of influenza broke out in 1918. Again, statistics are imprecise, but estimates range from twenty million to fifty million deaths from the flu. The estimate for American deaths is 548,000. This epidemic has been compared to the Black Death. Coupled with the losses of World War I, the loss of life during the influenza epidemic utterly devastated much of the world.

B. Responding to the Quotation

? Why is fear something to be feared? [Possible responses: Fear brings out the worst in people and makes them unable to make good judgments or think clearly; or if someone fears that something bad will happen, conditions might be ripe for that bad thing to happen.]

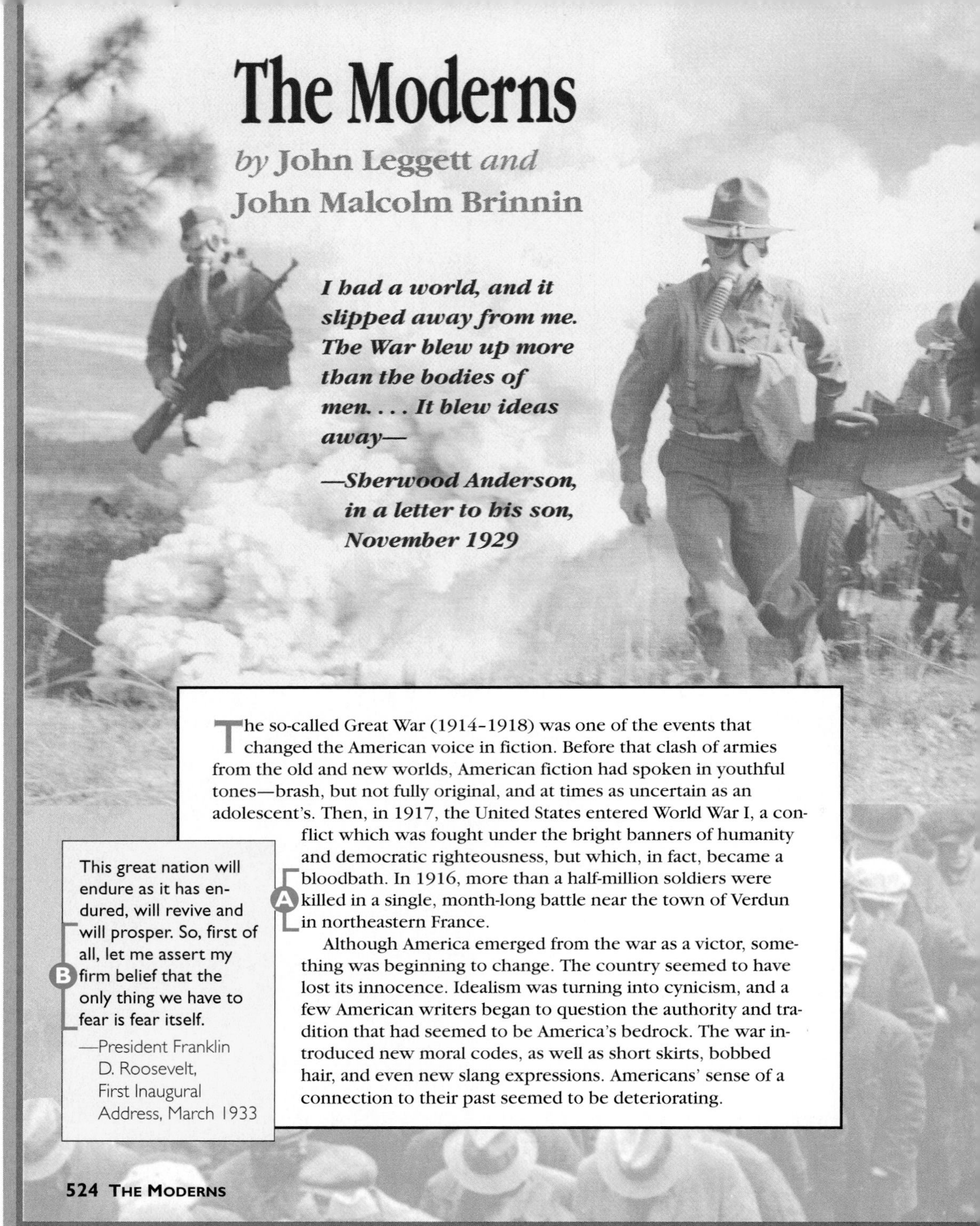

The Moderns

by John Leggett *and* John Malcolm Brinnin

I had a world, and it slipped away from me. The War blew up more than the bodies of men. . . . It blew ideas away—

—Sherwood Anderson, in a letter to his son, November 1929

The so-called Great War (1914–1918) was one of the events that changed the American voice in fiction. Before that clash of armies from the old and new worlds, American fiction had spoken in youthful tones—brash, but not fully original, and at times as uncertain as an adolescent's. Then, in 1917, the United States entered World War I, a conflict which was fought under the bright banners of humanity and democratic righteousness, but which, in fact, became a bloodbath. In 1916, more than a half-million soldiers were killed in a single, month-long battle near the town of Verdun in northeastern France. (A)

Although America emerged from the war as a victor, something was beginning to change. The country seemed to have lost its innocence. Idealism was turning into cynicism, and a few American writers began to question the authority and tradition that had seemed to be America's bedrock. The war introduced new moral codes, as well as short skirts, bobbed hair, and even new slang expressions. Americans' sense of a connection to their past seemed to be deteriorating.

This great nation will endure as it has endured, will revive and will prosper. So, first of all, let me assert my firm belief that the only thing we have to fear is fear itself. (B)

—President Franklin D. Roosevelt, First Inaugural Address, March 1933

Elements of Literature:
Videodisc Use the bar codes below to access information on the time period. For more information, see the Videodisc *Teacher's Manual.*

Videodisc Side B

Begin Play
English Track

Begin Play
Spanish Track

There were other reasons for this change in outlook. The Great Depression that followed the crash of the New York stock market in 1929 brought suffering to millions of Americans—to those same hard-working people who had put their faith in the boundless capacity of America to provide them with jobs and their children with brighter futures.

American writers, like their European counterparts, were also being profoundly affected by the **modernist** movement. This movement in literature, painting, music, and the other arts—swept along by disillusionment with traditions that seemed to have become spiritually empty—called for bold experimentation and a wholesale rejection of traditional themes and styles.

World War I was a turning point in American life, marking a loss of innocence and a strong disillusionment with tradition. American writers were profoundly affected by the ideas of modernism, which called for a break with traditional themes and styles.

The American Dream: Pursuit of a Promise

If we try to identify our uniquely American beliefs, we find three central ideas that we have come to call the **American dream.**

First, there is admiration for America as a new Eden: a land of beauty, bounty, and unlimited promise. Both the promise and the disappointment of this idea are reflected in one of the greatest American novels, *The Great Gatsby* (1925), by F. Scott Fitzgerald (page 584). This work appeared at a time when great wealth and the pursuit of pleasure had become ends in themselves for many people. The title character, Gatsby, is a self-made man whose wealth has mysterious and clearly illegal origins. Moving into a pretentious mansion near New York City, Gatsby tries to woo both society and the woman he loves with a series of lavish parties. His extravagant gestures are in pursuit of a dream. Unfortunately, Gatsby's capacity for dreaming is far greater than any opportunity offered by the Roaring Twenties, and he meets a grotesquely violent end. But Gatsby's greatness is bound up with his tragedy: He believes in an America that has virtually disappeared under the degradations of modern life.

It is left to Nick Carraway, the narrator, to reflect at the end of the novel on the original promise of the American dream that underlies all the vulgarities of modern life:

> . . . gradually I became aware of the old island here that flowered once for Dutch sailors' eyes—a fresh, green breast of the new world. Its vanished trees, the trees that had made way for Gatsby's house, had once pandered in whispers to the last and greatest of all human dreams; for a transitory enchanted moment man must have held his breath in the presence of this continent, compelled into an aesthetic contemplation he neither understood nor desired, face to face for the last time in history with something commensurate to his capacity for wonder.
>
> —F. Scott Fitzgerald, *from The Great Gatsby*

***The Victorious Allies* (c. 1918) by Newell Convers Wyeth. Oil on canvas. Cover, *The Red Cross Magazine*, March 1919.**

Delaware Art Museum, Gift of the Bank of Delaware, 1989.

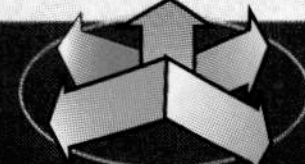

PROGRAM MANAGER

- **Planning Instruction** See **Teaching Notes, *Teaching Resources B*,** pp. 1–2, for additional teaching options about the Moderns.
- **Assessment** For assessment of the literary and historical events mentioned in the historical introduction, see **Literary Period Introduction Test, *Test Booklet*,** pp. 127–128.

Time Line

• 1900–1909

W.E.B. Du Bois was an important leader of the civil rights movement in the first half of the twentieth century. While the popular Booker T. Washington proposed that African Americans earn respect through sacrifice and self-restraint, Du Bois advocated that African Americans protest discrimination. Du Bois was the first African American to receive a Ph.D. from Harvard. He taught at Atlanta University and helped found the National Association for the Advancement of Colored People. His ideas are expressed in *The Souls of Black Folk.*

• 1920–1929

In *Main Street,* Sinclair Lewis satirized the narrow-mindedness of residents of small towns in the United States. The novel caused a sensation after it was published in 1920. In the novel, Carol Kennicott is unable to alert her town to its shortcomings. In *Babbitt* (1922), George Babbitt does become aware of the confines of his middle-class life, but he is unable to break free. Lewis won both the Pulitzer Prize in 1926, which he declined, and the Nobel Prize in literature in 1930.

The Moderns 1900–1950

LITERARY EVENTS

England's Joseph Conrad publishes the psychological novel *Heart of Darkness,* 1902

Frank Norris publishes *The Octopus,* a naturalistic novel about California wheat farmers fighting the railroad, 1901

William Carlos Williams's first collection of poems published, 1909

W.E.B. Du Bois publishes an influential collection of essays, *The Souls of Black Folk,* 1903

Jack London publishes *The Call of the Wild,* 1903

Carl Sandburg publishes *Chicago Poems,* 1916

Edgar Lee Masters publishes *Spoon River Anthology,* 1915

Willa Cather publishes *O Pioneers!,* 1913

Robert Frost publishes first poetry collection, 1913

Edna St. Vincent Millay wins Pulitzer Prize in poetry, 1923

T. S. Eliot publishes *The Waste Land,* 1922

Irish writer James Joyce publishes *Ulysses,* 1922

Sinclair Lewis publishes *Main Street,* a novel about small-town Minnesota, 1920

1900–1909 | **1910–1919** | **1920–1929**

CULTURAL/HISTORICAL EVENTS

Queen Victoria of England dies, 1901

South African (or Boer) War ends in costly British victory, 1902

Einstein formulates his theory of relativity, 1905

Earthquake and fire ravage San Francisco, 1906

Freud lectures on psychoanalysis in U.S., 1909

British ocean liner *Titanic* sinks after striking an iceberg off Newfoundland, 1912

Armory Show in New York City introduces modern art to U.S., 1913

Panama Canal opens, 1914

World War I begins in Europe, 1914

U.S. enters World War I, 1917

Russian Revolution ends czarist regime, 1917

Harlem Renaissance begins, 1920

19th Amendment to Constitution grants U.S. women the right to vote, 1920

Charles A. Lindbergh completes first transatlantic solo flight by airplane, 1927

Albert Einstein. The Granger Collection, New York.

Charles Lindbergh and the *Spirit of St. Louis.*

USING THE TIME LINE

Pair students, and assign each pair two events from the lower half of the time line. Ask students to create a banner head and to compose a newspaper headline for each event. Ask them to compose a lead story on the front page under the headline using as much information as they know about the event. Have students research their events to create more detailed lead stories. When they finish revising, circulate students' newspaper stories around the class to allow all students to read the "hot news" of the period.

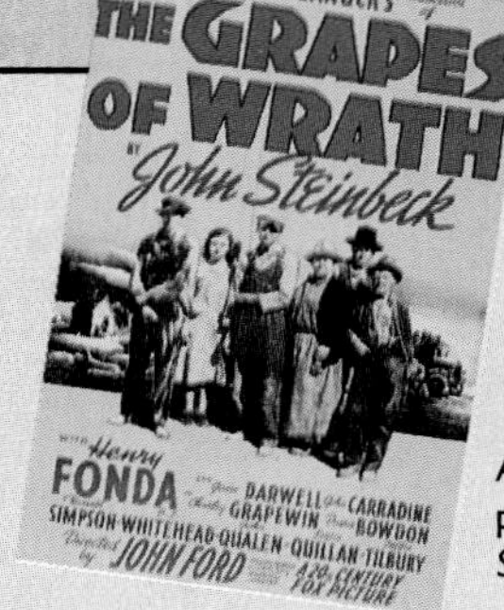

Ernest Hemingway publishes noted World War I novel, *A Farewell to Arms,* 1929

•

Langston Hughes publishes his first poetry collection, *The Weary Blues,* 1926

•

The novels *An American Tragedy,* by Theodore Dreiser, and *The Great Gatsby,* by **F. Scott Fitzgerald,** are published, 1925

John Steinbeck publishes *The Grapes of Wrath* and wins the Pulitzer Prize, 1939

•

Thornton Wilder's *Our Town* opens and wins Pulitzer Prize, 1938

•

Zora Neale Hurston publishes *Their Eyes Were Watching God,* 1937

•

Eugene O'Neill's dramatic trilogy *Mourning Becomes Electra* opens, 1931

Tennessee Williams's play *The Glass Menagerie* opens, 1945

•

Richard Wright publishes *Native Son,* 1940

Arthur Miller's play *Death of a Salesman* opens, 1949

•

William Faulkner publishes *Intruder in the Dust,* 1948

•

William Carlos Williams publishes first part of his long poem *Paterson,* 1946

1920–1929 | **1930–1939** | **1940–1950**

1920–1929

The Jazz Singer, one of the first sound films with dialogue, opens, 1927

•

U.S. stock market crashes, leading to Great Depression, 1929

1930–1939

Mohandas Gandhi leads protest against British salt tax in India, 1930

•

Franklin D. Roosevelt becomes U.S. president; New Deal program to counter Great Depression begins, 1933

•

Nazi leader Adolf Hitler comes to power in Germany, 1933

•

Nationalist forces of Francisco Franco win Spanish civil war, 1939

•

Germany invades Poland; World War II begins in Europe, 1939

1940–1950

U.S. enters World War II after Japan attacks Pearl Harbor in Hawaii, 1941

•

Oklahoma!, a groundbreaking musical play by Rodgers and Hammerstein, opens, 1943

•

Allies begin final drive against German forces on D-day, June 6, 1944

•

Germany surrenders, 1945

•

U.S. explodes atom bombs over Hiroshima and Nagasaki, Japan; Japan surrenders, 1945

United Nations established, 1945

•

India gains independence from British rule, 1947

•

State of Israel established, 1948

•

Communist forces under Mao Zedong win control of mainland China, 1949

•

Korean War begins, 1950

•

U.S. population is about 151 million, 1950

Franklin D. Roosevelt.

Pearl Harbor.

United Nations Building, New York City.

• 1930–1939

The worldwide depression of the 1930s created the context that partly explains Hitler's rise to power in Germany. With unemployment at high levels, Hitler gained political support by opposing the Young Plan of 1929, which required Germany to pay for damages it had inflicted in World War I. Using the emotional appeals of hate rhetoric to create an easy but completely false scapegoat, Hitler argued that Communists and Jews had caused Germany's defeat in the war and that the Young Plan was the further attempt of Communists and Jews to undo the life of "true" Germans. Hitler's Nazi party became Germany's leading political party after the 1932 elections and, with his promise to act lawfully, Hitler was named chancellor in 1933. Soon after, he moved to dictatorship, establishing laws that discriminated against Jews, eliminated individual rights, and allowed the Nazis to jail anyone without a trial. Hitler controlled German radio and newspapers, labor, and agriculture and industry. In full violation of the Versailles Treaty, Hitler rearmed the German military and, in 1938, he began his invasion of neighboring countries. Hitler stated that conquest was a right and a duty.

• 1940–1950

On May 14, 1948, the state of Israel was established as a homeland for Jews from all parts of the world. On the following day, May 15, 1948, Israel was attacked by troops from neighboring Arab nations—mainly Syria, Jordan, Egypt, Iraq, and Lebanon—who opposed the UN plan to divide Palestine into a Jewish state and an Arab state. Founded on a site sacred to Muslims and Christians as well as Jews, Israel remained embattled for four decades.

A. Expansion
In 1935, the WPA created Federal Project No. 1 and allocated about $300 million for it. This agency gave work to people in the fields of writing, theater, music, and the visual arts. The Federal Writers' Project, a beneficiary of these funds, hired some 6,600 writers for such projects as collecting oral histories of former slaves, producing state travel guides, and gathering folk tales. This project helped writers such as John Steinbeck (p. 606) and Richard Wright (p. 1012). The Federal Theatre Project, another recipient of this funding, enabled small towns to see live productions. The Federal Music Project presented some four thousand musical productions a month around the country. The Federal Arts Project hired artists to produce posters for New Deal programs, teach art in public schools, and paint murals on buildings constructed by the Public Works Administration.

B. Expansion
One aspect of the optimism inherent in the American dream is the belief that, through hard work and delayed gratification, ordinary people can improve their standards of living and achieve a degree of economic success. This idea is embodied in the novels of Horatio Alger, Jr. (1832–1899), who sold twenty million books about virtuous boys who were born into poverty and who became rich through hard work and sacrifice. World War I and the Great Depression both undermined these beliefs in the minds of many people.

C. Literary Connections
Ask students to re-read the selection from Emerson's "Self-Reliance" on pp. 224–225 and to discuss Emerson's definition of the American dream.

A CLOSER LOOK

The Best of Times, the Worst of Times

The era of the 1930s in the United States was marked by triumph and tragedy, growth and hardship. Between 1890 and 1940, the U.S. population more than doubled, rising from 63 million to 132 million. African Americans made up about 10 percent of the population, and other ethnic groups about 0.5 percent. Families were slightly larger than they are today, but people died younger—on average, around age sixty.

By 1933, the United States was in the depths of the Great Depression. Anywhere from one fourth to one third of American workers were unemployed. People waited in bread lines, foraged for food in garbage dumps, and slept in sewer pipes. Homeless families lived in tents and shacks in camps called Hoovervilles, named for President Herbert Hoover. In 1933, the new president, Franklin Delano Roosevelt (FDR), ignited a spark of hope with his promise to help the "forgotten man." True to his word, FDR launched a blizzard of agencies, such as the (A) Works Progress Administration and the Civilian Conservation Corps, that put millions of Americans back to work.

Despite hard times, human and technological marvels were a hallmark of the

FPG International

(B) The second element in the American dream is optimism, justified by the ever-expanding opportunity and abundance that many people have come to expect. Most of the time, Americans have believed in progress—that life keeps getting better and that we are moving toward an era of prosperity, justice, and joy that always seems just around the corner.

Finally, the third important element in the American dream has been the importance and ultimate triumph of the individual—the independent, self-reliant person. This ideal of the self-reliant individual was championed by Ralph Waldo Emerson (page 216), who probably deserves most of the credit for defining the essence of the (C) American dream, including its roots in the promise of the "new Eden" and its faith that "things are getting better all the time." Trust the universe and trust yourself, Emerson wrote. "If the single man plant himself indomitable on his instincts, and there abide, the huge world will come round to him."

OPTIONS FOR TEACHING

STRATEGIES FOR INCLUSION

Auditory Some students might find it beneficial to read the period introduction aloud in small groups. Divide students into groups of four for this activity, and, if possible, provide each reading group with an audiocassette recorder. Students can take turns reading aloud, or a single reader who has had a chance to practice reading the material orally can read for the group. Later, when students want to review the material, they can listen to the audiotape they made during the initial reading.

Visual Let students work with a transparency placed over the period introduction, and have them highlight information to help call it to their attention. They can use one color for main ideas and a second color for supporting details. After students have read and highlighted the first two sections of the material, allow them to compare their work with the work of others. Ask them to discuss any discrepancies that might exist in the highlighting and to make changes to their work as needed. If highlighting is not practical, students might create an outline of the material and compare outlines.

era. Amelia Earhart became the first woman to fly solo across the Atlantic (1932). Three famous structures were built during this decade: the Empire State Building in New York City (1931), Boulder (now Hoover) Dam on the Arizona-Nevada border (1936), and the Golden Gate Bridge in San Francisco (1937).

Happily, during a decade of severe shortages, there was no shortage of entertainment. Mystery fans devoured whodunits featuring Dashiell Hammett's hard-boiled investigator, Sam Spade, while both young and old listened to the Dorseys' jazz orchestra and danced to the swing music of Count Basie.

By the late 1930s, the Depression had eased, and people could again afford one of the most popular entertainments: movies. The golden age of motion pictures had begun. Each week, over a hundred million Americans flocked to watch cartoons, newsreels, and feature films at elaborate movie palaces with names such as the Bijou, the Roxy, and the Ritz. Audiences loved slapstick comics like Laurel and Hardy or the Marx brothers. Lines spoken by Mae West, such as "Come up and see me sometime," became household phrases. To top off the decade, audiences in 1939 thronged to behold the long-awaited blockbuster movie epic, *Gone with the Wind.*

But perhaps the most popular form of entertainment during the 1930s was the radio. By 1933, two thirds of American households owned at least one radio, and families gathered together to listen to comedies like *Fibber McGee and Molly* and adventures like *The Shadow.* People also relied on radios for news, as was demonstrated by a famous Halloween broadcast of 1938. Six million listeners tuned in to Orson Welles's radio play "Invasion from Mars"—a series of convincing but fictional news bulletins about a Martian invasion near New York City, based on H. G. Wells's science fiction novel *War of the Worlds.* At the time, some people feared that the German dictator Adolf Hitler might actually invade the United States. Believing that the broadcast was describing a real invasion, hundreds of people clogged eastern highways, fleeing for their lives.

> Fitzgerald's greatest work shows what happens to people who pursue illusory American dreams, and how society . . . fails to sustain them in their desperate hour.
>
> —Jeffrey Meyers, *Scott Fitzgerald: A Biography,* 1994

The three underpinnings of the American dream are a belief in the land as a bountiful new Eden, an unwavering faith in progress, and a confidence in the ultimate triumph of the individual. D E

A Crack in the World: Breakdown of Beliefs and Traditions

The cannonades of World War I and the economic crash a decade later severely damaged these inherited ideas of an Edenic land, an optimism in the future, and faith in individualism. Postwar writers became skeptical of the New England Puritan tradition and the gentility that had been central to the literary

The Tenets of the American Dream

- America is a new Eden, a "promised land" of beauty, unlimited resources, and endless opportunities.
- The American birthright is one of ever-expanding opportunity. Progress is a good thing, and we can optimistically expect life to keep getting better and better.
- The independent, self-reliant individual will triumph. Everything is possible for the person who places trust in his or her own powers and potential.

D. Reader's Response: First Thoughts

? How important do you think optimism and individualism are in the United States today? [Sample responses: It is hard to be optimistic considering tough international economic competition; or the self-reliant individual is still important in shaping the future of our country.]

E. Reader's Response: Connecting with the Text

? Do we still have a belief in the American dream today? [Sample responses: Yes, more people are better educated and more people can get better jobs than in the past; or no, the future does not hold as many opportunities as it once did.]

STRATEGIES FOR INCLUSION

Kinesthetic Some students might find it useful to create a map of the United States that contains the locations associated with the authors who are mentioned in the text. After they read each section of the period introduction, ask one student to write on an index card a summary about an author. Then, that student can attach the index card in the appropriate place on a large United States map. Leave the map on display in the classroom during the instruction of Collections 11–16 and invite students to add to it as new information is presented. ☞

A. Exploring the Historical Period

Karl Marx believed that the economic structure of a society was responsible for every aspect of life in that society. He also believed that the evils associated with the capitalist system could not be reformed from within; instead, the only alternative was the complete destruction of capitalism in favor of the creation of a classless society in which everyone is equal. His ideas greatly influenced Vladimir Ilyich Lenin, who became, in 1903, the head of the Bolshevik faction of the Social Democratic Party in Russia. In 1917, the Bolsheviks overthrew the government of the czar and established a Marxist version of socialism.

B. Expansion

A belief in free will is essential to Judeo-Christian religions and to the very concept of democracy. In these religions, people can be justly rewarded or punished only if they are free to enact the deeds that lead to reward or punishment. Similarly, in a democracy, people can govern themselves only if they are free to make choices. Freud's emphasis on the unconscious as a source of motivation for many of the choices people make tended, in the minds of some people, to undermine the freedom of the will that much of American society is based on.

ideal. In fact, the center of American literary life now finally started to shift away from New England, which had been the native region of America's most brilliant writers during the nineteenth century. Many of the modernist writers you will read in the collections that follow were born in the South, the Midwest, or the West.

> The liberty of the individual is no gift of civilization. It was greatest before there was any civilization.
>
> —Sigmund Freud, *Civilization and Its Discontents*, 1930

In the postwar period, two new intellectual trends or movements, **Marxism** and **psychoanalysis**, combined to increase the pressure on traditional beliefs and values. In Russia during World War I, a Marxist revolution had toppled and even murdered an anointed ruler, the czar. The socialistic beliefs of Karl Marx (1818–1883) that had powered the Russian Revolution in 1917 were in direct opposition to the American system of capitalism and free enterprise, and Marxists threatened to export their revolution everywhere. From Moscow, the American writer John Reed sent back the alarming message: "I have seen the future and it works." **(A)**

Sigmund Freud looking at a manuscript in the office of his Vienna home (c. 1930).
The Bettmann Archive.

In Vienna, there was another unsettling movement. Sigmund Freud (1856–1939), the founder of psychoanalysis, had opened the workings of the unconscious mind to scrutiny and called for a new understanding of human sexuality and the role it plays in our unconscious thoughts. Throughout America, there was a growing interest in this new field of psychology, and a resultant anxiety about the amount of freedom an individual really had. If our actions were influenced by our subconscious, and if we had no control over our subconscious, there seemed to be little room left for "free will." **(B)**

One literary result of this interest in the psyche was the narrative technique called **stream of consciousness.** This writing style abandoned chronology and attempted to imitate the moment-by-moment flow of a character's perceptions and memories. The Irish writer James Joyce (1882–1941) radically changed the very concept of the novel by using stream of consciousness in *Ulysses* (1922), his monumental "odyssey" set in Dublin. Soon afterward, the American writers Katherine Anne Porter (page 702) and William Faulkner (page 713) used the stream-of-consciousness technique in their works.

Two important trends, Marxism and psychoanalysis, were noteworthy factors in the breakdown of traditional beliefs and values. Psychoanalysis led to the literary technique of stream-of-consciousness narration.

James Joyce.
Archive Photos.

At Home and Abroad: The Jazz Age

In 1919, the Constitution was amended to prohibit the manufacture and sale of alcohol, which was singled out as a central social evil. But far from shoring up traditional values, Prohibition ushered in an age characterized by the bootlegger, the speakeasy, the cocktail, the short-skirted flapper, the new rhythms of jazz, and the dangerous but lucrative

Title page of the first edition of *Studies on Hysteria* (1895) by Joseph Breuer and Sigmund Freud.
The Granger Collection, New York.

OPTIONS FOR TEACHING

INTEGRATING THE LANGUAGE ARTS

Strategic Reading Encourage students to take notes on the main ideas as they read the period introduction by having them fill out a chart like the following. After students have filled out the chart, have them write a summary statement about the first writer or idea that they listed. Then, have several volunteers read their statements to the class, and discuss what constitutes a good summary statement. Finally, have students write summary statements for all the rows in their charts.

Period Introduction: The Moderns		
Writer or Idea	Importance of Writer/Idea	Class Notes and Explanations

profession of the gangster. Recording the Roaring Twenties and making the era a vivid chapter in our history, F. Scott Fitzgerald gave it its name: the Jazz Age. Other writers also became emblems of the era. The poet Edna St. Vincent Millay (page 697)—"Vincent" to her friends—became a symbol of the liberated woman of the era. Her bold, carefree public identity as a romantic, extravagant female Casanova made her a national celebrity while she was still in her twenties. In 1920, women had finally won the right to vote, and Millay's poems, as well as her public persona, assigned women social, intellectual, and romantic roles that society had previously reserved for men.

As energetic as the Roaring Twenties were in America, the pursuit of pleasure abroad was even more attractive to some than its enjoyment at home. F. Scott Fitzgerald was among the many American writers and artists who abandoned their own shores after the war for the expatriate life in France. After World War I, living was not only cheap in Paris and on the sunny French Riviera, but also somehow better; it was more exotic, more filled with grace and luxury, and there was no need to go down a cellar stairway to get a drink. This wave of expatriates was another signal that something had gone wrong with the American dream—with the idea that America was Eden, with our notion of inherent virtue, and especially with the conviction that America was a land of heroes. **C**

The Jazz Age at home was racy and unconventional. The same decade of the 1920s witnessed the flight of many American authors to an expatriate life abroad, especially in France.

The United States . . . is a country the right age to have been born in and the wrong age to live in. **D**

—Gertrude Stein, *transition* magazine, Fall 1928

Grace Under Pressure: The New American Hero

Disillusionment was a major theme in the fiction of the time. In 1920, Sinclair Lewis (1885–1951) lashed out satirically at the

Village Speakeasy, Closed for Violations (detail) (c. 1934) by Ben Shahn. Tempera on masonite (16½″ × 48″). Museum of the City of New York. Permanent Deposit of the Public Art Project through the Whitney Museum. © 1997 Estate of Ben Shahn/Licensed by VAGA, New York.

C. Expansion

One of the most compelling images of this period was created by the poet T. S. Eliot (pp. 661–662) in his masterpiece *The Waste Land.* In the opinion of some critics, the aridity and infertility of the landscape of this poem and of its characters' lives captured the mood of barrenness, pointlessness, and spiritual despair that many of the expatriates seemed to feel.

D. Responding to the Quotation

? What does Gertrude Stein imply about the development of American culture and the society of her day? [Possible responses: American culture and the society of her day are in their adolescence. Or it was good to have been born into that culture and society because of the freshness and vitality they imparted, but Stein needs a more mature culture and society now that she is an adult.]

INTEGRATING THE LANGUAGE ARTS

Language and Vocabulary Many of the concepts and movements described in the period introduction end with the suffix *–ism* or *–ist (modernism, individualism, Marxist, Symbolism, Imagism).* Ask students to look up the meanings of this suffix and to decide which definition applies to the words in the modernist collections. Then, ask students to make vocabulary posters of the *–ism* or *–ist* words, including their pronunciations and definitions. Put these on display around the classroom for the duration of the lessons on the Moderns.

Speaking and Listening The last two paragraphs of the period introduction have a decidedly triumphant tone. Ask several students to prepare oral readings of these paragraphs and to present them to the class. You might videotape the readings and have a committee of students judge which reading best captures the tone of the passage.

A. Literary Connections
Although Hemingway's style is traceable to the plain prose style of the Puritans, some critics believe his immediate stylistic predecessors are Mark Twain and Stephen Crane. Hemingway had a great admiration for Twain's *The Adventures of Huckleberry Finn,* in which Twain uses the same kind of colloquial speech and sentence patterns that Hemingway employs. Crane serves as a link between Twain and Hemingway, for Crane and Hemingway share the same dark view of the human condition.

narrow-mindedness of small-town life in his immensely popular novel, *Main Street.* In 1925, Theodore Dreiser (1871–1945) produced a literary landmark with his prototype of the realistic novel, *An American Tragedy,* the story of an ambitious but luckless man who takes a path that leads him not to the success he seeks, but to the execution chamber.

The most influential of all the post–World War I writers, however, was Ernest Hemingway (page 650). Hemingway is perhaps most famous for his literary style, which affected the style of American prose fiction for several generations. Like the Puritans who strove for a "plain style" centuries earlier, Hemingway reduced the flamboyance of literary language to a minimum, to the bare bones of the truth it must express.

Hemingway also introduced a new kind of hero to American fiction, a character type that many readers embraced as a protagonist and a role model. This Hemingway hero is a man of action, a warrior, and a tough competitor; he has a code of honor, courage, and endurance. He shows, in Hemingway's own words, "grace under pressure." But the most important trait of this Hemingway hero is that he is thoroughly disillusioned, a quality that reflected the author's own outlook. For Hemingway feared, a little like Herman Melville (page 311), that at the inscrutable center of creation lay nothing at all.

Hemingway found his own "answer" to this crisis of faith in a belief in the self and in such qualities as decency, bravery, competence, and skill. He clung to this conviction in spite of what he saw as the absolutely unbeatable odds ranged against us all. A further part of the Hemingway code was the importance of recognizing and snatching up the rare, good, rich moments that life offers before those moments elude us.

Hemingway summed up the values of many post–World War I writers, both in his spare, plain style and in his creation of a new kind of hero, disillusioned but also honorable and courageous.

Modernist Voices in Poetry: A Dazzling Period

After the deaths of Emily Dickinson (page 372) and Walt Whitman (page 348), American poetry went into something of a decline. But time would show that the comparatively uneventful period between 1890 and 1910 was but the trough of a wave that was about to break. The force of this wave, when it arrived, would be strong enough to wash away the last traces of British influence on American poetry and to carry our poets into their most dazzling period of variety and experimentation.

During this period, many poets began to explore the artistic life of Europe, especially Paris. With other writers, artists, and composers from all over the world, they

Gary Cooper as Robert Jordan in the 1943 movie *For Whom the Bell Tolls,* based on Hemingway's novel.

OPTIONS FOR TEACHING

CROSSING THE CURRICULUM

History The material in the period introduction presents numerous opportunities for students to investigate aspects of the history of the period. Divide the class into groups that will research and report on such areas as World War I, the Russian Revolution, the influenza epidemic of 1918, Prohibition, the Roaring Twenties, or the Great Depression. Students can investigate the political, economic, or social aspects of these topics and a number of others. Have them give a radio broadcast using the information they have discovered.

Fine Arts The text of the period introduction mentions Pablo Picasso and Henri Matisse. Some students might be interested in investigating their work, as well as the work of other modernist artists who were active during the first half of the twentieth century. Students can research biographical information about the artists and the artists' philosophies and techniques, and review photographs or reproductions of their works. An art teacher or a resource person from a local art gallery or museum might be willing to speak to your class and show slides of works of modern art. Ask students to create an exhibit of the artists' work and to conduct a museum tour that tells about the artists.

Guernica (1937) by Pablo Picasso. Museo del Prado, Madrid. Courtesy Giraudon/Art Resource.

> Literature is news that *stays* news.
> —Ezra Pound

absorbed the lessons of modernist painters like Henri Matisse and Pablo Picasso, who were exploring new ways to see and represent reality. In the same way, poets sought to create poems that invited new ways of seeing and thinking. Ezra Pound (page 773) and T. S. Eliot (page 661) used the suggestive techniques of **Symbolism** to fashion a new, modernist poetry (see page 770). Pound also spearheaded a related poetic movement called **Imagism.** Exemplified by brilliant poets like William Carlos Williams (page 778), Marianne Moore (page 787), E. E. Cummings (page 796), and Wallace Stevens (page 783), the Imagist and Symbolist styles would prevail in poetry until midway into the twentieth century.

After an uneventful period between 1890 and 1910, an explosion of modernist poetry, heavily influenced by developments in Europe, began. Ezra Pound and T. S. Eliot, associated with the Symbolist and Imagist movements, were especially important in charting a modernist direction for American poetry.

The Elements of Modernism in American Literature

- Emphasis on bold experimentation in style and form, reflecting the fragmentation of society
- Rejection of traditional themes and subjects
- Sense of disillusionment and loss of faith in the American dream
- Rejection of the ideal of a hero as infallible in favor of a hero who is flawed and disillusioned but shows "grace under pressure"
- Interest in the inner workings of the human mind, sometimes expressed through new narrative techniques such as stream of consciousness

B. Responding to the Quotation

What does Ezra Pound mean by comparing literature to news? How can news stay news? [Possible responses: Literature, like news, should inform people about something they do not already know; or news remains news as long as people do not know it; or literature does not age.]

C. Literary Connections

The Symbolist movement has had a significant effect on twentieth-century British and American literature. To the Symbolists, the proper subject matter of poetry is the unique, immediate, and intensely personal emotional reactions of poets to their experience. These reactions are essentially incommunicable, so poets must rely on a complex and highly personal web of symbols to express their feelings. Writers such as William Butler Yeats, John Millington Synge, James Joyce, and Eugene O'Neill have all used Symbolist techniques. For the Imagists, the **image** is a complex that includes intellectual and emotional content, with the visual component of the image relating to the intellectual content and the auditory component relating to the emotional content. Poets of the Imagist school wanted to find the precise word to express their experiences, to achieve intense concentration of effect, and to suggest rather than state directly.

CLASSROOM MANAGEMENT

Pacing Instruction The period introduction contains a large amount of information that students may not be familiar with. You might spread your treatment of this material over several days to give students a chance to absorb its content. Intersperse the segments of the period introduction with the study of the selections of this period.

Previewing Material Use the summaries between sections to preview the entire period introduction. Ask a volunteer to read each of these passages aloud for the class, and then ask the class to indicate what they already know about the subject of the passage. In addition, have them suggest questions that the summaries bring to mind, and these questions can serve as guides in focusing attention during the reading as students look for answers.

A. Expansion
Not all of the modernist poets left the United States. William Carlos Williams (p.778), for example, maintained a full-time medical practice in his native Rutherford, New Jersey. In fact, Williams, who has come to be one of the most influential poets of the twentieth century, scorned the decision of his friend Ezra Pound to become an expatriate.

B. Responding to the Quotation
? What does Robert Frost imply about the relationship between poetry and the culture that produces it? [Possible responses: Frost implies that poetry embodies the values of a particular culture and that by knowing the culture, one can anticipate what the poetry will be like. Or Frost implies that just as the country is diverse and complex, so too is its poetry essentially complex and difficult to know fully.]

C. Expansion
Other significant poets who were born in the Midwest include Vachel Lindsey (Springfield, Illinois); Archibald MacLeish (Glencoe, Illinois); Theodore Roethke (p.1001) (Saginaw, Michigan); Richard Eberhart (Austin, Minnesota); T. S. Eliot (pp. 661–662), Marianne Moore (p. 787), and Sara Teasdale (all in St. Louis, Missouri); and Hart Crane (Garrettsville, Ohio).

Voices of American Character: Poetry in New England and the Midwest

A Meanwhile, other American poets rejected modernist trends. While their colleagues found inspiration in Paris, these poets stayed at home, ignoring or defying the revolution of modernism. These poets preferred to say what they had to say in plain American speech. Their individual accents reveal the regional diversity of American life and character.

Edwin Arlington Robinson (page 644) lightly disguised the people of his own "Down East" home—Gardiner, Maine—as characters representing American "types" whose fates were manifestations of their characters.

B Tell me what America is and I'll tell you what its poetry is.
—Robert Frost

The greatest poetic voice in New England, however, was that of Robert Frost (page 558). Frost's independence was grounded in his ability to handle ordinary New England speech and in his surprising skill at taking the most conventional poetic forms and giving them a twist all his own. In an era when "good" was being equated by many artists with "new," the only new thing about Robert Frost was old: individual poetic genius. Using this gift to impose his own personality on the iambic line in verse, Frost created a poetic voice that was unique and impossible to imitate.

C At the same time, poets of the Midwest brought the American heartland to life in slightly more adventuresome verse forms. They used rougher stanzas and looser lines. Best known of these poets is Edgar Lee Masters (page 692), who assembled a sort of town biography in his *Spoon River Anthology* (1915). Masters took the lid off sentimentalized small-town life—the *coffin* lid, to be exact—and allowed the dead of Spoon River to speak their own shocking litanies of greed, frustration, and spiritual poverty. His best-selling collection of poems received the same kind of interest Americans were beginning to give to Freudian case histories.

Poets like Edwin Arlington Robinson and Robert Frost from New England and Edgar Lee Masters from the Midwest continued to use traditional verse forms and offered penetrating insights into a variety of American character types.

The Harlem Renaissance: Voices of the African American Experience

African American culture found expression in poetry in two different ways. The works of black poets who wrote in conventional forms, like Paul Laurence Dunbar (1872-1906), were most quickly accepted by white readers. These metrically regular and rhymed verse forms tended to make even the most urgent and desperate of African American concerns seem undisturbing. A second

Ernest Hemingway in Paris. Culver Pictures.

OPTIONS FOR TEACHING

PROFESSIONAL NOTES

Technology Tip Before students begin this Collection, ask them to report on the history of the period and to report on their findings in an electronic presentation to the class. For example, one group may choose to research the political forces behind World War I; another may choose to focus on family life during the Great Depression. For the electronic presentations, students will need access to an LCD projection system.

Paul Laurence Dunbar.

Culver Pictures.

group of black poets, however, focused directly on the unique contributions of African American culture to America. Their poetry based its rhythms on spirituals and jazz, its lyrics on songs known as the blues, and its diction on the street talk of the ghettos. D

Foremost among African American lyric poets were James Weldon Johnson (page 736), Claude McKay (page 743), Langston Hughes (page 760), and Countee Cullen (page 746). These poets brought literary distinction to the broad movement of artists known as the **Harlem Renaissance** (page 734). The geographical center of the movement was Harlem, the section of New York City north of 110th Street in Manhattan. But its spiritual center was a place in the consciousness of African Americans—a people too long ignored, patronized, or otherwise shuffled to the margins of American art. When African American poetry, hand in hand with the music echoing from New Orleans, Memphis, and Chicago, became part of the Jazz Age, it was a catalyst for a new appreciation of the role of black talent in American culture.

> . . . O, let America
> be America again—
> The land that never
> has been yet—
> And yet must be.
>
> —Langston Hughes

E

The poets of the Harlem Renaissance revolutionized the African American contribution to American literature by introducing ghetto speech and the rhythms of jazz and blues into their verse.

Against the Grain: Poetic Voices of the West and South

The most distinctive poetic voice from the West in the early twentieth century was that of Robinson Jeffers (page 580), who carved out an isolated and almost hermitlike existence in a California town by the Pacific shore. Jeffers steered a wavering course between convention and experiment: Sometimes he worked in meter and rhyme, but more often he wrote in long lines of free verse. He became widely known less for his craftsmanship than for his unorthodox attitudes toward progress, religion, and the nature of humanity. While his contemporaries celebrated democracy and the rise of the common man, Jeffers took a very dim view of both. After his death, his poems became an inspiration to the Beats and other West Coast literary groups in the 1960s.

The South offered an equally distinctive literary voice in John Crowe Ransom (page 577). Ransom stood for wit, gentility, subtle intellect, and the manners of an earlier century. Ransom's formal grace and polish intimidated some readers, but others found in him a gentle nature and a passionate concern for the beauty and elegance of the English language.

Poetic voices of the West and the South included Robinson Jeffers, who was skeptical of social progress, and John Crowe Ransom, a Southerner who wrote with the courtly grace of an earlier age.

(Background) Museum of African Art/Smithsonian Institution/Courtesy Aldo Tutino/Art Resource.

D. Exploring the Culture

Spirituals (see pp. 432–434) are religious folk songs of African American slaves. Many of the songs express the misery of slavery and the desire of people to be free, often in terms of Biblical imagery. Spirituals are typically sung by a chorus. The blues developed from African American folk songs sung solo. Blues songs typically have three-line stanzas that develop through repetition, and they express such feelings as resentment, loneliness, and grief. The third contribution of African Americans to American and world music is jazz, which grew out of a number of factors in the cultural, social, and racial context of the South. A combination of African rhythms, the rhythms of camp-meeting spirituals and gospel songs, the inflection of the blues, and the improvisations of "washboard bands" came together to produce the jazz sound.

E. Responding to the Quotation

? What does Hughes envision for the United States? [Possible responses: He sees that the country should be a land where hopes and dreams can come true; or the American dream can be hoped for and experienced by all the peoples living in the country.]

ASSESSMENT TOOLS

Peer Assessment To help the student committee evaluate the Speaking and Listening activity on p. T531, have each student on the committee use a chart like the following. Ask students to comment on each reader's performance in each category and then to rate each reader in every category using a 1 to 5 rating (5 being the highest). Students should add any additional comments they have in the space provided below the chart. Comments will provide student readers with an assessment of their performance; averaging the ratings will help indicate the preferred performance.

Criteria	Comments	Rating
Voice quality and tone		
Controlled rate of speaking to reflect meaning and mood of piece		
Stress and pauses to emphasize important words and ideas		

Additional comments:

A. Expansion

In the second half of the twentieth century, a number of forces converged to help expand the voices that make up the chorus of American literature. The civil rights movement of the 1950s and 1960s helped add the voices of African Americans in greater numbers. In the late 1960s, readers became increasingly attentive to the voices of Native Americans, who previously had been largely ignored. The women's movement of that same period made readers more conscious of the unique voices of women writers. A general awareness of cultural diversity opened the way for the literary voices of Spanish-speaking Americans, Asian Americans, and people of greatly diverse cultural backgrounds.

Quickwrite

Before students begin writing, ask them to make a list of the goals they hope to accomplish by the time they are forty years old. Then, suggest they try to arrive at a generalization or two that summarizes their aspirations. You can carry this activity a step further by asking volunteers to share their generalizations with the class and then discussing the common threads that run through the statements of various students. These common threads may be the skeleton of a definition of the American dream. *Remind students to choose goals they would not mind sharing with others.*

The American Dream Revised

Even though the modernists rejected Emerson's optimism, a belief in self-reliance persisted as the old idea of America as Eden. Hemingway is really telling us about Eden in his *Up in Michigan* stories, where he describes the lakes and streams and woods he knew as a boy and where he extols the restorative power of nature in a way that Emerson might have recognized. This is the same Edenic America that has come down to us through Mark Twain's Mississippi, through Faulkner's Yoknapatawpha County, and through John Steinbeck's Salinas Valley.

A As we explore this period of American writing—in some respects, the richest period since the flowering of New England in the first half of the nineteenth century—we stand at the threshold of our own time. Though this part of our own century has seen major changes in American attitudes, you'll recognize many concerns that are consistent with concerns of the past. These writers—some of the best that America has produced—experimented boldly with forms and subject matter. But they were also still trying to find the answers to the basic human questions: Who are we? Where are we going? And what values should guide us on that search for our human identity?

> I began to gather these impressions. There was a thing called happiness toward which men were striving. They never got to it. All of life was amazingly accidental. Love, moments of tenderness and despair, came to the poor and the miserable as to the rich and successful.
>
> It began to seem to me that what was most wanted by all people was love, understanding. Our writers, our storytellers, in wrapping life up into neat little packages, were only betraying life.
>
> —Sherwood Anderson, in a letter to George Freitag, August 27, 1938

American modernist writers both echoed and challenged the American dream. They constituted a broader, more resonant voice than ever before, resulting in a second American renaissance. With all the changes, however, writers continued to ask fundamental questions about the meaning and purpose of human existence.

Quickwrite

What Is Today's American Dream?

In 1929, Gertrude Stein, a leading modernist literary figure among the American expatriates in Paris, declared, "Everything is the same and everything is different." Apply her remark to the American dream today. How do you define the American dream now? (Is there even an American dream anymore?) How has it remained the same? How has it changed? Write your responses in your Reader's Log.

OPTIONS FOR TEACHING

ASSESSMENT TOOLS

Check Test: True-False

1. World War I marked the beginning of America's loss of innocence. [True]
2. Interest in psychoanalysis led to a general anxiety about the influences of the subconscious on people's actions. [True]
3. American writers were afraid to leave the country and live in Europe after World War I. [False]
4. Disillusionment was a major theme for many writers in the 1920s. [True]
5. Poets from New England continued to completely dominate American literature after World War I. [False]

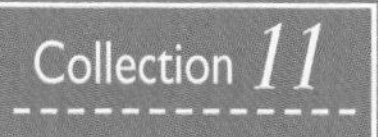

LOSS AND REDEMPTION

Theme: **In Search of Lost Times**
American writers in the first half of the twentieth century were obsessed with exploring a seemingly global loss of innocence in people; and they began to search within themselves and their art for meaning.

Thematic Focus

The protagonists of the selections in Collection 11 experience loss.

- **A Wagner Matinée** A concert rekindles Aunt Georgiana's passion for music.
- **His Father's Earth** The young narrator yearns for both adventure and stability.
- **Design** Nature appears innocent in this sonnet.
- **Nothing Gold Can Stay** Natural processes are temporal.
- **Once by the Pacific** The crashing ocean portends the end of the world.
- **Neither Out Far Nor In Deep** Humanity accepts its limitations.
- **Birches** Birches symbolize simple moral lessons and truths.
- **The Death of the Hired Man** "Home" is a sense of belonging to others.
- **Bells for John Whiteside's Daughter** The speaker expresses anger toward death.
- **Shine, Perishing Republic** The speaker addresses society's corrupting influence.

Literary Focus

Literary Element	Selection / Feature
Setting	**A Wagner Matinée**
Description	**His Father's Earth**
Parable	**Birches**
Dialogue in Verse/Blank Verse	**The Death of the Hired Man**
Tone	**Bells for John Whiteside's Daughter**

Writing Focus

The following chart shows how the writing assignment for each selection relates to and builds toward the culminating writing assignment presented in the Writer's Workshop at the end of the unit.

Selection	Work-in-Progress Assignment
A Wagner Matinée	Freewrite about the effect of music for a speculation about causes and effects p. 547
His Father's Earth	List questions to ask the subject of a biography for a speculation about causes and effects p. 557
Design/Nothing Gold Can Stay/ Once by the Pacific/Neither Out Far nor In Deep/Birches/ The Death of the Hired Man	Write questions about Frost's poems for a speculation about causes and effects p. 576
Bells for John Whiteside's Daughter	Freewrite a personal response for a speculation about causes and effects p. 579
Shine, Perishing Republic	List possible topics for a speculation about causes and effects p. 582
Writer's Workshop	Write a speculation about causes and effects pp. 685–689

Collection 11 **LOSS AND REDEMPTION**

Collection Planner

PUPIL'S EDITION

SELECTION/FEATURE	Literary Elements / Active Reading	Writing	Speaking and Listening	Language and Vocabulary
A Wagner Matinée Willa Cather (pp. 538–547)	• Reader's Log p. 539 • Setting p. 539	• Critical Writing: Write comparative essay p. 547 • Creative Writing: Write description p. 547		
His Father's Earth Thomas Wolfe (pp. 548–557)	• Reader's Log p. 549 • Description p. 549	• Critical Writing: Write comparative essay p. 557 • Creative Writing: Write description p. 557		
Design; Nothing Gold Can Stay; Once by the Pacific; Neither Out Far nor In Deep; Birches; The Death of the Hired Man Robert Frost (pp. 558–576) **Connections: Trying to Name What Doesn't Change** Naomi Shihab Nye (p. 563) Primary Sources: I must have the pulse beat of rhythm Robert Frost (p. 574)	• Reader's Log pp. 560, 562, 564, 565, 567, 569 • Parable p. 568 • Dialogue in verse p. 569 • Blank verse p. 575	• Critical Writing: Write essay exploring conflicts in Frost's poems p. 576 • Critical Writing: Write comparative essay p. 576 • Creative Writing: Write modern version of poem in verse or prose p. 576 • Art: Write explanations for visual images p. 576	• Speaking and Listening: Discuss Romantic and Puritan traditions in Frost's poems p. 576 • Music/Art: Create multimedia presentation p. 576	
Bells for John Whiteside's Daughter John Crowe Ransom (pp. 577–579)	• Reader's Log p. 577 • Tone p. 577	• Critical Writing: Write explanatory essay p. 579 • Critical Writing: Write comparative essay p. 579		
Shine, Perishing Republic Robinson Jeffers (pp. 580–582)	• Reader's Log p. 580	• Critical Writing: Write essay evaluating Jeffers's views p. 582		

Collection Resources

Teaching Resources B — Cross-Curricular Activity p. 31
Audiovisual Resources Binder — Fine Art Transparency 11.1
Test Booklet — Collection 11 Test pp. 137–140

 Computer disk or CD-ROM
 Audiocassette
 Overhead Transparency

PROGRAM RESOURCES

Electronic Media	Teaching Resources with Organizer: Teaching Resources B	Teaching Resources with Organizer: Other Resources	Audiovisual Resources Binder
• Language Workshop: Subject-verb agreement • Test Generator	• Teaching Notes pp. 3–4 • Reading Organizer p. 13 • Language Link pp. 14–15 • Words to Own p. 16	• Test Booklet: Selection Test pp. 129–130 • Language and Writing Skills Worksheets pp. 25–26 • Portfolio Management System pp. 39, 132	
• Test Generator • Language Workshop: Active voice	• Teaching Notes p. 4 • Reading Organizer p. 17 • Language Links pp. 18–21 • Words to Own p. 22	• Test Booklet: Selection Test pp. 131–132 • Language and Writing Skills Worksheets pp. 1–2, 4–5 • Portfolio Management System pp. 48–49, 133	
• Test Generator	• Teaching Notes pp. 5–8 • Reading Organizers pp. 23–28	• Test Booklet: Selection Test pp. 133–134 • Portfolio Management System pp. 52, 134–135	• Selected Readings Audiocassette 2, Side B • Elements of Literature Transparency 11.2
• Test Generator	• Teaching Notes pp. 8–9 • Reading Organizer p. 29	• Test Booklet: Selection Test pp. 135–136 • Portfolio Management System p. 136	• Selected Reading Audiocassette 2, Side B
• Test Generator	• Teaching Notes pp. 9–10 • Reading Organizer p. 30	• Test Booklet: Selection Test pp. 135–136 • Portfolio Management System pp. 54–55, 137	

Proofreading Warm-ups

You may use the following exercises to help students practice their proofreading skills. Copy a set of incorrect sentences onto the chalkboard, and have students find and correct the spelling, punctuation, usage, and mechanical errors in each sentence. Ask students to share and discuss their responses.

	Sentences with Errors	Sentences Corrected	Skills Covered
1	**a.** in 1917 america enterred world war I, 1914–1918, and sent troups to europ **b.** during the battle of Verdun (1916, the feilds of northern france had became a bloodbath	**a.** In 1917, America entered World War I (1914–1918) and sent troops to Europe. **b.** During the Battle of Verdun (1916), the fields of northern France became a bloodbath.	Capitalization, Comma usage, Spelling, Parenthesis usage, Verb tense, End marks
2	**a.** modernism effected american wrighters painters and musicans **b.** modernizm called for artists to experiment and rejecting traditional forms	**a.** Modernism affected American writers, painters, and musicians. **b.** Modernism called for artists to experiment and reject traditional forms.	Capitalization, Usage, Spelling, Comma usage, Verb form consistency (parallelism), End marks
3	**a.** the American dream was a optimist vision **b.** dissillusion caracterised the change in peoples' veiws	**a.** The American dream was an optimistic vision. **b.** Disillusionment characterized the change in people's views.	Capitalization, Articles, Adjective form, Noun form, Spelling, Possessives (plural noun), End marks
4	**a.** the idea of the united states as having nonlimited abundance felled away **b.** another tenant of the dream confidance in the individual remains an important literery theme	**a.** The idea of the United States as having unlimited abundance fell away. **b.** Another tenet of the dream—confi-dence in the individual—remains an important literary theme.	Capitalization, Usage, Verb tense, Dashes, Spelling, End marks
5	**a.** stream of consiousness a writting technic attemts at imitating a character's thouhts as they occur **b.** the work from Freud a Viennese Psichiatrist influinsed many novelists	**a.** Stream of consciousness, a writing technique, attempts to imitate a character's thoughts as they occur. **b.** The work of Freud, a Viennese psychia-trist, influenced many novelists.	Capitalization, Spelling, Comma usage, Prepositions, Verb form, End marks
6	**a.** among peoples' negative qualitys richard thinks hippocrisy is the most bad **b.** the constitution was amended in 1920 giveing women the rite to vote	**a.** Among people's negative qualities, Richard thinks hypocrisy is the worst. **b.** The Constitution was amended in 1920, giving women the right to vote.	Capitalization, Apostrophe errors (possessive), Plural nouns, Comma usage, Spelling, Superlative adjectives, End marks
7	**a.** both of sallys' parents work in circusses that are based at las vegas, Nev. **b.** didn't you never have the urge to travel	**a.** Both of Sally's parents work for circuses that are based in Las Vegas, Nevada. **b.** Didn't you ever have the urge to travel?	Capitalization, Apostrophe errors (possessive), Preposition, Plural nouns, Spelling out abbreviations, Double negatives, End marks
8	**a.** the poet edna st. Vincent Millay became a national cellebrity because of her libberated bold way of living **b.** prohibiting of alchol failed to titen moral values	**a.** The poet Edna St. Vincent Millay became a national celebrity because of her liberated, bold way of living. **b.** Prohibiting alcohol failed to tighten moral values.	Capitalization, Spelling, Comma usage, Usage, End marks
9	**a.** tho californian by birth poet Robert Frost moved to new england **b.** miranda and me researched the work of Jeffers a real pessimistical poet	**a.** Although Californian by birth, poet Robert Frost moved to New England. **b.** Miranda and I researched the work of Jeffers, a very pessimistic poet.	Capitalization, Standard usage, Comma usage, Pronoun case errors (nominative), Adjective form errors, End marks
10	**a.** between all the poets of the Harlem Rennassance i enjoy reading Langston hughes most, Chad said **b.** you read them poems good, Willa said to he	**a.** "Of all the poets of the Harlem Renais-sance, I enjoy reading Langston Hughes most," Chad said. **b.** "You read those poems well," Willa said to him.	Quotation marks, Capitalization, Usage, Spelling, Comma usage, Standard usage, Pronoun errors, End marks

Collection 11

LOSS AND REDEMPTION

Cather
Wolfe
Frost
Ransom
Jeffers

On the rough wet grass of the back yard my father and mother have spread quilts. We all lie there, my mother, my father, my uncle, my aunt, and I too am lying there. First we were sitting up, then one of us lay down, and then we all lay down, on our stomachs, or on our sides, or on our backs, and they have kept on talking. They are not talking much, and the talk is quiet, of nothing in particular, or nothing at all in particular, of nothing at all. The stars are wide and alive, they seem each like a smile of great sweetness, and they seem very near. All my people are larger bodies than mine, quiet, with voices gentle and meaningless like the voices of sleeping birds. One is an artist, he is living at home. One is a musician, she is living at home. One is my mother who is good to me. One is my father who is good to me. By some chance, here they are, all on this earth; and who shall ever tell the sorrow of being on this earth, lying, on quilts, on the grass, in a summer evening, among the sounds of the night. May God bless my people, my uncle, my aunt, my mother, my good father, oh, remember them kindly in their time of trouble; and in the hour of their taking away.

—James Agee (1909–1955),
from "Knoxville: Summer 1915,"
from A Death in the Family

Responding to the Quotation

? What does the quotation suggest about loss and redemption? [Possible responses: The speaker remembers his family. The quotation begins by showing how happy the speaker is with his or her life and family, and that loss is greatly felt when you love someone deeply. The last sentence indicates that he is thinking about their future deaths and is hopeful that they will not suffer. Or the speaker believes in spiritual redemption, as he prays for the deliverance of his family from any future pain.] Why might the editors have used this quotation to introduce the Collection? [Possible responses: The use of the quotation may indicate that the Collection will be about families and the pain of loss or about the deaths of others.]

PORTFOLIO ASSESSMENT

Parent/Guardian Involvement For forms that will help a parent or guardian review and respond to a student's portfolio, see the ***Portfolio Management System,*** pp. 62–63.

PROGRAM MANAGER

- **Integrated Assessment** For a summative assessment of the literature and language skills taught in this collection, see **Collection 11 Test, *Test Booklet,*** pp. 137–140.
- **Instructional Support** See **Fine Art Transparency** 11.1. Review teacher's notes for transparencies in the ***Audiovisual Resources Binder*** for suggestions on how to tie the transparencies to specific reading selections.
- **Extending Collection Theme** See **Cross-Curricular Activity: Loss and Redemption, *Teaching Resources B,*** p. 31, for an activity in other disciplines and for evaluation criteria.

QUICK PLANNING GUIDE

Into the Story

Through the Story

Beyond the Story

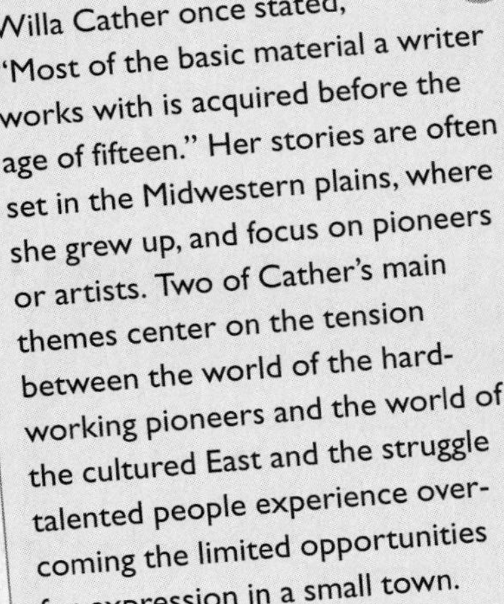

ABOUT THE AUTHOR

Willa Cather once stated, "Most of the basic material a writer works with is acquired before the age of fifteen." Her stories are often set in the Midwestern plains, where she grew up, and focus on pioneers or artists. Two of Cather's main themes center on the tension between the world of the hard-working pioneers and the world of the cultured East and the struggle talented people experience overcoming the limited opportunities for expression in a small town.

Willa Cather

(1873–1947)

Willa Cather, 1926 by Edward Steichen.

Courtesy George Eastman House. Reprinted with permission of Joanna T. Steichen.

Willa Cather was born in rural Virginia, the first of seven children. When she was nine, her father uprooted the family and headed for the untried lands of the West, settling in Webster County, Nebraska. She would later recall that this first encounter with the prairie was so striking that she felt "a kind of erasure of personality."

Nevertheless, Cather was stimulated by the hard life of the soil she saw around her, and she absorbed the stories of the immigrant families who were her neighbors. She read widely and became an outstanding student at the Red Cloud, Nebraska, school. In her boyish clothes and haircut, Willa was an unusual figure, and her teachers recognized in her an adolescent nonconformist.

While a freshman at the University of Nebraska, Cather published an essay in a Lincoln newspaper. She became a regular contributor to the newspaper and began to write poetry and stories. By the time Cather graduated in 1895, she had won a statewide reputation for brash, bright reviews. She moved to Pittsburgh and for a decade continued to work as a journalist. In 1903, she published her first book, a collection of verse entitled *April Twilights,* followed by *The Troll Garden,* a group of stories.

In 1906, the publisher S. S. McClure persuaded Cather to move to New York and join the staff of his dynamic, muckraking magazine, *McClure's.* For six years she served as a writer and editor, immersed in the social and political currents of the time; in 1912, she resigned from the magazine to give herself completely to writing fiction.

In 1908, Cather had met the Maine writer Sarah Orne Jewett (1849–1909), who had encouraged Cather to write about the themes and settings she knew best: the moral values of the hard-working immigrant families on the Midwestern prairie. Cather believed that these pioneers, who had sought to bring the wild, new land under cultivation, were heroic and that their era was the heart of the so-called American dream. She saw these immigrant settlers as contributing a cultural richness and an earthy love of life that were lacking in the pale, self-satisfied inhabitants of Eastern Seaboard cities. Cather developed these themes in *O Pioneers!* (1913), a novel whose title she borrowed from Walt Whitman, and in her novel *My Ántonia* (1918).

As Cather witnessed the decline of the agrarian ideal, her work became increasingly elegiac about the past and disillusioned with the present. *One of Ours* (1922), which was far from Cather's best novel but which won her the Pulitzer Prize, reflects Cather's dissatisfaction with the new people and machines who were betraying the pioneer ideal. "The world broke in two in 1922 or thereabout," Cather wrote, explaining that no one born in the twentieth century could grasp her own vision of America. She had seen her beloved Nebraska devastated by the machine, and she lamented the end of her epic vision of a noble society.

Cather reminds us of the novelist's duty to keep a wary eye on our relation to scientific progress. It was her profound intuition that a science that offers us new comfort, new speed, new security, and longer life will almost surely demand something of our spirit in return.

WORDS TO OWN

The following vocabulary words are defined in the Words to Own at the bottom of the pupil's page.

legacy p. 540	inert p. 543
grotesque p. 540	trepidation p. 543
eluding p. 542	obliquely p. 544
reverential p. 542	deluge p. 546
pious p. 542	myriad p. 546

PORTFOLIO ASSESSMENT

Portfolio Assessment For help with self- and teacher assessment of reading skills, see the ***Portfolio Management System,*** p. 39.

Before You Read
A Wagner Matinée

Reading Focus
Lost Pleasures
Most people can name at least one thing they enjoy that's a source of personal "bliss"—something they'd rather see, do, own, or listen to than anything else in the world. Sometimes circumstances in life force people to give up that beloved source of pleasure. Here is a story of a woman who has had to go without something important to her. As you will see, although Cather believed that Midwestern farm life fostered essential values, she was hardly a romantic who underestimated the hardships of that life, or the lost opportunities for some of the people who lived that life.

Quickwrite

Suppose you were deprived of your "bliss"—your favorite personal pleasure—for many years, and then you had the opportunity to experience it again, but only briefly. Write your ideas about how you would respond: whether you would seize the opportunity, or pass up the chance for fear that it would be too painful to realize what you had been missing.

Elements of Literature
Setting
As in most of Cather's works, **setting** plays a central role in this story. Here, however, there are really two settings: Rural Nebraska—in which the narrator, like Cather, spent his formative years—is contrasted with Boston and its thriving cultural life.

Setting is the time and location in which a story takes place.

For more on Setting, see the Handbook of Literary Terms.

Background
Willa Cather loved music and was herself an accomplished musician. The story's title refers to the German composer Richard Wagner (väg′nər) (1813–1883), the outstanding Romantic composer of the nineteenth century. A matinée is an afternoon performance of a play or concert.

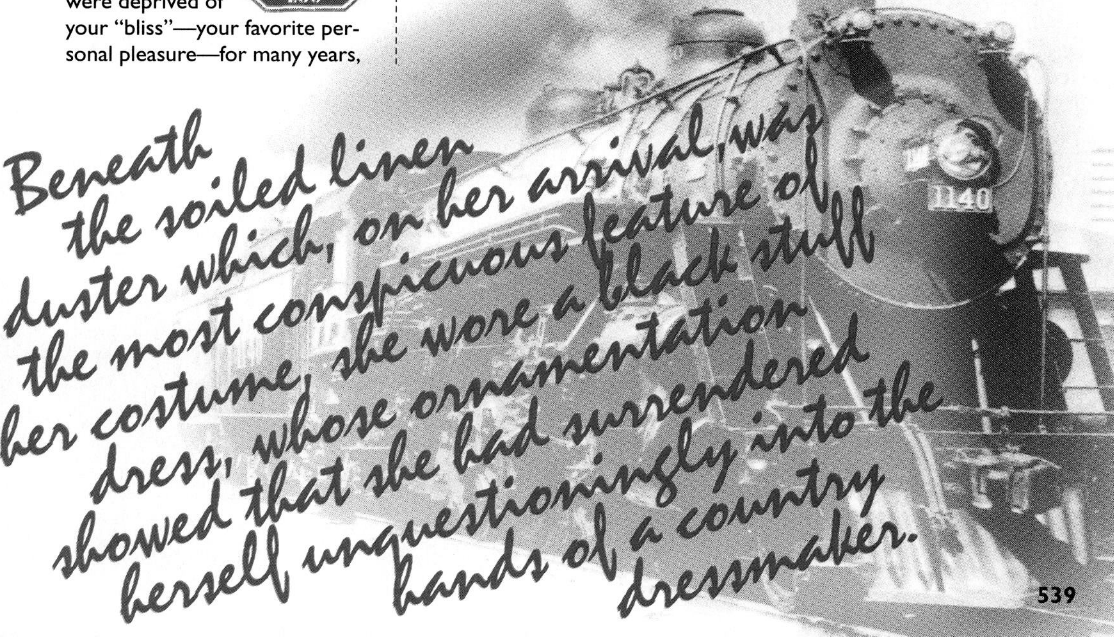

Beneath the soiled linen duster which, on her arrival, was the most conspicuous feature of her costume, she wore a black stuff dress, whose ornamentation showed that she had surrendered herself unquestioningly into the hands of a country dressmaker.

Using **Before You Read** p. 539

Elements of Literature
Although there are two settings for the story, the action takes place in only one of the settings—Boston. Through a series of flashbacks, the narrator familiarizes the reader with what Georgiana's life has been like in Nebraska. Tell students to consider how these flashbacks of life in Nebraska help them understand Georgiana's actions and reactions.

Background
Like the narrator of "A Wagner Matinée," Cather left Nebraska, after graduating from college, to experience the thriving cultural life of East Coast cities. Remind students that in those days there were no radios or compact discs and no nearby cities with orchestras; someone living on the frontier was isolated from music.

Program Manager
- **Planning Instruction** See Teaching Notes, *Teaching Resources B,* pp. 3–4, for objectives, a summary, literary elements, and additional information for this selection.
- **Instructional Support** Before beginning the instructional lesson, see Graphic Organizer for Active Reading, *Teaching Resources B,* p. 13, for an Into the Story activity.
- **Assessment** See Selection Test, *Test Booklet,* pp. 129–130.
- **Language Link** For instruction and practice in subject-verb agreement, see Language Link, *Teaching Resources B,* pp. 14–15, and *Language and Writing Skills Worksheets,* pp. 25–26.
- **Reinforcement** Use the Words to Own worksheet in *Teaching Resources B,* p. 16.

A. Literary Element: Character

? What do we learn about Uncle Howard in the first paragraph? [He is not a verbal man; still uses "blue-lined note paper" and "characteristically delayed writing"; lives in "a little Nebraska village"; and perhaps works outdoors since his pockets are "none too clean."]

B. Literary Element: Metaphor

? What is implied by the metaphor "a gulf of recollection so wide and deep"? [Possible answer: An almost overwhelming number of memories, rushing in like gulf waters.]

C. Critical Reading: Finding Details

? From the second paragraph, what can you learn about the narrator's present life and his former life? [Possible answer: In his present life he is comfortable in his study. In his former life he lived on a farm and would have felt uneasy in the city. His hands were scraped, cracked, and sore from cornhusking. He did play the organ, however awkwardly.]

D. Literary Element: Exposition

Call attention to the graceful manner in which Cather provides the necessary exposition in the three paragraphs beginning here.

A Wagner Matinée

Willa Cather

I received one morning a letter, written in pale ink on glassy, blue-lined note paper, and bearing the postmark of a little Nebraska village. This communication, worn and rubbed, looking as though it had been carried for some days in a coat pocket that was none too clean, was from my Uncle Howard and informed me that his wife had been left a small legacy by a bachelor relative who **A** had recently died, and that it would be necessary for her to go to Boston to attend to the settling of the estate. He requested me to meet her at the station and render her whatever services might be necessary. On examining the date indicated as that of her arrival, I found it no later than tomorrow. He had characteristically delayed writing until, had I been away from home for a day, I must have missed the good woman altogether.

The name of Aunt Georgiana called up not alone her own figure, at once pathetic and **B** grotesque, but opened before my feet a gulf of recollection so wide and deep, that, as the letter dropped from my hand, I felt suddenly a stranger to all the present conditions of my existence, wholly ill at ease and out of place amid the familiar surroundings of my study. I became, in short, **C** the gangling farmer-boy my aunt had known, scourged with chilblains[1] and bashfulness, my hands cracked and sore from the cornhusking. I felt the knuckles of my thumb tentatively, as though they were raw again. I sat again before her parlor organ, fumbling the scales with my stiff, red hands, while she, beside me, made canvas mittens for the huskers.

The next morning, after preparing my landlady somewhat, I set out for the station. When the train arrived I had some difficulty in finding my aunt. She was the last of the passengers to alight, and it was not until I got her into the carriage that she seemed really to recognize me. She had come all the way in a day coach; her linen duster had become black with soot and her black bonnet gray with dust during the journey. When we arrived at my boardinghouse the landlady put her to bed at once and I did not see her again until the next morning.

Whatever shock Mrs. Springer experienced at **D** my aunt's appearance, she considerately concealed. As for myself, I saw my aunt's misshapen figure with that feeling of awe and respect with which we behold explorers who have left their ears and fingers north of Franz Josef Land,[2] or their health somewhere along the upper Congo. My Aunt Georgiana had been a music teacher at

1. **chilblains** (chil′blānz′): inflammation of the hands and feet, caused by exposure to cold.

2. **Franz Josef Land:** group of islands in the Arctic Ocean.

WORDS TO OWN

legacy (leg′ə·sē) *n.:* inheritance.
grotesque (grō·tesk′) *adj.:* strange; absurd.

OPTIONS FOR TEACHING

STRATEGIES FOR INCLUSION

Visual Some students may volunteer to summarize the story with pictures. They can then write captions below the drawings to explain or summarize what happens in the drawings.

Less Proficient Readers To help readers organize what they learn from their reading, ask them to draw three columns on a sheet of paper and to take notes on the characters as they read: Aunt Georgiana, Clark, and Howard. After they finish the story, have them form groups of three and discuss what they noted about each character. Students should add any new information to their charts.

English Language Development To understand the story, students need to imagine the differences between the settings of Nebraska and Boston. Students who are not familiar with United States geography and history may not bring the background knowledge to the story that the author assumes readers have. Most students, however, will be able to imagine some differences between country life and city life. To help them activate prior knowledge, have students discuss differences between country and city. To help them build background, show them a map of the United States, pointing out Nebraska and Boston. Talk about the distance between the two locales, common means of travel at the time of the story, and the degree of difference between the two places.

Edith Mahon (1904) by Thomas Eakins. Oil on canvas.
Smith College Museum of Art, Northampton, Massachusetts. Purchased Drayton Hillyer Fund, 1931.

RESPONDING TO THE ART: ABOUT THE ARTIST

American painter Thomas Eakins (1844–1916) shocked the public and critics alike by painting too realistically. *The Gross Clinic* (1875), an early masterpiece depicting a surgical procedure performed in an operating amphitheater, spared none of the visual details of an operation and was rejected by the art jury for a Philadelphia exhibition celebrating the first century of American independence. Eakins's starkly realistic style is also evident in *Edith Mahon,* a portrait of a woman gazing emptily and off-center. Her head is tilted slightly, and she looks as though she is mesmerized or, as Aunt Georgiana may be, thinking of the past and what might have been.

INTEGRATING THE LANGUAGE ARTS

Strategic Reading To encourage reading for meaning, ask students to make predictions about what will happen in the story after reading the title, the introductory material, and the first paragraph. Then, ask them to read two pages and to verify the former prediction or alter it because of new information. Ask them to read another two pages and to verify and alter predictions. Have them continue this process until the story is finished.

Mechanics Point out that part of Cather's writing style includes placing adjectives after the noun they modify and that this usage requires commas to set off the adjectives. Example: "This communication, *worn and rubbed,* looking as though . . ." (Sentence 2, Paragraph 1). Ask them to find other examples and to try this syntax in the Writing activity on this page.

Writing: Character Journal After reading the story, which gives Clark's perspective, have students write a series of journal entries or a sequel from Aunt Georgiana's point of view after her visit to Boston. Assign students to write in pairs. ☞

A. Reader's Response: First Thoughts

? After reading the details of the courtship and marriage of Georgiana and Howard, what do you think their marriage will be like? [Sample responses: There may be problems with their differences in age, background, and education. Or even though her family and friends disapprove of the marriage, they will get along fine.]

B. Exploring the Historical Period

The Homestead Act, passed by Congress in 1862, provided for the transfer of 160 acres of public land to a homesteader occupying the land for five years. A small fee was charged. Each homestead occupied one fourth of a section (640 acres), the unit used to measure public land.

C. Humanities Connection

"The Joyous Farmer," a title often translated as "The Jolly Farmer," is one of a series of children's pieces composed by Robert Schumann (1810–1856). Students who have studied piano may have learned this or other Schumann pieces.

D. Humanities Connection

Euryanthe is an opera composed by Carl Maria von Weber (1786–1826), whose work was an early influence on Wagner. In the opera, the relationship between Euryanthe and her lover Adolar is nearly destroyed by a conniving count and Euryanthe's jealous companion Eglantine.

the Boston Conservatory, somewhere back in the latter sixties. One summer, while visiting in the little village among the Green Mountains where her ancestors had dwelt for generations, she had kindled the callow fancy of the most idle and shiftless of all the village lads, and had conceived for this Howard Carpenter one of those extravagant passions which a handsome country boy of twenty-one sometimes inspires in an angular, spectacled woman of thirty. When she returned to her duties in Boston, Howard followed her, and the upshot of this inexplicable infatuation was that she eloped with him, eluding the reproaches of her family and the criticisms of her friends by going with him to the Nebraska frontier. Carpenter, who, of course, had no money, had taken a homestead in Red Willow County, fifty miles from the railroad. There they had measured off their quarter section themselves by driving across the prairie in a wagon, to the wheel of which they had tied a red cotton handkerchief, and counting off its revolutions. They built a dugout in the red hillside, one of those cave dwellings whose inmates so often reverted to primitive conditions. Their water they got from the lagoons where the buffalo drank, and their slender stock of provisions was always at the mercy of bands of roving Indians. For thirty years my aunt had not been further than fifty miles from the homestead.

But Mrs. Springer knew nothing of all this, and must have been considerably shocked at what was left of my kinswoman. Beneath the soiled linen duster which, on her arrival, was the most conspicuous feature of her costume, she wore a black stuff[3] dress, whose ornamentation showed that she had surrendered herself unquestioningly into the hands of a country dressmaker. My poor aunt's figure, however, would have presented astonishing difficulties to any dressmaker. Originally stooped, her shoulders were now almost bent together over her sunken chest. She wore no stays,[4] and her gown, which trailed unevenly behind, rose in a sort of peak over her abdomen. She wore ill-fitting false teeth, and her skin was as yellow as a Mongolian's from constant exposure to a pitiless wind and to the alkaline water which hardens the most transparent cuticle into a sort of flexible leather.

I owed to this woman most of the good that ever came my way in my boyhood, and had a reverential affection for her. During the years when I was riding herd for my uncle, my aunt, after cooking the three meals—the first of which was ready at six o'clock in the morning—and putting the six children to bed, would often stand until midnight at her ironing board, with me at the kitchen table beside her, hearing me recite Latin declensions and conjugations, gently shaking me when my drowsy head sank down over a page of irregular verbs. It was to her, at her ironing or mending, that I read my first Shakespeare, and her old textbook on mythology was the first that ever came into my empty hands. She taught me my scales and exercises, too—on the little parlor organ, which her husband had bought her after fifteen years, during which she had not so much as seen any instrument, but an accordion that belonged to one of the Norwegian farmhands. She would sit beside me by the hour, darning and counting while I struggled with the "Joyous Farmer," but she seldom talked to me about music, and I understood why. She was a pious woman; she had the consolations of religion and, to her at least, her martyrdom was not wholly sordid. Once when I had been doggedly beating out some easy passages from an old score of *Euryanthe* I had found among her music books, she came up to me and, putting her hands over my eyes, gently drew my head back upon her shoulder, saying tremulously, "Don't love it so well, Clark, or it may be taken from you. Oh! dear boy, pray that whatever your sacrifice may be, it be not that."

When my aunt appeared on the morning after her arrival, she was still in a semisomnambulant[5] state. She seemed not to realize that she was in the city where she had spent her youth, the place longed for hungrily half a lifetime. She had been so wretchedly trainsick throughout the journey

3. **stuff:** cloth, usually woolen.

4. **stays:** a corset, or figure-enhancing women's undergarment, stiffened as with whalebone.

5. **semisomnambulant** (sem'ē·säm·nam'byo͞o·lənt): confused and unperceiving, as if sleepwalking.

Words to Own

eluding (ē·lo͞od'iŋ) *v.* used as *adj.:* escaping.
reverential (rev'ə·ren'shəl) *adj.:* deeply respectful.
pious (pī'əs) *adj.:* devoted to one's religion.

Options for Teaching

Classroom Management

Reading Positions Because few of us would choose stiff chairs to sit in while reading, give students some more comfortable options, such as throw rugs, beanbag pillows—or just the option of sitting on the floor, should that seem preferable.

Thought Chart Allow students to write their thoughts, questions, and comments about the story and related classroom activities on a large sheet of paper tacked to the wall. Other students can read these ideas, which may suggest new ways of thinking. Start them off by writing a few thoughts such as these: "Some things we never lose" and "Which life was better for Aunt Georgiana, her Nebraska life or her Boston life?"

Block Scheduling To help maintain student attention during the longer class time, record a story on tape for the class to hear (twenty to twenty-five minutes). After a general discussion, have students work with a partner to create an illustration based on some aspect of the story (twenty-five to thirty minutes). Then, conclude with students completing Making Meanings, or allow time for students to make Reader's Log notes (twenty to twenty-five minutes).

that she had no recollection of anything but her discomfort, and, to all intents and purposes, there were but a few hours of nightmare between the farm in Red Willow County and my study on Newbury Street. I had planned a little pleasure for her that afternoon, to repay her for some of the glorious moments she had given me when we used to milk together in the straw-thatched cowshed and she, because I was more than usually tired, or because her husband had spoken sharply to me, would tell me of the splendid performance of the *Huguenots*[6] she had seen in Paris, in her youth. **E** At two o'clock the Symphony Orchestra was to give a Wagner program, and I intended to take my **F** aunt; though, as I conversed with her, I grew doubtful about her enjoyment of it. Indeed, for her own sake, I could only wish her taste for such things quite dead, and the long struggle mercifully ended at last. I suggested our visiting the Conservatory and the Common before lunch, but she seemed altogether too timid to wish to venture out. **G** She questioned me absently about various changes in the city, but she was chiefly concerned that she had forgotten to leave instructions about feeding half-skimmed milk to a certain weakling calf, "old Maggie's calf, you know, Clark," she explained, evidently having forgotten how long I had been away. She was further troubled because she had neglected to tell her daughter about the freshly opened kit of mackerel in the cellar, which would spoil if it were not used directly.

I asked her whether she had ever heard any of the Wagnerian operas, and found that she had not, though she was perfectly familiar with their respective situations, and had once possessed the piano score of *The Flying Dutchman.* **H** I began to think it would have been best to get her back to Red Willow County without waking her, and regretted having suggested the concert.

From the time we entered the concert hall, however, she was a trifle less passive and inert, and for the first time seemed to perceive her surroundings. I had felt some trepidation lest she might become aware of the absurdities of her attire, or might experience some painful embarrassment at stepping suddenly into the world to which she had been dead for a quarter of a century. But, again, I found how superficially I had judged her. She sat looking about her with eyes as impersonal, almost as stony, as those with which the granite Ramses[7] in a museum watches the froth and fret[8] that ebbs and flows about his pedestal—separated from it by the lonely stretch of centuries. I have seen this same aloofness in old miners who drift into the Brown Hotel at Denver, their pockets full of bullion, their linen soiled, their haggard faces unshaven; standing in the thronged corridors as solitary as though they were still in a frozen camp on the Yukon, conscious that certain experiences have isolated them from their fellows by a gulf no haberdasher[9] could bridge.

We sat at the extreme left of the first balcony, facing the arc of our own and the balcony above us, veritable hanging gardens, brilliant as tulip beds. The matinée audience was made up chiefly of women. One lost the contour of faces and figures, indeed any effect of line whatever, and there was only the color of bodices past counting, the shimmer of fabrics soft and firm, silky and sheer; red, mauve, pink, blue, lilac, purple, ecru, rose, yellow, cream, and white, all the colors that an impressionist finds in a sunlit landscape, with here and there the dead shadow of a frock coat. My Aunt Georgiana regarded them as though they had been so many daubs of tube paint on a palette.

When the musicians came out and took their places, she gave a little stir of anticipation and looked with quickening interest down over the rail at that invariable grouping, perhaps the first wholly familiar thing that had greeted her eye since she had left old Maggie and her weakling calf. I could feel how all those details sank into her soul, for I had not forgotten how they had

6. ***Huguenots*** (hyo͞o′gə·näts): opera by Giacomo Meyerbeer about the violent struggle between Catholics and Protestants in sixteenth-century France.

7. **Ramses** (ram′sēz′): one of the kings of ancient Egypt.

8. **froth and fret:** agitated waters moving around obstacles.

9. **haberdasher** (hab′ər·dash′ər): one who sells men's clothing. A men's clothing store is sometimes called a haberdashery.

Words to Own

inert (in·urt′) *adj.:* dull; slow.

trepidation (trep′ə·dā′shən) *n.:* anxious uncertainty.

E. Critical Reading: Making Inferences

? What is significant about the reference to Georgiana's early life? [Mention of the fact that she had spent her youth in Boston and the later reference to her attending a performance of the *Huguenots* in Paris point up the deprivation she has endured on the isolated farm in Nebraska.]

F. Humanities Connection

Richard Wagner's operas, which were called "music dramas," expanded the music world's conception of opera. Wagner rejected the traditional Italian pattern of set arias separated by recitative, speechlike passages for exposition and advancing the plot. He substituted "endless melody"—that is, melody molded to the words of the libretto. Wagner also originated the leitmotif—a recurring musical phrase that symbolizes a character, emotion, or event in the musical drama.

G. Literary Element: Setting

? What further details do you have of the Nebraska setting? [They have cows, some of which Georgiana has to tend specially. They keep their food in a cellar and do not have good means for preserving food once a can, jar, or barrel has been opened.] What do these details let the reader know about Georgiana? [Possible answers: She has had a difficult life; or she feels responsibility toward her family.]

H. Critical Reading: Making Inferences

? What does Clark mean when he says he began to think it would be best "to get her back to Red Willow County without waking her"? [Possible answer: He does not want her to realize what she has missed in being away from the music and the Conservatory in Boston.]

COOPERATIVE LEARNING

Group Music Because this story may have made students more aware of their own responses to music, some groups may want to hold a music listening session to which the rest of the class may respond either in writing or in discussion. They should consider music they would not wish to leave behind should they have to move.

Technology Tip Have students form groups of three. Ask them to experiment with Wagner's music using multimedia editing software. Have them add special sound effects (feedback, echo) and corresponding visual images. One student could handle the music; a second, the sound effects; and a third, the visual images. Ask the group to present to the class what they compose and to describe changes in the music and the moods the music evokes.

A. Critical Reading: Metacognition

Have students consider what the author wants them to think about the events in this and the next four paragraphs. How did you arrive at your conclusions? [Possible answers: The author wants the reader to focus on Georgiana's reactions to the music, for there is a great deal of description devoted to her responses. Or the author wants the reader to focus on Clark's sympathetic response to Georgiana, for throughout the story, Cather tries to stress that readers should be careful what they sacrifice for love.]

B. Humanities Connection

Wagner's opera *Tannhäuser* (1845) is based on the adventures of a legendary German poet and minstrel of that name. Tannhäuser has been enticed to the Venusberg, a mountain, by the charms of Venus, the goddess of love. He longs to return to the real world and to his lover, Elisabeth. He wants to join the chorus of pilgrims on their way to Rome and to repent of allowing himself to be enticed into the Venusberg. The two motifs are the Pilgrim's chorus and the Venusberg theme. Ask students whether they believe Aunt Georgiana seeks a similar repentance.

C. Critical Reading: Drawing Conclusions

? Why might this line from Verdi's *Il Trovatore* be significant here? [Possible answers: It indicates how much Georgiana misses her home; or it is ironic that the narrator emphasizes his homesickness and fails to mention Georgiana's heartbreak.]

sunk into mine when I came fresh from plowing forever and forever between green aisles of corn, where, as in a treadmill, one might walk from daybreak to dusk without perceiving a shadow of change. The clean profiles of the musicians, the gloss of their linen, the dull black of their coats, the beloved shapes of the instruments, the (A) patches of yellow light thrown by the green shaded lamps on the smooth, varnished bellies of the cellos and the bass viols in the rear, the restless, wind-tossed forest of fiddle necks and bows—I recalled how, in the first orchestra I had ever heard, those long bow strokes seemed to draw the heart out of me, as a conjurer's stick reels out yards of paper ribbon from a hat.

(B) The first number was the *Tannhäuser*[10] overture. When the horns drew out the first strain of the Pilgrim's chorus, my Aunt Georgiana clutched my coat sleeve. Then it was I first realized that for her this broke a silence of thirty years; the inconceivable silence of the plains. With the battle between the two motives, with the frenzy of the Venusberg theme and its ripping of strings, there came to me an overwhelming sense of the waste and wear we are so powerless to combat; and I saw again the tall, naked house on the prairie, black and grim as a wooden fortress; the black pond where I had learned to swim, its margin pitted with sun-dried cattle tracks; the rain-gullied clay banks about the naked house, the four dwarf ash seedlings where the dishcloths were always hung to dry before the kitchen door. The world there was the flat world of the ancients; to the east, a cornfield that stretched to daybreak; to the west, a corral that reached to sunset; between, the conquests of peace, dearer bought than those of war.

The overture closed, my aunt released my coat sleeve, but she said nothing. She sat staring at the orchestra through a dullness of thirty years, through the films made little by little by each of the three hundred and sixty-five days in every one of them. What, I wondered, did she get from it? She had been a good pianist in her day I knew, and her musical education had been broader than that of most music teachers of a quarter of a century ago. She had often told me of Mozart's operas and Meyerbeer's, and I could remember hearing her sing, years ago, certain melodies of Verdi's. When I had fallen ill with a fever in her house she used to sit by my cot in the evening—when the cool, night wind blew in through the faded mosquito netting tacked over the window and I lay watching a certain bright star that burned red above the cornfield—and sing "Home to our (C) mountains, O, let us return!" in a way fit to break the heart of a Vermont boy near dead of homesickness already.

I watched her closely through the prelude to *Tristan and Isolde,* trying vainly to conjecture what that seething turmoil of strings and winds might mean to her, but she sat mutely staring at the violin bows that drove obliquely downward, like the pelting streaks of rain in a summer shower. Had this music any message for her? Had she enough left to at all comprehend this power which had kindled the world since she had left it? I was in a fever of curiosity, but Aunt Georgiana sat silent upon her peak in Darien.[11] She preserved this utter immobility throughout the number from *The Flying Dutchman,* though her fingers worked mechanically upon her black dress, as though, of themselves, they were recalling the piano score they had once played. Poor old hands! They had been stretched and twisted into mere tentacles to hold and lift and knead with; the palms unduly swollen, the fingers bent and knotted—on one of them a thin, worn band that had once been a wedding ring. As I pressed and gently quieted one of those groping hands, I remembered with quivering eyelids their services for me in other days.

(D) Soon after the tenor began the "Prize Song,"[12] I heard a quick drawn breath and turned to my aunt. Her eyes were closed, but the tears were glisten(E)ing on her cheeks, and I think, in a moment more, they were in my eyes as well. It never really died, then—the soul that can suffer so excruciatingly

10. ***Tannhäuser*** (tän′hoi′zər): Wagner's opera about German minstrels in the thirteenth century.

11. **silent . . . Darien:** allusion to John Keats's "On First Looking into Chapman's Homer," a poem about Keats's awe in the presence of a literary work of art.

12. **"Prize Song":** aria from the third act of Wagner's opera *Die Meistersinger von Nürnberg.*

Words to Own

obliquely (ō·blēk′lē) *adv.:* at a slant.

Options for Teaching

Crossing the Curriculum

Music Have student groups study the music mentioned in the story: Weber's *Euryanthe,* Meyerbeer's *Huguenots,* Verdi's *Il Trovatore,* and Wagner's *Tannhäuser, The Flying Dutchman, Tristan and Isolde, The Master Singer,* and *The Ring.* Have them determine how this music might have affected Georgiana and Clark or related to Georgiana's life. Ask them to play selections for the class and to relate their findings.

Geography Have student groups research the differences, physical and social, between Boston and Nebraska at the time the story takes place. Have each group examine an aspect (economy, climate, natural resources, population, or culture) of one of the two locations. Once they have completed their research, have groups report their findings to the class. Then, ask the class to discuss how these differences would have affected Georgiana and Clark.

Museum of Fine Arts, Boston. Charles Henry Hayden Fund (10.35). Photograph courtesy of Museum of Fine Arts, Boston.

At the Opera (1879) by Mary Cassatt. Oil on canvas (31½″ × 25½″).

RESPONDING TO THE ART: ABOUT THE ARTIST

Mary Cassatt (1844–1926) was a noted American painter and etcher. She lived most of her life in France, where she enjoyed the friendship and esteem of Edouard Manet and Edgar Degas. An Impressionist from early in her career, Cassatt is noted for her effective use of color and brushstroke technique. Note that the man in the upper left of the painting is gazing as intently at the woman in the foreground as she is at the performance on stage.

D. Humanities Connection
The "prize" of the midsummer singing festival is the hand of the coveted Eva. The tenor Walther defeats a rival by singing a song that takes music in a new and elevated direction.

E. Literary Element: Climax
? At what point in the story does Georgiana reveal that she has not lost her intense love of music? [When Clark sees the tears "glistening on her cheeks."] What realization does the narrator have at this moment? [That while the soul appears to wither, it may, given the right circumstances, flourish again.]

PROBLEM SOLVING/CRITICAL THINKING

To Go or Not to Go One question raised in this story concerns whether Georgiana made a good choice to go to Nebraska with Howard Carpenter. Ask students what factors Georgiana had to consider, and write these factors on the chalkboard as the students suggest them. Ask them to determine what was important to her and to decide whether she made a good decision. Then, ask students to form groups and to list what people have to choose between in life. Ask them to discuss and take notes on what factors influence each of those decisions. Then, have groups share their findings with the class.

PROFESSIONAL NOTES

Cultural Diversity People who have emigrated from other countries or who have moved from one region of the country to another can empathize with Aunt Georgiana's "culture shock" in moving from sophisticated Boston to 160 isolated acres in Nebraska. Encourage students to share how they feel people cope with leaving a familiar place behind when they move to a strange, new location. ☞

A. Critical Reading: Analyzing Symbolism

In *Twilight of the Gods,* the last part of the *Ring* cycle, Hagen plots against Siegfried, giving him a potion that makes him forget his bride Brünnhilde and think only of Gutrune. Hagen turns Brünnhilde against Siegfried, and she tells him Siegfried's back is unprotected by magic. In a cruel act, Hagen gives Siegfried a potion that restores his memory of Brünnhilde and his love for her. When Siegfried tells Hagen how he won Brünnhilde, Hagen stabs Siegfried in the back. Brünnhilde sacrifices herself on Siegfried's funeral pyre. Why does Cather close the program Georgiana and Clark view with Siegfried's funeral march? [Possible answer: Georgiana is about to return to the farm, and leaving the music behind a second time is metaphorically the death of something vital inside her. Like Siegfried, she awakens to a loss before experiencing the loss again.]

B. Reader's Response: Extending the Text

? What does Cather's story say about how people respond when they make sacrifices? [Sample responses: Like Georgiana, people usually live with their choices instead of making themselves miserable thinking about what might have been. Or although people may regret their choices, they find a way to carry on.]

C. Reader's Response: Challenging the Text

? Do you agree with the implication that Georgiana made the wrong decision? [Sample responses: Yes, she gave up her soul when she gave up her musical development. Or no, love is more important to her, for she could stay in Boston, but she returns to the one she loves.]

and so interminably; it withers to the outward eye only; like that strange moss which can lie on a dusty shelf half a century and yet, if placed in water, grows green again. She wept so throughout the development and elaboration of the melody.

During the intermission before the second half of the concert, I questioned my aunt and found that the "Prize Song" was not new to her. Some years before there had drifted to the farm in Red Willow County a young German, a tramp cowpuncher, who had sung the chorus at Bayreuth,[13] when he was a boy, along with the other peasant boys and girls. Of a Sunday morning he used to sit on his gingham-sheeted bed in the hands' bedroom which opened off the kitchen, cleaning the leather of his boots and saddle, singing the "Prize Song," while my aunt went about her work in the kitchen. She had hovered about him until she had prevailed upon him to join the country church, though his sole fitness for this step, in so far as I could gather, lay in his boyish face and his possession of this divine melody. Shortly afterward he had gone to town on the Fourth of July, been drunk for several days, lost his money at a faro[14] table, ridden a saddled Texan steer on a bet, and disappeared with a fractured collarbone. All this my aunt told me huskily, wanderingly, as though she were talking in the weak lapses of illness.

"Well, we have come to better things than the old *Trovatore*[15] at any rate, Aunt Georgie?" I queried, with a well-meant effort at jocularity.

Her lip quivered and she hastily put her handkerchief up to her mouth. From behind it she murmured, "And you have been hearing this ever since you left me, Clark?" Her question was the gentlest and saddest of reproaches.

A The second half of the program consisted of four numbers from the *Ring,*[16] and closed with Siegfried's funeral march. My aunt wept quietly, but almost continuously, as a shallow vessel overflows in a rainstorm. From time to time her dim eyes looked up at the lights which studded the ceiling, burning softly under their dull glass globes; doubtless they were stars in truth to her. I was still perplexed as to what measure of musical comprehension was left to her, she who had heard nothing but the singing of gospel hymns at Methodist services in the square frame schoolhouse on Section Thirteen for so many years. I was wholly unable to gauge how much of it had been dissolved in soapsuds, or worked into bread, or milked into the bottom of a pail.

The deluge of sound poured on and on; I never knew what she found in the shining current of it; I never knew how far it bore her, or past what happy islands. From the trembling of her face I could well believe that before the last numbers she had been carried out where the myriad graves are, into the gray, nameless burying grounds of the sea; or into some world of death vaster yet, where, from the beginning of the world, hope has lain down with hope and dream with dream and, renouncing, slept.

The concert was over; the people filed out of the hall chattering and laughing, glad to relax and find the living level again, but my kinswoman made no effort to rise. The harpist slipped its green felt cover over his instrument; the flute players shook the water from their mouthpieces; the men of the orchestra went out one by one, leaving the stage to the chairs and music stands, empty as a winter cornfield.

B I spoke to my aunt. She burst into tears and sobbed pleadingly. "I don't want to go, Clark, I don't want to go!"

C I understood. For her, just outside the door of the concert hall, lay the black pond with the cattle-tracked bluffs; the tall, unpainted house, with weather-curled boards; naked as a tower, the crook-backed ash seedlings where the dishcloths hung to dry; the gaunt, molting turkeys picking up refuse about the kitchen door.

13. **Bayreuth** (bī·roit′): Bavarian city that hosts an annual festival of Wagnerian music.
14. **faro** (fer′ō): gambling game played with cards.
15. ***Trovatore:*** opera by the Italian composer Giuseppe Verdi.
16. ***Ring:*** Wagner's *Der Ring des Nibelungen,* a cycle of four operas based on traditional Germanic, Scandinavian, and Icelandic myths and legends.

Words to Own

deluge (del′yo͞oj′) *n.:* rush; flood.
myriad (mir′ē·əd) *adj.:* countless.

Options for Teaching

Assessment Tools

Self-Reflection As a final learning activity for the story, give students these questions to answer.

1. What is important to remember about this story?
2. What helped me most to understand the story and to get ideas from it?
3. What did I learn about life that I had not thought about before?

Students may profit from sharing their ideas in small groups before they write.

Check Test: True-False

1. Clark lives in Boston. [True]
2. When Clark was young, Aunt Georgiana taught him to play the violin. [False]
3. Although she had never studied music formally, Aunt Georgiana had a natural gift. [False]
4. Clark had lived in Vermont. [True]
5. Clark persuades Aunt Georgiana to leave Nebraska and come to live in Boston. [False]

Making Meanings

First Thoughts

1. Georgiana says about music, "Don't love it so well, Clark, or it may be taken from you." How do you feel about her attitude?

> **Reviewing the Text**
>
> **a.** Numerous **flashbacks** in the story provide information about Aunt Georgiana's life after she moved to Nebraska. Describe some of her hardships and disappointments.
>
> **b.** Explain why the narrator feels he owes a great debt to Aunt Georgiana. What special treat has he planned for Aunt Georgiana in Boston? How does she react to this opportunity?

Shaping Interpretations

2. Locate passages in which Clark, the first-person narrator, actually acts as an **omniscient narrator.** How would you characterize Clark? Why do you think Cather didn't use a woman's voice to tell this story?

3. In contrast to the music and the concert hall is the emotional effect of the Nebraska frontier—the **setting** we hear about over and over again in the story. How does Cather want you to feel about the Nebraska setting? What specific images create this "feeling"?

4. Summarize in your own words what you think Clark "understands" at the end of the story.

5. What seems to be Cather's **theme** in the story? How would you say the central episode of the concert contributes to this theme?

Connecting with the Text

6. Would you have attended the concert or avoided it? Refer to the Quickwrite you wrote in your Reader's Log to explain your answer.

Extending the Text

7. If this story were told by a Romantic, how would Aunt Georgiana's visit to Boston have turned out? How do you think a Romantic writer would have described the Nebraska farm setting?

Choices: Building Your Portfolio

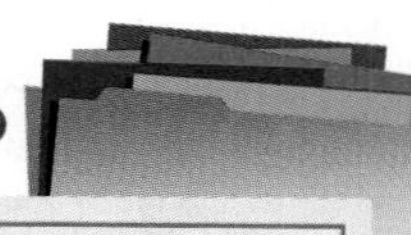

Writer's Notebook

1. Collecting Ideas for a Speculation About Causes and Effects

The powerful attraction of music is a theme that often recurs in Cather's fiction. Find recordings of some of the works of Richard Wagner. As you listen, write down your feelings about the emotional effects of this music. Speculate on the effect Wagner's music might have had on Georgiana's imagination and feelings. Do you think Cather succeeded in conveying the emotional effects anyone might experience in listening to any kind of music? Save your notes for possible use in the Writer's Workshop on page 685.

Critical Writing

2. Linked Lives

In what ways is Aunt Georgiana's experience like the experience of Mrs. Sommers in Kate Chopin's story "A Pair of Silk Stockings" (page 435)? Write a brief essay comparing the two women and their afternoons of escape. Consider each character's life when her story opens, her past life, her wants and needs, and her reactions to her "escape."

Creative Writing

3. The Power of a Setting

Cather's imagery creates a striking contrast between two very different settings—a bustling city with its rich cultural life, and an isolated, windswept farm. Write a description of two very different settings that you might create for a short story. Use vivid images and details to convey the distinct emotional impact of each setting.

Making Meanings

First Thoughts

1. Possible responses: It is better to experience something for a short time and then lose it than not to experience it at all. Or it is better to be protected from possible hurt.

Reviewing the Text

a. Georgiana washed, cleaned, and cooked. She cared for farm animals. The family lived in a dugout and had to get water from the lagoons where the buffalo drank. Her disappointment was being separated from the music she loved.

b. Aunt Georgiana helped bring him up and instilled in him a love of music and literature. To take her to hear the Symphony Orchestra. She seems impassive at first, but she begins to respond to the music and weeps in the second half of the concert.

Shaping Interpretations

2. Some of the passages describing Aunt Georgiana's feelings at the concert shift to an omniscient point of view. Clark is sensitive and supportive. Possible answer: As a male, Clark is freer to move about in society at the time and is, therefore, able to sympathize with the sacrifices Georgiana had made as wife and mother.

3. The setting is unfriendly, stark, and forbidding. Some images that support this effect are the "tall naked house," the "black pond," and "the gaunt molting turkeys picking up refuse about the kitchen door."

4. Possible response: That Georgiana knows she will not experience music in her life again.

5. One theme is people that have the capacity to endure great hardships and to experience a moment of joy again. The music at the matinée is the catalyst for Georgiana's joy in experiencing an afternoon of bittersweetness even though, as with a matinée, it lasts only for a brief time.

Connecting with the Text

6. Possible response: I would have attended since I could not hear such a concert in Nebraska.

Extending the Text

7. **(Synthesis)** Possible response: A Romantic would have likely allowed Georgiana to stay in Boston to enjoy more of the music she loved. The Nebraska setting would have been shown in a positive light rather than as a stark, dark, and unfriendly place.

Choices: Building Your Portfolio

1. **Writer's Notebook** Remind students to save their work. It could be used as prewriting for the Writer's Workshop on p. 685.

Choices: Assessment Criteria For help in evaluating these Choices assignments, see the criteria in the ***Portfolio Management System,*** p. 132.

QUICK PLANNING GUIDE

Into the Story

Author Biography p. 548
Before You Read p. 549
- **Reading Focus: Prior Knowledge** Students reflect on the circus.
- **A Dialogue with the Text: Set a Purpose** Monitor in Reader's Log response to the writer's fantasy
- **Elements of Literature: Description**

Through the Story

"His Father's Earth" pp. 550–556
Words to Own pp. 550–555
Making Meanings p. 557

Beyond the Story

Choices: Building Your Portfolio p. 557
- **Writer's Notebook:** Collect ideas for a speculation about causes and effects
- **Critical Writing:** Compare Wolfe's style and Whitman's style in a brief essay
- **Creative Writing:** Use a catalog of details to describe a setting

ABOUT THE AUTHOR

Thomas Wolfe had no trouble finding a title for his novel *You Can't Go Home Again.* This novel deals with George Webber's return to his hometown and is based on Wolfe's return to a somewhat hostile Asheville after the publication of *Look Homeward, Angel.* Wolfe told the story of his less-than-august experience to a dinner companion, who remarked, "But don't you know you can't go home again?" Thus, the title for his last book was born.

Thomas Wolfe

(1900–1938)

Thomas Wolfe is among the most autobiographical of all American writers. His fiction actually chronicles the events of his Southern upbringing and his later life in New York and Europe.

The youngest of eight children, Wolfe was born in the Smoky Mountains of Asheville, North Carolina. Much of his fiction centers on a character named Eugene Gant, who is the youngest child in a large Southern family and whose life parallels Wolfe's own. When Wolfe was six years old, his parents separated. His mother ran a boardinghouse, which she called The Old Kentucky Home; Wolfe's father, given to bouts of violent drinking, lived a few blocks away behind his stonecutting shop. The boy, very unhappy with the new situation, lived with his mother. Her boardinghouse appears repeatedly in Wolfe's fiction, usually depicted in an unpleasant light.

Culver Pictures.

Wolfe entered the University of North Carolina when he was sixteen. His extraordinary height, six feet six inches, was one reason he was so self-conscious all his life. After graduating in 1920, Wolfe studied playwriting at Harvard. In 1924, he moved to New York City, where he taught at New York University and tried, without success, to have his plays produced. That same year he made the first of seven trips to Europe that he would make during his lifetime.

In 1925, Wolfe became involved with Aline Bernstein, a woman much older than he was; he later wrote extensively about this affair in *The Web and the Rock.* Bernstein and Wolfe spent five years together, in England and in New York, where Wolfe continued to teach and to work on his first and best novel, *Look Homeward, Angel.*

Wolfe completed *Look Homeward, Angel* in 1928; the first draft is said to have filled up more than one suitcase. After several publishers rejected it, Scribner's showed interest. As a result, Wolfe began what would become a remarkable association with Maxwell Perkins, the famous editor who persuaded Wolfe to cut three hundred pages, or about one third, from his enormous story and saw the novel through to publication in 1929.

Wolfe eventually ended his association with Perkins and Scribner's. Before his sudden death in 1938 from an illness, Wolfe had signed up with another publisher, Harper's, and had delivered to them enormous chunks of a new manuscript. Another editor labored over the mass of material and, after Wolfe's death, published several posthumous books, including *You Can't Go Home Again* (1940).

Some readers believe that Wolfe's editors did Wolfe a disservice by reducing his manuscripts to the size of manageable novels. They think that Wolfe wanted to create one huge epic work of fiction based on his own life, just as Walt Whitman had crafted an American epic in "Song of Myself" (page 353). In many ways, Wolfe's greatness can be measured by the magnitude of what he tried, and failed, to accomplish. As William Faulkner (page 713) noted, Thomas Wolfe was "the best failure," a writer who dared "to throw away style, coherence, all the rules of preciseness, to try to put all the experience of the human heart on the head of a pin."

WORDS TO OWN

The following vocabulary words are defined in the Words to Own at the bottom of the pupil's page.

nominal p. 550	languid p. 554
prodigal p. 551	intermittent p. 554
garnished p. 551	frugal p. 555
exulted p. 552	opulent p. 555
vistas p. 554	surmise p. 555

PORTFOLIO ASSESSMENT

Portfolio Assessment For help with self- and teacher assessment of reading skills, see the *Portfolio Management System,* pp. 48–49.

BEFORE YOU READ
HIS FATHER'S EARTH

Reading Focus
When the Circus Comes to Town

In the past, when much of the United States was made up of small towns and rural areas, the most exciting annual event was the coming of the circus. It began with a parade—colorfully dressed band members, a calliope piping its shrill steam-whistle notes, wild animals roaring in rolling cages, elephants lumbering along in single file, bareback riders on prancing ponies, and a wild array of clowns, acrobats, and jugglers. No wonder many young observers harbored the secret dream of running away to join the circus—it was the embodiment of fantasy and adventure.

A Dialogue with the Text

The young dreamer in this story—perhaps Wolfe himself—imagines himself joining the circus to sell tickets, put up posters, and barter with farmers for fresh food. As you read, take notes on the effects his fantasy has on you. In what ways is it like a fairy tale? Do you feel pleasantly swept along in his fantasy, or does it create another response in you? As you read through to the end of the story, write your ideas about what "magic congruence" is shared by his "father's earth" and the circus as Wolfe describes it.

Elements of Literature
Description

Just as Napoleon realized the importance of food for his troops ("An army marches on its stomach"), so Wolfe, in this story, envisions a circus troupe eating its way through forty states. Wolfe's daydream, an exuberant **description** of the states' geographical features and abundant crops, coincides with the daydream of arriving at his father's house—a place that is not real but is pure fantasy. As you read, look for Wolfe's long descriptive lists of foods, people, and places.

> **Description** is a form of writing that uses sensory language to create images and to convey moods or emotions.
>
> *For more on Description, see the Handbook of Literary Terms.*

American circus posters from the 1920s and 1930s.

The Granger Collection, New York.

Into the Story

Using BEFORE YOU READ p. 549

Reading Focus
Have students brainstorm and list images that come to mind when they hear the word *circus*. Then, have students brainstorm a list of foods they usually associate with a circus. Tell students to watch for the connection between the circus and food as they read.

A Dialogue with the Text
As students read and take notes on how the fantasy affects them, have them consider the largely autobiographical nature of Wolfe's writing. Have them write down what Wolfe might be trying to say about the circus and "his father's earth."

Elements of Literature
Remind students of Walt Whitman's catalogs of descriptions. Point out that although this selection is prose, they might find some similarities between Wolfe's style and Whitman's style. Encourage students to jot down examples of poetic descriptions as they read.

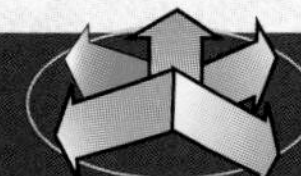

PROGRAM MANAGER

- **Planning Instruction** See Teaching Notes, *Teaching Resources B,* p. 4, for objectives, a summary, literary elements, and other information.
- **Instructional Support** See Graphic Organizer for Active Reading, *Teaching Resources B,* p. 17, for an Into the Story activity.
- **Instructional Support** See Fine Art Transparency 11.1. Review teacher's notes for transparencies in the *Audiovisual Resources Binder.*
- **Assessment** See Selection Test, *Test Booklet,* pp. 131–132.
- **Language Link** For practice in active voice and in identifying common usage problems, see Language Links, *Teaching Resources B,* pp. 18–21, and *Language and Writing Skills Worksheets,* pp. 1–2, 4–5.
- **Reinforcement** Use the Words to Own worksheet in *Teaching Resources B,* p. 22.

Through the Story

A. Expansion
Wolfe once wrote that the search for a father was the controlling **theme** of all his novels. In this story, the search embraces both an urge to wander and a yearning for home.

B. Critical Reading: Predicting
? After reading the title and the first two paragraphs, what do you think is going to happen in the story? [Possible answer: The boy only imagines he joins the circus.]

Metacognition How did you derive your answer? [Possible answer: In re-reading the first two paragraphs, one can find clues about imagination. In the first, images come to him in a "magic congruence." In the second, "He thought" and "in his vision" imply imagination.]

Fall Plowing (1931) by Grant Wood. Oil on canvas.
From the Deere & Company Art Collection, Moline, Illinois. © 1997 Estate of Grant Wood/Licensed by VAGA, New York.

His Father's Earth

Thomas Wolfe

A As the boy stood looking at the circus with his brother, there came to him two images, which had haunted his childhood and the life of every boy who ever lived, but were now for the first time seen together with an instant and magic congruence.[1] And these two images were the images of the circus and his father's earth.

B He thought then he had joined a circus and started on the great tour of the nation with it. It was spring: The circus had started in New England and worked westward and then southward as the summer and autumn came on. His nominal duties—for, in his vision, every incident, each face and voice and circumstance were blazing real as life itself—were those of ticket seller, but in this tiny show, everyone did several things: The performers helped put up and take down the tents, load and unload the wagons, and the roustabouts[2] and business people worked wherever they were needed.

The boy sold tickets, but he also posted bills and bartered with tradesmen and farmers in new places for fresh food. He became very shrewd and clever at this work, and loved to do it—some old, sharp, buried talent for shrewd trading, that had come to him from his mountain blood, now aided him. He could get the finest, freshest meats and vegetables at the lowest prices. The circus people were tough and hard, they always had a fierce and ravenous hunger, they would not accept bad food and cooking, they fed stupendously, and they always had the best of everything.

1. **congruence** (käŋ′gro͞o·əns): harmony.

2. **roustabouts** (roust′ə·bouts′): circus workers who handle various duties, including setting up and taking down tents.

Words to Own
nominal (näm′ə·nəl) *adj.*: very small.

Options for Teaching

Strategies for Inclusion

Less Proficient Readers Some readers may get bogged down in Wolfe's long sentences. Read the first paragraphs of the story aloud to them until they get accustomed to Wolfe's style. Ask them questions about the meaning of each paragraph after you read it. Make sure they understand that everything following the first paragraph is a daydream. Stop reading aloud when they answer your questions quickly and accurately. Have them finish the reading on their own.

Spatial Students talented in drawing may want to illustrate Wolfe's daydream in a single drawing or a series of drawings showing either the bounty of food or acres of land filling his imagination.

English Language Development To help prepare students for the descriptive catalogs of foods, ask them to write a grocery list with five to ten important foods on it. Initially, this exercise will allow you to gauge whether students have the basic vocabulary needed to understand the descriptions. Then, read aloud the fourth paragraph of the story (found on p. 551), which begins, "Usually the circus would arrive . . ." as they follow in their books. Point out to students that even though this paragraph is essentially a list, the descriptive language influences the way readers feel and is one way that Wolfe creates mood.

Usually the circus would arrive at a new town very early in the morning, before daybreak. He would go into town immediately: He would go to the markets, or with farmers who had come in for the circus. He felt and saw the purity of first light, he heard the sweet and sudden lutings of first birds, and suddenly he was filled with the earth and morning in new towns, among new men: He walked among the farmers' wagons, and he dealt with them on the spot for the prodigal plenty of their wares—the country melons bedded in sweet hay of wagons, the cool sweet prints of butter wrapped in clean wet cloths, with dew and starlight still on them, the enormous battered cans foaming with fresh milk, the new laid eggs which he bought by the gross and hundred dozens, the tender limy pullets by the score, the rude country wagons laden to the rim with heaped abundancies—with delicate bunches of green scallions, the heavy red ripeness of huge tomatoes, the sweet-leaved lettuces crisp as celery, the fresh podded peas and the succulent young beans, as well as the potatoes spotted with the loamy earth, the powerful winey odor of the apples, the peaches, and the cherries, the juicy corn stacked up in shocks of living green, and the heavy blackened rinds of home-cured hams and bacons.

As the market opened, he would begin to trade and dicker with the butchers for their finest cuts of meat: They would hold great roasts up in their gouted[3] fingers, they would roll up tubs of fresh ground sausage, they would smack with their long palms the flanks of beeves[4] and porks: He would drive back to the circus with a wagon full of meat and vegetables.

At the circus ground the people were already in full activity. He could hear the wonderful timed tattoo[5] of sledges on driven stakes, the shouts of men riding animals down to water, the slow clank and pull of mighty horses, the heavy rumble of the wagons as they rolled down off the circus flatcars. By now the eating table would be erected, and as he arrived, he could see the cooks already busy at their ranges, the long tables set up underneath the canvas with their rows of benches, their tin plates and cups, their strong readiness. There would be the amber indescribable pungency of strong coffee, and the smell of buckwheat batter.

And the circus people would come in for their breakfast: Hard and tough, for the most part decent and serious people, the performers, the men and women, the acrobats, the riders, the tumblers, the clowns, the jugglers, the contortionists, and the balancers would come in quietly and eat with a savage and inspired intentness.

The food they ate was as masculine and fragrant as the world they dwelt in: It belonged to the stained world of mellow sun-warmed canvas, the clean and healthful odor of the animals, and the mild sweet lyric nature of the land in which they lived as wanderers, and it was there for the asking with a fabulous and stupefying plenty, golden and embrowned: They ate stacks of buckwheat cakes, smoking hot, soaked in hunks of yellow butter which they carved at will with a wide free gesture from the piled prints on the table, and which they garnished (if they pleased) with ropes of heavy black molasses, or with the lighter, freer maple syrup.

They ate big steaks for breakfast, hot from the pan and lashed with onions, they ate whole melons, crammed with the ripeness of the deep pink meat, rashers of bacon, and great platters of fried eggs, or eggs scrambled with calves' brains, they helped themselves from pyramids of fruit piled up at intervals on the table—plums, peaches, apples, cherries, grapes, oranges, and bananas—they had great pitchers of thick cream to pour on everything, and they washed their hunger down with pint mugs of strong deep-savored coffee.

For their midday meal they would eat fiercely, hungrily, with wolfish gusts, mightily, with knit brows and convulsive movements of their corded throats. They would eat great roasts of beef with crackled hides, browned in their juices, rare and tender, hot chunks of delicate pork with hems of fragrant fat, delicate young boiled chickens, only a mouthful for these ravenous jaws, twelve-pound pot roasts cooked for hours in an iron pot with

3. **gouted** (gout′id): swollen as if suffering from gout, a kind of arthritis that affects the joints.
4. **beeves:** alternate plural of *beef.*
5. **tattoo:** pounding.

WORDS TO OWN

prodigal (präd′i·gəl) *adj.:* extremely abundant.
garnished (gär′nisht) *v.:* topped.

C. Literary Element: Alliteration
Point out Wolfe's use of alliteration ("prodigal plenty"), a device that can emphasize a point.

D. Literary Element: Catalog
Here begins the first catalog. What is the effect of this list of foods? [Possible answers: Wolfe does not simply name the foods but describes them at length—their size, texture, smell, taste, and color. The foods represent the area the circus visits.]

E. Literary Element: Description
? What senses has Wolfe appealed to thus far? [Taste—of the foods, sight—of the circus activities and of food, touch—of the sun and of the meat, sound—of the birds and of circus noises, smell—of the coffee.]

F. Expansion
Wolfe linked his writing with that of Walt Whitman, Mark Twain, and Sherwood Anderson, writers who had a poet's vision. Here, the land itself has a lyrical nature. In what sense are Wolfe's descriptions highly lyrical? [Possible answers: The rhythmic cadences; the profusion of sensory details.]

G. Reader's Response: First Thoughts
? Which foods particularly appeal to you? What would you list in your own catalog of favorite foods? [Sample responses: Steak, cherries, cobblers, artichokes, or sorbet.]

INTEGRATING THE LANGUAGE ARTS

Strategic Reading Demonstrate the power of Wolfe's lists with group readings of portions of the story. Divide the class into groups of six or seven and designate one student in each group to read the narrative material. When there is a list, ask others to read one item each, beginning with the student on the narrator's left. They should try to read without breaks between readers; their voices will indicate that a new item has been given. Students continue reading around the circle until the list is completed each time.

Language and Style Descriptive writing often evokes the reader's senses: sight, smell, taste, hearing, and touch. Ask students to look carefully at the sixth paragraph of the story (found on p. 551) and to answer these questions.

1. Which senses does Wolfe appeal to in this paragraph? [Hearing, sight, smell.]
2. What specific words evoke these senses? (Be sure the students know the appropriate definition of *tattoo.*) [Hearing: *tattoo, shouts, clank, rumble, rolled.* Sight: *busy cooks, tables, canvas, benches, tin plates, cups.* Smell: *pungency of strong coffee, smell of buckwheat batter.*]

Ask students to consider using vocabulary that appeals to the senses when they write their own descriptions in the Cooperative Learning: Group Writing activity on p. T553.

A. Humanities Connection
Have students compare Wolfe's vision of America with the Romantic view as described on pp. 138–150. [Like the Romantics, Wolfe rhapsodizes on the wonders of America—not its scenery or people, but its vast cornucopia of food. Later Wolfe glorifies Nature.]

B. Literary Element: Figures of Speech
? What figures of speech do you notice in this particularly poetic paragraph? [Metaphor—"the moon's man"; personification—"stars drown," "birth of light."]

C. Reader's Response: Shaping Interpretations
? Why does the boy find so much joy procuring food for the circus? [Sample responses: He is appreciated and loved; or he enjoys eating.]

D. Literary Element: Description
? What words suggest that the circus world is in conflict with the "real world"? ["phantasmal and unreal"; "the enemy"]

new carrots, onions, sprouts, and young potatoes, together with every vegetable that the season yielded: huge roasting ears of corn, smoking hot, stacked like cordwood on two-foot platters, tomatoes cut in slabs with wedges of okra and succotash, and raw onion, mashed potatoes whipped to a creamy smother, boats swimming with pure beef gravy, new carrots, turnips, fresh peas cooked in butter, and fat string beans seasoned with the flavor of big chunks of cooking-pork. In addition, they had every fruit that the place and time afforded: hot crusty apple, peach and cherry pies, encrusted with cinnamon, puddings and cakes of every sort, and blobbering cobblers inches deep.

Thus the circus moved across America, from town to town, from state to state, eating its way from Maine into the great plains of the West, eating its way along the Hudson and the Mississippi Rivers, eating its way across the prairies and from the North into the South, eating its way across the flat farmlands of the Pennsylvania Dutch colony, the eastern shore of Maryland and back again across the states of Virginia, North Carolina, Tennessee, and Florida—eating all good things that this enormous, this inevitably bountiful and abundant cornucopia[6] of a continent yielded.

They ate the cod, bass, mackerel, halibut, clams, and oysters of the New England coast, the terrapin[7] of Maryland, the fat beeves, porks, and cereals of the Middle West, and they had, as well, the heavy juicy peaches, watermelons, cantaloupes of Georgia, the fat sweet shad of the Carolina coasts, and the rounded and exotic citrus fruits of the tropics: the oranges, tangerines, bananas, kumquats, lemons, guavas down in Florida, together with a hundred other fruits and meats—the Vermont turkeys, the mountain trout, the bunched heaviness of the Concord grapes, the red winey bulk of the Oregon apples, as well as the clawed, shelled, and crusted dainties, the crabs, the clams, the pink-meated lobsters that grope their way along the sea floors of America.

The boy awoke at morning in three hundred towns with the glimmer of starlight on his face; he was the moon's man; then he saw light quicken in the east, he saw the pale stars drown, he saw the birth of light, he heard the lark's wing, the bird tree, the first liquorous liquefied lutings, the ripe-aired trillings, the plumskinned birdnotes, and he heard the hoof and wheel come down the streets of the nation. He exulted in his work as food-producer for the circus people, and they loved him for it. They said there had never been anyone like him—they banqueted exultantly, with hoarse gulpings and with joy, and they loved him.

Slowly, day by day, the circus worked its way across America, through forty states and through a dozen weathers. It was a little world that moved across the enormous loneliness of the earth, a little world that each day began a new life in new cities, and that left nothing to betray where it had been save a litter of beaten papers, the droppings of the camel and the elephant in Illinois, a patch of trampled grass, and a magical memory.

The circus men knew no other earth but this; the earth came to them with the smell of the canvas and the lion's roar. They saw the world behind the lights of the carnival, and everything beyond these lights was phantasmal and unreal to them; it lived for them within the circle of the tent as men and women who sat on benches, as the posts they came to, and sometimes as the enemy.

Their life was filled with the strong joy of food, with the love of traveling, and with danger and hard labor. Always there was the swift violence of change and movement, of putting up and tearing down, and sometimes there was the misery of rain and sleet, and mud above the ankles, of wind that shook their flimsy residence, that ripped the tent stakes from their moorings in the earth and lifted out the great center pole as if it were a match. Now they must wrestle with the wind and hold their dwelling to the earth; now they must fight the weariness of mud and push their heavy wagons through the slime; now, cold and wet and wretched, they must sleep on piles of canvas, upon the flatcars in a driving rain, and sometimes they must fight the enemy—the drunk, the savage, the violent enemy, the bloody man, who dwelt in every place. Sometimes it was the city

6. **cornucopia** (kôr′nyo͞o·kō′pē·ə): Also called a horn of plenty, a cornucopia is a symbol of fullness and abundance.
7. **terrapin** (ter′ə·pin): turtles.

Words to Own
exulted (eg·zult′id) *v.:* rejoiced greatly.

Options for Teaching

Integrating the Language Arts

Mechanics Review the punctuation rule for the use of a colon preceding a list (See Language Handbook, pp. 1244–1245). In the tenth paragraph (found on pp. 551–552), for example, Wolfe does not use the colon before the list because the items are direct objects that follow the verb of the main sentence. In the last sentence of the paragraph, however, the colon is used because the independent clause is completed before the list is given. Have students apply these rules to their own descriptions that they generate in the Cooperative Learning: Group Writing activity on p. T553.

Classroom Management

Exit Slips During the last five minutes of each class period, ask students to write down their most important observations and questions. Collect their notes as students leave class. You can use some of these ideas to begin the next class period.

RESPONDING TO THE PHOTOGRAPH: VISUAL LITERACY

To what part of the photograph is your attention drawn? [Possible response: First to the stage and then to the audience.] How did the photographer compose the picture and what effect does the composition have on the viewer? [Possible responses: He took the photograph from the back of the crowd, looking down at the stage. The camera was placed at the level of the heads of the people in front of him. The perspective conveys a feeling of actually being present because the view is the same that the audience has. Because the photograph was not taken from the stage or facing the audience, the viewer's own reaction is probably similar to the audience's reaction.]

COOPERATIVE LEARNING

Group Writing Ask student groups to write their own catalogs to describe an event or a place. Divide the class into small groups of three or four students each, asking each group to choose

- a leader (to keep things moving)
- a writer (to record the group's list)
- a timer (to keep students on task)
- a parallel structure expert (to make sure the items on the list are all the same part of speech)

Then, students should choose their topic and begin composing orally as the writer records what they decide to write. Display the finished products or have the groups read their catalogs aloud.

Group Reading Divide the class into pairs. Ask students to alternate reading aloud to each other, reading approximately a column each time. After one student reads, the other summarizes what has been read. The reader fills in any omitted information. Then the other student reads aloud, and they continue the same process until they finish the story.

A. Literary Element: Description
Striking contrasts are a hallmark of Wolfe's style. What dramatic contrasting picture of America does Wolfe present here? [The savage violence contrasts with the earlier picture of a bountifully productive land.]

B. Literary Element: Theme
? How can the boy recognize his father's land? [This is a daydream of wish fulfillment. His father's land is in the core of his being; it is his heart's desire.]

C. Language Note: Parallel Structure
Point out the parallel structure in this paragraph. Wolfe describes the father's land in prepositional phrases, most consisting of a preposition, pronoun, adjective, and noun. Twice he leaves out the adjective, but the structure is basically the same. Remind students that when they combine items in a series, the items should all be the same part of speech.

thug, sometimes the mill hands of the South, sometimes the miners in a Pennsylvania town—the circus people cried, "Hey, rube!"[8] and fought them with fist and foot, with pike and stake, and the boy saw and knew it all.

When the men in a little town barricaded the street against their parade, they charged the barricade with their animals, and once the sheriff tried to stop the elephant by saying: "Now, damn ye, if you stick your . . . damned trunk another inch, I'll shoot."

(A) The circus moved across America foot by foot, mile by mile. He came to know the land. It was rooted in his blood and his brain forever—its food, its fruit, its fields and forests, its deserts, and its mountains, its savage lawlessness. He saw the crimes and the violence of the people with pity, with mercy, and with tenderness: He thought of them as if they were children. They smashed their neighbors' brains out with an ax, they disembowelled one another with knives, they were murderous and lost upon this earth they dwelt upon as strangers.

The tongueless blood of the murdered men ran down into the earth, and the earth received it. Upon this enormous and indifferent earth the little trains rattled on over ill-joined rails that loosely bound the sprawling little towns together. Lost and lonely, brief sawings of wood and plaster and cheap brick ugliness, the little towns were scattered like encampments through the wilderness. Only the earth remained, which all these people had barely touched, which all these people dwelt upon but could not possess.

Only the earth remained, the savage and lyrical earth with its rude potency, its thousand vistas, its heights and slopes and levels, with all its violence and delicacy, the terrible fecundity,[9] decay, and growth, its fierce colors, its vital bite and sparkle, its exultancy of space and wandering. And the memory of this earth, the memory of all this universe of sight and sense, was rooted in this boy's heart and brain forever. It fed the hungers of desire and wandering, it breached the walls of his secret and withdrawn spirit. And for every memory of place and continent, of enormous coffee-colored rivers and eight hundred miles of bending wheat, of Atlantic coast and midland prairie, of (B) raw red Piedmont[10] and tropic flatness, there was always the small, fecund, perfect memory of his father's land, the dark side of his soul and his heart's desire, which he had never seen, but which he knew with every atom of his life, the strange phantasmal haunting of man's memory. It was a fertile, nobly swelling land, and it was large enough to live in, walled with fulfilled desire.

(C) Abroad in this ocean of earth and vision he thought of his father's land, of its great red barns and nobly swelling earth, its clear familiarity and its haunting strangeness, and its dark and secret heart, its magnificent, its lovely and tragic beauty. He thought of its smell of harbors and its rumors of the seas, the city, and the ships, its wine-red apples and its brown-red soil, its snug weathered houses, and its lyric unutterable ecstasy.

A wonderful thing happened. One morning he awoke suddenly to find himself staring straight up at the pulsing splendor of the stars. At first he did not know where he was, but he knew instantly, even before he looked about him, that he had visited this place before. The circus train had stopped in the heart of the country, for what reason he did not know. He could hear the languid and intermittent breathing of the engine, the strangeness of men's voices in the dark, the casual stamp of the horses in their cars, and all around him the attentive and vital silence of the earth.

Suddenly he raised himself from the pile of canvas on which he slept. It was the moment just before dawn: Against the east, the sky had already begun to whiten with the first faint luminosity of day, the invading tides of light crept up the sky, drowning the stars out as they went. The train had halted by a little river which ran swift and deep next to the tracks, and now he knew that what at first had been the sound of silence was the swift and ceaseless music of the river.

There had been rain the night before, and now

8. **rube:** unsophisticated person, usually from the country. The term is used as a taunt.
9. **fecundity** (fē·kun′də·tē): fertility.

10. **Piedmont** (pēd′mänt): hilly land east of the Appalachian Mountains.

Words to Own
vistas (vis′təz) *n. pl.:* views.
languid (laŋ′gwid) *adj.:* weak, as from exhaustion.
intermittent (in′tər·mit′'nt) *adj.:* pausing occasionally.

OPTIONS FOR TEACHING

CROSSING THE CURRICULUM

Music Ask students what music would be appropriate to complement this story. Ask them to explain their choices. Play that music as they work on projects or activities.

Geography Have groups of students trace the path of the circus as the boy imagines it. One student could plot the course on a map or create a map showing the course, a second could illustrate it with the various foods, and a third could draw the geographic features of each region. Display maps on a bulletin board.

Social Sciences Some students may be interested in researching the history of circuses in the United States and their impact on the lives of the people who enjoyed them. Have students create time capsules from various periods in circus history for the class to open. They should write magazine and newspaper articles as though they were written in the time period, draw illustrations, and include any small objects that may have been found at the circus at that time.

the river was filled with the sweet clean rain-drenched smell of earthy deposits. He could see the delicate white glimmer of young birch trees leaning from the banks, and on the other side he saw the winding whiteness of the road. Beyond the road, and bordering it, there was an orchard with a wall of lichened stone: A row of apple trees, gnarled and sweet, spread their squat twisted branches out across the road, and in the faint light he saw that they were dense with blossoms: The cool intoxication of their fragrance overpowered him.

As the wan light grew, the earth and all its contours emerged sharply, and he saw again the spare, gaunt loneliness of the earth at dawn, with all its sweet and sudden cries of spring. He saw the worn and ancient design of lichened rocks, the fertile soil of the baked fields, he saw the kept order, the frugal cleanliness, with its springtime overgrowth, the mild tang of opulent greenery. There was an earth with fences, as big as a man's heart, but not so great as his desire, and after his giant wanderings over the prodigal fecundity of the continent, this earth was like a room he once had lived in. He returned to it as a sailor to a small closed harbor, as a man, spent with the hunger of his wandering, comes home. **D**

Instantly he recognized the scene. He knew that he had come at last into his father's land. It was a magic that he knew but could not speak; he stood upon the lip of time, and all of his life now seemed the mirage of some wizard's spell—the spell of canvas and the circus ring, the spell of the tented world which had possessed him. Here was his home, brought back to him while he slept, like a forgotten dream. Here was the dark side of his soul, his heart's desire, his father's country, the earth his spirit dwelt on as a child. He knew every inch of the landscape, and he knew, past reason, doubt, or argument, that home was not three miles away. **E**

He got up at once and leaped down to the earth; he knew where he would go. Along the track there was the slow swing and dance of the brakemen's lamps, that moving, mournful, and beautiful cloud of light along the rails of the earth, that he had seen so many times. Already the train was in motion; its bell tolled and its heavy trucks rumbled away from him. He began to walk back along the tracks, for less than a mile away, he knew, where the stream boiled over the lip of a dam, there was a bridge. When he reached the bridge, a deeper light had come: The old red brick of the mill emerged sharply and with the tone and temper of deep joy fell sheer into bright shining waters.

He crossed the bridge and turned left along the road: Here it moved away from the river, among fields and through dark woods—dark woods bordered with stark poignancy of fir and pine, with the noble spread of maples, shot with the naked whiteness of birch. Here was the woodland maze: the sweet density of the brake[11] and growth. Sharp thrummings, woodland flitters broke the silence. His steps grew slow, he sat upon a wall, he waited.

Now rose the birdsong in first light, and suddenly he heard each sound the birdsong made. Like a flight of shot the sharp fast skaps of sound arose. With chittering bicker, fast-fluttering skirrs of sound, the palmy honeyed bird-cries came. Smooth drops and nuggets of bright gold they were. Now sang the birdtrees filled with lutings in bright air: The thrums, the lark's wing, and tongue-trilling chirrs arose now. The little nameless cries arose and fell with liquorous liquefied lutings, with lirruping chirp, plumbellied smoothness, sweet lucidity. **F**

And now there was the rapid kweet kweet kweet kweet kweet of homing birds and their pwee pwee pwee: others with sharp cricketing stitch, a mosquito buzz with thin metallic tongues, while some with rusty creakings, high shrew's caws, with eerie rasp, with harsh far calls—all birds that are awake in the sweet woodland tangles: And above, there passed the whirr of hidden wings, the strange lost cry of the unknown birds, in full flight now; in which the sweet confusion of their cries was mingled.

Then he got up and went along that road where, he knew, like the prophetic surmise of a dream, the house of his father's blood and kin lay hidden. At length, he came around a bending in

11. **brake:** thicket; marshy, overgrown area.

Words to Own

frugal (froo͞'gəl) *adj.:* thrifty; economical.
opulent (äp'yoo͞·lənt) *adj.:* abundant; plentiful.
surmise (sər·mīz') *n.:* guess.

D. Literary Element: Simile
Have students note the powerful similes; there are five in these two sentences. What conflict is expressed through them? [The conflict between home and wanderlust, between stability and freedom.]

E. Literary Element: Theme
This passage echoes a similar one in the fourth full paragraph on p. 554. Why do you think Wolfe repeats the idea? [Possible answer: The passage points to the theme and is a kind of refrain.]

F. Language Note: Diction
? What poetic technique dominates this passage? [Onomatopoeia, but note also the alliteration of "liquorous liquefied lutings," repeated from p. 552.] What unusual word choices and made-up words does Wolfe use? [*Skirrs, birdtrees, lutings,* and *chirrs.*] What is the overall effect of this passage? [It captures the sound of birdsong.] Is this legitimate use of language in a serious prose piece? [Possible answers: It is effective; or it is excessive.]

PROBLEM SOLVING/CRITICAL THINKING

Can You Go Home Again? The boy in Wolfe's story experiences a conflict between wanting to travel the country and longing to return home. Ask the class to list on a chart like the following the advantages and disadvantages of striking out on one's own and of remaining close to home. Invite students to consider whether one can have the best of both worlds.

	Traveling	Remaining
Advantages	[seeing new places]	[having security]
Disadvantages	[unpleasant accommodations]	[lack of change]

PROFESSIONAL NOTES

Cultural Diversity Invite students to research various professions and cultures that have a nomadic lifestyle. Ask them to consider how these groups select sites, make a living, and entertain themselves.

Thematic Connections: "Loss and Redemption" Have students discuss why the boy imagines he is part of the circus and what he may feel he has lost. Ask students to consider how this story differs from "A Wagner Matinée" and the extent to which the characters in each achieve redemption. Students may wish to compare Cather's use of music in her story to Wolfe's use of food in his narrative. ☞

A. Reader's Response: Shaping Interpretations

? What insight has the boy gained? [Sample responses: The boy sees that he cannot both have a home and travel all the time. Or he sees that his childhood has passed and he is no longer the same person.]

B. Critical Reading: Drawing Conclusions

? What wishes does the boy fulfill in these two fantasies? [To have a sense of love and belonging, of joy in work, of bounty.]

The Granger Collection, New York.

the road, he left the wooded land, he passed by hedges and saw the old white house, set in the shoulder of the hill, worn like care and habit in the earth; clean and cool, it sat below the clean dark shelter of its trees: A twist of morning smoke coiled through its chimney.

Then he turned in to the rutted road that led up to the house, and at this moment the enormous figure of a powerful old man appeared around the corner prophetically bearing a smoked ham in one huge hand. And when the boy saw the old man, a cry of greeting burst from his throat, and the old man answered with a roar of welcome that shook the earth.

Then the old man dropped his ham, and waddled forward to meet the boy: They met half down the road, and the old man crushed him in his hug; they tried to speak but could not; they embraced again and in an instant all the years of wandering, the pain of loneliness and the fierce hungers of desire, were scoured away like a scum of frost from a bright glass.

He was a child again, he was a child that had stood upon the lip and leaf of time and heard the quiet tides that move us to our death, and he knew that the child could not be born again, the book of the days could never be turned back, old errors and confusions never righted. And he wept with sorrow for all that was lost and could never be regained, and with joy for all that had been recovered.

A Suddenly he saw his youth as men on hilltops might look at the whole winding course of rivers to the sea, he saw the blind confusions of his wanderings across the earth, the horror of man's little stricken mote of earth against immensity, and he remembered the proud exultancy of his childhood when all the world lay like a coin between his palms, when he could have touched the horned rim of the moon, when heroes and great actions bent before him.

And he wept, not for himself, but out of love and pity for every youth that ever hoped and wandered and was alone. He had become a man, and he had in him unique glory that belongs to men alone, and that makes them great, and from which they shape their mightiest songs and legends. For out of their pain they utter first a cry for wounded self, then, as their vision deepens, widens, the universe of their marvelous sense leaps out and grips the universe; they feel contempt for gods, respect for men alone, and with the indifference of a selfless passion, enact earth out of a lyric cry.

At this moment, also, two young men burst from the house and came running down the road to greet him. They were powerful and heavy young men, already beginning to show signs of that epic and sensual grossness that distinguished their father. Like their father, they recognized the boy instantly, and in a moment he was engulfed in their mighty energies, borne up among them to the house. And they understood all he wanted to say, but could not speak, and they surrounded him with love and lavish heapings of his plate. **B** And the boy knew the strange miracle of return to the dark land of his heart's desire, the father's land which haunts men like a dream they never knew.

Such were the twin images of the circus and his father's land which were to haunt his dreams and waking memory and which now, as he stood there with his brother looking at the circus, fused instantly to a living whole and came to him in a blaze of light.

And in this way, before he had ever set foot upon it, he came for the first time to his father's earth.

OPTIONS FOR TEACHING

ASSESSMENT TOOLS

Self-Reflection Have students answer each of the following items and rate themselves according to the following scale: 1=rarely, 2=sometimes, or 3=always.

_____ **1.** I note words and ideas that interest me or puzzle me as I am reading.

_____ **2.** I try to predict what will happen next as I am reading.

_____ **3.** I jot down questions and ideas for discussion or writing as I am reading.

Check Test: Fill in the Blank

1. The two images that come to the boy as he stands looking at the circus are __________. [the circus and his father's earth]
2. The boy imagines that he spends some of his time selling tickets, but he spends most of his time __________. [buying or trading for food]
3. The circus people eat food that comes from __________. [all over America]
4. On his travels the boy arrives finally at __________. [his father's house (land)]
5. At the end of the story, the boy is greeted by three people: __________. [his father and his two brothers]

MAKING MEANINGS

First Thoughts

1. Look back over the notes you made in your Reader's Log. What words would you use to describe your response to this story?

Reviewing the Text

a. Which words or passages tell you that Wolfe is describing a fantasy and not reality?

b. What examples of **onomatopoeia, alliteration,** and other poetic devices give Wolfe's story the "sound" of poetry?

Shaping Interpretations

2. Wolfe depicts his father as a nurturer—a male version of the "earth mother." What details help create that picture?
3. How does the world of the circus differ from "his father's earth"? What similarities are there in what the boy does and what the father represents?
4. How do **descriptions** of birdsong bring together descriptions of circus life and of home?
5. Wolfe is famous for evocative descriptions that are presented like the **catalogs** of Walt Whitman (page 348). Select one passage of description in Wolfe's story, and identify the senses to which each image appeals: sight, taste, smell, hearing, or touch.

Extending the Text

6. Scenes in this story resemble other famous "reunion" scenes in literature. In Homer's *Odyssey,* Odysseus returns home after a twenty-year absence and is reunited with his aged father, who is tending vines. If you are familiar with the parable of the Prodigal Son in the New Testament (Luke 15:11–32), explain whether you think Wolfe's father-son reunion bears any resemblance to the reunion described there. Is the boy in this story a prodigal son? Why or why not?

CHOICES: Building Your Portfolio

Writer's Notebook

1. Collecting Ideas for a Speculation About Causes and Effects

WORK IN PROGRESS

Imagine that you are writing a biography of a writer. Brainstorm a list of questions you would ask your subject about his or her influences. (Recall how Wolfe was influenced by the setting in which he grew up and the relationships he had with other people.) Save your notes for possible use in the Writer's Workshop on page 685.

Critical Writing

2. Two Grand Styles

Re-read Walt Whitman's poetry (pages 352–362), especially the verses from "Song of Myself." In a brief essay, compare Whitman's style with Wolfe's. Gather details in a chart like the one below:

	Whitman	Wolfe
1. Use of descriptive catalogs		
2. Celebration of everyday people		
3. Celebration of America		
4. Emotional effect of writing		

Creative Writing

3. Details, Details

Write a Wolfe-like description of a place you know well. Include a wide variety of people or items, and build up a catalog of details that capture the atmosphere of the place. Use rich, sensory details to imitate Wolfe's exuberant style.

Making Meanings

First Thoughts

1. It made me hungry; or Wolfe paints a picture of the whole United States.

Reviewing the Text

a. "He thought then he had joined a circus. . . ."; "in his vision, every incident, each face . . . were blazing real as life itself. . . ."

b. Responses will vary. Examples include: **onomatopoeia:** "kweet," "pwee," "buzz," "whirr" **alliteration:** "sweet-leaved lettuces crisp as celery," "the first liquorous liquefied lutings" **repetition:** "Thus the circus moved across America, from town to town, from state to state, eating its way from Maine . . . eating its way along the Hudson . . . eating its way across the prairies . . . eating its way across the flat farmlands . . . eating all good things. . . ."

Shaping Interpretations

2. The father is linked with the fertile land and, by association, with its bounty. On his way to his father's place, springtime sights and sounds are described. When his father meets him, they hug each other.
3. The circus moves on, but his father's earth endures. The father represents the earth, which provides food, and the boy imagines himself feeding the circus.
4. The boy hears the birds first thing in the morning; on the way to his father's home, he catalogs the sounds of birds; this catalog is like the food catalogs.
5. Responses will vary. Students can work in small groups to analyze the images in different catalogs.

Extending the Text

6. **(Synthesis)** Possible responses: In both stories, the father welcomes the returning son with food. However, in the Bible the brother resents the father's forgiveness; in this story the brothers also embrace the returning brother. The boy is a prodigal son only in the sense that he at first fails to appreciate what he has at home.

Choices: Building Your Portfolio

1. **Writer's Notebook** Remind students to save their work. They may use it as prewriting for the Writer's Workshop on p. 685.

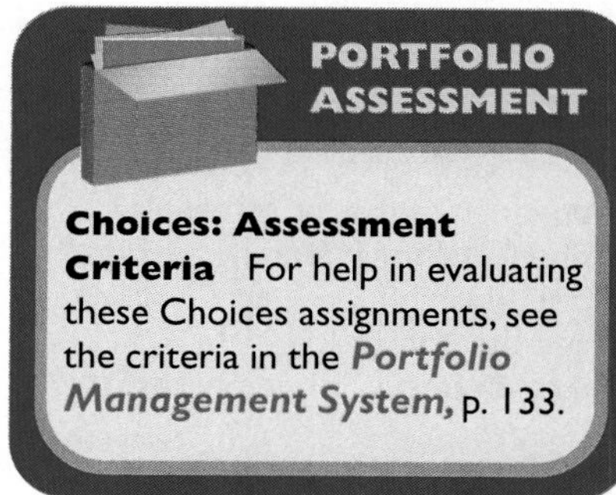

Choices: Assessment Criteria For help in evaluating these Choices assignments, see the criteria in the ***Portfolio Management System,*** p. 133.

QUICK PLANNING GUIDE

Into the Poems

Through the Poems

Beyond the Poems

Choices: Building Your Portfolio p. 576

- **Writer's Notebook:** Collect ideas for a speculation about causes and effects
- **Critical Writing:** Analyze dark conflicts in Frost's poetry in a brief essay
- **Critical Writing:** Compare Frost poem and Dickinson poem in a brief essay
- **Creative Writing:** Recast the poem in contemporary surroundings in a poem, narrative, or screenplay
- **Speaking and Listening:** Lead a discussion on Frost, the Puritans, and the Romantics
- **Art:** Create a collage of Frost's themes
- **Music/Art:** Prepare multimedia presentation of Frost's poetry

Robert Frost

(1874–1963)

Although Robert Frost is the poet whom Americans most closely identify with New England, he was born in San Francisco, California. Frost was about ten years old before he first saw the New England landscapes and knew the changing seasons that he would later describe with the familiarity of a native son. The boy's move across the country was the result of his father's early death and his mother's decision to settle in the industrial town of Lawrence, Massachusetts. After high school in Lawrence, Frost entered Dartmouth College in New Hampshire. He decided after a few months that he was not yet ready for higher education, and he returned to Lawrence to work in the cotton mills and to write. His verses, however, found little favor with magazine editors.

Married and with a growing family, Frost in his early twenties finally began to feel the need for a more formal education than his random reading could provide. He took his family to Cambridge, Massachusetts, where he entered Harvard and stayed for less than two years. He later wrote of his decision to leave: "Harvard had taken me away from the question of whether I could write or not."

Frost earned a living as a schoolteacher and as an editor before deciding to try farming. For ten years, Frost tilled the stony New Hampshire soil on thirty acres that his grandfather had bought for him. But he decided that the concentration necessary for writing poetry did not mix with the round-the-clock physical effort of working the land. Discouraged, he returned to teaching full time for a few years; then, in 1912, he sought a complete change of scene by taking his family to England.

From Scribbler to Scribe

The move turned out to be a wise one. Stimulated by meeting English poets, Frost continued to write poetry, though he found his subjects in

The Bettmann Archive.

New England. In the three years he spent in England, he completed the two volumes that would make him famous—*A Boy's Will* (1913) and *North of Boston* (1914). These collections included several poems that would stand among Frost's best-known works: "The Tuft of Flowers," "In Hardwood Groves," "Mending Wall," "The Death of the Hired Man," and "After Apple-Picking." These poems were marked by a flinty realism and an impressive mastery of iambic rhythm, narrative dialogue, and the dramatic monologue.

When Frost returned to New Hampshire in 1915, he was no longer an obscure scribbler intent on turning New England folkways into poetry; he was an accomplished writer who had already extended the scope and character of

PORTFOLIO ASSESSMENT

Portfolio Assessment For help with self- and teacher assessment of reading skills, see the ***Portfolio Management System,*** p. 52.

American literature into the twentieth century. In 1916, the publication of *Mountain Interval*—a collection that included such favorites as "The Road Not Taken," "'Out, Out—,'" and "Birches"—solidified his fame. Rewarded with many prizes (including four Pulitzer Prizes and a Congressional Medal), numerous honorary degrees, and the faithful attention of a wide readership, Frost spent the rest of his life as a lecturer at a number of colleges and as a public performer who, as he put it, liked to "say" rather than to recite his poetry.

Poet of the People

On stage, Frost in his later years became a character of his own creation—a lovable, fumbling old gent who could nevertheless pierce the minds and hearts of those able to see beyond his playacting. In private, he was apt to put aside this guileless character and become a sometimes wicked commentator on the pretensions of rival poets; and he could be just as cutting to gushing devotees, who were unaware that he held in contempt the very flattery he demanded.

On Inauguration Day, 1961, standing bareheaded in a bright, cold wind beside President John F. Kennedy on the Capitol steps in Washington, D.C., Frost recited "The Gift Outright." His art with words had brought him not only the friendship of a president (who was half his age) but also, by means of radio and television, the largest single audience in history for a poet up until that time.

In a period when poetry was being changed by verbal experiment and by exotic influences from abroad, Frost remained devoted to traditional forms and firmly rooted in American soil. If, at the time of his death, he seemed to belong more to the past than to the present, his reputation today is secure. Neither the cranky realism nor the homely philosophy of self-reliance and spiritual independence that mark his work have been forgotten. He was an artist who developed his talents with stubborn persistence, and he created a unique voice that remained unaffected by the clamor of modernism.

Literature and Science

Acquainted with the Night: Frost the Astronomer

In 1889, the teenage Robert Frost read a book titled *Our Place Among Infinities* by the British astronomer Richard Anthony Proctor. Something about Proctor's vision of the mysteries of the universe and of the place of science and religion in human life touched a chord in Frost, and he began to look to the night sky. He learned to identify the constellations and became familiar with the movements of the planets and stars. Shortly thereafter, when the magazine *The Youth's Companion* offered a telescope in exchange for a certain number of subscriptions sold, Frost set out on a door-to-door campaign. He failed to sell enough subscriptions on his own, but his mother pitched in, and together they made the magazine's quota. The telescope was his, marking the start of a serious and lifelong interest in astronomy.

Some forty years later, Robert Newdick, an English professor and friend of Frost's, testified to the poet's celestial knowledge: "When we stepped out-of-doors on that last night, or rather early in the morning, there was a strange light in the north. Could it be Northern Lights? We waited for our eyes to get used to the night. No; just a strange light on the underside of a cloud. Then F[rost] swept the heavens with his eyes and began to talk in intimate fashion of the stars, which were extraordinarily bright: the Northern Cross, Orion, the Pleiades—one constellation after another. He knows the stars as he knows flowers, botany."

Images of planets, stars, and constellations abound in Frost's poetry. Humans, Frost seems to say, should look to the sky not to see reflections of themselves, but to develop a broader—cosmic—perspective on the world and human affairs.

About the Author

Frost's friendship with Kennedy led him to take a trip to the Soviet Union in September 1962 along with Secretary of the Interior Stewart Udall. There Frost spoke at length with Khrushchev just a month before the Cuban Missile Crisis. The two men, who both thought of themselves as men of the soil, got along well, and Frost proposed a "noble rivalry" between the two nations that would be based on spurring each other to achieve their best rather than on destroying each other. Frost was soon disillusioned about the impact poetry can have on the actions of governments.

Literature and Science

Encourage students to discuss what they know about the stars. Ask students who study the stars to share what they have learned from observing them. Invite a science teacher or professor of astronomy to the class to talk about how the stars can broaden our perspective and what they can teach about the world and human affairs. If possible, take a field trip to an observatory, a local science museum, or a planetarium to see what it offers on stars. Follow up with a discussion on what students learned.

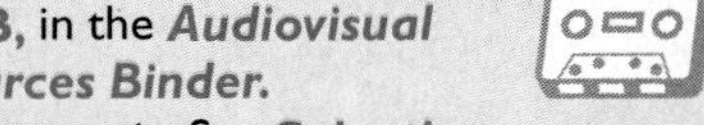

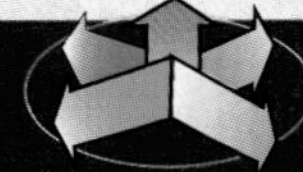

Program Manager

- **Planning Instruction** See Teaching Notes, *Teaching Resources B*, pp. 5–8, for objectives, summaries, literary elements, and additional historical and biographical information for the poems.
- **Instructional Support** Before beginning the instructional lesson, see Graphic Organizers for Active Reading, *Teaching Resources B*, pp. 23–28, for Into the Poem and Through the Poem activities.
- **Audiotaped Readings** To help less proficient readers or auditory learners through the lesson, use the Selected Readings, Audiocassette 2, Side B, in the *Audiovisual Resources Binder*.
- **Assessment** See Selection Test, *Test Booklet*, pp. 133–134.

Into the Poem

Using Before You Read p. 560

Background

This poem follows the conventions of the Petrarchan or Italian sonnet. The iambic pentameter lines are grouped into an octave with an *abba abba* rhyme scheme and a sestet with an *aca acc* rhyme. The octave contains four startling **similes,** and the sestet poses three rhetorical questions and ends with a wry comment.

Through the Poem

A. Literary Element: Ambiguity
This title may have a double meaning: it is *about* design, but as a well-made sonnet, it also *is* a design.

B. Reader's Response: Shaping Interpretations
Note the word *kindred.* What is Frost saying? [Sample responses: The spider and the moth are related; or they are related in that one preys on the other.]

C. Literary Element: Sonnet
Point out that the poem is divided into an octave and a sestet. Have students read the octave first to understand what Frost observes about the spider, the flower, and the moth. Then, have students read the sestet to understand the questions he poses about them.

Before You Read

Design

Reading Focus

Design of Darkness
Anyone who has had a direct experience of nature knows that sudden violence and grisly death are facts of life: The strong eat the weak; the slow are overcome by the quick; the healthy ultimately die and decay. By human standards, nature can be cold and merciless. To paraphrase Frost in this poem, nature can be "appalling."

Quickwrite

READER'S LOG

Read the first line of the poem, and write down your prediction about what the tone of the poem is going to be. What words lead you to that conclusion?

Background

Frost was particularly proud of his **sonnets,** and he often expressed regret that more of them were not reprinted in the hundreds of anthologies in which his work appeared. "Design" reveals how densely packed with ideas his sonnets can be. (For more about sonnets, see page 180 and the Handbook of Literary Terms.)

Butterflies (1950) by M. C. Escher. Wood engraving (28 cm × 26 cm).

Design

Robert Frost

I found a dimpled spider, fat and white,
On a white heal-all,° holding up a moth
Like a white piece of rigid satin cloth—
Assorted characters of death and blight
Mixed ready to begin the morning right,
Like the ingredients of a witches' broth—
A snowdrop spider, a flower like a froth,°
And dead wings carried like a paper kite.

What had that flower to do with being white,
The wayside blue and innocent heal-all?
What brought the kindred spider to that height,
Then steered the white moth thither° in the night?
What but design of darkness to appall?—
If design govern in a thing so small.

2. heal-all: flowering plant of the mint family. The flowers, leaves, and stems are used in folk medicine to treat sore throats and other minor ailments.
7. froth: foam.
12. thither: archaic for "there."

Options for Teaching

Strategies for Inclusion

Less Proficient Readers Some students may need help breaking up the long sentence of the octave to determine meaning. You can help them by reading up to each dash and then asking them to paraphrase what has been said. Then, ask them to paraphrase the three questions posed in the sestet. Finally, have them explain what the title means.

Visual The poem may become clearer to some students if they draw the details given in the poem: the fat white spider, the white moth, the white flower. Afterward, ask them to write in their Reader's Logs why Frost calls the event a "design of darkness."

Making Meanings

First Thoughts

1. Did your prediction about the **tone** of the poem prove correct, or did the poem surprise you? Review the notes you made in your Reader's Log to help explain your answer.

Shaping Interpretations

2. What **similes** occur in the octave (first eight lines) of this sonnet? How do they affect the **tone** of the poem?

3. Identify the three "characters" of the poem, and tell what is happening to each one. What color is each character? What justifies the poet's description of these things as "characters of death and blight"?

4. Look up the word *character* in a dictionary. Explain which definitions of the word Frost might be applying in line 4. How does each definition affect the meaning of the line?

5. Describe the **rhyme scheme** of the poem. In your view, how does Frost's use of a very limited number of rhymes affect the poem's **tone**?

6. In line 13, the poet answers his own questions with another question. Explain how his final question answers the previous ones. How would you define a "design of darkness"?

7. In line 14, Frost qualifies his answer with a reservation, beginning with a crucial "if." What is the reservation that remains in his mind?

8. How does the last line affect the whole **tone** and meaning of the poem?

Extending the Text

9. How do you think a Puritan (page 9) writer would have answered the questions Frost asks in this poem? How do you think a rationalist (page 13), or deist (page 16), would answer them?

Challenging the Text

10. The critic Laurence Perrine made this comment about "Design": "Frost's brief poem, like the wayside blue or white heal-all, seems from the outside innocent enough. But within its fourteen innocent-seeming lines, Frost chillingly poses the problem of evil." Do you agree or disagree with this comment? Give reasons for your response. If you disagree, state what *you* think is the poem's central issue.

Making Meanings

First Thoughts

1. Possible responses: The word "dimpled" made me think it would be an upbeat poem and it was not; or because the spider was "fat," I knew the poem would have a serious tone.

Shaping Interpretations

2. The moth is compared to "a white piece of rigid satin cloth" (l. 3); the combination of spider, moth, and flower is compared to "the ingredients of a witches' broth" (l. 6); the flower is "like a froth" (l. 7); the wings of the dead moth are compared to "a paper kite" (l. 8). The tone is serious, even somber, for satin should be soft, not rigid, and witches perform evil spells.

3. The spider, the moth, and the flower; the moth is trapped and killed by the spider on the flower. They are white. The spider kills the moth, and since the flower is white it camouflages the spider, thus contributing to the moth's death.

4. Possible responses: "A distinctive mark," "a mystic symbol," "a distinctive trait or quality," "a role in a story or play." Possible responses: They both mark the mint and are symbols of the cycle of nature; the spider embodies gluttony and the moth, fear; both play a role in the poem.

5. *abbaabba acaacc.* Possible reponse: The limited number of rhymes supports a serious rather than a playful tone.

6. The questions ask what brought the spider, moth, and flower together, and l. 13 answers nature's design. A "design of darkness" implies that nature has a sinister plan.

7. Frost is not sure that nature has a plan—evil or benevolent—at all.

8. It adds a note of cynicism to the poem; up until that point the spider, moth, and flower act out their parts in a cosmic plan; the last line implies that maybe there is no plan.

Extending the Text

9. (Synthesis) Possible responses: A Puritan would have said that all the events were part of a divine plan. A rationalist would have said that each behaved according to accepted scientific principles. A deist would have said that God had created an orderly universe.

Challenging the Text

10. (Evaluation) Possible responses: The poem is about evil, for the spider kills the moth and they are both part of a "witches' broth." Or the poem is not about evil; it is about the design of nature.

Into the Poem

Using BEFORE YOU READ p. 562

Reading Focus

The word *gold* often conjures up thoughts of great riches, but gold has many other associations also. Give students about three minutes to work in small groups to brainstorm as many word associations as they can for *gold.* After the groups have finished, make a cluster of their ideas such as the one below.

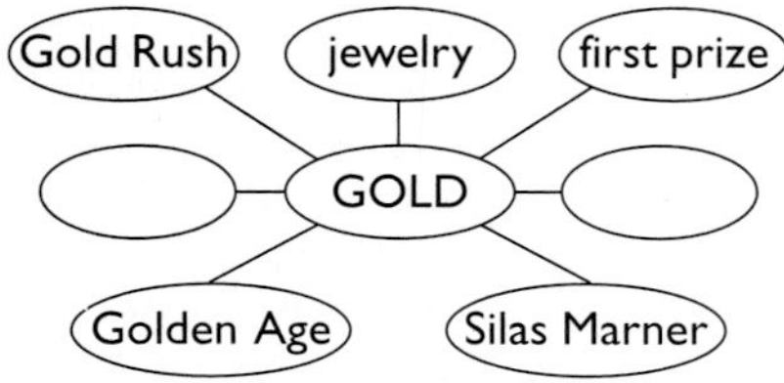

Through the Poem

A. Humanities Connection

Adam and Eve's loss of innocence and their expulsion from the Garden of Eden represent both the loss of innocence as one passes from childhood to adulthood and the loss of innocence of all humankind. According to Greek and Roman mythology, the Golden Age was a time of innocent happiness. Before Zeus (Jupiter) dethroned the Titan ruler Cronus (Saturn), the Titans lived in a land of great abundance, where there was no sickness or war. Like the expulsion of Adam and Eve from Eden, the loss of the Golden Age represents a loss of innocence.

This equating of "gold" or "golden" with innocence is echoed in Dylan Thomas's poem "Fern Hill," in which the speaker describes himself as "golden."

BEFORE YOU READ

NOTHING GOLD CAN STAY

Reading Focus

Good as Gold

"Gold," whether it refers to the metal or to the color, conjures up a myriad of images and meanings. Over the centuries, writers and artists have used gold as a symbol.

Quickwrite

READER'S LOG

Briefly write what you predict the poem is going to be about, based on its title.

Background

To understand this little lyric, you need to know about two other literary accounts: the Biblical account of Adam and Eve's loss of innocence and their expulsion from the Garden of Eden; and, in Greek mythology, the loss of the Golden Age, a time of innocent happiness that was an image of paradise for the ancient Greeks and Romans.

Nothing Gold Can Stay

Robert Frost

Nature's first green is gold,
Her hardest hue to hold.
Her early leaf's a flower;
But only so an hour.
A Then leaf subsides to leaf.
So Eden sank to grief,
So dawn goes down to day.
Nothing gold can stay.

MAKING MEANINGS

First Thoughts

1. Review your Quickwrite, and explain whether the title of the poem helped you predict its message.

Shaping Interpretations

2. Identify four specific things in the poem that cannot, or did not, "stay."
3. Think what the first buds of leaves look like in spring, and explain what line 1 means.
4. Explain the natural process described in line 5.
5. What Biblical event is alluded to in line 6? What state of mind or situation might "Eden" **symbolize** here?
6. What different ideas might "gold" **symbolize** in the poem? Why can't gold stay—or do you disagree?
7. Show how rhyme and rhythm contribute to this poem's compactness and completeness. How do **alliteration, slant rhyme,** and echoing **sound effects** contribute to the poem's tightly woven unity?

Making Meanings

First Thoughts

1. Possible responses: The title helped, because it shows that good things do not last. Or the title misled me, because I thought it would be about what does have value.

Shaping Interpretations

2. "Nature's first green," "early leaf," "Eden," and "dawn."
3. The first bud of leaves often have a golden tinge, so the first line means that the green leaves actually start as gold buds.
4. The first golden buds soon grow into leaves.
5. Adam and Eve were cast out of the Garden of Eden for disobeying God by eating from the tree of knowledge of good and evil; Eden symbolizes paradise and innocence—a lack of knowledge of evil—so the line symbolizes the loss of innocence.

Extending the Text

8. In Connections below, Naomi Shihab Nye tries to name things that don't change. How are her poem and Frost's poem alike and different in **tone** and **message**? Identify the central point you think each poet is trying to convey about change and loss.

Connections A POEM

Trying to Name What Doesn't Change

Naomi Shihab Nye

Roselva says the only thing that doesn't change
is train tracks. She's sure of it.
The train changes, or the weeds that grow up spidery
by the side, but not the tracks.
I've watched one for three years, she says,
and it doesn't curve, doesn't break, doesn't grow. **A**

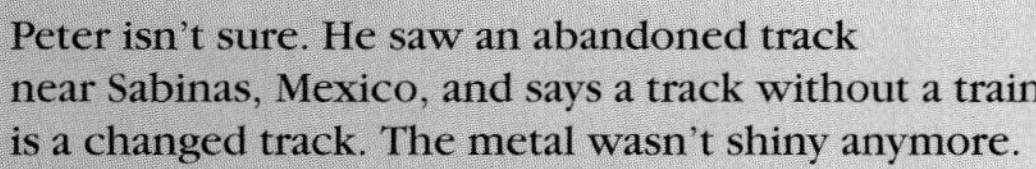

Peter isn't sure. He saw an abandoned track
near Sabinas, Mexico, and says a track without a train
is a changed track. The metal wasn't shiny anymore.
The wood was split and some of the ties were gone.

Every Tuesday on Morales Street
butchers crack the necks of a hundred hens.
The widow in the tilted house
spices her soup with cinnamon.
Ask her what doesn't change.

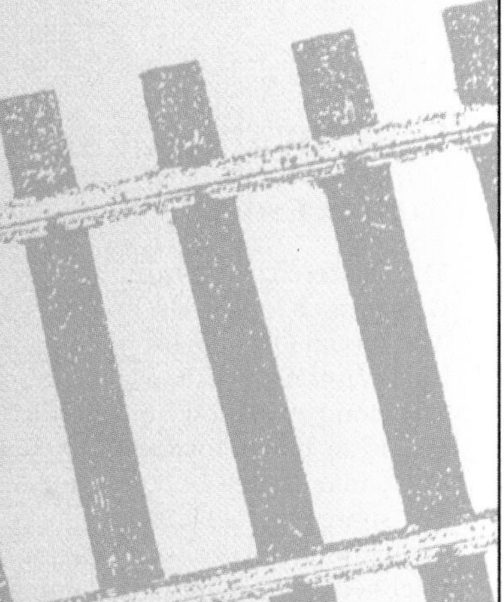

Stars explode. **B**
The rose curls up as if there is fire in the petals.
The cat who knew me is buried under the bush.

The train whistle still wails its ancient sound
but when it goes away, shrinking back
from the walls of the brain,
it takes something different with it every time.

6. Possible responses: Preciousness, perfection, paradise, value, nature's beauty, and material or spiritual wealth. The speaker implies that gold does not stay because of the transient nature of things: the seasons change, Eden was lost, dawn turns to day.
7. The poem's rhyming couplets keep the lines tight; the iambic trimeter only has variations in the first and last line, so the poem is regular, but emphasizes those two lines. Alliteration ("green is gold") and sound echoes ("only so") tightly relate words to each other. Slant rhyme ("dawn" and "down") connect words within a line.

Extending the Text

8. **(Analysis)** Possible responses: Frost's tone is bittersweet; his message might be to appreciate the "gold" in life because it never has stayed and never will stay. Nye's tone is forceful; her message might be that even those things that appear not to change do change, and people have to recognize and adjust to those changes.

A. Language Note: Repetition

? What is the effect of the repetition? [Possible answer: It gives emphasis to the idea that the tracks do not change.]

B. Reader's Response: Shaping Interpretations

? Why does the speaker include this image? [Sample responses: It shows that enormous objects change; or it shows that things we cannot see up close change; or things that seem stable and eternal to us change.]

CONNECTING WITH "NOTHING GOLD CAN STAY"

While both poems address the constancy of change, each varies in **tone, diction, rhyme scheme, rhythm, figures of speech,** and **imagery.** Ask students to discuss the ways in which the poems differ and how these variations contribute to the messages of the poems. Students may find a chart like the following helpful in analyzing the poems.

Literary Element	"Nothing Gold Can Stay"	"Trying to Name What Doesn't Change"
tone	[bittersweet]	[forceful]
diction	[formal]	[conversational]
rhyme scheme		
rhythm		
figures of speech		
imagery		

PROGRAM MANAGER

Audiotaped Readings To help auditory learners or readers having difficulty through the lesson, use the **Selected Reading, Audiocassette 2, Side B,** in the ***Audiovisual Resources Binder.***

Into the Poem

Using **Before You Read** p. 564

Reading Focus

Have students freewrite for two minutes what they believe to be the opposite of creation. Then, ask the class to discuss their responses.

Through the Poem

A. Literary Element: Personification

? How might the incoming waves and clouds be perceived as angry giants? [Possible answers: The larger waves look over other waves; the waves think about taking violent action; the clouds' eyes could foretell the evil that the waves contemplate.]

B. Literary Element: Parallel Structure

? What is the effect of the parallelism in these lines? [Possible answer: The parallelism of "in being backed by . . ." implies security, stability, and strength, and by this contrast, makes the force of the waves seem all the more threatening.]

Before You Read
Once by the Pacific

Reading Focus

The End of All Things

In the Bible, when God creates the universe, he says, "Let there be light." After each stage of creation, the Bible says, "And God saw that it was good." Keep these ideas in mind as you read Frost's vision of an event that is the opposite of creation.

A Dialogue with the Text

READER'S LOG

As you read the poem, list the words, phrases, or images that create a chilling effect or a feeling of doom.

Once by the Pacific

Robert Frost

The shattered water made a misty din.
Great waves looked over others coming in,
A And thought of doing something to the shore
That water never did to land before.
The clouds were low and hairy in the skies,
Like locks blown forward in the gleam of eyes.
You could not tell, and yet it looked as if
B The shore was lucky in being backed by cliff,
The cliff in being backed by continent;
It looked as if a night of dark intent
Was coming, and not only a night, an age.
Someone had better be prepared for rage.
There would be more than ocean-water broken
Before God's last *Put out the Light* was spoken.

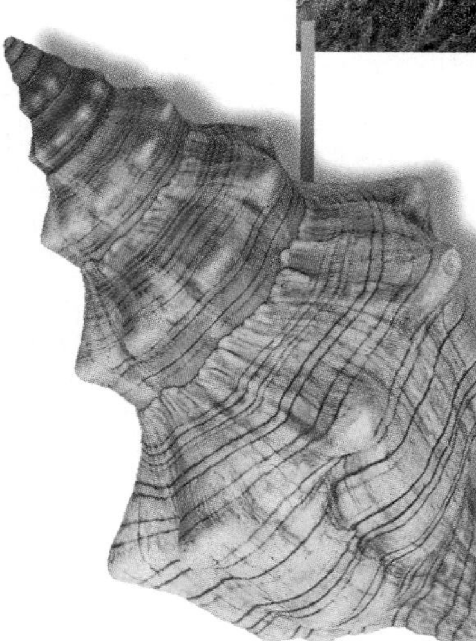

Options for Teaching

Strategies for Inclusion

Less Proficient Readers Read the poem aloud to the students. Then read it aloud again, stopping at each period or semicolon for students to summarize what has been said. In this way, students can gradually grasp the picture Frost paints and develop an understanding of the poem.

Visual Some students may find the meaning of the poem clearer if they draw a picture of the details: the rolling water, the low clouds, the cliff, and the shore.

The Pennsylvania Academy of the Fine Arts, Philadelphia.

Rocks and Breakers, California (1913) by William Ritschel. Oil on canvas.

Before You Read
Neither Out Far Nor In Deep

Reading Focus

Ocean Reveries

For some, the sea is an object of reverie, inspiring a sense of peace and oneness with the world. For others, the sea represents a powerful, mysterious force of nature. What other things might the sea symbolize?

Quickwrite

READER'S LOG

Before you read the poem, write down your guess as to the meaning of Frost's puzzling title.

Neither Out Far Nor In Deep

Robert Frost

The people along the sand
All turn and look one way.
They turn their back on the land.
They look at the sea all day.

As long as it takes to pass
A ship keeps raising its hull;
The wetter ground like glass
Reflects a standing gull.

The land may vary more;
But wherever the truth may be—
The water comes ashore,
And the people look at the sea.

They cannot look out far. **A**
They cannot look in deep.
But when was that ever a bar°
To any watch they keep?

15. **bar:** barrier; obstruction.

Into the Poem

Using **Before You Read** p. 565

Quickwrite

Before students guess about the meaning of the title, tell them to first consider what the phrases *out far* and *in deep* mean in relation to the sea. Then, they should think about how the conjunctions *neither* and *nor* affect the meaning of the title.

Through the Poem

A. Reader's Response: Shaping Interpretations

? What do "out far" and "in deep" mean in these lines? [Sample responses: People cannot see a great distance out to the water or down into the water; or the words might mean that people have little insight into the complexity of existence.]

Integrating the Language Arts

Speaking and Listening Students reluctant to read aloud for meaning may be encouraged by a choral reading activity. You might have the students read aloud together both when they first read the poem and after they have completed their discussion.

Crossing the Curriculum

Science Students interested in oceanography could report to the class on the life beneath the surface of the ocean, movement that seldom appears on the surface. The life of the ocean is "out far" and "in deep," its secrets impossible to learn by looking at the water. Then the analogy might be drawn between the hidden life of the ocean and the hidden mysteries of human existence.

Making Meanings "Once by the Pacific"

First Thoughts

1. Possible responses: The scene reminded me of the power of the film that shows the atomic bomb exploding; the poem made me feel the wrath of God.

Shaping Interpretations

2. Some future disaster or calamity, possibly the end of the world.
3. A terrible event will be set in motion and it will badly affect—or perhaps destroy—the future. God's or nature's intent.
4. All humankind. The rage of God or nature in the form of some natural disaster.
5. Buildings, land, cities, animals, and all humankind.
6. "Put out the light" is something everyone does every night, and everyone turns on the light in the morning. The speaker's use of the phrase is on the cosmic level and refers to a permanent putting out of the light—no one can turn it back on. The message is that human life could end.
7. The end of the world.

Connecting with the Text

8. Possible responses: Frost may be warning us that if people continue behaving as they do, life could end; or he may see life as a cycle of creation and destruction.

Making Meanings

Once by the Pacific

First Thoughts

1. Review the notes you made in your Reader's Log. How would you describe the scene that is presented in the poem? How did the poem make you feel?

Shaping Interpretations

2. What does the scene remind the speaker of?
3. Explain what you think the speaker means by "a night of dark intent /. . . not only a night, an age" (lines 10–11). Whose "intent" is he referring to?
4. Who do you think is the "someone" who "had better be prepared for rage" (line 12)? Whose "rage"?
5. Besides ocean water, what else might be "broken" during that rage?
6. "Put out the light" is something anyone might say on an ordinary evening at home. How does the use of this casual, domestic phrase make the poem's message even more chilling? What would you say that message is?
7. The poem's title suggests that Frost is describing a scene he once saw as he gazed at the Pacific Ocean. What larger event might this scene **symbolize**?

Connecting with the Text

8. Do you view this poem as a warning? Or do you think Frost is just expressing a certain philosophy of life? Explain what the warning might be, or discuss the philosophy revealed in the poem.

Neither Out Far Nor In Deep

First Thoughts

1. Review your Quickwrite. Why do you think Frost included the words *out far* and *in deep* in the poem's title?

Shaping Interpretations

2. What is the one **simile** that Frost uses in the poem? What effect does it have on the scene he describes?
3. In what way are lines 11–12 tinged with **irony**?
4. What might the sea and the land **symbolize** in this poem? What larger meaning might the "watch" (line 16) take on?
5. Comment on the poet's **tone** in the last line. Does he admire the watchers for keeping their vigil, or does he feel scorn or pity for their failure to recognize their limitations? Do you have another interpretation? Explain.
6. On a literal level, why is it that the people in the poem can look neither "out far" nor "in deep"? What more general human limitations might be **symbolized** by our inability to probe the distance and depth of the sea?

"Neither Out Far Nor In Deep"

First Thoughts

1. Possible responses: Frost wanted to emphasize what people do when they are at the ocean; or he wanted to emphasize how limited some people can be.

Shaping Interpretations

2. "The wetter ground like glass reflects a standing gull"; it gives an imaginative lift to a somewhat stark scene.
3. Although the water comes to the land, the people themselves are not interested in the land.
4. Possible response: The sea symbolizes the vastness of the unfamiliar—the future; the land symbolizes the familiar—the past and the present. A possible meaning of "watch" is that people are always looking toward what will happen next (the sea) instead of appreciating the here and now (the land).
5. Possible response: The tone is neither admiration nor pity but an acceptance of the human tendency to place more importance on the future than the present.
6. Possible response: The human eye cannot see far enough to observe the bounds of the ocean or the depths of the sea. Students might suggest that humans can never understand the larger picture of existence because they are always bound by their own experiences.

Before You Read
Birches

Reading Focus
Life Lessons

A **parable** is a short story in which an ordinary event from everyday life is used to teach a much wider moral or religious lesson. In this poem, Frost draws a lesson from nature—from the sight of the bent branches of birch trees.

A Dialogue with the Text
READER'S LOG

As you read the poem, note the points at which the poem shifts between fantasy and fact—between the poet's imaginings and a realistic description of the natural scene.

Background
As spindly and awkward as a giraffe's legs, the birch trees of Robert Frost's New England have white bark ringed with black. Their trunks are remarkably pliable—a fact that gives this poem its realistic base. Children do, in fact, climb and swing on birch trees.

Birches (A)
Robert Frost

When I see birches bend to left and right
Across the lines of straighter darker trees,
I like to think some boy's been swinging them.
But swinging doesn't bend them down to stay
As ice storms do. Often you must have seen them
Loaded with ice a sunny winter morning
After a rain. They click upon themselves
As the breeze rises, and turn many-colored
As the stir cracks and crazes their enamel.
Soon the sun's warmth makes them shed crystal shells
Shattering and avalanching on the snow crust—
Such heaps of broken glass to sweep away
You'd think the inner dome of heaven had fallen.
They are dragged to the withered bracken° by the load,
And they seem not to break; though once they are bowed
So low for long, they never right themselves:
You may see their trunks arching in the woods
Years afterwards, trailing their leaves on the ground
Like girls on hands and knees that throw their hair
Before them over their heads to dry in the sun.
But I was going to say when Truth broke in
With all her matter of fact about the ice storm,
I should prefer to have some boy bend them
As he went out and in to fetch the cows—
Some boy too far from town to learn baseball,
Whose only play was what he found himself,
Summer or winter, and could play alone.
One by one he subdued his father's trees
By riding them down over and over again
Until he took the stiffness out of them,
And not one but hung limp, not one was left
For him to conquer. He learned all there was
To learn about not launching out too soon
And so not carrying the tree away

14. bracken: large, coarse fern.

Into the Poem

Using Before You Read p. 567

A Dialogue with the Text
To help students get started, tell them that the first three lines tell what the speaker likes to think about when he sees bent birch trees. In l. 4 the speaker switches to the reality of the situation. Have them use a chart like the following to organize the shifts between fantasy and fact in the poem.

Fantasy (lines)	Fact (lines)
[thinks of boy swinging birches ll. 1–3]	[swinging does not bend birches permanently l. 4]

Through the Poem

A. Critical Reading: Finding Sequence
Point out the steps in the development of the meaning of the poem: ll. 1–3, introduction; ll. 4–20, damage caused by ice storms; ll. 21–40, the best way to swing on birches; ll. 41–47, yearning to swing on birches again; ll. 48–59, his wish to go away from Earth and then come back.

Options for Teaching
Strategies for Inclusion

Less Proficient Readers Make sure that all readers notice the transitional words that mark changes of thoughts in the poem: "When" (l. 1), "But" (l. 4), "But" (l. 21), and "So" (l. 41). To summarize: *When* he sees bent birches, he wants to think a boy's swinging pulled them down; *but* although a boy's play may bend the trees temporarily, ice storms forever damage them. *But,* to get to the point, he hopes a boy enjoyed playing in the trees. *So* did the narrator when he was a boy, and he would like to do so again.

Integrating the Language Arts

Writing: Poem, Expressive Piece, or Short Story This poem may remind students of games they played to escape life's troubles when they were younger: climbing trees, digging for treasure, looking for pirates, riding horses, or soaring on Ferris wheels. Invite them to write about those times and, like Frost, to try to give the games extra meaning. Students could write a poem, an expressive piece, or a short story.

A. Literary Element: Symbolism

? Is the speaker implying something symbolic in the fact that the tree must eventually set the swinger down? [Possible answer: Perhaps the speaker feels that the exercise is beneficial for people but that any prolonged restraint or tension can have permanent consequences.]

Making Meanings

First Thoughts

1. Possible response: It is interesting that he wants to get away from Earth for a time and then to come back later. Lots of people have felt like that.

Shaping Interpretations

2. When he sees the birch trees bend in a wind, the speaker likes to imagine a boy has been swinging on them. He realizes that, whereas the trees may bend back after someone swings on them, an ice storm bends them down permanently. The fact is the realistic description of an actual ice storm.
3. Examples of metaphor: "the stir cracks and crazes their enamel" (l. 9), the trees "shed crystal shells" (l. 10), the ice is "such heaps of broken glass" (l. 12). Examples of onomatopoeia: "click" (l. 7), "cracks" (l. 9), "swish" (l. 39).
4. The bent trunks are compared to girls on their hands and knees, who fling their wet hair over their heads to let it dry in the sun (ll. 18–20); life is compared to a wood where one's face feels the cobwebs as he or she walks through (ll. 44–46).
5. Possible responses: People rise to meet life's challenges and then take time to wind down; one can use imagination to soar to great heights.
6. Possible responses: People can periodically do their own "birch swinging"—they can be refreshed by breaking away from routine and reality and then going back. The speaker does not want to escape life permanently, although he is sensitive to life's pain and recognizes the need for respite.

Clear to the ground. He always kept his poise°
To the top branches, climbing carefully
With the same pains you use to fill a cup
Up to the brim, and even above the brim.
Then he flung outward, feet first, with a swish,
Kicking his way down through the air to the ground.
So was I once myself a swinger of birches.
And so I dream of going back to be.
It's when I'm weary of considerations,
And life is too much like a pathless wood
Where your face burns and tickles with the cobwebs
Broken across it, and one eye is weeping
From a twig's having lashed across it open.
I'd like to get away from earth awhile
And then come back to it and begin over.
May no fate willfully misunderstand me
And half grant what I wish and snatch me away
Not to return. Earth's the right place for love:
I don't know where it's likely to go better.
I'd like to go by climbing a birch tree,
And climb black branches up a snow-white trunk
Toward heaven, till the tree could bear no more,
But dipped its top and set me down again.
That would be good both going and coming back.
One could do worse than be a swinger of birches.

35. **poise:** balance.

Making Meanings

First Thoughts

1. Which passages of this poem do you think are especially interesting or true to life as you know it? Be sure to share your chosen lines in class.

Shaping Interpretations

2. Describe the scenario that the speaker imagines when he sees birch trees. What realistic objection to his idea does he recognize in lines 4–5? What "matter of fact" does "Truth" break in with in lines 5–10? Be sure to refer to your Reader's Log notes.
3. Find at least three examples of **metaphor** and **onomatopoeia** in the poem.
4. Two strong **similes** give the poem a richness that is both imaginative and the result of close observation. What are these similes?
5. What does the playful activity of birch swinging seem to **symbolize** in the poem?
6. Summarize in your own words what you think is the moral or message of Frost's **parable** about birch swinging. What complex, conflicting attitudes toward life does it reveal?

Extending the Text

7. If a Puritan writer were to come upon the bent birches, what response do you think he or she would have to the natural scene? What response would a Transcendentalist like Ralph Waldo Emerson (page 216) have had?

Challenging the Text

8. In a famous remark about the nature of poetry, Frost said that a poem "begins in delight and ends in wisdom." Do you agree or disagree that this applies to "Birches"? Explain your view, including what you think *delight* and *wisdom* mean.

Extending the Text

7. **(Synthesis)** Possible response: A Puritan might say that the bent trees are part of God's divine plan for rewards and punishment and that people who fail to follow God's law will also be bent (punished) by God. Someone like Emerson might say that he can feel God's presence in the birches and that he takes delight in them.

Challenging the Text

8. **(Evaluation)** Possible responses: Yes, because he first focuses on the boy and the fun the boy has, and he ends with a serious comment about life. Delight is anything that makes people happy. Wisdom is the knowledge people acquire with age.

Before You Read
The Death of the Hired Man

Reading Focus
Home Is Where the Heart Is
Embedded in this poem is one of Frost's most famous sayings, one often quoted by many people who probably have no idea where it comes from: "'Home is the place where, when you have to go there, / They have to take you in.'" Another definition of home is also offered in the poem: "'Something you somehow haven't to deserve.'" To some people, "home" is a definite place; to others, it is a state of mind, a sense of connectedness and belonging.

A Dialogue with the Text
READER'S LOG

Read this poem as if it were a short story. As you read, make notes about the feelings that exist between Warren and Mary and the feelings each of them has toward Silas, the hired man. Also, note your own feelings or impressions about each of these three characters.

Elements of Literature
Dialogue in Verse
Most of this poem is a **dialogue** in **blank verse** (page 575). The poem's main character never speaks for himself, yet his presence dominates the poem through the dialogue of the other characters. By the last line, we have heard enough about the hired man to understand his background, habits, and attitudes. In gradually coming to know him, we also come to know the personalities of the husband and wife whose dialogue carries the drama.

The Death of the Hired Man Ⓐ

Robert Frost

Mary sat musing on the lamp-flame at the table,
Waiting for Warren. When she heard his step,
She ran on tiptoe down the darkened passage
To meet him in the doorway with the news
And put him on his guard. "Silas is back."
She pushed him outward with her through the door
And shut it after her. "Be kind," she said.
She took the market things from Warren's arms
And set them on the porch, then drew him down
To sit beside her on the wooden steps. Ⓑ

"When was I ever anything but kind to him?
But I'll not have the fellow back," he said.
"I told him so last haying, didn't I?
If he left then, I said, that ended it.
What good is he? Who else will harbor° him
At his age for the little he can do?
What help he is there's no depending on.
Off he goes always when I need him most.
He thinks he ought to earn a little pay,
Enough at least to buy tobacco with,
So he won't have to beg and be beholden.°
'All right,' I say, 'I can't afford to pay

15. harbor: provide safe shelter for.

21. beholden: indebted.

Into the Poem

Using **Before You Read** p. 569

Reading Focus
Have students work in small groups to explore what home means to them. Suggest each group present its ideas in the form of a cluster, such as the one below, that can be shared with the class.

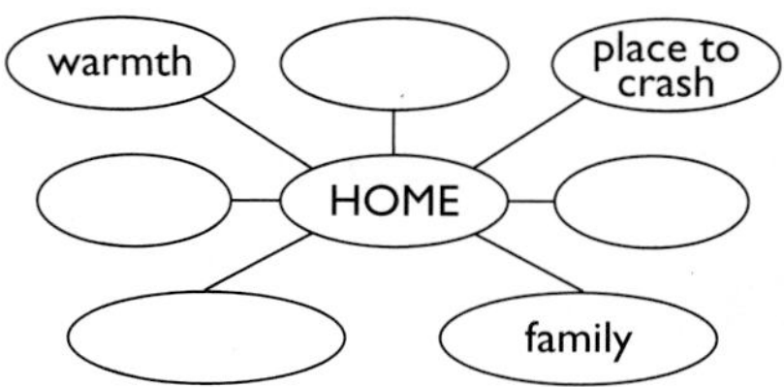

A. Literary Element: Blank Verse
This poem is written in blank verse, which is unrhymed iambic pentameter, a close imitation of normal speech patterns. One line flows into the next, producing a smoothness and creating a more subtle rhythm than found in poetry where pauses occur at the ends of lines.

B. Critical Reading: Speculating
? Who are Mary, Warren, and Silas? [Possible answers: Mary and Warren are married. Silas could be a son. Either he or Warren is the hired man.]

Strategies for Inclusion

Interpersonal Some students will be interested in the group dynamics among Mary, Warren, and Silas. Divide the class into groups to discuss these questions: (1) In what ways has Mary and Warren's farm become Silas's "home"? [They are people he can go to in times of need.] (2) Often people who view the world quite differently quarrel vehemently. What makes the relationship of Mary and Warren stable? [They respect each other. They talk; they communicate.]
(3) Why is it harder for Silas to go to his brother for help than to go to Mary and Warren? [They are more approachable.]

Advanced/Linguistic To understand the poem fully, a reader must visualize the prior conversation between Mary and Silas. Ask students to work in groups to write the scene of Silas's return; they should utilize all information gleaned from Mary and Warren's conversation (for example, Silas's changed looks, Mary's trying to get him to talk about his travels). They may want to write their scene in blank verse, as Frost has done.

Less Proficient Readers Some readers may find it difficult to tell who is speaking. Have them lay a transparency over the poem and ask them to underline Mary's words in one color and Warren's words in another.

A. Critical Reading: Drawing Conclusions

? What definitions of kindness do Mary and Warren have? [Possible answers: Mary thinks of kindness as being thoughtful and gentle. Warren thinks of kindness as putting up someone and offering him odd jobs for pay when Warren can afford it.]

B. Language Note: Quotation Marks

? What is the difference in the usage of double quotation marks and single quotation marks? [Double quotation marks are used for direct quotations and single quotation marks for a quotation within a quotation.]

C. Reader's Response: First Thoughts

? What are your feelings about Mary and Warren so far? [Sample responses: Mary seems warmer and softer than Warren; or Warren has been hardened by tough times.]

The Veteran in a New Field (1865) by Winslow Homer. Oil on canvas.
The Metropolitan Museum of Art; Bequest of Miss Adelaide Milton de Groot, 1967 (67.187.131).

(A) Any fixed wages, though I wish I could.'
'Someone else can.' 'Then someone else will have to.'
I shouldn't mind his bettering himself
If that was what it was. You can be certain,
(B) When he begins like that, there's someone at him
Trying to coax him off with pocket money—
In haying time, when any help is scarce.
In winter he comes back to us. I'm done."

"Sh! not so loud: He'll hear you," Mary said.

"I want him to: He'll have to soon or late."

"He's worn out. He's asleep beside the stove.
When I came up from Rowe's I found him here,
Huddled against the barn door fast asleep,
A miserable sight, and frightening, too—
You needn't smile—I didn't recognize him—
I wasn't looking for him—and he's changed.
Wait till you see."

(C) "Where did you say he'd been?"

"He didn't say. I dragged him to the house,
And gave him tea and tried to make him smoke.
I tried to make him talk about his travels.

OPTIONS FOR TEACHING

INTEGRATING THE LANGUAGE ARTS

Strategic Reading Model reading so that students will see that they should not necessarily pause at the end of each line. Point out the need to notice where there are periods and to read the poetic lines as complete sentences.

Mechanics To enable students to read and write conversation accurately, ask them to write a short conversation (sixteen to twenty lines, perhaps) that includes both double quotation marks and single quotation marks. (See Language Handbook, p. 1246, and *Language and Writing Skills Worksheets,* pp. 144–145.) Then, discuss the information given by quotation marks in the poem.

Writing: Dramatic Lyrics To help students understand dramatic lyrics, ask them to write lyrics, replaying the dialogue that might have occurred among Silas, Warren, and Mary. For example, students could have Warren find Silas alive, but near death.

Language and Style Ask students to discuss the difference between the descriptive interludes (ll. 103–110 and ll. 161–163) and the dialogue between Mary and Warren. [The descriptive lines use metaphors (the liquid moonlight in ll. 103–106, the silent music of the morning glories in ll. 107–110, the cloud ship in ll. 160–163). The dialogue uses conversational language.]

Nothing would do: He just kept nodding off."

"What did he say? Did he say anything?"

"But little."

"Anything? Mary, confess
He said he'd come to ditch° the meadow for me."

"Warren!"

"But did he? I just want to know."

"Of course he did. What would you have him say?
Surely you wouldn't grudge the poor old man
Some humble way to save his self-respect.
He added, if you really care to know,
He meant to clear the upper pasture, too.
That sounds like something you have heard before?
Warren, I wish you could have heard the way
He jumbled everything. I stopped to look
Two or three times—he made me feel so queer°—
To see if he was talking in his sleep.
He ran on° Harold Wilson—you remember—
The boy you had in haying four years since.
He's finished school, and teaching in his college.
Silas declares you'll have to get him back.
He says they two will make a team for work:
Between them they will lay this farm as smooth!
The way he mixed that in with other things.
He thinks young Wilson a likely lad, though daft
On education—you know how they fought
All through July under the blazing sun,
Silas up on the cart to build the load,
Harold along beside to pitch it on."

"Yes, I took care to keep well out of earshot."

"Well, those days trouble Silas like a dream.
You wouldn't think they would. How some things linger!
Harold's young college-boy's assurance piqued° him.
After so many years he still keeps finding
Good arguments he sees he might have used.
I sympathize. I know just how it feels
To think of the right thing to say too late.
Harold's associated in his mind with Latin.
He asked me what I thought of Harold's saying
He studied Latin, like the violin,
Because he liked it—that an argument!
He said he couldn't make the boy believe
He could find water with a hazel prong°—
Which showed how much good school had ever done him.
He wanted to go over that. But most of all
He thinks if he could have another chance

46. ditch: dig drainage channels in.

56. queer: uncomfortable; ill at ease.

58. ran on: kept talking in a rambling way about.

73. piqued: provoked.

83. hazel prong: forked branch used to find water underground.

D. Literary Element: Dialogue in Verse

? How would you describe Warren's tone here and the way he speaks with his wife? [Possible answers: Cynical, skeptical, knowing, demanding, or aggressive.]

E. Critical Reading: Making Inferences

? What does his reference to Harold Wilson suggest about Silas? [Possible answer: He has lost touch with reality. After working at the farm four summers before, Harold Wilson has gone on to college and teaching. Silas fails to understand that Wilson was working on a temporary basis.]

F. Reader's Response: First Thoughts

? How does this speech of Mary's make you feel? [Sample responses: I feel sorry for Silas; he is haunted by his failure both to teach Wilson to build a load of hay and to convince Wilson that Silas knew things too, in spite of his lack of education. Or I do not care for Silas; he fails to see the value of education or to understand that Harold does not need to know how to "witch" to make a living.]

COOPERATIVE LEARNING

Sharing Solutions After the students have finished reading and analyzing the poem, divide the class into small groups of three or four and ask each group to make a list of the social problems addressed in this poem (for example, homelessness, unemployment, and aging). Then, they should choose one problem and write an essay that defines the problem and proposes solutions. One student could take notes on the group's discussion, a second could be sure all students have a chance to speak, a third could lead the writing, and a fourth could conduct proofreading and editing. Students should use a chart like the following to help organize their ideas.

Problem	Situation	Solutions
[Relations between bosses and workers]	[Silas and Warren]	[Employ a mediator to encourage communication between parties]

A. Reader's Response: Extending the Text

? What modern dilemma does Silas's only achievement illustrate? [Sample responses: The world has moved on without him and there is no universal respect or need for his finest skill. Or those who ignore modern technology will find themselves left behind, no matter how outstanding their prior job performance has been.]

B. Literary Element: Style

Lines 103–110 present a particularly lovely description. Critic William H. Pritchard points out that even in his most simple farm narratives, like this poem, Frost has included passages of more elevated, lyrical style, possibly to relieve the monotony of being entirely colloquial.

C. Critical Reading: Making Connections

Lines 118–120 contain the two famous definitions of "home." Aside from the duty-mercy dichotomy, what other dichotomies might the two definitions represent? [Conservative-liberal and male-female.]

To teach him how to build a load of hay——"

"I know, that's Silas' one accomplishment.
He bundles every forkful in its place,
And tags and numbers it for future reference,
So he can find and easily dislodge it
In the unloading. Silas does that well.
He takes it out in bunches like big birds' nests.
You never see him standing on the hay
He's trying to lift, straining to lift himself."

"He thinks if he could teach him that, he'd be
Some good perhaps to someone in the world.
He hates to see a boy the fool of books.
Poor Silas, so concerned for other folk,
And nothing to look backward to with pride,
And nothing to look forward to with hope,
So now and never any different."

Part of a moon was falling down the west,
Dragging the whole sky with it to the hills.
Its light poured softly in her lap. She saw it
And spread her apron to it. She put out her hand
Among the harplike morning-glory strings,
Taut with the dew from garden bed to eaves,
As if she played unheard some tenderness
That wrought° on him beside her in the night.
"Warren," she said, "he has come home to die:
You needn't be afraid he'll leave you this time."

"Home," he mocked gently.

"Yes, what else but home?
It all depends on what you mean by home.
Of course he's nothing to us, any more
Than was the hound that came a stranger to us
Out of the woods, worn out upon the trail."

"Home is the place where, when you have to go there,
They have to take you in."

"I should have called it
Something you somehow haven't to deserve."

Warren leaned out and took a step or two,
Picked up a little stick, and brought it back
And broke it in his hand and tossed it by.
"Silas has better claim on us you think
Than on his brother? Thirteen little miles
As the road winds would bring him to his door.
Silas has walked that far no doubt today.
Why doesn't he go there? His brother's rich,
A somebody—director in the bank."

110. wrought: worked.

CLASSROOM MANAGEMENT

Managing the Reader's Response Classroom
Before beginning a classroom discussion of poetry, ask a student volunteer to read the poem(s) that will be discussed. Allowing a student to read will signal that you desire students participate in discussion, that they are responsible for participating, and that volunteers are welcome to speak. Furthermore, having a student read the poem aloud will help the class prepare for discussion by focusing student attention and setting a serious tone.

"He never told us that."

"We know it, though."

"I think his brother ought to help, of course.
I'll see to that if there is need. He ought of right
To take him in, and might be willing to—
He may be better than appearances.
But have some pity on Silas. Do you think
If he had any pride in claiming kin
Or anything he looked for from his brother,
He'd keep so still about him all this time?"

"I wonder what's between them."

"I can tell you.
Silas is what he is—we wouldn't mind him—
But just the kind that kinsfolk can't abide.
He never did a thing so very bad.

He don't know why he isn't quite as good
As anybody. Worthless though he is,
He won't be made ashamed to please his brother."

"*I* can't think Si ever hurt anyone."

"No, but he hurt my heart the way he lay
And rolled his old head on that sharp-edged chair-back.
He wouldn't let me put him on the lounge.
You must go in and see what you can do.
I made the bed up for him there tonight.
You'll be surprised at him—how much he's broken.
His working days are done; I'm sure of it."

"I'd not be in a hurry to say that."

"I haven't been. Go, look, see for yourself. E
But, Warren, please remember how it is:
He's come to help you ditch the meadow.
He has a plan. You mustn't laugh at him.
He may not speak of it, and then he may.
I'll sit and see if that small sailing cloud
Will hit or miss the moon."

It hit the moon.
Then there were three there, making a dim row,
The moon, the little silver cloud, and she.

Warren returned—too soon, it seemed to her—
Slipped to her side, caught up her hand and waited.

"Warren?" she questioned.

"Dead," was all he answered.

D. Critical Reading: Making Inferences

? Why hasn't Silas gone to his brother for help? [Possible answers: His brother would treat him like a failure, would be ashamed of him, and would humiliate him; or Silas has too much pride to ask for help.]

E. Critical Reading: Predicting

? What do you think will happen when Warren looks in on Silas? [Possible answers: Silas will be dead; or Warren will soften and take Silas in.] If students have read the poem at home, ask whether they felt suspense at this point.

F. Literary Element: Character

? What perhaps unexpected trait does Warren show at the end of the poem? [He shows tenderness and sensitivity as he takes hold of Mary's hand to tell her the bad news.]

CROSSING THE CURRICULUM

Health Have students research how people react to knowing they are about to die—and what is important to them. Ask these students to report to the class and to lead a discussion on the relevance of this information to the poem.

Social Sciences Invite students to research the changes in agricultural methods during the first half of this century. They should report their findings to the class by setting up an agricultural fair. Then, ask the class to discuss how these changes might affect Silas, whose skills are no longer in demand.

Primary Sources

Have students read or review the material on **blank verse** found in Elements of Literature on p. 575. Be sure students understand the difference between blank verse (poetry with unrhymed iambic pentameter) and **free verse** (poetry without regular rhyme or meter). Then, have them read Frost's commentary on free verse. To help students understand Frost's viewpoint, ask them to select one of his poems, such as "Once by the Pacific" on p. 564, and to turn it into free verse by paraphrasing the lines. Have students contrast the recast poem with Frost's original, and then have them compare their opinions to Frost's, based on his interview with Feld.

PRIMARY **Sources** AN INTERVIEW

"I must have the pulse beat of rhythm . . ."

These comments are from an interview held on October 21, 1923, with *New York Times* reporter Rose C. Feld. Not long after the interview, Frost won his first Pulitzer Prize. Here, Frost has been talking about American poetry.

. . . We're still a bit afraid. America, for instance, was afraid to accept Walt Whitman when he first sang the songs of democracy. His influence on American poetry began to be felt only after the French had hailed him as a great writer, a literary revolutionist. Our own poet had to be imported from France before we were sure of his strength.

Robert Frost at John F. Kennedy's inauguration, January 20, 1961.
Jim Brown/Black Star.

Today almost every man who writes poetry confesses his debt to Whitman. Many have gone very much further than Whitman would have traveled with them. They are the people who believe in wide straddling.

I, myself, as I said before, don't like it for myself. I do not write free verse; I write blank verse. I must have the pulse beat of rhythm, I like to hear it beating under the things I write.

That doesn't mean I do not like to read a bit of free verse occasionally. I do. It sometimes succeeds in painting a picture that is very clear and startling. It's good as something created momentarily for its sudden startling effect; it hasn't the qualities, however, of something lastingly beautiful.

And sometimes my objection to it is that it's a pose. It's not honest. When a man sets out consciously to tear up forms and rhythms and measures, then he is not interested in giving you poetry. He just wants to perform; he wants to show you his tricks. He will get an effect; nobody will deny that, but it is not a harmonious effect.

Sometimes it strikes me that the free-verse people got their idea from incorrect proof sheets. I have had stuff come from the printers with lines half left out or positions changed about. I read the poems as they stood, distorted and half finished, and I confess I get a rather pleasant sensation from them. They make a sort of nightmarish half-sense. . . .

—Robert Frost

STRATEGIES FOR INCLUSION

Less Proficient Readers Students will probably feel at ease with the conversational style of the interview but might have difficulty understanding some of the references. You might need to clarify the following.

- When Frost makes the reference to traveling with Whitman, he is speaking figuratively, not literally.
- When Frost submitted his poetry to a publisher, the printer would set the poem in type. Frost would receive a copy of his poem (a proof sheet) as it had been set by the printer so that he could correct any errors.

PROGRAM MANAGER

Application and Reinforcement For reinforcement of the elements of literature introduced in this lesson, see **Transparency 11.2** in the ***Audiovisual Resources Binder.***

Making Meanings

First Thoughts

1. Look back over the notes you made in your Reader's Log. How did you feel about each of the three characters in this poem?

Shaping Interpretations

2. What does the **dialogue** between Warren and Mary reveal about their individual characters?
3. Describe the basic problem facing Warren, Mary, and Silas. How does Warren's attitude toward Silas differ from Mary's? Do you think Warren's feelings about Silas are mixed? Give evidence from the poem to support your opinion.
4. Identify the details in lines 103–110 that create a vivid image of the **setting.** Besides contributing to atmosphere, what does this passage tell us about Mary's character?
5. Does the conclusion of this poem strike you as inevitable? Why or why not? What would your feelings have been if Warren, instead of answering "Dead" to Mary's question, had answered "Asleep," or "Sharpening his scythe"?
6. Find the two definitions of "home" offered in the poem. One critic has said that one definition is based on law and duty, the other definition on mercy. Which is which, and do you agree with the critic's observation? Which definition do you favor?

Extending the Text

7. State in your own words the poem's **message.** Do you think this message has any particular importance in today's world? How would it apply, for example, to the problem of homelessness in our society?

Elements of Literature

Blank Verse

"The poet goes in like a rope skipper to make the most of his opportunities," said Frost in an essay called "The Constant Symbol." "If he trips himself he stops the rope. He is of our stock and has been brought up by ear to choice of two meters, strict iambic and loose iambic (not to count varieties of the latter)." "The Death of the Hired Man" is written in **blank verse,** which is unrhymed iambic pentameter. It is called *blank* verse because the lines do not have end rhymes. Iambic pentameter means that there are five iambs to each line; an *iamb* is an unaccented syllable followed by an accented syllable: da DUM (˘´).

1. Scan the first ten lines, and recite them aloud to hear the meter.
2. Look over the poem, and find examples of strict iambic and loose iambic meter.
3. Do you think Frost ever "trips" himself in this poem?
4. Take ten lines from this poem, and rewrite them in the free-verse style of Walt Whitman (page 348). Where will you break the lines? What rearrangement of words will have to be made to break the iambic meter?
5. Look at Frost's comments on free verse in Primary Sources (page 574). What is *your* opinion of Frost's ideas?

C. Bradley Simmons/
Bruce Coleman, Inc.

Making Meanings

First Thoughts

1. Possible responses: Mary is likable, for she has a kind heart; Silas is a sad character, for he has no real home; or Warren is a disagreeable man, for he snaps at his wife as soon as he arrives home.

Shaping Interpretations

2. Warren is stubborn, but at the same time he is willing to listen to what Mary has to say. Mary is sympathetic to Silas's plight and knows how to sway her husband to soften his stance. Both are compassionate people.
3. Although he is old and ill, Silas wants to stay and work on Mary and Warren's farm. Mary regards Silas as an old man who has come home to die. Warren feels Silas is an unreliable nuisance; however, his feelings are mixed. He says Silas could build a good load of hay and admits that Silas would never hurt anyone.
4. The lines describe the setting moon whose light falls on Mary's apron in her lap. Mary extends her hand to the morning-glory strings as if she is playing a harp as she talks about Silas. Mary is compassionate and tactful.
5. Responses will vary, but most students will agree that the poem would not have closure with either of the other choices.
6. Warren's definition (ll. 118–119) is based on law and duty. Mary's definition (ll. 119–120) is based on mercy. Most students will agree with the critic's observation. Possible responses: Mercy, because it is humane. Or law and duty, because people will know how to act and what is expected of them.

Extending the Text

7. **(Analysis and Evaluation)** A possible message is that people need to have compassion for those less fortunate. In today's world homeless people need compassionate people who will help provide food and shelter.

Elements of Literature

Answers

1. Students are to recite the first ten lines aloud.
2. Strict iambic pentameter: ll. 4, 6, 7, 8, 9, 10; loose iambic pentameter: ll. 1, 2, 3, 5.
3. At times Frost ends a sentence in midline (for example, ll. 2, 5, and 7) or breaks a line into dialogue between two speakers (for example, ll. 39, 45, and 47). These seem to be deliberate stops rather than examples of Frost's tripping himself. He also uses loose iambic meter, but that is to keep a natural sound to the dialogue and so is not Frost's tripping himself. To force the meter would be to force the speech of the characters.
4. Lines chosen will vary. Some rearrangement of words and number of lines might occur, as in this revision of ll. 78–81:
   He mentally associates Harold
   with Latin.
   He asked me what I thought of
   Harold's claim
   To study Latin because he likes it,
   As he likes the violin—
   What kind of argument is that?
5. Possible answers: He may well be criticizing free verse as people criticized Whitman; or I agree with Frost, for I like a regular rhythm.

Choices: Building Your Portfolio

1. **Writer's Notebook** Remind students to save their work. They may use it as prewriting for the Writer's Workshop on p. 685.
2. **Critical Writing** Remind students that the Dark Romantics are Poe, Hawthorne, and Melville. To explore the conflicts students might focus on Frost's lyric poems.
3. **Critical Writing** Remind students that it is better not to depend on their memories. They should re-read the poems.
4. **Creative Writing** As students plan their works, encourage them to think about these issues.
   - What is the basic story of "The Death of the Hired Man"? How close should a modern story stay to Frost's story?
   - What was Frost's message in "The Death of the Hired Man"? In what way can my message be the same? Should it be the same?
5. **Speaking and Listening** To help students lead discussion, tell them to think of themselves as talk-show hosts. Their role is to keep the discussion on track, and so they should prepare questions and think about what to do if discussion falters.
6. **Art** Remind students that an effective collage often contains words as well as pictures.
7. **Music/Art** Before they get started, ask students to decide the tasks each will complete. Have one person make sure everyone has an assignment and that each student completes his or her task.

PORTFOLIO ASSESSMENT

Choices: Assessment Criteria For help in evaluating these Choices assignments, see the criteria in the ***Portfolio Management System,*** pp. 134–135.

CHOICES: Building Your Portfolio

Writer's Notebook

1. Collecting Ideas for a Speculation About Causes and Effects

WORK IN PROGRESS

Write down your own list of speculative questions suggested by the Frost poems you have read. What is the significance of the color white in "Design"? Why are the people in "Neither Out Far Nor In Deep" looking out to sea? What motivated Silas in "The Death of the Hired Man" to come back to Warren and Mary? Keep your notes for possible use in the Writer's Workshop on page 685.

Critical Writing

2. Frost Bites

The critic Louise Bogan pointed out the "tensions, dark conflicts, and passionate involvements" that appear in Frost's poetry and "pervade certain poems with almost nightmare intensity." In a brief essay, explore examples of the "dark conflicts" in Frost's poetry. What does Frost share with the Dark Romantics (page 213)? In what sense do Frost's poems have "bite"?

Critical Writing

3. Poetic Parallels

In a brief essay, compare and contrast "Design" and Emily Dickinson's poem "Apparently with no surprise" (page 385). Before you write, gather your data in a chart like the one below:

	Dickinson	Frost
Message in poem		
Use of symbols		
Tone		
Use of rhymes and rhythms		
Use of imagery		

Creative Writing

4. Making It Modern

In a poem, narrative, or screenplay, set "The Death of the Hired Man" in contemporary surroundings with modern characters. You might set the story in a city, in a rural area, in a suburb, on a modern-day farm, or in a migrant worker camp. Be sure to include **dialogue, conflict,** and **resolution** in your story.

Speaking and Listening

5. Reading Nature

The Puritans and later the Romantics "read" lessons into nature. Lead a class discussion about whether or not Frost's poems "Design" and "Birches" are part of this same tradition. Discuss whether Frost is more like the Puritans or the Romantics in his attitude.

Art

6. Dark Design

Create a collage that captures some of the central themes and images that you feel sum up Frost's poetry. In choosing appropriate visuals, consider similes, metaphors, and images from the Frost poems you have read. Write a brief explanation of the thought that went behind each image you chose.

Music / Art

7. Frost Three Ways

With a partner or a team, choose several Frost poems from this collection or from a book of Frost's poetry, and select music and works of art that relate to the poems' themes, images, and tones. Prepare slides, video, or overhead transparencies to show your accompanying visuals, and play recorded music (or perform your own compositions) as you read aloud Frost's poems, creating your own multimedia presentation.

STRATEGIES FOR INCLUSION

English Language Development Students often have a difficult time making inferences. Because they are unfamiliar with the cultural background of some stories and may have limited vocabularies that do not allow them to recognize connotations, they find it difficult to be sure that their interpretations of poetry and literature are accurate. Help these students complete activity #1 by generating a few of your own questions and explaining aloud the thought processes that led you to an answer.

Logical-Mathematical For activity #5, to help students determine whether Frost belongs to the same tradition as the Puritans and the Romantics, suggest they make a three-column chart like the following. In each column, they should list attitudes toward nature.

Attitudes Toward Nature

Puritans	Romantics	Frost

John Crowe Ransom

(1888–1974)

He was the son of a minister and perhaps the most intellectually elegant conservative of twentieth-century American writers, but John Crowe Ransom—poet, teacher, editor, and critic—was nevertheless an innovator in his own way. He was the founder of a group of renegade Southern poets. He helped form a new and innovative school of critical thought called New Criticism. He was also mentor to some of the most important young poets and critics of the time. His students—among them Randall Jarrell (page 932), Robert Lowell (page 948), Robert Penn Warren, and James Wright (page 151)—found a larger audience than their teacher ever did, but Ransom did more than any of them to keep alive the delicacy, beauty, and endless resources of the English language.

UPI/Bettmann.

Ransom was born in Pulaski, Tennessee. His illustrious teaching career at his alma mater, Vanderbilt University in Tennessee, lasted for more than twenty years, and it was during this stage of his life that he became a leader of the group of Southern writers called the "Fugitives." The Fugitives were determined to assert Southern cultural values, and they idealized a genteel, agrarian way of life that seemed to offer a more stable environment than Northern industrialism could. Their poetry was known for a combination of intellectual wit and the fatalism associated with Greek tragedy.

Changing times made Ransom's work, with its tone of wit, ironic detachment, and almost classical elegance of expression, seem like the echo of another age. But today Ransom is appreciated not only for his considerable influence on some of the best poets of the modern era, but also for the shining perfection of his small but memorable body of work.

Before You Read

Bells for John Whiteside's Daughter

Reading Focus

Preserved in Memory

Everyone experiences losses in life, but poets try to redeem, through their art, what we have lost.

A Dialogue with the Text

As you read the poem, note words or images that seem to express the speaker's emotions or attitudes. Then note in your own words what you think are the speaker's feelings about his subject.

Elements of Literature

Tone

Tone is the attitude a writer takes toward the subject of a work, the characters in it, or the audience. Ransom often combines two different tones—tenderness and detachment, for example—in one poem.

Quick Planning Guide

Into the Poem

Author Biography p. 577

Before You Read p. 577

- **Reading Focus:** Students discover memories help people.
- **A Dialogue with the Text: Set a Purpose** Note speaker's emotions and attitudes in Reader's Log
- **Elements of Literature: Tone**

Through the Poem

"Bells for John Whiteside's Daughter" p. 578

Making Meanings p. 579

Beyond the Poem

Choices: Building Your Portfolio p. 579

- **Writer's Notebook:** Collect ideas for a speculation about causes and effects
- **Critical Writing:** Support or refute a critic's claim in a brief essay
- **Critical Writing:** Compare two poems in a brief essay

Program Manager

- **Planning Instruction** See Teaching Notes, *Teaching Resources B,* pp. 8–9, for objectives, a summary, literary elements, and additional biographical information.
- **Instructional Support** See Graphic Organizer for Active Reading, *Teaching Resources B,* p. 29, for a Through the Poem activity.
- **Audiotaped Readings** To help learners through the lesson, use the Selected Reading, Audiocassette 2, Side B, in the *Audiovisual Resources Binder.*
- **Assessment** See Selection Test, *Test Booklet,* pp. 135–136.

Portfolio Assessment

Portfolio Assessment

For help with self- and teacher assessment of reading skills, see the *Portfolio Management System,* p. 53.

Into the Poem

Using **Before You Read** p. 577

A Dialogue with the Text

Work through the first verse of the poem with the students. Have them note words or images that express the speaker's emotions and have them identify those emotions. Then, ask them to continue reading and making notes on their own.

Through the Poem

A. Reader's Response: First Thoughts

? What is the occasion of the poem? [Sample responses: It marks a serious moment in the girl's life; or she has died.]

B. Literary Element: Tone

? What is the speaker's tone? [Possible response: Somber, but almost lighthearted.] What conveys this tone? [The bells, the speaker's being prevented from expressing displeasure, the body lying stretched out.]

Eleanor (1901) by Frank Benson.
Oil on canvas ($29\frac{1}{2}'' \times 25''$).
Museum of Art, Rhode Island School of Design; Gift of the Estate of Mrs. Gustav Radeke.

Bells for John Whiteside's Daughter

John Crowe Ransom

There was such speed in her little body,
And such lightness in her footfall,
It is no wonder that her brown study°
Astonishes us all.

Her wars were bruited° in our high window.
We looked among orchard trees and beyond.
Where she took arms against her shadow
Or harried° unto the pond

The lazy geese, like a snow cloud
Dripping their snow on the green grass,
Tricking and stopping, sleepy and proud,
Who cried in goose, Alas,

For the tireless heart within the little
Lady with rod that made them rise
From their noon apple-dreams, and scuttle
Goose-fashion under the skies!

But now go the bells, and we are ready;
In one house we are sternly stopped
To say we are vexed° at her brown study,
Lying so primly propped.

3. brown study: state of being lost in deep thought.
5. bruited (bro͞ot′id): reported.
8. harried (har′ēd): forced; pushed along.
19. vexed: disturbed; annoyed.

Options for Teaching

Strategies for Inclusion

Less Proficient Readers To help students determine the meaning of the poem, ask them to notice the punctuation of the poem, especially the periods. Point out, for example, that ll. 7–16 are all one sentence.

Auditory Read the poem aloud for the first reading, demonstrating that pauses need to come for meaning, not at the end of each line. After the students have studied the poem, lead them in a group reading.

Spatial/Visual Students may profit from drawing the two scenes from the poem, showing the little girl first playing in the orchard or driving off the geese, and then motionless in her casket. They will need to read the poem carefully to make their pictures accurate.

Learners Having Difficulty Students who have difficulty attending to or comprehending what they have read frequently require active participation to engage them in their reading. To meet their needs, have them visit a local graveyard with the assignment of collecting the most remarkable comments on gravestones. They may wish to make rubbings of gravestones they select. This activity should assist students in understanding that Ransom is not alone in his perception of death as not purely mournful.

Making Meanings

First Thoughts

1. How does the speaker feel about the little girl who died? How did the poet make *you* feel about the Whitesides' daughter and about death itself?

Shaping Interpretations

2. What characteristics of John Whiteside's daughter make the speaker astonished at her "brown study"?
3. What action of the little girl caused the geese to cry, "Alas"? What additional overtones does this cry take on, given the poem's subject?
4. What details in the last stanza make it clear what the speaker is looking at?
5. What do you associate with the verb *vexed* in the next to last line of the poem? What verb would you expect the speaker to use to describe his reaction to the dead child?

Challenging the Text

6. The critic Babette Deutsch once said of Ransom: "[W]hatever his subject . . . his tone is right. The glint of irony is there, deepened as well as softened by a sensitiveness without a grain of sentimentality." Look back over the notes you made in your Reader's Log. Do you think Ransom's **tone** is appropriate, given the highly emotional nature of the subject? Why or why not?

Choices: Building Your Portfolio

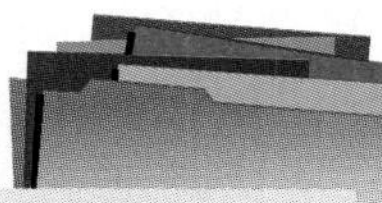

Writer's Notebook

1. Collecting Ideas for a Speculation About Causes and Effects

WORK IN PROGRESS

In Ransom's poem, the little girl is remembered after her death in a way that captures what she was like in life. Write down your feelings about the effects of memorial tributes to those who have died. Do works of art that honor the dead somehow help us to cope with loss? Why do you think artists throughout history have created tributes to those who have died? Do such tributes confer a kind of immortality? Save your notes for possible use in the Writer's Workshop on page 685.

Critical Writing

2. The Human Condition

The critic Thomas Daniel Young wrote that Ransom's poems emphasize such themes as "mortality and the fleetingness of youthful vigor and grace . . . [and] the disparity between the world as man would have it and as it actually is, between what [people] want and need emotionally and what is available for them. . . ." In a brief essay, explain whether or not you believe this comment is supported by the poem. Use specific references to the poem.

Critical Writing

3. Remembrances

Write a brief essay comparing "Bells for John Whiteside's Daughter" with Henry Wadsworth Longfellow's "The Cross of Snow" (page 178). Compare each poem's tone, imagery, and views of death. Support your comparison with specific examples from the poems.

Making Meanings

First Thoughts

1. Possible responses: The speaker is upset that the girl he liked died so young. She seems to have had a lot of fun and been very active. The poem makes death seem unfair.

Shaping Interpretations

2. She was always fast and lively.
3. She chased the geese with a rod. *Alas* has an overtone of sadness because the girl has died.
4. The bells ring and her body lies for display.
5. Possible answers: Frustrated; mourning, saddened, or crying.

Challenging the Text

6. **(Evaluation)** Possible response: The word *vexed* helps make the tone appropriate because it implies that the speaker and the speaker's companions cannot quite accept that a little girl so full of life is now dead.

Choices: Building Your Portfolio

2. **Critical Writing** Before students begin writing, have them work in a small group to discuss Young's quotation. To help focus their thoughts, suggest they consider these questions.

- What is the theme of "Bells for John Whiteside's Daughter"? What evidence can you find to support your statement?
- How, if at all, does this theme relate to the quotation?

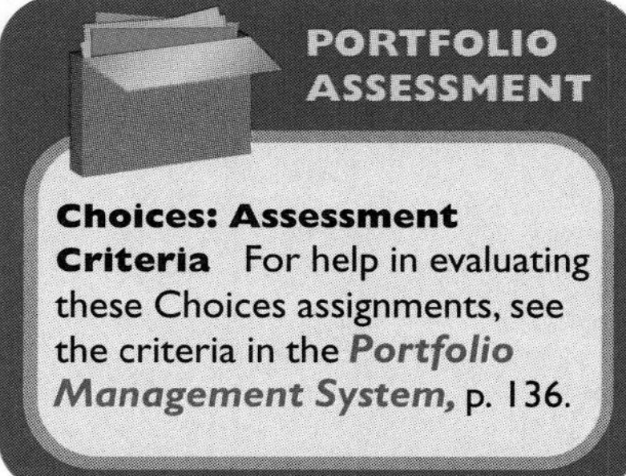

Choices: Assessment Criteria For help in evaluating these Choices assignments, see the criteria in the *Portfolio Management System,* p. 136.

STRATEGIES FOR INCLUSION

Visual Students who have photographs of the subject they wish to write about for activity #1 might like to bring them in. Studying the photographs can help jog students' memories and aid them in determining the overall impression the person made on them.

TECHNOLOGY

Advanced As an alternative to writing an essay in activity #3, have students create a multimedia performance in which they explore the **themes** in "Bells for John Whiteside's Daughter" and "The Cross of Snow." Have them combine music, images, and text to create a personal response to the poems.

QUICK PLANNING GUIDE

Into the Poem

Author Biography p. 580

Before You Read p. 580

- **Reading Focus: Scaffolding** Students discover nature is the teacher of truth.
- **Quickwrite:** Write about feelings for America in Reader's Log

Through the Poem

"Shine, Perishing Republic" pp. 581–582

Making Meanings p. 582

Beyond the Poem

Choices: Building Your Portfolio p. 582

- **Writer's Notebook:** Collect ideas for a speculation about causes and effects
- **Critical Writing:** Summarize and evaluate the poem in a brief essay

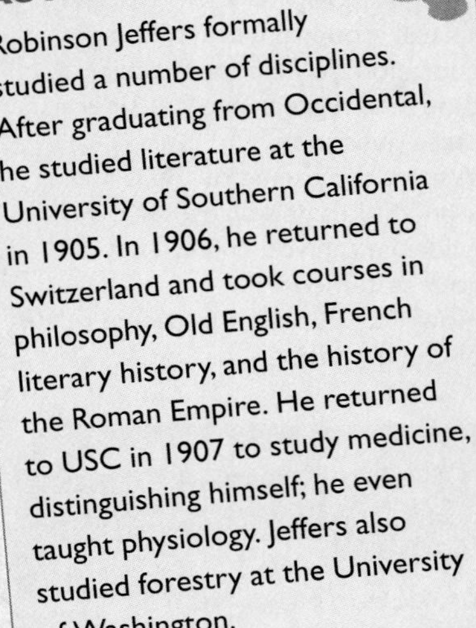

ABOUT THE AUTHOR

Robinson Jeffers formally studied a number of disciplines. After graduating from Occidental, he studied literature at the University of Southern California in 1905. In 1906, he returned to Switzerland and took courses in philosophy, Old English, French literary history, and the history of the Roman Empire. He returned to USC in 1907 to study medicine, distinguishing himself; he even taught physiology. Jeffers also studied forestry at the University of Washington.

Robinson Jeffers

(1887–1962)

Robinson Jeffers by Edward Weston.

The son of a theology teacher, Robinson Jeffers was born in Pittsburgh. His parents moved from place to place, and, by the time he was fifteen, he had already spent several years in Europe before the family settled in California. There Jeffers earned a degree from Occidental College and went on to do postgraduate work, including a term at medical school. But Jeffers did not pursue any of the careers he studied for. Fascinated with poetry, he found he could make no serious commitment to anything else.

In 1912, Jeffers inherited money from an uncle. This allowed him the freedom to live on his own terms and to provide for his wife and two sons without ever holding a job. Asserting his sudden independence, Jeffers bought property in the coastal village of Carmel, California. With his own hands he built a stone tower that would serve as a retreat and working studio for the rest of his life. As in the case of the Irish poet William Butler Yeats, the tower became symbolic for Jeffers of his worldview and his way of life; he lived a monklike existence apart from neighborly society and the literary world, marked by a lonely devotion to nature.

A man against the American grain, Jeffers had little confidence in the virtues of religion or democracy; he also kept a skeptical eye fixed on scientific progress and social advances. His philosophical outlook, combining fatalism with pessimism, was closer to that of the ancient Greeks than to that of the common American. For wayward humankind, aware of everything but its insignificance, he had little hope. He regarded awareness itself as a kind of disease to which natural forces are immune.

Much of Jeffers's poetic inspiration came from nature's power to endure and silently witness the absurdities of civilization. Rocks and the sea, hawks in the wind, sea creatures thrown upon the sea-washed ledges of the Pacific shore—these are Jeffers's recurring images and emblems. Although humorless, grandly isolated, and nourished by disgust, Jeffers was able to attract readers who were impressed by the integrity of his single-minded convictions and by his dark vision of the limited life of human beings.

BEFORE YOU READ

SHINE, PERISHING REPUBLIC

Reading Focus

Self-Sufficiency

This poem was written in the Big Sur region in California, where great mountains emerge like dripping shoulders out of the Pacific Ocean. The circumstance is that of a remote homestead built with the speaker's own hands. The speaker is a father determined to live apart from civilization and to have his children learn the lessons of nature rather than those of schoolbooks.

Quickwrite

READER'S LOG

Quickwrite your own feelings about America today. Do you consider it a "perishing republic" that has lost its positive qualities, or do you think the nation's values and strengths are still intact?

PROGRAM MANAGER

- **Planning Instruction** See Teaching Notes, *Teaching Resources B,* pp. 9–10, for objectives, a summary, literary elements, and additional biographical information for this selection.
- **Instructional Support** Before beginning the instructional lesson, see Graphic Organizer for Active Reading, *Teaching Resources B,* p. 30, for a Through the Poem activity.
- **Assessment** See Selection Test, *Test Booklet,* pp. 135–136.

Old Mill Big Sur (1933) by Millard Sheets. Watercolor on paper.
The E. Gene Crain Collection, Laguna Hills, California.

Shine, Perishing Republic

Robinson Jeffers

While this America settles in the mold of its vulgarity, heavily
  thickening to empire,
And protest, only a bubble in the molten mass, pops and sighs
  out, and the mass hardens,

I sadly smiling remember that the flower fades to make fruit,
  the fruit rots to make earth.
Out of the mother; and through the spring exultances,
  ripeness and decadence; and home to the mother.

Using BEFORE YOU READ p. 580

Reading Focus

Ask students to name some writers who looked to nature for truth. [Possible answers: Bryant, Emerson, Thoreau, Dickinson, Frost.] Robinson Jeffers also looked to nature for truth; like Thoreau, he moved to a remote location and lived in isolation. Ask students if they would do the same thing if they had the opportunity. Have them list the pros and cons of such an existence.

Pros	Cons
[no gangs]	[no friends]
[clean air]	[boredom]

Portfolio Assessment For help with teacher assessment of reading skills, see the ***Portfolio Management System,*** pp. 54–55.

OPTIONS FOR TEACHING

STRATEGIES FOR INCLUSION

English Language Development Check students' ability to recognize the pronoun antecedents in two important lines of the poem. In ll.5–6, "You making haste, haste on decay: not blameworthy; life is good, be it stubbornly long or suddenly / A mortal splendor," ask students what *it* refers to ["life"]. In the last line "There is the trap that catches noblest spirits, that caught–they say–God, when he walked on earth," ask them to identify the second *that* ["trap"].

Auditory Jeffers is one of the more difficult poets in this Collection, so you might read the poem aloud to the students. After you have read it aloud once, read it aloud again, pausing to allow volunteers to paraphrase Jeffers's thoughts. Then, have students work in pairs to read the poem to one another, alternating stanzas.

Through the Poem

A. Critical Reading: Identifying Main Ideas

? How does the speaker expect the children to avoid corruption? [They will leave the city and live close to nature in the mountains.]

B. Humanities Connection
The reference to God is to the historical figure of Jesus, who taught that people should love their neighbors as themselves and who was crucified despite his message of love.

Making Meanings

First Thoughts

1. Possible responses: Trust no one; or humankind even disappointed God. Jeffers says to be careful in loving other people.

Shaping Interpretations

2. Melted material is hardening into the rigidity of conformity (the mold). "Vulgarity" refers to undesirable choices of the majority. *Empire* implies a mass of people governed by one person rather than by individuals.
3. America's decadence is part of a natural cycle.
4. Cynical and pessimistic. Possible response: Yes, his tone is consistently cynical throughout the poem.
5. Conformity ("mold"), complacency ("settles in"), massiveness ("heavily thickening"), intolerance ("mass hardens").

Connecting with the Text

6. Possible responses: No, I still think the nation's values are intact; or I now think he may be right—it is time to move out of the cities.

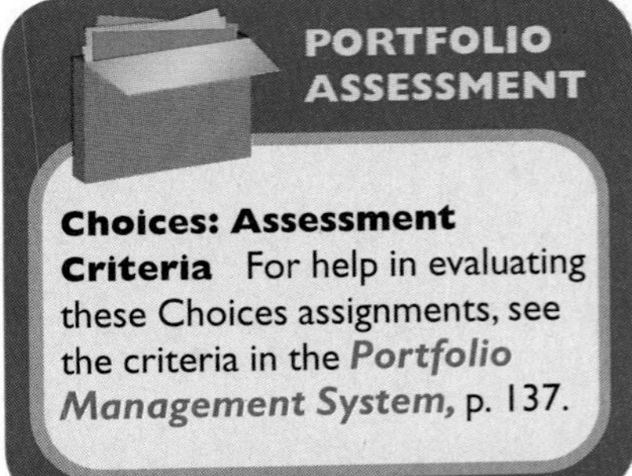

PORTFOLIO ASSESSMENT

Choices: Assessment Criteria For help in evaluating these Choices assignments, see the criteria in the ***Portfolio Management System,*** p. 137.

You making haste, haste on decay: not blameworthy; life is
good, be it stubbornly long or suddenly
A mortal splendor: meteors are not needed less than
mountains: shine, perishing republic.

A But for my children, I would have them keep their distance
from the thickening center; corruption
Never has been compulsory, when the cities lie at the
monster's feet there are left the mountains.

And boys, be in nothing so moderate as in love of man, a
clever servant, insufferable master.
B There is the trap that catches noblest spirits, that caught—
they say—God, when he walked on earth.

Making Meanings

First Thoughts

1. What thoughts or feelings did you have about the speaker's advice in the last stanza? In what ways is this advice quite the opposite of "love thy neighbor"?

Shaping Interpretations

2. The first stanza contains an **implied metaphor.** What is America compared to? What does "vulgarity" mean here, and why does the republic thicken to *empire?*
3. What attitude toward America does the second stanza express?
4. What is the speaker's attitude in the last stanza? Do you think he really means what he says in line 9?
5. What does the speaker seem to think is the cause of the republic's condition?

Connecting with the Text

6. Review the Quickwrite you wrote before reading the poem. Did the poem make you rethink any of your responses?

Choices: Building Your Portfolio

Writer's Notebook

1. Collecting Ideas for a Speculation About Causes and Effects

Brainstorm a list of possible topics suggested by Jeffers's poem: why a civilization might decay, why someone would choose to live apart from society, why someone would feel as Jeffers does about America. Save your notes for possible use in the Writer's Workshop on page 685.

Critical Writing

2. Taking Stock

This poem was published in 1925. In a brief essay, explain why you think Jeffers's view of the condition of American society is or is not still valid. Summarize the view expressed in the poem. Then tell whether or not you think this view applies to contemporary America. Support your position with specific references to the poem and to contemporary life.

Beyond the Poem

Choices: Building Your Portfolio

2. **Critical Writing** Have students suggest contemporary issues that support or refute Jeffers's position (terrorism, racism, crime, homeless shelters, food banks, or advances in medicine) before they determine their stand.

STRATEGIES FOR INCLUSION

Special Needs Students who have difficulty sorting through complicated reference material may benefit from computer-accessible information to assist them in preparing for activity #2. CD-ROM almanacs and encyclopedias contain a vast pool of written information, and some have photographs with written captions and video clips with sound. An easy-to-read text presented in a timetable format is *The Timetables of History* by Bernard Grun.

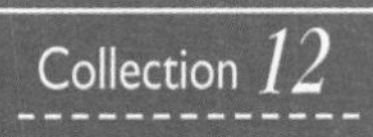

THE DREAM AND THE REALITY

Theme: **Illusions and Truth**

Dreams may take many forms—wistful expectations for the future, nostalgic longings for the past, escapist fantasies about the present—but all dreamers eventually find that they must reconcile their dreams with the facts of the real world.

Thematic Focus

Each short story in Collection 12 illustrates the conflict between dreams and reality.

- **Winter Dreams** A young man's dream girl finally disillusions him.
- **The Leader of the People** A grandfather and his grandson face the reality that the days of westward exploration and adventure are over.
- **The Secret Life of Walter Mitty** A henpecked husband leads a glamourous fantasy life.
- **A Worn Path** The habit of love prompts a journey fraught with difficulties.

Literary Focus

Literary Element	Selection / Feature
Motivation/Paradox	**Winter Dreams**
Conflict/Figures of Speech	**The Leader of the People**
Parody	**The Secret Life of Walter Mitty**
Theme	**A Worn Path**

Writing Focus

The following flowchart shows how the writing assignment for each selection relates to and builds toward the culminating writing assignment presented in the Writer's Workshop at the end of the unit.

Selection	Work-in-Progress Assignment
Winter Dreams	Write character interview questions and answers for a speculation about causes and effects p. 605
The Leader of the People	Write extension of the ending for a speculation about causes and effects p. 622
The Secret Life of Walter Mitty	Freewrite about Walter Mitty's daydreams for a speculation about causes and effects p. 632
A Worn Path	Take notes about segregation for a speculation about causes and effects p. 642
Writer's Workshop	Write a speculation about causes and effects pp. 685–689

Collection Planner

SELECTION / FEATURE	PUPIL'S EDITION: Literary Elements / Active Reading	Writing	Speaking and Listening	Language and Vocabulary
Winter Dreams F. Scott Fitzgerald (pp. 584–605) Primary Sources: A Letter (p. 603)	• Reader's Log p. 586 • Motivation p. 586 • Paradox p. 604	• Critical Writing: Write essay p. 605 • Creative Writing/Role-Playing: Create dialogue p. 605	• Crossing the Curriculum: Give oral report on period music p. 605	• Language and Style: Paradox p. 604
The Leader of the People John Steinbeck (pp. 606–622) Primary Sources: Nobel Prize Acceptance Speech, 1962 (pp. 620–621)	• Reader's Log p. 607 • External conflict p. 607 • Internal conflict p. 607 • Simile p. 622 • Metaphor p. 622 • Personification p. 622 • Oxymoron p. 622 • Hyperbole p. 622	• Critical Writing: Write comparison/contrast essay p. 622	• Speaking and Listening: Conduct panel discussion p. 622	• Language and Style: Figures of Speech p. 622
The Secret Life of Walter Mitty James Thurber (pp. 623–632) Primary Sources: *The New Yorker's* Farewell (p. 629) Connections: Snoopy as Beau Geste (p. 630)	• Reader's Log p. 624 • Parody p. 624	• Critical Writing: Write comparison/contrast essay p. 632 • Creative Writing: Write story episode p. 632 • Art/Creative Writing: Create cartoon p. 632 • Drama: Write script p. 632 • Creative Writing: Write letter to author p. 632	• Drama: Perform scene p. 632	
A Worn Path Eudora Welty (pp. 633–642) Primary Sources: Is Phoenix Jackson's Grandson Really Dead? (pp. 640–641)	• Reader's Log p. 634 • Theme p. 634	• Critical Writing: Write essay p. 642 • Creative Writing: Write story p. 642		

Collection Resources

Teaching Resources B	Audiovisual Resources Binder	Test Booklet
Cross-Curricular Activity p. 50	Fine Art Transparency 12.1	Collection 12 Test pp. 149–150

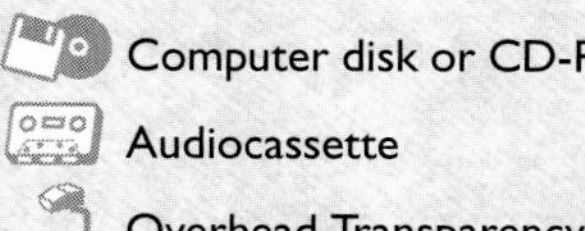

PROGRAM RESOURCES

Electronic Media	Teaching Resources with Organizer: Teaching Resources B	Teaching Resources with Organizer: Other Resources	Audiovisual Resources Binder
• Language Workshop: Antecedents • Test Generator	• Teaching Notes pp. 33–34 • Reading Organizer p. 36 • Language Link pp. 37–38 • Words to Own p. 39	• Test Booklet: Selection Test pp. 141–142 • Language and Writing Skills Worksheets pp. 31–32 • Portfolio Management System pp. 53, 138–139	• Elements of Literature Transparency 12.2
• Language Workshop: Personal pronouns • Test Generator	• Teaching Notes p. 34 • Reading Organizer p. 40 • Language Link pp. 41–42 • Words to Own p. 43	• Test Booklet: Selection Test pp. 143–144 • Language and Writing Skills Worksheets p. 13 • Portfolio Management System pp. 39, 140	
• Test Generator	• Teaching Notes pp. 34–35 • Reading Organizer p. 44 • Words to Own p. 45	• Test Booklet: Selection Test pp. 145–146 • Portfolio Management System pp. 54–55, 141–142	• Elements of Literature Transparency 12.3
• Language Workshop: Pronoun reference • Test Generator	• Teaching Notes p. 35 • Reading Organizer p. 46 • Language Link pp. 47–48 • Words to Own p. 49	• Test Booklet: Selection Test pp. 147–148 • Language and Writing Skills Worksheets pp. 57–58 • Portfolio Management System pp. 48–49, 143	• Elements of Literature Transparency 12.4

Proofreading Warm-ups

You may use the following exercises to help students practice their proofreading skills. Copy a set of incorrect sentences onto the chalkboard, and have students find and correct the spelling, punctuation, usage, and mechanical errors in each sentence. Ask students to share and discuss their responses.

	Sentences with Errors	Sentences Corrected	Skills Covered
1	**a.** judy jones sounds like a spoiled brat to me said Monica. **b.** I would of quit my job as a caddy to if I had had to put up with her.	**a.** "Judy Jones sounds like a spoiled brat to me," said Monica. **b.** I would have quit my job as a caddy too if I had had to put up with her.	Quotation marks, Capitalization, Comma usage, Nonstandard usage, Spelling
2	**a.** My father he owns his own business just like Dexter. **b.** Fitzgerald is the one about who we were talking.	**a.** My father owns his own business just like Dexter. **b.** Fitzgerald is the one about whom we were talking.	Nonstandard usage, Pronouns
3	**a.** Fitzgerald was the author whom wrote the storys. **b.** He also wrote the novel titled the great gatsby.	**a.** Fitzgerald was the author who wrote the stories. **b.** He also wrote the novel titled The Great Gatsby.	Pronouns, Spelling, Capitalization, Underline titles
4	**a.** My grandfather tells stories about emigrating to the United States. **b.** I would of made a grate wagon train leader.	**a.** My grandfather tells stories about immigrating to the United States. **b.** I would have made a great wagon train leader.	Spelling, Nonstandard usage
5	**a.** Steinbeck wrote about migrant workers in the grapes of wrath. **b.** That kind of a book is very realistick.	**a.** Steinbeck wrote about migrant workers in The Grapes of Wrath. **b.** That kind of book is very realistic.	Capitalization, Underline titles, Spelling
6	**a.** I'm planning to attend the Steinbeck Festival this august. **b.** Steinbeck won the pulitzer prize in fiction in 1940 and the nobel prize in literature in 1962	**a.** I'm planning to attend the Steinbeck Festival this August. **b.** Steinbeck won the Pulitzer Prize in fiction in 1940 and the Nobel Prize in literature in 1962.	Capitalization, End marks
7	**a.** While driving, Mitty imagines he is flying a navy hydroplane threw the worst storm in twenty years. **b.** As he drives his car past the hospital, it reminds him of another fantasy.	**a.** While driving, Mitty imagines he is flying a navy hydroplane through the worst storm in twenty years. **b.** As he drives his car past the hospital, the hospital reminds him of another fantasy.	Spelling, Pronoun reference
8	**a.** After hearing a newsboy, he becomes the defendent in a murder trial. **b.** james thurber wrote short stories and cartoons for the new yorker magazine.	**a.** After hearing a newsboy, Mitty becomes the defendant in a murder trial. **b.** James Thurber wrote short stories and cartoons for The New Yorker magazine.	Pronoun reference, Spelling, Capitalization, Underline titles
9	**a.** I think a worn path is a interesting short story said Shon. **b.** Phoenix is a good name for the mane careactor of this story because she always picks herself up and keeps on going no matter what happens to her.	**a.** "I think 'A Worn Path' is an interesting short story," said Shon. **b.** Phoenix is a good name for the main character of this story because she always picks herself up and keeps on going no matter what happens to her.	Quotation marks, Comma usage, Spelling
10	**a.** eudora welty won a prize for her book the optimists' daughter. **b.** Welty writes a kind of a southern short story.	**a.** Eudora Welty won a prize for her book The Optimist's Daughter. **b.** Welty writes a kind of Southern short story.	Capitalization, Underline titles, Apostrophes

Collection 12

THE DREAM AND THE REALITY

Fitzgerald
Steinbeck
Thurber
Welty

"Did you ever see an amusement park?"

"No, Father."

"Well, go and see an amusement park." The priest waved his hand vaguely. "It's a thing like a fair, only much more glittering. Go to one at night and stand a little way off from it in a dark place—under dark trees. You'll see a big wheel made of lights turning in the air, and a long slide shooting boats down into the water. A band playing somewhere, and a smell of peanuts—and everything will twinkle. But it won't remind you of anything, you see. It will all just hang out there in the night like a colored balloon—like a big yellow lantern on a pole."

Father Schwartz frowned as he suddenly thought of something.

"But don't get up close," he warned Rudolph, "because if you do you'll only feel the heat and the sweat and the life."

—F. Scott Fitzgerald, *from* "Absolution"

from "Absolution"

? What does Father Schwartz's warning about getting too close to the amusement park reveal about the role distance plays in the relationship between dream and reality? [Possible responses: A dream must be far away to sustain its beauty. Up close, a dream dissipates into the grime of real life. Or once you get too close to a fantasy, it loses its magic and becomes commonplace.]

PORTFOLIO ASSESSMENT

Parent/Guardian Involvement For forms that will help a parent or guardian review and respond to a student's portfolio, see ***Portfolio Management System,*** pp. 62–63.

PROGRAM MANAGER

- **Integrated Assessment** For a summative assessment of the literature and language skills taught in this collection, see **Collection 12 Test, *Test Booklet,*** pp. 149–150.
- **Instructional Support** See **Fine Art Transparency** 12.1. Review teacher's notes for transparencies in the ***Audiovisual Resources Binder*** for suggestions on how to tie the transparencies to specific reading selections.
- **Extending Collection Theme** See **Cross-Curricular Activity: *The Dream and the Reality, Teaching Resources B,*** p. 50, for an activity in another discipline and for evaluation criteria.

QUICK PLANNING GUIDE

Into the Story

Author Biography pp. 584–585
Before You Read p. 586
- **Reading Focus: Prior Knowledge** Students identify with a character's problems.
- **A Dialogue with the Text:** Analyze character in Reader's Log
- **Elements of Literature: Motivation**
- **Background: Scaffolding** Context of the story

Through the Story

"Winter Dreams" pp. 587–602
Words to Own pp. 588–602
Primary Sources p. 603
Making Meanings p. 604
Language and Style p. 604

Beyond the Story

Choices: Building Your Portfolio p. 605
- **Writer's Notebook:** List questions to analyze character motivation
- **Critical Writing:** Analyze fairy tale aspects in an essay
- **Creative Writing/Role-Playing:** Improvise conversation between characters
- **Crossing the Curriculum: Music** Report on songs from the era

F. Scott Fitzgerald

(1896–1940)

The Bettmann Archive.

If ever there was a writer whose life and fiction were one, it was F. Scott Fitzgerald. Fitzgerald—handsome, charming, and uncommonly gifted—was not only part of the crazy, wonderful, irresponsible era of the 1920s; he helped to name it the Jazz Age. He made a literary legend of it and, with his wife Zelda, lived it out in all of its excesses. He also almost certainly died of it.

Early Failures—and a Smash Hit

Fitzgerald was born in 1896 in St. Paul, Minnesota, the son of a father with claims to an aristocratic Maryland family. Scott was named for an ancestor, Francis Scott Key, the composer of "The Star-Spangled Banner." His mother was the daughter of a rich Irish immigrant. The young Scott was a spoiled boy, a failure at schoolwork and—to his own great disappointment—at sports. But he was a success at daydreaming and, while still in his teens, at writing stories and plays.

At Princeton University, which he entered in 1913, he wrote one of the Triangle Club musical shows, contributed to the *Nassau Literary Magazine,* and befriended the serious writers Edmund Wilson and John Peale Bishop. When the United States entered the First World War in 1917, Fitzgerald left college for officers' training school, yearning for heroic adventure on the battlefields of France. He was never sent overseas, but in camp he began to work on a novel, *The Romantic Egoist,* which was twice turned down by Scribner's.

While he was stationed at Camp Sheridan in Alabama, romance of a different sort overtook him. He fell deeply in love with Zelda Sayre, a high-spirited and gorgeous woman whose escapades had scandalized her hometown of Montgomery. Like Scott, Zelda hungered for new experiences. She was sure of her appeal and felt it was bound to bring her a full measure of luxury and gaiety. Although Scott courted her persistently, he had not nearly enough money to offer her the kind of marriage she wanted, and at first she turned him down.

Now out of the army, Fitzgerald took a low-paying job he hated; he sent his novel, rewritten and retitled *This Side of Paradise,* off to Scribner's for the third time. In 1919, they agreed to publish it.

"I was an empty bucket," he said of the experience, "so mentally blunted by the summer's writing that I'd taken a job repairing car roofs at the Northern Pacific shops. Then the postman rang, and that day I quit work and ran along the streets, stopping automobiles to tell friends and acquaintances about it—my novel *This Side of Paradise* was accepted for publication. That week the postman rang and rang, and I paid off my terrible small debts, bought a suit, and woke up every morning with a world of ineffable toploftiness and promise."

When it was published in 1920, *This Side of Paradise* was a sensation. The old, prewar world with its Victorian code of behavior had been dumped in favor of a great, gaudy spree of new

WORDS TO OWN

The following vocabulary words are defined in the Words to Own at the bottom of the pupil's page.

elation p. 588	mirth p. 593
perturbation p. 589	divergence p. 594
malicious p. 591	turbulence p. 597
reserve p. 592	ludicrous p. 601
petulance p. 593	plaintive p. 602

PORTFOLIO ASSESSMENT

Portfolio Assessment For help with self- and teacher assessment of reading skills, see the ***Portfolio Management System,*** p. 53.

freedoms. Girls bobbed their hair and shortened their skirts, while boys filled their flasks with bootleg gin. To the wail of saxophones, couples danced the Charleston across the nation's dance floors. In young Fitzgerald's novel, the Jazz Age had found its definition.

Taking Aim at the American Dream

Zelda married Scott in April of that year. The newlyweds moved to New York and became the center of a round of parties, while Scott turned out scores of stories. In the first years of the decade, he published two collections of stories and a second novel. After a stay in France, the Fitzgeralds returned to St. Paul, where their only child, a daughter named Frances, was born.

Scott announced to Maxwell Perkins, his editor at Scribner's, that he was going to write "something *new*—something extraordinary and beautiful and simple and intricately patterned." He fulfilled that ambition in *The Great Gatsby,* his nearly flawless masterpiece, which was published in 1925. It tells the story of James Gatz, a poor boy from the Middle West who dreams of success and elegance and finds their incarnation in a Louisville girl named Daisy Fay. When Gatz returns from the war, he learns that she has become Daisy Buchanan, married to a rich Chicagoan and leading a careless, sumptuous life on Long Island. The hero, now a successful bootlegger known as Jay Gatsby, hopes to win Daisy from what he believes is a loveless, unhappy marriage. The story ends in Gatsby's death, but we can see that his dreams, his vulnerability, and his feelings are admirable. The Buchanans, on the other hand, are insulated from life's possibilities by their wealth and self-indulgence.

The central triumph of *The Great Gatsby* was its revelation of the rich in all their seductive luxury and heedlessness, accompanied by an implicit condemnation of their way of life. It showed wealth as a numbing, dehumanizing force that can destroy the heart. In a remarkably concise work, Fitzgerald probed deeply the ambiguities of the American dream.

An Epitaph for the Jazz Age

The Great Gatsby won some critical praise, but it was a financial disappointment. Fitzgerald had to work even harder to keep up with the high cost of his and Zelda's international life. He turned out more potboiling short stories (mediocre in quality and written for money) and went to Hollywood to write movie scripts. In 1930, the tenth year of their marriage, Zelda suffered a mental breakdown and spent the rest of her life in and out of asylums. Hers was a search for both sanity and identity, an identity that seemed to have been devoured by Scott's productiveness. She aspired to be a dancer and a writer, and in 1932 produced her own novel, *Save Me the Waltz.* This was her thinly disguised account of her troubled marriage.

Scott's novel *Tender Is the Night,* published in 1934, was his rebuttal to Zelda's novel. Its hero, Dick Diver, is the protector and healer of the mad heroine, Nicole. However, the stock market crash of 1929 had put an end to Fitzgerald's era, and readers had lost interest in the problems of expatriates like Dick Diver. Still, the book displays Fitzgerald's hard-won experience of life, the commitment to early dreams, the self-destructiveness of charm, and a whole generation's craving for endless youth and irresponsibility. In its despair, *Tender Is the Night* is an epitaph for the Jazz Age.

It was Fitzgerald's epitaph as well. After its publication, he struggled with mounting debts, failing health, drinking, and depression. Zelda was hospitalized, and although Scott suffered under the drudgery of the Hollywood studios, he was bound to them. When he could, he continued to do serious work. Through his love affair with Sheilah Graham, a British journalist, he grew interested in the work of Hollywood producer Irving Thalberg and began to write a novel about him. He was at work on this novel, *The Last Tycoon,* in 1940 when he died of heart failure. *The Last Tycoon* was compiled and edited by his friend Edmund Wilson and was published to wide critical praise after Fitzgerald's death.

WRITERS ON WRITING

Fitzgerald rarely addressed his ideas or gave advice about writing. However, his fiction offers some insights into the inner workings of the writer. In *The Last Tycoon,* Fitzgerald wrote, "Writers aren't people exactly. Or, if they're any good, they're a whole lot of people trying so hard to be one person." In "The Crack-Up," Fitzgerald notes, "When the first-rate author wants an exquisite heroine or a lovely morning, he finds that all the superlatives have been worn shoddy by his inferiors. It should be a rule that bad writers must start with plain heroines and ordinary mornings, and, if they are able, work up to something better."

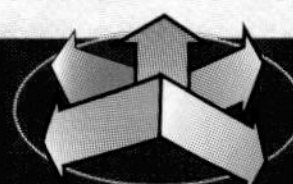

PROGRAM MANAGER

- **Planning Instruction** See Teaching Notes, *Teaching Resources B,* pp. 33-34, for additional information.
- **Instructional Support** See Graphic Organizer for Active Reading, *Teaching Resources B,* p. 36, for a Through the Story activity.
- **Application and Reinforcement** See Transparency 12.2 in the *Audiovisual Resources Binder.*
- **Assessment** See Selection Test, *Test Booklet,* pp. 141–142.
- **Language Link** For instruction and practice in pronouns, see Language Link, *Teaching Resources B,* pp. 37–38, and *Language and Writing Skills Worksheets,* pp. 31–32.
- **Reinforcement** Use the Words to Own worksheet in *Teaching Resources B,* p. 39.

Into the Story

Using BEFORE YOU READ p. 586

Reading Focus

Invite the class to brainstorm about things one might dream about but cannot easily get—a sports car, a date with a movie star, or a trip to Paris. Then, ask the class if the object itself is truly desired, or if it represents something larger, like success, achievement, or a certain lifestyle.

A Dialogue with the Text

Encourage students to acquire the habit of taking notes while they read. Fitzgerald's narrative may trigger associations between the characters' and the students' own ideas about life. These connective ideas are frequently discounted and forgotten; however, they can be the inspiration for creativity. Taking notes as they read will help students generate material and ideas for later writing.

Background

Many students will be unfamiliar with the Roaring Twenties or the Jazz Age. You might show a film to orient the class to this era, invite a speaker to share his or her memories, or bring in photographs and discuss the 1920s lifestyle. Some students may know people who were active in the 1920s and may interview them for more background information to share with the class.

BEFORE YOU READ

WINTER DREAMS

Reading Focus

You Can't Always Get What You Want

Have you ever met someone and thought, "That's the person I want to marry"? If you have had this thought—or if you ever do someday—you might find yourself facing the same kinds of problems that Dexter Green does. In fiction, as well as in life, what individuals hope for and yearn after is not always what they get.

A Dialogue with the Text

READER'S LOG

As you read this story, jot down your responses to these questions: How are Dexter's two ambitions—achieving material success and winning Judy's hand—tied together? What picture of Judy do you put together from what you learn about her? Why can't Dexter fully escape from Judy's magnetic charms?

Elements of Literature

Motivation

Motivation refers to the reasons for a character's behavior. Motivation can come from internal sources (ambition, insecurity, shyness) or from external factors (poverty, an ambitious parent, the crash of the stock market). In folk tales and simpler literature, motivation comes from a single cause. But in more sophisticated fiction, as in the complexity of life itself, motivation may come from many sources and is sometimes hard to pin down. In many stories, characters aren't even aware of their own motivation.

> **Motivation** refers to the reasons for a character's behavior.
>
> *For more on Motivation, see the Handbook of Literary Terms.*

Background

This story is one of several that Fitzgerald wrote about the dreams and illusions that marked the Jazz Age. "Winter Dreams" was written in 1922, when Fitzgerald's stories were commanding top prices at the *Saturday Evening Post* and other magazines. The story opens around 1911, when fourteen-year-old Dexter is caddying for wealthy golfers, and spans eighteen years of Dexter's life.

OPTIONS FOR TEACHING

STRATEGIES FOR INCLUSION

Learners Having Difficulty This story reflects the era of the Roaring Twenties. Ask a group of students to research this time in American history to provide a backdrop for the story, including the economy, society, the entertainment, the government, perhaps even the clothing styles. Then, students can present their findings to the rest of the class.

English Language Development "Winter Dreams" may be difficult for students who are struggling with new vocabulary, an unfamiliar setting, and characters who may represent unfamiliar stereotypes. Providing students with a framework on which to hang new information will be beneficial. Point out that the story is divided into six sections that move chronologically. If possible, do a quick comprehension check after students have read the first section.

A. Humanities Connection
Fitzgerald once noted that "Winter Dreams" (1922) was the first version of his novel *The Great Gatsby,* published in 1925. Students might enjoy reading the novel and comparing it with this story.

Winter Dreams (A)

F. Scott Fitzgerald

Some of the caddies were poor as sin and lived in one-room houses with a neurasthenic[1] cow in the front yard, but Dexter Green's father owned the second best grocery-store in Black Bear—the best one was "The Hub," patronized by the wealthy people from Sherry Island—and Dexter caddied only for pocket-money.

1. **neurasthenic** (no͞o′ras·then′ik): thin and weak, as though suffering from a nervous disorder.

STRATEGIES FOR INCLUSION

Special Needs Students who have difficulty composing written responses to literature may prefer an alternative method of demonstrating their comprehension of the material they have read. To demonstrate their understanding of the personalities of Dexter and Judy, students could create collages featuring the things that they feel were important to each character. Have students present their collages to the class with a verbal summary of the importance of each item.

Linguistic After students have read the story, have the class create a Found Poem. Divide the class into small groups, and instruct the students to look back at the story and to select eight words or phrases (not sentences) that they feel best communicate its essence. Then, have groups narrow their selections to no more than four words or phrases. After their selections are made, have each group read aloud one word or phrase. Write the words and phrases on the chalkboard to create the Found Poem.

A. Critical Reading: Identifying Main Ideas

? How does Dexter describe the changing seasons? [Possible answer: To Dexter, spring is dismal; summer is colorful; fall is gorgeous; and winter is melancholy, dreary, and desolate.]

B. Literary Element: Motivation

? What do Dexter's dreams indicate he wants in the future? [Sample responses: He wants to be a golf champion, wealthy and admired; or he wants to be a great athlete and showoff.]

C. Reader's Response: First Thoughts

? What kind of woman do you think eleven-year-old Judy will become? [Sample responses: She will be beautiful and tantalizing; or she will be insensitive and wild.]

Metacognition Ask students to describe the thought processes behind their answers. [The narrator uses the word "destined," so it seems as if he knows her future; the narrator says that she will bring "misery" to men, so he must mean that she will be cruel or insensitive.]

In the fall when the days became crisp and gray, and the long Minnesota winter shut down like the white lid of a box, Dexter's skis moved over the snow that hid the fairways[2] of the golf course. At these times the country gave him a feeling of profound melancholy—it offended him that the links should lie in enforced fallowness, haunted by ragged sparrows for the long season. It was dreary, too, that on the tees where the gay colors fluttered in summer there were now only the desolate sand-boxes knee-deep in crusted ice. (A) When he crossed the hills the wind blew cold as misery, and if the sun was out he tramped with his eyes squinted up against the hard dimensionless glare.

In April the winter ceased abruptly. The snow ran down into Black Bear Lake scarcely tarrying[3] for the early golfers to brave the season with red and black balls. Without elation, without an interval of moist glory, the cold was gone.

Dexter knew that there was something dismal about this Northern spring, just as he knew there was something gorgeous about the fall. Fall made him clinch his hands and tremble and repeat idiotic sentences to himself, and make brisk abrupt gestures of command to imaginary audiences and armies. October filled him with hope which November raised to a sort of ecstatic triumph, and in this mood the fleeting brilliant impressions of the summer at Sherry Island were ready grist to his mill.[4] He became a golf champion and defeated Mr. T. A. Hedrick in a marvellous match played a hundred times over the fairways of his imagination, a match each detail of which he changed about untiringly—sometimes he won with almost laughable ease, sometimes he came up magnifi- (B) cently from behind. Again, stepping from a Pierce-Arrow automobile, like Mr. Mortimer Jones, he strolled frigidly into the lounge of the Sherry Island Golf Club—or perhaps, surrounded by an admiring crowd, he gave an exhibition of fancy diving from the spring-board of the club raft. . . . Among those who watched him in open-mouthed wonder was Mr. Mortimer Jones.

And one day it came to pass that Mr. Jones—himself and not his ghost—came up to Dexter with tears in his eyes and said that Dexter was the ——best caddy in the club, and wouldn't he decide not to quit if Mr. Jones made it worth his while, because every other——caddy in the club lost one ball a hole for him—regularly——

"No, sir," said Dexter decisively, "I don't want to caddy any more." Then, after a pause: "I'm too old."

"You're not more than fourteen. Why the devil did you decide just this morning that you wanted to quit? You promised that next week you'd go over to the State tournament with me."

"I decided I was too old."

Dexter handed in his "A Class" badge, collected what money was due him from the caddy master, and walked home to Black Bear Village.

"The best——caddy I ever saw," shouted Mr. Mortimer Jones over a drink that afternoon. "Never lost a ball! Willing! Intelligent! Quiet! Honest! Grateful!"

The little girl who had done this was eleven—beautifully ugly as little girls are apt to be who are destined after a few years to be inexpressibly lovely and bring no end of misery to a great number of men. The spark, however, was perceptible. There was a general ungodliness in the way her (C) lips twisted down at the corners when she smiled, and in the—Heaven help us!—in the almost passionate quality of her eyes. Vitality is born early in such women. It was utterly in evidence now, shining through her thin frame in a sort of glow.

She had come eagerly out on to the course at nine o'clock with a white linen nurse and five small new golf-clubs in a white canvas bag which the nurse was carrying. When Dexter first saw her she was standing by the caddy house, rather ill at ease and trying to conceal the fact by engaging her nurse in an obviously unnatural conversation graced by startling and irrelevant grimaces from herself.

"Well, it's certainly a nice day, Hilda," Dexter heard her say. She drew down the corners of her

2. **fairways:** mowed parts of a golf course. The fairway of each hole starts at the tee and ends at the green.
3. **tarrying:** waiting.
4. **grist to his mill:** something that can be used to advantage.

WORDS TO OWN
elation (ē·lā′shən) *n.:* celebration.

OPTIONS FOR TEACHING

INTEGRATING THE LANGUAGE ARTS

Mechanics Review the rule for setting off essential and nonessential phrases and clauses: If the phrase identifies the noun it modifies (tells which one it is), then the phrase is essential and needs no commas. Otherwise, the phrase simply gives additional information and requires commas to set it off from the rest of the sentence. Here are two examples from the story:

1. "She swung her mashie impatiently and without interest, pitching the ball into a sand-pit on the other side of the green." (nonessential adverb clause)
2. ". . . within a year he was catering to the trade that wore knickerbockers." (essential adjective clause)

Ask students to find several examples of essential and nonessential elements in sentences and to write several examples of their own, being sure to punctuate them correctly.

mouth, smiled, and glanced furtively around, her eyes in transit falling for an instant on Dexter.

Then to the nurse:

"Well, I guess there aren't very many people out here this morning, are there?"

The smile again—radiant, blatantly artificial—convincing.

"I don't know what we're supposed to do now," said the nurse, looking nowhere in particular.

"Oh, that's all right. I'll fix it up."

Dexter stood perfectly still, his mouth slightly ajar. He knew that if he moved forward a step his stare would be in her line of vision—if he moved backward he would lose his full view of her face. For a moment he had not realized how young she was. Now he remembered having seen her several times the year before—in bloomers. (D)

Suddenly, involuntarily, he laughed, a short abrupt laugh—then, startled by himself, he turned and began to walk quickly away.

"Boy!"

Dexter stopped.

"Boy——"

Beyond question he was addressed. Not only that, but he was treated to that absurd smile, that preposterous smile—the memory of which at least a dozen men were to carry into middle age. (E)

"Boy, do you know where the golf teacher is?"

"He's giving a lesson."

"Well, do you know where the caddy-master is?"

"He isn't here yet this morning."

"Oh." For a moment this baffled her. She stood alternately on her right and left foot.

"We'd like to get a caddy," said the nurse. "Mrs. Mortimer Jones sent us out to play golf, and we don't know how without we get a caddy."

Here she was stopped by an ominous glance from Miss Jones, followed immediately by the smile.

"There aren't any caddies here except me," said Dexter to the nurse, "and I got to stay here in charge until the caddy-master gets here."

"Oh."

Miss Jones and her retinue[5] now withdrew, and at a proper distance from Dexter became involved in a heated conversation, which was concluded by Miss Jones taking one of the clubs and hitting it on the ground with violence. For further emphasis she raised it again and was about to bring it down smartly upon the nurse's bosom, when the nurse seized the club and twisted it from her hands.

"You damn little mean old *thing!*" cried Miss Jones wildly.

Another argument ensued. Realizing that the elements of the comedy were implied in the scene, Dexter several times began to laugh, but each time restrained the laugh before it reached audibility. He could not resist the monstrous conviction that the little girl was justified in beating the nurse. (F)

The situation was resolved by the fortuitous[6] appearance of the caddy-master, who was appealed to immediately by the nurse.

"Miss Jones is to have a little caddy, and this one says he can't go."

"Mr. McKenna said I was to wait here till you came," said Dexter quickly.

"Well, he's here now." Miss Jones smiled cheerfully at the caddy-master. Then she dropped her bag and set off at a haughty mince[7] toward the first tee.

"Well?" the caddy-master turned to Dexter. "What you standing there like a dummy for? Go pick up the young lady's clubs."

"I don't think I'll go out to-day," said Dexter.

"You don't——"

"I think I'll quit."

The enormity of his decision frightened him. He was a favorite caddy, and the thirty dollars a month he earned through the summer were not to be made elsewhere around the lake. But he had received a strong emotional shock, and his perturbation required a violent and immediate outlet.

It is not so simple as that, either. As so frequently would be the case in the future, Dexter was unconsciously dictated to by his winter dreams.

5. **retinue** (ret′'n·yo͞o′): group of followers or servants attending to a person of rank.

6. **fortuitous** (fôr·to͞o′ə·təs): fortunate.
7. **mince:** prim, affected walk.

WORDS TO OWN

perturbation (pur′tər·bā′shən) *n.:* feeling of alarm or agitation.

D. Literary Element: Character

? How does Dexter react to the little girl? [He is fascinated by her. When he realizes the spell, he is embarrassed and tries to break it.]

E. Critical Reading: Making Inferences

? How do you think Dexter feels when Judy calls him "Boy"? [He is appalled by her condescending attitude; or he is embarrassed.]

F. Reader's Response: Challenging the Text

? Is the girl justified in trying to beat the nurse? [Sample responses: No, she is a spoiled brat; or yes, the nurse is too bossy.]

INTEGRATING THE LANGUAGE ARTS

Language and Style To increase students' sentence composing skills, ask them to imitate several sentences written by Fitzgerald. Here are some possible sentences for imitation, followed by models of imitative writing.

1. "Dexter stood perfectly still, his mouth slightly ajar." [The new Chevy truck idled softly, its power momentarily caged.]
2. "Perhaps from so much youthful love, so many youthful lovers, she had come, in self-defense, to nourish herself wholly from within." [Doubtless in response to so many homework assignments, so little free time, they had asked, in desperation, to postpone the date for the test.]

After explaining the process, let students choose and imitate sentences they particularly like.

A. Language Note: Pronoun Reference

? What is the antecedent of the pronoun *they?* [*They* refers to the word *dreams*. His dreams influenced him to choose the eastern school over the state university.] This may be a good time to review pronoun reference and the importance of reading and writing pronouns carefully.

B. Critical Reading: Analyzing Character

? Does Dexter seek only objects that represent success? [Possible answer: No, this passage suggests that there is a core of true idealism in Dexter, which is translated into a longing for the beauty of upper-class life.]

C. Critical Reading: Identifying Main Ideas

? What is the theme of the story, as stated in these two sentences? [Possible answers: Some things may be denied us through no fault of our own; or despite human efforts, it is destiny that controls our fate.]

D. Humanities Connection

Dexter's life is, in some ways, a Horatio Alger story. Alger (1832–1899) wrote more than one hundred books for boys, many of them about bootblacks or newsboys who earn success through hard work, pluck, and virtue. Alger's name has thus become associated with the American dream: overcoming poverty and achieving success through self-reliance and hard work.

II

Now, of course, the quality and the seasonability of these winter dreams varied, but the stuff of (A) them remained. They persuaded Dexter several years later to pass up a business course at the State university—his father, prospering now, would have paid his way—for the precarious[8] advantage of attending an older and more famous university in the East, where he was bothered (B) by his scanty funds. But do not get the impression, because his winter dreams happened to be concerned at first with musings on the rich, that there was anything merely snobbish in the boy. He wanted not association with glittering things and glittering people—he wanted the glittering things themselves. Often he reached out for the best without knowing why he wanted it— (C) and sometimes he ran up against the mysterious denials and prohibitions in which life indulges. It is with one of those denials and not with his career as a whole that this story deals.

He made money. It was rather amazing. After college he went to the city from which Black Bear Lake draws its wealthy patrons. When he was only twenty-three and had been there not quite two years, there were already people who liked to say: "Now *there's* a boy—" All about him rich men's sons were peddling bonds precariously, or investing patrimonies[9] precariously, or plodding through the two dozen volumes of the "George Washington Commercial Course," but Dexter borrowed a thousand dollars on his college degree and his confident mouth, and bought a partnership in a laundry.

(D) It was a small laundry when he went into it but Dexter made a specialty of learning how the English washed fine woolen golf-stockings without shrinking them, and within a year he was catering to the trade that wore knickerbockers. Men were insisting that their Shetland hose and sweaters go to his laundry just as they had insisted on a caddy who could find golf-balls. A little later he was doing their wives' lingerie as well—and running five branches in different parts of the city. Before he was twenty-seven he owned the largest string of laundries in his section of the country. It was then that he sold out and went to New York. But the part of his story that concerns us goes back to the days when he was making his first big success.

When he was twenty-three Mr. Hart—one of the gray-haired men who like to say "Now there's a boy"—gave him a guest card to the Sherry Island Golf Club for a week-end. So he signed his name one day on the register, and that afternoon played golf in a foursome with Mr. Hart and Mr. Sandwood and Mr. T. A. Hedrick. He did not consider it necessary to remark that he had once carried Mr. Hart's bag over this same links, and that he knew every trap and gully with his eyes shut—but he found himself glancing at the four caddies who trailed them, trying to catch a gleam or gesture that would remind him of himself, that would lessen the gap which lay between his present and his past.

It was a curious day, slashed abruptly with fleeting, familiar impressions. One minute he had the sense of being a trespasser—in the next he was impressed by the tremendous superiority he felt toward Mr. T. A. Hedrick, who was a bore and not even a good golfer any more.

Then, because of a ball Mr. Hart lost near the fifteenth green, an enormous thing happened. While they were searching the stiff grasses of the rough there was a clear call of "Fore!"[10] from behind a hill in their rear. And as they all turned abruptly from their search a bright new ball sliced abruptly over the hill and caught Mr. T. A. Hedrick in the abdomen.

"By Gad!" cried Mr. T. A. Hedrick, "they ought to put some of these crazy women off the course. It's getting to be outrageous."

A head and a voice came up together over the hill:

"Do you mind if we go through?"

"You hit me in the stomach!" declared Mr. Hedrick wildly.

"Did I?" The girl approached the group of men. "I'm sorry. I yelled 'Fore!'"

Her glance fell casually on each of the men—then scanned the fairway for her ball.

"Did I bounce into the rough?"

It was impossible to determine whether this

8. **precarious:** uncertain.
9. **patrimonies:** inheritances.
10. **fore:** warning cry that a golfer gives before hitting a ball down the fairway.

OPTIONS FOR TEACHING

INTEGRATING THE LANGUAGE ARTS

Writing: Poem Invite students to write a poem in which they examine a time when they reached out for something glittering and ran up against denials and prohibitions as Dexter did. Ask them to reflect upon what they might have learned from being denied. *Remind students to select subject matter they would not mind sharing with others.*

question was ingenuous[11] or malicious. In a moment, however, she left no doubt, for as her partner came up over the hill she called cheerfully:

"Here I am! I'd have gone on the green except that I hit something."

As she took her stance for a short mashie[12] shot, Dexter looked at her closely. She wore a blue gingham dress, rimmed at throat and shoulders with a white edging that accentuated her tan. The quality of exaggeration, of thinness, which had made her passionate eyes and down-turning mouth absurd at eleven, was gone now. She was arrestingly beautiful. The color in her cheeks was centered like the color in a picture—it was not a "high" color, but a sort of fluctuating and feverish warmth, so shaded that it seemed at any moment it would recede and disappear. This color and the mobility of her mouth gave a continual impression of flux, of intense life, of passionate vitality—balanced only partially by the sad luxury of her eyes.

She was arrestingly beautiful. The color in her cheeks was centered like the color in a picture —

She swung her mashie impatiently and without interest, pitching the ball into a sand-pit on the other side of the green. With a quick, insincere smile and a careless "Thank you!" she went on after it. **E**

"That Judy Jones!" remarked Mr. Hedrick on the next tee, as they waited—some moments—for her to play on ahead. "All she needs is to be turned up and spanked for six months and then to be married off to an old-fashioned cavalry captain." **F**

"My God, she's good-looking!" said Mr. Sandwood, who was just over thirty.

"Good-looking!" cried Mr. Hedrick contemptuously, "she always looks as if she wanted to be kissed! Turning those big cow-eyes on every calf in town!"

It was doubtful if Mr. Hedrick intended a reference to the maternal instinct.

"She'd play pretty good golf if she'd try," said Mr. Sandwood.

"She has no form," said Mr. Hedrick solemnly.

"She has a nice figure," said Mr. Sandwood.

"Better thank the Lord she doesn't drive a swifter ball," said Mr. Hart, winking at Dexter.

Later in the afternoon the sun went down with a riotous swirl of gold and varying blues and scarlets, and left the dry, rustling night of Western summer. Dexter watched from the veranda of the Golf Club, watched the even overlap of the waters in the little wind, silver molasses under the harvest-moon. Then the moon held a finger to her lips and the lake became a clear pool, pale and quiet. Dexter put on his bathing-suit and swam out to the farthest raft, where he stretched dripping on the wet canvas of the springboard.

There was a fish jumping and a star shining and the lights around the lake were gleaming. Over on a dark peninsula a piano was playing the songs of last summer and of summers before that—songs from "Chin-Chin" and "The Count of Luxemburg" and "The Chocolate Soldier"—and because the sound of a piano over a stretch of water had always seemed beautiful to Dexter he lay perfectly quiet and listened. **G**

The tune the piano was playing at that moment had been gay and new five years before when Dexter was a sophomore at college. They had played it at a prom once when he could not afford the luxury of proms, and he had stood outside the gymnasium and listened. The sound of the tune precipitated in him a sort of ecstasy and it was with that ecstasy he viewed what happened to him now. It was a mood of intense appreciation, a sense that, for once, he was magnificently attuned to life and that everything about him was radiating a brightness and a glamour he might never know again. **H**

A low, pale oblong detached itself suddenly from the darkness of the Island, spitting forth the reverberate sound of a racing motor-boat. Two white streamers of cleft water rolled themselves out behind it and almost immediately the boat

11. **ingenuous** (in·jen′yoo̅·əs): innocent; without guile.
12. **mashie:** a number 5 iron golf club.

WORDS TO OWN
malicious (mə·lish′əs) *adj.:* intentionally hurtful.

E. Reader's Response: Shaping Interpretations

? What does Judy's behavior here suggest about her character? [Sample responses: She is arrogant and self-absorbed; or she is irresistible in her innocence. The word *careless* is probably the key to her character.]

F. Critical Reading: Making Inferences

? How do the men evaluate Judy? Why doesn't Dexter voice an opinion? [Possible answers: Mr. Hedrick seems immune to her charms, but Mr. Sandwood finds her very attractive. Dexter is too sharply drawn to her to risk saying something that would betray his emotions.]

G. Exploring the Culture

Chin-Chin, The Count of Luxemburg, and *The Chocolate Soldier* were all popular musicals of the time.

H. Literary Element: Theme

? How does Dexter's mood relate to the story's theme? [Possible answer: He feels intensely appreciative and harmonious with the world around him.] Is this moment a realization of his winter dreams? [Possible answer: To some extent, yes; he feels himself a part of the beauty and glamour of life.]

INTEGRATING THE LANGUAGE ARTS

Strategic Reading Ask students to make notes as they read, using a chart like the one at right. Have them draw a line down the middle of a sheet of paper and label the columns *Story Notes* and *My Comments*. They may take notes during or after reading each section of the story. For *Story Notes*, have them write down what happened; for *My Comments*, have them respond to the notes in several ways: with personal comments, questions, predictions, notations about literary elements such as figurative language and character development, and comparisons with other readings. Follow up this note-taking with class discussion; each student should have at least one idea to offer.

Story Notes	My Comments

A. Critical Reading: Finding Cause and Effect

? Why did she leave? [Possible answers: She left because she felt repulsed; she left to tease him because he cares so much; or since she knows herself better than anyone else, she knows that she is not ideal, and feels overwhelmed by his expectations.]

B. Literary Element: Character

? What do these passages reveal about Dexter's self-image? [He acknowledges his own accomplishments but realizes they are not enough to gain him full entry into the world he yearns for.]

C. Language Note: Repetition

Key words are repeated for emphasis. Notice Fitzgerald's repeated use of the words *careful, careless,* and *carelessness.* This carelessness is dangerous to Dexter, who must be careful in order to achieve his dreams.

was beside him, drowning out the hot tinkle of the piano in the drone of its spray. Dexter raising himself on his arms was aware of a figure standing at the wheel, of two dark eyes regarding him over the lengthening space of water—then the boat had gone by and was sweeping in an immense and purposeless circle of spray round and round in the middle of the lake. With equal eccentricity one of the circles flattened out and headed back toward the raft.

"Who's that?" she called, shutting off her motor. She was so near now that Dexter could see her bathing-suit, which consisted apparently of pink rompers.

The nose of the boat bumped the raft, and as the latter tilted rakishly, he was precipitated[13] toward her. With different degrees of interest they recognized each other.

"Aren't you one of those men we played through this afternoon?" she demanded.

He was.

"Well, do you know how to drive a motor-boat? Because if you do I wish you'd drive this one so I **(A)** can ride on the surf-board behind. My name is Judy Jones"—she favored him with an absurd smirk—rather, what tried to be a smirk, for, twist her mouth as she might, it was not grotesque, it was merely beautiful—"and I live in a house over there on the Island, and in that house there is a man waiting for me. When he drove up at the door I drove out of the dock because he says I'm his ideal."

There was a fish jumping and a star shining and the lights around the lake were gleaming. Dexter sat beside Judy Jones and she explained how her boat was driven. Then she was in the water, swimming to the floating surf-board with a sinuous[14] crawl. Watching her was without effort to the eye, watching a branch waving or a sea-gull flying. Her arms, burned to butternut, moved sinuously among the dull platinum ripples, elbow appearing first, casting the forearm back with a cadence of falling water, then reaching out and down, stabbing a path ahead.

They moved out into the lake; turning, Dexter saw that she was kneeling on the low rear of the now uptilted surf-board.

"Go faster," she called, "fast as it'll go."

13. **precipitated:** thrown headlong.
14. **sinuous:** curving back and forth; snakelike.

Obediently he jammed the lever forward and the white spray mounted at the bow. When he looked around again the girl was standing up on the rushing board, her arms spread wide, her eyes lifted toward the moon.

"It's awful cold," she shouted. "What's your name?"

He told her.

"Well, why don't you come to dinner tomorrow night?"

His heart turned over like the fly-wheel[15] of the boat, and, for the second time, her casual whim gave a new direction to his life.

III

Next evening while he waited for her to come down-stairs, Dexter peopled the soft deep summer room and the sun-porch that opened from it with the men who had already loved Judy Jones. **(B)** He knew the sort of men they were—the men who when he first went to college had entered from the great prep schools with graceful clothes and the deep tan of healthy summers. He had seen that, in one sense, he was better than these men. He was newer and stronger. Yet in acknowledging to himself that he wished his children to be like them he was admitting that he was but the rough, strong stuff from which they eternally sprang.

When the time had come for him to wear good clothes, he had known who were the best tailors in America, and the best tailors in America had made him the suit he wore this evening. He had acquired that particular reserve peculiar to his university, that set it off from other universities. He recognized the value to him of such a manner- **(C)** ism and he had adopted it; he knew that to be careless in dress and manner required more confidence than to be careful. But carelessness was for his children. His mother's name had been Krimslich. She was a Bohemian of the peasant class and she had talked broken English to the end of her days. Her son must keep to the set patterns.

15. **fly-wheel:** wheel that regulates the speed of a machine.

WORDS TO OWN
reserve (ri·zurv′) *n.:* self-restraint.

OPTIONS FOR TEACHING

COOPERATIVE LEARNING

Group Reports Arrange the class in five groups, asking each group to read for one of the following purposes.

1. Character development of Judy Jones
2. Character development of Dexter Green
3. Fitzgerald's use of figurative language
4. The Jazz Age as the setting for the story
5. The plot development of the story

After all students have read the story and the groups have prepared their presentations, each group can teach the class about its assigned topic.

At a little after seven Judy Jones came downstairs. She wore a blue silk afternoon dress, and he was disappointed at first that she had not put on something more elaborate. This feeling was accentuated when, after a brief greeting, she went to the door of a butler's pantry and pushing it open called: "You can serve dinner, Martha." He had rather expected that a butler would announce dinner, that there would be a cocktail. Then he put these thoughts behind him as they sat down side by side on a lounge and looked at each other.

"Father and mother won't be here," she said thoughtfully.

He remembered the last time he had seen her father, and he was glad the parents were not to be here to-night—they might wonder who he was. He had been born in Keeble, a Minnesota village fifty miles farther north, and he always gave Keeble as his home instead of Black Bear Village. Country **D** towns were well enough to come from if they weren't inconveniently in sight and used as footstools by fashionable lakes.

> *During dinner she slipped into a moody depression which gave Dexter a feeling of uneasiness.*

They talked of his university, which she had visited frequently during the past two years, and of the near-by city which supplied Sherry Island with its patrons, and whither Dexter would return next day to his prospering laundries.

During dinner she slipped into a moody depression which gave Dexter a feeling of uneasiness. Whatever petulance she uttered in her throaty voice worried him. Whatever she smiled at—at him, at a chicken liver, at nothing—it disturbed him that her smile could have no root in mirth, or even in amusement. When the scarlet corners of her lips curved down, it was less a smile than an invitation to a kiss.

Then, after dinner, she led him out on the dark sun-porch and deliberately changed the atmosphere.

"Do you mind if I weep a little?" she said.

"I'm afraid I'm boring you," he responded quickly.

"You're not. I like you. But I've just had a terrible afternoon. There was a man I cared about, and this afternoon he told me out of a clear sky that he was poor as a church-mouse. He'd never even hinted it before. Does this sound horribly mundane?"[16]

"Perhaps he was afraid to tell you."

"Suppose he was," she answered. "He didn't start right. You see, if I'd thought of him as poor—well, I've been mad about loads of poor men, and fully intended to marry them all. But in this case, I **E** hadn't thought of him that way, and my interest in him wasn't strong enough to survive the shock. As if a girl calmly informed her fiancé that she was a widow. He might not object to widows, but——

"Let's start right," she interrupted herself suddenly. "Who are you, anyhow?"

For a moment Dexter hesitated. Then:

"I'm nobody," he announced. "My career is largely a matter of **F** futures."

"Are you poor?"

"No," he said frankly, "I'm probably making more money than any man my age in the Northwest. I know that's an obnoxious remark, but you advised me to start right."

There was a pause. Then she smiled and the corners of her mouth drooped and an almost imperceptible sway brought her closer to him, looking up into his eyes. A lump rose in Dexter's throat, and he waited breathless for the experiment, facing the unpredictable compound that would form mysteriously from the elements of their lips. Then he saw—she communicated her excitement to him, lavishly, deeply, with kisses that were not a promise but a fulfillment. They aroused in him not hunger demanding renewal but surfeit that would demand more surfeit . . . kisses that were like charity, creating want by holding back nothing at all.

It did not take him many hours to decide that he had wanted Judy Jones ever since he was a proud, desirous little boy.

16. **mundane:** ordinary; everyday.

WORDS TO OWN

petulance (pech′ə·ləns) *n.:* irritability; impatience.
mirth (murth) *n.:* joyfulness.

D. Literary Element: Motivation

? Why does Dexter lie about his hometown? [Possible answers: A home in Black Bear Village would emphasize the social distance between himself and the lake residents. Keeble is far enough away to be anonymous. Dexter's social aspirations make him secretive about his origins.]

E. Critical Reading: Drawing Conclusions

? Is Judy exaggerating, or is she speaking literally? [Possible answers: Since Fitzgerald's portrait is sympathetic, her comments are exaggerated because of her romantic nature; or perhaps at the time, she believed she would marry each one.]

F. Critical Reading: Evaluating an Interpretation

? What does Dexter mean when he says his career is a matter of futures? [Possible answer: He is using the term *futures,* which refers to stocks and agricultural trading, ironically. He does not work in a family business or have family money, but he has a promising future that he is creating himself.]

COOPERATIVE LEARNING

Task Assignment To help groups function smoothly, ask each group to assign tasks to its members. For example: Leader—leads discussion and makes assignments; Writer—takes notes and writes down reports; Printer—makes final copies of materials to be produced, either written or audiovisual; Timer—keeps group on task and on schedule. If groups are larger, any of the members in these roles could have an assistant. ☞

A. Critical Reading: Expressing an Opinion

? Does this declaration confirm or challenge your own opinion of Judy? [Possible answers: This comment will confirm the negative view that some students have of Judy, while others will see it as a challenge to their positive view of her character.] Why doesn't Dexter want to change her? [Possible answer: Judy as she is—lovely and confident, defining her own life without regard to others—is what he sees as glamorous and vital.]

B. Reader's Response: Challenging the Text

? Does the character of Judy Jones seem realistic and consistent to you? [Sample responses: I have known someone like her and see her as realistic and consistent, a well-drawn character; nobody is that simple; or she is a stereotype.]

IV

It began like that—and continued, with varying shades of intensity, on such a note right up to the dénouement.[17] Dexter surrendered a part of himself to the most direct and unprincipled personality with which he had ever come in contact. Whatever Judy wanted, she went after with the full pressure of her charm. There was no divergence of method, no jockeying for position or premeditation of effects—there was a very little mental side to any of her affairs. She simply made men conscious to the highest degree of her physical loveliness. Dexter had no desire to change her. Her deficiencies were knit up with a passionate energy that transcended and justified them.

When, as Judy's head lay against his shoulder that first night, she whispered, "I don't know what's the matter with me. Last night I thought I was in love with a man and to-night I think I'm in love with you——" —it seemed to him a beautiful and romantic thing to say. It was the exquisite excitability that for the moment he controlled and owned. But a week later he was compelled to view this same quality in a different light. She took him in her roadster to a picnic supper, and after supper she disappeared, likewise in her roadster, with another man. Dexter became enormously upset and was scarcely able to be decently civil to the other people present. When she assured him that she had not kissed the other man, he knew she was lying—yet he was glad that she had taken the trouble to lie to him.

He was, as he found before the summer ended, one of a varying dozen who circulated about her. Each of them had at one time been favored above all others—about half of them still basked in the solace of occasional sentimental revivals. Whenever one showed signs of dropping out through long neglect, she granted him a brief honeyed hour, which encouraged him to tag along for a year or so longer. Judy made these forays[18] upon the helpless and defeated without malice, indeed half unconscious that there was anything mischievous in what she did.

When a new man came to town every one dropped out—dates were automatically cancelled.

The helpless part of trying to do anything about it was that she did it all herself. She was not a girl who could be "won" in the kinetic[19] sense—she was proof against[20] cleverness, she was proof

17. **dénouement** (dā'no͞o·män'): final outcome.

18. **forays** (fôr'āz): raids.
19. **kinetic:** coming about through action or energy.
20. **proof against:** able to withstand.

Words to Own

divergence (dī·vur'jəns) *n.:* variance; difference.

OPTIONS FOR TEACHING

CLASSROOM MANAGEMENT

Block Scheduling In planning for a longer class period, many teachers avoid trying to teach two complete lessons because students may become confused or lose interest due to information overload. Appropriate enrichment/reteaching activities often give more depth to a single lesson and fill out the longer class period in place of a second lesson.

Managing the Reader's Response Classroom Call attention to comments in the Reader's Log that express an opinion or judgment. Assure students that they are free to verbalize their opinions, but that they should listen willingly to others and use the text to support their judgments.

against charm; if any of these assailed her too strongly she would immediately resolve the affair to a physical basis, and under the magic of her physical splendor the strong as well as the brilliant played her game and not their own. She was entertained only by the gratification of her desires and by the direct exercise of her own charm. Perhaps from so much youthful love, so many youthful lovers, she had come, in self-defense, to nourish herself wholly from within. C

Succeeding Dexter's first exhilaration came restlessness and dissatisfaction. The helpless ecstasy of losing himself in her was opiate rather than tonic.[21] It was fortunate for his work during the winter that those moments of ecstasy came infrequently. Early in their acquaintance it had seemed for a while that there was a deep and spontaneous mutual attraction—that first August, for example—three days of long evenings on her dusky veranda, of strange wan kisses through the late afternoon, in shadowy alcoves or behind the protecting trellises of the garden arbors, of mornings when she was fresh as a dream and almost shy at meeting him in the clarity of the rising day. There was all the ecstasy of an engagement about it, sharpened by his realization that there was no engagement. It was during those three days that, for the first time, he had asked her to marry him. She said "maybe some day," she said "kiss me," she said "I'd like to marry you," she said "I love you"—she said—nothing. D

21. opiate . . . tonic: calming rather than stimulating.

C. Reader's Response: Shaping Interpretations

? Why does Dexter put up with Judy's behavior? Why do all the other young men do so as well? [Sample responses: Dexter and the rest of Judy's suitors endure her toying with them because they find her irresistible; or they hope that she will finally reject the rest of the pack and choose one of them. Perhaps, too, for Dexter, her carelessness is part of the society he aspires to belong to.]

D. Critical Reading: Making Inferences

? What does the narrator mean when he says that Judy says nothing? [Possible answers: She avoids answering the questions; or her answers come so glibly that they cannot be taken seriously.]

CROSSING THE CURRICULUM

Geography Point out Minnesota and New York City on a map so students will have a mental image of the two settings in the story. Have students research and create collages illustrating the differences between the two areas. Display the collages around the classroom.

Art Some students will enjoy illustrating the story, perhaps with one picture for each section. They may research the clothing and hairstyles of the era for their drawings or paintings. Ask students to share their illustrations with the class.

A. Literary Element: Theme

? Have Dexter's dreams changed? [Possible answer: Dexter has by now achieved material success, but the actual fulfillment of his dreams lies with Judy.]

B. Reader's Response: Challenging the Text

? Is Judy a worthy object of Dexter's idealism? [Sample responses: Yes, her beauty and desirability make her worthy; or no, because of her arrogance and erratic behavior she is not worthy.]

C. Reader's Response: Connecting with the Text

? Does access to the finer things in life—books, music, art—still differentiate the upper class from the rest of society? [Sample responses: The fine arts—especially opera and theater—are still beyond the reach of most people; or local arts organizations, public libraries, and museums, along with televised concerts and theatrical productions, have made the finer things in life accessible to everyone.]

The three days were interrupted by the arrival of a New York man who visited at her house for half September. To Dexter's agony, rumor engaged them. The man was the son of the president of a great trust company. But at the end of a month it was reported that Judy was yawning. At a dance one night she sat all evening in a motorboat with a local beau, while the New Yorker searched the club for her frantically. She told the local beau that she was bored with her visitor, and two days later he left. She was seen with him at the station, and it was reported that he looked very mournful indeed.

(A) On this note the summer ended. Dexter was twenty-four, and he found himself increasingly in a position to do as he wished. He joined two clubs in the city and lived at one of them. Though he was by no means an integral part of the stag-lines[22] at these clubs, he managed to be on hand at dances where Judy Jones was likely to appear. He could have gone out socially as much as he liked—he was an eligible young man, now, and popular with down-town fathers. His confessed devotion to Judy Jones had rather solidified his position. But he had no social aspirations and rather despised the dancing men who were always on tap for the Thursday or Saturday parties and who filled in at dinners with the younger married set. Already he was playing with the idea of going East to New York. He wanted to take Judy Jones with him. No disillusion as to the world in which she had grown up could cure his illusion as to her desirability.

Remember that—for only in the light of it can what he did for her be understood.

Eighteen months after he first met Judy Jones he became engaged to another girl. Her name was Irene Scheerer, and her father was one of the men who had always believed in Dexter. Irene was light-haired and sweet and honorable, and a little stout, and she had two suitors whom she pleasantly relinquished when Dexter formally asked her to marry him.

Summer, fall, winter, spring, another summer, another fall—so much he had given of his active life to the incorrigible[23] lips of Judy Jones. She had treated him with interest, with encouragement, with malice, with indifference, with contempt. She had inflicted on him the innumerable little slights and indignities possible in such a case—as if in revenge for having ever cared for him at all. She had beckoned him and yawned at him and beckoned him again and he had responded often with bitterness and narrowed eyes. She had brought him ecstatic happiness and intolerable agony of spirit. She had caused him untold inconvenience and not a little trouble. She had insulted him, and she had ridden over him, and she had played his interest in her against his interest in his work—for fun. She had done everything to him except to criticize him—this she had not done—it seemed to him only because it might have sullied the utter indifference she manifested and sincerely felt toward him.

(B) When autumn had come and gone again it occurred to him that he could not have Judy Jones. He had to beat this into his mind but he convinced himself at last. He lay awake at night for a while and argued it over. He told himself the trouble and the pain she had caused him, he enumerated her glaring deficiences as a wife. Then he said to himself that he loved her, and after a while he fell asleep. For a week, lest he imagined her husky voice over the telephone or her eyes opposite him at lunch, he worked hard and late, and at night he went to his office and plotted out his years.

At the end of a week he went to a dance and cut in on her once. For almost the first time since they had met he did not ask her to sit out with him or tell her that she was lovely. It hurt him that she did not miss these things—that was all. He was not jealous when he saw that there was a new man to-night. He had been hardened against jealousy long before.

(C) He stayed late at the dance. He sat for an hour with Irene Scheerer and talked about books and about music. He knew very little about either. But he was beginning to be master of his own time now, and he had a rather priggish[24] notion that he—the young and already fabulously successful Dexter Green—should know more about such things.

That was in October, when he was twenty-five. In January, Dexter and Irene became engaged. It

22. **stag-lines:** lines of unaccompanied men at a dance, waiting for available dance partners.
23. **incorrigible:** incapable of correction or reform.

24. **priggish:** annoyingly precise and proper.

OPTIONS FOR TEACHING

CROSSING THE CURRICULUM

History The Jazz Age is a memory to some adults, a complete blank for many students. Have groups of three students go on scavenger hunts (with parents' or guardians' approval) for items that were new in the Jazz Age. When students present the items to the class, each group must also present a brief history of its item or an oral report gleaned from the item's owner regarding its manufacture, use or function, cost, and desirability. Or groups may make a poster and present a report of a 1920s invention that interests them.

was to be announced in June, and they were to be married three months later.

The Minnesota winter prolonged itself interminably, and it was almost May when the winds came soft and the snow ran down into Black Bear Lake at last. For the first time in over a year Dexter was enjoying a certain tranquility of spirit. Judy Jones had been in Florida, and afterward in Hot Springs, and somewhere she had been engaged, and somewhere she had broken it off. At first, when Dexter had definitely given her up, it had made him sad that people still linked them together and asked for news of her, but when he began to be placed at dinner next to Irene Scheerer people didn't ask him about her any more—they told him about her. He ceased to be an authority on her.

May at last. Dexter walked the streets at night when the darkness was damp as rain, wondering that so soon, with so little done, so much of ecstasy had gone from him. May one year back had been marked by Judy's poignant, unforgivable, yet forgiven turbulence—it had been one of those rare times when he fancied she had grown to care for him. That old penny's worth of happiness he had spent for this bushel of content. He knew that Irene would be no more than a curtain spread behind him, a hand moving among gleaming tea-cups, a voice calling to children . . . fire and loveliness were gone, the magic of nights and the wonder of the varying hours and seasons . . . slender lips, down-turning, dropping to his lips and bearing him up into a heaven of eyes. . . . The thing was deep in him. He was too strong and alive for it to die lightly. (D)

In the middle of May when the weather balanced for a few days on the thin bridge that led to deep summer he turned in one night at Irene's house. Their engagement was to be announced in a week now—no one would be surprised at it. And to-night they would sit together on the lounge at the University Club and look on for an hour at the dancers. It gave him a sense of solidity to go with her—she was so sturdily popular, so intensely "great."

He mounted the steps of the brownstone house and stepped inside.

"Irene," he called.

Mrs. Scheerer came out of the living-room to meet him.

"Dexter," she said, "Irene's gone up-stairs with a splitting headache. She wanted to go with you but I made her go to bed."

"Nothing serious, I——"

"Oh, no. She's going to play golf with you in the morning. You can spare her for just one night, can't you, Dexter?"

Her smile was kind. She and Dexter liked each other. In the living-room he talked for a moment before he said good-night.

Returning to the University Club, where he had rooms, he stood in the doorway for a moment and watched the dancers. He leaned against the door-post, nodded at a man or two—yawned.

"Hello, darling."

The familiar voice at his elbow startled him. Judy Jones had left a man and crossed the room to him—Judy Jones, a slender enamelled doll in cloth of gold: gold in a band at her head, gold in two slipper points at her dress's hem. The fragile glow of her face seemed to blossom as she smiled at him. (E) A breeze of warmth and light blew through the room. His hands in the pockets of his dinner-jacket tightened spasmodically. He was filled with a sudden excitement.

"When did you get back?" he asked casually.

"Come here and I'll tell you about it."

She turned and he followed her. She had been away—he could have wept at the wonder of her return. She had passed through enchanted streets, doing things that were like provocative music. All mysterious happenings, all fresh and quickening hopes, had gone away with her, come back with her now.

She turned in the doorway.

"Have you a car here? If you haven't, I have."

"I have a coupé."

In then, with a rustle of golden cloth. He slammed the door. Into so many cars she had stepped—like this—like that—her back against the leather, so—her elbow resting on the door—waiting. She would have been soiled long since had there been anything to soil her—except herself—but this was her own self outpouring.

With an effort he forced himself to start the car and back into the street. This was nothing, he

Words to Own

turbulence (tur'byoo·ləns) *n.:* irregular behavior.

D. Critical Reading: Analyzing Theme

? What does Dexter imagine his future with Irene will be like? What will be missing? [Possible answer: He imagines a calm, orderly, contented life; but charm, glamour, and beauty will be missing.] How do the last two sentences of this paragraph hint at what is coming? [Possible answer: Dexter seems to be rebelling at the future he envisions.]

E. Literary Element: Symbol

? Why is Judy pictured all in gold? [Possible answers: The color symbolizes Dexter's dreams, his own Golden Fleece—the wealth he longed for, achieved, and found wanting. It also symbolizes the still-elusive goal of Judy herself and the glamour that she represents.]

PROFESSIONAL NOTES

Technology Tip To enhance their understanding of the Jazz Age, invite students to find supplementary historical documents on the American Studies home page at **http://pantheon.cis.yale.edu/~davidp/amstud.html**. Or, to help you prepare lessons for this Collection, browse the Teaching American Literature Web page at **http://www.georgetown.edu/tamlit/tamlit-home.html**. *You may want to preview any Internet activity that you suggest to students. Because these resources are sometimes public forums, their content can be unpredictable.*

A. Critical Reading: Predicting

? Do you think that Dexter will call off his engagement to Irene Scheerer? [Possible answer: Some students will predict that he will call off the engagement, especially if they remember Fitzgerald's earlier admonition on p. 596: "Remember that—for only in the light of it can what he did for her be understood."]

A must remember. She had done this before, and he had put her behind him, as he would have crossed a bad account from his books.

He drove slowly down-town and, affecting abstraction, traversed the deserted streets of the business section, peopled here and there where a movie was giving out its crowd or where consumptive[25] or pugilistic[26] youth lounged in front of pool halls. The clink of glasses and the slap of hands on the bars issued from saloons, cloisters of glazed glass and dirty yellow light.

She was watching him closely and the silence was embarrassing, yet in this crisis he could find no casual word with which to profane the hour. At a convenient turning he began to zigzag back toward the University Club.

"Have you missed me?" she asked suddenly.

"Everybody missed you."

25. **consumptive:** destructive; wasteful.
26. **pugilistic** (pyo͞o′jil·is′tik): quarrelsome; competitive.

OPTIONS FOR TEACHING

PROFESSIONAL NOTES

Cultural Diversity Few students will know about the country-club lifestyle of the early 1900s described here, yet they should be able to appreciate the theme and plot of this story. What may be more problematic is Judy's perplexing behavior. Because she is both aggressive and alluring with the zaniness of a flapper, some students may be facing an unfamiliar and unbelievable personality type. Make clear to students that Judy Jones is a complex character, not easily categorized. Remind students not to reject the character without first making an effort to understand her with patient analysis.

He wondered if she knew of Irene Scheerer. She had been back only a day—her absence had been almost contemporaneous with his engagement.

"What a remark!" Judy laughed sadly—without sadness. She looked at him searchingly. He became absorbed in the dashboard.

"You're handsomer than you used to be," she said thoughtfully. "Dexter, you have the most rememberable eyes."

He could have laughed at this, but he did not laugh. It was the sort of thing that was said to sophomores. Yet it stabbed at him.

"I'm awfully tired of everything, darling." She called every one darling, endowing the endearment with careless, individual comraderie. "I wish you'd marry me."

The directness of this confused him. He should have told her now that he was going to marry another girl, but he could not tell her. He could as easily have sworn that he had never loved her.

"I think we'd get along," she continued, on the same note, "unless probably you've forgotten me and fallen in love with another girl."

Her confidence was obviously enormous. She had said, in effect, that she found such a thing impossible to believe, that if it were true he had merely committed a childish indiscretion—and probably to show off. She would forgive him, because it was not a matter of any moment but rather something to be brushed aside lightly.

"Of course you could never love anybody but me," she continued. "I like the way you love me. Oh, Dexter, have you forgotten last year?"

"No, I haven't forgotten."

"Neither have I!"

Was she sincerely moved—or was she carried along by the wave of her own acting?

"I wish we could be like that again," she said, and he forced himself to answer:

"I don't think we can."

"I suppose not. . . . I hear you're giving Irene Scheerer a violent rush."

There was not the faintest emphasis on the name, yet Dexter was suddenly ashamed.

"Oh, take me home," cried Judy suddenly; "I don't want to go back to that idiotic dance—with those children."

Then, as he turned up the street that led to the residence district, Judy began to cry quietly to herself. He had never seen her cry before.

The dark street lightened, the dwellings of the rich loomed up around them, he stopped his coupé in front of the great white bulk of the Mortimer Joneses house, somnolent,[27] gorgeous, drenched with the splendor of the damp moonlight. Its solidity startled him. The strong walls, the steel of the girders, the breadth and beam and pomp of it were there only to bring out the

27. **somnolent:** sleepy.

B. Language Note: Repetition
Notice that the word *careless* appears again. This seems to be Fitzgerald's one-word summation of the rich in the 1920s; *careless* also describes Tom and Daisy in Fitzgerald's novel *The Great Gatsby.*

C. Critical Reading: Making Inferences
? Why does Judy make a renewed play for Dexter? [Possible answers: She wants to test her power to get Dexter back; she is jealous; or she really cares for him.]

PROBLEM SOLVING/CRITICAL THINKING

Defining the Problem Divide the class into groups of three, and ask each group to come up with three possible sources of Dexter's difficulties. After each group has reported to the class, the class may decide whether these problems exist today as obstacles to their own dreams.

[Possible responses: His poverty in a wealthy country, the fact that every day he saw how the rich lived, his natural appreciation for beauty, his ambition to be or have the best, his pride, his belief in the American dream—that one who works hard enough can get anything—all contribute to his dissatisfaction. Students will probably say that greed is an obstacle in any era.]

A. Literary Element: Theme
When students finish reading, have them come back to this page. Based on the story's theme, what is ironic about Judy's promise here? [Possible answer: She promises Dexter the beauty he longs for—but that is precisely what she will lose. And when she does, Dexter will lose his ideal of beauty.]

B. Critical Reading: Analyzing Character
? Does the story's narrator sympathize with Dexter or consider him a fool for falling for Judy's trick? [Possible answers: The narrator sympathizes with Dexter. Here and elsewhere, comments on Dexter's essential strength and worth are made; or while understanding his dreams, the narrator also considers Dexter foolish.]

contrast with the young beauty beside him. It was sturdy to accentuate her slightness—as if to show what a breeze could be generated by a butterfly's wing.

He sat perfectly quiet, his nerves in wild clamor, afraid that if he moved he would find her irresistibly in his arms. Two tears had rolled down her wet face and trembled on her upper lip.

"I'm more beautiful than anybody else," she said brokenly, "why can't I be happy?" Her moist eyes tore at his stability—her mouth turned slowly downward with an exquisite sadness: "I'd like to marry you if you'll have me, Dexter. I suppose you think I'm not worth having, but I'll be so beautiful for you, Dexter."

A million phrases of anger, pride, passion, hatred, tenderness fought on his lips. Then a perfect wave of emotion washed over him, carrying off with it a sediment of wisdom, of convention,[28] of doubt, of honor. This was his girl who was speaking, his own, his beautiful, his pride.

"Won't you come in?" He heard her draw in her breath sharply.

Waiting.

"All right," his voice was trembling, "I'll come in."

"I'm more beautiful than anybody else . . . why can't I be happy?"

V

It was strange that neither when it was over nor a long time afterward did he regret that night. Looking at it from the perspective of ten years, the fact that Judy's flare for him endured just one month seemed of little importance. Nor did it matter that by his yielding he subjected himself to a deeper agony in the end and gave serious hurt to Irene Sheerer and to Irene's parents, who had befriended him. There was nothing sufficiently pictorial about Irene's grief to stamp itself on his mind.

Dexter was at bottom hard-minded. The attitude of the city on his action was of no importance to him, not because he was going to leave the city, but because any outside attitude on the situation seemed superficial. He was completely indifferent to popular opinion. Nor, when he had seen that it was no use, that he did not possess in himself the power to move fundamentally or to hold Judy Jones, did he bear any malice toward her. He loved her, and he would love her until the day he was too old for loving—but he could not have her. So he tasted the deep pain that is reserved only for the strong, just as he had tasted for a little while the deep happiness.

Even the ultimate falsity of the grounds upon which Judy terminated the engagement, that she did not want to "take him away" from Irene—Judy, who had wanted nothing else—did not revolt him. He was beyond any revulsion or any amusement.

He went East in February with the intention of selling out his laundries and settling in New York—but the war came to America in March and changed his plans. He returned to the West, handed over the management of the business to his partner, and went into the first officers' training-camp in late April. He was one of those young thousands who greeted the war with a certain amount of relief, welcoming the liberation from webs of tangled emotion.

VI

This story is not his biography, remember, although things creep into it which have nothing to do with those dreams he had when he was young. We are almost done with them and with him now. There is only one more incident to be related here, and it happens seven years farther on.

28. **convention:** accepted practices of social behavior.

OPTIONS FOR TEACHING

ASSESSMENT TOOLS

Check Test: Multiple Choice

1. Dexter first sees Judy at (a) the lake (b) the golf course (c) a dance [b]
2. The business that makes Dexter wealthy is (a) stocks and bonds (b) a boat-rental shop (c) a string of laundries [c]
3. When he next sees Judy, she is (a) in a boat (b) on the golf course (c) at a dinner [b]
4. Dexter's courtship of Judy finally ends when (a) she drops him (b) he drops her (c) they get married [a]
5. When Dexter hears of her again, she is (a) playing golf (b) in college (c) married with children [c]

It took place in New York, where he had done well—so well that there were no barriers too high for him. He was thirty-two years old, and, except for one flying trip immediately after the war, he had not been West in seven years. A man named Devlin from Detroit came into his office to see him in a business way, and then and there this incident occurred, and closed out, so to speak, this particular side of his life.

"So you're from the Middle West," said the man Devlin with careless curiosity. "That's funny—I thought men like you were probably born and raised on Wall Street. You know—wife of one of my best friends in Detroit came from your city. I was an usher at the wedding."

Dexter waited with no apprehension of what was coming.

"Judy Simms," said Devlin with no particular interest; "Judy Jones she was once."

"Yes, I knew her." A dull impatience spread over him. He had heard, of course, that she was married—perhaps deliberately he had heard no more.

"Awfully nice girl," brooded Devlin meaninglessly, "I'm sort of sorry for her."

"Why?" Something in Dexter was alert, receptive, at once.

"Oh, Lud Simms has gone to pieces in a way. I don't mean he ill-uses her, but he drinks and runs around——"

"Doesn't she run around?"

"No. Stays at home with her kids."

"Oh."

"She's a little too old for him," said Devlin.

"Too old!" cried Dexter. "Why, man, she's only twenty-seven."

He was possessed with a wild notion of rushing out into the streets and taking a train to Detroit. He rose to his feet spasmodically.

"I guess you're busy," Devlin apologized quickly. "I didn't realize——"

"No, I'm not busy," said Dexter, steadying his voice. "I'm not busy at all. Not busy at all. Did you say she was—twenty-seven? No, I said she was twenty-seven."

"Yes, you did," agreed Devlin dryly.

"Go on, then. Go on."

"What do you mean?"

"About Judy Jones."

Devlin looked at him helplessly.

"Well, that's—I told you all there is to it. He treats her like the devil. Oh, they're not going to get divorced or anything. When he's particularly outrageous she forgives him. In fact, I'm inclined to think she loves him. She was a pretty girl when she first came to Detroit."

A pretty girl! The phrase struck Dexter as ludicrous.

"Isn't she—a pretty girl, any more?"

"Oh, she's all right."

"Look here," said Dexter, sitting down suddenly, "I don't understand. You say she was a 'pretty girl' and now you say she's 'all right.' I don't understand what you mean—Judy Jones wasn't a pretty girl, at all. She was a great beauty. Why, I knew her, I knew her. She was——"

Devlin laughed pleasantly.

"I'm not trying to start a row," he said. "I think Judy's a nice girl and I like her. I can't understand how a man like Lud Simms could fall madly in love with her, but he did." Then he added: "Most of the women like her."

Dexter looked closely at Devlin, thinking wildly that there must be a reason for this, some insensitivity in the man or some private malice.

"Lots of women fade just like *that*," Devlin snapped his fingers. "You must have seen it happen. Perhaps I've forgotten how pretty she was at her wedding. I've seen her so much since then, you see. She has nice eyes."

A sort of dulness settled down upon Dexter. For the first time in his life he felt like getting very drunk. He knew that he was laughing loudly at something Devlin had said, but he did not know what it was or why it was funny. When, in a few minutes, Devlin went he lay down on his lounge and looked out the window at the New York skyline into which the sun was sinking in dull lovely shades of pink and gold.

He had thought that having nothing else to lose he was invulnerable at last—but he knew that he had just lost something more, as surely as if he had married Judy Jones and seen her fade away before his eyes.

The dream was gone. Something had been taken from him. In a sort of panic he pushed the

Words to Own

ludicrous (lo͞o′di·krəs) *adj.:* laughable; absurd.

C. Literary Element: Irony

? What is ironic about Devlin's comment? [Possible answer: Dexter sees himself as a trespasser in the world of the rich, yet another outsider sees him as being part of it.]

D. Expansion

New York City's Wall Street is the home of the stock exchange and thus often associated with the rich and powerful.

E. Critical Reading: Finding Cause and Effect

? What brought about the changes in Judy? Are they believable? [Possible answers: The change in her appearance could be the result of disappointment in a sour marriage or natural aging. It seems likely that she would not be as stunningly beautiful as she ages; or perhaps she was only incredibly beautiful to Dexter.]

Assessment Tools

Peer Assessment When groups give reports to the class, the best evaluation often comes from other students, based on whether or not their understanding of the story has grown. Provide each student with a checklist like the following one.

Scale: 1=Low	5=High
Informative	______
Easy to understand	______
Organized	______
Interesting	______

A. Literary Connections
In *The Snows of Kilimanjaro,* Ernest Hemingway wrote, "He thought they [the very rich] were a special glamorous race and when he found they weren't it wrecked him just as much as any other thing that wrecked him." Ask students how this comment applies to Dexter Green.

The dream was gone. Something had been taken from him.

palms of his hands into his eyes and tried to bring up a picture of the waters lapping on Sherry Island and the moonlit veranda, and gingham on the golf-links and the dry sun and the gold color of her neck's soft down. And her mouth damp to his kisses and her eyes plaintive with melancholy and her freshness like new fine linen in the morning. Why, these things were no longer in the world! They had existed and they existed no longer.

For the first time in years the tears were streaming down his face. But they were for himself now. He did not care about mouth and eyes and moving hands. He wanted to care, and he could not care. For he had gone away and he could never go back any more. The gates were closed, the sun was gone down, and there was no beauty but the gray beauty of steel that withstands all time. Even the grief he could have borne was left behind in the country of illusion, of youth, of the richness of life, where his winter dreams had flourished.

A "Long ago," he said, "long ago, there was something in me, but now that thing is gone. Now that thing is gone, that thing is gone. I cannot cry. I cannot care. That thing will come back no more."

WORDS TO OWN
plaintive (plān′tiv) *adj.:* expressing sadness.

PRIMARY **Sources** A LETTER

A Letter to His Daughter

La Paix, Rodgers' Forge,
Towson, Maryland,
August 8, 1933

Dear Pie:

I feel very strongly about you doing duty. Would you give me a little more documentation about your reading in French? I am glad you are happy—but I never believe much in happiness. I never believe in misery either. Those are things you see on the stage or the screen or the printed page, they never really happen to you in life.

All I believe in in life is the rewards for virtue (according to your talents) and the *punishments* for not fulfilling your duties, which are doubly costly. If there is such a volume in the camp library, will you ask Mrs. Tyson to let you look up a sonnet of Shakespeare's in which the line occurs *"Lilies that fester smell far worse than weeds."*

Have had no thoughts today, life seems composed of getting up a *Saturday Evening Post* story. I think of you, and always pleasantly; but if you call me "Pappy" again I am going to take the White Cat out and beat his bottom *hard, six times for every time you are impertinent.* Do you react to that?

I will arrange the camp bill.

Halfwit, I will conclude. Things to worry about:

Worry about courage
Worry about cleanliness
Worry about efficiency
Worry about horsemanship . . .

Things not to worry about:

Don't worry about popular opinion
Don't worry about dolls
Don't worry about the past
Don't worry about the future
Don't worry about growing up
Don't worry about anybody getting ahead of you
Don't worry about triumph
Don't worry about failure unless it comes through your own fault
Don't worry about mosquitoes
Don't worry about flies
Don't worry about insects in general
Don't worry about parents
Don't worry about boys
Don't worry about disappointments
Don't worry about pleasures
Don't worry about satisfactions

Things to think about:

What am I really aiming at?
How good am I really in comparison to my contemporaries in regard to:
(a) Scholarship
(b) Do I really understand about people and am I able to get along with them?
(c) Am I trying to make my body a useful instrument or am I neglecting it?

With dearest love,

Culver Pictures.

F. Scott Fitzgerald with his daughter, Scottie.

Primary Sources

Fitzgerald was always keen on giving self-improvement advice to others, and his only daughter, Scottie, was a natural recipient. The litany of things to worry about or not to worry about that ends this letter to Scottie at camp is basically serious advice with a few bits of jocular counsel thrown in. Have students consider how they would feel if they received such a letter from a loved one. Students might also discuss what advice they agree with and how they might change the list.

Making Meanings questions begin on p. 604

Making Meanings

First Thoughts

1. Most students will probably sympathize with Dexter if they are aware of the phenomenon in which people are often attracted to people who are bad for them.

Reviewing the Text

a. Dexter refuses to caddy for the wealthy, arrogant little girl who rudely calls him "Boy."
b. Dexter is playing golf with men he once caddied for, and Judy, still arrogant, plays through.
c. During another chance encounter, Judy says she wants to marry Dexter. He succumbs, putting aside wisdom, doubt, and honor.
d. Judy has married Lud Simms, who treats her badly, and her spirit and beauty are gone.

Shaping Interpretations

2. Responses will vary. As a boy, Dexter dreams of success and a glamorous life. Though poor, he attends a prestigious eastern university. He takes risks to buy a laundry. Mr. Jones and Mr. Hart talk about Dexter's great promise. The narrator comments several times on Dexter's unrealistic dreams, which seem to be in conflict with his essential strength and worth.

STRATEGIES FOR INCLUSION

Intrapersonal Ask students to write in their journals their own lists of things to worry about, not to worry about, and to think about.

Kinesthetic Have student groups of two to three pantomime a skit illustrating one of Fitzgerald's things to worry or not worry about. [Example: Worrying about horsemanship might be pantomimed by pretending to ride a horse, holding reins, crouching over a horse approaching a jump, and so forth.] Let the rest of the class guess which aphorism is being pantomimed as each group performs.

Answers to Making Meanings begin on p. T603.

3. Dexter's winter dreams reflect his discontent because they reveal his longing for the magical, golden life he believes the wealthy live. Becoming rich does not satisfy him because he does not possess the symbol of that life—Judy.
4. Judy represents the beauty, glamour, carelessness, and confidence of the wealthy. Some students may feel Dexter really loves her; others may argue that he loves what she represents.
5. The urgency of Dexter's ambitions and his working-class background make him more willing to take risks and to actually involve himself in business. Dexter wants his children to have what he cannot: an innate sense of belonging to the upper class.
6. Students might suggest that Fitzgerald's American dream was based on success, wealth, and elegance, symbolized by Judy, and achieved through self-reliance, ambition, and opportunity. Some students may feel that Fitzgerald overlooked the need for moral or spiritual fortitude in his vision.
7. Judy's loss of beauty signals the irretrievable loss of his youth and "the richness of life." With the death of his idealism, he faces his own mortality.

Connecting with the Text

8. Students need to be true to Fitzgerald's description of both characters—Judy's direct and unprincipled personality, her vitality, independence, and seductive charms; and Dexter's idealism, ambition, romanticism, and sensitivity.
9. Some students might feel that Dexter would not have been happier because Judy herself would have eventually corrupted his idealism. Other students might feel that Dexter would have been happy because he would have had the woman he truly loved and he would also have felt a part of the upper class, thus fulfilling his aspirations.

Challenging the Text

10. **(Evaluation)** Most students will probably agree that the themes are universal and that people are still idealistic and ambitious.

Making Meanings

First Thoughts

1. Did you sympathize with Dexter Green in his tangled feelings for Judy Jones? Explain why or why not.

Reviewing the Text

a. How does his first meeting with Judy Jones lead Dexter to quit his job?

b. How does Dexter encounter Judy again after nearly a decade?

c. Why does Dexter break his engagement to Irene? Is he sorry later?

d. At the end of the story, what has happened to Judy?

Shaping Interpretations

2. What details does Fitzgerald use to persuade us that Dexter is an ambitious young man? What does the story suggest are Dexter's **motivations**? Explain how Dexter's actions reveal his deepest motivations and conform to what the narrator and the other characters say about him.
3. In *Richard III,* Shakespeare refers to "the winter of our discontent." How do Dexter's "winter dreams" reflect his discontent? Does his sense of deprivation subside when he fulfills his ambition to become rich? Explain.
4. When they meet again as adults, Dexter decides that he has "wanted Judy Jones ever since he was a proud, desirous little boy" (page 593). What does Judy represent to Dexter? (Refer to the notes you made in your Reader's Log.) Explain why you think he really does—or does not—love her.
5. What makes Dexter "newer and stronger" (page 592) than the wealthy people he meets? Why, then, does he want his children to be like those people?
6. A recurring **theme** of Fitzgerald's work is the pursuit of the American dream. Based on this story, explain what you think Fitzgerald saw as the American dream. (Be sure to include Dexter's quest for Judy as part of your answer.) What, if anything, do you think is left out of his vision?
7. Why do you think Dexter feels a profound sense of loss when he hears about Judy at the end of the story?

Connecting with the Text

8. According to the story, Dexter and Judy did not know each other during their high school years. Imagine that they did, and that they asked you for advice. What would you tell Judy about Dexter's crush on her? What would you advise Dexter to do about Judy's coolness?
9. Do you think Dexter would have been happier in the end if Judy had married him? Why or why not?

Challenging the Text

10. Do you think the **themes** of this story are universal and timeless, or is this a story that could only have happened in its specific time and place? Explain.

Language and Style

Fitzgerald's Paradoxes

A **paradox** is a seemingly contradictory statement which may, upon closer inspection, prove to illuminate a deeper truth. F. Scott Fitzgerald uses paradox frequently in "Winter Dreams," particularly in his descriptions of Judy Jones. For example:

> "The smile again—radiant, blatantly artificial—convincing." (page 589)
>
> ". . . kisses that were like charity, creating want by holding back nothing at all." (page 593)

Find three more paradoxical descriptions of Judy's behavior. How does this method of phrasing help convey the enigmatic complexity Dexter perceives in her?

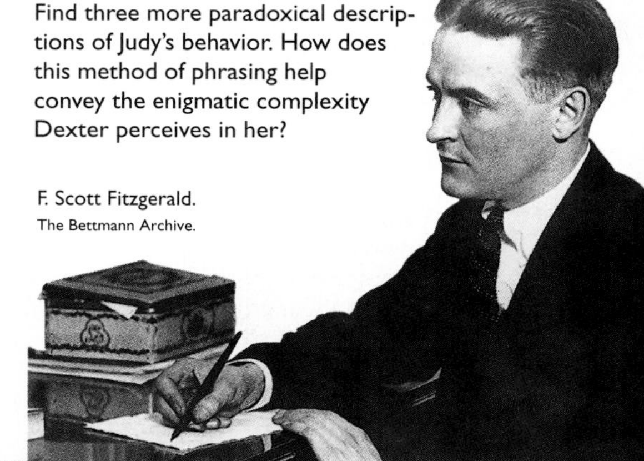

F. Scott Fitzgerald.
The Bettmann Archive.

Language and Style

Answers

Three additional paradoxical descriptions include "beautifully ugly" (p. 588), "quick, insincere smile and a careless 'Thank you!'" (p. 591), and ". . . it was not grotesque, it was merely beautiful . . ." (p. 592). This method of conveying Judy's enigmatic complexity works by illustrating all the opposing and conflicting aspects of her paradoxical nature.

CHOICES: Building Your Portfolio

Writer's Notebook

1. Collecting Ideas for a Speculation About Causes and Effects

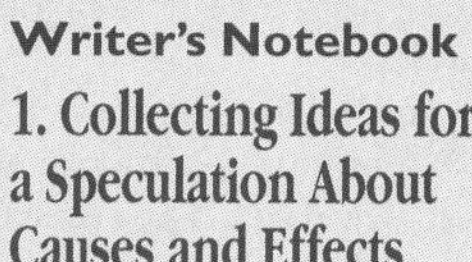

In the Writer's Workshop on page 685, you'll write an essay that speculates about causes and effects. One of your choices will be to analyze the **motivations** of a fictional character that interests you. Record a series of questions you'd like to ask either Judy Jones or Dexter Green. (For example, you could ask Judy questions such as these: "Were you in love with all, some, or none of your suitors? Was your main goal to be the center of attention, or was it something else? Did you enjoy making your boyfriends jealous? Did you intend to hurt anyone?") Then record the answers you'd expect to receive from the character. Keep your notes for possible use in the Writer's Workshop.

Critical Writing

2. Jazz-Age Fairy Tale?

In a book review of Fitzgerald's stories, the novelist Jay McInerney wrote the following:

> . . . the young (poor) boy's quest for the hand of the beautiful, rich princess is undoubtedly Fitzgerald's best plot, the fairy-tale skeleton of his jazz age tales. One supposes that magazine editors preferred the stories in which the quest is successful, but in the better ones, like "Winter Dreams" (1922) and "The Sensible Thing" (1924), the success is qualified or the quest ends in failure.
>
> —Jay McInerney

In a brief essay, analyze the ways in which "Winter Dreams" is like and unlike a fairy tale. Consider the story's **plot, atmosphere, tone,** and **characterization**.

Creative Writing/ Role-Playing

3. Dexter and Judy Get Real

Imagine that it is a year after the end of "Winter Dreams." Dexter and Judy meet by chance in a railroad station, where they are waiting for different trains. In their few minutes together, they discuss their past and present feelings and what they have learned about life. With a partner, briefly plan the content and direction of the conversation. Then improvise the conversation in front of the class.

Crossing the Curriculum: Music

4. Jazzing It Up

"Winter Dreams" mentions three musical works, *Chin-Chin, The Count of Luxemburg,* and *The Chocolate Soldier.* Learn about the "soundtrack" of Dexter's and Judy's life by listening to music composed from 1900 to 1930. Try the jazz, blues, operetta, and popular vocals sections of your public library or music store. Report your findings to the class. Your report might focus on a particular aspect—for example, how the genres of jazz and blues music emerged during this era. Bring recordings to share.

Louis Armstrong.
Culver Pictures.

Choices: Building Your Portfolio

1. **Writer's Notebook** Remind students to save their work. They may use it as prewriting for the Writer's Workshop p. 685.
2. **Critical Writing** To help them analyze the story, have students fill in a chart like the following one before starting their essays.

	Fairy tale: like	Fairy tale: unlike
Plot		
Atmosphere		
Tone		
Characterization		

3. **Creative Writing/Role-Playing** Before students write their dialogues, have them adopt the persona of each character in their journals. They may write about each other, their feelings, and what they have learned about life. Then students may share these journal responses and develop a conversation for improvisation.
4. **Crossing the Curriculum: Music** Have a jazz day after students have had time to research 1920s music. In addition to bringing music to share with the class, students might present brief reports or demonstrations of popular dances such as the Charleston, the Black Bottom, and the fox trot.

PORTFOLIO ASSESSMENT

Choices: Assessment Criteria For help in evaluating these Choices assignments, see the criteria in the ***Portfolio Management System,*** pp. 138–139.

STRATEGIES FOR INCLUSION

Visual For activity #1, suggest that students collect notes for their Writer's Notebooks and the essay by using a graphic organizer. Consider using Transparency 5: Venn Diagram in the Transparency Package.

Auditory To help students role-play in activity #3, have them dramatize several sections of the story. Choose parts with dialogue that reveals or suggests the characters' attitudes and motivations. Then, have students read the roles of Dexter, Judy, and the narrator. Ask students to offer different interpretations of the same dialogue in order to reach a consensus as to the appropriate characterization, especially of Judy. Then, discuss how these characters might react to each other after the story ends.

QUICK PLANNING GUIDE

Into the Story

Through the Story

Beyond the Story

John Steinbeck
(1902–1968)

Most writers would probably agree that fiction that delivers a political message may be effective propaganda, but it is unlikely to be art. John Steinbeck would *not* have agreed with this precept, and he is a notable exception to it.

During the 1930s, the Great Depression cost millions of people their jobs and shook their faith in the American dream. But big business and the corporate farm seemed untouched by hard times; they were angrily perceived by many as impersonal and indifferent to human hardship.

Many novelists of the time were moved by this sense of injustice and turned their pens to a by-product of the Depression known as "the protest novel." Among these writers, John Steinbeck was the most widely praised and successful.

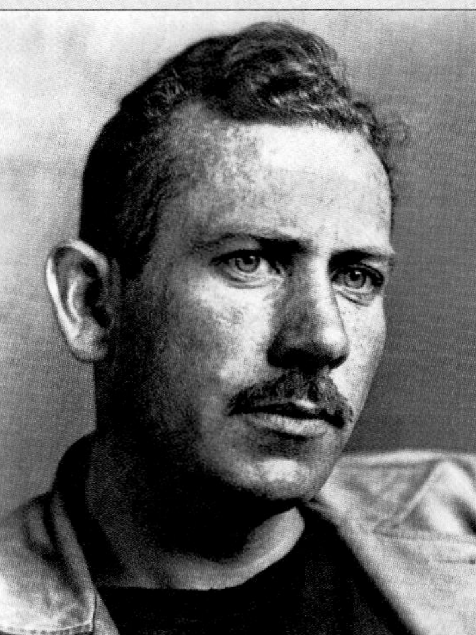

UPI/Bettmann.

Steinbeck was born in California's Salinas Valley in 1902, the son of a county treasurer and a schoolteacher. Although he graduated from high school and spent some time at Stanford University, he took more pride in the many jobs he held as a young man than in his formal education. He worked as a hod carrier, fruit picker, apprentice painter, laboratory assistant, caretaker, surveyor, and journalist. He also wrote seventeen novels, in addition to stories, plays, and screenplays.

Steinbeck's first major success came in 1937 with *Of Mice and Men,* a short, best-selling novel that Steinbeck himself adapted into a Broadway play. It is a tale of two itinerant farmhands: George and the powerful but simple-minded Lennie. Steinbeck took a pathetic situation and transformed it into an affirmative acceptance of life's brutal conflicts, along with life's possibilities for fellowship and courage.

He followed this success by living and working with some Oklahoma farmers—known as "Okies"—over the next two years. The result was his strongest and most enduring novel, *The Grapes of Wrath* (1939). It tells of the Joad family and their forced migration from the Dust Bowl of Oklahoma to California, the region that promised work at decent wages and a chance to buy land. Once in California, however, the Joads find only the exploitation and poverty of labor camps. Gradually they learn what "Okies" really means—people who never even had a chance.

The Grapes of Wrath was an angry book that spoke out on behalf of the migrant workers. Steinbeck sharply criticized a system that bankrupted thousands of farmers and turned them from their own land, making them into paid help for the big growers. When the novel appeared, it was greeted with outbursts of praise and condemnation, and it became the most widely read of all the protest novels of the 1930s.

The Grapes of Wrath won the Pulitzer Prize in 1940. After this major success, however, Steinbeck's eminence waned. Toward the end of his life, Steinbeck achieved a gratifying success with the award of the Nobel Prize in literature in 1962 and with the publication in that year of *Travels with Charley,* a nostalgic account of his odyssey across America with his aged poodle Charley. But Steinbeck's reputation is grounded on those earlier novels that portray California as the real and symbolic land of American promise.

PROGRAM MANAGER

- **Planning Instruction** See *Teaching Notes, Teaching Resources B,* p. 34, for objectives, a summary, and literary elements for this selection.
- **Instructional Support** See **Graphic Organizer for Active Reading,** *Teaching Resources B,* p. 40, for a Through the Story activity.
- **Assessment** See **Selection Test,** *Test Booklet,* pp. 143–144.
- **Language Link** For instruction and practice in personal pronouns, see **Language Link,** *Teaching Resources B,* pp. 41-42 and *Language and Writing Skills Worksheets,* p.13.
- **Reinforcement** Use the Words to Own worksheet in *Teaching Resources B,* p. 43.

BEFORE YOU READ
THE LEADER OF THE PEOPLE

Reading Focus

The Golden Age

It seems that in every generation older people say to younger people, "It was different in my day." Most people feel nostalgic about the past, dreaming of it as a "golden age" that was somehow cleaner or more heroic or happier than the present. In fact, some people end up living mainly in memories of a past that might never have existed.

Quickwrite

READER'S LOG

There's a certain point of view that holds that the time of heroes is long past. Who are our heroes today? Would you consider them role models? What opportunities do you see for heroism today? Quickwrite your thoughts.

Elements of Literature

Conflict

"The Leader of the People" shows three generations of a family in conflict because of differences in age, gender, personal histories, and the roles they play on the family ranch. Some conflicts in the story are **external conflicts:** They occur between two or more people. Others are **internal conflicts,** occurring inside one person's mind. One conflict involves a close look at that recurring dream of a more heroic American past.

Conflict is a struggle between opposing forces or characters in a story. Conflict can be internal (a character struggles with conscience, for example) or external (a character struggles against a blizzard).

For more about Conflict, see the Handbook of Literary Terms.

Background

In "The Leader of the People," John Steinbeck explores the conflict between dream and reality at the heart of so much American fiction. This story appears as the fourth and final part of Steinbeck's novel *The Red Pony* (1945). Each part of this "novel" was published as a complete short story. The stories, all connected by their characters and settings, are called "The Gift," "The Great Mountains," "The Promise," and "The Leader of the People."

Into the Story

Using **BEFORE YOU READ** p. 607

Reading Focus

Many students will have heard stories about the "good old days" from relatives, novels, or movies. Divide the class into groups of four and have them tell each other some of these stories. Afterward, lead a class discussion about the conflict between dreams and reality inherent in these tales. Was it really so great back then? Are modern times devoid of meaning and opportunities for heroic deeds and happiness? The class need not reach consensus for the discussion to be enriching.

Quickwrite

Remind students that their heroes or role models do not have to be larger-than-life movie or sports stars. Anyone whom they admire or would like to emulate will be a suitable subject for their Quickwrites.

Elements of Literature

Ask students if conflicts must be resolved in an effective story. Then, as students read the story, have them identify the internal and external conflicts. Students should respond to the following questions: Which conflict seems most important? Is this conflict resolved? Would you describe the resolution as satisfying, or would you describe its effect in some other way?

WORDS TO OWN

The following vocabulary words are defined in the Words to Own at the bottom of the pupil's page.

arrogant p. 609	convened p. 611
immune p. 609	unseemly p. 612
cleft p. 610	humoring p. 613
contemptuously p. 610	marshaling p. 617
rancor p. 611	disconsolately p. 619

PORTFOLIO ASSESSMENT

Portfolio Assessment For help with self-assessment of reading skills, see the ***Portfolio Management System,*** p. 39.

ABOUT THE AUTHOR

John Steinbeck wrote about California's Salinas Valley in some of his most famous works, from *The Red Pony* to *East of Eden*. He used not only local settings to inspire these stories, but also the local citizens. The residents of his hometown of Salinas were not totally flattered. Some even burned *The Grapes of Wrath* in 1939. However, before the author died, the townsfolk changed their minds, and now Salinas has the Steinbeck Festival every August. Along with speakers and workshops, the festival includes tours of the John Steinbeck Library and the Steinbeck historic district, in which the writer's boyhood home still stands.

Ranch Near San Luis Obispo, Evening Light (c. 1935) by Phil Paradise. Oil on canvas (28″ × 34″).

OPTIONS FOR TEACHING

STRATEGIES FOR INCLUSION

Advanced Ask students to independently research the westward movement in the mid-nineteenth century and the difficulties experienced by those who took part. They should then present their research either as a report to the rest of the class or as a research paper.

Spatial Give students the option of summarizing the story with drawings of main events in the plot. Below each picture, other students should write what is happening. Or students might work in pairs, one drawing the pictures and the other writing the summaries.

Less Proficient Readers Because there is so much dialogue in this story, you may want to assign parts, including a narrator, to read all or parts of the selection. Other students should listen and write plot summaries after each reading session. Ask the students to include at least five comments on what happens in the story, a question about an action, a discussion of the reason for an action, or a personal experience related to an action.

The Buck Collection, Laguna Hills, California.

The Leader of the People

John Steinbeck

On Saturday afternoon Billy Buck, the ranch-hand, raked together the last of the old year's haystack and pitched small forkfuls over the wire fence to a few mildly interested cattle. High in the air small clouds like puffs of cannon smoke were driven eastward by the March wind. The wind could be heard whishing in the brush on the ridge crests, but no breath of it penetrated down into the ranch-cup.

The little boy, Jody, emerged from the house eating a thick piece of buttered bread. He saw Billy working on the last of the haystack. Jody tramped down scuffing his shoes in a way he had been told was destructive to good shoe-leather. A flock of white pigeons flew out of the black cypress tree as Jody passed, and circled the tree and landed again. A half-grown tortoise-shell[1] cat leaped from the bunkhouse porch, galloped on stiff legs across the road, whirled and galloped back again. Jody picked up a stone to help the game along, but he was too late, for the cat was under the porch before the stone could be discharged. He threw the stone into the cypress tree and started the white pigeons on another whirling flight. **A**

Arriving at the used-up haystack, the boy leaned against the barbed wire fence. "Will that be all of it, do you think?" he asked.

The middle-aged ranch-hand stopped his careful raking and stuck his fork[2] into the ground. He took off his black hat and smoothed down his hair. "Nothing left of it that isn't soggy from ground moisture," he said. He replaced his hat and rubbed his dry leathery hands together.

"Ought to be plenty mice," Jody suggested.

"Lousy with them," said Billy. "Just crawling with mice."

"Well, maybe, when you get all through, I could call the dogs and hunt the mice."

"Sure, I guess you could," said Billy Buck. He lifted a forkful of the damp ground-hay and threw it into the air. Instantly three mice leaped out and burrowed frantically under the hay again.

Jody sighed with satisfaction. Those plump, sleek, arrogant mice were doomed. For eight months they had lived and multiplied in the haystack. They had been immune from cats, from traps, from poison and from Jody. They had grown smug in their security, overbearing and fat. Now the time of disaster had come; they would not survive another day.

1. **tortoise-shell:** having a pattern of brown and yellow markings, as commonly seen on the shell of a tortoise.
2. **fork:** pitchfork.

WORDS TO OWN

arrogant (ar′ə·gənt) *adj.:* proud and overly confident.
immune (im·myo͞on′) *adj.:* protected.

A. Literary Element: Point of View
Steinbeck uses the third-person-limited point of view. Events are viewed through the eyes of Jody, the young farm boy, a perspective that allows the reader to share Jody's thoughts and feelings.

STRATEGIES FOR INCLUSION

Special Needs Students for whom written compositions require a great deal of time and effort may prefer an alternative to a written response for this selection. These students could make an audio recording of an interview with their grandparents or a person they view as heroic. Questions should be prepared and organized before the interview and may be similar to the following.

1. What is the most important contribution you have made to humanity in your life so far?
2. Do you feel that society today still values that contribution?
3. What people do you feel are having a powerful impact on society today?

The recordings can be reviewed by the teacher and portions shared with the class for discussion.

English Language Development Make sure that all students are aware of the deeply rooted tradition of moving, especially west, in order to find greater opportunity. Ask students if they can think of various situations in which people take a great risk to move for a better life. If appropriate, mention refugees who have taken great risks to reach the United States. Ask students if they have any memories of other "leaders of the people."

A. Critical Reading: Analyzing Conflict

? What is there in this conversation between Jody and Billy that hints at a conflict between Jody and his father? [Possible answers: Jody slumps against the fence post and responds that his father doesn't care about the mice. Also, the word *ominously* hints at a problem between them.]

B. Literary Element: Point of View

? Does the last part of this sentence sound like something Jody would say or think? What happened to the third-person limited point of view? [Possible answer: Steinbeck momentarily drops into the omniscient point of view to make an observation about dogs, characteristic of him but not likely to occur to Jody. Steinbeck resumes the limited point of view in the next paragraph.]

C. Reader's Response: First Thoughts

? What does this first picture of Carl Tiflin suggest to you about the man? [Sample responses: He is clearly defined as a man in charge; or he is to be feared because the dog stiffens.]

Billy looked up at the top of the hills that surrounded the ranch. "Maybe you better ask your father before you do it," he suggested.

"Well, where is he? I'll ask him now."

"He rode up to the ridge ranch after dinner. He'll be back pretty soon."

A Jody slumped against the fence post. "I don't think he'd care."

As Billy went back to his work he said ominously, "You'd better ask him anyway. You know how he is."

Jody did know. His father, Carl Tiflin, insisted upon giving permission for anything that was done on the ranch, whether it was important or not. Jody sagged farther against the post until he was sitting on the ground. He looked up at the little puffs of wind-driven cloud. "Is it like to rain, Billy?"

"It might. The wind's good for it, but not strong enough."

"Well, I hope it don't rain until after I kill those damn mice." He looked over his shoulder to see whether Billy had noticed the mature profanity. Billy worked on without comment.

Jody turned back and looked at the side-hill where the road from the outside world came down. The hill was washed with lean March sunshine. Silver thistles, blue lupins[3] and a few poppies bloomed among the sage bushes. Halfway up the hill Jody could see Doubletree Mutt, the black dog, digging in a squirrel hole. He paddled for a while and then paused to kick bursts of dirt out between his hind legs, and he dug with an earnestness which belied the knowledge he must have had that no dog had ever caught a squirrel by digging in a hole. B

Suddenly, while Jody watched, the black dog stiffened, and backed out of the hole and looked up the hill toward the cleft in the ridge where the road came through. Jody looked up too. For a moment Carl Tiflin on horseback stood out against the pale sky and then he moved down the road toward the house. He carried something white in his hand. C

The boy started to his feet. "He's got a letter," Jody cried. He trotted away toward the ranch house, for the letter would probably be read aloud and he wanted to be there. He reached the house before his father did, and ran in. He heard Carl dismount from his creaking saddle and slap the horse on the side to send it to the barn where Billy would unsaddle it and turn it out.

Jody ran into the kitchen. "We got a letter!" he cried.

His mother looked up from a pan of beans. "Who has?"

"Father has. I saw it in his hand."

Carl strode into the kitchen then, and Jody's mother asked, "Who's the letter from, Carl?"

He frowned quickly. "How did you know there was a letter?"

She nodded her head in the boy's direction. "Big-Britches Jody told me."

Jody was embarrassed.

His father looked down at him contemptuously. "He *is* getting to be a Big-Britches," Carl said. "He's minding everybody's business but his own. Got his big nose into everything."

Mrs. Tiflin relented a little. "Well, he hasn't enough to keep him busy. Who's the letter from?"

Carl still frowned on Jody. "I'll keep him busy if he isn't careful." He held out a sealed letter. "I guess it's from your father."

Mrs. Tiflin took a hairpin from her head and slit open the flap. Her lips pursed judiciously. Jody saw her eyes snap back and forth over the lines. "He says," she translated, "he says he's going to drive out Saturday to stay for a little while. Why, this is Saturday. The letter must have been delayed." She looked at the postmark. "This was mailed day before yesterday. It should have been here yesterday." She looked up questioningly at her husband, and then her face darkened angrily. "Now what have you got that look on you for? He doesn't come often."

Carl turned his eyes away from her anger. He could be stern with her most of the time, but when occasionally her temper arose, he could not combat it.

"What's the matter with you?" she demanded again.

3. **lupins** (lo͞o′pinz): flowering plants of the bean family; more often spelled *lupines.*

Words to Own

cleft (kleft) *n.:* opening.

contemptuously (kən·temp′cho͞o·əs·lē) *adv.:* scornfully.

Options for Teaching

Integrating the Language Arts

Strategic Reading Ask students to read in pairs. After reading each page, have each student write down a prediction of what will happen next and why. Then, have the pairs discuss their predictions and read the next page, checking the predictions made earlier and predicting once more. This method should help them to develop the habit of thinking while reading.

Vocabulary and Language Begin with the first paragraph and point out that Steinbeck narrates from a third-person point of view. Ask what changes might be made if Jody were the narrator. Model this activity by working with the whole class to change the language of the first paragraph to the first person, in Jody's voice. Then ask the students to rewrite a narrative section of the story using Jody's voice and vocabulary.

Writing: Paragraph Ask students to take notes several times during the reading of the story. They could use these notes to write a paragraph about their own heroes, about the accomplishments of their own parents or grandparents, and about new frontiers faced by people today.

In his explanation there was a tone of apology Jody himself might have used. "It's just that he talks," Carl said lamely. "Just talks."

"Well, what of it? You talk yourself."

"Sure I do. But your father only talks about one thing."

"Indians!" Jody broke in excitedly. "Indians and crossing the plains!"

Carl turned fiercely on him. "You get out, Mr. Big-Britches! Go on, now! Get out!" **D**

Jody went miserably out the back door and closed the screen with elaborate quietness. Under the kitchen window his shamed, downcast eyes fell upon a curiously shaped stone, a stone of such fascination that he squatted down and picked it up and turned it over in his hands.

The voices came clearly to him through the open kitchen window. "Jody's damn well right," he heard his father say. "Just Indians and crossing the plains. I've heard that story about how the horses got driven off about a thousand times. He just goes on and on, and he never changes a word in the things he tells."

When Mrs. Tiflin answered her tone was so changed that Jody, outside the window, looked up from his study of the stone. Her voice had become soft and explanatory. Jody knew how her face would have changed to match the tone. She said quietly, "Look at it this way, Carl. That was the big thing in my father's life. **E** He led a wagon train clear across the plains to the coast, and when it was finished, his life was done. It was a big thing to do, but it didn't last long enough. Look!" she continued, "it's as though he was born to do that, and after he finished it, there wasn't anything more for him to do but think about it and talk about it. If there'd been any farther west to go, he'd have gone. He's told me so himself. But at last there was the ocean. He lives right by the ocean where he had to stop."

She had caught Carl, caught him and entangled him in her soft tone. **F**

"I've seen him," he agreed quietly. "He goes down and stares off west over the ocean." His voice sharpened a little. "And then he goes up to the Horseshoe Club in Pacific Grove, and he tells people how the Indians drove off the horses."

She tried to catch him again. "Well, it's everything to him. You might be patient with him and pretend to listen."

Carl turned impatiently away. "Well, if it gets too bad, I can always go down to the bunkhouse and sit with Billy," he said irritably. He walked through the house and slammed the front door after him.

Jody ran to his chores. He dumped the grain to the chickens without chasing any of them. He gathered the eggs from the nests. He trotted into the house with the wood and interlaced it so carefully in the wood-box that two armloads seemed to fill it to overflowing.

His mother had finished the beans by now. She stirred up the fire and brushed off the stove-top with a turkey wing. Jody peered cautiously at her to see whether any rancor toward him remained. "Is he coming today?" Jody asked.

"That's what his letter said."

"Maybe I better walk up the road to meet him."

Mrs. Tiflin clanged the stove-lid shut. "That would be nice," she said. "He'd probably like to be met."

"I guess I'll just do it then."

Outside, Jody whistled shrilly to the dogs. "Come on up the hill," he commanded. The two dogs waved their tails and ran ahead. Along the roadside the sage had tender new tips. Jody tore off some pieces and rubbed them on his hands until the air was filled with the sharp wild smell. With a rush the dogs leaped from the road and yapped into the brush after a rabbit. That was the last Jody saw of them, for when they failed to catch the rabbit, they went back home.

Jody plodded on up the hill toward the ridge top. When he reached the little cleft where the road came through, the afternoon wind struck him and blew up his hair and ruffled his shirt. He looked down on the little hills and ridges below and then out at the huge green Salinas Valley. He could see the white town of Salinas far out in the flat and the flash of its windows under the waning sun. Directly below him, in an oak tree, a crow congress had convened. The tree was black with crows all cawing at once. **G**

Then Jody's eyes followed the wagon road down from the ridge where he stood, and lost it

WORDS TO OWN

rancor (raŋ′kər) *n.:* anger.
convened (kən·vēnd′) *v.:* assembled.

D. Critical Reading: Drawing Conclusions

? What is Jody's position in the family? What would he like it to be? [Possible answers: By calling Jody Big-Britches, his parents indicate that he is nosy, trying to be a part of things when he's still too young. Jody is embarrassed; he wants their respect.]

E. Language Note: Dialogue

? How does Steinbeck indicate the manner in which words were spoken? [Possible answer: He frequently uses adverbs to indicate a speaker's way of talking; for example, *lamely, excitedly,* and *fiercely.*]

F. Reader's Response: Shaping Interpretations

? What does Steinbeck mean when he says that Jody's mother "had caught Carl, caught him and entangled him in her soft tone"? [Sample responses: Her soft, gentle manner defuses Carl's anger; or by contrast, her voice shows him how harsh and unfair he is being.]

G. Literary Element: Setting

These two paragraphs contain a number of details about the setting. How many different senses does Steinbeck appeal to? [Possible answers: Four: *smell*—rubbing the sage buds; *hearing*—the dogs' yapping, the wind singing on the hilltops; *sight*—the white town of Salinas in the green valley, the tree black with crows; *touch*—the wind striking Jody, ruffling his shirt and blowing his hair.]

INTEGRATING THE LANGUAGE ARTS

Mechanics Have students turn to p. 616 and read the last paragraph, made up of seven sentences. (The paragraph continues on p. 617) Ask them to write the numbers 1–7 on a sheet of paper and to explain the functions of the commas in each sentence. Remind students that commas can be used singly (to separate) or in pairs (to enclose). Here are the answers:

1. To separate a nonessential appositive phrase
2. To separate two independent clauses
3. A pair of commas to enclose an interrupting phrase
4. A pair of commas to enclose a nonessential appositive phrase
5. None
6. To separate a nonessential participial phrase
7. To separate two independent clauses

A. Language Note: Vocabulary
Here, *flirted* means "moved in a rapid and jerky manner."

B. Reader's Response: Shaping Interpretations
? How does this description of the grandfather reveal what kind of person he is? [Sample responses: His giant shadow and his reputation, which flicker darkly behind him, indicate that his greatest achievements are in the past; or his granite dignity makes him unable to adjust to changes—once he starts in a direction, he never wavers.]

C. Literary Element: Theme
? How does Jody's grandfather react to the idea of the mouse hunt? [Possible answers: He doesn't think much of it; or he makes a joke about it.] What do you begin to learn about the grandfather's relationships to the people of this generation? [Possible answers: He doesn't have much respect for them; or it is difficult for him to relate to them.]

behind a hill, and picked it up again on the other side. On that distant stretch he saw a cart slowly pulled by a bay[4] horse. It disappeared behind the hill. Jody sat down on the ground and watched the place where the cart would reappear again. The wind sang on the hilltops and the puff-ball clouds hurried eastward.

Then the cart came into sight and stopped. A man dressed in black dismounted from the seat and walked to the horse's head. Although it was so far away, Jody knew he had unhooked the check-rein, for the horse's head dropped forward. The horse moved on, and the man walked slowly up the hill beside it. Jody gave a glad cry and ran down the road toward them. The squirrels bumped along off the road, and a road-runner flirted its tail and raced over the edge of the hill and sailed out like a glider. (A)

Jody tried to leap into the middle of his shadow at every step. A stone rolled under his foot and he went down. Around a little bend he raced, and there, a short distance ahead, were his grandfather and the cart. The boy dropped from his unseemly running and approached at a dignified walk.

The horse plodded stumble-footedly up the hill and the old man walked beside it. In the lowering sun their giant shadows flickered darkly behind them. The grandfather was dressed in a black broadcloth suit and he wore kid congress gaiters[5] and a black tie on a short, hard collar. He carried his black slouch hat in his hand. His white beard was cropped close and his white eyebrows overhung his eyes like mustaches. The blue eyes were sternly merry. About the whole face and figure there was a granite dignity, so that every motion seemed an impossible thing. Once at rest, it seemed the old man would be stone, would never move again. His steps were slow and certain. Once made, no step could ever be retraced; once headed in a direction, the path would never bend nor the pace increase nor slow. (B)

When Jody appeared around the bend, Grandfather waved his hat slowly in welcome, and he called, "Why, Jody! Come down to meet me, have you?"

4. **bay:** reddish brown.
5. **kid congress gaiters:** high leather boots with elastic inserts in each side.

Jody sidled[6] near and turned and matched his step to the old man's step and stiffened his body and dragged his heels a little. "Yes, sir," he said. "We got your letter only today."

"Should have been here yesterday," said Grandfather. "It certainly should. How are all the folks?"

"They're fine, sir." He hesitated and then suggested shyly, "Would you like to come on a mouse hunt tomorrow, sir?"

"Mouse hunt, Jody?" Grandfather chuckled. "Have the people of this generation come down to hunting mice? They aren't very strong, the new people, but I hardly thought mice would be game for them." (C)

"No, sir. It's just play. The haystack's gone. I'm going to drive out the mice to the dogs. And you can watch, or even beat the hay a little."

The stern, merry eyes turned down on him. "I see. You don't eat them, then. You haven't come to that yet."

Jody explained, "The dogs eat them, sir. It wouldn't be much like hunting Indians, I guess."

"No, not much—but then later, when the troops were hunting Indians and shooting children and burning teepees, it wasn't much different from your mouse hunt."

They topped the rise and started down into the ranch cup, and they lost the sun from their shoulders. "You've grown," Grandfather said. "Nearly an inch, I should say."

"More," Jody boasted. "Where they mark me on the door, I'm up more than an inch since Thanksgiving even."

Grandfather's rich throaty voice said, "Maybe you're getting too much water and turning to pith and stalk. Wait until you head out, and then we'll see."[7]

Jody looked quickly into the old man's face to see whether his feelings should be hurt, but there was no will to injure, no punishing nor putting-in-your-place light in the keen blue eyes. "We might kill a pig," Jody suggested.

6. **sidled** (sīd′'ld): approached slyly.
7. **Maybe . . . we'll see:** Like an overwatered plant, Jody may grow tall but not be very productive. Not until he "heads out" will anyone know what he is capable of.

WORDS TO OWN
unseemly (un·sēm′lē) *adj.:* improper.

OPTIONS FOR TEACHING

CROSSING THE CURRICULUM

Geography Use a large map to trace the westward expansion of the nineteenth century. Students can research a particular wagon train excursion and create a map tracing its route and events along the way.

Social Sciences Jody's grandfather's experiences were shared by many people. You may want to make available information about the western migration the story refers to, perhaps from an encyclopedia. Or a group of students may volunteer to report on this phase of the history of the United States.

Health Invite students to investigate the aging process to better understand the needs of older people. They might talk to their own grandparents or other older persons about the aging process, a topic they may not have discussed before.

"Oh, no! I couldn't let you do that. You're just humoring me. It isn't the time and you know it."

"You know Riley, the big boar, sir?"

"Yes. I remember Riley well."

"Well, Riley ate a hole into that same haystack, and it fell down on him and smothered him."

"Pigs do that when they can," said Grandfather.

"Riley was a nice pig, for a boar, sir. I rode him sometimes, and he didn't mind."

A door slammed at the house below them, and they saw Jody's mother standing on the porch waving her apron in welcome. And they saw Carl Tiflin walking up from the barn to be at the house for the arrival.

The sun had disappeared from the hills by now. The blue smoke from the house chimney hung in flat layers in the purpling ranch-cup. The puff-ball clouds, dropped by the falling wind, hung listlessly in the sky.

Billy Buck came out of the bunkhouse and flung a wash basin of soapy water on the ground. He had been shaving in mid-week, for Billy held Grandfather in reverence, and Grandfather said that Billy was one of the few men of the new generation who had not gone soft. Although Billy was in middle age, Grandfather considered him a boy. Now Billy was hurrying toward the house too. **D**

When Jody and Grandfather arrived, the three were waiting for them in front of the yard gate.

Carl said, "Hello, sir. We've been looking for you."

Mrs. Tiflin kissed Grandfather on the side of his beard, and stood still while his big hand patted her shoulder. Billy shook hands solemnly, grinning under his straw mustache. "I'll put up your horse," said Billy, and he led the rig away.

Grandfather watched him go, and then, turning back to the group, he said as he had said a hundred times before, "There's a good boy. I knew his father, old Mule-tail Buck. I never knew why they called him Mule-tail except he packed mules." **E**

Mrs. Tiflin turned and led the way into the house. "How long are you going to stay, Father? Your letter didn't say."

"Well, I don't know. I thought I'd stay about two weeks. But I never stay as long as I think I'm going to."

In a short while they were sitting at the white oilcloth table eating their supper. The lamp with the tin reflector hung over the table. Outside the dining-room windows the big moths battered softly against the glass.

Grandfather cut his steak into tiny pieces and chewed slowly. "I'm hungry," he said. "Driving out here got my appetite up. It's like when we were crossing. We all got so hungry every night we could hardly wait to let the meat get done. I could eat about five pounds of buffalo meat every night."

"It's moving around does it," said Billy. "My father was a government packer. I helped him when I was a kid. Just the two of us could about clean up a deer's ham."

"I knew your father, Billy," said Grandfather. "A fine man he was. They called him Mule-tail Buck. I don't know why except he packed mules."

"That was it," Billy agreed. "He packed mules."

Grandfather put down his knife and fork and looked around the table. "I remember one time we ran out of meat—" His voice dropped to a curious low sing-song, dropped into a tonal groove the story had worn for itself. "There was no buffalo, no antelope, not even rabbits. The hunters couldn't even shoot a coyote. That was the time for the leader to be on the watch. I was the leader, and I kept my eyes open. Know why? Well, just the minute the people began to get hungry they'd start slaughtering the team oxen. Do you believe that? I've heard of parties that just ate up their draft cattle. Started from the middle and worked toward the ends. Finally they'd eat the lead pair, and then the wheelers. The leader of a party had to keep them from doing that." **F**

In some manner a big moth got into the room and circled the hanging kerosene lamp. Billy got up and tried to clap it between his hands. Carl struck with a cupped palm and caught the moth and broke it. He walked to the window and dropped it out.

"As I was saying," Grandfather began again, but Carl interrupted him. "You'd better eat some more meat. All the rest of us are ready for our pudding."

Jody saw a flash of anger in his mother's eyes. Grandfather picked up his knife and fork. "I'm pretty hungry, all right," he said. "I'll tell you about that later."

WORDS TO OWN

humoring (hyo͞o′mər·iŋ) *v.:* indulging.

D. Literary Element: Irony

? What is ironic about Grandfather's feeling that Billy was one of the few men who had not gone soft? [Possible answers: Billy is a hired hand who is told what to do, who takes no risks and makes no decisions; or he is neither a leader nor influential.]

E. Language Note: Vocabulary

Billy's father had been a mule packer—that is, someone who transports goods and supplies by mule.

F. Literary Element: Theme

Here Grandfather reveals his importance as the leader of a party. Much of his dissatisfaction is probably due to the frustrations related to the lack of a significant role in life, a major theme in this story.

COOPERATIVE LEARNING

Group Writing/Acting Students may enjoy performing this short story as a drama. Divide the class into four or five groups, and assign each group one section of the story to dramatize. They might add lines in order to eliminate the narrator or cast someone to be the narrator. Then, each group can perform its assigned section as reader's theater.

Fielding Questions Put up a large sheet of butcher paper or blank newsprint on which students can write questions as they read, leaving room between questions for other students to answer. Periodically check to make sure that misconceptions are cleared up. Leave a few minutes at the beginning or end of class to discuss the posted questions and answers or to allow students to add or answer new questions. ☞

A. Critical Reading: Making Connections

? Do people in our society today still react as Jody's grandfather does when they are deprived of a significant role because of age and perhaps technological developments? [Although answers may vary, most students will agree that yes, people today feel frustrated too; the grandfather's need to relive the old days is understandable.]

B. Critical Reading: Finding Details

? Who is listening to the grandfather's stories? [Possible answer: Nobody except Jody, not even Billy Buck.]

C. Reader's Response: Shaping Interpretations

? If Jody's grandfather isn't interested in the stories himself, why does he tell them? [Sample responses: Perhaps because he feels his present life is so limited that he has nothing else to contribute; or perhaps because he needs to remind himself and others of what he once was.]

When supper was over, when the family and Billy Buck sat in front of the fireplace in the other room, Jody anxiously watched Grandfather. He saw the signs he knew. The bearded head leaned forward; the eyes lost their sternness and looked wonderingly into the fire; the big lean fingers laced themselves on the black knees. "I wonder," he began, "I just wonder whether I ever told you how those thieving Piutes[8] drove off thirty-five of our horses."

"I think you did," Carl interrupted. "Wasn't it just before you went up into the Tahoe country?"

Grandfather turned quickly toward his son-in-law. "That's right. I guess I must have told you that story."

"Lots of times," Carl said cruelly, and he avoided his wife's eyes. But he felt the angry eyes on him, and he said, "'Course I'd like to hear it again."

A Grandfather looked back at the fire. His fingers unlaced and laced again. Jody knew how he felt, how his insides were collapsed and empty. Hadn't Jody been called a Big-Britches that very afternoon? He arose to heroism and opened himself to the term Big-Britches again. "Tell about Indians," he said softly.

Grandfather's eyes grew stern again. "Boys always want to hear about Indians. It was a job for men, but boys want to hear about it. Well, let's see. Did I ever tell you how I wanted each wagon to carry a long iron plate?"

Everyone but Jody remained silent. Jody said, "No. You didn't."

"Well, when the Indians attacked, we always put the wagons in a circle and fought from between the wheels. I thought that if every wagon carried a long plate with rifle holes, the men could stand the plates on the outside of the wheels when the wagons were in the circle and they would be protected. It would save lives and that would make up for the extra weight of the iron. But of course the party wouldn't do it. No party had done it before and they couldn't see why they should go to the expense. They lived to regret it, too."

B Jody looked at his mother, and knew from her expression that she was not listening at all. Carl picked at a callus on his thumb and Billy Buck watched a spider crawling up the wall.

Grandfather's tone dropped into its narrative groove again. Jody knew in advance exactly what words would fall. The story droned on, speeded up for the attack, grew sad over the wounds, struck a dirge[9] at the burials on the great plains. **C** Jody sat quietly watching Grandfather. The stern blue eyes were detached. He looked as though he were not very interested in the story himself.

When it was finished, when the pause had been politely respected as the frontier of the story, Billy Buck stood up and stretched and hitched his trousers. "I guess I'll turn in," he said. Then he faced Grandfather. "I've got an old powder horn and a cap and ball pistol down to the bunkhouse. Did I ever show them to you?"

Grandfather nodded slowly. "Yes, I think you did, Billy. Reminds me of a pistol I had when I was leading the people across." Billy stood politely

National Museum of American Art, Washington D.C./Courtesy Art Resource.

8. **Piutes** (pī'yo͞ots'): more correctly spelled *Paiutes.* The Paiutes are an American Indian people who originally lived in Utah, Arizona, Nevada, and California.
9. **dirge** (durj): sad song that accompanies a funeral or expresses grief.

OPTIONS FOR TEACHING

CLASSROOM MANAGEMENT

Managing the Reader's Response Classroom If students' comments are not supported by the material, urge them to return to the text to explain how they reached their conclusions. Guide them to make adjustments in their conclusions if they cannot find support.

Responding to Reader's Logs To save time reading and responding to Reader's Logs each week, ask students to exchange Reader's Logs and respond to each other's comments. Rotate your own responses so that you read Reader's Logs of only one or two classes each week. *Remind students not to write anything in their Reader's Logs that they would mind sharing with others.*

Pioneers of the West (1934) by Helen Lundeberg. Oil on canvas (40″ × 50 ¼″).

RESPONDING TO THE ART: VISUAL LITERACY

Ask students what words they would use to describe the people in the illustration. [Possible responses: *Hopeful; determined; proud.*]

PROBLEM SOLVING/CRITICAL THINKING

Finding Solutions After students have discussed one of the problems presented in the story—such as living in the past, helping someone retain self-respect, earning treatment as an adult in a family—they can then brainstorm to suggest several possible solutions to that problem. Each solution should make clear who will act, what will be done, and how it will be done. Have students fill in a chart like the following after the discussion.

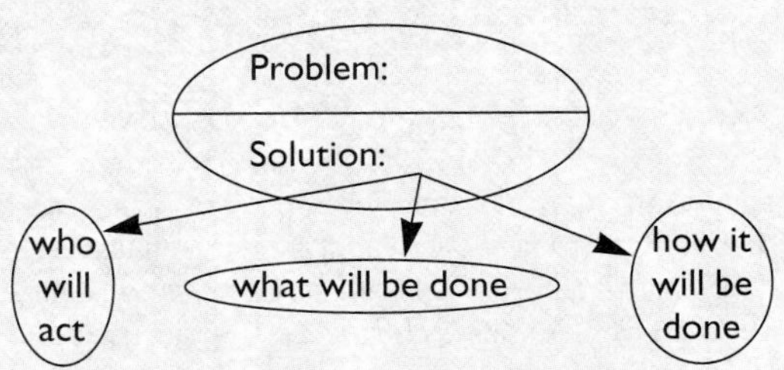

LITERATURE AND FILM

Show in class, or reserve in the school library, videos or films that depict the myth of the West or a revisionist look at it. After they have viewed some of the Westerns, have student groups of five script their own. They can glorify the myth, revise history, or create a comedy. Assist students in borrowing school video cameras and equipment to use for taping their scripts. While each group should write its script together, separate roles should be assigned for the taping. Director, camera person, set or location designer, and lighting and costume designer are some of the necessary roles. Groups may want to recruit other students as actors. Remind students to keep their videos short—ten to fifteen minutes. Your class might invite others to view the final videos. Groups should develop a rationale for their approach to the Western and prepare for a question-and-answer period after the screening.

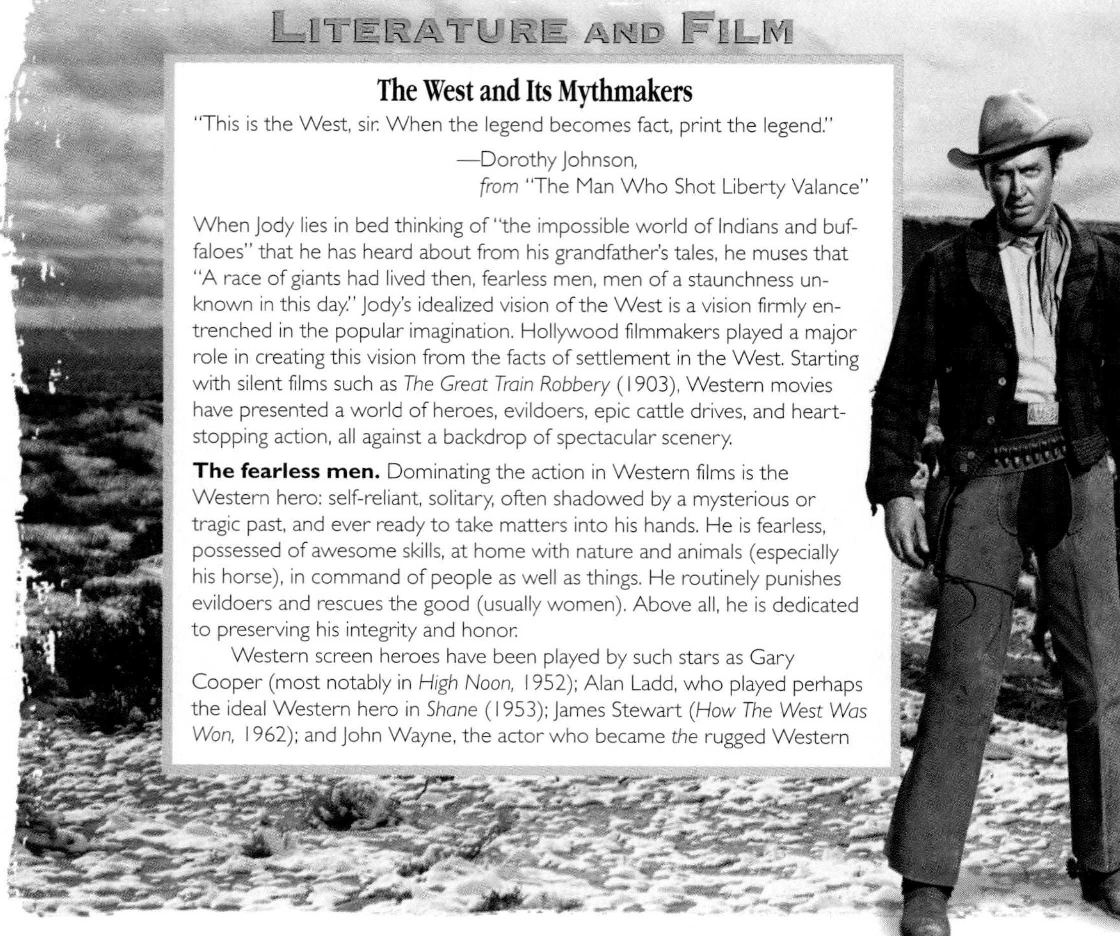

Literature and Film

The West and Its Mythmakers

"This is the West, sir. When the legend becomes fact, print the legend."

—Dorothy Johnson,
from "The Man Who Shot Liberty Valance"

When Jody lies in bed thinking of "the impossible world of Indians and buffaloes" that he has heard about from his grandfather's tales, he muses that "A race of giants had lived then, fearless men, men of a staunchness unknown in this day." Jody's idealized vision of the West is a vision firmly entrenched in the popular imagination. Hollywood filmmakers played a major role in creating this vision from the facts of settlement in the West. Starting with silent films such as *The Great Train Robbery* (1903), Western movies have presented a world of heroes, evildoers, epic cattle drives, and heart-stopping action, all against a backdrop of spectacular scenery.

The fearless men. Dominating the action in Western films is the Western hero: self-reliant, solitary, often shadowed by a mysterious or tragic past, and ever ready to take matters into his hands. He is fearless, possessed of awesome skills, at home with nature and animals (especially his horse), in command of people as well as things. He routinely punishes evildoers and rescues the good (usually women). Above all, he is dedicated to preserving his integrity and honor.

Western screen heroes have been played by such stars as Gary Cooper (most notably in *High Noon,* 1952); Alan Ladd, who played perhaps the ideal Western hero in *Shane* (1953); James Stewart (*How The West Was Won,* 1962); and John Wayne, the actor who became *the* rugged Western

until the little story was done, and then he said, "Good night," and went out of the house.

Carl Tiflin tried to turn the conversation then. "How's the country between here and Monterey? I've heard it's pretty dry."

"It is dry," said Grandfather. "There's not a drop of water in the Laguna Seca. But it's a long pull from '87. The whole country was powder then, and in '61 I believe all the coyotes starved to death. We had fifteen inches of rain this year."

"Yes, but it all came too early. We could do with some now." Carl's eye fell on Jody. "Hadn't you better be getting to bed?"

Jody stood up obediently. "Can I kill the mice in the old haystack, sir?"

"Mice? Oh! Sure, kill them all off. Billy said there isn't any good hay left."

Jody exchanged a secret and satisfying look with Grandfather. "I'll kill every one tomorrow," he promised.

Jody lay in his bed and thought of the impossible world of Indians and buffaloes, a world that had ceased to be forever. He wished he could have been living in the heroic time, but he knew he was not of heroic timber.[10] No one living now,

10. **timber:** character.

OPTIONS FOR TEACHING

PROFESSIONAL NOTES

Thematic Connections: "The Dream and the Reality" Remind students of the title of this collection; then, ask them how this story fits into that category. Have them analyze each character, defining the difference between dream and reality for each one. To bring closure to the discussion, emphasize the importance of both dreams (imagination, vision) and reality (practicality, common sense) in a complete world, and ask students to write about their own dreams and realities.

Cultural Diversity Set on a small ranch in California in the early part of the twentieth century, this story presents a lifestyle unfamiliar to many young readers. Ask students to notice ways in which Jody's life differs from theirs and ways in which his life resembles theirs. They could also discuss the advantages and disadvantages of urban and rural life, both in the early 1900s and now.

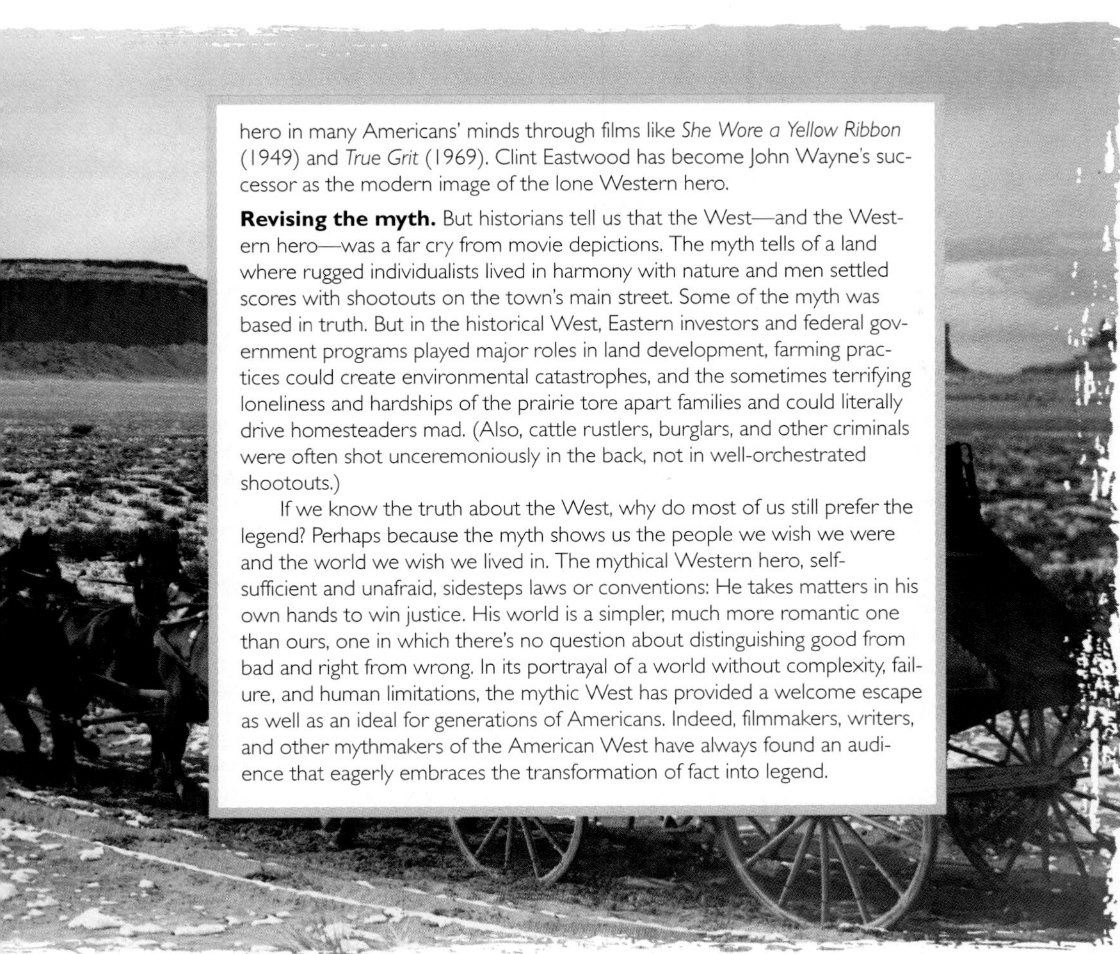

hero in many Americans' minds through films like *She Wore a Yellow Ribbon* (1949) and *True Grit* (1969). Clint Eastwood has become John Wayne's successor as the modern image of the lone Western hero.

Revising the myth. But historians tell us that the West—and the Western hero—was a far cry from movie depictions. The myth tells of a land where rugged individualists lived in harmony with nature and men settled scores with shootouts on the town's main street. Some of the myth was based in truth. But in the historical West, Eastern investors and federal government programs played major roles in land development, farming practices could create environmental catastrophes, and the sometimes terrifying loneliness and hardships of the prairie tore apart families and could literally drive homesteaders mad. (Also, cattle rustlers, burglars, and other criminals were often shot unceremoniously in the back, not in well-orchestrated shootouts.)

If we know the truth about the West, why do most of us still prefer the legend? Perhaps because the myth shows us the people we wish we were and the world we wish we lived in. The mythical Western hero, self-sufficient and unafraid, sidesteps laws or conventions: He takes matters in his own hands to win justice. His world is a simpler, much more romantic one than ours, one in which there's no question about distinguishing good from bad and right from wrong. In its portrayal of a world without complexity, failure, and human limitations, the mythic West has provided a welcome escape as well as an ideal for generations of Americans. Indeed, filmmakers, writers, and other mythmakers of the American West have always found an audience that eagerly embraces the transformation of fact into legend.

save possibly Billy Buck, was worthy to do the things that had been done. A race of giants had lived then, fearless men, men of a staunchness unknown in this day. Jody thought of the wide plains and of the wagons moving across like centipedes. He thought of Grandfather on a huge white horse, marshaling the people. Across his mind marched the great phantoms, and they marched off the earth and they were gone.

He came back to the ranch for a moment, then. He heard the dull rushing sound that space and silence make. He heard one of the dogs, out in the doghouse, scratching a flea and bumping his elbow against the floor with every stroke. Then the wind arose again and the black cypress groaned and Jody went to sleep.

He was up half an hour before the triangle sounded for breakfast. His mother was rattling the stove to make the flames roar when Jody went through the kitchen. "You're up early," she said. "Where are you going?"

"Out to get a good stick. We're going to kill the mice today."

WORDS TO OWN

marshaling (mär′shəl·iŋ) *v.* used as *adj.*: leading; guiding.

ASSESSMENT TOOLS

Check Test: Fill-in-the-Blank

1. As a younger man, Jody's grandfather was the leader of a __________. [wagon train]
2. Jody is looking forward to killing the __________ that live under the haystack. [mice]
3. Billy Buck is the name of a __________ on Jody's father's ranch. [ranch hand or hand]
4. The people in the wagon train used steel plates as protection against __________. [Indians]
5. Jody's grandfather overhears __________ saying that nobody wants to hear his stories over and over again. [Carl or Jody's father]

A. Reader's Response: First Thoughts

? Why does Jody's mother say this to him? [Sample responses: She doesn't like him and is always putting him down; she is a serious woman who expects a lot from her son; or Jody is always trying to blame others for his mistakes.]

B. Critical Reading: Making Inferences

? Why does Billy's statement stagger Jody? [Possible answers: It has never occurred to him that people can't predict their own destinies, that life is truly fragile and uncontrollable. Perhaps he thinks, too, of his grandfather, who had participated in a grand event but had lost his power and his purpose.]

C. Literary Element: Conflict

? In what tone of voice do you think Carl makes this remark about his father-in-law? [Possible answer: In a sarcastic tone—Carl resents the grandfather acting as if all eyes were on the former pioneer leader.]

D. Reader's Response: Shaping Interpretations

? Why do you suppose Carl becomes so angry toward Grandfather? [Sample responses: Probably because for Carl the world of reality is one of grueling sunrise-to-sunset labor on a farm; or it may be that he resents the grandfather's dreams. He could be jealous, or he has become increasingly annoyed at hearing the same stories repeatedly.]

"Who is 'we'?"

"Why, Grandfather and I."

A "So you've got him in it. You always like to have someone in with you in case there's blame to share."

"I'll be right back," said Jody. "I just want to have a good stick ready for after breakfast."

He closed the screen door after him and went out into the cool blue morning. The birds were noisy in the dawn and the ranch cats came down from the hill like blunt snakes. They had been hunting gophers in the dark, and although the four cats were full of gopher meat, they sat in a semi-circle at the back door and mewed piteously for milk. Doubletree Mutt and Smasher moved sniffing along the edge of the brush, performing the duty with rigid ceremony, but when Jody whistled, their heads jerked up and their tails waved. They plunged down to him, wriggling their skins and yawning. Jody patted their heads seriously, and moved on to the weathered scrap pile. He selected an old broom handle and a short piece of inch-square scrap wood. From his pocket he took a shoelace and tied the ends of the sticks loosely together to make a flail.[11] He whistled his new weapon through the air and struck the ground experimentally, while the dogs leaped aside and whined with apprehension.

Jody turned and started down past the house toward the old haystack ground to look over the field of slaughter, but Billy Buck, sitting patiently on the back steps, called to him, "You better come back. It's only a couple of minutes till breakfast."

Jody changed his course and moved toward the house. He leaned his flail against the steps. "That's to drive the mice out," he said. "I'll bet they're fat. I'll bet they don't know what's going to happen to them today."

"No, nor you either," Billy remarked philosophically, "nor me, nor anyone."

B Jody was staggered by this thought. He knew it was true. His imagination twitched away from the mouse hunt. Then his mother came out on the back porch and struck the triangle, and all thoughts fell in a heap.

11. **flail:** farm tool for hand threshing grain. A flail is made of a short stick fastened with a leather strap to a longer handle. The user lets the short stick swing freely from the handle to knock the heads from the grain stalks.

Grandfather hadn't appeared at the table when they sat down. Billy nodded at his empty chair. "He's all right? He isn't sick?"

"He takes a long time to dress," said Mrs. Tiflin. "He combs his whiskers and rubs up his shoes and brushes his clothes."

C Carl scattered sugar on his mush. "A man that's led a wagon train across the plains has got to be pretty careful how he dresses."

Mrs. Tiflin turned on him. "Don't do that, Carl! Please don't!" There was more of threat than of request in her tone. And the threat irritated Carl.

D "Well, how many times do I have to listen to the story of the iron plates, and the thirty-five horses? That time's done. Why can't he forget it, now it's done?" He grew angrier while he talked, and his voice rose. "Why does he have to tell them over and over? He came across the plains. All right! Now it's finished. Nobody wants to hear about it over and over."

The door into the kitchen closed softly. The four at the table sat frozen. Carl laid his mush spoon on the table and touched his chin with his fingers.

Then the kitchen door opened and Grandfather walked in. His mouth smiled tightly and his eyes were squinted. "Good morning," he said, and he sat down and looked at his mush dish.

Carl could not leave it there. "Did—did you hear what I said?"

Grandfather jerked a little nod.

"I don't know what got into me, sir. I didn't mean it. I was just being funny."

Jody glanced in shame at his mother, and he saw that she was looking at Carl, and that she wasn't breathing. It was an awful thing that he was doing. He was tearing himself to pieces to talk like that. It was a terrible thing to him to retract a word, but to retract it in shame was infinitely worse.

Grandfather looked sidewise. "I'm trying to get right side up," he said gently. "I'm not being mad. I don't mind what you said, but it might be true, and I would mind that."

"It isn't true," said Carl. "I'm not feeling well this morning. I'm sorry I said it."

"Don't be sorry, Carl. An old man doesn't see things sometimes. Maybe you're right. The crossing is finished. Maybe it should be forgotten, now it's done."

OPTIONS FOR TEACHING

ASSESSMENT TOOLS

Ongoing Assessment: Response to Literature Use the following criteria to assess students' written or oral responses to literature.

Key: A=always S=sometimes R=rarely N=never

Characteristic	Date	Rating
Shows involvement with literature		
Makes personal and universal connections to the literature		
Gets beyond superficial judgement of the literature		
Interprets the literature, giving evidence of multiple meanings		
Discusses author's control of elements in creating the literature		

Carl got up from the table. "I've had enough to eat. I'm going to work. Take your time, Billy!" He walked quickly out of the dining-room. Billy gulped the rest of his food and followed soon after. But Jody could not leave his chair.

"Won't you tell any more stories?" Jody asked.

"Why, sure I'll tell them, but only when—I'm sure people want to hear them."

"I like to hear them, sir."

"Oh! Of course you do, but you're a little boy. It was a job for men, but only little boys like to hear about it."

Jody got up from his place. "I'll wait outside for you, sir. I've got a good stick for those mice."

He waited by the gate until the old man came out on the porch. "Let's go down and kill the mice now," Jody called.

"I think I'll just sit in the sun, Jody. You go kill the mice."

"You can use my stick if you like."

"No, I'll just sit here a while."

Jody turned disconsolately away, and walked down toward the old haystack. He tried to whip up his enthusiasm with thoughts of the fat juicy mice. He beat the ground with his flail. The dogs coaxed and whined about him, but he could not go. Back at the house he could see Grandfather sitting on the porch, looking small and thin and black.

Jody gave up and went to sit on the steps at the old man's feet.

"Back already? Did you kill the mice?"

"No, sir. I'll kill them some other day."

E

The morning flies buzzed close to the ground and the ants dashed about in front of the steps. The heavy smell of sage slipped down the hill. The porch boards grew warm in the sunshine.

Jody hardly knew when Grandfather started to talk. "I shouldn't stay here, feeling the way I do." He examined his strong old hands. "I feel as though the crossing wasn't worth doing." His eyes moved up the side-hill and stopped on a motionless hawk perched on a dead limb. "I tell those old stories, but they're not what I want to tell. I only know how I want people to feel when I tell them.

F

"It wasn't Indians that were important, nor adventures, nor even getting out here. It was a whole bunch of people made into one big crawling beast. And I was the head. It was westering and westering. Every man wanted something for himself, but the big beast that was all of them wanted only westering. I was the leader, but if I hadn't been there, someone else would have been the head. The thing had to have a head.

"Under the little bushes the shadows were black at white noonday. When we saw the mountains at last, we cried—all of us. But it wasn't getting here that mattered, it was movement and westering.

"We carried life out here and set it down the way those ants carry eggs. And I was the leader. The westering was as big as God, and the slow steps that made the movement piled up and piled up until the continent was crossed.

"Then we came down to the sea, and it was done." He stopped and wiped his eyes until the rims were red. "That's what I should be telling instead of stories."

When Jody spoke, Grandfather started and looked down at him. "Maybe I could lead the people some day," Jody said.

The old man smiled. "There's no place to go. There's the ocean to stop you. There's a line of old men along the shore hating the ocean because it stopped them."

"In boats I might, sir."

"No place to go, Jody. Every place is taken. But that's not the worst—no, not the worst. Westering has died out of the people. Westering isn't a hunger any more. It's all done. Your father is right. It is finished." He laced his fingers on his knee and looked at them.

Jody felt very sad. "If you'd like a glass of lemonade I could make it for you."

Grandfather was about to refuse, and then he saw Jody's face. "That would be nice," he said. "Yes, it would be nice to drink a lemonade."

Jody ran into the kitchen where his mother was wiping the last of the breakfast dishes. "Can I have a lemon to make a lemonade for Grandfather?"

His mother mimicked—"And another lemon to make a lemonade for you."

"No, ma'am. I don't want one."

"Jody! You're sick!" Then she stopped suddenly. "Take a lemon out of the cooler," she said softly. "Here, I'll reach the squeezer down to you."

G

Words to Own

disconsolately (dis·kän′sə·lit·lē) *adv.:* unhappily.

E. Critical Reading: Making Inferences

? Why does Jody decide not to kill the mice? [Possible answers: He is depressed because his grandfather is depressed; all the fun has gone out of it; or he has matured.]

F. Reader's Response: Shaping Interpretations

? How does the grandfather want people to feel when he tells them about westering? [Sample responses: He wants them to feel part of a historic event in the recent past of the United States; he wants people to recognize that he was a leader and that the people never gave up.]

G. Critical Reading: Expressing an Opinion

? Why does Jody's mother speak "softly" to him in the last paragraph? [Possible answer: She recognizes his unselfishness, his mature motivation for making the lemonade: He wants to make his grandfather feel better.]

Primary Sources

Steinbeck sees literature as a medium for understanding, which he hopes can bring about the perfectibility of humans. Indeed, Steinbeck says that a writer who does not believe that the perfectibility of humans is possible "has no dedication nor any membership in literature." The statement reflects Steinbeck's warm, somewhat sentimental view of human nature, but some will agree that the requirement he sets for membership in literature is extreme. It would exclude many great writers—Hawthorne, Melville, and Faulkner, to name only a few American writers. Ask student groups to create collages that illustrate whether or not the perfectibility of humans is possible. Have each group present its collage to the class and explain its position.

PRIMARY **Sources** A SPEECH

Nobel Prize Acceptance Speech, 1962

I thank the Swedish Academy for finding my work worthy of this highest honor.

In my heart there may be doubt that I deserve the Nobel award over other men of letters whom I hold in respect and reverence—but there is no question of my pleasure and pride in having it for myself.

It is customary for the recipient of this award to offer personal or scholarly comment on the nature and the direction of literature. At this particular time, however, I think it would be well to consider the high duties and the responsibilities of the makers of literature.

Such is the prestige of the Nobel award and of this place where I stand that I am impelled, not to squeak like a grateful and apologetic mouse, but to roar like a lion out of pride in my profession and in the great and good men who have practiced it through the ages.

Literature was not promulgated by a pale and emasculated critical priesthood singing their litanies in empty churches—nor is it a game for the cloistered elect, the tinhorn mendicants of low-calorie despair.

Literature is as old as speech. It grew out of human need for it, and it has not changed except to become more needed.

The skalds, the bards, the writers are not separate and exclusive. From the beginning, their functions, their duties, their responsibilities have been decreed by our species.

Humanity has been passing through a gray and desolate time of confusion. My great predecessor, William Faulkner, speaking here, referred to it as a tragedy of universal fear so long sustained that there were no longer problems of the spirit, so that only the human heart in conflict with itself seemed worth writing about.

Faulkner, more than most men, was aware of human strength as well as of human weakness. He knew that the understanding and the resolution of fear are a large part of the writer's reason for being.

This is not new. The ancient commission of the writer has not changed. He is charged with exposing our many grievous faults and failures, with dredging up to the light our dark and dangerous dreams for the purpose of improvement.

Furthermore, the writer is delegated to declare and to celebrate man's proven capacity for greatness of heart and spirit—for gallantry in defeat—for courage, compassion, and love. In the endless war against weakness and despair, these are the bright rally-flags of hope and of emulation.

I hold that a writer who does not passionately believe in the perfectibility of man has no dedication nor any membership in literature.

The present universal fear has been the result of a forward surge in our knowledge and manipulation of certain dangerous factors in the physical world.

It is true that other phases of understanding have not yet caught up with this great step, but there is no reason to presume that they cannot or will not draw abreast. Indeed, it is a part of the writer's responsibility to make sure that they do.

With humanity's long, proud history of standing firm against natural enemies, sometimes in the face of almost certain defeat and extinction, we would be cowardly and stupid to leave the field on the eve of our greatest potential victory.

Understandably, I have been reading the life of Alfred Nobel—a solitary man, the books say, a thoughtful man. He perfected the release of explosive forces, capable of creative good or of destructive evil, but lacking choice, ungoverned by conscience or judgment.

STRATEGIES FOR INCLUSION

Less Proficient Readers Pair students for reading Steinbeck's speech so that they may read aloud and exchange interpretations, questions, and concerns. As students take turns reading, they should express any thoughts about content, problems they encounter with language and vocabulary and how to resolve them, connections to their lives, or judgments they are making. Pairs can then share their ideas with other pairs.

Auditory Ask interested students to prepare and present this speech orally as they imagine Steinbeck might have given it.

Nobel saw some of the cruel and bloody misuses of his inventions. He may even have foreseen the end result of his probing—access to ultimate violence—to final destruction. Some say that he became cynical, but I do not believe this. I think he strove to invent a control, a safety valve. I think he found it finally only in the human mind and the human spirit. To me, his thinking is clearly indicated in the categories of these awards.

They are offered for increased and continuing knowledge of man and of his world—for understanding and communication, which are the functions of literature. And they are offered for demonstrations of the capacity for peace—the culmination of all the others.

Less than fifty years after his death, the door of nature was unlocked and we were offered the dreadful burden of choice.

We have usurped many of the powers we once ascribed to God.

Fearful and unprepared, we have assumed lordship over the life or death of the whole world—of all living things.

The danger and the glory and the choice rest finally in man. The test of his perfectibility is at hand.

Having taken Godlike power, we must seek in ourselves for the responsibility and the wisdom we once prayed some deity might have.

Man himself has become our greatest hazard and our only hope.

So that today, Saint John the apostle may well be paraphrased: In the end is the Word, and the Word is Man—and the Word is with Men.

—John Steinbeck

MAKING MEANINGS

First Thoughts

1. How does Grandfather's statement "Westering has died out of the people" make Jody feel? How did it make *you* feel?

Reviewing the Text

a. Why does Jody look forward to his grandfather's visit, while his father dreads it? How does Jody feel about his grandfather?

b. What are Grandfather's stories about? In what way was he "the leader of the people"?

Shaping Interpretations

2. What seems to have been the significance of "the crossing" for Jody's grandfather?
3. There are several **conflicts** in the story—between Carl Tiflin and his wife, between Jody and his father, and between Jody's father and his grandfather. Describe the source of each conflict. Would you say this story is more about family relationships or more about the changing attitudes of each new generation?
4. The story is full of **ironies.** How does Steinbeck ironically characterize the modern age by his use of the mouse hunt?
5. What would you say is the **theme** of the story? What does it say about the relation between dreams and reality and the loss of the heroic ideal?
6. Is Jody right to want to listen to the same stories over and over, or is Carl right in wanting the past to be forgotten? Or are these two characters both right *and* wrong? Give reasons to support your views.

Extending the Text

7. Look back at the notes you took in your Reader's Log. Do you believe, as Jody's grandfather does, that there are no longer any frontiers for young Americans? Where do you think young people today should look for frontiers?

Making Meanings

First Thoughts

1. Students might use the following descriptions: sad, nostalgic, relieved.

Reviewing the Text

a. Jody enjoys his grandfather's company and looks forward to hearing again the exciting stories about Indians and crossing the plains. Jody's father dreads having to listen to the same old stories over again.

b. Grandfather tells about leading a wagon train across the plains to the West Coast. He was entrusted by the other settlers with overall responsibility for the crossing. Steinbeck indirectly suggests that Grandfather was also a leader in a metaphorical sense—as an aspiring, daring young man, he had participated in a heroic age of the American past.

Shaping Interpretations

2. In Grandfather's mind, westering seems symbolic of the frontier dream—and, in a larger sense, of an aspiring state of mind among Americans. Both he and Jody, in contrast to Carl, have the intuition that such aspirations were linked to heroism.
3. The source of conflict between Carl and his wife is Grandfather's visit. Although Mrs. Tiflin does not pay attention anymore to her father's stories, she insists that her husband show the old man some respect. The source of the conflict between Jody and his father is Carl's determination to control his son and to keep him in his place. Jody's evident pleasure in Grandfather's visit and in his stories also annoys Carl. The source of the conflict between Carl and Grandfather is that Carl is bored and annoyed by Grandfather's obsession with the past. His anger may be due to jealousy—he has no heroic past.
4. Steinbeck has Grandfather imply the softness and puniness of the modern age by making him say, "Have the people of this generation come down to hunting mice?"
5. Responses will vary. One statement of the theme might be as follows: The imaginative hunger of the human spirit for heroism and greater achievement must inevitably clash with harsh, almost brutal, realities that often do not allow opportunities for heroism.
6. Students might say Jody is right to encourage his grandfather because he makes an old man feel needed and appreciated and because the stories fuel Jody's dreams of doing something heroic. Others may feel Carl is right because Grandfather's obsession with the past keeps him from adjusting to the realities of the present and from finding his niche in a modern world. Both characters might have valid viewpoints.

Extending the Text

7. **(Evaluation)** Some students will agree that there are no longer any frontiers; others may say that space is the present-day frontier.

Language and Style

Answers

Paraphrases will vary. The figures of speech should be identified as follows.

1. oxymoron/personification
2. metaphor
3. simile
4. oxymoron
5. metaphor
6. metaphor
7. simile
8. hyperbole/metaphor

Beyond the Story

Choices: Building Your Portfolio

1. **Writer's Notebook** Remind students to save their work. They may use it as prewriting for the Writer's Workshop on p. 685.
2. **Critical Writing** Have students work in small groups to think of appropriate stories and themes and help each other collect details to support their ideas for the essays.
3. **Speaking and Listening** Choose a leader who can keep students on track and maintain balance among group members. Formulate the topic into a question: "Do heroes exist today, and if so, who are they and what makes them heroic?"

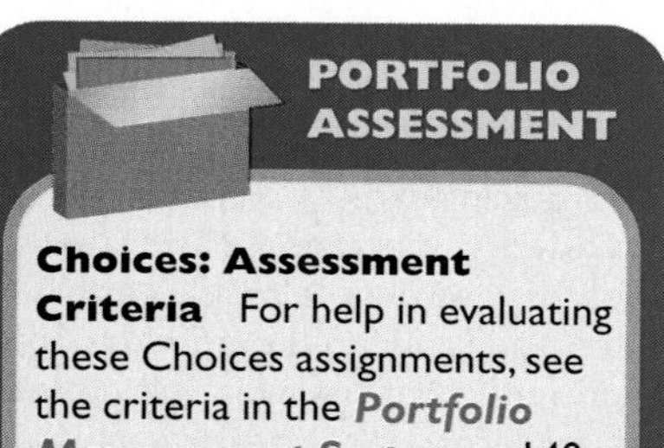

PORTFOLIO ASSESSMENT

Choices: Assessment Criteria For help in evaluating these Choices assignments, see the criteria in the ***Portfolio Management System,*** p. 140.

LANGUAGE AND STYLE

Steinbeck's Figures of Speech

Scholars have defined over three hundred different figures of speech, but most people are familiar with five types: **(1) simile,** which compares two unlike things by using words of specific comparison (such as *like, as,* or *resembles*); **(2) metaphor,** which identifies two unlike things directly without using a specific word of comparison; **(3) personification,** a type of metaphor that speaks of an animal or something nonhuman as if it were human and alive; **(4) oxymoron,** a combination of words that seem to contradict each other (*wise fool, death in life, sweet sorrow*); and **(5) hyperbole,** which uses exaggeration for effect.

Read the following figures of speech from the story, and see if you can identify the type being used from the list above. Then, paraphrase the literal meaning of each phrase in your own words.

1. "plump, sleek, arrogant mice" (page 609)
2. "a crow congress had convened" (page 611)
3. "a road-runner . . . sailed out like a glider" (page 612)
4. "blue eyes were sternly merry" (page 612)
5. "a granite dignity" (page 612)
6. "a race of giants had lived then" (page 617)
7. "wagons moving across like centipedes" (page 617)
8. "a whole bunch of people made into one big crawling beast" (page 619)

CHOICES: Building Your Portfolio

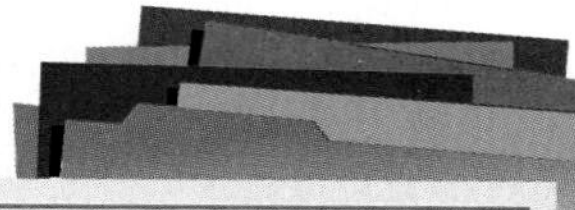

Writer's Notebook

1. Collecting Ideas for a Speculation About Causes and Effects

WORK IN PROGRESS

Re-read the story's ending, this time thinking about what Jody and his mother are feeling and what their quiet words and actions signify. Then, write an extension of the ending, speculating on something Jody does afterward. You may continue the scene in the story, or skip to a new scene. In your scene, speculate on how Jody has been affected by his experiences with his grandfather and his father. Save your notes for possible use in the Writer's Workshop on page 685.

Critical Writing

2. Same Theme, Different Story

Identify one of the basic **themes** of Steinbeck's story. It may have to do with the contrast between dream and reality, the loss of heroism, conflicts between generations, disillusionment, the limitations of the American dream, or some other theme. Choose another story from this textbook that deals with a similar theme. Write an essay comparing and contrasting the ways each story develops the theme. Focus on the stories' similarities and differences in **plot, character, setting,** and **tone.**

Speaking and Listening

3. Heroes Are Hard to Find

With several students, organize a panel to discuss whether there are heroes today, and if so, who they are and what makes them heroic. For historical and cultural insight on heroes and heroism, see if you can find a video recording of Bill Moyers's interviews with the anthropologist Joseph Campbell titled "The Hero's Adventure" (part of the *Joseph Campbell and the Power of Myth* PBS series).

STRATEGIES FOR INCLUSION

Visual For activity #2, students should use note cards to help them collect details for their essay. They should take notes about the theme, plot, characters, and setting. Students should put the theme on a one card, the title "Leader of the People" on a second card, and the title of their other story on a third card. Have students list one detail for each literary element, for each story. Then, ask students to place the cards for each story side by side to look for differences and similarities and possible organizational patterns.

Interpersonal For activity #3, have students evaluate their panel discussions by considering the following questions and writing a brief summary in response to these questions.

a. What new information did you learn?
b. In what new ways do you now look at the topic?

James Thurber

(1894–1961)

James Thurber is generally acknowledged to be the foremost American humorist of the twentieth century. He was a supremely gifted cartoonist and a writer of essays, sketches, and stories. He once mocked the typical puffed-up biographies of literary figures by presenting this self-portrait:

> James Thurber was born in Columbus, Ohio, where so many awful things happened to him, on December 8, 1894. He was unable to keep anything on his stomach until he was seven years old, but grew to six feet one and a quarter inches tall and to weigh a hundred and fifty-four pounds fully dressed for winter. He began to write when he was ten years old . . . and to draw when he was fourteen. . . . Quick to arouse, he is very hard to quiet and people often just go away. . . . He never listens when anybody else is talking, preferring to keep his mind a blank until they get through, so he can talk. His favorite book is *The Great Gatsby.* His favorite author is Henry James. He wears excellent clothes very badly and can never find his hat. . . . He is Sagittarius with the moon in Aries and gets along fine with persons born between the 20th and 24th of August.

UPI/Bettmann.

Thurber did grow up in Columbus, where he attended Ohio State University. He worked as a reporter in Columbus and Chicago for a number of years. He moved east, went to work for *The New Yorker* magazine in 1927, and remained on the staff for the rest of his life. Thurber's literary career peaked in the 1940s, even as his eyesight, damaged in a boyhood accident, worsened despite a series of operations. In addition to many collections of essays, stories, and children's books, he collaborated on a successful Broadway play.

His humor often turned on the chaos of contemporary American life. Thurber focused on the "little man," who cannot quite assert himself in a confusing world where women seem surer of their way. Walter Mitty, the antihero of Thurber's most famous story, seeks in fantasy a release from a wife who overwhelms him.

In many of his stories and cartoons, Thurber focused on relationships between men and women. While Thurber claimed to hope the feminist movement would seize power and prevent men from blowing the world to bits, he viewed women with a certain ambivalence—as intimidating to their mates, and as mother figures rather than partners. (His attitude toward women is comically revealed in the cartoons that illustrate his stories.)

Thurber defined humor as "a kind of emotional chaos told about calmly and quietly in retrospect." But humor is not subject to rational explanation. Perhaps this was in the mind of Thurber's friend, the writer Mark Van Doren, when he said of Thurber: "He was an extraordinary man . . . with so many quick changes: gentle and fierce, fascinating and boring, sophisticated and boorish, kind and cruel, broadminded and parochial. You can't explain Thurber."

QUICK PLANNING GUIDE

Into the Story

Through the Story

Beyond the Story

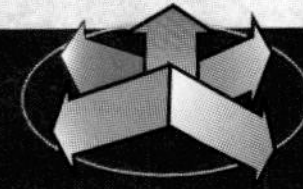

PROGRAM MANAGER

- **Planning Instruction** See Teaching Notes, *Teaching Resources B,* pp. 34–35, for objectives, a summary, and literary elements for this selection.
- **Instructional Support** See Graphic Organizer for Active Reading, *Teaching Resources B,* p. 44, for a Through the Story activity.
- **Application and Reinforcment** See Transparency 12.3 in the *Audiovisual Resources Binder.*

- **Assessment** See Selection Test, *Test Booklet,* pp. 145–146.
- **Reinforcement** Use the Words to Own worksheet in *Teaching Resources B,* p. 45.

Into the Story

Using **Before You Read** p. 624

Elements of Literature

Point out to students that **parody** often achieves its humorous effect through the use of exaggeration or mockery. As students read, have them note how Thurber exaggerates or mocks **character, plot, setting, dialogue,** or other story elements.

WORDS TO OWN

The following vocabulary words are defined in the Words to Own at the bottom of the pupil's page.

rakishly p. 625	insinuatingly p. 627
distraught p. 626	pandemonium p. 627
haggard p. 626	bedlam p. 627
craven p. 626	cannonading p. 628
insolent p. 626	rending p. 628

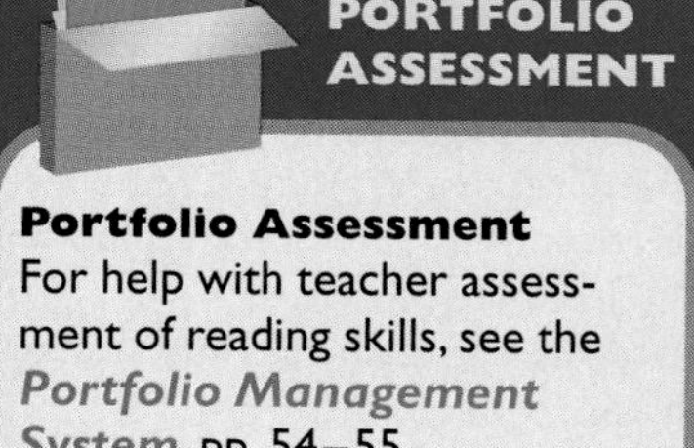

PORTFOLIO ASSESSMENT

Portfolio Assessment
For help with teacher assessment of reading skills, see the ***Portfolio Management System,*** pp. 54–55.

Before You Read
The Secret Life of Walter Mitty

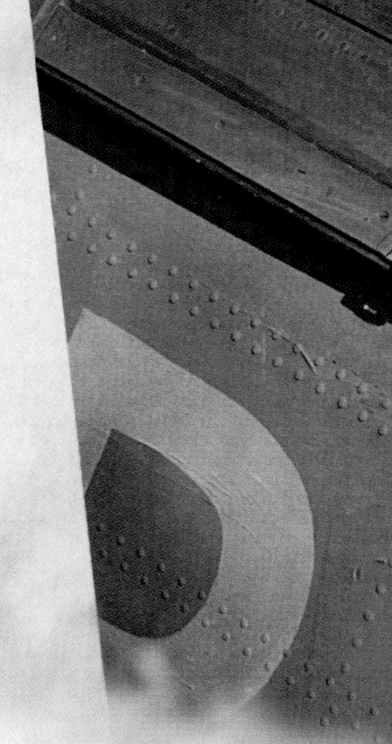

Reading Focus

Daydream Believer

The name "Walter Mitty" has entered our language as the epitome of the "little guy" who is dominated by an assertive wife. You might recognize Mitty and the formidable Mrs. Mitty—they are character types that have formed the basis of many TV situation comedies. Mitty is based on a stereotype of the henpecked husband, but Mitty himself is an original. In fact, the term "Walter Mitty" is found in *Webster's Third New International Dictionary,* where it is defined as "a commonplace unadventurous person who seeks escape from reality through daydreaming and typically imagines himself leading a glamorous life and becoming famous."

A Dialogue with the Text

READER'S LOG

As you read this story, jot down the event that triggers each of Mitty's daydreams.

Elements of Literature

Parody

A **parody** makes fun of another work by imitating aspects of its style or contents. You've probably encountered parodies of shows, songs, and movies in humor magazines, TV sitcoms, commercials, and movies.

After you've read the first paragraph of this story, ask yourself what kind of movie it parodies.

> A **parody** is a work that makes fun of another work by imitating some aspect of its style or content.
>
> *For more about Parody, see the Handbook of Literary Terms.*

"Why don't you let *me* know what it is, if it's so pleasant?"

OPTIONS FOR TEACHING

STRATEGIES FOR INCLUSION

Visual To help students understand the structure of the story better, especially the relationship between actions and daydreams, have them map out the plot on a sheet of paper divided into two columns. Ask them to record real action on the left and daydreams on the right. Then, have them discuss possible causes for each daydream.

Advanced Assign students to write a story with interior and exterior action. Encourage them to use teenagers like themselves as characters. Students might prefer to work in small groups for this project.

All photos pages 625, 627, 628 from the movie *The Secret Life of Walter Mitty* with Danny Kaye (1947).
Photofest.

The Secret Life of Walter Mitty

James Thurber

"We're going through!" The commander's voice was like thin ice breaking. He wore his full-dress uniform, with the heavily braided white cap pulled down rakishly over one cold gray eye. "We can't make it, sir. It's spoiling for[1] a hurricane, if you ask me." "I'm not asking you, Lieutenant Berg," said the commander. "Throw on the power lights! Rev her up to 8,500! We're going through!" The pounding of the cylinders increased: ta-pocketa-pocketa-pocketa-*pocketa-pocketa*. The commander stared at the ice forming on the pilot window. He walked over and twisted a row of complicated dials. "Switch on No. 8 auxiliary!" he shouted. "Switch on No. 8 auxiliary!" repeated Lieutenant Berg. "Full strength in No. 3 turret!" shouted the commander. "Full strength in No. 3 turret!" The crew, bending to their various tasks in the huge, hurtling eight-engined navy hydroplane, looked at each other and grinned. "The Old Man'll get us through," they said to one another. "The Old Man ain't afraid of Hell!" . . . **A**

"Not so fast! You're driving too fast!" said Mrs. Mitty. "What are you driving so fast for?"

"Hmm?" said Walter Mitty. He looked at his wife, in the seat beside him, with shocked astonishment. She seemed grossly unfamiliar, like a strange woman who had yelled at him in a crowd. "You were up to fifty-five," she said. "You know I don't like to go more than forty. You were up to fifty-five." Walter Mitty drove on toward Waterbury in silence, the roaring of the SN202 through

1. **it's spoiling for:** slang for "conditions are right for."

Words to Own
rakishly (rāk′·ish·lē) *adv.:* dashingly; jauntily.

About the Author

James Thurber depicted the modern world—its confusions and frustrations—in two books that he also illustrated, *Fables for Our Time* (1940) and *Further Fables for Our Time* (1956). The fables show animals talking and acting like Thurber's Americans. They include Thurber's special brand of moral humor, such as "It is better to have the ring of freedom in your ears than in your nose."

A. Literary Element: Parody
? What details in this scene reveal exaggeration, or **parody**? [Sample responses: An officer wouldn't wear a full-dress uniform while flying a plane; or a hydroplane doesn't have a turret, much less three turrets.]

INTEGRATING THE LANGUAGE ARTS

Strategic Reading This story is fun to read aloud. Ask for volunteers to write the story in the form of a play and then perform it in a reader's theater format. So that the performance will be more polished, provide rehearsal time. You might want to give students a chance to perform for other classes.

Mechanics Review the use of the semicolon to separate two independent clauses. Then, ask students to find at least three semicolons in Thurber's story and explain how the rule applies in each case. After this review, ask students to write at least three sentences about the short story that require semicolons.

Vocabulary and Language After reviewing with the class the meaning of **onomatopoeia,** point out its use in this story: "ta-pocketa-pocketa. . . ." Then, ask students for other examples of onomatopoeia. They may want to make up some of their own. ☞

A. Critical Reading: Finding Cause and Effect

? What makes Mitty so tense? [Possible answer: Probably his wife's harping. So far she has complained about his driving. Ask students to notice what else she complains about during the rest of the story.]

B. Reader's Response: Shaping Interpretations

? Why does Mitty put his gloves back on when the traffic cop yells at him? [Sample responses: Momentarily flustered, he thinks the policeman is reprimanding him for not following his wife's orders about wearing the gloves; or he is just used to obeying orders.]

C. Critical Reading: Finding Details

? What stimulus brings on Mitty's great surgeon fantasy? [Driving past the hospital.]

D. Critical Reading: Making Connections

? How does Mitty's performance in his operating room fantasy contrast with his real performance in the parking lot? [Possible answer: He repairs a complicated machine and takes over delicate surgery from two great specialists. In the parking lot, Mitty almost hits another car, and the attendant has to park his car.]

the worst storm in twenty years of navy flying fading in the remote, intimate airways of his mind. (A) "You're tensed up again," said Mrs. Mitty. "It's one of your days. I wish you'd let Dr. Renshaw look you over."

Walter Mitty stopped the car in front of the building where his wife went to have her hair done. "Remember to get those overshoes while I'm having my hair done," she said. "I don't need overshoes," said Mitty. She put her mirror back into her bag. "We've been all through that," she said, getting out of the car. "You're not a young man any longer." He raced the engine a little. "Why don't you wear your gloves? Have you lost your gloves?" Walter Mitty reached in a pocket and brought out the gloves. He put them on, but after she had turned and gone into the building and he had driven on to a red light, he took them (B) off again. "Pick it up, brother!" snapped a cop as the light changed, and Mitty hastily pulled on his gloves and lurched ahead. He drove around the (C) streets aimlessly for a time, and then he drove past the hospital on his way to the parking lot.

. . . "It's the millionaire banker, Wellington McMillan," said the pretty nurse. "Yes?" said Walter Mitty, removing his gloves slowly. "Who has the case?" "Dr. Renshaw and Dr. Benbow, but there are two specialists here, Dr. Remington from New York and Mr. Pritchard-Mitford from London. He flew over." A door opened down a long, cool corridor and Dr. Renshaw came out. He looked distraught and haggard. "Hello, Mitty," he said. "We're having the devil's own time with McMillan, the millionaire banker and close personal friend of Roosevelt. Obstreosis of the ductal tract. Tertiary. Wish you'd take a look at him." "Glad to," said Mitty.

In the operating room there were whispered introductions: "Dr. Remington, Dr. Mitty. Mr. Pritchard-Mitford, Dr. Mitty." "I've read your book on streptothricosis," said Pritchard-Mitford, shaking hands. "A brilliant performance, sir." "Thank you," said Walter Mitty. "Didn't know you were in the States, Mitty," grumbled Remington. "Coals to Newcastle,[2] bringing Mitford and me up here for a tertiary." "You are very kind," said Mitty. A huge, complicated machine, connected to the operating table, with many tubes and wires, began at this moment to go pocketa-pocketa-pocketa. "The new anesthetizer is giving way!" shouted an intern. "There is no one in the East who knows how to fix it!" "Quiet, man!" said Mitty, in a low, cool voice. He sprang to the machine, which was now going pocketa-pocketa-queep-pocketa-queep. He began fingering delicately a row of glistening dials. "Give me a fountain pen!" he snapped. Someone handed him a fountain pen. He pulled a faulty piston out of the machine and inserted the pen in its place. "That will hold for ten minutes," he said. "Get on with the operation." A nurse hurried over and whispered to Renshaw, and Mitty saw the man turn pale. "Coreopsis has set in," said Renshaw nervously. "If you would take over, Mitty?" Mitty looked at him and at the craven figure of Benbow, who drank, and at the grave, uncertain faces of the two great specialists. "If you wish," he said. They slipped a white gown on him; he adjusted a mask and drew on thin gloves; nurses handed him shining . . .

(D) "Back it up, Mac! Look out for that Buick!" Walter Mitty jammed on the brakes. "Wrong lane, Mac," said the parking-lot attendant, looking at Mitty closely. "Gee. Yeh," muttered Mitty. He began cautiously to back out of the lane marked "Exit Only." "Leave her sit there," said the attendant. "I'll put her away." Mitty got out of the car. "Hey, better leave the key." "Oh," said Mitty, handing the man the ignition key. The attendant vaulted into the car, backed it up with insolent skill, and put it where it belonged.

They're so damn cocky, thought Walter Mitty, walking along Main Street; they think they know everything. Once he had tried to take his chains[3] off, outside New Milford, and he had got them wound around the axles. A man had had to come out in a wrecking car and unwind them, a young, grinning garageman. Since then Mrs. Mitty always made him drive to a garage to have the chains

2. **coals to Newcastle:** an unnecessary effort. Newcastle, England, was a major coal-producing city.

3. **chains:** chains attached to automobile tires to increase traction in snow and ice.

WORDS TO OWN

distraught (di·strôt′) *adj.:* troubled.
haggard (hag′ərd) *adj.:* wasted or worn in appearance.
craven (krā′vən) *adj.:* very fearful; cowardly.
insolent (in′sə·lənt) *adj.:* arrogant.

OPTIONS FOR TEACHING

COOPERATIVE LEARNING

Group Writing Divide the class into groups of three, and ask each group to write its own story about how stress can push a person into daydreams. To help groups function more smoothly, suggest that although they work together, they divide the responsibilities: Writer—puts together the group's story; Discussion Leader—leads discussion as group writes the story; and Editor—revises the first draft, using suggestions from the whole group.

CROSSING THE CURRICULUM

Science Because Mitty is not really an expert pilot or surgeon or marksman, he does not use correct terms, and he describes machines as complicated. Ask students to check the real meanings of the terms he uses.

taken off. The next time, he thought, I'll wear my right arm in a sling; they won't grin at me then. I'll have my right arm in a sling, and they'll see I couldn't possibly take the chains off myself. He kicked at the slush on the sidewalk. "Overshoes," he said to himself, and he began looking for a shoe store.

When he came out into the street again, with the overshoes in a box under his arm, Walter Mitty began to wonder what the other thing was his wife had told him to get. She had told him, twice, before they set out from their house for Waterbury. In a way he hated these weekly trips to town—he was always getting something wrong. Kleenex, he thought, Squibb's,[4] razor blades? No. Toothpaste, toothbrush, bicarbonate, carborundum, initiative and referendum? He gave it up. But she would remember it. "Where's the what's-its-name?" she would ask. "Don't tell me you forgot the what's-its-name." A newsboy went by shouting something about the Waterbury trial.

E

. . . "Perhaps this will refresh your memory." The district attorney suddenly thrust a heavy automatic at the quiet figure on the witness stand. "Have you ever seen this before?" Walter Mitty took the gun and examined it expertly. "This is my Webley-Vickers 50.80," he said calmly. An excited buzz ran around the courtroom. The judge rapped for order. "You are a crack shot with any sort of firearms, I believe?" said the district attorney, insinuatingly. "Objection!" shouted Mitty's attorney. "We have shown that the defendant could not have fired the shot. We have shown that he wore his right arm in a sling on the night of the fourteenth of July." Walter Mitty raised his hand briefly and the bickering attorneys were stilled. "With any known make of gun," he said evenly, "I could have killed Gregory Fitzhurst at three hundred feet *with my left hand.*" Pandemonium broke loose in the courtroom. A woman's scream rose above the bedlam and suddenly a lovely, dark-haired girl was in Walter Mitty's arms. The district attorney struck at her savagely. Without rising from his chair, Mitty let the man have it on the point of the chin. "You miserable cur!"[5] . . .

"Puppy biscuit," said Walter Mitty. He stopped walking and the buildings of Waterbury rose up out of the misty courtroom and surrounded him again. A woman who was passing laughed. "He said 'Puppy biscuit,'" she said to her companion. "That man said 'Puppy biscuit' to himself." Walter Mitty hurried on. He went into an A & P, not the first one he came to but a smaller one farther up the street. "I want some biscuit for small, young dogs," he said to the clerk. "Any special brand, sir?" The greatest pistol shot in the world thought a moment. "It says 'Puppies Bark for It' on the box," said Walter Mitty.

"A brilliant performance, sir." "Thank you," said Walter Mitty.

Photofest.

His wife would be through at the hairdresser's in fifteen minutes, Mitty saw in looking at his watch, unless they had trouble drying it; sometimes they had trouble drying it. She didn't like to get to the hotel first; she would want him to be there waiting for her as usual. He found a big

4. **Squibb's:** Squibb was a U.S. pharmaceutical company, established in 1858, that manufactured a variety of prescription drugs and health-care products, such as cough and cold medicines and vitamins. It is not clear which specific product Mitty is thinking about here.

5. **cur:** a cowardly or contemptible person; also, a mongrel dog.

WORDS TO OWN

insinuatingly (in·sin′yo͞o·āt′iŋ·lē) *adv.:* suggestively.
pandemonium (pan′də·mō′nē·əm) *n.:* wild confusion.
bedlam (bed′ləm) *n.:* place or condition of noise and confusion.

E. Critical Reading: Making Connections

? What elements from real life send Mitty into the courtroom fantasy?

[Possible answers: The newsboy shouting about the Waterbury trial; forgetting an item on his wife's shopping list, which gives rise to "Perhaps this will refresh your memory," a cliché of courtroom dramas.]

CROSSING THE CURRICULUM

Health Some students may be interested in forming an expert group to do research on daydreams. Others might want to form a group to study the causes and results of stress and low self-esteem. Both groups could then report to the entire class in a panel discussion.

PROFESSIONAL NOTES

Cultural Diversity Point out that Mitty's daydreams reflect his culture; the story was published in 1939. His heroes—the Navy pilot, the surgeon, the expert shot, the bomber pilot—reflect the years before World War II. Ask students to discuss what heroes they might daydream of becoming now, sixty years later.

A. Reader's Response: Connecting with the Text

? How is Mitty like the grandfather in "The Leader of the People," pp. 609–619? [Sample responses: Both men escape the reality of their lives by telling stories that restore their dignity—though the grandfather's stories are true and Mitty's are made up.]

B. Reader's Response: Extending the Text

? How does this story relate to one of Thurber's favorite themes, the battle of the sexes? [Sample responses: When the real world becomes too critical or negative, a person may create an imaginary world that gives needed approval; or it shows how a lack of communication and an inability to understand the person you live with may lead to unhappiness.]

C. Critical Reading: Expressing an Opinion

? Is the ending humorous or tragic? Explain. [Possible answers: Mitty's imaginary escape from his wife to the firing squad is humorous; it is also tragically sad because he lacks the courage required for a real solution.]

Photofest.

A leather chair in the lobby, facing a window, and he put the overshoes and the puppy biscuit on the floor beside it. He picked up an old copy of *Liberty* and sank down into the chair. "Can Germany Conquer the World Through the Air?" Walter Mitty looked at the pictures of bombing planes and of ruined streets.

. . . "The cannonading has got the wind up in young Raleigh, sir," said the sergeant. Captain Mitty looked up at him through tousled hair. "Get him to bed," he said wearily. "With the others. I'll fly alone." "But you can't, sir," said the sergeant anxiously. "It takes two men to handle that bomber and the Archies[6] are pounding hell out of the air. Von Richtman's circus[7] is between here and Saulier." "Somebody's got to get to that ammunition dump," said Mitty. "I'm going over. Spot of brandy?" He poured a drink for the sergeant and one for himself. War thundered and whined around the dugout and battered at the door. There was a rending of wood and splinters flew through the room. "A bit of a near thing," said Captain Mitty carelessly. "The box barrage is closing in," said the sergeant. "We only live once, Sergeant," said Mitty, with his faint, fleeting smile. "Or do we?" He poured another brandy and tossed it off. "I never see a man could hold his brandy like you, sir," said the sergeant. "Begging your pardon, sir." Captain Mitty stood up and strapped on his huge Webley-Vickers automatic. "It's forty kilometers through hell, sir," said the sergeant. Mitty finished one last brandy. "After all," he said softly, "what isn't?" The pounding of the cannon increased; there was the rat-tat-tatting of machine guns, and from somewhere came the menacing pocketa-pocketa-pocketa of the new flamethrowers. Walter Mitty walked to the door of the dugout humming "Auprès de Ma Blonde,"[8] He turned and waved to the sergeant. "Cheerio!" he said. . . .

B Something struck his shoulder. "I've been looking all over this hotel for you," said Mrs. Mitty. "Why do you have to hide in this old chair? How did you expect me to find you?" "Things close in," said Walter Mitty vaguely. "What?" Mrs. Mitty said. "Did you get the what's-its-name? The puppy biscuit? What's in that box?" "Overshoes," said Mitty. "Couldn't you have put them on in the store?" "I was thinking," said Walter Mitty. "Does it ever occur to you that I am sometimes thinking?" She looked at him. "I'm going to take your temperature when I get you home," she said.

They went out through the revolving doors that made a faintly derisive whistling sound when you pushed them. It was two blocks to the parking lot. At the drugstore on the corner she said, "Wait here for me. I forgot something. I won't be a minute." She was more than a minute. Walter Mitty lighted a cigarette. It began to rain, rain with sleet in it. He stood up against the wall of the drugstore, smoking. . . . C He put his shoulders back and his heels together. "To hell with the handkerchief," said Walter Mitty scornfully. He took one last drag on his cigarette and snapped it away. Then, with that faint, fleeting smile playing about his lips, he faced the firing squad; erect and motionless, proud and disdainful, Walter Mitty the Undefeated, inscrutable[9] to the last.

6. **Archies:** German antiaircraft guns or gunners in World War I.
7. **circus:** squadron of planes.

8. **Auprès de Ma Blonde:** French song. The title means "Near My Blonde."
9. **inscrutable** (in·skrōōt′ə·bəl): mysterious.

WORDS TO OWN

cannonading (kan′ən·ād′iŋ) *v.* used as *n.*: artillery fire.
rending (rend′iŋ) *v.* used as *n.*: violent ripping apart.

OPTIONS FOR TEACHING

ASSESSMENT TOOLS

Check Test: True-False

1. Mrs. Mitty reminds Walter to buy a snow shovel. [False]
2. As Dr. Mitty, Walter repairs the anesthetizer with a metal coat hanger. [False]
3. One item on Walter's shopping list is puppy biscuits. [True]
4. One of the roles Walter imagines himself in is that of a crusading district attorney. [False]
5. An article about German air power triggers Mitty's fantasy about flying. [True]

PRIMARY **Sources** A TRIBUTE

Thurber's longtime associate on *The New Yorker,* E. B. White, wrote this parting tribute to his friend on November 11, 1961.

The New Yorker's Farewell

I am one of the lucky ones; I knew him before blindness hit him, before fame hit him, and I tend always to think of him as a young artist in a small office in a big city, with all the world still ahead. It was a fine thing to be young and at work in New York for a new magazine when Thurber was young and at work, and I will always be glad that this happened to me.

It was fortunate that we got on well; the office we shared was the size of a hall bedroom. There was just room enough for two men, two typewriters, and a stack of copy paper. The copy paper disappeared at a scandalous rate—not because our production was high (although it was) but because Thurber used copy paper as the natural receptacle for discarded sorrows, immediate joys, stale dreams, golden prophecies, and messages of good cheer to the outside world and to fellow workers. His mind was never at rest, and his pencil was connected to his mind by the best conductive tissue I have ever seen in action. The whole world knows what a funny man he was, but you had to sit next to him day after day to understand the extravagance of his clowning, the wildness and subtlety of his thinking, and the intensity of his interest in others and his sympathy for their dilemmas—dilemmas that he instantly enlarged, put in focus, and made immortal, just as he enlarged and made immortal the strange goings-on in the Ohio home of his boyhood. His waking dreams and his sleeping dreams commingled shamelessly and uproariously. Ohio was never far from his thoughts, and when he received a medal from his home state in 1953, he wrote, "The clocks that strike in my dreams are often the clocks of Columbus." It is a beautiful sentence and a revealing one.

He was both a practitioner of humor and a defender of it. The day he died, I came on a letter from him, dictated to a secretary and signed in pencil with his sightless and enormous "Jim." "Every time is a time for humor," he wrote. "I write humor the way a surgeon operates, because it is a livelihood, because I have a great urge to do it, because many interesting challenges are set up, and because I have the hope it may do some good." Once, I remember, he heard someone say that humor is a shield, not a sword, and it made him mad. He wasn't going to have anyone beating his sword into a shield. That "surgeon," incidentally, is pure Mitty. During his happiest years, Thurber did not write the way a surgeon operates, he wrote the way a child skips rope, the way a mouse waltzes.

Although he is best known for "Walter Mitty" and *The Male Animal,* the book of his I like best is *The Last Flower.* In it you will find his faith in the renewal of life, his feeling for the beauty and fragility of life on earth. Like all good writers, he fashioned his own best obituary notice. Nobody else can add to the record, much as he might like to. And of all the flowers, real and figurative, that will find their way to Thurber's last resting place, the one that will remain fresh and wiltproof is the little flower he himself drew, on the last page of that lovely book.

—E. B. White

Primary Sources

White's tribute suggests the scope of Thurber's comic genius without falling into extravagance or sentimentality. The last sentence in the third paragraph (about skipping rope and dancing mice) is pure White; it is one that Thurber might have admired.

STRATEGIES FOR INCLUSION

Advanced Ask students to write personal tributes, either to themselves or to someone else. Volunteers may share their tributes with the class.

Visual Have students draw self-portraits or cartoons about themselves like Thurber's. They should provide captions that add crucial details or humor. Students may then create a display of their drawings in the room or self-publish a newspaper or flyer featuring their cartoons.

CROSSING THE CURRICULUM

Journalism Have students research the career field of journalism and make brief reports to the class. Students might focus on how they imagine this occupation has changed since Thurber's day. Also, you might invite a local journalist to speak to the class.

Connections A CARTOON

One of the most familiar Walter Mitty–like characters in popular culture is Snoopy, Charles M. Schulz's (1922–) beloved creation from the famous "Peanuts" comic strip.

CONNECTING WITH "THE SECRET LIFE OF WALTER MITTY"

Ask students to describe characters in other comic strips, movies, or television shows who escape from reality by daydreaming or pretending to be other people. [Possible responses: Calvin in the comic strip "Calvin and Hobbes," various characters from TV sitcoms.]

Making Meanings

First Thoughts

1. Do you think there's a little of Mitty in everyone? Explain.

> **Reviewing the Text**
>
> **a.** List the errands Mitty is doing in real life.
>
> **b.** In contrast, what deeds does Mitty perform in his fantasy life?

Shaping Interpretations

2. What is the central **irony** of Mitty's life? Is this irony humorous, serious, or partly both?
3. Thurber's story uses a technique called free association, in which words and sounds from real life become associated with elements of Mitty's daydreams. Review the notes you made in your Reader's Log, and identify what sends Mitty into each daydream. What decidedly unheroic event snaps him out of each episode?
4. Where does Thurber use **parody** in the story? Who or what are the targets of his satire? (To help identify the targets, look especially at the jargon being bandied about in each daydream.)
5. Why do you think Mitty daydreams so much, and about these specific events? Do you think that his daydreaming enriches his life, or does it work as a handicap? Why?

He always half suspected that something would get him.

Some nights she threw them all.

Extending the Text

6. Walter Mitty could be seen as one of a line of archetypal American characters, beginning with Benjamin Franklin's "self-made man." What does Mitty's life reveal about the opportunities for heroism and "self making" today? Do you agree with Thurber's assessment of modern life?
7. Walter Mitty and the formidable Mrs. Mitty have become **stock character** types in American popular culture. Brainstorm a list of popular movies and TV sitcoms in which similar husbands and wives can be found. Why do these character types endure? Do you think changing views of gender roles will eventually make these stock characters obsolete? Explain.

Making Meanings

First Thoughts

1. Most students will probably agree that many people have fantasies or dreams of leading lives vastly different from their actual lives.

Reviewing the Text

a. His errands include buying overshoes and puppy biscuits.

b. He commands a war plane, performs a tricky surgical procedure, testifies at a murder trial, and executes a critical military mission.

Shaping Interpretations

2. The central irony in Mitty's life is the contrast between his mousey true existence and his heroic daydreams. It is both humorous and sad.
3. Mrs. Mitty's unheroic reproach about driving too fast connects to Mitty's fantasy of the Navy plane. Gloves are associated with surgical gloves in the operating room episode. This episode ends with the parking lot attendant's yell. A sling is associated with the courtroom episode. The insult about the "miserable cur" leads Mitty to remember the puppy biscuits. An article about the German air force leads into the bomber fantasy, which Mrs. Mitty ends by slapping his shoulder.
4. Thurber parodies technical jargon in the hospital fantasy. Mitty's fantasies target stereotypical situations and characters—the flight commander leading his crew through a storm.
5. In fantasy, Mitty can be dashing, competent, and admirable, which might help him cope with unpleasant circumstances. However, by daydreaming so much, he may lose interest in his real life.

Extending the Text

6. **(Synthesis)** For Thurber, heroism exists primarily in the realm of fantasy. Some students may feel that we need to change our perception of heroism to include common acts of bravery that make the world a better place.
7. **(Synthesis)** Students may find exaggerated characters funny because they parody real people, actions, and desires. Others may say that new stock characters will evolve as media portray more nontraditional families.

Choices: Building Your Portfolio

1. **Writer's Notebook** Remind students to save their work. They may use it as prewriting for the Writer's Workshop on p. 685.
2. **Critical Writing** Before writing their essays, have students share their ideas in small groups. Remind students to explore enough details to support descriptions for each character.
3. **Creative Writing** Model a cluster on the chalkboard. Have student volunteers come to the chalkboard and try to complete it so that students may see the variety of ideas that may be generated through clustering.

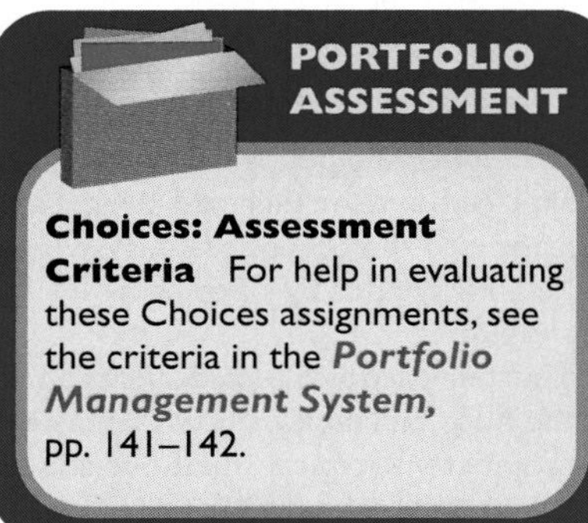

Choices: Assessment Criteria For help in evaluating these Choices assignments, see the criteria in the ***Portfolio Management System,*** pp. 141–142.

CHOICES: Building Your Portfolio

Writer's Notebook

1. Collecting Ideas for a Speculation About Causes and Effects

WORK IN PROGRESS

Imagine that you are a psychological counselor who has been assigned to the Walter Mitty case. Freewrite your speculations about the causes of Mitty's tendency to daydream and the possible effects if he continues to rely on fantasy. You'll want to consider these points:

- What is Mitty's problem? Is he a potential psychopath, or merely a timid, disappointed romantic—or something else?
- What are some factors in Mitty's life that cause him to seek refuge in fantasy? What evidence or reasons make you think this?
- What will be the result(s) if Mitty continues his daydreaming?
- What's your recommendation? Should Mitty give up his daydreams, try to make some of them come true, or do something else?

Keep your notes for possible use in the Writer's Workshop on page 685.

Critical Writing

2. The Gender Gap

Thurber has been accused of being "tough" on women, a criticism that has also been leveled against Washington Irving for his portrait of Dame Van Winkle (page 154). In a brief essay, compare and contrast these two famous American couples—Rip and Dame Van Winkle, and Walter and Mrs. Mitty. At the end of your essay, describe your response to the character types used in each story to make us laugh.

Creative Writing

3. The Secret Life of Mrs. Mitty

Everybody has fantasies in which they escape from their everyday lives. What do you think *Mrs.* Mitty daydreams about? Brainstorm a list of elements you would include in a story about Mrs. Mitty's everyday experiences and her contrasting daydreams. Use your list to write an episode in "The Secret Life of Mrs. Mitty."

Art/Creative Writing

4. Thoroughly Modern Mitty

Charles M. Schulz's character Snoopy (Connections, page 630) is truly cast in the Walter Mitty mold. Try creating your own cartoon version of a contempory Walter Mitty. What heroic fantasies might he or she escape to?

Drama

5. Coming to a Theater Near You

Because it contains five different fantasy settings and a recurring real-life setting, this story is packed with material for dramatic action. (In fact, the story was made into a 1947 movie starring Danny Kaye.) Work with a group of classmates to adapt a short play or video drama from the story. Assign parts, and create costumes and props. Perform the scene for your class, or videotape it.

Creative Writing

6. Dear Mr. Thurber

In his lifetime, James Thurber sometimes complained that he received too many letters from students. Yet he answered such letters graciously and candidly. Write a letter in which you tell Thurber what you think of his story, giving reasons for your opinion.

STRATEGIES FOR INCLUSION

Learners Having Difficulty For activity #2, examine models of comparison/contrast essays so that students may see how to use details to support ideas, how to organize the material, and what kinds of transition words and phrases to use for coherence.

Interpersonal For activity #5, have students decide who will take on the responsibilities of director, stage manager, prop person, and costume person for their productions. After the performance, students should evaluate how well they performed their responsibilities.

Eudora Welty

(1909–)

Eudora Welty was born in the quintessentially Southern city of Jackson, Mississippi, and she has lived in Jackson almost her whole life. As the daughter of an insurance man and a schoolteacher, she enjoyed a conventional girlhood. She recalls pleading with her brothers to teach her golf, sharing their enthusiasm for baseball, and bicycling to the library in *two* petticoats to forestall the librarian's caustic remark, "I can practically see through you."

Welty attended Mississippi State College for Women, graduated from the University of Wisconsin, and did graduate work at Columbia University, anticipating a career in advertising. However, the Depression sent her home to Jackson with a belief, which did not fail her, that she would succeed as a writer of fiction.

Welty's widely recognized triumph is a painstaking accuracy in colloquial speech. The exactly right word always matters to her. She has always been fascinated by words, by the *way* people say things, by snatches of overheard dialogue. She was once delighted to hear a country woman confess to "a gnawing and a craving" for something. Telling a friend about it, Welty added, "Wasn't that a wonderful way of putting it? A gnawing and a craving!"

She greatly admires the work of Katherine Anne Porter (page 702), who befriended her when she was sending out stories and getting back rejection slips. It was the literary agent Diarmuid Russell who shared Welty's belief in an ultimate success. He not only took her on as a client, but also said of a certain Welty story that if the editor didn't accept it, the two ought to "horsewhip the offending editor for his insult to literature." (The editor in question bought the story.)

Welty's first collections of stories, *A Curtain of Green* and *The Wide Net,* appeared in the 1940s. These were followed by *The Golden Apples* (1949), one of her best-known volumes of short stories. Then came a novella, *The Ponder Heart* (1954), which was made into a Broadway play. *Losing Battles,* Welty's fine comic novel about a family reunion in the rural South, was published in 1970. Two years later, Welty produced *The Optimist's Daughter,* a poignant short novel about family conflicts; this book won her the Pulitzer Prize. An autobiographical memoir entitled *One Writer's Beginnings,* based on lectures Welty gave at Harvard University, was published in 1983 to wide critical acclaim.

© Rollie McKenna.

Welty admits to being blessed with a visual mind, and she says that this gift makes for "the best shorthand a writer can have." She once wrote, "To watch everything about me I regarded grimly and possessively as a *need.*" Clearly, that need became an enviable artistic vision.

QUICK PLANNING GUIDE

Into the Story

Author Biography p. 633
Before You Read p. 634

- **Reading Focus: Scaffolding** Students redefine the hero's journey.
- **Quickwrite:** Write character prediction in Reader's Log
- **Elements of Literature: Theme**
- **Background: Set a Purpose** Examine race and social status

Through the Story

"A Worn Path" pp. 635–639
Words to Own pp. 635–638
Primary Sources pp. 640–641
Making Meanings p. 642

Beyond the Story

Choices: Building Your Portfolio p. 642

- **Writer's Notebook:** Take notes on causes and effects of segregation
- **Critical Writing:** Identify and analyze the parts of a journey
- **Creative Writing:** Write a story about a person who endures a hardship

PROGRAM MANAGER

- **Planning Instruction** See Teaching Notes, *Teaching Resources B,* p. 35, for objectives, a summary, and literary elements for this selection.
- **Instructional Support** See Graphic Organizer for Active Reading, *Teaching Resources B,* p. 46, for a Through the Story activity.
- **Application and Reinforcement** See Transparency 12.4 in the *Audiovisual Resources Binder.*
- **Assessment** See Selection Test, *Test Booklet,* pp. 147–148.
- **Language Link** For instruction and practice in pronoun reference, see Language Link, *Teaching Resources B,* pp. 47–48 and *Language and Writing Skills Worksheets,* pp. 57–58.
- **Reinforcement** Use the Words to Own worksheet in *Teaching Resources B,* p. 49.

Into the Story

Using Before You Read p. 634

Elements of Literature

To help students understand the theme of "A Worn Path," have them create a two-column dialectical journal in their Reader's Logs. In one column, students should write down details about **characters**, **plot**, and **setting**. In the second column, students should write personal comments, symbolic responses, or comparisons for each detail.

PORTFOLIO ASSESSMENT

Portfolio Assessment
For help with self-assessment of reading skills, see the ***Portfolio Management System,*** pp. 48–49.

WORDS TO OWN

The following vocabulary words are defined in the Words to Own at the bottom of the pupil's page.

pendulum p. 635	appointed p. 635
persistent p. 635	furrow p. 636
meditative p. 635	radiation p. 637
illumined p. 635	ceremonial p. 638
intent p. 635	solemn p. 638

Before You Read
A Worn Path

Reading Focus

The Perilous Journey

From earliest times storytellers have used the perilous journey as a metaphor for life. When we think of a perilous journey, we might conjure up images of a steely, larger-than-life hero or heroine who endures incredible hardships and faces monstrous adversaries. But a perilous journey can be a much more ordinary—even an everyday—affair, on a road as modest and simple as a worn path.

Quickwrite

READER'S LOG

The major character in this story is named Phoenix Jackson. Before you read, look up the word *phoenix* in a dictionary. Then, write down your prediction of what a character named Phoenix might be like.

Elements of Literature

Theme

The plot of the story you are about to read is very simple, but its **themes**—its main insights into life—are subtle and complex. You may need a second reading to be sure you have grasped what Eudora Welty is implying in her low-key narrative about Phoenix Jackson's walk down a worn path.

To get a handle on the theme, first visualize the story and characters in a literal sense: who they are, where they are, and what they are doing. Then visualize people and circumstances that are very different—perhaps your own life or the lives of other people you know. Ask yourself how knowing about Phoenix Jackson's path might help you understand your own path or that of someone you know.

The **theme** of a story is its main idea or insight into life.

For more on Theme, see the Handbook of Literary Terms.

Background

Phoenix makes her journey in rural Mississippi, late in the Depression era of the 1930s. This story offers several clues to how a person's race determined his or her social status in that time and place.

Pages 634 and 640: A woman of the thirties, Hinds County (1935) by Eudora Welty. Photograph.

Eudora Welty Collection, Mississippi Department of Archives and History.

A Worn Path

Eudora Welty

634 The Moderns

OPTIONS FOR TEACHING

STRATEGIES FOR INCLUSION

Advanced Ask students to choose one other story that uses a journey as a metaphor for life—perhaps the *Odyssey* or *Adventures of Huckleberry Finn*—and compare and contrast it with "A Worn Path." Suggest that they begin by comparing themes, types of obstacles, and sources of strength.

Special Needs Before reading, invite the class to discuss difficult or challenging things they have done out of the "habit of love." Have they made sacrifices or gone through uncomfortable experiences for the benefit of someone they love? If not, have they been the recipient of such a gift from someone else? This discussion will establish an emotional climate and mood of anticipation for the selection. *Remind students to select experiences they would not mind sharing with others.*

It was December—a bright frozen day in the early morning. Far out in the country there was an old Negro woman with her head tied in a red rag, coming along a path through the pinewoods. Her name was Phoenix Jackson. She was very old and small and she walked slowly in the dark pine shadows, moving a little from side to side in her steps, with the balanced heaviness and lightness of a pendulum in a grandfather clock. She carried a thin, small cane made from an umbrella, and with this she kept tapping the frozen earth in front of her. This made a grave and persistent noise in the still air, that seemed meditative like the chirping of a solitary little bird. **A**

She wore a dark striped dress reaching down to her shoe tops, and an equally long apron of bleached sugar sacks, with a full pocket: all neat and tidy, but every time she took a step she might have fallen over her shoelaces, which dragged from her unlaced shoes. She looked straight ahead. Her eyes were blue with age. Her skin had a pattern all its own of numberless branching wrinkles and as though a whole little tree stood in the middle of her forehead, but a golden color ran underneath, and the two knobs of her cheeks were illumined by a yellow burning under the dark. Under the red rag her hair came down on her neck in the frailest of ringlets, still black, and with an odor like copper. **B**

> *Finally, trembling all over, she stood free, and after a moment dared to stoop for her cane.*

Now and then there was a quivering in the thicket. Old Phoenix said, "Out of my way, all you foxes, owls, beetles, jack rabbits, coons, and wild animals! . . . Keep out from under these feet, little bobwhites. . . . Keep the big wild hogs out of my path. Don't let none of those come running in my direction. I got a long way." Under her small black-freckled hand her cane, limber as a buggy whip, would switch at the brush as if to rouse up any hiding things. **C**

On she went. The woods were deep and still. The sun made the pine needles almost too bright to look at, up where the wind rocked. The cones dropped as light as feathers. Down in the hollow was the mourning dove—it was not too late for him. **D**

The path ran up a hill. "Seem like there is chains about my feet, time I get this far," she said, in the voice of argument old people keep to use with themselves. "Something always take a hold of me on this hill—pleads I should stay."

After she got to the top she turned and gave a full, severe look behind her where she had come. "Up through pines," she said at length. "Now down through oaks."

Her eyes opened their widest, and she started down gently. But before she got to the bottom of the hill a bush caught her dress.

Her fingers were busy and intent, but her skirts were full and long, so that before she could pull them free in one place they were caught in another. It was not possible to allow the dress to tear. "I in the thorny bush," she said. "Thorns, you doing your appointed work. Never want to let folks pass, no sir. Old eyes thought you was a pretty little *green* bush." **E**

Finally, trembling all over, she stood free, and after a moment dared to stoop for her cane.

"Sun so high!" she cried, leaning back and

Words to Own

pendulum (pen′dyoo͞·ləm) *n.:* freely swinging weight suspended from a fixed point to regulate a clock's movement.
persistent (pər·sist′ənt) *adj.:* continuing.
meditative (med′ə·tāt′iv) *adj.:* deeply thoughtful; reflective.
illumined (i·lo͞o′mənd) *v.:* lighted up.
intent (in·tent′) *adj.:* purposeful.
appointed (ə·point′id) *v.* used as *adj.:* assigned.

Through the Story

A. Humanities Connection
From earliest times storytellers have used journeys as metaphors for life: Ulysses' journey home, Gulliver's travels to strange worlds, and Huck Finn's raft trip down the Mississippi are only a few examples. Ask students to consider in what ways Phoenix Jackson's journey is a symbolic one.

B. Literary Element: Sensory Images
? Which senses does Welty use in describing Phoenix Jackson? [Sight, smell, touch, hearing—all except taste.]

C. Reader's Response: First Thoughts
? What kind of person do you think Phoenix Jackson is? [Sample responses: Old and poor; or determined and courageous.]

D. Critical Reading: Speculating
? What do you think she is referring to? [Possible answers: To a boy or man who must be in trouble. She takes the dove as a sign of hope. Or she is referring to the dove—that it is not too late in the day for it to be out.]

E. Reader's Response: Shaping Interpretations
? How would you describe Phoenix's relationship with the natural world? [Sample responses: She seems to feel a kinship with the trees, animals, and even the thorn bush; or she fusses at everything.]

INTEGRATING THE LANGUAGE ARTS

Writing: Diary Entry Invite students to keep a diary as if they were Phoenix. Have them write entries for the day the story covers, beginning in the morning before she begins her journey; entries on the different events and encounters of the journey; town entries; and one entry to reflect on the entire day after she returns home that evening.

Language and Style Point out that Welty's style includes meticulous attention to imagery. She does this by engaging many senses and using figurative language. Ask students to find as many different kinds of images as possible, along with examples of **figurative language—metaphors, similes,** and **personification.**

Usage After reviewing the conventions for setting off nouns of direct address, ask students to look in the story for examples of correct usage of this punctuation rule. ☞

A. Reader's Response: First Thoughts

? Do you ever talk to yourself? When are you most likely to do so?

[Sample responses: I talk to myself usually when I am concentrating on a difficult task; or no, I never talk to myself.]

B. Critical Reading: Finding Details

? What obstacles has Phoenix Jackson overcome so far?

[Possible answers: The cold; the need for a cane; unlaced shoelaces; wild animals; hills; a thorny bush; log across creek; fantasies of cake; barbed wire.]

C. Reader's Response: Shaping Interpretations

? What makes the journey a little easier for Phoenix Jackson?

[Sample responses: She has made the trip before and has last summer's experience to guide her; or she is determined and has a purpose.]

looking, while the thick tears went over her eyes. "The time getting all gone here."

At the foot of this hill was a place where a log was laid across the creek.

(A) "Now comes the trial," said Phoenix.

Putting her right foot out, she mounted the log and shut her eyes. Lifting her skirt, leveling her cane fiercely before her, like a festival figure in some parade, she began to march across. Then she opened her eyes and she was safe on the other side.

"I wasn't as old as I thought," she said.

But she sat down to rest. She spread her skirts on the bank around her and folded her hands over her knees. Up above her was a tree in a pearly cloud of mistletoe. She did not dare to close her eyes, and when a little boy brought her a plate with a slice of marble cake on it she spoke to him. "That would be acceptable," she said. But when she went to take it there was just her own hand in the air.

(B) So she left that tree, and had to go through a barbed-wire fence. There she had to creep and crawl, spreading her knees and stretching her fingers like a baby trying to climb the steps. But she talked loudly to herself: She could not let her dress be torn now, so late in the day, and she could not pay for having her arm or her leg sawed off if she got caught fast where she was.

At last she was safe through the fence and risen up out in the clearing. Big dead trees, like black men with one arm, were standing in the purple stalks of the withered cotton field. There sat a buzzard.

"Who you watching?"

In the furrow she made her way along.

(C) "Glad this not the season for bulls," she said, looking sideways, "and the good Lord made his snakes to curl up and sleep in the winter. A pleasure I don't see no two-headed snake coming around that tree, where it come once. It took a while to get by him, back in the summer."

She passed through the old cotton and went into a field of dead corn. It whispered and shook and was taller than her head. "Through the maze now," she said, for there was no path.

Then there was something tall, black, and skinny there, moving before her.

At first she took it for a man. It could have been a man dancing in the field. But she stood still and listened, and it did not make a sound. It was as silent as a ghost.

"Ghost," she said sharply, "who be you the ghost of? For I have heard of nary death close by."

But there was no answer—only the ragged dancing in the wind.

She shut her eyes, reached out her hand, and touched a sleeve. She found a coat and inside that an emptiness, cold as ice.

"You scarecrow," she said. Her face lighted. "I ought to be shut up for good," she said with laughter. "My senses is gone. I too old. I the oldest people I ever know. Dance, old scarecrow," she said, "while I dancing with you."

She kicked her foot over the furrow, and with mouth drawn down, shook her head once or twice in a little strutting way. Some husks blew down and whirled in streamers about her skirts.

Then she went on, parting her way from side to side with the cane, through the whispering field. At last she came to the end, to a wagon track where the silver grass blew between the red ruts. The quail were walking around like pullets, seeming all dainty and unseen.

"Walk pretty," she said. "This the easy place. This the easy going."

She followed the track, swaying through the quiet bare fields, through the little strings of trees silver in their dead leaves, past cabins silver from weather, with the doors and windows boarded shut, all like old women under a spell sitting there. "I walking in their sleep," she said, nodding her head vigorously.

In a ravine she went where a spring was silently flowing through a hollow log. Old Phoenix bent and drank. "Sweet gum makes the water sweet," she said, and drank more. "Nobody know who made this well, for it was here when I was born."

The track crossed a swampy part where the moss hung as white as lace from every limb. "Sleep on, alligators, and blow your bubbles." Then the track went into the road.

Deep, deep the road went down between the high green-colored banks. Overhead the live oaks met, and it was as dark as a cave.

Words to Own

furrow (fʉr'ō) *n.:* groove in the land made by a plow.

OPTIONS FOR TEACHING

COOPERATIVE LEARNING

Jigsaw Reading Have students work in small groups. Each member should concentrate on how one of the following literary elements is important in the story: **setting, motivation, conflict,** and **suspense.** After ten minutes, ask students who worked on the same element to form new groups to discuss their findings. After five minutes of discussion, ask students to return to their original groups to share their information with the other members.

CROSSING THE CURRICULUM

Geography Ask students to go back to the story to find details of the country landscape and then to draw a map of the journey that Welty created for Phoenix Jackson.

Science Invite students to take a nature walk in their community, as a class or in supervised groups. Have them keep journal entries on the plants, insects, and animals they see. Then, have them compare their entries with the flora and fauna Phoenix encounters on her walk.

A black dog with a lolling tongue came up out of the weeds by the ditch. She was meditating, and not ready, and when he came at her she only hit him a little with her cane. Over she went in the ditch, like a little puff of milkweed.

Down there, her senses drifted away. A dream visited her, and she reached her hand up, but nothing reached down and gave her a pull. So she lay there and presently went to talking. "Old woman," she said to herself, "that black dog come up out of the weeds to stall you off, and now there he sitting on his fine tail, smiling at you."

A white man finally came along and found her—a hunter, a young man, with his dog on a chain. "Well, Granny!" he laughed. "What are you doing there?"

"Lying on my back like a June bug waiting to be turned over, mister," she said, reaching up her hand.

He lifted her up, gave her a swing in the air, and set her down. "Anything broken, Granny?"

"No sir, them old dead weeds is springy enough," said Phoenix, when she had got her breath. "I thank you for your trouble."

"Where do you live, Granny?" he asked, while the two dogs were growling at each other.

"Away back yonder, sir, behind the ridge. You can't even see it from here."

"On your way home?"

"No sir, I going to town."

"Why, that's too far! That's as far as I walk when I come out myself, and I get something for my trouble." He patted the stuffed bag he carried, and there hung down a little closed claw. It was one of the bobwhites, with its beak hooked bitterly to show it was dead. "Now you go on home, Granny!"

"I bound to go to town, mister," said Phoenix. "The time come around."

He gave another laugh, filling the whole landscape. "I know you old colored people! Wouldn't miss going to town to see Santa Claus!" **D**

But something held old Phoenix very still. The deep lines in her face went into a fierce and different radiation. Without warning, she had seen with her own eyes a flashing nickel fall out of the man's pocket onto the ground.

"How old are you, Granny?" he was saying.

"There is no telling, mister," she said, "no telling."

Then she gave a little cry and clapped her hands and said, "Git on away from here, dog! Look! Look at that dog!" She laughed as if in admiration. "He ain't scared of nobody. He a big black dog." She whispered, "Sic him!" **E**

"Watch me get rid of that cur," said the man. "Sic him, Pete! Sic him!"

Phoenix heard the dogs fighting, and heard the man running and throwing sticks. She even heard a gunshot. But she was slowly bending forward by that time, further and further forward, the lids stretched down over her eyes, as if she were doing this in her sleep. Her chin was lowered almost to her knees. The yellow palm of her hand came out from the fold of her apron. Her fingers slid down and along the ground under the piece of money with the grace and care they would have in lifting an egg from under a setting hen. Then she slowly straightened up, she stood erect, and the nickel was in her apron pocket. A bird flew by. Her lips moved. "God watching me the whole time. I come to stealing."

The man came back, and his own dog panted about them. "Well, I scared him off that time," he said, and then he laughed and lifted his gun and pointed it at Phoenix.

She stood straight and faced him.

"Doesn't the gun scare you?" he said, still pointing it.

"No, sir, I seen plenty go off closer by, in my day, and for less than what I done," she said holding utterly still.

He smiled, and shouldered the gun. "Well, Granny," he said, "you must be a hundred years old, and scared of nothing. I'd give you a dime if I had any money with me. But you take my advice and stay home, and nothing will happen to you."

"I bound to go on my way, mister," said Phoenix. She inclined her head in the red rag. Then they went in different directions, but she could hear the gun shooting again and again over the hill.

She walked on. The shadows hung from the oak trees to the road like curtains. Then she smelled woodsmoke, and smelled the river, and she saw a steeple and the cabins on their steep

---

WORDS TO OWN

radiation (rā′dē·ā′shən) *n.:* pattern; arrangement.

D. Literary Element: Irony
The young hunter's condescending notion that Phoenix would make the arduous trip to see Santa Claus becomes very ironic when the reader learns the real reason for her journey.

E. Critical Reading: Making Inferences
? Why does Phoenix clap her hands and call attention to the black dog?
[Possible answer: She hopes to divert the hunter's attention so that she will have a chance to pick up the nickel.]

CLASSROOM MANAGEMENT

Managing the Reader's Response Classroom To encourage students to see that there is not just one way to look at material, allow several students to express opinions on each topic. Encourage students to amend their responses after they have considered other input.

Block Scheduling After reading the last story in a unit, take the class to the library and allow students time to check out a book related to the unit's theme. At a later date, students may present book reports to the class. ☞

A. Reader's Response: Connecting with the Text

? Why do you suppose the author chose to set this story during Christmas? [Sample responses: The fact that Phoenix makes her journey at this time adds a spiritual dimension to it; or one would think people would be kinder to Phoenix at that time of year, and it is ironic that they are not.]

B. Reader's Response: Shaping Interpretations

? How does this young woman's attitude toward Phoenix compare with the hunter's? [Sample responses: She helps Phoenix without condescension; or calling her "Grandma" is patronizing, too.]

C. Critical Reading: Speculating

? Why is the reason for Phoenix's journey not revealed earlier in the story? [Possible answer: Without a specific reason for the journey, it seems more a journey of the archetypal human being, a journey through life that we all share.]

D. Critical Reading: Analyzing Character

Phoenix's loss of recent memory is not uncommon in people of her age. She has not forgotten her grandson; she has only momentarily forgotten what brings her to these relatively strange surroundings.

steps. Dozens of little black children whirled around her. There ahead was Natchez shining. Bells were ringing. She walked on.

A In the paved city it was Christmas time. There were red and green electric lights strung and crisscrossed everywhere, and all turned on in the daytime. Old Phoenix would have been lost if she had not distrusted her eyesight and depended on her feet to know where to take her.

She paused quietly on the sidewalk where people were passing by. A lady came along in the crowd, carrying an armful of red-, green-, and silver-wrapped presents; she gave off perfume like the red roses in hot summer, and Phoenix stopped her.

"Please, missy, will you lace up my shoe?" She held up her foot.

"What do you want, Grandma?"

"See my shoe," said Phoenix. "Do all right for out in the country, but wouldn't look right to go in a big building."

B "Stand still then, Grandma," said the lady. She put her packages down on the sidewalk beside her and laced and tied both shoes tightly.

"Can't lace 'em with a cane," said Phoenix. "Thank you, missy. I doesn't mind asking a nice lady to tie up my shoe, when I gets out on the street."

Moving slowly and from side to side, she went into the big building, and into a tower of steps, where she walked up and around and around until her feet knew to stop.

She entered a door, and there she saw nailed up on the wall the document that had been stamped with the gold seal and framed in the gold frame, which matched the dream that was hung up in her head.

"Here I be," she said. There was a fixed and ceremonial stiffness over her body.

"A charity case, I suppose," said an attendant who sat at the desk before her.

But Phoenix only looked above her head. There was sweat on her face, the wrinkles in her skin shone like a bright net.

"Speak up, Grandma," the woman said. "What's your name? We must have your history, you know. Have you been here before? What seems to be the trouble with you?"

Old Phoenix only gave a twitch to her face as if a fly were bothering her.

"Are you deaf?" cried the attendant.

But then the nurse came in.

C "Oh, that's just old Aunt Phoenix," she said. "She doesn't come for herself—she has a little grandson. She makes these trips just as regular as clockwork. She lives away back off the Old Natchez Trace." She bent down. "Well, Aunt Phoenix, why don't you just take a seat? We won't keep you standing after your long trip." She pointed.

The old woman sat down, bolt upright in the chair.

"Now, how is the boy?" asked the nurse.

Old Phoenix did not speak.

"I said, how is the boy?"

But Phoenix only waited and stared straight ahead, her face very solemn and withdrawn into rigidity.

"Is his throat any better?" asked the nurse. "Aunt Phoenix, don't you hear me? Is your grandson's throat any better since the last time you came for the medicine?"

With her hands on her knees, the old woman waited, silent, erect and motionless, just as if she were in armor.

"You mustn't take up our time this way, Aunt Phoenix," the nurse said. "Tell us quickly about your grandson, and get it over. He isn't dead, is he?"

At last there came a flicker and then a flame of comprehension across her face, and she spoke.

D "My grandson. It was my memory had left me. There I sat and forgot why I made my long trip."

"Forgot?" The nurse frowned. "After you came so far?"

Then Phoenix was like an old woman begging a dignified forgiveness for waking up frightened in the night. "I never did go to school, I was too old at the Surrender," she said in a soft voice. "I'm an old woman without an education. It was my memory fail me. My little grandson, he is just the same, and I forgot it in the coming."

"Throat never heals, does it?" said the nurse, speaking in a loud, sure voice to old Phoenix. By

WORDS TO OWN

ceremonial (ser′ə·mō′nē·əl) *adj.:* formal.
solemn (säl′əm) *adj.:* serious.

OPTIONS FOR TEACHING

ASSESSMENT TOOLS

Check Test: True-False

1. The story takes place in winter. [True]
2. Phoenix often talks to herself as she walks along. [True]
3. Her destination is a general store in a nearby town. [False]
4. A hunter gives Phoenix some money. [False]
5. Her grandson suffers from a throat ailment. [True]

Informal Assessment As students discuss the selection, write in their Reader's Logs, and work in learning groups, observe to make sure that all students are participating. Take short notes on students who are not participating and save the notes for a future student or parent conference.

Courthouse town, Grenada (1935), by Eudora Welty. Photograph. Eudora Welty Collection, Mississippi Department of Archives and History.

now she had a card with something written on it, a little list. "Yes. Swallowed lye. When was it?—January—two-three years ago—"

Phoenix spoke unasked now. "No, missy, he not dead, he just the same. Every little while his throat begin to close up again, and he not able to swallow. He not get his breath. He not able to help himself. So the time come around, and I go on another trip for the soothing medicine."

"All right. The doctor said as long as you came to get it, you could have it," said the nurse. "But it's an obstinate case."

"My little grandson, he sit up there in the house all wrapped up, waiting by himself," Phoenix went on. "We is the only two left in the world. He suffer and it don't seem to put him back at all. He got a sweet look. He going to last. He wear a little patch quilt and peep out holding his mouth open like a little bird. I remembers so plain now. I not going to forget him again, no, the whole enduring time. I could tell him from all the others in creation."

"All right." The nurse was trying to hush her now. She brought her a bottle of medicine. "Charity," she said, making a check mark in a book.

Old Phoenix held the bottle close to her eyes, and then carefully put it into her pocket.

"I thank you," she said.

"It's Christmas time, Grandma," said the attendant. "Could I give you a few pennies out of my purse?"

"Five pennies is a nickel," said Phoenix stiffly.

"Here's a nickel," said the attendant.

Phoenix rose carefully and held out her hand. She received the nickel and then fished the other nickel out of her pocket and laid it beside the new one. She stared at her palm closely, with her head on one side.

Then she gave a tap with her cane on the floor.

"This is what come to me to do," she said. "I going to the store and buy my child a little windmill they sells, made out of paper. He going to find it hard to believe there such a thing in the world. I'll march myself back where he waiting, holding it straight up in this hand."

She lifted her free hand, gave a little nod, turned around, and walked out of the doctor's office. Then her slow step began on the stairs, going down.

E. Critical Reading: Finding Details

The plight of Phoenix's grandson is made poignantly clear here—he depends completely on Phoenix, who is old and does not have a very firm grip on life herself.

F. Reader's Response: Extending the Text

? What does Phoenix Jackson's generosity here—giving all that she has—contribute to the theme of the story? [Sample responses: She maintains what Welty calls the habit of love, which cuts through confusion; or she is a woman who finds her way through all manner of obstacles, time after time, because of her love.]

G. Literary Element: Theme

? Does traveling the worn path work effectively in this story as a metaphor for the theme of going through life? [Possible answer: Yes, there are obstacles to overcome and sometimes people lose the way; or no, life is different and more complicated.]

RESPONDING TO THE ART: VISUAL LITERACY

What qualities does the face and posture of the woman in this illustration bring to mind? [Possible responses: Grace, dignity, courage, determination.]

Fayette (1930s), by Eudora Welty. Photograph.
Eudora Welty Collection, Mississippi Department of Archives and History.

The path is the thing that matters.
—Eudora Welty

PRIMARY Sources | **AN ESSAY**

"Is Phoenix Jackson's Grandson Really Dead?"

A story writer is more than happy to be read by students; the fact that these serious readers think and feel something in response to his work he finds life-giving. At the same time he may not always be able to reply to their specific questions in kind. I wondered if it might clarify something, for both the questioners and myself, if I set down a general reply to the question that comes to me most often in the mail, from both students and their teachers, after some classroom discussion. The unrivaled favorite is this: "Is Phoenix Jackson's grandson really *dead*?"

. . . I had not meant to mystify readers by withholding any fact; it is not a writer's business to tease. The story is told through Phoenix's mind as she undertakes her errand. As the author at one with the character as I tell it, I must assume that the boy is alive. As the reader, you are free to think as you like, of course: The story invites you to believe that no matter what happens, Phoenix for as long as she is able to walk and can hold to her purpose

STRATEGIES FOR INCLUSION

Auditory Have students take turns reading the above essay aloud, using the KWL process: They divide a piece of paper into three columns and complete the "What do I know?" (K) and "What do I want to know?" (W) columns before reading. After the reading, students should discuss "What did I learn?" (L) and record their answers in the L column. Groups should share their insights with other groups.

Logical-Mathematical Have students develop a sentence outline of the above essay to help them categorize Welty's major ideas. Their outline should also include the thesis of the essay.

Courthouse steps, Fayette (1930s), by Eudora Welty. Photograph.

Eudora Welty Collection, Mississippi Department of Archives and History.

will make her journey. The *possibility* that she would keep on even if he were dead is there in her devotion and its single-minded, single-track errand. Certainly the *artistic* truth, which should be good enough for the fact, lies in Phoenix's own answer to that question. When the nurse asks, "He isn't dead, is he?" she speaks for herself: "He still the same. He going to last."

The grandchild is the incentive. But it is the journey, the going of the errand, that is the story, and the question is not whether the grandchild is in reality alive or dead. It doesn't affect the outcome of the story or its meaning from start to finish. But it is not the question itself that has struck me as much as the idea, almost without exception implied in the asking, that for Phoenix's grandson to be dead would somehow make the story "better."

. . . The grandson's plight was real and it made the truth of the story, which is the story of an errand of love carried out. If the child no longer lived, the truth would persist in the "wornness" of the path. But his being dead can't increase the truth of the story, can't affect it one way or the other. I think I signal this, because the end of the story has been reached before old Phoenix gets home again: she simply starts back. To the question "Is the grandson really dead?" I could reply that it doesn't make any difference. I could also say that I did not make him up in order to let him play a trick on Phoenix. But my best answer would be: "*Phoenix* is alive."

The origin of a story is sometimes a trustworthy clue to the author—or can provide him with the clue—to its key image; maybe in this case it will do the same for the reader. One day I saw a solitary old woman like Phoenix. She was walking; I saw her, at middle distance, in a winter country landscape, and watched her slowly make her way across my line of vision. That sight of her made me write the story. I invented an errand for her, but that only seemed a living part of the figure she was herself: What errand other than for someone else could be making her go? And her going was the first thing, her persisting in her landscape was the real thing, and the first and the real were what I wanted and worked to keep. I brought her up close enough, by imagination, to describe her face, make her present to the eyes, but the full-length figure moving across the winter fields was the indelible one and the image to keep, and the perspective extending into the vanishing distance the true one to hold in mind.

I invented for my character, as I wrote, some passing adventures—some dreams and harassments and a small triumph or two, some jolts to her pride, some flights of fancy to console her, one or two encounters to scare her, a moment that gave her cause to feel ashamed, a moment to dance and preen—for it had to be a *journey,* and all these things belonged to that, parts of life's uncertainty.

. . . What I hoped would come clear was that in the whole surround of this story, the world it threads through, the only certain thing at all is the worn path. The habit of love cuts through confusion and stumbles or contrives its way out of difficulty, it remembers the way even when it forgets, for a dumbfounded moment, its reason for being. The path is the thing that matters.

—Eudora Welty

Primary Sources

The essay gives students a rare opportunity to analyze an author's own explanation of a story's origin and meaning. Some schools of literary criticism would not place importance on Welty's comments about her story. Some critics would say that a reader can independently analyze the elements of the story to derive a meaning different from Welty's. Other critics would say that the experience of reading the text will be unique for each reader, and that these unique experiences are more important than what Welty intended. Have students discuss these viewpoints in light of their own experiences with literature.

Making Meanings questions begin on p. 642

Making Meanings

First Thoughts

1. Responses will vary. The story may seem too subtle to some.

Reviewing the Text

a. Phoenix travels from her country home to Natchez for medicine for her grandson. She faces obstacles of the terrain: walking uphill, crossing a creek on a log, getting through a barbed-wire fence, and fending off a dog.

b. She is successful; she gets the medicine and prepares to buy her grandson a gift.

Shaping Interpretations

2. The phoenix is a mythical bird that is periodically reborn from its own ashes; it is thus a symbol of renewal and regeneration. It is an appropriate name for the old woman who travels to town over and over again in an act of love and healing.

3. She is identified with time because of her great age. By comparing the wrinkles of Phoenix's forehead to a small tree, the author suggests natural growth.

4. The imagined encounter with the little boy offering marble-cake shows that Phoenix is polite and gracious. The questions she asks the buzzard indicate she is imaginative. The encounter with the scarecrow shows that she has a sense of humor. The encounter with the bush suggests that Phoenix is inclined to be optimistic and to look on the bright side of things. Finally, her encounter with the hunter shows that Phoenix is courageous, dignified, and a bit sly, as she creates a diversion so that she can pick up the dropped nickel.

5. It is ironic because the hunter suggests that Phoenix is going to town to see Santa Claus, a frivolous errand. In reality, Phoenix is on a difficult errand of love. Ageism or racism may explain her treatment.

6. Phoenix's act of charity is performed at great sacrifice, whereas the nurse equates charity with poverty.

Answers to Making Meanings begin on p. T641.

7. Students might recognize that the term implies a steady, long-term commitment filled with daily, often mundane, loving acts. The other images might suggest more recent or glamorous pathways.
8. Metaphorically, the title suggests the habitual path of love in Phoenix's mind and heart. This, in turn, suggests Welty's theme: The path of love—worn because it entails sacrifice and repetition—is open to all of us.

Beyond the Story

Choices: Building Your Portfolio

1. **Writer's Notebook** Remind students to save their work. They may use it as prewriting for the Writer's Workshop on p. 685.
2. **Critical Writing** Before students begin their essays, review with the class some of the similarities between Odysseus's quest and Phoenix's journey. Identify parts of the Odyssey that correspond to the lettered list in the activity description.
2. **Creative Writing** Review the distinction between **flat** and **round characters** and ask students to include details that make their characters seem real. Also, suggest that students choose a character name that suggests something about the character's personal qualities or **motivation**.

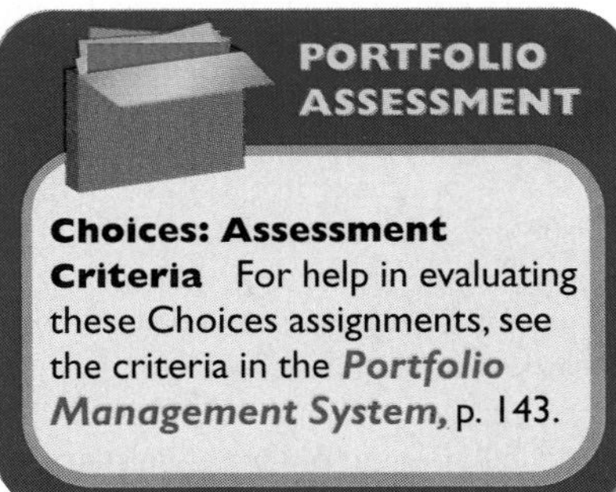

PORTFOLIO ASSESSMENT

Choices: Assessment Criteria For help in evaluating these Choices assignments, see the criteria in the ***Portfolio Management System,*** p. 143.

MAKING MEANINGS

First Thoughts

1. What was your first reaction to the story: "Good story!" or "I don't get it"—or another response? What questions do you have about the story?

Reviewing the Text

a. Describe the purpose of Phoenix Jackson's journey, and list the obstacles she overcomes.
b. At the end of Phoenix's perilous journey, does she get what she wants? Explain.

Shaping Interpretations

2. Why is Phoenix an appropriate name for the main character? (Review your Quickwrite notes.)
3. How do Welty's **descriptions** of Phoenix's appearance, speech, and behavior identify her with the world of nature and with time itself?
4. Describe what Phoenix's encounters with the little boy, the buzzard, the scarecrow, the thorny bush, and the hunter tell us about her **character.** Is she a heroine in the traditional sense of the word? Why or why not?
5. What is **ironic** about the reason the hunter suggests for Phoenix's long journey? Many people treat Phoenix in a condescending manner. Why would they do this?
6. When the nurse gives Phoenix the medicine, she says, "Charity," and makes a check mark in her book. Given the character of Phoenix, what is **ironic** about the nurse's statement and action?
7. Welty says that the worn path is a **metaphor** for the habit of love. Explain what Welty means by "the habit of love," and tell why this habit might be compared with a worn path (and not with a new road, or the shining path of a rocket, or a crystal stairway).
8. What do you consider Welty's major **theme** in "A Worn Path"? Put another way, what "worn path" is open to us all?

CHOICES: Building Your Portfolio

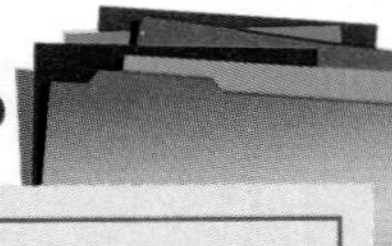

Writer's Notebook

1. Collecting Ideas for a Speculation About Causes and Effects

This story reveals in an indirect way the effects of racism and segregation. Take notes on what you can infer about the *effects* of segregation on people like Phoenix—and on the white hunter. Or, you might want to approach the situation from another perspective: Take notes on what you infer to be the *causes* of segregation in Phoenix's community—why would people want to separate themselves from other people? Save your notes for the Writer's Workshop on page 685.

Critical Writing

2. The Perils of the Journey

In her comment on the story (page 640), Welty summarizes the purposes of the adventures she invented for Phoenix. In an essay, identify the specific parts of the journey that can be characterized as **(a)** dreams, **(b)** harassments, **(c)** small triumphs, **(d)** some jolts to the traveler's pride, **(e)** some flights of fancy to console the traveler, **(f)** encounters to scare the traveler, **(g)** cause to be ashamed, and **(h)** a moment to dance and preen. In your essay, explain how Phoenix's journey takes on mythic significance. How is it like the quests of heroes like Odysseus or fairy-tale heroes and heroines?

Creative Writing

3. Another Worn Path

Write a story of your own about a person who travels a worn path over and over again without complaint. Open your story with a description of your setting: the time and place of the action. Let us see your main traveler as clearly as Welty shows us Phoenix. Your story may be fiction, or it may be based on fact.

STRATEGIES FOR INCLUSION

Advanced For activity #1, hold an informal debate. One group should argue that Phoenix's grandson is dead and the other group should argue that he is alive. In an informal debate, each group should collect support for their side and choose a spokesperson to present their case. After each side has argued the issue, conduct a question-and-answer period between each of the groups and then a brief summation from each spokesperson.

Learners Having Difficulty Before students begin activity # 3, ask them to list the details from the story that provide information about its setting. Then, have the class brainstorm various places or time periods they might research in the library. Finally, review with students the use of the reference materials that might help them in their research.

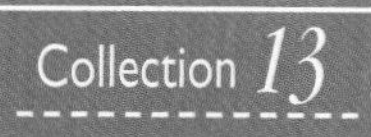

NO TIME FOR HEROES

Theme: **A Lost Generation**

Literature produced after World War I reflected mounting disillusionment with values and goals that had gone unquestioned in times past. As writers explored themselves and the people they observed, they created characters who were not courageous, active heroes, but shadowy antiheroes.

Thematic Focus

The protagonists of the selections in Collection 13 embody characteristics of the modern antihero.

- **Richard Cory** The speaker creates a profile of a man who has everything, but the ironic last line of the poem undercuts that illusion.
- **Miniver Cheevy** The poet describes a man who so longs for the distant past that he despises the present.
- **Soldier's Home** Harold Krebs returns home from World War I a disillusioned outsider without purpose.
- **The Love Song of J. Alfred Prufrock** The speaker of this modern monologue is a passive antihero.
- **The Life You Save May Be Your Own** Ideals of romance and heroism are turned upside down in this story of innocence confronted by evil.

Literary Focus

Literary Element	Selection / Feature
Dramatic Monologue	**The Love Song of J. Alfred Prufrock**
Foreshadowing/The Four "Modes" of Fiction	**The Life You Save May Be Your Own**

Writing Focus

The following chart shows how the writing assignment for each selection relates to and builds toward the culminating writing assignment presented in the Writer's Workshop at the end of the unit.

Selection	Work-in-Progress Assignment
Richard Cory/Miniver Cheevy	List possible causes for a speculation about causes and effects p. 649
Soldier's Home	Freewrite on the protagonist's future for a speculation about causes and effects p. 660
The Love Song of J. Alfred Prufrock	Speculate on causes of Prufrock's isolation and paralysis p. 671
The Life You Save May Be Your Own	Speculate about causes for not writing about great heroes p. 684
Writer's Workshop	Write a persuasive essay about causes and effects pp. 685–689

Collection Planner

SELECTION / FEATURE	PUPIL'S EDITION			
	Literary Elements / Active Reading	Writing	Speaking and Listening	Language and Vocabulary
Richard Cory **Miniver Cheevy** Edwin Arlington Robinson (pp. 644–649) Primary Sources: Robinson's Ruminations (p. 648)	• Reader's Log pp. 645, 646	• Critical Writing: Write essay p. 649 • Creative Writing/ Performance: Write dramatic monologue p. 649	• Creative Writing/ Performance: Present dramatic monologue p. 649	
Soldier's Home Ernest Hemingway (pp. 650–660) Primary Sources: Nobel Prize Acceptance Speech, 1954 (p. 659)	• Reader's Log p. 652	• Critical Writing: Write essay p. 660 • Critical Writing: Write explanatory essay p. 660 • Creative Writing/ Performance: Write script p. 660	• Creative Writing/ Performance: Perform scripted discussion p. 660	
The Love Song of J. Alfred Prufrock T. S. Eliot (pp. 661–671) Critical Comment (p. 668)	• Reader's Log p. 663 • Dramatic Monologue p. 663	• Critical Writing: Write essay in response p. 671 • Critical Writing: Write comparative essay p. 671 • Creative Writing: Write dramatic monologue p. 671 • Critical Writing: Write essay p. 671 • Creative Writing/ Performance: Write dialogue p. 671	• Creative Writing/ Performance: Present dialogue p. 671	• Language and Style: Rhythm, Rhymes, Metaphors, and Allusions p. 670
The Life You Save May Be Your Own Flannery O'Connor (pp. 672–684) Primary Sources: The Adventures of Mr. Shiftlet (p. 682)	• Reader's Log p. 673 • Foreshadowing p. 673 • Tragedy p. 683 • Comedy p. 683 • Romance p. 683 • Irony pp. 683-684	• Critical Writing: Write essay p. 684 • Creative Writing: Write epilogue p. 684 • Creative Writing/Art: Write motto p. 684	• Critical Thinking/ Speaking and Listening: Lead analytical discussion p. 684	
Writer's Workshop: Speculating About Causes and Effects (pp. 685–689)		• Writing process: Speculating about causes and effects (pp. 685–689)		
Language Workshop: Showing Relationships: Using Subordinating Conjunctions (p. 690)				• Subordination p. 690

Collection Resources

Teaching Resources B	Audiovisual Resources Binder	Test Booklet
Cross-Curricular Activity p. 68	Fine Art Transparency 13.1	Collection 13 Test pp. 158–160

 Computer disk or CD-ROM

 Audiocassette

 Overhead Transparency

PROGRAM RESOURCES

Electronic Media	Teaching Resources with Organizer		Audiovisual Resources Binder
	Teaching Resources B	Other Resources	
• Test Generator	• Teaching Notes pp. 51–52 • Reading Organizers pp. 55–56	• Test Booklet: Selection Test pp. 151–152 • Portfolio Management System pp. 39, 144	• Selected Reading Audiocassette 2, Side B
• Language Workshop: Wordiness • Test Generator	• Teaching Notes p. 52 • Reading Organizer p. 57 • Language Link pp. 58–59 • Words to Own p. 60	• Test Booklet: Selection Test pp. 153–154 • Language and Writing Skills Worksheets p. 107 • Portfolio Management System pp. 48-49, 145	
• Test Generator	• Teaching Notes p. 53 • Reading Organizer p. 61	• Test Booklet: Selection Test p. 155 • Portfolio Management System pp.53, 146-147	
• Language Workshop: Usage • Test Generator	• Teaching Notes pp. 53–54 • Reading Organizer p. 62 • Language Link p. 63–64 • Words to Own p. 65	• Test Booklet: Selection Test pp. 156–157 • Language and Writing Skills Worksheets pp. 1–2, 6–8 • Portfolio Management System pp. 54-55, 148, 149	• Selected Reading Audiocassette 3, Side A • Elements of Literature Transparency 13.2
• Writer's Workshop 2: Cause and Effect		• Portfolio Management System pp. 150–152	• Revision Transparencies 13.3–13.4
• Language Workshop: Subordinating conjunctions	• Language Workshop pp. 66–67	• Language and Writing Skills Worksheets p. 98	

Proofreading Warm-ups

You may use the following exercises to help students practice their proofreading skills. Copy a set of incorrect sentences onto the chalkboard, and have students find and correct the spelling, punctuation, usage, and mechanical errors in each sentence. Ask students to share and discuss their responses.

	Sentences with Errors	Sentences Corrected	Skills Covered
1	**a.** solitery by temperment poet Edwin Arlington Robinson mostley kept to hisself **b.** one of the poets fans were president Theodore Roosevelt	**a.** Solitary by temperament, poet Edwin Arlington Robinson mostly kept to himself. **b.** One of the poet's fans was President Theodore Roosevelt.	Capitalization, Spelling, Comma usage, Pronouns (reflexive), Apostrophes (possessives), Agreement (subject-verb), End marks
2	**a.** are people allways what they seem, in all ways **b.** a hippocrite is someone that say one thing and do an other	**a.** Are people always what they seem, in all ways? **b.** A hypocrite is someone that says one thing and does another.	Capitalization, Spelling, Agreement (subject-verb), End marks
3	**a.** liz use to live in a small, new england town **b.** forshadowing is a tecknike that creates suspence by giving suttle hints of whats to come	**a.** Liz used to live in a small New England town. **b.** Foreshadowing is a technique that creates suspense by giving subtle hints of what's to come.	Capitalization, Nonstandard usage, Comma errors, Spelling, Apostrophes (contractions), End marks
4	**a.** an avid hunter fisherman and aventurer writer Ernest Hemingway became nown for his exiting life **b.** in the 1960's the songwriting team of simon and garfunkel perform a song inspired by the poem Richard Cory	**a.** An avid hunter, fisherman, and adventurer, writer Ernest Hemingway became known for his exciting life. **b.** In the 1960s, the songwriting team of Simon and Garfunkel performed a song inspired by the poem "Richard Cory."	Capitalization, Comma usage, Spelling, Apostrophe errors, Verb tense consistency, Titles, End marks
5	**a.** the transendentalists championned ideals of self relianse and indevidulism **b.** emily rased her hand and ansered ms. Chongs question confidantly	**a.** The Transcendentalists championed ideals of self-reliance and individualism. **b.** Emily raised her hand and answered Ms. Chong's question confidently.	Capitalization, Spelling, Hyphens, Apostrophes (possessives), End marks
6	**a.** some novels begin with a quoting, or epigraph **b.** hemingway's prose stile is caracterized by short sentences	**a.** Some novels begin with a quotation, or epigraph. **b.** Hemingway's prose style is characterized by short sentences.	Capitalization, Noun form, Spelling, End marks
7	**a.** Shiftlets' mother in law ought to of been carefuller **b.** theres a prestige literary prize for short stories named in honor of the writer Flannery O'connor	**a.** Shiftlet's mother-in-law ought to have been more careful. **b.** There's a prestigious literary prize for short stories named in honor of the writer Flannery O'Connor.	Capitalization, Apostrophe errors, Hyphen usage, Nonstandard usage, Adjectives (comparative, form), End marks
8	**a.** some critisize Flannery o'connors' work for it's vilent imagrey **b.** like the caracters she created the author lived in The South	**a.** Some criticize Flannery O'Connor's work for its violent imagery. **b.** Like the characters she created, the author lived in the South.	Capitalization, Spelling, Apostrophe errors, Comma usage, End marks
9	**a.** is kim custumed as a flapper from the 20s **b.** world war one effected a generation's out-look	**a.** Is Kim costumed as a flapper from the 1920s? **b.** World War I affected a generation's outlook.	Capitalization, Spelling, Abbreviation/Usage, Numeral usage, Hyphen errors, End marks
10	**a.** even if niether of the actors show up," said the directer we will go ahaed with the performance" **b.** don't nobody know where the theater is at	**a.** "Even if neither of the actors shows up," said the director, "we will go ahead with the performance." **b.** Doesn't anybody know where the theater is?	Punctuating quotations, Capitalization, Spelling, Agreement (subject-verb), Double negatives, Nonstandard usage, End marks

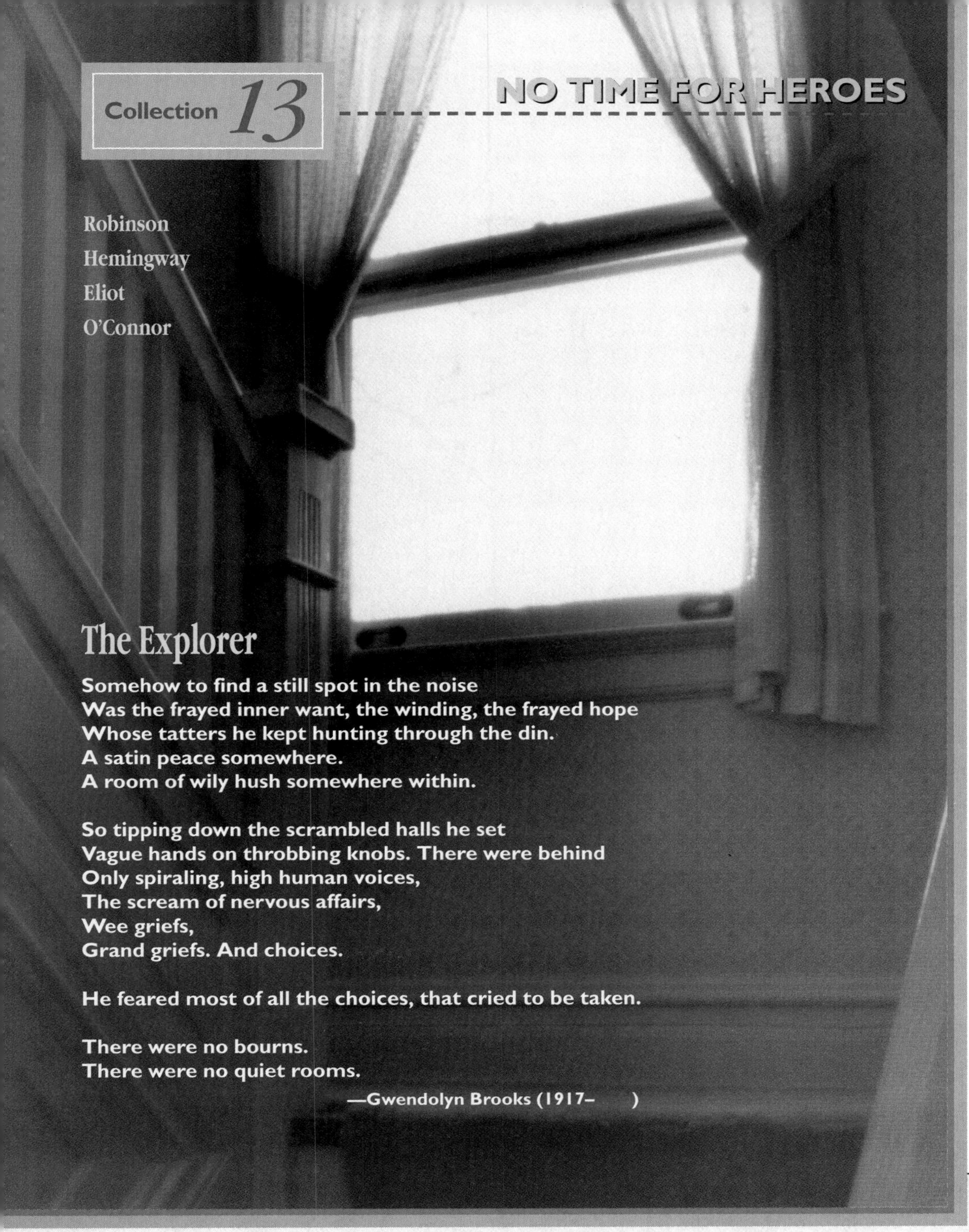

Collection 13

NO TIME FOR HEROES

Robinson
Hemingway
Eliot
O'Connor

The Explorer

Somehow to find a still spot in the noise
Was the frayed inner want, the winding, the frayed hope
Whose tatters he kept hunting through the din.
A satin peace somewhere.
A room of wily hush somewhere within.

So tipping down the scrambled halls he set
Vague hands on throbbing knobs. There were behind
Only spiraling, high human voices,
The scream of nervous affairs,
Wee griefs,
Grand griefs. And choices.

He feared most of all the choices, that cried to be taken.

There were no bourns.
There were no quiet rooms.

—Gwendolyn Brooks (1917–   )

"The Explorer"
Inform students that the term *bourns* is an archaic term for "limits" or "boundaries" and can also refer to a small stream or rivulet. As the world becomes increasingly chaotic and full of tension, people have difficulty determining an identity or establishing clear-cut definitions of *heroism*. In Brooks's poem, what is the explorer looking for? [Possible responses: A quiet place, peace, and relief from making choices.] What themes might this poem introduce? [Possible response: The stories and poems in this Collection may focus on the difficulties people face in dealing with society's pressures or in coping with making hard choices. There may be no heroes in modern life, or *heroism* may be redefined or may no longer exist in modern society.]

Parent/Guardian Involvement For forms that will help a parent or guardian review and respond to a student's portfolio, see the ***Portfolio Management System,*** pp. 62–63.

PROGRAM MANAGER

- **Integrated Assessment** For a summative assessment of the literature and language skills taught in this collection, see **Collection 13 Test, *Test Booklet,*** pp. 158–160.
- **Instructional Support** See **Fine Art Transparency** 13.1. Review teacher's notes for transparencies in the ***Audiovisual Resources Binder*** for suggestions on how to tie the transparencies to specific reading selections.
- **Extending Collection Theme** See **Cross-Curricular Activity: No Time for Heroes, *Teaching Resources B,*** p. 68, for an activity in other disciplines and for evaluation criteria.

QUICK PLANNING GUIDE

Into the Poems

Through the Poems

Beyond the Poems

- **Writer's Notebook:** Collect ideas for a speculation about causes and effects
- **Critical Writing:** Write an essay comparing and contrasting characters to ideals
- **Creative Writing/Performance:** Write and present a dramatic monologue

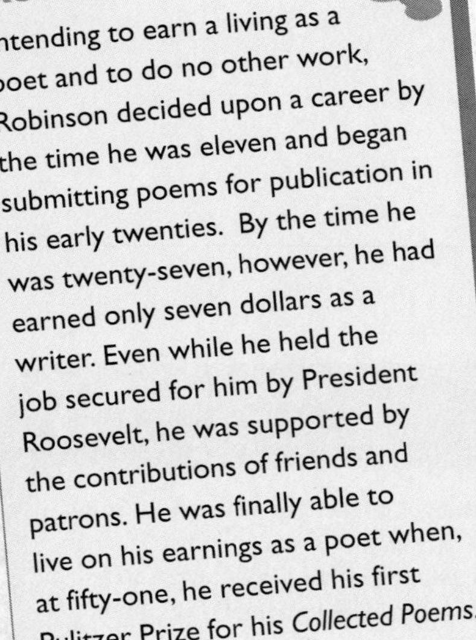

ABOUT THE AUTHOR

Intending to earn a living as a poet and to do no other work, Robinson decided upon a career by the time he was eleven and began submitting poems for publication in his early twenties. By the time he was twenty-seven, however, he had earned only seven dollars as a writer. Even while he held the job secured for him by President Roosevelt, he was supported by the contributions of friends and patrons. He was finally able to live on his earnings as a poet when, at fifty-one, he received his first Pulitzer Prize for his *Collected Poems.*

Edwin Arlington Robinson

(1869–1935)

By the 1890s, the vitality of the nineteenth century seemed exhausted, and the gathering forces of modernism were still scattered and obscure. Between 1890 and 1910, many poets were churning out the same old rhymes and meters of Romanticism. But in those two decades, one voice spoke out in traditional forms enlivened with an authentic, contemporary American accent: the voice of Edwin Arlington Robinson.

The strengths that distinguish Robinson are his native voice and his wise and ironic view of human behavior. Robinson's bedrock realism informs even the most formal of his carefully wrought poems. In some of his poetic portraits of individuals, he anticipates by a decade the more loosely drawn portraits found in Edgar Lee Masters's *Spoon River Anthology* (page 692). In his skill with meter, Robinson foreshadows Robert Frost's gift for bending the strictly counted line to accommodate the ease and flow of vernacular speech.

Robinson was a Yankee from the rocky coast of Maine. Born at Head Tide in 1869, he lived for the next twenty-seven years in the town of Gardiner, except for the two years when he attended Harvard as a special student. Gardiner became the Tilbury Town of his poems, the home of some of his most famous characters. When he was in his late twenties, Robinson moved to New York City and published his first book. There he supported himself at various jobs, including one as a timekeeper at the construction site of the new subway system.

After a year of such work, Robinson's fortunes took a surprising turn for the better. Among the young poet's readers was none other than the president of the United States, Theodore Roosevelt. When Roosevelt learned that the poet he admired was barely scraping by on a laborer's salary, he arranged to have the New York Custom House hire him as a clerk, a position Robinson held for almost five years. One year after Robinson resigned, he published *The Town Down the River* (1910) and dedicated the volume to Roosevelt.

AP/Wide World Photos.

Another form of assistance came in an invitation from the famous MacDowell Colony in Peterborough, New Hampshire. The colony was a center for composers, artists, and writers, established by the widow of the American composer Edward MacDowell. There Robinson spent long, working summers for the greater part of his life.

Robinson, a loner by temperament, became an increasingly popular poet. Even in a modernist age, Robinson's poetry, which was traditional in form, continued to be read and admired, and he was awarded the Pulitzer Prize three times. At the time of his death, Robinson's reputation had survived the tide of modernism that had once threatened to wash it away.

PROGRAM MANAGER

- **Planning Instruction** See Teaching Notes, *Teaching Resources B,* pp. 51–52, for objectives, a summary, literary elements, and additional biographical information.
- **Instructional Support** Before beginning the lesson, see Graphic Organizer for Active Reading, *Teaching Resources B,* pp. 55–56, for Into the Poem activities.
- **Audiotaped Readings** To help less proficient readers or auditory learners through the lesson, use the Selected Reading, Audiocassette 2, Side B, in the *Audiovisual Resources Binder.*
- **Assessment** See Selection Test, *Test Booklet,* pp. 151–152.

Before You Read
Richard Cory

Reading Focus

Things Aren't Always What They Seem

One of the persistent themes of early-twentieth-century American poetry is that the conventions of small-town life are a façade that often obscures unpleasant realities. In this famous poem, which contains a harsh, surprise ending, an unidentified speaker tells what happened to a prominent citizen.

A Dialogue with the Text

When you have finished reading the poem, write down your thoughts about what "real" story remains untold about Richard Cory.

Winter Twilight (1930) by Charles Burchfield. Oil on composition board (27 3/4" × 30 1/2").

Collection of Whitney Museum of American Art, New York.

Richard Cory

Edwin Arlington Robinson

Whenever Richard Cory went downtown,
We people on the pavement looked at him:
He was a gentleman from sole to crown,
Clean favored, and imperially slim.

And he was always quietly arrayed,
And he was always human when he talked;
But still he fluttered pulses when he said,
"Good morning," and he glittered when he walked.

And he was rich—yes, richer than a king—
And admirably schooled in every grace:
In fine, we thought that he was everything
To make us wish that we were in his place. **A**

So on we worked, and waited for the light, **B**
And went without the meat, and cursed the bread;
And Richard Cory, one calm summer night,
Went home and put a bullet through his head.

Into the Poem

Using BEFORE YOU READ p. 645

Reading Focus

Ask students to brainstorm works of literature or movies in which a pleasant façade is torn away to reveal something unexpected.

Through the Poem

A. Reader's Response: Shaping Interpretations

? What assumptions do people make about Richard Cory because he is wealthy? [Sample responses: They assume that he has everything; in fact, they wish they were in his place; or because he has a lot of money, they think he is happy.]

B. Language Note: Connotations

Glittered in l. 8 may mean "dispensing light." How does use of this word in l. 8 contrast with the word *light* in l. 13? [Cory gives off light, the word *glittered* in l. 8 perhaps symbolizing success, by walking. The townspeople, on the other hand, must struggle for the light.]

Options for Teaching

Strategies for Inclusion

Special Needs If possible, have students who have difficulty with sound discrimination and word decoding listen with headphones to an audiotape of one of the poems as they highlight specific information. For example, have students place a blank transparency sheet over the poem "Richard Cory" in their books. As the students listen to the tape, have them highlight with a colored marker the words that describe outward appearances.

Visual Have students create a visual representation of Richard Cory or Miniver Cheevy. Students may use magazine clippings or create original artwork. Have students explain to the class how their visual reflects Robinson's image of Cory or Cheevy.

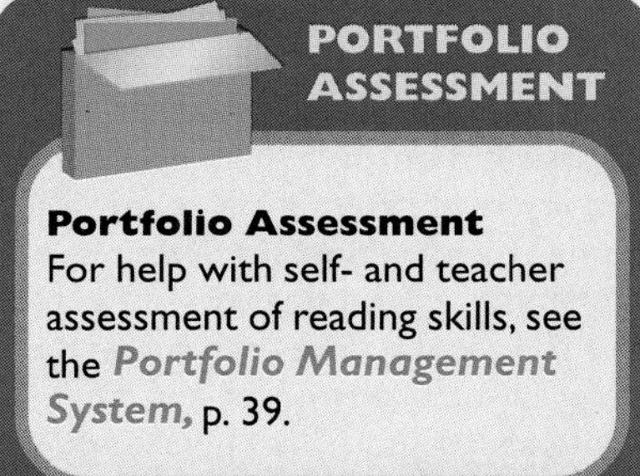

Portfolio Assessment

Portfolio Assessment

For help with self- and teacher assessment of reading skills, see the *Portfolio Management System*, p. 39.

Into the Poem

Using **BEFORE YOU READ** p. 646

Reading Focus

Ask students to brainstorm what people might find charming about bygone days and what might make those people wish they lived then instead of now.

A Dialogue with the Text

Ask students, when they have finished reading, to list important negative aspects of the past that Miniver Cheevy overlooks.

Through the Poem

A. Literary Elements: Rhyme and Meter

? Would you describe the rhyme and meter as regular or irregular? [Very regular.] How does this singsong quality affect your expectations of the poem? [Possible answer: Such poems are usually comic rather than tragic.] Based on your reading of "Richard Cory," do you think that this poet is likely to compose a comic poem? [No, the poet is likely to have something serious in store for us.]

BEFORE YOU READ
MINIVER CHEEVY

Reading Focus

Long Ago and Far Away

The glory and glamour of bygone days hold an irresistible charm for many people. But sometimes a longing for the past makes people sorely disappointed with the present.

A Dialogue with the Text

READER'S LOG

As you read the poem, list Miniver Cheevy's reasons for loving the past and for feeling he was "born too late."

Background

The title of this poem is not simply a man's name: It contains a clue to the poem's meaning. "Miniver" is the white fur trim, sometimes ermine, seen on the costumes of royalty in medieval and Renaissance portraits. The subjects of such portraits include rich and powerful members of the Medici family of Renaissance Italy. Other references in the poem also evoke heroic eras of the past.

Miniver Cheevy

Edwin Arlington Robinson

(A)
Miniver Cheevy, child of scorn,
  Grew lean while he assailed the seasons;
He wept that he was ever born,
  And he had reasons.

Miniver loved the days of old
  When swords were bright and steeds were prancing:
The vision of a warrior bold
  Would set him dancing.

Miniver sighed for what was not,
  And dreamed, and rested from his labors;
He dreamed of Thebes° and Camelot,°
  And Priam's° neighbors.

Miniver mourned the ripe renown
  That made so many a name so fragrant;
He mourned Romance, now on the town,°
  And Art, a vagrant.

11. Thebes: city in ancient Greece associated with several myths. **Camelot:** legendary site of King Arthur's court.
12. Priam's: In Homer's epic poem *The Iliad,* Priam (prī′əm) is the king of Troy during the Trojan War.
15. on the town: dependent on charity.

OPTIONS FOR TEACHING

STRATEGIES FOR INCLUSION

Kinesthetic To help students focus their attention, have them do a tactile activity in which they can be involved in some type of action. For example, have students work on one verse in pairs or in small groups. Give each student a different-colored marker and some sentence strips (24" x 4" pieces of poster board for sentences to be run lengthwise and to be seen when displayed), and have them write each rhyming line on a separate strip with the same colored marker. Have students read the poem aloud. As their line is read they should hold up their strip. Students will also get practice identifying rhyming words.

English Language Development Timed reading is a practice technique that can help readers increase their reading speed. While this technique is usually used with prose reading, the structure of "Richard Cory" and "Miniver Cheevy" leads the reader quickly to the end, and curiosity about where the poems are going will help motivate students to read quickly. Set a reasonable time limit for each poem, based on students' skill level. An approximate judgment of level indicates that reading time of twenty-five wpm (words per minute) or less is basic reading, twenty-five to fifty wpm is beginning level, seventy-five wpm is intermediate, and one hundred wpm or more is advanced.

The Sentimental Yearner (1936) by Grant Wood. Pencil, black and white conté crayon, painted white around image.

RESPONDING TO THE ART: ABOUT THE ARTIST

Grant Wood (1892–1942), an American painter, began his career painting camouflage in World War I. After spending a year at the Académie Julian in Paris, he returned home to Iowa. A mortician provided him with a studio and living space. Wood painted coldly realisitic portrayals of rural life. Some of his early works were not very successful, but *American Gothic* caused quite a stir when it was exhibited in Chicago in 1930.

Technology Tip

In response to "Richard Cory," ask students to research the incidence of suicide in the United States. They may want to consult with sociologists via e-mail to discover the underlying causes of suicide. Similarly, they may wish to have a psychologist or psychiatrist evaluate Richard Cory's case based solely on what is known about him from the poem. Finally, they may wish to inquire what may help people with clinical depression today.

INTEGRATING THE LANGUAGE ARTS

Strategic Reading Have students in groups of four present an oral reading of "Richard Cory" or "Miniver Cheevy." Give students advance notice and time to practice. Assign each student an equal number of stanzas to read aloud.

Writing: Advice Column Have students write a letter in response to Cheevy as though they were advice columnists. Ask them to advise Cheevy on how to free himself from nostalgic thoughts. Be sure students refer to the poem in their letters.

CROSSING THE CURRICULUM

Music Have students compare Robinson's "Richard Cory" to Simon and Garfunkel's song of the same name. Give each student a copy of the words to the song; then, play it for the class. Ask students to point out the similarities and differences between the song and the poem. Then, ask students to discuss which version they preferred.

History Have students research and report on some of the following historical allusions in "Miniver Cheevy": Thebes, Priam, the Medici, medieval armor, Camelot, chivalry. Students should present the information as though they were people from the time period.

A. Critical Reading: Making Inferences

? What might Cheevy feel is missing in his life? [Possible answers: Heroism, romance, beauty.]

Metacognition How did you arrive at your answer? [Possible answer: The speaker makes references to Thebes, Camelot, Priam, and the Medici. These words called up prior knowledge from past courses I have taken and from books I have read.]

B. Reader's Response: Shaping Interpretations

? Why do you suppose the poet reveals Cheevy's drinking only in the final stanza? [Sample responses: To increase the effect on the reader of Cheevy's drinking to cope with his lot in life. Or the speaker first shows why Cheevy drinks so that the reader will understand Cheevy's behavior.]

Primary Sources

Ask students to work in pairs, speculating on what Edith Brower might have written to Robinson that prompted the second excerpt. Ask them to speculate about Brower's reasons for disliking "Richard Cory." Have them write a letter from Brower based on their guesses. You might have them read "Reuben Bright" before they write. The poem focuses on Bright's grief upon his wife's death.

Miniver loved the Medici,°
    Albeit° he had never seen one;
He would have sinned incessantly
    Could he have been one.

Miniver cursed the commonplace
    And eyed a khaki suit with loathing;
He missed the medieval grace
    Of iron clothing.°

Miniver scorned the gold he sought,
    But sore annoyed was he without it;
Miniver thought, and thought, and thought,
    And thought about it.

Miniver Cheevy, born too late,
    Scratched his head and kept on thinking;
Miniver coughed, and called it fate,
    And kept on drinking.

17. Medici (med′ə chē′): members of a powerful Italian family of the fourteenth to sixteenth centuries. They were famous for their wealth, their sponsorship of the arts, and their control of the city of Florence.
18. albeit (ôl·bē′it): even though. The word combines and condenses "although it be."

24. iron clothing: armor worn by medieval knights.

PRIMARY **Sources** LETTERS

Robinson's Ruminations

I've written a nice little thing called "Richard Cory"—"Whenever Richard Cory went downtown, we people on the pavement looked at him . . . And Richard Cory, one calm summer night, went home and put a bullet through his head." There isn't any idealism in it, but there's lots of something else—humanity, maybe.

. . .

Why don't you like "Richard Cory"? You say it makes you feel cold, but that statement doesn't seem to agree with my impression of your character. It can't be you are squeamish after all. If you are, don't read "Reuben Bright" or he will knock you down. I used to read about clearness, force, and elegance in the rhetoric books, but I'm afraid I go in chiefly for force. So you will not be offended if I'm not always elegant. There are too many elegant men in the world just now, and they seem to be increasing.

. . .

I don't have trances, furors, or ecstasies. My poetic spells are of the most prosaic sort. I just sit down and grind it out and use a trifle more tobacco than is good for me.

. . .

You may call me anything you like—anything but Eddie. I had an aunt who called me Eddie and now she doesn't call me at all.

—Edwin Arlington Robinson,
from Letters to Edith Brower

STRATEGIES FOR INCLUSION

Less Proficient Readers Preview some of the more difficult vocabulary before students read the Primary Sources feature. Some of these words include *idealism, squeamish, rhetoric, trances, furors, ecstasies, prosaic,* and *trifle.*

English Language Development Lead a brief discussion contrasting Edith Brower's reaction to "Richard Cory" and Edwin Arlington Robinson's defense of the poem. Ask students whether they agree with Brower (that the poem is cold) or with Robinson (that the poem has humanity in it). Invite them to consider whether they have ever known anyone like Richard Cory, who appears to have everything but is very unhappy.

MAKING MEANINGS

Richard Cory

First Thoughts

1. How did you respond to the ending of the poem?

Shaping Interpretations

2. What is **ironic** in the fact that Richard Cory takes his own life?
3. Find five words or phrases in "Richard Cory" that connote kingliness or royalty. How does the poet's choice of these words contribute to the contrast between the townspeople and Richard Cory?
4. What aspects of Richard Cory's life are *not* mentioned? How might these hidden or overlooked areas account for his fate? Review the notes you made in your Reader's Log to explain your answer.
5. Read Robinson's comments on "Richard Cory" (page 648). What do you think he means when he says there is a lot of "humanity" in the poem? Why do you think it made his correspondent feel "cold"? How did it make you feel?

Miniver Cheevy

First Thoughts

1. Review the notes you made in your Reader's Log. What were your thoughts or feelings about Cheevy and his attitude toward life?

Shaping Interpretations

2. Do Cheevy's problems really stem from his having been "born too late"? Explain. How does the disappointed Cheevy cope with his lot in life?
3. "Romance" and "Art" are **personified** in the fourth stanza. What does Cheevy think has happened to romance and art in his own time?
4. How would you describe the change of **tone** in the last stanza? How does this change affect the poem's meaning?

Extending the Text

5. Explain whether or not you think the tales of Richard Cory and Miniver Cheevy have a moral or message for us today. Where can you find Corys and Cheevys in today's world?

CHOICES: Building Your Portfolio

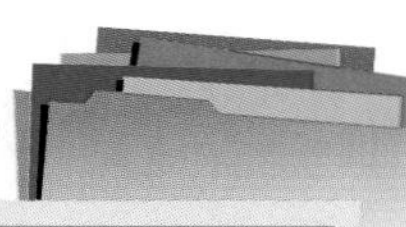

Writer's Notebook

1. Collecting Ideas for a Speculation About Causes and Effects

WORK IN PROGRESS

Why does Richard Cory kill himself? Why does Miniver Cheevy suffer so much? Brainstorm a list of causes you could speculate on to answer these questions. With each cause, list details from the poem that might support your speculation. Save your notes for possible use in the Writer's Workshop on page 685.

Critical Writing

2. Lives of Quiet Desperation?

Robinson has been described as "a sober Transcendentalist who dealt primarily with the ethical conflicts within the individual." In a brief essay, show how either Richard Cory or Miniver Cheevy demonstrates, or fails to demonstrate, the Transcendentalist ideals of self-reliance and individualism championed by Emerson (page 216) and Thoreau (page 230). As the focus of your essay, choose an appropriate quotation from either of these Transcendentalist writers.

Creative Writing / Performance

3. From Page to Stage

In prose or verse, let Richard Cory tell his own story in the first person. Reveal the reasons for Cory's unhappiness and his true thoughts about the townspeople. Then, present his story to the class in a dramatic monologue. (For more on dramatic monologue, see page 663 and the Handbook of Literary Terms.)

"Miniver Cheevy"

First Thoughts

1. Possible responses: Other people also idealize the past; or why did he not try to find something to focus on in the present?

Shaping Interpretations

2. Possible responses: No, no matter when he lived, he would be wanting something else. Or yes, some people just are not in touch with the times and would fit better in a different era. He sighs, makes money, and drinks too much.
3. He may think that they have been neglected.
4. It is only in the last stanza that the reader learns Cheevy's health is deteriorating. Robinson combines the irony of previous stanzas with a note of sympathy in the last stanza.

Extending the Text

5. **(Synthesis)** Responses will vary. The moral of "Richard Cory" might be that appearances can be deceiving. People today still can be fooled by appearances. The moral of "Miniver Cheevy" might be to grow where you are planted. Corys today include people who are successful but unhappy. Cheevys today could be people who are frightened by technology.

Choices: Building Your Portfolio

1. **Writer's Notebook** Remind students to save their work. They may use it as prewriting for the Writer's Workshop on p. 685.

Making Meanings "Richard Cory"

First Thoughts

1. Possible responses: I was shocked. Or after reading the Reading Focus, I expected something bad to happen, so I was not surprised.

Shaping Interpretations

2. Cory seems to have everything, yet he is inwardly unhappy. There is also an ironic contrast between the calm night and his sudden, violent act.
3. *Crown, imperially, arrayed, glittered, rich, king, grace.* The connotations of royalty contrast with the connotations of the commonplace nature of the words that characterize the townspeople: *downtown, pavement, meat,* and *bread.*
4. Possible responses: His work, home, friends, parents, and whether he has a wife or children. Perhaps he has some deep personal trouble that makes him miserable. He may have no friends or family and so is lonely.
5. Possible response: That people see only Cory's success, but do not see his pain. She may not have liked the abruptness of the last lines. It made me feel sorry for Cory.

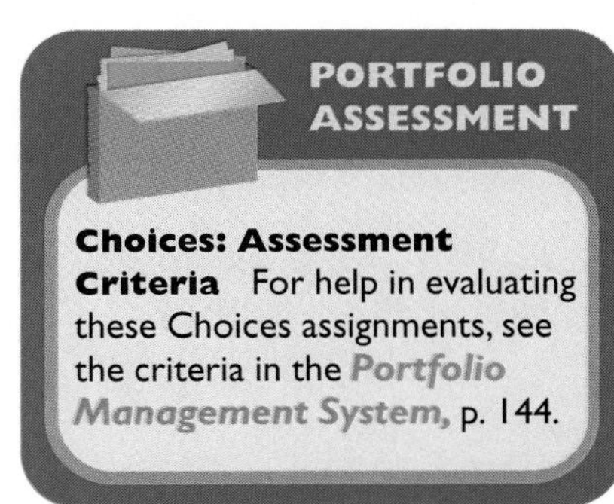

PORTFOLIO ASSESSMENT

Choices: Assessment Criteria For help in evaluating these Choices assignments, see the criteria in the *Portfolio Management System,* p. 144.

WRITERS ON WRITING

Hemingway's comments on writing "the truest sentence" came in a discussion of what some call writer's block: "Sometimes when I was starting a new story and I could not get it going, I would sit in front of the fire and squeeze the peel of the little oranges into the edge of the flame and watch the sputter of blue that they made. I would stand and look out over the roofs of Paris and think, 'Do not worry. You have always written before and you will write now. All you have to do is write one true sentence. Write the truest sentence that you know.' So finally I would write one true sentence, and then go on from there. It was easy then because there was always one true sentence that I knew or had seen or had heard someone say."

Technology Tip

The Ernest M. Hemingway Home Page is sponsored by the University of Florida's English Department. The Web site address is **http://www.afn.org~afn27906/hem.html**. *You may want to preview any Internet activity that you suggest to students. Because these resources are sometimes public forums, their content can be unpredictable.*

Ernest Hemingway

(1899–1961)

Karsh/Woodfin Camp and Associates.

Few American authors have offered as powerful a definition of the twentieth-century hero as Ernest Hemingway has. Hemingway's fiction presents a strict code of contemporary heroism. His vision centers on disillusionment with the conventions of an optimistic, patriotic society and a belief that the essence of life is violence, from which there is no refuge. As Hemingway saw it, the only victory that can be won from life lies in a graceful stoicism, a willingness to accept gratefully life's few moments of pleasure.

Although this image of rugged machismo now seems radically oversimplified, it powerfully affected generations of American readers. Moreover, Hemingway launched a new style of writing so forceful in its simplicity that it became a measure of excellence around the world.

Hemingway's life, like F. Scott Fitzgerald's, bore a notable resemblance to the lives of his fictional characters. He was born in the Chicago suburb of Oak Park on July 21, 1899. His father, a doctor, initiated him early into a love for the Michigan woods and the hunting and fishing that could be found there. Growing up, Hemingway boxed and played football devotedly, but he also wrote poetry, short stories, and a column for the school newspaper. Graduating from high school just as the United States entered World War I in 1917, he yearned to enlist, but he was rejected by the army because of a boxing injury to his eye. He landed a job as a reporter for the *Kansas City Star.* Hemingway reached the war a year later as an ambulance driver for the Red Cross in Italy, but after six weeks he was wounded in the knee, seriously enough to require a dozen operations. This wound was a central episode in both Hemingway's real and creative life. During his long convalescence in an Italian hospital, he fell in love with a nurse who became the model for the heroine of his novel *A Farewell to Arms.*

After the armistice in 1918, Hemingway returned to Michigan. His experience of coming to terms with the war is reflected in his story "Big Two-Hearted River." In the story, Nick Adams, a war veteran, camps and fishes alone in the woods, escaping from the world in order to heal himself from both a physical and psychological shattering.

An American in Paris

In 1921, newly married and with a commission as a roving reporter for the *Toronto Star,* Hemingway set off for Paris. It was the era of the American expatriates, when writers and painters crowded the cafes of the Left Bank of the Seine. Here Hemingway worked at the craft of fiction and met other important writers, among them F. Scott Fitzgerald, James Joyce, and Ezra Pound. But most important, he met the American writer Gertrude Stein (1874–1946). She read all his work and advised him to prune his descriptions and to "concentrate." Hemingway took her advice and spoke fervently of writing "the truest sentence that you know," and of arriving through straight presentation of unvarnished fact at a "true, simple declarative sentence."

Hemingway's first book, *Three Stories and Ten Poems* (1923), along with *The Torrents of Spring* (1926), a parody of his friend Sherwood Anderson's work, drew scant notice. Then, late in 1926, he published *The Sun Also Rises,* a novel based on his life in Paris but transplanted to Pamplona, the Spanish town famous for its annual running of the bulls through the streets. The novel brought Hemingway widespread critical attention on both sides of the Atlantic. Gertrude Stein's remark, "You are all a lost generation," was the novel's epigraph, or opening quotation, and the book did reveal the postwar epoch to itself. Many American readers of Hemingway's age embraced it as a portrait of their shattered lives.

Hemingway, around thirty years old and married for the second time, went on to write an even more powerful and successful novel, *A Farewell to Arms* (1929). This is the moving story of a wounded ambulance driver, disillusioned with the war, who falls in love with an English nurse and flees with her to Switzerland, where she dies in childbirth. The novel contains one of the most famous passages in American fiction, juxtaposing the writer's cynicism about the human experience with the characters' romantic love.

Author and Adventurer

After the major success of *A Farewell to Arms,* Hemingway established himself as a worldwide adventurer, as though a heroic style was as important to his life as to his fiction. He fished and hunted wherever new seas and continents beckoned. And he periodically resumed his role as war correspondent, most notably during the Spanish civil war (1936–1939).

During the early 1930s, Hemingway brought out two nonfiction books that revealed his fascination with bullfighting and with big-game hunting—*Death in the Afternoon* (1932) and *Green Hills of Africa* (1935). Significantly, both books centered on the art of killing. In 1940, just as the literary world was writing Hemingway off as a has-been novelist, he presented another triumph, *For Whom the Bell Tolls.*

The outbreak of World War II drew Hemingway back into uniform. Although officially a correspondent, he gathered around himself a small army of adventurers. During one battle, a First Army commander reported that Hemingway's band was sixty miles in front of the Americans' advancing line. When the Allies at last reached Paris in 1944, they found that Hemingway had already "liberated" the bar at the Ritz Hotel.

By 1952, Hemingway's celebrated literary accomplishments and his continuous pursuit of excitement and danger had made him as famous as any film star. In spite of his flamboyant exploits, he produced yet another widely acclaimed novel in that year, *The Old Man and the Sea,* which won the 1953 Pulitzer Prize. It tells of an old Cuban fisherman who hooks a giant marlin far out at sea and battles the fish for two days and nights. Although he finally succeeds in subduing the great fish and lashing it to the side of his boat, sharks tear at the carcass until the man is left with only the marlin's skeleton. The tale has been interpreted as Hemingway's metaphor for life: a vision of the hero, weighed down by the years, but still able to use his skill to taunt fate and so win a kind of victory from it.

In 1954, Hemingway won the Nobel Prize in literature. He now divided his time between his house in Ketchum, Idaho, and his restless travels all over the world: to Cuba, China, Venice, Spain, and Africa. His health deteriorated, and periods of elation alternated with episodes of severe depression. After a visit to the Mayo Clinic for treatment, he returned to Idaho. On the morning of July 2, 1961, he rose early, and with two charges of a double-barreled shotgun, he killed himself.

"He put life back on the page," wrote the critic Alfred Kazin, "made us see, feel, and taste the gift of life. . . . To read Hemingway was always to feel more alive."

ABOUT THE AUTHOR

The heroes in Hemingway's short stories are often wounded men—physically and psychologically. They carry with them their memories of violence. Facing a hypocritical world, they seek to find some code by which to live, some way to accept their reality. When Hemingway was recuperating from his knee injury, he wrote his family from a Milan hospital: "Wounds don't matter. I wouldn't mind being wounded again so much because I know just what it is like . . . and it does give you an awfully satisfactory feeling to be wounded." During his lifetime Hemingway was repeatedly injured—in car crashes, airplane crashes, shooting accidents, and fires. Like many of the heroes in his novels, he, too, was a wounded man.

QUICK PLANNING GUIDE

Into the Story

Through the Story

Beyond the Story

- **Writer's Notebook:** Collect ideas for a speculation about causes and effects
- **Critical Writing:** Write a brief essay applying a quotation to a character
- **Critical Writing:** Write a brief essay applying a principle to a story
- **Creative Writing/Performance:** Write and present a scene

BEFORE YOU READ
SOLDIER'S HOME

Reading Focus

A Hero's Welcome

World War I was greeted as the "war to end all wars," and songs like "Over There" celebrated the heroism of hundreds of thousands of American soldiers who were shipped off to fight in the trenches of Europe. But advances in weaponry made the Great War more devastating than any previous war, both physically and psychologically. Returning soldiers sometimes proved unable to readjust to life back home, which seemed to offer little they could relate to or believe in. Some became disillusioned, cynical, isolated, and overwhelmed by hopelessness. They became the most "lost" of Gertrude Stein's lost generation.

A Dialogue with the Text

As you read the story, try to piece together a character profile of the returned soldier Harold Krebs. Take notes on Krebs's feelings, attitudes, and views on the following: the war, his return home, his family, other people, his hometown, and his future.

Background

Soldiers who returned home from World War I were often described as shellshocked—suffering from a mental and emotional condition of confusion, exhaustion, anxiety, and depression. In the past, the condition—now termed *post-traumatic stress disorder*—was not well understood, and friends and relatives often found themselves at a loss. They expected returning soldiers to plunge directly back into civilian life and could not understand why some young men seemed unable to do so.

(Left and opposite page) Photos of Ernest Hemingway in Italy and France during World War I (1918).

Department of Rare Books and Special Collections/Princeton University Libraries.

Leib Image Archives.

WORDS TO OWN

The following vocabulary words are defined in the Words to Own at the bottom of the pupil's page.

PORTFOLIO ASSESSMENT

Portfolio Assessment For help with self- and teacher assessment of reading skills, see the *Portfolio Management System,* pp. 48–49.

John F. Kennedy Library, Boston, Massachusetts.

Department of Rare Books and Special Collections/Princeton University Libraries.

Soldier's Home

Ernest Hemingway

Krebs went to the war from a Methodist college in Kansas. There is a picture which shows him among his fraternity brothers, all of them wearing exactly the same height and style collar. He enlisted in the Marines in 1917 and did not return to the United States until the second division returned from the Rhine[1] in the summer of 1919.

There is a picture which shows him on the Rhine with two German girls and another corporal. Krebs and the corporal look too big for their uniforms. The German girls are not beautiful. The Rhine does not show in the picture. **A**

By the time Krebs returned to his home town in Oklahoma the greeting of heroes was over. He came back much too late. The men from the town who had been drafted had all been welcomed elaborately on their return. There had been a great deal of hysteria. Now the reaction had set in. People seemed to think it was rather ridiculous for Krebs to be getting back so late, years after the war was over.

At first Krebs, who had been at Belleau Wood, Soissons, the Champagne, St. Mihiel and in the Argonne[2] did not want to talk about the war at all. Later he felt the need to talk but no one wanted to hear about it. His town had heard too many atrocity stories to be thrilled by actualities. Krebs found that to be listened to at all he had to lie, and after he had done this twice he, too, had a reaction against the war and against talking about it. A distaste for everything that had happened to him in the war set in because of the lies he had told.

1. **Rhine:** river that flows through Germany into the North Sea.

2. **Belleau** (be·lō′) **Wood . . . Argonne** (är′gän′): sites of World War I battles that demonstrated the Allies' superior strength against the Germans.

WORDS TO OWN

elaborately (ē·lab′ə·rit·lē) *adv.:* with great care.
hysteria (hi·ster′ē·ə) *n.:* uncontrolled excitement.
atrocity (ə·träs′ə·tē) *n.* used as *adj.:* horrible; brutal.

Into the Story

Using BEFORE YOU READ p. 652

A Dialogue with the Text

Have students use a web like the following to help them generate and organize their ideas about Krebs.

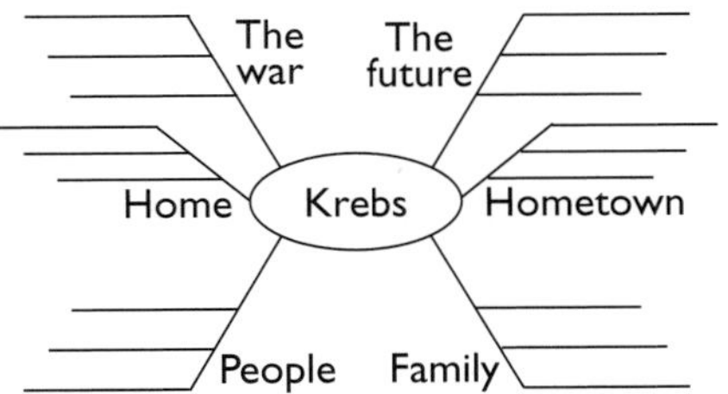

Through the Story

A. Language Note: Style

Hemingway is noted for his plain literary style. How is his attempt to arrive at the "truest sentence that you know" evident here? [Each of the last three sentences in this second paragraph is a simple sentence beginning with the subject. There are no transition words between sentences and there are no modifying clauses.]

PROGRAM MANAGER

- **Planning Instruction** See *Teaching Notes, Teaching Resources B,* p. 52, for objectives, a summary, and literary elements for this selection.
- **Instructional Support** See *Graphic Organizer for Active Reading, Teaching Resources B,* p. 57, for a Through the Story activity.
- **Instructional Support** See Fine Art Transparency 13.1. Review notes for transparencies in the *Audiovisual Resources Binder* for teaching suggestions.
- **Reinforcement** Use the *Words to Own* worksheet in *Teaching Resources B,* p. 60.
- **Assessment** See *Selection Test, Test Booklet,* pp. 153–154.
- **Language Link** For instruction in identifying repetition and wordiness and practice in revising, see *Language Link, Teaching Resources B,* pp. 58–59, and *Language and Writing Skills Worksheets,* p. 107.

A. Critical Reading: Speculating

? What do you think was "the one thing, the only thing for a man to do"? [Possible answers: The act of killing another person in battle, running away from the fight, avoiding killing someone else in battle, or avoiding being killed.]

B. Reader's Response: First Thoughts

? Why does Krebs fall into an "easy pose of the old soldier" only when he is with other soldiers? [Sample responses: The soldiers have shared similar experiences that civilians have not had; he knows what kind of behavior other soldiers expect; or they can be honest with each other about their fears during wartime.] How has he lost everything? [Sample responses: Krebs loses everything by focusing on the fear he felt; or he fails to adjust to civilian life because he associates with other soldiers.]

C. Literary Element: Symbol

? What is the significance of his father's still having the same car? [The car is a symbol that while Krebs has been altered by events in the war, the family has not. The father still drives the same car he drove before the war began.]

D. Reader's Response: Shaping Interpretations

? What is the effect of the repetition in the first three sentences of this paragraph? [Sample responses: The narrator emphasizes Krebs's feeling of exhaustion; or the emphasis indicates that Krebs wants to live his life without concerning himself with consequences.]

(A) All of the times that had been able to make him feel cool and clear inside himself when he thought of them; the times so long back when he had done the one thing, the only thing for a man to do, easily and naturally, when he might have done something else, now lost their cool, valuable quality and then were lost themselves.

His lies were quite unimportant lies and consisted in attributing to himself things other men had seen, done or heard of, and stating as facts certain apocryphal incidents familiar to all soldiers. Even his lies were not sensational at the pool room. His acquaintances, who had heard detailed accounts of German women found chained to machine guns in the Argonne forest and who could not comprehend, or were barred by their patriotism from interest in, any German machine gunners who were not chained, were not thrilled by his stories.

(B) Krebs acquired the nausea in regard to experience that is the result of untruth or exaggeration, and when he occasionally met another man who had really been a soldier and they talked a few minutes in the dressing room at a dance he fell into the easy pose of the old soldier among other soldiers: that he had been badly, sickeningly frightened all the time. In this way he lost everything.

During this time, it was late summer, he was sleeping late in bed, getting up to walk down town to the library to get a book, eating lunch at home, reading on the front porch until he became bored and then walking down through the town to spend the hottest hours of the day in the cool dark of the pool room. He loved to play pool.

In the evening he practised on his clarinet, strolled down town, read and went to bed. He was still a hero to his two young sisters. His mother would have given him breakfast in bed if he had wanted it. She often came in when he was in bed and asked him to tell her about the war, but her attention always wandered. His father was non-committal.

Before Krebs went away to the war he had never been allowed to drive the family motor car. His father was in the real estate business and always wanted the car to be at his command when he required it to take clients out into the country to show them a piece of farm property. The car always stood outside the First National Bank building where his father had an office on the second floor. (C) Now, after the war, it was still the same car.

Nothing was changed in the town except that the young girls had grown up. But they lived in such a complicated world of already defined alliances and shifting feuds that Krebs did not feel the energy or the courage to break into it. He liked to look at them, though. There were so many good-looking young girls. Most of them had their hair cut short. When he went away only little girls wore their hair like that or girls that were fast. They all wore sweaters and shirt waists with round Dutch collars. It was a pattern. He liked to look at them from the front porch as they walked on the other side of the street. He liked to watch them walking under the shade of the trees. He liked the round Dutch collars above their sweaters. He liked their silk stockings and flat shoes. He liked their bobbed hair and the way they walked.

When he was in town their appeal to him was not very strong. He did not like them when he saw them in the Greek's ice cream parlor. He did not want them themselves really. They were too complicated. There was something else. Vaguely he wanted a girl but he did not want to have to work to get her. He would have liked to have a girl but he did not want to have to spend a long time getting her. He did not want to get into the intrigue and the politics. He did not want to have to do any courting. He did not want to tell any more lies. It wasn't worth it.

(D) He did not want any consequences. He did not want any consequences ever again. He wanted to live along without consequences. Besides he did not really need a girl. The army had taught him that. It was all right to pose as though you had to have a girl. Nearly everybody did that. But it

Words to Own

apocryphal (ə·päk′rə·fəl) *adj.:* of questionable authority; false.
exaggeration (eg·zaj′ər·ā·shən) *n.:* overstatement.
alliances (ə·lī′əns·iz) *n. pl.:* close associations for common objectives.
intrigue (in′trēg′) *n.:* scheming.
consequences (kän′si·kwens·iz) *n. pl.:* results of an action.

Options for Teaching

Strategies for Inclusion

Less Proficient Readers To motivate students to read the story, have them predict what the story will be about, based on the title and the first four paragraphs of the story. Ask them to verify their hypotheses as they read and to continue predicting what may occur next in the story.

Visual After students have read the first three pages of the story, have them work in pairs to create a character attribute cluster for Krebs. Ask students to add new attributes to the cluster as they gain additional insight into the character in the last half of the story. Demonstrate how to begin by reading aloud the first paragraph to the class and then asking students to name attributes. Use Transparency 3: Cluster Diagram in the Transparency Package and list students' responses on it as they offer them.

English Language Development As students read "Soldier's Home," they will encounter difficult passages. Suggest that they try making notes in their Reader's Logs of any difficult passage and what they think it is about. Then, encourage them to complete the reading, coming back to the difficult passages and trying to understand them in the context of the whole story.

wasn't true. You did not need a girl. That was the funny thing. First a fellow boasted how girls mean nothing to him, that he never thought of them, that they could not touch him. Then a fellow boasted that he could not get along without girls, that he had to have them all the time, that he could not go to sleep without them.

That was all a lie. It was all a lie both ways. You did not need a girl unless you thought about them. He learned that in the army. Then sooner or later you always got one. When you were really ripe for a girl you always got one. You did not have to think about it. Sooner or later it would come. He had learned that in the army.

Now he would have liked a girl if she had come to him and not wanted to talk. But here at home it was all too complicated. He knew he could never get through it all again. It was not worth the trouble. That was the thing about French girls and German girls. There was not all this talking. You couldn't talk much and you did not need to talk. It was simple and you were friends. He thought about France and then he began to think about Germany. On the whole he had liked Germany better. He did not want to leave Germany. He did not want to come home. Still, he had come home. He sat on the front porch.

He liked the girls that were walking along the other side of the street. He liked the look of them much better than the French girls or the German girls. But the world they were in was not the world he was in. He would like to have one of them. But it was not worth it. They were such a nice pattern. He liked the pattern. It was exciting. But he would not go through all the talking. He did not want one badly enough. He liked to look at them all, though. It was not worth it. Not now when things were getting good again.

He sat there on the porch reading a book on the war. It was a history and he was reading about all the engagements he had been in. It was the most interesting reading he had ever done. He wished there were more maps. He looked forward with a good feeling to reading all the really good histories when they would come out with good detail maps. Now he was really learning about the war. He had been a good soldier. That made a difference.

One morning after he had been home about a month his mother came into his bedroom and sat on the bed. She smoothed her apron.

"I had a talk with your father last night, Harold," she said, "and he is willing for you to take the car out in the evenings."

"Yeah?" said Krebs, who was not fully awake. "Take the car out? Yeah?"

"Yes. Your father has felt for some time that you should be able to take the car out in the evenings whenever you wished but we only talked it over last night."

"I'll bet you made him," Krebs said.

"No. It was your father's suggestion that we talk the matter over."

"Yeah. I'll bet you made him," Krebs sat up in bed.

"Will you come down to breakfast, Harold?" his mother said.

"As soon as I get my clothes on," Krebs said.

His mother went out of the room and he could hear her frying something downstairs while he washed, shaved and dressed to go down into the dining-room for breakfast. While he was eating breakfast his sister brought in the mail.

"Well, Hare," she said. "You old sleepy-head. What do you ever get up for?"

Krebs looked at her. He liked her. She was his best sister.

"Have you got the paper?" he asked.

She handed him *The Kansas City Star* and he shucked off its brown wrapper and opened it to the sporting page. He folded *The Star* open and propped it against the water pitcher with his cereal dish to steady it, so he could read while he ate.

"Harold," his mother stood in the kitchen doorway, "Harold, please don't muss up the paper. Your father can't read his *Star* if it's been mussed."

"I won't muss it," Krebs said.

His sister sat down at the table and watched him while he read.

"We're playing indoor over at school this afternoon," she said. "I'm going to pitch."

"Good," said Krebs. "How's the old wing?"[3]

"I can pitch better than lots of the boys. I tell them all you taught me. The other girls aren't much good."

3. **wing:** arm.

WORDS TO OWN
engagements (en·gāj′mənts) *n. pl.:* battles.

E. Critical Reading: Drawing Conclusions
Hemingway describes Krebs's thoughts. What do you think of Krebs at this point in the story? [Possible answers: He is confused. He can become lost in thought.]

F. Literary Element: Irony
? Why is this scene ironic? [Krebs, who has just returned from the war, is finally learning about the war from books.]

G. Reader's Response: Shaping Interpretations
? Why do you think Krebs's father is now willing to allow Krebs to take out the car? [Sample responses: Krebs's father feels Krebs is now mature enough to drive the car after participating in the war; or his father is worried about Krebs's lack of direction, and he feels that driving the car will somehow help Krebs become active.]

INTEGRATING THE LANGUAGE ARTS

Language and Style To keep readers engaged, writers change tempo by varying sentence length and using a variety of sentence structures and beginnings. Point out that although Hemingway uses a plain journalistic style, readers would promptly fall asleep if every sentence in his story had the same length and structure. Ask students to focus on the paragraph that begins "At first Krebs . . ." on p. 653. Have them look carefully at sentence lengths, noticing how several short sentences contrast with longer sentences. Next, have them examine sentence structure to locate examples of simple, compound, complex, and compound-complex sentences. Then, have students focus on sentence beginnings. Have students analyze sentence variety in other paragraphs.

Strategic Reading Students will benefit both by hearing Hemingway's story read aloud and by reading it aloud themselves. Have students try Break-In Reading. Have one person read aloud while others follow along. When another student wants to read aloud, he or she "breaks in" and the other reader stops and follows along with the group.

Writing: Poem Have students write a stream-of-consciousness poem from Krebs's point of view. Ask students to write ideas on images, moments, and memory flashes that Krebs might experience. Then, have them organize their ideas into a poem. ☞

LITERATURE AND POPULAR CULTURE

Have students read the material on the Roaring Twenties. Ask students to consider whether Krebs's postwar experience may have been a reflection of the changing times. Invite students to discuss what other periods in the United States may have been similar to the Roaring Twenties and how current times compare and contrast to the 1920s.

LITERATURE AND POPULAR CULTURE

UPI/Bettmann.

Charleston endurance contest (1926).

The Decade That Roared

Harold Krebs finds his hometown much the same as he left it before the war, except for new styles in women's hair and clothing. He especially notices girls' short, bobbed hair—a style that marked a girl as "fast" only a few years earlier when he shipped out to the trenches of France.

The flap over flappers. Krebs was right on target. As the slick, sophisticated ads of the era show, nothing symbolized the decade after World War I so well as the "flapper"—a liberated young woman who cropped her hair into a caplike shape, wore half the amount of clothing of her Victorian-era counterpart, and boldly wore rouge and lipstick. The flapper abandoned the confines of the corset and opted instead for loose, long-waisted dresses that ended at or above the knee. She showed off her legs in the new silk or rayon stockings that were affordable at every income level. And she kicked, shimmied, and swayed in a wild, new dance called the Charleston.

An era of excess. Tired of war and disillusioned with political and social causes, city dwellers and even small-town residents yearned for fun and excitement in the Roaring Twenties. Millions of Americans purchased automobiles and took to the road on touring

"Yeah?" said Krebs.

"I tell them all you're my beau.[4] Aren't you my beau, Hare?"

"You bet."

"Couldn't your brother really be your beau just because he's your brother?"

"I don't know."

"Sure you know. Couldn't you be my beau, Hare, if I was old enough and if you wanted to?"

"Sure. You're my girl now."

"Am I really your girl?"

"Sure."

"Do you love me?"

"Uh, huh."

"Will you love me always?"

"Sure."

"Will you come over and watch me play indoor?"

"Maybe."

"Aw, Hare, you don't love me. If you loved me, you'd want to come over and watch me play indoor."

Krebs's mother came into the dining-room from the kitchen. She carried a plate with two fried eggs and some crisp bacon on it and a plate of buckwheat cakes.

"You run along, Helen," she said. "I want to talk to Harold."

4. **beau:** boyfriend.

OPTIONS FOR TEACHING

COOPERATIVE LEARNING

Duologue To encourage students to develop an in-depth understanding of the thoughts and actions of the characters of this story, have pairs of students participate in a Duologue between Krebs and his father. Have one student assume the persona of Krebs; and the other, that of his father. Students should begin talking and develop a conversation as it might have taken place if it were incorporated into the story. All student pairs should conduct this Duologue at the same time, so that it is not a performance to be given in front of the class, but rather an exercise to be undertaken simultaneously by all the students. After pairs have conducted the Duologue, hold a class discussion and ask students what new insights about the characters they may have.

CLASSROOM MANAGEMENT

Managing the Reader's Response Classroom To encourage students to see that there is more than one way to look at material, allow several students to express their ideas on each topic. Then, help students to respond to one another and to amend their interpretations after they have considered other interpretations and have verified their ideas with the text.

vacations. Consumerism grew by leaps and bounds, fueled by abundant advertising and easy credit plans. Popular entertainment filled people's leisure time: Commercial radio and the movies changed American life by forming a national mass culture. People devoured the sensational stories of the day—vivid reports of scandals, crimes, freak disasters, and sports exploits. Young and old alike reveled in learning details of the private lives of movie stars like Rudolph Valentino, writers like Edna St. Vincent Millay (page 697), sports figures like Babe Ruth and the American Indian athlete Jim Thorpe, and celebrities like the pilot Charles Lindbergh. Crazes spread throughout the country—manias for the Chinese game of mahjong, six-day bicycle races, dance marathons, and even flagpole sitting. Jazz, one of the great African American contributions to popular culture, provided the exciting soundtrack to the era.

The young rebels. Women and men alike became more aware of modernist thought and the psychological theories of Sigmund Freud, calling for new social freedoms. Young people rebelled against the tight moral codes and even the good manners of the prewar years. They scoffed at the prohibition on alcohol by inventing the private cocktail party. With the new availability of motorcars, people roared off to dances in places where no one knew them, where they could feel free of their inhibitions. Couples danced closer together than ever before, tangoing and fox-trotting cheek to cheek to the sound of the saxophone.

The twenties' emphasis on youth and openness is recognizably "modern." At the time, many Americans were shocked and outraged by what they saw as the deterioration of culture and values. The 1920s were a rowdy, roisterous time—a decade that roared.

Archive Photos.

She put the eggs and bacon down in front of him and brought in a jug of maple syrup for the buckwheat cakes. Then she sat down across the table from Krebs.

"I wish you'd put down the paper a minute, Harold," she said.

Krebs took down the paper and folded it.

"Have you decided what you are going to do yet, Harold?" his mother said, taking off her glasses. **A**

"No," said Krebs.

"Don't you think it's about time?" His mother did not say this in a mean way. She seemed worried.

"I hadn't thought about it," Krebs said.

"God has some work for every one to do," his mother said. "There can be no idle hands in His Kingdom."

"I'm not in His Kingdom," Krebs said.

"We are all of us in His Kingdom."

Krebs felt embarrassed and resentful as always.

"I've worried about you so much, Harold," his mother went on. "I know the temptations you must have been exposed to. I know how weak men are. I know what your own dear grandfather, my own father, told us about the Civil War and I have prayed for you. I pray for you all day long, Harold."

Krebs looked at the bacon fat hardening on his plate.

A. Literary Element: Theme

? Why has Krebs not made a decision about what he is going to do? [Krebs's experience in the war has changed his outlook on life; he no longer shares the same values as his parents. Pursuing the American dream, which is so important to his parents, seems alien to him.]

CROSSING THE CURRICULUM

History Have students work in pairs or in small groups to research the following questions.

- When and why did the United States enter World War I?
- With what countries did the United States form an alliance? What countries fought against these allies?
- How many soldiers lost their lives in the war? How many of these soldiers were from the United States?
- Why did the war end? Who won?

After students have reported their findings to the class, ask them to discuss why the generation surviving the war might have lost the optimism and innocence of prewar years.

Geography Give students a map of Europe, and have them locate the Rhine River and the battle sites mentioned in the story—Belleau Wood, Soissons, the Champagne, St. Mihiel, and the Argonne. Ask students to research these battles and to record an audiotape as though they were war correspondents reporting from the front. Play these tapes for the class.

Psychology To give students a better understanding of the psychological effects of war, invite a psychologist or psychiatrist who specializes in post-traumatic stress disorder to visit the class.

A. Literary Element: Conflict

? What conflict does this passage suggest? [Harold will now be forced to make a decision: either get a job or leave his parents' home.]

B. Literary Element: Character

? Why does Krebs say that he does not love anybody? [Possible answers: His experience in the war seems to have left him detached and disinterested. Perhaps seeing the death of so many dulled his emotions, making him immune to feeling; or perhaps he is angry with his mother, who does not understand how he feels, and he is trying to hurt her.]

Technology Tip

Students can discuss their reading of "Soldier's Home" with others on the Hemingway mailing list. Instruct students to send the message *sub Ernest* followed by the student's name to **listserv@cfrvm.cfr.usf.edu**. *You may want to preview any Internet activity that you suggest to students. Because these resources are sometimes public forums, their content can be unpredictable.*

East Wind over Weehawken (1934) by Edward Hopper. Oil on canvas (34″ × 50 1/4″).

The Pennsylvania Academy of the Fine Arts. Collections Fund.

"Your father is worried, too," his mother went on. "He thinks you have lost your ambition, that you haven't got a definite aim in life. Charley Simmons, who is just your age, has a good job and is going to be married. The boys are all settling down; they're all determined to get somewhere; you can see that boys like Charley Simmons are on their way to being really a credit to the community."

Krebs said nothing.

A "Don't look that way, Harold," his mother said. "You know we love you and I want to tell you for your own good how matters stand. Your father does not want to hamper your freedom. He thinks you should be allowed to drive the car. If you want to take some of the nice girls out riding with you, we are only too pleased. We want you to enjoy yourself. But you are going to have to settle down to work, Harold. Your father doesn't care what you start in at. All work is honorable as he says. But you've got to make a start at something. He asked me to speak to you this morning and then you can stop in and see him at his office."

"Is that all?" Krebs said.

"Yes. Don't you love your mother, dear boy?"

"No," Krebs said.

His mother looked at him across the table. Her eyes were shiny. She started crying.

B "I don't love anybody," Krebs said.

It wasn't any good. He couldn't tell her, he couldn't make her see it. It was silly to have said it. He had only hurt her. He went over and took hold of her arm. She was crying with her head in her hands.

"I didn't mean it," he said. "I was just angry at something. I didn't mean I didn't love you."

His mother went on crying. Krebs put his arm on her shoulder.

"Can't you believe me, mother?"

His mother shook her head.

"Please, please, mother. Please believe me."

"All right," his mother said chokily. She looked up at him. "I believe you, Harold."

Krebs kissed her hair. She put her face up to him.

OPTIONS FOR TEACHING

ASSESSMENT TOOLS

Informal Assessment: Reading Be aware of whether students are using the story to respond to questions and to participate in class discussion. Rate students on a scale of one to five (five points being the highest), using the following three criteria:

____ Students refer to events in the story to support their points.

____ Students make interpretations about the story that can be justified by the text.

____ Students quote from the story to support their points.

Check Test: True-False

1. Krebs did not return from the war until the summer of 1919. [True]
2. Krebs's acquaintances at the pool room are impressed by his war stories. [False]
3. Krebs first discovers he was a "good soldier" when he reads a book about the war. [True]
4. Krebs's father eventually gives him permission to drive the car. [True]
5. At the end of the story, Krebs decides to go down to his father's office to discuss his future plans. [False]

"I'm your mother," she said. "I held you next to my heart when you were a tiny baby."

Krebs felt sick and vaguely nauseated.

"I know, Mummy," he said. "I'll try and be a good boy for you."

"Would you kneel and pray with me, Harold?" his mother asked.

They knelt down beside the dining-room table and Krebs's mother prayed.

"Now, you pray, Harold," she said.

"I can't," Krebs said.

"Try, Harold."

"I can't."

"Do you want me to pray for you?"

"Yes."

So his mother prayed for him and then they stood up and Krebs kissed his mother and went out of the house. He had tried so to keep his life from being complicated. Still, none of it had touched him. He had felt sorry for his mother and she had made him lie. He would go to Kansas City and get a job and she would feel all right about it. There would be one more scene maybe before he got away. He would not go down to his father's office. He would miss that one. He wanted his life to go smoothly. It had just gotten going that way. Well, that was all over now, anyway. He would go over to the schoolyard and watch Helen play indoor baseball.

C

WORDS TO OWN

nauseated (nô′zhē·āt′id) *v.* used as *adj.:* feeling sickness or discomfort in the stomach.

PRIMARY **Sources** A SPEECH

Nobel Prize Acceptance Speech, 1954

Having no facility for speech making and no command of oratory nor any domination of rhetoric, I wish to thank the administrators of the generosity of Alfred Nobel for this prize.

No writer who knows the great writers who did not receive the prize can accept it other than with humility. There is no need to list these writers. Everyone here may make his own list according to his knowledge and his conscience.

It would be impossible for me to ask the ambassador of my country to read a speech in which a writer said all of the things which are in his heart. Things may not be immediately discernible in what a man writes, and in this sometimes he is fortunate; but eventually they are quite clear and by these and the degree of alchemy[1] that he possesses he will endure or be forgotten.

1. **alchemy:** magical power to transform the ordinary into the extraordinary. Alchemy was a branch of medieval science in which one aim was to change common metals such as lead into gold.

Writing, at its best, is a lonely life. Organizations for writers palliate[2] the writer's loneliness, but I doubt if they improve his writing. He grows in public stature as he sheds his loneliness, and often his work deteriorates. For he does his work alone, and if he is a good enough writer he must face eternity, or the lack of it, each day.

For a true writer each book should be a new beginning where he tries again for something that is beyond attainment. He should always try for something that has never been done or that others have tried and failed. Then sometimes, with great luck, he will succeed.

How simple the writing of literature would be if it were only necessary to write in another way what has been well written. It is because we have had such great writers in the past that a writer is driven far out past where he can go, out to where no one can help him.

I have spoken too long for a writer. A writer should write what he has to say and not speak it. Again I thank you.

—Ernest Hemingway

2. **palliate:** ease; lessen.

C. Reader's Response: Challenging the Text

? Is this a good ending for the story? [Sample responses: Yes, Krebs does not seem to make any move toward getting a job or doing anything differently, and that behavior fits his character. Or no, the reader has no idea what becomes of Krebs.]

Primary Sources

After students have read the speech or have heard it read, ask them to reevaluate "Soldier's Home." Ask them what things in his heart Hemingway is trying to express in the story. Have them discuss whether Krebs's loneliness as a veteran relates to Hemingway's loneliness as a writer. Finally, invite them to talk about what Hemingway might have tried to do in "Soldier's Home" that had not been done before in literature.

Technology Tip

TECHNOLOGY An audio clip of Hemingway's Nobel Prize acceptance speech is available from the Internet Town Hall via the World Wide Web at **http://town.hall.org/Archives/radio/IMS/HarperAudio/012494_harp_ITH.html**. *You may want to preview any Internet activity that you suggest to students. Because these resources are sometimes public forums, their content can be unpredictable.*

STRATEGIES FOR INCLUSION

Learners Having Difficulty Talk with students about the first paragraph in Hemingway's speech. Hemingway, acknowledged as a fine writer, says he is uncomfortable making speeches. Remind and reassure students that people have different areas of expertise and skill. Encourage them to understand that people can work on their weaknesses by building on their strengths.

English Language Development To find out if the language of the Nobel Prize Acceptance Speech is appropriate for students, have one or two students read the first two paragraphs aloud to you. A rule of thumb for this kind of quick analysis is that if students can read eighty-five percent of the words correctly, the level of the reading is probably appropriate. This quick strategy can be used with other reading materials as well.

Interpersonal Have students discuss the fourth paragraph of the speech. Ask them to focus on why writers are lonely or whether loneliness is a necessary part of the profession.

Making Meanings

First Thoughts

1. Possible responses: Krebs has problems readjusting; he needs a job; or he needs psychiatric care.

Reviewing the Text

a. He gets up late, goes to the library to get a book, eats lunch, reads until he is bored, spends time in the pool room, practices the clarinet, and takes walks.
b. Possible responses: It validates his experience in the war. He feels it teaches him things that he did not know about the war. It makes his war experience matter.
c. He is a hero to her.
d. His conversation with his mother.

Shaping Interpretations

2. People do not understand why he is returning so long after the war ended. They are not interested in hearing any more stories about the war. First Krebs tells lies to interest his audience. Then, because of the lies he tells, the war and his experiences in it become distasteful and no longer have value for him.
3. He likes to look at them and wishes for one, but only if he does not have to put forth the effort to have a relationship with one. He has experienced a lot of stress.
4. Krebs does not want to deal with the consequences of his actions. He feels concern or guilt about his actions in the war, so he does not want to do anything for which he will be responsible.
5. His parents want him to get a job, but he does not want one. His mother wants displays of affection, and he rebuffs her at first. Krebs has lost his faith, his ambition, and his interest in actively engaging in life.
6. Possible responses: War makes it impossible for some soldiers to rejoin society. War disconnects soldiers from their home life because it requires them to act against the values they have learned at home.

Extending the Text

7. **(Synthesis)** Possible responses: Krebs fits the description of an antihero, for he does little when he returns from the war. Or he fits the traditional hero image, for he has sacrificed by going to war. He may be different from antiheroes in that he may change his listless behavior.

MAKING MEANINGS

First Thoughts

1. Review the notes you made in your Reader's Log. What were your thoughts and feelings about Krebs's view of life? What advice would you give him?

Reviewing the Text

a. Describe the way Krebs spends his days.
b. What is Krebs's reaction to reading a history of all the battles he had been in?
c. How does Krebs's younger sister Helen feel about him?
d. What makes Krebs decide he should leave home?

Shaping Interpretations

2. By the time Krebs returns, his hometown has quit "the greeting of heroes" and "the reaction had set in." What is this reaction, and how does it affect Krebs?
3. What does Krebs's attitude toward the girls in town reveal about his state of mind?
4. What does Krebs mean when he says he wants "to live along without consequences"? Why do you suppose he feels that way?
5. Describe the **conflicts** expressed in the conversation between Mrs. Krebs and Harold at the end of the story. From this talk, what do we learn about the losses Harold has experienced?
6. How would you state the **theme** of "Soldier's Home"? What does the story reveal to you about the effects of war on the young?

Extending the Text

7. The "antihero" is a type of **protagonist** found in much modern literature. In contrast to the traditional hero, who responds to fate with strength and self-sacrifice, the antihero is generally disillusioned, passive, and defeated by life. Explain whether or not you consider Krebs to be an antihero. What does he have in common with antiheroes portrayed in contemporary books and movies? How is he different?

CHOICES: Building Your Portfolio

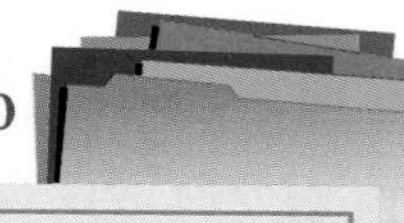

Writer's Notebook

1. Collecting Ideas for a Speculation About Causes and Effects

Freewrite your speculation about the effects that Krebs's war experience and homecoming will have on his future. Will he leave home after all? If so, where will he go, and what will he do? Will he maintain contact with his family? Save your notes for possible use in the Writer's Workshop on page 685.

Critical Writing

2. The Lost Generation

Gertrude Stein's remark "You are all a lost generation" summarized her perception of the pain and disillusionment experienced by many young people after World War I. In a brief essay, explain how Stein's quotation applies to Krebs. Is Krebs like or unlike someone you could meet today? Why or why not?

Critical Writing

3. The Tip of the Iceberg

Ernest Hemingway once remarked of his writing style: "I always try to write on the principle of the iceberg. There is seven-eighths of it under water for every part that shows." In a brief essay, explain what you think Hemingway means, and tell whether or not you feel that "Soldier's Home" illustrates the "iceberg principle."

Creative Writing / Performance

4. What Can We Do About Harold?

With another student, write and perform a script of the discussion between Krebs's parents that leads to Mrs. Krebs's talk with Harold. Why are Mr. and Mrs. Krebs worried about Harold? After your performance, tell how you think his parents should have dealt with Krebs's problems.

Beyond the Story

Choices: Building Your Portfolio

1. **Writer's Notebook** Remind students to save their work. They may use it as prewriting for the Writer's Workshop on p. 685.

PORTFOLIO ASSESSMENT

Choices: Assessment Criteria For help in evaluating these Choices assignments, see the criteria in the ***Portfolio Management System,*** p. 145.

T. S. Eliot

(1888–1965)

UPI/Bettmann.

At the time when he was regarded as America's most eminent living poet, T. S. Eliot announced that he was a "classicist in literature, royalist in politics, and Anglo-Catholic in religion." In 1927, Eliot gave up his U.S. citizenship and became a subject of the king of England. The same year he was received into the Church of England. By a kind of poetic justice, this loss to America was later to be made up for: W. H. Auden (1907–1973), the leading British poet of his time, became a naturalized American citizen in 1946. But residence in an adopted country does not necessarily change the philosophy or the style of a poet. Eliot continued to speak in a voice first heard in the Puritan pulpits of Massachusetts. And Auden retained a British sense of language unaffected by the inroads of American speech.

Thomas Stearns Eliot's family was rooted in New England, though he was born in St. Louis, Missouri, where his grandfather had been a founder and chancellor of Washington University. Eliot's childhood awareness of his native city would show itself in his poetry, but only after he had moved far away from St. Louis. He graduated from Harvard and went on to postgraduate work at the Sorbonne in Paris.

Just before the outbreak of World War I, Eliot took up residence in London, the city that would become his home for the rest of his life. There he worked for a time in a bank, suffered a nervous breakdown, married an emotionally troubled Englishwoman, and finally took up the business of literature. He became active as a publisher in the outstanding firm of Faber and Faber and, on his own, edited *The Criterion,* a literary magazine. As a critic, he was responsible for reviving interest in many neglected poets, notably the seventeenth-century English poet John Donne.

Poet and Scholar

Long before he decided to live abroad permanently, Eliot had developed a taste for classical literature. He was as familiar with European and Eastern writings as he was with the masterpieces of English. But the most crucial influence upon his early work came from the late-nineteenth-century French poets who, as a group, came to be known as the Symbolists. (For more on the Symbolists, see page 770.) When he was nineteen, Eliot came upon a book by the British critic Arthur Symons titled *The Symbolist Movement in Literature*. "I myself owe Mr. Symons a great debt," wrote Eliot. "But for having read his book, I should not . . . have heard of Laforgue and Rimbaud; I should probably not have begun to read Verlaine; and but for reading Verlaine, I should not have heard of Corbière. So the Symons book is one of those which have affected the course of my life."

The poets Eliot mentions were men of distinctly different talents. Yet they all believed

ABOUT THE AUTHOR

I. A. Richards, an important literary critic of his time, knew Eliot when Eliot worked for Lloyd's Bank in London. Richards recalls meeting a senior banker who asked Richards whether he thought Eliot was a good poet. When Richards said yes, the banker was relieved, for he and his staff had argued whether poetry and banking mixed. The banker felt that having a hobby helped people in their work. He added that if Eliot continued doing as well as he had been at the bank, he might even become a branch manager some day. Richards loved to tease Eliot with the banker's pronouncement.

WRITERS ON WRITING

T. S. Eliot thought that poetry had a social function, and wrote, "For I think it is important that every people should have its own poetry, not simply for those who enjoy poetry . . . but because it actually makes a difference to the society as a whole, and that means to people who do not enjoy poetry. . . . We may say that the duty of the poet, as poet, is . . . to his *language,* first to preserve, and second to extend and improve. . . . [U]nless [people] go on producing great authors, and especially great poets, their language will deteriorate, their culture will deteriorate and perhaps become absorbed in a stronger one."

QUICK PLANNING GUIDE

Into the Poem

Author Biography pp. 661–662
Before You Read p. 663

- **Reading Focus: Scaffolding** Students reflect on the antihero.
- **A Dialogue with the Text:** Record thoughts in Reader's Log about how the poem reflects spiritual emptiness and an unheroic view of life
- **Elements of Literature: Dramatic Monologue**

Through the Poem

"The Love Song of J. Alfred Prufrock" pp. 663–667
Critical Comment p. 668
Making Meanings pp. 669–670
Language and Style p. 670

Beyond the Poem

Choices: Building Your Portfolio p. 671

- **Writer's Notebook:** Collect ideas for a speculation about causes and effects
- **Critical Writing:** Write a brief essay responding to critical comment
- **Critical Writing:** Compare two poems in a short essay
- **Art:** Draw a line from the poem in cartoon form
- **Creative Writing:** Write a dramatic monologue
- **Critical Writing:** Compare three characters in a brief essay
- **Creative Writing/Performance:** Write and present a dialogue

in poetry as an art of suggestion rather than statement. They saw poetry as an art of re-creating states of mind and feeling, as opposed to reporting or confessing them. These beliefs became the basis of Eliot's own poetic methods. When people complained that this poetic method of suggestion was complex and difficult to understand, Eliot retorted that poetry had to be complex to express the complexities of modern life. More or less ignoring the still undervalued contribution of Walt Whitman, Eliot and other American poets also believed that, divorced from British antecedents, they would once and for all bring the peculiar rhythms of their native speech into the mainstream of world literature. Eliot and these other poets are often referred to as modernists.

Words for a Wasteland

Eliot had an austere view of poetic creativity; he disagreed with those who regarded a poem as a means of self-expression, as a source of comfort, or as a kind of spiritual pep talk. Practicing what he preached, Eliot startled his contemporaries with "The Love Song of J. Alfred Prufrock" in 1915 and "Portrait of a Lady" in 1917. Then, in 1922, with the editorial advice and encouragement of Ezra Pound, Eliot published *The Waste Land,* a long work that would become the most significant poem of the early twentieth century. The poem was so influential that the word *wasteland* entered common usage from Eliot's work. The word suggests a civilization that is spiritually empty and paralyzed by indecision and anxiety.

Assembled in the manner of a painter's collage or a moviemaker's montage, *The Waste Land* proved that it was possible to write an epic poem of classical scope in the space of 434 lines. Critics pored over the poem's complex structure and its dense network of allusions to world literature, Oriental religion, and anthropology. A few years after *The Waste Land* appeared, Eliot published a series of notes identifying many of his key references. (He was dismayed to find that some of his more ardent admirers were more interested in the notes than in the poem itself.)

In 1925, Eliot published a kind of lyrical postscript to *The Waste Land* called *The Hollow Men,* which predicted in its somber conclusion that the world would end not with a bang but with a whimper. In *The Hollow Men,* Eliot repeats and expands some of the themes of his longer poem and arrives at that point of despair beyond which lie but two alternatives: renewal or annihilation.

Faith and Fame

For critics surveying Eliot's career, it has become commonplace to say that, after the spiritual dead end of *The Hollow Men,* Eliot chose hope over despair, and faith over the world-weary cynicism that marked his early years. But there is much evidence in his later poems to indicate that, for Eliot, hope and faith were not conscious choices. Instead, they were the consequences of a submission, even a surrender, to that "peace which passeth understanding" referred to in the last line of *The Waste Land.*

Eliot spent the remainder of his poetic career in an extended meditation upon the limits of individual will and the limitless power of faith in the presence of grace.

Cited for his work as a pioneer of modern poetry, Eliot was awarded the Nobel Prize in literature in 1948. In the decades that followed, he came frequently to the United States to lecture and to read his poems, sometimes to audiences so large that he had to appear in football stadiums. Some of those who fought to buy tickets on the fifty-yard line were probably unaware of the irony in all of this: that a man once regarded as the most difficult and obscure poet of his era had achieved the drawing power of a rock star.

Ezra Pound (who called Eliot "Possum") wrote a few final words on the death of his old friend, ending with this passage:

"Am I to write 'about' the poet Thomas Stearns Eliot? Or my friend 'the Possum'? Let him rest in peace, I can only repeat, but with the urgency of fifty years ago: READ HIM."

PORTFOLIO ASSESSMENT

Portfolio Assessment
For help with self- and teacher assessment of reading skills, see the ***Portfolio Management System,*** p. 53.

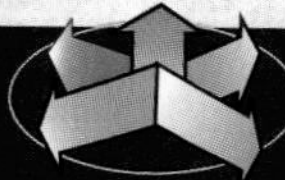

PROGRAM MANAGER

- **Planning Instruction** See **Teaching Notes, *Teaching Resources B,*** p. 53, for objectives, a summary, literary elements, and additional historical and biographical information for this selection.
- **Instructional Support** Before beginning the instructional lesson, see **Graphic Organizer for Active Reading, *Teaching Resources B,*** p. 61, for a Through the Poem activity.
- **Assessment** See **Selection Test, *Test Booklet,*** p. 155.

BEFORE YOU READ
THE LOVE SONG OF J. ALFRED PRUFROCK

Reading Focus

Where Have All the Heroes Gone?

In the PBS television series *The Power of Myth,* the famous mythologist Joseph Campbell says, "The hero is today running up against a hard world that is in no way responsive to his spiritual need." Modern society has become a "stagnation of inauthentic lives and living . . . that evokes nothing of our spiritual life, our potentialities, or even our physical courage." According to Campbell, the times we live in are hostile to heroism. Heroes are people of action, but the drudgery of modern life has made many people observers rather than participants in life's adventures. The "hero" of this poem is a person of profound self-absorption and passivity, who fits the profile of "antihero," the disillusioned and ineffectual protagonist we find in much modern and contemporary literature.

A Dialogue with the Text

Read the poem through twice. The first time, aim for a general sense of Prufrock's thoughts. As you read the poem again, write down examples of how his thoughts reflect the following ideas about his own time (the poem was published in 1915, during World War I), and perhaps about our time as well: (1) the idea that people are spiritually empty, and (2) the idea that contemporary life is unromantic and unheroic. Use your Reader's Log to answer the questions in the side notes.

Elements of Literature

Dramatic Monologue

This poem is written as a **dramatic monologue**—a poem in which a character speaks directly to one or more listeners. The words are being spoken by a man named Prufrock.

In a dramatic monologue, we must learn everything about the setting, situation, other characters, and the personality of the speaker through what the speaker tells us. Sometimes Prufrock's line of reasoning is interrupted by an unexpected thought. You will often have to supply the missing connections in the speaker's stream of thoughts and associations.

A **dramatic monologue** is a poem in which a character speaks directly to one or more listeners.

For more on Dramatic Monologue, see the Handbook of Literary Terms.

The Love Song of J. Alfred Prufrock

T. S. Eliot

S'io credessi che mia risposta fosse
a persona che mai tornasse al mondo,
questa fiamma staria senza più scosse.
Ma per ciò che giammai di questo fondo
non tornò vivo alcun, s'i'odo il vero,
senza tema d'infamia ti rispondo.

Let us go then, you and I,
When the evening is spread out against the sky
Like a patient etherized upon a table;
Let us go, through certain half-deserted streets,
The muttering retreats

Epigraph: This quotation is from Dante's epic poem *The Divine Comedy* (1321). The speaker is Guido da Montefeltro, a man consigned to Hell for dispensing evil advice. He speaks from a flame that quivers when he talks: "If I thought my answer were to one who ever could return to the world, this flame should shake no more; but since none ever did return alive from this depth, if what I hear be true, without fear of infamy I answer this." (*Inferno,* Canto 27, lines 61–66) Think of Prufrock as speaking from his own personal hell.

? **3.** *What is the evening compared with?*

Using BEFORE YOU READ p. 663

A Dialogue with the Text

To help students organize their ideas when they re-read the poem, have them use a table like the following.

Line(s)	Spiritual Emptiness	Life Is Unromantic/ Unheroic
2–3	[People are emotionally numb.]	

A. Literary Element: Dramatic Monologue

A dramatic monologue is frequently addressed to a specific audience. Whom does Prufrock address? [Possible answers: A companion or the reader.]

Answer to Margin Question

Line 3. With a patient under ether, lying on a table.

OPTIONS FOR TEACHING

STRATEGIES FOR INCLUSION

Visual To help students analyze Prufrock's character, have them use a chart like the one that follows to take notes as they read. Students should each divide their paper into two columns. In the first column, have them write down key quotations from the text, and in the second, ask them to make generalizations about Prufrock's personality.

Key Quotations	Generalizations
["Do I dare / Disturb the universe?"]	[He seems timid and afraid.]

Advanced The failure of communication between a man and woman is a major theme in Eliot's work. Have students look for evidence of this theme in some of Eliot's other works like *The Waste Land,* "Portrait of a Lady," or "Hysteria." Ask students to read the poems, or portions of them, and to report their findings to the class.

A. Literary Element: Conceit

? In this famous extended metaphor, what is the fog compared to? [It is compared to a cat.] What is the effect of the conceit? [Possible answer: It makes the fog seem gentle and warm.]

B. Reader's Response: Connecting with the Text

? How do we "prepare a face" to meet people? [Sample responses: Women often use makeup; or people think about how they want to present themselves.] How are our "faces" different at school, at home, at work, around strangers? [Sample responses: People change their posture and speech depending on the people they meet; or people are more relaxed at home, but are very careful about what they say at school and how they say it.]

Answers to Margin Questions

Line 7. Through half-deserted streets, to one-night cheap hotels, and to restaurants with sawdust on the floor. To someone who might accompany him.

Line 22. Pools stand in drains; soot falls from chimneys. The house has a terrace. It is autumn.

Line 27. Prufrock is acutely self-conscious about how he might look to others. He wants to present himself well.

Line 34. *There will be time* is repeated four times; the word *time* occurs eight times in all; and four lines begin with the word *And.*

Line 38. On one level, he may want to interact with other people; on another, he may wish to do other things in life than what he is doing.

Line 41. People who, in Prufrock's mind, are observing him closely and criticizing him.

Line 42. He seems to be appropriately dressed, but has thinning hair and thin limbs. His age is uncertain.

Of restless nights in one-night cheap hotels
And sawdust restaurants with oyster-shells:
Streets that follow like a tedious argument
Of insidious intent
To lead you to an overwhelming question . . .
Oh, do not ask, "What is it?"
Let us go and make our visit.

In the room the women come and go
Talking of Michelangelo.°

The yellow fog that rubs its back upon the window-panes,
The yellow smoke that rubs its muzzle on the window-panes,
Licked its tongue into the corners of the evening,
Lingered upon the pools that stand in drains,
Let fall upon its back the soot that falls from chimneys,
Slipped by the terrace, made a sudden leap,
And seeing that it was a soft October night,
Curled once about the house, and fell asleep.

And indeed there will be time
For the yellow smoke that slides along the street
Rubbing its back upon the window-panes;
There will be time, there will be time
To prepare a face to meet the faces that you meet;
There will be time to murder and create,
And time for all the works and days of hands
That lift and drop a question on your plate;
Time for you and time for me,
And time yet for a hundred indecisions,
And for a hundred visions and revisions,
Before the taking of a toast and tea.

In the room the women come and go
Talking of Michelangelo.

And indeed there will be time
To wonder, "Do I dare?" and, "Do I dare?"
Time to turn back and descend the stair,
With a bald spot in the middle of my hair—
(They will say: "How his hair is growing thin!")
My morning coat, my collar mounting firmly to the chin,
My necktie rich and modest, but asserted by a simple pin—
(They will say: "But how his arms and legs are thin!")
Do I dare
Disturb the universe?
In a minute there is time
For decisions and revisions which a minute will reverse.

For I have known them all already, known them all—

? **7.** *Where does the speaker want to take his companion? Whom could he be talking to?*

14. Michelangelo: Michelangelo Buonarroti (1475–1564), the great artist of the Italian Renaissance.

? **22.** *What details are you given about this setting? What season is it?*

? **27.** *What could this line mean?*

? **34.** *What words are repeated in this stanza?*

? **38.** *What could he want to dare to do?*

? **41.** *Who are "they"?*

? **42.** *A morning coat is formal daytime dress for men. What does Prufrock look like? Is he young, middle-aged, or elderly?*

OPTIONS FOR TEACHING

STRATEGIES FOR INCLUSION

Less Proficient Readers To help students understand Eliot's use of sensory details, have them complete a description chart such as the following. Ask them to divide a piece of notebook paper into five columns and to label them with the five senses. Have students fill in the details as they read.

Hearing	Sight	Smell	Taste	Touch
[Muttering]	[Cheap hotels]	[Perfume]	[Toast, tea]	[Smoothed by long fingers]

Learners Having Difficulty Ask students who have difficulty comprehending abstract information to do an activity that presents the information in a concrete manner. Divide the class into groups of three or four. Give each group a small portion or stanza of the poem. Ask students to cut out magazine photographs or to make drawings that illustrate the concept in their portion of the poem and to paste their illustrations onto a sheet of poster board. In the lower right-hand corner, have students rewrite the portion or stanza in their own words. Display the posters.

Have known the evenings, mornings, afternoons,
I have measured out my life with coffee spoons;
I know the voices dying with a dying fall°
Beneath the music from a farther room.
So how should I presume?

And I have known the eyes already, known them all—
The eyes that fix you in a formulated° phrase,
And when I am formulated, sprawling on a pin,
When I am pinned and wriggling on the wall,
Then how should I begin
To spit out all the butt-ends of my days and ways?
And how should I presume?

And I have known the arms already, known them all—
Arms that are braceleted and white and bare
(But in the lamplight, downed with light brown hair!)
Is it perfume from a dress
That makes me so digress?
Arms that lie along a table, or wrap about a shawl.
And should I then presume?
And how should I begin?

. . . . .

Shall I say, I have gone at dusk through narrow streets
And watched the smoke that rises from the pipes
Of lonely men in shirt-sleeves, leaning out of windows? . . .

I should have been a pair of ragged claws
Scuttling across the floors of silent seas.

. . . . .

And the afternoon, the evening, sleeps so peacefully!
Smoothed by long fingers,
Asleep . . . tired . . . or it malingers,
Stretched on the floor, here beside you and me.
Should I, after tea and cakes and ices,
Have the strength to force the moment to its crisis?
But though I have wept and fasted, wept and prayed,
Though I have seen my head (grown slightly bald) brought in
upon a platter,°
I am no prophet—and here's no great matter;
I have seen the moment of my greatness flicker,
And I have seen the eternal Footman hold my coat, and
snicker,
And in short, I was afraid.

And would it have been worth it, after all,
After the cups, the marmalade, the tea,
Among the porcelain, among some talk of you and me,
Would it have been worth while,

? **51.** *Has a life that is measured in coffee spoons been very exciting or heroic?*

52. dying fall: in music, notes that fade away.

56. formulated: reduced to a formula and made insignificant.

? **58.** *What do you see here?*

? **60.** *What are his days compared to? Is this a positive or a negative image?*

? **72.** *What has Prufrock done at night?*

? **74.** *What is the speaker comparing himself to here?*

? **77.** Malingers *means "pretends to be sick." How is this image of the evening connected to the one that opens the poem?*

82. my head . . . a platter: allusion to the execution of John the Baptist (Mark 6:17–28 and Matthew 14:3–11). The dancing of Salome so pleased Herod Antipas, ruler of ancient Galilee, that he offered her any reward she desired. Goaded by her mother, who hated John, Salome asked for John's head. Herod ordered the prophet beheaded and his head delivered on a serving plate.

? **85.** *The "eternal Footman" is death. What does this line tell you about Prufrock's confidence?*

C. Reader's Response: First Thoughts

? What do you know about Prufrock so far? [Sample responses: He is insecure; he worries about what others will say of him. He is timid; he believes that revealing his feelings might "disturb the universe." He is indecisive; he seems to vacillate, unable to make a decision whether or not to speak to someone.]

Answers to Margin Questions

Line 51. It has been dull.
Line 58. A mounted but still living specimen, perhaps an insect.
Line 60. Cigarette or cigar stubs. A negative image, unpleasant and sad.
Line 72. He has walked through streets and seen lonely men leaning out of their windows, smoking.
Line 74. A crab.
Line 77. The evening's seeming ill relates to the opening lines, which compare the evening to a patient etherized on a table.
Line 85. His life will amount to nothing; he lacks confidence. Even death laughs at Prufrock's anxiety.

INTEGRATING THE LANGUAGE ARTS

Strategic Reading Provide a large sheet of kraft paper on which the class can keep track of figurative language found in the poem, such as **metaphors, similes,** and **personification.** Have students use check marks to note figures of speech that are repeated later in the poem.

Speaking and Listening As an alternative to reading the poem aloud yourself, have students follow along in their texts as you play a recording of Eliot reading the poem (Harvard Vocarium, Spoken Literature Series, recorded for the Poetry Room, Harvard College Library, 1930 and 1945.)

RESPONDING TO THE ART: ABOUT THE ARTIST

Tea Leaves by William Paxton (1869–1941) is a painting by a contemporary of T. S. Eliot. Paxton was born in Baltimore, studied at the Ecole des Beaux-Arts, Paris, and spent most of his working life in Boston. From 1906 to 1913 he taught at the Boston Museum of Fine Arts School. Paxton's paintings are exhibited at many of America's major art museums, including the Cincinnati Art Museum, the Detroit Institute of Arts, the Wadsworth Atheneum in Hartford, and the Metropolitan Museum of Art in New York City.

Tea Leaves (1909) by William M. Paxton. Oil on canvas (36 1/8″ × 28 3/4″).

The Metropolitan Museum of Art, Gift of George A. Hearn, 1910 (10.64.8).

OPTIONS FOR TEACHING

COOPERATIVE LEARNING

Consensus-Building Activity To offer students an opportunity to discuss the poem with their peers and to evaluate each other's reasoning, try a collaborative consensus-building activity. Have each student work individually to come up with a thematic statement for the poem. Divide the class into small groups and have them discuss each member's statement. Appoint a discussion leader, scribe, and spokesperson for each group. Ask students to choose one thematic statement as the best response or to combine their statements into one best response. Have each spokesperson share the group's chosen thematic statement with the class.

CROSSING THE CURRICULUM

Music Remind students that popular musicians often make use of literary allusions. Make an enlarged transparency of the words to the Crash Test Dummies' song "Afternoons and Coffeespoons" and, as you play the song for the class, point out the allusions to l. 51 of the poem.

Art After students finish reading the poem, have them synthesize the themes in the poem by creating a graphic organizer. Place students in small groups and have them use words, lines, colors, charts, or pictures to illustrate the important themes and symbols in the poem. Their graphic organizer should make sense of the poem in a new and different way. Have them share their organizers with the class.

To have bitten off the matter with a smile,
To have squeezed the universe into a ball
To roll it towards some overwhelming question,
To say: "I am Lazarus, come from the dead,
Come back to tell you all, I shall tell you all"—
If one, settling a pillow by her head,
Should say: "That is not what I meant at all.
That is not it, at all."

And would it have been worth it, after all,
Would it have been worth while,
After the sunsets and the dooryards and the sprinkled streets,
After the novels, after the teacups, after the skirts that trail
along the floor—
And this, and so much more?—
It is impossible to say just what I mean!
But as if a magic lantern° threw the nerves in patterns on a
screen:
Would it have been worth while
If one, settling a pillow or throwing off a shawl,
And turning toward the window, should say:
"That is not it at all,
That is not what I meant, at all."
. . . . .

No! I am not Prince Hamlet, nor was meant to be;
Am an attendant lord, one that will do
To swell a progress,° start a scene or two,
Advise the prince; no doubt, an easy tool,
Deferential, glad to be of use,
Politic, cautious, and meticulous;
Full of high sentence,° but a bit obtuse;
At times, indeed, almost ridiculous—
Almost, at times, the Fool.

I grow old . . . I grow old . . .
I shall wear the bottoms of my trousers rolled.

Shall I part my hair behind? Do I dare to eat a peach?
I shall wear white flannel trousers, and walk upon the beach.
I have heard the mermaids singing, each to each.

I do not think that they will sing to me.

I have seen them riding seaward on the waves
Combing the white hair of the waves blown back
When the wind blows the water white and black.

We have lingered in the chambers of the sea
By sea-girls wreathed with seaweed red and brown
Till human voices wake us, and we drown.

? **94.** *In the Bible, a man named Lazarus is raised from the dead by Jesus (John 11:38–44). How do these lines connect with the opening quote from Dante?*

? **95.** *What is he afraid will happen if he tells them "all"?*

105. magic lantern: early type of projector that could magnify and project opaque photographs or book pages as well as transparent slides.

? **110.** *Who do you think might say this to Prufrock?*

? **111.** *Hamlet is the hero of Shakespeare's tragedy about a prince of Denmark. What is Prufrock saying "No!" to?*

113. swell a progress: fill out a scene in a play or pageant by serving as an extra.

117. high sentence: pompous talk.

? **119.** *How does Prufrock feel about himself?*

? **121.** *The style of the time called for fashionable young men to turn up the cuffs of their trousers. What is Prufrock hoping for here?*

? **125.** *If the mermaids do not sing to him, what will he miss in life?*

? **128.** *What does he see here?*

? **131.** *What breaks the romantic spell cast by the sight of the mermaids? What could "drown" mean here?*

Answers to Margin Questions

Line 94. Like Guido, Prufrock lives in a kind of spiritual and mental hell. If he could rise like Lazarus, he could leave his personal hell and warn the world.

Line 95. He fears being misunderstood and rejected.

Line 110. A woman to whom Prufrock is attracted.

Line 111. He is not princely but instead attends his superiors.

Line 119. He feels ridiculous; he has low self-esteem.

Line 121. He is hoping to look like a fashionable young man, even though he feels as if he is growing old.

Line 125. He will spend his life without love or fulfillment.

Line 128. He sees the mermaids riding out to sea on whitecaps.

Line 131. Human voices. *Drown* may mean "to lose hope."

A. Reader's Response: Challenging the Text

? Should Eliot have used a genre other than poetry to reveal Prufrock's thoughts? [Sample responses: No, because poetry allows the speaker to be expressive. Yes, because Prufrock's inability to do anything other than question better fits prose, rather than poetry, which seems more suited to lofty ideals and bright minds.]

PROFESSIONAL NOTES

Critical Comment: Prufrock's Failure
Stephen Spender does not condone Prufrock's inaction: "His [Prufrock's] failure, for which he despises himself, is failure to relate either with another person or with the Absolute. He is isolated, he cannot communicate. Although the fact that he is *conditioned* by the society in which he lives may account for his spiritual and sexual enervation, this does not excuse his moral cowardice. The fact that he is able to see his character as the projection of circumstances is still no excuse for his inertia." Have students discuss the issue that Spender raises and to what extent a person should be expected to rise above the circumstances of birth, upbringing, and environment.

Thematic Connections: "No Time for Heroes" Ask students how Prufrock may be like other characters who lack heroic qualities in the Collection. Students may feel that Prufrock resembles Miniver Cheevy, for although both seem to despise their present circumstances, both remain paralyzed, unable to move beyond the realm of thought and indecision to affect any change in their worlds. Miniver Cheevy drinks and calls it fate, while Prufrock only wonders whether he dares. Students may also suggest that Prufrock is similar to Krebs, since both experience inertia. Krebs, however, may not want to do anything different about his situation, and Prufrock at least wonders about changing.

A. Reader's Response: Shaping Interpretations

? What do you think Prufrock is a victim of? [Sample responses: Himself; a society that does not value "sensitive" men; or a society that overemphasizes heroism.]

B. Expansion

Readers need to fill in gaps to make these psychological connections. The monologue includes interrupting thoughts and observations on events or occurrences superimposed on the speaker's stream-of-consciousness thinking. Readers have to work hard to reconstruct events, to fill in gaps in thinking and in plot, and to make sense of the cyclical and sporadic thought patterns.

C. Expansion

This is a reference to one of Eliot's theories about how poetry works—the objective correlative. Eliot explains the idea as a set of objects, a chain of events, or a single situation that evokes a certain emotion when it is stated or written.

Critical Comment

The Oddest Love Song

Of all the love songs ever written, this must be one of the oddest and most pathetic. The man who "sings" it has feelings but no one to share them with and ideas that are realized nowhere but in his own mind. Sensitive emotions and sophisticated thoughts do nothing to help him come to grips with the real world of the streets. He knows that life is "out there," but he also knows that he will never join it, and so he takes refuge in self-dramatization and heroic fantasy. Yet the man himself is not pitiful. He has sufficient knowledge of himself to control his longings and enough of a sense of humor to portray himself as a victim without being victimized. **A**

"I am not Prince Hamlet," he says; and yet, he shares with Hamlet a breadth of vision to see two sides or more of every issue and the inability to act decisively upon any of his insights. If, in the jargon of today, we'd ask, "What's his problem?" the answer might be "self-consciousness—the egocentric trap that keeps an extraordinarily sophisticated man from enjoying the pleasures of this world that simpler men and women pursue and embrace without a thought."

One way to read the poem is to think of it as a movie—scenes follow one another immediately, without the connections or transitions that a conventional writer would provide. Consequently, the poem is demanding. What it demands is that, in the absence of logical connections, the reader must make the *psychological* connections that underlie the poem's structure and content. **B**

"Let us go then," says the speaker, and so invites us (or someone) to join him on a "visit." But, instead of going wherever it is he has in mind, we soon find ourselves observers in the course of the man's search. Our companion seems to be looking for answers to the meaning of life and the nature of romantic love. He tries, without success, to find some place for himself even in the world he knows well. In line 10, we read that he has an "overwhelming question." But he impatiently brushes us aside before we can ask what it is.

Quick as a flash, we're confronted with something unexpected: women passing back and forth in a room and discussing Michelangelo, one of the greatest artists of all time. This little glimpse from the corner of the eye, so to speak, introduces an aspect of Prufrock's character that we'll find illustrated time and again. Focusing on one thing, he can't help thinking of something else. Everything actual has its counterpart in an image or a metaphor or a situation, by means of which Eliot can dramatize the dilemma of a man suffering a kind of emotional paralysis. **C** As for the women who "come and go," they may be in an art gallery or in a museum or at a party or someplace else. The importance of their early and sudden appearance is to prepare us for the *method* of the poem. It is made up of a sequence of disjointed scenes that are psychologically related to the speaker's half-formed thoughts.

Time is a motif that recurs throughout the poem. Prufrock is conscious of time, and toward the end of his "love song," he makes his preoccupation clear: "I grow old . . . I grow old. . . ." Oppressed by time, he makes fun of his own obsession with it when he says, "There will be time . . . for a hundred visions." This statement might make us think of a religious revelation and the promise of salvation. But only for a moment. Prufrock soon drops us back into reality by the workaday word *revisions*—as if he is suggesting that the grandeur of imagination could be edited with a blue pencil, and that this would all take place before teatime.

STRATEGIES FOR INCLUSION

Special Needs Have students who have difficulty focusing their attention listen to an audiotape of the Critical Comment with headphones while noting information that gives more insight into Prufrock's character.

INTEGRATING THE LANGUAGE ARTS

Strategic Reading Students will have better recall for this Critical Comment if they organize the information it presents paragraph by paragraph in a chart like the following.

Paragraph Number	Topic

Making Meanings

First Thoughts

1. What words would you use to describe Prufrock's emotional difficulty in the poem?

Shaping Interpretations

2. What hints does the name "J. Alfred Prufrock" give us about the **character** of the "hero"?
3. How could the famous **simile** in lines 2–3 reveal that the speaker's mind or will is paralyzed?
4. What is the speaker inviting someone to do in lines 1–12? What is suggested by the **images** of the place they are going to travel through?
5. What does the name Michelangelo contribute in lines 13–14? What would be the effect if, for instance, the women were "talking of Joe DiMaggio" or "discussing detergents"?
6. In lines 15–22, we have one of the most famous **extended metaphors** in modern poetry. What is being indirectly compared with what? How many details extend the metaphor?
7. The self-consciousness of the speaker is nowhere more evident than in lines 37–44. What do you think he is self-conscious and worried about in these lines?
8. What does line 51 imply about the way Prufrock has lived? (Coffeehouses have long been an important feature of life in England and on the European continent.) What other "measuring devices" would suggest a more exciting life?
9. What references to women does Prufrock make in the poem? How do you think he feels about women and his attractiveness to them?
10. How are the **setting** and people described in lines 70–72 different from those familiar to Prufrock? What might this experience with another segment of city life tell us about Prufrock?
11. In lines 73–74, the speaker creates a **metaphor** to pointedly dramatize his sense of alienation from the rest of the world. Can you explain why Prufrock thinks he should have been a crab at the bottom of the sea?
12. Lines 87–98 echo the widely heard complaint that a "lack of communication" between people is the cause of misunderstanding. What do you think Prufrock would like to tell people?
13. In lines 99–104, Prufrock summarizes his life and reaches a point of exasperation that seems close to surrender: "It is impossible to say just what I mean!" What sort of life does he seem to have led?

Drawing by C. Barsotti. © 1987 The New Yorker Magazine, Inc.

6. The fog or smoke is being compared to a cat. It rubs its back and muzzle on the windowpanes, licks the evening with its tongue, lingers on pools in drains, allows soot to fall on it, leaps, slips by the terrace, observes the night, curls up, and falls asleep.
7. He is worried about doing something different from what he has done in the past. He is also worried about his physical appearance and dress.
8. Possible responses: He has been an observer of life rather than an active participant. He may be lonely. Airline tickets or award certificates would suggest excitement.
9. Lines 13–14, 35–36, the women talking of Michelangelo; ll. 62–69, women's arms, jewelry, perfume, and dress; ll. 75–110, the speaker sees himself having tea with a woman, and women twice tell him that he has totally misunderstood what they meant; ll. 124–131, the mermaids and sea-girls. Possible responses: He feels unsure of their reactions to him, both physically and intellectually. He fears rejection and mockery.
10. Possible responses: He tells of having visited the poor side of town, and he is familiar with more upper-class settings. It might suggest that Prufrock is not comfortable with anyone and feels alienated.
11. Possible response: He feels lonely, alienated, and frustrated.
12. Possible response: He would like to talk to people about his hopes and fears and to be understood.
13. He seems to have led a dull, lonely, alienated life.

Making Meanings

First Thoughts

1. Possible responses: He is afraid that if he does try to do things differently, he will be misunderstood. He is frozen—unable to act.

Shaping Interpretations

2. Possible responses: The use of an initial with a middle name seems pompous and self-conscious. *Alfred* sounds old-fashioned. *Prufrock* reminds one of *prude* and *frock,* the garment a priest would wear, making Prufrock seem to be a prudish man, removed from the world and from interactions with women.
3. When people are etherized, they are numb to feeling.
4. To take a mental and spiritual journey. The images suggest a sordid section of a city.
5. It suggests a sophisticated, intellectual society. Such conversation would give the women a mundane, more commonplace character.

14. The metaphor compares his inner thoughts and emotions to patterns projected onto a screen. He is afraid of misunderstanding and rejection.
15. Possible responses: He would like to try new things and to be daring; however, he feels his role is to remain reserved. He is still doubtful, for his next line is a question. He may yet overcome his doubts by changing small things and working up to bigger issues.
16. Possible responses: Too self-concerned; neurotic; or overly concerned with others' opinions of him.
17. Possible responses: He wants to believe in romance. They might represent love, which is so foreign to him that he might as well be trying to woo mermaids. He believes they will not sing for him because they reject him.
18. Possible responses: People are happy dreaming and hoping until they realize that their dreams and hopes have no chance of materializing. People drown in indecision and in the monotony of their lives.

Connecting with the Text

19. Possible responses: The journey leads to a realization that people will lead dull lives if they do not try to interact with others. Or it is an experience in that the reader sees the despair of one man.

Extending the Text

20. **(Evaluation)** Possible responses: It reflects spiritual emptiness because Prufrock makes no true effort to change his life and only dwells at length on its emptiness. It is a depiction of only one person's life. Or it does reveal how difficult it is for people to communicate in today's world.

Challenging the Text

21. **(Synthesis)** Possible responses: The title is ironic. Rather than declaring love for someone, the speaker expresses his alienation from the world. The title reflects his frustration at not being loved. Or the title should be "Do I Dare?" because that is the central question in Prufrock's mind.

14. In a poem loaded with **irony,** Prufrock does exactly what he believes is "impossible" by stating what he means in a brilliant visual **metaphor** that exposes him (line 105) with the force of an X-ray. What is the metaphor? How does he think people will respond to his exposure?
15. The speaker seems to finally arrive at decisiveness in line 121. Explain how he sees his role in life. Do you think he has overcome his doubts, or is he now just ignoring them?
16. How would you characterize someone who worries about the part in his hair and about what he should dare to eat (line 122)?
17. In lines 125–128, the speaker thinks that the mermaids are indifferent to him, yet he is held by this romantic vision. Why do you think he is so fascinated by these mythological creatures, and what might they represent for him? Why do you think he believes they will not sing to him?
18. By means of **paraphrase,** can you restate the meaning of lines 129–131? When "human voices wake us," what do we "drown" in?

Connecting with the Text

19. Think about this poem as a journey, a quest that begins with an invitation to join the man who makes it. What do you think the journey has finally led us to? Or do you think that the point of the poem is not so much an answer arrived at as an experience lived? Explain.

Extending the Text

20. Review the notes you made in your Reader's Log. Explain why this poem—one of the most famous poems of the twentieth century—has been described as a reflection of spiritual emptiness and emotional paralysis. Do you think its depiction of modern life is accurate? Why or why not?

Challenging the Text

21. Why do you think Eliot called this a "love song"? How is it different from the usual love song? If you were titling it, would you keep "love song" or use some other phrase?

LANGUAGE AND STYLE

Rhythm, Rhymes, Metaphors, and Allusions

"No *vers* [verse] is *libre* [free] for the man who wants to do a good job," Eliot once remarked. Though Eliot's poem is written in free verse (page 355), it makes use of rhythm, rhyme, and, of course, figurative language.

1. Re-read the first stanza, and identify the lines that conform to a particular **metrical pattern.**
2. How does repetition in the first thirty-four lines help create **rhythm** in the poem?
3. How many **end rhymes** can you find in the poem? How many **internal rhymes**?
4. Make a list of at least five **figures of speech** in the poem that you think are particularly original and memorable.
5. Note the terms of comparison in the figures of speech. Has Eliot based his comparison on "things" from modern life? Or has he used comparisons based mostly on elements from the world of nature?

It is characteristic of many poets who are highly educated and intimately aware of the history of their art to make use of **allusions.** Eliot expects that, just at a glance, his readers will identify his references and see their relationship to the poem. Here is a list of a few of the allusions in "Prufrock." What do you think each one means in the context of the poem?

1. Dante's *Inferno,* a section of *The Divine Comedy* (opening quotation)
2. Michelangelo (line 14)
3. Salome and John the Baptist (line 82)
4. The raising of Lazarus from the dead in the New Testament (line 94)
5. Hamlet, Prince of Denmark, in Shakespeare's play (line 111)

Language and Style

Answers

Rhythm, Rhymes, Figurative Language

1. Lines 6 and 7 are iambic pentameter. Lines 1 and 12 are trochaic tetrameter.
2. The repetition within stanzas unifies them.
3. End rhymes occur throughout the poem. Stanza one uses *I/sky, streets/retreats, hotels/shells, argument/intent, is it/visit.* Internal rhymes are less frequent, but include "decisions and revisions" (l. 48) and "days and ways" (l. 60).
4. Choices will vary. Possible answers: Synecdoche—"I should have been a pair of ragged claws" (l. 73); simile—"When the evening is spread out against the sky/Like a patient etherized upon a table" (ll. 2–3); metaphor—"The yellow fog that rubs its back upon the window-panes . . ." (ll. 15–22); personification—"I have seen the eternal Footman hold my coat, and snicker"(l. 85).
5. Answers will depend on responses to question #4. Students may find a mixture in the comparisons.

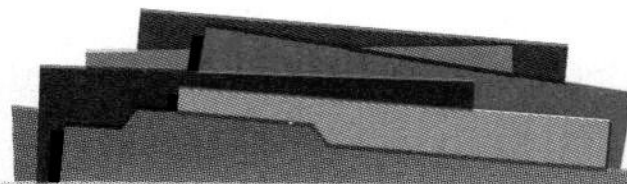

Choices: Building Your Portfolio

Writer's Notebook

1. Collecting Ideas for a Speculation About Causes and Effects

What is wrong with J. Alfred Prufrock? Join the critics who have been speculating for years on answers to that question. Take notes of your own about the possible causes of Prufrock's isolation and his inability to act on or commit himself to anything. You could collect your speculations in a cluster diagram or other graphic organizer. Be sure to cite lines from the poem that seem to support your speculations. Save your notes for possible use in the Writer's Workshop on page 685.

Critical Writing

2. Triumph or Tragedy?

Ezra Pound made the following comment about Prufrock in a letter to Harriet Monroe, the editor of *Poetry* magazine. Monroe must have mentioned that Prufrock ends in some kind of triumph (that he "goes off at the end"). In a brief essay, respond to Pound's comments.

> Now as to Eliot: "Mr. Prufrock" does not "go off at the end." It is a portrait of failure, or of a character which fails, and it would be false art to make it end on a note of triumph. I dislike the paragraph about Hamlet, but it is an early and cherished bit and T. E. won't give it up, and as it is the only portion of the poem that most readers will like at first reading, I don't see that it will do much harm. . . .
>
> —Ezra Pound

Critical Writing

3. Soul Searching

Write a short essay in which you compare "the explorer" in Gwendolyn Brooks's poem (page 643) to Prufrock. Consider how the explorer's search differs from Prufrock's, the fears each of them has, and the discoveries they each make. What does each poem have to say about the difficulty of making choices in today's world?

Art

4. Prufrock in Cartoons

Take a line from the poem, and draw it in cartoon form. You will probably get best results if you focus on a figure of speech, as the artist of the cartoon on page 669 did.

Creative Writing

5. "Let Us Go Then . . ."

Write a **dramatic monologue** spoken by someone who wants to invite another person to do something. Let your monologue reflect the random process of the speaker's thoughts. Try to find **images** that suggest your speaker's feeling and state of mind. Open with Eliot's words: "Let us go then, you and I."

Critical Writing

6. Blood Brothers?

Is J. Alfred Prufrock like Walter Mitty in James Thurber's story (page 625)? Is he like Miniver Cheevy in Edwin Arlington Robinson's poem (page 646)? In a brief essay, compare and contrast these three characters. In what ways are they different? In what ways are they all "types" of the modern hero?

Creative Writing / Performance

7. Talking It Through

Write a dialogue between Prufrock and another person. Include in your dialogue some references to topics in the poem that concern Prufrock. You might even imagine the conversation as being with Ralph Waldo Emerson (page 216), with references to Emerson's advice in the essay "Self-Reliance" (page 224). With another student, present your dialogue to the class.

Choices: Building Your Portfolio

1. **Writer's Notebook** Remind students to save their work. They may use it as prewriting for the Writer's Workshop on p. 685. Have students use a chart such as Transparency 2: Drawing Conclusions from Information Chart in the Transparency Package to organize their ideas on which view is most accurate.
2. **Critical Writing** Before students attempt this assignment, have them try to reconstruct what they think Harriet Monroe thought the ending meant and why she considered it triumphant. This will help them create a better argument.
3. **Critical Writing** Before students attempt this short essay, they should clearly articulate what they think each speaker is searching for, what problems are encountered in the search, and whether or not each is successful.

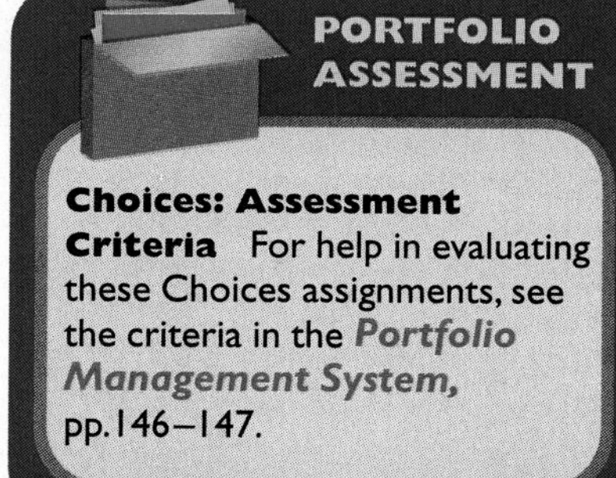

Choices: Assessment Criteria For help in evaluating these Choices assignments, see the criteria in the ***Portfolio Management System,*** pp. 146–147.

Allusions

1. The speaker lives in his own kind of hell. The speaker is afraid of revealing what he knows.
2. Knowledge of the great Italian Renaissance sculptor and painter suggests sophisticated, cultured women or women who have chosen this topic to present themselves as refined.
3. Prufrock feels that his head has been separated from his body and presented to the company.
4. These blasé women would not be interested even in the observations of someone who came back from the dead.
5. Hamlet asks the "overwhelming question" ("To be or not to be") and answers it in the affirmative—the false king must die. But Prufrock answers in the negative (l. 111)—it is not worthwhile to pursue the question and risk the exposure (kill the false king).

QUICK PLANNING GUIDE

Into the Story

Author Biography p. 672

Before You Read p. 673

- **Reading Focus: Scaffolding** Students reflect on a classic theme and discover three vivid characters.
- **A Dialogue with the Text:** Record predictions and outcomes in Reader's Log
- **Elements of Literature: Foreshadowing**

Through the Story

"The Life You Save May Be Your Own" pp. 674–681

Words to Own pp. 674–681

Primary Sources p. 682

Making Meanings p. 683

Elements of Literature pp. 683-684

- Tragedy
- Comedy
- Romance
- Irony

Beyond the Story

Choices: Building Your Portfolio p. 684

- **Writer's Notebook:** Collect ideas for a speculation about causes and effects
- **Critical Writing:** Write a brief essay defending a critical analysis
- **Critical Thinking/Speaking and Listening:** Lead a class discussion analyzing O'Connor's comments
- **Creative Writing:** Write a screenplay, narrative, magazine interview, or newspaper article
- **Creative Writing/Art:** Design a bumper sticker

Flannery O'Connor

(1925–1964)

The Bettmann Archive.

Flannery O'Connor with self-portrait.

Flannery O'Connor was born in Savannah, Georgia, and spent her short life almost entirely in nearby Milledgeville, where her family had lived since before the Civil War. Although she limited herself to a rural, Southern literary terrain and the body of her work was small, her place in American literature is secure.

O'Connor wrote steadily from 1948 until her death sixteen years later. For fourteen of those sixteen years, she was plagued by lupus, a painful, wasting disease that she had inherited from her father and that kept her ever more confined and immobile. "I have never been anywhere but sick," she wrote. "In a sense sickness is a place, more instructive than a long trip to Europe, and it's always a place where there's no company, where nobody can follow. Sickness before death is a very appropriate thing and I think those who don't have it miss one of God's mercies."

O'Connor graduated from the Women's College of Georgia in 1945. She then went to the Writer's Workshop at the University of Iowa. Her first novel, *Wise Blood,* was published in 1952. She followed that novel with a short-story collection, *A Good Man Is Hard to Find,* in 1955; a second novel, *The Violent Bear It Away,* in 1960; and a second collection of stories, *Everything That Rises Must Converge,* in 1965.

Always disciplined as a writer, O'Connor forced herself to sit at her desk without conscious distraction of any sort at the same time every day for two hours, even if no inspiration came. "Sometimes I work for months and have to throw everything away," she commented, "but I don't think any of that was time wasted." While her central concern in her fiction was the abstract idea of good and evil, she felt compelled to confine herself to the concrete. She noted that the short-story writer has "only a short space" to "reveal as much of the mystery of existence as possible" and must therefore "do it by showing, not by saying, and by showing the concrete. . . ."

From the first, O'Connor was recognized as a satirist of astonishing originality and vigor, whose targets were smugness, optimism, and self-righteousness. However, the essential element of O'Connor's life and work is that she remained a Roman Catholic without the slightest wavering of faith throughout her thirty-nine years. A thunder-and-lightning Christian belief pervades every story and novel she wrote. Her attraction to the grotesque and the violent puts off many critics and readers. They fail to appreciate that the violent motifs in her fiction grow from her passionate, Christian vision of our secular times.

What O'Connor wants to tell us is that, in our rationality, we have lost the one essential—a spiritual center for our lives. "Redemption is meaningless," O'Connor wrote, "unless there is cause for it in the actual life we live, and for the last few centuries there has been operating in our culture the secular belief that there is no such cause."

In her works, O'Connor seems to be saying that we have become so accustomed to the lack of God in our lives that a writer must use violent means to make a point. Just as we are made to feel comfortable, enjoying O'Connor's carnival show, the comedy is miraculously transcended, and we realize that the situation has a philosophical meaning. All the freaks and clowns have taken on God's meaning. God is here, and the devil is, too.

WORDS TO OWN

The following vocabulary words are defined in the Words to Own at the bottom of the pupil's page.

gaunt p. 674	volley p. 678
listed p. 674	morose p. 679
amble p. 674	sultry p. 680
irked p. 676	rued p. 680
ravenous p. 677	guffawing p. 681

PORTFOLIO ASSESSMENT

Portfolio Assessment For help with teacher assessment of reading skills, see the ***Portfolio Management System,*** pp. 54–55.

BEFORE YOU READ
THE LIFE YOU SAVE MAY BE YOUR OWN

Reading Focus
Truth in the Grotesque

The characters in this story act out a classic **theme**—that of innocence beset by evil. But, from the very beginning, we are confronted with dark hints that this is no comforting fairy tale or noble heroic epic. In this exquisite piece of storytelling, ideals of romance and heroism are turned upside down.

There are three vivid characters here, each one a masterful portrait from the rural South. With all their peculiarities, O'Connor's characters are disturbingly familiar. They are homespun figures, as real as any Georgia barnyard or roadside cafe, drawn with a kind of humor that balances on the edge of terror. They find themselves in a situation that is both tragic and comic, an odd mixture that O'Connor often used in order to communicate her points.

A Dialogue with the Text

You won't have to read very far to discover that this story is both disturbing and funny. Pay special attention to the way the characters speak, but don't let their casual, down-home voices fool you.

As you read, fill in a prediction chart like the one below. Record events or details from the story, along with your predictions about what these events or details suggest might happen later in the story. As you continue reading, write down what actually happens.

Detail or Event in Story	Your Prediction	Actual Outcome

Elements of Literature
Foreshadowing

Writers often **foreshadow** what will happen later on in a story by giving hints or clues. These hints, which often create **suspense** and arouse curiosity, can carry potentially ominous or menacing undertones, so subtle sometimes as to escape notice on a first reading.

Foreshadowing is the use of hints and clues to suggest what will happen later in a plot.

For more on Foreshadowing, see the Handbook of Literary Terms.

Bob Leroy/ProFiles West.

Into the Story

Using BEFORE YOU READ p. 673

A Dialogue with the Text

Students may find O'Connor's writing wildly unpredictable. Tell them not to worry about how outlandish or far from the truth their predictions might seem. Ask them to base their ideas on details from the story and on the knowledge that the story is both tragic and comic.

WRITERS ON WRITING

Flannery O'Connor practiced her craft unflaggingly, but could be reluctant to talk about it: "I have very little to say about short-story writing. It's one thing to write short stories and another thing to talk about writing them, and I hope you realize that your asking me to talk about story-writing is just like asking a fish to lecture on swimming. The more stories I write, the more mysterious I find the process and the less I find myself capable of analyzing it. Before I started writing stories, I suppose I could have given you a pretty good lecture on the subject, but nothing produces silence like experience, and at this point I have very little to say about how stories are written."

PROGRAM MANAGER

- **Planning Instruction** See Teaching Notes, *Teaching Resources B,* pp. 53–54, for information.
- **Instructional Support** See Graphic Organizer for Active Reading, *Teaching Resources B,* p. 62, for an Into the Story activity.
- **Application and Reinforcement** For reinforcement of the elements of literature introduced in this lesson, see Transparency 13.2 in the *Audiovisual Resources Binder.*
- **Audiotaped Readings** To help readers through the lesson, use the Selected Reading, Audiocassette 3, Side A in the *Audiovisual Resources Binder.*
- **Assessment** See Selection Test, *Test Booklet,* pp. 156–157.
- **Language Link** For instruction in correcting common usage problems, see Language Link, *Teaching Resources B,* pp. 63–64, and *Language and Writing Skills Worksheets,* pp. 1–2, 6–8.
- **Reinforcement** Use the Words to Own worksheet in *Teaching Resources B,* p. 65.

A. Critical Reading: Analyzing Character

? What does Mr. Shiftlet's name suggest about him? [It suggests that he is shifty or shiftless.]

Lilacs (1924–1927) by Charles Burchfield. Oil on board.

The Life You Save May Be Your Own

Flannery O'Connor

(A) The old woman and her daughter were sitting on their porch when Mr. Shiftlet came up their road for the first time. The old woman slid to the edge of her chair and leaned forward, shading her eyes from the piercing sunset with her hand. The daughter could not see far in front of her and continued to play with her fingers. Although the old woman lived in this desolate spot with only her daughter and she had never seen Mr. Shiftlet before, she could tell, even from a distance, that he was a tramp and no one to be afraid of. His left coat sleeve was folded up to show there was only half an arm in it and his gaunt figure listed slightly to the side as if the breeze were pushing him. He had on a black town suit and a brown felt hat that was turned up in the front and down in the back and he carried a tin toolbox by a handle. He came on, at an amble, up her road, his face turned toward the sun which appeared to be balancing itself on the peak of a small mountain.

The old woman didn't change her position until he was almost into her yard; then she rose

Words to Own

gaunt (gônt) *adj.:* very thin.
listed (list′id) *v.:* tilted.
amble (am′bəl) *n.:* leisurely pace.

OPTIONS FOR TEACHING

STRATEGIES FOR INCLUSION

Learners Having Difficulty After students have finished reading the story, have them work in small groups of mixed ability to determine how the title of the story relates to the **theme.** Have each group choose a spokesperson to share their analysis with the class.

Less Proficient Readers Some students may fail to appreciate the ironic humor in this story. Reading part of the story aloud yourself or playing the audiocassette of the entire story will help students become familiar with the tone.

Visual Before reading this story, discuss how the author uses figurative language and descriptive details to create vivid characters that one can see in one's mind. As you read the opening passages of the story, ask students to close their eyes and to create a personal "mind picture" of the main characters in this story. Then, have them draw the images they have pictured.

with one hand fisted on her hip. The daughter, a large girl in a short blue organdy dress, saw him all at once and jumped up and began to stamp and point and make excited speechless sounds.

Mr. Shiftlet stopped just inside the yard and set his box on the ground and tipped his hat at her as if she were not in the least afflicted; then he turned toward the old woman and swung the hat all the way off. He had long black slick hair that hung flat from a part in the middle to beyond the tips of his ears on either side. His face descended in forehead for more than half its length and ended suddenly with his features just balanced over a jutting steel-trap jaw. He seemed to be a young man but he had a look of composed dissatisfaction as if he understood life thoroughly.

"Good evening," the old woman said. She was about the size of a cedar fence post and she had a man's gray hat pulled down low over her head. **B**

The tramp stood looking at her and didn't answer. He turned his back and faced the sunset. He swung both his whole and his short arm up slowly so that they indicated an expanse of sky and his figure formed a crooked cross. **C** The old woman watched him with her arms folded across her chest as if she were the owner of the sun, and the daughter watched, her head thrust forward and her fat helpless hands hanging at the wrists. She had long pink-gold hair and eyes as blue as a peacock's neck.

He held the pose for almost fifty seconds and then he picked up his box and came on to the porch and dropped down on the bottom step. "Lady," he said in a firm nasal voice, "I'd give a fortune to live where I could see me a sun do that every evening."

"Does it every evening," the old woman said and sat back down. The daughter sat down too and watched him with a cautious sly look as if he were a bird that had come up very close. He leaned to one side, rooting in his pants pocket, and in a second he brought out a package of chewing gum and offered her a piece. She took it and unpeeled it and began to chew without taking her eyes off him. He offered the old woman a piece but she only raised her upper lip to indicate she had no teeth.

Mr. Shiftlet's pale sharp glance had already passed over everything in the yard—the pump near the corner of the house and the big fig tree that three or four chickens were preparing to roost in—and had moved to a shed where he saw the square rusted back of an automobile. "You ladies drive?" he asked.

"That car ain't run in fifteen year," the old woman said. "The day my husband died, it quit running."

"Nothing is like it used to be, lady," he said. "The world is almost rotten."

"That's right," the old woman said. "You from around here?"

"Name Tom T. Shiftlet," he murmured, looking at the tires.

"I'm pleased to meet you," the old woman said. "Name Lucynell Crater and daughter Lucynell Crater. What you doing around here, Mr. Shiftlet?"

He judged the car to be about a 1928 or '29 Ford. "Lady," he said, and turned and gave her his full attention, "lemme tell you something. There's one of these doctors in Atlanta that's taken a knife and cut the human heart—the human heart," he repeated, leaning forward, "out of a man's chest and held it in his hand," and he held his hand out, palm up, as if it were slightly weighted with the human heart, "and studied it like it was a day-old chicken, and lady," he said, allowing a long significant pause in which his head slid forward and his clay-colored eyes brightened, "he don't know no more about it than you or me." **D**

"That's right," the old woman said.

"Why, if he was to take that knife and cut into every corner of it, he still wouldn't know no more than you or me. What you want to bet?"

"Nothing," the old woman said wisely. "Where you come from, Mr. Shiftlet?" **E**

He didn't answer. He reached into his pocket and brought out a sack of tobacco and a package of cigarette papers and rolled himself a cigarette, expertly with one hand, and attached it in a hanging position to his upper lip. Then he took a box of wooden matches from his pocket and struck one on his shoe. He held the burning match as if he were studying the mystery of flame while it traveled dangerously toward his skin. The daughter began to make loud noises and to point to his hand and shake her finger at him, but when the flame was just before touching him, he leaned down with his hand cupped over it as if he were going to set fire to his nose and lit the cigarette.

He flipped away the dead match and blew a stream of gray into the evening. A sly look came

B. Literary Element: Description

? How does O'Connor use descriptive language to enable the reader to visualize her characters? [She describes the old woman as "about the size of a cedar fence post"; later, O'Connor describes the daughter as having "fat helpless hands hanging at the wrists" and "eyes as blue as a peacock's neck."]

C. Critical Reading: Drawing Conclusions

? What might the "crooked cross" symbolize? [Possible answers: That Shiftlet may be corrupt; or that he may be like one of the thieves crucified with Jesus.]

D. Literary Element: Point of View

? How would you describe the point of view from which this story is told—first person, limited third person, or omniscient? [Omniscient; here, readers are told what Shiftlet is thinking. Elsewhere, readers are told what the old woman is thinking.]

E. Literary Element: Foreshadowing

? What have you learned so far about Tom T. Shiftlet? [The name *Shiftlet* seems appropriate for the tramp. He has no possessions. At first meeting, Shiftlet appears to be a clever con man. He flatters the old woman by praising her sunset and by equating his and her knowledge to that of a doctor. He quickly spots the old automobile and seems to size up the situation, including young Lucynell's mental retardation.] What might these details reveal about what is to come? [Possible answer: The old woman is about to be conned out of the car or money or both.]

INTEGRATING THE LANGUAGE ARTS

Language and Vocabulary Before class begins, write a sentence on the chalkboard about the day's reading. The sentence should contain two or three new vocabulary words, with some contextual clues to their meanings—for example, "A gaunt man who may not have eaten for quite some time ambles up to an old woman's house." When students arrive, ask them to write a paraphrase of the sentence without using the new vocabulary words. Discuss their responses, asking what context clues they used.

Strategic Reading As they read the story, have students note the main events in the plot. Students should list the events in boxes drawn on a sheet of paper with the events linked in order by arrows between them, as shown in the following diagram. Advise students that they should list the events in the order in which they occur. Have students label each box with the terms *exposition, complications, climax,* and *resolution* or *denouement* to indicate which plot element each event represents.

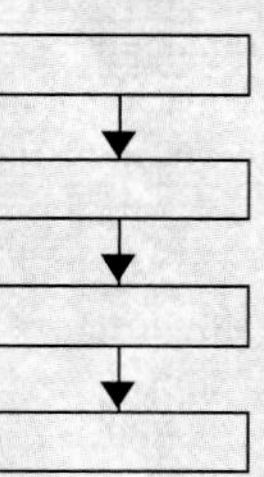

A. Reader's Response: First Thoughts

? Do you believe Shiftlet when he tells about his life? [Sample responses: No; Shiftlet mispronounces *Armed Services* and although he continues to say that he was raised to care about how he does things, he seems to be a con artist. Or some of it may be true; he could have worked for the railroad and lost his arm there.]

B. Reader's Response: Shaping Interpretations

? What does "a moral intelligence" mean? [Sample responses: An understanding of the rightness or wrongness of something; or acting according to moral principles.] How can this be an "impossible truth" for Shiftlet? [Sample responses: He does not follow a moral code; or Shiftlet cares only about what he can get.]

over his face. "Lady," he said, "nowadays, people'll do anything anyways. I can tell you my name is Tom T. Shiftlet, and I come from Tarwater, Tennessee, but you never have seen me before: How you know I ain't lying? How you know my name ain't Aaron Sparks, lady, and I come from Singleberry, Georgia, or how you know it's not George Speeds and I come from Lucy, Alabama, or how you know I ain't Thompson Bright from Toolafalls, Mississippi?"

"I don't know nothing about you," the old woman muttered, irked.

"Lady," he said, "people don't care how they lie. Maybe the best I can tell you is, I'm a man; but listen lady," he said and paused and made his tone more ominous still, "what is a man?"

The old woman began to gum a seed. "What you carry in that tin box, Mr. Shiftlet?" she asked.

"Tools," he said, put back. "I'm a carpenter."

"Well, if you come out here to work, I'll be able to feed you and give you a place to sleep but I can't pay. I'll tell you that before you begin," she said.

There was no answer at once and no particular expression on his face. He leaned back against the two-by-four that helped support the porch roof. "Lady," he said slowly, "there's some men that some things mean more to them than money." The old woman rocked without comment and the daughter watched the trigger that moved up and down in his neck. He told the old woman then that all most people were interested in was money, but he asked what a man was made for. He asked her if a man was made for money, or what. He asked her what she thought she was made for but she didn't answer, she only sat rocking and wondered if a one-armed man could put a new roof on her garden house. (A) He asked a lot of questions that she didn't answer. He told her that he was twenty-eight years old and had lived a varied life. He had been a gospel singer, a foreman on the railroad, an assistant in an undertaking parlor, and he come over the radio for three months with Uncle Roy and his Red Creek Wranglers. He said he had fought and bled in the Arm Service of his country and visited every foreign land and that everywhere he had seen people that didn't care if they did a thing one way or another. He said he hadn't been raised thataway.

A fat yellow moon appeared in the branches of the fig tree as if it were going to roost there with the chickens. He said that a man had to escape to the country to see the world whole and that he wished he lived in a desolate place like this where he could see the sun go down every evening like God made it to do.

"Are you married or are you single?" the old woman asked.

There was a long silence. "Lady," he asked finally, "where would you find you an innocent woman today? I wouldn't have any of this trash I could just pick up."

The daughter was leaning very far down, hanging her head almost between her knees watching him through a triangular door she had made in her overturned hair; and she suddenly fell in a heap on the floor and began to whimper. Mr. Shiftlet straightened her out and helped her get back in the chair.

"Is she your baby girl?" he asked.

"My only," the old woman said, "and she's the sweetest girl in the world. I would give her up for nothing on earth. She's smart too. She can sweep the floor, cook, wash, feed the chickens, and hoe. I wouldn't give her up for a casket of jewels."

"No," he said kindly, "don't ever let any man take her away from you."

"Any man come after her," the old woman said, " 'll have to stay around the place."

Mr. Shiftlet's eye in the darkness was focused on a part of the automobile bumper that glittered in the distance. "Lady," he said, jerking his short arm up as if he could point with it to her house and yard and pump, "there ain't a broken thing on this plantation that I couldn't fix for you, one-arm jackleg[1] or not. I'm a man," he said with a sullen dignity, (B) "even if I ain't a whole one. I got," he said, tapping his knuckles on the floor to emphasize the immensity of what he was going to say, "a moral intelligence!" and his face pierced out of the darkness into a shaft of doorlight and he stared at her as if he were astonished himself at this impossible truth.

The old woman was not impressed with the

1. **jackleg:** not properly trained; amateur. O'Connor is possibly playing on the word's other meaning: "dishonest."

Words to Own

irked (ʉrkt) *v.* used as *adj.:* annoyed; irritated.

OPTIONS FOR TEACHING

COOPERATIVE LEARNING

Debate To engage students' feelings and stimulate critical thinking, stage a debate in your classroom. Have students take sides on the question "Is Shiftlet an evil character?" Divide the class on each side into smaller groups for developing supporting arguments. Ask half the members of each group to propose the arguments; have the other half think of how the opposing side would object to these arguments. Have the group develop a reply to the objections. Ask each group's spokesperson to present one supporting argument to the class. Allow time for rebuttals and discussion of each group's argument.

Reader's Theater The **dialogue** in the story lends itself well to Reader's Theater. Have students work in groups of three or four to adapt a scene from the story. Ask students to script a scene (for example, the opening scene between Shiftlet and the old woman) as a drama and then to read their script aloud dramatically. Ask each group member to take a role: reading a part, directing, or providing costumes, props, or sound effects. Be sure that students know that the readers should sit or stand in front of the audience and read from the book.

phrase. "I told you you could hang around and work for food," she said, "if you don't mind sleeping in that car yonder."

"Why listen, lady," he said with a grin of delight, "the monks of old slept in their coffins!"

"They wasn't as advanced as we are," the old woman said.

The next morning he began on the roof of the garden house while Lucynell, the daughter, sat on a rock and watched him work. He had not been around a week before the change he had made in the place was apparent. He had patched the front and back steps, built a new hog pen, restored a fence, and taught Lucynell, who was completely deaf and had never said a word in her life, to say the word "bird." The big rosy-faced girl followed him everywhere, saying "Burrttddt ddbirrrttdt," and clapping her hands. The old woman watched from a distance, secretly pleased. She was ravenous for a son-in-law.

In the evenings he sat on the steps and talked while the old woman and Lucynell rocked violently in their chairs on either side of him.

Mr. Shiftlet slept on the hard narrow back seat of the car with his feet out the side window. He had his razor and a can of water on a crate that served him as a bedside table and he put up a piece of mirror against the back glass and kept his coat neatly on a hanger that he hung over one of the windows.

In the evenings he sat on the steps and talked while the old woman and Lucynell rocked violently in their chairs on either side of him. The old woman's three mountains were black against the dark blue sky and were visited off and on by various planets and by the moon after it had left the chickens. Mr. Shiftlet pointed out that the reason he had improved this plantation was because he had taken a personal interest in it. He said he was even going to make the automobile run.

He had raised the hood and studied the mechanism and he said he could tell that the car had been built in the days when cars were really built. You take now, he said, one man puts in one bolt and another man puts in another bolt and another man puts in another bolt so that it's a man for a bolt. That's why you have to pay so much for a car: you're paying all those men. Now if you didn't have to pay but one man, you could get you a cheaper car and one that had had a personal interest taken in it, and it would be a better car. The old woman agreed with him that this was so.

Mr. Shiftlet said that the trouble with the world was that nobody cared, or stopped and took any trouble. He said he never would have been able to teach Lucynell to say a word if he hadn't cared and stopped long enough.

"Teach her to say something else," the old woman said.

"What you want her to say next?" Mr. Shiftlet asked.

The old woman's smile was broad and toothless and suggestive. "Teach her to say 'sugarpie,'" she said.

Mr. Shiftlet already knew what was on her mind.

The next day he began to tinker with the automobile and that evening he told her that if she would buy a fan belt, he would be able to make the car run.

The old woman said she would give him the money. "You see that girl yonder?" she asked, pointing to Lucynell who was sitting on the floor a foot away, watching him, her eyes blue even in the dark. "If it was ever a man wanted to take her away, I would say, 'No man on earth is going to take that sweet girl of mine away from me!' but if he was to say, 'Lady, I don't want to take her away, I want her right here,' I would say, 'Mister, I don't blame you none. I wouldn't pass up a chance to live in a permanent place and get the sweetest girl

Words to Own

ravenous (rav'ə·nəs) *adj.:* very eager.

C. Literary Element: Irony

? What is ironic about the old woman's response to Shiftlet's comment about monks sleeping in their coffins? [Neither Shiftlet nor the old woman considers sleeping in an old car to be "advanced." Both, however, consider themselves to be among the "advanced."]

D. Critical Reading: Expressing an Opinion

? Do you think Mr. Shiftlet really cares about Lucynell? [Possible answers: No, he is working the old woman to get her car. Or yes, in some strange way he does, for he does teach her to say *bird.*]

Metacognition How did you derive your answer? [Possible answers: I remembered what I read in the story; or my own experience tells me that people who take the time to teach usually care in some way.]

E. Critical Reading: Drawing Conclusions

? Why does the old woman suggest that Shiftlet teach Lucynell to say *sugarpie?* [Possible answer: She hopes that having Lucynell master this term of endearment will encourage Shiftlet to marry her daughter.]

CLASSROOM MANAGEMENT

Reader's Theater Strategies To facilitate the Reader's Theater presentations described on p. T676, ask group members to decide on a scene and to mark the beginning and ending of the scene in their books with self-stick notes. Ask students to read over the dialogue, noting any narration that indicates the movement or emotions of the characters in the scene. They should decide whether they would like a narrator to read the movements and emotions, or whether the reading of movements should be omitted and the character readers should reveal the emotions through their voices. Assign parts and have students practice in their groups before they present their scene to the class.

Block Scheduling To maintain student enthusiasm during a longer class period, vary activities every twenty to twenty-five minutes. Combine differing activities such as short lecture, pair share, small-group discussion, and activities which involve some student movement. These varied activities are important to keep students focused, on task, and actively engaged during the longer time span.

A. Literary Element: Simile

To whom is Shiftlet being compared? [Jesus, who raised Lazarus from the dead.] **Why is this a particularly ironic comparison?** [Possible answers: Because Shiftlet appears to be a con artist and not at all Christlike. Or because inanimate objects cannot have life, and therefore the car cannot be raised from the dead.]

B. Critical Reading: Making Inferences

Why does the old woman suddenly aim such language at Shiftlet? [She shifts tactics. Instead of enticing him to marry Lucynell with promises of a deep well and a permanent house, she reminds him of his prospects without her daughter.]

C. Literary Element: Irony

What is ironic about Shiftlet's statement? [Shiftlet's purpose is to repair the automobile so that his body can move on. Shiftlet's spirit, on the other hand, is static.]

D. Literary Element: Simile

What does O'Connor's use of the snake simile tell you about Shiftlet? [*Snake* implies deceit, treachery, and evil. A serpent was also the deceiver of Adam and Eve.]

in the world myself. You ain't no fool,' I would say."

"How old is she?" Mr. Shiftlet asked casually.

"Fifteen, sixteen," the old woman said. The girl was nearly thirty but because of her innocence it was impossible to guess.

"It would be a good idea to paint it too," Mr. Shiftlet remarked. "You don't want it to rust out."

"We'll see about that later," the old woman said.

The next day he walked into town and returned with the parts he needed and a can of gasoline. Late in the afternoon, terrible noises

In the darkness, Mr. Shiftlet's smile stretched like a weary snake waking up by a fire.

issued from the shed and the old woman rushed out of the house, thinking Lucynell was somewhere having a fit. Lucynell was sitting on a chicken crate, stamping her feet and screaming, "Burrddttt! bddurrddtttt!" but her fuss was drowned out by the car. With a volley of blasts it emerged from the shed, moving in a fierce and stately way. Mr. Shiftlet was in the driver's seat, sitting very erect. He had an expression of serious (A) modesty on his face as if he had just raised the dead.

That night, rocking on the porch, the old woman began her business, at once. "You want you an innocent woman, don't you?" she asked sympathetically. "You don't want none of this trash."

"No'm, I don't," Mr. Shiftlet said.

"One that can't talk," she continued, "can't sass you back or use foul language. That's the kind for you to have. Right there," and she pointed to Lucynell sitting cross-legged in her chair, holding both feet in her hands.

"That's right," he admitted. "She wouldn't give me any trouble."

"Saturday," the old woman said, "you and her and me can drive into town and get married."

Mr. Shiftlet eased his position on the steps.

"I can't get married right now," he said. "Everything you want to do takes money and I ain't got any."

"What you need with money?" she asked.

"It takes money," he said. "Some people'll do anything anyhow these days, but the way I think, I wouldn't marry no woman that I couldn't take on a trip like she was somebody. I mean take her to a hotel and treat her. I wouldn't marry the Duchesser Windsor," he said firmly, "unless I could take her to a hotel and giver something good to eat.

"I was raised thataway and there ain't a thing I can do about it. My old mother taught me how to do."

"Lucynell don't even know what a hotel is," the (B) old woman muttered. "Listen here, Mr. Shiftlet," she said, sliding forward in her chair, "you'd be getting a permanent house and a deep well and the most innocent girl in the world. You don't need no money. Lemme tell you something: there ain't any place in the world for a poor disabled friendless drifting man."

The ugly words settled in Mr. Shiftlet's head like a group of buzzards in the top of a tree. He didn't answer at once. He rolled himself a cigarette and lit it and then he said in an even voice, "Lady, a man is divided into two parts, body and spirit."

The old woman clamped her gums together.

"A body and a spirit," he repeated. "The body, (C) lady, is like a house: it don't go anywhere; but the spirit, lady, is like a automobile: always on the move, always . . ."

"Listen, Mr. Shiftlet," she said, "my well never goes dry and my house is always warm in the winter and there's no mortgage on a thing about this place. You can go to the courthouse and see for yourself. And yonder under that shed is a fine automobile." She laid the bait carefully. "You can have it painted by Saturday. I'll pay for the paint."

In the darkness, Mr. Shiftlet's smile stretched (D) like a weary snake waking up by a fire. After a second he recalled himself and said, "I'm only saying

Words to Own

volley (väl'ē) *n.:* firing of many shots at once.

OPTIONS FOR TEACHING

CROSSING THE CURRICULUM

Industrial Arts Ask students to consider the condition of the car and to research reasons why it may not have run. Have them explain to the class what Shiftlet may have repaired to get the car running.

Music Flannery O'Connor sold the television rights to this story. Ask students to imagine that they are staging the television production of the story. What music would they choose as the theme song? Have students explain their choices.

Social Sciences Have students research mental retardation. They should consider such topics as the past treatment of people with mental retardation, the degrees of retardation, and current theories on how to help or teach people with mental retardation. Ask students to report their findings to the class.

a man's spirit means more to him than anything else. I would have to take my wife off for the weekend without no regards at all for cost. I got to follow where my spirit says to go."

"I'll give you fifteen dollars for a weekend trip," the old woman said in a crabbed voice. "That's the best I can do."

"That wouldn't hardly pay for more than the gas and the hotel," he said. "It wouldn't feed her."

"Seventeen-fifty," the old woman said. "That's all I got so it isn't any use you trying to milk me. You can take a lunch."

Mr. Shiftlet was deeply hurt by the word "milk." He didn't doubt that she had more money sewed up in her mattress but he had already told her he was not interested in her money. "I'll make that do," he said and rose and walked off without treating[2] with her further.

On Saturday the three of them drove into town in the car that the paint had barely dried on and Mr. Shiftlet and Lucynell were married in the Ordinary's[3] office while the old woman witnessed. As they came out of the courthouse, Mr. Shiftlet began twisting his neck in his collar. He looked morose and bitter as if he had been insulted while someone held him. "That didn't satisfy me none," he said. "That was just something a woman in an office did, nothing but paperwork and blood tests. What do they know about my blood? If they was to take my heart and cut it out," he said, "they wouldn't know a thing about me. It didn't satisfy me at all."

"It satisfied the law," the old woman said sharply.

"The law," Mr. Shiftlet said and spit. "It's the law that don't satisfy me."

He had painted the car dark green with a yellow band around it just under the windows. The three of them climbed in the front seat and the old woman said, "Don't Lucynell look pretty? Looks like a baby doll." Lucynell was dressed up in a white dress that her mother had uprooted from a trunk and there was a Panama hat on her head with a bunch of red wooden cherries on the brim. Every now and then her placid expression was changed by a sly isolated little thought like a shoot of green in the desert. "You got a prize!" the old woman said.

Mr. Shiftlet didn't even look at her. **E**

They drove back to the house to let the old woman off and pick up the lunch. When they were ready to leave, she stood staring in the window of the car, with her fingers clenched around the glass. Tears began to seep sideways out of her eyes and run along the dirty creases in her face. "I ain't ever been parted with her for two days before," she said.

Mr. Shiftlet started the motor.

"And I wouldn't let no man have her but you because I seen you would do right. Good-bye, Sugarbaby," she said, clutching at the sleeve of the white dress. Lucynell looked straight at her and didn't seem to see her there at all. Mr. Shiftlet eased the car forward so that she had to move her hands.

The early afternoon was clear and open and surrounded by pale blue sky. Although the car would go only thirty miles an hour, Mr. Shiftlet imagined a terrific climb and dip and swerve that went entirely to his head so that he forgot his morning bitterness. He had always wanted an automobile but he had never been able to afford one before. He drove very fast because he wanted to make Mobile by nightfall.

Occasionally he stopped his thoughts long enough to look at Lucynell in the seat beside him. She had eaten the lunch as soon as they were out

Occasionally he stopped his thoughts long enough to look at Lucynell in the seat beside him.

2. **treating:** dealing; negotiating.
3. **Ordinary's:** judge's.

WORDS TO OWN
morose (mə·rōs′) *adj.:* gloomy.

E. Critical Reading: Drawing Conclusions

? What does this sentence suggest about Mr. Shiftlet's feelings for Lucynell? [Mr. Shiftlet's refusal even to look at Lucynell suggests that he does not really care for her. He probably married her to obtain a permanent home and access to an automobile.]

PROFESSIONAL NOTES

Critical Comment: Valiant Foes According to critic Michael D. True, "The paradox of keeping Christ alive by making heroes of His most formidable antagonists lies in the center of Miss O'Connor's fiction." In her stories, "the weak in spirit, the vulgar in speech, the superficial and even insipid in moral and religious values, the demonic characters often stand out clearly as the ones to be preferred. . . . In a chaotic world, plagued by casual violence and meaningless pursuits, she finds much to admire in those valiant foes who take the devil's part knowingly and enthusiastically, bent on the annihilation of a world without meaning. . . ."

Thematic Connections: "No Time for Heroes" Have students think of this story in relation to the other stories in this Collection. Ask them whether there are any heroes in this story. Students should note that both Shiftlet and the older Lucynell are motivated by self-interest. The young Lucynell may be too unaware of her circumstances to be considered a hero.

A. Critical Reading: Speculating

? When does Shiftlet decide to desert Lucynell? [Possible answers: He has planned to desert her all along; he gets the idea when he decides to stop; or he gets the idea when she is sitting sleeping at the counter and the boy says she looks like an angel.]

B. Literary Element: Irony

? What makes this statement ironic? [Possible answers: Shiftlet's feeling responsible for others does not prevent him from abandoning his wife. He has just left someone he called a hitchhiker.] How is the warning sign also ironic? [Possible answers: Just like Shiftlet, the warning seems to combine a public-spirited concern for highway safety with a certain selfishness. Note the emphasis on saving one's own life instead of another's. Or the sign points out Shiftlet's lack of moral scruples.]

C. Critical Reading: Making Connections

? Who has just been similarly described? [Lucynell, asleep at the diner.] What is the difference in the purposes of the two similar descriptions? [The young man's description of Lucynell is an honest response to her innocence; Shiftlet's description of his mother is for effect.]

of the yard and now she was pulling the cherries off the hat one by one and throwing them out the window. He became depressed in spite of the car. He had driven about a hundred miles when he decided that she must be hungry again and at the next small town they came to, he stopped in front of an aluminum-painted eating place called The Hot Spot and took her in and ordered her a plate of ham and grits. The ride had made her sleepy and as soon as she got up on the stool, she rested her head on the counter and shut her eyes. There was no one in The Hot Spot but Mr. Shiftlet and the boy behind the counter, a pale youth with a greasy rag hung over his shoulder. Before he could dish up the food, she was snoring gently.

A "Give it to her when she wakes up," Mr. Shiftlet said. "I'll pay for it now."

The boy bent over her and stared at the long pink-gold hair and the half-shut sleeping eyes. Then he looked up and stared at Mr. Shiftlet. "She looks like an angel of Gawd," he murmured.

"Hitchhiker," Mr. Shiftlet explained. "I can't wait. I got to make Tuscaloosa."

The boy bent over again and very carefully touched his finger to a strand of the golden hair and Mr. Shiftlet left.

He was more depressed than ever as he drove on by himself. The late afternoon had grown hot and <u>sultry</u> and the country had flattened out. Deep in the sky a storm was preparing very slowly and without thunder as if it meant to drain every drop of air from the earth before it broke. There were times when Mr. Shiftlet preferred not to be alone. He felt too that a man with a car had a responsibility to others and he kept his eye out for B a hitchhiker. Occasionally he saw a sign that warned: "Drive carefully. The life you save may be your own."

Occasionally he saw a sign that warned: "Drive carefully. The life you save may be your own."

The narrow road dropped off on either side into dry fields and here and there a shack or a filling station stood in a clearing. The sun began to set directly in front of the automobile. It was a reddening ball that through his windshield was slightly flat on the bottom and top. He saw a boy in overalls and a gray hat standing on the edge of the road and he slowed the car down and stopped in front of him. The boy didn't have his hand raised to thumb the ride, he was only standing there, but he had a small cardboard suitcase and his hat was set on his head in a way to indicate that he had left somewhere for good. "Son," Mr. Shiftlet said, "I see you want a ride."

The boy didn't say he did or he didn't but he opened the door of the car and got in, and Mr. Shiftlet started driving again. The child held the suitcase on his lap and folded his arms on top of it. He turned his head and looked out the window away from Mr. Shiftlet. Mr. Shiftlet felt oppressed. "Son," he said after a minute, "I got the best old mother in the world so I reckon you only got the second best."

The boy gave him a quick dark glance and then turned his face back out the window.

"It's nothing so sweet," Mr. Shiftlet continued, "as a boy's mother. She taught him his first prayers at her knee, she give him love when no other would, she told him what was right and what wasn't, and she seen that he done the right thing. Son," he said, "I never <u>rued</u> a day in my life like the one I rued when I left that old mother of mine."

The boy shifted in his seat but he didn't look at Mr. Shiftlet. He unfolded his arms and put one hand on the door handle.

C "My mother was a angel of Gawd," Mr. Shiftlet said in a very strained voice. "He took her from heaven and giver to me and I left her." His eyes

Words to Own

sultry (sul′trē) *adj.:* humid and still.
rued (ro͞od) *v.:* regretted.

OPTIONS FOR TEACHING

ASSESSMENT TOOLS

Observation Assessment: Reading

As students discuss the short story, use the following checklist to assess and evaluate students' critical reading skills.

1=Rarely 2=Sometimes 3=Always

___ Attends to multiple levels of meaning.
___ Uses the text to verify and clarify ideas.
___ Makes connections between the text and other works.
___ Makes personal connections.
___ Challenges the text.

Check Test: True-False

1. Tom Shiftlet is interested in the Crater car even though it has not run in fifteen years. [True]
2. Lucynell, the daughter, is just over sixteen years old. [False]
3. Shiftlet claims to have been a gospel singer at one time. [True]
4. The first word that young Lucynell learns how to say is *sugarpie*. [False]
5. Shiftlet tells Mrs. Crater that he needs money to buy a suit to get married. [False]

Williams College Museum of Art, Gift of Cole Porter (47.1.3). © 1997 Estate of Grant Wood/Licensed by VAGA, New York.

Death on the Ridge Road (1935) by Grant Wood.
Oil on masonite (39″ × 46 1/16″).

were instantly clouded over with a mist of tears. The car was barely moving.

The boy turned angrily in the seat. "You go to the devil!" he cried. "My old woman is a fleabag and yours is a stinking polecat!" and with that he flung the door open and jumped out with his suitcase into the ditch.

Mr. Shiftlet was so shocked that for about a hundred feet he drove along slowly with the door still open. A cloud, the exact color of the boy's hat and shaped like a turnip, had descended over the sun, and another, worse looking, crouched behind the car. Mr. Shiftlet felt that the rottenness of the world was about to engulf him. He raised his arm and let it fall again to his breast. "Oh Lord!" he prayed. "Break forth and wash the slime from this earth!"

The turnip continued slowly to descend. After a few minutes there was a guffawing peal of thunder from behind and fantastic raindrops, like tin-can tops, crashed over the rear of Mr. Shiftlet's car. **D** Very quickly he stepped on the gas and with his stump sticking out the window he raced the galloping shower into Mobile.

WORDS TO OWN

guffawing (gu·fô′iŋ) *v.* used as *adj.*: like a loud burst of laughter. "Guffaw" is an echoic word—one that imitates the sound it stands for.

D. Critical Reading: Drawing Conclusions

? What is the significance of the image of the thunderstorm racing Shiftlet to Mobile? [It stresses the irony in the story, since Shiftlet represents the very slime he has prayed to be washed from this earth.]

Primary Sources

Before students read Primary Sources, ask them what they think happens when a writer signs over a short story, play, or novel to a television producer. Invite them to talk about novels or short stories they have read that have been turned into movies or television shows, and to what extent the print version may have been altered in the film or television version. After the discussion, have students read O'Connor's comments on the dramatization of "The Life You Save May Be Your Own."

PRIMARY **Sources** LETTERS

The Adventures of Mr. Shiftlet

The following comments are from *The Habit of Being* (1979), a collection of O'Connor's letters.

I am going to New York on the 30th to be, if you please, interviewed by Mr. Harvey Breit (on the 31st) on a program he is starting over at NBC-TV [called *Galley-Proof*]. They are also going to dramatize the opening scene from "The Life You Save" etc. Do you reckon this is going to corrupt me? I already feel like a combination of Msgr. Sheen[1] and Gorgeous George [a wrestler]. Everybody who has read *Wise Blood* thinks I'm a hillbilly nihilist, whereas I would like to create the impression over the television that I'm a hillbilly Thomist,[2] but I will probably not be able to think of anything to say to Mr. Harvey Breit but "Huh?" and "Ah dunno." When I come back I'll probably have to spend three months day and night in the chicken pen to counteract these evil influences.

. . .

I have just sold the television rights to "The Life You Save May Be Your Own" to what I understand is called the General Electric Playhouse. All I know about television is hearsay but somebody told me that this was a production conducted by Ronald Regan (?). I don't know if this means RR will be Mr. Shiftlet or not. A staggering thought. Mr. Shiftlet and the idiot daughter will no doubt go off in a Chrysler and live happily ever after. Anyway, on account of this, I am buying my mother a new refrigerator. While they make hash out of my story, she and me will make ice in the new refrigerator.

. . .

I have just learned via one of those gossip columns that the story I sold for a TV play is going to be put on in the spring and that a *tap-dancer* by the name of Gene Kelly is going to make his tellyvision debut in it. The punishment always fits the crime. They must be going to make a musical out of it.

. . .

A letter from my agent today announces that "The Life You Save" will be presented February 1 on the Schlitz Playhouse at 9:30 New York time. My eager beaver friend in NY keeps sending me clippings of gossip columns, one announcing that Kelly will star in Flannery O'Connor's "backwoods love story." Another saying Kelly says "It's a kind of hillbilly thing in which I play a guy who *befriends* a deaf-mute girl in the hills of Kentucky. It gives me a great chance to do some straight acting, something I really have no opportunity to do in movies." See? He ain't had the opportunity before. There'll be no singing & dancing, Kelly says. I think it's channel 5 and people tell me you can't get it very good here, so I hope you will absolutely be in front of your set this time at the correct hour, as I must have some representative there to give Kelly a good leer every now and then for me. I don't know who his leading lady will be, but doubtless my NY friend will be providing that information before long. She thinks this is all hilariously funny and keeps writing me, "Has dignity no value for you?" etc. It will probably be appropriate to smoke a corncob pipe while watching this. All my kinfolks are going to think that it is a great improvement over the original story.

. . .

Someone has just called my attention to the fact that this . . . text which has "The Life You Save" in it has it with the last paragraph omitted. I would be much obliged if you would call Harcourt [O'Connor's publisher] and tell them. I think some kind of protest ought to be lodged. I suppose there is nothing that can be done about it now but I certainly don't like the idea of my story being in a textbook and the last paragraph omitted. . . ."

—Flannery O'Connor

1. **Msgr. Sheen:** Monsignor Fulton J. Sheen, a Catholic priest who had a popular TV show in the early days of television.
2. **Thomist:** someone who follows the thinking of the thirteenth-century philosopher Thomas Aquinas.

STRATEGIES FOR INCLUSION

Advanced Have students discuss how they would cast the story if they were television producers today. Ask them to write the characteristics they would look for when casting actors in each role. Invite them to post a list of actors they might consider for each role.

Special Needs Ask students who have difficulty with reading comprehension to listen to an audiotape of excerpts from O'Connor's letters while highlighting specific information. Give students transparency sheets to place over the text selection. As students listen, have them highlight the passages that tell them how the Playhouse is going to produce O'Connor's story.

Linguistic Ask students to discuss the story's ending. Have them consider how the story would be different without its last paragraph as O'Connor discusses in her letter. Have them write their responses in their Reader's Logs.

English Language Development Students may need some assistance with O'Connor's use of dialect (for example, "Do you reckon" and "Ah dunno") and her sarcastic tone. Read the letters aloud to help students understand O'Connor's tone and attitude. Students can then read the letters themselves and more fully appreciate O'Connor's use of dialect and sarcasm.

MAKING MEANINGS

First Thoughts

1. Were you surprised at the way the story ended? Review the notes you made in your Reader's Log, and explain how the story's outcome affected you.

> **Reviewing the Text**
>
> **a.** Describe the improvements Mr. Shiftlet makes in the Craters' place during his first week there.
>
> **b.** Explain how Mr. Shiftlet seems to want to exploit the Craters.
>
> **c.** How does the older Lucynell want to exploit Mr. Shiftlet?
>
> **d.** What has become of young Lucynell and Mr. Shiftlet by the story's end?

Shaping Interpretations

2. In the opening pages of the story, what details of setting, of characterization, and of dialogue carry menacing undertones and seem to **foreshadow** later events? (Look back over your Reader's Log notes.)
3. What is the significance of the remarks made by the hitchhiker just before he leaps from the moving car?
4. What are we to make of the fact that Mr. Shiftlet feels that "the rottenness of the world" (page 681) is about to engulf him? What **irony** do you sense in Mr. Shiftlet's realization?
5. Find four **figures of speech** and several words with strongly connotative meanings that reveal O'Connor's attitude toward Mr. Shiftlet. Consider, for example, why O'Connor says that Shiftlet's "figure formed a crooked cross" (page 675) and why she describes his eyes as "clay-colored" (page 675). How does O'Connor want us to regard Mr. Shiftlet? Is he a prophet or a demon?
6. What do you think is the significance of the peculiar clouds and storm that pursue Mr. Shiftlet toward Mobile at the end of the story?
7. Do you sense **irony** in the story's title? How would you state the story's **theme,** based on the warning implied in the title?
8. Are there any heroes in this story? Do you think it is a story about innocence versus evil, or is it a story about a world in which everyone is a rogue? Explain.

ELEMENTS OF LITERATURE

The Four "Modes" of Fiction

According to some critics, all narrative literature can be more or less described in terms of four basic "modes," or story patterns. These modes are tragedy, comedy, romance, and irony. Tragedy and comedy are opposites, as are romance and irony.

In a typical **tragedy,** the hero is a noble, admirable character who falls from a position of some prominence to disaster or even death. This tragic hero is overcome by evil, but in the course of the struggle, he or she gains self-knowledge and wisdom. Watching a tragedy, we feel exhilarated, for we have seen the best that human beings are capable of in the face of overwhelming adversity. Greek tragedies such as *Antigone* and Shakespearean plays such as *Hamlet* best exemplify the tragic mode.

In a **comedy,** on the other hand, the central characters are often two lovers who want to marry despite parental and societal obstacles. By the end of a comedy, the young lovers have triumphed over the forces blocking them and are to be married. Many comedies end with a wedding, suggesting the renewal of life and love. Shakespeare's comedies, such as *Much Ado About Nothing* and *A Midsummer Night's Dream,* are perfect examples of comedy.

In the typical **romance** story, a hero undertakes a quest, during which his or her heroic qualities are put to the test. The hero is usually successful and returns having learned something of value. In such a story, beauty, innocence, and goodness prevail over evil, often with the help of magic or supernatural intervention. If you've ever read a fairy tale or a superhero comic, watched *Star Wars* or *Star Trek,* or gotten caught up in an adventure like *Raiders of the Lost Ark,* you've encountered the world of romance.

In the world of **irony,** as opposed to romance, there are no heroes and no triumphs. The world is a place where injustice, crime, and general foolishness prevail. The characters who triumph in such a

Making Meanings

First Thoughts

1. Possible responses: It was not surprising that he cons the Craters; it was surprising that nothing bad happens to him and that he drives off in a storm.

Reviewing the Text

a. He patches the front and back steps, builds a hog pen, fixes a fence, and teaches Lucynell to say *bird.*

b. He is interested in fixing the car and bargaining for money.

c. She does not pay him money for his work and wants him to marry her daughter, who is deaf and mentally retarded.

d. Shiftlet leaves Lucynell sleeping in a diner. He tries to outrun the storm to Mobile.

Shaping Interpretations

2. Setting: The sunset is "piercing"; the Lucynells live alone in a "desolate spot"; the sun appears precariously balanced on the peak of a small mountain. Characterization: The strange behavior of young Lucynell; the characterization of Shiftlet as a tramp; old Lucynell's fist; Shiftlet's "steel-trap jaw"; his look of "composed dissatisfaction" and his figure's forming "a crooked cross"; Shiftlet's "pale sharp glance" and his frequent notice of the automobile; his actions with the burning match; "the trigger that moved up and down in his neck." Dialogue: Shiftlet's reference to monks sleeping in coffins; his dwelling on surgery on the human heart; his statements that "the world is almost rotten," "people'll do anything anyways," and "people don't care how they lie"; old Lucynell's lying about her daughter's age.
3. He is the first to confront Shiftlet for lying.
4. Shiftlet cannot see the rottenness in himself. His realization is ironic because his own rottenness is about to engulf him and his prayer will be answered.
5. Some include "jutting steel-trap jaw"; "his clay-colored eyes"; "the trigger that moved up and down in his neck"; "smile stretched like a weary snake." Possible responses: These details show he is evil or that his actions are not true to his words. He is neither a prophet nor demon (because demons know they are evil); but his actions are evil.
6. They are a judgment on Mr. Shiftlet.
7. Possible responses: The warning on the road sign reflects an almost casual selfishness—it shows that people care more about themselves than about others. The theme is that most people, whatever they say to the contrary, are really preoccupied with their own interests.
8. Possible responses: There are no heroes. Young Lucynell is truly innocent, but since she does not know what is truly evil, she cannot know to fight it. Both old Lucynell and Shiftlet are evil and try to get something out of the other. Not everyone is a rogue, for the boy in the diner seems kind.

Elements of Literature

Answers

Tragedy: "A Wagner Matinée," "Winter Dreams," "The Leader of the People," "Soldier's Home"
Comedy: from *Dust Tracks on a Road*
Romance: "His Father's Earth," "A Worn Path"
Irony: "The Secret Life of Walter Mitty," "The Jilting of Granny Weatherall," "A Rose for Emily"

Beyond the Story

Choices: Building Your Portfolio

1. **Writer's Notebook** Remind students to save their work. They may use it as prewriting for the Writer's Workshop on p. 685.

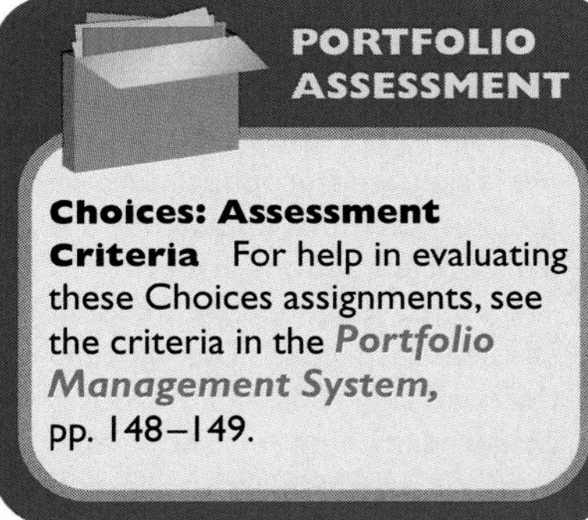

PORTFOLIO ASSESSMENT

Choices: Assessment Criteria For help in evaluating these Choices assignments, see the criteria in the *Portfolio Management System,* pp. 148–149.

world are often crafty rascals and even con artists—people who learn how to manipulate the world for their own gain. In other forms of irony, the characters are ordinary human beings like ourselves and are caught in a world that offers little opportunity for heroism. Walter Mitty (page 625) is an example of this type of character, one who longs for heroism but is limited to shopping for puppy biscuits in Waterbury, Connecticut. The characters in ironic fiction often find themselves in settings that are confining, that offer no opportunities for free choice: prisons, totalitarian societies, or even madhouses.

What modes are used in the stories you have read in the modern literature collections thus far?

Choices: Building Your Portfolio

Writer's Notebook

1. Collecting Ideas for a Speculation About Causes and Effects

The dominant mode in today's stories, novels, and plays is irony. In Arthur Miller's famous play *The Death of a Salesman,* for example, the characters and their problems are very ordinary. No longer do we find larger-than-life heroes struggling admirably against some malign fate, emerging with increased self-knowledge, even if the conflict ends in death. In Miller's play, the main character is an antihero named, appropriately, Loman. He is not a king or superman, but a failed salesman. His troubles are not caused by the gods or by fate, but by a boss who wants to make more money. Think of other ironic stories or novels you've read or ironic movies or plays you've seen. Then take notes speculating on why the dominant mode in literature today is irony. In other words, why don't we write about great heroes any more? Save your notes for possible use in the Writer's Workshop on page 685.

WORK IN PROGRESS

Critical Writing

2. Romantic Reversal

In a brief essay, analyze O'Connor's story as an ironic parody of a romance. (See Elements of Literature on page 683.) Account for these ironic reversals of the typical romance story: (a) the nurturing mother; (b) the beautiful, innocent young woman; (c) the hero who rescues the young woman; and (d) the romantic setting in a fairy-tale kingdom.

Critical Thinking / Speaking and Listening

3. Have Things Changed?

Lead a discussion in class analyzing O'Connor's comments about this story in Primary Sources (page 682). Consider (a) why TV producers would change the story, (b) whether the story would be popular if it were dramatized on TV today or made into a movie, and (c) why a textbook would omit the last paragraph (it is not omitted here).

Creative Writing

4. What Fate Awaits?

What becomes of Lucynell, asleep in the Hot Spot, and Mr. Shiftlet, driving on toward Mobile? In the form of a screenplay, narrative, magazine interview, or newspaper article, relate what befalls them.

Creative Writing / Art

5. Mr. Shiftlet's Motto

Design a bumper sticker for Mr. Shiftlet that, in a very few words, expresses his philosophy of life. Include an appropriate logo or graphic to accompany his saying.

"The world is almost rotten."

STRATEGIES FOR INCLUSION

Advanced/Auditory Before students begin activity #3, discuss several books and movies, and have students analyze the changes that were made to move from a print to a film format. If time permits, have students read portions of a selection, and show corresponding film clips. Possible titles include *The Wizard of Oz, The Jungle Book,* and *Little Women.*

Learners Having Difficulty/Auditory Students who have difficulty writing or who prefer speaking may want to create a live news broadcast from The Hot Spot rather than a written product for activity #4.

English Language Development Students from various cultures may not be familiar with bumper stickers. As preparation for activity #5, send students outside to write down slogans from bumper stickers they see. Ask them to find out what the slogans mean by interviewing native speakers. This preparation will allow them to understand some of the references and the wordplay that appear on some stickers, in addition to giving them a sense of the format for writing bumper stickers.

EXPOSITORY WRITING

Speculating About Causes and Effects

In our everyday lives, we frequently speculate on what caused a given event to occur, or we predict the outcome of another event or phenomenon. Whether we're discussing why the basketball team lost last week's game, deciding what electives will most benefit us in our school careers, or speculating about why there's been an increase in crime in our neighborhood, we are thinking about causes and effects. In fact, the world would make almost no sense to us unless we made these connections between cause and effect. Thus, when you write a cause-and-effect essay, you're simply doing in a more formal and careful way what you informally or even unconsciously do much of the time.

A cause-and-effect essay is one in which the writer speculates about either the causes or the effects of an event, a phenomenon, or a trend. (An *event* is a specific occurrence, such as a realignment of NCAA football conferences; a *phenomenon* is a continuing state of affairs, such as annual school performance on a nationwide academic test; and a *trend* is a changing pattern over time, such as an increased number of home computers.) To successfully write a cause-and-effect essay, you must present reasons, evidence, and examples to convince your readers that your particular arguments are plausible. A good way to think of the cause-and-effect essay is that it answers either *How did . . . ?* (by speculating about causes) or *What if . . . ?* (by predicting effects).

Prewriting

1. **Examining change.** Changes often give rise to speculations about causes and effects. Perhaps there has been a change in the number of homeless people in a city park. Or perhaps there has been a change in state automobile insurance laws. Change is also involved when we predict the effects or results of an event, phenomenon, or trend—for example, what the results may be of the school's new policy on locker searches.

   WORK IN PROGRESS

   Puzzling issues also lend themselves to speculations about causes or effects. Literary works, for example, can suggest many possible topics for speculation: Why did Richard Cory take his own life? Why is J. Alfred Prufrock so self-conscious and paralyzed? In F. Scott Fitzgerald's "Winter Dreams," why does Judy Jones change from a popular, carefree young girl to a neglected wife? If you kept your Writer's Notebook jottings from Collections 11–13, you may already have some ideas for a speculative essay about a literary topic.

Technology HELP

See Writer's Workshop 2 CD-ROM. *Assignment: Cause and Effect.*

ASSIGNMENT

Write a cause-and-effect essay speculating on the causes and/or effects of an event, phenomenon, situation, or trend.

AIM

To explain or inform; to persuade; to explore.

AUDIENCE

Your teacher, classmates, and perhaps the readership of a particular magazine or newspaper.

QUICK PLANNING GUIDE

Speculating About Causes and Effects

Motivation

Bring to class a local newspaper or the most recent issue of the school newspaper. Write on the chalkboard several headlines from stories that deal with recent events in your community or school. Ask students to suggest reasons (causes) for these events. After several students have volunteered possible causes, read one or two of the articles aloud to determine whether students' speculations were accurate. Point out that students already possess the thinking skills they need to write the essay and that this Writer's Workshop will help them refine these skills as they apply them to a topic that interests them.

PROGRAM MANAGER

Computer Guided Instruction For a related cause-and-effect assignment that students may use as additional instruction, see ***Writer's Workshop 2.***

PORTFOLIO ASSESSMENT

- **Generating Ideas** To help students in prewriting, use the heuristic in the *Portfolio Management System,* p. 150.
- **Portfolio Assessment** For a rubric that can be used to assess writing, see the *Portfolio Management System,* p. 152.

Teaching the Lesson

Remind students to focus on the most compelling arguments. An event, phenomenon, or trend (effects) can have a number of different causes, but there are usually one or two causes that are most important. Similarly, a cause can have several effects, one or two of which are most significant.

This lesson includes instruction for each stage of the writing process. Guide students through the process by modeling each step of the process with your own writing.

Prewriting

- Encourage students to think about recent changes at school or in the community that will have a direct effect on them. Then, ask them to consider why the changes occurred (the causes) or how the school or community will be affected (the effects).
- Point out that it might be possible for students to interview school or community officials to determine why the changes occurred. Students should keep in mind that officials may be somewhat reluctant to address all of the causes, especially if specific individuals are involved. Students might also interview classmates or others in the community to find out what these people think the results (or effects) of the changes will be. *You may want to obtain permission from parents or guardians and from the parties students will contact before they begin work on this activity.*

Try It Out

In brainstorming topics, it is useful to consider different categories of change. Changes can occur, for example, in physical, social, economic, ecological, political, cultural, educational, and technological spheres.

Choose two topics from any of the categories mentioned above. For each topic, explore possible causes and effects by completing these sentence beginnings:

- Because this (event, phenomenon, trend) happened, the result has been that ________________.
- If (a particular event, phenomenon, or trend) occurred, the result would be ________________.

If you don't have any ideas for an essay topic, brainstorm a list of possible topics by listing events, phenomena, and trends you would enjoy speculating about. If you are not truly interested in your topic, then you'll probably have trouble engaging your reader.

After you have a list of five or more topics, participate in a classwide brainstorming session led by the teacher or a classmate. Write as many topics as possible on the chalkboard where everyone can see them. Seeing the ideas of others may prompt you to think of additional topics you would like to explore. For each topic you seriously consider, make sure you can ask either *Why?* (causes) or *What's the result?* (effects) about it.

2. **Charting causes and effects.** Look at your list, and choose the topic that you find most interesting. Decide whether you are going to address causes, effects, or both. Depending on your topic, you can organize your information using a table, cluster diagram, or other graphic organizer. To make a table, form two columns on a piece of paper. On the left, list possible causes or effects related to your topic. On the right, record your explanations and reasons for these causes or effects. As you consider causes and effects, try to go beyond the obvious.

Model

Topic: *What are the causes of decreasing voter turnout in local elections?*

Causes	Possible explanations
People are not interested in local issues.	*The issues have become so complicated that people are confused.* *People don't have time to watch local news programs or read newspaper articles on local issues.*
Voting locations are not conveniently located.	*Working people often must vote during a lunch hour or short break; if it takes too long to get to a voting location, many people may not have the time or energy.* *The downtown voting locations often have long lines, while the voting locations near people's homes are hardly used.*
People don't trust local politicians.	*The media has portrayed all politicians as dishonest. The city population is so large that few people have a chance to meet politicians personally.*
People are apathetic.	*People feel that someone else can make the decision for them.* *People feel powerless to bring about desired changes; this becomes a self-fulfilling prophecy.*
Lately, the platforms of local candidates are a lot alike.	*People may feel that there is no real choice in the candidates. In reality, there is a choice, but people may not be aware of differences.*

OPTIONS FOR TEACHING

STRATEGIES FOR INCLUSION

Visual Some students might find it useful to use a flowchart to organize chains of causes and effects. As the first chart indicates, some effects have multiple causes. As the second chart indicates, some causes have multiple effects. Encourage students to experiment with the flowchart format to capture the relationships that exist among the ideas they are writing about.

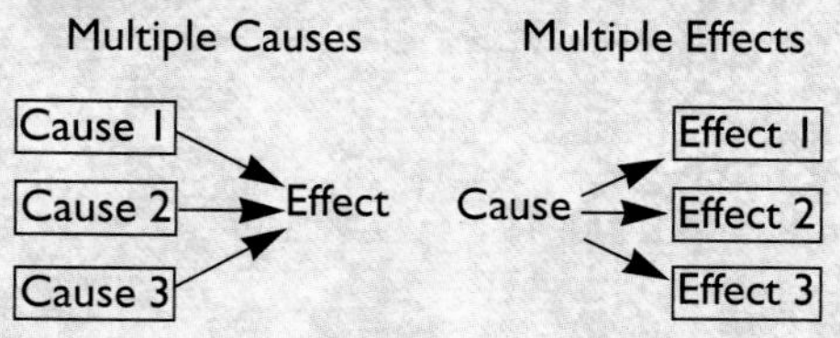

Multiple Causes

Cause 1 → Effect
Cause 2 → Effect
Cause 3 → Effect

Multiple Effects

Cause → Effect 1
Cause → Effect 2
Cause → Effect 3

Kinesthetic/Spatial Students can use index cards with information written on them to organize their essays. Ask students to write causes and effects on separate index cards and to color-code them by highlighting the causes in one color and the effects in another. Some index cards may contain information about an event, phenomenon, or trend that is both a cause and an effect, and these should be highlighted in a third color. Ask students to arrange the index cards in various orders until they are satisfied with an order that reflects the causes and effects as they understand them. They can then use the order they perceive to organize their essays.

Study your table or diagram, and select the elements you want to include in your essay. Make an outline of the major structure of your essay. If possible, meet with one or two classmates and exchange outlines. Briefly discuss your outlines, pointing out to each other any major causes or effects that may have been overlooked.

3. **Swaying the crowd.** If you're speculating about a social issue, will your audience be citizens of your town? members of the student body? readers of a particular magazine or newspaper in which your essay might be published? If you are speculating about the causes or reasons for a character's actions in a piece of literature, will your audience be other students who have read this literary work? Once you have identified your audience and its needs, think about necessary background information you may need to provide. Remember that your purpose is to make your explanation clear and persuasive to your readers. To this end, you will have to provide sound evidence or reasoning for your explanation or prediction.

Inductive Thinking: Drawing Conclusions

Speculating about causes and effects requires that you use a sound critical thinking process called **induction.** When you use induction to figure out something, you begin with a specific set of facts or observations, study them carefully, and then draw a general conclusion from them. In other words, induction is a kind of thinking in which you reason from the specific to the general. Here's an inductive model:

Evidence: A local defense plant with 10,000 employees has closed down in our city.

Evidence: The jobless rate in our area has climbed by almost 2 percent.

Evidence: Local retail sales are off significantly from the same time last year. Retailers are worried.

Generalization: The closing of a defense plant has had a noticeably negative effect on our local economy.

You need to be sure of the validity of the generalization you've made. Here are some questions to ask yourself in order to test the validity of your conclusion:

1. Do I have enough evidence to support my generalization? Is the sample I have selected truly representative of a larger population, or have I jumped to a conclusion based on insufficient evidence?
2. Is the source of my evidence trustworthy? Have I used a mixture of sound research sources—published statistics, opinions of authorities, eyewitness testimonies—and not just personal observations?
3. Does all my evidence lead to the generalization, or does some evidence refute it? What can I make of such discrepancies?

With a partner, study the inductive statements below, and brainstorm possible sources for gathering the necessary evidence to support or refute each generalization.

1. Traffic fatalities will increase if the speed limit on Highway 1 is raised to 70 miles per hour.
2. Passage of a law allowing people to carry concealed weapons with a permit will reduce crime in our state.
3. Students who have above-average aptitude in mathematics will have higher earning potential in their future careers.

Questions for Gathering Information

Here are some questions you can use as you search for causes, effects, and evidence.

Causes
- What are the obvious causes?
- Are there any hidden causes?
- Is there a main, or most important, cause? What is it?
- What is the most recent cause?
- Did any of the causes occur in the distant past?

Effects
- What are the obvious effects?
- Are there any hidden effects?
- What was (or will be) the first effect?
- What effect(s) might occur in the distant future?

Evidence
- What facts or statistics show that this cause (or effect) exists?
- What expert(s) acknowledges that this cause (or effect) exists?
- What constitutes sufficient evidence?

Communications Handbook HELP

Taking notes and documenting sources: pages 1210–1213.

Try It Out: Possible Answers

- Because airplane highjackings have happened, the result has been that airports have had to take extensive security measures.
- If pollution increased, the result would be that the environment would suffer.

INTEGRATING THE LANGUAGE ARTS

Strategic Reading Some students might find it useful when they read the Writer's Workshop material to summarize the main ideas of each section in a chart like the following. They can use the chart as they work through the stages of the writing process.

Summarizing Main Ideas

Section of Text	Main Ideas	Class Notes

Mechanics Students may want to use an acronym to stand for an organization or agency, such as NCAA for National Collegiate Athletic Association. Point out to students that acronyms are acceptable as long as they associate the initials with the full title of the organization or agency. Students should spell out the full name of the organization or agency the first time it is used and give the initials in parentheses immediately afterward. Besides identifying the acronyms, this method will also signal readers that the acronyms will be used in the essay. ☞

Drafting

- Some students might find it useful to read and study models of cause-and-effect essays. Letters to the editor of a newspaper or magazine are often short cause-and-effect essays, so you might consider using these as models.
- Encourage students who are having trouble writing an attention-grabbing lead to skip ahead to the introductions, bodies, and conclusions of their essays. The act of drafting most of the essay might give a student fresh ideas about how to start it.

Evaluating and Revising

- Encourage students to use the questions listed under Peer Review and the Evaluation Criteria to evaluate their own writing, as well as that of other students.
- As students revise their work, encourage them to use subordinating conjunctions to show the relationships between their points and make the organization of the paper clear to readers. Refer students to the Language Workshop on p. 690.

Proofreading

Remind students that careful proofreading is one way to help their readers understand precisely what they want to communicate.

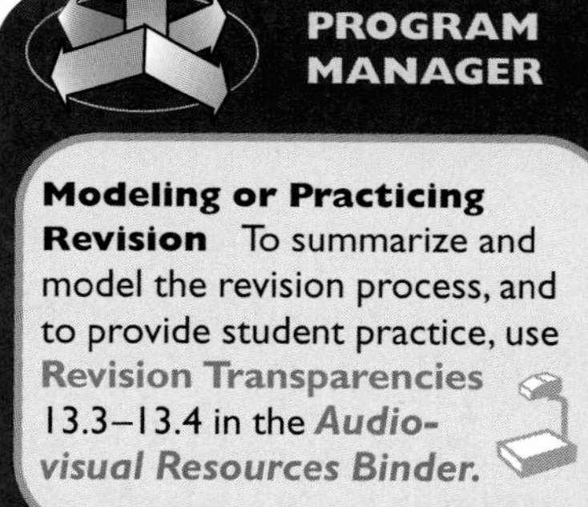

PROGRAM MANAGER

Modeling or Practicing Revision To summarize and model the revision process, and to provide student practice, use **Revision Transparencies** 13.3–13.4 in the ***Audio-visual Resources Binder.***

PORTFOLIO ASSESSMENT

Peer Evaluation During evaluating and revising, students can use the peer evaluation sheet found in the ***Portfolio Management System,*** p. 151.

Strategies for Elaboration

- Can you cite historical evidence, statistics, analogous cases, or other facts to develop your topic?
- Can you cite experts in order to support your speculations? Can you interview someone in your community for information?
- Can you provide interesting examples and details to support your statements?
- Can you use observations or anecdotes from your experience or from the experience of people you know? Try interviewing people to obtain interesting testimonials and insights.
- If you are writing about a literary work, can you cite evidence from the text of the story, novel, or play to which you are referring?
- Have you included less obvious causes and effects along with more obvious ones?
- Have you provided convincing support for each cause and effect you discuss?

Drafting

With your audience firmly in mind, begin drafting your essay.

1. **Lead.** Begin by grabbing your reader's attention. You might open with a startling observation, an anecdote, an interesting situation, or a vivid "what if" scenario. If you interviewed someone, try opening with an arresting quotation. If you are writing about a literary character, begin by zeroing in on a particular action, or decision, made by that character.
2. **Introduction.** State the event, phenomenon, or trend that you are going to analyze through cause and/or effect. If you have chosen an event or situation, you need to describe this briefly. If you have chosen a phenomenon or a trend, you must provide sufficient evidence that such a phenomenon or trend actually exists. If you are writing about a literary character, briefly provide the context within which this character acts. Then, briefly state your topic as a **thesis statement.** In your thesis, be sure you say whether you're going to discuss causes, effects, or both.
3. **Body.** In the body of your paper, present a sequence of causes and/or effects based on your speculations. In a cause-and-effect essay, you are almost always dealing with uncertainties, not with facts. Therefore, what you are presenting are plausible reasons and/or plausible results. These are reasonable hypotheses which you have constructed. For each cause or effect, you must elaborate—explaining the cause or effect and providing logical and convincing evidence. It's important to demonstrate that you've asked yourself plenty of "what if" questions and anticipated any objections or counterarguments your audience might have—and formulated valid rebuttals to them.

   You may organize your arguments in order of importance or, in some cases, chronological order. Use separate paragraphs to make your organization clear to the reader. Another way to make your essay clear is to use **subordinating conjunctions** when you are discussing cause and effect. (For more on subordinating conjunctions, see the Language Workshop on page 690.)
4. **Conclusion.** Conclude your essay by summarizing your main points. You can wrap up your essay with a thought-provoking comment or a prediction of future changes or effects, based on your analysis.

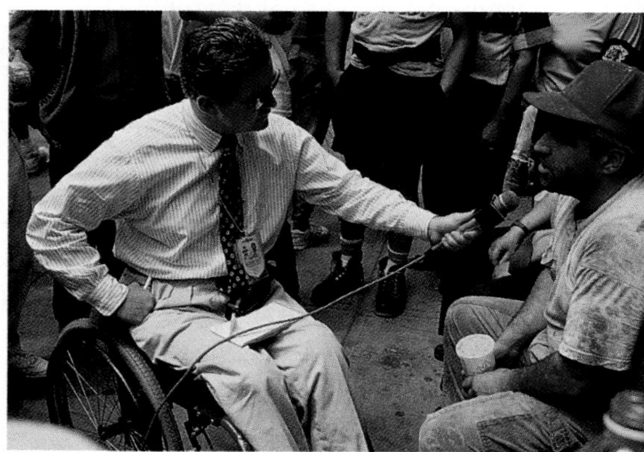

OPTIONS FOR TEACHING

COOPERATIVE LEARNING

Causal Analysis If students are writing about changes at school or in the community, have them work in groups of four to share ideas about the causes and effects of these changes. Each student should select a subject before joining a group. In the group, each student should present his or her subject in turn, and the other members of the group should suggest causes, effects, or both. Students can then work individually with these ideas as they draft their essays.

CLASSROOM MANAGEMENT

Block Scheduling Brainstorm causes and effects on one issue for ten or fifteen minutes. Using a stopwatch, allow pairs of students one minute to generate on paper as many causes and effects as possible. Ask volunteers to share with the class. Have students brainstorm on two to three additional issues, sharing after each brainstorming session. This activity may be used at any time during the longer class period to create student enthusiasm and to serve as a warm-up for other class activities.

Evaluating and Revising

1. **Peer review.** Share your draft with a classmate, and have him or her answer these questions:
   - Is the event, phenomenon, or trend clear and well defined? Has the writer provided enough elaboration to convince the reader that the situation really exists?
   - Is the thesis statement—the focus of the essay—clear?
   - Has the writer provided several causes, effects, or causes and effects—depending upon the overall aim of the essay? Are there too many elements? too few?
   - Are the causes and/or effects presented in a clear and convincing way?
   - Has the writer overlooked any important causes and/or effects? Has he or she failed to address counterarguments?
   - Has the writer presented the speculations in a logical order—for example, in order of importance? Would some other order than the one chosen be better?
   - Are the introduction and conclusion original and engaging?
   - Are there any weak or imprecise words, sentences, or paragraphs that can be deleted or improved in order to make the essay more persuasive?
2. **Self-evaluation.** Review your critical reader's comments, and make any revisions you feel are necessary. Use the list above to evaluate your own work.

Proofreading

If your essay includes technical or difficult words, check to make sure that you have spelled these correctly and defined them for your readers. Be sure that you have used subordinate conjunctions correctly to clearly indicate cause-and-effect relationships. Then, check spelling, punctuation, and usage, as usual.

Publishing

To decide how and where to publish your essay, let the intended audience for your essay be your guide. You can

- submit your essay to your school or community newspaper, or to newsletters or magazines whose readers have an interest in your topic
- form a discussion panel together with other students who have written speculations about the same topic
- read your essay to the class, especially if your topic is literary
- send your essay to your student council, or the appropriate local or state agency or legislator

Reflecting on Your Writing

Did you choose a topic that truly interested you? Did you learn something new about the topic? Did you engage in creative thinking and come up with some original ideas? Was feedback from your peers helpful? Did the *writing* process help your *thinking* process? Write a reflection for your portfolio.

Language Handbook HELP

Subordinate clauses: pages 1231–1232; combining sentences by subordinating ideas: page 1238.

Revision STRATEGIES

Review the solutions you have proposed to problems. Think about whether there are other, better solutions you can propose.

Evaluation Criteria

A good cause-and-effect essay has

1. *a well-defined topic presented in a clear thesis statement*
2. *clear explanations of plausible and logical causes and/or effects*
3. *appropriate evidence and examples, including references to personal experience or observation, or, if a literary essay, references to the text itself*
4. *acknowledgment of potential counterarguments and sucessful rebuttals*
5. *clear, coherent organization and appropriate transitions*
6. *an attention-getting introduction and an engaging conclusion*

Publishing

Some Usenet newsgroups on the Internet might be appropriate for student essays, and your school might be receptive to publishing students' writing on Web home pages that it maintains. *You may want to preview any Internet activity that you suggest to students. Because these resources are public forums, their content can be unpredictable.*

Closure

Once students have completed their assignments, ask them what steps they followed in writing their essays. You might make three columns on the chalkboard: one for those who wrote about causes, one for those who wrote about effects, and one for those who wrote about both causes and effects. After students have volunteered the essential steps of writing the essay and you have written the steps on the chalkboard, ask students to compare the three columns and to note differences and similarities in the processes for the different purposes of writing.

Enrichment

Social Sciences Connection

Historians frequently speculate about the causes of historical events. Ask students to examine how the causes of a particular event are described in several different history books. If different books give different causes, ask students to speculate about why this might be so.

Portfolio

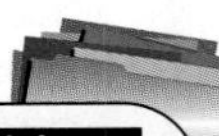

Reflecting on Your Writing

- Have students write answers to the questions on p. 689 and attach these to their essays when they include the essays in their portfolios.

CROSSING THE CURRICULUM

Science Many chemical reactions are essentially sequences of causes and effects. Ask a chemistry teacher or some of your students who are taking chemistry to demonstrate for the class a series of related chemical reactions. Ask the students in your class to create a cause-and-effect flowchart to capture the events as they witness them. After the demonstration, ask students to summarize the causes and effects in a paragraph.

ASSESSMENT TOOLS

Self-Assessment Have students use the following rubric to evaluate their writing.

3=Clearly Evident 2=Evident 1=Not Evident

Does the essay have the following elements?

1. A well-defined topic presented in a clear thesis statement _____
2. Clear explanations of plausible and logical causes and/or effects _____
3. Appropriate evidence and examples, or references to the text _____
4. An acknowledgment of potential counterarguments and successful rebuttals of them _____
5. Clear, coherent organization and appropriate transitions _____
6. An attention-getting introduction and an engaging conclusion _____

Language Workshop

Connecting to Students' Writing

Ask students to select a piece of writing from their portfolios and to work through it looking for sentences that have been joined by the simple conjunction *and.* Have them determine whether each conjunction adequately expresses the relationship between the ideas in the joined clauses. If not, have them revise each sentence by using a subordinating conjunction that more accurately reflects the relationship between the clauses.

Try It Out: Answers

1. Although Mr. Shiftlet claimed to be honest, he betrayed the old woman and her daughter.
2. The old woman gave Mr. Shiftlet the car so that he would marry her daughter.
3. Mr. Shiftlet worked hard at fixing up the old woman's place because he planned to con her.

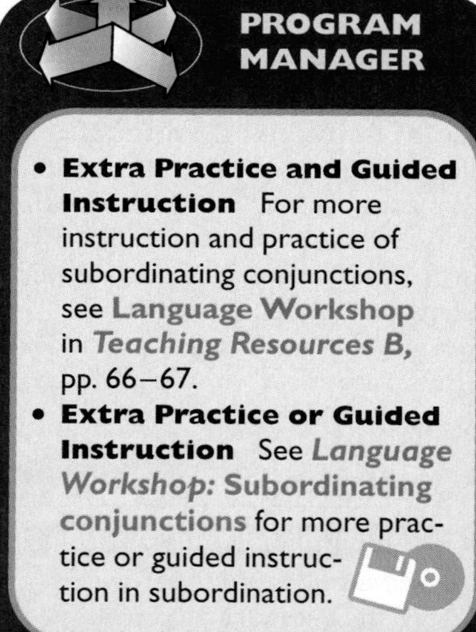

PROGRAM MANAGER

- **Extra Practice and Guided Instruction** For more instruction and practice of subordinating conjunctions, see **Language Workshop** in ***Teaching Resources B,*** pp. 66–67.
- **Extra Practice or Guided Instruction** See ***Language Workshop:* Subordinating conjunctions** for more practice or guided instruction in subordination.

Technology HELP

See Language Workshop CD-ROM. *Key word entry: subordinating conjunctions.*

Language Handbook HELP

Subordinating ideas: pages 1235 and 1238.

Try It Out

Rewrite these sentences, replacing *and* with a subordinating conjunction that more precisely explains the relationship between the two clauses.

1. Mr. Shiftlet claimed to be honest, and he betrayed the old woman and her daughter.
2. The old woman gave Mr. Shiftlet her car, and he married her daughter.
3. Mr. Shiftlet worked hard at fixing up the old woman's place, and he planned to con her.

Showing Relationships: Using Subordinating Conjunctions

When you write, part of your job is to sort out and define for your readers the relationships between the ideas you present. In the following sentence, two clauses are joined with the simple conjunction *and.* As you will see, this conjunction fails to indicate the relationship between the two clauses.

EXAMPLE Flannery O'Connor was sick for sixteen years, and she wrote critically acclaimed novels and short stories.

By using a subordinating conjunction instead, you can join the same clauses above in a way that more clearly conveys the relationship between the ideas expressed:

EXAMPLE *Although* Flannery O'Connor was sick for sixteen years, she wrote critically acclaimed novels and short stories.

A **subordinating conjunction** begins a subordinate clause and indicates the relationship of this clause to an independent clause in the same sentence. A subordinating conjunction may come between two clauses, or it may appear at the beginning of a sentence. The chart below shows some common subordinating conjunctions.

Subordinating Conjunctions		
although	in order that	until
as	since	when
because	so that	whereas
before	that	why

Writer's Workshop Follow-Up: Revising

In writing your cause-and-effect essay for the Writer's Workshop on page 685, you speculated on the relationships between ideas. Specifically, you joined ideas in terms of causes and effects. Now, review your essay to see whether you can better define relationships between ideas by inserting subordinating conjunctions.

✔ QUICK CHECK: Using Subordinating Conjunctions

Replace the simple conjunction *and* with a subordinating conjunction that better expresses the relationship between the two clauses.

[1] People think well of Richard Cory, and he shoots himself.
[Although people think well of Richard Cory, he shoots himself.]

[2] Krebs suffers from shell shock, and he does nothing all day.
[Since Krebs suffers from shell shock, he does nothing all day.]

[3] Lucynell falls asleep in the diner, and Mr. Shiftlet leaves her.
[When Lucynell falls asleep in the diner, Mr. Shiftlet leaves her.]

[4] Prufrock worries about his appearance, and he avoids talking to women.
[Prufrock avoids talking to women because he worries about his appearance.]

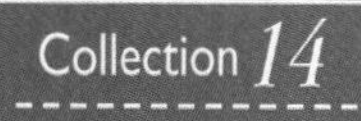

SHADOWS OF THE PAST

Theme: Memory, The Original Time Machine

In memories, people relive past events and sensations vividly, as if they are traveling back in time. Many realist and naturalistic writers in the twentieth century have tried, in their narratives, to represent the mind's ability to traverse barriers of time and place; using stream-of-consciousness techniques, they explore a character's disjointed thoughts, and let events in their stories unfold without regard to the conventional rules of storytelling that writers had honored in earlier times.

Thematic Focus

The protagonists of the selections in Collection 14 experience conflicts in which memory plays a key role.

- **Richard Bone** A stonecutter confesses his guilt candidly from beyond the grave: Most of the epitaphs he carved were flattering falsehoods.
- **Lucinda Matlock** An old woman tells of her full but hard life, and chides the younger generation for its self-indulgent whining.
- **Recuerdo** The speaker recalls one sparkling night on a ferry when she and her companion had too much happiness to keep to themselves.
- **The Jilting of Granny Weatherall** The thoughts of an old woman on her deathbed revolve around one traumatic incident in her youth.
- **A Rose for Emily** In this small Southern town, folks knew everything about eccentric Miss Emily—except for her horrible crime.
- **The Feather Pillow** A new bride suffers from an inexplicable sickness that seems to be drawing her life away through her dreams.

Literary Focus

Literary Element	Selection / Feature
Stream of Consciousness	**The Jilting of Granny Weatherall**
Setting	**A Rose for Emily**

Writing Focus

The following chart shows how the writing assignment for each selection relates to and builds toward the culminating writing assignment presented in the Writer's Workshop at the end of the Collection.

Selection	Work-in-Progress Assignment
Richard Bone/ Lucinda Matlock	Freewrite notes comparing and contrasting two characters p. 696
Recuerdo	Freewrite a personal response for an interpretation p. 701
The Jilting of Granny Weatherall	List questions speculating about meaning for an interpretation p. 712
A Rose for Emily	Write a character analysis for an interpretation p. 725
Writer's Workshop	Write an interpretation pp. 804–807

Collection 14 **SHADOWS OF THE PAST**

Collection Planner

SELECTION/ FEATURE	PUPIL'S EDITION			
	Literary Elements / Active Reading	Writing	Speaking and Listening	Language and Vocabulary
Richard Bone Edgar Lee Masters (pp. 692–693, 696) Primary Sources: The Genesis of Spoon River (p. 693) **Lucinda Matlock** Edgar Lee Masters (pp. 694–696) **Connections: Don Arturo Says:** Víctor Hernández Cruz (p. 695)	• Reader's Log p. 692; p. 694	• Critical Writing: Write essay p. 696 • Creative Writing: Compose epitaph p. 696		
Recuerdo Edna St. Vincent Millay (pp. 697–701) Primary Sources: "The brawny male sends his picture" (p. 700)	• Reader's Log p. 698	• Critical Writing: Contrast two poems p. 701 • Creative Writing: Write poem p. 701		• Language and Style: Millay's Imagery p. 701
The Jilting of Granny Weatherall Katherine Anne Porter (pp. 702–712) **Connections: Aunt Jennifer's Tigers** Adrienne Rich (p. 711)	• Reader's Log p. 703 • Stream of consciousness p. 703	• Critical Writing: Write essay p. 712 • Creative Writing: Write monologue p. 712		
A Rose for Emily William Faulkner (pp. 713–726) Primary Sources: Nobel Prize Acceptance Speech, 1950 (p. 723)	• Reader's Log p. 715 • Setting p. 715	• Critical Writing: Write analytical essay p. 725 • Creative Writing: Write short-short story p. 725	• Speaking and Listening: Debate in response to prompt p. 725	• How to Own a Word: Distinguishing Connotations of Synonyms p. 726
Literature of the Americas: The Feather Pillow Horacio Quiroga (pp. 727–731)	• Reader's Log p. 728		• Finding Common Ground: Discuss issues or reactions p. 732	

Collection Resources

Teaching Resources B
Cross-Curricular Activity p. 82

Audiovisual Resources Binder
Fine Art Transparency 14.1

Test Booklet
Collection 14 Test pp. 167–170

 Computer disk or CD-ROM

Audiocassette

Overhead Transparency

PROGRAM RESOURCES

Electronic Media	Teaching Resources with Organizer		Audiovisual Resources Binder
	Teaching Resources B	Other Resources	
• Test Generator	• Teaching Notes p. 69 • Reading Organizer pp. 72–73	• Test Booklet: Selection Test pp. 161–162 • Language and Writing Skills Worksheet p. 174 • Portfolio Management System p. 39, p. 153	• Selected Reading, Audiocassette 2, Side B
• Test Generator	• Teaching Notes p. 70 • Reading Organizer p. 74	• Test Booklet: Selection Test pp. 161–162 • Portfolio Management System p. 154	• Selected Reading, Audiocassette 2, Side B
• Test Generator	• Teaching Notes pp. 70–71 • Reading Organizer p. 75 • Language Link pp. 76–77 • Words to Own p. 78	• Test Booklet: Selection Test pp. 163–164 • Portfolio Management System pp. 48–49, p. 155	• Selected Reading, Audiocassette 2, Side B
• Test Generator	• Teaching Notes p. 71 • Reading Organizer p. 79 • Words to Own pp. 80–81	• Test Booklet: Selection Test pp. 165–166 • Portfolio Management System pp. 54–55, p. 156	• How to Own a Word Transparency 14.2
	• Teaching Notes p. 71		

Proofreading Warm-ups

You may use the following exercises to help students practice their proofreading skills. The proofreading exercises are designed to reinforce the language skills introduced in the previous collections. Copy a set of incorrect sentences onto the chalkboard, and have students find and correct the spelling, punctuation, usage, and mechanical errors in each sentence. Ask students to share and discuss their responses.

	Sentences with Errors	Sentences Corrected	Skills Covered
1	**a.** lucinda allways balls we kids out, edward said angryly **b.** her's is the borded up house	**a.** "Lucinda always bawls out us kids," Edward said angrily. **b.** Hers is the boarded-up house.	Quotation marks, Capitalization, Spelling, Usage, Pronouns, Comma usage, Apostrophe, Hyphens, Homonyms, End marks
2	**a.** modernists favered flawed heros who showed what writer Ernest Hemingway called "grace under pressure **b.** acording to Hemingway, the strong perservere irregardless of the odds against them	**a.** Modernists favored flawed heroes who showed what writer Ernest Hemingway called "grace under pressure." **b.** According to Hemingway, the strong persevere regardless of the odds against them.	Capitalization, Spelling, Plural nouns, Nonstandard usage, End marks
3	**a.** in Spoon River Anthology poet Edgar Lee Masters offers penatrating insites into human psicology **b.** "theres nothing special about my family to write on, rosalie complaned	**a.** In <u>Spoon River Anthology</u>, poet Edgar Lee Masters offers penetrating insights into human psychology. **b.** "There's nothing special about my family to write about," Rosalie complained.	Capitalization, Underlining book titles, Comma usage, Spelling, Apostrophes, Prepositions, Quotation marks, End marks
4	**a.** works in the Symbolist Style are more suggestive and suttle then obvious **b.** edna st vincent millay was called "Vincent by her frends	**a.** Works in the Symbolist style are more suggestive and subtle than obvious. **b.** Edna St. Vincent Millay was called "Vincent" by her friends.	Capitalization, Spelling, Usage, Abbreviations, Quotation marks, End marks
5	**a.** 2 of the ideas central to the american dream was optimism and self reliance **b.** some of the most great post war writers left the U.S. for europe	**a.** Two of the ideas central to the American dream were optimism and self-reliance. **b.** Some of the greatest postwar writers left the United States for Europe.	Capitalization, Spelling out numbers, Subject-verb agreement, Hyphens, Superlative adjectives, Spelling out abbreviations, End marks
6	**a.** like the poet Millay him and his sisters Chandra and Elise are brite opinionnated and nonconventional **b.** for many people the pursuit of welth and happyness has become an end in themselves	**a.** Like the poet Millay, he and his sisters, Chandra and Elise, are bright, opinionated, and unconventional. **b.** For many people, the pursuit of wealth and happiness has become an end in itself.	Capitalization, Comma usage, Pronouns, Spelling, Usage, Agreement (in number), End marks
7	**a.** is everything possibel for people who trusts in themself **b.** tho his works are universal in scoap novelist william Faulkner's voice remained true to it's southern heratidge	**a.** Is everything possible for people who trust in themselves? **b.** Though his works are universal in scope, novelist William Faulkner's voice remained true to its Southern heritage.	Capitalization, Spelling, Verb agreement, Pronouns, Comma usage, Apostrophes, End marks
8	**a.** I could care less about you either replide hauty priscilla **b.** each of the essays have a topic	**a.** "I couldn't care less about you, either," replied haughty Priscilla. **b.** Each of the essays has a topic.	Quotation marks, Nonstandard usage, Comma usage, Spelling, Capitalization, Verb agreement, End marks
9	**a.** when the stock market crashed in 1929 the nation plunges into a period nown as the great depression **b.** millions were layed off nearly 1/3 of the country was unemployed	**a.** When the stock market crashed in 1929, the nation plunged into a period known as the Great Depression. **b.** Millions were laid off; about one-third of the country was unemployed.	Capitalization, Comma usage, Verb tense, Spelling, Semicolons, Usage, Spelling out fractions, End marks
10	**a.** while granny lied in bed her dauhter called the doctor **b.** no she had not forgot that humiliating day after all	**a.** While Granny lay in bed, her daughter called the doctor. **b.** No, she had not forgotten that humiliating day, after all.	Capitalization, Usage, Comma usage, Spelling, Past participles, End marks

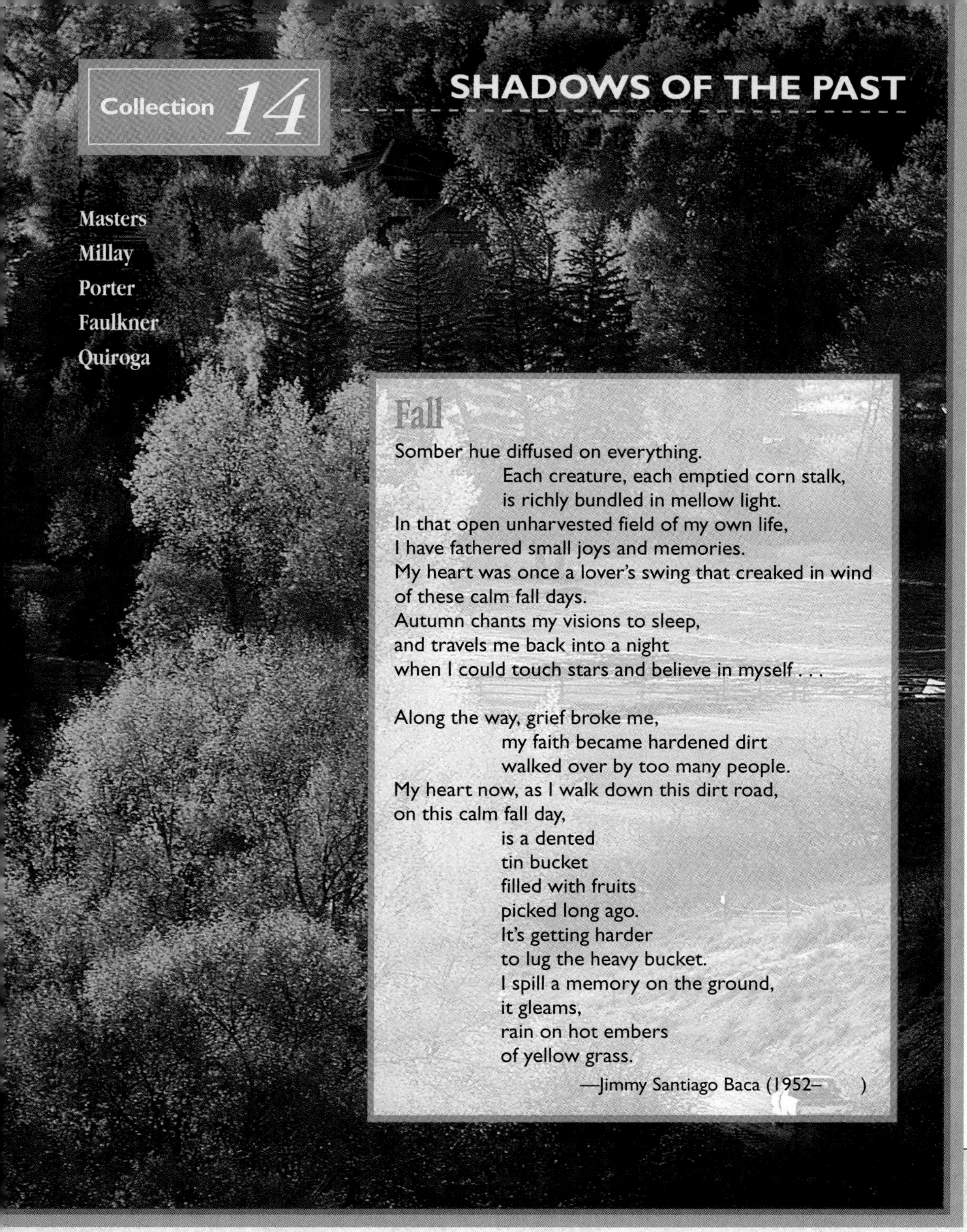

Collection 14

SHADOWS OF THE PAST

Masters
Millay
Porter
Faulkner
Quiroga

Fall

Somber hue diffused on everything.
Each creature, each emptied corn stalk,
is richly bundled in mellow light.
In that open unharvested field of my own life,
I have fathered small joys and memories.
My heart was once a lover's swing that creaked in wind
of these calm fall days.
Autumn chants my visions to sleep,
and travels me back into a night
when I could touch stars and believe in myself . . .

Along the way, grief broke me,
my faith became hardened dirt
walked over by too many people.
My heart now, as I walk down this dirt road,
on this calm fall day,
is a dented
tin bucket
filled with fruits
picked long ago.
It's getting harder
to lug the heavy bucket.
I spill a memory on the ground,
it gleams,
rain on hot embers
of yellow grass.

—Jimmy Santiago Baca (1952–)

"Fall"

? How does the speaker feel about his own "shadows of the past"? [Possible responses: The speaker feels haunted by the happiness he experienced in the past. The speaker is trying to stir himself by remembering the hopes he once had.] What is the tone of the poem? [Meditative, sad, nostalgic.]

- **Integrated Assessment** For a summative assessment of the literature and language skills taught in this collection, see **Collection 14 Test, *Test Booklet,*** pp. 167–170.
- **Extending Collection Theme** See **Cross-Curricular Activity: Shadows of the Past, *Teaching Resources B,*** p. 82, for activities in other disciplines and for evaluation criteria.

Parent/Guardian Involvement For forms that will help a parent or guardian review and respond to a student's portfolio, see the ***Portfolio Management System,*** pp. 62–63.

QUICK PLANNING GUIDE

Into the Poems

Through the Poems

Beyond the Poems

Choices: Building Your Portfolio p. 696
- **Writer's Notebook:** Students analyze characters' names.
- **Critical Writing:** Compare and contrast two poems
- **Creative Writing:** Write an epitaph

Into the Poem

Using **Before You Read** p. 692

Reading Focus

Discuss with students how a guilty conscience may cause a person's past to affect his or her present. Ask students for examples from films, TV shows, or works of literature whose characters have guilty consciences. Why do they feel guilty? Do they do anything about their feelings? Write students' ideas on the chalkboard.

Edgar Lee Masters

(1868–1950)

AP/Wide World Photos.

Edgar Lee Masters was born in Garnett, Kansas. Like Carl Sandburg (page 792), he was a product of that part of the Middle West known as the Corn Belt or Bible Belt. Also like Sandburg, he found his voice in the free verse that characterized the second decade of the twentieth century. But unlike Sandburg, Masters produced just one book in a spare style that served his homely subject matter. After that he reverted to a more conventional poetic style: pretty, romantic, and wordy.

Yet this one book, *Spoon River Anthology* (1915), was a landmark in American literature, and it made Masters famous. It is a collection of more than two hundred epitaphs—memorial inscriptions on gravestones—spoken by the inhabitants of a cemetery in the fictional town of Spoon River: drunkards, bankers, judges, poets, atheists, preachers, gamblers, druggists, and housewives.

The dramatic device of having dead people speak their own epitaphs served Masters brilliantly. Drawing upon his memories of Petersburg and Lewistown—the Illinois towns he knew during his first twenty years—he used these epitaphs to show the hidden underside of American life. Victims of that life, freed by death to speak without fear of consequences, tell their stories. Bit by bit, they fill in a picture of small-town life that is vastly different from the folksy, sentimental magazine cover images of the time. Masters's speakers from beyond the grave bring buried truth into the daylight.

Spoon River Anthology became one of the most widely read books of an age that was fascinated by psychology. Better than any scientific study, it revealed how the conventions of society warred with people's real needs and beliefs. By turning psychological "case histories" into lyric poems, Masters gave speech to the inarticulate and, at the same time, brought a new kind of realism to poetry.

Before You Read
Richard Bone

Reading Focus

Cutting to the Bone

Like many other citizens presented in *Spoon River Anthology,* Richard Bone is troubled by past deeds. The name Masters gives his speaker is itself a clue to Bone's profession and his nature. As a stonecutter in life, Richard Bone engraved words that identified skeletons. As a spokesman for his own conscience, he speaks words that "cut to the bone."

A Dialogue with the Text

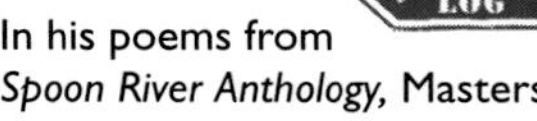

In his poems from *Spoon River Anthology,* Masters captured the sounds and rhythms of American English spoken by ordinary people. Read "Richard Bone" aloud in order to appreciate both how Masters imitates real speech and how he conveys a sense of the person who is speaking. Jot down in your Reader's Log what tone of voice would successfully convey Bone's attitude and feelings.

PROGRAM MANAGER

- **Planning Instruction** See Teaching Notes, *Teaching Resources B,* p. 69, for objectives, a summary, literary elements, and biographical information for this selection.
- **Instructional Support** Before beginning the instructional lesson, see Graphic Organizer for Active Reading, *Teaching Resources B,* pp. 72–73, for a Through the Poems and an Into the Poems activity.
- **Audiotaped Readings** To help less proficient readers or auditory learners through the lesson, use the Selected Reading, Audiocassette 2, Side B, in the *Audiovisual Resources Binder.*
- **Assessment** See Selection Test, *Test Booklet,* pp. 161–162.

Richard Bone Ⓐ

Edgar Lee Masters

When I first came to Spoon River
I did not know whether what they told me
Was true or false.
They would bring me the epitaph° Ⓑ
And stand around the shop while I worked
And say "He was so kind," "He was wonderful,"
"She was the sweetest woman," "He was a consistent Christian."
And I chiseled for them whatever they wished,
All in ignorance of its truth.
But later, as I lived among the people here,
I knew how near to the life
Were the epitaphs that were ordered for them as they died.
But still I chiseled whatever they paid me to chisel
And made myself party to the false chronicles° Ⓒ
Of the stones,
Even as the historian does who writes
Without knowing the truth,
Or because he is influenced to hide it. Ⓓ

4. epitaph: inscription on a tombstone or grave marker.

14. chronicles: historical accounts.

PRIMARY SOURCES — AN AUTOBIOGRAPHY

The Genesis of Spoon River [1914]

About the 20th of May my mother came to visit us, and we had many long talks. . . . In our talks now we went over the whole past of Lewistown and Petersburg, bringing up characters and events that had passed from my mind. We traced these persons to their final fates, to the positions in life that they were then in. We had many sessions at this recalling of old days. . . .

The psychological experience of this was truly wonderful. Finally on the morning she was leaving for Springfield we had a last and a rather sobering talk. It was Sunday, too, and after putting her on the train at 53rd Street I walked back home full of strange pensiveness. The little church bell was ringing, but spring was in the air. I went to my room and immediately wrote "The Hill," and two or three of the portraits of *Spoon River Anthology.* Almost at once the idea came to me: Why not make this book the book I had thought about in 1906, in which I should draw the macrocosm by portraying the microcosm? Why not put side by side the stories of two characters interlocked in fate, thus giving both misunderstood souls a chance to be justly weighed? . . .

People ask me over and over where the town of Spoon River is located. As there is no such town, I have to answer that there is only a river. And what a river! What a small stream winding its way through flatlands, amid hills that only distance lifts into any beauty, through jungles of weeds and thickets and melancholy cottonwoods. It goes by little towns as ugly and lonely as the tin-roofed hamlets of Kansas. Yet this is the town, or one of the towns, and this is the river and the country from which I extracted whatever beauty there is in that part of *Spoon River Anthology* which relates to a village depiction, and is not concerned with a world view.

—Edgar Lee Masters, *from Across Spoon River: An Autobiography*

Through the Poem

A. Reader's Response: First Thoughts

? What is your impression of the character's name? [Sample responses: The name *Richard* is ordinary enough, but *Bone* sounds morbid; it reminds me of skeletons. The name is so simple and bare that it makes me think of someone who isn't very complicated.]

B. Critical Reading: Making Inferences

? Who are "they"? [The family and friends of the person who has died, bringing the person's epitaph to the stonecutter.]

C. Literary Element: Metaphor

? How are epitaphs like chronicles? [Possible answers: Both tell a story, usually from a limited point of view, both are meant to be authoritative, to be taken as the truth, and both have people who are dead as their subjects.]

D. Literary Element: Simile

? Does this comparison seem appropriate to you? Explain. [Possible answers: Yes, because an epitaph is like a history, and sometimes the official version of something is not the truth. No, because an epitaph is just a private note for friends and family to remember a loved one by, while a history is a public account of important events.]

PORTFOLIO ASSESSMENT

Portfolio Assessment
For help with self-assessment of reading skills, see the ***Portfolio Management System,*** p. 39.

STRATEGIES FOR INCLUSION

Auditory Have students read the poem aloud with partners. Ask the partners to concentrate on the **tone** and **style** of the lines as they take turns reading them. What picture of the speaker do the elements give? Have the pairs of students share observations.

INTEGRATING THE LANGUAGE ARTS

Strategic Reading Have students organize their impressions of Richard Bone's character by using a graphic similar to the one on Transparency 3: Cluster Diagram in the Transparency Package.

Using **BEFORE YOU READ** p. 694

Reading Focus

Ask students to make a list of some of the "scoldings" they have heard directed at their generation. Students can list the criticisms, their sources, and their own replies in a table of three columns. Have students complete their tables with a partner.

A Dialogue with the Text

Have students re-read the poem with a partner. Partners should take turns reading the poem aloud, pausing frequently during the re-readings to share their thoughts about the speaker's tone of voice. Ask for volunteers to give an expressive reading of the poem for the class.

BEFORE YOU READ
LUCINDA MATLOCK

Reading Focus

My Generation

Masters based Lucinda Matlock on his grandmother, Lucinda Masters. In the pages of *Spoon River Anthology,* Lucinda Matlock's voice emerges as unique. She seems both to scold and to boast. The boasting is implicit; we pick it up by reading between the lines. But the scolding is quite explicit—it is directed at "sons and daughters," whose lax attitudes toward the serious business of life she regards as "degenerate," or fallen to a low moral standard.

What are some of the things you have heard older people say about your generation? What would you like to have a chance to say in your defense?

A Dialogue with the Text

READER'S LOG

After you have read this poem, re-read it, imagining that Lucinda Matlock is actually speaking it. Where and how might her tone of voice change? What words or phrases might she emphasize? Jot down what you notice when you read the poem aloud.

Portrait of Mother (1940) by Nan Phelps. Oil on canvas (43 1/4″ × 37″).
Collection of the Museum of American Folk Art, New York; Donated by Robert Phelps in loving memory of his wife, Nan Phelps (1992.18.3).

OPTIONS FOR TEACHING
INTEGRATING THE LANGUAGE ARTS

Strategic Reading Have students review "Lucinda Matlock" to divide it into a number of sections. Each section should cover a certain area or theme. For example, the first five lines describe Lucinda's life before she met her husband, and thus could be considered one section. Students should note the main idea of each section and then write a comment on how each section connects with the next. Students can record the information in interlocking boxes, alternating main ideas with the connecting ideas, and then compare their results in a small group. Students can use the graphic below as model.

Main Idea	Transition	Main Idea	Transition

Lucinda Matlock

Edgar Lee Masters

I went to dances at Chandlerville,
And played snap-out at Winchester. A
One time we changed partners,
Driving home in the moonlight of middle
June,
And then I found Davis.
We were married and lived together for
seventy years,
Enjoying, working, raising the twelve B
children,
Eight of whom we lost
Ere I had reached the age of sixty.
I spun, I wove, I kept the house, I nursed the
sick,
I made the garden, and for holiday
Rambled over the fields where sang the larks,
And by Spoon River gathering many a shell,
And many a flower and medicinal weed—
Shouting to the wooded hills, singing to the
green valleys.
At ninety-six I had lived enough, that is all,
And passed to a sweet repose.
What is this I hear of sorrow and weariness,
Anger, discontent, and drooping hopes? C
Degenerate sons and daughters,
Life is too strong for you—
It takes life to love Life. D

Connections — A Poem

Víctor Hernández Cruz (1949–) was born in a small mountain town in Puerto Rico; he now lives and writes in San Francisco.

Don Arturo Says:

Víctor Hernández Cruz

When I was young
there was no difference
Between the way I danced
and the way tomatoes E
Converted themselves
Into sauce
I did the waltz or a
guaguancó°
Which every one your rhythm
which every one your song
The whole town was caressed
to sleep with my two-tone
Shoes
Everyone
had to leave me alone
On the dirt or on the wood
they used to come from afar
and near F
Just to say look at Arturo
disappear.

8. ***guaguancó*** (gwä·gwän·kō′): type of rumba.

A. Critical Reading: Finding Details

? How did the speaker in the poem spend her youth? [She spent the time dancing, playing games, and socializing.]

B. Language Note: Repetition

? What does the repetition in the line express about the character's life? [Possible answer: It emphasizes the repetitiveness of her many chores.]

C. Critical Reading: Speculating

? To whom is the speaker responding? [Pessimistic and cynical people around her.]

D. Reader's Response: Shaping Interpretations

? What does the speaker mean by the statement "It takes life to love Life"? [Sample responses: To love life, one has to love all the simple or difficult things about it. She means that to get anything out of life, one has to exert energy and work hard.]

E. Reader's Response: Shaping Interpretations

? What does the speaker mean by this comparison? [Sample responses: The speaker means that he had danced so much that the movements had become instinctual, like a cook making a basic sauce. The comparison means that dancing is like cooking, which is creative and transformative.]

F. Literary Element: Diction

? How does the speaker "disappear"? [Possible answers: The speaker loses himself in the music. The speaker becomes another person in the observers' eyes, a person with no cares or worries.]

CONNECTING WITH "LUCINDA MATLOCK"

Have students discuss how Don Arturo and Lucinda Matlock are similar. [Both characters look back fondly on their enthusiastic, active pasts. They are proud of their accomplishments, and both boast about themselves.]

Questions to Making Meanings begin on p. 696

Making Meanings "Richard Bone"

First Thoughts

1. Possible responses: Richard Bone is too hard on himself, because he lied for a good reason. Or Bone should feel guilty because he lied.

Answers to Making Meanings begin on p. T695.

Shaping Interpretations

2. He realizes that the epitaphs are often false. Since Bone's living depends on his clients, he does not comment.
3. "How near to the life" ironically emphasizes the gap between illusion and reality represented by the idealized epitaphs. The phrase "how far from the life" would not be as effective, since it would not emphasize Bone's cynicism.
4. Bone compares himself to a historian.

"Lucinda Matlock"

First Thoughts

1. Possible responses: Lucinda Matlock's message made me feel guilty for worrying about petty things. Her message moved and inspired me to live life fully.

Shaping Interpretations

2. Dancing, playing "snap-out," walking in the fields. She has raised twelve children and lost eight, performed household chores, and nursed the sick.
3. She accuses the young of complaining too much and of yielding to discontent. Students may say that her criticism is unfair because younger people face different problems than she experienced.
4. Students should support their answers with evidence. The idea of "life" may refer to everyday life, and "Life" could refer to a deeper appreciation for life's beauty.
5. Masters seems to admire Lucinda Matlock's enthusiasm and her stoicism. Her view that both happiness and sadness are inevitably part of life is wise. Her condemnation of the younger generation does seem harsh, however.

Extending the Texts

6. **(Synthesis and Analysis)** Remorse and pride are two universal emotions. Modern-day Richard Bones may include employees who carry out the questionable business practices of their employers; today's Lucinda Matlocks might have lived through the Depression or fought in a war. They may have similiar tales to tell.

MAKING MEANINGS

Richard Bone

First Thoughts

1. Is Richard Bone being too critical of himself, or do you think he is right to be disturbed about creating "false chronicles"?

Shaping Interpretations

2. What does Richard Bone come to realize about the people of Spoon River? Why does he keep on carving sentiments that he knows to be false?
3. In line 11, Richard Bone says that he knew "how near to the life" were his epitaphs. Review the notes you made in your Reader's Log. How do you know he really means "how *far from* the life"? Why is "near to" more effective than "far from" would be?
4. What **analogy,** or comparison, does Richard Bone draw in the poem's last three lines?

Lucinda Matlock

First Thoughts

1. How did Lucinda Matlock's message make you feel?

Shaping Interpretations

2. List the simple pleasures and pastimes Lucinda Matlock enjoyed in her life. What hardships did she experience?
3. Why does Lucinda Matlock consider the younger generation "degenerate"? Is it fair of Lucinda Matlock to imply that if younger people are unhappy, it's their own fault? Explain your response.
4. Explain the meaning of the last line, especially the difference between "life" and "Life."
5. Does Masters mean to present Lucinda Matlock as a judgmental person, or as a voice of wisdom? Review the notes you made in your Reader's Log, and give evidence from the poem to support your view.

Extending the Texts

6. In what ways do Richard Bone's remorse and Lucinda Matlock's pride suggest more universal **themes,** or messages? Who are the Richard Boneses and Lucinda Matlocks of today, and what would they have to say?

CHOICES: Building Your Portfolio

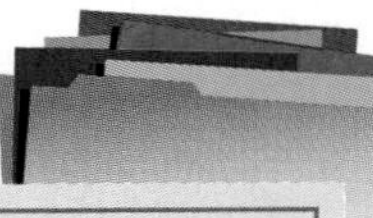

Writer's Notebook

1. Collecting Ideas for an Interpretive Essay

WORK IN PROGRESS

Writers often give their characters names that hint at inner qualities or at an important theme in a story or poem. Write down all the associations you make to the names Richard Bone and Lucinda Matlock. What are some of the connotations of these names? In each case, what does the name reveal about the character or the meaning of the poem? Save your notes for possible use in the Writer's Workshop on page 804.

Critical Writing

2. Lovers of Life

In a brief essay, compare and contrast the poems "Lucinda Matlock" and "Don Arturo Says:" (Connections, page 695). Consider, especially, the similarities and differences in the poems' **themes, tones,** and **speakers** and in their poetic forms. What do these poems have to say about the thoughts an older person might have in looking back on his or her youth?

Creative Writing

3. Carved in Stone

Try making up an original epitaph—in prose or poetry—that reveals a truth about a subject's life. You can write an epitaph for yourself, for someone you know personally, or for a celebrity. See if you can reveal character "between the lines" in your epitaph.

696 THE MODERNS

Beyond the Poems

Choices: Building Your Portfolio

1. **Writer's Notebook** Students can use their work as prewriting for the Writer's Workshop on p. 804.

PORTFOLIO ASSESSMENT

Choices: Assessment Criteria For help in evaluating these Choices assignments, see the criteria in the *Portfolio Management System,* p. 153.

Edna St. Vincent Millay

(1892–1950)

Like Edwin Arlington Robinson (page 644), Edna St. Vincent Millay was born on the granite coast of Maine and established her poetic reputation in New York. Also like Robinson, she lived to see the day when, despite many honors and the devotion of a wide audience, she had to realize that her reputation had barely withstood the onslaught of modernism.

AP/Wide World Photos.

Millay achieved fame even before she graduated from Vassar College, with the publication of her first collection of verse, *Renascence and Other Poems* (1917). After World War I, she moved to Greenwich Village. This was an era when that section of New York City was not only a haven for artists, but also a place where women were as free as men to speak their minds, to live by their own rules, and to pursue careers—activities that most Americans still considered improper for women. Taking advantage of this liberated atmosphere, Millay became one of its leading voices—a free spirit who wrote saucy and slightly scandalous lyrics in a style that occasionally evoked Elizabethan verse. Millay's philosophy might best be described in her own words:

First Fig

My candle burns at both ends;
    It will not last the night;
But ah, my foes, and oh, my friends—
    It gives a lovely light!

Millay also became caught up in the radical dissent of the time, and she worked passionately, if vainly, to save the anarchists Sacco and Vanzetti, who were executed in Massachusetts in 1927 after a celebrated trial.

"Vincent," as she was familiarly known, was a skilled actress and speaker with the flair of a seasoned performer. She gave recitals during long, nationwide tours in which she won a degree of celebrity seldom associated with poets.

Both shocking and fascinating to her audiences, Millay grew in popularity even as her poetic achievements began to decline. Her most productive period was between the two world wars, when she published seven collections of poetry, as well as a series of dramas written for the Provincetown Players in New York. In 1923, she became the first woman to win the Pulitzer Prize in poetry.

During World War II, Millay determined to write "public" poetry to contribute to the Allied cause. She produced scores of poems which, although widely read, proved that outrage and passion could not substitute for the verbal artistry that poetry demands. The lyricist had been overtaken by the propagandist.

One of the brightest literary stars of a generation was all but faded from sight when, in her fifty-eighth year, Edna St. Vincent Millay died alone at her home, Steepletop.

QUICK PLANNING GUIDE

Into the Poem

Through the Poem

Beyond the Poem

ABOUT THE AUTHOR

The publication of her poem "Renascence" was partly responsible for Edna St. Vincent Millay's being awarded a scholarship to attend Vassar College. She studied theater and literature and pursued both interests throughout her life, writing plays as well as poetry and establishing herself as a respected actress. Her best-known work expresses much of the freedom and creative discovery of the Jazz Age of the 1920s. She won the Pulitzer Prize in poetry for her book *The Ballad of the Harp-Weaver.*

PROGRAM MANAGER

- **Planning Instruction** See **Teaching Notes, *Teaching Resources B,*** p. 70, for objectives, a summary, literary elements, and additional biographical information for this selection.
- **Instructional Support** Before beginning the instructional lesson, see **Graphic Organizer for Active Reading, *Teaching Resources B,*** p. 74, for a Through the Poem activity.
- **Audiotaped Readings** To help less proficient readers or auditory learners through the lesson, use the **Selected Reading, Audiocassette 2, Side B,** in the ***Audiovisual Resources Binder.***
- **Assessment** See **Selection Test, *Test Booklet,*** pp. 161–162.

Into the Poem

Using Before You Read p. 698

Reading Focus

Point out to students that a bad memory from the past can often haunt someone as regret or guilt. Ask students if they think there is an opposite emotion to regret or guilt, that allows a past experience to be remembered in a positive way. Challenge students to describe the emotion and to give it a name. *Caution students that they do not have to discuss anything they would feel uncomfortable sharing with other students.*

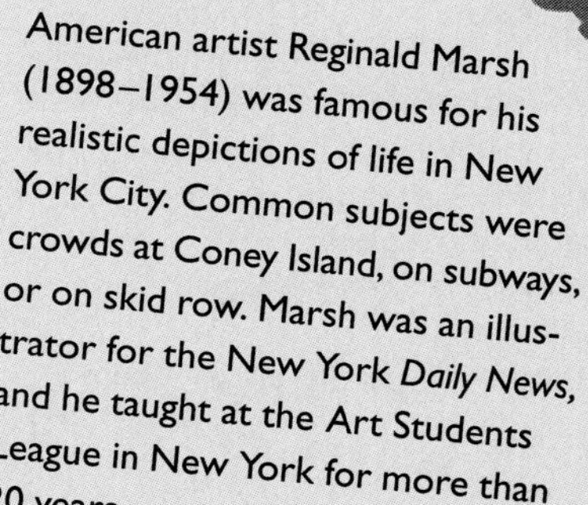

Responding to the Art: About the Artist

American artist Reginald Marsh (1898–1954) was famous for his realistic depictions of life in New York City. Common subjects were crowds at Coney Island, on subways, or on skid row. Marsh was an illustrator for the New York *Daily News*, and he taught at the Art Students League in New York for more than 20 years.

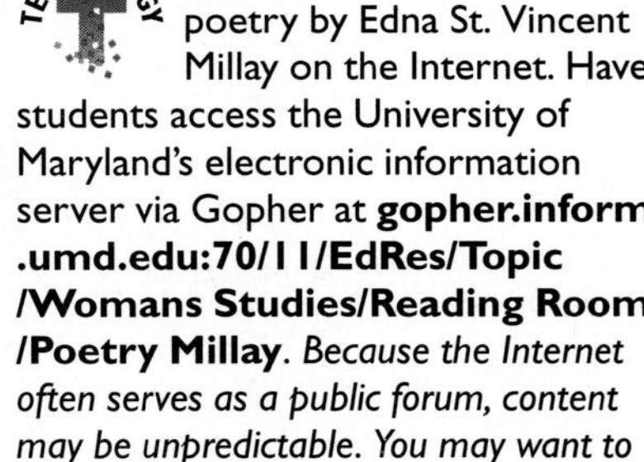

Technology Tip

Students can find more poetry by Edna St. Vincent Millay on the Internet. Have students access the University of Maryland's electronic information server via Gopher at **gopher.inform.umd.edu:70/11/EdRes/Topic/Womans Studies/Reading Room/Poetry Millay**. *Because the Internet often serves as a public forum, content may be unpredictable. You may want to check the content of this site before having students access it.*

Before You Read
Recuerdo

Reading Focus

Happy Memories

Remembering a happy event can cast a sudden glow over our lives. The title of this poem is a Spanish word meaning "remembrance" or "souvenir." Here the poet evokes a happy memory of youth: a carefree night spent riding one of the ferry boats that once connected the island of Manhattan with the rest of New York.

Quickwrite

Without pausing for critical thought, freewrite a list of three or four memories of happiness that pop into your mind.

The Normandie (1938) by Reginald Marsh. Watercolor (30″ × 50″).

The Butler Institute of American Art, Youngstown, Ohio. Purchased 1962.

INTEGRATING THE LANGUAGE ARTS

Strategic Reading Have students use a graphic to help them distinguish between the scenes and events in the poem, and to help them place the elements in order. Students can make a time line that covers the period treated in the poem and list each of the different scenes in the order in which they happen.

Then, ask students to study their time lines and to decide if the scenes show a progression of ideas or a certain **theme**. Students can compare their time lines and their observations.

Recuerdo

Edna St. Vincent Millay

We were very tired, we were very merry—
We had gone back and forth all night on the ferry.
It was bare and bright, and smelled like a stable— (A)
But we looked into a fire, we leaned across a table,
We lay on a hill-top underneath the moon;
And the whistles kept blowing, and the dawn came soon.

We were very tired, we were very merry— (B)
We had gone back and forth all night on the ferry;
And you ate an apple, and I ate a pear,
From a dozen of each we had bought somewhere; (C)
And the sky went wan, and the wind came cold,
And the sun rose dripping, a bucketful of gold.

We were very tired, we were very merry,
We had gone back and forth all night on the ferry.
We hailed, "Good morrow, mother!" to a shawl-covered head,
And bought a morning paper, which neither of us read;
And she wept, "God bless you!" for the apples and pears,
And we gave her all our money but our subway fares. (D)

Through the Poem

A. Literary Element: Imagery
? What image of the ferry does this brief description give you? [The phrase "bare and bright" indicates that the ferry is pleasingly plain, functional without being decorative, but the smell indicates that the ferry is old and overused.]

B. Literary Element: Refrain
Point out to students that refrains usually come at the end of a stanza. What effect does the refrain at the beginning of each stanza have on the reader? [Possible answer: The refrain emphasizes the couple's weariness and introduces the different scenes.]

C. Critical Reading: Making Generalizations
? What can you tell about the couple's mood by their wealth of apples and pears? [Possible answer: The abundance of fruit seems to indicate the couple's enthusiasm and carefree spirit, their feeling of richness in their good moods, and their passion for sensation.]

D. Reader's Response: Shaping Interpretations
? Why should this particular scene stand out among the couple's experiences of the night? [Sample responses: It shows the two people sharing their overflowing happiness with someone else, which makes the happy experience even better. The scene is representative of the couple's generosity and passionate feeling.]

STRATEGIES FOR INCLUSION

Auditory Have pairs of students take turns reading the poem aloud to each other. Direct students to pay attention to the poem's **rhythm** and to determine the effect the rhythm has on the reader. Partners can record their ideas and then share them with the class.

ASSESSMENT TOOLS

Check Test: Questions and Answers

1. What does the ferry smell like? [A stable.]
2. What has the couple bought to eat? [A dozen apples and a dozen pears.]
3. To whom does the couple speak in the morning? [An older woman on the ferry.]
4. What do they do for the person they meet? [They give the woman their fruit and all the money they have except for their subway fares.]

Primary Sources

Ask students if they think the writing style of an author reflects the author's personality. Students should think about the authors whose works they have read and about whose lives they have heard or read. Is Stephen King, for example, as bizarre as his writing? Have students discuss their views, and encourage them to incorporate Edna St. Vincent Millay's letter into their discussion.

PRIMARY SOURCES | **A LETTER**

In 1912, one of the judges for a poetry contest remarked that "Renascence," the poem submitted by E. St. Vincent Millay, Esq., must surely be the work of a forty-five-year-old brawny male. When she heard of this remark, Edna St. Vincent Millay sent this letter.

"The brawny male sends his picture"

[December 5, 1912]

To Mr. Ficke and Mr. Bynner:

Mr. Earle has acquainted me with your wild surmises. Gentlemen: I must convince you of your error; my reputation is at stake. I simply will not be a "brawny male." Not that I have an aversion to brawny males; *au contraire, au contraire.* But I cling to my femininity!

Is it that you consider brain and brawn so inseparable?—I have thought otherwise. Still, that is all a matter of personal opinion. But, gentlemen: When a woman insists that she is twenty, you must not, must not call her forty-five. That is more than wicked; it is indiscreet.

Mr. Ficke, you are a lawyer. I am very much afraid of lawyers. Spare me, kind sir! Take into consideration my youth—for I am indeed but twenty—and my fragility—for "I do protest I am a maid"—and—sleuth me no sleuths!

Seriously: I thank you also for the compliment you have unwittingly given me. For tho I do not yet aspire to be forty-five and brawny, if my verse so represents me, I am more gratified than I can say. When I was a little girl, this is what I thought and wrote:

Let me not shout into the world's great ear
Ere I have something for the world to hear.
Then let my message like an arrow dart
And pierce a way into the world's great heart.

You cannot know how much I appreciate what you have said about my *Renascence*.

If you should care to look up the April, 1907, number of *Current Literature,* you would find a review of my *Land of Romance* (near a review of Mr. Bynner's *Fair of My Fancy*). And you might be interested in Mr. Edward Wheeler's comment: "The poem which follows (by E. St. Vincent Millay) seems to me to be phenomenal. The author, whether boy or girl we do not know, is just fourteen years of age."

E. St. V. M.

P. S. The brawny male sends his picture. I *have* to laugh.

Portrait of Edna St. Vincent Millay (1934) by Charles Ellis. National Portrait Gallery, Washington, D.C./Courtesy Art Resource.

STRATEGIES FOR INCLUSION

Interpersonal Arrange students in small groups, and ask them what kinds of elements in a piece of writing could indicate that it was written by a "brawny male." Have them keep in mind the ideas and preconceptions of the time period in which Edna St. Vincent Millay lived. How could the comment be a compliment? How could it be an insult? Groups can compare their ideas with Millay's comments in her letter and then choose a spokesperson to deliver their ideas to the rest of the class.

CROSSING THE CURRICULUM

Art Have students research paintings and photographs of a number of authors they have read. Do the writers look the way students expect them to appear? Have students share their more surprising discoveries with the class.

MAKING MEANINGS

First Thoughts

1. Do you recognize the feelings described in this poem? When have you ever had similar feelings?

Shaping Interpretations

2. Whom do you think the "we" in the poem refers to? What do lines 4–5 suggest about their feelings for each other?
3. Why do you think the people in the poem gave their money to the "shawl-covered head"? What does this action say about the power of love?
4. Identify the **metaphor** in line 12. What does this image reveal about the speaker's feelings?
5. Describe the poem's **meter** and **rhyme scheme.** How would you describe the **tone** of "Recuerdo"? (You may find it easier to answer this question if you first read the poem aloud.)

LANGUAGE AND STYLE

Millay's Imagery

Imagery in poetry is more than decoration. It helps express the poet's feelings, and it evokes feelings in the reader. Imagery depends a great deal on the **connotations** of words—their suggestive power. For example, "smelled like a stable" in line 3 of "Recuerdo" might create a feeling of distaste in someone who despises the odor of stables. But for other readers, the image might evoke something pleasant—earthiness, the warmth of animals, the coziness of a place protected from the out-of-doors. The image would have been quite different if the poet had said "smelled of manure."

Try your hand at changing the effect Millay created with her words and images in the poem "Recuerdo."

a. In line 6, replace "blowing" with a verb that creates a negative or unpleasant feeling.
b. In line 12, think of an image to replace "a bucketful of gold" that would make the rising sun seem unpleasant.
c. Think of the image suggested by the phrase "shawl-covered head." Replace that image with one that makes the old woman sound threatening or dangerous.

CHOICES: Building Your Portfolio

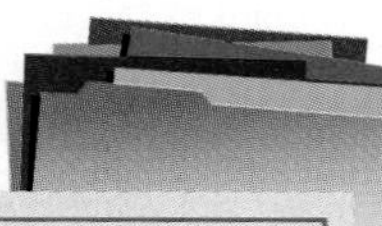

Writer's Notebook

1. Collecting Ideas for an Interpretive Essay

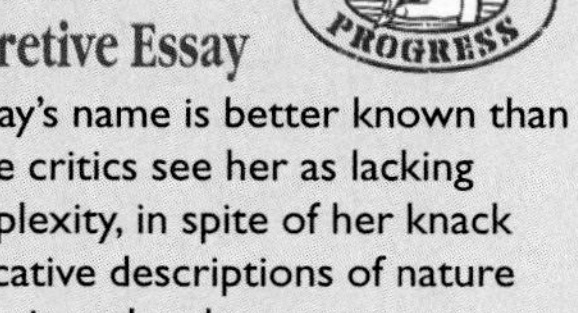

Nowadays, Millay's name is better known than her work. Some critics see her as lacking depth and complexity, in spite of her knack for simple, evocative descriptions of nature and human emotions. Jot down your own reactions to Millay, based on the poem you have read. Save your notes for possible use in the Writer's Workshop on page 804.

Critical Writing

2. Two Styles

The contrasts between America's most famous early-twentieth-century female poet (Millay) and America's most famous nineteenth-century female poet (Emily Dickinson) are interesting. Dickinson—quiet, reserved, and a social hermit—was an experimenter in poetry, a true original. Millay—socially unconventional and adventuresome—was more imitative and conservative poetically. In a brief essay, contrast "Recuerdo" with at least one of Dickinson's poems (perhaps "Heart! We will forget him!" on page 374). Consider differences in messages, imagery, rhymes, meter, and tone.

Creative Writing

3. Merry Memory

Review the Reader's Log entry you made before reading "Recuerdo," and use it as a springboard for your own poem about a happy memory in your life. Your poem can be in any format you like, rhymed or unrhymed, but it should have a **tone** and **rhythm** that convey joy and lightheartedness.

5. The rhythm of the poem is regular, strong, and lilting. The rhyme scheme is *aabbcc aaddee aaffgg.* Its tone is nostalgic, ecstatic, and passionate.

Language and Style

Possible Answers

a. Shrieking, howling, cutting.
b. The sun rose like a spreading fire, or the distant explosion of a bomb.
c. The covered face from which glared an angry eye.

Choices: Building Your Portfolio

1. **Writer's Notebook** Remind students to react to Millay's poem and not to what they think they know about her life and personality. Students should save their work to use as prewriting for the Writer's Workshop on p. 804.
2. **Critical Writing** Encourage students to use graphic organizers to assemble their thoughts before beginning to write their essays. Students can use a graphic such as Transparency 5: Venn Diagram in the Transparency Package to compare and contrast the poems, or students can list the poems' elements in a graphic such as Transparency 6: Comparison and Contrast Chart. Students can use their graphics to make an outline of their planned essays.

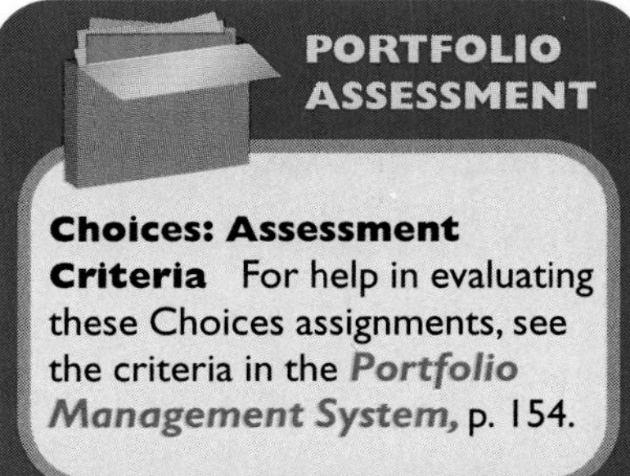

Choices: Assessment Criteria For help in evaluating these Choices assignments, see the criteria in the ***Portfolio Management System,*** p. 154.

Making Meanings

First Thoughts

1. Possible responses: The feelings of idle, wandering happiness in the poem are common. I have felt as happy as the couple in the poem, but usually it is when I am doing something fun, like riding my bike.

Shaping Interpretations

2. The speaker is never specific about the other person, but the context suggests that he is a man with whom she is romantically involved. The lines give the reader a picture of two lovers enjoying activities together.
3. The couple are in a happy, generous mood. The scene implies that love can inspire sympathy and generosity.
4. The sun is compared to a bucket that rises slowly from the sea, containing gold rather than water. The image contributes to a portrait of the speaker as romantic and highly emotional.

QUICK PLANNING GUIDE

Into the Story

Through the Story

Beyond the Story

- **Writer's Notebook:** List questions about the story's meaning
- **Critical Writing:** Compare characters from two different works
- **Creative Writing:** Write a monologue

© Rollie McKenna.

Katherine Anne Porter

(1890–1980)

Katherine Anne Porter was born in a Texas log cabin. She was raised, mostly by her grandmother, as a member of a sprawling family on close terms with hardship and deprivation. Her schooling was fragmentary. In later life, Porter tended to embroider these plain origins with a certain romantic opulence, as though her past could be revised like a novel in progress.

The first of Porter's four marriages took place when she was sixteen. She was consistently impatient with lasting marital relationships, and yet she disliked being alone. Her early years were a struggle to define herself as an individual, as a Southern woman, and as the writer that, so very slowly, she was becoming.

After her Texas youth, Porter traveled widely, living at various times in the West, New York City's Greenwich Village, New England, Washington, Mexico, Paris, and Berlin. She supported herself as a newspaper reporter and editor and as a translator of French and Spanish literature.

As a creative writer, Porter was largely self-taught. She became well read and had a natural talent for clear, flowing language. She could tell a seemingly effortless story, combining a searching intelligence, honesty, sound psychology, a flawless memory, and a vivid sense of scene. The grace of her objective style concealed the labor that went into it. Porter worked slowly and painstakingly, and she did not begin publishing until she was over thirty. Her first book of stories, *Flowering Judas* (1930), grew out of her recollections of her experiences in Mexico immediately after World War I. This collection won her a critical reputation as a stylist.

Much of Porter's work presents Southern women caught up in a web of custom and obligation. Her main themes include the burden of past evil and the strain with which that evil holds us captive in the present. Miranda, the clearly autobiographical central figure of so many of her stories, is forever trying to separate the fictions of family legend from objective truth. She knows that people do not always tell the truth, and she is skeptical of the romantic sheen with which they disguise the realities of poverty and sexuality.

With the publication of her finest story collection, *Pale Horse, Pale Rider* (1939), Porter's growing audience eagerly awaited a promised novel. In 1941, Porter began her novel, titled *Ship of Fools*. The novel takes place during the early days of Hitler's rise to power and chronicles the passage of a steamer ship whose passengers, in escaping their loneliness, search for fantasy rather than friendship or love. *Ship of Fools* is really about the seeds of World War II—a bitter portrait of the Nazi state and the human race's capacity for cruelty. When it finally appeared in 1962, the novel enjoyed a wide popular success. It was followed by the many awards and tributes (including the National Book Award and the Pulitzer Prize) that embellished the final years of Porter's long life.

PROGRAM MANAGER

- **Planning Instruction** See **Teaching Notes, *Teaching Resources B,*** pp. 70–71, for objectives, a summary, and literary elements for this selection.
- **Instructional Support** See **Graphic Organizer for Active Reading, *Teaching Resources B,*** p. 75, for a Through the Story activity.
- **Audiotaped Readings** To help auditory learners with Rich's poem on p. 711, use the **Selected Reading, Audiocassette 2, Side B,** in the ***Audiovisual Resources Binder.***
- **Assessment** See **Selection Test, *Test Booklet,*** p. 163–164.
- **Language Link** For practice in identifying and using stream of consciousness and flashback, see **Language Link, *Teaching Resources B,*** pp. 76–77.
- **Reinforcement** Use the **Words to Own** worksheet in ***Teaching Resources B,*** p. 78.

Before You Read
The Jilting of Granny Weatherall

Reading Focus
Alive in Memory
Most of the people we know and come across in the course of a day are looking ahead. Even for those in middle or old age, much of life seems to lie before them. What's the weather going to be next Sunday? Where shall we go on vacation?

Often, older persons can vividly recall events of long ago but have more difficulty remembering the recent past. That is surely true of Ellen Weatherall. Ellen is eighty years old, and she has little interest in the future, which she knows is over for her. But the past! Now *there's* something to think about.

The point of this very perceptive story is what Granny Weatherall recalls most vividly of all. It happened sixty years ago, Granny tells us, and the memory still hurts.

A Dialogue with the Text
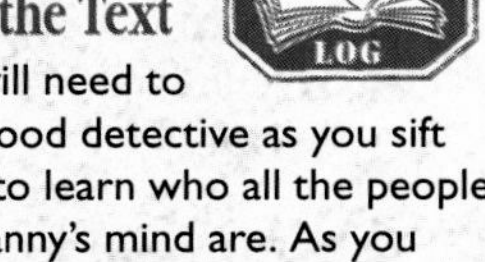

You will need to be a good detective as you sift clues to learn who all the people in Granny's mind are. As you meet them, note in your Reader's Log what their relationships to Granny are and whether they are living or dead.

Here are some suggestions: Pay careful attention to tenses of verbs, since they help distinguish past from present. Also, pay attention to the use of quotation marks. They enclose words actually spoken as opposed to unspoken thoughts. Finally, be patient. If a character is mentioned but not immediately identified, wait until more clues are given.

Elements of Literature
Stream of Consciousness
Although this story uses some dialogue, it mostly employs a modernist narrative technique called **stream of consciousness.** This technique allows the reader to overhear Granny's thoughts and memories. These occur to her in no special order, her mind switching back and forth from what is going on around her to what happened long ago, including the central episode of the story.

Stream of consciousness is a style of writing that conveys the inner—and sometimes chaotic—workings of a character's mind.

For more on Stream of Consciousness, see the Handbook of Literary Terms.

Into the Story

Using Before You Read p. 703

Reading Focus
Ask students to reflect on memories they have that are particularly vivid. Have students discuss why some memories are more vivid than others. Does a memory's clarity depend only on how recently the event happened? Challenge students to think of a number of other factors that make memories stand out in one's mind.

A Dialogue with the Text
Suggest to students that they use the chart like the one below to keep track of the characters in the story. Using the same chart will allow students to compare their evaluations more easily.

Character	Relationship to Granny	Living or Dead?

About the Author
Katherine Anne Porter is thought by many to be one of the greatest American short-fiction writers of the century. In her work, she often draws from her personal experience of growing up in the American South. The protagonist of *Pale Horse, Pale Rider* is Miranda, a recurring character in Porter's fiction that many feel to be her fictional counterpart. Porter's fiction often centers on an epiphany, or sudden dramatic realization, rather than on action.

Words to Own
The following vocabulary words are defined in the Words to Own at the bottom of the pupil's page.

tactful p. 706
margin p. 706
clammy p. 706
plague p. 706
vanity p. 708
jilted p. 708
disputed p. 708
frippery p. 710
nimbus p. 710
dwindled p. 711

Portfolio Assessment
Portfolio Assessment For help with self-assessment of reading skills, see the *Portfolio Management System,* pp. 48–49.

A. Critical Reading: Making Inferences

? Why would Granny Weatherall refer to Doctor Harry as a "brat"? [He is much younger than she, and she remembers him when he was just a boy. His professional sense of self-importance rankles her.]

The Jilting of Granny Weatherall

Katherine Anne Porter

A She flicked her wrist neatly out of Doctor Harry's pudgy careful fingers and pulled the sheet up to her chin. The brat ought to be in knee breeches. Doctoring around the country with spectacles on his nose! "Get along now, take your schoolbooks and go. There's nothing wrong with me."

Doctor Harry spread a warm paw like a cushion on her forehead where the forked green vein danced and made her eyelids twitch. "Now, now, be a good girl, and we'll have you up in no time."

"That's no way to speak to a woman nearly eighty years old just because she's down. I'd have you respect your elders, young man."

"Well, Missy, excuse me." Doctor Harry patted her cheek. "But I've got to warn you, haven't I? You're a marvel, but you must be careful or you're going to be good and sorry."

"Don't tell me what I'm going to be. I'm on my feet now, morally speaking. It's Cornelia. I had to go to bed to get rid of her."

Her bones felt loose, and floated around in her skin, and Doctor Harry floated like a balloon around the foot of the bed. He floated and pulled down his waistcoat and swung his glasses on a cord. "Well, stay where you are, it certainly can't hurt you."

OPTIONS FOR TEACHING

STRATEGIES FOR INCLUSION

Less Proficient Readers The stream-of-consciousness narrative may confuse students. Point out that the story is told through the eyes of Granny Weatherall. Other characters' viewpoints come from dialogue. Work with students as they read to help them differentiate among the various **points of view** and to determine who is the speaker.

Advanced Have students look for other examples of the **stream-of-consciousness** style. Encourage students to research the term and to read other stories, novels, or poems that make use of interior monologue. Students should compare the examples they find to Porter's story. Ask students to share their comparisons with the class.

Learners Having Difficulty Students must have a clear understanding of the concept of being jilted, for it plays a vital part in the story. Ask a student to look up the word *jilt* in a dictionary and to dictate the definition to you as you write it on the chalkboard. Then, ask students to read the title and to make predictions about the story. After students have finished reading, you might ask them to explain the significance of the title in relation to the events in the story.

New England Woman (1895) by Cecilia Beaux. Oil on canvas (43″ × 24¼″).

Courtesy of The Museum of American Art of The Pennsylvania Academy of the Fine Arts, Philadelphia; Temple Fund Purchase.

RESPONDING TO THE ART: VISUAL LITERACY

What is the mood of this painting, and which details create the mood? [Possible responses: The mood is quiet, contemplative, and lonely; the painting's single figure, her interrupted actions, her steady gaze, and the candle's light create the effect.] **Challenge students to guess what the woman is thinking about, and to support their answers.** [Possible response: She is reliving a memory—she is obviously not paying attention to her present surroundings.]

STRATEGIES FOR INCLUSION

Special Needs The **stream-of-consciousness** narrative technique may confuse students about the relationships between the story's characters. Ask students to make a list as they read the characters' names and to note beside each name the character's relationship to Granny Weatherall. Encourage students to be as specific as possible in their notes.

CROSSING THE CURRICULUM

Health Granny Weatherall is almost eighty when she dies, but her husband and at least one of her children died when they were much younger. Have students research and report on life expectancy, death rates, and infant mortality rates in the United States in the 1800s. They can then compare the statistics with birth and death rates in today's society. Students can graph or chart their findings and explain them to the class.

Social Science Have students research the "Forty Acres" that Granny worries about as she is dying. Why is the number specifically forty? Students can research individually and share their findings in small groups.

A. Reader's Response: First Thoughts

? What are your impressions of Granny Weatherall from this paragraph? [Sample responses: Granny is obstinate and opinionated; she shouts at the doctor as he is leaving because she cannot stand not having her own way. The old woman is strong-willed and honest, and she has her own rigid sense of right and wrong.]

B. Literary Element: Stream of Consciousness

The description is from Granny's point of view, and since she is slipping in and out of sleep the sounds are hard to pin down. This is an example of the stream-of-consciousness technique.

C. Critical Reading: Drawing Conclusions

? Why should Granny be concerned with order right now, with "tuck[ing] in the edges orderly"? [She knows she is going to die soon and does not want to leave important things left undone.]

D. Reader's Response: Shaping Interpretations

? Why do you think Granny is uneasy about the possibility of the children reading the letters? [Sample responses: The letters are probably love letters, and she does not want her children to know about her romances. The letters might contain information that would cause her children to think of Granny differently after she is dead.]

(A) "Get along and doctor your sick," said Granny Weatherall. "Leave a well woman alone. I'll call for you when I want you. . . . Where were you forty years ago when I pulled through milk leg[1] and double pneumonia? You weren't even born. Don't let Cornelia lead you on," she shouted, because Doctor Harry appeared to float up to the ceiling and out. "I pay my own bills, and I don't throw my money away on nonsense!"

She meant to wave goodbye, but it was too much trouble. Her eyes closed of themselves, it was like a dark curtain drawn around the bed. The pillow rose and floated under her, pleasant as a hammock in a light wind. (B) She listened to the leaves rustling outside the window. No, somebody was swishing newspapers: No, Cornelia and Doctor Harry were whispering together. She leaped broad awake, thinking they whispered in her ear.

"She was never like this, *never* like this!" "Well, what can we expect?" "Yes, eighty years old. . . ."

Well, and what if she was? She still had ears. It was like Cornelia to whisper around doors. She always kept things secret in such a public way. She was always being tactful and kind. Cornelia was dutiful; that was the trouble with her. Dutiful and good: "So good and dutiful," said Granny, "that I'd like to spank her." She saw herself spanking Cornelia and making a fine job of it.

"What'd you say, Mother?"

Granny felt her face tying up in hard knots.

"Can't a body think, I'd like to know?"

"I thought you might want something."

"I do. I want a lot of things. First off, go away and don't whisper."

She lay and drowsed, hoping in her sleep that the children would keep out and let her rest a minute. It had been a long day. Not that she was tired. It was always pleasant to snatch a minute now and then. There was always so much to be done, let me see: tomorrow.

Tomorrow was far away and there was nothing to trouble about. Things were finished somehow when the time came; thank God there was always a little margin over for peace: (C) Then a person could spread out the plan of life and tuck in the edges orderly. It was good to have everything clean and folded away, with the hairbrushes and tonic bottles sitting straight on the white embroidered linen: the day started without fuss and the pantry shelves laid out with rows of jelly glasses and brown jugs and white stone-china jars with blue whirligigs and words painted on them: coffee, tea, sugar, ginger, cinnamon, allspice: and the bronze clock with the lion on top nicely dusted off. The dust that lion could collect in twenty-four hours! The box in the attic with all those letters tied up, well, she'd have to go through that tomorrow. (D) All those letters—George's letters and John's letters and her letters to them both—lying around for the children to find afterward made her uneasy. Yes, that would be tomorrow's business. No use to let them know how silly she had been once.

While she was rummaging around she found death in her mind and it felt clammy and unfamiliar. She had spent so much time preparing for death there was no need for bringing it up again. Let it take care of itself now. When she was sixty she had felt very old, finished, and went around making farewell trips to see her children and grandchildren, with a secret in her mind: This is the very last of your mother, children! Then she made her will and came down with a long fever. That was all just a notion like a lot of other things, but it was lucky too, for she had once for all got over the idea of dying for a long time. Now she couldn't be worried. She hoped she had better sense now. Her father had lived to be one hundred and two years old and had drunk a noggin[2] of strong hot toddy[3] on his last birthday. He told the reporters it was his daily habit, and he owed his long life to that. He had made quite a scandal and was very pleased about it. She believed she'd just plague Cornelia a little.

"Cornelia! Cornelia!" No footsteps, but a sudden hand on her cheek. "Bless you, where have you been?"

1. **milk leg:** painful swelling of the leg, usually as a result of an infection during childbirth.

2. **noggin:** mug.

3. **hot toddy:** drink made of liquor mixed with hot water, sugar, and spices.

WORDS TO OWN

tactful (takt′fəl) *adj.:* skilled in saying the right thing.
margin (mär′jən) *n.:* extra amount.
clammy (klam′ē) *adj.:* cold and damp.
plague (plāg) *v.:* annoy.

OPTIONS FOR TEACHING

COOPERATIVE LEARNING

Time-Line Activity Have students work in groups of four or five to make a time line of key events in the story. Students should cooperate to list the events in chronological order, distinguishing between events that happened in the past and those that happen in the present of the story. Then, each student can draw a connection between two of the events, either a connection Granny realizes or a parallel that students discover. Groups can present their time lines to the class on a poster board. Finally, students can share their individual observations about their time lines.

Extending Dialogues To give students further insight into character development, have them work in groups of four on Speaking-Thinking Dialogues. Each group should choose a piece of dialogue from the selection. One student reads what the first character is saying, and the second student says what the character is thinking. The other two students present what the second character is saying and thinking. Each group should share its results with the class.

"Here, Mother."

"Well, Cornelia, I want a noggin of hot toddy."

"Are you cold, darling?"

"I'm chilly, Cornelia. Lying in bed stops the circulation. I must have told you that a thousand times."

Well, she could just hear Cornelia telling her husband that Mother was getting a little childish and they'd have to humor her. The thing that most annoyed her was that Cornelia thought she was deaf, dumb, and blind. Little hasty glances and tiny gestures tossed around her and over her head saying, "Don't cross her, let her have her way, she's eighty years old," and she sitting there as if she lived in a thin glass cage. Sometimes Granny almost made up her mind to pack up and move back to her own house where nobody could remind her every minute that she was old. Wait, wait, Cornelia, till your own children whisper behind your back! (E)

In her day she had kept a better house and had got more work done. She wasn't too old yet for Lydia to be driving eighty miles for advice when one of the children jumped the track, and Jimmy still dropped in and talked things over: "Now, Mammy, you've a good business head, I want to know what you think of this? . . ." Old. Cornelia couldn't change the furniture around without asking. Little things, little things! They had been so sweet when they were little. (F) Granny wished the old days were back again with the children young and everything to be done over. It had been a hard pull, but not too much for her. When she thought of all the food she had cooked, and all the clothes she had cut and sewed, and all the gardens she had made—well, the children showed it. There they were, made out of her, and they couldn't get away from that. Sometimes she wanted to see John again and point to them and say, Well, I didn't do so badly, did I? But that would have to wait. That was for tomorrow. She used to think of him as a man, but now all the children were older than their father, and he would be a child beside her if she saw him now. It seemed strange and there was something wrong in the idea. Why, he couldn't possibly recognize her. (G) She had fenced in a hundred acres once, digging the postholes herself and clamping the wires with just a Negro boy to help. That changed a woman. John would be looking for a young woman with the peaked Spanish comb in her hair and the painted fan. Digging postholes changed a woman. Riding country roads in the winter when women had their babies was another thing: sitting up nights with sick horses and sick Negroes and sick children and hardly ever losing one. John, I hardly ever lost one of them! John would see that in a minute, that would be something he could understand, she wouldn't have to explain anything!

It made her feel like rolling up her sleeves and putting the whole place to rights again. No matter if Cornelia was determined to be everywhere at once, there were a great many things left undone on this place. She would start tomorrow and do them. It was good to be strong enough for everything, even if all you made melted and changed and slipped under your hands, so that by the time you finished you almost forgot what you were working for. What was it I set out to do? she asked herself intently, but she could not remember. A fog rose over the valley, she saw it marching across the creek swallowing the trees and moving up the hill like an army of ghosts. (H) Soon it would be at the near edge of the orchard, and then it was time to go in and light the lamps. Come in, children, don't stay out in the night air. (I)

Lighting the lamps had been beautiful. The children huddled up to her and breathed like little calves waiting at the bars in the twilight. Their eyes followed the match and watched the flame rise and settle in a blue curve, then they moved away from her. The lamp was lit, they didn't have to be scared and hang on to mother any more. Never, never, never more. God, for all my life I thank Thee. Without Thee, my God, I could never have done it. Hail, Mary, full of grace.

I want you to pick all the fruit this year and see that nothing is wasted. There's always someone who can use it. Don't let good things rot for want of using. You waste life when you waste good food. Don't let things get lost. It's bitter to lose things. Now, don't let me get to thinking, not when I am tired and taking a little nap before supper. . . .

The pillow rose about her shoulders and pressed against her heart and the memory was being squeezed out of it: Oh, push down the pillow, somebody: It would smother her if she tried to hold it. Such a fresh breeze blowing and such a green day with no threats in it. But he had not

E. Cultural Connections
Point out to students that Granny is complaining about being treated like a child by her own children. Have students discuss how older people are treated in various cultures. Then, ask students to think of how they would like to be treated when they are older.

F. Language Note: Transition
? How does the word *little* connect two separate trains of thought in Granny's mind? [She first thinks of how her children need her help doing "little things," and then she begins to remember when her children were little themselves.]

G. Critical Reading: Drawing Conclusions
? What does this section reveal about John? [John was Granny's husband who died at an age younger than the age at which their children are now. Granny thinks it is strange to think of him as so young.]

H. Literary Element: Stream of Consciousness
? The fog is part of the setting of the next scene, but how does it also connect with Granny's preceding thoughts? [She is lost in the vagueness of her memories, which are lost as if in a fog; the "army of ghosts" is the past moments in Granny's life.]

I. Literary Element: Symbol
? How is Granny's lighting of a lamp symbolic of her caring for her children? [Possible answers: The light represents the wisdom, love, security, and confidence she gives to her children.]

CLASSROOM MANAGEMENT

Individual Accountability in Collaborative Learning A group is not cooperative if some members do not participate or contribute. The following suggestions are ways to structure individual accountability in group activities.

- Choose one student from the group to explain the group's answers.
- Randomly choose one paper from the group to grade.
- Have each member of a group teach the group one thing that he or she has learned.
- Monitor and assess each group's performance frequently.

Managing the Reader's Response Classroom
Encourage students to consider different ways of responding to a story. After students have read a selection, have volunteers express their opinions about the work on a number of topics. Challenge students to change and broaden their responses after they have listened to others' views.

Block Scheduling After students have read the story, ask pairs of students to write five to ten questions about the story (twenty minutes). Use the student-generated questions and answers to quiz the class (fifteen minutes). Close the block by having students relate the story to their own knowledge and experience (fifteen minutes).

A. Literary Element: Metaphor

? Where, for Granny, is hell located? [For Granny, hell is the memory of the day she was jilted and the anger and resentment she feels for the man who jilted her.]

B. Critical Reading: Drawing Conclusions

? What is wrong with Cornelia? [She has been crying, probably because Granny's condition is worsening.]

Metacognition Have students explain the reasoning by which they arrived at their answers.

C. Critical Reading: Making Inferences

? Why does nobody answer Granny? [Students may say that Granny is hallucinating, or that everyone is shocked by Granny's ironic insistence on lying "in peace."]

D. Critical Reading: Analyzing Character

? Who is George, and what feelings does Granny have for him? [George is the man who jilted her. She regrets not being able to tell him that she bears him no ill will and has had a good life without him.]

come, just the same. What does a woman do when she has put on the white veil and set out the white cake for a man and he doesn't come? She tried to remember. No, I swear he never harmed me but in that. He never harmed me but in that . . . and what if he did? There was the day, the day, but a whirl of dark smoke rose and covered it, crept up and over into the bright field where everything was planted so carefully in orderly rows. That was hell, she knew hell when she saw it. For sixty years she had prayed against remembering him and against losing her soul in the deep pit of hell, and now the two things were mingled in one and the thought of him was a smoky cloud from hell that moved and crept in her head when she had just got rid of Doctor Harry and was trying to rest a minute. Wounded vanity, Ellen, said a sharp voice in the top of her mind. Don't let your wounded vanity get the upper hand of you. Plenty of girls get jilted. You were jilted, weren't you? Then stand up to it. Her eyelids wavered and let in streamers of blue-gray light like tissue paper over her eyes. She must get up and pull the shades down or she'd never sleep. She was in bed again and the shades were not down. How could that happen? Better turn over, hide from the light, sleeping in the light gave you nightmares. "Mother, how do you feel now?" and a stinging wetness on her forehead. But I don't like having my face washed in cold water!

Hapsy? George? Lydia? Jimmy? No, Cornelia, and her features were swollen and full of little puddles. "They're coming, darling, they'll all be here soon." Go wash your face, child, you look funny.

Instead of obeying, Cornelia knelt down and put her head on the pillow. She seemed to be talking but there was no sound. "Well, are you tongue-tied? Whose birthday is it? Are you going to give a party?"

Cornelia's mouth moved urgently in strange shapes. "Don't do that, you bother me, daughter."

"Oh, no, Mother. Oh, no . . ."

Nonsense. It was strange about children. They disputed your every word. "No what, Cornelia?"

"Here's Doctor Harry."

"I won't see that boy again. He just left five minutes ago."

"That was this morning, Mother. It's night now. Here's the nurse."

"This is Doctor Harry, Mrs. Weatherall. I never saw you look so young and happy!"

"Ah, I'll never be young again—but I'd be happy if they'd let me lie in peace and get rested."

She thought she spoke up loudly, but no one answered. A warm weight on her forehead, a warm bracelet on her wrist, and a breeze went on whispering, trying to tell her something. A shuffle of leaves in the everlasting hand of God, He blew on them and they danced and rattled. "Mother, don't mind, we're going to give you a little hypodermic."[4] "Look here, daughter, how do ants get in this bed? I saw sugar ants yesterday." Did you send for Hapsy too?

It was Hapsy she really wanted. She had to go a long way back through a great many rooms to find Hapsy standing with a baby on her arm. She seemed to herself to be Hapsy also, and the baby on Hapsy's arm was Hapsy and himself and herself, all at once, and there was no surprise in the meeting. Then Hapsy melted from within and turned flimsy as gray gauze and the baby was a gauzy shadow, and Hapsy came up close and said, "I thought you'd never come," and looked at her very searchingly and said, "You haven't changed a bit!" They leaned forward to kiss, when Cornelia began whispering from a long way off, "Oh, is there anything you want to tell me? Is there anything I can do for you?"

Yes, she had changed her mind after sixty years and she would like to see George. I want you to find George. Find him and be sure to tell him I forgot him. I want him to know I had my husband just the same and my children and my house like any other woman. A good house too and a good husband that I loved and fine children out of him. Better than I hoped for even. Tell him I was given back everything he took away and more. Oh, no, oh, God, no, there was something else besides the house and the man and the children. Oh, surely they were not all? What was it? Something not given back. . . . Her breath crowded down under

4. **hypodermic:** injection of medicine.

Words to Own

vanity (van′ə·tē) *n.:* excessive pride.
jilted (jilt′id) *v.* used as *adj.:* rejected after being previously accepted.
disputed (di·spyo͞ot′id) *v.:* contested.

Options for Teaching

Integrating the Language Arts

Language and Style Ask students to look at one of the ways Porter manipulates language toward her own ends by having students study her use of sentence fragments. Have students read the eleven-sentence paragraph on p. 710 that begins "Her eyes opened very wide. . . ." Ask students to find sentence fragments. [Sentences 2, 6, and 9 are fragments.] Ask students why the author has used unusual syntax in the paragraph. [To mirror Granny's wandering, faltering thoughts as she falls in and out of sleep.]

Writing: Narration Ask students to choose two or three incidents in the life of Granny Weatherall and to rewrite them in another form of narration. Students should put the events in chronological order and use the third-person **point of view**. Direct students to keep their narratives to no more than four pages in length. Then, have students compare their writing with Porter's method, and discuss the advantages and disadvantages of the style that Porter uses.

Cincinnati Art Museum, Kate Banning Fund.

Evening Light (1908) by Frank Benson. Oil on canvas (25 ¼″ × 30 ½″).

her ribs and grew into a monstrous frightening shape with cutting edges; it bored up into her head, and the agony was unbelievable: Yes, John, get the Doctor now, no more talk, my time has come.

When this one was born it should be the last. The last. It should have been born first, for it was the one she had truly wanted. Everything came in good time. Nothing left out, left over. She was strong, in three days she would be as well as ever. Better. A woman needed milk in her to have her full health. **E**

"Mother, do you hear me?"

"I've been telling you—"

"Mother, Father Connolly's here."

"I went to Holy Communion only last week. Tell him I'm not so sinful as all that."

"Father just wants to speak to you."

He could speak as much as he pleased. It was like him to drop in and inquire about her soul as if it were a teething baby, and then stay on for a cup of tea and a round of cards and gossip. He always had a funny story of some sort, usually about an Irishman who made his little mistakes and confessed them, and the point lay in some absurd thing he would blurt out in the confessional showing his struggles between native piety and original sin.[5] Granny felt easy about her soul. Cornelia, where are your manners? Give Father Connolly a chair. She had her secret comfortable understanding with a few favorite saints who cleared a straight road to God for her. All as surely signed and sealed as the papers for the new Forty Acres. **F** Forever . . . heirs and assigns forever. Since the day the wedding cake was not cut, but thrown

5. **original sin:** in Christian theology, the sin of disobedience committed by Adam and Eve, the first man and woman, which is passed on to all persons.

E. Reader's Response: Connecting with the Text

? In what other works that you have read has a character expressed a similar bittersweet satisfaction with life? Do you agree with such a statement? [Sample responses: Characters such as Lucinda Matlock teach that one learns to appreciate what one has in life; I agree that a person has to come to a happy conclusion about his or her life. I disagree that life always works out for the best—Richard Bone did not get a chance to correct his mistakes, and Granny Weatherall will never get a chance to speak to George.]

F. Critical Reading: Analyzing Simile

? What does Granny compare to her deed for the "Forty Acres"? [She compares the deed to her "understanding" with saints that she will go to heaven when she dies.] What does the comparison reveal about Granny's character? [Students may say that the simile shows how confident Granny is in going to heaven, or that it shows how much importance she places on material possessions.]

INTEGRATING THE LANGUAGE ARTS

Strategic Reading Have students read this selection in pairs. Partners can take turns reading the story, the first student reading until the second student calls out "stop." The second student summarizes what the first student has read. The first student can then ask questions about the second student's summary. Next, partners reverse their roles, and the second student reads until the first student calls out "stop."

PROBLEM SOLVING/CRITICAL THINKING

Dealing with the Past Ask students to discuss the ways in which Granny Weatherall deals with a painful event in her past. Have students identify her various reactions, attitudes, and strategies for overcoming the pain she feels. Write students' observations on the chalkboard, and then have them say what they would do or feel if they were in Granny's place. Also, ask students to discuss the situations and strategies of characters from other works who have trouble with their past. Students can use the graphic from Transparency 1: Problem-Solution Chart in the Transparency Package to organize their ideas for alternative courses of action. ☞

A. Reader's Response: Extending the Text

? In what other ways does Granny show her appreciation for "honest" things? [Sample responses: Granny values honest, simple things such as family and self-reliance. Granny is concerned with honesty because she wants to die with a clean conscience.]

B. Reader's Response: Connecting with the Text

? How does this image of death compare to images of death in other works? [Sample responses: In her poem "Because I could not stop for Death—," Emily Dickinson also compares death to a driver in a horse-drawn carriage. Porter's comparison is more mundane than most images of death in literary works; for example, Lucinda Matlock finds death a "sweet repose."]

C. Literary Element: Ambiguity

? To what does the pronoun *it* refer? [Students may say that "it" is Granny's last grasp at life, that she needs to feel someone's touch on her hand before she can die.]

out and wasted. The whole bottom dropped out of the world, and there she was blind and sweating with nothing under her feet and the walls falling away. His hand had caught her under the breast, she had not fallen, there was the freshly polished floor with the green rug on it, just as before. He had cursed like a sailor's parrot and said, "I'll kill him for you." Don't lay a hand on him, for my sake leave something to God. "Now, Ellen, you must believe what I tell you. . . ."

So there was nothing, nothing to worry about any more, except sometimes in the night one of the children screamed in a nightmare, and they both hustled out shaking and hunting for the matches and calling, "There, wait a minute, here we are!" John, get the doctor now, Hapsy's time has come. But there was Hapsy standing by the bed in a white cap. "Cornelia, tell Hapsy to take off her cap. I can't see her plain."

Her eyes opened very wide and the room stood out like a picture she had seen somewhere. Dark colors with the shadows rising toward the ceiling in long angles. The tall black dresser gleamed with nothing on it but John's picture, enlarged from a little one, with John's eyes very black when they should have been blue. You never saw him, so how do you know how he looked? But the man insisted the copy was perfect, it was very rich and handsome. For a picture, yes, but it's not my husband. The table by the bed had a linen cover and a candle and a crucifix. The light was blue from Cornelia's silk lampshades. No sort of light at all, just frippery. You had to live forty (A) years with kerosene lamps to appreciate honest electricity. She felt very strong and she saw Doctor Harry with a rosy nimbus around him.

"You look like a saint, Doctor Harry, and I vow that's as near as you'll ever come to it."

"She's saying something."

"I heard you, Cornelia. What's all this carrying-on?"

"Father Connolly's saying—"

Cornelia's voice staggered and bumped like a cart in a bad road. It rounded corners and turned back again and arrived nowhere. Granny stepped up in the cart very lightly and reached for the reins, (B) but a man sat beside her and she knew him by his hands, driving the cart. She did not look in his face, for she knew without seeing, but looked instead down the road where the trees leaned over and bowed to each other and a thousand birds were singing a Mass. She felt like singing too, but she put her hand in the bosom of her dress and pulled out a rosary, and Father Connolly murmured Latin in a very solemn voice and tickled her feet.[6] My God, will you stop that nonsense? I'm a married woman. What if he did run away and leave me to face the priest by myself? I found another a whole world better. I wouldn't have exchanged my husband for anybody except St. Michael[7] himself, and you may tell him that for me with a thank you in the bargain.

Light flashed on her closed eyelids, and a deep roaring shook her. Cornelia, is that lightning? I hear thunder. There's going to be a storm. Close all the windows. Call the children in. . . . "Mother, here we are, all of us." "Is that you, Hapsy?" "Oh, no, I'm Lydia. We drove as fast as we could." Their faces drifted above her, drifted away. The rosary fell out of her hands and Lydia put it back. Jimmy tried to help, their hands fumbled together, and Granny closed two fingers around Jimmy's thumb. (C) Beads wouldn't do, it must be something alive. She was so amazed her thoughts ran round and round. So, my dear Lord, this is my death and I wasn't even thinking about it. My children have come to see me die. But I can't, it's not time. Oh, I always hated surprises. I wanted to give Cornelia the amethyst[8] set—Cornelia, you're to have the amethyst set, but Hapsy's to wear it when she wants, and, Doctor Harry, do shut up. Nobody sent for you. Oh, my dear Lord, do wait a minute. I meant to do something about the Forty Acres, Jimmy doesn't need it and Lydia will later on, with that worthless husband of hers. I meant to finish the altar cloth and send six bottles of wine to Sister Borgia for her dyspepsia.[9] I want to send six

6. **murmured . . . feet:** The priest is performing the sacramental last rites of the Roman Catholic Church, which include anointing the dying person's feet with oil.
7. **St. Michael:** most powerful of the four archangels in Jewish and Christian doctrine. In art, he is usually depicted as a handsome knight in white armor.
8. **amethyst:** purple or violet quartz gemstone, used in jewelry.
9. **dyspepsia** (dis·pep'sē·ə): indigestion.

WORDS TO OWN

frippery (frip'ər·ē) *n.:* something showy, frivolous, or unnecessary.
nimbus (nim'bəs) *n.:* aura; halo.

OPTIONS FOR TEACHING

PROFESSIONAL NOTES

Cultural Diversity Have students work in small groups to explore issues about the treatment of older people in their own culture and in various cultures. Are children expected to care for their older parents at home? Why might people choose to seek other options for housing their older relatives? Have students form groups that include members from various cultural backgrounds to report on their ideas and to discuss similarities and differences in attitudes about older people among cultures.

ASSESSMENT TOOLS

Check Test: Multiple Choice

1. The author gives us the viewpoint and thoughts of (a) Dr. Harry (b) Granny Weatherall (c) Cornelia [b]
2. The occasion of the story is a (a) wedding (b) birth (c) death [c]
3. The person responsible for the jilting was (a) John (b) George (c) Hapsy [b]
4. Granny Weatherall's religion is (a) Roman Catholic (b) Protestant (c) Jewish [a]
5. The man that Granny Weatherall did marry was (a) John (b) George (c) Dr. Harry [a]

bottles of wine to Sister Borgia, Father Connolly, now don't let me forget.

Cornelia's voice made short turns and tilted over and crashed. "Oh, Mother, oh, Mother, oh, Mother . . ."

"I'm not going, Cornelia. I'm taken by surprise. I can't go."

You'll see Hapsy again. What about her? "I thought you'd never come." Granny made a long journey outward, looking for Hapsy. What if I don't find her? What then? Her heart sank down and down, there was no bottom to death, she couldn't come to the end of it. The blue light from Cornelia's lampshade drew into a tiny point in the center of her brain, it flickered and winked like an eye, quietly it fluttered and dwindled. Granny lay curled down within herself, amazed and watchful, staring at the point of light that was herself; her body was now only a deeper mass of shadow in an endless darkness and this darkness would curl around the light and swallow it up. God, give a sign!

For the second time there was no sign. Again no bridegroom and the priest in the house. She could not remember any other sorrow because this grief wiped them all away. Oh, no, there's nothing more cruel than this—I'll never forgive it. She stretched herself with a deep breath and blew out the light.

Words to Own
dwindled (dwin′dəld) *v.*: diminished.

Connections — A Poem

Adrienne Rich (1929–) is one of the most prominent poets in the United States, a feminist who addresses larger questions of personal and political relationships as she explores the situations of individual women.

Aunt Jennifer's Tigers

Adrienne Rich

Aunt Jennifer's tigers prance across a screen,
Bright topaz denizens of a world of green.
They do not fear the men beneath the tree;
They pace in sleek chivalric° certainty.

Aunt Jennifer's fingers fluttering through her wool
Find even the ivory needle hard to pull.
The massive weight of Uncle's wedding band
Sits heavily upon Aunt Jennifer's hand.

When Aunt is dead, her terrified hands will lie
Still ringed with ordeals she was mastered by.
The tigers in the panel that she made
Will go on prancing, proud and unafraid.

4. **chivalric** (shiv′əl·rik′): suggesting the noble qualities associated with medieval knighthood, such as honor, fearlessness, and protectiveness.

Bengal Tiger Rug (c. 1820). Handspun wool yarns sewn on handwoven wool ground (41 ¼″ × 67″).
The Shelburne Museum, Shelburne, Vermont. Photo by Ken Burris.

D. Critical Reading: Making Connections
? How is this scene like the one that still haunts Granny? [Students' answers will vary, but correlations to Granny's jilting include a priest but no husband, the waiting of her family, and the presence of much pain.]

E. Critical Reading: Analyzing Character and Plot
? What is Aunt Jennifer doing? [She is sewing a pattern into a piece of fabric, a picture of tigers in a jungle.] What can you tell about Aunt Jennifer from her drawing of the ivory needle? [That it is hard to pull indicates she may be older or ill.]

F. Reader's Response: Shaping Interpretations
? Why does the poet focus on the image of Aunt Jennifer's heavy wedding band? [Sample responses: The detail adds to the picture, but it also indicates that married life is a burden to Aunt Jennifer. The image is a symbol for how her husband stifles Aunt Jennifer's creativity.]

G. Reader's Response: Connecting with the Text
? What about Aunt Jennifer lives and survives only in her work? Can you think of other characters in similar situations? [Sample responses: Aunt Jennifer's creativity and passion live only in her needlework, which many might dismiss as a simple housekeeping task; her situation is much like that of Granny Weatherall, who tries to pass down to her children her simple passion for life.]

ASSESSMENT TOOLS

Self Reflection: Reading Ask students to use the following prompts to evaluate their reading of the story.

1. One strategy that helped me make meanings when reading was ____________________.
2. One strategy that helped me follow the story clearly was ____________________.
3. One thing I could do better next time is ____________________.

CONNECTING WITH "THE JILTING OF GRANNY WEATHERALL"

Discuss with students the correlations between the characters of Granny Weatherall and Aunt Jennifer from the poem above. Emphasize particularly the parallels on the subject of marriage. Students can use Transparency 5: Venn Diagram in the Transparency Package to organize their comparisons.

Students can use the following example as a model.

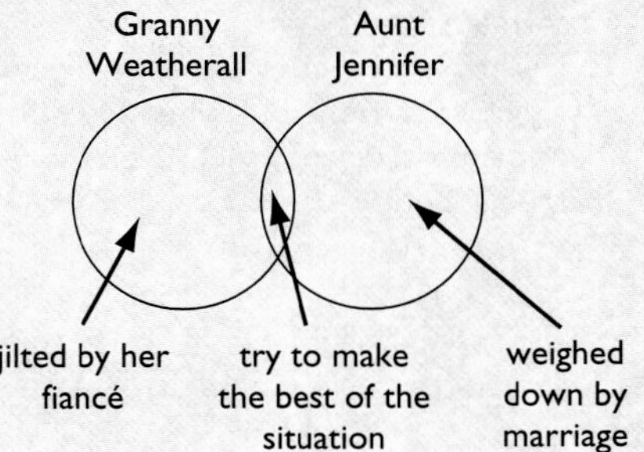

Making Meanings

First Thoughts

1. Possible responses: Yes, it is believable because this is an event that affected Granny deeply. No, too much time has passed for something so distant to be so clear.

Reviewing the Text

a. Granny is staying at her daughter Cornelia's house. Dr. Harry and Cornelia are with her.

b. Granny's children are Hapsy, Lydia, Jimmy, and Cornelia.

c. Granny's favorite child is Hapsy. She is either dead or imaginary because Granny thinks about seeing her again when she dies.

d. The title refers to Granny's memory of being jilted.

Shaping Interpretations

2. It is ironic because Granny clearly remembers George well. George's betrayal has affected Granny so much that she compares her husband and family to what she could have had with George.
3. Responses will vary, but some possible things "not given back" are her trust in people and her dream of what her life would have been with George. One ambiguity is her daughter Hapsy—does she even exist? Another ambiguity is Granny's alternating acceptance and denial of her own death. The use of stream of consciousness adds ambiguity through its limited and personal point of view.
4. The point of view is third-person limited. A change in the point of view to omniscient would cause the reader to lose the insight (and the ambiguity) of Granny's understanding of reality.
5. Granny experienced hell on the day she was jilted. Granny envisions heaven as a place where she will be reunited with lost loved ones from her life.
6. Granny blows out the "light" of her own life.
7. Granny is expecting Jesus, the heavenly bridegroom, but when He does not appear, Granny feels even more cruelly betrayed.

MAKING MEANINGS

First Thoughts

1. Granny's last thoughts revolve around a rejection that occurred six decades before. Do you find this believable? Why or why not?

Reviewing the Text

a. When the story opens, who is with Granny?

b. What are the names of Granny's children? (Review the notes you made in your Reader's Log.)

c. Which child was Granny's favorite? Is she still alive—or did she even exist at all?

d. What does the title of the story refer to?

Shaping Interpretations

2. When Granny recalls George, she thinks, "Find him and be sure to tell him I forgot him" (page 708). What is **ironic** in Granny's thought? How did George really affect her life?
3. **Ambiguity** is a technique by which a writer deliberately suggests two or more different, and possibly conflicting, meanings in a work. Granny feels that she was "given back everything" that was taken away by the jilting. Yet, she then says that something was "not given back." Identify what that something might be. What other ambiguities do you find in the story? How does Porter's use of **stream of consciousness** contribute to these ambiguities?
4. From what **point of view** is this story told? How would the effect of the story have been different if another point of view had been used?
5. What does Granny mean when she thinks, "That was hell, she knew hell when she saw it" (page 708)? How does she feel about heaven?
6. What is the significance of the light Granny blows out at the end of the story?
7. The end of the story suggests that Granny is jilted again. Who jilts her this time? How does Granny feel at this moment of revelation?

Extending the Text

8. Read Adrienne Rich's poem "Aunt Jennifer's Tigers" (Connections, page 711). How are Aunt Jennifer and Granny Weatherall alike and different? In what ways might both women have been "mastered by" events in their lives?

CHOICES: Building Your Portfolio

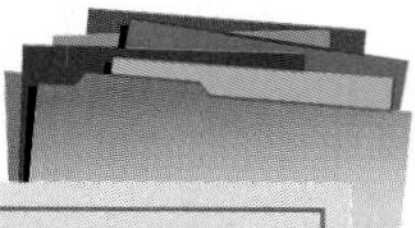

Writer's Notebook

1. Collecting Ideas for an Interpretive Essay

Porter's story contains enough **ambiguities** to give a reader plenty of food for thought. Jot down some questions you have about the possible meanings of this story. Keep your notes for possible use in the Writer's Workshop on page 804.

Critical Writing

2. Weathering It All

Granny Weatherall and Lucinda Matlock (in Masters's poem on page 695) have certain "family" resemblances. In a brief essay, tell how the two women are similar and, more important, how they are different. You might want to organize your details in a chart:

	Granny	Lucinda
1. Kind of life she led		
2. Attitude toward other people		
3. Tragedies in her life		
4. Feelings about death		

Creative Writing

3. Too Late the Bridegroom

George, now eighty years old, has returned just in time to see Ellen at her bedside. Write a brief **monologue** in which you reproduce George's thoughts as he looks at the woman he jilted sixty years earlier. Use **stream of consciousness** to show George's flow of thoughts.

Extending the Text

8. **(Synthesis)** Possible answers: Both women have experienced hard times, Aunt Jennifer because of her husband and Granny Weatherall because of a man who did not become her husband. Students should determine that each character's life has been deeply affected by the actions of this other person.

Beyond the Story

Choices: Building Your Portfolio

2. **Critical Writing** Tell students to include in their charts details that support their observations about each woman. After students have completed their charts, they can use the graphics as an outline for their essays.

William Faulkner

(1897–1962)

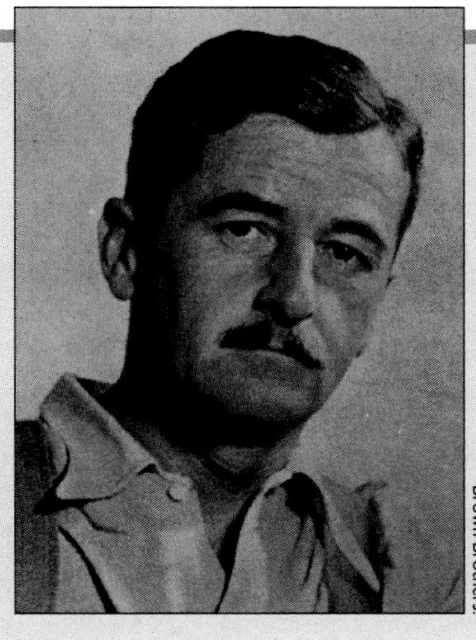
Brown Brothers.

Yoknapatawpha County, Mississippi, is surely the hardest of American literary place names to pronounce. Still, it is wise to learn how (yäk'nə·pə·tô'fə), for it is famous as the imagined world of William Faulkner, the scene of his most celebrated novels and stories. Imaginary Yoknapatawpha is similar in many ways to the actual impoverished farmland, with its red clay hills, that rings Oxford, Mississippi, home of the state's university. It was there that William's father, Murray Falkner (William added the "u" to the family name), ran a livery stable and later became the university's business manager. William Faulkner lived and wrote there throughout most of his life.

The South Provides a Theme

Faulkner was a mediocre student and quit high school in the tenth grade, but he read widely and he wrote poetry. At the outbreak of World War I, the United States Army rejected him because he failed to meet their height and weight requirements. However, he enlisted in the Royal Air Force of Canada and trained for flight duty, only to see the war end before he was commissioned. Returning to Oxford after the war, he took some courses at the university and did poorly in English. With neither profession nor skill, and a marked distaste for regular employment, he seemed a moody and puzzling young man to his neighbors.

Faulkner took several short-lived jobs, among them that of postmaster for the university. Resigning from this job, he wrote, "I will be damned if I propose to be at the beck and call of every itinerant scoundrel who has two cents to invest in a postage stamp."

In 1924, Faulkner left Oxford for New Orleans, where he met Sherwood Anderson, who had attracted much attention with the publication of *Winesburg, Ohio* (1919), his study of small-town life. Impressed and encouraged by Anderson, Faulkner tried his hand at fiction. In five months, he completed a first novel, *Soldier's Pay,* a self-conscious story about the lost generation. Thereafter, Faulkner wrote with a tireless energy.

Within the next three years, Faulkner found his great theme: the American South as a microcosm for the universal themes of time, the passions of the human heart, and the destruction of the wilderness. Faulkner saw the South as a nation unto itself, with a strong sense of its noble past and an array of myths by which it clung to its pride, despite the humiliating defeat of the Civil War and the acceptance of the distasteful values of an industrial North. Faulkner started to explore these themes in *Sartoris* (the first story set in mythical Yoknapatawpha) and *The Sound and the Fury,* two novels published within months of each other in 1929. *The Sound and the Fury* was a milestone in American literature, owing to Faulkner's bold manipulation of point of view and its stream-of-consciousness narrative technique.

In the decade that followed, Faulkner produced a succession of dazzling books: *As I Lay Dying* (1930), *Sanctuary* (1931), *Light in August* (1932), *Absalom! Absalom!* (1936)—considered by many readers to be his finest work—*The Unvanquished* (1938), and *The Hamlet* (1940). These works reveal Faulkner as equally skillful in the tragic or comic mode. He portrayed the South accurately, perceptively, and with a poignant ambivalence—on the one hand affectionate, on the other critical. He once said of the South, "Well, I love it and I hate it."

WRITERS ON WRITING

Here are some of Faulkner's thoughts about being a Southern writer: "[In the South, we] need to talk, to tell, since oratory is our heritage. We seem to try in the simple furious breathing (or writing) span of the individual to draw a savage indictment of the contemporary scene or to escape from it into a make-believe region of swords and magnolias and mockingbirds which perhaps never existed anywhere. Both of the courses are rooted in sentiment. . . . That cold intellect which can write with calm and complete detachment and gusto of its contemporary scene is not among us; I do not believe there lives the Southern writer who can say without lying that writing is any fun to him. Perhaps we do not want it to be."

PORTFOLIO ASSESSMENT

Choices: Assessment Criteria For help in evaluating the Choices assignments on p. 712, see the criteria in the ***Portfolio Management System,*** p. 155.

QUICK PLANNING GUIDE

Into the Story

Through the Story

Beyond the Story

Faulkner's Fictional Families

Faulkner described his South through fictional families who often reappear from novel to novel. They resemble trees, attaining grandeur, casting much shade, and then growing old and dry, crumbling as the seedlings of social change grow up around their fallen limbs and stumps.

There are the aristocratic Sartorises, who resemble Faulkner's own ancestors. Colonel John Sartoris, for example, was patterned after Faulkner's great-grandfather, who rose from rural poverty to command the Second Mississippi Regiment, built a railroad, wrote a best-selling novel, and was murdered on the street by his business partner.

There are also the Compsons, who incorporate some characteristics of the author's immediate family. They form the centerpiece of *The Sound and the Fury,* which records the decline of a once great clan, and with it the passing of a traditionally Southern world.

As I Lay Dying tells of the poor-white Bundren family and its efforts to bring the body of its matriarch, Addie, back to the town of Jefferson for burial. The novel reveals these humble people as more enduring than their social betters. *Light in August* concerns other Southern families and explores the problem of racism through the character of the protagonist, Joe Christmas. Although he appears white, Joe's racial heritage is mixed. His failure to find a place in either white or black society leads to his murder.

And, finally, there is Faulkner's unforgettable portrayal of the Snopeses—a sprawling clan of irresponsible, depraved, socially ambitious varmints who rise from the dust and cheat their way to respectability and wealth, destroying the old values of aristocracy and peasantry alike.

Faulkner often forces the reader to piece together events from a seemingly random and fragmentary series of impressions experienced by a variety of narrators. Faulkner's style often strains conventional syntax; he might pile up clause upon clause in an effort to capture the complexity of thought. In *The Sound and the Fury,* for example, he entrusts part of the narrative to the chaotic intelligence of one of the sons, Benjy Compson. But the efforts of patient readers are richly repaid, as they discover in book after book a mythical universe in which the moral dilemmas are the perennial mysteries of human existence.

"The Dream of Perfection"

By the time he received the Nobel Prize in literature in 1950, Faulkner's best work was behind him. After his richly productive period (1929–1942), he wrote many more stories and novels, including *Intruder in the Dust* (1948), *Requiem for a Nun* (1951), *A Fable* (1954), *The Town* (1957), *The Mansion* (1959), and *The Reivers* (1962). All these works displayed his characteristic virtuosity and willingness to experiment, but his powers were clearly diminished. His critics noted this and tended to underestimate his lasting importance.

Faulkner's writing surely diverged from that of his realist contemporaries—notably Ernest Hemingway, whom he put at the bottom of his own list of the best American contemporary writers. "I said we were all failures. All of us had failed to match the dream of perfection. . . . I rated Hemingway last because he stayed within what he knew. He did it fine, but he didn't try for the impossible."

Faulkner had this to say about the qualities of a novel: "The only mistake with any novel is if it fails to create pleasure. That it is not true is irrelevant; a novel is to be enjoyed. A book that fails to create enjoyment is not a good one."

Debate will always rage about the position of figures in our literary pantheon, but critics are now unanimous in their opinion that Faulkner is one of the greatest of all American novelists. There is certainly no argument over William Faulkner's preeminence among Southern writers. As Flannery O'Connor once put it: "The presence alone of Faulkner in our midst makes a great difference in what the writer can and cannot permit himself to do. Nobody wants his mule and wagon stalled on the same track the Dixie Limited is roaring down."

PORTFOLIO ASSESSMENT

Portfolio Assessment For help with teacher assessment of reading skills, see the ***Portfolio Management System,*** pp. 54–55.

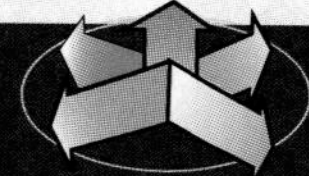

PROGRAM MANAGER

- **Planning Instruction** See **Teaching Notes, *Teaching Resources B,*** p. 71, for objectives, a summary, and literary elements for this selection.
- **Instructional Support** Before beginning the instructional lesson, see **Graphic Organizer for Active Reading, *Teaching Resources B,*** p. 79, for a Through the Story activity.
- **Assessment** See **Selection Test, *Test Booklet,*** pp. 165–166.
- **Reinforcement** Use the **Words to Own** worksheet in ***Teaching Resources B,*** pp. 80–81.

Before You Read
A Rose for Emily

Reading Focus

Skeletons in the Closet

Faulkner, the master of the Southern Gothic tale, knew firsthand the American South and all its powerful social traditions. It's all here in "A Rose for Emily"—the small-town social castes, the changes in a society's values, the politeness with which people go about the routine of life, and the struggles they undergo to find joy in it.

The core of this story is a lurid tale, as sensational as any you will see headlined in those scandal sheets displayed at the supermarket checkout counter. But what turns this account of outrageous human behavior into literature is the relation between the event and its setting. As the story of one eccentric woman unfolds, we learn some important truths about the rest of her community: its loyalty to family and the past, its pride, its faithfulness to old values, its fierce independence, and its scorn for all that is new and widely accepted.

A Dialogue with the Text

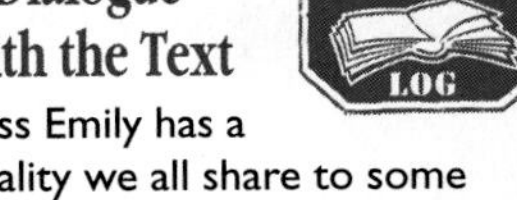

Miss Emily has a quality we all share to some degree: a tendency to retreat from a reality we don't like into an unreality where we can have things all our own way. But is her bizarre behavior merely madness, or an extension of qualities admired in her community? As you read the story, take notes on Miss Emily's characteristics, and write your ideas about the motives for her strange actions.

Elements of Literature

Setting

Setting is the time and location where a story takes place. Setting also includes the customs and social conditions of a time—including, in this case, such things as racial stereotyping. If parts of this story give off an offensive odor, it comes only in part from Miss Emily's house and her horrible deed: It comes also from the racial slurs used by some of the characters. Although we find this language offensive, we must remember that Faulkner used it to portray as realistically as possible a racially segregated town of the rural South in the early part of the twentieth century.

> **Setting** is the time and location where a story takes place.
>
> *For more on Setting, see the Handbook of Literary Terms.*

Using Before You Read p. 715

Reading Focus

Ask students to think of images of the American South from films, TV shows, or other literary works. List students' examples on the chalkboard, and have them create a generalized picture of the region from the details they mention. Challenge students to be wary of stereotypes.

A Dialogue with the Text

Have students freewrite for a few minutes about ways in which people attempt to escape reality. Students may base their answers on fictional characters they have seen or read about. Students can organize their ideas in the form of a diagram such as the one in Transparency 3: Cluster Diagram in the Transparency Package.

Elements of Literature

Have students discuss their own setting. Challenge students to describe as precisely as they can their situation and to organize the details into categories such as time, place, and social conditions. Students can use as a model Transparency 4: Category Chart in the Transparency Package.

WORDS TO OWN

The following vocabulary words are defined in the Words to Own at the bottom of the pupil's page.

perpetuity p. 716	virulent p. 721
archaic p. 716	tranquil p. 722
vindicated p. 719	doddering p. 722
pauper p. 719	acrid p. 722
circumvent p. 721	valance p. 722

A. Critical Reading: Making Generalizations

? What can you tell about the townspeople's attitude toward Miss Emily from their reaction to her death? [Possible answers: The townspeople treasure Miss Emily as a representative of the Old Guard, not as an individual human being. They view her as a curiosity, an anachronism, and an eccentric.]

B. Literary Element: Setting

? What is the impression created by the description of the house and its neighborhood? [Students will probably say that the house is the last remnant of a vanished era, and that it stubbornly resists all change. Its obstinacy and overblown, heavy design might reflect the stubbornness and delusion of its owner.]

C. Cultural Connections

Discuss with students why a colonel from the old days and a woman might both approve of this story. Point out to students that an obsession with maintaining a proper appearance is part of the culture explored in the story. Ask students how societal roles have changed or stayed the same.

A Rose for Emily

William Faulkner

I

When Miss Emily Grierson died, our whole town went to her funeral: the men through a sort of respectful affection for a fallen monument, the women mostly out of curiosity to see the inside of her house, which no one save an old manservant—a combined gardener and cook—had seen in at least ten years.

It was a big, squarish frame house that had once been white, decorated with cupolas[1] and spires and scrolled balconies in the heavily lightsome style of the seventies,[2] set on what had once been our most select street. But garages and cotton gins had encroached and obliterated even the august names of that neighborhood; only Miss Emily's house was left, lifting its stubborn and coquettish decay above the cotton wagons and the gasoline pumps—an eyesore among eyesores. And now Miss Emily had gone to join the representatives of those august names where they lay in the cedar-bemused cemetery among the ranked and anonymous graves of Union and Confederate soldiers who fell at the battle of Jefferson.

Alive, Miss Emily had been a tradition, a duty, and a care; a sort of hereditary obligation upon the town, dating from that day in 1894 when Colonel Sartoris, the mayor—he who fathered the edict that no Negro woman should appear on the streets without an apron—remitted[3] her taxes, the dispensation dating from the death of her father on into perpetuity. Not that Miss Emily would have accepted charity. Colonel Sartoris invented an involved tale to the effect that Miss Emily's father had loaned money to the town, which the town, as a matter of business, preferred this way of repaying. Only a man of Colonel Sartoris' generation and thought could have invented it, and only a woman could have believed it.

When the next generation, with its more modern ideas, became mayors and aldermen, this arrangement created some little dissatisfaction. On the first of the year they mailed her a tax notice. February came, and there was no reply. They wrote her a formal letter, asking her to call at the sheriff's office at her convenience. A week later the mayor wrote her himself, offering to call or to send his car for her and received in reply a note on paper of an archaic shape in a thin, flowing calligraphy in faded ink, to the effect that she no longer went out at all. The tax notice was also enclosed, without comment.

They called a special meeting of the Board of Aldermen. A deputation waited upon her, knocked at the door through which no visitor had passed since she ceased giving china-painting lessons eight or ten years earlier. They were admitted by the old Negro into a dim hall from which a stairway mounted into still more shadow. It smelled of dust and disuse—a close, dank smell. The Negro led them into the parlor. It was furnished in heavy, leather-covered furniture. When

1. **cupolas** (kyo͞o′pə·ləz): small, dome-shaped structures built on a roof.
2. **the seventies:** the 1870s.

3. **remitted:** refrained from enforcing payment of.

WORDS TO OWN

perpetuity (pʉr′pə·to͞o′ə·tē) *n.:* eternity.
archaic (är·kā′ik) *adj.:* old-fashioned.

OPTIONS FOR TEACHING

STRATEGIES FOR INCLUSION

Less Proficient Readers Direct students to the subtleties of the story by asking them to stop reading when they come to mysterious or suggestive details and to make inferences about how the details are significant. Students can use a two-column version of Transparency 2: Drawing Conclusions from Information in the Transparency Package. In one column students can list the details, and in the other the inferences they make. Allow students time to compare inferences with a partner.

Learners Having Difficulty Students may have trouble keeping track of the chronology of the story. Pair each student with a more proficient reader, and have them read the story together. Partners should note every instance of the story's flashing back or leaping forward in time as they read, and then they should discuss the important events within each time period. After reading the story, partners can make a summary of the events.

Spatial After students have read Part V of the story, have them reenact the scene. Students can arrange desks as the bed and use two other desks for the doorway. Volunteers can go through the motions of the characters' actions while another volunteer slowly reads the description of the scene.

My Mother (1921)
by George Wesley Bellows.
American (1882–1925).
Oil on canvas
(210.9 cm × 124.5 cm).

CLASSROOM MANAGEMENT

Structuring Interdependence When students work in cooperative groups, you might use some of the following ideas to help structure positive interdependence within the groups.

- Limit the resources of the group (one paper or one pencil per group).
- Require all members to achieve a certain mastery level of the material.
- Choose randomly to evaluate the worksheet or report of one member for the group's grade.
- Choose randomly one member to represent the group and to explain its answers.
- Assign each member of the group a role.

Organizational Tip Each week, assign a different student the task of saving extra copies of handouts, transparencies, notes, or any other materials that you use in class. Direct students to keep these notes and handouts in a designated place in the classroom. This procedure will save time if you want to use the material again or if a student who needs to make up work needs to refer to the resources. ☞

A. Reader's Response: First Thoughts

? What is your first impression of Miss Emily? [Sample responses: The woman is exactly what I would expect from the description of her house: decrepit, elegant, and somehow far away. The physical details of the description are surprising, because they hint that Miss Emily has decayed into a "lump of dough" or "bloated" like a drowning victim.]

B. Cultural Connections

Point out that though the word *nigger* is an extremely offensive term, it is vital to the realistic setting of the story. Tell students that the author uses the racial epithet objectively, as would a reporter documenting an event. Ask students what they think the significance is of the term coming from the mouth of a respected judge. Discuss students' reactions to the term, their expectations of the person who uses it, and their view of the time and place of the story.

C. Critical Reading: Speculating

? What is the smell that is coming from Miss Emily's house? [Possible answers: The smell is the result of neglect of the house, the spoilage of food, or some dead animal.]

the Negro opened the blinds of one window they could see that the leather was cracked; and when they sat down, a faint dust rose sluggishly about their thighs spinning with slow motes in the single sun-ray. On a tarnished gilt easel before the fireplace stood a crayon portrait of Miss Emily's father.

(A) They rose when she entered—a small, fat woman in black, with a thin gold chain descending to her waist and vanishing into her belt, leaning on an ebony cane with a tarnished gold head. Her skeleton was small and spare; perhaps that was why what would have been merely plumpness in another was obesity in her. She looked bloated, like a body long submerged in motionless water, and of that pallid hue. Her eyes, lost in the fatty ridges of her face, looked like two small pieces of coal pressed into a lump of dough as they moved from one face to another while the visitors stated their errand.

She did not ask them to sit. She just stood in the door and listened quietly until the spokesman came to a stumbling halt. Then they could hear the invisible watch ticking at the end of the gold chain.

Her voice was dry and cold. "I have no taxes in Jefferson. Colonel Sartoris explained it to me. Perhaps one of you can gain access to the city records and satisfy yourselves."

"But we have. We are the city authorities, Miss Emily. Didn't you get a notice from the sheriff, signed by him?"

"I received a paper, yes," Miss Emily said. "Perhaps he considers himself the sheriff . . . I have no taxes in Jefferson."

"But there is nothing on the books to show that, you see. We must go by the—"

"See Colonel Sartoris. I have no taxes in Jefferson."

"But, Miss Emily—"

"See Colonel Sartoris." (Colonel Sartoris had been dead almost ten years.) "I have no taxes in Jefferson. Tobe!" The Negro appeared. "Show these gentlemen out."

II

So she vanquished them, horse and foot, just as she had vanquished their fathers thirty years before about the smell. That was two years after her father's death and a short time after her sweetheart—the one we believed would marry her—had deserted her. After her father's death she went out very little; after her sweetheart went away, people hardly saw her at all. A few of the ladies had the temerity[4] to call, but were not received, and the only sign of life about the place was the Negro man—a young man then—going in and out with a market basket.

"Just as if a man—any man—could keep a kitchen properly," the ladies said; so they were not surprised when the smell developed. It was another link between the gross, teeming world and the high and mighty Griersons.

A neighbor, a woman, complained to the mayor, Judge Stevens, eighty years old.

"But what will you have me do about it, madam?" he said.

"Why, send her word to stop it," the woman said. "Isn't there a law?"

(B) "I'm sure that won't be necessary," Judge Stevens said. "It's probably just a snake or a rat that nigger of hers killed in the yard. I'll speak to him about it."

The next day he received two more complaints, one from a man who came in diffident deprecation.[5] "We really must do something about it, Judge. I'd be the last one in the world to bother Miss Emily, but we've got to do something." That night the Board of Aldermen met—three graybeards and one younger man, a member of the rising generation.

"It's simple enough," he said. "Send her word to have her place cleaned up. Give her a certain time to do it in, and if she don't . . ."

"Dammit, sir," Judge Stevens said, "will you accuse a lady to her face of smelling bad?"

(C) So the next night, after midnight, four men crossed Miss Emily's lawn and slunk about the house like burglars, sniffing along the base of the brickwork and at the cellar openings while one of them performed a regular sowing motion with his hand out of a sack slung from his shoulder. They broke open the cellar door and sprinkled lime there, and in all the outbuildings. As they recrossed the lawn, a window that had been dark was lighted and Miss Emily sat in it, the light

4. **temerity:** foolish boldness; rashness.
5. **diffident deprecation:** timid disapproval.

OPTIONS FOR TEACHING

COOPERATIVE LEARNING

Newspaper Activity Have students work in groups as the staff of the Jefferson newspaper to prepare a special edition reporting the death of Miss Emily and the discovered murder. Ask group members to choose an editor in chief and to decide on reporting assignments. Each group should cover not only the main stories but also other news by including features on fashion, society, and other related topics. Encourage students to be creative but to keep in mind what they know about their audience, the townspeople from the story. Students in groups of five or six can cover the events from several angles, or smaller groups can be used to encourage students to keep to the main ideas of the story. Ask the groups to organize their articles in newspaper format on a piece of poster board. Groups should display their work in the classroom.

CROSSING THE CURRICULUM

Social Sciences Write on the chalkboard *Setting: Small Town in Mississippi, 1920s–1930s*, and have students share anything they know about this time period and place. If students cannot think of many items, have them research a topic about the setting in a single source such as an encyclopedia, a history book, or a film based on fact. Students can then report their findings and summarize their information together in a cluster diagram on the chalkboard.

behind her, and her upright torso motionless as that of an idol. They crept quietly across the lawn and into the shadow of the locusts that lined the street. After a week or two the smell went away.

That was when people had begun to feel really sorry for her. People in our town, remembering how old lady Wyatt, her great-aunt, had gone completely crazy at last, believed that the Griersons held themselves a little too high for what they really were. None of the young men were quite good enough for Miss Emily and such. We had long thought of them as a tableau,[6] Miss Emily a slender figure in white in the background, her father a spraddled silhouette in the foreground, his back to her and clutching a horsewhip, the two of them framed by the back-flung front door. So when she got to be thirty and was still single, we were not pleased exactly, but vindicated; even with insanity in the family she wouldn't have turned down all of her chances if they had really materialized.

When her father died, it got about that the house was all that was left to her; and in a way, people were glad. At last they could pity Miss Emily. Being left alone, and a pauper, she had become humanized. Now she too would know the old thrill and the old despair of a penny more or less.

The day after his death all the ladies prepared to call at the house and offer condolence and aid, as is our custom. Miss Emily met them at the door, dressed as usual and with no trace of grief on her face. She told them that her father was not dead. She did that for three days, with the ministers calling on her, and the doctors, trying to persuade her to let them dispose of the body. Just as they were about to resort to law and force, she broke down, and they buried her father quickly.

We did not say she was crazy then. We believed she had to do that. We remembered all the young men her father had driven away, and we knew that with nothing left, she would have to cling to that which had robbed her, as people will.

III

She was sick for a long time. When we saw her again, her hair was cut short, making her look like a girl, with a vague resemblance to those angels in colored church windows—sort of tragic and serene.

The town had just let the contracts for paving the sidewalks, and in the summer after her father's death they began the work. The construction company came with niggers and mules and machinery, and a foreman named Homer Barron, a Yankee—a big, dark, ready man, with a big voice and eyes lighter than his face. The little boys would follow in groups to hear him cuss the niggers, and the niggers singing in time to the rise and fall of picks. Pretty soon he knew everybody in town. Whenever you heard a lot of laughing anywhere about the square, Homer Barron would be in the center of the group. Presently we began to see him and Miss Emily on Sunday afternoons driving in the yellow-wheeled buggy and the matched team of bays from the livery stable.

At first we were glad that Miss Emily would have an interest, because the ladies all said, "Of course a Grierson would not think seriously of a Northerner, a day laborer." But there were still others, older people, who said that even grief could not cause a real lady to forget *noblesse oblige*[7]—without calling it *noblesse oblige.* They just said, "Poor Emily. Her kinsfolk should come to her." She had some kin in Alabama; but years ago her father had fallen out with them over the estate of old lady Wyatt, the crazy woman, and there was no communication between the two families. They had not even been represented at the funeral.

And as soon as the old people said, "Poor Emily," the whispering began. "Do you suppose it's really so?" they said to one another. "Of course it is. What else could . . ." This behind their hands; rustling of craned[8] silk and satin behind jalousies[9]

6. **tableau:** set scene, as in the theater.

7. ***noblesse oblige*** (nō·bles′ ô·blēzh′): French for "nobility obliges"; that is, the supposed obligation of the upper classes to act nobly or kindly toward the lower classes.
8. **craned:** stretched.
9. **jalousies** (jal′ə·sēz′): doors or windows covered with adjustable slats.

Words to Own

vindicated (vin′də·kāt′id) *v.* used as *adj.:* proved correct.
pauper (pô′pər) *n.:* extremely poor person.

D. Literary Element: Imagery

? What do you make of the "tableau" of the woman and her father? [Possible answers: The scene is the typical result of suitors' attempts to court Miss Emily. The scene shows the two set against the community, Miss Emily untouchable in pure white, her father violently protective.]

E. Reader's Response: Shaping Interpretations

? Why is the community's reaction to the death of Miss Emily's father one of satisfaction? [Sample responses: They take delight, out of envy and spite, in seeing Miss Emily brought down from the untouchable status she enjoyed. The community wants everyone to be on the same level, and they recognize that without her father Miss Emily will have to face reality.]

F. Critical Reading: Evaluating an Interpretation

? What excuse does the narrator give for Miss Emily's bizarre behavior? [He states that she clings to that which robbed her—her father—because that is all she has.] Do you agree with the interpretation? Explain. [Possible answers: The interpretation is wrong because her clinging has nothing to do with her father's actions toward her. The interpretation is right because driving away all of Miss Emily's suitors only made her father more important to her.]

G. Critical Reading: Making Inferences

? What are the townspeople saying about Miss Emily? [They are speculating about a romantic involvement between her and Homer Barron, and they are delighted by the scandal.]

CROSSING THE CURRICULUM

Mathematics Have students take particular note of the mention of dates and references to the passing of years in the story. Challenge them to create a time line of events in the story by placing significant incidents in chronological order. Students can then compare their work and think of reasons that explain any differences their time lines show.

Art Have students draw a picture of their favorite scene in the story. Students can gather in small groups to discuss their depictions of the scenes, especially their renditions of the **characters** and the **setting**.

INTEGRATING THE LANGUAGE ARTS

Strategic Reading Pair each student with a partner, and have the partners take turns reading each of the five parts of the story. After each section, the student who did not read can ask his or her partner questions. The reader should answer as many questions as possible, and then the other student should give a summary of the section. Students can then exchange roles and continue reading the story.

A. Literary Element: Imagery

? What kind of look is described here? [The look hints that Miss Emily is trying to preserve her dignity.]

B. Reader's Response: Shaping Interpretations

? Why does Miss Emily not answer the pharmacist's question? [Sample responses: She is insulted that someone should take the liberty of asking her motive for an action. She does not want to talk about the poison because she has a secret purpose for it.]

C. Reader's Response: Extending the Text

? Do you think the community's response to Miss Emily's purchase of the poison is appropriate? Explain. [Sample responses: The community's reaction is not appropriate, because they do not care whether or not Miss Emily kills herself. The neighbors' reaction is not tasteful, but it is rational, because they feel that death is preferable to public degradation.]

That Which I Should Have Done I Did Not Do (1931–1941) by Ivan Le Lorraine Albright (1897–1983). American. Oil on canvas (246.5 cm × 91.5 cm).

closed upon the sun of Sunday afternoon as the thin, swift, clop-clop-clop of the matched team passed: "Poor Emily."

She carried her head high enough—even when we believed that she was fallen. It was as if she demanded more than ever the recognition of her dignity as the last Grierson; as if it had wanted that touch of earthiness to reaffirm her imperviousness. Like when she bought the rat poison, the arsenic. That was over a year after they had begun to say "Poor Emily," and while the two female cousins were visiting her.

"I want some poison," she said to the druggist. She was over thirty then, still a slight woman, though thinner than usual, with cold, haughty black eyes in a face the flesh of which was strained across the temples and about the eye-sockets as you imagine a lighthouse-keeper's face ought to look. "I want some poison," she said.

"Yes, Miss Emily. What kind? For rats and such? I'd recom—"

"I want the best you have. I don't care what kind."

The druggist named several. "They'll kill anything up to an elephant. But what you want is—"

"Arsenic," Miss Emily said. "Is that a good one?"

"Is . . . arsenic? Yes, ma'am. But what you want—"

"I want arsenic."

(A) The druggist looked down at her. She looked back at him, erect, her face like a strained flag. "Why, of course," the druggist said. "If that's what you want. But the law requires you to tell what you are going to use it for."

(B) Miss Emily just stared at him, her head tilted back in order to look him eye for eye, until he looked away and went and got the arsenic and wrapped it up. The Negro delivery boy brought her the package; the druggist didn't come back. When she opened the package at home there was written on the box, under the skull and bones: "For rats."

IV

(C) So the next day we all said, "She will kill herself"; and we said it would be the best thing. When she had first begun to be seen with Homer Barron, we had said, "She will marry him." Then we said, "She will persuade him yet," because Homer himself

OPTIONS FOR TEACHING

INTEGRATING THE LANGUAGE ARTS

Speaking and Listening Ask for volunteers to read sections from the story in which the narrator refers explicitly, with the words *we* or *our*, to the opinions of a group. Have students respond to each section with ideas and opinions they have of the community. Challenge students to characterize the group. Make sure each student responds to at least one section and that students take each other's opinions into consideration while making their comments.

Language and Style Ask students to analyze the language and style of one of the story's many minor details. For example, on the first page the aldermen pause in their request for Miss Emily's taxes and listen to "the invisible watch ticking at the end of the gold chain." The detail emphasizes the silence of the scene, the aldermen's confusion, and the contrasting timelessness of Miss Emily's world. The word "invisible" also evokes mystery.

Writing: Description of a Scene Ask students to choose a particular scene from the story and to retell it from Miss Emily's **point of view**. Students can use the stream-of-consciousness style that Katherine Anne Porter uses in "The Jilting of Granny Weatherall," or they can frame their narratives as a diary entry. Before students begin writing, they should focus on Miss Emily's feelings and thoughts at the specific point in the story. Encourage students to keep their narratives to no more than four pages.

had remarked—he liked men, and it was known that he drank with the younger men in the Elks' Club—that he was not a marrying man. Later we said, "Poor Emily," behind the jalousies as they passed on Sunday afternoon in the glittering buggy, Miss Emily with her head high and Homer Barron with his hat cocked and a cigar in his teeth, reins and whip in a yellow glove.

Then some of the ladies began to say that it was a disgrace to the town and a bad example to the young people. The men did not want to interfere, but at last the ladies forced the Baptist minister—Miss Emily's people were Episcopal—to call upon her. He would never divulge what happened during that interview, but he refused to go back again. The next Sunday they again drove about the streets, and the following day the minister's wife wrote to Miss Emily's relations in Alabama.

So she had blood-kin under her roof again and we sat back to watch developments. At first nothing happened. Then we were sure that they were to be married. We learned that Miss Emily had been to the jeweler's and ordered a man's toilet set[10] in silver, with the letters H. B. on each piece. Two days later we learned that she had bought a complete outfit of men's clothing, including a nightshirt, and we said, "They are married." We were really glad. We were glad because the two female cousins were even more Grierson than Miss Emily had ever been.

So we were not surprised when Homer Barron—the streets had been finished some time since—was gone. We were a little disappointed that there was not a public blowing-off, but we believed that he had gone on to prepare for Miss Emily's coming, or to give her a chance to get rid of the cousins. (By that time it was a cabal,[11] and we were all Miss Emily's allies to help circumvent the cousins.) Sure enough, after another week they departed. And, as we had expected all along, within three days Homer Barron was back in town. A neighbor saw the Negro man admit him at the kitchen door at dusk one evening.

And that was the last we saw of Homer Barron. And of Miss Emily for some time. The Negro man went in and out with the market basket, but the front door remained closed. Now and then we would see her at a window for a moment, as the men did that night when they sprinkled the lime, but for almost six months she did not appear on the streets. Then we knew that this was to be expected too; as if that quality of her father which had thwarted her woman's life so many times had been too virulent and too furious to die.

When we next saw Miss Emily, she had grown fat and her hair was turning gray. During the next few years it grew grayer and grayer until it attained an even pepper-and-salt iron-gray, when it ceased turning. Up to the day of her death at seventy-four it was still that vigorous iron-gray, like the hair of an active man.

From that time on her front door remained closed, save for a period of six or seven years, when she was about forty, during which she gave lessons in china-painting. She fitted up a studio in one of the downstairs rooms, where the daughters and granddaughters of Colonel Sartoris' contemporaries were sent to her with the same regularity and in the same spirit that they were sent to church on Sundays with a twenty-five-cent piece for the collection plate. Meanwhile her taxes had been remitted.

Then the newer generation became the backbone and the spirit of the town, and the painting pupils grew up and fell away and did not send their children to her with boxes of color and tedious brushes and pictures cut from the ladies' magazines. The front door closed upon the last one and remained closed for good. When the town got free postal delivery, Miss Emily alone refused to let them fasten the metal numbers above her door and attach a mailbox to it. She would not listen to them.

Daily, monthly, yearly we watched the Negro grow grayer and more stooped, going in and out with the market basket. Each December we sent her a tax notice, which would be returned by the post office a week later, unclaimed. Now and then we would see her in one of the downstairs windows—she had evidently shut up the top floor of

10. **toilet set:** set of grooming aids, such as a hand mirror, hairbrush, and comb.

11. **cabal** (kə·bäl'): small group involved in a secret intrigue.

WORDS TO OWN

circumvent (sur'kəm·vent') *v.:* to get the better of by craft or ingenuity.

virulent (vir'yoo·lənt) *adj.:* full of hate; venomous.

D. Reader's Response: Connecting with the Text

? What does this comment tell you about the people referred to as "we"? [Sample responses: They protect their own fellow townspeople. They are highly sensitive to social position.] In what other works that you have read has there been a similar group identity that comments on the story? [Sample responses: The technique is similar to the use of a chorus in a play. The group is like the couple in "Recuerdo" that does everything together.]

Metacognition Have students describe the ways in which they found connections between the texts they mentioned.

E. Language Note: Style

? What is the style of the passage that describes the malignant force that lives on in Miss Emily? [Students may say that the style of the passage is mysterious, suggestive, evocative, and fanciful.]

F. Critical Reading: Drawing Conclusions

? Why do the daughters and granddaughters of the older generation take china-painting lessons from Miss Emily? [They are sent to help Miss Emily without seeming to be giving her charity.] Why does the newer generation not send pupils? [The newer generation is less concerned about Miss Emily.]

PROBLEM SOLVING/CRITICAL THINKING

Conflict Resolution Point out to students that Miss Emily's bizarre behavior is simply an exaggeration of the real human desire to hold on to the people we love. Ask students to think of possible alternatives for Miss Emily's actions. Ask them also to think of similar situations about which they have heard, seen in films or TV shows, or read in other works. *Tell students that they do not need to talk about anything they would mind sharing with other students.* Ask students to arrange the problems and solutions they discuss in a graphic organizer similar to Transparency 1: Problem-Solution Chart in the Transparency Package.

PROFESSIONAL NOTES

Thematic Connections: "Shadows of the Past" Both Miss Emily and Granny Weatherall are thwarted in love. Have students compare how each deals with the experience. Then, have students compare the **points of view** of each story: Miss Emily's is told from the outside perspective of a narrator, Granny Weatherall's in an interior monologue. Ask students how each point of view affects the telling of the story.

A. Critical Reading: Making Inferences

? How did the townspeople know there was a room that would have to be forced open? [Like the reader, they have picked up on the clues and guessed what has happened.]

B. Critical Reading: Drawing Conclusions

? Who is the dead man? [Homer Barron.]

C. Reader's Response: Challenging the Text

? Knowing what you do about Miss Emily, do you find this ending plausible? Why or why not? [Sample responses: The story makes sense because only by murdering Homer Barron was Emily able to be with him, and she always had to have everything her own way. The story is too realistic to have such a fantastic ending, because no matter how crazy Miss Emily is, the townspeople should have been able to figure out what had happened.]

the house—like the carven torso of an idol in a niche, looking or not looking at us, we could never tell which. Thus she passed from generation to generation—dear, inescapable, impervious, tranquil, and perverse.

And so she died. Fell ill in the house filled with dust and shadows, with only a doddering Negro man to wait on her. We did not even know she was sick; we had long since given up trying to get any information from the Negro. He talked to no one, probably not even to her, for his voice had grown harsh and rusty, as if from disuse.

She died in one of the downstairs rooms, in a heavy walnut bed with a curtain, her gray head (B) propped on a pillow yellow and moldy with age and lack of sunlight.

V

The Negro met the first of the ladies at the front door and let them in, with their hushed, sibilant[12] voices and their quick, curious glances, and then he disappeared. He walked right through the house and out the back and was not seen again.

The two female cousins came at once. They held the funeral on the second day, with the town coming to look at Miss Emily beneath a mass of bought flowers, with the crayon face of her father musing profoundly above the bier[13] and the ladies sibilant and macabre;[14] and the very old men—some in their brushed Confederate uniforms—on the porch and the lawn, talking of Miss Emily as if she had been a contemporary of theirs, believing that they had danced with her and courted her perhaps, confusing time with its mathematical progression, as the old do, to whom all the past is not a diminishing road but, instead, a huge meadow which no winter ever quite touches, divided from them now by the narrow bottle-neck of the most recent decade of years.

(A) Already we knew that there was one room in that region above stairs which no one had seen in forty years, and which would have to be forced. They waited until Miss Emily was decently in the ground before they opened it.

The violence of breaking down the door seemed to fill this room with pervading dust. A thin, acrid pall as of the tomb seemed to lie everywhere upon this room decked and furnished as for a bridal: upon the valance curtains of faded rose color, upon the rose-shaded lights, upon the dressing table, upon the delicate array of crystal and the man's toilet things backed with tarnished silver, silver so tarnished that the monogram was obscured. Among them lay a collar and tie, as if they had just been removed, which, lifted, left upon the surface a pale crescent in the dust. Upon a chair hung the suit, carefully folded; beneath it the two mute shoes and the discarded socks.

The man himself lay in the bed.

For a long while we just stood there, looking down at the profound and fleshless grin. The body had apparently once lain in the attitude of an embrace, but now the long sleep that outlasts love, that conquers even the grimace of love, had cuckolded[15] him. What was left of him, rotted beneath what was left of the nightshirt, had become inextricable from the bed in which he lay; and upon him and upon the pillow beside him lay that even coating of the patient and biding dust.

(C) Then we noticed that in the second pillow was the indentation of a head. One of us lifted something from it, and leaning forward, that faint and invisible dust dry and acrid in the nostrils, we saw a long strand of iron-gray hair.

12. **sibilant:** hissing.
13. **bier** (bir): coffin and its platform.
14. **macabre** (mə·käb′rə): focused on the gruesome; horrible.
15. **cuckolded** (kuk′əld·id): betrayed, as in the sense of a husband whose wife has been unfaithful.

Words to Own

tranquil (tran′kwil) *adj.:* calm; quiet.
doddering (däd′ər·iŋ) *adj.:* shaky; trembling from old age.
acrid (ak′rid) *adj.:* bitter; irritating.
valance (val′əns) *n.* used as *adj.:* short decorative drapery.

Options for Teaching

Assessment Tools

Check Test: True-False

1. Miss Emily refuses to tell the local druggist why she wants to purchase arsenic. [True]
2. When Homer Barron comes calling, Emily's father sends him away. [False]
3. By the time she becomes overweight, Miss Emily's hair has become iron gray. [True]
4. Townspeople find Miss Emily's body behind a locked door that has to be forced open. [False]
5. Miss Emily asks the druggist to sprinkle lime around her house because of an offensive smell. [False]

Self-Reflection: Reading To check students' reading comprehension and to encourage students to reflect on what they have read, have them respond to one of the following questions.

- Are you like any character in this work? Why?
- Does anyone in this work remind you of someone you know? Why?
- Do you like this work? Why or why not?
- What do you feel is the most important scene, dialogue, or passage in this work? Why?

PRIMARY Sources | **A SPEECH**

Nobel Prize Acceptance Speech, 1950

I feel that this award was not made to me as a man, but to my work—a life's work in the agony and sweat of the human spirit, not for glory and least of all for profit, but to create out of the materials of the human spirit something which did not exist before. So this award is only mine in trust. It will not be difficult to find a dedication for the money part of it commensurate with the purpose and significance of its origin. But I would like to do the same with the acclaim too, by using this moment as a pinnacle from which I might be listened to by the young men and women already dedicated to the same anguish and travail, among whom is already that one who will someday stand here where I am standing.

Our tragedy today is a general and universal physical fear so long sustained by now that we can even bear it. There are no longer problems of the spirit. There is only the question: When will I be blown up? Because of this, the young man or woman writing today has forgotten the problems of the human heart in conflict with itself which alone can make good writing because only that is worth writing about, worth the agony and the sweat.

He must learn them again. He must teach himself that the basest of all things is to be afraid; and, teaching himself that, forget it forever, leaving no room in his workshop for anything but the old verities and truths of the heart, the old universal truths lacking which any story is ephemeral and doomed—love and honor and pity and pride and compassion and sacrifice. Until he does so, he labors under a curse. He writes not of love but of lust, of defeats in which nobody loses anything of value, of victories without hope and, worst of all, without pity or compassion. His griefs grieve on no universal bones, leaving no scars. He writes not of the heart but of the glands.

William Faulkner (right) receiving the Nobel Prize (1950).
AP/Wide World Photos.

Until he relearns these things, he will write as though he stood among and watched the end of man. I decline to accept the end of man. It is easy enough to say that man is immortal simply because he will endure: that when the last dingdong of doom has clanged and faded from the last worthless rock hanging tideless in the last red and dying evening, that even then there will still be one more sound: that of his puny inexhaustible voice, still talking. I refuse to accept this. I believe that man will not merely endure: he will prevail. He is immortal, not because he alone among creatures has an inexhaustible voice, but because he has a soul, a spirit capable of compassion and sacrifice and endurance. The poet's, the writer's, duty is to write about these things. It is his privilege to help man endure by lifting his heart, by reminding him of the courage and honor and hope and pride and compassion and pity and sacrifice which have been the glory of his past. The poet's voice need not merely be the record of man, it can be one of the props, the pillars to help him endure and prevail.

—William Faulkner

Primary Sources

As students read the speech, ask them to take notes on Faulkner's ideas about the purposes of writing in modern times. Then, discuss these notes with students. Ask them to apply the criteria to "A Rose for Emily" and to evaluate the story by Faulkner's own standards. Make sure students provide supporting details from the speech for their evaluations.

Technology Tip

Encourage students to explore the Internet for more information about William Faulkner and his writing. The World Wide Web address of the William Faulkner home page is **http://www.mcsr.olemiss.edu/~egjbp/faulkner/faulkner.html.** *You may want to preview any Internet activity that you suggest to students. Because these resources are sometimes public forums, their content can be unpredictable.*

STRATEGIES FOR INCLUSION

Special Needs In the speech above, students may not understand some of Faulkner's allusions to the concerns of the time. Review with students Faulkner's comments, and have them pool their knowledge of the era to identify the allusions. Discuss with students particularly why a U.S. citizen in the 1950s might worry about being "blown up."

Linguistic Discuss with students the purposes of a speech. Then, ask them to reflect on the **style** of Faulkner's speech. Challenge students to determine how the style supports the purposes of the speech; direct them to pay particular attention to **tone, rhythm,** and **diction**.

Advanced Have students write their own speeches, no longer than Faulkner's above. Students' speeches should reflect the concerns of their era and their own thoughts on the value of writing. Ask volunteers to read their speeches to the class.

Making Meanings

First Thoughts

1. Possible responses: The story contains enough clues that the ending is not a surprise. The ending is surprising because it is a bizarre conclusion.

Reviewing the Text

a. The townspeople assume that the odor is a dead rat or snake. It is later discovered that it is Homer Barron's corpse.

b. Emily says that her father is still alive and refuses to let his body be buried. This foreshadows the townspeople's discovery that Emily has lived with Homer Barron's corpse.

c. The minister's wife sends for Emily's cousins because the community does not approve of Homer Barron.

d. Homer Barron, the Yankee foreman of a construction company, is Miss Emily's lover. He disappears because Miss Emily kills him.

Shaping Interpretations

2. Miss Emily was dominated by her father. Her father's pose with the horsewhip implies that he was ready to fend off suitors with force.
3. After the death of Emily's father, Colonel Sartoris remits her taxes to avoid the possibility that she might not have enough money. Judge Stevens keeps the city authorities from telling Emily that her house stinks. As the South becomes more developed, the old class barriers dissolve, and the city authorities do not feel restrained by social mores from asking her for her taxes.
4. Emily's hair turns gray after she has killed Homer Barron. It is as if she has suddenly withdrawn from the living.
5. Emily sleeps in the same bed as Homer Barron's body, as if they were a married couple.
6. Tobe had to have known about the corpse in the upstairs room, but being a loyal servant, he does what Emily tells him.
7. The narrator is the voice of the community and as such is male and female, rich and poor, old and young. The narrator regards Miss Emily with pity, admiration, curiosity, and respect.

MAKING MEANINGS

First Thoughts

1. Did the ending of this story surprise you, or were you prepared for it? Explain.

Reviewing the Text

a. What do people think is causing Miss Emily's house to smell? What really causes the odor?

b. How does Miss Emily's odd behavior when her father dies **foreshadow** the end of the story?

c. Why does the minister's wife send for Miss Emily's relations?

d. Who is Homer Barron? What makes him disappear?

Shaping Interpretations

2. The community thought of Emily and her father "as a tableau"—a kind of dramatic picture. This tableau suggests conflict. What **conflicts** do you think existed between Emily and her father? (For whom or what was that horsewhip intended?)
3. How is Colonel Sartoris's white lie to Miss Emily about her taxes an attempt to spare her any embarrassment? Explain how, one generation later, Judge Stevens takes steps to avoid embarrassing her. How do the changes in attitude toward Miss Emily's taxes reflect wider social and economic changes in the South?
4. Why do you think Faulkner emphasizes the way Miss Emily's hair turned gray—and what do you think is significant about the time it started to happen?
5. What significance do you see in the strand of iron-gray hair found on the second pillow?
6. What part do you think Tobe, the manservant, plays in Miss Emily's history?
7. What sort of person do you think the **narrator** of this story is? Is it a man or a woman? Does the narrator pity Miss Emily? admire her? hold her in contempt?
8. The critics Cleanth Brooks, R.W. B. Lewis, and Robert Penn Warren noted of this story: "The community is nearly everywhere in Faulkner's work as an important force and, diffused and anonymous though it be, it becomes one of the most important elements in the story. . . . Miss Emily Grierson is one of the numerous characters in Faulkner's work who are warped by their inheritance from the past and who are cut off from the community—sometimes by their own will—to their detriment." Do you agree with these critics? Why or why not?
9. Another observation made by critics Cleanth Brooks, R.W. B. Lewis, and Robert Penn Warren is that Faulkner's story has significance far beyond its horror-story-like shock ending: "To read 'A Rose for Emily' as merely a piece of cheap Southern Gothicism, an attempt to shock and horrify, would be to miss the point." Do you agree or disagree with these critics? What is the point of the story, in your opinion?

Extending the Text

10. Historical details in this story reveal a great deal about its **setting.** What do you learn about the times from the townspeople's attitude toward the African Americans who live in Jefferson? In our time, have such attitudes changed or stayed much the same? Discuss how Faulkner might have changed his story if he'd written it today.

Challenging the Text

11. Faulkner once explained the title "A Rose for Emily" this way:

> "Oh, it's simply the poor woman had had no life at all. Her father had kept her more or less locked up and then she had a lover who was about to quit her, she had to murder him. It was just 'A Rose for Emily'—that's all."

Faulkner's answer is not very helpful. Consider what roses usually **symbolize.** Then defend the title of the story, or propose a more appropriate title.

8. Possible responses: Yes, Miss Emily's separation from the community causes the tragedy in the story. No, the community around Emily is no more healthy than she is.
9. Students should support their opinions with details from the story. If they agree with the critics, students should identify the main ideas of the story; if students disagree, they should provide evidence to support the view that the tale is just a horror story.

Extending the Text

10. **(Evaluation and Synthesis)** The town regards African Americans as second-class citizens. Attitudes have changed dramatically, and if Faulkner were writing the story today he might pay more attention to race.

Challenging the Text

11. **(Evaluation)** The flower's associations with romantic love, health and vitality, and death and funerals allow for many interpretations. Students should support their answers with specific citations from the story.

Choices: Building Your Portfolio

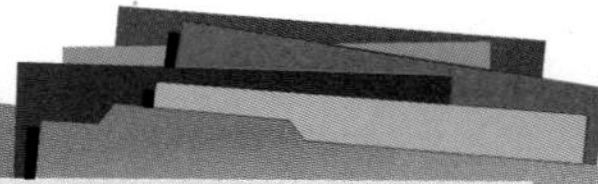

Writer's Notebook

1. Collecting Ideas for an Interpretive Essay

In order to fully understand a **character,** you must analyze him or her. Review the places in this story where the narrator directly describes what the townspeople thought of Miss Emily. For example, in part IV, he says they thought of her as "dear, inescapable, impervious, tranquil, and perverse" (page 722). Use these descriptions, together with your Reader's Log notes, to make a chart, perhaps something like the one below. When you have finished your chart, write a few sentences summarizing your insights into Miss Emily, including why you think she acted as she did. Save your work for possible use in the Writer's Workshop on page 804.

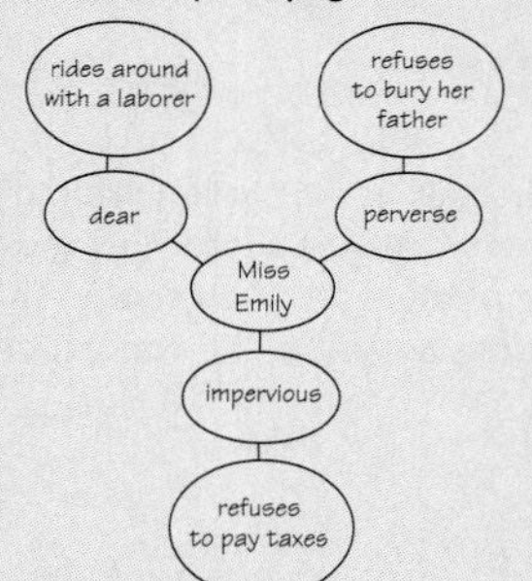

Critical Writing

2. Untangling the Plot

The order in which the narrator *mentions* events in this story differs from the order in which they actually occurred. Go through the story, listing these events and other key events as they are mentioned: Homer's arriving in town, Emily's buying the poison, the death of Emily's father, and so on. Rearrange your list in chronological order. Compare the lists, and write a brief essay in which you analyze Faulkner's **plot sequence** and speculate on why he presented events this way.

Creative Writing

3. Nightmare on *Your* Street

Write a short-short story (no more than 1,200 words) about a fictional solitary person who lives in your neighborhood. A shocking secret should lie hidden in this person's past. Before you begin writing, decide what the secret is and what events occur in the plot of your story. Include vivid, descriptive details that create a mysterious **atmosphere** and a believable **setting.** Save the startling truth for the last sentence, as Faulkner does in "A Rose for Emily."

Speaking and Listening

4. Literary Likenesses

With a small group, choose one of the statements below. Divide your group in half, and decide which side will argue in support of and in opposition to each statement. Do whatever research is needed (in this book or in the library) before deciding which side you can argue most convincingly.

a. Miss Emily's house is like Roderick Usher's house in "The Fall of the House of Usher" by Edgar Allan Poe (page 263). (You could also compare it with Julio Cortázar's "House Taken Over" on page 291.)

b. Miss Emily and Richard Cory in the poem by Edwin Arlington Robinson (page 645) are both victims of their extreme isolation from their communities.

c. Miss Emily is haunted by a lost love in much the same way that Granny Weatherall in Katherine Anne Porter's story (page 704) turns out to be haunted by the memory of the man who jilted her.

d. Miss Emily's room, as it is finally discovered after her death, is like Miss Havisham's apartment in the novel *Great Expectations* by Charles Dickens.

Beyond the Story

Choices: Building Your Portfolio

1. **Writer's Notebook** Encourage students to keep in mind the point of view of each description of Miss Emily. Students may find that some of the narrator's observations are faulty or biased. Remind students to save their work for use as prewriting for the Writer's Workshop on p. 804.
2. **Critical Writing** Students can use a graphic organizer such as the one on Transparency 12: Sequence Chart in the Transparency Package to track the progression of events in the story. Students can make two such charts: one to show the connections between the events as they are arranged in the story, and one to show the events in chronological order.
3. **Creative Writing** Students might create a map to note important qualities of each character and outline the story's events. Each student can share his or her map with a partner and talk the partner through the story. Partners can then help each other revise their maps, and students can begin writing their stories individually.
4. **Speaking and Listening** Divide the topics among an equal number of groups, and allow the groups adequate time to organize their arguments. Direct each group to record its main points, along with supporting details from the texts, on note cards. Groups can then use the cards to stage a debate for the rest of the class.

Options for Teaching

Strategies for Inclusion

Visual Encourage students to use other graphic organizers of their choice to collect ideas for activity #1. Students could use flow charts to record the character's changes and actions or use quick sketches with quotations from the story to visualize the scenes.

Kinesthetic For activity #3, have students act out scenes from their stories with a partner. Acting out scenes will help students to revise their dialogue so that it sounds more natural, and it should help them to better visualize action in the story.

Portfolio Assessment

Choices: Assessment Criteria For help in evaluating these Choices assignments, see the criteria in the ***Portfolio Management System,*** p. 156.

How to Own a Word

Mini-Lesson: Distinguishing Connotations of Synonyms

Have students work with a partner to check the table given for the words *tradition, duty, care,* and *obligation.* Each team should have a thesaurus and should make a suggestion about how the table could be different (another denotation used, for example). Then, have the partners choose their own words for a semantic features analysis. The terms could be adjectives used by the author in a series, such as in the example, or they could be terms used at different times for the same character or setting. To make students' charts easier to check, have them label each row and column of their charts with a citation that gives the word's location in the text or the denotation's source in the thesaurus.

Try It Out: Possible Answers

Students can use semantic features analysis to examine similar words in a selection in this collection or in another collection. One possibility is an analysis of the terms describing the younger generation in ll. 18–19 of "Lucinda Matlock": "What is this I hear of sorrow and weariness, / Anger, discontent, and drooping hopes?" Challenge students to use their charts to examine a deeper meaning in the poem. The terms in "Lucinda Matlock," for example, combine to paint a wholly despairing way of looking at the world. Have students share their charts and observations in small groups.

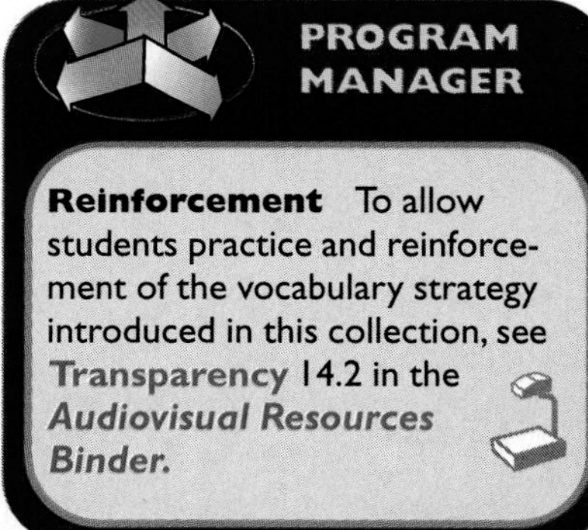

PROGRAM MANAGER

Reinforcement To allow students practice and reinforcement of the vocabulary strategy introduced in this collection, see **Transparency** 14.2 in the ***Audiovisual Resources Binder.***

HOW TO OWN A WORD

Distinguishing Connotations of Synonyms: Semantic Features Analysis

Semantic features analysis is a way of analyzing related words or **synonyms**—words having nearly the same meaning—to highlight their similarities and differences. A good way to see distinctions between terms that have overlapping meanings or subtle differences in **connotation** (the idea suggested by a specific word) is to analyze their semantic features.

Here's an example of an occasion when you might want to use this technique. Near the beginning of "A Rose for Emily," William Faulkner writes, "Alive, Miss Emily had been a tradition, a duty, and a care; a sort of hereditary obligation upon the town. . . ." You can be sure that Faulkner precisely chose the words *tradition, duty, care,* and *obligation* and made a considered decision to use all four to describe Miss Emily. Why? A semantic features analysis might help you understand why, and make you more sensitive to the author's choice of words.

To make a semantic features chart, list the words being analyzed down the left-hand side. From a thesaurus and a dictionary, gather various definitions, meanings, or features of the words to list along the top. (A thesaurus is a compilation of synonyms and antonyms. Many writers use a thesaurus to add variety to their work or, like Faulkner, to emphasize a point by using words with similar connotations.)

If a word has or suggests a particular meaning or connotation, mark +. If the word does *not* have that meaning or connotation, mark –. If a word potentially, but not necessarily, has a specific connotation, you may want to mark it *.

For the four words from "A Rose for Emily," you might need to begin with a dictionary definition to help you be sure you know the exact meaning—or **denotation**—of each word. Then you would choose features, and you might create a chart like the one below.

The following analysis shows that each word listed emphasizes a different aspect of responsibility. *Tradition* is the only word that suggests something that is necessarily passed along over generations. *Duty* emphasizes requirement. *Care* implies a burden. *Obligation* emphasizes the contractual nature of the responsibility. Thus, it could be argued, Faulkner has used these four words together to build a composite, or combined, meaning that is richer than the meaning of any one or two of the words alone.

	felt as burdensome	something long-established	something that is required	suggests a social obligation	has aspects of a law or contract
tradition	*	+	*	+	*
duty	+	*	+	*	+
care	+	*	–	–	–
obligation	+	*	+	*	+

Try It Out

Choose words with similar meanings from one or more selections to form an appropriate group for semantic features analysis. Make a chart, and use a thesaurus and dictionary definitions to help you identify features. Then, fill in the chart. Finally, try to describe in your own words the similarities and differences in meaning of the words you chose. Think about the connotations as well as the denotations.

OPTIONS FOR TEACHING

CROSSING THE CURRICULUM

Science Have students use the technique of semantic features analysis to analyze a system of scientific categorization. Students can choose a system such as animals' scientific names or the periodic table of the elements. Students can then use semantic features analysis to explore how the different terms used to describe an item in the system work together without redundancy. For example, the different terms of an animal's scientific name place the animal in different categories and groups; the separate parts of an element's notation give different information about the element. Have students share their findings with the class, and discuss with students why accurate, concise description is a valuable scientific tool.

Horacio Quiroga

(1878–1937)

Courtesy of the Consulate of Uruguay, New York.

Horacio Quiroga (kē·rō′gä) was one of Latin America's finest and most celebrated short-story writers, a master of the taut, suspenseful, well-crafted tale. Born in Salto, Uruguay, Quiroga was an avid admirer of Edgar Allan Poe's fiction. Like Poe, Quiroga wrote stories that blend horror with psychological suspense. Also like Poe, Quiroga developed a philosophy of short-story writing. In his essay "Manual of the Perfect Short Story Writer," Quiroga presents an approach to writing not unlike Poe's theory of the "single effect": the idea that every word and detail in a story should build to a single, unified emotional effect. Quiroga warns writers to avoid unnecessary words and details and never to begin a story without knowing exactly where it is heading. He felt that in the perfect short story the first few sentences are as important as the last few, and inevitably lead to them. In his best stories—among which is "The Feather Pillow" (first published in 1907)—Quiroga achieves a compressed, sustained effect with every word and sentence. By the time of his death, he had written about two hundred works of fiction, including the classic story collections *Jungle Tales* (1918) and *The Decapitated Chicken and Other Stories* (1925).

A master of dramatic technique, Quiroga was also superb at creating setting. In his stories, as in the stories of William Faulkner and other American writers who explore in depth certain real or fictionalized regions, Quiroga makes setting almost a character in itself. He spent a good portion of his life in San Ignacio, a jungle province in Misiones (in northern Argentina) that provided inspiration for his settings. In many of his stories, he deals with fundamental conflicts between human beings and the world of nature—conflicts in which nature is invariably the victor. Many of his jungle stories illustrate his uncompromising vision of life as an eternal, often brutal, struggle for survival, not unlike some of the tales of Jack London, to whom Quiroga has also been compared.

Quiroga's Poe-like obsession with death and the grotesque is not surprising, given that his life was a patchwork of nightmares as disturbing as the tales he crafted. Quiroga came face to face with gruesome death early in his life. First, his father accidentally killed himself with a shotgun. When he was twenty-three, Quiroga accidentally shot to death one of his closest friends. There were more personal tragedies: Quiroga's attempts to start a business in the rugged and dangerous Argentine jungle failed; his first wife, in despair over their living conditions in the jungle, took her own life; and his second marriage ended unhappily in separation. Quiroga ended his own tragic life in 1937, after discovering that he was dying of cancer.

ABOUT THE AUTHOR

Quiroga was born in Uruguay, and he spent most of his youth there, but the jungle frontier of northern Argentina was where he made his home. His jungle fables were written for children and adults, and they often featured animals as the main characters. Perhaps his greatest *cuento*, or tale, is *Anaconda* (1921), which tells of the struggles between the jungle snakes, the anaconda and the viper. As with much of his work, the tale can be read on many levels, realistic, symbolic, and philosophical.

PROFESSIONAL NOTES

Technology Tip Have Spanish-speaking students find out more about Horacio Quiroga's native country of Uruguay by accessing resources on the Internet. Students can begin their exploration with the address **http://bilbo.edu.uy/uruguay.html.** *Because the Internet often serves as a public forum, content may be unpredictable. You may want to check this and other sites and prepare a list of suitable addresses before having students access them.*

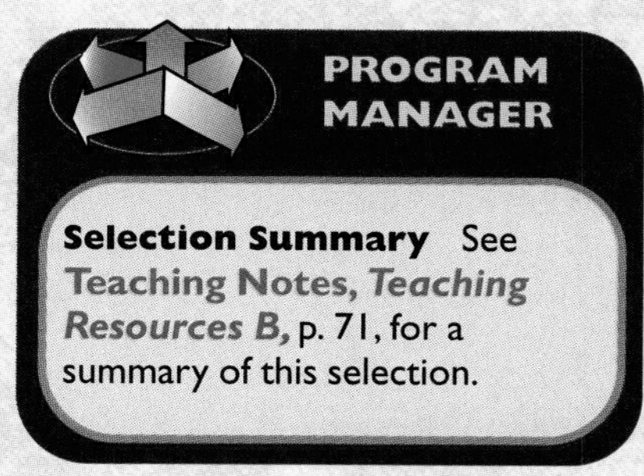

PROGRAM MANAGER

Selection Summary See Teaching Notes, *Teaching Resources B,* p. 71, for a summary of this selection.

Background

Ask students if they have read any works by the authors listed as using Gothic elements in their writing. Discuss with students what the authors have in common. Write students' ideas on the chalkboard as they discuss what makes a tale Gothic.

A Dialogue with the Text

Encourage students to stop to write a comment whenever they feel themselves pausing during their reading to reflect on a particular point. Tell students to make the notes quickly and then to resume their reading. They can review their notes after they have finished the story.

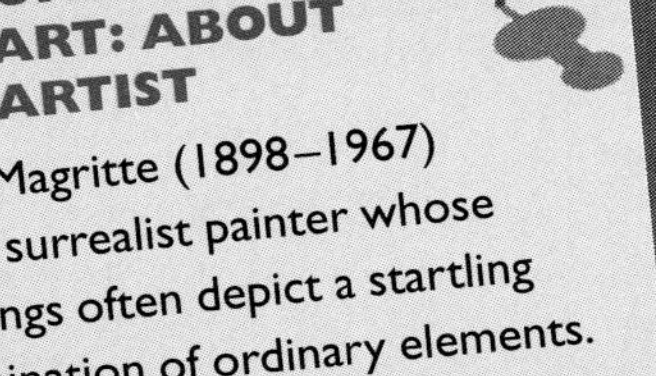

RESPONDING TO THE ART: ABOUT THE ARTIST

René Magritte (1898–1967) was a surrealist painter whose paintings often depict a startling combination of ordinary elements. For example, his painting *Golconda* is composed of outlines of men in bowler hats suspended in mid-air. This mixture of a realistic style and imaginative, dreamlike juxtapositions is frequently referred to as *magic realism*.

Before You Read

The Feather Pillow

Background

The Gothic tale has been well represented in literature of the United States, starting with Edgar Allan Poe, moving to Southern Gothic writers like William Faulkner and Flannery O'Connor, and continuing into the present with best-selling writers like Stephen King and Anne Rice.

Like their counterparts in the United States, many Latin American writers have used Gothic conventions to craft unsettling tales of the fantastic. One of the most successful of these writers is Horacio Quiroga, who used his fascination with the dark side of the human mind to craft a number of powerful stories with Gothic horror overtones. A typical Quiroga story quickly reaches its terrible conclusion with not a word or detail wasted.

Be warned: The story you are about to read is one you won't soon forget. After you come to the stunning conclusion of this tale, you may never look at feather pillows the same way again.

A Dialogue with the Text

As you read this story, pause at least three or four times to jot down any of the following:

- a question that has occurred to you
- an emotional reaction you have to the story
- a prediction you have about where the story is heading
- a thought you have about characters, details of the plot, or issues the story raises

The Lovers (1928) by René Magritte. Oil on canvas (21⅜″ × 28⅞″).

The Feather Pillow

Horacio Quiroga

***translated from the Spanish by* Margaret Sayers Peden**

Her entire honeymoon gave her hot and cold shivers. A blond, angelic, (A) and timid young girl, the childish fancies she had dreamed about being a bride had been chilled by her husband's rough character. She loved him very much, nonetheless, although sometimes she gave a light shudder when, as they returned home through the streets together at night, she cast a furtive glance at the impressive stature of her Jordan, who had been silent for an hour. He, for his part, loved her profoundly but never let it be seen.

For three months—they had been married in April—they lived in a special kind of bliss. Doubtless she would have wished less severity in the rigorous sky of love, more expansive and less cautious tenderness, but her husband's impassive manner always restrained her.

The house in which they lived influenced her chills and shuddering to no small degree. The whiteness of the silent patio—friezes,[1] columns, and marble statues—produced the wintry impression of an enchanted palace. Inside, the glacial brilliance of stucco, the completely bare walls, affirmed the (B) sensation of unpleasant coldness. As one crossed from one room to another, the echo of his steps reverberated throughout the house, as if long abandonment had sensitized its resonance.

Alicia passed the autumn in this strange love nest. She had determined, however, to cast a veil over her former dreams and live like a sleeping beauty in the hostile house, trying not to think about anything until her husband arrived each evening.

It is not strange that she grew thin. She had a light attack of influenza that dragged on insidiously for days and days: After that Alicia's health never returned. Finally one afternoon she was able to go into the garden, supported on her husband's arm. She looked around listlessly. Suddenly Jordan, with deep tenderness, ran his hand very slowly over her head, and Alicia instantly burst into sobs, throwing her arms around his neck. For a long time she cried out all the fears she had kept silent, redoubling her weeping at Jordan's

1. **friezes** (frēz′iz): decorative, ornamental bands around a room or along a wall.

A. Reader's Response: First Thoughts

? What does the first sentence tell the reader about the main character and her situation? [Sample responses: The main character is a woman who has some reservations about her recent marriage. The woman is sometimes excited about her honeymoon and sometimes scared, which is a strange reaction to one's marriage.]

B. Literary Element: Setting

? How does the setting reflect the character's state of mind? [The house is as reserved as her husband, and its coldness and its oversensitivity to sound correspond with the woman's fear and nervousness.]

OPTIONS FOR TEACHING

INTEGRATING THE LANGUAGE ARTS

Strategic Reading Ask students to pause frequently as they read to make predictions about the causes and outcomes of the mysterious events in the story. Students can arrange their predictions with confirmations and descriptions of their reasoning in a chart with three columns: Prediction, Reasons for Prediction, and Outcome. After students have finished reading the story, have them review their charts with a partner.

Writing: A Play Have groups of students turn Quiroga's short story into a one-act play. Arrange students in groups of four or five, and tell each group that its play should be no longer than ten minutes. The group members can collaborate on writing the play, sticking as closely as they wish to the original story, and then divide up roles such as those of actors, director, and stage manager. The groups can then take turns performing their plays for the rest of the class. ☞

A. Literary Element: Diction

? What is the effect of the author's use of the word *swallowed* in this sentence? [The word gives the carpet the quality of a living, hungry being; the effect is sinister and unnerving.]

B. Critical Reading: Making Inferences

? What is the significance of Alicia's most persistent hallucination? [Students may say that it shows that the cause of her worry is a combination of the inhuman coldness of her husband and something else, something even more inhuman.]

slightest caress. Then her sobs subsided, and she stood a long while, her face hidden in the hollow of his neck, not moving or speaking a word.

This was the last day Alicia was well enough to be up. On the following day she awakened feeling faint. Jordan's doctor examined her with minute attention, prescribing calm and absolute rest.

"I don't know," he said to Jordan at the street door. "She has a great weakness that I am unable to explain. And with no vomiting, nothing . . . if she wakes tomorrow as she did today, call me at once."

When she awakened the following day, Alicia was worse. There was consultation. It was agreed there was an anemia of incredible progression, completely inexplicable. Alicia had no more fainting spells, but she was visibly moving toward death. The lights were lighted all day long in her bedroom, and there was complete silence. Hours went by without the slightest sound. Alicia dozed. Jordan virtually lived in the drawing room, which was also always lighted. With tireless persistence he paced ceaselessly from one (A) end of the room to the other. The carpet swallowed his steps. At times he entered the bedroom and continued his silent pacing back and forth alongside the bed, stopping for an instant at each end to regard his wife.

Suddenly Alicia began to have hallucinations, vague images, at first seeming to float in the air, then descending to floor level. Her eyes excessively wide, she stared continuously at the carpet on either side of the head of her bed. One night she suddenly focused on one spot. Then she opened her mouth to scream, and pearls of sweat suddenly beaded her nose and lips.

"Jordan! Jordan!" she clamored, rigid with fright, still staring at the carpet.

Jordan ran to the bedroom, and, when she saw him appear, Alicia screamed with terror.

"It's I, Alicia, it's I!"

Alicia looked at him confusedly; she looked at the carpet; she looked at him once again; and after a long moment of stupefied confrontation, she regained her senses. She smiled and took her husband's hand in hers, caressing it, trembling, for half an hour.

(B) Among her most persistent hallucinations was that of an anthropoid[2] poised on his fingertips on the carpet, staring at her.

The doctors returned, but to no avail. They saw before them a diminishing life, a life bleeding away day by day, hour by hour, absolutely without their knowing why. During their last consultation Alicia lay in a stupor while they took her pulse, passing her inert wrist from one to another. They observed her a long time in silence and then moved into the dining room.

"Phew . . ." The discouraged chief physician shrugged his shoulders. "It is an inexplicable case. There is little we can do . . ."

"That's my last hope!" Jordan groaned. And he staggered blindly against the table.

Alicia's life was fading away in the subdelirium[3] of anemia, a delirium which grew worse throughout the evening hours but which let up somewhat after dawn. The illness never worsened during the daytime, but

2. **anthropoid** (an′thrə·poid′): humanlike creature, such as an ape.
3. **subdelirium** (sub·di·lir′ē·əm): restless, feverish state in which a person hallucinates.

ASSESSMENT TOOLS

Self-Reflection: Reading Have students use the rubric provided to evaluate their reading after they have finished "The Feather Pillow." You can review the self-reflections to offer individual improvement plans.

Always = 4 Seldom = 2
Usually = 3 Never = 1

____ I understand most of the reading assignment.
____ I can use techniques to find meanings for unfamiliar words.
____ I easily remember information I have read.
____ I take organized notes on assignments.
____ I review my notes frequently.

Check Test: True-False

1. Alicia feels a sudden calm after her marriage. [False]
2. Alicia is disturbed by the house's strange noises. [False]
3. Jordan frequently expresses his love for Alicia. [False]
4. Alicia's health begins to slip after she and her husband fight. [False]
5. The creature that kills Alicia is an overgrown bird parasite. [True]

each morning she awakened pale as death, almost in a swoon. It seemed only at night that her life drained out of her in new waves of blood. Always when she awakened she had the sensation of lying collapsed in the bed with a million-pound weight on top of her. Following the third day of this relapse she never left her bed again. She could scarcely move her head. She did not want her bed to be touched, not even to have her bedcovers arranged. Her crepuscular[4] terrors advanced now in the form of monsters that dragged themselves toward the bed and laboriously climbed upon the bedspread. C

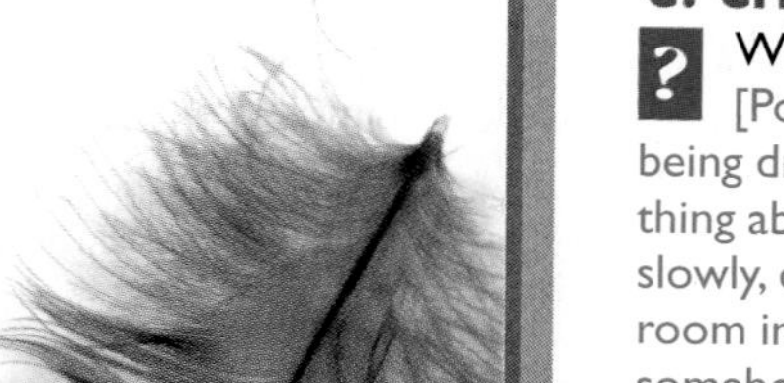

Then she lost consciousness. The final two days she raved ceaselessly in a weak voice. The lights funereally illuminated the bedroom and drawing room. In the deathly silence of the house the only sound was the monotonous delirium from the bedroom and the dull echoes of Jordan's eternal pacing.

Finally, Alicia died. The servant, when she came in afterward to strip the now empty bed, stared wonderingly for a moment at the pillow. D

"Sir!" she called Jordan in a low voice. "There are stains on the pillow that look like blood."

Jordan approached rapidly and bent over the pillow. Truly, on the case, on both sides of the hollow left by Alicia's head, were two small, dark spots.

"They look like punctures," the servant murmured after a moment of motionless observation.

"Hold it up to the light," Jordan told her.

The servant raised the pillow but immediately dropped it and stood staring at it, livid and trembling. Without knowing why, Jordan felt the hair rise on the back of his neck. E

"What is it?" he murmured in a hoarse voice.

"It's very heavy," the servant whispered, still trembling.

Jordan picked it up; it was extraordinarily heavy. He carried it out of the room, and on the dining room table he ripped open the case and the ticking with a slash. The top feathers floated away, and the servant, her mouth opened wide, gave a scream of horror and covered her face with her clenched fists: In the bottom of the pillowcase, among the feathers, slowly moving its hairy legs, was a monstrous animal, a living, viscous ball. It was so swollen one could scarcely make out its mouth.

Night after night, since Alicia had taken to her bed, this abomination had stealthily applied its mouth—its proboscis[5] one might better say—to the girl's temples, sucking her blood. The puncture was scarcely perceptible. The daily plumping of the pillow had doubtlessly at first impeded its progress, but as soon as the girl could no longer move, the suction became vertiginous.[6] In five days, in five nights, the monster had drained Alicia's life away.

These parasites of feathered creatures, diminutive in their habitual environment, reach enormous proportions under certain conditions. Human blood seems particularly favorable to them, and it is not rare to encounter them in feather pillows. F

4. crepuscular (kri·pus′kyo͞o·lər): happening at or related to twilight.
5. proboscis (prō·bäs′is): tubular mouthpart used by parasites to attach to a host and withdraw blood.
6. vertiginous (vər·tij′ə·nəs): causing vertigo; dizzying.

C. Critical Reading: Speculating

? What is happening to Alicia? [Possible answers: Her blood is being drained nightly, there is something about the night that is killing her slowly, or something sneaks in her bedroom in the darkness and harms her somehow.]

D. Reader's Response: Shaping Interpretations

? Why is the tone of the announcement of Alicia's death so dull and matter-of-fact? [Sample responses: The tone is flat and lifeless because it reflects the cold reality of the woman's death. The tone is understated because the outcome is predetermined—the reader already knows that Alicia is going to die.]

E. Critical Reading: Drawing Conclusions

? Why should the servant be afraid of a heavy pillow? [There is something inside the pillow that makes it heavy, something unexpected and strange.]

F. Reader's Response: Challenging the Text

? Does this explanation succeed in making you think, if only just for a moment, that such a story is possible in real life? Explain. [Sample responses: Yes, the ending is convincing because it gives an almost scientific reason for the mysterious events, which makes the story's eeriness seem even more real. No, the ending is not plausible because it is out of place with the tone of the rest of the story; the ending feels tacked on and false.]

CLASSROOM MANAGEMENT

Block Scheduling After students have read the last story in a collection (twenty to twenty-five minutes), take the class to the library, and allow them time to check out a book related to the Collection's **theme** (twenty-five to thirty minutes). After returning to class, give students time to begin reading (thirty to forty minutes). At a later date, students may present book reports to the class.

CONNECTING WITH "SHADOWS OF THE PAST"

Point out to students that this story, unlike the others in the Collection, does not focus on memories of events in the past. Challenge students to determine what it does have in common with the other selections. Have students especially focus on **mood, tone, character,** and the significance of **setting**. Discuss the elements with students, and write their ideas on the chalkboard. Students may find it useful to work with a graphic organizer such as Transparency 6: Comparison and Contrast Chart in the Transparency Package.

Finding Common Ground

Arrange students in groups of three or four. Allow the groups adequate time to discuss their notes, and then direct them to discuss their comparisons of the story to "A Rose for Emily" and "The Fall of the House of Usher." Then, give each group some markers and a sheet of poster board, and have each group graphically illustrate its comparisons on the board. Groups can use their poster boards as a visual aid while presenting their ideas to the class.

Literature and Pop Culture

Have students discuss some of the legends they have heard. Tell students that a good way of differentiating between legends and factual accounts is to examine the story's structure. Legends often are passed along orally, in the fashion of rumors. They usually involve someone the teller vaguely knows (such as a friend of a friend), and they often have an ironic twist at the end. Ask students to compile a collection of legends they know and then to research their favorites. They may find that their stories have been told elsewhere in different versions.

Finding Common Ground

Now that you've read the story, meet in small groups, and share the questions and comments you recorded in your log.

- Read aloud your notes, or pass the notes around so that everyone can read one another's comments.
- Identify and discuss three or four issues, comments, or reactions that seem most interesting or widely shared within your group.
- Compare the effect of this story to that of "A Rose for Emily." For example, both stories end on a shocking note. But Faulkner does not spell out what happens to Miss Emily and Homer Barron; Quiroga, on the other hand, reveals Alicia's fate in graphic detail. In what other ways are Faulkner's and Quiroga's stories alike and different?
- Quiroga also has much in common with Edgar Allan Poe. Like Poe, he was fascinated by madness and obsession, and he mastered the short-story format, creating a single sustained effect in each story. What does "The Feather Pillow" have in common with "The Fall of the House of Usher" and other Poe stories you have read?
- Reconvene as a class, and share the results of your discussion.

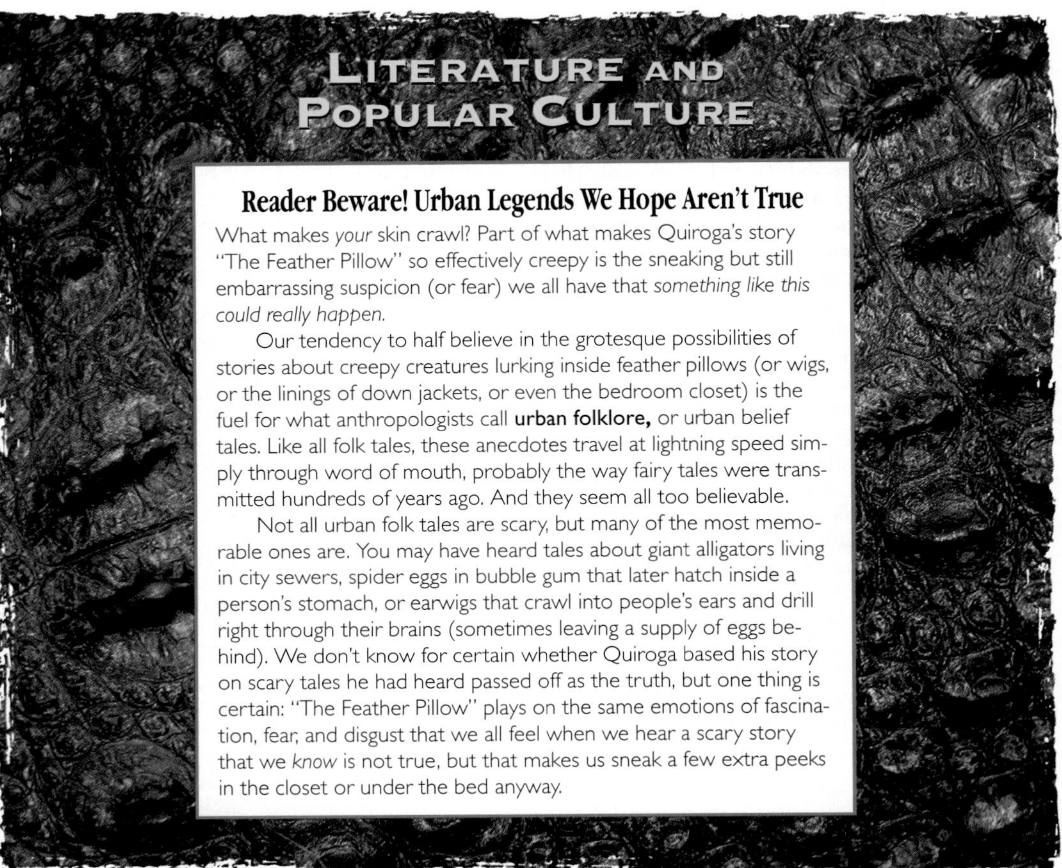

Literature and Popular Culture

Reader Beware! Urban Legends We Hope Aren't True

What makes *your* skin crawl? Part of what makes Quiroga's story "The Feather Pillow" so effectively creepy is the sneaking but still embarrassing suspicion (or fear) we all have that *something like this could really happen.*

Our tendency to half believe in the grotesque possibilities of stories about creepy creatures lurking inside feather pillows (or wigs, or the linings of down jackets, or even the bedroom closet) is the fuel for what anthropologists call **urban folklore,** or urban belief tales. Like all folk tales, these anecdotes travel at lightning speed simply through word of mouth, probably the way fairy tales were transmitted hundreds of years ago. And they seem all too believable.

Not all urban folk tales are scary, but many of the most memorable ones are. You may have heard tales about giant alligators living in city sewers, spider eggs in bubble gum that later hatch inside a person's stomach, or earwigs that crawl into people's ears and drill right through their brains (sometimes leaving a supply of eggs behind). We don't know for certain whether Quiroga based his story on scary tales he had heard passed off as the truth, but one thing is certain: "The Feather Pillow" plays on the same emotions of fascination, fear, and disgust that we all feel when we hear a scary story that we *know* is not true, but that makes us sneak a few extra peeks in the closet or under the bed anyway.

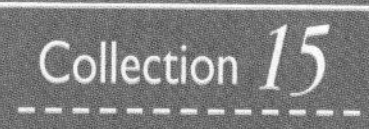

I, TOO, SING AMERICA

Theme: **All That Jazz**

During the 1920s and 1930s, many African American writers, musicians, and performers were part of a great post–World War I migration to the industrial, urban north. Drawn to Harlem, a vibrant New York City neighborhood, creative individuals affirmed the inestimable value of African American talent and forever changed the cultural landscape of America with their unique contributions to the movement known as the Harlem Renaissance.

Thematic Focus

The protagonists of the selections in Collection 15 illustrate aspects of African American culture in the early twentieth century.

- **Go Down, Death** The speaker delivers a comforting funeral sermon in the style of an old-time African American preacher in the Deep South.
- **America** This country is a harsh, voracious, yet vigorous inferno, which the speaker embraces with defiant courage.
- **Tableau** A victory against racism is celebrated in a scene of two young friends—one black, one white—casually walking arm in arm.
- **Incident** The speaker reflects upon the power of a racial slur to shatter a child's joy.
- *from* **Dust Tracks on a Road** In this autobiographical excerpt, the author recollects the beginnings of her lifelong love affair with culture and books.
- **The Weary Blues** The poet describes a blues pianist in language that captures the rhythm, form, and melancholy mood of the soulful music.
- **Harlem** Ironically detached and bitter, the speaker tells of the poverty and racial injustices suffered by African Americans in Harlem.

Literary Focus

Literary Element	Selection / Feature
Personification	**Go Down, Death**
Rhythm	**The Weary Blues**
Tone	**Harlem**

Writing Focus

The following chart shows how the writing assignment for each selection relates to and builds toward the culminating writing assignment presented in the Writer's Workshop at the end of the unit.

Selection	Work-in-Progress Assignment
Go Down, Death	Make a comparison/contrast chart for an interpretive essay p. 742
America	Create a diagram to compare and contrast for an interpretive essay p. 745
Tableau/Incident	Take notes on language for an interpretive essay p. 749
Dust Tracks on a Road	Freewrite a personal response for an interpretive essay p. 759
The Weary Blues/Harlem	Create a chart for an interpretive essay p. 768
Writer's Workshop	Write an interpretive essay pp. 804–807

Collection 15 **I, TOO, SING AMERICA**

Collection Planner

PUPIL'S EDITION

SELECTION/ FEATURE	Literary Elements / Active Reading	Writing	Speaking and Listening	Language and Vocabulary
Go Down, Death James Weldon Johnson (pp. 736–742) Primary Sources: Preface to *God's Trombones* James Weldon Johnson (p. 740) **Connections: of DeWitt Williams on his way to Lincoln Cemetery** Gwendolyn Brooks (p. 741)	• Reader's Log p. 737 • Personification p. 737	• Critical Writing: Write essay p. 742		• Language and Style: Free Verse and the Orator's Style p. 742
America Claude McKay (pp. 743–745)	• Reader's Log p. 744	• Creative Writing/Art: Write slogan p. 745		
Tableau **Incident** Countee Cullen (pp. 746–749)	• Reader's Log p. 747 • Reader's Log p. 748	• Creative Writing: Write conversation p. 749 • Critical Writing/Music: Write film treatment (summary) p. 749	• Critical Writing/ Music: Create soundtrack p. 749	
from **Dust Tracks on a Road** Zora Neale Hurston (pp. 750–759) Primary Sources: In Search of a Story Zora Neale Hurston (p. 758)	• Reader's Log p. 751	• Critical Writing: Write essay p. 759 • Creative Writing/ Performance: Write script p. 759	• Creative Writing/ Performance: Create theatrical adaptation p. 759	
The Weary Blues **Harlem** Langston Hughes (pp. 760–768) Primary Sources: Heyday in Harlem Langston Hughes (pp. 766–767)	• Reader's Log p. 761 • Reader's Log p. 764 • Rhythm p. 761 • Tone p. 764	• Critical Writing: Write essay p. 768 • Creative Writing: Write opening paragraph p. 768 • Creative Writing/ Research: Write liner notes p. 768	• Music/Performance: Perform musical accompaniment p. 768	

Collection Resources

Teaching Resources B
Cross-Curricular Activity p. 99

Audiovisual Resources Binder
Fine Art Transparency 15.1

Test Booklet
Collection 15 Test pp. 179–182

 Computer disk or CD-ROM

 Audiocassette

 Overhead Transparency

PROGRAM RESOURCES

Electronic Media	Teaching Resources with Organizer: Teaching Resources B	Teaching Resources with Organizer: Other Resources	Audiovisual Resources Binder
• Test Generator	• Teaching Notes p. 83 • Reading Organizer p. 87	• Test Booklet: Selection Test pp. 171–172 • Portfolio Management System pp. 39, 157	• Selected Reading Audiocassette 2, Side B
• Test Generator	• Teaching Notes pp. 83–84 • Reading Organizer p. 88	• Test Booklet: Selection Test pp. 171–172 • Portfolio Management System pp. 48–49, 158	• Selected Reading Audiocassette 3, Side A
• Test Generator	• Teaching Notes p. 84 • Reading Organizers pp. 89–90	• Test Booklet: Selection Test pp. 173–174 • Portfolio Management System pp. 53, 159	• Selected Reading Audiocassette 3, Side A
• Language Workshop: Commas • Test Generator	• Teaching Notes p. 85 • Reading Organizer p. 91 • Language Link pp. 92–93 • Words to Own p. 94	• Test Booklet: Selection Test pp. 175–176 • Language and Writing Skills Worksheets pp. 131–135 • Portfolio Management System pp. 48–49, 160	• Selected Reading Audiocassette 2, Side B
• Language Workshop: End marks • Test Generator	• Teaching Notes pp. 85–86 • Reading Organizers pp. 95–96 • Language Link pp. 97–98	• Test Booklet: Selection Test pp. 177–178 • Language and Writing Skills Worksheets p. 129 • Portfolio Management System pp. 54–55, 161–162	• Selected Reading Audiocassette 3, Side A • Elements of Literature Transparencies 15.2–15.3

Proofreading Warm-ups

You may use the following exercises to help students practice their proofreading skills. Copy a set of incorrect sentences onto the chalkboard, and have students find and correct the spelling, punctuation, usage, and mechanical errors in each sentence. Ask students to share and discuss their responses.

	Sentences with Errors	Sentences Corrected	Skills Covered
1	**a.** one of the formost poet of the harlem renessance james Weldon Johnson was also a teacher, and a lawyer **b.** a principle theme of hims work was black pride	**a.** One of the foremost poets of the Harlem Renaissance, James Weldon Johnson was also a teacher and a lawyer. **b.** A principal theme of his work was black pride.	Capitalization, Spelling, Agreement (in number), Comma usage, Pronoun errors, End marks
2	**a.** josephine sings good but she need a voice coach **b.** each blues singer developes their unieqe style	**a.** Josephine sings well, but she needs a voice coach. **b.** Each blues singer develops his or her unique style.	Capitalization, Usage, Comma usage, Agreement (subject-verb), Spelling, Agreement (in number), End marks
3	**a.** whose the importentest poet alive in your opinion **b.** of all them stories we read in class Latishas is the bestest	**a.** Who's the most important poet alive, in your opinion? **b.** Of all the stories we read in class, Latisha's is the best.	Capitalization, Usage, Superlative adjectives, Comma usage, Standard usage, Apostrophes (possessive), End marks
4	**a.** poet claude McKay used to be born in jamaica, a iland in the carribbean **b.** francine had put pierres' letter in a envelop, but she forgets the stamp	**a.** Poet Claude McKay was born in Jamaica, an island in the Caribbean. **b.** Francine had put Pierre's letter in an envelope, but she forgot the stamp.	Capitalization, Verb tense errors, Articles, Spelling, Apostrophe errors, End marks
5	**a.** singing and playing the blues make me feel melancoly **b.** chease grits with ham are my moms breakfast speciality	**a.** Singing and playing the blues makes me feel melancholy. **b.** Cheese grits with ham is my mom's breakfast specialty.	Capitalization, Subject-verb agreement (compound subjects), Spelling, Apostrophes (possessive), End marks
6	**a.** zora likes to read books and telling stories **b.** jason admitts that he does not know nothing on greek and roman mythlogy	**a.** Zora likes to read books and to tell stories. **b.** Jason admits that he does not know anything about Greek and Roman mythology.	Capitalization, Verb form errors (parallelism), Spelling, Double negatives, Preposition errors, End marks
7	**a.** "please sit that bundle of mail on the hall table mr Calhoun said **b.** oh Hennie is just jellous at you" Stella said	**a.** "Please set that bundle of mail on the hall table," Mr. Calhoun said. **b.** "Oh, Hennie is just jealous of you," Stella said.	Capitalization, Usage, Comma usage, Quotation marks, Abbreviations, Spelling, Preposition errors, End marks
8	**a.** caroline will derect the film Ted will act in it **b.** its not your turn Kali was here first	**a.** Caroline will direct the film; Ted will act in it. **b.** It's not your turn; Kali was here first.	Capitalization, Spelling, Semicolon usage, Apostrophes, End marks
9	**a.** neither of their ansers were acurrate **b.** the comittee will nomenate either Jorge or she as their candadate	**a.** Neither of their answers was accurate. **b.** The committee will nominate either Jorge or her as its candidate.	Capitalization, Spelling, Subject-verb agreement, Pronoun errors, End marks
10	**a.** the great depression ended funding to much art's organizations **b.** lenox ave. is a bussling street in N.Y.C.	**a.** The Great Depression ended funding to many arts organizations. **b.** Lenox Avenue is a bustling street in New York City.	Capitalization, Usage, Apostrophes, Spelling out abbreviations, Spelling, End marks

Collection 15

I, TOO, SING AMERICA

Johnson
McKay
Cullen
Hurston
Hughes

I, Too

I, too, sing America.

I am the darker brother.
They send me to eat in the kitchen
When company comes,
But I laugh,
And eat well,
And grow strong.

Tomorrow,
I'll be at the table
When company comes.
Nobody'll dare
Say to me,
"Eat in the kitchen,"
Then.

Besides,
They'll see how beautiful I am
And be ashamed—

I, too, am America.

—Langston Hughes (1902–1967)

"I, Too"

? How might people feel when they experience exclusion—such as being omitted from group activities or being forbidden membership in an organization? [Possible responses: Loneliness, unworthiness, shame, or depression.] What do the Collection theme and "I, Too" suggest about the selections to come? [Possible responses: The Collection theme indicates that various peoples make up the United States and that they all have voices and wish to be heard. The poem indicates that their voices may not always be heard, but that these people have much to contribute. The Collection will include various definitions of life in the United States.]

PORTFOLIO ASSESSMENT

Parent/Guardian Involvement For forms that will help a parent or guardian review and respond to a student's portfolio, see *Portfolio Management System,* pp. 62–63.

PROGRAM MANAGER

- **Integrated Assessment** For a summative assessment of the literature and language skills taught in this collection, see Collection 15 Test, *Test Booklet,* pp. 179–182.
- **Instructional Support** See Fine Art Transparency 15.1. Review teacher's notes for transparencies in the *Audiovisual Resources Binder* for suggestions on how to tie the transparencies to specific reading selections.
- **Extending Collection Theme** See Cross-Curricular Activity: I, Too, Sing America, *Teaching Resources B,* p. 99, for an activity in another discipline and for evaluation criteria.

A. Cultural Connections
The word *renaissance,* meaning "rebirth or revival," usually designates the Renaissance that flourished in Europe between 1300 and 1600, an era characterized by a spirit of discovery, curiosity, and adventure in many fields from architecture to science to fine art. The European Renaissance was considered a flowering rebirth of the Golden Age of Athens, Greece, some two thousand years earlier. What happened in Harlem, New York, in the 1920s occurred with such compelling vibrance that it became known as the Harlem Renaissance.

B. Expansion
Marcus Garvey (1887–1940) was a Jamaican-born American who exhorted blacks to consider Africa as their homeland and urged them to return to Africa.

C. Humanities Connection
Jazz is commonly considered a truly original American art form that evolved from African American folk music. Its roots lie in African rhythms, European harmonies, American gospel sounds, and work songs that flourished during slavery. This musical "melting pot" became known as jazz, an improvisational music that originated in New Orleans in the early 1900s. The blues that contributed to the jazz sound evolved from the work songs and "field hollers" that functioned as a form of musical communication among plantation workers after the Civil War. Blues lyrics typically evoked life's troubles, but often in a humorous way. Both jazz and blues have continued to develop and remain immensely popular among listeners worldwide. The English rock band the Rolling Stones was, for instance, heavily influenced by American bluesman Muddy Waters.

The Harlem Renaissance

In the early 1920s, African American artists, writers, musicians, and performers were part of a great cultural movement known as the Harlem Renaissance. The huge migration to the north after World War I brought African Americans of all ages and walks of life to the thriving New York City neighborhood called Harlem. Doctors, singers, students, musicians, shopkeepers, painters, and writers congregated, forming a vibrant mecca of cultural affirmation and inspiration.

As Langston Hughes wrote, "It was the period when the Negro was in vogue." Marcus Garvey's "Back to Africa" movement was in full swing. The blues were vibrantly alive; jazz was just beginning. An all-black show, *Shuffle Along,* opened on Broadway with the performers Josephine Baker, Paul Robeson, and Florence Mills, and music composed by Eubie Blake. And mainstream America was developing a new respect for African art and culture, thanks in part to its reflection in the work of the modernist artists Pablo Picasso and Georges Braque.

Against this backdrop, Harlem Renaissance artists insisted that the African American be accepted as "a collaborator and participant in American civilization," in the words of the educator and critic Alain Locke. Writers such as Jean Toomer and Zora Neale Hurston (page 750) wrote about the African American experience. Artists such as Aaron Douglas and William H. Johnson painted it. The photographer James Van Der Zee recorded it with his camera. The trumpeter Louis Armstrong and the pianist Fletcher Henderson set it to music, and vocalists Bessie Smith and Ma Rainey sang it.

Harlem newspapers and journals, such as *Crisis* and *Opportunity,* published the work of both new and established African American writers. To encourage and support intellectually gifted young people, the journals sponsored literary contests that encouraged creative production and rewarded it with cash prizes and social introductions to the top writers of the time.

In autobiographies, poetry, short stories, novels, and folklore, African American writers affirmed the role of black talent in American culture and focused on different aspects of black life in Harlem, the South, Europe, the

Bessie Smith.
Brown Brothers.

OPTIONS FOR TEACHING

STRATEGIES FOR INCLUSION

Auditory "The Harlem Renaissance" can be read aloud in about five minutes. If you have students who might grasp the material better if they were to hear it read, call on one or more volunteers to present the selection orally. As students listen, they may take notes about details that they want to discuss and remember.

CHICAGO NEW YORK ST. LOUIS

The Phillips Collection, Washington, D.C. Acquired 1942.

The Migration of the Negro, Panel No. 1 (1940–1941) by Jacob Lawrence. Tempera on masonite (12″ × 18″).

Caribbean, and even Russia. They addressed issues of race, class, religion, and gender. Some writers focused entirely on black characters, while others addressed relationships among people of different races. Some writers attacked racism; others addressed issues within black communities. A by-product of African American writing was the affirmation that black dialects were as legitimate as standard English.

Unfortunately, by the early 1930s, the Great Depression had depleted many of the funds that had provided financial support to individual African American writers, institutions, and publications. Nevertheless, Harlem and African American culture were forever changed. The foundation was laid for Ralph Ellison, James Baldwin, Gwendolyn Brooks, Alice Walker, Toni Morrison, Maya Angelou, Terry McMillan, Rita Dove, and thousands of other African American writers, painters, composers, and singers to make their feelings and experiences part of American artistic expression: "I, too, sing America. . . ."

Louis Armstrong.

Brown Brothers.

Technology Tip

Before you begin this Collection, guide your students to Harlem Renaissance resources on the Internet. A good Web site to suggest is the Reference Center at the University of Southern California at **http://www.usc.edu/Library/Ref/Ethnic/harlem.html**. To find African American studies resources on the World Wide Web, access the list of links available from the African American Studies Center at the University of Pennsylvania at **http://www.sas.upenn.edu/African_Studies/K-12/menu_EduAFAM.html**. You may also want to refer to the African American literature resources at the Voice of the Shuttle, a Web site for humanities research, at **http://humanitas.ucsb.edu/shuttle/eng-min.html**.

You may want to preview any Internet activity that you suggest to students. Because these resourses are sometimes public forums, their content can be unpredictable.

INTEGRATING THE LANGUAGE ARTS

Strategic Reading Have students work in groups to discuss reading strategies. Structure this as Jigsawing. Ask students to discuss and compare the skills they would use for the following purposes when reading the introduction: enjoyment, fact finding, and preparation for a test of recall questions. Have students use different paragraphs from the introduction to model these different skills. Then, as a class, discuss ways students can use these strategies to strengthen their own personal reading skills.

QUICK PLANNING GUIDE

Into the Poem

Through the Poem

Beyond the Poem

ABOUT THE AUTHOR

The Autobiography of an Ex-Colored Man takes a very light-skinned black youth through a variety of experiences, from the rural South to New York honky-tonks to chic locales in Europe, before he bitterly decides to pass as white. The narrative voice was so convincing to readers that many assumed it was a genuine autobiography. Johnson later wrote his real autobiography partly to rebut this belief.

James Weldon Johnson (c. 1925) by Winold Reiss. Pastel on artist board (30 1/16″ × 21 9/16″).

National Portrait Gallery, Washington, D.C. Courtesy Art Resource.

James Weldon Johnson

(1871–1938)

James Weldon Johnson—poet, teacher, and lawyer—was born in Jacksonville, Florida. Educated at Atlanta University in Georgia and Columbia University in New York City, he was the first African American to be admitted to the Florida bar after Reconstruction. Throughout his career, Johnson was an energetic exponent of civil rights, and in his writing he constantly sought recognition for the contributions that African Americans had made to American culture.

After serving as U.S. consul to Venezuela and then to Nicaragua (1907–1913), Johnson worked as field secretary of the National Association for the Advancement of Colored People (NAACP) for four years and then served as the association's general secretary for the following ten years. In 1931, he was appointed professor of creative literature at Fisk University. Seven years later, he died in an automobile accident.

Although some of Johnson's early poems are in dialect, he soon abandoned that style for standard English, which he felt was capable of greater variety and power. His principal theme was black pride, which he celebrated in such poems as "Fifty Years," written on the fiftieth anniversary of the Emancipation Proclamation, and "O Black and Unknown Bards," a tribute to the anonymous authors of African American spirituals. With his brother, the composer John Rosamond Johnson, he wrote a number of very successful light operas and songs for Tin Pan Alley, and the brothers collaborated in editing two collections of spirituals.

Johnson was an important leader of the first phase of the Harlem Renaissance. His anthology, *The Book of American Negro Poetry* (1922), was one of the significant early collections of poems by African Americans. In addition to poetry, Johnson wrote fiction (most notably *The Autobiography of an Ex-Colored Man,* published in 1912), nonfiction studies of black life, and an autobiography, *Along This Way* (1933).

It was Johnson's extensive research for one collection, *The Book of American Negro Spirituals* (1925), that inspired his poem "Go Down, Death." Describing this experience, he said: "The research which I did in collecting the spirituals and gathering the data for my introductory essay had an effect on me similar to what I received from hearing the Negro evangelist preach. . . . I was in touch with the deepest revelation of the Negro's soul that has yet been made, and I felt myself attuned to it. I made an outline of the second poem that I wrote of this series. It was to be a 'funeral sermon.' I decided to call it 'Go Down, Death.'

"On Thanksgiving Day, 1926, I was at home. After breakfast I went to my desk and began work in earnest on the poem. As I worked, my own spirit rose till it reached a degree almost of ecstasy. The poem shaped itself easily and before the hour for dinner I had written it as it stands published."

736 THE MODERNS

PORTFOLIO ASSESSMENT

Portfolio Assessment For help with self- and teacher assessment of reading skills, see the ***Portfolio Management System,*** p. 39.

BEFORE YOU READ
GO DOWN, DEATH

Reading Focus

Death at the Doorstep

Every religion has its own view of what happens when we die, and countless storytellers, philosophers, and writers have added their views to the sum of our understanding of the great mystery we call death. Is death a source of pain and sorrow, or is it a comfort—perhaps even a joyous affirmation of life?

A Dialogue with the Text

This poem is one of seven "sermons" written by Johnson in the style of the old-time African American preachers. He collected the sermons in a book called *God's Trombones*—the trombone being "of just the tone and timbre to represent the old-time Negro preacher's voice."

Johnson tells us that the person reading "Go Down, Death" would intone, moan, plead, blare, crash, and thunder. In your Reader's Log, jot down the words, lines, or stanzas that have the strongest emotional effect on you.

Elements of Literature

Personification

Personification is a figure of speech in which an animal, object, or abstract concept is portrayed with human qualities. In this poem, Johnson invites readers to see and understand Death as a character rather than as an abstract concept.

Go Down, Death

A Funeral Sermon

James Weldon Johnson

Weep not, weep not,
She is not dead;
She's resting in the bosom of Jesus.
Heart-broken husband—weep no more;
Grief-stricken son—weep no more;
Left-lonesome daughter—weep no more;
She's only just gone home.

Day before yesterday morning,
God was looking down from his great, high heaven,
Looking down on all his children,
And his eye fell on Sister Caroline,
Tossing on her bed of pain.
And God's big heart was touched with pity,
With the everlasting pity.

And God sat back on his throne,
And he commanded that tall, bright angel standing at his right hand:
Call me Death!
And that tall, bright angel cried in a voice
That broke like a clap of thunder:
Call Death!—Call Death!
And the echo sounded down the streets of heaven
Till it reached away back to that shadowy place,
Where Death waits with his pale, white horses.° 

And Death heard the summons,
And he leaped on his fastest horse,
Pale as a sheet in the moonlight.
Up the golden street Death galloped,
And the hoofs of his horse struck fire from the gold,
But they didn't make no sound.
Up Death rode to the Great White Throne,
And waited for God's command.

And God said: Go down, Death, go down,
Go down to Savannah, Georgia,
Down in Yamacraw,

23. Death waits . . . horses: allusion to Revelation 6:8, "And I looked, and behold a pale horse: and his name that sat on him was Death."

Using **BEFORE YOU READ** p. 737

Reading Focus

Ask students to write down the first five feelings and emotions that come to mind when they hear the word *death*. As a class, compile student responses on the chalkboard and classify them under the heads "Comforting" or "Painful." Have students determine which is the class's dominant response to death.

A. Literary Element: Allusion

Have students note the reference to Revelation 6:8. In Johnson's poem, why is Death associated with "pale, white horses," and why would Death himself be "pale as a sheet in the moonlight"? [Possible answers: White tends to symbolize goodness and purity, and Death on a horse calls to mind valiant medieval knights. These images make death seem helpful and gallant. Or white may symbolize the absence of life, and the horses, the power of death.]

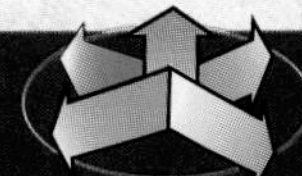

PROGRAM MANAGER

- **Planning Instruction** See Teaching Notes, *Teaching Resources B,* p. 83, for objectives, a summary, and literary elements for this selection.
- **Instructional Support** See Graphic Organizer for Active Reading, *Teaching Resources B,* p. 87, for an Into the Poem activity.
- **Audiotaped Readings** To help auditory learners, use the Selected Reading, Audiocassette 2, Side B, in the *Audiovisual Resources Binder.*
- **Instructional Support** See Fine Art Transparency 15.1. Review teacher's notes for transparencies in the *Audiovisual Resources Binder* for suggestions on how to tie the transparencies to specific reading selections.
- **Assessment** See Selection Test, *Test Booklet,* pp. 171–172.

RESPONDING TO THE ART: ABOUT THE ARTIST

Aaron Douglas (born 1899) was a leader of the Harlem Renaissance. He studied African art in the 1920s and became one of the first American painters to be considered an Africanist, one who studies African cultures and customs. His use of both classical and African forms set him apart from other artists. Douglas felt he did not know enough about Africa to treat it as his central subject and chose instead to paint African Americans. He illustrated works by African American authors such as Countee Cullen and Langston Hughes. The series of illustrations he created for James Weldon Johnson's *God's Trombones* is considered a masterpiece.

Collection of Professor and Mrs. David Driskell, Hyattsville, Maryland.

Go Down Death (1927) by Aaron Douglas. Oil on masonite.

OPTIONS FOR TEACHING

STRATEGIES FOR INCLUSION

Musical Have students listen to a recording of the spiritual "Go Down, Moses" and review the section on spirituals (pp. 432–434). Ask them to consider how this spiritual might have affected Johnson's writing of the poem. Play the song for the class and have them explain any connections they make between the song and the poem.

Auditory To gain the full impact of this powerful oration, have students read silently along with the audiocassette recording. Point out to students that this is an oration in the voice of a preacher, not a narration in the voice of an impersonal narrator. Ask students to imagine that the preacher knew Sister Caroline and is addressing a church audience who also knew her.

English Language Development After the first reading, focus students' attention on the sixth, seventh, and eighth stanzas and ask students to write down any words or phrases that they believe describe the character of Death. They may choose to look up these words to confirm their understanding. An activity such as this makes the reading more manageable and provides "in-depth" reading rather than reading for main idea or general impression. Both are necessary skills but are difficult to do during a single reading as students develop skills in a second language.

And find Sister Caroline.
She's borne the burden and heat of the day,
She's labored long in my vineyard,
And she's tired—
She's weary—
Go down, Death, and bring her to me. **A**

And Death didn't say a word,
But he loosed the reins on his pale, white horse, **B**
And he clamped the spurs to his bloodless sides,
And out and down he rode,
Through heaven's pearly gates,
Past suns and moons and stars;
On Death rode,
And the foam from his horse was like a comet in the sky;
On Death rode,
Leaving the lightning's flash behind;
Straight on down he came.

While we were watching round her bed,
She turned her eyes and looked away,
She saw what we couldn't see;
She saw Old Death. She saw Old Death **C**
Coming like a falling star.
But Death didn't frighten Sister Caroline;
He looked to her like a welcome friend.
And she whispered to us: I'm going home,
And she smiled and closed her eyes.

And Death took her up like a baby,
And she lay in his icy arms,
But she didn't feel no chill.
And Death began to ride again—
Up beyond the evening star,
Out beyond the morning star,°
Into the glittering light of glory,
On to the Great White Throne.
And there he laid Sister Caroline
On the loving breast of Jesus.

And Jesus took his own hand and wiped away her tears,
And he smoothed the furrows from her face,
And the angels sang a little song,
And Jesus rocked her in his arms,
And kept a-saying: Take your rest,
Take your rest, take your rest.

Weep not—weep not,
She is not dead;
She's resting in the bosom of Jesus.

D

66. evening star . . . morning star: the planet Venus, which is traditionally referred to as both the morning star and the evening star. Its orbital path makes it visible for no more than about three hours after sunset and three hours before sunrise.

A. Critical Reading: Making Connections

? What does the phrase "Go down, Death" mean here? What additional meaning might it have in the title? [Here it refers to God's commandment to Death to go to Earth for Sister Caroline. In the title, it might also mean the subjugation of death through the knowledge and acceptance of life after death, as it does in John Donne's "Death Be Not Proud" (1633): "And death shall be no more, Death thou shalt die."]

B. Literary Element: Personification

Note that the poet uses capitalization to indicate that death is being personified.

C. Reader's Response: Shaping Interpretations

? Why might Death be portrayed as old? [Sample responses: Death has always been present throughout time. Or for centuries, people have attempted to understand and accept death.]

D. Reader's Response: Connecting with the Text

? What is the poem's attitude toward Sister Caroline? [Sample responses: Sorry for her passing. Or respectful of her long, productive life.] What is its attitude toward death and toward God? [Sample responses: Death is not to be feared, for it brings the soul to rest in heaven, in the arms of a loving God. Or death is the reliever of pain.] Does Johnson make you share those attitudes? [Sample responses: The funeral sermon is uplifting; or death still seems horrible.]

INTEGRATING THE LANGUAGE ARTS

Writing: Essay Ask students to write a short essay describing the use of the language of death in this poem. Begin by brainstorming how our culture, in general, treats death in terms of avoidance and talks about it in euphemisms and slang, from "passed on," "kicked the bucket," and "bought the farm" to "funeral director" and "funeral home." Have students list and analyze the death images and death language in the poem "Go Down, Death," discussing the emotional connotations that are associated with specific words in the poem and that are associated with Death. Encourage students to discuss how Johnson handles death and the cultural expectations toward death in this poem.

Language and Style Many students confuse colons and semicolons and use them incorrectly or not at all. This poem gives students a chance to see both punctuation marks in action. Remind them that a semicolon marks a pause between parts that already have commas. Have students look at lines 2, 4, 5, and 6 and state what effect these semicolons have. Then direct students to lines 16 and 59 and ask students how colons are used in this poem. [To set off a quotation, instead of quotation marks.] Have students find other examples. [Lines 19, 32, and 75] Ask students to write four sentences containing colons and semicolons. Have students exchange papers and check to see whether they have been used correctly.

Primary Sources

Oratory is the art of public speaking. An orator speaks to influence listeners through skillful and artful eloquence. Inform students that the history of oratory stretches to ancient Greece and its democratic assemblies, where public policy was formed and justice was administered through open debate. The great importance of effective public speaking led philosophers to study the process of speechmaking, or oratory. Have students listen to tapes of speeches or sermons by Martin Luther King, Jr., Jesse Jackson, or Ralph Abernathy. Have them compare these speakers' styles with the one Johnson describes. Ask them to what extent these speakers belong to the "old-time preacher" tradition. Invite students to evaluate the effectiveness of the speeches. Ask students to demonstrate the effectiveness of these techniques by playing portions of the speeches for the class.

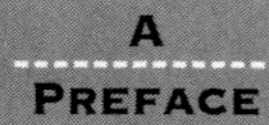

PRIMARY **Sources** A PREFACE

God's Trombones

In his preface to *God's Trombones,* from which "Go Down, Death" is taken, Johnson describes the origin of his idea for his collection of poems.

The old-time preacher was generally a man far above the average in intelligence; he was, not infrequently, a man of positive genius. The earliest of these preachers must have virtually committed many parts of the Bible to memory through hearing the scriptures read or preached from in the white churches which the slaves attended. They were the first of the slaves to learn to read, and their reading was confined to the Bible, and specifically to the more dramatic passages of the Old Testament. A text served mainly as a starting point and often had no relation to the development of the sermon. Nor would the old-time preacher balk at any text within the lids of the Bible. There is the story of one who after reading a rather cryptic passage took off his spectacles, closed the Bible with a bang and by way of preface said, "Brothers and sisters, this morning—I intend to explain the unexplainable—find out the undefinable—ponder over the imponderable—and unscrew the inscrutable."

The old-time Negro preacher of parts was above all an orator, and in good measure an actor. He knew the secret of oratory, that at bottom it is a progression of rhythmic words more than it is anything else. Indeed, I have witnessed congregations moved to ecstasy by the rhythmic intoning of sheer incoherencies. He was a master of all the modes of eloquence. He often possessed a voice that was a marvelous instrument, a voice he could modulate from a sepulchral whisper to a crashing thunder clap. His discourse was generally kept at a high pitch of fervency, but occasionally he dropped into colloquialisms and, less often, into humor. He preached a personal and anthropomorphic God, a sure-enough heaven and a red-hot hell. His imagination was bold and unfettered. He had the power to sweep his hearers before him; and so himself was often swept away. At such times his language was not prose but poetry. It was from memories of such preachers there grew the idea of this book of poems.

—James Weldon Johnson

Prayer Meeting (1951) by Samella Sanders Lewis. Watercolor (17″ × 14¾″).

Hampton University Museum, Hampton, Virginia.

STRATEGIES FOR INCLUSION

Special Needs Have students who have difficulty with word recognition and reading comprehension make a graphic to help understand the selection. For example, have students use a cluster like the following and fill in information as they read.

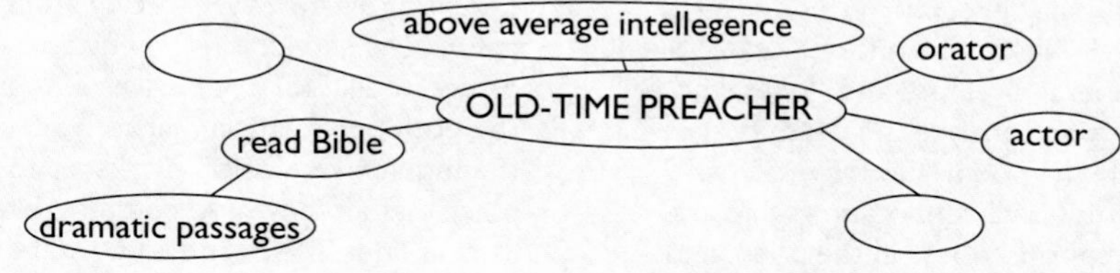

A POEM

Borrowing from the spiritual "Swing Low, Sweet Chariot," the African American poet Gwendolyn Brooks (1917–) creates a poem that also has the rhythm of a song. (For more on spirituals, see page 432.) Lincoln Cemetery is in Chicago.

of De Witt Williams on his way to Lincoln Cemetery (A)

Gwendolyn Brooks

He was born in Alabama.
He was bred in Illinois.
He was nothing but a
Plain black boy.

Swing low swing low sweet sweet chariot. (B)
Nothing but a plain black boy.

Drive him past the Pool Hall.
Drive him past the Show.
Blind within his casket,
But maybe he will know.

Down through Forty-seventh Street:
Underneath the L, (C)
And—Northwest Corner, Prairie,
That he loved so well.

Don't forget the Dance Halls—
Warwick and Savoy,
Where he picked his women, where
He drank his liquid joy.

Born in Alabama.
Bred in Illinois.
He was nothing but a
Plain black boy. (D)

Swing low swing low sweet sweet chariot.
Nothing but a plain black boy.

Haitian Funeral Procession (c. 1950s) by Ellis Wilson. Oil on canvas (30½″ × 29¼″).
Aaron Douglas Collection, Amistad Research Center, Tulane University, New Orleans, Louisiana.

A. Reader's Response: Shaping Interpretations

? How might the title be significant? [Sample responses: It indicates that the speaker will talk about De Witt's life. De Witt is now freed from this life, since he is going to be buried in Lincoln Cemetery and Lincoln was known as the Great Emancipator.]

B. Literary Element: Allusion

This line refers to the spiritual "Swing Low, Sweet Chariot" in which a chariot and a band of angels arrive to take a dying person to heaven. A chariot was a French vehicle that resembled a sled and was used to transport tobacco. African American slaves may have sung this song out of a desire to mount such a vehicle and be carried away from slavery and from North America.

C. Expansion

The L is Chicago's elevated railway. Forty-seventh Street and Northwest Corner, Prairie are part of the city's South Side.

D. Literary Element: Tone

? What is the tone of these lines? [Possible answers: Ironic, because people are complicated. Or sad, because a life has been wasted.]

Technology Tip

Both "Go Down, Death" and "of De Witt Williams on his way to Lincoln Cemetery" have musical overtones. Have your students create gospel songs out of the poems using traditional instruments, synthesizers, and computer recording and editing software. Invite them to share their songs with the class.

CONNECTING WITH "GO DOWN, DEATH"

The content and style of Brooks's poem and "Go Down Moses" are similar. Both focus on the death of an individual. Both have a songlike rhythm, use repetition and parallel structure, alternate long and short lines for effect, and use simple language.

Have students talk about the specific ways in which these poems resemble each other and the ways in which they differ. Then, have them discuss how these poems reflect the African American experience at the time of the Harlem Renaissance.

Making Meanings

First Thoughts

1. Possible response: Seeing Death come on his foaming horse, because death frightens us all.

Shaping Interpretations

2. God is in heaven, and Death is waiting in a "shadowy place" (l. 22). Sister Caroline lies in bed in Savannah, Georgia. Death was welcome to her, as a friend would be.
3. The comparison of the angel's voice to a clap of thunder (l. 19), of the foam from Death's horse to a comet (l. 48), and of Death himself to a falling star (l. 56).
4. Most students will agree that the portrait of God and Jesus stresses mercy and gentleness. Supporting details include the pity that touches God's heart (ll. 13–14), God's compassion for Sister Caroline's weariness (ll. 36–39), the mention of the "loving breast" of Jesus (l. 70), and the portrait of Jesus rocking Sister Caroline in his arms (ll. 71–76).
5. Possible responses: The pallor may indicate the absence of life in death or white may symbolize goodness and peace. In contrast, in *Moby-Dick,* Melville uses white to describe the whale that brings death and destruction (pp. 313–327).

Extending the Text

6. **(Synthesis)** Possible responses: Johnson portrays Death as quite gentle and comforting. He acts as God's servant, brings relief from pain, handles Caroline gently, and reunites her with God and Jesus. In Dickinson's poem death is also portrayed as gentle.

Language and Style

Answers

1. For example: In stanza 1, "weep not" and "weep no more" are repeated. In stanza 4, "Death heard . . . Death galloped . . . Death rode" is parallel.
2. For example: "Straight on down" (l. 51) is everyday language, and "she didn't feel no chill" (l. 63) represents a use of double negatives that is heard in some informal speech.
3. For example: Lines 16 (long) and 17 (short); ll. 70 (short) and 71 (long).
4. For example: "clap of thunder" (l. 19), "clamped the spurs" (l. 43).

MAKING MEANINGS

First Thoughts

1. Review the notes you made in your Reader's Log. Which words, lines, or stanzas in this poem had the strongest effect on you? Why?

Shaping Interpretations

2. Identify where God is in stanza 2, and where Death is in stanza 3. According to stanza 5, where is Sister Caroline? How does Sister Caroline respond to Death's arrival in stanza 6?
3. Find three **similes** that help to suggest the magnificence of the workings of heaven.
4. Does the speaker portray God and Jesus as distant, forbidding figures, or as familiar, gentle ones? Point out at least four details that support your interpretation.
5. Why do you think Death rides a "pale," or white, horse? Where else have you seen the color white used in a similar **symbolic** way?

Extending the Text

6. While many of the traditional representations of death are fearful, the one in this poem is not. Discuss the ways Johnson **personifies** death in this poem. Then compare Johnson's image with images you have encountered in literature (see especially Emily Dickinson's "Because I could not stop for Death" on page 391) or on film.

LANGUAGE AND STYLE

Free Verse and the Orator's Style

When Johnson was working on the poems that would eventually become *God's Trombones,* he talked with the African American poet Paul Laurence Dunbar (1872–1906).

> I showed Paul the things I had done under the sudden influence of Whitman. He read them through and, looking at me with a queer smile, said, "I don't like them, and I don't see what you are driving at." He may have been justified, but I was taken aback. I got out my copy of *Leaves of Grass* and read him some of the things I admired most. There was, at least, some personal consolation in the fact that his verdict was the same on Whitman himself.
>
> —James Weldon Johnson

Examine "Go Down, Death," and see if you can identify the influence of Whitman (page 348). Look for these elements of Whitman's style: **(1) repetition** and **parallel structure** to create rhythm; **(2)** the simple language of everyday conversation, including slang; **(3)** variation of line length, from very long to very short, to create a rolling cadence; **(4)** other **sound effects.**

CHOICES: Building Your Portfolio

Writer's Notebook

1. Collecting Ideas for an Interpretive Essay

Explore the similarities and differences in the attitudes toward death expressed in Johnson's "Go Down, Death" and Gwendolyn Brooks's "of De Witt Williams on his way to Lincoln Cemetery" (page 741). Take notes in a double-column comparison/contrast chart. Save your notes for possible use in the Writer's Workshop on page 804.

Critical Writing

2. Sermons Side by Side

Extracts from another famous sermon in American literature are on page 79—Jonathan Edwards's "Sinners in the Hands of an Angry God." In a brief essay, compare and contrast Johnson's sermon with Edwards's. Consider these elements of each sermon: (a) imagery, (b) figures of speech, (c) message, (d) tone, (e) audience, and (f) purpose.

Beyond the Poem

Choices: Building Your Portfolio

1. **Writer's Notebook** Remind students to save their work. They may use it as prewriting for the Writer's Workshop on p. 804.

PORTFOLIO ASSESSMENT

Choices: Assessment Criteria For help in evaluating these Choices assignments, see the criteria in the *Portfolio Management System,* p. 157.

Claude McKay (1941) by Carl Van Vechten.

The Beinecke Rare Book and Manuscript Library, Yale University, New Haven, Connecticut. Estate of Carl Van Vechten, Joseph Solomon, Executor.

Claude McKay

(1890–1948)

Claude McKay was born and raised on the Caribbean island of Jamaica, the eighth child of farmers. When he was nine, he went to live with his eldest brother, who was a schoolmaster, and his early education came chiefly from his brother's classroom and library. McKay apprenticed as a wheelwright and cabinetmaker, then worked as a constable. All the while, he was writing poems in a Jamaican dialect of English. In 1912, with the help of an English friend, he published his first two collections of verse, *Songs of Jamaica* and *Constab Ballads,* then traveled to the United States to study agriculture. After briefly enrolling at Tuskegee Institute in Alabama, McKay transferred to Kansas State College, where he studied for two years.

In 1914, McKay moved to Harlem and opened a restaurant with a friend. When this venture failed, he supported himself with a variety of jobs, from janitor to butler, while he continued to refine his craft and publish poems in periodicals. In 1920, his third book, *Spring in New Hampshire,* was published. His most important book of poetry, *Harlem Shadows,* appeared in 1922.

By this time, McKay was a major figure in the Harlem Renaissance. He had served as an editor of the radical newspapers the *Liberator* and *The Masses*. Like many writers of the period, he was drawn to the "noble experiment" of communism. In 1922, he signed on as a stoker for a merchant ship and toured Russia for a year.

McKay lived abroad, principally in France, until 1934. During this time he concentrated on writing fiction and essays rather than poetry, and he published four novels, including the best-selling *Home to Harlem* (1928). Disillusioned with communism, in 1942 he converted to Roman Catholicism. McKay spent the rest of his life teaching in Catholic schools in Chicago.

Despite the use of Jamaican dialect early in his career, much of McKay's poetry shows the influence of the English Romantic poets, especially Wordsworth, Keats, and Shelley. In subject matter, however, the Romantics and McKay diverge widely: McKay's sonnets voice his ambivalent and often defiant feelings about African American life in the United States.

QUICK PLANNING GUIDE

Into the Poem

- **Reading Focus: Scaffolding** Students discover the complexity of the African American experience.
- **A Dialogue with the Text: Set a Purpose** Note in Reader's Log changing impressions of the speaker

Through the Poem

Beyond the Poem

- **Writer's Notebook:** Collect ideas for an interpretive essay
- **Creative Writing/Art:** Design a poster or bumper sticker

PORTFOLIO ASSESSMENT

Portfolio Assessment
For help with self- and teacher assessment of reading skills, see the *Portfolio Management System,* pp. 48–49.

PROGRAM MANAGER

- **Planning Instruction** See Teaching Notes, *Teaching Resources B,* pp. 83–84, for objectives, a summary, literary elements, and additional biographical information for this selection.
- **Instructional Support** Before beginning the instructional lesson, see Graphic Organizer for Active Reading, *Teaching Resources B,* p. 88, for an Into the Poem activity.
- **Audiotaped Readings** To help less proficient readers or auditory learners through the lesson, use the Selected Reading, Audiocassette 3, Side A, in the *Audiovisual Resources Binder.*
- **Assessment** See Selection Test, *Test Booklet,* pp. 171–172.

Using **Before You Read** p. 744

A Dialogue with the Text

Have students track their impressions of the speaker using the following organizer:

Line No.	My impression	No change (check box)	Line No.	My impression changes to
[2]	[Speaker is bitter toward the country.]		[4]	[Speaker has a love/hate feeling toward the country.]

A. Critical Reading: Analyzing Poetry

? What is the rhyme scheme of the poem? [*abab cdcd efef gg*] What is the rhythm? [Iambic pentameter] What type of poem is this? [Shakespearean sonnet] Some sonnets were written in praise of an unattainable woman. How is the subject of this poem a variation on this theme? [The speaker of this poem personifies the United States as a woman but has mixed feelings about her.]

Before You Read
America

Reading Focus

America the Beautiful?

By expressing defiance as well as love, McKay reveals the complexity of the African American experience in the United States—an experience that requires a large measure of strength and courage.

A Dialogue with the Text

READER'S LOG

As you read this sonnet, write down your impressions of the speaker, and note whether your ideas change over the course of the poem.

National Museum of American Art, Washington, D.C. Courtesy Art Resource.

Lower East Side from *Scenes of New York* (Mural study, Madison Square Postal Station, New York City) by Kindred McLeary. Tempera on fiberboard (23¾″ × 20″).

America

Claude McKay

Although she feeds me bread of bitterness,°
And sinks into my throat her tiger's tooth,
Stealing my breath of life, I will confess
I love this cultured hell that tests my youth!
Her vigor flows like tides into my blood,
Giving me strength erect against her hate.
Her bigness sweeps my being like a flood.
Yet as a rebel fronts° a king in state,
I stand within her walls with not a shred
Of terror, malice, not a word of jeer.
Darkly I gaze into the days ahead,
And see her might and granite wonders there,
Beneath the touch of Time's unerring hand,
Like priceless treasures sinking in the sand.

1. **bread of bitterness:** allusion to Psalm 80:5, "Thou feedest them with the bread of tears; and givest them tears to drink in great measure."
8. **fronts:** confronts.

Options for Teaching

Strategies for Inclusion

Learners Having Difficulty Creating paraphrases will aid students who may be daunted by the richness of the poem's imagery. Have students work with partners to paraphrase each line of the poem, explaining all similes and metaphors. Have students compare their paraphrases with those written by other students.

Special Needs Some students may have difficulty understanding the poem if they take the figures of speech literally. Have these students listen to an audiotape of the poem with headphones while highlighting a transparency overlaid on the text. Ask them to look for specific information. For example, ask them to highlight the passages that personify America. After they have read the poem, have them list the words that make America sound like a human.

English Language Development A skill that must be reinforced for low beginning level students is the ability to read in meaningful units rather than reading word by word. Help students identify meaningful units by pointing out the periods (and other closing punctuation), which signal the end of a sentence and the end of an idea.

Making Meanings

First Thoughts

1. Review the notes you made in your Reader's Log. What picture did you form of the poem's speaker?

Shaping Interpretations

2. In lines 1–3, what treatment does the poet say he receives from America? What qualities of America cause the speaker to love the country anyway?
3. America is **personified** in this poem as an entity both cruel and powerful. What **images** suggest America's cruelty and injustice? What images convey her power?
4. A rebel with "not a shred / Of terror, malice, not a word of jeer" might seem to be a rebel without a rebellion. How does the poem resolve this **paradox,** or apparent contradiction?

Extending the Text

5. What does this speaker see happening to America as he gazes into "the days ahead"? What messages about America's future do you hear today in various sources—films, TV shows, news programs, magazines, and other media?

Choices: Building Your Portfolio

Writer's Notebook

1. Collecting Ideas for an Interpretive Essay

WORK IN PROGRESS

Using a chart like the one below, compare McKay's "America" to Robinson Jeffers's "Shine, Perishing Republic" (page 581). Consider the **form, subject, point of view,** and **tone** of each poem. List similarities in the overlapping space. Use the remaining spaces to list the differences. Save your notes for possible use with the Writer's Workshop on page 804.

America | Shine, Perishing Republic

Creative Writing / Art

2. Get the Message

Design a poster or write a bumper sticker that the speaker in "America" might display. Try to capture in a phrase or two the main idea expressed in the poem.

Markets in the streets of Harlem.

UPI/Bettmann.

Making Meanings

First Thoughts

1. Possible responses: A vigorous man with a strong jaw or an angry, defiant man.

Shaping Interpretations

2. The country threatens to kill him. Its culture, vigor, and size.
3. Images of cruelty: "bread of bitterness" (l. 1), "tiger's tooth" (l. 2), and the mention of hate (l. 6). Images of power: "Tides" of vigor (l. 5), the country's "bigness" sweeping "like a flood" (l. 7), and "king in state" (l. 8).
4. The speaker is a philosophical rebel who combines nonviolence with protest against injustice and cruelty.

Extending the Text

5. **(Synthesis)** Possible responses: He sees the United States being destroyed by Time. The first seven lines of the poem depict the country as a land of bitterness and hatred. Some news programs report the United States is in trouble because of internal strife. Some magazines paint a positive image because of American advances in technology.

Choices: Building Your Portfolio

1. **Writer's Notebook** Remind students to save their work. They may use it as prewriting for the Writer's Workshop on p. 804.
2. **Creative Writing/Art** Pair students of differing learning styles, and have them work together on the project. For example, pair a visual learner and a student favoring linguistic intelligence.

STRATEGIES FOR INCLUSION

Interpersonal To help students create their Venn diagrams in activity #1, first have them meet in small groups. Have students list one difference in each category (subject, point of view, and tone) to get them started.

Learners Having Difficulty Help students generate ideas for activity #2. Bring a variety of posters and bumper stickers to class so that students may see and study them. They should pay attention to content and design.

PORTFOLIO ASSESSMENT

Choices: Assessment Criteria
For help in evaluating these Choices assignments, see the criteria in the *Portfolio Management System,* p. 158.

QUICK PLANNING GUIDE

Into the Poems

Through the Poems

Beyond the Poems

- **Writer's Notebook** Collect ideas for an interpretive essay
- **Creative Writing** Write a conversation between three boys
- **Critical Writing/Music** Write a short film treatment of a poem

WRITERS ON WRITING

Countee Cullen said that "good poetry is a lofty thought beautifully expressed," a thing that "should not be too intellectual" but should "deal more . . . with the emotions." As a writer, his objectives seem more poetic than political. It has been noted that while Cullen's poetic purpose aimed to transcend the issue of race through forms that struck the universal heart of all human beings, his poems never abandoned the issue of race, in particular, the predicaments faced by African Americans living in a largely hostile world. It is this tension between the universal and the everyday that gives his poetry its greatness.

Countee Cullen

(1903–1946)

Countee Cullen grew up in New York City, raised by the childless Reverend and Mrs. Frederick Cullen. He was a brilliant student, and during high school he was already writing accomplished poems in traditional forms. He graduated Phi Beta Kappa from New York University in 1925. While in college, Cullen won the Witter Bynner Poetry Prize; that same year, *Color,* his first volume of poetry, was published. This collection won a gold medal from the Harmon Foundation and established the young poet's reputation.

After earning his master's degree from Harvard in 1926, Cullen worked as an assistant editor of the important African American magazine *Opportunity.* His poems were published in such influential periodicals as *Harper's, Poetry,* and *Crisis.* In 1927, he published *Copper Sun,* a collection of poems, and *Caroling Dusk,* an anthology of poetry by African Americans. *Caroling Dusk* was a significant contribution to the Harlem Renaissance, but the introduction Cullen wrote for the book was controversial. He called for black poets to write traditional verse and to avoid the restrictions of solely racial themes.

At the peak of his career, Cullen married the daughter of the famous black writer W.E.B. Du Bois and published a third collection of poems, *The Ballad of the Brown Girl.* In 1929, he published a fourth volume, *The Black Christ.* Although he continued to write prose until the end of his life, this was his last collection of poetry. During the Great Depression of the 1930s, unable to make a living solely from writing, he began teaching in Harlem public schools, a job that he held until his early death.

Countee Porter Cullen (c. 1925) by Winold Reiss. Pastel on artist board (30 1/16" × 21 1/2").

Cullen's verse was heavily influenced by the poetry of the English Romantics, especially John Keats. He thought of himself primarily as a lyric poet in the Romantic tradition, not as a black poet writing about social and racial themes. Nevertheless, Cullen found himself repeatedly drawn to such themes: "Somehow or other I find my poetry of itself treating of the Negro, of his joys and his sorrows—mostly of the latter—and of the heights and depths of emotion which I feel as a Negro."

PROGRAM MANAGER

- **Planning Instruction** See **Teaching Notes, *Teaching Resources B,*** p. 84, for objectives, a summary, and literary elements for these selections.
- **Instructional Support** Before beginning the instructional lesson, see **Graphic Organizer for Active Reading, *Teaching Resources B,*** pp. 89–90, for Into and Through the Poem activities.
- **Audiotaped Readings** To help less proficient readers or auditory learners through the lesson, use the **Selected Reading, Audiocassette 3, Side A,** of "Tableau" in the ***Audiovisual Resources Binder.***
- **Assessment** See **Selection Test, *Test Booklet,*** pp. 173–174.

Before You Read
Tableau

Reading Focus
Still Life

Usually, *tableau* means a scene or an action stopped cold, like a still picture in a reel of film. Here we have a *tableau vivant;* that is, a little scene in which figures silently pose, a significant moment caught and preserved. This preserved moment is a disarmingly simple glimpse of a friendship—a friendship that speaks silently but forcefully of a much larger issue.

A Dialogue with the Text

After you've read the poem once, re-read it and jot down the images that help you see this vivid scene.

Tableau
(For Donald Duff)
Countee Cullen

Locked arm in arm they cross the way,
The black boy and the white,
The golden splendor of the day,
The sable pride of night.

From lowered blinds the dark folk stare,
And here the fair folk talk,
Indignant that these two should dare
In unison to walk.

Oblivious to look and word
They pass, and see no wonder
That lightning brilliant as a sword
Should blaze the path of thunder.

Tony Galindo/The Image Bank

Using **Before You Read** p. 747

Reading Focus
Invite students to write a work order stating specifications for an artist who will be drawing a tableau. Tell students to envision and describe a tableau that captures figures expressing friendship. Explain that work orders must specify precisely what is to be drawn, including the details of the physical scene and the settings, poses, attitudes, emotional expressions, and actions of the human figure. Have students share their work orders in groups of three.

A. Reader's Response: Shaping Interpretations

? What do you see in this image? [Sample responses: People are suspicious of change and progress. Or people gossip and criticize.]

B. Language Note: Inversion

Ordinarily "to walk" would precede "in unison." Why might Cullen invert them here? [Possible answer: To place emphasis on the words "in unison."]

Portfolio Assessment

For help with self- and teacher assessment of reading skills, see the ***Portfolio Management System,*** p. 53.

STRATEGIES FOR INCLUSION

Special Needs Some students learn and remember better when they can make a visual graphic to illustrate a poem. For example, since *tableau* means "scene" or "action stopped cold," illustrating this poem will reinforce the understanding of the title. Have students, draw, cut out magazine photographs, or use a computer to draw their interpretation of the poem. Then have them choose the line or lines that go best with their picture and write them on the back.

INTEGRATING THE LANGUAGE ARTS

Language and Style Have students work in groups to re-read the poems and focus on the economy of language. Have them determine the speaker's message. Ask them what each stanza contributes to each poem's total effect. Have them decide whether any one stanza could be omitted. Ask them how the poem would be different had Cullen not written in such a concise fashion.

Using **BEFORE YOU READ** p. 748

Quickwrite

If students have difficulty getting started, have them quickly complete a map like the following for each word. Have students jot down on the appropriate spoke the emotions, questions, and images they associate with the word.

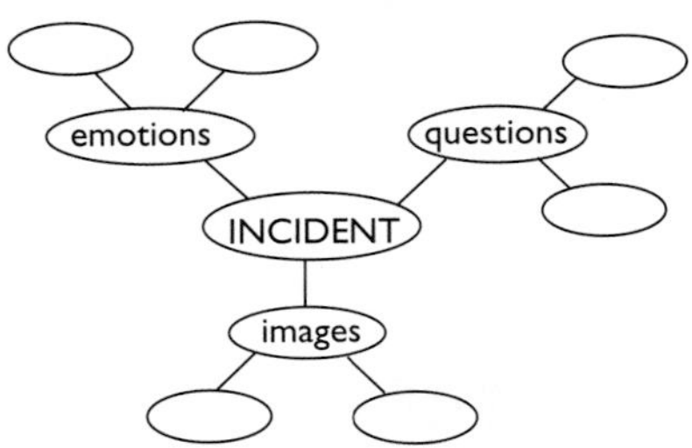

A. Literary Element: Rhythm
Iambic tetrameter alternates with iambic trimeter. How does the singsong style of the poem befit the subject? [Possible answers: It complements the age of the young boy. It makes the racial slur stand out in stark contrast.]

BEFORE YOU READ
INCIDENT

Reading Focus

A Word Remembered
The power of a word to taunt, to criticize, to dehumanize can't be underestimated. You might be shaken by the offensive word in this poem—imagine how it would affect a child.

Quickwrite

READER'S LOG

Before you read "Incident," quickwrite your response to the poem's title. Does it suggest something serious, or something relatively minor? How would you react if the title were "Catastrophe"?

Passengers (1953) by Raphael Soyer. Oil on canvas.

Incident

Countee Cullen

Once, riding in old Baltimore,
  Heart-filled, head-filled with glee,
I saw a Baltimorean
  Keep looking straight at me.

Now I was eight and very small,
  And he was no whit bigger,
And so I smiled, but he poked out
  His tongue, and called me "Nigger."

I saw the whole of Baltimore
  From May until December;
Of all the things that happened there
  That's all that I remember.
A

OPTIONS FOR TEACHING

STRATEGIES FOR INCLUSION

Intrapersonal/Interpersonal To help students understand the poem's last stanza—primarily the psychological imprint that significant moments can create in the mind—have them brainstorm memorable incidents from their own lives, things they have never forgotten because of the strong impression, either positive or negative, those things made. Have them select one of these incidents and remember concrete details of what surrounded them at that moment—sights, sounds, smells, tastes, textures, and feelings. Encourage a richly detailed record of the incident. Then have students share their results in small groups. *Remind students to choose a situation they would not mind sharing with others.*

CROSSING THE CURRICULUM

Social Sciences Both of Cullen's poems were written during a period in American history when the races were segregated and boys of different races walking together would draw stares. The Civil Rights movement that began in the 1960s was aimed at ending segregation and racist attitudes. Have students research and report on the following aspects of the movement in the 1960s:

- Montgomery bus boycott
- "I Have a Dream" speech
- Voting Rights Act of 1965 and registering black voters
- passive resistance
- Civil Rights Act of 1964

MAKING MEANINGS

Tableau

First Thoughts

1. What is the tableau—the stopped and still picture?

Shaping Interpretations

2. Review the notes you made in your Reader's Log. What **metaphors** describe the two boys in the first stanza?
3. In the third stanza, who or what is "lightning brilliant as a sword"? Who or what is the "path of thunder"?
4. Why should such a commonplace thing as the friendship between two boys evoke such a dramatic response? What larger topic do you think the poem is really about?

Incident

First Thoughts

1. Review the notes you made in your Reader's Log. Was this really only an "incident"?

Shaping Interpretations

2. What might lead a child to insult an eight-year-old boy in the way described here? In what ways is a child's prejudice even more disturbing than an adult's?
3. What **ironic** overtones does the title have? Review your response to First Thoughts, as well as your Reader's Log notes.
4. The speaker never directly states his emotional response to the experience. How does the last stanza indirectly make clear the impression the event had on him?

Extending the Text

5. Do you think that the content and message of "Tableau" and "Incident" are outdated, or are the scenes described in these poems still occurring today? Explain.

CHOICES: Building Your Portfolio

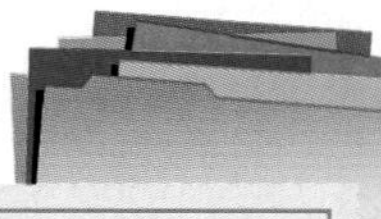

Writer's Notebook

1. Collecting Ideas for an Interpretive Essay

Compare and contrast the **diction** and **sentence structure** in "Tableau" and "Incident." Take notes that show how Cullen uses language to create two different effects in poems that are about very similar subjects. Save your notes for possible use in the Writer's Workshop on page 804.

Creative Writing

2. Worlds of Difference

Write a conversation in which the two boys who appear in "Tableau" discuss what happens in "Incident" with the eight-year-old boy who was the victim of the "incident."

Critical Writing / Music

3. Incident on Film

Suppose you were going to make a short film based on the poem "Incident." To convince a producer that you have a good idea, write a list of planned camera shots, in the order in which they would appear on screen. Then write a treatment, or summary, of your vision of the film. If you wish, find or compose music that you would use as an appropriate soundtrack for your film, and include a recording of that music with your film treatment.

Making Meanings "Tableau"

First Thoughts

1. Possible response: Two boys, one black and one white, walking arm in arm, being observed by dark people in one house and by "fair" people elsewhere.

Shaping Interpretations

2. The white boy is indirectly compared to the "golden splendor of the day" (l. 3), while the black boy is called "the sable pride of night" (l. 4).
3. Possible responses: The lightning refers to the boys' unexpected courage in risking an interracial friendship; the poet indirectly compares their boldness to the brilliance of a lightning bolt. The "path of thunder" also refers to the example of the boys' friendship. Their boldness clearly runs the risk of upsetting established conventions—and such boldness, although commendable, may be ominous.
4. Possible responses: It goes against the social expectations of the times. The larger topic is racial relations in the country as a whole.

"Incident"

First Thoughts

1. Possible responses: Since the speaker continues to remember it, it was obviously much more than a minor incident. It was important, for the boy was unable to remember anything else about his trip.

Shaping Interpretations

2. Parental example, peer pressure, or social experience. A child's prejudice suggests that prejudice is learned early and is handed down through generations.
3. To call it a mere "incident" is ironic—since such a title understates the trauma that the speaker suffered.
4. By telling us that this incident was the only thing he could remember about Baltimore in his seven months there, the speaker indirectly emphasizes his profound sense of injury.

Extending the Text

5. **(Synthesis)** Possible responses: Both poems capture the racial prejudice that continues today. Or the poem may be outdated, for some children do worse things than just stick out their tongues.

Choices: Building Your Portfolio

1. **Writer's Notebook** Remind students to save their work. They may use it as prewriting for the Writer's Workshop on p. 804.

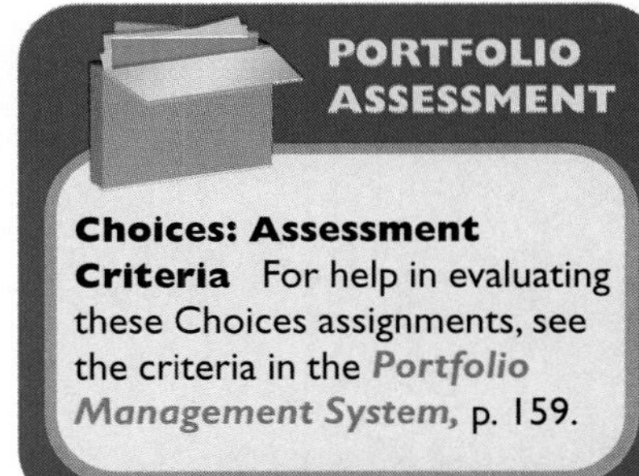

Choices: Assessment Criteria For help in evaluating these Choices assignments, see the criteria in the *Portfolio Management System,* p. 159.

QUICK PLANNING GUIDE

Into the Selection

Author Biography p. 750

Before You Read p. 751

- **Reading Focus: Scaffolding** Students discover writers' early interests.
- **A Dialogue with the Text: Set a Purpose** Note in Reader's Log details about Hurston's early interest in people and story
- **Background** Historical and cultural meanings as well as personal insight in story

Through the Selection

from Dust Tracks on a Road pp. 752–757

Words to Own pp. 753–757

Primary Sources p. 758

Making Meanings p. 759

Beyond the Selection

Choices: Building Your Portfolio p. 759

- **Writer's Notebook:** Collect ideas for an interpretive essay
- **Critical Writing:** Compare autobiographies in a brief essay
- **Creative Writing/Performance:** Adapt selection for play

Zora Neale Hurston

(c. 1891–1960)

Zora Neale Hurston was born in the all-black town of Eatonville, Florida. Her father was a preacher, and her mother, a schoolteacher, urged her talented daughter to "jump at the sun."

In her autobiography, Hurston recalls that as a young girl, "I used to climb to the top of one of the huge chinaberry trees which guarded our front gate and look out over the world. The most interesting thing that I saw was the horizon. . . . It grew upon me that I ought to walk out to the horizon and see what the end of the world was like."

Zora Neale Hurston (1935) by Carl Van Vechten.

When Hurston was nine, her mother died, and Zora was passed among relatives and family friends, supporting herself from her early teens on. Eventually, she enrolled at Howard University in Washington, D.C., where she published her first story in 1921.

Four years later, she set out for New York City to attend Barnard College, arriving with a dollar and a half in her pocket. Hurston was soon in the midst of the Harlem Renaissance, writing stories and plays that celebrated her African American heritage. She wore big hats and turbans, danced, gave parties, and sometimes shocked other African American artists, especially male writers like James Weldon Johnson and Langston Hughes.

Enrolling at prestigious Barnard College, Hurston met the famous anthropologist Franz Boas. Boas believed that Hurston's interest was really in his field, the study of human social and cultural behavior. Indeed, Hurston, who became his protégé, did eventually make her reputation not just as a fiction writer, but also as a folklorist. She traveled through Alabama, Florida, and Louisiana to gather folklore material, using a scholar's eye to evaluate oral tales, many of which were familiar to her from earliest childhood. Eventually, she gathered enough folklore to fill two groundbreaking collections, *Mules and Men* (1935) and *Tell My Horse* (1938). Alice Walker (page 1101) says that the stories in *Mules and Men* gave back to her own relatives in the South all the stories they'd forgotten or grown ashamed of.

Hurston also wrote musical revues portraying black folk-culture, and these brought her initial success. But it was *Story* magazine's publication of her short story "The Gilded Six Bits" that launched her literary career. When the Philadelphia publisher J. B. Lippincott asked if she had a novel, Hurston promptly sat down and wrote *Jonah's Gourd Vine,* published in 1934. Three years later, Hurston published her best novel, *Their Eyes Were Watching God,* the story of a young African American woman who strikes out for a life beyond a conventional marriage, much as Hurston herself had done.

Throughout the last twenty years of her life, Hurston continued to produce fiction and nonfiction, including her autobiography, *Dust Tracks on a Road.* But she began to have difficulty finding a market for her work, some of which was criticized in the African American community for celebrating the life of black people in the United States rather than confronting the white community for its discrimination.

In the late 1940s, Hurston left New York and returned to Florida. In 1960, she died, broke, in a Florida welfare home. A collection had to be taken up to pay for her funeral. Ironically, in the years since her death, much of her work has been brought back into print, and Hurston is now recognized as the forerunner of such celebrated contemporary writers as Toni Morrison and Alice Walker.

WORDS TO OWN

The following vocabulary words are defined in the Words to Own at the bottom of the pupil's page.

hail p. 753	avarice p. 756
brazenness p. 753	tread p. 757
caper p. 754	profoundly p. 757
exalted p. 754	resolved p. 757
realm p. 755	conceive p. 757

PORTFOLIO ASSESSMENT

Portfolio Assessment For help with self- and teacher assessment of reading skills, see the ***Portfolio Management System,*** pp. 48–49.

BEFORE YOU READ
FROM DUST TRACKS ON A ROAD

Reading Focus

Looking for the Threads
It's no surprise that the autobiographies of writers often include lovingly detailed memories of childhood interests and discoveries that paved the way for the adult writer. In her autobiography, *One Writer's Beginnings,* Eudora Welty (page 633) notes, "Writing fiction has developed in me an abiding respect for the unknown in a human lifetime and a sense of where to look for the threads, how to follow, how to connect, find in the thick of the tangle what clear line persists. The strands are all there: To the memory nothing is ever really lost." Here, Zora Neale Hurston connects some of her own threads by recounting what is surely every writer's first experience of falling in love: the passion for hearing and reading stories.

Woven through these recollections of Hurston's childhood are her impressions of racial segregation, economic conditions, education, social customs, and family, as well as general attitudes of Southerners in the early 1900s.

A Dialogue with the Text

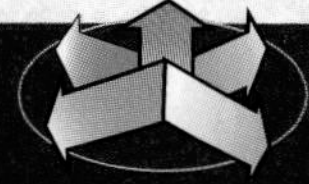

As you read, write down what you learn about Hurston's character from her thoughts and actions, as well as any details that suggest Hurston's early interest in people, her fascination with storytelling, and her later devotion to anthropology and folklore research.

Background

Zora Neale Hurston's *Dust Tracks on a Road* is rich with cultural and historical meaning, as well as personal insight and data.

I used to take a seat on top of the gatepost and watch the world go by.

Her World (1948) by Philip Evergood. Oil on canvas (48″ × 35⅝″).

The Metropolitan Museum of Art, Arthur Hoppock Hearn Fund, 1950 (50.29).

Into the Selection

Using BEFORE YOU READ p. 751

A Dialogue with the Text

Have students draw a center line down each of two facing pages in their Reader's Logs. At the top of each column, they should write the headings listed below and record observations and supporting details as they read.

Character	Interests in people	Fascination with storytelling research	Devotion to anthropology and folklore

WRITERS ON WRITING

Hurston says the folk tradition she was born into was so familiar it fit her "like a tight chemise" that she could not see because she was wearing it. "It was only when I was off in college," she says, "away from my native surroundings, that I could see myself like somebody else and stand off and look at my garment. Then I had to have the spy-glass of Anthropology to look through at that."

PROGRAM MANAGER

- **Planning Instruction** See Teaching Notes, *Teaching Resources B,* p. 85, for objectives, a summary, literary elements, and additional information.
- **Instructional Support** See Graphic Organizer for Active Reading, *Teaching Resources B,* p. 91, for an Into the Selection activity.
- **Audiotaped Readings** To help readers through the lesson, use the Selected Reading, Audiocassette 2, Side B, in the *Audiovisual Resources Binder.*
- **Assessment** See Selection Test, *Test Booklet,* pp. 175–176.
- **Language Link** For instruction and practice in commas, see Language Link, *Teaching Resources B,* pp. 92–93, and *Language and Writing Skills Worksheets,* pp. 131–135.
- **Reinforcement** Use the Words to Own worksheet in *Teaching Resources B,* p. 94.

RESPONDING TO THE PHOTOGRAPH: VISUAL LITERACY

Have students compare and contrast this photograph of Hurston's school with their own school. Ask them to list and discuss differences and similarities between the two. [Possible responses: Students might note that all of the students in the photograph are black, but that their own school is more integrated or that students at their own school are all African Americans. The students in the photograph range in age from about six years old to about eighteen, but most schools now are divided into smaller groups according to age. Some students might identify with the photograph because it reflects a community based on a particular culture.]

from Dust Tracks on a Road

Zora Neale Hurston

Dunbar High School, Quincy, Florida (pages 752–753, 755, 756).
Florida State Archives.

OPTIONS FOR TEACHING

STRATEGIES FOR INCLUSION

Advanced Invite students to read the full text of *Dust Tracks on a Road.* After students finish the autobiography, have them work together to prepare a storytelling session using incidents from Hurston's life and to connect the stories with narration about her life. Have them give their presentation to the class.

Interpersonal Have students turn to a person near them and share their thoughts about the two women in the selection. Have them discuss why the women pick Hurston to visit them and what motivates them to give her gifts. After students talk with each other, ask volunteers to share thoughts with the entire class.

Learners Having Difficulty If students experience difficulties in making inferences about Hurston's character, have them work with partners to identify passages where her character is revealed through her thoughts, words, or actions. Students can use the following chart.

Passage from Text	What It Reveals
["But I knew better than to bring that up right here, so I said yes, I *loved* school."]	[She is savvy, perceptive.]

I used to take a seat on top of the gatepost and watch the world go by. One way to Orlando ran past my house, so the carriages and cars would pass before me. The movement made me glad to see it. Often the white travelers would hail me, but more often I hailed them, and asked, "Don't you want me to go a piece of the way with you?"

They always did. I know now that I must have caused a great deal of amusement among them, but my self-assurance must have carried the point, for I was always invited to come along. I'd ride up the road for perhaps a half-mile, then walk back. I did not do this with the permission of my parents, nor with their foreknowledge. When they found out about it later, I usually got a whipping. My grandmother worried about my forward ways a great deal. She had known slavery and to her my brazenness was unthinkable.

She had known slavery and to her my brazenness was unthinkable.

"Git down offa dat gatepost! You li'l sow, you! Git down! Setting up dere looking dem white folks right in de face! They's gowine[1] to lynch you, yet. And don't stand in dat doorway gazing out at 'em neither. Youse too brazen to live long." **A**

1. **gowine:** dialect for "going."

Words to Own

hail (hāl) *v.:* greet.
brazenness (brā'zən·nis) *n.:* boldness.

A. Language Note: Dialect
Here is an example of Hurston's use of dialect to reproduce the southern African American pattern of speech she grew up with. Readers should note that Richard Wright resented her use of dialogue, believing that it perpetuated the minstrel stereotype and promoted racism.

INTEGRATING THE LANGUAGE ARTS

Strategic Reading The conversational tone of this selection will be more apparent when it is read aloud. So that each student has a chance to read a portion of the text aloud, have students work in groups of four or five. Have the first student read until he or she comes to a natural "break" in the selection. That student will stop and the second student will begin to read until the next "break" in the text.

Writing: Letter Have students assume the persona of the main character and write a letter to the two women in the selection. Remind students that the thoughts and language of the letter should be consistent with the student's view of Hurston's character documented in his or her Reader's Log.

A. Literary Connections
Remind students of Thoreau's famous words in *Walden:* "If a man does not keep pace with his companions, perhaps it is because he hears a different drummer. Let him step to the music which he hears, however measured or far away" (p. 244).

B. Exploring the Culture
At the time Zora Neale Hurston was growing up in the South, schools and towns were often segregated by race. Eatonville, the town she grew up in, was an all-black town in Florida. The whites who came down from the North were curious about an all-black school.

C. Literary Element: Figure of Speech
? What does Hurston mean when she says the children were "sent home to lick the calf over again?" [She compares a child's scrubbing by his or her mother or father to a calf's being licked clean by its mother.] What does this expression contribute to the story's effectiveness? [Such expressions lend an authentic voice to the narrative. They make the writing informal and personal.]

D. Critical Reading: Drawing Conclusions
? What does this passage reveal about Zora Neale Hurston's relationship with whites? [Possible answer: Her fascination with the two white women and her curiosity about what their hands must feel like reveal that except for the travelers who passed by her house, she did not have many dealings with white people.]

Nevertheless, I kept right on gazing at them, and "going a piece of the way" whenever I could make it. The village seemed dull to me most of the time. If the village was singing a chorus, I must have missed the tune.

Perhaps a year before the old man[2] died, I came to know two other white people for myself. They were women.

It came about this way. The whites who came down from the North were often brought by their friends to visit the village school. A Negro school was something strange to them, and while they were always sympathetic and kind, curiosity must have been present, also. They came and went, came and went. Always, the room was hurriedly put in order, and we were threatened with a prompt and bloody death if we cut one caper while the visitors were present. We always sang a spiritual, led by Mr. Calhoun himself. Mrs. Calhoun always stood in the back, with a palmetto switch[3] in her hand as a squelcher. We were all little angels for the duration, because we'd better be. She would cut her eyes[4] and give us a glare that meant trouble, then turn her face toward the visitors and beam as much as to say it was a great privilege and pleasure to teach lovely children like us. They couldn't see that palmetto hickory in her hand behind all those benches, but we knew where our angelic behavior was coming from.

Usually, the visitors gave warning a day ahead and we would be cautioned to put on shoes, comb our heads, and see to ears and fingernails. There was a close inspection of every one of us before we marched in that morning. Knotty heads, dirty ears, and fingernails got hauled out of line, strapped, and sent home to lick the calf[5] over again.

This particular afternoon, the two young ladies just popped in. Mr. Calhoun was flustered, but he put on the best show he could. He dismissed the class that he was teaching up at the front of the room, then called the fifth grade in reading. That was my class.

So we took our readers and went up front. We stood up in the usual line, and opened to the lesson. It was the story of Pluto and Persephone.[6] It was new and hard to the class in general, and Mr. Calhoun was very uncomfortable as the readers stumbled along, spelling out words with their lips, and in mumbling undertones before they exposed them experimentally to the teacher's ears.

Then it came to me. I was fifth or sixth down the line. The story was not new to me, because I had read my reader through from lid to lid, the first week that Papa had bought it for me.

That is how it was that my eyes were not in the book, working out the paragraph which I knew would be mine by counting the children ahead of me. I was observing our visitors, who held a book between them, following the lesson. They had shiny hair, mostly brownish. One had a looping gold chain around her neck. The other one was dressed all over in black and white with a pretty finger ring on her left hand. But the thing that held my eyes were their fingers. They were long and thin, and very white, except up near the tips. There they were baby pink. I had never seen such hands. It was a fascinating discovery for me. I wondered how they felt. I would have given those hands more attention, but the child before me was almost through. My turn next, so I got on my mark, bringing my eyes back to the book and made sure of my place. Some of the stories I had reread several times, and this Greco-Roman myth was one of my favorites. I was exalted by it, and that is the way I read my paragraph.

"Yes, Jupiter[7] had seen her (Persephone). He had seen the maiden picking flowers in the field. He had seen the chariot of the dark monarch pause by the maiden's side. He had seen him when he seized Persephone. He had seen the

2. **old man:** a white farmer who knew Hurston's family, took her fishing, and gave her advice.
3. **palmetto switch:** whip made from the stem of a large, fanlike leaf of a kind of palm tree. Teachers sometimes used them to discipline students.
4. **cut her eyes:** slang for "look at scornfully."
5. **lick the calf:** slang for "get cleaned up."
6. **Pluto and Persephone** (pər·sef′ə·nē): In classical mythology, Pluto, or Hades, is the god who rules the underworld; Persephone, also known as Proserpina, is his wife, queen of the underworld. In this version of the origin of the seasons, Hurston uses the names of Roman and Greek gods interchangeably.
7. **Jupiter:** in Roman mythology, king of the gods.

WORDS TO OWN
caper (kā′pər) *n.:* foolish prank.
exalted (eg·zôlt′id) *v.:* lifted up.

OPTIONS FOR TEACHING

CLASSROOM MANAGEMENT

Block Scheduling Give students the opportunity to become involved with computer technology within the scope of the selection. Students can devote an entire class period to activities involving electronic mail, CD-ROM, laser disc, videodisc, interactive video, or other recent technology. This is an excellent way to take advantage of the longer class period to enrich, enhance, and re-teach any concept.

Managing the Reader's Response Classroom
Before ending a discussion, allow students to comment on it. Vary the way in which you end discussion in one of the following ways.

- Ask students to take turns telling the most important thing they learned from the discussion.
- Have them evaluate the discussion, explaining what they thought went well and what could be improved.
- Have them state what they, as individuals or as a class, might do differently if they were to hold the same discussion.

black horses leap down Mount Aetna's[8] fiery throat. Persephone was now in Pluto's dark realm and he had made her his wife."

The two women looked at each other and then back to me. Mr. Calhoun broke out with a proud smile beneath his bristly moustache, and instead of the next child taking up where I had ended, he nodded to me to go on. So I read the story to the end, where flying Mercury, the messenger of the Gods, brought Persephone back to the sunlit earth and restored her to the arms of Dame Ceres, her mother, that the world might have springtime and summer flowers, autumn and harvest. But because she had bitten the pomegranate while in Pluto's kingdom, she must return to him for three months of each year, and be his queen. Then the world had winter, until she returned to earth.

The class was dismissed and the visitors smiled us away and went into a low-voiced conversation with Mr. Calhoun for a few minutes. They glanced my way once or twice and I began to worry. Not only was I barefooted, but my feet and legs were dusty. My hair was more uncombed than usual, and my nails were not shiny clean. Oh, I'm going to catch it now. Those ladies saw me, too. Mr. Calhoun is promising to 'tend to me. So I thought.

Then Mr. Calhoun called me. I went up thinking how awful it was to get a whipping before company. Furthermore, I heard a snicker run over the room. Hennie Clark and Stell Brazzle did it out loud, so I would be sure to hear them. The smart aleck was going to get it. I slipped one hand behind me and switched my dress tail at them, indicating scorn.

"Come here, Zora Neale," Mr. Calhoun cooed as I reached the desk. He put his hand on my shoulder and gave me little pats. The ladies smiled and held out those flower-looking fingers toward me. I seized the opportunity for a good look.

"Shake hands with the ladies, Zora Neale," Mr. Calhoun prompted and they took my hand one after the other and smiled. They asked me if I loved school, and I lied that I did. There was *some* truth in it, because I liked geography and reading, and I liked to play at recess time. Whoever it was invented writing and arithmetic got no thanks from me. Neither did I like the arrangement where the teacher could sit up there with a palmetto stem and lick me whenever he saw fit. I hated things I couldn't do anything about. But I knew better than to bring that up right there, so I said yes, I *loved* school. (E)

The ladies smiled and held out those flower-looking fingers toward me.

"I can tell you do," Brown Taffeta gleamed. (F) She patted my head, and was lucky enough not to get sandspurs in her hand. Children who roll and tumble in the grass in Florida are apt to get sandspurs in their hair. They shook hands with me again and I went back to my seat.

When school let out at three o'clock, Mr. Calhoun told me to wait. When everybody had gone, he told me I was to go to the Park House, that was the hotel in Maitland, the next afternoon to call upon Mrs. Johnstone and Miss Hurd. I must tell Mama to see that I was clean and brushed from head to feet, and I must wear shoes and stockings. The ladies liked me, he said, and I must be on my best behavior.

The next day I was let out of school an hour early, and went home to be stood up in a tub of suds and be scrubbed and have my ears dug into. My sandy hair sported a red ribbon to match my red and white checked gingham dress, starched until it could stand alone. Mama saw to it that my shoes were on the right feet, since I was

WORDS TO OWN

realm (relm) *n.:* kingdom.

8. **Mount Aetna's:** Mount Aetna (also spelled Etna) is a volcanic mountain in eastern Sicily.

E. Literary Element: Character

? What does this passage show about Zora Neale Hurston's character? [She is perceptive, for she understands that this is not the moment to discuss what she does not like about school; she does not like things she cannot do anything about; she has strong opinions about the subjects she enjoys at school and those she does not.]

F. Literary Element: Metonymy

Inform students that "Brown Taffeta" is an instance of metonymy, a figure of speech in which a person, place, or thing is referred to by something closely associated with it. What is the effect of equating the woman with brown taffeta? [Possible answer: It reveals Hurston's fascination with the fabric the woman wears and Hurston's affinity with her own color. It also indicates how foreign the woman seems to her.]

CROSSING THE CURRICULUM

Art Have students create identity collages of Hurston as a child. Ask them to draw or paint or use pictures, words, and letters from magazines and newspapers to portray Hurston's character—her personality, appearance, likes, dislikes, interests. Invite students to explain their identity collages to the class. Post the collages around the classroom.

Social Sciences Have students work in small groups to do research and to prepare short presentations on one of the mythological or biblical figures Hurston mentions in the selection—Pluto, Persephone, Ceres, Odin, Hercules, or David. Have each group explain the relationship between the figures and Hurston's autobiography and use drawings, illustrations, or fine art in their presentation.

COOPERATIVE LEARNING

Speaking the Language Have students in groups of three find examples of idioms, colloquial expressions, and dialect in the selection. Have each student in the group bring an example of each for group discussion. Assign each student a role: scribe, discussion leader, or spokesperson. Ask students to discuss how each example is used and what effect it has on the telling of the selection. Have them choose their favorite and share it with the class.

A. Reader's Response: Shaping Interpretations

? What does Hurston mean when she says "I stood on the mountain"? [Sample responses: When she sees the heap of shiny new pennies, she feels like the person at the top of the mountain—at the height of joy. Or she is happy, surveying the beauty of the scene.]

B. Expansion

Zora Neale Hurston presents elements of African American folk culture in her writings. She uses the blues, street language, and spirituals. Here she refers to the songs she liked "where the words marched to a throb [she] could feel."

careless about left and right. Last thing, I was given a handkerchief to carry, warned again about my behavior, and sent off, with my big brother John to go as far as the hotel gate with me.

First thing, the ladies gave me strange things, like stuffed dates and preserved ginger, and encouraged me to eat all that I wanted. Then they showed me their Japanese dolls and just talked. I was then handed a copy of *Scribner's Magazine,* and asked to read a place that was pointed out to me. After a paragraph or two, I was told with smiles, that that would do.

I was led out on the grounds and they took my picture under a palm tree. They handed me what was to me then a heavy cylinder done up in fancy paper, tied with a ribbon, and they told me goodbye, asking me not to open it until I got home.

My brother was waiting for me down by the lake, and we hurried home, eager to see what was in the thing. It was too heavy to be candy or anything like that. John insisted on toting it for me.

My mother made John give it back to me and let me open it. Perhaps, I shall never experience such joy again. The nearest thing to that moment was the telegram accepting my first book. One hundred goldy-new pennies rolled out of the cylinder. Their gleam lit up the world. It was not (A) avarice that moved me. It was the beauty of the thing. I stood on the mountain. Mama let me play with my pennies for a while, then put them away for me to keep.

That was only the beginning. The next day I received an Episcopal hymnbook bound in white leather with a golden cross stamped into the front cover, a copy of *The Swiss Family Robinson,* and a book of fairy tales.

I set about to commit the song words to memory. There was no music written there, just the words. But there was to my consciousness music in between them just the same. "When I survey the Wondrous Cross" seemed the most beautiful to me, so I committed that to memory first of all. (B) Some of them seemed dull and without life, and I pretended they were not there. If white people liked trashy singing like that, there must be something funny about them that I had not noticed before. I stuck to the pretty ones where the words marched to a throb I could feel.

Of the Greeks, Hercules moved me most.

Words to Own

avarice (av′ə·ris) *n.:* greed.

OPTIONS FOR TEACHING — **PROFESSIONAL NOTES**

Thematic Connections: "I, Too, Sing America" In their poetry, Johnson, Cullen, McKay, and Hughes all present their interpretation of the country. In this story, Hurston presents a picture of life in the community of Eatonville, Florida. Ask students to describe the world Hurston sees and how her description compares with that of the poets in the Collection. Invite them to discuss how each contributes to the various "songs" of the United States.

A month or so after the two young ladies returned to Minnesota, they sent me a huge box packed with clothes and books. The red coat with a wide circular collar and the red tam pleased me more than any of the other things. My chums pretended not to like anything that I had, but even then I knew that they were jealous. Old Smarty had gotten by them again. The clothes were not new, but they were very good. I shone like the morning sun.

But the books gave me more pleasure than the clothes. I had never been too keen on dressing up. It called for hard scrubbings with Octagon soap suds getting in my eyes, and none too gentle fingers scrubbing my neck and gouging in my ears.

In that box were *Gulliver's Travels, Grimm's Fairy Tales, Dick Whittington, Greek and Roman Myths,* and best of all, *Norse Tales.* Why did the Norse tales strike so deeply into my soul? I do not know, but they did. I seemed to remember seeing Thor swing his mighty short-handled hammer as he sped across the sky in rumbling thunder, lightning flashing from the tread of his steeds and the wheels of his chariot. The great and good Odin, who went down to the well of knowledge to drink, and was told that the price of a drink from that fountain was an eye. Odin drank deeply, (C) then plucked out one eye without a murmur and handed it to the grizzly keeper, and walked away. That held majesty for me.

Of the Greeks, Hercules moved me most. I followed him eagerly on his tasks. The story of the choice of Hercules as a boy when he met Pleasure and Duty, and put his hand in that of Duty and followed her steep way to the blue hills of fame and glory, which she pointed out at the end, moved me profoundly. I resolved to be like him. The tricks and turns of the other gods and goddesses left me cold. There were other thin books about this and that sweet and gentle little girl who gave up her heart to Christ and good works. Almost always they died from it, preaching as they passed. I was utterly indifferent to their deaths. In the first place I could not conceive of death, and in the next place they never had any funerals that amounted to a hill of beans, so I didn't care how soon they rolled up their big, soulful, blue eyes and kicked the bucket. They had no meat on their bones.

But I also met Hans Andersen[9] and Robert Louis Stevenson.[10] They seemed to know what I wanted to hear and said it in a way that tingled me. Just a little below these friends was Rudyard Kipling in his Jungle Books.[11] I loved his talking snakes as much as I did the hero.

I came to start reading the Bible through my mother. She gave me a licking one afternoon for repeating something I had overheard a neighbor telling her. She locked me in her room after the whipping, and the Bible was the only thing in there for me to read. I happened to open to the place where David was doing some mighty smiting, and I got interested. David went here and he went there, and no matter where he went, he smote 'em hip and thigh. Then he sung songs to his harp awhile, and went out and smote some (D) more. Not one time did David stop and preach about sins and things. All David wanted to know from God was who to kill and when. He took care of the other details himself. Never a quiet moment. I liked him a lot. So I read a great deal more in the Bible, hunting for some more active people like David. Except for the beautiful language of Luke and Paul, the New Testament still plays a poor second to the Old Testament for me. The Jews had a God who laid about Him[12] when they needed Him. I could see no use waiting till Judgment Day to see a man who was just crying for a (E) good killing, to be told to go and roast.[13] My idea was to give him a good killing first, and then if he got roasted later on, so much the better.

9. **Andersen:** Hans Christian Andersen, Danish writer known primarily for his fairy tales.
10. **Robert Louis Stevenson:** Scottish writer of adventure stories such as *Kidnapped* and *Treasure Island.*
11. **Kipling . . . Books:** Kipling was an English writer born in India. His *The Jungle Book* (1894) and *The Second Jungle Book* (1895) are stories of the adventures of Mowgli, a boy raised by animals in the jungles of India.
12. **laid about Him:** slang for "struck blows in every direction."
13. **roast:** slang for "burn in hell."

WORDS TO OWN

tread (tred) *n.:* stepping.
profoundly (prō·found′lē) *adv.:* deeply.
resolved (rē·zälvd′) *v.:* made a decision; determined.
conceive (kən·sēv′) *v.:* think; imagine.

C. Reader's Response: Connecting with the Text

? Have you ever felt admiration for a literary character in this way? Explain. [Sample responses: Yes, when Jerry in *The Chocolate War* refuses to sell the chocolates that the school requires him to sell. Or no, but I felt that way about Rocky in the movie *Rocky* when he finished the fight with the world champion.]

D. Literary Element: Irony

? What is ironic about this scene? [After being punished for repeating something that was told to her mother, Zora is left in a room with the Bible. Ironically, instead of reading a passage delineating the wages of sin, she turns to passages in 1 and 2 Samuel where David kills enemies of his faith or tribe. Zora notices that never once does he preach about his sins. She decides that she likes David, for reasons her mother would never have approved of, and begins to read more of the Bible, not because of the virtues preached there, but because she is looking for adventurous people like David.]

E. Language Note: Exaggeration

Point out to students Hurston's humorous use of exaggeration in this passage. What does this passage reveal about her character as a child? [She has no patience with the meek or timid. She admires boldness and action in others.]

ASSESSMENT TOOLS

Informal Assessment As students work in groups, observe their behavior and note the following on a scale that includes high, medium, and low values.

1. Do all students in each group seem engaged?
2. Are students performing assigned group roles (recorder, reporter, monitor)?
3. Are students staying on the assigned task?
4. Are all contributing to the group task?
5. Does the atmosphere of the group seem conducive to participation by all members?

Check Test: Questions and Answers

1. Why does Zora like to sit on top of the gatepost? [She likes to hail the travelers who go by and get a ride with them up the road.]
2. What does Zora find so fascinating about the two white women who visit the school? [She is enthralled by the women's hands.]
3. Why does she come to the attention of the two women? [She reads fluently from a difficult text.]
4. What is inside the cylinder that the two women give Zora? [One hundred new pennies.]
5. Why does Zora like the stories about David? [He was an active person and took care of things himself.]

Primary Sources

In her work as an anthropologist, Zora Neale Hurston gained prominence as a recorder of African American folktales. One challenge the folklorist confronts as a field researcher is to capture *naturally* the stories that people tell. To record such "naturalistic data," including not just the stories themselves but the meanings conveyed by a storyteller's gestures and voice, it is crucial for folklorists to gain the trust of their subjects so they will feel comfortable and be willing to speak naturally. Hurston's account shows how her sophisticated way of talking worked against her in gathering naturalistic data. Her proper speech created a mistrust among the largely uneducated country folk whose stories she wanted to collect, making them "clam up" rather than openly and naturally sharing their stories. Have students think of times when people have been unable to get what they liked because they did not speak the "lingo" of a particular group. Have students choose a particular group of people, such as friends, neighbors, relatives, or local folklorists or historians, and think of how to get them to tell stories. Ask each student to collect three stories. Encourage students to use an audiotape recorder. Invite them to share these stories in a special class storytelling session. *You may want to obtain permission from parents or guardians and from the people students will contact before they begin work on this activity.*

Primary Sources | **An Autobiography**

In Search of a Story

In another section of *Dust Tracks on a Road,* Zora Neale Hurston tells of her passion, as a child, for hearing stories from the African American tradition.

For me, the store porch was the most interesting place that I could think of. I was not allowed to sit around there, naturally. But, I could and did drag my feet going in and out, whenever I was sent there for something, to allow whatever was being said to hang in my ear. I would hear an occasional scrap of gossip in what to me was adult double talk, but which I understood at times. . . .

But what I really loved to hear was the menfolks holding a "lying" session. That is, straining against each other in telling folks tales. God, Devil, Brer Rabbit, Brer Fox, Sis Cat, Brer Bear, Lion, Tiger, Buzzard, and all the wood folk walked and talked like natural men. The wives of the storytellers might yell from back yards for them to come and tote some water, or chop wood for the cookstove and never get a move out of the men. The usual rejoinder was, "Oh, she's got enough to go on. No matter how much wood you chop, a woman will burn it all up to get a meal. If she got a couple of pieces, she will make it do. If you chop up a whole boxful, she will burn every stick of it. Pay her no mind." So the storytelling would go right on.

• • •

This passion for listening to stories from the oral tradition led Hurston to collect folklore as a field researcher. In this section of her autobiography, Hurston tells of studying anthropology at Barnard College in New York City and of how she went out among African Americans to gather their folk tales. In her first attempts as a folklore collector, she did not succeed. She had to learn the hard way that a folklorist must use just the right approach with his or her sources.

Mecklenburg Evening (1984) by Romare Bearden. Collage and watercolor on board.
Courtesy Estate of Romare Bearden/ ACA Galleries, New York.

Research is formalized curiosity. It is poking and prying with a purpose. It is a seeking that he who wishes may know the cosmic secrets of the world and they that dwell therein. . . .

My first six months were disappointing. I found out later that it was not because I had no talents for research, but because I did not have the right approach. The glamour of Barnard College was still upon me. I dwelt in marble halls. I knew where the material was all right. But, I went about asking, in carefully accented Barnardese, "Pardon me, but do you know any folk tales or folk songs?" The men and women who had whole treasuries of material just seeping through their pores looked at me and shook their heads. No, they had never heard of anything like that around there. Maybe it was over in the next county. Why didn't I try over there? I did, and got the selfsame answer. Oh, I got a few little items. But compared with what I did later, not enough to make a flea a waltzing jacket.

—Zora Neale Hurston

STRATEGIES FOR INCLUSION

Learners Having Difficulty Some students need personal involvement or a personal way to relate to the information in a story in order to focus their attention. Have these students share some personal experience where a family or group story has been passed on through the generations. Have them describe how they became familiar with the story. Then, have the students read the selection and find out how Hurston finally went about collecting African American folklore. *Remind students to choose a story they would not mind sharing with others.*

CROSSING THE CURRICULUM

Social Sciences Students can work in small groups to explore gender relations in various cultures. If possible, form groups that include students from various cultural backgrounds. Ask them to select two cultures to study. Have them inquire what each gender does in each culture that the other is not allowed to do. Have them ask what each gender talks about that excludes the other gender, how men's and women's ways of talking differ, and whether men and women respond to each other differently. Have them report their findings.

MAKING MEANINGS

First Thoughts

1. Did you identify with Hurston's love of books? What were your feelings about books when you were younger?

Reviewing the Text

- **a.** Why is Hurston's grandmother afraid of Zora's boldness?
- **b.** Why do white Northerners visit the school?
- **c.** What do the two young ladies send the narrator from Minnesota?
- **d.** What are the narrator's favorite books?

Shaping Interpretations

2. How would you **characterize** the narrator? Look back over your Reader's Log entries, and find examples from the text to support your view of Hurston.
3. What qualities does the young Hurston exhibit when she reads aloud in class?
4. What does Hurston think about the two women who visit? How do you know?
5. Why do you think the visitors invite Hurston to their hotel?
6. Why does the young Hurston treasure the books the ladies from Minnesota send her?

Challenging the Text

7. Hurston was criticized by some of her contemporaries because they felt she did not place enough emphasis on the racial oppression of African Americans by the white community. Using references from this autobiographical excerpt, explain whether you agree or disagree with this criticism.

CHOICES: Building Your Portfolio

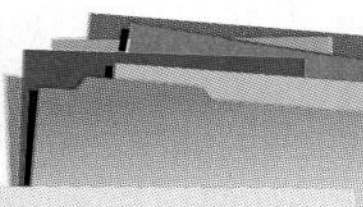

Writer's Notebook

1. Collecting Ideas for an Interpretive Essay

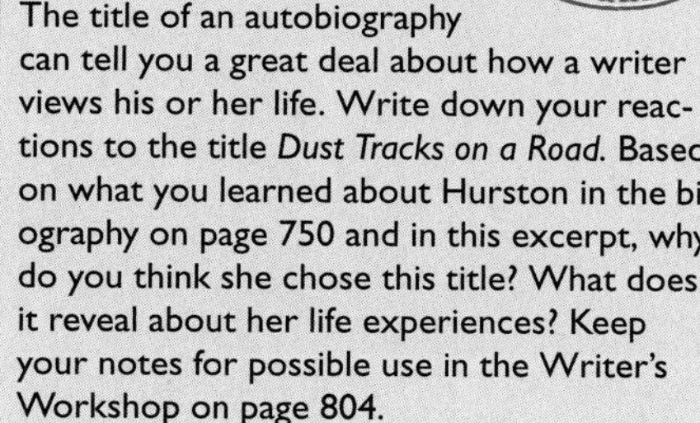

The title of an autobiography can tell you a great deal about how a writer views his or her life. Write down your reactions to the title *Dust Tracks on a Road.* Based on what you learned about Hurston in the biography on page 750 and in this excerpt, why do you think she chose this title? What does it reveal about her life experiences? Keep your notes for possible use in the Writer's Workshop on page 804.

Critical Writing

2. Real Life Stories

In a brief essay, compare this passage from Hurston's autobiography with the selection from Benjamin Franklin's *Autobiography* (page 86). You might compare (a) the narrator's actions and motives; (b) the narrator's relationship with other people described; (c) the incidents described, and why the narrator might have chosen to write about them.

Creative Writing / Performance

3. Dust Tracks Onstage

Autobiographies are often successfully adapted and dramatized for the stage. Working with a group, prepare this excerpt from *Dust Tracks on a Road* for performance. You will have to assign scriptwriters, a director, actors, costume designers, and set designers. You might also need a narrator to tell the parts of the story that are not told directly in dialogue. Consider using music (rock, folk, blues, jazz, or rap) to emphasize important moments.

Making Meanings

First Thoughts

1. Possible responses: Yes, except the books I read as a child were a lot different. Or I always liked books as a child because my father read them to me and used different voices.

Reviewing the Text

- **a.** Her memories from the days of slavery make her worry that Zora's boldness will be misinterpreted and that Zora will be punished by whites.
- **b.** Out of curiosity to see an all-black school.
- **c.** A box packed with books and clothes.
- **d.** *Norse Tales, Greek and Roman Myths,* Rudyard Kipling's *Jungle Books,* the Bible, and books by Robert Louis Stevenson and Hans Christian Anderson.

Shaping Interpretations

2. As self-assured, bright, and strong-willed. Supporting examples: Her independence in hitching rides with white travelers in spite of her parents' wishes; her reading ability, demonstrated in class; her attitudes toward stories in the Bible.
3. Her self-assurance, her dramatic flair, and her intelligence, shown by her passionate reading and deep understanding and appreciation of the text.
4. At first she is fascinated by their difference. She later fears that they are displeased with her appearance, for she thinks that the teacher is about to punish her.
5. Possible response: They appreciate her talent and wish to show their appreciation for her.
6. Because the books spoke to her so profoundly.

Challenging the Text

7. **(Evaluation)** Possible responses: She does not place enough emphasis on oppression, for she has her grandmother cower before white people; she does not question the sentimental good works of the white women from Minnesota. Or she presents a realistic view of racial oppression as experienced by African Americans living in the rural South by focusing on her own lack of knowledge about whites at the time, which points up the segregation of the times.

Choices: Building Your Portfolio

1. **Writer's Notebook** Remind students to save their work. They may use it as prewriting for the Writer's Workshop on p. 804.

Choices: Assessment Criteria For help in evaluating these Choices assignments, see the criteria in the *Portfolio Management System,* p. 160.

QUICK PLANNING GUIDE

Into the Poems

Through the Poems

Beyond the Poems

- **Writer's Notebook:** Collect ideas for an interpretive essay
- **Critical Writing:** Compare poems in a brief essay
- **Creative Writing:** Write introduction and portion of interview for newspaper article or TV news special.
- **Critical Writing/Research:** Write liner notes for recording of classic blues songs
- **Music/Performance:** Set passage to music or adapt blues song to poem

Springer/Bettmann.

Langston Hughes

(1902–1967)

One evening toward the end of 1925, the poet Vachel Lindsay was eating dinner in the Wardman Park Hotel in Washington, D.C. The busboy, a twenty-three-year-old African American, left three poems near Lindsay's plate. Lindsay was so impressed by the poems that he presented them in his reading that night, telling the audience that he had discovered a true poet—a young black man who was working as a busboy in the hotel restaurant. Over the next few days, articles about the "busboy poet" appeared in newspapers up and down the East Coast.

The busboy, Langston Hughes, was no beginning writer. In fact, when he shyly approached Lindsay, Hughes's first book of poetry, *The Weary Blues,* was about to be published by a prestigious New York company, and individual poems had appeared in numerous places. Lindsay warned the young poet about literary "lionizers" who might exploit him for their own purpose: "Hide and write and study and think. I know what factions do. Beware of them. I know what lionizers do. Beware of them." In response to Lindsay, Hughes wrote back: "If anything is important, it is my poetry, not me. I do not want folks to know me, but if they know and like some of my poems I am glad. Perhaps the mission of an artist is to interpret beauty to the people—the beauty within themselves. That is what I want to do, if I consciously want to do anything with poetry."

Before this encounter, Hughes had attended Columbia University and worked his way to Africa and back as a crew member on an ocean freighter. Ambitious and energetic, Hughes had learned early to rely on himself. He spoke German and Spanish; he had lived in Mexico, France, and Italy. In the years that followed his "overnight" celebrity, he earned his degree at Lincoln University, wrote fifteen volumes of poetry, six novels, three books of short stories, eleven plays, and a variety of nonfiction works.

Born in Joplin, Missouri, Hughes spent most of his childhood in Lawrence, Kansas, with his grandmother. When he was thirteen, she died, and he moved to Lincoln, Illinois, and then to Cleveland, Ohio, to live with his mother and stepfather.

Hughes began writing poems in the eighth grade, and he began publishing his work as a high school student in his school literary magazine. He read voraciously and greatly admired the work of Edgar Lee Masters, Vachel Lindsay, Amy Lowell, Carl Sandburg, and Walt Whitman.

The most important influences on Hughes's poetry were Walt Whitman and Carl Sandburg. Both poets broke from traditional poetic forms and used free verse to express the humanity of all people regardless of their age, gender, race, and class. Encouraged by the examples of Whitman and Sandburg, Hughes celebrated the experiences of African Americans, often using jazz rhythms and the repetitive structure of the blues in his poems. Toward the end of his life, he wrote poems specifically for jazz accompaniment. He was also responsible for the founding of several black theater companies, and he wrote and translated a number of dramatic works. His work, he said, was an attempt to "explain and illuminate the Negro condition in America." It succeeded in doing that with both vigor and compassion.

WRITERS ON WRITING

In his autobiography, Langston Hughes wrote about his early writing, "I had been . . . a writer who wrote mostly because, when I felt bad, writing kept me from feeling worse; it put my inner emotions into exterior form, and gave me an outlet for words that never came in conversation." In his twenties, he shunned the popular "slick" writing commercial writers produced and worked to earn a living writing seriously about African Americans.

PORTFOLIO ASSESSMENT

Portfolio Assessment For help with teacher assessment of reading skills, see the *Portfolio Management System,* pp. 54–55.

BEFORE YOU READ
THE WEARY BLUES

Reading Focus
Sweet Blues
Among the great contributions of American culture to the world is the music produced by African Americans: blues, ragtime, jazz, rap, and new musical expressions that are still evolving.

The kind of music known as the "blues" started to attract attention at the turn of the century, eventually becoming widely popular in the United States and abroad and making stars out of such blues singers as Bessie Smith and Ethel Waters. In this poem, Hughes tries both to report the experience of a "sad raggy tune" and to capture some of its rhythms in words.

Quickwrite
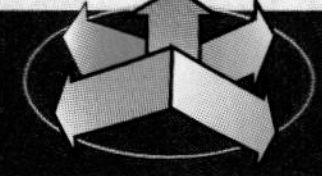

Blues music has influenced all kinds of popular music, from rock and soul to country, folk, and jazz. Jot down any associations you make to the word *blues*. What do you already know about blues music? Is there any blues influence in the kinds of music you like?

Elements of Literature
Rhythm
Rhythm in poetry is the rise and fall of the voice, produced by the alternation of stressed and unstressed syllables. Langston Hughes uses several different kinds of rhythms in "The Weary Blues." As he says in the first line, he uses the "syncopated tune" of a piano. He also uses the rhythm of everyday speech, the soulful rhythm of the blues, and even the formal meter of traditional poetry. His poems are true originals.

Background
On a March night in 1922, Langston Hughes sat in a small Harlem cabaret and wrote "The Weary Blues." In this poem, Hughes incorporated the many elements of his life—the music of Southern black speech, the lyrics of the first blues he ever heard, and conventional poetic forms he learned in school. While the body of the poem took shape quickly, it took the poet two years to get the ending right: "I could not achieve an ending I liked, although I worked and worked on it." When he at last completed the poem, "The Weary Blues" marked the beginning of his literary career.

The Weary Blues
Langston Hughes

Droning a drowsy syncopated tune,°
Rocking back and forth to a mellow croon,
   I heard a Negro play.
Down on Lenox Avenue° the other night
By the pale dull pallor of an old gas light
   He did a lazy sway . . .
   He did a lazy sway . . . **A**
To the tune o' those Weary Blues.
With his ebony hands on each ivory key
He made that poor piano moan with melody.
   O Blues!
Swaying to and fro on his rickety stool
He played that sad raggy tune like a musical fool. **B**
   Sweet Blues!

1. **syncopated tune:** melody in which accents are placed on normally unaccented beats.
4. **Lenox Avenue:** street in Harlem.

Using **BEFORE YOU READ** p. 761

Quickwrite
To help students understand the questions, play examples of the blues-influenced musical styles that are listed. The early Rolling Stones, for instance, are strongly blues influenced. The song "Roll Over Beethoven," recorded by the Beatles and written by Chuck Berry, is strongly influenced by the blues. Also influenced are rhythm and blues artists such as B. B. King and Eric Clapton. Let students listen and discuss their observations before they quickwrite responses.

A. Literary Element: Rhythm
? What does the repetition contribute to the rhythm of these lines? [Possible answers: It makes the lines more emphatic. The player's tune seems to sway lazily.] Have students note other instances of rhythmic repetition. ["O Blues!" "Weary Blues," and "Ain't got nobody . . . "]

B. Expansion
The word *fool* is used affectionately.

PROGRAM MANAGER

- **Planning Instruction** See Teaching Notes, *Teaching Resources B,* pp. 85–86, for information.
- **Audiotaped Readings** To help auditory learners, use the Selected Reading, Audiocassette 3, Side A, of "Harlem" in the *Audiovisual Resources Binder.*
- **Instructional Support** See Graphic Organizer for Active Reading, *Teaching Resources B,* pp. 95–96, for Through the Poem activities.
- **Application and Reinforcement** For reinforcement of the elements of literature, see Transparencies 15.2–15.3 in the *Audiovisual Resources Binder.*

- **Assessment** See Selection Test, *Test Booklet,* pp. 177–178.
- **Language Link** For instruction and practice in end punctuation see Language Link, *Teaching Resources B,* pp. 97–98, and *Language and Writing Skills Worksheets,* p. 129.

A. Literary Element: Dialect
Point out that the song-within-the-poem is in dialect while the bulk of the poem is in standard English.

B. Reader's Response: Shaping Interpretations

? What troubles might the musician be experiencing? [Sample responses: He could have lost his girlfriend, or he could need money.]

C. Literary Element: Theme
The poem contains two blues "songs." One is sung by the piano player about his troubles. Students should note the traditional blues themes—isolation and a wish for death—that are expressed in his song. The other song is the frame of the poem and focuses on the piano player and on the blues itself.

Out Chorus by Romare Bearden. Silkscreen (12⅜″ × 16½″).

Coming from a black man's soul.
    O Blues!
In a deep song voice with a melancholy tone
I heard that Negro sing, that old piano moan—
    "Ain't got nobody in all this world,
    Ain't got nobody but ma salf.
    I's gwine to quit ma frownin'
    And put ma troubles on the shelf."
Thump, thump, thump, went his foot on the floor.
He played a few chords then he sang some more—
    "I got the Weary Blues
    And I can't be satisfied.
    Got the Weary Blues
    And can't be satisfied—
    I ain't happy no mo'
    And I wish that I had died."
And far into the night he crooned that tune.
The stars went out and so did the moon.
The singer stopped playing and went to bed
While the Weary Blues echoed through his head.
He slept like a rock or a man that's dead.

OPTIONS FOR TEACHING

STRATEGIES FOR INCLUSION

Auditory Have students read along while you play an audiocassette recording of this poem, or have a small group of students rehearse and present a choral reading of the poem.

English Language Development Students may need to look up the definition of many of the vocabulary words in "The Weary Blues." As they do this, encourage them to include as part of their personal definition whether the new word describes the man, his music, the setting, or how he feels. This will help students incorporate the new vocabulary in a meaningful way into their own personal vocabularies.

Special Needs Have students who have difficulty reading with expression and rhythm listen to an audiotape of the poem with headphones while highlighting specific information. Give the students a clear transparency sheet to place over the poem in their book. Also give them two different colored highlighters. Have the students use one color to highlight the part of the poem that gives the musical rhythm and another color for the part that provides information. Have them circle the words that rhyme.

LITERATURE AND MUSIC

Birth of the Blues

When asked about the origins of the blues, a veteran New Orleans fiddler once said: "The blues? Ain't no first blues! The blues always been." The first form of blues, country blues, developed in several parts of the United States, most notably the Mississippi Delta, around 1900. Country blues tunes were typically sung by men—usually sharecroppers. The subject was often the relationship between men and women. As the contemporary blues singer B. B. King once said, the blues is about a man losing his woman.

From the start, blues music was improvisational—it changed with every singer and performance. Parts of lyrics were freely borrowed from other songs or based on folk songs or figures of speech. Lines might be repeated two or three times, then answered or completed by a rhyming line:

> Black cat on my doorstep, black cat on my window sill. (repeat)
> If some black cat don't cross me, some other black cat will.
>
> —Ma Rainey

The blues catch on. The earliest blues singers, among them Charley Patton, Robert Johnson, and Blind Lemon Jefferson, played at country stores, at Friday and Saturday night dances, at cafes, and at picnics. The first popular blues recordings, made in the 1920s, featured female singers such as Ma Rainey and Bessie Smith, who performed onstage, backed by a piano or a jazz band.

When rural Southern African Americans migrated after World War I to cities like Chicago, New York, Detroit, St. Louis, and Memphis, the blues sound evolved further. Musicians sang about their experiences in the city, adding the electric guitar, amplified harmonica, bass, and drums to blues ensembles. Musicians such as Sunnyland Slim, T-Bone Walker, and Memphis Minnie pioneered the urban blues sound in the 1930s and 1940s; the next generation included the blues greats Muddy Waters, Howlin' Wolf, and B. B. King. Since then, blues music has influenced virtually every genre of music, including folk, country and western, and—most profoundly—rock. Elvis Presley, Bob Dylan, the Rolling Stones, Eric Clapton, and Bonnie Raitt have all borrowed freely from the blues tradition. Today, blues music is still being played and created by such artists as Buddy Guy, Etta James, Otis Rush, Koko Taylor, and Robert Cray. They are carrying on a musical tradition that was invented at a particular time and place—the American South in the early 1900s—to express the African American experience. The genius of the blues is that it has honored its origins even as it expresses universal hopes, fears, and sorrows.

LITERATURE AND MUSIC

Ask students to identify the kinds of music they like, and ask them to determine whether each kind has any blues influence in it. Have students bring in cassette tapes of music that has such an influence and play a song for the class. Discuss the influence of blues on each selection.

PROFESSIONAL NOTES

Cultural Diversity The content of the blues frequently deals with disappointment. The repetition and pattern of the lines help emphasize the disappointment. The blues have a pattern of one long line, a second line that repeats the first or some variation of it, and a third line that rhymes with the first two. Hughes sometimes varies his lines so that two lines may equal one line of the blues. In the first stanza sung by the piano player, the second line is a variation of the first, and the third and fourth lines are combined to equal the third line of the blues pattern. In the piano player's second stanza, the first two lines equal the first line of the blues, the third and fourth equal the second line, and the fifth and sixth equal the third.

Critical Comment: Hughes and the Blues The critic Edward E. Waldron made the following comments: "Many writers/poets have attempted for years to incorporate the essence of the blues into works outside the reference of music—i.e., into stories and poetry. One of the most successful poets in this endeavor was Langston Hughes, the 'Poet Laureate' of Black America. In his blues poetry Langston Hughes captures the mood, the feel, and the spirit of the blues; his poems have the rhythm and the impact of the musical form they incorporate. Indeed, the blues poems of Langston Hughes are blues as well as poetry. . . ."

Into the Poem

Using Before You Read p. 764

Elements of Literature

Ask students to select words and phrases from each stanza that suggest the speaker's attitude and list them on the chart below. In the appropriate columns, they should state the literal meaning as well as the implied meaning. For each word or phrase, discuss how the implied meaning might suggest the speaker's attitude.

Word or Phrase	Literal Meaning	Implied Meaning
["Edge of hell"]	[Place of punishment after death]	[Misery, poverty, inability to improve one's life]

Through the Poem

A. Literary Element: Tone

? What is the tone of these lines? [Possible answers: Anger, frustration, bitterness.]

Metacognition How did you derive your answer? [Possible answers: Anger because the repeated negatives "never," "never," and "can't" build on each other and the emphasis makes the speaker seem angry. Frustration because the speaker cites an unjust reason that African Americans have heard before. Or bitterness because things are getting worse.]

Before You Read
Harlem

Reading Focus

Feeling Trapped

The Harlem Renaissance writers created many poems that were responses to the feeling of oppression that pervaded the lives of Harlem residents. Hughes himself wrote several poems called "Harlem." (Another one is on page 828.) This poem is set during the Great Depression, a time when even a one-cent increase in the price of bread could be disastrous, when being black and poor meant that there were limited opportunities.

A Dialogue with the Text

As you read this poem, look for signs of the speaker's emotional state. Is he angry, amused, baffled? Can he be described by more than one of these adjectives? Write down your thoughts.

Elements of Literature

Tone

Tone is the attitude a writer takes toward the subject of a literary work, the characters or events in it, or the audience that it is directed to. Some early African American writers conveyed their real emotions under masks of carefully shaped observations, images, and thoughts. In "Harlem," Langston Hughes manipulates the poem's tone to both hide and reveal his feelings.

Harlem

Langston Hughes

Here on the edge of hell
Stands Harlem—
Remembering the old lies,
The old kicks in the back,
The old "Be patient"
They told us before.

Sure, we remember.
Now when the man at the corner store
Says sugar's gone up another two cents,
And bread one,
And there's a new tax on cigarettes—
We remember the job we never had,
Never could get,
And can't have now
Because we're colored.

So we stand here
On the edge of hell
In Harlem
And look out on the world
And wonder
What we're gonna do
In the face of what
We remember.

Options for Teaching

Strategies for Inclusion

Special Needs Have students who have difficulty with visual perception, word decoding, and auditory reception do an activity that involves listening and speaking. First, have the students listen to the audiotape of the poem. Then, have each student read a stanza in the poem and summarize that stanza.

Advanced/Auditory Use "Harlem" to help students develop a sense of English stress patterns. Read the poem aloud and have them mark which syllables are stressed. Use this activity as a springboard for a discussion of the differences between stressed and unstressed syllables and the importance of this distinction, not only to poetry in English but also to ordinary speech.

Courtesy of the artist and Francine Seders Gallery, Seattle, Washington. Photo by Spike Mafford.

Harlem Street Scene (1975) by Jacob Lawrence. Serigraph (27″ × 24″).

RESPONDING TO THE ART: ABOUT THE ARTWORK

Harlem Street Scene by Jacob Lawrence is a serigraph, a color silk-screen print. The silk-screen process involves printing a flat color design through a piece of silk or fine cloth. A stencil regulates the flow of ink to different parts of the design, which is then printed on a surface beneath the cloth.

Technology Tip

TECHNOLOGY Selected poetry of Langston Hughes can be obtained from the Web server of the University of Windsor at **http://ie.uwindsor.ca/jazz/hughes.html**.

COOPERATIVE LEARNING

Multimedia Students should work together in groups of four to prepare a multimedia presentation that interprets Hughes's poem. One group member should be chosen to direct the group's progress and coordinate the final presentation. Each of the other three members will focus on a particular medium—art, photography, music, dance, video, or theater—to interpret the poem. Students may create their own drawings, paintings, photographs, musical compositions, dances, videotapes, or scenes, or they may use works by established artists.

PROFESSIONAL NOTES

Thematic Connections: "I, Too, Sing America" "Harlem" is a poem about the African American experience in the United States. Have students compare "Harlem" to Cullen's poems "Tableau" and "Incident." Ask students to evaluate which poem they think most effectively protests oppression and to explain why.

Primary Sources

Besides their obvious social value and function, house-rent parties were frequently necessary in Harlem culture. Economic conditions for black Americans during the 1920s were far from ideal. Job opportunities in most Northern cities were restricted and housing was severely strained. A small apartment, for instance, would often house two or three families, including friends and relatives, in conditions that were frequently unsafe, unhealthy, and overcrowded. Rents were high, and crime rates, even then, were rising. Saturday night house-rent parties were thus extremely important to the psychological health of the community, giving residents of Harlem a chance to momentarily forget the pressures of daily life and celebrate being alive.

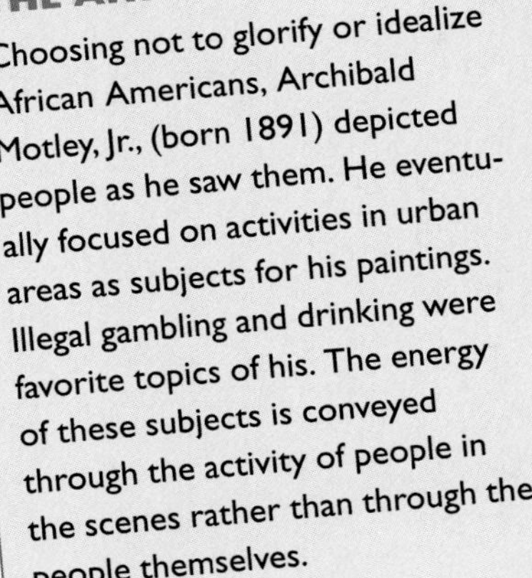

RESPONDING TO THE ART: ABOUT THE ARTIST

Choosing not to glorify or idealize African Americans, Archibald Motley, Jr., (born 1891) depicted people as he saw them. He eventually focused on activities in urban areas as subjects for his paintings. Illegal gambling and drinking were favorite topics of his. The energy of these subjects is conveyed through the activity of people in the scenes rather than through the people themselves.

PRIMARY **Sources** — AN ESSAY

Heyday in Harlem

Langston Hughes describes the vigor and excitement of Harlem in the 1920s and 1930s.

White people began to come to Harlem in droves. For several years they packed the expensive Cotton Club on Lenox Avenue. But I was never there, because the Cotton Club was a Jim Crow club[1] for gangsters and monied whites. They were not cordial to Negro patronage, unless you were a celebrity like Bojangles.[2] So Harlem Negroes did not like the Cotton Club and never appreciated its Jim Crow policy in the very heart of their dark community. . . .

It was a period when, at almost every Harlem upper-crust dance or party, one would be introduced to various distinguished white

1. **Jim Crow club:** segregated nightclub.

2. **Bojangles:** Bill "Bojangles" Robinson, star of black musical comedies and vaudeville.

Jockey Club (1929) by Archibald John Motley, Jr. Oil on canvas.

Schomburg Center for Research in Black Culture. Art and Artifacts Division. The New York Public Library, Astor, Lenox and Tilden Foundations.

STRATEGIES FOR INCLUSION

Special Needs Have students who have difficulty organizing information do an activity with the Primary Sources selection in which they can classify and group information as they read. Have students divide a sheet of 8 ½" x 11" notebook paper in half, vertically. Have them label one column People Who Came to Harlem and the other column Harlem Locals. As they read the excerpt, have them write down information that would match the appropriate category.

People Who Came to Harlem	Harlem Locals
[Celebrities, expensive Cotton Club, distinguished, visiting royalty]	[House-rent parties, bootleg whiskey, truck drivers, maids, fried fish]

celebrities there as guests. It was a period when almost any Harlem Negro of any social importance at all would be likely to say casually: "As I was remarking the other day to Heywood—," meaning Heywood Broun.[3] Or: "As I said to George—," referring to George Gershwin.[4] It was a period when local and visiting royalty were not at all uncommon in Harlem. And when the parties of A'Lelia Walker, the Negro heiress, were filled with guests whose names would turn any Nordic[5] social climber green with envy. . . . It was a period when every season there was at least one hit play on Broadway acted by a Negro cast. And when books by Negro authors were being published with much greater frequency and much more publicity than ever before or since in history. It was a period when white writers wrote about Negroes more successfully (commercially speaking) than Negroes did about themselves. It was the period (God help us!) when Ethel Barrymore[6] appeared in blackface in *Scarlet Sister Mary*! It was the period when the Negro was in vogue. . . .

Then it was that house-rent parties began to flourish—and not always to raise the rent either. But, as often as not, to have a get-together of one's own, where you could do the black-bottom[7] with no stranger behind you trying to do it, too. Nontheatrical, nonintellectual Harlem was an unwilling victim of its own vogue. It didn't like to be stared at by white folks. But perhaps the downtowners never knew this—for the cabaret owners, the entertainers, and the speakeasy[8] proprietors treated them fine—as long as they paid.

3. **Heywood Broun:** American journalist during the 1920s and 1930s.
4. **George Gershwin:** American composer of Broadway musicals and popular music.
5. **Nordic:** white.
6. **Ethel Barrymore:** American stage and movie actress.
7. **black-bottom:** popular dance of the late 1920s.
8. **speakeasy:** slang for club where alcoholic drinks were sold illegally during Prohibition.

The Saturday night rent parties that I attended were often more amusing than any night club, in small apartments where God knows who lived—because the guests seldom did—but where the piano would often be augmented by a guitar, or an odd cornet, or somebody with a pair of drums walking in off the street. And where awful bootleg whiskey and good fried fish or steaming chitterling[9] were sold at very low prices. And the dancing and singing and impromptu entertaining went on until dawn came in at the windows.

These parties, often termed whist[10] parties or dances, were usually announced by brightly colored cards stuck in the grille of apartment house elevators. Some of the cards were highly entertaining in themselves:

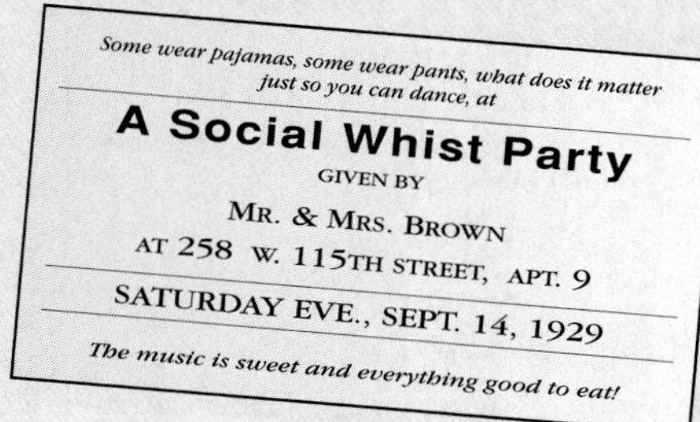
Some wear pajamas, some wear pants, what does it matter just so you can dance, at

A Social Whist Party

GIVEN BY

MR. & MRS. BROWN

AT 258 W. 115TH STREET, APT. 9

SATURDAY EVE., SEPT. 14, 1929

The music is sweet and everything good to eat!

Almost every Saturday night when I was in Harlem I went to a house-rent party. I wrote lots of poems about house-rent parties, and ate thereat many a fried fish and pig's foot—with liquid refreshments on the side. I met ladies' maids and truck drivers, laundry workers and shoeshine boys, seamstresses and porters. I can still hear their laughter in my ears, hear the soft slow music, and feel the floor shaking as the dancers danced.

—Langston Hughes,
from "When the Negro Was in Vogue,"
from The Big Sea

9. **chitterling** (chit′lin): food made from small intestines of pigs, deep-fried in hot oil.
10. **whist:** card game.

CROSSING THE CURRICULUM

Social Sciences Ask students to research and report on the Prohibition Era and bootlegging. Have small groups work collaboratively to write reports. As part of their presentation, a group may choose to focus on particular aspects or persons associated with the era: the Volstead Act; Al Capone; the "local option"; bathtub gin, white lightning, and near beer; repeal of the Volstead Act; the Woman's Christian Temperance Union; and life during Prohibition, for example.

Health Have student pairs research acute alcohol poisoning to understand more clearly the consequences that consumers of unregulated liquor were subject to during Prohibition. Have students give an oral report to the class. Ask them to explain and illustrate how alcohol affects the body and how this effect changes depending on whether alcohol intake is mild or extreme. In particular, have them explain and illustrate bodily responses during acute alcohol poisoning.

Making Meanings "The Weary Blues"

First Thoughts

1. Possible response: The man playing the piano; because of his sadness.

Shaping Interpretations

2. The first stresses individualism and optimism; the speaker says he is going to put aside his troubles. But in the second, the singer despairs, saying he wishes that he were dead.
3. Such words include "droning" and "drowsy" (l. 1), "rocking" and "mellow" (l. 2), "pale dull pallor" (l. 5), "lazy sway" (l. 6), "Weary Blues" (l. 8), "moan" (ll. 10 and 18), "melancholy" (l. 17), "troubles" (l. 22).
4. The repetition of words and phrases and the syncopation of longer lines when combined with shorter ones contribute to the rhythmic effect. Examples include "droning a drowsy" (l. 1), "Pale dull pallor of an old gas light" (l. 5), "lazy sway" (l. 6), "poor piano moan with melody" (l. 10), "sad raggy tune like a musical fool" (l. 13), "thump, thump, thump" (l. 23).
5. Ominous and foreboding; the extinction of the stars and the moon seems to hint that the singer dies, either literally or figuratively.
6. The singer sleeps "like a rock" or like "a man that's dead." The singer has given up hope; his spirit is dead.

"Harlem"

First Thoughts

1. Possible responses: Anger or frustration.

Shaping Interpretations

2. The lies they were told, physical abuse, poverty, and their inability to get a job because of their race.
3. Possible responses: It suggests misery, with no relief or escape. Or it contains a warning: In the boiling resentment of its citizens, Harlem is close to a violent destruction, which might resemble "hell."
4. Possible responses: Anger, frustration, or bitterness.
5. Possible responses: Powerlessness; they seem unable to decide what to do. Or a threat; they sound tired of doing with less and less.
6. Possible response: Sadly, to echo the weariness.

MAKING MEANINGS

The Weary Blues

First Thoughts

1. What would you say is the most powerful **image** in "The Weary Blues"? Why?

Shaping Interpretations

2. How does the message of the blues singer's first verse contrast with that of his second?
3. What are some of the words in the poem that help to create a slow, weary, melancholy **mood**?
4. Go back to your Reader's Log to see how well this poem fits your concept of blues music. Describe how the poem's structure suggests the rhythms of blues music. Point out examples of **alliteration** and **onomatopoeia** that also add to the poem's wailing, musical effect.
5. How would you describe the emotional effect of the **image** in line 32?
6. What **similes** in the poem's last line describe how the singer sleeps? What do you think the last five words suggest?

Harlem

First Thoughts

1. Review the notes you made in your Reader's Log. What one word would you use to describe the feelings of the speaker in this poem?

Shaping Interpretations

2. Name the specific hardships and injustices that the people of Harlem remember, according to the speaker in the poem.
3. In "Harlem," what does the speaker suggest when he says "Here on the edge of hell / Stands Harlem—"?
4. What **tone** does the repetition of "remember" create?
5. Do you interpret the poem's final stanza as an expression of powerlessness, or as a threat? Defend your opinion.
6. How would you read this poem and "The Weary Blues" aloud to express the **tones** you hear in them?

CHOICES: Building Your Portfolio

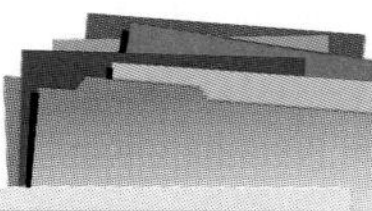

Writer's Notebook

1. Collecting Ideas for an Interpretive Essay

WORK IN PROGRESS

Create a chart analyzing the attitudes of the speakers in "Harlem" and "I, Too" (page 733). Note the ways the speakers are similar and the ways they are different. Save your notes for possible use in the Writer's Workshop on page 804.

Critical Writing

2. Echoes of Whitman

In a brief essay, compare and contrast Walt Whitman's "I Celebrate Myself and Sing Myself" (page 347) with Hughes's "I, Too" (page 733).

Creative Writing

3. The Harlem Beat

Write the opening paragraph for a newspaper article or TV news special about the Harlem described in "Harlem." Include a portion of an interview with an imagined resident of Hughes's Harlem.

Critical Writing / Research

4. Liner Notes

Write brief liner notes (400 to 800 words) for a recording of classic blues songs. Your notes should briefly explain what the blues are and how they developed, as well as tell a bit about each of the classic blues musicians (your choice) represented in the anthology.

Music / Performance

5. Blues Riff

Choose any passage in "The Weary Blues," and set it to a rhythmic or other musical accompaniment. Or, adapt an existing blues melody to the poem. Perform your work.

Choices: Building Your Portfolio

1. **Writer's Notebook** Remind students to save their work. They may use it as prewriting for the Writer's Workshop on p. 804.

PORTFOLIO ASSESSMENT

Choices: Assessment Criteria
For help in evaluating these Choices assignments, see the criteria in the *Portfolio Management System,* pp. 161–162.

MAKE IT NEW!

Theme: **Innovative Images**
American poets boldly established a new poetic order in the early twentieth century. Rejecting the artificial language and forced metrics of earlier verse, they sought to create a more concentrated form of poetry that relied on the raw power of pure images.

Thematic Focus

Each poem in this Collection reflects the influence of modernism on American poetry.

- **The River Merchant's Wife: A Letter** Using a series of scenes, the speaker recalls several stages of her life as she comments on time, love, and longing.
- **The Red Wheelbarrow/The Great Figure** Both of these short poems are snapshots that capture the starkness and simplicity of pure images.
- **Anecdote of the Jar** This Wallace Stevens poem centers on the image of a solitary jar that first energizes and then tames the wilderness that surrounds the hill on which it stands.
- **Poetry** The speaker suggests that genuine images are significant because they are useful, not because they can be manipulated to seem profound.
- **Chicago** Addressing the city as he would another human being, the speaker presents a series of descriptions that capture its life and exuberance in detail.
- **what if a much of a which of a wind** The speaker contrasts descriptions of the wind as a destroyer with a description of the steadfast, enduring power of the human spirit.

Literary Focus

Literary Element	Selection / Feature
Objective correlative	**The River Merchant's Wife: A Letter**
Imagery	**The Red Wheelbarrow/ The Great Figure**
Apostrophe	**Chicago**

Writing Focus

The following chart shows how the writing assignment for each selection relates to the writing assignment presented in the Writer's Workshop at the end of the unit.

Selection	Work-in-Progress Assignment
The River Merchant's Wife: A Letter	Compare two poems p. 777
The Red Wheelbarrow/ The Great Figure	Jot down notes about the use of concrete objects p. 782
Anecdote of the Jar	Analyze a poem p. 786
Poetry	Paraphrase criteria for good poetry p. 791
Chicago	Write notes comparing and contrasting two poems p. 795
what if a much of a which of a wind	Paraphrase a poem p. 799
Writer's Workshop	Write an interpretive essay pp. 804–807

Collection Planner

SELECTION/ FEATURE	PUPIL'S EDITION			
	Literary Elements / Active Reading	Writing	Speaking and Listening	Language and Vocabulary
The River Merchant's Wife: A Letter Ezra Pound (pp. 773–777) Primary Sources: A Few Don'ts by an Imagist (p. 776)	• Reader's Log p. 774 • Objective Correlative p. 777	• Critical Writing: Explain images from poem p. 777 • Creative Writing: Describe concrete image p. 777		
The Red Wheelbarrow/ The Great Figure William Carlos Williams (pp. 778–782) Critical Comment: (pp. 780–781) Primary Sources: Williams Talks about Poetry (p. 781)	• Reader's Log p. 779 • Imagery p. 779	• Critical Writing: Write essay p. 782 • Creative Writing: Write poem p. 782	• Speaking and Listening/Art: Present oral report p. 782	
Anecdote of the Jar Wallace Stevens (pp. 783–786) Primary Sources: Poetry and Meaning (p. 785)	• Reader's Log p. 784 • Symbolism p. 785	• Critical Reading: Write essay on images p. 786 • Creative Writing: Write "Anecdote of the ____" p. 786		
Poetry Marianne Moore (pp. 787–791) **Connections: Ars Poetica** Archibald MacLeish (p. 790)	• Reader's Log p. 787	• Critical Writing: Write comparative essay p. 791 • Critical Writing: Write letter to Moore p. 791 • Creative Writing: Write poem p. 791	• Performance: Record or perform different renditions of "Poetry" p. 791	
Chicago Carl Sandburg (pp. 792–795)	• Reader's Log p. 792 • Apostrophe p. 792	• Creative Writing: Write apostrophe p. 795	• Performance: Perform poem with group p. 795	
what if a much of a which of a wind E. E. Cummings (pp. 796–799) Primary Sources: Miracles are to come (p. 798) Student to Student (p. 798)	• Reader's Log p. 797 • Rhyme p. 799	• Critical Writing: Write essay p. 799 • Critical Writing: Write comparison-contrast essay p. 799	• Music: Create melody to accompany poem p. 799	
The American Language: American Slang Gary Q. Arpin (pp. 801–803)				• Try It Out: List slang words p. 803
Writer's Workshop: Interpretative Essay (pp. 804–807)		• Writing process: Interpretive essay pp. 804–807		
Language Workshop: Using the Literary Present (p. 808)				• Language Handbook: Tenses pp. 1224–1225 • Using the Literary Present p. 808
Learning for Life (p. 809)		• Design a brochure p. 809	• Create video documentary p. 809	

Collection Resources

Teaching Resources B	Audiovisual Resources Binder	Test Booklet
Cross-Curricular Activitiy p. 116	Fine Art Transparency 16.1	Collection 16 Test pp. 192–194

 Computer disk or CD-ROM

Audiocassette

Overhead Transparency

PROGRAM RESOURCES

Electronic Media	Teaching Resources with Organizer: Teaching Resources B	Teaching Resources with Organizer: Other Resources	Audiovisual Resources Binder
• Test Generator	• Teaching Notes p. 101 • Reading Organizer p. 104	• Test Booklet: Selection Test p. 183 • Portfolio Management System pp. 39, 163	• Selected Reading, Audiocassette 3, Side A
• Test Generator • Language Workshop: Run-on sentences	• Teaching Notes pp. 101–102 • Reading Organizer p. 105 • Language Link pp. 106–107	• Test Booklet: Selection Test pp. 184–185 • Portfolio Management System pp. 48–49, 164	
• Test Generator	• Teaching Notes p. 102 • Reading Organizer p. 108	• Test Booklet: Selection Test pp. 186–187 • Portfolio Management System pp. 53, 165	
• Test Generator	• Teaching Notes p. 102 • Reading Organizer p. 109	• Test Booklet: Selection Test pp. 186–187 • Portfolio Management System pp. 39, 166–167	• Selected Reading, Audiocassette 3, Side A
• Test Generator	• Teaching Notes p. 103 • Reading Organizer p. 110	• Test Booklet: Selection Test pp. 188–189 • Portfolio Management System pp. 53, 168	• Elements of Literature Transparency 16.2 • Selected Reading, Audiocassette 3, Side A
• Test Generator	• Teaching Notes p. 103 • Reading Organizer p. 111 • Words to Own pp. 112–113	• Test Booklet: Selection Test pp. 188–189 • Portfolio Management System pp. 54–55, 169	• Selected Reading, Audiocassette 3, Side A
	• Teaching Notes p. 103	• Test Booklet: Selection Test pp. 190–191	
• Writer's Workshop 2: Interpretation		• Portfolio Management System pp. 170–172	• Revision Transparencies 16.3–16.4
• Language Workshop: Consistency of tense	• Language Workshop pp. 114–115		
		• Portfolio Management System p. 173	

Proofreading Warm-ups

You may use the following exercises to help students practice their proofreading skills. Copy a set of incorrect sentences onto the chalkboard, and have students find and correct the spelling, punctuation, usage, and mechanical errors in each sentence. Ask students to share and discuss their responses.

	Sentences with Errors	Sentences Corrected	Skills Covered
1	**a.** after a uneventful Period between 1890 and 1910 a explosion of modernist poetry begun **b.** during this period many poets had began to explore the artistic life	**a.** After an uneventful period between 1890 and 1910, an explosion of modernist poetry began. **b.** During this period, many poets had begun to explore the artistic life.	Capitalization, Nonstandard usage, Comma usage, Verb tense, End marks
2	**a.** symbolism poets convay emotions through objects **b.** symbolists seeked a diffrent reality	**a.** Symbolist poets convey emotions through objects. **b.** Symbolists sought a different reality.	Capitalization, Spelling, Nonstandard usage, End marks
3	**a.** ezra pound, used objective correlatives in his works **b.** it is a set of objects used as a formula for an emotion	**a.** Ezra Pound used objective correlatives in his works. **b.** It is a set of objects used as a formula for an emotion.	Capitalization, Comma usage, Nonstandard usage, Spelling, End marks
4	**a.** william carlos williams was a medical Dr. he also happened to be a Poet **b.** williams early poetry was influenced by Pounds theorys of Imagism	**a.** William Carlos Williams was a medical doctor; he also happened to be a poet. **b.** Williams's early poetry was influenced by Pound's theories of Imagism.	Capitalization, Write out abbreviations, Semicolon usage, Run-on sentences, Apostrophes, Spelling, Comma usage, End marks
5	**a.** wallace stevens not only a poet but also Vice president of a co. **b.** stevens poem Anecdote of the Jar challenges the reader quiet a bit	**a.** Wallace Stevens was not only a poet, but also vice president of a company. **b.** Stevens's poem "Anecdote of the Jar" challenges the reader quite a bit.	Capitalization, Sentence fragments, Write out abbreviations, Apostrophes, Quotation marks, Spelling, End marks
6	**a.** archibald MacLeishs title Ars Poetica translates as "the art of poetry" **b.** of all sports it has been marianne moores favorite sport baseball that has more engaged poets imaginations	**a.** Archibald MacLeish's title "Ars Poetica" translates as "the art of poetry." **b.** Of all sports, it has been Marianne Moore's favorite sport, baseball, that has most engaged poets' imaginations.	Capitalization, Apostrophes, Quotation marks, Comma usage, Nonstandard usage, End marks
7	**a.** apostrophe is a literary technique in which a writer adresses a inanimate object or an idea **b.** carl sandburgs poem Chicago uses apostrophe to address the "City of the Big Shoulders"	**a.** Apostrophe is a literary technique in which a writer addresses an inanimate object or an idea. **b.** Carl Sandburg's poem "Chicago" uses apostrophe to address the "City of the Big Shoulders."	Capitalization, Indefinite articles, Spelling, Comma usage, Apostrophes, Quotation marks, Punctuation, End marks
8	**a.** poet E E Cummings altared english syntax (word order in his poetry **b.** notice the lack of capitol letters, and unconventional punctuation	**a.** Poet E. E. Cummings altered English syntax (word order) in his poetry. **b.** Notice the lack of capital letters and unconventional punctuation.	Capitalization, Periods for abbreviations, Spelling, Parentheses usage, Comma usage, End marks
9	**a.** slang marks members of a group and assert's the group's relatedness **b.** slang as we know it today used to be called cant and argot	**a.** Slang marks members of a group and asserts the group's relatedness. **b.** Slang as we know it today used to be called <u>cant</u> and <u>argot</u>.	Capitalization, Indefinite articles, Apostrophes, Comma usage, Underline words, End marks
10	**a.** the word cant referred to the secret language of thiefs **b.** the word argot referred to the specialized vocab. of people, such as sailers and farmers	**a.** The word <u>cant</u> referred to the secret language of thieves. **b.** The word <u>argot</u> referred to the specialized vocabulary of people such as sailors and farmers.	Capitalization, Underline words, Write out abbreviations, End marks

Collection 16

MAKE IT NEW!

Pound
Williams
Stevens
Moore
Sandburg
Cummings

Oread

Whirl up, sea—
whirl your pointed pines,
splash your great pines
on our rocks,
hurl your green over us,
cover us with your pools of fir.

—H. D. [Hilda Doolittle]
(1886–1961)

Make it new! Art is a joyous thing.
—Ezra Pound

"Oread"

? What is the sea compared to in this poem? What is striking or unusual about the image it presents? [Possible response: The poet compares the turbulent waters of the sea to the spreading green shapes of fir and pine trees. The image is unusual because it associates the dynamic movement of waves with the relatively static foliage of trees.]

PORTFOLIO ASSESSMENT

Parent/Guardian Involvement For forms that will help a parent or guardian review and respond to a student's portfolio, see the ***Portfolio Management System,*** pp. 62–63.

PROGRAM MANAGER

- **Integrated Assessment** For a summative assessment of the literature and language skills taught in this collection, see Collection 16 Test, *Test Booklet,* pp. 192–194.
- **Instructional Support** See Fine Art Transparency 16.1. Review teacher's notes for transparencies in the *Audiovisual Resources Binder* for suggestions on how to tie the transparencies to specific reading selections.
- **Extending Collection Theme** See Cross-Curricular Activity: Make It New! *Teaching Resources B,* p. 116, for an activity in another discipline and for evaluation criteria.

A. Literary Connections
The French writer Charles Baudelaire (1821–1867) was a very important forerunner of both the Symbolists and the Imagists. Baudelaire was strongly influenced by the writings of Edgar Allan Poe (1809–1849). In Poe's poetic theory, which emphasizes the conscious choice of sounds, images, and atmosphere to create an overall emotional effect, Baudelaire found inspiration for the development of his own theory of poetry.

B. Critical Reading: Making Inferences
? What effect might relying on imagination instead of reason have on the interpretation of a poem? [Possible answer: It might make the interpretation a subjective, personal experience rather than an objective analysis.]

C. Literary Connections
Briefly review the definition of Romanticism. Ask students to look back at the table of contents at the beginning of the book to skim the names of some of the authors and major works in the Romantic tradition.

Symbolism, Imagism, and Beyond

by John Malcolm Brinnin

Sometime in the early twentieth century, Americans awoke to a sense that their own national culture had come of age. This was true in poetry and in painting, in music and in dance, even in the new architecture of the skyscraper. Ironically, American poets found their new inspiration in Paris rather than their homeland. Learning from the French Symbolist (A) poets, who dominated French literature from about 1875 to 1895, Americans were able to produce a new type of poetry through which the true American genius could speak.

Symbolism: The Search for a New Reality

Symbolism is a form of expression in which the world of appearances is violently rearranged by artists who seek a different and more truthful version of reality. The Symbolist poets did not merely describe objects; they tried to portray the emotional effects that objects can suggest. But don't be misled by the term *symbolism.* It has nothing to do with the religious, national, or psychological symbols we are all familiar with. In fact, the Symbolists were concerned with getting rid of such symbols, which they saw as having become dull and meaningless through overuse. The Symbolists stressed instead the need for a trust in the nonrational. (B) Imagination is more reliable than reason, the Symbolists argued, and just as precise. With their emphasis on the mysterious and the intuitive, Symbolists hoped to bring revelation—self-discovery—to the reader through poems that lead the imagination to discover truths.

(C) Symbolism was a new manifestation of the **Romanticism** that had swept over Europe and the United States in the nineteenth century. The Romantics had stressed the importance of feeling and the independence of the individual, and they had made a great stand against the mechanization of human life. In the natural world, the Romantics found messages that spoke to the soul and gave it strength.

The Symbolists, however, could find neither solace nor spiritual renewal in nature. By the start of the twentieth century, nature had been subjected to so much scientific classification and interpretation that it had been stripped of much of its mystery. Artists now faced the onslaught of the modern world, which in spite of advances in science and technology suffered increased poverty, violence, and conflict. The Symbolist poets saw this new world as spiritually debased, and they faced it with a distaste amounting to outrage. They knew they could not transform or erase the modern world, though, so their revolt was spiritual. They tried to redefine what it meant to be human in a time when individualism was succumbing to the power of mass culture.

OPTIONS FOR TEACHING

STRATEGIES FOR INCLUSION

Interpersonal Place students into groups of three, and ask them to think of a popular media image that they consider dated or distorted. Then, have them brainstorm ways to update it or to make it more realistic.

Musical/Auditory Ask students to think of musical groups that are innovative and to list these groups' innovative qualities. Students may then compile a tape of innovative music and another of more conventional music and play them for the class, comparing the two and pointing out how they are different. Explain to the class that the Symbolists and Imagists were also poetic innovators who were distinguished by the striking originality of their images.

Visual Ask students to design visual symbols to represent issues important to them. Students may redesign a symbol to replace a well-known symbol (like the peace sign), or they may make up their own symbols for new issues. Ask students to explain their choices.

Night Fires (c. 1919) by Joseph Stella. Pastel on paper (22 ½″ × 29″).
Milwaukee Art Museum, Gift of Friends of Art.

Imagism: "The *Exact* Word"

The two Americans who first came into close contact with Symbolism and introduced the techniques of the movement to the United States were Ezra Pound (page 773) and T. S. Eliot (page 661). With the help of several British poets, a group of Americans led by Pound founded a school perhaps better known and understood in the United States than Symbolism itself. This was **Imagism,** which flourished in the years 1912–1917.

Like the Symbolists, Imagists believed that poetry can be made purer by concentration on the precise, clear, unqualified image. Imagery alone, the Imagists believed, could carry a poem's emotion and message. It could do this almost instantly, without all the elaborate metrics and

A. Expansion

Ezra Pound recalled his inspiration for this poem: "Three years ago in Paris I got out of a 'metro' train at La Concorde, and saw suddenly a beautiful face, and then another and another, and then a beautiful child's face, and then another beautiful woman, and I tried all that day to find words for what this had meant to me, and I could not find any words that seemed to me worthy, or as lovely as that sudden emotion." Point out to students that this extremely short poem took a long time to write. Pound's first attempt contained thirty lines; his second, fifteen. He did not produce the final, two-line poem until a year had passed.

stanza patterns that were part of poetry's traditional mode. The Imagists—including Pound, H. D. (Hilda Doolittle), and Amy Lowell—took on the role of reformers. They would rid poetry of its prettiness, sentimentality, and artificiality, concentrating instead on the raw power of the image to communicate feeling and thought.

The Imagists issued a "manifesto," or public declaration, proposing "to use the language of common speech," as well as "the *exact* word, not merely the decorative word." In the same spirit, they called for a poetry "hard and clear, never blurred or indefinite." Some of the Imagists' inspiration was drawn from Eastern art forms, particularly Japanese **haiku,** a verse form that juxtaposes two distinct images and invites the reader to experience the emotion created by the juxtaposition.

Pound defined an *image* as "that which presents an intellectual and emotional complex in an instant of time." Here is a famous Imagist poem that illustrates this concept:

In a Station of the Metro

(A) The apparition of these faces in the crowd;
Petals on a wet, black bough.

—Ezra Pound

A New Poetic Order

Today, poems with imagistic technique are commonplace. But at the time the Imagists published their manifesto on poetry's nature and function, their theory created a great stir. It insisted that the range of poetic subject matter might include the kitchen sink as well as the rising of the moon, the trash can as well as the Chinese porcelain vase. The strongest opposition to the Imagists was caused by their proposal "to create new rhythms—as the expression of new moods. . . . We do believe that the individuality of a poet may often be better expressed in free verse than in conventional forms." To tradition-minded poets, this **free verse**—poetry without regular rhyming and metrical patterns—was deplorable. It meant a loosening of poetic standards and an assault on the very craft of poetry. These poets did not yet realize that successful free verse was at least as difficult to create as verse written in traditional forms.

Although Imagism was a short-lived movement, it gave rise to some of our greatest poets. Many in the forefront of Imagism went beyond the movement's limitations and expanded its insights. Besides Pound, H. D., and Lowell, these included William Carlos Williams (page 778), Marianne Moore (page 787), E. E. Cummings (page 796), and Wallace Stevens (page 783). Eventually, Imagism came to stand for a whole new order of poetry in the United States. Most Americans became familiar with the movement mainly as the school of "free verse." But the Imagist program was not only a call for a new method of organizing lines and stanzas; it was also an invitation to a new way of seeing and experiencing the world.

Ezra Pound

(1885–1972)

Boris De Rachewiltz/New Directions Publishing.

Ezra Pound is remembered by many people as the man who was charged with treason during World War II and who spent many years in a psychiatric hospital. This notoriety has tended to obscure Pound's impact on American poetry. But his influence is still apparent everywhere; the generations of poets who have come after Pound have kept alive a complex memory of a man whose career wavered between brilliance and episodic madness.

Pound was born in Hailey, Idaho, and grew up in Pennsylvania. He taught at a conservative religious college for a while but his bohemian lifestyle was out of tune with his surroundings.

In search of greater personal freedom and contacts with European poets, Pound settled in London in 1908. There he became a self-appointed spokesperson for the new poetic movement known as Imagism. He also became a self-exiled critic of American life and torchbearer for any art that challenged the complacent middle class.

Pound—whose slogan was "Make it new!"—was a born teacher whose advice was sought by the most brilliant writers of the period. T. S. Eliot acknowledged Pound's valuable advice when he dedicated his great poem *The Waste Land* (1922) to Pound.

After World War I, Pound felt the need for even broader horizons than London offered him. He moved to Paris in 1921, and to Italy three years later, where he continued to write poetry and criticism. And now came a tragic turning point in Pound's life. His interest in economics and social theory led him to support Benito Mussolini, the Fascist dictator of Italy.

When World War II broke out, Pound stayed in Italy and turned propagandist for Mussolini's policies. In his radio broadcasts from Italy, Pound denounced the struggle of the United States and its allies against Germany, Italy, and Japan. Many of these broadcasts were viciously antisemitic.

When the American army advanced northward up the Italian peninsula in 1945, Pound was taken prisoner. He was confined to a cage on an airstrip near Pisa and eventually returned to the United States to be tried for treason. But psychiatrists judged him to be mentally incompetent, and in 1946 the poet was committed to St. Elizabeth's, at the time designated as a hospital for the criminally insane, in Washington, D.C.

Twelve years later, he was released through the intercession of writers, including Archibald MacLeish and Robert Frost, who argued that his literary contributions outweighed his disastrous lack of judgment and his notorious bigotry. Pound returned to Italy, where he lived the rest of his life. During these last years of exile, a reporter once asked Pound where he was living. "In hell," Pound answered. "Which hell?" the reporter asked. "Here," said Pound, pressing his heart. "Here."

When he died in Venice, Pound left behind a body of work extending from the delicate lyrics he wrote at the turn of the century to *The Cantos,* an enormous epic he did not complete until well over fifty years later. He also left a public record that still uncomfortably involves scholars and historians in "The Case of Ezra Pound."

QUICK PLANNING GUIDE

Into the Poem

- **Reading Focus: Scaffolding** Students consider the poem's speaker.
- **A Dialogue with the Text:** Take notes about the poem's setting

Through the Poem

Beyond the Poem

- **Writer's Notebook:** Collect ideas on tone and imagery
- **Critical Writing:** Write about images
- **Creative Writing:** Write paragraph that expresses feelings indirectly

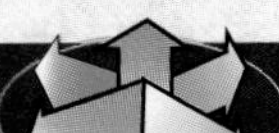

PROGRAM MANAGER

- **Planning Instruction** See Teaching Notes, *Teaching Resources B,* p. 101, for objectives, a summary, and literary elements for this selection.
- **Instructional Support** Before beginning the instructional lesson, see Graphic Organizer for Active Reading, *Teaching Resources B,* p. 104, for a Through the Poem activity.
- **Audiotaped Readings** To help auditory learners, use the Selected Reading, Audiocassette 3, Side A, in the *Audiovisual Resources Binder.*
- **Assessment** See Selection Test, *Test Booklet,* p. 183.
- **Reinforcement** Use the Words to Own worksheet in *Teaching Resources B,* pp. 112–113.

Using **BEFORE YOU READ** p. 774

Reading Focus

Have student pairs create a cluster diagram of commonly used expressions or clichés that might appear in a love letter.

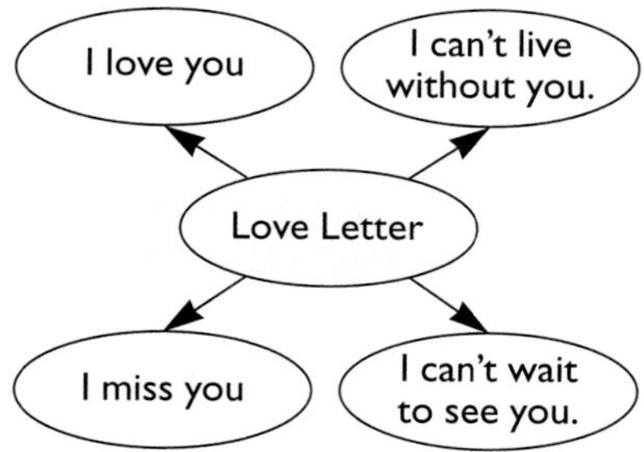

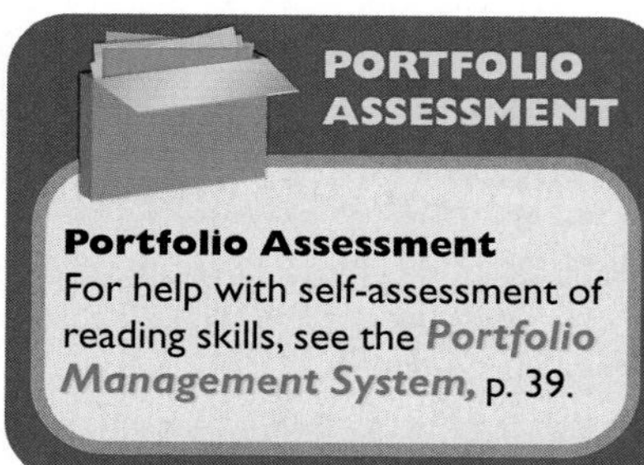

Portfolio Assessment
For help with self-assessment of reading skills, see the ***Portfolio Management System,*** p. 39.

BEFORE YOU READ
THE RIVER-MERCHANT'S WIFE: A LETTER

Reading Focus

I Sent a Letter to My Love
Have you ever been moved to write a letter to someone you loved and missed? In this letter-poem, Pound assumes the voice of a river merchant's wife as she contemplates her life, love, and longing. This poem is a tribute to Li Po (701–762), one of the greatest Chinese poets. Though Pound crosses generations, cultures, continents, and gender, the intimate tone of the poem creates a bridge for the reader, inviting understanding and even identification with the eighth-century Chinese speaker.

A Dialogue with the Text

READER'S LOG

This poem is not a word-for-word translation of Li's poem but an adaptation based on the feelings and images that Pound experienced when reading translations of the original poem. As you read, jot down **images** that identify the geographical and cultural location of the poem. Take notes also about the tone, the mood, the concerns of the speaker, and images that seem to suggest specific emotions.

Handscroll: *Wang Hsi-chih Watching Geese* (detail) (c. 1235—before 1307) by Ch'ien Hsüan. Ink and color on paper (9 1/8″ × 36 1/2″).
The Metropolitan Museum of Art, Gift of The Dillon Fund, 1973 (1973.120.6).

The River-Merchant's Wife: A Letter

Li T'ai Po

Ezra Pound

While my hair was still cut straight across my forehead
Played I about the front gate, pulling flowers.
(A) You came by on bamboo stilts, playing horse,
You walked about my seat, playing with blue plums.
And we went on living in the village of Chokan:
Two small people, without dislike or suspicion.

(B) At fourteen I married My Lord you.
I never laughed, being bashful.
Lowering my head, I looked at the wall.
Called to, a thousand times, I never looked back.

At fifteen I stopped scowling,
I desired my dust to be mingled with yours

OPTIONS FOR TEACHING

STRATEGIES FOR INCLUSION

Spatial To help students organize information about Imagism before they read the selection, have them record in a cluster diagram some of these descriptive terms found in the Collection introduction on pp. 770–772: symbols, imagination, images, emotions, free verse.

Auditory Ask students to close their eyes and to visualize the images in Pound's poem as you read it aloud to them. Then, have students describe the images to partners as the partners sketch them. Then, ask students to choose one of the sketched images and to write a short explanation of why they believe the image is important to the poem.

Visual Ask students to think of a particularly effective image from an advertisement. Ask them to describe the strategy that makes the image work. Then, ask students to sketch their own images for advertisements and to explain the strategies they used to create them. Then, ask students to choose an image from the poem and to explain how it might be used effectively in an advertisement.

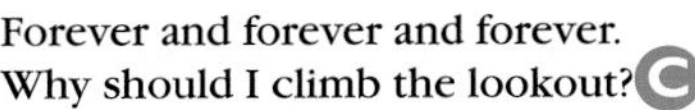

Forever and forever and forever.
Why should I climb the lookout? C

At sixteen you departed,
You went into far Ku-to-yen, by the river of swirling eddies,
And you have been gone five months.
The monkeys make sorrowful noise overhead.

You dragged your feet when you went out.
By the gate now, the moss is grown, the different mosses,
Too deep to clear them away!
The leaves fall early this autumn, in wind.
The paired butterflies are already yellow with August
Over the grass in the West garden;
They hurt me. I grow older.
If you are coming down through the narrows of the river Kiang,
Please let me know beforehand.
And I will come out to meet you
As far as Cho-fu-Sa. D

A. Critical Reading: Drawing Conclusions

? At what point in her life does the speaker meet her future husband? [When they are children.]

Metacognition How did you reach this conclusion? [Possible answer: I could tell by the way the speaker's hair is cut and by the fact that they are playing.]

B. Critical Reading: Making Inferences

? Why does the wife call her husband "My Lord"? [Possible answers: To show respect; or to show her love for him.]

C. Reader's Response: Shaping Interpretations

? How would you paraphrase this line? [Sample responses: Why should I look back on my old life now that I am married; or why look for more in life now that I am satisfied?]

D. Reader's Response: First Thoughts

? What emotions does this poem call to mind? [Sample responses: Thoughts of love, nostalgia, longing; or thoughts of pain, bitterness, despair.]

INTEGRATING THE LANGUAGE ARTS

Strategic Reading Help students monitor their own reading by demonstrating how you would read the poem. Begin by reading aloud the first stanza. Talk about any images it suggests, remark on the connotations of specific words, and explain how you react to the poem as you read. Then, have student pairs take turns reading the rest of the poem together. Each student should read a stanza, pause, and talk to the other students using the monitoring strategies you demonstrated.

CLASSROOM MANAGEMENT

Managing the Reader's Response Classroom Students are often reluctant to make oral responses because the worry about being wrong. Help students feel comfortable by encouraging a wide variety of response and interpretations and by offering sincere praise to students for the thoughtfulness of their interpretations, not just for their accuracy. After a variety of responses has been offered, ask students to return to the text to find support for their own interpretations.

Primary Sources

In "A Retrospect," Pound comments about the dangers poets face in writing free verse: "[Free verse] has brought faults of its own. The actual language and phrasing is often as bad as that of our elders without even the excuse that the words are shovelled in to fill a metric pattern or to complete the noise of a rhyme-sound."

Making Meanings

First Thoughts

1. Yes, because of the wife's request at the end of the poem; or no, the request is wishful thinking.

Shaping Interpretations

2. (1) The girl and boy play together as children. (2) The girl is married to the boy. (3) The girl stops scowling. (4) A year later, the husband leaves on a long river voyage.
3. Her change from shy silence to deep commitment. She may be expressing a fear that her husband will not return.
4. He drags his feet when he leaves.
5. The fall season contributes to the mood of regret and sadness.
6. The "paired butterflies" contrast with her own sense of separation. The five-month separation seems much longer because of her loneliness; she becomes more conscious of the passage of time.
7. If her husband will send advance news of his return, she will come to meet him as far as Cho-fu-Sa.
8. The husband may have left for business. His journey may have been long and dangerous; or he might have been delayed (or killed) by an accident.

An Article

Ezra Pound wrote the following "rules" for poets in an article in the March 1913 issue of *Poetry* magazine. Many of them are useful to all writers.

A Few Don'ts by an Imagiste

It is better to present one Image in a lifetime than to produce voluminous works. . . .

Pay no attention to the criticism of men who have never themselves written a notable work. Consider the discrepancies between the actual writing of the Greek poets and dramatists, and the theories of the Greco-Roman grammarians, concocted to explain their meters.

Language

Use no superfluous word, no adjective, which does not reveal something.

Don't use such an expression as "dim lands of peace." It dulls the image. It mixes an abstraction with the concrete. It comes from the writer's not realizing that the natural object is always the *adequate* symbol.

Go in fear of abstractions. Don't retell in mediocre verse what has already been done in good prose. Don't think any intelligent person is going to be deceived when you try to shirk all the difficulties of the unspeakably difficult art of good prose by chopping your composition into line lengths. . . .

Don't imagine that the art of poetry is any simpler than the art of music, or that you can please the expert before you have spent at least as much effort on the art of verse as the average piano teacher spends on the art of music.

Be influenced by as many great artists as you can, but have the decency either to acknowledge the debt outright, or to try to conceal it. . . .

Rhythm and Rhyme

. . . Let the neophyte know assonance and alliteration, rhyme immediate and delayed, simple and polyphonic, as a musician would expect to know harmony and counterpoint and all the minutiae of his craft. No time is too great to give to these matters or to any one of them, even if the artist seldom have need of them. . . .

Consider the way of the scientists rather than the way of an advertising agent for a new soap.

The scientist does not expect to be acclaimed as a great scientist until he has *discovered* something. He begins by learning what has been discovered already. He goes from that point onward. He does not bank on being a charming fellow personally. He does not expect his friends to applaud the results of his freshman classwork. Freshmen in poetry are unfortunately not confined to a definite and recognizable classroom. They are "all over the shop." Is it any wonder "the public is indifferent to poetry"?

Don't chop your stuff into separate *iambs.* Don't make each line stop dead at the end, and then begin every next line with a heave. Let the beginning of the next line catch the rise of the rhythm wave, unless you want a definite longish pause. . . .

If you are using a symmetrical form, don't put in what you want to say and then fill up the remaining vacuums with slush.

—Ezra Pound

OPTIONS FOR TEACHING

STRATEGIES FOR INCLUSION

Logical-Mathematical Have students organize Pound's "Don'ts" into a diagram web.

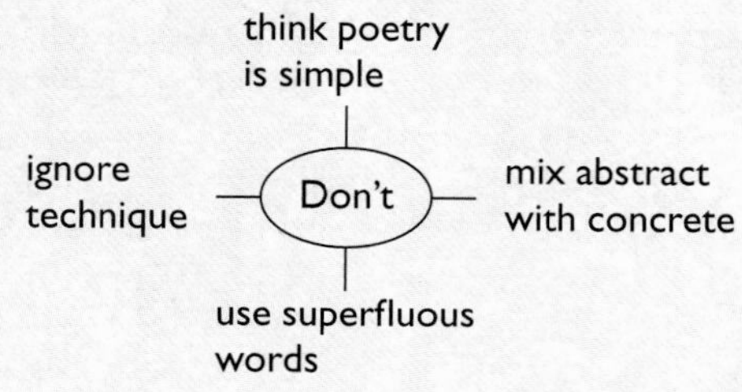

Special Needs To help students stay focused and find Pound's main ideas, have them create two-column organizers. Ask students to divide a sheet of notebook paper in vertical halves. Have them label one side "Do" and the other side "Don't." As the students read the rules, they should copy them into the appropriate column.

Making Meanings

First Thoughts

1. Do you think this letter-poem was ever sent? Why or why not?

Shaping Interpretations

2. What events are referred to in the first four stanzas?
3. How is the third stanza a turning point in the poem? What do you think the wife expresses in line 14?
4. What **image** suggests that the husband was reluctant to leave home?
5. How is the season appropriate to the **mood** of the poem? (Refer to your Reader's Log.)
6. What hurts the young wife in line 25, and why? Why does she say, after only five months, that she grows "older" (line 25)?
7. What does the wife promise to do?
8. Think of possible reasons why the husband left. Do you think he is ever going to return? What may have delayed him?

Elements of Literature

The Objective Correlative

Throughout Pound's poem, the letter writer's feelings are expressed more often by references to objects and activities than by direct statements. This is a method often practiced by Pound and identified by T. S. Eliot as the **objective correlative.** Eliot defined this term as "a set of objects, a situation, a chain of events which shall be the formula of [a] *particular* emotion." According to Eliot, the only valid way to express an emotion in art is to find such an objective correlative.

The term *objective correlative* soon became a permanent part of the vocabulary of poetic analysis. Several years earlier, however, Pound had anticipated the essence of the term, when he referred to poetry as "a sort of inspired mathematics" that gives us "equations for the human emotions."

Both Eliot and Pound believed that poetry is a means of expressing emotions *indirectly* but precisely. Poetry does this by finding the images and actions that best embody a feeling. (An example in Pound's poem might be the "river of swirling eddies.") This kind of poetic shorthand leaves the reader without the connections that usually join the parts of an argument, a story, or even most poems. Readers are forced to supply these connections and find the logic of a poem by themselves.

Not every poem deals in objective correlatives. Most poems have a logical or narrative sequence that is easy to recognize. But other poems are organized, not by a logical sequence, but by a *psychological* one. Such poems will make no logical sense until you supply the connecting links. These are the poems that can be analyzed according to Eliot's definition of the objective correlative.

Choices: Building Your Portfolio

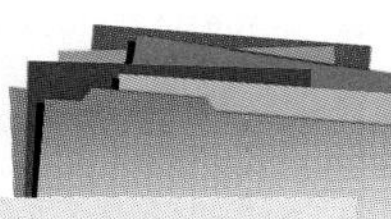

Writer's Notebook

1. Collecting Ideas for an Interpretive Essay

WORK IN PROGRESS

Re-read Emily Dickinson's poem "If you were coming in the Fall" (page 376), and compare it to "The River-Merchant's Wife: A Letter." Jot down the ways that Dickinson's poem is like and unlike Pound's poem in reference to its speaker's expectations, its tone, and its imagery. Save your notes for possible use in the Writer's Workshop on page 804.

Critical Writing

2. Indirect Expression

Choose at least three images from the poem, and, in a paragraph, explain how each image is used as an **objective correlative** to convey emotion indirectly.

Creative Writing

3. Tell It Slant

Choose a topic you feel strongly about. Then, think of a single concrete image that suggests your feelings. In a paragraph, describe your image in a way that communicates your feelings but doesn't express them directly.

Elements of Literature

Mini-Lesson: Objective Correlative

Students may find the term *objective correlative* easier to relate to film. Movie directors frequently use images and sounds to trigger specific emotions in viewers.

Choices: Building Your Portfolio

1. **Writer's Notebook** Remind students to save their work. They may use it as prewriting for the Writer's Workshop on p. 804. Have students work in pairs to create a Venn diagram that shows the similarities and differences between the two poems

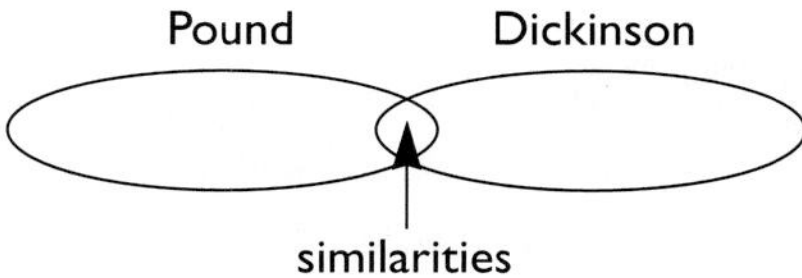

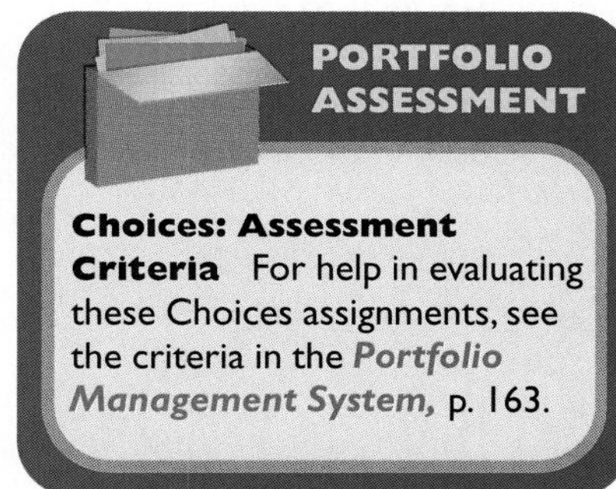

Choices: Assessment Criteria For help in evaluating these Choices assignments, see the criteria in the ***Portfolio Management System,*** p. 163.

Strategies for Inclusion

Visual For activity #1, have students fill out a graphic organizer like the following:

	image	tone	expectation
Dickinson	action (brushing, winding)	anxious	uncertain of outcome
Pound	quiet observations of garden in autumn	understated	becoming less hopeful

Special Needs To help students learn to interpret directions in activity #2, explain that it is important to follow instructions and not to do more or less than is asked for. This activity asks students to choose three images and respond in a paragraph.

Linguistic For activity #3, allow students to write a poem instead of a paragraph, as long as the poem contains a single concrete image that conveys a strong feeling.

QUICK PLANNING GUIDE

Into the Poems

Author Biography p. 778
Before You Read p. 779
- **Reading Focus: Scaffolding** Students note Williams's adaptation of the Imagist credo.
- **A Dialogue with the Text:** Describe images from the poems.
- **Elements of Literature: Imagery**

Through the Poems

"The Red Wheelbarrow" p. 779
"The Great Figure" p. 780
Critical Comment pp. 780–781
Primary Sources p. 781
Making Meanings p. 782

Beyond the Poems

Choices: Building Your Portfolio, p. 782
- **Writer's Notebook:** Takes notes on the author's technique
- **Critical Writing:** Write an essay about color and imagery
- **Creative Writing:** Write a poem
- **Speaking and Listening/Art:** Report on art

William Carlos Williams
(1883–1963)

William Carlos Williams was born in Rutherford, New Jersey, where he lived and practiced medicine as a pediatrician and obstetrician for most of his adult life. While studying medicine at the University of Pennsylvania, he came in contact with Ezra Pound (page 773). Pound's theories of Imagism had a considerable influence on Williams's early verse, which was published in *Poems* (1909) and *The Tempers* (1913). During the next two decades, however, Williams went on to evolve his own distinctive poetic style, which he called *objectivism*.

Williams defined the source of his poetry as "the local," by which he meant a strict focus on the reality of individual life and its surroundings. Williams looked for a return to the barest essentials in poetry. In this respect, he opposed such contemporaries as T. S. Eliot (page 661) and, to a certain extent, Pound himself, in their frequent use of allusions to art, history, religion, and foreign cultures. (Williams and Eliot, in fact, made no secret of their dislike of each other's work.)

In addition to poetry, Williams produced novels, plays, essays, and several autobiographical memoirs. His influence on twentieth-century American poetry, especially since World War II, has been considerable, and he was awarded the Pulitzer Prize in 1963. His masterpiece is the long epic *Paterson,* a poem that appeared in five volumes over a twelve-year span (1946–1958). In this partly autobiographical epic, a poet wanders the neighborhoods of Paterson, New Jersey, an industrial town near Williams's home, and meditates on the variegated experiences of urban life.

In his insistence on local topics and colloquial speech, Williams was allying himself with the kind of poetic revolution championed by the English Romantics a century earlier. William Wordsworth, in his preface to the second edition of *Lyrical Ballads* (1802), had written that poetry should treat "incidents and situations from common life . . . in a selection of language really used by men."

Pach/Bettmann.

Williams deliberately wrote in a spare, detached style about commonplace subjects, the very opposite of what many nineteenth-century American writers had thought of as poetic material. Using as his slogan "No ideas but in things," Williams wrote of such sights and events as animals at the zoo, schoolgirls walking down a street, a piece of paper blowing down a street, or a raid on the refrigerator. As Marianne Moore, an admirer, pointed out, Williams's topics are "American"—crowds at the movies, turkey nests, mushrooms among fir trees, mist rising from a duck pond, a ballgame.

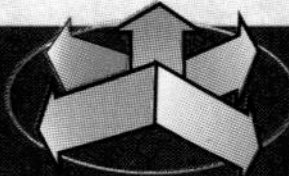

PROGRAM MANAGER

- **Planning Instruction** See Teaching Notes, *Teaching Resources B,* pp. 101–102, for additional information.
- **Instructional Support** See Graphic Organizer for Active Reading, *Teaching Resources B,* p. 105, for a Through the Poems activity.
- **Assessment** See Selection Test, *Test Booklet,* pp. 184–185.
- **Language Link** For instruction and practice in identifying and using prepositional phrases, see Language Link, *Teaching Resources B,* pp. 106–107 and *Language and Writing Skills Worksheets,* p. 103.
- **Reinforcement** Use the Words to Own worksheet in *Teaching Resources B,* pp. 112–113.

Before You Read
The Red Wheelbarrow
The Great Figure

Reading Focus
What You See Is What You Get
The Imagists placed primary importance on details that render particular objects or scenes just as they are, without symbolic or metaphorical meaning. As is evident in the following two poems, Williams adapted the Imagist credo to bring a realistic new dimension to American poetry.

A Dialogue with the Text
READER'S LOG
Immediately after you read each poem that follows, write down what it made you see.

Elements of Literature
Imagery
Imagery is the use of language to evoke a picture or concrete sensation of a person, thing, experience, or place. While many images appeal to the senses of sight, they may also appeal to the senses of hearing, taste, touch, and smell. William Carlos Williams's poems rely on clear and simple imagery that is described in direct, everyday speech.

National Museum of American Art, Smithsonian Institution. Transfer from the U.S. Department of Labor. Courtesy Art Resource.

Wheelbarrow (1934) by Morris Graves. Oil on canvas (31⅛″ × 35⅛″).

The Red Wheelbarrow
William Carlos Williams

so much depends
upon

a red wheel
barrow

glazed with rain
water

beside the white
chickens.

A

Using **Before You Read** p. 779

Elements of Literature
As students read each poem, have them consider these questions:
- Is Williams's imagery in this poem primarily visual?
- What other senses does this poem appeal to?
- Is anything about this poem difficult to understand?

A. Literary Element: Imagery
Point out to students that in a poem this short, diction becomes especially important. Which words are crucial to the imagery? [Answers may vary. Each word is important, but critics often focus on the color words, *red* and *white*, and on the words *glazed* and *beside*.]

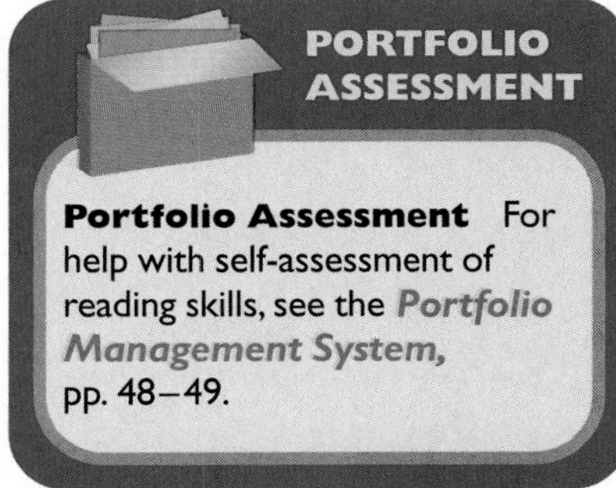

Portfolio Assessment For help with self-assessment of reading skills, see the ***Portfolio Management System,*** pp. 48–49.

Options for Teaching
Strategies for Inclusion

English Language Development To evaluate comprehension after students have finished reading, ask them to write alternative titles for each of the poems along with short explanations of their reasons for choosing the new titles. Then, provide discussion-skills practice by asking students to explain orally to partners which specific parts of the poems influenced their choices of titles. Remind students to ask their partners to clarify any words or phrases they do not clearly understand.

Special Needs Visual prereading activities often work well with students who have difficulty evaluating poetry. Before students begin the poem, have them look at the illustrations on pp. 779–780. Then, divide the class into mixed-ability pairs, and give students five minutes to brainstorm and jot down ideas for original poems based on the illustrations. After students have finished their poems, ask them to compare their poems to the ideas they developed from the illustrations. ☞

A. Reader's Response: First Thoughts

? Based on the title, what do you think the poem might be about? [Sample responses: It might be about a great person or a hero; or it might be about a famous statue.]

B. Critical Reading: Expressing an Opinion

Ask students to compare this poem to "The Red Wheelbarrow." Ask them which is the more purely Imagist poem and why. [Possible answer: This poem is more purely Imagist because the author presents an image without comment. In "The Red Wheelbarrow," the words "so much depends" color the image.]

C. Literary Element: Rhythm

This poem follows an irregular rhythm that shapes the poem to reflect the movement of the thoughts and actions it describes. Have students read the poem aloud, pausing slightly at the end of each line. Ask students how the pauses help to suggest movement. [Possible answer: The pauses help to make the number 5 on the truck seem to move with tension and deliberation, as though on a mission.]

D. Expansion

Point out that many poets of the last half of the twentieth century look to Williams—not to Pound or Eliot—as the writer who did the most to free modern American poetry from some of the artificial conventions of earlier verse.

The title of this small poem plays a joke on readers: What do you associate with a "great figure"? The American painter Charles Demuth (1883–1935) was so moved by the dynamic imagery in this poem that he was inspired to create his famous painting *The Figure 5 in Gold.*

The Figure 5 in Gold (1928) by Charles Henry Demuth. Oil on composition board (36″ × 29¾″).

The Metropolitan Museum of Art, Alfred Stieglitz Collection, 1949 (49.59.1).

The Great Figure

William Carlos Williams

Among the rain
and lights
I saw the figure 5
in gold
on a red
fire truck
moving
tense
unheeded
to gong clangs
siren howls
and wheels rumbling
through the dark city.

Critical Comment

So Much Depends

Williams's "The Red Wheelbarrow" at first glance seems to be very slight. But it has proved to have the leverage power that the ancient Greek inventor and mathematician Archimedes spoke of when he said, "Give me a place to stand, and I will move the world." Where William Carlos Williams stood was a place where ordinary things were *not* used as symbols or metaphors; they were simply ordinary things. The world he moved was the world of poetry. Before Williams, poets saw things not as things in themselves, but as objects to be used (to be compared, to be endowed with alien meaning, or to be played with); in themselves, things meant nothing.

How do we talk about this poem? When we consider analyzing it, where do we begin? Trying to answer these questions leads only to frustration. And perhaps frustrating our expectations is exactly what Williams had in mind.

OPTIONS FOR TEACHING

INTEGRATING THE LANGUAGE ARTS

Mechanics After students have read the poem, point out that it is actually a single sentence broken into separate lines. Ask students to write the poem out in sentence form and to add punctuation where they think it is needed. After students have finished, ask them to compare their punctuation choices. Remind the class that there are a variety of ways in which the sentence might be correctly punctuated.

CLASSROOM MANAGEMENT

Block Scheduling If you are working through this Collection with a block schedule, you may have difficulty teaching two complete lessons in one period. Use class time more efficiently by enhancing a single lesson with high-interest enrichment, reteaching, or cross-curricular activities such as the ones on p. 782. By not overloading students with too much information, this in-depth approach prevents confusion, and the added activities provide a stronger sense of wholeness and closure.

This poem is a composition of words so complete and simple that it denies all attempts to treat it as a poem.

And yet, there is the temptation to ask what happens in the brief course of the poem that has made it so durable. It was, after all, not a typographical accident; it was composed, and as such it can be analyzed. But our analysis must be concerned with the modest premises of the poem; we must not attempt to give it meanings that it does not claim.

The first line contains a vague but enormously suggestive phrase that leads the reader to expect an answer. (*What* depends on *what*?) But, except for the metaphorical lift of the word *glazed* in line 5, what the reader gets is only bare, flat reality—a moment captured as permanently as if it had been photographed. If the poem can be said to have some movement, some progress, from its first word to its last, it would be in what we call "reverse action." Our yearning toward what might be implicit in "so much depends" is quietly checked by the homely beauty of what *is*.

In many other poems like this one, Williams brought a realistic new dimension into American poetry. Williams showed us a way of recording the visible world in all its stark, simple reality, without filtering it through the Romantic imagination.

PRIMARY **Sources** | AN AUTOBIOGRAPHY

Williams Talks About Poetry

I'll never forget the dream I had a few days after he [Williams's father] died, after a wasting illness, on Christmas Day, 1918. I saw him coming down a peculiar flight of exposed steps, steps I have since identified as those before the dais of Pontius Pilate in some well-known painting. But this was in a New York office building, Pop's office. He was bare-headed and had some business letters in his hand on which he was concentrating as he descended. I noticed him and with joy cried out, "Pop! So, you're *not* dead!" But he only looked up at me over his right shoulder and commented severely, "You know all that poetry you're writing. Well, it's no good." I was left speechless and woke trembling.

• • •

What were we seeking? No one knew consistently enough to formulate a "movement." We were restless and constrained, closely allied with the painters. Impressionism, dadaism, surrealism applied to both painting and the poem. What a battle we made of it merely getting rid of capitals at the beginning of every line! The immediate image, which was impressionistic, sure enough, fascinated us all. We had followed Pound's instructions, his famous "Don'ts," eschewing inversions of the phrase. . . . Literary allusions, save in very attenuated form, were unknown to us. Few had the necessary reading.

We were looked at askance by scholars and those who turned to scholarship for their norm. To my mind the thing that gave us most a semblance of a cause was not Imagism, as some thought, but the line: the poetic line and our hopes for its recovery from stodginess. I say recovery in the sense that one recovers a salt from solution by chemical action. We were destroyers, vulgarians, obscurantists to most who read; though occasionally a witty line, an unusual reference, or a wrench of the simile to force it into approximation with experience rather than reading—bringing a whole proximate "material" into view—found some response from the alert.

—William Carlos Williams, *from The Autobiography*

Primary Sources

In the foreword to his autobiography, Williams talks about finding time to write:

"Five minutes, ten minutes, can always be found. I had my typewriter in my office desk. All I needed to do was to pull up the leaf to which it was fastened and I was ready to go. I worked at top speed. If a patient came in at the door while I was in the middle of a sentence, bang would go the machine—I was a physician. When the patient left, up would come the machine. My head developed a technique: something growing inside me demanded reaping. It had to be attended to. Finally, after eleven at night, when the last patient had been put to bed, I could always find the time to bang out ten or twelve pages. In fact, I couldn't rest until I had freed my mind from the obsessions which had been tormenting me all day. Cleansed of that torment, having scribbled, I could rest."

STRATEGIES FOR INCLUSION

Linguistic To help students relate to the author's comments in Primary Sources, have them develop an imaginary dialogue between Williams and his father. The dialogue should explain why the father thinks Williams's poetry is "no good," and it should indicate what Williams would say in response.

CROSSING THE CURRICULUM

Fine Arts Have students work in groups of three to research and prepare brief reports on the artistic movements—impressionism, dadaism, and surrealism—that Williams mentions in this Primary Sources excerpt. Have them present their reports to the class and provide visual examples of each artistic style, using slides or art books.

Making Meanings The Red Wheelbarrow

First Thoughts

1. Some may like the simplicity of the poem; others may find it puzzling.

Shaping Interpretations

2. Pleasure in the beauty of a simple scene.
3. Possible responses: The speaker; the speaker's happiness.
4. Students' images will vary in detail.

The Great Figure

First Thoughts

1. Most students will choose the image of the figure 5 itself because of its direct relation to the title.

Shaping Interpretations

2. The word is *tense*.
3. The images include rain and lights, the gold figure 5 and red truck, the gong clangs, the siren howls, the wheels rumbling, and the dark city.
4. Many students will be surprised to discover that the title refers to a number and not to a person.
5. The speaker may be excited about the images.

Beyond the Poems

Choices: Building Your Portfolio

1. **Writer's Notebook** Remind students to save their work. They may use it as prewriting for the Writer's Workshop on p. 804.

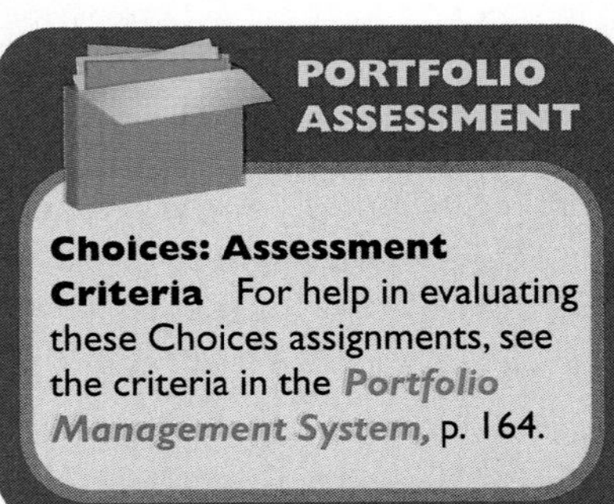

PORTFOLIO ASSESSMENT

Choices: Assessment Criteria For help in evaluating these Choices assignments, see the criteria in the *Portfolio Management System*, p. 164.

Making Meanings

The Red Wheelbarrow

First Thoughts

1. Do you like or dislike this poem? Why?

Shaping Interpretations

2. What emotion does "The Red Wheelbarrow" suggest?
3. Who or what do you think *depends* on the wheelbarrow and chickens?
4. Refer to the notes you made after reading this poem. Compare your mental images in class. Did you all see the same things?

The Great Figure

First Thoughts

1. Review the notes you took in your Reader's Log. What do you think is the most vivid **image** in this poem? Why did it stand out for you?

Shaping Interpretations

2. What one word is used **metaphorically** to describe the fire truck as if it were a person?
3. What **images** re-create specific sights and sounds?
4. Did you think the "great figure" was going to be the numeral 5 on an ordinary fire truck? What did you expect it to be? What is suggested by the term "great figure"?
5. How do you think the speaker feels about this brief scene?

Choices: Building Your Portfolio

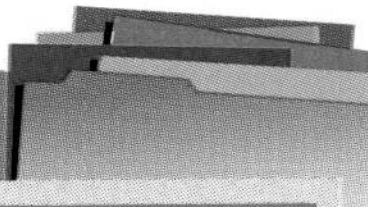

Writer's Notebook

1. Collecting Ideas for an Interpretive Essay

Jot down some notes about Williams's use of concrete objects to make you think in new ways about people, art, or life in general. Save your notes for possible use in the Writer's Workshop on page 804.

Critical Writing

2. In Living Color

Replace the colors Williams uses in "The Great Figure" and "The Red Wheelbarrow" with other colors (purple, hot pink, black, orange, and so on). In a brief essay, describe how the new colors change the **images** and feelings suggested by the poems.

Creative Writing

3. Picture a Poem

Find a painting or photograph that interests you. Write a six-line poem describing the images you see in the picture. Like Williams, you should try to record details exactly as they are, without using them as symbols or ascribing any significance to them beyond the fact that they simply are what they are.

Speaking and Listening / Art

4. Image Inspiration

Williams was a great admirer of the Renaissance Flemish painter Pieter Brueghel (1525?–1569); he was even awarded the Pulitzer Prize for his collection *Pictures from Brueghel.* Do some research to discover more about the links between poetry and painting. Research poems by Williams and others based on works of art, or works of art based on poems. Prepare an oral report of your findings. Read one or two poems aloud to the class, accompanied by a reproduction of the artwork that inspired them—or that they inspired.

OPTIONS FOR TEACHING

STRATEGIES FOR INCLUSION

Visual Encourage students to make use of multimedia resources when they do their research for activity #4. Most electronic encyclopedias contain a large number of images that can be scanned quickly, and the search engine of a computer-based reference source will help students to find links between famous poets and painters more easily.

Auditory Before students begin activity #3, remind them that sound remains an important element in modern poetry and that most poems are still meant to be read aloud. After students finish writing, allow some time for them to read their poems aloud to partners. Then, ask students to describe to the class the effects of some of the sounds in their partners' poems.

Wallace Stevens

(1879–1955)

The Bettmann Archive.

Americans are often surprised to learn that one of their greatest poets was a business executive who walked to his downtown office, sat on boards of directors, served as a vice president of a major insurance company, and became one of the pillars of a local society dedicated to the collection, investment, and distribution of money. Wallace Stevens was all of these and, almost incidentally, a genius of such magnitude that his place in American literature is still being reassessed and the depth of his vision ever more closely examined. Yet Stevens's life was a remarkably quiet, undramatic, and private one.

Stevens was born in Reading, Pennsylvania. He was educated at Harvard College and the New York Law School. Married in 1909 (to a woman who modeled for the image on the liberty-head dime), he and his wife had one child, Holly, who after his death assumed the editorship of his letters and other posthumously published works.

When he was thirty-six, Stevens moved to Hartford, Connecticut, where he entered the insurance business. He kept his creative life completely apart from his preoccupations as a business executive and maintained his literary friendships almost exclusively by correspondence. Happy with routine, a connoisseur of wines and French painting, and a lover of music, Stevens traveled to Cuba and often to Key West. Unlike most of his equally eminent contemporaries, he refused all invitations (until the last years of his life) to give interviews or to recite his poetry in public.

Almost forty-four when he published his first book of verse, *Harmonium* (1923)—a volume that sold a meager few hundred copies—Stevens came late and very quietly onto a scene already occupied by two quite different kinds of poetic expression: the colloquial rhythms and down-to-earth concerns of Carl Sandburg and Edgar Lee Masters, and the intellectual style exemplified by Ezra Pound and T. S. Eliot. Stevens shared the aspirations of both movements; yet he made his way along a path that avoided the extreme practices of either. His sense of place and American character kept him firmly rooted on native ground, but his grasp of metaphysical precision allowed him to soar into realms of "pure" poetry. Stevens went beyond where any other American poet had gone before.

Stevens admired the work of many contemporary American poets with whom he would seem to have little in common. Long before critics or the reading public were aware of William Carlos Williams's common speech and of his flat, almost casual rendering of everyday experience, Stevens knew exactly what his friend was up to. His respect and affection for Marianne Moore, his beloved "Marianna," was lifelong, as was his admiration for the precisely intricate structures that were the hallmark of her poetry. Toward Robert Frost, his attitude was one of friendly rivalry. "The trouble with you, Robert," Stevens once remarked in the course of one of their meetings, "is that [all of your poems] have *subjects*." That statement contains a clue to the distinctive originality of Stevens's work: For him, objects are important only as touchstones for the play of the imagination.

In 1955, Stevens's *Collected Poems* won the Pulitzer Prize in poetry. In a poem called "Of Modern Poetry," Stevens said this of his craft:

> It has to be living, to learn the speech of the place.
> It has to face the men of the time and to meet
> The women of the time. It has to think about war
> And it has to find what will suffice. It has
> To construct a new stage.

QUICK PLANNING GUIDE

Into the Poem

Through the Poem

Beyond the Poem

- **Writer's Notebook:** Freewrite on poem's meaning
- **Critical Writing:** Write an essay on the symbolism of the jar
- **Creative Writing:** Write a poem

ABOUT THE AUTHOR

Stevens struggled with the dilemma of how to be a writer and earn a living at the same time. After graduation from Harvard, he worked in journalism, became a lawyer, and worked in the insurance business.

Toward the end of his life, he commented, "It gives a man character as a poet to have this daily contact with a job."

PROGRAM MANAGER

- **Planning Instruction** See Teaching Notes, *Teaching Resources B,* p. 102, for objectives, a summary, and literary elements for this selection.
- **Instructional Support** See Graphic Organizer for Active Reading, *Teaching Resources B,* p. 108, for an Into the Poem activity.
- **Assessment** See Selection Test, *Test Booklet,* pp. 186–187.
- **Reinforcement** Use the Words to Own worksheet in *Teaching Resources B,* pp. 112–113.

PORTFOLIO ASSESSMENT

Portfolio Assessment
For help with self- and teacher assessment of reading skills, see the *Portfolio Management System,* p. 53.

Using **Before you Read** p. 784

Reading Focus

Write the meaning of *anecdote* on the chalkboard. Help students write a brief anecdote illustrating an aspect of another person's behavior to help them better understand what an anecdote is. *Remind them to write about an incident they would not mind sharing with you or the class.*

A. Reader's Response: First Thoughts

? In what way is this poem an anecdote? [Sample responses: It tells a pointed, allegorical story; or it is brief.]

B. Literary Element: Symbolism
Point out that the jar may symbolize the way art orders chaotic nature or it may symbolize human interference with nature.

Before You Read

Anecdote of the Jar

Reading Focus

More Than Meets the Eye

An **anecdote** is a brief story, usually one that illustrates an odd or amusing example of human behavior. The anecdote in "Anecdote of the Jar," in contrast, tells a big story. Stevens invites us to make our own emotional and visual associations in order to supply the details that lift this cryptic poetic anecdote out of the ordinary.

A Dialogue with the Text

READER'S LOG

As you read "Anecdote of the Jar," pay attention to the contrast between the scenes described in the first two stanzas. Then, write down what you associate with each scene, or image.

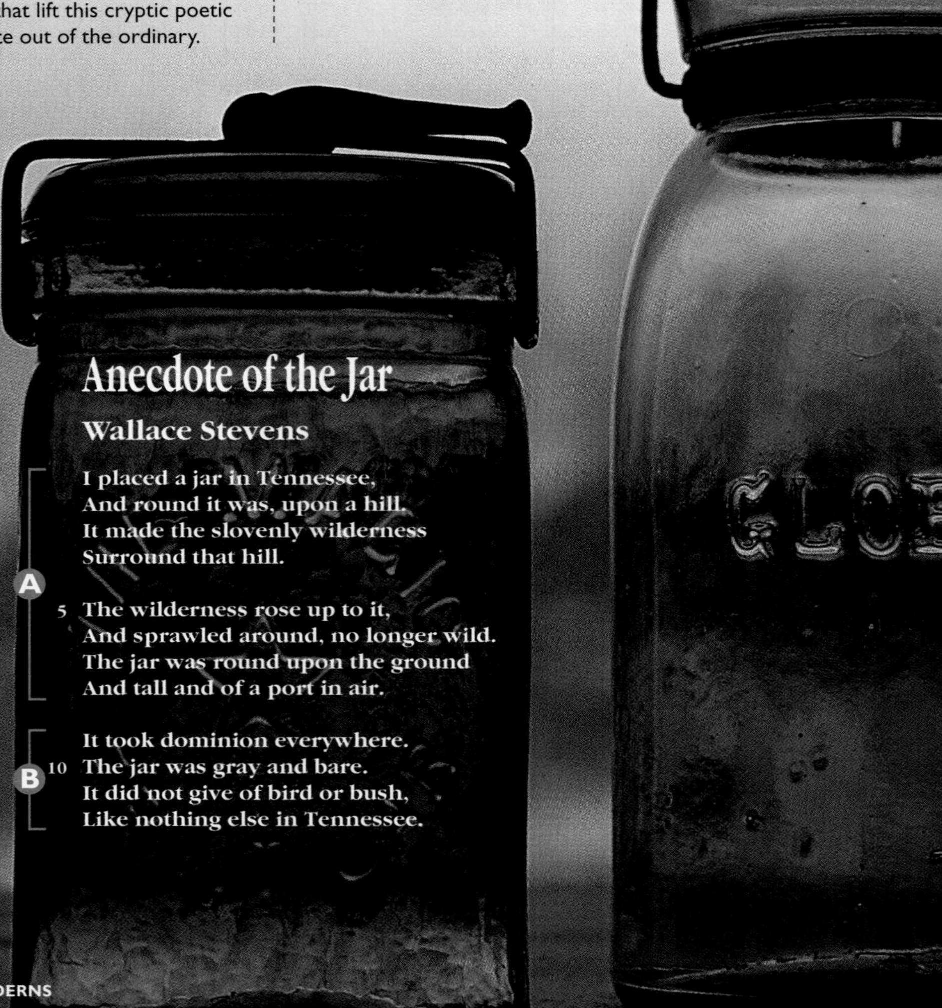

Anecdote of the Jar

Wallace Stevens

A

I placed a jar in Tennessee,
And round it was, upon a hill.
It made the slovenly wilderness
Surround that hill.

The wilderness rose up to it,
And sprawled around, no longer wild.
The jar was round upon the ground
And tall and of a port in air.

B

It took dominion everywhere.
The jar was gray and bare.
It did not give of bird or bush,
Like nothing else in Tennessee.

Options for Teaching

Strategies for Inclusion

Less Proficient Readers Ask students to create a cluster diagram like the following for each of these words from the poem: *jar, Tennessee, hill,* and *wilderness.* Ask students to use the diagram to record questions, associations, and ideas that each word brings to mind. After students have completed their diagrams, ask them to compare them in small groups.

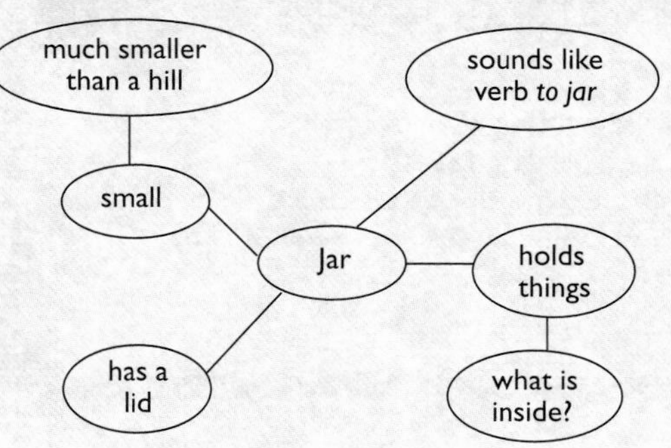

Integrating the Language Arts

Strategic Reading Ask students to investigate the precise meaning of specific words used in Stevens's poem. Have them concentrate on the words *jar, slovenly,* and *port.* Ask them to look up each word in the dictionary, suggest other words that might be used, and determine whether the poet may be suggesting a double meaning for each word.

PRIMARY Sources — LETTERS

The following statements are from letters Stevens wrote in the 1930s and 1940s.

Poetry and Meaning

Poetry is like anything else; it cannot be made suddenly to drop all its rags and stand out naked, fully disclosed. Everything is complicated; if that were not so, life and poetry and everything else would be a bore.

• • •

Obviously, it is not possible to tell one what one's own poems mean, or were intended to mean. On the other hand, it is not the simplest thing in the world to explain a poem. I thought of it this way this morning: A poem is like a man walking on the bank of a river, whose shadow is reflected in the water. If you explain a poem, you are quite likely to do it either in terms of the man or in terms of the shadow, but you have to explain it in terms of the whole. When I said recently that a poem was what was on a page, it seems to me now that I was wrong because that is explaining in terms of the man. But the thing and its double always go together.

—Wallace Stevens

MAKING MEANINGS

First Thoughts

1. Do any details in this poem puzzle you? If so, explain what they are.

Shaping Interpretations

2. Describe what the speaker does in the first stanza. What adjective does the speaker use to describe the jar? How does he describe the wilderness in which he places the jar?
3. In the second stanza, what effect does the jar have on the wilderness?
4. What does the jar *take* in the last stanza? What does it not *give*?
5. How would you paraphrase lines 11–12?
6. The jar is, on one level, a vessel designed by human ingenuity and shaped by human hands. (Some critics think Stevens was referring to a specific kind of glass jar, like a Mason jar, that was embossed with the brand-name "Dominion.") The jar contrasts with what simply arises out of the vast abundance of nature. What, in your view, is the meaning of the jar's "dominion" over the wilderness (line 9)? What might the wilderness **symbolize**?
7. Review the notes you made in your Reader's Log. In what sense might the jar **symbolize** anything made or devised by humans—including poetry, religion, law, and other human endeavors?

Connecting with the Text

8. Which details in this poem still puzzle you? Consider what you have learned about the poem, and explain why these details still puzzle you.

Primary Sources

Point out that Stevens felt complexity and irrationality were essential to the meanings of his poems. In his lecture "The Irrational Element in Poetry," Stevens suggests that poets select subjects as much by chance as by choice, and that the development of a poem often hinges on fortuitous and unbidden thoughts. Irrationality, he felt, was an involuntary and inevitable product of the creative process.

Making Meanings

First Thoughts

1. Many students will be puzzled by the description of action.

Shaping Interpretations

2. The speaker places a jar on a hill in Tennessee. The adjective he uses is *round*. The speaker says the wilderness is *slovenly*.
3. It civilizes or tames the wilderness.
4. The jar takes dominion—it rules its environment. It has no connection with the untamed wilderness.
5. The jar, unlike everything else in the natural environment, has no connection with its surroundings.
6. The jar's dominion is a civilizing force that threatens the natural world around it. The wilderness symbolizes the raw life force.
7. The jar may symbolize intrusion into nature by humankind.

Connecting with the Text

8. Students may remain puzzled about the poet's choice of symbols and by the lack of resolution in the poem.

OPTIONS FOR TEACHING

CROSSING THE CURRICULUM

Fine Arts To expand Stevens's ideas presented above in Primary Sources, have students work in groups of three to find a reproduction of a famous painting and two different critical interpretations of it. Then, have each group present its results: One student should display the painting, while the other two members read the interpretations out loud. Ask the class if they can think of more interpretations of the painting.

STRATEGIES FOR INCLUSION

Less Proficient Readers Read aloud the simile in the second Primary Sources paragraph. Point out that the man in Stevens's simile may be thought of as the words on a page that come together to make a poem, while the shadow of the man may be thought of as the associations—words, questions, symbols, and so on—that the poem brings to mind. Then, this simile might be seen as a suggestion that a poem should not be explained without referring to both the words of the poem themselves, and to the subjective associations they evoke.

Beyond the Poem

Choices: Building Your Portfolio

1. **Writer's Notebook** Remind students to save their work. They may use it as prewriting for the Writer's Workshop on p. 804.
2. **Critical Writing** Have students list on notecards specific images, ideas, and words that support their views.
3. **Creative Writing** It may help some students to look through photography books or news magazines for ideas about subject matter, specific imagery, and powerful symbols.

PORTFOLIO ASSESSMENT

Choices: Assessment Criteria For help in evaluating these Choices assignments, see the *Portfolio Management System*, p. 165.

Choices: Building Your Portfolio

Writer's Notebook

1. Collecting Ideas for an Interpretive Essay

WORK IN PROGRESS

Use the questions listed in the following guidelines to analyze any poem in this collection. Then, freewrite a paragraph explaining how all the elements work together to help create the poem's meaning. Save your notes for possible use in the Writer's Workshop on page 804.

Guidelines for Analyzing a Poem

1. What is the **subject** of the poem?
2. What is the **tone** of the poem?
3. What **images** does the poet use? What is their emotional effect?
4. What **figures of speech** does the poem contain?
5. What **symbols,** if any, does the poem contain? What do they represent?
6. How does the poet use **rhyme, meter,** and other **sound effects**? How does the poem's sound affect its sense?
7. Which elements are most important in the poem? Which are least important?
8. What does the poem's **title** mean?
9. What is the poem's **theme** or **main idea**?
10. What is your emotional response to the text?

Critical Writing

2. A Jarring Image

Some people think Stevens's jar symbolizes the way art gives order and meaning to "slovenly" nature. Others think the jar symbolizes human interference with nature. In a brief essay, explain which view you agree with, using evidence from the poem.

Creative Writing

3. Small Poem, Big Story

Write your own "Anecdote of the ______" poem. First, choose a familiar, simple object that **symbolizes** some larger concept, such as human endeavor, ingenuity, or love. Then, show that object in a landscape or other surroundings that somehow contrast with it. Use simple, straightforward imagery that nevertheless "tells a big story." Make your poem mysterious and out of the ordinary.

Peanuts reprinted by permission of United Feature Syndicate, Inc.

OPTIONS FOR TEACHING

STRATEGIES FOR INCLUSION

Interpersonal To help students start activity #1, place them into teams of five—two pairs and one team leader working on a single poem. The leader will organize and assign the specific questions to the student pairs. Team members will present their responses to the leader who will share them with the entire group before students write their paragraphs.

Special Needs For activity #3, have students choose an object with which they are familiar. Ask them to create a drawing, painting, collage, or three-dimensional object to illustrate their object. Have them either present their project to the class and describe the imagery that goes with it or attach two or three lines of verse, describing the imagery.

Marianne Moore

(1887–1972)

Esther Bubley/Life Magazine © Time, Inc.

Marianne Moore is remembered by many people as the woman who wrote a poem in 1955 celebrating the only World Series the Brooklyn Dodgers ever won. Moore spent almost half her life in Brooklyn, where she became one of the most famous supporters of the local baseball team.

She was born in Kirkwood, a suburb of St. Louis, Missouri. After graduating from Bryn Mawr College in Philadelphia, Moore worked as a teacher and a librarian, and later served as the editor of *The Dial,* a magazine that encouraged young writers. She spent a good part of her life caring for her brother and mother. When her mother died, Moore lost her best friend—and her toughest critic.

All the while, Moore was writing and publishing her poems in the prestigious journals of the time. By 1921, she was living in New York City and had just published her first collection of poetry, *Poems*. Among the literary celebrities in New York, she was easily identifiable by her antique capes and other nineteenth-century touches in costume.

Behind the costume, however, Moore was a serious poet of meticulous detail, clarity, and humor. Mixing with the *literati* did not mean that she endorsed their tolerance in matters of personal behavior or their embrace of anything in the arts that seemed new, or bold, or simply amusing.

In fact, the only thing "modern" about Moore was her poetry. Like a bird building an intricate nest, she carefully pieced together her poems by combining her own writing with quotations and excerpts from social science and natural history journals. It has been said of her that no one was ever more indebted to other writers for material and, at the same time, more original. Her poetry reflects some of the influence of the Imagists, and it also makes constant use of the concrete in the tradition of William Carlos Williams. Williams himself assessed his colleague's achievement when he said, "The magic name, Marianne Moore . . . I don't think there is a better poet writing in America today or one who touches so deftly a great range of our thought."

Like the graphic artists of the twentieth century, Moore was able to join apparently unrelated elements of what she observed and bring them into a "picture" with a single focus. In some of her poems, Moore works like a painter whose nervous strokes and jagged edges capture a hundred details in one moment stopped in time. What she says in one famous poem, "The Steeple-Jack," might apply to readers approaching her work for the first time: "[I]t is a privilege to see so much confusion."

Before You Read

Poetry

Reading Focus

All This Fiddle

Without even really knowing why, many people throw up their hands and say, "I hate poetry! I never understand it." In the following poem, Moore directly and humorously explains the usefulness and the characteristics of good poetry. She takes the role of the critic explaining her own work, as well as the critic confronting the entire genre. When we've finished reading Moore's thoughts on poetry, we might be a bit more inclined to admit that we really can find something interesting, genuine, and even exciting in "all this fiddle."

Quickwrite

READER'S LOG

Before you read, jot down your thoughts about poetry. Be honest: What do you like about poetry, and what don't you like? What, to you, should a poem be?

Quick Planning Guide

Into the Poem

Author Biography p. 787
Before You Read p. 787
- **Reading Focus: Scaffolding** Students consider dislike of poetry.
- **Quickwrite:** Take notes about poetry preferences

Through the Poem

"Poetry" pp. 788–789
Literature and Sports p. 789
Connections: A Poem
"Ars Poetica" **p. 790**
Making Meanings p. 791

Beyond the Poem

Choices: Building Your Portfolio p. 791
- **Writer's Notebook:** Paraphrase criteria for good poetry
- **Critical Writing:** Write comparison essay
- **Critical Writing:** Write a letter to the poet
- **Creative Writing:** Write list defining poetry
- **Creative Writing:** Write poem about nature
- **Performance:** Perform a poetry reading

Program Manager

- **Planning Instruction** See **Teaching Notes, *Teaching Resources B,*** p. 102, for objectives, a summary, and literary elements for this selection.
- **Instructional Support** See **Graphic Organizer for Active Reading, *Teaching Resources B,*** p. 109, for an Into the Poem activity.
- **Audiotaped Readings** To help auditory learners, use the **Selected Reading, Audiocassette 3, Side A,** in the ***Audiovisual Resources Binder.***
- **Assessment** See **Selection Test, *Test Booklet,*** pp. 186–187.
- **Reinforcement** Use the **Words to Own** worksheet in ***Teaching Resources B,*** pp. 112–113.

Using **BEFORE YOU READ** p. 787

Reading Focus

Ask students to write the word *poetry* in the middle of a sheet of paper and to make a cluster diagram around it of reasons why people enjoy poetry.

A. Reader's Response: First Thoughts

? Do you think the poet really dislikes poetry? [Sample responses: No, she is probably just agreeing that poetry is simply not as important as life; or yes, even though she writes poetry, she can still dislike it.]

Portfolio Assessment
For help with self-assessment of reading skills, see the ***Portfolio Management System,*** p. 39.

Baseball at Night (1934) by Morris Kantor. Oil on linen (37″ × 47 ¼″).

National Museum of American Art, Smithsonian Institution. Courtesy Art Resource.

Poetry

Marianne Moore

(A) I, too, dislike it: there are things that are important beyond all this fiddle.°
  Reading it, however, with a perfect contempt for it, one discovers in
  it after all, a place for the genuine.
    Hands that can grasp, eyes
    that can dilate, hair that can rise
      if it must, these things are important not because a

high-sounding interpretation can be put upon them but because they are
  useful. When they become so derivative° as to become unintelligible,
  the same thing may be said for all of us, that we
    do not admire what
    we cannot understand: the bat
      holding on upside down or in quest of something to

1. **fiddle:** slang for "nonsense."
8. **derivative:** based so much on the work of others as to show no originality.

OPTIONS FOR TEACHING

STRATEGIES FOR INCLUSION

English Language Development Students may find this poem more difficult to read than the poems that precede it in this Collection. Before students read this poem, briefly review the usage rules for the punctuation marks it contains. Point out that a colon signals an explanation or a list to follow; a period signals a full stop, while a comma signals a pause; a dash may also signal a pause, but it often signals an abrupt change in thought; and a semicolon signals a pause between two sentences that are more closely related than sentences separated by a period. Help students to read and understand "Poetry" by asking them to look for punctuation as they read and to pause at the end marks in the poem, not just at the end of each line.

INTEGRATING THE LANGUAGE ARTS

Writing: Poem Point out that by choosing the form of a poem to comment on poetry, Moore is able to present her ideas in a concise and interesting way. Ask students to write their own poems about poetry, modeled on Moore's poem. Have students read their poems aloud, and lead a discussion about the similarities and difference between students' views.

eat, elephants pushing, a wild horse taking a roll, a tireless wolf under
a tree, the immovable critic twitching his skin like a horse that feels a flea, the base-
ball fan, the statistician—
nor is it valid
to discriminate against 'business documents and

school-books'; all these phenomena are important. One must make a distinction
however: when dragged into prominence by half poets, the result is not poetry,
nor till the poets among us can be
'literalists of
the imagination'—above
insolence and triviality and can present

for inspection, 'imaginary gardens with real toads in them,' shall we have
it. In the meantime, if you demand on the one hand,
the raw material of poetry in
all its rawness and
that which is on the other hand
genuine, then you are interested in poetry.

Literature and Sports

This Writing Life, This Sporting Life

Of all sports, it has been Marianne Moore's favorite sport, baseball (she was a passionate Brooklyn Dodgers fan), that has most engaged the imagination of modern American writers. Why? Perhaps partly because of baseball's long history in the United States (the first game played under modern rules was in 1846); perhaps because of the mystery of its simultaneous simplicity and complexity; or perhaps because its amazing feats and bizarre anecdotes make the game and its players almost larger than life (think of the New York Yankees' Dave Winfield beaning a sea gull as he returned a ball from the outfield).

Possibly the most popular and enduring literary memorial to baseball in verse came from Ernest Lawrence Thayer, whose mock-heroic poem "Casey at the Bat" was first published in 1888. Some three decades later, newspaper writers like Ring Lardner and Damon Runyon were writing vividly and humorously about the sport. Bernard Malamud's *The Natural* (1952) tells the story of Roy Hobbs, a rookie of prodigious abilities who, victimized by those around him, ends up a loser both professionally and personally. (The 1984 film, which gives the story a happy ending, features Robert Redford as Hobbs.) More recently, the Canadian writer W. P. Kinsella mixed fantasy and reality in *Shoeless Joe* (1982), later made into the film *Field of Dreams* (1989) with Kevin Costner. Kinsella tells the story of a fan who builds a baseball diamond in an Iowa cornfield, magically bringing back members of the 1919 White Sox team.

In the words of *The New Yorker*'s staff writer Roger Angell, himself a graceful chronicler of the game: "Always, it seems, there is something more to be discovered about this game." No wonder Marianne Moore found a kind of poetry in baseball.

B. Humanities Connection
Moore alludes to a quotation from the *Diary of Tolstoy,* in which Tolstoy writes that "poetry is everything with the exception of business documents and school books."

C. Reader's Response: Shaping Interpretations
? What does Moore finally tell the person who dislikes poetry?
[Sample responses: If you are interested in life itself and what is genuine, poetry has something to offer you; or you may be someone who would like poetry if exposed to poets.]

LITERATURE AND SPORTS

Point out that a variety of baseball terms are often used as **metaphors** and **similes** in conversation, in prose, and sometimes in poetry. Ask students to explain some of the metaphorical meanings of the following baseball terms: big leagues, curve ball, heavy hitter, whiff, squeeze play, hit one out of the park, steal home, clutch player.

PROFESSIONAL NOTES

Critical Comment: Moore's Poetry T. S. Eliot once wrote of Moore's poetry: "She seems to have saturated her mind in the perfections of prose, in its precision rather than its purple; and to have found her rhythm, her poetry, her appreciation of the individual word, for herself."

ASSESSMENT TOOLS

Observation Assessment: Speaking Use this scale to assess students' speaking performances when they present oral reports before the class.

1=Good 2=Fair 3=Needs Improvement

_____ Appears self-assured
_____ Shows good pronunciation and grammar skills
_____ Speaks clearly, uses pleasant voice, and projects to audience
_____ Has accurate, well-organized material
_____ Has logical, interesting introduction and conclusion
_____ Holds audience's attention

A. Reader's Response: Shaping Interpretations

? In what sense must a poem be "not true"? [Sample responses: It must suggest rather than state literal facts; or it can lie about reality while containing its own inner truth.]

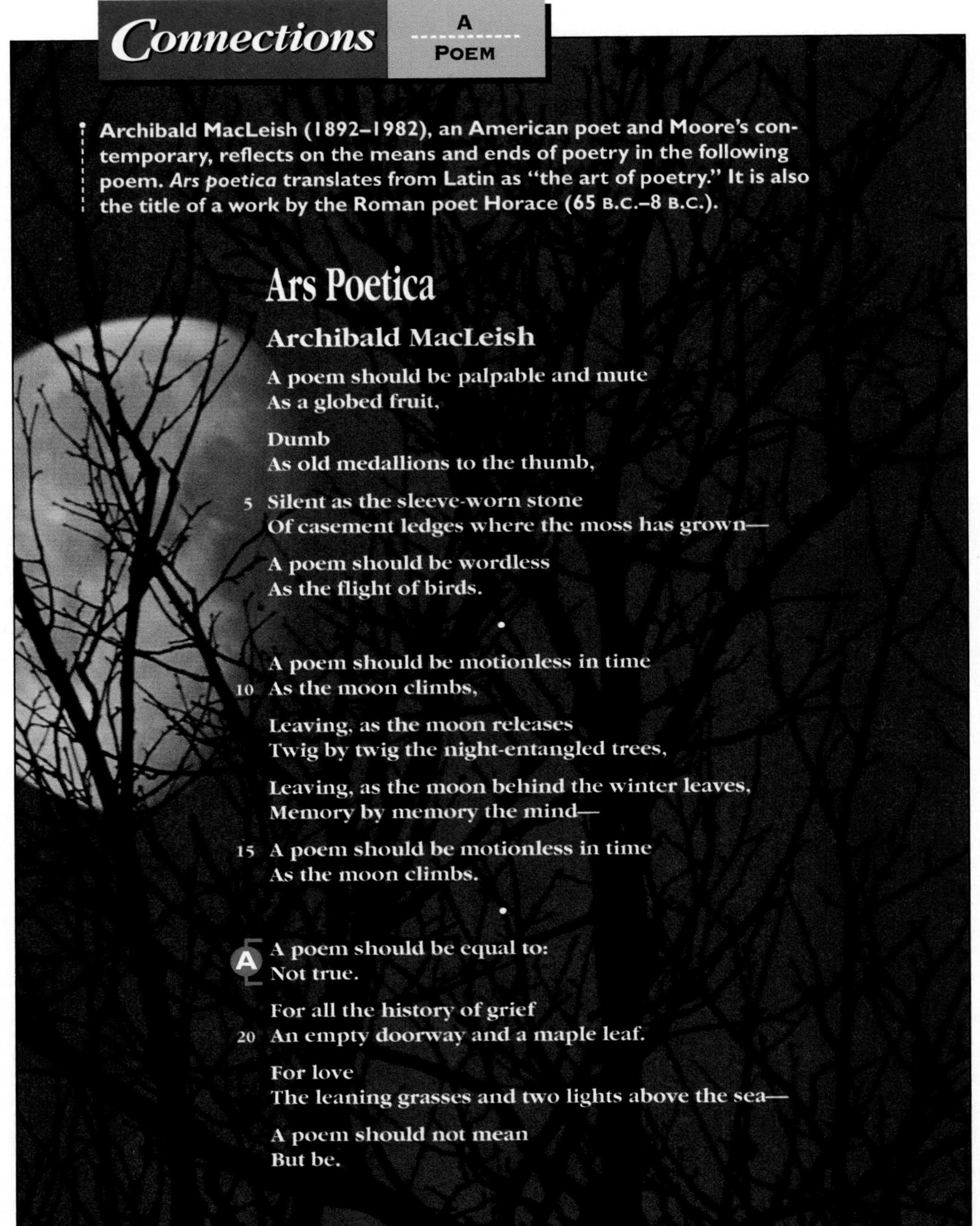

Connections

A POEM

Archibald MacLeish (1892–1982), an American poet and Moore's contemporary, reflects on the means and ends of poetry in the following poem. *Ars poetica* translates from Latin as "the art of poetry." It is also the title of a work by the Roman poet Horace (65 B.C.–8 B.C.).

Ars Poetica

Archibald MacLeish

A poem should be palpable and mute
As a globed fruit,

Dumb
As old medallions to the thumb,

Silent as the sleeve-worn stone
Of casement ledges where the moss has grown—

A poem should be wordless
As the flight of birds.

•

A poem should be motionless in time
As the moon climbs,

Leaving, as the moon releases
Twig by twig the night-entangled trees,

Leaving, as the moon behind the winter leaves,
Memory by memory the mind—

A poem should be motionless in time
As the moon climbs.

•

A A poem should be equal to:
Not true.

For all the history of grief
An empty doorway and a maple leaf.

For love
The leaning grasses and two lights above the sea—

A poem should not mean
But be.

CONNECTING WITH "POETRY"

Poetics, the aesthetic theory of poetry, is extremely important to both Moore and MacLeish, who have definite ideas about what poetry should be. Ask the class how MacLeish's requirement that a poem be "palpable and mute" is like Moore's urging for "imaginary gardens with real toads in them." Have the class brainstorm images from the poems that are similar or that recall each other in some way, while you cluster the images on the chalkboard. The entire class may contribute drawings, magazine illustrations or photographs, or found objects to a group collage that combines the poets' ideas on poetics.

MAKING MEANINGS

First Thoughts

1. How do *you* feel about poetry? Do you agree with Moore about what "real" poetry is? Review the notes you made in your Reader's Log Quick-write.

Shaping Interpretations

2. Whom do you think Moore addresses in this poem?
3. What kind of poetry does Moore dislike?
4. What elements does Moore think useful poetry should contain?
5. Moore says "'literalists of the imagination'" are necessary for true poetry. What do you think she means? How is this idea related to those "imaginary gardens with real toads in them"?
6. How might the kind of poetry Moore describes in the last stanza be useful in our lives?

Connecting with the Text

7. List five experiences or activities from your own life that you believe Moore would consider the "raw material of poetry" and "genuine."

CHOICES: Building Your Portfolio

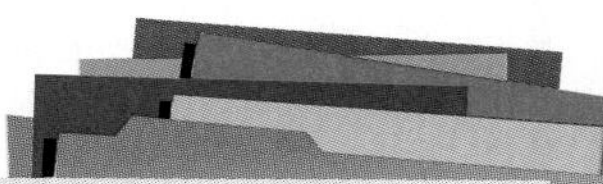

Writer's Notebook

1. Collecting Ideas for an Interpretive Essay

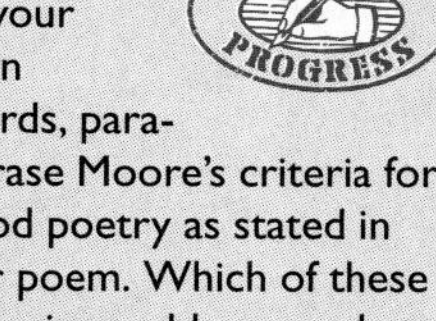

In your own words, paraphrase Moore's criteria for good poetry as stated in her poem. Which of these criteria would you apply to your own interpretation of a poem? Which of the criteria would you change or expand? Keep your notes for possible use in the Writer's Workshop on page 804.

Critical Writing

2. Poems About Poetry

In a brief essay, compare Marianne Moore's ideas about poetry with Archibald MacLeish's ideas presented in "Ars Poetica" (page 790). What does each poet require in a poem? What do their descriptions of poetry have in common?

Critical Writing

3. But No E-Mail, Please

Write a letter to Marianne Moore, describing your response to "Poetry." Let her know if she has persuaded you about the merits of poetry or reinforced your own feelings—whether positive or negative—about the genre. Cite specific passages from her poem.

Creative Writing

4. Poetry Is . . .

The most famous line in this poem is the one that says that poetry should show us imaginary gardens with real toads in them. Write your own list of what poetry is. Start with the words: "Poetry is . . . ." (Another famous American poet, Carl Sandburg [page 792], wrote a whole poem on this subject. One of the things he said is that poetry is the synthesis of hyacinths and biscuits.)

Creative Writing

5. Moore's Method

Marianne Moore often used information that she took from science and nature publications. Look through nature magazines or journals, and find an article that includes illustrations of animals, insects, birds, or fish that interest you. Write a poem about your chosen subject. Incorporate quotations from the article into your poem.

Performance

6. "Poetry" Reading

With a partner, take turns reading "Poetry" aloud. Pay attention to line and stanza breaks and to the alternation of long and short lines. Note also the punctuation: Where would you read quickly, and where would you slow down for emphasis? Record or perform two or three renditions for your class, and discuss how responses and interpretations differ for each reading.

Making Meanings

First Thoughts

1. Responses will vary. Poetry is not just nonsense, or Moore would not go to the trouble of defending it; or poetry is trivial and less important than other human activities like growing food or earning a living.

Shaping Interpretations

2. She addresses readers who think they dislike poetry; or she addresses other poets who may doubt the value of their work.
3. She dislikes poetry that is derivative and unintelligible.
4. Useful poetry includes elements of genuineness and rawness.
5. Moore means that the imagined symbols or images of poetry must be so concretely described that readers can see the toad's warts, toe pads, and sticky tongue.
6. Our awareness of life is heightened when we recognize our own experience and thought in poetry.

Connecting with the Text

7. *Remind students to choose situations they would not mind sharing.*

Choices: Building Your Portfolio

1. **Writer's Notebook** Remind students to save their work. They may use it as prewriting for the Writer's Workshop on p. 804.

Choices: Assessment Criteria For help in evaluating these Choices assignments, see the *Portfolio Management System*, pp. 166–167.

STRATEGIES FOR INCLUSION

Less Proficient Readers For activity #2, have students work in groups of four, with two students listing Moore's ideas, requirements for a good poem, description of poetry, tone, and imagery. The other two students should list the same features of MacLeish. Then, all four may compare and contrast their findings about each poet before writing their essays.

Learners Having Difficulty Perhaps the most evocative line of the poem, certainly the line that has been most often cited by critics since the poem's publication is the line about "imaginary gardens." For activity #3, use this line to focus student attention on what Moore says a good poem should be able to do.

QUICK PLANNING GUIDE

Into the Poem

Through the Poem

Beyond the Poem

- **Writer's Notebook:** Contrast Whitman's poetry with Sandburg's
- **Creative Writing:** Write an apostrophe
- **Performance:** Perform choral reading
- **Art:** Create a collage

WRITERS ON WRITING

In his *Complete Poems,* Carl Sandburg concludes that any definition of poetry has to reside in the work itself: "A poet explains for us what for him is poetry by what he presents to us in his poems. . . . We go to it, read it, look at it, perhaps go back to it many a time and it is for each of us what we make of it."

Carl Sandburg

(1878–1967)

Brown Brothers.

When he died in his ninetieth year, Carl Sandburg was already an American myth. Sandburg's deeply lined, leathery face and his boyish shock of hair had been familiar to the American public for more than five decades. As the author of two of the most popular poems of the first half of the century—"Chicago" (1914) and "Fog" (1916)—and a six-volume biography of Abraham Lincoln, Sandburg had carved a place for himself in modern literature. As a poetic spokesperson for the American laborer, he had become part of the folklore from which he drew his inspiration. While he seemed on the page to be the roughest of American poets, Sandburg was actually a gentle and contemplative man. He found his most characteristic voice in the vernacular—in slang, street talk, and the common speech of clichés and plain expressions.

A descendant of Swedes who had settled in Galesburg, Illinois, where he was born, Sandburg was not so much schooled in a classroom as in the proverbial "school of hard knocks." Before he was twenty, he had ranged the Middle West from Illinois to Nebraska. He thus came in contact with workers in the fields and factories that would one day provide his own poetic landscape. Sandburg volunteered, more from restlessness than from patriotism, to fight in the Spanish-American War that broke out in 1898, and he served in the first Puerto Rican campaign. When the war ended, he was finally ready to go back to school. He attended Lombard College in his hometown, where he was captain of the basketball team and editor of the college newspaper. It was at Lombard that Sandburg first began to think of himself as a writer. But his first professional writing was in advertising, politics, and journalism.

After a succession of jobs, Sandburg became nationally known as a poet at the age of thirty-six when *Poetry* magazine published some of his shorter poems, including "Chicago." Sandburg's audacious use of colloquialism and free verse (suggesting the influence of Walt Whitman) involved him in critical controversy and established his reputation as a major literary figure.

Sandburg's affirmation of American democracy and of the inherent nobility of labor and the working person culminated in one of his best-known collections of poems, *The People, Yes* (1936), a Whitmanesque panorama of American life that expressed its author's profound social faith. Besides poetry and his epic biography of Lincoln, Sandburg wrote folk songs and ballads, memoirs, and children's books.

BEFORE YOU READ

CHICAGO

Reading Focus

Cityspeak

Free verse with a ring of oratory in its cadences is characteristic of Sandburg's poetry. Be sure to read the following poem aloud to hear the echoes of Whitman.

A Dialogue with the Text

READER'S LOG

Sandburg uses vivid words and **images** to portray a city of enormous energy. As you read, jot down words or passages that capture the city's energy. Also, make note of the image in the poem that is most surprising to you.

Elements of Literature

Apostrophe

Apostrophe is a technique in which a writer addresses an inanimate object, an idea, or a person who is either dead or absent. In this poem, Sandburg addresses an entire city as though it were a kind of intelligent being, capable of understanding what he says.

PROGRAM MANAGER

- **Planning Instruction** See **Teaching Notes, *Teaching Resources B,*** p. 103, for additional information.
- **Instructional Support** See **Graphic Organizer for Active Reading, *Teaching Resources B,*** p. 110, for a Through the Poem activity.
- **Audiotaped Readings** To help auditory learners, use the **Selected Reading, Audiocassette 3, Side A** in the ***Audiovisual Resources Binder.***
- **Application and Reinforcement** For reinforcement of the literary elements introduced in this lesson, see **Transparency** 16.2 in the ***Audiovisual Resources Binder.***

- **Assessment** See **Selection Test, *Test Booklet,*** pp. 188–189.

Private Collection, Washington, D.C.

Chicago (1923) by Louis Lozowick. Oil on canvas.

Chicago

Carl Sandburg

Hog Butcher for the World,
Tool Maker, Stacker of Wheat,
Player with Railroads and the Nation's Freight Handler;
Stormy, husky, brawling,
City of the Big Shoulders:

Using **BEFORE YOU READ** p. 792

Reading Focus

Read aloud some stanzas from Whitman's "I Hear America Singing" on p. 352 to remind students of his long lines and catalogs.

Elements of Literature

Although many poems use apostrophe in a formal way, we frequently use this element of literature informally in our daily lives. For instance, if a soda machine does not work, we may demand that it give us our money back. Ask students for other informal examples of apostrophe.

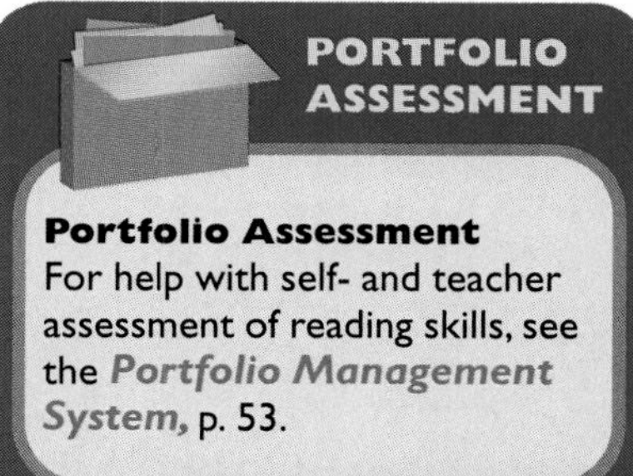

Portfolio Assessment
For help with self- and teacher assessment of reading skills, see the ***Portfolio Management System,*** p. 53.

OPTIONS FOR TEACHING

STRATEGIES FOR INCLUSION

Auditory Have students make a KWL chart for the poem. Students should divide a paper into three parts labeled "What I already know about Chicago," "What I would like to learn," "What I learned about Chicago." Ask them to fill in the first two parts before the poem is read and the last part after the reading is complete. Follow this activity with a discussion about the city.

Special Needs To help students remain focused on the poem, have them create a cluster diagram describing the sights and sounds of Chicago as they listen to you read the poem aloud.

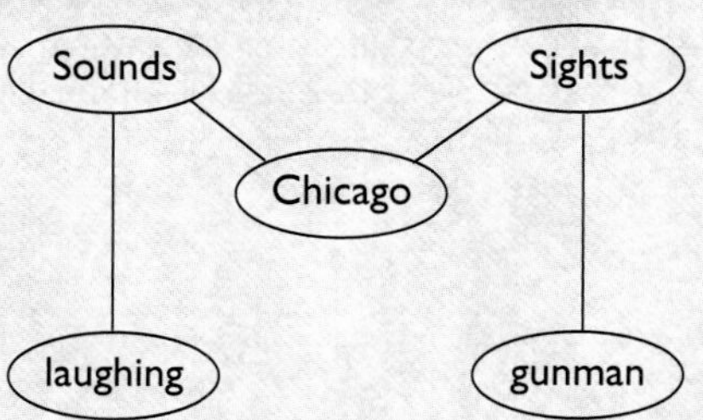

A. Literary Element: Setting
This poem first appeared in 1914. What clue does the poet give about the period of time to which this poem refers? [Possible answer: He refers to "gas lamps," an old-fashioned kind of street lighting.]

B. Literary Element: Apostrophe
Point out that the poet personifies and addresses the city by using the pronoun *you* in these lines.

C. Reader's Response: Challenging the Text
? What do you think the poet really thinks about Chicago? [Sample responses: He recognizes that the city has flaws, but its strengths and vitality far outweigh any deficiencies; or he admires it as the embodiment of the American city.]

They tell me you are wicked and I believe them, for I have seen your painted women under the gas lamps luring the farm boys.
And they tell me you are crooked and I answer: Yes, it is true I have seen the gunman kill and go free to kill again.
And they tell me you are brutal and my reply is: On the faces of women and children I have seen the marks of wanton hunger.
And having answered so I turn once more to those who sneer at this my city, and I give them back the sneer and say to them:
Come and show me another city with lifted head singing so proud to be alive and coarse and strong and cunning.
Flinging magnetic curses amid the toil of piling job on job, here is a tall bold slugger set vivid against the little soft cities;
Fierce as a dog with tongue lapping for action, cunning as a savage pitted against the wilderness,
    Bareheaded,
    Shoveling,
    Wrecking,
    Planning,
    Building, breaking, rebuilding.
Under the smoke, dust all over his mouth, laughing with white teeth,
Under the terrible burden of destiny laughing as a young man laughs,
Laughing even as an ignorant fighter laughs who has never lost a battle,
Bragging and laughing that under his wrist is the pulse, and under his ribs the heart of the people,
        Laughing!
Laughing the stormy, husky, brawling laughter of Youth, half-naked, sweating, proud to be Hog Butcher, Tool Maker, Stacker of Wheat, Player with Railroads and Freight Handler to the Nation.

OPTIONS FOR TEACHING

INTEGRATING THE LANGUAGE ARTS

Strategic Reading So that all students participate in reading aloud, even if they are reluctant, place students in small groups of mixed abilities. Ask students to read out loud each line of the poem in succession in a Round-Robin reading. This strategy removes the pressure of reading in public for a long period of time.

CROSSING THE CURRICULUM

Social Sciences Have students update Sandburg's look at Chicago by researching and delivering oral presentations about an aspect of Chicago mentioned in the poem. Suggested topics: stockyards, railroads, construction, urban development, poverty, crime.

Making Meanings

First Thoughts

1. How does Sandburg make you feel about the city he describes?

Shaping Interpretations

2. Sandburg opens with a series of **epithets,** or descriptive phrases, about Chicago. What does each of these epithets reveal about the city and the various activities that make up its economy?
3. What do people tell the speaker about Chicago? What is the speaker's answer to each of these comments about the city?
4. Many different **images** contribute to this portrait of Chicago, but its central image is never named. To what is Chicago really being compared? How is this image introduced and extended? (Review your Reader's Log.)
5. What are the city's main strengths and main weaknesses, according to Sandburg? What seems to be the poet's attitude toward the city?

Extending the Text

6. Which features of Chicago do you think have changed since this poem was written in 1914?

Challenging the Text

7. What would you say to those critics who have claimed that Sandburg's poetry is full of bluster and proclamation at the expense of thought?

Choices: Building Your Portfolio

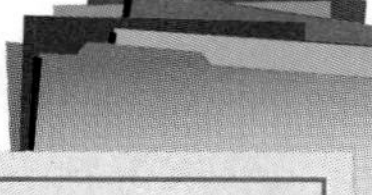

Writer's Notebook

1. Collecting Ideas for an Interpretive Essay

Re-read Walt Whitman's "I Hear America Singing" (page 352). Then, write some notes comparing and contrasting Whitman's poem with Sandburg's "Chicago." Gather your data in a chart like the following one.

Save your notes for possible use in the Writer's Workshop on page 804.

	Whitman	Sandburg
Subject		
Imagery		
Figures of speech		
Rhythm		
Catalogs of details		
Slang and colloquial language		
Tone		

Creative Writing

2. Apt Epithets

Review the **epithets,** or descriptive phrases, Sandburg uses in addressing Chicago in the opening stanza. Then, choose a city, town, or other area you know well. Write an **apostrophe**—a direct address to an inanimate object—using at least five epithets about the place you have chosen.

Performance

3. Sing It Out

Prepare this famous poem for a group performance. Your first task will be to decide how many speakers you will need and whether you will use a group of voices to recite some passages. You will also want to decide whether you will use sound effects, even music. Perform the poem for your class.

Art

4. Chicago Illustrated

Using pictures from magazines and newspapers, create a collage to illustrate Sandburg's "Chicago." Look for references to specific images in the poem as you select drawings and photographs for the collage.

Making Meanings

First Thoughts

1. Some students may say that Sandburg makes them interested in or makes them want to visit the city.

Shaping Interpretations

2. l. 1 = meat-packing center; l. 2 = heavy industry and; l. 3 = grain processing; railway hub.
3. People say the city is wicked, crooked, and brutal. The speaker agrees, mentioning murderers and hungry children.
4. The central image of a strong, exuberant young man is introduced in the opening lines and extended with a variety of other dynamic descriptions.
5. The city's main strengths are vitality, industry, pride, and endurance. Its weaknesses include wickedness, crime, and brutality. Sandburg likes the city despite its flaws.

Extending the Text

6. **(Evaluation)** The stockyards are now an industrial park. Financing and wholesaling are important now. Heavy industry is less important. The gas lamps are gone.

Challenging the Text

7. **(Evaluation)** Possible response: The poem is built around a strong image and is not intended to be a thoughtful argument.

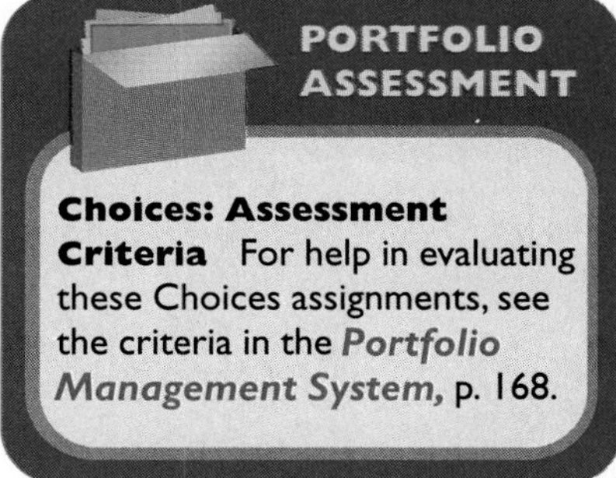

Choices: Assessment Criteria For help in evaluating these Choices assignments, see the criteria in the *Portfolio Management System,* p. 168.

Strategies for Inclusion

Musical/Kinesthetic To help students plan their performance and absorb the poem's musicality for activity #3, have them first read the poem aloud while lightly tapping out the rhythm of the lines. Their production can grow and evolve from the basic rhythms.

English Language Development For activity #4, have students choose a city that they are familiar with and illustrate the atmosphere of that city by making a drawing, painting, or a collage. On the back of their illustration, have them write at least four descriptive phrases to go with it.

QUICK PLANNING GUIDE

Into the Poem

Author Biography p. 796
Before You Read p. 797
- **Reading Focus: Scaffolding** Students listen for tone.
- **Quickwrite:** Take notes about predictions

Through the Poem

"what if a much of a which of a wind" p. 797
Primary Sources p. 798
Student to Student p. 798
"rollerskating"
Making Meanings p. 799

Beyond the Poem

Choices: Building Your Portfolio p. 799
- **Writer's Notebook**: Paraphrase thought groupings in a paragraph
- **Critical Writing:** Write an essay on Cummings's attitude toward life
- **Critical Writing:** Compare Cummings and Frost poems
- **Music:** Create a melody

ABOUT THE AUTHOR

Cummings's unusual typography may appear arbitrary to some students, just as it did to some early critics. But in fact the punctuation was intentional, precise, and extremely important to Cummings.

Self-Portrait by E. E. Cummings.

Berg Collection, New York Public Library.

E. E. Cummings

(1894–1962)

Edward Estlin (E. E.) Cummings was born in Cambridge, Massachusetts, the son of a Unitarian minister. After a childhood spent within walking distance of Harvard, he attended the university at a time when French Symbolism and free verse were major new influences on American poetry. Like other poets, Cummings found in the Imagist manifesto guidelines that allowed him to experiment and to break old rules.

If there is such a thing as "rugged individualism" in poetry, Cummings may be its prime example. All by himself, he altered conventional English syntax and made typography and the division of words part of the shape and meaning of a poem. And—in the age of celebration of the common person—he went against the grain by championing the virtues of elitism. "So far as I am concerned," he wrote, "poetry and every other art was and is and forever will be strictly and distinctly a question of individuality. . . . Poetry is being, not doing. If you wish to follow, even at a distance, the poet's calling . . . you've got to come out of the measurable doing universe into the immeasurable house of being. . . . Nobody else can be alive for you; nor can you be alive for anybody else."

Graduating from college in the midst of World War I, Cummings became part of the conflict well before American soldiers appeared on European battlefields in 1917. He volunteered for an ambulance corps privately financed by Americans and staffed by young men like himself. Crossing to Bordeaux on a French troop ship threatened by German U-boats, Cummings had hardly begun his duties when a French censor, intercepting one of his typographically odd letters, imprisoned him on suspicion of espionage. Released within three months, Cummings drew on the experience to produce his first important book of prose, *The Enormous Room* (1922).

After World War I, Cummings returned to France. He was one of the American literary expatriates who found in Paris the freedom and inspiration they felt were denied them by the restrictive Puritan climate of their own country. During this period, Cummings refined the eccentric shifts of syntax and typography that would become his trademark. In 1923, he published his first collection of verse, *Tulips and Chimneys,* which was followed by & (1925), *XLI Poems* (1925), and *is 5* (1926). His poetry is often marked by jubilant lyricism, as he celebrates love, nature's beauty, and an almost Transcendentalist affirmation of the individual. He reserved his mischievous wit for the satire of the "unman," by which he meant the unthinking, unfeeling temperament of urban "humans."

"Back in the United States,"Cummings split his time between an apartment in Greenwich Village in New York City and a house in Silver Lake, New Hampshire. He died still believing that "when skies are hanged and oceans drowned, / the single secret will still be man."

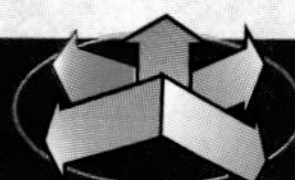

PROGRAM MANAGER

- **Planning Instruction** See **Teaching Notes, *Teaching Resources B,*** p. 103, for objectives, a summary, and literary elements for this selection.
- **Instructional Support** Before beginning the instructional lesson, see **Graphic Organizer for Active Reading, *Teaching Resources B,*** p. 111, for a Through the Poem activity.
- **Audiotaped Readings** To help auditory learners use the **Selected Reading, Audiocassette 3, Side A,** in the ***Audiovisual Resources Binder.***
- **Assessment** See **Selection Test, *Test Booklet,*** pp. 188–189.

Before You Read
WHAT IF A MUCH OF A WHICH OF A WIND

Reading Focus
The Prevailing Spirit
Modern literature is full of bleak images of destruction and the wane of civilization. At the same time, an extraordinary number of writers explore the determination of the human spirit to prevail in spite of hardship and even devastation. What tone about the future of this planet do you hear in Cummings's poem?

Quickwrite
Before you read this poem, jot down some of your predictions about the future of the planet. You could focus your thoughts on "What if . . . ?"

what if a much of a which of a wind (A)

E. E. Cummings

what if a much of a which of a wind
gives the truth to summer's lie;
bloodies with dizzying leaves the sun
and yanks immortal stars awry?°
Blow king to beggar and queen to seem
(blow friend to fiend:blow space to time)
—when skies are hanged and oceans drowned,
the single secret will still be man

what if a keen of a lean wind flays°
screaming hills with sleet and snow:
strangles valleys by ropes of thing
and stifles forests in white ago?
Blow hope to terror;blow seeing to blind
(blow pity to envy and soul to mind) (B)
—whose hearts are mountains,roots are trees,
it's they shall cry hello to the spring

what if a dawn of a doom of a dream
bites this universe in two,
peels forever out of his grave
and sprinkles nowhere with me and you?
Blow soon to never and never to twice
(blow life to isn't:blow death to was)
—all nothing's only our hugest home;
the most who die,the more we live

4. **awry** (ə·rī′): out of place.
9. **flays:** literally, strips the skin or outer layer from.

Into the Poem

Using **Before You Read** p. 797

Reading Focus
Many news stories focus on life-affirming acts of kindness. Brainstorm with the class to create a list of life-affirming stories recently in the news.

Through the Poem

A. Reader's Response: First Thoughts
? Judging by the title, what do you expect this poem to be about?
[Sample responses: The power of the wind; nonsense.]

B. Language Note: Diction
Ask students to find several examples of unusual wording in these lines.
[Possible answers: Line 5, *seem;* l. 12, *ago;* l. 13, *blind;* l. 21, *soon;* l. 21, *never;* l. 22, *isn't;* l. 22, *was.*]

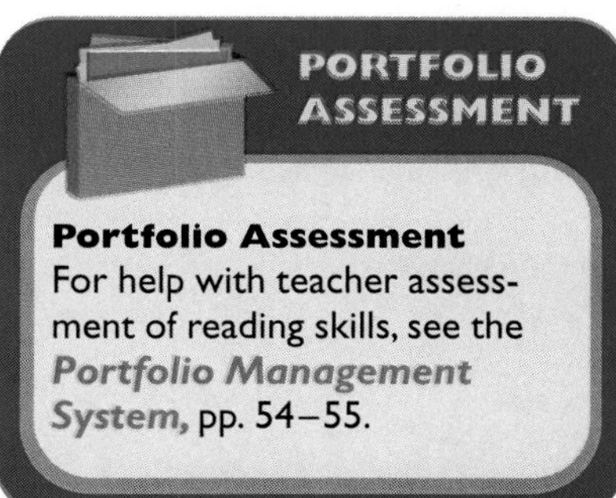

PORTFOLIO ASSESSMENT

Portfolio Assessment
For help with teacher assessment of reading skills, see the ***Portfolio Management System,*** pp. 54–55.

OPTIONS FOR TEACHING

STRATEGIES FOR INCLUSION

Linguisitic Before they read the poem, have students work in teams to create on the chalkboard, on a large sheet of canvas, or on poster board, cluster diagrams or other visual organizers listing nouns, adjectives, and verbs they associate with the wind.

Special Needs Have students who have difficulty with reading comprehension listen with headphones to an audio recording of the poem while they highlight specific information. Give each student a clear transparency sheet and two highlighting markers of different colors. As they listen to the poem, have them lay the clear sheet over the book page and highlight all the positive phrases in the poem in one color and the negative phrases in another color.

Primary Sources

Ask students why Cummings runs together the phrase "mostpeople." [Possible answer: Cummings shows his contempt for the phrase *most people* and the idea that anyone should worry about what "mostpeople" think or do.]

A. Expansion
Ask students to compare this poem to Cummings' poem "Buffalo Bill's." Ask them to identify any similar elements. Encourage students to write their own poems modeled on Cummings's original or the student poem.

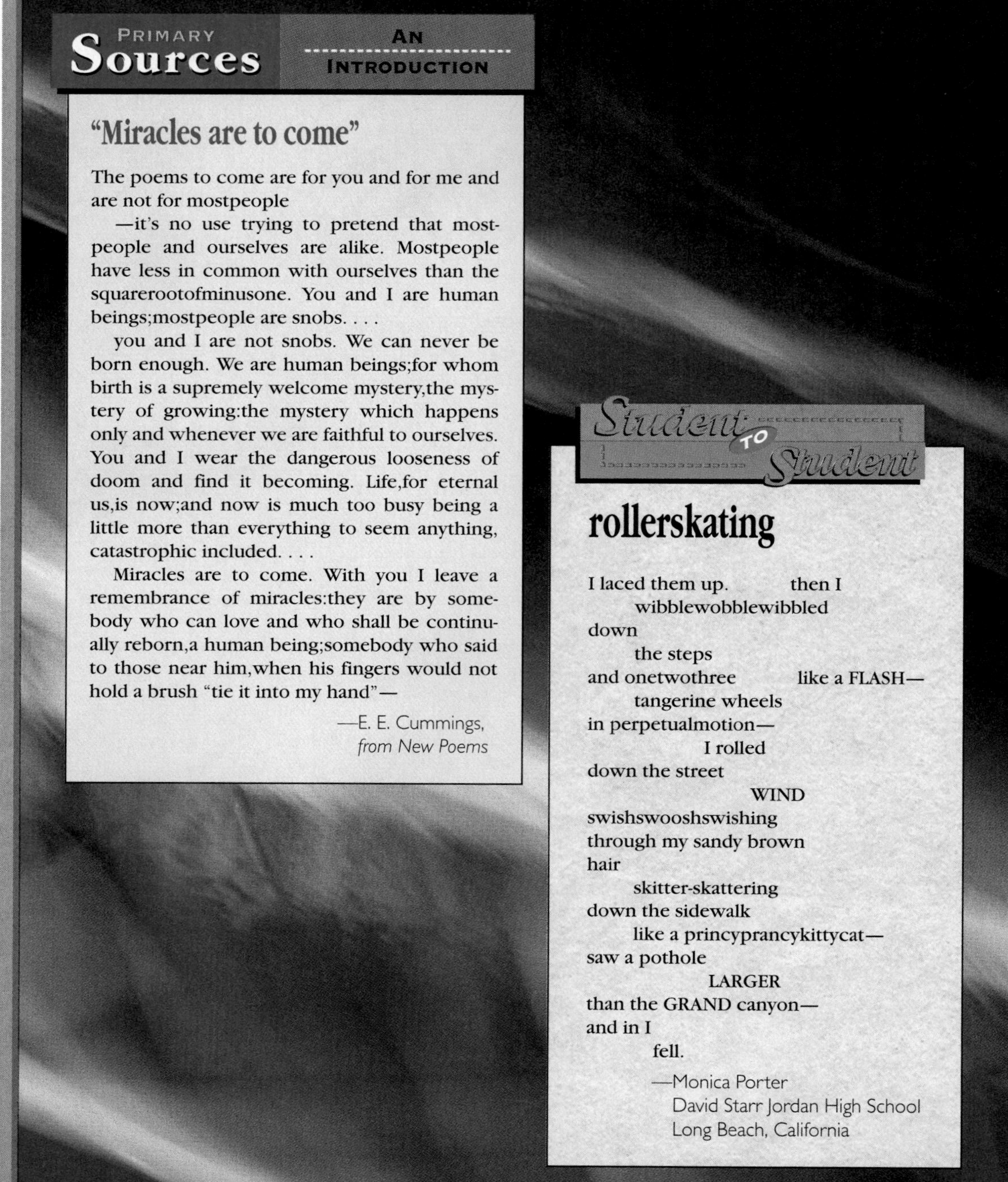

PRIMARY **Sources** AN INTRODUCTION

"Miracles are to come"

The poems to come are for you and for me and are not for mostpeople

—it's no use trying to pretend that mostpeople and ourselves are alike. Mostpeople have less in common with ourselves than the squarerootofminusone. You and I are human beings;mostpeople are snobs. . . .

you and I are not snobs. We can never be born enough. We are human beings;for whom birth is a supremely welcome mystery,the mystery of growing:the mystery which happens only and whenever we are faithful to ourselves. You and I wear the dangerous looseness of doom and find it becoming. Life,for eternal us,is now;and now is much too busy being a little more than everything to seem anything, catastrophic included. . . .

Miracles are to come. With you I leave a remembrance of miracles:they are by somebody who can love and who shall be continually reborn,a human being;somebody who said to those near him,when his fingers would not hold a brush "tie it into my hand"—

—E. E. Cummings,
from New Poems

Student TO Student

rollerskating

I laced them up.   then I
        wibblewobblewibbled
down
        the steps
and onetwothree   like a FLASH—
        tangerine wheels
in perpetualmotion—
                I rolled
down the street
                        WIND
swishswooshswishing
through my sandy brown
hair
        skitter-skattering
down the sidewalk
        like a princyprancykittycat—
saw a pothole
                LARGER
than the GRAND canyon—
and in I
        fell.

—Monica Porter
David Starr Jordan High School
Long Beach, California

OPTIONS FOR TEACHING

STRATEGIES FOR INCLUSION

Spatial Have students create cluster charts for the Primary Sources feature showing what qualities Cummings associates with "mostpeople" and "you and I." Ask them to consider what Cummings means by "snob." Ask students if he is snobbish himself in distinguishing himself from mostpeople.

Intrapersonal Ask students to copy one or two sentences from "Miracles" at the top of a piece of paper. Then, ask them to quickwrite a personal response in the form of a letter to Cummings. Ask students to share their responses in small groups.

CONNECTING WITH "WHAT IF A MUCH OF A WHICH OF A WIND"

Point out that in "rollerskating," the student poet runs words together for special effects and meanings, just as Cummings does in "what if a much of a which of a wind." Place students into pairs and ask them to look at the words that are run together in each poem. Have students discuss with their partners the possible reasons that each poet may have had for merging certain words and not others.

Making Meanings

First Thoughts

1. How did you react to the message of Cummings's poem?

Shaping Interpretations

2. If the world is destroyed, what will still survive?
3. Who "shall cry hello to the spring" if the world freezes over?
4. What will happen if the universe is blown up?
5. What **images** describe the seasons of the year in the first two stanzas? How does the third stanza deal with time on a different scale?
6. Describe the **rhyme scheme** of the poem. How does Cummings make use of **slant rhyme**? (For information on slant rhyme, see page 380.)
7. What common human fears does Cummings refer to in the first six lines of each stanza? How does he comment on those fears in the last two lines of each stanza?
8. What is the effect of the direct reference to "me and you" in line 20?
9. What do you think Cummings means by the last two lines? Is he celebrating life or death?

Connecting with the Text

10. Look back at the notes you made for the Quickwrite before reading this poem. Do you share Cummings's attitude about the future of planet Earth? Explain.

Choices: Building Your Portfolio

Writer's Notebook

1. Collecting Ideas for an Interpretive Essay

Cummings's style can be challenging because he uses a difficult syntax consisting of thought groupings that often don't have any punctuation or that use unusual punctuation. He also often uses verbs, adjectives, and adverbs as nouns. Go back over "what if a much of a which of a wind," and determine where thought groupings begin and end. Paraphrase these thought groupings in a brief paragraph. Save your notes for possible use in the Writer's Workshop on page 804.

Critical Writing

2. Snobs, Look Elsewhere

In the preceding Primary Sources (page 798), from the introduction to his collection called *New Poems,* Cummings makes several statements about poetry and his audience, and at the same time reveals an attitude toward life itself. In a brief essay, tell whether you find any of these statements related to the messages in "what if a much of a which of a wind." Use specific lines from the poem to support your opinions.

Critical Writing

3. That Which Survives

In a brief essay, compare and contrast Cummings's poem with Robert Frost's "Once by the Pacific" (page 564). Consider in your essay the theme or message, imagery, tone, and structure of the poems.

Music

4. Wind Song

Create a melody to accompany "what if a much of a which of a wind." With two or three classmates, perform the song for your class.

Making Meanings

First Thoughts

1. Some students may find the poem to be dark; others may find it life-affirming.

Shaping Interpretations

2. The secret of human existence.
3. People "whose hearts are mountains, roots are trees."
4. The human spirit will remain.
5. Images in the first two stanzas involve the cycle of the seasons; the third stanza focuses on eternity ("dawn of a doom"), using such words as *forever* and *nowhere.*
6. The rhyme scheme of each stanza is *abcbddac.* Examples of slant rhyme include ll. 3 and 8, ll. 5 and 6, ll. 1 and 7, ll. 9 and 15, ll. 19 and 24, and ll. 17 and 23.
7. Fears of loss, disappointment, death, oblivion. In the last two lines of each stanza, he counters the fears with a positive image.
8. It makes the poem personal.
9. Possible response: Even though many people die every day, those people who are alive must live life to the fullest. Cummings celebrates life.

Connecting with the Text

10. Some students may express concern about the planet's future; Others may express faith that human wisdom will protect the planet.

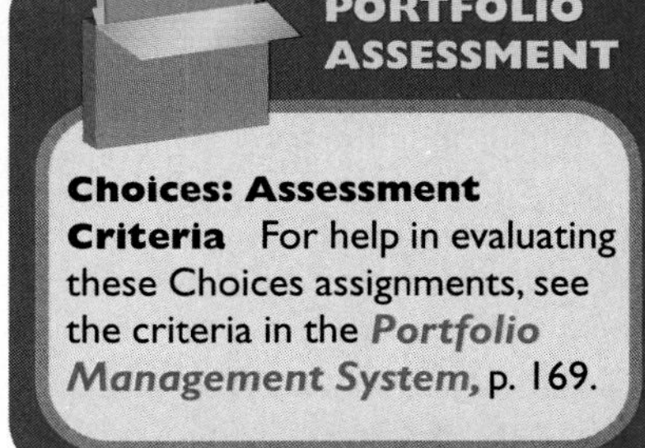

Choices: Assessment Criteria For help in evaluating these Choices assignments, see the criteria in the *Portfolio Management System,* p. 169.

STRATEGIES FOR INCLUSION

Leaners Having Difficulty Ask students to use this chart to record notes for activity #3.

Element	Cummings Poem	Frost Poem
Theme	[life will survive destruction]	[dark night is coming]
Imagery	[wind]	[ocean]
Tone	[celebration]	[warning]
Structure	[some rhyme]	[all couplets]

Musical Encourage students to make use of computer software and electronic instruments when they compose their melodies for activity #4. Students may create their own songs by starting with existing compositions and manipulating their tempo, pitch, instrument sounds, and other elements using a music program or electronic keyboard.

Lifestyles of the Rich and Famous

He's rich, he's handsome, he throws great parties—so why does Jay Gatsby stand outside his opulent Long Island mansion, gazing at a light across the water? The narrator Nick Carraway tries to unlock the puzzle in *The Great Gatsby* (Scribner's), F. Scott Fitzgerald's novel of American dreams and disappointments during the Jazz Age. A movie adaptation is available on video.

Small-Town Americana

Like Edwin Arlington Robinson's Tilbury Town and Edgar Lee Masters's Spoon River, Sherwood Anderson's Winesburg is a typical American small town. In *Winesburg, Ohio* (Viking), Anderson explores the splendid hopes and stifled dreams of Winesburg's inhabitants in a series of interconnected stories set in the early decades of this century. For another, more sentimental view of the archetypal small town, read Thornton Wilder's classic play *Our Town.*

Wounds of War

Ernest Hemingway was famous for his unemotional, almost journalistic accounts of the triumphs and tragedies of warfare. In *A Farewell to Arms* (Scribner's), he sets a tragic romance against the backdrop of World War I Italy. In *For Whom the Bell Tolls* (Scribner's), the backdrop changes to the Spanish civil war. Both novels have been adapted as films.

Take the "A" Train

From 1919 to 1932, Harlem was a cultural mecca at the center of an African American renaissance. Langston Hughes, Zora Neale Hurston, and James Weldon Johnson are just three of the many creative talents featured in *When Harlem Was in Vogue* (Random House), a highly readable social history by David Levering Lewis.

Two Sisters Have Their Say

The Delany sisters, Sarah Louise and Annie Elizabeth, were 104 and 102 in 1993 when they wrote *Having Our Say* (Dell). Their father was born into slavery; the sisters lived through the northern migration of African Americans, the Harlem Renaissance, and the civil rights movement of the 1960s. Their story gives a unique perspective of life in the United States over the last hundred years. This nonfiction best-seller has been adapted as a stage play.

Read On

Portfolio Assessment Options

The following projects can help you evaluate and assess your students' reading accomplishments outside of class. Videotapes or audiotapes of completed projects may be included in students' portfolios.

- **Present a Play** After students have read *The Great Gatsby,* ask them to select a pivotal scene to use as the basis for a Readers' Theater presentation. Have students write a script based on the narrative, cast the parts, and rehearse their presentations. Invite students to perform their plays for the class, and videotape their productions.
- **Draw a Character** After students have read one or more of the stories from *Winesburg, Ohio,* ask them to select the character that interests them most. Then, have students draw or paint a picture of what they think the character looks like. If drawing or painting isn't practical, ask students to look through old newspapers and magazines and find a photograph of a person they think resembles their character.
- **Make a Collage** As students read either of the Hemingway novels, ask them to pay particular attention to the images of battle and its aftermath that the author presents. Then, ask students to make a collage based on these images and to write a statement explaining it. After displaying the collages in the classroom, include them in the students' portfolios.
- **Create a Summary Chart** As students read *When Harlem Was in Vogue,* ask them to make notes for a summary chart. The chart should include the names of writers and other important figures in the Harlem Renaissance, their works, and major social and historical events.

FOR FURTHER EXPLORATION

Novel

The Enormous Room by E. E. Cummings

Poems

What's O'Clock by Amy Lowell
Collected Poems 1912–1944 by H. D. (Hilda Doolittle)

Nonfiction

The Necessary Angel by Wallace Stevens
Imagism: A Chapter from the History of Modern Poetry by Stanley K. Coffman, Jr.

Films

The Cabinet of Dr. Caligari (1919)
Nosferatu (1922)
The Battleship Potemkin (1925)

The American Language

American Slang

by Gary Q. Arpin

Most people think of slang as a kind of corrupt English, the product of ignorance and laziness. They see slang as a sort of linguistic disease that flourishes in the poorest and worst-maintained neighborhoods of the language. Slang, they feel, should be stamped out for the health and well-being of the general public.

But slang is as old as language itself. In fact, many words that at one time were considered slang later entered the language and are now used by all speakers. Perhaps Carl Sandburg (page 792) sized up the appeal of slang best: "Slang is language that rolls up its sleeves, spits on its hands, and goes to work."

Before the middle of the eighteenth century, slang as we know it today was called *cant* and *argot. Cant* referred to the secret language of thieves and beggars. *Argot* referred to the specialized vocabulary of occupations (sailors and farmers, for example). Gradually, the word *slang* came to refer to any informal, nonstandard, specialized language. Today, slang specifically refers to a kind of colorful, irreverent, lively language that quickly becomes popular and often just as quickly drops out of use. It has always been popular among the young. **A**

Why Do We Use Slang?

Why do people use slang? Not usually out of ignorance, despite popular misconceptions. Most slang terms are substitutes for fairly common words or phrases. A waiter who calls out the food order "Adam and Eve on a raft—wreck 'em," knows how to say "two scrambled eggs on toast." She is just using the **jargon,** or specialized vocabulary, of her occupation.

We ordinarily think of language only as a means of communication. But anthropologists point out that it has a more subtle function as well—marking relatedness. Members of a family or other group reinforce their connections by their language. If you think about it for a moment, you will probably realize that your family or group of friends does the same thing by using key words or unusual pronunciations. This is the most important function of slang: It marks members of a group and asserts the group's relatedness, thereby helping to keep it together.

> Walt Whitman claimed that slang produced poets and poetry.

The group can be of any size and come from any social class. It can be a single family or a large and widespread profession. Teenagers, athletes, actors, truck drivers, doctors, criminals, filmmakers, and soldiers all have their own slang. People outside the group who try to use its slang often appear ridiculous.

Walt Whitman (page 348) claimed that slang produced poets and poetry. This is an exaggeration, but it might point to another explanation for the persistence of slang. **B** Slang may be used for the sheer pleasure of making sounds. It may also be a way to create new metaphors, sometimes just for the fun of it, sometimes to capture attention. Perhaps slang is used because as humans we have an impulse to be wordsmiths. Certainly, people have persisted in making up new slang terms for concepts that already have more than enough terms to name them. Even some forty-five years ago, there were 180 slang terms for "having no money," 400 slang terms for "failing," and 200 slang terms for "getting angry." By now, who can tell how many new slang terms have been added to those lists?

People who do not speak a particular slang often are highly critical of it. This can be because some slang is vulgar or is a pointless corruption of standard

A. Expansion
Slang makes communication less formal. Since members of groups often wish to speak informally to one another, they frequently rely on slang.

B. Literary Connections
Whitman isn't the only writer who was fond of slang. The British novelist G. K. Chesterton is reputed to have said, "The one stream of poetry which is constantly flowing is slang. Every day some nameless poet weaves some fairy tracery of popular language . . . All slang is metaphor, and all metaphor is poetry."

OPTIONS FOR TEACHING

STRATEGIES FOR INCLUSION

English Language Development Remind students that if they are uncertain about whether a slang term should be used in formal writing, they may check the entry for the word in a good college or unabridged dictionary. Explain that the entry for informal terms will generally be preceded or followed by a descriptor such as *slang, informal,* or *vulgar.* Explain that words marked *slang* or *informal* may sometimes be appropriate in writing, while words marked *vulgar* are usually inappropriate and potentially offensive.

Advanced Ask students to do independent research on an obsolete slang term that appears in a work of literature from a previous era. Especially rich sources for these terms include the plays of Shakespeare and the works of other sixteenth- or seventeenth-century playwrights. Each student should select a different term and create a dictionary-style entry that includes a definition, a quotation from a period source showing how the word was used in context, and a brief etymology, if possible. *Remind students to choose terms that would be appropriate to share aloud in the classroom.*

A. Expansion
Most slang is short-lived, but some slang terms have existed for centuries. For examples, *bones,* meaning "dice," has been used since the Middle Ages.

speech with no apparent justification other than novelty. Some slang can also be criticized for being imprecise. Often, however, naysayers are simply annoyed at not being part of the in-group associated with the slang they are criticizing.

Origins of American Slang

America has always been a fertile ground for the development of slang, especially since the 1830s, when informality began to be considered an almost essential aspect of democracy. The country's cowboys, railroad workers, politicians, and members of hundreds of new occupations introduced many slang terms, often to name things for which there were no existing words. The media then helped to popularize the new terms.

Slang words and phrases develop in the same ways as other additions to standard English.

1. Existing words may be given a new meaning. *Sack,* during World War II, became the almost universal slang word for "bed." It helped to create countless new phrases for "sleep": *hit the sack, sack out, sack time, sack duty,* and *sack drill.*
2. Two or more words may be combined to form a new expression. Americans' love affair with cars, for example, gave us the marvelously inventive *rattletrap* and the more recent *gas guzzler.* One witty compound verb, *to rubberneck,* meaning to stretch one's neck to see an accident or traffic tie-up, was once said to be the best slang term ever coined.
3. A word may be "clipped" to form a shortened word. *Fan,* as in *baseball fan,* was clipped from the word *fanatic.*
4. Words may also be borrowed from other languages. (These are often called *loanwords.*) During the westward expansion, for example, *bronco* was borrowed from the Spanish for "rough" and *mustang* from the Spanish for "stray."
5. Some slang words are simply invented. Among American backwoodsmen of the nineteenth century, the wilder the invention, the better. If you were *puckerstoppled,* you were embarrassed; confusion was *conbobberation;* and a heavy blow, in a fight or from the weather, was a *sockdologer.* Those words have disappeared, but other invented words have remained. *Blizzard,* for example, was first defined as a violent blow, perhaps from the German word *blitz,* for "lightning." In 1870, *blizzard* was applied by newspapers to violent snowstorms and was found to be so useful that it became standard English.

From Slang to Standard English

(A) Most slang terms die quickly. There is a constant turnover, especially among "in" words. *Lounge lizard, hootchie-kootchie,* and *goo-goo eyes* came and went as fast as *cool cat, squaresville,* and *hep.* (*Hep's* offspring, *hip,* is still with us, however.) Terms that fill a need in standard English sometimes make the transition from slang to standard. *Plunder, fix, all right,* and *rough-*

OPTIONS FOR TEACHING

INTEGRATING THE LANGUAGE ARTS

Strategic Reading Students probably know more about slang than they realize. In order to draw on the background they already have, ask students to fill out the following KWL chart before (columns 1 and 2) and after (column 3) they read the material on pp. 801–803.

Know	Want to know	Have learned

Spelling Because slang terms are more often heard than read, some students might have trouble spelling them when they want to use them in writing. Ask students to create a list of slang terms whose spellings they are unsure of. Discuss these terms with the class, attempting to arrive at a consensus about their spellings. Point out that the spellings of many slang terms can be found by remembering the spelling of other words with similar sounds.

neck all started as slang and were once condemned by one *highbrow* or another.

Who decides what is slang and what is standard usage? The answer to this is that we all do. Native speakers of a language have a finely tuned sense of the distinction between formal and informal language. As some slang words achieve wide popular usage, though, that distinction may blur. For example, which of these words would you say are slang, and which are standard: *corny, scrumptious, pinhead*? You might say, "Look it up in the dictionary." But the answer depends on which dictionary you use. Dictionaries whose primary purpose is to *describe* the language are apt to provide fewer usage distinctions than dictionaries prepared by lexicographers who feel that it is important to *prescribe* usage. The chart below shows the verdicts of three popular American dictionaries on whether or not our three test words are slang.

Obviously, lexicographers disagree on when a word becomes widely enough used to qualify as "standard." Some words, in fact, never make the jump at all. Terms that fill a real informal need often remain as slang for generations. Terms like *rubberneck, to squeal, baloney,* and *nifty* have endured, although regarded as slang for years. These words seem so informal that they resist incorporation into standard English, but they survive to remind us of our capacity for making poetry out of the commonplace.

Harbaugh/Rothco.

"Failure to do your homework on proper grammatical usage will result in a final grade of zero, zip, zilch . . ."

	Corny	Scrumptious	Pinhead
Webster's Second International	No	Yes	No
Webster's Third International	No	No	No
American Heritage Dictionary	No	No	Yes

Try It Out

1. There are hundreds of slang terms for some common experiences or things. With two or three other students, list as many slang terms as you can for the following.

a. an automobile
b. failing a test
c. getting angry
d. stealing

Once you've completed the lists, talk about the **metaphors** on which the slang terms are based.

2. Here are some clipped forms of words in current use. Identify their full forms, referring to a dictionary if necessary.

ad lib	flu	pep
bus	gas	prom
cello	gym	prop

3. Join with the rest of the class in compiling a list of slang words that you believe are used only in your particular school or community. Try to explain the origin of each word.

Try It Out: Possible Answers

1. Remind students to list only those slang expressions that would be appropriate to share aloud in the classroom.

a. wheels, ride, machine, chariot
b. flunk, crash and burn, bomb
c. burn, boil, see red, get sore
d. swipe, pinch, lift, rip off, nick

2. ad lib [ad libitum], bus [omnibus], cello [violincello], flu [influenza], gas [gasoline], gym [gymnasium], pep [pepper], prom [promenade], prop [property]

3. There may be some disagreement among students over the origin of certain words.

ASSESSMENT TOOLS

Check Test: True-False

1. The term *slang* refers to colorful, irreverent, lively language that quickly becomes popular and quickly disappears. [True]

2. The main function of slang is to show membership in a group. [True]

3. Americans did not start using slang until the 1960s. [False]

4. The term *fan,* as in baseball fan, is a shortened version of *fanatic* and is called a "clipped" form of a word. [True]

5. Dictionary makers are the only people who decide whether or not a word is slang. [False]

QUICK PLANNING GUIDE

Interpretive Essay

PROGRAM MANAGER

Computer Guided Instruction For a related interpretation assignment that students may use as additional instruction, see ***Writer's Workshop 2.***

BUILDING YOUR PORTFOLIO

Writer's Workshop

Technology HELP

See Writer's Workshop 2 CD-ROM. *Assignment: Interpretation.*

ASSIGNMENT
Write an essay interpreting any work of literature: a poem, story, novel, essay, or play.

AIM
To inform; to explain; to persuade.

AUDIENCE
Your teacher, members of your class, or members of a literary or reading group.

EXPOSITORY WRITING

INTERPRETIVE ESSAY

Every day you interpret information you receive from your environment and arrive at conclusions based on evidence presented to you. You might see dark clouds and infer that it's going to rain, or notice how shy a classmate is and infer that he may have difficulty making friends. Interpreting a literary work isn't as straightforward as inferring the meaning of an event, but it can be a fascinating exercise in making sense of a text and in getting others to see the meanings you see.

Prewriting

WORK IN PROGRESS

1. **What hooks your interest?** When you write an interpretation, it's important to care deeply about the work you're interpreting. Perhaps one poem or story in this book or in your outside reading moved you in a way no other literary work has. If you haven't had that kind of emotional response to a work, review your Writer's Notebook entries for Collections 14–16; you may have already made a head start on prewriting for an interpretive essay. You can also review selections you've studied in other collections. Re-read the titles, the Before You Read pages and Making Meanings questions, and the beginnings and endings of the works. Re-read your notes to see which works you have already said the most about. Be sure the work you choose is something you don't mind reading more than once and spending time analyzing critically.
2. **Ask yourself about the work.** "What does this mean to me?" is perhaps the most productive question to ask yourself after reading a literary work. This question can take you anywhere: into your own life experience; into the society around you; into historical events; into other subject areas; into other literary works, films, and other works of art; or into an examination of the author's life and personality. Spend time developing your answers to that question. Write in your journal or Reader's Log. Talk to other students who have read the same work. Discuss your ideas with your teacher. Read literary criticism as well as background on the writer.
3. **Use a double-entry journal.** A double-entry or dialectical journal is one of the simplest and best literary response tools you can use. Divide a page into two columns. In the left column, copy quotations from the work you're analyzing, or perhaps a summary of a section. In the right column, write your response to each quotation or summary. Choose quotations or passages you strongly agree or disagree with, respond to emotionally, or sense are crucial to the work's meaning. Think of the double-entry journal as a written

PORTFOLIO ASSESSMENT

- **Generating Ideas** To help students in prewriting, use the heuristic in the ***Portfolio Management System,*** p. 170.
- **Assessment Rubric** For a rubric that can be used to assess students progress in writing, see the ***Portfolio Management System,*** p. 172.

dialogue with yourself, full of questions, dead ends, and unexpected discoveries. In addition to this double-entry journal, you might wish to use other prewriting strategies, such as note-taking, clustering, or freewriting.

Model: A Double-Entry Journal

"A Rose for Emily" by William Faulkner

"A Rose for Emily"	*The title seems kind of romantic, maybe sentimental and nostalgic.*
"stubborn and coquettish decay"; "an eyesore among eyesores"	*I had to look up the word "coquettish." It comes from the word coquette, a vain girl or woman who tries to get the attention of admirers. A clue to Miss Emily's personality? The house reminds me of the house in Poe's "Fall of the House of Usher." It's creepy.*
"Miss Emily had been a tradition, a duty, and a care; a sort of hereditary obligation upon the town."	*She sounds like a burden. I wonder if anyone really liked her? Sounds like they probably didn't.*

4. **Make interpretive claims.** Begin thinking in general terms about what the work means. For fiction, consider character, plot, setting, point of view, style, and theme; for poetry, consider diction, imagery, symbolism, figurative language, sound, rhythm, repetition, speaker, and theme. Try to list at least one generalization for each element that is important to the work. For Faulkner's "A Rose for Emily," for example, these might include "Events in the story are related out of sequence so that Faulkner can explore the effects of the past on the present" (plot). Such generalizations are **interpretive claims** that you make about the work. Avoid unsupportable opinions such as "I like this poem" or "I have mixed feelings about this story." The focus must be on an analytical understanding of the literary work.
5. **Focus on a thesis.** Choose the interpretive claim that you feel is the strongest or most interesting or has the most validity, and make it your thesis: the central idea that will unify your essay. A thesis statement might be, "Faulkner's 'A Rose for Emily' seems on the surface to be a shocking horror story, but it is ultimately a serious work of literature that explores what can happen to people who cling too much to the past and tradition."

   As you re-read the work and gather more evidence, you may find that your thesis is only partly justified and needs revision or even replacement. Outlining before you draft is a good way of checking how well your interpretive claims fit together with one another and with your central thesis.

Try It Out

With a partner or a small group, choose a poem or short story you have read in this text. Identify two or three of the most important literary elements in the work, and discuss how they relate to the work's theme. Then develop three or four interpretive claims you can make about the work.

Motivation

Write the following topics on the chalkboard: Hobbies, Politics, People, News Events, and Sports. Ask students to consider the popularity of these topics among their families and friends and to rank them in order from most often to least often discussed. Ask students to describe what they talk about when they discuss people. Point out that many conversations about people concern what people do and why they do it. Conclude by asking students to write their interpretive essays using skills similar to those they use in conversation when discussing people.

Teaching the Lesson

Be sure that students understand the purpose of the writing they will be doing and that interpretation involves understanding how a literary work applies to human beings, including themselves. Ask students to read the model double-entry journal. Then, discuss the Strategies for Elaboration in the side margin on p. 806. This lesson includes instructions for each stage of the writing process. You may want to guide students by modeling each stage with your own writing.

Prewriting

As students work on their double-entry journals, encourage them to ask the question "why" and to speculate on reasons behind events or characters' decisions. The answers to these "why" questions may provide valuable insight that could lead to a thesis statement.

Try It Out

Students' interpretive claims should be capable of serving as thesis statements for whole essays and they should be based on literary elements.

OPTIONS FOR TEACHING

STRATEGIES FOR INCLUSION

Auditory Students might find it useful to participate in an oral reading of the literary works they plan to interpret. They may read aloud independently or take turns reading in small groups. In either case, suggest that students tape-record the reading so they can listen to it as they draft their papers. Students may also dictate their double-entry journals entries so they can play back what they have written.

Visual The double-entry journal can serve as a powerful visual aid for students as they draft their essays. Students might use horizontal and vertical lines to produce squares or rectangles that they can use to represent paragraphs, stanzas, or other major divisions of the literary work. They can then write their observations and ideas in the corresponding spaces.

Drafting

Provide a model of an interpretive essay. Share one that you have written or show examples from other writers. With students' help, highlight the thesis statement, the major points and evidence, and the restatement of the thesis.

Evaluating and Revising

Ask students to use the Evaluation Criteria on p. 807.

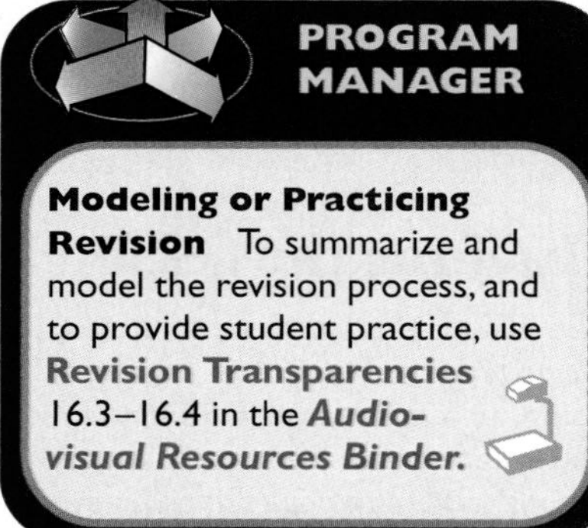

Modeling or Practicing Revision To summarize and model the revision process, and to provide student practice, use **Revision Transparencies** 16.3–16.4 in the ***Audiovisual Resources Binder.***

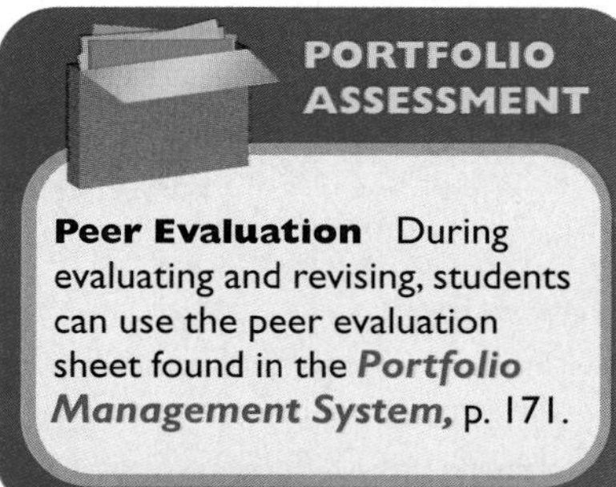

Peer Evaluation During evaluating and revising, students can use the peer evaluation sheet found in the ***Portfolio Management System,*** p. 171.

Strategies for Elaboration

Arranging and unifying all your evidence requires not only critical thinking but also a readable style. To make your essay read well:

- Use transitional words and phrases.
- Use concrete language as well as anecdotes, examples, and figures of speech.
- Use a consistent tense throughout. When writing about literature, use the literary present. (See Language Workshop, page 808.)
- Your tone should be relatively formal. Avoid contractions and colloquialisms and (unless your teacher suggests otherwise) the first-person point of view (*I* or *we*).

Communications Handbook HELP

Taking notes and documenting sources: pages 1210–1213.

6. **Support your claims.** Types of supporting evidence include quotations and paraphrases from the text, quotations and paraphrases from related reading, and your own knowledge and experience. Interpretive essays are usually most persuasive when they use a combination of these types of support rather than just one. You are also much more likely to persuade readers when each claim is backed up by more than one item of evidence.

Drafting

1. **Choosing a point of departure.** At the beginning of your essay, identify the work you are writing about (by title and author), and give necessary background information. You also need to give your readers a sense of where the essay as a whole is going. You might do that by stating your thesis directly, or by describing a section of the work that bears directly upon your thesis; or you might briefly discuss the author's life or career in such a way that the thesis flows naturally from that information.
2. **Organizing your thoughts.** Choose a sensible order for presenting your ideas. An interpretive essay may be organized in one of several ways.
   - **Chronological order.** You can organize your essay chronologically, showing the order in which certain things occur in the work you're analyzing. This organizational pattern is especially useful if you want to show how a character changes during the course of a story or if you want to make a point about a writer's handling of plot sequence.
   - **Order of importance.** Move from your least important point to your most important point, or vice versa.
   - **Logical order.** Group related ideas together. If, for example, you're focusing on two literary elements, such as plot and setting, present all your points about plot together in one section and all your points about setting in another section.

   If you've chosen to compare and contrast two works in your interpretive essay, you can either treat each of the elements of one work first before turning to elements of the other work (block method) or alternate between the works as you discuss each element in turn (point-by-point organization).
3. **Being aware of your audience.** Since your purpose is to convince readers that your claims are sound, you should be mindful of your audience and what they already know about the work you're analyzing. Decide whether you need to provide background information to fill in gaps for your audience.
4. **Presenting and developing your interpretive claims.** The heart of your essay is an organized presentation of your claims about the work. Your generalizations may only require a sentence or two, while many more sentences are devoted to evidence for your claims, including quotations from the text and related works. You'll need to credit your sources in two places—in parenthetical citations and in the list of Works Cited at the end of your essay. For more information on documenting sources, see pages 518 and 1211–1213.
5. **Adopting a stance.** To persuade the reader that your essay is based on sound reasoning, it's important to adopt a consistent **stance** throughout.

OPTIONS FOR TEACHING

INTEGRATING THE LANGUAGE ARTS

Vocabulary As students consider aspects of the literary work, especially when they create their double-entry journals, assist them by reviewing the difference between denotation and connotation. Using the following examples, ask students to identify the synonym with the most positive connotation.

house	<u>home</u>	domicile
<u>fragrance</u>	scent	smell
thin	<u>lean</u>	skinny

Mechanics Students will be using the titles of short stories and poems in their essays. Review with students the correct punctuation of titles for literary works. Remind students that although the titles of their own essays require neither quotation marks nor underlinings, any title of a literary work used within their own essays should be punctuated correctly.

Keep your thesis in mind at all times; never lose the thread of your analysis; include only relevant points, and clarify the relevance wherever it seems doubtful; be specific and concrete. Conclude your essay with an insight that either sums up your thesis or leads to intriguing new questions about literature or life.

Language Handbook HELP

Punctuation with quotation marks: page 1246.

Evaluating and Revising

1. **Peer review.** Exchange papers with one or more classmates, and answer the following questions about the paper you read:
   - Can you clearly identify the writer's thesis? Does the writer provide enough background information about the work to enable you to follow the ideas?
   - Does the writer present enough evidence to support his or her interpretive claims? Were you convinced of the writer's position?
   - What aspects of the essay are particularly effective? Are there passages that are difficult to understand? If so, how might they be strengthened?
   - Does the essay come to a conclusion that ties all the writer's ideas together and reinforces the thesis?
2. **Self-evaluation.** Read your peers' comments; then re-read your own essay as if you were not the author. Assess whether your essay needs more of something (more supporting evidence, more focus on ideas) or less of something (less padding, less personal opinion). Then make appropriate revisions.

Revision STRATEGIES

Re-read your conclusion to see if it wraps up your essay satisfactorily. If your essay seems to sputter at the end, leaving loose threads, go back and tie together all your strands of thought. Ask a peer to review your conclusion.

Proofreading

Correct all errors in spelling, usage, and mechanics. Be certain that you have correctly documented your sources, both in the text and in your list of Works Cited. Check that all quotations are exact, including line breaks for poems. Check for consistency of tense and the appropriate use of the literary present.

Publishing

One way to publish an interpretive essay is to share it with classmates who are interested in literature; perhaps a small circle of students would like to read their works aloud, with discussion following. Your school literary magazine might be interested in your essay. Try sending your essay to a publication devoted to the writing of high school students, or even to an appropriate academic journal or literary publication.

Reflecting on Your Writing

Include this essay (with the date on it) in your portfolio. Accompany it with a brief written reflection that addresses the following questions:

1. How did my writing process increase my understanding of the work I selected?
2. What problems did I have understanding the literary work, and how did I solve them? Did I end up changing my thesis once or more than once?
3. What will I do differently the next time I write an interpretive essay? How did this assignment help me in general with writing about literature?

Evaluation Criteria

A good interpretive essay

1. *identifies the title and author of the work and provides a point of departure that defines the subject and context*
2. *focuses on a central thesis that is clearly stated*
3. *presents a coherent series of interpretive claims that are relevant to the main thesis*
4. *provides specific support for each claim with evidence from the text or other valid sources*
5. *is clearly and consistently organized*
6. *maintains a consistent interpretive stance*
7. *has a conclusion that reinforces the thesis*

Proofreading

Remind students to proofread for errors in tense. Refer students to the Language Workshop on p. 808 for help on using the literary present and on achieving consistency of tense.

Reteaching

Some students may have difficulty arriving at thesis statements that meet the requirements of the assignment. Work with small groups and use students' double-entry journals as the basis for discussion. Show students how to form their journal notes into valid thesis statements.

Closure

After students have written their essays, have them list the most significant steps they followed during the writing process. Have volunteers read their lists aloud, and make a master list on the chalkboard.

Portfolio

Reflecting on Your Writing

As a starting point for reflections about their own writing, have students write answers to the questions on p. 807, and attach these to their essays when they file the essays in their portfolios.

COOPERATIVE LEARNING

Interpretive Teams Allow several students who write about the same literary work to work together as an interpretive team. Students may discuss possible topics, brainstorm ideas for supporting details, discuss entries in their journals, and listen for the tone and clarity of their drafts. During evaluation and revision, they may work together as a peer-review group. Each group member should produce a paper. These papers need not take similar viewpoints—some groups may wish to present their papers together as a thorough analysis and interpretation of the work.

ASSESSMENT TOOLS

Self-Assessment After students have completed their work, have them evaluate their essays using the following criteria.

1=Needs work; 2=Adequate; 3=Superior

___ Identifies the title and author of the work and provides a point of departure that defines the subject and context and attracts the reader's interest.

___ Focuses on a central thesis that is clearly stated.

___ Presents a coherent series of interpretive claims that are relevant to the main thesis.

___ Provides specific support for each claim with evidence from the text or other valid sources.

___ Is clearly and consistently organized.

___ Maintains a consistent interpretive stance.

___ Has a conclusion that reinforces the thesis.

Language Workshop

Connecting to Students' Writing

Ask students to select from their portfolios an essay about a literary work. Using the four Strategies for Achieving Consistency of Tense listed in the Language Workshop, students should then carefully re-read and revise their essays to correct the tense of any verbs that are not in the literary present. Then, divide the class into pairs and ask students to read their revised essays aloud to their partners. The partners should listen for any inconsistencies in tense and suggest further corrections.

Try It Out: Answers

(Verbs that have been changed to the present tense are underlined.)

"A Rose for Emily" **is** a complex story that **can** be interpreted on several levels. On one level, the story is about the conflict between the individual and the community. It **is** also about the conflicts between tradition and modern life. Faulkner, a modernist, **contrasts** the "New South" with the "Old South," which **is** symbolized by Miss Emily's old-style, crumbling house.

PROGRAM MANAGER

- **Extra Practice and Guided Instruction** For more instruction and practice in using the literary present, see **Language Workshop** in ***Teaching Resources B,*** pp. 114–115.
- **Extra Practice or Guided Instruction** See ***Language Workshop:*** **Consistency of tense** for more practice or guided instruction in using the literary present.

Language Workshop

The history of the written word is rich and

The Right Tense for Sense: Using the Literary Present

Technology HELP

See Language Workshop CD-ROM. *Key word entry: consistency of tense.*

Language Handbook HELP

Tenses and their uses: pages 1224–1225.

When you write, you can help your readers to understand the order in which things occurred by using verb tenses correctly—and consistently. Each of the six basic verb tenses—present, past, future, present perfect, past perfect, and future perfect—has its own applications. The present tense, for example, is used to express an action or state of being that is current, that is happening right now. Nowadays, much more so than in the past, some works of fiction and nonfiction are written in the present tense. A more common use of the present tense, however, is in literary criticism.

When you write about literature, you'll want to use a form of present tense called the **literary present.** You may write, for example, "'A Rose for Emily' *is* a story about a solitary individual with a shocking secret." The use of the literary present expresses the idea that a work of literature is continually alive, re-created each time someone reads it.

Try It Out

Revise the paragraph below to achieve a consistent use of the literary present.

"A Rose for Emily" was a complex story that could be interpreted on several levels. On one level, the story is about the conflict between the individual and the community. It was also about the conflicts between tradition and modern life. Faulkner, a modernist, contrasted the "New South" with the "Old South," which was symbolized by Miss Emily's old-style, crumbling house.

Strategies for Achieving Consistency of Tense

1. In general, consistently use the same tense throughout any piece you write.
2. At times you'll make valid exceptions to Strategy 1. For example, you would use the present tense when analyzing a story or paraphrasing the author's ideas, but the past tense when the characters themselves use the past tense. In other words, when you're quoting directly from a work, use the same tense the author uses. Otherwise, keep your essay in the literary present.
3. Sometimes, you can achieve consistency by deleting the verb in a subordinate clause, creating an appositive. The inconsistent sentence "Faulkner, who *was* a Southerner, *is* intimate with customs and traditions of the South" can become the consistent sentence "Faulkner, a Southerner, *is* intimate with customs and traditions of the South."
4. Check consistency of tense during revision and proofreading.

Writer's Workshop Follow-Up: Revising

Re-read the interpretive essay you wrote for the Writer's Workshop on page 804, and make sure your verb tenses are consistent. If you ever change tense, make sure you follow a consistently applied, sensible policy. If you have not used the literary present, try rewriting a sample passage in that tense.

✔ QUICK CHECK: Using the Literary Present

Change the verbs in the following sentences to the literary present. If a sentence is already in the literary present, write "correct."

[1] William Faulkner, the author of "A Rose for Emily," wrote about a wide variety of people in his works. [writes]

[2] For example, in his novel *As I Lay Dying*, Faulkner shows the tribulations of a poor family. [correct]

[3] In another novel, *The Sound and the Fury*, he presented the saga of an aristocratic family, the Compsons. [presents]

[4] Many readers and critics believe that Faulkner captured the whole spectrum of Southern life in his writings. [captures]

CREATIVE PROBLEM SOLVING

LEARNING FOR LIFE

Planning for the Future

Problem

Many of the stories and poems in the collections you have just read are told from the perspective of people looking back on their lives from the vantage point of old age. How do people in our society make fulfilling lives for themselves as they grow older? How can you plan for your later years so that life is meaningful and enjoyable?

Project

Research contemporary issues pertaining to aging: geriatric health care, the future of Social Security and retirement benefits, increases in life expectancy, older employees returning to the work force, changing perspectives of older adults, and so on.

Preparation

1. With a group, brainstorm a list of questions you have about the topic of aging.
2. Make a list of current books, periodicals, and other sources for information on aging.

Procedure

1. You might want to interview an older relative or friend about individual perspectives on aging and retirement. You might also choose to
   - interview a geriatric doctor or nurse about the medical aspects of aging
   - investigate retirement options by contacting the American Association of Retired Persons (AARP)
   - examine retirement financing with a financial planning expert
   - discuss social and emotional aspects of aging with a social worker or psychologist

   Set a time for your interview, and prepare a list of questions.
2. Study current social views of aging and the elderly by paying attention to media representations. You might take notes on news programs devoted to the topic of the elderly, keep track of the number of older adult characters on TV shows and note how they are portrayed, and watch popular films such as *The Trip to Bountiful* and *Driving Miss Daisy*. What positive and negative messages about aging is society giving us?

Presentation

Present your information on aging in one of the following formats (or another that your teacher approves):

1. **Retirement Brochure**
   Write and design a brochure describing the ideal retirement plan for you. Be sure to include the following:
   - whether you plan to continue working part time, perform community service, and so on
   - a description of the living situation you would prefer
   - recreational activities you hope to participate in
2. **In Praise of Old Age**
   Put together a video documentary or a photo-essay of interviews with older adults. Show as many sides of the realities of aging as you can. If you wish, include interviews with people who work with the aged or who live with or know the particular persons you have interviewed.
3. **Graphic Communication**
   Share your findings about aging (what happens to the body as it ages, life expectancy in the twenty-first century, media depictions of the elderly, economic trends among retired people, and so on) in a visual display that combines two or more types of graphic communication: charts, graphs, diagrams, illustrations, and so on. Set up your graphic display in your school.

Processing

What did you learn about aging by completing this project? What can people do to develop more realistic ideas of what growing older entails? What can you do now to make sure that your own later years are meaningful and enjoyable? Write a reflection for your portfolio.

Learning for Life

Technology Tip

Using a computer station at school, students may research the topic of aging over the Internet. Refer students to **http://www.yahoo.com/Health/Geriatrics_and_Aging** for a directory of resources available on the World Wide Web. The American Association of Retired Persons (AARP), a membership organization for people over fifty, provides information about travel opportunities, discounts, and issues related to aging. Students may use a search engine and the keywords *AARP*, *Gray Panthers*, or *aging* to search the World Wide Web for additional information. *Preview any Internet activity that you suggest to students. Because these resources are sometimes public forums, their content can be unpredictable.* When completing video documentation or photo essays, remind students that they must ask for permission from older adults before taping interviews and that they must stop taping at any time they are asked to do so.

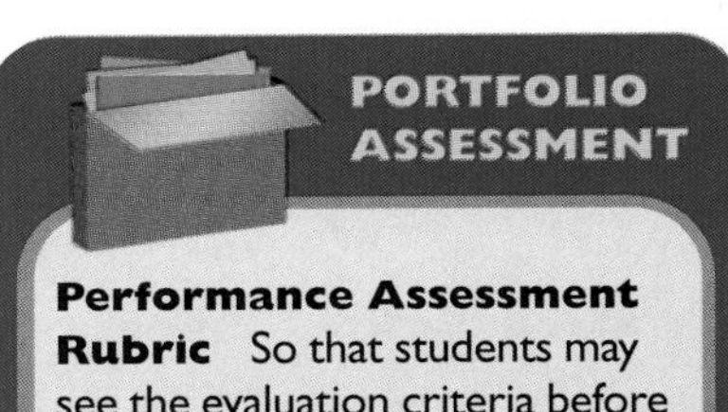

Performance Assessment Rubric So that students may see the evaluation criteria before they begin working on these projects, share the rubric provided in the ***Portfolio Management System***, p. 173.

DEVELOPING WORKPLACE COMPETENCIES

Preparation	Procedure	Presentation
Makes decisions Works on teams Demonstrates individual responsibility Works with people from diverse backgrounds	Acquires data Evaluates data Applies technology to specific tasks Improves systems	Thinks creatively Teaches others Selects equipment Communicates ideas and information

American Drama

Scene from Rodgers and Hammerstein's *Carousel.* Lincoln Center, New York City, 1994.
Photofest.

811

PROGRAM MANAGER

- **Summative Assessment** See **Test: Literary Period Test: American Drama,** ***Test Booklet,*** pp. 209–214, for a test on an additional text from the same historical era.
- **Application** For practice of a reading strategy for this unit, see **Becoming a Strategic Reader** worksheet, ***Teaching Resources B,*** pp. 121–122.
- **Performance Assessment** Use **Assessment** 4 in the ***Integrated Performance Assessment,*** Level F, to evaluate reading and writing skills covered in collections 17–21. For help with evaluation, see ***Holistic Scoring Workshop*** software.

Responding to the Quotation
Even students who have never attended live theater have experienced a kind of theater in television and movies. Encourage students to share examples of times when seeing a story helped them to understand or enjoy it better than reading it would have. Then, ask students to put the second sentence of Mann's comment in their own words. [Possible responses: Theater helps us understand the world around us; or theater helps people see why they feel and behave as they do.]

Technology Tip

Invite your school's drama teacher or a local thespian to discuss the history of American theater with your students. Discuss whether the history of the theater parallels the history of the United States and the history of literature and the arts. Videotape the conversation for use with other classes.

American Drama

by **Robert Anderson**

Theater is one of the most emotionally satisfying experiences imaginable. It touches our inner core, and gives insight into who we are.

—Theodore Mann

Drama is probably the most difficult form of writing; it certainly seems to take the longest to learn. According to a saying, young poets are eighteen, young novelists are twenty-four, and young playwrights are thirty.

George S. Kaufman, a noted American writer of comedies during the 1920s and 1930s, said that writing plays was not an art but a trick. Art or trick, it is difficult, possibly because when a play is written, it is not finished in the same way that a poem or novel is. There remains the painful and pleasurable process of bringing the play to life on stage, with the help of a director, actors, set designer, costume designer, lighting technician, stagehands, musicians—and a responsive audience. Producing a play is a team effort, and much can go wrong. A beautifully written and acted scene, for example, can be ruined if the lighting technician dims the lights too rapidly. **A**

> . . . [W]hile I am working I toss papers right and left; at the end of each day I gather them helter-skelter and pile them together. So that the ultimate arrangement is a colossal job, which I do with actual groans and muttered curses, sitting on the floor with papers all about me, gradually going into little separate stacks, some order finally emerging, but not till I have died a thousand deaths. . . . Writing is not a happy profession.
>
> —Tennessee Williams

Another difference between drama and other literary forms is that movement and gesture are essential elements in drama. Some of the high points in a play may even be nonverbal. In *The Diary of Anne Frank,* **B** for example, Mr. Frank realizes that the Nazis are downstairs and that the family's hiding place is about to be discovered. He turns to his family and friends and spreads his hands in resignation. This heartbreaking moment is conceived by the playwright, but its achievement on the stage—the exact gesture—requires the close and creative cooperation of actor and director.

Young writers are often drawn to the stage by the theatrical trappings: the gestures, the colorful sets, and the magical effects that drama can achieve. But playwrights soon learn that theatrical effects are rarely enough in themselves. The effects and gestures are there only to serve a story, and it must be a story that engages the passions of the collaborators—the director, the actors, and dozens of others who work to produce a play. Stage technicians may dazzle our senses with intricate and fascinating effects, but if a play doesn't have a significant story, we find nothing moving in the end, because our emotions have not been touched.

A. Expansion

Commenting on this process, Donald C. Farber, the author of several books about play production and theater law, writes that the people a producer selects are all equally important. "I can't and won't say that any one thing or person is more important than any other. . . . I have participated in discussions into the wee hours of the night as to whether the director is more important than the star, or whether the stage manager is more important than the set designer. This is utter nonsense. They are all critically important and it behooves you to select all wisely for therein may lie the difference between a flop and a smash hit."

B. Expansion

The Diary of Anne Frank, written by Frances Goodrich and Albert Hackett, is based on the diary kept by Anne Frank, a real-life teenage Jewish girl, as she hid with her family and a few other Jewish people in an Amsterdam attic during the Nazi occupation of Holland. The play won many awards, and its first production ran for 717 performances. The play was not universally applauded; for example, Arthur Miller found it powerful but complained that it lacked a far-reaching vision. Still, *The Diary of Anne Frank* continues to touch audiences around the world.

Elements of Literature:* Videodisc** Use the bar codes below to access information American drama. For more information, see the Videodisc ***Teacher's Manual.

Videodisc Side B

Begin Play, English Track

Begin Play, Spanish Track

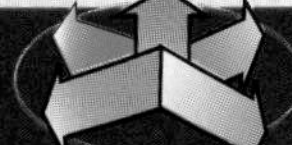

PROGRAM MANAGER

- **Planning Instruction** See **Teaching Notes, *Teaching Resources B,*** pp. 117–118, for additional teaching options about American Drama.
- **Assessment** For assessment of the literary and historical events mentioned in the historical introduction, see **Literary Period Introduction Test, *Test Booklet,*** pp. 199–200.

A. Exploring the Historical Period

Our Town was innovative for its era. It did away with the proscenium curtain and scenery, relying instead on a few props and descriptions by the stage manager to establish **setting.**

B. Exploring the Culture

Baseball has itself been a topic for playwrights exploring ideas that are part of U.S. culture. For example, *Damn Yankees* (1955), a musical comedy about a man who sells his soul to the Devil to become an outstanding baseball player, is periodically revived. On a serious note, a main character in August Wilson's *Fences* (1986) lives with the frustration of having missed a baseball career.

C. Reader's Response: First Thoughts

? How do people respond to a sporting event? [Sample responses: By getting involved with the action—cheering favorite teams and players; or getting passionate about the game's outcome.] How is this like the way people respond to a play? [Sample responses: People get involved with the characters and story of a play; what happens to the characters has an emotional effect on the audience.]

D. Expansion

Conflict is vital to effective drama. The U.S. playwright David Mamet (whose works include *Glengarry Glen Ross* [1983; 1984 Pulitzer Prize]) speaks of the dynamics in acting: "It's all about two people who want something different. . . . If the two people don't want something from each other, then why are you having the scene? . . . If two people don't want something different, the audience is going to go to sleep. Power, that's just another way of putting it."

Structure: Organizing Our Emotions

When a play goes wrong, it is almost always because the writer has failed to conceive the story in dramatic terms. There are, of course, some plays (such as (A) Thornton Wilder's *Our Town*) that work in the theater even though they ignore the usual principles of drama. But over the centuries certain principles have developed, and they are usually observed by playwrights who want to catch, hold, and reward the attention of an audience.

The analogy is slightly oversimplified, but we respond to a play in very much the way we respond (B) to a sports event. Let's assume that one summer (C) evening you go to a professional baseball game. For some reason, you take a liking to one of the pitchers. Then someone sitting next to you says that the pitcher has been out for several weeks with an injured elbow and is trying to make a comeback. If he fails in this game, he is finished. You start rooting for him. He gets some bad calls from the plate umpire, and you boo or whistle. Then your neighbor tells you that the pitcher is not pitching his best. Unless he stops protecting his injured elbow and starts putting more speed in his pitches, he will not win.

> You have to hit the public when it is not looking . . . you have to make it real to them the way the subway is real. You can't depend on their embracing your work because it is art, but only because it somehow reaches into the part of them that is still alive and questing.
>
> —Arthur Miller

Most plays have more psychological complexity than this situation does. With a little imagination, however, we can add to the pitcher's problems. Suppose, for instance, that the pitcher's wife is afraid that if he throws too hard, he will ruin his elbow and be unable to play. She tells him that if he damages his elbow further, she will leave him; but, to him, the glory of winning transcends practical matters. To his wife, he is a ball-playing "boy," careless and immature. And so forth. . . . What has happened in this scenario is what happens in almost every play. Early on, the playwright organizes our emotions behind some character or group of characters: We are "for" them. The playwright has placed these characters in a situation involving **conflict** and then has made us understand that it is not just any conflict: The character or characters have something vital at stake. They want to win, and they need to win in order to survive. In the baseball game, the (D) situation is made difficult for the pitcher, who is the **protagonist** (the major character who wants something and who drives the action forward). The pitcher struggles against

NEIL SIMON'S
New Comedy
BRIGHTON BEACH MEMOIRS
MATTHEW BRODERICK
ELIZABETH FRANZ
PETER MICHAEL GOETZ
MANDY INGBER
ŽELJKO IVANEK
JODI THELEN
JOYCE VAN PA

JED HARRIS presents
OUR TOWN
A PLAY BY THORNTON WILDER

PLAYBILL
Winter Garden
WEST SIDE STORY

OPTIONS FOR TEACHING

STRATEGIES FOR INCLUSION

Advanced As time permits, supplement the discussion in the text by asking students to research and report on any of the following topics:

- the history of comedy on the American stage
- the history of Broadway musicals
- today's best-known playwrights
- stock and repertory companies
- regional theater
- drama in your community

Kinesthetic/Spatial To help students apply the idea that a play exists in the interaction between actors and audience, have several students present a scene from a play (*A Raisin in the Sun,* pp. 828–886, or another play of your choosing). After they have done so, have the actors and the audience describe, with examples from the performance, how the people onstage responded not only to each other but also to the audience.

Interpersonal Ask students to imagine that they are producing a new play. In whole-class or small-group discussion, have them explain what their tasks would be, how they would establish good working relationships among the parties involved, and how they would produce the play efficiently. Also, ask them to explain what they would do if the play had poor ticket sales and received mixed or unfavorable reviews.

both **external conflict** (the opposing side) and **internal conflict** (his fears of damaging his arm, his feelings about the pressure from his wife). The fan sitting next to you has given us the background information, or **exposition** (who the pitcher is, what he wants to do, and what he has at stake). The story of a character who, against the odds, wants something meaningful has been set in motion. The tension mounts as the innings pass; we are witnessing, or participating in and enjoying, a drama.

> . . . I would say that the whole notion of going into a theater and sitting with a lot of other people and watching a spectacle, especially now when you can watch television or the movies with greater convenience, tells me that, apart from the fact that it's a little more exciting to see a live actor on the stage, it's also exciting to sit next to human beings.
>
> —Arthur Miller

The word *participation* is important. We have all heard ballplayers say how encouraged they are by the response of the spectators. Actors, too, may say as they come offstage after a scene, "That's a wonderful audience out there tonight!" And because of the audience, performances often rise to a higher level. It has often been said that a play exists halfway between the stage and the audience. What an audience gets from a performance is directly related to what it brings to the performance, not only in the way of understanding and feeling but also in enthusiasm. In successful dramatic performances, a note is sounded onstage, and a chord of recognition or responsiveness echoes back from the audience. A play performed in an empty theater is not a play.

The basic elements of drama include exposition, to give us information, and a protagonist, the major character who struggles against internal conflict and external conflict.

How a Play Is Produced (It's a Miracle!)

The English plays of the late Middle Ages were called miracle plays because they often dealt with stories of miracles from the Bible or the lives of the saints. Any modern-day American play might also be called a miracle play, because it is a miracle that it was written and even more of a miracle that it was produced. In the United States today, drama is dependent on money. Only a few institutional theaters are able to present plays with little or no regard for profit. Most of the plays that are produced (and that therefore stand a chance of becoming part of our dramatic literature) are put on with the idea that they will make money.

To produce any writer's new play on Broadway costs a minimum of half a million dollars (at this writing). The **producers** (people who advance the money) willing to take such a risk are rare, although such risks *are* taken every season. Even though it operates in a very costly manner, the professional Broadway theater, to its credit, has been the launching pad for most of the distinguished plays in American dramatic literature.

E. Expansion

The power of a dramatic performance often can be measured by its ability to transcend the audience's background. For example, the first time *Waiting for Godot* was presented at San Quentin penitentiary (in November, 1957, by the San Francisco Actors' Workshop), there was concern over how it would be received. The prison newspaper reported the response as follows: "[The] San Francisco company had its audience of captives in its collective hand. . . . Those that had felt a less controversial vehicle should be attempted as a first play here had their fears allayed a short five minutes after the Samuel Beckett piece began to unfold. . . . We're still waiting for Godot, and shall continue to wait. When the scenery gets too drab and the action too slow, we'll call each other names and swear to part forever—but then, there's no place to go!" For some time afterward, names and phrases from the play remained a part of the private language of San Quentin.

STRATEGIES FOR INCLUSION

Visual/Auditory If possible, watch excerpts from film versions of the plays mentioned in the text. The following (with years of the recommended film versions in parentheses) are available on videocassette:

- *All My Sons* by Arthur Miller (1986)
- *Death of a Salesman* by Arthur Miller (1985)
- *The Glass Menagerie* by Tennessee Williams (1987)
- *Our Town* by Thornton Wilder (1940; 1980)
- *Strange Interlude* by Eugene O'Neill (1932; 1988)
- *A Streetcar Named Desire* by Tennessee Williams (1951)

Special Needs Tell students that drama is a literary form that demands a collaborative process. The author's message is interpreted through the actors, coloring the way the audience reacts. Have students create a mobile to illustrate the balance necessary between the people on and behind the stage and those in the audience. Each element of the mobile, whether a word or a picture, should present one aspect of this creative participation. Ask students to begin with the collaborators discussed in "Structure" on pp. 814–815 and "How a Play Is Produced" on pp. 815–817, but have students add to this list from their own knowledge about plays.

A. Expansion
Explain to students the differences among these terms:
Broadway: A group of New York theaters (34 in all, seating more than 800 people each), on or near Broadway in Manhattan.
Off-Broadway: A group of New York theaters (seating less than 300 people each) that arose in the 1950s beyond the Broadway theater district and that features more experimental and less expensive productions.
Off-Off-Broadway: A still more experimental and often not-for-profit group of approximately 125 theaters.
Regional theater: Dramatic production—especially year-round, professional drama—occurring outside New York City.

B. Expansion
The fact that a producer is interested in a play does not guarantee that the play will go before an audience. Often, a producer will negotiate only for an option—exclusive rights to produce the play within a given time, if he or she decides to do so. Even a good producer cannot guarantee that a play will be a hit and will turn a profit. Broadway history abounds with stories of critically acclaimed, award-winning plays that closed very quickly because of poor ticket sales.

C. Expansion
The producer's tasks go far beyond choosing the play and working with the playwright to selecting a director and cast. Most important, the producer works with backers, or investors, to arrange for the financing of the production. The producer also secures a theater; hires a stage manager and set, costume, and lighting designers; and makes final decisions about how to promote the production.

(A) Recently, regional theaters throughout the country have been presenting new plays by both new and established playwrights. The Broadway producers often visit, look, and take whatever they want for production. For the most part, only a successful Broadway production gives a playwright enough income to plunge in and take the years necessary to write the next play. For that reason, Broadway remains the goal of most playwrights.

There are many stops on the way to New York, some of which become full stops. Over ten thousand plays are copyrighted every year; this probably represents only half of the plays that are actually written. Perhaps several hundred new plays are produced onstage *somewhere* around the country; maybe ten appear on Broadway.

> To a certain extent I imagine a play is completely finished in my mind—in my case, at any rate—without my knowing it, before I sit down to write. So in that sense, I suppose, writing a play is *finding out* what the play is.
>
> —Edward Albee

Producers could not hope to cope with reading thousands and thousands of plays, so playwrights must generally find an **agent** who will handle their work. The agent is the producer's first line of defense. Knowing their various tastes, the agent submits a play to likely producers, who (B) may take three months to a year to read it. They may admire the play but still be unwilling to produce it. One playwright used to say, "If they take you to lunch, they're not going to invest in your play." A good lunch is a consolation prize, and many playwrights have eaten very well off plays that were never produced.

(C) But if the producer should decide to finance the play, he or she then sits down with the playwright to go over changes suggested for the script or ideas for directors and actors. Authors maintain control over their scripts, and the playwright is very much involved in the selection of the director and the actors. Of course, since theater is a collaborative medium, the playwright tries to get along with the producer. But if the playwright and producer discover during these preliminary talks that they have incompatible ideas, they can shake hands and part.

The director becomes the playwright's surrogate at rehearsals. In a sense, the director takes the play away from the playwright, and, finally, the actors take it away from both of them.

Rehearsals involve both pleasure and tension. Many temperaments must mesh as the actors move forward to the climactic moment of opening night. (Note that all the elements of drama itself are also present at play rehearsals: striving for a goal, having something at stake, dealing with internal and external conflicts, etc.)

OPTIONS FOR TEACHING

INTEGRATING THE LANGUAGE ARTS

Strategic Reading Help students summarize the introduction's main points by dividing the class into five groups, each group focusing on one of these sections:

- Introduction and "Structure"
- "How a Play Is Produced"
- "The History of American Drama" and "The Influence of Europe"
- The discussions of Eugene O'Neill, Arthur Miller, and Tennessee Williams
- "The Revolt Against Realism"

Ask each group to place each section title in the center of a cluster diagram and to record the section's main points on the spokes. Demonstrate the process using Transparency 3: Cluster Diagram in the Transparency Package. Ask groups to explain and share their clusters so that everyone in the class has a complete set.

Writing: Letter Invite groups of students to write a letter designed to secure an agent's interest in their original play. The letter should include a summary of the play as well as a persuasive appeal about why such a play would be successful. After students have presented their letters, have the class choose the play in which they think an agent would be most interested.

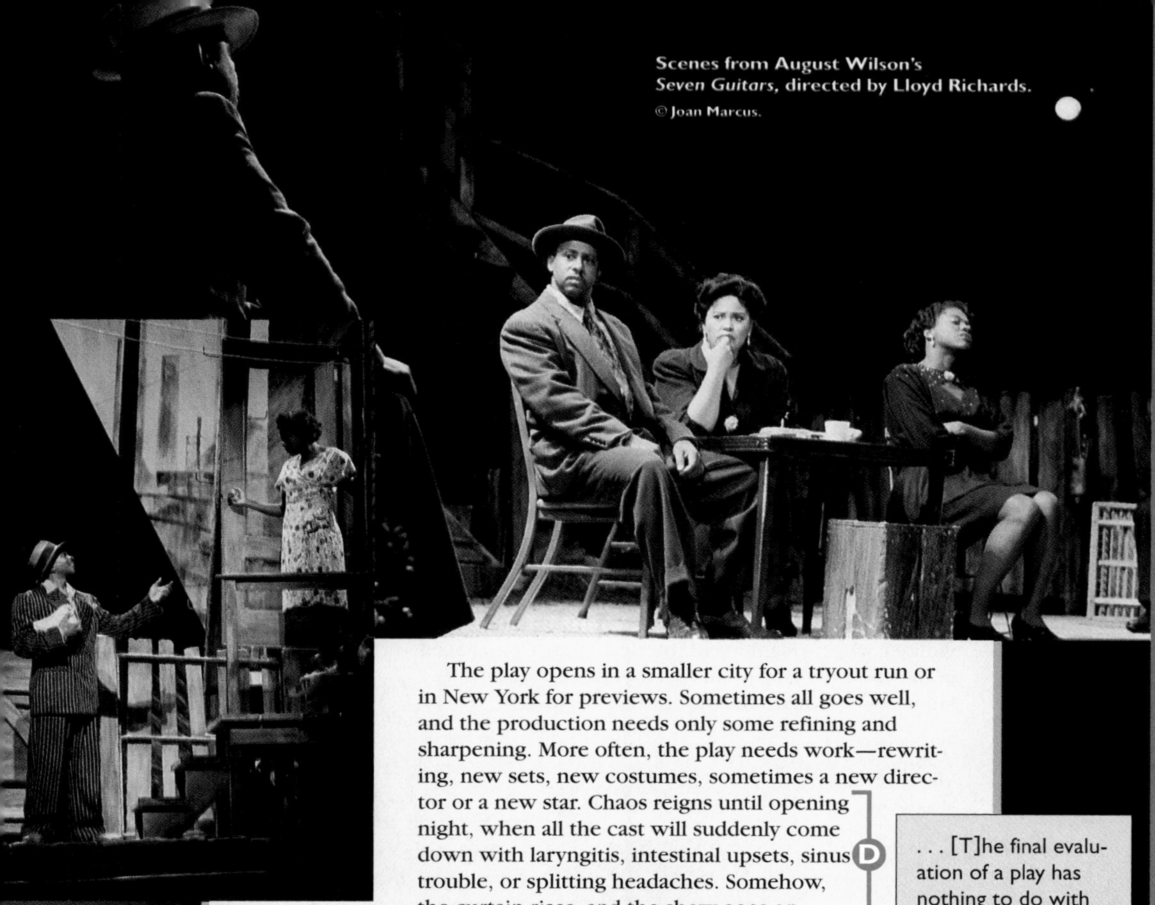

Scenes from August Wilson's *Seven Guitars*, directed by Lloyd Richards.
© Joan Marcus.

The play opens in a smaller city for a tryout run or in New York for previews. Sometimes all goes well, and the production needs only some refining and sharpening. More often, the play needs work—rewriting, new sets, new costumes, sometimes a new director or a new star. Chaos reigns until opening night, when all the cast will suddenly come down with laryngitis, intestinal upsets, sinus trouble, or splitting headaches. Somehow, the curtain rises, and the show goes on. **D**

The day after the opening, there may or may not be a line of eager theatergoers at the box office. If there is, the playwright has created what may later be called an American classic, which will be performed around the world and will find its way into the anthologies you study in school. If there isn't a line, the playwright will quickly look around for a way to make a living while writing the next play—if he or she has the courage. The second instance is the more usual. The theater has been called the "fabulous invalid," always teetering on the edge of extinction. If so, playwrights themselves might be called the walking wounded—working, barely surviving, but finally enduring to try once again.

The production of a play depends on a successful working relationship between the playwright, the producer, the director, and the actors.

> . . . [T]he final evaluation of a play has nothing to do with immediate audience or critical response. The playwright, along with any writer, composer, painter in this society, has got to have a terribly private view of his own value, of his own work. He's got to listen to his own voice primarily.
>
> —Edward Albee

D. Critical Reading: Expressing an Opinion

? What do you think causes these sudden illnesses? [Possible answers: opening-night jitters; the buildup of stress over weeks or months of preparation.] What is ironic about the humor in this comment? [Possible answer: The writer first suggests that opening night brings an end to the chaos of preparation; but to have a cast become so ill on opening night would itself produce chaos.]

INTEGRATING THE LANGUAGE ARTS

Speaking and Listening Refer students to the discussion of O'Neill's experimental techniques on p. 820. Then, have small groups improvise scenes that show how masks might be used to distinguish between a character's social and private personalities, how asides might be used to reveal inner feelings, and how two actors might be used to portray the same character. Students could improvise scenes such as applying for a job, asking for a date, or attending a party with someone they do not like. Follow up each improvisation with class discussion.

Vocabulary The following words relate to the production of plays in the United States today. Have students use a dictionary or a book about stagecraft to discover their meaning.

blocking	method acting
crew	properties
drop	roadshow
extras	run
grips	stage manager
house	understudy
loft	upstage

A. Expansion

O'Neill's grim and moving psychological plays marked a radical departure from the romantic convention of theater as entertainment. With no uniquely American tradition to guide him, O'Neill introduced many techniques that have become staples: repetition of actions or phrases to underscore dramatic intent; use of symbolic masks or costumes; use of archetypal themes from classical religion and myth; and revival of the Elizabethan devices of soliloquy and aside to reveal a character's inner state. Like Whitman and Twain, O'Neill gained material from the many odd jobs he held as he moved around the country before he began to write. Although several American novelists have won the Nobel Prize in literature, at the time of publication of this textbook, O'Neill is the only American playwright to have done so, in 1936.

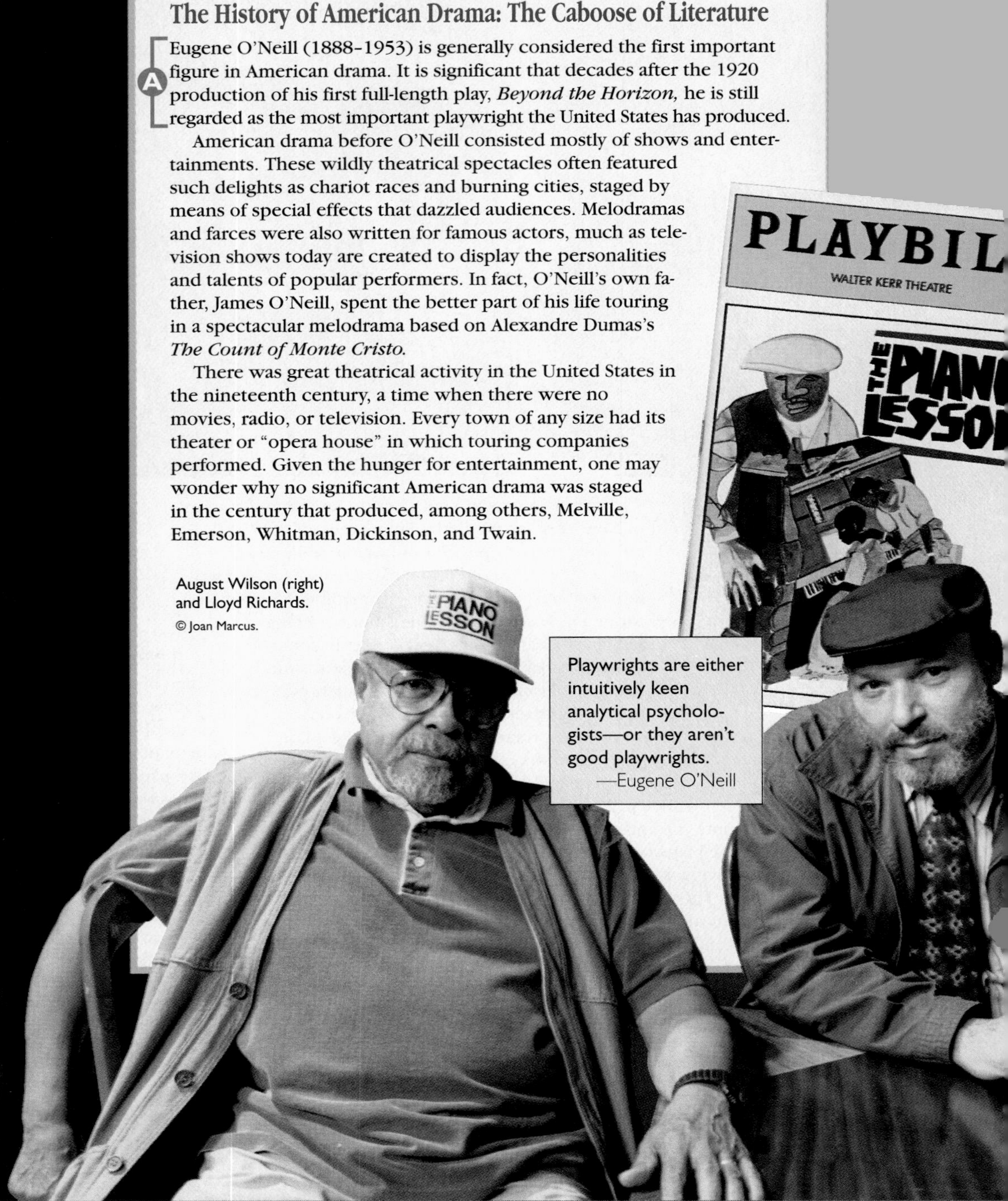

The History of American Drama: The Caboose of Literature

A Eugene O'Neill (1888–1953) is generally considered the first important figure in American drama. It is significant that decades after the 1920 production of his first full-length play, *Beyond the Horizon,* he is still regarded as the most important playwright the United States has produced.

American drama before O'Neill consisted mostly of shows and entertainments. These wildly theatrical spectacles often featured such delights as chariot races and burning cities, staged by means of special effects that dazzled audiences. Melodramas and farces were also written for famous actors, much as television shows today are created to display the personalities and talents of popular performers. In fact, O'Neill's own father, James O'Neill, spent the better part of his life touring in a spectacular melodrama based on Alexandre Dumas's *The Count of Monte Cristo.*

There was great theatrical activity in the United States in the nineteenth century, a time when there were no movies, radio, or television. Every town of any size had its theater or "opera house" in which touring companies performed. Given the hunger for entertainment, one may wonder why no significant American drama was staged in the century that produced, among others, Melville, Emerson, Whitman, Dickinson, and Twain.

August Wilson (right) and Lloyd Richards.

Playwrights are either intuitively keen analytical psychologists—or they aren't good playwrights.
—Eugene O'Neill

OPTIONS FOR TEACHING

COOPERATIVE LEARNING

Corners Query Designate each corner of the classroom as a "query corner" for one of the following topics:

- How plays create meaning
- How plays are produced
- The history of American drama
- American drama today

Send students to the corner dealing with the subject in which they are most interested. Have each group choose a discussion leader, a secretary, and a spokesperson to present the group's list of questions to the class. Students should brainstorm three to five questions that they hope to have answered in the introductory material. Compile a class list of questions, and have students vote on the five questions that they deem most important. Then, have them read the introduction to find the answers to the five questions. If the text does not answer a question to students' satisfaction, have them conduct original research to find an answer.

One explanation is that theater has usually followed the other arts, rather than pointing the way toward new directions. Robert Sherwood, one of a group of notable American playwrights between 1920 and 1940, once said, "Drama travels in the caboose of literature." Theater seems to take up new attitudes, subject matter, and forms only after they have been explored in the other arts. For the most part, theater tends to dramatize accepted attitudes and values. **B**

The reason for this is that theater is a social art, one we attend as part of a large group; we seem to respond to something new much more slowly as a group than we do as individuals. When you laugh or cry in the theater, your response is noticed. You are, in a sense, giving your approval, and this approval may be subject to criticism or condemnation by those sitting around you who are not laughing or crying. Furthermore, you may not be shocked to *read* about your secret thoughts, dreams, and desires; but if you *see* them shown on stage as you sit among a thousand people, you may refuse to respond, refuse to acknowledge them. You may even rise up and stalk out of the theater.

Thus, the novel and, to some extent, the poetry of the nineteenth and early twentieth centuries were more daring than the theater in giving us a record of experience, in showing us life as it *is* lived rather than as it *should be* lived.

During the period before Eugene O'Neill, American drama tended to be mild and sentimental, rarely questioning the life and attitudes it depicted, almost never challenging the accepted traditions of its times.

The Influence of Europe: Psychology and Taboo Subjects

European drama, which was to influence modern American drama profoundly, matured in the last third of the nineteenth century with the achievements of three playwrights: the Norwegian Henrik Ibsen, the Swede August Strindberg, and the Russian Anton Chekhov. **C** Ibsen deliberately tackled subjects such as guilt, sexuality, and mental illness—subjects that had never before been so realistically and disturbingly portrayed on stage. Strindberg brought to his characterizations an unprecedented level of psychological complexity. And Chekhov, along with Ibsen and Strindberg, shifted the subject matter of drama from wildly theatrical displays of external action to inner action and emotions and the concerns of everyday life. Chekhov once remarked, "People don't go to the North Pole and fall off icebergs. They go to the office and quarrel with their wives and eat cabbage soup."

Ibsen, Strindberg, and Chekhov bequeathed to their American heirs plays about life as it is actually lived. They presented characters and situations more or less realistically, in what has been called the "slice-of-life" dramatic technique.

B. Expansion
Robert Sherwood (1896–1955), wounded in World War I, resolved to do all that he could to stop future wars—an attitude evident in his first Broadway play, *The Road to Rome* (1927), and in his Pulitzer Prize–winning play *Idiot's Delight* (1936). He won another Pulitzer Prize in 1940 for *There Shall Be No Light,* a play about the Soviet Union's invasion of Finland. Extremely vocal in warning of the dangers of European totalitarianism, Sherwood also served at times as a special assistant in the War Department (now the Department of Defense), and he was a speech writer for President Franklin D. Roosevelt.

C. Literary Connections
Notable plays by these authors include the following:
Henrik Ibsen: *Peer Gynt* (1867), *A Doll's House* (1879), *Ghosts* (1881), *An Enemy of the People* (1882), *The Wild Duck* (1884), *Hedda Gabler* (1890), *The Master Builder* (1892)
August Strindberg: *The Father* (1887), *The Dance of Death* (1901), *Easter* (1901), *A Dream Play* (1902)
Anton Chekhov: *The Seagull* (1896), *Uncle Vanya* (1899), *The Three Sisters* (1901), *The Cherry Orchard* (1904)

CLASSROOM MANAGEMENT

Gallery Give students who have completed the Art activity on p. T820 a chance to display their artwork in a classroom gallery. Work with them to set up stations around the classroom for groups of related artwork, and have each student write an informational card about his or her piece. Ask groups of students to tour all the stations, to make notes about each piece of art, and to share their thoughts in a class discussion.

Teacher's Reflection While students are reading the introduction or working on activities related to it, do a self-assessment of your goals in teaching drama. Rate each of the following goals from 1 (absolutely) to 5 (certainly not).

____ Have students enact dramatic scenes in class.
____ Explore in detail the play's **conflicts** and **themes.**
____ Supplement the play with excerpts from other plays dealing with similar conflicts and themes.
____ Focus on elements of stagecraft.
____ Have students spend time recording personal responses to drama in their Reader's Logs.

A. Exploring the Historical Period

- The Provincetown Players—a group of actors, producers, and playwrights—organized in Provincetown, Massachusetts, and moved to New York the following year; they worked there until 1929. The group produced almost one hundred plays by many playwrights of the period.
- The Washington Square Players was a shorter-lived group, several of whose members founded the Theatre Guild in 1918. The Guild specialized in contemporary productions, particularly the plays of O'Neill and of the Irish dramatist George Bernard Shaw (1856–1950). The Guild also helped develop musical theater; for example, it produced George Gershwin's *Porgy and Bess* (1935) and brought together Richard Rodgers and Oscar Hammerstein II for *Oklahoma!* (1943).

B. Expansion

David Sievers points out that O'Neill wrote his most Freudian plays after undergoing psychoanalysis in 1927. O'Neill was influenced not only by Freud but also by Jung. Jung defined *character-splitting*, a phenomenon in which a person deceives others about his or her true character. The person puts on a figurative mask. O'Neill used actual masks to symbolize this splitting. He wrote that masks would allow the playwright to explore psychological conflicts.

Realism and Eugene O'Neill: Putting American Drama on the Map

Realistic drama is based on the illusion that when we watch a play, we are looking at life through a "fourth wall" that has been removed so that we can see the action. Soon after the beginning of the twentieth century, realism became the dominant mode of American drama.

As with all theatrical revolutions, the movement toward realism began apart from the commercial theater. But very soon after the new drama succeeded in the little theaters off Broadway (about 1916), the commercial theater adopted realism, too.

> Sure, I'll write about happiness if I ever happen to meet up with that luxury and find it sufficiently dramatic and in harmony with any deep rhythm of life. But happiness is a word. What does it mean? Exaltation, an intensified feeling of the significant worth of man's being and becoming? Well, if it means that—and not a mere smirking contentment with one's lot—I know that there is more of it in one real tragedy than in all the happy ending plays ever written.
>
> —Eugene O'Neill

Goodspeed Opera House, East Haddam, Connecticut.

Inge Morath/Magnum.

A In 1916 and 1917, two small theater groups in New York—the Provincetown Players and the Washington Square Players—began to produce new American plays. They provided a congenial home for new American playwrights, notably Eugene O'Neill, whose first one-act plays about the sea were produced by the Provincetown Players in Greenwich Village in 1916. (New movements in the theater have often begun with one-act plays. In addition to O'Neill, Tennessee Williams, Clifford Odets, and Edward Albee all started with short plays.)

These theater groups seemed to have no program. They were not sure what they were for, but they were sure what they were against: the established commercial theater. They would produce any play, in any style, that commercial theater would not touch.

B O'Neill gravitated there naturally. Well aware of Sigmund Freud and his new theories about the complex self, O'Neill tried especially hard to reveal more than realism—or Naturalism—could normally reveal. "The old naturalism," he wrote, "no longer applies. We have taken too many snapshots of each other in every graceless position; we have endured too much from the banality of surfaces."

In *The Great God Brown* (1926), O'Neill experimented with using masks to differentiate between two sides of a personality. In *Days Without End* (1934), he had two actors play one character to achieve the same end. And in *Strange Interlude* (1928), characters spoke in asides to the audience, revealing thoughts and feelings that could not be expressed in dialogue to other characters.

OPTIONS FOR TEACHING

CROSSING THE CURRICULUM

Art Invite students to capture artistically an image that (1) depicts some aspect of stagecraft or play presentation (which may include the creation of a thematic symbol for the set of an original play), (2) represents some era of American theatrical history, or (3) relates to a specific play discussed in the introduction. Students may work individually or cooperatively; encourage the use of a variety of mediums.

Industrial Arts Have interested students research (by meeting with technicians at a local playhouse, if possible) and report on ways in which lighting and sound effects are achieved in plays. *You may want to obtain permission from parents or guardians and from the parties students will contact before they begin work on this activity.* Alternatively, allow students to find out how some special effects (such as burning a building, crossing a raging river, or staging a chariot race) might be achieved without endangering the theater, actors, or audience.

Social Sciences Invite a team of students to present an oral report about a play that has been a milestone in its dealings with social issues of the past or present. Some plays they might consider are:

- *The Crucible* (Arthur Miller) and McCarthyism
- *A Doll's House* (Henrik Ibsen) and the women's movement
- *Rhinoceros* (Eugene Ionesco) and Nazism

With his experimental flair, his enormous output, and his high aspirations for the theater, Eugene O'Neill dominated American drama in his generation; he can be said to have put it on the map. His plays were widely produced abroad, and he was awarded the Nobel Prize in literature in 1936.

Scene from *Death of a Salesman* by Arthur Miller.
Photofest.

> Americans fancy themselves . . . to be openhanded, on the side of justice, a little bit careless about what they buy, wasteful, but essentially good guys, optimistic. But under that level of awareness there is another one, which gets expressed in very few movies and very few plays, but in more plays in proportion than in the movies: the level which confronts our bewilderment, our lonely naïveté, our hunger for purpose.
>
> —Arthur Miller

Arthur Miller: Playwright of Our Social Conscience

The post–World War II years brought two important figures to prominence in American drama: Arthur Miller (1915–) and Tennessee Williams (1911–1983). Although other playwrights, such as William Inge (1913–1973), have contributed striking and effective plays, Miller and Williams remain the dominant figures of the second half of the century. Miller and Williams represent the two principal movements in modern American drama: realism, and realism combined with an attempt at something more imaginative. From the beginning, American playwrights have tried to break away from realism or to blend it with more poetic expression, as in Miller's *Death of a Salesman* (1949), Williams's *The Glass Menagerie* (1944), and Thornton Wilder's *Our Town* (1938) and *The Skin of Our Teeth* (1942).

ASSESSMENT TOOLS

Check Test: Questions and Answers

1. Why is it desirable for an audience to participate in a play? [Not only do actors tend to respond better to an involved audience, but the audience gains a better understanding of what the production is trying to convey.]
2. What control do playwrights have over their plays? [They have control over their scripts and are involved in the selection of the director and the actors.]
3. How did Eugene O'Neill change the character of American drama? [He set a new standard by focusing on human psychology and experimenting with realistic drama.]
4. How did the concerns explored in Arthur Miller's plays differ from those explored by Tennessee Williams? [Miller generally focused on social issues, whereas Williams focused on personal ones.]
5. How is the Theater of the Absurd different from other kinds of drama? [It is more experimental and expressionistic, meant to portray the minds of characters through poetic images.] ☞

A. Literary Connections
Much of the complexity in Williams's plays centers on family relationships. In *The Glass Menagerie,* Amanda and Laura are mother and daughter. Amanda speaks constantly of her popularity as a young woman and seeks a gentleman caller for her shy daughter. In *A Streetcar Named Desire,* Blanche relies heavily on her sister, Stella, for emotional support.

Arthur Miller's best work, *Death of a Salesman,* is one of the most successful in fusing the realistic and the imaginative; in all of his other plays, however, Miller is the master of realism. He is a true disciple of Henrik Ibsen, not only in his realistic technique but also in his concern about society's impact on his characters' lives.

In Miller's plays, the course of the action and the development of characters depend not only on the characters' psychological makeup but also on the social, philosophical, and economic atmosphere of their times. Miller's most notable character, Willy Loman in *Death of a Salesman,* is a self-deluded man; but he is also a product of the American dream of success and a victim of the American business machine, which disposes of him when he has outlived his usefulness.

Miller is a writer of high moral seriousness, whether he is dealing with personal versus social responsibility, as in *All My Sons* (1947), or with witch hunts past and present, as in *The Crucible* (1953). Miller writes a plain and muscular prose that under the force of emotion often becomes eloquent, as in Linda Loman's famous speech in *Death of a Salesman,* in which she talks to her two sons about their father:

> I don't say he's a great man. Willy Loman never made a lot of money. His name was never in the paper. He's not the finest character that ever lived. But he's a human being, and a terrible thing is happening to him. So attention must be paid. He's not to be allowed to fall into his grave like an old dog. Attention, attention must finally be paid to such a person.
>
> —Arthur Miller,
> *from Death of a Salesman*

death of a Salesma

The PLAYBILL *for the Morosco*

Tennessee Williams: Playwright of Our Souls

A Although Tennessee Williams was Miller's contemporary, his concern was not with social matters, but with personal ones. If Miller was often the playwright of our social conscience, then Williams was the playwright of our souls. In play after play, he probed the psychological complexities of his characters, especially of his female characters: Amanda and Laura in *The Glass Menagerie* (1944), Blanche in *A Streetcar Named Desire* (1947), and Alma in *Summer and Smoke* (1948).

In contrast to Miller's spare, plain language, Williams's writing is delicate and sensuous; it is often colored with lush imagery and evocative rhythms. Miller's characters are, by and large, ordinary people with whom we identify because they are caught up in the social tensions of our times. Williams's characters are often women who are lost ladies, drowning in their own neuroses, but somehow mirroring a part of our own complex psychological selves.

OPTIONS FOR TEACHING

ASSESSMENT TOOLS

Self-Reflection Have students briefly explain (orally or in writing) what they knew about American drama before they read this introductory article. Then, ask them to respond to one or both of these questions.

- What would a play have to do or be to hold and reward your attention?
- What ideas do you think American drama should address today?

Invite students to share their responses; assess informally.

The actual scenes in Williams's plays are usually purely realistic, even though these scenes may deal with colorful and extreme characters. But Williams usually theatricalized the realism with "music in the wings" or symbolic props, such as Laura's unicorn in *The Glass Menagerie* or the looming statue of Eternity in *Summer and Smoke.* He always conceived his plays in visually arresting, colorful, theatrical environments—an effort in which he was aided by the imaginative designer Jo Mielziner, who designed the sets for many of his plays. B

In the works of Arthur Miller and Tennessee Williams, we see the two strongest strands in American drama: pure realism, and realism blended with an imaginative, poetic sensibility.

The Revolt Against Realism: Theater of Fragmentation

In the mid-nineteenth century, realism in drama was conceived as a revolt against crude theatricalism. Currently, there is a revolt against realism itself in American drama. Naturally, the movement is toward theatricalism again, with its emphasis on stage effects and imaginative settings. This revolt does not confine itself to a particular manner of staging; instead, it extends to the texture of language and plot in the scripts themselves.

The moral and religious certainties that once bound people together exert little or no force on many modern audiences. Some people believe that survival itself depends on a willingness to accept life as formless or meaningless.

Some American playwrights found this new outlook on life impossible to express in the orderly "beginning, middle, end" format of realism. They borrowed, again from Europe, a theater of fragmentation, impressions, and stream of consciousness that was called "expressionist." **Expressionist drama** aimed at the revelation of characters' interior consciousness without reference to a logical sequence of surface actions. Many writers who used expressionist techniques in drama came to be called playwrights of the Theater of the Absurd. Samuel Beckett (1906–1989) and Eugene Ionesco (1912–1994) were among the founders of the Theater of the Absurd. C The drama critic Martin Esslin has written this about the Absurdists: D

> The action of a play of the Theater of the Absurd is not intended to tell a story but to communicate a pattern of poetic images. E To give but one example: Things happen in [Samuel Beckett's] *Waiting*

Scene from *The Glass Menagerie* by Tennessee Williams. Long Wharf Theater, New Haven, Connecticut, 1986.

B. Humanities Connection
Jo Mielziner was perhaps Broadway's most innovative stage designer. Mielziner has said of Tennessee Williams and *The Glass Menagerie,* "My use of translucent and transparent scenic interior walls was not just another trick. It was a true reflection of the contemporary playwright's interest in—and at times obsession with—the exploration of the inner man." And of *A Streetcar Named Desire,* Mielziner writes "The magic of light opened up a fluid and poetic world of story telling. . . . Throughout the play the brooding atmosphere is like an impressionistic X-ray."

C. Expansion
Samuel Beckett's best-known plays are *Waiting for Godot* (1952), *Endgame* (1957), and *Krapp's Last Tape* (1958); he was awarded the Nobel Prize in literature in 1969. Eugene Ionesco is best remembered for *The Bald Soprano* (1950; his first play) and for *Rhinoceros* (1959).

D. Expansion
As the word *absurd* suggests, some aspects of this movement stress comedy. For example, the first New York production of *Waiting for Godot* featured the film comedian Bert Lahr, and its 1988 Lincoln Center revival starred Steve Martin and Robin Williams.

E. Responding to the Quotation
? In what ways might you see Esslin's comment about the Theater of the Absurd at work on television or at the movies? [Possible response: A pattern of images may be seen in dream sequences in television and movies, in music videos, or even in some commercials.]

Quickwrite

Before students write in their Reader's Logs, have them talk about what issues are important today and what they predict will happen to those issues. Then, have them jot down their ideas on how the predicted changes in these issues will affect American drama.

So, I would say, our main tradition from O'Neill to the present revolves around the question of integrity—not moral integrity alone, but the integrity of the personality. The difficulty is to locate the forces of disintegration. I have to believe they exist and can be unveiled.

—Arthur Miller

for Godot, but these things do not constitute a plot or a story; they are an image of Beckett's intuition that *nothing really ever happens* in man's existence.

—Martin Esslin

The trouble with a static play that mirrors a static life is that it is static. It is an image, a picture; and a picture can absorb our interest for only so long because it lacks the progression and development of a dramatic story. We can observe a situation without development for about the length of a one-act play. Perhaps this is why so many of the Absurdist plays *are* only one act, such as Beckett's *Krapp's Last Tape* and Ionesco's *The Bald Soprano.*

The most significant Absurdist in the United States has been Edward Albee (1928–). Albee is not a pure Absurdist, since, like all innovative playwrights, he experiments with many forms. From 1959 to 1970, Albee produced a play a year. These works ranged from his startling one-act debut, *The Zoo Story* (1959), through the Absurdist play *The American Dream* (1961), to the savage and electrifying domestic drama *Who's Afraid of Virginia Woolf?* (1962), which made Albee world famous.

Scene from *Happy Days* by Samuel Beckett. The entire play takes place while the actors are half buried in a pile of sand.

Experimental drama has increased the options that are open to playwrights. There are practically no conventions in the theater anymore; there is simply a stage and an audience. Playwrights are free to load the stage with scenery, lights, and special effects; but they are equally free—as the playwright was in the age of Shakespeare—to have an actor gesture toward one side of an utterly bare stage and say, "This is the Forest of Arden."

Dramatists now have the freedom to express their deepest feelings in almost any form they choose—provided that their approach can be made comprehensible to an audience and touch their emotions.

READER'S LOG

Quickwrite

What do you predict will happen to American drama in the next ten years with regard to subject matter, sets and costume design, popularity, and competition with movies and television? Jot down your thoughts, and then compare notes with those of your classmates.

REACHING FOR THE DREAM

Theme: **Deferred Dreams**

Hansberry's play reflects modern trends in theater. Both the psychology of the characters and the larger sociological picture are explored in this drama of conflicting dreams and hopes of one family living in mid-twentieth-century America.

Thematic Focus

The effects of a dream deferred are explored in this modern American drama.

- **A Raisin in the Sun** Members of an African American family struggle to retain their dignity in the face of personal as well as societal obstacles.

Literary Focus

Literary Element	Selection / Feature
Conflict/Characterization/Static and Dynamic Characters	**A Raisin in the Sun**

Writing Focus

The following flowchart shows how the writing assignment for the selection relates to and builds toward the culminating writing assignment presented in the Writer's Workshop at the end of the unit.

Selection	Work-in-Progress Assignment
A Raisin in the Sun	Collect ideas for a problem-solution essay p. 889
Writer's Workshop	Write a problem-solution essay pp. 895–899

Collection Planner

SELECTION/ FEATURE	PUPIL'S EDITION: Literary Elements / Active Reading	Writing	Speaking and Listening	Language and Vocabulary
A Raisin in the Sun Lorraine Hansberry (pp. 826–890) Primary Sources: A Letter from the Playwright (p. 887) Student to Student (p. 887)	• Reader's Log pp. 827, 851, 876 • Conflict p. 827 • Characterization p. 851 • Static and Dynamic Characters p. 876	• Critical Writing: Write essay on universal significance of play p. 889 • Critical Writing: Write opinion essay on importance of heritage p. 889 • Creative Writing: Write poem that could be used as new epigraph for play p. 889	• Performance: Act out scene or do group reading p. 889	• Language and Style: Patterns of Speech: Realistic Dialogue p. 888 • How to Own a Word: Analogies: Thought-Provoking Comparisons p. 890 • Try It Out: Write analogy exercise p. 890
The American Language: Euphemisms Gary Q. Arpin (pp. 892–894)				• Try It Out p. 894
Writer's Workshop: Problem-Solution Essay (pp. 895–899)		• Writing Process: Problem-solution essay pp. 895–899		
Language Workshop: Using Transitional Expressions (p. 900)				• Language Handbook: Commas pp. 1243–1244 • Using Transitional Expressions p. 900
Learning for Life: The Play's the Thing (p. 901)		• Write letter of recommendation p. 901	• Discuss plays p. 901	

Collection Resources

Teaching Resources B
Cross-Curricular Activity p. 132

Audiovisual Resources Binder
Fine Art Transparency 17.1

 Computer disk or CD-ROM

 Audiocassette

 Overhead Transparency

PROGRAM RESOURCES

Electronic Media	Teaching Resources with Organizer: Teaching Resources B	Teaching Resources with Organizer: Other Resources	Audiovisual Resources Binder
• Language Workshop: Punctuation, Capitalization, Spelling, Usage • Test Generators	• Teaching Notes pp. 118–120 • Reading Organizers pp. 123, 125, 128 • Language Link p. 126 • Words to Own pp. 124, 127, 129	• Test Booklet: Selection Tests pp. 201–206 • Language and Writing Skills Worksheets pp. 127–128, 140–142, 169–170 • Portfolio Management System pp. 39, 174–175	• Elements of Literature Transparency 17.2 • How to Own a Word Transparency 17.3
• Test Generator	• Teaching Notes p. 120	• Test Booklet: The American Language pp. 207–208	
		• Portfolio Management System pp. 176–178	• Revision Transparencies 17.4–17.5
• Language Workshop: Transitional expressions	• Language Workshop pp. 130–131		
		• Portfolio Management System p. 179	

Proofreading Warm-ups

You may use the following exercises to help students practice their proofreading skills. Copy a set of incorrect sentences onto the chalkboard, and have students find and correct the spelling, punctuation, usage, and mechanical errors in each sentence. Ask students to share and discuss their responses.

	Sentences with Errors	Sentences Corrected	Skills Covered
1	**a.** drama is probably the difficultest form of writing it certainly seem's to take the longest to learn **b.** george s. kaufman a noted american writer said that writing plays was a trick not an art	**a.** Drama is probably the most difficult form of writing; it certainly seems to take the longest to learn. **b.** George S. Kaufman, a noted American writer, said that writing plays was a trick, not an art.	Capitalization, Superlative modifiers, Semicolon usage, Apostrophe usage, Comma usage, End marks
2	**a.** a difference between drama and other literary forms is that movment and jesture is essential elements in drama **b.** jestures are their only to serve a story	**a.** A difference between drama and other literary forms is that movement and gesture are essential elements in drama. **b.** Gestures are there only to serve a story.	Capitalization, Spelling, Subject-verb agreement, End marks
3	**a.** theater dramatises attitudes, and values already excepted by society **b.** robert sherwood stated, drama travels in the caboose of literature	**a.** Theater dramatizes attitudes and values already accepted by society. **b.** Robert Sherwood stated, "Drama travels in the caboose of literature."	Capitalization, Spelling, Quotation marks, End marks
4	**a.** the dramatists, Ibsen Strindberg and Chekhov, gave to their heirs play's of great psychological insight **b.** thay presented true to life people and conflict's	**a.** The dramatists Ibsen, Strindberg, and Chekhov gave to their heirs plays of great psychological insight. **b.** They presented true-to-life people and conflicts.	Capitalization, Comma usage, Apostrophe usage, Spelling, Hyphen usage, End marks
5	**a.** two playrights used expressionistic techniques Beckett and Ionesco **b.** arthur millers best work was the play Death of a Salesman	**a.** Two playwrights used expressionistic techniques: Beckett and Ionesco. **b.** Arthur Miller's best work was the play Death of a Salesman.	Capitalization, Spelling, Colon usage, Apostrophe usage, Underline play titles, End marks
6	**a.** what queried Ms. Dancause do you predict will happen to American drama in the next 10 years **b.** i am not sure but i bet it will be quiet dramatic cracked Clarence	**a.** "What," queried Ms. Dancause, "do you predict will happen to American drama in the next ten years?" **b.** "I am not sure, but I bet it will be quite dramatic," cracked Clarence.	Quotation marks, Capitalization, Comma usage, Write out cardinal numbers, Spelling, End marks
7	**a.** hansberrys father protested restricted covenant's **b.** when it opened in 1959 Hansberrys play was a instant success	**a.** Hansberry's father protested restricted covenants. **b.** When it opened in 1959, Hansberry's play was an instant success.	Capitalization, Apostrophe usage, Comma usage, Standard usage, End marks
8	**a.** hansberry uses hughes poem Harlem as an epigraph for her play **b.** an epigraph as you may know is a opening quotation	**a.** Hansberry uses Hughes's poem "Harlem" as an epigraph for her play. **b.** An epigraph, as you may know, is an opening quotation.	Capitalization, Apostrophe usage, Quotation marks for poem titles, Comma usage, Standard usage, End marks
9	**a.** in A Raisin in the Sun, Beneatha dresses' in Yoruban cloths **b.** in the Yoruban Culture, woman hold important positions as chieftain's	**a.** In A Raisin in the Sun, Beneatha dresses in Yoruban clothes. **b.** In the Yoruban culture, women hold important positions as chieftains.	Capitalization, Underline play titles, Apostrophe usage, Spelling, End marks
10	**a.** analogies is a spacific kinda comparison **b.** they offen appear as a Logic problem in Standardized Tests	**a.** Analogies are a specific kind of comparison. **b.** They often appear as logic problems in standardized tests.	Capitalization, Subject-verb agreement, Spelling, Standard usage, End marks

Collection 17

REACHING FOR THE DREAM

Hansberry

I say to you today, my friends, that in spite of the difficulties and frustrations of the moment I still have a dream. It is a dream deeply rooted in the American dream.

I have a dream that one day this nation will rise up and live out the true meaning of its creed: "We hold these truths to be self-evident; that all men are created equal."

—Martin Luther King, Jr., *from* "I Have a Dream"

Responding to the Quotation

? From what you know about Dr. King and from this part of his famous speech, what dream do you see him encouraging in his listeners? [Possible responses: The dream of racial equality or the dream that the United States will be true to the Declaration of Independence.] At the time he spoke, King said that the "true meaning" of his dream was yet to be realized. What "difficulties and frustrations of the moment" were keeping it from coming true? [Possible responses: Legislation that denied African Americans some of the opportunities (in education, employment, and housing) enjoyed by white Americans; the efforts of groups such as the Ku Klux Klan; intolerant attitudes among individuals as well as groups of people.] What might this quotation reveal about the play in this Collection? [Possible responses: It will be about racial tension or about difficulties in actualizing a dream.]

PORTFOLIO ASSESSMENT

Parent/Guardian Involvement For forms that will help a parent or guardian review and respond to a student's portfolio, see the ***Portfolio Management System,*** pp. 62–63.

PROGRAM MANAGER

- **Instructional Support** See **Fine Art Transparency** 17.1. Review teacher's notes for transparencies in the ***Audiovisual Resources Binder*** for suggestions on how to tie the transparency to specific reading selections.
- **Extending Collection Theme** See **Cross-Curricular Activity: Reaching for the Dream, *Teaching Resources B,*** p. 132, for an activity in another discipline and for evaluation criteria.

QUICK PLANNING GUIDE

Into the Play

Through the Play

Beyond the Play

Lorraine Hansberry

(1930–1965)

Lorraine Hansberry grew up on Chicago's South Side, the youngest of four children. Her father was a successful businessman, and her family was relatively wealthy by neighborhood standards. When she was eight, Hansberry's family moved into a hostile white neighborhood because her father, in conjunction with the NAACP (National Association for the Advancement of Colored People), was protesting against the "restrictive covenants" that segregated housing.

Hansberry was educated in Chicago's public schools and showed an early talent for both writing and drawing. She wrote plays and short stories while she was in high school and when she later attended the University of Wisconsin and the Art Institute of New York.

When *A Raisin in the Sun* opened in 1959, it was an instant success. This play marked the beginning of a vigorous black theater movement, which became one of the most vital forces in the modern American theater.

> How to describe the effect *A Raisin in the Sun* had on most of us when it opened in 1959! There I was in Detroit's Cass Theater, a young man who had never seen anywhere a black man express all the things I felt but never had the courage to express. . . . The power of the play had made us all aware of our uniqueness as blacks and had encouraged us to pursue our dreams. Indeed, the play had confirmed that our dreams were possible.
>
> —Woodie King, Jr.

Lloyd Richards directed a superb cast, which included Sidney Poitier, Claudia McNeil, Diana Sands, Ruby Dee, and Louis Gossett. The play was translated into thirty languages and won the New York Drama Critics' Circle Award. At twenty-nine, Lorraine Hansberry became the youngest person—and the first African American playwright—ever to win this award.

Lorraine Hansberry (c. 1960) by David Moses Attie. Photograph, gelatin silver print (13⅝″ × 10¾″).

National Portrait Gallery, Washington, D.C. Courtesy Art Resource.

After the success of *A Raisin in the Sun,* Lorraine Hansberry continued to write plays. Her second Broadway play, *The Sign in Sidney Brustein's Window,* opened just three weeks before she died of cancer, at the age of thirty-four. *To Be Young, Gifted, and Black,* a collection of letters, journal entries, speeches, and play excerpts, was published in 1969.

In 1959, just two weeks before *A Raisin in the Sun* opened, someone asked Hansberry why she was so sure that human life should go on:

> I wish to live because life has within it that which is good, that which is beautiful, and that which is love. Therefore, since I have known all of these things, I have found them to be reason enough and—I wish to live. Moreover, because this is so, I wish others to live for generations and generations and generations. . . .

WORDS TO OWN

The following vocabulary words from Act One are defined in the Words to Own at the bottom of the pupil's page.

drily p. 831	permeated p. 834
oppression p. 832	unobtrusively p. 836
ally p. 833	furtively p. 838
mutual p. 833	reflective p. 838
anguish p. 834	raucous p. 839

PORTFOLIO ASSESSMENT

Portfolio Assessment For help with self- and teacher assessment of reading skills, see the ***Portfolio Management System,*** p. 39.

Before You Read
A Raisin in the Sun
Act One

Reading Focus
Dreams Deferred

The American dream has been described in many different ways, but it always has at its core the promise that, with hard work, every American can make his or her dreams come true. It also carries the promise that opportunities are unlimited, and that we can constantly improve our lives, looking forward to bigger and better things. But what happens when our dreams don't seem to be materializing? How long are we willing to have our dreams deferred or postponed?

Quickwrite

Read the Langston Hughes poem "Harlem" on page 828, which Hansberry uses as an epigraph—an opening quotation—for her play. Then write your answer to the question Hughes poses: What *does* happen to a deferred, or postponed, dream? What do you predict will be some of the themes and concerns of this play?

Elements of Literature
Conflict

A **conflict** is the central struggle between opposing forces or characters in a story. A $10,000 life insurance payment to Mama Younger generates the conflict in this play. As she and her family dream of how to use the money, they cope with both **internal conflicts,** battling their own inner desires, and **external conflicts,** struggling with one another and with the American society of the mid-1950s.

> **Conflict** is the struggle between opposing forces or characters. A conflict can be either **internal,** involving opposing forces within a person's mind, or **external,** involving outside forces in the form of other people, nature, or an entire society.
>
> *For more on Conflict, see the Handbook of Literary Terms.*

Background

A Raisin in the Sun is in the tradition of the family play. Eugene O'Neill once said that a play should focus on the most intense and basic human relationships, and playwrights throughout the ages have found that stories about families do just that. *A Raisin in the Sun* is about a poor family in a desperate situation. Each family member struggles to realize a dream that conflicts with the hopes and dreams of other family members. Hansberry is interested in both the psychology of her characters and the larger sociological picture. Her characters' problems are not only personal; they also stem from the fact that the characters are African American and living in the United States in the mid–twentieth century.

The events of this play occur during the mid-1950s: a time when $10,000 was double the yearly salary of most Americans, and a time when African American families who moved into some all-white neighborhoods would be threatened or intimidated into leaving.

About the Author

In 1938, Hansberry's father, Carl Hansberry, was sued by residents of an all-white area in which he had bought a house. He fought back, and in 1940, the case of *Hansberry* v. *Lee* went before the U.S. Supreme Court. The case focused on restrictive covenants—private contracts in which property owners in an area agreed not to sell to African Americans. The NAACP and other watchers of civil-rights law hoped that the Court would declare restrictive covenants unconstitutional; but the Court ruled in Hansberry's favor on a technicality, bypassing the broader issue of restrictive covenants. Soured by the experience, Carl Hansberry was preparing to move his family to Mexico when he died suddenly in 1946. *A Raisin in the Sun,* which also raises the issue of restrictive covenants, thus can be seen as a tribute to the life of Carl Hansberry. Not until 1948, in the case of *Shelley* v. *Kramer,* did the Court rule that lower courts cannot uphold restrictive covenants.

Program Manager

- **Planning Instruction** See Teaching Notes, *Teaching Resources B,* pp. 118–119, for objectives, a summary, literary elements, and additional information.
- **Instructional Support** See Graphic Organizer for Active Reading, *Teaching Resources B,* p. 123, for an Into the Play activity.
- **Application and Reinforcement** For reinforcement of the elements of literature introduced in this lesson, see Transparency 17.2 in the *Audiovisual Resources Binder.*
- **Assessment** See Selection Test, *Test Booklet,* pp. 201–202.
- **Reinforcement** Use the Words to Own worksheet in *Teaching Resources B,* p. 124.

Into the Play

Using **Before You Read** p. 827

Reading Focus

Give students five minutes to list a few goals or dreams under these headings: "One-Year Dreams," "Five-Year Dreams," "Twenty-five-Year Dreams." Have students choose the goal or dream that seems most important right now; then, ask them to imagine that making the dream come true would take ten years longer than they had imagined. Have them discuss or freewrite how they would deal with feelings of disappointment and how the postponement of the dream would affect their family and friends.

Background

Offer these other facts about life for African Americans at this time in American history:

- Not until 1949 did any state ban all segregation of public accommodations. New Jersey and Connecticut passed such laws that year.
- In 1954, the Supreme Court, in the case of *Brown* v. *Board of Education of Topeka,* ruled that segregation in public education was unconstitutional.
- In 1957, New York passed the first ordinance against discrimination in private as well as public housing.

A Raisin in the Sun

Lorraine Hansberry

What happens to a dream deferred?
Does it dry up
like a raisin in the sun?
Or fester like a sore—
And then run?
Does it stink like rotten meat?
Or crust and sugar over—
like a syrupy sweet?

Maybe it just sags
like a heavy load.

Or does it explode?

—Langston Hughes, "Harlem"

Scenes from 1989 production of *A Raisin in the Sun* (pages 828, 832, 841, 842, 847, 852, 857, 860, 866, 871, 876, 879, 882–883, 885). © Mitzi Trumbo for PBS American Playhouse, KCET Los Angeles.

Options for Teaching

Strategies for Inclusion

Kinesthetic Enacting scenes can be a teaching tool as well as a way to integrate the language arts. Students who can speak and move as the Youngers will gain valuable insights into their characters. Have students enact Walter and Ruth's breakfast discussion on pp. 833–834, Walter's argument with Beneatha just before Mama's entrance on pp. 835–836, Mama's reminiscence with Ruth about Mr. Younger on p. 838, Beneatha's visit with Joseph Asagai on pp. 844–845, and Mama's confrontation with Walter about buying a liquor store on pp. 848–850.

Linguistic In the stage directions that introduce Walter Lee on p. 830, Hansberry notes his movements and speech patterns. Challenge students to focus on Walter's dialogue in Act One, looking for examples of his accusatory tone and explaining changes in his way of speaking to his family from the beginning of the act to the end.

Spatial After students have read Act One, have them work in groups to sketch the set. Remind them that all the action takes place on one set. (For example, the play opens in the living room, which dominates throughout, but there also is a kitchen with a window. Furthermore, students should decide how much of the bedrooms need to be seen and how to indicate the hallway outside the apartment's front door.) Ask students to exchange plans with another group and to evaluate that group's design.

A Raisin in the Sun was first presented by Philip Rose and David J. Cogan at the Ethel Barrymore Theatre, New York City, March 11, 1959, with the following cast:

(In order of appearance)

Ruth Younger	Ruby Dee
Travis Younger	Glynn Turman
Walter Lee Younger (Brother)	Sidney Poitier
Beneatha Younger	Diana Sands
Lena Younger (Mama)	Claudia McNeil
Joseph Asagai	Ivan Dixon
George Murchison	Louis Gossett
Karl Lindner	John Fiedler
Bobo	Lonne Elder III
Moving Men	Ed Hall, Douglas Turner Ward

Directed by Lloyd Richards

Designed and lighted by Ralph Alswang

Costumes by Virginia Volland

The action of the play is set in Chicago's South Side, sometime between World War II and the present.

Act One

Scene 1. Friday morning.
Scene 2. The following morning.

Act Two

Scene 1. Later, the same day.
Scene 2. Friday night, a few weeks later.
Scene 3. Moving day, one week later.

Act Three

An hour later.

The photographs illustrating the play are from the American Playhouse production of *A Raisin in the Sun* first broadcast on February 1, 1989. The production was directed by Bill Duke, based on the Twenty-fifth Anniversary stage production produced by the Roundabout Theatre Company and Robert Nemiroff, directed by Harold Scott. The American Playhouse television production features Danny Glover as Walter Lee Younger, Esther Rolle as Lena Younger (Mama), Starletta DuPois as Ruth Younger, Kim Yancey as Beneatha Younger, and Lou Ferguson as Joseph Asagai.

Act One

Scene 1

The YOUNGER *living room would be a comfortable and well-ordered room if it were not for a number of indestructible contradictions to this state of being. Its furnishings are typical and undistinguished and their primary feature now is that they have clearly had to accommodate the living of too many people for too many years—and they are tired. Still, we can see that at some time, a time probably no longer remembered by the family (except perhaps for* MAMA*), the furnishings of this room were actually selected with care and love and even hope—and brought to this apartment and arranged with taste and pride.*

That was a long time ago. Now the once loved pattern of the couch upholstery has to fight to show itself from under acres of crocheted doilies and couch covers which have themselves finally come to be more important than the upholstery. And here a table or a chair has been moved to disguise the worn places in the carpet; but the carpet has fought back by showing its weariness, with depressing uniformity, elsewhere on its surface. (A)

Weariness has, in fact, won in this room. Everything has been polished, washed, sat on, used, scrubbed too often. All pretenses but living itself have long since vanished from the very atmosphere of this room.

Moreover, a section of this room, for it is not really a room unto itself, though the landlord's lease would make it seem so, slopes backward to provide a small kitchen area, where the family prepares the meals that are eaten in the living room proper, which must also serve as dining room. The single window that has been provided for these "two" rooms is located in this kitchen area. The sole natural light the family may enjoy in the course of a day is only that which fights its way through this little window. (B)

At left, a door leads to a bedroom which is shared by MAMA *and her daughter,* BENEATHA. *At right, opposite, is a second room (which in the beginning of the life of this apartment was probably a breakfast room) which serves as a bedroom for* WALTER *and his wife,* RUTH. (C)

A. Critical Reading: Predicting

? Given Hansberry's description of the apartment's furnishings, what might you expect from the people who live in this apartment? [Possible answer: They, too, are tired from having been used for so long, yet they retain a certain nobility.]

Metacognition How might you be able to verify your prediction? [Possible answer: By seeing how the Youngers act when trouble arises.]

B. Language Note: Connotation

Ask students to look back over this paragraph and the two that precede it. Which word repeatedly describes things in the room? *[Fight.]* What does that word suggest about the family's life? [Possible answers: Everything about it is a struggle. The Youngers are willing to fight to maintain their identity.]

C. Reader's Response: First Thoughts

The audience later learns that Walter is thirty-five years old and that Beneatha is twenty. If you were their ages, how would you feel about sharing a bedroom or an apartment with your mother? If you were married (and had been married for eleven years), how would you feel about living in your mother's home? [Sample responses: Uncomfortable; stressed by the lack of privacy; angry that things were this way; or eager to make a change.]

Technology Tip

Download audio clips of the play from the Internet Town Hall at **http://town.hall.org/Archives/radio/IMS/HarperAudio/355_harp_00_ITH.html**. *You may want to preview any Internet activity that you suggest to students. Because these resources are sometimes public forums, their content can be unpredictable.*

STRATEGIES FOR INCLUSION

Learners Having Difficulty If students seem concerned about reading a story that takes more than fifty pages to tell, or if they are unfamiliar with the format of a script, have them approach the play by looking at the photographs from start to finish. Have students talk in small groups about the clues they find to the action and what they infer from the various characters' facial expressions. Encourage students to choose two or three photographs that particularly interest them and to pay special attention to the text that relates to those photographs.

Visual/Auditory Both the 1961 film adaptation and the 1988 made-for-television presentation of *A Raisin in the Sun* (recommended by Robert Nemiroff, Hansberry's literary executor, as being truer to the original play) are available on videocassette. Watching and listening to the first ten minutes from Act One may help students grasp the tensions that drive Walter, Ruth, and Beneatha as well as the influence that Mama has over them all.

A. Critical Reading: Drawing Conclusions
Walter's question immediately creates a sense of anticipation. What makes it obvious that the check is important? [Possible answer: Although he is barely awake, he already is thinking about the check.]

B. Language Note: Dialect
? What are some characteristics of Ruth's dialect? [The use of *ain't;* dropped syllables; double negatives; third person singular verb used with first person singular subject.]

C. Reader's Response: Shaping Interpretations
? Why does Ruth scramble the eggs after Walter has asked for them not to be scrambled? [Sample responses: She is angry with him; or she is not paying attention to him.]

D. Exploring the Historical Period
Students should remember that in the late 1950s the civil rights movement was still in its relative infancy. The social changes created by demands for an end to segregation often resulted in violence. Lynchings still took place on occasion, as did bombings and burnings; more common was a refusal by some local governments to comply with federal antidiscrimination laws.

Time: Sometime between World War II and the present.

Place: Chicago's South Side.

At rise: It is morning dark in the living room. TRAVIS *is asleep on the make-down bed at center. An alarm clock sounds from within the bedroom at right, and presently* RUTH *enters from that room and closes the door behind her. She crosses sleepily toward the window. As she passes her sleeping son she reaches down and shakes him a little. At the window she raises the shade and a dusky South Side morning light comes in feebly. She fills a pot with water and puts it on to boil. She calls to the boy, between yawns, in a slightly muffled voice.*

RUTH *is about thirty. We can see that she was a pretty girl, even exceptionally so, but now it is apparent that life has been little that she expected, and disappointment has already begun to hang in her face. In a few years, before thirty-five even, she will be known among her people as a "settled woman."*

She crosses to her son and gives him a good, final, rousing shake.

Ruth. Come on now, boy, it's seven-thirty! (*Her son sits up at last, in a stupor of sleepiness.*) I say hurry up, Travis! You ain't the only person in the world got to use a bathroom! (*The child, a sturdy, handsome little boy of ten or eleven, drags himself out of the bed and almost blindly takes his towels and "today's clothes" from drawers and a closet and goes out to the bathroom, which is in an outside hall and which is shared by another family or families on the same floor.* RUTH *crosses to the bedroom door at right and opens it and calls in to her husband.*) Walter Lee! . . . It's after seven-thirty! Lemme see you do some waking up in there now! (*She waits.*) You better get up from there, man! It's after seven-thirty I tell you. (*She waits again.*) All right, you just go ahead and lay there and next thing you know Travis be finished and Mr. Johnson'll be in there and you'll be fussing and cussing round here like a madman! And be late too! (*She waits, at the end of patience.*) Walter Lee—it's time for you to GET UP!

[*She waits another second and then starts to go into the bedroom, but is apparently satisfied that her husband has begun to get up. She stops, pulls the door to, and returns to the kitchen area. She wipes her face with a moist cloth and runs her fingers through her sleep-disheveled hair in a vain effort and ties an apron around her housecoat. The bedroom door at right opens and her husband stands in the doorway in his pajamas, which are rumpled and mismated. He is a lean, intense young man in his middle thirties, inclined to quick nervous movements and erratic speech habits—and always in his voice there is a quality of indictment.*[1]]

Walter. Is he out yet?

Ruth. What you mean *out*? He ain't hardly got in there good yet.

Walter (*wandering in, still more oriented to sleep than to a new day*). Well, what was you doing all that yelling for if I can't even get in there yet? (*Stopping and thinking*) Check coming today? **A**

B **Ruth.** They *said* Saturday and this is just Friday and I hopes to God you ain't going to get up here first thing this morning and start talking to me 'bout no money—'cause I 'bout don't want to hear it.

Walter. Something the matter with you this morning?

Ruth. No—I'm just sleepy as the devil. What kind of eggs you want?

C **Walter.** Not scrambled. (RUTH *starts to scramble eggs.*) Paper come? (RUTH *points impatiently to the rolled up* Tribune *on the table, and he gets it and spreads it out and vaguely reads the front page.*) Set off another bomb yesterday.

D **Ruth** (*maximum indifference*). Did they?

Walter (*looking up*). What's the matter with you?

Ruth. Ain't nothing the matter with me. And don't keep asking me that this morning.

Walter. Ain't nobody bothering you. (*Reading the news of the day absently again*) Say Colonel McCormick[2] is sick.

Ruth (*affecting tea-party interest*). Is he now? Poor thing.

Walter (*sighing and looking at his watch*). Oh, me. (*He waits.*) Now what is that boy doing in

1. **indictment:** accusation; complaint.
2. **Colonel McCormick:** Robert R. McCormick (1880–1955), publisher of the *Chicago Tribune.*

OPTIONS FOR TEACHING

INTEGRATING THE LANGUAGE ARTS

Strategic Reading Before students begin to read the play, ask them to look at the cast list on p. 829 and to consider this introductory premise: *Three generations of an African American family live under one roof on the South Side of Chicago. The family members dream of a better life, but a dream is all it seems—until the patriarch of the family dies, leaving a life insurance policy.* Have students use the first column of a three-column chart like the following to write three to five questions that this premise suggests.

As students read Act One, they should make predictions related to as many of their questions as possible, listing their predictions in the second column of the chart. By the time students finish reading the play, they should have used the third column of the chart to note how their predictions played out; they also might have made additional reading predictions and noted their actual outcomes.

Prereading Questions	Reading Predictions	Actual Outcomes
[Do the children share similar dreams?]		

that bathroom all this time? He just going to have to start getting up earlier. I can't be being late to work on account of him fooling around in there.

Ruth (*turning on him*). Oh, no he ain't going to be getting up no earlier no such thing! It ain't his fault that he can't get to bed no earlier nights 'cause he got a bunch of crazy good-for-nothing clowns sitting up running their mouths in what is supposed to be his bedroom after ten o'clock at night . . .

Walter. That's what you mad about, ain't it? The things I want to talk about with my friends just couldn't be important in your mind, could they?

[*He rises and finds a cigarette in her handbag on the table and crosses to the little window and looks out, smoking and deeply enjoying this first one.*]

Ruth (*almost matter-of-factly, a complaint too automatic to deserve emphasis*). Why you always got to smoke before you eat in the morning?

Walter (*at the window*). Just look at 'em down there . . . Running and racing to work . . . (*He turns and faces his wife and watches her a moment at the stove, and then, suddenly*) You look young this morning, baby.

Ruth (*indifferently*). Yeah?

Walter. Just for a second—stirring them eggs. Just for a second it was —you looked real young again. (*He reaches for her; she crosses away. Then, drily*) It's gone now—you look like yourself again!

Ruth. Man, if you don't shut up and leave me alone.

Walter (*looking out to the street again*). First thing a man ought to learn in life is not to talk love to no colored woman first thing in the morning. You all some eeeevil people at eight o'clock in the morning.

[TRAVIS *appears in the hall doorway, almost fully dressed and quite wide awake now, his towels and pajamas across his shoulders. He opens the door and signals for his father to make the bathroom in a hurry.*]

Travis (*watching the bathroom*). Daddy, come on!

[WALTER *gets his bathroom utensils and flies out to the bathroom.*]

Ruth. Sit down and have your breakfast, Travis.

Travis. Mama, this is Friday. (*Gleefully*) Check coming tomorrow, huh?

Ruth. You get your mind off money and eat your breakfast.

Travis (*eating*). This is the morning we supposed to bring the fifty cents to school.

Ruth. Well, I ain't got no fifty cents this morning.

Travis. Teacher say we have to.

Ruth. I don't care what teacher say. I ain't got it. Eat your breakfast, Travis.

Travis. I *am* eating.

Ruth. Hush up now and just eat!

[*The boy gives her an exasperated look for her lack of understanding, and eats grudgingly.*]

Travis. You think Grandmama would have it?

Ruth. No! And I want you to stop asking your grandmother for money, you hear me?

Travis (*outraged*). Gaaaleee! I don't ask her, she just gimme it sometimes!

Ruth. Travis Willard Younger—I got too much on me this morning to be—

Travis. Maybe Daddy—

Ruth. *Travis!*

[*The boy hushes abruptly. They are both quiet and tense for several seconds.*]

Travis (*presently*). Could I maybe go carry some groceries in front of the supermarket for a little while after school then?

Ruth. Just hush, I said. (*Travis jabs his spoon into his cereal bowl viciously, and rests his head in anger upon his fists.*) If you through eating, you can get over there and make up your bed.

[*The boy obeys stiffly and crosses the room, almost mechanically, to the bed and more or less folds the bedding into a heap, then angrily gets his books and cap.*]

Travis (*sulking and standing apart from her unnaturally*). I'm gone.

Ruth (*looking up from the stove to inspect him automatically*). Come here. (*He crosses to her*

WORDS TO OWN

drily (drī′lē) *adv.*: matter-of-factly; without emotion.

E. Literary Element: Conflict

? What aspects of Walter's behavior create conflict between him and Ruth? [Smoking as soon as he gets up and keeping Travis up too late.]

F. Literary Element: Tone

? How would you describe the attitude that Walter expresses through these comments? [Possible answer: Critical, even sarcastic, which is the basis for his humor.]

G. Critical Reading: Making Connections

Students may smile at the way in which Travis tries to get his fifty cents, but they also may recognize themselves in him. Ask students how common they think it is for a child to play one relative off another like this. [Possible answers: Everybody does it; or it depends on the family.]

INTEGRATING THE LANGUAGE ARTS

Language and Vocabulary Playwrights often provide stage directions that indicate how an actor's voice should sound when speaking the dialogue. These stage directions appear in italics and are enclosed in either brackets or parentheses. Note that these stage directions often take the form of well-chosen adverbs, modifying the understood verb *says* or *speaks*. Have students find examples of some of the adverbs that Hansberry uses in the stage directions for Act One, Scene 1. Volunteers should try reading lines aloud in the manner that the adverb specifies. Have different volunteers read the same line. Alternatively, ask students to suggest adverbs for dialogue for which Hansberry has *not* specified stage directions. Students may work together in small groups on different sections of the play—perhaps a scene for each group. Students should think of adverbs for stage directions, practice reading the lines aloud, and then perform the scene for the class.

Grammar and Usage Although English is the official language of Nigeria, Asagai may well have grown up speaking Yoruba. His English certainly seems more formal than that of the Youngers. Students might look for grammatical and usage differences between the two types of English found in Act One and discuss what they feel Hansberry was trying to suggest through the contrast. ☞

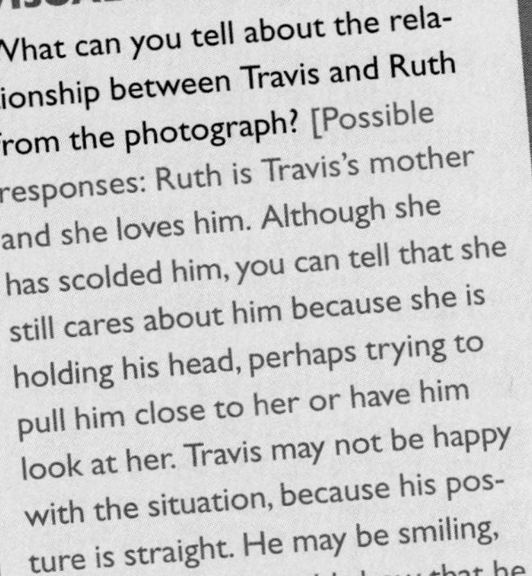
RESPONDING TO THE PHOTOGRAPH: VISUAL LITERACY

What can you tell about the relationship between Travis and Ruth from the photograph? [Possible responses: Ruth is Travis's mother and she loves him. Although she has scolded him, you can tell that she still cares about him because she is holding his head, perhaps trying to pull him close to her or have him look at her. Travis may not be happy with the situation, because his posture is straight. He may be smiling, however, which would show that he appreciates his mother's teasing.]

A. Critical Reading: Metacognition

? If you were watching this play—that is, if you did not have stage directions to help you—how would you know that Ruth is imitating Travis? [Possible answers: By the tone of her voice; by the way she looks in Travis's direction as she speaks; by his reactions to what she says; by ways in which she imitates how a child would stand or gesture.]

and she studies his head.) If you don't take this comb and fix this here head, you better! (TRAVIS *puts down his books with a great sigh of oppression, and crosses to the mirror. His mother mutters under her breath about his "slubbornness."*) 'Bout to march out of here with that head looking just like chickens slept in it! I just don't know where you get your slubborn ways . . . And get your jacket, too. Looks chilly out this morning.

Travis (*with conspicuously brushed hair and jacket*). I'm gone.

Ruth. Get carfare and milk money—(*waving one finger*)—and not a single penny for no caps, you hear me?

Travis (*with sullen politeness*). Yes'm.

[*He turns in outrage to leave. His mother watches after him as in his frustration he approaches the door almost comically. When she speaks to him, her voice has become a very gentle tease.*]

Ruth (*mocking; as she thinks he would say it*). Oh, Mama makes me so mad sometimes, I don't know what to do! (*She waits and continues to his back as he stands stock-still in front of the door.*) I wouldn't kiss that woman goodbye for nothing in this world this morning! (*The boy finally turns around and rolls his eyes at her, knowing the mood has changed and he is vindicated; he does not, however, move toward her yet.*) Not for nothing in this world! (*She finally laughs aloud at him and holds out her arms to him and we see that it is a way between them, very old and practiced. He crosses to her and allows her to embrace him warmly but keeps his face fixed with masculine rigidity. She holds him back from her presently and looks at him and runs her fingers over the features of his face. With utter gentleness—*) Now—whose little old angry man are you?

Travis (*The masculinity and gruffness start to fade at last.*). Aw gaalee—Mama . . .

Ruth (*mimicking*). Aw—gaaaaalleeeee, Mama! (*She pushes him, with rough playfulness and finality, toward the door.*) Get on out of here or you going to be late.

WORDS TO OWN

oppression (ə·presh'ən) *n.:* feeling of being tyrannized.

OPTIONS FOR TEACHING

COOPERATIVE LEARNING

Character Sociograms After students have read Act One, divide the class into small groups to discuss the Youngers in greater detail. Have them create a diagram that represents the relationships between the characters so far: Mama, Beneatha, Travis, Walter, Ruth, and Asagai. Diagrams may use a variety of designs and symbols to express the characters' hopes, concerns, and thoughts about other characters (such as a map of Nigeria between Beneatha and Asagai, or a house floor plan that has bedrooms labeled with the occupants' names to demonstrate Mama's wishes for her family). If you have students display and compare their diagrams, ask a representative from each group to explain the group's analysis.

Grouping Students For group reading or some of the small-group activities relating to Act One, assign to each group a student with an interest in theater (a student actor, for example, or a student who demonstrates critical thinking when discussing television programs or films). His or her comments may be of particular help to students who are having trouble reading drama.

Travis *(in the face of love, new aggressiveness).* Mama, could I *please* go carry groceries?
Ruth. Honey, it's starting to get so cold evenings.
Walter *(coming in from the bathroom and drawing a make-believe gun from a make-believe holster and shooting at his son).* What is it he wants to do?
Ruth. Go carry groceries after school at the supermarket.
Walter. Well, let him go . . .
Travis *(quickly, to the ally).* I *have* to—she won't gimme the fifty cents . . .
Walter *(to his wife only).* Why not?
Ruth *(simply, and with flavor).* 'Cause we don't have it.
Walter *(to* RUTH *only).* What you tell the boy things like that for? *(Reaching down into his pants with a rather important gesture)* Here, son—

[*He hands the boy the coin, but his eyes are directed to his wife's.* TRAVIS *takes the money happily.*]

Travis. Thanks, Daddy.

[*He starts out.* RUTH *watches both of them with murder in her eyes.* WALTER *stands and stares back at her with defiance, and suddenly reaches into his pocket again on an afterthought.*]

Walter *(without even looking at his son, still staring hard at his wife).* In fact, here's another fifty cents . . . Buy yourself some fruit today—or take a taxicab to school or something!
Travis. Whoopee—

[*He leaps up and clasps his father around the middle with his legs, and they face each other in mutual appreciation; slowly* WALTER LEE *peeks around the boy to catch the violent rays from his wife's eyes and draws his head back as if shot.*]

Walter. You better get down now—and get to school, man.
Travis *(at the door).* O.K. Goodbye.

[*He exits.*]

Walter *(after him, pointing with pride).* That's *my* boy. *(She looks at him in disgust and turns back to her work.)* You know what I was thinking 'bout in the bathroom this morning?
Ruth. No.
Walter. How come you always try to be so pleasant!
Ruth. What is there to be pleasant 'bout!
Walter. You want to know what I was thinking 'bout in the bathroom or not!
Ruth. I know what you thinking 'bout.
Walter *(ignoring her).* 'Bout what me and Willy Harris was talking about last night.
Ruth *(immediately—a refrain).* Willy Harris is a good-for-nothing loudmouth.
Walter. Anybody who talks to me has got to be a good-for-nothing loudmouth, ain't he? And what you know about who is just a good-for-nothing loudmouth? Charlie Atkins was just a "good-for-nothing loudmouth" too, wasn't he! When he wanted me to go in the dry-cleaning business with him. And now—he's grossing a hundred thousand a year. A hundred thousand dollars a year! You still call *him* a loudmouth!
Ruth *(bitterly).* Oh, Walter Lee . . .

[*She folds her head on her arms over the table.*]

Walter *(rising and coming to her and standing over her).* You tired, ain't you? Tired of everything. Me, the boy, the way we live—this beat-up hole—everything. Ain't you? *(She doesn't look up, doesn't answer.)* So tired—moaning and groaning all the time, but you wouldn't do nothing to help, would you? You couldn't be on my side that long for nothing, could you?
Ruth. Walter, please leave me alone.
Walter. A man needs for a woman to back him up . . .
Ruth. Walter—
Walter. Mama would listen to you. You know she listen to you more than she do me and Bennie. She think more of you. All you have to do is just sit down with her when you drinking your coffee one morning and talking 'bout things like you do and—*(He sits down beside her and demonstrates graphically what he thinks her methods and tone should be.)*—you just sip your coffee, see, and say easy like that you been thinking 'bout that deal Walter Lee is so interested in, 'bout the

Words to Own

ally (al'ī) *n.:* supporter; friend.
mutual (myo͞o'cho͞o·əl) *adj.:* shared.

B. Literary Element: Conflict

? What further conflict between Walter and Ruth is revealed here? [They have differences about the right way to raise their son; in particular, Walter subverts what she has told Travis by giving the boy not just one half-dollar but two. They have different ideas about what money is available in the family and how it should be spent.] Based on what you know of this husband-wife relationship thus far, do you think these conflicts will be easy to resolve? Why or why not? [Possible answer: They will be difficult to resolve, for they arise from issues that both Walter and Ruth consider important.]

C. Critical Reading: Analyzing Character

? What does this exchange suggest about Walter's goals? [He would like to be rich and to receive the respect that prosperous people enjoy.] How does the exchange make you feel about Willy Harris, and why? [Possible answers: Somewhat suspicious, for Walter becomes very defensive of the man when Ruth criticizes him; or he may be all right, and Ruth may be speaking out against him only because she is tired.] Do you think that Ruth is being fair in her assessment of Walter's friends? Explain. [Possible answers: It may be too soon to tell, but perhaps Ruth senses something about them that Walter does not. Or she may not be fair, for she continues to criticize Charlie Atkins even after his success.]

CLASSROOM MANAGEMENT

Budgeting Time If there is not enough time for students to read aloud all of Act One in class, read to the point just before Mama's entrance, ending the reading with Ruth's giving Walter fifty cents on p. 836. Offer the following questions to guide students as they continue reading independently.

- Why is Ruth so unhappy about Walter's friends?
- Why does Walter overturn Ruth's decisions concerning Travis?
- Does Mama support Beneatha's desire to become a doctor? Will she use part of the money to help Beneatha?
- What family conflicts will intensify when the check arrives?

Managing the Reader's Response Classroom
Some students tend to dominate classroom discussion. To allow more students an opportunity to speak, appoint a monitor to help lead discussion. First, advise students that the monitor's task is to permit all who want to speak an opportunity to do so and that the monitor will praise eager students when they have already spoken several times and politely ask them to allow someone else to speak. Advise students to give way gracefully to others at the monitor's suggestion. Then, select a monitor from the group. Change monitors for each discussion, and consider giving the task to students who seem more reluctant to speak than the more dominant speakers.

A. Literary Element: Plot

? What plan does Walter have for the check? [Investment in a liquor store with his friends Willy and Bobo.] Why might this plan create greater conflict in the Younger home?[Possible answers: Ruth already has expressed distrust of Willy; it is not clear what Mama may have planned to do with the money.]

B. Reader's Response: Extending the Text

? If Walter is right, what would have to change for the system to stop being so corrupt? [Sample responses: The people who work for "the system" would need a change of heart—that is, to stop being greedy. Or everyone could refuse to pay them off.]

C. Literary Element: Irony

? Do you sense any irony in Walter's blanket statement about "the colored woman"? Explain. [Walter wants to become someone important, someone who stands out, but he seems quite willing to classify Ruth in a stereotyped, demeaning way.] How does Ruth use Walter's comment to her own advantage? [She snipes at him, using his stereotype and his form of sarcastic humor to exclude herself from blame.]

store and all, and sip some more coffee, like what you saying ain't really that important to you—And the next thing you know, she be listening good and asking you questions and when I come home—I can tell her the details. This ain't no fly-by-night proposition, baby. I mean we figured it out, me and Willy and Bobo.

Ruth (*with a frown*). Bobo?

Walter. Yeah. You see, this little liquor store we got in mind cost seventy-five thousand and we figured the initial investment on the place be 'bout thirty thousand, see. That be ten thousand each. Course, there's a couple of hundred you got to pay so's you don't spend your life just waiting for them clowns to let your license get approved—

Ruth. You mean graft?

Walter (*frowning impatiently*). Don't call it that. See there, that just goes to show you what women understand about the world. Baby, don't *nothing* happen for you in this world 'less you pay *somebody* off!

Ruth. Walter, leave me alone! (*She raises her head and stares at him vigorously—then says, more quietly*) *Eat* your eggs, they gonna be cold.

Walter (*straightening up from her and looking off*). That's it. There you are. Man say to his woman: I got me a dream. His woman say: Eat your eggs. (*Sadly, but gaining in power*) Man say: I got to take hold of this here world, baby! And a woman will say: Eat your eggs and go to work. (*Passionately now*) Man say: I got to change my life, I'm choking to death, baby! And his woman say—(*in utter anguish as he brings his fists down on his thighs*)—Your eggs is getting cold!

Ruth (*softly*). Walter, that ain't none of our money.

Walter (*not listening at all or even looking at her*). This morning, I was lookin' in the mirror and thinking about it . . . I'm thirty-five years old; I been married eleven years and I got a boy who sleeps in the living room—(*very, very quietly*)—and all I got to give him is stories about how rich white people live . . .

Ruth. Eat your eggs, Walter.

Walter (*slams the table and jumps up*).—DAMN MY EGGS—DAMN ALL THE EGGS THAT EVER WAS!

Ruth. Then go to work.

Walter (*looking up at her*). See—I'm trying to talk to you 'bout myself—(*shaking his head with the repetition*)—and all you can say is eat them eggs and go to work.

Ruth (*wearily*). Honey, you never say nothing new. I listen to you every day, every night and every morning, and you never say nothing new. (*Shrugging*) So you would rather *be* Mr. Arnold than be his chauffeur. So—I would *rather* be living in Buckingham Palace.

Walter. That is just what is wrong with the colored woman in this world . . . Don't understand about building their men up and making 'em feel like they somebody. Like they can do something.

Ruth (*drily, but to hurt*). There *are* colored men who do things.

Walter. No thanks to the colored woman.

Ruth. Well, being a colored woman, I guess I can't help myself none.

[*She rises and gets the ironing board and sets it up and attacks a huge pile of rough-dried clothes, sprinkling them in preparation for the ironing and then rolling them into tight fat balls.*]

Walter (*mumbling*). We one group of men tied to a race of women with small minds!

[*His sister* BENEATHA *enters. She is about twenty, as slim and intense as her brother. She is not as pretty as her sister-in-law, but her lean, almost intellectual face has a handsomeness of its own. She wears a bright-red flannel nightie, and her thick hair stands wildly about her head. Her speech is a mixture of many things; it is different from the rest of the family's insofar as education has permeated her sense of English—and perhaps the Midwest rather than the South has finally—at last—won out in her inflection; but not altogether, because over all of it is a soft slurring and transformed use of vowels which is the decided influence of the South Side. She passes through the room without looking at either* RUTH *or* WALTER *and goes to the outside door and looks, a little blindly, out to the bathroom. She sees that it has been lost to the Johnsons. She*

WORDS TO OWN

anguish (aŋ′gwish) *n.:* pain and suffering; heartache.

permeated (pʉr′mē·āt′id) *v.:* spread through and affected every part of.

OPTIONS FOR TEACHING

CROSSING THE CURRICULUM

Health/Social Sciences In Scene 1, Mama expresses her disapproval of selling liquor, and Beneatha applauds her. Have students research health and social problems related to alcohol abuse. Ask them to inquire how Mama and Beneatha's opinions might have been formed. Ask students to report to the class as though they were psychiatrists, social workers, or police officers.

Art Ask students to choose a member of the Younger family and to create a piece of artwork that captures the character's personality—his or her dreams, fears, and conflicts. If possible, try to have all five Youngers represented. Students may work in the medium and style of their choice. Have them create a gallery display of their pieces. Ask students to create a small sign to be placed by each piece of art. It should give the name of the piece, the date, the artist's name, and a brief description of the artwork.

Mathematics A check for ten thousand dollars might not sound like much today; however, its value was far greater in the 1950s. Invite students to research prices during the 1950s (for example, the cost of a dozen eggs and of a new car, the minimum hourly wage, and the average cost of college tuition) and to determine what an average paycheck might have been able to buy. Then, have them create a budget proposal showing how the Youngers might get the most for their money.

"That money belongs to Mama, Walter, and it's for her to decide how she wants to use it."

closes the door with a sleepy vengeance and crosses to the table and sits down a little defeated.]

Beneatha. I am going to start timing those people.

Walter. You should get up earlier.

Beneatha (*her face in her hands. She is still fighting the urge to go back to bed.*). Really—would you suggest dawn? Where's the paper?

Walter (*pushing the paper across the table to her as he studies her almost clinically, as though he has never seen her before*). You a horrible-looking chick at this hour.

Beneatha (*drily*). Good morning, everybody.

Walter (*senselessly*). How is school coming?

Beneatha (*in the same spirit*). Lovely. Lovely. And you know, biology is the greatest. (*Looking up at him*) I dissected something that looked just like you yesterday.

Walter. I just wondered if you've made up your mind and everything.

Beneatha (*gaining in sharpness and impatience*). And what did I answer yesterday morning—and the day before that?

Ruth (*from the ironing board, like someone disinterested and old*). Don't be so nasty, Bennie.

Beneatha (*still to her brother*). And the day before that and the day before that!

Walter (*defensively*). I'm interested in you. Something wrong with that? Ain't many girls who decide—

Walter *and* **Beneatha** (*in unison*). —"to be a doctor."

[*Silence*]

Walter. Have we figured out yet just exactly how much medical school is going to cost?

Ruth. Walter Lee, why don't you leave that girl alone and get out of here to work?

Beneatha (*exits to the bathroom and bangs on the door*). Come on out of there, please!

[*She comes back into the room.*]

Walter (*looking at his sister intently*). You know the check is coming tomorrow.

Beneatha (*turning on him with a sharpness all her own*). That money belongs to Mama, Walter, and it's for her to decide how she wants to use it. I don't care if she wants to buy a house or a rocket ship or just nail it up somewhere and look at it. It's hers. Not ours—*hers.* **D**

Walter (*bitterly*). Now ain't that fine! You just got your mother's interest at heart, ain't you, girl? You such a nice girl—but if Mama got that money she can always take a few thousand and help you through school too—can't she?

Beneatha. I have never asked anyone around here to do anything for me!

Walter. No! And the line between asking and just accepting when the time comes is big and wide—ain't it! **E**

Beneatha (*with fury*). What do you want from me, Brother—that I quit school or just drop dead, which!

Walter. I don't want nothing but for you to stop acting holy 'round here. Me and Ruth done made some sacrifices for you—why can't you do something for the family?

Ruth. Walter, don't be dragging me in it.

Walter. You are in it—Don't you get up and go work in somebody's kitchen for the last three years to help put clothes on her back?

Ruth. Oh, Walter—that's not fair . . .

Walter. It ain't that nobody expects you to get on your knees and say thank you, Brother; thank you, Ruth; thank you, Mama—and thank you, Travis, for wearing the same pair of shoes for two semesters— **F**

Beneatha (*dropping to her knees*). Well—I *do*—all right?—thank everybody! And forgive me for ever wanting to be anything at all! (*Pursuing him on her knees across the floor*) FORGIVE ME, FORGIVE ME, FORGIVE ME!

Ruth. Please stop it! Your mama'll hear you.

Walter. What fool told you you had to be a doctor? If you so crazy 'bout messing 'round with sick people—then go be a nurse like other women—or just get married and be quiet . . .

D. Critical Reading: Expressing an Opinion

? What do you think Mama should do with the money? [Possible answers: Retire; find a better place for the family to live; help with Beneatha's education; help Walter finance his business.]

E. Critical Reading: Summarizing

? How could you express all of Walter's thoughts thus far about the check in one sentence? [He thinks he needs financial help if he is ever going to make something out of his life; but he thinks Mama probably is going to give the money to Beneatha and ignore him.]

F. Critical Reading: Analyzing Character

? What new information about Ruth is revealed in this passage? [She works as a domestic servant and has helped support Beneatha financially.] What does Beneatha's dropping to her knees suggest about her personality? [She has a flair for the dramatic; she has felt the pressure of being the only nonworking adult in the household; she has been criticized like this before.]

PROBLEM SOLVING/CRITICAL THINKING

Exploring Options Act One can be said to focus on discussions about the wise use of money. Several options are mentioned, but the act closes before the money actually is spent. Students can apply the problem-solving skill of exploring options to the following similar situation, using a graphic like the following to describe and rank the options. Also, use Transparency 1: Problem-Solving Chart in the Transparency Package to help students assess pros and cons for each option.

For your eighteenth birthday you receive a one-hundred-dollar bill. The card in which it is enclosed says, "Use this for books when you start college." This money, however, plus money that you've been setting aside, will enable you to buy a camera that you have been admiring. When your friends hear about the gift, they urge you to buy concert tickets. What will happen to that one-hundred-dollar bill?

[1] Option:
[2] Option:
[3] Option:

A. Reader's Response: Challenging the Text

? What do you think Beneatha's comment adds to the exchange? [Sample responses: It gives her the last word; or it strengthens her definition of Walter as crazy by picturing him as a misguided prophet.]

B. Critical Reading: Making Inferences

? What details in this paragraph most strongly suggest the kind of person Mama will prove to be? [Possible answer: Her erect carriage, lively eyes, and soft voice suggest a quiet strength that strongly contrasts with Walter's bombast. Her carriage also resembles that of women in southwest Africa and contrasts with Walter's more Western deportment.]

C. Literary Element: Symbolism

? How might a plant "growing doggedly" symbolize the people in this play? [The family shows strength and determination; everyone tries to combat poverty; they have not abandoned their hopes for a better life.]

Beneatha. Well—you finally got it said . . . It took you three years but you finally got it said. Walter, give up; leave me alone—it's Mama's money.

Walter. *He was my father, too!*

Beneatha. So what? He was mine, too—and Travis' grandfather—but the insurance money belongs to Mama. Picking on me is not going to make her give it to you to invest in any liquor stores—(*underbreath, dropping into a chair*)—and I for one say, God bless Mama for that!

Walter (*to* RUTH). See—did you hear? Did you hear!

Ruth. Honey, please go to work.

Walter. Nobody in this house is ever going to understand me.

Beneatha. Because you're a nut.

Walter. Who's a nut?

Beneatha. You—you are a nut. Thee is mad, boy.

Walter (*looking at his wife and his sister from the door, very sadly*). The world's most backward race of people, and that's a fact.

A **Beneatha** (*turning slowly in her chair*). And then there are all those prophets who would lead us out of the wilderness—(WALTER *slams out of the house.*)—into the swamps!

Ruth. Bennie, why you always gotta be pickin' on your brother? Can't you be a little sweeter sometimes? (*Door opens.* WALTER *walks in. He fumbles with his cap, starts to speak, clears throat, looks everywhere but at* RUTH. *Finally:*)

Walter (*to* RUTH). I need some money for carfare.

Ruth (*looks at him, then warms; teasing, but tenderly*). Fifty cents? (*She goes to her bag and gets money.*) Here—take a taxi!

B [WALTER *exits.* MAMA *enters. She is a woman in her early sixties, full-bodied and strong. She is one of those women of a certain grace and beauty who wear it so* <u>*unobtrusively*</u> *that it takes a while to notice. Her dark-brown face is surrounded by the total whiteness of her hair, and, being a woman who has adjusted to many things in life and overcome many more, her face is full of strength. She has, we can see, wit and faith of a kind that keep her eyes lit and full of interest and expectancy. She is, in a word, a beautiful woman. Her bearing is perhaps most like the noble bearing of the women of the Hereros*[3] *of South West Africa—rather as if she imagines that as she walks she still bears a basket or a vessel upon her head. Her speech, on the other hand, is as careless as her carriage is precise—she is inclined to slur everything—but her voice is perhaps not so much quiet as simply soft.*]

Mama. Who that 'round here slamming doors at this hour?

C [*She crosses through the room, goes to the window, opens it, and brings in a feeble little plant growing doggedly in a small pot on the windowsill. She feels the dirt and puts it back out.*]

Ruth. That was Walter Lee. He and Bennie was at it again.

Mama. My children and they tempers. Lord, if this little old plant don't get more sun than it's been getting it ain't never going to see spring again. (*She turns from the window.*) What's the matter with you this morning, Ruth? You looks right peaked. You aiming to iron all them things? Leave some for me. I'll get to 'em this afternoon. Bennie honey, it's too drafty for you to be sitting 'round half dressed. Where's your robe?

Beneatha. In the cleaners.

Mama. Well, go get mine and put it on.

Beneatha. I'm not cold, Mama, honest.

Mama. I know—but you so thin . . .

Beneatha (*irritably*). Mama, I'm not cold.

Mama (*seeing the make-down bed as* TRAVIS *has left it*). Lord have mercy, look at that poor bed. Bless his heart—he tries, don't he?

[*She moves to the bed* TRAVIS *has sloppily made up.*]

Ruth. No—he don't half try at all 'cause he knows you going to come along behind him and fix everything. That's just how come he don't know how to do nothing right now—you done spoiled that boy so.

Mama (*folding bedding*). Well—he's a little boy. Ain't supposed to know 'bout housekeeping. My baby, that's what he is. What you fix for his breakfast this morning?

Words to Own

unobtrusively (un·əb·tro͞o′siv·lē) *adv.:* inconspicuously; quietly.

3. **Hereros:** a Bantu-speaking ethnic group in Namibia (formerly called South West Africa).

OPTIONS FOR TEACHING

PROFESSIONAL NOTES

Critical Comment: Themes In his review of *A Raisin in the Sun* on its opening in 1959, critic Brooks Atkinson wrote that the play is "about human beings who want, on the one hand, to preserve their family pride and, on the other hand, to break out of the poverty that seems to be their fate." Atkinson saw the situations of the play as ranging from "hilarious" to "painful in the extreme." Hansberry made her points, he said, by showing "how character is controlled by environment." Have students record in their Reader's Logs five headings that are based on Atkinson's comments—"Family Pride," "Escape from Poverty," "Humor," "Pain," and "Influence of Environment on Character"—and to jot down comments as they read Act One.

Thematic Connections: "Reaching for the Dream" By the end of Act One, each of the adult Youngers has voiced some kind of dream. Ask students to rank those characters from least to most likely to succeed in "reaching for the dream" by the play's end. [Possible response: Walter is least likely; he is pinning his dream on a gift of money that Mama refuses to give him. Perhaps Beneatha is somewhat less likely to succeed; even if she has the money for medical school, she has to prove herself capable of the demanding work. Mama is most likely to be successful; the insurance money is hers to do with as she pleases.]

Ruth (*angrily*). I feed my son, Lena!

Mama. I ain't meddling—(*underbreath; busy-bodyish*) I just noticed all last week he had cold cereal, and when it starts getting this chilly in the fall a child ought to have some hot grits or something when he goes out in the cold—

Ruth (*furious*). I gave him hot oats—is that all right!

Mama. I ain't meddling. (*Pause*) Put a lot of nice butter on it? (RUTH *shoots her an angry look and does not reply.*) He likes lots of butter.

Ruth (*exasperated*). Lena—

Mama (*to* BENEATHA. MAMA *is inclined to wander conversationally sometimes.*). What was you and your brother fussing 'bout this morning?

Beneatha. It's not important, Mama.

[*She gets up and goes to look out at the bathroom, which is apparently free, and she picks up her towels and rushes out.*]

Mama. What was they fighting about?

Ruth. Now you know as well as I do.

Mama (*shaking her head*). Brother still worrying hisself sick about that money?

Ruth. You know he is.

Mama. You had breakfast?

Ruth. Some coffee.

Mama. Girl, you better start eating and looking after yourself better. You almost thin as Travis.

Ruth. Lena—

Mama. Un-hunh?

Ruth. What are you going to do with it?

Mama. Now don't you start, child. It's too early in the morning to be talking about money. It ain't Christian. **D**

Ruth. It's just that he got his heart set on that store— **E**

Mama. You mean that liquor store that Willy Harris want him to invest in?

Ruth. Yes—

Mama. We ain't no business people, Ruth. We just plain working folks.

Ruth. Ain't nobody business people till they go into business. Walter Lee say colored people ain't never going to start getting ahead till they start gambling on some different kinds of things in the world—investments and things.

Mama. What done got into you, girl? Walter Lee done finally sold you on investing.

Ruth. No. Mama, something is happening between Walter and me. I don't know what it is—but he needs something—something I can't give him any more. He needs this chance, Lena.

Mama (*frowning deeply*). But liquor, honey—

Ruth. Well—like Walter say—I spec people going to always be drinking themselves some liquor.

Mama. Well—whether they drinks it or not ain't none of my business. But whether I go into business selling it to 'em *is*, and I don't want that on my ledger this late in life. (*Stopping suddenly and studying her daughter-in-law*) **F** Ruth Younger, what's the matter with you today? You look like you could fall over right there.

Ruth. I'm tired.

Mama. Then you better stay home from work today.

Ruth. I can't stay home. She'd be calling up the agency and screaming at them, "My girl didn't come in today—send me somebody! My girl didn't come in!" Oh, she just have a fit . . .

Mama. Well, let her have it. I'll just call her up and say you got the flu— **G**

Ruth (*laughing*). Why the flu?

Mama. 'Cause it sounds respectable to 'em. Something white people get, too. They know 'bout the flu. Otherwise they think you been cut up or something when you tell 'em you sick.

Ruth. I got to go in. We need the money.

Mama. Somebody would of thought my children done all but starved to death the way they talk about money here late. Child, we got a great big old check coming tomorrow.

Ruth (*sincerely, but also self-righteously*). Now that's your money. It ain't got nothing to do with me. We all feel like that—Walter and Bennie and me—even Travis.

Mama (*thoughtfully, and suddenly very far away*). Ten thousand dollars—

Ruth. Sure is wonderful.

Mama. Ten thousand dollars.

Ruth. You know what you should do, Miss Lena? You should take yourself a trip somewhere. To Europe or South America or someplace—

Mama (*throwing up her hands at the thought*). Oh, child!

Ruth. I'm serious. Just pack up and leave! Go on away and enjoy yourself some. Forget about the family and have yourself a ball for once in your life—

Mama (*drily*). You sound like I'm just about ready

D. Literary Connections

The Bible has a great deal to say about the use and abuse of money. When Mama frowns on Ruth's question by saying, "It ain't Christian," she may be thinking of I Timothy 6:10: "For the love of money is the root of all evil."

E. Reader's Response: First Thoughts

? Are you surprised that Ruth suggests Walter's idea to his mother? Explain. [Sample responses: Her suggestion may be somewhat surprising; still, she loves Walter and is willing to support him, even when she does not fully agree with his ideas. Or it is not too surprising—perhaps his earlier criticism has made her want to try harder to prove her support.]

F. Literary Element: Imagery

? What image does Mama evoke by her "ledger"? [The image of a recording angel, listing in a book the good and bad deeds of her life.] What does the image suggest about her? [Religious beliefs are important to her.]

G. Reader's Response: Extending the Text

? Why do you think people are so often willing to believe the worst about others? [Sample responses: The worst may be more fascinating than the truth; or they find it easier to fall back on a stereotype or on hearsay than to find out the facts.]

ASSESSMENT TOOLS

Check Test: Questions and Answers

1. Why are the Youngers so excited about the arrival of the mail? [It is supposed to contain a ten-thousand-dollar check—the death benefit on Walter and Beneatha's father—and each member of the family has dreams that the money would help to fulfill.]
2. What dream does each adult Younger have? [Walter dreams of investing in a liquor store; Beneatha of becoming a doctor; Mama of providing for Beneatha's education and buying a house.]
3. How does Walter feel about Ruth's practicality? About Beneatha's aspirations? [Possible response: He finds Ruth's practicality stifling to his dreams; he seems to feel that Beneatha is not doing enough to support the family, and he may be jealous that Mama supports her dreams but not his own.]
4. Why is Beneatha attracted to George Murchison? To Joseph Asagai? [George is rich and shows her a good time; Asagai is more intellectual and, being Nigerian, more exciting.]
5. When Mama finally has the check, what conflict is resurrected? What new conflict is revealed? [The older conflict is that Mama does not want Walter to invest in a liquor store and that she is generally concerned about Walter's dissatisfaction with his life; the new conflict is that Ruth is pregnant —news that stuns Walter.]

A. Reader's Response: Extending the Text

? How strong a dream do you think home ownership is to most people? [Sample responses: If money were not a major consideration, most people would want a place that they could consider their own; or people who live in a city may not see the need to own a home.]

B. Critical Reading: Identifying Main Ideas

? How does Mama's reminiscence capture the idea of a "dream deferred"? [She reveals that she and Big Walter had to defer their dream of a home in Morgan Park when they first married; then, as the years went by, the dream slipped further and further away. In short, she has had to live with a "dream deferred" since before anyone in her present household was born.]

C. Literary Element: Character

? How does Mama characterize her late husband? [As a man who had his faults and who mourned his life in many ways but who also had a fierce love for his children.] How do her words help to characterize herself? [They show that Mama is tolerant, loyal, and able to love someone whose ways are not her own.]

to die. Who'd go with me? What I look like wandering 'round Europe by myself?

Ruth. Shoot—these here rich white women do it all the time. They don't think nothing of packing up they suitcases and piling on one of them big steamships and—swoosh!—they gone, child.

Mama. Something always told me I wasn't no rich white woman.

Ruth. Well—what are you going to do with it then?

Mama. I ain't rightly decided. (*Thinking. She speaks now with emphasis.*) Some of it got to be put away for Beneatha and her schoolin'—and ain't nothing going to touch that part of it. Nothing. (*She waits several seconds, trying to make up her mind about something, and looks at* RUTH *a little tentatively before going on.*) Been thinking that we maybe could meet the notes on a little old two-story somewhere, with a yard where Travis could play in the summertime, if we use part of the insurance for a down payment and everybody kind of pitch in. I could maybe take on a little day work again, few days a week—

(A)

Ruth (*studying her mother-in-law furtively and concentrating on her ironing, anxious to encourage without seeming to*). Well, Lord knows, we've put enough rent into this here rat trap to pay for four houses by now . . .

Mama (*looking up at the words "rat trap" and then looking around and leaning back and sighing—in a suddenly reflective mood—*). "Rat trap"—yes, that's all it is. (*Smiling*) I remember just as well the day me and Big Walter moved in here. Hadn't been married but two weeks and wasn't planning on living here no more than a year. (*She shakes her head at the dissolved dream.*) We was going to set away, little by little, don't you know, and buy a little place out in Morgan Park. We had even picked out the house. (*Chuckling a little*) Looks right dumpy today. But Lord, child, you should know all the dreams I had 'bout buying that house and fixing it up and making me a little garden in the back—(*She waits and stops smiling.*) And didn't none of it happen.

[*Dropping her hands in a futile gesture*]

(B)

Ruth (*keeps her head down, ironing*). Yes, life can be a barrel of disappointments, sometimes.

Mama. Honey, Big Walter would come in here some nights back then and slump down on that couch there and just look at the rug, and look at me and look at the rug and then back at me—and I'd know he was down then . . . really down. (*After a second very long and thoughtful pause; she is seeing back to times that only she can see.*) And then, Lord, when I lost that baby—little Claude—I almost thought I was going to lose Big Walter too. Oh, that man grieved hisself! He was one man to love his children.

Ruth. Ain't nothin' can tear at you like losin' your baby.

Mama. I guess that's how come that man finally worked hisself to death like he done. Like he was fighting his own war with this here world that took his baby from him.

Ruth. He sure was a fine man, all right. I always liked Mr. Younger.

Mama. Crazy 'bout his children! God knows there was plenty wrong with Walter Younger—hard-headed, mean, kind of wild with women—plenty wrong with him. But he sure loved his children. Always wanted them to have something—be something. That's where Brother gets all these notions, I reckon. Big Walter used to say, he'd get right wet in the eyes sometimes, lean his head back with the water standing in his eyes and say, "Seem like God didn't see fit to give the black man nothing but dreams—but He did give us children to make them dreams seem worth while." (*She smiles.*) He could talk like that, don't you know.

Ruth. Yes, he sure could. He was a good man, Mr. Younger.

(C)

Mama. Yes, a fine man—just couldn't never catch up with his dreams, that's all.

[BENEATHA *comes in, brushing her hair and looking up to the ceiling, where the sound of a vacuum cleaner has started up.*]

Beneatha. What could be so dirty on that woman's rugs that she has to vacuum them every single day?

Ruth. I wish certain young women 'round here who I could name would take inspiration about

Words to Own

furtively (fur'tiv·lē) *adv.:* secretly; stealthily.
reflective (ri·flek'tiv) *adj.:* thoughtful; contemplative.

Options for Teaching

Assessment Tools

Self-Reflection Have students briefly explain orally or in writing what they know about inner-city poverty and the status of race relations in the 1950s before they begin reading *A Raisin in the Sun.* Then, offer these questions for them to answer in their Reader's Logs:

- Do you find these characters believable?
- Which character is the most sympathetic?
- What do you make of the difficulties that the Youngers face? Which one do you think will cause the greatest frustration, and why?

Invite students to share their responses; assess informally.

certain rugs in a certain apartment I could also mention.

Beneatha (*shrugging*). Well, good God, how much cleaning can a house need.

Mama (*not liking the Lord's name used thus*). Bennie!

Ruth. Just listen to her—just listen!

Beneatha. Oh, . . .

Mama. If you use the Lord's name just one more time—

Beneatha (*a bit of a whine*). Oh, Mama—

Ruth. Fresh—just fresh as salt, this girl!

Beneatha (*drily*). Well—if the salt loses its savor[4]—

Mama. Now that will do. I just ain't going to have you 'round here reciting the scriptures in vain—you hear me?

Beneatha. How did I manage to get on everybody's wrong side by just walking into a room?

Ruth. If you weren't so fresh—

Beneatha. Ruth, I'm twenty years old.

Mama. What time you be home from school today?

Beneatha. Kind of late. (*With enthusiasm*) Madeline is going to start my guitar lessons today.

[MAMA *and* RUTH *look up with the same expression.*]

Mama. Your *what* kind of lessons?

Beneatha. Guitar.

Ruth. Oh, Father!

Mama. How come you done taken it in your mind to learn to play the guitar?

Beneatha. I just want to, that's all.

Mama (*smiling*). Lord, child, don't you know what to get tired of this now—like you got tired of that little do with yourself? How long it going to be before you play-acting group you joined last year? (*Looking at* RUTH) And what was it the year before that?

Ruth. The horseback-riding club for which she bought that fifty-five-dollar riding habit that's been hanging in the closet ever since!

Mama (*to* BENEATHA). Why you got to flit so from one thing to another, baby?

Beneatha (*sharply*). I just want to learn to play the guitar. Is there anything wrong with that?

Mama. Ain't nobody trying to stop you. I just wonders sometimes why you has to flit so from one thing to another all the time. You ain't never done nothing with all that camera equipment you brought home—

Beneatha. I don't flit! I—I experiment with different forms of expression—

Ruth. Like riding a horse?

Beneatha. —People have to express themselves one way or another.

Mama. What is it you want to express?

Beneatha (*angrily*). Me! (MAMA *and* RUTH *look at each other and burst into* raucous *laughter.*) Don't worry—I don't expect you to understand.

Mama (*to change the subject*). Who you going out with tomorrow night?

Beneatha (*with displeasure*). George Murchison again.

Mama (*pleased*). Oh—you getting a little sweet on him?

Ruth. You ask me, this child ain't sweet on nobody but herself—(*Underbreath*) Express herself!

[*They laugh.*]

Beneatha. Oh—I like George all right, Mama. I mean I like him enough to go out with him and stuff, but—

Ruth (*for devilment*). What does *and stuff* mean?

Beneatha. Mind your own business.

Mama. Stop picking at her now, Ruth. (*She chuckles—then a suspicious sudden look at her daughter as she turns in her chair for emphasis.*) What DOES it mean?

Beneatha (*wearily*). Oh, I just mean I couldn't ever really be serious about George. He's—he's so shallow.

Ruth. Shallow—what do you mean he's shallow? He's *Rich*!

Mama. Hush, Ruth.

Beneatha. I know he's rich. He knows he's rich, too.

4. **salt . . . savor:** reference to Matthew 5:13: "Ye are the salt of the earth: but if the salt have lost his savor, wherewith shall it be salted? It is thenceforth good for nothing, but to be cast out, and to be trodden under foot of men."

WORDS TO OWN

raucous (rô′kəs) *adj.:* loud; boisterous.

D. Critical Reading: Finding Cause and Effect

? **What causes Mama to be concerned for Beneatha?** [Possible answers: Beneatha goes from one form of expression to another very quickly; after spending money to start a hobby, she then abandons it. Mama probably worries that Beneatha may never settle down.] **Why do you think Mama and Ruth laugh when Beneatha says she wants to express herself?** [Possible answers: Perhaps the search for self-expression seems frivolous or childish to them; perhaps they feel that Beneatha's personality is so unusual that anything artistic that she creates will be bizarre.]

E. Critical Reading: Making Inferences

? **What does Beneatha mean when she calls George Murchison "shallow"?** [Possible answers: He does not think on a deep level; he is emotionally immature; he does not share her interests.]

A. Literary Element: Character

? What differences exist between Ruth and Beneatha when it comes to marrying a man with money? [Ruth may be joking but seems to think it would be worth marrying a nice rich man even if he were shallow; Beneatha disagrees. This may stem from the fact that Ruth has worked hard and sacrificed all her married life and Beneatha has been financially able to do things she would like to do.]

B. Critical Reading: Evaluating an Interpretation

? How does Beneatha justify her view of "rich colored people"? [She points to the example of George's mother, whom she considers snobbish, and she claims that "everybody" knows that what she has said is true. She also justifies her view by claiming that if people can look down on the poor, then people should be able to look down on the rich.] Do you think that Beneatha has justified her view? [Possible answer: No, she bases her view on one example; then, she supports her view by identifying herself with a vague "everybody" and by claiming, in essence, that two wrongs make a right.]

C. Literary Element: Tone

? What kind of tone is "a wisdom-of-the-ages manner"? How is Ruth meant to sound? [The tone is knowledgeable yet consoling. She is meant to sound like Mama's equal—perhaps like Mama herself.]

D. Reader's Response: First Thoughts

? What are your reactions to Mama and Beneatha's argument? [Sample responses: Beneatha needs to find a more tactful way to express her views. Mama reacts too harshly by slapping her child; she could have found a better way to make her point. Or Beneatha should know what Mama's reaction will be and keep her ideas to herself.]

Ruth. Well—what other qualities a man got to have to satisfy you, little girl?

Beneatha. You wouldn't even begin to understand. Anybody who married Walter could not possibly understand.

Mama (*outraged*). What kind of way is that to talk about your brother?

Beneatha. Brother is a flip—let's face it.

Mama (*to* RUTH, *helplessly*). What's a flip?

Ruth (*glad to add kindling*). She's saying he's crazy.

Beneatha. Not crazy. Brother isn't really crazy yet—he—he's an elaborate neurotic.

Mama. Hush your mouth!

Beneatha. As for George. Well. George looks good—he's got a beautiful car and he takes me to nice places and, as my sister-in-law says, he is probably the richest boy I will ever get to know and I even like him sometimes—but if the Youngers are sitting around waiting to see if their little Bennie is going to tie up the family with the Murchisons, they are wasting their time.

Ruth. You mean you wouldn't marry George Murchison if he asked you someday? That pretty, rich thing? Honey, I knew you was odd—

Beneatha. No I would not marry him if all I felt for him was what I feel now. Besides, George's family wouldn't really like it.

Mama. Why not?

Beneatha. Oh, Mama—The Murchisons are (A) honest-to-God-real-*live*-rich colored people, and the only people in the world who are more snob-(B)bish than rich white people are rich colored people. I thought everybody knew that. I've met Mrs. Murchison. She's a scene!

Mama. You must not dislike people 'cause they well off, honey.

Beneatha. Why not? It makes just as much sense as disliking people 'cause they are poor, and lots of people do that.

Ruth (*a wisdom-of-the-ages manner. To* MAMA). (C) Well, she'll get over some of this—

Beneatha. Get over it? What are you talking about, Ruth? Listen, I'm going to be a doctor. I'm not worried about who I'm going to marry yet—if I ever get married.

Mama *and* **Ruth.** *If!*

Mama. Now, Bennie—

Beneatha. Oh, I probably will . . . but first I'm going to be a doctor, and George, for one, still thinks that's pretty funny. I couldn't be bothered with that. I am going to be a doctor and everybody around here better understand that!

Mama (*kindly*). 'Course you going to be a doctor, honey, God willing.

Beneatha (*drily*). God hasn't got a thing to do with it.

Mama. Beneatha—that just wasn't necessary.

Beneatha. Well . . . I get sick of hearing about God.

Mama. Beneatha!

Beneatha. I mean it! I'm just tired of hearing about God all the time. What has He got to do with anything? Does he pay tuition?

Mama. You 'bout to get your fresh little jaw slapped!

Ruth. That's just what she needs, all right!

Beneatha. Why? Why can't I say what I want to around here, like everybody else?

Mama. It don't sound nice for a young girl to say things like that—you wasn't brought up that way. Me and your father went to trouble to get you and Brother to church every Sunday.

Beneatha. Mama, you don't understand. It's all a matter of ideas, and that is just one idea I don't accept. It's not important. I am not going out and be immoral or commit crimes because I don't believe (D) in God. I don't even think about it. It's just that I get tired of Him getting credit for all the things the human race achieves through its own stubborn effort. There simply is no God—there is only man and it is *he* who makes miracles!

[MAMA *absorbs this speech, studies her daughter, and rises slowly and crosses to* BENEATHA *and slaps her powerfully across the face. After, there is only silence and the daughter drops her eyes from her mother's face, and* MAMA *is very tall before her.*]

Mama. Now—you say after me, in my mother's house there is still God. (*There is a long pause and* BENEATHA *stares at the floor wordlessly.* MAMA *repeats the phrase with precision and cool emotion.*) In my mother's house there is still God.

Beneatha. In my mother's house there is still God.

[*A long pause*]

Mama (*walking away from* BENEATHA, *too disturbed for triumphant posture. Stopping and turning back to her daughter*). There are some ideas we ain't going to have in this house. Not long as I am at the head of this family.

Beneatha. Yes, ma'am.

[MAMA *walks out of the room.*]

Ruth (*almost gently, with profound understanding*). You think you a woman, Bennie—but you still a little girl. What you did was childish—so you got treated like a child.

Beneatha. I see. (*Quietly*) I also see that everybody thinks it's all right for Mama to be a tyrant. But all the tyranny in the world will never make her right!

[*She picks up her books and goes out. Pause.*]

Ruth (*goes to* MAMA'S *door*). She said she was sorry.

Mama (*coming out, going to her plant*). They frightens me, Ruth. My children.

Ruth. You got good children, Lena. They just a little off sometimes—but they're good.

Mama. No—there's something come down between me and them that don't let us understand each other and I don't know what it is. One done almost lost his mind thinking 'bout money all the time and the other done commence to talk about things I can't seem to understand in no form or fashion. What is it that's changing, Ruth? E

Ruth (*soothingly, older than her years*). Now . . . you taking it all too seriously. You just got strong-willed children and it takes a strong woman like you to keep 'em in hand.

Mama (*looking at her plant and sprinkling a little water on it*). They spirited all right, my children. Got to admit they got spirit—Bennie and Walter. Like this little old plant that ain't never had enough sunshine or nothing—and look at it . . . F

[*She has her back to* RUTH, *who has had to stop ironing and lean against something and put the back of her hand to her forehead.*] G

Ruth (*trying to keep* MAMA *from noticing*). You . . . sure . . . loves that little old thing, don't you? . . .

Mama. Well, I always wanted me a garden like I used to see sometimes at the back of the houses down home. This plant is close as I ever got to having one. (*She looks out of the window as she replaces the plant.*) Lord, ain't nothing as dreary as the view from this window on a dreary day, is there? Why ain't you singing this morning, Ruth? Sing that "No Ways Tired." That song always lifts me up so—(*She turns at last to see that* RUTH *has slipped quietly to the floor, in a state of semiconsciousness.*) Ruth! Ruth honey—what's the matter with you . . . Ruth!

Curtain

"No—there's something come down between me and them that don't let us understand each other...."

E. Critical Reading: Identifying Main Ideas

? What barriers have come between Mama and her children? [Mama cannot understand Walter's obsession with money. Beneatha talks about subjects to which Mama has had no exposure.]

F. Literary Element: Symbolism

? What comparison does Mama draw between the plant and her children? [Possible answers: By speaking of the plant as never having "had enough sunshine or nothing," she implies that her children never have had all the things that they needed.]

G. Critical Reading: Finding Details

? What other clues have there been that Ruth is not feeling well? [She has been irritated all morning. She is so tired that Mama has suggested she stay home from work.]

RESPONDING TO THE PHOTOGRAPH: VISUAL LITERACY

Describe the expressions on the faces of the women in this photograph. [Possible responses: Shocked, sad, concerned, serious.] How is the quotation ironic for this situation? [Possible responses: The statement is very sarcastic. There are no happy faces, but instead, faces bearing expressions of sad feelings.] How is tension created in this photograph? [Possible responses: Mama and Beneatha are facing Ruth and holding onto her as if they are scared of what she might say. Their postures reveal that they are anxious. Ruth's hand is to her throat and her arm is pulled in.]

"Well, I guess from all the happy faces—everybody knows."

Scene 2

It is the following morning; a Saturday morning, and housecleaning is in progress at the YOUNGERS. *Furniture has been shoved hither and yon and* MAMA *is giving the kitchen-area walls a washing down.* BENEATHA, *in dungarees, with a handkerchief tied around her face, is spraying insecticide into the cracks in the walls. As they work, the radio is on and a South Side disc-jockey program is inappropriately filling the house with a rather exotic saxophone blues.* TRAVIS, *the sole idle one, is leaning on his arms, looking out of the window.*

Travis. Grandmama, that stuff Bennie is using smells awful. Can I go downstairs, please?
Mama. Did you get all them chores done already? I ain't seen you doing much.
Travis. Yes'm—finished early. Where did Mama go this morning?
Mama (*looking at* BENEATHA). She had to go on a little errand.

[*The phone rings.* BENEATHA *runs to answer it and reaches it before* WALTER, *who has entered from bedroom.*]

Travis. Where?
Mama. To tend to her business.
Beneatha. Haylo . . . (*Disappointed*) Yes, he is. (*She tosses the phone to* WALTER, *who barely catches it.*) It's Willy Harris again.
Walter (*as privately as possible under* MAMA'*s gaze*). Hello, Willy. Did you get the papers from the lawyer? . . . No, not yet. I told you the mailman doesn't get here till ten-thirty . . . No, I'll come there . . . Yeah! Right away. (*He hangs up and goes for his coat.*)
Beneatha. Brother, where did Ruth go?
Walter (*as he exits*). How should I know!
Travis. Aw come on, Grandma. Can I go outside?
Mama. Oh, I guess so. You stay right in front of the house, though, and keep a good lookout for the postman.

Travis. Yes'm. (*He darts into bedroom for stickball and bat, reenters, and sees* BENEATHA *on her knees spraying under sofa with behind upraised. He edges closer to the target, takes aim, and lets her have it. She screams.*) Leave them poor little cockroaches alone, they ain't bothering you none! (*He runs as she swings the spray gun at him viciously and playfully.*) Grandma! Grandma!
Mama. Look out there, girl, before you be spilling some of that stuff on that child!
Travis (*safely behind the bastion of* MAMA). That's right—look out, now! (*He exits.*)
Beneatha (*drily*). I can't imagine that it would hurt him—it has never hurt the roaches.
Mama. Well, little boys' hides ain't as tough as South Side roaches. You better get over there behind the bureau. I seen one marching out of there like Napoleon yesterday.
Beneatha. There's really only one way to get rid of them, Mama—
Mama. How?
Beneatha. Set fire to this building! Mama, where did Ruth go?
Mama (*looking at her with meaning*). To the doctor, I think.
Beneatha. The doctor? What's the matter? (*They exchange glances.*) You don't think—
Mama (*with her sense of drama*). Now I ain't saying what I think. But I ain't never been wrong 'bout a woman neither.

[*The phone rings.*]

Beneatha (*at the phone*). Hay-lo . . . (*Pause, and a moment of recognition*) Well—when did you get back! . . . And how was it? . . . Of course I've missed you—in my way . . . This morning? No . . . housecleaning and all that and Mama hates it if I let people come over when the house is like this . . . You *have*? Well, that's different . . . What is it—Oh, what the heck, come on over . . . Right, see you then. *Arrivederci.*

[*She hangs up.*]

Mama (*who has listened vigorously, as is her habit*). Who is that you inviting over here with this house looking like this? You ain't got the pride you was born with!
Beneatha. Asagai doesn't care how houses look, Mama—he's an intellectual.
Mama. *Who?*
Beneatha. Asagai—Joseph Asagai. He's an African boy I met on campus. He's been studying in Canada all summer.
Mama. What's his name?
Beneatha. Asagai, Joseph. Ah-sah-guy . . . He's from Nigeria.[5]
Mama. Oh, that's the little country that was founded by slaves way back . . .
Beneatha. No, Mama—that's Liberia.[6]
Mama. I don't think I never met no African before.
Beneatha. Well, do me a favor and don't ask him a whole lot of ignorant questions about Africans. I mean, do they wear clothes and all that—
Mama. Well, now, I guess if you think we so ignorant 'round here maybe you shouldn't bring your friends here—
Beneatha. It's just that people ask such crazy things. All anyone seems to know about when it comes to Africa is Tarzan—
Mama (*indignantly*). Why should I know anything about Africa?
Beneatha. Why do you give money at church for the missionary work?
Mama. Well, that's to help save people.
Beneatha. You mean save them from *heathenism*—
Mama (*innocently*). Yes.
Beneatha. I'm afraid they need more salvation from the British and the French.

[RUTH *comes in forlornly and pulls off her coat with dejection. They both turn to look at her.*]

Ruth (*dispiritedly*). Well, I guess from all the happy faces—everybody knows.
Beneatha. You pregnant?
Mama. Lord have mercy, I sure hope it's a little old girl. Travis ought to have a sister.

[BENEATHA *and* RUTH *give her a hopeless look for this grandmotherly enthusiasm.*]

Beneatha. How far along are you?
Ruth. Two months.

5. **Nigeria:** one of the largest and most populous countries on the western coast of Africa. Nigeria, a British dependency when this play opened, gained its independence in 1960.
6. **Liberia:** nation on the west coast of Africa, established as a republic in 1847 by freed American slaves.

A. Language Note: Humor

? What purpose does humor serve in this passage? [Possible answers: It offers some comic relief, a respite from the high emotion in Scene 1; it also serves as a counterpoint for Walter's furtive telephone conversation.]

A. Critical Reading: Making Generalizations

Consider the **conflicts** that have driven the play thus far. How would you define *ghetto-itus*? [Possible answers: A mix of financial worries, frustration about limited educational and employment opportunities, the tensions of too many people living too close together, and the problems created by doing without for too long.]

B. Literary Element: Character

Asagai acts as a foil, clarifying differences in attitudes between Africans and African Americans. Have students notice that Asagai speaks an almost stilted variety of English. How do you account for Asagai's dialect of English? [Possible answers: He may have been taught it as a second language. English speakers in Africa at the time were mostly British, not American.]

C. Reader's Response: First Thoughts

? How does Asagai differ from the Youngers? [Sample responses: He is more worldly; he is more proud of his heritage and his physical features, particularly his naturally coarse hair.] What does he find difficult to understand? [Sample responses: Assimilationism, mutilating one's hair, or that many kinds of feelings can exist between a man and a woman.] What do you think of Asagai's view that there need be only one kind of feeling between a man and a woman? [Sample responses: It is outdated thinking; it is thinking that may reflect Asagai's culture; or in their attitudes toward women, Asagai and Walter have some similarities.]

Beneatha. Did you mean to? I mean did you plan it or was it an accident?

Mama. What do you know about planning or not planning?

Beneatha. Oh, Mama.

Ruth (*wearily*). She's twenty years old, Lena.

Beneatha. Did you plan it, Ruth?

Ruth. Mind your own business.

Beneatha. It is my business—where is he going to live, on the *roof*? (*There is silence following the remark as the three women react to the sense of it.*) Gee—I didn't mean that, Ruth, honest. Gee, I don't feel like that at all. I—I think it is wonderful.

Ruth (*dully*). Wonderful.

Beneatha. Yes—really.

Mama (*looking at* RUTH, *worried*). Doctor say everything going to be all right?

Ruth (*far away*). Yes—she says everything is going to be fine . . .

Mama (*immediately suspicious*). "She"—What doctor you went to?

[RUTH *folds over, near hysteria.*]

Mama (*worriedly hovering over* RUTH). Ruth honey—what's the matter with you—you sick?

[RUTH *has her fists clenched on her thighs and is fighting hard to suppress a scream that seems to be rising in her.*]

Beneatha. What's the matter with her, Mama?

Mama (*working her fingers in* RUTH*'s shoulders to relax her*). She be all right. Women gets right depressed sometimes when they get her way. (*Speaking softly, expertly, rapidly*) Now you just relax. That's right . . . just lean back, don't think 'bout nothing at all . . . nothing at all—

Ruth. I'm all right . . .

[*The glassy-eyed look melts and then she collapses into a fit of heavy sobbing. The bell rings.*]

Beneatha. Oh . . . that must be Asagai.

Mama (*to* RUTH). Come on now, honey. You need to lie down and rest awhile . . . then have some nice hot food.

[*They exit,* RUTH*'s weight on her mother-in-law.* BENEATHA, *herself profoundly disturbed, opens the door to admit a rather dramatic-looking young man with a large package.*]

Asagai. Hello, Alaiyo—

Beneatha (*holding the door open and regarding him with pleasure*). Hello . . . (*Long pause*) Well—come in. And please excuse everything. My mother was very upset about my letting anyone come here with the place like this.

Asagai (*coming into the room*). You look disturbed too . . . Is something wrong?

Beneatha (*still at the door, absently*). Yes . . . we've all got acute ghetto-itus. (*She smiles and comes toward him, finding a cigarette and sitting.*) So—sit down! No! Wait! (*She whips the spray gun off sofa where she had left it and puts the cushions back. At last perches on arm of sofa. He sits.*) So, how was Canada?

Asagai (*a sophisticate*). Canadian.

Beneatha (*looking at him*). Asagai, I'm very glad you are back.

Asagai (*looking back at her in turn*). Are you really?

Beneatha. Yes—very.

Asagai. Why?—you were quite glad when I went away. What happened?

Beneatha. You went away.

Asagai. Ahhhhhhhh.

Beneatha. Before—you wanted to be so serious before there was time.

Asagai. How much time must there be before one knows what one feels?

Beneatha (*stalling this particular conversation. Her hands pressed together, in a deliberately childish gesture*). What did you bring me?

Asagai (*handing her the package*). Open it and see.

Beneatha (*eagerly opening the package and drawing out some records and the colorful robes of a Nigerian woman*). Oh, Asagai! . . . You got them for me! . . . How beautiful . . . and the records too! (*She lifts out the robes and runs to the mirror with them and holds the drapery up in front of herself.*)

Asagai (*coming to her at the mirror*). I shall have to teach you how to drape it properly. (*He flings the material about her for the moment and stands back to look at her.*) Ah—*Oh-pay-gay-day, oh-gbah-mu-shay.* (*A Yoruba*[7] *exclamation for admiration*) You wear it well . . . very well . . . mutilated hair and all.

7. **Yoruba:** a people living in southwestern Nigeria and parts of Benin and Togo, and the language they speak.

Beneatha (*turning suddenly*). My hair—what's wrong with my hair?
Asagai (*shrugging*). Were you born with it like that?
Beneatha (*reaching up to touch it*). No . . . of course not.

[*She looks back to the mirror, disturbed.*]

Asagai (*smiling*). How then?
Beneatha. You know perfectly well how . . . as crinkly as yours . . . that's how.
Asagai. And it is ugly to you that way?
Beneatha (*quickly*). Oh, no—not ugly . . . (*More slowly, apologetically*) But it's so hard to manage when it's, well—raw.
Asagai. And so to accommodate that—you mutilate it every week?
Beneatha. It's not mutilation!
Asagai (*laughing aloud at her seriousness*). Oh . . . please! I am only teasing you because you are so very serious about these things. (*He stands back from her and folds his arms across his chest as he watches her pulling at her hair and frowning in the mirror.*) Do you remember the first time you met me at school? . . . (*He laughs.*) You came up to me and you said—and I thought you were the most serious little thing I had ever seen—you said: (*He imitates her.*) "Mr. Asagai—I want very much to talk with you. About Africa. You see, Mr. Asagai, I am looking for my *identity*!"

[*He laughs.*]

Beneatha (*turning to him, not laughing*). Yes—

[*Her face is quizzical, profoundly disturbed.*]

Asagai (*still teasing and reaching out and taking her face in his hands and turning her profile to him*). Well . . . it is true that this is not so much a profile of a Hollywood queen as perhaps a queen of the Nile—(*A mock dismissal of the importance of the question*) But what does it matter? Assimilationism[8] is so popular in your country.
Beneatha (*wheeling, passionately, sharply*). I am not an assimilationist!
Asagai (*The protest hangs in the room for a moment and* ASAGAI *studies her, his laughter fading.*). Such a serious one. (*There is a pause.*) So—you like the robes? You must take excellent care of them—they are from my sister's personal wardrobe.
Beneatha (*with incredulity*). You—you sent all the way home—for me?
Asagai (*with charm*). For you—I would do much more . . . Well, that is what I came for. I must go.
Beneatha. Will you call me Monday?
Asagai. Yes . . . We have a great deal to talk about. I mean about identity and time and all that.
Beneatha. Time?
Asagai. Yes. About how much time one needs to know what one feels.
Beneatha. You see! You never understood that there is more than one kind of feeling which can exist between a man and a woman—or, at least, there should be.
Asagai (*shaking his head negatively but gently*). No. Between a man and a woman there need be only one kind of feeling. I have that for you . . . Now even . . . right this moment . . .
Beneatha. I know—and by itself—it won't do. I can find that anywhere.
Asagai. For a woman it should be enough.
Beneatha. I know—because that's what it says in all the novels that men write. But it isn't. Go ahead and laugh—but I'm not interested in being someone's little episode in America or—(*with feminine vengeance*)—one of them! (ASAGAI *has burst into laughter again.*) That's funny . . . , huh!
Asagai. It's just that every American girl I have known has said that to me. White—black—in this you are all the same. And the same speech, too!
Beneatha (*angrily*). Yuk, yuk, yuk!
Asagai. It's how you can be sure that the world's most liberated women are not liberated at all. You all talk about it too much!

[MAMA *enters and is immediately all social charm because of the presence of a guest.*]

Beneatha. Oh—Mama—this is Mr. Asagai.
Mama. How do you do?
Asagai (*total politeness to an elder*). How do you do, Mrs. Younger. Please forgive me for coming at such an outrageous hour on a Saturday.
Mama. Well, you are quite welcome. I just hope you understand that our house don't always look like this. (*Chatterish*) You must come again. I

8. **assimilationism** (ə·sim′ə·lā′shən·iz′əm): belief that minority groups should drop their ethnic, racial, and religious identities and be absorbed into the majority culture.

D. Critical Reading: Finding Sequence

? How would you trace the progress of Mama's comments to Asagai in this scene? [Possible answer: She begins nervously, parroting things that she has heard Beneatha say. When Asagai begins to relax, however, so does she. She becomes more motherly in her comments, sympathizing with him for being away from home and even inviting him back for meals.]

A. Reader's Response: Challenging the Text

? Do you think that Alaiyo is a good name for Beneatha? [Sample responses: Yes, it seems to fit her perfectly, for she refuses to be satisfied with the basic assumptions about what her life should be. Or no, it makes her sound as though she lacks something.]

B. Literary Element: Character

? How similar are Beneatha and her brother Walter? Could a masculine form of the same name apply to him? [Possible answers: They are alike in their ambitions to be successful, but they are not alike in how they choose to attain their goals. The name could apply to him, but Walter's interests are materialistic and Beneatha's are spiritual.]

would love to hear all about—(*not sure of the name*)—your country. I think it's so sad the way our American Negroes don't know nothing about Africa 'cept Tarzan and all that. And all that money they pour into these churches when they ought to be helping you people over there drive out them French and Englishmen done taken away your land.

[*The mother flashes a slightly superior look at her daughter upon completion of the recitation.*]

Asagai (*taken aback by this sudden and acutely unrelated expression of sympathy*). Yes . . . yes . . .

Mama (*smiling at him suddenly and relaxing and looking him over*). How many miles is it from here to where you come from?

Asagai. Many thousands.

Mama (*looking at him as she would* WALTER). I bet you don't half look after yourself, being away from your mama either. I spec you better come 'round here from time to time to get yourself some decent home-cooked meals . . .

Asagai (*moved*). Thank you. Thank you very much. (*They are all quiet, then—*) Well . . . I must go. I will call you Monday, Alaiyo.

Mama. What's that he call you?

Asagai. Oh—"Alaiyo." I hope you don't mind. It is what you would call a nickname, I think. It is a Yoruba word. I am a Yoruba.

Mama (*looking at* BENEATHA). I—I thought he was from— (*Uncertain*)

Asagai (*understanding*). Nigeria is my country. Yoruba is my tribal origin—

Beneatha. You didn't tell us what Alaiyo means . . . for all I know, you might be calling me Little Idiot or something . . .

Asagai. Well . . . let me see . . . I do not know how just to explain it . . . The sense of a thing can be so different when it changes languages.

Beneatha. You're evading.

A **Asagai.** No—really it is difficult . . . (*Thinking*) It means . . . it means One for Whom Bread—Food—Is Not Enough. (*He looks at her.*) Is that all right? B

Beneatha (*understanding, softly*). Thank you.

Mama (*looking from one to the other and not understanding any of it*). Well . . . that's nice . . . You must come see us again—Mr. ——

Asagai. Ah-sah-guy . . .

Mama. Yes . . . Do come again.

Asagai. Goodbye.

[*He exits.*]

Mama (*after him*). Lord, that's a pretty thing just went out here! (*Insinuatingly, to her daughter*) Yes, I guess I see why we done commence to get so interested in Africa 'round here. Missionaries my aunt Jenny!

[*She exits.*]

Beneatha. Oh, Mama! . . .

[*She picks up the Nigerian dress and holds it up to her in front of the mirror again. She sets the headdress on haphazardly and then notices her hair again and clutches at it and then replaces the headdress and frowns at herself. Then she starts to wriggle in front of the mirror as she thinks a Nigerian woman might.* TRAVIS *enters and stands regarding her.*]

Travis. What's the matter, girl, you cracking up?

Beneatha. Shut up.

[*She pulls the headdress off and looks at herself in the mirror and clutches at her hair again and squinches her eyes as if trying to imagine something. Then, suddenly, she gets her raincoat and kerchief and hurriedly prepares for going out.*]

Mama (*coming back into the room*). She's resting now. Travis, baby, run next door and ask Miss Johnson to please let me have a little kitchen cleanser. This here can is empty as Jacob's kettle.

Travis. I just came in.

Mama. Do as you told. (*He exits and she looks at her daughter.*) Where you going?

Beneatha (*halting at the door*). To become a queen of the Nile!

[*She exits in a breathless blaze of glory.* RUTH *appears in the bedroom doorway.*]

Mama. Who told you to get up?

Ruth. Ain't nothing wrong with me to be lying in no bed for. Where did Bennie go?

Mama (*drumming her fingers*). Far as I could make out—to Egypt. (RUTH *just looks at her.*) What time is it getting to?

Ruth. Ten-twenty. And the mailman going to ring that bell this morning just like he done every morning for the last umpteen years.

[TRAVIS *comes in with the cleanser can.*]

Travis. She say to tell you that she don't have much.

Mama (*angrily*). Lord, some people I could name sure is tight-fisted! (*Directing her grandson*) Mark two cans of cleanser down on the list there. If she that hard up for kitchen cleanser, I sure don't want to forget to get her none!

Ruth. Lena—maybe the woman is just short on cleanser—

Mama (*not listening*). —Much baking powder as she done borrowed from me all these years, she could of done gone into the baking business!

[*The bell sounds suddenly and sharply and all three are stunned—serious and silent—mid-speech. In spite of all the other conversations and distractions of the morning, this is what they have been waiting for, even* TRAVIS, *who looks helplessly from his mother to his grandmother.* RUTH *is the first to come to life again.*] C

Ruth (*to* TRAVIS). *Get down them steps, boy!*

[TRAVIS *snaps to life and flies out to get the mail.*]

Mama (*her eyes wide, her hand to her breast*). You mean it done really come?

Ruth (*excited*). Oh, Miss Lena!

Mama (*collecting herself*). Well . . . I don't know what we all so excited about 'round here for. We known it was coming for months.

Ruth. That's a whole lot different from having it come and being able to hold it in your hands . . . a piece of paper worth ten thousand dollars . . . (TRAVIS *bursts back into the room. He holds the envelope high above his head, like a little dancer, his face is radiant, and he is breathless. He moves to his grandmother with sudden slow ceremony and puts the envelope into her hands. She accepts it, and then merely holds it and looks at it.*) Come on! Open it . . . Lord have mercy, I wish Walter Lee was here!

Travis. Open it, Grandmama!

Mama (*staring at it*). Now you all be quiet. It's just a check.

Ruth. Open it . . .

Mama (*still staring at it*). Now don't act silly . . . We ain't never been no people to act silly 'bout no money— D

Ruth (*swiftly*). We ain't never had none before—

OPEN IT!

[MAMA *finally makes a good strong tear and pulls out the thin blue slice of paper and inspects it closely. The boy and his mother study it raptly over* MAMA*'s shoulders.*]

Mama. *Travis!* (*She is counting off with doubt.*) Is that the right number of zeros.

Travis. Yes'm . . . ten thousand dollars. Gaalee, Grandmama, you rich.

Mama (*She holds the check away from her, still looking at it. Slowly her face sobers into a mask of unhappiness.*). Ten thousand dollars. (*She hands it to* RUTH.) Put it away somewhere, Ruth. E (*She does not look at* RUTH; *her eyes seem to be seeing something somewhere very far off.*) Ten thousand dollars they give you. Ten thousand dollars.

C. Reader's Response: Connecting with the Text

Ask students to think about a scene from a book, movie, or television program in which characters' dreams seem about to come true. [Sample responses: Dorothy before the Wizard in *The Wizard of Oz*, or Pip at Jagger's in *Great Expectations*.] Based on what you remember about that scene, what emotions would you guess the Youngers are feeling at this moment? [Sample responses: Joy; fear; excitement; or hesitation, because the feeling of the moment will be lost.]

D. Critical Reading: Expressing an Opinion

? Do you think Mama's assessment of her family is accurate? Explain. [Possible answer: Perhaps it was true in the past—before the insurance check became available—but Walter's behavior, at least, is diminishing that assessment.]

E. Critical Reading: Making Inferences

? With the long-awaited check finally in her hands, why is Mama sad? [She remembers Big Walter, who was worth far more to her than any amount of money.]

A. Literary Element: Character

? What does this exchange suggest about Mama's personality and about Big Walter's importance to her? [Possible answers: She is generous enough that she might give away all her money to the church; although she seems strong, she can be indecisive; she depended on Big Walter more than has been suggested thus far.]

B. Critical Reading: Speculating

Mama rejects Walter's plan. Can you think of anything that might change her mind? [Possible answer: If he went into a different kind of business, she might reconsider.] What reactions on Walter's part do you predict as a result of her rejection of his plan? [Possible answer: Walter may become angry or withdrawn.]

C. Language Note: Repetition

Have students re-read Walter's speech, perhaps aloud. Encourage them to notice how repetition tightens and strengthens his language—the repeated *you* (sometimes stated, sometimes understood) and especially the repeated *and tell it.*

D. Reader's Response: Extending the Text

? How do you think that most adults would feel about being spoken to as Walter is spoken to here by Mama? [Sample responses: They would feel frustrated, embarrassed, or bitter. They would feel belittled, as if the person speaking had no faith in them.]

Travis (*to his mother, sincerely*). What's the matter with Grandmama—don't she want to be rich?
Ruth (*distractedly*). You go on out and play now, baby. (TRAVIS *exits.* MAMA *starts wiping dishes absently, humming intently to herself.* RUTH *turns to her, with kind exasperation.*) You've gone and got yourself upset.
Mama (*not looking at her*). I spec if it wasn't for you all . . . I would just put that money away or give it to the church or something.
Ruth. Now what kind of talk is that. Mr. Younger would just be plain mad if he could hear you talking foolish like that.
Mama (*stopping and staring off*). Yes . . . he sure would. (*Sighing*) We got enough to do with that money, all right. (*She halts then, and turns and looks at her daughter-in-law hard;* RUTH *avoids her eyes and* MAMA *wipes her hands with finality and starts to speak firmly to* RUTH.) Where did you go today, girl?
Ruth. To the doctor.
Mama (*impatiently*). Now, Ruth . . . you know better than that. Old Doctor Jones is strange enough in his way but there ain't nothing 'bout him make somebody slip and call him "she"—like you done this morning.
Ruth. Well, that's what happened—my tongue slipped.
Mama. You went to see that woman, didn't you?
Ruth (*defensively, giving herself away*). What woman you talking about?
Mama (*angrily*). That woman who—

[WALTER *enters in great excitement.*]

Walter. Did it come?
Mama (*quietly*). Can't you give people a Christian greeting before you start asking about money?
Walter (*to* RUTH). Did it come? (RUTH *unfolds the check and lays it quietly before him, watching him intently with thoughts of her own.* WALTER *sits down and grasps it close and counts off the zeros.*) Ten thousand dollars—(*He turns suddenly, frantically to his mother and draws some papers out of his breast pocket.*) Mama—look. Old Willy Harris put everything on paper—
Mama. Son—I think you ought to talk to your wife . . . I'll go out and leave you alone if you want—
Walter. I can talk to her later—Mama, look—
Mama. Son—
Walter. WILL SOMEBODY PLEASE LISTEN TO ME TODAY!
Mama (*quietly*). I don't 'low no yellin' in this house, Walter Lee, and you know it—(WALTER *stares at them in frustration and starts to speak several times.*) And there ain't going to be no investing in no liquor stores.
Walter. But, Mama, you ain't even looked at it.
Mama. I don't aim to have to speak on that again.

[*A long pause*]

Walter. You ain't looked at it and you don't aim to have to speak on that again? You ain't even looked at it and *you* have decided—(*Crumpling his papers*) Well, *you* tell that to my boy tonight when you put him to sleep on the living-room couch . . . (*Turning to* MAMA *and speaking directly to her*) Yeah—and tell it to my wife, Mama, tomorrow when she has to go out of here to look after somebody else's kids. And tell it to *me,* Mama, every time we need a new pair of curtains and I have to watch *you* go out and work in somebody's kitchen. Yeah, you tell me then!

[WALTER *starts out.*]

Ruth. Where you going?
Walter. I'm going out!
Ruth. Where?
Walter. Just out of this house somewhere—
Ruth (*getting her coat*). I'll come too.
Walter. I don't want you to come!
Ruth. I got something to talk to you about, Walter.
Walter. That's too bad.
Mama (*still quietly*). Walter Lee—(*She waits and he finally turns and looks at her.*) Sit down.
Walter. I'm a grown man, Mama.
Mama. Ain't nobody said you wasn't grown. But you still in my house and my presence. And as long as you are—you'll talk to your wife civil. Now sit down.
Ruth (*suddenly*). Oh, let him go on out and drink himself to death! He makes me sick to my stomach! (*She flings her coat against him and exits to bedroom.*)
Walter (*violently flinging the coat after her*). And you turn mine too, baby! (*The door slams behind her.*) That was my biggest mistake—
Mama (*still quietly*). Walter, what is the matter with you?

Walter. Matter with me? Ain't nothing the matter with *me*!

Mama. Yes there is. Something eating you up like a crazy man. Something more than me not giving you this money. The past few years I been watching it happen to you. You get all nervous acting and kind of wild in the eyes—(WALTER *jumps up impatiently at her words.*) I said sit there now, I'm talking to you!

Walter. Mama—I don't need no nagging at me today.

Mama. Seem like you getting to a place where you always tied up in some kind of knot about something. But if anybody ask you 'bout it you just yell at 'em and bust out the house and go out and drink somewheres. Walter Lee, people can't live with that. Ruth's a good, patient girl in her way—but you getting to be too much. Boy, don't make the mistake of driving that girl away from you.

Walter. Why—what she do for me?

Mama. She loves you.

Walter. Mama—I'm going out. I want to go off somewhere and be by myself for a while.

Mama. I'm sorry 'bout your liquor store, son. It just wasn't the thing for us to do. That's what I want to tell you about—

Walter. I got to go out, Mama—

[*He rises.*]

Mama. It's dangerous, son.

Walter. What's dangerous?

Mama. When a man goes outside his home to look for peace.

Walter (*beseechingly*). Then why can't there never be no peace in this house then?

Mama. You done found it in some other house?

Walter. No—there ain't no woman! Why do women always think there's a woman somewhere when a man gets restless. (*Picks up the check*) Do you know what this money means to me? Do you know what this money can do for us? (*Puts it back*) Mama—Mama—I want so many things . . .

Mama. Yes, son—

Walter. I want so many things that they are driving me kind of crazy . . . Mama—look at me.

Mama. I'm looking at you. You a good-looking boy. You got a job, a nice wife, a fine boy, and—

Walter. A job. (*Looks at her*) Mama, a job? I open and close car doors all day long. I drive a man around in his limousine and I say, "Yes, sir; no, sir; very good, sir; shall I take the Drive, sir?" Mama, that ain't no kind of job . . . that ain't nothing at all. (*Very quietly*) Mama, I don't know if I can make you understand.

Mama. Understand what, baby?

Walter (*quietly*). Sometimes it's like I can see the future stretched out in front of me—just plain as day. The future, Mama. Hanging over there at the edge of my days. Just waiting for me—a big, looming blank space—full of *nothing*. Just waiting for *me*. But it don't have to be. (*Pause. Kneeling beside her chair*) Mama—sometimes when I'm downtown and I pass them cool, quiet-looking restaurants where them white boys are sitting back and talking 'bout things . . . sitting there turning deals worth millions of dollars . . . sometimes I see guys don't look much older than me—

Mama. Son—how come you talk so much 'bout money?

Walter (*with immense passion*). Because it is life, Mama!

Mama (*quietly*). Oh—(*Very quietly*) So now it's life. Money is life. Once upon a time freedom used to be life—now it's money. I guess the world really do change . . .

Walter. No—it was always money, Mama. We just didn't know about it.

Mama. No . . . something has changed. (*She looks at him.*) You something new, boy. In my time we was worried about not being lynched and getting to the North if we could and how to stay alive and still have a pinch of dignity too . . . Now here come you and Beneatha—talking 'bout things we ain't never even thought about hardly, me and your daddy. You ain't satisfied or proud of nothing we done. I mean that you had a home; that we kept you out of trouble till you was grown; that you don't have to ride to work on the back of nobody's streetcar—You my children—but how different we done become.

Walter (*a long beat. He pats her hand and gets up.*). You just don't understand, Mama, you just don't understand.

Mama. Son—do you know your wife is expecting another baby? (WALTER *stands, stunned, and absorbs what his mother has said.*) That's what she wanted to talk to you about. (WALTER *sinks down into a chair.*) This ain't for me to be telling—but you ought to know. (*She waits.*) I think Ruth is

E. Critical Reading: Identifying Main Ideas

? What main ideas of the play are addressed in this exchange? [The frustration that builds up in people who see their dreams go unfulfilled; friction between parent and child; the importance of communication among family members.]

F. Reader's Response: First Thoughts

? Do you agree with Walter that money "is life"? [Sample responses: Money is a useful tool, but many other values define life; or when you do not have it, money seems to be everything.]

G. Literary Element: Climax

? What tensions come to a boiling point as Act One reaches its climax? [Possible answers: Mama's "meddling" in Walter's life; Walter's lack of demonstrative affection for Ruth; the tension over Ruth's pregnancy.] Are any of the Youngers exempt from these tensions? [Possible answers: Beneatha and Travis are not directly involved in the climax of Act One, but they suffer from the conflicts among the other characters; Beneatha, too, has conflicts of her own regarding George Murchison and Joseph Asagai.]

Making Meanings Act One

First Thoughts

1. Possible responses: The poem is appropriate for Walter because he is drying up like a raisin in the sun. Walter's dream seems deferred. Beneatha will get the money for tuition.

Reviewing the Text

The centrality of the check is established with Walter's entrance; even before the amount and source of the money are explained, the check sparks arguments between Walter and Ruth and between Beneatha and Walter, showing the clash of their dreams as well as their personalities. Mama's dream of using the money for a home of their own is meant for the good of all, but her determination that money be set aside for Beneatha's schooling and her refusal to back Walter's liquor store deal increase the conflict. When the check finally arrives, the arguments resurface.

Shaping Interpretations

2. We are told that Mama is about to receive the check; Walter implies that Mama is more open to Ruth than she is to Walter and that an indirect approach to Mama is best; Ruth tells Travis not to bother his grandmother for money. Mama expresses concern about the signs of an argument. She shows that she is indeed a concerned, loving mother: She worries over Ruth's physical condition, offering to iron some of the clothes, and she reminds Beneatha to put on her robe to avoid the cold. Mama even expresses concern over a plant.
3. When Beneatha announces no God exists, Mama reacts with surprising firmness and a strong reminder that as long as Mama is head of the family, Beneatha will acknowledge God. Hansberry also suggests Mama's faith through her refusal to have a liquor store and through her love for spirituals.
4. Asagai, a Nigerian student in Chicago, represents a different, more international viewpoint. He is well traveled, liberal, and passionately convinced that the true roots and identity of African Americans are to be found in Africa. Asagai believes that African Americans should not yield to assimilationism.

thinking 'bout doing something to that child.

Walter (*slowly understanding*). —No—no—Ruth wouldn't do that.

Mama. When the world gets ugly enough—a woman will do anything for her family. *The part that's already living.*

Walter. You don't know Ruth, Mama, if you think she would do that.

[RUTH *opens the bedroom door and stands there a little limp.*]

Ruth (*beaten*). Yes I would too, Walter. (*Pause*) . . .

[*There is total silence as the man stares at his wife and the mother stares at her son.*]

Mama (*presently*). Well— (*Tightly*) Well—son, I'm waiting to hear you say something . . . (*She waits.*) I'm waiting to hear how you be your father's son. Be the man he was . . . (*Pause. The silence shouts.*) Your wife say she going to destroy your child. And I'm waiting to hear you talk like him and say we a people who give children life, not who destroys them—(*She rises.*) I'm waiting to see you stand up and look like your daddy and say we done give up one baby to poverty and that we ain't going to give up nary another one . . . I'm waiting.

Walter. Ruth— (*He can say nothing.*)

Mama. If you a son of mine, tell her! (WALTER *picks up his keys and his coat and walks out. She continues, bitterly.*) You . . . you are a disgrace to your father's memory. Somebody get me my hat!

Curtain

MAKING MEANINGS

Act One

First Thoughts

1. Review the notes you made in your Reader's Log. So far, how does the play connect with Hughes's poem "Harlem" on page 828? Whose dreams are being deferred, and where do you predict the play is going to go from here?

> **Reviewing the Text**
> Trace the significance of the check in this act as it moves from something that arouses our curiosity to something that becomes the play's central plot issue and source of **conflict.**

Shaping Interpretations

2. There has been a considerable buildup for Mama's entrance, which occurs in the middle of Scene 1. What are we told about Mama before she appears? In a play, showing is better than telling. When she makes her entrance, Mama immediately shows us in small ways what kind of woman and mother she is. What does she do, and what do her actions reveal about her **character**?
3. It is important that we know the strength of Mama's religious beliefs because it is these beliefs that influence her decision not to give Walter the money. How does the playwright show us how strong Mama's beliefs are?
4. The character of Asagai, introduced in Scene 2, gives us a different perspective on life in the Younger household. What does Asagai represent? How is he contrasted with George Murchison, Beneatha's other admirer?
5. What dramatic questions have been posed in this first act? What possible answers could each question have?

Connecting with the Text

6. It has been said that to enjoy a play we must believe what is happening and care about the characters. Is the action of the play believable so far? Explain. Which characters are you rooting for most, and why?

On the other hand, the goals and interests of George Murchison—the child of wealthy and successful African American parents—show that he has joined the mainstream of American society.

5. Possible questions: How will the conflict over the insurance money be resolved? Will Mama succeed in her efforts to keep the family together? Possible answers: Beneatha will receive money for her education, and Mama will use the rest of the money to help Walter. The family will stay together.

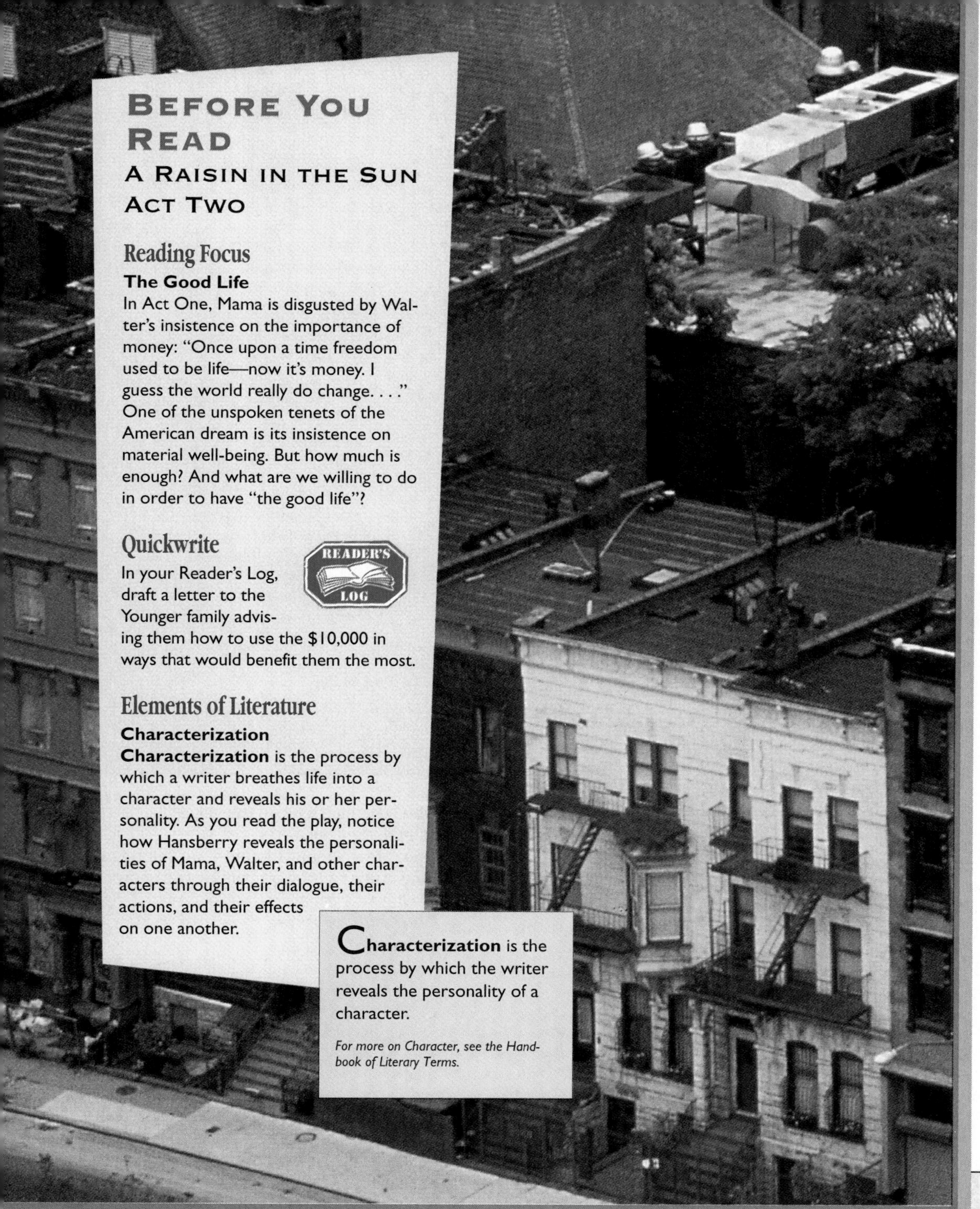

BEFORE YOU READ

A RAISIN IN THE SUN ACT TWO

Reading Focus

The Good Life

In Act One, Mama is disgusted by Walter's insistence on the importance of money: "Once upon a time freedom used to be life—now it's money. I guess the world really do change. . . ." One of the unspoken tenets of the American dream is its insistence on material well-being. But how much is enough? And what are we willing to do in order to have "the good life"?

Quickwrite

In your Reader's Log, draft a letter to the Younger family advising them how to use the $10,000 in ways that would benefit them the most.

Elements of Literature

Characterization

Characterization is the process by which a writer breathes life into a character and reveals his or her personality. As you read the play, notice how Hansberry reveals the personalities of Mama, Walter, and other characters through their dialogue, their actions, and their effects on one another.

Characterization is the process by which the writer reveals the personality of a character.

For more on Character, see the Handbook of Literary Terms.

Into the Play

Using BEFORE YOU READ p. 851

Quickwrite

Have students consider the following questions before writing their letters to the Youngers:

- Would everyone in the family agree with my plan for using this money?
- If other people knew what the Younger family did with the money, what would they say?
- Five years after using the money in this way, what benefits might the Youngers still be experiencing?

PROGRAM MANAGER

- **Planning Instruction** See Teaching Notes, *Teaching Resources B,* pp. 119–120, for objectives, and a summary for this act.
- **Instructional Support** Before beginning the instructional lesson, see Graphic Organizer for Active Reading, *Teaching Resources B,* p. 125, for a Through the Play activity.
- **Assessment** See Selection Test, *Test Booklet,* pp. 203–204.
- **Language Link** For instruction and practice in correcting errors in usage, spelling, punctuation, and capitalization, see Language Link, *Teaching Resources B,* p. 126, and *Language and Writing Skills Worksheets,* pp. 127–128, 140–142, 169–170.
- **Reinforcement** Use the Words to Own worksheet in *Teaching Resources B,* p. 127.

WORDS TO OWN

The following vocabulary words from Act Two are defined in the Words to Own at the bottom of the pupil's page.

fraternal p. 853	imploring p. 858
dominant p. 854	vigor p. 859
sobriety p. 855	exuberant p. 859
resignation p. 856	saucily p. 869
revelation p. 858	taut p. 874

PORTFOLIO ASSESSMENT

Portfolio Assessment For help with self- and teacher assessment of reading skills, see the *Portfolio Management System,* p. 53.

Through the Play

A. Humanities Connection
African music varies from culture to culture, but some generalizations can be made.

- The distinguishing feature is rhythmic complexity, achieved by claps, xylophones, rattles, and a variety of tuned and untuned drums.
- Polyphony exists in overlapping solo and choral parts, with occasional simultaneous melodies.
- Besides the human voice, wind and string instruments are used, including bamboo flutes, ivory trumpets, and the one-string ground bow (which uses a hole in the ground as a resonator).

B. Language Note: Style
Encourage students to try sounding out these song lyrics, savoring the feel of the language. Ask what students think Hansberry accomplishes by mixing languages here. [Possible answer: The sound of the Yoruban song makes the moment exotic; it also underscores Beneatha's search for an African identity.]

"What kind of dance is that?"

Act Two

Scene 1

Time: Later the same day.

At rise: RUTH *is ironing again. She has the radio going. Presently* BENEATHA*'s bedroom door opens and* RUTH*'s mouth falls and she puts down the iron in fascination.*

Ruth. What have we got on tonight!

Beneatha (*emerging grandly from the doorway so that we can see her thoroughly robed in the costume Asagai brought*). You are looking at what a well-dressed Nigerian woman wears—(*She parades for* RUTH, *her hair completely hidden by the headdress; she is coquettishly fanning herself with an ornate oriental fan, mistakenly more like Butterfly*[1] *than any Nigerian that ever was.*) Isn't it beautiful? (*She promenades to the radio and, with an arrogant flourish, turns off the good loud blues that is playing.*) Enough of this assimilationist junk! (RUTH *follows her with her eyes as she goes to the phonograph and puts on a record and turns and waits ceremoniously for the music to come up. Then, with a shout—*) OCOMOGOSIAY![2]

A [RUTH *jumps. The music comes up, a lovely Nigerian melody.* BENEATHA *listens, enraptured, her eyes far away—"back to the past." She begins to dance.* RUTH *is dumbfounded.*]

Ruth. What kind of dance is that?

Beneatha. A folk dance.

Ruth (*Pearl Bailey*[3]). What kind of folks do that, honey?

Beneatha. It's from Nigeria. It's a dance of welcome.

Ruth. Who you welcoming?

Beneatha. The men back to the village.

Ruth. Where they been?

Beneatha. How should I know—out hunting or something. Anyway, they are coming back now . . .

Ruth. Well, that's good.

Beneatha (*with the record*).

B
Alundi, alundi
Alundi alunya
Jop pu a jeepua
Ang gu soooooooooo

Ai yai yae . . .
Ayehaye—alundi . . .[4]

1. **Butterfly:** Madama Butterfly, the heroine in the opera of the same name by Giacomo Puccini.
2. ***ocomogosiay:*** shout of triumph in battle. It is a coined word, combining syllables from the Yoruban, Swahili, and Zulu languages.
3. **Pearl Bailey** (1918–1990): American entertainer, singer, and actress. Ruth is imitating her.
4. ***alundi . . . alundi:*** Yoruban harvest festival song. *Alundi* is Yoruba for "happy holiday."

OPTIONS FOR TEACHING

STRATEGIES FOR INCLUSION

Advanced In Act Two, the members of the Younger family will be confronted with what may be the greatest challenges of their lives. As students follow the action in Act Two, have them make notes in their Reader's Logs of any evidence that supports or refutes any one or all of the following statements.

- A college education may not make a person ready to face life's realities.
- Even the best of relationships can turn sour.
- Loving others sometimes may mean letting them make mistakes.
- People are blind to their own destructive tendencies.

Intrapersonal Students who often work independently already may have commented on Walter's tendency to deal with his feelings alone. By the end of Act Two, Walter will have become even more isolated. In their Reader's Logs, encourage students to trace the development of Walter's character in this act, focusing on the chances he has to strengthen his family relationships and determining what he does with these opportunities.

[WALTER *comes in during this performance; he has obviously been drinking. He leans against the door heavily and watches his sister, at first with distaste. Then his eyes look off—"back to the past"—as he lifts both his fists to the roof, screaming.*]

Walter. YEAH . . . AND ETHIOPIA STRETCH FORTH HER HANDS AGAIN! . . .

Ruth (*drily, looking at him*). Yes—and Africa sure is claiming her own tonight. (*She gives them both up and starts ironing again.*)

Walter (*all in a drunken, dramatic shout*). Shut up! . . . I'm digging them drums . . . them drums move me! . . . (*He makes his weaving way to his wife's face and leans in close to her.*) In my *heart of hearts*—(*He thumps his chest.*)—I am much warrior!

Ruth (*without even looking up*). In your heart of hearts you are much drunkard.

Walter (*coming away from her and starting to wander around the room, shouting*). Me and Jomo[5] . . . (*Intently, in his sister's face. She has stopped dancing to watch him in this unknown mood.*) That's my man, Kenyatta. (*Shouting and thumping his chest*) FLAMING SPEAR! . . . (*He is suddenly in possession of an imaginary spear and actively spearing enemies all over the room.*) *OCOMOGOSIAY* . . .

Beneatha (*to encourage* WALTER, *thoroughly caught up with this side of him*). *OCOMOGOSIAY,* FLAMING SPEAR!

Walter. THE LION IS WAKING . . . OWIMOWEH![6] (*He pulls his shirt open and leaps up on the table and gestures with his spear.*)

Beneatha. OWIMOWEH!

Walter (*on the table, very far gone, his eyes pure glass sheets. He sees what we cannot, that he is a leader of his people, a great chief, a descendant of Chaka,[7] and that the hour to march has come.*). Listen, my black brothers—

Beneatha. OCOMOGOSIAY!

Walter. —Do you hear the waters rushing against the shores of the coastlands—

Beneatha. OCOMOGOSIAY!

Walter. —Do you hear the screeching of the cocks in yonder hills beyond where the chiefs meet in council for the coming of the mighty war—

Beneatha. OCOMOGOSIAY!

[*And now the lighting shifts subtly to suggest the world of* WALTER'S *imagination, and the mood shifts from pure comedy. It is the inner* WALTER *speaking; the South Side chauffeur has assumed an unexpected majesty.*]

Walter. —Do you hear the beating of the wings of the birds flying low over the mountains and the low places of our land—

Beneatha. OCOMOGOSIAY!

Walter. —Do you hear the singing of the women, singing the war songs of our fathers to the babies in the great houses? Singing the sweet war songs! (*The doorbell rings.*) OH, DO YOU HEAR, MY *BLACK* BROTHERS!

Beneatha (*completely gone*). We hear you, Flaming Spear—

[RUTH *shuts off the phonograph and opens the door.* GEORGE MURCHISON *enters.*]

Walter. Telling us to prepare for the GREATNESS OF THE TIME! (*Lights back to normal. He turns and sees* GEORGE.) Black Brother!

[*He extends his hand for the fraternal clasp.*]

George. Black Brother, . . .

Ruth (*having had enough, and embarrassed for the family*). Beneatha, you got company—what's the matter with you? Walter Lee Younger, get down off that table and stop acting like a fool . . .

[WALTER *comes down off the table suddenly and makes a quick exit to the bathroom.*]

Ruth. He's had a little to drink . . . I don't know what her excuse is.

George (*to* BENEATHA). Look honey, we're going *to* the theater—we're not going to be *in* it . . . so go change, huh?

5. **Jomo:** Jomo Kenyatta, leader and first president of Kenya (1964–1978). Jomo means "flaming spear."
6. ***owimoweh:*** variation of a Zulu word meaning "lion."
7. **Chaka:** more correctly, Shaka. Shaka (1787?–1828) was a great Zulu chief and military leader. He was given his name Shaka (meaning "early pregnancy") because he was born before his parents were married.

WORDS TO OWN

fraternal (frə·tʉrn′əl) *adj.:* brotherly; friendly.

C. Reader's Response: Shaping Interpretations

? If you were portraying Walter, how would you interpret the stage direction *"back to the past"*? [Sample responses: By changing my gaze from a casual focus on Beneatha to an intent stare at something offstage, as at a great distance; or by gradually stiffening my posture, as if being controlled by something else.]

D. Language Note: Humor

Ruth's wry commentary on the activity around her helps to deflate its high emotion.

E. Literary Element: Repetition

After students have read through this exchange, ask them if it in any way reminds them of a litany, prayer, or sermon. [Possible answer: Walter's repeated "Do you hear" sounds like something that a preacher might say, and Beneatha's repeated "OCOMOGOSIAY!" is like an "Amen!"] You might point out that the alternation between statements and responses is often found in folk and worship songs. (For example, see "Go Down, Moses" and "Follow the Drinking Gourd" on p. 434.)

F. Literary Element: Tone

? What tone does George use? [Possible answers: Sarcastic; disdainful.] What does that tone suggest about George's values? [Possible answers: He does not think much of Africa or African tradition; he finds nothing wrong in insulting a woman whom he is dating.]

STRATEGIES FOR INCLUSION

Musical/Auditory Encourage students with an ear for the power of speech and sound effects to present and comment on the scene that opens Act Two (up to, but not including, the first words by George Murchison). Ask them to discuss why they think the drums, the song lyrics, and "OCOMOGOSIAY!" and other cries move Beneatha and, to an even greater extent, Walter.

Spatial Good and bad news enters the Youngers' lives through the door to their apartment. Students might plot their progress through Act Two by drawing a series of "open door" diagrams like the one that follows. Outside each door, they should note who comes into the Youngers' home in this act; inside the door, they should note how the person's news affects the family.

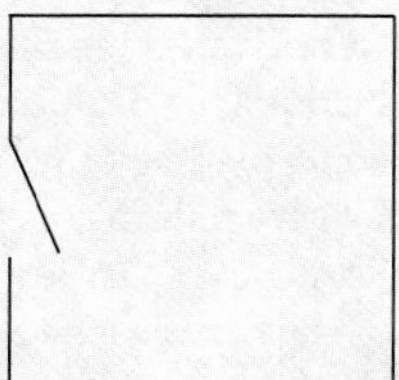

A. Reader's Response: Connecting with the Text

George's ridicule of African heritage and Beneatha's response to his ridicule may be of great relevance in your classroom—not only to African American students but also to any of your students who are immigrants and perhaps to any others who feel that they know too little about their own ethnic or cultural heritage. You might encourage students to record their responses to this passage in their Reader's Logs. *Remind students to choose responses they would not mind sharing with others.*

B. Exploring the Historical Period

The bombs that Ruth is talking about are not the bombs that Walter read about at the beginning of Act One on p. 830; rather, she is referring to the possible effects of nuclear weapons testing. *A Raisin in the Sun* opened during the height of the Cold War. By 1959, the United States had had nuclear weapons technology for fourteen years and the Soviet Union had had it for ten years. It would be another ten years before the first Strategic Arms Limitation Talks between these superpowers would begin.

[BENEATHA *looks at him and slowly, ceremoniously, lifts her hands and pulls off the headdress. Her hair is close-cropped and unstraightened.* GEORGE *freezes mid-sentence and* RUTH*'s eyes all but fall out of her head.*]

George. What in the name of—

Ruth (*touching* BENEATHA*'s hair*). Girl, you done lost your natural mind!? Look at your head!

George. What have you done to your head—I mean your hair!

Beneatha. Nothing—except cut it off.

Ruth. Now that's the truth—it's what ain't been done to it! You expect this boy to go out with you with your head all nappy like that?

Beneatha (*looking at* GEORGE). That's up to George. If he's ashamed of his heritage—

George. Oh, don't be so proud of yourself, Bennie—just because you look eccentric.

Beneatha. How can something that's natural be eccentric?

George. That's what being eccentric means—being natural. Get dressed.

Beneatha. I don't like that, George.

Ruth. Why must you and your brother make an argument out of everything people say?

Beneatha. Because I hate assimilationist Negroes!

Ruth. Will somebody please tell me what assimila-whoever means!

George. Oh, it's just a college girl's way of calling people Uncle Toms—but that isn't what it means at all.

Ruth. Well, what does it mean?

Beneatha (*cutting* GEORGE *off and staring at him as she replies to* RUTH). It means someone who is willing to give up his own culture and submerge himself completely in the dominant, and in this case *oppressive* culture!

A **George.** Oh, dear, dear, dear! Here we go! A lecture on the African past! On our Great West African Heritage! In one second we will hear all about the great Ashanti[8] empires; the great Songhay[9] civilizations; and the great sculpture of Benin[10]—and then some poetry in the Bantu[11]—and the whole monologue will end with the word *heritage*! (*Nastily*) Let's face it, baby, your heritage is nothing but a bunch of raggedy . . . spirituals and some grass huts!

Beneatha. GRASS HUTS! (RUTH *crosses to her and forcibly pushes her toward the bedroom.*) See there . . . you are standing there in your splendid ignorance talking about people who were the first to smelt iron on the face of the earth! (RUTH *is pushing her through the door.*) The Ashanti were performing surgical operations when the English—(RUTH *pulls the door to, with* BENEATHA *on the other side, and smiles graciously at* GEORGE. BENEATHA *opens the door and shouts the end of the sentence defiantly at* GEORGE.)—were still tattooing themselves with blue dragons! (*She goes back inside.*)

Ruth. Have a seat, George. (*They both sit.* RUTH *folds her hands rather primly on her lap, determined to demonstrate the civilization of the family.*) Warm, ain't it? I mean for September. (*Pause*) Just like they always say about Chicago weather: If it's too hot or cold for you, just wait a minute and it'll change. (*She smiles happily at* B *this cliché of clichés.*) Everybody say it's got to do with them bombs and things they keep setting off. (*Pause*) Would you like a nice cold beer?

George. No, thank you. I don't care for beer. (*He looks at his watch.*) I hope she hurries up.

Ruth. What time is the show?

George. It's an eight-thirty curtain. That's just Chicago, though. In New York standard curtain time is eight-forty.

[*He is rather proud of this knowledge.*]

Ruth (*properly appreciating it*). You get to New York a lot?

George (*offhand*). Few times a year.

Ruth. Oh—that's nice. I've never been to New York.

8. **Ashanti:** people in West Africa who had a powerful empire in the eighteenth and nineteenth centuries. The Ashanti Empire was once a British protectorate and is now part of Ghana.

9. **Songhay:** more correctly Songhai, a West African empire in the fifteenth and sixteenth centuries.

10. **Benin:** West African kingdom (c. mid-1400s–mid-1600s) known for its beautiful sculpture, metalwork, and carved ivory.

11. **Bantu:** family of languages including Zulu and Swahili, spoken in central and southern Africa.

WORDS TO OWN

dominant (däm′ə·nənt) *adj.:* prevailing; principal.

OPTIONS FOR TEACHING

INTEGRATING THE LANGUAGE ARTS

Strategic Reading Act Two spotlights some sensitive issues related to multiculturalism, racial prejudice, and alcohol abuse. Providing time for small-group cooperative talk may help students in exploring these issues. Students might share their responses to the passages in which the issues are explored. Ask students to discuss why they think Hansberry chose to focus on these issues rather than on others.

Speaking and Listening Call on pairs of volunteers to present improvised **dialogues** based on Act Two. Each dialogue should be a spontaneous conversation between characters such as Mama and Walter, Ruth and Walter, Walter and Beneatha, George and Beneatha, or Walter and Travis. These characters may have different (even conflicting) attitudes about the Younger family and its future. After each dialogue, have the class discuss which character seemed to reflect the play more accurately, and why.

Language and Style Karl Lindner's talk to the Youngers on pp. 867–869 is filled with double talk and innuendo. Before students reach this passage in class discussion, you might invite interested students to analyze it—to highlight Lindner's key points, to distinguish between what he says and what he implies, and to draw conclusions about his persuasive appeal. Consider having these students teach this part of Act Two to the class.

[WALTER *enters. We feel he has relieved himself, but the edge of unreality is still with him.*]

Walter. New York ain't got nothing Chicago ain't. Just a bunch of hustling people all squeezed up together—being "Eastern." C

[*He turns his face into a screw of displeasure.*]

George. Oh—you've been?
Walter. *Plenty* of times.
Ruth (*shocked at the lie*). Walter Lee Younger!
Walter (*staring her down*). Plenty! (*Pause*) What we got to drink in this house? Why don't you offer this man some refreshment. (*To* GEORGE) They don't know how to entertain people in this house, man.
George. Thank you—I don't really care for anything.
Walter (*feeling his head; sobriety coming*). Where's Mama?
Ruth. She ain't come back yet.
Walter (*looking* MURCHISON *over from head to toe, scrutinizing his carefully casual tweed sports jacket over cashmere V-neck sweater over soft eyelet shirt and tie, and soft slacks, finished off with white buckskin shoes*). Why all you college boys wear them funny-looking white shoes?
Ruth. Walter Lee!

[GEORGE MURCHISON *ignores the remark.*] D

Walter (*to* RUTH). Well, they look crazy . . . white shoes, cold as it is.
Ruth (*crushed*). You have to excuse him—
Walter. No he don't! Excuse me for what? What you always excusing me for! I'll excuse myself when I needs to be excused! (*A pause*) They look as funny as them black knee socks Beneatha wears out of here all the time.
Ruth. It's the college *style,* Walter.
Walter. Style?! She looks like she got burnt legs or something!
Ruth. Oh, Walter—
Walter (*an irritable mimic*). Oh, Walter! Oh, Walter! (*To* MURCHISON) How's your old man making out? I understand you all going to buy that big hotel on the Drive? (*He finds a beer in the refrigerator, wanders over to* MURCHISON, *sipping and wiping his lips with the back of his hand, and straddling a chair backwards to talk to the other man.*) Shrewd move. Your old man is all right, E man. (*Tapping his head and half winking for emphasis*) I mean he knows how to operate. I mean he thinks *big,* you know what I mean, I mean for a *home,* you know? But I think he's kind of running out of ideas now. I'd like to talk to him. Listen, man, I got some plans that could turn this city upside down. I mean think like he does. *Big.* Invest big, gamble big, shoot, lose *big* if you have to, you know what I mean. It's hard to find a man on this whole South Side who understands my kind of thinking—you dig? (*He scrutinizes* MURCHISON *again, drinks his beer, squints his eyes, and leans in close, confidential, man to man.*) Me and you ought to sit down and talk sometimes, man. Man, I got me some ideas . . .
Murchison (*with boredom*). Yeah—sometimes we'll have to do that, Walter.
Walter (*understanding the indifference, and offended*). Yeah—well, when you get the time, man. I know you a busy little boy.
Ruth. Walter, please—
Walter (*bitterly, hurt*). I know ain't nothing in this world as busy as you colored college boys with your fraternity pins and white shoes . . .
Ruth (*covering her face with humiliation*). Oh, Walter Lee—
Walter. I see you all all the time—with the books tucked under your arms—going to your (*British A—a mimic*) "clahsses." And for what! What in the world you learning over there? Filling up your heads—(*counting off on his fingers*)—with the sociology and the psychology—but they teaching you how to be a man? How to take over and run the world? They teaching you how to run a rubber plantation or a steel mill? Naw—just to talk proper and read books and wear them funny-looking white shoes . . .
George (*looking at him with distaste, a little above it all*). You're all wacked up with bitterness, man.
Walter (*intently, almost quietly, between the teeth, glaring at the boy*). And you—ain't you bitter, man? Ain't you just about had it yet? Don't you see no stars gleaming that you can't reach out and grab? You happy?—You contented turkey—you

WORDS TO OWN
sobriety (sə·brī′ə·tē) *n.:* state or quality of being sober.

C. Critical Reading: Making Inferences

? What do you think Walter means by New Yorkers being "Eastern"? [Possible answers: Being snobbish, showing off their education, or disliking people who are not like themselves.]

D. Expansion

Walter's comment is based on the fashion tradition that white shoes are appropriate for summer wear but are put away after Labor Day. Walter may just be trying to be contentious: He complains that the weather is cold; but just a few lines earlier, Ruth commented that the weather was warm for September.

E. Critical Reading: Finding Cause and Effect

? How has Mama's refusal to fund the liquor store venture affected Walter? [Possible answers: It has led him to get drunk, to lie, and to be abrasive toward others—including George, who may be able to help him.]

COOPERATIVE LEARNING

Team Word-Webbing Divide the class into three or four teams; provide each team with a large sheet of paper on which the word *dream* is written in a circle in the center. Have team members collaborate, branching from the circle to jot down words and images that they associate with the word *dream* (such as various kinds of dreams, feelings associated with reaching for dreams, and responses to Langston Hughes's poem). For each group, assign a discussion leader; a scribe; a task manager, whose role is to see that everyone shares equally in the work; and a monitor, whose role is to see that all group members have an opportunity to speak. When students are finished, ask them to comment on which responses remind them of events and emotions related to Act Two, and why.

Grouping Students As students discuss the play in small groups, suggest that they gather on the basis of a shared interest in a particular character. To determine interest, you might designate an area of the room for each character; if a large number of students gather to discuss a particular character (Walter, for example), you can divide that group. ☞

A. Humanities Connection
Ask students to read the footnote about Prometheus; then, ask students to speculate about why George chooses to insult Walter in this way. [Possible answers: Walter has just claimed to be "a giant—surrounded by ants," and Prometheus was a giant; Walter has called himself "a volcano," and Prometheus is associated with fire. Walter may see himself as bringing something important to the "ants." George also may dislike Walter enough to wish on him something of Prometheus's fate.]

B. Literary Element: Conflict
At this point, the pain that Ruth and Walter share in their conflict comes to a head, and it looks as though the two may achieve a reconciliation. Why does the line ending "have babies" strike even Walter as being "too bitter"? [Possible answer: He suddenly must have recalled that his own wife is pregnant.] How do you feel about Ruth's attempt to defuse the intensity of the moment by apologizing for her pregnancy? [Possible answers: She still knows how to soften him; or Walter is equally responsible for the baby.]

happy? You got it made? Bitter? Man, I'm a volcano. Bitter? Here I am a giant—surrounded by ants! Ants who can't even understand what it is the giant is talking about.
Ruth (*passionately and suddenly*). Oh, Walter—ain't you with nobody!
Walter (*violently*). No! 'Cause ain't nobody with me! Not even my own mother!
Ruth. Walter, that's a terrible thing to say!

[BENEATHA *enters, dressed for the evening in a cocktail dress and earrings, hair natural.*]

George. Well—hey—(*Crosses to* BENEATHA; *thoughtful, with emphasis, since this is a reversal*) You look great!
Walter (*seeing his sister's hair for the first time*). What's the matter with your head?
Beneatha (*tired of the jokes now*). I cut it off, Brother.
Walter (*coming close to inspect it and walking around her*). Well, I'll be damned. So that's what they mean by the African bush . . .
Beneatha. Ha ha. Let's go, George.
George (*looking at her*). You know something? I like it. It's sharp. I mean it really is. (*Helps her into her wrap*)
Ruth. Yes—I think so, too. (*She goes to the mirror and starts to clutch at her hair.*)
Walter. Oh no! You leave yours alone, baby. You might turn out to have a pin-shaped head or something!
Beneatha. See you all later.
Ruth. Have a nice time.
George. Thanks. Good night. (*Half out the door, he reopens it. To* WALTER) Good night, Prometheus![12] **A**

[BENEATHA *and* GEORGE *exit.*]

Walter (*to* RUTH). Who is Prometheus?
Ruth. I don't know. Don't worry about it.
Walter (*in fury, pointing after* GEORGE). See there—they get to a point where they can't insult you man to man—they got to go talk about something ain't nobody never heard of!

12. **Prometheus:** in Greek mythology, a Titan who steals fire from the gods and gives it to humans. Zeus, king of the gods, punishes Prometheus by chaining him to a mountain, where each day an eagle eats his liver. Each night Zeus causes the liver to regrow so that the torture is excruciatingly repetitive. Prometheus is finally freed by Hercules.

Ruth. How do you know it was an insult? (*To humor him*) Maybe Prometheus is a nice fellow.
Walter. Prometheus! I bet there ain't even no such thing! I bet that simple-minded clown—
Ruth. Walter—

[*She stops what she is doing and looks at him.*]

Walter (*yelling*). Don't start!
Ruth. Start what?
Walter. Your nagging! Where was I? Who was I with? How much money did I spend?
Ruth (*plaintively*). Walter Lee—why don't we just try to talk about it . . .
Walter (*not listening*). I been out talking with people who understand me. People who care about the things I got on my mind.
Ruth (*wearily*). I guess that means people like Willy Harris.
Walter. Yes, people like Willy Harris.
Ruth (*with a sudden flash of impatience*). Why don't you all just hurry up and go into the banking business and stop talking about it!
Walter. Why? You want to know why? 'Cause we all tied up in a race of people that don't know how to do nothing but moan, pray, and have babies!

[*The line is too bitter even for him and he looks at her and sits down.*]

Ruth. Oh, Walter . . . (*Softly*) Honey, why can't you stop fighting me?
Walter (*without thinking*). Who's fighting you? Who even cares about you? **B**

[*This line begins the retardation of his mood.*]

Ruth. Well—(*She waits a long time, and then with resignation starts to put away her things.*) I guess I might as well go on to bed . . . (*More or less to herself*) I don't know where we lost it . . . but we have . . . (*Then, to him*) I—I'm sorry about this new baby, Walter. I guess maybe I better go on and do what I started . . . I guess I just didn't realize how bad things was with us . . . I guess I just didn't really realize—(*She starts out to the bedroom and stops.*) You want some hot milk?

WORDS TO OWN
resignation (rez′ig·nā′shən) *n.:* acquiescence; reluctant acceptance.

OPTIONS FOR TEACHING

CLASSROOM MANAGEMENT

Cooperative Learning For students working on the Cooperative Learning: Team Word-Webbing activity on p. T855, have one or two groups work under the direction of a team leader while the remaining groups work simultaneously and without leadership. Which team's resulting diagram is easiest to follow? What advantages, if any, are there to the more spontaneous work atmosphere?

Timesaver If time for covering *A Raisin in the Sun* is running out, ask each student to submit, on a slip of paper, one question that he or she hopes will be answered in Act Three. When you discuss Act Three, focus on the questions asked most often or the questions that seem to have the widest application.

Block Scheduling Have students read the play in class for twenty to thirty minutes. After discussion, reinforce the elements of drama by allowing students time to rehearse or perform portions of the play for forty-five to sixty minutes. Allow time for prop and costume gathering, set placement, and room rearrangement. If possible, take the class to the auditorium to give them a feel for the stage.

Walter. Hot milk?
Ruth. Yes—hot milk.
Walter. Why hot milk?
Ruth. 'Cause after all that liquor you come home with you ought to have something hot in your stomach.
Walter. I don't want no milk.
Ruth. You want some coffee then?
Walter. No, I don't want no coffee. I don't want nothing hot to drink. (*Almost plaintively*) Why you always trying to give me something to eat?
Ruth (*standing and looking at him helplessly*). What *else* can I give you, Walter Lee Younger?

[*She stands and looks at him and presently turns to go out again. He lifts his head and watches her going away from him in a new mood which began to emerge when he asked her "Who cares about you?"*]

Walter. It's been rough, ain't it, baby? (*She hears and stops but does not turn around and he continues to her back.*) I guess between two people there ain't never as much understood as folks generally thinks there is. I mean like between me and you—(*She turns to face him.*) How we gets to the place where we scared to talk softness to each other. (*He waits, thinking hard himself.*) Why you think it got to be like that? (*He is thoughtful, almost as a child would be.*) Ruth, what is it gets into people ought to be close?
Ruth. I don't know, honey. I think about it a lot.
Walter. On account of you and me, you mean? The way things are with us. The way something done come down between us.
Ruth. There ain't so much between us, Walter . . . Not when you come to me and try to talk to me. Try to be with me . . . a little even.
Walter (*total honesty*). Sometimes . . . sometimes . . . I don't even know how to try.
Ruth. Walter—
Walter. Yes?
Ruth (*coming to him, gently and with misgiving, but coming to him*). Honey . . . life don't have to be like this. I mean sometimes people can do things so that things are better . . . You remember how we used to talk when Travis was born . . . about the way we were going to live . . . the kind of house . . . (*She is stroking his head.*) Well, it's all starting to slip away from us . . .

[*He turns her to him and they look at each other and kiss, tenderly and hungrily. The door opens and* MAMA *enters*—WALTER *breaks away and jumps up. A beat*]

Walter. Mama, where have you been?
Mama. My—them steps is longer than they used to be. Whew! (*She sits down and ignores him.*) How you feeling this evening, Ruth?

[RUTH *shrugs, disturbed at having been interrupted and watching her husband knowingly.*]

Walter. Mama, where have you been all day?
Mama (*still ignoring him and leaning on the table and changing to more comfortable shoes*). Where's Travis?
Ruth. I let him go out earlier and he ain't come back yet. Boy, is he going to get it!
Walter. Mama!
Mama (*as if she has heard him for the first time*). Yes, son?
Walter. Where did you go this afternoon?
Mama. I went downtown to tend to some business that I had to tend to.
Walter. What kind of business?

C. Critical Reading: Making Connections

Speaking to Mama in Act One, Ruth said that Walter "needs something—something I can't give him any more" (p. 837). What does Ruth believe that Walter needs? [The chance for success—primarily through the liquor store partnership.] What other needs do you think Ruth may sense at a deeper level? [Possible answers: Walter's need for self-esteem, for greater compassion for others, and for greater recognition of others' support for him.]

D. Reader's Response: Extending the Text

? How do you think people get to the point where they are scared to talk to each other? [Sample responses: Through anger with each other or through an unresolved conflict; through a long period of spending time on other things and neglecting the relationship; or through selfishness.]

E. Reader's Response: Shaping Interpretations

? If Ruth alone could spend the insurance money, what do you think she would do with it? [Sample responses: Buy a house or help Walter invest in a business she approves of.]

F. Literary Element: Suspense

Walter's question is the first of a string of questions that Mama will try to evade. With each round of questioning, suspense builds and the action of the scene rises closer to its **climax**.

CROSSING THE CURRICULUM

Architecture On p. 858 Mama describes the house in Clybourne Park merely as "just a plain little old house—but it's made good and solid." Invite interested students to research urban housing styles of the 1950s and to sketch a floor plan and an external view of 406 Clybourne Street.

Industrial Arts/Social Sciences Early in Act Two, Beneatha challenges George Murchison with information about technology—specifically, the smelting of iron and the advanced state of surgical procedure—in ancient Africa. Ask individuals or groups of students to present oral reports that give more information about Beneatha's references and that offer additional examples of ancient African technology.

History At the beginning of Act Two, Walter expresses admiration for Jomo Kenyatta, and Hansberry refers to Walter as "a descendant of Chaka." Have students find out about these two African leaders and how they both—despite being separated by more than a century—inspired African Americans at the time that *A Raisin in the Sun* first was performed.

A. Critical Reading: Drawing Conclusions

? Why do you think Mama insists on first breaking her momentous news to Travis? [Possible answers: She is manipulating the scene, for by speaking to Travis, she makes it almost impossible for Walter and Ruth to say anything judgmental in his presence. She may not wish to directly confront Walter's disappointment and anger. She thinks that Travis will welcome the news.]

B. Critical Reading: Making Inferences

? Why is Mama acting in a childlike way? [Possible answers: She loves Walter and knows that he is unhappy about her action; a house has been her dream since before Walter was born, and now that the dream has been fulfilled, she does not want Walter to ruin it.]

C. Exploring the Historical Period

Suburban building increased dramatically after World War II, many builders following the example of housebuilders Levitt & Sons, who introduced the near assembly-line production of row upon row of identical houses in Long Island. Levitt houses, snapped up at prices ranging from approximately seven thousand to eight thousand dollars, featured four rooms, radiant heat, electric kitchens, and basements that the buyers could finish. Levitt imitators cut corners more and more, eliminating such amenities as porches and garages and often doing shoddy work. Even in the late 1950s Mama would have had to shop carefully to get the best value and to find a house in which basic construction had been done properly.

Mama. You know better than to question me like a child, Brother.

Walter (*rising and bending over the table*). Where were you, Mama? (*Bringing his fists down and shouting*) Mama, you didn't do something with that insurance money, something crazy?

[*The front door opens slowly, interrupting him, and* TRAVIS *peeks his head in, less than hopefully.*]

Travis (*to his mother*). Mama, I—

Ruth. "Mama I" nothing! You're going to get it, boy! Get on in that bedroom and get yourself ready!

Travis. But I—

Mama. Why don't you all never let the child explain hisself.

Ruth. Keep out of it now, Lena.

[MAMA *clamps her lips together, and* RUTH *advances toward her son menacingly.*]

Ruth. A thousand times I have told you not to go off like that—

A **Mama** (*holding out her arms to her grandson*). Well—at least let me tell him something. I want him to be the first one to hear . . . Come here, Travis. (*The boy obeys, gladly.*) Travis—(*She takes him by the shoulder and looks into his face.*)—you know that money we got in the mail this morning?

Travis. Yes'm—

Mama. Well—what you think your grandmama gone and done with that money?

Travis. I don't know, Grandmama.

Mama (*putting her finger on his nose for emphasis*). She went out and she bought you a house! (*The explosion comes from* WALTER *at the end of the revelation and he jumps up and turns away from all of them in a fury.* MAMA *continues, to* TRAVIS.) You glad about the house? It's going to be yours when you get to be a man.

Travis. Yeah—I always wanted to live in a house.

Mama. All right, gimme some sugar then—(TRAVIS *puts his arms around her neck as she watches her son over the boy's shoulder. Then, to* TRAVIS, *after the embrace*) Now when you say your prayers tonight, you thank God and your grandfather—'cause it was him who give you the house—in his way.

Ruth (*taking the boy from* MAMA *and pushing him toward the bedroom*). Now you get out of here and get ready for your beating.

Travis. Aw, Mama—

Ruth. Get on in there—(*Closing the door behind him and turning radiantly to her mother-in-law*) So you went and did it!

Mama (*quietly, looking at her son with pain*). Yes, I did.

Ruth (*raising both arms classically*). PRAISE GOD! (*Looks at* WALTER *a moment, who says nothing. She crosses rapidly to her husband.*) Please, honey—let me be glad . . . you be glad too. (*She has laid her hands on his shoulders, but he shakes himself free of her roughly, without turning to face her.*) Oh, Walter . . . a home . . . *a home.* (*She comes back to* MAMA.) Well—where is it? How big is it? How much it going to cost?

Mama. Well—

Ruth. When we moving?

Mama (*smiling at her*). First of the month.

Ruth (*throwing back her head with jubilance*). *Praise God!*

Mama (*tentatively, still looking at her son's back turned against her and* RUTH). It's—it's a nice house too . . . B (*She cannot help speaking directly to him. An imploring quality in her voice, her manner, makes her almost like a girl now.*) Three bedrooms—nice big one for you and Ruth. . . . Me and Beneatha still have to share our room, but Travis have one of his own—and (*with difficulty*) I figure if the—new baby—is a boy, we could get one of them double-decker outfits . . . And there's a yard with a little patch of dirt where I could maybe get to grow me a few flowers . . . And a nice big basement . . .

Ruth. Walter honey, be glad—

Mama (*still to his back, fingering things on the table*). C 'Course I don't want to make it sound fancier than it is . . . It's just a plain little old house—but it's made good and solid—and it will be *ours.* Walter Lee—it makes a difference in a man when he can walk on floors that belong to *him* . . .

Ruth. Where is it?

WORDS TO OWN

revelation (rev′ə·lā′shən) *n.:* disclosure; something made known.

imploring (im·plôr′iŋ) *v.* used as *adj.:* pleading; entreating.

OPTIONS FOR TEACHING

CROSSING THE CURRICULUM

Music Hearing some African folk music might enhance students' appreciation of Act Two. Challenge pairs or groups of students to complete one or more of the following activities:

- Locate (through a public or college library, a knowledgeable record dealer, or the resources of an African American cultural organization) and play a recording of Nigerian or other African folk songs. Students should write liner notes to accompany the recording. These notes should include a summary of the content of each piece, the instruments used, the names of the musicians or groups, and a description of the pieces and their importance in the field of music.
- Perform an African folk song learned from a recording, found in a book, recalled from memory, or learned from a relative.
- Write and perform a folk song, based on a study of African folk melodies and rhythms.

As time permits, have students evaluate the effectiveness of this activity in terms of understanding the characters of Beneatha and Walter.

Mama (*frightened at this telling*). Well—well—it's out there in Clybourne Park—

[RUTH'S *radiance fades abruptly, and* WALTER *finally turns slowly to face his mother with incredulity and hostility.*]

Ruth. Where?
Mama (*matter-of-factly*). Four o six Clybourne Street, Clybourne Park.
Ruth. Clybourne Park? Mama, there ain't no colored people living in Clybourne Park.
Mama (*almost idiotically*). Well, I guess there's going to be some now. **D**
Walter (*bitterly*). So that's the peace and comfort you went out and bought for us today!
Mama (*raising her eyes to meet his finally*). Son—I just tried to find the nicest place for the least amount of money for my family.
Ruth (*trying to recover from the shock*). Well—well—'course I ain't one never been 'fraid of no crackers, mind you—but—well, wasn't there no **E** other houses nowhere?
Mama. Them houses they put up for colored in them areas way out all seem to cost twice as much as other houses. I did the best I could.
Ruth (*Struck senseless with the news, in its various degrees of goodness and trouble, she sits a moment, her fists propping her chin in thought, and then she starts to rise, bringing her fists down with* vigor, *the radiance spreading from cheek to cheek again.*). Well—well!—All I can say is—if this is my time in life—*MY* TIME—to say goodbye—(*and she builds with momentum as she starts to circle the room with an* exuberant, *almost tearfully happy release.*)—to these . . . cracking walls!—(*She pounds the walls.*)—and these marching roaches!—(*She wipes at an imaginary army of marching roaches.*)—and this cramped little closet which ain't now or never was no kitchen! . . . then I say it loud and good, HALLELUJAH! AND GOODBYE MISERY . . . I DON'T NEVER WANT TO SEE YOUR UGLY FACE AGAIN! (*She laughs joyously, having practically destroyed the apartment, and flings her arms up and lets them come down happily, slowly, reflectively, over her abdomen, aware for the first time perhaps that the life therein pulses with happiness and not despair.*) Lena?
Mama (*moved, watching her happiness*). Yes, honey?
Ruth (*looking off*). Is there—is there a whole lot of sunlight?
Mama (*understanding*). Yes, child, there's a whole lot of sunlight.

[*Long pause*]

Ruth (*collecting herself and going to the door of the room* TRAVIS *is in*). Well—I guess I better see 'bout Travis. (*To* MAMA) Lord, I sure don't feel like whipping nobody today!

[*She exits.*]

Mama (*The mother and son are left alone now and the mother waits a long time, considering deeply, before she speaks.*). Son—you—you understand what I done, don't you? (WALTER *is silent and sullen.*) I—I just seen my family falling apart today . . . just falling to pieces in front of my eyes . . . We couldn't of gone on like we was today. We was going backwards 'stead of forwards—talking 'bout not wanting babies and wishing each other was dead . . . When it gets like that in life—you just got to do something different, push on out and do something bigger . . . (*She waits.*) I wish you say something, son . . . I wish you'd say how deep inside you you think I done the right thing—
Walter (*crossing slowly to his bedroom door and finally turning there and speaking measuredly*). What you need me to say you done right for? *You* the head of this family. You run our lives like you want to. It was your money and you did what you wanted with it. So what you need for **F** me to say it was all right for? (*Bitterly, to hurt her as deeply as he knows is possible*) So you butchered up a dream of mine—you—who always talking 'bout your children's dreams . . .
Mama. Walter Lee—

[*He just closes the door behind him.* MAMA *sits alone, thinking heavily.*]

Curtain

WORDS TO OWN

vigor (vig'ər) *n.:* intense strength; vitality.
exuberant (eg·zo͞o'bər·ənt) *adj.:* intensely happy; visibly enthusiastic.

D. Critical Reading: Analyzing Plot

? If Mama's announcement that she has bought a house is the **climax** of this scene, how does this news push the climax even higher? [It reveals that Mama not only has used the money (perhaps all of it) but that she has used it in a way that is bound to bring the entire family more trouble—this time, racial conflict.]

E. Language Note: Epithet

Cracker originally referred disparagingly to a poor white person of the rural South, but here it is used as a term of derision for whites in general.

F. Language Note: Diction

Walter's measured speaking consists almost exclusively of simple, monosyllabic words. When his tone turns bitter, however, the words become more complex, and the verb *butchered* is shocking in the way it leaps out of its context.

PROBLEM SOLVING/CRITICAL THINKING

Analyzing Behavior Walter Lee Younger is a puzzle—to his mother, his wife, his employer, and probably others. In real life, one way to begin understanding people is to try to analyze why they act as they do—a problem-solving skill with many applications. Have groups of students use the graphic like the one provided to analyze the puzzling person in the following hypothetical situation:

A new playmate of your younger sister acts quite hostile. She always seems to yell at people or to go off by herself and glare silently. Occasionally she has been known to push or take a swing at those around her. Your parents are starting to wonder if they should let your sister associate with this girl.

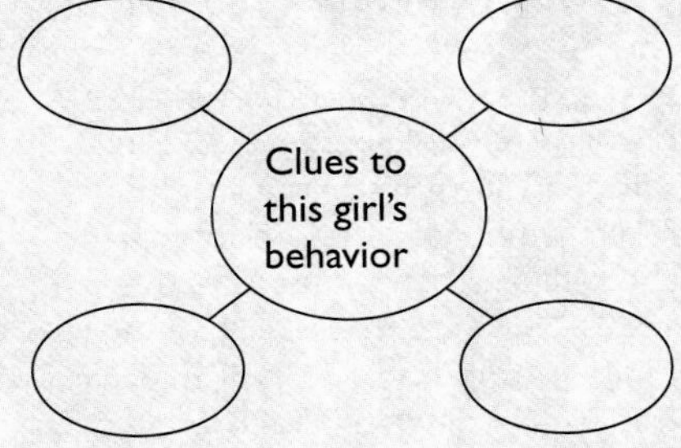

A. Critical Reading: Summarizing

A few weeks pass between Scene I and Scene 2. What **conflicts** have been at work during that time? [The clash between Walter and Mama over the use of the insurance money has not been resolved, and it may have soured the reconciliation between Walter and Ruth. In addition, Beneatha has had to face her own changing feelings toward both Asagai and George.]

B. Reader's Response: Connecting with the Text

? What kind of person does George want for a girlfriend? [Sample responses: a person who is pretty and sophisticated but who does not think or talk too seriously about life; or someone who makes him look good but who does not look for much consideration in return.] Do you think George would have much trouble finding that kind of girlfriend today? [Sample responses: No, there are women who do not want to talk seriously about life; some would be willing to put up with his views for the sake of his money. Or yes, most women want to be taken seriously.]

C. Critical Reading: Drawing Conclusions

? How do George's and Beneatha's views on books differ? [Beneatha wants to be stimulated to think and learn; George reads books only for grades.] What do you think will be the result of George's words? [Possible answer: He will drive Beneatha away, once and for all.]

"Thank you....For understanding me this time."

Scene 2

A *Time: Friday night. A few weeks later.*

At rise: Packing crates mark the intention of the family to move. BENEATHA *and* GEORGE *come in, presumably from an evening out again.*

George. O.K. . . . O.K., whatever you say . . . (*They both sit on the couch. He tries to kiss her. She moves away.*) Look, we've had a nice evening; let's not spoil it, huh? . . .

[*He again turns his head and tries to nuzzle in and she turns away from him, not with distaste but with momentary lack of interest; in a mood to pursue what they were talking about.*]

Beneatha. I'm *trying* to talk to you.

George. We always talk.

Beneatha. Yes—and I love to talk.

George (*exasperated; rising*). I know it and I don't mind it sometimes . . . I want you to cut it out, see—The moody stuff, I mean. I don't like it. You're a nice-looking girl . . . all over. That's all you need, honey, B forget the atmosphere. Guys aren't going to go for the atmosphere—they're going to go for what they see. Be glad for that. Drop the Garbo[13] routine. It doesn't go with you. As for myself, I want a nice—(*groping*)—simple (*thoughtfully*)—sophisticated girl . . . not a poet—O.K.?

[*He starts to kiss her, she rebuffs him again, and he jumps up.*]

Beneatha. Why are you angry, George?

George. Because this is stupid! I don't go out with you to discuss the nature of "quiet desperation"[14] or to hear all about your thoughts—because the world will go C on thinking what it thinks regardless—

Beneatha. Then why read books? Why go to school?

George (*with artificial patience, counting on his fingers*). It's simple. You read books—to learn facts—to get grades—to pass the course—to get a degree. That's all—it has nothing to do with thoughts.

[*A long pause*]

Beneatha. I see. (*He starts to sit.*) Good night, George.

[GEORGE *looks at her a little oddly, and starts to exit. He meets* MAMA *coming in.*]

George. Oh—hello, Mrs. Younger.

Mama. Hello, George, how you feeling?

13. **Garbo:** Greta Garbo, Swedish star of American films, who was famous for her moodiness and for the often misquoted line "I want to be let alone."

14. **"quiet desperation":** George is referring to a line from Henry David Thoreau's *Walden* (page 230): "The mass of men lead lives of quiet desperation."

OPTIONS FOR TEACHING

PROFESSIONAL NOTES

Critical Comment: The Spirit of the Youngers Discussing *A Raisin in the Sun* in *African American Writers,* Margaret B. Wilkerson notes, "The spirit and struggles of the Younger family symbolized the social progress and setbacks characteristic of the 1950s. . . . The newly militant mood of black Americans, born of anger, frustration, and deferred dreams, had been captured in the explosive and desperate Walter Lee. The sudden decision of Rosa Parks, whose refusal to move to the back of a bus precipitated the historic Montgomery bus boycott, was mirrored in Lena Younger's apolitical decision to live in Clybourne Park and her consequent challenge to the restrictive covenants of the day. The rise of independent African nations was reflected in the presence of the African student Asagai, who brought to the play the reality of his people's struggle for liberation; Beneatha's adulation of things Africaine anticipated a new wave of hair and dress styles that black Americans would soon adopt. . . . The play touched the vibrating nerve of a country on the verge of change and a people on the move." Encourage students to see how many of these comments are reflected in Act Two.

George. Fine—fine, how are you?
Mama. Oh, a little tired. You know them steps can get you after a day's work. You all have a nice time tonight?
George. Yes—a fine time. A fine time.
Mama. Well, good night.
George. Good night. (*He exits.* MAMA *closes the door behind her.*) Hello, honey. What you sitting like that for?
Beneatha. I'm just sitting.
Mama. Didn't you have a nice time?
Beneatha. No.
Mama. No? What's the matter?
Beneatha. Mama, George is a fool—honest. (*She rises.*)
Mama (*bustling around unloading the packages she has entered with. She stops.*). Is he, baby?
Beneatha. Yes.

[BENEATHA *makes up* TRAVIS*'s bed as she talks.*]

Mama. You sure?
Beneatha. Yes.
Mama. Well—I guess you better not waste your time with no fools.

[BENEATHA *looks up at her mother, watching her put groceries in the refrigerator. Finally she gathers up her things and starts into the bedroom. At the door she stops and looks back at her mother.*]

Beneatha. Mama—
Mama. Yes, baby—
Beneatha. Thank you.
Mama. For what?
Beneatha. For understanding me this time.

D

[*She exits quickly and the mother stands, smiling a little, looking at the place where* BENEATHA *just stood.* RUTH *enters.*]

Ruth. Now don't you fool with any of this stuff, Lena—
Mama. Oh, I just thought I'd sort a few things out. Is Brother here?
Ruth. Yes.
Mama (*with concern*). Is he—
Ruth (*reading her eyes*). Yes.

[MAMA *is silent and someone knocks on the door.* MAMA *and* RUTH *exchange weary and knowing glances and* RUTH *opens it to admit the neighbor,* MRS. JOHNSON,* *who is a rather squeaky wide-eyed lady of no particular age, with a newspaper under her arm.*]

Mama (*changing her expression to acute delight and a ringing cheerful greeting*). Oh—hello there, Johnson.
Johnson (*This is a woman who decided long ago to be enthusiastic about EVERYTHING in life and she is inclined to wave her wrist vigorously at the height of her exclamatory comments.*). Hello there, yourself! H'you this evening, Ruth?
Ruth (*not much of a deceptive type*). Fine, Mis' Johnson, h'you?
Johnson. Fine. (*Reaching out quickly, playfully, and patting* RUTH*'s stomach*) Ain't you starting to poke out none yet! (*She mugs with delight at the overfamiliar remark and her eyes dart around looking at the crates and packing preparation;* MAMA*'s face is a cold sheet of endurance.*) Oh, ain't we getting ready round here, though! Yessir! Lookathere! I'm telling you the Youngers is really getting ready to "move on up a little higher!"—Bless God!
Mama (*a little drily, doubting the total sincerity of the Blesser*). Bless God.
Johnson. He's good, ain't He?
Mama. Oh yes, He's good.
Johnson. I mean sometimes He works in mysterious ways . . . but He works, don't He!
Mama (*the same*). Yes, He does.
Johnson. I'm just soooooo happy for y'all. And this here child—(*about* RUTH) looks like she could just pop open with happiness, don't she. Where's all the rest of the family?
Mama. Bennie's gone to bed—
Johnson. Ain't no . . . (*The implication is pregnancy.*) sickness done hit you—I hope . . . ?
Mama. No—she just tired. She was out this evening.
Johnson (*All is a coo, an emphatic coo.*). Aw—ain't that lovely. She still going out with the little Murchison boy?
Mama (*drily*). Ummmm huh.
Johnson. That's lovely. You sure got lovely children, Younger. Me and Isaiah talks all the time

*This character and the scene of her visit were cut from the original production and early editions of the play.

D. Critical Reading: Finding Details

? What details in this passage suggest change both on Beneatha's part and on Mama's part in an attempt to resolve earlier **conflicts**? [Possible answers: Beneatha does not argue; Mama, after checking to make sure that Beneatha is serious, simply accepts her daughter's judgment. Beneatha's final, quiet remark underscores the change.]

PROFESSIONAL NOTES

Cultural Diversity Act Two begins with Beneatha's joyous recall of her African heritage, but feelings quickly go so out of control that the restoration of order is accomplished only at the cost of embarrassment and hurt feelings. Use this scene as a springboard to discuss how students honor their own national or ethnic heritages and whether the call to assimilate is felt as strongly in the United States today as it was when *A Raisin in the Sun* first was performed.

Thematic Connections: "Reaching for the Dream" Ask students what obstacles stand in the way of these people who are "reaching for the dream." Have students brainstorm as many answers as possible, considering obstacles imposed on the family from the outside and obstacles that they may create themselves. [Possible responses: Many Americans still expressed hostility toward ideas of racial integration; Walter's anger at life thwarts his attempts to take charge of his future; or Beneatha is so contemptuous of assimilationism that she may overlook people who could help the family.] ☞

Technology Tip

Ask students to research the history behind present housing antidiscrimination laws. They may begin their search using an on-line encyclopedia, an American history CD-ROM, or key word searched on the Internet. *You may want to preview any Internet activity that you suggest to students. Because these resources are sometimes public forums, their content can be unpredictable.*

'bout what fine children you was blessed with. We sure do.

Mama. Ruth, give Mis' Johnson a piece of sweet potato pie and some milk.

Johnson. Oh honey, I can't stay hardly a minute—I just dropped in to see if there was anything I could do. (*Accepting the food easily*) I guess y'all seen the news what's all over the colored paper this week . . .

Mama. No—didn't get mine yet this week.

Johnson (*lifting her head and blinking with the spirit of catastrophe*). You mean you ain't read 'bout them colored people that was bombed out their place out there?

[RUTH *straightens with concern and takes the paper and reads it.* JOHNSON *notices her and feeds commentary.*]

Johnson. Ain't it something how bad these here white folks is getting here in Chicago! Lord, getting so you think you right down in Mississippi! (*With a tremendous and rather insincere sense of melodrama*) 'Course I thinks it's wonderful how our folks keeps on pushing out. You hear some of those Negroes round here talking 'bout how they don't go where they ain't wanted and all that—but not me, honey! (*This is a lie.*) Wilhemenia Othella Johnson goes anywhere, any time she feels like it! (*With head movement for emphasis*) Yes I do! Why if we left it up to these here crackers, the poor niggers wouldn't have nothing—(*She clasps her hand over her mouth.*) Oh, I always forgets you don't 'low that word in your house.

Mama (*quietly, looking at her*). No—I don't 'low it.

Johnson (*vigorously again*). Me neither! I was just telling Isaiah yesterday when he come using it in front of me—I said, "Isaiah, it's just like Mis' Younger says all the time—"

Mama. Don't you want some more pie?

Johnson. No—no thank you; this was lovely. I got to get on over home and have my midnight coffee. I hear some people say it don't let them sleep but I finds I can't close my eyes right lessen I done had that laaaast cup of coffee . . . (*She waits. A beat. Undaunted*) My Good-night coffee, I calls it!

Mama (*with much eye-rolling and communication between herself and* RUTH). Ruth, why don't you give Mis' Johnson some coffee.

[RUTH *gives* MAMA *an unpleasant look for her kindness.*]

Johnson (*accepting the coffee*). Where's Brother tonight?

Mama. He's lying down.

Johnson. MMmmmmm, he sure gets his beauty rest, don't he? Good-looking man. Sure is a good-looking man! (*Reaching out to pat* RUTH*'s stomach again*) I guess that's how come we keep on having babies around here. (*She winks at* MAMA.) One thing 'bout Brother, he always know how to have a *good* time. And soooooo ambitious! I bet it was his idea y'all moving out to Clybourne Park. Lord—I bet this time next month y'all's names will have been in the papers plenty—(*Holding up her hands to mark off each word of the headline she can see in front of her*) "NEGROES INVADE CLYBOURNE PARK—BOMBED!"

Mama (*She and* RUTH *look at the woman in amazement.*). We ain't exactly moving out there to get bombed.

Johnson. Oh, honey—you know I'm praying to God every day that don't nothing like that happen! But you have to think of life like it is—and these here Chicago peckerwoods[15] is some baaaad peckerwoods.

Mama (*wearily*). We done thought about all that Mis' Johnson.

[BENEATHA *comes out of the bedroom in her robe and passes through to the bathroom.* MRS. JOHNSON *turns.*]

Johnson. Hello there, Bennie!

Beneatha (*crisply*). Hello, Mrs. Johnson.

Johnson. How is school?

Beneatha (*crisply*). Fine, thank you. (*She goes out.*)

Johnson (*insulted*). Getting so she don't have much to say to nobody.

Mama. The child was on her way to the bathroom.

Johnson. I know—but sometimes she act like ain't got time to pass the time of day with nobody ain't been to college. Oh—I ain't criticizing her

15. **peckerwoods:** disparaging term for poor whites.

OPTIONS FOR TEACHING

ASSESSMENT TOOLS

Observation Assessment As you observe students discussing Act Two in class, participating in small-group work, or writing in their Reader's Logs, use the following statements to rate their reading performance.

1=Rarely 2=Sometimes 3=Never

____ Understands the basic issues of the play

____ Shows a growing appreciation for the complexities of each character

____ Draws on knowledge of elements of drama when making meaning

____ Makes personal connections

____ Challenges the text

none. It's just—you know how some of our young people gets when they get a little education. (MAMA *and* RUTH *say nothing, just look at her.*) Yes—well. Well, I guess I better get on home. (*Unmoving*) 'Course I can understand how she must be proud and everything—being the only one in the family to make something of herself. I know just being a chauffeur ain't never satisfied Brother none. He shouldn't feel like that, though. Ain't nothing wrong with being a chauffeur.
Mama. There's plenty wrong with it.
Johnson. What?
Mama. Plenty. My husband always said being any kind of servant wasn't a fit thing for a man to have to be. He always said a man's hands was made to make things, or to turn the earth with—not to drive nobody's car for 'em—or—(*She looks at her own hands.*) carry they slop jars. And my boy is just like him—he wasn't meant to wait on nobody.
Johnson (*rising, somewhat offended*). Mmmm-mmmmm. The Youngers is too much for me! (*She looks around.*) You sure one proud-acting bunch of colored folks. Well—I always thinks like Booker T. Washington said that time—"Education has spoiled many a good plow hand"—
Mama. Is that what old Booker T. said?
Johnson. He sure did.
Mama. Well, it sounds just like him. The fool.
Johnson (*indignantly*). Well—he was one of our great men.
Mama. Who said so?
Johnson (*nonplussed*). You know, me and you ain't never agreed about some things, Lena Younger. I guess I better be going—
Ruth (*quickly*). Good night.
Johnson. Good night. Oh—(*Thrusting it at her*) You can keep the paper! (*With a trill*) 'Night.
Mama. Good night, Mis' Johnson.

[MRS. JOHNSON *exits.*]

Ruth. If ignorance was gold . . .
Mama. Shush. Don't talk about folks behind their backs.
Ruth. You do.
Mama. I'm old and corrupted. (BENEATHA *enters.*) You was rude to Mis' Johnson, Beneatha, and I don't like it at all.
Beneatha (*at her door*). Mama, if there are two things we, as a people, have got to overcome, one is the Klu Klux Klan—and the other is Mrs. Johnson. (*She exits.*)
Mama. Smart aleck.

[*The phone rings.*]

Ruth. I'll get it.
Mama. Lord, ain't this a popular place tonight.
Ruth (*at the phone*). Hello—Just a minute. (*Goes to door*) Walter, it's Mrs. Arnold. (*Waits. Goes back to the phone. Tense*) Hello. Yes, this is his wife speaking . . . He's lying down now. Yes . . . well, he'll be in tomorrow. He's been very sick. Yes—I know we should have called, but we were so sure he'd be able to come in today. Yes—yes, I'm very sorry. Yes . . . Thank you very much. (*She hangs up.* WALTER *is standing in the doorway of the bedroom behind her.*) That was Mrs. Arnold.
Walter (*indifferently*). Was it?
Ruth. She said if you don't come in tomorrow that they are getting a new man . . .
Walter. Ain't that sad—ain't that crying sad.
Ruth. She said Mr. Arnold has had to take a cab for three days . . . Walter, you ain't been to work for three days! (*This is a revelation to her.*) Where you been, Walter Lee Younger? (WALTER *looks at her and starts to laugh.*) You're going to lose your job.
Walter. That's right . . . (*He turns on the radio.*)
Ruth. Oh, Walter, and with your mother working like a dog every day—

[*A steamy, deep blues pours into the room.*]

Walter. That's sad too— Everything is sad.
Mama. What you been doing for these three days, son?
Walter. Mama—you don't know all the things a man what got leisure can find to do in this city . . . What's this—Friday night? Well—Wednesday I borrowed Willy Harris's car and I went for a drive . . . just me and myself and I drove and drove . . . Way out . . . way past South Chicago, and I parked the car and I sat and looked at the steel mills all day long. I just sat in the car and looked at them big black chimneys for hours. Then I drove back and I went to the Green Hat. (*Pause*) And Thursday—Thursday I borrowed the car again and I got in it and I pointed it the other way and I drove the other way—for hours—way, way up to Wiscon-

A. Expansion
Mama's and Mrs. Johnson's remarks demonstrate the historical debate over the best way for African Americans to advance their civil rights. In 1881, Booker T. Washington was asked to found Tuskegee Institute, a school for African Americans. Washington felt that the way for African Americans to advance was through vocational education. He implied that African Americans should earn their rights as citizens by proving that they could be successful financially. He promoted restraint and self-sacrifice. In contrast, W.E.B. Du Bois, an organizer of the National Association for the Advancement of Colored People, called for political activism as a way for African Americans to advance. He supported broad education that went beyond vocational schooling.

B. Literary Element: Mood
Until Walter appears in this scene, the audience has been uncertain about where his anger with Mama, at the end of Scene 1, would take him. His indifferent and then sarcastic tone sets a mood for Scene 2 that well could be defined as "quiet desperation"—an idea that George Murchison already has noted as being in Beneatha's thoughts.

ASSESSMENT TOOLS

Check Test: Questions and Answers

1. How does George Murchison respond to Walter and Beneatha's "African act"? [He disapproves, and he ridicules them.]
2. What news from Mama infuriates Walter? [That she has used 3,500 dollars of the insurance money to buy a house in the all-white community of Clybourne Park.]
3. What does Mama do with the remaining 6,500 dollars? [She gives it all to Walter, instructing him to put 3,000 dollars into a savings account for Beneatha's education and to use the rest as he sees fit.]
4. Why does Karl Lindner visit the Youngers? [As a representative of the Clybourne Park Improvement Association, he has come with an offer to buy them out to keep them from integrating the area.]
5. What news does Bobo bring? [That Willy Harris, their partner in the liquor store venture, has run off with their money, including the 3,000 dollars that was supposed to go for Beneatha's education.]

A. Critical Reading: Drawing Conclusions

? How has Walter been spending most of his time? [Hanging out at the Green Hat club, driving in the country, and walking around the city.] What consequences may result? [He may lose his job; the family may not be able to make house payments; they may have to do without necessities.]

B. Literary Element: Characterization

It takes just a moment's action to transform Walter. As students read Walter's ensuing conversation with Travis, encourage them to look for ways in which Walter has changed as well as areas in which some of his previously voiced opinions come out. [Possible answers: He can afford to be generous. He places value on a college education. He encourages his son to be whatever he wants to be, whereas previously he has criticized Beneatha's desire to be a doctor. He includes Ruth in his dreams. He is still preoccupied with money, status, and material things.]

C. Critical Reading: Making Inferences

? What traits of Walter's do you think Ruth does and does not want to see in Travis? [Possible answers: Ruth might want Travis to have Walter's energy but not his obsession, his occasional tenderness but not his abusiveness, his reaching for dreams but not his frustration with life.] What connection might there be between Ruth's wishes and the major ideas of *A Raisin in the Sun*? [Possible answers: Reaching for a dream is a major idea of the play, and Ruth is concerned for her son's future.]

sin, and I looked at the farms. I just drove and looked at the farms. Then I drove back and I went to the Green Hat. (*Pause*) And today—today I didn't get the car. Today I just walked. All over the South Side. And I looked at the Negroes and they looked at me and finally I just sat down on the curb at Thirty-ninth and South Parkway and I just sat there and watched the Negroes go by. And then I went to the Green Hat. You all sad? You all depressed? And you know where I am going right now—

[RUTH *goes out quietly.*]

Mama. Oh, Big Walter, is this the harvest of our days?

Walter. You know what I like about the Green Hat? I like this little cat they got there who blows a sax . . . He blows. He talks to me. He ain't but 'bout five feet tall and he's got a conked[16] head and his eyes is always closed and he's all music—

Mama (*rising and getting some papers out of her handbag*). Walter—

Walter. And there's this other guy who plays the piano . . . and they got a sound. I mean they can work on some music . . . They got the best little combo in the world in the Green Hat . . . You can just sit there and drink and listen to them three men play and you realize that don't nothing matter in this whole world, but just being there—

Mama. I've helped do it to you, haven't I, son? Walter I been wrong.

Walter. Naw—you ain't never been wrong about nothing, Mama.

Mama. Listen to me, now. I say I been wrong, son. That I been doing to you what the rest of the world been doing to you. (*She turns off the radio.*) Walter—(*She stops and he looks up slowly at her and she meets his eyes pleadingly.*) What you ain't never understood is that I ain't got nothing, don't own nothing, ain't never really wanted nothing that wasn't for you. There ain't nothing as precious to me . . . There ain't nothing worth holding on to, money, dreams, nothing else—if it means—if it means it's going to destroy my boy. (*She takes an envelope out of her handbag and puts it in front of him and he watches her without speaking or moving.*) I paid the man thirty-five hundred dollars down on the house. That leaves sixty-five hundred dollars. Monday morning I want you to take this money and take three thousand dollars and put it in a savings account for Beneatha's medical schooling. The rest you put in a checking account—with your name on it. And from now on any penny that come out of it or that go in it is for you to look after. For you to decide. (*She drops her hands a little helplessly.*) It ain't much, but it's all I got in the world and I'm putting it in your hands. I'm telling you to be the head of this family from now on like you supposed to be.

Walter (*stares at the money*). You trust me like that, Mama?

Mama. I ain't never stop trusting you. Like I ain't never stop loving you.

[*She goes out, and* WALTER *sits looking at the money on the table. Finally, in a decisive gesture, he gets up, and, in mingled joy and desperation, picks up the money. At the same moment,* TRAVIS *enters for bed.*]

Travis. What's the matter, Daddy? You drunk?

Walter (*sweetly, more sweetly than we have ever known him*). No, Daddy ain't drunk. Daddy ain't going to never be drunk again. . . .

Travis. Well, good night, Daddy.

[*The* FATHER *has come from behind the couch and leans over, embracing his son.*]

Walter. Son, I feel like talking to you tonight.

Travis. About what?

Walter. Oh, about a lot of things. About you and what kind of man you going to be when you grow up. . . . Son—son, what do you want to be when you grow up?

Travis. A bus driver.

Walter (*laughing a little*). A what? Man, that ain't nothing to want to be!

Travis. Why not?

Walter. 'Cause, man—it ain't big enough—you know what I mean.

Travis. I don't know then. I can't make up my mind. Sometimes Mama asks me that too. And sometimes when I tell her I just want to be like you—she says she don't want me to be like that and sometimes she says she does. . . .

Walter (*gathering him up in his arms*). You know what, Travis? In seven years you going to be

16. **conked:** African American hairstyle in which the hair is chemically straightened and smoothed.

seventeen years old. And things is going to be very different with us in seven years, Travis. . . . One day when you are seventeen I'll come home—home from my office downtown somewhere—

Travis. You don't work in no office, Daddy.

Walter. No—but after tonight. After what your daddy gonna do tonight, there's going to be offices—a whole lot of offices. . . .

Travis. What you gonna do tonight, Daddy?

Walter. You wouldn't understand yet, son, but your daddy's gonna make a transaction . . . a business transaction that's going to change our lives. . . . That's how come one day when you 'bout seventeen years old I'll come home and I'll be pretty tired, you know what I mean, after a day of conferences and secretaries getting things wrong the way they do . . . 'cause an executive's life is hard, man—(*The more he talks the farther away he gets.*) And I'll pull the car up on the driveway . . . just a plain black Chrysler, I think, with white walls—no—black tires. More elegant. Rich people don't have to be flashy . . . though I'll have to get something a little sportier for Ruth—maybe a Cadillac convertible to do her shopping in. . . . And I'll come up the steps to the house and the gardener will be clipping away at the hedges and he'll say, "Good evening, Mr. Younger." And I'll say, "Hello, Jefferson, how are you this evening?" And I'll go inside and Ruth will come downstairs and meet me at the door and we'll kiss each other and she'll take my arm and we'll go up to your room to see you sitting on the floor with the catalogues of all the great schools in America around you. . . . All the great schools in the world! And—and I'll say, all right son—it's your seventeenth birthday, what is it you've decided? . . . Just tell me where you want to go to school and you'll *go.* Just tell me, what it is you want to be—and you'll *be* it. . . . Whatever you want to be—Yessir! (*He holds his arms open for* TRAVIS.) You just name it, son . . . (TRAVIS *leaps into them.*) and I hand you the world!

[WALTER*'s voice has risen in pitch and hysterical promise and on the last line he lifts* TRAVIS *high.*]

[*Blackout*]

Scene 3

Time: Saturday, moving day, one week later.

Before the curtain rises, RUTH*'s voice, a strident, dramatic church alto, cuts through the silence.*

It is, in the darkness, a triumphant surge, a penetrating statement of expectation: "Oh, Lord, I don't feel no ways tired! Children, oh, glory hallelujah!"

As the curtain rises we see that RUTH *is alone in the living room, finishing up the family's packing. It is moving day. She is nailing crates and tying cartons.* BENEATHA *enters, carrying a guitar case, and watches her exuberant sister-in-law.*

Ruth. Hey!

Beneatha (*putting away the case*). Hi.

Ruth (*pointing at a package*). Honey—look in that package there and see what I found on sale this morning at the South Center. (RUTH *gets up and moves to the package and draws out some curtains.*) Lookahere—hand-turned hems!

Beneatha. How do you know the window size out there?

Ruth (*who hadn't thought of that*). Oh—Well, they bound to fit something in the whole house. Anyhow, they was too good a bargain to pass up. (RUTH *slaps her head, suddenly remembering something.*) Oh, Bennie—I meant to put a special note on that carton over there. That's your mama's good china and she wants 'em to be very careful with it.

Beneatha. I'll do it.

[BENEATHA *finds a piece of paper and starts to draw large letters on it.*]

Ruth. You know what I'm going to do soon as I get in that new house?

Beneatha. What?

Ruth. Honey—I'm going to run me a tub of water up to here . . . (*With her fingers practically up to her nostrils*) And I'm going to get in it—and I am going to sit . . . and sit . . . and sit in that hot water and the first person who knocks to tell *me* to hurry up and come out—

Beneatha. Gets shot at sunrise.

Ruth (*laughing happily*). You said it, sister! (*Noticing how large* BENEATHA *is absent-mindedly*

D. Reader's Response: Connecting with the Text

? Do you think Walter's idea of an executive's job is accurate? [Sample responses: Yes, executives have to meet with various people frequently; or no, secretaries do not always get things wrong—otherwise they would be fired.] How do you think Walter got that picture? [Sample responses: He has seen what Mr. Arnold does and overheard him talking; or he may have been influenced by television, movies, and hearsay.]

E. Critical Reading: Making Inferences

? Do you think Travis believes his father? [Possible answer: He seems to believe, for he already has expressed an admiration for Walter. His jumping into Walter's arms underscores his trust.]

F. Exploring the Culture

As Scene 3 opens, Ruth finally can sing the song that Mama requested at the end of Act One, Scene 1—"No Ways Tired." The line is a testament to Ruth's religious faith but perhaps even more so to her African American heritage.

G. Critical Reading: Drawing Conclusions

? Why is Ruth so eager for a bath? [An uninterrupted bath is a luxury that is virtually impossible when two families share a bathroom, as do the Youngers and the Johnsons.]

A. Reader's Response: Connecting with the Text

? Is Ruth's observation that Walter and Beneatha share the same philosophy of life correct? [Sample responses: Yes, both Walter and Beneatha have big dreams: Beneatha wants to become a doctor and Walter wants to become a successful businessman; or yes, both have a dramatic flair when they talk or move.]

B. Literary Element: Symbolism

At the beginning of Scene 3, Ruth proudly displayed a package of curtains; now Walter comes in with a package. What do the packages suggest about the results of Walter's new self-confidence? [Possible answer: It has given Ruth an increased sense of security, so that she no longer feels the need to hoard every penny. It has made Walter generous and more interested in others, and it has inspired generosity in his family.]

making the note) Honey, they ain't going to read that from no airplane.

A **Beneatha** (*laughing herself*). I guess I always think things have more emphasis if they are big, somehow.

Ruth (*looking up at her and smiling*). You and your brother seem to have that as a philosophy of life. Lord, that man—done changed so 'round here. You know—you know what we did last night? Me and Walter Lee?

Beneatha. What?

Ruth (*smiling to herself*). We went to the movies. (*Looking at* BENEATHA *to see if she understands*) We went to the movies. You know the last time me and Walter went to the movies together?

Beneatha. No.

Ruth. Me neither. That's how long it been. (*Smiling again*) But we went last night. The picture wasn't much good, but that didn't seem to matter. We went—and we held hands.

Beneatha. Oh, Lord!

Ruth. We held hands—and you know what?

Beneatha. What?

Ruth. When we come out of the show it was late and dark and all the stores and things was closed up . . . and it was kind of chilly and there wasn't many people on the streets . . . and we was still holding hands, me and Walter.

Beneatha. You're killing me.

B [WALTER *enters with a large package. His happiness is deep in him; he cannot keep still with his newfound exuberance. He is singing and wiggling and snapping his fingers. He puts his package in a corner and puts a phonograph record, which he has brought in with him, on the record player. As the music, soulful and sensuous, comes up he dances over to* RUTH *and tries to get her to dance with him. She gives in at last to his raunchiness and in a fit of giggling allows herself to be drawn into his mood. They dip and she melts into his arms in a classic, body-melding "slow drag."*]

Beneatha (*regarding them a long time as they dance, then drawing in her breath for a deeply exaggerated comment which she does not particularly mean*). Talk about—olddddddddd fashionedddddd—Negroes!

Walter (*stopping momentarily*). What kind of Negroes?

[*He says this in fun. He is not angry with her today, nor with anyone. He starts to dance with his wife again.*]

Beneatha. Old-fashioned.

Walter (*as he dances with* RUTH). You know, when these *New Negroes* have their convention—(*pointing at his sister*)—that is going to be the chairman of the Committee on Unending Agitation. (*He goes on dancing, then stops.*) Race, race, race! . . . Girl, I do believe you are the first person in the history of the entire human race to successfully brainwash yourself. (BENEATHA *breaks up and he goes on dancing. He stops again, enjoying his tease.*) Shoot, even the N double A C P takes a holiday sometimes! (BENEATHA *and* RUTH *laugh. He dances with* RUTH *some more and starts to laugh and stops and pantomimes someone over an operating table.*) I can just see that chick someday looking down at some poor cat on an operating table and before she starts to slice him, she says . . . (*Pulling his sleeves back maliciously*) "By the way, what are your views on civil rights down there? . . ."

[*He laughs at her again and starts to dance happily. The bell sounds.*]

Beneatha. Sticks and stones may break my bones but . . . words will never hurt me!

[BENEATHA *goes to the door and opens it as* WALTER *and* RUTH *go on with the clowning.* BENEATHA *is somewhat surprised to see a quiet-looking middle-aged white man in a business suit holding his hat and a briefcase in his hand and consulting a small piece of paper.*]

Man. Uh—how do you do, miss. I am looking for a Mrs.—(*He looks at the slip of paper.*) Mrs. Lena Younger? (*He stops short, struck dumb at the sight of the oblivious* WALTER *and* RUTH.)

Beneatha (*smoothing her hair with slight embarrassment*). Oh—yes, that's my mother. Excuse me. (*She closes the door and turns to quiet the other two.*) Ruth! Brother! (*Enunciating precisely but soundlessly: "There's a white man at the door!" They stop dancing,* RUTH *cuts off the phonograph,* BENEATHA *opens the door. The man casts a curious quick glance at all of them.*) Uh—come in please.

Man (*coming in*). Thank you.

Beneatha. My mother isn't here just now. Is it business?

Man. Yes . . . well, of a sort.

Walter (*freely, the Man of the House*). Have a seat. I'm Mrs. Younger's son. I look after most of her business matters.

[RUTH *and* BENEATHA *exchange amused glances.*]

Man (*regarding* WALTER, *and sitting*). Well—My name is Karl Lindner . . .

Walter (*stretching out his hand*). Walter Younger. This is my wife—(RUTH *nods politely.*)—and my sister.

Lindner. How do you do.

Walter (*amiably, as he sits himself easily on a chair, leaning forward on his knees with interest and looking expectantly into the newcomer's face*). What can we do for you, Mr. Lindner!

Lindner (*some minor shuffling of the hat and briefcase on his knees*). Well—I am a representative of the Clybourne Park Improvement Association—

Walter (*pointing*). Why don't you sit your things on the floor?

Lindner. Oh—yes. Thank you. (*He slides the briefcase and hat under the chair.*) And as I was saying—I am from the Clybourne Park Improvement Association and we have had it brought to our attention at the last meeting that you people—or at least your mother—has bought a piece of residential property at—(*He digs for the slip of paper again.*)—four o six Clybourne Street . . .

Walter. That's right. Care for something to drink? Ruth, get Mr. Lindner a beer.

Lindner (*upset for some reason*). Oh—no, really. I mean thank you very much, but no thank you.

C. Expansion

The National Association for the Advancement of Colored People (NAACP), established in 1910 to work for the end of racial discrimination and segregation, was formed following the 1908 lynching of two African Americans in Springfield, Illinois (a city relevant to the plot of this play, as will be revealed at the end of Scene 3). As early as 1915, the NAACP worked to suppress a movie about the rise of the Ku Klux Klan, D. W. Griffith's *The Birth of a Nation.* Other early efforts were directed, successfully, against lynchings. By the late 1950s, with this worst example of racism virtually wiped out, the NAACP had turned to other civil rights issues.

D. Literary Element: Characterization

Walter has taken Mama's exhortation to be "the head of this family" seriously. Even if Hansberry had not included "*the Man of the House*" in her stage directions, Walter's actions would demonstrate that he has grown into the role that Mama envisioned for him.

E. Literary Element: Suspense

? Why does the announcement of Lindner's affiliation create suspicion? [Possible answers: The name and purpose of the organization are not explained at first; the announcement makes the audience wonder about whether an organization related to the Youngers' new home will consider their arrival an improvement.]

A. Literary Element: Connotation

? What double meanings are suggested by Lindner's explanations? [Possible answers: "Improvement Association" suggests both landscaping enhancements and keeping out people they do not care for. "New Neighbors Orientation Committee" implies both welcoming and screening out. "Give them the lowdown on the way we do things" implies both how the community is run and who the community prefers not to do business with. "Special community problems" could refer to such activities as crime watches but also to preventing people the community considers undesirable from moving in.]

B. Critical Reading: Making Generalizations

? How would you characterize the attitude that Lindner seems to be promoting? [Possible answer: He appears to promote a community spirit, for he seems to feel that all people are about the same and that there is no problem that cannot be overcome if people will work together.] Why do Ruth and Beneatha respond to it as they do? [Possible answer: Ruth believes in community with a religious intensity; Beneatha is surprised to hear such talk from a white man, especially given her first suspicions about Lindner.]

C. Literary Element: Tone

Notice how Beneatha reacts to these words. What tone is Lindner conveying (perhaps without realizing it) as he compliments the Youngers? [Possible answers: Doubt or insincerity; Beneatha's frown is perhaps a reaction to the negative tone insinuated in the "this thing."]

Ruth (*innocently*). Some coffee?

Lindner. Thank you, nothing at all.

[BENEATHA *is watching the man carefully.*]

Lindner. Well, I don't know how much you folks know about our organization. (*He is a gentle man; thoughtful and somewhat labored in his manner.*) It is one of these community organizations set up to look after—oh, you know, things like block upkeep and special projects and we also have what we call our New Neighbors Orientation Committee . . .

Beneatha (*drily*). Yes—and what do they do?

Lindner (*turning a little to her and then returning the main force to* WALTER). Well—it's what you might call a sort of welcoming committee, I guess. I mean they, we—I'm the chairman of the committee—go around and see the new people who move into the neighborhood and sort of give them the lowdown on the way we do things out in Clybourne Park.

Beneatha (*with appreciation of the two meanings, which escape* RUTH *and* WALTER). Un-huh.

Lindner. And we also have the category of what the association calls—(*He looks elsewhere.*)—uh—special community problems . . .

Beneatha. Yes—and what are some of those?

Walter. Girl, let the man talk.

Lindner (*with understated relief*). Thank you. I would sort of like to explain this thing in my own way. I mean I want to explain to you in a certain way.

Walter. Go ahead.

Lindner. Yes. Well. I'm going to try to get right to the point. I'm sure we'll all appreciate that in the long run.

Beneatha. Yes.

Walter. Be still now!

Lindner. Well—

Ruth (*still innocently*). Would you like another chair—you don't look comfortable.

Lindner (*more frustrated than annoyed*). No, thank you very much. Please. Well—to get right to the point I—(*A great breath, and he is off at last.*) I am sure you people must be aware of some of the incidents which have happened in various parts of the city when colored people have moved into certain areas—(BENEATHA *exhales heavily and starts tossing a piece of fruit up and down in the air.*) Well—because we have what I think is going to be a unique type of organization in American community life—not only do we deplore that kind of thing—but we are trying to do something about it. (BENEATHA *stops tossing and turns with a new and quizzical interest to the man.*) We feel—(*gaining confidence in his mission because of the interest in the faces of the people he is talking to*)—we feel that most of the trouble in this world, when you come right down to it—(*He hits his knee for emphasis.*)—most of the trouble exists because people just don't sit down and talk to each other.

Ruth (*nodding as she might in church, pleased with the remark*). You can say that again, mister.

Lindner (*more encouraged by such affirmation*). That we don't try hard enough in this world to understand the other fellow's problem. The other guy's point of view.

Ruth. Now that's right.

[BENEATHA *and* WALTER *merely watch and listen with genuine interest.*]

Lindner. Yes—that's the way we feel out in Clybourne Park. And that's why I was elected to come here this afternoon and talk to you people. Friendly like, you know, the way people should talk to each other and see if we couldn't find some way to work this thing out. As I say, the whole business is a matter of *caring* about the other fellow. Anybody can see that you are a nice family of folks, hard working and honest I'm sure. (BENEATHA *frowns slightly, quizzically, her head tilted regarding him.*) Today everybody knows what it means to be on the outside of *something.* And of course, there is always somebody who is out to take advantage of people who don't always understand.

Walter. What do you mean?

Lindner. Well—you see our community is made up of people who've worked hard as the dickens for years to build up that little community. They're not rich and fancy people; just hard-working, honest people who don't really have much but those little homes and a dream of the kind of community they want to raise their children in. Now, I don't say we are perfect and there is a lot wrong in some of the things they want. But you've got to admit that a man, right or wrong, has the right to want to have the neighborhood he lives in a certain kind of way. And at the moment the overwhelming majority of our people out there feel that people get along better, take more of a common interest in the life of the community, when they share a common background. I want you to believe me when I tell you that race prejudice simply doesn't enter into it. It is a matter of the people of Clybourne Park believing, rightly or wrongly, as I say, that for the happiness of all concerned that our Negro families are happier when they live in their *own* communities.

Beneatha (*with a grand and bitter gesture*). This, friends, is the Welcoming Committee!

Walter (*dumbfounded, looking at* LINDNER). Is this what you came marching all the way over here to tell us?

Lindner. Well, now we've been having a fine conversation. I hope you'll hear me all the way through.

Walter (*tightly*). Go ahead, man.

Lindner. You see—in the face of all the things I have said, we are prepared to make your family a very generous offer . . .

Beneatha. Thirty pieces and not a coin less![17]

Walter. Yeah?

Lindner (*putting on his glasses and drawing a form out of the briefcase*). Our association is prepared, through the collective effort of our people, to buy the house from you at a financial gain to your family.

Ruth. Lord have mercy, ain't this the living gall!

Walter. All right, you through?

Lindner. Well, I want to give you the exact terms of the financial arrangement—

Walter. We don't want to hear no exact terms of no arrangements. I want to know if you got any more to tell us 'bout getting together?

Lindner (*taking off his glasses*). Well—I don't suppose that you feel . . .

Walter. Never mind how I feel—you got any more to say 'bout how people ought to sit down and talk to each other? . . . Get out of my house, man.

[*He turns his back and walks to the door.*]

Lindner (*looking around at the hostile faces and reaching and assembling his hat and briefcase*). Well—I don't understand why you people are reacting this way. What do you think you are going to gain by moving into a neighborhood where you just aren't wanted and where some elements—well—people can get awful worked up when they feel that their whole way of life and everything they've ever worked for is threatened.

Walter. Get out.

Lindner (*at the door, holding a small card*). Well—I'm sorry it went like this.

Walter. Get out.

Lindner (*almost sadly regarding* WALTER). You just can't force people to change their hearts, son.

[*He turns and puts his card on a table and exits.* WALTER *pushes the door to with stinging hatred, and stands looking at it.* RUTH *just sits and* BENEATHA *just stands. They say nothing.* MAMA *and* TRAVIS *enter.*]

Mama. Well—this all the packing got done since I left out of here this morning. I testify before God that my children got all the energy of the *dead*! What time the moving men due?

Beneatha. Four o'clock. You had a caller, Mama.

[*She is smiling, teasingly.*]

Mama. Sure enough—who?

Beneatha (*her arms folded saucily*). The Welcoming Committee.

[WALTER *and* RUTH *giggle.*]

Mama (*innocently*). Who?

Beneatha. The Welcoming Committee. They said they're sure going to be glad to see you when you get there.

Walter (*devilishly*). Yeah, they said they can't hardly wait to see your face.

[*Laughter*]

Mama (*sensing their facetiousness*). What's the matter with you all?

Walter. Ain't nothing the matter with us. We just telling you 'bout the gentleman who came to see you this afternoon. From the Clybourne Park Improvement Association.

Mama. What he want?

17. **Thirty . . . less:** reference to the thirty pieces of silver Judas Iscariot received for betraying Jesus (Matthew 26:14–15).

WORDS TO OWN

saucily (sô′sə·lē) *adv.:* sassily; impertinently.

D. Reader's Response: First Thoughts

? What is your initial reaction to hearing the offer? [Sample responses: I thought he was going to ask them to sell the house. It is surprising that they offer to buy it. Beneatha will tell him off. Or I wonder whether the house will be bombed if they move in.]

E. Critical Reading: Making Inferences

? What advice is Lindner implicitly giving the Youngers? [Possible answer: Do not move into our community, or you may face violence from some of your new neighbors.]

F. Reader's Response: Extending the Text

? How true is Lindner's view today? [Sample responses: Many people do not want to change or do not see the need to do so. Civil wars are still being fought all over the world; some groups do not get along. Or laws can force people to change their actions if not their hearts.]

G. Critical Reading: Speculating

? Why are Beneatha, Walter, and Ruth laughing? [Possible answers: As a natural reaction to the passing of a tense moment; to relieve their nervousness about what to do as a result of Lindner's visit; to mock Lindner and the Clybourne Park Improvement Association; in enjoyment of the way they are teasing Mama.]

A. Literary Element: Tone

? How does Beneatha's remark precisely catch the hypocrisy of the association's offer? [The association claims it is acting in a civil and generous fashion, but it disobeys the Biblical admonition to love one another.]

B. Critical Reading: Analyzing Humor

? What is both comical and exactly right about Mama's defense of her plant? [Possible answers: Mama uses Beneatha's own words from earlier in the play as her defense. The plant is a good symbol of Mama's doggedness and hope for the future.]

C. Reader's Response: First Thoughts

? How do you respond to this stage direction? [Sample responses: They really are struggling financially if they do not give gifts to each other other than at Christmas; or Mama must really be surprised.]

Ruth (*in the same mood as* BENEATHA *and* WALTER). To welcome you, honey.

Walter. He said they can't hardly wait. He said the one thing they don't have, that they just *dying* to have out there is a fine family of fine colored people! (*To* RUTH *and* BENEATHA) Ain't that right!

Ruth (*mockingly*). Yeah! He left his card—

Beneatha (*handing card to* MAMA). In case.

[MAMA *reads and throws it on the floor—understanding and looking off as she draws her chair up to the table on which she has put her plant and some sticks and some cord.*]

Mama. Father, give us strength. (*Knowingly—and without fun*) Did he threaten us?

A **Beneatha.** Oh—Mama—they don't do it like that any more. He talked Brotherhood. He said everybody ought to learn how to sit down and hate each other with good Christian fellowship.

[*She and* WALTER *shake hands to ridicule the remark.*]

Mama (*sadly*). Lord, protect us . . .

Ruth. You should hear the money those folks raised to buy the house from us. All we paid and then some.

Beneatha. What they think we going to do—eat 'em?

Ruth. No, honey, marry 'em.

Mama (*shaking her head*). Lord, Lord, Lord . . .

Ruth. Well—that's the way the crackers crumble. (*A beat*) Joke.

Beneatha (*laughingly noticing what her mother is doing*). Mama, what are you doing?

Mama. Fixing my plant so it won't get hurt none on the way . . .

B **Beneatha.** Mama, you going to take *that* to the new house?

Mama. Un-huh—

Beneatha. That raggedy-looking old thing?

Mama (*stopping and looking at her*). It expresses ME!

Ruth (*with delight, to* BENEATHA). So there, Miss Thing!

[WALTER *comes to* MAMA *suddenly and bends down behind her and squeezes her in his arms with all his strength. She is overwhelmed by the suddenness of it and, though delighted, her manner is like that of* RUTH *and* TRAVIS.]

Mama. Look out now, boy! You make me mess up my thing here!

Walter (*His face lit, he slips down on his knees beside her, his arms still about her.*). Mama . . . you know what it means to climb up in the chariot?

Mama (*gruffly, very happy*). Get on away from me now . . .

Ruth (*near the gift-wrapped package, trying to catch* WALTER'*s eye*). Psst—

Walter. What the old song say, Mama . . .

Ruth. Walter—Now?

[*She is pointing at the package.*]

Walter (*speaking the lines, sweetly, playfully, in his mother's face*).

I got wings . . . you got wings . . .
All God's children got wings . . .

Mama. Boy—get out of my face and do some work . . .

Walter.

When I get to heaven gonna put on my wings,
Gonna fly all over God's heaven . . .

Beneatha (*teasingly, from across the room*). Everybody talking 'bout heaven ain't going there!

Walter (*to* RUTH, *who is carrying the box across to them*). I don't know, you think we ought to give her that . . . Seems to me she ain't been very appreciative around here.

Mama (*eyeing the box, which is obviously a gift*). What is that?

Walter (*taking it from* RUTH *and putting it on the table in front of* MAMA). Well—what you all think? Should we give it to her?

Ruth. Oh—she was pretty good today.

Mama. I'll good you—

[*She turns her eyes to the box again.*]

Beneatha. Open it, Mama.

[*She stands up, looks at it, turns and looks at all of them, and presses her hands together and does not open the package.*]

C **Walter** (*sweetly*). Open it, Mama. It's for you. (MAMA *looks in his eyes. It is the first present in her life without its being Christmas. Slowly she opens her package and lifts out, one by one, a brand-new sparkling set of gardening tools.*

WALTER *continues, prodding.*) Ruth made up the note—read it . . .

Mama (*picking up the card and adjusting her glasses*). "To our own Mrs. Miniver[18]—Love from Brother, Ruth, and Beneatha." Ain't that lovely . . .

Travis (*tugging at his father's sleeve*). Daddy, can I give her mine now?

Walter. All right, son. (TRAVIS *flies to get his gift.*)

Mama. Now I don't have to use my knives and forks no more . . .

Walter. Travis didn't want to go in with the rest of us, Mama. He got his own. (*Somewhat amused*) We don't know what it is . . .

Travis (*racing back in the room with a large hatbox and putting it in front of his grandmother*). Here!

18. **Mrs. Miniver:** title character and genteel English heroine played by Greer Garson in the 1942 movie based on Jan Struther's novel *Mrs. Miniver.*

Mama. Lord have mercy, baby. You done gone and bought your grandmother a hat?

Travis (*very proud*). Open it!

[*She does and lifts out an elaborate, but very elaborate, wide gardening hat, and all the adults break up at the sight of it.*]

Ruth. Travis, honey, what is that?

Travis (*who thinks it is beautiful and appropriate*). It's a gardening hat! Like the ladies always have on in the magazines when they work in their gardens.

Beneatha (*giggling fiercely*). Travis—we were trying to make Mama Mrs. Miniver—not Scarlett O'Hara![19]

19. **Scarlett O'Hara:** flamboyant heroine of *Gone with the Wind* (1936), Margaret Mitchell's Pulitzer Prize-winning novel about the South during the Civil War and Reconstruction, and a classic Hollywood movie (1939).

"You done gone and bought your grandmother a hat?"

D. Humanities Connection

The Youngers' reference to *Mrs. Miniver* takes on deeper meaning when one realizes that Mrs. Miniver's heroism was demonstrated in the way she held her family together during the difficult days of World War II. Encourage students to make the connection.

LITERATURE AND CULTURE

Ask students to discuss similarities and differences between Yoruban culture and current American culture, particularly women's roles, fashions, hairstyles, and approaches to naming children. Put students in small groups to research other African cultures, instructing each group to create its own set of categories on a chart comparing and contrasting cultural features. Discuss the lines of influence in contemporary American culture. Students can create visual displays and hold a Cultural Celebration event where they visit, examine, and discuss each display. In addition, encourage students to dress in traditional clothing and to bring in representative objects and music.

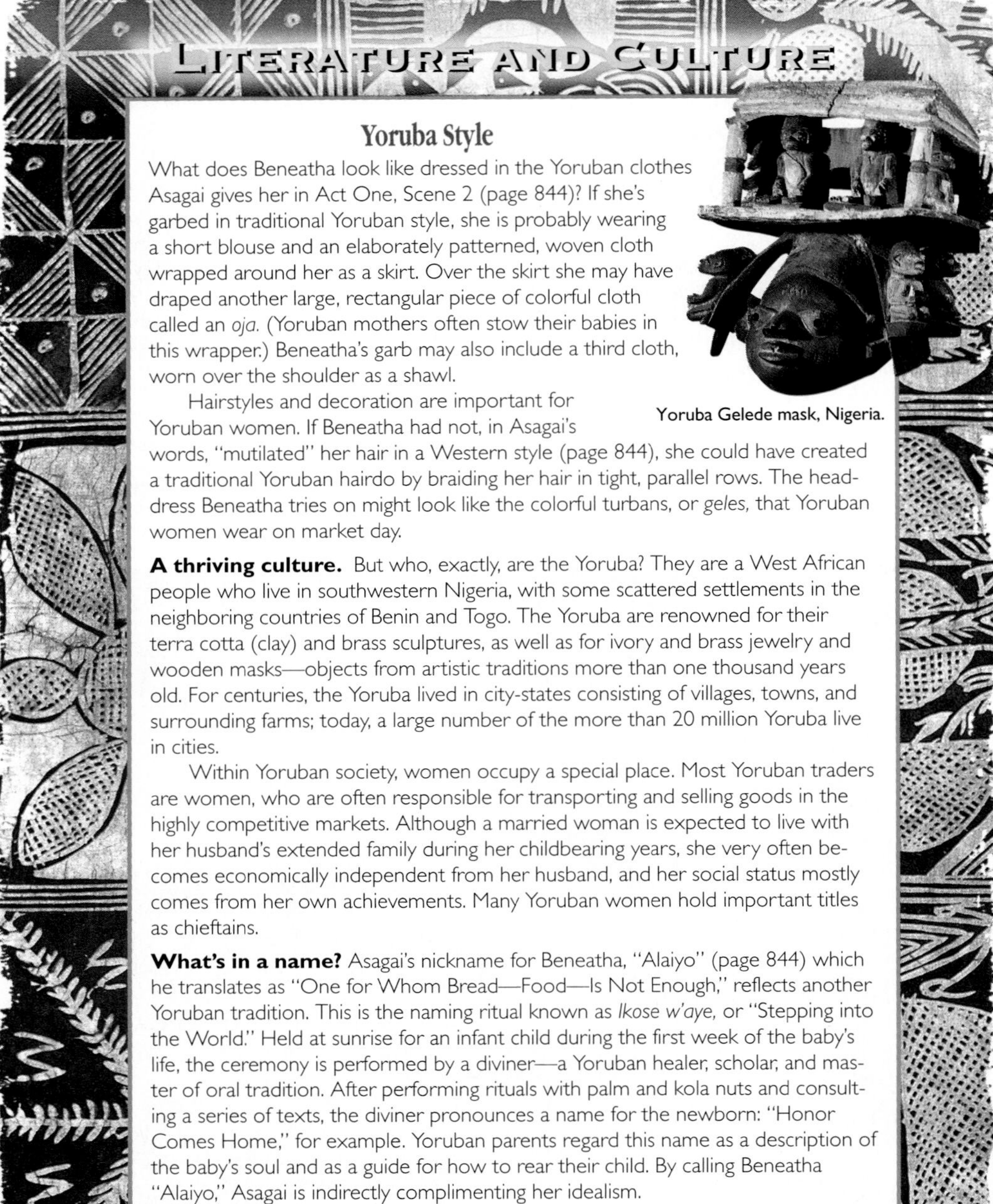

LITERATURE AND CULTURE

Yoruba Style

What does Beneatha look like dressed in the Yoruban clothes Asagai gives her in Act One, Scene 2 (page 844)? If she's garbed in traditional Yoruban style, she is probably wearing a short blouse and an elaborately patterned, woven cloth wrapped around her as a skirt. Over the skirt she may have draped another large, rectangular piece of colorful cloth called an *oja.* (Yoruban mothers often stow their babies in this wrapper.) Beneatha's garb may also include a third cloth, worn over the shoulder as a shawl.

Yoruba Gelede mask, Nigeria.

Marc & Evelyne Bernheim/Woodfin Camp & Associates.

Hairstyles and decoration are important for Yoruban women. If Beneatha had not, in Asagai's words, "mutilated" her hair in a Western style (page 844), she could have created a traditional Yoruban hairdo by braiding her hair in tight, parallel rows. The headdress Beneatha tries on might look like the colorful turbans, or *geles,* that Yoruban women wear on market day.

A thriving culture. But who, exactly, are the Yoruba? They are a West African people who live in southwestern Nigeria, with some scattered settlements in the neighboring countries of Benin and Togo. The Yoruba are renowned for their terra cotta (clay) and brass sculptures, as well as for ivory and brass jewelry and wooden masks—objects from artistic traditions more than one thousand years old. For centuries, the Yoruba lived in city-states consisting of villages, towns, and surrounding farms; today, a large number of the more than 20 million Yoruba live in cities.

Within Yoruban society, women occupy a special place. Most Yoruban traders are women, who are often responsible for transporting and selling goods in the highly competitive markets. Although a married woman is expected to live with her husband's extended family during her childbearing years, she very often becomes economically independent from her husband, and her social status mostly comes from her own achievements. Many Yoruban women hold important titles as chieftains.

What's in a name? Asagai's nickname for Beneatha, "Alaiyo" (page 844) which he translates as "One for Whom Bread—Food—Is Not Enough," reflects another Yoruban tradition. This is the naming ritual known as *Ikose w'aye,* or "Stepping into the World." Held at sunrise for an infant child during the first week of the baby's life, the ceremony is performed by a diviner—a Yoruban healer, scholar, and master of oral tradition. After performing rituals with palm and kola nuts and consulting a series of texts, the diviner pronounces a name for the newborn: "Honor Comes Home," for example. Yoruban parents regard this name as a description of the baby's soul and as a guide for how to rear their child. By calling Beneatha "Alaiyo," Asagai is indirectly complimenting her idealism.

Mama (*indignantly*). What's the matter with you all! This here is a beautiful hat! (*Absurdly*) I always wanted me one just like it!

[*She pops it on her head to prove it to her grandson, and the hat is ludicrous and considerably oversized.*]

Ruth. Hot dog! Go, Mama!
Walter (*doubled over with laughter*). I'm sorry, Mama—but you look like you ready to go out and chop you some cotton sure enough!

A

[*They all laugh except* MAMA, *out of deference to* TRAVIS'S *feelings.*]

Mama (*gathering the boy up to her*). Bless your heart—this is the prettiest hat I ever owned—(WALTER, RUTH, *and* BENEATHA *chime in—noisily, festively, and insincerely congratulating* TRAVIS *on his gift.*) What are we all standing around here for? We ain't finished packin' yet. Bennie, you ain't packed one book.

[*The bell rings.*]

Beneatha. That couldn't be the movers . . . it's not hardly two good yet—

[BENEATHA *goes into her room.* MAMA *starts for door.*]

B

Walter (*turning, stiffening*). Wait—wait—I'll get it.

[*He stands and looks at the door.*]

Mama. You expecting company, son?
Walter (*just looking at the door*). Yeah—yeah . . .

[MAMA *looks at* RUTH, *and they exchange innocent and unfrightened glances.*]

Mama (*not understanding*). Well, let them in, son.
Beneatha (*from her room*). We need some more string.
Mama. Travis—you run to the hardware and get me some string cord.

[MAMA *goes out and* WALTER *turns and looks at* RUTH. TRAVIS *goes to a dish for money.*]

Ruth. Why don't you answer the door, man?
Walter (*suddenly bounding across the floor to embrace her*). 'Cause sometimes it hard to let the future begin! (*Stooping down in her face*)

I got wings! You got wings!
All God's children got wings!

(*He crosses to the door and throws it open. Standing there is a very slight little man in a not too prosperous business suit and with haunted frightened eyes and a hat pulled down tightly, brim up, around his forehead.* TRAVIS *passes between the men and exits.* WALTER *leans deep in the man's face, still in his jubilance.*)

C

When I get to heaven gonna put on my
wings,
Gonna fly all over God's heaven . . .

(*The little man just stares at him.*)

Heaven—

(*Suddenly he stops and looks past the little man into the empty hallway.*) Where's Willy, man?

Bobo. He ain't with me.
Walter (*not disturbed*). Oh—come on in. You know my wife.
Bobo (*dumbly, taking off his hat*). Yes—h'you, Miss Ruth.
Ruth (*quietly, a mood apart from her husband already, seeing* BOBO). Hello, Bobo.
Walter. You right on time today . . . Right on time. That's the way! (*He slaps* BOBO *on his back.*) Sit down . . . lemme hear.

[RUTH *stands stiffly and quietly in back of them, as though somehow she senses death, her eyes fixed on her husband.*]

Bobo (*his frightened eyes on the floor, his hat in his hands*). Could I please get a drink of water, before I tell you about it, Walter Lee?

[WALTER *does not take his eyes off the man.* RUTH *goes blindly to the tap and gets a glass of water and brings it to* BOBO.]

Walter. There ain't nothing wrong, is there?
Bobo. Lemme tell you—
Walter. Man—didn't nothing go wrong?
Bobo. Lemme tell you—Walter Lee. (*Looking at* RUTH *and talking to her more than to* WALTER) You know how it was. I got to tell you how it was. I

A. Reader's Response: First Thoughts

? What do you think of the various reactions to the gardening hat? [Sample responses: Travis has a right to be proud of his gift, for he gave it out of love; his parents and aunt should not make such fun of it; or Mama shows great graciousness in her admiration for Travis's gift.]

B. Critical Reading: Predicting

? Who will be the person at the door? [Possible answers: Someone who wishes the Youngers harm; Asagai, to congratulate them.]

C. Critical Reading: Metacognition

? What questions do these stage directions raise? [Possible answers: Why is the little man frightened? When will Walter realize that something bad has happened?]

A. Critical Reading: Finding Cause and Effect

? Why do you think Walter keeps suggesting causes for Willy's absence? [Possible answer: He is desperately hoping that one of the causes will be true, for he does not want to deal with the possibility that Willy has disappeared with the money.]

Making Meanings Act Two

First Thoughts

1. Possible responses: Mama made a mistake in giving the money to Walter. He already had expressed a willingness to break the law to speed up approval of a liquor license; he also disapproved of Beneatha becoming a doctor. Or Mama did the right thing, for she felt that she had to make up for failing to treat Walter as an adult; she felt Walter would become a better person if she trusted him with the money.

Reviewing the Text

Scene 1: Beneatha and a drunken Walter get in touch with their African heritage, but the excitement ends with the arrival of George Murchison. Walter ridicules this guest. When George and Beneatha leave, Walter and Ruth talk with genuine sadness about the state of their relationship. Mama returns with the news that she has bought a house in Clybourne Park, an all-white area.
Scene 2: The family prepares to move. The others discover that Walter has been skipping work and spending time in a bar. Mama tells him that she has spent 3,500 dollars on the down payment for the house but that he is to take charge of the remainder, setting aside 3,000 dollars for Beneatha's schooling and using the rest as he sees fit. Made confident by Mama's trust, Walter promises Travis a good life in the years to come.
Scene 3: Walter's new assurance revives his marriage. Then, on moving day, the Youngers receive a visit from Karl Lindner, representing the Clybourne Park Improvement Association. Lindner brings a buyout offer; Walter, Ruth, and Beneatha refuse. When Mama comes home, they joke to her about the offer and give her presents. The merriment is cut short, however, when Bobo brings the news that Willy has left town with all of the money for the liquor store venture (including the money that Walter had failed to set aside for Beneatha's education).

"Man, please, not with that money...Oh, God...Don't let it be true...."

mean first I got to tell you how it was all the way . . . I mean about the money I put in, Walter Lee . . .

Walter (*with taut agitation now*). What about the money you put in?

Bobo. Well—it wasn't much as we told you—me and Willy—(*He stops.*) I'm sorry, Walter. I got a bad feeling about it. I got a real bad feeling about it . . .

Walter. Man, what you telling me about all this for? . . . Tell me what happened in Springfield . . .

Bobo. Springfield.

Ruth (*like a dead woman*). What was supposed to happen in Springfield?

Bobo (*to her*). This deal that me and Walter went into with Willy—Me and Willy was going to go down to Springfield and spread some money 'round so's we wouldn't have to wait so long for the liquor license . . . That's what we were going to do. Everybody said that was the way you had to do, you understand, Miss Ruth?

Walter. Man—what happened down there?

Bobo (*a pitiful man, near tears*). I'm trying to tell you, Walter.

Walter (*screaming at him suddenly*). THEN TELL ME, DAMMIT . . . WHAT'S THE MATTER WITH YOU?

Bobo. Man . . . I didn't go to no Springfield, yesterday.

Walter (*halted, life hanging in the moment*). Why not?

Bobo (*the long way, the hard way to tell*). 'Cause I didn't have no reasons to . . .

Walter. Man, what are you talking about!

Bobo. I'm talking about the fact that when I got to the train station yesterday morning—eight o'clock like we planned . . . Man—*Willy didn't never show up.*

Walter. Why . . . where was he . . . where is he?

Bobo. That's why I'm trying to tell you . . . I don't know . . . I waited six hours . . . I called his house . . . and I waited . . . six hours . . . I waited in that train station six hours . . . (*Breaking into tears*) That was all the extra money I had in the world . . . (*Looking up at* WALTER *with the tears running down his face*) Man, *Willy is gone.*

A **Walter.** Gone, what you mean Willy is gone? Gone where? You mean he went by himself. You mean he went off to Springfield by himself—to take care of getting the license—(*Turns and looks anxiously at* RUTH) You mean maybe he didn't want too many people in on the business down there? (*Looks to* RUTH *again, as before*) You know Willy got his own ways. (*Looks back to* BOBO) Maybe you was late yesterday and he just went on down there without you. Maybe—maybe—he's been callin' you at home tryin' to tell you what happened or something. Maybe—maybe—he just got sick. He's somewhere—he's got to be somewhere. We just got to find him—me and you got to find him. (*Grabs* BOBO *senselessly by the collar and starts to shake him*) We got to!

Bobo (*in sudden angry, frightened agony*). What's the matter with you, Walter! *When a cat take off with your money he don't leave you no road maps!*

Walter (*turning madly, as though he is looking for* WILLY *in the very room*). Willy! . . . Willy . . . don't do it . . . Please don't do it . . . Man, not with that money . . . Man, please, not with that money . . . Oh, God . . . Don't let it be true . . . (*He is wandering around, crying out for* WILLY *and looking for him or perhaps for help from God.*) Man . . . I trusted you . . . Man, I put my life in your hands . . . (*He starts to crumple down on the floor as* RUTH *just covers her face in horror.* MAMA *opens the door and comes into the room, with* BENEATHA *behind her.*) Man . . . (*He starts to pound the floor with his fists, sobbing wildly.*) THAT MONEY IS MADE OUT OF MY FATHER'S FLESH——

Bobo (*standing over him helplessly*). I'm sorry, Walter . . . (*Only* WALTER*'s sobs reply.* BOBO *puts on his hat.*) I had my life staked on this deal, too . . .

[*He exits.*]

Words to Own
taut (tôt) *adj.:* tense; rigid.

Shaping Interpretations

2. Prometheus was a mythical Greek giant, and Walter has spoken of himself as a giant. Prometheus brought fire to humanity; Walter has called himself "a volcano." Since Prometheus suffered torture as a result of such defiance of the gods, George implies that Walter's rantings are wrongheaded and that his dreams are fated to fail.
3. Responses may vary, but students should note that the basic conflict between Walter and Ruth is largely the result of Walter's ambition, which has nearly overwhelmed his feelings of responsibility and love as a husband and father.
4. Beneatha's ambition to become a doctor is serious, and students probably will sympathize with her. Yet it also is clear that Beneatha is immature, allowing herself to become passionately involved in various passing fancies (as in the photography lessons). In her eagerness to learn about her African heritage, Beneatha's dressing in Nigerian costume and her rigidity in discussions with the rest of the family seem

Mama (*to* WALTER). Son—(*She goes to him, bends down to him, talks to his bent head.*) Son . . . Is it gone? Son, I gave you sixty-five hundred dollars. Is it gone? All of it? Beneatha's money too?

Walter (*lifting his head slowly*). Mama . . . I never . . . went to the bank at all . . .

Mama (*not wanting to believe him*). You mean . . . your sister's school money . . . you used that too . . . Walter? . . .

Walter. Yessss! All of it . . . It's all gone . . .

[*There is total silence.* RUTH *stands with her face covered with her hands;* BENEATHA *leans forlornly against a wall, fingering a piece of red ribbon from the mother's gift.* MAMA *stops and looks at her son without recognition and then, quite without thinking about it, starts to beat him senselessly in the face.* BENEATHA *goes to them and stops it.*]

Beneatha. Mama!

[MAMA *stops and looks at both of her children and rises slowly and wanders vaguely, aimlessly away from them.*]

Mama. I seen . . . him . . . night after night . . . come in . . . and look at that rug . . . and then look at me . . . the red showing in his eyes . . . the veins moving in his head . . . I seen him grow thin and old before he was forty . . . working and working and working like somebody's old horse . . . killing himself . . . and you—you give it all away in a day—(*She raises her arms to strike him again.*)

Beneatha. Mama—

Mama. Oh, God . . . (*She looks up to Him.*) Look down here—and show me the strength.

Beneatha. Mama—

Mama (*folding over*). Strength . . .

Beneatha (*plaintively*). Mama . . .

Mama. Strength!

Curtain

Making Meanings

Act Two

> **Reviewing the Text**
> In your own words, summarize the main events in Scenes 1, 2, and 3.

First Thoughts

1. Compare Mama's action with the recommendation you made in your Reader's Log (page 851). Do you think she did the right thing with the money? If not, then what should she have done?

Shaping Interpretations

2. In Scene 1, why does George address Walter as "Prometheus"?

3. Walter asks, "Ruth, what is it gets into people ought to be close?" When they try to talk about why they are having such problems, they reach no conclusion. What do you think the playwright wants us to understand as the cause of their problems?

4. Beneatha is a serious character, but she also becomes comic through her excesses. Discuss how she can be seen as a comic **character.** Is she a believable character, or a stereotype? Explain.

5. To which character does Mama first tell her news in Scene 1? Why?

6. In Scene 2, why do you think Walter has stopped going to work?

7. What kind of person does Mrs. Johnson represent? What do her comments **foreshadow** about the Youngers' move?

8. Scene 3 is full of **reversals,** in which sudden shifts take place in the fortunes of the main characters. Discuss the reversals in this scene. What is the mood at the beginning of this scene and at the end?

Connecting with the Text

9. How do you feel about the various characters at this point in the play? Are you still rooting for any particular character? Have your sympathies switched from one character to another? Explain.

more than a bit comic. Overall, students generally will agree that the relatively complex and convincing characterization of Beneatha keeps her from becoming a mere stereotype.

5. Mama tells the news to Travis, her grandson. Her reason appears to be linked with one of her major goals: the stability and continuity of family life (seen, in part, in her promise that the house will be his someday).

6. When confronted by Mama, Walter implies that he has been finding out what leisure time (which he sees as a byproduct of financial success) is like. He is depressed and feeling hopeless. At the end of Act One, he speaks of the restlessness he feels when he sees nothing in his future and realizes how slim a chance he has to make his dreams a reality; he also tells Mama that the restlessness makes him "want to go off somewhere" and be alone—which, basically, is what he has been doing for the past three days when Scene 2 opens.

7. Possible responses: Mrs. Johnson seems to represent several things that the Youngers are not: She is falsely enthusiastic, whereas the Youngers are emotionally honest; she loves to snoop and gossip, whereas the Youngers exhibit a quiet pride; her ideas and language suggest attitudes of the past, whereas the Youngers look for a better future. Her comments foreshadow potential trouble—perhaps even violence—should the Youngers move to Clybourne Park.

8. At the beginning of Scene 3, the mood is joyful and expectant; by the scene's end, all seems to have been lost. The first major reversal occurs in conjunction with Lindner's visit. Although it first appears that Lindner's purpose is to welcome the Youngers to their new neighborhood, it turns out that his true goal is to propose a buyout of their house, since they are not welcome in Clybourne Park. When informed of this development, Mama is disturbed at first, but her consternation turns to pleasure and joy when Walter, Ruth, Beneatha, and Travis give her their presents. This light moment, however, is soon shattered when Bobo enters with the terrible news that Willy Harris has stolen the money that Bobo and Walter had entrusted to him. Walter admits to Mama that he never deposited Beneatha's money in the bank; Mama responds by beating Walter. Remembering her dead husband, Mama prays to God for strength and then crumples to the floor in despair.

Connecting with the Text

9. Possible responses: Mama and Ruth are the most thoughtful. Beneatha seems somewhat selfish. It would be good if things worked out for Walter because he can be a good husband and father and needs so much to succeed. He is more sympathetic in the second act than in the first.

Into the Play

Using Before You Read p. 876

Quickwrite

Using the chalkboard, work with the class to develop a pro and con chart like the one provided before having students do the Quickwrite. Encourage students to suggest not only the potential risks of living in the new neighborhood but also the dreams that seem impossible to fulfill without moving. As students develop their Quickwrites, have them expand on the pro and con chart. Some students may want to focus on their feelings regarding either one pro or one con; others may prefer to weigh both and present their conclusions in a persuasive appeal. Invite students to share their Quickwrites in small groups. Allow volunteers to relate to the class what they think the deciding factor would be in such a case.

Pro-Moving	Con-Moving

Before You Read

A Raisin in the Sun Act Three

Reading Focus

What Price a Dream?

No dream—no goal or ambition—comes without a price: sacrifices, struggles, setbacks. The American dream is not within easy reach of everyone, and the attempt to grasp even a portion of it sometimes requires exceptional courage and persistence.

Quickwrite

Suppose that in order to fulfill their dreams a family must not only move but move to a neighborhood where they may be disliked or intimidated. Should they make the move? Why or why not? Jot down your thoughts about this problem.

Elements of Literature

Static and Dynamic Characters

Characters in fiction can be classified as static or dynamic. A **static character** does not change during the course of a story. A **dynamic character,** on the other hand, changes in some important way as a result of the events of a story. As you read Act Three, think about which characters change and grow as a result of their experiences.

A **dynamic character** changes in some important way as a result of a story's action. A **static character** stays the same during the course of a story.

For more on Character, see the Handbook of Literary Terms.

Words to Own

The following vocabulary words are defined in the Words to Own at the bottom of the pupil's page.

flippancy p. 879	epitaph p. 884
wrought p. 880	negotiate p. 884
monologue p. 880	groping p. 885
gait p. 880	reverie p. 885
agitated p. 883	bustling p. 886

Portfolio Assessment

Portfolio Assessment For help with teacher assessment of reading skills, see the ***Portfolio Management System,*** pp. 54–55.

"...maybe I'll just get down on my black knees..."

Act Three

An hour later.

At curtain, there is a sullen light of gloom in the living room, gray light not unlike that which began the first scene of Act One. At left we can see WALTER *within his room, alone with himself. He is stretched out on the bed, his shirt out and open, his arms under his head. He does not smoke, he does not cry out, he merely lies there, looking up at the ceiling, much as if he were alone in the world.*

In the living room BENEATHA *sits at the table, still surrounded by the now almost ominous packing crates. She sits looking off. We feel that this is a mood struck perhaps an hour before, and it lingers now, full of the empty sound of profound disappointment. We see on a line from her brother's bedroom the sameness of their attitudes. Presently the bell rings and* BENEATHA *rises without ambition or interest in answering. It is* ASAGAI, *smiling broadly, striding into the room with energy and happy expectation and conversation.*

Asagai. I came over . . . I had some free time. I thought I might help with the packing. Ah, I like the look of packing crates! A household in preparation for a journey! It depresses some people . . . but for me . . . it is another feeling. Something full of the flow of life, do you understand? Movement, progress . . . It makes me think of Africa.
Beneatha. Africa!
Asagai. What kind of a mood is this? Have I told you how deeply you move me?
Beneatha. He gave away the money, Asagai . . .
Asagai. Who gave away what money?
Beneatha. The insurance money. My brother gave it away.
Asagai. Gave it away?
Beneatha. He made an investment! With a man even Travis wouldn't have trusted with his most worn-out marbles.
Asagai. And it's gone?
Beneatha. Gone!
Asagai. I'm very sorry . . . And you, now?
Beneatha. Me? . . . Me? . . . Me, I'm nothing . . . (A) Me. When I was very small . . . we used to take our sleds out in the wintertime and the only hills we had were the ice-covered stone steps of some houses down the street. And we used to fill them in with snow and make them smooth and slide down them all day . . . and it was very dangerous, you know . . . far too steep . . . and sure enough one day a kid named Rufus came down too fast and hit the sidewalk and we saw his face just split open right there in front of us . . . And I remember standing there looking at his bloody open face thinking that was the end of Rufus. But the ambulance came and they took him to the hospital and they fixed the broken bones and they sewed it all up . . . and the next time I saw Rufus he just had a little line down the middle of his face . . . I never (B) got over that . . .
Asagai. What?
Beneatha. That that was what one person could do for another, fix him up—sew up the problem, make him all right again. That was the most marvelous thing in the world . . . I wanted to do that. I always thought it was the one concrete thing in the world that a human being could do. Fix up the sick, you know—and make them whole again. This was truly being God . . .
Asagai. You wanted to be God?
Beneatha. No—I wanted to cure. It used to be so important to me. I wanted to cure. It used to matter. I used to care. I mean about people and how their bodies hurt . . .
Asagai. And you've stopped caring?
Beneatha. Yes—I think so.
Asagai. Why?
Beneatha (*bitterly*). Because it doesn't seem deep enough, close enough to what ails mankind! It was a child's way of seeing things—or an idealist's. (C)
Asagai. Children see things very well sometimes—and idealists even better.

A. Reader's Response: First Thoughts

? Why might people who face a great loss, as Beneatha does, be tempted to think of themselves as nothing? [Sample responses: They feel foolish for having spent so much emotion on something that did not last; or having lost something that was so much a part of their identity, they now are challenged to redefine themselves.]

B. Reader's Response: Shaping Interpretations

? Prior to this monologue, how serious did you think Beneatha was about becoming a doctor? [Sample responses: It was another whim, like taking up the guitar or horseback riding; or she seemed to build her life around it.] How does her story about "a kid named Rufus" affect your view? [Sample responses: It shows that her desire to become a doctor is much stronger than her other interests; or it shows where her desire came from.]

C. Literary Element: Characterization

? What does Asagai's response to Beneatha's comment suggest about his character? [Possible answers: He is wise; he is sensitive to the frustration she feels; he is clever, for he turns Beneatha's own words back on her; he is appealingly childlike and idealistic.]

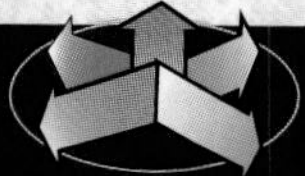

PROGRAM MANAGER

- **Planning Instruction** See *Teaching Notes, Teaching Resources B,* p. 120, for objectives and a summary for this act.
- **Instructional Support** Before beginning the instructional lesson, see *Graphic Organizer for Active Reading, Teaching Resources B,* p. 128, for a Through the Play activity.
- **Assessment** See *Selection Test, Test Booklet,* pp. 205–206.
- **Reinforcement** Use the *Words to Own* worksheet in *Teaching Resources B,* p. 129.

A. Humanities Connection

? How does Beneatha's speech summarize the philosophy of naturalism? (See p. 421, the third paragraph of the section "Realism and Naturalism.") [Beneatha feels that human beings have no control over their lives.] Do you think Hansberry is using this exchange to promote naturalism? Explain. [Possible answer: No; through Asagai she repudiates naturalism, offering in its place a realism that sees the bad but works for improvement.]

B. Critical Reading: Expressing an Opinion

? Do you agree with Asagai that Beneatha is giving up too easily? Is her life over because of the money, as she seems to feel? What advice might you offer? [Possible answer: Although Beneatha feels her situation hopeless, she still can become a doctor. She can work hard to attain her goal.]

Metacognition How did you come to your answer? [Possible answer: From practical and personal experience. I know that people can get money for college by working for it and applying for scholarships.]

C. Reader's Response: Connecting with the Text

? Does Asagai's willingness to die for his cause remind you of any historical or literary figure about whom you have read? [Sample responses: Dr. Martin Luther King, Jr.; Mohandas Ghandi; Malcolm X; or soldiers at war.]

Beneatha. I know that's what you think. Because you are still where I left off. You with all your talk and dreams about Africa! You still think you can patch up the world. Cure the Great Sore of Colonialism—(*loftily, mocking it*) with the Penicillin of Independence—!

Asagai. Yes!

Beneatha. Independence *and then what*? What about all the crooks and thieves and just plain idiots who will come into power and steal and plunder the same as before—only now they will be black and do it in the name of the new Independence—WHAT ABOUT THEM?!

Asagai. That will be the problem for another time. First we must get there.

Beneatha. And where does it end?

Asagai. End? Who even spoke of an end? To life? To living?

Beneatha. An end to misery! To stupidity! Don't you see there isn't any real progress, Asagai, there is only one large circle that we march in, around and around, each of us with our own little picture in front of us—our own little mirage that we think is the future.

Asagai. That is the mistake.

A **Beneatha.** What?

Asagai. What you just said—about the circle. It isn't a circle—it is simply a long line—as in geometry, you know, one that reaches into infinity. And because we cannot see the end—we also cannot see how it changes. And it is very odd but those who see the changes—who dream, who will not give up—are called idealists . . . and those who see only the circle—we call *them* the "realists"!

Beneatha. Asagai, while I was sleeping in that bed in there, people went out and took the future right out of my hands! And nobody asked me, nobody consulted me—they just went out and changed my life!

Asagai. Was it your money?

Beneatha. What?

Asagai. Was it your money he gave away?

Beneatha. It belonged to all of us.

Asagai. But did you earn it? Would you have had it at all if your father had not died?

Beneatha. No.

Asagai. Then isn't there something wrong in a house—in a world—where all dreams, good or bad, must depend on the death of a man? I never thought to see *you* like this, Alaiyo. You! Your brother made a mistake and you are grateful to him so that now you can give up the ailing human B race on account of it! You talk about what good is struggle, what good is anything! Where are we all going and why are we bothering!

Beneatha. AND YOU CANNOT ANSWER IT!

Asagai (*shouting over her*). *I LIVE THE ANSWER!* (*Pause*) In my village at home it is the exceptional man who can even read a newspaper . . . or who ever sees a book at all. I will go home and much of what I will have to say will seem strange to the people of my village. But I will teach and work and things will happen, slowly and swiftly. At times it will seem that nothing changes at all . . . and then again the sudden dramatic events which make history leap into the future. And then quiet again. Retrogression[1] even. Guns, murder, revolution. And I even will have moments when I wonder if the quiet was not better than all that death and hatred. But I will look about my village at the illiteracy and disease and ignorance and I will not wonder long. And perhaps . . . perhaps I will be a great man . . . I mean perhaps I will hold on to the substance of truth and find my way always with C the right course . . . and perhaps for it I will be butchered in my bed some night by the servants of empire . . .

Beneatha. *The martyr!*

Asagai (*He smiles.*). . . . or perhaps I shall live to be a very old man, respected and esteemed in my new nation . . . And perhaps I shall hold office and this is what I'm trying to tell you, Alaiyo: Perhaps the things I believe now for my country will be wrong and outmoded, and I will not understand and do terrible things to have things my way or merely to keep my power. Don't you see that there will be young men and women—not British soldiers then, but my own black countrymen—to step out of the shadows some evening and slit my then useless throat? Don't you see they have always been there . . . that they always will be. And that such a thing as my own death will be an advance? They who might kill me even . . . actually replenish all that I was.

Beneatha. Oh, Asagai, I know all that.

Asagai. Good! Then stop moaning and groaning and tell me what you plan to do.

Beneatha. Do?

1. **retrogression:** degeneration; backward movement.

OPTIONS FOR TEACHING

STRATEGIES FOR INCLUSION

Linguistic Encourage students who demonstrate a sensitivity to the nuances of words to pay special attention to Mama's short but powerful "measure him right" speech on p. 884. In particular, invite them to make comments in their Reader's Logs on Mama's questioning technique and her use of **figurative language**.

Interpersonal Students who enjoy working with others may find much to comment on as several **conflicts** in *A Raisin in the Sun* find a resolution. In particular, ask them to write in their Reader's Log responses to Asagai's "I live the answer" speech to Beneatha on p. 878; to Ruth's insistence that they not abandon the move on p. 881; to Mama's "Measure him right" speech to Beneatha on p. 884; and to Walter's "We are very proud people" speech to Lindner on p. 885.

Logical-Mathematical Students who enjoy making predictions may want to do some second-guessing before reading Act Three. Work with students to create a list of **conflicts** and tensions revealed by the end of Act Two. Ask them to predict which ones will be resolved, and how. Have them consider whether the Youngers will continue to follow their dreams, or whether the loss of the money—and the stress that the loss creates—will prove too strong an obstacle.

Asagai. I have a bit of a suggestion.
Beneatha. What?
Asagai (*rather quietly for him*). That when it is all over—that you come home with me—
Beneatha (*staring at him and crossing away with exasperation*). Oh—Asagai—at this moment you decide to be romantic!
Asagai (*quickly understanding the misunderstanding*). My dear, young creature of the New World—I do not mean across the city—I mean across the ocean: home—to Africa.
Beneatha (*slowly understanding and turning to him with murmured amazement*). To Africa?
Asagai. Yes! . . . (*Smiling and lifting his arms playfully*) Three hundred years later the African Prince rose up out of the seas and swept the maiden back across the middle passage over which her ancestors had come—
Beneatha (*unable to play*). To—to Nigeria?
Asagai. Nigeria. Home. (*Coming to her with genuine romantic flippancy*) I will show you our mountains and our stars; and give you cool drinks from gourds and teach you the old songs and the ways of our people—and, in time, we will pretend that—(*very softly*)—you have only been away for a day. Say that you'll come—(*He swings*

Words to Own
flippancy (flip′ən·sē) *n.:* impertinence; glibness.

D. Critical Reading: Analyzing Dialogue

? How does Asagai try to persuade Beneatha to come with him?
[Asagai appeals to the first thing he understood about Beneatha—that she was searching for her identity. Consequently, he uses a historical reference to the middle passage and mentions Beneatha's African ancestry; then he fills her mind with images of the sights and culture of Nigeria.]

INTEGRATING THE LANGUAGE ARTS

Strategic Reading Although *A Raisin in the Sun* is accessible to students with a wide range of abilities, you might ensure comprehension by having pairs of students work through Act Three using Reciprocal Teaching. As they read, have pairs of students summarize each exchange of ideas and perhaps any piece of dialogue of more than six lines or so. Have one student ask the other student two or three questions about the material; the second student will ask questions of the first after the next section of the text is read and summarized. Ask pairs to continue reading and to alternate asking questions and responding until they have finished the selection.

Speaking and Listening The conclusion of the play makes for powerful oral reading. Depending on class time and the number of students you want to involve, you might begin with Mama's speech beginning "Son—I come from five generations . . . " on p. 882. Have students take turns portraying Mama, Walter, Beneatha, Ruth, Travis, and Lindner.

Language and Style Have students compare Asagai's comments about Africa on pp. 878–880 to Walter's in Act Two on p. 853. Ask students to consider what makes both speakers—one African born, the other separated from Africa by several generations—speak so poetically on the subject of Africa.

A. Critical Reading: Predicting

? Do you think Beneatha will go with Asagai? [Possible answers: No, she will stay and go to medical school. Or yes, she will be able to leave trouble behind to find her identity.]

B. Critical Reading: Drawing Conclusions

? Why do you think Mama sets her plant outside? [Possible answers: Mama is continuing to do what she previously did with the plant, meaning that the family will not be moving; or she is giving the plant light, meaning that the family will be moving.]

her around and takes her full in his arms in a kiss which proceeds to passion.)

Beneatha (*pulling away suddenly*). You're getting me all mixed up—

Asagai. Why?

A **Beneatha.** Too many things—too many things have happened today. I must sit down and think. I don't know what I feel about anything this minute.

[*She promptly sits down and props her chin on her fist.*]

Asagai (*charmed*). All right, I shall leave you. No—don't get up. (*Touching her, gently, sweetly*) Just sit awhile and think . . . Never be afraid to sit awhile and think. (*He goes to door and looks at her.*) How often I have looked at you and said, "Ah—so this is what the New World hath finally wrought . . ."

[*He exits.* BENEATHA *sits alone. Presently* WALTER *enters from his room and starts to rummage through things, feverishly looking for something. She looks up and turns in her seat.*]

Beneatha (*hissingly*). Yes—just look at what the New World hath wrought! . . . Just look! (*She gestures with bitter disgust.*) There he is! *Monsieur le petit bourgeois noir*[2]—himself! There he is—Symbol of a Rising Class! Entrepreneur! Titan[3] of the system! (WALTER *ignores her completely and continues frantically and destructively looking for something and hurling things to floor and tearing things out of their place in his search.* BENEATHA *ignores the eccentricity of his actions and goes on with the monologue of insult.*) Did you dream of yachts on Lake Michigan, Brother? Did you see yourself on that Great Day sitting down at the Conference Table, surrounded by all the mighty bald-headed men in America? All halted, waiting, breathless, waiting for your pronouncements on industry? Waiting for you—Chairman of the Board! (WALTER *finds what he is looking for—a small piece of white paper—and pushes it in his pocket and puts on his coat and rushes out without ever having looked at her. She shouts after him.*) I look at you and I see the final triumph of stupidity in the world!

[*The door slams and she returns to just sitting again.* RUTH *comes quickly out of* MAMA*'s room.*]

Ruth. Who was that?

Beneatha. Your husband.

Ruth. Where did he go?

Beneatha. Who knows—maybe he has an appointment at U.S. Steel.

Ruth (*anxiously, with frightened eyes*). You didn't say nothing bad to him, did you?

Beneatha. Bad? Say anything bad to him? No—I told him he was a sweet boy and full of dreams and everything is strictly peachy keen, as the ofay[4] kids say!

B [MAMA *enters from her bedroom. She is lost, vague, trying to catch hold, to make some sense of her former command of the world, but it still eludes her. A sense of waste overwhelms her gait; a measure of apology rides on her shoulders. She goes to her plant, which has remained on the table, looks at it, picks it up, and takes it to the windowsill and sits it outside, and she stands and looks at it a long moment. Then she closes the window, straightens her body with effort, and turns around to her children.*]

Mama. Well—ain't it a mess in here, though? (*A false cheerfulness, a beginning of something*) I guess we all better stop moping around and get some work done. All this unpacking and everything we got to do. (RUTH *raises her head slowly in response to the sense of the line; and* BENEATHA *in similar manner turns very slowly to look at her mother.*) One of you all better call the moving people and tell 'em not to come.

Ruth. Tell 'em not to come?

Mama. Of course, baby. Ain't no need in 'em coming all the way here and having to go back.

2. ***Monsieur le petit bourgeois noir:*** "Mister black lower middle class." The *petit bourgeois* are owners of shops and small businesses.

3. **Titan:** In Greek mythology, the Titans are a race of giants. In modern usage, a titan is someone of great power.

4. **ofay:** former African American slang for a white person. Derived from a pig Latin form of "foe."

Words to Own

wrought (rôt) *v.:* created; made.
monologue (män′ə·lôg′) *n.:* speech given by one person.
gait (gāt) *n.:* way of walking; stride.

OPTIONS FOR TEACHING

COOPERATIVE LEARNING

Cluster After students have read and discussed Act Three, have them work in small groups to complete two sets of cluster diagrams similar to Transparency 3: Cluster Diagram in the Transparency Package:

- In one diagram, students should brainstorm words and phrases that capture one character's thoughts and beliefs as presented over the course of the play; in the other, they should do the same for a character whose thoughts and beliefs are different.
- In one diagram, students should brainstorm words and phrases that capture one character's thoughts and beliefs as seen in Act One; in the other, they should show the changes in that character's thinking by the end of Act Three.

Assign students the roles of discussion leader, scribe, and task manager. Encourage groups to present and discuss their completed diagrams. Then, hang the diagrams on a classroom wall or bulletin board.

Grand Conversation Have small groups of five to seven students gather for a Grand Conversation about *A Raisin in the Sun* as a whole. Each leader might begin by saying to the group, "The poem that prefaces the play asks, 'What happens to a dream deferred?' In this play, what does happen?" The secretary records their ideas and the spokesperson shares with the class the main ideas discussed.

They charges for that too. (*She sits down, fingers to her brow, thinking.*) Lord, ever since I was a little girl, I always remembers people saying, "Lena—Lena Eggleston, you aims too high all the time. You needs to slow down and see life a little more like it is. Just slow down some." That's what they always used to say down home—"Lord, that Lena Eggleston is a high-minded thing. She'll get her due one day!" [C]

Ruth. No, Lena . . .

Mama. Me and Big Walter just didn't never learn right.

Ruth. Lena, no! We gotta go. Bennie—tell her . . . (*She rises and crosses to* BENEATHA *with her arms outstretched.* BENEATHA *doesn't respond.*) Tell her we can still move . . . the notes ain't but a hundred and twenty-five a month. We got four grown people in this house—we can work . . .

Mama (*to herself*). Just aimed too high all the time— [D]

Ruth (*turning and going to* MAMA *fast—the words pouring out with urgency and desperation*). Lena—I'll work . . . I'll work twenty hours a day in all the kitchens in Chicago . . . I'll strap my baby on my back if I have to and scrub all the floors in America and wash all the sheets in America if I have to—but we got to MOVE! We got to get OUT OF HERE!!

[MAMA *reaches out absently and pats* RUTH'S *hand.*]

Mama. No—I sees things differently now. Been thinking 'bout some of the things we could do to fix this place up some. [E] I seen a secondhand bureau over on Maxwell Street just the other day that could fit right there. (*She points to where the new furniture might go.* RUTH *wanders away from her.*) Would need some new handles on it and then a little varnish and it look like something brand-new. And—we can put up them new curtains in the kitchen . . . Why this place be looking fine. Cheer us all up so that we forget trouble ever come . . . (*To* RUTH) And you could get some nice screens to put up in your room round the baby's bassinet . . . (*She looks at both of them, pleadingly.*) Sometimes you just got to know when to give up some things . . . and hold on to what you got. . . .

[WALTER *enters from the outside, looking spent and leaning against the door, his coat hanging from him.*]

Mama. Where you been, son?

Walter (*breathing hard*). Made a call.

Mama. To who, son?

Walter. To The Man. (*He heads for his room.*)

Mama. What man, baby?

Walter (*stops in the door*). The Man, Mama. Don't you know who The Man is? [F]

Ruth. Walter Lee?

Walter. *The Man.* Like the guys in the streets say—The Man. Captain Boss—Mistuh Charley . . . Old Cap'n Please Mr. Bossman . . .

Beneatha (*suddenly*). Lindner!

Walter. That's right! That's good. I told him to come right over.

Beneatha (*fiercely, understanding*). For what? What do you want to see him for!

Walter (*looking at his sister*). We going to do business with him.

Mama. What you talking 'bout, son?

Walter. Talking 'bout life, Mama. You all always telling me to see life like it is. Well—I laid in there on my back today . . . and I figured it out. Life just like it is. Who gets and who don't get. (*He sits down with his coat on and laughs.*) Mama, you know it's all divided up. Life is. Sure enough. Between the takers and the "tooken." (*He laughs.*) I've figured it out finally. (*He looks around at them.*) Yeah. Some of us always getting "tooken." (*He laughs.*) People like Willy Harris, they don't never get "tooken." And you know why the rest of us do? 'Cause we all mixed up. Mixed up bad. We get to looking 'round for the right and the wrong; and we worry about it and cry about it and stay up nights trying to figure out 'bout the wrong and the right of things all the time . . . And all the time, man, them takers is out there operating, just taking and taking. Willy Harris? Shoot—Willy Harris don't even count. He don't even count in the big scheme of things. But I'll say one thing for old Willy Harris . . . he's taught me something. He's taught me to keep my eye on what counts in this world. Yeah—(*Shouting out a little*) Thanks, Willy!

Ruth. What did you call that man for, Walter Lee?

Walter. Called him to tell him to come on over to the show. Gonna put on a show for the man. Just what he wants to see. You see, Mama, the man

C. Critical Reading: Making Connections

? In Act One, what does Mama remember Big Walter saying? [That God did not give the African American anything but dreams.] How does she compare herself to him here? [Possible answer: She suggests that sorrow has come to them both because they dared to dream too big.] Do you think that the two of them have passed along this trait to their children? [Possible answer: Walter and Beneatha, having grown up with such dreamers for parents, have learned to dream big themselves.]

D. Critical Reading: Finding Cause and Effect

? Why is Ruth frantic to keep Mama from calling off the move? [Possible answers: After years of living in the apartment, Ruth's nerves are almost ready to snap; she fears that if they do not make a major change in their lives, neither she and Walter nor Travis will have a future.]

E. Literary Element: Plot

? What decision has Mama made about the new house? [Not to move.] Why do you think she made this decision? [Ruth's protest about how she will help earn the monthly payments makes it clear that the Youngers do not have the money to make the payments.]

F. Language Note: Slang

The Man came into use during the 1950s as a slang reference to federal law-enforcement officers; by the end of the decade it was commonly used among African Americans to refer to whites in positions of authority. As used by Hansberry, the term prefaces a list of slang terms for white authority figures that increasingly shows Walter's bitter frustration.

CLASSROOM MANAGEMENT

Cooperative Learning Cooperative learning need not be limited to a method of completing an assignment; at times it can arise from the way in which a completed assignment is shared. You might try having two students who completed the same activity for Act Three compare their responses. Then, have them report (to you or to the class) what they learned from seeing another person's approach to the same material.

Teacher's Reflection While students are working on activities related to the close of *A Raisin in the Sun,* do a self-check to assess your feelings about teaching drama and longer selections. Use the following statements as a guide.

1=Certain 2=Uncertain 3=Doubt

____ The next time I teach a play, I will give students more time to enact it in class.

____ For our next play, I will focus more on **character** and **conflict** and less on stagecraft.

____ As we work through another play or other lengthy piece, I will spend more time focusing on personal responses to the literature.

____ As we approach another lengthy piece, I will plan a wider variety of ways to individualize instruction.

____ When we next read a longer selection, I will break it up into smaller segments for reading and discussion.

A. Reader's Response: Shaping Interpretations

? What is "that old-time stuff"? [Sample responses: Pride; the ambition of African Americans to make a better future for themselves; the determination not to give in to racist pressure; or the goals of the civil rights movement to end bigotry.]

B. Critical Reading: Making Inferences

? Do you think Mama will agree to this? Support your answers with details from the play. [Possible answer: Mama will be unwilling to take the money because that will imply that her family has no scruples and that social prejudice against African Americans is acceptable.]

C. Literary Element: Theme

? How does Mama's response reflect a major theme in this play? [Possible answer: In speaking against accepting Lindner's offer, Mama emphasizes that the issue is human dignity, not money. Although materialism is a topic in the play, it is overshadowed by the issue of defining and defending human worth in the face of trouble.]

came here today and he told us that them people out there where you want us to move—well they so upset they willing to pay us *not* to move! (*He laughs again.*) And—and oh, Mama—you would of been proud of the way me and Ruth and Bennie acted. We told him to get out . . . Lord have mercy! (A) We told the man to get out! Oh, we was some proud folks this afternoon, yeah. (*He lights a cigarette.*) We were still full of that old-time stuff . . .

(B) **Ruth** (*coming toward him slowly*). You talking 'bout taking them people's money to keep us from moving in that house?

Walter. I ain't just talking 'bout it, baby—I'm telling you that's what's going to happen!

Beneatha. Oh, God! Where is the bottom! Where is the real honest-to-God bottom so he can't go any farther!

Walter. See—that's the old stuff. You and that boy that was here today. You all want everybody to carry a flag and a spear and sing some marching songs, huh? You wanna spend your life looking into things and trying to find the right and the wrong part, huh? Yeah. You know what's going to happen to that boy someday—he'll find himself sitting in a dungeon, locked in forever—and the takers will have the key! Forget it, baby! There ain't no causes—there ain't nothing but taking in this world, and he who takes most is smartest—and it don't make a bit of difference *how.*

Mama. You making something inside me cry, son. Some awful pain inside me.

Walter. Don't cry, Mama. Understand. That white man is going to walk in that door able to write checks for more money than we ever had. It's important to him and I'm going to help him . . . I'm going to put on the show, Mama.

(C) **Mama.** Son—I come from five generations of people who was slaves and sharecroppers—but ain't nobody in my family never let nobody pay 'em no money that was a way of telling us we wasn't fit to walk the earth. We ain't never been that poor. (*Raising her eyes and looking at him*) We ain't never been that—dead inside.

Beneatha. Well—we are dead now. All the talk about dreams and sunlight that goes on in this house. It's all dead now.

Walter. What's the matter with you all! I didn't make this world! It was give to me this way! Lord, yes, I want me some yachts someday! Yes, I want

"Don't cry, Mama. Understand."

OPTIONS FOR TEACHING

CROSSING THE CURRICULUM

Fine Arts In 1973, *Raisin*—a musical based on *A Raisin in the Sun,* with music by Judd Woldin and lyrics by Robert Brittain—opened on Broadway. It won the 1974 Tony Award for best musical. Have a group of students find and listen to the original cast recording of *Raisin;* then, have them report on it to the class. Their presentation might focus on three types of songs in the musical:

- Songs that capture key passages of dialogue (such as "Man Say," the musical treatment of Walter's "eat your eggs" speech to Ruth; "Alaiyo," Asagai's love song for Beneatha; "You Done Right," Walter's angry response to Mama's purchase of the house; "Not Anymore," the Youngers' recounting of Lindner's visit; and "Measure the Valleys," Mama's "measure him right" speech)
- Songs that expand on other elements (such as "Whose Angry Little Man," Ruth's song to Travis; "A Whole Lotta Sunlight," Mama's symbolic song about her plant; and "It's a Deal," Walter's song about his liquor store venture)
- Songs that add new elements to the story (such as "He Come Down This Morning," a gospel song sung at Mama's church; and "Sidewalk Tree," Travis's lament about leaving his neighborhood)

Students also might discuss whether they think the same **themes** from Hansberry's original come across in *Raisin.* Have students illustrate their points by playing excerpts from the recording.

to hang some real pearls 'round my wife's neck. Ain't she supposed to wear no pearls? Somebody tell me—tell me, who decides which women is suppose to wear pearls in this world. I tell you I am a *man*—and I think my wife should wear some pearls in this world!

[*This last line hangs a good while and* WALTER *begins to move about the room. The word "Man" has penetrated his consciousness; he mumbles it to himself repeatedly between strange agitated pauses as he moves about.*]

Mama. Baby, how you going to feel on the inside?
Walter. Fine! . . . Going to feel fine . . . a man . . .
Mama. You won't have nothing left then, Walter Lee.
Walter (*coming to her*). I'm going to feel fine, Mama. I'm going to look that man in the eyes and say—(*He falters.*)—and say, "All right, Mr. Lindner—(*He falters even more.*)—that's *your* neighborhood out there! You got the right to keep it like you want! You got the right to have it like you want! Just write the check and—the house is yours." And—and I am going to say—(*His voice almost breaks.*) "And you—you people just put the money in my hand and you won't have to live next to this bunch of stinking . . ." (*He straightens up and moves away from his mother, walking around the room.*) And maybe—maybe I'll just get down on my black knees . . . (*He does so;* RUTH *and* BENNIE *and* MAMA *watch him in frozen horror.*) "Captain, Mistuh, Bossman—(*Groveling and grinning and wringing his hands in profoundly anguished imitation of the slow-witted movie stereotype*) A-hee-hee-hee! Oh, yassuh boss! Yasssssuh! Great white—(*Voice breaking, he forces himself to go on.*)—Father, just gi' ussen de money, fo' God's sake, and we's—we's ain't gwine come out deh and dirty up yo' white folks neighborhood . . ." (*He breaks down completely.*) And I'll feel fine! Fine! FINE! (*He gets up and goes into the bedroom.*)
Beneatha. That is not a man. That is nothing but a toothless rat.
Mama. Yes—death done come in this here house.

WORDS TO OWN
agitated (aj'i·tāt'id) *adj.:* anxious; frantic.

D. Literary Element: Irony
Point out Walter's sarcasm in saying that having Lindner's money will make him feel like a man. What is the irony of his statement? [Possible answer: Walter asserts that the money or the power the money can buy for him will make him a man; to get that money, however, he is willing to demean himself so far that he acts unethically and almost loses his humanity.]

E. Reader's Response: Shaping Interpretations
? Will Walter "feel fine"? [Sample responses: No, he intends this sarcastically; or yes, he will be glad to have the money although he will have to demean himself and his family to get it.]

PROBLEM SOLVING/CRITICAL THINKING

Pros and Cons Implied in the decisions of Act Three—whether or not to go ahead with the move, whether or not to accept Lindner's offer—is some "pro and con" thinking. To help students put that problem-solving skill to work, offer the following hypothetical situation, and encourage them to use a chart such as the one provided to jot down their ideas. Ask students to discuss what Kelly should do based on their charts.

Kelly is looking ahead to the summer, and she has some options. Two are especially appealing—either working full time at a day-care center or taking an intensive Spanish workshop at the community college. "Both of these could come in handy in the future," she thinks, "but I can't do both."

	pro	con
Working		
Learning Spanish		

A. Critical Reading: Identifying Main Ideas

? What is the main idea of this passage? [That love is compassionate, and that those who love think of the one they love before they think of themselves, especially when the loved one has suffered a setback.] In a larger sense, how have you seen this idea at work throughout the play? [Possible answer: Mama has demonstrated this idea in the way she has spoken of her children and her late husband; it is a key to her strength—a strength that has held the Younger family together.]

B. Literary Element: Plot

Because the movers and Lindner arrive simultaneously, a decision must be made immediately. The action of the play now will build quickly to the **climax**.

C. Critical Reading: Making Inferences

? What do Walter's actions, described in these stage directions, suggest he is thinking at this moment? [Possible answer: Despite his seeming assurance about how to face Lindner, now that the moment has arrived, Walter is nervous about going through with his plan. Perhaps he is reconsidering.]

D. Critical Reading: Making Inferences

? How does Mama attempt to change Walter's thinking? [Possible answer: She challenges Walter to break out of the kind of thinking and acting that he would be perpetuating if he accepted Lindner's offer—and to do it for the sake of his son.]

(*She is nodding, slowly, reflectively.*) Done come walking in my house on the lips of my children. You what supposed to be my beginning again. You—what supposed to be my harvest. (*To* BENEATHA) You—you mourning your brother?

Beneatha. He's no brother of mine.

Mama. What you say?

Beneatha. I said that that individual in that room is no brother of mine.

Mama. That's what I thought you said. You feeling like you better than he is today? (BENEATHA *does not answer.*) Yes? What you tell him a minute ago? That he wasn't a man. Yes? You give him up for me? You done wrote his epitaph too—like the rest of the world? Well, who give you the privilege?

Beneatha. Be on my side for once! You saw what he just did, Mama! You saw him—down on his knees. Wasn't it you who taught me to despise any man who would do that? Do what he's going to do?

Mama. Yes—I taught you that. Me and your daddy. But I thought I taught you something else too . . . I thought I taught you to love him.

Beneatha. Love him? There is nothing left to love.

A **Mama.** There is *always* something left to love. And if you ain't learned that, you ain't learned nothing. (*Looking at her*) Have you cried for that boy today? I don't mean for yourself and for the family 'cause we lost the money. I mean for him: what he been through and what it done to him. Child, when do you think is the time to love somebody the most? When they done good and made things easy for everybody? Well then, you ain't through learning—because that ain't the time at all. It's when he's at his lowest and can't believe in hisself 'cause the world done whipped him so! When you starts measuring somebody, measure him right, child, measure him right. Make sure you done taken into account what hills and valleys he come through before he got to wherever he is.

[TRAVIS *bursts into the room at the end of the speech, leaving the door open.*]

B **Travis.** Grandmama—the moving men are downstairs! The truck just pulled up.

Mama (*turning and looking at him*). Are they, baby? They downstairs?

[*She sighs and sits.* LINDNER *appears in the doorway. He peers in and knocks lightly, to gain attention, and comes in. All turn to look at him.*]

Lindner (*hat and briefcase in hand*). Uh—hello . . .

[RUTH *crosses mechanically to the bedroom door and opens it and lets it swing open freely and slowly as the lights come up on* WALTER *within, still in his coat, sitting at the far corner of the room. He looks up and out through the room to* LINDNER.]

Ruth. He's here.

[*A long minute passes and* WALTER *slowly gets up.*]

Lindner (*coming to the table with efficiency, putting his briefcase on the table and starting to unfold papers and unscrew fountain pens*). C Well, I certainly was glad to hear from you people. (WALTER *has begun the trek out of the room, slowly and awkwardly, rather like a small boy, passing the back of his sleeve across his mouth from time to time.*) Life can really be so much simpler than people let it be most of the time. Well—with whom do I negotiate? You, Mrs. Younger, or your son here? (MAMA *sits with her hands folded on her lap and her eyes closed as* WALTER *advances.* TRAVIS *goes closer to* LINDNER *and looks at the papers curiously.*) Just some official papers, sonny.

Ruth. Travis, you go downstairs—

D **Mama** (*opening her eyes and looking into* WALTER'S). No. Travis, you stay right here. And you make him understand what you doing, Walter Lee. You teach him good. Like Willy Harris taught you. You show where our five generations done come to. (WALTER *looks from her to the boy, who grins at him innocently.*) Go ahead, son—(*She folds her hands and closes her eyes.*) Go ahead.

Walter (*at last crosses to* LINDNER, *who is reviewing the contract*). Well, Mr. Lindner. (BENEATHA *turns away.*) We called you—(*There is a pro-*

Words to Own

epitaph (ep'ə·taf') *n.:* memorable or descriptive phrase written on a tombstone or in memory of the dead.

negotiate (ni·gō'shē·āt') *v.:* make a bargain; come to an agreement.

OPTIONS FOR TEACHING

PROFESSIONAL NOTES

Critical Comment: The Heroic Dimension In speaking of Walter's final refusal to accept Lindner's offer, literary scholar Julius Lester says, "Our heroes are more difficult to recognize only because they appear so small beside the overwhelming enemies they must slay. But because they appear small does not mean that they are, and it does not make their acts less heroic. Walter Lee Younger has his contemporary historic counterpart in the person of a small, quiet black woman named Rosa Parks who refused to get out of a seat on a bus in Montgomery, Alabama. It would have been so easy for her to have relinquished her seat to a white person that day—as it would have been easy for Walter to have taken the money. But something in her, as in him, said No. And in that quiet dissent, both of them said Yes to human dignity. They said No to those who would define them and thereby deny their existence, and by saying No, they began to define themselves. There have been many Rosa Parks, but few of them have mysteriously set in motion a whole movement for social change. Walter Lee Younger is one of those whose act probably set nothing in motion. And that only increases its heroic dimension." Invite students to respond to this comment; in particular, ask them how the Rosa Parks analogy helps them better understand the significance of Walter's action.

found, simple groping quality in his speech.)—because, well, me and my family *(He looks around and shifts from one foot to the other.)* Well—we are very plain people . . .

Lindner. Yes—

Walter. I mean—I have worked as a chauffeur most of my life—and my wife here, she does domestic work in people's kitchens. So does my mother. I mean—we are plain people . . .

Lindner. Yes, Mr. Younger—

Walter *(really like a small boy, looking down at his shoes and then up at the man).* And—uh—well, my father, well, he was a laborer most of his life. . . .

Lindner *(absolutely confused).* Uh, yes—yes, I understand. *(He turns back to the contract.)*

Walter *(a beat; staring at him).* And my father—*(With sudden intensity)* My father almost *beat a man to death* once because this man called him a bad name or something, you know what I mean? E

Lindner *(looking up, frozen).* No, no, I'm afraid I don't—

Walter *(a beat. The tension hangs; then* WALTER *steps back from it.).* Yeah. Well—what I mean is that we come from people who had a lot of *pride.* I mean—we are very proud people. And that's my sister over there and she's going to be a doctor—and we are very proud— F

Lindner. Well—I am sure that is very nice, but—

Walter. What I am telling you is that we called you over here to tell you that we are very proud and that this—*(Signaling to* TRAVIS*)* Travis, come here. (TRAVIS *crosses and* WALTER *draws him before him facing the man.)* This is my son, and he makes the sixth generation our family in this country. And we have all thought about your offer—

Lindner. Well, good . . . good—

Walter. And we have decided to move into our house because my father—my father—he earned it for us brick by brick. *(*MAMA *has her eyes closed and is rocking back and forth as though she were in church, with her head nodding the Amen yes.)* We don't want to make no trouble for nobody or fight no causes, and we will try to be good neighbors. And that's *all* we got to say about that. *(He looks the man absolutely in the eyes.)* We don't want your money. *(He turns and walks away.)* G

Lindner *(looking around at all of them).* I take it then—that you have decided to occupy . . .

Beneatha. That's what the man said.

Lindner *(to* MAMA *in her reverie).* Then I would like to appeal to you, Mrs. Younger. You are older and wiser and understand things better I am sure . . .

Mama. I am afraid you don't understand. My son said we was going to move and there ain't nothing left for me to say. *(Briskly)* You know how these young folks is nowadays, mister. Can't do a thing with 'em. *(As he opens his mouth, she rises.)* Goodbye. H

Lindner *(folding up his materials).* Well—if you are that final about it . . . there is nothing left for me to say. *(He finishes, almost ignored by the family, who are concentrating on* WALTER LEE. *At*

WORDS TO OWN

groping (grōp′iŋ) *v.* used as *adj.:* searching; fumbling.
reverie (rev′ər·ē) *n.:* thought; musing.

E. Reader's Response: Shaping Interpretations

? Is Walter threatening Lindner? [Sample responses: It does not seem to be a direct threat of violence, for Walter's demeanor is calm, even humbled. Or yes, Walter is saying the Youngers do not take well to being demeaned.]

F. Exploring the Culture

As the play already has suggested, at this time many people thought that African Americans should be happy to work at menial tasks, and the concept of pride was not widely encouraged. How does Walter react to those views? [He emphasizes the Younger family's pride and points in particular to Beneatha, who is planning a professional career.]

G. Reader's Response: Extending the Text

? Which of Walter's reasons for moving into the house do you think is the most important? [Sample responses: Providing Travis with an opportunity for the future; or honoring the heritage of his ancestors.]

H. Literary Element: Tone

? What tone does Hansberry use in Mama's reply? [Ironic, since Mama, of all people, does a great deal with the young people in her household—especially because she has just taken exactly the right approach to help her son do what she hoped he would do.]

ASSESSMENT TOOLS

Peer Assessment Have students use the following criteria to rate the group they were part of in any of the Cooperative Learning activities on p. T880.

1=Strong 2=Average 3=Weak

_____ The group was serious about the assigned task.
_____ The group respected each member's opinions.
_____ Everyone contributed to the group effort.

Check Test: Questions and Answers

1. Why does Beneatha think that she no longer cares about becoming a doctor? [She feels that healing sickness does not go far enough toward fixing the greater, moral ills of humanity.]
2. What proposition does Asagai offer to Beneatha? [That she come with him to Nigeria to live and work.]
3. Why does Walter call Karl Lindner? [Walter has decided that now they should accept the buyout offer from the Clybourne Park Improvement Association.]
4. Why does Mama say she stops Travis from going downstairs when the movers and Karl Lindner arrive? [She says she wants Travis to stay and listen to his father.]
5. What does Walter do to cause Mama to feel her son has become a man? [He refuses Lindner's offer.]

A. Literary Elements: Static and Dynamic Characters

? Is Ruth a dynamic or static character? Support your answer. [Possible answers: Static, because her character does not change; she is for the move throughout the play. Or dynamic, for she has had doubts about the move and has had to make a decision about the baby. She has also come to understand and attend to Walter's needs.]

B. Critical Reading: Identifying Main Ideas

? How does the concept of human dignity—a major idea in this play—figure into Mama's comment to Ruth? [Possible answer: Mama's view of manhood (unlike Walter's earlier view, which linked manhood with financial power and business success) is based on human dignity. By refusing Lindner's offer, Walter has reasserted a belief in human dignity and restored Mama's faith.]

C. Reader's Response: Shaping Interpretations

? What is the "great heaving thing" that causes Mama's final moment in the apartment to seem less than joyous? [Sample responses: The recognition that the family came very close to losing the chance to leave; the realization that Big Walter is not there to share this dreamed-of moment with her; or a flood of memories, good and bad, that involve the apartment.]

"LET'S GET THIS BLESSED FAMILY OUT OF HERE!"

the door LINDNER *halts and looks around.*) I sure hope you people know what you're getting into.

[*He shakes his head and exits.*]

A **Ruth** (*looking around and coming to life*). Well, for God's sake—if the moving men are here—LET'S GET THIS BLESSED FAMILY OUT OF HERE!

Mama (*into action*). Ain't it the truth! Look at all this here mess. Ruth, put Travis' good jacket on him . . . Walter Lee, fix your tie and tuck your shirt in, you look like somebody's hoodlum! Lord have mercy, where is my plant? (*She flies to get it amid the general bustling of the family, who are deliberately trying to ignore the nobility of the past moment.*) You all start on down . . . Travis child, don't go empty-handed . . . Ruth, where did I put that box with my skillets in it? I want to be in charge of it myself . . . I'm going to make us the biggest dinner we ever ate tonight . . . Beneatha, what's the matter with them stockings? Pull them things up, girl . . .

[*The family starts to file out as two moving men appear and begin to carry out the heavier pieces of furniture, bumping into the family as they move about.*]

Beneatha. Mama, Asagai asked me to marry him today and go to Africa—

Mama (*in the middle of her getting-ready activity*). He did? You ain't old enough to marry nobody—(*Seeing the moving men lifting one of her chairs precariously*) Darling, that ain't no bale of cotton, please handle it so we can sit in it again! I had that chair twenty-five years . . .

[*The movers sigh with exasperation and go on with their work.*]

Beneatha (*girlishly and unreasonably trying to pursue the conversation*). To go to Africa, Mama—be a doctor in Africa . . .

Mama (*distracted*). Yes, baby—

Walter. *Africa!* What he want you to go to Africa for?

Beneatha. To practice there . . .

Walter. Girl, if you don't get all them silly ideas out your head! You better marry yourself a man with some loot . . .

Beneatha (*angrily, precisely as in the first scene of the play*). What have you got to do with who I marry!

Walter. Plenty. Now I think George Murchison—

Beneatha. *George Murchison!* I wouldn't marry him if he was Adam and I was Eve!

[WALTER *and* BENEATHA *go out yelling at each other vigorously and the anger is loud and real till their voices diminish.* RUTH *stands at the door and turns to* MAMA *and smiles knowingly.*]

Mama (*fixing her hat at last*). Yeah—they something all right, my children . . .

Ruth. Yeah—they're something. Let's go, Lena.

Mama (*stalling, starting to look around at the house*). Yes—I'm coming. Ruth—

Ruth. Yes?

B **Mama** (*quietly, woman to woman*). He finally come into his manhood today, didn't he? Kind of like a rainbow after the rain . . .

Ruth (*biting her lip lest her own pride explode in front of* MAMA). Yes, Lena.

[WALTER*'s voice calls for them raucously.*]

Walter (*offstage*). Y'all come on! These people charges by the hour, you know!

Mama (*waving* RUTH *out vaguely*). All right, honey—go on down. I be down directly.

[RUTH *hesitates, then exits.* MAMA *stands, at last alone in the living room, her plant on the table before her as the lights start to come down. She looks around at all the walls and ceilings and* C *suddenly, despite herself, while the children call below, a great heaving thing rises in her and she puts her fist to her mouth to stifle it, takes a final desperate look, pulls her coat about her, pats her hat, and goes out. The lights dim down. The door opens and she comes back in, grabs her plant, and goes out for the last time.*]

Curtain

WORDS TO OWN

bustling (bus′liŋ) *v.* used as *n.:* busyness; energetic activity.

PRIMARY Sources | A LETTER

Lorraine Hansberry wrote the following letter to her mother on January 19, 1959, just before *A Raisin in the Sun* opened in New Haven, Connecticut.

A Letter from the Playwright

Dear Mother,

Well—here we are. I am sitting alone in a nice hotel room in New Haven, Conn. Downstairs, next door in the Shubert Theatre, technicians are putting the finishing touches on a living room that is supposed to be a Chicago living room. Wednesday the curtain goes up at 8 P.M. The next day the New Haven papers will say what they think about our efforts. A great deal of money has been spent and a lot of people have done some hard, hard work, and it may be the beginning of many different careers.

The actors are very good and the director is a very talented man—so if it is a poor show I won't be able to blame a soul but your youngest daughter.

Mama, it is a play that tells the truth about people, Negroes, and life and I think it will help a lot of people to understand how we are just as complicated as they are—and just as mixed up—but above all, that we have among our miserable and downtrodden ranks—people who are the very essence of human dignity. That is what, after all the laughter and tears, the play is supposed to say. I hope it will make you very proud. See you soon. Love to all.

—Lorraine Hansberry

The Skaters

No one expected anything of us.
I struggled and fought and fell
Until we began to dream
While performing small miracles.
But golden dreams turned to nothing.
Neither gold, nor silver, nor bronze,
The flag, the song
It isn't mine.
My country, my family
I didn't want to disappoint you.

But all is forgiven
You are no disappointment.
We have seen the beauty
That you possess.
The blood, the bruises, the brotherhood
No one could ask for more.
In your eyes there is a flame
That burns despite defeat
It doesn't matter.
You always carry the flame.

—Maggie Shi
Madison High School
Madison, New Jersey

Primary Sources

Ask students to consider in what ways Hansberry is like or unlike her characters. [Possible answers: She has a bond with her mother and wants to please her, which is similar to the feelings Beneatha, Ruth, and Walter have toward Mama. She is deeply moved by important issues, just as Beneatha and Asagai are. She has dreams of having a successful play, just as the characters have their own dreams. Or unlike Walter, her dreams do not focus on money.]

A. Critical Reading: Drawing Conclusions

? What dream does the skater have? [Winning a medal in a skating competition.]

B. Reader's Response: Challenging the Text

? Do these two lines hurt or contribute to the poem? [Sample responses: They take away from the poem, for to forgive someone implies that injury was done, and there is no apparent injury committed here. They contribute because the speaker of the second stanza reaches out to the speaker of the first.]

C. Literary Element: Point of View

The point of view in the second stanza is different from the point of view in the first stanza. Who is speaking in the second stanza? [Possible answers: Parents, skating fans.]

STRATEGIES FOR INCLUSION

English Language Development In her letter, Hansberry writes about the dreams she hopes to realize. Ask students to discuss what dreams are revealed in the letter and what dreams members of the Younger family have. Invite students to talk about what dreams Hansberry and the Youngers would have for the world at large. Ask students to what extent these dreams have been realized several decades later. Encourage students to consider in what ways the play may have helped fulfill these dreams.

Linguistic Have students write the letter Hansberry might have received from her mother. Ask them to include a response to the diligence of the people who worked on the play and to Hansberry's description of the content of the play. Post their letters on the class bulletin board.

CONNECTING WITH *A RAISIN IN THE SUN*

Like Beneatha and Walter in *A Raisin in the Sun,* the first speaker of Shi's poem dreams of an outstanding personal achievement. Ask students to identify the specific dreams expressed in the poem and to discuss to what extent these dreams have been realized and whether they resemble the dreams members of the Younger family have.

Making Meanings Act Three

First Thoughts

1. Possible responses: The Youngers are heroic and brave; or they are in serious danger. Yes, I listed danger.

Reviewing the Text

a. Walter stands up for his own dignity and that of his family. He puts aside material ambition to assert his essential humanity.

b. By having Mama linger to look around the apartment, Hansberry suggests that Mama is somewhat nostalgic about the past and her memories of Big Walter.

Shaping Interpretations

2. Both Mama and Walter are dynamic characters. Mama learns to understand Walter's torment, and she changes as she trusts and supports him more vigorously. Walter learns that he must stand up for his own dignity and must pay more attention to the needs of his wife and child. Students probably will agree that the minor characters in the play—Travis, Asagai, George, Mrs. Johnson, Lindner, and Bobo—are static, but they may have varying views of Ruth and Beneatha.
3. Mama's plant; it represents the constant, loving care with which Mama nurtures those who surround her.
4. The poem implies that a dream too long postponed may be the cause of torment, suffering, or violence. The play's major theme—that dignity and love can endure and triumph—is somewhat different from that of the poem, which ends ominously and even menacingly. Most of the characters in *A Raisin in the Sun* have had their dreams deferred: Walter, Mama, Ruth, and Beneatha. By the end of the play, none of these characters has fully achieved his or her dream; but it is implied that the dream shared by Mama and Ruth is to be fulfilled.
5. She values religion, human dignity, and love. She reveals her religious beliefs in Act One, when she reprimands Beneatha for saying God does not exist. In Act Three, she tells Walter that members of her family have never allowed anyone to rob them of their dignity. A little later in Act Three, Mama reminds Beneatha that there is always something to love in a person.
6. Suspense is driven by fear that Walter will sell out by making the deal with Lindner. Hansberry shows Walter frantically searching for a piece of paper, possibly the card with Lindner's telephone number. Walter reveals his plan and bitterly parodies the actions of a defeated man begging a master for mercy. As he breaks down and retires to the bedroom, the audience is almost convinced that Walter is unbalanced and that he will not heed Mama's words about human dignity. When the movers and Lindner arrive almost simultaneously, the suspense is intensified because of the need for a decision. Mama orders Travis to remain in the room as Walter faces Lindner—a signal that the critical moment, the moment of greatest suspense, has arrived. Walter starts with an apologetic, almost humble tone; but then he rejects Lindner's offer, asserting the family's pride and resolving the tension of the climax.
7. Walter realizes his own dignity and pride. Mama helps make this realization possible, and finds rescue in her strong sense of love and support for her children.

MAKING MEANINGS

Act Three

Reviewing the Text

a. The scene with Mr. Lindner is the **climax** of the play. What happens during this scene that ends our doubts about the Younger family's decision?

b. What do the closing stage directions suggest about Mama's frame of mind just before the final curtain?

First Thoughts

1. How did you feel about the family's decision to move to the all-white neighborhood? Did their experiences relate to anything you wrote in your Reader's Log? Explain.

Shaping Interpretations

2. In a play, certain characters change and grow as a result of their experiences. These are **dynamic characters. Static characters** remain essentially the same throughout the play; they do not change in any important way. Which characters in this play are dynamic? Which are static? Cite passages from the play to support your answer.
3. A movable object on stage is called a *prop* (short for *property*). A prop may serve as a **symbol** that stands for much more than the object itself. There is such a prop in this play. What is it, and what does it symbolize?
4. Explain how the play's **title** and the poem by Langston Hughes (page 828) support the play's **theme.** Which characters in the play have had their dreams "deferred"? Which characters have dreams that come true?
5. During the course of the play, we learn that Mama believes there are several absolutely essential things in life. What would you say Mama's values are?
6. Discuss the playwright's use of **suspense** in Act Three. What is it that we fear will happen? How does the playwright draw out the action so that our suspense is heightened?
7. Both Mama and Walter seem defeated for a while in Act Three. However, we know from the play's general tone that it cannot end in defeat for these good people. In a way, we "enjoy" their defeat and despair because we sense that the playwright is preparing us for another **reversal.** What is it that rouses each character from defeat to the joyful, triumphant note on which the play ends?

Extending the Text

8. What do you predict will happen to the Younger family in the years ahead?
9. The movie director Spike Lee writes, "We all have to ask ourselves, have things gotten any better than when the play was written? I have to say I think they've gotten worse." Tell why you agree or disagree with Lee's statement. Are the issues raised by the play still pertinent in the United States, or is the play outdated?

Challenging the Text

10. The content and attitude of this play derive from the realistic school of drama exemplified by Henrik Ibsen and Arthur Miller. Sometimes plays of this school, or genre, are accused of being didactic or preachy. All good plays teach or reveal something significant about the human condition, but they usually do so subtly; the point, or message, arises naturally from the characters and the action. Do you think that *A Raisin in the Sun* sends its message in a subtle way, or is it preachy and obvious? Explain.

LANGUAGE AND STYLE

Patterns of Speech: Realistic Dialogue

In his book *Hansberry's Drama,* Steven Carter notes that Hansberry makes her characters seem convincing by giving them diverse speech patterns.

1. Find examples of dialogue spoken by Beneatha, Mama, Walter, and Mrs. Johnson that characterize them and make them seem real.
2. Based on his speech, how would you characterize Karl Lindner?

CHOICES: Building Your Portfolio

Writer's Notebook

1. Collecting Ideas for a Problem-Solution Essay

WORK IN PROGRESS

Think of a social problem suggested by *A Raisin in the Sun.* To analyze the problem, answer as many of these questions as you can.

Description:
What is the problem?
How widespread is it?

Narration:
What is its history?
What are its causes? What are its effects?

Classification:
How is the problem similar to other problems?
How is the problem different from other problems?
What are the major parts of the problem?

Evaluation:
Why is the problem important?
What solutions have already been tried?
Which solution is most practical?
Which solution does the most good for the most people?
What are the advantages and disadvantages of your solution?

Keep your notes for possible use in the Writer's Workshop on page 895.

Critical Writing

2. Universal Significance

Hansberry has said this about playwriting:

> I believe that one of the most sound ideas in dramatic writing is that in order to create the universal, you must pay very great attention to the specific.
>
> —Lorraine Hansberry

Do you think that *A Raisin in the Sun* says something universal about human beings? Or do you think that the play focuses in such realistic detail—on a specific family living at a particular time on the South Side of Chicago—that it fails in its attempt to say something universal about human beings? Discuss these questions in a brief essay.

Critical Writing

3. Do Yourself Proud

In the characters of Beneatha and Asagai, Hansberry deals with the relationship of African Americans to their African heritage. How important do you think it is for a person to know about his or her cultural, ethnic, racial, or religious background? Is pride in one's heritage necessary for a person to have a positive sense of identity and self-esteem? Or should assimilation be the goal of Americans? In a brief essay, explore what you think about these questions, and give reasons to support your answers.

Performance

4. Bring It to Life

With a group, prepare a scene of the play for performance. You can act out the scene, or you can do a group reading. In a reading, the performers do not have to memorize the lines; they read from scripts. Lighting and costumes might be used in a reading to help create atmosphere. Whichever kind of presentation you decide on, you will have to appoint a director and prepare scripts for your actors.

Creative Writing

5. An Apt Epigraph

Write an original poem that could be used as a new epigraph—an opening quotation—for *A Raisin in the Sun,* as Lorraine Hansberry used Langston Hughes's poem "Harlem" on page 828. Your poem can address one of the age-old themes dealt with in the play: human beings' inhumanity to one another, the frustrations of being unable to achieve a dream, people's ability to summon courage to overcome adversity. For inspiration, read the student poem "The Skaters" on page 887.

Language and Style

Answers

1. Possible examples:
   Beneatha: "GRASS HUTS! See there . . . you are standing there in your splendid ignorance talking about people who were the first to smelt iron on the face of the earth!" (p. 854).
   Mama: "What you ain't never understood is that I ain't got nothing, don't own nothing, ain't never really wanted nothing that wasn't for you." (p. 864)
   Walter: "Bitter? Man, I'm a volcano. Bitter? Here I am a giant—surrounded by ants! Ants who can't even understand what it is the giant is talking about." (p. 856)
   Mrs. Johnson: "Oh, ain't we getting ready round here, though! Yessir! Lookathere! I'm telling you the Youngers is really getting ready to 'move on up a little higher!'—Bless God!" (p. 861)
2. The gentle evenness of his speech, his politeness, and his attempts to put the best face on everything suggest that Lindner does not like trouble. His pauses suggest nervousness; his clichés and platitudes suggest that he is satisfied with the status quo of his community and not eager for change.

Choices: Building Your Portfolio

1. **Writer's Notebook** Remind students to save their work. They may use it as prewriting for the Writer's Workshop on p. 895.

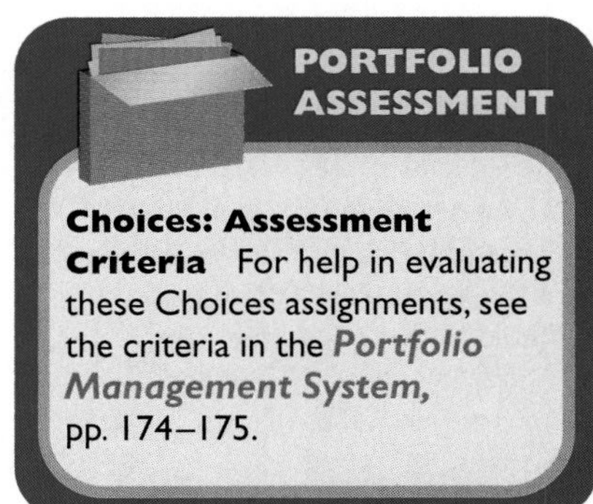

Choices: Assessment Criteria For help in evaluating these Choices assignments, see the criteria in the ***Portfolio Management System,*** pp. 174–175.

Extending the Text

8. **(Synthesis)** Possible responses: They will move and experience some trouble, but they will stay. Ruth will have her baby. Beneatha will go to Africa with Asagai and will go to medical school there. Walter will eventually start a business.
9. **(Evaluation)** Possible response: Things have gotten better in that more educational and employment opportunities are available to minorities today than when the play was written. Things have gotten worse in that racial tension continues. All parents and their adult children, regardless of race, still must figure out how to get along, as must husbands and wives; dreams and goals continue to drive us; any dream postponed remains a source of frustration and conflict.

Challenging the Text

10. **(Evaluation)** Possible responses: Subtle, for it focuses on the interaction between several believable characters; or preachy, because it keeps returning to one theme.

How to Own a Word

Mini-Lesson: Analogies

- One of the pitfalls in solving analogies is focusing solely on the word to which the correct answer is related. Offer this example:
  HOUSE : SHELTER : : sweater : ___
  A student focusing on *sweater* probably would answer with *wool* or *heavy* before selecting *warmth*, a far better response.
- Similarly, students should remember that a word can have several meanings. Offer this example:
  LOAF : LAZINESS : : gorge : _____
  A student thinking of *loaf* and *gorge* as nouns might be unable to find a relationship, whereas a student who considers the words as verbs suggesting kinds of behavior would be correct in choosing *gluttony* to complete the analogy.

Try It Out: Possible Answers

Classification
BAGEL : BREAD :: pork : [meat]
Performer and related object
BRICK : MASON :: pipe : [plumber]
Characteristic quality
FURRY : KITTEN :: scaly : [fish]
Cause and effect
BLEACH : WHITENESS :: dye : [dye color]
Part and whole
DROPLETS : SEA :: grains : [desert]
Synonym
ROUND : CIRCULAR :: strong : [muscular]
Antonym
PATRIOT : TRAITOR :: loyal : [unfaithful]
Function
DESK : STUDY :: bed : [sleep]
Degree
COLOSSAL : LARGE :: microscopic : [small]
Performer and related action
AUTHOR : WRITE :: Violinist : [play]

HOW TO OWN A WORD

Analogies: Thought-Provoking Comparisons

Langston Hughes's poem "Harlem" on page 828 suggests five things that a "dream deferred" might resemble: a raisin in the sun, drying up from the heat; a sore that is festering; a stinking piece of rotten meat; a syrupy sweet that is crusting over; a heavy load that is sagging. He ends by suggesting that none of these comparisons is adequate—a dream deferred is likely to explode.

A specific kind of comparison called an **analogy** often appears as a logic problem in standardized tests. This kind of analogy begins with a related pair of words or phrases. The goal is to create or identify a second pair that has a similar relationship.

Analogies appearing on tests are always written in a set form. Often, the last word is omitted, and you will have to supply it.

TREE : FLORA :: mammal : _______

The colon (:) stands for the phrase "is related to." The double colon (::) between the capitalized word pair and the first word of the incomplete pair can be read as "in the same way that." Thus, you'd read the above analogy like this: "Tree is related to flora in the same way that mammal is related to . . ."

Now you have to do two things: Identify the relationship between the first two elements as precisely as possible, and choose a word that will make the final pair have a parallel relationship. In this case, you could say TREE **is a type of** FLORA. **Is a type of** is the relationship. Now read the first word of the second pair, supplying the same relationship: "mammal **is a type of** _______." The only word that fits this blank adequately is "fauna," a term often paired with "flora."

TREE : FLORA :: mammal : fauna

The chart in the next column shows the relationships that are most frequently used in formal analogies. In reading an analogy, you can substitute the phrasing of the relationship—"is a type of," for example, or "is similar in meaning to"—for the colon.

Sometimes only the first pair of an analogy will be presented, and you will have to choose a parallel second pair. If you are doing this type of analogy exercise, keep the following guidelines in mind:

1. Look for a second pair with a clear, precise relationship.
2. Compare the relationship, not the words.
3. Knowing the precise meanings of words will help. Consult a dictionary frequently.
4. Don't be tricked by choices in which the order is reversed. For example, if the first pair has first the part and then the whole, the second pair must appear in the same order.

TYPES OF ANALOGY RELATIONSHIPS

TYPE	RELATIONSHIP	EXAMPLE
Classification	. . . is a type of . . .	TREE : FLORA
Performer and related object	. . . is the tool of . . .	BATON : CONDUCTOR
Characteristic quality	. . . is characteristic of . . .	SURLINESS : CURMUDGEON
Cause and effect	. . . is a cause or indication of . . .	SMOKE : FIRE
Part and whole	. . . is a part of . . .	STOMACH : DIGESTIVE TRACT
Synonym	. . . is similar in meaning to . . .	DRY : ARID
Antonym	. . . is opposite in meaning to . . .	KIND : CRUEL
Function	. . . is used to . . .	PEN : WRITE
Degree	. . . is a small or large . . .	CHUCKLE : LAUGH
Performer and related action	. . . does/performs . . .	CHEF : COOKS

Try It Out

Write an analogy exercise for each of the ten relationships defined above. Leave out the last word in each analogy, and trade papers with a partner. See if you can complete each other's exercises. Discuss the answers and any differences between the responses expected and those given.

PROGRAM MANAGER

Reinforcement To allow students practice and reinforcement of the vocabulary strategy introduced in this collection, see **Transparency 17.3** in the ***Audiovisual Resources Binder.***

STRATEGIES FOR INCLUSION

Logical-Mathematical/Visual Have students who demonstrate an ability to grasp the abstract relationships in analogies work together with students who have a keen visual awareness to analyze the sample analogies in the text and to prepare visual representations of the relationships. (They might start with Part and whole and Cause and effect, moving on to more complex types.) Encourage them to present their work to the class.

COOPERATIVE LEARNING

Peer Teaching Have interested students review and expand on the information as if they were presenting it in an SAT preparation class. Students will need to analyze examples of various relationships among the words in analogies; they also might come up with a list of test-taking tips. Have the class decide which presentation was most helpful and why.

READ ON

Lessons and Legacies

Would you part with a cherished family heirloom if you thought that by selling it you could make a better life for your family? This is the question the Charles family must answer in August Wilson's 1990 Pulitzer Prize–winning play *The Piano Lesson.* An antique piano becomes the catalyst for discovery of their African American heritage. *The Piano Lesson* is one of a series of award-winning plays by Wilson, each one exploring the lives of ordinary families who represent the roles African Americans have played in American history.

Walk a Mile in My Shoes

What was it like to be African American in the segregated South of the 1950s? To find out, the white reporter John Howard Griffin darkened his skin and traveled through the South. His exposé, *Black Like Me* (Houghton Mifflin) and its 1964 film adaptation (available on video) helped gain support for the civil rights movement. For a fine account of the civil rights movement itself, consider *Eyes on the Prize,* a six-part PBS series available on video.

A Long Drive Together

For twenty-five years in midcentury Atlanta, Hoke Coleburn, an African American, works as the chauffeur for Daisy Werthan, an elderly Jewish woman. Their growing friendship is traced in *Driving Miss Daisy* (Theatre Communications), a gentle depiction of prejudice and aging that won the playwright Alfred Uhry the 1988 Pulitzer Prize. The multiple Academy Award–winning film adaptation (Best Picture, Best Actress, Best Adapted Screenplay, 1989) is available on video.

After Pearl Harbor

During World War II, thousands of Japanese Americans, unjustly suspected of disloyalty, were uprooted from their West Coast homes and forced to live in internment camps like the one at Manzanar in California. Jeanne Wakatsuki Houston recalls her family's unjust incarceration in *Farewell to Manzanar* (Houghton Mifflin), an acclaimed memoir cowritten with her husband, the author James D. Houston.

More American Drama

Shy young Laura Wingfield finds it easier to talk to her collection of glass animals than to other people, but her mother still insists that Laura prepare for "gentleman callers." Their poignant story is recounted in Tennessee Williams's *The Glass Menagerie* (New Directions), one of the most beloved dramas of the American stage. A film adaptation is available on video. Also on video are two versions of *A Raisin in the Sun,* a 1961 film adaptation with an all-star cast and the 1989 American Playhouse production shown in this text's illustrations.

FOR FURTHER EXPLORATION

Short Stories
"Dry September" by William Faulkner
"Delta Autumn" by William Faulkner
"The Demonstrators" by Eudora Welty

Novel
The Reivers by William Faulkner

Drama
Death of a Salesman by Arthur Miller

Poetry
"The Fortress" by Anne Sexton
"The Eskimo National Anthem" by William Stafford
"The Chicago Defender Sends a Man to Little Rock" by Gwendolyn Brooks
"Life's Tragedy" by Paul Laurence Dunbar
"Justice Denied in Massachusetts" by Edna St. Vincent Millay

Nonfiction
The Fire Next Time by James Baldwin

Read On

Portfolio Assessment Options

The following projects can help you evaluate and assess your students' reading accomplishments outside class. Videotapes, audiotapes, or slides of completed projects may be included in students' portfolios.

- **Develop a Script** Have students work in pairs or groups to develop a script for a news broadcast that reports on a **character's** actions and motivations. Two of the students could function as anchors presenting the news to the class. As on a genuine news broadcast, a video or slides of characters discussed, including interviews, action shots, or setting, can form the background. Slides can be made from pictures in magazines and from other texts relevant to the events and setting of the book.
- **Design a Book Jacket** On the front cover, have students include the title, the author, and an appropriate graphic or drawing that represents the book's **theme.** On the spine, ask them to identify the publisher. On the back, have them write a biography of the author and a favorable review. Students can use any medium in their work: crayons, colored pencils, felt-tipped pens, or paints. Ask them to display their covers to the class, to explain their design choices, and to read the biography or review.
- **Research the Author's Life** Have students research the author's background, especially as it relates to the book. The students' findings could be used in a short report or in an oral presentation. They may explain what their research contributed to their understanding of the book, how and why it changed or reaffirmed their original understanding, what it revealed about the author's impetus for writing the book, and what it revealed about the **themes** of the author's other works.

A. Expansion
Sometimes words that once seemed perfectly acceptable become unpopular almost overnight. When the United States entered World War I in 1917, for example, German words and German place names suddenly seemed unpatriotic. *Sauerkraut* became *liberty cabbage*. *Brandenburg,* Texas, became *Old Glory. Thalheim,* California, was translated into *Valley Home*. But Germans form a large immigrant group in the United States, and many German names stayed the same. *Kindergarten* and *hamburger* remained, as did *Berlin,* New Hampshire, and *Bismarck,* North Dakota.

B. Language Note: Euphemism
Stress the symbolic nature of language as you discuss taboo words. As the passage points out, there is nothing inherently good or bad about any word. The relationship of words to things is an arbitrary one. Once a word becomes established, emotions attach to it. For example, there are people who avoid using the word *cancer.* Instead, they may say "the big C." Although these people realize that *cancer* could have been called *zingdot* or *renster* or *blivery,* in fact it was not, and they wish to avoid speaking of the thing, the affliction, that the word *cancer* represents. So they use a euphemism.

PROGRAM MANAGER

- **Assessment** See **The American Language, *Test Booklet,*** pp. 207–208.
- **Planning Instruction** See **Teaching Notes, *Teaching Resources B,*** p. 120, for objectives for this feature.

The American Language

Euphemisms

by Gary Q. Arpin

One day in 1837, Captain Frederick Marryat, a British naval officer visiting the United States, was escorting a young lady in Niagara Falls, New York. She slipped and grazed her shin, and Marryat asked, "Did you hurt your leg much?" What he said seemed to offend her.

"She turned from me," Marryat wrote, "evidently much shocked." Puzzled, he asked her what he had done wrong. The word *leg,* she told him, was never used in the presence of ladies. What word was used for "such articles," the captain asked her. "Her reply," he wrote, "was that the word *limb* was used."

Victorian Prudery

The young lady did not invent the delicacy that had caused a leg to become a limb. The year 1837 marked the beginning of the long reign of Queen Victoria in England. One of the meanings of the adjective formed from her name—*Victorian*—is "having excessively severe standards of respectability." The Victorian Age became known for its prudery, an attitude that was as common in some American social circles as it was in England.

During this period in America, the only polite word for women's stockings was *hose,* and undergarments were referred to as *unmentionables*. Even the word *woman* was considered vulgar; *female* and *lady* became its acceptable substitutes.

Victorians were so offended by the names of body parts that they developed a new vocabulary for meals. A chicken or turkey leg became a *drumstick* or a *first joint;* the *thigh* became the *second joint;* chicken or turkey breast came to be called simply *white meat.*

Euphemisms for Taboo Words

A **euphemism** is a word or phrase that is substituted for another word or phrase considered offensive or upsetting. The word *euphemism* comes from a Greek term meaning "to use words of good omen." People use euphemisms in an attempt to hide a reality they find unpleasant, or to politely communicate something that another person might find offensive.

People use euphemisms in an attempt to hide a reality they find unpleasant, or to politely communicate something that another person might find offensive.

Why do certain words become taboo or forbidden, while other words with the same meaning are acceptable? There is no simple answer, because the role that language plays in our lives is so complex. One thing is certain, though. [A] There is nothing inherent in any word that [B] makes it good or bad. Words become acceptable or offensive only because people give them those qualities.

Some words become taboo because they refer to experiences we find psychologically overwhelming. The more terrifying the experience, the more euphemisms we are likely to devise for it. For example, we have dozens of ways of talking about death without using that word. Some of our euphemisms for death are respectful, such as *departed, breathed her last, went to her final reward,* and *met his Maker.* Some are neutral, like *passed on, passed away,* and *deceased.* Others are humorous: *kicked the bucket, went West, bought the farm,* and *cashed in his chips* are flippant ways of reducing the horror of death.

Euphemisms and "Civilized Behavior"

For a number of reasons, Americans have been especially prone to using euphemisms. The early Puritans were concerned with

OPTIONS FOR TEACHING

STRATEGIES FOR INCLUSION

Linguistic Ask students to generate additional pairs of plain and fancy terms, such as the ones in Try It Out, and to look up their etymologies. They can record their findings in their Reader's Logs.

Auditory Set up an oral reading center in a remote corner of the classroom, and have a volunteer read the selection aloud to any auditory learners who would like to listen. Alternatively, provide individuals with cassette players, headphones, and the selection on tape. This setup will enable students to replay sections they do not grasp on the first hearing.

Learners Having Difficulty After students have read the selection, guide them through a review of the material by having them write a brief summary of each section. Prompt them by writing the key ideas on the chalkboard: euphemisms, euphemisms for taboo words, euphemisms for "civilized behavior," "language of anticipation," euphemisms and democracy, Latinate words and Anglo-Saxon words, and euphemism and distortion. Ask them to read the first section and to write a brief summary of it. Invite volunteers to share their summaries. Then, ask students to confirm the summaries, and discuss any questions they have about the section. Continue the process until all sections have been read, summarized, and discussed.

purifying language as well as religious practice. While they did not completely eradicate profanity, they certainly created an atmosphere hostile to vulgar speech. Though Americans who later moved westward were not averse to using profanity, it was in the pioneer communities that linguistic delicacy often was most prevalent. "The essentially English word *bull,*" William Bartlett wrote, "is refined beyond the mountains . . . into *cow-creature, male-cow, and even gentleman-cow*!"

"The Language of Anticipation"

Another aspect of the need to provide a kind of instant civilization through gentility in language is what the historian Daniel Boorstin has called "the language of anticipation." This form of "good speaking" described things as they were to be in the future, rather than as they actually were at the time. Wealthy City, Kansas, which never fulfilled the promise of its name and dwindled into extinction, is an example of this kind of positive thinking. This linguistic optimism was a common phenomenon in a country where someone confronting a muddy, stump-filled plain might imagine a prosperous farm in its place. As Boorstin points out, even the country's name, "United States of America," which appears in the Constitution, was anticipatory. "It expressed hope that the new nation be *united,* that the components really be *states,* and that somehow they could be identified with the whole of *America.*" (*State,* until that time, referred only to sovereign nations.)

C

Examples of this kind of anticipatory euphemism abound in American history. Americans needed to talk "big." For instance, *city* was preferred over the more modest (if more accurate) *town* or *village.* Many cities boasted an *opera house,* even if it usually was only a tiny auditorium that presented troupes of traveling jugglers. "The elegant *hotel,*" Boorstin writes, "was widely applied to ramshackle, flea-bitten inns and taverns. Americans thought they were not exaggerating but only anticipating—describing things which had not quite yet 'gone through the formality of taking place.'"

D

Euphemisms and Democracy

A love of inflated descriptive terms has a long history in America. Relentlessly democratic, Americans declared every man a "gentleman," while the British restricted the term to men of a particular social standing. Proud of being a nation with no inherited titles, Americans almost immediately began to generate countless acquired titles.

E

A British traveler in New York in 1744 remarked on the great many colonels he encountered. "It is a common saying here," he wrote, "that a man has no right to that dignity unless he has killed a rattlesnake." Governors of states were later empowered to bestow the title (along with *captain* and *major*) on virtually anyone they wished, and many did so with great zeal, notably in Kentucky.

Americans applied a similar principle to occupations. Any occupation that was in danger of falling below a certain level of acceptability was usually yanked up by its linguistic bootstraps. This relentless linguistic upgrading of occupational titles is especially popular today. At times, this upgrading is very subtle; at other times, very obvious.

What is the difference, for example, between a *teacher* and an *educator?* Most people would agree that *educator* has a slightly more prestigious ring to it. This can be accounted for by taking a look at where English words come from.

English is composed primarily of Anglo-Saxon and Latin-based words. Historically, the Anglo-Saxon words have been the property of the common people, while the Latinate words have filtered down from the upper classes. This was especially the case following the Norman conquest of England in 1066. After that invasion, French (which is derived ultimately from Latin) was the official language of England for generations. Most people in England, however, continued to speak their own Anglo-Saxon language. During this bilingual period, the language was further enriched with synonyms. In most cases, the French word became the genteel word, while the Anglo-Saxon word became the common word. This explains the difference between the Latin *educare* (to educate) and the Anglo-Saxon word *taecan* (to teach).

C. Language Note: Names and Their Significance

Ask students to look at a map of their state (or of the United States) and to find at least five place names that they consider to be examples of anticipatory naming. For example, Columbia Cross Roads, a tiny community in northern Pennsylvania, did not become the hub of the nation that its name suggests. The gold-mining community in the foothills of the Sierras in California changed its name from Hangtown to Placerville. Explain that a *placer* is a deposit of sand or gravel in the bed of a stream that contains particles of gold or other valuable minerals. The connotation of *Placerville* is much more positive than that of *Hangtown,* so named, legend suggests, for the executions that occurred there.

D. Exploring the Culture

Point out to students that builders and developers often try to choose impressive names for their projects. Miller's Swamp becomes Fairview Acres. Apartment buildings take names such as Royal Palm Court and Barchester Arms. Ordinary streets are elevated to boulevards or parkways. What are some places in your community whose names are euphemistic in that they are pleasant or impressive designations for fairly ordinary sites? Where, for example, do your "sanitation workers" take your "refuse"?

E. Exploring the Culture

What are some of the inherited titles in Great Britain? [King, queen, prince, princess, duke, duchess, marquess, earl, viscount, viscountess, baron, baroness.]

INTEGRATING THE LANGUAGE ARTS

Strategic Reading Preview the material with students by using the following steps:

- Define the term *euphemism* for students. [A word that is substituted for one considered upsetting.] Offer them an example. Then, ask students to share euphemisms they have heard or used.
- Ask students to read the headings, review the quotations, and look at the illustrations. Have them predict what the selection will be about.
- Have students generate questions from the headings, quotations, and illustrations. Tell them to refer to these questions as they read to see whether the questions have been answered, whether different questions should be generated as they read, or whether these questions helped them pay attention to their reading.

A. Literary Element: Diction

What is a shorter, easier word for each of the following Latinate words? Check the dictionary to see if the shorter word is Old English (OE). Some possible answers are shown.

acrimonious ["bitter"—OE]
homicide ["murder"—OE]
iniquitous ["evil"—OE]
velocity ["speed"—OE]
veracity ["truth"—OE]

Which group of words, Latinate or Old English, would be used in the context of the legal, academic, or scientific communities?

Try It Out: Answers

1. Answers will vary. Some examples include "disposal service" for "garbage collection"; "funeral director" for "undertaker;" "administrative assistant" for "secretary."
2. Plain words: eat, spit, love, cheap, win, cow, pig, work, calf, father—all classified as AS.
   Fancy words: dine, expectorate, cherish, inexpensive, achieve, beef, pork, career, veal, parent—classified as L except for *achieve* (OF).
   The Latin words are "fancy" words, whereas the "plain" words are Anglo-Saxon. The Latin words are also usually longer than the Anglo-Saxon words. Most of the Anglo-Saxon words have one syllable while several of the Latinate words have two or more syllables.
3. More direct words or phrases are (a) toilet or bathroom, (b) died, (c) poor, (d) older people, (e) janitor, (f) garbage collectors, (g) strike, (h) pregnant, and (i) graveyards.

A Latinate words usually have more syllables than Anglo-Saxon words. Hence, a greater number of syllables often indicates a slide up the scale of acceptability. A *profession* (Latinate) somehow seems more important than a *job* (Anglo-Saxon). American job titles (or "career designations") have undergone frequent upgradings as a result of this tendency toward linguistic respectability. Thus, *mortician* (Latinate) was coined in the 1890s as a more dignified term than *undertaker* (Anglo-Saxon) for a person who manages a funeral home.

Euphemism and Distortion

Euphemisms can demonstrate sensitivity to the feelings of others. But euphemisms can also obscure meaning. Language can provide a veil to hide behind.

A boss would rather "excess" an employee than "fire" her, not because it makes the employee feel any better but because it makes the boss feel better. A government does not like to think of itself as "invading" another country, for example. It will make an *incursion,* or *liberate* the country instead. It is wrong to be the aggressor in a war, and *invasion* is a very aggressive word.

Many people have attacked the bureaucratic tendency to use long Latinate words where a short Anglo-Saxon word would serve just as well. The state and federal governments are particularly creative in generating euphemisms: prison guards have become "correctional officers," budget deficits are "negative growth," and taxes are sometimes called "revenue enhancement." This tendency has also spilled over to the general public in the language of advertising. Secondhand clothes are now sold as "vintage clothing," and used cars are called "previously owned" or "pre-driven." Even in this so-called modern age, softening blunt or distasteful names for things sometimes seems as prevalent now as in those prudish Victorian times.

Try It Out

1. With another student, look through the local Yellow Pages or another business directory. Find at least three examples of euphemistic titles for occupations or businesses. Write the titles on a sheet of paper, and next to each write the ordinary word it is replacing. (For example, "resale boutique" is a euphemism that sometimes replaces "thrift shop.")
2. Make two columns on a sheet of paper. Write the column titles *Plain* and *Fancy* at the top of the page. Decide which word in each of the following pairs belongs in each column. Then find each word in a dictionary. Write *L* next to the word if it is derived from Latin. Write *OE* if it is derived from Old English—that is, if it has Anglo-Saxon roots. What patterns do you notice?
   eat / dine
   spit / expectorate
   love / cherish
   cheap / inexpensive
   achieve / win
   beef / cow
   pig / pork
   work / career
   veal / calf
   father / parent
3. The following words are commonly used euphemisms. See if you can come up with a word or phrase that is a more direct way of saying the same thing.
   a. restroom
   b. passed on
   c. underprivileged
   d. senior citizens
   e. custodian
   f. sanitation engineers
   g. work stoppage
   h. expecting
   i. resting places

OPTIONS FOR TEACHING

ASSESSMENT TOOLS

Check Test: True-False

1. During the Victorian period, the word *woman* was considered vulgar. [True]
2. The word *euphemism* comes from Anglo-Saxon terms meaning "good saying." [False]
3. In pioneer communities, the language spoken was often delicate. [True]
4. The United States has a long tradition of using euphemisms. [True]
5. French was the official language of England for generations. [True]

BUILDING YOUR PORTFOLIO

Writer's Workshop

PERSUASIVE WRITING

Problem-Solution Essay

If you've ever tried to work out a problem or dilemma by writing about it in a diary, journal, or letter, you know how the simple act of writing can help you think through problems and possible solutions. When you write a **problem-solution essay,** you thoroughly explore a problem and its possible solutions in a formal, methodical way. In a problem-solution essay, you identify and describe a problem and then propose one or more solutions to that problem.

Technology HELP

See Writer's Workshop 2 CD-ROM. *Assignment: Controversial Issue.*

Assignment
Describe a problem, and then propose and defend the solution or solutions you believe are best.

Aim
To explore; to explain; to persuade.

Audience
People who are affected by the problem; people who can carry out your suggested solution; your teacher and classmates.

Prewriting

1. Looking for problems. The problems you think about in a given day may range from how to save enough money for a new bicycle to how to implement world peace. The problem of saving money is probably going to be too personal and specific to be of interest to a general audience. The problem of world peace is, on the other hand, far too broad for an essay. In selecting a topic for a problem-solution essay, think of a problem that is interesting to other people and manageable in a short paper.

You might already have an idea for a problem to explore if you completed the Writer's Notebook assignment on page 889. If you are starting from scratch, you might begin by thinking of problems that affect the everyday life of yourself, your family, and your friends. Think about problems you have observed firsthand in your school or community. Are students having a problem getting access to computers? Does your community need to do more to respond to the needs of people with disabilities by improving wheelchair access and increasing handicapped parking? Are families failing to participate fully in your local recycling program? Quickwrite a list of problems you would like to write about. Even if you are more interested in a national or global problem, such as health care or unemployment, you might want to focus on how that problem affects your community.

WORK IN PROGRESS

In selecting a problem to write about, consider these questions:

- Which problem do I care most about solving?
- Which problem do I most want to learn about?
- Which problem could I, or others, act on?

Portfolio Assessment

- **Generating Ideas** To help students in prewriting, use the heuristic in the *Portfolio Management System,* p. 176.
- **Assessment Rubric** For a rubric that can be used to assess students' progress in writing, see the *Portfolio Management System,* p 178.

Quick Planning Guide

WW **Problem-Solution Essay**

Motivation

Bring copies of recent local newspapers to class, and ask each student to read at least one editorial that deals with a local problem. After students have read the editorials, ask volunteers each to briefly outline the problems addressed and the solutions proposed in one of the editorials. Then, ask students whether they found the editorials convincing. Have them identify at least one reason they were or were not convinced. After several volunteers have made comments, point out that they encounter problem-solution writing almost every time they read an editorial. Tell students that the Writer's Workshop will help them fine-tune their own skills of identifying problems and stating solutions. They will become better readers of persuasive writing by learning to recognize good problem-solution writing.

Teaching the Lesson

Remind students that problems often are more complex than they first appear and that people often have objections to even the simplest solutions.

This lesson includes instructions for each stage of the writing process. You may guide students by modeling each stage with your own writing.

Prewriting

Encourage students to choose problems they have observed firsthand. Students should also consider whether information on the problem can be readily obtained. The school environment is a good place to begin looking because students are probably most familiar with school problems, and they can discuss the problems and solutions with other students and with school personnel. The local community is also a good place to identify problems.

2. **Defining the problem.** Once you've chosen a problem to write about, you need to define it: You can't solve a problem that you don't understand. To define the problem you want to write about, ask yourself these questions:

   - Why is it a problem?
   - What causes this problem?
   - What or whom does the problem affect?
   - How does it affect them?

   If you don't have the answers to all these questions, you'll want to do some research, which will probably involve reading, interviewing, viewing, or listening. For example, if you are interested in the effectiveness of neighborhood crime-prevention efforts in your community, you might want to interview local police officers.

3. **Brainstorming solutions.** Once you have thoroughly investigated your problem, you can move on to finding some answers. Remember, don't censor yourself. Often, viable solutions come from seemingly offbeat or improbable ideas.

   One way to thoroughly explore multiple solutions is to make a chart in which you list the advantages and disadvantages of each solution. Don't forget to include solutions that have already been tried, perhaps in other schools or communities, and to note how effective these solutions have been. The chart below explores the topic of community recycling.

Model

Problem: *Families in the community do not recycle cans, glass, and newspapers.*

Possible Solutions	Advantages	Disadvantages
Give an award to one family each week, on the basis of that family's recycling	*Encourages family participation; enhances public awareness of problem*	*Cost of awards; people who don't win awards promptly may lose interest*
Provide recycling containers and pickup service	*Makes participation easier; can use existing volunteer groups*	*Expense of containers and pickup service; requires long-term supervision and management*
Fine people who do not recycle	*Provides incentive to recycle; only those who don't cooperate need pay money*	*Requires regulatory staff; may foster negative feelings about recycling.*

Review your chart, and ask these questions to help you evaluate all possible solutions and select the best one:

- What are possible objections to these solutions?
- What are the counterarguments to these objections?
- Which solutions seem better than others?
- Is one solution more practical than the others?
- Does one solution do the most good for the most people?

4. **Outlining.** Once you have decided on a solution, pull all the information you've gathered together, and plan your essay. Outline the following items:

OPTIONS FOR TEACHING

STRATEGIES FOR INCLUSION

Auditory Some students might feel comfortable composing their essays orally. Suggest that they imagine themselves giving a speech to the audience they select for the essay. Have them make a brief outline of the ideas they wish to cover in the order in which they want to cover them. Then, have each deliver the speech to an audience of classmates. Students can make audiotapes or videotapes of themselves delivering their speeches, and they can later use these tapes to transcribe their speeches as their essays.

Kinesthetic Some of the solutions that students recommend might lend themselves to model-building. For example, if a student tackles the problem of how to ease the parking situation at school, it might be possible to illustrate the solution by creating a model of how the parking lot could be laid out differently. Some students might wish to think through their solutions by building models and then to describe the solutions, by describing their models, in writing.

Visual After students have completed a list of ideas for their essays, encourage them to highlight related ideas with the same color. When they have developed an outline for the essay, have them color-code the outline to match the colors on the list.

- the problem
- your proposed solution
- the steps necessary to implement your solution
- evidence to support your solution, including reasons, facts, examples, and statistics (If you need more support, now is the time to gather it.)
- possible objections to your solution
- other possible solutions and the reasons you rejected them

5. **Targeting your audience.** When you write a problem-solution essay, it's crucial to know who your audience is: Remember, you are trying to convince people that (1) your problem is serious and (2) your proposed solution is the best one. To convince your readers, you have to know what point of view and what concerns they bring to your essay.

   Your audience may be your teacher and your classmates, or it may be people who are affected by your problem. You may decide that individuals with the power or authority to solve the problem are your target audience. Your target audience could even be people who are responsible for causing the problem.

   After you decide who your audience is, ask these questions: Are your target readers aware that there is a problem? If so, what do they already know about it? In other words, what background information do you need to provide? Throughout the writing process, be aware of your audience's concerns and viewpoint. Your approach, tone, and even your word choice should be adapted to these target readers.

Drafting

A problem-solution essay can take many different forms. One effective pattern is as follows:

1. **Introducing the problem.** Think about how you can best engage your readers' interest. If you're confident that your readers share your interest in the problem, you might simply introduce it directly, together with a statement of its importance. Or, you might start with an anecdote or attention-getting fact. For example, in an essay about recycling, you might open with this detail: "Every day, thousands of pounds of newspapers, glass jars, and aluminum cans are needlessly thrown into our town dump."
2. **Stating the problem.** State the problem clearly. In a recycling essay, you might write, "Most of the families in our community are simply not recycling their newspapers, glass jars, and cans." In describing the problem, you might want to use anecdotes or testimonies from interviews to engage the readers' interest. You might also want to use **connotative language**—words and phrases that create a specific emotional response.
3. **More on the problem.** If you think your readers might be skeptical about the seriousness of the problem, you'll need to convince them that your problem is serious and worth their attention. To do this, use pertinent evidence, facts, statistics, and examples you gathered in the prewriting stage. In the recycling essay, for example, you might tell about negative consequences if a solution is not found: how much land will be used for landfill

Try It Out

You can use many kinds of graphic organizers to explore solutions to problems. Together with one or more classmates, choose a problem from the Quickwrite list you made while prewriting, and use a cluster diagram, map, double-entry journal, or other graphic organizer to list possible solutions. On your graph, also answer the questions listed below the model chart on page 896.

Drafting

- Some students like to see models of the kinds of writing they are asked to do, and you can provide models of problem-solution essays in several ways. Write one yourself for students to study. Let students read good examples of this kind of essay from other classes. Direct students to editorials and letters to the editor in newspapers and magazines. Not all editorials and letters to the editor are problem-solution essays, nor are all equally well written. However, you can ask students to bring in examples they find, and you can help them evaluate these examples.
- Remind students that opening paragraphs are important in catching the reader's attention. If students have difficulty developing good opening paragraphs at the start of the drafting phase, suggest they postpone writing the introductory paragraph until they have written the rest of the essay.

Try It Out

Responses will vary. The following guidelines may help to evaluate students' responses.

1. The graphic organizer should include all the ideas students generate.
2. The graphic organizer should be self-explanatory.
3. The graphic organizer should be logical and appropriate for the ideas students generate.
4. The graphic organizer should illustrate relationships among ideas. The answers to the questions should be complete, adequately addressing all aspects of the questions.

INTEGRATING THE LANGUAGE ARTS

Strategic Reading As students read the Writer's Workshop, encourage them to take notes on the main ideas by using a chart like the following. They can supplement the main ideas in the text with class notes. Have them organize the chart according to the stages of the writing process.

Stages	Main Ideas	Class Notes
[Prewriting]	[Make sure topic is not too personal or too broad.]	[Test the idea on another student.]

Speaking and Listening As students define the problem they are going to work on, it might be useful for them to conduct interviews with school or public officials or with other people who can provide information about the problem or reactions to the students' proposed solutions. Ask each to prepare an interview protocol before the interview. The protocol should contain planned questions and a place to write answers. Have each student take notes on one protocol sheet for each person interviewed. Ask students to practice by interviewing one another. Let them videotape their practice sessions and then review their tapes to see where the interview went well and to spot places where they can improve. *You may want to obtain permission from parents or guardians and from the parties students will contact before they begin work on this activity.* ☞

Evaluating and Revising

- Students should use the questions in the Evaluation Criteria and in Peer review.
- Ask students to pay particular attention to their use of transitional expressions. They can turn to the Language Workshop on p. 900 for guidance.

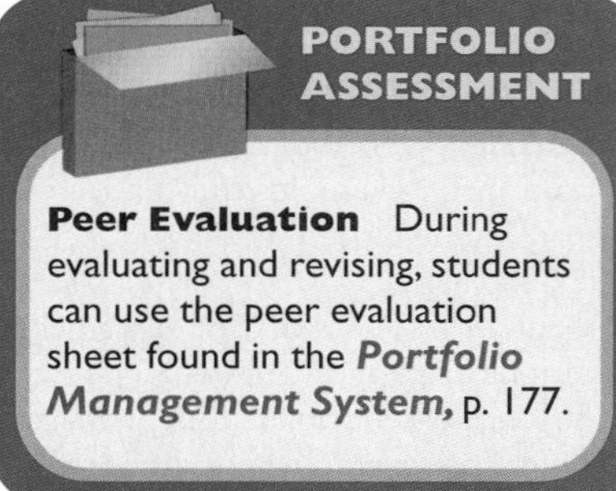

PORTFOLIO ASSESSMENT

Peer Evaluation During evaluating and revising, students can use the peer evaluation sheet found in the ***Portfolio Management System,*** p. 177.

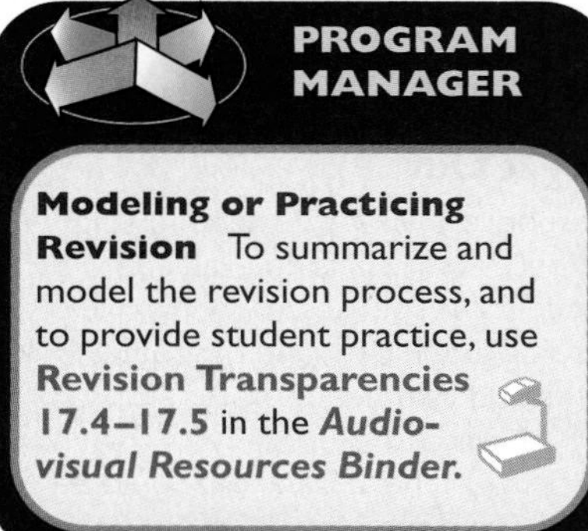

PROGRAM MANAGER

Modeling or Practicing Revision To summarize and model the revision process, and to provide student practice, use **Revision Transparencies 17.4–17.5** in the ***Audio-visual Resources Binder.***

Reteaching

If students have difficulty arriving at a topic that is appropriate for the assignment, encourage them to brainstorm with other students to generate a list of possible problems. Then, have them classify the problems on their list, using a chart like the following. After students have filled out the chart, encourage them to consider as topics for their papers the problems listed in the second and third columns of the chart. They can then use a chart like the model in Brainstorming Solutions on p. 896 to generate further ideas.

Personal	School	Local	National	International

Strategies for Elaboration

When you evaluate something, you measure it against certain standards. The evidence you plan to use in your problem-solution essay should be evaluated based on these standards, or **criteria:**

1. Is the evidence **trustworthy**? That is, is it from a reliable source with a reputation for integrity or from an acknowledged expert?
2. Is the evidence **accurate**? Question the information you've gathered. If it seems suspect, check it against other sources. Also, make sure you copy facts, statistics, and other data correctly.
3. Is the evidence **useful**? That is, is it logically connected to your problem or your solution? Will it make your essay more persuasive?

Communications Handbook HELP

Taking notes and documenting sources: pages 1210–1213.

in coming years if recycling does not increase, information on the biodegrading rates of certain materials, and anticipated shortages of papers and metals. You might also discuss the unnecessary destruction of forests or the variety of uses to which recycled materials can now be put.

Hold your readers' interest by providing vivid details. You might write, "I went to the town dump and was sickened by the waste that I saw. The mound of moldy garbage was full of newspapers, cans, and glass—all items that could have been recycled. Meanwhile, this week the newspaper included an article reporting that more land will soon be needed for garbage dumping if these wasteful habits persist."

4. **Discussing the solutions.** Use your chart as a guide to briefly touch on two or three solutions that have been suggested or tried. You might choose the solutions you think your audience is inclined to favor. Discuss the disadvantages of these solutions in a balanced, fair way, being as thorough and persuasive as you can.

   Devote about a paragraph to describing your solution and how it would be implemented. Be sure to outline the steps involved in implementing your solution. Remember that one purpose of your essay is to persuade your reader that, having considered all factors, you have chosen the best solution. Think of arguments you might make for your solution—for example, on the basis of its practicality, feasibility, low cost, easy implementation, or other benefits.
5. **Producing the evidence.** Use the most persuasive reasoning and information you've collected to show your readers that your solution is the best. Bolster your argument, if possible, with evidence from some other community or school that has tried this solution. You may even be able to locate statistics that back up your claim that this is an effective solution.

   Remember that you will want to credit your sources with full documentation. In your essay, you'll credit sources in two places—in parenthetical citations and in the list of Works Cited at the end of your essay. (For more information on documenting sources, see page 518.)
6. **Answering possible objections.** In presenting your solution, you will have to respond to the logical arguments your readers may raise against it. What concerns and objections to your solution might your audience raise? Your paper will be most persuasive if you directly address all possible disadvantages to your solution that you can think of. Explain why you consider these disadvantages negligible compared to the advantages.
7. **Tending to tone.** You'll want the tone of your problem-solution essay to be objective, in order to convince your readers that your reasoning is sound. On the other hand, you want to convey to your readers that your paper reflects a committed, personal exploration of the problem you present. If your teacher approves, consider using the first-person pronoun *I* to convey this tone.
8. **In conclusion.** Conclude by again stating your solution and briefly restating its advantages. You might conclude your essay with your personal conviction that this solution should be implemented, or end with a clear call to action—advice about what readers themselves can do.

OPTIONS FOR TEACHING

COOPERATIVE LEARNING

Presenting Solutions Have students work in groups of four to test their solutions. Have one student in the group present a problem and its potential solutions. Ask the other group members to tell the student whether each solution will work and why it will or will not succeed. Then, have the group members suggest other possible solutions and counterarguments for each solution presented. Have each student take a turn.

CLASSROOM MANAGEMENT

Portfolio Management Students' portfolios may become quite large, especially if you have them include artwork and audio- and videotapes. One way to store portfolios is to have each student use a box, such as a standard gift box, to hold items. Students can place their names on a side edge. Store the boxes on a bookshelf. Develop a contents form for students to place inside the boxes. On the form, they may write each item they include in their portfolios.

Evaluating and Revising

1. **Peer review.** After you have a rough draft, ask one or more classmates who are interested in the problem to read your essay. Then ask them the following questions.
   - Did I help you to understand the problem, and did I convince you that it is a significant one? If not, how can I persuade you to care about this problem as I do?
   - Do you think I clearly and fully described my proposed solution? Did I provide sound reasons for adopting my solution? If not, what reasons should I add?
   - Which solution is the most convincing? the least convincing? Should any proposed solutions be omitted?
   - Do you feel I have overlooked a potential solution? If so, how can I address this other solution while still showing why I think my solution is preferable?
   - Is my tone and approach appropriate for the subject?
   - What is the strongest aspect of my essay? What parts of the essay need more work?
2. **Self-evaluation.** Revise your essay according to the feedback that you find most helpful, then do your own critique using the same list of questions. Eliminate any unnecessary words in your essay so that your arguments are forceful and easy to grasp.

Proofreading

Since you are trying to persuade people that your solution is sound and should be enacted, you'll want to do everything you can to have your audience take you seriously. Errors in grammar and punctuation can erode your credibility, so be sure to proofread your essay. If possible, have a friend proofread it, too.

Publishing

Your class could publish these essays in a class book with a title such as "Building a Better World," "Creative Problem Solving," or some other title you invent. You might also choose to send your essay to the school or local paper, to be published as an expanded letter to the editor or as a "guest editorial." You might send your suggestion to a local agency, or to your student council or city council, if you think they might be interested.

Reflecting on Your Writing

In a democracy, it is important for citizens to feel that their ideas can help improve people's quality of life. In this assignment, you pondered problems in the "real world." Have you enjoyed this process? Did you find that you came up with more solutions than you thought you would? Did the problems discourage you, or did you feel hopeful about finding workable solutions? Do you feel that writing about problems can be a significant part of inventing solutions? Do you think sharing your essay will result in your solution being enacted? Write a reflection for your portfolio.

Revision STRATEGIES

Re-read your essay from the viewpoint of your readers. Ask yourself: Have I presented the problem in a compelling way? How strong a case have I made for my solution? Have I responded to all likely objections? Have I addressed alternative solutions?

Language Handbook HELP

Revising to reduce wordiness: page 1237.

Evaluation Criteria

A good problem-solution essay

1. *has a catchy opening that elicits interest in the topic*
2. *clearly states the problem and its importance*
3. *addresses solutions other than your own, and explains their disadvantages*
4. *clearly explains your solution, and supports it with evidence*
5. *addresses possible objections to your proposed solution*
6. *takes into account the reader's point of view*
7. *has an objective, authoritative tone that reflects your commitment to your solution*
8. *leaves the reader feeling convinced of the soundness of the solution*

Closure

When all the essays have been completed, ask students to write a brief outline of the steps they followed in writing their papers. Then, ask them to compare the steps they followed with the steps outlined in the Writer's Workshop. Have them write brief reasons they added or deleted steps, and have volunteers share their reasons with the class.

Enrichment

History Connection

Bring to class transcripts of famous persuasive speeches from American history. Ask students to evaluate the speeches, using the criteria in the Assessment Tools on p. T899. Ask students to write down their ratings and comments for each speech. Then, have students discuss their ratings. An American history teacher in your school might be able to suggest speeches that would be useful for this activity, and you might explore making this activity a collaborative effort with teachers of American history.

Portfolio

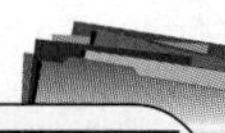

Reflecting on Your Writing

- Help students reflect on their writing by suggesting they base their reflections on the questions in the text. Ask them to write a paragraph or two about the experience of writing the essay, or have them write answers to the questions.
- Ask them to attach their reflections to their essays when they file the essays in their portfolios.

CROSSING THE CURRICULUM

Art Ask students to transform the ideas in their essays into words and images and to place them on a poster or in a full-page advertisement for a newspaper. If students have access to a desktop publishing program on a computer, encourage them to use it to design and create their posters or ads. If not, encourage them to illustrate their posters or ads with drawings, paintings, calligraphy, and other decorative features that catch a reader's eye and support points made in their essays.

ASSESSMENT TOOLS

Self-Assessment Have students rate their papers on each item according to the following scale.

1=Strong 2=Moderate 3=Weak

______ Has a catchy opening that elicits interest in the topic.
______ Clearly states the problem and its importance.
______ Addresses the disadvantages of other solutions.
______ Clearly explains the solution and supports it with evidence.
______ Addresses possible objections to the proposed solution.
______ Takes into account the reader's point of view.
______ Has an objective, authoritative tone.
______ Convinces reader that the solution is sound.

Language Workshop

Connecting To Students' Writing

To help students identify and use transitional words, have students highlight the transitions on their revised problem-solution essays. Instruct students to classify those transitions that fit under the categories covered in the language workshop: comparing ideas, contrasting ideas, showing cause and effect, showing time, showing place, and showing importance. Ask students each to work with a partner to improve transitions or to add transitions where needed in their essays.

Try It Out: Answers

1. Possible answer: As *A Raisin in the Sun* opens, Mama is about to receive ten thousand dollars. Consequently, her children plan how they can use this money.
2. Mama anticipates how the family will find happiness in their new home. However, the Clybourne Park Improvement Association plans to stop the family from moving.

PROGRAM MANAGER

- **Extra Practice and Guided Instruction** For more instruction and practice in using transitional expressions, see **Language Workshop** in ***Teaching Resources B,*** pp. 130–131.
- **Extra Practice or Guided Instruction** See ***Language Workshop:* Transitional expressions** for more practice or guided instruction in using transitions.

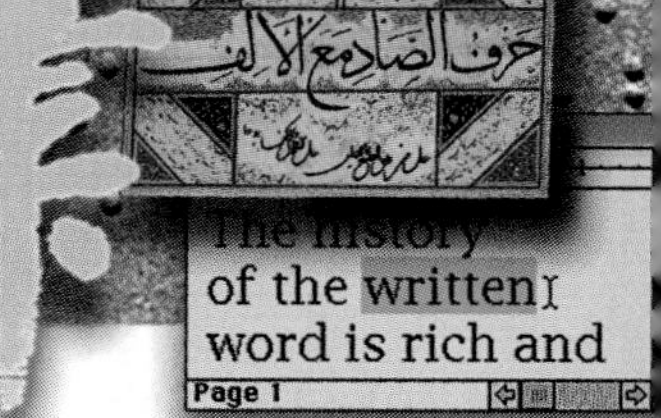

Technology HELP

See Language Workshop CD-ROM. *Key word entry: transitional expressions.*

Language Handbook HELP

Commas: pages 1243–1244.

Try It Out

Add transitional words or phrases to the following sentences in order to link the ideas they express.

1. As *A Raisin in the Sun* opens, Mama is about to receive ten thousand dollars. Her children plan how they can use this money.
2. Mama anticipates how the family will find happiness in their new home. The Clybourne Park Improvement Association plans to stop the family from moving.

Fitting It All Together: Using Transitional Expressions

Transitional expressions are words or phrases that provide a transition between ideas, making writing more coherent. Often these expressions show chronological or spatial relationships. They may also show relationships of cause and effect, definition, or contrast.

EXAMPLE *A Raisin in the Sun* was an instant success when it opened in 1959. *As a result,* an African American theater movement began. (*As a result* indicates a cause-and-effect relationship.)

TRANSITIONAL WORDS AND PHRASES		
Comparing Ideas / Classification and Definition		
also	another	similarly
and	moreover	too
Contrasting Ideas / Classification and Definition		
although	in spite of	on the other hand
but	instead	still
however	nevertheless	yet
Showing Cause and Effect / Narration		
as a result	consequently	so that
because	since	therefore
Showing Time / Narration		
after	eventually	next
at last	finally	then
at once	first	thereafter
before	meanwhile	when
Showing Place / Description		
above	down	next
across	here	over
around	in	there
before	inside	to
beyond	into	under
Showing Importance / Evaluation		
first	mainly	then
last	more important	to begin with

Writer's Workshop Follow-Up: Revising

Re-read the problem-solution essay you wrote for the Writer's Workshop on page 895. If some of your ideas seem disconnected, or if cause-effect and other relationships are unclear, revise your essay by adding transitions for coherence.

✔ QUICK CHECK: Transitional Expressions

Fill in the blanks with appropriate transitional expressions. [Possible answers in brackets.]

[1] Mama disapproves of Walter's owning a liquor store; ____, he makes arrangements to get a liquor license. [nevertheless]

[2] _____ she becomes pregnant, Ruth wonders how the family will manage. [After]

[3] Asagai speaks eloquently to Beneatha of Africa; _____ Beneatha may find her identity. [there]

[4] Ruth is uneasy about Walter's potential business deal; ____, she encourages Mama to support Walter's plans. [however]

[5] Walter loses the insurance money; ____, he calls Lindner with the intent of accepting the buyout offer. [as a result]

CREATIVE PROBLEM SOLVING

LEARNING FOR LIFE

The Play's the Thing

Problem

Evaluating a drama means more than just saying "I liked that play" or "It stinks." Sometimes we may need to evaluate a play's suitability for a specific purpose, or its appropriateness for a certain audience, setting, or physical location. A play that addresses adult themes would be suitable for a professional theater but inappropriate in a middle school. One that calls for elaborate costumes, special effects, and a huge stage belongs on Broadway—not in a small community playhouse. How can we evaluate a play's suitability for a particular situation, purpose, and audience?

Project

Collect and evaluate information on a number of plays in order to recommend one to be performed next year by your school.

Preparation

1. Form a team of evaluators.
2. In your school or community library, research eight to ten plays to evaluate. You can consult with a librarian, your English teacher, or the school drama teacher for guidance in getting your research under way. Start with plays that are commonly taught and/or performed in high schools.
3. Decide the role each team member will play in evaluating the eight to ten plays.
4. Come to a consensus on the criteria you will use to evaluate the plays you're researching. Some criteria you might use are
   - general quality and value
   - number and types of roles
   - staging requirements
   - subject matter and language suitability for high school students

   Include any other criteria you think are important in making your recommendation.
5. Prepare an evaluation form that each team member will fill out for each play that is being considered. Your form should list the various criteria your team agreed upon.

Procedure

1. Read the plays and any critical literature you can find about them. Fill out your evaluation forms.
2. As a group, convene to discuss the plays and your evaluations.
3. Reach consensus on one play you will recommend as being suitable for your school to perform next year.

Presentation

Present your drama evaluations and recommendations in one of the following formats (or another your teacher approves):

1. **Letter to the Drama Teacher**
   Working as a group, compose a detailed, persuasive letter to a drama or English teacher in your school, describing your project and the evaluation process, listing the plays you examined, and justifying your recommendation.
2. **Informational Display**
   As a group, create an informational display about the plays and your evaluation of them. Include excerpts from your evaluations, dialogue from the plays, photographs of the playwrights or scenes from performances of the plays, and any other elements that will make your display attractive and informative. Exhibit your display in your school or your community library.
3. **Critics' Corner**
   Prepare a "Sneak Previews"–style presentation of your reviews. Each member of your group should orally present his or her evaluation of a play. If individuals from different groups evaluated the same play, you could pair reviewers from the different groups and have them present a spirited "thumbs up, thumbs down" discussion of the play.

Processing

What did this project teach you about evaluating drama? How could you apply techniques you used to make decisions and choose from various alternatives in your everyday life? Write a reflection for your portfolio.

Learning for Life

Technology Tip

Students may videotape the presentations of reviewers giving "Sneak Previews." Pairs of reviewers could alternate their comments in a lively interaction or simply present two full reviews, one following the other. Before students begin, have them look at sets used for television talk shows. Encourage students to furnish their reviewers with props arranged in unique settings for their taped performances. They should also pay close attention to any logos, icons, or sound effects that are used to indicate the reviewer's evaluation of the play. For example, miniature tragedy or comedy masks could be used as part of the evaluations, with four masks indicating an outstanding evaluation, and one mask indicating a less favorable reaction.

PORTFOLIO ASSESSMENT

Performance Assessment Rubric So that students may see the evaluation criteria before they begin working on these projects, share the rubric provided in the ***Portfolio Management System***, p. 179.

DEVELOPING WORKPLACE COMPETENCIES

Preparation	Procedure	Presentation
Uses resources well Makes decisions Works on teams Evaluates data	Communicates ideas and information Works well with people from diverse backgrounds Reasons	Thinks creatively Demonstrates individual responsibility Exhibits self-esteem

Contemporary Literature
1950 to Present

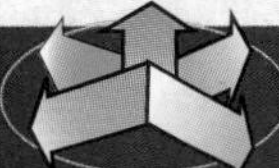

PROGRAM MANAGER

- **Summative Assessment** See **Literary Period Test: Contemporary Literature, *Test Booklet,*** pp. 276–279 for a test on an additional text from the same historical era.
- **Application** For practice of a reading strategy for this unit, see **Becoming a Strategic Reader** worksheet, ***Teaching Resources B,*** pp. 140–141.

Responding to the Quotation

? What does the description of Catch–22 say about life in combat? Does the catch apply to other aspects of contemporary life? Explain. [Catch–22 embodies the senseless contradictions of life during wartime. Students' responses will vary; make sure they give specific examples.]

Contemporary Literature

by John Leggett, Susan Allen Toth, John Malcolm Brinnin, *and* Thomas Hernacki

"You mean there's a catch?"

"Sure there's a catch," Doc Daneeka replied. "Catch-22. Anyone who wants to get out of combat duty isn't really crazy."

There was only one catch and that was Catch-22, which specified that a concern for one's own safety in the face of dangers that were real and immediate was the process of a rational mind. Orr was crazy and could be grounded. All he had to do was ask; and as soon as he did, he would no longer be crazy and would have to fly more missions. Orr would be crazy to fly more missions and sane if he didn't, but if he was sane he had to fly them. If he flew them he was crazy and didn't have to; but if he didn't want to he was sane and had to. Yossarian was moved very deeply by the absolute simplicity of this clause of Catch-22 and let out a respectful whistle.

"That's some catch, that Catch-22," he observed.

"It's the best there is," Doc Daneeka agreed.

—Joseph Heller, from Catch-22

Elements of Literature:

Videodisc Use the following bar codes to build background knowledge. For more information, see the Videodisc *Teacher's Manual.*

Videodisc Side B

Begin Play English Track

Begin Play Spanish Track

Whaam! (1963) by Roy Lichtenstein. Acrylic on canvas (172.7cm × 406.4cm).

On August 6, 1945, at 8:15 A.M., an atomic bomb was dropped on the Japanese city of Hiroshima from the U.S. airplane *Enola Gay.* Within seconds, the center of Hiroshima had disappeared. The bomb, in effect, ended World War II, and its mushroom cloud has cast a shadow over each generation since. **A**

Although many Americans disapproved of the use of the atomic bomb to end World War II, most Americans agreed with the purpose of the war itself. They were fighting against tyranny, against regimes that would destroy the American way of life. Only twenty years later, however, the United States became deeply involved in another overseas war—this time in Vietnam—that would sharply divide the nation. In the 1960s, demonstrations, both peaceful and violent, became commonplace. To some writers, such as Kurt Vonnegut, Jr., the madness of the war-torn world was an inescapable condition of modern life, and the only appropriate response was hard-edged laughter at life's tragic ironies. The term *gallows humor*—ironic humor arising from an acknowledgment of the absurd or grotesque—was often used to describe Vonnegut's work, as well as that of Joseph Heller, Terry Southern, and others. Heller's novel *Catch-22* (1961) is set in World War II, but the absurdities it describes belong to postwar life. In *Catch-22,* madness and war are inextricably mixed, not because madness is a result of war but because war is the result of our madness.

> At all times, an old world is collapsing and a new world arising; we have better eyes for the collapse than the rise, for the old one is the world we know. The artist, in focusing on his own creation, finds, and offers, relief from the tension and sadness of being burdened not just with consciousness but with historical consciousness. . . . **B**
>
> —John Updike, *from Hugging the Shore*

A. Expansion
When the atomic bomb detonated over Hiroshima, nearly every building within a half-mile radius of ground zero (the ground directly below the detonation) was demolished. Twelve-inch-thick brick walls a mile away were cracked, and homes two miles away were damaged. About 92,000 people died in the blast, and many more died later as a result of radioactive fallout.

B. Critical Reading: Evaluating an Opinion

? According to Updike, what is the role of the artist in society? Do you agree? Explain. [The role of the artist, according to Updike, is to offer society relief from the stress of constant historical upheaval. Students may agree or may think artists should have another primary role such as to entertain. Make sure that students provide support for their opinions.]

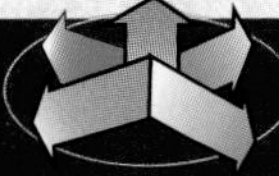

PROGRAM MANAGER

- **Planning Instruction** See Teaching Notes, *Teaching Resources B,* pp. 133–134 for additional teaching options about contemporary literature.
- **Assessment** For assessment of the literary and historical events mentioned in the historical introduction, see **Literary Period Introduction Test, *Test Booklet,*** pp. 215–216.

•1950–1959
Lorraine Hansberry died from cancer in 1965 at the age of thirty-four, six years after she had won the New York Drama Critics Circle Award for her first completed play, *A Raisin in the Sun.* Two other plays, *The Sign in Sidney Brustein's Window* and *Les Blancs,* have been published, and some of Hansberry's letters appeared in the book *To Be Young, Gifted and Black.*

•1960–1964
King's "I Have a Dream" speech reached an audience of over two hundred thousand people gathered in Washington, D.C.—and millions more watching on television—in a passionate demonstration for civil rights and racial justice. Standing on the steps of the Lincoln Memorial, King proclaimed the need for change through nonviolent political action and peaceful demonstration. He said: "I have a dream that one day this nation will rise up and live out the true meaning of its creed: 'We hold these truths to be self-evident; that all men are created equal.'" King's contribution helped lead to the passage of the Civil Rights Act of 1964 and the Voting Rights Act of 1965, two landmark pieces of legislation that guaranteed all Americans, regardless of color or creed, equal access to the political process.

•1965–1969
Bernard Malamud wrote primarily about Jews in America, creating memorable characters through humor, pathos, and a sensitivity to human suffering. He published several collections of short stories, including *The Magic Barrel* and *Idiots First,* plus the novels *Dubin's Lives, The Assistant,* and *The Fixer.* In 1984, his early novel about a gifted baseball player, *The Natural,* was the basis for a motion picture starring Robert Redford.

•1970–1974
To this day, Americans remain emotionally torn on the question of U.S. involvement in Vietnam. In all, about 57,000 U.S. soldiers, 254,000 South Vietnamese soldiers, and 1,027,000 North Vietnamese and Viet Cong troops were killed between 1957 and 1975.

Contemporary Literature 1950 to Present

Literary Events

1950–1959
- *A Raisin in the Sun,* a play by Lorraine Hansberry, opens, 1959
- Wallace Stevens publishes his *Collected Poems,* 1954
- J. D. Salinger publishes the novel *The Catcher in the Rye,* 1951

1960–1964
- Thomas Pynchon publishes the mysterious novel *V.,* 1963
- *Who's Afraid of Virginia Woolf?,* a play by Edward Albee, opens, 1962
- Joseph Heller publishes *Catch-22,* a darkly humorous novel satirizing military illogic, 1961

1965–1969
- **N. Scott Momaday** publishes the novel *House Made of Dawn,* 1968
- Colombian **Gabriel García Márquez** publishes *One Hundred Years of Solitude,* 1967
- **Bernard Malamud** publishes *The Fixer,* a novel about Jewish life in czarist Russia, 1966

1970–1974
- Aleksandr Solzhenitsyn publishes the first volume of *The Gulag Archipelago,* documenting oppression in the Soviet Union, 1973
- James Dickey publishes *Deliverance,* a novel about an ill-fated canoe trip in Georgia, 1970

Cultural/Historical Events

1950–1959
- Korean War ends, 1953
- U.S. Supreme Court rules that racial segregation in public schools is unconstitutional, 1954
- Soviet Union launches first artificial satellite, *Sputnik I,* thereby energizing the U.S. space-exploration program and beginning the "space race" between the two countries, 1957
- Federal troops enforce the integration of Central High School in Little Rock, Arkansas, 1957

1960–1964
- U.S. population is about 179 million, 1960
- Many African countries, including Nigeria and Senegal, achieve independence, 1960
- Rev. Martin Luther King, Jr., delivers "I Have a Dream" speech during the March on Washington, 1963
- President John F. Kennedy is assassinated, 1963

1965–1969
- U.S. escalates involvement in Vietnam War, 1965
- Israel occupies nearby territory as a result of Six-Day War with Arab countries, 1967
- Rev. Martin Luther King, Jr., and Senator Robert F. Kennedy are assassinated, 1968
- Two U.S. astronauts become first humans to walk on the moon, 1969

1970–1974
- Peace treaty provides for cease-fire in Vietnam and withdrawal of U.S. forces, 1973
- World economy is jolted by a sharp rise in petroleum prices, 1973
- Watergate scandal forces Richard M. Nixon to resign as U.S. president, 1974

President JohnF.Kennedy's funeral procession, November 25, 1963.

Arkansas student heckled during enforced integration, September 4, 1957.

The Nixon family, August 1974.

Amy Tan.

Alex Haley publishes *Roots,* a history of his family from its origins in Africa, 1976

•

The Awful Rowing Toward God, a collection of poems by **Anne Sexton,** is published, 1975

•

E. L. Doctorow publishes *Ragtime,* a novel mixing fictional and real characters, 1975

Paul Theroux publishes the novel *The Mosquito Coast;* **Alice Walker** publishes the novel *The Color Purple;* **James Merrill** publishes the long poem *The Changing Light at Sandover,* 1982

•

John Updike publishes the novel *Rabbit Is Rich,* 1981

Amy Tan publishes the novel *The Joy Luck Club,* 1989

•

Richard Wilbur publishes *New and Collected Poems,* 1988

•

Anne Tyler publishes the novel *Breathing Lessons,* 1988

•

Larry McMurtry publishes the novel *Lonesome Dove,* 1985

Garrett Hongo publishes *Volcano: A Memoir of Hawaii,* 1995

•

Yusef Komunyakaa publishes the poetry collection *Neon Vernacular,* 1993

•

Tim O'Brien publishes *The Things They Carried,* 1990

1975–1979

Israel and Egypt agree to a landmark peace treaty, 1978–1979

•

Iranian militants seize the U.S. embassy in Tehran and take 52 Americans hostage, thus beginning 444-day "hostage crisis," 1979

•

Soviet Union invades Afghanistan, 1979

1980–1984

Eight-year war between Iran and Iraq begins, 1980

•

Sandra Day O'Connor becomes the first female justice on U.S. Supreme Court, 1981

•

United States invades Grenada after a military coup there, 1983

1985–1989

Era of great change in Soviet Union begins as Mikhail Gorbachev rises to power, 1985

•

U.S. space shuttle *Challenger* explodes soon after liftoff, 1986

•

U.S. stock market crashes, 1987

•

United States and Soviet Union sign treaty reducing medium-range nuclear weapons, 1987

•

Berlin Wall comes down, 1989

1990–

U.S. population is about 249 million, 1990

•

Iraq invades neighboring Kuwait but is forced to retreat by Operation Desert Storm, a short, powerful military action led by the United States, 1990–1991

•

West Germany and East Germany unite, 1991

•

Soviet Union is dissolved; Russia becomes the largest successor state, 1991

•

United States helps implement peace accords in Bosnia and Herzegovina, 1995

Fall of the Berlin Wall, November 1989.

Berlin Wall coming down.

•1975–1979

In 1979, the Ayatollah Ruhollah Khomeini led Islamic fundamentalists to overthrow the shah of Iran because of the shah's secular and pro-Western policies. Under the shah, laws gave women equal rights, including the right to vote and work, and imported many Western styles and technologies. Ayatollah Khomeini declared Iran an Islamic state with laws based on the teachings of Islam. When the shah fled and later entered the United States for medical treatment, the Ayatollah's forces seized the U.S. Embassy in Tehran and took a group of U.S. citizens hostage, refusing to release them until the United States returned the shah for trial. When the United States refused, a "hostage crisis" ensued, lasting more than fourteen months. Finally, six months after the shah died in Egypt from natural causes, the hostages were released.

•1990–1995

The United States is not only a growing nation, but also a nation of people growing older. Census figures in 1990 showed the median age to be 32.9 years, up 2.9 years from 1980. The percentage of people over age 65 increased from 11 percent to 13 percent between 1980 and 1990, part of which may be due to the increasing number of young adults delaying marriage. In 1970, the median age at first marriage was 23.2 years for males and 20.8 for females; in 1990, it was 26.1 for males and 23.9 for females. In 1970, the marriage rate was 10.6 percent and the divorce rate 3.5 percent, while in 1990 the marriage rate was 9.8 percent and the divorce rate 4.7 percent. In 1990, a survey showed 77 percent of those between 18 and 24 were not married, with 66 percent still living with their parents.

USING THE TIME LINE

Arrange students in small groups and instruct the groups to classify events from the lower half of the time line in one of the following categories: political, economic, socio-cultural, geographical, scientific, or artistic. Have groups share classifications with the whole class. Ask each group to choose two events and collaborate to write a paragraph answering the following question for each event: What would be the effects today if the event had never happened? How would the world be different? Have groups share their paragraphs to prompt class discussion.

A. Exploring the Historical Period

President Richard M. Nixon resigned from the presidency on August 9, 1974, after the House Judiciary Committee voted to recommend three articles of impeachment against Nixon. The recommendations were based on evidence from the Watergate scandal, which began with the arrest and conviction of several of Nixon's 1972 campaign employees for a burglary at the Democratic Party headquarters in the Watergate building in Washington, D.C. Nixon was charged with obstructing justice, abusing presidential powers, and disobeying subpoenas. Vice President Gerald Ford was sworn in as his successor.

A CLOSER LOOK

ATOMIC ANXIETY

Things are probably going to look different when you get outside.

—*from How to Survive an Atomic Bomb* (1950)

At the end of World War II, Americans confronted two unsettling new facts of life: the atomic bomb and the cold war with the Soviet Union. U.S. scientists published chilling calculations of what would happen if atomic (and later, hydrogen) bombs were dropped on American cities. Meanwhile, a vivid image of a malignant Soviet leadership with its collective finger poised over the red button that would launch a nuclear attack was created in the American psyche—an image memorably evoked in the 1963 film *Dr. Strangelove: or, How I Learned to Stop Worrying and Love the Bomb.* Politicians warned that war would come, in the words of New York Governor Thomas E. Dewey, "whenever the fourteen evil men in Moscow decide to have it break out." It was high time, experts of various stripes agreed, to devise a new national civil defense plan.

The possible responses to nuclear attack were succinctly described by one U.S. government official as "dig, die, or get out." The second option aside, "getting out" meant leaving big cities, which presumably would be targets of Soviet bombs. Some policymakers urged that major cities be relocated under mountain ranges or in 30-foot strips alongside highways. Government officials ultimately rejected these and other relocation schemes. Even the less ambitious idea of evacuating cities drove planners to despair as they pondered maps of New York City and Los Angeles.

What was left but to dig? The notion of burrowing underground took root, partly because it allowed every citizen a personal response to nuclear war: Build a bomb shelter. Companies selling shelters proliferated in the 1950s, and marketing creativity soared. Using fictitious "protection factor" ratings, shelter ads boasted blastproof rooms; one ad featured a decontamination room for latecomers to the shelter. Aesthetic considerations came into play in one prefab shelter that featured a window with a woodland view painted on one wall. Ingenious designs and vigorous advertising

By permission of the artist. National Museum of American Art, Washington, D.C.

Miss Liberty (1987) by Malcah Zeldis. Oil on corrugated cardboard.

A The 1970s saw the winding down of the Vietnam War, but another focus of disillusion filled the news: the Watergate scandal that in 1974 forced the only resignation of an American president. On the other hand, the celebration in 1976 of the bicentennial of the Declaration of Independence witnessed a prideful restatement of fundamental American values.

Then came the 1980s, which many Americans now regard as the time of the Me Generation, when individual enjoyment and material success seemed to overshadow other concerns.

OPTIONS FOR TEACHING

STRATEGIES FOR INCLUSION

Less Proficient Readers To help students learn strategies for actively constructing meaning as they read, pair them for a Think Aloud activity. As students take turns reading one paragraph at a time, instruct them to pause occasionally to express any thoughts about the text's content, interpretation, problems and resolutions in interpretation, or connections with real-life situations. Encourage students to work together to discuss and construct meaning from the text as they read.

Visual To help students understand the extent of cultural change that occurred decade by decade from 1940 to 1990, gather popular periodicals from each decade so students can study the American way of life represented in each decade. Bring in a current periodical (*Life* or *People,* for example) and compare the images. Ask the class to come up with generalizations that capture the essence of each decade (for example, "The decade of the 1980s was the 'Me Generation' —people were focused on personal wealth and status.") Tell students to select images from periodicals that best represent the generalizations for each decade.

were essential, because bomb shelters were a considerable investment: Models typically cost several hundred dollars (a large sum in those days), and that didn't include the requisite first-aid kit, flashlights, sandbags, periscope, supply of water and canned food, and pliers (in case of toothache). Economy-minded citizens were encouraged to improvise a shelter in their homes by stacking brick-filled dresser drawers on a table, and to crawl underneath in the event of a nuclear strike. (Helpful instructions warned the builder to "be careful not to overload the table to the point where it will collapse.") Bomb shelters generated so much enthusiasm that, by the end of 1960, industrious Americans had constructed about one million of them.

Bomb shelter in New York, 1952.

Although shelters and other civil defense schemes of the fifties sound far-fetched today, the fears that inspired them were entirely justified. In fact, interest in civil defense waned in the early 1960s partly because people began to understand just how disastrous nuclear war could be. Antiradiation suits and community loudspeaker systems began to seem ridiculous in light of dangerously high and long-lived radiation levels. Moreover, weapons delivery systems had been improved so that bombs could reach the United States in minutes—hardly time to alert entire communities. The final blow to civil defense programs, however, was a positive development: The signing of the Limited Test Ban Treaty in 1963 officially ended above-ground nuclear testing—and thus the fallout that had aroused so much alarm. The bomb shelters of the fifties have long since been converted into toolsheds and wine cellars—or storage spaces for the home Geiger counters and antiradiation pills of another era.

As the 1980s ended, so did the cold war, the struggle between the United States and the Soviet Union that had dominated international politics since shortly after the end of World War II. The Soviet Union collapsed as its republics and satellite nations declared independence. The end of the cold war reduced but did not end the threat of nuclear warfare.

In many ways, the nuclear bomb is the dramatic symbol of the last half of the twentieth century. Its infamous mushroom cloud represents the proliferation of science and technology, the purpose of which was, ironically enough, to benefit humankind, to make life richer and easier for all.

In some ways, science and technology have fulfilled their promise. They have increased the life spans of many and have fed and housed many people better. They have moved us faster from place to place—even allowing a few of us to stroll on the surface of the moon.

But at the same time, poverty and crime have increased, not diminished. Science and technology have standardized and "assembly-lined" our lives and displaced countless workers. The era of the computer chip has

Peace Today **by Rube Goldberg.**

The Granger Collection, New York.

Neil Armstrong on the moon, 1969.

STRATEGIES FOR INCLUSION

Musical Have students compare a number of popular songs from different eras. Students can look up old singles charts or ask their older relatives and friends to suggest songs from the times. Play a few examples in class and challenge students to express an opinion about the time periods based on their music.

INTEGRATING THE LANGUAGE ARTS

Strategic Reading Have students use a chart such as Transparency 11: Analysis Chart in the Transparency Package to record supporting information for inferences they make as they read this introduction to the time period. Encourage students to make one or two inferences for each page of the introduction. The inferences should express an observation that is based on the information in the essay. After students have finished reading, ask them to review each inference and use metacognition to identify the thought processes that they used in making their inferences.

A. Literary Connection
Ralph Waldo Emerson's idea of the individual is grounded in a transcendentalist philosophy that focuses on human individuality rather than human society. In his essay "Self-Reliance," he wrote: "Nothing is at last sacred but the integrity of your own mind."

B. Humanities Connection
Many people point out that postmodern movements have appeared in several fields besides the visual and literary arts, including politics, philosophy, and theology. Rather than defining it as a style, some think of postmodernism as a sensibility defined by a set of tastes and attitudes. In the visual arts, the postmodern sensibility can be seen as having four interrelated characteristics— *pluralism* (a profusion of styles and modes); *eclecticism* (consisting of borrowed fragments); *self-consciousness* (emphasis on the codes used to transmit content rather than the content itself); and *contextualism* (awareness of historical roots).

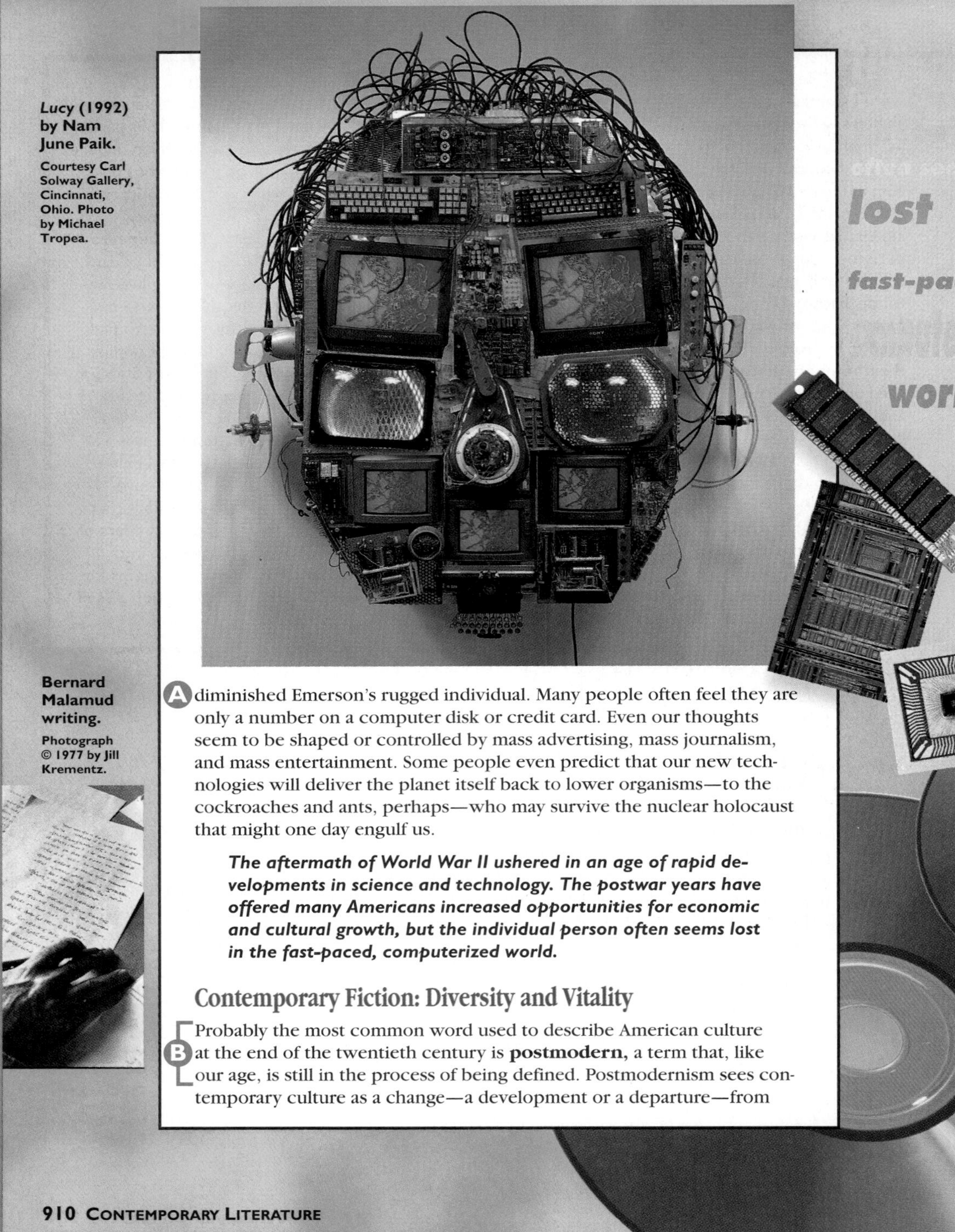

***Lucy* (1992) by Nam June Paik.**
Courtesy Carl Solway Gallery, Cincinnati, Ohio. Photo by Michael Tropea.

Bernard Malamud writing.
Photograph © 1977 by Jill Krementz.

(A) diminished Emerson's rugged individual. Many people often feel they are only a number on a computer disk or credit card. Even our thoughts seem to be shaped or controlled by mass advertising, mass journalism, and mass entertainment. Some people even predict that our new technologies will deliver the planet itself back to lower organisms—to the cockroaches and ants, perhaps—who may survive the nuclear holocaust that might one day engulf us.

The aftermath of World War II ushered in an age of rapid developments in science and technology. The postwar years have offered many Americans increased opportunities for economic and cultural growth, but the individual person often seems lost in the fast-paced, computerized world.

Contemporary Fiction: Diversity and Vitality

(B) Probably the most common word used to describe American culture at the end of the twentieth century is **postmodern**, a term that, like our age, is still in the process of being defined. Postmodernism sees contemporary culture as a change—a development or a departure—from

OPTIONS FOR TEACHING

CROSSING THE CURRICULUM

Architecture/Art/Fine Arts Ask students to research examples of modernism and postmodernism in artistic fields other than literature. Encourage students to find prints or photographs of artwork and architecture, and display students' findings around the classroom. Discuss with students how changes in the art reflect those that occurred in the literature of the same era.

Science Ask students to think of scientific advancements other than the discovery of atomic energy that have changed people's lives. Have students research a development (for example, with computers) and, in a brief oral presentation, tell the class how they think the advancement has changed people's lives. Challenge students to think of ways the changes in science parallel changes in literature.

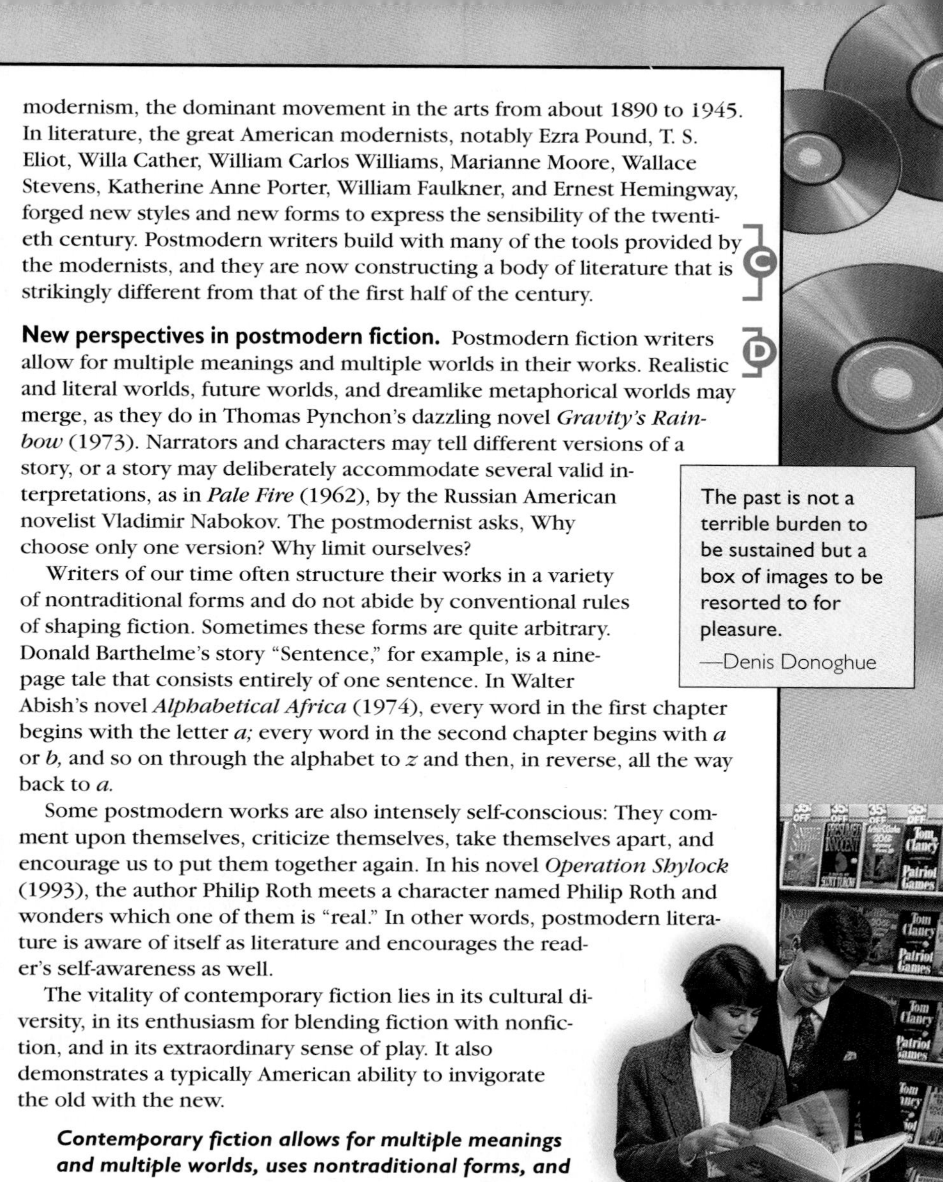

modernism, the dominant movement in the arts from about 1890 to 1945. In literature, the great American modernists, notably Ezra Pound, T. S. Eliot, Willa Cather, William Carlos Williams, Marianne Moore, Wallace Stevens, Katherine Anne Porter, William Faulkner, and Ernest Hemingway, forged new styles and new forms to express the sensibility of the twentieth century. Postmodern writers build with many of the tools provided by the modernists, and they are now constructing a body of literature that is strikingly different from that of the first half of the century. C

New perspectives in postmodern fiction. Postmodern fiction writers allow for multiple meanings and multiple worlds in their works. Realistic and literal worlds, future worlds, and dreamlike metaphorical worlds may merge, as they do in Thomas Pynchon's dazzling novel *Gravity's Rainbow* (1973). Narrators and characters may tell different versions of a story, or a story may deliberately accommodate several valid interpretations, as in *Pale Fire* (1962), by the Russian American novelist Vladimir Nabokov. The postmodernist asks, Why choose only one version? Why limit ourselves? D

> The past is not a terrible burden to be sustained but a box of images to be resorted to for pleasure.
>
> —Denis Donoghue

Writers of our time often structure their works in a variety of nontraditional forms and do not abide by conventional rules of shaping fiction. Sometimes these forms are quite arbitrary. Donald Barthelme's story "Sentence," for example, is a nine-page tale that consists entirely of one sentence. In Walter Abish's novel *Alphabetical Africa* (1974), every word in the first chapter begins with the letter *a;* every word in the second chapter begins with *a* or *b,* and so on through the alphabet to *z* and then, in reverse, all the way back to *a.*

Some postmodern works are also intensely self-conscious: They comment upon themselves, criticize themselves, take themselves apart, and encourage us to put them together again. In his novel *Operation Shylock* (1993), the author Philip Roth meets a character named Philip Roth and wonders which one of them is "real." In other words, postmodern literature is aware of itself as literature and encourages the reader's self-awareness as well.

The vitality of contemporary fiction lies in its cultural diversity, in its enthusiasm for blending fiction with nonfiction, and in its extraordinary sense of play. It also demonstrates a typically American ability to invigorate the old with the new.

Contemporary fiction allows for multiple meanings and multiple worlds, uses nontraditional forms, and comments upon itself. But it embraces traditional storytellers as well as postmodern risk-takers. It features cultural diversity, crisscrosses the boundaries between fiction and nonfiction, and uses subjects, images, and themes from the past fearlessly.

C. Literary Connections

Narrative forms of traditional fiction are usually driven by content, such as the events in a character's life. Narrative forms of postmodern fiction are often driven by elements of form itself, the conventions associated with the act of storytelling. Traditional realistic narrative may be seen as depending for coherence on the created illusion of a character's life by portraying events and emotional responses to events as they unfold in that life. Postmodern narrative, on the other hand, may consciously call attention to, comment on, and manipulate the very techniques the writer uses to create those illusions. Instead of writing to paint a picture of reality, as a traditional storyteller might, the postmodern storyteller may write to paint a picture of himself or herself painting a picture of reality.

D. Humanities Connection

Pastiche is a term that is useful to describe the postmodern tendency to appropriate ideas and forms from the past and use them again in new creations. Although this process may sound like plagiarism, pastiche involves stripping ideas and forms from their original contexts and replacing them in surprising new contexts. It is this contextual upheaval that distinguishes pastiche from plagiarism. The postmodern artist's object is the effect created by recontextualizing the image rather than the effect created by the image itself. The appearance of Leonardo da Vinci's *Mona Lisa* on a necktie is a playful example of postmodern pastiche.

ASSESSMENT TOOLS

Check Test: Questions and Answers

1. What does the phrase "dig, die, or get out" refer to? [Possible responses to nuclear attack.]
2. List two characteristics of postmodern literature. [Any two of the following: Multiple meanings/multiple worlds; nontraditional forms; self-reflexivity; cultural diversity; blending of fiction and nonfiction; borrowing or manipulating ideas from the past.]
3. What is the New Journalism? [An approach to writing nonfiction—also called *literary journalism*—that adds personal and fictional elements.]
4. What was the long poem that launched the Beat Generation and became known as its bible? Who wrote it? ["Howl"; Allen Ginsberg.]
5. What school of poets was influenced by Robert Lowell's *Life Studies?* [The Confessional School.]

Contemporary Nonfiction: Breaking the Barriers

> . . . [N]onfiction is the place where much of the best writing of the day is being done. Yet many writers and teachers of writing continue to feel vaguely guilty if they prefer it to fiction—nonfiction is the slightly disreputable younger brother in the royal house of literature. No such guilt is necessary. While the keepers of the temple weren't looking, nonfiction crept in and occupied the throne.
>
> —William Zinsser

Until fairly recently, "nonfiction" meant whatever was *not* fiction—suggesting that nonfiction was a nonliterary form and a nonart. Nonfiction writers were lumped together with journalists, who were in turn defined as nonliterary folk whose work was quickly written, read, and discarded. Critics tended to concentrate on the search for the elusive Great American Novel, which was thought to be more important than anything a nonfiction writer could produce.

Since the 1970s, however, nonfiction has come into its own. Featured reviews now discuss the art (not just the factual content) of books on computers, architecture, travel, history, film, and other subjects. Best-seller lists, which have always included self-help books, cookbooks, and exercise manuals, now also regularly feature memoirs, biographies, and histories.

Questions of terminology and accuracy. Critics, however, are still uncertain about the terminology we should apply to nonfiction. For instance, when discussing fiction, we can talk about point of view, character, plot, theme, and setting; with more complex fiction, we can analyze irony, metaphors, symbols, and levels of meaning. But these traditional literary terms don't always apply to nonfiction.

More troubling is the problem of accuracy. No one expects a novel to be true, although it may be based on verifiable facts. But truth or accuracy is often a test applied to nonfiction, with frequently unsatisfactory results. A class recently read Peter Matthiessen's *The Snow Leopard* (1978), a travel memoir about wildlife in the Himalayas and the writer's search for the meaning of life. The class praised the book for its penetrating observations, philosophical depth, and narrative technique. Students were then asked if they would like it just as much if they learned that it was fiction, that Matthiessen had done extensive library research but had never gone to the Himalayas at all. (This is, of course, *not* the case.) No, many students said, they would not

Jimmy Santiago Baca at the Dodge Poetry Festival, Waterloo, New Jersey.

OPTIONS FOR TEACHING

ASSESSMENT TOOLS

Peer Assessment After students have worked together in their small groups, ask each student to write a paragraph assessing the group's activities in response to the following questions.

1. What did the group do effectively? Why do you think this was effective?
2. What could the group do next time to improve its effectiveness?
3. Why do you think this would improve the group's effectiveness?

like the book as well. It would no longer be true. Wasn't truth what distinguished nonfiction from fiction?

Characteristics of Postmodern Literature

- Allows for multiple meanings and multiple worlds
- Structures works in nontraditional forms
- Comments upon itself
- Features cultural diversity
- Blends and overlaps fiction and nonfiction
- Uses the past fearlessly

The New Journalism. This question was often raised in the 1960s when the New Journalism (also called Literary Journalism) began to appear. Truman Capote, Tom Wolfe, Joan Didion, Norman Mailer, and others attracted attention by describing contemporary culture and actual events in strongly individual voices. They employed many of the devices of fiction, including complex characterization, plot, suspense, setting, symbolism, and irony.

A New Journalist did not feel obliged to keep personal opinion and his or her presence out of the writing; in fact, presence and participation were often crucial. Joan Didion bought a dress for a defendant in a trial she was covering as a journalist. Truman Capote befriended the murderers he was writing about in his book *In Cold Blood,* which he called a nonfiction novel—a perfect example of the overlapping of genres. Readers wanted to know just what the writer was thinking or feeling about the subject, and so the tone of a book became nearly as important as its facts. **A**

If facts alone do not distinguish nonfiction from fiction, what does? No one is sure. What readers *are* sure about is their interest in nonfiction that uses the traditional attractions of accomplished fiction: characters

Truman Capote in his office signing several copies of his new book *In Cold Blood.*

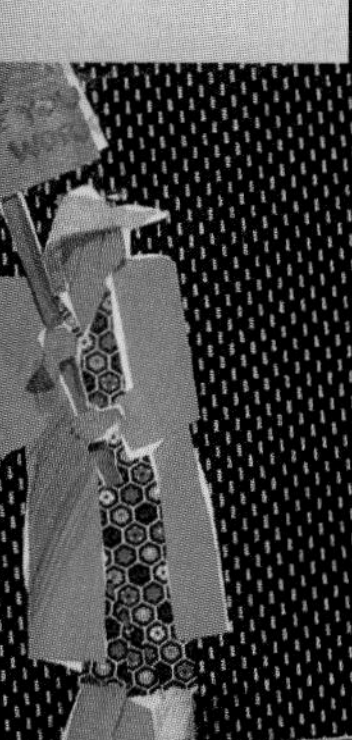

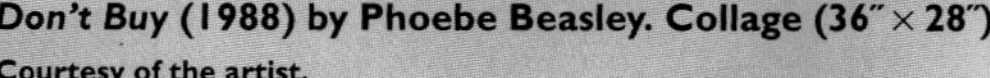

Don't Buy **(1988) by Phoebe Beasley. Collage (36″ × 28″)**
Courtesy of the artist.

A. Literary Connections
A distinctly Southern writer, Truman Capote has written novels bearing the hallmarks of Southern Gothic fiction: eccentric characters and settings full of strangely grotesque and supernatural elements. His work includes three novels (*Other Voices, Other Rooms; The Grass Harp;* and *Breakfast at Tiffany's*), two short-story collections (*A Tree of Night and Other Stories* and *Music for Chameleons*), and an unfinished novel, *Answered Prayers.*

A. Exploring the Culture
Some attribute the increasing numbers of Americans writing poetry to graduate M.F.A. programs in creative writing that have proliferated on university campuses. The master of fine arts degree is awarded for, generally, a two-year course of study in the art and craft of creative writing. M.F.A. programs graduate hundreds of poets who not only write and publish, but also have credentials to teach the writing of poetry. The M.F.A. is a creative degree, meaning students produce a portfolio of creative work—usually a book-length manuscript of poems—in lieu of a traditional master's thesis.

B. Literary Connection
T. S. Eliot was born in St. Louis, Missouri, but moved to London and eventually became a British subject, calling himself "Anglo-Catholic in religion, royalist in politics, and classicist in literature." In his most famous poem, *The Waste Land,* Eliot expresses classicist interest in myths to contrast what he perceives to be the utter spiritual bankruptcy of modern Europe with the absolute values that unified life in the past. Eliot won the Nobel Prize in literature in 1948.

to care about, suspense, and compelling use of language. Many readers, eager for literature that will illuminate their lives, enrich their knowledge, and entertain them, have become as willing to pursue those goals in nonfiction as they are in fiction. They find what they are looking for in the works of the writers mentioned above and many others, including Annie Dillard, Lewis Thomas, Paul Theroux, Alice Walker, and Barry Lopez.

Contemporary nonfiction has become a field equal to fiction, though questions about terminology and accuracy still give rise to controversy. New Journalism (or Literary Journalism) has added personal and fictional elements to nonfiction, enhancing its popularity with today's readers.

Contemporary Poetry: Varied and Intensely Personal

It is difficult to describe the course of American poetry since 1945, because recent trends are still too close to be viewed objectively. Moreover, in recent years, unprecedented numbers of Americans have been writing poetry, so it is a special challenge to determine which poets and which movements will last.

The decline of modernism. There are a number of clear, significant differences between American poetry written before 1945 and the poetry written in the decades since. The twenty years between World War I and World War II marked the flowering and near monopoly of modernist poetry. This was the kind of poetry defined, by and large, by the theory and practice of T. S. Eliot, Ezra Pound, and, somewhat later, W. H. Auden.

In 1917, Eliot had called for an impersonal, objective poetry that would transcend the subjective emotions of the poet. The poem, said Eliot, should be impersonal, allusive (it should make references, or allusions, to other works), and intellectually challenging. Modernist writers followed Ezra Pound's insistence that the image was all-important and that all unnecessary words should be omitted; but in doing this, they often eliminated material that could have made their poetry more accessible to readers.

By the early 1950s, though, there was a growing sense that modernism was somehow becoming played out, that it was no longer appropriate for the times. The era itself may have had something to do with the shift away from modernism. A generation had returned from war to a country where conformity and material success were predominant values. The Soviet Union and the atomic bomb worried Americans in the late

Maya Angelou reciting her poem "On the Pulse of Morning" at President Bill Clinton's inauguration.

1940s and early 1950s, but acquiring a house and a car and making money were generally of more immediate importance. "These are the tranquilized *Fifties,*" Robert Lowell wrote in a poem toward the end of that decade, as he ironically described the complacent scene around him:

I hog a whole house on Boston's
"hardly passionate Marlborough Street,"
where even the man
scavenging filth in the back alley trash cans,
has two children, a beach wagon, a helpmate,
and is a "young Republican."

—Robert Lowell, *from*
"Memories of West Street and Lepke"

By the early 1950s, many writers and readers felt that modernist poetry—impersonal, allusive, difficult—was no longer appropriate. The times called for a more personal and accessible approach that challenged complacency and convention.

Cast from *Leave It to Beaver,* a late 1950s TV show often associated with the fifties stereotype of the "typical American family."

The Beat poets. In 1956, a long poem called *Howl* was published by Allen Ginsberg, who could by no stretch of the imagination be described as dull. A cry of outrage against the conformity of the 1950s, *Howl* was as far removed from the safe confines of modernism as could be imagined. It begins, "I saw the best minds of my generation destroyed by madness, starving hysterical naked," and it continues at the same intense pitch for hundreds of lines. C

Student reading at the 1995 Dodge Poetry Festival.

C. Exploring the Culture
The Beat movement of the 1950s maintained a critical stance toward mainstream American culture. Also known as "Beatniks," the Beats were seen by many as praising individuality and speaking out against social injustice and conventional middle-class conformity. The Beats declared mainstream America morally bankrupt and in their literature, planted the seed of protest that germinated in the rebellious youth culture of the 1960s.

A. Literary Connections
The Confessional poets listed all won the Pulitzer Prize in poetry, an annual award given for a distinguished book of verse by an American author. The prizes were awarded to John Berryman (1965, 77 *Dream Songs*); Anne Sexton (1967, *Live or Die*); and Sylvia Plath (1982, *The Collected Poems*).

Poetry today is anything but impersonal. Poetry today is anything but impersonal. Poetry tod

American Flag: A Mosaic of Faces is part of an exhibit at the Ellis Island Immigration Museum. From 1891 to 1954 this New York Harbor island processed over 16 million immigrants.

Together with *On the Road* (1957), Jack Kerouac's novel celebrating the bohemian life, *Howl* quickly became a kind of bible for young nonconformists known as the Beat Generation. Beat poetry and the Beat lifestyle of poetry readings, jazz, and late-night coffeehouses in San Francisco and New York's Greenwich Village had an immediate impact on American popular culture. *Life* magazine even ran illustrated stories about the new bohemians.

> One judges an age, just as one judges a poet, by its best poems.
> —Randall Jarrell

Howl provided the first clear alternative to academic poetry—intellectual poetry that seemed to be written for analysis in the classroom rather than poetry that addressed the real concerns of contemporary life. Many of Ginsberg's concerns—the injustices of modern life, the importance of the imagination—would become the principal themes of poetry a decade later.

Poetry and personal experience. In 1959, Robert Lowell published *Life Studies,* one of the most important and influential volumes of verse to appear since World War II. These poems are about personal experiences that modernist poets had avoided dealing with directly: emotional problems, alcoholism, illness, and depression. In *Life Studies,* Lowell clearly and decisively broke with Eliot's theory that poetry should be impersonal; in doing so, he helped to reunite, both for himself and for other writers, "the man who suffers and the mind which creates."

Shortly after *Life Studies* appeared, a critic described Lowell's poems as "confessional." The label stuck, and the **Confessional School** of poets, mostly friends or students of Lowell, was officially born. These poets—(A) including Sylvia Plath, Anne Sexton, and John Berryman—wrote frank,

mes
uld be
he times
hanging
but not in lyrical phrases
phrases
Dylan's lyrical songs

sometimes brutal poems about their private lives. Nothing could have been further from Eliot's model.

By the mid-1970s, many of the first generation of major postwar poets were dead, as were some of the second generation. William Carlos Williams, Theodore Roethke, and Plath all died in 1963. The 1970s saw the deaths of Berryman, Sexton, and Lowell. With Lowell's death, the American literary world was again without a major poet to provide it with definition and a common sense of direction.

Landmarks in the revolt against modernist poetry include Allen Ginsberg's* Howl *(1956) and Robert Lowell's* Life Studies *(1959), both of which deal vividly with the poets' personal experience. The Confessional School of poets, which included Lowell, Sylvia Plath, and Anne Sexton, wrote frank and revealing poems about their private lives.

Lava lamps.

A time of diversity. Since the 1970s, American poetry has been characterized by diversity. Extraordinary variety in style and attitude has attracted large new audiences to poetry. Oral performance of poetry has increased, with live poetry "slams" at such places as the Nuyorican Poets Cafe in New York City. Technology has made available thousands of readings on audiotape and videotape, and even some television broadcasts devoted to poetry. B

Much contemporary poetry reflects a democratic quality, often influenced by the works of Walt Whitman and William Carlos Williams. Poetry lives in the people, contemporary poets seem to say, and any walk of life, any everyday experience, any style of expression can result in authentic poetry. C These poets often write in the vernacular, the language of common speech, and do not hesitate to surprise or even shock with their language, attitudes, and details of their private lives.

Poetry today is anything but impersonal.

Where the Present Meets the Past on the Way to the Future

The literature that captures a wide audience often does so by offering a fresh voice and a new attitude, for these are the powerful needs of each new generation. Yet much of contemporary American literature still deals with the same themes that concerned our greatest writers of the nineteenth century: Poe, Hawthorne, Whitman, Dickinson, Melville, Emerson, and Thoreau. The characters of the

***Electro-Symbio Phonics for Phoenix* (detail) (1992) by Nam June Paik. Video sculpture and neon installation.**

Courtesy Carl Solway Gallery, Cincinnati, Ohio.

B. Exploring the Culture

Poetry "slams" are popular in many U.S. cities, usually occurring in coffee houses where avant-garde self-expression is the norm. The slam format is often "open mike," meaning anyone can take the floor and read. Poets may read from table tops with great verve and passion. The tone is often not that of a gentle offering of poems for the pleasure of a polite, mannered audience, but more that of a deeply moved, impassioned voice "slamming" poems with a boldness intended to bring the audience to life.

C. Expansion

The democratic qualities of this poetry may extend to the audience, as well. The degree of confidence with which readers can engage the language and form of a poem is an important measure of its accessibility. The accessibility of "democratic" poetry, shown in the audience interaction at "slams," contrasts with that of academic poetry, which tends to be accessible mostly to highly trained readers.

Quickwrite

Have students use the following chart to compare their images. Students can then share their comparisons in small groups. Ask each group to compile a list of postmodern characteristics to add to those listed in the book.

Similarities	Differences

There are good reasons for suggesting that the modern age has ended. Many things indicate that we are going through a transitional period, when it seems that something is on the way out and something else is painfully being born. It is as if something were crumbling, decaying, and exhausting itself, while something else, still indistinct, were arising from the rubble.

The distinguishing features of transitional periods are a mixing and blending of cultures and a plurality or parallelism of intellectual and spiritual worlds. These are periods when all consistent value systems collapse, when cultures distant in time and space are discovered or rediscovered. New meaning is gradually born from the encounter, or the intersection, of many different elements.

Today, this state of mind, or of the human world, is called postmodernism. For me, a symbol of that state is a Bedouin mounted on a camel and clad in traditional robes under which he is wearing jeans, with a transistor radio in his hands and an ad for Coca-Cola on the camel's back.

—Vaclav Havel, on receiving the Philadelphia Liberty Medal, July 4, 1994

Today, this state of mind, or of the human world, is called postmodernism.

novelist John Updike, for example, seek spiritual revelations in ordinary life. "The invariable mark of wisdom," Emerson wrote, "is to find the miraculous in the common." But it is more difficult to find transcendent spiritual values in the cheap clutter of modern life than it was in the woods around Emerson's Concord. Still, Updike's characters continue the search. "I find myself . . . circling back to man's religious nature," Updike has written of his own work, "and the real loss to man and art alike when that nature has nowhere to plug itself in. . . ." These words could serve to describe the work of a great number of contemporary writers whose intellectual roots can be traced to the Transcendentalists of the nineteenth century, and even further back to those hardy, practical Puritans who braved that two-month voyage in a tiny wooden boat.

Quickwrite

Read the quote about postmodernism by Vaclav Havel at the top of this page. How do you think contemporary literature bears out his assertion that new meanings arise from the meeting of a variety of old and new elements? What striking image—like Havel's camel-riding, jeans-clad Bedouin listening to a radio—can you think of that would symbolize the qualities of contemporary American culture?

Collection 18 THE WAGES OF WAR

Theme: **Seeking Resolution in Conflict**
Many postmodern writers have turned their attention to war, drawing from personal experience or their imagination, or recounting the experiences of others. The authors explore idealism, hope, and courage alongside the dehumanizing horror and absurdity of modern warfare.

Thematic Focus

Each selection examines the nature of war and its impact upon humanity.

- **Tamar** The narrator discovers beauty in London on the brink of war.
- **The Death of the Ball Turret Gunner** A shocking account of a soldier's death.
- **A Noiseless Flash** Six survivors' experiences of the atomic bombing of Hiroshima, Japan.
- **For the Union Dead** A poet reflects on the idealistic sacrifices of war.
- **Game** The absurd, nightmare reality of two soldiers cut off from the outside world.
- **Speaking of Courage** A Vietnam vet wrestles with the truths he has learned.
- **Monsoon Season** Rain evokes a soldier's painful Vietnam experience.

Literary Focus

Literary Element	Selection / Feature
Irony	**Tamar**
Subjectivity and Objectivity	**A Noiseless Flash**
Imagery	**Union Dead/Monsoon Season**
Satire	**Game**
Conflict	**Speaking of Courage**

Writing Focus

The following chart shows how the writing assignment for each selection relates to and builds toward the assignment presented in the Writer's Workshop at the end of the unit.

Selection	Work-in-Progress Assignment
Tamar	Judge the fictional characters p. 931
Ball Turret Gunner	Note the real-world context p. 934
A Noiseless Flash	Find objective and subjective reporting p. 947
For the Union Dead	Take notes of the poem's context p. 954
Game	Take notes on the theme of this selection p. 963
Speaking of Courage	Judge the character Paul Berlin p. 973
Monsoon Season	Record visual images from the poem p. 978
Writer's Workshop	Write an evaluation of a work pp. 1181–1185

Collection Planner

SELECTION / FEATURE	PUPIL'S EDITION: Literary Elements / Active Reading	Writing	Speaking and Listening	Language and Vocabulary
Tamar Mark Helprin (pp. 920–931) **Connections: Nobel Prize Acceptance Speech** Isaac Bashevis Singer (pp. 929–930)	• Reader's Log p. 921 • Irony p. 921	• Critical Writing: Explain a statement made by the narrator p. 931 • Creative Writing: Write journal entry from Tamar's point of view p. 931		• Language and Style: Helprin's Figurative Language p. 931
The Death of the Ball Turret Gunner Randall Jarrell (pp. 932–934) Primary Sources: The Ball Turret (p. 933)	• Reader's Log p. 932	• Critical Writing: Explain the poem's extended metaphor p. 934 • Creative Writing: Write poem/paragraph p. 934	• Speaking and Listening: Perform the poem before the class p. 934	
A Noiseless Flash John Hersey (pp. 935–947)	• Reader's Log p. 936 • Subjectivity and Objectivity p. 936	• Critical Writing: Write essay p. 947 • Crossing the Curriculum: History: Research and write essay p. 947 • Critical Writing: Write essay on Hersey's use of Japanese terms p. 947		
For the Union Dead Robert Lowell (pp. 948–954) Critical Comment: A Vision of Blacks and Whites United (p. 953)	• Reader's Log p. 949 • Imagery p. 949	• Critical Writing: Compare and contrast poems p. 954		
Game Donald Barthelme (pp. 955–963) Critical Comment: Absurd World (p. 961)	• Reader's Log p. 956 • Satire p. 962	• Critical Writing: Compare Barthelme's story to Auden's "The Unknown Citizen" p. 963		
Speaking of Courage Tim O'Brien (pp. 964–973)	• Reader's Log p. 965 • Conflict p. 965	• Critical Writing: Discuss contrast in this selection and "Tamar" p. 973 • Critical Writing: Compare two characters p. 973 • Creative Writing/ Performance: Write dialogue p. 973	• Creative Writing/ Performance: Perform dialogue p. 973	
Monsoon Season Yusef Komunyakaa (pp. 974–978) **Connections: Poetry Emotion** Anna Quindlen (p. 977)	• Reader's Log p. 975 • Imagery p. 975	• Critical Writing: Write essay evaluating symbols in this selection p. 978	• Critical Thinking/ Speaking and Listening: Take a stand on a statement by the author p. 978	

Collection Resources

Teaching Resources B	Audiovisual Resources Binder	Test Booklet
Cross-Curricular Activities p. 155	Fine Art Transparency 18.1	Collection Test pp. 226–228

 Computer disk or CD-ROM
Audiocassette
Overhead Transparency

PROGRAM RESOURCES

Electronic Media	Teaching Resources with Organizer: Teaching Resources B	Teaching Resources with Organizer: Other Resources	Audiovisual Resources Binder
• Test Generator	• Teaching Notes p. 135 • Reading Organizer p. 142 • Words to Own p. 143	• Test Booklet: Selection Test pp. 217–218 • Portfolio Management System p. 180	
• Test Generator	• Teaching Notes p. 136 • Reading Organizer p. 144	• Test Booklet: Selection Test pp. 219–220 • Portfolio Management System p. 181	
• Test Generator	• Teaching Notes pp. 136–137 • Reading Organizer p. 145 • Words to Own p. 146	• Test Booklet: Selection Test pp.219–220 • Portfolio Management System pp. 54–55, p. 182	• Elements of Literature Transparency 18.2
• Test Generator	• Teaching Notes p. 137 • Reading Organizer p. 147	• Test Booklet: Selection Test pp. 221–222 • Portfolio Management System p. 39, p. 183	
• Test Generator	• Teaching Notes p. 138 • Reading Organizer p. 148 • Words to Own p. 149	• Test Booklet: Selection Test pp. 221–222 • Portfolio Management System pp. 54–55, p. 184	
• Language Workshop: Punctuation • Test Generator	• Teaching Notes pp. 138–139 • Reading Organizer p. 150 • Language Link pp. 151–152 • Words to Own p. 153	• Test Booklet: Selection Test pp. 223–224 • Portfolio Management System p. 185	
• Test Generator	• Teaching Notes p. 139 • Reading Organizer p. 154	• Test Booklet: Selection Test p. 225 • Portfolio Management System p. 39, p. 186	• Selected Reading, Audiocassette 3, Side B

Proofreading Warm-ups

You may use the following exercises to help students practice their proofreading skills. Copy a set of incorrect sentences onto the chalkboard, and have students find and correct the spelling, punctuation, usage, and mechanical errors in each sentence. Ask students to share and discuss their responses.

	Sentences with Errors	Sentences Corrected	Skills Covered
1	**a.** one commonest word used to describe american culture at the end of the twentieth-century is postmodern **b.** postmodernism is a term that, is still in the process of, being defined	**a.** One of the most common words used to describe American culture at the end of the twentieth century is postmodern. **b.** Postmodernism is a term that is still in the process of being defined.	Capitalization, Comparison of modifiers, Hyphen usage, Underline word used as word, Comma usage, End marks
2	**a.** new journalism appear in the 1960s w/ such writers as Truman Capote **b.** new journalists did not keep personnel opinions out of thier writing	**a.** New Journalism appeared in the 1960s with such writers as Truman Capote. **b.** New Journalists did not keep personal opinions out of their writing.	Capitalization, Verb error, Write out abbreviations, Spelling, End marks
3	**a.** in 1956, a long poem called Howl was published, by Allen Ginsberg **b.** howl was a cry off outrage against the conformity, of the 1950s	**a.** In 1956, a long poem called Howl was published by Allen Ginsberg. **b.** Howl was a cry of outrage against the conformity of the 1950s.	Capitalization, Underline title of long poems, Spelling, Comma usage, End marks
4	**a.** mark helprins short story Tamar first appeared in the collection titled Ellis Island and Other Stories **b.** tamar a story set in london just before the outbreak of World War II contain's many examples of irony	**a.** Mark Helprin's short story "Tamar" first appeared in the collection titled Ellis Island and Other Stories. **b.** "Tamar," a story set in London just before the outbreak of World War II, contains many examples of irony.	Capitalization, Apostrophe usage, Quotation marks for short story titles, Underline book title, Comma usage, End marks
5	**a.** the 5 lines of The Death of the Ball Turret Gunner makes up one of the most famous World War II poems **b.** the poem written by Randall Jarrell has a extended metaphor	**a.** The five lines of "The Death of the Ball Turret Gunner" make up one of the most famous World War II poems. **b.** The poem, written by Randall Jarrell, has an extended metaphor.	Capitalization, Write out numerals, Quotation marks for poem titles, Subject-verb agreement, Comma usage, Nonstandard usage, End marks
6	**a.** john herseys Hiroshima details the lifes of six survivors of the atomic blast **b.** the enola gay is the airplane that droped the bomb on Hiroshima	**a.** John Hersey's Hiroshima details the lives of six survivors of the atomic blast. **b.** The Enola Gay is the airplane that dropped the bomb on Hiroshima.	Capitalization, Apostrophe usage, Underline book title, Spelling, Underline aircraft names, End marks
7	**a.** you explained that poem good Ms. Kaatz observed Kevin **b.** you mean she explained it well corrected Jan with emphasis	**a.** "You explained that poem well, Ms. Kaatz," observed Kevin. **b.** "You mean she explained it well," corrected Jan with emphasis.	Quotation marks, Capitalization, Nonstandard usage, Comma usage, End marks
8	**a.** should one lay a book on the table, or lie it on the table **b.** since lay means "to put or place something" and it usually takes an object use lay instead of lie	**a.** Should one lay a book on the table or lie it on the table? **b.** Since lay means "to put or place something" and it usually takes an object, use lay instead of lie.	Capitalization, Comma usage, Underline word used as word, End marks
9	**a.** do ya wanna lie down, on the sofa **b.** lie means "to stay to recline or to remain in a certain position"	**a.** Do you want to lie down on the sofa? **b.** Lie means "to stay, to recline, or to remain in a certain position."	Capitalization, Nonstandard usage, Comma usage, Underline word used as word, End marks
10	**a.** a internal conflict in the story Speaking of Courage involves Paul Berlins regret about a incident in Vietnam **b.** berlin looking back on what he experianced and learned in Vietnam	**a.** An internal conflict in the story "Speaking of Courage" involves Paul Berlin's regret about an incident in Vietnam. **b.** Berlin looks back on what he experienced and learned in Vietnam.	Capitalization, Nonstandard usage, Quotation marks for short story titles, Apostrophe usage, Spelling, Fragment, End marks

Collection 18

THE WAGES OF WAR

Helprin
Jarrell
Hersey
Lowell
Barthelme
O'Brien
Komunyakaa

At the Bomb Testing Site

At noon in the desert a panting lizard
waited for history, its elbows tense,
watching the curve of a particular road
as if something might happen.

It was looking at something farther off
than people could see, an important scene
acted in stone for little selves
at the flute end of consequences.

There was just a continent without much on it
under a sky that never cared less.
Ready for a change, the elbows waited.
The hands gripped hard on the desert.

—William Stafford
(1914–1993)

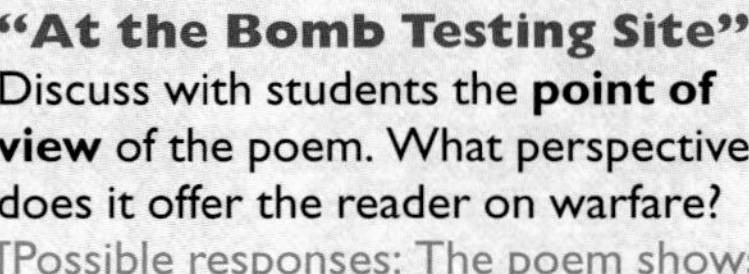

"At the Bomb Testing Site" Discuss with students the **point of view** of the poem. What perspective does it offer the reader on warfare? [Possible responses: The poem shows the development of the atomic bomb from the point of view of nature, which until the bomb's development has not been in as much danger from humans. The poem shows how fragile life is, and it implies that now warfare can end everything.]

PORTFOLIO ASSESSMENT

Parent/Guardian Involvement For forms that will help a parent or guardian review and respond to a student's portfolio, see the *Portfolio Management System,* pp. 62–63.

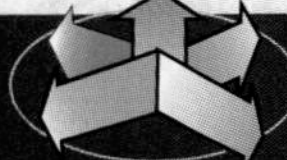

PROGRAM MANAGER

- **Integrated Assessment** For a summative assessment of the literature and language skills taught in this collection, see Collection 18 Test, *Test Booklet,* pp. 226–228.
- **Instructional Support** See Fine Art Transparency 18.1. Review teacher's notes for transparencies in the *Audiovisual Resources Binder* for suggestions on how to tie the transparency to specific reading selections.
- **Extending Collection Theme** See Cross-Curricular Activity: The Wages of War, *Teaching Resources B,* p. 155, for an activity in another discipline and for evaluation criteria.

QUICK PLANNING GUIDE

Into the Story

Through the Story

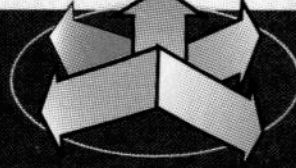

Beyond the Story

© Nancy Crampton.

Mark Helprin

(1947–   )

"I write in service of illumination and memory. I write to reach into 'the blind world where no one can help.' I write because it is a way of glimpsing the truth. And I write to create something of beauty."

This is the many-layered reply of Mark Helprin to one of the most basic questions asked of a writer: Why do you write? Helprin does not say that he writes to demonstrate a critical theory or to communicate a set of political or social ideas. His answer, instead, has the sound of a poet and the yearning of a visionary.

Helprin grew up in New York City and in nearby Ossining. He graduated from Harvard College and later earned a master's degree from Harvard in Middle Eastern studies. When he was twenty-five, he enlisted in the Israeli army and served for a year in its infantry and air force. He has also worked for a time as a merchant seaman, a farm laborer, a teacher, an editor, and a security guard. His turn to professional writing took place after *The New Yorker* published a short story he had written while under the spell of the great American writer Henry James.

Helprin's fiction is highly readable, marked by a lyrical grace of language and a delight in the extravagant and the fabulous. Many of his stories possess a thoroughly contemporary blend of the real and the fantastic. His first book, published in 1975, was a collection called *A Dove of the East and Other Stories*. *Ellis Island and Other Stories* followed in 1980. "Tamar" is from that collection.

Helprin's first novel, *Refiner's Fire,* published in 1977, is a picaresque tale that opens with the central character dying of wounds he received as a soldier in the battle for the Golan Heights on the border of Israel and Syria during the Arab-Israeli war of 1973.

Helprin's second novel, *Winter's Tale* (1983), is set just before the year 2000 and tells of a burglar-hero who leads a group of people across the snowdrifts of time in search of the Promised Land of Justice, which they must discover by December 1999. One of the novel's unusual features is a flying white horse, a fugitive from a Brooklyn milk wagon. Helprin has also published *A Soldier of the Great War* (1991), a novel about an Italian soldier of World War I, and *Memoir from Antproof Case* (1995), a novel written from the perspective of an American expatriate in Brazil. In addition, Helprin regularly contributes essays on political and social matters to *The Wall Street Journal.*

PROGRAM MANAGER

- **Planning Instruction** See **Teaching Notes, *Teaching Resources B,*** p. 135, for objectives, a summary, literary elements, and additional historical information for this selection.
- **Instructional Support** Before beginning the instructional lesson, see **Graphic Organizer for Active Reading, *Teaching Resources B,*** p. 142, for a Through the Story activity.
- **Assessment** See **Selection Test, *Test Booklet,*** pp. 217–218.
- **Reinforcement** Use the **Words to Own** worksheet in ***Teaching Resources B,*** p. 143.

Before You Read
TAMAR

Reading Focus

A World of Contradictions
Many writers and other artists see the world we live in as a world of contradictions. Our lives, which are so full of beauty and innocence, can also be marked by ugliness and horror. How can we reconcile these contradictory aspects of the human condition?

Quickwrite

READER'S LOG

Before you read this story set in a world on the brink of war, write your own thoughts on the contradictions you see in life. Do you think people could ever create a totally peaceful and innocent world? Save your notes.

Elements of Literature

Irony
In general, irony is a discrepancy between appearance and reality. "Tamar" contains many examples of two of the main types of irony. **Situational irony** takes place when there is a discrepancy between what is expected to happen, or what would be appropriate to happen, and what really does happen. As you read, compare the expectations of the characters with the reality of the world that engulfs them. In **dramatic irony,** a character thinks one thing is true, but the reader (and in this case the narrator) knows better. In "Tamar," the narrator understands in retrospect a great deal that he and the other characters in the story did not understand in 1938.

Irony is a discrepancy between appearances or expectations and reality.

For more on Irony, see the Handbook of Literary Terms.

The Girl with Peaches (1887) by Valentin Serov. Oil on canvas (37¾″ × 33½″).

Collection Tretiakov Gallery, Moscow. Courtesy Sovfoto.

Background

"Tamar" takes place in London, just before the outbreak of World War II. On September 1, 1939, Nazi Germany invaded Poland, and soon thereafter Britain and France declared war on Germany. The story presumes that the reader is aware of the Holocaust—the murder of some six million Jewish men, women, and children by the Nazis.

Using **Before You Read** p. 921

Elements of Literature

Point out to students that TV situational comedies, or "sitcoms," rely heavily on **irony** for their humor. Ask students to think of a number of examples of both situational and dramatic irony from such shows. Then, challenge students to name instances of both in literary works they have read.

Background

Ask students to share what they know about the Holocaust from films, TV shows, or books and articles on the subject. Challenge students to think of how they would have felt if they had lived through the era and found out about the Holocaust after it had happened. How would the knowledge change their views of the time? Have students record their ideas and compare them with the author's attitude after they have read the story.

PORTFOLIO ASSESSMENT

Portfolio Assessment For help with self-assessment of reading skills, see the *Portfolio Management System,* p. 39.

WORDS TO OWN

The following vocabulary words are defined in the Words to Own at the bottom of the pupil's page.

vulnerability p. 923	theologians p. 925
superficial p. 923	gregariousness p. 925
précis p. 924	interjected p. 926
disheveled p. 924	guilelessly p. 927
hierarchy p. 924	lucidity p. 929

A. Expansion
Jews in Germany began to be stripped of their rights as soon as the Nazis seized control of the government. The Nuremberg Laws, passed on September 15, 1935, deprived Jews of full German citizenship. By November 1938, as many as 150,000 of Germany's half-million Jews had succeeded in leaving the country, some only to fall back under Nazi rule with the advance of the German army across Europe.

Aftermath of *Kristallnacht* in Germany, 1938.
AP/Wide World Photos.

Tamar

Mark Helprin

[A] Before the War, in London, I was trying to arrange a system whereby the Jews of Germany and Austria could sell their paintings and other works of art without depressing demand. It was very serious business, for our primary aim was to require that twenty-five percent of each sale go into an escape fund to provide transport for those who could not make it on their own. We thought that we could exact this price if we managed to keep market values steady. But all of Europe was on edge about the political situation, and no one was in the mood to buy anything. And then, after *Kristallnacht,*[1] every Jew in Germany came forward, wanting to sell precious objects.

1. ***Kristallnacht*** (kris·täl′nakht′): German for "crystal night"; in English, sometimes called "Night of Broken Glass." On November 9, 1938, there was widespread Nazi destruction of Jewish property and brutal attacks on Jews throughout Germany and Austria. (See photo above.)

OPTIONS FOR TEACHING

STRATEGIES FOR INCLUSION

Advanced Have students work in pairs to read aloud and discuss the last paragraph of the selection. Tell students to analyze the paragraph sentence by sentence by freely expressing their thoughts about its content, by discussing any problems they find and questions they have, and by making connections to real-life characters or situations. Then, have the pairs think of similar situations from other literary works to share.

Musical Ask students to work in teams of two or three to discuss the kind of music that the falling snow might have suggested on the night of the story. Students may expand the activity to think of a soundtrack for a film version of "Tamar." Students may share their song lists with the rest of the class and describe the feelings the music evokes.

Less Proficient Readers After students have read the selection, have them summarize the story. Call on a volunteer to summarize the first few paragraphs of the story, and ask the class "Then what happened?" Have another student summarize the next few paragraphs, and continue the process until the story has been accurately summarized.

At the time of our greatest hope, my job was to set up fronts for selling what we expected would be a flood of art coming in from Middle Europe. If it had appeared that English collectors were opening their storerooms to take advantage of a favorable market, the excitement might well have pushed values upward. So we tried to get the cooperation of those prominent collectors who had the foresight to see what was about to happen on the Continent and were in sympathy with our cause. Excepting a very few, these were Jews. The others simply were not interested, and, anyway, we did not want to divulge the plan in too many places. **B**

Soon I found myself deeply involved in the high society of Jews in London and in their great houses throughout the countryside. My conviction was then, as it is now, that it is not possible for Jews to be in "society" but that their efforts to be so are (except when immoderate or in bad taste) courageous, for the mechanisms of high social status are encouragements of vulnerability, safe only for those who can afford to lose themselves in pursuits superficial and deep and not fear that their fundamental positions will drop out from under them as a result of their inattention. My attitude toward the Jewish peers[2] and the Jewish upper class in general was mixed, and had complex roots. I admired their bravery while occasionally chafing at their blindness. I knew that, in spite of their learning and culture, they were isolated in such a way as to make me—a young man of thirty-two—far better a judge of certain things than were they. I had been in the ghetto[3] in Warsaw not a month before, and the people there had confided to me that they felt the end was near. They said, "Tell them, in England, that in Poland they are killing Jews." I had been in Berlin, Munich, Vienna, and Prague. I had passed through Jewish villages from Riga to Bucharest,[4] where I had seen a temple about to fall. How misty and beautiful it was, that autumn. I cannot describe the quiet. It was as if the nineteenth century—indeed, all the past—were in hiding and feared to give itself away. The whole world of the Jews in Central Europe looked outward with the saddest eyes. What could *I* do? I tried my best. I was working for the Jewish Agency, and had just come from two years in Palestine, in the desert, and thought that my responsibility was to save the Jews of Europe. Like all young men, I was full of speeches that I could not deliver. Somehow, I imagined that the art scheme would be everything. I have since forgiven myself. **C**

Visions of the Jews in the forests, in green pine valleys as sharp as chevrons,[5] in villages marked by silent white ribbons of wood smoke, never left me as I undertook to master the intricacies of the London social season. I cannot remember when I have enjoyed myself more. Sometimes I became as lost and trusting as my hosts, and, even when I did not, the contrast between the Eastern European *Heimat*[6] and the drawing rooms of modern London was incalculably enlivening. I was suspended between two dream-worlds.

Just before Christmas, that time in all capitals when the city flares most brightly, I was oppressed with invitations. I had a blue pad upon which I listed my engagements, and one terrible, lovely week it had sixteen entries. I met so many **D** dukes, duchesses, M.P.s,[7] industrialists, and academics that my eyes began to cross. But we had begun to succeed in hammering out a network for art sales, and I was confident and happy.

Then a magical power in the Jewish Agency must have decided that these several score dinners had made me into a diplomat, for I received an invitation to a dinner party on the twenty-first at the house of the most eminent Jew in all the British Empire. Only that summer, I had scrubbed pots, guarded at night, and lived in a tent, in a

2. **peers:** members of the nobility.
3. **ghetto:** section of some cities in Europe where Jews had to live, even before the Nazi occupation. The Nazis moved Jews into a ghetto in Warsaw, Poland, before transporting them to concentration camps during World War II.
4. **Riga** (rē′gə) **to Bucharest** (bo͞o′kə·rest′): capital cities of, respectively, Latvia and Romania, countries in Eastern Europe.
5. **chevrons:** V-shaped designs in heraldic devices or military insignia.
6. ***Heimat*** (hī′mät): German for "home" or "homeland."
7. **M.P.s:** in Great Britain, members of Parliament.

Words to Own

vulnerability (vul′ner·ə·bil′ə·tē) *n.:* state of being open for attack.
superficial (so͞o′pər·fish′əl) *adj.:* obvious; shallow.

B. Critical Reading: Summarizing

? What plan is the author a part of? [He and a group of others are trying to sell the artwork collected by Central European Jews who now need money to escape the Nazi regime in Germany. They must sell the works quietly to avoid swamping the market and drastically altering the market value of the works.]

C. Literary Element: Dramatic Irony

? What is the author's attitude toward his past self and his high hopes for the plan? [He knows better now and considers his enthusiasm for the plan as naïve or idealistic at best, and perhaps even something for which he should seek forgiveness, as if it were a crime to have such beliefs.]

D. Reader's Response: Shaping Interpretations

? How can a week be both "terrible" and "lovely"? [Sample responses: The week was terrible for him because it was so busy and draining, but it was lovely because it was exciting. At the time, the week was lovely because he believed in the cause, but now he sees his excitement over the week's events as terribly misguided.]

Strategies for Inclusion

Interpersonal Help students explore the contradictions at the end of the story by having groups of students apply the ideas to the narrator's remembrance of Tamar. Have groups especially focus on the contradictory phrases "great contexts remained unbroken" and "all connections are temporary." What details of the narrator's interaction with Tamar support one or the other of these statements? Have the pairs share their ideas.

Integrating the Language Arts

Writing: Diary Entry Ask students to write a diary entry for the narrator that describes the events of the evening. Students can write the diary entry from the **point of view** of the time, without knowledge of the impending war and Holocaust. Have students compare their completed entries to the story, taking note particularly of the differences in tone. Ask volunteers to read their work to the class.

A. Literary Element: Imagery

? What does the image tell you about the mood of the setting? [Possible answer: The falling snow adds an air of disquietude and a beautiful, but sinister or oppressive, feeling to the dignified grace of the neighborhood.]

B. Reader's Response: First Impressions

? What does the description of the narrator's arrival tell you about the narrator and the people he is visiting? [Sample responses: Both the narrator and the people already at the house are frightened and aloof because of the importance of their meeting. The people at the house are overcautious because of their experiences as European Jews, and the narrator, not having had the same experiences, does not know how to treat them.]

collective settlement in the Negev.[8] Now I ballooned with pride. The entire seventeenth century could not have produced enough frills to clothe the heavy monster of my pomposity. Sure that all my troubles were over forever, I spent every bit of my money on the most beautiful three-piece suit in London. When the tailor—who was himself a knight—heard where I was going, he set his men to work, and they finished it in three days. London became, for me, the set of a joyous light opera.

On the night of the twentieth, just twenty-four hours before what I assumed would be my apotheosis[9] (it was said that the Prime Minister would be there, and I imagined myself declaring to him a leaden diplomatic précis along the lines of the Magna Carta or the Treaty of Vienna),[10] I had yet another engagement, this one at the house of a Jewish art dealer whom I had recently regarded as a big fish. I was so overconfident that I left my hotel without his address, thinking that I would manage to find it anyway, since I knew its approximate location in Chelsea.[11]

I was due at six-thirty. For an hour and a half I rushed through Chelsea in this direction and that, trying to find the house. Everyone, it seemed, was having a dinner party, and all the buildings looked alike. When, finally, I arrived at the right square, I stood in a little park and stared at the house. It was five stories tall and it was lit like a theater. Through the sparkling windows came firelight, candlelight, (A) and glimpses of enormous chandeliers—while the snow fell as if in time to sad and troubling music. Red and disheveled from running about, I stood in my splendid suit, frightened to go in. In that square, the coal smoke was coiling about like a great menagerie of airborne snakes, and occasionally it caught me and choked me in its unbearable fumes. But I remember it with fondness, because it was the smell of Europe in the winter; and, though it was devilish and foul, it seemed to say that, underneath everything, another world was at work, that the last century was alive in its clumsiness and warmth, signaling that all was well and that great contexts[12] remained unbroken.

I was afraid to go in, because I was so late and because I knew what a fool I had been in judging these people according to the hierarchy in which they believed, and thus underrating them in comparison to the plutocrats[13] of the next night. But I took hold of myself and rang their bell. I heard conversation stop. A servant came to the door. (B) Each of his steps shot through the wood like an X-ray. I was taken upstairs to a magnificent room in which were five tables of well-dressed people completely motionless and silent, like a group of deer surprised by a hunter. Every eye was upon me. Though frightened of fainting, I remained upright and seemingly composed. My host stood to greet me. Then he took me about like a roast, and introduced me to each and every guest, all of whom had a particular smile that can be described only as simultaneously benevolent, sadistic, and amused. I don't know why, but I broke into German, though my German was not the best. They must have been thinking, Who is this strange red-faced German who does not speak his own language well? Or perhaps they thought that I was confused as to my whereabouts. I suppose I was.

Then Herr Dennis, as I called him, took me by the arm and explained that, since they had readjusted the seating in my absence, I (who, the next day, would be waltzing with the Prime Minister) would have to sit at the children's table. It was a very great blow, especially since the poor children were bunched up all by themselves in a little ell of the room that led to the kitchen. I was in no position to protest; in fact, I was, by that time, quite numb.

8. **collective . . . Negev** (neg′ev′): farms or other enterprises where members work together, renting or owning property and the means of production as a group. A number of these settlements are located in the Negev, a desert region in present-day southern Israel.
9. **apotheosis** (ə·päth′ē·ō′sis): glorification.
10. **Magna Carta . . . Vienna:** Signed by England's King John in 1215, the Magna Carta (Latin for "great charter") guaranteed certain civil and political liberties. The Treaty of Vienna, also known as the Final Act of the Congress of Vienna, helped reorganize Europe in 1815, near the end of the Napoleonic wars.
11. **Chelsea:** district of London.
12. **contexts:** settings; situations.
13. **plutocrats:** people whose wealth gives them power.

Words to Own

précis (prā·sē′) *n.:* summary.
disheveled (di·shev′əld) *adj.:* rumpled; messed up.
hierarchy (hī′ər·är′kē) *n.:* class system of social ranking.

OPTIONS FOR TEACHING

INTEGRATING THE LANGUAGE ARTS

Speaking and Listening Ask students to read the selection silently and highlight words, phrases, or sentences that create an unforgettable mental picture of the story's **theme, characters, setting,** or **subject.** Ask students to read aloud the portions of text they have highlighted. Then, have other students respond with their own highlighted passages. Encourage students to draw connections between their examples.

Language and Style Call on a volunteer to explain the meaning of **tone.** Remind students that **tone** is a result of a number of elements such as **diction, imagery,** and **style.** Ask students to identify the tone Helprin uses in this selection and to provide examples from the text.

Strategic Reading Before they read the story, have students draw on their knowledge about World War II and the experiences of Jews during the war. Ask them to record on the following chart what they know and what they want to know about the time. After they finish reading the selection, have them complete the third column.

What I Know	What I Want to Know	What I Learned

As he led me, in a daze, toward the children's table, I imagined myself sitting with five or ten infants in bibs, staring down at them as if from a high tower, eating sullenly like a god exiled from Olympus. But when we rounded the corner of the ell, I discovered that the children were adolescents; and their charm arose to envelop me. First, there were four red-headed girl cousins, all in white. They were from thirteen to sixteen; they had between them several hundred million freckles; and they were so disturbed by my sudden arrival that they spent the next half hour swallowing, darting their eyes about, clearing their throats, and adjusting fallen locks of hair. They spoke as seriously as very old theologians, but ever so much more delicately; they pieced together their sentences with great care, the way new skaters skate, and when they finished they breathed in relief, not unlike students of a difficult Oriental language, who must recite in class. At the end of these ordeals, they looked at each other with the split-second glances common to people who are very familiar. Then, there was a boy with dark woolly hair and the peculiarly adolescent animal-lost-out-on-the-heath expression common to young men whose abilities greatly exceed their experience. At my appearance, he lowered his horns, knowing that he was going to spend the rest of the evening bashing himself against a castle wall. I admired his courage; I liked him; I remembered. Next to him was a fat boy who wanted to be an opera singer. He was only fourteen, and when he saw that the threat presented by the woolly-haired boy was neutralized, he went wild with excitement, blooming at the four cousins with a gregariousness of which he had probably never been aware.

I liked these children. They seemed somewhat effete,[14] and sheltered, but I knew that this was because I was used to the adolescents of our collective, who were much older than their years, and that these young people were the products of an ultra-refined system of schooling. I knew that, if protected during this vulnerability, they might emerge with unmatched strength. I had been through the same system, and had seen my schoolmates undergo miraculous transformations. I knew as well that they were destined for a long and terrible war, but, then again, so were we all. Yes, I liked these children, and I enjoyed the fact that I had left those years behind.

I have not described everyone at that table. One remains. She was the daughter of my host, the eldest, the tallest, the most beautiful. Her name was Tamar, and as I had turned the corner she had seemed to rise in the air to meet me, while the others were lost in the dark. Tamar and I had faced one another in a moment of silence that I will not ever forget. Sometimes, on a windy day, crosscurrented waves in the shallows near a beach will spread about, trapped in a caldron of bars and brakes, until two run together face to face and then fall back in shocked tranquility. So it was with Tamar. It was as if I had run right into her. I was breathless, and I believe that she was, too.

I immediately took command of myself, and did not look at her. In fact, I studied every face before I studied hers—black eyes; black hair; her mouth and eyes showing her youth and strength in the way they were set, in the way they moved, not ever having been tried or defeated or abused. She wore a rich white silk blouse that was wonderfully open at the top, and a string of matched pearls. For a moment, I was convinced that she was in her twenties, but when she smiled I saw a touching thin silver wire across her upper teeth, and I knew that she was probably no more than seventeen. She *was* seventeen, soon to be eighteen, soon to take off the wire, soon (in fact) to become a nurse with the Eighth Army in Egypt. But at that time she was just on the verge of becoming a woman, and she virtually glowed with the fact.

As soon as I saw the wire, I felt as if I could talk with her in a way that could be managed, and I did. Unlike the four red-headed cousins, she was fearless and direct. She laughed out loud without the slightest self-consciousness, and I felt as if in our conversation we were not speaking but dancing. Perhaps it was because she was so clear of voice, so alert, and so straightforward. She was old enough to parry, and she did, extraordinarily well.

14. **effete** (e·fēt'): overrefined; delicate.

WORDS TO OWN

theologians (thē'ə·lō'jənz) *n. pl.:* scholars of religious doctrine.
gregariousness (grə·ger'ē·əs·nis) *n.:* sociability.

C. Literary Element: Situational Irony

? What is ironic about the narrator's seat for dinner? [He expects to be an important guest, but because he is late he is seated at the children's table.]

D. Literary Element: Imagery

? What does the image of the skaters suggest about the children's speech? [Students may say that the children speak unnaturally—very slowly, carefully, and stiffly.]

E. Critical Reading: Making Inferences

? Why is the boy so happy? [He realizes that the narrator will have to deal with the other boy's willfulness, not him, so the boy begins to relax and enjoy himself.]

F. Reader's Response: Connecting with the Text

? In what other works have you read such a description of a meeting between two people? What is happening between the two characters? [Sample responses: The description is like that in a story of romance; the two characters are attracted to each other. The description records an important event, much like the clashing of two armies; the two characters will affect each other's life in some important way.]

CLASSROOM MANAGEMENT

Recording Thoughts with a Quickwrite To solidify an impression or thoughts about any subject before, during, or after a learning experience, have students do a quickwrite. Students should quickwrite for a given amount of time, such as two or three minutes. They should write anything they can think of on the topic with no concern for punctuation, spelling, or grammar. They can use these notes for activities following their reading.

Student Interaction One purpose of cooperative learning and small group discussion is to encourage students to interact with each other with minimal input from the teacher. Here are some tips for maximizing student interaction.

- Ask another student to respond to a student's statement or question.
- Seat students in a circle so that they can face each other.
- Try to minimize teacher talk or suggestions.
- Encourage students to call on one another.

Block Scheduling In order to work successfully within a longer class period, plan for approximately twice as much material as would be taught in a shorter period of time. Enhance a lesson with a variety of shorter activities. This variety is important in setting the pace of lessons in block scheduling. ☞

LITERATURE AND HISTORY

Ask students to discuss their knowledge or experience of the works discussed in the feature. Have students compare the different perspectives on the Holocaust. What do they have in common? How are they different? Students can record their ideas in a graphic organizer like that on Transparency 5: Venn Diagram in the Transparency Package.

A. Critical Reading: Expressing an Opinion

? Why does the narrator say "Tamar" instead of "you" when he speaks to her? [Possible responses: He is teasing Tamar or mimicking the red-haired girl's announcement of Tamar's travel plans.]

LITERATURE AND HISTORY

Never Again: Witnesses to the Holocaust

The Holocaust (or, in Hebrew, *Sho'ah*) was the systematic murder of six million Jews by the German Nazi dictatorship across Europe between 1933 and 1945. Determined to exalt "racial purity," the Nazi tyranny exterminated Jews along with Gypsies and Slavs, homosexuals, people with disabilities, political enemies, and others deemed undesirable by the Nazis. By the end of World War II, two thirds of European Jews had perished, victims of the largest known genocide in human history.

The Nobel Peace Prize–winning writer Elie Wiesel has said that the Holocaust "defies language and art." Nevertheless, since 1945, artists have tried to use words and images to express the inexpressible anguish of victims and survivors. In 1947, *The Diary of a Young Girl,* the first widely read work to come out of the Holocaust, was published. Anne Frank, a teenage Jewish girl, had kept the diary while she and her family hid from the Nazis in Amsterdam. Their hiding place discovered, Anne was sent to the German concentration camp at Belsen, where she died less than one year later. Anne's story touched readers throughout the world and reached an even larger audience when it was later dramatized as a play and a film. Eleven years later came one of the most powerful and moving accounts of the Holocaust: Elie Wiesel's *Night* (1960). Wiesel, who had been arrested by the Nazis in 1944 at the age of fifteen and deported from Romania to the concentration camp at Auschwitz, wrote eloquently of his experiences in order to, as he has said, "bear witness" to the atrocities perpetrated against Jews and other victims of the Nazis. "Never shall I forget these things," Wiesel wrote in *Night,* "even if I am condemned to live as long as God Himself. Never."

"Tamar is going to Brussels[15] next year," volunteered one of the red-haired girls, in the manner of a handmaiden at court, "to study at the Royal Laboratory for Underzek and Verpen."

"No, no, no," said Tamar. "What you're thinking of, Hannah, is called the Koninklijk Laboratorium voor Onderzoek van Voorwerpen van Kunst en Wetenschap, and it's in The Hague."[16] She glided over the minefield of Dutch words without hesitation and in a perfect accent.

(A) "Does Tamar speak Dutch?" I asked, looking right at her.

"Yes," she answered, "Tamar speaks Dutch, because she learnt it at her Dutch grandmother's knee—Daddy's mother. But," she continued, shaking a finger gently at Hannah, though really speaking to me, "I'm going to Brussels, to study restoration at the Institut Central des Beaux-Arts, or, if Fascism[17] flies out the window in Italy between now and next year, to the Istituto Nazionale per il Restauro, in Rome."

When she realized that her recitation of the names of these formidable institutes, each in its own language, might have seemed ostentatious, she blushed.

Emboldened nearly to giddiness, the fat boy interjected, "We went to Rome. We ate shiski ba there, and the streets are made of water."

15. **Brussels:** capital of Belgium.
16. **The Hague** (hāg): city in western Netherlands; seat of national government.

17. **Fascism** (fash'iz'm): dictatorial system of government, instituted in Italy in 1922.

WORDS TO OWN

interjected (in'tər·jekt'id) *v.:* interrupted with; inserted.

OPTIONS FOR TEACHING

CROSSING THE CURRICULUM

Social Sciences Ask students to research and report on a memorial in the United States or abroad for the victims of the Holocaust. Discuss with students how the memorial serves as an important preservation of the memory of Holocaust victims. Then, challenge students to think of other purposes it serves.

Geography/Social Sciences Ask students to research the geography of the Central European countries in which Jews were threatened by the armies of Nazi Germany. Students can find information on the Jewish population of the countries, their responses to the Nazi threat, and the international response to the plight of Central European Jews. Have students share their findings in a round-table discussion.

Art Ask students to find prints and photographs of art that they think express the narrator's feelings for Tamar. Have each student present one photograph or print to the rest of the class. Students should explain how the art they find relates to the story.

As the firsthand memory of the Holocaust dwindles in our time with the deaths of the survivors, the idea of "witness" has become even more powerful. In 1985, the almost nine-hour-long French documentary film *Shoah* riveted audiences with its uncompromising interviews with survivors of the Holocaust—and some of the Nazi perpetrators. Art Spiegelman's two-part Pulitzer Prize–winning graphic novel *Maus* (1986) used a cartoon format to tell, with poignancy and ironic force, the grim, true story of his parents' experiences in a concentration camp.

A "witness" of a different sort is the United States Holocaust Memorial Museum, which opened in 1993 in Washington, D.C. The museum's mission is to preserve concrete evidence of the Holocaust and to prompt reflection about the tragedy. In the same year, the movie director Steven Spielberg adapted Thomas Keneally's novel *Schindler's Ark.* As *Schindler's List,* the Academy Award–winning film recounts a non-Jewish businessman's risky efforts to save hundreds of Jews from certain death.

Artists, politicians, and thoughtful people the world over hold on to the hope that words and images will serve to prevent repetition of the horror of the Holocaust. Perhaps this bleak tale by a German pastor, Martin Niemöller, one of those who found the courage to resist the Nazis during World War II, sums up the importance of acting courageously on behalf of all human beings:

> In Germany, the Nazis first came for the Communists and I didn't speak up because I wasn't a Communist. Then they came for the Jews and I did not speak up because I was not a Jew. Then they came for the trade unionists and I didn't speak up because I was not a trade unionist. Then they came for the Catholics and I was a Protestant so I didn't speak up. Then they came for me: by that time there was no one left to speak up.

"That's *Venice, stupid,*" said one of the red-haired girls. "And what is shiski ba?"

"Shiski ba," answered the fat boy, guilelessly, "is roasted meat on a stick. The Turks sell it in the park."

"Bob,"[18] I offered, by way of instruction. A silence followed, during which the poor boy looked at me blankly.

"Richard," he said, sending the four cousins (who knew him well) into a fit of hysteria. Tamar tried not to laugh, because she knew that he hung on her every gesture and word. **B**

To change the subject, I challenged Tamar. "Do you really think," I said, "that you will be able to study on the Continent?"

She shrugged her shoulders and smiled in a way that belied her age. "I'll do the best I can," she answered. "Even if there is a war, it will have an end. I'll still be young, and I'll start again."

My eyes opened at this. I don't know exactly why; perhaps it was that I imagined her in the future and became entranced with the possibility that I might encounter her then—in some faraway place where affection could run unrestrained. But I wanted to steer things away from art, war, and love.

So, while constantly fending off the quixotic[19] charges of the woolly-haired boy (without ever

18. **bob:** The narrator is correcting the boy's pronunciation of "shish kebab."

19. **quixotic** (kwiks·ät′ik): extremely idealistic and impractical, like the hero of *Don Quixote* (dän kē·hōt′ē), a novel by the Spanish writer Miguel de Cervantes (1547–1616).

WORDS TO OWN

guilelessly (gīl′lis·lē) *adv.:* innocently or frankly; without slyness.

B. Critical Reading: Drawing Conclusions

? What has happened that is so funny? [The narrator tries to correct the boy's pronunciation of *shish kebab,* but the boy, thinking the narrator is calling him "Bob," replies that his name is Richard.]

PROBLEM SOLVING/CRITICAL THINKING

Dealing with Disappointment Point out to students that the narrator in the story deals with at least two instances of disappointment in the story—the failure of his great plan for saving Central European Jews and his youthful obsession with the opera singer. Ask students to name the strategies the narrator uses to deal with these disappointments. Then, have students brainstorm for other strategies for similar situations from film, literature, or TV. Students can discuss and compare the merit of the strategies.

PROFESSIONAL NOTES

Cultural Diversity The narrator tells the children tales of his days in Palestine. Following World War I, the League of Nations gave Britain a provisional mandate over Palestine so that Britain could prepare Palestine for future self-rule and the establishment of a Jewish national home. Jewish immigration to Palestine greatly increased in the 1930s as Hitler instituted programs to persecute Jews. As early as the 1920s, however, Arabs opposed the action, and it may have been in one of these early conflicts that the narrator was involved. Discuss with students the status of Jewish/Arab relations in the Middle East today.

A. Critical Reading: Analyzing Character

? What does this statement tell you about the narrator's **character?** [Possible answers: The narrator is playful, creative, and he likes to entertain; he also does not have any qualms about making up stories.]

B. Literary Element: Metaphor

? What does the metaphor reveal about Tamar's reaction to the narrator's stories? [She changes her mind often about the veracity of his tales, each time becoming more skeptical and on guard.]

C. Critical Reading: Identifying Main Ideas

? What is the narrator's assessment of the situation? [He realizes that he has embarrassed himself as well as Tamar, but his experience with romance allows him to shrug off the confusion because his comment was only part of a minor flirtation.]

D. Literary Element: Anecdote

? How is the narrator's situation with Tamar similar to his experience with the opera singer? [Both women are beautiful but out of reach, for different reasons; he must admire both from a distance and be content with the slightest involvement with their lives.]

really looking at him), I told a long story about Palestine. Because they were children, more or less, I told them anything I wanted to tell them. Until long after the adults had left for the living room, I spoke of impossible battles between Jews and Bedouins,[20] of feats of endurance which made me reel merely in imagining them, of horses that flew, and golden shafts of light, pillars of fire, miracles here and there, the wonders of spoken Hebrew, and the lions that guarded the banks and post offices of Jerusalem—in short, anything which seemed as if it might be believed.

Tamar alternated between belief and disbelief with the satisfying rhythm of a blade turning back and forth over a whetstone.[21] She was weaving soft acceptance and sparkling disdain together in a tapestry which I feared she would throw right over my head. She did this in a most delicate cross-examination, the object of which was to draw out more of the tale for the sake of the children, to satisfy her own curiosity, to mock me gently, and to continue—by entrapment and release—the feeling we had that, though we were still, we were dancing.

"Why," she asked, "did you not get water from the Bedouins that you captured, if you had already gone without it for ten days?"

"Ah!" I said, holding up my finger in the same way she had done with Hannah. "I was only able to capture them because they themselves had run out of water, and were thirstier than I was. And I did not capture them with a gun but by giving a graphic dissertation on European fountains; they were especially taken with my description of the Diana fountain in Bushy Park, and I believe that they would have followed me anywhere after I told them what goes on in the Place de la Concorde."[22]

"What is it like to be a British Jew in Palestine?" asked Hannah, earnestly, and with such *Weltschmerz*[23] that it was as if an alpine storm cloud had rolled over the table.

"What is it like? It's like being an Italian Negro in Ethiopia, or"—I looked at Tamar—"like living in a continuous production of *Romeo and Juliet*."

I had meant the allusion to *Romeo and Juliet* to be purely illustrative, but with a life of its own it turned Tamar as red as a throbbing coal, and I, a generation apart, nearly followed suit. I was caught in my own springe,[24] enchanted—yet never really in danger, for not only did her father come to fetch me back into the world of adults but I had run those rapids before, and knew the still and deep water at their end.

I recall exactly how the children were sitting when I left them, poised to explode in gossip as soon as I had disappeared—it is likely that in my absence I was cut to ribbons by the woolly-haired boy, and perhaps deservedly so. As Tamar's father and I climbed a broad staircase to the library, where we would discuss business, I remembered the opera singer with whom I had once fallen in love. Her voice was like liquid or a jewel. I have not since heard such a beautiful voice. But she was, oddly enough, almost unknown. I went to Covent Garden[25] to find out in what productions she would sing. Her name was Erika, and when I inquired of the old man at the ticket office I found that he, too, was in love with her.

"I'm too old," he said, "and you're too young." I knew that this was true, and I must have looked pained, because he grabbed me through the ticket window and said, "Don't you see, it's much better that way!"

"I see nothing," I said. "If that's better, then I'm sorry to be alive."

"Wait," he said, and laughed. "You'll see. It's sweeter, much sweeter."

I went to the opera that season two dozen times just to see and hear Erika of the liquid voice. I wanted, despite the fact that I was fifteen, to marry her immediately, to run away to Brazil or Argentina, to take her with me to the South Seas, etc., etc., etc. It had been unspeakable torture to watch her on a brilliantly lighted stage, singing in a way that fired up all my emotions.

But by the time I met Tamar, I knew that a lighted stage is often best left untouched, and I knew, further, that all connections are temporary, and, therefore, can be enjoyed in their fullness

20. **Bedouins:** Arabs who primarily live as nomads in the desert.
21. **whetstone:** stone used to sharpen tools.
22. **Place de la Concorde** (plas dë lä cōn·côrd'): large square with beautiful fountains, in Paris.
23. ***Weltschmerz*** (velt'shmerts'): German for "world-weariness."
24. **springe** (sprinj): device with a noose used to trap small animals.
25. **Covent Garden:** site of the Royal Opera House, in London.

COOPERATIVE LEARNING

Enact a Skit Have students work in groups of four to research a specific event in the history of the Holocaust. Then ask students to write and perform a skit in which the narrator of "Tamar" tells of the horror that would come for the European Jews. Each student should have a speaking role, with one actor portraying the narrator and the others enacting or adding to his story.

ASSESSMENT TOOLS

Check Test: Questions and Answers

1. What is the story's setting? [London, before World War II.]
2. What is the goal of the narrator's plan in the story? [To help Jews obtain money to escape from the increasing oppression of the Nazi government.]
3. Who is the person the story is named after? [Tamar is the teenage daughter of a Jewish art dealer in London.]
4. What sight makes the narrator easier about talking to the girl? [He sees the silver wire of her braces, which indicate her much younger age.]
5. Whom does the narrator remember after leaving Tamar? [Erika, an opera singer with whom he had fallen in love when he was much younger.]

even after the most insubstantial touch—if only one knows how. I was, that night, in a dream within a dream. I was young again in a room of bright colors and laughter; and all the time the dark image of a smoky continent called me away and threatened to tear me apart. I did not know then that there is no contradiction in such contradictions; they are made for one another; without **E** them, we would have nothing to lose and nothing to love.

Tamar was the most lovely girl—and had it not been for that delicate and slim bit of silver wire, I might not have known her as well as I did. Her father agreed to the scheme, but then the scheme collapsed, and the world collapsed soon after. Six years of war. Most of the Jews did not survive. Most of the paintings did. In six years of war, there was probably not a day when I did not think of the time when I had had to sit at the children's table, in a world of vulnerable beauty. Perhaps things are most beautiful when they are not quite real; when you look upon a scene as an outsider, and come to possess it in its entirety and forever; when you live the present with the lucidity and feeling of memory; when, for want of connection, **F** the world deepens and becomes art.

WORDS TO OWN

lucidity (lo͞o·sid′i·tē) *n.:* clarity; rationality.

Connections — A Speech

Isaac Bashevis Singer (1904–1991) grew up in Poland as the son of a rabbi. He immigrated to the United States in 1935, alarmed by the rise of violent antisemitism in Europe (also a somber concern of the narrator of "Tamar"). The greatest modern writer in Yiddish, Singer became known for stories in which unseen forces—both divine and demonic—are at work. He was awarded the Nobel Prize in literature in 1978. Among the best known of his works (many translated into English) are the novel *The Family Moskat* (1950) and the short-story collections *Gimpel the Fool and Other Stories* (1961), *The Spinoza of Market Street and Other Stories* (1961), *A Crown of Feathers* (1973), and *The Death of Methuselah* (1985).

Nobel Prize Acceptance Speech, 1978

The storyteller and poet of our time, as in any other time, must be an entertainer of the spirit in the full sense of the word, not just a preacher of social or political ideals. There is no paradise for bored readers and no excuse for tedious literature that does not intrigue the reader, uplift his spirit, give him the joy and the escape that true art always grants. Nevertheless, it is also true that the serious writer of our time must be deeply concerned about the problems of his generation. He cannot but see that the power of religion, especially belief in revelation, is weaker today than it was in any other epoch in human history. More and more children grow up without faith in God, without belief in reward and punishment, in the immortality of the soul, and even in the validity of ethics. The genuine writer cannot ignore the fact that the family is losing its spiritual foundation. All the dismal prophecies of Oswald Spengler have become realities since the **G** Second World War. No technological achievements can mitigate the disappointment of modern man, his loneliness, his feeling of inferiority, and his fear of war, revolution, and terror. Not only has our generation lost faith in Providence, but also in man himself, in his institutions, and often in those who are nearest to him.

In their despair a number of those who no longer have confidence in the leadership of

CONNECTING WITH "TAMAR"

Do Singer and the narrator of "Tamar" have similar ideas about art's role in the survival of humanity? Explain. [Possible responses: Yes, the two have similar ideas about the way art clarifies life and makes it more meaningful and profound. No, because the narrator of "Tamar" sees art as being something separate from life, something experienced only by an individual at a particular place and time, while for Singer art is public and purposeful.]

E. Reader's Response: Extending the Text

? Judging from your own life or other works you have read, do you think that there are essential contradictions in life? [Sample responses: There is really no contradiction in what the narrator describes; as Updike points out in the quotation that opens the unit, things always seem like they're coming into existence and being destroyed at the same time. Or yes, there are essential contradictions, because even in the happiest moments there is a touch of sadness, as the narrator realizes.]

F. Reader's Response: Challenging the Text

? Has the story demonstrated how life can suddenly deepen and become art? Explain. [Sample responses: No; the story has shown how a chance encounter can affect someone deeply, but the experience doesn't become art until the author writes about it. Yes; the story depicts a moment in which life suddenly takes on layers of contradictions and meanings, like a work of art.]

Metacognition Ask students to share the strategies they used to come to conclusions about the contradictions addressed by the narrator at the end of the story. Students can also draw parallels to the "art" in their own lives and compare their insights to Helprin's. *Remind students that they do not have to share anything they feel uncomfortable discussing with other students.*

G. Humanities Connection

Oswald Spengler (1880–1936) was a German philosopher who became famous in 1918 when he published the first volume of his *The Decline of the West* (two volumes, 1918–22). Spengler's pessimistic philosophy held that history grew and decayed in systematic ways that may be studied by people in the changes in their own culture.

A. Literary Connections
Charles Baudelaire (1821–1867), the French poet, examined shocking and disturbing topics, but also fundamental subjects such as the nature of truth. Paul Verlaine (1844–1896), another French poet, was one of the most gifted writers of his age. For Poe (1809–1849), see pp. 260–261. August Strindberg (1849–1912) was a Swedish playwright and novelist who exerted enormous influence on the international theater of the twentieth century.

B. Humanities Connection
A major work of ancient Greek philosophy, *The Republic* (c. 370 B.C.) advanced many of Plato's principal ideas on government and justice. It describes the ideal state, which should be ruled by "philosopher-kings."

our society look up to the writer, the master of words. They hope against hope that the man of talent and sensitivity can perhaps rescue civilization. Maybe there is a spark of the prophet in the artist after all.

As the son of a people who received the worst blows that human madness can inflict, I have many times resigned myself to never finding a true way out. But a new hope always emerges, telling me that it is not yet too late for all of us to take stock and make a decision. I was brought up to believe in free will. Although I came to doubt all revelation, I can never accept the idea that the universe is a physical or chemical accident, a result of blind evolution. Even though I learned to recognize the lies, the clichés, and the idolatries of the human mind, I still cling to some truths which I think all of us might accept someday. There must be a way for man to attain all possible pleasures, all the powers and knowledge that nature can grant him, and still serve God—a God who speaks in deeds, not in words, and whose vocabulary is the universe.

I am not ashamed to admit that I belong to those who fantasize that literature is capable of bringing new horizons and new perspectives—philosophical, religious, aesthetical, and even social. In the history of old Jewish literature there was never any basic difference between the poet and the prophet. Our ancient poetry often became law and a way of life.

Some of my cronies in the cafeteria near the *Jewish Daily Forward* in New York call me a pessimist and a decadent, but there is always a background of faith behind resignation. [A] I found comfort in such pessimists and decadents as Baudelaire, Verlaine, Edgar Allan Poe, and Strindberg. My interest in psychic research made me find solace in such mystics as your Swedenborg and in our own Rabbi Nachman Bratzlaver, as well as in a great poet of my time, my friend Aaron Zeitlin, who died a few years ago and left a spiritual inheritance of high quality, most of it in Yiddish.

The pessimism of the creative person is not decadence, but a mighty passion for the redemption of man. While the poet entertains he continues to search for eternal truths, for the essence of being. In his own fashion he tries to solve the riddle of time and change, to find an answer to suffering, to reveal love in the very abyss of cruelty and injustice. Strange as these words may sound, I often play with the idea that when all the social theories collapse and wars and revolutions leave humanity in utter [B] gloom, the poet—whom Plato banned from his Republic—may rise up to save us all.

—Isaac Bashevis Singer

Making Meanings

First Thoughts

1. Possible response: Tamar and the narrator of the story are likable because they are open to the beauty of experiences around them. Students' examples of similar people they know will vary.

Reviewing the Text

The narrator visits the house of a Jewish art dealer in London as part of a plan to sell Central European Jews' art so that they may have money to escape the growing Nazi threat. He is late, and has to sit at the children's table, where he meets Tamar. He tells the children fantastical tales of his experiences in Palestine. At the end of the story, he compares his attraction to Tamar to his youthful love for an opera singer, and then tells of the deaths of many of the Jews he tried to save.

Shaping Interpretations

2. She responds to the special attention he pays her. The blush at the reference to *Romeo and Juliet* probably means she compares the star-crossed lovers to the narrator and herself.

MAKING MEANINGS

First Thoughts

1. What is your reaction to Tamar and the narrator? Do you like them? Do they resemble any people you know?

Reviewing the Text

Summarize the events that bring the narrator to Tamar's house, his dinner conversation with the children, and the events the narrator relates at the end of the story.

Shaping Interpretations

2. How would you explain Tamar's attraction to the narrator? What can we infer when Tamar blushes at the reference to *Romeo and Juliet?*
3. What does the story of Erika, the opera singer, have to do with the story of Tamar?
4. What effect does Helprin achieve by wrapping the story of Tamar inside an account of the Nazis and the war? What passage in the story reminds us, with deep **irony,** of what is about to happen in Europe?
5. What larger group of people might be represented by Herr Dennis and his family and

3. In each case, the narrator has been attracted to a woman who is unattainable because of an age difference.
4. Responses will vary. The setting highlights the theme of vulnerability. The narrator's meeting with Tamar and his ignorance of her future are poignant because of his later knowledge of the Holocaust. Several passages are ironic. The third and last paragraphs are ironic reminders of what will happen to the Jews in Europe.
5. Responses will vary. The narrator's comment about the Jewish upper classes' "bravery" and "blindness" suggests that Dennis and his family are symbolic of many Jews who failed to heed the warning signs of persecution in Europe. The children's table evinces the vulnerability of innocence and youth.

friends? What do you think the children's table itself stands for in the narrator's memory?

6. The narrator uses **paradoxes,** or apparent contradictions, to sum up the story in the last two paragraphs. Identify each paradox, and tell how they affect your emotional response to the end of the story.
7. Explain what you think "the world deepens and becomes art" means. What outlook on life could the narrator be describing in the last passage? How do you respond to his words?
8. In Connections on page 929, Isaac Bashevis Singer says that he finds hope in the creative person's search "to find an answer to suffering." How do you feel about this idea? Be sure to check the notes you took before reading this story.
9. Why do you think Helprin chose to title this story "Tamar"? How might Tamar be central to the point of Helprin's story?
10. Is this a romantic love story? a story about war? a story about the redemptive power of beauty? Explain your views.

Extending the Text

11. Compare the impact of this story with that of another book or a movie that deals with the Jewish experience before or during World War II.

Language and Style

Helprin's Figurative Language

Helprin's writing is distinguished by a style rich in **figurative language**. Read each figure of speech below in context. What two different things is Helprin comparing in each passage? The most significant figure of speech in the story is the long extended simile describing the narrator's meeting with Tamar. Find this simile and explain in your own words what it reveals about the significance of this encounter.

1. "Visions of the Jews in the forests, in green pine valleys as sharp as chevrons . . ." (page 923).
2. "The entire seventeenth century could not have produced enough frills to clothe the heavy monster of my pomposity" (page 924).
3. "London became, for me, the set of a joyous light opera" (page 924).
4. ". . . well-dressed people completely motionless and silent, like a group of deer surprised by a hunter" (page 924).

Choices: Building Your Portfolio

Writer's Notebook

1. Collecting Ideas for an Evaluation

What are your criteria for deciding whether a writer has succeeded in creating a believable fictional character? (You might require, for example, that characters have plausible motivations and authentic-sounding speech.) Do the characters of Tamar and the narrator meet your criteria? Be sure to note details from the story that support your judgments. Save your notes. You might want to use some of them for the Writer's Workshop on page 1181.

Critical Writing

2. Forgive—But Forget?

On page 923, at the end of a paragraph telling how he felt about the Jews of London and Europe, and explaining his mission, the narrator says, "I have since forgiven myself." In a paragraph, explain what you think this statement means. Before you write, look for other passages that reveal how the narrator feels about that time in London.

Creative Writing

3. Shifting Point of View

Imagine that Tamar kept a journal. Write an entry she might have recorded on the day after she met the narrator at the dinner party.

8. Responses will vary. Students may share Singer's hope. Student's responses should draw from their prereading notes.
9. Students may say that Tamar's beauty and hope best embodies Helprin's ironic observations about the European Jewish community before World War II.
10. Students should support their choice with specific references from the text: A love story should describe two emotionally engaged characters; a story about human vulnerability should describe mistakes or regrets; and a story about beauty should have an aesthetic focus.

Extending the Text

11. **(Synthesis)** Responses will vary. Have students refer to specific scenes in the works for comparison, and ask them to share their reactions.

Language and Style

1. The simile compares valleys and chevrons.
2. Pomposity is personified as a monster.
3. This metaphor compares London with a light opera.
4. This simile compares people with deer. The narrator's meeting Tamar is compared to two waves crashing together; the simile suggests the meeting is dramatic, almost violently passionate, overwhelming, and beautiful.

6. The narrator remarks on the lasting effects of temporary connections. He notes the contradiction between the beauty of his surroundings and the horror of Europe on the verge of war. He speculates that "perhaps things are most beautiful when they are not quite real." Students will probably react both emotionally and thoughtfully to the paradoxes.

7. Responses will vary. In general, the narrator uses the beautiful memory of Tamar as the antithesis of the horrors of the ensuing war. She becomes associated with art, which expands and enriches the cold, hard facts of reality.

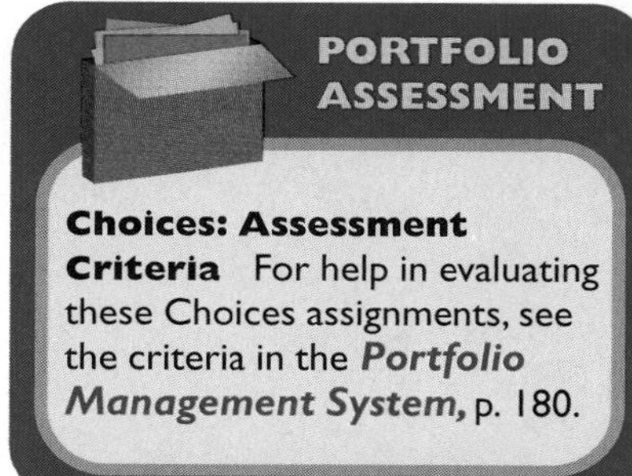

PORTFOLIO ASSESSMENT

Choices: Assessment Criteria For help in evaluating these Choices assignments, see the criteria in the ***Portfolio Management System,*** p. 180.

QUICK PLANNING GUIDE

Into the Poem

Author Biography p. 932

Before You Read p. 932

- **Reading Focus:** Students read five famous lines.
- **Quickwrite: Prior Knowledge** Examine shock value in poetry

Through the Poem

"The Death of the Ball Turret Gunner" p. 933

Primary Sources p. 933

Making Meanings p. 934

Beyond the Poem

Choices: Building Your Portfolio p. 934

- **Writer's Notebook:** Students make notes for an evaluation.
- **Critical Writing:** Write an essay
- **Creative Writing:** Write a paragraph or poem
- **Speaking and Listening:** Perform the poem aloud

Into the Poem

Using BEFORE YOU READ p. 932

Reading Focus

Ask students how they think it would have felt to be a gunner in a World War II bomber. Students can record their thoughts and review them after they have finished reading the poem.

Randall Jarrell

(1914–1965)

One of the most careful and erudite readers of contemporary poetry, Randall Jarrell was, at the same time, both an abrasive critic and a generous promoter of the art of poetry.

Born in Nashville, Tennessee, Jarrell was brought up in California. His childhood experiences included close observation of the gaudy remnants of the old Hollywood, a personal acquaintance with the MGM lion, and an appreciation of the difference between fantasy and fact—between life and myths about life—that would provide him with themes for poetry for years to come.

Elliott Erwitt/Magnum.

After graduating from Vanderbilt University in his native city, Jarrell began a career that led to positions in the English departments of many colleges and universities from Texas to New York. In 1942, he joined the Army Air Corps and served for a time as a pilot and then, for a longer time, as Celestial Navigation Trainer of pilots assigned to fly the famous B-29 bombers of World War II. Out of this experience came two notable books of poetry, *Little Friend, Little Friend* (1945) and *Losses* (1948). Many critics say these books rank among the best American contributions to the literature of World War II.

A man of extraordinary wit, Jarrell gave full play to his gifts in his often caustic and devastating critical articles and essays, particularly in the collection *A Sad Heart at the Supermarket* (1962). In poetry, however, his faculty for contemptuous criticism is kept under wraps: His wit shows itself only in mellow good humor ("I feel like the first men who read Wordsworth. / It's so simple I can't understand it.") and in a resigned toleration of the more absurd aspects of American life.

Jarrell died when struck by a car while walking on a North Carolina highway in 1965. His tragic death raised a question: Was it actually a suicide? But of his loss to American letters and to the poets who had counted upon him to explain, judge, and celebrate their art, there was no question at all.

BEFORE YOU READ
THE DEATH OF THE BALL TURRET GUNNER

Reading Focus

Five Famous Lines

These five lines, written in 1945, make up the most famous poem to come out of World War II.

Quickwrite

READER'S LOG

Write your thoughts on these questions: What attitude toward war do you expect to find in most literature and films produced today? Is war literature today more cynical than it used to be?

PROGRAM MANAGER

- **Planning Instruction** See Teaching Notes, *Teaching Resources B,* p. 136, for objectives, a summary, literary elements, and additional biographical information for this selection.
- **Instructional Support** Before beginning the instructional lesson, see Graphic Organizer for Active Reading, *Teaching Resources B,* p. 144, for an Into the Poem activity.
- **Assessment** See Selection Test, *Test Booklet,* pp. 219–220.

The Death of the Ball Turret Gunner

Randall Jarrell

From my mother's sleep I fell into the State,
And I hunched in its belly till my wet fur froze.
Six miles from earth, loosed from its dream of life, **A**
I woke to black flak and the nightmare fighters.
When I died they washed me out of the turret with a hose. **B**

PRIMARY Sources | **A COMMENT**

The Ball Turret

A ball turret was a plexiglass sphere set into the belly of a B-17 or B-24, and inhabited by **C** two .50 caliber machine guns and one man, a short small man. When this gunner tracked with his machine guns a fighter attacking his bomber from below, he revolved with the turret; hunched upside down in his little sphere, he looked like the fetus in the womb. The fighters which attacked him were armed with cannon firing explosive shells. The hose was a steam hose.

—Randall Jarrell

A. Critical Reading: Making Connections
The phrases "dream of life" and "nightmare fighters" are in contrast. What do these phrases suggest? [The first phrase suggests the dreamy innocence and stability the young soldier felt at home; the second phrase implies a harsh initiation into brutal realities of war—danger, violence, and lack of concern for life.]

B. Reader's Response: Challenging the Text
? Do you think the last line has a meaning beyond simple shock value? Why or why not? [Sample responses: The line is meaningful because it emphasizes the horror and humiliation of warfare. Or, the line is simply shocking because it doesn't add any new ideas, it only tries to provoke the reader.]

C. Expansion
During World War II, bombers of the American Eighth Air Force, based in England, flew more than 260,000 bombing missions against targets in Germany and occupied Europe.

STRATEGIES FOR INCLUSION

Visual Have students draw a political cartoon in which they express the same **point of view** as the speaker in the poem with regard to the tragedy of war. Students can choose any of the images from the poem. Ask volunteers to present their cartoons to the class.

INTEGRATING THE LANGUAGE ARTS

Strategic Reading Encourage students to focus on the **diction** in the poem. Direct them to concentrate on the **style** of the poem rather than on its content. Have students select five key words, and have them note the effect of the words on the poem's **tone**. Have students also consider substitutes for their five key words, noting the effect of the new words on the overall tone of the poem. Students can then compare their findings in small groups.

Portfolio Assessment
For help with self-assessment of reading skills, see the ***Portfolio Management System,*** pp. 48–49.

Making Meanings

First Thoughts

1. Possible responses: The poem is not shocking, because war is pointless and gruesome. The poem is shocking because its tone is so detached.

Shaping Interpretations

2. "Belly" suggests two extremes: The protection of a mother's womb and the exposed, lonely isolation of the ball turret.
3. "I fell" (l. 1) implies he was drafted or thoughtlessly enlisted.
4. Answers will vary. The "wet fur" could be the fleece-lined flight suit that crewmen wore, sweat-soaked from fear. Fear reduces the gunner to an animal frozen in the sights of an adversary, and the nature of war dehumanizes comrades and enemies alike.
5. Answers will vary. Some may say he is a hero because he died for his country, others might insist that because he does not decide his own fate, he is not a hero.
6. If students decide that the poem is about dissent, they should summarize its protest; if they decide that the poem focuses on mechanization, they should contrast the human with the machine; and if they decide it concerns destruction of the innocent, they should describe the loss of innocence.

Extending the Text

7. **(Synthesis)** Answers will vary. Ask students to name war movies and write them on the chalkboard. Then, discuss the films in the context of the poem.

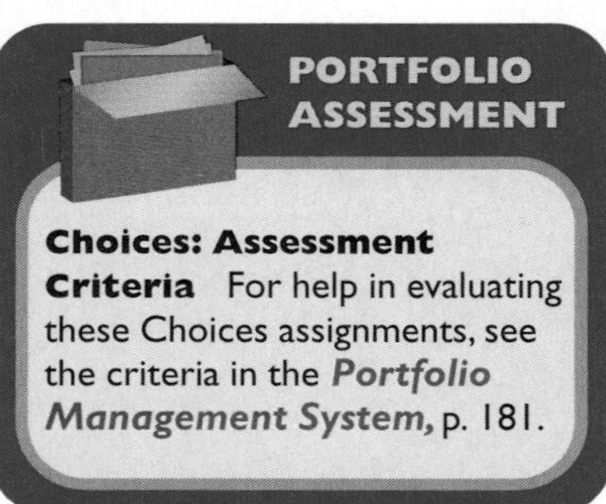

Choices: Assessment Criteria For help in evaluating these Choices assignments, see the criteria in the ***Portfolio Management System,*** p. 181.

MAKING MEANINGS

First Thoughts

1. Do you find this poem shocking? Why or why not?

Shaping Interpretations

2. "Belly" here can be read on two levels. What two bellies is the speaker talking about?
3. How do you know that the speaker didn't enter the army on the basis of a rational decision?
4. What is the speaker's "wet fur"? Why do you think he compares himself to an animal?
5. Do you think the speaker is a hero? Explain.
6. What, in the long run, do you think this poem is about? Is it about political dissent? Is it a statement about the way things in the world are regimented and mechanized? Is it about the destruction of the innocent? Explain your views.

Extending the Text

7. Hollywood has produced hundreds of movies about war. These movies reflect a wide spectrum of attitudes. Some show soldiers as heroes, some as victims; some evoke pride in one's country, some hatred of another country; some summon nostalgia for a past era. Think of some war movies you have seen, and analyze their attitudes toward war. (Be sure to check your Quickwrite notes.)

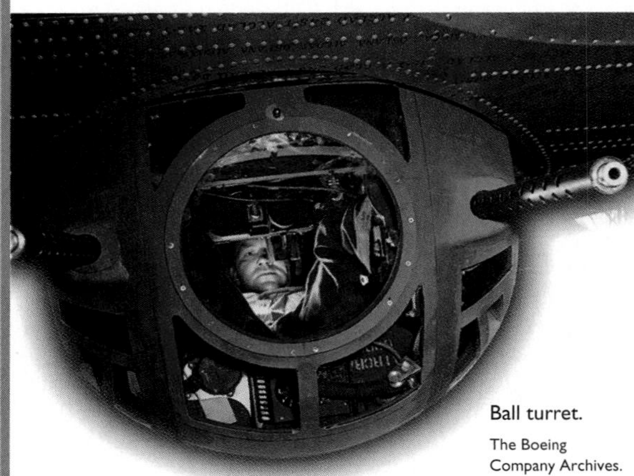

Ball turret.

The Boeing Company Archives.

CHOICES: Building Your Portfolio

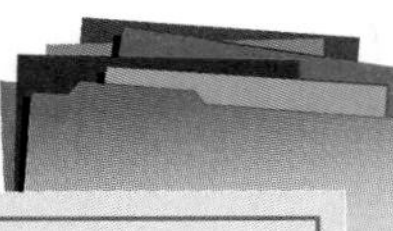

Writer's Notebook

1. Collecting Ideas for an Evaluation

WORK IN PROGRESS

If you were writing an evaluation of "The Death of the Ball Turret Gunner," what facts would a general audience need to know? Write down aspects of the real-world context of the poem—relevant information about World War II, the ball turret, and Jarrell's experiences. Keep your notes for possible use in the Writer's Workshop on page 1181.

Critical Writing

2. Hunched in the Belly

In a brief essay, explain the **extended metaphor** that runs through the poem. Is there something **ironic** about the metaphor? Explain your interpretation.

Creative Writing

3. Speaking Out

Find a newspaper article about someone who has died. Write a paragraph or a short poem from the point of view of that person as you imagine him or her. Imitate the style of "The Death of the Ball Turret Gunner." Speak as "I."

Speaking and Listening

4. Whose Emphasis?

Poems are musical. They are meant to be read aloud or recited from memory. When performing a poem aloud, each of us tends to emphasize different words as we give our particular spin to the poem. Together with another student, perform "The Death of the Ball Turret Gunner" before the class. The class should try to spot differences, even small differences, between the performances, and discuss how different interpretations affect the meaning of the poem.

STRATEGIES FOR INCLUSION

Logical-Mathematical/Advanced For activity #2, have students make a copy of the poem with plenty of space between each line. In the space above each element in the poem's extended metaphor, have students write the literal meaning of that specific part of the metaphor. In the space below each element in the extended metaphor, students should write the element's metaphorical meaning—the connotations that fit in with the extended metaphor of the poem.

Bodily-Kinesthetic When students perform the poem for activity #4, encourage them to use gestures, poses, and expressions to add to their readings. Students can practice their deliveries in front of a mirror before performing for the class.

John Hersey

(1914–1993)

Brown Brothers.

What book was considered so extraordinary that the great scientist Albert Einstein ordered one thousand copies? What book was thought so compelling that the Book-of-the-Month Club distributed free copies because no book "could be of more importance at this moment to the human race"? The book is *Hiroshima,* by John Hersey.

Hersey was born in China, where he lived until he was ten. He later graduated from Yale and studied at Cambridge University in England, served as private secretary to the American novelist Sinclair Lewis, and reported from the South Pacific and the Mediterranean during World War II for *Time* and *Life* magazines.

But journalism (if that means objective, factual reporting) could not contain Hersey's passionate concern about contemporary events. In 1945, he won the Pulitzer Prize for his novel *A Bell for Adano,* based on what he had seen of American military government in Italy. Some critics saw this novel as a troubling examination of democracy, its ideals, and the difficulties of putting it into practice.

In 1946, Hersey published *Hiroshima.* Combining techniques of a novel and the factual air of journalism to describe a real event, *Hiroshima* began what some critics call the genre of the "nonfiction novel." (Other examples include Truman Capote's *In Cold Blood* [1966] and Norman Mailer's *The Executioner's Song* [1979].) Hersey took an almost incomprehensible act, the dropping of an atomic bomb on a civilian population, and showed how it affected the lives of six survivors. Through their eyes, Americans could experience this catastrophe as if it were happening to them and to their friends and neighbors. Through Hersey's vivid narrative and his gift for characterization, the unimaginable became horrifyingly real.

Hiroshima became a national event, a precursor of the kind of celebrity status that best-sellers often enjoy today, with attention paid to the authors on talk shows and in interviews in magazines and newspapers. *Hiroshima* first appeared in *The New Yorker,* which devoted an entire issue to the book—a startling commitment for a magazine. The American Broadcasting Company had the book read aloud on its radio stations. *Hiroshima* has since been called the most significant piece of reportage in modern times.

After *Hiroshima,* Hersey became famous as a writer who could make history understandable. While serving as a teacher and mentor at Yale, he continued to dramatize issues and events, dealing with the Holocaust, racism, fascism, and other evils of modern life. He called his type of fiction "the novel of contemporary history" and wrote that "this kind of novel should make anyone who reads it better able to meet life in his generation—whenever that generation may be." He produced books in a steady stream from the 1940s to the 1990s, sending his publisher a manuscript of new short stories, *Key West Tales,* six weeks before his death. His books include the highly acclaimed novel *The Wall* (1950), about the annihilation of Polish Jews in the Warsaw ghetto, and *Blues* (1987), a brilliant meditation on Hersey's favorite sport, fishing. (The book, of course, turns out to be about much more than fly-casting and trolling).

None of Hersey's other works achieved the impact of *Hiroshima.* The book continues to force readers to face the horrifying realities of nuclear war. In half a century, no book on nuclear warfare has come close to *Hiroshima*'s impact on our moral and ethical sensibilities.

QUICK PLANNING GUIDE

Into the Selection

Author Biography p. 935

Before You Read p. 936

- **Reading Focus:** Students examine attitudes about modern warfare.
- **A Dialogue with the Text: Set a Purpose** Note the author's use of details
- **Elements of Literature:** Discriminate between objective and subjective reporting
- **Background: Scaffolding** Review the story's context

Through the Selection

"A Noiseless Flash" pp. 937–946

Words to Own pp. 938–944

Making Meanings pp. 946–947

Beyond the Selection

Choices: Building Your Portfolio p. 947

- **Writer's Notebook:** Record examples of objective and subjective reporting from the story
- **Critical Writing:** Examine the author's use of suspense
- **Crossing the Curriculum: History:** Research the decision to drop the bomb
- **Critical Writing:** Analyze the use of a specific term

WORDS TO OWN

The following vocabulary words are defined in the Words to Own at the bottom of the pupil's page.

rendezvous p. 938	debris p. 942
abstinence p. 938	hedonistic p. 942
obsessed p. 938	sustained p. 942
philanthropies p. 939	convivial p. 943
incendiary p. 941	idealist p. 944

Into the Selection

Using BEFORE YOU READ p. 936

Reading Focus

Ask students what Hersey's personal interest might be in writing about such a destructive event. Students can review their ideas after they have read the selection.

Elements of Literature

Suggest to students that the **point of view** often offers a clue to a writer's position. Ask students if they think first-person reports are usually subjective and third-person reports usually objective. Challenge students to support and refute the statement.

Background

Since the massive firebombing of Toyko in March, 1945, Japanese cities had been repeatedly devastated by U.S. bombing raids. Because Hiroshima was one of the few cities to escape bombing, its citizens expected an attack, but no one could have anticipated this magnitude of destruction. Ask students to discuss the decision to use the atomic bomb.

PORTFOLIO ASSESSMENT

Portfolio Assessment
For help with teacher assessment of reading skills, see the ***Portfolio Management System,*** pp. 54–55.

BEFORE YOU READ

A NOISELESS FLASH

Reading Focus

The Human Element
Modern war, waged with highly sophisticated weaponry, is often described in *numerical* terms: how many missiles fired, how many targets annihilated, how many people killed. In the face of such abstraction, writers and artists force us to confront the personal element in war. By telling us about the details of other people's lives, writers remind us that, even in war, we are all—friend and foe—human beings first and foremost.

A Dialogue with the Text

READER'S LOG

As you read this account of the effects of the atomic bomb explosion on six people in Hiroshima, note the many precise details Hersey uses to lend his account authenticity. Pick one of the six people, and write down details about that person as you read.

Elements of Literature

Subjectivity and Objectivity
In **subjective reporting,** the writer openly expresses personal emotions and attitudes toward the events and characters he or she is writing about. In **objective reporting,** such as John Hersey's, the writer presents mainly observable, verifiable facts and keeps his or her own feelings at a distance. At times, the only way we can discover how such a writer feels about an event is by analyzing the details specifically chosen for inclusion or omission.

In **subjective reporting,** the writer openly expresses emotions and attitudes toward events and characters. In **objective reporting,** the writer keeps his or her feelings at a distance.

Background

War between the United States and Japan began on December 7, 1941, when the Japanese suddenly attacked the U.S. naval base at Pearl Harbor, in Hawaii. By mid-1945, after many costly battles, the United States and its allies were nearing the final victory in World War II as they pressed toward an invasion of the main Japanese islands. As part of the endgame against Japan, the United States used its newest and most powerful weapon, the atomic bomb, twice—first to destroy Hiroshima, and then, three days later, to devastate another Japanese city, Nagasaki.

First photo taken of Hiroshima after the atomic explosion, August 6, 1945.
Matsushige/Sygma.

PROGRAM MANAGER

- **Planning Instruction** See **Teaching Notes, *Teaching Resources B,*** pp. 136–137, for objectives, a summary, literary elements, and additional historical information for this selection.
- **Instructional Support** Before beginning the instructional lesson, see **Graphic Organizer for Active Reading, *Teaching Resources B,*** p. 145, for a Through the Story activity.
- **Assessment** See **Selection Test, *Test Booklet,*** pp. 219–220.
- **Reinforcement** Use the **Words to Own** worksheet in ***Teaching Resources B,*** p. 146.
- **Application and Reinforcement** For reinforcement of the elements of literature introduced in this lesson, see **Transparency** 18.2 in the ***Audiovisual Resources Binder.***

A Noiseless Flash

from Hiroshima

John Hersey

At exactly fifteen minutes past eight in the morning, on August 6, 1945, Japanese time, at the moment when the atomic bomb flashed above Hiroshima, Miss Toshiko Sasaki, a clerk in the personnel department of the East Asia Tin Works, had just sat down at her place in the plant office and was turning her head to speak to the girl at the next desk. At that same moment, Dr. Masakazu Fujii was settling down cross-legged to read the Osaka *Asahi*[1] on the porch of his private hospital, overhanging one of the seven deltaic rivers which divide Hiroshima; Mrs. Hatsuyo Nakamura, a tailor's widow, stood by the window of her kitchen, watching a neighbor tearing down his house because it lay in the path of an air-raid-defense fire lane; Father Wilhelm Kleinsorge, a German priest of the Society of Jesus,[2] reclined in his underwear on a cot on the top floor of his order's three-story mission house, reading a Jesuit magazine, *Stimmen der Zeit;*[3] Dr. Terufumi Sasaki, a young member of the surgical staff of the city's large, modern Red Cross Hospital, walked along one of the hospital corridors with a blood specimen for a Wassermann test[4] in his hand; and the

1. ***Asahi:*** Japanese for "morning sun." The Osaka *Asahi* is the city newspaper.

2. **Society of Jesus:** Roman Catholic religious order of priests and brothers, also known as the Jesuit (jezh′o͞o·it) order.

3. ***Stimmen der Zeit*** (shtim′ən der tsīt): German for "Voices of the Times."

4. **Wasserman test:** blood test used to diagnose syphilis.

A. Reader's Response: First Thoughts

? What is your reaction to the first sentence? What do you expect of the selection? [Sample responses: The first sentence is eerie because it names the precise time the atomic bomb drops and focuses on a specific person's actions in Hiroshima at that moment; the combination of looming destruction and details about a specific person in Hiroshima creates suspense. The selection will probably be suspenseful. Or the first sentence is matter-of-fact and reads like a newspaper report; the selection will probably be full of facts and details.]

OPTIONS FOR TEACHING

STRATEGIES FOR INCLUSION

Linguistic Ask students to list any Japanese words or phrases as they read, along with their English translations. Discuss with students the effect of the Japanese words in the story. Do they add to the authenticity of the description or to the realism of the narration?

Visual/Spatial Ask students to make diagrams that depict the survivors' locations in Hiroshima in relation to the blast center. Students can refer to the text for information on direction and distance. Have students compare their maps with a partner's.

English Language Development Have students concentrate on the details vital to an objective account of the survivors' experiences. Ask pairs of students to choose a survivor and make a chart in which to write the details they find. Charts should have columns labeled *who, what, why, when,* and *where,* with the details listed in rows underneath. ☞

A. Critical Reading: Identifying Main Ideas

? What one thing do the six people described in this paragraph have in common? [By chance, they were all among the survivors.]

B. Expansion

When the *Enola Gay*—the B-29 that dropped the first atomic bomb, called Little Boy—lifted off the runway and headed for Japan on August 6, 1945, its destination was not yet determined. Weather reports it received while airborne dictated its course. Of three possible targets—Hiroshima, Kokura, and Nagasaki—Hiroshima had the best weather.

C. Cultural Connection: The Japanese Language

In Japan, the suffix *–san* is often attached to a noun as a way of showing respect. Why is it ironic that the people would attach the suffix to the B-29? [Possible response: Although they had a grave respect for the plane and the destruction it could cause, it was never a welcome sight.]

Reverend Mr. Kiyoshi Tanimoto, pastor of the Hiroshima Methodist Church, paused at the door of a rich man's house in Koi, the city's western suburb, and prepared to unload a handcart full of things he had evacuated from town in fear of the massive B-29 raid which everyone expected Hiroshima to suffer. (A) A hundred thousand people were killed by the atomic bomb, and these six were among the survivors. (B) They still wonder why they lived when so many others died. Each of them counts many small items of chance or volition—a step taken in time, a decision to go indoors, catching one streetcar instead of the next—that spared him. And now each knows that in the act of survival he lived a dozen lives and saw more death than he ever thought he would see. At the time, none of them knew anything.

The Reverend Mr. Tanimoto got up at five o'clock that morning. He was alone in the parsonage, because for some time his wife had been commuting with their year-old baby to spend nights with a friend in Ushida, a suburb to the north. Of all the important cities of Japan, only two, Kyoto[5] and Hiroshima, had not been visited in strength by (C) *B-san,* or Mr. B, as the Japanese, with a mixture of respect and unhappy familiarity, called the B-29; and Mr. Tanimoto, like all his neighbors and friends, was almost sick with anxiety. He had heard uncomfortably detailed accounts of mass raids on Kure, Iwakuni, Tokuyama, and other nearby towns; he was sure Hiroshima's turn would come soon. He had slept badly the night before, because there had been several air-raid warnings. Hiroshima had been getting such warnings almost every night for weeks, for at that time the B-29s were using Lake Biwa, northeast of Hiroshima, as a rendezvous point, and no matter what city the Americans planned to hit, the Superfortresses streamed in over the coast near Hiroshima. The frequency of the warnings and the continued abstinence of Mr. B with respect to Hiroshima had made its citizens jittery; a rumor was going around that the Americans were saving something special for the city.

Mr. Tanimoto is a small man, quick to talk, laugh, and cry. He wears his black hair parted in the middle and rather long; the prominence of the frontal bones just above his eyebrows and the smallness of his moustache, mouth, and chin give him a strange, old-young look, boyish and yet wise, weak and yet fiery. He moves nervously and fast, but with a restraint which suggests that he is a cautious, thoughtful man. He showed, indeed, just those qualities in the uneasy days before the bomb fell. Besides having his wife spend the nights in Ushida, Mr. Tanimoto had been carrying all the portable things from his church, in the close-packed residential district called Nagaragawa, to a house that belonged to a rayon manufacturer in Koi, two miles from the center of town. The rayon man, a Mr. Matsui, had opened his then unoccupied estate to a large number of his friends and acquaintances, so that they might evacuate whatever they wished to a safe distance from the probable target area. Mr. Tanimoto had had no difficulty in moving chairs, hymnals, Bibles, altar gear, and church records by pushcart himself, but the organ console and an upright piano required some aid. A friend of his named Matsuo had, the day before, helped him get the piano out to Koi; in return, he had promised this day to assist Mr. Matsuo in hauling out a daughter's belongings. That is why he had risen so early.

Mr. Tanimoto cooked his own breakfast. He felt awfully tired. The effort of moving the piano the day before, a sleepless night, weeks of worry and unbalanced diet, the cares of his parish—all combined to make him feel hardly adequate to the new day's work. There was another thing, too: Mr. Tanimoto had studied theology at Emory College, in Atlanta, Georgia; he had graduated in 1940; he spoke excellent English; he dressed in American clothes; he had corresponded with many American friends right up to the time the war began; and among a people obsessed with a fear of being spied upon—perhaps almost obsessed himself—he found himself growing increasingly uneasy. The police had questioned him several times, and just a few days before, he had heard that an influential acquaintance, a Mr. Tanaka, a retired

5. **Kyoto:** city some 200 miles east of Hiroshima.

Words to Own

rendezvous (rän′dā·vo͞o′) *adj.:* meeting.
abstinence (ab′stə·nəns′) *n.:* staying away.
obsessed (əb·sest′) *v.* used as *adj.:* preoccupied; haunted.

Options for Teaching

Integrating the Language Arts

Grammar Remind students that an *appositive* is a noun (with its modifiers) that identifies a preceding noun. Appositives give more information about the preceding noun. Ask students to find and record four examples of appositive phrases in the first thirty-one lines of the selection that give more information about a person. Students can indicate, in parentheses, who the appositive gives more information about. [Possible answers include: "a clerk . . . Works" (Miss Toshiko Sasaki); "a tailor's widow" (Mrs. Hatsuyo Nakamura); "a German priest . . . Jesus" (Father Wilhelm Kleinsorge); "a young member . . . Hospital" (Dr. Terufumi Sasaki); and "pastor . . . Church" (the Reverend Mr. Kiyoshi Tanimoto).]

Speaking and Listening Have students work in groups of six, with each student assuming the role of any one of the characters in the selection. The groups should initiate a conversation in which they share their individual experiences just before and after the blast. Encourage students to ask questions of each other and to step into character to share their emotions.

officer of the Toyo Kisen Kaisha steamship line, an anti-Christian, a man famous in Hiroshima for his showy philanthropies and notorious for his personal tyrannies, had been telling people that Tanimoto should not be trusted. In compensation, to show himself publicly a good Japanese, Mr. Tanimoto had taken on the chairmanship of his local *tonarigumi,* or Neighborhood Association, and to his other duties and concerns this position had added the business of organizing air-raid defense for about twenty families.

Before six o'clock that morning, Mr. Tanimoto started for Mr. Matsuo's house. There he found that their burden was to be a *tansu,* a large Japanese cabinet, full of clothing and household goods. The two men set out. The morning was perfectly clear and so warm that the day promised to be uncomfortable. A few minutes after they started, the air-raid siren went off—a minute-long blast that warned of approaching planes but indicated to the people of Hiroshima only a slight degree of danger, since it sounded every morning at this time, when an American weather plane came over. The two men pulled and pushed the handcart through the city streets. Hiroshima was a fan-shaped city, lying mostly on the six islands formed by the seven estuarial[6] rivers that branch out from the Ota River; its main commercial and residential districts, covering about four square miles in the center of the city, contained three-quarters of its population, which had been reduced by several evacuation programs from a wartime peak of 380,000 to about 245,000. Factories and other residential districts, or suburbs, lay compactly around the edges of the city. To the south were the docks, an airport, and the island-studded Inland Sea. A rim of mountains runs around the other three sides of the delta. Mr. Tanimoto and Mr. Matsuo took their way through the shopping center, already full of people, and across two of the rivers to the sloping streets of Koi, and up them to the outskirts and foothills. As they started up a valley away from the tight-ranked houses, the all-clear sounded. (The Japanese radar operators, detecting only three planes, supposed that they comprised a reconnaissance.)[7] Pushing the handcart up to the rayon man's house was tiring, and the men, after they had maneuvered their load into the driveway and to the front steps, paused to rest awhile. They stood with a wing of the house between them and the city. Like most homes in this part of Japan, the house consisted of a wooden frame and wooden walls supporting a heavy tile roof. Its front hall, packed with rolls of bedding and clothing, looked like a cool cave full of fat cushions. Opposite the house, to the right of the front door, there was a large, finicky rock garden. There was no sound of planes. The morning was still; the place was cool and pleasant.

Then a tremendous flash of light cut across the sky. Mr. Tanimoto has a distinct recollection that it traveled from east to west, from the city toward the hills. It seemed a sheet of sun. Both he and Mr. Matsuo reacted in terror—and both had time to react (for they were 3,500 yards, or two miles, from the center of the explosion). Mr. Matsuo dashed up the front steps into the house and dived among the bedrolls and buried himself there. Mr. Tanimoto took four or five steps and threw himself between two big rocks in the garden. He bellied up very hard against one of them. As his face was against the stone, he did not see what happened. He felt a sudden pressure, and then splinters and pieces of board and fragments of tile fell on him. He heard no roar. (Almost no one in Hiroshima recalls hearing any noise of the bomb. But a fisherman in his sampan[8] on the Inland Sea near Tsuzu, the man with whom Mr. Tanimoto's mother-in-law and sister-in-law were living, saw the flash and heard a tremendous explosion; he was nearly twenty miles from Hiroshima, but the thunder was greater than when the B-29s hit Iwakuni, only five miles away.)

When he dared, Mr. Tanimoto raised his head and saw that the rayon man's house had collapsed. He thought a bomb had fallen directly on it. Such clouds of dust had risen that there was a sort of twilight around. In panic, not thinking for the moment of Mr. Matsuo under the ruins, he dashed out into the street. He noticed as he ran that the

6. **estuarial** (es'tyo͞o·er'ē·əl): on the estuary, or mouth of a river, where freshwater meets saltwater.

7. **reconnaissance** (ri·kän'ə·səns): exploratory mission.

8. **sampan:** small, flat-bottomed boat.

WORDS TO OWN

philanthropies (fə·lan'thrə·pēz) *n. pl.:* charitable gifts.

D. Critical Reading: Metacognition

Hersey uses Japanese words throughout this story. How do you figure out what these words mean? [Possible answers: The author uses restatement—giving the English equivalent right after the Japanese word or expression—but you can also make a good guess based on the context.]

E. Literary Element: Subjectivity and Objectivity

? What do the exact descriptions and statistics add to the description of the scene? [The precise, objective reporting helps the reader get an overview of the town and the situation of its inhabitants.]

F. Critical Reading: Drawing Conclusions

? What is ironic about the sounding of the all-clear? [The radar operators think that they are safe because there are only three planes, but the reader knows that the three planes are more dangerous than waves of bombers with conventional explosives.]

G. Literary Element: Subjectivity and Objectivity

? What are some elements of subjectivity in the description of the garden and the morning? What do the elements add to the scene? [Elements of subjectivity include the description of the garden as "finicky," and the description of the place as "cool and pleasant." The elements make the scene more vivid than would objective reporting.]

INTEGRATING THE LANGUAGE ARTS

Strategic Reading To aid students in keeping track of the experiences of the six characters, ask them to notice the main points as they read and enter the information in a chart. Students can use a graphic organizer such as is found on Transparency 4: Category Chart in the Transparency Package. They can organize the characters by occupation, distance from the blast, and experience of the explosion. Students can compare their charts in small groups.

Writing: Poem Have students write a stream-of-consciousness poem about the bombing of Hiroshima. Encourage students to use one character's experience as a guide or as the point of view of their poems. Students can brainstorm for a few minutes to think of the emotions and thoughts of one of the survivors, and then use their brainstorming notes as they write their poems. Ask volunteers to share their work with the class.

CLASSROOM MANAGEMENT

Managing the Reader's Response Classroom Call students' attention to comments in their Reader's Logs that express opinions or judgments. Assure students that they are free to express their opinions, but remind them that they should consider other points of view as well. Students should return to the text to support their assertions.

Hiroshima after the atomic explosion, August 6, 1945.
Matsumoto/Sygma.

OPTIONS FOR TEACHING

CLASSROOM MANAGEMENT

Grading Cooperative Learning Students need to know that both individual and group efforts in cooperative learning situations are important. Here are some suggestions for grading cooperative projects to emphasize individual accountability.

- Giving each group member an individual score plus bonus points if all members of the group fulfill certain criteria
- Giving each member an individual score plus points based on the group average
- Taking the average of members' individual scores
- Giving a group score for a single product

concrete wall of the estate had fallen over—toward the house rather than away from it. In the street, the first thing he saw was a squad of soldiers who had been burrowing into the hillside opposite, making one of the thousands of dugouts in which the Japanese apparently intended to resist invasion, hill by hill, life for life; the soldiers were coming out of the hole, where they should have been safe, and blood was running from their heads, chests, and backs. They were silent and dazed.

Under what seemed to be a local dust cloud, the day grew darker and darker.

At nearly midnight, the night before the bomb was dropped, an announcer on the city's radio station said that about two hundred B-29s were approaching southern Honshu[9] and advised the population of Hiroshima to evacuate to their designated "safe areas." Mrs. Hatsuyo Nakamura, the tailor's widow, who lived in the section called Nobori-cho and who had long had a habit of doing as she was told, got her three children—a ten-year-old boy, Toshio, an eight-year-old girl, Yaeko, and a five-year-old girl, Myeko—out of bed and dressed them and walked with them to the military area known as the East Parade Ground, on the northeast edge of the city. There she unrolled some mats and the children lay down on them. They slept until about two, when they were awakened by the roar of the planes going over Hiroshima.

As soon as the planes had passed, Mrs. Nakamura started back with her children. They reached home a little after two-thirty and she immediately turned on the radio, which, to her distress, was just then broadcasting a fresh warning. When she looked at the children and saw how tired they were, and when she thought of the number of trips they had made in past weeks, all to no purpose, to the East Parade Ground, she decided that in spite of the instructions on the radio, she simply could not face starting out all over again. She put the children in their bedrolls on the floor, lay down herself at three o'clock, and fell asleep at once, so soundly that when the planes passed over later, she did not waken to their sound.

9. **Honshu:** largest island of Japan. Hiroshima is in southern Honshu.

The siren jarred her awake at about seven. She arose, dressed quickly, and hurried to the house of Mr. Nakamoto, the head of her Neighborhood Association, and asked him what she should do. He said that she should remain at home unless an urgent warning—a series of intermittent blasts of the siren—was sounded. She returned home, lit the stove in the kitchen, set some rice to cook, and sat down to read that morning's Hiroshima *Chugoku.*[10] To her relief, the all-clear sounded at eight o'clock. She heard the children stirring, so she went and gave each of them a handful of peanuts and told them to stay on their bedrolls, because they were tired from the night's walk. She had hoped that they would go back to sleep, but the man in the house directly to the south began to make a terrible hullabaloo of hammering, wedging, ripping, and splitting. The prefectural government,[11] convinced, as everyone in Hiroshima was, that the city would be attacked soon, had begun to press with threats and warnings for the completion of wide fire lanes, which, it was hoped, might act in conjunction with the rivers to localize any fires started by an incendiary raid; and the neighbor was reluctantly sacrificing his home to the city's safety. Just the day before, the prefecture had ordered all able-bodied girls from the secondary schools to spend a few days helping to clear these lanes, and they started work soon after the all-clear sounded.

Mrs. Nakamura went back to the kitchen, looked at the rice, and began watching the man next door. At first, she was annoyed with him for making so much noise, but then she was moved almost to tears by pity. Her emotion was specifically directed toward her neighbor, tearing down his home, board by board, at a time when there was so much unavoidable destruction, but undoubtedly she also felt a generalized, community pity, to say nothing of self-pity. She had not had an easy time. Her husband, Isawa, had gone into the

10. ***Chugoku:*** newspaper named for the region where Hiroshima is located.

11. **prefectural government:** the regional administration of each Japanese district, called a prefecture.

WORDS TO OWN

incendiary (in·sen′dē·er′ē) *adj.:* designed to cause fires.

A. Literary Element: Irony

? Why does Hersey put "safe areas" in quotation marks? [When the atomic bomb is dropped on Hiroshima, there is no safe area in the whole city.]

B. Critical Reading: Analyzing Character

? How would you describe Mrs. Nakamura? [Possible answers: Mrs. Nakamura is responsible, dutiful, careful, kind, industrious, respectful of authority, and a person of habit.]

C. Literary Element: Imagery

? What impression of the town does the image of the man tearing down his house give you? [Possible answers: The townspeople are trying to work together to get through the trial of war. The inhabitants have a strong sense of duty and respect for the community.]

COOPERATIVE LEARNING

Front Page Mock-Up Have students work in groups of four or five to design the front page of an American newspaper dated August 7, 1945. Students should research statistics and general information about the bombing of Hiroshima, then write an appropriate banner headline, headlines of related stories that might appear, and captions for photos and/or other graphics. Students should appoint a managing editor to oversee the project, a layout artist to provide art to accompany the stories, and reporters to provide research and background information. Have the groups display their work.

Interview Have students work in groups of four or five to interview older relatives or acquaintances, both American and Japanese, who remember or have family stories about the bombing of Hiroshima. *You may want to obtain permission from parents and from the interviewees before students begin work on this activity.* Encourage students to tape-record or videotape their interviews. Then, have each group present its findings to the class in the form of an eyewitness account or an oral report.

A. Reader's Response: Connecting with the Text

? How does Mrs. Nakamura's experience of the blast compare to that of Mr. Tanimoto? [Possible responses: Since she is closer to the explosion, she has less time to react to the warning flash and is caught in midstep. In Mrs. Nakamura's case, her own children are injured, which adds a further sadness to the confusion of what has happened.]

B. Cultural Connections: Family Unity

? What does the family involvement in Dr. Fujii's hospital say about the Japanese family unit? [Possible response: In Japan, the family is a close unit in which each person takes care of and assumes responsibility for the others.] Discuss with students the ways in which various cultures demonstrate their regard for family ties.

C. Critical Reading: Drawing Conclusions

? Why is the direction in which Dr. Fujii's porch faces important? [The fact that it faces away from the center of the city might have saved his life.]

Army just after Myeko was born, and she had heard nothing from or of him for a long time, until, on March 5, 1942, she received a seven-word telegram: "Isawa died an honorable death at Singapore." She learned later that he had died on February 15th, the day Singapore fell, and that he had been a corporal. Isawa had been a not particularly prosperous tailor, and his only capital was a Sankoku sewing machine. After his death, when his allotments stopped coming, Mrs. Nakamura got out the machine and began to take in piecework[12] herself, and since then had supported the children, but poorly, by sewing.

As Mrs. Nakamura stood watching her neighbor, everything flashed whiter than any white she had ever seen. She did not notice what happened to the man next door; the reflex of a mother set her in motion toward her children. She had taken a single step (the house was 1,350 yards, or three-quarters of a mile, from the center of the explosion) when something picked her up and she seemed to fly into the next room over the raised sleeping platform, pursued by parts of her house. **A**

Timbers fell around her as she landed, and a shower of tiles pummeled her; everything became dark, for she was buried. The debris did not cover her deeply. She rose up and freed herself. She heard a child cry, "Mother, help me!," and saw her youngest—Myeko, the five-year-old—buried up to her breast and unable to move. As Mrs. Nakamura started frantically to claw her way toward the baby, she could see or hear nothing of her other children.

In the days right before the bombing, Dr. Masakazu Fujii, being prosperous, hedonistic, and at the time not too busy, had been allowing himself the luxury of sleeping until nine or nine-thirty, but fortunately he had to get up early the morning the bomb was dropped to see a house guest off on a train. He rose at six, and half an hour later walked with his friend to the station, not far away, across two of the rivers. He was back home by seven, just as the siren sounded its sustained warning. He ate breakfast and then, because the morning was already hot, undressed down to his underwear and went out on the porch to read the paper. This porch—in fact, the whole building—was curiously constructed. Dr. Fujii was the proprietor of a peculiarly Japanese institution: a private, single-doctor hospital. This building, perched beside and over the water of the Kyo River, and next to the bridge of the same name, contained thirty rooms for thirty patients and their kinfolk—for, according to Japanese custom, when a person falls sick and goes to a hospital, one or more members of his family go and live there with him, to cook for him, bathe, massage, and read to him, and to offer incessant familial sympathy, without which a Japanese patient would be miserable indeed. **B** Dr. Fujii had no beds—only straw mats—for his patients. He did, however, have all sorts of modern equipment: an X-ray machine, diathermy[13] apparatus, and a fine tiled laboratory. The structure rested two-thirds on the land, one-third on piles over the tidal waters of the Kyo. This overhang, the part of the building where Dr. Fujii lived, was queer-looking, but it was cool in summer and from the porch, **C** which faced away from the center of the city, the prospect of the river, with pleasure boats drifting up and down it, was always refreshing. Dr. Fujii had occasionally had anxious moments when the Ota and its mouth branches rose to flood, but the piling was apparently firm enough and the house had always held.

Dr. Fujii had been relatively idle for about a month because in July, as the number of untouched cities in Japan dwindled and as Hiroshima seemed more and more inevitably a target, he began turning patients away, on the ground that in case of a fire raid he would not be able to evacuate them. Now he had only two patients left—a woman from Yano, injured in the shoulder, and a young man of twenty-five recovering from burns he had suffered when the steel factory near Hiroshima in which he worked had been hit. Dr. Fujii had six nurses to tend his patients. His wife and children were safe; his wife

12. **piecework:** work paid at a fixed rate for each piece completed.

13. **diathermy:** heat treatment.

Words to Own

debris (də·brē′) *n.:* rubble; broken pieces.
hedonistic (hē′də·nis′tik) *adj.:* pleasure-loving; self-indulgent.
sustained (sə·stānd′) *v.* used as *adj.:* prolonged.

OPTIONS FOR TEACHING

CROSSING THE CURRICULUM

Science Ask students to research and report on the development of the atomic bomb. Students can focus on a significant individual or a single event in the bomb's development. Students can present their information to the class as oral reports.

Health Have students look up information on radiation illnesses and other lingering effects of the atomic bomb blast on the people of Hiroshima. Students should report their findings to the class, along with copies of photos, reports, charts, or other graphic illustrations.

Social Sciences/Art Have students work in groups of two or three to research and write about Peace Memorial Park, which was created in memory of the bombing. Ask each group to describe what they find most interesting, significant, or moving about the park. Groups can share their ideas in a class discussion.

and one son were living outside Osaka, and another son and two daughters were in the country on Kyushu.[14] A niece was living with him, and a maid and a manservant. He had little to do and did not mind, for he had saved some money. At fifty, he was healthy, convivial, and calm, and he was pleased to pass the evenings drinking whiskey with friends, always sensibly and for the sake of conversation. Before the war, he had affected brands imported from Scotland and America; now he was perfectly satisfied with the best Japanese brand, Suntory.

Dr. Fujii sat down cross-legged in his underwear on the spotless matting of the porch, put on his glasses, and started reading the Osaka *Asahi.* He liked to read the Osaka news because his wife was there. He saw the flash. To him—faced away from the center and looking at his paper—it seemed a brilliant yellow. Startled, he began to rise to his feet. In that moment (he was 1,550 yards from the center), the hospital leaned behind his rising and, with a terrible ripping noise, toppled into the river. The doctor, still in the act of getting to his feet, was thrown forward and around and over; he was buffeted and gripped; he lost track of everything, because things were so speeded up; he felt the water.

Dr. Fujii hardly had time to think that he was dying before he realized that he was alive, squeezed tightly by two long timbers in a V across his chest, like a morsel suspended between two huge chopsticks—held upright, so that he could not move, with his head miraculously above water and his torso and legs in it. The remains of his hospital were all around him in a mad assortment of splintered lumber and materials for the relief of pain. His left shoulder hurt terribly. His glasses were gone.

Father Wilhelm Kleinsorge, of the Society of Jesus, was, on the morning of the explosion, in rather frail condition. The Japanese wartime diet had not sustained him, and he felt the strain of being a foreigner in an increasingly xenophobic[15] Japan; even a German, since the defeat of the Fatherland,[16] was unpopular. Father Kleinsorge had, at thirty-eight, the look of a boy growing too fast—thin in the face, with a prominent Adam's apple, a hollow chest, dangling hands, big feet. He walked clumsily, leaning forward a little. He was tired all the time. To make matters worse, he had suffered for two days, along with Father Cieslik, a fellow-priest, from a rather painful and urgent diarrhea, which they blamed on the beans and black ration bread they were obliged to eat. Two other priests then living in the mission compound, which was in the Noboricho section—Father Superior LaSalle and Father Schiffer—had happily escaped this affliction.

Father Kleinsorge woke up about six the morning the bomb was dropped, and half an hour later—he was a bit tardy because of his sickness—he began to read Mass in the mission chapel, a small Japanese-style wooden building which was without pews, since its worshipers knelt on the usual Japanese matted floor, facing an altar graced with splendid silks, brass, silver, and heavy embroideries. This morning, a Monday, the only worshipers were Mr. Takemoto, a theological student living in the mission house; Mr. Fukai, the secretary of the diocese;[17] Mrs. Murata, the mission's devoutly Christian housekeeper; and his fellow-priests. After Mass, while Father Kleinsorge was reading the Prayers of Thanksgiving, the siren sounded. He stopped the service and the missionaries retired across the compound to the bigger building. There, in his room on the ground floor, to the right of the front door, Father Kleinsorge changed into a military uniform which he had acquired when he was teaching at the Rokko Middle School in Kobe and which he wore during air-raid alerts.

After an alarm, Father Kleinsorge always went out and scanned the sky, and in this instance, when he stepped outside, he was glad to see only the single weather plane that flew over Hiroshima each day about this time. Satisfied that nothing

14. **Kyushu:** southernmost of the principal islands of Japan.
15. **xenophobic** (zen'ō·fō'bik): fearing or disliking foreigners.

16. **defeat of the Fatherland:** Germany surrendered to the Allies on May 7, 1945, approximately three months before the bombing of Hiroshima.
17. **diocese** (dī'ə·sis): church district administered by a bishop.

WORDS TO OWN

convivial (kən·viv'ē·əl) *adj.:* jovial; sociable.

D. Literary Element: Imagery

? Why is the description of Dr. Fujii's being pinned by the timbers a particularly strange or ironic image? [The image compares his position to the common Japanese experience of eating with chopsticks, and this time he finds himself between the "chopsticks."]

E. Exploring the Culture

There was not a large number of Christians in Japan at the time. The majority of Japanese practiced Buddhism, which was introduced from China in about the sixth century. Many Japanese also practiced Shintoism, a religion closely related to Buddhism; it was the ancient Japanese and former state religion. Confucianism, which was introduced to Japan during the fourth century, also had many followers.

PROBLEM SOLVING/CRITICAL THINKING

Making a Crucial Decision Point out to students that President Truman was faced with a critical decision about whether to use the atomic bomb. He had to consider the number of lives to be saved in avoiding an invasion of Japan—and to consider the devastation that would be brought about by the bomb's use. Ask students to think of strategies they use when making important decisions. Do they speak to informed people, use graphic organizers, or meditate on the decision? Encourage students to share their strategies, and tell what they would have done in Truman's position.

PROFESSIONAL NOTES

Thematic Connections: "The Wages of War" Ask students to list words that come to mind when they think about war, such as *soldiers, battles, destruction,* and *death.* Then, discuss with students how Hersey's presentation of the effects war has on specific individuals brings a new perspective to the images of war students have come to expect.

A. Critical Reading: Summarizing

? What happens to Father Kleinsorge immediately after he thinks a bomb has fallen directly on the compound? [The force of the explosion levels the buildings, and somehow he finds his way into the garden, where the housekeeper is crying out to Jesus for pity.]

B. Expansion

Tsingtao (ching dou'), now spelled Qingdao, is a large city on the Yellow Sea in China. It was occupied by Japan at the time Dr. Sasaki trained there.

C. Reader's Response: Extending the Text

? What is the significance of the detail in parentheses? [Sample responses: The detail shows the role that chance plays in life. The detail shows how ordinary people can get caught in extraordinary events.]

would happen, he went in and breakfasted with the other Fathers on substitute coffee and ration bread, which, under the circumstances, was especially repugnant to him. The Fathers sat and talked awhile, until, at eight, they heard the all-clear. They went then to various parts of the building. Father Schiffer retired to his room to do some writing. Father Cieslik sat in his room in a straight chair with a pillow over his stomach to ease his pain, and read. Father Superior LaSalle stood at the window of his room, thinking. Father Kleinsorge went up to a room on the third floor, took off all his clothes except his underwear, and stretched out on his right side on a cot and began reading his *Stimmen der Zeit.*

After the terrible flash—which, Father Kleinsorge later realized, reminded him of something he had read as a boy about a large meteor colliding with the earth—he had time (since he was 1,400 yards from the center) for one thought: A bomb has fallen directly on us. Then, for a few seconds or minutes, he went out of his mind.

(A) Father Kleinsorge never knew how he got out of the house. The next things he was conscious of were that he was wandering around in the mission's vegetable garden in his underwear, bleeding slightly from small cuts along his left flank; that all the buildings round about had fallen down except the Jesuits' mission house, which had long before been braced and double-braced by a priest named Gropper, who was terrified of earthquakes; that the day had turned dark; and that Murata-*san,* the housekeeper, was nearby, crying over and over, "*Shu Jesusu, awaremi tamai!* Our Lord Jesus, have pity on us!"

On the train on the way into Hiroshima from the country, where he lived with his mother, Dr. Terufumi Sasaki, the Red Cross Hospital surgeon, thought over an unpleasant nightmare he had had the night before. His mother's home was in Mukai-hara, thirty miles from the city, and it took him two hours by train and tram to reach the hospital. He had slept uneasily all night and had wakened an hour earlier than usual, and, feeling sluggish and slightly feverish, had debated whether to go to the hospital at all; his sense of duty finally forced him to go, and he had started out on an earlier train than he took most mornings. The dream had particularly frightened him because it was so closely associated, on the surface at least, with a disturbing actuality. He was only twenty-five years old and had just completed his training at the Eastern Medical University, in (B) Tsingtao, China. He was something of an idealist and was much distressed by the inadequacy of medical facilities in the country town where his mother lived. Quite on his own, and without a permit, he had begun visiting a few sick people out there in the evenings, after his eight hours at the hospital and four hours' commuting. He had recently learned that the penalty for practicing without a permit was severe; a fellow-doctor whom he had asked about it had given him a serious scolding. Nevertheless, he had continued to practice. In his dream, he had been at the bedside of a country patient when the police and the doctor he had consulted burst into the room, seized him, dragged him outside, and beat him up cruelly. On the train, he just about decided to give up the work in Mukai-hara, since he felt it would be impossible to get a permit, because the authorities would hold that it would conflict with his duties at the Red Cross Hospital.

At the terminus, he caught a streetcar at once. (C) (He later calculated that if he had taken his customary train that morning, and if he had had to wait a few minutes for the streetcar, as often happened, he would have been close to the center at the time of the explosion and would surely have perished.) He arrived at the hospital at seven-forty and reported to the chief surgeon. A few minutes later, he went to a room on the first floor and drew blood from the arm of a man in order to perform a Wassermann test. The laboratory containing the incubators[18] for the test was on the third floor. With the blood specimen in his left hand, walking in a kind of distraction he had felt all morning, probably because of the dream and his restless night, he started along the main corridor on his way toward the stairs. He was one step beyond an open window when the light of the bomb was reflected, like a gigantic photographic

18. **incubators:** equipment providing a favorable environment for the growth of cell cultures.

WORDS TO OWN

idealist (ī·dē'əl·ist) *n.:* one who believes in noble, though often impractical, goals; dreamer.

OPTIONS FOR TEACHING

PROFESSIONAL NOTES

Critical Comment In the July 31, 1995, issue of *The New Yorker,* Roger Angell tries to give an idea of the impact of the piece that was published in its entirety in the magazine almost fifty years before. "John Hersey's 'Hiroshima'," he writes, ". . . is a work of sustained silence. Its appearance . . . offered one of the first detailed accounts of the effects of nuclear warfare on its survivors, in a prose so stripped of mannerism, sentimentality, and even minimal emphasis as to place each reader alone within scenes laid bare of all but pain." Angell points out that the work's emotional effect is even stronger because its words "abstain from the smallest judgment or moral positioning, and leave the reader to deal with the consequences and the questions." Hersey's work had tremendous impact when it was first published, but it has also had a long-term effect, for as soon as people began to understand the destruction and horror of the first atomic bombings, they began to work toward making them the last.

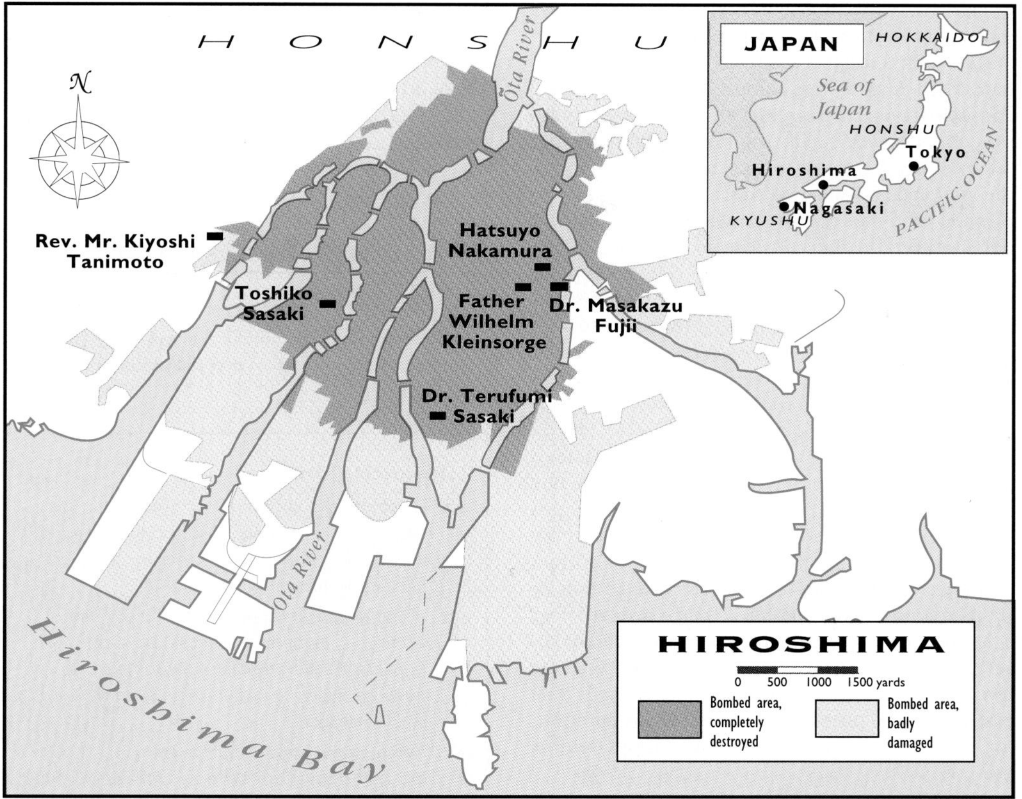

flash, in the corridor. He ducked down on one knee and said to himself, as only a Japanese would, (D) "Sasaki, *gambare!* Be brave!" Just then (the building was 1,650 yards from the center), the blast ripped through the hospital. The glasses he was wearing flew off his face; the bottle of blood crashed against one wall; his Japanese slippers zipped out from under his feet—but otherwise, thanks to where he stood, he was untouched.

Dr. Sasaki shouted the name of the chief surgeon and rushed around to the man's office and found him terribly cut by glass. The hospital was in horrible confusion: Heavy partitions and ceilings had fallen on patients, beds had overturned, windows had blown in and cut people, blood was spattered on the walls and floors, instruments were everywhere, many of the patients were running about screaming, many more lay dead. (A colleague working in the laboratory to which Dr. Sasaki had been walking was dead; Dr. Sasaki's patient, whom he had just left and who a few moments before had been dreadfully afraid of syphilis, was also dead.) Dr. Sasaki found himself the only doctor in the hospital who was unhurt.

Dr. Sasaki, who believed that the enemy had hit only the building he was in, got bandages and began to bind the wounds of those inside the hospital; while outside, all over Hiroshima, maimed and dying citizens turned their unsteady steps toward the Red Cross Hospital to begin an invasion that was to make Dr. Sasaki forget his private nightmare for a long, long time.

Miss Toshiko Sasaki, the East Asia Tin Works clerk, who is not related to Dr. Sasaki, got up at three o'clock in the morning on the day the bomb fell. (E)

D. Reader's Response: Shaping Interpretations

? Why does Hersey use the phrase "as only a Japanese would" in describing Dr. Sasaki's behavior? [Sample responses: Honor is very important to the Japanese, and Dr. Sasaki would feel his honor to be jeopardized by cowardly behavior, even though no one was there to witness it. The phrase shows the importance that the Japanese place on contributing to the war effort, and that somehow Dr. Sasaki can help just by being brave.]

E. Language Note: Transition

The narration again abruptly shifts to another person. What provides the link between the two strangers' experiences? [They were both mentioned at the beginning as survivors of the bomb.]

OBSERVATION ASSESSMENT

Observation Assessment Use the following points to assess how well students interact with each other in cooperative learning situations.

1=Rarely 2=Sometimes 3=Often

_____ Participates willingly
_____ Takes a leadership role
_____ Listens attentively to other students' ideas
_____ Easily grasps the task or problem at hand
_____ Offers innovative approaches to the task
_____ Accepts and works with group decisions

ASSESSMENT TOOLS

Check Test: True-False

1. The two characters named Sasaki are brother and sister. [False]
2. Hiroshima is left relatively unharmed before the atomic blast. [True]
3. Mrs. Nakamura hears only one of her three children after the blast. [True]
4. The Japanese call B-29's "the big guys." [False]
5. Dr. Sasaki is the only doctor in the hospital who is unhurt. [True]

A. Critical Reading: Predicting

? What do you expect of Miss Sasaki's experience of the blast, given her distance from its center? [Students will probably expect that the woman will be severely injured by the explosion, since it is so close.]

B. Reader's Response: Challenging the Text

Hersey's account of the survivors' stories abounds with **irony.** Do you think it is ironic or significant that "in the first moment of the atomic age, a human being was crushed by books"? Why or why not? [Sample responses: The detail is ironic because books are symbols of civilization, while the dropping of the bomb may be seen as an act of violence against humanity. The detail is ironic because the atomic bomb could end history, which is contained in the books.]

There was extra housework to do. Her eleven-month-old brother, Akio, had come down the day before with a serious stomach upset; her mother had taken him to the Tamura Pediatric Hospital and was staying there with him. Miss Sasaki, who was about twenty, had to cook breakfast for her father, a brother, a sister, and herself, and—since the hospital, because of the war, was unable to provide food—to prepare a whole day's meals for her mother and the baby, in time for her father, who worked in a factory making rubber earplugs for artillery crews, to take the food by on his way to the plant. When she had finished and had cleaned and put away the cooking things, it was nearly seven. The family lived in Koi, and she had a forty-five-minute trip to the tin works, in the section of town called Kannon-machi. She was in charge of the personnel records in the factory. She left Koi at seven, and as soon as she reached the plant, she went with some of the other girls from the personnel department to the factory auditorium. A prominent local Navy man, a former employee, had committed suicide the day before by throwing himself under a train—a death considered honorable enough to warrant a memorial service, which was to be held at the tin works at ten o'clock that morning. In the large hall, Miss Sasaki and the others made suitable preparations for the meeting. This work took about twenty minutes.

Miss Sasaki went back to her office and sat down at her desk. She was quite far from the windows, which were off to her left, and behind her were a couple of tall bookcases containing all the books of the factory library, which the personnel department had organized. She settled herself at her desk, put some things in a drawer, and shifted papers. She thought that before she began to make entries in her lists of new employees, discharges, and departures for the Army, she would chat for a moment with the girl at her right. Just as she turned her head away from the windows, the room was filled with a blinding light. She was paralyzed by fear, fixed still in her chair for a long moment (the plant was 1,600 yards from the center). **A**

Everything fell, and Miss Sasaki lost consciousness. The ceiling dropped suddenly and the wooden floor above collapsed in splinters and the people up there came down and the roof above them gave way; but principally and first of all, the bookcases right behind her swooped forward and the contents threw her down, with her left leg horribly twisted and breaking underneath her. **B** There, in the tin factory, in the first moment of the atomic age, a human being was crushed by books.

Making Meanings

First Thoughts

1. What aspect of *Hiroshima* did you focus on most intently as you read—what character, image, or idea?

Reviewing the Text

a. Describe the six people presented in this section of *Hiroshima.* Besides surviving the atomic bomb explosion, what do they have in common?
b. What simple **images** does Hersey use to help us imagine the actual physical impact of the bomb? For example, how does he describe the flash as seen by each character?
c. What small, commonplace human-interest details does Hersey give about his characters so that they come alive and seem like people we might know? (Refer to your Reader's Log.)
d. How does Hersey explain the **ironic** fact that an all-clear signal sounded just before the bomb was dropped?

Shaping Interpretations

2. What **ironies** can you find in each character's story—including the irony of the last image?
3. While mostly recounting facts **objectively,** Hersey communicates a **subjective** attitude toward war. How does he accomplish that? How would you describe his attitude toward the Japanese? toward the Americans?
4. During World War II, most Americans felt that the Japanese, like the Germans, were enemies to be destroyed no matter what the cost. How do

Making Meanings

First Thoughts

1. Possible response: Mrs. Nakamura's experience moved me most because of her struggle to protect her children on her own.

Reviewing the Text

a. Answers will vary. Each is a civilian, each was taken by surprise by the blast, none worked directly for the war effort (in a munitions factory, for example), and they all attribute their survival to chance.
b. All the images are a variation of a flash. Mr. Tanimoto remembers a "sheet of sun" that traveled across the sky. Mrs. Nakamura recalls the flash as "whiter than any white she had ever seen." Dr. Fujii, looking away from the sky, remembered a brilliant yellow. Father Kleinsorge thought of a meteor colliding with the earth. Dr. Sasaki saw the light reflected, like a gigantic photographic flash. Miss Sasaki's office was filled with a "blinding light."
c. Possible response: The first paragraph offers many such details. Miss Sasaki, sitting at her desk, had just turned to talk to the girl next to her. Dr. Fujii was sitting cross-legged to read the newspaper. Father Kleinsorge sat in his underwear reading a magazine. Mr. Tanimoto is helping a friend move. Some may say Hersey's use of Japanese words helps make the scenes realistic.
d. The Japanese radar operators, detecting only three planes, thought that the number was too small for an air raid and supposed it was a reconnaissance flight.

Shaping Interpretations

2. Each story shares a common irony. The daily routine of each character, even by wartime standards, becomes drastically unreal. The city expected a "massive B-29 raid," yet only one bomb was dropped and caused more destruction than anyone could imagine. In the last image, irony lies in the fact that books, symbols of civilization, crush Miss Sasaki. This suggests that the advent of the atomic age calls for a reevaluation of civilization.

you respond to Hersey's treatment of the Japanese in this account? How do you think readers in 1946—one year after the war had ended—would have responded?

5. What other methods might a historian or journalist have used to tell this story? What do you think of Hersey's method?

Extending the Text

6. From what you know of history and from what you have read here, tell why, in human and political terms, the explosion at Hiroshima was a central event in the twentieth century. How has this distant event affected your life?

CHOICES: Building Your Portfolio

Writer's Notebook

1. Collecting Ideas for an Evaluation

Write down some of the facts and events in this excerpt from *Hiroshima* that are striking examples of **objective reporting.** Then choose examples of vivid **subjective reporting** and personal involvement by the author. Which type of reporting dominates, and how effective is it? Keep your notes for possible use in the Writer's Workshop on page 1181.

Critical Writing

2. "I want to read on!"

Readers of Hersey's *Hiroshima* know the outcome of the narrative before they open the book. In a brief essay, show how in this excerpt Hersey manages, nevertheless, to create **suspense.** What questions does he plant in your mind? When does he answer them?

Crossing the Curriculum: History

3. To Use the Bomb

Research the decision by U.S. President Harry S Truman to use the atomic bomb against Japan. You will find facts and opinions in biographies and memoirs of Truman and other U.S. and British government officials, in government reports, and in a wide variety of additional works by historians and journalists. In an essay, describe how the decision was made and what factors were considered. End the essay with your own reflections about whether Truman made the correct decision.

Critical Writing

4. What's in a Word?

Hersey notes that the Japanese had a nickname for the B-29 bomber planes that regularly damaged their cities: "*B-san,* or Mr. B" (page 938). The appositive (which is a context clue that directly defines the word) also gives us an idea of what *–san* means when attached to a noun. Hersey almost always helps his readers by including strong **context clues** with Japanese terms. In a brief essay, describe how Hersey's use of Japanese terms helps to establish the authenticity of his report, and explain the insight these terms provide into the people, the culture, or the events described. (For example, the information about the Japanese nickname "B-san" for the B-29 bomber might tell you something about how some Japanese were coping psychologically with the frequent bombings.)

3. The facts he chooses to relate communicate his subjective attitude. He presents the horrors of war, not the glories, by reporting its effects on ordinary, innocent people. Hersey is sympathetic toward the Japanese. Answers will vary regarding Hersey's attitude toward the Americans. He neither justifies nor condemns the attack.

4. Students may say that a 1946 audience would have been shocked by Hersey's sympathetic treatment of the Japanese so soon after the war. Students should support their responses, and may point out that Hersey downplays political and military issues and focuses on typical Japanese citizens.

5. Historians or journalists would probably have focused on reporting the facts and numbers. Students' opinions on Hersey's method will vary. Ask students to support their responses and offer alternative approaches.

Extending the Text

6. **(Evaluation)** Possible response: Hiroshima was the first use of the ultimate weapon. The technology of war had progressed to the point where it could destroy the world. It raised the question of whether there were limits to the human capacity for destruction. Students will have different responses to how this event affects their lives.

Choices: Building Your Portfolio

2. **Critical Writing** Ask students to work with a partner to examine the strategies Hersey uses to sustain **suspense** in the description of the survivors' experiences. Pairs should make a list of the strategies they find, and then use the list to write their essays individually.
3. **Crossing the Curriculum: History** Arrange students in small groups for the research project, and encourage each student in a group to use a different source of information. Group members can pool their findings and then trade their opinions and reasons on the question. After their discussions, group members can use their notes while individually writing their essays.

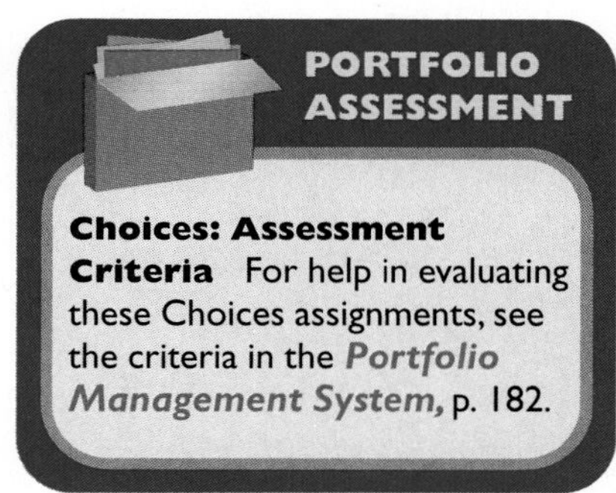

Choices: Assessment Criteria For help in evaluating these Choices assignments, see the criteria in the ***Portfolio Management System,*** p. 182.

QUICK PLANNING GUIDE

Into the Poem

Through the Poem

Beyond the Poem

UPI/Bettmann.

Robert Lowell

(1917–1977)

From virtually the beginning of his career, Robert Lowell was a major presence in American poetry. He was born into an aristocratic Boston family whose ancestors went back to the *Mayflower.* The nineteenth-century poet James Russell Lowell (1819–1891) was his great-uncle; the early-twentieth-century poet Amy Lowell (1874–1925), a promoter of Imagism, was his cousin. Lowell felt he had to rebel against his family's conservative, traditional background in order to carve out his own identity as an individual and as a poet.

Lowell left Harvard after two years to attend Kenyon College in Ohio, where the poet John Crowe Ransom was teaching. The summer before enrolling at Kenyon, Lowell lived in a tent on the poet Allen Tate's lawn in Nashville, Tennessee, soaking up all he could learn from Tate about writing poetry. Ransom and Tate were both supporters of what is called the New Criticism. They admired densely packed, "formal, difficult poems," as Lowell later put it, and Lowell began writing poems in this style.

Lowell graduated from Kenyon in 1940, married the novelist Jean Stafford, and started what would be a distinguished career of teaching and writing. Shortly thereafter, in what was at least partly another rebellious act against his family's Protestant roots, he converted to Roman Catholicism.

In the early days of World War II, Lowell tried several times to enlist in the Navy, but was rejected for his poor eyesight. By 1943, appalled at the destruction caused by American bombing in Europe, he refused induction into the Army and served a five-month prison sentence. His poems of this period—in the collections *Land of Unlikeness* (1944), *Lord Weary's Castle* (1946) (which won a Pulitzer Prize), and *The Mills of the Kavanaughs* (1951)—were tight, formal, and intellectually challenging. They usually presented a grim vision of a world about to end.

In the 1950s, Lowell's style and subject matter gradually changed. At poetry readings with Allen Ginsberg (page 1008), whose loose and freewheeling style immediately touched audiences, Lowell, an endless reviser, would sometimes simplify some of his own poems as he read them. He began writing a looser, freer verse, with more natural rhythms and more personal subject matter.

All his life, Lowell suffered great bouts of mental instability. In 1959, he published *Life Studies,* in which he wrote frankly about his condition. His tone was neither self-pitying nor self-indulgent. Instead, he described his suffering with a light irony.

Life Studies became one of the most influential works of poetry written after World War II. It helped to make acceptable the highly personal poetry being written by Sylvia Plath (page 1148), Anne Sexton (page 1088), and John Berryman (1914–1972)—the group now referred to as the Confessional School of poets.

In the 1960s, Lowell became more and more of a public figure. Like many writers of the time, he expressed opposition to the war in Vietnam. His poetry remained deeply personal, however, and he wrote a great many unrhymed sonnets, first published as *Notebooks* in 1969 and then revised as *History* in 1973. He also wrote several well-received plays, notably *The Old Glory* (1965), based on stories by Herman Melville and Nathaniel Hawthorne.

In 1977, returning to New York from London, Robert Lowell died of a heart attack in a taxi taking him home from the airport.

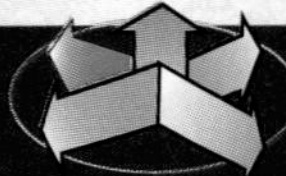

PROGRAM MANAGER

- **Planning Instruction** See *Teaching Notes, Teaching Resources B,* p. 137, for objectives, a summary, literary elements, and additional historical and biographical information for this selection.
- **Instructional Support** Before beginning the instructional lesson, see *Graphic Organizer for Active Reading, Teaching Resources B,* p. 147, for a Through the Poem activity.
- **Assessment** See *Selection Test, Test Booklet,* pp. 221–222.

BEFORE YOU READ
FOR THE UNION DEAD

Reading Focus

What Have We Gained?

After all the wars that Americans have fought, after all the suffering and loss and sacrifice, what kind of a world have we created? Poets and politicians, sages and students ask this question in different ways every day: Are we satisfied with our world?

A Dialogue with the Text

READER'S LOG

As you read "For the Union Dead," keep a record of your questions and uncertainties about the poem. If a passage seems confusing or obscure, try to write down exactly what you need to learn in order to understand the passage. Remember, no great work of art gives up all its secrets upon first acquaintance.

Elements of Literature

Imagery

"For the Union Dead" resonates with powerful **imagery**—language that evokes a picture or a concrete sensation of a person, a thing, a place, or an experience. Lowell wants us to do more than simply think about his ideas; he gives us the opportunity to *feel* what he means—in our noses, in our throats, and on our fingertips.

> **Imagery** is language that evokes a picture or a concrete sensation of a person, a thing, a place, or an experience.
>
> *For more on Imagery, see the Handbook of Literary Terms.*

Background

"They give up everything to serve the Republic," says the Latin inscription preceding this poem. "They" are all the Union soldiers who served during the Civil War. But, more specifically, "they" are the members of the first regiment of African American soldiers from a free state, in this case Massachusetts. Under a white commander, Robert Gould Shaw, this regiment stormed Fort Wagner, South Carolina, in an assault resulting in many deaths, including that of the commander himself. The event is dramatized in the award-winning film *Glory*.

The subject of the poem is not that event, however, but its memorial—the bronze monument by the great sculptor Augustus Saint-Gaudens, which stands in Boston Common, the park directly across from the State House.

Today, Boston has a new aquarium that is a major tourist attraction. In 1960, when "For the Union Dead" was written, an older aquarium in South Boston—empty, deserted, and dilapidated—provided just the right image to set up the relationship between past and present.

Because this is a complex poem, you should read it at least twice. A comment follows the poem.

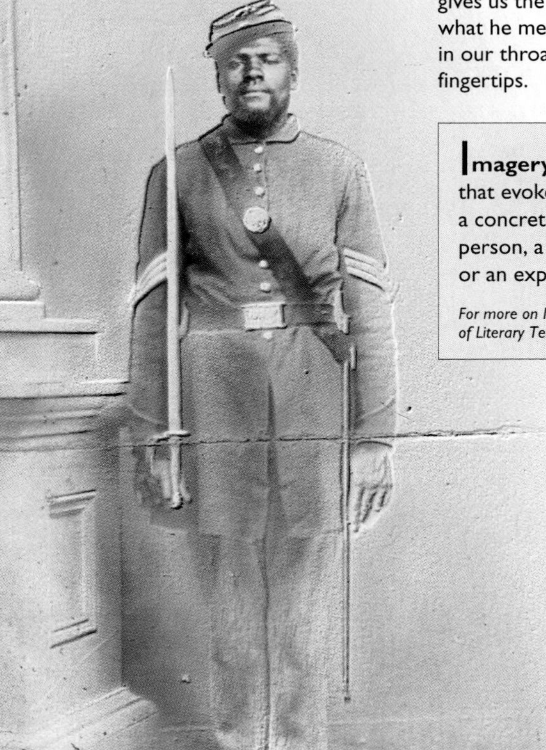

Henry Steward, Sergeant, Fifty-fourth Massachusetts Infantry Regiment, Company E.

Massachusetts Historical Society, Boston.

Using BEFORE YOU READ p. 949

Reading Focus

Ask students to think about the following wars in U.S. history: the American Revolution, the War of 1812, the Mexican War, the Civil War, the Spanish-American War, World War I, World War II, the Korean War, and the Vietnam War. Have the class form several groups and allow each group to choose a war for consideration. Ask each group to list the reasons why the United States entered the conflict and to illustrate how the world (or the country) did, or did not, change as a result. Groups may share their results with the class.

Elements of Literature

While **imagery** often appeals to the sense of sight, it can appeal to the other senses as well. Ask students to look for words or phrases that appeal to the senses. Students can organize their notes in the form of a cluster diagram such as that on Transparency 3 in the Transparency Package.

Background

Suggest to students that the poem on one level compares the social and racial ideals of the Union in 1863 with those of American society nearly one hundred years later. Ask students to list on the left side of a sheet of paper some of the ideals of the Union during the Civil War (such as an undivided nation and freedom for African Americans). On the right side of the paper, have students list what they know about American society in the late 1950s and early 1960s (for example, marches for civil rights, the Red scare, fear of nuclear war, and big cars). Students should try to make connections between the two time periods as they read and analyze the poem.

PORTFOLIO ASSESSMENT

Portfolio Assessment For help with self-assessment of reading skills, see the *Portfolio Management System*, p. 39.

A. Reader's Response: Shaping Interpretations

? What does the **metaphor** suggest about the setting? [Sample responses: The abandoned aquarium is a wasteland. The setting is paradoxical and mixed-up, because it conjures images of snow and a desert.]

B. Literary Element: Imagery

? What does this image suggest about the speaker's attention? [Comparing the speaker's nose to a crawling snail emphasizes the speaker's intense concentration on the fish.]

William Johnson/Stock Boston.

Civil War monument by Augustus Saint-Gaudens honoring the Fifty-fourth Regiment of Black Soldiers, led by Col. Robert Gould Shaw, Boston Common.

For the Union Dead

"Relinquunt Omnia Servare Rem Publicam."

Robert Lowell

The old South Boston Aquarium stands
(A) in a Sahara of snow now. Its broken windows are boarded.
The bronze weathervane cod has lost half its scales.
The airy tanks are dry.

(B) Once my nose crawled like a snail on the glass;
my hand tingled
to burst the bubbles
drifting from the noses of the cowed, compliant fish.

My hand draws back. I often sigh still
for the dark downward and vegetating kingdom
of the fish and reptile. One morning last March,
I pressed against the new barbed and galvanized

fence on the Boston Common. Behind their cage,
yellow dinosaur steamshovels were grunting

OPTIONS FOR TEACHING

STRATEGIES FOR INCLUSION

Less Proficient Readers Have students use a chart as they read to help them recognize the poem's imagery. Students should write the names of the five senses at the tops of the columns. Ask students to pause at every image and determine in which of the five categories it belongs. Students can compare their charts.

English Language Development Encourage students to read beyond the literal meaning of important terms and images in the poem. Have students focus on the words "aquarium," "cage," "compass needle," "graveyards," and "statues." Ask students to define the literal use of the words but also to explore how each word creates an image that applies both to the poem's setting and to its theme.

Special Needs Have students work in small groups to examine closely lines in the poem that contain dense or confusing imagery. Students should take turns describing to each other their perceptions of the imagery; they can also make sketches of what the lines make them "see." Have the groups share their drawings and thoughts with the class.

as they cropped up tons of mush and grass
to gouge their underworld garage.

Parking spaces luxuriate like civic
sandpiles in the heart of Boston.
A girdle of orange, Puritan-pumpkin colored girders
braces the tingling Statehouse,

shaking over the excavations, as it faces Colonel Shaw
and his bell-cheeked Negro infantry
on St. Gaudens' shaking Civil War relief, C D
propped by a plank splint against the garage's earthquake.

Two months after marching through Boston,
half the regiment was dead;
at the dedication,
William James° could almost hear the bronze Negroes breathe.

Their monument sticks like a fishbone E
in the city's throat.
Its Colonel is as lean
as a compass-needle.

He has an angry wrenlike vigilance,
a greyhound's gentle tautness;
he seems to wince at pleasure,
and suffocate for privacy.

He is out of bounds now. He rejoices in man's lovely,
peculiar power to choose life and die—
when he leads his black soldiers to death,
he cannot bend his back.

On a thousand small town New England greens,
the old white churches hold their air
of sparse, sincere rebellion; frayed flags
quilt the graveyards of the Grand Army of the Republic.

The stone statues of the abstract Union Soldier
grow slimmer and younger each year—
wasp-wasted, they doze over muskets
and muse through their sideburns . . .

Shaw's father wanted no monument
except the ditch,
where his son's body was thrown
and lost with his "niggers." F

The ditch is nearer.
There are no statues for the last war° here;

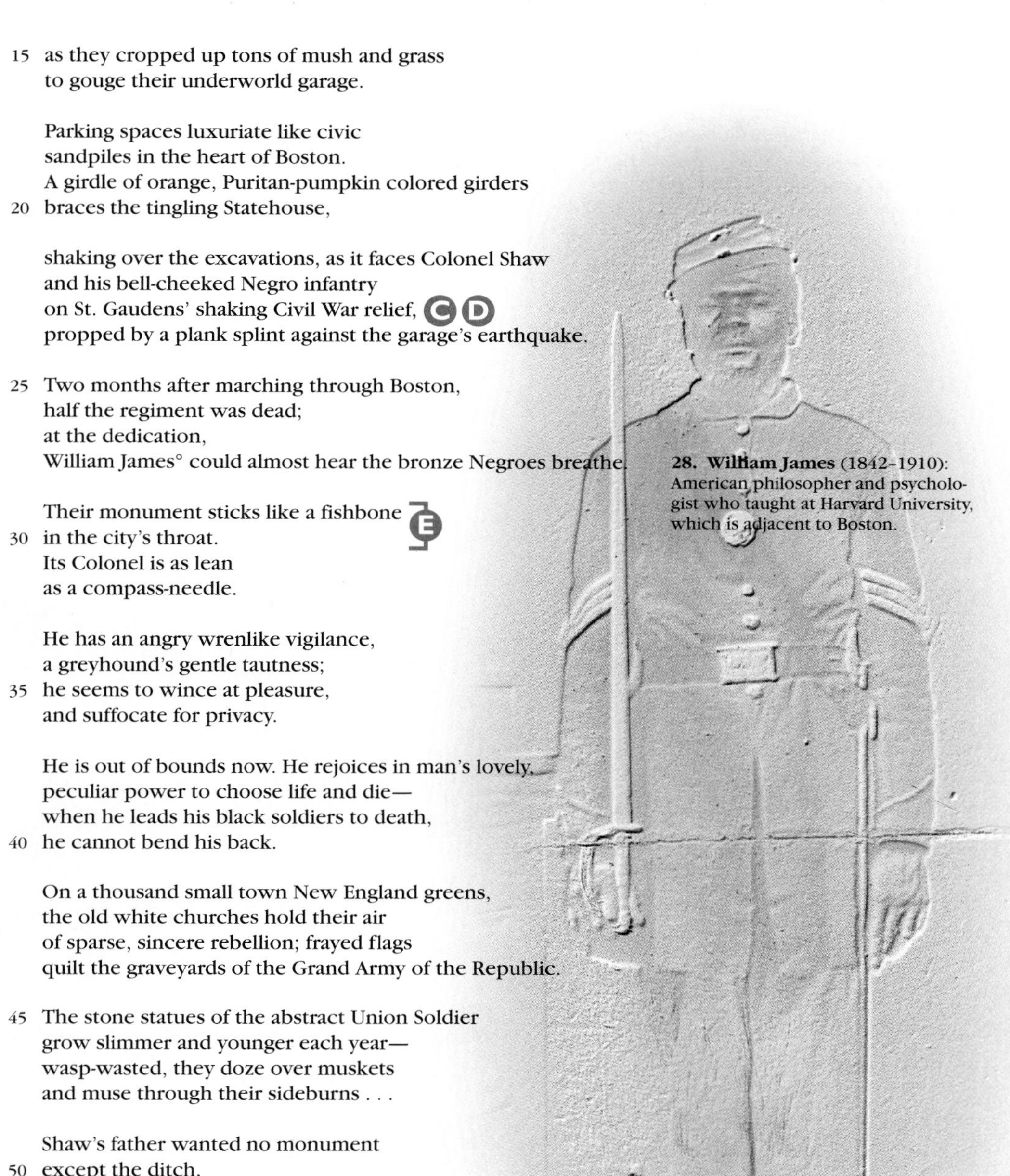

28. William James (1842–1910): American philosopher and psychologist who taught at Harvard University, which is adjacent to Boston.

54. the last war: World War II.

C. Expansion

Lowell's grandfather, Robert Traill Spence Lowell, had a nephew, Colonel Charles Russell Lowell, who married Josephine Shaw, the sister of Colonel Shaw. Robert Lowell's great uncle, James Russell Lowell, was grief-stricken at the death of his nephew-in-law and wrote a poem to commemorate the twenty-five-year-old colonel's heroism, "Memoriae Positum" (1863). The Saint-Gaudens monument bears an inscription written by the nineteenth-century Lowell.

D. Humanities Connection

Augustus Saint-Gaudens (1848–1907) was the most noted American sculptor of the nineteenth century. In addition to the Shaw Memorial, he crafted two memorials of Lincoln.

E. Reader's Response: Shaping Interpretations

? Why is the monument "a fishbone / in the city's throat"? [Sample responses: The monument commemorates an ideal of racial equality that the city is ashamed of not having fulfilled. The statue is like a fishbone because it has been worn by weather and because it clashes with its modern surroundings.]

F. Language Note: Quotation Marks

? Why is this word in quotation marks? [The word is spoken by Shaw's father, who apparently is a racist, unlike his son.]

INTEGRATING THE LANGUAGE ARTS

Language and Style Have students analyze the phrases below to see how Lowell uses language to convey unfulfilled hope. Ask students to discuss the images each of the phrases evokes, the word choices that evoke the imagery, and the relation of the image to the poem's theme.

l. 4: "The airy tanks are dry"
l. 18: "sandpiles in the heart of Boston"
l. 35: "he seems to wince at pleasure"
ll. 37-38: "He rejoices in man's lovely, / peculiar power to choose life and die—"
l. 60: "the drained faces of Negro school-children rise like balloons"

Strategic Reading Have pairs of students read the poem by taking turns reading two or three stanzas. After one student in each pair has read a section of the poem aloud, the other partner can ask the reader questions that came to mind during the reading. The questions may relate directly to the poem, to selections from other lessons or classes, or to anything that the reading brought to mind. The second student should answer as many questions as possible. Then, have students reverse roles and continue their reading. When the partners are finished, have them summarize the poem.

A. Reader's Response: First Thoughts

? Why do you think the word *is* is emphasized in the sentence? [Sample responses: The emphasis conclusively establishes that the Aquarium is gone. Times have changed, even though it may seem that the times have stayed the same.]

on Boylston Street, a commercial photograph
shows Hiroshima boiling

over a Mosler Safe, the "Rock of Ages"
that survived the blast. Space is nearer.
When I crouch to my television set,
the drained faces of Negro school-children rise like balloons.

Colonel Shaw
is riding on his bubble,
he waits
for the blesséd break.

(A) The Aquarium *is* gone. Everywhere,
giant finned cars nose forward like fish;
a savage servility
slides by on grease.

Courtesy of the Bostonian Society, Old State House.

Aerial view of excavation site for Boston Common garage. Lowell's poem was inspired by the scene of this razing—a deep scar on a landscape that once boasted the old South Boston Aquarium.

OPTIONS FOR TEACHING

CROSSING THE CURRICULUM

Social Sciences Have students explore specific developments in race relations in the United States between the time of Shaw's regiment and the setting of the poem. Students can work in groups of four or five to research a single topic concerning race relations in the United States, such as a Supreme Court ruling or a civil rights leader. Each group can present its information in an oral report to the rest of the class.

ASSESSMENT TOOLS

Check Test: Questions and Answers

1. What is the setting of the poem? [Boston during the late 1950s.]
2. What is the monument on which the poet meditates? [A monument to Colonel Shaw and his African American infantry in the Civil War.]
3. What is the other central structure in the poem? [The old South Boston Aquarium.]
4. To what are the cars in the last stanza compared? [Fish.]

Critical Comment

A Vision of Blacks and Whites United

A good poem can withstand anything said about it. Understanding "For the Union Dead" depends on the knowledge and experiences you bring to it as much as it depends upon what the poem itself offers. After you read the poem, try to paraphrase it in order to clarify some of its references and to open possibilities of interpretation. (A)

Looking at the ruined aquarium in its desert of snow, the poet remembers how, as a child, he used to press his nose right up against the glass of the great fish tanks; he recalls how his hand itched to get inside the tanks and play with the rising bubbles and all the marvelous sea creatures. But he is no longer a child. He draws back his hand, even though something in his nature still hungers to explore another order of life—that subconscious region where all beings in the "vegetating kingdom" had their beginnings.

The grown man presses himself against the fence that makes a "cage" in which steamshovels are gouging out space for an underground parking garage. The tremors of excavation work are so thunderous that both the State House and the bronze monument facing it have to be braced for protection. The jeopardy in which "progress" has placed both State House and monument brings the poet's central subject—the black regiment—into focus.

Having paraded through Boston as heroes on their way to the battlefield, half of these soldiers were dead within two months. When the monument to them was dedicated in 1897, the memory of these men was so much alive, and their faces and figures so faithfully rendered in bronze, that the great American psychologist William James felt that they almost breathed.

But now the poet observes that the monument "sticks like a fishbone/in the city's throat," meaning that it is an irritant. Ironically, Boston is not only one of the cities where the abolitionist movement was strongest; it is also, like many places in the United States, a place where racism has persisted. The poet compares Colonel Shaw, the regiment's leader, to the needle on a compass; this characterization suggests that Shaw pointed the way—a way in which whites and blacks united might become part of a nation's most honorable history. But Shaw is now "out of bounds" in a time and place where his special kind of vision and integrity are conspicuously lacking.

Then, instantaneously, like a change of scene in a movie, the poet's eye suddenly "pans" over the New England landscape (lines 41–48). Churches on village greens remind him of the Revolutionary War; cemeteries with their "quilt" of ragged flags recall the Civil War; the young soldiers of the Union, "stone statues" all alike, remain young and slim as their nation grows older and fatter.

Colonel Shaw's father, we learn, felt that the monument to his son was unnecessary; people had only to remember the ditch where the young commander's body was thrown with those of his soldiers. "The ditch," that common boneyard of blacks and whites, "is nearer." Why? Because nuclear holocaust threatens a world more preoccupied with sales and profits than with its own survival. (B)

The bubbles that rose in the fish tanks of the old aquarium return at the end of the poem. They are now "balloons" that are compared to the "drained faces" of young African Americans. They also appear as the buried dream of Colonel Shaw that, like a bubble, may burst forth when idealism explodes into reality. (C)

The old aquarium and everything it stood for in the speaker's childhood imagination no longer exist. "Finned" luxury cars now "slide by," just as the marvelous fish once glided through the bubbly depths of their tanks. To the speaker, the chrome-laden automobiles represent a "savage servility." They move "on grease," the by-product of the oil that supplies the modern world's energy, and the end product and sludgy residue of the world's great power.

A. Critical Reading: Metacognition

? How do the strategies the author mentions help a reader understand a poem? Can you think of other useful strategies? [Possible answers: Paraphrasing a literary work helps a reader understand the work's main points, and making interpretations allows a reader to make sense of ambiguities or subtle, easily overlooked points. Bringing prior knowledge to a poem is unavoidable because a reader must use prior knowledge to understand a poem's context.]

B. Critical Reading: Evaluating an Interpretation

? Do you think this evaluation of the poem's view of the world is valid? Explain. [Possible answers: The evaluation is valid because it is a logical conclusion based on the poem's references to Hiroshima and luxuries of modern society. The evaluation is shaky because the poem concerns itself more with humanity's distancing of people different from themselves.]

C. Reader's Response: Challenging the Text

? Do you agree with the way the author has united the **imagery** of the poem into a central message? Explain. [Sample responses: The unity of the images makes sense because it shows how the poem, which displays a wide range of ideas, actually has a tight thematic focus: The difference between an idealism of race and the more sordid reality of materialism. The unity of the images does not make sense because it simplifies the poem too much; the poem is not so much about idealism as it is about real people's need to acknowledge each other as equals.]

STRATEGIES FOR INCLUSION

Less Proficient Readers Students may be confused by the many different connections the critic makes between the ideas in the poem. Encourage students to keep track of the connections by using a graphic organizer such as the one on Transparency 3: Cluster Diagram in the Transparency Package. As they read, students can periodically compare their organizers with those of other students.

INTEGRATING THE LANGUAGE ARTS

Strategic Reading Have the class read the essay aloud, with a different volunteer reading each paragraph. After each paragraph has been read, ask students for their thoughts on the author's ideas and conclusions. Encourage students especially to test the author's ideas by reviewing evidence from the poem. Direct students to cite specific passages in agreement or disagreement with the author. After the class has finished reading the essay, ask students to summarize and evaluate the author's critique of the poem.

Making Meanings

First Thoughts

1. Possible answers may include observations on the decay of American ideals, greed, racism, progress, or materialism.

Reviewing the Text

a. The aquarium stands in a Sahara of snow; it has broken and boarded windows; its airy tanks are dry.
b. The speaker sees yellow steam shovels that look like dinosaurs gouging up the earth to build an underground parking garage.
c. The monument is shaking (l. 23); its bronze infantrymen are bell-cheeked (l. 22). Shaw is compared with a compass-needle (l. 32), an angry wren (l. 33), and a taut grey-hound (l. 34).
d. Half the regiment was dead two months after marching through Boston (ll. 25–26); their bodies were thrown into a ditch (ll. 50–51).

Shaping Interpretations

2. Lowell suggests that only humanity has the ability to choose to risk life for important values.
3. The events occurred in the nation-wide struggle for the desegregation of schools brought about by the Supreme Court decision in the case of *Brown v. Board of Education of Topeka* (1954).
4. The word "savage" suggests that Americans now respond to base instincts, rather than to cultivated principles. Servility to materialism is compared unfavorably with the service to a higher calling, such as the cause of the Union during the Civil War.
5. "Union" read as an adjective and "dead" read as a noun indicate the title refers to soldiers who died for the Union. "Union" read as a noun with "dead" as its adjective implies that the Union and its ideals are now dead.
6. Students may agree the tone is mixed—nostalgic, ironic, meditative, and disillusioned.

Making Meanings

First Thoughts

1. What basic **message** does this poem suggest to you? Explain it briefly.

Reviewing the Text

a. What **images** describe the old South Boston Aquarium?
b. What **images** describe what the speaker saw on Boston Common?
c. What **images** describe the Saint-Gaudens monument? How many things is the colonel compared with?
d. What details tell you what happened to Colonel Shaw and his men?

Shaping Interpretations

2. What do you think the poet means by saying Colonel Shaw "rejoices in man's lovely, / peculiar power to choose life and die" (lines 37–38)?
3. What historical events in Boston and other American cities might the poet be referring to with the mention of the "drained faces" of African American children on television (line 60)?
4. What do you think is the "savage servility" mentioned in the last stanza?
5. Explain how the **title** of the poem could have at least two meanings.
6. How would you describe the poem's **tone**?

Choices: Building Your Portfolio

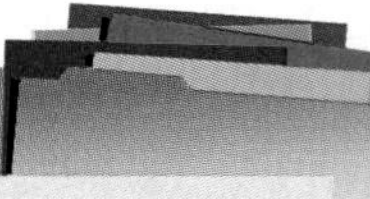

Writer's Notebook

1. Collecting Ideas for an Evaluation

When you write an evaluation, you need to be aware of your readers—the knowledge and experience they bring to a reading of the text. Review the notes you made in your Reader's Log. Then make a list of the historical information, allusions, vocabulary, and other data you would need to include in an evaluation of this poem written for students your own age who are not in your class. Save your notes for possible use in the Writer's Workshop on page 1181.

Critical Writing

2. Monuments and Messages

In an essay, explain how the following poem by Henry Timrod (1828–1867) is like or unlike Lowell's poem in terms of (a) theme, (b) tone, (c) diction, and (d) form.

Ode on the Confederate Dead

Sung on the Occasion of Decorating the Graves of the Confederate Dead, at Magnolia Cemetery, Charleston, S.C., 1867

Sleep sweetly in your humble graves,
  Sleep, martyrs of a fallen cause;
Though yet no marble column craves
  The pilgrim here to pause.

In seeds of laurel in the earth
  The blossom of your fame is blown,
And somewhere, waiting for its birth,
  The shaft is in the stone!°

Meanwhile, behalf the tardy years
  Which keep in trust your storied tombs,
Behold! your sisters bring their tears,
  And these memorial blooms.

Small tributes! but your shades will smile
  More proudly on these wreaths today,
Than when some cannon-molded pile
  Shall overlook this bay.

Stoop, angels, hither from the skies!
  There is no holier spot of ground
Than where defeated valor lies,
  By mourning beauty crowned!

8. **shaft . . . stone:** allusion to Arthurian legend. Arthur proved he was the rightful king by pulling a sword out of a stone.

Beyond the Poem

PORTFOLIO ASSESSMENT

Choices: Assessment Criteria For help in evaluating these Choices assignments, see the criteria in the ***Portfolio Management System,*** p. 183.

Donald Barthelme

(1931–1989)

© Nancy Crampton.

Donald Barthelme (bär′thəl·mē) was an experimenter in fiction and a true member of the avant-garde. Sometimes known as a postmodernist, he is widely regarded as one of the ablest and most versatile American stylists—witty, adventurous, and profound.

In broad terms, Barthelme believed that while literature of the past functioned to revitalize the imagination, storytelling had largely lost the power to inspire, persuade, or even entertain us. He felt that our language had gone bankrupt. Since words no longer effectively communicated feelings, he said, they had lost the power to move us. Contemporary language, Barthelme asserted, is thick with sludge and stuffing. Its use of clichés and its verbosity obscure truth rather than reveal it. As Snow White, the title character of Barthelme's 1967 novel, says, "Oh I wish there were some words in the world that were not the words I always hear!"

Barthelme saw the problems with language as a reflection of a society so dehumanized, so lacking in quality, that it could no longer sustain the kinds of myths that once gave us our identity. Thus, he felt, the whole point of storytelling was lost.

In his fiction, Barthelme set out to create a banal world that fails to make distinctions of quality in people, things, and ideas. Then, since he felt it was no longer possible to write about real life or the real world, he took writing itself for his subject—the art of making art out of language. His interest lay in the form and sound of language, and he tended to play with words, to make art out of fragments, much as some contemporary sculptors fashion works out of everyday objects and some pop artists transform cartoons into art.

Barthelme's plots are also unconventional. They are episodic, a clutter of styles, absurdities, and slapstick. "Fragments are the only forms I trust," says one of his narrators. His characters are types rather than fully developed individuals.

In Barthelme's hands, myth may turn into realism and realism into absurdity; readers can lose their way as they try to identify with the proceedings and wonder about the writer's point. Barthelme explained to the puzzled: "Art is not difficult because it wishes to be difficult, rather because it wishes to be art. However much the writer might long to be, in his work, simple, honest, straightforward, these virtues are no longer available to him. He discovers that in being simple, honest, straightforward, nothing much happens. . . . We are looking for the as yet unspeakable, the as yet unspoken."

Barthelme was born in Philadelphia, the son of an avant-garde architect, and was raised and educated in Texas. After serving with the U.S. Army, he worked as a reporter for the *Houston Post,* as a museum director, as the editor of an art and literature review, as a professor of English at the City University of New York, and as a teacher of creative writing at the University of Houston. He was a regular contributor to *The New Yorker* magazine. Collections of his stories include *Come Back, Dr. Caligari* (1964), *Unspeakable Practices, Unnatural Acts* (1968), in which "Game" appears, *Sixty Stories* (1981), and *Overnight to Many Distant Cities* (1983).

QUICK PLANNING GUIDE

Into the Story

Through the Story

Beyond the Story

ABOUT THE AUTHOR

Donald Barthelme began writing in high school, but did not become fully comfortable with his style until he moved to New York in 1962. He was influenced by the French Symbolists, and borrowed words and phrases from a variety of sources, including songs and advertisements. His first novel, *Snow White,* amazed its audience, and Barthelme continued to delight readers with his experimentation until his death.

PORTFOLIO ASSESSMENT

Portfolio Assessment For help with teacher assessment of reading skills, see the ***Portfolio Management System,*** pp. 54–55.

WORDS TO OWN

The following vocabulary words are defined in the Words to Own at the bottom of the pupil's page.

console p. 956	exemplary p. 959
sated p. 956	sensors p. 959
ruse p. 958	acrimoniously p. 959
precedence p. 958	nether p. 959
simultaneously p. 958	overtures p. 960

Using **BEFORE YOU READ** p. 956

Reading Focus

Discuss with students how perspective shapes reality. Give students the example of a professional athlete. To the spectator, the game is merely a pastime, entertainment, but to the athlete, the game is work. Challenge students to think of other examples of events that mean different things from different perspectives.

A Dialogue with the Text

To help organize reading responses, have students map the ideas, associations, and meanings that come up for them in relation to the word *game*. Students can use a graphic organizer such as Transparency 3: Cluster Diagram in the Transparency Package.

BEFORE YOU READ
GAME

Reading Focus

Games People Play

We are all part of the physical and social world around us. How we view that world determines in large measure how we live our lives. The following story offers a rather quirky view of our times. "Game" won't give you a clear picture of your world, but it may start you thinking.

A Dialogue with the Text

How many distinct meanings can you think of for the word *game*? What does it mean to a child? to a professional athlete? to a hunter? Jot down the meanings of the word that occur to you as you read the story.

And don't forget: Barthelme said that art is difficult, and "Game" is no exception. Read the story slowly, and don't expect everything to be immediately understandable.

If I behave strangely Shotwell is supposed to shoot me.

Game

Donald Barthelme

Shotwell keeps the jacks and the rubber ball in his attaché case and will not allow me to play with them. He plays with them, alone, sitting on the floor near the console hour after hour, chanting "onesies, twosies, threesies, foursies" in a precise, well-modulated voice, not so loud as to be annoying, not so soft as to allow me to forget. I point out to Shotwell that two can derive more enjoyment from playing jacks than one, but he is not interested. I have asked repeatedly to be allowed to play by myself, but he simply shakes his head. "Why?" I ask. "They're mine," he says. And when he has finished, when he has sated himself, back they go into the attaché case.

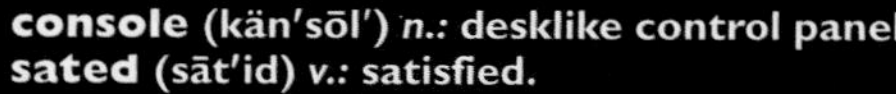

WORDS TO OWN

console (kän′sōl′) *n.:* desklike control panel.
sated (sāt′id) *v.:* satisfied.

PROGRAM MANAGER

- **Planning Instruction** See Teaching Notes, *Teaching Resources B,* p. 138, for objectives, a summary, and literary elements for this selection.
- **Instructional Support** Before beginning the instructional lesson, see Graphic Organizer for Active Reading, *Teaching Resources B,* p. 148, for a Through the Story activity.
- **Assessment** See Selection Test, *Test Booklet,* pp. 221–222.
- **Reinforcement** Use the Words to Own worksheet in *Teaching Resources B,* p. 149.

RESPONDING TO THE ART: VISUAL LITERACY

Ask students to describe their impressions of the story, based on the art. Encourage students to provide specific details that support their reactions. [Possible responses: The art is spooky and disturbing, because it makes the viewer wonder where the person is who sits in the chair; the story will probably be about a strange person who is absent in some way. Or the art is dark and confined—only a jagged piece of sky shows through; the story will probably be about a type of prison or trap.] Have students discuss their ideas before they begin to read the story.

A. Language Note: Jargon

? What does the phrase "the bird flies" mean? Where are the two men? [The phrase is military jargon for the launching of a missile. The two men are in an underground bunker connected to a missile silo.]

B. Language Note: Repetition

? What does the repetition in these lines reflect about the speaker's state of mind? [Possible answers: The obsessive repetition of key words and phrases indicate that the speaker is nervous or paranoid, or that he distrusts language and feels awkward speaking.]

C. Literary Element: Irony

? What is ironic about the agreement? [The two men have to come to an agreement to eat when they are hungry and sleep when they are tired, a state that should be natural.]

D. Reader's Response: First Thoughts

? What picture of the two men do you get from their pastimes? [Sample responses: The two men are regressing to a childlike state, playing silly games and writing on the walls. The men are so bored that they will do anything to amuse themselves.]

It is unfair but there is nothing I can do about it. I am aching to get my hands on them.

Shotwell and I watch the console. Shotwell and I live under the ground and watch the console. If certain events take place upon the console, we are to insert our keys in the appropriate locks and turn our keys. Shotwell has a key and I have a key. **A** If we turn our keys simultaneously the bird flies, certain switches are activated and the bird flies. But the bird never flies. In one hundred thirty-three days the bird has not flown. Meanwhile Shotwell and I watch each other. We each wear a .45 and if Shotwell behaves strangely I am supposed to shoot him. If I behave strangely Shotwell is supposed to shoot me. We watch the console and think about shooting each other and think about the bird. Shotwell's behavior with the jacks is strange. Is it strange? I do not know. Perhaps he is merely selfish . . . perhaps his character is flawed, perhaps his childhood was twisted. I do not know.

Each of us wears a .45 and each of us is supposed to shoot the other if the other is behaving strangely. How strangely is strangely? I do not know. In addition to the .45 I have a .38 which Shotwell does not know about concealed in my attaché case, and Shotwell has a .25 caliber Beretta which I do not know about strapped to his right calf. Sometimes instead of watching the console I pointedly watch Shotwell's .45, but this is simply a ruse, simply a maneuver, in reality I am watching his hand when it dangles in the vicinity of his right calf. If he decides I am behaving strangely he will shoot me not with the .45 but **B** with the Beretta. Similarly, Shotwell pretends to watch my .45 but he is really watching my hand resting idly atop my attaché case, my hand resting idly atop my attaché case, my hand. My hand resting idly atop my attaché case.

In the beginning I took care to behave normally. So did Shotwell. Our behavior was painfully normal. Norms of politeness, consideration, speech, and personal habits were scrupulously observed. But then it became apparent that an error had been made, that our relief was not going to arrive. Owing to an oversight. Owing to an oversight we have been here for one hundred thirty-three days. When it became clear that an error had been made, that we were not to be relieved, the norms were relaxed. Definitions of normality were redrawn in the agreement of January 1, called by us, The Agreement. Uniform regulations were relaxed, and mealtimes are no longer **C** rigorously scheduled. We eat when we are hungry and sleep when we are tired. Considerations of rank and precedence were temporarily put aside, a handsome concession on the part of Shotwell, who is a captain, whereas I am only a first lieutenant. One of us watches the console at all times rather than two of us watching the console at all times, except when we are both on our feet. One of us watches the console at all times and if the bird flies then that one wakes the other and we turn our keys in the locks simultaneously and the bird flies. Our system involves a delay of perhaps twelve seconds but I do not care because I am not well, and Shotwell does not care because he is not himself. After the agreement was signed Shotwell produced the jacks and the rubber ball from his attaché case, and I began to write a series of descriptions of forms occurring in nature, such as a shell, a leaf, a stone, an animal. On the walls.

D Shotwell plays jacks and I write descriptions of natural forms on the walls.

Shotwell is enrolled in a USAFI[1] course which leads to a master's degree in business administration from the University of Wisconsin (although we are not in Wisconsin, we are in Utah, Montana or Idaho). When we went down it was in either Utah, Montana or Idaho, I don't remember. We have been here for one hundred thirty-three days owing to an oversight. The pale green reinforced concrete walls sweat and the air conditioning zips on and off erratically and Shotwell reads *Introduction to Marketing* by Lassiter and Munk, making notes with a blue ballpoint pen. Shotwell is not himself but I do not know it, he presents a calm

1. **USAFI:** United States Armed Forces Information, an organization that supervises courses taken by service members.

Words to Own

ruse (ro͞oz) *n.:* trick; deception.
precedence (pres′ə·dəns) *n.:* order.
simultaneously (sī′məl·tā′nē·əs·lē) *adv.:* at the same time.

Options for Teaching

Strategies for Inclusion

Linguistic Have students read the story aloud with a partner. Encourage partners to comment on the ways the speaker's paranoia and obsessiveness come through in the patterns of his speech. Students can take notes on specific examples and share them with the class after they have read the story.

Spatial/Kinesthetic Encourage students to imagine the situation of the speaker in the story. Ask them how they would feel being trapped underground in a bunker about the size of the classroom. How would the confinement affect them? Students can use their responses to help them understand the games that go on in the story.

Less Proficient Readers Students may have trouble identifying the conflict in the story and differentiating between the **character** of the narrator and that of Shotwell. Have students keep notes in a two-columned chart as they read. In one column, students can list the details of the narrator's position, and in the other column, students can describe Shotwell. Students can then compare the two columns to determine the pair's similarities and differences.

aspect and reads *Introduction to Marketing* and makes his exemplary notes with a blue ballpoint pen, meanwhile controlling the .38 in my attaché case with one-third of his attention. I am not well.

We have been here one hundred thirty-three days owing to an oversight. Although now we are not sure what is oversight, what is plan. Perhaps the plan is for us to stay here permanently, or if not permanently at least for a year, for three hundred sixty-five days. Or if not for a year for some number of days known to them and not known to us, such as two hundred days. Or perhaps they are observing our behavior in some way, sensors of some kind, perhaps our behavior determines the number of days. It may be that they are pleased with us, with our behavior, not in every detail but in sum. Perhaps the whole thing is very successful, perhaps the whole thing is an experiment and the experiment is very successful. I do not know. But I suspect that the only way they can persuade sun-loving creatures into their pale green sweating reinforced concrete rooms under the ground is to say that the system is twelve hours on, twelve hours off. And then lock us below for some number of days known to them and not known to us. We eat well although the frozen enchiladas are damp when defrosted and the frozen devil's food cake is sour and untasty. We sleep uneasily and acrimoniously. I hear Shotwell shouting in his sleep, objecting, denouncing, cursing sometimes, weeping sometimes, in his sleep. When Shotwell sleeps I try to pick the lock on his attaché case, so as to get at the jacks. Thus far I have been unsuccessful. Nor has Shotwell been successful in picking the locks on my attaché case so as to get at the .38. I have seen the marks on the shiny surface. I laughed, in the latrine, pale green walls sweating and the air conditioning whispering, in the latrine.

I write descriptions of natural forms on the walls, scratching them on the tile surface with a diamond. The diamond is a two and one-half carat solitaire I had in my attaché case when we went down. It was for Lucy. The south wall of the room containing the console is already covered. I have described a shell, a leaf, a stone, animals, a baseball bat. I am aware that the baseball bat is not a natural form. Yet I described it. "The baseball bat," I said, "is typically made of wood. It is typically one meter in length or a little longer, fat at one end, tapering to afford a comfortable grip at the other. The end with the handhold typically offers a slight rim, or lip, at the nether extremity, to prevent slippage." My description of the baseball bat ran to 4500 words, all scratched with a diamond on the south wall. Does Shotwell read what I have written? I do not know. I am aware that Shotwell regards my writing-behavior as a little strange. Yet it is no stranger than his jacks-behavior, or the day he appeared in black bathing trunks with the .25 caliber Beretta strapped to his right calf and stood over the console, trying to span with his two arms outstretched the distance between the locks. He could not do it, I had already tried, standing over

WORDS TO OWN

exemplary (eg·zem′plə·rē) *adj.:* serving as a model.
sensors (sen′sərz) *n. pl.:* detecting devices.
acrimoniously (ak′ri·mō′nē·əs·lē) *adv.:* bitterly; harshly.
nether (ne*th*′ər) *adj.:* lower.

E. Critical Reading: Drawing Conclusions

? What does this passage tell you about the men's assessment of their situation? [The men do not know much about their situation. They suspect that they are being watched, and that their actions affect their situation in ways they do not understand.]

F. Critical Reading: Finding Details

? What is the effect of the detail about the men's food? [The detail is humorous because it is out of place. It reflects the men's obsession with the details, however insignificant, of their situation.]

G. Reader's Response: Shaping Interpretations

? Why does Shotwell try to reach both locks at once? [Sample responses: He does not trust the narrator, and wants to know if he can launch the missile on his own. He wants to get rid of the narrator, and is checking to see if he can launch the missile alone so that he can kill the other man.]

INTEGRATING THE LANGUAGE ARTS

Strategic Reading Have students make inferences about subtle details and mysterious suggestions in the story. Students should make a number of inferences as they read and record their inferences in a chart such as the one below. In the fourth column, students can use metacognitive skills to evaluate the thought processes that went into their inferences.

Inference	Textual support	Outcome	Evaluation of inference

CROSSING THE CURRICULUM

Social Sciences Ask students to research the topic of U.S. nuclear weapons. How many are there? How can they be launched? Form students in groups of four with each member responsible for a distinct question to research. Have the groups share their findings with the class.

A. Critical Reading: Predicting

? What do you think will happen to the two men? Explain. [Possible responses: They will launch the missile because they are bored and paranoid. They will argue about the launching and end up killing each other.]

B. Literary Element: Imagery

? What does this image of the two men tell you? [Possible responses: The men are scared and helpless, like babies. Even though they do not trust each other, the men comfort each other because they are lonely.]

C. Reader's Response: Challenging the Text

? Do the last two sentences give the reader an idea of what will happen? Is this a suitable ending? Explain. [Sample responses: The ending is a good one because it hints that the men will begin a nuclear holocaust out of mere boredom and confusion. The ending is not suitable because it just takes the reader back to the story's beginning; nothing has happened and nothing will.]

the console with my two arms outstretched, the distance is too great. I was moved to comment but did not comment, comment would have provoked counter-comment, comment would have led God knows where. They had in their infinite patience, in their infinite foresight, in their infinite wisdom already imagined a man standing over the console with his two arms outstretched, trying to span with his two arms outstretched the distance between the locks.

Shotwell is not himself. He has made certain overtures. The burden of his message is not clear. It has something to do with the keys, with the locks. Shotwell is a strange person. He appears to be less affected by our situation than I. He goes about his business stolidly, watching the console, studying *Introduction to Marketing,* bouncing his rubber ball on the floor in a steady, rhythmical, conscientious manner. He appears to be less affected by our situation than I am. He is stolid. He says nothing. But he has made certain overtures, certain overtures have been made. I am not sure that I understand them. They have something to do with the keys, with the locks. Shotwell has something in mind. Stolidly he shucks the shiny silver paper from the frozen enchiladas, stolidly he stuffs them into the electric oven. But he has something in mind. But there [A] must be a quid pro quo.[2] I insist on a quid pro quo. I have something in mind.

I am not well. I do not know our target. They do not tell us for which city the bird is targeted. I do not know. That is planning. That is not my responsibility. My responsibility is to watch the console and when certain events take place upon the console, turn my key in the lock. Shotwell bounces the rubber ball on the floor in a steady, stolid, rhythmical manner. I am aching to get my hands on the ball, on the jacks. We have been here one hundred thirty-three days owing to an oversight. I write on the walls. Shotwell chants "onesies, twosies, threesies, foursies" in a precise, well-modulated voice. Now he cups the jacks and the rubber ball in his hands and rattles them suggestively. I do not know for which city the bird is targeted. Shotwell is not himself.

Sometimes I cannot sleep. Sometimes Shotwell cannot sleep. Sometimes when Shotwell cradles me in his arms and rocks me to sleep, singing [B] Brahms' "Guten Abend, gute Nacht,"[3] or I cradle Shotwell in my arms and rock him to sleep, singing, I understand what it is Shotwell wishes me to do. At such moments we are very close. But only if he will give me the jacks. That is fair. There is something he wants me to do with my key, while he does something with his key. But only if [C] he will give me my turn. That is fair. I am not well.

2. **quid pro quo:** Latin for "something for something." The phrase is used here to mean an even exchange.

3. **Guten Abend, gute Nacht** (go͞ot′'n ä′bənt go͞ot′ə näkht): German for "good evening, good night." This line is from the musical composition popularly known as "Brahms' Lullaby" by Johannes Brahms (1833–1897).

WORDS TO OWN

overtures (ō′vər·chərz) *n. pl.:* approaches; offers.

CROSSING THE CURRICULUM

Health Have groups of students research the effects on human beings of being confined underground or being shut off from the sun for a long period of time. Each group can present the results of its study to the class and speculate on how the results may have practical applications.

PROBLEM SOLVING/ CRITICAL THINKING

Diffusing Conflict The agreement drawn up by the two men in the story has not successfully brought peace between them. Ask students to name the missing elements of a possible truce. Then, challenge students to compare the men in the story to warring factions currently in the news. Students can apply their peace-keeping strategies both to the story and to the current events.

ASSESSMENT TOOLS

Check Test: True-False

1. Each of the men has a hidden weapon. [True]
2. Each of the men has tried to reach both locks at once. [True]
3. The narrator writes poetry on the walls. [False]
4. The men agree to launch the missile. [False]

Critical Comment

Absurd World

Almost every element of Barthelme's story contributes to its satirical, absurdist tone. As in the plays of the Theater of the Absurd, such as those composed by Samuel Beckett and Eugene Ionesco, statements either do not follow each other logically, or they are connected by pseudologic. The narrator's constant repetition suggests the mind of someone on the brink of a precipice, desperately trying to hold on to words as symbols of reality and sanity.

The two characters, Shotwell and the unnamed narrator, are confined underground for an indefinite period. We never learn the exact details of the mission they may be called to carry out, but it seems to involve nuclear warfare and so could result in world destruction.

The first-person narration underscores the horror, as we know only what the speaker can tell us about his situation. Both he and Shotwell have been reduced to infantilism as they wait for the terrible contingency on the console: Childlike pastimes alternate with petty jealousies and disturbing nightmares. The two men's gradual dehumanization is relieved only when they rock each other to sleep. The men's eccentric behavior is portrayed as a desperate attempt to blot out the horror of their circumstances, but the story makes it clear that they are on the edge of madness: Note that Shotwell seems determined to destroy them by activating the two locks that apparently will launch a destructive event.

As you read Barthelme's vignette of life in the nuclear age, it may be easy to dismiss the particulars of his vision as exaggerated or surrealistic. But consider that a serious theme may underlie this apparently absurdist story. Our modern methods of warfare, Barthelme seems to be suggesting, are horrible not only because of their potential for physical destruction, but also because of the way their very existence corrodes and perverts humanity.

MAKING MEANINGS

First Thoughts

1. What was your emotional reaction to "Game"?

Reviewing the Text

a. Despite his experimentation, Barthelme still uses essential elements of fiction. Who is the **narrator** of this story? What is the **setting**?

b. What is the narrator's problem, or **conflict**? Is there a **resolution** to it? If so, describe it.

Shaping Interpretations

2. Which details in the first three paragraphs suggest the state of Shotwell's and the narrator's minds?
3. How would you explain the strange behavior of the men? What do you think happened before the story begins?
4. How would you explain what the "bird" is?
5. What might be the "oversight" that has led to the men's confinement?
6. The narrator is apprehensive that Shotwell "has something in mind." What might that something be? How can you tell?
7. Barthelme uses a great deal of repetition in this story. What phrases are most often repeated? How does the repetition contribute to the **characterization**?
8. What would you say is Barthelme's **theme** in this story? Review the notes you made in your Reader's Log. How does the **title** suggest the theme?

Challenging the Text

9. Is the world as absurd as Barthelme describes it? Describe your response to the world Barthelme has created.

Making Meanings

First Thoughts

1. Possible responses: The story frustrated me because it was so strange and nothing happened. The story made me laugh with its absurdist view of the universe.

Reviewing the Text

a. The narrator of the story is a first lieutenant in the U.S. armed forces and a commander in a missile silo. The setting of the story is the underground silo.

b. The narrator's problems are many: He does not know how much longer he will be in the bunker; he does not trust his partner, Shotwell; he does not feel well; and he wants to play with Shotwell's jacks. The story does not resolve these problems.

Shaping Interpretations

2. The narrator's fascination with Shotwell's game of jacks and Shotwell's selfishness reveal the childishness of the two men's minds.
3. The men are suffering from their isolation and their lack of knowledge about their situation. The sanity of the two probably broke down slowly before the story began.
4. The "bird" is the missile the two men command.
5. The "oversight" is never clarified, but it is implied that the men have been forgotten.
6. Shotwell wants to launch the missile. His plan is suggested by his desire to turn both keys in the console.
7. The narrator repeats key phrases such as "owing to an oversight" and "I am not well." The phrases underscore the narrator's mental distress.
8. Barthelme's central theme is that life is a game, even in matters of life and death such as nuclear warfare.

Challenging the Text

9. **(Synthesis and Evaluation)** Students' responses will vary, but they probably will say that their world is not as absurd as the one Barthleme describes, and that the author's absurdities are exaggerations for artistic effect. They may react to Barthelme's vision of the world with a mixture of horror, surprise, amazement, amusement, and disgust.

Elements of Literature

Mini-Lesson: Satire

Review with students the definitions of the terms *satire, irony, hyperbole,* and *fantasy.* Encourage students to think of examples of each from other works of literature or from other sources, such as films or newspaper editorials. Write students' suggestions on the chalkboard and discuss with students how their suggestions meet the definitions of the terms.

Elements of Literature

Satire

Satire—ridiculing human foolishness or wrongdoing—ultimately holds a moral. The sting of satire is meant to cure the human race of its pretensions and blindness. While a realistic, ironic writer wants us to come to terms with the world as it is, the satirist wants to reform that world. The satirist's premise is that when an unacceptable situation is exposed to ridicule and laughter, it cannot last very long.

Satire requires two ingredients to be successful: (1) either wit, humor based on fantasy, or humor based on a sense of the absurd and (2) a target.

The humor of the satirist almost always involves some use of **irony**—that is, it involves a discrepancy between what is said and what is actually meant, or between what we expect to happen and what actually happens. Satirists also use **hyperbole,** or exaggeration, for effect, and **incongruity,** a kind of irony that brings together two ideas (or events or people) that do not belong together (*incongruous* means "not fitting together"). Donald Barthelme uses all three devices in "Game."

One of the greatest satirists of all time was the Irish-born writer Jonathan Swift. In *Gulliver's Travels* (1726), Swift took as his target the narrow-minded, hypocritical, and cruel English society of his time. Swift mocked his fellow citizens' pretensions to superiority by describing, among other wonders, a race of noble horses who are unquestionably superior to the English in intellect and in morals. In 1729, Swift published a satiric essay called *A Modest Proposal,* in which his fictional narrator suggests that the English could solve their vexing "Irish problem" (and also their food shortages) by serving poor Irish children up as food for the rich landlords, "who, as they have already devoured most of the parents, seem to have the best title to the children."

One of the greatest weapons of a certain type of satire is **fantasy,** the creation of a world where common sense has collapsed. Two of the most famous fantasies in the English language are Lewis Carroll's *Alice's Adventures in Wonderland* (1865) and *Through the Looking-Glass* (1871). In these books, the whole world is turned on its head. Even language itself no longer means what we think it means. "When *I* use a word," proclaims Humpty Dumpty, "it means just what I choose it to mean—neither more nor less." This world of satiric fantasy is also found in *Gulliver's Travels.* There, for example, the horses not only speak, but also govern themselves in a way far superior to human governments.

At times, a satirist's fantasy will turn to the absurd or grotesque, and we can get what is known as *gallows humor,* an Americanism that means "morbid or cynical humor" (literally, humor when facing the executioner). Swift's *A Modest Proposal* becomes grotesque when the narrator dares to suggest cannibalism as a solution to an economic problem.

Satire has a long history in American literature. The shrewd counsels of prudence we hear from Benjamin Franklin's Poor Richard (page 95) are a kind of satire, in which the writer suggests practical ways to succeed in a world that is less than ideal. Mark Twain (page 450) was more of a satirist than he generally receives credit for; his Mr. Bixby in *Life on the Mississippi* is part of a long line of boasters and rogues in literature who use wit and verbal exuberance to survive in an imperfect world. James Thurber created in Walter Mitty (page 625) an American version of the man bullied by a woman, an archetypal character popular in satire at least from the days of ancient Rome. And, of course, the daily newspapers are filled with biting editorial cartoons built on satire.

What absurd ideas do you find in Barthelme's satire? Do the narrator and Shotwell respond to their limited world with bravado and bluster, like a Twain character, or are they more like Walter Mitty?

The Mad Hatter at the tea party, after Sir John Tenniel's design for the first edition of Lewis Carroll's *Alice's Adventures in Wonderland* (1865).

The Granger Collection, New York.

Integrating the Language Arts

Strategic Reading As students read the feature, have them record elements and examples of **satire** in a cluster diagram. Encourage students to start by defining the term *satire* in a central circle drawn on a page. In connecting circles, students can write examples of the elements and also words and phrases that they associate with each element. Have volunteers share their diagrams with the class.

Strategies for Inclusion

Visual Have students make a chart for examining the elements of satire in the story. Students can check off each element and list its examples on their charts as they review the story. Have students compare their charts with a partner's.

CHOICES: Building Your Portfolio

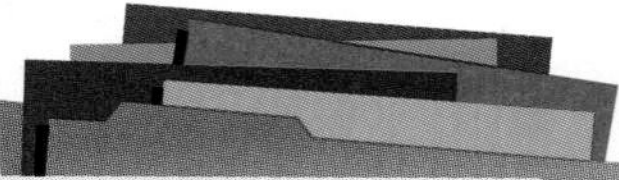

Writer's Notebook

1. Collecting Ideas for an Evaluation

Suppose you want to evaluate the theme of "Game." Take notes now that you might use later in an essay of evaluation. First, try to state the theme as accurately as you can. Then, describe your responses to the theme. Here are some questions you can cover: Is the theme clearly presented, or is it ambiguous? Do I agree with the theme? Is the theme popular in contemporary literature and film? How does its presentation in "Game" compare with its presentation in other texts? What does the theme reveal about the writer's view of the world? Jot down evidence to support your responses. Save your work for possible use in the Writer's Workshop on page 1181.

Critical Writing

2. The World According to Barthelme, Auden, and You

In the following famous poem, W. H. Auden (1907–1973) describes a citizen of the modern world. In a brief essay, tell whether you think Barthelme's characters and Auden's citizen live in the same world. Has society taken away their freedom and ignored their humanity? Do you agree with these views of the world?

The Unknown Citizen

To JS/07/M/378
This Marble Monument Is Erected by the State

He was found by the Bureau of Statistics to be
One against whom there was no official complaint,
And all the reports on his conduct agree
That, in the modern sense of an old-fashioned word,
he was a saint,
For in everything he did he served the Greater Community.
Except for the War till the day he retired
He worked in a factory and never got fired,
But satisfied his employers, Fudge Motors Inc.
Yet he wasn't a scab or odd in his views,
For his Union reports that he paid his dues,
(Our report on his Union shows it was sound)
And our Social Psychology workers found
That he was popular with his mates and liked a drink.
The Press are convinced that he bought a paper every day
And that his reactions to advertisements were normal in
every way.
Policies taken out in his name prove that he was fully insured,
And his Health-card shows he was once in hospital but
left it cured.
Both Producers Research and High-Grade Living declare
He was fully sensible to the advantages of the Installment Plan
And had everything necessary to the Modern Man,
A gramophone, a radio, a car, and a frigidaire.
Our researchers into Public Opinion are content
That he held the proper opinions for the time of year;
When there was peace, he was for peace; when there
was war, he went.
He was married and added five children to the population,
Which our Eugenist says was the right number for a parent of
his generation,
And our teachers report that he never interfered with
their education.
Was he free? Was he happy? The question is absurd:
Had anything been wrong, we should certainly have heard.

Beyond the Story

Choices: Building Your Portfolio

1. **Writer's Notebook** Remind students to save their work as possible prewriting for the Writer's Workshop on p. 1181.
2. **Critical Writing** Tell students to freewrite an emotional response to the poem as soon as they have read it. Direct students to use their initial responses to compare the effects on the reader of the two works.

STRATEGIES FOR INCLUSION

Learners Having Difficulty Students may have trouble expressing the **theme** of the story. For activity #1, ask students to imagine themselves describing the point of the story to a friend. How would they explain the story's basic idea? Students can write down their descriptions and compare their assessments of the story's theme.

Visual For activity #2, ask students to use a graphic organizer to compare the two works. Students can use a Venn diagram such as the one on Transparency 5 in the Transparency Package. Have students compare their graphic organizers in small groups before they begin writing.

PORTFOLIO ASSESSMENT

Choices: Assessment Criteria For help in evaluating these Choices assignments, see the criteria in the ***Portfolio Management System,*** p. 184.

QUICK PLANNING GUIDE

Into the Story

Author Biography p. 964
Before You Read p. 965
- **Reading Focus:** Students define courage.
- **A Dialogue with the Text: Set a Purpose** In Reader's Log, track changes in the story
- **Elements of Literature: Conflict**
- **Background: Scaffolding** Discuss the story's character

Through the Story

"Speaking of Courage" pp. 966–972
Words to Own pp. 967–972
Making Meanings p. 973

Beyond the Story

Choices: Building Your Portfolio p. 973
- **Writer's Notebook:** Evaluate a character
- **Critical Writing:** Compare two stories' use of contrast
- **Critical Writing:** In an essay, compare and contrast two characters' similar experiences
- **Creative Writing/Performance:** Write and perform a dialogue

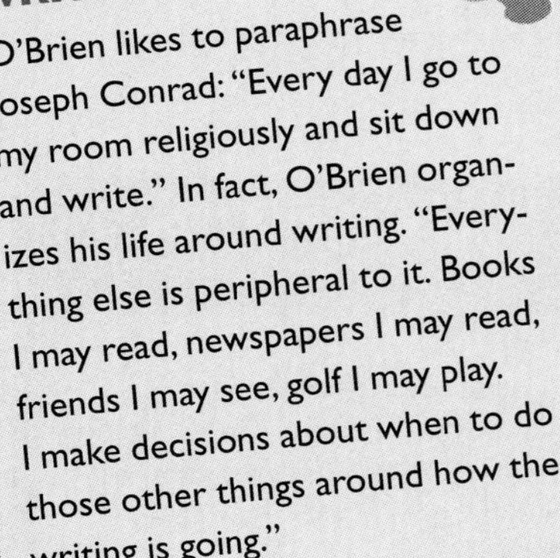

WRITERS ON WRITING

O'Brien likes to paraphrase Joseph Conrad: "Every day I go to my room religiously and sit down and write." In fact, O'Brien organizes his life around writing. "Everything else is peripheral to it. Books I may read, newspapers I may read, friends I may see, golf I may play. I make decisions about when to do those other things around how the writing is going."

Tim O'Brien

(1946–)

© Jerry Bauer.

"All my work has been somewhat political in that it's been directed at big issues," Tim O'Brien once said. "My concerns have to do with the abstractions: What's courage and how do you get it? What's justice and how do you achieve it? How does one do right in an evil situation?" O'Brien turned those questions into powerful artistic tools in his gripping war novel *Going After Cacciato* (1978).

O'Brien was born in Austin, Minnesota, and graduated from Macalester College. In 1968, he was drafted and served with the U.S. Army in Vietnam, where he attained the rank of sergeant. Returning from the war, he went to Harvard for graduate work in English. A summer internship on the *Washington Post* led to a job as national affairs reporter for that newspaper.

O'Brien had been writing stories since childhood, and even in the midst of his academic work, he knew he wanted to write full time. It was his military experience in Vietnam that provided much of the material for his fiction and personal narratives. *If I Die in a Combat Zone, Box Me Up and Ship Me Home* (1973) is a collection of anecdotes and observations of his duty in Vietnam. The book drew widespread praise, particularly from veterans, as an authentic re-creation of the foot soldier's experience in an unpopular war.

O'Brien's first novel, *Northern Lights,* appeared in 1974 and dealt with a veteran returned to civilian life. *Going After Cacciato,* his second novel, followed four years later. This novel returned to the jungle war and depicted a soldier's fantasy of quitting the battle and walking off across the mountains to find Paris. *Cacciato* was acclaimed as one of the few novels to have captured the essence of the Vietnam experience, and it won a prestigious National Book Award in 1979.

O'Brien has said of his novel, "It's not really Vietnam that I was concerned about when I wrote *Cacciato;* rather it was to have readers care about what's right and wrong and about the difficulty of doing right, the difficulty of saying no to a war."

In 1990, O'Brien published *The Things They Carried,* another remarkable book dealing with the Vietnam War and its human effects. At publication, he told an interviewer:

> My life is storytelling. I believe in stories, in their incredible power to keep people alive, to keep the living alive, and the dead. And if I have started now to play with the stories, inside the stories themselves, well, that's what people do all the time.
>
> Storytelling is the essential human activity. The harder the situation, the more essential it is. In Vietnam men were constantly telling one another stories about the war. Our unit lost a lot of guys around My Lai, but the stories they told stay around after them. I would be mad not to tell the stories I know.

O'Brien keeps the Vietnam experience at the core of his psychological thriller *In the Lake of the Woods* (1994). This is a novel about a politician who attempts to conceal his past involvement in the massacre of Vietnamese civilians by American soldiers at My Lai in 1968.

PORTFOLIO ASSESSMENT

Portfolio Assessment For help with self-assessment of reading skills, see the ***Portfolio Management System,*** pp. 48–49.

WORDS TO OWN

The following vocabulary words are defined in the Words to Own at the bottom of the pupil's page.

affluent p. 967	valor p. 968
tepid p. 967	municipal p. 969
mesmerizing p. 967	mortars p. 970
drone p. 968	profundity p. 971
recede p. 968	tactile p. 972

Three Flags (1958) by Jasper Johns. Encaustic on canvas (30⅞″ × 45½″ × 5″).

BEFORE YOU READ
SPEAKING OF COURAGE

Reading Focus

Courage and Common Sense

What is courage? At what point does it become foolhardiness? In retrospect, Paul Berlin wishes he had been *really* courageous in war, especially during a particular incident. Maybe he was following good common sense, however, in acting as he did.

A Dialogue with the Text

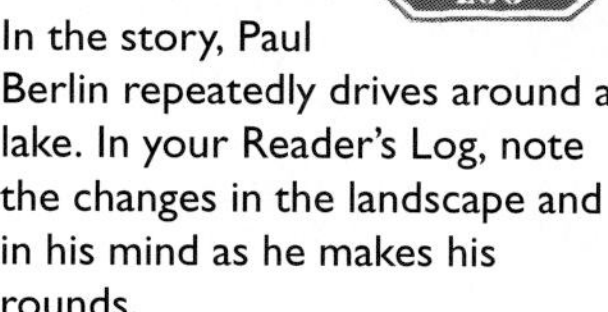

In the story, Paul Berlin repeatedly drives around a lake. In your Reader's Log, note the changes in the landscape and in his mind as he makes his rounds.

Elements of Literature

Conflict

A **conflict** is a struggle between opposing forces or characters. An **external conflict** can involve two people, a person and nature, a person and a machine, and many other situations. An **internal conflict** involves opposing forces within a person's mind. "Speaking of Courage" is largely about an internal conflict in Paul Berlin's mind.

A **conflict** is a struggle between opposing forces or characters.

For more on Conflict, see page 607 and the Handbook of Literary Terms.

Background

Before he published the full novel *Going After Cacciato,* O'Brien published portions of it as short stories in magazines. This story, which appeared in a different form in the novel, was named one of the O. Henry Prize Stories of 1978.

The novel about Cacciato is told through the eyes and sensibilities of a young soldier from Iowa named Paul Berlin. In this story, Paul has recently returned from battle duty in Vietnam. Like many veterans of that war, he is confused over the meaning of his experience. He is also vaguely dissatisfied with his performance in the war.

Into the Story

Using BEFORE YOU READ p. 965

Reading Focus

Discuss the following quotations with the class. Ask students to think about the different definitions of courage in each passage.

"He wished that he, too, had a wound, a red badge of courage."
Stephen Crane, *The Red Badge of Courage* (1895), Chapter 9

"Life shrinks or expands in proportion to one's courage."
The Diary of Anaïs Nin, vol. II (1967), June 1941

"He who has courage and faith will never perish in misery!"
Anne Frank: The Diary of a Young Girl (1952), March 7, 1944

A Dialogue with the Text

In the first paragraph and throughout the story, the narrator speaks of many aspects of the lake that have remained the same. To help students think more clearly about the changes in the landscape, ask them also to record as they read details that remain the same for Paul on this Fourth of July afternoon.

Elements of Literature

Challenge students to think of other literary works that contain **internal conflict**. Give students the examples of the solitary speaker in Emily Dickinson poems such as "Heart! We will forget him!" or the title character in Thurber's "The Secret Life of Walter Mitty." Students may also want to expand the discussion to include characters from films or TV shows.

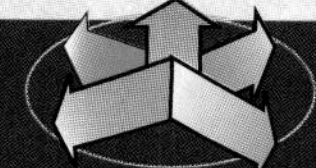

PROGRAM MANAGER

- **Planning Instruction** See Teaching Notes, *Teaching Resources B,* pp. 138–139, for objectives, a summary, literary elements, and additional historical information for this selection.
- **Instructional Support** Before beginning the instructional lesson, see Graphic Organizer for Active Reading, *Teaching Resources B,* p. 150, for an Into the Story activity.
- **Assessment** See Selection Test, *Test Booklet,* pp. 223–224.
- **Language Link** For instruction and practice in punctuating dialogue, see Language Link, *Teaching Resources B,* pp. 151–152, and *Language and Writing Skills Worksheets,* pp. 144–145.
- **Reinforcement** Use the Words to Own worksheet in *Teaching Resources B,* p. 153.

Speaking of Courage

Tim O'Brien

OPTIONS FOR TEACHING

STRATEGIES FOR INCLUSION

Visual Have students draw a picture of the lake around which Paul keeps driving. Ask students to include in their drawings all the places, events, and people Paul sees along the way. Have students compare their maps with a partner's.

Less Proficient Readers To help students develop an effective description of the **main character** in the story, pair less proficient with more advanced readers. Ask pairs to first mark with a self-stick note anything in the text that gives information about Paul Berlin. Then, the pairs can summarize what they have marked in a single word or phrase. After they are finished reviewing the story, the partners can work together to combine their words into a unified character description.

Spatial Have students define the relationship between Paul and his father by using a graphic organizer such as the one on Transparency 5: Venn Diagram in the Transparency Package. As students read the story, they can list words or ideas that relate to both characters or words that express how one character feels about the other. Ask students to compare their diagrams in small groups and discuss how significant the distance between the two characters is in the story.

The war was over, and there was no place in particular to go. Paul Berlin followed the tar road in its seven-mile loop around the lake, then he started all over again, driving slowly, feeling safe inside his father's big Chevy, now and again looking out onto the lake to watch the boats and waterskiers and scenery. It was Sunday and it was summer, and things seemed pretty much the same. The lake was the same. The houses were the same, all low-slung and split level and modern, porches and picture windows facing the water. The lots were spacious. On the lake-side of the road, the houses were handsome and set deep in, well-kept and painted, with docks jutting out into the lake, and boats moored and covered with canvas, and gardens, and sometimes even gardeners, and stone patios with barbecue spits and grills, and wooden shingles saying who lived where. On the other side of the road, to his left, the houses were also handsome, though less expensive and on a smaller scale and with no docks or boats or wooden shingles. The road was a sort of boundary between the affluent and the almost affluent, and to live on the lake-side of the road was one of the few natural privileges in a town of the prairie—the difference between watching the sun set over cornfields or over the lake.

It was a good-sized lake. In high school he'd driven round and round and round with his friends and pretty girls, talking about urgent matters, worrying eagerly about the existence of God and theories of causation,[1] or wondering whether Sally Hankins, who lived on the lake-side of the road, would want to pull into the shelter of Sunset Park. Then, there had not been a war. But there had always been the lake. It had been dug out by the southernmost advance of the Wisconsin glacier. Fed by neither springs nor streams, it was a tepid, algaed lake that depended on fickle prairie rains for replenishment. Still, it was the town's only lake, the only one in twenty-six miles, and at night the moon made a white swath across its waters, and on sunny days it was nice to look at, and that evening it would dazzle with the reflections of fireworks, and it was the center of things from the very start, always there to be driven around, still mesmerizing and quieting and a good audience for silence, a seven-mile flat circumference that could

1. **theories of causation:** philosophical theories holding that events are connected through cause-and-effect relationships.

WORDS TO OWN

affluent (af'lo͞o·ənt) *adj.* used as *n.:* well-to-do people.
tepid (tep'id) *adj.:* lukewarm.
mesmerizing (mez'mər·īz'iŋ) *v.* used as *adj.:* hypnotic.

A. Reader's Response: Shaping Interpretations

? What do you know about the narrator from the first sentence? [Sample responses: The narrator has just been in a war and has mixed feelings or regrets about his experience. The narrator is a soldier returned home to discover that nothing is like it was when he left.]

B. Literary Element: Internal Conflict

? What is the conflict in the narrator's repeated observation that everything is the same? [The repetition reflects the narrator's boredom, idleness, and disillusionment; it suggests ironically that perhaps the problem is that everything is *not* the same—the narrator has changed.]

C. Literary Element: Figures of Speech

? Which figures of speech are involved in the narrator's description of the lake being "a good audience for silence"? [The phrase is a metaphor (a comparison of unlike objects: the lake and an audience), an example of personification (the nonhuman lake talked about as if it were human), and an example of paradox (an audience for silence).]

STRATEGIES FOR INCLUSION

English Language Development Help students investigate the significance of repeated ideas in the story. Ask students to each choose a repeated word or phrase and use a cluster diagram to record ideas and images associated with it. For example, students can write the first sentence from the story in a central circle on a sheet of paper and then include in surrounding circles repetitions or elaborations of the idea of "no place in particular to go." Challenge students to include examples of the character's actions in their diagrams. Students can compare diagrams with a partner.

INTEGRATING THE LANGUAGE ARTS

Writing: Personal Letter Have students write a letter from Paul to his father that expresses everything he thinks of saying in the story. Students should review the story and take notes of Paul's imaginary conversations with his father. Then, students can brainstorm for a list of emotions Paul might feel toward his father. Students should use both sets of notes to write their letters. Ask volunteers to share their work with the class.

A. Reader's Response: Shaping Interpretations

? What is the truth that the narrator's father also knows from being in a war but will not talk about? [Sample responses: Paul's father knows that war is a shameful, humiliating horror that cannot be expressed in words. The truth is a general one about the absurdity of human life, that comes out especially in the senseless destruction of war.]

B. Critical Reading: Analyzing Details

? How does the image of the man trying to fix his boat change the **tone** of the description of the scene on the lake? [The detail adds a note of frustration to the quiet scene.]

C. Literary Element: Diction

? What does the word *might* reveal about the conversation? [That the conversation is imagined or hypothetical.]

be traveled by slow car in twenty-five minutes. It was not such a good lake for swimming. After college, he'd caught an ear infection that had almost kept him out of the war. And the lake had drowned Max Arnold, keeping him out of the war entirely. Max had been one who liked to talk about the existence of God. "No, I'm not saying *that,*" he would say carefully against the drone of the engine. "I'm saying it is possible as an idea, even necessary as an idea, a final cause in the whole structure of causation." Now he knew, perhaps. Before the war, they'd driven around the lake as friends, but now Max was dead and most of the others were living in Des Moines or Sioux City, or going to school somewhere, or holding down jobs. None of the girls was left. Sally Hankins was married. His father would not talk. His father had been in another war, so he knew the truth already, and he would not talk about it, and there was no one left to talk with.

He turned on the radio. The car's big engine fired machinery that blew cold air all over him. Clockwise, like an electron spinning forever around its nucleus, the big Chevy circled the lake, and he had little to do but sit in the air-conditioning, both hands on the wheel, letting the car carry him in orbit. It was a lazy Sunday. The town was small. Out on the lake, a man's motorboat had stalled, and the fellow was bent over the silver motor with a wrench and a frown, and beyond him there were waterskiers and smooth July waters and two mud hens.

The road curved west. The sun was low in front of him, and he figured it was close to five o'clock. Twenty after, he guessed. The war had taught him to figure time. Even without the sun, waking from sleep, he could usually place it within fifteen minutes either way. He wished his father were there beside him, so he could say, "Well, looks about five-twenty," and his father would look at his watch and say, "Hey! How'd you do that?" "One of those things you learn in the war," he would say. "I know exactly what you mean," his father would then say, and the ice would be broken, and then they would be able to talk about it as they circled the lake.

He drove past Slater Park and across the causeway and past Sunset Park. The radio announcer sounded tired. He said it was five-thirty. The temperature in Des Moines was eighty-one degrees, and "All you on the road, drive carefully now, you hear, on this fine Fourth of July." Along the road, kicking stones in front of them, two young boys were hiking with knapsacks and toy rifles and canteens. He honked going by, but neither boy looked up. Already he'd passed them six times, forty-two miles, nearly three hours. He watched the boys recede in his rearview mirror. They turned purply colored, like clotted blood, before finally disappearing.

"How many medals did you win?" his father might have asked.

"Seven," he would have said, "though none of them were for valor."

"That's all right," his father would have answered, knowing full well that many brave men did not win medals for their bravery, and that others won medals for doing nothing. "What are the medals you won?"

And he would have listed them, as a kind of starting place for talking about the war: the Combat Infantryman's Badge, the Air Medal, the Bronze Star (without a V-device for valor), the Army Commendation Medal, the Vietnam Campaign Medal, the Good Conduct Medal, and the Purple Heart, though it wasn't much of a wound, and there was no scar, and it didn't hurt and never had. While none of them was for valor, the decorations still looked good on the uniform in his closet, and if anyone were to ask, he would have explained what each signified, and eventually he would have talked about the medals he did not win, and why he did not win them, and how afraid he had been.

"Well," his father might have said, "that's an impressive list of medals, all right."

"But none were for valor."

"I understand."

And that would have been the time for telling his father that he'd almost won the Silver Star, or maybe even the Medal of Honor.

"I almost won the Silver Star," he would have said.

"How's that?"

Words to Own

drone *n.:* monotonous hum.

recede (ri·sēd′) *v.:* become more distant and indistinct.

valor (val′ər) *n.:* great courage.

OPTIONS FOR TEACHING

INTEGRATING THE LANGUAGE ARTS

Language and Style Discuss with students O'Brien's effective use of short, simple sentences. Draw attention to the paragraph on p. 971 that begins "He passed the sprawling. . . ." Ask students how many simple sentences they can find. [Seven; the fourth sentence is a compound sentence.] Then, discuss with students what they think O'Brien's use of simple sentences tells the reader about Paul's **character**. Challenge students also to relate the style to the story's **theme**. [Possible answers: The simple sentences reflect the basic nature and honesty of the character's search for answers about bravery. The style's simplicity also mirrors the theme's basic problem of how to go on with life after such experiences.]

Strategic Reading To give every student a chance to take part in the reading of this selection, try Popcorn Reading. Have one student read aloud while the rest of the class follows along. After a paragraph or a number of sentences, the reader should call out "popcorn" and the name of someone else in the class. This person then reads aloud and "pops" to someone else. Set a minimum number of lines to be read each time before students begin, and make sure everyone gets a turn.

"Oh, it's just a war story."

"What's wrong with war stories?" his father would have said.

"Nothing, except I guess nobody wants to hear them."

"Tell me," his father would have said.

And then, circling the lake, he would have started the story by saying what a crazy hot day it had been when Frenchie Tucker crawled like a snake into the clay tunnel and got shot in the neck, going on with the story in great detail, telling how it smelled and what the sounds had been, everything, then going on to say how he'd almost won the Silver Star for valor. **D**

"Well," his father would have said, "that's not a very pretty story."

"I wasn't very brave."

"You have seven medals."

"True, true," he would have said, "but I might have had eight," but even so, seven medals was pretty good, hinting at courage with their bright colors and heavy metals. "But I wasn't brave," he would have admitted.

"You weren't a coward, either," his father would have said.

"I might have been a hero."

"But you weren't a coward," his father would have insisted.

"No," Paul Berlin would have said, holding the wheel slightly right of center to produce the constant clockwise motion, "no, I wasn't a coward, and I wasn't brave, but I had the chance." He would have explained, if anyone were there to listen, that his most precious medal, except for the one he did not win, was the Combat Infantryman's Badge. While not strictly speaking a genuine medal—more an insignia of soldierdom—the CIB meant that he had seen the war as a real soldier, on the ground. It meant he'd had the opportunity to be brave, it meant that. It meant, too, that he'd . . . seen Frenchie Tucker crawl into the tunnel so that just his feet were left showing, and heard the sound when he got shot in the neck. With its crossed rifles and silver and blue colors, the CIB was really not such a bad decoration, not as good as the Silver Star or Medal of Honor, but still evidence that he'd once been there with the chance to be very brave. "I wasn't brave," he would have said, "but I might have been." **E**

The road descended into the outskirts of town, turning northwest past the junior college and tennis courts, then past the city park where tables were spread with sheets of colored plastic as picnickers listened to the high school band, then past the municipal docks where a fat woman stood in pedal-pushers and white socks, fishing for bullheads.[2] There were no other fish in the lake, excepting some perch and a few worthless carp. It was a bad lake for swimming and fishing both.

He was in no great hurry. There was no place in particular to go. **F** The day was very hot, but inside the Chevy the air was cold and oily and secure, and he liked the sound of the big engine and the radio and the air-conditioning. Through the windows, as though seen through one-way glass, the town shined like a stop-motion photograph, or a memory. The town could not talk, and it would not listen, and it was really a very small town anyway. "How'd you like to hear about the time I almost won the Silver Star for valor?" he might have said. The Chevy seemed to know its way around the lake.

It was late afternoon. Along an unused railway spur, four men were erecting steel launchers for the evening fireworks. They were dressed alike in khaki trousers, work shirts, visored caps and black boots. They were sweating. Two of them were unloading crates of explosives from a city truck, stacking the crates near the steel launchers. They were talking. One of them was laughing. "How'd you like to hear about it?" he might have murmured, but the men did not look up. Later they would blow color into the sky. The lake would be like a mirror, and the picnickers would sigh. The colors would open wide. "Well, it was this crazy hot day," he would have said to anyone who asked, "and Frenchie Tucker took off his helmet and pack and crawled into the tunnel with a forty-five and a knife, and the whole platoon stood in a circle around the mouth of the tunnel to watch him go down. 'Don't get blowed away,' said Stink Harris, but Frenchie was already inside and he didn't hear. You could see his feet wiggling,

2. **bullheads:** A bullhead is a type of freshwater catfish with hornlike growths near its mouth.

Words to Own

municipal (myo͞o·nis′ə·pəl) *adj.:* belonging to a city or town.

D. Reader's Response: First Thoughts

? What are your impressions of the narrator's story from his summary of it? [Sample responses: It sounds like a strange, disturbing story that he might not want to tell because recalling it is painful. Or the story must not be that important if the narrator simply summarizes it instead of telling it with all its details.]

E. Critical Reading: Comparing and Contrasting

? How are the medals similar, and how are they different? [All three medals can only be won by "real soldiers," those fighting the war on the front lines. The Silver Star or Medal of Honor are proofs of valor, however, while the Combat Infantryman's Badge only implies that its bearer had the chance to be brave.]

F. Literary Element: Analyzing Repetition

? How does the author's repetition of certain words and phrases, such as "There was no place in particular to go," emphasize Paul's aimlessness? [Possible responses: Verbal repetition, like the physical repetition of Paul's circling the lake, underscores the fact that Paul has nothing to do—his old friends are gone, and the war seems to have sapped his desire for involvement in the community. The repetition mirrors the narrator's obsession with the past—he is not engaged in the present, only in verbally repeating the past.]

INTEGRATING THE LANGUAGE ARTS

Speaking and Listening What might take place if Paul were to stop and talk to one of the many characters he sees? Ask volunteers to write and act out a scene in which Paul and the other characters engage in conversation. Have students refer to the text to conclude how the characters may have responded to Paul. The rest of the class can serve as audience and critics, discussing after each scene the believability and creativity of each conversation.

COOPERATIVE LEARNING

Create A Memorial Have students work in mixed-ability groups of four to six to create a memorial to the soldiers who fought in the Vietnam War. Encourage students to make their memorials address and attempt to unify the divisions of the time that would cause a veteran such as Paul to feel so isolated. Challenge groups also to make their memorials creative. Groups can present their ideas in drawings and oral descriptions. To make sure each student takes part, have each group member submit a brief description of his or her contribution to the project. ☞

A. Critical Reading: Analyzing a Symbol

? What is symbolic about the sprinkler that Paul observes?

[Possible response: The rotating sprinkler symbolizes futility. Its circular motion is comparable to Paul's circling the lake. Moreover, because the grass is so dry, the sprinkling is "hopeless." Likewise, Paul's activity is getting him nowhere.]

B. Cultural Connections

Students may not understand why "nobody believed it was really a war at all." One reason is that, like the Korean War of the early 1950s, the Vietnam War was undeclared. In addition, it was an unpopular war. Some Americans felt that the U.S. presence in South Vietnam only served to continue the corrupt government left over from the country's former colonial status under the French. Finally, when U.S. troops withdrew and North and South Vietnam were unified under communist rule, many Americans preferred to forget the war.

and you could smell the dirt and clay, and then, when he got shot through the neck, you could smell the gunpowder and you could see Frenchie's feet jerk, and that was the day I could have won the Silver Star for valor."

The Chevy rolled smoothly across the old railroad spur. To his right, there was only the open lake. To his left, the lawns were scorched dry like October corn. Hopelessly, round and round, a rotating sprinkler scattered water into Doctor Mason's vegetable garden. In August it would get worse. The lake would turn green, thick with bacteria and decay, and the golf course would dry up, and dragonflies would crack open for lack of good water. The summer seemed permanent.

The big Chevy curled past the A&W[3] and Centennial Beach, and he started his seventh revolution around the lake.

He followed the road past the handsome low-slung houses. Back to Slater Park, across the causeway, around to Sunset Park, as though riding on tracks.

Out on the lake, the man with the stalled motorboat was still fiddling with the engine.

The two boys were still trudging on their hike. They did not look up when he honked.

The pair of mud hens floated like wooden decoys. The waterskiers looked tan and happy, and the spray behind them looked clean.

It was all distant and pretty.

Facing the sun again, he figured it was nearly six o'clock. Not much later the tired announcer in Des Moines confirmed it, his voice seeming to rock itself into a Sunday afternoon snooze.

Too bad, he thought. If Max were there, he would say something meaningful about the announcer's fatigue, and relate it to the sun low and red now over the lake, and the war, and courage. Too bad that all the girls had gone away. And his father, who already knew the difficulties of being brave, and who preferred silence.

Circling the lake, with time to talk, he would have told the truth. He would not have faked it. Starting with the admission that he had not been truly brave, he would have next said he hadn't been a coward, either. "I almost won the Silver Star for valor," he would have said, and, even so, he'd learned many important things in the war. Like telling time without a watch. He had learned to step lightly. He knew, just by the sound, the difference between friendly and enemy mortars, and with time to talk and with an audience, he could explain the difference in great detail. He could tell people that the enemy fired 82-millimeter mortar rounds, while we fired 81's, and that this was a real advantage to the enemy since they could steal our rounds and shoot them from their own weapons. He knew many lies. Simple, unprofound things. He knew it is a lie that only stupid men are brave. He knew that a man can die of fright, literally, because it had happened just that way to Billy Boy Watkins after his foot had been blown off. Billy Boy had been scared to death. Dead of a heart attack caused by fright, according to Doc Peret, who would know. He knew, too, that it is a lie, the old saying that you never hear the shot that gets you, because Frenchie Tucker was shot in the neck, and after they dragged him out of the tunnel he lay there and told everyone his great discovery; he'd heard it coming the whole way, he said excitedly; and then he raised his thumb and bled through his mouth, grinning at the great discovery. So the old saying was surely a lie, or else Frenchie Tucker was lying himself, which under the circumstances was hard to believe. He knew a lot of things. They were not new or profound, but they were true. He knew that he might have won a Silver Star, like Frenchie, if he'd been able to finish what Frenchie started in the foul tunnel. He knew many war stories, a thousand details, smells and the confusion of the senses, but nobody was there to listen, and nobody knew a damn about the war because nobody believed it was really a war at all. It was not a war for war stories, or talk of valor, and nobody asked questions about the details, such as how afraid you can be, or what the particular sounds were, or whether it hurts to be shot, or what you think about and hear and see on ambush, or whether you can really tell in a firefight which way to shoot, which you can't, or how you become brave enough to win the Silver Star, or how it smells of sulfur against your cheek after firing

3. **A&W:** chain of drive-in, fast-food restaurants.

WORDS TO OWN

mortars (môrt′ərz) *n. pl.:* cannons used to fire explosive shells.

OPTIONS FOR TEACHING

COOPERATIVE LEARNING

Critique Have students work in groups of four or five to present a television literary review show. Groups should consist of a host asking questions and guests expressing their opinions, with support from the text. Encourage groups to begin by drawing up a list of questions for the show and thinking of different positions that could be taken on each topic. The host's questions should concern the **theme** of the story, the author's **style**, or the **main character**. Guests can analyze these elements, express their opinions, or make connections with other works. Each group should then practice their discussions and take notes that they can use when performing their review show for the class.

Cooperative Zone You might not use cooperative reading strategies with the entire class. One way to help students focus on their work in the classroom, and to minimize distractions, is to set aside a part of the classroom (such as a row of seats along one side of the room) as a Cooperative Zone for students participating in a cooperative reading activity. Over the course of a unit or grading period, try to give each student a chance to work in that area.

eighteen fast rounds, or how you crawl on hands and knees without knowing direction, and how, after crawling into the red-mouthed tunnel, you close your eyes like a mole and follow the tunnel walls and smell Frenchie's fresh blood and know a bullet cannot miss in there, and how there is nowhere to go but forward or backward, eyes closed, and how you can't go forward, and lose all sense, and are dragged out by the heels, losing the Silver Star. All the details, without profundity, simple and age old, but nobody wants to hear war stories because they are age old and not new and not profound, and because everyone knows already that it hadn't been a war like other wars. If Max or his father were ever to ask, or anybody, he would say, "Well, first off, it was a war the same as any war," which would not sound profound at all, but which would be the truth. Then he would explain what he meant in great detail, explaining that, right or wrong or win or lose, at root it had been a real war, regardless of corruption in high places or politics or sociology or the existence of God. His father knew it already, though. Which was why he didn't ask. And Max could not ask. It was a small town, but it wasn't the town's fault, either.

Bill Hickey/The Image Bank.

Vietnam Veterans Memorial (detail), Washington, D.C.

He passed the sprawling ranch-style homes. He lit a cigarette. He had learned to smoke in the war. He opened the window a crack but kept the air-conditioner going full, and again he circled the lake. His thoughts were the same. Out on the lake, the man was frantically yanking the cord to his stalled outboard motor. Along the causeway, the two boys marched on. The pair of mud hens sought sludge at the bottom of the lake, heads under water and tails bobbing.

Six-thirty, he thought. The lake had divided into two halves. One half still glistened. The other was caught in shadow. Soon it would be dark. The crew of workers would shoot the sky full of color, for the war was over, and the town would celebrate independence. He passed Sunset Park once again, and more houses, and the junior college and tennis courts, and the picnickers and the high school band, and the municipal docks where the fat woman patiently waited for fish.

Already, though it wasn't quite dusk, the A&W was awash in neon lights.

He maneuvered his father's Chevy into one of the parking slots, let the engine idle, and waited. The place was doing a good holiday business. Mostly kids in their fathers' cars, a few farmers in for the day, a few faces he thought he remembered, but no names. He sat still. With the sound of the engine and air-conditioning and radio, he could not hear the kids laughing, or the cars coming and going and burning rubber. But it didn't matter, it seemed proper, and he sat patiently and watched while mosquitoes and June bugs swarmed off the lake to attack the orange-colored lighting. A slim, hipless, deft young blonde delivered trays of food, passing him by as if the big Chevy were invisible, but he waited. The tired announcer in Des Moines gave the time, seven

WORDS TO OWN

profundity (prō·fun′də·tē) *n.:* intellectual depth.

C. Language Note: Style
Paul concludes that the truth is not necessarily profound. How does the **style** of his thoughts reflect that position? [Possible response: His thoughts are wandering, obsessive, and focused on almost forgotten details, and his ideas are simple and simply put. But his outrage and pain are real and plainly show in his insistence on the unadulterated truth about the war.]

D. Literary Element: Symbol
? How is Paul's situation like that of the boys? [Paul too is still "marching," in his memories of being a soldier during the war.]

CLASSROOM MANAGEMENT

Managing the Reader's Response Classroom
After students have expressed their own reactions to a selection, encourage them to expand the possibilities. One way they can do this is to consider the possible responses of people with various backgrounds and experiences.

PROBLEM SOLVING/ CRITICAL THINKING

Conflict Resolution In this story, the narrator sees no outlet for addressing inner conflicts that developed from his experience with war. Ask students how they would advise Paul if they knew him personally. Then, have students work in small groups to discuss other traumatic experiences that a person may find difficult to face, such as serious illness or moving to a new neighborhood or country. Ask each group to come up with possible solutions. Have groups compare their answers.

PROFESSIONAL NOTES

Thematic Connections: "The Wages of War" Ask students to scan the selection and use their notes to determine the **theme** of the story. Then, discuss with students how this story shows a number of possible "wages" of war. ☞

A. Critical Reading: Expressing an Opinion

? How would going forward in the tunnel have helped Paul to go forward with his life? [He thinks that if he had been brave he would be happier now with his role in the war, and he would not be trapped in the past.]

B. Critical Reading: Making Inferences

? Considering Paul's thoughts and experiences, what is ironic about his exchange with the order taker? [The dialogue over the speaker mimics a military situation.]

C. Reader's Response: Challenging the Text

? How do you feel about the ending of this story? Is it an effective ending? [Sample responses: The ending is a good one because it ends on a note of hope that Paul can come to appreciate and live in the present. The ending is ironic because Paul is viewing a patriotic celebration and has not been rewarded for his service for the country, but it is too abrupt and doesn't answer any of the reader's questions about Paul's future.]

o'clock. He could trace the fall of dusk in the orange lights which grew brighter and sharper. It was a bad war for medals. But the Silver Star would have been nice. Nice to have been brave. (A) The tactile, certain substance of the Silver Star, and how he could have rubbed his fingers over it, remembering the tunnel and the smell of clay in his nose, going forward and not backward in simple bravery. He waited patiently. The mosquitoes were electrocuting themselves against a Pest-Rid machine. The slim young carhop ignored him, chatting with four boys in a Firebird, her legs in nylons even in mid-summer.

He honked once, a little embarrassed, but she did not turn. The four boys were laughing. He could not hear them, or the joke, but he could see their bright eyes and the way their heads moved. She patted the cheek of the driver.

He honked again, twice. He could not hear the sound. The girl did not hear, either.

He honked again, this time leaning on the horn. His ears buzzed. The air-conditioning shot cold air into his lap. The girl turned slowly, as though hearing something very distant, not at all sure. She said something to the boys, and they laughed, then she moved reluctantly toward him. EAT MAMA BURGERS said the orange and brown button on her chest. "How'd you like to hear about the war," he whispered, feeling vengeful. "The time I almost won the Silver Star."

She stood at the window, straight up so he could not see her face, only the button that said, EAT MAMA BURGERS. "Papa Burger, root beer, and french fries," he said, but the girl did not move or answer. She rapped on the window.

"Papa Burger, root beer, and french fries," he said, rolling it down.

She leaned down. She shook her head dumbly. Her eyes were as lovely and fuzzy as cotton candy.

"Papa Burger, root beer, and french fries," he said slowly, pronouncing the words separately and distinctly for her.

She stared at him with her strange eyes. "You blind?" she chirped suddenly. She gestured toward an intercom attached to a steel post. "You blind or something?"

"Papa Burger, root beer, and french fries."

"Push the button," she said, "and place your order." Then, first punching the button for him, she returned to her friends in the Firebird.

"Order," commanded a tinny voice.

"Papa Burger, root beer, and french fries."

"Roger-dodger," the voice said. "Repeat: one Papa, one beer, one fries. Stand by. That's it?"

(B) "Roger," said Paul Berlin.

"Out," said the voice, and the intercom squeaked and went dead.

"Out," said Paul Berlin.

When the slim carhop brought him his tray, he ate quickly, without looking up, then punched the intercom button.

"Order," said the tinny voice.

"I'm done."

"That's it?"

"Yes, all done."

"Roger-dodger, over n' out," said the voice.

"Out."

On his ninth revolution around the lake he passed the hiking boys for the last time. The man with the stalled motorboat was paddling toward shore. The mud hens were gone. The fat woman was reeling in her line. The sun had left a smudge of watercolor on the horizon, and the bandshell[4] was empty, and Doctor Mason's sprinkler went round and round.

On his tenth revolution, he switched off the air-conditioning, cranked open a window, and rested his elbow comfortably on the sill, driving with one hand. He could trace the contours of the tunnel. He could talk about the scrambling sense of being lost, though he could not describe it even in his thoughts. He could talk about the terror, but he could not describe it or even feel it anymore. He could talk about emerging to see sunlight, but he could not feel the warmth, or see the faces of the men who looked away, or talk about his shame. There was no one to talk to, and nothing to say.

On his eleventh revolution, the sky went crazy with color.

(C) He pulled into Sunset Park and stopped in the shadow of a picnic shelter. After a time, he got out and walked down to the beach and stood with his arms folded and watched the fireworks. For a small town, it was a pretty good show.

4. **bandshell:** open-air stage with a rear sounding board shaped like the shell of a scallop.

WORDS TO OWN

tactile (tak'təl) *adj.:* able to be perceived by touch.

CROSSING THE CURRICULUM

Geography Have students research photographs and sketches of the Vietnamese countryside. Students can use the images to imagine the setting of Paul's opportunity for bravery and to contrast the appearance of the country with that of his hometown.

ASSESSMENT TOOLS

Check Test: True-False

1. Paul is amazed at how much everything has changed in his hometown. [False]
2. Paul received seven medals in the war, but none of them was for valor. [True]
3. The day Paul could have won his Silver Star was the day Frenchie Tucker was shot through the neck. [True]
4. In Vietnam, Paul learned that a man can die from fright. [True]
5. The man whose motorboat stalls finally gets the engine going. [False]

Making Meanings

First Thoughts

1. How would you have felt if you had been in Paul Berlin's shoes?

Reviewing the Text

a. Describe the story's **setting.** In contrast, what sights, sounds, and smells does Paul remember from his time in Vietnam?

b. What does Paul wish his father would do?

c. List the things Paul has learned as a result of the war. According to Paul, why don't people want to hear about the war?

d. What does Paul wish he had done in Vietnam? What does he want to tell his father?

Shaping Interpretations

2. Explain why it is so difficult for Paul and his father to talk. What do you think Paul means when he says that his father "knew the truth already"? What truth does his father know, and how does he know it?
3. Discuss the **symbolic** meaning of the repeated circular action in the story and of the repeated references to time. (Be sure to review your Reader's Log.)
4. What is the **symbolic** meaning of the date in the story's context?
5. Given his experiences, what is **ironic** about the military language in Paul's conversation with the disembodied voice on the drive-in restaurant's intercom system?
6. Find the passages in which Paul mentions conversations about God. What purpose do you think these passages serve?
7. Do you think Paul's **internal conflict** has been resolved by the end of the story? Explain.
8. Do you think Paul is or is not a courageous person? Explain your answer.

Extending the Text

9. What will happen to Paul next? Share your predictions about Paul's future, and explain your reasons.

Choices: Building Your Portfolio

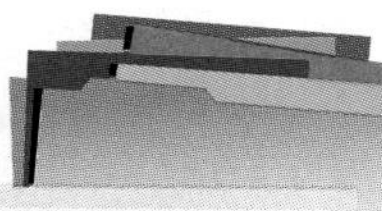

Writer's Notebook

1. Collecting Ideas for an Evaluation

What are your criteria for judging whether a writer has been successful in creating a character? List some qualities you expect to find in a well-conceived character. Then note whether Paul Berlin meets those criteria. Save your notes for possible use in the Writer's Workshop on page 1181.

Critical Writing

2. War and Peace, Peace and War

Both "Speaking of Courage" and Mark Helprin's "Tamar" (page 922) deal indirectly with the horror of warfare. In a brief essay, explain how both stories use contrast to deal with this subject. In planning your essay, consider how contrast is evident in each story's **setting, characterization,** and **tone.**

Critical Writing

3. Soldiers' Homes

In a brief essay, compare and contrast the situations and characters of Paul Berlin in this story and Harold Krebs in Ernest Hemingway's "Soldier's Home" (page 653). What can you infer about the similarities and differences in the experiences of soldiers returning from World War I and those returning from Vietnam?

Creative Writing / Performance

4. "What Did You Do in the War?"

Write the dialogue for a television interview about Vietnam with Paul Berlin to be broadcast on a July 4 newscast. Then ask two students to perform the dialogue, with you as director. Instruct them in how to speak and what gestures and facial expressions to use. Allow them to ad-lib a little as well.

Making Meanings

First Thoughts

1. Answers will vary. Some students may offer comparable examples of missed opportunities from their own experiences.

Reviewing the Text

a. The story takes place on a Sunday, the Fourth of July, around the lake in Paul's hometown near Des Moines, Iowa, after his tour of duty in Vietnam. Paul sees the blackness of the tunnel and Frenchie bleeding through his mouth; he remembers the sounds of enemy mortars and the shot to Frenchie's neck, the smell of sulfur, dirt, clay, gunpowder, and blood.

b. Paul wishes his father would talk to him about the war and courage.

c. Possible answers include: He learned how to tell time without a watch; he learned to step lightly; he learned to differentiate between sounds of friendly and enemy fire. Nobody believes it was a war like other wars.

d. Paul wishes he had won medals for valor. He wants to tell his father how he almost won the Silver Star.

Shaping Interpretations

2. Possible responses: Perhaps his father is disappointed in Paul, or his own wartime experience may be too painful to relive with his son. His father already knows the grim facts of war because he served in a war himself.
3. The repetitive circular action and references to time emphasize Paul's inertia.
4. The Fourth of July celebrates national pride and freedom. No one acknowledges Paul's contribution to this ideal.
5. Nobody wants to hear Paul's war stories, yet people use the language of war in peaceful contexts.
6. The passages in the second paragraph juxtapose the philosophical conversations about God with the reality of war and Max's death.
7. Nothing in the story indicates a resolution; it is left open-ended.
8. Answers will vary, but most will agree he is courageous. He did fight and survive, and he tries to make sense of his experience and go on.

Extending the Text

9. **(Synthesis)** Students may point to Paul's strong inertia and the lack of resolution in the story and predict no change or even a decline for Paul. Others will point to the final note of hope and predict that Paul will recover.

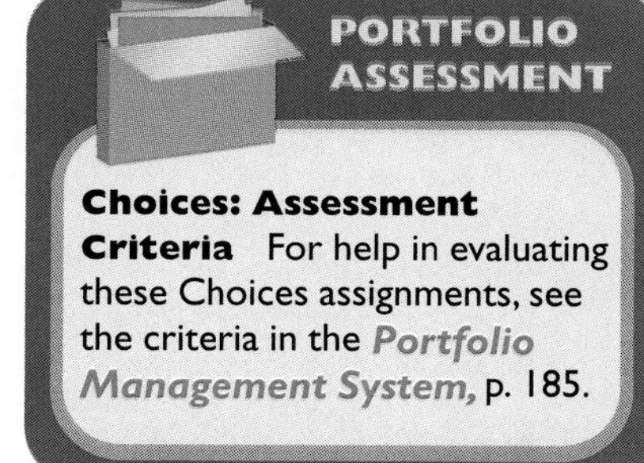

Choices: Assessment Criteria For help in evaluating these Choices assignments, see the criteria in the *Portfolio Management System,* p. 185.

QUICK PLANNING GUIDE

Into the Poem

Through the Poem

Beyond the Poem

- **Writer's Notebook:** Evaluate the poem's imagery
- **Critical Writing:** Evaluate the poem's symbolism
- **Critical Thinking/Speaking and Listening:** Express an opinion about a statement by the author

PORTFOLIO ASSESSMENT

Portfolio Assessment
For help with self-assessment of reading skills, see the ***Portfolio Management System,*** p. 39.

© Nancy Crampton.

Yusef Komunyakaa
(1947–   )

"Vietnam helped me to look at the horror and terror in the hearts of people and realize how we can't aim guns and set booby traps for people we have never spoken a word to. That kind of impersonal violence mystifies me." These are the heartfelt reflections of one of the finest poets to emerge from the Vietnam conflict, Yusef Komunyakaa (kō·mun·yä'kə), the soldier-writer-teacher who was awarded a Pulitzer Prize in 1994 for his poetry collection *Neon Vernacular.*

A poet of both unflinching honesty and emotional restraint, Komunyakaa was born and raised in Bogalusa, Louisiana. His impulse to write, he recalls, first came when he was sixteen and read a copy of James Baldwin's *Nobody Knows My Name,* which he had found in a tiny church library. After high school, he served as a soldier in Vietnam and was awarded the Bronze Star. He then worked as a military "information specialist," corresponding from the front for a service newspaper. After the war, Komunyakaa earned advanced degrees: a master's from Colorado State University in 1979 and a master's in creative writing from the University of California, Irvine, in 1980.

Like so many American poets, Komunyakaa has made his living as a teacher. He has taught at the University of New Orleans and Indiana University, and he has given special poetry classes to elementary school students. Essentially a private and even shy man, Komunyakaa once said, "I'm happier talking about the process of writing, yes. . . . I'm even happier to have people read my work. I'm uncomfortable with the focus on the poet and not on the poem." Nevertheless, he gives poetry readings across America and in other countries. One critic, Kirkland C. Jones, points out the close connection for Komunyakaa between the written and the spoken word:

> In his Vietnam verse he keeps before the world what it meant and still means to be American, black, and a soldier, and what the painful inequities of this combination add up to. His poetry is as rhythmic and fluid as his speaking voice, and just as mellow and introspective.

Komunyakaa's collections include *Lost in the Bonewheel Factory* (1979); *Copacetic* (1983), in which critics have noted jazzlike poems that recall the poems of Langston Hughes and Jean Toomer; *I Apologize for the Eyes in My Head* (1986); and *Magic City* (1992). His poems cluster around themes of violent conflict and loss, of family and racial identity, of survival and memory, and of facing up to the harsh facts of life and death. In 1988, Komunyakaa published a powerful volume devoted entirely to his Vietnam experience, *Dien Cai Dau.* Kirkland Jones ranks this among the most highly accomplished books generated by the war, because Komunyakaa

> focuses on the mental horrors of war—the anguish shared by the soldiers, those left at home to keep watch, and other observers, participants, objectors, who are all part of the "psychological terrain," as he has termed it, "that makes us all victims" and rages behind the eyes long after the actual fighting has ceased.

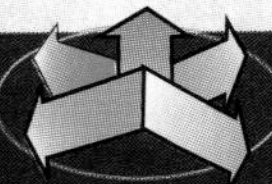

PROGRAM MANAGER

- **Planning Instruction** See **Teaching Notes, *Teaching Resources B,*** p. 139, for objectives, a summary, and literary elements for this selection.
- **Instructional Support** Before beginning the instructional lesson, see **Graphic Organizer for Active Reading, *Teaching Resources B,*** p. 154, for an Into the Poem activity.
- **Audiotaped Readings** To help less proficient readers or auditory learners through the lesson, use the **Selected Reading, Audiocassette 3, Side B,** in the ***Audiovisual Resources Binder.***
- **Assessment** See **Selection Test, *Test Booklet,*** p. 225.

Before You Read
Monsoon Season

Reading Focus

Living with Dying

Memories of violence last far longer than the physical pain. Sometimes the most common things—a leaf, a breeze, a drop of rain—can trigger those memories and bring seemingly forgotten experiences back to life.

A Dialogue with the Text

As you read, write down the **images** the speaker uses to express his memories and emotions.

Elements of Literature

Imagery

Images in literature use language to evoke a picture or a sensation of a person or thing. Poetry is closely related to music, so it is not surprising that many poems contain **images** of sound. "Monsoon Season" includes several. Try to spot them as you read. It will probably help to read the poem aloud.

Background

U.S. soldiers fighting the ground war during the Vietnam conflict had to contend with conditions completely alien to them. The moist, hot, tropical climate of Vietnam, its extensive jungles and mountains, and the ever-present threat of an often invisible enemy made fighting conditions unusually hazardous and frightening. And then there were the monsoons—year-round winds bringing torrents of seemingly unending rain in the hot summer and lighter but still frequent showers in the somewhat cooler winter.

Monsoon Season

Yusef Komunyakaa

A river shines in the jungle's
wet leaves. The rain's finally
let up but whenever wind shakes
the foliage it starts to fall.
The monsoon uncovers troubled
seasons we tried to forget. A
Dead men slip through bad weather,
stamping their muddy boots to wake us, B
their curses coming easier.
There's a bend in everything,
in elephant grass & flame trees,
raindrops pelting the sand-bagged
bunker like a muted gong.

Into the Poem

Using **Before You Read** p. 975

Reading Focus

Ask students to think of sensory stimuli that have caused them to relive memories. Challenge students to think of one memory for each of the five senses. *Caution students that they do not have to discuss with the class anything they would not feel comfortable sharing.*

A Dialogue with the Text

Direct students to include in their lists of images the sense that each image evokes. Remind students that an image can appeal to more than one sense.

Elements of Literature

Pair students with a partner to read the poem. Each student in a pair can read through the poem once while the other listens for sound **imagery**. The listener should take notes on the imagery. When both students have read the poem, they can compare their notes.

Through the Poem

A. Reader's Response: First Thoughts

? How can the monsoon bring back forgotten seasons? [Sample responses: The rain may remind the speaker of times long ago. The repetitiveness of the falling rain might lull the speaker into meditating on unpleasant memories.]

B. Critical Reading: Drawing Conclusions

? How can dead men walk? [Possible answers: The speaker is simply remembering men who have died. The speaker is looking at soldiers who will not last long in the war—in a way, they are dead already.]

Integrating the Language Arts

Strategic Reading Have students read the poem in pairs. Partners can take turns reading the poem aloud and discussing the layers in the work. After a first reading, partners can discuss the **setting**, characters, and events in the poem. After a second reading, partners can discuss the literary elements used by the poet, including **imagery**. Then, after a third reading, partners can discuss the **theme** and ideas in the poem. The partners should take notes on their discussions.

Strategies for Inclusion

Visual Have students draw pictures of the images they encounter in the poem. Students can sketch to elucidate the text as they read, or they can choose a significant scene from the poem and illustrate it for display in the classroom. Encourage students to include captions from the poem on their drawings.

A. Literary Element: Imagery

? What does this metaphor say about the natural world that is the setting of the poem? [Possible answers: Nature is out of place in a war, just like stars not in the sky. After the shocking experiences of war, everything seems alien to the speaker; nature is now unnatural.]

B. Reader's Response: Shaping Interpretations

? In what ways has the poem shown how the monsoon brings up the dead? [Sample responses: The soldiers' idleness leads inevitably to thoughts about dead comrades. It is only when the fighting pauses that the men realize the extent of the war's destruction.]

WRITERS ON WRITING

Speaking of the black soldier who is a central figure in his work, Komunyakaa says he is "just one black face connected to a parade of others who have risked their lives for this enigma we call America. This black soldier in Vietnam, however, seems rather uncomfortable with his role. Maybe the agent of free will lurks like a specter in his psyche. Or perhaps he feels guilty, because he has a sense of history and he knows that he's merely a cog in the whole contradictory machinery some might call democracy or even manifest destiny."

White phosphorus° washed from the air,
wind sways with violet myrtle,°
beating it naked. Soaked to the bone,
jungle rot brings us down to earth.
We sit in our hooches°
with too much time,
where grounded choppers
can't fly out the wounded.
Somewhere nearby a frog
begs a snake.
I try counting droplets,
stars that aren't in the sky.
My poncho feels like a body bag.
I lose count. Red leaves
whirl by, the monsoon
unburying the dead.

14. white phosphorus: poisonous, highly flammable chemical element used in weapons during the Vietnam War.
15. myrtle: type of evergreen shrub.
18. hooches: U.S. military slang for huts and other simple buildings in which soldiers lived while at base camps.

U.S. soldier of the Second Battalion in Mekong Delta, Vietnam, 1967.
Larry Burrows © 1967 Time, Inc.

ASSESSMENT TOOLS

Check Test: True-False

1. The setting of the poem is by a river in the jungle, during a lull in a monsoon. [True]
2. White phosphorus is a natural coating on jungle plants. [False]
3. The rain on the hut sounds like cymbals. [False]
4. The speaker compares his poncho to a body bag. [True]
5. The speaker sees a snake eating a frog. [False]

Connections — A Newspaper Column

Poetry Emotion

ANNA QUINDLEN

Yusef Komunyakaa won the Pulitzer Prize this week, but he does not expect to become a household name, and not because his name itself, phonetically simple once parsed out bit by bit, looks at first glance so unpronounceable. Mr. Komunyakaa won the prize for poetry, and there is little premium in poetry in a world that thinks of Pound and Whitman as a weight and sampler, not an Ezra, a Walt, a thing of beauty, a joy forever.

It's hard to figure out why this should be true, why poetry has been shunted onto a siding at a time, a place, so in need of brevity and truth. We still use the word as a synonym for a kind of lovely perfection, for an inspired figure skater, an accomplished ballet dancer. Many of the finest books children read when young are poetry: "The Cat in the Hat," "Goodnight Moon," the free verse of "Where the Wild Things Are."

And then suddenly, just as their faces lose the soft curves of babyhood, the children harden into prose, and leave verse behind, or reject it entirely. Their summer reading lists rarely include poetry, only stories; *The Red Badge of Courage,* not Mr. Komunyakaa's spare and evocative poems about his hitch in Vietnam:

He danced with tall grass
for a moment, like he was
swaying
with a woman. Our gun barrels
glowed white-hot.
When I got to him,
a blue halo
of flies had already claimed
him.

For some of those children who once were lulled to sleep by the rhythms of Seuss and Sendak, poetry comes now set to music: Nirvana and Arrested Development, Tori Amos and the Indigo Girls. Many readers are scared off young, put off by the belief that poetry is difficult and demanding. We complain that it doesn't sound like the way we talk, but if it sounds like the way we talk, we complain that it doesn't rhyme.

A poet who teaches in the schools tells of how one boy told him he couldn't, wouldn't write poetry. Then one day in class he heard Hayden Carruth's "Cows at Night" and cried, "I didn't know we were allowed to write poems about cows."

Or to write a poem about two women talking in the kitchen:

Crazy as a bessy bug.
Jack wasn't cold
In his grave before
She done up & gave all
The insurance money
To some young pigeon
Who never hit a lick
At work in his life.
He cleaned her out & left
With Donna Faye's girl.
Honey, hush. You don't
Say . . .

That's Mr. Komunyakaa, from the collection, *Neon Vernacular,* that won the Pulitzer. His publisher originally printed 2,500 copies, which is fairly large for poetry but a joke to the folks who stock those racks at the airport. Few are the parents who leap up with soundless joy when a son or daughter announces, "Mom, Dad, I've decided to become a poet."

People who are knowledgeable about poetry sometimes discuss it in that knowing, rather hateful way in which enophiles talk about wine: robust, delicate, muscular. This has nothing to do with how most of us experience it, the heart coming around the corner and unexpectedly running into the mind. Of all the words that have stuck to the ribs of my soul, poetry has been the most filling. Robert Frost, Robert Lowell, Elizabeth Bishop, Emily Dickinson, the divine W. B. Yeats. April is the cruellest month. O World, I cannot hold thee close enough! After the first death, there is no other. A terrible beauty is born. (A)

Poems are now appearing on posters in subway trains; one commuter said of a Langston Hughes poem, "I can't express it, but I get it." Now rolling through the soot-black dark of the tunnels and the surprising sunshine where the subways suddenly shoot aboveground: Marianne Moore, William Carlos Williams, Audre Lorde, May Swenson, Rita Dove, and Gwendolyn Brooks, who wrote that exquisite evocation of *carpe diem*, and perhaps of poetry too:

Exhaust the little moment.
Soon it dies.
And be it gash or gold it will
not come
Again in this identical
disguise.

Says Mr. Komunyakaa, who teaches, "I never really approached it from the perspective of making a living. It was simply a need." Maybe it's a need for us all and we just forget it, as we move past bedtime-story rhythms and into a world without rhyme or reason.

—*New York Times,* April 16, 1994

A. Literary Connections
"April is the cruellest month" T. S. Eliot (1888–1965), *The Waste Land*
"O World, I cannot hold thee close enough!" Edna St. Vincent Millay (1892–1950), "God's World"
"After the first death, there is no other" Dylan Thomas (1914–1953), "A Refusal to Mourn the Death, by Fire, of a Child in London"
"A terrible beauty is born." William Butler Yeats (1865–1939), "Easter 1916"

CONNECTING WITH "MONSOON SEASON"

After students have read the column, ask them to review the poem and discuss how Quindlen's views affect their re-reading. Do they appreciate Komunyakaa's skill more? Do they find an increase in meaning in the poem? Challenge students to recite lines from poetry that they have found stirring and inspirational.

Making Meanings

First Thoughts

1. Answers will vary. The tone suggests the narrator is gloomy, depressed, disheartened, and disillusioned. Acceptable supporting passages include: "The monsoon uncovers troubled / seasons we tried to forget," "Soaked to the bone," "jungle rot brings us down to earth," and "My poncho feels like a body bag."

Shaping Interpretations

2. The jungles of Vietnam during the war. Answers will vary, but may include earlier monsoons and moments of destruction.
3. Significantly; milder weather would likely lighten their moods—but it would also allow more fighting.
4. The monsoon (the rain and wind). Some students might suggest the unburied dead as well.
5. Answers will vary, but should describe a muffled, heavy sound.
6. Raindrops. The implication is that he is counting dead soldiers or wasted moments.

Extending the Text

7. **(Evaluation)** Responses will vary. The statement describes a feeling put into words in a way that enables readers to see something in a new way. Students may say that this observation is too romantic or carefree for "Monsoon Season."

Choices: Building Your Portfolio

3. **Critical Thinking/Speaking and Listening** Suggest that students begin their statement by defining what they mean by *hero.* Ask them to make a list of at least five heroes. The list can include historical figures as well as characters from film and fiction. Have them determine whether all these "heroes have blood on their hands." Make sure students support their positions.

Making Meanings

First Thoughts

1. How would you characterize the speaker's mood? Cite passages to support your opinion.

Shaping Interpretations

2. Where is the speaker in the poem? What are the "troubled / seasons we tried to forget"?
3. The monsoon rain forces the soldiers to "sit in our hooches / with too much time." How might the weather have influenced the speaker's thoughts and feelings?
4. What specifically triggers the speaker's memory of past experiences?
5. In an **image** of sound, the speaker of "Monsoon Season" says the raindrops pelted the bunker "like a muted gong." In your own words, tell what the sound of the raindrops was like to the speaker. Why is it surprising to hear rain described this way?
6. When the speaker says, "I lose count," what does he *explicitly* say he is counting? What does he *imply* he has been counting?

Extending the Text

7. In Connections on page 977, Anna Quindlen describes most people's experience of poetry as "the heart coming around the corner and unexpectedly running into the mind." Choose this or another observation of Quindlen's, and tell what you think it means and whether it seems to fit your experience of "Monsoon Season."

U.S. Army helmet, Vietnam.
Henri Bureau / Sygma

Choices: Building Your Portfolio

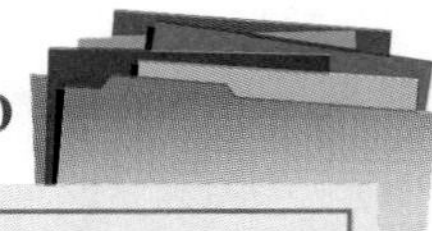

Writer's Notebook

1. Collecting Ideas for an Evaluation

One criterion for evaluating a poem is the success with which it uses **imagery.** Reviewing your Reader's Log, list some of the visual images in "Monsoon Season," and jot down some notes evaluating whether the poet uses them effectively. Save your notes for possible use in the Writer's Workshop on page 1181.

Critical Writing

2. Frogs and Snakes

Poets frequently use **symbols**—persons, places, things, or events that have meaning in themselves but also stand for something more. In the passage "Somewhere nearby a frog / begs a snake," what might the frog and the snake symbolize? Do you think the poet has chosen his symbols wisely? Present your answers in a short essay.

Critical Thinking / Speaking and Listening

3. "I have a real problem with that."

Komunyakaa struggles to understand the contemporary legacy of violence. He once said in an interview, "In our culture we celebrate violence. All of our heroes have blood on their hands. I have a real problem with that." Imagine that you are present at the interview in which Komunyakaa delivers this opinion. In a brief statement of your own, with no wasted words, tell him—and your class—why you agree or disagree with his statement.

STRATEGIES FOR INCLUSION

Linguistic For activity #2, ask students to freewrite for a few minutes for words they associate with the animals. Students can then review their notes to think of how the animals symbolize the soldiers.

Learners Having Difficulty To help students consider the issue more clearly for activity #3, have them answer the questions by using a graphic organizer such as Transparency 11: Analysis Chart in the Transparency Package.

PORTFOLIO ASSESSMENT

Choices: Assessment Criteria For help in evaluating these Choices assignments, see the criteria in the ***Portfolio Management System,*** p. 185.

DISCOVERIES AND AWAKENINGS

Theme:

Theme: In Search of Meaning

Contemporary literature shows people striving for some sort of meaning in life, a struggle that is reflected in the ways people define the universe and each other. Because personal epiphanies and insights are as varied as the population, each selection reflects an individual type of revelation or awareness.

Literary Focus

Literary Element	Selection / Feature
Static and Dynamic Characters	**The Magic Barrel**
Figures of Speech	**Elegy for Jane: My Student, Thrown by a Horse**
Ambiguity/Sound Effects	**The Beautiful Changes**
Extended Metaphor	**Homework**
Dialogue	**Black Boy**
Style	**Everything Stuck to Him**
Personification	**The Fish**
Conflict	**The Girl Who Wouldn't Talk**
Dialect	**Blue Highways**

Writing Focus

The following flowchart shows how the writing assignment for each selection relates to the Writer's Workshop at the end of the unit.

Selection	Work-in-Progress Assignment
The Magic Barrel	Create a chart to evaluate characters p. 994
Elegy for Jane	Write an informal outline p. 1004
The Beautiful Changes	List criteria for a good lyric poem p. 1007
Homework	Plan evaluation of a poem p. 1011
Black Boy	Write down two experiences p. 1025
Everything Stuck to Him	Interview classmates and record opinions p. 1033
The Fish	Compare a poem to another work p. 1038
Remember	Jot down personal experiences p. 1042
The Girl Who Wouldn't Talk	Write sentences evaluating use of imagery p. 1053
Blue Highways	Make a chart comparing works p. 1066
Writer's Workshop	Write an evaluation pp. 1181–1185

Collection 19 **DISCOVERIES AND AWAKENINGS**

Collection Planner

SELECTION / FEATURE	PUPIL'S EDITION: Literary Elements / Active Reading	Writing	Speaking and Listening	Language and Vocabulary
The Magic Barrel Bernard Malamud (pp. 980–994) Critical Comment: A Tale of Self-Discovery (p. 993)	• Reader's Log p. 981 • Static and Dynamic Characters p. 981	• Critical Writing: Write response essay p. 994 • Creative Writing: Write dialogue p. 994		
The Handsomest Drowned Man in the World Gabríel García Márquez (pp. 995–1000)	• Reader's Log p. 996		• Finding Common Ground: Discuss story in groups p. 1000	
Elegy for Jane: My Student, Thrown by a Horse Theodore Roethke (pp. 1001–1004)	• Reader's Log p. 1002 • Figures of Speech p. 1002	• Critical Writing: Write comparison essay p. 1004		
The Beautiful Changes Richard Wilbur (pp. 1005–1007)	• Reader's Log p. 1006 • Ambiguity p. 1006 • Language and Style: Sound Effects p. 1007	• Critical Writing: Write essay p. 1007	• Crossing the Curriculum: Science: Present findings to class in oral report p. 1007	• Language and Style: Wilbur's Sound Effects p. 1007
Homework Allen Ginsberg (pp. 1008–1011)	• Reader's Log p. 1009 • Extended Metaphor p. 1009	• Critical Writing: Write comparison essay p. 1011 • Creative Writing: Write short poem p. 1011		
from **Black Boy** Richard Wright (pp. 1012–1025)	• Reader's Log p. 1013 • Dialogue p. 1013	• Critical Writing: Write essay p. 1025	• Speaking and Listening/ Performance: Present oral reading p. 1025	
Everything Stuck to Him Raymond Carver (pp. 1026–1033) Primary Sources: Paddle-wheel of Days (p. 1032)	• Reader's Log p. 1027 • Style p. 1027	• Critical Writing: Write opinion essay p. 1033 • Creative Writing: Write monologue p. 1033		
The Fish Elizabeth Bishop (pp. 1034–1038)	• Reader's Log p. 1035 • Personification p. 1035	• Critical Writing: Write essay p. 1038 • Creative Writing: Write short poem p. 1038		
Remember Joy Harjo (pp. 1039–1042)	• Reader's Log p. 1040	• Critical Writing: Write essay p. 1042 • Creative Writing: Write poem p. 1042	• Creative Writing: Read personal "Remember" poem to class p. 1042	
The Girl Who Wouldn't Talk Maxine Hong Kingston (pp. 1043–1053)	• Reader's Log p. 1044 • Conflict p. 1044	• Critical Writing: Write essay p. 1053 • Creative Writing: Write story p. 1053		
from **Blue Highways** William Least Heat-Moon (pp. 1054–1066) **Connections:** from **Let Us Now Praise Famous Men** James Agee (pp. 1064–1065)	• Reader's Log p. 1055 • Dialect p. 1055	• Critical Writing: Write opinion essay p. 1066 • Crossing the Curriculum: Geography: Write essay about place names p. 1066		• Language and Style: Heat-Moon's Metaphors p. 1066

Collection Resources

Teaching Resources B	Audiovisual Resources Binder	Test Booklet
Cross-Curricular Activity p. 182	Fine Art Transparency 19.1	Collection 19 Test pp. 243–246

 Computer disk or CD-ROM

 Audiocassette

 Overhead Transparency

PROGRAM RESOURCES

Electronic Media	Teaching Resources with Organizer: Teaching Resources B	Teaching Resources with Organizer: Other Resources	Audiovisual Resources Binder
• Language Workshop: Semicolons, Colon • Test Generator	• Teaching Notes p. 157 • Reading Organizer p. 163 • Language Link pp. 164–165 • Words to Own p. 166	• Test Booklet: Selection Test pp. 229–230 • Language and Writing Skills Worksheets pp. 138–139 • Portfolio Management System pp. 39, 187	• Elements of Literature Transparency 19.2
	• Teaching Notes p. 158		
• Test Generator	• Teaching Notes p. 158 • Reading Organizer p. 167	• Test Booklet: Selection Test pp. 231–232 • Portfolio Management System pp. 48–49, 188	
• Test Generator	• Teaching Notes p. 159 • Reading Organizer p. 168	• Test Booklet: Selection Test pp. 231–232 • Portfolio Management System p. 189	
• Test Generator	• Teaching Notes p. 159 • Reading Organizer p. 169	• Test Booklet: Selection Test pp. 231–232 • Portfolio Management System pp. 53, 190	
• Language Workshop: Sentence style • Test Generator	• Teaching Notes p. 160 • Reading Organizer p. 170 • Language Link pp. 171–172 • Words to Own p. 173	• Test Booklet: Selection Test pp. 233–234 • Language and Writing Skills Worksheets p. 116 • Portfolio Management System pp. 54–55, 191	• Elements of Literature Transparency 19.3
• Test Generator	• Teaching Notes pp. 160–161 • Reading Organizer p. 174 • Words to Own p. 175	• Test Booklet: Selection Test pp. 235–236 • Portfolio Management System pp. 53, 192	
• Test Generator	• Teaching Notes p. 161 • Reading Organizer p. 176	• Test Booklet: Selection Test pp. 237–238 • Portfolio Management System pp. 53, 193	• Selected Reading Audiocassette 3, Side B
• Test Generator	• Teaching Notes p. 161 • Reading Organizer p. 177	• Test Booklet: Selection Test pp. 237–238 • Portfolio Management System pp. 53, 194	
• Test Generator	• Teaching Notes p. 162 • Reading Organizer p. 178 • Words to Own p. 179	• Test Booklet: Selection Test pp. 239–240 • Portfolio Management System pp. 39, 195	
• Test Generator	• Teaching Notes p. 162 • Reading Organizer p. 180 • Words to Own p. 181	• Test Booklet: Selection Test pp. 241–242 • Portfolio Management System pp. 54–55, 196	

Proofreading Warm-ups

You may use the following exercises to help students practice their proofreading skills. Copy a set of incorrect sentences onto the chalkboard, and have students find and correct the spelling, punctuation, usage, and mechanical errors in each sentence. Ask students to share and discuss their responses.

	Sentences with Errors	Sentences Corrected	Skills Covered
1	**a.** bernard malamud a important contemporary american jewish writter **b.** the short story the magic barrel has a dynamic main character who change's	**a.** Bernard Malamud is an important contemporary American Jewish writer. **b.** The short story "The Magic Barrel" has a dynamic main character who changes.	Capitalization, Fragments, Spelling, Quotation marks for short story titles, Apostrophe usage, End marks
2	**a.** marquezs novel one hundred years of solitude published in english in 1970 **b.** thus exposed new readers to magic realism the technique of mixing realistic detail and fantasy	**a.** Marquez's novel One Hundred Years of Solitude was published in English in 1970. **b.** The book exposed new readers to magic realism, the technique of mixing realistic detail and fantasy.	Capitalization, Apostrophe usage, Underline titles, Fragments, Comma usage, End marks
3	**a.** roethke a native of saginaw michigan spent his childhood close to nature **b.** roethkes Father owned the largest greenhouse complex in the State	**a.** Roethke, a native of Saginaw, Michigan, spent his childhood close to nature. **b.** Roethke's father owned the largest greenhouse complex in the state.	Capitalization, Comma usage, Apostrophe usage, End marks
4	**a.** ambiguity an expression that deliberately suggest's different and sometimes conflicting meanings **b.** for instance Wilburs poem The Beautiful Changes contains ambiguity	**a.** Ambiguity is an expression that deliberately suggests different, and sometimes conflicting, meanings. **b.** For instance, Wilbur's poem "The Beautiful Changes" contains ambiguity.	Capitalization, Fragments, Apostrophe usage, Comma usage, Quotation marks for poem titles, End marks
5	**a.** allen ginsbergs poem Homework contain's a extended metaphor **b.** a extended metaphor is one, that is extended beyond a single comparison	**a.** Allen Ginsberg's poem "Homework" contains an extended metaphor. **b.** An extended metaphor is one that is extended beyond a single comparison.	Capitalization, Apostrophe usage, Quotation marks for poem titles, Standard usage, Comma usage, End marks
6	**a.** wright often described as the first african american writer to expose racism to a white audience **b.** black boy wrights autobiography secured his fame as a writer	**a.** Wright is often described as the first African American writer to expose racism to a white audience. **b.** Black Boy, Wright's autobiography, secured his fame as a writer.	Capitalization, Fragments, Underline book titles, Comma usage, Apostrophe usage, End marks
7	**a.** style is one of the most strikeing elements of Raymond Carvers writing **b.** sometimes he dont even give his character's names	**a.** Style is one of the most striking elements of Raymond Carver's writing. **b.** Sometimes he doesn't even give his characters names.	Capitalization, Spelling, Apostrophe usage, Subject-verb agreement, End marks
8	**a.** stephen please identify one use of personification in Elizabeth Bishop's poem The Fish said Ms. Hebert **b.** the pronoun I because it refers to a person he answered	**a.** "Stephen, please identify one use of personification in Elizabeth Bishop's poem 'The Fish,'" instructed Ms. Hebert. **b.** "The pronoun I, because it refers to a person," he answered.	Quotation marks (single and double), Capitalization, Comma usage, Underline words used as words, End marks
9	**a.** a refrain is a word phrase line or group of lines that are repeated for affect **b.** identify the refrain in Joy Harjos poem Remember	**a.** A refrain is a word, phrase, line, or group of lines that is repeated for effect. **b.** Identify the refrain in Joy Harjo's poem "Remember."	Capitalization, Comma usage, Subject-verb agreement, Spelling, Apostrophe usage, Quotation marks for poem titles, End marks
10	**a.** maxine hong kingston born in California, of chinese immigrant parents **b.** kingston recieved literary acclaim in 1976 w/ her 1st book	**a.** Maxine Hong Kingston was born in California of Chinese immigrant parents. **b.** Kingston received literary acclaim in 1976 with her first book.	Capitalization, Fragments, Comma usage, Spelling, Write out abbreviations, End marks

Collection 19

DISCOVERIES AND AWAKENINGS

Malamud
García Márquez
Roethke
Wilbur
Ginsberg
Wright
Carver
Bishop
Harjo
Kingston
Heat-Moon

Pine Tree Tops

In the blue night
frost haze, the sky glows
with the moon
pine tree tops
bend snow-blue, fade
into sky, frost, starlight.
The creak of boots.
Rabbit tracks, deer tracks,
what do we know.

—Gary Snyder (1930–)

"Pine Tree Tops"
Invite students to comment on what discoveries the speaker in this poem makes while looking at the pine trees. Ask them how they interpret the last three lines. Then, have them discuss what they think the focus of the Collection will be.

PORTFOLIO ASSESSMENT

Parent/Guardian Involvement For forms that will help a parent or guardian review and respond to a student's portfolio, see *Portfolio Management System,* pp. 62–63.

PROGRAM MANAGER

- **Integrated Assessment** For a summative assessment of the literature and language skills taught in this collection, see Collection 19 Test, *Test Booklet,* pp. 243–246.
- **Instructional Support** See Fine Art Transparency 19.1. Review teacher's notes for transparencies in the *Audiovisual Resources Binder* for suggestions on how to tie the transparencies to specific reading selections.
- **Extending Collection Theme** See Cross-Curricular Activity: Discoveries and Awakenings, *Teaching Resources B,* p. 182, for an activity in other disciplines and for evaluation criteria.

QUICK PLANNING GUIDE

Into the Story

Author Biography p. 980
Before You Read p. 981
- **Reading Focus: Scaffolding** Students discover seemingly mismatched couples can have deep emotional connections.
- **Quickwrite: Prior Knowledge** Freewrite on the nature of love
- **Elements of Literature: Static and Dynamic Characters**

Through the Story

"The Magic Barrel" pp. 982–993
Words to Own pp. 983–988
Critical Comment p. 993
Making Meanings p. 994

Beyond the Story

Choices: Building Your Portfolio p. 994
- **Writer's Notebook:** Collect ideas for an evaluation
- **Critical Writing:** Write a brief essay in response to a critical comment
- **Creative Writing:** Write dialogue between Leo and Stella

ABOUT THE AUTHOR

Malamud was born in Brooklyn, the son of a grocer and of a woman who came from a theatrical family. During his early years, Malamud moved from community to community with his family as they tried to improve their lot. During the Depression, eking out a living was difficult, and he spent many hours working behind the counter of the grocery store his parents ran. His early experiences may explain why he created characters who strive to achieve a better life.

Bernard Malamud

(1914–1986)

© Nancy Crampton.

Bernard Malamud is a principal figure in the group of Jewish writers whose work has enriched contemporary American literature. Yet Malamud preferred not to be easily pigeonholed. He did write *about* Jews, but he wrote *for* all people.

Malamud's characters usually live at a level of bare physical subsistence. Though we may feel compassion for them, they do not display the least self-pity. If their plight is sad, it is also triumphant, because they survive in heroic fashion against the odds all humans face.

"As you are grooved, so you are grieved," Malamud once wrote as preamble to an account of his own bleak upbringing. He was the older of two sons of a Russian immigrant storekeeper. His mother died when he was fourteen. He grew up in Brooklyn in a household without books, music, or pictures on the walls. During the Great Depression, he worked at a census office and a yarn factory to help support his family, but he felt these experiences were important to him as a writer. Getting down to essential needs and "turning inward," Malamud believed, are the best preparation for writing.

It was the suffering of European Jews during World War II that convinced Malamud he had something to say as a writer. "I for one believe that not enough has been made of the tragedy of the destruction of six million Jews," he said. "Somebody has to cry—even if it's just a writer, twenty years later."

Malamud's unique drama is spun out of the commonplace, the tragicomedy of survival in a brutal world. But his stories are always informed by love, and, indeed, his characters are largely redeemed by love. Philip Roth, whose own notable writing covers some of the same ground as Malamud's, wrote the following analysis:

> "Malamud wrote of a meager world of pain in a language all his own. [It was] an English that often appeared, even outside the idiosyncratic dialogue, to have in large part been clipped together from out of what one might have thought to be the least promising stockpile, most unmagical barrel, around: the locutions, inversions, and diction of Jewish immigrant speech, a heap of broken verbal bones that looked, until he came along in those early stories to make them dance to his sad tune, to be of no use to anyone any longer other than the Borscht Belt comic and the professional nostalgia-monger."

Malamud taught English in New York City high schools and fiction at Oregon State University and Bennington College in Vermont. His first novel, *The Natural* (1952), whose central character is a baseball player, was made into a popular film in 1984. His other books include *The Assistant* (1957), a novel set in Brooklyn, considered by some critics to be his best work; the short-story collections *The Magic Barrel* (1958; National Book Award) and *Idiots First* (1963); and the novels *The Fixer* (1966; National Book Award and Pulitzer Prize), set in czarist Russia, and *The Tenants* (1971).

Malamud was a firm believer in the power of story. "The story will be with us as long as man is," he once said. "You know that, in part because of its effect on children. It's through story they realize that mystery won't kill them. Through story they learn they have a future."

WORDS TO OWN

The following vocabulary words are defined in the Words to Own at the bottom of the pupil's page.

meager p. 983	clientele p. 985
suppress p. 983	nuptial p. 987
ascetic p. 983	traditional p. 987
dowry p. 984	machinations p. 988
upbraided p. 985	evident p. 988

Before You Read
The Magic Barrel

Reading Focus

"When I fall in love . . ."

"Unbelievable!" "You're kidding!" Many of us react with exclamations like these when we hear of two seemingly mismatched people falling in love. After all, what do they have in common? A great deal, apparently. It may happen to friends or people in our families, to a famous actress who marries a quiet intellectual, to a king who gives up his throne for a commoner—to ourselves, even. Suddenly, deep emotional connections are made between people who, on the surface, inhabit different worlds.

Quickwrite

Why do people fall in love? Poets, philosophers, playwrights, and just about everybody else have been offering answers to that question for thousands of years. Yet we are still not sure about the answer. Is love purely emotional? Does it involve the mind as well as the heart? Write down some of your ideas on the subject.

Elements of Literature

Static and Dynamic Characters

A **static character** does not change much over the course of a story. A **dynamic character,** on the other hand, changes in an important way as the story unfolds. As you read, ask yourself: Which type of character is Leo Finkle? Which type is Pinye Salzman?

A **static character** does not change much over the course of a story. A **dynamic character** changes in an important way as a result of the story's action.

For more on Character, see the Handbook of Literary Terms.

Phyllis Seated (1952) by Moses Soyer. Oil on canvas (42″ × 36″).

Courtesy ACA Gallery, New York.

Into the Story

Using Before You Read p. 981

Elements of Literature

Using a graphic organizer like the one following, have students note the characteristics, thoughts, actions, and words of Finkle and Salzman as the story progresses. Students will be able to see changes in characteristics, action, thought, and words, which will indicate dynamic character. Little or no change will reveal a static character.

	Finkle		
	Beginning	Middle	End
Characteristics Actions Thoughts Words			

	Salzman		
	Beginning	Middle	End
Characteristics Actions Thoughts Words			

Portfolio Assessment

Portfolio Assessment
For help with self- and teacher assessment of reading skills, see the ***Portfolio Management System,*** p. 39.

Program Manager

- **Planning Instruction** See **Teaching Notes, *Teaching Resources B,*** p. 157, for information.
- **Instructional Support** See **Graphic Organizer for Active Reading, *Teaching Resources B,*** p. 163, for a Through the Story activity.
- **Application and Reinforcement** For reinforcement of the elements of literature introduced in this lesson, see **Transparency** 19.2 in the ***Audiovisual Resources Binder.***
- **Instructional Support** See **Fine Art Transparency** 19.1. Review teacher's notes for transparencies in the ***Audiovisual Resources Binder.***
- **Assessment** See **Selection Test, *Test Booklet,*** pp. 229–230.
- **Language Link** For practice in semicolons and colons, see **Language Link, *Teaching Resources B,*** pp. 164–165 and ***Language and Writing Skills Worksheets,*** pp. 138–139.
- **Reinforcement** Use the **Words to Own** worksheet in ***Teaching Resources B,*** p. 166.

RESPONDING TO THE ART: ABOUT THE ARTIST

Birthday by Marc Chagall (1887–1985) conveys the festive gaiety that the Russian-born artist felt about his approaching marriage to Bella, the woman in the picture. He regarded this painting as symbolic of the happiness that awaited the couple. Art critics in 1915 generally objected to the simplifications and distortions of anatomy in the painting. What is your reaction? Do you find the figures crude and childish? Or do you agree with modern critics who find them charming, naive, and lyrical? Explain. [Possible responses: Their floating seems appropriate for people in love; the figures are charming and lyrical. The rendering of the woman's eye seems childish to me.]

Technology Tip

Before they read the story, have students research the history behind Jewish traditions by accessing an on-line encyclopedia or database. They may also do key word searches on the Internet. *You may want to preview any Internet activity that you suggest to students. Because these resources are sometimes public forums, their content can be unpredictable.* If possible, invite a local rabbi or scholar in to discuss the history of the Jewish people. Be sure to videotape the session for use with other classes.

Birthday (*L'Anniversaire*) (1915) by Marc Chagall. Oil on canvas (31¾″ × 39¼″).

The Magic Barrel

Bernard Malamud

"Love comes with the right person, not before."

OPTIONS FOR TEACHING

STRATEGIES FOR INCLUSION

Less Proficient Readers To help students organize details from the story, have them use a graphic organizer like the one following. Ask them to list in the first column details that support the idea that Salzman is not prosperous and in the second column, details that support that he is likable.

Not Prosperous	Likable
[Worn Portfolio Old hat Overcoat too small Smells of fish Missing teeth]	[Enjoys eating Not displeasing manner Amiable Animated features]

Visual Have students draw or paint their impressions of Salzman on a book cover and include the most important quotation from the story. Make sure they include details and images that portray him as unprosperous but likable.

Not long ago there lived in uptown New York, in a small, almost meager room, though crowded with books, Leo Finkle, a rabbinical student in the Yeshivah University.[1] Finkle, after six years of study, was to be ordained in June and had been advised by an acquaintance that he might find it easier to win himself a congregation if he were married. Since he had no present prospects of marriage, after two tormented days of turning it over in his mind, he called in Pinye Salzman, a marriage broker whose two-line advertisement he had read in the *Forward.*[2]

The matchmaker appeared one night out of the dark fourth-floor hallway of the graystone rooming house where Finkle lived, grasping a black, strapped portfolio that had been worn thin with use. Salzman, who had been long in the business, was of slight but dignified build, wearing an old hat, and an overcoat too short and tight for him. He smelled frankly of fish, which he loved to eat, and although he was missing a few teeth, his presence was not displeasing, because of an amiable manner curiously contrasted with mournful eyes. His voice, his lips, his wisp of beard, his bony fingers were animated, but give him a moment of repose and his mild blue eyes revealed a depth of sadness, a characteristic that put Leo a little at ease although the situation, for him, was inherently tense.

He at once informed Salzman why he had asked him to come, explaining that his home was in Cleveland, and that but for his parents, who had married comparatively late in life, he was alone in the world. He had for six years devoted himself almost entirely to his studies, as a result of which, understandably, he had found himself without time for a social life and the company of young women. Therefore he thought it the better part of trial and error—of embarrassing fumbling—to call in an experienced person to advise him on these matters. He remarked in passing that the function of the marriage broker was ancient and honorable, highly approved in the Jewish community, because it made practical the necessary without hindering joy. Moreover, his own parents had been brought together by a matchmaker. They had made, if not a financially profitable marriage—since neither had possessed any worldly goods to speak of—at least a successful one in the sense of their everlasting devotion to each other. Salzman listened in embarrassed surprise, sensing a sort of apology. Later, however, he experienced a glow of pride in his work, an emotion that had left him years ago, and he heartily approved of Finkle.

The two went to their business. Leo had led Salzman to the only clear place in the room, a table near a window that overlooked the lamp-lit city. He seated himself at the matchmaker's side but facing him, attempting by an act of will to suppress the unpleasant tickle in his throat. Salzman eagerly unstrapped his portfolio and removed a loose rubber band from a thin packet of much-handled cards. As he flipped through them, a gesture and sound that physically hurt Leo, the student pretended not to see and gazed steadfastly out the window. Although it was still February, winter was on its last legs, signs of which he had for the first time in years begun to notice. He now observed the round white moon, moving high in the sky through a cloud menagerie, and watched with half-open mouth as it penetrated a huge hen, and dropped out of her like an egg laying itself. Salzman, though pretending through eyeglasses he had just slipped on, to be engaged in scanning the writing on the cards, stole occasional glances at the young man's distinguished face, noting with pleasure the long, severe scholar's nose, brown eyes heavy with learning, sensitive yet ascetic lips, and a certain, almost hollow quality of the dark cheeks. He gazed around at shelves upon shelves of books and let out a soft, contented sigh.

When Leo's eyes fell upon the cards, he counted six spread out in Salzman's hand.

1. **Yeshivah** (ye·shē′və) **University:** prominent New York City school serving both as a general college and as a seminary for Orthodox Jewish rabbis.
2. ***Forward:*** formerly the *Jewish Daily Forward,* a newspaper published in New York City.

WORDS TO OWN

meager (mē′gər) *adj.:* poor; inadequate.
suppress (sə·pres′) *v.:* to restrain; hold back.
ascetic (ə·set′ik) *adj.:* severe; stern.

A. Exploring the Historical Period
This story was first published in 1954. "Not long ago" probably refers to the post–World War II period after 1945, a time of sorrow for Jews still deeply tied to their European roots and to memories of the Holocaust.

B. Literary Element: Exposition
Modern short stories typically begin with action or dialogue, but this one starts with exposition—information about the protagonist (Leo Finkle) and his problem.

C. Critical Reading: Analyzing Character
? What do the details describing Salzman tell us about him?
[That he is old and poor, perhaps not a successful matchmaker. He is sad, yet dignified and likable.]

D. Reader's Response: First Thoughts
? Why does Salzman feel renewed pride in his work and approve of Finkle? [Sample responses: Because he thinks Finkle is already a rabbi, an esteemed person in the Jewish community, and because Finkle praises matchmaking as an old, honorable profession. Or Finkle calls him experienced and says his parents' successful marriage was due to a matchmaker.]

STRATEGIES FOR INCLUSION

Learners Having Difficulty To help students understand the plot, have them fill in a series of events chain like the following.

[Leo contacts matchmaker.]
[Leo rejects prospective brides.]
[Salzman convinces Leo to meet Lily.]
[Lily prods Leo into admitting he does not love God.]
[Salzman leaves photos.]

English Language Development Finkle grows from a lonely, isolated student to someone with a more honest understanding of himself and his life choices. Place students in pairs and have each pair create a chart listing the individuals in the story who have a forceful hand in Finkle's dynamic change. Beginning with Pinye Salzman, list the actions or conversations which affect Leo. Ask students to discuss how many people are needed for Leo to see what changes he needs in his life.

	Actions	Conversations
Salzman	[Withholds information]	[Tells him that love comes with the right person]
Lily		

A. Literary Element: Character

? What differences do you note between Finkle and Salzman? [Possible answers: Finkle is interested in the physical qualities of his future bride; Salzman is interested in social standing. Or Finkle is interested in an actual person; Salzman is more interested in financial qualifications.]

B. Reader's Response: Shaping Interpretations

? Why had Salzman not given the teacher's age or mentioned a dowry? [Sample responses: He suspects Leo wants an attractive, younger bride. Finkle does not seem interested in the widow's wealth, either. Or Salzman has learned to withhold information that he thinks will cause Finkle to reject a potential match.]

C. Literary Element: Dialect

? What elements does Malamud use to create the dialect that characterizes Salzman? [The rhythm and unusual syntax help us hear his distinctive New York Jewish accent. Other techniques are inversion and using questions instead of direct statements.] What contribution does dialect make to the story? [Characterization, local color, cultural identification.]

"So few?" he asked in disappointment.

"You wouldn't believe me how much cards I got in my office," Salzman replied. "The drawers are already filled to the top, so I keep them now in a barrel, but is every girl good for a new rabbi?"

Leo blushed at this, regretting all he had revealed of himself in a curriculum vitae[3] he had sent to Salzman. He had thought it best to acquaint him with his strict standards and specifications, but in having done so, felt he had told the marriage broker more than was absolutely necessary.

(A) He hesitantly inquired, "Do you keep photographs of your clients on file?"

"First comes family, amount of dowry, also what kind promises," Salzman replied, unbuttoning his tight coat and settling himself in the chair. "After comes pictures, rabbi."

"Call me Mr. Finkle. I'm not yet a rabbi."

Salzman said he would, but instead called him doctor, which he changed to rabbi when Leo was not listening too attentively.

Salzman adjusted his horn-rimmed spectacles, gently cleared his throat and read in an eager voice the contents of the top card:

"Sophie P. Twenty four year. Widow one year. No children. Educated high school and two years college. Father promises eight thousand dollars. Has wonderful wholesale business. Also real estate. On the mother's side comes teachers, also one actor. Well known on Second Avenue."

Leo gazed up in surprise. "Did you say a widow?"

"A widow don't mean spoiled, rabbi. She lived with her husband maybe four months. He was a sick boy she made a mistake to marry him."

"Marrying a widow has never entered my mind."

"This is because you have no experience. A widow, especially if she is young and healthy like this girl, is a wonderful person to marry. She will be thankful to you the rest of her life. Believe me, if I was looking now for a bride, I would marry a widow."

Leo reflected, then shook his head.

Salzman hunched his shoulders in an almost imperceptible gesture of disappointment. He placed the card down on the wooden table and began to read another:

"Lily H. High school teacher. Regular. Not a substitute. Has savings and new Dodge car. Lived in Paris one year. Father is successful dentist thirty-five years. Interested in professional man. Well Americanized family. Wonderful opportunity."

"I knew her personally," said Salzman. "I wish you could see this girl. She is a doll. Also very intelligent. All day you could talk to her about books and theyater and what not. She also knows current events."

(B) "I don't believe you mentioned her age?"

"Her age?" Salzman said, raising his brows. "Her age is thirty-two years."

Leo said after a while, "I'm afraid that seems a little too old."

Salzman let out a laugh. "So how old are you, rabbi?"

"Twenty-seven."

"So what is the difference, tell me, between twenty-seven and thirty-two? My own wife is seven years older than me. So what did I suffer?—Nothing. If a Rothschild's[4] daughter wants to marry you, would you say on account her age, no?"

"Yes," Leo said dryly.

(C) Salzman shook off the no in the yes. "Five years don't mean a thing. I give you my word that when you will live with her for one week you will forget her age. What does it mean five years—that she lived more and knows more than somebody who is younger? On this girl, God bless her, years are not wasted. Each one that it comes makes better the bargain."

"What subject does she teach in high school?"

"Languages. If you heard the way she speaks French, you will think it is music. I am in the business twenty-five years, and I recommend her

3. ***curriculum vitae*** (kə·rik′yoo̅·ləm vīt′ē): Latin for "course of life"; that is, a résumé or summary of one's career and qualifications.

4. **Rothschild's:** The Rothschilds are a wealthy banking family.

Words to Own

dowry (dou′rē) *n.:* money or goods a bride brings with her in a marriage.

Options for Teaching

Integrating the Language Arts

Writing: Film Scripts Have student groups create film scripts of the story. Assign one student in each group to write one scene; for example, the scene in which Finkle and Salzman meet, or the scene between Lily and Finkle. Have groups enact and film the scenes.

Language and Style Malamud provides a wealth of details to help us picture Finkle, his room, Salzman, and the bridal candidates. Many of the details are provided by adjectives. Have students turn to the descriptions of the main characters—Finkle, Salzman, and Stella—and think of some additional adjectives, including participles, that Malamud might have used. Have them share these with the class.

Strategic Reading To help students explore the story in depth and gain greater understanding, as they read have them record in their Reader's Logs answers to the following questions. Then, have students work with partners to discuss their responses.

1. Why do Stella's eyes seem familiar? [Because of a family resemblance—she is Salzman's daughter.]
2. Why does Finkle swear he has seen Salzman's wife before? [Stella also resembles her mother.]
3. Finkle's running forward with flowers before him is similar to what previous image? [Finkle's imagining Pan throwing flowers in front of him and Lily.]

with my whole heart. Believe me, I know what I'm talking, rabbi."

"What's on the next card?" Leo said abruptly.

Salzman reluctantly turned up the third card:

"Ruth K. Nineteen years. Honor student. Father offers thirteen thousand cash to the right bridegroom. He is a medical doctor. Stomach specialist with marvelous practice. Brother-in-law owns own garment business. Particular people."

Salzman looked as if he had read his trump card.

"Did you say nineteen?" Leo asked with interest.

"On the dot."

"Is she attractive?" He blushed. "Pretty?"

Salzman kissed his finger tips. "A little doll. On this I give you my word. Let me call the father tonight and you will see what means pretty."

But Leo was troubled. "You're sure she's that young?"

"This I am positive. The father will show you the birth certificate."

"Are you positive there isn't something wrong with her?" Leo insisted.

"Who says there is wrong?"

"I don't understand why an American girl her age should go to a marriage broker." D

A smile spread over Salzman's face.

"So for the same reason you went, she comes."

Leo flushed. "I am pressed for time."

Salzman, realizing he had been tactless, quickly explained. "The father came, not her. He wants she should have the best, so he looks around himself. When we will locate the right boy he will introduce him and encourage. This makes a better marriage than if a young girl without experience takes for herself. I don't have to tell you this."

"But don't you think this young girl believes in love?" Leo spoke uneasily.

Salzman was about to guffaw but caught himself and said soberly, "Love comes with the right person, not before."

Leo parted dry lips but did not speak. Noticing that Salzman had snatched a glance at the next card, he cleverly asked, "How is her health?"

"Perfect," Salzman said, breathing with difficulty. "Of course, she is a little lame on her right foot from an auto accident that it happened to her when she was twelve years, but nobody notices on account she is so brilliant and also beautiful."

Leo got up heavily and went to the window. He felt curiously bitter and upbraided himself for having called in the marriage broker. Finally, he shook his head. E

"Why not?" Salzman persisted, the pitch of his voice rising.

"Because I detest stomach specialists."

"So what do you care what is his business? After you marry her do you need him? Who says he must come every Friday night in your house?" F

Ashamed of the way the talk was going, Leo dismissed Salzman, who went home with heavy, melancholy eyes.

Though he had felt only relief at the marriage broker's departure, Leo was in low spirits the next day. He explained it as arising from Salzman's failure to produce a suitable bride for him. He did not care for his type of clientele. But when Leo found himself hesitating whether to seek out another matchmaker, one more polished than Pinye, he wondered if it could be—his protestations to the contrary, and although he honored his father and mother—that he did not, in essence, care for the matchmaking institution? This thought he quickly put out of mind yet found himself still upset. All day he ran around in the woods—missed an important appointment, forgot to give out his laundry, walked out of a Broadway cafeteria without paying and had to run back with the ticket in his hand; had even not recognized his landlady in the street when she passed with a friend and courteously called out, "A good evening to you, Doctor Finkle." By nightfall, however, he had regained sufficient calm to sink his nose into a book and there found peace from his thoughts.

Almost at once there came a knock on the door. Before Leo could say enter, Salzman, commercial cupid, was standing in the room. His face was gray and meager, his expression hungry, and

WORDS TO OWN

upbraided (up·brād′id) *v.:* severely criticized.
clientele (klī′ən·tel′) *n.:* customers.

D. Cultural Connections

? Why does Leo think that a young American girl would not go to a matchmaker? [Possible answers: She would be too modern, would want to marry for love, and would be young enough to be able to choose from a variety of men. His thinking that a young American would not do what he is doing suggests his discomfort with the matchmaking tradition.]

E. Literary Element: Plot

Complications are integral to the success of a story's plot. What complication occurs here? [Leo, dissatisfied with Salzman's prospective brides, sees his marriage-broker plan is not working out.]

F. Cultural Connections

Salzman's mention of Friday night refers to the Jewish Sabbath, which begins at sundown on Friday. Traditions include the lighting of the menorah, a candelabrum with seven branches; males wearing a yarmulke, or skullcap; and the cessation of work from sundown on Friday until sundown on Saturday, the Jewish Sabbath day.

COOPERATIVE LEARNING

Duologue To help students understand conflict in the story, pair students, and ask one student in each pair to take the role of Leo Finkle and the other to take the role of Pinye Salzman. Have the student playing Finkle ask the one playing Salzman for advice based upon a conflict in the story. Have the one playing Salzman offer counsel. Then, have the students switch roles. They repeat the process (asking for advice appropriate to their new roles) and then complete the following statements and record them in their Reader's Logs:

My problem is ________________.
I was advised to ________________.
I will/will not take the advice because ________________.

A. Critical Reading: Analyzing Character

Malamud is famous for his *schlemiels*. A *schlemiel* is a habitual bungler, a person who is always doing or saying the wrong thing. Is Salzman a *schlemiel?* [Yes. His arriving uninvited, eating his fish, and asking for tomato and tea are the typically inappropriate acts of a *schlemiel.*]

he looked as if he would expire on his feet. Yet the marriage broker managed, by some trick of the muscles, to display a broad smile.

"So good evening. I am invited?"

Leo nodded, disturbed to see him again, yet unwilling to ask the man to leave.

Beaming still, Salzman laid his portfolio on the table. "Rabbi, I got for you tonight good news."

"I've asked you not to call me rabbi. I'm still a student."

"Your worries are finished. I have for you a first-class bride."

"Leave me in peace concerning this subject." Leo pretended lack of interest.

"The world will dance at your wedding."

"Please, Mr. Salzman, no more."

"But first must come back my strength," Salzman said weakly. He fumbled with the portfolio straps and took out of the leather case an oily paper bag, from which he extracted a hard, seeded roll and a small, smoked whitefish. With a quick motion of his hand he stripped the fish out of its skin and began ravenously to chew. "All day in a rush," he muttered.

Leo watched him eat.

"A sliced tomato you have maybe?" Salzman hesitantly inquired.

"No."

The marriage broker shut his eyes and ate. When he had finished he carefully cleaned up the crumbs and rolled up the remains of the fish, in the paper bag. His spectacled eyes roamed the room until he discovered, amid some piles of books, a one-burner gas stove. Lifting his hat he humbly asked, "A glass tea you got, rabbi?"

Conscience-striken, Leo rose and brewed the tea. He served it with a chunk of lemon and two cubes of lump sugar, delighting Salzman.

After he had drunk his tea, Salzman's strength and good spirits were restored.

"So tell me, rabbi," he said amiably, "you considered some more the three clients I mentioned yesterday?"

"There was no need to consider."

"Why not?"

"None of them suits me."

"What then suits you?"

Leo let it pass because he could give only a confused answer.

Without waiting for a reply, Salzman asked, "You remember this girl I talked to you—the high school teacher?"

"Age thirty-two?"

But, surprisingly, Salzman's face lit in a smile. "Age twenty-nine."

Leo shot him a look. "Reduced from thirty-two?"

"A mistake," Salzman avowed. "I talked today with the dentist. He took me to his safety deposit box and showed me the birth certificate. She was twenty-nine years last August. They made her a party in the mountains where she went for her vacation. When her father spoke to me the first time I forgot to write the age and I told you thirty-two, but now I remember this was a different client, a widow."

"The same one you told me about? I thought she was twenty-four?"

"A different. Am I responsible that the world is filled with widows?"

"No, but I'm not interested in them, nor for that matter, in school teachers."

Salzman pulled his clasped hands to his breast. Looking at the ceiling he devoutly exclaimed, "Yiddishe kinder,[5] what can I say to somebody that he is not interested in high school teachers? So what then you are interested?"

Leo flushed but controlled himself.

"In what else will you be interested," Salzman went on, "if you not interested in this fine girl that she speaks four languages and has personally in the bank ten thousand dollars? Also her father guarantees further twelve thousand. Also she has a new car, wonderful clothes, talks on all subjects, and she will give you a first-class home and children. How near do we come in our life to paradise?"

"If she's so wonderful, why wasn't she married ten years ago?"

"Why?" said Salzman with a heavy laugh. "—Why? Because she is *partikiler.* This is why. She wants the *best.*"

Leo was silent, amused at how he had entangled himself. But Salzman had aroused his interest in Lily H., and he began seriously to consider

5. ***Yiddishe kinder:*** Yiddish for "Jewish children."

OPTIONS FOR TEACHING

CLASSROOM MANAGEMENT

Cooperative Learning Students who work cooperatively will learn more—and enjoy learning more—if they observe certain courtesies. Encourage students to keep these pointers in mind.

- If your partner or group drifts away from the subject, speak up and get back on track. If the distracting subject sounds interesting, make a note of it for future consideration.
- When other participants are speaking, listen. Take notes; ask questions.
- Don't monopolize the conversation or activity. Encourage everyone to contribute.
- Participants do not have to agree on issues. Make compromises to finish an activity and respect participants with whom you may disagree.

Discipline Positive reinforcement can motivate students. Give out good behavior tickets for staying on task, working quietly in groups, even coming prepared for the student who never has pen and paper. Use awards appropriate to your school and student, such as three tickets equal a hall pass, a free homework assignment grade, or bonus points on a test.

calling on her. When the marriage broker observed how intently Leo's mind was at work on the facts he had supplied, he felt certain they would soon come to an agreement.

Late Saturday afternoon, conscious of Salzman, Leo Finkle walked with Lily Hirschorn along Riverside Drive. He walked briskly and erectly, wearing with distinction the black fedora he had that morning taken with trepidation out of the dusty hat box on his closet shelf, and the heavy black Saturday coat he had thoroughly whisked clean. Leo also owned a walking stick, a present from a distant relative, but quickly put temptation aside and did not use it. Lily, petite and not unpretty, had on something signifying the approach of spring. She was au courant,[6] animatedly, with all sorts of subjects, and he weighed her words and found her surprisingly sound—score another for Salzman, whom he uneasily sensed to be somewhere around, hiding perhaps high in a tree along the street, flashing the lady signals with a pocket mirror; or perhaps a cloven-hoofed Pan,[7] piping nuptial ditties as he **B** danced his invisible way before them, strewing wild buds on the walk and purple grapes in their path, symbolizing fruit of a union, though there was of course still none.

Lily startled Leo by remarking, "I was thinking of Mr. Salzman, a curious figure, wouldn't you say?"

Not certain what to answer, he nodded.

She bravely went on, blushing, "I for one am grateful for his introducing us. Aren't you?"

He courteously replied, "I am."

"I mean," she said with a little laugh—and it was all in good taste, or at least gave the effect of being not in bad—"do you mind that we came together so?"

He was not displeased with her honesty, recognizing that she meant to set the relationship aright, and understanding that it took a certain amount of experience in life, and courage, to want to do it quite that way. One had to have some sort of past to make that kind of beginning.

He said that he did not mind. Salzman's function was traditional and honorable—valuable for what it might achieve, which, he pointed out, was frequently nothing.

Lily agreed with a sigh. They walked on for a while and she said after a long silence, again with a nervous laugh, "Would you mind if I asked you something a little bit personal? Frankly, I find the subject fascinating." Although Leo shrugged, she went on half embarrassedly, "How was it that you came to your calling? I mean was it a sudden passionate inspiration?"

Leo, after a time, slowly replied, "I was always interested in the Law."[8]

"You saw revealed in it the presence of the Highest?"

He nodded and changed the subject. "I understand that you spent a little time in Paris, Miss Hirschorn?"

"Oh, did Mr. Salzman tell you, Rabbi Finkle?" Leo winced but she went on, "It was ages ago and almost forgotten. I remember I had to return for my sister's wedding."

And Lily would not be put off. "When," she asked in a trembly voice, "did you become enamored of God?"

He stared at her. Then it came to him that she was talking not about Leo Finkle, but of a total stranger, some mystical figure, perhaps even passionate prophet that Salzman had dreamed up for her—no relation to the living or dead. Leo trembled with rage and weakness. The trickster had obviously sold her a bill of goods, just as he had him, who'd expected to become acquainted with a young lady of twenty-nine, only to behold, the moment he laid eyes upon her strained

6. ***au courant*** (ō ko͞o·*rän*): French for "in the current," that is, up-to-date on news or events.

7. **Pan:** in Greek mythology, a god associated with forests, pastures, flocks, and shepherds. Pan is usually pictured as having the legs, horns, and ears of a goat, and the head and upper body of a man. He plays music on reed pipes.

8. **Law:** first five books of the Bible, the most sacred texts of Judaism. These books are also called the Torah or the Five Books of Moses.

Words to Own

nuptial (nup′shəl) *adj.:* related to weddings or marriage.

traditional (trə·dish′ə·nel) *adj.:* established; customary.

B. Reader's Response: Challenging the Text

? What is Malamud's purpose in having Leo suspect that Salzman is up in a tree watching him or having Leo imagine Pan? [Sample responses: He could be exaggerating for comic effect or showing how strong an impression Salzman has made on Leo. These two images also foreshadow the story's final scene.]

CROSSING THE CURRICULUM

Social Sciences To help students understand the historical and cultural context of the story, assign student groups to research and make an oral presentation on:

1. The post–World War II period for Jews in New York
2. Yeshivah University
3. *Jewish Daily Forward*

Group leaders should assign a different section of the report to each student.

Fine Arts To help students analyze the image of the winged loaves of bread or other images from the story, bring in posters or art books to show examples of surreal paintings. Assign student pairs to research and give oral reports on one of the surrealist painters: Magritte, Dali, Miró, Ernst, or Chagall.

A. Literary Element: Point of View

? Why do you think Malamud chose a third-person point of view in this story rather than first person, even though everything is seen through the eyes of Finkle? [Possible answer: A third-person limited point of view distances the author from the protagonist, whereas first person may have made the reader identify too closely with the protagonist.]

and anxious face, a woman past thirty-five and aging rapidly. Only his self-control had kept him this long in her presence.

"I am not," he said gravely, "a talented religious person," and in seeking words to go on, found himself possessed by shame and fear. "I think," he said in a strained manner, "that I came to God not because I loved Him, but because I did not."

This confession he spoke harshly because its unexpectedness shook him.

Lily wilted. Leo saw a profusion of loaves of bread go flying like ducks high over his head, not unlike the winged loaves by which he had counted himself to sleep last night. Mercifully, then, it snowed, which he would not put past Salzman's machinations.

He was infuriated with the marriage broker and swore he would throw him out of the room the minute he reappeared. But Salzman did not come that night, and when Leo's anger had subsided, an unaccountable despair grew in its place. At first he thought this was caused by his disappointment in Lily, but before long it became evident that he had involved himself with Salzman without a true knowledge of his own intent. He gradually realized—with an emptiness that seized him with six hands—that he had called in the broker to find him a bride because he was incapable of doing it himself. This terrifying insight he had derived as a result of his meeting and conversation with Lily Hirschorn. Her probing questions had somehow irritated him into revealing—to himself more than her—the true nature of his relationship to God, and from that it had come upon him, with shocking force, that apart from his parents, he had never loved anyone. Or perhaps it went the other way, that he did not love God so well as he might, because he had not loved man. It seemed to Leo that his whole life stood starkly revealed and he saw himself for the first time as he truly was—unloved and loveless. This bitter but somehow not fully unexpected revelation brought him to a point of panic, controlled only by extraordinary effort. He covered his face with his hands and cried.

A The week that followed was the worst of his life. He did not eat and lost weight. His beard darkened and grew ragged. He stopped attending seminars and almost never opened a book. He seriously considered leaving the Yeshivah, although he was deeply troubled at the thought of the loss of all his years of study—saw them like pages torn from a book, strewn over the city—and at the devastating effect of this decision upon his parents. But he had lived without knowledge of himself, and never in the Five Books and all the Commentaries—mea culpa[9]—had the truth been revealed to him. He did not know where to turn, and in all this desolating loneliness there was no *to whom,* although he often thought of Lily but not once could bring himself to go downstairs and make the call. He became touchy and irritable, especially with his landlady, who asked him all manner of personal questions; on the other hand, sensing his own disagreeableness, he waylaid her on the stairs and apologized abjectly, until mortified, she ran from him. Out of this, however, he drew the consolation that he was a Jew and that a Jew suffered. But gradually, as the long and terrible week drew to a close, he regained his composure and some idea of purpose in life: to go on as planned. Although he was imperfect, the ideal was not. As for his quest of a bride, the thought of continuing afflicted him with anxiety and heartburn, yet perhaps with this new knowledge of himself he would be more successful than in the past. Perhaps love would now come to him and a bride to that love. And for this sanctified seeking who needed a Salzman?

The marriage broker, a skeleton with haunted eyes, returned that very night. He looked, withal, the picture of frustrated expectancy—as if he had steadfastly waited the week at Miss Lily Hirschorn's side for a telephone call that never came.

Casually coughing, Salzman came immediately to the point: "So how did you like her?"

9. ***mea culpa*** (mā′ä ko͞ol′pä): Latin for "by my fault."

WORDS TO OWN

machinations (mak′ə·nā′shənz) *n. pl.:* plots; schemes.

evident (ev′ə·dənt) *adj.:* clear; obvious.

OPTIONS FOR TEACHING

PROBLEM SOLVING/CRITICAL THINKING

A Little Disagreement Finkle and Salzman disagree about the characteristics Finkle's bride should possess. Their negotiations do not go well, in part because Salzman has a preconceived idea of the kind of woman a rabbi should marry. Salzman also has ideas of what a rabbi should be and projects these ideas onto Finkle. However, Finkle feels that he should determine what he wants in a bride and that people should not make him out to be someone he is not. Have the class discuss what people should do when others fail to see them for who they are, and how they could better communicate their needs.

The Rabbi by Marc Chagall.

RESPONDING TO THE ART: ABOUT THE ARTIST

Marc Chagall was born into a Hasidic Jewish family. In paintings such as *The Rabbi,* he calls up images he remembers from his Jewish heritage. His realistic images are rendered surrealistically; his scenes carry a pictorial symbolism. How might *The Rabbi* be representative of Finkle in "The Magic Barrel"? [Possible responses: It shows a rabbi lost in thought and worry as Finkle might have been. It shows the rabbi alone and isolated from the world as Finkle may have been before meeting Salzman. The star of David and the book, possibly a Bible or commentary, may show how devoted the rabbi is to the study of God. Finkle, too, has been devoted to such a study.]

PROFESSIONAL NOTES

Critical Comment: The Sorrow of a Generation Mark Shechner, reviewing *The Stories of Bernard Malamud* (1983) emphasizes Malamud's attention to the "sad music of humanity": "It is a commonplace of criticism that [Malamud's characters] are ruined by circumstance, but it is less often observed that those circumstances are helped along by their own narrowness and rigidity.

"So deeply ingrained is this woe that it seems virtually biological. . . . But in the first postwar decade, it had the full sanction of the times and was well-nigh universal among Jewish writers and intellectuals. The sorrow that penetrates to the bone in Malamud was the mood of a generation of Jewish writers who had been raised on immigrant poverty and worldwide depression and brought abruptly to adulthood by the holocaust. Low spirits came as naturally to them as hunger or ambition or breath."

Cultural Diversity Leo seems to be honoring his Jewish heritage while accommodating his New York identity. This situation provides an opportunity to discuss the multiplicity of cultures that influence people and American society. Have students discuss the cultures that have influenced their lives. *Remind students to choose information they would not mind sharing with others.*

A. Literary Element: Metaphor

? Why is the metaphorical snow on Salzman effective in this situation? [Salzman is a *schlemiel,* who always encounters disasters; here, Malamud uses a snowstorm image. Salzman's face turns white when he is accused of lying by his "rabbi" client.]

B. Reader's Response: Shaping Interpretations

? Why does Salzman hurry away after leaving the manila envelope? [Sample responses: He knows Finkle wants nothing more to do with him, but hopes that Finkle will find someone marriageable in the packet. Or Salzman has learned that the way to arrange a match with Finkle is to show him what Finkle is interested in—pictures.]

Leo's anger rose and he could not refrain from chiding the matchmaker: "Why did you lie to me, Salzman?" (A)

Salzman's pale face went dead white, the world had snowed on him.

"Did you not state that she was twenty-nine?" Leo insisted.

"I give you my word—"

"She was thirty-five, if a day. *At least* thirty-five."

"Of this don't be too sure. Her father told me—"

"Never mind. The worst of it was that you lied to her."

"How did I lie to her, tell me?"

"You told her things about me that weren't true. You made me out to be more, consequently less than I am. She had in mind a totally different person, a sort of semi-mystical Wonder Rabbi."

"All I said, you was a religious man."

"I can imagine."

Salzman sighed. "This is my weakness that I have," he confessed. "My wife says to me I shouldn't be a salesman, but when I have two fine people that they would be wonderful to be married, I am so happy that I talk too much." He smiled wanly. "This is why Salzman is a poor man."

Leo's anger left him. "Well, Salzman, I'm afraid that's all."

The marriage broker fastened hungry eyes on him.

"You don't want any more a bride?"

"I do," said Leo, "but I have decided to seek her in a different way. I am no longer interested in an arranged marriage. To be frank, I now admit the necessity of premarital love. That is, I want to be in love with the one I marry."

"Love?" said Salzman, astounded. After a moment he remarked, "For us, our love is our life, not for the ladies. In the ghetto they—"

"I know, I know," said Leo. "I've thought of it often. Love, I have said to myself, should be a by-product of living and worship rather than its own end. Yet for myself I find it necessary to establish the level of my need and fulfill it."

Salzman shrugged but answered, "Listen, rabbi, if you want love, this I can find for you also. I have such beautiful clients that you will love them the minute your eyes will see them."

Leo smiled unhappily. "I'm afraid you don't understand."

But Salzman hastily unstrapped his portfolio and withdrew a manila packet from it.

"Pictures," he said, quickly laying the envelope on the table. (B)

Leo called after him to take the pictures away, but as if on the wings of the wind, Salzman had disappeared.

March came. Leo had returned to his regular routine. Although he felt not quite himself yet—lacked energy—he was making plans for a more active social life. Of course it would cost something, but he was an expert in cutting corners; and when there were no corners left he would make circles rounder. All the while Salzman's pictures had lain on the table, gathering dust. Occasionally as Leo sat studying, or enjoying a cup of tea, his eyes fell on the manila envelope, but he never opened it.

The days went by and no social life to speak of developed with a member of the opposite sex—it was difficult, given the circumstances of his situation. One morning Leo toiled up the stairs to his room and stared out the window at the city. Although the day was bright his view of it was dark. For some time he watched the people in the street below hurrying along and then turned with a heavy heart to his little room. On the table was the packet. With a sudden relentless gesture he tore it open. For a half-hour he stood by the table in a state of excitement, examining the photographs of the ladies Salzman had included. Finally, with a deep sigh he put them down. There were six, of varying degrees of attractiveness, but look at them long enough and they all became Lily Hirschorn: all past their prime, all starved behind bright smiles, not a true personality in the lot. Life, despite their frantic yoohooings, had passed them by; they were pictures in a briefcase that stank of fish. After a while, however, as Leo attempted to return the photographs into the envelope, he found in it another, a snapshot of the type taken by a machine for a quarter. He gazed at it a moment and let out a cry.

Her face deeply moved him. Why, he could at first not say. It gave him the impression of youth—spring flowers, yet age—a sense of

OPTIONS FOR TEACHING

ASSESSMENT TOOLS

Peer Assessment In the same groups that wrote the film scripts described in Integrating the Language Arts on p. T984, have students exchange scripts with another group and rate the scripts one to five (five being the highest) for the following criteria:

- Action and dialogue that are faithful to the story.
- Believable characters with clearly motivated actions.
- Stage and camera directions that add to the dialogue.

Ask peer groups to write additional comments on these criteria and to return their evaluations to the script writers. Have groups revise scripts after receiving the evaluations.

Check Test: Fill-in-the-Blank

1. The favorite food of Pinye Salzman, the matchmaker, is __________. [fish]
2. Finkle wants Pinye to call him "Mr. Finkle" because he has not yet become __________. [a rabbi]
3. At first Finkle is not interested in Lily, the high school teacher, saying that she is ________. [too old]
4. In response to Lily's questions, Finkle says that he decided to study at Yeshivah because he was not enamored of ______. [God]
5. At the very end of the story, Pinye Salzman is chanting prayers for ___________. [the dead]

having been used to the bone, wasted; this came from the eyes, which were hauntingly familiar, yet absolutely strange. He had a vivid impression that he had met her before, but try as he might he could not place her although he could almost recall her name, as if he had read it in her own handwriting. No, this couldn't be; he would have remembered her. It was not, he affirmed, that she had an extraordinary beauty—no, though her face was attractive enough; it was that *something* about her moved him. Feature for feature, even some of the ladies of the photographs could do better; but she leaped forth to his heart—had *lived,* or wanted to—more than just wanted, perhaps regretted how she had lived—had somehow deeply suffered: It could be seen in the depths of those reluctant eyes, and from the way the light enclosed and shone from her, and within her, opening realms of possibility: This was her own. Her he desired. His head ached and eyes narrowed with the intensity of his gazing, then as if an obscure fog had blown up in the mind, he experienced fear of her and was aware that he had received an impression, somehow, of evil. He shuddered, saying softly, it is thus with us all. Leo brewed some tea in a small pot and sat sipping it without sugar, to calm himself. But before he had finished drinking, again with excitement he examined the face and found it good: good for Leo Finkle. Only such a one could understand him and help him seek whatever he was seeking. She might, perhaps, love him. How she had happened to be among the discards in Salzman's barrel he could never guess, but he knew he must urgently go find her.

Leo rushed downstairs, grabbed up the Bronx[10] telephone book, and searched for Salzman's home address. He was not listed, nor was his office. Neither was he in the Manhattan[11] book. But Leo remembered having written down the address on a slip of paper after he had read Salzman's advertisement in the "personals" column of the *Forward.* He ran up to his room and tore through his papers, without luck. It was exasperating. Just when he needed the matchmaker he was nowhere to be found. Fortunately Leo remembered to look in his wallet. There on a card he found his name written and a Bronx address. No phone number was listed, the reason—Leo now recalled—he had originally communicated with Salzman by letter. He got on his coat, put a hat on over his skullcap and hurried to the subway station. All the way to the far end of the Bronx he sat on the edge of his seat. He was more than once tempted to take out the picture and see if the girl's face was as he remembered it, but he refrained, allowing the snapshot to remain in his inside coat pocket, content to have her so close. When the train pulled into the station he was waiting at the door and bolted out. He quickly located the street Salzman had advertised.

The building he sought was less than a block from the subway, but it was not an office building, nor even a loft, nor a store in which one could rent office space. It was a very old tenement house. Leo found Salzman's name in pencil on a soiled tag under the bell and climbed three dark flights to his apartment. When he knocked, the door was opened by a thin, asthmatic, gray-haired woman, in felt slippers.

"Yes?" she said, expecting nothing. She listened without listening. He could have sworn he had seen her, too, before but knew it was an illusion.

"Salzman—does he live here? Pinye Salzman," he said, "the matchmaker?"

She stared at him a long minute. "Of course."

He felt embarrassed. "Is he in?"

"No." Her mouth, though left open, offered nothing more.

"The matter is urgent. Can you tell me where his office is?"

"In the air." She pointed upward.

"You mean he has no office?" Leo asked.

"In his socks."

He peered into the apartment. It was sunless and dingy, one large room divided by a half-open curtain, beyond which he could see a sagging metal bed. The near side of the room was crowded with rickety chairs, old bureaus, a three-legged table, racks of cooking utensils, and all the apparatus of a kitchen. But there was no

10. Bronx: borough of New York City.
11. Manhattan: borough of New York City, south of the Bronx.

C. Literary Element: Foreshadowing

? What is the effect of Finkle's thinking that the woman's eyes are familiar and that he has met her before? [Possible answers: It foreshadows a connection with Salzman; a sense of recognition is an indication of true love.]

D. Reader's Response: Shaping Interpretations

? What does Finkle see in this woman that matches what he is looking for in a wife? [Sample responses: Finkle wants a younger woman, someone who can help him find what he wants in life. Her suffering and youth may help her love him for who he is, not for what he does or for how much he is worth.]

E. Critical Reading: Finding Cause and Effect

? What do Salzman's lack of a telephone number and the very old tenement in which he lives tell about his matchmaking business? [Possible answers: It is not prospering. Or business is not good for matchmakers in general.]

F. Literary Element: Foreshadowing

? How does Finkle's feeling that he has seen Mrs. Salzman before heighten the tension in the story? [It provides further foreshadowing and increases the reader's feelings that something momentous is about to happen to Finkle.]

A. Critical Reading: Predicting
? Why is Salzman unable to tell Finkel the identity of the woman in the picture? [Possible answers: It is a woman who has done something wrong. It is someone related to Salzman.]

sign of Salzman or his magic barrel, probably also a figment of the imagination. An odor of frying fish made Leo weak to the knees.

"Where is he?" he insisted. "I've got to see your husband."

At length she answered, "So who knows where he is? Every time he thinks a new thought he runs to a different place. Go home, he will find you."

"Tell him Leo Finkle."

She gave no sign she had heard.

He walked downstairs, depressed.

But Salzman, breathless, stood waiting at his door.

Leo was astounded and overjoyed. "How did you get here before me?"

"I rushed."

"Come inside."

They entered. Leo fixed tea, and a sardine sandwich for Salzman. As they were drinking he reached behind him for the packet of pictures and handed them to the marriage broker.

Salzman put down his glass and said expectantly, "You found somebody you like?"

"Not among these."

The marriage broker turned away.

"Here is the one I want." Leo held forth the snapshot.

Salzman slipped on his glasses and took the picture into his trembling hand. He turned ghastly and let out a groan.

"What's the matter?" cried Leo.

"Excuse me. Was an accident this picture. She isn't for you."

Salzman frantically shoved the manila packet into his portfolio. He thrust the snapshot into his pocket and fled down the stairs.

Leo, after momentary paralysis, gave chase and cornered the marriage broker in the vestibule. The landlady made hysterical outcries but neither of them listened.

"Give me back the picture, Salzman."

"No." The pain in his eyes was terrible.

A "Tell me who she is then."

"This I can't tell you. Excuse me."

He made to depart, but Leo, forgetting himself, seized the matchmaker by his tight coat and shook him frenziedly.

"Please," sighed Salzman. "*Please.*"

Leo ashamedly let him go. "Tell me who she is," he begged. "It's very important for me to know."

"She is not for you. She is a wild one—wild, without shame. This is not a bride for a rabbi."

"What do you mean wild?"

"Like an animal. Like a dog. For her to be poor was a sin. This is why to me she is dead now."

"In God's name, what do you mean?"

"Her I can't introduce to you," Salzman cried.

"Why are you so excited?"

"Why, he asks," Salzman said, bursting into tears. "This is my baby, my Stella, she should burn in hell."

Leo hurried up to bed and hid under the covers. Under the covers he thought his life through. Although he soon fell asleep he could not sleep her out of his mind. He woke, beating his breast. Though he prayed to be rid of her, his prayers went unanswered. Through days of torment he endlessly struggled not to love her; fearing success, he escaped it. He then concluded to convert her to goodness, himself to God. The idea alternately nauseated and exalted him.

He perhaps did not know that he had come to a final decision until he encountered Salzman in a Broadway cafeteria. He was sitting alone at a rear table, sucking the bony remains of a fish. The marriage broker appeared haggard, and transparent to the point of vanishing.

Salzman looked up at first without recognizing him. Leo had grown a pointed beard and his eyes were weighted with wisdom.

"Salzman," he said, "love has at last come to my heart."

"Who can love from a picture?" mocked the marriage broker.

"It is not impossible."

"If you can love her, then you can love anybody. Let me show you some new clients that they just sent me their photographs. One is a little doll."

"Just her I want," Leo murmured.

"Don't be a fool, doctor. Don't bother with her."

"Put me in touch with her, Salzman," Leo said humbly. "Perhaps I can be of service."

Salzman had stopped eating and Leo understood with emotion that it was now arranged.

Leaving the cafeteria, he was, however, afflicted by a tormenting suspicion that Salzman had planned it all to happen this way.

Leo was informed by letter that she would meet him on a certain corner, and she was there one spring night, waiting under a street lamp. He appeared, carrying a small bouquet of violets and rosebuds. Stella stood by the lamppost, smoking. She wore white with red shoes, which fitted his expectations, although in a troubled moment he had imagined the dress red, and only the shoes white. She waited uneasily and shyly. From afar he saw that her eyes—clearly her father's—were filled with desperate innocence. He pictured, in her, his own redemption. Violins and lit candles revolved in the sky. Leo ran forward with flowers outthrust. 

Around the corner, Salzman, leaning against a wall, chanted prayers for the dead. 

Critical Comment

A Tale of Self-Discovery

At the opening of this story, a lonely young rabbinical student decides to contact a marriage broker through a newspaper ad. Leo Finkle has been immersed in his studies for six years, he is painfully shy, and he can think of no other way to meet suitable young women. (If the custom seems strange, think of the thousands of people today who use dating services.)

Finkle's attitudes have been shaped by years of study and theological debate. It is not surprising that he has had very little time to think about his social life. The tradition of the marriage broker, seemingly exotic in America, was familiar to European Jews in the early part of this century. Brokers fulfilled a genuine social function by negotiating between families and easing embarrassment. It was inevitable that, in some of these arranged marriages, the chief feature was not the partners' mutual devotion but the financial or social advantages to the families involved. (D)

Finkle is portrayed as wavering between two worlds. In the old world of his parents (who owed their marriage to a broker), social criteria for marriage were more important than love. Leo himself is originally impelled to look for a wife by an acquaintance's suggestion that "he might find it easier to win himself a congregation if he were married." In his first conversations with Salzman, Finkle is preoccupied by external, superficial criteria. But a profound change is at work in Leo, and he reaches a turning point when he suddenly finds himself admitting to the pleasant but superficial Lily that "I came to God not because I loved Him, but because I did not." The story then shows him dramatically, even transcendentally, caught up in love at first sight. As you think about the story, consider the possibility that Malamud's real interest is not in the probability—or even the future consequences—of Leo's change of heart. Perhaps the writer wants us to witness Leo Finkle's process of self-discovery: his initiation into a new world, where he can exist as an authentic person, capable of love.

Italian Passover plate (c. 1850). Faience pottery.
The Granger Collection, New York.

STRATEGIES FOR INCLUSION

Intrapersonal Have students write in their Reader's Logs what Finkle discovers about himself as discussed in Critical Comment. [Possible answers: Finkle learns that if he is going to be an "authentic" person he must look deeper inside himself. He knows at the end of the story that he is now capable of love because he now loves who he is.]

Interpersonal To help make the tradition of the marriage broker less strange, after reading Critical Comment, have students discuss modern concepts of matchmaking such as personal ads and dating services. Ask them to talk about how each works and whether they believe these systems can successfully bring people together. Then, have them compare these ways of finding a suitable partner with matchmaking.

B. Literary Element: Climax
The first climax occurs when Finkle confesses to Lily that he does not believe in God. What is the second of the two climaxes in the story? [Finkle's rush toward Stella.] What effect on the reader do the two climaxes have? [Emotional impact and excitement; the two climaxes reveal the changes in Finkle—first he is devastated by realizing his feelings toward God. However, this realization enables him to embrace love at the end.]

C. Literary Element: Static and Dynamic Characters
? Is Salzman a static or dynamic character? [Possible answers: Dynamic, for he now hopes that Leo will be able to return Stella to her family by redeeming her. Or static, because he still considers Stella as "dead."]

D. Exploring the Culture
? What might have intensified this need for a broker? [The Jewish culture throughout history is a story of a culture nearly wiped out. Consistency, via happy marriages between Jews, would preserve social, cultural, and religious practices. The broker took the guesswork out of seeking a suitable partner.]

Making Meanings questions begin on p. 994

Making Meanings

First Thoughts

1. Possible responses: She somehow brought "disgrace" upon her family, perhaps by running off with a man or by having a child out of wedlock.

Reviewing the Text

a. A young rabbinical student named Leo Finkle, who lives in New York City. About to be ordained, he thinks it will be easier to find employment if he is married.
b. He appears one night in the dark, perhaps implying adverse circumstances or a tragic past. His hat is old and his overcoat fits badly. He smells of fish, and his eyes are mournful and sad.
c. He discovers a truth about himself when he admits to Lily that he came to God because he did *not* love Him. Finkle also realizes that he has never loved anyone, apart from his parents.
d. It seems to Finkle that this woman, like him, has suffered

Answers to Making Meanings begin on p. T993

deeply somehow. He feels this woman might understand and possibly even love him.

Shaping Interpretations

2. Finkle may be saying that he is trying to atone for his sins by undertaking his studies or that some divine grace attracted him to the service of God. The theme of the story involves the power of love and the onset of maturity. To love sincerely, one must first be honest about what one loves and does not love. Finkle's confession provides him with sudden answers to unasked questions about his relation to God and his relation to women. He opts for a deeper relationship rather than a superficial one.
3. Possible responses: He has found someone he can love. He may want to be redeemed from alienation and loneliness.
4. Possible responses: That he can love. That love may be found in places where we least expect it. That which we think is opposite to us may be the exact thing we are seeking. He no longer feels he needs a broker to pick an ideal wife.
5. Possible responses: Stella seems nice enough; she does show up and is even nervous about the meeting. Salzman is still sincere in his opposition to their meeting. Or her picture is included in the packet Salzman leaves with Finkle; he did arrange for the meeting.
6. Possible responses: On a positive note, for by saying prayers for the dead, Salzman hopes his daughter will be redeemed. Or on a negative note, for he still thinks of Stella as dead to him.
7. In a literal sense, the barrel (which may not exist) is the place where the broker keeps pictures and related information about potential mates. In a figurative sense it contains the "magic" of love, for out of the barrel marriages are made. In a broader sense, the title symbolizes the strange way in which chance or Salzman's cleverness has brought together Stella and Finkle.

Extending the Text

8. **(Synthesis)** Possible responses: They may stay together because Finkle has learned valuable lessons about love, life, and happiness. Or they will not stay together because Stella is wild.

Making Meanings

First Thoughts

1. What do you think caused Stella's father to regard her as dead?

Reviewing the Text

a. According to the first paragraph, who is the story's protagonist, and what does he want?
b. Another character—Pinye Salzman—is introduced in the second paragraph. Find the descriptive details that hint of something tragic in his past.
c. Explain what Finkle discovers about himself after the experience with Lily.
d. Why does Finkle fall in love with the woman in the photograph?

Shaping Interpretations

2. Finkle confesses to Lily, "I came to God not because I loved Him, but because I did not." How would you explain this **paradox,** or seeming contradiction?
3. Why do you think Finkle pictures in Stella his own redemption? What does he want to be redeemed *from*?
4. Summarize what you think Finkle has learned about love and about himself by the end of the story. Has he changed in an important way?
5. What do you think of the scene with Finkle and Stella near the end of the story? Do you think Salzman arranged a marriage for Finkle after all?
6. Does Malamud end the story on a positive or a negative note? How would you explain the last sentence of the story: "Around the corner, Salzman, leaning against a wall, chanted prayers for the dead"?
7. Explain the story's **title.**

Extending the Text

8. What do you think will happen to Leo and Stella once they learn more about each other? Will they marry? Will they drift apart? Consult your Quickwrite notes for ideas.

Choices: Building Your Portfolio

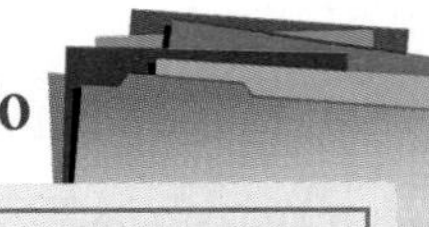

Writer's Notebook

1. Collecting Ideas for an Evaluation

What makes for skillful characterization? Create a chart to organize the criteria you'd use to evaluate the characters Leo Finkle and Pinye Salzman in "The Magic Barrel." In column one, enter five or six qualities that make for skillful characterization. (Two criteria might be that a character be **believable** and **dynamic.**) In columns two and three (headed "Leo" and "Pinye"), list specific examples from the text that show how each character meets (or does not meet) each criterion. Save your notes for possible use in the Writer's Workshop on page 1181.

Critical Writing

2. What's at the Heart of Malamud?

Select one of the following comments about Bernard Malamud's fiction, and write a brief essay responding to it. Tell whether or not the comment has to do with the **plot, characters,** or **theme** of "The Magic Barrel."

a. "Malamud has always had a fondness for telling tales arranged for the purpose of a specific moral lesson." (Alan Lelchuk)
b. "What it is to be human, and to be humane, is his [Malamud's] deepest concern." (Philip Roth)

Creative Writing

3. Stella by Starlight

One spring night, Leo runs toward Stella "with flowers outthrust." That's about where "The Magic Barrel" ends. What might they say to each other? Write some lines of dialogue—with no other commentary—that you imagine Leo and Stella might say as they meet for the first time. Who speaks first?

Choices: Building Your Portfolio

1. **Writer's Notebook** Remind students to save their work. They may use it as prewriting for the Writer's Workshop on p. 1181.

PORTFOLIO ASSESSMENT

Choices: Assessment Criteria For help in evaluating these Choices assignments, see the criteria in the ***Portfolio Management System,*** p. 187.

LITERATURE OF THE AMERICAS
COLOMBIA

Gabriel García Márquez
(1928–   )

Gabriel García Márquez (gä′brē·el′ gär·sē′ä mär′kes) was born in Aracataca, Colombia, the town that became the model for the fictional village of Macondo in his popular novel *One Hundred Years of Solitude* (1970). He spent his early years with his maternal grandparents, whom he regards as "wonderful beings." According to García Márquez, "They had an enormous house, full of ghosts. They were people of great imagination and superstitions. In every corner there were dead people and memories, and after six o'clock in the [evening] the house was untraversable. It was a world prodigious with terror. There were conversations in code."

After attending universities in Bogotá and Cartagena, García Márquez worked as a journalist in Colombia and in Rome, Paris, Barcelona, Caracas, and New York. Newspaper work helped García Márquez (like Ernest Hemingway) develop a style of writing fiction. Even after ending his newspaper career in 1965, García Márquez considered himself to be at heart a journalist, which is one reason for the factual or realistic basis for his fiction. It also accounts for his occasional books and articles on contemporary politics. Because of serious political differences with the Colombian government, he lives in self-imposed exile in Mexico City.

García Márquez has achieved international renown mainly for his fiction, which includes, besides *One Hundred Years of Solitude, The Autumn of the Patriarch* (1976), *Love in the Time of Cholera* (1988), *Strange Pilgrims* (1993), and *Of Love and Other Demons* (1995). He was awarded the Nobel Prize in literature in 1982.

Carlos Angel/Gamma Liaison.

Gabriel García Márquez signing autographs in the streets of Cartagena.

Technology Tip

Students can locate links to resources about García Márquez on the Internet by accessing **http://www.microserve.net/~thequail/libyrinth/garcia.marquez.html.** *You may want to preview any Internet activity that you suggest to students. Because these resources are sometimes public forums, their content can be unpredictable.*

PROGRAM MANAGER

Planning Instruction See **Teaching Notes, *Teaching Resources B*,** p. 158, for objectives and a summary.

Background

Ask students to look for the mythical elements of magic realism as they read the story. They may discover such features as a focus on a superhuman character, the occurrence of supernatural events, or characters that transform shape. Have students write in their Reader's Logs the mythical elements they discover in the story.

A Dialogue with the Text

Students may wish to work together to be sure they have found answers to the questions. Have pairs meet to compare notes after reading two or three paragraphs and writing about them. Have them continue the process until the entire story is read.

Technology Tip

TECHNOLOGY García Márquez is known for a style of writing known as magic realism. Have students create their own brand of magic realism using computer technology. Ask them to write original stories in hypertext on the computer and to include links to sounds, pictures, and movie clips.

Before You Read

The Handsomest Drowned Man in the World

Background

Gabriel García Márquez blends **realism** with playful imagination to create a type of literature known as **magic realism.** Developed in Latin America around the middle of the twentieth century, the genre has proved popular and influential in much of the world. You can see echoes of magic (also called marvelous) realism in works by such noted U.S. authors as Donald Barthelme (page 955), Thomas Pynchon, and Kurt Vonnegut, Jr., and in the writing of Günter Grass of Germany and John Fowles of England. A key novel of magic realism is García Márquez's best-selling *Cien años de soledad* (1967), translated into English as *One Hundred Years of Solitude* (1970).

According to a perceptive analysis by the literary critic David Young, "One way to understand magic realism is as a kind of pleasant joke on realism, suggesting as it does a new kind of fiction, produced in reaction to the confining assumptions of realism. [Magic realism is] a hybrid that somehow manages to combine the truthful and verifiable aspects of realism with the magical effects we associate with myth, folk tale, tall story, and that being in all of us—our childhood self, perhaps—who loves the spell that narrative casts even when it is perfectly implausible." The critic James Park Sloan observes that an essential element of García Márquez's magic realism is "a steadily toneless background in which everyday events become marvelous and marvelous events are assimilated without comment into everyday life."

García Márquez identifies an additional important aspect of his writing: "There's no doubt nostalgia is one of the important ingredients of my books and life. I make decisions, basic decisions, out of sheer nostalgia. Nostalgia gives my books the distance they bear from reality."

A Dialogue with the Text

As you read this story by García Márquez, write down your responses to the following questions. Where appropriate, back up your responses by quoting passages from the story.

- The author subtitles the story "A Tale for Children." In what ways do you need to become childlike again in order to really enjoy this work?
- Which passages remind you in general of a **myth,** legend, or folk tale? Are you reminded at any point of a specific myth or tale?
- How does the villagers' attitude toward the drowned man change over the course of the story?
- What ultimate effect does the arrival of the drowned man have on the villagers' lives?
- What did you find puzzling or difficult to understand about this story?

Art on pages 996, 997, 999 by Sergio Bustamente/Photo by Clint Clemens.

Connecting with "Discoveries and Awakenings"

In Márquez's story the villagers live essentially mundane and unexamined lives until the drowned man appears; afterward, their world is never the same. The villagers create the identity of the drowned man much as Salzman tries to create an image of Finkle that does not exist. Finkle, however, discovers himself when talking with Lily and after seeing Stella's photograph. Like the villagers, Finkle changes dramatically as he begins to examine his life. Ask students to discuss the discoveries the characters in these stories make and the discoveries the speakers, characters, and authors make in the other selections in the Collection.

The Handsomest Drowned Man in the World

Gabriel García Márquez

***translated by* Gregory Rabassa**

A Tale for Children

The first children who saw the dark and slinky bulge approaching through the sea let themselves think it was an enemy ship. Then they saw it had no flags or masts and they thought it was a whale. But when it was washed up on the beach, they removed the clumps of seaweed, the jellyfish tentacles, and the remains of fish and flotsam, and only then did they see that it was a drowned man. (A)

They had been playing with him all afternoon, burying him in the sand and digging him up again, when someone chanced to see them and spread the alarm in the village. The men who carried him to the nearest house noticed that he weighed more than any dead man they had ever known, almost as much as a horse, and they said to each other that maybe he'd been floating too long and the water had got into his bones. When they laid him on the floor they said he'd been taller than all other men because there was barely enough room for him in the house, but they thought that maybe the ability to keep on growing after death was part of the nature of certain drowned men. He had the smell of the sea about him and only his shape gave one to suppose that it was the corpse of a human being, because the skin was covered with a crust of mud and scales.

They did not even have to clean off his face to know that the dead man was a stranger. The village was made up of only twenty-odd wooden houses that had stone courtyards with no flowers and which were spread about on the end of a desertlike cape. There was so little land that mothers always went about with the fear that the wind would carry off their children and the few dead that the years had caused among them had to be thrown off the cliffs. But the sea was calm and bountiful and all the men fit into seven boats. So when they found the drowned man they simply had to look at one another to see that they were all there. (B)

That night they did not go out to work at sea. While the men went to find out if anyone was missing in neighboring villages, the women stayed behind to care for the drowned man. They took the mud off with grass swabs, they removed the underwater stones entangled in his hair, and they scraped the crust off with tools used for scaling fish. As they were doing that they noticed that the vegetation on him came from faraway oceans and deep water and that his clothes were in tatters, as if he had sailed through labyrinths of coral. They noticed too that he bore his death with pride, for he did not have the lonely look of other drowned men who came out of the sea or that haggard, needy look of men who drowned in rivers. But only when they finished cleaning him off did they become aware of the kind of man he

A. Reader's Response: First Thoughts

? What would your response be to finding a drowned man on the shore? [Sample responses: I would call 911. Or I would be too scared to go near him.] Why do you think García Márquez has the children play with him? [Sample responses: To make the scene playful, odd, funny, and grotesque. It is partly believable and partly unbelievable.]

B. Critical Reading: Making Inferences

The villagers' looking at each other to determine that none of them is the drowned man is a humorous moment. How would people normally find out that a corpse was not someone they had known? [They would look at the body and see that they did not recognize it.]

OPTIONS FOR TEACHING

STRATEGIES FOR INCLUSION

Spatial To help conceptualize the drowned man's physical size and dimension, put students into small groups and assign each group a section of the story to scrutinize for details that describe or refer to Esteban's size. When groups finish, compile their results on the chalkboard and work with the whole class to determine the drowned man's exact dimensions. Once computed, have a student draw an outline to scale on large art paper. Ask students to stand around it in a circle to get a sense of his size.

English Language Development Because the magic realism in this story may be difficult for students to understand, have students work in pairs to find the parts of the story that could not be true. Elicit students' results and write them on the chalkboard. Discuss with the class why García Márquez put the unreal parts into his story and what they might mean.

A. Expansion

The man's size is an example of magic realism. Its use here may stem from gigantism, a condition caused by a disorder of the pituitary gland that can cause people to grow as tall as nine feet. Most people who are extraordinarily tall are not so because of gigantism, but because of an inherited gene trait. A hormone usually regulates the growth of bones and this growth stops between the ages of eighteen and twenty-four. In gigantism, the body increases its output of this hormone and bone growth is increased. Treatment to control gigantism is available and can begin in early childhood.

B. Reader's Response: Shaping Interpretations

? Why do they say he could not be Lautaro? [Sample responses: The villagers may think a religious martyr has more power and majesty than a political hero. Or the villagers are looking for a hero of global renown rather than national renown.]

C. Critical Reading: Drawing Conclusions

? How do the men's reactions differ from the women's? [Possible answer: The women create a past for him and imagine how he might have felt; they feel sorry for him and are attracted to him. The men see the body as an inconvenience that creates more work for them; they do not attribute a past to him.]

was and it left them breathless. Not only was he the tallest, strongest, most virile, and best-built man they had ever seen, but even though they were looking at him there was no room for him in their imagination.

They could not find a bed in the village large enough to lay him on nor was there a table solid enough to use for his wake. The tallest men's holiday pants would not fit him, not the fattest ones' Sunday shirts, nor the shoes of the one with the biggest feet. Fascinated by his huge size and his beauty, the women then decided to make him some pants from a large piece of sail and a shirt from some bridal brabant linen[1] so that he could continue through his death with dignity. As they sewed, sitting in a circle and gazing at the corpse between stitches, it seemed to them that the wind had never been so steady nor the sea so restless as on that night and they supposed that the change had something to do with the dead man. They thought that if that magnificent man had lived in the village, his house would have had the widest doors, the highest ceiling, and the strongest floor, his bedstead would have been made from a midship frame held together by iron bolts, and his wife would have been the happiest woman. They thought that he would have had so much authority that he could have drawn fish out of the sea simply by calling their names and that he would have put so much work into his land that springs would have burst forth from among the rocks so that he would have been able to plant flowers on the cliffs. They secretly compared him to their own men, thinking that for all their lives theirs were incapable of doing what he could do in one night, and they ended up dismissing them deep in their hearts as the weakest, meanest, and most useless creatures on earth. They were wandering through that maze of fantasy when the oldest woman, who as the oldest had looked upon the drowned man with more compassion than passion, sighed:

"He has the face of someone called Esteban."[2]

It was true. Most of them had only to take another look at him to see that he could not have any other name. The more stubborn among them, who were the youngest, still lived for a few hours with the illusion that when they put his clothes on and he lay among the flowers in patent leather shoes his name might be Lautaro.[3] But it was a vain illusion. There had not been enough canvas, the poorly cut and worse sewn pants were too tight, and the hidden strength of his heart popped the buttons on his shirt. After midnight the whistling of the wind died down and the sea fell into its Wednesday drowsiness.[4] The silence put an end to any last doubts: he was Esteban. The women who had dressed him, who had combed his hair, had cut his nails and shaved him were unable to hold back a shudder of pity when they had to resign themselves to his being dragged along the ground. It was then that they understood how unhappy he must have been with that huge body since it bothered him even after death. They could see him in life, condemned to going through doors sideways, cracking his head on crossbeams, remaining on his feet during visits, not knowing what to do with his soft, pink, sea lion hands while the lady of the house looked for her most resistant chair and begged him, frightened to death, sit here, Esteban, please, and he, leaning against the wall, smiling, don't bother, ma'am, I'm fine where I am, his heels raw and his back roasted from having done the same thing so many times whenever he paid a visit, don't bother, ma'am, I'm fine where I am, just to avoid the embarrassment of breaking up the chair, and never knowing perhaps that the ones who said don't go, Esteban, at least wait till the coffee's ready, were the ones who later on would whisper the big boob finally left, how nice, the handsome fool has gone. That was what the women were thinking beside the body a little before dawn. Later, when they covered his face with a handkerchief so that the light would not bother him, he looked so forever dead, so defenseless, so much

1. **brabant** (brə·bant′) **linen:** linen from Brabant, a province of Belgium known for its fine lace and cloth.
2. **Esteban** (es·te′bän): Spanish equivalent for "Stephen." In Christian tradition, Stephen was the first martyr. He was stoned to death because of his beliefs.
3. **Lautaro** (lou·tä′rô): leader of Araucanian Indian people who resisted the Spanish conquistadors entering their land, in what is now Chile, during the sixteenth century. Lautaro is now seen as a Chilean national hero.
4. **Wednesday drowsiness** (and later **Wednesday meat** and **Wednesday dead body**): *Wednesday* is a colloquial expression for "tiresome." In many fishing villages, fishers returned from the sea on Thursday, so by Wednesday, people began running out of food and were generally weary and bored.

OPTIONS FOR TEACHING

INTEGRATING THE LANGUAGE ARTS

Strategic Reading Some students may have difficulty with the shifts in the story between third-person omniscient and first-person points of view. Before reading the story, alert students to these shifts and discuss why an author may alternate points of view. As they read the story, have students note in their Reader's Logs where these shifts occur and write down any questions they may have.

Writing: Found Poem Ask students to review the story and to choose eight words or phrases that best represent Esteban or the villagers. Then, ask them to meet in groups of three and to narrow their choices to four words or phrases. Then, ask each group to read one word or phrase, without pausing between groups. Continue in this fashion until all words or phrases have been read. The groups will have composed a Found Poem.

blind and divers die of nostalgia, and bad currents would not bring him back to shore, as had happened with other bodies. But the more they hurried, the more the women thought of ways to waste time. They walked about like startled hens, pecking with the sea charms[6] on their breasts, some interfering on one side to put a scapular[7] of the good wind on the drowned man, some on the other side to put a wrist compass on him, and after a great deal of *get away from there, woman, stay out of the way, look, you almost made me fall on top of the dead man,* the men began to feel mistrust in their livers and started grumbling about why so many main-altar decorations for a stranger, because no matter how many nails and holy-water jars he had on him, the sharks would chew him all the same, but the women kept piling on their junk relics, running back and forth, stumbling, while they released in sighs what they did not in tears, so that the men finally exploded with *since when has there ever been such a fuss over a drifting corpse, a drowned nobody, a piece of cold Wednesday meat.* One of the women, mortified by so much lack of care, then removed the handkerchief from the dead man's face and the men were left breathless too.

like their men that the first furrows of tears opened in their hearts. It was one of the younger ones who began the weeping. The others, coming to, went from sighs to wails, and the more they sobbed the more they felt like weeping, because the drowned man was becoming all the more Esteban for them, and so they wept so much, for he was the most destitute, most peaceful, and most obliging man on earth, poor Esteban. So when the men returned with the news that the drowned man was not from the neighboring villages either, the women felt an opening of jubilation in the midst of their tears.

"Praise the Lord," they sighed, "he's ours!"

The men thought the fuss was only womanish frivolity. Fatigued because of the difficult nighttime inquiries, all they wanted was to get rid of the bother of the newcomer once and for all before the sun grew strong on that arid, windless day. They improvised a litter with the remains of foremasts and gaffs,[5] tying it together with rigging so that it would bear the weight of the body until they reached the cliffs. They wanted to tie the anchor from a cargo ship to him so that he would sink easily into the deepest waves, where fish are

He was Esteban. It was not necessary to repeat it for them to recognize him. If they had been told Sir Walter Raleigh, even they might have been impressed with his gringo accent, the macaw[8] on his shoulder, his cannibal-killing blunderbuss,[9] but there could be only one Esteban in the world and there he was, stretched out like a sperm whale, shoeless, wearing the pants of an undersized child, and with those stony nails that had to be cut with a knife. They only had to take the handkerchief off his face to see that he was ashamed, that it was not his fault that he was so big or so heavy or so handsome, and if he had known that this

5. **gaffs:** poles used on a boat to support a sail.

6. **sea charms:** magic charms worn to protect the wearer from dangers at sea.
7. **scapular** (skap′yə·lər): a pair of small cloth squares joined at the shoulders by string, worn under clothing on the chest and back, usually worn by Catholics as a symbol of religious devotion or for good luck.
8. **macaw:** large, brightly colored parrot.
9. **blunderbuss:** a now-obsolete gun with a short, flaring muzzle.

D. Literary Element: Style

? Why might García Márquez run the men's words together and write them in italics and without quotation marks? [Possible answer: He might run them together to show the unity of the men's thinking; he might use italics to signal that these are the characters' words; he might not use quotation marks to preserve the tone of magic realism.]

ASSESSMENT TOOLS

Self-Reflection Ask students to write a paragraph assessing their own understanding of this story. Tell them to use the following format to specify what they do and do not understand about the story and to assess their overall understanding.

Circle one:

I feel (very confident, okay, not very confident, like I'm missing something crucial) about my understanding of the story because:

____

____

Check Test: Questions and Answers

1. How did the children respond to the drowned man? [They played with him all afternoon, almost as if he were a toy.]
2. How did the women's response to the drowned man change in the course of the story? [Before cleaning him up, he was just another drowned man; afterward, their imaginations created an identity for him.]
3. What name was the drowned man called and why? [Esteban, because they felt he had the face someone called Esteban.]
4. What kind of funeral was the drowned man given? [Elegant and elaborate, rich with flowers and honor.]

A. Literary Element: Point of View

Have students note the shift from third-person to first-person point of view. What is the effect of this shift? [Possible answers: The narrator comments on the action. Or the narrator almost seems to be one of the villagers. Or it plays up the magic realism of the story; the intrusion of the narrator appears to make the story seem more realistic, which contrasts strongly with the reader's knowledge that the story is fantastic.]

B. Critical Reading: Drawing Conclusions

? What do the villagers realize about their environment? [They live in a poor, desolate area and do not have momentous dreams or goals. They have been satisfied with comparatively little.]

C. Reader's Response: Shaping Interpretations

? How does the drowned man's appearance change the village? [Sample responses: They take more pride and better care of the things they have. Or the people find something that gives their lives meaning.]

Finding Common Ground

Have groups use their discussion notes to write a paragraph that states and supports the strongest conclusion that group members reached in discussing the story. Ask a member from each group to share the group's paragraph with the class. Then have the class discuss the points made in the paragraphs.

(A) was going to happen, he would have looked for a more discreet place to drown in, seriously, I even would have tied the anchor off a galleon around my neck and staggered off a cliff like someone who doesn't like things in order not to be upsetting people now with this Wednesday dead body, as you people say, in order not to be bothering anyone with this filthy piece of cold meat that doesn't have anything to do with me. There was so much truth in his manner that even the most mistrustful men, the ones who felt the bitterness of endless nights at sea fearing that their women would tire of dreaming about them and begin to dream of drowned men, even they and others who were harder still shuddered in the marrow of their bones at Esteban's sincerity.

That was how they came to hold the most splendid funeral they could conceive of for an abandoned drowned man. Some women who had gone to get flowers in the neighboring villages returned with other women who could not believe what they had been told, and those women went back for more flowers when they saw the dead man, and they brought more and more until there were so many flowers and so many people that it was hard to walk about. At the final moment it pained them to return him to the waters as an orphan and they chose a father and mother from among the best people, and aunts and uncles and cousins, so that through him all the inhabitants of the village became kinsmen. Some sailors who heard the weeping from a distance went off course and people heard of one who had himself tied to the mainmast, remembering ancient fables about sirens.[10] (B) While they fought for the privilege of carrying him on their shoulders along the steep escarpment by the cliffs, men and women became aware for the first time of the desolation of their streets, the dryness of their courtyards, the narrowness of their dreams as they faced the splendor and beauty of their drowned man. They let him go without an anchor so that he could come back if he wished and whenever he wished, and they all held their breath for the fraction of centuries the body took to fall into the abyss. They did not need to look at one another to realize that they were no longer all present, that they (C) would never be. But they also knew that everything would be different from then on, that their houses would have wider doors, higher ceilings, and stronger floors so that Esteban's memory could go everywhere without bumping into beams and so that no one in the future would dare whisper the big boob finally died, too bad, the handsome fool has finally died, because they were going to paint their house fronts gay colors to make Esteban's memory eternal and they were going to break their backs digging for springs among the stones and planting flowers on the cliffs so that in future years at dawn the passengers on great liners would awaken, suffocated by the smell of gardens on the high seas, and the captain would have to come down from the bridge in his dress uniform, with his astrolabe,[11] his polestar, and his row of war medals and, pointing to the promontory of roses on the horizon, he would say in fourteen languages, look there, where the wind is so peaceful now that it's gone to sleep beneath the beds, over there, where the sun's so bright that the sunflowers don't know which way to turn, yes, over there, that's Esteban's village.

10. **sirens:** In Greek mythology, the sirens are sea maidens whose seductive singing lures men to wreck their boats on coastal rocks. Odysseus, hero of Homer's *Odyssey,* fills his crew's ears with wax so that they can pass the sirens safely. But Odysseus wants to hear the sirens' songs and has his crew tie him to the ship's mast so he can listen without plunging into the sea.

11. **astrolabe** (as'trō·lāb'): instrument used to find a star's altitude and to help navigators determine their position at sea.

Finding Common Ground

Meet in small groups to discuss "The Handsomest Drowned Man in the World." As you talk about the story, refer to the notes you made in your Reader's Log.

- First, decide how to run your discussion group. If you want a moderator, choose a group member to fill that role.
- Second, draw up an agenda of topics for consideration. (Refer to your Reader's Log for some ideas.) It will be helpful for a group member to act as a recorder, writing down the agenda as well as the main points brought up in the discussion.

UPI/Bettmann.

Theodore Roethke

(1908–1963)

"Everything that lives is holy: I call upon these holy forms of life." These words of Theodore Roethke (ret'kē), which sound like the words of a religious ceremony, are at the core of his intense vision. For Roethke, the function of poetry is to represent in words the sanctified forms and experiences of life.

A native of Saginaw, Michigan, Roethke grew up in a family situation that had an enormous influence on his poetry. His father owned the largest greenhouse complex in the state, and Roethke's childhood was spent close to nature, nurturing cuttings and small plants and walking in the vast acres of woodlands owned by his family. This childhood world provided the foundation for much of his poetry, which often looks at the smallest aspects of nature—worms, snails, tiny seedlings—through the eyes of a child. "I have a genuine love of nature," he wrote when he was a sophomore in college. "When I get alone under an open sky where man isn't too evident—then I'm tremendously exalted and a thousand vivid ideas and sweet visions flood my consciousness."

Roethke studied law and worked in public relations for some time after graduating from college, but his desire to become a writer finally led him to graduate school. He began a teaching career at Lafayette College in Easton, Pennsylvania (where he also coached the tennis team); taught at Pennsylvania State University; and, from 1947 until his death, taught at the University of Washington.

A passionate and dedicated teacher, Roethke brought the same energy to the classroom that he brought to poetry. In teaching, he sought the same rewards he searched for in his writing: transcendence and illumination. "Most teaching is visceral," he wrote, "and the genial uproar that constitutes a verse class, especially so. It is as ephemeral as the dance. . . . [Teaching] is what is left after all the reading and thinking and reciting: the residue, the illumination."

The search for illumination and ecstasy was a fundamental concern for Roethke in life as well as in poetry. This search brought with it a psychological imbalance that he tried to face openly and employ honestly in his verse. "My heart keeps open house," he wrote in an early poem.

My truths are all foreknown,
This anguish self-revealed.
I'm naked to the bone,
With nakedness my shield.

—*from* "Open House"

Between 1947 and 1958, Roethke published four volumes of poetry and received a number of honors, including a Pulitzer Prize, a National Book Award, and a Bollingen Prize. A poet of both pain and joy, the dark and the light, Roethke tried to find in both extremes the same transcendent moment, "a consciousness beyond the mundane," as he once put it, "a purity, a final innocence."

ABOUT THE AUTHOR

Roethke struggled all his life with self-doubt. In high school, he wanted to be accepted by his peers, who thought people who read a great deal, as Roethke did, were "sissies." When he began to compose poetry as an undergraduate, he wrote in secret. Succumbing to peer pressure and mounting insecurity, he began to drink while at the University of Michigan. He drank heavily for the rest of his life; some of his friends attributed his drinking to a desire for oblivion. His drinking contributed to his being hospitalized several times. Doubt plagued him about his family as well. Even as an adult, Roethke felt he could do nothing to win his father's approval. He married Beatrice O'Connell, one of his former students, who helped him through his troubles and provided the companionship he needed.

QUICK PLANNING GUIDE

Into the Poem

Author Biography p. 1001

Before You Read p. 1002

- **Reading Focus: Scaffolding** Students learn that in intense moments people concentrate on small things.
- **Quickwrite: Prior Knowledge** Write characteristics of a person held dear
- **Elements of Literature: Figures of Speech**

Through the Poem

"Elegy for Jane" p. 1002

Making Meanings p. 1004

Beyond the Poem

Choices: Building Your Portfolio p. 1004

- **Writer's Notebook:** Collect ideas for an evaluation
- **Critical Writing:** Write a brief comparison essay on figures of speech and tone
- **Art:** Draw or paint a picture of Jane

PORTFOLIO ASSESSMENT

Portfolio Assessment
For help with self- and teacher assessment of reading skills, see the ***Portfolio Management System,*** pp. 48–49.

BEFORE YOU READ
ELEGY FOR JANE

Reading Focus

In Moments of Intensity

At the most intense and concentrated moments of our lives, we often focus on the tiniest things. Like one of Shakespeare's great tragic kings musing on a straw or a worm, people in crisis seem to search for a comforting balance between the infinite and the infinitesimal. On the one hand, we face love and death and grief and fate; on the other hand, we take note of a bird, a smile, a leaf, a strand of hair.

Quickwrite

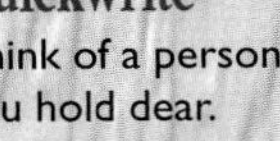
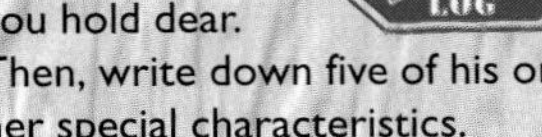

Think of a person you hold dear. Then, write down five of his or her special characteristics.

Elements of Literature

Figures of Speech

A **figure of speech** is a word or phrase that describes one thing in terms of another and that is not meant to be taken literally. It always involves a comparison of two things that are very dissimilar. Many such figures of speech have been identified by scholars. Among the most common are the **simile,** which makes an explicit comparison, using *like, as, than, resembles,* or another connective; **metaphor,** which (in contrast to a simile) makes a comparison without using a connective; and **personification,** in which an object or animal is given human feelings, thoughts, or attitudes. Watch for all three figures of speech in "Elegy for Jane."

Elegy for Jane
My Student, Thrown by a Horse

Theodore Roethke

I remember the neckcurls, limp and damp as tendrils,°
And her quick look, a sidelong pickerel° smile;
And how, once startled into talk, the light syllables leaped
  for her,
And she balanced in the delight of her thought,
A wren, happy, tail into the wind,
Her song trembling the twigs and small branches.
The shade sang with her;
The leaves, their whispers turned to kissing;
And the mold sang in the bleached valleys under the rose.

Oh, when she was sad, she cast herself down into such a
  pure depth,
Even a father could not find her:
Scraping her cheek against straw;
Stirring the clearest water.

My sparrow, you are not here,
Waiting like a fern, making a spiny shadow.
The sides of wet stones cannot console me,
Nor the moss, wound with the last light.

If only I could nudge you from this sleep,
My maimed darling, my skittery pigeon.
Over this damp grave I speak the words of my love:
I, with no rights in this matter,
Neither father nor lover.

1. **tendrils:** coiled strands, as of a climbing plant.
2. **pickerel:** small, North American pike fish.

PROGRAM MANAGER

- **Planning Instruction** See Teaching Notes, *Teaching Resources B,* p. 158, for objectives, a summary, and literary elements for this selection.
- **Instructional Support** Before beginning the instructional lesson, see Graphic Organizer for Active Reading, *Teaching Resources B,* p. 167, for an Into the Poem activity.
- **Assessment** See Selection Test, *Test Booklet,* pp. 231–232.

Enchantment (c. 1922) by Joseph Kleitsch. Oil on canvas (22″ × 18″). The Irvine Museum, Irvine, California.

Into the Poem

Using **BEFORE YOU READ** p. 1002

Reading Focus

Have students recall a moment in their lives when they were in crisis. Ask them to list what small things they may have been thinking about. *Remind students to choose a situation they would not mind sharing with others.* After they complete the list, have students discuss how intense moments help people to focus attention on the infinitesimal.

Through the Poem

A. Literary Element: Figures of Speech

? How do the figures of speech in these first lines characterize Jane? [Possible answers: Pickerels have long mouths. When they are seen from the side they look as though they are smiling, so perhaps she has a big smile. Her speech seems lighthearted and her thoughts happy. She seems to enjoy the thinking process. She might rather think than talk.]

OPTIONS FOR TEACHING

STRATEGIES FOR INCLUSION

English Language Development This poem was written by a teacher after the unexpected death of a student. Tell students to re-read ll. 5–9, lines in which the speaker describes his student's personality by comparing her to a bird. From this metaphor, ask them to choose five adjectives which might illustrate the personality of this student. Work with the students to help them arrange the five words as a poem, beginning and ending the poem with the student's name, Jane.

INTEGRATING THE LANGUAGE ARTS

Strategic Reading Have students look for the speaker's mood swings as they read. Ask them to point out at what point he makes these shifts and what elements of the poem reveal the shifts. Have students work in pairs to discuss how his varying moods affect the content of the poem and whether these shifts are appropriate in an elegy, a poem of mourning for someone who has died.

Making Meanings

First Thoughts

1. Possible responses: Jane is happy and full of hope. She has moments of sadness like the person I wrote about.

Shaping Interpretations

2. Jane is compared to a wren, a sparrow, and a pigeon. The wren makes her seem happy and energetic. The sparrow makes her seem tiny and fleeting. The pigeon makes her seem excitable or nervous.
3. Roethke personifies the shade and mold as singing and the leaves as whispering and kissing. The personification implies that Jane instills joy.
4. Possible responses: It focuses on the death of one of his students. Or Roethke uses Jane's death to reflect on the tragedy of death.
5. Possible responses: Like a father, Roethke seeks her out when she is sad. Like a lover, he focuses on the happiness she instilled. Or his reserve in the last lines indicates that he is just speaking as her teacher.
6. Possible responses: Literally, he has no legal claims to her for she is not his daughter or wife. However, he does grieve over her absence.

Challenging the Text

7. **(Synthesis)** Possible responses: Because of the highly romantic quality of the poem, how she died would not be appropriate in the poem itself and is better left in the title. Or including the information in the poem would intensify the reader's feelings about her loss.
8. **(Evaluation)** Possible responses: There are too many comparisons and the reader can get confused. Or a variety of comparisons helps the reader see the different sides of her character.

Choices: Building Your Portfolio

1. **Writer's Notebook** Remind students to save their work. They may use it as prewriting for the Writer's Workshop on p. 1181.

Making Meanings

First Thoughts

1. Describe Jane's personality. Has Roethke focused on characteristics that you might focus on in a person you love? Explain. (Review your Reader's Log.)

Shaping Interpretations

2. In the poem, Jane is compared to three birds. Name them, and tell how the comparisons help build an overall impression of the young woman.
3. Identify an instance of **personification** in the first stanza. What does it add to the overall effect of the poem?
4. An **elegy** is a poem of mourning. Some elegies concentrate fully on the person who has died; others extend their subject to reflect on general matters, such as life, death, beauty, even politics. Which type of elegy is Roethke's poem? Explain.
5. A critic has written that in "Elegy for Jane" a sensitive and caring man who is "neither father nor lover" shares some of the feelings of both. Do you agree? Explain.
6. The poem's speaker says he has "no rights in this matter." In your own words, explain what he means. Do you think he is correct? Why or why not?

Challenging the Text

7. Unlike most poems, "Elegy for Jane" has a subtitle, one that conveys important information to the reader. Do you think the poem would be better if the information were incorporated directly into the poem? Give specific reasons to support your opinion.
8. Do you think the speaker uses too many comparisons to describe Jane? Should he have concentrated on one or two? Explain your answer.

Choices: Building Your Portfolio

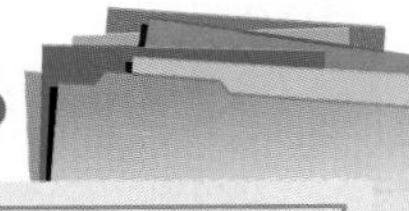

Writer's Notebook

1. Collecting Ideas for an Evaluation

WORK IN PROGRESS

A well-written evaluation of a work of literature includes an *orientation* for the audience, a clearly stated *judgment,* identification of the *criteria* used in judging, and *evidence* to back up the judgment. Make an informal outline for an evaluation of "Elegy for Jane." What would your readers need to know? What specific aspects of the poem would you evaluate—**figures of speech, theme, form, emotional effect**, something else? What criteria would you apply? What evidence (examples, experiences, authorities) would you cite? Save your notes for possible use in the Writer's Workshop on page 1181.

Critical Writing

2. Jane and the Little Lady

Write a brief essay comparing and contrasting "Elegy for Jane" with John Crowe Ransom's "Bells for John Whiteside's Daughter" (page 578). Consider especially the **figures of speech** and **tone** used in each elegy.

Art

3. Picturing Jane

Draw or paint a picture of the poem's Jane engaged in an activity you think she would have liked. Be as true as possible to the speaker's description of her.

STRATEGIES FOR INCLUSION

Visual For activity #2, students may wish to chart information in a table like the one following to make the information easier to categorize and analyze.

Element of Literature	"Elegy"	"Bells"
Metaphor		
Simile		
Personification		
Tone		

PORTFOLIO ASSESSMENT

Choices: Assessment Criteria For help in evaluating these Choices assignments, see the criteria in the ***Portfolio Management System,*** p. 188.

Richard Wilbur

(1921–)

"No poetry can have any strength unless it continually bashes itself against the reality of things." This poetic credo of Richard Wilbur has given us some of the strongest poems of our time—rock hard at the center, subtle and delicate on the edges.

© Nancy Crampton.

From the time of his first book, *The Beautiful Changes and Other Poems* (1947), Wilbur was recognized as one of the most graceful and technically adept poets in the generation then coming of age. His poetry reminds us of the meters and natural speech of Robert Frost and of the metaphysical elegance and emotional reticence of Wallace Stevens.

But the influences of Frost and Stevens are merely overtones. Wilbur's poetic character is forged of his own unassertive religious devotion, his political liberalism, and his irrepressible delight in "the things of this world." Wilbur writes at a time when poetry has often been marked by self-promotion and seeming formlessness, as well as by uneasy borrowings from the paintings of minimalists and surrealists. But Wilbur has continued to write lyrics demanding scrupulous care and skill. His inward vision of delight finds expression in measured speech and indelible metaphor.

Wilbur was born in New York City but grew up in suburban New Jersey. He attended Amherst College in Massachusetts, served with combat troops in Europe during World War II, and went to graduate school at Harvard. There he prepared for the illustrious teaching career that has taken him to long-term appointments at Wellesley, Wesleyan (Connecticut), and Smith. During 1987–1988, Wilbur served as poet laureate of the United States.

When Wilbur is not embarked on reading tours that take him across the breadth of the continent, he divides his time between Cummington, Massachusetts, the Berkshire village where he lives within a stone's throw of the homestead where William Cullen Bryant (page 169) lived, and Key West, Florida.

In addition to poetry, Wilbur has produced sparkling translations of the plays of Molière, including *The Misanthrope* (1955) and *Tartuffe* (1963). These rhymed verse versions of the great French playwright are both elegant and earthy, as well as practical enough to have been successfully produced on the stage.

Two of Wilbur's poetry collections, *Things of This World: Poems* (1956) and *New and Collected Poems* (1988), won Pulitzer Prizes. He has also published several noted books for children, including *A Bestiary* (1955), illustrated by Alexander Calder. Wilbur's fondness for wordplay is evident in his book *Pedestrian Flight: Twenty-one Clerihews for the Telephone* (1981). A *clerihew* is a humorous poem made up of two rhymed couplets that give some real and some imagined biographical information about a famous person.

QUICK PLANNING GUIDE

Into the Poem

Through the Poem

Beyond the Poem

ABOUT THE AUTHOR

Richard Wilbur began writing poetry in earnest while he was a soldier during World War II. The war took him to Monte Cassino, Anzio, and the Siegfried Line, where the destruction and chaos had a profound effect on him. He turned to poetry to make sense out of the disorder he witnessed. Wilbur, borrowing a Robert Frost phrase, said that poetry provided a moment of reprieve from confusion.

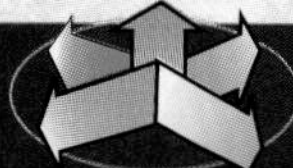

PROGRAM MANAGER

- **Planning Instruction** See **Teaching Notes, *Teaching Resources B,*** p. 159, for objectives, a summary, and literary elements for this selection.
- **Instructional Support** Before beginning the instructional lesson, see **Graphic Organizer for Active Reading, *Teaching Resources B,*** p. 168, for a Through the Poem activity.
- **Assessment** See **Selection Test, *Test Booklet,*** pp. 231–232.

Using **BEFORE YOU READ** p. 1006

Quickwrite

Encourage students to think about a person's actions as well. Their gestures or deeds may reflect beauty. Students may also describe objects that are considered symbols; what they symbolize may be beautiful.

A. Literary Element: Ambiguity

? Why would the author begin with an ambiguous title? [Possible answers: Both meanings add to the understanding of this poem. Both meanings are true.]

B. Reader's Response: Shaping Interpretations

? How does the field relate to the title? [Sample responses: Fall is a time of change. Or a field moving like water represents constant change, as does water.]

BEFORE YOU READ
THE BEAUTIFUL CHANGES

Reading Focus

The Eye of the Beholder

Beauty often seems to have something magical about it. "Now you see it, now you don't" is a magician's cliché that could just as easily be a poet's catch phrase. The poet, like the magician, knows that beauty can be ever-shifting, forged in a fleeting moment by combining everyday people and things with the artist's creative eye.

Quickwrite

Think about a person or a thing you consider beautiful. Then, write down some of the special characteristics of this person or thing. For instance, a beautiful person might radiate a sense of kindness.

Elements of Literature

Ambiguity

The title of Wilbur's poem presents us with an **ambiguity**—an expression that deliberately suggests two or more different, and sometimes conflicting, meanings. Does "the beautiful changes" mean that our idea of the beautiful changes? Or is the poem about beautiful transformations? Do both meanings apply?

Background

Queen Anne's lace (or wild carrot) is a common weed. Its flower looks like a crocheted doily with a tiny ruby at its center. "Lucernes" (lo͞o · surnz′) is a reference to the glacier-fed Lake of Lucerne in Switzerland.

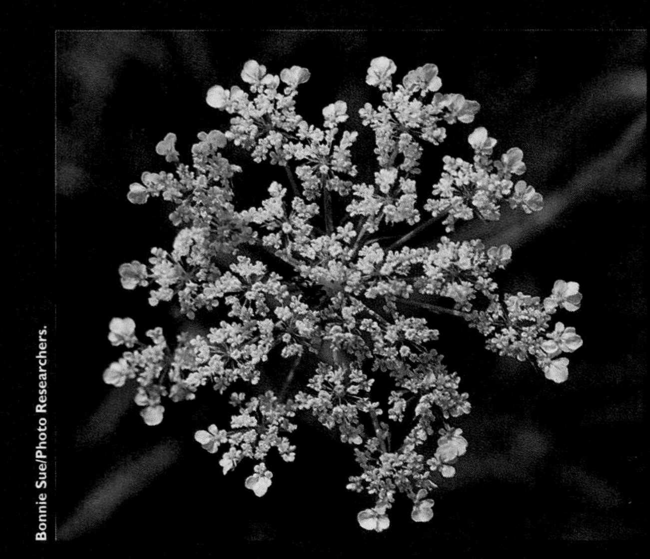
Bonnie Sue/Photo Researchers.

(A) The Beautiful Changes

Richard Wilbur

(B)
One wading a Fall meadow finds on all sides
The Queen Anne's Lace lying like lilies
On water; it glides
So from the walker, it turns
Dry grass to a lake, as the slightest shade of you
Valleys my mind in fabulous blue Lucernes.

The beautiful changes as a forest is changed
By a chameleon's tuning his skin to it;
As a mantis, arranged
On a green leaf, grows
Into it, makes the leaf leafier, and proves
Any greenness is deeper than anyone knows.

Your hands hold roses always in a way that says
They are not only yours; the beautiful changes
In such kind ways,
Wishing ever to sunder
Things and things' selves for a second finding, to lose
For a moment all that it touches back to wonder.

OPTIONS FOR TEACHING

STRATEGIES FOR INCLUSION

Kinesthetic Have students create mobiles that show change. Ask them to present their mobiles and have the class talk about the types of change that the mobiles illustrate. Invite student artists to share why they made the choices they did.

Musical Ask students to bring in recordings of music that have changes in key or rhythm. Or invite them to play such pieces. Have them point out to the class what changes are made and invite the class to share what responses they have to these changes and how the changes enhance the composition.

INTEGRATING THE LANGUAGE ARTS

Writing: Recasting Have the students rewrite this poem into prose. As they write they should be aware of the processes that they use to create the prose. After they have completed their prose pieces, have the students respond to the process in their journals. Have them decide whether the rewrite created new meaning or took away from the meaning in the poem and then, have them explain their decisions.

Making Meanings

First Thoughts

1. Is anything in the poem similar to your own experience? Can you make a connection between the poem and anything you noted in your Reader's Log?

Shaping Interpretations

2. According to the poem's speaker, in what way does Queen Anne's lace change a meadow?
3. Who is "you"? In what way is the effect of "you" similar to the effect of Queen Anne's lace?
4. In the second stanza, what similar effect do the chameleon and mantis have? What does "Any greenness is deeper than anyone knows" mean?
5. With great delicacy the third stanza makes a strong statement. Paraphrase that statement, and tell what you think the "second finding" might be.
6. In your own words, explain the **ambiguity** of the title. Does the poem as a whole support one meaning or the other, or both?
7. Is this a love poem? If so, who or what does the speaker love? Pick out the lines that support your answer.

Language and Style

Wilbur's Sound Effects

Wilbur's poems often have the effect of **free verse,** but they are written with the most careful attention to **rhyme** and other **sound effects.** This is the verbal "magic" that creates the *music* of the poem.

1. What is the **rhyme scheme** of "The Beautiful Changes"?
2. What examples of **alliteration** can you find?
3. What examples of **assonance** and **consonance** can you find?

Choices: Building Your Portfolio

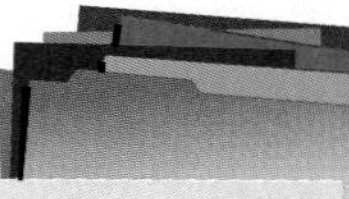

Writer's Notebook

1. Collecting Ideas for an Evaluation

"The Beautiful Changes" is a **lyric poem,** a poem that expresses the personal feelings and thoughts of a speaker. List some of your criteria for a good lyric poem. In your opinion, what makes such a poem effective? Consider elements like **message, language, form,** and **tone**. Then, note how Wilbur's poem meets or does not meet each of your criteria. Save your notes for possible use in the Writer's Workshop on page 1181.

Critical Writing

2. "Glorious Energy"

In an interview, Wilbur made this statement: "To put it simply, I feel that the universe is full of glorious energy, that the energy tends to take pattern and shape, and that the ultimate character of things is comely and good." In a brief essay, discuss how "The Beautiful Changes" demonstrates what Wilbur means in this statement. Do you agree or disagree with the poet?

Crossing the Curriculum: Science

3. Weasel Brown, Ermine White

A leopard may not change its spots, but several other animals do change their skin color or design for a variety of reasons. A chameleon, mentioned in "The Beautiful Changes," is a lizard that alters its skin color. Some weasels are brown most of the year but white in winter, when they are known as ermine. Join with two or three class members to identify several animals that change color, and explain why they do so. Start your research with a biology or zoology textbook. Present your findings to the class in a well-organized oral report.

Making Meanings

First Thoughts

1. Possible responses: I have walked through fields before. Or I also wrote about the beauty of roses.

Shaping Interpretations

2. It changes a meadow of dry grass into a wonderful blue lake.
3. Possible responses: A loved one or the reader of the poem. Both create images of beauty. The "you" establishes valleys surrounded by even more water—establishing beauty and change. The "you" refers to the change the reader experiences when seeing beauty or reading a poem about it.
4. Both blend into and increase the beauty of their environment. Beauty is deeper than what is perceived at first sight.
5. Beautiful things can be appreciated anew; beauty can lead to other discoveries or "findings."
6. Beautiful things and people change; the changes in nature are beautiful. Possible responses: The poem supports both; the poem focuses on how quickly beauty changes; and the poem emphasizes the changes in beauty.
7. Possible responses: References to "the slightest shade of you" and "your hands" suggest a love poem about a particular person. Or the speaker's reference to "the beautiful" indicates a general love of beauty.

Language and Style

Answers

1. a,b,a,c,d,c / e,f,e,g,h,g / i,j,i,k,l,k
2. Line 2 "lace lying like lilies," l. 5 "slightest shade," and l. 13 "hands hold." Other examples occur on ll. 1, 10, 11, and 17.
3. Assonance: Line 6 "fabulous blue Lucernes," l. 12 "greenness is deeper," and l. 13 "hold roses." Consonance: Line 1 "wading a Fall meadow," and l. 2 "lying like lilies." Assonance and consonance: Line 1 "finds on all sides."

Choices: Building Your Portfolio

1. **Writer's Notebook** Remind students to save their work. They may use it as prewriting in the Writer's Workshop on p. 1181.
2. **Critical Writing** Have students respond to each of Wilbur's three statements: that the universe is full of energy, that energy has shape and pattern, and that ultimately the character of things is good.

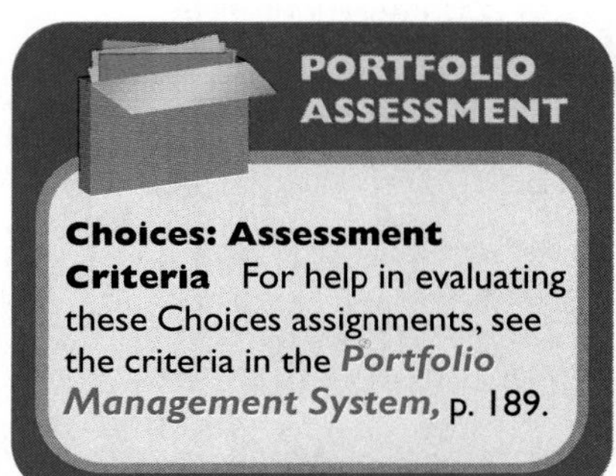

Choices: Assessment Criteria For help in evaluating these Choices assignments, see the criteria in the ***Portfolio Management System,*** p. 189.

QUICK PLANNING GUIDE

Into the Poem

Author Biography p. 1008

Before You Read p. 1009

- **Reading Focus: Scaffolding** Students discover that poetry can convey a social or political statement.
- **A Dialogue with the Text: Set a Purpose** Draw in Reader's Log pictures of poetic images
- **Elements of Literature: Extended Metaphor**

Through the Poem

"Homework" p. 1010

Making Meanings p. 1010

Beyond the Poem

Choices: Building Your Portfolio p. 1011

- **Writer's Notebook:** Collect ideas for an evaluation
- **Critical Writing:** Compare poems in a brief essay
- **Creative Writing:** Write a short poem using extended metaphor

ABOUT THE AUTHOR

Allen Ginsberg recognized his parents as a great influence on his writing. His father had published three volumes of verse. Father and son even gave poetry readings together, though they differed greatly in demeanor and dress. Ginsberg's father believed in order, tradition, and restraint, and these values came through in his poetry. His mother, however, had strong leftist political beliefs. She felt alienated from the mainstream and hoped for a major transformation of life in the United States.

Allen Ginsberg

(1926–1997)

Sophie Bassouls/Sygma.

Allen Ginsberg, like most poets, wrote poetry as a very personal exercise. It's "a form of discovering who I am," he said, "and getting beyond who I am to free awakeness of consciousness, to a self that isn't who I am. It's a form of discovering my own nature, and my own identity, or my own ego. . . ."

The son of Louis Ginsberg, a schoolteacher and poet of conventional tendencies and modest reputation, Ginsberg was born in Newark, New Jersey. He was brought up in nearby Paterson, the industrial town given literary prominence by William Carlos Williams, the poet who came to be young Ginsberg's spiritual father and poetic master. Like Williams, Ginsberg was at first attracted to the great poets of England. But in what amounted to a 180-degree turn in his thought and practice, Ginsberg soon became one of the staunchest promoters of the American idiom and of poetry that echoed the rhythms of American speech. He saw himself as a direct descendant of the great nineteenth-century American writers Henry David Thoreau, Ralph Waldo Emerson, Herman Melville, and Walt Whitman.

At Columbia College, Ginsberg associated with the novelist Jack Kerouac and with other young writers who would eventually constitute the literary movement known as the Beat Generation. In footloose travels "on the road" (as Kerouac's popular novel was called), Ginsberg typified the restless and alienated nature of the Beat Generation and its subculture. When, at the age of thirty, he published his long poem *Howl,* Ginsberg became one of the Beats' most famous members.

Ginsberg and other Beats eventually joined Lawrence Ferlinghetti, Gary Snyder, and other writers with similar ideologies or techniques and established a group known as the San Francisco Renaissance. Ginsberg's influence broadened, and his role as a kind of literary, philosophical, and political guru made him the standard-bearer of dissent in the conduct of life as well as in the practice of his art.

Open-minded and inquiring, Ginsberg explored Eastern and Western mysticism from Buddha to the English writer William Blake as part of his effort to understand the human psyche and to attain self-fulfillment. Though intensely concerned with the life of the mind, he also played influential roles in practical efforts to end American involvement in the Vietnam War, protect the natural environment, and prevent curbs on human freedom. All in all, he was a person "in the tradition of the oldtime American transcendentalist individual," as Ginsberg once classified himself.

Ginsberg was a prolific poet, as his *Collected Poems: 1947–1980* (1984), *White Shroud: Poems, 1980–1985* (1986), and *Snapshot Poetics* (1993) attest. Besides *Howl,* a well-known Ginsberg poem is "Kaddish" (1961), an elegy for his mother, Naomi; the poem is based on a Jewish prayer for the dead. Ginsberg also published many of his notebooks, letters, essays, lectures, and journals. He died in New York City, his longtime home, in 1997.

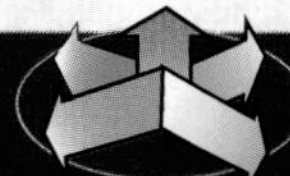

PROGRAM MANAGER

- **Planning Instruction** See **Teaching Notes, *Teaching Resources B,*** p. 159, for objectives, a summary, and literary elements for this selection.
- **Instructional Support** Before beginning the instructional lesson, see **Graphic Organizer for Active Reading, *Teaching Resources B,*** p. 169, for a Through the Poem activity.
- **Assessment** See **Selection Test, *Test Booklet,*** pp. 231–232.

Before You Read
Homework

Reading Focus
The Politics of Poetry
A poem can set forth a social, environmental, or political position just as effectively as a speech or an essay—sometimes even more so. You can probably think of several contemporary issues that could form the basis for a powerful poetic statement.

A Dialogue with the Text
READER'S LOG

"Homework" has a double focus (pollution and politics) and a single point of view. You might think of the poem as a series of exaggerated visual cartoons. After you have read the poem, try drawing pictures of a few of the poem's visual **images.**

Elements of Literature
Extended Metaphor
An **extended metaphor** is a metaphor that is extended beyond a single comparison and developed as far as the writer wants to take it. It may extend from a few lines to an entire poem. One of the delights of an extended metaphor is watching how the poet works out its details, sometimes surprising us with ingenious turns of language.

Using **Before You Read** p. 1009

Reading Focus
Begin with the whole class brainstorming contemporary social, environmental, and political issues. Have small groups select an issue from the list. Have them write one position statement in support of the issue and another against it. Have groups use a web to brainstorm visual images that might communicate or support each statement.

A Dialogue with the Text
Remind students that one way to express criticism indirectly is through sarcasm and satire. Show them political cartoons from an editorial page of a current newspaper and point out examples of visual exaggeration. Encourage students to use the political cartoons as models for their own drawings.

Elements of Literature
Have students use the following chart to trace the poem's use of extended metaphor, focusing on and recording the verbs and verb phrases that carry the metaphor.

Metaphors	Verbs that carry the metaphor
[Cleaning the environment compared to cleaning clothes]	[To do, to wash]

STRATEGIES FOR INCLUSION

Visual Bring in magazines, newspapers, posterboard, glue, and magic markers. Have students create a giant collage that illustrates the "dirty linen" that exists around the world.

Special Needs Have students who have difficulty staying focused and organizing information complete the following chart as they read the poem. Ask them to label one column Action Words and the other column Descriptive Words. Have them place words from the poem in the appropriate column of each category.

	Action Words	Descriptive Words
Wash		
Rinse		
Rub		
Cleanse		
Dry		

Portfolio Assessment
For help with self- and teacher assessment of reading skills, see the ***Portfolio Management System,*** p. 53.

A. Reader's Response: First Thoughts

? After having read the title, what do you believe this poem will be about? [Sample responses: Something that must be looked at closely or studied, or something that must be dealt with at home.]

B. Language Note: Capitalization

? Why would the author capitalize "Laundry"? [By capitalizing a word that is not normally capitalized the poet draws the reader's attention to the word, giving it enhanced value. In this case the "Laundry" includes countries, bodies of water, and land areas that must be cleaned in some way.]

C. Element of Literature: Extended Metaphor

? How does Ginsberg extend the metaphor of doing the laundry in these lines? [Ginsberg has compared doing the laundry to ridding the world of pollution. Here, he also refers to ending war and violence.]

Homework

Homage Kenneth Koch

Allen Ginsberg

If I were doing my Laundry I'd wash my dirty Iran
I'd throw in my United States, and pour on the Ivory Soap, scrub up Africa, put all the birds and elephants back in the jungle,
I'd wash the Amazon river and clean the oily Carib & Gulf of Mexico,
Rub that smog off the North Pole, wipe up all the pipelines in Alaska,
Rub a dub dub for Rocky Flats and Los Alamos, Flush that sparkly Cesium out of Love Canal
Rinse down the Acid Rain over the Parthenon & Sphinx, Drain the Sludge out of the Mediterranean basin & make it azure again,
Put some blueing back into the sky over the Rhine, bleach the little Clouds so snow return white as snow,
Cleanse the Hudson Thames & Neckar, Drain the Suds out of Lake Erie
Then I'd throw big Asia in one giant Load & wash out the blood & Agent Orange,
Dump the whole mess of Russia and China in the wringer, squeeze out the tattletale Gray of U.S. Central American police state,
& put the planet in the drier & let it sit 20 minutes or an Aeon till it came out clean.

Making Meanings

First Thoughts

1. How would you describe the attitude of the speaker in "Homework"? Do you share this attitude? Explain.

Shaping Interpretations

2. What **extended metaphor** underlies the whole poem?
3. Identify at least five of the social and environmental ills that the poem singles out. What would you say these contemporary problems have in common?
4. What do you think the poem's **title** means?
5. Refer to the sketches you made in your Reader's Log, and draw a series of cartoons that illustrate what Ginsberg might have done about the state of the world. Be sure to compare your visual interpretations in class.

Challenging the Text

6. Notice that the poem does not spell out any of its solutions in practical detail. Do you think the poem would be better or worse if the poet had tried to specify particular programs of action?

Making Meanings

First Thoughts

1. Possible responses: Frustration and impatience with social and political forces. Or anger at the dirty mess. I share his frustration: Pollution should be prevented.

Shaping Interpretations

2. The speaker is purifying the world, just as one might stuff dirty laundry into a washing machine, clean it, and then put it in the drier.
3. Possible responses: Violent revolution, political oppression, environmental damage, air pollution, and chemical warfare. All are destructive.
4. Possible responses: The title ironically suggests that the speaker may be a student trying to solve a few problems for next day's class. Perhaps Ginsberg is suggesting that the world's problems are not intractable; with good will and serious effort, they may be resolved as quickly and easily as a homework assignment, or as cleaning laundry in a washing machine. Or perhaps Ginsberg means to imply that working to eradicate evil in the world should be a homework assignment, a daily obligation, for all concerned citizens on the planet.
5. Drawings will vary.

Challenging the Text

6. **(Synthesis)** Possible responses: Solutions would make the poem better because without them, the poem only complains about problems and does not help to solve them. Or solutions would make the poem worse because the power of the poem lies in getting people first to see the need for reform.

Choices: Building Your Portfolio

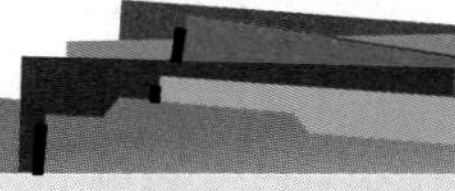

Writer's Notebook

1. Collecting Ideas for an Evaluation

A criteria-reasons-evidence chart, like the one shown below, can help you plan your evaluation of a text. One thing that some people might say about Ginsberg's poem is that it isn't poetry. In the left-hand column, list your criteria for evaluating "Homework" as poetry. You should focus on the elements of poetry: **meter, imagery, metaphor, sound effects.** In the middle column, give at least one reason why the poem either meets or does not meet each criterion. When relevant, write specific passages from the poem in the right-hand column to support your evaluations. Save your notes for possible use in the Writer's Workshop on page 1181.

Criterion	Meets Criterion? Reasons	Evidence? Passages

Critical Writing

2. Kindred Spirits

Allen Ginsberg dedicated "Homework" to Kenneth Koch (1925–), a noted poet who teaches at Columbia University in New York City. Read the following poem by Koch (pronounced "coke"), and then write a brief essay comparing the **tone, diction,** and use of **extended metaphor** in "Homework" and "Permanently." Do you prefer one poem over the other? Explain.

Creative Writing

3. Your Own Spin on the World

Write a short poem describing, as Ginsberg does, what you would "wash" in the world if you could. Open with the line "If I were doing my laundry, I'd wash . . ." Try to imitate Ginsberg's use of **extended metaphor** and **repetition.** It may help to draw up a list of words related to doing laundry before you begin your poem.

Permanently

One day the Nouns were clustered in the street.
An Adjective walked by, with her dark beauty.
The Nouns were struck, moved, changed.
The next day a Verb drove up, and created the Sentence.

Each Sentence says one thing—for example, "Although it was a dark rainy day when the Adjective walked by, I shall remember the pure and sweet expression on her face until the day I perish from the green, effective earth."
Or, "Will you please close the window, Andrew?"
Or, for example, "Thank you, the pink pot of flowers on the window sill has changed color recently to a light yellow, due to the heat from the boiler factory which exists nearby."

In the springtime the Sentences and the Nouns lay silently on the grass.
A lonely Conjunction here and there would call, "And! But!"
But the Adjective did not emerge.

As the adjective is lost in the sentence,
So I am lost in your eyes, ears, nose, and throat—
You have enchanted me with a single kiss
Which can never be undone
Until the destruction of language.

—Kenneth Koch

Choices: Building Your Portfolio

1. **Writer's Notebook** Remind students to save their work. They may use it as prewriting in the Writer's Workshop on p. 1181. Pair students with opposing viewpoints. Have them test each other's arguments to see whether they are viable. Remind students that they do not have to agree with their partners' viewpoints, but must check to see whether their arguments are adequately supported.
2. **Critical Writing** Put students in pairs and have them construct three Venn diagrams, one each for tone, diction, and extended metaphor. This should help them locate and discuss points of comparison and contrast.
3. **Creative Writing** Remind students that first attempts, especially in creative work, should be treated as *very* rough drafts. The aim of the first draft is to discover possibilities for exploration in subsequent drafts.

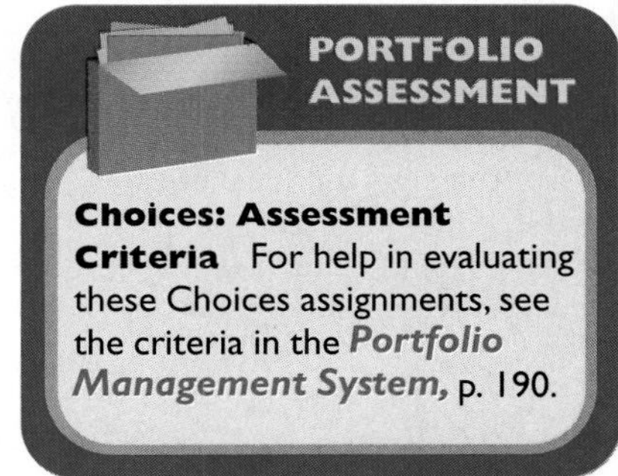

Choices: Assessment Criteria For help in evaluating these Choices assignments, see the criteria in the ***Portfolio Management System,*** p. 190.

STRATEGIES FOR INCLUSION

Visual For activity #2 have students read Koch's poem, paraphrasing the meaning of each stanza as they read. After they have read the poem, have them use a chart like the following to work through Koch's extended metaphor.

Element	Comparison
["Nouns"]	[Men]
["Adjective"]	[An attractive woman]

Learners Having Difficulty Give students who will work on activity #3 a supply of relatively recent newspapers and newsmagazines to tap into as they brainstorm a list of world, national, state, and local problems that need "cleaning up." Have each student find an article that discusses the problem they want to address in their poems. Have them write a one-paragraph summary of the problem. Ask them to attach it to the poem when they have finished the assignment.

QUICK PLANNING GUIDE

Into the Selection

Through the Selection

Beyond the Selection

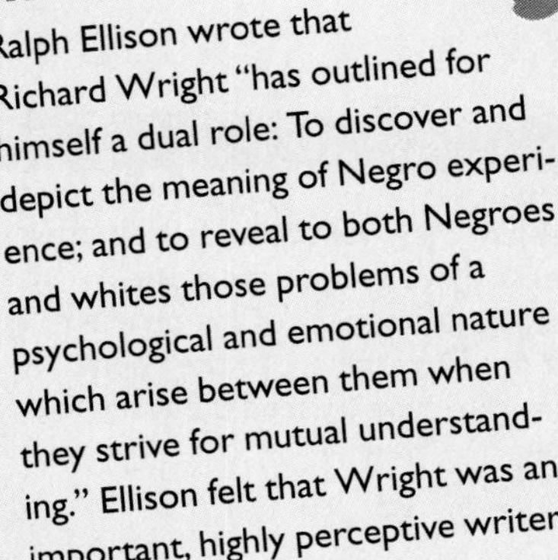

ABOUT THE AUTHOR

Ralph Ellison wrote that Richard Wright "has outlined for himself a dual role: To discover and depict the meaning of Negro experience; and to reveal to both Negroes and whites those problems of a psychological and emotional nature which arise between them when they strive for mutual understanding." Ellison felt that Wright was an important, highly perceptive writer.

Richard Wright

(1908–1960)

"It had been only through books—at best, no more than vicarious cultural transfusions—that I had managed to keep myself alive. . . ." Richard Wright *did* keep himself alive, and he became a writer with a gift for conveying the intensity of his struggle. He is typically described as the first African American writer to expose American racism to a large white audience. But this cool academic assessment fails to capture the angry, relentless drive of his most famous novel, *Native Son* (1940), or of his autobiography, *Black Boy* (1945).

Critics have labored to justify Wright's twelve-year membership in the Communist Party and explain his self-exile in Paris for the last fourteen years of his life. Full of contradictions, Wright is hard to label, yet it is clear that African American writers who have followed him have had to emerge from his shadow.

When the University of Mississippi organized a symposium on Wright in 1985, it was front-page news. Part of the poignancy of such posthumous recognition comes from the fact that Wright had remembered his home state of Mississippi with "ambivalence." We can only speculate on how Wright might have reacted to an authority on Southern culture who told *The New York Times:* "Faulkner is considered the top Mississippi writer, but I would put Wright with Eudora Welty and Tennessee Williams in their international reputation."

Wright's life began in poverty. His father, a Mississippi sharecropper, abandoned his family when Wright was five; when the boy was twelve, his mother could no longer support the family. Raised by various relatives, Wright early learned the bitter lessons of survival on ghetto streets. He remembered living with "the sustained expectation of violence." By borrowing a white man's library card, he was finally able to gain access to books.

Richard Wright by Carl Van Vechten.

Before he was twenty, Wright fled the South forever, moving to Chicago and then to New York. He joined the WPA Federal Writers Project, a Depression-era government organization that provided a livelihood for unemployed writers. He began to explore Marxism and eventually joined the Communist Party at a time when many people thought it offered hope for a more equitable reorganization of society (and before the horrors of the Stalinist purges of the 1930s became public). Eventually disillusioned, Wright left the party in 1944.

Wright achieved his first real recognition with *Native Son,* a tale of a victimized black man, Bigger Thomas, who accidentally kills once, then murders again to avoid betrayal. *Black Boy* secured Wright's fame and became a best-seller. But in the fifteen years between its publication and his death, Wright wrote no other book that equaled its success. He struggled to understand the historical and cultural place of African Americans in modern life, visiting Africa and recording his observations in *Black Power* (1954) and *White Man, Listen!* (1957). But he felt as much an alien in Africa as anywhere else. He died in Paris, where he had found as much of a home as he could.

WORDS TO OWN

The following vocabulary words are defined in the Words to Own at the bottom of the pupil's page.

enthralled p. 1016	ardently p. 1018
lurk p. 1016	galled p. 1018
clamor p. 1016	futile p. 1020
dispirited p. 1017	elapse p. 1024
frenzy p. 1018	withering p. 1024

PORTFOLIO ASSESSMENT

Portfolio Assessment For help with teacher assessment of reading skills, see the ***Portfolio Management System,*** pp. 54–55.

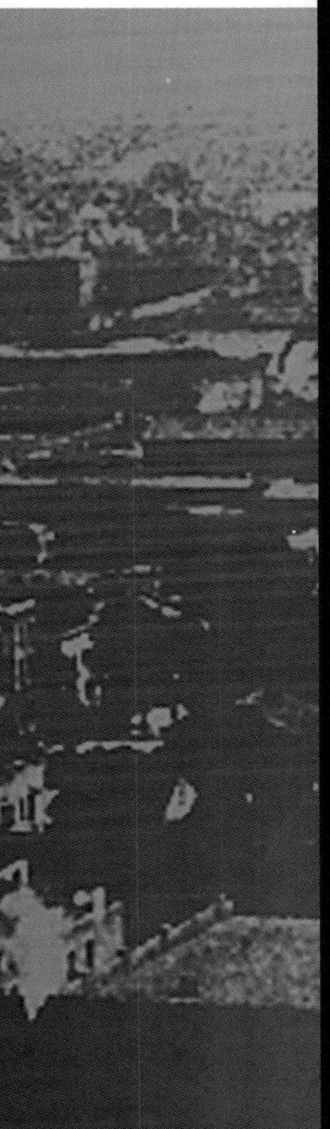

Before You Read

from Black Boy

Reading Focus

The Child Is Father to the Man

What does it mean to grow up, to put away our toys, and to participate in the world as mature and responsible adults? What elements of childhood do we carry with us forever? The discoveries we make as children, awakening to what the world is really like, can be harsh or sweet, shocking or gradual, depending on the specific circumstances of our lives. Yet in one way or another, we are all deeply affected by our childhood awakenings.

A Dialogue with the Text

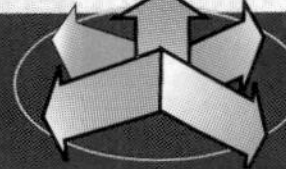

In this excerpt, images of "home" are associated mainly with physical and emotional hunger. As you read, make note of details that express the two kinds of hunger the young Wright feels—physical, gnawing hunger and another, emotional kind of hunger. Which hunger do you think Wright feels most acutely?

Elements of Literature

Dialogue

We often think of dialogue, or the directly quoted words of conversation between two or more people, as the property of drama and fiction. But dialogue can also play a significant role in nonfiction.

In nonfiction, though, dialogue can be controversial. Reporters and biographers are often challenged in court to prove that the conversations they put in quotation marks really occurred. In this excerpt from Wright's autobiography, most scenes are dramatized through dialogue. By presenting conversations, Wright *shows,* rather than describes, his own thoughts and feelings. With dialogue, he creates vivid pictures of the people in his life.

Dialogue is the directly quoted words of conversation between two or more people.

For more on Dialogue, see the Handbook of Literary Terms.

Into the Selection

Using **Before You Read** p. 1013

Reading Focus

Ask students to reflect on their experiences as children. Ask them to remember a critical event from their early years that awakened them to the realities of life. *Remind them to choose experiences they would not mind sharing with others.* Have them write in their Reader's Logs about the event and what they learned from it.

A Dialogue with the Text

Encourage students to use a chart like the following one to note details from the selection. Ask them to look at the number of details in each column and at the significance of those details to help them determine which hunger Wright feels most acutely.

Physical hunger	Emotional hunger
[Hunger stares at him.]	[He pauses to think of what is happening to him.]

Elements of Literature

Have students select dialogue from the story that best describes Wright's feelings about his own childhood. Have students rewrite the dialogue in prose form. Ask them to discuss what the effect would be of eliminating dialogue from the autobiography.

Program Manager

- **Planning Instruction** See Teaching Notes, *Teaching Resources B,* p. 160, for objectives, a summary, and literary elements for this selection.
- **Instructional Support** Before beginning the instructional lesson, see Graphic Organizer for Active Reading, *Teaching Resources B,* p. 170, for an Into the Story activity.
- **Application and Reinforcement** For reinforcement of the elements of literature introduced in this lesson, see Transparency 19.3 in the *Audiovisual Resources Binder.*
- **Assessment** See Selection Test, *Test Booklet,* pp. 233–234.
- **Language Link** For instruction and practice in varying sentence length, see Language Link, *Teaching Resources B,* pp. 171–172 and *Language and Writing Skills Worksheets,* p. 116.
- **Reinforcement** Use the Words to Own worksheet in *Teaching Resources B,* p. 173.

RESPONDING TO THE ART: ABOUT THE ARTIST

Hughie Lee-Smith was born in 1914 in Eustis, Florida, to parents who supported his passion for art. As a young child, he moved with his family to Cleveland where he studied at Karamu House, a community center renowned for its art program. He chose to paint the urban ghetto, a setting far distant from his birthplace. Lee-Smith's moody paintings address the contradictions of contemporary American life: loneliness and community, and poverty and wealth. They evoke a sense of understanding of human beings in isolated and alienated situations, treating them with sympathy, not sentiment.

Technology Tip

A teacher's guide to Richard Wright's *Black Boy* is available from PBS Online at **http://www.pbs.org:80/rwbb/teachgd.html.** The guide includes questions and activities for students and a photo archive. *You may want to preview any Internet activity that you suggest to students. Because these resources are sometimes public forums, their content can be unpredictable.*

Boy with Tire (1952) by Hughie Lee-Smith. Oil on prestwood panel (60.3 cm × 82.6 cm).

OPTIONS FOR TEACHING

STRATEGIES FOR INCLUSION

Auditory Have students read aloud portions of the dialogue. Assign different parts to different students and have a student read the narrative passages that introduce the dialogue.

Interpersonal Help students see literature as a reflection of society by having them discuss Wright's treatment of his childhood experiences in his writing. Wright had a difficult childhood that left him with great anger. However, he was able to succeed as a writer in the city which had failed his family.

Ask students to discuss the personal strengths Wright developed as a child to succeed in spite of the difficulties he faced. Have students in groups of three develop a list of skills people need to succeed today.

The Detroit Institute of Arts, Gift of Dr. S. B. Milton, Dr. James A. Owen, Dr. B. F. Seabrooks, and Dr. A. E. Thomas, Jr.

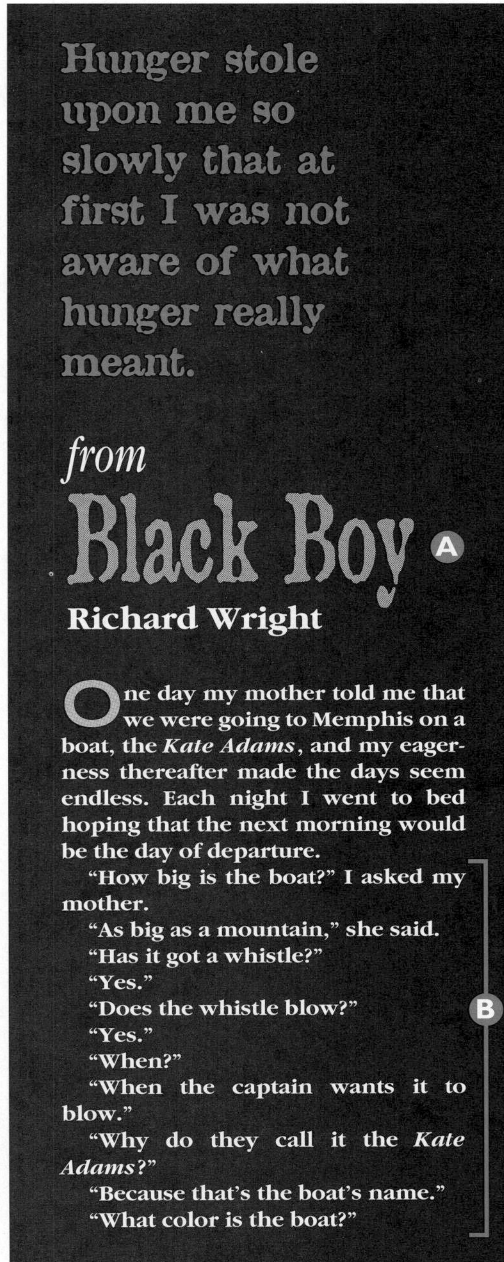

Hunger stole upon me so slowly that at first I was not aware of what hunger really meant.

from

Black Boy (A)

Richard Wright

One day my mother told me that we were going to Memphis on a boat, the *Kate Adams*, and my eagerness thereafter made the days seem endless. Each night I went to bed hoping that the next morning would be the day of departure.

"How big is the boat?" I asked my mother.

"As big as a mountain," she said.

"Has it got a whistle?"

"Yes."

"Does the whistle blow?" (B)

"Yes."

"When?"

"When the captain wants it to blow."

"Why do they call it the *Kate Adams*?"

"Because that's the boat's name."

"What color is the boat?"

Through the Selection

A. Reader's Response: First Thoughts

? As a title for an autobiography, what does *"Black Boy"* tell us about the author and about the themes he might explore in the book? [Sample responses: The use of *boy* indicates that this will be the story of a young black child growing up. Or the book will focus on the African American experience.]

B. Literary Element: Dialogue
Wright had a good ear for the rhythms of speech, and he uses dialogue effectively throughout his autobiography to involve the reader in whatever scene he is depicting.

STRATEGIES FOR INCLUSION

Visual There are several times in this excerpt when Richard cannot act; he is literally frozen. Then there are times when he is able to react to a situation. Have the students use a chart like the following to identify the incidents and to determine what causes the action or the lack of action.

Incident	Result	Rationale

Special Needs Pair students, and have each pair write a dialogue about everyday activities in the lives of teenagers. Ask that one character be a teenager and another be an adult. Let them first record the dialogue as they improvise it, then write it down and edit it, and finally read it to the class. Have the class talk about each character and ask the writers to confirm whether the class's perceptions of each character match what they were trying to convey. Many students have trouble with oral as well as written expression. This exercise will help the students check their perceptions against those of others.

A. Critical Reading: Expressing an Opinion

? Why do you think that he could not tell his mother the problem? [Possible answers: Young children dream and do not know how to cope when the dream does not come true. Or young children do not know how to express what might be wrong with them. Or he may not have understood the extent of the problem himself.]

B. Expansion

This is the one agreeable experience involving Wright's father.

C. Literary Element: Diction

? What are the implications of the word *tenement?* [The family is renting an apartment in a run-down building. It connotes hopelessness and depression.]

D. Critical Reading: Analyzing Character

? What does this paragraph tell the reader about the relationship between father and son? [Possible answers: The father does not foster a relationship with his son. Or the son fears his father.]

Metacognition How did you determine your answer? [Possible answers: Wright writes that he cannot make noise and that he does not laugh in his father's presence. He writes that he feels his father is a stranger. The biography on p. 1012 says his father left the family when Wright was five.]

E. Literary Element: Personification

? What is the effect of giving hunger human qualities? [Possible answer: It makes hunger seem more threatening and evil.]

"White."

"How long will we be on the boat?"

"All day and all night."

"Will we sleep on the boat?"

"Yes, when we get sleepy, we'll sleep. Now, hush."

(A) For days I had dreamed about a huge white boat floating on a vast body of water, but when my mother took me down to the levee on the day of leaving, I saw a tiny, dirty boat that was not at all like the boat I had imagined. I was disappointed and when time came to go on board I cried and my mother thought that I did not want to go with her to Memphis, and I could not tell her what the trouble was. Solace came when I wandered about the boat and gazed at Negroes throwing dice, drinking whiskey, playing cards, (B) lolling on boxes, eating, talking, and singing. My father took me down into the engine room and the throbbing machines enthralled me for hours.

(C) In Memphis we lived in a one-story brick tenement. The stone buildings and the concrete pavements looked bleak and hostile to me. The absence of green, growing things made the city seem dead. Living space for the four of us—my mother, my brother, my father, and me—was a kitchen and a bedroom. In the front and rear were paved areas in which my brother and I could play, but for days I was afraid to go into the strange city streets alone.

(D) It was in this tenement that the personality of my father first came fully into the orbit of my concern. He worked as a night porter in a Beale Street drugstore and he became important and forbidding to me only when I learned that I could not make noise when he was asleep in the daytime. He was the lawgiver in our family and I never laughed in his presence. I used to lurk timidly in the kitchen doorway and watch his huge body sitting slumped at the table. I stared at him with awe as he gulped his beer from a tin bucket, as he ate long and heavily, sighed, belched, closed his eyes to nod on a stuffed belly. He was quite fat and his bloated stomach always lapped over his belt. He was always a stranger to me, always somehow alien and remote. . . .

(E) Hunger stole upon me so slowly that at first I was not aware of what hunger really meant. Hunger had always been more or less at my elbow when I played, but now I began to wake up at night to find hunger standing at my bedside, staring at me gauntly. The hunger I had known before this had been no grim, hostile stranger; it had been a normal hunger that had made me beg constantly for bread, and when I ate a crust or two I was satisfied. But this new hunger baffled me, scared me, made me angry and insistent. Whenever I begged for food now my mother would pour me a cup of tea which would still the clamor in my stomach for a moment or two; but a little later I would feel hunger nudging my ribs, twisting my empty guts until they ached. I would grow dizzy and my vision would dim. I became less active in my play, and for the first time in my life I had to pause and think of what was happening to me.

"Mama, I'm hungry," I complained one afternoon.

"Jump up and catch a kungry," she said, trying to make me laugh and forget.

"What's a *kungry?*"

"It's what little boys eat when they get hungry," she said.

"What does it taste like?"

"I don't know."

"Then why do you tell me to catch one?"

"Because you said that you were hungry," she said, smiling.

I sensed that she was teasing me and it made me angry.

"But I'm hungry. I want to eat."

"You'll have to wait."

"But I want to eat now."

"But there's nothing to eat," she told me.

"Why?"

"Just because there's none," she explained.

"But I want to eat," I said, beginning to cry.

"You'll just have to wait," she said again.

"But why?"

"For God to send some food."

"When is He going to send it?"

"I don't know."

"But I'm hungry!"

WORDS TO OWN

enthralled (en·thrôld′) *v.:* fascinated.
lurk (lurk) *v.:* to hide unnoticed.
clamor (klam′ər) *n.:* loud noise; uproar.

OPTIONS FOR TEACHING

INTEGRATING THE LANGUAGE ARTS

Language and Style Tell students if every sentence were the same length and had the same structure, readers would promptly fall asleep. To keep readers alert and to create a desired effect, writers change tempo by varying sentence structure. Ask students to focus on the paragraph that begins, "She slammed . . ." on p. 1018. Have them look carefully at sentence lengths, noticing how several short sentences provide contrast with longer sentences. Next, have them examine sentence structure to locate examples of simple, compound, complex, and compound-complex sentences. (Review the definitions and examples on pp. 1234–1235 in the Language Handbook.) Then, have student pairs analyze sentence variety in other paragraphs.

Strategic Reading Divide the class into reading pairs. Have one student read a portion of the selection while the other student listens and thinks of questions; the questions can focus on content, interpretation, or style. Ask the listener to ask questions of the reader, and have the reader respond. After one passage is complete, the students will switch roles and continue the process until the assigned material is read.

She was ironing and she paused and looked at me with tears in her eyes.

"Where's your father?" she asked me.

I stared in bewilderment. Yes, it was true that my father had not come home to sleep for many days now and I could make as much noise as I wanted. Though I had not known why he was absent, I had been glad that he was not there to shout his restrictions at me. But it had never occurred to me that his absence would mean that there would be no food. **F**

"I don't know," I said.

"Who brings food into the house?" my mother asked me.

"Papa," I said. "He always brought food."

"Well, your father isn't here now," she said.

"Where is he?"

"I don't know," she said.

"But I'm hungry," I whimpered, stomping my feet.

"You'll have to wait until I get a job and buy food," she said.

As the days slid past, the image of my father became associated with my pangs of hunger, and whenever I felt hunger I thought of him with a deep biological bitterness. **G**

My mother finally went to work as a cook and left me and my brother alone in the flat each day with a loaf of bread and a pot of tea. When she returned at evening she would be tired and dispirited and would cry a lot. Sometimes, when she was in despair, she would call us to her and talk to us for hours, telling us that we now had no father, that our lives would be different from those of other children, that we must learn as soon as possible to take care of ourselves, to dress ourselves, to prepare our own food; that we must take upon ourselves the responsibility of the flat while she worked. Half frightened, we would promise solemnly. We did not understand what had happened between our father and our mother and the most that these long talks did to us was to make us feel a vague dread. Whenever we asked why father had left, she would tell us that we were too young to know.

One evening my mother told me that thereafter I would have to do the shopping for food. She took me to the corner store to show me the way. I was proud; I felt like a grownup. The next afternoon I looped the basket over my arm and went down the pavement toward the store. When I reached the corner, a gang of boys grabbed me, knocked me down, snatched the basket, took the money, and sent me running home in panic. **H** That evening I told my mother what had happened, but she made no comment; she sat down at once, wrote another note, gave me more money, and sent me out to the grocery again. I crept down the steps and saw the same gang of boys playing down the street. I ran back into the house.

"What's the matter?" my mother asked.

"It's those same boys," I said. "They'll beat me."

"You've got to get over that," she said. "Now, go on."

"I'm scared," I said. **I**

"Go on and don't pay any attention to them," she said.

I went out of the door and walked briskly down the sidewalk, praying that the gang would not molest me. But when I came abreast of them someone shouted.

"There he is!"

They came toward me and I broke into a wild run toward home. They overtook me and flung me to the pavement. I yelled, pleaded, kicked, but they wrenched the money out of my hand. They yanked me to my feet, gave me a few slaps, and sent me home sobbing. My mother met me at the door.

"They b-beat m-me," I gasped. "They t-t-took the m-money."

I started up the steps, seeking the shelter of the house.

"Don't you come in here," my mother warned me.

I froze in my tracks and stared at her.

"But they're coming after me," I said.

"You just stay right where you are," she said in a deadly tone. "I'm going to teach you this night to stand up and fight for yourself."

She went into the house and I waited, terrified, wondering what she was about. Presently she returned with more money and another note; she also had a long heavy stick.

"Take this money, this note, and this stick," she said. "Go to the store and buy those groceries. If those boys bother you, then fight."

WORDS TO OWN

dispirited (di·spir′it·id) *adj.:* discouraged.

F. Expansion

Explain that when Wright was a young child, there was no welfare, food stamp program, or public day care similar to what the United States has today to mitigate the suffering caused by poverty.

G. Critical Reading: Making Connections

? What image displaces Wright's past image of his father? [He is no longer an alien lawgiver, but is closely associated with Wright's hunger.]

H. Critical Reading: Making Connections

Just as hunger "stole" from Wright earlier in the passage, his peers now steal from him. Both thefts have similar results: He feels he has no control over his situation.

I. Reader's Response: Connecting with the Text

Even with his father gone, Richard still has fear—the fear of surviving on his own. Do you believe that this kind of fear is true for young people today? [Sample responses: If you live in a large city, being on your own is probably frightening. Or if you are educated and experienced you may not have a strong fear.]

COOPERATIVE LEARNING

Time Line Have student groups research government social services from 1910 to the present. Assign each group a range in dates of five to ten years. After each group has researched its time period, draw a time line on the chalkboard or on large art paper. Have a member from the group researching the earliest dates write the information on the time line as another member from the group shares his or her findings with the class. Continue having each group write and present information until all groups have finished reporting. Have group members decide who will be lead researcher, information organizer, speaker, and time line scribe.

A. Critical Reading: Drawing Conclusions

? Why is the mother so focused on teaching Richard to stand up for himself? [Possible answers: She is unable to protect him from the evils of poverty and urban crime, and she wants him to be able to take care of himself so he does not get hurt. Or previously she had relied on her husband; now she does not have him. She hopes her son will be able to help out with the family.]

B. Critical Reading: Finding Sequence

? How has Wright changed as a result of this encounter? [Possible answers: He realizes that to survive on the streets, people have to take extreme measures. Or he realizes that he has won his rights, but that he had to do so by fighting.]

A I was baffled. My mother was telling me to fight, a thing that she had never done before.

"But I'm scared," I said.

"Don't you come into this house until you've gotten those groceries," she said.

"They'll beat me; they'll beat me," I said.

"Then stay in the streets; don't come back here!"

I ran up the steps and tried to force my way past her into the house. A stinging slap came on my jaw. I stood on the sidewalk, crying.

"Please, let me wait until tomorrow," I begged.

"No," she said. "Go now! If you come back into this house without those groceries, I'll whip you!"

She slammed the door and I heard the key turn in the lock. I shook with fright. I was alone upon the dark, hostile streets and gangs were after me. I had the choice of being beaten at home or away from home. I clutched the stick, crying, trying to reason. If I were beaten at home, there was absolutely nothing that I could do about it; but if I were beaten in the streets, I had a chance to fight and defend myself. I walked slowly down the sidewalk, coming closer to the gang of boys, holding the stick tightly. I was so full of fear that I could scarcely breathe. I was almost upon them now.

"There he is again!" the cry went up.

They surrounded me quickly and began to grab for my hand.

"I'll kill you!" I threatened.

They closed in. In blind fear I let the stick fly, feeling it crack against a boy's skull. I swung again, lamming another skull, then another. Realizing that they would retaliate if I let up for but a second, I fought to lay them low, to knock them cold, to kill them so that they could not strike back at me. I flayed with tears in my eyes, teeth clenched, stark fear making me throw every ounce of my strength behind each blow. I hit again and again, dropping the money and the grocery list. The boys scattered, yelling, nursing their heads, staring at me in utter disbelief. They had never seen such frenzy. I stood panting, egging them on, taunting them to come on and fight. When they refused, I ran after them and they tore out for their homes, screaming. The parents of the boys rushed into the streets and threatened me, and for the first time in my life I shouted at grownups, telling them that I would give them the same if they bothered me. I finally found my grocery list and the money and went to the store. On my way back I kept my stick poised for instant B use, but there was not a single boy in sight. That night I won the right to the streets of Memphis. . . .

After my father's desertion, my mother's ardently religious disposition dominated the household and I was often taken to Sunday school where I met God's representative in the guise of a tall, black preacher. One Sunday my mother invited the tall, black preacher to a dinner of fried chicken. I was happy, not because the preacher was coming but because of the chicken. One or two neighbors also were invited. But no sooner had the preacher arrived than I began to resent him, for I learned at once that he, like my father, was used to having his own way. The hour for dinner came and I was wedged at the table between talking and laughing adults. In the center of the table was a huge platter of golden-brown fried chicken. I compared the bowl of soup that sat before me with the crispy chicken and decided in favor of the chicken. The others began to eat their soup, but I could not touch mine.

"Eat your soup," my mother said.

"I don't want any," I said.

"You won't get anything else until you've eaten your soup," she said.

The preacher had finished his soup and had asked that the platter of chicken be passed to him. It galled me. He smiled, cocked his head this way and that, picking out choice pieces. I forced a spoonful of soup down my throat and looked to see if my speed matched that of the preacher. It did not. There were already bare chicken bones on his plate, and he was reaching for more. I tried eating my soup faster, but it was no use; the other people were now serving themselves chicken and the platter was more than half empty. I gave up and sat staring in despair at the vanishing pieces of fried chicken.

"Eat your soup or you won't get anything," my mother warned.

I looked at her appealingly and could not answer. As piece after piece of chicken was eaten, I

Words to Own

frenzy (fren′zē) *n.:* frantic behavior; wildness.
ardently (ärd′'nt·lē) *adv.:* intensely; eagerly.
galled (gôld) *v.:* irritated; angered.

OPTIONS FOR TEACHING

CLASSROOM MANAGEMENT

Sources Available Give students constant access to research or collage materials so that they can work on extended projects when time allows. Permit them to go to the library as needed and supply the classroom with discarded magazines. These can frequently be found at libraries that purge their periodical holdings or can be donated by parents. Doctors or dentists who provide magazines for patients in waiting rooms also may give you their old ones.

Expectations Have the goals or expectations for the daily lesson written on the chalkboard, overhead projector, or giant tablet as the students enter the classroom. This procedure gives students an immediate understanding of what will occur during the class that day as well as an understanding of what should be mastered for that lesson.

Smith College Museum of Art, Northampton, Massachusetts.

My Brother (1942) by John Wilson. Oil on panel (12″ × 10⅝″).

was unable to eat my soup at all. I grew hot with anger. The preacher was laughing and joking and the grownups were hanging on his words. My growing hate of the preacher finally became more important than God or religion and I could no longer contain myself. I leaped up from the table, knowing that I should be ashamed of what I was doing, but unable to stop, and screamed, running blindly from the room.

"That preacher's going to eat *all* the chicken!" I bawled.

The preacher tossed back his head and roared with laughter, but my mother was angry and told me that I was to have no dinner because of my bad manners.

When I awakened one morning my mother told me that we were going to see a judge who

RESPONDING TO THE ART: ABOUT THE ARTIST

Racism in his hometown of Boston became the drive and inspiration for the socially conscious works of John Wilson, who was born in 1922. His teacher and advisor at the Boston Art Museum, who recognized Wilson's desire for justice and equality, encouraged him to respond to the problems of racism and oppression through social art. Artists whose works inspired him include Honoré Daumier, a French printmaker and social critic, as well as José Clemente Orozco, Diego Rivera, and Ben Shahn. He was too young to be identified with the Harlem Renaissance, but his works are reminiscent of the philosophy and style of the time.

C. Reader's Response: Shaping Interpretations

Like the incident at the boat and Wright's initial fight on the streets, he panics. Why has he lost control at dinner? [Sample responses: The soup does not satisfy him and reminds him of his hunger. He wants more substantial food—the fried chicken. He does not know how to get want he wants, so he loses control.] Do you find his lack of control understandable? Explain. [Sample responses: Yes, people can get so upset and frustrated that they lose control. Or no, he could ask them to save him a piece of chicken.]

CROSSING THE CURRICULUM

Economics Have students research what a nickel could buy in 1917 in order to determine what Wright was refusing when he did not take his father's nickel. Have them chart the change in what a nickel can buy over the years on a time line. In addition, ask them to investigate what the poverty level was then and how it has changed. Ask them to report their findings to the class.

Social Sciences Wright was placed in an orphanage at an early age. Have students research orphanages as an institution in the United States in the 1910s and 1920s. Students should consider the administration of orphanages, the conditions of orphanages, and the children who lived in them and their prospects for adoption. Have students report their findings to the class and relate them to the selection.

A. Critical Reading: Main Ideas

? Why does Wright value taking action over talking? [Possible answer: Wright has only found relief when he took action, as he did when the fight in the streets gave access to the grocery store. Wright does not verbally express his needs well, and when he does, as at the dinner table, he fails. He also sees that talk in court did not help them get food.]

B. Critical Reading: Making Generalizations

? Why do the streets seem simple to him? [Possible answer: The streets are where he has control. He can fight successfully for what he needs. At home things become much more complicated because people only talk and fail to act. No one can get what is needed.]

C. Expansion

Point out that advances in social welfare since Wright's childhood make the sending of a child to an orphanage so that the mother can work seem outlandish. However, in 1912, when this incident takes place, there were few other options for Wright's mother.

would make my father support me and my brother. An hour later all three of us were sitting in a huge crowded room. I was overwhelmed by the many faces and the voices which I could not understand. High above me was a white face which my mother told me was the face of the judge. Across the huge room sat my father, smiling confidently, looking at us. My mother warned me not to be fooled by my father's friendly manner; she told me that the judge might ask me questions, and if he did I must tell him the truth. I agreed, yet I hoped that the judge would not ask me anything.

For some reason the entire thing struck me as being useless; I felt that if my father were going to feed me, then he would have done so regardless of what a judge said to him. And I did not want my father to feed me; I was hungry, but my thoughts of food did not now center about him. I waited, growing restless, hungry. My mother gave me a dry sandwich and I munched and stared, longing to go home. Finally I heard my mother's name called; she rose and began weeping so copiously that she could not talk for a few moments; at last she managed to say that her husband had deserted her and two children, that her children were hungry, that they stayed hungry, that she worked, that she was trying to raise them alone. Then my father was called; he came forward jauntily, smiling. He tried to kiss my mother, but she turned away from him. I only heard one sentence of what he said.

"I'm doing all I can, Your Honor," he mumbled, grinning.

It had been painful to sit and watch my mother crying and my father laughing and I was glad when we were outside in the sunny streets. Back at home my mother wept again and talked complainingly about the unfairness of the judge who had accepted my father's word. After the court scene, I tried to forget my father; I did not hate him; I simply did not want to think of him. Often when we were hungry my mother would beg me to go to my father's job and ask him for a dollar, a dime, a nickel . . . But I would never consent to go. I did not want to see him.

My mother fell ill and the problem of food became an acute, daily agony. Hunger was with us always. Sometimes the neighbors would feed us or a dollar bill would come in the mail from my grandmother. It was winter and I would buy a dime's worth of coal each morning from the corner coalyard and lug it home in paper bags. For a time I remained out of school to wait upon my mother, then Granny came to visit us and I returned to school.

At night there were long, halting discussions about our going to live with Granny, but nothing came of it. Perhaps there was not enough money for railroad fare. Angered by having been hauled into court, my father now spurned us completely. I heard long, angrily whispered conversations between my mother and grandmother to the effect that "that woman ought to be killed for breaking up a home." **(A)** What irked me was the ceaseless talk and no action. If someone had suggested that my father be killed, I would perhaps have become interested; if someone had suggested that his name never be mentioned, I would no doubt have agreed; if someone had suggested that we move to another city, I would have been glad. But there **(B)** was only endless talk that led nowhere and I began to keep away from home as much as possible, preferring the simplicity of the streets to the worried, futile talk at home.

Finally we could no longer pay the rent for our dingy flat; the few dollars that Granny had left us **(C)** before she went home were gone. Half sick and in despair, my mother made the rounds of the charitable institutions, seeking help. She found an orphan home that agreed to assume the guidance of me and my brother provided my mother worked and made small payments. My mother hated to be separated from us, but she had no choice.

The orphan home was a two-story frame building set amid trees in a wide, green field. My mother ushered me and my brother one morning into the building and into the presence of a tall, gaunt, mulatto woman who called herself Miss Simon. At once she took a fancy to me and I was frightened speechless; I was afraid of her the moment I saw her and my fear lasted during my entire stay in the home.

The house was crowded with children and there was always a storm of noise. The daily routine was blurred to me and I never quite grasped it. The most abiding feeling I had each day was

WORDS TO OWN

futile (fyo͞ot''l) *adj.:* useless; pointless.

OPTIONS FOR TEACHING

PROBLEM SOLVING/CRITICAL THINKING

Research Poverty and Hunger

Ask students to research the extent of poverty and hunger in the United States today and how many Americans live with the pain of hunger as Richard Wright did. In addition have students research and create a chart that shows the changes in poverty over the past eighty years. Once students have looked at the extent of poverty over the years, ask them to conduct research on the solutions that are being proposed or used today. Invite them to share those possible solutions with the entire class. Ask students what individuals can do to prevent children from living with hunger. If possible and appropriate, have students develop a project to contribute to the fight against hunger. The class could adopt a child through one of the national agencies such as CARE or hold a fund drive to donate to an appropriate charity.

hunger and fear. The meals were skimpy and there were only two of them. Just before we went to bed each night we were given a slice of bread smeared with molasses. The children were silent, hostile, vindictive, continuously complaining of hunger. There was an overall atmosphere of nervousness and intrigue, of children telling tales upon others, of children being deprived of food to punish them.

The home did not have the money to check the growth of the wide stretches of grass by having it mown, so it had to be pulled by hand. Each morning after we had eaten a breakfast that seemed like no breakfast at all, an older child would lead a herd of us to the vast lawn and we would get to our knees and wrench the grass loose from the dirt with our fingers. At intervals Miss Simon would make a tour of inspection, examining the pile of pulled grass beside each child, scolding or praising according to the size of the pile. Many mornings I was too weak from hunger to pull the grass; I would grow dizzy and my mind would become blank and I would find myself, after an interval of unconsciousness, upon my hands and knees, my head whirling, my eyes staring in bleak astonishment at the green grass, wondering where I was, feeling that I was emerging from a dream . . .

During the first days my mother came each night to visit me and my brother, then her visits stopped. I began to wonder if she, too, like my father, had disappeared into the unknown. I was rapidly learning to distrust everything and everybody. When my mother did come, I asked her why had she remained away so long and she told me that Miss Simon had forbidden her to visit us, that Miss Simon had said that she was spoiling us with too much attention. I begged my mother to take me away; she wept and told me to wait, that soon she would take us to Arkansas. She left and my heart sank.

Miss Simon tried to win my confidence; she asked me if I would like to be adopted by her if my mother consented and I said no. She would take me into her apartment and talk to me, but her words had no effect. Dread and mistrust had already become a daily part of my being and my memory grew sharp, my senses more impressionable; I began to be aware of myself as a distinct personality striving against others. I held myself in, afraid to act or speak until I was sure of my surroundings, feeling most of the time that I was suspended over a void. My imagination soared; I dreamed of running away. Each morning I vowed that I would leave the next morning, but the next morning always found me afraid.

One day Miss Simon told me that thereafter I was to help her in the office. I ate lunch with her and, strangely, when I sat facing her at the table, my hunger vanished. The woman killed something in me. Next she called me to her desk where she sat addressing envelopes.

"Step up close to the desk," she said. "Don't be afraid."

I went and stood at her elbow. There was a wart on her chin and I stared at it.

"Now, take a blotter from over there and blot each envelope after I'm through writing on it," she instructed me, pointing to a blotter that stood about a foot from my hand.

I stared and did not move or answer.

"Take the blotter," she said.

I wanted to reach for the blotter and succeeded only in twitching my arm.

"Here," she said sharply, reaching for the blotter and shoving it into my fingers.

She wrote in ink on an envelope and pushed it toward me. Holding the blotter in my hand, I stared at the envelope and could not move.

"Blot it," she said.

I could not lift my hand. I knew what she had said; I knew what she wanted me to do; and I had heard her correctly. I wanted to look at her and say something, tell her why I could not move; but my eyes were fixed upon the floor. I could not summon enough courage while she sat there looking at me to reach over the yawning space of twelve inches and blot the wet ink on the envelope.

"Blot it!" she spoke sharply.

Still I could not move or answer.

"Look at me!"

I could not lift my eyes. She reached her hand to my face and I twisted away.

"What's wrong with you?" she demanded.

I began to cry and she drove me from the room. I decided that as soon as night came I would run away. The dinner bell rang and I did not go to the table, but hid in a corner of the hallway. When I heard the dishes rattling at the table, I opened the door and ran down the walk to the street. Dusk

D. Critical Reading: Summarizing

? What happens to the children placed in the orphanage? [They feel they have no one to trust. They are still hungry and feel unsafe. To survive they begin to use any means to get more food and some security; they turn on each other and lie.]

E. Literary Connections

The scene of the children pulling up tufts of grass has a Dickensian grimness.

F. Critical Reading: Making Connections

Compare this description of Richard's hunger to the earlier description on p. 1016. How are they alike? How are they different? [In the initial passage Wright's hunger causes pain, dizziness, and blurry vision. Now the hunger is so intense that he actually passes out; he is unaware of where he is.]

PROFESSIONAL NOTES

Critical Comments: Suffering and Cruelty Orville Prescott wrote in his review of *Black Boy*, "Mr. Wright in this explosive autobiography does not suggest any constructive means for improving the lot of the Negro in this country. . . . [H]e can only display suffering and cruelty with harsh dramatic power, he can only arouse anger and sympathy. If enough such books are written, if enough millions of people read them, maybe, some day, in the fullness of time, there will be a greater understanding and a more true democracy." In a class discussion, ask students to evaluate Prescott's statements.

Cultural Diversity Have students address the following questions in their journals: Does culture affect the number of times a family moves? Explain. What might the effects be on young people who constantly move? Does moving often affect the development of an identity within a culture? Ask students to discuss their answers to these questions in small groups. Then, hold a class discussion on these issues.

A. Critical Reading: Finding Cause and Effect

? Why would Richard think that a "white" police officer would beat him? [He has been told stories about a white man who beat an African American boy. He has no reason to think he will be treated any differently.]

B. Literary Element: Irony

? What is ironic about this situation? [He is hungry at home and at the orphanage, but he is fed at the police station. The police officers seem to understand what he needs.]

C. Language Note: Repetition

? What is the point of the repeated use of *white* in quotation marks in this paragraph? [At first, Richard sees the police officer only as different and as someone who potentially beats African Americans. The sympathetic officer gains his confidence and makes him forget the difference in color.]

was falling. Doubt made me stop. Ought I go back? No; hunger was back there, and fear. I went on, coming to concrete sidewalks. People passed me. Where was I going? I did not know. The farther I walked the more frantic I became. In a confused and vague way I knew that I was doing more running *away* from than running *toward* something. I stopped. The streets seemed dangerous. The buildings were massive and dark. The moon shone and the trees loomed frighteningly. No, I could not go on. I would go back. But I had walked so far and had turned too many corners and had not kept track of the direction. Which way led back to the orphan home? I did not know. I was lost.

I stood in the middle of the sidewalk and cried. A "white" policeman came to me and I wondered if he was going to beat me. He asked me what was the matter and I told him that I was trying to find (A) my mother. His "white" face created a new fear in me. I was remembering the tale of the "white" man who had beaten the "black" boy. A crowd gathered and I was urged to tell where I lived. Curiously, I was too full of fear to cry now. I wanted to tell the "white" face that I had run off from an orphan home and that Miss Simon ran it, but I was (B) afraid. Finally I was taken to the police station where I was fed. I felt better. I sat in a big chair (C) where I was surrounded by "white" policemen, but they seemed to ignore me. Through the window I could see that night had completely fallen and that lights now gleamed in the streets. I grew sleepy and dozed. My shoulder was shaken gently and I opened my eyes and looked into a "white" face of another policeman who was sitting beside me. He asked me questions in a quiet, confidential tone, and quite before I knew it he was not "white" any more. I told him that I had run away from an orphan home and that Miss Simon ran it.

It was but a matter of minutes before I was walking alongside a policeman, heading toward the home. The policeman led me to the front gate and I saw Miss Simon waiting for me on the steps. She identified me and I was left in her charge. I begged her not to beat me, but she yanked me upstairs into an empty room and lashed me thoroughly. Sobbing, I slunk off to bed, resolved to run away again. But I was watched closely after that.

My mother was informed upon her next visit that I had tried to run away and she was terribly upset.

"Why did you do it?" she asked.

"I don't want to stay here," I told her.

"But you must," she said. "How can I work if I'm to worry about you? You must remember that you have no father. I'm doing all I can."

"I don't want to stay here," I repeated.

"Then, if I take you to your father . . ."

"I don't want to stay with him either," I said.

"But I want you to ask him for enough money for us to go to my sister's in Arkansas," she said.

Again I was faced with choices I did not like, but I finally agreed. After all, my hate for my father was not so great and urgent as my hate for the orphan home. My mother held to her idea and one night a week or so later I found myself standing in a room in a frame house. My father and a strange woman were sitting before a bright fire that blazed in a grate. My mother and I were standing about six feet away, as though we were afraid to approach them any closer.

"It's not for me," my mother was saying. "It's for your children that I'm asking you for money."

"I ain't got nothing," my father said, laughing.

"Come here, boy," the strange woman called to me.

I looked at her and did not move.

"Give him a nickel," the woman said. "He's cute."

"Come here, Richard," my father said, stretching out his hand.

I backed away, shaking my head, keeping my eyes on the fire.

"He is a cute child," the strange woman said.

"You ought to be ashamed," my mother said to the strange woman. "You're starving my children."

"Now, don't you-all fight," my father said, laughing.

"I'll take that poker and hit you!" I blurted at my father.

He looked at my mother and laughed louder.

"You told him to say that," he said.

"Don't say such things, Richard," my mother said.

"You ought to be dead," I said to the strange woman.

The woman laughed and threw her arms about my father's neck. I grew ashamed and wanted to leave.

"How can you starve your children?" my mother asked.

OPTIONS FOR TEACHING

ASSESSMENT TOOLS

Peer Assessment After cooperative groups work together, have each member evaluate the other members in the group. Each evaluator should be given forms with the following criteria printed on them. A space should be left at the bottom of the form for an evaluator to comment further on a student's performance.

1=frequently 2=seldom 3=never

The member was an active participant. ____
The member gave suggestions. ____
The member completed assignments. ____
The member attended group meetings. ____
The member benefited the team. ____
Comments:

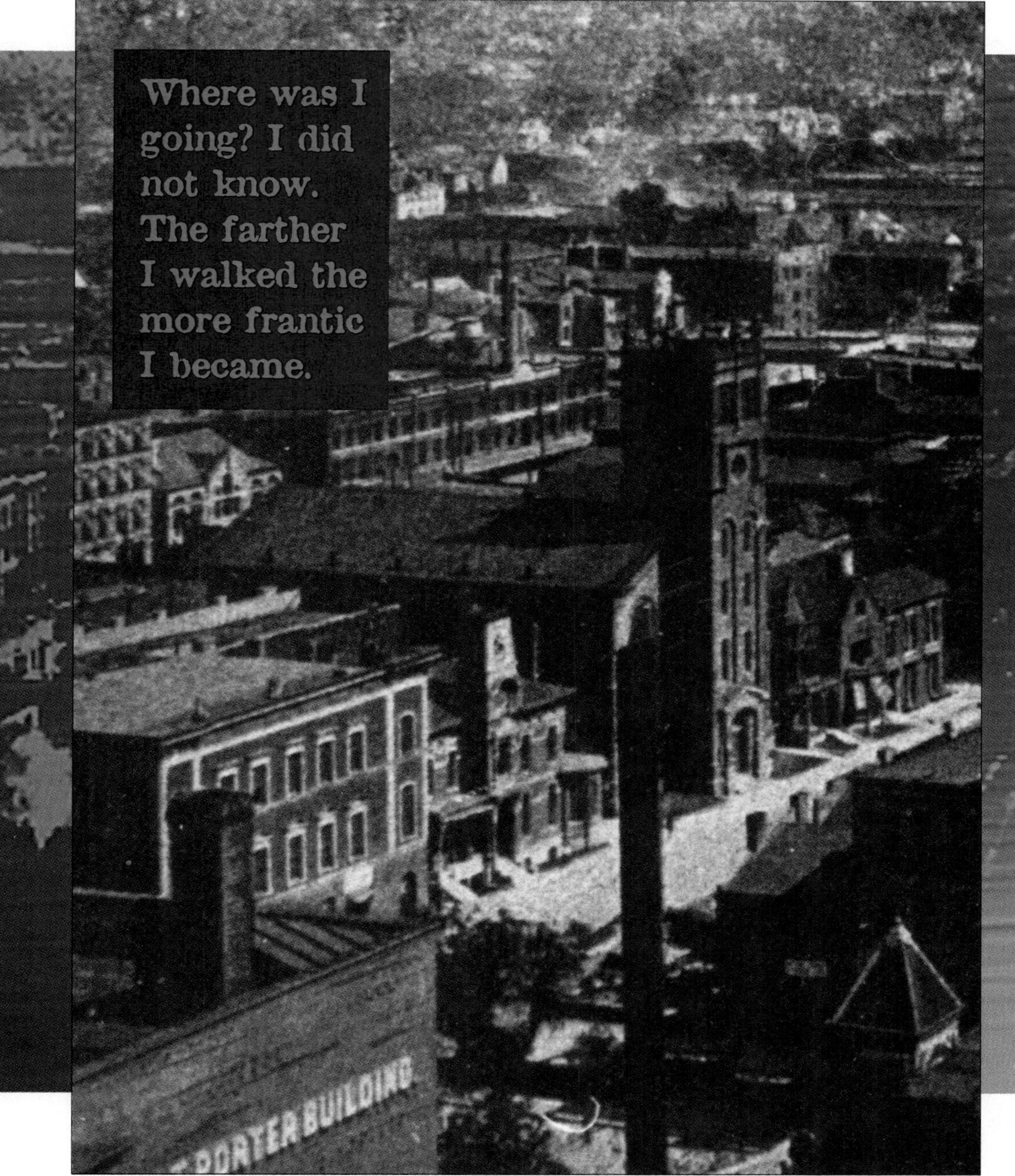

RESPONDING TO THE PHOTOGRAPH: VISUAL LITERACY

What impressions do you have of this street scene? [Possible responses: It seems large, empty, and uninviting.] Which details demonstrate this impression? [Possible responses: A number of lines in the photograph are vertical, making the cityscape seem tall. The buildings are packed closely together, and the aerial perspective shows that they extend quite a distance. No one is on the street, so the city seems empty. Both the size and the emptiness as well as the dark lower right foreground make the town seem uninviting.]

ASSESSMENT TOOLS

Check Test: True-False

1. This selection takes place in Atlanta, Georgia. [False]
2. Wright's mother would not let him back in the house until he faced down the bullies. [True]
3. The judge ordered Wright's father to contribute money to his family's support. [False]
4. As a bedtime snack, the orphanage children were given bread and molasses. [True]
5. Richard's mother told him not to take the nickel his father offered him. [True]

A. Literary Element: Character

? What impression is created by the fact that Richard's father laughs continually throughout this serious confrontation? [Possible answer: It makes him appear weak, irresponsible, and unfeeling.]

B. Critical Reading: Drawing Conclusions

? What is the effect of ending this statement with the thought that his father has no hope? [Possible answers: It makes his father seem as though he is an empty shell. It makes him pathetic. He has given up and represents defeat. If one does not have hope, one does not have a future.]

C. Literary Element: Symbolism

? Does Wright talk only about his father here? [No. He sees his father as a symbol for rural African Americans whose culture is ill-suited to urban life.]

"Let Richard stay with me," my father said.

"Do you want to stay with your father, Richard?" my mother asked.

"No," I said.

"You'll get plenty to eat," he said.

"I'm hungry now," I told him. "But I won't stay with you."

"Aw, give the boy a nickel," the woman said.

My father ran his hand into his pocket and pulled out a nickel.

"Here, Richard," he said.

"Don't take it," my mother said.

"Don't teach him to be a fool," my father said. "Here, Richard, take it."

I looked at my mother, at the strange woman, at my father, then into the fire. I wanted to take the nickel, but I did not want to take it from my father.

"You ought to be ashamed," my mother said, weeping. "Giving your son a nickel when he's hungry. If there's a God, He'll pay you back."

A "That's all I got," my father said, laughing again and returning the nickel to his pocket.

We left. I had the feeling that I had had to do with something unclean. Many times in the years after that the image of my father and the strange woman, their faces lit by the dancing flames, would surge up in my imagination so vivid and strong that I felt I could reach out and touch it; I would stare at it, feeling that it possessed some vital meaning which always eluded me.

A quarter of a century was to elapse between the time when I saw my father sitting with the strange woman and the time when I was to see him again, standing alone upon the red clay of a Mississippi plantation, a sharecropper,[1] clad in ragged overalls, holding a muddy hoe in his gnarled, veined hands—a quarter of a century during which my mind and consciousness had become so greatly and violently altered that when I tried to talk to him I realized that, though ties of blood made us kin, though I could see a shadow of my face in his face, though there was an echo of my voice in his voice, we were forever strangers, speaking a different language, living on vastly distant planes of reality. That day a quarter of a century later when I visited him on the plantation—he was standing against the sky, smiling toothlessly, his hair whitened, his body bent, his eyes glazed with dim recollection, his fearsome aspect of twenty-five years ago gone forever from him—I was overwhelmed to realize that he could never understand me or the scalding experiences that had swept me beyond his life and into an area of living that he could never know. I stood before him, poised, my mind aching as it embraced the simple nakedness of his life, feeling how completely his soul was imprisoned by the slow flow of the seasons, by wind and rain and sun, how fastened were his memories to a crude and raw past, how chained were his actions and emotions to the direct, animalistic impulses of his withering body . . .

From the white landowners above him there had not been handed to him a chance to learn the meaning of loyalty, of sentiment, of tradition. Joy was as unknown to him as was despair. As a creature of the earth, he endured, hearty, whole, B seemingly indestructible, with no regrets and no hope. He asked easy, drawling questions about me, his other son, his wife, and he laughed, amused, when I informed him of their destinies. I forgave him and pitied him as my eyes looked past C him to the unpainted wooden shack. From far beyond the horizons that bound this bleak plantation there had come to me through my living the knowledge that my father was a black peasant who had gone to the city seeking life, but who had failed in the city; a black peasant whose life had been hopelessly snarled in the city, and who had at last fled the city—that same city which had lifted me in its burning arms and borne me toward alien and undreamed-of shores of knowing.

1. **sharecropper:** farmer who works a piece of land for its owner and gets a small portion of the crop in return.

Words to Own

elapse (ē·laps′) *v.:* to pass by; slip away.
withering (with′ər·iŋ) *v.* used as *adj.:* drying up; weakening.

Making Meanings

First Thoughts

1. Wright works in swift strokes to draw sharp images of his life. Which images stand out most clearly in your mind?

Reviewing the Text

a. What details does Wright use to make the reader feel the physical and emotional hunger he experienced as a boy? (Check your Reader's Log.)

b. How did Richard win the right to the streets of Memphis?

c. How does Wright's father behave in the courtroom scene and in the meeting with Richard, his mother, and the strange woman?

d. How is the city's effect on his father different from its effect on Wright?

Shaping Interpretations

2. When his mother gives Richard a stick and sends him back to confront the bullies, what lesson is she trying to teach? Was there anything else she could have done?
3. Why can't Richard eat his soup when the preacher is devouring the chicken? What does this reveal about the boy's **character**?
4. Remembering his father and the strange woman, "their faces lit by the dancing flames," Wright says this **image** "possessed some vital meaning which always eluded me" (page 1024). What do you think he means?

Connecting with the Text

5. The **image** of the boy pulling grass at the orphanage is a powerful one, although Wright makes no comment on it. Do you wish he had commented, or do you think it wasn't necessary? How does this scene make you feel?

Choices: Building Your Portfolio

Writer's Notebook

1. Collecting Ideas for an Evaluation

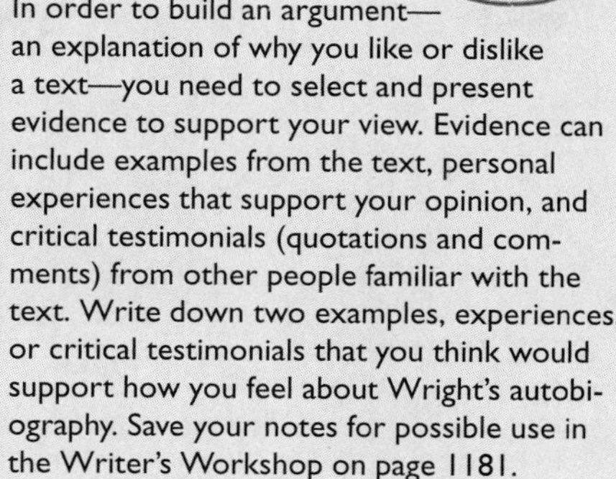

In order to build an argument—an explanation of why you like or dislike a text—you need to select and present evidence to support your view. Evidence can include examples from the text, personal experiences that support your opinion, and critical testimonials (quotations and comments) from other people familiar with the text. Write down two examples, experiences, or critical testimonials that you think would support how you feel about Wright's autobiography. Save your notes for possible use in the Writer's Workshop on page 1181.

Critical Writing

2. "The simple nakedness of his life . . ."

The father changes tremendously in this excerpt from *Black Boy.* In a short essay, characterize the father when he lives in Memphis and, twenty-five years later, when he lives as a sharecropper. Why does he change? Does he see his son in a different light?

Speaking and Listening / Performance

3. Wright Aloud

Select a section of *Black Boy,* and present it as an oral reading. (Be sure to choose a passage with dialogue.) In preparing for your performance, consider the following: How many speakers will you use? Will you include sound or visual effects, such as music or dramatic lighting?

4. Possible responses: They are people foreign to him. Or they are people who have wronged him.

Connecting with the Text

5. Possible responses: The image is powerful by itself and does not need explanation. Or a brief sentence of comment would have given the scene more emphasis. The scene makes me realize how poor they are and how harsh Miss Simon is.

Choices: Building Your Portfolio

1. **Writer's Notebook** Remind students to save their work. They may use it as prewriting for the Writer's Workshop on p. 1181. First, ask students to determine how they feel about the selection. Then, have students use an organizer like the following to help them present the reasons for their opinions.

Opinion about selection:	
Reason	
Examples from text	
Personal experience	
Critical comments	
Quotations	

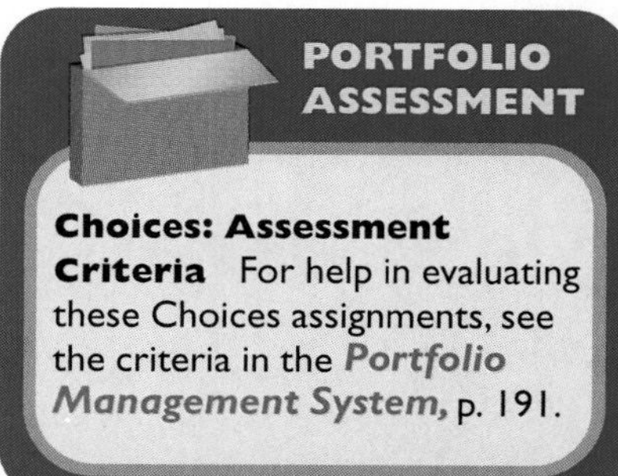

Choices: Assessment Criteria For help in evaluating these Choices assignments, see the criteria in the ***Portfolio Management System,*** p. 191.

Making Meanings

First Thoughts

1. Possible responses: His vivid images of hunger or the description of the orphanage.

Reviewing the Text

a. Waking up at night, the clamor in his stomach, his dizziness and listlessness.

b. He fought back with a stick against boys in a gang.

c. In an offhand, irresponsible fashion. He mumbles he is doing what he can and grins.

d. Whereas his father failed there, the city has given him great knowledge.

Shaping Interpretations

2. Possible responses: She is trying to teach him that he will have to defend himself. She could have confronted the gang herself. She could have taught him how to avoid them. She could have called the police.
3. Possible responses: He resents the preacher's greed and selfishness. It shows how Richard can be angry, self-righteous, or unable to overcome his rage.

QUICK PLANNING GUIDE

Into the Story

Author Biography p. 1026

Before You Read p. 1027

- **Reading Focus: Scaffolding** Students find that great fiction enables readers to discover depths of feeling.
- **A Dialogue with the Text: Set a Purpose** List in Reader's Log questions about characters
- **Elements of Literature: Style**

Through the Story

"Everything Stuck to Him" pp. 1028–1032

Words to Own pp. 1028–1030

Primary Sources p. 1032

Making Meanings p. 1033

Beyond the Story

Choices Building Your Portfolio p. 1033

- **Writer's Notebook:** Collect ideas for an evaluation
- **Critical Writing:** Analyze statement in short essay
- **Creative Writing:** Write an interior monologue

Raymond Carver

(1938–1988)

AP/Wide World Photos.

"We didn't have any youth," Raymond Carver remembered in a 1983 interview. He was thinking of the tough days he spent growing up in a working-class family in the Pacific Northwest. Carver was born in Oregon and raised in Yakima, Washington, where his father worked in a lumber mill and his mother worked periodically as a waitress and a clerk. Carver married soon after graduating from high school, and by the time he turned twenty he and his wife were raising two children. To support his family, he worked at a variety of blue-collar jobs: pumping gas, sweeping hospital corridors, picking tulips.

Given Carver's experiences, it is no surprise that in his stories—as the critic Thomas R. Edwards has commented—"people worry about whether their old cars will start, [and] unemployment or personal bankruptcy are present dangers." Carver's characters typically work as mechanics, factory workers, waitresses, or door-to-door salespeople in an America where making a living can be difficult and uncertain. Characters often survive their difficulties, however, and there is a sense of hope in many Carver stories. "I have a great deal of sympathy with [characters in my stories]," Carver once said. "They're my people. I know them. I could never write down to them."

In the late 1950s, the Carvers moved to California, where Raymond enrolled in college, taking a course in fiction writing with the novelist John Gardner. In 1963, he earned a college degree and then attended the University of Iowa's highly regarded Writers' Workshop.

In the 1960s and early 1970s, Carver published stories and poems, some dealing with favorite topics like hunting and fishing. A breakthrough came in 1976 with the publication of a collection of his stories, *Will You Please Be Quiet, Please?* The lavish praise bestowed upon this book earned Carver wide recognition as a hugely talented writer. The critic Margo Johnson noted that the stories "are filled with glass-sharp details, images and conversations, meticulously arranged." In 1977, Carver won a prestigious Guggenheim fellowship. Yet as he succeeded professionally, his personal life deteriorated, and his marriage ended.

In 1981, Carver published another collection of stories, *What We Talk About When We Talk About Love,* and in 1983, his story collection *Cathedral* enjoyed enormous critical and popular success. By now critics were talking of Carver's permanent place in American literature. The critic Irving Howe compared his work to that of Stephen Crane and Ernest Hemingway. The *Washington Post* book reviewer Jonathan Yardley called Carver "a writer of astonishing compassion and honesty, utterly free of pretense and affectation, his eye set only on describing and revealing the world as he sees it. His eye is so clear, it almost breaks your heart."

Carver's personal life brightened in the years before his early death from lung cancer. He formed a close relationship with the poet and short-story writer Tess Gallagher, who eventually became his wife. Since his death, Carver's reputation as a preeminent poet and short-story writer has remained firm. His work has been translated into more than twenty languages.

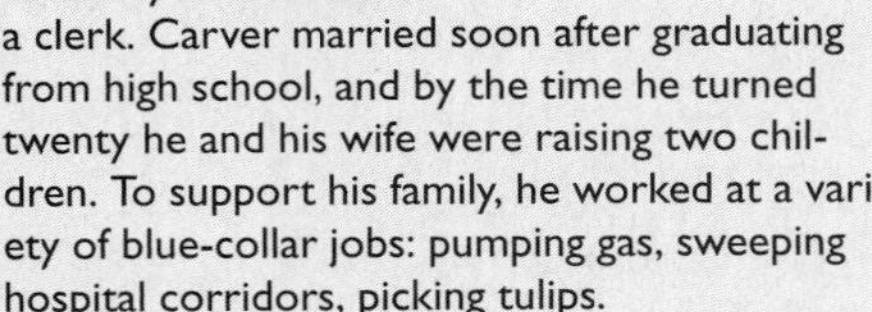

WORDS TO OWN

The following vocabulary words are defined in the Words to Own at the bottom of the pupil's page.

coincide p. 1028	striking p. 1030
correspondence p. 1028	overcast p. 1030
	fitfully p. 1030

PORTFOLIO ASSESSMENT

Portfolio Assessment For help with self- and teacher assessment of reading skills, see the ***Portfolio Management System,*** p. 53.

Into the Story

Using **Before Your Read** p. 1027

Reading Focus

Ask students to discuss other stories they have read that may have appeared simple on the surface. Remind students of Hemingway's story "Soldier's Home" on pp. 653–659. Discuss how the story reveals the complexity of interactions between people.

Elements of Literature

Have students note in their Reader's Logs elements of Carver's writing style. Students may also discover other features of Carver's minimalist style (short sentence structure, one sentence paragraphs for emphasis, extensive use of dialogue) and note examples of them.

L. (1986) by Mike & Doug Starn. Toned silver print on polyester, tape, wood (48″ × 48″).

Before You Read

Everything Stuck to Him

Reading Focus

Life's Give-and-Take

If we think in simple terms about human feelings, reducing them to clear-cut patterns and easy definitions, we may be tricked into believing that feelings themselves are simple. Great fiction, no matter how simple on the surface, enables us to discover the depths of feelings. We respond to such fiction because we recognize in it the give-and-take of real experience, the gains and the losses, the complex interactions of people who defy stereotyping.

A Dialogue with the Text

As you read "Everything Stuck to Him," make a list of questions that occur to you about the characters. You might ask, for instance, about their feelings, and what they are *not* saying to each other.

Elements of Literature

Style

One of the most striking elements of Raymond Carver s writing is its **style,** the unique way in which he uses language. Carver's prose has a chiseled quality, as if he has chipped away every unnecessary word. There are some oddities, however. No quotation marks surround dialogue. Most of the characters aren't given names. You need to read very carefully to catch every turn of Carver's meticulously crafted prose.

> **Style** is the unique way in which a writer uses language.
>
> *For more on Style, see the Handbook of Literary Terms.*

About the Author

Carver's work was nominated for both a Pulitzer Prize and a National Book Critics Circle Award. Carver never expected to be financially successful with his writing: "I never figured I'd make a living writing short stories. How far in this world are you going to get writing short stories? I never had stars in my eyes. I never had the big-score mentality." Fame, he says, "never ceases to amaze me. And that's not false modesty, either. I'm pleased and happy with the way things have turned out. But I was surprised."

Program Manager

- **Planning Instruction** See Teaching Notes, *Teaching Resources B,* pp. 160–161, for objectives, a summary, and literary elements.
- **Instructional Support** Before beginning the instructional lesson, see Graphic Organizer for Active Reading, *Teaching Resources B,* p. 174, for a Through the Story activity.
- **Assessment** See Selection Test, *Test Booklet,* pp. 235–236.
- **Reinforcement** Use the Words to Own worksheet in *Teaching Resources B,* p. 175.

A. Reader's Response: First Thoughts

? What is the relationship between these two characters? [Sample responses: A daughter is asking her father to talk about her childhood. She may not have had a close relationship with him over the years. She may be questioning his role as a father. Or she may be nostalgic about a past she does not clearly remember.]

B. Literary Element: Point of View

The man talks in the third person about himself and his wife. What is the point of view in this selection? [Third-person omniscient; the narrator tells a story within a story.]

C. Critical Reading: Predicting

? Why might this detail be important? [Possible answer: There will be some conflict over hunting.]

D. Literary Element: Style

? Who are the people listed? [The boy, husband, and father are one and the same. The girl, wife, and mother are also the same.] Why describe their relationship in successive pairs? [Possible answers: Carver is showing progressing maturity and responsibility. He is revealing the complexities of the variety of roles and responsibilities one person can have.]

Everything Stuck to Him

Raymond Carver

They were kids themselves, but they were crazy in love.

(A) She's in Milan[1] for Christmas and wants to know what it was like when she was a kid.

Tell me, she says. Tell me what it was like when I was a kid. She sips Strega, waits, eyes him closely.

She is a cool, slim, attractive girl, a survivor from top to bottom.

That was a long time ago. That was twenty years ago, he says.

You can remember, she says. Go on.

What do you want to hear? he says. What else can I tell you? I could tell you about something that happened when you were a baby. It involves you, he says. But only in a minor way.

Tell me, she says. But first fix us another so you won't have to stop in the middle.

He comes back from the kitchen with drinks, settles into his chair, begins.

(B) They were kids themselves, but they were crazy in love, this eighteen-year-old boy and this seventeen-year-old girl when they married. Not all that long afterwards they had a daughter.

The baby came along in late November during a cold spell that just happened to (C) coincide with the peak of the waterfowl season. The boy loved to hunt, you see. That's part of it.

(D) The boy and girl, husband and wife, father and mother, they lived in a little apartment under a dentist's office. Each night they cleaned the dentist's place upstairs in exchange for rent and utilities. In summer they were expected to maintain the lawn and the flowers. In winter the boy shoveled snow and spread rock salt on the walks. Are you still with me? Are you getting the picture?

I am, she says.

That's good, he says. So one day the dentist finds out they were using his letterhead for their personal correspondence. But that's another story.

He gets up from his chair and looks out the window. He sees the tile rooftops and the snow that is falling steadily on them.

Tell the story, she says.

1. **Milan** (mi·lan′): city in northwestern Italy.

Words to Own

coincide (kō′in·sīd′) *v.*: to occur at the same time.

correspondence (kôr′ə·spän′dəns) *n.*: communication by letters.

Options for Teaching

Strategies for Inclusion

English Language Development To help students understand the theme, explain that when someone is committed to another person, he or she will "stick" with the relationship. Ask students to list four actions of the boy/husband/father that demonstrate his commitment to his family.

Learners Having Difficulty Point out to students that this story is about love. Before they read, ask them to call out definitions and examples of love. Then, as they read the story, have them locate examples of the demonstration of love that would satisfy their definitions as well as those that might redefine them. Ask students to share those definitions in small groups.

Special Needs To illustrate the concept of frame story and inner story, have the students draw a picture frame like the one that follows and list the characters in the frame story within the frame and then the characters in the inner story inside the frame.

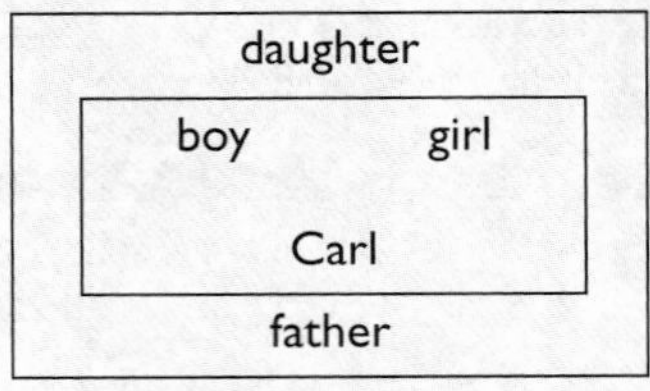

Courtesy Sidney Janis Gallery, New York. © 1997 George Segal/Licensed by VAGA, New York.

Couple in Open Doorway (1977) by George Segal. Painted plaster, wood, and metal (96″ × 69″ × 52″).

RESPONDING TO THE ART: ABOUT THE ARTWORK

American sculptor George Segal (born 1924) began his artistic career as a painter but gained recognition for his experimental sculptures in the late 1950s. These sculptures were made of plaster, chicken wire, burlap, and molds of live models, and were placed in "environments" defined by objects such as chairs, tables, and beds. Later, he began to cast in plaster of paris directly from human forms, producing mummy-like molds that look as though they might still contain bodies. The figures of Segal's sculptures never communicate with each other, but instead, remain motionless and disaffected. The overall effect of his works is a silent, melancholy environment in which only objects communicate and reveal themselves to be hostile masters of the emotionless humans who use them.

INTEGRATING THE LANGUAGE ARTS

Strategic Reading As they study Carver's story, have students keep a double-entry chart in their Reader's Logs. In the left column, they should note words and phrases that catch their attention. In the right column, they should offer comments or interpretations as they read.

Speaking and Listening Students can practice listening skills for the Crossing the Curriculum: Health feature on p. T1030. Have them listen for the speaker's main purpose, which usually will be stated in the opening remarks. Tell students to keep that purpose in mind as they listen to the talk so that they will be able to follow the speaker's points and evaluate what they hear.

Writing: Character Letter Have students write a letter from the girl to her father, expressing her feelings and reactions about the story her father tells. Have students exchange and read letters in class.

A. Reader's Response: First Thoughts

? What might be wrong with the baby? [Sample responses: She could be sick. Or she might want to be held. Or she might be lonely.]

The two kids were very much in love. On top of this they had great ambitions. They were always talking about the things they were going to do and the places they were going to go.

Now the boy and girl slept in the bedroom, and the baby slept in the living room. Let's say the baby was about three months old and had only just begun to sleep through the night.

On this one Saturday night after finishing his work upstairs, the boy stayed in the dentist's office and called an old hunting friend of his father's.

Carl, he said when the man picked up the receiver, believe it or not, I'm a father.

Congratulations, Carl said. How is the wife?

She's fine, Carl. Everybody's fine.

That's good, Carl said, I'm glad to hear it. But if you called about going hunting, I'll tell you something. The geese are flying to beat the band. I don't think I've ever seen so many. Got five today. Going back in the morning, so come along if you want to.

I want to, the boy said.

The boy hung up the telephone and went downstairs to tell the girl. She watched while he laid out his things. Hunting coat, shell bag, boots, socks, hunting cap, long underwear, pump gun.

What time will you be back? the girl said.

Probably around noon, the boy said. But maybe as late as six o'clock. Would that be too late?

It's fine, she said. The baby and I will get along fine. You go and have some fun. When you get back, we'll dress the baby up and go visit Sally.

The boy said, Sounds like a good idea.

Sally was the girl's sister. She was striking. I don't know if you've seen pictures of her. The boy was a little in love with Sally, just as he was a little in love with Betsy, who was another sister the girl had. The boy used to say to the girl, If we weren't married, I could go for Sally.

What about Betsy? the girl used to say. I hate to admit it, but I truly feel she's better looking than Sally and me. What about Betsy?

Betsy too, the boy used to say.

After dinner he turned up the furnace and helped her bathe the baby. He marveled again at the infant who had half his features and half the girl's. He powdered the tiny body. He powdered between fingers and toes.

He emptied the bath into the sink and went upstairs to check the air. It was overcast and cold. The grass, what there was of it, looked like canvas, stiff and gray under the street light.

Snow lay in piles beside the walk. A car went by. He heard sand under the tires. He let himself imagine what it might be like tomorrow, geese beating the air over his head, shotgun plunging against his shoulder.

Then he locked the door and went downstairs.

In bed they tried to read. But both of them fell asleep, she first, letting the magazine sink to the quilt.

It was the baby's cries that woke him up.

The light was on out there, and the girl was standing next to the crib rocking the baby in her arms. She put the baby down, turned out the light, and came back to the bed.

He heard the baby cry. This time the girl stayed where she was. The baby cried fitfully and stopped. The boy listened, then dozed. But the baby's cries woke him again. The living-room light was burning. He sat up and turned on the lamp.

I don't know what's wrong, the girl said, walking back and forth with the baby. I've changed her and fed her, but she keeps on crying. I'm so tired I'm afraid I might drop her. **(A)**

You come back to bed, the boy said. I'll hold her for a while.

He got up and took the baby, and the girl went to lie down again.

Just rock her for a few minutes, the girl said from the bedroom. Maybe she'll go back to sleep.

The boy sat on the sofa and held the baby. He jiggled it in his lap until he got its eyes to close, his own eyes closing right along. He rose carefully and put the baby back in the crib.

It was a quarter to four, which gave him forty-five minutes. He crawled into bed and dropped off. But a few minutes later the baby was crying again, and this time they both got up.

WORDS TO OWN

striking *adj.:* impressive; attractive.
overcast *adj.:* cloudy; gloomy.
fitfully *adv.:* irregularly; in stops and starts.

OPTIONS FOR TEACHING

CLASSROOM MANAGEMENT

Managing the Reader's Response Classroom Have students direct their questions about Carver's work to their fellow students instead of to you. You may wish to set aside a part of a class period for a question and answer session. Encourage students to cooperate in making the sessions a free exchange of ideas.

CROSSING THE CURRICULUM

Health Have students research the difficulties facing new parents in their early twenties. Ask students to talk with obstetricians, pediatricians, and nurses specializing in these fields, as well as to consult references in the library. Have students present their findings as though they were speaking to couples preparing for their first child. *You may want to obtain permission from parents or guardians and from the parties the students will contact before they begin work on this activity.*

Art Have students illustrate the concept of love. Tell them they cannot depict people or draw scenes, but must illustrate love in an abstract fashion using colors, shapes, forms, objects, and symbols. Have them write a caption explaining what the art says about love. Display their illustrations.

The boy did a terrible thing. He swore.

For God's sake, what's the matter with you? the girl said to the boy. Maybe she's sick or something. Maybe we shouldn't have given her the bath.

The boy picked up the baby. The baby kicked its feet and smiled.

Look, the boy said, I really don't think there's anything wrong with her.

How do you know that? the girl said. Here, let me have her. I know I ought to give her something, but I don't know what it's supposed to be.

The girl put the baby down again. The boy and the girl looked at the baby, and the baby began to cry.

The girl took the baby. Baby, baby, the girl said with tears in her eyes.

Probably it's something on her stomach, the boy said.

The girl didn't answer. She went on rocking the baby, paying no attention to the boy.

The boy waited. He went to the kitchen and put on water for coffee. He drew his woolen underwear on over his shorts and T-shirt, buttoned up, then got into his clothes.

What are you doing? the girl said.

Going hunting, the boy said.

I don't think you should, she said. I don't want to be left alone with her like this.

Carl's planning on me going, the boy said. We've planned it.

I don't care about what you and Carl planned, she said. And I don't care about Carl, either. I don't even know Carl.

B

You've met Carl before. You know him, the boy said. What do you mean you don't know him?

That's not the point and you know it, the girl said.

What is the point? the boy said. The point is we planned it.

The girl said, I'm your wife. This is your baby. She's sick or something. Look at her. Why else is she crying?

I know you're my wife, the boy said.

The girl began to cry. She put the baby back in the crib. But the baby started up again. The girl dried her eyes on the sleeve of her nightgown and picked the baby up.

The boy laced up his boots. He put on his shirt, his sweater, his coat. The kettle whistled on the stove in the kitchen.

You're going to have to choose, the girl said. Carl or us. I mean it.

What do you mean? the boy said.

You heard what I said, the girl said. If you want a family, you're going to have to choose.

They stared at each other. Then the boy took up his hunting gear and went outside. He started the car. He went around to the car windows and, making a job of it, scraped away the ice.

He turned off the motor and sat awhile. And then he got out and went back inside.

The living-room light was on. The girl was asleep on the bed. The baby was asleep beside her.

The boy took off his boots. Then he took off everything else. In his socks and his long underwear, he sat on the sofa and read the Sunday paper.

The girl and the baby slept on. After a while, the boy went to the kitchen and started frying bacon.

The girl came out in her robe and put her arms around the boy.

Hey, the boy said.

I'm sorry, the girl said.

It's all right, the boy said.

I didn't mean to snap like that.

It was my fault, he said.

You sit down, the girl said. How does a waffle sound with bacon?

Sounds great, the boy said.

She took the bacon out of the pan and made waffle batter. He sat at the table and watched her move around the kitchen.

She put a plate in front of him with bacon, a waffle. He spread butter and poured syrup. But when he started to cut, he turned the plate into his lap.

I don't believe it, he said, jumping up from the table.

If you could see yourself, the girl said.

The boy looked down at himself, at everything stuck to his underwear.

I was starved, he said, shaking his head.

You were starved, she said, laughing.

He peeled off the woolen underwear and threw it at the bathroom door. Then he opened his arms and the girl moved into them.

B. Critical Reading: Metacognition

Ask students to quickwrite in their Reader's Logs their predictions of whether the boy will go hunting or stay home. Then, have them write what evidence they have for their predictions. After finishing the story have them read what they wrote. If the actual outcome differed from their prediction, ask them to analyze what evidence they might have considered instead.

ASSESSMENT TOOLS

Observation Assessment: Response to Literature Use the following criteria to assess students' written or oral responses to the selection.

Key: A=Always S=Sometimes
R=Rarely N=Never

Characteristic	Date	Rating
Shows enjoyment/involvement of/with selection		
Makes personal and universal connections to the selection		
Interprets the selection, giving evidence of multiple meanings		
Discusses author's control of elements in creating the selection		

Check Test: Fill-in-the-Blank

1. The conversation takes place between a man and ____. [his daughter]
2. The husband wants to go ____. [hunting]
3. He is awakened one night by ____. [his baby's crying]
4. After thinking over his position, the husband decides ____. [not to go hunting and to stay with his wife and sick child]
5. The couple agrees to ____. [never argue again]

A. Reader's Response: Shaping Interpretations

? What do you think happened to the boy and girl? [Sample responses: Their love was wonderful for awhile, but it did not last long. Or his wife died.]

Primary Sources

Have students compare their own writing process to Carver's. Ask them what they can learn from his process that they can apply in their own. Invite students to discuss whether they think most writers write as he does.

We won't fight anymore, she said.
The boy said, We won't.

He gets up from his chair and refills their glasses.

That's it, he says. End of story. I admit it's not much of a story.

I was interested, she says.

He shrugs and carries his drink over to the window. It's dark now but still snowing.

A Things change, he says. I don't know how they do. But they do without your realizing it or wanting them to.

Yes, that's true, only——But she does not finish what she started.

She drops the subject. In the window's reflection he sees her study her nails. Then she raises her head. Speaking brightly, she asks if he is going to show her the city, after all.

He says, Put your boots on and let's go.

But he stays by the window, remembering. They had laughed. They had leaned on each other and laughed until the tears had come, while everything else—the cold, and where he'd go in it—was outside, for a while anyway.

PRIMARY **Sources** AN INTERVIEW

When Raymond Carver was interviewed by *The Paris Review* in 1983, he was asked, "What are your writing habits like? Are you always working on a story?" This was his reply.

"Paddlewheel of Days"

When I'm writing, I write every day. It's lovely when that's happening. One day dovetailing into the next. Sometimes I don't even know what day of the week it is. The "paddlewheel of days," John Ashbery has called it. When I'm not writing, like now, when I'm tied up with teaching duties as I have been the last while, it's as if I've never written a word or had any desire to write. I fall into bad habits. I stay up too late and sleep in too long. But it's okay. I've learned to be patient and to bide my time. I had to learn that a long time ago. Patience. If I believed in signs, I suppose my sign would be the sign of the turtle. I write in fits and starts. But when I'm writing, I put in a lot of hours at the desk, ten or twelve or fifteen hours at a stretch, day after day. I love that, when that's happening. Much of this work time, understand, is given over to revising and rewriting. There's not much that I like better than to take a story that I've had around the house for a while and work it over again. It's the same with the poems I write. I'm in no hurry to send something off just after I write it, and I sometimes keep it around the house for months doing this or that to it, taking this out and putting that in. It doesn't take that long to do the first draft of the story, that usually happens in one sitting, but it does take a while to do the various versions of the story. I've done as many as twenty or thirty drafts of a story. Never less than ten or twelve drafts. It's instructive, and heartening both, to look at the early drafts of great writers. I'm thinking of the photographs of galleys belonging to Tolstoy, to name one writer who loved to revise. I mean, I don't know if he loved it or not, but he did a great deal of it. He was always revising, right down to the time of page proofs. He went through and rewrote *War and Peace* eight times and was still making corrections in the galleys. Things like this should hearten every writer whose first drafts are dreadful, like mine are.

—Raymond Carver

STRATEGIES FOR INCLUSION

Advanced Have students research other writers' writing habits and revision practices in addition to those of Carver mentioned in Primary Sources. Ask them to compare the writers' various methods of writing and revising. Then, have them report their findings to the class before beginning the next Writer's Workshop.

INTEGRATING THE LANGUAGE ARTS

Writing: Revision Have students select one of their own pieces of writing and ask them to revise it over time as Carver did. Have them revise it once or twice a week over the next six weeks. After they have rewritten the piece several times, have them write an evaluation of what they learned in the process. Have them include the piece, the revisions, and the evaluation in their portfolios.

MAKING MEANINGS

First Thoughts

1. What was your emotional reaction to "Everything Stuck to Him"?

Reviewing the Text

a. What is the **setting** and who are the **characters** in the **frame story**?

b. What is the **setting** and who are the main **characters** in the **inner story**? Which characters appear in both the frame and inner stories?

c. What happened during the night when the baby kept crying?

d. What promise did the couple make on Sunday morning?

Shaping Interpretations

2. What is the effect of not giving names to the main characters? Why do you think Carver uses the terms *boy* and *girl* rather than *man* and *woman* or *father* and *mother?*
3. How would you describe the main **conflict** between the husband and wife in the inner story?
4. What thoughts and emotions do you think the boy experienced as he "sat awhile" in the car?
5. The man, having told the tale of the boy and the girl, says that "things change." What has changed since the time of the inner story? What has the man discovered?
6. Near the end of the story, after the man offers statements about change, the woman replies "Yes, that's true, only—— " She does not finish. What do you think she intended to say, and why did she stop?
7. The story's **title** refers to an incident in the inner story. Explain how the title also refers to something much more important to the man.

Challenging the Text

8. The Carver **style** is the result of much revising, as he says in Primary Sources on page 1032. What scenes, speeches, or comments do you think might have been deleted from earlier drafts of this story? Do you think Carver should have provided more details? Refer to the notes you made in your Reader's Log for ideas.

CHOICES: Building Your Portfolio

Writer's Notebook

1. Collecting Ideas for an Evaluation

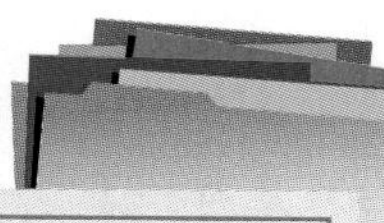

One strategy you might use in evaluating a text is to consider the reading experience of others. Interview three or four class members who have read "Everything Stuck to Him," and record their opinions of Carver's **characters, themes,** and **style.** Did you learn from their opinions? Save your notes for possible use in the Writer's Workshop on page 1181.

Critical Writing

2. Major or Minor?

Early on, the man says the inner story involves the woman, "but only in a minor way." Do you take this comment at face value, or is it an **understatement,** a statement that downplays the importance or magnitude of something? Explain your opinion in a short essay, defending it with evidence from the text.

Creative Writing

3. Words Unspoken

Write a **monologue** revealing the unspoken thoughts and feelings of one of the characters in "Everything Stuck to Him." Use the personal pronoun *I.* Choose one of the following scenes in the story to step into the character's mind: (a) the girl sitting up alone with the crying baby, (b) the boy sitting alone in the car, or (c) the woman looking at her fingernails after hearing the story.

Making Meanings

First Thoughts

1. Possible responses: I was glad they decided not to argue anymore. Or I was disappointed the boy did not get to go hunting.

Reviewing the Text

a. The setting is Milan, Italy at Christmas and the characters are a father and daughter.

b. It is November during waterfowl season. The characters of the inner story are a husband and wife and their baby. The husband is the father of the frame story and the baby is the daughter.

c. The husband and wife keep taking turns trying to rock the baby to sleep. They argue.

d. They promise not to fight anymore.

Shaping Interpretations

2. Not naming the characters helps the reader to personally identify with the characters. It also makes them seem more universal. Using these terms connotes a kind of immaturity and innocence.
3. Possible response: The boy wants a moment of relief from the frustrations that come with raising a family, while the girl feels it important to make personal sacrifices if one wants a family.
4. It is possible he felt a sense of guilt. It is also likely he realized that his family needed him. He knows now that his personal needs must become secondary to the needs of his family.
5. Possible responses: The man has grown older and his daughter has grown up. The man realizes the value of having children. In the inner story he discovers that he must put the needs of his child before himself.
6. Possible responses: Things do not always change for the better. Or I wish you and mother had stayed together. Or that is not the story I wanted to hear.
7. What sticks to him refers literally to the breakfast that falls on his lap. The figurative meaning is deeper: The boy tries to pull away from his family, but family needs tug at his soul and "stick" to him and become more important than escaping for a time.

Challenging the Text

8. **(Synthesis)** Possible responses: He may have omitted what the daughter said at the end of the story. Carver might have told what had become of the man's wife. Or he said enough; it is more interesting for the reader to fill in the details that Carver leaves out.

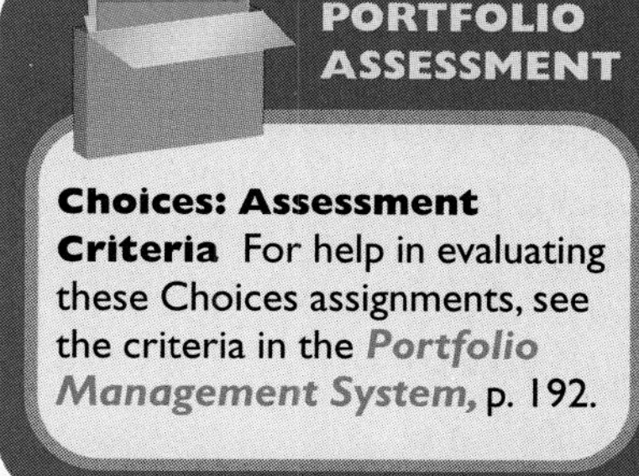

Choices: Assessment Criteria For help in evaluating these Choices assignments, see the criteria in the ***Portfolio Management System,*** p. 192.

QUICK PLANNING GUIDE

Into the Poem

Author Biography p. 1034
Before You Read p. 1035
- **Reading Focus: Scaffolding** Students discover writers use creatures to illustrate human behavior.
- **Quickwrite: Set a Purpose** Write a prediction in Reader's Log
- **Elements of Literature: Personification**

Through the Poem

"The Fish" pp. 1035–1037
Making Meanings p. 1038

Beyond the Poem

Choices: Building Your Portfolio p. 1038
- **Writer's Notebook:** Collect ideas for an evaluation
- **Critical Writing:** Explain the speaker's actions in a brief essay
- **Creative Writing:** Write a short poem from the fish's point of view

ABOUT THE AUTHOR

Her peers at the Natick, Massachusetts boarding school remarked on Bishop's genius. She had read widely, thought deeply, and was extremely funny. She knew ballads and sea chants and could produce wonderful songs for school occasions. When Bishop began attending Vassar, she thought to major in music, but the mere thought of piano recitals terrified her, and she switched her major to English.

UPI/Bettmann.

Elizabeth Bishop

(1911–1979)

A "poet's poet," Elizabeth Bishop has been, for many important poets of our time, an acknowledged master of the highest art and most meticulous craft. She has also been an unacknowledged inspiration for many others still trying to solve the mystery of her impenetrable simplicity. Her poetry has won wide formal recognition, including a Pulitzer Prize for *Poems: North and South—A Cold Spring* (1955) and a National Book Award for *Complete Poems* (1969).

Born in Worcester, Massachusetts, Bishop spent her early years in a Nova Scotia village—a childhood marked by the early death of her father and darkened by the long illness of her mother. These circumstances, in effect, made her an orphan whose upbringing was entrusted to relatives.

At the time of her mother's death in a psychiatric hospital, Bishop was a student at Vassar College. After graduation, she embarked on a career quietly devoted to poetry and, by means of a private income, to travels. During these travels, she discovered two places congenial enough to detain her for years—Key West, Florida, and Rio de Janeiro. *Questions of Travel* (1965), the title she gave to one of her books, might serve as an index to the story of a life told in poems that are always "letters from abroad." In these poems, places—near or far—provide temporary settings for an endless inquiry into the nature of perception and reality.

In the final years of her life, Bishop lived in a condominium on a Boston Harbor wharf and spent her summers on an island off the coast of Maine. These changes of scene came about when her close friend Robert Lowell (page 948) became ill, and Harvard University invited her to take over the classes he had been scheduled to teach. She continued to teach at Harvard until her death.

A shy woman with a taste for the exotic as well as a love of the ordinary, Bishop surrounded herself with artifacts acquired in the course of her travels. She conducted herself with a scrupulous conventionality much at odds with the audacity and profundity of her imagination. Her poems most truly reveal her character: a combination of the conservatism and moral rectitude many associate with "the North" and the casual sensuousness and cheerfully untidy sprawl many associate with nature and the everyday outdoor life of "the South." For Elizabeth Bishop, geography was less a matter of maps and place names than of states of mind and areas of feeling.

PORTFOLIO ASSESSMENT

Portfolio Assessment For help with self- and teacher assessment of reading skills, see the ***Portfolio Management System,*** p. 53.

Before You Read
The Fish

Reading Focus
Creature Teachers
Since ancient times, writers and storytellers have used creatures from the natural world to illustrate all aspects of human behavior, from the wisest to the most absurd. Ancient Greek myths, Aesop's fables, and Grimms' fairy tales contain famous examples. American literature also includes many notable examples, such as "The Chambered Nautilus" by Oliver Wendell Holmes (page 189) and *Moby-Dick; or The Whale* by Herman Melville (page 313).

Quickwrite
Read the first nine lines of the poem, and then stop: Write what you predict the poem's speaker will do with the fish.

Elements of Literature
Personification
A metaphor is a comparison between two unlike things. **Personification** is a kind of metaphor in which a nonhuman thing or quality is talked about as if it were human. It may be given human feelings, thoughts, or attitudes. In the poem that follows, the speaker uses many metaphors and similes to describe the fish. Watch for instances of personification.

The Fish
Elizabeth Bishop

I caught a tremendous fish
and held him beside the boat
half out of water, with my hook
fast in a corner of his mouth.
He didn't fight.
He hadn't fought at all.
He hung a grunting weight,
battered and venerable
and homely. Here and there
his brown skin hung in strips
like ancient wall-paper,
and its pattern of darker brown
was like wall-paper:
shapes like full-blown roses
stained and lost through age. (A)
He was speckled with barnacles,
fine rosettes of lime,
and infested
with tiny white sea-lice,
and underneath two or three
rags of green weed hung down.
While his gills were breathing in
the terrible oxygen
—the frightening gills
fresh and crisp with blood,
that can cut so badly—
I thought of the coarse white flesh
packed in like feathers,
the big bones and the little bones,
the dramatic reds and blacks
of his shiny entrails,
and the pink swim-bladder
like a big peony.
I looked into his eyes
which were far larger than mine
but shallower, and yellowed,
the irises backed and packed
with tarnished tinfoil
seen through the lenses
of old scratched isinglass.
They shifted a little, but not
to return my stare.

Into the Poem

Using **Before You Read** p. 1035

Elements of Literature
Have students recall poems and stories they have read that use personification. (In "Thanatopsis," pp. 171–172, nature is personified; in "The Fall of the House of Usher," pp. 262–279, the house is personified; in "Because I could not stop for Death," p. 391, and in "Go Down, Death," on pp. 737–739, death is personified.) Discuss how personification enhances the quality of the works.

Through the Poem

A. Reader's Response: First Thoughts
? How does this description make you feel toward the fish? [Sample responses: I do not care for him; he seems old and ugly. Or I like him; he looks tough.]

PROGRAM MANAGER

- **Planning Instruction** See Teaching Notes, *Teaching Resources B,* pp. 161, for objectives, a summary, and literary elements for this selection.
- **Instructional Support** Before beginning the instructional lesson, see Graphic Organizer for Active Reading, *Teaching Resources B,* p. 176, for an Into the Poem activity.
- **Audiotaped Readings** To help less proficient readers or auditory learners through the lesson, use the Selected Reading, Audiocassette 3, Side B, in the *Audiovisual Resources Binder.*

- **Assessment** See Selection Test, *Test Booklet,* pp. 237–238.

RESPONDING TO THE ART: ABOUT THE ARTIST

American artist Winslow Homer (1836–1910) established himself as a realistic and straightforward illustrator of the Civil War. At the same time, he painted oils of country life. He took up watercolors in 1873. He spent two years in the early 1880s in Tynemouth, England on the North Sea coast painting nature, especially the sea. His transparent washes lend a dramatic quality to his works and reflect a sense of light.

OPTIONS FOR TEACHING

STRATEGIES FOR INCLUSION

Learners Having Difficulty To help students better understand the use of symbolism in the poem, have them do a quickwrite about another living thing that could represent survival in the face of adversity, such as a neglected plant or an endangered animal. Then, have them read the poem.

English Language Development In the eyes of the poet, the fish changes character from the beginning of the poem to the end. From l. 45 on, have students discuss in pairs how the poet develops a personality for the fish and how it earns the speaker's respect. Have them decide whether it was necessary for the poet to give the fish human qualities to show respect. Invite students to share other works in which such **personification** occurs.

Special Needs Pass out pictures of all types of fish and work with students to develop **similes** and **metaphors** to describe the fish as well as a person who might be like the fish. Have the students then draw the fish, embellishing it with items from their comparisons, if possible. Ask them to find a picture of a person who is like their fish, thus giving them a concrete example of **personification.** Have them attach the picture to their drawing. Display their work in the classroom.

—It was more like the tipping
of an object toward the light.
I admired his sullen face,
the mechanism of his jaw,
and then I saw
that from his lower lip
—if you could call it a lip—
grim, wet, and weapon-like,
hung five old pieces of fish-line,
or four and a wire leader
with the swivel still attached,
with all their five big hooks
grown firmly in his mouth.
A green line, frayed at the end
where he broke it, two heavier lines,
and a fine black thread
still crimped from the strain and snap
when it broke and he got away.
Like medals with their ribbons
frayed and wavering,
a five-haired beard of wisdom
trailing from his aching jaw.
I stared and stared
and victory filled up
the little rented boat,
from the pool of bilge
where oil had spread a rainbow
around the rusted engine
to the bailer rusted orange,
the sun-cracked thwarts,
the oarlocks on their strings,
the gunnels—until everything
was rainbow, rainbow, rainbow!
And I let the fish go.

Leaping Trout (1889) by Winslow Homer. Watercolor on paper (14″ × 19¾″).

Portland Museum of Art, Portland, Maine. Bequest of Charles Shipman Payson (1988.55.7). Photo by Melville McLean.

A. Critical Reading: Drawing Conclusions

? What do these pieces of line and leader reveal about the fish's history? [It has been caught at least five times before and has escaped several times. It is a survivor.]

B. Literary Element: Personification

? What is the effect of personification of the fish at this point? [Possible answers: The speaker admires the fish. Or the speaker feels it is wise and experienced in the ways of survival.]

INTEGRATING THE LANGUAGE ARTS

Language and Vocabulary Tell students that many English words have long histories—they may have been borrowed from the French, who borrowed from the Romans, who in turn borrowed from the Greeks. In this poem, three words have histories that can be traced back to Greek or Roman gods and goddesses. Have students use a dictionary to answer the following questions:

1. From what Roman goddess is the word *venerable* derived? [The Latin word for Venus, the goddess of love.] Explain the connection between the meaning of *venerable* and this goddess. [To show respect is one way to show love.]
2. From what Greek goddess is the word *iris* derived? [The goddess of the rainbow.] Explain the connection between one meaning of this word and the goddess. [Iris is the pigmented part of the eye; the flower iris comes in many colors.]
3. The word *peony* is derived from another name for the Greek god Apollo. What is that name? [Paion, an epithet for Apollo, physician of the gods; the peony was once used for medicinal purposes.]

Making Meanings

First Thoughts

1. Possible responses: No, I predicted the speaker would let it go. Or yes, I thought the fish would be kept as a prize.

Shaping Interpretations

2. Simile: Lines 10–11, the fish's skin hung like strips of wallpaper; ll. 14–15, the skin was like old roses; ll. 27–28, flesh packed like feathers; ll. 32–33, the fish's bladder compared to a peony. Metaphor: Line 7, the fish is compared to a weight; ll. 39–40, lenses of isinglass.
3. The simile on l. 61 refers to wearing medals and the metaphoric reference to a beard and jaw compare the fish to an old war hero.
4. Possible responses: The speaker is overwhelmed by the realization that letting the fish go would be a victory. Literally, the angler is the victor for catching the fish. The deeper meaning suggests that the captured fish, in its heroic description, causes the speaker—and perhaps previous anglers—to have a more profound respect for living things. In this case the fish is the "victor," for he continues to live and provides the speaker with a better sense of the world.
5. Possible responses: The fish's living so long might symbolize longevity. Or his beard may symbolize wisdom.
6. Possible responses: The number of colors mentioned indicate that the fish might symbolize the rainbow. In the Bible, God sends a rainbow after the Flood as His promise never to destroy the earth again. The rainbow is a symbol of victory over tragedy, of hope over despair. Or the fact that the speaker lets go of the fish indicates that it might represent freedom or tenacity in the face of adversity.

Connecting with the Text

7. Possible responses: I felt similarly when I could have shot a deer, but I let it go. Or looking down from Mt. Washington, I felt a sense of majesty.
8. Possible responses: The fish should be let go, for it has survived a great deal, and can remind other anglers of its strength and nature's beauty. Or I would have kept the fish as a trophy to remind me of its strength.

Making Meanings

First Thoughts

1. Did the ending of "The Fish" surprise you? (Review your Reader's Log notes.) Explain.

Shaping Interpretations

2. As the speaker examines the fish, a series of **similes** and **metaphors** are used to describe it. Find at least six figures of speech in lines 1–40 that help you see the fish.
3. Identify the two figures of speech in lines 61–64 that **personify** the fish. How would you characterize the type of person these comparisons suggest?
4. As the speaker stares at the fish, "victory filled up" the boat. What does this expression mean? Whose "victory" is it, and who or what was the enemy?
5. What clues suggest that the fish might have **symbolic** meaning? What might it symbolize?
6. As the speaker thinks "rainbow, rainbow, rainbow," she sees the pool of oil, the "rusted engine," and the "sun-cracked thwarts" in a totally new way. Why do you think she lets the fish go?

Connecting with the Text

7. Have you ever experienced a moment when the ordinary suddenly seemed full of beauty and wonder? Describe your experience.
8. What do you think of the speaker's decision to let the old fish go? What would you have done?

Choices: Building Your Portfolio

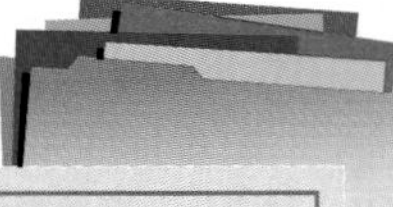

Writer's Notebook

1. Collecting Ideas for an Evaluation

Comparing "The Fish" to another literary work could be an effective strategy for arriving at an evaluation of this poem. List several American works that center around the conflict between a main character and an animal, such as Ernest Hemingway's *The Old Man and the Sea* or William Faulkner's "The Bear." Jot down your thoughts on **themes, plots, characters,** or **images** that each work might have in common with Bishop's "The Fish," or tell how each work might be different. Keep your notes for possible use in the Writer's Workshop on page 1181.

Critical Writing

2. What Happened?

The first line of "The Fish" is a simple statement: "I caught a tremendous fish." So is the last line: "And I let the fish go." Between the moment the speaker announces the catch and the moment the fish is let go, something important happens, and that is what the poem is all about. Make a list of the speaker's actions in the poem. Then, in a brief essay, recount these actions in chronological order. At the conclusion of your essay, identify the moment when something happens that makes the speaker give up what any other fisher would be only too happy to keep. Explain this moment of discovery in a few sentences.

Creative Writing

3. A Fish's Story

Write a short poem telling the poem's story from the fish's point of view. You might begin with the line "I was caught," and end with the line "I was let go." How does the fish feel about being caught? about being set free? What does the fish think of the speaker? Try to imitate the style of "The Fish."

Beyond the Poem

Choices: Building Your Portfolio

1. **Writer's Notebook** Remind students to save their work. They may use it as prewriting for Writer's Workshop on p. 1181.

PORTFOLIO ASSESSMENT

Choices: Assessment Criteria For help in evaluating these Choices assignments, see the criteria in the ***Portfolio Management System,*** p. 193.

Joy Harjo

(1951–)

And I write it to you
at this moment
never being able to get
the essence
    the true breath
in words, because we exist
not in words, but in the motion
set off by them. . . .

—*from* "Motion"

© Paul Abdoo.

Joy Harjo is a poet who puts words in their place, who doesn't let them take over life itself. Stymied, she says, by the limitations of language, she has written that "all poets / understand the final uselessness of words." Nevertheless, she produces vibrant poetry and screenplays, teaches Native American literature and creative writing, edits poetry journals, and holds a master's degree from the University of Iowa Writers' Workshop.

Harjo is mostly of mixed Muscogee Creek and Cherokee descent. She grew up in Oklahoma in difficult circumstances, as her divorced mother struggled to feed and clothe four children. Partly in response to the poverty and frustration of her mother's life, Harjo has said, she "wanted something different" for herself and for her son and her daughter. "I obtained two degrees as a single mother. I wrote poetry, screenplays, became a professor, and tried to live a life that would be a positive influence for both of my children." In addition to being a poet, the multitalented Harjo is an editor, filmmaker, painter, and jazz saxophonist.

Harjo's first collection of poems, *The Last Song,* appeared in 1975, when she was still a student at the University of New Mexico. Her 1983 volume, *She Had Some Horses,* met with particular acclaim, and she issued another poetry collection, *In Mad Love and War,* in 1990. Her ability to invest the contemporary scene with American Indian myths is evident in *The Woman Who Fell from the Sky* (1994), a book accompanied by an audiocassette of Harjo reading her words.

Harjo's work is rooted in the past and the present of her fellow Native Americans. She has written that "my work in this life has to do with reclaiming the memory stolen from our peoples when we were dispossessed from our lands east of the Mississippi; it has to do with restoring us. I am proud of our history." As she asks in her poem "Anchorage,"

    who would believe
the fantastic and terrible story of all of our
        survival
those who were never meant to survive?

As an American Indian and as a contemporary woman, Harjo continues to use poetry as a vehicle for moving beyond survival to success. She writes, she tells us, because "if Indian people, Indian women, keep silent, then we will disappear."

QUICK PLANNING GUIDE

Into the Poem

- **Reading Focus: Scaffolding** Students discover that poets remind people of their connections with others and with the world.
- **Quickwrite: Prior Knowledge** Freewrite about connections

Through the Poem

Beyond the Poem

- **Writer's Notebook:** Collect ideas for an evaluation
- **Critical Writing:** Compare in a short essay two authors' messages
- **Creative Writing/Speaking and Listening:** Write a poem

PORTFOLIO ASSESSMENT

Portfolio Assessment
For help with self- and teacher assessment of reading skills, see the *Portfolio Management System,* p. 53.

PROGRAM MANAGER

- **Planning Instruction** See Teaching Notes, *Teaching Resources B,* p. 161, for objectives, a summary, and literary elements.
- **Instructional Support** Before beginning the instructional lesson, see Graphic Organizer for Active Reading, *Teaching Resources B,* p. 177, for a Through the Poem activity.
- **Assessment** See Selection Test, *Test Booklet,* pp. 237–238.

Using **BEFORE YOU READ** p. 1040

Reading Focus

Ask students to brainstorm a list of varied and unusual ways people make connections with other people and with the world. Have students discuss methods of establishing and maintaining connections, and how people used to communicate when computers and television were not available.

A. Cultural Connections
Connections to the past, respect for ancestors, and reverence for the earth and one's homeland are vital elements of the poem. How does the speaker want readers to remember their cultural roots? [By remembering how closely connected we are to the earth, the wind, the trees, and, ultimately, the universe.]

B. Literary Element: Refrain
? Why does Harjo repeat the refrain at the beginning of each of these lines? [Possible answers: The repetition emphasizes the theme. It adds to the rhythm of the poem.]

BEFORE YOU READ
REMEMBER

Reading Focus

Connected
In this age of isolated computer modems, the impersonal information superhighway, and lonely flickering TV screens, it is easy to overlook the many ways we can connect with fellow humans and with the world around us. One of the main functions of poets through the ages has been to remind us of connections we have forgotten or take for granted and to show us new connections.

Quickwrite

READER'S LOG

Freewrite all the associations you make to the word *connection.* How many possible connections can human beings make to one another and to the world around them?

Remember

Joy Harjo

Remember the sky that you were born under,
know each of the star's stories.
Remember the moon, know who she is.
Remember the sun's birth at dawn, that is the
strongest point of time. Remember sundown
and the giving away to night.
Remember your birth, how your mother struggled
to give you form and breath. You are evidence of
her life, and her mother's, and hers.
Remember your father. He is your life, also.
Remember the earth whose skin you are:
red earth, black earth, yellow earth, white earth
brown earth, we are earth.
Remember the plants, trees, animal life who all have their
tribes, their families, their histories, too. Talk to them,
listen to them. They are alive poems.
Remember the wind. Remember her voice. She knows the
origin of this universe.
Remember that you are all people and that all people
are you.
Remember that you are this universe and that this
universe is you.
Remember that all is in motion, is growing, is you.
Remember that language comes from this.
Remember the dance that language is, that life is.
Remember.

OPTIONS FOR TEACHING

STRATEGIES FOR INCLUSION

Musical Have students take a favorite work of instrumental music and use it as a background for an oral reading of the poem. Or students may wish to research American Indian music and choose selections to play as background to their reading.

Advanced Have students develop a personal response to the poem's theme. The speaker asks the reader to remember the connections among all living creatures and calls plants, trees, and animals "alive poems." Have students share what a plant, tree, or animal might say should be remembered about these connections. Ask them to present their response as a conversation, song, poster, or poem.

Learners Having Difficulty Many of the songs and poems students have read in this book contain **refrains**. To help students identify Harjo's refrain and understand its purpose, share examples of refrains from familiar literature or songs. Ask students to bring in other examples and have them explain why they think Harjo decided to use a refrain.

RESPONDING TO THE ART: ABOUT THE ARTWORK

Abstract art is a general term used to describe contemporary schools that include art "abstracted," or drawn apart from reality. *Sun* by Arthur G. Dove (1880–1946), an American painter, exemplifies the abstract art of his generation. Restricted to geometric forms, *Sun* nevertheless conveys the warmth of the sun and expresses Dove's love and praise of nature.

Sun (1943) by Arthur G. Dove. Wax emulsion on canvas (24″ × 32″).

National Museum of American Art, Washington, D.C. Bequest of Suzanne M. Smith. By permission of D. Mullett Smith Trust. © 1976 by Suzanne Mullett Smith. Courtesy Art Resource.

INTEGRATING THE LANGUAGE ARTS

Strategic Reading Explain to students the fact that American Indians often use chant in dances and prayers. Have the class do a choral reading of the poem. Discuss the effect of everyone reading the poem together as opposed to one person reading aloud and how choral reading may help establish connections between people. Discuss the chantlike quality of this poem and, in particular, how the refrain adds to its rhythmic quality.

Making Meanings

First Thoughts

1. Possible responses: Lines 8–10 on birth because of the tradition of passing on life. Or ll. 23–24 because it is powerful to think we are one with the universe.

Shaping interpretations

2. Possible responses: The speaker may be an American Indian tribal elder who is addressing a younger person. Or the speaker may be someone about to die who addresses younger family members.
3. Possible response: The importance of remembering the connection people have to each other, to the earth, and to the universe.
4. The moon is personified in ll. 3 and 4; the sun in l. 5; the plants, trees, and animals in ll. 14–16; the wind in ll. 17–18. By personifying them, the poet gives life to objects considered inanimate and places them in high regard.
5. "Remember." It adds emphasis to the poem's message: the importance of remembering connections to others and to the earth.

Connecting with the Text

6. Possible responses: Yes, if we listen to plants, trees, and animals, we will come to a greater appreciation of what surrounds us and feel a stronger connection to the universe. Or no, I do not know how to go about listening to trees.

Choices: Building Your Portfolio

1. **Writer's Notebook** Remind students to save their work. They may use it as prewriting for the Writer's Workshop on p. 1181. *Also remind students to choose an experience they would not mind sharing with others.* You may wish to have students recall others' experiences.

MAKING MEANINGS

First Thoughts

1. Which passage in the poem had the strongest effect on you? Why?

Shaping Interpretations

2. Who do you think is the **speaker** of "Remember"? Whom is the speaker addressing?
3. How would you state the main **theme** of the poem in your own words?
4. In the poem, there are several instances of **personification** (a figure of speech in which an object or animal is given human attributes). Identify two such instances, and explain what they add to the poem.
5. Identify the **refrain** of the poem. What does it contribute to the poem's message?

Connecting with the Text

6. The speaker asks the reader to talk to and listen to plants, trees, and animal life. Does this request make sense to you? Explain, referring to your Quickwrite notes.

David L. Brown/The Stock Market.

CHOICES: Building Your Portfolio

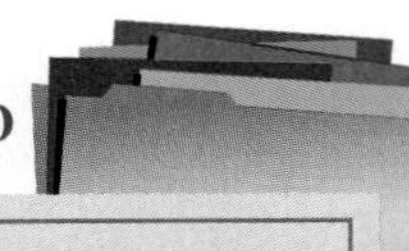

Writer's Notebook

1. Collecting Ideas for an Evaluation

When writing an evaluation, you can cite your own experience to support your judgment of a text. Jot down experiences you can recall that relate to Harjo's "Remember." Do any match the speaker's? Based on your own experience, which of the speaker's requests could you follow easily? Which would be more difficult or even impossible to follow? Save your notes for possible use in the Writer's Workshop on page 1181.

Critical Writing

2. The American Tradition

Though Ralph Waldo Emerson was born in a very different era, almost 150 years before Joy Harjo, the two writers share a keen appreciation of the natural world. In a short essay, compare the messages of Harjo's "Remember" and the excerpt from Emerson's *Nature* (page 219). How are they similar? How are they different?

Creative Writing / Speaking and Listening

3. All Your Yesterdays

Write a "Remember" poem, in which you relate some of your own memories and experiences. Start each line or stanza with "Remember" or "I remember":

Remember ____________________
____
____

Remember ____________________
____
____

If you wish, read your poem before the class.

STRATEGIES FOR INCLUSION

Linguistic To help students in the prewriting stage of activity #2, suggest that they imagine what Harjo and Emerson would say to each other. For example, have students take notes on what Harjo and Emerson might say about maintaining connections with nature and retiring from society.

PORTFOLIO ASSESSMENT

Choices: Assessment Criteria For help in evaluating these Choices assignments, see the criteria in the *Portfolio Management System,* p. 194.

Maxine Hong Kingston

(1940–)

© Nancy Crampton.

Maxine Hong Kingston burst onto the literary scene in 1976 with an extraordinary and innovative book—*The Woman Warrior: Memoirs of a Girlhood Among Ghosts.* Kingston, who was born in California of Chinese immigrant parents, uses a mixture of autobiography, myth, poetic meditation, and fiction to convey her memories and feelings about growing up in a strange world (the United States) populated by what she and her family thought of as white-skinned "ghosts."

The book received immediate acclaim. William McPherson of the *Washington Post* wrote: "*The Woman Warrior* is a strange, sometimes savagely terrifying and, in the literal sense, wonderful story about growing up caught between two highly sophisticated and utterly alien cultures, both vivid, often menacing, and equally mysterious." Paul Gray said in *Time:* "Exiles and refugees tell sad stories of the life they left behind. Even sadder, sometimes, is the muteness of their children. They are likely to find the old ways and old language excess baggage, especially if their adopted homeland is the United States, where the race is to the swift and the adaptable. Thus a heritage of centuries can die in a generation of embarrassed silence. *The Woman Warrior* gives that silence a voice."

When *The Woman Warrior* won the National Book Critics Circle Award for general nonfiction in 1976, Kingston gained national attention. The suddenness of her appearance as an important literary figure was startling.

Where had Kingston been until the age of thirty-six? Named for an American woman in the gambling house where her father worked for a time, Maxine Hong grew up in the Chinatown of Stockton, California. She earned a B.A. from the University of California at Berkeley in 1962 and married the actor Earll Kingston. After their son was born, the Kingstons lived in Hawaii for a time, where Maxine taught English at the high school and college levels, before returning to California.

In 1980, Kingston published a companion piece to *The Woman Warrior,* a kind of ancestral history called *China Men.* The critic Susan Currier has described this book as "a sort of vindication of all the Chinese who helped build America but who were rewarded with abuse and neglect." In 1988, Kingston published an extravagant novel called *Tripmaster Monkey: His Fake Book,* blending Chinese history and myth and vivid storytelling in the adventures of a young Chinese American named Wittman Ah Sing. The noted novelist Anne Tyler called *Tripmaster Monkey* "a novel of satisfying complexity and bite and verve." In the early 1990s, Kingston taught creative writing at the University of California at Berkeley and worked on a book of nonfiction.

Despite the attention given to her books, Kingston has remained relatively private. She seldom gives interviews or appears at public readings. In her two memoirs, she does not answer all of the personal questions raised by her writing. In the passage that follows, even a careful reader will not be able to decide what is truth, what is fiction, and what is simply left unsaid. This ambiguity gives Kingston's work much of its haunting quality.

ABOUT THE AUTHOR

Kingston's parents married in China. Her father emigrated to New York City and worked in a laundry for fifteen years to send his wife money to study for certifications in medicine and midwifery in China. She established a practice in China, but gave it up when her husband sent for her to come to the United States. In the United States she worked as a laundress and a field hand. Kingston may have found in her mother a model for some of the women in her writing.

QUICK PLANNING GUIDE

Into the Story

Author Biography p. 1043

Before You Read p. 1044

- **Reading Focus:** Students discover different avenues of expression.
- **A Dialogue with the Text: Set a Purpose** List the character's unexpressed thoughts and feelings in Reader's Log
- **Elements of Literature: Conflict**
- **Background: Scaffolding** Chinese voices and American ghosts

Through the Story

"The Girl Who Wouldn't Talk" pp. 1045–1052

Words to Own pp. 1047–1049

Literature and Society pp. 1050–1051

Making Meanings p. 1053

Beyond the Story

Choices: Building Your Portfolio p. 1053

- **Writer's Notebook:** Collect ideas for an evaluation
- **Critical Writing:** Discuss the character of the narrator in a short essay
- **Creative Writing:** Discuss what might have happened to the narrator in an essay

BEFORE YOU READ
THE GIRL WHO WOULDN'T TALK

Reading Focus

Things Left Unspoken

It happens just about every day to all of us: For one reason or another, we don't tell others about something important we know or feel. Out of self-doubt, politeness, love, fear, or many other reasons, we don't express in conversation certain thoughts or feelings that are near to us. Instead, we sometimes express them in writing, painting, dance, song, or some other art form.

A Dialogue with the Text

As you read "The Girl Who Wouldn't Talk," write down what you think the silent girl is not saying—that is, what her unexpressed thoughts and feelings are. You might also jot down what you think the *narrator* is not saying.

Elements of Literature

Conflict

Conflict—the struggle between opposing forces or characters in a story—can be either external or internal. **External conflict** can take many forms. For example, it can involve two people, a person and a force of nature, a person and a machine, or a person and a society or community. **Internal conflict** involves opposing forces within a person's mind. Kingston's story presents both external and internal conflicts centering around childhood cruelty, a problem that knows no cultural or linguistic barriers.

> **Conflict** is the struggle between opposing forces or characters in a story.
>
> *For more on Conflict, see page 607 and the Handbook of Literary Terms.*

Background

The Chinese American family in this extract from *The Woman Warrior* lives in Stockton, California. Just before the episode starts, the narrator talks about speech and Chinese voices, which she says are louder than American voices. Describing her own voice, the narrator says: "You could hear splinters in my voice, bones rubbing jagged against one another. I was loud, though. I was glad I didn't whisper."

The "ghosts" mentioned by the narrator are white Americans, who seemed so strange to this Chinese family.

WORDS TO OWN

The following vocabulary words are defined in the Words to Own at the bottom of the pupil's page.

loitered p. 1047	sarcastic p. 1048
nape p. 1048	temples p. 1049
habitually p. 1048	

PORTFOLIO ASSESSMENT

Portfolio Assessment For help with self- and teacher assessment of reading skills, see the *Portfolio Management System,* p. 39.

The Girl Who Wouldn't Talk

Maxine Hong Kingston

Using **BEFORE YOUR READ** p. 1044

Reading Focus

Have students discuss reasons why certain things are left unsaid. Ask them also to talk about the importance of having other activities, hobbies, or pastimes as a way to say those things people cannot put into words.

A Dialogue with the Text

Remind the class that authors let the reader know what characters are thinking even though the characters (and the author) leave certain things unsaid. Have students offer ways of knowing what characters think or feel. [Through their actions or gestures, physical appearance, and interactions with others.]

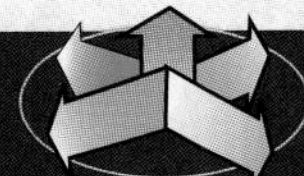

PROGRAM MANAGER

- **Planning Instruction** See Teaching Notes, *Teaching Resources B,* p. 162, for objectives, a summary, and literary elements for this selection.
- **Instructional Support** Before beginning the instructional lesson, see Graphic Organizer for Active Reading, *Teaching Resources B,* p. 178, for a Through the Story activity.
- **Assessment** See Selection Test, *Test Booklet,* pp. 239–240.
- **Reinforcement** Use the Words to Own worksheet in *Teaching Resources B,* p. 179.

A. Cultural Connections

? How does the narrator describe the various ways of talking? [Chinese women's voices are loud. American women's voices are soft.] How do the Chinese girls feel about changing their voices? [Some gave up; some could not talk; others invented an American woman's way of talking. One could not speak at all. The narrator feels ambivalent about talking like American women.]

B. Reader's Response: First Thoughts

? What do you think about the two girls? [Sample responses: The narrator may be angry at having had to start school so early. The quiet girl and her sister may have come from a well-to-do family since they did not have to work. The narrator may resent this.]

C. Literary Element: Conflict

? What clues does the narrator provide here as to the reasons for her animosity toward the quiet girl? [Possible answers: The narrator recognizes similarities between herself and the girl. Or she sees in the girl aspects of the "Chinese feminine" personality she wishes to suppress in herself.]

Normal Chinese women's voices are strong and bossy. We American-Chinese girls had to whisper to make ourselves American-feminine. Apparently we whispered even more softly than the Americans. Once a year the teachers referred my sister and me to speech therapy, but our voices would straighten out, unpredictably normal, for the therapists. Some of us gave up, shook our heads, and said nothing, not one word. Some of us could not even shake our heads. At times shaking my head no is more self-assertion than I can manage. Most of us eventually found some voice, however faltering. We invented an American-feminine speaking personality, except for that one girl who could not speak up even in Chinese school. **A**

She was a year older than I and was in my class for twelve years. During all those years she read aloud but would not talk. Her older sister was usually beside her; their parents kept the older daughter back to protect the younger one. They were six and seven years old when they began school. Although I had flunked kindergarten, I was the same age as most other students in our class; my parents had probably lied about my age, so I had had a head start and came out even. My younger sister was in the class below me; we were normal ages and normally separated. The parents of the quiet girl, on the other hand, protected both daughters. When it sprinkled, they kept them home from school. The girls did not work for a living the way we did. But in other ways we were the same. **B**

We were similar in sports. We held the bat on our shoulders until we walked to first base. (You got a strike only when you actually struck at the ball.) Sometimes the pitcher wouldn't bother to throw to us. "Automatic walk," the other children would call, sending us on our way. By fourth or fifth grade, though, some of us would try to hit the ball. "Easy out," the other kids would say. I hit the ball a couple of times. Baseball was nice in that there was a definite spot to run to after hitting the ball. Basketball confused me because when I caught the ball I didn't know whom to throw it to. "Me. Me," the kids would be yelling. "Over here." Suddenly it would occur to me I hadn't memorized which ghosts were on my team and which were on the other. When the kids said, "Automatic walk," the girl who was quieter than I kneeled with one end of the bat in each hand and placed it carefully on the plate. Then she dusted her hands as she walked to first base, where she rubbed her hands softly, fingers spread. She always got tagged out before second base. She would whisper-read but not talk. Her whisper was as soft as if she had no muscles. She seemed to be breathing from a distance. I heard no anger or tension.

I joined in at lunchtime when the other students, the Chinese too, talked about whether or not she was mute, although obviously she was not if she could read aloud. People told how *they* had tried *their* best to be friendly. *They* said hello, but if she refused to answer, well, they didn't see why they had to say hello anymore. She had no friends of her own but followed her sister everywhere, although people and she herself probably thought I was her friend. I also followed her sister about, who was fairly normal. She was almost two years older and read more than anyone else.

I hated the younger sister, the quiet one. I hated her when she was the last chosen for her team and I, the last chosen for my team. I hated her for her China doll hair cut. I hated her at music time for the wheezes that came out of her plastic flute. **C**

One afternoon in the sixth grade (that year I was arrogant with talk, not knowing there were going to be high school dances and college seminars to set me back), I and my little sister and the quiet girl and her big sister stayed late after school for some reason. The cement was cooling, and the tetherball poles made shadows across the gravel. The hooks at the rope ends were clinking against the poles. We shouldn't have been so late; there was laundry work to do and Chinese school to get to by 5:00. The last time we had stayed late, my mother had phoned the police and told them we had been kidnapped

OPTIONS FOR TEACHING

STRATEGIES FOR INCLUSION

Intrapersonal Have students make an entry in a personal journal about a time when someone they knew felt tormented because he or she was not accepted. Have them relate that experience to that of the narrator and the girl who would not talk. Ask them to share the entry with you. *Remind students to use situations they would not mind sharing with others.*

English Language Development Although the narrator says she hated the girl who would not talk, she herself refused to give voice to many of her own feelings. She does not name the "ghosts" she goes to school with and cannot recognize their faces. Her anger with the quiet girl reflects her own conflicts. To help students express a personal understanding of internal and external conflicts, have them draw a visual representation of the internal and external conflicts the narrator might have. Ask them to choose colors, lines, and movement which illustrate this division. Have them share the image with a classmate.

Advanced Invite students to read Kingston's novel *The Woman Warrior.* Ask them to look for other times the narrator experiences conflict between adapting American customs and dealing with Chinese customs. Have them talk about the book with the rest of the class.

by bandits. The radio stations broadcast our descriptions. I had to get home before she did that again. But sometimes if you loitered long enough in the schoolyard, the other children would have gone home and you could play with the equipment before the office took it away. We were chasing one another through the playground and in and out of the basement, where the playroom and lavatory were. During air raid drills (it was during the Korean War, which you knew about because every day the front page of the newspaper printed a map of Korea with the top part red and going up and down like a window shade), we curled up in this basement. Now everyone was gone. The playroom was army green and had nothing in it but a long trough with drinking spigots in rows. Pipes across the ceiling led to the drinking fountains and to the toilets in the next room. When someone flushed you could hear the water and other matter, which the children named, running inside the big pipe above the drinking spigots. There was one playroom for girls next to the girls' lavatory and one playroom for boys next to the boys' lavatory. The stalls were open and the toilets had no lids, by which we knew that ghosts have no sense of shame or privacy.

Inside the playroom the lightbulbs in cages had already been turned off. Daylight came in x-patterns through the caging at the windows. I looked out and, seeing no one in the schoolyard, ran outside to climb the fire escape upside down, hanging on to the metal stairs with fingers and toes.

I did a flip off the fire escape and ran across the schoolyard. The day was a great eye, and it was not paying much attention to me now. I could disappear with the sun; I could turn quickly sideways and slip into a different world. It seemed I could run faster at this time, and by evening I would be able to fly. As the afternoon wore on we could run into the forbidden places—the boys' big yard, the boys' playroom. We could go into the boys' lavatory and look at the urinals. The only time during school hours I had crossed the boys' yard was when a flatbed truck with a giant thing covered with canvas and tied down with ropes had parked across the street. The children had told one another that it was a gorilla in captivity; we couldn't decide whether the sign said "Trail of the Gorilla" or "Trial of the Gorilla." The thing was as big as a house. The teachers couldn't stop us from hysterically rushing to the fence and clinging to the wire mesh. Now I ran across the boys' yard clear to the Cyclone fence and thought about the hair that I had seen sticking out of the canvas. It was going to be summer soon, so you could feel that freedom coming on too.

I ran back into the girls' yard, and there was the quiet sister all by herself. I ran past her, and she followed me into the girls' lavatory. My footsteps rang hard against cement and tile because of the taps I had nailed into my shoes. Her footsteps were soft, padding after me. There was no one in the lavatory but the two of us. I ran all around the rows of twenty-five open stalls to make sure of that. No sisters. I think we must have been playing hide-and-go-seek. She was not good at hiding by herself and usually followed her sister; they'd hide in the same place. They must have gotten separated. In this growing twilight, a child could hide and never be found.

I stopped abruptly in front of the sinks, and she came running toward me before she could stop herself, so that she almost collided with me. I walked closer. She backed away, puzzlement, then alarm in her eyes.

"You're going to talk," I said, my voice steady and normal, as it is when talking to the familiar, the weak, and the small. "I am going to make you talk, you sissy-girl." She stopped backing away and stood fixed.

I looked into her face so I could hate it close up. She wore black bangs, and her cheeks were pink and white. She was baby-soft. I thought that I could put my thumb on

Words to Own

loitered (loit′ərd) *v.:* spent time; hung around.

D. Exploring the Historical Period

The top of the newspaper map was red to mark North Korean territory. The red portion went up and down, reflecting the rapid changes in the fortunes of that war: At first the North Koreans occupied most of South Korea; then they were driven back almost to the Chinese border; then Chinese soldiers entered the fighting on the North Korean side, and the South Koreans and Americans were pushed back down again.

E. Critical Reading: Speculating

? Why does the narrator check all the stalls? [Possible answer: She is going to do something cruel to the younger sister. Or she is going to try to make the younger sister talk.]

INTEGRATED LANGUAGE ARTS

Strategic Reading As students read the story, have them note in their Reader's Logs why the selection is titled "The Girl Who Wouldn't Talk." After they have finished reading the story, students should return to their logs and explain whether they think the title is appropriate for the story. If they think it is not, they should suggest and defend new titles.

Grammar and Mechanics Point out that the title contains an adjective clause—a subordinate clause that modifies a noun or pronoun. Remind students that adjective clauses often begin with the words *that, which, who,* or *whom.* Then ask them to identify the adjective clause in the title and the noun it modifies. [*Who wouldn't talk* modifies *girl.*] Sometimes adjective clauses provide more information about the noun or pronoun they modify (nonessential clauses); at other times they pin down a specific person or object (essential clauses). In this case ask, "Which girl?" Since the answer is "Not just any girl, but the one who wouldn't talk," the clause is essential. Most people are insecure about comma usage when punctuating an adjective clause. If you want to deal with this punctuation problem, have students turn to p. 1243, rule 12i. Then, have students write three sentences that contain adjective clauses, adding commas where necessary. ☞

A. Critical Reading: Drawing Conclusions

? What does the narrator admire about the Mexican American and African American girls she has seen fighting? [They seem tough. The quiet girl, in contrast, has too many passive, gentle qualities that the narrator does not like to see in herself.]

B. Literary Element: Similes

? What unpleasant similes in this long paragraph suggest how repulsive the narrator finds the quiet girl? [Her skin is like squid; her arms like tracing paper; and her ears like white cutworms.]

her nose and push it bonelessly in, indent her face. I could poke dimples into her cheeks. I could work her face around like dough. She stood still, and I did not want to look at her face anymore; I hated fragility. I walked around her, looked her up and down the way the Mexican and Negro girls did when they fought, so tough. I hated her weak neck, the way it did not support her head but let it droop; her head would fall backward. I stared at the curve of her nape. I wished I was able to see what my own neck looked like from the back and sides. I hoped it did not look like hers; I wanted a stout neck. I grew my hair long to hide it in case it was a flower-stem neck. I walked around to the front of her to hate her face some more.

I reached up and took the fatty part of her cheek, not dough, but meat, between my thumb and finger. This close, and I saw no pores. "Talk," I said. "Are you going to talk?" Her skin was fleshy, like squid out of which the glassy blades of bones had been pulled. I wanted tough skin, hard brown skin. I had callused my hands; I had scratched dirt to blacken the nails, which I cut straight across to make stubby fingers. I gave her face a squeeze. "Talk." When I let go, the pink rushed back into my white thumbprint on her skin. I walked around to her side. "Talk!" I shouted into the side of her head. Her straight hair hung, the same all these years, no ringlets or braids or permanents. I squeezed her other cheek. "Are you? Huh? Are you going to talk?" She tried to shake her head, but I had hold of her face. She had no muscles to jerk away. Her skin seemed to stretch. I let go in horror. What if it came away in my hand? "No, huh?" I said, rubbing the touch of her off my fingers. "Say 'No,' then," I said. I gave her another pinch and a twist. "Say 'No.'" She shook her head, her straight hair turning with her head, not swinging side to side like the pretty girls'. She was so neat. Her neatness bothered me. I hated the way she folded the wax paper from her lunch; she did not wad her brown paper bag and her school papers. I hated her clothes—the blue pastel cardigan, the white blouse with the collar that lay flat over the cardigan, the homemade flat, cotton skirt she wore when everybody else was wearing flared skirts. I hated pastels; I would wear black always. I squeezed again, harder, even though her cheek had a weak rubbery feeling I did not like. I squeezed one cheek, then the other, back and forth until the tears ran out of her eyes as if I had pulled them out. "Stop crying," I said, but although she habitually followed me around, she did not obey. Her eyes dripped; her nose dripped. She wiped her eyes with her papery fingers. The skin on her hands and arms seemed powdery-dry, like tracing paper, onion paper. I hated her fingers. I could snap them like breadsticks. I pushed her hands down. "Say 'Hi,'" I said. "'Hi.' Like that. Say your name. Go ahead. Say it. Or are you stupid? You're so stupid, you don't know your own name, is that it? When I say, 'What's your name?' you just blurt it out, O.K.? What's your name?" Last year the whole class had laughed at a boy who couldn't fill out a form because he didn't know his father's name. The teacher sighed, exasperated and was very sarcastic, "Don't you notice things? What does your mother call him?" she said. The class laughed at how dumb he was not to notice things. "She calls him father of me," he said. Even we laughed although we knew that his mother did not call his father by name, and a son does not know his father's name. We laughed and were relieved that our parents had had the foresight to tell us some names we could give the teachers. "If you're not stupid," I said to the quiet girl, "what's your name?" She shook her head, and some hair caught in the tears; wet black hair stuck to the side of the pink and white face. I reached up (she was taller than I) and took a strand of hair. I pulled it. "Well, then,

Words to Own

nape (nāp) *n.:* back of the neck.
habitually (hə · bich′o͞o · əl · lē) *adv.:* usually; by habit.
sarcastic (sär · kas′tik) *adj.:* scornful; mocking.

OPTIONS FOR TEACHING

COOPERATIVE LEARNING

Jigsaw Reading Have students work in small groups for ten minutes. Each member should concentrate on a different one of the following literary elements, and write ideas about how the elements are important in the story: **tone, motivation, external conflict,** and **internal conflict.** After ten minutes, ask students who worked on the same element to form new groups to discuss their findings. After five minutes of discussion, ask students to return to their original groups to share their information with the other members.

Assessing Characters Have students work in pairs to write one-sentence character assessments of the narrator and the quiet girl. Students may refer to the information on **character** in the Handbook of Literary Terms. After five minutes, ask a speaker from each group to read the sentences the group wrote. Discuss differences among the groups' assessments of the characters.

let's honk your hair," I said. "Honk. Honk." Then I pulled the other side—"ho-o-n-nk"—a long pull; "ho-o-n-n-nk"—a longer pull. I could see her little white ears, like white cutworms curled underneath the hair. "Talk!" I yelled into each cutworm.

I looked right at her. "I know you talk," I said. "I've heard you." Her eyebrows flew up. Something in those black eyes was startled, and I pursued it. "I was walking past your house when you didn't know I was there. I heard you yell in English and in Chinese. You weren't just talking. You were shouting. I heard you shout. You were saying, 'Where are you?' Say that again. Go ahead, just the way you did at home." I yanked harder on the hair, but steadily, not jerking. I did not want to pull it out. "Go ahead. Say, 'Where are you?' Say it loud enough for your sister to come. Call her. Make her come help you. Call her name. I'll stop if she comes. So call. Go ahead."

She shook her head, her mouth curved down, crying. I could see her tiny white teeth, baby teeth. I wanted to grow big strong yellow teeth. "You do have a tongue," I said. "So use it." I pulled the hair at her temples, pulled the tears out of her eyes. "Say, 'Ow'" I said. "Just 'Ow.' Say, 'Let go.' Go ahead. Say it. I'll honk you again if you don't say, 'Let me alone.' Say, 'Leave me alone,' and I'll let you go. I will. I'll let go if you say it. You can stop this anytime you want to, you know. All you have to do is tell me to stop. Just say, 'Stop.' You're just asking for it, aren't you? You're just asking for another honk. Well then, I'll have to give you another honk. Say, 'Stop.'" But she didn't. I had to pull again and again.

Sounds did come out of her mouth, sobs, chokes, noises that were almost words. Snot ran out of her nose. She tried to wipe it on her hands, but there was too much of it. She used her sleeve. "You're disgusting," I told her. "Look at you, snot streaming down your nose, and you won't say a word to stop it. You're such a nothing." I moved behind her and pulled the hair growing out of her weak neck. I let go. I stood silent for a long time. Then I screamed, "Talk!" I would scare the words out of her. If she had had little bound feet, the toes twisted under the balls, I would have jumped up and landed on them—crunch!—stomped on them with my iron shoes. She cried hard, sobbing aloud. "Cry, 'Mama,'" I said. "Come on. Cry, 'Mama.' Say, 'Stop it.'"

I put my finger on her pointed chin. "I don't like you. I don't like the weak little toots you make on your flute. Wheeze. Wheeze. I don't like the way you don't swing at the ball. I don't like the way you're the last one chosen. I don't like the way you can't make a fist for tetherball. Why don't you make a fist? Come on. Get tough. Come on. Throw fists." I pushed at her long hands; they swung limply at her sides. Her fingers were so long, I thought maybe they had an extra joint. They couldn't possibly make fists like other people's. "Make a fist," I said. "Come on. Just fold those fingers up; fingers on the inside, thumbs on the outside. Say something. Honk me back. You're so tall, and you let me pick on you.

"Would you like a hanky? I can't get you one with embroidery on it or crocheting along the edges, but I'll get you some toilet paper if you tell me to. Go ahead. Ask me. I'll get it for you if you ask." She did not stop crying. "Why don't you scream, 'Help'?" I suggested. "Say, 'Help.' Go ahead." She cried on. "O.K. O.K. Don't talk. Just scream, and I'll let you go. Won't that feel good? Go ahead. Like this." I screamed not too loudly. My voice hit the tile and rang it as if I had thrown a rock at it. The stalls opened wider and the toilets wider and darker. Shadows leaned at angles I had not seen before. It was very late. Maybe a janitor had locked me in with this girl for the night. Her black eyes blinked and stared, blinked and stared. I felt dizzy from hunger. We had been in this lavatory together forever. My mother would call

WORDS TO OWN

temples (tem′pəlz) *n. pl.:* sides of the forehead, just above and in front of the ears.

C. Critical Reading: Making Inferences

? What is it that particularly startles the quiet girl? [The narrator's claim that she has heard the quiet girl talk.]

D. Exploring the Historical Period

? What makes the narrator think of bound feet? [The narrator makes a connection between the custom of binding young girls' feet and what she would have done to the little girl's feet had they been bound. The thought may be symbolic of what the narrator hates about Chinese traditions of submissiveness and silence.]

CLASSROOM MANAGEMENT

Managing the Reader's Response Classroom About five minutes before the end of class, ask students to write down a comment or an idea resulting from reading this story. They can give these comments to you on slips of paper as they exit. You may want to ask a few students to read their ideas aloud the next day. This procedure provides thoughtful closure after each story.

Constructive Peer Feedback Encourage students to develop an atmosphere of trust and cooperation in the classroom. At every available opportunity, have students meet in small groups, varying the members each time. In these groups, students can provide constructive feedback on a project or assignment that is still being revised. As students become used to remarks from their peers, they will be better able to collaborate in group efforts and discussions. ☞

LITERATURE AND SOCIETY

Have student groups research and report in detail on a particular Chinese custom or facet of Chinese culture. The report could focus on one custom mentioned here, such as reverence toward ancestors or the Chinese New Year, or it could focus on a subject of the group's own choosing, such as Confucianism, calligraphy, Chinese characters, Taoism, or the Cultural Revolution. Be sure each group chooses a different subject. Have the groups hold Chinese school, where they teach the class about Chinese life and customs.

Technology Tip

Ask students to research principles of *feng-shui*. Have them use CAD software and redesign your classroom or school based on this Chinese tradition.

Literature and Society

The Chinese American Family

In her story, Maxine Hong Kingston mentions that the girl who wouldn't talk was supported and protected by her family. This isn't surprising, given the importance of family relationships in Chinese culture. As the Chinese American writer Leslie Li notes, solitude is not a coveted state among most Chinese people. "They love their family and friends and want them around, along with the *renao* they bring, the heat and noise of human relationships."

Family ties. In Chinese culture, "name" does not so much signify individual identity as relationship to others, such as daughter, son, aunt, uncle, and so on. In Chinese tradition, the family name is given first—for example, "Chung Connie," not the Americanized "Connie Chung"—and family members are often introduced not by their names but by their family relationships. Children may address family members not by name but as Aunt, Second Older Brother, Grandfather, and so on. In Kingston's story, a boy is laughed at in class because he doesn't know his father's name; at home, he says, his father is called only "father of me." In the story "Rules of the Game" by the Chinese American writer Amy Tan (page 1111), the character Waverly is called "Waverly" for the benefit of outsiders, but at home she is "Meimei" (Little Sister).

Bridging two worlds. Ultimately, many Chinese Americans choose to integrate the cultures of both China and the United States in their family life. They embrace some traditional beliefs of their immigrant parents or grandparents, but they also take part in mainstream American traditions. They may celebrate both Chinese and American holidays, for example, or enjoy traditional Chinese foods one day, grilled steak the next. They may use American names with outsiders but their Chinese middle names at home. In addition to attending regular public or private school all day, some Chinese American children spend three or four hours at Chinese school (often held on Saturdays), where their

the police again if I didn't bring my sister home soon. "I'll let you go if you say just one word," I said. "You can even say 'a' or 'the,' and I'll let you go. Come on. Please." She didn't shake her head anymore, only cried steadily, so much water coming out of her. I could see the two duct holes where the tears welled out. Quarts of tears but no words. I grabbed her by the shoulder. I could feel bones. The light was coming in queerly through the frosted glass with the chicken wire embedded in it. Her crying was like an animal's—a seal's—and it echoed around the basement. "Do you want to stay here all night?" I asked. "Your mother is wondering what happened to her baby. You wouldn't want to have her mad at you. You'd better say something." I shook her shoulder. I pulled her hair again. I squeezed her face. "Come on! Talk! Talk! Talk!" She didn't seem to feel it anymore when I pulled her hair. "There's nobody here but you and me. This isn't a classroom or a playground or a crowd. I'm just one person. You can talk in front of one person. Don't make me pull harder and harder until you talk." But her hair seemed to stretch; she did not say a word. "I'm going to pull harder. Don't make me pull anymore, or your hair will come out and you're going to be bald. Do you want to be bald? You don't want to be bald, do you?"

Far away, coming from the edge of town, I

OPTIONS FOR TEACHING

CROSSING THE CURRICULUM

Health Have students research what the narrator's mysterious illness could have been. They may wish to look into the possibility of psychosomatic illness. Ask students to research the traumatic effect this interaction could have had on her health over a long period. Have students present their findings to the class.

History Have student pairs research the Korean War. Ask them to write several newspaper stories about the war and include maps of North and South Korea reflecting shifting boundaries during the war. Post the articles and illustrations on bulletin boards in the classroom.

PROBLEM SOLVING/CRITICAL THINKING

Cultural Change The narrator observes that some of the Chinese girls tape their eyelids. Ask students to identify things that people do to be accepted into another culture at the expense of their own. Have groups discuss how people can learn to accept themselves and how individuals can learn to accept others as they are. Ask them what communities might do to encourage the acceptance of a variety of cultures and cultural practices.

parents expect them to learn Chinese language, literature, history, and philosophy.

Reverence toward ancestors, a cornerstone of Chinese tradition, has been an important feature of traditional Chinese American family life. A memorial plaque inscribed with ancestors' names is sometimes displayed in the home, and one tradition requires family members to read the names aloud while bowing to the plaque. Some families make ritual visits to ancestors' graves each spring, honoring the spirits of the dead by bringing gifts of food and cleaning the graves. And, when the Chinese New Year arrives, families may rearrange their living quarters *feng-shui* style—that is, move the furniture around to achieve maximum harmony with nature. The belief behind *feng-shui* is that proper balancing of elements will pump *ch'i* (vital energy) throughout the home and enhance the family's experience of harmony and success during the coming year.

heard whistles blow. The cannery was changing shifts, letting out the afternoon people, and still we were here at school. It was a sad sound—work done. The air was lonelier after the sound died.

"Why won't you talk?" I started to cry. What if I couldn't stop, and everyone would want to know what happened? "Now look what you've done," I scolded. "You're going to pay for this. I want to know why. And you're going to tell me why. You don't see (A) I'm trying to help you out, do you? Do you want to be like this, dumb (do you know what dumb means?), your whole life? Don't you ever want to be a cheerleader? Or a pompom girl? What are you going to do for a living? Yeah, you're going to have to work because you can't be a housewife. Somebody has to marry you before you can be a housewife. And you, you are a plant. Do you know that? That's all you are if you don't talk. If you don't talk, you can't have a personality. You'll have no personality and no hair. You've got to let people know you have a personality and a brain. You think somebody is going to take care of you all your stupid life? You think you'll always have your big sister? You think somebody's going to marry you, is that it? Well, you're not the type that gets dates, let alone gets married. Nobody's going to notice you. And you have to talk for interviews, speak right up in front

A. Expansion
This paragraph is an example of a harangue. The narrator goes on and on as she buries the little girl in a sea of disparaging remarks which are physically and psychologically damaging to herself and the little girl.

PROFESSIONAL NOTES

Critical Comment: Finding Voice Scholar Amy Ling writes: "A major theme in Kingston's *Woman Warrior* is the importance of articulateness. Finding one's voice and telling one's stories represents power, just as having one's stories buried is powerlessness." Ask students to discuss how this quotation relates to "The Girl Who Wouldn't Talk."

Thematic Connections: "Discoveries and Awakenings" The narrator of the story not only learns about the character of the quiet girl, but also awakens to her own character. She discovers the power of culture, over society in general, and over individuals, including herself, in particular. Have students list what the narrator discovers. Ask them to meet in groups and to discuss what they have listed. Then, have them compare the discoveries and awakenings in this story to those in the other selections in this unit. Ask group members what they have discovered in the process.

of the boss. Don't you know that? You're so dumb. Why do I waste my time on you?" Sniffling and snorting, I couldn't stop crying and talking at the same time. I kept wiping my nose on my arm, my sweater lost somewhere (probably not worn because my mother said to wear a sweater). It seemed as if I had spent my life in that basement, doing the worst thing I had yet done to another person. "I'm doing this for your own good," I said. "Don't you dare tell anyone I've been bad to you. Talk. Please talk."

I was getting dizzy from the air I was gulping. Her sobs and my sobs were bouncing wildly off the tile, sometimes together, sometimes alternating. "I don't understand why you won't say just one word," I cried, clenching my teeth. My knees were shaking, and I hung on to her hair to stand up. Another time I'd stayed too late, I had had to walk around two Negro kids who were bonking each other's head on the concrete. I went back later to see if the concrete had cracks in it. "Look. I'll give you something if you talk. I'll give you my pencil box. I'll buy you some candy. O.K.? What do you want? Tell me. Just say it, and I'll give it to you. Just say, 'yes,' or, 'O.K.,' or, 'Baby Ruth.'" But she didn't want anything.

I had stopped pinching her cheek because I did not like the feel of her skin. I would go crazy if it came away in my hands. "I skinned her," I would have to confess.

Suddenly I heard footsteps hurrying through the basement, and her sister ran into the lavatory calling her name. "Oh, there you are," I said. "We've been waiting for you. I was only trying to teach her to talk. She wouldn't cooperate, though." Her sister went into one of the stalls and got handfuls of toilet paper and wiped her off. Then we found my sister, and we walked home together. "Your family really ought to force her to speak," I advised all the way home. "You mustn't pamper her."

The world is sometimes just, and I spent the next eighteen months sick in bed with a mysterious illness. There was no pain and no symptoms, though the middle line in my left palm broke in two. Instead of starting junior high school, I lived like the Victorian recluses[1] I read about. I had a rented hospital bed in the living room, where I watched soap operas on TV, and my family cranked me up and down. I saw no one but my family, who took good care of me. I could have no visitors, no other relatives, no villagers. My bed was against the west window, and I watched the seasons change the peach tree. I had a bell to ring for help. I used a bedpan. It was the best year and a half of my life. Nothing happened.

But one day my mother, the doctor, said, "You're ready to get up today. It's time to get up and go to school." I walked about outside to get my legs working, leaning on a staff I cut from the peach tree. The sky and trees, the sun were immense—no longer framed by a window, no longer grayed with a fly screen. I sat down on the sidewalk in amazement—the night, the stars. But at school I had to figure out again how to talk. I met again the poor girl I had tormented. She had not changed. She wore the same clothes, hair cut, and manner as when we were in elementary school, no make-up on the pink and white face, while the other Asian girls were starting to tape their eyelids. She continued to be able to read aloud. But there was hardly any reading aloud anymore, less and less as we got into high school.

I was wrong about nobody taking care of her. Her sister became a clerk-typist and stayed unmarried. They lived with their mother and father. She did not have to leave the house except to go to the movies. She was supported. She was protected by her family, as they would normally have done in China if they could have afforded it, not sent off to school with strangers, ghosts, boys.

1. **Victorian recluses:** like characters in Victorian novels who, because of some illness or incapacity, lived shut away from the world.

A. Critical Reading: Drawing Conclusions

? How important is it for the narrator to make the girl talk? [Extremely important.]

Metacognition On what do you base your assertion? [Possible answer: She says that the last time she was late, she had to walk around people who were fighting; her checking the scene later may indicate how worried she was. She also talks about the inconvenience of her mother's calling the police and telling them her daughters had been kidnapped. She says she does not want to go through that again. And she is horrified by her own actions, worrying that the girl's skin might come away in her hands. She cannot stop tormenting the girl.]

B. Reader's Response: Connecting with the Text

? Do you see any relationship between the previous scene and the narrator's illness? [Sample responses: No, it could be coincidental. Or yes, it could be psychosomatic—she could be suffering from guilt. Or yes, she could be so upset from worrying about assimilating into American culture that it made her ill.]

C. Reader's Response: Challenging the Text

? Is the ending a good one for this story? [Sample response: No, the narrator does not seem to resolve her internal conflict. Or yes, the end continues to show how life is complex and that there are no simple solutions to cultural conflicts.]

OPTIONS FOR TEACHING

ASSESSMENT TOOLS

Self-Reflection: Reading Have students answer the following questions about how they read the story.

1. What predictions did you make about the selection as you read?
2. What unfamiliar words did you look up or try to figure out from context clues?
3. What questions did you jot down during your reading?
4. How did you account for the actions of the silent girl and the narrator?

Check Test: True-False

1. The girl who wouldn't talk does use her voice when she reads aloud. [True]
2. The quiet girl and the narrator are different in every way. [False]
3. One day the narrator catches the quiet girl in the school lavatory. [True]
4. The narrator torments the girl by pinching her and trying to make her talk. [True]
5. Soon after the incident with the narrator, the quiet girl becomes ill with a mysterious paralysis. [False]

MAKING MEANINGS

First Thoughts

1. What is your reaction to the silent girl? How do you feel about the narrator?

Reviewing the Text

a. What reasons does the narrator give for hating the silent girl?
b. What do the other students think of the silent girl?
c. How does the narrator try to make the silent girl talk? (Note the physical and the psychological torments she applies.) What is the girl's response?
d. What happens to the narrator to make her say that "the world is sometimes just"?

Shaping Interpretations

2. The narrator's deep undercurrent of anger seems directed solely at the silent girl. What else do you think the narrator could be angry about? Is she affected by an **internal conflict**? Explain.
3. The silent girl was obviously able to speak. Review the notes you made in your Reader's Log. Why do you think the girl did *not* speak? What **external** or **internal conflicts** might have caused her to remain silent?
4. What inference do you draw from the fact that the narrator says that her time in bed "was the best year and a half of my life"? What discoveries about herself or about the silent girl might she have made during this time?
5. This episode comes from a chapter called "A Song for a Barbarian Reed Pipe." What could be the significance of that **title**? How is this story of the silent girl related to that title?
6. At times, Kingston's **images** can evoke powerful responses from us and can reveal the narrator's strong feelings as well. Find the images describing the silent girl's skin, her fingers, the skin of her hands and arms, her ears, and her crying. What feelings about the girl do these images reveal? How do they make you respond to the girl and to her tormentor, the narrator?

Connecting with the Text

7. Why do you think the narrator cares so intensely about making the silent girl talk? Do her feelings strike you as believable—have you experienced or observed feelings like these?

CHOICES: Building Your Portfolio

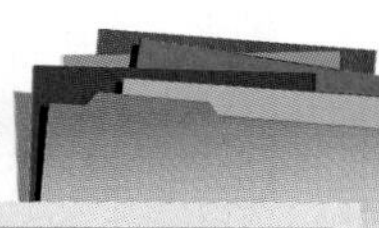

Writer's Notebook

1. Collecting Ideas for an Evaluation

WORK IN PROGRESS

A well-written evaluation maintains a consistent and confident **tone.** Whether stating your judgment or offering evidence, express your thoughts clearly and with confidence. As practice, write several sentences evaluating the use of **imagery** in Kingston's work. Make sure your tone is crystal clear and consistent. Save your sentences for possible use in the Writer's Workshop on page 1181.

Critical Writing

2. Tortured Tormentor

In a short essay, discuss the **character** of the narrator in this excerpt. Consider these basic elements of characterization: (a) appearance, (b) speech, (c) actions, (d) private thoughts and feelings, and (e) responses of other people to the character. Conclude your essay by discussing your personal response to the narrator.

Creative Writing

3. Time Out

The narrator says that "nothing happened" during her time sick in bed. But something must have happened, because one day her mother said that she was "ready" to return to school. In a brief story, reveal what you think happened to prepare the narrator to rejoin the world.

Making Meanings

First Thoughts

1. Possible responses: I feel angry with the silent girl. Or the narrator is cruel.

Reviewing the Text

a. She regards her as weak, fragile, delicate, and too "Chinese."
b. They say that they try to be friendly but get no response from her.
c. She pushes, pinches, and shakes her, pulls her hair, taunts her, shouts at her, calls her stupid and disgusting, and she tells her that she will never be married. The silent girl is alarmed and puzzled, but she endures the narrator's torments without ever speaking.
d. She falls ill and is forced to spend a year and a half at home in bed.

Shaping Interpretations

2. She seems angry at her own family, at the "ghosts" of American society, at herself, and at the conflicts posed by loyalty to her own family and community on the one hand, and the pressures to become assimilated to the "ghost" society on the other. Her internal conflict is wrestling with being accepted by the "ghost" society.
3. Possible responses: The girl is probably terrified. Or Chinese culture may demand a silent acceptance on the part of the younger girl. The external forces are the demands by Chinese society for a particular reaction; the internal forces are trying to decide for herself how to act.
4. Possible response: She says that during this period "nothing happened." Perhaps she means that she is temporarily spared the tension of growing up "between two cultures." The narrator realizes how cruel she has been, that cultural beliefs are deeply embedded, and that she is part of the same culture as the silent girl.
5. Possible responses: The narrator refers to the "wheezes" that the silent girl makes on her flute. Perhaps part of the narrator's motivation in writing the essay is as belated atonement for her cruelty to the silent girl.
6. The silent girl's cheeks are pink and white. Her skin is fleshy like squid. Her fingers are "papery" and her eyes and nose "dripped." Possible responses: The images evoke her revulsion or pity for the silent girl. They make the girl seem weak.

Connecting with the Text

7. Possible responses: The narrator feels the girl represents the delicate, traditional Chinese image of femininity and submission—an image the narrator has rejected. Her feelings seem believable. I have not experienced such hatred.

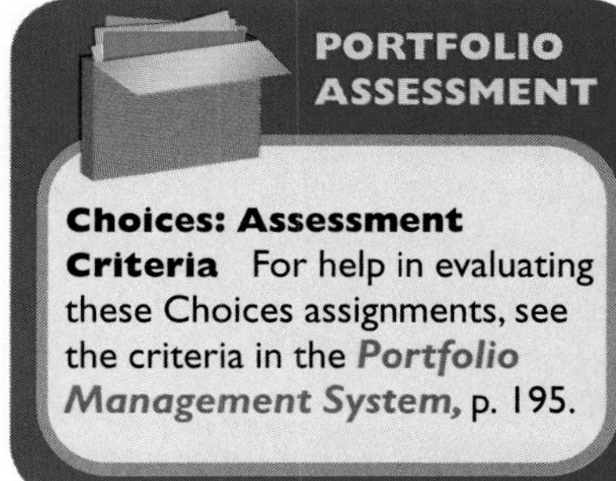

QUICK PLANNING GUIDE

Into the Story

Author Biography pp. 1054–1055
Before You Read p. 1055
- **Reading Focus: Scaffolding** Students discover that harmony is created, not found.
- **A Dialogue with the Text: Set a Purpose** Write in Reader's Log details that are intriguing
- **Elements of Literature: Dialect**

Through the Story

from Blue Highways **pp. 1057–1063**
Words to Own pp. 1057–1063
Connections: An Essay pp. 1064–1065
from Let Us Now Praise Famous Men
Making Meanings p. 1066
Language and Style p. 1066

Beyond the Story

Choices: Building Your Portfolio p. 1066
- **Writer's Notebook:** Collect ideas for an evaluation
- **Critical Writing:** Write a short essay on whether Heat-Moon finds harmony
- **Crossing the Curriculum: Geography:** Write an essay on place names

ABOUT THE AUTHOR

One of Heat-Moon's ancestors, an Englishman, emigrated to North Carolina and was killed by Tories for giving food to rebel colonists during the American Revolution. The first leg of Heat-Moon's journey, from Missouri to North Carolina, retraced in reverse the journey his forebears had made.

© Robert M. Lindholm.

William Least Heat-Moon

(1939–)

Some of the finest insights into American ways of life have appeared in the nonfiction accounts of travelers. As early as 1835, Alexis de Tocqueville, a visiting Frenchman, wrote *Democracy in America,* still treasured as a profound commentary on the American character. Traveling Americans turned their journals into such classics as Henry David Thoreau's *The Maine Woods* (1864), Mark Twain's *Roughing It* (1872) and *Life on the Mississippi* (1883), and Henry James's *The American Scene* (1907). Modern writers have explored America—Jack Kerouac, in *On the Road* (1957); John Steinbeck, in *Travels with Charley* (1962); and Robert Pirsig, in *Zen and the Art of Motorcycle Maintenance* (1974). William Least Heat-Moon's *Blue Highways: A Journey into America* (1982) thus takes its place in a vital American literary tradition. In fact, the writer says that Steinbeck's *Charley* inspired him to embark on the journey described in *Blue Highways*.

William Least Heat-Moon is the pen name of William Trogdon, who is descended mainly from the Osage people in Missouri. His given name, he explains, comes from an immigrant English ancestor eight generations back, and the name Heat-Moon comes from his Osage father (William added the hyphen). "My father calls himself Heat Moon"—the name for the seventh month in the Osage calendar—"[and] my elder brother Little Heat Moon. I, coming last, am therefore Least. It has been a long lesson of a name to learn."

When Heat-Moon was thirty-eight, his first marriage was ending and he was laid off from a teaching job, so he left Missouri in a converted van that became both transport and home. He called his van *Ghost Dancing,* after the name the Plains Indians gave to ceremonies of the 1890s

WORDS TO OWN

The following vocabulary words are defined in the Words to Own at the bottom of the pupil's page.

saturated p. 1057	lore p. 1062
infallible p. 1057	incised p. 1063
translucent p. 1058	chronologically p. 1063
recollect p. 1059	transcribed p. 1063
vouch p. 1059	
commenced p. 1061	

PORTFOLIO ASSESSMENT

Portfolio Assessment For help with teacher assessment of reading skills, see the ***Portfolio Management System,*** pp. 54–55.

in which they prayed for the return of their old life. And in a sense, Heat-Moon's trip was such a ceremony. "I took to the open road in search of places where change did not mean ruin and where time and men and deeds connected." At the start of the trip, he decided to use his Osage last name rather than Trogdon.

Blue Highways, the edited journal of his travels, shows that Heat-Moon found what he sought. He stayed on the back roads, the ones printed in blue on old highway maps, not the main routes printed in red. His quest took him east from Missouri to North Carolina, south to Louisiana, then west across Texas to New Mexico, north through Utah and California to Washington State, back across the northernmost boundary of the United States all the way to Maine, south again to New Jersey, and finally west back to Missouri. The roughly circular trip, he thought, "would give a purpose—to come around again."

Some contemporary travelers have found a sad, petty-minded, and materialistic America. But Heat-Moon usually liked the people he met in such places as Lookingglass and Simplicity, New Hope and New Freedom, Cutthroat Gulch and Calamity River, Why and Whynot. He found the inhabitants as vigorous, imaginative, and astonishing as the names of their towns. His journal celebrates these people—their struggles, their poverty, their spiritual wealth, and their dignity. They treated him well, and he admired them.

In 1991, Heat-Moon continued that celebration with *PrairyErth (a deep map).* Instead of offering a wide-ranging view of America, *PrairyErth* delves into the landscape and the people of one Kansas county.

Heat-Moon returned to a broader view of the United States in 1995, when he undertook an approximately 5,200-mile coast-to-coast journey of North America's inland waterways, almost all on a 22-foot cruiser named *Nikawa.* The four-month voyage began in New York and ended in Oregon. Perhaps we can look forward to a Heat-Moon celebration of America's "blue" waterways and the people who live along them.

BEFORE YOU READ

FROM **BLUE HIGHWAYS**

Reading Focus

Discovering Harmony

"Where are you going?" We hear that question often, and the answer is usually something like "the gym" or "shopping" or "Omaha." Heat-Moon goes out to discover *harmony.* In music, harmony is the sounding of separate tones in a satisfying combination. In human experience, its definition is much more elusive. We search for harmony in our individual lives, families, communities, and nations. Perhaps the real discovery is that harmony has to be created, not found.

A Dialogue with the Text

READER'S LOG

As you read, jot down details that you find particularly intriguing or unusual in Heat-Moon's narrative. Note whether you would like to know more about some of them.

Elements of Literature

Dialect

As he travels across America, Heat-Moon *listens* to the people he meets. By accurately transferring their dialects to the printed page, he lets us hear them too. **Dialect** is a way of speaking that is characteristic of a certain social group or of the inhabitants of a certain geographical area. It is an authentic link between people and the places they have made their own.

Dialect is a way of speaking that is characteristic of a certain social group or of the inhabitants of a certain geographical area.

For more on Dialect, see page 512 and the Handbook of Literary Terms.

Into the Story

Using BEFORE YOU READ p. 1055

A Dialogue with the Text

Have students complete the following chart. In the first column, they should write the page number on which the detail occurs; in the second column, the detail(s); in the third, what they would like to know about details that intrigue them. They may make notes or write questions.

Page	Detail(s)	Would like more information

PROGRAM MANAGER

- **Planning Instruction** See Teaching Notes, *Teaching Resources B,* p.162, for objectives, a summary, and literary elements for this selection.
- **Instructional Support** Before beginning the instructional lesson, see Graphic Organizer for Active Reading, *Teaching Resources B,* p. 180, for an Into the Story activity.
- **Assessment** See Selection Test, *Test Booklet,* pp. 241–242.
- **Reinforcement** Use the Words to Own worksheet in *Teaching Resources B,* p. 181.

RESPONDING TO THE ART: ABOUT THE ARTWORK

Photo-realism is a form of painting based on and often imitating still photographs. As a Photo-realist, American painter Ralph Goings (born 1928) has concerned himself with perceptions of things in his paintings, rather than their underlying structure or meaning. Rejecting the idea that art must be about art, Goings's works are about subject matter. His meticulous and accurate replications of everyday things and people are objective depictions of his perception. He hopes these depictions will lead the viewer to discovery.

Courtesy OK Harris Gallery, New York.

Pee Wee's Diner, Warnerville, N.Y. (1977) by Ralph Goings. Oil on canvas (48″ × 48″).

OPTIONS FOR TEACHING

STRATEGIES FOR INCLUSION

Auditory Begin by sharing with the class the story of an unusual place you have visited. Include the cultural variations; then, ask students to think about places that they have been and to share with the class an experience that they had while visiting a new place. *Remind students to choose an experience they would not mind sharing with others.*

Logical-Mathematical Give the students different state maps that show the transportation infrastructure of that state. Have students pick two locations in the state or one in one state and one in another that have some distance between them. Then, have them calculate the miles from the first location to the second. Ask the students to choose several different routes from the first location to the second, and to determine the difference in distance. Once they have determined the difference in distance, ask them to discuss what factors besides distance might affect the time it takes to travel from the first location to the second location. Have them decide which route would be the best route to take and why.

Ⓐ

Had it not been raining hard that morning on the Livingston square, I never would have learned of Nameless, Tennessee. Waiting for the rain to ease, I lay on my bunk and read the atlas to pass time rather than to see where I might go. In Kentucky were towns with fine names like Boreing, Bear Wallow, Decoy, Subtle, Mud Lick, Mummie, Neon; Belcher was just down the road from Mouthcard, and Minnie only ten miles from Mousie.

I looked at Tennessee. Turtletown eight miles from Ducktown. Ⓑ And also: Peavine, Wheel, Milky Way, Love Joy, Dull, Weakly, Fly, Spot, Miser Station, Only, McBurg, Peeled Chestnut, Clouds, Topsy, Isoline. And the best of all, Nameless. The logic! I was heading east, and Nameless lay forty-five miles west. I decided to go anyway.

The rain stopped, but things looked saturated, even bricks. In Gainesboro, a hill town with a square of businesses around the Jackson County Courthouse, I stopped for directions and breakfast. There is one almost infallible way to find honest food at just prices in blue-highway America: Count the wall calendars in a cafe.

No calendar: Same as an interstate pit stop.
One calendar: Preprocessed food assembled in New Jersey.
Two calendars: Only if fish trophies present. Ⓒ
Three calendars: Can't miss on the farm-boy breakfasts.
Four calendars: Try the ho-made pie too.
Five calendars: Keep it under your hat, or they'll franchise.

One time I found a six-calendar cafe in the Ozarks, which served fried chicken, peach pie, and chocolate malts, that left me searching for another ever since. I've never seen a seven-calendar place. But old-time travelers—road men in a day when cars had running Ⓓ

Words to Own

saturated (sach′ə·rāt′id) *adj.:* completely soaked.
infallible (in·fal′ə·bəl) *adj.:* sure; never wrong.

A. Reader's Response: First Thoughts

? From the title what do you think this excerpt from Heat-Moon's book will be about? [Sample responses: It will be about his travels. Or the word blue indicates that it might be about sad times.]

B. Critical Reading: Analyzing Names

? Why do you think that people would name their towns like this? [Possible answer: These may have been places where bears wallowed or where there had been an early neon sign.]

C. Critical Reading: Expressing an Opinion

? Why would the number of wall calendars be a measure of a restaurant's quality? [Possible answers: The presence of calendars seems to promise a homey, unsophisticated atmosphere. They would not be found in a slick, fast-food restaurant. Or the people who work there like to be surrounded by the pretty pictures one finds in calendars. Such people usually take pride in their service and like to make their customers happy.]

D. Language Note: Punctuation

The use of the dash in this case is like the use of comma around an appositive. The dash calls for a longer pause than a comma and gives greater emphasis to the information between the dashes.

STRATEGIES FOR INCLUSION

Musical To help students make connections with the text, ask a music teacher to bring in music that the Watts might have played on their old Edison phonograph. Ask the teacher to talk about the music.

Special Needs Heat-Moon uses a rating system to rate cafes as he travels. Have students make a rating system for restaurants. They may wish to rate restaurants based on decor, prices, quality of food, or whatever criteria they choose. Have the students develop the criteria, list restaurants, and then rate them. Ask them to create a chart. Display it in the classroom.

A. Critical Reading: Making Inferences

? Why would it be important that these people not be present in the restaurant? [Possible answer: Heat-Moon is looking for the atmosphere of small towns throughout America. Travelers and truckers taint the view of the local town because they bring with them the attitudes and concerns of other communities.]

B. Reader's Response: Shaping Interpretations

? What does Heat-Moon mean when he says that he is looking for "harmony"? [Sample responses: He is searching the back roads of this country for people who are happy with their lives. Or he is looking for something that has been missing from his own life.]

C. Critical Reading: Making Generalizations

? Why would the waitress want to take a dog? [Possible answers: For companionship or protection.]

boards and lunchroom windows said AIR COOLED in blue letters with icicles dripping from the tops—those travelers have told me the golden legends of seven-calendar cafes.

To the rider of back roads, nothing shows the tone, the voice of a small town more quickly than the breakfast grill or the five-thirty tavern. Much of what the people do and believe and share is evident then. The City Cafe in Gainesboro had three calendars that I could see from the walk. Inside were no interstate refugees with full bladders and empty tanks, no wild-eyed children just released from the glassy cell of a station-wagon backseat, no long-haul truckers talking in CB numbers.[1] There were only townspeople wearing overalls, or catalog-order suits with five-and-dime ties, or uniforms. That is, here were farmers and mill hands, bank clerks, the dry goods merchant, a policeman, and chiropractor's receptionist. Because it was Saturday, there were also mothers and children.

Welcome to Dull

I ordered my standard on-the-road breakfast: two eggs up, hash browns, tomato juice. The waitress, whose pale, almost translucent skin shifted hue in the gray light like a thin slice of mother of pearl, brought the food. Next to the eggs was a biscuit with a little yellow Smiley button stuck in it. She said, "You from the North?"

"I guess I am." A Missourian gets used to Southerners thinking him a Yankee, a Northerner considering him a cracker, a Westerner sneering at his effete Easternness, and the Easterner taking him for a cowhand.

"So whata you doin' in the mountains?"

"Talking to people. Taking some pictures. Looking mostly."

"Lookin' for what?"

"A three-calendar cafe that serves Smiley buttons on the biscuits."

"You needed a smile. Tell me really."

"I don't know. Actually, I'm looking for some jam to put on this biscuit now that you've brought one."

She came back with grape jelly. In a land of quince jelly, apple butter, apricot jam, blueberry preserves, pear conserves, and lemon marmalade, you always get grape jelly.

"Whata you lookin' for?"

Like anyone else, I'm embarrassed to eat in front of a watcher, particularly if I'm getting interviewed. "Why don't you have a cup of coffee?"

"Cain't right now. You gonna tell me?"

"I don't know how to describe it to you. Call it harmony."

She waited for something more. "Is that it?" Someone called her to the kitchen. I had managed almost to finish by the time she came back. She sat on the edge of the booth. "I started out in life not likin' anything, but then it grew on me. Maybe that'll happen to you." She watched me spread the jelly. "Saw your van." She watched me eat the biscuit. "You sleep in there?" I told her I did. "I'd love to do that, but I'd be scared spitless."

"I don't mind being scared spitless. Sometimes."

"I'd love to take off cross country. I like to look at different license plates. But I'd take a dog. You carry a dog?"

"No dogs, no cats, no budgie birds. It's a one-man campaign to show Americans a person can travel alone without a pet."

"Cain't travel without a dog!"

"I like to do things the hard way."

"Shoot! I'd take me a dog to talk to. And for protection."

"It isn't traveling to cross the country and talk to your pug instead of people along the way. Besides, being alone on the road makes you ready to meet someone when you stop. You get sociable traveling alone."

She looked out toward the van again. "Time I get the nerve to take a trip, gas'll cost five dollars a gallon."

"Could be. My rig might go the way of the

1. **CB numbers:** Users of CB (citizens' band) shortwave radios substitute numbers for simple messages (such as "10-4" for "message received").

WORDS TO OWN

translucent (trans·lo͞o′sənt) *adj.:* allowing light to pass through.

OPTIONS FOR TEACHING

INTEGRATING THE LANGUAGE ARTS

Strategic Reading Have students read a portion of the assignment; then, ask them to stop and predict what will happen. As they continue reading, have them verify their predictions and if they cannot, ask them to make new predictions or adjust old ones. Have students continue the process until they have finished reading the assignment.

Speaking and Listening Ask students to interview newcomers to their community. Before they conduct the interviews, discuss interviewing skills with them and have the class prepare several questions that would be appropriate to ask. The focus should be on the differences between the communities. Students may wish to ask questions about holidays, celebrations, and education. Have the students record the interview on audiotape and take notes during the interview. Have each student write up the interview for presentation to the class. The presentation should include a report of what they discovered. Ask them to play a portion of the tape of the person interviewed. *You may want to obtain permission from parents or guardians and from the parties students will contact before they begin work on this activity.*

steamboat." I remembered why I'd come to Gainesboro. "You know the way to Nameless?"

"Nameless? I've heard of Nameless. Better ask the amlance driver in the corner booth." She pinned the Smiley on my jacket. "Maybe I'll see you on the road somewhere. His name's Bob, by the way."

"The ambulance driver?"

"The Smiley. I always name my Smileys—otherwise they all look alike. I'd talk to him before you go."

"The Smiley?"

"The amlance driver."

And so I went looking for Nameless, Tennessee, with a Smiley button named Bob.

"I don't know if I got directions for where you're goin'," the ambulance driver said. "I *think* there's a Nameless down the Shepardsville Road."

"When I get to Shepardsville, will I have gone too far?"

"Ain't no Shepardsville."

"How will I know when I'm there?"

"Can't say for certain."

"What's Nameless look like?"

"Don't recollect."

"Is the road paved?"

"It's possible."

Those were the directions. I was looking for an unnumbered road named after a nonexistent town that would take me to a place called Nameless that nobody was sure existed.

Clumps of wild garlic lined the county highway that I hoped was the Shepardsville Road. It scrimmaged with the mountain as it tried to stay on top of the ridges; the hillsides were so steep and thick with oak, I felt as if I were following a trail through the misty treetops. Chickens, doing more work with their necks than legs, ran across the road, and, with a battering of wings, half leapt and half flew into the lower branches of oaks. A vicious pair of mixed-breed German shepherds raced along trying to eat the tires. After miles, I decided I'd missed the town—assuming there truly *was* a Nameless, Tennessee. It wouldn't be the first time I'd qualified for the Ponce de Leon[2] Believe Anything Award. **D**

I stopped beside a big man loading tools in a pickup. "I may be lost."

"Where'd you lose the right road?"

"I don't know. Somewhere around nineteen sixty-five." **E**

"Highway fifty-six, you mean?"

"I came down fifty-six. I think I should've turned at the last junction."

"Only thing down that road's stumps and huckleberries, and the berries ain't there in March. Where you tryin' to get to?"

"Nameless. If there is such a place."

"You might not know Thurmond Watts, but he's got him a store down the road. That's Nameless at his store. Still there all right, but I might not vouch you that tomorrow." He came up to the van. "In my army days, I wrote Nameless, Tennessee, for my place of birth on all the papers, even though I lived on this end of the ridge. All these ridges and hollers got names of their own. That's Steam Mill Holler over yonder. Named after the steam engine in the gristmill. Miller had him just one arm but done a good business."

"What business you in?"

"I've always farmed, but I work in Cookeville now in a heatin' element factory. Bad back made me go to town to work." He pointed to a wooden building not much bigger than his truck. By the slanting porch, a faded Double Cola sign said J M WHEELER STORE. "That used to be my business. That's me—Madison Wheeler. Feller came by one day. From Detroit. He wanted to buy the sign because he carried my name too. But I didn't sell. Want to keep my name up." He gave a cigarette a good slow smoking. "Had a decent business for **F**

2. **Ponce de Leon:** Juan Ponce de Leon, Spanish explorer and discoverer of Florida. According to legend, he searched for a fountain said to have the power to restore youth.

WORDS TO OWN

recollect (rek'ə·lekt') *v.:* remember.
vouch (vouch) *v.:* guarantee.

D. Critical Reading: Making Inferences

? What does Least Heat-Moon mean when he writes that he has been the recipient of "the Ponce de Leon" award? [Ponce de Leon looked for something that does not exist. Heat-Moon thinks that Nameless, Tennessee may not exist. But during his travels he has looked for many places and things that did not exist.]

E. Critical Reading: Drawing Conclusions

? What does Heat-Moon mean by his response? [He is saying, metaphorically, that his life took a wrong turn around 1965—that is, when Heat-Moon was about twenty-six.]

F. Critical Reading: Making Inferences

? Why doesn't Madison Wheeler want to sell the sign that has his name? [Possible answers: The store is very important to him. He likes having his name on the sign. It reminds him of a time in his life that he enjoyed.]

COOPERATIVE LEARNING

Touring Divide the class into five-member cooperative teams. Give the teams access to different types of maps: city maps, state maps, or travel atlases. Each group should plan a trip using the map given to their group. Along with the map, give each group information about its trip: for example, time allotted for travel, budget, family size, and access to various modes of transportation. The students will need to research the destination and places along the way. They could use the library, consult a travel agency or an automobile club, and write to the tourist bureau of that city or state. Once they have researched the area and planned the trip, they should present the proposed trip to the class, and include visuals. Assign students one of the following responsibilities: team leader (to organize the project), art coordinator (to locate and display visual aids), research expert (to assign students different research areas), secretary (to send letters of request, make phone calls, and keep notes), and process observer (to analyze the process and everyone's participation in the project). All members should work on all aspects of the project. *You may want to obtain permission from parents or guardians and from the parties students will contact before they begin work on this activity.*

A. Literary Element: Dialect
A "briar blade" is a scythe. How does the use of dialect characterize Wheeler? [The terms and expressions he uses demonstrate the importance of the region in shaping his character. His dropping letters from words and grammatical errors reveal an openness.]

Virginia Museum of Fine Arts, Richmond, Virginia. Gift of Sydney and Frances Lewis. Photo by Ron Jennings.

Highway US 1, Panel 3 (1963) by Allan D'Arcangelo. Acrylic on canvas ($69\frac{1}{2}'' \times 81''$).

five years, but too much of it was in credit. Then them supermarkets down in Cookeville opened, and I was buyin' higher than they was sellin'. With these hard roads now, everybody gets out of the hollers to shop or work. Don't stay up in here anymore. This tar road under my shoes done my business in, and it's likely to do Nameless in."

"Do you wish it was still the old way?"

"I got no debts now. I got two boys raised, and they never been in trouble. I got a brick house and some corn and tobacco and a few Hampshire hogs and Herefords. A good bull. Bull's pumpin' better blood than I do. Real generous man in town let me put my cow in with his stud. I couldna paid the fee on that specimen otherwise." He took another long, meditative pull on his filter tip. "If you're satisfied, that's all they are to it. I'll tell you, people from all over the nation—Florida, Mississippi—are comin' in here to retire because it's good country. But our young ones don't stay on. Not much way to make a livin' in here anymore. Take me. I been beatin' on these stumps all my life, tryin' to farm these hills. They don't give much up to you. Fightin' rocks and briars all the time. (A) One of the first things I recollect is swingin' a briar blade—filed out of an old saw it was. Now they come in with them crawlers and push out a pasture in a day. Still, it's a grudgin' land—like the gourd. Got to hard cuss gourd seed, they say, to get it up out of the ground."

OPTIONS FOR TEACHING

CLASSROOM MANAGEMENT

Choosing Groups Prior to giving out the maps for the Touring Cooperative Learning project on p. T1059, have the students fill out interest surveys. On the survey ask questions that deal with the students' interests in the different regions or cities for which you have maps. From the information on the surveys, determine the groups for the projects.

Block Scheduling Take a tour of a local library so students may become acquainted with community resources. The extended class period can allow students to conduct in-depth research, check out books, read, or learn how to use the library's computer network. The block allows enough time for students to get to the library, conduct research, and return to class for discussion and closure.

The whole time, my rig sat in the middle of the right lane while we stood talking next to it and wiped at the mist. No one else came or went. Wheeler said, "Factory work's easier on the back, and I don't mind it, understand, but a man becomes what he does. Got to watch that. That's why I keep at farmin', although the crops haven't ever throve. It's the doin' that's important." He looked up suddenly. "My apologies. I didn't ask what you do that gets you into these hollers."

I told him. I'd been gone only six days, but my account of the trip already had taken on some polish.

He nodded. "Satisfaction is doin' what's important to yourself. A man ought to honor other people, but he's got to honor what he believes in too."

As I started the engine, Wheeler said, "If you get back this way, stop in and see me. Always got beans and taters and a little piece of meat."

Down along the ridge, I wondered why it's always those who live on little who are the ones to ask you to dinner.

Nameless, Tennessee, was a town of maybe ninety people if you pushed it, a dozen houses along the road, a couple of barns, same number of churches, a general merchandise store selling Fire Chief gasoline, and a community center with a lighted volleyball court. Behind the center was an open-roof, rusting metal privy with PAINT ME on the door; in the hollow of a nearby oak lay a full pint of Jack Daniel's Black Label. From the houses, the odor of coal smoke.

Welcome to Nameless

Next to a red tobacco barn stood the general merchandise with a poster of Senator Albert Gore, Jr.,[3] smiling from the window. I knocked. The door opened partway. A tall, thin man said, "Closed up. For good," and started to shut the door.

"Don't want to buy anything. Just a question for Mr. Thurmond Watts."

The man peered through the slight opening. He looked me over. "What question would that be?"

"If this is Nameless, Tennessee, could he tell me how it got that name?"

The man turned back into the store and called out, "Miss Ginny! Somebody here wants to know how Nameless come to be Nameless."

Miss Ginny edged to the door and looked me and my truck over. Clearly, she didn't approve. She said, "You know as well as I do, Thurmond. Don't keep him on the stoop in the damp to tell him." Miss Ginny, I found out, was Mrs. Virginia Watts, Thurmond's wife.

I stepped in and they both began telling the story, adding a detail here, the other correcting a fact there, both smiling at the foolishness of it all. It seems the hilltop settlement went for years without a name. Then one day the Post Office Department told the people if they wanted mail up on the mountain they would have to give the place a name you could properly address a letter to. The community met; there were only a handful, but they commenced debating. Some wanted patriotic names, some names from nature, one man recommended in all seriousness his own name. They couldn't agree, and they ran out of names to argue about. Finally, a fellow tired of the talk; he didn't like the mail he received anyway. "Forget the durn Post Office," he said. "This here's a nameless place if I ever seen one, so leave it be." And that's just what they did.

Watts pointed out the window. "We used to have signs on the road, but the Halloween boys keep tearin' them down."

"You think Nameless is a funny name," Miss Ginny said. "I see it plain in your eyes. Well, you take yourself up north a piece to Difficult or Defeated or Shake Rag. Now them are silly names."

The old store, lighted only by three fifty-watt bulbs, smelled of coal oil and baking bread. In the middle of the rectangular room, where the oak floor sagged a little, stood an iron stove. To the right was a wooden table with an unfinished

3. **Senator Albert Gore, Jr.** (1948–): United States senator from Tennessee, 1985–1992; elected vice president of the United States in 1992.

WORDS TO OWN
commenced (kə·mensd′) *v.:* started.

B. Reader's Response: Connecting with the Text

? Do you agree with Wheeler when he says that "It's the doin' that's important"? [Sample responses: Yes; you have to enjoy the work you do because you spend so much time doing it. Or no, the results are more important: Seeing a finished product, like a harvested crop, or receiving a paycheck is more satisfying.]

C. Reader's Response: Extending the Text

? How does one "honor other people" and still "honor what he believes in too"? [Sample responses: A person should respect others for what they believe but should personally stick to his or her own beliefs. Or people should not change their beliefs to suit the beliefs of others.]

D. Critical Reading: Drawing Conclusions

? What do these statements in this paragraph say about the people's feelings toward the government? [Possible answer: They feel the government requires them to do things they do not believe need to be done.]

E. Critical Reading: Finding Details

The description in this paragraph creates a vivid impression of the country store in the reader's mind. To how many senses does this description appeal? [Three—sight, smell, hearing.]

CROSSING THE CURRICULUM

Social Sciences Have students, individually or in pairs, interview an older person from their community. Students should choose someone who has lived in the community a long time and can discuss how the community has changed. After students have created several questions that would be appropriate to ask, have them record the interview on audiotape or videotape. If students record the interview, ask them to take photographs if the interviewee permits. After students report on the interviews and play portions of the tapes, collect the reports and tapes to establish an archive of oral histories about their community. The library or local historical museum may wish to house the students' interviews. If neither institution is able to house the histories, check with your high school librarian or college librarian. You can also create a local history library within your classroom. *You may want to obtain permission from parents or guardians and from the parties students will contact before they begin work on this activity.*

Architecture Ask students to study different types of architecture from various regions of the country. They could focus on either residential or business architecture. Have them conduct library research or examine local buildings. Using a large map of the country posted on the wall, have the students post pictures of the different types of architecture on the appropriate part of the map.

A. Critical Reading: Drawing Conclusions

? According to Watts what is the difference between what has been forgotten and modern medicine? [Possible answers: Some of the contemporary medicines actually make people more ill than the original illness. But more importantly he believes that the old cures are forgotten because there is little commercial profit in them. He believes that modern medicine is concerned with making profits, not providing cures.]

B. Reader's Response: Shaping Interpretations

? How is Watts's remark a "defense" of Heat-Moon's practice of sleeping in his van? [Sample responses: People's ideas of comfort depend on what they are accustomed to. Or the shell for a clam is a source of protection; Heat-Moon can pull himself into his van whenever he needs to.]

game of checkers and a stool made from an apple-tree stump. On shelves around the walls sat earthen jugs with corncob stoppers, a few canned goods, and some of the two thousand old clocks and clockworks Thurmond Watts owned. Only one was ticking; the others he just looked at. I asked how long he'd been in the store.

"Thirty-five years, but we closed the first day of the year. We're hopin' to sell it to a churchly couple. Upright people. No athians."[4]

"Did you build this store?"

"I built this one, but it's the third general store on the ground. I fear it'll be the last. I take no pleasure in that. Once you could come in here for a gallon of paint, a pickle, a pair of shoes, and a can of corn."

"Or horehound candy," Miss Ginny said. "Or corsets and salves. We had cough syrups and all that for the body. In season, we'd buy and sell blackberries and walnuts and chestnuts, before the blight got them. And outside, Thurmond milled corn and sharpened plows. Even shoed a horse sometimes."

"We could fix up a horse or a man or a baby," Watts said.

"Thurmond, tell him we had a doctor on the ridge in them days."

"We had a doctor on the ridge in them days. As good as any doctor alivin'. He'd cut a crooked toenail or deliver a woman. Dead these last years."

"I got some bad ham meat one day," Miss Ginny said, "and took to vomitin'. All day, all night. Hangin' on the drop edge of yonder. I said to Thurmond, 'Thurmond, unless you want shut of me, call the doctor.'"

"I studied on it," Watts said.

"You never did. You got him right now. He come over and put three drops of iodeen in half a glass of well water. I drank it down and the vomitin' stopped with the last swallow. Would you think iodeen could do that?"

4. **athians:** Mr. Watts means "atheists," people who deny the existence of God.

"He put Miss Ginny on one teaspoon of spirits of ammonia in well water for her nerves. Ain't nothin' works better for her to this day."

"Calms me like the hand of the Lord."

Hilda, the Wattses' daughter, came out of the backroom. "I remember him," she said. "I was just a baby. Y'all were talkin' to him, and he lifted me up on the counter and gave me a stick of Juicy Fruit and a piece of cheese."

A "Knew the old medicines," Watts said. "Only drugstore he needed was a good kitchen cabinet. None of them antee-beeotics that hit you worsen your ailment. Forgotten lore now, the old medicines, because they ain't profit in iodeen."

Miss Ginny started back to the side room where she and her sister Marilyn were taking apart a duck-down mattress to make bolsters. She stopped at the window for another look at *Ghost Dancing*.[5] "How do you sleep in that thing? Ain't you all cramped and cold?"

B "How does the clam sleep in the shell?" Watts said in my defense.

"Thurmond, get the boy a piece of buttermilk pie afore he goes on."

"Hilda, get him some buttermilk pie." He looked at me. "You like good music?" I said I did. He cranked up an old Edison phonograph, the kind with the big morning-glory blossom for a speaker, and put on a wax cylinder. "This will be 'My Mother's Prayer,'" he said.

While I ate buttermilk pie, Watts served as disc jockey of Nameless, Tennessee. "Here's 'Mountain Rose.'" It was one of those moments that you know at the time will stay with you to the grave: the sweet pie, the

5. ***Ghost Dancing:*** Least Heat-Moon's van, named for the Plains Indian ceremony performed for the restoration of the buffalo and old ways of life.

WORDS TO OWN

lore (lôr) *n.:* traditional knowledge or teachings.

OPTIONS FOR TEACHING

PROBLEM SOLVING/ CRITICAL THINKING

Discovering This Country Ask students to list the things that they have learned about the people in the excerpt from *Blue Highways*. Ask them to refer to their Reader's Logs and to list other things that they would like to know about the people Heat-Moon meets. Have students discuss whether it would be beneficial to interview the citizens of their city in the same manner that Heat-Moon interviews people in small towns. Ask them to discuss how a book on city people would differ from Heat-Moon's work.

PROFESSIONAL NOTES

Thematic Connections: "Discoveries and Awakenings" Ask students why this selection belongs in this Collection. Divide the class into cooperative groups to debate whether it fits this theme. Allow each group to decide whether it fits. Then, ask for two volunteer groups on opposite sides to debate the issue in front of the class. Have the class determine the winner of the debate.

gaunt man playing the old music, the coals in the stove glowing orange, the scent of kerosene and hot bread. "Here's 'Evening Rhapsody.'" The music was so heavily romantic we both laughed. I thought: It is for this I have come.

Feathered over and giggling, Miss Ginny stepped from the side room. She knew she was a sight. "Thurmond, give him some lunch. Still looks hungry."

Hilda pulled food off the woodstove in the backroom: home-butchered and canned whole-hog sausage, home-canned June apples, turnip greens, coleslaw, potatoes, stuffing, hot cornbread. All delicious. C D

Watts and Hilda sat and talked while I ate. "Wish you would join me."

"We've ate," Watts said. "Cain't beat a woodstove for flavorful cookin'."

He told me he was raised in a one-hundred-fifty-year-old cabin still standing in one of the hollows. "How many's left," he said, "that grew up in a log cabin? I ain't the last surely, but I must be climbin' on the list."

Hilda cleared the table. "You Watts ladies know how to cook."

"She's in nursin' school at Tennessee Tech. I went over for one of them football games last year there at Coevul." To say *Cookeville,* you let the word collapse in upon itself so that it comes out "Coevul."

"Do you like football?" I asked.

"Don't know. I was so high up in that stadium, I never opened my eyes."

Watts went to the back and returned with a fat spiral notebook that he set on the table. His expression had changed. "Miss Ginny's *Deathbook.*"

The thing startled me. Was it something I was supposed to sign? He opened it but said nothing. There were scads of names written in a tidy hand over pages incised to crinkliness by a ballpoint. Chronologically, the names had piled up: wives, grandparents, a stillborn infant, relatives, friends close and distant. Names, names. After each, the date of *the* unknown finally known and transcribed. The last entry bore yesterday's date.

"She's wrote out twenty years' worth. Ever day she listens to the hospital report on the radio and puts the names in. Folks come by to check a date. Or they just turn through the books. Read them like a scrapbook."

Hilda said, "Like Saint Peter at the gates inscribin' the names."

Watts took my arm. "Come along." He led me to the fruit cellar under the store. As we went down, he said, "Always take a newborn baby upstairs afore you take him downstairs, otherwise you'll incline him downwards."

The cellar was dry and full of cobwebs and jar after jar of home-canned food, the bottles organized as a shopkeeper would: sausage, pumpkin, sweet pickles, tomatoes, corn relish, blackberries, peppers, squash, jellies. He held a hand out toward the dusty bottles. "Our tomorrows."

Upstairs again, he said, "Hope to sell the store to the right folk. I see now, though, it'll be somebody offen the ridge. I've studied on it, and maybe it's the end of our place." He stirred the coals. "This store could give a comfortable livin', but not likely get you rich. But just gettin' by is dice rollin' to people nowadays. I never did see my day guaranteed."

When it was time to go, Watts said, "If you find anyone along your way wants a good store—on the road to Cordell Hull Lake—tell them about us."

I said I would. Miss Ginny and Hilda and Marilyn came out to say goodbye. It was cold and drizzling again. "Weather to give a man the weary dismals," Watts grumbled. "Where you headed from here?"

"I don't know."

"Cain't get lost then." E

Miss Ginny looked again at my rig. It had worried her from the first as it had my mother. "I hope you don't get yourself kilt in that durn thing gallivantin' around the country."

"Come back when the hills dry off," Watts said. "We'll go lookin' for some of them round rocks all sparkly inside."

I thought a moment. "Geodes?"[6]

"Them's the ones. The county's properly full of them." F

6. **geodes** (jē′ōdz′): stones having cavities lined with crystals or minerals.

WORDS TO OWN

incised (in·sīzd′): *v.* used as *adj.:* deeply marked.
chronologically (krän′ō·läj′i·kə·lē) *adv.:* arranged in order of occurrence.
transcribed (tran·skrībd′) *v.* used as *adj.:* written down.

C. Cultural Connections

? Why does Heat-Moon emphasize the food in this passage? [He is pointing to the cultural differences that he has discovered on his back-road journey. People in the city probably would not have invited a stranger in and offered food. And the food offered would not have been prepared on a woodstove, nor have been home-butchered and home-preserved.]

D. Reader's Response: Connecting with the Text

? What other works might the description remind you of? [Sample responses: Woolf's "His Father's Earth"; Arnold Adoff's *Eats* poems.]

E. Literary Element: Paradox

? How is this statement contradictory yet true? [Possible answers: Anyone can get lost, but it is impossible to get lost if you do not care where you are going. Or wandering around the country purposefully lost is not truly lost but is a quest to discover the unknown; once you know the previously unknown, you know where you are and you are no longer lost. Or Heat-Moon was lost while looking for Nameless, but he was on the correct path. Once he found the community, he knew exactly where he was.]

F. Literary Element: Irony

It is ironic that Watts has access to all of the geodes one could want, yet he does not know the term. Heat-Moon knows the name. The man from Nameless, Tennessee does not have to name things; the man from the city, looking for harmony, has a need to name even the rocks that sparkle inside.

ASSESSMENT TOOLS

Check Test: Multiple Choice

1. The author says that best way to find a good cafe is to (a) count the trucks in the lot (b) count the wall calendars (c) see if the cook is fat or skinny. [b]
2. What town is the author trying to find? (a) Peavine, Kentucky (b) Bear Wallow, North Carolina (c) Nameless, Tennessee. [c]
3. The author feels that those most likely to invite a traveler to supper are (a) those who have plenty to spare (b) those who are superstitious (c) those who have little. [c]
4. Thurmond Watts (a) has just bought his store (b) is trying to sell his store (c) has built another store. [b]
5. Ginny Watts keeps (a) a wedding book (b) a death book (c) a wish book. [b]

A. Reader's Response: First Thoughts

? Given that Agee met the Gudgers during the Great Depression when much was scarce, what do their actions say about the Gudgers? [Sample responses: They are extremely generous. Or they place more value on people than on material goods.]

Connections

AN ESSAY

James Agee (1909–1955) was a Tennessee-born author who is now remembered primarily for his Pulitzer Prize–winning autobiographical novel, *A Death in the Family* (1957). He also wrote poetry, much-admired movie criticism for *The Nation* and *Time* magazines, and several screenplays, including adaptations of two of Stephen Crane's short stories.

In 1936, during the Great Depression, *Fortune* magazine assigned Agee to write about sharecroppers in the South. The result was too passionate for the magazine, but was eventually published as a book, *Let Us Now Praise Famous Men* (1941), one of the lesser-known masterpieces of American literature. Like Heat-Moon, Agee wrote about the people he discovered along back roads in rural America. Issued with photographs by Walker Evans, *Let Us Now Praise Famous Men* is Agee's dignified and heart-rending portrait of three Alabama families.

In the following passage, the young journalist shares a meal with a family he calls the Gudgers. As you read, notice how Agee's meditative style adds a layer of personal interpretation over the spare reality he is observing. He avoids quotation marks, and his long sentences and stream of thoughts are reminiscent of the modernist style of William Faulkner.

from Let Us Now Praise Famous Men

James Agee

So it was there was neither any fake warmth and heartiness nor any coldness in his saying, Sure, come on in, to my asking could he put me up for the night after all, and he added, Better eat some supper. I was in fact very hungry, but I did all I was able to stop this, finally trying to compromise it to a piece of bread and some milk, that needn't be prepared; I'm making you enough bother already; but no; Can't go to bed without no supper; you just hold on a second or two; and he leans his head through the bedroom door and speaks to his wife, explaining, **A** and lights the lamp for her. After a few moments, during which I hear her breathing and a weary shuffling of her heels, she comes out barefooted carrying the lamp, frankly and profoundly sleepy as a child; feeling disgusted to wake her further with so many words I say, Hello, Mrs. Gudger: say I want to tell you I'm *aw*ful sorry to give you all this bother: you just, honest I don't need much of anything, if you'd just tell me where a piece of bread is, it'll be *plenty,* I'd hate for you to bother to cook anything up for me: but she answers me while passing, looking at me, trying to get me into focus from between her sticky eyelashes, that 'tain't no bother at all, and for me not to worry over that, and goes on into the kitchen; and how quickly I don't understand, for I am too much occupied to see, with Gudger, and with holding myself from the cardinal error of hovering around her, or of offering to help her, she has built a pine fire and set in front of me, on the table in the hall, warmed-over biscuit and butter and blackberry jam and a jelly-glass full of buttermilk, and warmed field peas, fried pork, and four fried eggs, and she sits a little away from the table out of courtesy, trying to hold her head up and her eyes open, until I shall have finished eating, saying at one time how it's an awful poor sort of supper and at another how it's awful plain, mean food; I tell her different, and eat as rapidly as possible and a good deal more than I can hold, in fact, all the eggs, a second large plateful of peas, most of the biscuit, feeling it is better to keep them awake and to eat too much than in the least to let them continue to believe I am what they

CONNECTING WITH *BLUE HIGHWAYS*

Both Heat-Moon and Agee recount their experiences encountering strangers in small towns. Have students list what each writer discovers about people on a chart like the following one. Have them compare what the two have discovered. Then, ask students to discuss what differences they have found and to account for these differences.

People's characteristics	Heat-Moon	Agee	Similar or different
[Friendly to strangers.]	[The Watts invite him in for dinner.]	[Mr. Gudger gets his wife up to serve Agee dinner.]	[Similar—both couples trouble themselves to serve a stranger. The Gudgers may go to a bit more trouble.]

assume I must be: 'superior' to them or to their food, eating only so much as I need to be 'polite'; and I see that they are, in fact, quietly surprised and gratified in my appetite.

But somehow I have lost hold of the reality of all this, I scarcely can understand how; a loss of the reality of simple actions upon the specific surface of the earth. This country, these roads, these odors and noises, the action of walking the dark in mud, the approach, just what a slow succession of certain trees past your walking can implant in you, can mean to you, the house as it stands there dark in darkness, the indecisiveness and the bellowing dog, the conversations of questioning, defense, assurance, acceptance, the subtle yet strong distinctions of attitude, the walking between the walls of wood and the sitting and eating, the tastes of the several foods, the weights of our bodies in our chairs, the look of us in the lamplight in the presence of the walls of the house and of the country night, the beauty and the stress of our tiredness, how we held quietness, gentleness, and care toward one another like three mild lanterns held each at the met heads of strangers **B** in darkness: such things, and these are just a few, I have not managed to give their truth in words, which are a soft, plain-featured, and noble music, each part in the experience of it and in the memory so cleanly and so simply defined in its own terms, striking so many chords and relationships at once, which I can but have blurred in the telling at all.

Depression-era photo of living room by Walker Evans.
Library of Congress.

B. Literary Elements: Figures of Speech

? How do the figures of speech at the end of this paragraph add to Agee's writing? [Possible answers: They ennoble the sharecroppers and their generosity. They add an elegance to the recounting of events.]

Making Meanings

First Thoughts

1. Possible responses: Were you ever worried? Or What was your favorite moment in your travels?

Reviewing the Text

a. The food that people choose to eat tells a lot about what they like. How they eat it tells a lot about their station in life and about their mental and physical condition.
b. Something that can be called harmony.
c. The Post Office Department insisted that the community have a name so that mail could be delivered. When the inhabitants met to name the town, they could not agree, so the place went by the name "Nameless."
d. Their food.

Shaping Interpretations

2. The sharing of food suggests that the Watts are cordial, good-natured, honest people.
3. Numerous passages suggest poor economic conditions. The paragraph that begins with "The old store, lighted only by three fifty-watt bulbs . . ." suggests mean conditions. The Watts's cheerfulness and generosity, despite their circumstances, keep the story from being depressing.
4. Possible response: image: "like Saint Peter at the gates inscribin' names"; expression: "I ain't the last surely, but I must be climbin' on the list"; proverb: "Always take a newborn baby upstairs afore you take him downstairs, otherwise you'll incline him downwards"; uncommon grammar: "We've ate."
5. Heat-Moon finds tranquility in sharing the evening with the Watts. They have a simple, pleasant lifestyle and they welcome strangers as friends. He finds the harmony he seeks.
6. Agee does not want to insult the Gudgers by not eating their food. Heat-Moon feels that eating food is a good way to understand people.

Language and Style

Answers

1. The actual road he missed to the course his life has taken.
2. a. Near death.
   b. A creature is comfortable in its own environment.

MAKING MEANINGS

First Thoughts

1. Review the notes in your Reader's Log. What would you most like to ask Heat-Moon about his travels?

Reviewing the Text

a. What can you learn about a small town by observing people eating breakfast at a restaurant?
b. According to what he tells the waitress, what is Heat-Moon searching for?
c. Explain how Nameless, Tennessee, got its name.
d. What does the Watts family share with the narrator?

Shaping Interpretations

2. Heat-Moon knows that food tells a lot about the people who serve and eat it. Where in this excerpt does food tell us about **character**?
3. What concrete details help paint a vivid picture of the Wattses' home? What details keep the Wattses' story from being a depressing one?
4. Heat-Moon captures the flavor of the country in recreating the **dialect** of Madison Wheeler and the Watts family. Find examples of images, expressions, proverbs, and uncommon grammar that tell us who and what these people are.
5. Heat-Moon eats buttermilk pie while an old man plays music on a hand-cranked phonograph. Heat-Moon thinks, "It is for this I have come." What does he mean?
6. In Connections on page 1064, James Agee spends the night with the Gudger family in Alabama. Why does Agee eat so heartily there? Does Heat-Moon eat a huge meal at the Wattses' for the same reasons? Explain.

LANGUAGE AND STYLE

Heat-Moon's Metaphors

When a man asks Heat-Moon, "Where'd you lose the right road?" his reply is "Somewhere around nineteen sixty-five" (page 1059). This befuddles the man, because he doesn't grasp that Heat-Moon is using a **metaphor,** a figure of speech in which one thing is compared to another thing, as in "the voyage of life."

1. In the metaphor of "the right road," what two things is Heat-Moon comparing?
2. Explain what is meant by these metaphors:
   a. "Hangin' on the drop edge of yonder" (page 1062)
   b. "How does the clam sleep in the shell?" (page 1062)

CHOICES: Building Your Portfolio

Writer's Notebook

1. Collecting Ideas for an Evaluation

Comparing and contrasting are effective methods of evaluation. Try comparing or contrasting Heat-Moon's narrative with the excerpt from Thoreau's *Walden* (page 233). Make a chart in which you compare the two works in terms of **topics, tone, style,** and each narrator's **quest.** Save your notes for possible use in the Writer's Workshop on page 1181.

Critical Writing

2. "Tell Them About Us"

Heat-Moon sets out to find harmony—places "where time and men and deeds connected." Do you think he finds harmony in Nameless, Tennessee? In a short essay, state your opinion, and support it with evidence from the selection.

Crossing the Curriculum: Geography

3. What's in a Name?

Heat-Moon delights in the names of American towns, rivers, and mountains. Find a detailed map of your state, and write an essay about the place names that amuse or please you, telling why they do so. What do the names suggest about the people in the state or about the state's physical geography or history?

Beyond the Story

Choices: Building Your Portfolio

1. **Writer's Notebook** Remind students to save their work. They may use it as prewriting or the Writer's Workshop on p. 1181.

PORTFOLIO ASSESSMENT

Choices: Assessment Criteria
For help in evaluating these Choices assignments, see the criteria in the *Portfolio Management System,* p. 196.

Collection 20

FROM GENERATION TO GENERATION

Theme: **The Ties that Bind**
In going through the process of self-discovery, many people find that they begin to understand and appreciate the lives and legacies of family members from earlier generations.

Thematic Focus

Each selection in the Collection examines bonds between members of different generations.

- **Son** The vignettes in this story span the lives of four generations of sons.
- **Daughter of Invention** A young girl has the chance to deliver a speech that might win her acceptance at school, but the opportunity brings about a family crisis at home.
- **The Bells** A tattered poster evokes memories of the enjoyment and sense of comfort the poem's speaker experienced at a circus she watched with her father.
- *from* **The Way to Rainy Mountain** In this lyrical, elegiac excerpt, the author remembers his grandmother, her home, and the history of her people, the Kiowa.
- *from* **In Search of Our Mothers' Gardens** The author writes about generations of unacknowledged mothers who have handed down the creative spirit to their daughters.
- *from* **Rules of the Game** A young girl becomes a champion chess player, but her success provokes an emotional confrontation with her mother.
- **What For** The speaker of this poem pays tribute to his father and grandparents and recalls memories of a childhood marked by the healing power of words.

Literary Focus

Literary Element	Selection / Feature
Internal and External Conflict	**Daughter of Invention**
Imagery	**The Bells**
Setting	**The Way to Rainy Mountain**
Personal Essay	**In Search of Our Mothers' Gardens**
Motivation	**Rules of the Game**
Refrain	**What For**

Writing Focus

The following flow chart shows how the writing assignment for each selection relates to the culminating writing assignment presented in the Writer's Workshop at the end of the unit.

Selection	Work-in-Progress Assignment
Son	Use cluster to analyze theme p. 1075
Daughter of Invention	Chart thoughts about conflict p. 1087
The Bells	List qualities of images p. 1091
The Way to Rainy Mountain	Evaluate use of setting p. 1100
In Search of Our Mothers' Gardens	Evaluate essay p. 1108
Rules of the Game	Respond to critical evaluation p. 1119
What For	Establish criteria for evaluation p. 1126
Writer's Workshop	Write evaluation pp. 1181–1185

Collection Planner

SELECTION / FEATURE	PUPIL'S EDITION: Literary Elements / Active Reading	Writing	Speaking and Listening	Language and Vocabulary
Son John Updike (pp. 1068–1075) **Connections:** from **Still Just Writing** Anne Tyler (p. 1074)	• Reader's Log p. 1069	• Critical Writing: Write essay p. 1075 • Creative Writing: Write episodes of story titled "Daughter" p. 1075		
Daughter of Invention Julia Alvarez (pp. 1076–1087)	• Reader's Log p. 1077 • Conflict p. 1077	• Critical Writing: Write essay explaining title p. 1087 • Creative Writing/ Speaking and Listening: Write first page of speech p. 1087	• Creative Writing/ Speaking and Listening: Read speech aloud p. 1087	
The Bells Anne Sexton (pp. 1088–1091)	• Reader's Log p. 1089 • Imagery p. 1089	• Critical Writing: Write essay about end rhymes p. 1091	• Music/Performance: Record appropriate soundtrack p. 1091	
from **The Way to Rainy Mountain** N. Scott Momaday (pp. 1092–1100)	• Reader's Log p. 1093 • Setting p. 1093	• Critical Writing: Write essay p. 1100 • Creative Writing: Write description of childhood place p. 1100		
from **In Search of Our Mothers' Gardens** Alice Walker (pp. 1101–1108)	• Reader's Log p. 1102 • Personal Essay p. 1102	• Critical Writing: Write essay about figures of speech p. 1108 • Creative Writing/Art: Write character sketch p. 1108		
from **Rules of the Game** from **The Joy Luck Club** Amy Tan (pp. 1109–1120) Primary Sources: An Interview with Amy Tan (p. 1118)	• Reader's Log p. 1110 • Motivation p. 1110	• Critical Writing: Write essay p. 1119	• Speaking and Listening: Prepare oral report p. 1119	• How to Own a Word: Base Words, Roots, and Word Families p. 1120 • Try It Out: Identify word roots p. 1120
What For Garrett Hongo (pp. 1121–1126) Primary Sources: A Different Story (p. 1125)	• Reader's Log p. 1122 • Refrain p. 1122	• Critical Writing: Write essay p. 1126 • Critical Writing: Write comparison-contrast essay p. 1126 • Creative Writing: Write poem from father's point of view p. 1126		

Collection Resources

Teaching Resources B	Audiovisual Resources Binder	Test Booklet
Cross-Curricular Activity p. 202	Fine Art Transparency 20.1	Collection Test pp. 257–259

Computer disk or CD-ROM

Audiocassette

Overhead Transparency

PROGRAM RESOURCES

Electronic Media	Teaching Resources with Organizer: Teaching Resources B	Teaching Resources with Organizer: Other Resources	Audiovisual Resources Binder
• Test Generator	• Teaching Notes p. 183 • Reading Organizer p. 188 • Words to Own p. 189	• Test Booklet: Selection Test pp. 247–248 • Portfolio Management System pp. 39, 197	
• Test Generator	• Teaching Notes pp. 183–184 • Reading Organizer p. 190 • Words to Own p. 191	• Test Booklet: Selection Test pp. 249–250 • Portfolio Management System pp. 48–49, 198	
• Test Generator	• Teaching Notes p. 184 • Reading Organizer p. 192	• Test Booklet: Selection Test pp. 251–252 • Portfolio Management System pp. 39, 199	• Selected Readings, Audiocassette 3, Side B
• Test Generator	• Teaching Notes p. 185 • Reading Organizer p. 193 • Words to Own p. 194	• Test Booklet: Selection Test pp. 251–252 • Portfolio Management System pp. 52–53, 200	• Selected Readings, Audiocassette 3, Side B
• Test Generator	• Teaching Notes p. 185 • Reading Organizer p. 195 • Words to Own p. 196	• Test Booklet: Selection Test pp. 253–254 • Portfolio Management System pp. 54–55, 201	• Elements of Literature Transparency 20.2
• Test Generator • Language Workshop: Irregular verbs	• Teaching Notes p. 186 • Reading Organizer p. 197 • Language Link pp. 198–199 • Words to Own p. 200	• Test Booklet: Selection Test pp. 255–256 • Portfolio Management System p. 202 • Language and Writing Skills Worksheets pp. 36–38	• How to Own a Word Transparency 20.3
• Test Generator	• Teaching Notes p. 187 • Reading Organizer p. 201	• Test Booklet: Selection Test pp. 255–256 • Portfolio Management System pp. 54–55, 203	• Selected Readings, Audiocassette 3, Side B

Proofreading Warm-ups

You may use the following exercises to help students practice their proofreading skills. Copy a set of incorrect sentences onto the chalkboard, and have students find and correct the spelling, punctuation, usage, and mechanical errors in each sentence. Ask students to share and discuss their responses.

	Sentences with Errors	**Sentences Corrected**	**Skills Covered**
1	**a.** john updike has wrote real good novels and short stories for along time **b.** Updike portrays the conflict between generations real good	**a.** John Updike has written really good novels and short stories for a long time. **b.** Updike portrays the conflict between generations really well.	Capitalization, Verb tense, Nonstandard usage, Spelling, End marks
2	**a.** a aphorism is a breif wise saying **b.** in the story Daughter of Invention the mother uses aphorisms but she gets them slightly wrong	**a.** An aphorism is a brief, wise saying. **b.** In the story "Daughter of Invention," the mother uses aphorisms, but she gets them slightly wrong.	Capitalization, Indefinite articles, Spelling, Comma usage, Quotation marks, End marks
3	**a.** anne sexton earned numerus poetry prizes; including a Pulitzer prize **b.** anne sextons poem The Bells has alot of imagery in it	**a.** Anne Sexton earned numerous poetry prizes including a Pulitzer Prize. **b.** Anne Sexton's poem "The Bells" has a lot of imagery in it.	Capitalization, Spelling, Semicolon usage, Apostrophe usage, Quotation marks, End marks
4	**a.** n. scott momaday write's memores about his travels & his discoverys **b.** there is a Kiowa Legend that was created at the base of devils tower	**a.** N. Scott Momaday writes memoirs about his travels and his discoveries. **b.** There is a Kiowa legend that was created at the base of Devil's Tower.	Capitalization, Apostrophe usage, Spelling, Nonstandard usage, Plural nouns, Misplaced modifiers, End marks
5	**a.** alice walker, celebrates in her writing, the creativity of unsung women **b.** her pome about women contains a paradox; or apparant contradiction	**a.** Alice Walker celebrates in her writing the creativity of unsung women. **b.** Her poem about women contains a paradox, or apparent contradiction.	Capitalization, Comma usage, Spelling, Semicolon usage, End marks
6	**a.** amy tan had not planed to become a Fiction-Writer but she ended up writing stories anyway **b.** her and her mother disagreed, over what Tan should study, in collage	**a.** Amy Tan had not planned to become a fiction writer, but she ended up writing stories anyway. **b.** She and her mother disagreed over what Tan should study in college.	Capitalization, Spelling, Nonstandard Usage, Hyphens, Comma usage, Pronoun usage, End marks
7	**a.** class today we are going to study base words roots and word familys announced ms. Doerr **b.** do you mean base as in low words Ms. Doerr queried Joel earnestly	**a.** "Class, today we are going to study base words, roots, and word families," announced Ms. Doerr. **b.** "Do you mean base as in low words, Ms. Doerr?" queried Joel earnestly.	Quotation marks, Capitalization, Comma usage, Plural nouns, Question marks, End marks
8	**a.** inflectional suffixs are one's that change person number or tense **b.** example's include, the endings –s –ed and ing	**a.** Inflectional suffixes are ones that change person, number, or tense. **b.** Examples include the endings –s, –ed, and –ing.	Capitalization, Plural nouns, Apostrophe usage, Comma usage, Hyphens, Underlining, End marks
9	**a.** garrett hongo born in volcano hawaii growed up on Oahu **b.** his poems overflow w/ the common details of Contemporary American Culture; such as television shows	**a.** Garrett Hongo, born in Volcano, Hawaii, grew up on Oahu. **b.** His poems overflow with the common details of contemporary American culture, such as television shows.	Capitalization, Comma usage, Verbs, Write out abbreviations, Semicolon usage, End marks
10	**a.** a refrain is a word phrase line or group of line's that are repeated several times **b.** sometime's as in Garrett Hongos poem What For refrains appear at the beginnings of lines	**a.** A refrain is a word, phrase, line, or group of lines that is repeated several times. **b.** Sometimes, as in Garrett Hongo's poem "What For," refrains appear at the beginnings of lines.	Capitalization, Comma usage, Apostrophe usage, Subject-Verb agreement, Quotation marks, End marks

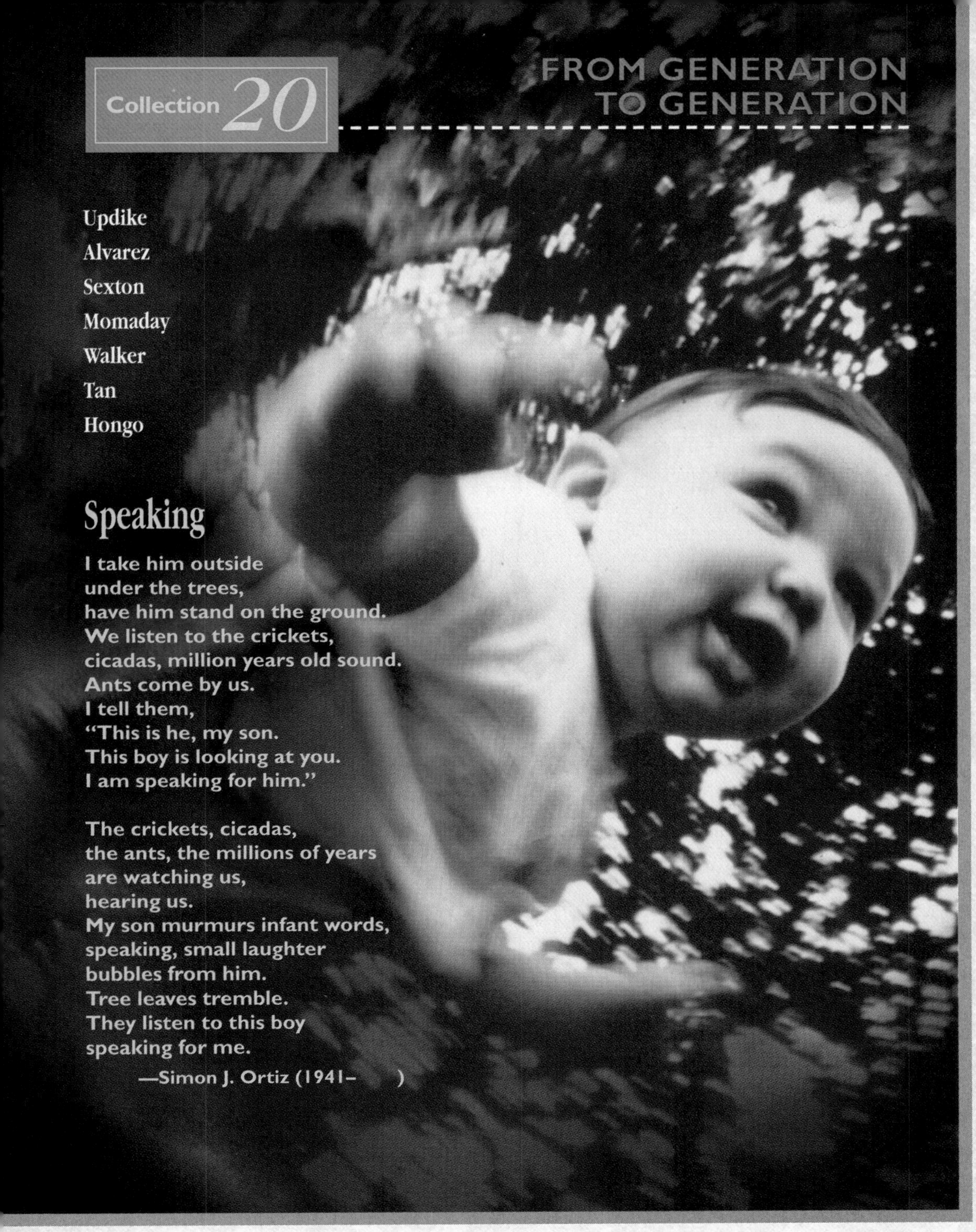

Collection 20

FROM GENERATION TO GENERATION

Speaking

I take him outside
under the trees,
have him stand on the ground.
We listen to the crickets,
cicadas, million years old sound.
Ants come by us.
I tell them,
"This is he, my son.
This boy is looking at you.
I am speaking for him."

The crickets, cicadas,
the ants, the millions of years
are watching us,
hearing us.
My son murmurs infant words,
speaking, small laughter
bubbles from him.
Tree leaves tremble.
They listen to this boy
speaking for me.

—Simon J. Ortiz (1941–)

"Speaking"

? How does this poem relate to the theme of this Collection, "From Generation to Generation"? [Possible responses: The poem is about two generations, a father and his infant son, each of whom speaks to nature in his own way.]

PROGRAM MANAGER

- **Integrated Assessment** For a summative assessment of the literature and language skills taught in this collection, see **Collection 20 Test, *Test Booklet,*** pp. 257–259.
- **Instructional Support** See **Fine Art Transparency** 20.1. Review teacher's notes for transparencies in the ***Audiovisual Resources Binder*** for suggestions on how to tie the transparency to specific reading selections.
- **Extending Collection Theme** See **Cross-Curricular Activity: From Generation to Generation, *Teaching Resources B,*** p. 202, for an activity in another discipline and for evaluation criteria.

PORTFOLIO ASSESSMENT

Parent/Guardian Involvement For forms that will help a parent or guardian review and respond to a student's portfolio, see the ***Portfolio Management System,*** pp. 62–63.

QUICK PLANNING GUIDE

Into the Story

Author Biography p. 1068
Before You Read p. 1069

- **Reading Focus:** Students consider father-son relationships.
- **A Dialogue with the Text: Set a Purpose** Describe personality traits of main characters

Through the Story

"Son" pp. 1070–1073
Words to Own pp. 1070–1073
Connections: An Essay p. 1074
from "Still Just Writing"
Making Meanings p. 1075

Beyond the Story

Choices: Building Your Portfolio p. 1075

- **Writer's Notebook:** Create a cluster diagram that conveys the story's theme
- **Critical Writing:** Write about a critic's statement
- **Creative Writing:** Write an original story

WRITERS ON WRITING

On being a writer, Updike says, ". . . I distrust prolific writers. I think that if they'd write half as much, they might be twice as good. I think of myself as writing at a stately pace—a few pages a day. That's really less than a thousand words—a very modest quota compared with that which many writers have set for themselves."

John Updike
(1932–)

© Nancy Crampton.

Accepting the National Book Award in 1982, John Updike offered this advice to young writers: "Have faith. May you surround yourselves with parents, editors, mates, and children as supportive as mine have been. But the essential support and encouragement of course come from within, arising out of the mad notion that your society needs to know what only you can tell it." That "mad notion" has generated some of our finest contemporary short stories.

John Updike spent his youth in the small town of Shillington in rural Pennsylvania. Gifted with what seems like total recall of growing up in the American middle class, Updike also displays a skill with language that can evoke responses to the most ordinary and familiar events, endowing them with importance.

In his memoir, "The Dogwood Tree: A Boyhood" (published in *Assorted Prose* in 1965), Updike crafts an image of his youthful artistic ambition: ". . . riding a thin pencil line out of Shillington, out of time altogether, into an infinity of unseen and even unborn hearts." As a mature and successful writer, he confronts that image and senses disappointment: "Like some phantom conjured by this child from a glue bottle, I have executed his commands; acquired pencils, paper, and an office. Now I wait apprehensively for his next command, or at least a nod of appreciation, and he smiles through me as if I am already transparent with failure."

After graduating *summa cum laude* from Harvard University in 1954, Updike studied drawing in England for a year, and on his return to the United States went to work for *The New Yorker* magazine. After two years, he made the courageous decision to support his young family entirely by writing. He left New York for Massachusetts and has since produced a long shelf of impressive novels, stories, poems, memoirs, and critical essays.

Although critics are a cantankerous lot, nearly all agree with Rachael C. Burchard that Updike's "style is superb. His work is worth reading if for no reason other than to enjoy the piquant phrase, the lyric vision, the fluent rhetoric." Among his successful novels have been the tales in the Rabbit series—*Rabbit, Run* (1960), *Rabbit Redux* (1971), *Rabbit Is Rich* (1981; Pulitzer Prize), and *Rabbit at Rest* (1990).

The Rabbit novels mark the ends of four consecutive decades and embody the concerns of their time. They chronicle the life of Harry "Rabbit" Angstrom, who lives, as his creator might have, an outwardly conventional life in a small Pennsylvania town. In revealing Rabbit's yearnings and disappointments and the fluctuations of his relationships, Updike gives us a portrait of forty years of American social behavior. As always with an Updike novel, readers enjoy the feel of life—the sights, smells, and sounds that bring life into focus.

Among Updike's other novels are *The Centaur* (1963; National Book Award) and a trilogy, *A Month of Sundays* (1975), *Roger's Version* (1986), and *S.* (1988), which make up a modern version of Nathaniel Hawthorne's *The Scarlet Letter.* In 1996 he published *In the Beauty of the Lilies*, a novel that spans the twentieth century and focuses, in Updike's characteristic way, on generations of a family and on the mysteries of faith – and, as something new, on the American love affair with the movies.

WORDS TO OWN

The following vocabulary words are defined in the Words to Own at the bottom of the pupil's page.

symmetrical p. 1070	docile p. 1070
jocular p. 1070	anarchy p. 1072
irksome p. 1070	seminary p. 1072
mincingly p. 1070	jaunty p. 1072
antagonists p. 1070	siblings p. 1073

Photograph Copyright © 1995 Whitney Museum of American Art, New York. Gift of Mr. and Mrs. Herbert Fischbach. Photography by Bill Jacobson. © 1997 Alex Katz/Licensed by VAGA/Marlborough Gallery, New York.

Eli (1963) by Alex Katz. Oil on canvas (72″ × 86″).

BEFORE YOU READ
SON

Reading Focus

Fathers and Sons

"Fathers and sons"—simple words that hide complex, mystifying, and aching relationships. Why do a father's good intentions and thoughts go astray? Why does a son feel antagonized and trapped by a well-meaning father? These are age-old questions that always intrigue us and never seem to receive satisfactory answers.

A Dialogue with the Text

READER'S LOG

This story deals with several different generations in the same family, so the title has more meanings than you might at first expect. As you begin each section, read slowly to make sure you know which son the narrator is talking about. Stop after each section, and write down the main personality traits of the principal characters in the section. Be brief; use just a word or two to describe each trait.

Using BEFORE YOU READ
p. 1069

Reading Focus

Have students draw in their Reader's Logs sketches or icons representing a father and a son. Ask them to write responses, in dialogue bubbles above the appropriate figures, about any of these subjects: money, home, sports, work, or music.

A Dialogue with the Text

To help students understand which son the narrator is talking about in each section, draw on the chalkboard a chart like the one following, using the dates given in the story.

1889	Narrator's grandfather
1913	Narrator's father
1949	Narrator
1973	Narrator's son

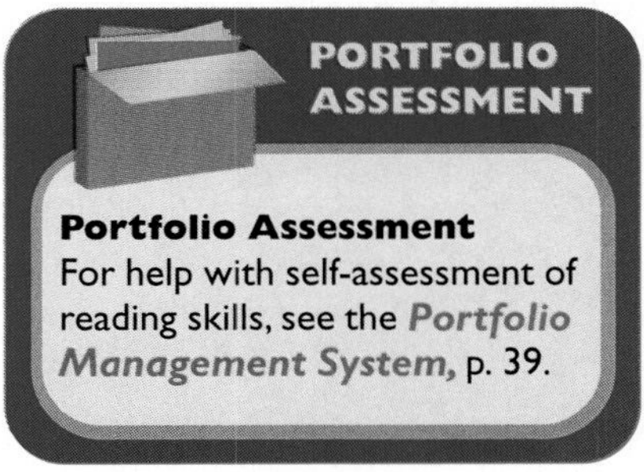

Portfolio Assessment

For help with self-assessment of reading skills, see the *Portfolio Management System,* p. 39.

PROGRAM MANAGER

- **Planning Instruction** See Teaching Notes, *Teaching Resources B,* p. 183, for objectives, a summary, and literary elements for this selection.
- **Instructional Support** Before beginning the instructional lesson, see Graphic Organizer for Active Reading, *Teaching Resources B,* p. 188, for a Through the Story activity.
- **Assessment** See Selection Test, *Test Booklet,* pp. 247–248.
- **Reinforcement** Use the Words to Own worksheet in *Teaching Resources B,* p. 189.

Through the Story

A. Literary Element: Point of View
Because several sons are described in this story, students should be careful to notice details (such as dates) that indicate the narrator is describing a different son. Explain that the boy in this paragraph is the fifteen-year-old son of the narrator, and the year is 1973. Point out that a different son is described in the next paragraph.

B. Literary Element: Irony
? What is ironic about this marital relationship? [Possible answer: Society at the time expected men to be more aggressive than their wives; in this relationship, though, the wife seems more aggressive.]

C. Critical Reading: Finding Cause and Effect
? What effect does his parents' relationship have on the son? [Possible answers: He may feel angry, confused, or depressed by their conflict. He probably wishes for a calmer home life in which adults are kind to one another. He may long for the time when he can pursue his own dreams.]

SON

John Updike

He is often upstairs, when he has to be home. He prefers to be elsewhere. He is almost sixteen, though beardless still, a man's mind indignantly captive in the frame of a child. I love touching him, but don't often dare. The other day, he had the flu, and a fever, and I gave him a back rub, marvelling at the symmetrical knit of muscle, the organic tension. He is high-strung. Yet his sleep is so solid he sweats like a stone in the wall of a well. He wishes for perfection. He would like to destroy us, for we are, variously, too fat, too jocular, too sloppy, too affectionate, too grotesque and heedless in our ways. His mother smokes too much. His younger brother chews with his mouth open. His older sister leaves unbuttoned the top button of her blouses. His younger sister tussles with the dogs, getting them overexcited, avoiding doing her homework. Everyone in the house talks nonsense. He would be a better father than his father. But time has tricked him, has made him a son. After a quarrel, if he cannot go outside and kick a ball, he retreats to a corner of the house and reclines on the beanbag chair in an attitude of strange—infantile or leonine—torpor.[1] We exhaust him, without meaning to. He takes an interest in the newspaper now, the front page as well as the sports, in this tiring year of 1973. **A**

He is upstairs, writing a musical comedy. It is a Sunday in 1949. He has volunteered to prepare a high-school assembly program; people will sing. Songs of the time go through his head, as he scribbles new words. *Up in de mornin', down at de school, work like a debil for my grades.* Below him, irksome voices grind on, like machines working their way through tunnels. His parents each want something from the other. "Marion, you don't understand that man like I do; he has a heart of gold." His father's charade is very complex: the world, which he fears, is used as a flail[2] on his wife. But from his cringing attitude he would seem to an outsider the one being flailed. With burning red face, the woman accepts the role of aggressor as penance for the fact, the incessant shameful fact, that *he* has to wrestle with the world while she hides here, in solitude, at home. This is normal, but does not seem to them to be so. **B** Only by convolution[3] have they arrived at the dominant/submissive relationship society has assigned them. For the man is maternally kind and with a smile hugs to himself his jewel, his certainty of being victimized; it is the mother whose tongue is sharp, who sometimes strikes. "Well, he gets you out of the house, and I guess that's gold to you." His answer is "Duty calls," pronounced mincingly. "The social contract is a balance of compromises." This will infuriate her, the son knows; **C** as his heart thickens, the downstairs overflows with her hot voice. "*Don't* wear that smile at me! And *take* your hands off your hips; you look like a sissy!" Their son tries not to listen. When he does, visual details of the downstairs flood his mind: the two antagonists, circling with their coffee cups; the shabby mismatched furniture; the hopeful books; the docile framed photographs of the dead, docile and still like cowed students. This matrix of pain that bore him—he

1. **torpor** (tôr′pər): sluggishness; dormancy.

2. **flail:** farm tool for hand threshing grain.
3. **convolution:** twisting together until distinctions are obscured.

Words to Own

symmetrical (si·me′tri·kəl) *adj.:* equally balanced.
jocular (jäk′yo͞o·lər) *adj.:* joking; comical.
irksome (ʉrk′səm) *adj.:* irritating.
mincingly (mins′iŋ·lē) *adv.:* in an affectedly dainty manner.
antagonists (an·tag′ə·nists) *n. pl.:* adversaries; opponents.
docile (däs′əl) *adj.:* passive.

Options for Teaching

Strategies for Inclusion

Advanced Have students locate descriptions of father-son relationships in literary works from the late nineteenth century through the 1970s. Ask students to evaluate how the fathers and sons are portrayed in the works and how the portrayals have changed over time. Ask students to create their own poems or short stories containing descriptions of contemporary father-son relationships.

Visual Before the class reads the story, ask small groups of students to find or to create illustrations depicting men in the three stages of life described in the story: a teenage boy, a father, and a grandfather. Suggest that students use original sketches, computer clip art, photographs, or magazine clippings for their illustrations. Ask students to write original captions describing each illustration.

Interpersonal Ask students to conduct interviews about what it is like to be a son or father. Encourage students to tape-record their interviews to share with the class. *Before students begin this activity, you may want to obtain written permission from parents or guardians and from the parties students will interview. Remind students to choose interview topics that they would not mind sharing with others.*

The Parrish Art Museum, Southampton, New York. Gift of the Estate of Fairfield Porter. Photo by Noel Rowe.

Laurence Typing (1952) by Fairfield Porter. Oil on canvas (40″ × 30 1/8″).

RESPONDING TO THE ART: VISUAL LITERACY

Which son is this illustration meant to represent? Why do you think so? [Possible response: It is probably meant to represent the son who is writing the musical comedy in 1949, because the boy in the illustration is typing and the date of the painting (1952) is close to the date in the story.]

INTEGRATING THE LANGUAGE ARTS

Strategic Reading Divide the class into pairs, and ask students to read or re-read the story with their partners, one section at a time. (See the answers to Making Meanings: Reviewing the Text on p. T1074 for a breakdown of the eight sections of the story.) Have students stop reading at the end of each section to discuss the events with their partners and to write a one- to three-sentence summary before reading the next section.

Speaking and Listening To help students develop a better understanding of the characters in the story, ask them to create Duologues. Divide the class into pairs, and ask students to choose a scene from the story in which a conversation could have taken place between a father and son but did not. Have students make notes about what the characters might have said. Then, ask students to improvise the conversation aloud, with one student playing the role of the son and one student playing the role of the father.

A. Literary Element: Setting

? How does the holiday setting contrast with the plight of the narrator's father? [Possible answer: It is Christmas, a time of the year that should be happy; yet money is scarce, and the narrator's father must work to provide for the family.]

B. Critical Reading: Making Connections

? What pattern seems to be unfolding from one vignette to the next? [Possible answers: The sons and fathers have similar feelings of dissatisfaction. The narrator's father feels trapped as a paperboy and later as a teacher. The narrator's grandfather, who is unhappy at his Missouri seminary, knows he is preparing for the wrong vocation.]

C. Reader's Response: Shaping Interpretations

? Why is the narrator's father so depressed by his visit to the seminary town of his father? [Sample responses: Perhaps by visiting the scene he is reminded of his own dissatisfaction in life; or he may feel angry with his father for the choices he made.]

feels he is floating above it, sprawled on the bed as on a cloud, stealing songs as they come into his head (*Across the hallway from the guidance room / Lives a French instructor called Mrs. Blum*), contemplating the view from the upstairs window (last summer's burdock[4] stalks like the beginnings of an alphabet, an apple tree holding three rotten apples as if pondering why they failed to fall), yearning for Monday, for the ride to school with his father, for the bell that calls him to homeroom, for the excitements of class, for Broadway, for fame, for the cloud that will carry him away, out of this, out.

He returns from his paper-delivery route and finds a few Christmas presents for him on the kitchen table. I must guess at the year. 1913? Without opening them, he knocks them to the floor, puts his head on the table, and falls asleep. He must have been consciously dramatizing his plight: His father was sick, money was scarce, he had to work, to win food for the family when he was still a child. In his dismissal of Christmas, he touched a nerve: his love of anarchy, his distrust of the social contract. He treasured this moment of revolt; else why remember it, hoard a memory so bitter, and confide it to his son many Christmases later? He had a teaching instinct, though he claimed that life miscast him as a schoolteacher. I suffered in his classes, feeling the confusion as a persecution of him, but now wonder if his rebellious heart did not court confusion, not as Communists do, to intrude their own order, but, more radical still, as an end pleasurable in itself, as truth's very body. Yet his handwriting (an old pink permission slip recently fluttered from a book where it had been marking a page for twenty years) was always considerately legible, and he was sitting up doing arithmetic the morning of the day he died.

And letters survive from that yet prior son, written in brown ink, in a tidy tame hand, home to his mother from the Missouri seminary where he was preparing for his vocation. The dates are 1887, 1888, 1889. Nothing much happened: He missed New Jersey, and was teased at a church social for escorting a widow. He wanted to do the right thing, but the little sheets of faded penscript exhale a dispirited calm, as if his heart already knew he would not make a successful minister, or live to be old. His son, my father, when old, drove hundreds of miles out of his way to visit the Missouri town from which those letters had been sent. Strangely, the town had not changed; it looked just as he had imagined, from his father's descriptions: tall wooden houses, rain-soaked, stacked on a bluff. The town was a sepia[5] postcard mailed homesick home and preserved in an attic. My father cursed: His father's old sorrow bore him down into depression, into hatred of life. My mother claims his decline in health began at that moment.

He is wonderful to watch, playing soccer. Smaller than the others, my son leaps, heads, dribbles, feints, passes. When a big boy knocks him down, he tumbles on the mud, in his green-and-black school uniform, in an ecstasy of falling. I am envious. Never for me the jaunty pride of the school uniform, the solemn ritual of the coach's pep talk, the camaraderie of shook hands and slapped backsides, the shadow-striped hush of late afternoon and last quarter, the solemn vaulted universe of official combat, with its cheering mothers and referees exotic as zebras and the bespectacled timekeeper alert with his claxon.[6] When the boy scores a goal, he runs into the arms of his teammates with upraised arms and his face alight as if blinded by triumph. They lift him from the earth in a union of muddy hugs. What spirit! What valor! What skill! His father, watching from the sidelines, inwardly registers only one complaint: He feels the boy, with his talent, should be more aggressive.

4. **burdock:** coarse, hairy weed with thick stalks, heart-shaped leaves, and prickly purple flowers.

5. **sepia** (sē′pē·ə): brownish ink used in artwork and photography.

6. **claxon** (klaks′ən): more correctly, Klaxon, the trademark for a type of electric horn with a distinctively loud, shrill sound. Such a horn is often used to mark the end of a time period in sporting events.

Words to Own

anarchy (an′ər·kē) *n.:* complete disorder.
seminary (sem′ə·ner′ē) *n.:* school for training ministers, priests, or rabbis.
jaunty (jônt′ē) *adj.:* confident; carefree.

OPTIONS FOR TEACHING

PROFESSIONAL NOTES

Critical Comments: Negative Criticism Point out that many well-known writers have had to deal with adverse criticism of their work, particularly their earlier writing. In 1963, critic Norman Podhoretz wrote of Updike, "His short stories . . . strike me as all windup and no delivery, and I am alternately bored and exasperated by the verbal pyrotechnics they specialize in. . . . " A few years later, in 1967, another critic, Richard H. Rupp, wrote, "At worst . . . [his] style leaves an empty husk. At best, it reveals characters only potentially interesting. One does not remember them by name, only collectively—the young husband, the student abroad, the long-suffering wife." Point out that "Son" was published in 1973, more than fifteen years into Updike's career. Ask students to respond to Podhoretz's and Rupp's criticisms by writing a short evaluation of the **characterization** and **style** in "Son." In particular, ask students to state whether or not "Son" has the faults the critics saw in Updike's earlier writing. Remind students to include specific examples from the story as support.

They drove across the Commonwealth of Pennsylvania to hear their son read in Pittsburgh. But when their presence was announced to the audience, they did not stand; the applause groped for them and died. My mother said afterwards she was afraid she might fall into the next row if she tried to stand in the dark. Next morning was sunny, and the three of us searched for the house where once they had lived. They had been happy there; I imagined, indeed, that I had been conceived there, just before the slope of the Depression steepened and fear gripped my family. We found the library where she used to read Turgenev,[7] and the little park where the bums slept close as paving stones in the summer night; but their street kept eluding us, though we circled in the car. On foot, my mother found the tree. She claimed she recognized it, the sooty linden tree she would gaze into from their apartment windows. The branches, though thicker, had held their pattern. But the house itself, and the entire block, was gone. Stray bricks and rods of iron in the grass suggested that the demolition had been recent. We stood on the empty spot and laughed. They knew it was right, because the railroad tracks were the right distance away. In confirmation, a long freight train pulled itself east around the curve, its great weight gliding as if on a river current; then a silver passenger train came gliding as effortlessly in the other direction. The curve of **D** the tracks tipped the cars slightly toward us. The Golden Triangle,[8] gray and hazed, was off to our left, beyond a forest of bridges. We stood on the grassy rubble that morning, where something once had been, beside the tree still there, and were intensely happy. Why? We knew.

"'No,' Dad said to me, 'the Christian ministry isn't a job you choose, it's a vocation for which you got to receive a call.' I could tell he wanted me to ask him. We never talked much, but we understood **E** each other, we were both scared devils, not like you and the kid. I asked him, Had he ever received the call? He said No. He said No, he never had. Received the call. That was a terrible thing, for him to admit. And I was the one he told. As far as I knew he never admitted it to anybody, but he admitted it to me. He felt like hell about it, I could tell. That was all we ever said about it. That was enough."

He has made his younger brother cry, and justice must be done. A father enforces justice. I corner **F** the rat in our bedroom; he is holding a cardboard mailing tube like a sword. The challenge flares white-hot; I roll my weight toward him like a rock down a mountain, and knock the weapon from his hand. He smiles. Smiles! Because my facial expression is silly? Because he is glad that he can still be overpowered, and hence is still protected? Why? I do not hit him. We stand a second, father and son, and then as nimbly as on the soccer field he steps around me and out the door. He slams the door. He shouts obscenities in the hall, slams all the doors he can find on the way to his room. Our moment of smilingly shared silence was the moment of compression; now the explosion. The whole house rocks with it. Downstairs, his siblings and mother come to me and offer advice and psychological analysis. I was too aggressive. He is spoiled. What they can never know, my grief alone to treasure, was that lucid many-sided second of his smiling and my relenting, before the world's wrathful pantomime of power resumed.

As we huddle whispering about him, my son takes his revenge. In his room, he plays his guitar. He has greatly improved this winter; his hands getting bigger is the least of it. He has found in the guitar an escape. He plays the Romanza[9] wherein repeated notes, with a sliding like the heart's valves, let themselves fall along the scale:

The notes fall, so gently he bombs us, drops feathery notes down upon us, our visitor, our prisoner.

7. **Turgenev** (toor·gān′əf): Ivan Turgenev (1818–1883), Russian writer.

8. **The Golden Triangle:** wedge-shaped piece of land formed by the junction of the Allegheny and Monongahela Rivers in Pittsburgh, Pennsylvania. The two rivers join to form the Ohio River at this point.

9. **Romanza** (rō·män′zə): musical term. Italian for "romance."

WORDS TO OWN

siblings (sib′liŋz) *n. pl.:* brothers or sisters.

D. Reader's Response: Shaping Interpretations

? Why are the narrator and his parents happy even though the house they were trying to find is now gone? [Sample responses: Maybe they realize that their happiness isn't tied to the old house—that they could be just as happy without it; or maybe they are laughing at themselves for the comic picture they make standing on the rubble of their old home.]

E. Literary Element: Point of View

First, point out that this entire paragraph is enclosed in quotation marks; then, ask students to identify the speaker in the paragraph. [The speaker is the narrator's father; the person who failed to receive the call for the ministry is the narrator's grandfather.]

F. Reader's Response: Challenging the Text

Point out that the father compares confronting his son to cornering a rat. Ask students whether they think this is an effective comparison, and have them explain why or why not. [Sample responses: It is effective because the father is using the word *rat* in an affectionate way; or it is not effective because the comparison seems humorous and does not fit the serious tone of the story.]

ASSESSMENT TOOLS

Check Test: Fill-in-the-Blank

1. The sections in the story are written in the __________ person. [third]
2. The son in 1949 is disturbed when his mother and father ________. [argue]
3. One father enters the _________ in the late 1800s. [seminary]
4. During Christmas in or around the year ________, a son must work to help his family. [1913]
5. A father is watching his son play ________ in one of the sections of the story. [soccer]

Ongoing Assessment: Reading Use this scale and list of criteria to evaluate each student's prereading notes, comments, and Reader's Log.

A=Always U=Usually O=Occasionally

____ Makes reasonable predictions based on prereading information and discussion
____ Connects personal experience and prior knowledge with prereading information
____ Applies prereading strategies that have been discussed previously in class
____ Keeps a record of prereading responses

A. Reader's Response: First Thoughts

? What do you think it would be like to make your living as a writer? Why? [Sample responses: It would be a good job because the hours would be flexible, and you could work at home; or it would be stressful because you might run out of ideas or not know where your next paycheck is coming from.]

Connections — An Essay

One of contemporary America's best fiction writers, Anne Tyler (1941–   ) has written several widely read novels, including *Dinner at the Homesick Restaurant* (1982), *The Accidental Tourist* (1985), which was made into a popular film, and *Breathing Lessons* (1988). In the following passage, Tyler talks about writing as a craft and about how she discovered that one can write interestingly about ordinary people. "Even the most ordinary person, in real life," she says, "will turn out to have something unusual at his center."

from "Still Just Writing"

Anne Tyler

I was standing in the schoolyard waiting for a child when another mother came up to me. "Have you found work yet?" she asked "Or are you still just writing?"

Now, how am I supposed to answer that?

A I could take offense, come to think of it. Maybe the reason I didn't is that I halfway share her attitude. They're *paying* me for this? For just writing down untruthful stories? I'd better look around for more permanent employment. For I do consider writing to be a finite job. I expect that any day now, I will have said all I have to say; I'll have used up all my characters, and then I'll be free to get on with my real life. When I make a note of new ideas on index cards, I imagine I'm clearing out my head, and that soon it will be empty and spacious. I file the cards in a little blue box, and I can picture myself using the final card one day—ah! through at last!—and throwing the blue box away. I'm like a dentist who continually fights tooth decay, working toward the time when he's conquered it altogether and done himself out of a job. But my head keeps loading up again; the little blue box stays crowded and messy. Even when I feel I have no ideas at all, and can't possibly start the next chapter, I have a sense of something still bottled in me, trying to get out. . . .

Walker/Gamma Liaison.

I spent my adolescence planning to be an artist, not a writer. After all, books had to be about major events, and none had ever happened to me. All I knew were tobacco workers, stringing the leaves I handed them and talking up a storm. Then I found a book of Eudora Welty's short stories in the high school library. She was writing about Edna Earle, who was so slow-witted she could sit all day just pondering how the tail of the *C* got through the loop of the *L* on the Coca-Cola sign. Why, I knew Edna Earle. You mean you could *write* about such people? I have always meant to send Eudora Welty a thank-you note, but I imagine she would find it a little strange.

Making Meanings

First Thoughts

1. Some students may say they understand their parents better after reading the story.

Reviewing the Text

a. (1) Narrator's teenage son is described (1973). (2) Narrator appears as a teen dreaming of becoming a playwright (1949). (3) Narrator's father appears as a young paperboy (1913). (4) Narrator's grandfather speaks through old letters (1889). (5) Narrator's teenage son appears again (1973). (6) Narrator's parents hear their grown son read from his work (probably after 1960). (7) Narrator's father tells him about a talk he had with his own father (no date). (8) Narrator again describes his son (1973).

b. Students may identify a variety of passages from pp. 1070, 1072, and 1073.

c. The narrator tries to discipline his son, but his son defies him.

d. Son and father share a smile; then the son rushes out, slams the door, shouts, and goes off to play his guitar in revenge.

Making Meanings

First Thoughts

1. What thoughts about parents and children did you have as you read "Son"?

> **Reviewing the Text**
>
> a. For each of the story's eight sections, identify the time period and the characters.
>
> b. Find passages in each section in which the narrator reveals private thoughts of the characters.
>
> c. What test does the father-narrator face in the last section?
>
> d. How does the son respond to the father's discipline?

Shaping Interpretations

2. This story includes a variety of incidents that range over several different periods. What **thematic** thread unifies the story?
3. In the long line of the generations, hope keeps reappearing. In what ways are the characters' hopes for each other disappointed? How are they fulfilled?
4. In the context of the story, what do you think Updike means by the phrase "the social contract"? Would he say that this contract is or is not honored between fathers and sons? Explain.
5. At the end of the story, why does the narrator refer to his son as "our visitor, our prisoner"?
6. Why do you think Updike gave the story the title "Son" instead of "Father"? Would you read the story differently if it had been called "Father"?
7. How would you describe the narrator's **tone** in telling this story? How does he feel about the people in this family?

Extending the Text

8. What discovery about writing, described by Anne Tyler in Connections on page 1074, is also apparent in "Son"? Explain.

Challenging the Text

9. Review the notes you made in your Reader's Log. Do you find Updike's portrayal of the characters and their relationships believable? Are these portrayals sentimental or realistic? Explain.

Choices: Building Your Portfolio

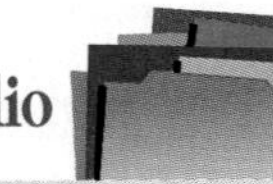

Writer's Notebook

1. Collecting Ideas for an Evaluation

WORK IN PROGRESS

When you evaluate a short story, you need to show how separate elements work (or do not work) together. Use a graphic organizer, such as a cluster diagram, to demonstrate how the eight sections of Updike's "Son" contribute to the story's main theme. Write the theme in the center of the cluster, and, in each of the eight bubbles, identify the words, images, characters, or ideas that help convey the theme. Save your notes for possible use in the Writer's Workshop on page 1181.

Critical Writing

2. "A contact barely reached"

Analyzing Updike's book *Problems and Other Stories* (1979), in which "Son" appears, the critic Donald J. Greiner wrote:

> The stories were written from 1971 to 1978, a period of unsettling family conditions for Updike himself. Although the tales are not autobiography, the specter of domestic loss, of love moving forward from all sides toward a contact barely reached, hovers around most of them. It is not that love is denied but that it is difficult to sustain.

Write a brief essay applying Greiner's statement to "Son." What does this story have to say about loss, love, and "a contact barely reached"?

Creative Writing

3. "Daughter"

Imitating the structure of "Son," write some episodes of a story called "Daughter." Let your narrator reveal the thoughts and feelings of at least three generations of one family.

Extending the Text

8. **(Synthesis)** Possible response: The realization that ordinary people—not just major events—can be the subjects of interesting stories.

Challenging the Text

9. **(Evaluation)** Possible responses: Updike writes realistically; his fathers and sons are very round characters; or Updike's portrayal seems sentimental—not all father-son relationships are so emotional.

Choices: Building Your Portfolio

1. **Writer's Notebook** Remind students to save their work. They may use it as prewriting for the Writer's Workshop on p. 1181.
2. **Critical Writing** Have students work in pairs to brainstorm thesis statements for their essays and to gather details from the story that support their statements.
3. **Creative Writing** Suggest that students base their episodes on the first four sections of the story. Before students write, have them analyze each section carefully.

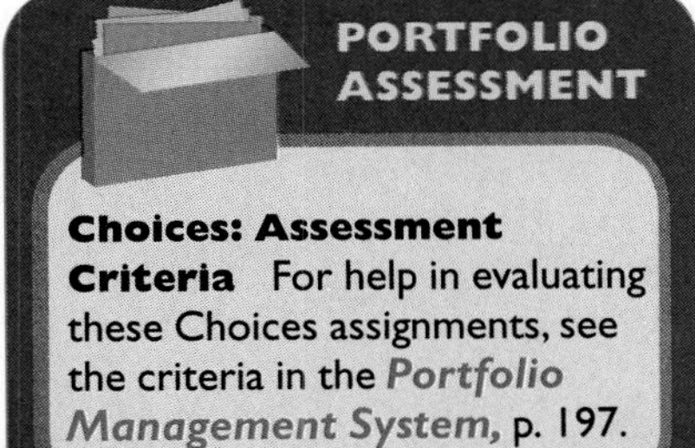

Choices: Assessment Criteria For help in evaluating these Choices assignments, see the criteria in the *Portfolio Management System*, p. 197.

Shaping Interpretations

2. The relationships between fathers and sons.
3. Disappointed hope: the narrator's grandfather becomes a minister even though he receives no call and knows he will be unsuccessful. Fulfilled hope: the narrator admires his son's athletic accomplishments.
4. The narrator's father refers to the social contract as "a balance of compromises." The author might say it is honored between sons and fathers when they try to balance their needs for power, love, and independence.
5. His son is like a visitor because the narrator knows he will leave home in a few short years. He is like a prisoner because, until he does leave, he is restricted by a family arrangement that he is starting to outgrow.
6. Students may suggest that Updike wanted readers to focus on the sons' points of view. If the story were titled "Father," the reader would focus on the fathers rather than on the sons.
7. The tone is nostalgic or bittersweet. The narrator feels strongly about the people in his family; he loves them, yet he sees their flaws as well as his own.

QUICK PLANNING GUIDE

Into the Story

Author Biography p. 1076

Before You Read p. 1077

- **Reading Focus: Prior Knowledge** Students discuss how parents and children struggle to make peace with each other.
- **A Dialogue with the Text: Scaffolding** Take notes on how the characters adjust

Elements of Literature: Conflict

Through the Story

"Daughter of Invention" pp. 1079–1086

Words to Own pp. 1079–1086

Literature and Techonology pp. 1084–1085

Making Meanings p. 1087

Beyond the Story

Choices: Building Your Portfolio p. 1087

- **Writer's Notebook:** Make a conflict chart
- **Critical Writing:** Write an essay about the title
- **Creative Writing/Speaking and Listening:** Write the first page of a speech

Julia Alvarez

(1950–)

"All my childhood I had dressed like an American, eaten American foods, and befriended American children. I had gone to an American school and spent most of the day speaking and reading English. At night, my prayers were full of blond hair and blue eyes and snow. . . . All my childhood I had longed for this moment of arrival. And here I was, an American girl, coming home at last."

With these words, Julia (pronounced "hoolia") Alvarez describes stepping back into America. Although born in New York City, Alvarez spent her early childhood in the Dominican Republic. In 1960, just before her father was to be arrested for his involvement in a secret plot to overthrow the dictator Rafael Trujillo Molina, Alvarez and her family were tipped off by an American agent and escaped to the United States.

Paradoxically, her homecoming was filled with all the difficulties of adjusting to a brand-new life. Learning contemporary American English was only part of the adjustment. Alvarez also had to learn to compromise in order to resolve conflicts between American customs and her parents' more traditional views. This theme is at the heart of her fiction—particularly her short stories and her best-known work, the novel *How the Garcia Girls Lost Their Accents* (1991).

Before concentrating on writing fiction, Alvarez taught courses in poetry for twelve years in schools in Kentucky, California, Vermont, Illinois, and Washington, D.C. Her first collection of poems, appropriately titled *Homecoming,* was published in 1984. Alvarez has also won the American Academy of Poetry Prize, but it is as a novelist that she has received the most notice.

How the Garcia Girls Lost Their Accents is a novel of fifteen interlocking stories with engaging and memorable characters. The Garcia family, with its four daughters, struggles to overcome a variety of cultural and generational conflicts, and comparisons with Alvarez's own family make it clear that the novel is highly autobiographical. Her 1994 novel, *In the Time of the Butterflies,* is a fictionalized account of the lives and deaths of three sisters, Patria, Minerva, and María Teresa Mirabal, the wives of political prisoners in the Dominican Republic. In a case that became notorious throughout Latin America, the women, who had been visiting their husbands, were murdered in 1960 by thugs connected to the Trujillo regime.

It is clear that Alvarez has forged, out of memory and imagination, a novelist's sensibility. As one critic said about *Garcia Girls,* Alvarez has "beautifully captured the threshold experience of the new immigrant, where the past is not yet a memory and the future remains an anxious dream."

Theo Westenberger/Gamma Liaison.

WORDS TO OWN

The following vocabulary words are defined in the Words to Own at the bottom of the pupil's page.

disembodied p. 1079	florid p. 1082
labyrinth p. 1080	ultimatum p. 1083
communal p. 1080	vengeful p. 1084
disclaimer p. 1080	misnomers p. 1086
eulogy p. 1081	reconcile p. 1086

Before You Read
Daughter of Invention

Reading Focus

Generations

From the Biblical parable of the prodigal son to a short story written this morning, literature will probably never end its chronicle of children and parents struggling to understand and make peace with each other. "Experience is the greatest teacher, so trust us," says the older generation. "We want to live our own lives, not yours," say the children. Both have valid points, of course, and the search for equilibrium goes on.

A Dialogue with the Text

It is fascinating to see how the three characters in the following story have adapted so differently to the liberty the family enjoys in its new country. As you read, jot down notes on how Cukita, Mami, and Papi have adjusted to the United States, their new homeland.

Elements of Literature

Conflict

Do you doubt that a story runs on **conflict**? Here is a splendid example that takes its strength and much of its fun from the clash between the anxious values of Latin American parents and the liberated ones of their New York–raised daughter. Each major character in this story experiences both **external conflict** (with other people, a government, or society in general) and **internal conflict** (within his or her own mind).

External conflict exists between two people, between a person and a thing, or between a person and society. **Internal conflict** involves opposing forces within a person's mind.

For more on Conflict, see the Handbook of Literary Terms.

Into the Story

Using Before You Read
p. 1077

Reading Focus

Have students work in pairs to create two cluster diagrams—one centered on the word *parents* and the other on the word *children.* Ask students to write words, images, thoughts, and special concerns related to each group.

Elements of Literature

Ask students to consider the following questions as they read: What are the **external conflicts** between the two generations in the story? What internal conflicts take place within each character?

Portfolio Assessment

Portfolio Assessment
For help with self-assessment of reading skills, see the *Portfolio Management System,* pp. 48–49.

Program Manager

- **Planning Instruction** See Teaching Notes, *Teaching Resources B,* pp. 183–184, for objectives, a summary, literary elements, and additional historical and biographical information for this selection.
- **Instructional Support** Before beginning the instructional lesson, see Graphic Organizer for Active Reading, *Teaching Resources B,* p. 190, for a Through the Story activity.
- **Assessment** See Selection Test, *Test Booklet,* pp. 249–250.
- **Reinforcement** Use the Words to Own worksheet in *Teaching Resources B,* p. 191.

RESPONDING TO THE ART: VISUAL LITERACY

What might the placement of the two figures in the illustration suggest about their attitude toward one another? [Possible response: They are not facing toward each other, so it may indicate that the two of them are not communicating.]

OPTIONS FOR TEACHING

STRATEGIES FOR INCLUSION

Linguistic If possible, bring in a book, such as *Brewer's Dictionary of Phrase and Fable,* that contains a variety of aphorisms or clichés. Write a few of the expressions on the chalkboard, and ask students to create fractured versions of them, as Mami unintentionally does. Suggest that students change key words in the sayings, or substitute rhyming words, such as *home* for *Rome*. Ask them to read the original and the fractured versions aloud. Ask the class to discuss how the changes affect the meanings of the sayings.

Logical-Mathematical Before students read the story, discuss a few inventions from the past and the problems that they were designed to solve. Then, ask students to work independently to come up with an idea for an original invention that might be used to solve a problem that exists today. Ask students to present their ideas to the class, using scale drawings or other visual aids. After students have read the story, review the narrator's descriptions of Mami's invention ideas, and ask students to compare them with their own ideas.

Daughter of Invention

Julia Alvarez

She wanted to invent something, my mother. There was a period after we arrived in this country, until five or so years later, when my mother was inventing. They were never pressing, global needs she was addressing with her pencil and pad. She would have said that was for men to **A** do, rockets and engines that ran on gasoline and turned the wheels of the world. She was just fussing with little house things, don't mind her.

She always invented at night, after settling her house down. On his side of the bed my father would be conked out for an hour already, his Spanish newspaper draped over his chest, his glasses, propped up on his bedside table, looking out eerily at the darkened room like a disembodied guard. But in her lighted corner, like some devoted scholar burning the midnight oil, my mother was inventing, sheets pulled to her lap, pillows propped up behind her, her reading glasses riding the bridge of her nose like a schoolmarm's. On her lap lay one of those innumerable pads of paper my father always brought home from his office, compliments of some pharmaceutical company, advertising tranquilizers or antibiotics or skin cream; in her other hand, my mother held a pencil that looked like a pen with a little cylinder of lead inside. She would work on a sketch of something familiar, but drawn at such close range so she could attach a special nozzle or handier handle, the thing looked peculiar. Once, I mistook the spiral of a corkscrew for a nautilus shell, but it could just as well have been a galaxy forming.

It was the only time all day we'd catch her sitting down, for she herself was living proof of the *perpetuum mobile*[1] machine so many inventors had sought over the ages. My sisters and I would seek her out now when she seemed to have a moment to talk to us: We were having trouble at school or we wanted her to persuade my father to give us permission to go into the city or to a shopping mall or a movie—in broad daylight! My mother would wave us out of her room. "The problem with you girls . . ." I can tell you right now what the problem always boiled down to: We wanted to become Americans and my father—and my mother, at first—would have none of it.

"You girls are going to drive me crazy!" She always threatened if we kept nagging. "When I end up in Bellevue,[2] you'll be safely sorry!"

She spoke in English when she argued with us, even though, in a matter of months, her daughters were the fluent ones. Her English was much better than my father's, but it **B** was still a mishmash of mixed-up idioms and sayings that showed she was "green behind the ears," as she called it.

If my sisters and I tried to get her to talk in Spanish, she'd snap, "When in Rome, do unto the Romans . . ."

I had become the spokesman for my sisters, and I would stand my ground in that bedroom. "We're not going to that school anymore, Mami!"

"You have to." Her eyes would widen with worry. "In this country, it is against the law not to go to school. You want us to get thrown out?"

"You want us to get killed? Those kids were throwing stones today!"

"Sticks and stones don't break bones . . ." she chanted. I could tell, though, by the look on her face, it was as if one of those stones the kids had aimed at us had hit her. But she always pretended we were at fault. "What did you do to provoke them? It takes two to tangle, you know."

"Thanks, thanks a lot, Mom!" I'd storm out of that room and into mine. I never called her *Mom* except when I wanted her to feel how much she **C** had failed us in this country. She was a good enough Mami, fussing and scolding and giving advice, but a terrible girlfriend parent, a real failure of a Mom.

Back she'd go to her pencil and pad, scribbling and tsking and tearing off paper, finally giving up,

1. ***perpetuum mobile*** (per·pe'to͞o·əm' mō'bi·le): Latin for "perpetual motion."

2. **Bellevue:** large New York City hospital known for its psychiatric department.

Madre e hija (1995) by Oscar Pardo. Pastel on paper (19″ × 12½″). Courtesy of the artist.

WORDS TO OWN

disembodied (dis'im·bäd'ēd) *v.* used as *adj.*: separated from the body.

A. Reader's Response: First Thoughts

What do you think of the narrator's mother's ideas about the division of labor for men and women? [Sample responses: Her mother's view—that men should be concerned with the outside world and women with the home—is traditional; or her mother's views are outdated.]

B. Language Note: Idioms

What clichés or idioms does the narrator's mother mangle or combine in these paragraphs? ["You'll be sorry" combined with "Better safe than sorry;" "Green" (meaning "inexperienced") with "Wet behind the ears;" "When in Rome, do as the Romans do" with "Do unto others as you would have them do unto you."]

C. Critical Reading: Summarizing

What does the narrator say is the difference between a Mami and a Mom? [Possible answer: To the narrator, a Mami is a traditional mother who corrects her children and gives them guidance, but a Mom is more like a friend who offers her support.]

INTEGRATING THE LANGUAGE ARTS

Strategic Reading After the class has read the story once, call on students to answer the question "What is the first (or last) thing that happens in the story?" After an initial answer, prompt students forward or backward in the story by asking, "Then what happens?" or "What happens before that?" Allow students to refer to the story and to re-read passages when they are unsure about details. Continue until students have completely and accurately retold the story. This activity is also appropriate for students working together in small groups.

Writing: Telegram After students have read the story, show them an example of a message written in the style of a telegram. Then, ask students to write a telegram that the narrator might send to a relative or pen pal in another country. The telegram should briefly describe the conflict the narrator has with her father about her speech. Ask students to limit their message to a certain number of words, but ask them to try to summarize the problem and to describe the narrator's feelings about it. Also, discuss the possible difficulties a recipient would have in reading such a condensed message.

A. Literary Element: Conflict
Point out the conflict between mother and daughter in this paragraph. The narrator's need for time alone to explore and write about her feelings conflicts with her mother's need to share the excitement of a new idea.

B. Critical Reading: Analyzing Conflict

? What do the narrator and her sisters want from their mother? [Possible answers: They want her to pay more attention to their needs and to help them adjust to life in America more easily. Instead, she spends her time thinking up ideas for inventions to make life easier for other people.]

and taking up her *New York Times.* Some nights, though, she'd get a good idea, and she'd rush into my room, a flushed look on her face, her tablet of paper in her hand, a cursory knock on the door she'd just thrown open: "Do I have something to show you, Cukita!"

(A) This was my time to myself, after I'd finished my homework, while my sisters were still downstairs watching TV in the basement. Hunched over my small desk, the overhead light turned off, my lamp shining poignantly on my paper, the rest of the room in warm, soft, uncreated darkness, I wrote my secret poems in my new language.

"You're going to ruin your eyes!" My mother would storm into my room, turning on the overly bright overhead light, scaring off whatever shy passion I had just begun coaxing out of a labyrinth of feelings with the blue thread of my writing.

"Oh Mami!" I'd cry out, my eyes blinking up at her. "I'm writing."

"Ay, Cukita." That was her communal pet name for whoever was in her favor. "Cukita, when I make a million, I'll buy you your very own typewriter." (I'd been nagging my mother for one just like the one father had bought her to do his order forms at home.) "Gravy on the turkey" was what she called it when someone was buttering her up. She'd butter and pour. "I'll hire you your very own typist."

Down she'd plop on my bed and hold out her pad to me. "Take a guess, Cukita?" I'd study her rough sketch a moment: soap sprayed from the nozzle head of a shower when you turned the knob a certain way? Coffee with creamer already mixed in? Time-released water capsules for your plants when you were away? A key chain with a timer that would go off when your parking meter was about to expire? (The ticking would help you find your keys easily if you mislaid them.) The famous one, famous only in hindsight, was the stick person dragging a square by a rope—a suitcase with wheels? "Oh, of course," we'd humor her. "What every household needs: a shower like a car wash, keys ticking like a bomb, luggage on a leash!" By now, as you can see, it'd become something of a family joke, our Thomas Edison Mami, our Benjamin Franklin Mom.

Her face would fall. "Come on now! Use your head." One more wrong guess, and she'd tell me, pressing with her pencil point the different highlights of this incredible new wonder. "Remember that time we took the car to Bear Mountain, and we re-ah-lized that we had forgotten to pack an opener with our pick-a-nick?" (We kept correcting her, but she insisted this is how it should be said.) "When we were ready to eat we didn't have any way to open the refreshments cans?" (This before fliptop lids, which she claimed had crossed her mind.) "You know what this is now?" A shake of my head. "Is a car bumper, but see this part is a removable can opener. So simple and yet so necessary, no?"

"Yeah, Mami. You should patent it." I'd shrug. She'd tear off the scratch paper and fold it, carefully, corner to corner, as if she were going to save it. But then, she'd toss it in the wastebasket on her way out of the room and give a little laugh like a disclaimer. "It's half of one or two dozen of another . . ."

(B) I suppose none of her daughters was very encouraging. We resented her spending time on those dumb inventions. Here, we were trying to fit in America among Americans; we needed help figuring out who we were, why these Irish kids whose grandparents were micks two generations ago, why they were calling us spics. Why had we come to the country in the first place? Important, crucial, final things, you see, and here was our own mother, who didn't have a second to help us puzzle any of this out, inventing gadgets to make life easier for American moms. Why, it seemed as if she were arming our own enemy against us!

One time, she did have a moment of triumph. Every night, she liked to read *The New York Times* in bed before turning off her light, to see what the Americans were up to. One night, she let out a yelp to wake up my father beside her, bolt upright, reaching for his glasses which, in his haste, he knocked across the room. *"Que pasa? Que pasa?"*[3] What is wrong? There was terror in

3. ***Que pasa?*** (kā pä′sä): Spanish for "What's going on?"

Words to Own

labyrinth (lab′ə·rinth′) *n.:* place full of intricate passageways; maze.
communal (kə·myo͞on′əl) *adj.:* belonging to an entire group (in this case, Mami's daughters).
disclaimer (dis·klām′ər) *n.:* a giving up of a claim or connection.

Options for Teaching

Cooperative Learning

Designing a Board Game Students may find both **internal** and **external conflict** in this story. Ask groups of four to six students to identify the conflicts and to create a board game based on matching the characters with their internal and external conflicts. Students should write identifying descriptors or dialogue on various squares of the game board as examples of conflict. During the game, players should take turns matching conflicts with the corresponding characters. Students should design the game board and players' cards, write rules for the game, assign points for correct answers, and play the game to identify and correct flaws in the game's design.

his voice, fear she'd seen in his eyes in the Dominican Republic before we left. We were being watched there; he was being followed; he and mother had often exchanged those looks. They could not talk, of course, though they must have whispered to each other in fear at night in the dark bed. Now in America, he was safe, a success even; his Centro Medico in Brooklyn was thronged with the sick and the homesick. But in dreams, he went back to those awful days and long nights, and my mother's screams confirmed his secret fear: We had not gotten away after all; they had come for us at last.

"Ay, Papi, I'm sorry. Go back to sleep, Cukito. It's nothing, nothing really." My mother held up the *Times* for him to squint at the small print, back page headline, one hand tapping all over the top of the bedside table for his glasses, the other rubbing his eyes to wakefulness.

"Remember, remember how I showed you that suitcase with little wheels so we would not have to carry those heavy bags when we traveled? Someone stole my idea and made a million!" She shook the paper in his face. She shook the paper in all our faces that night. "See! See! This man was no *bobo*![4] He didn't put all his pokers on a back burner. I kept telling you, one of these days my ship would pass me by in the night!" She wagged her finger at my sisters and my father and me, laughing all the while, one of those eerie laughs crazy people in movies laugh. We had congregated in her room to hear the good news she'd been yelling down the stairs, and now we eyed her and each other. I suppose we were all thinking the same thing: Wouldn't it be weird and sad if Mami did end up in Bellevue as she'd always threatened she might?

"*Ya, ya*! Enough!" She waved us out of her room at last. "There is no use trying to drink spilt milk, that's for sure."

(C) It was the suitcase rollers that stopped my mother's hand; she had weather vaned a minor brainstorm. She would have to start taking herself seriously. That blocked the free play of her ingenuity. Besides, she had also begun working at my father's office, and at night, she was too tired and busy filling in columns with how much money they had made that day to be fooling with gadgets!

4. ***bobo:*** Spanish for "fool."

She did take up her pencil and pad one last time to help me out. In ninth grade, I was chosen by my English teacher, Sister Mary Joseph, to deliver the teacher's day address at the school assembly. Back in the Dominican Republic, I was a terrible student. No one could ever get me to sit down to a book. But in New York, I needed to settle somewhere, and the natives were unfriendly, the country inhospitable, so I took root in the language. By high school, the nuns were reading my stories and compositions out loud to my classmates as examples of imagination at work.

(D) This time my imagination jammed. At first I didn't want and then I couldn't seem to write that speech. I suppose I should have thought of it as a "great honor," as my father called it. But I was mortified. I still had a pronounced lilt to my accent, and I did not like to speak in public, subjecting myself to my classmates' ridicule. Recently, they had begun to warm toward my sisters and me, and it took no great figuring to see that to deliver a eulogy for a convent full of crazy, old overweight nuns was no way to endear myself to the members of my class.

But I didn't know how to get out of it. Week after week, I'd sit down, hoping to polish off some quick, noncommittal little speech. I couldn't get anything down.

The weekend before our Monday morning assembly I went into a panic. My mother would just have to call in and say I was in the hospital, in a coma. I was in the Dominican Republic. Yeah, that was it! Recently, my father had been talking about going back home to live.

My mother tried to calm me down. "Just remember how Mister Lincoln couldn't think of anything to say at the Gettysburg, but then, Bang! 'Four score and once upon a time ago,'" she began reciting. Her version of history was half invention and half truths and whatever else she needed to prove a point. "Something is going to come if you just relax. You'll see, like the Americans say, 'Necessity is the daughter of invention.' I'll help you."

All weekend, she kept coming into my room with help. "Please, Mami, just leave me alone, please," I pleaded with her. But I'd get rid of the

WORDS TO OWN

eulogy (yo͞o'lə·jē) *n.:* public speech of praise.

C. Reader's Response: Shaping Interpretations

? What does Mami's final reaction to the suitcase headline suggest about her? [Sample responses: Maybe, by seeing that someone else actually pursued a crazy idea and made it work, she realizes that inventing is serious business that she isn't ready for; or she enjoyed inventing when it was just a dream, but the discovery that it is real takes the fun out of it for her.]

D. Reader's Response: Connecting with the Text

? Do you think most people fear public speaking? Why or why not? [Sample responses: People don't like to speak in front of an audience because they aren't sure how the audience will react; or many people like to speak in front of others because it gives them a chance to get extra attention.]

CLASSROOM MANAGEMENT

Initiating Group Dynamics Before members of a group sit down to work together, have them do some kinesthetic warm-up activities. Group members should stand in a circle and shake out their limbs or do light stretches together. Then, one member from each group should initiate a mirroring activity in which he or she makes a simple movement that the rest of the group may copy. After a few moments, another member should create a new movement that the others mirror. The activity should continue until all members have initiated a movement at least once. Performing kinesthetic warm-ups together should help to develop a rapport and sense of cooperation among students who may not be accustomed to collaborating on assignments.

A. Literary Element: Irony
Point out the irony in this paragraph. Mami is usually the one who mangles clichés, but in this paragraph, the narrator is the one who mixes up the idiom "What's good for the goose is good for the gander."

B. Critical Reading: Analyzing Character
? What impresses the narrator about Whitman's poetry? How does it help her write her speech? [Possible answers: The poems, unlike the ones she reads in school, are about a person who seems very real. Whitman's words help her to find a prose voice that expresses her true self.]

C. Critical Reading: Finding Details
? What contrasts between the narrator's mother and father are revealed in this paragraph? [Possible answer: Her father still reads Dominican newspapers and considers moving back because the dictatorship has fallen; her mother reads *The New York Times* and no longer has any interest in going back because she enjoys her life in America more.]

(A) goose only to have to contend with the gander. My father kept poking his head in the door just to see if I had "fulfilled my obligations," a phrase he'd used when we were a little younger, and he'd check to see whether we had gone to the bathroom before a car trip. Several times that weekend around the supper table, he'd recite his valedictorian speech from when he graduated from high school. He'd give me pointers on delivery, on the great orators and their tricks. (Humbleness and praise and falling silent with great emotion were his favorites.)

My mother sat across the table, the only one who seemed to be listening to him. My sisters and I were forgetting a lot of our Spanish, and my father's formal, florid diction was even harder to understand. But my mother smiled softly to herself, and turned the Lazy Susan at the center of the table around and around as if it were the prime mover,[5] the first gear of attention.

(B) That Sunday evening, I was reading some poetry to get myself inspired: Whitman in an old book with an engraved cover my father had picked up in a thrift shop next to his office a few weeks back. "I celebrate myself and sing myself . . ." "He most honors my style who learns under it to destroy the teacher." The poet's words shocked and thrilled me. I had gotten used to the nuns, a literature of appropriate sentiments, poems with a message, expurgated texts. But here was a flesh and blood man, belching and laughing and sweating in poems. "Who touches this book touches a man."

That night, at last, I started to write, recklessly, three, five pages, looking up once only to see my father passing by the hall on tiptoe. When I was done, I read over my words, and my eyes filled. I finally sounded like myself in English!

As soon as I had finished that first draft, I called my mother to my room. She listened attentively, as she had to my father's speech, and in the end, her eyes were glistening too. Her face was soft and warm and proud. "That is a beautiful, beautiful speech, Cukita. I want for your father to hear it before he goes to sleep. Then I will type it for you, all right?"

Down the hall we went, the two of us, faces flushed with accomplishment. Into the master bedroom where my father was propped up on his pillows, still awake, reading the Dominican papers, already days old. He had become interested in his country's fate again. The dictatorship had been toppled. The interim government was going to hold the first free elections in thirty years. There was still some question in his mind whether or not we might want to move back. History was in the making, freedom and hope were (C) in the air again! But my mother had gotten used to the life here. She did not want to go back to the old country where she was only a wife and a mother (and a failed one at that, since she had never had the required son). She did not come straight out and disagree with my father's plans. Instead, she fussed with him about reading the papers in bed, soiling those sheets with those poorly printed, foreign tabloids. "*The Times* is not that bad!" she'd claim if my father tried to humor her by saying they shared the same dirty habit.

The minute my father saw my mother and me, filing in, he put his paper down, and his face brightened as if at long last his wife had delivered a son, and that was the news we were bringing him. His teeth were already grinning from the glass of water next to his bedside lamp, so he lisped when he said, "Eh-speech, eh-speech!"

"It is so beautiful, Papi," my mother previewed him, turning the sound off on his TV. She sat down at the foot of the bed. I stood before both of them, blocking their view of the soldiers in helicopters landing amid silenced gun reports and explosions. A few weeks ago it had been the shores of the Dominican Republic. Now it was the jungles of Southeast Asia they were saving. My mother gave me the nod to begin reading.

I didn't need much encouragement. I put my nose to the fire, as my mother would have said, and read from start to finish without looking up. When I was done, I was a little embarrassed at my pride in my own words. I pretended to quibble with a phrase or two I was sure I'd be talked out of changing. I looked questioningly to my mother. Her face was radiant. She turned to share her pride with my father.

5. **prime mover:** in philosophy, the self-moved being that is the source of all motion; in machinery, the source of power, such as a windmill or an engine.

WORDS TO OWN
florid (flôr′id) *adj.:* showy.

OPTIONS FOR TEACHING

CROSSING THE CURRICULUM

Social Sciences Ask students to write a bill of rights for a country where a dictatorship has been overthrown and a new election has been held. Students should use ideas from the Bill of Rights in the United States Constitution and discuss the reasons behind each item in the U.S. Bill of Rights. Discuss the new freedoms the country might offer and the adjustments that the government and citizens might need to make. Ask students to keep in mind the consequences associated with the freedoms guaranteed to people in the United States, such as freedom of speech.

Geography/History Ask students to do independent research on the Dominican Republic. Have them consult an encyclopedia or other source to locate information about the history of the country just before and just after the year in which "Daughter of Invention" is set (probably 1961 or 1962). Discuss as a class the information students collect, and ask students to write a short paragraph describing what effect the events may have had on the narrator's father. Follow up by asking students to look through recent newspapers and magazines for information about current events in that country.

Courtesy Rachel Adler Gallery, New York.

Uno (1920) by Alejandro Xul Solar. Watercolor and pencil on paper on card (5 9/32″ × 7 1/2″).

But the expression on his face shocked us both. His toothless mouth had collapsed into a dark zero. His eyes glared at me, then shifted to my mother, accusingly. In barely audible Spanish, as if secret microphones or informers were all about, he whispered, "You will permit her to read *that*?"

My mother's eyebrows shot up, her mouth fell open. In the old country, any whisper of a challenge to authority could bring the secret police in their black V.W.'s. But this was America. People could say what they thought. "What is wrong with her speech?" my mother questioned him.

"What ees wrrrong with her eh-speech?" My father wagged his head at her. His anger was always more frightening in his broken English. As if he had mutilated the language in his fury—and now there was nothing to stand between us and his raw, dumb anger. "What is wrong? I will tell you what is wrong. It shows no gratitude. It is boastful. 'I celebrate myself'? 'The best student learns to destroy the teacher'?" He mocked my plagiarized words. "That is insubordinate. It is improper. It is disrespecting of her teachers—" In his anger he had forgotten his fear of lurking spies: Each wrong he voiced was a decibel higher than the last outrage. Finally, he was yelling at me, "As your father, I forbid you to say that eh-speech!" (D)

My mother leapt to her feet, a sign always that she was about to make a speech or deliver an ultimatum. She was a small woman, and she spoke all her pronouncements standing up, either for more protection or as a carry-over from her girlhood in convent schools where one asked for, and literally took, the floor in order to speak. She stood by my side, shoulder to shoulder; we looked down at my father. "That is no tone of voice, Eduardo—" she began.

By now, my father was truly furious. I suppose it was bad enough I was rebelling, but here was

WORDS TO OWN

ultimatum (ul′tə·māt′əm) *n.:* last offer; final proposition.

D. Literary Element: Irony

? What is ironic about Papi's reaction to the narrator's speech? [Possible answer: He supports the renewal of independence and personal freedom in his home country, but he wants to forbid his daughter from giving a speech that is a free expression of her ideas.]

PROBLEM SOLVING/CRITICAL THINKING

Resolving Conflict Discuss with the class the conflicts the narrator experiences in the story: her struggle for acceptance at school, her conflict with her mother over her need for support and attention, and her conflict with her father over her speech. Ask students to consider the various methods that the narrator, Mami, and Papi use to try to resolve these conflicts. Then, show students an example of an advice column from a newspaper or magazine. Using the column as a model, ask students to write a short letter to an advice columnist, in the narrator's voice, asking for other suggestions on how the conflicts might be resolved. After they have written their letters, ask students to draft a brief reply from the advice columnist. Invite students to read their letters and replies aloud. Then, discuss as a class the similarities and differences among students' responses.

☞

LITERATURE AND TECHNOLOGY

A variety of information related to patents may be found at the home page of the Source Translation and Optimization Internet Patent Search System on the World Wide Web at **http://sunsite.unc.edu/patents/intropat.html**. *Preview any Internet activity that you suggest to students. Because these resources are sometimes public forums, their content can be unpredictable.*

LITERATURE AND TECHNOLOGY

Patently American Inventions

Have an invention of your own you'd like to protect? Consider patenting it. A U.S. patent gives you the right to exclude all others from making, using, or selling your invention within the United States for a limited number of years. To start, put your idea in writing, illustrate your device or process, and sign and date the document (use indelible ink). But before you reach for pad and pen, you might want to learn a little more about patents and inventions.

Patents are granted by the U.S. Patent and Trademark Office, in Arlington, Virginia. The Patent Office is flooded with over 150,000 applications a year, each of which takes about two years to process. If you can convince the patent officer that your invention is (1) new, (2) useful, and (3) original, a patent is yours. But be warned: You'll need deep pockets, since patent fees typically exceed $1,000.

Patented inventions we haven't seen in stores. Anyone wanting an afternoon's—or a lifetime's—entertainment could do worse than browse through the five million patents on record at the Patent Office. Ideas on record include these:

- eye protectors for chickens
- suspenders that convert into ropes in case the wearer needs to escape a burning building
- a device combining a plow and a gun
- a locket for storing used chewing gum
- a wake-up device consisting of suspended wood blocks that fall on the sleeper's face
- a device to create or maintain dimples
- balloons powered by large birds
- farms that rest on giant saucers floating in the sea

my mother joining forces with me. Soon he would be surrounded by a house full of independent American women. He too leapt from his bed, throwing off his covers. The Spanish newspapers flew across the room. He snatched my speech out of my hands, held it before my panicked eyes, a vengeful, mad look in his own, and then once, twice, three, four, countless times, he tore my prize into shreds.

"Are you crazy?" My mother lunged at him. "Have you gone mad? That is her speech for tomorrow you have torn up!"

"Have *you* gone mad?" He shook her away. "You were going to let her read that . . . that insult to her teachers?"

"Insult to her teachers!" My mother's face had crumpled up like a piece of paper. On it was written a love note to my father. Ever since they had come to this country, their life together was a constant war. "This is America, Papi, America!" she reminded him now. "You are not in a savage country any more!"

I was on my knees, weeping wildly, collecting all the little pieces of my speech, hoping that I could put it back together before the assembly tomorrow morning. But not even a sibyl[6] could

6. **sibyl** (sib′əl): in ancient Greece and Rome, a woman who foretold the future.

WORDS TO OWN

vengeful (venj′fəl) *adj.:* intent on revenge.

OPTIONS FOR TEACHING

PROFESSIONAL NOTES

Cultural Diversity This story provides a starting point for a discussion about the challenges many families face after making a long-distance move. Point out that family conflict may often take place when some family members—like the narrator's father in "Daughter of Invention"—show a desire to return home, but other family members want to remain where they are. Have students discuss this problem in small groups, and ask them to work together to create short lists of other short stories or novels in which it occurs.

Thematic Connections: "From Generation to Generation" Ask students to compare the narrator's description of the first draft of her speech with her description of the final version. Encourage students to comment on the different roles that the narrator's father and mother play in the success of her speech. Extend the discussion to include comments about the value of lessons that are passed down from older family members. Remind students that although some of these lessons may not immediately be accepted by younger family members, they often prove valuable later in life.

Did you know . . . ? The narrator's mother in "Daughter of Invention" is one in a long list of female American inventors. Since 1793, U.S. patents have been granted to women for inventions ranging from the brown paper bag, the modern coffeepot, and the disposable diaper to the first computer program, cancer treatments, and construction methods for dams and reservoirs. And here are some other patently interesting facts:

- The U.S. patent code forbids the patenting of devices with "no utility"—loosely speaking, no evident usefulness. One interesting category under the "no utility" banner is devices that defy the laws of nature. Inventors of antigravity boots, flying saucers, and other sci-fi devices needn't bother to apply for patents.
- The typewriter bombed when it was first brought out by E. Remington and Sons in 1874. Some recipients of typewritten letters felt insulted, and others, assuming the letters were junk mail, threw them away. And who could tell if typed letters had been forged? It wasn't until Remington targeted businesses that sales skyrocketed and the typewriter became an indispensable piece of office equipment.
- After returning from a nature walk one day, a Swiss inventor noticed that the cockleburs clinging to his jacket had tiny hooks that attached themselves to the fabric. He imitated the design in the first version of Velcro™ (from *vel*vet and *cro*chet).
- One day in 1958, Willy Higinbotham, a physicist bored with his work, devised a game involving two players and a tiny five-inch screen which displayed a net along with a ball each player could control with a button and a knob: video tennis. Despite the fact that people literally stood in line to play his game, Higinbotham saw no commercial value in it. The holder of twenty patents, he didn't bother to patent a device that launched the billion-dollar video-game industry.

have made sense of all those scattered pieces of paper. All hope was lost. "He broke it, he broke it," I moaned as I picked up a handful of pieces.

Probably, if I had thought a moment about it, I would not have done what I did next. I would have realized my father had lost brothers and comrades to the dictator Trujillo.[7] For the rest of his life, he would be haunted by blood in the streets and late night disappearances. Even after he had been in the states for years, he jumped if a black Volkswagen passed him on the street. He feared anyone in uniform: the meter maid giving out parking tickets, a museum guard approaching to tell him not to touch his favorite Goya at the Metropolitan.[8]

I took a handful of the scraps I had gathered, stood up, and hurled them in his face. "Chapita!" I said in a low, ugly whisper. "You're just another Chapita!"

(A) It took my father only a moment to register the hated nickname of our dictator, and he was after me. Down the halls we raced, but I was quicker than he and made it to my room just in time to lock the door as my father threw his weight

7. **Trujillo** (trōō·hē′yō): Rafael Leonidas Trujillo Molina, general who took over as president of the Dominican Republic and ruled oppressively from 1930 to 1938 and from 1942 until he was assassinated in 1961.

8. **Goya . . . Metropolitan:** a painting by the Spanish artist Francisco José de Goya y Lucientes at the Metropolitan Museum of Art in New York City.

A. Expansion
During Trujillo's regime, the people of the Dominican Republic had virtually no civil or political freedom—dissent and even suspected opposition were dealt with harshly. The mention of Trujillo's nickname probably evokes memories of oppression, terror, and brutality in the narrator's father.

ASSESSMENT TOOLS

Check Test: Multiple Choice

1. The narrator's family emigrates from (a) Puerto Rico (b) Colombia (c) Mexico (d) the Dominican Republic [d]
2. The narrator's father runs (a) a large law office (b) an elementary school (c) a medical center (d) a small restaurant [c]
3. The narrator and her sisters attend a (a) public school (b) parochial school (c) small school in the country (d) prep school [b]
4. The narrator's mother designs her inventions (a) at the kitchen table (b) using the computer (c) with pencil and paper (d) at a drafting table [c]
5. The narrator's mother is continually getting her (a) clichés wrong (b) names wrong (c) inventions confused (d) countries mixed up [a]

A. Critical Reading: Finding Cause and Effect

? What change in the relationship between the narrator and her mother is suggested in this paragraph, and what causes the change? [Possible answer: The narrator's mother was once too absorbed in her own ideas for inventions to notice when her daughter needed her support. But when Papi destroys the speech, he brings the narrator and Mami closer together; Mami finally helps by rewriting the speech when the narrator is too upset to work on it by herself.]

B. Reader's Response: First Thoughts

? Who is responsible for the success of the narrator's speech? [Sample responses: Her mother helps her the most by writing the speech; or her mother and father both help—her mother by composing the speech, and her father by contributing the critical ending for the speech.]

C. Critical Reading: Making Inferences

? What does Papi's gift suggest about his new attitude toward the narrator? [Possible answer: The gift is his way of showing that he knew the speech he destroyed was very important to the narrator; perhaps it also shows that even though he was shocked by what he saw as a disrespectful tone in the speech, he also saw the talent the speech revealed and he wants to nurture her talent by giving her the typewriter.]

D. Reader's Response: Extending the Text

? What does the narrator's mother pass on to her? What does the narrator do with her gift? [Sample responses: Her mother passes on her creativity or inventiveness. The narrator uses her gift to create ideas for the stories, such as this one, that she writes.]

against it. He called down curses on my head, ordered me on his authority as my father to open that door this very instant! He throttled that doorknob, but all to no avail. My mother's love of gadgets saved my hide that night. She had hired a locksmith to install good locks on all the bedroom doors after our house had been broken into while we were away the previous summer. In case burglars broke in again, and we were in the house, they'd have a second round of locks to contend with before they got to us.

"Eduardo," she tried to calm him down. "Don't you ruin my new locks."

He finally did calm down, his anger spent. I heard their footsteps retreating down the hall. I heard their door close, the clicking of their lock. Then, muffled voices, my mother's peaking in anger, in persuasion, my father's deep murmurs of explanation and of self-defense. At last, the house fell silent, before I heard, far off, the gun blasts and explosions, the serious, self-important voices of newscasters reporting their TV war.

A little while later, there was a quiet knock at my door, followed by a tentative attempt at the doorknob. "Cukita?" my mother whispered. "Open up, Cukita."

"Go away," I wailed, but we both knew I was glad she was there, and I needed only a moment's protest to save face before opening that door.

(A) What we ended up doing that night was putting together a speech at the last moment. Two brief pages of stale compliments and the polite commonplaces on teachers, wrought by necessity without much invention by mother for daughter late into the night in the basement on the pad of paper and with the same pencil she had once used for her own inventions, for I was too upset to compose the speech myself. After it was drafted, she typed it up while I stood by, correcting her misnomers and mis-sayings.

She was so very proud of herself when I came home the next day with the success story of the assembly. The nuns had been flattered, the audience had stood up and given "our devoted teachers a standing ovation," what my mother had suggested they do at the end of my speech.

She clapped her hands together as I recreated the moment for her. "I stole that from your father's speech, remember? (B) Remember how he put that in at the end?" She quoted him in Spanish, then translated for me into English.

That night, I watched him from the upstairs hall window where I'd retreated the minute I heard his car pull up in front of our house. Slowly, my father came up the driveway, a grim expression on his face as he grappled with a large, heavy cardboard box. At the front door, he set the package down carefully and patted all his pockets for his house keys—precisely why my mother had invented her ticking key chain. I heard the snapping open of the locks downstairs. Heard as he struggled to maneuver the box through the narrow doorway. Then, he called my name several times. But I would not answer him.

"My daughter, your father, he love you very much," he explained from the bottom of the stairs. "He just want to protect you." Finally, my mother came up and pleaded with me to go down and reconcile with him. "Your father did not mean to harm. You must pardon him. Always it is better to let bygones be forgotten, no?"

(C) I guess she was right. Downstairs, I found him setting up a brand new electric typewriter on the kitchen table. It was even better than the one I'd been begging to get like my mother's. My father had outdone himself with all the extra features: a plastic carrying case with my initials, in decals, below the handle, a brace to lift the paper upright while I typed, an erase cartridge, an automatic margin tab, a plastic hood like a toaster cover to keep the dust away. Not even my mother, I think, could have invented such a machine!

But her inventing days were over just as mine were starting up with my schoolwide success. That's why I've always thought of that speech my mother wrote for me as her last invention rather than the suitcase rollers everyone else in the family remembers. (D) It was as if she had passed on to me her pencil and pad and said, "Okay, Cukita, here's the buck. You give it a shot."

Words to Own

misnomers (mis·nō′merz) *n. pl.:* wrong terms or names.

reconcile (rek′ən·sīl′) *v.:* to make peace.

Making Meanings

First Thoughts

1. In the beginning, Mami seems selfish and unconcerned, but in the end, she shows concern for the narrator by helping her daughter and husband understand one another, and by helping her daughter write the speech.

Reviewing the Text

a. Luggage with wheels.
b. Her daughters think she cares more about thinking up ideas for inventions than she does about helping her children adjust to life in their new country.
c. Possible responses: "It's half of one or two dozen of another"—Six of one, half a dozen of another; "There is no use trying to drink spilt milk"—There is no use crying over spilt milk; "Necessity is the daughter of invention"—Necessity is the mother of invention. See also annotation B on p. T1079.
d. She throws scraps of paper from the speech in his face and calls him the nickname of the dictator Trujillo.

Making Meanings

First Thoughts

1. Did your feelings about any of the characters change as you read the story? Explain.

Shaping Interpretations

2. The narrator wants to use Whitman's words: "He most honors my style who learns under it to destroy the teacher" (page 1082). How does the girl's father interpret the words? What do you think Whitman was really saying?
3. The narrator says, "She was a good enough Mami, fussing and scolding and giving advice, but a terrible girlfriend parent, a real failure of a Mom" (page 1079). What does the narrator mean?
4. What **conflicts** does the father face in this story? Why do you think the father does not want his daughter to challenge authority?
5. Review the notes you made in your Reader's Log, and compare and contrast how Cukita, Mami, and Papi have adjusted to life in the United States. What adjustments occur over the course of the story?

Extending the Text

6. In this story, the father's experience of politics in his country of origin clearly influences his behavior in the United States. Can you identify other contemporary or past immigrants who have vivid memories of politics in their native lands?

Reviewing the Text

a. Which of the mother's ideas for an invention is a huge success for somebody else?

b. Why did the daughters resent the time the mother spent on inventions?

c. The narrator's mother is fond of English-language **aphorisms** (brief, wise sayings), but she gets them slightly wrong. Provide corrected versions of her sayings.

d. How does the daughter insult her father after he destroys her speech?

Choices: Building Your Portfolio

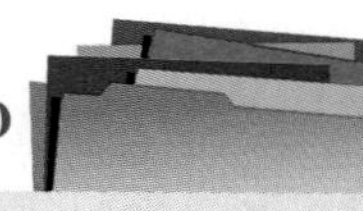

Writer's Notebook

1. Collecting Ideas for an Evaluation

Readers often evaluate a story according to the power of its conflicts. "Daughter of Invention" offers a variety of **external** and **internal conflicts.** Make a chart to help organize your thoughts about them. In the first column, list all the conflicts you can identify, such as interpersonal, social, cultural, and political conflicts. In the second column, tell who is involved in each conflict: for example, mother/daughter, father/daughter, husband/wife. In the third column, describe the resolution—if any—of each conflict in the story. In the fourth column, evaluate each conflict's power to hold your interest and to evoke emotions and thoughts. Save your chart for possible use in the Writer's Workshop on page 1181.

Critical Writing

2. Resonance

A good title often has what might be called resonance—it echoes with meaning. In an essay, explain how Alvarez's title touches on (a) a humorous detail of the story, (b) a **theme** of the story, and (c) the **climax** of the story.

Creative Writing / Speaking and Listening

3. "All these I feel or am"

The narrator's Walt Whitman–inspired speech ends up as little pieces of paper on the floor. Re-read the Whitman selections in this book (beginning on page 352), and then write the first page of the speech the narrator might have written. You can use the Whitman lines she uses or any other appropriate Whitman lines. If you like, read the opening of your speech to the class.

Extending the Text

6. **(Synthesis)** Students may identify immigrants from a variety of countries that have experienced political and social turmoil.

Choices: Building Your Portfolio

1. **Writer's Notebook** Remind students to save their work. They may use it as prewriting for the Writer's Workshop on p. 1181.
2. **Critical Writing** Before students begin the assignment, discuss as a class the meaning of the expression "Necessity is the mother of invention" and ask students to name situations to which it might apply.
3. **Creative Writing/Speaking and Listening** Ask students to consider the purpose and intended audience for the speech. Briefly review the Whitman poems in this book and ask volunteers to choose other lines that the narrator might have quoted in her speech. Tell students that the speech should include an interesting beginning and that the theme of the speech—its main idea—should be clearly expressed. Encourage students to include personal anecdotes or other details designed to engage the attention of their audience.

Choices: Assessment Criteria For help in evaluating these Choices assignments, see the criteria in the *Portfolio Management System,* p. 198.

Shaping Interpretations

2. Papi thinks that the words insult teachers by expressing contempt for them. Whitman may have been saying that a good teacher gives students the skills to think independently.
3. The narrator seems to imply that her mother was fine as a traditional stern Mami in the Dominican Republic, but she was a failure as the helpful, supportive Mom they needed in the United States. See also annotation C on p. T1079.
4. The narrator's father faces a conflict between his traditional values and his daughter's need to freely express her own ideas. Also, his family's desire to remain in the United States conflicts with his own yearnings to return to his home country. He may not want his daughter to challenge authority because his experiences in his home country have taught him that the response to such a challenge will be harsh.
5. In the course of the story, the narrator becomes accepted at school, develops an appreciation for Whitman's poetry, and gains a better understanding of her parents. Mami reads *The New York Times* and becomes more of a "Mom" for her daughter. Papi still reads the Dominican papers, but he learns to acknowledge and support his daughter's differences.

QUICK PLANNING GUIDE

Into the Poem

Author Biography p. 1088
Before You Read p. 1089
- **Reading Focus:** Students consider what they remember of long-ago events.
- **Quickwrite: Prior Knowledge** Write about a memory
- **Elements of Literature: Imagery**

Through the Poem

"The Bells" p. 1089
Making Meanings p. 1091

Beyond the Poem

Choices: Building Your Portfolio p. 1091
- **Writer's Notebook:** Evaluate Sexton's images
- **Critical Writing:** Write an essay on end rhymes in "The Bells"
- **Music/Performance:** Create and perform a musical setting

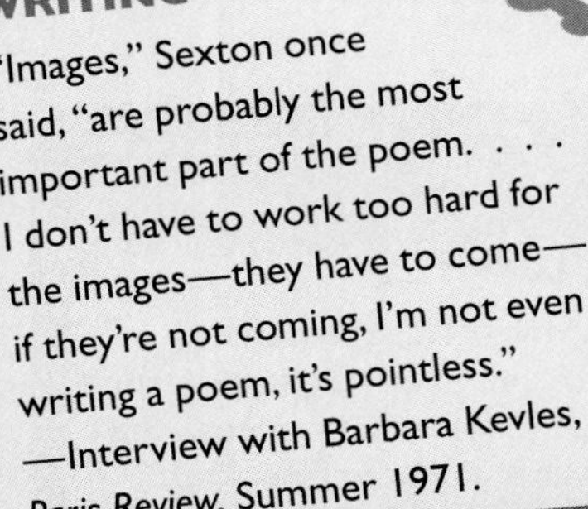

WRITERS ON WRITING

"Images," Sexton once said, "are probably the most important part of the poem. . . . I don't have to work too hard for the images—they have to come—if they're not coming, I'm not even writing a poem, it's pointless."
—Interview with Barbara Kevles, *Paris Review,* Summer 1971.

Anne Sexton

(1928–1974)

© Rollie McKenna.

From the very beginning of her literary career, Anne Sexton was recognized as a spirit in turmoil. The writer James Dickey (1923–   ) put it this way: "Anne Sexton's poems so obviously come out of deep, painful sections of the author's life that one's literary opinions scarcely seem to matter; one feels tempted to drop them furtively into the nearest ashcan, rather than be caught with them in the presence of so much naked suffering."

Sexton's poetry was an eruption into art of her stormy emotional life. The titles of her most gripping volumes indicate a preoccupation with bouts of mental illness and anxiety and with the need to confront ultimate questions: *To Bedlam and Part Way Back* (1960), *Live or Die* (1966), *The Death Notebooks* (1974), and *The Awful Rowing Toward God* (1975).

Anne Gray Harvey was born in Newton, Massachusetts, and attended the public schools in nearby Wellesley. In 1947, she enrolled in the Garland School, a finishing school for women, and in 1948 married Alfred Sexton. Anne Sexton worked for a time as a fashion model, gave birth to two daughters, and then, at age 28, began writing poetry.

Sexton studied with Robert Lowell (page 948) in his graduate writing seminar at Boston University, and developed friendships with other important poets, including Sylvia Plath (page 1148), Maxine Kumin, and George Starbuck. One of the strongest influences on her was the work of her friend W. D. Snodgrass, whose volume of poetry, *Heart's Needle* (1959), traced the emotional consequences of a difficult midlife divorce.

Sexton traveled to Europe and Africa, taught at Boston University, gave readings, and earned several honorary doctorates and numerous poetry prizes, including a Pulitzer Prize for *Live or Die.* In 1968, she formed a rock music group called Anne Sexton and Her Kind. In performance, Sexton read her poems while musicians accompanied her on guitar, flute, saxophone, drums, bass, and keyboards. She believed, she said, that the music "opens up my poems in a new way, by involving them in the sound of rock music."

Sexton's poetry was intended to be, as she said, "a shock to the senses." In her second book, *All My Pretty Ones* (1962), she quoted Franz Kafka: ". . . the books we need are the kind that act upon us like a misfortune, that make us suffer like the death of someone we love more than ourselves . . . [A] book should serve as the ax for the frozen sea within us." Her books were personal axes, but they also opened up a wider vision of contemporary women. Many of her poems are dramatic monologues that portray women in moments of crisis.

The general public as well as other poets responded enthusiastically to Sexton's poems. But artistic success did not strengthen her fragile personality. As her close friend Robert Lowell remembered: "At a time when poetry readings were expected to be boring, no one ever fell asleep at Anne's. I see her as having the large, transparent, breakable, and increasingly ragged wings of a dragonfly—her poor, shy, driven life, the blind terror behind her bravado, her deadly increasing pace . . . her bravery while she lasted."

PROGRAM MANAGER

- **Planning Instruction** See Teaching Notes, *Teaching Resources B,* p. 184, for objectives, a summary, literary elements, and additional biographical information for this selection.
- **Instructional Support** Before beginning the instructional lesson, see Graphic Organizer for Active Reading, *Teaching Resources B,* p. 192, for a Through the Poem activity.
- **Audiotaped Readings** To help less proficient readers or auditory learners through the lesson, use the Selected Reading, Audiocassette 3, Side B, in the *Audiovisual Resources Binder.*
- **Assessment** See Selection Test, *Test Booklet,* pp. 251–252.

Before You Read
The Bells

Reading Focus

Remembrance of Things Past

Some events, major or minor at the time, stick in our minds many years later. A parade, a kiss, a word, a bell—it could be anything that brings back the past for us, reminding us of our younger selves.

Quickwrite

READER'S LOG

Jot down an experience from the past that makes you feel joy. What image or sound prompts your memory of the experience?

Elements of Literature

Imagery

Imagery is the use of language to evoke a picture or a concrete sensation of a person, place, thing, or experience. Most images in literature appeal to our sense of sight. An image can, however, also appeal to our senses of taste, smell, hearing, and touch. In the following poem, look for images of sight, hearing, and touch.

The Bells

Anne Sexton

Today the circus poster
is scabbing off the concrete wall
and the children have forgotten
if they knew at all.
Father, do you remember?
Only the sound remains,
the distant thump of the good elephants,
the voice of the ancient lions
and how the bells
trembled for the flying man. A
I, laughing,
lifted to your high shoulder
or small at the rough legs of strangers,
was not afraid.
You held my hand
and were instant to explain
the three rings of danger.
Oh see the naughty clown
and the wild parade
while love love
love grew rings around me.
This was the sound where it began;
our breath pounding up to see
the flying man breast out
across the boarded sky
and climb the air.
I remember the color of music
and how forever
all the trembling bells of you
were mine.

Into the Poem

Using Before You Read

p. 1089

Quickwrite

Ask students to explain the ties between their memories and the images or sounds they evoke. Also, have students describe in detail the thoughts or feelings they associate with the memories.

Elements of Literature

Remind students that **imagery** may be used to evoke a dynamic sense of action or movement instead of just a static picture. Tell students that in this poem there is one particularly effective action verb ("trembled") that is used to describe movement or sound. Ask students to look for it as they read.

Through the Poem

A. Literary Element: Imagery

Point out the verb *trembled* in this line. Discuss some of the connotations of the word and ask students why the poet might have chosen it. Call on students to name other verbs the poet might have used in place of *trembled* here. [Possible answers: *Shook, rang, jingled, shuddered.*]

Options for Teaching

Strategies for Inclusion

Less Proficient Readers Read the poem aloud to the class. Then, have pairs of students take turns reading the poem aloud to one another. Before the pairs begin reading, point out that sentences in poetry often continue for several lines. Remind students to look for punctuation—especially end marks—as they read.

Integrating the Language Arts

Writing: Description Using descriptions from the poem as a guide, ask students to write a poem or paragraph using imagery to describe a happy memory of a childhood visit to a circus or similar place. Allow students to include descriptive details from their imaginations along with the actual details that they can remember. *Remind students to choose memories they would not mind sharing with the class.*

RESPONDING TO THE ART: VISUAL LITERACY

What word would you use to describe the feeling this illustration creates? [Possible responses: Danger, excitement, anticipation, gracefulness.]

PORTFOLIO ASSESSMENT

Portfolio Assessment
For help with self-assessment of reading skills, see the *Portfolio Management System*, p. 39.

The Flying Codonas (1932) by John Steuart Curry. Tempera and oil on composition board (36″ × 30″).
Collection of Whitney Museum of American Art, New York. Purchase.

Making Meanings

First Thoughts

1. Possible responses: Happiness, nostalgia, or sadness.

Shaping Interpretations

2. She sees an old circus poster. Responses from Quickwrite notes will vary.
3. The sound remains in her memory. The loud sounds may have seemed especially overwhelming and unusual to her as a small child, so she might remember them more vividly.
4. The "flying man" was probably a trapeze artist. The speaker recalls him because he may have been the first one she saw and because she remembers fearing for his safety.
5. She remembers being frightened, happy, and excited. Students may use a variety of terms to describe the poem's tone— nostalgic and excited, or sad and regretful.

Making Meanings

First Thoughts

1. What emotions did you feel as you read "The Bells"?

Shaping Interpretations

2. What prompts the speaker to remember the scene from her past? (How do her memories compare with your own, as recorded in your Quickwrite notes?)
3. According to line 6, what "remains"? Where does it remain, and why do you think it does so?
4. Who could "the flying man" have been? Why do you think the speaker particularly recalls "the flying man"?
5. What feelings does the poem's speaker remember? How would you describe the **tone** of the poem?
6. "Rings" are mentioned twice in the poem. At first they are "rings of danger." What do they become, and what is it that transforms them?
7. Line 22 states, "This was the sound where it began." What do you think this sound was? What is "it" that began with the sound?
8. Describing a perception of one sense in terms of another sense is called **synesthesia.** This figure of speech hides in many everyday expressions, such as *a warm voice* and *a quiet sunset.* What senses does Sexton mix in line 27? Why do you think this device is especially effective in this kind of memory poem?
9. One **theme** of the poem is conveyed with childlike simplicity in the last two lines. How would you state this message in your own words?

Challenging the Text

10. Sexton once remarked, "There is some very bad writing in some of my best poems, and yet those flaws seem to me to make them even better. They are with all their flaws, a little more human, you might say." Do you think this statement applies to "The Bells"? Explain.

Choices: Building Your Portfolio

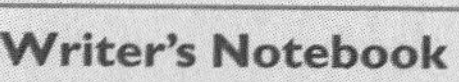

Writer's Notebook

1. Collecting Ideas for an Evaluation

WORK IN PROGRESS

What are your criteria for evaluating **images** in a poem? Do they need to be powerful? If so, what gives them power? Must they be universal, or can they be personal? List the qualities that you think an image ought to have, and then apply your criteria to several of Sexton's images. Save your notes for possible use in the Writer's Workshop on page 1181.

Critical Writing

2. The Poet's Craft

In "The Bells," Sexton uses **end rhymes** very subtly and very skillfully. Many are **approximate rhymes** (words that have some correspondence in sound but not an exact one), and therefore they may not be apparent at first. (Reading the poem aloud should help reveal these "hidden" rhymes.) In a short essay, identify some of the end rhymes in "The Bells," and explain their effect in the poem.

Music / Performance

3. Set It to Music

"The Bells," with all its imagery of sound, lends itself naturally to a musical setting. Using a tape recorder or other electronic device, combine parts of appropriate recordings of music (or compose your own music) and sounds from the world around you (including appropriate bells) to accompany a reading of the poem. Perform your setting for the class.

Choices: Building Your Portfolio

1. **Writer's Notebook** Remind students to save their work. They may use it as prewriting for the Writer's Workshop on p. 1181.
2. **Critical Writing** Have small groups of students work together to locate and discuss the **rhymes** in the poem. Remind students that they may want to compare this poem to the work of another poet, such as Emily Dickinson, who uses approximate, or "slant," rhyme.
3. **Music/Performance** Remind students that Sexton sometimes read her poems to musical accompaniment. Ask students to consider the variety of sounds one might hear at a circus.

PORTFOLIO ASSESSMENT

Choices: Assessment Criteria For help in evaluating these Choices assignments, see the criteria in the *Portfolio Management System*, p. 199.

6. Possible response: At first, the "rings of danger" are the three rings in which the circus acts are performed. Expect a variety of interpretations of the rings mentioned in l. 21—from tree-like growth rings to prisoner's restraints.
7. Possible response: The sound of bells probably signals feelings of danger and excitement.
8. Sexton mixes sight and sound. Synesthesia is effective in this kind of poem because the poem describes a memory, and most memories are a complex mixture of senses and emotions.
9. The intensity of the experience of the circus and the strong presence of her father are linked forever in the speaker's memory.

Challenging the Text

10. **(Evaluation)** Many students will not see flaws in this poem. Some students may question why the poet includes ll. 3–4 or why the speaker describes the lions as "ancient." You might ask students to suggest revisions for any lines they consider flawed.

QUICK PLANNING GUIDE

Into the Selection

Through the Selection

Beyond the Selection

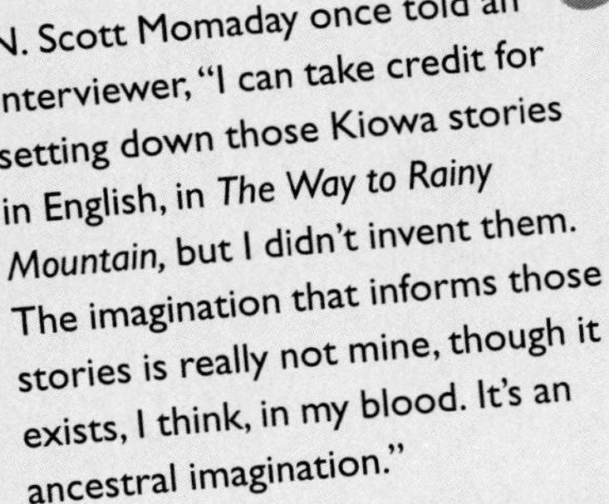

WRITERS ON WRITING

N. Scott Momaday once told an interviewer, "I can take credit for setting down those Kiowa stories in English, in *The Way to Rainy Mountain*, but I didn't invent them. The imagination that informs those stories is really not mine, though it exists, I think, in my blood. It's an ancestral imagination."

N. Scott Momaday

(1934–   )

Among American voices, one of the most poignant and powerful to make itself heard at long last has been that of the Native American. In the past, the American Indian appeared in literature and the other arts mostly in the baldest of stereotypes, either as a noble, primitive warrior or as a fearsome, ignorant savage. One has only to look at Western movies from the 1940s and 1950s to see how blatant the stereotypes were. Even American history textbooks seldom questioned the popular view that the white settlers' gradual "winning" of the West was a virtuous struggle against the unwarranted resistance of American Indians. Few Americans gave much thought either to the moral basis on which the United States expanded or to the history of the American Indians.

Courtesy N. Scott Momaday.

When the civil rights movement of the 1950s and 1960s brought discrimination against African Americans to the forefront of public discussion, other minority groups began to demand a fairer social and political standing for themselves. Native Americans spoke loudly and clearly of loss, injustice, and prejudice. Among the notable books on the Native American experience are Vine Deloria, Jr.'s novel *Custer Died for Your Sins* (1969), the historian Dee Brown's *Bury My Heart at Wounded Knee* (1970), Louise Erdrich's novel *Love Medicine* (1984), and the works of N. Scott Momaday.

Navarre Scott Momaday was born in Lawton, Oklahoma, of Kiowa ancestry on his father's side, and some Cherokee on his mother's. After receiving an undergraduate degree from the University of New Mexico in 1958, Momaday studied creative writing at Stanford University, where he earned a Ph.D. in 1963.

But Momaday broke loose from the standard academic mold with three works grounded in his knowledge of American Indian life: a Pulitzer Prize–winning novel, *House Made of Dawn* (1968), and two memoirs, *The Way to Rainy Mountain* (1969) and *The Names* (1976).

The Way to Rainy Mountain is part legend, part history, and part poetry, with an artistic addition of striking illustrations by Momaday's father, Alfred Momaday. Following the introduction, Momaday describes Kiowa history in a form that is associative and imagistic; it works on the reader's imagination in subtle ways that do not depend on a straightforward narrative. On one page, he sets down a Kiowa myth or legend; on the facing page, he places a short excerpt from a traditional history and then a personal memory of his own. In the mind of the reader, the inner truth blends with the outer; emotion mixes with fact.

The Kiowas' journey to Rainy Mountain begins in the hidden mists of time, when a tribe of unknown origin descends from the headwaters of the Yellowstone River eastward to the Black Hills (in present-day South Dakota) and south to the Wichita Mountains. It ends in a cemetery where many of Momaday's Kiowa relatives are buried. Momaday says that "the journey is an evocation of three things in particular: a landscape that is incomparable, a time that is gone forever, and the human spirit, which endures."

The incomparable landscape is the Great Plains, wind-swept and lonely, in turn brilliant with summer sun and buried in winter snows. Momaday's love of the land where he grew up suffuses everything he writes. He reminds us of both the spiritual richness and the rigors of living close to the land, under a wide, open sky, in harmony with the changing seasons. In his work, Momaday has looked at his own particular landscape from so many angles that his pictures often shimmer like prisms.

WORDS TO OWN

The following vocabulary words are defined in the Words to Own at the bottom of the pupil's page.

infirm p. 1095	disperse p. 1097
preeminently p. 1095	opaque p. 1099
luxuriant p. 1096	vital p. 1099
tenuous p. 1096	enmities p. 1099
wariness p. 1096	indulge p. 1099

Before You Read

from The Way to Rainy Mountain

Reading Focus

Knowledge of Ancient Days

What is it that we honor about the generations that preceded us? Perhaps it's the realization that not only did they build civilizations and give us life—but also that they *knew* something. We search in thousands of ways for the secret of what they must have known. We search in history, archaeology, anthropology, art, linguistics, architecture, music, mythology, literature. In many ways, we search for knowledge of ourselves as we search the past.

A Dialogue with the Text

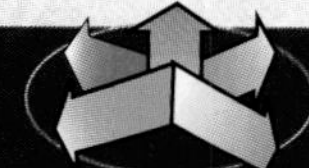

As you read, take notes on Momaday's grandmother—her appearance, feelings, and actions.

Elements of Literature

Setting

Momaday is a master at describing **setting,** the time and location in which events take place or in which characters are placed. The following extract contains descriptions of numerous settings, which help to create mood and atmosphere. In some cases, the description is made up of just one or two well-chosen images.

> **Setting** is the time and location in which events take place or in which characters are placed.
>
> *For more on Setting, see the Handbook of Literary Terms.*

Background

This excerpt from *The Way to Rainy Mountain* is not a simple narrative. Momaday uses frequent flashbacks to earlier times and often omits transitional passages. The text is like a poem in which the narrator traces, in his imagination, the heroic and ultimately tragic history of his people, the Kiowas. Keep in mind Momaday's telling comment at the end of the book: "Once in his life a man ought to concentrate his mind upon the remembered earth. . . ."

Using Before You Read

p. 1093

Reading Focus

Ask students if they believe that lost knowledge exists in the past—that people in an earlier century might have known something that has now been forgotten. Have students suppose that they could go back in time and ask someone from the past a question about a problem or mystery that exists today. Ask how far back in time they would go, what question they would ask, and to whom they would direct the question.

Elements of Literature

Ask students to consider the following questions about **setting**: What images help you visualize the setting? What mood or atmosphere does the setting create? How does the setting help reveal character?

Background

Explain that the excerpt starts with a description of the author's visit to his grandmother's grave near Rainy Mountain in Oklahoma. Focusing on the past, the narrator then describes his grandmother's life and the history of the Kiowa people by tracing their migration from Yellowstone to the south and east.

Program Manager

- **Planning Instruction** See Teaching Notes, *Teaching Resources B,* p. 185, for objectives, a summary, literary elements, and additional historical and biographical information for this selection.
- **Instructional Support** Before beginning the instructional lesson, see Graphic Organizer for Active Reading, *Teaching Resources B,* p. 193, for a Through the Selection activity.
- **Audiotaped Readings** To help less proficient readers or auditory learners through the lesson, use the Selected Reading, Audiocassette 3, Side B, in the *Audiovisual Resources Binder.*

- **Assessment** See Selection Test, *Test Booklet,* pp. 251–252.
- **Reinforcement** Use the Words to Own worksheet in *Teaching Resources B,* p. 194.

RESPONDING TO THE PHOTOGRAPH

Why do you think the woman in this photograph is sitting alone rather than socializing with the people in the background? [Possible responses: Maybe she is resting after a walk; perhaps she has already socialized with the others and now wants some time to herself; she may simply be posing for the photograph.]

PORTFOLIO ASSESSMENT

Portfolio Assessment
For help with self- and teacher assessment of reading skills, see the *Portfolio Management System,* pp. 52–53.

from The Way to Rainy Mountain

N. Scott Momaday

Blind Kiowa woman at Carnegie, Oklahoma, powwow (1946). Photo by P. Tartoue.

Archives and Manuscripts Division of the Oklahoma Historical Society.

OPTIONS FOR TEACHING

STRATEGIES FOR INCLUSION

Logical-Mathematical Show the class the map on p. 1098 and ask students to use it to measure the distance the Kiowa traveled on their journey from western Montana to Rainy Mountain in southern Oklahoma. Point out that the Kiowa migration was gradual; but to give students a sense of the difficulty of journey, ask them to calculate roughly how long it would take to travel the distance on foot.

Advanced Before students read the selection, review the definition of the literary term **elegy.** Read aloud a famous elegy such as Milton's *Lycidas,* Shelley's "Adonais," or Tennyson's *In Memoriam.* Ask students to write a paragraph describing the **tone** of the elegy. Point out that while most elegies are written in verse, the mournful, pensive tone that is common to them may also be captured in prose.

Devils Tower, Wyoming.

A single knoll rises out of the plain in Oklahoma north and west of the Wichita Range. For my people, the Kiowas, it is an old landmark, and they gave it the name Rainy Mountain. The hardest weather in the world is there. Winter brings blizzards, hot tornadic winds arise in the spring, and in summer the prairie is an anvil's edge. The grass turns brittle and brown, and it cracks beneath your feet. There are green belts along the rivers and creeks, linear groves of hickory and pecan, willow and witch hazel. At a distance in July or August the steaming foliage seems almost to writhe in fire. Great green and yellow grasshoppers are everywhere in the tall grass, popping up like corn to sting the flesh, and tortoises crawl about on the red earth, going nowhere in the plenty of time. Loneliness is an aspect of the land. All things in the plain are isolate; there is no confusion of objects in the eye, but *one* hill or *one* tree or *one* man. To look upon that landscape in the early morning, with the sun at your back, is to lose the sense of proportion. Your imagination comes to life, and this, you think, is where Creation was begun.

I returned to Rainy Mountain in July. My grandmother had died in the spring, and I wanted to be at her grave. She had lived to be very old and at last infirm. Her only living daughter was with her when she died, and I was told that in death her face was that of a child.

I like to think of her as a child. When she was born, the Kiowas were living that last great moment of their history. For more than a hundred years they had controlled the open range from the Smoky Hill River to the Red, from the headwaters of the Canadian to the fork of the Arkansas and Cimarron. In alliance with the Comanches, they had ruled the whole of the southern Plains. War was their sacred business, and they were among the finest horsemen the world has ever known. But warfare for the Kiowas was preeminently a matter of disposition rather than of survival, and they never understood the grim, unrelenting advance of the U.S. Cavalry. When at last, divided and ill-provisioned, they were driven onto the Staked Plains in the cold rains of autumn, they fell into panic. In Palo Duro Canyon they abandoned their crucial stores to pillage and had nothing then but their lives. In order to save themselves, they surrendered to the soldiers at Fort Sill and were imprisoned in the old stone corral that now stands as a military museum. My grandmother was spared the humiliation of those high gray walls by eight or ten years, but she must have known from birth the affliction of defeat, the dark brooding of old warriors.

Her name was Aho, and she belonged to the last culture to evolve in North America. Her forebears came down from the high country in western Montana nearly three centuries ago. They were a mountain people, a mysterious tribe of hunters whose language has never been positively classified in any major group. In the late seventeenth century they began a long migration to the south and east. It was a journey toward the dawn, and it led to a golden age. Along the way the Kiowas were befriended by the Crows, who gave them the culture and religion of the Plains. They acquired horses, and their ancient nomadic spirit was suddenly free of the ground. They acquired Tai-me, the sacred Sun Dance doll, from that moment the object and symbol of their worship, and so shared in the divinity of the sun. Not least, they acquired the sense of destiny, therefore courage and pride. When they entered upon the southern Plains they had been transformed. No longer were they slaves to the simple necessity of survival; they were a lordly and dangerous society of fighters and thieves, hunters and priests of the sun. According to their origin myth, they entered the world through a hollow log. From one point of view, their migration was the fruit of an old prophecy, for indeed they emerged from a sunless world.

Although my grandmother lived out her long life in the shadow of Rainy Mountain, the immense landscape of the continental interior lay like memory in her blood. She could tell of the Crows, whom she had never seen, and of the

WORDS TO OWN

infirm (in·fʉrm′) *adj.:* physically weak.
preeminently (prē·em′ə·nənt·lē) *adv.:* above all else.

Through the Selection

A. Literary Element: Setting

? What word would you use to describe the setting the author portrays in this paragraph? [Possible answers: Rugged, harsh, desolate, lonely.]

Metacognition What details in the selection influenced your choice? [Possible response: The author mentions blizzards, hot winds, brown grass, and stinging grasshoppers.]

B. Literary Element: Tone

The author sets the somber, reflective tone of the excerpt by his use of sentences such as these throughout the excerpt.

C. Critical Reading: Summarizing

? In what ways does the author say the Kiowas' journey changes them? [Possible answer: He says that the journey gives them pride and a sense of place and purpose in the world.]

INTEGRATING THE LANGUAGE ARTS

Strategic Reading Ask students to create a three-column KWL Chart to organize their knowledge of the Kiowas. Before they read, they should use the first (K) column to record notes about what they already know, and the second (W) column to record what they would like to know. After they have finished reading the excerpt, they should fill in the third (L) column with notes about what they learned while reading the excerpt.

Writing: Legends Discuss the legend of the seven sisters and the Big Dipper. Then, ask students to write their own legends based on natural phenomena. Ask students to try to create a legend, such as the one in the story, that might help a certain group of people give meaning to something in their world that is otherwise unexplainable. Also, point out that many legends involve metamorphosis, and encourage students to include transformations in their legends.

A. Reader's Response: Shaping Interpretations

? What does the author mean when he says that the Kiowas were "bent and blind" in their first home? [Sample responses: He means that life in the mountains restrained the Kiowas and limited their vision of themselves and their future.]

B. Cultural Connections

In the legend, seven Kiowa sisters become the stars in the Big Dipper. Ask students why this legend might be important to the Kiowas. [Possible answer: The author says that the Kiowas judged themselves by how far around them they could see, so it makes sense that the far-off stars they saw would be important to them. By placing "kinsmen" in the sky to look down over the whole earth, they gained stature as a people.]

Black Hills, where she had never been. I wanted to see in reality what she had seen more perfectly in the mind's eye, and traveled fifteen hundred miles to begin my pilgrimage.

Yellowstone, it seemed to me, was the top of the world, a region of deep lakes and dark timber, canyons and waterfalls. But, beautiful as it is, one might have the sense of confinement there. The skyline in all directions is close at hand, the high wall of the woods and deep cleavages of shade. There is a perfect freedom in the mountains, but it belongs to the eagle and the elk, the badger and the bear. The Kiowas reckoned their stature by **A** the distance they could see, and they were bent and blind in the wilderness.

Descending eastward, the highland meadows are a stairway to the plain. In July the inland slope of the Rockies is luxuriant with flax and buckwheat, stonecrop and larkspur. The earth unfolds and the limit of the land recedes. Clusters of trees, and animals grazing far in the distance, cause the vision to reach away and wonder to build upon the mind. The sun follows a longer course in the day, and the sky is immense beyond all comparison. The great billowing clouds that sail upon it are shadows that move upon the grain like water, dividing light. Farther down, in the land of the Crows and Blackfeet, the plain is yellow. Sweet clover takes hold of the hills and bends upon itself to cover and seal the soil. There the Kiowas paused on their way; they had come to the place where they must change their lives. The sun is at home on the plains. Precisely there does it have the certain character of a god. When the Kiowas came to the land of the Crows, they could see the dark lees of the hills at dawn across the Bighorn River, the profusion of light on the grain shelves, the oldest deity ranging after the solstices.[1] Not yet would they veer southward to the caldron of the land that lay below; they must wean their blood from the northern winter and hold the mountains a while longer in their view. They bore Tai-me in procession to the east.

A dark mist lay over the Black Hills, and the land was like iron. At the top of a ridge I caught sight of Devils Tower upthrust against the gray sky as if in the birth of time the core of the earth had broken through its crust and the motion of the world was begun. There are things in nature that engender an awful quiet in the heart of man; Devils Tower is one of them. Two centuries ago, because they could not do otherwise, the Kiowas made a legend at the base of the rock. My grandmother said:

B *Eight children were there at play, seven sisters and their brother. Suddenly the boy was struck dumb; he trembled and began to run upon his hands and feet. His fingers became claws, and his body was covered with fur. Directly there was a bear where the boy had been. The sisters were terrified; they ran, and the bear after them. They came to the stump of a great tree, and the tree spoke to them. It bade them climb upon it, and as they did so it began to rise into the air. The bear came to kill them, but they were just beyond its reach. It reared against the tree and scored the bark all around with its claws. The seven sisters were borne into the sky, and they became the stars of the Big Dipper.*

From that moment, and so long as the legend lives, the Kiowas have kinsmen in the night sky. Whatever they were in the mountains, they could be no more. However tenuous their well-being, however much they had suffered and would suffer again, they had found a way out of the wilderness.

My grandmother had a reverence for the sun, a holy regard that now is all but gone out of mankind. There was a wariness in her, and an an-

1. **solstices:** The solstices are the points where the sun is farthest north and farthest south of the celestial equator, creating the longest day (June 21) and the shortest day (December 21) of sunlight in the Northern Hemisphere.

WORDS TO OWN

luxuriant (lug·zhoor'ē·ənt) *adj.:* rich; abundant.
tenuous (ten'yoo·əs) *adj.:* slight; insubstantial; not firm.
wariness (wer'ē·nis) *n.:* caution; carefulness.

COOPERATIVE LEARNING

Write a Screenplay Have students work in groups of three to draft a film script based on the selection. Ask students to include, as voice-over, three quotations from the selection. Since the selection contains no dialogue, ask students to use camera directions to indicate what details viewers would see and from what angles they would see them. Encourage students to suggest music and sound effects that would be appropriate to the author's **tone** and to the **atmosphere** of the selection.

CLASSROOM MANAGEMENT

Managing the Reader's Response Classroom If students' comments about a particular passage are not supported by any information in the selection, ask students to reexamine their conclusions after they have read the passage a second time. Help all students to adjust their conclusions as they read a selection and discuss it in class. Remind students that even the best readers sometimes need to re-read a challenging selection and to ask for ideas or help from other readers.

John Stevens/The Stock Solution.

cient awe. She was a Christian in her later years, but she had come a long way about, and she never forgot her birthright. As a child she had been to the Sun Dances; she had taken part in those annual rites, and by them she had learned the restoration of her people in the presence of Tai-me. She was about seven when the last Kiowa Sun Dance was held in 1887 on the Washita River above Rainy Mountain Creek. The buffalo were gone. In order to consummate the ancient sacrifice—to impale the head of a buffalo bull upon the medicine tree—a delegation of old men journeyed into Texas, there to beg and barter for an animal from the Goodnight herd. She was ten when the Kiowas came together for the last time as a living Sun Dance culture. They could find no buffalo; they had to hang an old hide from the sacred tree. Before the dance could begin, a company of soldiers rode out from Fort Sill under orders to disperse the tribe. Forbidden without cause the essential act of their faith, having seen the wild herds slaughtered and left to rot upon the ground, the Kiowas backed away forever from the medicine tree. That was July 20, 1890, at the great bend of the Washita. My grandmother was there. Without bitterness, and for as long as she lived, she bore a vision of deicide.[2]

2. **deicide** (dē′ə·sīd′): murder of a god.

WORDS TO OWN
disperse (di·spurs′) *v.:* to scatter.

C. Reader's Response: Shaping Interpretations

Why was the Sun Dance so important to the Kiowas, and why would the government have sent soldiers to stop it? [Sample responses: The Sun Dance brought the Kiowas together and reaffirmed their pride in themselves as a people; perhaps the government wanted to stop it because they did not understand it and thought it was dangerous.]

CROSSING THE CURRICULUM

History In this excerpt, Momaday refers to the destructive role that the United States Cavalry played in the history of the Kiowas. Ask students to do independent research on the part that the Cavalry played in the wars against the Indians throughout the West between 1850 and 1890. After students have completed their research, ask them to report the information to the class, using informational handouts and charts, maps, photographs, or other visual aids.

PROFESSIONAL NOTES

TECHNOLOGY

Technology Tip More details about the author are available on the World Wide Web at **http://users.mwci.net/~lapoz/N.Scott.Momaday.html**. Or, to find other information, search the Web using a search engine and the key word **Momaday**. *You may want to preview any Internet activity that you suggest to students. Because these resources are sometimes public forums, their content can be unpredictable.*

A. Expansion
Point out the shift in narrative time that this paragraph marks. Remind students that at the beginning of this piece, the author says that he has returned to Rainy Mountain to visit his grandmother's grave; then, he shifts the focus to a description of the Kiowa people and the Kiowa values that shaped his grandmother's life. Now he begins a more personal description of her.

Now that I can have her only in memory, I see my grandmother in the several postures that were peculiar to her: standing at the wood stove on a winter morning and turning meat in a great iron skillet; sitting at the south window, bent above her beadwork, and afterwards, when her vision failed, looking down for a long time into the fold of her hands; going out upon a cane, very slowly as she did when the weight of age came upon her; praying. I remember her most often at prayer. She made long, rambling prayers out of suffering and hope, having seen many things. I was never sure that I had the right to hear, so exclusive were they of all mere custom and company. The last time I saw her she prayed standing by the side of her bed at night, naked to the waist, the light of a kerosene lamp moving upon her dark skin. Her long, black hair, always drawn and braided in the day, lay upon her shoulders and against her breasts like a shawl. I do not speak Kiowa, and I never understood her prayers, but there was something inherently sad in the sound, some merest hesitation upon the syllables of sorrow. She began in a high and descending pitch, exhausting her breath to silence; then again and again—and always the same intensity of effort, of something that is, and is not, like urgency in the human voice. Transported so in the dancing light among the shadows of her room, she seemed beyond the reach of time. But that was illusion; I think I knew then that I should not see her again.

Houses are like sentinels in the plain, old keepers of the weather watch. There, in a very little while, wood takes on the appearance of great age. All colors wear soon away in the wind and rain, and then the wood is burned gray and the grain appears

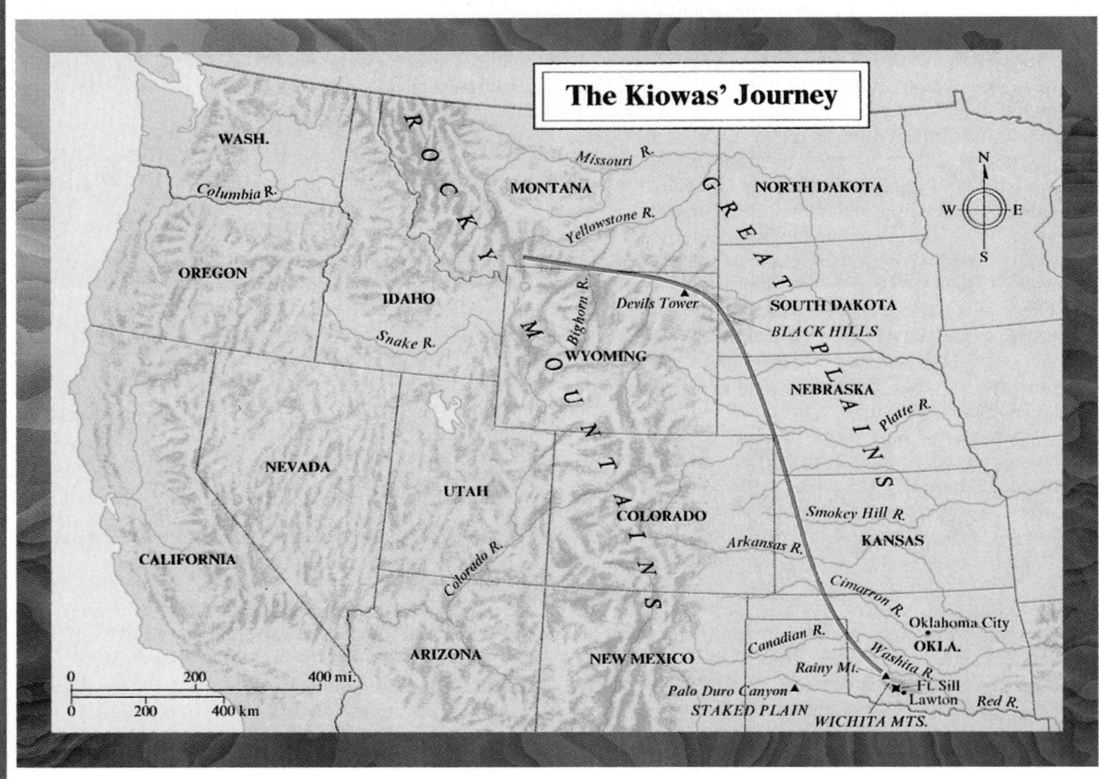

OPTIONS FOR TEACHING

ASSESSMENT TOOLS

Check Test: True-False

1. The American Indians described in the essay are Sioux. [False]
2. The narrator recalls a legend about a fire god. [False]
3. The sacred animal associated with the Sun Dance is the buffalo. [True]
4. The Kiowas are described as excellent horse trainers. [True]
5. At the end, the author climbs Rainy Mountain. [False]

Ongoing Assessment Use this assessment scale to record the progress of students as you observe them working in groups or individually on assignments for this selection.

1=Never 2=Sometimes 3=Always

_____ Asks appropriate questions
_____ Stays on task unreminded
_____ Completes work on time
_____ Maintains positive attitude
_____ Participates actively

and the nails turn red with rust. The windowpanes are black and opaque; you imagine there is nothing within, and indeed there are many ghosts, bones given up to the land. They stand here and there against the sky, and you approach them for a longer time than you expect. They belong in the distance; it is their domain.

Once there was a lot of sound in my grandmother's house, a lot of coming and going, feasting and talk. The summers there were full of excitement and reunion. The Kiowas are a summer people; they abide the cold and keep to themselves, but when the season turns and the land becomes warm and vital they cannot hold still; an old love of going returns upon them. The aged visitors who came to my grandmother's house when I was a child were made of lean and leather, and they bore themselves upright. They wore great black hats and bright ample shirts that shook in the wind. They rubbed fat upon their hair and wound their braids with strips of colored cloth. Some of them painted their faces and carried the scars of old and cherished enmities. They were an old council of warlords, come to remind and be reminded of who they were. Their wives and daughters served them well. The women might indulge themselves; gossip was at once the mark and compensation of their servitude. They made loud and elaborate talk among themselves, full of jest and gesture, fright and false alarm. They went abroad in fringed and flowered shawls, bright beadwork and German silver. They were at home in the kitchen, and they prepared meals that were banquets.

There were frequent prayer meetings, and great nocturnal feasts. When I was a child I played with my cousins outside, where the lamplight fell upon the ground and the singing of the old people rose up around us and carried away into the darkness. There were a lot of good things to eat, a lot of laughter and surprise. And afterwards, when the quiet returned, I lay down with my grandmother and could hear the frogs away by the river and feel the motion of the air.

Now there is a funeral silence in the rooms, the endless wake of some final word. The walls have closed in upon my grandmother's house. When I returned to it in mourning, I saw for the first time in my life how small it was. It was late at night, and there was a white moon, nearly full. I sat for a long time on the stone steps by the kitchen door. From there I could see out across the land; I could see the long row of trees by the creek, the low light upon the rolling plains, and the stars of the Big Dipper. Once I looked at the moon and caught sight of a strange thing. A cricket had perched upon the handrail, only a few inches away from me. My line of vision was such that the creature filled the moon like a fossil.[3] It had gone there, I thought, to live and die, for there, of all places, was its small definition made whole and eternal. A warm wind rose up and purled[4] like the longing within me.

The next morning I awoke at dawn and went out on the dirt road to Rainy Mountain. It was already hot, and the grasshoppers began to fill the air. Still, it was early in the morning, and the birds sang out of the shadows. The long yellow grass on the mountain shone in the bright light, and a scissortail[5] hied above the land. There, where it ought to be, at the end of a long and legendary way, was my grandmother's grave. Here and there on the dark stones were ancestral names. Looking back once, I saw the mountain and came away.

3. **fossil:** hardened remains of plant or animal life from a previous geological time period.
4. **purled** (purld): moved in ripples.
5. **scissortail:** a species of flycatcher bird. The bird's distinctive tail is an average of thirteen inches long and is divided like scissors near its end.

WORDS TO OWN

opaque (ō·pāk') *adj.:* not transparent; not letting light pass through.
vital (vīt''l) *adj.:* filled with life.
enmities (en'mə·tēz) *n. pl.:* hatreds.
indulge (in·dulj') *v.:* satisfy; please; humor.

B. Language Note: Description
Point out the similarities between the descriptive language the author uses in this paragraph to portray houses on the plain and the language he uses in the first paragraph of the excerpt to describe the plain itself.

C. Reader's Response: Shaping Interpretations
? Why does the narrator see his grandmother's house as small "for the first time"? [Sample responses: It was so important to him as a child that it grew large in his memory; or now that his grandmother is gone, the life has left it, and it has become just another house on the plain.]

D. Literary Element: Imagery
Ask students to try to visualize this image as they read. Looking outside, the author sees a cricket in silhouette against the moon. Because of his viewing angle, the cricket looks as if it is framed or enclosed like a fossil within the moon.

E. Critical Reading: Analyzing Setting
? How is the author's **tone** here appropriate to the **setting** he describes? [Possible answer: His somber, reflective tone is especially appropriate because it captures in words the rugged, expansive quality of the land where his grandmother lived.]

Making Meanings questions begin on p. 1100.

Making Meanings

First Thoughts

1. Possible response: The image of Devils Tower, because it combines elements of myth, magic, geology, and history.

Reviewing the Text

a. He returns to visit his grandmother's grave.
b. The Kiowas acquired a sacred Sun Dance doll on their journey and centered their religious ceremonies around the sun.
c. To escape from their brother, who had become a bear, seven sisters climbed a tree and were lifted into the sky to form the Big Dipper. Devils Tower looks like a huge tree trunk and is made of columns that come together to look like cuts made by giant bear claws.
d. Their culture is forever changed when they are prevented from practicing the Sun Dance.

Shaping Interpretations

2. Possible response: The journey led to a "golden age" for the Kiowas before their eventual dispersal. It was also a journey to the east, the direction from which the sun rises.

Choices: Building Your Portfolio

1. **Writers's Notebook** Remind students to save their work. They may use it as prewriting for the Writer's Workshop on p. 1181.
2. **Critical Writing** Read aloud the paragraph from the excerpt in which the sentence occurs. Remind students that Momaday is referring to Devils Tower. Before they write, ask students to take another look at the photo of Devils Tower on p. 1096, or, if possible, show them a larger photo of the tower.
3. **Creative Writing** Suggest to students that they may want to choose a place from childhood that is connected in some way to a certain person, as Rainy Mountain is associated in the narrator's memory with his grandmother.

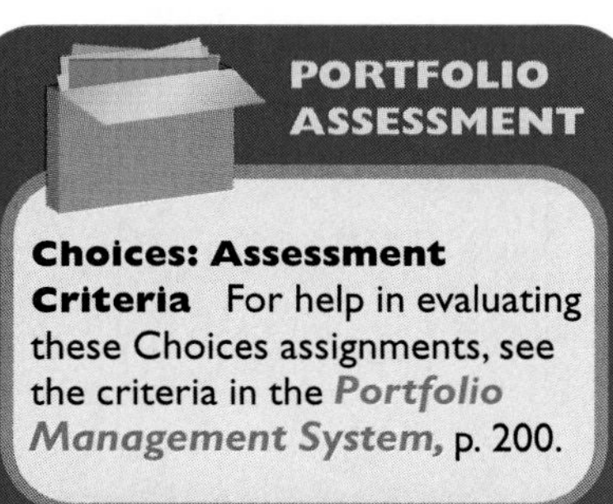

Choices: Assessment Criteria For help in evaluating these Choices assignments, see the criteria in the *Portfolio Management System,* p. 200.

Making Meanings

First Thoughts

1. What single visual image in Momaday's text strikes you as the most memorable? Why?

Reviewing the Text

a. Why does the narrator return to Rainy Mountain?
b. What does this memoir tell about the Kiowa religion and the role of the sun in their rituals?
c. According to Kiowa legend, what is the origin of the Big Dipper? How does this myth explain the peculiar formation called Devils Tower?
d. What eventually happens to the Kiowa?

Shaping Interpretations

2. What do you think Momaday means when he calls the Kiowa migration "a journey toward the dawn" (page 1095)?
3. Review the notes in your Reader's Log, and describe Momaday's grandmother Aho, noting her physical appearance and her thoughts. What is Momaday's attitude toward her?
4. When Momaday tells of a cricket near the end of the extract, he says: "It had gone there, I thought, to live and die, for there, of all places, was its small definition made whole and eternal." How do you interpret this comment? What do you think the cricket might **symbolize**?
5. List **images** that Momaday uses to convey strongly contrasting feelings of light and life, darkness and death. Is the overall **mood** of this essay light or dark? Explain your answer.
6. Momaday writes in gracefully evocative poetic prose. Re-read the paragraph on page 1096 beginning "Descending eastward . . . ." Then, identify at least three figures of speech (**metaphor, simile, personification**) in the paragraph that refer to the **setting.** How do they contribute to the overall effect of the writing?
7. *The Way to Rainy Mountain* is in part an **elegy,** a song or poem contemplating a dead person—or, by extension, a way of life that has been destroyed. What does Momaday praise about the Kiowas? What does he mourn?
8. Do you think Momaday and the Kiowas, like earlier Puritans and Romantics, read lessons in nature? Explain.

Choices: Building Your Portfolio

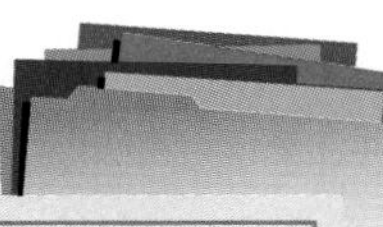

Writer's Notebook

1. Collecting Ideas for an Evaluation

WORK IN PROGRESS

Just about every work of literature has at least one **setting.** One criterion for evaluating a work is the skill with which setting is evoked. In a few sentences, evaluate Momaday's success in describing setting, giving specific reasons for your judgment. Save your notes for possible use in the Writer's Workshop on page 1181.

Critical Writing

2. "An awful quiet"

Momaday writes (page 1096), "There are things in nature that engender an awful quiet in the heart of man." In a two-paragraph essay, explain in your own words what the writer means by this statement, and then tell whether you agree with him.

Creative Writing

3. Your Remembered Earth

For Momaday, the land around Rainy Mountain is associated with childhood and ancestral memories. Think of a place you associate with your own childhood—a store, a park, a play area. Write a description of this place, using vivid imagery to describe what it looked like and to suggest what it meant to you.

Answers to Making Meanings begin on p. T1099.

3. Momaday reveres his grandmother and respects her cultural heritage.
4. The cricket may symbolize Momaday's grandmother, who lived her whole life and died on the same land where she was born—land that gave her life meaning.
5. Light and life images: Sun, sky, yellow plain. Darkness and death images: Dark mist, night, dark stones of the cemetery. Images of darkness and light are balanced, but the **tone** of the meditative excerpt is somewhat dark.
6. Metaphor: Meadows are a stairway. Simile: Shadows moving like water. Personification: Clover taking hold of the hills. The images make the setting more vivid.
7. Momaday praises the Kiowas' pride, fighting abilities, and sense of freedom. He mourns the assault on their religion and the loss of many of their cultural traditions.
8. The Kiowas read a lesson in the Big Dipper, and they probably look to nature for other truths and explanations. In his description of the cricket near the end of the excerpt, Momaday also reads a lesson in nature.

Alice Walker

(1944–)

© Jeff Reinking.

In her poetry, essays, and novels, Alice Walker has celebrated the endurance, the strength, and the creativity of African American women like her mother—unsung women who carried immense familial and social burdens even as they struggled against low status and a complete lack of recognition.

Walker was born in Eatonton, Georgia, and grew up on a succession of farms in the area. Her father was a sharecropper, and her mother labored side-by-side with him in the fields, cared for their eight children, and still never failed, wherever they were living, to cultivate a large and beautiful flower garden. Her mother's hard work and determination to enrich her own life have served as an inspiration to Walker throughout her career.

A childhood accident that blinded Walker in one eye made her feel for a time disfigured and outcast. Seeking solace, she turned to writing poetry and reading, and also to closely observing people around her. Walker later attended Spelman College in Atlanta for two and a half years, before transferring to Sarah Lawrence College, near New York City. There she studied with the noted poet Muriel Rukeyser (1913–1980) before graduating in 1965.

During her college years, Walker was active in the civil rights movement in Georgia and Mississippi, and she traveled in Africa. Many of the poems in her first published collection, *Once: Poems* (1968), were inspired by these activities. The poems were written in a burst of creativity while Walker was at Sarah Lawrence. As quickly as she completed a poem, she would rush over to Muriel Rukeyser's classroom (a converted gardener's cottage in the center of the campus) and shove it under the door, then go back to her own room and write some more. This immense outpouring of creative energy continued night and day for the short period it lasted, but Walker didn't even care what Rukeyser did with the poems—the point was the creative surge of expression, not the end goal of publication. But the result was that Rukeyser gave the poems to her agent, and *Once: Poems* was published a few years later.

After graduating from college, Walker began a career of teaching and writing. She was among the first to teach university courses on the work of African American women writers, and she has since brought an understanding of their work to a wider audience. For example, Walker edited a collection of the writing of Zora Neale Hurston (page 750) called *I Love Myself When I Am Laughing . . .* (1979). In addition to poetry, short stories, and essays, Walker has written a number of well-received novels, including *Meridian* (1976), the Pulitzer Prize–winning *The Color Purple* (1982), *The Temple of My Familiar* (1989), and *Possessing the Secret of Joy* (1992).

According to the critic Donna Haisty Winchell, Walker "comes across in her writing from the 1980s and 1990s as a woman at peace with herself and with the universe. Some of the anger of her youth remains, but it is more tempered and more focused." This mellowing is evident in her 1983 collection of essays, *In Search of Our Mothers' Gardens*. In the title essay, Walker celebrates not just the few black women who managed, against all odds, to become recognized as artists, but also the unknown and unsung thousands, including her own mother, whose creativity flowered in their everyday lives.

QUICK PLANNING GUIDE

Into the Selection

Author Biography p. 1101

Before You Read p. 1102

- **Reading Focus: Scaffolding** Students learn about questions the author addresses in the selection.
- **Quickwrite:** Define *creative* and describe feelings about undeveloped abilities

Elements of Literature: Personal Essay

Through the Selection

from "In Search of Our Mothers' Gardens" pp. 1102–1107

Words to Own pp. 1103–1107

Making Meanings p. 1108

Beyond the Selection

Choices: Building Your Portfolio p. 1108

- **Writer's Notebook:** Identify and apply evaluation criteria
- **Critical Writing:** Write essay comparing metaphor and simile
- **Creative Writing/Art:** Write a character sketch

WORDS TO OWN

The following vocabulary words are defined in the Words to Own at the bottom of the pupil's page.

vibrant p. 1103
medium p. 1104
profusely p. 1104
conception p. 1107
ingenious p. 1107

Into the Selection

Using Before You Read

p. 1102

Quickwrite

Before students write what the word *creative* means to them, ask them to write a short list of other words or phrases that they associate with the word *creative.*

Elements of Literature

Write the following list of questions on the chalkboard for students to consider as they read the selection.

- What is the purpose of this essay?
- What is the writer's attitude toward the subject of the essay?
- Does the essay appeal primarily to the emotions or to the intellect?
- What techniques does the writer use to achieve her purpose?

PORTFOLIO ASSESSMENT

Portfolio Assessment
For help with teacher assessment of reading skills, see the *Portfolio Management System,* pp. 54–55.

Before You Read

from In Search of Our Mothers' Gardens

Reading Focus

Creativity Close to Home

The selection that follows is the second part of an essay about the creative spirit of African American women. In this section of her personal essay, Walker attempts to answer some questions she raised earlier:

- What did it mean for black women of previous generations to be artists?
- How were black women able to be creative in spite of limited opportunity and constrained freedom?

Walker explores these questions by examining her own mother's life. In doing so, she finds the answers very close to home.

Quickwrite

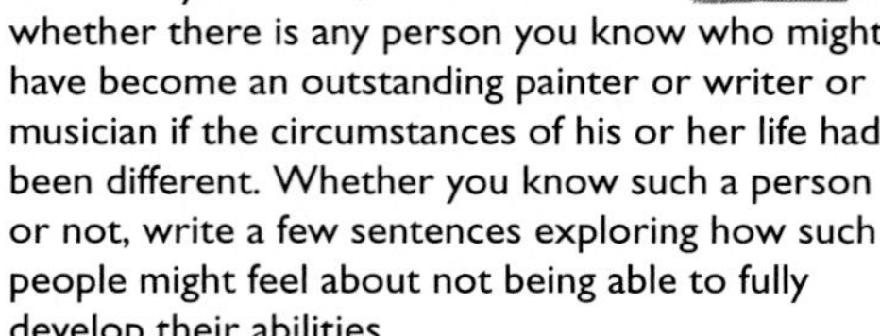

Write down what the word *creative* means to you. Then, consider whether there is any person you know who might have become an outstanding painter or writer or musician if the circumstances of his or her life had been different. Whether you know such a person or not, write a few sentences exploring how such people might feel about not being able to fully develop their abilities.

Elements of Literature

Personal Essay

A **personal essay** (also called an **informal essay**) is a short work of nonfiction prose with a personal slant. Although the subject of a personal essay can be almost anything, some of the best personal essays reveal a relationship between matters involving the writer personally and larger, more universal concerns. Such essays often refer to personal experiences and anecdotes to make a point, and typically reveal deeply felt emotional involvement.

> A **personal** or **informal essay** is a short work of nonfiction prose with a personal slant.
>
> *For more on the Essay, see the Handbook of Literary Terms.*

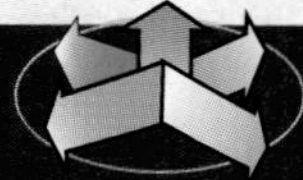

PROGRAM MANAGER

- **Planning Instruction** See Teaching Notes, *Teaching Resources B,* p. 185, for objectives, a summary, and literary elements for this selection.
- **Instructional Support** Before beginning the instructional lesson, see Graphic Organizer for Active Reading, *Teaching Resources B,* p. 195, for a Through the Selection activity.
- **Assessment** See Selection Test, *Test Booklet,* pp. 253–254.
- **Reinforcement** Use the Words to Own worksheet in *Teaching Resources B,* p. 196.
- **Application and Reinforcement** For reinforcement of the elements of literature introduced in this lesson, see Transparency 20.2 in the *Audiovisual Resources Binder.*

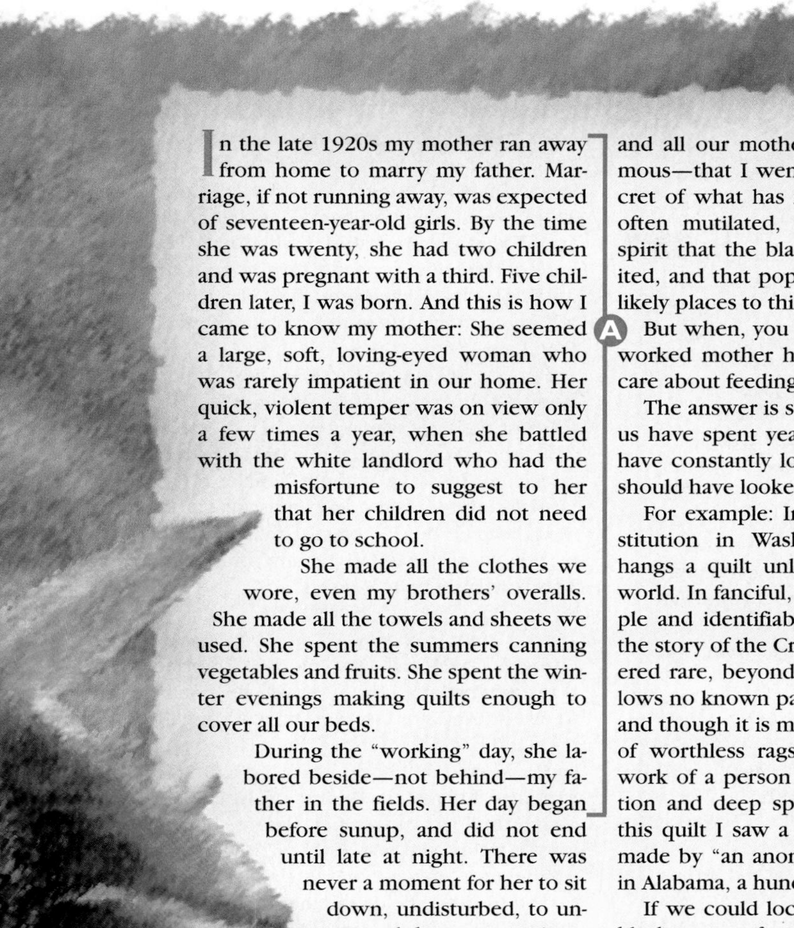

In the late 1920s my mother ran away from home to marry my father. Marriage, if not running away, was expected of seventeen-year-old girls. By the time she was twenty, she had two children and was pregnant with a third. Five children later, I was born. And this is how I came to know my mother: She seemed a large, soft, loving-eyed woman who was rarely impatient in our home. Her quick, violent temper was on view only a few times a year, when she battled with the white landlord who had the misfortune to suggest to her that her children did not need to go to school. **A**

She made all the clothes we wore, even my brothers' overalls. She made all the towels and sheets we used. She spent the summers canning vegetables and fruits. She spent the winter evenings making quilts enough to cover all our beds.

During the "working" day, she labored beside—not behind—my father in the fields. Her day began before sunup, and did not end until late at night. There was never a moment for her to sit down, undisturbed, to unravel her own private thoughts; never a time free from interruption—by work or the noisy inquiries of her many children. And yet, it is to my mother—and all our mothers who were not famous—that I went in search of the secret of what has fed that muzzled and often mutilated, but vibrant, creative spirit that the black woman has inherited, and that pops out in wild and unlikely places to this day. **B**

But when, you will ask, did my overworked mother have time to know or care about feeding the creative spirit?

The answer is so simple that many of us have spent years discovering it. We have constantly looked high, when we should have looked high—and low.

For example: In the Smithsonian Institution in Washington, D.C., there hangs a quilt unlike any other in the world. In fanciful, inspired, and yet simple and identifiable figures, it portrays the story of the Crucifixion. It is considered rare, beyond price. Though it follows no known pattern of quilt-making, and though it is made of bits and pieces of worthless rags, it is obviously the work of a person of powerful imagination and deep spiritual feeling. Below this quilt I saw a note that says it was made by "an anonymous Black woman in Alabama, a hundred years ago." **C**

If we could locate this "anonymous" black woman from Alabama, she would turn out to be one of our grandmothers—an artist who left her mark in the

WORDS TO OWN
vibrant (vī′brənt) *adj.:* full of energy.

A. Reader's Response: First Thoughts

? What is your first impression of the author's mother? [Sample responses: It sounds as if the author's mother had a very difficult life when she was raising her children; or the author's mother must have really cared a lot about raising her children well.]

B. Literary Element: Personal Essay

? What purpose for her essay does the author reveal here? [Possible answer: She suggests that the essay will explore the secret of African American women's "creative spirit," and she implies that she wants to understand the force that enables that spirit to survive.]

C. Critical Reading: Making Inferences

? Why does the author mention this quilt at this point in the essay? [Possible answer: She offers it as an example of one of the "unlikely places" where she found an example of the creative spirit that is the subject of her essay.]

OPTIONS FOR TEACHING

STRATEGIES FOR INCLUSION

Visual Before students read the essay, display or distribute a color photograph of a small flower garden and ask students to freewrite responses to it. Then, discuss with the class the skill and attention that goes into creating and caring for a garden, and ask students to list a few of the regular tasks that would be necessary in order to successfully maintain a garden such as the one in the photograph.

Bodily-Kinesthetic Ask students to think for a few moments about a movement they associate with the word *creative*. Then, call on students to pantomime or to describe aloud the movements the word evokes for them. [Possible responses: A flower opening, a person dancing, a hand writing with a pencil or painting with a brush, a movement like a sunrise.] Discuss as a class the similarities and differences among students' responses. ☞

A. Literary Element: Figures of Speech

Point out the **metaphor** and **simile** the author uses in this paragraph and ask students what she suggests about the "creative spark" by these figures of speech. [Possible answer: She suggests that even though many mothers were not able to fully explore their own creativity and see it blossom—or to spend enough time being creative to be able to open and decipher the "sealed letter" that held the answer to their own creativity—they were able to pass on their creative spirit to children who might finally make full use of it.]

B. Critical Reading: Predicting

? Based on what the author has already written, what information do you think she will provide next? [Possible answer: She suggests that her mother is a creative person, so perhaps she will give a more specific example of something that her mother created.]

only materials she could afford, and in the only medium her position in society allowed her to use.

As Virginia Woolf[1] wrote further, in *A Room of One's Own:*

> Yet genius of a sort must have existed among women as it must have existed among the working class. [Change this to "slaves" and "the wives and daughters of sharecroppers."] Now and again an Emily Brontë[2] or a Robert Burns[3] [change this to "a Zora Hurston or a Richard Wright"] blazes out and proves its presence. But certainly it never got itself on to paper. When, however, one reads of a witch being ducked, of a woman possessed by devils [or "Sainthood"[4]], of a wise woman selling herbs [our root workers], or even a very remarkable man who had a mother, then I think we are on the track of a lost novelist, a suppressed poet, of some mute and inglorious Jane Austen. . . .[5] Indeed, I would venture to guess that Anon, who wrote so many poems without signing them, was often a woman. . . .

A And so our mothers and grandmothers have, more often than not anonymously, handed on the creative spark, the seed of the flower they themselves never hoped to see: or like a sealed letter they could not plainly read.

And so it is, certainly, with my own mother. Unlike "Ma" Rainey's[6] songs, which retained their creator's name even while blasting forth from Bessie Smith's[7] mouth, no song or poem will bear my mother's name. Yet so many of the stories that I write, that we all write, are my mother's stories. Only recently did I fully realize this: that through years of listening to my mother's stories of her life, I have absorbed not only the stories themselves, but something of the manner in which she spoke, something of the urgency that involves the knowledge that her stories—like her life—must be recorded. It is probably for this reason that so much of what I have written is about characters whose counterparts in real life are so much older than I am.

But the telling of these stories, which came from my mother's lips as naturally as breathing, was not the only way my mother showed herself as an artist. For stories, too, were subject to being distracted, to dying without conclusion. Dinners must be started, and cotton must be gathered before the big rains. B The artist that was and is my mother showed itself to me only after many years. This is what I finally noticed:

Like Mem, a character in *The Third Life of Grange Copeland,*[8] my mother adorned with flowers whatever shabby house we were forced to live in. And not just your typical straggly country stand of zinnias, either. She planted ambitious gardens—and still does—with over fifty different varieties of plants that bloom profusely from early March until late November. Before she left home for the fields, she watered her flowers, chopped up the grass, and laid out new beds. When she returned from the fields she might divide clumps of bulbs, dig a cold pit,[9] uproot and replant roses, or prune branches from her taller bushes or trees—until night came and it was too dark to see.

1. **Virginia Woolf:** English novelist and critic. In *A Room of One's Own* (1929), Woolf says that, in order to write, a woman must have a room of her own (privacy) and the means to support herself (money).
2. **Emily Brontë:** English novelist and poet, best known for her novel *Wuthering Heights* (1847).
3. **Robert Burns:** eighteenth-century Scottish poet.
4. **"Sainthood":** In the early part of this essay, Walker talks about certain black women in the South called Saints. Intensely spiritual, these women were driven to madness by their creativity, for which they could find no release.
5. **Jane Austen:** English novelist, best known for *Pride and Prejudice* (1813).
6. **"Ma" Rainey:** nickname of Gertrude Malissa Nix Pridgett Rainey. She was the first great African American professional blues vocalist and is considered to be the mother of the blues.
7. **Bessie Smith:** One of the greatest of blues singers, Smith was helped to professional status by Ma Rainey. She became known in her lifetime as "Empress of the Blues."
8. ***The Third Life of Grange Copeland:*** Alice Walker's first novel, published in 1970.
9. **cold pit:** shallow pit, usually covered with glass, that is used for rooting plants or sheltering young plants from temperature variations in the spring.

WORDS TO OWN

medium (mē′dē·əm) *n.:* material for an artist.
profusely (prō·fyo͞os′lē) *adv.:* in great quantities.

OPTIONS FOR TEACHING

INTEGRATING THE LANGUAGE ARTS

Strategic Reading Ask students working in groups of three or four to take turns reading aloud sections of the essay. After a reader has finished a section, each student in the group should write a one-sentence summary of the section; then, another student should begin reading aloud the next section. After the whole essay has been read aloud, students should review it in their groups by comparing and discussing with one another their one-sentence summaries for each section.

Writing: Poetic Tribute After students have read this essay, read aloud the poem on p. 1107. Ask students to choose as the subject of a poem a person or group that has made an important but overlooked contribution to the world. Give the class time to record a few notes about their people or groups. Then, using Walker's poem for her mother as a model, ask students to write their own poetic tributes to the people or groups they chose. Encourage students to read their poems aloud in class.

Courtesy ACA Gallery, New York.

Sunset and Moonrise with Maudell Sleet (1978) by Romare Bearden. From the *Profile/Part 1: The Twenties* series (Mecklenburg County). Collage on board (41″ × 29″).

RESPONDING TO THE ART: VISUAL LITERACY

Why might the artist have decided to depict both a sunset and moonrise in the same collage? [Possible response: Perhaps he wanted to indicate the passage of time.]

CLASSROOM MANAGEMENT

Parental Involvement Students' parents or guardians may be especially interested in the theme of this Collection and may be able to offer ideas about how it could be made more relevant to your students. Contact parents or guardians to enlist their cooperation and seek their participation in an in-class presentation program. Some may be able to come to the classroom and talk about the significance in family life of heirlooms such as quilts, books, letters, and photographs. A scheduled career-exploration day or week may be a good time for parents or guardians to attend class and give presentations. Parents or guardians who cannot attend in person may be able to videotape or audiotape a short presentation. ☞

RESPONDING TO THE ART: VISUAL LITERACY

Which person in the selection is this illustration meant to depict? Why do you think so? [Possible response: It is meant to depict the author's mother, because she works in her garden just as the woman in the illustration does.]

Courtesy Sheldon Ross Gallery, Birmingham, Michigan.

Maudell Sleet's Magic Garden (1978) by Romare Bearden. From the *Profile/Part 1: The Twenties* series (Mecklenburg County). Collage on board ($10\frac{1}{8}'' \times 7''$).

OPTIONS FOR TEACHING

ASSESSMENT TOOLS

Check Test: Questions and Answers

1. To which of her relatives does Walker pay tribute in this essay? [Her mother.]
2. According to Virginia Woolf, who probably wrote many anonymous poems? [Women.]
3. Why do strangers visit Walker's house in Georgia? [To see her mother's garden.]
4. In the short poem Walker includes in the essay, what does she suggest that women of her mother's generation valued above all for their children? [Education.]

Informal Assessment Ask students to write responses in their journal to the following questions.

- I have really improved at _______ because _______.
- I am not doing as well at _______ because _______.
- My favorite assignment is _______ because _______.

Collect the journals, and read the entries without writing comments. Use the responses to make adjustments for individual problems or to create mini-lessons for the class.

Whatever she planted grew as if by magic, and her fame as a grower of flowers spread over three counties. Because of her creativity with her flowers, even my memories of poverty are seen through a screen of blooms—sunflowers, petunias, roses, dahlias, forsythia, spirea, delphiniums, verbena . . . and on and on.

And I remember people coming to my mother's yard to be given cuttings from her flowers; I hear again the praise showered on her because whatever rocky soil she landed on, she turned into a garden. A garden so brilliant with colors, so original in its design, so magnificent with life and creativity, that to this day people drive by our house in Georgia—perfect strangers and imperfect strangers—and ask to stand or walk among my mother's art.

I notice that it is only when my mother is working in her flowers that she is radiant, almost to the point of being invisible—except as Creator: hand and eye. She is involved in work her soul must have. Ordering the universe in the image of her personal conception of Beauty.

(A) Her face, as she prepares the Art that is her gift, is a legacy of respect she leaves to me, for all that illuminates and cherishes life. She has handed down respect for the possibilities—and the will to grasp them.

For her, so hindered and intruded upon in so many ways, being an artist has still been a daily part of her life. This ability to hold on, even in very simple ways, is work black women have done for a very long time.

This poem is not enough, but it is something, for the woman who literally covered the holes in our walls with sunflowers:

They were women then
My mama's generation
Husky of voice—Stout of
Step
With fists as well as
Hands
How they battered down
Doors
And ironed
Starched white
Shirts
How they led
Armies
Headragged Generals
Across mined
Fields
Booby-trapped
Kitchens
To discover books
Desks
A place for us
How they knew what we
Must know
Without knowing a page
Of it
Themselves.

Guided by my heritage of a love of beauty and a respect for strength—in search of my mother's garden, I found my own.

(B) And perhaps in Africa over two hundred years ago, there was just such a mother; perhaps she painted vivid and daring decorations in oranges and yellows and greens on the walls of her hut; perhaps she sang—in a voice like Roberta Flack's[10]—*sweetly* over the compounds of her village; perhaps she wove the most stunning mats or told the most ingenious stories of all the village storytellers. Perhaps she was herself a poet—though only her daughter's name is signed to the poems that we know.

Perhaps Phillis Wheatley's mother was also an artist.

Perhaps in more than Phillis Wheatley's biological life is her mother's signature made clear.

10. **Roberta Flack's:** Roberta Flack is a popular African American singer-songwriter.

WORDS TO OWN

conception (kən·sep′shən) *n.:* mental formation of ideas.
ingenious (in·jēn′yəs) *adj.:* clever.

A. Reader's Response: Connecting with the Text

? What other valuable legacies or gifts are handed down to children by their parents or guardians? [Sample response: Parents also pass down family traditions, attitudes toward life, and important values.]

B. Reader's Response: Shaping Interpretations

? Why do you think the author includes these final examples? [Sample responses: She includes them in order to emphasize the important role that anonymous women may have played in bringing lasting beauty into the world; or she includes them in order to remind the reader that even though not all women artists of the past were famous, they were able to pass down their creativity to their children.]

Making Meanings questions begin on p. 1108.

Making Meanings

First Thoughts

1. Possible responses: She never became bitter or discouraged; she brought beauty into the world; she passed on her creative spirit.

Reviewing the Text

a. It was a hard life; she worked in the fields all day, made all of her family's clothes, raised eight children, and helped her children by sending them to school instead of work.
b. The source of their creative spirit.
c. Through her stories and her flower gardens.
d. She becomes radiantly creative as she brings order and beauty to her garden.

Shaping Interpretations

2. Her mother's art has given Walker a respect for the potential in everyone, and she writes because she feels her mother's stories must be recorded. She probably feels regret that no creative works carry her mother's name.
3. Possible response: Walker's mother taught her daughter that whatever one does in life can and should be done with love and respect for beauty and order.

Answers to Making Meanings begin on p. T1107.

4. Even though they were uneducated, the mothers knew that educating their children was important.
5. She means that in searching to understand the force that drove her mother to create her gardens, she discovered the same creative spirit behind her own works.

Challenging the Text

6. **(Evaluation)** Possible response: The essay is a tribute to Walker's mother, written in a **tone** of wonder at what she was able to accomplish. Quotations from Walker's mother might have altered that tone of wonder and made it a different type of essay.

Choices: Building Your Portfolio

1. **Writer's Notebook** Remind students to save their work. They may use it as prewriting for the Writer's Workshop on p. 1181.
2. **Critical Writing** See annotation A on p. T1104. Point out that Woolf is suggesting that many famous men may have had very creative, extraordinary mothers.
3. **Creative Writing/Art** Ask students to use cluster diagrams to list details about their subject.

PORTFOLIO ASSESSMENT

Choices: Assessment Criteria For help in evaluating these Choices assignments, see the criteria in the *Portfolio Management System*, p. 201.

MAKING MEANINGS

First Thoughts

1. What do you find most admirable about Alice Walker's mother? Do you think she might have shared some of the feelings you outlined in your Reader's Log?

Reviewing the Text

a. Describe the kind of life Walker's mother led while Walker was growing up.
b. What secret does Walker hope to discover from examining her mother's life and the lives of other women like her mother?
c. In what two ways does Walker's mother express her creativity?
d. What happens to Walker's mother when she works in her garden?

Shaping Interpretations

2. As a writer, how does Walker feel she has been enriched by her mother's storytelling? How do you think Walker feels about the fact that her mother's name will never be associated with a poem, song, or other creative work?
3. What do you think Walker the writer has learned from her mother the gardener?
4. In the last five lines of the poem in the essay, Walker presents a **paradox,** or apparent contradiction. State the paradox in your own words, and tell what kinds of knowledge you think Walker is talking about.
5. What do you think Walker means when she says that she found her own "garden" in the process of searching for her mother's?

Challenging the Text

6. Walker describes her mother's life and feelings but never allows her mother to speak for herself. Would the essay be improved if it included quotations from Walker's mother, telling us about her life and thoughts? Explain.

CHOICES: Building Your Portfolio

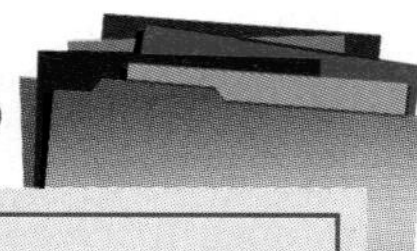

Writer's Notebook

1. Collecting Ideas for an Evaluation

WORK IN PROGRESS

When you evaluate a **personal essay,** you might want to consider such criteria as interest of topic, clarity of theme, and emotional effect. Apply such criteria to Walker's essay, citing specific passages to support your evaluation. Save your notes for possible use in the Writer's Workshop on page 1181.

Critical Writing

2. A Priceless Legacy

On page 1104, Walker uses a **metaphor** and a **simile** to describe how African American women have handed down their creative spark over the generations. In a short essay, tell what these figures of speech have in common. Also, discuss how they relate to Virginia Woolf's ideas about the mothers of "very remarkable" men.

Creative Writing / Art

3. Quiet Strengths

Write a **character sketch** about someone you admire who is not at all famous and who might even be regarded by some as a failure. In your sketch, be sure to indicate exactly what you admire about this person. Try to include the person's occupation and a description of what he or she looks like. If you wish, draw a picture of the person.

STRATEGIES FOR INCLUSION

Learners Having Difficulty For activity #2, ask students to use a chart like the following to record notes on the two figures of speech.

Creative Spark

Figure of Speech from Story	flower seed	like a sealed letter
Type	metaphor	simile
Qualities	potential for growth	has information that cannot be read

Spatial/Auditory For activity #3, ask pairs of students to work together to produce cluster diagrams based on their partners' oral descriptions of the subjects they have chosen for their character sketches. As one student describes his or her subject, the other student should write words or draw symbols that immediately come to mind. Ask students to use the finished cluster diagrams their partners produce to create three- or four-panel "character strip" graphic organizers or outlines for their written character sketches.

Reuters/Bettmann.

Amy Tan

(1952–)

Amy Tan had not planned to become a fiction writer. In fact, for years she worked as a freelance writer for high-technology companies, a career in which flights of imagination are not permitted. To ease the pressures of her job, she decided to take jazz piano lessons—and she began writing fiction. The result was the release of a dazzling new storyteller.

Tan's parents had fled Communist China and had come to the United States shortly before she was born in Oakland, California. Her mother, a nurse, was originally from Shanghai; her father, an engineer and a Baptist minister, came from Beijing.

After her father and young brother both died of brain tumors when Amy Tan was just fifteen, her mother took her away from the "diseased" house to Switzerland, where she finished high school. Her mother expected her talented daughter to become a neurosurgeon, as well as a pianist, in her spare time. When they returned to the United States, Tan enrolled as a premed student at Linfield College, a Baptist school in Oregon, which had been selected by her mother. But she defied her mother by leaving Linfield to join her boyfriend at San Jose State University, where she changed her major from premed to English. Tan's mother took this defiance as a sort of death between them, and mother and daughter did not speak for six months.

Tan was well aware of her mother's narrative gift (she says her mother can talk for three hours straight), and perhaps it was this which eventually prompted her own desire to write. However, she was thirty-three before she wrote her first story. Called "Endgame" (retitled "Rules of the Game") and written for a Squaw Valley writers' conference, it was the first of many Tan stories that would explore the dynamic relationship between daughters and their mothers.

These stories were collected in 1989 in one volume, the now widely known best-seller *The Joy Luck Club* (also made into a popular movie). In it, stories about Chinese American daughters are interwoven with stories of their four Chinese mothers, who are members of a mah-jongg club in San Francisco.

Tan's 1991 novel, *The Kitchen God's Wife,* was hailed by some critics as even more artistically successful than *The Joy Luck Club.* In this second book, a mother tells her grown daughter what life was like in China during World War II—and the daughter begins to see both her mother and herself with enlightened eyes. A third novel, *The Hundred Secret Senses* (1995), also explores a familial relationship—this time between two sisters whose lives are transformed during a visit to a small village in China.

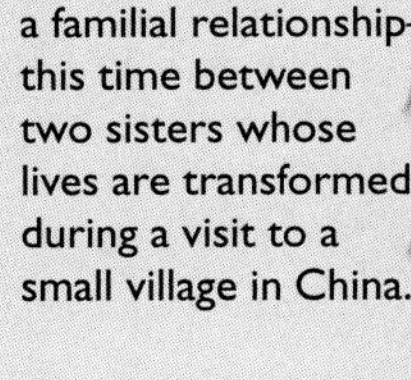

WORDS TO OWN

The following vocabulary words are defined in the Words to Own at the bottom of the pupil's page.

intricate p. 1112	prodigy p. 1116
ancestral p. 1112	malodorous p. 1116
obscured p. 1113	concessions p. 1117
retort p.1113	careened p. 1117
touted p. 1116	successive p. 1118

QUICK PLANNING GUIDE

Into the Story

Author Biography p. 1109

Before You Read p. 1110

- **Reading Focus: Scaffolding** Students learn about the forces behind the conflict in the selection.
- **Quickwrite: Prior Knowledge** Compare the rules of a game to rules of human relationships
- **Elements of Literature: Motivation**

Through the Story

from "Rules of the Game" pp. 1110–1118

Words to Own p. 1112–1118

Primary Sources p. 1118

Making Meanings p. 1119

Beyond the Story

Choices: Building Your Portfolio p. 1119

- **Writer's Notebook:** Comment on a critical evaluation of the story
- **Critical Writing:** Switch a character with one from another story
- **Speaking and Listening:** Prepare an oral report on a game

How to Own a Word p. 1120

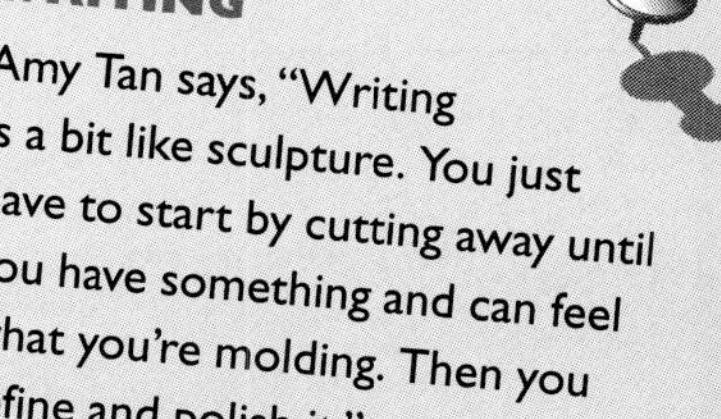

WRITERS ON WRITING

Amy Tan says, "Writing is a bit like sculpture. You just have to start by cutting away until you have something and can feel what you're molding. Then you refine and polish it."

Into the Story

Using Before You Read

p. 1110

Reading Focus

Ask student groups to discuss some of the differences between parents' expectations and children's needs. *Remind students that they are not required to talk about anything they would feel uncomfortable sharing and discussing with others.*

Elements of Literature

Ask students to consider the following questions as they read.

- Are the characters' actions consistent?
- Can you understand the reasons behind the characters' actions?
- How are the reasons behind the characters' action revealed?

PORTFOLIO ASSESSMENT

Portfolio Assessment
For help with self-assessment of reading skills, see the *Portfolio Management System,* pp. 48–49.

Before You Read

from Rules of the Game

Reading Focus

Parents and Children

At first, the following story appears to be about a Chinese American girl who stumbles into the forbidding world of championship chess and becomes an absolute whiz at it. But presently we come to understand that the story is about a matter far more familiar to us: the clash between a mother's authority over her children and her ambition for them, and a child's need to find his or her own way.

Quickwrite

Think about the rules of chess or another game you know. Then, write down some ways a game's rules might be similar to rules of human relations, especially between parents and children. What do you think the title of this story might mean? (Might it have more than one meaning?)

Elements of Literature

Motivation

Motivation refers to the reasons for a character's behavior. A writer can reveal motivation directly by telling us what makes a character tick. In many works, however, the writer shows us characters talking and acting but does not tell us the reasons for their behavior: We must sift through the details and then infer motivation. Tan's story fits into this second category. Pay particular attention to how the beat-up chess set arrives in the Jong family, how Waverly becomes interested in the game while her brothers play, and how her interest grows as theirs wanes. Then ask yourself: What's really going on in that final match between Waverly and her true adversary and coach?

> **Motivation** refers to the underlying reasons for a character's behavior.
>
> *For more on Motivation, see the Handbook of Literary Terms.*

from Rules of the Game
from The Joy Luck Club
Amy Tan

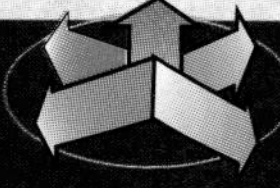

PROGRAM MANAGER

- **Planning Instruction** See Teaching Notes, *Teaching Resources B,* p. 186, for objectives, a summary, literary elements and additional historical and biographical information for this selection.
- **Instructional Support** Before beginning the instructional lesson, see Graphic Organizer for Active Reading, *Teaching Resources B,* p. 197, for Through the Story activities.
- **Assessment** See Selection Test, *Test Booklet,* pp. 255–256.
- **Language Link** For instruction and practice in identifying and using irregular verbs, see Language Link, *Teaching Resources B,* pp. 198–199, and *Language and Writing Skills Worksheets,* pp. 36–38.
- **Reinforcement** Use the Words to Own worksheet in *Teaching Resources B,* p. 200.

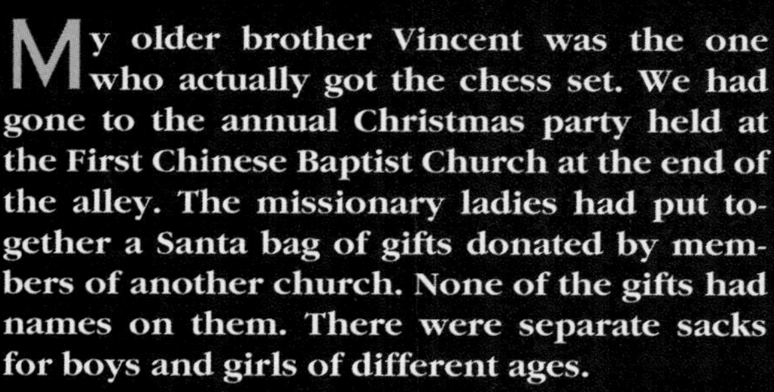

My older brother Vincent was the one who actually got the chess set. We had gone to the annual Christmas party held at the First Chinese Baptist Church at the end of the alley. The missionary ladies had put together a Santa bag of gifts donated by members of another church. None of the gifts had names on them. There were separate sacks for boys and girls of different ages. **A**

One of the Chinese parishioners had donned a Santa Claus costume and a stiff paper beard with cotton balls glued to it. I think the only children who thought he was the real thing were too young to know that Santa Claus was not Chinese. When my turn came up, the Santa man asked me how old I was. I thought it was a trick question; I was seven according to the American formula and

A. Literary Element: Point of View
Point out to students that the story is written from the first-person point of view of a narrator looking back on episodes from her childhood.

OPTIONS FOR TEACHING

STRATEGIES FOR INCLUSION

Logical-Mathematical Before students begin reading the story, discuss as a class the rules of chess. Ask a student volunteer to describe the moves that the various pieces are permitted to make and to briefly explain how computer programs are created to compete at the tournament level against highly skilled players. Ask the volunteer to describe also the thought process that occurs during a chess game.

TECHNOLOGY **Visual** Ask students to locate or create a photograph, drawing, or other illustration that best represents for them the **conflict** between the narrator and her mother that takes place in the selection. Call on students to display their illustrations for the class and to explain their connection to the story. Encourage students to use slides or computer presentation programs to display their images.

A. Reader's Response: First Thoughts

? What type of gift would you have hoped to select from a bag of gifts when you were seven or eight? [Sample responses: A book, a doll, baseball cards, a compact disc, a video game.]

B. Critical Reading: Expressing an Opinion

? Do you think it would have been better to start the narration of this episode with this sentence, or with the one the author uses on p. 1111? Why? [Possible answers: This sentence would be better because it is more of an attention-getter; or if this sentence were at the beginning, it would be more confusing than the sentence that the author uses.]

eight by the Chinese calendar. I said I was born on March 17, 1951. That seemed to satisfy him. He then solemnly asked if I had been a very, very good girl this year and did I believe in Jesus Christ and obey my parents. I knew the only answer to that. I nodded back with equal solemnity.

Having watched the other children opening their gifts, I already knew that the big gifts were not necessarily the nicest ones. One girl my age got a large coloring book of biblical characters, while a less greedy girl who selected a smaller box received a glass vial of lavender toilet water.[1] The sound of the box was also important. A ten-year-old boy had chosen a box that jangled when he shook it. It was a tin globe of the world with a slit for inserting money. He must have thought it was full of dimes and nickels, because when he saw that it had just ten pennies, his face fell with such undisguised disappointment that his mother slapped the side of his head and led him out of the church hall, apologizing to the crowd for her son who had such bad manners he couldn't appreciate such a fine gift.

(A) As I peered into the sack, I quickly fingered the remaining presents, testing their weight, imagining what they contained. I chose a heavy, compact one that was wrapped in shiny silver foil and a red satin ribbon. It was a twelve-pack of Life Savers and I spent the rest of the party arranging and rearranging the candy tubes in the order of my favorites. My brother Winston chose wisely as well. His present turned out to be a box of intricate plastic parts; the instructions on the box proclaimed that when they were properly assembled he would have an authentic miniature replica of a World War II submarine.

(B) Vincent got the chess set, which would have been a very decent present to get at a church Christmas party, except it was obviously used and, as we discovered later, it was missing a black pawn and a white knight. My mother graciously thanked the unknown benefactor, saying, "Too good. Cost too much." At which point, an old lady with fine white, wispy hair nodded toward our family and said with a whistling whisper, "Merry, merry Christmas."

When we got home, my mother told Vincent to throw the chess set away. "She not want it. We not want it," she said, tossing her head stiffly to the side with a tight, proud smile. My brothers had deaf ears. They were already lining up the chess pieces and reading from the dog-eared instruction book.

1. **toilet water:** perfumed after-bath skin freshener.

A little knowledge withheld is a great advantage one should store for future use. That is the power of chess. It is a game of secrets in which one must show and never tell.

I watched Vincent and Winston play during Christmas week. The chess board seemed to hold elaborate secrets waiting to be untangled. The chessmen were more powerful than Old Li's magic herbs that cured ancestral curses. And my brothers wore such serious faces that I was sure something was at stake that was greater than avoiding the tradesmen's door to Hong Sing's.

"Let me! Let me!" I begged between games when one brother or the other would sit back with a deep sigh of relief and victory, the other annoyed, unable to let go of the outcome. Vincent at first refused to let me play, but when I offered my Life Savers as replacements for the buttons that filled in for the missing pieces, he relented. He chose the flavors: wild cherry for the black pawn and peppermint for the white knight. Winner could eat both.

As our mother sprinkled flour and rolled out small doughy circles for the steamed dumplings that would be our dinner that night, Vincent explained the rules, pointing to each piece. "You

WORDS TO OWN

intricate (in′tri·kit) *adj.:* complicated.
ancestral (an·ses′trəl) *adj.:* inherited.

OPTIONS FOR TEACHING

INTEGRATING THE LANGUAGE ARTS

Strategic Reading Help students monitor their own reading by demonstrating how you would read the selection. Begin by reading aloud the first paragraph. Talk about any images it suggests, remark on any confusing words or phrases, and explain how you adjust your thinking as you read. Then, ask student pairs to take turns reading the selection together. Each student should read a paragraph, pause, and talk to the other student, using the monitoring strategies that you demonstrated.

Writing: Essay Remind the class that the title of this selection is meant to refer to more than just the rules of chess. Ask students to write a short essay in which they (1) describe the other game that takes place in the story, and (2) explain the rules of this other game. Remind students to use information or quotations from Tan's story to support their explanations. If students have trouble getting started, write the following prompt on the chalkboard as an example.
Game: [bring honor to the family while maintaining harmony]
Rules: [work hard, win, sacrifice to allow family members to win]

have sixteen pieces and so do I. One king and queen, two bishops, two knights, two castles, and eight pawns. The pawns can only move forward one step, except on the first move. Then they can move two. But they can only take men by moving crossways like this, except in the beginning, when you can move ahead and take another pawn."

"Why?" I asked as I moved my pawn. "Why can't they move more steps?"

"Because they're pawns," he said.

"But why do they go crossways to take other men. Why aren't there any women and children?"

"Why is the sky blue? Why must you always ask stupid questions?" asked Vincent. "This is a game. These are the rules. I didn't make them up. See. Here. In the book." He jabbed a page with a pawn in his hand. "Pawn. P-A-W-N. Pawn. Read it yourself."

My mother patted the flour off her hands. "Let me see book," she said quietly. She scanned the pages quickly, not reading the foreign English symbols, seeming to search deliberately for nothing in particular.

"This American rules," she concluded at last. "Every time people come out from foreign country, must know rules. You not know, judge say, Too bad, go back. They not telling you why so you can use their way go forward. They say, Don't know why, you find out yourself. But they knowing all the time. Better you take it, find out why yourself." She tossed her head back with a satisfied smile.

I found out about all the whys later. I read the rules and looked up all the big words in a dictionary. I borrowed books from the Chinatown library. I studied each chess piece, trying to absorb the power each contained.

I learned about opening moves and why it's important to control the center early on; the shortest distance between two points is straight down the middle. I learned about the middle game and why tactics between two adversaries are like clashing ideas; the one who plays better has the clearest plans for both attacking and getting out of traps. I learned why it is essential in the endgame to have foresight, a mathematical understanding of all possible moves, and patience; all weaknesses and advantages become evident to a strong adversary and are obscured to a tiring opponent. I discovered that for the whole game one must gather invisible strengths and see the endgame before the game begins. **C**

I also found out why I should never reveal "why" to others. A little knowledge withheld is a great advantage one should store for future use. That is the power of chess. It is a game of secrets in which one must show and never tell.

I loved the secrets I found within the sixty-four black and white squares. I carefully drew a handmade chessboard and pinned it to the wall next to my bed, where at night I would stare for hours at imaginary battles. Soon I no longer lost any games or Life Savers, but I lost my adversaries. Winston and Vincent decided they were more interested in roaming the streets after school in their Hopalong Cassidy[2] cowboy hats.

On a cold spring afternoon, while walking home from school, I detoured through the playground at the end of our alley. I saw a group of old men, two seated across a folding table playing a game of chess, others smoking pipes, eating peanuts, and watching. I ran home and grabbed Vincent's chess set, which was bound in a cardboard box with rubber bands. I also carefully selected two prized rolls of Life Savers. I came back to the park and approached a man who was observing the game.

"Want to play?" I asked him. His face widened with surprise and he grinned as he looked at the box under my arm.

"Little sister, been a long time since I play with dolls," he said, smiling benevolently. I quickly put the box down next to him on the bench and displayed my retort. **D**

Lau Po, as he allowed me to call him, turned out to be a much better player than my brothers. I lost many games and many Life Savers. But over the weeks, with each diminishing roll of candies, I added new secrets. Lau Po gave me the names. The Double Attack from the East and West Shores. Throwing Stones on the Drowning Man. The Sudden Meeting of the Clan. The Surprise from

2. **Hopalong Cassidy:** cowboy hero of movies and television from the 1930s through the early 1950s.

Words to Own

obscured (əb·skyoord') *v.:* concealed.
retort (ri·tôrt') *n.:* quick answer.

C. Reader's Response: Connecting with the Text

? How might the narrator's comments about chess strategy apply to life as well? [Sample responses: To be successful, a person needs to make long-term plans—to anticipate success before it comes; or the people with the clearest plans for the future are the ones who have the best chance for success.]

D. Critical Reading: Finding Details

? Which of the narrator's earlier comments about chess is echoed in her unspoken retort to the man's taunt? [Possible answer: The narrator said earlier that chess is a game of showing, not telling. Here, she does not answer the man in words; instead she attempts to show him her skill.]

COOPERATIVE LEARNING

Hot Seat Place students in pairs, and ask them each to choose a character to portray—either the narrator or her mother. Ask each student to create a short list of the character's attributes.

- Narrator: [embarrassed by her mother; unsure about how to react]
- Mother: [proud of her daughter; confused and hurt by her embarrassment]

Then, ask students to give their partners two minutes on the Hot Seat to respond in character to questions about the story's conflict.

Group Sketches Ask students to work in groups of four to prepare dramatic sketches based on scenes from the story. Allow students to base their sketches on dialogue or on action. Suggest that the groups select one member to act as a narrator who introduces and explains the sketch. Encourage students to include sound effects and background music when they perform their sketches. Remind the class that the sketches may be interpretations based only loosely on actual events in the story. ☞

RESPONDING TO THE ILLUSTRATION: VISUAL LITERACY

What might the girl in the illustration be thinking? [Possible response: She may be planning her next move, or she may be thinking about what her opponent plans to do.]

OPTIONS FOR TEACHING

CLASSROOM MANAGEMENT

Managing the Reader's Response Classroom Encourage students to explore a variety of interpretations by asking them to consider how various people might respond to a selection. For example, after students have expressed their initial reactions to a question about a selection, ask them what kinds of responses they would expect from someone older or younger than they are. If students are writing their responses, encourage them to include these other perspectives in their final responses.

Block Scheduling At the end of a unit or collection, use the longer class time provided by a block schedule to show a video related to an important aspect or theme (in this case, family relationships or conflicts) covered in the unit or collection. Because of the longer time available, many videos may be viewed in just one or two periods. The schedule also provides enough time for an in-depth discussion and for an appropriate follow-up writing assignment, reteaching activity, or enrichment activity. See p. 1119 for some activities that relate to this selection.

the Sleeping Guard. The Humble Servant Who Kills the King. Sand in the Eyes of Advancing Forces. A Double Killing Without Blood. (A)

There were also the fine points of chess etiquette. Keep captured men in neat rows, as well-tended prisoners. Never announce "Check" with vanity, lest someone with an unseen sword slit your throat. Never hurl pieces into the sandbox after you have lost a game, because then you must find them again, by yourself, after apologizing to all around you. By the end of the summer, Lau Po had taught me all he knew, and I had become a better chess player.

A small weekend crowd of Chinese people and tourists would gather as I played and defeated my opponents one by one. My mother would join the crowds during these outdoor exhibition games. She sat proudly on the bench, telling my admirers with proper Chinese humility, "Is luck."

A man who watched me play in the park suggested that my mother allow me to play in local chess tournaments. My mother smiled graciously, an answer that meant nothing. I desperately wanted to go, but I bit back my tongue. I knew she would not let me play among strangers. So as we walked home I said in a small voice that I didn't want to play in the local tournament. They would have American rules. If I lost, I would bring shame on my family. (B)

"Is shame you fall down nobody push you," said my mother.

During my first tournament, my mother sat with me in the front row as I waited for my turn. I frequently bounced my legs to unstick them from the cold metal seat of the folding chair. When my name was called, I leapt up. My mother unwrapped something in her lap. It was her *chang,* a small tablet of red jade which held the sun's fire. "Is luck," she whispered, and tucked it into my dress pocket. I turned to my opponent, a fifteen-year-old boy from Oakland. He looked at me, wrinkling his nose.

As I began to play, the boy disappeared, the color ran out of the room, and I saw only my white pieces and his black ones waiting on the other side. A light wind began blowing past my ears. It whispered secrets only I could hear.

Scene from the movie *The Joy Luck Club.*
Buena Vista Pictures Distribution, Inc.

A. Expansion
Point out that Lau Po's colorful names for strategies suggest that a chess is a challenging game that may be won—or lost—in a great variety of ways.

B. Reader's Response: Shaping Interpretations
Point out the trick that the narrator uses to convince her mother to let her play in the chess tournament. Ask students what this action might reveal about the narrator. [Sample responses: It shows that the narrator can apply to her relationship with her mother some of the ingenuity she uses to win at chess.]

CROSSING THE CURRICULUM

Art Games and competition in general have been a common subject of art for centuries. Have students do independent research to locate drawings, paintings, photographs, or other works that depict competition or specific games. Ask students to bring in the works and to share them with the rest of the class. Call on students to compare the works aloud and to point out details that are common elements in them.

History Ask students to research and prepare a news report on chess prodigy Bobby Fischer and his career, based on encyclopedia articles, news stories, or information from other news media. Suggest that students include a discussion about how Fischer's personal conflicts may have affected his chess playing. If copies of photographs or illustrations are available, encourage students to include them with their reports. ☞

A. Critical Reading: Drawing Conclusions

? What might the wind represent to the narrator? [Possible answers: Quiet strength, silent strategy.] How does the wind's advice echo the narrator's earlier comments about chess? [Possible answers: She keeps her opponent guessing, avoids his traps, and effectively distracts him.]

B. Expansion

Bobby Fischer, also a child prodigy, became at age fifteen the youngest chess player ever ranked as an international grand master. Born in 1943, he won the first of many United States championships at age fourteen. The match that won him the world championship in 1972 generated enormous worldwide interest in chess.

A "Blow from the South," it murmured. "The wind leaves no trail." I saw a clear path, the traps to avoid. The crowd rustled. "Shhh! Shhh!" said the corners of the room. The wind blew stronger. "Throw sand from the East to distract him." The knight came forward ready for the sacrifice. The wind hissed, louder and louder. "Blow, blow, blow. He cannot see. He is blind now. Make him lean away from the wind so he is easier to knock down."

"Check," I said, as the wind roared with laughter. The wind died down to little puffs, my own breath.

My mother placed my first trophy next to a new plastic chess set that the neighborhood Tao society had given to me. As she wiped each piece with a soft cloth, she said, "Next time win more, lose less."

"Ma, it's not how many pieces you lose," I said. "Sometimes you need to lose pieces to get ahead."

"Better to lose less, see if you really need."

At the next tournament, I won again, but it was my mother who wore the triumphant grin.

"Lost eight piece this time. Last time was eleven. What I tell you? Better off lose less!" I was annoyed, but I couldn't say anything.

I attended more tournaments, each one farther away from home. I won all games, in all divisions. The Chinese bakery downstairs from our flat displayed my growing collection of trophies in its window, amidst the dust-covered cakes that were never picked up. The day after I won an important regional tournament, the window encased a fresh sheet cake with whipped-cream frosting and red script saying, "Congratulations, Waverly Jong, Chinatown Chess Champion." Soon after that, a flower shop, headstone engraver, and funeral parlor offered to sponsor me in national tournaments. That's when my mother decided I no longer had to do the dishes. Winston and Vincent had to do my chores.

"Why does she get to play and we do all the work," complained Vincent.

"Is new American rules," said my mother. "Meimei[3] play, squeeze all her brains out for win chess. You play, worth squeeze towel."

By my ninth birthday, I was a national chess champion. I was still some 429 points away from grand-master status,[4] but I was touted as the Great American Hope, a child prodigy and a girl to boot. B They ran a photo of me in *Life* magazine next to a quote in which Bobby Fischer said, "There will never be a woman grand master." "Your move, Bobby," said the caption.

The day they took the magazine picture I wore neatly plaited braids clipped with plastic barrettes trimmed with rhinestones. I was playing in a large high school auditorium that echoed with phlegmy coughs and the squeaky rubber knobs of chair legs sliding across freshly waxed wooden floors. Seated across from me was an American man, about the same age as Lau Po, maybe fifty. I remember that his sweaty brow seemed to weep at my every move. He wore a dark, malodorous suit. One of his pockets was stuffed with a great white kerchief on which he wiped his palm before sweeping his hand over the chosen chess piece with great flourish.

In my crisp pink-and-white dress with scratchy lace at the neck, one of two my mother had sewn for these special occasions, I would clasp my hands under my chin, the delicate points of my elbows poised lightly on the table in the manner my mother had shown me for posing for the press. I would swing my patent leather shoes back and forth like an impatient child riding on a school bus. Then I would pause, suck in my lips, twirl my chosen piece in midair as if undecided, and then firmly plant it in its new threatening place, with a triumphant smile thrown back at my opponent for good measure.

I no longer played in the alley of Waverly Place. I never visited the playground where the pigeons and old men gathered. I went to school, then directly home to learn new chess secrets, cleverly concealed advantages, more escape routes.

But I found it difficult to concentrate at home. My mother had a habit of standing over me while

3. **Meimei** (mā·mā): Chinese for "little sister."

4. **grand-master status:** top rank in international chess competition.

Words to Own

touted (tout'id) *v.:* highly praised.
prodigy (präd'ə·jē) *n.:* extremely gifted person.
malodorous (mal'ō'dər·əs) *adj.:* bad-smelling.

Options for Teaching

Professional Notes

Technology Tip An interview with the author may be found on the World Wide Web at **http://www.salon1999.com/12nov1995/feature/tan.html**. Or, for other information on the author, search the Web using a search engine and the key words **Amy Tan**. *You may want to preview any Internet activity that you suggest to students. Because these resources are sometimes public forums, their content can be unpredictable.*

Critical Comment: Tan's Characters Critic Nancy Willard writes about Tan's "ability to show how . . . mothers and daughters . . . love . . . and forgive each other." Discuss the conflict between the narrator and her mother in "Rules of the Game." Then, ask students to write predictions about how the narrator and her mother might resolve their conflict by showing their love and forgiveness to one another.

I plotted out my games. I think she thought of herself as my protective ally. Her lips would be sealed tight, and after each move I made, a soft "Hmmmmph" would escape from her nose.

"Ma, I can't practice when you stand there like that," I said one day. She retreated to the kitchen and made loud noises with the pots and pans. When the crashing stopped, I could see out of the corner of my eye that she was standing in the doorway. "Hmmmph!" Only this one came out of her tight throat.

My parents made many concessions to allow me to practice. One time I complained that the bedroom I shared was so noisy that I couldn't think. Thereafter, my brothers slept in a bed in the living room facing the street. I said I couldn't finish my rice; my head didn't work right when my stomach was too full. I left the table with half-finished bowls and nobody complained. But there was one duty I couldn't avoid. I had to accompany my mother on Saturday market days when I had no tournament to play. My mother would proudly walk with me, visiting many shops, buying very little. "This my daughter Wave-ly Jong," she said to whoever looked her way.

C

One day, after we left a shop I said under my breath, "I wish you wouldn't do that, telling everybody I'm your daughter." My mother stopped walking. Crowds of people with heavy bags pushed past us on the sidewalk, bumping into first one shoulder, then another.

"Aiii-ya. So shame be with mother?" She grasped my hand even tighter as she glared at me.

I looked down. "It's not that, it's just so obvious. It's just so embarrassing."

"Embarrass you be my daughter?" Her voice was cracking with anger.

"That's not what I meant. That's not what I said."

"What you say?"

I knew it was a mistake to say anything more, but I heard my voice speaking. "Why do you have to use me to show off? If you want to show off, then why don't you learn to play chess."

My mother's eyes turned into dangerous black slits. She had no words for me, just sharp silence.

I felt the wind rushing around my hot ears. I jerked my hand out of my mother's tight grasp and spun around, knocking into an old woman. Her bag of groceries spilled to the ground.

"Aii-ya! Stupid girl!" my mother and the woman cried. Oranges and tin cans careened down the sidewalk. As my mother stooped to help the old woman pick up the escaping food, I took off.

I raced down the street, dashing between people, not looking back as my mother screamed shrilly, "Meimei! Meimei!" I fled down an alley, past dark curtained shops and merchants washing the grime off their windows. I sped into the sunlight, into a large street crowded with tourists examining trinkets and souvenirs. I ducked into another dark alley, down another street, up another alley. I ran until it hurt and I realized I had nowhere to go, that I was not running from anything. The alleys contained no escape routes.

My breath came out like angry smoke. It was cold. I sat down on an upturned plastic pail next to a stack of empty boxes, cupping my chin with my hands, thinking hard. I imagined my mother, first walking briskly down one street or another looking for me, then giving up and returning home to await my arrival. After two hours, I stood up on creaking legs and slowly walked home.

The alley was quiet and I could see the yellow lights shining from our flat like two tiger's eyes in the night. I climbed the sixteen steps to the door, advancing quietly up each so as not to make any warning sounds. I turned the knob; the door was locked. I heard a chair moving, quick steps, the locks turning—click! click! click!—and then the door opened.

"About time you got home," said Vincent. "Boy, are you in trouble."

He slid back to the dinner table. On a platter were the remains of a large fish, its fleshy head still connected to bones swimming upstream in vain escape. Standing there waiting for my punishment, I heard my mother speak in a dry voice.

"We are not concerning this girl. This girl not have concerning for us."

D

Nobody looked at me. Bone chopsticks clinked against the insides of bowls being emptied into hungry mouths.

I walked into my room, closed the door, and lay down on my bed. The room was dark, the ceiling

Words to Own

concessions (kən·sesh′ənz) *n. pl.:* acts of giving in.
careened (kə·rēnd′) *v.:* lurched sideways.

C. Literary Element: Motivation

? What does this passage suggest about the difference between the motivations of the narrator and those of her mother? [Possible answer: It may show that the narrator's mother enjoys the narrator's success because of the attention and respect it brings to the family. In contrast, the narrator does not seem to want the attention.]

D. Critical Reading: Making Inferences

? What does this comment reveal about the narrator's mother's feelings? [Possible answers: The comment shows that she was hurt by the way the narrator spoke to her earlier; she thinks the narrator is not concerned about her feelings.]

ASSESSMENT TOOLS

Check Test: True-False

1. The narrator receives her new chess set at a Christmas party. [False]
2. The narrator's first chess games were with her brothers. [True]
3. Other players are intimidated by the narrator and her appearance. [False]
4. Her brothers willingly help with chores so that Waverly may practice chess. [False]
5. The conflict in the story is about the money the narrator spends on chess. [False]

Observation Assessment Use the following scale and list of criteria to evaluate students' responses for the assignments for this selection.
1=Weak 2=Average 3=Strong

_____ Oral responses during class discussion
_____ Creative responses (other than writing)
_____ Written responses (formal or informal)
_____ Responses during small-group discussion

Then, write a short list of specific strategies that might be used to help students in each of the categories marked as weak.

A. Literary Element: Imagery
Point out that the narrator once again associates the wind with strategy and strength, as she did earlier in the story when she was describing her thought process during a chess game—but this time she uses the image to describe her struggle with her mother.

Primary Sources

Tan has said that her mother, who wanted her to be financially successful, worried about her future after she switched her major to English in college. It was only after Tan and her husband were able to buy Tan's mother a house that she began to feel better. Tan says, "That's really what success is about in Chinese families—it's not success for yourself, it's success so you can take care of your family."

filled with shadows from the dinnertime lights of neighboring flats.

In my head, I saw a chessboard with sixty-four black and white squares. Opposite me was my opponent, two angry black slits. She wore a triumphant smile. "Strongest wind cannot be seen," she said.

A

Her black men advanced across the plane, slowly marching to each successive level as a single unit. My white pieces screamed as they scurried and fell off the board one by one. As her men drew closer to my edge, I felt myself growing light. I rose up into the air and flew out the window. Higher and higher, above the alley, over the tops of tiled roofs, where I was gathered up by the wind and pushed up toward the night sky until everything below me disappeared and I was alone.

I closed my eyes and pondered my next move.

WORDS TO OWN
successive (sək·ses′iv) *adj.:* consecutive.

PRIMARY Sources | **AN INTERVIEW**

An Interview with Amy Tan

In a magazine interview, Amy Tan answered questions about her stories of mothers and daughters in *The Joy Luck Club.* Here are some of her responses:

Q: Do you have advice to offer aspiring novelists?

A: You have to develop a discipline, and you have to learn that you can't always wait for inspiration. Also, I think young writers try to imitate the people they admire, and that's dangerous. No matter how well you imitate Tama Janowitz or Jay McInerney, it doesn't work. You have to find your own voice.

Q: How do Chinese Americans like your book?

A: My feelings were so personal; I didn't think anyone else felt that way. The surprise is how many Chinese people have said, "Your stories are so much like my family." They thought I had been eavesdropping in their living rooms.

Q: How does your mother feel about your success?

A: The day the book was number four on *The New York Times* Best Seller List, I showed the list to my mother. She looked at it, laid her finger across the line, and asked, "Who's number three? And two? And one?" She's very proud, but none of this impresses her too much, and she doesn't think that I should be impressed either. But she was also saying, "I think you should be number one."

—Joan Chatfield Taylor,
"Cosmo Talks to Amy Tan"

Archive Photos.

Making Meanings

First Thoughts

1. Possible response: It is believable because it shows both the ups and the downs of their interaction with one another.

Reviewing the Text

a. Vincent receives the chess set at a church Christmas party.
b. She offers candy as replacements for the missing pieces.
c. She tells her to lose fewer pieces, relieves her from chores so that she can practice, and introduces her to people on the street.
d. Her mother's uninformed advice conflicts with Waverly's knowledge of chess. Waverly is embarrassed when her mother shows her off to people on the street.

Shaping Interpretations

2. She means that she does not want to accept anything that someone else would not value. Her children do not share her view; the boys ignore her order to throw the chess set away.

MAKING MEANINGS

First Thoughts

1. Did you find the relationship between mother and daughter believable? Why or why not?

Reviewing the Text

a. How did the Jongs get their first chess set?

b. Explain how young Waverly came to be allowed to play with her brothers.

c. Point out some of the ways in which Waverly's mother shows she is ambitious for her daughter and proud of her accomplishments.

d. As a result of Waverly's success at chess, what **conflicts** arise between her and her mother?

Shaping Interpretations

2. What does Waverly's mother mean when she says, on page 1112, "She not want it. We not want it"? How do the boys' actions show cultural and generational **conflicts** between the mother and her children?
3. Review the notes you made in your Reader's Log. How does the "power of chess" relate to the relationship between Waverly and her mother?
4. What do you think is Mrs. Jong's **motivation** for showing off Waverly? Why does Waverly resent her mother's actions?
5. Near the end of the story, Waverly's imaginary opponent says, "Strongest wind cannot be seen." Where else in the story is that statement used? Explain what you think it means.
6. What do you think is the meaning of Waverly's fantasy at the story's end? What do you predict will be her "next move"?
7. Find passages in the story where rules of various sorts are talked about. What multiple meanings might the **title** have?

CHOICES: Building Your Portfolio

Writer's Notebook

1. Collecting Ideas for an Evaluation

In a review of *The Joy Luck Club,* the critic Susan Dooley wrote: "These women from China find trying to talk to their daughters like trying to plug a foreign appliance into an American outlet. The current won't work. Impulses collide and nothing flows through the wires except anger and exasperation." Write your thoughts on how well this critical evaluation applies to "Rules of the Game." Use specific examples from the story as well as your personal comments. Save your notes for possible use in the Writer's Workshop on page 1181.

Critical Writing

2. Switch 'em!

In a brief essay, tell what you think would happen if Mrs. Jong and Cukita's mother (from Julia Alvarez's story on page 1079) were to enter each other's story. If Mrs. Jong could be brought into Alvarez's story, whose side would she take—the mother's or the father's? If Cukita's mother could be introduced to Mrs. Jong, what advice would she give Mrs. Jong?

Speaking and Listening

3. End Around, Slam-Dunk, Endgame

Choose a sport or game familiar to you and other class members. Working in groups, prepare oral reports on the etiquette of the game—its unwritten rules, examples of gamesmanship, and the terms used to describe its special maneuvers or plays. Before you begin, review Tan's discussion of the "language" of chess on page 1113.

Choices: Building Your Portfolio

1. **Writer's Notebook** Remind students to save their work. They may use it as prewriting for the Writer's Workshop on p. 1181.
2. **Critical Writing** Briefly review as a class the descriptions of the narrator's mother in "Daughter of Invention." Ask students to use a two-column chart or cluster diagram to organize information about both characters.
3. **Speaking and Listening** Brainstorm as a class to create a list of games and their rules. Encourage students to consider a variety of games, including computer games and television quiz shows, with which they might be familiar.

Choices: Assessment Criteria For help in evaluating these Choices assignments, see the criteria in the *Portfolio Management System,* p. 202.

3. Waverly tricks her mother into letting her play in the tournament by using a chess-like strategy to anticipate how she will react.
4. Mrs. Jong's motives probably center on pride in her daughter's accomplishments and a desire to share in her victories. Waverly resents her mother's actions because she is embarrassed by all of the attention.
5. The wind uses a similar expression when giving advice to her during her first tournament. Perhaps the statement refers to the importance of keeping strategies or feelings secret from an opponent.
6. Waverly may be trying to understand her conflict with her mother by comparing it to something at which she is skilled: chess. Her next move may be to try to use the conflict to strengthen their relationship.
7. Many unspoken rules may be found in the story: how to talk to Santa Claus, how to communicate with parents, and how to deal with conflict. The title could refer to chess, to family relationships, or to life.

How to Own a Word

Mini-Lesson: Base Words, Roots, and Word Families

Remind the class that not all roots come from Greek or Latin. Point out that learning the meanings of roots, prefixes, and suffixes is one of the best ways to prepare to read more challenging materials and to study for standardized tests. Emphasize to students that every time they learn a new prefix, suffix or root word, they are acquiring a key that will help them unlock the meanings of many words.

Try It Out: Possible Answers

1. *–bene–;* benefit, benign
2. *–audi–;* audience, audible
3. *–ver–;* invert, vertex
4. *–pos–;* position; oppose
5. *–sacr–, –sanc–;* sacrament; sanctify

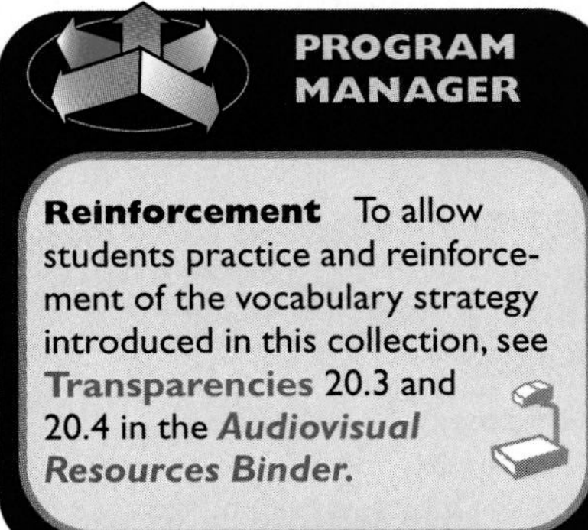

Reinforcement To allow students practice and reinforcement of the vocabulary strategy introduced in this collection, see **Transparencies** 20.3 and 20.4 in the ***Audiovisual Resources Binder.***

How to Own a Word

Base Words, Roots, and Word Families

Amy Tan opens "Rules of the Game" with a Christmas party at which the narrator receives a gift after satisfactorily answering a set of questions.

> He then *solemnly* asked if I had been a very, very good girl this year and did I believe in Jesus Christ and obey my parents. I knew the only answer to that. I nodded back with equal *solemnity.*

Notice the appropriateness of the narrator's answer. Tan uses a noun to describe the manner of the answer (*solemnity*) that is nearly identical to the adverb used to describe the tone of the question (*solemnly*). The two words, *solemnly* and *solemnity,* belong to the same word family.

In general, there are two broad categories of words in English: those that can be divided into smaller parts (*unkind, repackage*) and those that cannot (*proud, high*). Words that stand alone and are complete by themselves are called **base words:** *solemn, answer, equal.* Words that can be divided (*solemnity, equality*) are made up of two or more of these three word parts: **roots, prefixes, suffixes.** Roots are word parts that carry the core meaning of a word, but usually do not stand alone (the root *graph* is an exception). Most often, they are combined with a prefix and/or suffix to form a word. Words that share the same root or base word can be considered word families.

In the English language, many words are formed from Greek and Latin roots. To the right are some examples of common word roots.

Common Word Roots		
Root	**Meaning**	**Examples**
GREEK		
–anthrop–	human	anthropology
–chrom–	color	monochrome
–dem–	people	demagogue, democrat
–derm–	skin	dermatology
–log–, –logy–	study, word	logic, theology
–ortho–	straight	orthodox, orthography
–phil–	like, love	philanthropy
LATIN		
–audi–	hear	audio, auditorium
–ben–, –bene–	good	benign, beneficial
–cogn–	know	recognize
–duc–, –duct–	draw, lead	induce, deduct
–loc–	place	locality, locate
–magn–	large, grand	magnify, magnitude
–mor–, –mort–	death	moribund, mortal
–omni–	all	omniscient
–pon–, –pos–	place	impose, postpone
–prim–	early	primeval, primitive
–sacr–, –sanc–	sacred, holy	sacrilege
–spir–	breath	expire, inspire
–uni–	one	unify, universe
–ver–	turn	reverse, aversion

Try It Out

Following are some other words that Amy Tan uses in "Rules of the Game." Identify the word roots. Then find at least two other words that belong to the same word family, using a dictionary if necessary. Do not include forms whose only difference is an **inflectional suffix**—a suffix that changes person, number, or tense (*–s, –ed, –ing*). Compare your answers with a partner's responses.

1. benefactor
2. auditorium
3. adversaries
4. opponent
5. sacrifice

Options for Teaching

Strategies for Inclusion

Advanced Ask students to use the list of roots above and prefixes or suffixes of their own choice to build neologisms that make creative use of the word parts' meanings or connotations. Encourage students to create puns or other humorous words, but remind them to develop only words that would be appropriate to share aloud in class.

Crossing the Curriculum

Science Assign pairs of students to review different pages from a science textbook or dictionary of scientific terms. Ask each pair to find five words on their assigned page that are based on Greek or Latin roots, prefixes, or suffixes. Ask them to list any nonscientific words that may use the same word parts. Create a class master list of students' terms.

Garrett Hongo

(1951–)

"For me, one voice among so many others, a voice I've tried to train as much out of a passion for English and American poetry as out of my loyalties to the Japanese American past of four generations and to the landscape of Hawaii, the place of my birth, it has been a *feeling* for language and its beauty that has brought me to poetry and kept me at it."

In this one long sentence, Garrett Hongo seems to unite all the most vital elements that characterize his work: a distinctive voice, a passion for poetry, loyalty to past generations, a sense of place, and a love of language itself.

Garrett Hongo was born in Volcano, Hawaii, and grew up on the North Shore of Oahu and in the Los Angeles area. He graduated from Pomona College in 1973 and earned a Master of Fine Arts degree from the University of California, Irvine, in 1980. His first poetry collection, *Yellow Light,* was published in 1982. But it was his second collection, *The River of Heaven* (1988), that made a strong impression on literary critics. The book was chosen as the Lamont Poetry Selection of the Academy of American Poets and was a finalist for a Pulitzer Prize. While writing, Hongo taught at the University of Missouri and the University of Houston before becoming professor of English at the University of Oregon. In 1995, he published a well-received prose work, *Volcano: A Memoir of Hawaii.*

Garrett Hongo's poems often center on the complexities facing Americans of Asian descent as they labor to establish a personal identity, interact with people of other backgrounds, and express themselves artistically. His poems also overflow with the common details of contemporary American popular culture, such as television shows and pop music, all delivered in a language and style that blends passion and delicacy.

Hongo says that he strives for "emotional nobility of some kind, the idea that poems might help produce and reveal our 'better nature.'" He reaches for "the *jen* of Confucianism which was a notion of the innate moral and spiritual 'good' in people that impressed Ezra Pound as one of the highest poetic values; and the idea of *samadhi,* or sensate and sentient calm, that we get from Buddhism."

Charles Wright.

Hongo's wife, his friends, his fellow poets, all those who share his ideals—these are his audience, he tells us. Yet he adds with pride, "I think I must say that I write for my father, Albert Kazuyoshi Hongo, in a very personal way. I want to be his witness, to testify to his great and noble life, in struggle against anger, in struggle against his own loneliness and isolation for being a Hawaiian Japanese who emigrated to Los Angeles without much family or community. He was a great example to me of a man who refused to hate, or, being different himself, to be afraid of difference, who accepted the friendship of all the strange and underprivileged ostracized by the rest of 'normal' society—Vietnamese, Mexicans, Southern blacks, reservation Indians relocated to the city—and I want my poems to be equal to his heart." The following poem certainly is devoted to that goal.

QUICK PLANNING GUIDE

Into the Poem

Through the Poem

Beyond the Poem

WRITERS ON WRITING

Garrett Hongo says that when he was a freshman in college, he made the important discovery that the poets he heard at readings were "the truth-tellers, the passionate ones. . . . There was something in their speaking that changed me. There was an integrity to it, and also an incredible willingness to face difficult issues. . . . There was a greatness to it that impressed and stirred me."

PORTFOLIO ASSESSMENT

Portfolio Assessment For help with teacher assessment of reading skills, see the ***Portfolio Management System,*** pp. 54–55.

Using **Before You Read**
p. 1122

Reading Focus

Ask students to think about the ways in which language is used to express a variety of feelings and ideas. To start a discussion, ask volunteers to suggest expressions: compliments, warnings, insults, sayings, stories, teachings, prayers, and jokes. Ask students to explain the purposes of each type of expression.

A Dialogue with the Text

Remind students that details in a poem take the form of images that re-create the speaker's emotions or experiences. As students read, ask them to list the senses to which the images in this poem appeal.

A. Expansion
Point out that in the early years of this century, many Japanese citizens came to Hawaii to work on sugar cane plantations, where they endured difficult living and working conditions. Hongo's family worked in the fields for two generations before his parents, his grandparents, and he came to live and work in California.

Before You Read
What For

Reading Focus

Language Matters
Sometimes we forget that language matters—it affects us in many important ways, whether it is spoken or written. The poem that follows zeroes in on spoken language—old Hawaiian chants, Buddhist mantras, the stories and songs of grandparents. We learn from language, the poem's speaker tells us, and we try to change the world with spoken words and syllables passed from generation to generation.

A Dialogue with the Text

As you read, write down details from the poem that you feel are particularly vivid or interesting.

Elements of Literature

Refrain
A **refrain** is a word, phrase, line, or group of lines that is repeated several times in a poem. A poet may use a refrain to help establish rhythm, to emphasize a point, or to achieve some other effect. Short refrains typically appear at the ends of lines, but in the following poem they appear at the beginnings of lines.

What For

Garrett Hongo

At six I lived for spells:
how a few Hawaiian words could call
up the rain, could hymn like the sea
in the long swirl of chambers
curling in the nautilus of a shell,
how Amida's° ballads of the Buddhaland
in the drone of the priest's liturgy
could conjure money from the poor
and give them nothing but mantras,°
the strange syllables that healed desire.

A I lived for stories about the war
my grandfather told over *hana* cards,°
slapping them down on the mats
with a sharp Japanese *kiai.*°

6. Amida's: *Amida* is Japanese for "Amitābha," Sanskrit for "infinite light." Amida is the great savior worshiped by members of the Pure Land sect, one of the most popular forms of Buddhism in eastern Asia.
9. mantras: hymns or other portions of sacred Hindu text, chanted or intoned as incantations or prayers.
12. *hana* cards: cards used in a Japanese game in which players attempt to match pairs of flower patterns. *Hana* is Japanese for "flower."
14. *kiai:* a Japanese onomatopoeic word for the sound made by slapping down *hana* cards.

PROGRAM MANAGER

- **Planning Instruction** See Teaching Notes, *Teaching Resources B,* p. 187, for objectives, a summary, and literary elements for this selection.
- **Instructional Support** Before beginning the instructional lesson, see Graphic Organizer for Active Reading, *Teaching Resources B,* p. 201, for a Through the Poem activity.
- **Audiotaped Readings** To help less proficient readers or auditory learners through the lesson, use the Selected Reading, Audiocassette 3, Side B, in the *Audiovisual Resources Binder.*

- **Assessment** See Selection Test, *Test Booklet,* pp. 255–256.

I lived for songs my grandmother sang
stirring curry into a thick stew,
weaving a calligraphy of Kannon's° love
into grass mats and straw sandals.

I lived for the red volcano dirt
staining my toes, the salt residue
of surf and sea wind in my hair,
the arc of a flat stone skipping
in the hollow trough of a wave.

I lived a child's world, waited
for my father to drag himself home,
dusted with blasts of sand, powdered rock,
and the strange ash of raw cement,
his deafness made worse by the clang
of pneumatic drills, sore in his bones

17. Kannon's: In Japanese Buddhism, Kannon is the bodhisattva ("Buddha to be") of infinite compassion and mercy.

B. Reader's Response: First Thoughts

? What attitudes toward his grandparents does the speaker reveal in this and the previous stanza? [Sample responses: His tone and the details he gives about them show that he cares for them and respects their legacy; or he sees them as examples of the way that language is used to pass down family traditions.]

C. Literary Element: Refrain

Point out the repeated phrase "*I lived*" in the second, third, fourth, and fifth stanzas. Ask students to look for another refrain ("*I wanted to*") in the final stanzas of poem.

OPTIONS FOR TEACHING

STRATEGIES FOR INCLUSION

Special Needs Students who have difficulty understanding the concentrated imagery in poetry often benefit from prereading activities that introduce images or ideas from the poems they will read. Help students prepare to read and respond to this poem by showing them photographs or illustrations of some of its images before they begin to read. Discuss the illustrations as a class.

English Language Development Before students read, give them this list of words from the poem: *liturgy* and *conjure* (p. 1122), *calligraphy* (p. 1123), and *fragrant* (p. 1124). Read aloud the phrases from the poem in which the words occur. Ask students to write possible definitions for the words. Then, ask students to look up definitions for the words and to compare them to their predicted definitions.

A. Critical Reading: Finding Details

? What details in this stanza suggest the importance of language in the speaker's relationship with his father? [Possible answer: He is concerned about the effect that work has on his father's hearing; he invents names for his father and tells them to him when he comes home.]

B. Critical Reading: Summarizing

? How does the speaker want to heal his father? [Possible answer: He says that he wants to ease his father's pain by using magic words and chanted blessings.]

from the buckings of a jackhammer.
(A) He'd hand me a scarred lunchpail,
let me unlace the hightop G.I. boots,
call him the new name I'd invented
that day in school, write it for him
on his newspaper. He'd rub my face
with hands that felt like gravel roads,
tell me to move, go play, and then he'd
walk to the laundry sink to scrub,
rinse the dirt of his long day
from a face brown and grained as koa° wood.

(B) I wanted to take away the pain
in his legs, the swelling in his joints,
give him back his hearing,
clear and rare as crystal chimes,
the fins of glass that wrinkled
and sparked the air with their sound.

I wanted to heal the sores that work
and war had sent to him,
let him play catch in the backyard
with me, tossing a tennis ball
past papaya trees without the shoulders
of pain shrugging back his arms.

I wanted to become a doctor of pure magic,
to string a necklace of sweet words
fragrant as pine needles and plumeria,°
fragrant as the bread my mother baked,
place it like a lei of cowrie shells
and *pikake*° flowers around my father's neck,
and chant him a blessing, a sutra.°

40. koa: Hawaiian mimosa tree valued for its wood and bark.

55. plumeria: classification of fragrant, flowering, tropical American trees.
58. *pikake:* Hawaiian for "Arabian jasmine."
59. sutra: in general, one of the sacred scriptures of Buddhism.

OPTIONS FOR TEACHING

INTEGRATING THE LANGUAGE ARTS

Strategic Reading Divide the class into groups of four. Ask each group to perform a collaborative reading of the poem for the class. Let students determine how the poem will be read, deciding who will read which lines and how the readers will communicate ideas and feelings. Emphasize that everyone in the group must participate in the reading and in the decision-making process.

CROSSING THE CURRICULUM

Geography Before students read the poem, prepare and distribute a handout containing information about the Hawaiian Islands, including historical and cultural details that will help students to better understand the poem. After students have read the poem, ask them to re-read the handout and to write a short paragraph explaining what information in the handout helped them to appreciate the poem more.

PRIMARY **Sources** | AN ESSAY

A Different Story

In this excerpt from a personal essay, Garrett Hongo remembers his maternal grandfather, who was known by his last name, Kubota. During most of Hongo's childhood and adolescence, Kubota lived with the poet's family near Los Angeles, California. The grandfather is also remembered in "What For."

I was a teenager and, though I was bored listening to stories I'd heard often enough before at holiday dinners, I was dutiful. I took my spot on the couch next to Kubota and heard him out. Usually, he'd tell me about his schooling in Japan where he learned judo along with mathematics and literature. He'd learned the *soroban* there—the abacus, which was the original pocket calculator of the Far East—and that, along with his strong, judo-trained back, got him his first job in Hawaii. This was the moral. "Study *ha-ahd,*" he'd say with pidgin emphasis. "Learn read good. Learn speak da kine *good* English." The message is the familiar one taught to any children of immigrants: succeed through education. And imitation. But this time, Kubota reached down into his past and told me a different story. I was thirteen by then, and I suppose he thought me ready for it. He told me about Pearl Harbor, how the planes flew in wing after wing of formations over his old house in La'ie in Hawaii, and how, the next day, after Roosevelt had made his famous "Day of Infamy" speech about the treachery of the Japanese, the FBI agents had come to his door and taken him in, hauled him off to Honolulu for questioning, and held him without charge for several days. I thought he was lying. I thought he was making up a kind of horror story to shock me and give his moral that much more starch. But it was true. I asked around. I brought it up during history class in junior high school, and my teacher, after silencing me and stepping me off to the back of the room, told me that it was indeed so. I asked my mother and she said it was true. I asked my schoolmates, who laughed and ridiculed me for being so ignorant. We lived in a Japanese-American community, and the parents of most of my classmates were the *nisei* who had been interned as teenagers all through the war. . . .

I was not made yet, and [Kubota] was determined that his stories be part of my making. He spoke quietly at first, mildly, but once into his narrative and after his drink was down, his voice would rise and quaver with resentment and he'd make his accusations. He gave his testimony to me and I held it at first cautiously in my conscience like it was an heirloom too delicate to expose to strangers and anyone outside of the world Kubota made with his words. "I give you story now," he once said, "and you learn speak good, eh?" It was my job, as the disciple of his preaching I had then become, Ananda to his Buddha, to reassure him with a promise. "You learn speak good like the Dillingham," he'd say another time, referring to the wealthy scion of the grower family who had once run, unsuccessfully, for one of Hawaii's first senatorial seats. Or he'd then invoke a magical name, the name of one of his heroes, a man he thought particularly exemplary and righteous. "Learn speak dah good Ing-rish like *Mistah Inouye,*" Kubota shouted. "He *lick* dah Dillingham even in debate. I saw on *terre-bision* myself." He was remembering the debates before the first senatorial election just before Hawaii was admitted to the Union as its fiftieth state. "You *tell* story," Kubota would end. And I had my injunction.

—Garrett Hongo
from "Kubota"

Primary Sources

After students have read the excerpt, ask them to re-read "What For" and to make notes on the lines in which Hongo mentions songs, stories or other special uses of language. Point out that in both this excerpt and the poem, Hongo writes about how his parents' and grandparents' words and stories have shaped his life and his work.

OPTIONS FOR TEACHING

STRATEGIES FOR INCLUSION

Less Proficient Readers Before reading the Primary Sources excerpt with the class, discuss the definitions, synonyms, and connotations of these important words from it: *heirloom, disciple, testimony,* and *injunction.* After students read the excerpt, ask them to copy the sentences from the story which contain the words. Then, ask them to paraphrase each sentence in their own words. Call on students to read their new sentences aloud.

Interpersonal After students have read the Primary Sources excerpt, place students in small groups and ask them to discuss these questions.

- Why might Hongo's grandfather Kubota place such a value on learning to speak English well?
- In what way is Hongo's writing and poetry a response to his grandfather's injunction?

Call on a member from each group to read aloud the group's responses to the questions.

Beyond the Poem

Choices: Building Your Portfolio

1. **Writer's Notebook** Remind students to save their work. They may use it as prewriting for the Writer's Workshop on p. 1181.
2. **Critical Writing** Before students begin the activity, discuss the difference between concrete detail and abstract generalizations. Point out that most images are generally made up of concrete details.
3. **Critical Writing** Briefly review the elements that go into a writer's style: sentence length and complexity, diction, use of figurative language, imagery, repetition, and concrete details.
4. **Creative Writing** Ask students to brainstorm about what the father might have wanted to do for his son. If they find this too difficult, ask them to imagine that they are fathers (or mothers) writing about what they would want for their children.

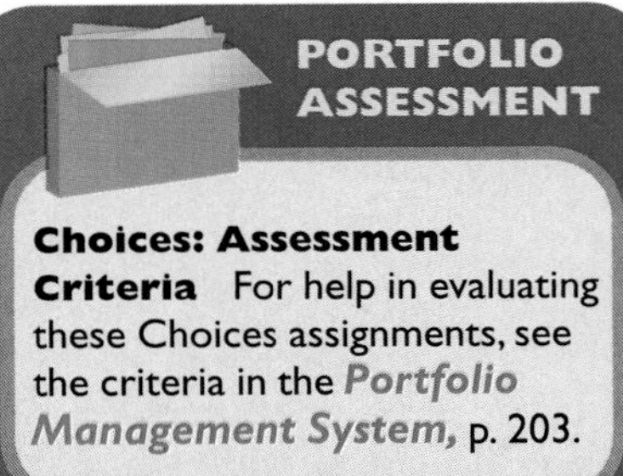

PORTFOLIO ASSESSMENT

Choices: Assessment Criteria For help in evaluating these Choices assignments, see the criteria in the *Portfolio Management System,* p. 203.

Making Meanings

First Thoughts

1. What **images** stood out for you as you read the poem? Why were they so effective?

Shaping Interpretations

2. What do you think the speaker means in the line "I wanted to become a doctor of pure magic"?
3. What does the title of the poem mean?
4. Identify the two **refrains** of the poem. What effects do each of them have?

Extending the Text

5. In Primary Sources (page 1125), Garrett Hongo remembers holding his grandfather's "testimony" in his mind "like it was an heirloom." How do you think the testimony of previous generations comes down to us?

Left, A. K. Hongo (Garrett Hongo's father) on the docks of Honolulu Harbor, shipping out to Oakland, then boot camp, then Italy (1944).

Courtesy Garrett Hongo.

Choices: Building Your Portfolio

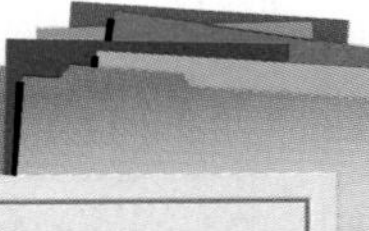

Writer's Notebook

1. Collecting Ideas for an Evaluation

Establishing criteria for evaluating the emotional impact of a poem (or other work of art) is not easy. You might consider the power of the emotional effect, whether it appeals to sentiment or to more complex feelings, or whether it changes you in any way. Establish your own criteria for evaluating emotional impact, and then apply them to Hongo's "What For." Save your notes for possible use in the Writer's Workshop on page 1181.

Critical Writing

2. Concretions of Detail

Hongo includes an amazing amount of concrete detail in "What For." Review the notes you made in your Reader's Log. Then write a short essay in which you discuss the effect of supplying so much detail. Would the poem be very different if it were made up mainly of abstract generalizations? Why or why not?

Critical Writing

3. Walt Whitman Redux?

Some critics say Garrett Hongo's style is similar to Walt Whitman's, partly because both poets frequently repeat words, word order, and phrasing and often include catalogs of concrete items. Do you agree? Pick a poem or two by Whitman (pages 352–362), and in a brief essay compare and contrast Whitman's style with Hongo's style in "What For."

Creative Writing

4. The Father's Poem

What might the father in Hongo's poem have thought of his son and his son's attitude toward him? Have the father tell us in a poem whose structure and style resemble the final three stanzas of "What For."

Making Meanings

First Thoughts

1. Possible responses: The ocean, sea shells, card games, flowers, and the descriptions of the father as he comes home from work. They are effective because they are so vivid.

Shaping Interpretations

2. Possible response: He wants to heal his father's pain with words, perhaps by writing a poem that would express his love for him.
3. It may indicate that the speaker is explaining what his father and grandparents lived for or what was important about them. It may also be an idiomatic expression.
4. The refrain in the first part of the poem is "I lived." The refrain of the final three stanzas is "I wanted." The "I lived" stanzas introduce a child who passively takes in images and words. The "I wanted" stanzas show the child wanting to use words to heal his father.

Extending the Text

5. **(Evaluation)** Possible responses: Through stories, legends, traditions, and prayers.

THE CREATED SELF

Theme: Establishing Identity

Personal identity is shaped by several factors: where we came from, what we experience on a daily basis, and what we wish to do or become. All these circumstances play an integral part in defining who we are.

Thematic Focus

The following selections illustrate ways in which individuals have forged their unique selves.

- **New African** A young girl's stand is part of her entry into adulthood.
- **Autobiographical Notes** For a writer, self-assessment is a part of self-creation.
- **Mirror** A personified mirror reveals a woman's hopes and fears.
- **Literature of the Americas: Borges and Myself** The author playfully explores the line between the existing and the created self.
- **The Fifteenth Summer** A boy ponders the world's immensity and his place in it.
- **Straw into Gold** The author finds herself transforming raw material of life into literature.
- **The Latin Deli: An Ars Poetica** Language and culture are vital to self-expression.
- **The Satisfaction Coal Company** Remembered moments illuminate identity.

Literary Focus

Literary Element	Selection / Feature
Internal Conflict	**New African**
Personification	**Mirror**
Rhyme Scheme	**The Fifteenth Summer**
Allusion	**Straw into Gold**
Concrete and Abstract Language	**The Latin Deli: An Ars Poetica**

Writing Focus

The following flow chart shows how the writing assignment for each selection builds toward the culminating writing assignment in the Writer's Workshop at the end of the unit.

Selection	Work-in-Progress Assignment
New African	Evaluate three details from a story p. 1140
Autobiographical Notes	Examine Baldwin's objectivity p. 1147
Mirror	Provide background information p. 1151
The Fifteenth Summer	Evaluate Merrill's poem p. 1157
Straw into Gold	List criteria for an autobiography p. 1165
The Latin Deli: An Ars Poetica	Compare definitions of poetry p. 1169
The Satisfaction Coal Company	Make a judgment p. 1176
Writer's Workshop	Write an evaluation of a work pp. 1181–1185

Collection Planner

SELECTION/ FEATURE	PUPIL'S EDITION			
	Literary Elements / Active Reading	Writing	Speaking and Listening	Language and Vocabulary
New African Andrea Lee (pp. 1128–1140)	• Reader's Log p. 1129 • Internal Conflict p. 1129	• Critical Writing: Write essay describing Sarah or her father p. 1140 • Creative Writing: Write first-person narrative from young person's point of view p. 1140	• Creative Writing: Read your narrative aloud for the class p. 1140	
Autobiographical Notes James Baldwin (pp. 1141–1147)	• Reader's Log p. 1142	• Critical Writing: Write essay on the effect of the past on the present p. 1147 • Critical Writing: Compare diction and tone of Baldwin's selection to Emerson selection (p. 224) p. 1147 • Creative Writing/ Speaking and Listening: Respond to point in Baldwin selection p. 1147	• Creative Writing/ Speaking and Listening: Share with class your response to point in selection p. 1147	
Mirror Sylvia Plath (pp. 1148–1151) **Connections: A Strange Beautiful Woman** Marion Nelson Waniek **The Face in the Mirror** Robert Graves (p. 1150)	• Reader's Log p. 1149 • Personification p. 1149	• Critical Writing: Write comparison-contrast essay about poems p. 1151 • Creative Writing: Write poem or prose paragraph describing your version of talking mirror p. 1151	• Art: Draw, paint, or make collage of what you see in mirror p. 1151	
Literature of the Americas: Borges and Myself Jorge Luis Borges (pp. 1152–1154)			• Finding Common Ground: Discuss selection in small groups p. 1154	
The Fifteenth Summer James Merrill (pp. 1155–1157)	• Reader's Log p. 1156 • Rhyme Scheme p. 1156	• Critical Writing: Write essay discussing use of rhyme in this selection p. 1157 • Creative Writing: Write poem reflecting on past experience p. 1157	• Creative Writing: Share with class your poem about past experience p. 1157	
Straw into Gold Sandra Cisneros (pp. 1158–1165)	• Reader's Log p. 1159 • Allusion p. 1159	• Critical Writing: Write essay discussing main idea of selection p. 1165 • Critical Writing: Write essay describing examples of multicultural combinations p. 1165		

Collection Resources

Teaching Resources B	Audiovisual Resources Binder	Test Booklet
Cross-Curricular Activity p. 222	Fine Art Transparency 21.1	Collection Test pp. 273–275

 Computer disk or CD-ROM
 Audiocassette
 Overhead Transparency

PROGRAM RESOURCES

Electronic Media	Teaching Resources with Organizer: Teaching Resources B	Teaching Resources with Organizer: Other Resources	Audiovisual Resources Binder
• Test Generator (Computer disk or CD-ROM)	• Teaching Notes p. 203 • Reading Organizer p. 207 • Words to Own p. 208	• Test Booklet: Selection Test pp. 261–262 • Portfolio Management System pp. 39, 204	
• Test Generator (Computer disk or CD-ROM)	• Teaching Notes pp. 203–204 • Reading Organizer p. 209 • Language Link pp. 210–211 • Words to Own p. 212	• Test Booklet: Selection Test pp. 263–264 • Portfolio Management System pp. 48–49, 205	• Selected Reading Audiocassette 3, Side B (Audiocassette)
• Test Generator (Computer disk or CD-ROM)	• Teaching Notes p. 204 • Reading Organizer p. 213	• Test Booklet: Selection Test pp. 265–266 • Portfolio Management System p. 206	• Selected Reading Audiocassette 3, Side B (Audiocassette)
	• Teaching Notes pp. 204–205		• Selected Reading Audiocassette 3, Side B (Audiocassette)
• Test Generator (Computer disk or CD-ROM)	• Teaching Notes p. 205 • Reading Organizer p. 214	• Test Booklet: Selection Test pp. 265–266 • Portfolio Management System pp. 54–55, 207	
• Test Generator (Computer disk or CD-ROM)	• Teaching Notes p. 205 • Reading Organizer p. 215 • Words to Own p. 216	• Test Booklet: Selection Test pp. 267–268 • Portfolio Management System pp. 39, 208	• Elements of Literature Transparency 21.2 (Overhead Transparency)

Collection 21 **THE CREATED SELF**

Collection Planner

SELECTION/ FEATURE	PUPIL'S EDITION			
	Literary Elements / Active Reading	Writing	Speaking and Listening	Language and Vocabulary
The Latin Deli: An Ars Poetica Judith Ortiz Cofer (pp. 1166–1169)	• Reader's Log p. 1167 • Concrete and Abstract Language p. 1167	• Critical Writing/ Music: Write essay analyzing musical qualities of Cofer's poem p. 1169	• Art: Make collage or painting that unites numerous images of one subject p. 1169	
The Satisfaction Coal Company Rita Dove (pp. 1170–1176) Student to Student (p. 1175)	• Reader's Log p. 1171	• Critical Writing: Write essay explaining how moment of discovery applies to selection p. 1176	• Research/ Speaking and Listening: Organize panel discussion with other students on position of U.S. poet laureate p. 1176	
The American Language High Tech's Influence Gary Q. Arpin (pp. 1178–1180)				• Try It Out: Technological terms p. 1180
Writer's Workshop: Evaluation (pp. 1181–1185)		• Writing process: Evaluation pp. 1181–1185		
Language Workshop: Using Effective Diction (p. 1186)				• Language Handbook: Glossary of usage pp. 1252–1257 • Using effective diction p. 1186
Learning for Life: Celebrating Cultural Diversity (p. 1187)		• Write feature article p. 1187 • Develop advertising campaign p. 1187	• Make multimedia presentation p. 1187	

Collection Resources

Teaching Resources B	Audiovisual Resources Binder	Test Booklet
Cross-Curricular Activity p. 222	Fine Art Transparency 21.1	Collection Test pp. 273–275

 Computer disk or CD-ROM

 Audiocassette

 Overhead Transparency

PROGRAM RESOURCES

Electronic Media	Teaching Resources with Organizer		Audiovisual Resources Binder
	Teaching Resources B	Other Resources	
• Test Generator	• Teaching Notes p. 206 • Reading Organizer p. 217	• Test Booklet: Selection Test pp. 269–270 • Portfolio Management System pp. 53, 209	• Selected Reading Audiocassette 3, Side B
• Test Generator	• Teaching Notes p. 206 • Reading Organizer p. 218	• Test Booklet: Selection Test pp. 269–270 • Portfolio Management System p. 210	
• Test Generator	• Teaching Notes p. 206	• Test Booklet: Selection Test pp. 271–272	
• Writer's Workshop 2: Evaluation		• Portfolio Management System pp. 211–213	• Revision Transparencies 21.3–21.4
	• Language Workshop p. 219–221		
		• Portfolio Management System p. 214	

COLLECTION PLANNER

Proofreading Warm-ups

You may use the following exercises to help students practice their proofreading skills. Copy a set of incorrect sentences onto the chalkboard, and have students find and correct the spelling, punctuation, usage, and mechanical errors in each sentence. Ask students to share and discuss their responses.

	Sentences with Errors	Sentences Corrected	Skills Covered
1	**a.** upon reading the poem Autobiographia Literaria the last stanza was delightful **b.** has you ever imagined yourself, as a wrighter of poems, like Frank O'Hara	**a.** Upon reading the poem "Autobiographia Literaria," I thought that the last stanza was delightful. **b.** Have you ever imagined yourself as a writer of poems like Frank O'Hara?	Capitalization, Quotation marks for poem titles, Comma usage, Dangling modifiers, Subject-verb agreement, Spelling, End marks
2	**a.** andrea lee a well educated contemperary writer **b.** she has contributed regular to The New Yorker a weekly magazine for along time	**a.** Andrea Lee is a well-educated contemporary writer. **b.** She has contributed regularly to The New Yorker, a weekly magazine, for a long time.	Capitalization, Fragments, Hyphen usage, Spelling, Nonstandard usage, Underline magazine titles, Comma usage, End marks
3	**a.** the Philosopher Socrates beleived that only the examined life was worth liveing intoned Ms. Phillips **b.** as you will see upon reading todays assignment James Baldwin took Socrates dictum to heart she said	**a.** "The philosopher Socrates believed that only the examined life was worth living," intoned Ms. Phillips. **b.** "As you will see upon reading today's assignment, James Baldwin took Socrates' dictum to heart," she said.	Quotation marks, Capitalization, Spelling, Comma usage, Apostrophe usage, End marks
4	**a.** between you and I confided Tawana I think the poem Mirror is real good **b.** "i especially like Sylvia Plaths use of personification its so effective" she said	**a.** "Between you and me," confided Tawana, "I think the poem 'Mirror' is really good." **b.** "I especially like Sylvia Plath's use of personification; it's so effective," she said.	Quotation marks, Capitalization, Pronoun usage, Comma usage, Quotation marks for poem titles, Single quotation marks, Nonstandard usage, Apostrophe usage, Semicolon usage, End marks
5	**a.** jorge luis borges, born in Buenos Aires the capitol of Argentina **b.** his long list of publications include the poetry collection "Elogio de la sombra"	**a.** Jorge Luis Borges was born in Buenos Aires, the capital of Argentina. **b.** His long list of publications includes the poetry collection Elogio de la sombra.	Capitalization, Comma usage, Fragments, Spelling, Subject-verb agreement, Underline book titles, End marks
6	**a.** james merrill an american poet uses Rhyme scheme good **b.** the rhyme scheme of The Fifteenth Summer is a integral part of the poems overall affect	**a.** James Merrill, an American poet, uses rhyme scheme well. **b.** The rhyme scheme of "The Fifteenth Summer" is an integral part of the poem's overall effect.	Capitalization, Comma usage, Nonstandard usage, Quotation marks for poem titles, Apostrophe usage, Spelling, End marks
7	**a.** is a reference to someone or something a allusion or a illusion **b.** its allusion spelled w/ a a	**a.** Is a reference to someone or something an allusion or an illusion? **b.** It's allusion, spelled with an a.	Capitalization, Nonstandard usage, Question marks, Apostrophe usage, Comma usage, Write out abbreviations, Underline letters, End marks
8	**a.** ars poetica is latin for "the art of poetry **b.** in anceint Rome the poet Horace (65–8 B.C. wrote a treatise called Ars Poetica	**a.** Ars poetica is Latin for "the art of poetry." **b.** In ancient Rome the poet Horace (65–8 B.C.) wrote a treatise called Ars Poetica.	Capitalization, Underline foreign words and phrases, Quotation marks, Spelling, Comma usage, Parentheses usage, Underline book titles, End marks
9	**a.** a large amount of writers hope to have thier poems published, and appreciated **b.** rita dove a poet laureate of The United States beleives our Country thrives on symbolism	**a.** A large number of writers hope to have their poems published and appreciated. **b.** Rita Dove, a poet laureate of the United States, believes our country thrives on symbolism.	Capitalization, Number/Amount usage, Spelling, Comma usage, End marks
10	**a.** alot of acronyms, have sprang, from computer technology **b.** RAM an acronym for "random access memory is but won example	**a.** A lot of acronyms have sprung from computer technology. **b.** RAM, an acronym for "random access memory," is but one example.	Capitalization, Spelling, Comma usage, Verb errors, Quotation marks, End marks, Homonyms

Collection 21

THE CREATED SELF

Lee
Baldwin
Plath
Borges
Merrill
Cisneros
Cofer
Dove

Autobiographia Literaria

When I was a child
I played by myself in a
corner of the schoolyard
all alone.

I hated dolls and I
hated games, animals were
not friendly and birds
flew away.

If anyone was looking
for me I hid behind a
tree and cried out "I am
an orphan."

And here I am, the
center of all beauty!
writing these poems!
Imagine!

—Frank O'Hara (1926–1966)

"Autobiographia Literaria"

? How does the speaker say he has changed since he was a child? What is the cause of the change? [Possible response: The speaker was a shy, uncertain, and lonely child, but now he is confident and proud because he writes poetry.]

PORTFOLIO ASSESSMENT

Parent/Guardian Involvement For forms that will help a parent or guardian review and respond to a student's portfolio, see the *Portfolio Management System,* pp. 62–63.

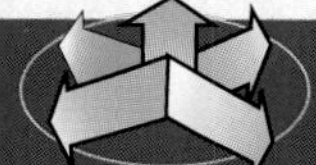

PROGRAM MANAGER

- **Integrated Assessment** For a summative assessment of the literature and language skills taught in this collection, see Collection 21 Test, *Test Booklet,* pp. 273–275.
- **Extending Collection Theme** See Cross-Curricular Activity: The Created Self, *Teaching Resources B,* p. 222, for an activity in other disciplines and for evaluation criteria.
- **Instructional Support** See Fine Art Transparency 21.1. Review teacher's notes for transparencies in the *Audiovisual Resources Binder* for suggestions on how to tie the transparencies to specific reading selections.

QUICK PLANNING GUIDE

Into the Story

Through the Story

Beyond the Story

ABOUT THE AUTHOR

Lee's quiet, affluent upbringing forms the background of her first novel, *Sarah Phillips,* whose heroine observes the old-fashioned black middle class that "has carried on with cautious pomp for years in eastern cities and suburbs, using its considerable fund to attempt poignant imitations of high society. . . ." In *Sarah Phillips,* the heroine's father is a prosperous Baptist minister and her mother a prim ex-schoolteacher.

Andrea Lee

(1953–   )

Andrea Lee grew up in Yeadon, a prosperous Philadelphia suburb favored by African American professionals. It was a place where grounds were well kept, children were sent off to good schools, and prejudice was something the residents knew only from books and television.

"Yeadon . . . was as solid a repository of American virtues and American flaws as any other close-knit suburban community," Lee wrote in the early 1980s. "It had, and still has, its own peculiar flavor—a lively mixture of materialism, idealism, and ironic humor that prevents the minds of its children from stagnating."

In 1978, Lee went to Russia with her husband, a graduate student in Russian history, for eight months' study at Moscow State University and for another two months in Leningrad (now St. Petersburg). The young Americans stood in lines and rode the subways with ordinary Russians. They absorbed, as Lee wrote, "a view of life in Moscow and Leningrad that was very different from that of the diplomats and journalists we knew." This yearlong trip resulted in a series of articles that were collected in her well-received book *Russian Journal,* nominated for a National Book Award in 1981.

Lee's novel *Sarah Phillips* was published in 1984. The title character shares with the author a prosperous upbringing and a Harvard education. Sarah is the daughter of an African American minister who combines old-fashioned Baptist charisma with a contemporary dedication to the civil rights movement. The reviewer Bruce Van Wyngarden praised *Sarah Phillips* as a "coming-of-age remembrance in which detail and insight are delightfully, and sometimes poignantly, blended." The story that follows is an excerpt from that novel.

© Jerry Bauer.

A longtime contributor to *The New Yorker,* Lee, who now lives in Italy, has proved herself as both a journalist and a novelist. Her style manifests the craft essential to both nonfiction and fiction. She combines the pinpoint accuracy of observation that we expect of nonfiction with the warmth that gives life to fictional characters. One critic called her writing "luminous," a word that suggests her appealing clarity and grace.

PROGRAM MANAGER

- **Planning Instruction** See Teaching Notes, *Teaching Resources B,* p. 203, for objectives, a summary, and literary elements for this selection.
- **Instructional Support** Before beginning the instructional lesson, see Graphic Organizer for Active Reading, *Teaching Resources B,* p. 207, for a Through the Story activity.
- **Assessment** See Selection Test, *Test Booklet,* pp. 261–262.
- **Reinforcement** Use the Words to Own worksheet in *Teaching Resources B,* p. 208.

BEFORE YOU READ
NEW AFRICAN

Reading Focus
Coming of Age

"New African" is about the love and conflicts in an African American family. The story is in particular about how a girl establishes a place for herself in the family, and at the same time takes a huge step toward forging her own identity. Watch for the give-and-take as the narrator tries to come to terms with her father and her father's world.

A Dialogue with the Text

"New African" is in large part a character study of the narrator's father. As you read, write down details and descriptive passages that give you insight into Reverend Phillips.

Elements of Literature
Internal Conflict

An **internal conflict** is a struggle between opposing forces within a person's mind. Much of the power and suspense of "New African" derives from several internal conflicts the narrator experiences as she struggles to make her own place in the world.

> An **internal conflict** is a struggle between opposing forces within a person's mind.
>
> *For more on Conflict, see the Handbook of Literary Terms.*

Background
Before you read "New African," you might review the section on Puritan religious beliefs in the "Beginnings" introduction (see page 10). This story, set in Philadelphia in 1963, deals with a Baptist church whose members believe that baptism should be given only to those people who ask for it after receiving a special call from God.

WORDS TO OWN

The following vocabulary words are defined in the Words to Own at the bottom of the pupil's page.

discreet p. 1132	sedate p. 1137
affected p. 1132	mortal p. 1139
dispelling p. 1133	sacrilege p. 1139
wistfulness p. 1134	ambiguousness p. 1139
defiantly p. 1136	
omniscient p. 1137	

PORTFOLIO ASSESSMENT

Portfolio Assessment For help with self-assessment of reading skills, see the *Portfolio Management System,* p. 39.

Into the Story

Using BEFORE YOU READ
p. 1129

Reading Focus
Have students brainstorm ways a young person can establish a place in a family and ways the person can forge an identity. Students may record their ideas to review after they have read the story. Then, have students meet with a partner to discuss their ideas and the ideas' connection to the story. *Tell students that they do not have to share anything they would feel uncomfortable discussing with other students.*

A Dialogue with the Text
Have students record their notes in a chart as they read. Headings for the chart should include elements of personality, such as thoughts and ideals, emotions, and behavior, or other related topics. Students may list their notes under the appropriate columns and then, after they have read the story, combine the notes into a brief description of Sarah's father.

Elements of Literature
Ask students how a person can have a conflict within himself or herself. Tell students that an inner conflict can be as simple as being tempted to act in a way they know is not right, such as telling a lie. Have students provide examples of other internal conflicts from real life, literature, film, or TV. *Remind students to choose an example they would not mind sharing with others.*

Background
Ask students to review the section on Puritan religious beliefs and then to prepare a Venn diagram such as the one on Transparency 5 in the Transparency Package. Before they read, students may record in the diagram similarities and differences they anticipate between the two religious groups. After they have read the story, students may expand and revise their diagrams.

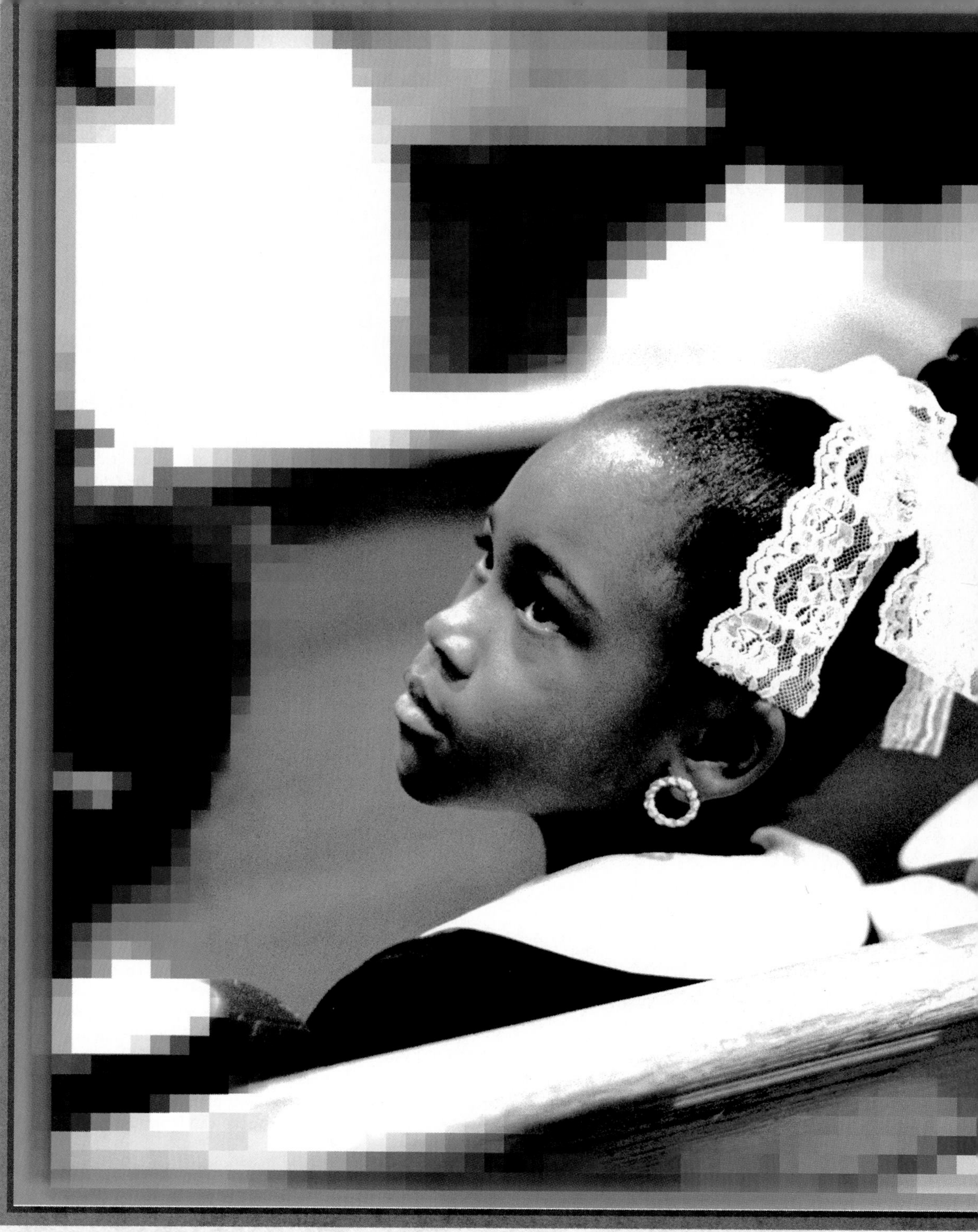

OPTIONS FOR TEACHING

STRATEGIES FOR INCLUSION

Special Needs Students may be better able to focus on the story if they are told to locate specific information as they read. Give students a list of the characters in the story, and have them take notes as they read about the narrator's relation to each character. Students may also record the narrator's thoughts and feelings about each character. Have students discuss their notes with a partner after they finish the story.

Visual Ask students to collect and share with the class various pictures of churches. Have students discuss the differences in the appearances of the churches and how those differences affect their perceptions of the congregation and the ceremonies. Remind students to be respectful of others' beliefs.

New African

Andrea Lee

On a hot Sunday morning in the summer of 1963, I was sitting restlessly with my mother, my brother Matthew, and my aunts Lily, Emma, and May in a central pew of the New African Baptist Church. It was mid-August, and the hum of the big electric fans at the back of the church was almost enough to muffle my father's voice from the pulpit; behind me I could hear Mrs. Gordon, a stout, feeble old woman who always complained of dizziness, remark sharply to her daughter that at the rate the air-conditioning fund was growing, it might as well be for the next century. Facing the congregation, my father—who was Reverend Phillips to the rest of the world—seemed hot himself; he mopped his brow with a handkerchief and drank several glasses of ice water from the heavy pitcher on the table by the pulpit. I looked at him critically. He's still reading the text, I thought. Then he'll do the sermon, then the baptism, and it will be an hour, maybe two.

I rubbed my chin and then idly began to snap the elastic band that held my red straw hat in place. What I would really like to do, I decided, would be to go home, put on my shorts, and climb up into the treehouse I had set up the day before with Matthew. We'd nailed an old bushel basket up in the branches of the big maple that stretched above the sidewalk in front of the house; it made a sort of crow's nest where you could sit comfortably, except for a few splinters, and read, or peer through the dusty leaves at the cars that passed down the quiet suburban road. There was shade and wind and a feeling of high adventure up in the treetop, where the air seemed to vibrate with the dry rhythms of the cicadas; it was as different as possible from church, where the packed congregation sat in a near-visible miasma of emotion and cologne, and trolleys[1] passing in the city street outside set the stained-glass windows rattling.

I slouched between Mama and Aunt Lily and felt myself going limp with lassitude and boredom, as if the heat had melted my bones; the only thing about me with any character seemed to be my firmly starched eyelet dress. Below the scalloped hem, my legs were skinny and wiry,

1. **trolleys:** mass-transit vehicles that run along tracks set into the street.

Through the Story

A. Reader's Response: First Thoughts

? Just from reading the title, what would you expect this short story to be about? [Sample responses: It could be about a person who has just moved to Africa. Or it could be about a person rediscovering his or her African roots.]

B. Expansion

During the summer of 1963, an African American church in Birmingham, Alabama, was bombed, killing four girls. Dr. Martin Luther King, Jr., led the March on Washington that same summer. His famous "I Have a Dream" speech contributed to the eventual passage of the Civil Rights Act in 1964.

C. Critical Reading: Analyzing Details

? What do the details tell the reader about the speaker? [She is bored and not paying attention in church, even though her father is the minister. The details suggest that she likes to daydream and is impatient.]

D. Critical Reading: Metacognition

? Judging by the word's context, what do you think *miasma* means? [Possible answers: That it is a mixture of "emotion and cologne" suggests that a miasma is like a fog or cloud. It sounds like something unhealthy, because it is contrasted with the fresh air outside.]

STRATEGIES FOR INCLUSION

Logical-Mathematical Have students list each example of Sarah's conflicting or contradictory thoughts or emotions. Next to each example, have students note the subject or cause of the conflict. After students have finished the story, they may review their notes and draw connections between the conflicts. Challenge students to find a pattern in the development of the conflicts, and have volunteers share their ideas with the class.

INTEGRATING THE LANGUAGE ARTS

Strategic Reading Have each student read the story aloud with a partner. Encourage students to pause frequently in their reading to discuss with their partners the connections they make with the story or the elements of the story that they find interesting or confusing. Partners should take notes on their discussions and, after reading the story, choose one item to share with the rest of the class.

A. Literary Element: Irony

? What is unexpected or surprising about the fans? [The congregation of the church is predominately black, but the fans in use depict a white Jesus with "pink-cheeked" children. The fans bearing the image of a black child praying are not in use.] Why are the fans with black children not used? [Possible answers: People may have kept the fans at home to keep them like new, or they might prefer the ones they are using because they have come to accept the idea of Jesus as a white, blond man.]

B. Critical Reading: Summarizing

? What has happened to the church and the surrounding neighborhood? What is the effect on the congregation? [The church has maintained its respectable stature, but the neighborhood around it has declined. The members of its congregation now come in from the suburbs, and as a result no longer feel at home at the church.]

C. Critical Reading: Drawing Conclusions

? Why do the children feel both "pride and animosity"? [Their pride comes from the fact that their father is the respected minister of the church. Their animosity comes from having to leave the suburbs to travel into an area of the city that has become run-down.]

D. Literary Element: Diction

? What is suggested by the use of the word *primitive*? [Something primitive can be characterized by simplicity or a lack of sophistication. The word relates to the physical state of the neighborhood around the church and the decline of the community. It is a strong word, and it emphasizes the embarrassment of the children.]

the legs of a ten-year-old amazon,[2] scarred from violent adventures with bicycles and skates. A fingernail tapped my wrist; it was Aunt Emma, reaching across Aunt Lily to press a piece of butterscotch into my hand. When I slipped the candy into my mouth, it tasted faintly of Arpège;[3] my mother and her three sisters were monumental women, ample of bust and slim of ankle, with a weakness for elegant footwear and French perfume. As they leaned back and forth to exchange discreet tidbits of gossip, they fanned themselves and me with fans from the Byron J. Wiggins Funeral Parlor. The fans, which were fluttering throughout the church, bore a depiction of the Good Shepherd: a hollow-eyed blond Christ holding three fat pink-cheeked children. This Christ resembled the Christ who stood among apostles on the stained-glass windows of the church. Deacon Wiggins, a thoughtful man, had also provided New African with a few dozen fans bearing the picture of a black child praying, but I rarely saw those in use. (A)

There was little that was new or very African about the New African Baptist Church. The original congregation had been formed in 1813 by three young men from Philadelphia's large community of free blacks, and before many generations had passed, it had become spiritual home to a collection of prosperous, conservative, generally light-skinned parishioners. The church was a gray Gothic structure, set on the corner of a rundown street in South Philadelphia a dozen blocks below Rittenhouse Square and a few blocks west of the spare, clannish Italian neighborhoods that produced Frankie Avalon[4] and Frank Rizzo.[5] At the turn of the century, the neighborhood had been a tidy collection of brick houses with scrubbed marble steps—the homes of a group of solid citizens whom Booker T. Washington,[6] in a centennial address to the church, described as "the ablest Negro businessmen of our generation." Here my father had grown up aspiring to preach to the congregation of New African—an ambition encouraged by my grandmother Phillips, a formidable churchwoman. Here, too, my mother and her sisters had walked with linked arms to Sunday services, exchanging affected little catch phrases of French and Latin they had learned at Girls' High.

In the 1950s many of the parishioners, seized by the national urge toward the suburbs, moved to newly integrated towns outside the city, leaving the streets around New African to fill with bottles and papers and loungers. (B) The big church stood suddenly isolated. It had not been abandoned—on Sundays the front steps overflowed with members who had driven in—but there was a tentative feeling in the atmosphere of those Sunday mornings, as if through the muddle of social change, the future of New African had become unclear. Matthew and I, suburban children, felt a mixture of pride and animosity toward the church. (C) On the one hand, it was a marvelous private domain, a richly decorated and infinitely suggestive playground where we were petted by a congregation that adored our father; on the other hand, it seemed a bit like a dreadful old relative in the city, one who forced us into tedious visits and who linked us to a past that came to seem embarrassingly primitive as we grew older. (D)

I slid down in my seat, let my head roll back, and looked up at the blue arches of the church ceiling. Lower than these, in back of the altar, was an enormous gilded cross. Still lower, in a semicircle near the pulpit, sat the choir, flanked by two tall golden files of organ pipes, and below the choir was a somber crescent of dark-suited deacons. In front, at the center of everything, his bald head gleaming under the lights, was Daddy. On summer Sundays he wore white robes, and when he raised his arms, the heavy material fell in curving folds like the ridged petals of an Easter lily. Usually when I came through the crowd to kiss him after the service, his cheek against my lips felt wet and gravelly with sweat and a new growth of beard sprouted since morning. Today, however, was a baptismal Sunday, and I wouldn't have a chance to kiss him until he was freshly shaven and

2. **amazon:** strong, athletic woman. The Amazons of Greek mythology were a race of female warriors.
3. **Arpège** (är·pezh′): brand of perfume.
4. **Frankie Avalon** (1940–): popular 1960s singer.
5. **Frank Rizzo** (1920–1991): mayor of Philadelphia from 1972 to 1980.
6. **Booker T. Washington** (1856–1915): noted African American author and educator.

WORDS TO OWN

discreet (di·skrēt′) *adj.:* wisely cautious.
affected (a·fekt′id) *v.* used as *adj.:* put on for show.

OPTIONS FOR TEACHING

INTEGRATING THE LANGUAGE ARTS

Language and Style Draw students' attention to Lee's precise and vivid diction in the story. Have them consider the paragraph on p. 1133 that begins "For a Baptist minister and his wife . . ." Ask students to find three examples of especially vivid and effective diction in the paragraph and to tell why they find each example so impressive. Students may share their findings in small groups.

Writing: Diary Entry Ask students to write a diary entry that Sarah might have written after the climactic scene in the church. Encourage students to explore Sarah's point of view. What are her hopes and fears? What is her understanding of her refusal to be baptized and its consequences? Students may consider such questions and take notes on possible answers, brainstorming the character's thoughts and emotions at the time. Then, they should review the story and write their diary entries.

cool from the shower he took after the ceremony. The baptismal pool was in an alcove to the left of the altar; it had mirrored walls and red velvet curtains, and above it, swaying on a string, hung a stuffed white dove.

Daddy paused in the invocation and asked the congregation to pray. The choir began to sing softly:

> Blessed assurance,
> Jesus is mine!
> Oh what a foretaste
> Of glory divine!

In the middle of the hymn, I edged my head around my mother's cool, muscular arm (she swam every day of the summer) and peered at Matthew. He was sitting bolt upright holding a hymnal and a pencil, his long legs inside his navy-blue summer suit planted neatly in front of him, his freckled thirteen-year-old face that was so like my father's wearing not the demonic grin it bore when we played alone but a maddeningly composed, attentive expression. "Two hours!" I mouthed at him, and pulled back at a warning pressure from my mother. Then I joined in the singing, feeling disappointed: Matthew had returned me a glance of scorn. Just lately he had started acting very superior and tolerant about tedious Sunday mornings. A month before, he'd been baptized, marching up to the pool in a line of white-robed children as the congregation murmured happily about Reverend Phillips's son. Afterward Mrs. Pinkston, a tiny, yellow-skinned old woman with a blind left eye, had come up to me and given me a painful hug, whispering that she was praying night and day for the pastor's daughter to hear the call as well.

I bit my fingernails whenever I thought about baptism; the subject brought out a deep-rooted balkiness in me. Ever since I could remember, Matthew and I had made a game of dispelling the mysteries of worship with a gleeful secular eye: We knew how the bread and wine were prepared (E) for Communion, and where Daddy bought his robes (Ekhardt Brothers, in North Philadelphia, makers also of robes for choirs, academicians, and judges). Yet there was an unassailable magic about an act as public and dramatic as baptism. I felt toward it the slightly exasperated awe a stagehand might feel on realizing that although he can identify with professional exactitude the minutest components of a show, there is still something indefinable in the power that makes it a cohesive whole. Though I could not have put it into words, I believed that the decision to make a frightening and embarrassing backward plunge into a pool of sanctified water meant that one had received a summons to Christianity as unmistakable as the blare of an automobile horn. I believed this with the same fervor with which, already, I believed in the power of romance, especially in the miraculous efficacy of a lover's first kiss. I had never been kissed by a lover, nor had I heard the call to baptism.

For a Baptist minister and his wife, my father and mother were unusually relaxed about religion; Matthew and I had never been required to read the Bible, and my father's sermons had been criticized by some older church members for omitting the word "sin." Mama and Daddy never tried to push me toward baptism, but a number of other people did. Often on holidays, when I had retreated from the noise of the family dinner table and sat trying to read in my favorite place (the window seat in Matthew's room, with the curtains drawn to form a tent), Aunt Lily would come and find me. Aunt Lily was the youngest of my mother's sisters, a kindergarten teacher with the fatally overdeveloped air of quaintness that is the infallible mark of an old maid. Aunt Lily hoped and hoped again with various suitors, but even I knew she would never find a husband. I re- (F) spected her because she gave me wonderful books of fairy tales, inscribed in her neat, loopy hand; when she talked about religion, however, she assumed an anxious, flirtatious air that made me cringe. "Well, Miss Sarah, what are you scared of?" she would ask, tugging gently on one of my braids and bringing her plump face so close to mine that I could see her powder, which was, in accordance with the custom of fashionable colored ladies, several shades lighter than her olive skin. "God isn't anyone to be afraid of!" she'd continue as I looked at her with my best deadpan expression. "He's someone nice, just as nice as your daddy"—I had always suspected Aunt Lily of

Words to Own
dispelling (di·spel′iŋ) *v.* used as *n.:* driving away.

E. Literary Element: Internal Conflict

? What is Sarah's internal conflict? [She is skeptical about the church's ceremonies, especially baptism, because she knows the mundane details that go into the spectacle; but she also feels attracted by the drama and magic of the ceremonies. She does not know whether she wants to be baptized or not.]

F. Critical Reading: Analyzing Character

? How would you describe Aunt Lily? [Possible answers: She is dreamy, disconnected, eccentric, and aristocratic. The aunt tries to put on a show of being elegant and knowledgeable, but really she seems lonely and unsatisfied with her life.]

COOPERATIVE LEARNING

Skit Arrange students in groups of four. Have each group write a skit that illustrates the climactic scene in the story and adds insight into the characters. The groups could retell the story from another point of view, such as the father's, the brother's, or Aunt Bessie's. Or students may use stage conventions, such as soliloquies, to reveal characters' thoughts and emotions. Each group should present its skit to the class. Each group member should participate in the writing of the skit and in its performance, by taking on the role of a character.

Student Involvement As students work on a collaborative activity such as a skit or group story, encourage individual involvement by having students work on a give-and-take basis with each other. Tell students that when someone in the group suggests an idea, it is the job of someone else in the group to respond or expand on the idea. Direct group members to focus on having every item of their project be the result of everyone's efforts. Suggest, for example, that if they are writing a skit, each scene should incorporate ideas from each group member. ☞

A. Literary Element: Internal Conflict

? What is bothering the speaker? [She feels guilty because she does not know if her parents are angry with her for not being baptized. She cannot remove the guilt because her parents do not give her the opportunity; they never talk about baptism with her.]

B. Reader's Response: Shaping Interpretations

? Who might these white students be? [Sample responses: They are probably participants in the civil rights movement who have come to hear Sarah's father preach on the subject. They might simply be adventurous students who want to try new things.]

C. Literary Element: Irony

? Why do the students view going to jail in Alabama as "almost miraculous"? [Civil rights leaders at the time in the South were frequently jailed—it was part of their plan, and no stigma was attached to being arrested. The students admire the courage and convictions of Sarah's father.]

D. Reader's Response: Shaping Interpretations

? What do the questions tell you about Sarah's father? [Sample responses: The questions are irrelevant—they demonstrate that her father would talk and argue about anything at all. The questions show that he has a quick mind and that he likes puzzles and games.]

having a crush on my father—"and he loves you, in the same way your daddy does!"

"You would make us all so happy!" I was told at different times by Aunt Lily, Aunt Emma, and Aunt May. The only people who said nothing at all were Mama and Daddy, but I sensed in them a thoughtful, suppressed wistfulness that maddened me.

After the hymn, Daddy read aloud a few verses from the third chapter of Luke, verses I recognized in the almost instinctive way in which I was familiar with all of the well-traveled parts of the Old and New Testaments. "Prepare the way of the Lord, make his paths straight," read my father in a mild voice. "Every valley shall be filled, and every mountain and hill shall be brought low, and the crooked shall be made straight, and the rough paths made smooth, and all flesh shall see the salvation of God."

He had a habit of pausing to fix his gaze on part of the congregation as he read, and that Sunday he seemed to be talking to a small group of strangers who sat in the front row. These visitors were young white men and women, students from Philadelphia colleges, who for the past year had been coming to hear him talk. It was hard to tell them apart: All the men seemed to have beards, and the women wore their hair long and straight. Their informal clothes stood out in that elaborate assembly, and church members whispered angrily that the young women didn't wear hats. I found the students appealing and rather romantic, with their earnest eyes and timid air of being perpetually sorry about something. It was clear that they had good intentions, and I couldn't understand why so many of the adults in the congregation seemed to dislike them so much. After services, they would hover around Daddy. "Never a more beautiful civil rights sermon!" they would say in low, fervent voices. Sometimes they seemed to have tears in their eyes.

I wasn't impressed by their praise of my father; it was only what everyone said. People called him a champion of civil rights; he gave speeches on the radio, and occasionally he appeared on television. (The first time I'd seen him on Channel 5, I'd been gravely disappointed by the way he looked: The bright lights exaggerated the furrows that ran between his nose and mouth, and his narrow eyes gave him a sinister air; he looked like an Oriental villain in a Saturday afternoon thriller.) During the past year he had organized a boycott that integrated the staff of a huge frozen-food plant in Philadelphia, and he'd been away several times to attend marches and meetings in the South. I was privately embarrassed to have a parent who freely admitted going to jail in Alabama, but the students who visited New African seemed to think it almost miraculous. Their conversations with my father were peppered with references to places I had never seen, towns I imagined as being swathed in a mist of darkness visible: Selma, Macon, Birmingham, Biloxi.[7]

Matthew and I had long ago observed that what Daddy generally did in his sermons was to speak very softly and then surprise everyone with a shout. Of course, I knew that there was more to it than that; even in those days I recognized a genius of personality in my father. He loved crowds, handling them with the expert good humor of a man entirely in his element. At church banquets, at the vast annual picnic that was held beside a lake in New Jersey, or at any gathering in the backyards and living rooms of the town where we lived, the sound I heard most often was the booming of my father's voice followed by shouts of laughter from the people around him. He had a passion for oratory; at home, he infuriated Matthew and me by staging absurd debates at the dinner table, verbal melees[8] that he won quite selfishly, with a loud crow of delight at his own virtuosity. "Is a fruit a vegetable?" he would demand. "Is a zipper a machine?" Matthew and I would plead with him to be quiet as we strained to get our own points across, but it was no use. When the last word had resounded and we sat looking at him in irritated silence, he would clear his throat, settle his collar, and resume eating, his face still glowing with an irrepressible glee.

When he preached, he showed the same private delight. A look of rapt pleasure seemed to broaden and brighten the contours of his angular face until it actually appeared to give off light as

7. Selma . . . Biloxi: Selma, Alabama; Macon, Georgia; Birmingham, Alabama; and Biloxi, Mississippi: sites of significant civil rights protests during the 1960s.
8. melees (mā′lāz′): battles.

Words to Own

wistfulness (wist′fəl·nes) *n.:* vague longing.

Options for Teaching

Classroom Management

Managing the Reader's Response Classroom Emphasize to students that there is more than one way of looking at a topic. During a discussion, have a number of students express their opinions on a single subject. Ask students to consider the benefits of alternate viewpoints, and have them revise their own responses if they find merit in another student's point of view.

Block Scheduling After reading the story in class for thirty minutes, engage students in a discussion relating the story to current events (fifteen to twenty minutes). Then, arrange students in groups of three, and have each group brainstorm possible newspaper or magazine articles on the ideas discussed (fifteen to twenty minutes). Conclude by asking volunteers to share their article ideas with the class.

he spoke. He could preach in two very different ways. One was the delicate, sonorous idiom of formal oratory, with which he must have won the prizes he held from his seminary days. The second was a hectoring,[9] insinuating, incantatory tone, full of the rhythms of the South he had never lived in, linking him to generations of thunderous Baptist preachers. When he used this tone, as he was doing now, affectionate laughter rippled through the pews.

"I know," he said, looking out over the congregation and blinking his eyes rapidly, "that there are certain people in this room—oh, I don't have to name names or point a finger—who have ignored that small true voice, the voice that is the voice of Jesus calling out in the shadowy depths

9. **hectoring:** bullying.

E. Critical Reading: Comparing and Contrasting

? How do the two styles of oratory differ? How are they similar? [The two styles differ in that one is calm, well-argued, and rational, and the other is more passionate and moving. They are similar in that both have an identifiable rhythm and an entrancing quality.]

CROSSING THE CURRICULUM

Social Sciences Have students locate the cities mentioned in the story, where civil rights struggles were especially intense. Then, ask students to research events associated with each city at the time. Students may meet in small groups to share their observations on the events in the cities and their importance to the civil rights movement of the 1960s.

Music Ask students to investigate the musical conflict between the choirmaster and the choir in the story. Students may research recordings of Handel and Paul Robeson, or you may play recordings of both musicians in class. Have students discuss the differences between the two musicians, and challenge students to relate the differences to the conflict in the congregation. Ask student pairs to write a proposal to the choirmaster recommending the kind of music the choir should sing.

History Point out to students that Sarah feels she has little in common with her slave ancestors. Ask students to research the topic of the spiritual in African American history. Then, have students apply the ideas and expressions of the spiritual to the civil rights movement. Challenge students to apply the topic to Sarah's own life: Are there parallels between the ideas and emotions of the songs and Sarah's ideas and emotions? Have students create a video using spirituals, describing how they were used by African Americans, and drawing parallels between the songs and Sarah's ideas.

A. Critical Reading: Drawing Conclusions

? How does Sarah's father feel about the behavior of the church members? [He is disappointed yet amused by their restraint, and he privately pokes fun at them.]

B. Reader's Response: Extending the Text

? If someone goes against a group's code of behavior, do you think it is right to label such a person as "barbarous"? Why or why not? [Sample responses: It is not right to call someone who acts differently barbarous, because what is improper in one place (such as shouting in the New African Church) may be proper somewhere else (such as at another Baptist church). It is right to judge a person's behavior when it goes against that of a group because an organized group has to have standards.]

C. Literary Element: Simile

? What makes this simile—"like carvings on a scarab"—especially appropriate? [The creases on Deacon West's brow are an indication of his age; an ancient Egyptian scarab is an artifact. Also, a scarab is mysterious and may be seen as a symbol of ancient or forgotten knowledge; Deacon West's age makes him mysterious, because he was personally involved in past events (such as the Spanish-American War) that nearly everyone has forgotten.]

D. Reader's Response: Shaping Interpretations

? Why might Sarah be so affected by this event? [Sample responses: Sarah takes baptism very seriously; it awes her, as it does the other children. Sarah feels she is expected to join in the ceremony—she is excited by the spectacle but does not know if she wants to be involved.]

of the soul. And while you all are looking around and wondering just who those 'certain people' are, I want to tell you all a secret: They are you and me, and your brother-in-law, and every man, woman, and child in this room this morning. All of us listen to our bellies when they tell us it is time to eat, we pay attention to our eyes when they grow heavy from wanting sleep, but when it comes to the sacred knowledge our hearts can offer, we are deaf, dumb, blind, and senseless. Throw away that blindness, that deafness, that sulky indifference. When all the world lies to you, Jesus will tell you what is right. Listen to him. Call on him. In these times of confusion, when there are a dozen different ways to turn, and Mama and Papa can't help you, trust Jesus to set you straight. Listen to him. The Son of God has the answers. Call on him. Call on him. Call on him."

The sermon was punctuated with an occasional loud "Amen!" from Miss Middleton, an excitable old lady whose eyes flashed defiantly at the reproving faces of those around her. New African was not the kind of Baptist church where (A) shouting was a normal part of the service; I occasionally heard my father mock the staid congregation by calling it Saint African. Whenever Miss (B) Middleton loosed her tongue (sometimes she went off into fits of rapturous shrieks and had to be helped out of the service by the church nurse), my mother and aunts exchanged grimaces and shrugged, as if confronted by incomprehensibly barbarous behavior.

When Daddy had spoken the final words of the sermon, he drank a glass of water and vanished through a set of red velvet curtains to the right of the altar. At the same time, the choir began to sing what was described in the church bulletin as a "selection." These selections were always arenas for the running dispute between the choirmaster and the choir. Jordan Grimes, the choirmaster, was a Curtis[10] graduate who was partial to Handel,[11] but the choir preferred artistic spirituals performed in the lush, heroic style of Paul Robeson.[12] Grimes had triumphed that Sunday. As the choir gave a spirited but unwilling rendition of Agnus Dei,[13] I watched old Deacon West smile in (C) approval. A Spanish-American War veteran, he admitted to being ninety-four but was said to be older; his round yellowish face, otherwise unwrinkled, bore three deep, deliberate-looking horizontal creases on the brow, like carvings on a scarab.[14] "That old man is as flirtatious as a boy of twenty!" my mother often said, watching his stiff, courtly movements among the ladies of the church. Sometimes he gave me a dry kiss and a piece of peppermint candy after the service; I liked his crackling white collars and smell of bay rum.[15]

The selection ended; Jordan Grimes struck two deep chords on the organ, and the lights in the church went low. A subtle stir ran through the congregation, and I moved closer to my mother. (D) This was the moment that fascinated and disturbed me more than anything else at church: the prelude to the ceremony of baptism. Deacon West rose and drew open the draperies that had been closed round the baptismal pool, and there stood my father in water to his waist. The choir began to sing:

> We're marching to Zion,
> Beautiful, beautiful Zion,
> We're marching upward to Zion,
> The beautiful city of God!

Down the aisle, guided by two church mothers, came a procession of eight children and adolescents. They wore white robes, the girls with white ribbons in their hair, and they all had solemn expressions of terror on their faces. I knew each one of them. There was Billy Price, a big, slow-moving boy of thirteen, the son of Deacon Price. There were the Duckery twins. There was Caroline Piggee, whom I hated because of her long, soft black curls, her dimpled pink face, and her lisp that ravished grown-ups. There was

10. **Curtis:** Curtis Institute of Music in Philadelphia.
11. **Handel:** George Frideric Handel, eighteenth-century British composer.
12. **Paul Robeson:** twentieth-century African American actor and singer.
13. **Agnus Dei** (äg′noos dā′ē′): Latin for "lamb of God." The Agnus Dei is a prayer sung in the Roman Catholic Mass and in many Protestant services.
14. **scarab** (skar′əb): beetle-shaped religious symbol of ancient Egypt.
15. **bay rum:** fragrant after-shave lotion.

Words to Own

defiantly (dē·fī′ənt·lē) *adv.:* strongly and openly resisting.

OPTIONS FOR TEACHING

PROFESSIONAL NOTES

Thematic Connections: "The Created Self" Ask students to identify the central event in the story that affected the speaker's life. Then, have them discuss how Sarah's life is changed by the encounter with Aunt Bessie. How could Sarah be said to have created herself? [Possible answer: By standing up for her own sense of right and wrong, and by trusting in her own feelings, Sarah becomes an assertive individual. Even her father has to realize that she is maturing.]

Cultural Diversity Ask students to reflect on the close-knit community of the church, shown especially in the character of Bessie Gray. Ask students to consider various cultures and to discuss ways in which cultures express their community ties. Challenge students also to think of the different groups that make up a community, such as churches, neighborhood organizations, and school groups.

Georgie Battis and Sue Anne Ivory, and Wendell and Mabel Cullen.

My mother gave me a nudge. "Run up to the side of the pool!" she whispered. It was the custom for unbaptized children to watch the ceremony from the front of the church. They sat on the knees of the deacons and church mothers, and it was not unusual for a child to volunteer then and there for next month's baptism. I made my way quickly down the dark aisle, feeling the carpet slip under the smooth soles of my patent-leather shoes.

When I reached the side of the pool, I sat down in the bony lap of Bessie Gray, an old woman who often took care of Matthew and me when our parents were away; we called her Aunt Bessie. She was a fanatically devout Christian whose strict ideas on child rearing had evolved over decades of domestic service to a rich white family in Delaware. The link between us, a mixture of hostility and grudging affection, had been forged in hours of pitched battles over bedtimes and proper behavior. Her worshipful respect for my father, whom she called "the Rev," was exceeded only by her pride—the malice-tinged pride of an omniscient family servant—in her "white children," to whom she often unflatteringly compared Matthew and me. It was easy to see why my mother and her circle of fashionable matrons described Bessie Gray as "archaic"—one had only to look at her black straw hat attached with three enormous old-fashioned pins to her knot of frizzy white hair. Her lean, brown-skinned face was dominated by a hawk nose inherited from some Indian ancestor and punctuated by a big black mole; her eyes were small, shrewd, and baleful. She talked in ways that were already passing into history and parody, and she wore a thick orange face powder that smelled like dead leaves.

I leaned against her spare bosom and watched the other children clustered near the pool, their bonnets and hair ribbons and round heads outlined in the dim light. For a minute it was very still. Somewhere in the hot, darkened church a baby gave a fretful murmur; from outside came the sound of cars passing in the street. The candidates for baptism, looking stiff and self-conscious, stood lined up on the short stairway leading to the pool. Sue Anne Ivory fiddled with her sleeve and then put her fingers in her mouth.

Daddy spoke the opening phrases of the ceremony: "In the Baptist Church, we do not baptize infants, but believe that a person must choose salvation for himself." **E**

I didn't listen to the words; what I noticed was the music of the whole—how the big voice darkened and lightened in tone, and how the grand architecture of the Biblical sentences ennobled the voice. **F** The story, of course, was about Jesus and John the Baptist. **G** One phrase struck me newly each time: "This is my beloved son, in whom I am well pleased!" Daddy sang out these words in a clear, triumphant tone, and the choir echoed him. Ever since I could understand it, this phrase had made me feel melancholy; it seemed to expose a hard knot of disobedience that had always lain inside me. When I heard it, I thought enviously of Matthew, for whom life seemed to be a sedate and ordered affair: He, not I, was a child in whom a father could be well pleased. **H**

Daddy beckoned to Billy Price, the first baptismal candidate in line, and Billy, ungainly in his white robe, descended the steps into the pool. In soft, slow voices the choir began to sing:

Wade in the water,
Wade in the water, children,
Wade in the water,
God gonna trouble
The water.

In spite of Jordan Grimes's efforts, the choir swayed like a gospel chorus as it sang this spiritual; the result was to add an eerie jazz beat to the minor chords. The music gave me goose flesh. Daddy had told me that this was the same song that the slaves had sung long ago in the South, when they gathered to be baptized in rivers and streams. Although I cared little about history, and found it hard to picture the slaves as being any ancestors of mine, I could clearly imagine them coming together beside a broad muddy river that wound away between trees drooping with strange vegetation. They walked silently in lines, their faces very black against their white clothes, leading their children. The whole scene was bathed in

Words to Own

omniscient (äm·nish′ənt) *adj.:* all-knowing.
sedate (si·dāt′) *adj.:* calm and composed.

E. Cultural Connections

The age of the person to be baptized, as well as the method of baptism, is important to an understanding of this story. In many Christian churches, Sarah would have been baptized as an infant by being sprinkled with a small amount of water. In a Baptist church, on the other hand, the person to be baptized is old enough to have made the decision to be baptized and may be an adult. Moreover, the Baptists require total immersion— that is, the person's entire body must be briefly underwater. Thus, a large baptismal pool—or, in rural regions, a river or creek—is necessary.

F. Critical Reading: Evaluating an Interpretation

? What is the music that so entrances Sarah? [The music is her father's voice while he is performing the baptism ceremony. Sarah sees the beauty in the event as well as her own fear of the event.] How can a person's voice be like music? [Students might point to the tone, timbre, and rhythm of a voice as its spoken music.]

G. Humanities Connection

John the Baptist was a notable preacher and prophet in Judea famous for baptizing his followers. John also baptized Jesus. In later years, John the Baptist angered Herodias, the wife of Herod, and at the direct request of Herodias's daughter Salome, John was beheaded.

H. Literary Element: Internal Conflict

Sarah's comments about her brother give the reader a deeper understanding of her conflict. How would you describe her conflict now? [Possible answer: Sarah is jealous of her brother's comfort with being baptized and of his ability to please their father. She wants very much to make her father proud of her.]

PROBLEM SOLVING/CRITICAL THINKING

Facing Consequences Point out to students that the main characters in the story, Sarah and her father, each face the consequences of their actions. The father is jailed for his participation in civil rights protests. The daughter faces the possibility of her parents' anger for not being baptized. Challenge students to name people from real life and characters in other works of literature to support their opinions about the importance of facing consequences. Then, ask students to think of ways they have to face consequences in their own lives. *Emphasize to students that they do not have to discuss anything that they would feel uncomfortable in sharing with other students.* ☞

A. Critical Reading: Expressing an Opinion

? What significance do these details have? [Possible answers: The details give a better picture of Sarah's everyday life. Or the details show that Sarah is musing about conflicts and worries.]

B. Literary Element: Symbol

The stuffed dove hanging over the pool has been mentioned before. What does it symbolize? [It symbolizes "the Spirit of God" (Matthew 3:16), or "the Holy Ghost" (Luke 3:22). In the context of this story, it probably does not symbolize peace, since a dove is expressly associated in the Biblical passages above with the baptism of Jesus.]

C. Literary Element: Climax

? What brings about the climax of the story? [When Aunt Bessie says, "Go on up and accept Jesus," she sets off a clash of wills with Sarah. The struggle deepens when Aunt Bessie compares Sarah to her brother and says that her father wants her to be baptized.]

the heavy golden light that meant age and solemnity, the same light that seemed to weigh down the Israelites in illustrated volumes of Bible stories, and that shone now from the baptismal pool, giving the ceremony the air of a spectacle staged in a dream.

All attention in the darkened auditorium was now focused on the pool, where between the red curtains my father stood holding Billy Price by the shoulders. Daddy stared into Billy's face, and the boy stared back, his lips set and trembling. "And now, by the power invested in me," said Daddy, "I baptize you in the name of the Father, the Son, and the Holy Ghost." As he pronounced these words, he conveyed a tenderness as efficient and impersonal as a physician's professional manner; beneath it, however, I could see a strong private gladness, the same delight that transformed his face when he preached a sermon. He paused to flick a drop of water off his forehead, and then, with a single smooth, powerful motion of his arms, he laid Billy Price back into the water as if he were putting an infant to bed. I caught my breath as the boy went backward. When he came up, sputtering, two church mothers helped him out of the pool and through a doorway into a room where he would be dried and dressed. Daddy shook the water from his hands and gave a slight smile as another child entered the pool.

One by one, the baptismal candidates descended the steps. Sue Anne Ivory began to cry and had to be comforted. Caroline Piggee blushed and looked up at my father with such a coquettish air that I jealously wondered how he could stand it. After a few baptisms my attention wandered, and I began to gnaw the edge of my thumb and to peer at the pale faces of the visiting college students. Then I thought about Matthew, who had punched me in the arm that morning and had shouted, "No punchbacks!" I thought as well about a collection of horse chestnuts I meant to assemble in the fall, and about two books, one whose subject was adults and divorces, and another, by E. Nesbit, that continued the adventures of the Bastable children.

After Wendell Cullen had left the water (glancing uneasily back at the wet robe trailing behind him), Daddy stood alone among the curtains and the mirrors. The moving reflections from the pool made the stuffed dove hanging over him seem to flutter on its string. "Dear Lord," said Daddy, as Jordan Grimes struck a chord, "bless these children who have chosen to be baptized in accordance with your teaching, and who have been reborn to carry out your work. In each of them, surely, you are well pleased." He paused, staring out into the darkened auditorium. "And if there is anyone out there—man, woman, child—who wishes to be baptized next month, let him come forward now." He glanced around eagerly. "Oh, do come forward and give Christ your heart and give me your hand!"

Just then Aunt Bessie gave me a little shake and whispered sharply, "Go on up and accept Jesus!"

I stiffened and dug my bitten fingernails into my palms. The last clash of wills I had had with Aunt Bessie had been when she, crazily set in her old southern attitudes, had tried to make me wear an enormous straw hat, as her "white children" did, when I played outside in the sun. The old woman had driven me to madness, and I had ended up spanked and sullen, crouching moodily under the dining-room table. But this was different, outrageous, none of her business, I thought. I shook my head violently and she took advantage of the darkness in the church to seize both of my shoulders and jounce me with considerable roughness, whispering, "Now, listen, young lady! Your daddy up there is calling you to Christ. Your big brother has already offered his soul to the Lord. Now Daddy wants his little girl to step forward."

"No, he doesn't." I glanced at the baptismal pool, where my father was clasping the hand of a strange man who had come up to him. I hoped that this would distract Aunt Bessie, but she was tireless.

"Your mama and your aunt Lily and your aunt May all want you to answer the call. You're hurting them when you say no to Jesus."

"No, I'm not!" I spoke out loud and I saw the people nearby turn to look at me. At the sound of my voice, Daddy, who was a few yards away, faltered for a minute in what he was saying and glanced over in my direction.

Aunt Bessie seemed to lose her head. She stood up abruptly, pulling me with her, and, while I was still frozen in a dreadful paralysis, tried to drag me

OPTIONS FOR TEACHING

ASSESSMENT TOOLS

Check Test: Fill-in-the-Blank

1. The New African Baptist Church is located ________. [in Philadelphia]
2. Sarah feels that a person needs only a slight nudge toward religion in order to be ________. [baptized]
3. Reverend Phillips seems to direct his sermon toward ________ in the congregation. [white college students]
4. Sarah observes the baptism from ________. [the front pew of the church]
5. Aunt Bessie wants Sarah to ________. [step foward to be baptized]

Self-Reflection Ask students to write a paragraph expressing what they have learned from the story and the work they have done in making meanings from it. Encourage students to describe things they could do better next time. Students should review their notes before beginning the next subject of study.

down the aisle toward my father. The two of us began a brief struggle that could not have lasted for more than a few seconds but that seemed an endless mortal conflict—my slippery patent-leather shoes braced against the floor, my straw hat sliding cockeyed and lodging against one ear, my right arm twisting and twisting in the iron circle of the old woman's grip, my nostrils full of the dead-leaf smell of her powder and black skirts. In an instant I had wrenched my arm free and darted up the aisle toward Mama, my aunts, and Matthew. As I slipped past the pews in the darkness, I imagined that I could feel eyes fixed on me and hear whispers. "What'd you do, dummy?" whispered Matthew, tugging on my sash as I reached our pew, but I pushed past him without answering. Although it was hot in the church, my teeth were chattering: It was the first time I had won a battle with a grown-up, and the earth seemed to be about to cave in beneath me. I squeezed in between Mama and Aunt Lily just as the lights came back on in the church. In the baptismal pool, Daddy raised his arms for the last time. "The Lord bless you and keep you," came his big voice. "The Lord be gracious unto you, and give you peace."

What was curious was how uncannily subdued my parents were when they heard of my skirmish with Aunt Bessie. Normally they were swift to punish Matthew and me for misbehavior in church and for breaches in politeness toward adults; this episode combined the two, and smacked of sacrilege besides. Yet once I had made an unwilling apology to the old woman (as I kissed her she shot me such a vengeful glare that I realized that forever after it was to be war to the death between the two of us), I was permitted, once we had driven home, to climb up into the green shade of the big maple tree I had dreamed of throughout the service. In those days, more than now, I fell away into a remote dimension whenever I opened a book; that afternoon, as I sat with rings of sunlight and shadow moving over my arms and legs, and winged yellow seeds plopping down on the pages of *The Story of the Treasure Seekers,* I felt a vague uneasiness floating in the back of my mind—a sense of having misplaced something, of being myself misplaced. I was holding myself quite aloof from considering what had happened, as I did with most serious events, but through the adventures of the Bastables I kept remembering the way my father had looked when he'd heard what had happened. He hadn't looked severe or angry, but merely puzzled, and he had regarded me with the same puzzled expression, as if he'd just discovered that I existed and didn't know what to do with me. "What happened, Sairy?" he asked, using an old baby nickname, and I said, "I didn't want to go up there." I hadn't cried at all, and that was another curious thing.

After that Sunday, through some adjustment in the adult spheres beyond my perception, all pressure on me to accept baptism ceased. I turned twelve, fifteen, then eighteen without being baptized, a fact that scandalized some of the congregation; however, my parents, who openly discussed everything else, never said a word to me. The issue, and the episode that had illuminated it, was surrounded by a clear ring of silence that, for our garrulous[16] family, was something close to supernatural. I continued to go to New African—in fact, continued after Matthew, who dropped out abruptly during his freshman year in college; the ambiguousness in my relations with the old church gave me at times an inflated sense of privilege (I saw myself as a romantically isolated religious heroine, a sort of self-made Baptist martyr) and at other times a feeling of loss that I was too proud ever to acknowledge. I never went up to take my father's hand, and he never commented upon that fact to me. It was an odd pact, one that I could never consider in the light of day; I stored it in the subchambers of my heart and mind. It was only much later, after he died, and I left New African forever, that I began to examine the peculiar gift of freedom my father—whose entire soul was in the church, and in his exuberant, bewitching tongue—had granted me through his silence.

16. **garrulous** (gar′ə·ləs): talkative.

WORDS TO OWN

mortal (môr′təl) *adj.:* life-threatening; extreme.
sacrilege (sak′rə·lij) *n.:* violation of something sacred.
ambiguousness (am·big′yo͞o·əs·nes) *n.:* lack of clarity; uncertainty.

D. Reader's Response: Shaping Interpretations

? Why was Sarah not punished? [Sample responses: Her parents decided that the decision to be baptized was their daughter's and not their own. Her parents thought that Aunt Bessie was wrong to try to force their daughter to be baptized, believing that baptism is a personal, spiritual choice.]

E. Critical Reading: Summarizing

? Why does Sarah's father look at her differently after the incident with Aunt Bessie? [Possible answer: Her father has had to change from viewing her as a little girl. He realizes suddenly that she is beginning to grow up.]

F. Literary Element: Denouement

? What is the denouement, or resolution, of the story? [All efforts to get Sarah to accept baptism cease. After the episode with Aunt Bessie, her parents never say another word about it. Later in her life, Sarah is pleased because she feels that her father granted her a "peculiar gift of freedom" through his patience and understanding.]

G. Literary Element: Irony

? What is the irony in Sarah's note about her brother? [Matthew went forward to be baptized and saw himself as superior to his sister because she did not hear the call. Then Matthew left the church once he left home. Even though she did not meet the congregation's expectations of baptism, Sarah stayed with the church.]

H. Reader's Response: Shaping Interpretations

? What is the "gift of freedom" that Sarah's father gave her? [Sample responses: Her father allowed her to choose her own actions within the traditions of the church. His "gift of freedom" was showing her that being an adult means having the power to make decisions; he allowed her to grow up instead of babying her.]

Making Meanings

First Thoughts

1. Possible responses: Yes, her determination to stand up for herself is part of growing up. No, the conflict between herself and Aunt Bessie is too melodramatic.

Reviewing the Text

a. It is a hot summer day in 1963 in the New African Baptist Church in Philadelphia. The electric fans, Reverend Phillips's mopping his brow and drinking ice water, and Sarah's wish to put on shorts and go outside are evidence of the heat.

b. Matthew projects a superior attitude now that he has been baptized. She suspects her father addresses the phrase "This is my beloved son, in whom I am well pleased!" especially to her brother.

c. Sarah is bored and daydreams. She is awed and frightened by the baptism ceremony, but she clearly admires her father the pastor and she wants to please him.

d. Most students will agree that there is a resolution. Sarah is grateful that her father did not force his expectations upon her.

Shaping Interpretations

2. She is objecting to having important decisions made for her. She feels disoriented because her parents do nothing to punish her for her "misconduct" in church.

3. He is an inspiring preacher, a social activist, a gifted debater. She is thankful for his patience and trust.

4. There are many conflicts between children and parents, traditional attitudes and social changes, and old Southern values and modern views.

5. Possible response: Both the daughter and father are "new" Africans in that each shows a willingness to challenge many traditional expectations. Sarah's father fights for civil rights for African Americans, while Sarah tries to be an individual.

6. Possible response: The story shows both a specific record of an individual experience and an elaboration on a theme. Asserting herself is a turning point in Sarah's life. Also, growing up as an African American in the 1960s meant fighting against traditional and oppressive expectations to create oneself as an individual. Both experiences result in greater freedom, as Sarah herself states at the end of the story.

MAKING MEANINGS

First Thoughts

1. Do you find the narrator's attitudes and feelings believable? Why or why not?

Reviewing the Text

a. Describe the **setting** as it is presented in the opening of "New African." What details in the first three paragraphs help you feel the summer heat of the city?

b. In what ways does Sarah feel her brother growing away from her? What passages show that she regards him as more "acceptable" than she is?

c. What passages throughout the story reveal Sarah's **inner conflict** about her father's church?

d. Is there a **resolution** to Sarah's conflict by story's end? Explain.

Shaping Interpretations

2. In refusing to be baptized, what do you think Sarah is really objecting to? How would you explain the feeling of being misplaced that she experiences at the end of the story?

3. Referring to the notes in your Reader's Log, how would you **characterize** Sarah's father? What does Sarah mean in the tribute she pays to her father in the story's last sentence?

4. What **conflicts** between generations and cultures can you identify in the story?

5. The **title** of a work of art often is a key to its meaning. In what ways is the father a "new" African? In what ways is Sarah?

6. Is Lee's main purpose in this story to present a realistic record of a single experience in 1963, or is she presenting a broader **theme** about coming of age as an African American woman in the early sixties? Support your answer with specific references to the story.

CHOICES: Building Your Portfolio

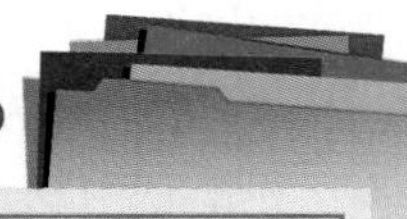

Writer's Notebook

1. Collecting Ideas for an Evaluation

WORK IN PROGRESS

One characteristic of almost all good writing is the inclusion of interesting details. The details should be relevant to the work, not just tossed in for no apparent reason. "New African" contains many details about the setting and characters. Pick out at least three details, and write notes evaluating their contribution to the story's overall effect. Save your notes for possible use in the Writer's Workshop on page 1181.

Critical Writing

2. Father and Daughter

In a brief essay, describe the **character** of either Sarah or her father. Remember that character can be revealed by these methods: (a) describing physical appearance; (b) describing actions; (c) quoting spoken words; (d) showing people's responses to the character; (e) revealing private thoughts and feelings; and (f) direct comments by the author.

Creative Writing

3. A Face in the Crowd

Write a first-person narrative told from the **point of view** of a young person (who might or might not be yourself) who is a member of a large audience attending a public function. Imitating Lee's style in the opening paragraphs of this story, have your narrator describe the setting and reveal what he or she sees, hears, smells, and thinks about the setting and audience. Before you write, decide what tone your narrator will adopt in describing the situation. Then, read your narrative aloud for the class.

Beyond the Story

Choices: Building Your Portfolio

1. **Writer's Notebook** Remind students to save their work. They may use it as prewriting for the Writer's Workshop on p. 1181.

PORTFOLIO ASSESSMENT

Choices: Assessment Criteria For help in evaluating these Choices assignments, see the criteria in the *Portfolio Management System*, p. 204.

James Baldwin

(1924–1987)

Y. Coatsaliou/Sygma.

James Baldwin felt compelled to write at length about being an African American "because it was the gate I had to unlock before I could hope to write about anything else." His essays flow from his conviction that a writer's duty is "to examine attitudes, to go beneath the surface, to tap the source."

One of the most controversial and stirring writers of the twentieth century, James Baldwin was born and raised in New York City's Harlem, where his stepfather was the minister of a small evangelical church. As a young man, Baldwin read voraciously and served as a junior minister for a few years at the Fireside Pentecostal Assembly. At the age of twenty-four, he used funds from a fellowship to move to Europe. While living in Paris, he completed his first—and some say best—novel, *Go Tell It on the Mountain* (1953). *Notes of a Native Son,* a collection of autobiographical essays published in 1955, established Baldwin as an American writer of the first rank. The critic Irving Howe said Baldwin was among "the two or three greatest essayists this country has ever produced."

Although he lived much of his life in France, Baldwin never relinquished his U.S. citizenship, and in later years he traveled back to his homeland so often that he considered himself a transatlantic commuter. While abroad, he wrote in a variety of forms, including novels, plays, essays, poetry, and book reviews. Two of Baldwin's plays, *The Amen Corner* (1955) and *Blues for Mister Charlie* (1964), were produced on Broadway.

In the 1950s, the decade that witnessed the early growth of the American civil rights movement, Baldwin's audacious, searing scrutiny of racial injustice played a major role in forcing leaders, black and white, to come to terms with one of the nation's most anguishing problems—the treatment of African Americans. He saw himself as a "disturber of the peace," and some chided him for his unrelenting criticism. For instance, Benjamin DeMott wrote in the *Saturday Review,* "To function as a voice of outrage month after month for a decade and more strains heart and mind, and rhetoric as well; the consequence is a writing style ever on the edge of being winded by too many summonses to intensity."

In the early sixties, Baldwin's reputation grew with the publication of additional essays, *Nobody Knows My Name: More Notes of a Native Son* (1961) and *The Fire Next Time* (1963), a groundbreaking book on race relations that had wide influence. He later published several novels, participated in TV documentaries, and remained a prominent, humane advocate of racial justice in American life.

At the time of his death in France, Baldwin was working on a biography of the Reverend Martin Luther King, Jr. Soon after Baldwin died, two noted African American writers praised his lifework. Orde Coombs wrote, "Because he existed we felt that the racial miasma that swirled around us would not consume us, and it is not too much to say that this man saved our lives." Juan Williams of the *Washington Post* said, "America and the literary world are far richer for [Baldwin's] witness. The proof of a shared humanity across the divides of race, class, and more is the testament that the preacher's son, James Arthur Baldwin, has left us."

QUICK PLANNING GUIDE

Into the Selection

Author Biography p. 1141

Before You Read p. 1142

- **Reading Focus:** Students examine self-assessment as part of self-creation.
- **A Dialogue with the Text: Set a Purpose** Take notes on the problems faced by African Americans

Through the Selection

"Autobiographical Notes" pp. 1142–1146

Words to Own pp. 1144–1146

Making Meanings p. 1147

Beyond the Selection

Choices: Building Your Portfolio p. 1147

- **Writer's Notebook:** Examine the writer's objectivity
- **Critical Writing:** Write an essay on the effects of the past on the present
- **Critical Writing:** Compare the diction and tone of two pieces of writing
- **Creative Writing/Speaking and Listening:** Respond to James Baldwin's points

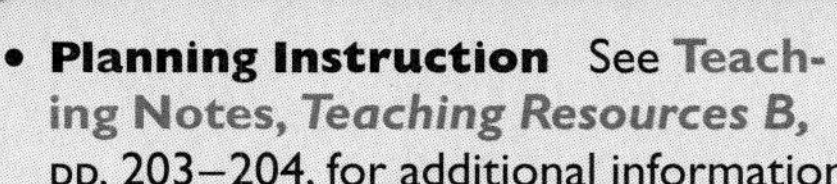

PROGRAM MANAGER

- **Planning Instruction** See **Teaching Notes, *Teaching Resources B,*** pp. 203–204, for additional information for this selection.
- **Instructional Support** See **Graphic Organizer for Active Reading, *Teaching Resources B,*** p. 209, for a Through the Selection activity.
- **Assessment** See **Selection Test, *Test Booklet,*** pp. 263–264.
- **Language Link** For revising weak words and clichés, see **Language Link, *Teaching Resources B,*** pp. 210–211.
- **Reinforcement** Use the **Words to Own** worksheet in ***Teaching Resources B,*** p. 212.
- **Audiotaped Readings** To help less proficient readers, use the **Selected Reading, Audiocassette 3, Side B** in the ***Audiovisual Resources Binder.***

Into the Selection

Using Before You Read
p. 1142

Reading Focus

Ask students to think of times when they assess themselves and their own lives. Are there certain times that they find they look at themselves and at life more critically than at other times? *Caution students that they do not have to share any ideas they would feel uncomfortable discussing with other students.* Then, have students speculate on the causes of and reasons for Baldwin's examination of his own life.

A Dialogue with the Text

Direct students to keep their notes in two columns. In one column, students may describe the particular aspect of "the Negro problem" that Baldwin is discussing. In the other column, students may record how the specific problem creates difficulties for the African American writer. After students have finished reading, have them compare their notes with a partner.

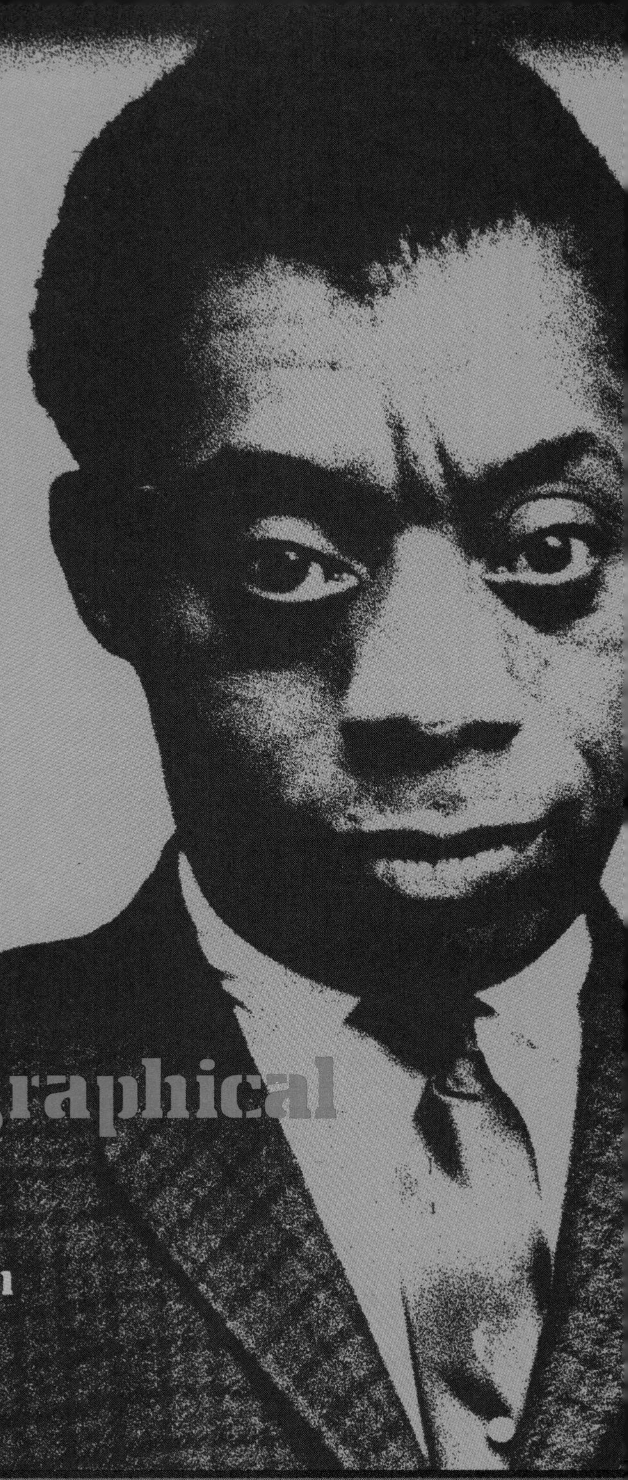

Before You Read
Autobiographical Notes

Reading Focus
Know Thyself

The ancient Greek philosopher Socrates believed that only an *examined* life is worth living. What exactly does it mean to live an examined life? At the least, it means stepping back from the whirl of daily activities and gaining some perspective on who you are, where you have been, and where you are heading. It means creating new angles of vision, asking questions, proposing answers. It means self-assessment as a part of self-creation. As you will see, James Baldwin certainly took Socrates' dictum to heart. He is especially interested in the role of the writer as an examiner of outlooks and attitudes. The autobiographical notes that follow first appeared as a preface to *Notes of a Native Son*.

A Dialogue with the Text
READER'S LOG

As you read, jot down Baldwin's observations on how what he calls "the Negro problem" creates difficulties for the African American writer.

Autobiographical Notes
James Baldwin

Portfolio Assessment For help with self-assessment of reading skills, see the *Portfolio Management System*, pp. 48–49.

ABOUT THE AUTHOR

After graduating from De Witt Clinton High School in 1942, James Baldwin held a number of jobs in order to support himself while writing book reviews for such national publications as *The New Leader* and *The Nation*. He was befriended by Richard Wright (p. 1012), who helped him obtain a writing fellowship. Like Wright, Baldwin based much of his writing on his own experiences.

WORDS TO OWN

The following vocabulary words are defined in the Words to Own at the bottom of the pupil's page.

bleak p. 1144	crucial p. 1145
censored p. 1144	interloper p. 1145
assess p. 1145	appropriate p. 1146
conundrum p. 1145	explicit p. 1146
coherent p. 1145	pulverized p. 1146

Through the Selection

A. Critical Reading: Identifying Main Ideas

? What does the second line of the essay tell you about the role of writing in Baldwin's life? [Writing is central to his life and bound up with his image of himself.]

B. Reader's Response: Shaping Interpretations

? What can you tell about James Baldwin from his writing style in this passage? [Sample responses: Baldwin seems contrary or belligerent, because he didn't read the book everyone wanted him to read, but he also has a sense of humor. Baldwin is fiercely independent—he doesn't like to be censored—but he is also very thoughtful of others, which is shown in his care for his siblings.]

C. Critical Reading: Making Inferences

? What can you infer from Baldwin's statement about his poetry? [He does not like the poetry that he wrote and obviously feels more comfortable with other genres of writing.]

D. Exploring the Culture

In the 1940s and 1950s, many African American writers left the United States for Paris, seeking a community that was less prejudiced and racially divided than the ones they left behind. Among the expatriates were James Baldwin and Richard Wright.

Danny Lyon/Magnum.

(A) I was born in Harlem thirty-one years ago. I began plotting novels at about the time I learned to read. The story of my childhood is the usual bleak fantasy, and we can dismiss it with the restrained observation that I certainly would not consider living it again. In those days my mother was given to the exasperating and mysterious habit of having babies. As they were born, I took them over with one hand and held a book with (B) the other. The children probably suffered, though they have since been kind enough to deny it, and in this way I read *Uncle Tom's Cabin* and *A Tale of Two Cities* over and over and over again; in this way, in fact, I read just about everything I could get my hands on—except the Bible, probably because it was the only book I was encouraged to read. I must also confess that I wrote—a great deal—and my first professional triumph, in any case, the first effort of mine to be seen in print, occurred at the age of twelve or thereabouts, when a short story I had written about the Spanish revolution won some sort of a prize in an extremely short-lived church newspaper. I remember the story was censored by the lady editor, though I don't remember why, and I was outraged.

(C) Also wrote plays, and songs, for one of which I received a letter of congratulations from Mayor La Guardia,[1] and poetry, about which the less said, the better. My mother was delighted by all these goings-on, but my father wasn't; he wanted me to be a preacher. When I was fourteen I became a preacher, and when I was seventeen I stopped. Very shortly thereafter I left home. For God knows how long I struggled with the world of commerce and industry—I guess they would say they struggled with *me*—and when I was about twenty-one I had enough done of a novel to get a Saxton Fellowship. When I was twenty-two the fellowship was over, the novel turned out to be unsalable, and I started waiting on tables in a Village[2] restaurant and writing book reviews—mostly, as it turned out, about the Negro problem, concerning which the color of my skin made me automatically an expert. Did another book, in company with photographer Theodore Pelatowski, about the store-front churches in Harlem. This book met exactly the same fate as my first—fellowship, but no sale. (It (D) was a Rosenwald Fellowship.) By the time I was twenty-four I had decided to stop reviewing books about the Negro problem—which, by this time, was only slightly less horrible in print than it was in life—and I packed my bags and went to France, where I finished, God knows how, *Go Tell It on the Mountain.*

Any writer, I suppose, feels that the world into which he was born is nothing less than a conspiracy against the cultivation of his talent—which attitude certainly has a great deal to support it. On

1. **Mayor La Guardia:** Fiorello La Guardia, mayor of New York City from 1934 to 1945.
2. **Village:** Greenwich Village, a section of Manhattan noted as a center for writers and other artists.

WORDS TO OWN

bleak (blēk) *adj.:* cheerless.
censored (sen′sərd) *v.:* cut or changed to remove material deemed objectionable.

OPTIONS FOR TEACHING

STRATEGIES FOR INCLUSION

Intrapersonal Before students read the essay, have them consider the title and apply it to themselves. What would "autobiographical notes" of their own lives be like? Encourage students to think of their future as well as their past for their notes. *Emphasize that students do not have to share anything with the class that they would not feel comfortable discussing with other students.*

Auditory If possible, obtain an audio tape of James Baldwin reading or discussing his writing, and play the tape for the class. In a library, you may also be able to find a videotape of his speeches, such as the one he gave after Dr. Martin Luther King, Jr., was assassinated. Ask students for their impressions of the author based on the audiotape or videotape.

Musical Point out to students that Baldwin, on p. 1146, compares African American prose and music. Ask students to think of African American styles of music. Then, discuss with students why Baldwin might complain that African American prose is "pallid and harsh" in contrast.

the other hand, it is only because the world looks on his talent with such a frightening indifference that the artist is compelled to make his talent important. So that any writer, looking back over even so short a span of time as I am here forced to assess, finds that the things which hurt him and the things which helped him cannot be divorced from each other; he could be helped in a certain way only because he was hurt in a certain way; and his help is simply to be enabled to move from one conundrum to the next—one is tempted to say that he moves from one disaster to the next. When one begins looking for influences one finds them by the score. I haven't thought much about my own, not enough anyway; I hazard that the King James Bible, the rhetoric of the storefront church, something ironic and violent and perpetually understated in Negro speech—and something of Dickens' love for bravura[3]—have something to do with me today; but I wouldn't stake my life on it. Likewise, innumerable people have helped me in many ways; but finally, I suppose, the most difficult (and most rewarding) thing in my life has been the fact that I was born a Negro and was forced, therefore, to effect some kind of truce with this reality. (Truce, by the way, is the best one can hope for.)

One of the difficulties about being a Negro writer (and this is not special pleading, since I don't mean to suggest that he has it worse than anybody else) is that the Negro problem is written about so widely. The bookshelves groan under the weight of information, and everyone therefore considers himself informed. And this information, furthermore, operates usually (generally, popularly) to reinforce traditional attitudes. Of traditional attitudes there are only two—For or Against—and I, personally, find it difficult to say which attitude has caused me the most pain. I am speaking as a writer; from a social point of view I am perfectly aware that the change from ill-will to good-will, however motivated, however imperfect, however expressed, is better than no change at all.

But it is part of the business of the writer—as I see it—to examine attitudes, to go beneath the surface, to tap the source. From this point of view the Negro problem is nearly inaccessible. It is not only written about so widely; it is written about so badly. It is quite possible to say that the price a Negro pays for becoming articulate is to find himself, at length, with nothing to be articulate about. ("You taught me language," says Caliban to Prospero,[4] "and my profit on't is I know how to curse.") Consider: the tremendous social activity that this problem generates imposes on whites and Negroes alike the necessity of looking forward, of working to bring about a better day. This is fine, it keeps the waters troubled; it is all, indeed, that has made possible the Negro's progress. Nevertheless, social affairs are not generally speaking the writer's prime concern, whether they ought to be or not; it is absolutely necessary that he establish between himself and these affairs a distance which will allow, at least, for clarity, so that before he can look forward in any meaningful sense, he must first be allowed to take a long look back. In the context of the Negro problem neither whites nor blacks, for excellent reasons of their own, have the faintest desire to look back; but I think that the past is all that makes the present coherent, and further, that the past will remain horrible for exactly as long as we refuse to assess it honestly.

I know, in any case, that the most crucial time in my own development came when I was forced to recognize that I was a kind of bastard of the West; when I followed the line of my past I did not find myself in Europe but in Africa. And this meant that in some subtle way, in a really profound way, I brought to Shakespeare, Bach, Rembrandt, to the stones of Paris, to the cathedral at Chartres, and to the Empire State Building, a special attitude. These were not really my creations, they did not contain my history; I might search in them in vain forever for any reflection of myself. I was an interloper; this was not my heritage. At the

3. **bravura** (brə·vyoor'ə): florid, brilliant style.

4. **Caliban to Prospero:** Caliban, a rough creature, is Prospero's slave, whom Prospero tries to civilize in *The Tempest* by William Shakespeare. The quotation is from Act I, Scene 2, lines 363–364.

WORDS TO OWN

assess (ə·ses') *v.:* to evaluate; judge the value of.
conundrum (kə·nun'drəm) *n.:* riddle.
coherent (kō·hir'ənt) *adj.:* clear, logical, and consistent.
crucial (kro͞o'shəl) *adj.:* critical; decisive.
interloper (in'tər·lō'pər) *n.:* intruder or meddler.

E. Literary Element: Paradox

? What is the central paradox that Baldwin finds as an African American writer? [What hurts him nevertheless serves as material for his writing; the prejudice and hate that he faces fuel his creative fires.]

F. Reader's Response: Challenging the Text

? Do you agree that a truce is the best an African American can hope for? [Sample responses: Yes, because there will always be racial bias, and a person cannot change the color of his or her skin. No, there have been great strides made in racial relations since the essay was written, and more than just a truce is possible.]

G. Critical Reading: Making Inferences

? How can even the actions of those who support African Americans cause pain? [Possible answer: Baldwin suggests that an overeager desire to help may hurt when it is condescending, motivated by the wrong reasons, or expressed in an awkward way.]

H. Reader's Response: Extending the Text

? Do you agree with what Baldwin is saying about the effect of not facing up to our history? Why or why not? [Sample responses: I agree; just as a person must address a personal past in order to deal with his or her present and future, a society must address the past, or it will repeat its mistakes. Or I disagree, because it is very easy to get stuck in the past; the important thing about race relations is to concentrate on people's common situation and common goals.]

I. Critical Reading: Summarizing

? What is the special attitude that Baldwin brought to these people and things? [He felt that he was alien to the culture that had produced these artists and works, but he did not belong to any other culture. He had to consciously make European culture his own.]

INTEGRATING THE LANGUAGE ARTS

Strategic Reading Using information from the text, have students make inferences from the reading. After they have recorded their inferences, ask them to support their inferences by writing information from the text. After completing their reading, they can note the actual outcome and compare it with their inferences. Help students to identify the thought processes used while they were making inferences and to use metacognitive strategies to evaluate the processes.

Inferences	Support	Outcome

Writing: Magazine Article Ask students to imagine themselves in the future, successful at the careers they now envision for themselves. How would they describe the struggles that got them to the top? How would they have had to "create" themselves? Direct students to write their descriptions in the form of a brief magazine article. Ask volunteers to share their articles with the class. *Remind students to choose a situation they would not mind sharing with others.*

A. Critical Reading: Finding Cause and Effect

? How could Baldwin's hatred of the world prevent him from writing? [Possible answers: If he hated and feared the world, he could not understand it, and thus could not write about it. Or if he hated the world, he hated himself too, and he could not create—he could only destroy.]

B. Critical Reading: Evaluating an Interpretation

? Do you agree that art is the making of order out of personal experience? Explain. [Possible answers: Yes, because one has to come to some conclusions about things before one can write about them. No, because art just as easily can reflect life's disorder without organizing it.]

C. Literary Connections

In 1949, William Faulkner (pp. 713–714) received the Nobel Prize in literature. Robert Penn Warren was the first poet laureate of the United States. Ralph Ellison wrote of the African American search for identity in his novel *Invisible Man.*

D. Critical Reading: Analyzing Character

? How does this passage make you revise your understanding of Baldwin? [Possible answers: The passage shows a more fun-loving side of the author. The passage shows hope, too.]

E. Language Note: Paragraph

? Why is this sentence set alone at the end of the essay, instead of being at the end of the previous paragraph? [Possible answer: Setting the sentence by itself emphasizes it as the main idea of the essay and gives it a dramatic weight.]

same time I had no other heritage which I could possibly hope to use—I had certainly been unfitted for the jungle or the tribe. I would have to appropriate these white centuries, I would have to make them mine—I would have to accept my special attitude, my special place in this scheme—otherwise I would have no place in *any* scheme. What was the most difficult was the fact that I was forced to admit something I had always hidden from myself, which the American Negro has had to hide from himself as the price of his public progress; that I hated and feared white people. This did not mean that I loved black people; on the contrary, I despised them, possibly because they failed to produce Rembrandt. In effect, I hated and feared the world. And this meant, not only that I thus gave the world an altogether murderous power over me, but also that in such a self-destroying limbo[5] I could never hope to write.

One writes out of one thing only—one's own experience. Everything depends on how relentlessly one forces from this experience the last drop, sweet or bitter, it can possibly give. This is the only real concern of the artist, to recreate out of the disorder of life that order which is art. The difficulty then, for me, of being a Negro writer was the fact that I was, in effect, prohibited from examining my own experience too closely by the tremendous demands and the very real dangers of my social situation.

I don't think the dilemma outlined above is uncommon. I do think, since writers work in the disastrously explicit medium of language, that it goes a little way toward explaining why, out of the enormous resources of Negro speech and life, and despite the example of Negro music, prose written by Negroes has been generally speaking so pallid and so harsh. I have not written about being a Negro at such length because I expect that to be my only subject, but only because it was the gate I had to unlock before I could hope to write about anything else. I don't think that the Negro problem in America can be even discussed coherently without bearing in mind its context; its context being the history, traditions, customs, the moral assumptions and preoccupations of the country; in short, the general social fabric. Appearances to the contrary, no one in America escapes its effects and everyone in America bears some responsibility for it. I believe this the more firmly because it is the overwhelming tendency to speak of this problem as though it were a thing apart. But in the work of Faulkner, in the general attitude and certain specific passages in Robert Penn Warren, and, most significantly, in the advent of Ralph Ellison, one sees the beginnings—at least—of a more genuinely penetrating search. Mr. Ellison, by the way, is the first Negro novelist I have ever read to utilize in language, and brilliantly, some of the ambiguity and irony of Negro life.

About my interests: I don't know if I have any, unless the morbid desire to own a sixteen-millimeter camera and make experimental movies can be so classified. Otherwise, I love to eat and drink—it's my melancholy conviction that I've scarcely ever had enough to eat (this is because it's *impossible* to eat enough if you're worried about the next meal)—and I love to argue with people who do not disagree with me too profoundly, and I love to laugh. I do *not* like bohemia,[6] or bohemians, I do not like people whose principal aim is pleasure, and I do not like people who are *earnest* about anything. I don't like people who like me because I'm a Negro; neither do I like people who find in the same accident grounds for contempt. I love America more than any other country in the world, and, exactly for this reason, I insist on the right to criticize her perpetually. I think all theories are suspect, that the finest principles may have to be modified, or may even be pulverized by the demands of life, and that one must find, therefore, one's own moral center and move through the world hoping that this center will guide one aright. I consider that I have many responsibilities, but none greater than this: to last, as Hemingway says, and get my work done.

I want to be an honest man and a good writer.

5. **limbo:** borderland state of uncertainty and oblivion.

6. **bohemia:** any nonconformist, unconventional community, often made up of writers and other artists.

WORDS TO OWN

appropriate (ə·prō′prē·āt) *v.:* to take over.
explicit (eks·plis′it) *adj.:* clear; definite.
pulverized (pul′vər·īzd′) *v.:* crushed; destroyed.

OPTIONS FOR TEACHING

CROSSING THE CURRICULUM

Social Sciences Remind students that James Baldwin was an active member of the civil rights movement. Arrange students in small groups, and have the groups research his role in the movement. What issues were important to him? How did he become involved? What are some of his works that address the topic of civil rights? Have the groups share their findings with the class.

ASSESSMENT TOOLS

Check Test: True-False

1. James Baldwin is the youngest in a family of many children. [False]
2. Baldwin was encouraged as a child to read the Bible. [True]
3. As a young man, Baldwin lived for a while in Mexico. [False]
4. Baldwin accuses both blacks and whites of dwelling too much on their past conflicts. [False]
5. Baldwin says that above all he loves the bohemian life. [False]

Making Meanings

First Thoughts

1. What do you think were James Baldwin's main goals in writing "Autobiographical Notes"? Do you think he achieved his purpose? Explain.

Shaping Interpretations

2. Describe Baldwin's **tone** toward his subject matter. What specific words or details helped you to identify the tone? Do you share his attitude?
3. How do you think Baldwin feels about himself?
4. Baldwin says that Ralph Ellison was the first African American novelist "to utilize in language, and brilliantly, some of the ambiguity and irony of Negro life." What do you think he means?
5. Review the notes you made in your Reader's Log. Why does Baldwin say his "social situation" as an African American creates a dilemma for Baldwin the writer?

Challenging the Text

6. Do you agree with Baldwin's statement that "the world looks on [the artist's] talent with such a frightening indifference"? Back up your opinion with examples of contemporary writers, painters, musicians, or other artists.

Reviewing the Text

a. According to the essay, what was the most crucial time in Baldwin's development? What did he learn about himself then?
b. How does Baldwin describe the business of the writer, and what does this have to do with what he calls "the Negro problem"?
c. According to Baldwin, how does a writer make use of his or her experiences?
d. What does Baldwin say is his greatest responsibility?

Choices: Building Your Portfolio

Writer's Notebook

1. Collecting Ideas for an Evaluation

When you evaluate nonfiction, you can focus on the writer's objectivity. That is, you can examine how balanced the writer is, how much evidence the writer uses to support his or her opinions and judgments. Examine Baldwin's essay to see if he offers examples, facts, and reasons for his views. Does he try to be objective in all his statements? Or are some statements purely subjective and emotional and not supported by hard evidence? Take notes on the ways Baldwin presents his views, and save your notes for the Writer's Workshop on page 1181.

Critical Writing

2. The Past Is Prologue

Baldwin believes that "the past is all that makes the present coherent." In a short essay, discuss the implications of this belief. You may want to consider the effects of the past on education, government, the arts, or an individual's intellectual or spiritual growth.

Critical Writing

3. Echoes of Emerson

Re-read the excerpt from Ralph Waldo Emerson's "Self-Reliance" (page 224) closely. Then, in a few paragraphs, compare the **diction** and **tone** of Emerson's famous essay with Baldwin's "Autobiographical Notes."

Creative Writing / Speaking and Listening

4. Response to a Native Son

In the form of a letter, poem, newspaper Op-Ed article, or dialogue, respond to one or more of Baldwin's points in "Autobiographical Notes." You might call your piece "Letter to a Native Son, ____ Years Later." Present your response orally to the class.

Making Meanings

First Thoughts

1. Possible response: Baldwin's main goal was to give the reader an idea of how he viewed himself as an African American writer; he succeeded by describing in detail the "Negro problem" and the reality he faced as an African American writer.

Reviewing the Text

a. Baldwin says that the most crucial time in his development was when he realized that he had to approach Western culture with an African American perspective. He learned that he hated and feared the world.
b. Baldwin says that the business of the writer is going beneath the surfaces and examining attitudes. He writes that the "Negro problem" is inaccessible, because, although it is written about widely, it is analyzed badly. He says that although an honest assessment of the past may be painful for members of both races, such an assessment is vital.
c. A writer makes use of his or her experiences by relentlessly analyzing and utilizing the past.
d. He says that his greatest responsibility is to last and to get his work done.

Shaping Interpretations

2. Baldwin's tone may be described as good-humored, passionate, direct, creative, and critical. This tone is established from the first paragraph in the description of his childhood memories. Students may respond that they do not feel as comfortable as Baldwin viewing matters of race so directly and with such easy shifts between strong emotions and objectivity.
3. Baldwin's attitude toward himself is objective: He understands the dilemma that he faces as an African American, and he considers himself honest and hard-working.
4. Students may say that Ellison is able to express in fiction the complex and contradictory reality of life as an African American.
5. Baldwin's "social situation" as an African American resulted in his hating and fearing the world. He could not write, filled as he was with so much hate.

Challenging the Text

6. **(Evaluation)** Possible response: Most artists live in states of relative poverty as they struggle to produce their work. Public funding for the arts is minimal. Some artists do well, however; some writers, such as Stephen King, make a lot of money and gain worldwide fame.

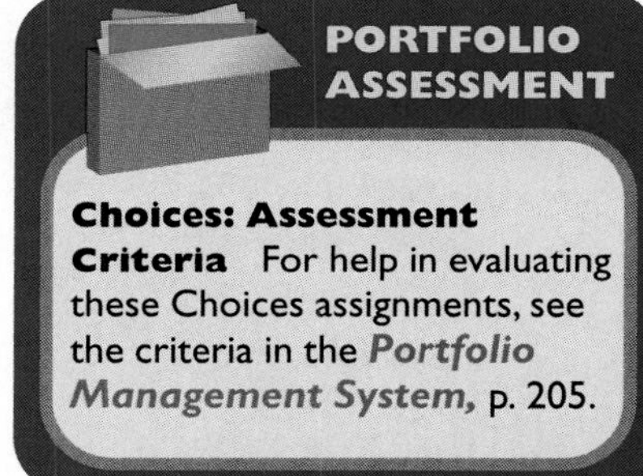

Choices: Assessment Criteria For help in evaluating these Choices assignments, see the criteria in the ***Portfolio Management System,*** p. 205.

QUICK PLANNING GUIDE

Into the Poem

Author Biography p. 1148
Before You Read p. 1149

- **Reading Focus:** Students consider a mirror's point of view.
- **Quickwrite: Scaffolding** Think of observations a mirror would make
- **Elements of Literature: Personification**

Through the Poem

"Mirror" p. 1149
Connections: Two Poems p. 1150
Making Meanings p. 1151

Beyond the Poem

Choices: Building Your Portfolio p. 1151

- **Writer's Notebook:** Write a paragraph giving background information
- **Critical Writing:** Compare and contrast two poems
- **Creative Writing:** Write a poem from the point of view of a mirror
- **Art:** Make a piece of artwork representing a view in a mirror

ABOUT THE AUTHOR

Though her writing career was short, Sylvia Plath is considered one of the most important American writers of the post–World War II period. Plath did not achieve fame until *Ariel* was published after her death. Another arrangement of poems, *The Collected Poems,* won the Pulitzer Prize in poetry in 1981, eighteen years after her death. A collection of her short stories, *Johnny Panic and the Bible of Dreams,* was published in 1977.

Sylvia Plath

(1932–1963)

Until her death in 1963, Sylvia Plath's life was, to most outward appearances, a model of achievement. This success, however, could not fully mask nor calm a fearsome inner turmoil. Plath was born in Boston and spent her early years in the nearby seaside town of Winthrop. Both her parents were immigrants—her father, a professor of biology, from Poland; her mother, a teacher of office skills, from Austria. According to the critic A. Alvarez, Plath later seemed convinced that the reason for her emotional suffering as an adult was her father's death from diabetes when she was only eight.

© Rollie McKenna.

Plath started writing poems and stories in elementary school, and she first published a poem in a Boston newspaper around the time of her father's death. From an early age, she was persistent in finding a publisher for her work; for instance, she persevered through forty-five rejection slips from *Seventeen* magazine before landing a story there in 1950. Plath was awarded a scholarship to Smith College, where she flourished academically and continued to pursue creative writing. She won a much-coveted fiction prize from *Mademoiselle* magazine in her junior year and spent that summer as a guest editor in the magazine's New York office.

The first serious sign of dangerous turbulence in Plath's emotional life came at the end of that seemingly storybook summer, when she was overcome by depression and attempted suicide, an experience that became the basis for her novel *The Bell Jar*. After psychiatric treatment and electroshock therapy—"the painful agony of slow rebirth and psychic regeneration," as she called it—she returned to college. But she was ill with manic depression, years before effective drug therapy was available.

After graduating from Smith, Plath attended Cambridge University in England on a Fulbright fellowship. At Cambridge, she met the noted English poet Ted Hughes, whom she married in 1956. They lived in Boston during most of the late 1950s and moved to London at the end of 1959. The following year, Plath's first book of poetry, *The Colossus,* was published, and their daughter Frieda was born; their son Nicholas was born in 1962. "Mirror," the selection that follows, was written in 1961.

In January 1963, Plath's famous autobiographical novel, *The Bell Jar,* was published. In the few weeks between its publication and her death, Plath wrote poetry at a furious pace—sometimes two or three poems a day. The subject matter and style of these poems, published posthumously in *Ariel* (1965), were different from her earlier work. Most poems in *The Colossus* were relatively restrained and formal, influenced by a number of poetic styles, from the classicism of John Crowe Ransom (page 577) to the exuberance of Theodore Roethke (page 1001). But the *Ariel* poems, especially the bitter poems about her father and her attempts at suicide, showed a violence and a frankness absent from her earlier work. Robert Lowell (page 948) wrote in the book's foreword, "These poems are playing Russian roulette with six cartridges in the cylinder, a game of 'chicken,' the wheels of both cars locked and unable to swerve." The poems were, he said, an "appalling and triumphant fulfillment" of her talents. Anne Sexton (page 1088) observed, "These last poems stun me. They eat time."

By 1963, Plath was separated from her husband and caring for their two young children in an unheated London flat. In February, during a very cold London winter, Plath's depression returned. She attempted suicide again. This time she succeeded.

PROGRAM MANAGER

- **Planning Instruction** See **Teaching Notes, *Teaching Resources B,*** p. 204, for objectives, a summary, and literary elements for this selection.
- **Instructional Support** Before beginning the instructional lesson, see **Graphic Organizer for Active Reading, *Teaching Resources B,*** p. 213, for a Through the Poem activity.
- **Audiotaped Readings** To help less proficient readers or auditory learners through the lesson, use the **Selected Reading, Audiocassette 3, Side B,** in the ***Audiovisual Resources Binder.***

- **Assessment** See **Selection Test, *Test Booklet,*** pp. 265–266.

BEFORE YOU READ
MIRROR

Reading Focus
Reflections
We all do it: We check our appearance in a mirror, partly to make sure we are appropriately groomed, partly in order to discover and polish our self-image. What might a mirror—"silver and exact"—think of the person peering into it?

Quickwrite
READER'S LOG

If a mirror could talk, what might it say about the concerns of the people passing before it? In your Reader's Log, write a few observations that a "talking" mirror might make.

Elements of Literature
Personification
Personification is a figure of speech in which an object (such as a mirror) or an animal is given human qualities, such as feelings, thoughts, and attitudes. At its heart, personification is a type of metaphor in which two dissimilar things are compared. For instance, if you say "A mirror tells no lies," you are comparing a mirror to a person by giving it a human attribute.

Courtesy Marisa Del Re Gallery, New York.

Mirror IV (1976–1979) by George Tooker. Egg tempera on gesso panel (24″ × 20″).

Mirror
Sylvia Plath

I am silver and exact. I have no preconceptions.
Whatever I see I swallow immediately
Just as it is, unmisted by love or dislike.
I am not cruel, only truthful— **A**
The eye of a little god, four-cornered.
Most of the time I meditate on the opposite wall.
It is pink, with speckles. I have looked at it so long
I think it is a part of my heart. But it flickers.
Faces and darkness separate us over and over.
Now I am a lake. A woman bends over me,
Searching my reaches for what she really is. **B**
Then she turns to those liars, the candles or the moon.
I see her back, and reflect it faithfully.
She rewards me with tears and an agitation of hands. **C**
I am important to her. She comes and goes.
Each morning it is her face that replaces the darkness.
In me she has drowned a young girl, and in me an old woman
Rises toward her day after day, like a terrible fish. **D**

Using BEFORE YOU READ
p. 1149

Quickwrite
Ask students to imagine themselves in a mirror's position. What would they think of the people or things that passed in front of them? Encourage students to begin their writing by brainstorming ideas.

A. Literary Element: Personification

? How does the mirror assess itself? Do you agree with the mirror? [The mirror sees itself as honest and perfect. Students may say that the mirror's lack of emotion does in fact make it cruel.]

B. Humanities Connection
In Greek mythology, Narcissus was a handsome young man who was so enamored with his own image in a lake's surface that he was turned into a flower beside the lake. This myth is the origin of the term *narcissism*, meaning "exclusive love of self." Alert students to pay attention to how the poet uses the myth in the poem.

C. Critical Reading: Making Inferences

? Why does the woman "reward" the mirror by crying and being upset? [She does not like what she sees in the mirror. Students may infer that she thinks she is ugly or that she is losing her beauty.]

D. Cultural Connections
Ask students why the woman may be upset to find herself growing older. Then, encourage students to think of ways that age is valued and respected in various cultures. Challenge students also to name people who have proven the stereotypes about aging wrong by what people might consider their more youthful actions and attitudes.

STRATEGIES FOR INCLUSION

Spatial/Kinesthetic As students read the poem, encourage them to keep in mind the perspective of the speaker. Suggest students imagine themselves first as a mirror in the classroom, staring out at eye level from a position they cannot change. They may wish to practice reading in front of a mirror. Then, have students imagine the mirror in the specific setting of the poem. Students may read the poem aloud in the posture of the speaker: rigid, speaking unemotionally and evenly.

INTEGRATING THE LANGUAGE ARTS

Strategic Reading Have students take notes on the connection between the poem's speaker and subject. Students may write their notes in two columns. In the right column, students should write the mirror's thoughts and feelings, and in the left column, the thoughts and feelings of the woman. Direct students to connect the notes on both sides and to label each connection. Is it cause and effect? A similarity? A contrast? Have students compare their work.

A. Literary Elements: Tone and Style

? Judging by the line of dialogue in the first poem, how would you describe the poem's style and tone? [The poem's style is simple, direct, and casual; its tone is breezy, confident, and upbeat.]

B. Critical Reading: Identifying Main Ideas

? What does the first poem's final sentence tell you about the speaker's experience of looking in the mirror? [For her, looking in the mirror is a very positive, affirming experience. She likes the way she looks.]

C. Critical Reading: Making Generalizations

? How would you characterize the face in the mirror? [Possible answer: The face is battered by experience but animated, feisty, and determined.]

D. Reader's Response: Challenging the Text

? Do you think the last two lines are an appropriate end to the poem? Explain. [Sample responses: The lines are not appropriate because the poem has nothing to do with a lady, only the speaker; or the lines are appropriate because they contrast the speaker's face with what the speaker expects to be faced with in life.]

Connections — Two Poems

The following poems by Marilyn Nelson Waniek (1946–   ) and Robert Graves (1895–1985) explore other encounters with reflections.

A Strange Beautiful Woman

Marilyn Nelson Waniek

A strange beautiful woman
met me in the mirror
the other night.
Hey,
I said,
What you doing here?
She asked me
the same thing.

The Face in the Mirror

Robert Graves

Grey haunted eyes, absent-mindedly glaring
From wide, uneven orbits; one brow drooping
Somewhat over the eye
Because of a missile fragment still inhering,
Skin deep, as a foolish record of old-world fighting.

Crookedly broken nose—low tackling caused it;
Cheeks, furrowed; coarse grey hair, flying frenetic;
Forehead, wrinkled and high;
Jowls, prominent; ears, large; jaw, pugilistic;
Teeth, few; lips, full and ruddy; mouth, ascetic.

I paused with razor poised, scowling derision
At the mirrored man whose beard needs my attention,
And once more ask him why
He still stands ready, with a boy's presumption,
To court the queen in her high silk pavilion.

CONNECTING TO "MIRROR"

Ask students how the poems above compare to "Mirror." Then, have students discuss whether the difference in the points of view of the poems' speakers accounts for the difference in their tones. [Part of the cruelty of "Mirror" comes from the objective, overly critical perspective of the inhuman mirror. The exuberant human speaker of "A Strange Beautiful Woman" looks at herself much more compassionately and understandingly. The speaker of "The Face in the Mirror" falls in between; he assesses himself honestly and critically but manages to do so with some humor and hope.]

MAKING MEANINGS

First Thoughts

1. What thoughts or feelings did "Mirror" evoke in you? Did you find the poem surprising in any way? Explain.

Shaping Interpretations

2. Identify the **speaker** of the poem. In what ways does Plath **personify** the speaker?
3. Describe the qualities that the speaker claims to possess. Are any of these qualities implausible, or hard to believe? What does the speaker imply by saying "the eye of a little god" (line 5)?
4. What comparison is Plath making between the mirror and "the candles or the moon" (line 12)? What is the significance of this comparison in the poem?
5. The last line of "Mirror" contains the striking **image** of "a terrible fish." How would you explain the significance of this image in the poem? What associations and emotional overtones does the image have for you?

Extending the Text

6. Plath frequently alludes to myths in her poems. "Mirror" recalls the ancient Greek myth of Narcissus. Find and read the story of Narcissus, and identify ways in which you think the woman in the poem is like and unlike that mythical character.

Challenging the Text

7. "A mirror tells no lies" is a common saying. Referring to the notes in your Reader's Log, discuss whether you think the speaker of the poem is "exact" (line 1) and "truthful" (line 4) about the woman, or omits mention of her more important aspects.

CHOICES: Building Your Portfolio

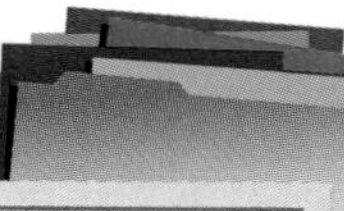

Writer's Notebook

1. Collecting Ideas for an Evaluation

When you evaluate a work of literature, you must decide how much background information you'll need to supply—either on the writer or on the text. If readers are new to the subject, you'll need to provide considerable background; if readers are already knowledgeable, you should provide much less. Draft the opening paragraph of an evaluation of Plath's "Mirror," in which you present some background information about the poet. (Your essay should be targeted at readers with some knowledge of poetry but no familiarity with Plath.) Save your draft for possible use in the Writer's Workshop on page 1181.

Critical Writing

2. Reflections

In a brief essay, compare and contrast either Marilyn Nelson Waniek's or Robert Graves's poem in Connections (page 1150) to "Mirror." What points does each poem make about personal identity? How does each poem present the relationship between the observer and the observed? Explain the different meanings of the word *reflection* that these poems suggest.

Creative Writing

3. "Mirror, mirror, on the wall . . ."

Write a poem or prose paragraph from the point of view of a talking mirror. Your mirror might comment on or reflect a person or place you know.

Art

4. Mirroring Images

Imagine that a piece of paper (or poster board, or canvas, or another surface of your choice) is a mirror. Draw, paint, or make a collage of what you see in that "mirror."

Making Meanings

First Thoughts

1. Possible response: I first thought of human vanity—how much we look outside ourselves to confirm who we are—but the horror of the poem's ending surprised me. The poem is not about vanity but its opposite, a kind of overly critical cruelty.

Shaping Interpretations

2. The speaker of the poem is the mirror. Plath personifies the mirror by giving it a speaking voice, uses the first person pronoun *I*, and gives it human attributes of thought, vision, and intention.
3. The speaker claims to possess the human capacity to see and to analyze experience, both of which are plausibly realistic qualities. The mirror's claim to perfection is harder to believe. In the phrase "the eye of a little god," the speaker implies that an honest, objective perspective allows one a godlike view of the world.
4. The comparison concerns the conflicting human qualities of objectivity and romantic imagination. The mirror calls the candles and moon "liars" because they evoke romantic self-images in the speaker. They provide more flattering light in which to be seen.
5. The image of "a terrible fish" conveys the deepening pain and anguish that accompanies loss of self. The image is so monstrous that it suggests that aging is unnatural and that it destroys a person. Students may say that the image is shocking and depressing.

Extending the Text

6. **(Synthesis)** Possible response: The woman is like Narcissus in that both look at the outside themselves for their own self-image. They are dissimilar in that Narcissus falls in love with his self-image while the woman is destroyed by her reflection.

Challenging the Text

7. **(Evaluation)** Possible response: The mirror is truthful about what it sees, but it is not exact because it does not know the whole truth. The mirror does not know anything about the woman's thoughts and feelings; it makes judgments based only on appearances and so misses very important aspects of life.

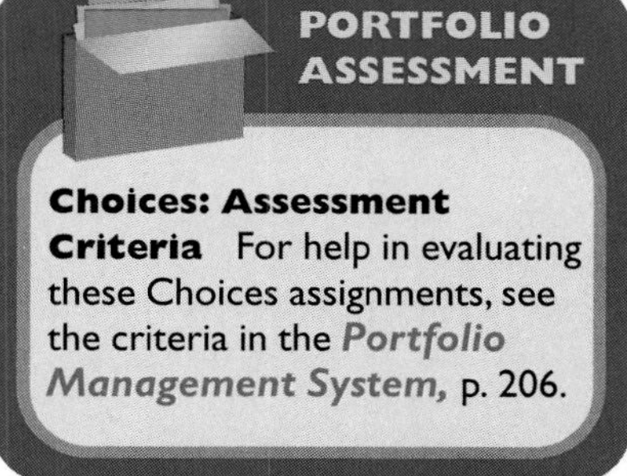

Choices: Assessment Criteria For help in evaluating these Choices assignments, see the criteria in the *Portfolio Management System,* p. 206.

ABOUT THE AUTHOR

Jorge Luis Borges was one of the primary figures of the Ultraista movement in Spanish and Spanish American literature after World War I. The Ultraistas were a group of avant-garde poets who were influenced heavily by the French Symbolists, and they were distinguished by their use of free verse and unconventional imagery. Borges's first published work was *Fervor de Buenos Aires* (1923), a collection of poems. His writing has been compared to that of Franz Kafka. In 1961, he and Samuel Beckett shared the Formentor Prize.

LITERATURE OF THE AMERICAS
ARGENTINA

Jorge Luis Borges
(1899–1986)

Jorge Luis Borges (bôr′hes) was born in Buenos Aires, the capital of Argentina. As a youth, Borges spent many hours reading in his father's large collection of Spanish and English books. He later wrote, "If I were asked to name the chief event in my life, I should say my father's library." Borges lived in Europe with his family from 1914 to 1921, attending school for four of those years in Geneva, Switzerland.

Returning to Buenos Aires, the highly educated Borges soon turned to writing and to editing literary journals. Beginning in the late 1930s, he earned a living mostly as a librarian and teacher, serving from 1955 to 1973 as director of Argentina's national library. Borges continued to write, and in the early 1960s he gained wide recognition as one of the world's great contemporary writers. He subsequently taught at leading universities (including Harvard) and was awarded high honors by numerous countries and educational institutions.

Borges's long list of publications (some translated into English) includes the remarkable stories in *Ficciones, 1935–1944* (1944); the prose and poetry of *El hacedor* (1960); the poetry collection *Elogio de la sombra* (1969); and the subtle stories of *El libro de arena* (1975). Borges also translated into Spanish the writings of Herman Melville, Walt Whitman, Virginia Woolf, William Faulkner, Franz Kafka, and other noted authors. Translations into English of Borges's writing include *Selected Poems, 1923–1967* (1972) and *Borges: A Reader* (1981).

S. Bassouls/Sygma.

Borges began to lose his eyesight in his twenties, and as he grew into total blindness in his fifties, he took to dictating his works. Late in life, when Borges learned he was suffering from cancer, he returned to Switzerland. He married his longtime assistant and collaborator Maria Kodama just seven weeks before he died.

Background

Ask students to characterize the work of Poe and Whitman, two influences on Borges. Encourage students to speculate on the style that might emerge from such influences. Discuss also with students what they expect of the piece of writing. Students may make notes of their expectations to review after they have finished reading.

BEFORE YOU READ
BORGES AND MYSELF

Background

Few writers create a body of literature so distinctive that its characteristics are immediately recognizable, widely imitated, and ultimately turned into an adjective—for example, *Dantean, Shakespearean, Emersonian, Whitmanesque, Kafkaesque.* In our time, *Borgesian* is an adjective frequently applied to writing that is mysterious, playful, ambiguous, and profoundly concerned with questions of identity, fate, time, and language.

Perhaps the writer who most fully exemplifies the experimental side of postmodern literature, Jorge Luis Borges has produced fictionlike essays, nonfiction-like stories, essaylike poems, and other hybrid, unclassifiable works. His characters are as

PROGRAM MANAGER

- **Selection Summary** See Teaching Notes, *Teaching Resources B,* pp. 204–205, for a summary of this selection.
- **Audiotaped Readings** To help less proficient readers or auditory learners through the lesson, use the Selected Reading, Audiocassette 3, Side B, in the *Audiovisual Resources Binder.*

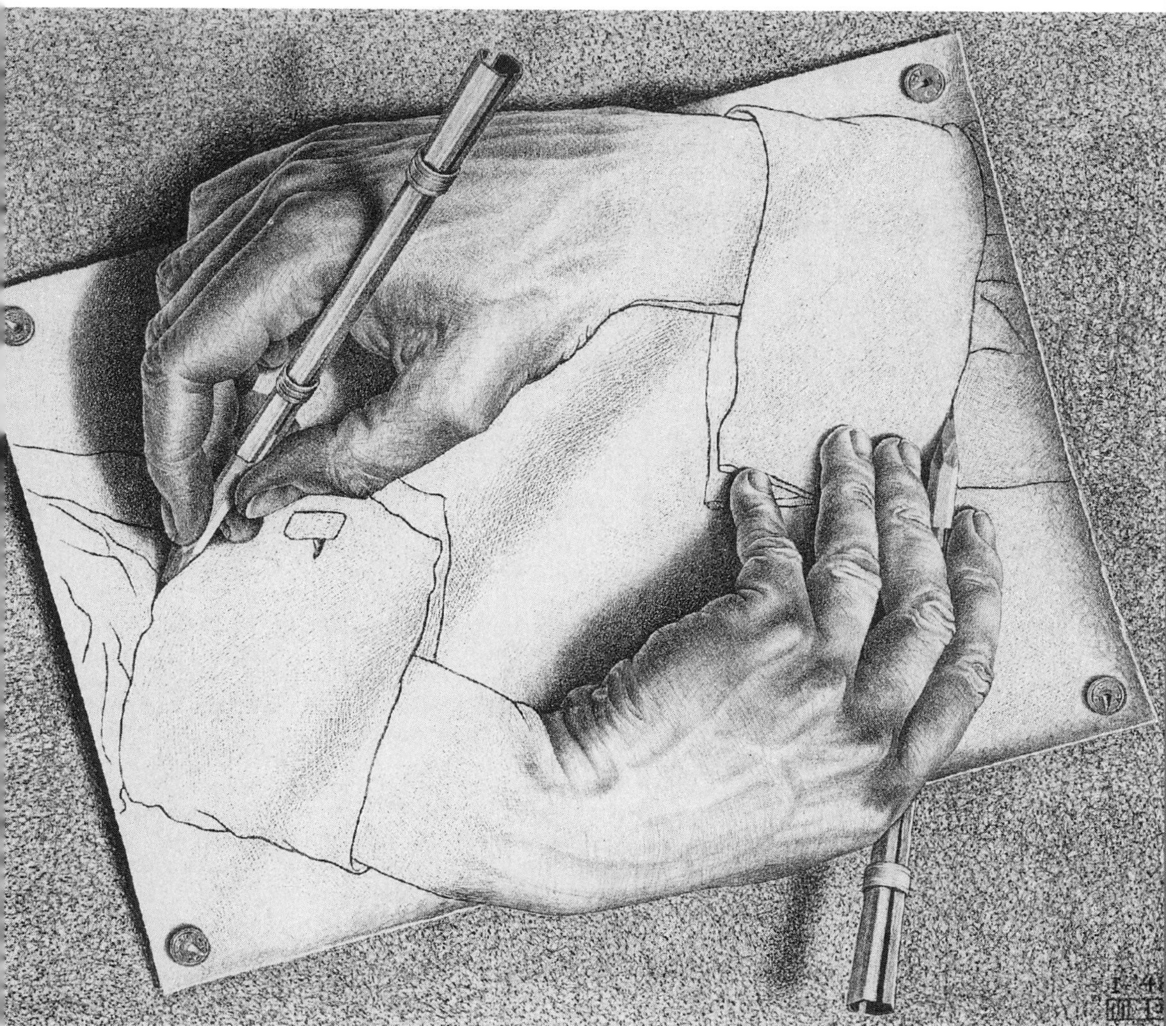

Drawing Hands (1948) by M. C. Escher. Lithograph (11 ⅛″ × 13 ⅛″).

hybrid as his forms. People meet their doubles and often don't know whether they are coming or going, literally, in the labyrinth of the universe. Borgesian time can be circular, events can be endlessly repeated, and the boundaries between dream and reality are often erased.

Influenced by Edgar Allan Poe's sense of fantasy and by Walt Whitman's vision of universality, Borges in his turn has had an enormous influence on contemporary literature. His stories-within-stories approach, his concern with personal identity, and the self-conscious literariness of his fiction have become part of the common literary vocabulary of our age.

RESPONDING TO THE ART: ABOUT THE ARTIST

Maurits Cornelius Escher (1898–1971) was a Dutch artist known for lithographs and woodcuts that make use of optical illusions and geometric patterns. In an Escher print, water may flow uphill and staircases may spiral continuously upward and yet lead back to their starting points. Escher's work often contains repeated interlocking designs.

A Dialogue with the Text

Students may add to notes in their Reader's Logs by organizing their notes into a Venn diagram such as the one on Transparency 5 in the Transparency Package. Students may also use the diagram to look more closely at the connections between the "narrator" and "Borges."

A. Reader's Response: Shaping Interpretations

? What connection does this "other man" have to Borges the narrator? [Sample responses: The other man is the same as Borges but more showy and observable—maybe the other man is Borges's public persona. Or the other man is Borges the writer, his reputation and work habits, while Borges himself is just an ordinary person.]

B. Critical Reading: Making Inferences

? Why would Borges not recognize himself very well in his own books? [Possible answers: His writing is a kind of game or acting, but his life is real and more ambiguous and unruly. Or his writing is imaginative and abstract, while his life is centered on concrete sensory experiences.]

C. Reader's Response: Challenging the Text

? Does the text of Borges's writing suggest why the doubt might be important? Do you agree with the perspective? Explain. [Sample responses: The piece of writing suggests that the doubt is important because Borges feels like a stranger to his own work, and I think that would be a strange way to look at things. Or Borges is just playing a game; there have never been two men, only Borges and the power of his imagination.]

Finding Common Ground

Have each group use its discussion notes to write a paragraph stating and supporting the strongest conclusion that group members reached—that is, the conclusion that had greatest consensus. Have groups read their paragraphs aloud. Then, have the groups work to find their own common ground in their reactions to Borges's piece of writing.

A Dialogue with the Text

READER'S LOG

The following famous piece by Jorge Luis Borges is a very short investigation of personal identity and personal psychology. Like a great poem, however, it is so packed with subtleties and connections and surprises that you could profitably spend hours—even days—analyzing its contents. In fact, many scholarly essays have been written about the last sentence alone.

Divide a page in your Reader's Log into two columns, one headed "Narrator," the other "Borges." As you read, write down the key characteristics of each in the appropriate column. After you finish reading the piece, write a paragraph discussing what the puzzling last sentence might mean.

Borges and Myself

Jorge Luis Borges
translated by **Norman Thomas di Giovanni** *and* **Jorge Luis Borges**

It's to the other man, to Borges, that things happen. I walk along the streets of Buenos Aires, stopping now and then—perhaps out of habit—to look at the arch of an old entranceway or a grillwork gate; of Borges I get news through the mail and glimpse his name among a committee of professors or in a dictionary of biography. I have a (A) taste for hourglasses, maps, eighteenth-century typography, the roots of words, the smell of coffee, and Stevenson's[1] prose; the other man shares these likes, but in a showy way that turns them into stagy mannerisms. It would be an exaggeration to say that we are on bad terms; I live, I let myself live, so that Borges can weave his tales and poems, and those tales and poems are my justification. It is not hard for me to admit that he has managed to write a few worthwhile pages, but these pages cannot save me, perhaps because what is good no longer belongs to anyone—not even the other man—but rather to speech or tradition. In any case, I am fated to become lost once and for all, and only some moment of myself will survive in the other man. Little by little, I have been surrendering everything to him, even though I have evidence of his stubborn habit of falsification and exaggerating. Spinoza[2] held that all things try to keep on being themselves; a stone wants to be a stone and the tiger, a tiger. I shall remain in Borges, not in myself (if it is so that I am (B) someone), but I recognize myself less in his books than in those of others or than in the laborious tuning of a guitar. Years ago, I tried ridding myself of him and I went from myths of the outlying slums of the city to games with time and infinity, but those games are now part of Borges and I will have to turn to other things. And so, my life is a running away, and I lose everything and everything is left to oblivion or to the other man.

(C) Which of us is writing this page I don't know.

1. **Stevenson's:** Robert Louis Stevenson (1850–1894), Scottish writer.

2. **Spinoza** (spi·nō′zə): Baruch Spinoza (1632–1677), Dutch philosopher.

Finding Common Ground

Form a discussion group with four or five other students, with one student acting as recording secretary. Before you begin discussing Borges's piece, review the notes in your Reader's Logs. Then refer to them as necessary during the exchange of views.

- First, each person should present his or her overall reaction to the work. Then begin to pin down the main characteristics of the story's narrator and of Borges.
- As the group comes to an agreement on a characteristic, the recording secretary should write it down. The secretary should also note separately whenever group members can't agree on whether a particular characteristic applies.
- Finally, discuss the meaning of the selection's last sentence. Can you determine with some certainty who exactly wrote "Borges and Myself"? What do you think this selection is saying about questions of identity and self-creation?

CONNECTING WITH "THE CREATED SELF"

Tell students that the human body constantly produces new cells. Ask students to think of things that stay the same about a person through this constant physical change. Then, have students consider the questions that arise in Borges's piece of writing: What is the self? Is it constituted by what a person is or what a person does?

INTEGRATING THE LANGUAGE ARTS

Strategic Reading Students may easily be confused by the differences between Borges and his alter ego. Have students read the piece with a partner, and encourage students to pause in their reading to share their observations and questions. Direct students to read the piece two or three times, and then have the partners discuss their notes with the rest of the class.

ASSESSMENT TOOLS

Check Test: Questions and Answers

1. Who is "the other man" the narrator speaks of? [Borges the writer or public figure.]
2. Who is the narrator? [Borges the regular person.]
3. How does the narrator feel about Borges's writing? [It is his "justification," but he does not think too much of it.]
4. Which writer does Borges say he admires? [Robert Louis Stevenson.]

James Merrill

(1926–1995)

The influential poetry critic Helen Vendler once praised James Merrill in this way:

> The time eventually comes, in a good poet's career, when readers actively long for his books: to know that someone out there is writing down your century, your generation, your language, your life—under whatever terms of difference—makes you wish for news of yourself, for those authentic tidings of invisible things, as Wordsworth called them, that only come in the interpretation of life voiced by poetry.

Merrill had become, as Vendler said, "one of our indispensable poets"; when he died in 1995, many people, not only poets and not only Americans, felt a heartbreaking loss.

James Ingram Merrill was born in New York City, a son of a founder of Merrill Lynch, the giant financial-services company. He spent his early years in New York City and on the eastern part of Long Island, attended the Lawrenceville School in New Jersey, and graduated *summa cum laude* from Amherst College in 1947. In the 1950s, after living for extensive periods in Paris and Rome, Merrill began a practice (that lasted more than two decades) of dividing his years between Athens, Greece, and the seaside village of Stonington, Connecticut.

Merrill was an elegant stylist and a skilled craftsperson with words, whose earliest work showed signs of mastery. He avoided free verse, saying "I by and large put my faith in forms. The attention they require at once frees and channels the unconscious. . . . Even if your poem turns out badly, you've learned something about proportion and concision and selflessness."

Merrill published volumes of increasingly impressive poetry, beginning with *The Black Swan and Other Poems* (1946) and *First Poems* (1951) and later including *Nights and Days* (1966), *The Fire Screen* (1969), and *Braving the Elements* (1972). He then turned his attention to the slow and artful composition of a highly praised but controversial epic, *The Changing Light at Sandover* (1982). This unsettling work tells of sessions at a Ouija board that Merrill and a friend said they conducted with otherworldly spirits. One critic compared the book favorably to the visionary poems of William Blake and William Butler Yeats. Another said, "The verse never impedes the narrative; it enhances it with its exuberance of puns, amazing condensations of ideas and observations, feats of beautiful lyric sound."

Photograph © 1997 by Jill Krementz.

Soon after the publication of his epic, Merrill returned to writing lyrics that detailed his engagement with life as lived in Stonington and his winter residence in the historic "old town" of Key West, Florida. *A Scattering of Salts* (1995), the last poetry collection Merrill oversaw, appeared just after he died. He won numerous honors and awards for his poetry, including a Bollingen Prize, a Pulitzer Prize, and two National Book Awards.

Over the years, Merrill included more and more personal matters in his verse, but he never became as open and raw as Anne Sexton, Sylvia Plath, and other "confessional" poets of his time. In contrast, according to one reviewer, a principal characteristic of Merrill's poetry was the "transformation of the natural, autobiographical, narrative events and tone into the magical, universal, sonorous, [and] eternal."

PROGRAM MANAGER

- **Planning Instruction** See Teaching Notes, *Teaching Resources B,* p. 205, for objectives, a summary, and literary elements for this selection.
- **Instructional Support** Before beginning the instructional lesson, see Graphic Organizer for Active Reading, *Teaching Resources B,* p. 214, for a Through the Poem activity.
- **Assessment** See Selection Test, *Test Booklet,* pp. 265–266.

QUICK PLANNING GUIDE

Into the Poem

Author Biography p. 1155
Before You Read p. 1156

- **Reading Focus: Scaffolding** Students examine their place in the world.
- **A Dialogue with the Text: Set a Purpose** Record the thoughts of the speaker as a youth and as an adult
- **Elements of Literature: Rhyme Scheme**

Through the Poem

"The Fifteenth Summer" p. 1156
Making Meanings p. 1157

Beyond the Poem

Choices: Building Your Portfolio p. 1157

- **Writer's Notebook:** Use a rating scale to evaluate a poem
- **Critical Writing:** Write an essay on the poem's rhyme
- **Creative Writing:** Write a poem that reflects on a past experience

PORTFOLIO ASSESSMENT

Portfolio Assessment
For help with teacher assessment of reading skills, see the *Portfolio Management System,* pp. 54–55.

Using Before You Read
p. 1156

Reading Focus
Have students reflect on specific experiences in which they have contemplated the view from a high place. Volunteers may express their thoughts in a situation similar to that of the poet.

A. Reader's Response: First Thoughts

? What is your first impression of the boy? [Sample responses: The boy is daring, but he is also thoughtful. Or the boy is foolhardy.]

B. Literary Element: Imagery

? To what is the world compared in the poem, and what is the image's effect? [Possible answer: The world is compared to a scale. The image suggests the speaker is judging his experience.]

C. Literary Element: Rhyme Scheme

? What is the rhyme scheme of this stanza? [abcba] How is Merrill's ryhme scheme an integral part of the poem's effect? [Possible answer: It interweaves the ideas and images in the poem.]

Before You Read
The Fifteenth Summer

Reading Focus
Where Do I Fit in?
What do you think about when you look over a wide vista from high up in a building or on a mountain or from another lofty vantage point? You might well think about the immensity of the world and your place in it. That's what James Merrill remembers doing at age fifteen, from the heights of a tall tree.

A Dialogue with the Text
READER'S LOG

Divide a page in your Reader's Log into two columns, one headed "At Age Fifteen," the other "As an Adult." Then, as you read the poem, write down in the proper column the speaker's thoughts and feelings as a youth and as an adult. It'll take some thought to differentiate between the two.

Elements of Literature
Rhyme Scheme
The pattern of end rhymes in a poem is called a **rhyme scheme.** A rhyme scheme is commonly indicated with letters of the alphabet, each different rhyming sound at the end of a line represented by a different letter—for instance, *ababcc.* For a careful poet like Merrill, rhyme scheme is an integral part of the poem's overall effect, not merely window dressing.

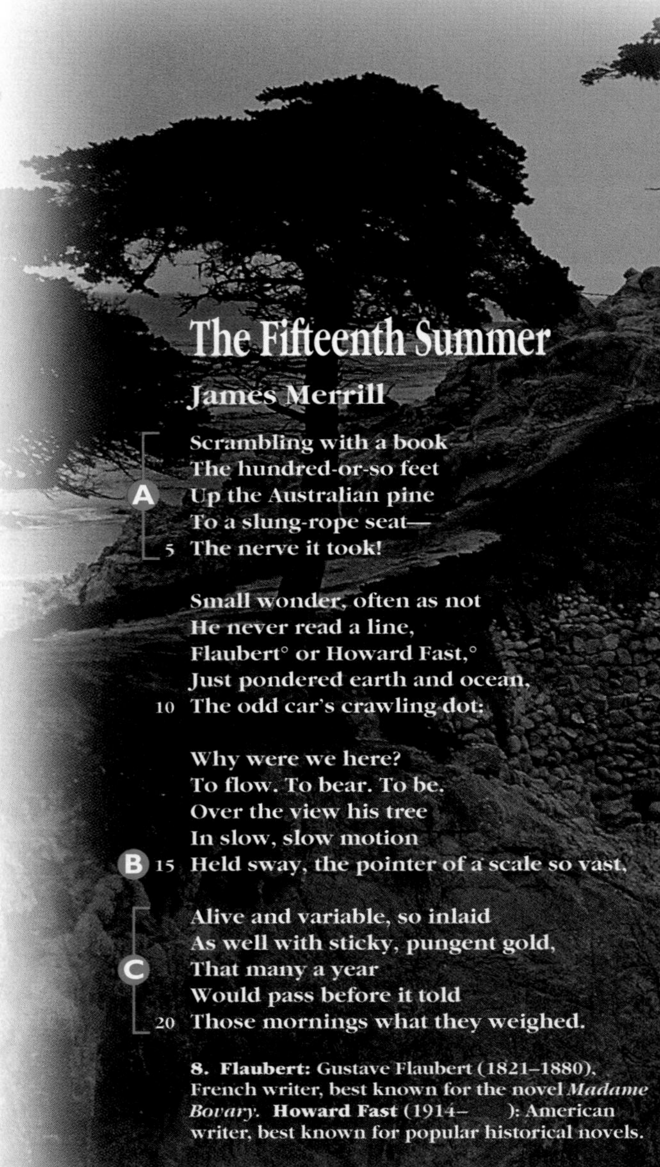

The Fifteenth Summer
James Merrill

Scrambling with a book
The hundred-or-so feet
Up the Australian pine
To a slung-rope seat—
The nerve it took!

Small wonder, often as not
He never read a line,
Flaubert° or Howard Fast,°
Just pondered earth and ocean,
The odd car's crawling dot:

Why were we here?
To flow. To bear. To be.
Over the view his tree
In slow, slow motion
Held sway, the pointer of a scale so vast,

Alive and variable, so inlaid
As well with sticky, pungent gold,
That many a year
Would pass before it told
Those mornings what they weighed.

8. Flaubert: Gustave Flaubert (1821–1880), French writer, best known for the novel *Madame Bovary.* **Howard Fast** (1914–): American writer, best known for popular historical novels.

STRATEGIES FOR INCLUSION

Visual To help students visualize the scene and the poem's metaphorical language, ask them to make a sketch of the poem's setting. Students may draw the scene depicted in the poem and then turn the picture into a diagram of a scale with a pointer, the metaphor in ll. 13–20. Have students share their drawings and their thoughts on the central metaphor in the poem.

INTEGRATING THE LANGUAGE ARTS

Strategic Reading Have students use a three-column chart to record, confirm, and evaluate predictions they make about the poem. Before students read the poem, have them read the title and record in the first column what they think will happen in the poem or what they think the poem will be about. In the second column, they may confirm the predictions with specific references to the text. In the third column, students should evaluate the thinking that went into each prediction. Challenge students to think of five predictions.

MAKING MEANINGS

First Thoughts

1. Have you ever felt the way the young man in this poem feels? Explain.

Shaping Interpretations

2. According to the first two stanzas of the poem, where does the young man go and what does he do there?
3. Tell in your own words the meaning of the lines "Why were we here? / To flow. To bear. To be."
4. Review the notes in your Reader's Log, and then describe the ways in which the adult's perspective differs from the youth's. Cite specific passages to support your analysis.

Connecting with the Text

5. Do you ever retreat to a special place for reading or thinking or just being alone? Why do you think people often find a place like that vitally important?

CHOICES: Building Your Portfolio

Writer's Notebook

1. Collecting Ideas for an Evaluation

WORK IN PROGRESS

When you evaluate a text, one of your criteria might be "The text should be accessible—that is, it should communicate meaning to me." Evaluate Merrill's poem in terms of how well it communicates a meaning to you. Support your judgment of the poem with details from the text. If there is any passage in the text that puzzles you, note it and describe the problem you have with it. Sometimes in an evaluation you might want to use a rating scale: See if you can rate Merrill's poem on a scale of one to five, *one* meaning that it is too difficult or ambiguous to interpret and *five* meaning that it is very accessible to you. Save your notes for possible use in the Writer's Workshop on page 1181.

Critical Writing

2. The Reason for the Rhyme

In a brief essay, discuss the use of rhyme in "The Fifteenth Summer." Before you begin writing, assign letters of the alphabet to indicate the **rhyme scheme** of each stanza. In your essay, describe how the rhymes contribute to the overall musical effect of the poem. Mention anything else about the end rhymes that you find interesting.

Creative Writing

3. Then and Now

Write a poem in which you reflect on an experience of several years ago. Try imitating the form of "The Fifteenth Summer," though you might choose not to include end rhymes. If you like, read your poem before the class.

Making Meanings

First Thoughts

1. Possible responses: Yes, I share his feelings, because experiencing something is far more interesting and exciting than reading a book. I too wonder why we are here, as the boy does, and I think the answer will get clearer when I'm older.

Shaping Interpretations

2. He climbs a hundred feet to the top of a pine tree with a book in hand and watches the world below.
3. Possible response: The lines pose a question concerning the purpose of human life, and suggest that our purpose is to fulfill our duty ("flow"), create new life ("bear"), and not expect answers to higher questions ("be").
4. Possible response: The perspectives of the adult and the young person differ in their views of risk (the nerve of youth to climb such heights mentioned in l. 2) and in their abilities to think abstractly (the youth cannot concentrate enough to read with such a view, l. 7). The adult also seems to value the experience more now that he is older (the "weight" of l. 20).

Connecting with the Text

5. Possible response: A quiet place to contemplate life is important because humans need to pause occasionally to make meaning of their lives.

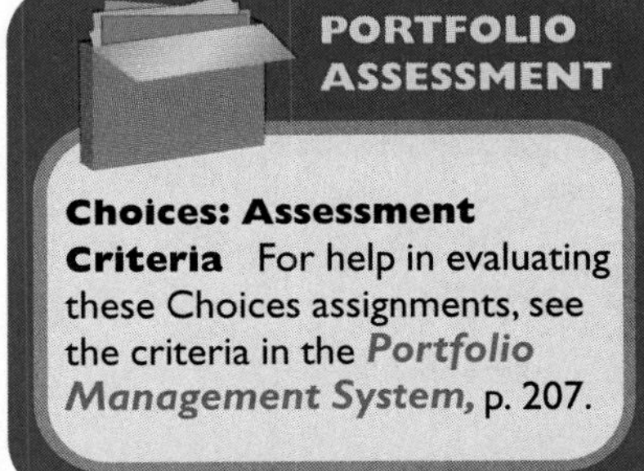

Choices: Assessment Criteria For help in evaluating these Choices assignments, see the criteria in the ***Portfolio Management System,*** p. 207.

STRATEGIES FOR INCLUSION

Learners Having Difficulty To help students gain a clear sense of the poem's musical effects as requested in activity #2, put students in pairs to take turns reading the poem aloud, identifying its rhyme scheme from their listening, and noting their responses to its musical effects. Encourage repeated readings and listenings.

Auditory Emphasize to students the benefit of thinking aloud as they compose their poems for activity #3. Students may try out lines, play with rhymes, or just get a better feel for their poems by speaking the lines aloud. Students should work with pen or pencil in hand so that they do not forget any discoveries.

QUICK PLANNING GUIDE

Into the Selection

Author Biography p. 1158
Before You Read p. 1159
- **Reading Focus:** Students examine the everyday in literature.
- **Quickwrite: Scaffolding** List reasons that writers write about early experiences
- **Elements of Literature: Allusion**

Through the Selection

"Straw into Gold: The Metamorphosis of the Everyday" pp. 1160–1164
Words to Own pp. 1160–1164
Making Meanings p. 1165

Beyond the Selection

Choices: Building Your Portfolio p. 1165
- **Writer's Notebook:** Make a list of evaluation criteria for an autobiographical work
- **Critical Writing:** Identify the writer's purpose and main idea
- **Critical Writing:** Examine multiculturalism in art

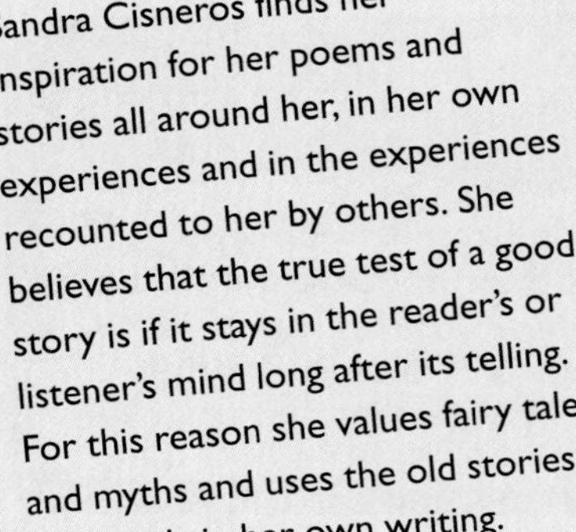

ABOUT THE AUTHOR

Sandra Cisneros finds her inspiration for her poems and stories all around her, in her own experiences and in the experiences recounted to her by others. She believes that the true test of a good story is if it stays in the reader's or listener's mind long after its telling. For this reason she values fairy tales and myths and uses the old stories frequently in her own writing.

Sandra Cisneros

(1954–)

Sandra Cisneros remembers her Chicago childhood as solitary, even though, she says, her parents would be hard pressed to remember it that way. The nine members of her Mexican American family lived in cramped apartments where the only room with any privacy was the bathroom. But as the only female child in a family of six sons, Cisneros often felt as solitary as an only child.

To Cisneros, solitude proved important. If she had had a sister or a best friend, Cisneros thinks, she would not have buried herself in books. She read voraciously—lives of the saints, Horatio Alger's office-boy-makes-good stories, Doctor Dolittle books, Alice in Wonderland, and fairy tales. (She imagined herself as the lone sister in "Six Swans." Coincidentally, her family name is translated as "keeper of swans.")

Cisneros received a bachelor's degree from Loyola University, in Chicago, and then earned a master's at The Writers' Workshop at the University of Iowa. There she found her subject matter in her own life, and she began writing in earnest. Finding her own voice did not come easily or quickly for Cisneros; she did not realize for a long time that her best writer's voice was the voice of the home she grew up in, a voice that was a combination of her mother's South Side Chicago "tough" street English and her father's gentle, lulling Spanish. The result is a style that suggests a unique synthesis of the disparate languages of her childhood. Cisneros writes in English, but it is an English often heavily informed by Spanish diction and grammatical structure.

Cisneros's first book of poetry is called *Bad Boys* (1980); her first novel, *The House on Mango Street* (1983), won the American Book Award of the Before Columbus Foundation. The title of her second book of poetry, *My Wicked Wicked Ways* (1987), alludes to the title of the autobiography of Errol Flynn, a movie star of the 1930s and 1940s. In 1991, she published another prose collection—*Woman Hollering Creek and Other Stories.* As the following selection tells you, Cisneros has lived in many places. In 1995, she was awarded a prestigious long-term fellowship by the John D. and Catherine T. MacArthur Foundation.

© Rubén Guzmán.

Growing up and attending college in Chicago, Cisneros led a circumscribed life and, like many young people (not just writers), desperately yearned to break away. She took solace from the thought of Emily Dickinson (page 372), who seldom left her house, let alone her hometown, but still managed to create a magnificent legacy of creative work. Dickinson became Cisneros's source of inspiration, the image to which she hitched her dreams of becoming a professional writer. Only years later did Cisneros, all too aware of the struggles of working-class people (especially women), realize that Dickinson lived a uniquely privileged existence in circumstances any aspiring writer would envy: She had money, a fine education, her own room in her own house, and even household help to take care of time-consuming chores. Cisneros, growing up, had none of these advantages. Yet, like Dickinson, Cisneros has been able to take both the possibilities and the constraints of her unique situation and weave them into art.

WORDS TO OWN

The following vocabulary words are defined in the Words to Own at the bottom of the pupil's page.

subsisting p. 1160	nomadic p. 1162
intuitively p. 1162	nostalgia p. 1162
edible p. 1162	obsess p. 1162
ventured p. 1162	flourished p. 1163
taboo p. 1162	prestigious p. 1164

PORTFOLIO ASSESSMENT

Portfolio Assessment For help with self-assessment of reading skills, see the ***Portfolio Management System,*** p. 39.

BEFORE YOU READ
STRAW INTO GOLD

Reading Focus

Transforming the Everyday
One of the oldest bits of advice to an aspiring author is simply to "write about what you know." Taking that advice, just about every good writer discovers that personal experience is what gives vitality and authenticity to literature. Some of the best writers have an uncanny ability to discover the essential that is hidden in the everyday, the universal that is hidden in the local. In the following autobiographical essay, Sandra Cisneros tells us about some of the raw material she has transformed into literature.

Quickwrite

It is a characteristic of most American writers that they turn to their childhoods for the subjects of their early works (and, sometimes, all their works). In your Reader's Log, write down a few reasons why writers might go back to their early years for subjects to write about.

Elements of Literature

Allusion
An **allusion** is a reference to someone or something that is known from history, literature, religion, politics, sports, science, or some other branch of culture. Cisneros builds an allusion into the title of this essay. To what old folk tale is she referring? What do you think she is suggesting through this allusion?

> An **allusion** is a reference to someone or something from history, literature, the arts, politics, or some other branch of culture.
>
> *For more on Allusion, see the Handbook of Literary Terms.*

Into the Selection

Using **BEFORE YOU READ**
p. 1159

Reading Focus

Point out to students that authors are not the only people to transform the everyday—many scientists, for example, have found inspiration for great discoveries in trivial events. Discuss with students how the mundane may take on importance with a flash of insight or emotion.

Quickwrite

Ask students to think of some authors who draw on their past experiences in their work. Write students' ideas on the chalkboard. Then, discuss with students what the authors found so important in their lives that they felt they had to share with their readers.

Elements of Literature

Ask students to think of some common allusions that they encounter in everyday life. Point out to students, for example, that an intelligent person may often be compared to Einstein, or a strong person to Hercules. Have students identify the allusions they share.

PROGRAM MANAGER

- **Planning Instruction** See Teaching Notes, *Teaching Resources B,* p. 205, for objectives, a summary, and literary elements for this selection.
- **Instructional Support** Before beginning the instructional lesson, see Graphic Organizer for Active Reading, *Teaching Resources B,* p. 215, for a Through the Selection activity.
- **Assessment** See Selection Test, *Test Booklet,* pp. 267–268.
- **Reinforcement** Use the Words to Own worksheet in *Teaching Resources B,* p. 216.
- **Application and Reinforcement** For reinforcement of the elements of literature introduced in this selection, see Transparency 21.2 in the *Audiovisual Resources Binder.*

Through the Selection

A. Reader's Response: First Thoughts

? Were the author's hosts wrong to have expected her to know how to make tortillas? Why or why not? [Sample responses: It depends on how they asked; if they were polite, it might have been a natural mistake, like a person in another country expecting an American to know how to make a hamburger. Or her hosts stereotyped her because of her family origins, and this attitude would have been offensive to anyone.]

Straw into Gold: The Metamorphosis of the Everyday

Sandra Cisneros

When I was living in an artists' colony in the south of France, some fellow Latin-Americans who taught at the university in Aix-en-Provence invited me to share a home-cooked meal with them. I had been living abroad almost a year then on an NEA[1] grant, subsisting mainly on French bread and lentils so that my money could last longer. So when the invitation to dinner arrived, I accepted without hesitation. Especially since they had promised Mexican food.

What I didn't realize when they made this invitation was that I was supposed to be involved in preparing the meal. I guess they assumed I knew how to cook Mexican food because I am Mexican. They wanted specifically tortillas, though I'd never made a tortilla in my life. (A)

It's true I had witnessed my mother rolling the little armies of dough into perfect circles, but my mother's family is from Guanajuato; they are *provincianos,* country folk. They only know how to make flour tortillas. My father's family, on the other hand, is *chilango*[2] from Mexico City. We ate corn tortillas but we didn't make them. Someone was sent to the corner tortilleria to buy some. I'd never seen anybody make corn tortillas. Ever.

Somehow my Latino hosts had gotten a hold of a packet of corn flour, and this is what they tossed my way with orders to produce tortillas. *Así como sea.* Any ol' way, they said and went back to their cooking.

1. **NEA:** National Endowment for the Arts, a federal agency that grants money to organizations and individuals so they may engage in creative pursuits.
2. ***chilango:*** variation of "*Shilango,*" Veracruz name for people who live inland, especially the poor people of Mexico.

WORDS TO OWN

subsisting (səb·sist′iŋ) *v.* used as *adj.:* staying alive.

OPTIONS FOR TEACHING

STRATEGIES FOR INCLUSION

Auditory Read the fairy tale "Rumpelstiltskin" to the class. Afterward, discuss the lesson that the tale teaches. Alert students to look for parallels between the story and Cisneros' essay as they read.

Less Proficient Readers Students may have trouble keeping track of the essay's central metaphor. Have these students keep notes as they read the essay listing details of Cisneros' unpromising early life under the heading "Straw" and details about her later successes under the heading "Gold." Encourage students to study their notes to see how the writer progressed from humble beginnings to a life of fulfillment and success.

English Language Development Point out to students before they read the selection that the author grew up in two cultures, with two languages. Suggest to students that the selection may contain strategies that Cisneros uses to maintain connections to both cultures and languages and to handle the demands and expectations each one places on her. After students have read the selection, ask them to share what they learned from it that is applicable to their own lives. *Tell students that they do not have to share anything they would feel uncomfortable discussing in class.*

Woman Making Tortillas (1945) by Diego Rivera. Watercolor (12″ × 15¾″).
Courtesy of Mary-Anne Martin/Fine Art, New York.

RESPONDING TO THE ART: VISUAL LITERACY

What do you think the woman's attitude is toward making the tortillas? Explain. [Possible responses: The woman looks meditative and calm with her closed eyes and her faint smile; she probably takes great pride in her work.] How do the colors of the painting affect the mood of the scene? [Possible responses: The bright colors give the scene a warm, homelike feel; the vivid colors reflect the woman's creative energy in her work.]

STRATEGIES FOR INCLUSION

Linguistic Challenge students to read the essay for evidence of the gold in the straw that the author describes. For example, ask students if there is anything in Cisneros' description of herself as an eleven-year-old that indicates she would make a good writer. Encourage students to focus on a particular passage about the writer's early life. Have students share their findings.

INTEGRATING THE LANGUAGE ARTS

Strategic Reading Have students read the essay with a partner. Tell students to take turns reading and to switch roles after each paragraph. Encourage partners to stop periodically in order to exchange their views and questions about the essay. Partners may make notes of their discussions and share their ideas with the class after the essay is read. ☞

A. Literary Element: Allusion

? To which fairy tale does Cisneros refer, and why? [She refers to the tale about Rumpelstiltskin because she feels as if she has been given a task as impossible as that given the woman in the story. The allusion helps to describe her feeling of being overwhelmed by expectations.]

B. Critical Reading: Making Inferences

? Why would Cisneros be glad that her mother was not there to see her first tortillas? [Her mother, unlike her hosts, knows how tortillas are supposed to be made, and she would not have been impressed with her daughter's tortillas.]

C. Cultural Connections

Discuss with students the taboo that Cisneros broke, and ask students to think of similar taboos in various cultures. You might also ask students to think of how the movement to end discrimination against women causes changes in various cultures. Encourage students to listen to other viewpoints without rushing to judgment.

D. Critical Reading: Summarizing

? What has the writer inherited from her parents? [From her father, a love of wandering and a "sappy heart." From her mother, a "tough, streetwise voice."]

E. Critical Reading: Making Connections

? What does Cisneros mean by the expression "odd woman out"? [On the return of her older brother, Kiki transfers his allegiance from her to him. They have each other, but she is left to herself.]

(A) Why did I feel like the woman in the fairy tale who was locked in a room and ordered to spin straw into gold? I had the same sick feeling when I was required to write my critical essay for the MFA[3] exam—the only piece of noncreative writing necessary in order to get my graduate degree. How was I to start? There were rules involved here, unlike writing a poem or story, which I did intuitively. There was a step by step process needed and I had better know it. I felt as if making tortillas—or writing a critical paper, for that matter—were tasks so impossible I wanted to break down into tears.

Somehow though, I managed to make tortillas—crooked and burnt, but edible nonetheless. My hosts were absolutely ignorant when it came to Mexican food; they thought my tortillas were (B) delicious. (I'm glad my mama wasn't there.) Thinking back and looking at an old photograph documenting the three of us consuming those lopsided circles I am amazed. Just as I am amazed I could finish my MFA exam.

I've managed to do a lot of things in my life I didn't think I was capable of and which many others didn't think I was capable of either. Especially because I am a woman, a Latina, an only daughter in a family of six men. My father would've liked to have seen me married long ago. In our culture men and women don't leave their father's house except by way of marriage. I crossed my father's threshold with nothing carrying me but my own two feet. A woman whom no one came for and no one chased away.

To make matters worse, I left before any of my (C) six brothers had ventured away from home. I broke a terrible taboo. Somehow, looking back at photos of myself as a child, I wonder if I was aware of having begun already my own quiet war.

I like to think that somehow my family, my Mexicanness, my poverty, all had something to do with shaping me into a writer. I like to think my parents were preparing me all along for my life as (D) an artist even though they didn't know it. From my father I inherited a love of wandering. He was born in Mexico City but as a young man he traveled into the U.S. vagabonding. He eventually was drafted and thus became a citizen. Some of the stories he has told about his first months in the U.S. with little or no English surface in my stories in *The House on Mango Street* as well as others I have in mind to write in the future. From him I inherited a sappy heart. (He still cries when he watches Mexican soaps—especially if they deal with children who have forsaken their parents.)

My mother was born like me—in Chicago but of Mexican descent. It would be her tough streetwise voice that would haunt all my stories and poems. An amazing woman who loves to draw and read books and can sing an opera. A smart cookie.

When I was a little girl we traveled to Mexico City so much I thought my grandparents' house on La Fortuna, number 12, was home. It was the only constant in our nomadic ramblings from one Chicago flat to another. The house on Destiny Street, number 12, in the colonia Tepeyac would be perhaps the only home I knew, and that nostalgia for a home would be a theme that would obsess me.

My brothers also figured greatly in my art. Especially the older two; I grew up in their shadows. Henry, the second oldest and my favorite, appears often in poems I have written and in stories which at times only borrow his nickname, Kiki. He played a major role in my childhood. We were bunk-bed mates. We were co-conspirators. We (E) were pals. Until my oldest brother came back from studying in Mexico and left me odd woman out for always.

What would my teachers say if they knew I was a writer now? Who would've guessed it? I wasn't a very bright student. I didn't much like school because we moved so much and I was always new and funny looking. In my fifth-grade report card I have nothing but an avalanche of C's and D's, but I don't remember being that stupid. I was good at art and I read plenty of library books and Kiki laughed at all my jokes. At home I was fine, but at

3. **MFA:** Master of Fine Arts.

Words to Own

intuitively (in·to͞o'i·tiv·lē) *adv.:* without conscious reasoning.
edible (ed'ə·bəl) *adj.:* capable of being eaten.
ventured (ven'chərd) *v.:* dared or risked going.
taboo (ta·bo͞o') *n.:* something that is forbidden.
nomadic (nō·mad'ik) *adj.:* wandering.
nostalgia (näs·tal'jə) *n.:* longing.
obsess (əb·ses') *v.:* take all of one's attention.

Options for Teaching

Integrating the Language Arts

Language and Style Discuss with students how varying sentence structure can create interest and draw a reader's attention to a particular point. In the paragraph beginning "My brothers also figured . . ." Cisneros uses a variety of sentences: a long detailed sentence to describe how her brother appears in her writing, and later, three short parallel sentences that describe her relationship to her brother. Have students find other examples of varied sentence structure in the essay, and have them describe the resulting effect.

Classroom Management

Missed Assignments Near the front of the classroom, place a folder for each class that you have. As you pass out materials for each class, place a copy of the material for each absent student into the class's folder. When the students return to school, be sure they know to go to the folder to pick up the materials that they have missed during their absence.

La Llorona (The Crying Woman) by Carmen Lomas Garza. Gouache (18″ × 26″).

school I never opened my mouth except when the teacher called on me.

When I think of how I see myself it would have to be at age eleven. I know I'm thirty-two on the outside, but inside I'm eleven. I'm the girl in the picture with skinny arms and a crumpled skirt and crooked hair. I didn't like school because all they saw was the outside me. School was lots of rules and sitting with your hands folded and being very afraid all the time. I liked looking out the window and thinking. I liked staring at the girl across the way writing her name over and over again in red ink. I wondered why the boy with the dirty collar in front of me didn't have a mama who took better care of him. (F)

I think my mama and papa did the best they could to keep us warm and clean and never hungry. We had birthday and graduation parties and things like that, but there was another hunger that had to be fed. There was a hunger I didn't even have a name for. Was this when I began writing?

In 1966 we moved into a house, a real one, our first real home. This meant we didn't have to change schools and be the new kids on the block every couple of years. We could make friends and not be afraid we'd have to say goodbye to them and start all over. My brothers and the flock of boys they brought home would become important characters eventually for my stories—Louie and his cousins, Meme Ortiz and his dog with two names, one in English and one in Spanish.

My mother flourished in her own home. She took books out of the library and taught herself to garden—to grow flowers so envied we had to put a lock on the gate to keep out the midnight flower thieves. My mother has never quit gardening.

This was the period in my life, that slippery age when you are both child and woman and neither, I was to record in *The House on Mango Street.* I was still shy. I was a girl who couldn't come out of her shell.

Words to Own

flourished (flʉr′ishd) *v.:* did well; blossomed.

F. Critical Reading: Analyzing Character

? What can you tell about Cisneros from her description of herself?

[She feels younger than her years and still sees herself as having a lot of questions and a roving eye for detail.]

PROFESSIONAL NOTES

Cultural Diversity Like Cisneros, Cesar Chavez also attended many schools as a young child. He attended over thirty elementary schools because his father was a migrant farm worker. In 1962, he began to organize the United Farm Workers, or UFW, a union to help protect migrant farm workers. In an attempt to stop the grape growers from using pesticides while the pickers were in the vineyards, Chavez organized a national boycott of table grapes. His efforts have led to some important steps toward protecting the migrant farm workers.

ASSESSMENT TOOLS

Check Test: Questions and Answers

1. Cisneros is asked ________. [to make tortillas]
2. Cisneros is the only daughter in a family of ______ children. [seven]
3. Cisneros was not an especially bright student and felt ________ at school. [uncomfortable]
4. As an adult, Cisneros studied with ________. [famous writers]

A. Reader's Response: Shaping Interpretations

? What can you tell about Cisneros from the list of things of which she is proud? [Sample responses: She is proud of her accomplishments as a writer and all the places she has been; she is an active, energetic person. Or she speaks about the variety of her experience because she appreciates diversity and adventure.]

B. Critical Reading: Making Inferences

? How has Texas brought Mexico back to her? [Texas was formerly a part of Mexico and is still heavily influenced by Mexican culture. By living in Texas, Cisneros has come back to the ideas that influenced her during her stable times with her grandmother in Mexico.]

C. Reader's Response: Challenging the Text

? Has the essay shown how the author has made gold from straw? Explain. [Sample responses: Cisneros' essay does show how she has made gold from straw, because in spite of her unpromising beginnings she has managed to have many great experiences, and she has written about her life to make art. Or the essay hints at how she has made gold from straw, but it really doesn't give a single concrete example, such as a poem or story that is based on a specific incident in her life.]

How was I to know I would be recording and documenting the women who sat their sadness on an elbow and stared out a window? It would be the city streets of Chicago I would later record, as seen through a child's eyes.

I've done all kinds of things I didn't think I could do since then. I've gone to a prestigious university, studied with famous writers, and taken an MFA degree. I've taught poetry in schools in Illinois and Texas. I've gotten an NEA grant and run away with it as far as my courage would take me. (A) I've seen the bleached and bitter mountains of the Peloponnesus.[4] I've lived on an island. I've been to Venice twice. I've lived in Yugoslavia. I've been to the famous Nice[5] flower market behind the opera house. I've lived in a village in the pre-Alps and witnessed the daily parade of promenaders.

I've moved since Europe to the strange and wonderful country of Texas, land of polaroid-blue skies and big bugs. I met a mayor with my last name. I met famous Chicana and Chicano artists and writers and *políticos.*

Texas is another chapter in my life. It brought with it the Dobie-Paisano Fellowship, a six-month (B) residency on a 265-acre ranch. But most important, Texas brought Mexico back to me.

In the days when I would sit at my favorite people-watching spot, the snakey Woolworth's counter across the street from the Alamo (the Woolworth's which has since been torn down to make way for progress), I couldn't think of anything else I'd rather be than a writer. I've traveled and lectured from Cape Cod to San Francisco, to Spain, Yugoslavia, Greece, Mexico, France, Italy, and now today to Texas. Along the way there has (C) been straw for the taking. With a little imagination, it can be spun into gold.

4. **Peloponnesus** (pel′ə·pə·nē′səs): large peninsula on the mainland of Greece.
5. **Nice** (nēs): port city in southern France.

WORDS TO OWN

prestigious (pres·tij′əs) *adj.:* impressive; having distinction.

J. Frank Dobie's Paisano Ranch.

Alan Pogue/University of Texas, Austin.

Making Meanings

First Thoughts

1. Possible response: I want to know exactly how Cisneros changed from an unremarkable little girl to a talented and successful professional writer. She doesn't tell how in the essay.

Reviewing the Text

a. Writing the critical essay for the MFA exam is a step-by-step process with rigid rules, just like the procedure for making tortillas. She finds herself overwhelmed with the demands involved in both.

b. Her school experiences were not positive because she moved a lot and because school was geared to seeing a person's outside instead of a person's inside. She fearfully obeyed the rules but got average and below-average grades, spending much of her time lost in her imagination.

c. From her father, Cisneros inherited a love for traveling and storytelling and a certain amount of sentimentality. From her mother, she inherited a streetwise voice.

d. As a child, Cisneros moved around a lot, and she did not have a constant home until her early teens.

Shaping Interpretations

2. The subtitle suggests Cisneros has made something out of nothing, namely a success out of herself when she had no promise as a child. Her stories also make art of her everyday experiences.

Making Meanings

First Thoughts

1. What do you still want to know about Cisneros after reading this essay?

Reviewing the Text

a. How do the writer's feelings about making the tortillas connect to her feelings about writing the MFA essay?
b. Describe Cisneros's experiences at school.
c. Exactly how did her family help shape Cisneros into a writer?
d. Why does Cisneros think nostalgia for a home is a **theme** that obsesses her?

Shaping Interpretations

2. How would you interpret the essay's subtitle, "The Metamorphosis of the Everyday"?
3. Review the notes in your Reader's Log about why writers turn to their childhoods for subject matter. In what ways do your notes explain Cisneros's interest in her childhood experiences? What new reasons have you discovered from reading her essay?
4. Describe the **tone** of Cisneros's essay. Do you think it is appropriate for the subject matter?
5. Describe in your own words the kind of writer that Cisneros believes she has become. What qualities as a writer has she developed from the raw material of her personal experience?
6. What do you think Cisneros means when she says she documented the women "who sat their sadness on an elbow and stared out a window" (page 1164)?
7. Identify some fresh **images** and **figures of speech** in the essay that reveal Cisneros as an accomplished writer. How would you describe her style?
8. The title of the essay includes an **allusion** to the folk tale about Rumpelstiltskin. In the essay itself, how does Cisneros use that magical story as a metaphor for her writing? What do you think of the metaphor?

Choices: Building Your Portfolio

Writer's Notebook

1. Collecting Ideas for an Evaluation

What qualities give life to the story of a life? In other words, what are your criteria for evaluating an autobiographical work? Think of autobiographies you have enjoyed, and make a list of their key characteristics. Among your criteria might be that an autobiography be honest and that it include interesting details describing the writer's feelings. Save your notes for possible use in the Writer's Workshop on page 1181.

Critical Writing

2. To What End?

Cisneros's essay is the revised version of a speech delivered at Texas Lutheran College. In a brief essay, discuss the following questions: What is the writer's principal **purpose**? What is her **main idea**? If you had been a member of her audience, how would this speech have affected you?

Critical Writing

3. Multicultural Celebrations

In essays and lectures Cisneros has told of dual cultural influences on her writing. This mix of cultures is a common feature of the arts in a multicultural society like that of the United States. The writer Bernard Malamud, for example (page 980), often included Yiddish expressions in his English-language text, thus combining two heritages. In a brief essay, identify and describe two or three specific examples of contemporary arts—writing, dance, music, painting, fashion, or another art form—that fuse elements of two or more cultural heritages. In what ways do such fusions of cultural influences enrich contemporary artistic expression? What predictions can you make about multicultural fusions in the years to come?

3. Possible response: Writers turn to their childhoods for subject matter because those years are typically filled with fond memories of an almost magical time of life. Cisneros seems fascinated by who she was as a child and by how unlikely it seemed that she could ever turn into a writer.

4. Cisneros' tone is heartfelt, sincere, enthusiastic, and full of wonder. It is an appropriate tone for an autobiographical account of becoming a surprising success.

5. Possible response: Cisneros believes she has become an imaginative, compassionate, and honest writer. She depends on her past experiences for material, but she has also acquired qualities that help her as a writer, such as the distinctive voice she got from her mother.
6. Possible response: Cisneros observed the women and wondered about them so much that their worries, dreams, actions—everything about them—have not left her, and she uses them often in her writing.
7. Cisneros' poetic ability is revealed in the images and figures of speech she uses to describe places she has traveled to ("daily parade of promenaders"), her descriptions of herself as an eleven-year-old schoolgirl (the image of the girl writing her name), and her descriptions of the women "who sat their sadness on an elbow and stared out a window."
8. Cisneros uses the Rumpelstiltskin tale metaphorically in two ways. The overwhelming task of spinning straw into gold is a metaphor used to describe Cisneros' feelings when she was faced with a "step-by-step" task. The actual transformation of the straw into gold is a metaphor for the writer's belief that all of life's experiences can be used as raw material for art. Students will probably appreciate the metaphor's usefulness.

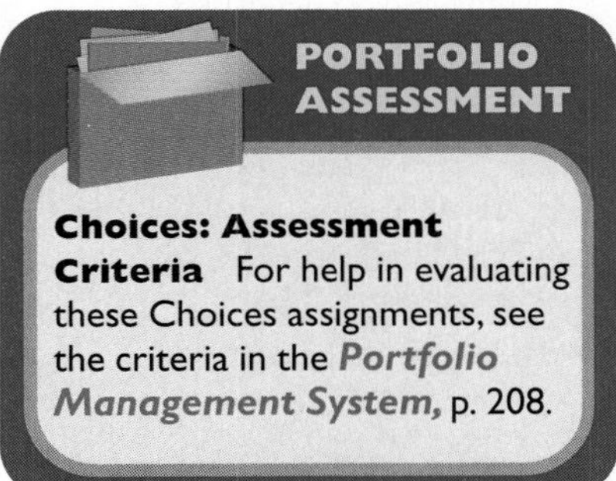

Choices: Assessment Criteria For help in evaluating these Choices assignments, see the criteria in the ***Portfolio Management System,*** p. 208.

QUICK PLANNING GUIDE

Into the Poem

Through the Poem

Beyond the Poem

- **Writer's Notebook:** Compare and contrast three poets' views of poetry
- **Critical Writing/Music:** Analyze the musical qualities of the poem
- **Art:** Make a piece of art with many images

ABOUT THE AUTHOR

The writing of Judith Ortiz Cofer is situated on a bridge between two cultures; her feet are planted linguistically and culturally in the soil of both. The lyrical qualities of her English prose reflect what one reviewer called a "vigorous elegance." The precision of her poet's eye reveals a cultural knowledge that understands life on the streets as deeply as it understands the human heart, regardless of which side of the bridge it occupies.

Judith Ortiz Cofer

(1952–)

According to Judith Ortiz Cofer, "My family is one of the main topics of my poetry; the ones left behind on the island of Puerto Rico, and the ones who came to the United States. In tracing their lives, I discover more about mine." This impulse toward self-discovery and self-definition emerges in Cofer's stories, essays, and poems. By delving into her past, she clarifies her place in the present; by writing of those who shaped her life, she shapes her own life.

"We lived in Puerto Rico until my brother was born in 1954," Cofer has written. "Soon after, because of economic pressures on our growing family, my father joined the United States Navy. He was assigned to duty on a ship in Brooklyn [Navy] Yard . . . that was to be his home base in the States until his retirement more than twenty years later." Subsequently, Cofer's childhood was divided between a mainland American urban environment and Puerto Rico. She lived mostly in Paterson, New Jersey, but moved temporarily to Puerto Rico with her mother and brother when her father was at sea.

Cofer earned a master's degree in English from Florida Atlantic University in 1977 and then taught at the University of Miami and the University of Georgia, conducting poetry workshops on the side. Her first publication, *Latin Women Pray,* appeared in 1980. Since then she has published several additional volumes of poetry, including *Peregrina* (1986) and *Terms of Survival* (1987). Her semiautobiographical first novel, *The Line of the Sun* (1989), traces a family that moves from Puerto Rico to Paterson and is then caught between two cultural heritages. A reviewer of the novel describes Cofer as "a prose writer of evocatively lyrical authority." She has also published a volume of personal essays called *Silent Dancing: A Partial Remembrance of a Puerto Rican Childhood* (1990) and *An Island Like You: Stories from the Barrio* (1995).

Some consider Cofer's *The Latin Deli* (1993), a collection of poetry and prose, her most powerful book. It is a mosaic of responses to cultural differences, an evocation of places past and present, and an engaging blend of poetry and lyrical prose. As Cofer has said, "The place of birth itself becomes a metaphor for the things we all must leave behind; the assimilation of a new culture is the coming into maturity by accepting the terms necessary for survival. My poetry is a study of this process of change, assimilation, and transformation."

Language, of course, plays a major role in such a transformation. In one interview, Cofer summed up what the dynamic force of language has meant to her: "The 'infinite variety' and power of language interest me. I never cease to experiment with it. As a native Puerto Rican, my first language was Spanish. It was a challenge, not only to learn English, but to master it enough to teach it and—the ultimate goal—to write poetry in it."

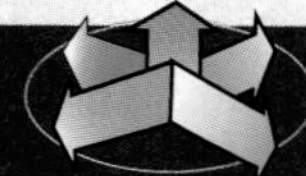

PROGRAM MANAGER

- **Planning Instruction** See Teaching Notes, *Teaching Resources B,* p. 206, for objectives, a summary, and literary elements for this selection.
- **Instructional Support** Before beginning the instructional lesson, see Graphic Organizer for Active Reading, *Teaching Resources B,* p. 217, for a Through the Poem activity.
- **Audiotaped Readings** To help less proficient readers or auditory learners through the lesson, use the Selected Reading, Audiocassette 3, Side B, in the *Audiovisual Resources Binder.*
- **Assessment** See Selection Test, *Test Booklet,* pp. 269–270.

Before You Read
The Latin Deli: An Ars Poetica

Reading Focus
Native Tongue
Language is our most common tool of self-expression. Hidden in the words we say, beneath the immediate practical meanings, are layers of personal associations, complex social implications, and even cultural histories. This is especially true of immigrants, who try to adjust to a new country but are still drawn to their former homelands. You may know recent immigrants who intermix words of their native language with English.

Quickwrite
In your Reader's Log, write some of the things an immigrant might remember with fondness about his or her native country. Be as precise as possible.

Elements of Literature
Concrete and Abstract Language
In literature, **concrete language** involves the use of well-chosen sensory details to evoke and describe a particular subject. In contrast, **abstract language** deals with a subject in general terms and emphasizes intangible concepts like qualities and values. Sensory words are few, and details do not play a large role. The following poem is a striking example of the effective use of concrete language. (*Ars poetica,* by the way, is Latin for "the art of poetry.")

PORTFOLIO ASSESSMENT

Portfolio Assessment For help with self-assessment of reading skills, see the *Portfolio Management System,* p. 53.

Into the Poem

Using Before You Read
p. 1167

Reading Focus
Ask students to think of how they change the ways they speak to fit different situations. They might speak differently to a principal, for example, than to a fellow student. Then, have students think of how it would be to alternate between two or more languages. Ask for bilingual volunteers to share their views on speaking more than one language. *Emphasize to students that they do not have to discuss anything they would feel uncomfortable sharing with other students.*

Quickwrite
Have students imagine that they are moving to a different country. What would they miss about their home in the United States? Students may find it easier to write if they imagine themselves in the position of an immigrant.

Elements of Literature
Direct students to note examples of each type of language as they read. After students have read the poem, have them share their findings.

A. Reader's Response: First Thoughts

? What do you think the "canned memories" consist of? [Sample responses: For the immigrants, eating the food sold at the deli will evoke memories of times, places, and people in their native countries. Or just being surrounded by familiar sights and smells brings back preserved or "canned" memories for the immigrants.]

B. Exploring the Culture

Following Fidel Castro's rise to power in 1959, many Cubans left family, homes, and friends to forge a new life in the United States. The speeches of "glorious return" refer to their hopes for Castro's downfall so that they can return home to a democratic form of government.

C. Literary Element: Imagery

? What image is produced by the detail that the immigrants read the labels as if "they were the names of lost lovers"? [The image is one of dreamy longing, of being lost in fond memories.]

D. Literary Element: Concrete and Abstract Language

The detailed, concrete description of the deli's version of a ham-and-cheese sandwich leads to a more abstract conclusion about the immigrants. What is the conclusion? [The immigrants need items that remind them of their native countries as much as they need food itself.]

The Latin Deli:

An Ars Poetica

Judith Ortiz Cofer

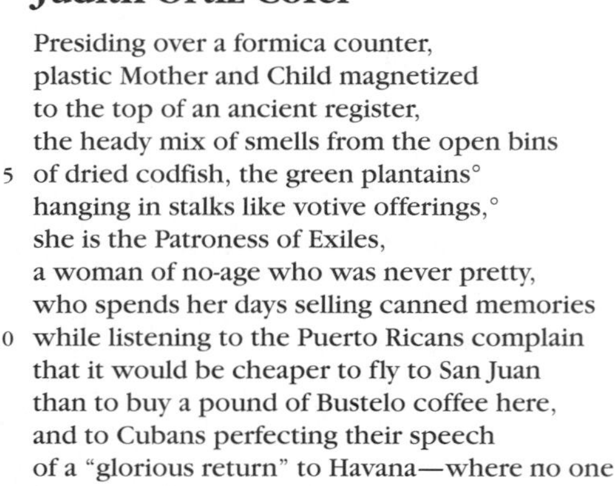

Presiding over a formica counter,
plastic Mother and Child magnetized
to the top of an ancient register,
the heady mix of smells from the open bins
of dried codfish, the green plantains°
hanging in stalks like votive offerings,°
she is the Patroness of Exiles,
a woman of no-age who was never pretty,
A who spends her days selling canned memories
while listening to the Puerto Ricans complain
that it would be cheaper to fly to San Juan
than to buy a pound of Bustelo coffee here,
B and to Cubans perfecting their speech
of a "glorious return" to Havana—where no one
has been allowed to die and nothing to change until then;
to Mexicans who pass through, talking lyrically
of *dólares* to be made in El Norte—
all wanting the comfort
of spoken Spanish, to gaze upon the family portrait
of her plain wide face, her ample bosom
resting on her plump arms, her look of maternal interest
as they speak to her and each other
of their dreams and their disillusions—
how she smiles understanding,
when they walk down the narrow aisles of her store
reading the labels of packages aloud, as if
C they were the names of lost lovers: *Suspiros,*°
Merengues,° the stale candy of everyone's childhood.
She spends her days
slicing *jamón y queso*° and wrapping it in wax paper
tied with string: plain ham and cheese
D that would cost less at the A&P, but it would not satisfy
the hunger of the fragile old man lost in the folds
of his winter coat, who brings her lists of items
that he reads to her like poetry, or the others,
whose needs she must divine, conjuring up products
from places that now exist only in their hearts—
closed ports she must trade with.

5. plantains: type of banana.
6. votive offerings: sacrifices made to fulfill a vow, or offered in devotion.
27. *Suspiros* (sōōs·pē′rōs): type of small spongecake.
28. *Merengues* (mā·rān′gās): meringue candy.
30. *jamón y queso* (khä·mōn′ ē kā′sō): Spanish for "ham and cheese."

OPTIONS FOR TEACHING

Linguistic Challenge students to determine why the poet uses Spanish words in the way she does. Would the words not be as effective if they were translated into English? Why or why not? Have students work in pairs to examine each of the words in context. Have the pairs share their observations with the rest of the class.

STRATEGIES FOR INCLUSION

Interpersonal As students read the poem, have them share their impressions of the main character with a partner. Encourage the pairs of students to record everything they know about the character, and what they can infer about her from the poem's details.

INTEGRATING THE LANGUAGE ARTS

Strategic Reading Have students make a diagram of the details in the poem. Students may use a graphic organizer such as the one on Transparency 3: Cluster Diagram in the Transparency Package. Students may group details with common themes and jot down observations about the details next to their places in the diagram. Encourage students to investigate how the specific details work to support more general or abstract ideas in the poem.

MAKING MEANINGS

First Thoughts

1. What do you think of the woman who runs the deli? What does she do for her customers?

Shaping Interpretations

2. Describe in your own words the feelings of the customers in the deli.
3. Were you surprised that the proprietor of a deli and the things she sells could have so many important associations for the customers? Explain your answer.
4. The poem contains many sensory **images.** Identify at least one image each of sight, hearing, taste, smell, and touch.
5. What **concrete details** help make this poem very specific—and rooted in a particular time and place?

Extending the Text

6. Language is important to the deli's customers. Review the notes in your Reader's Log, and discuss the various ways immigrants to this country might have a perspective on language and culture that is different from the perspective of Americans who have lived their whole lives here.

Challenging the Text

7. In ancient Rome, the poet Horace (65–8 B.C.) wrote a treatise called *Ars Poetica,* or *The Art of Poetry,* setting forth his own rules for writing poetry. Since Horace's time, many poets have explored ideas about what makes a good poem. Why do you think Cofer subtitles her poem "An Ars Poetica"? In what sense might this poem reflect her ideas about what constitutes good poetry?

CHOICES: Building Your Portfolio

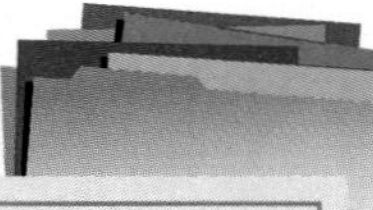

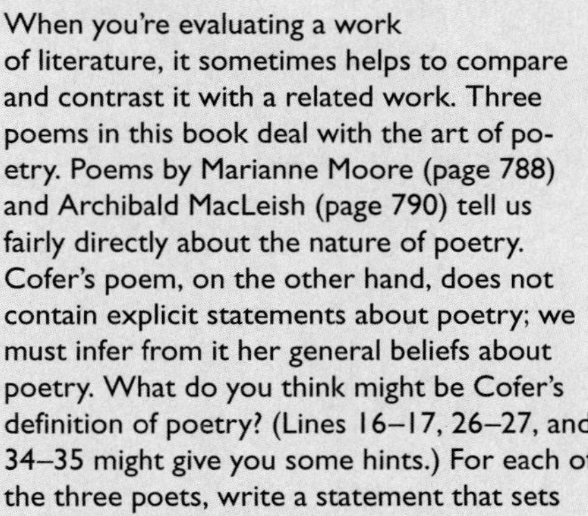

Writer's Notebook

1. Collecting Ideas for an Evaluation

When you're evaluating a work of literature, it sometimes helps to compare and contrast it with a related work. Three poems in this book deal with the art of poetry. Poems by Marianne Moore (page 788) and Archibald MacLeish (page 790) tell us fairly directly about the nature of poetry. Cofer's poem, on the other hand, does not contain explicit statements about poetry; we must infer from it her general beliefs about poetry. What do you think might be Cofer's definition of poetry? (Lines 16–17, 26–27, and 34–35 might give you some hints.) For each of the three poets, write a statement that sets forth the poet's definition of *ars poetica.* How are these poets' views of poetry alike and different? Save your notes for possible use in the Writer's Workshop on page 1181.

Critical Writing / Music

2. The Music of Words

In a brief essay, analyze the musical qualities of Cofer's poem: its rhythm, assonance, alliteration, and other sound effects. If this poem were a piece of music, what musical qualities would it have? Describe the kind of music you associate with this poem, and, if possible, accompany your essay with a recording of vocal or instrumental music that "sounds" like the poem.

Art

3. Many Parts to the Whole

Cofer uses many images to craft this poem. Transfer her technique to the visual arts by making a collage or painting that unites numerous images in one work. You may want to follow Cofer's lead and use a deli as your subject; you could also assemble images of a restaurant, a ballgame, a city, or another subject.

Making Meanings

First Thoughts

1. Possible response: The woman in the deli is probably an immigrant herself, and she is more than helpful. She provides a spiritual and emotional haven for the immigrants.

Shaping Interpretations

2. Possible response: The customers in the deli seem full of longing for something lost. They seem unsatisfied with their new home.
3. Possible response: No, I wasn't surprised, because certain sensory experiences can bring back strong memories.
4. Possible responses: Sight: "a formica counter, / plastic Mother and Child magnetized / to the top of an ancient register"; hearing: "reading the labels of packages aloud . . . *Suspiros, / Merengues"*; taste: "Bustelo coffee"; smell: "the heady mix of smells . . . open bins / of dried codfish, the green plantains / hanging"; touch: "slicing *jamón y queso* and wrapping it in wax paper / tied with string."
5. Concrete details that make the setting specific include the description of the woman who runs the deli and names like "*Merengues*" and "A&P." The details evoke a certain time, place, and group of people.

Extending the Text

6. **(Synthesis)** Possible response: An immigrant's experience of language is likely to be more emotional—both positively and negatively—than a native speaker's. Positively, language can provoke a rich store of memories associated with one's native country and native culture. Negatively, it can present obstacles to a smooth, successful assimilation into the new culture. Native speakers are more likely to experience language as transparent, that is, something they see through and simply do not notice.

Challenging the Text

7. **(Synthesis)** Cofer's subtitle suggests that one finds poetry in ordinary, everyday places. The language of good poetry is emotionally charged and rich in imagery that leads one to deep and poignant feeling.

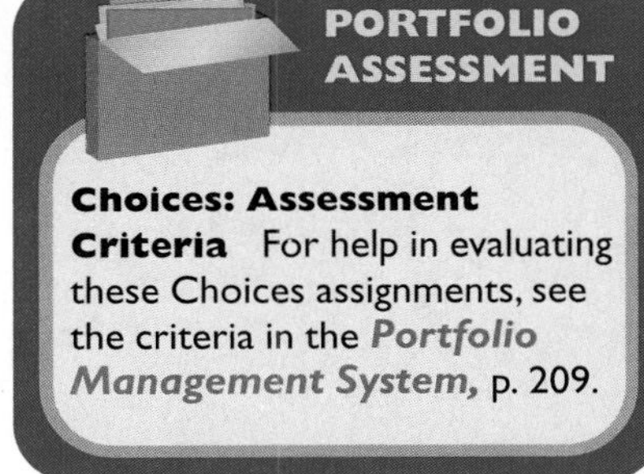

Choices: Assessment Criteria For help in evaluating these Choices assignments, see the criteria in the ***Portfolio Management System,*** p. 209.

QUICK PLANNING GUIDE

Into the Poem

Through the Poem

Beyond the Poem

Robert Severi/Gamma Liaison.

Rita Dove

(1952–)

Rita Dove's best-known work, *Thomas and Beulah* (1986), is a sequence of poems (including the following selection) loosely based on the lives of her maternal grandparents. Dove described the poems in an interview:

> I know that when I was writing the poems that went into *Thomas and Beulah,* . . . I realized that what I was trying to tell, let's say, was not a narrative as we know narratives but actually the moments that matter most in our lives. I began to think, how do we remember our lives? How do we think of our lives or shape our lives in our own consciousnesses, and I realized that we don't actually think of our lives in very cohesive strands but we remember as beads on a necklace, moments that matter to us, come to us in flashes, and the connections are submerged.

This statement expresses the central concern of much of Dove's poetry: how memory shapes who we are—in other words, how we become ourselves.

In addition to *Thomas and Beulah,* Dove's books of poetry include *The Other Side of the House* (1988), *Grace Notes* (1989), *Selected Poems* (1993), and *Mother Love* (1995), a book largely inspired by the ancient Greek myths of Demeter and Persephone. The esteemed poetry critic Helen Vendler, writing in *The New Yorker,* has praised Dove's "laser glance" and "remarkable objectivity." Dove has also written short stories, a novel, and a verse play, but it is her poetry that has brought her renown. From 1993 to 1995, she served as poet laureate of the United States.

Born and raised in Akron, Ohio, Dove graduated *summa cum laude* from Miami University (in Ohio), studied literature at the University of Tübingen in Germany, and attended the noted Writers' Workshop at the University of Iowa, where she received a master's degree in 1977. After teaching at several universities, Dove became professor of English at the University of Virginia, Charlottesville, in 1989.

The joys and trials of raising a family play as large a part in Dove's life as they do in her writing. Dove says that after her daughter, Aviva, was born, she felt she was living "the story of many women who all have three full-time jobs: You teach, you do parenting, and you try to write, too. I just was tired all the time. I remember days when I came back home and fell asleep over dessert."

Besides writing on personal subjects, Dove interweaves historical themes, including race relations, into her verse. As she told the *Washington Post,* "Obviously, as a black woman, I am concerned with race. But certainly not every poem of mine mentions the fact of being black. They are poems about humanity, and sometimes humanity happens to be black. I cannot run from, I *won't* run from any kind of truth." This honesty, strength, and vision of universality are the very qualities that distinguish Dove's work.

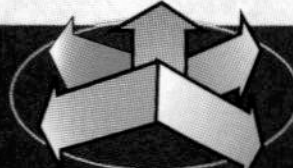

PROGRAM MANAGER

- **Planning Instruction** See Teaching Notes, *Teaching Resources B,* p. 206, for objectives, a summary, and literary elements.
- **Instructional Support** Before beginning the instructional lesson, see Graphic Organizer for Active Reading, *Teaching Resources B,* p. 218, for a Through the Poem activity.
- **Assessment** See Selection Test, *Test Booklet,* pp. 269–270.

Before You Read
The Satisfaction Coal Company

Reading Focus

Moments That Matter
Rita Dove once said, "I think all of us have moments, particularly in our childhood, where we come alive, maybe for the first time. And we go back to those moments and think, 'This is when I became myself.'" These remembered moments, however common and ordinary they may seem, illuminate who we are—they reveal the layers of experience that create our selves.

A Dialogue with the Text

READER'S LOG

This poem is divided into three sections. As you read, keep a log of your responses to each section: Describe what is happening, identify whether the actions being described take place in the present or the past, and note any emotional reactions you have to particular words, phrases, or images.

Background

"The Satisfaction Coal Company" is the second-to-last poem in the section of *Thomas and Beulah* devoted to Thomas, a character who represents Rita Dove's maternal grandfather. Thomas found part-time work during the Great Depression of the 1930s as a cleaner at the offices of the Satisfaction Coal Company, in Akron, Ohio. In those days, coal was still widely used to heat homes, which explains the importance of the coal scraps Thomas carries home. The poem that appears in *Thomas and Beulah* before "The Satisfaction Coal Company" tells of the stroke Thomas suffered; the section's next, and final, poem tells of Thomas's death in 1963.

Aaron by Thomas Hart Benton. Oil-tempera on canvas ($30\frac{1}{4}'' \times 20\frac{1}{4}''$).

The Satisfaction Coal Company

Rita Dove

1.

What to do with a day.
Leaf through *Jet.* Watch T.V.
Freezing on the porch
but he goes anyhow, snow too high (A)
for a walk, the ice treacherous.
Inside, the gas heater takes care of itself;
he doesn't even notice being warm.

Everyone says he looks great.
Across the street a drunk stands smiling (B)
at something carved in a tree.

Using Before You Read
p. 1171

Reading Focus

Challenge students to name other works of literature in which a character realizes something important about himself or herself. What did the character find out? Write students' examples on the chalkboard, and ask them what they expect of the poem.

Background

Ask students to share their knowledge about the Great Depression. They may draw on their discussion when analyzing the last two sections of the poem.

A. Reader's Response: First Thoughts

? What is your first impression of Thomas's character? [Sample responses: He is dutiful and preoccupied. Or he does not notice things around him and is just passing time.]

B. Literary Element: Irony

? What irony is there in this stanza? [The observation that "Everyone says he looks great," the similar distraction of the drunk, and the posing of the neighbor are all unexpected, quirky details that reveal the extent of Thomas's distraction.]

Options for Teaching

Strategies for Inclusion

Less Proficient Readers Have students read the poem with a partner. Each partner may take a turn reading the poem aloud, and then the partners may discuss their impressions, observations, and interpretations of the poem. The pairs should take notes of their discussions and then review parts of the poem that still confuse them. Ask the pairs to share their notes on any difficulties they had with the poem, strategies they used to resolve those difficulties, and their final interpretations of the poem.

Advanced Have students read the rest of *Thomas and Beulah*. Ask them to make a presentation to the class. Have them describe Thomas's character and read passages from the book that illustrate his character traits.

A. Critical Reading: Making Inferences

? What attitude did Thomas bring to his work? [He looked at his work as a reflection of himself, and he did it with great care.]

B. Exploring the Historical Period

The year 1934 marked the midpoint in the worst economic depression in world history. Five years earlier, the Great Depression started as an extended slump in business activity that continued well into the 1930s. Huge numbers of people lost their life savings when the stock market crashed. Bank failures caused depositor savings to evaporate. Thousands of Americans lost jobs and homes, and many were forced to live on charity. Unemployment reached epidemic proportions with about thirteen million people in the United States out of work by 1933. During the Great Depression, a job was something highly cherished.

C. Reader's Response: Shaping Interpretations

? What can you tell about the speaker from his use of the phrase "*I'm listening*"? [Sample responses: Thomas doesn't like to have attention directed toward himself, so he avoids voicing his own opinion. Or Thomas gets easily annoyed by people prying into his work or his life.]

The new neighbor with the floating hips
scoots out to get the mail
and waves once, brightly,
storm door clipping her heel on the way in.

2.

Twice a week he had taken the bus down Glendale hill
to the corner of Market. Slipped through
the alley by the canal and let himself in.
Started to sweep
with terrible care, like a woman
brushing shine into her hair,
same motion, same lullaby.
No curtains—the cop on the beat
stopped outside once in the hour
to swing his billy club and glare.

It was better on Saturdays
when the children came along:
he mopped while they emptied
ashtrays, clang of glass on metal
then a dry scutter. Next they counted
nailheads studding the leather cushions.
Thirty-four! they shouted,
that was the year and
they found it mighty amusing.

But during the week he noticed more—
lights when they gushed or dimmed
at the Portage Hotel, the 10:32
picking up speed past the B & O switchyard,°
floorboards trembling and the explosive
kachook kachook kachook kachook
and the oiled rails ticking underneath.

3.

They were poor then but everyone had been poor.
He hadn't minded the sweeping,
just the thought of it—like now
when people ask him what he's thinking
and he says *I'm listening.*

Those nights walking home alone,
the bucket of coal scraps banging his knee,
he'd hear a roaring furnace
with its dry, familiar heat. Now the nights
take care of themselves—as for the days,

37. B & O switchyard: yard of the Baltimore and Ohio Railroad where train cars are switched from one track to another to make up trains.

OPTIONS FOR TEACHING

INTEGRATING THE LANGUAGE ARTS

Strategic Reading As students read, encourage them to take an active role by making inferences as they go along. Students may make one inference for each stanza and record their inferences in a chart such as the following one. After students have finished reading the poem, ask them to share their inferences and the thinking that went into making them.

Inference	Textual Support

Language and Style Alert students to the vivid sensory imagery in the poem. Have them record examples of the imagery in a graphic organizer such as the one on Transparency 7: Sensory Details Chart in the Transparency Package. Then, challenge students to relate the imagery to the theme of the poem. Are the sensory images more vivid and frequent in certain passages? Do any images stand out? Have students discuss their charts and ideas in small groups.

there is the canary's sweet curdled song,
the wino smiling through his dribble.
Past the hill, past the gorge
choked with wild sumac in summer,
the corner has been upgraded.
Still, he'd like to go down there someday
to stand for a while, and get warm.

D. Critical Reading: Drawing Conclusions

? How would standing at the corner make Thomas warm? [His memories of working for the coal company make him warmer than his own heater does, because it was a time that meant a lot to him.]

CROSSING THE CURRICULUM

Social Sciences Ask students to research one or more personal accounts of life during the Great Depression. Ask students to concentrate on finding out how a specific person survived the era: What strategies did the person use? How did he or she adapt to changes in surroundings? Have volunteers briefly share their findings with the class. Ask students to speculate on how they would have lived through the time period.

ASSESSMENT TOOLS

Check Test: True-False

1. The poem is set in the time of the Great Depression. [False]
2. Thomas worked briefly for the railroad after quitting his job sweeping. [False]
3. The year Thomas remembers is 1934. [True]
4. Thomas's life is harder now than it has ever been. [False]
5. When people ask him what he is thinking, Thomas replies, "I'm remembering." [False]

LITERATURE AND CULTURE

Ask students to name the most recent recipients of the three awards. Have students research the names of the winners if they do not know them. Ask if anyone in the classroom is familiar with any of the recipients' work, or set aside part of a class period to have students read excerpts from the winners' works.

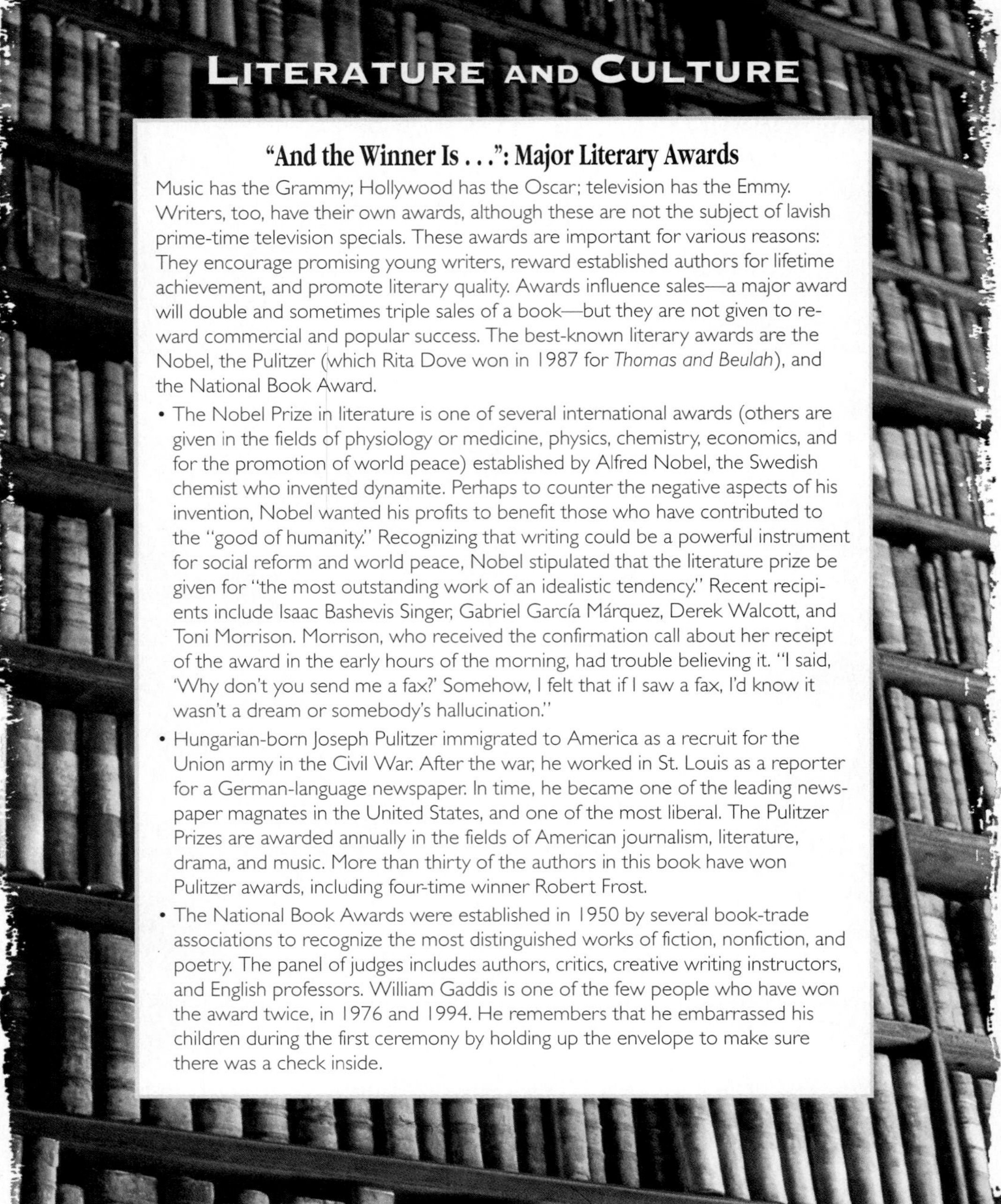

LITERATURE AND CULTURE

"And the Winner Is . . .": Major Literary Awards

Music has the Grammy; Hollywood has the Oscar; television has the Emmy. Writers, too, have their own awards, although these are not the subject of lavish prime-time television specials. These awards are important for various reasons: They encourage promising young writers, reward established authors for lifetime achievement, and promote literary quality. Awards influence sales—a major award will double and sometimes triple sales of a book—but they are not given to reward commercial and popular success. The best-known literary awards are the Nobel, the Pulitzer (which Rita Dove won in 1987 for *Thomas and Beulah*), and the National Book Award.

- The Nobel Prize in literature is one of several international awards (others are given in the fields of physiology or medicine, physics, chemistry, economics, and for the promotion of world peace) established by Alfred Nobel, the Swedish chemist who invented dynamite. Perhaps to counter the negative aspects of his invention, Nobel wanted his profits to benefit those who have contributed to the "good of humanity." Recognizing that writing could be a powerful instrument for social reform and world peace, Nobel stipulated that the literature prize be given for "the most outstanding work of an idealistic tendency." Recent recipients include Isaac Bashevis Singer, Gabriel García Márquez, Derek Walcott, and Toni Morrison. Morrison, who received the confirmation call about her receipt of the award in the early hours of the morning, had trouble believing it. "I said, 'Why don't you send me a fax?' Somehow, I felt that if I saw a fax, I'd know it wasn't a dream or somebody's hallucination."
- Hungarian-born Joseph Pulitzer immigrated to America as a recruit for the Union army in the Civil War. After the war, he worked in St. Louis as a reporter for a German-language newspaper. In time, he became one of the leading newspaper magnates in the United States, and one of the most liberal. The Pulitzer Prizes are awarded annually in the fields of American journalism, literature, drama, and music. More than thirty of the authors in this book have won Pulitzer awards, including four-time winner Robert Frost.
- The National Book Awards were established in 1950 by several book-trade associations to recognize the most distinguished works of fiction, nonfiction, and poetry. The panel of judges includes authors, critics, creative writing instructors, and English professors. William Gaddis is one of the few people who have won the award twice, in 1976 and 1994. He remembers that he embarrassed his children during the first ceremony by holding up the envelope to make sure there was a check inside.

from An Interview with Rita Dove: Poet Laureate of the United States

We stood in a cool, dimly lit room in the Library of Congress with a nervousness to be expected when meeting the poet laureate of the United States. In our minds, we were reviewing possible questions and camera angles and hoping we would not seem immature or unprepared. When Rita Dove appeared, her energy and friendliness—together with her M & M multicolored fingernails—put us in a creative, relaxed frame of mind and led us to a fascinating interview with a remarkable writer.

Heritage: Why do you think it's important for the United States to have a poet laureate?

Rita Dove: Our country thrives on symbolism. Because it's so large and spread out, we get our energy when there are people to focus on. A poet laureate reminds us that the cultural life in this country is necessary. Practically speaking, it gives people someone to write to when they have questions. I can't tell you how many letters I get from people who simply say, "Here I am in Idaho, and I like to write poetry and I don't even know if there's anyone else around me who writes poetry." Then I am able to tell them how they can find someone: where they can go, what community centers there are, and how they can find out about poetry readings.

H: How do you see your appointment as poet laureate in terms of your career?

R. D.: It has given me incredible exposure and publicity that I did not count on at this point in my life. It has changed my life in the sense that I'm not going to have as much private time ever again, probably. But in terms of writing my poems, I'm trying very hard not to let it affect that. When I sit down to write, I don't think, "Well, there are all these people waiting. . . ." I'm in my room; it's just me and a circle of light and the page. The main difference now is that it is harder to get to the room. Critics and reporters ask, "Won't it just give you pressure to do better on your next work?" I think that's not the point. The point is to write the poem, then let people think of it what they may.

H: Do you feel strongly about writing as an African American woman?

R. D.: It's extremely important for writers to write fully about their own experience and about whatever other experiences strike their fancy. It is important for all the stories to be told. I don't feel a particular obligation to write only about the African American experience or the experience of being a woman. I would not want to limit myself, and I don't think anyone should. But I also feel very, very lucky to be writing in a time when people are beginning to understand, to realize, that the experience of an African American woman could also have relevance to their life.

H: From where do you get your inspiration?

R. D.: I get it from everywhere: from other authors, from just walking down the street. Sometimes I think of myself as a giant sponge; I just keep soaking all this stuff up. I think that anything, *anything* that interests one is worthy of a poem. I don't cut things out by saying, "Well, this is math; there's nothing I can do with poetry and math." You never know.

—Moira Haney and Catherine Nicholas
Heritage, Spring 1994
James Madison High School
Vienna, Virginia

Questions to Making Meanings begin on p.1176.

Making Meanings

First Thoughts

1. Possible response: Thomas is a quiet man and a careful listener, dutiful yet uninspired. He doesn't say much or respond visibly but seems to notice a lot and says he's listening. He does what he has to do, with little emotion, yet notices details very acutely.

Reviewing the Text

a. Winter. The last stanza also refers to summer.

b. His going to work at the coal company building to sweep up. Thomas notices the hotel lights through the window and the sounds of the trains.

c. A drunk smiling at a tree; a woman retrieving mail and waving; a cop swinging his billy club and glaring; children cleaning ashtrays and counting nailheads in a leather chair; a wino smiling through his dribble.

d. He doesn't really mind the sweeping. At the end of the poem, he'd like to stand and listen to the familiar old sounds again and let his memories warm him.

Shaping Interpretations

2. Possible examples: "the ice treacherous" (l. 5), "brushing shine" (l. 20), "the canary's sweet curdled song" (l. 51).

CONNECTING WITH "THE SATISFACTION COAL COMPANY"

Discuss with students whether the interview gives them a different perspective on the poem they have just read. Ask students if they can find evidence of Dove's methods and ideas in the poem. Encourage students to refer to specific passages for support.

Technology Tip

TECHNOLOGY Have students use the Internet to research Dove's other works. Students can hear the author read "Lady Freedom Among Us" by accessing the University of Virginia Internet Library at **http://www.lib.virginia.edu/etext/fourmill/DovLady.html**. *You may want to preview any Internet activity that you suggest to students. Because these resources are sometimes public forums, their content can be unpredictable.*

Making Meanings answers begin on p.T1175.

3. Possible responses: Line 1: "What to do with a day" suggests the simple dimensions of a working life. Line 4: "snow" is characteristic of winter, which is part of the inescapable and inevitable yearly cycle of seasons. Line 12: "the mail" is a daily event that brings small pleasure in an otherwise simple life. Line 15: "Twice a week" suggests the plodding regularity of work and duty. Line 25: "Saturdays" are a brief moment of pleasure in the weekly routine. Lines 31–32: "*Thirty-four!* . . . the year" is ironic because the children find amusing this year of severe economic depression.
4. Possible response: Thomas's response to his circumstances seems sober and unemotional. His reminiscence suggests little sense of larger purpose, little intention other than surviving. The opening line "What to do with a day" reinforces the feeling of aimlessness, as does the ambiguity of Thomas's plans for the future in the final lines.
5. Possible response: Dove's central theme seems to be that no matter how repressive the circumstances of life, there is pleasure in the simple act of perceiving and responding. Part 3 develops this theme by juxtaposing the phrase "*I'm listening*" with the richness of life and Thomas's restrained desire to someday "go down there." The title foreshadows the theme by combining "satisfaction" and "coal company," seemingly disparate elements (like hard times and happiness) that Dove's poem unites.

Connecting with the Text

6. The phrase "struggling to sing in his chains" fits Thomas because he quietly finds satisfaction in hard times. He does not speak much, but he has a fine appreciation of life around him that must struggle to be expressed.

Making Meanings

First Thoughts

1. What words would you use to describe Thomas? Why?

Reviewing the Text

a. In the first and last stanzas of the poem, what seasons of the year are referred to?
b. What actions and events are described in part 2 of the poem? What things does Thomas notice during the week (lines 34–40)?
c. Aside from Thomas, what things do we see other people doing in the poem?
d. In part 3, what are Thomas's feelings about the sweeping? What does he want to do at the end of the poem?

Shaping Interpretations

2. One of this poem's strengths is its **diction**—the poet's choice of words. For instance, the poet writes that lights "gushed" rather than "brightened." What other examples of unusual diction can you find in the poem?
3. Dove's poem is full of **images** and phrases related to time, such as days of the week and seasons of the year. Review the notes you made in your Reader's Log, and identify some of these images. Explain their significance in the poem.
4. How would you describe Thomas's response to the circumstances of his life? What do his reminiscences tell us about him? Support your interpretation with specific evidence from the poem.
5. State what you think is the central **theme** or message of Dove's poem. In what ways does part 3 further develop this theme? Does the poem's title suggest a clue?

Connecting with the Text

6. Dove has said that some individuals in her poems "are struggling to sing in their chains." How do you think this statement applies to Thomas, if at all? How does it describe his response to the circumstances of his life?

Choices: Building Your Portfolio

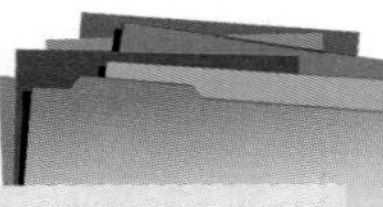

Writer's Notebook

1. Collecting Ideas for an Evaluation

One way to make a judgment about a work you're reviewing is by evaluating how it supports—or does not support—a comment made by a critic or by the work's author. Re-read the biography of Rita Dove on page 1170, as well as comments Dove made to the student interviewers (Student to Student, page 1175). Using a quotation from Dove as a starting point, make some notes on how well "The Satisfaction Coal Company" reflects or fails to reflect Dove's comments about "moments that matter" and other aspects of poetry. Save your notes for possible use in the Writer's Workshop on page 1181.

Critical Writing

2. Moments of Discovery

One critic has written, "Dove's poems enter the mysterious by opening themselves to the moment of discovery. Usually that discovery is not rational, but emotional or physical." In a brief essay, explain how this statement applies to "The Satisfaction Coal Company."

Research / Speaking and Listening

3. Laurels for a Poet

Rita Dove once commented, "I'm hoping that by the end of my term people will think of a poet laureate as someone who's out there with her sleeves rolled up and working. . . ." With three or four other students, organize a panel discussion on the position of U.S. poet laureate. Panel members should report on (a) how the poet laureate is chosen; (b) the main functions of the post; (c) which poets have held the post in the past and who holds it now; and (d) how it compares with the similarly named post in Great Britain. After the panel discussion, field questions and comments from the class.

Beyond the Poem

Choices: Building Your Portfolio

1. **Writer's Notebook** Remind students to save their work. They may use it as prewriting for the Writer's Workshop on p. 1181.

PORTFOLIO ASSESSMENT

Choices: Assessment Criteria For help in evaluating these Choices assignments, see the criteria in the ***Portfolio Management System,*** p. 210.

Many works of contemporary literature use realistic language and graphic depictions of characters in crises and conflict. Be sure to check with your teacher and parent or guardian before reading any of the following books.

There's Always a Catch

"Orr was crazy and could be grounded. All he had to do was ask; and as soon as he did, he would no longer be crazy." Paradoxical military rules and the madness of war become a metaphor for life's absurdities in Joseph Heller's sharp satire *Catch-22* (Simon and Schuster). *Closing Time* (Simon and Schuster) is Heller's recently published, long-awaited sequel.

Yiddish Yarns

Isaac Bashevis Singer's work is rooted in the Polish-Jewish culture of his youth. Singer, whose work was translated from the Yiddish, was awarded the Nobel Prize in literature in 1982 for his novels, memoirs, children's books, and, most notably, his dozens of short stories. *Collected Stories* (Farrar, Straus and Giroux) reveals the range and scope of this master storyteller.

Both Sides of the Story

Another consummate storyteller is Toni Morrison, winner of the 1993 Nobel Prize in literature. Morrison writes of the debilitating effects of oppression against African Americans on victim and perpetrator alike; she also explores the other side of the coin, writing about the richness of African American community and traditions. *Beloved* (Knopf) tells the story of a mother's desperate attempt to prevent her children from being enslaved.

Stylist Extraordinaire

For anyone interested in the craft of writing, E. B. White is essential reading. For most of his life, White wrote for *The New Yorker* magazine, though he also wrote several classic books for children, including *Charlotte's Web.* White's easy, gently humorous style is displayed in abundance in *The Essays of E. B. White* (HarperCollins).

A Nation of Poets

More people are writing poetry than ever before, and, happily, the audience for poetry is also growing—especially for coffeehouse readings. *Contemporary American Poetry,* edited by Donald Hall (Penguin), samples work published through the early 1970s. To explore the more recent work of poets such as Charles Olson, Denise Levertov, and Jimmy Santiago Baca, see *Postmodern American Poetry,* edited by Paul Hoover (Norton).

Read On

Portfolio Assessment Options

The following projects can help you evaluate and assess your student's reading accomplishments outside class. Videotapes or photographs of completed projects themselves may be included in student's portfolios.

- **Design a Book Jacket** Have students design and create a book jacket for a book they read. The cover should include an illustration; the book's title, author, and publisher; and an original blurb to encourage reader interest.
- **Make a Map** Ask students to create a map based on a novel. They can use symbols to designate important locations. They can also trace the route of the main character(s).
- **Take a Photograph** Ask students to choose a high point from a novel and to set up a photograph to represent it. Encourage students to help each other to provide the needed subjects for the pictures. Some students may also be willing to help find or lend props or costumes.
- **Film Adaptation** Have students work in pairs to rewrite important scenes as movie scripts. Remind students that scripts focus more on dialogue and action than on description. Suggest that students read their scripts aloud before reading or performing them for the class.

FOR FURTHER EXPLORATION

Fiction

Catch-22 by Joseph Heller
Slaughterhouse Five by Kurt Vonnegut
The Heart is a Lonely Hunter by Carson McCullers
On the Road by Jack Kerouac
House Made of Dawn by N. Scott Momaday

Short Stories

Cosmicomics by Italo Calvino
Nine Stories by J. D. Salinger
Selected Short Stories of Raymond Carver by Raymond Carver
Borges: A Reader by Jorge Luis Borges

Poetry

"The Explorer" by Gwendolyn Brooks
"Running" by Richard Wilbur
"Eleven" by Archibald MacLeish
"Song" by Adrienne Rich

Nonfiction

Aké: The Years of Childhood by Wole Soyinka
Barrio Boy by Ernesto Galarza
American Hunger by Richard Wright
Hugging the Shore by John Updike
Bury my Heart at Wounded Knee by Dee Brown

A. Humanities Connection
Derivational morphology is a subfield of linguistics that studies rules governing word formation. Morphologists recognize four processes of word formation in English: prefixation, adding a prefix; suffixation, adding a suffix; conversion, by which a word changes class without changing form (for example, *radio* the noun becomes *radio* the verb); and compounding, by which two base forms combine (such as *goldfish*). Less common processes of English word formation are reduplication (compounding with the same or similar elements, such as *buddy-buddy* or *wishy-washy*); clipping (shortening a longer form, such as *advertising* to *ad*); and blending (merging two words, such as *tangerine* and *orange* to form *tangelo*).

B. Humanities Connection
In addition to developing the first electric telegraph in the United States and inventing the Morse code, Samuel Morse was a successful artist. In 1813, he won the Adelphi Society of Arts Medal for a clay sculpture of Hercules. After exhibiting paintings in London at the Royal Academy of Art, Morse returned to the United States and became established as a well-known portrait painter. His portrait of the Marquis de Lafayette hangs in the New York City Hall. Morse entered work in a competition for four paintings to hang in the rotunda of the Capitol in Washington, D.C. When his entries were not accepted, Morse started work on the telegraph.

C. Expansion
Technically, a telegraph message is called a telegram or wire if it is transmitted over a land circuit and a cablegram if it is transmitted via underwater cable. In 1861, the first transcontinental telegraph line connected California and Washington, D.C. The first telegraph message was sent by California Chief Justice Stephen Field to President Abraham Lincoln declaring California's loyalty to the embattled Union. The first successful cablegram between England and the United States was sent in 1866.

The American Language

High Tech's Influence

by Gary Q. Arpin

Before *high tech,* there was just plain *technology*. The nineteenth-century British author Richard Burton used the word *technology* in his book *Travels in Arabia and Africa* (1829) to refer to fairly simple practical arts, such as extracting dye from plants. In 1829, an American, Professor Jacob Bigelow, first used the word in its present meaning of "applied science" when he published *The Elements of Technology* (subtitled *On the Application of the Sciences to the Useful Arts*).

Training for New Vocabulary

The advanced technology of the early nineteenth century was chiefly steam, and the steam engine entered people's lives in the form of factories, steamboats, and train locomotives. The railroad's impact on American lives was speedy and unprecedented. In 1830, there were just 73 miles of railroad tracks in the United States. By 1850, the number had increased to some 8,900 miles, and by 1860, to about 30,600 miles. "The world has seen nothing like it before," Daniel Webster wrote. "The progress of the age has almost outstripped human belief."

The new application of steam technology required a host of new words. Where did these terms come from? The same processes of word formation applied to railroad terms as had applied to Americanisms in general. Some new words celebrated innovators; for instance, the *Pullman car,* a railroad car with berths for sleeping, was named after George Pullman, who invented it in 1865. Many other terms were formed by combining existing words, such as *redcap* and *whistle-stop*.

A substantial number of railroad terms were borrowed from earlier forms of transportation. Sailing ships and steamboats provided the railroad with terms like *berth, caboose, crew, gondola,* and *all aboard*. The stagecoach provided *car, coach, conductor,* and *station*. This process continues today, as one technology lends its words to a successor.

Most technological terms have a well-defined and specific job to do. Some terms find a broader popularity, usually through metaphor, and enter standard usage. To be *under pressure,* for example, is a phrase borrowed from the steam engine. Most of us use the term only in its metaphoric sense, without thinking about its origin. The train gave people something to do—watch the train come in—and it also gave rise to a new social designation, "the wrong side of the tracks," as well as such terms as *right of way* and *sidetrack*.

New Words from *Tele* and *Graph*

About the same time the railroad was crisscrossing the American continent, the telegraph was doing so, too. The word *telegraph* (coined from two Greek terms, *tele,* "afar," and *graphein,* "to write"), had been used in England since the eighteenth century to refer to various forms of semaphores (systems of signaling). However, it became popular only with the invention of the Morse telegraph in the mid–nineteenth century—another example of one technology lending its words to another.

Telegram is a true Americanism, coined in Albany, New York, in 1852. "A friend desires us to give notice," wrote an Albany *Evening Journal* reporter, "that he will ask leave . . . to introduce a new word. It is *telegram,* instead of *telegraphic dispatch*." The word, so politely brought into the world, encountered some vigorous opposition before being accepted. The reason? It was not a proper combination of Greek words. The proper word, purists argued, would be *telegrapheme*.

OPTIONS FOR TEACHING

STRATEGIES FOR INCLUSION

Advanced Challenge students to think of other high-tech terms that pertain to specific areas of contemporary life. Students may go a step further and research words that have just been formed and that are finding a place in circulation. Have students share their results with the class.

Visual To help students form a picture of how words with common roots and affixes are related, have students make drawings that show the relationships among words with common elements. Words with a common root such as *graphein,* Greek for "to write," can be shown in a graphic organizer as branches on a tree labeled with the root.

Tele and *graph* have been busy root words since the early nineteenth century. *Photograph* appeared in 1839 (*photo* is Greek for "light"). For a number of years, *photographist* fought it out with *photographer* before disappearing. Late in the nineteenth century came the *cinematograph* (*kinema* is Greek for "motion"). It was shortened to *cinema* in England, but changed to *moving picture* in the United States and later shortened to *movie*.

The *telephone* was invented in 1876 and the *phonograph* in 1877 (*phono* is Greek for "sound" or "voice"). The technology for wireless communication led to the *radiotelegraph* in 1903, which was shortened to *radio*.

Television first achieved commercial success in the late 1940s. The British shortened *television* to *telly*, while Americans abbreviated it to *TV*. (As we shall see, initials and acronyms became especially popular during this period in the United States.) D

Acronyms: Convenient Abbreviations

One method of forming new words, now so popular that it almost threatens to overwhelm us, is the use of acronyms. The word *acronym* is probably an Americanism, although the practice is ancient. The term comes from the Greek words for "top" and "name," and refers to a word formed from the combination of the first letters of the words in a phrase. *Radar* was a technological acronym (from "radio detecting and ranging"), and it quickly knocked out the British candidate, *radiolocator*. *Sonar* ("sound navigation and ranging") followed, as did *laser* ("light amplification by stimulated emission of radiation").

The acronym device was not the sole property of scientists and technologists. In the twentieth century, the military and other bureaucracies have bred many acronyms, from AWOL ("absent without leave"), coined in World War I, to NATO (North Atlantic Treaty Organization) to *snafu* (situation normal, all fouled up). World War II saw the development of a great many acronyms, such as WAVES and WAC ("Women Appointed for Voluntary Emergency Service" and "Women's Army Corps"), the women's branches of the U.S. Navy and Army.

> One method of forming new words, now so popular that it almost threatens to overwhelm us, is the use of acronyms.

Airplane Argot

The airplane had an effect on American culture in the twentieth century similar to the effect of the railroad in the nineteenth. When the Wright brothers patented their flying machine in 1906, the word *airplane* was already there, waiting for them. The new technology of *aeronautics* borrowed part of its name from sailing technology (*nautes* is Greek for "sailor"), and it borrowed a number of technical terms from sailing as well. *Cockpit, cabin, steward, rudder,* and many other terms were adapted from the ocean liners that the airplane would eventually make almost obsolete. New words and combinations, like *barnstorm, tailspin,* and *Mayday* (from the French *m'aidez,* "help me"), came into common usage as a result of the airplane.

Nautes, by the way, connects the ancient and the modern worlds in a strikingly direct way. In Greek mythology, the *Argonauts* sailed with Jason in a ship called the *Argo* in search of the Golden Fleece. The U.S. *astronauts* ("star sailors") sail to outer space in the twentieth century, as do the Russian *cosmonauts* ("universe sailors").

Terms like *countdown, blastoff, malfunction,* and *put on hold* are the legacy of jargon, or argot, from the space program. E Airplane flyers had long had a number of colorful terms for unexplained malfunctions. The word *gremlin* was commonly used by pilots during World War II, but was later replaced by *bug,* which is still in use. The word today's astronauts probably use most often, though, is *glitch,* a term taken over by computer experts.

Computerspeak

Much of the language associated with computers is highly specific and may never be extended to a noncomputer field. Such computer terms include *RAM, ROM,* and *DOS,* acronyms for "random access memory," "read only memory," and "disk operating system." People in the computer

D. Exploring the Culture
Television (from *tele,* "afar," and *videre,* "to see") did not become popular in the United States until after World War II. Between 1945 and 1960, the number of television sets in the United States skyrocketed from a few thousand to nearly sixty million. In the second half of the twentieth century, television clearly established itself as a powerful and pervasive force. The year 1960 marked the first televised presidential campaign debates, between Richard Nixon and John F. Kennedy, a significant event that extended the influence of television in the United States from cultural to political life.

E. Exploring the Culture
Jargon is any specialized language used by a specific social group. Doctors, sportscasters, sailors, educators, and countless other groups all use jargon when communicating with colleagues and other specialists.

Assessment See *The American Language, Test Booklet,* pp. 271–272.

STRATEGIES FOR INCLUSION

Interpersonal Arrange students in small groups and tell each group to compose a list of jargon with which its members are familiar. Direct group members to begin by thinking of their common interests and activities. Encourage the groups to compete with each other to compose the longest list. Each term on the list should be accompanied by its area of specialty.

INTEGRATING THE LANGUAGE ARTS

Strategic Reading Ask students to construct a KWL chart to show what they know, what they want to know, and what they learn about the influence of technology on the American language. Students may complete the first two columns individually before they read the essay. Encourage students to think of at least five items for each column. After they have read the article, they may then meet with a partner to discuss and record in the third column of their charts what they have learned about the subject. Partners may share their surprising discoveries with the class.

Try It Out: Possible Answers

1. | | | |
|---|---|---|
| sidetrack | railroad | to divert |
| stopover | stagecoach | an interruption in the course of a journey |
| bailout | boating | to parachute from an aircraft |
| tank town | railroad | a town where trains refilled boilers with water |
| tailspin | aircraft | a loss of control |
| nose dive | aircraft | any sudden, swift downward plunge |

2. CAT scan (computerized axial tomography); COBOL (common business oriented language); CAD/CAM (Computer-Aided Design /Computer-Aided Manufacturing); NASA (National Aeronautics and Space Administration); and SCUBA (self-contained underwater breathing apparatus).
3. SURFS, Surfers United to Reclaim Fouled Seas (an environmental clean up group comprised of surfers)

industry have adapted many standard English words to technical uses, though, and a number of these terms are edging back into the noncomputer world with slightly different meanings. The most notable are nouns that have been changed to verbs. *Access, format, interface,* and *program* are being used as verbs with some frequency today. *Program* has already produced an offspring, *deprogram,* referring to "reverse brainwashing."

Computer language is often lively and whimsical. If a programmer interferes with someone else's program, for example, he or she is said to *bomb the program* (not a nice thing to do). Programs that stop working unexpectedly *hang* or *crash,* sometimes as the result of a *spike,* or a surge in electricity. When we start a computer, we *boot* it. *Boot* is a shortening of *bootstrap,* which comes from the familiar expression "to pull yourself up by your bootstraps," meaning "to succeed on your own without the help of others," or, in computer jargon, "to be self-initiating."

Try It Out

1. The following terms, once associated only with trains, automobiles, or airplanes, have entered general usage. For each term, (1) identify the technology with which it was originally associated, and (2) give its meaning in general usage. You might want to refer to a dictionary.

   sidetrack
   stopover
   bailout
   tank town
   tailspin
   nose dive
2. Look at some newspapers or newsmagazines to find five acronyms related to technology that are in current usage. Remember that an acronym is an abbreviation that is pronounced like a word, not as separate letters.
3. An acronym can be especially effective if it is the same as a word whose meaning is related to the phrase the acronym stands for. An example would be *SEEP* (standing for "Student Environmental Education Program"), since environmentalists are often concerned with chemicals that seep into the water supply. Try inventing this kind of meaningful acronym. Share your creation with the rest of the class.

"You've learned to respond to verbal commands. Now let's test your computer literacy."

Rothco Cartoons.

OPTIONS FOR TEACHING

ASSESSMENT TOOLS

Check Test: Questions and Answers

1. What is the present meaning of *technology*? [Applied science.]
2. What is an acronym? Give an example. [A word formed by the first letters of words in a phrase; AWOL (Absent Without Leave).]
3. What does Jason of ancient Greek mythology share with NASA's space exploration program? [Jason and the Argonauts sailed the *Argo* in quest of the Golden Fleece; NASA astronauts "sail" through space in quest of knowledge; the root word *nautes* means "sailor."]
4. What are two ways words come into existence? [Any two of the following: A word can celebrate an innovator (Pullman cars), combine existing words (whistle-stop), borrow from related fields (caboose), be used metaphorically (under pressure), shorten a longer word (television to TV), be an acronym (NASA), or be created in a new field (computer interface).]

BUILDING YOUR PORTFOLIO

Writer's Workshop

The history of the written word is rich

PERSUASIVE WRITING

EVALUATION

When you evaluate something, you present a well-considered judgment about its worth, offering reasons that support your stance and evidence that those reasons are valid. In English classes, you are often asked to evaluate works of literature; in life, you may need to evaluate anything from the color scheme of a room to a politician's voting record to your own job performance.

Prewriting

1. **Choose a literary work.** Of the stories and poems you have read in the Contemporary Literature collections, which moved you most strongly, either to delight or to distaste? Which seemed to be the most flawless—or most flawed—examples of their art forms? Which stayed in your mind the longest? Quickwrite a list of outstanding works from the Contemporary Literature collections. The ones that first spring to mind may be the ones that left the strongest impression; however, take a few moments to allow less obvious choices to emerge from the back of your mind. Circle two or three titles that seem promising. Then skim over the circled works, and decide which to write about. If you completed and kept any of the Writer's Notebook activities from these collections, you may already have a head start on a topic for evaluation. Of course, you can always choose to evaluate a literary work you've encountered on your own, outside this textbook.
2. **Reacquaint yourself with the work.** Re-read the work, the prereading and postreading materials, and your notes, immersing yourself in the work's content and your own response to it. Take new notes as you go along. You'll continue consulting the work as you move through the writing process.
3. **Explore the work in writing.** Put your thoughts and feelings about the work on paper in a quick paragraph or two. State your opinion of the work, and mention as many specific reasons for your stance as you can. Note passages, scenes, characters, or other literary elements that make strong impressions on you. Include both positive and negative responses to the work.
4. **Decide on your criteria.** To evaluate something, you must apply standards to it. These standards, or **criteria,** are objective rather than personal. Criteria are used to assess whether

Technology HELP

See Writer's Workshop 2 CD-ROM. *Assignment: Evaluation.*

ASSIGNMENT
Write an essay evaluating a short story, essay, or poem.

AIM
To inform; to explain; to persuade.

AUDIENCE
Your classmates and teacher or a specialized audience interested in the subject of your evaluation.

Try It Out

In a small group, come up with as many valid criteria as you can for evaluating any of the following:

1. What are the qualities of a good elective course?
2. What makes a first-rate film?
3. What are the qualities of good conversation?
4. What qualities do you look for in a good teacher?
5. What are the qualities of an excellent radio station?

QUICK PLANNING GUIDE

Evaluation

Motivation

Ask students to write down the title of their favorite movie or album. Then ask students to make a list of some reasons they like the work. Ask volunteers to share their titles and their lists of reasons, and have the class discuss whether they agree or disagree with the volunteers' choices and support. Point out to students that they have just been using the process of evaluation to judge a work's worth.

OPTIONS FOR TEACHING

STRATEGIES FOR INCLUSION

Visual As students reacquaint themselves with a literary work, allow them to use self-stick notes to mark points in the work that could provide support for their evaluations. Students can review their self-stick notes and record the location of important passages in one column of a two-column chart. In the other column, students should note how the material would support their argument.

Auditory Before students review each other's drafts, ask students to read their papers softly to themselves. Alert students to pay attention to times in their reading where their voices falters, wanders, or sounds more tentative. Point out that these changes in their reading will help them identify weak points in their papers. Students can mark the points in their papers and revise them before exchanging papers.

PROGRAM MANAGER

Computer Guided Instruction For a related evaluation assignment that students may use as additional instruction, see ***Writer's Workshop 2.***

Teaching The Lesson

Remind students that they are expressing their opinions in their essays and that their opinions will only be taken seriously by others if they are backed up by strong reasons and examples that prove their points.

This lesson includes instructions for each stage of the writing process. You may want to guide students by modeling each stage with your own writing.

Prewriting

- Point out to students that their evaluations can concern why they didn't like a work; the important point is that students choose a work to which they have a strong reaction.
- Students who have difficulty choosing a work to write about can review the table of contents of this book and rate each work they've read on a scale of 1 to 5, with the higher number indicating a greater liking for the work. Then they can only consider as possible subjects of evaluation the works with the highest and lowest ratings.
- Point out to students that the model criterion-assessment-evidence chart is based on four prominent literary elements and that there are other elements, such as symbolism, setting, and point of view, that might also be useful in evaluating the works they have chosen. You can remind them that A Handbook of Literary Terms at the back of their textbooks contains definitions and examples of the literary elements, and you can suggest they review these terms.

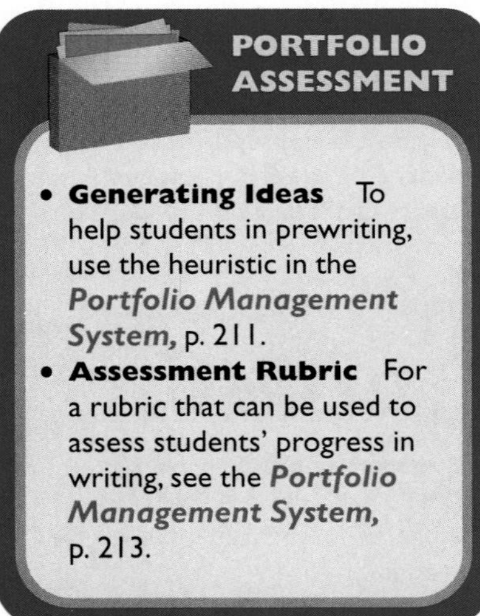

PORTFOLIO ASSESSMENT

- **Generating Ideas** To help students in prewriting, use the heuristic in the ***Portfolio Management System,*** p. 211.
- **Assessment Rubric** For a rubric that can be used to assess students' progress in writing, see the ***Portfolio Management System,*** p. 213.

something is an excellent example of its type or kind. For example, if a car is what you wish to evaluate, cost, gas mileage, repair record, and structural integrity might be among the traditional, or expected, criteria you would use. Similarly, the criteria you would apply to a literary work should agree, on the whole, with accepted critical standards of what makes a literary work successful or unsuccessful. It's important, of course, to develop criteria that are relevant to the unique characteristics of the subject you are evaluating. You might give a thumbs up to a popular science fiction novel because it is fast-paced, contains innovative ideas, and has interesting, larger-than-life characters. But the criteria you'd use to judge a more reflective, overtly "literary" novel would be quite different. You may also choose to weigh a given criterion more heavily than another criterion. For example, although both style and plot are important and basic aspects of literary works in general, you may decide to give little weight to literary style when evaluating a popular novel and instead evaluate the work almost entirely on its plot and characterization.

5. **Make a criterion-assessment-evidence chart.** Make a list of several criteria you think are important in the genre of literature you've chosen to evaluate. Then make a three-column criteria evaluation chart. In the left column, list your criteria. In the middle column, assess how you think the work either meets or does not meet each criterion, giving a brief reason for your judgment. In the right column, give factual evidence for each evaluation. Most of the evidence you will use in evaluating a literary work will be specific passages, quotations, or scenes. For example, if you feel the simple, straightforward style of Amy Tan's "Rules of the Game" perfectly suits the subject matter, a sample passage could be one piece of evidence; another piece of evidence might be the relatively small number of words per sentence in the story; another might be the large number of simple sentences. To generate evidence for your chart, you might
   - compare and/or contrast two works
   - relate the work to your own experience
   - cite the evaluations and judgments of experts

   Use any of the strategies above to fill in a chart like the one below.

Model

"Rules of the Game"

Criterion	Assessment	Evidence
style	very readable; appropriate to narrator's voice	many short, simple sentences; colloquial language
theme	timeless: conflict between generations & cultures	Waverly & her mother have different responses to her chess victories
characterization	individuality of mother & daughter overcomes possible stereotypes	the mother's speeches in dialect are sometimes wise, sometimes not—she's complex
plot	a success story with a twist	the story is open-ended; ends with a question

OPTIONS FOR TEACHING

STRATEGIES FOR INCLUSION

Interpersonal Throughout the writing process, students may benefit from working with a group of students with whom they can discuss any unclear points. Group members can also help each other by discussing particularly involved steps or by providing examples for each other, such as examples of hasty generalizations or overstatement ror the fourth item in Drafting.

Spatial Students may want to organize their ideas for their papers by using a graphic organizer. Point out that a pyramid-shaped organizer may be useful. Students can place at the top of the pyramid their evaluation conclusions and then list under the top their supporting reasons. Encourage students to make connecting lines on their graphics between connecting ideas, such as cause-effect relationships.

6. **Choose your final criteria.** You may not want to discuss every single one of your criteria when you draft your essay, and within a criterion you may not need to cite every aspect you evaluated or every piece of evidence. Mark or highlight the entries on your chart that seem strongest. Add new elements to your chart as you think of them.

Strategies for Elaboration

Use these strategies to find evidence from the text to support your literary evaluation:

- Keep re-reading the work, and give yourself time to ponder what you've read.
- Go from a general question or issue to specific evidence. You may ask yourself, "Where can I find evidence for the characterization of Mrs. Jong?" and then search the story for any passages that contain her thoughts, spoken words, or vivid actions.
- Move from a specific point or question to an assessment or conclusion. You may wonder, "What does the last paragraph mean?" and then draw a conclusion about Waverly's possible future and her changing attitudes toward her mother and herself.
- Remember that in a strong work of literature, every word and action serves a purpose. Focus not only on the things you understand in the story or poem but also on the things you don't. Ask yourself, "Why did the author put that there?" When you find the answer, you'll have both a reason and the evidence for it.

Drafting

1. **Present your subject and judgment.** Think about how you can capture your reader's attention at the start of your essay—perhaps by opening with an anecdote, a description, a personal observation, or simply an arresting statement of your evaluation. Identify the work of literature you're evaluating, and express your basic judgment of it, if you haven't done so in your opening sentence. Your readers want to know from the start what you're discussing and what your thumbs-up or thumbs-down verdict is.

   Make your evaluation statement—your claim—specific and fresh. "'Rules of the Game' is one of the best stories I've ever read" does not give the reader any concrete idea of why you think Amy Tan's story is a good one. Indicate what you see in the literary work and why: "'Rules of the Game' is about a Chinese American girl who becomes a chess champion, but anyone who has ever been a teenager in conflict with a parent can identify with it."

2. **Clarify your criteria.** Your criteria should become apparent to the reader as you explore the reasons for your judgment. If your reasons for liking a story include its plot, characterization, and theme, for instance, readers who are familiar with literature will recognize those criteria. You might need to state your criteria explicitly, however, if you have omitted some that readers might have expected, if you have included unusual criteria, or if you give a different weight to certain criteria than your readers might.

3. **Develop your reasons coherently.** Most of your essay will be devoted to your reasons for your overall judgment of the literary work. Evidence to support your reasoning usually comes immediately after, or immediately before, each reason. Use your prewriting chart as a guide, and add details that a chart can't contain. Using transitional words and phrases (*in addition, moreover, likewise*) is one way to create a coherent flow from point to point. Even more important is the placement of your points. For instance, if you discuss plot first, then characterization, then theme, the reader should sense that you ordered those elements thoughtfully rather than just tossing them in the air and seeing which fell first. Their placement should reflect your understanding of the literary work. In evaluating Amy Tan's story, for example, you might show how characterization grows out of plot and how both elements lead to thematic insight.

Language Handbook HELP

Ways to achieve clarity: pages 1235–1236.

Drafting

- Have students start work on their drafts in class. Check their evaluation statements so you can offer advice about the statements' specificity and clarity before students begin writing.
- Remind students first to concentrate on brainstorming for ideas for their supporting reasons. Students should not worry too much at this stage about spelling, punctuation, and other items that can be taken care of during the revision stage of the writing process. Encourage students to make an outline of their argument. Students can meet briefly with a partner to discuss their outlines.
- If students are writing their essays on a computer, have them print a copy of their outline and later their paper for a peer to review.

INTEGRATING THE LANGUAGE ARTS

Strategic Reading As students read the descriptions of the steps in the writing process, have them keep notes on the main ideas of the steps. Ask them also to note the purpose or goal of each step. Students can organize their notes in the form of a three-column chart like the one shown below.

Writing Process Stage	Main Ideas	Goal or Purpose

Speaking and Listening Students can engage in a panel discussion on the topic of appropriate evaluation criteria. Have students meet in small groups and use their criterion-assessment-evidence charts as a guide in a discussion of what makes a successful literary work. Give students a focus for their discussions by telling them to offer at least three insights and to discover at least three insights of others that they find useful. Students can record the insights on a sheet of paper. Groups can share their conclusions.

CROSSING THE CURRICULUM

Art Bring to class photographs of art works. Ask volunteers to share their brief evaluations of a particular work with the class. Then ask students to list at least two ways in which evaluating art is a very useful activity. Does it help them consider different points of view? Does it help them expand their ideas about art?

Evaluating and Revising

- Students should read their papers at least once while pretending they have never seen the essay before. This "cold read" may help them look at their work from an impersonal distance.
- Have students read their evaluations once through to concentrate solely on their diction. Students will further review and revise their diction in the Language Workshop.

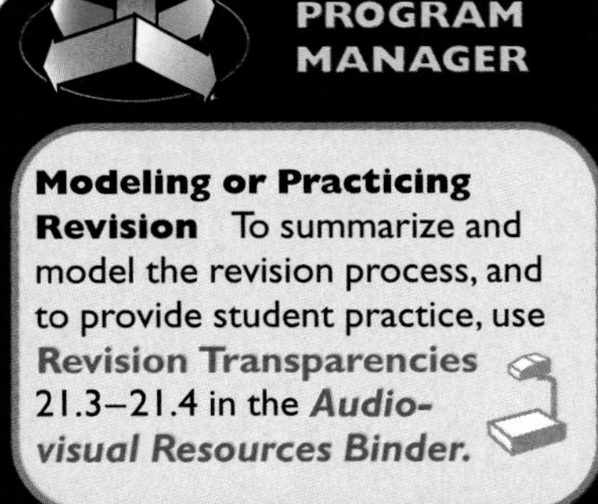

PROGRAM MANAGER

Modeling or Practicing Revision To summarize and model the revision process, and to provide student practice, use **Revision Transparencies** 21.3–21.4 in the ***Audiovisual Resources Binder.***

PROGRAM MANAGER

Peer Evaluation During evaluation and revising, students can use the peer evaluation sheet found in the ***Portfolio Management System,*** p. 212.

Proofreading

Remind students that their papers' tone should be appropriate but also consistent. Have students pay special attention to possible lapses in tone. Students should look for similar lapses in their arguments to make sure their papers have a specific conclusion for their focus.

Publishing

If your school has access to the Internet, students can explore the possibilities of posting their stories to bulletin boards or to homepages on the World Wide Web that concern the authors or the subjects of their papers. Or have students use their evaluations to create a class literary magazine.

Communications Handbook HELP

Taking notes and documenting sources: pages 1210–1213.
Preparing for the debate: logical fallacies: pages 1215–1216.

Incorporating Supporting Evidence

In a literary evaluation, your main supporting evidence will be in the form of direct quotations and paraphrases from the work you're evaluating. Here are ways to smoothly incorporate supporting evidence into your evaluation:

1. If you're using a direct quotation, make it a seamless part of your sentence structure. A passage you're quoting directly should match the tense and number of the sentence it's being woven into. Although you should try to avoid it, you may need to use brackets to indicate slight alterations you've made in the quotation to make it fit smoothly with the rest of your sentence.
2. Enclose a direct quotation in double quotation marks. If part of your quotation includes a character's dialogue, place that in single quotation marks. Be sure that you've copied the quote word-for-word as it appears in the original work.
3. Use ellipsis points (. . .) to indicate the omission of any part of the quotation.
4. For both direct quotations and paraphrases, cite the page number from which the quotation is taken. For poetry, cite line numbers.

   EXAMPLE Waverly, the story's narrator, "learn[s] why it is essential in the endgame to have foresight, a mathematical understanding of all possible moves, and patience . . ." (page 1113).
5. When you're quoting poetry, use a slash (/) with a space before and after it to indicate the end of a line.

Revision STRATEGIES

When you find a broad statement in your evaluation, such as "This is a fine story" or "This is a great poem," be suspicious. Cross out this generalization, and, in lively language, write about a specific aspect of the work.

4. **Avoid logical fallacies.** Your evaluation will be more convincing if readers are impressed by its intellectual honesty. Avoid
   - *hasty generalizations* (praising or condemning a work without weighing sufficient evidence)
   - *overstatement* (giving the work an artificially high or low rating in order to make your evaluation seem dramatic)
   - *either/or fallacy* (acting as if the work is all good or all bad)
   - *straw-man arguments* (stacking the deck in favor of or against a work by comparing it to something that is clearly inferior or superior to it. A "straw man" is something that can be easily knocked down.)
5. **Set a tone.** Remember that your purpose is to persuade your readers that they should take your evaluation seriously. Therefore, your tone should be authoritative, confident, and consistent. If you have supported your assertions with relevant, accurate evidence, you are already on your way to projecting this tone. Using somewhat formal language, including the third person (*he, she*), will help maintain an authoritative tone.
6. **End decisively.** You can conclude your essay by restating your judgment, summarizing your reasons, or doing both. Your conclusion should bring the essay to a definite close, leaving your reader with a clear idea of your evaluation and the reasons behind it.

Evaluating and Revising

1. **Peer review.** Exchange papers with one or more classmates. Ask questions such as the following:

OPTIONS FOR TEACHING

CLASSROOM MANAGEMENT

Writing-Process Log Have students use a chart to log their completion of the different steps of the writing process. The log can serve as a reminder for students of the steps involved in the process, and of the work remaining for them to do, and it can also serve as a way for you to keep track of students' progress. You can have students use the chart at the right as a model.

Writing-Process Step	Work Done
Prewriting	
Drafting	
Evaluating and Revising	
Proofreading	
Publishing	

- What are the writer's criteria? Do they seem valid and well-chosen?
- Are the reasons for the evaluation adequate and convincing?
- Are the reasons backed up by detailed, specific evidence?
- Does the essay help you understand the literary work better?

2. Self-evaluation. Consider your peers' comments carefully. Act on those you agree with, and set aside those you don't. Try reading the literary work one more time to see what new insights emerge. You'll be revising both for content (to strengthen your reasons and evidence) and for style (to make your essay more readable).

Proofreading

Have a partner read your essay both to discover mechanical errors and to make sure that your reasons are clearly stated and that your tone is appropriate to an evaluative essay.

Publishing

Since you are writing about a literary work, your English class is the most natural venue for publication. You may choose to read your paper aloud, display it, or exchange papers with a classmate. Perhaps your class would be interested in compiling all its evaluation essays into a publication called *The Review of Contemporary American Literature*. You might also submit the essay to a school literary magazine or another publication interested in literary reviews.

Reflecting on Your Writing

Date your essay, and write a brief reflection addressing the following questions:

- What did you discover about the literary work as you evaluated it?
- The next time you write an evaluation of a literary work, how might you improve your method of doing the assignment?
- Given its intellectually serious subject matter, how can an evaluation of literature be made enjoyable to read?
- How might this writing experience help you in evaluating subjects other than literary works? For example, how could you use your experience in evaluating a work of literature to help you review a film, assess the merits of an extracurricular club, or evaluate the qualities of a new restaurant?

Evaluation Criteria

A good evaluative essay

1. *identifies the subject of your evaluation*
2. *presents your criteria, either explicitly or implicitly*
3. *provides factual evidence to support your views*
4. *makes its points in a coherent order*
5. *avoids logical fallacies*
6. *concludes effectively*
7. *has an authoritative, confident tone*

Shoe by Jeff MacNelly, reprinted by permission: Tribune Media Services.

ASSESSMENT TOOLS

Self-Assessment: Writing Have students use the following rubric to evaluate their writing.

Assessment Criteria

1	2	3	4	5	6
needs improvement					superior

Content:

_____ identifies the subject of your evaluation
_____ presents your criteria, either explicitly or implicitly
_____ provides reasons to support your views based on factual evidence
_____ makes its points in a coherent order
_____ avoids logical fallacies
_____ concludes effectively
_____ has an authoritative, confident tone

Reteaching

If students have difficulty providing a clear argument, have them discuss with a partner a movie or TV show they would recommend. Partners should take notes on each other's "pitch" and then discuss each other's reasons. Which reasons were convincing, and which were not? Point out to students that they use the process of evaluation every day, and that they would not accept another's recommendation or advice unless they had good reasons.

Closure

After students have completed their essays, ask them to jot down the most important steps and activities they used in the writing process. Have volunteers share their ideas with the class and write the ideas on the chalkboard. Then lead students in a discussion of how each step contributes to the goal of evaluation: not only to provide a judgment on a topic, but to provide a judgment that is well-reasoned enough to be convincing to an objective reader.

Extension

Ask each student to bring to class an example of an evaluation such as a review of a recent book, movie, TV show, or album. Ask for volunteers to share their reactions to the evaluations. Then, have students meet in small groups, and have each group examine one of its evaluations and answer the following questions. Did the evaluations provide a strong argument? Were the evaluations convincing? Why or why not?

Portfolio

Reflecting on Your Writing

- Encourage students to provide specific examples in their answers. Students can mention the benefits of a specific step in the writing process, or refer to a particular discussion they had while writing their papers.
- Have students include these questions and their answers in their portfolios, attached to their evaluations.

Language Workshop

Connecting to Students' Writing

Ask students to select a piece of writing from their portfolios and to review the diction in it. Have students replace any vague or approximate words and any phrases that don't say quite what students intended to say. Remind students to choose words that are consistent with the overall tone of their writing. Ask for volunteers to share their examples with the class.

Try It Out: Possible Answers

1. casual or informal
   "pretty good show"
2. formal, poetic
   "first came fully"
   "orbit of my concern"

Language Handbook HELP

Glossary of usage: pages 1252–1257.

Words to the Wise: Using Effective Diction

Consider the difference between these two sentences:

> He is almost sixteen, and though he doesn't have a beard yet, he has a man's mind in a boy's body.
>
> He is almost sixteen, *though beardless still,* a man's mind *indignantly captive* in *the frame of a child.*

In the second sentence (from John Updike's story "Son"), the italicized phrases create a more formal and poetic feeling than the phrases in the first sentence. The difference is in **diction,** or word choice. Diction may be plain or ornate, formal or informal, and so on. In this example, from Julia Alvarez's "Daughter of Invention," the informal, colloquial phrases are in italics:

> She was *just fussing* with *little house things, don't mind her.*

To use diction effectively in your writing, pay attention to the following:

1. Choose words that are appropriate to your subject. You would use technical words in a science report, for example, but informal colloquial language in a letter to a friend.
2. Choose words that are appropriate to your audience. Your word choice when addressing third-grade students would differ from diction you would use with a group of high school students, for example.
3. Choose words that are appropriate to your purpose. If you are formally introducing a guest of honor at a dinner, for instance, you'll choose different words than if you are delivering a humorous description of a friend.
4. Use precise words instead of approximate ones.
5. Use vivid words instead of vague ones.
6. Use figures of speech when they are fresh and meaningful.
7. When choosing among synonyms, consider their different connotations.

Try It Out

For each sentence below, write a word or phrase describing the diction. Then state which words or phrases in the sentence led you to that conclusion.

1. For a small town, it was a pretty good show.
   —Tim O'Brien, *from* "Speaking of Courage"
2. It was in this tenement that the personality of my father first came fully into the orbit of my concern.
   —Richard Wright, *from Black Boy*

Writer's Workshop Follow-Up: Revising

Re-read the evaluation you wrote for the Writer's Workshop (page 1181). Search carefully for vague or approximate words and for phrases that don't quite say what you intended. Work carefully to improve your diction, using a dictionary and a thesaurus to help you choose the most precise words.

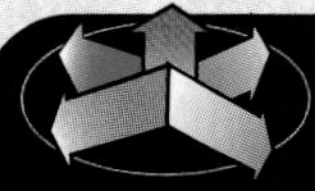

PROGRAM MANAGER

Extra Practice and Guided Instruction For more instruction and practice in using effective diction, see **Language Workshop** in ***Teaching Resources B,*** pp. 219–221.

✔ QUICK CHECK: Correct Common Usage Problems

State a word or phrase that describes the diction of the following expressions.

[1] her cool car [colloquial]
[2] your considerable fortitude in the face of near disaster [formal, ornate]
[3] The computer printer spat out my essay. [using figure of speech, colorful or poetic]
[4] What did you say? [informal]
[5] I beg your pardon; kindly repeat your statement. [formal]

CREATIVE PROBLEM SOLVING

LEARNING FOR LIFE

State of the Arts: Celebrating Cultural Diversity

Problem

The vitality and diversity of contemporary American literature is shared by other contemporary American art forms, from the visual arts to dance to theater. How can people be made more aware of the range and richness of multiculturally diverse arts available in their communities?

Project

Recommend ways that your school or community can promote awareness and appreciation of multiculturally diverse contemporary arts.

Preparation

1. Work with a partner or a small group to brainstorm a list of various art forms available in your community: dance, drama, poetry, storytelling, sculpture, opera, painting, and so on.
2. Formulate a list of *5W-How?* questions (*Who? What? When? Where? Why? How?*) about one or more of these art forms.

Procedure

1. Research local museums, galleries, performing arts centers, playhouses, writers' groups, poetry readings and storytelling sessions, and other sources of art and culture in your community or city. Collect brochures, advertisements, mission statements, program notes, and the like from your sources.
2. Research local newspapers, magazines, newsletters, and other publications for write-ups or reviews of your local arts scene. Focus especially on arts from specific cultural groups: African American and Latino theater groups, galleries, or museums; traveling art exhibitions; local or visiting dance troupes; community spaces for poetry readings celebrating ethnic diversity; and so on.
3. Arrange interviews with local museum directors, theater directors, gallery owners, arts reviewers, or any others who make their living from the arts (painters, writers, actors, and so on). Ask the people you interview about multicultural diversity in their area, their predictions about where the arts are heading, local audience response to and participation in multicultural arts, and other questions relevant to your research.

Presentation

Present your findings in one of the following formats (or another that your teacher approves):

1. **Feature Article**
   Write a feature article on some aspect of multicultural art in your community, such as a Latino art gallery, a local American Indian craftsperson, or multicultural poetry readings at a community center. Submit your article to your school or local newspaper. Provide quotations from any interviews you've conducted.
2. **Multimedia Presentation**
   Working in a small group, create and present a multimedia exhibit showcasing examples of drama, music, visual art, dance, and other art forms available in your community. Demonstrate the variety of art forms available to the public, with an emphasis on multicultural diversity.
3. **Advertising Campaign**
   With a small group, develop and present a "State of the Arts" advertising campaign for your school. Create posters, brochures, slogans, and other visual and written advertising tools. Emphasize multiculturalism in the arts, and highlight appropriate examples available in your community.

Processing

What did you learn about the importance of the arts to a community? How are multicultural trends in all the arts changing our cultural climate? In the years to come, what roles do you think the arts will fulfill in both celebrating diversity and uniting people of diverse backgrounds? Write a reflection for your portfolio.

Learning for Life

Technology Tip

If your community offers few sources of art and culture or has limited resources for researching the arts scene, you might have students work on the Internet to gather their information. The following Web sites will give students access to information on Cuban art, Caribbean art, Mexican art, Native American art, contemporary Southwest art, dance of various cultures, Mexican Reggae music, and Caribbean music among many other topics:

Chicano/Latino Net at **http://latino.sscnet.ucla.edu/MUSEUM.HTML**
Native Web at **http://web.maxwell.syr.edu/nativeweb/**
Latino Web at **http://www.latinoweb.com/favision/art.htm**
Culturefinder at **http://www.culturefinder.com/**
CLNET Diversity Page at **http://latino.sscnet.ucla.edu/diversity1.html**

Performance Assessment Rubric So that students may see the evaluation criteria before they begin working on these projects, share the rubric provided in the ***Portfolio Management System,*** p. 214.

DEVELOPING WORKPLACE COMPETENCIES

Preparation	Procedure	Presentation
Thinks creatively Works on teams Exhibits sociability Uses self-management skills Designs systems	Uses resources well Acquires data Communicates ideas and information Demonstrates individual responsibility Selects equipment	Evaluates data Interprets information Monitors and corrects performance Reasons Solves problems

RESOURCE CENTER

HANDBOOK OF LITERARY TERMS

HANDBOOK OF LITERARY TERMS

You will find more information about the terms in this Handbook on the pages given at the ends of the entries. To learn more about **Allusion,** for example, turn to pages 39, 186, 670, and 1159 in this book.

Cross-references at the ends of some entries refer to other entries in the Handbook containing related information. For instance, at the end of **Antagonist,** you are referred to **Protagonist.**

ALLEGORY **A story or poem in which characters, settings, and events stand for other people or events or for abstract ideas or qualities.** An allegory can be read on one level for its literal meaning and on a second level for its symbolic, or allegorical, meaning. The most famous allegory in the English language is *The Pilgrim's Progress* (1678) by the English Puritan writer John Bunyan, in which Christian, on his journey to the Celestial City, meets such personages as Mr. Worldly Wiseman, Hopeful, and Giant Despair and travels to such places as the Slough of Despond, the Valley of Humiliation, and Doubting Castle. Puritans were trained to see their own lives as allegories of Biblical experiences. Nathaniel Hawthorne's and Edgar Allan Poe's fictions are often called allegorical.

See page 280.

ALLITERATION **The repetition of the same or similar consonant sounds in words that are close together.** Alliteration is used to create musical effects and to establish mood. In the following line from "The Tide Rises, the Tide Falls" by Henry Wadsworth Longfellow, the repetition of the *s* sound is an example of alliteration:

> But the sea, the sea in the darkness calls

See pages 288, 355.

ALLUSION **A reference to someone or something that is known from history, literature, religion, politics, sports, science, or some other branch of culture.** T. S. Eliot drew on his knowledge of the Bible when he alluded to the raising of Lazarus from the dead in "The Love Song of J. Alfred Prufrock" (page 667). The title of Sandra Cisneros's essay "Straw into Gold" (page 1160) is an allusion to the folk tale about Rumpelstiltskin.

You won't understand the cartoon to the right unless you recognize the fairy tale it alludes to.

See pages 39, 186, 670, 1159.

AMBIGUITY **A technique by which a writer deliberately suggests two or more different, and sometimes conflicting, meanings in a work.** Langston Hughes's poem "Harlem" (page 764) has an ambiguous ending; the title of Richard Wilbur's "The Beautiful Changes" (page 1006) is also deliberately ambiguous.

See page 493.

ANALOGY **A comparison made between two things to show how they are alike.** In "The Crisis, No. 1" (page 108), Thomas Paine draws an analogy between a thief breaking into a house and the king of England interfering in the affairs of the American Colonies.

See page 112.

ANAPEST **A metrical foot that has two unstressed syllables followed by one stressed syllable.** The word *coexist* (˘ ˘ ʹ) is an example of an anapest.

See also *Dactyl.*

ANECDOTE **A very brief story, told to illustrate a point or serve as an example of something.** In Thomas Paine's "The Crisis, No. 1," the tale of the Tory tavern keeper and his child (page 108) is an anecdote.

See pages 465, 784.

ANTAGONIST **The opponent who struggles against or blocks the hero, or protagonist, in a story.** In *The Narrative of the Life of Frederick Douglass,* Mr. Covey is Douglass's antagonist. In Herman Melville's *Moby-Dick,* the white whale is Ahab's antagonist.

See also *Protagonist.*

"They're offering a deal—you can pay court costs and damages, they drop charges of breaking and entering."
Drawing by Maslin. © 1988 The New Yorker Magazine, Inc.

ANTHROPOMORPHISM Attributing human characteristics to an animal or inanimate object. Writers often anthropomorphize animals or objects in order to achieve humorous or satirical effects.

See also *Personification.*

APHORISM A brief, cleverly worded statement that makes a wise observation about life. Benjamin Franklin's *Poor Richard's Almanack* is a book of aphorisms. Ralph Waldo Emerson's style is **aphoristic**—he incorporates many pithy sayings into his essays (which is why he is so quotable).

See pages 95, 222, 1087.

APOSTROPHE A technique by which a writer addresses an inanimate object, an idea, or a person who is either dead or absent. Sor Juana Inés de la Cruz apostrophizes her critics in "World, in Hounding Me . . ." (page 76). Oliver Wendell Holmes apostrophizes a shell and his soul in "The Chambered Nautilus" (page 189).

See pages 188, 792, 795.

ARGUMENT A form of persuasion that appeals to reason, rather than emotion, to convince an audience to think or act in a certain way. The Declaration of Independence provides some famous examples of argument.

See page 112.
See also *Persuasion.*

ASSONANCE The repetition of similar vowel sounds followed by different consonant sounds, especially in words that are close together. Notice the repeated sound of *i* in the following lines by Henry Wadsworth Longfellow:

> The tide rises, the tide falls,
> The twilight darkens, the curlew calls

See page 355.
See also *Alliteration, Onomatopoeia, Rhyme.*

ATMOSPHERE The mood or feeling created in a piece of writing. A story's atmosphere might be peaceful, festive, menacing, melancholy, and so on. Edgar Allan Poe's "The Fall of the House of Usher," for example, conveys an atmosphere of gloom.

See page 262.

AUTOBIOGRAPHY An account of the writer's own life. Benjamin Franklin's autobiography (page 86) is one of the most famous autobiographies in American literature. A selection from Richard Wright's autobiography, *Black Boy,* is on page 1015.

See pages 57, 97.

BALLAD A song or poem that tells a story. The typical ballad tells a tragic story in the form of a monologue or dialogue. Ballads usually have a simple, steady rhythm, a rhyme pattern, and a refrain, all of which make them easy to memorize. Ballads composed by unknown singers and passed on orally from one generation to the next are called **folk ballads. Literary ballads** are written to imitate the sounds and subjects of folk ballads. A strong tradition of folk ballads and of literary ballads exists in the United States. Country-and-western music, for example, frequently features songs written to imitate the older ballads.

BIOGRAPHY An account of someone's life written by another person. One of the most famous biographies in American literature is Carl Sandburg's multivolume life of Abraham Lincoln.

BLANK VERSE Poetry written in unrhymed iambic pentameter. Blank verse has a long history in English literature. It was used notably by such poets as Shakespeare and Milton in the sixteenth and seventeenth centuries and by Robert Frost in the twentieth.

See pages 569, 575.
See also *Iambic Pentameter.*

CADENCE The natural, rhythmic rise and fall of a language as it is normally spoken. Cadence is different from **meter,** in which the stressed and unstressed syllables of a poetic line are carefully counted to conform to a regular pattern. Walt Whitman was a master at imitating the cadences of spoken American English in his free verse.

See pages 344, 355.
See also *Free Verse, Meter, Rhythm.*

CAESURA A pause or break within a line of poetry. Some pauses are indicated by punctuation; others are suggested by phrasing or meaning. In the lines below, the caesuras are marked by double vertical lines. These pauses are indicated by punctuation.

> Announced by all the trumpets of the sky,
> Arrives the snow, || and, || driving o'er the fields,
> Seems nowhere to alight: || the whited air
> Hides hills and woods . . .
>
> —Ralph Waldo Emerson,
> *from* "The Snow-Storm"

CATALOG A list of things, people, or events. Cataloging was a favorite device of Walt Whitman, who included long, descriptive lists throughout *Leaves of Grass.*

See page 351.

CHARACTER An individual in a story or play. A character always has human traits, even if the character is an animal, as in Aesop's fables, or a god, as in the Greek and Roman myths.

The process by which the writer reveals the personality of a character is called **characterization.** A writer can reveal a character in the following ways:

- by telling us directly what the character is like: sneaky, generous, mean to pets, and so on
- by describing how the character looks and dresses
- by letting us hear the character speak
- by revealing the character's private thoughts and feelings
- by revealing the character's effect on other people—showing how other characters feel or behave toward the character
- by showing the character in action

The first method of revealing a character is called **direct characterization.** When a writer uses this method, we do not have to figure out what a character's personality is like—the writer tells us directly. The other five methods of revealing a character are known as **indirect characterization.** When a writer uses these methods, we have to exercise our own judgment, putting clues together to infer what a character is like—just as we do in real life when we are getting to know someone.

Characters are often classified as static or dynamic. A **static character** is one who does not change much in the course of a story. A **dynamic character,** on the other hand, changes in some important way as a result of the story's action. Characters can also be classified as flat or round. **Flat characters** have only one or two personality traits. They are one-dimensional, like a piece of cardboard; they can be summed up by a single phrase: the loyal sidekick, the buffoon, the nosy neighbor. In contrast, **round characters** have more dimensions to their personalities—they are complex, just as real people are.

See pages 313, 851, 876, 888, 981.

CLICHÉ A word or phrase, often a figure of speech, that has become lifeless because of overuse. Some examples of clichés are "green with envy," "quiet as a mouse," and "pretty as a picture."

CLIMAX That point in a plot that creates the greatest intensity, suspense, or interest. The climax is usually the point at which the conflict in the story is resolved.

See also *Plot.*

COMEDY In general, a story that ends with a happy resolution of the conflicts faced by the main character or characters. In many comedies, the conflict is provided when a young couple who wish to marry are blocked by adults. In many comedies, the main character at the end has moved into a world of greater freedom; this is the kind of comedy we see in Washington Irving's "Rip Van Winkle" (page 154). In literature, the word *comedy* is not synonymous with *humor.* Some comedies are humorous; some are not.

See page 683.

CONCEIT An elaborate metaphor or other figure of speech that compares two things that are startlingly different. Often a conceit is also a very lengthy comparison. The conceit was a popular figure of speech in seventeenth-century English metaphysical poetry. In American literature, the poems of Edward Taylor (page 72) and Emily Dickinson (page 372) are known for their conceits. T. S. Eliot, in more recent literary history, also used conceits (page 661).

See page 74.
See also *Figure of Speech, Metaphor.*

CONCRETE POEM A poem in which the words are arranged on a page to suggest a visual representation of the subject. In English poetry in the seventeenth century, poets wrote concrete poems in the shapes of such things as crosses, altars, and wings; today, poets write concrete poems in every conceivable shape: waves, hearts, cats, flowers.

See page 65.

CONFLICT The struggle between opposing forces or characters in a story. A conflict can be **internal,** involving opposing forces within a person's mind. In James Thurber's "The Secret Life of Walter Mitty" (page 625), for example, the title character has a comical internal conflict between his desire for heroism and his cowardice in the face of a formidable spouse. **External** conflicts can exist between two people, between a person and nature or a machine, or between a person and a whole society. In one segment of "Son" (page 1070), for example, John Updike shows the narrator in conflict with his son. Many stories have both internal and external conflict.

See pages 607, 814, 827, 965, 1044, 1077, 1129.

CONNOTATION **The associations and emotional overtones that have become attached to a word or phrase, in addition to its strict dictionary definition.** The words *determined, firm, rigid, stubborn,* and *pigheaded* have similar dictionary definitions, but widely varying connotations, or overtones of meaning. *Determined* and *firm* both suggest an admirable kind of resoluteness; *rigid* suggests an inability to bend and a kind of mindless refusal to change. *Stubborn* and *pigheaded,* on the other hand, have even more negative connotations. *Stubborn* has associations with a mule, and *pigheaded* with the pig, which, wrongly or not, is an animal often associated with mindless willfulness. Here are some other words that are more or less synonymous but which have vastly different connotations: *fastidious* and *fussy; daydreamer* and *escapist; scent, odor, smell,* and *stink.* Words with strong connotations are often called **loaded words** or **suggestive words.**

See pages 46, 281, 701, 726.

CONSONANCE **The repetition of the same or similar final consonant sounds on accented syllables or in important words.** The words *ticktock* and *singsong* contain examples of consonance. Some modern poets use consonance in place of rhyme.

COUPLET **Two consecutive rhyming lines of poetry.** If the two rhyming lines express a complete thought, they are called a **closed couplet.** The following lines are from a poem built on a series of closed couplets.

If ever wife was happy in a man,
Compare with me, ye women, if you can.

—Anne Bradstreet, *from* "To My Dear and Loving Husband"

DACTYL **A metrical foot of three syllables in which the first syllable is stressed and the next two are unstressed.** The word *tendency* (′ ˘ ˘) is a dactyl.

See also *Anapest.*

DENOUEMENT (dā′noo·män′) **The conclusion (or resolution) of a story.** In French, the word means "unraveling." At this point in a story, all the mysteries are unraveled, the conflicts are resolved, and all the questions raised by the plot are answered. Much modern fiction ends without a denouement, so that the story leaves us with a sense of incompleteness.

See also *Plot.*

DESCRIPTION **One of the four major forms of discourse, in which language is used to create a mood or emotion.** Description does this by the use of words that appeal to our senses: sight, hearing, touch, smell, taste. Walt Whitman gives a wonderful description of a Civil War battlefield in *Specimen Days* (page 363).

See page 549.

DIALECT **A way of speaking that is characteristic of a certain social group or of the inhabitants of a certain geographical area.** Dialects may differ from one another in vocabulary, pronunciation, and grammar. One dialect has become dominant in America, and it is known as Standard English. This is the dialect used most often on national radio news and television news broadcasts. Many writers try to capture dialects to give their stories local color, humor, or an air of authenticity. Among the writers in this book who make skilled use of dialect are Mark Twain, Eudora Welty, Flannery O'Connor, William Faulkner, and Langston Hughes.

See pages 512, 1055, 1066.

DICTION **A speaker or writer's choice of words.** Diction can be formal, informal, colloquial, full of slang, poetic, ornate, plain, abstract, concrete, and so on. Diction depends on the writer's subject, purpose, and audience. Some words, for example, are suited to informal conversations but are inappropriate in a formal speech. Diction has a powerful effect on the **tone** of a piece of writing.

See pages 107, 113, 1176.

DRAMATIC MONOLOGUE **A poem in which a character speaks to one or more listeners.** The reactions of the listener must be inferred by the reader. From the speaker's words, the reader learns about the setting, the situation, the identity of the other characters, and the personality of the speaker. The outstanding dramatic monologue in American literature is T. S. Eliot's "The Love Song of J. Alfred Prufrock." The poems in Edgar Lee Masters's *Spoon River Anthology* (page 692) are also dramatic monologues.

See page 663.

ELEGY **A poem of mourning, usually about someone who has died.** Most elegies are written to mark a person's death, but some extend their subject to reflect on life, death, and the fleeting nature of beauty. The elegies in this book include William Cullen Bryant's "Thanatopsis" (page 171), John Crowe Ransom's "Bells for John Whiteside's Daughter" (page 578), and Theodore Roethke's "Elegy for Jane" (page 1002).

See pages 1004, 1100.

EPIC **A long narrative poem, written in heightened language, which recounts the deeds of a heroic character who embodies the values of a particular society.** Epics in English include *Beowulf* (c. 700) and John Milton's *Paradise Lost* (1667). Some critics view Walt Whitman's *Leaves of Grass* as an American epic in which the hero is the questing poet.

See page 350.

EPITHET **A descriptive word or phrase that is frequently used to characterize a person or thing.** The epithet "the father of his country" is often used to characterize George Washington. New York City's popular epithet, "the Big Apple," is frequently used by advertisers. Epics such as Homer's *Odyssey* and *Iliad* frequently use **stock epithets** over and over again to describe certain characters or places: "patient Penelope," "wily Odysseus," and "earthshaker" (for Poseidon).

See page 795.

ESSAY **A short piece of nonfiction prose in which the writer discusses some aspect of a subject.** The word *essay* comes from the French *essai,* meaning "to try," a derivation that suggests that the essay form is not an exhaustive treatment of a subject. Essays are sometimes classified as formal or informal, or as formal or personal (or familiar). The essay form has been especially popular in the twentieth century, particularly among American writers. Some famous American essayists of the past include Thomas Paine (page 106), Ralph Waldo Emerson (page 216), and Henry David Thoreau (page 230). More recent essayists include E. B. White, Alice Walker (page 1101), James Baldwin (page 1141), Annie Dillard, Joan Didion, Lewis Thomas, and Edward Abbey.

See page 1102.

EXPOSITION **One of the four major forms of discourse, in which something is explained or "set forth."** Exposition is most commonly used in nonfiction. The word *exposition* also refers to that part of a plot in which the reader is given important background information on the characters, their setting, and their problems. Such exposition is usually provided at the opening of a story or play. See Washington Irving's "Rip Van Winkle" for an example (page 155, starting second paragraph).

See page 815.
See also *Plot.*

FABLE **A very short story told in prose or poetry that teaches a practical lesson about how to succeed in life.** In many fables, the characters are animals that behave like people. The most ancient fabulist is the Greek Aesop; the most famous American fabulist is James Thurber (page 623), who produced two collections: *Fables for Our Time* and *Further Fables for Our Time.*

FARCE **A type of comedy in which ridiculous and often stereotyped characters are involved in silly, far-fetched situations.** The humor in a farce is often physical and slapstick, with characters being hit in the face with pies or running into closed doors. The American cinema has produced many farces, including those starring Laurel and Hardy, Abbott and Costello, and the Marx brothers.

FIGURE OF SPEECH **A word or phrase that describes one thing in terms of another and that is not meant to be taken literally.** Figures of speech always involve a comparison of two things that are basically very dissimilar. Hundreds of figures of speech have been identified by scholars; the most common ones are **simile, metaphor, personification,** and **symbol.** Figures of speech, also called, more generally, **figurative language,** are basic to everyday speech. Statements like "She is a tower of strength" and "He is a pain in the neck" are figures of speech.

See pages 78, 224, 228, 622, 931, 1002.
See also *Conceit, Metaphor, Simile, Personification, Symbol.*

FLASHBACK **A scene that interrupts the normal chronological sequence of events in a story to depict something that happened at an earlier time.** Although the word was coined to describe a technique used by movie makers, the technique itself is at least as old as ancient Greek literature. Much of Homer's epic poem the *Odyssey* is a flashback. Willa Cather uses frequent flashbacks to reveal the past of Georgiana in "A Wagner Matinée" (page 540).

FOIL **A character who acts as a contrast to another character.** In Herman Melville's *Moby-Dick,* First Mate Starbuck is a foil to Captain Ahab.

FOOT **A metrical unit of poetry.** A foot always contains at least one stressed syllable, and, usually, one or more unstressed syllables. An **iamb** is a common foot in English poetry: It consists of an unstressed syllable followed by a stressed syllable (˘ ʹ).

See also *Anapest, Dactyl, Iamb, Spondee, Trochee.*

FORESHADOWING **The use of hints and clues to suggest what will happen later in a plot.** A writer might use foreshadowing to create suspense or to prefigure later events. In "To Build a Fire," for example, Jack London foreshadows the conclusion of his story by placing hints throughout the story.

See page 673.

FREE VERSE **Poetry that does not conform to a regular meter or rhyme scheme.** Poets who write in free verse try to reproduce the natural rhythms of the spoken language. Free verse uses the traditional poetic elements of **imagery, figures of speech, repetition, internal rhyme, alliteration,** and **onomatopoeia.** The first American practitioner of free verse was Walt Whitman (page 348). Some of Whitman's heirs are William Carlos Williams (page 778), Carl Sandburg (page 792), and Allen Ginsberg (page 1008).

See pages 344, 355, 742, 772.

HYPERBOLE **A figure of speech that uses an incredible exaggeration, or overstatement, for effect.** In *Life on the Mississippi,* Mark Twain uses hyperbole for comic effect. An example is Twain's response when Mr. Bixby tells him he must learn the shape of the Mississippi River throughout its course:

> Have I got to learn the shape of the river according
> to all these five hundred thousand different ways?
> If I tried to carry all that cargo in my head it
> would make me stoop-shouldered.
>
> —Mark Twain, *from Life on the Mississippi*

See pages 463, 622, 962.

IAMB **A metrical foot in poetry that has an unstressed syllable followed by a stressed syllable, as in the word *protect.*** The iamb (˘ ′) is a common foot in poetry written in English.

See page 180.
See also *Spondee, Trochee.*

IAMBIC PENTAMETER **A line of poetry that contains five iambic feet.** The iambic pentameter line is the most common in English and American poetry. Shakespeare and John Milton, among others, used iambic pentameter in their major works. So did such American poets as William Cullen Bryant, Ralph Waldo Emerson, Robert Frost, and Wallace Stevens. Here, for example, are the opening lines of a poem by Emerson:

> ˘ ′ ˘ ′ ˘ ′ ˘ ′˘ ′
> In May, when sea-winds pierced our solitudes,
> ˘ ′ ˘ ′ ˘ ′˘ ′ ˘ ′
> I found the fresh Rhodora in the woods
>
> —Ralph Waldo Emerson,
> *from* "The Rhodora"

See page 180.

IMAGERY **The use of language to evoke a picture or a concrete sensation of a person, a thing, a place, or an experience.** Although most images appeal to the sense of sight, they also sometimes appeal to the senses of taste, smell, hearing, and touch as well.

See pages 218, 355, 701, 779, 949, 1089.

IMAGISM **A twentieth-century movement in European and American poetry that advocated the creation of hard, clear images, concisely expressed in everyday speech.** The leading Imagist poets in America were Ezra Pound (page 773), Amy Lowell, H. D. [Hilda Doolittle], and William Carlos Williams (page 778).

See pages 533, 771.

IMPRESSIONISM **A nineteenth-century movement in literature and art that advocated a recording of the artist's personal impressions of the world, rather than a strict representation of reality.** Some of the famous American Impressionists in art were Mary Cassatt, Maurice Prendergast, and William Merritt Chase. In fiction, Stephen Crane pioneered a kind of literary impressionism in which he portrayed not objective reality but a specific character's impressions of reality. Crane's impressionistic technique is best seen in his novel *The Red Badge of Courage.*

See page 484.

INCONGRUITY **The deliberate joining of opposites or of elements that are not appropriate to each other.** T. S. Eliot's famous opening simile in "The Love Song of J. Alfred Prufrock" (page 663) joins two incongruous elements: a sunset and a patient knocked out by ether on an operating table. Incongruity can also be used for humor: We laugh at the sight of an elephant dressed in a pink tutu because the two elements are incongruous. Writers also use incongruity for dramatic effect. In Donald Barthelme's "Game" (page 956), the childish actions of the characters are in sharp contrast with the devastation they can cause by turning a key.

See page 962.

INTERIOR MONOLOGUE **A narrative technique that records a character's internal flow of thoughts, memories, and ideas.** Parts of James Joyce's *Ulysses* and William Faulkner's *The Sound and the Fury* are written as interior monologues.

INTERNAL RHYME **Rhyme that occurs within a line of poetry or within consecutive lines.** The first line of the following couplet includes an internal rhyme.

> And so, all the night-*tide,* I lie down by the *side*
> Of my darling—my darling—my life and my bride
>
> —Edgar Allan Poe, *from* "Annabel Lee"

See page 288.
See also *Rhyme.*

INVERSION **The reversal of the normal word order in a sentence or phrase.** An English sentence normally is built on subject-verb-complement, in that order. An inverted sentence reverses one or more of those elements. In poetry written many years ago, writers often inverted word order as a matter of course, in order to have the words conform to the meter, or to create rhymes. The poetry of Anne Bradstreet (page 68) contains many inversions, as in the first line of the poem on the burning of her house:

> In silent night when rest I took

In prose, inversion is often used for emphasis, as when Patrick Henry, in his fiery speech to the Virginia Convention (page 102), said "Suffer not yourselves to be betrayed with a kiss" (instead of "Do not suffer [allow] yourselves," etc.).

See pages 69, 174.

IRONY **In general, a discrepancy between appearances and reality.** There are three main types of irony:

1. **Verbal irony** occurs when someone says one thing but really means something else. Oliver Wendell Holmes uses irony when, in "Old Ironsides" (page 190), he urges that the warship be destroyed.
2. **Situational irony** takes place when there is a discrepancy between what is expected to happen, or what would be appropriate to happen, and what really does happen. A famous use of situational irony is in Stephen Crane's "A Mystery of Heroism" (page 487), in which a soldier risks his life to get water but fails to bring it back to anyone living.
3. **Dramatic irony** is so called because it is often used on stage. In this kind of irony, a character in the play or story thinks one thing is true, but the audience or reader knows better. In Edwin Arlington Robinson's "Miniver Cheevy" (page 646), Miniver thinks he is too refined for his age, but in the reader's eyes, he seems foolish and somewhat pathetic.

See pages 422, 485, 683, 921.

LYRIC POEM **A poem that does not tell a story but expresses the personal feelings or thoughts of a speaker.** Lyric poems in this textbook range from the philosophic "Thanatopsis" by William Cullen Bryant (page 171) to the satiric "Homework" by Allen Ginsberg (page 1010).

See page 1007.

MAGIC REALISM **A genre developed in Latin America which juxtaposes the everyday with the marvelous or magical.** Myths, folk tales, religious beliefs, and tall tales are the raw material for many magic realist writers. Gabriel García Márquez's work, particularly his novel *One Hundred Years of Solitude* (1970), established him as a master of the genre. Other prominent Latin American magic realists include Jorge Luis Borges, Julio Cortázar, and Isabel Allende. Among American writers, Donald Barthelme and Thomas Pynchon have been influenced by magic realism.

See page 996.

METAPHOR **A figure of speech that makes a comparison between two unlike things without the use of such specific words of comparison as *like, as, than,* or *resembles.*** There are several kinds of metaphor:

1. A **directly stated metaphor** states the comparison explicitly: "Fame is a bee" (Emily Dickinson).
2. An **implied metaphor** does not state explicitly the two terms of the comparison: "I like to see it lap the Miles" (Emily Dickinson) is an implied metaphor in which the verb *lap* implies a comparison between "it" (which is a train) and some animal that "laps" up water.
3. An **extended metaphor** is a metaphor that is extended or developed as far as the writer wants to take it. Dickinson's poem beginning "Fame is a bee" is an extended metaphor: The comparison between fame and a bee is extended through four lines:

> Fame is a bee.
>   It has a song—
> It has a sting—
>   Ah, too, it has a wing.

4. A **dead metaphor** is a metaphor that has been used so often that the comparison is no longer vivid: "The head of the house," "the seat of government," "a knotty problem" are all dead metaphors.
5. A **mixed metaphor** is a metaphor that has gotten out of control and mixes its terms so that they are visually or imaginatively incompatible. If you say, "The President is a lame duck who is running out of gas," you've lost control of your metaphor and have produced a statement that is ridiculous (ducks do not run out of gas).

See pages 74, 188, 246, 431, 452, 463, 622, 1002, 1009, 1066.
See also *Conceit.*

METER **A pattern of stressed and unstressed syllables in poetry.** The meter of a poem is commonly indicated by using the symbol (ʹ) for stressed syllables and the symbol (˘) for unstressed syllables. This is called **scanning** the poem.

Meter is described as **iambic, trochaic, dactylic,** or **anapestic.** These scanned lines from "Richard Cory" are iambic because they are built on iambs—an unstressed syllable followed by a stressed syllable.

˘ ʹ ˘ ʹ ˘ ʹ ˘ ʹ ˘ ʹ
And he was always quietly arrayed

˘ ʹ ˘ ʹ ˘ ʹ ˘ ʹ ˘ ʹ
And he was always human when he talked

See pages 69, 355, 396.
See also *Scanning.*

METONYMY **A figure of speech in which a person, place, or thing is referred to by something closely associated with it.** Referring to a king or queen as "the crown" is an example of metonymy, as is calling a car "wheels."

See also *Synecdoche.*

MODERNISM **A term for the bold new experimental styles and forms that swept the arts during the first third of the twentieth century.** Modernism called for changes in subject matter, in fictional styles, in poetic forms, and in attitudes. T. S. Eliot (page 661) and Ezra Pound (page 773) are associated with the modernist movement in poetry. Their aim was to rid poetry of its nineteenth-century "prettiness" and sentimentality.

See pages 525, 533.
See also *Imagism, Symbolism.*

MOTIVATION **The reasons for a character's behavior.** In order for us to understand why characters act the way they do, their motivation has to be believable, at least in terms of the story. At times, a writer will directly reveal motivation; in subtler fiction, we have to use details from the story to infer motivation.

See pages 586, 1110.
See also *Character.*

MYTH **An anonymous traditional story that is basically religious in nature and that usually serves to explain a belief, ritual, or mysterious natural phenomenon.** Most myths have grown out of religious rituals, and almost all of them involve the exploits of gods and humans. Works of magic realism often draw on myths or mythlike tales.

See page 996.

NARRATIVE **The form of discourse that tells about a series of events.** Narration is used in all kinds of literature: fiction, nonfiction, and poetry. Usually a narrative is told in **chronological order**—in the order in which the events occurred. The other three major forms of discourse are **description, exposition,** and **persuasion.**

NATURALISM **A nineteenth-century literary movement that was an extension of realism and that claimed to portray life exactly as it was.** The naturalists relied heavily on the new fields of psychology and sociology, and they tended to dissect human behavior with complete objectivity, the way a scientist would dissect a specimen in the laboratory. The naturalists were also influenced by Darwinian theories of the survival of the fittest. Naturalists believed that human behavior is determined by heredity and environment; they felt that people have no recourse to supernatural forces and that human beings, like animals, are subject to laws of nature beyond their control. The outstanding naturalists among American writers are Theodore Dreiser, Stephen Crane (page 484), and Frank Norris. Some people consider John Steinbeck's *The Grapes of Wrath* a naturalistic novel, in which characters are the pawns of economic conditions.

See pages 421, 484, 496.
See also *Realism.*

OBJECTIVE CORRELATIVE **An object, a situation, or a chain of events that serves as the formula for a specific emotion.** The term was first used in an essay by T. S. Eliot.

See page 777.

OCTAVE **An eight-line poem, or the first eight lines of a Petrarchan, or Italian, sonnet.** In a Petrarchan sonnet, the octave states the subject of the sonnet, or poses a problem or question.

See page 180.
See also *Sestet, Sonnet.*

ODE A lyric poem, usually long, on a serious subject and written in dignified language. In ancient Greece and Rome, odes were written to be read in public at ceremonial occasions. In modern literature, odes tend to be more private, informal, and reflective. Robert Lowell's "For the Union Dead" (page 950) and Henry Timrod's "Ode on the Confederate Dead" (page 954) are examples of the personal, meditative ode.

ONOMATOPOEIA The use of a word whose sound imitates or suggests its meaning. The word *buzz* is an onomatopoeic word; it imitates the sound it names.

See pages 288, 355.

OXYMORON A figure of speech that combines opposite or contradictory terms in a brief phrase. "Sweet sorrow," "deafening silence," and "living death" are common oxymorons. (Some jokesters claim that phrases like "jumbo shrimp," "congressional leadership," and "limited nuclear war" are also oxymorons.)

See page 622.

PARABLE A relatively short story that teaches a moral, or lesson, about how to lead a good life. The most famous parables are those told by Jesus in the Gospels.

See pages 308, 567.

PARADOX A statement that appears self-contradictory but that reveals a kind of truth. Many writers like to use paradox because it allows them to express the complexity of life by showing how opposing ideas can be both contradictory and true. Emily Dickinson often used paradoxes, as in this line: "I taste a liquor never brewed" (page 382).

See pages 229, 248, 604, 1108.

PARALLEL STRUCTURE (also called *parallelism*) The repetition of words or phrases that have similar grammatical structures. In his Gettysburg Address (page 479), Lincoln used several memorable examples of parallel structure, as when he refers to "government of the people, by the people, for the people."

See pages 115, 355.

PARODY A work that makes fun of another work by imitating some aspect of the writer's style. Parodies often achieve their effects by humorously exaggerating certain features in the original work.

See pages 289, 320, 624.

PERSONIFICATION A figure of speech in which an object or animal is given human feelings, thoughts, or attitudes. Personification is a type of metaphor in which two dissimilar things are compared. In "To the Fringed Gentian," William Cullen Bryant personifies a flower by giving it an eye and eyelashes:

> Then doth thy sweet and quiet eye
> Look through its fringes to the sky.

See pages 622, 737, 1002, 1035, 1042, 1151.
See also *Anthropomorphism, Apostrophe.*

PERSUASION One of the four forms of discourse, which uses reason and emotional appeals to convince a reader to think or act in a certain way. Persuasion is used in the Declaration of Independence (page 116), in Patrick Henry's "Give me liberty, or give me death" speech (page 102), and in Thomas Paine's "The Crisis, No. 1" (page 108). Persuasion is almost exclusively used in nonfiction, particularly in essays and speeches.

See pages 101, 112.
See also *Argument.*

PLAIN STYLE A way of writing that stresses simplicity and clarity of expression. The plain style was favored by most Puritan writers, who avoided unnecessary ornamentation in all aspects of their lives, including church ritual. Simple sentences, everyday words from common speech, and clear and direct statements characterize the plain style. The plain style eliminates elaborate figures of speech and imagery. One of the chief exponents of the plain style in recent American literature was Ernest Hemingway (page 650).

See pages 12, 27, 35.

PLOT The series of related events in a story or play, sometimes called the *story line.* Most short-story plots contain the following elements: **exposition,** which tells us who the characters are and introduces their conflict; **complications,** which arise as the characters take steps to resolve their conflicts; the **climax,** that exciting or suspenseful moment when the outcome of the conflict is imminent; and a **resolution** or **denouement,** when the story's problems are all resolved and the story ends.

The plots of dramas and novels are somewhat more complex because of their length. A schematic representation of a typical dramatic plot follows. It is based on a "pyramid" developed by the nineteenth-century German critic Gustav Freitag. The **rising action** refers to all the actions that take place before the **turning point** (sometimes called the **crisis**). This is the point at which the hero experiences a reversal of fortune: In a comedy, things begin to work out well; in a tragedy, they get worse and worse. (In Shakespeare's plays, the turning point takes place in the third act. In *Romeo and Juliet,* for example, after he kills Tybalt in the third act, Romeo experiences one disaster after another.) All the action after the turning point is called **falling action** because it is leading to the final resolution (happy or unhappy) of the conflict. The major **climax** in most plays and novels takes place just before the ending; in Shakespeare's plays, it takes place in the fifth, or last, act. (In *Romeo and Juliet,* the major climax takes place when the two young people kill themselves.)

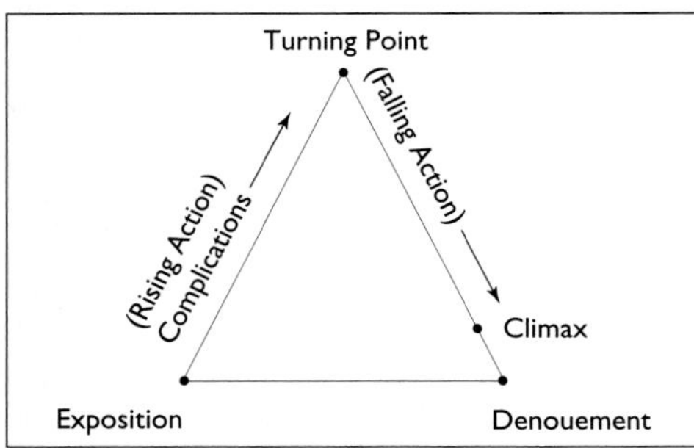

See page 994.

POINT OF VIEW The vantage point from which the writer tells a story. In broad terms, there are four main points of view: **first-person, third-person limited, omniscient,** and **objective.**

1. In the **first-person point of view,** one of the characters in the story tells the story, using first-person pronouns such as *I* and *we.* With this point of view, we can know only what the narrator knows. Mark Twain's novel *Adventures of Huckleberry Finn* is told from the first-person point of view, by the novel's main character, a boy named Huck Finn. One of the great pleasures of that novel, in fact, is that its point of view allows us to hear Huck's very distinct voice and dialect.
2. In the **third-person limited point of view,** an unknown narrator (usually thought of as the author) tells the story, but this narrator zooms in to focus on the thoughts and feelings of only one character. (This point of view gets its name because the narrator refers to all the characters as *he, she,* and *they;* this narrator does not use the first-person pronoun *I.*) Like the first-person point of view, however, this point of view also limits us to the perceptions of one character, but in this case the narrator can tell us many things about the character, things that the character himself (or herself) might be unaware of. For example, Eudora Welty tells "A Worn Path" (page 634) from the third-person limited point of view of her protagonist, an old woman named Phoenix Jackson. At one point, Welty's narrator tells us that Phoenix was "like an old woman begging a dignified forgiveness."
3. In the **omniscient point of view,** an omniscient, or "all-knowing," narrator tells the story, also using the third-person pronouns. However, this narrator, instead of focusing on one character only, often tells us everything about many characters: their motives, weaknesses, hopes, childhoods, and sometimes even their futures. This narrator can also comment directly on the character's actions. Washington Irving's "Rip Van Winkle" (page 154) is told from the omniscient point of view.
4. In the **objective point of view,** a narrator who is totally impersonal and objective tells the story, with no comment on any characters or events. The objective point of view is like the point of view of a movie camera; it is totally impersonal, and what we know is only what the camera might see. This narrator never gives any direct revelation of the characters' thoughts or motives. Ernest Hemingway (page 650) uses this objective point of view, which is why his stories often seem so puzzling to readers. "What happened?" we ask. The *reader* must infer what happens in Hemingway's stories, just as in real life we have to infer the motives, thoughts, and feelings of people we meet.

See pages 232, 467.

POSTMODERNISM A term for the dominant trend in the arts since 1945. Postmodern writing typically experiments with nontraditional forms and allows for multiple meanings. The lines between real and imaginary worlds are often blurred, as is the boundary between fiction and nonfiction. Other characteristics of postmodern literature are cultural diversity and an often playful self-consciousness: that is, an acknowledgment that literature is not a mirror that accurately reflects the world, but a created world unto itself.

See page 910.

PROTAGONIST The central character in a story, the one who initiates or drives the action. The protagonist might or might not be the story's hero; some protagonists are actually the villains in the story.

See page 814.
See also *Antagonist.*

PROVERB A short, well-known statement that expresses a common truth or experience. Many of Benjamin Franklin's sayings have become proverbs in American culture.

See page 465.

PUN A "play on words" based on the multiple meanings of a single word or on words that sound alike but mean different things. An example of the first type of pun is a singer explaining her claim that she was locked out of an audition because she couldn't find the right key. The second kind of pun can be found in the opening lines of Shakespeare's *Julius Caesar,* where a man who repairs shoes claims to be a mender of men's souls (soles). Puns are often used for humor, but some puns are a serious element in poetry.

See page 390.

QUATRAIN A poem consisting of four lines, or four lines of a poem that can be considered as a unit. The typical ballad stanza, for example, is a quatrain.

RATIONALISM A movement that began in Europe in the seventeenth century, which held that we can arrive at truth by using our reason rather than relying on the authority of the past, on the authority of the Church, or on intuition. The rationalists believed that all people were born with an innate ethical sense and had the ability to regulate and improve their own lives.

See pages 13, 18, 143.

REALISM A style of writing, developed in the nineteenth century, that attempts to depict life accurately without idealizing or romanticizing it. Instead of writing about the long ago or far away, the realists concentrated on contemporary life and on middle- and lower-class lives in particular. Among the outstanding realistic novelists in America are Stephen Crane (page 484), Willa Cather (page 538), and John Steinbeck (page 606). European playwrights who wrote realistic dramas, including Henrik Ibsen, August Strindberg, and Anton Chekov, discarded artificial plots in favor of themes centering on contemporary society. They also rejected extravagant language in favor of simpler, everyday diction.

See pages 418, 820, 996.
See also *Naturalism, Romanticism.*

REFRAIN A word, phrase, line, or group of lines that is repeated, for effect, several times in a poem. Refrains are often used in ballads and other narrative poems. "Nevermore" is a refrain in Poe's "The Raven" (page 282).

See pages 288, 1122.

REGIONALISM Literature that emphasizes a specific geographic setting and that reproduces the speech, behavior, and attitudes of the people who live in that region. Among the great regional writers of the twentieth century are Sinclair Lewis (Midwest); John Steinbeck (California); and William Faulkner, Flannery O'Connor, and Eudora Welty (the South).

See page 419.

RESOLUTION The conclusion of a story, when all or most of the conflicts have been settled. The resolution is also often called the *denouement.*

See also *Denouement, Plot.*

RHETORICAL QUESTION A question asked for an effect, not actually requiring an answer. In his speech to the Virginia Convention, Patrick Henry asks several rhetorical questions. Such questions presume the audience agrees with the speaker on the answers.

See page 105.

RHYME The repetition of vowel sounds in accented syllables and all succeeding syllables. *Listen* and *glisten* rhyme, as do *chime* and *sublime.* When words within the same line of poetry have repeated sounds, we have an example of **internal rhyme. End rhyme** refers to rhyming words at the ends of lines.

The pattern of rhymes in a poem is called a **rhyme scheme.** Rhyme scheme is commonly indicated with letters of the alphabet, each rhyming sound represented by a different letter of the alphabet. For example, the rhyme scheme of the following lines is *abab.*

Tell me not, in mournful numbers, *a*
Life is but an empty dream!— *b*
For the soul is dead that slumbers, *a*
And things are not what they seem. *b*

—Henry Wadsworth Longfellow,
from "A Psalm of Life"

Approximate rhymes (also called **off rhymes, half rhymes, imperfect rhymes,** or **slant rhymes**) are words that have some correspondence in sound but not an exact one. Examples of approximate rhymes are often found in Emily Dickinson's poems. *Flash* and *flesh* are approximate rhymes, as are *stream* and *storm,* and *early* and *barley.* Approximate rhyme has the effect of catching the reader off guard: Where you expect a perfect rhyme, you get only an approximation. The emotional effect is something like that of the sound of a sharp or flat note in music.

See pages 288, 380, 1156.
See also *Internal Rhyme, Slant Rhyme.*

RHYTHM **A rise and fall of the voice produced by the alternation of stressed and unstressed syllables in language.** When rhythm is tightly controlled and the stressed and unstressed syllables fall into a pattern, it is called **meter.**

See pages 670, 761.
See also *Cadence, Meter.*

ROMANCE **In general, a story in which an idealized hero or heroine undertakes a quest and is successful.** In a romance, beauty, innocence, and goodness usually prevail over evil. Romances are traditionally set in the distant past and use a great deal of fantasy. The laws of nature are often suspended in a romance, so that the hero often has supernatural powers, as we see in the adventures of King Arthur and his knights. Stories set in the American West are in the romance mode, except that the supernatural elements are eliminated (though the sheriff-hero usually has a nearly magical skill with his gun). Today we also use the word *romance* to refer to a kind of popular escapist love story, which often takes place in an exotic setting.

See page 683.

ROMANTICISM **A revolt against rationalism that affected literature and the other arts, beginning in the late eighteenth century and remaining strong throughout most of the nineteenth century.** Romanticism is marked by these characteristics: (1) a conviction that intuition, imagination, and emotion are superior to reason; (2) a conviction that poetry is superior to science; (3) a belief that contemplation of the natural world is a means of discovering the truth that lies behind mere reality; (4) a distrust of industry and city life and an idealization of rural life and of the wilderness; (5) an interest in the more "natural" past and in the supernatural. Romanticism affected so many creative people that it was bound to take many different forms; the result is that it is difficult to define the word in a way that includes everyone who might be called a Romantic. In the nineteenth century, for example, Romantics were outspoken in their love of nature and contempt for technology. In this century, however, as nature has been taken over by developers and highways, some writers have taken a romantic view of machines, buildings, and other products of technology.

See pages 143, 144, 212, 770.

SATIRE **A type of writing that ridicules the shortcomings of people or institutions in an attempt to bring about a change.** Satire can cover a wide range of tones, from gentle spoofing to savage mockery. In "Rip Van Winkle" (page 154), for example, Washington Irving pokes good-natured fun at the Van Winkles and the townspeople. In Donald Barthelme's "Game" (page 956), the satire is harsher, as it points up the absurdity and illogic of nuclear war games. Satire is always intensely moral in its purpose. Mark Twain, in *Adventures of Huckleberry Finn*, satirizes a whole spectrum of American life, but the thrust of the novel is moral: Twain is making us see things that should not be permitted to exist (slavery is one of them).

See pages 50, 962.

SCANNING **The analysis of a poem to determine its meter.** When you scan a poem, you describe the pattern of stressed and unstressed syllables in each line. Stresses or accents are indicated by the symbol (′) and unstressed syllables by the symbol (˘).

To him who in the love of Nature holds
Communion with her visible forms, she speaks
A various language: for his gayer hours
She has a voice of gladness, and a smile

—William Cullen Bryant,
from "Thanatopsis"

See also *Iambic Pentameter, Meter.*

SESTET **Six lines of poetry, especially the last six lines of a Petrarchan, or Italian, sonnet.** In the Petrarchan sonnet, the sestet offers a comment on the subject or problem presented in the first eight lines (the octave) of the poem.

See page 180.
See also *Octave, Sonnet.*

SETTING **The time and location where a story takes place.** Setting can have several functions in fiction:

1. Setting is often used to create **conflict.** In the purest and often simplest form of story, a character is in conflict with some element of a setting: The narrator in Jack London's "To Build a Fire" (page 497) is in conflict with extreme cold (the cold wins).
2. Often the setting helps to create **atmosphere** or **mood,** as does Edgar Allan Poe's setting of a decaying mansion in "The Fall of the House of Usher" (page 263).
3. Setting can also create and delineate **character:** In William Faulkner's "A Rose for Emily" (page 716), Miss Emily Grierson's old-fashioned house with its musty rooms reflects her refusal to live in the present.

See pages 153, 539, 715, 1093.

SIMILE **A figure of speech that makes an explicit comparison between two unlike things, using a word such as *like, as, than,* or *resembles.***

Helen, thy beauty is to me
Like those Nicéan barks of yore

—Edgar Allan Poe, *from* "To Helen"

See pages 622, 1002.
See also *Figure of Speech, Metaphor.*

SLANT RHYME **A rhyming sound that is not exact.** *Follow/fellow* and *mystery/mastery* are examples of slant or approximate rhyme. Emily Dickinson frequently used the subtleties of slant rhyme in her poetry.

See page 380.
See also *Rhyme.*

SOLILOQUY **A long speech made by a character in a play while no other characters are on stage.** A soliloquy is different from a monologue in that the speaker appears to be thinking aloud, not addressing a listener.

SONNET **A fourteen-line poem, usually written in iambic pentameter, that has one of two basic structures.** The **Petrarchan sonnet,** also called the **Italian sonnet,** is named after the fourteenth-century Italian poet Petrarch. Its first eight lines, called the **octave,** ask a question or pose a problem. These lines have a rhyme scheme of *abba, abba.* The last six lines, called the **sestet,** respond to the question or problem. These lines have a rhyme scheme of *cde, cde.*

The form used to such perfection by William Shakespeare is known as the **English, Elizabethan,** or **Shakespearean sonnet.** It has three four-line units, or **quatrains,** and it concludes with a **couplet.** The most common rhyme scheme for the Shakespearean sonnet is *abab, cdcd, efef, gg.*

Longfellow wrote many sonnets, such as "The Cross of Snow" (page 178), as did Edna St. Vincent Millay (page 697), Robert Frost (page 558), and E. E. Cummings (page 796).

See page 180.
See also *Octave, Sestet.*

SOUND EFFECTS **The use of sounds to create specific literary effects.** Writers use devices such as **rhythm, rhyme, meter, alliteration, onomatopoeia, assonance, consonance,** and **repetition** to make the sounds of a work convey and enhance its meaning.

See pages 282, 288, 1007.

SPONDEE **A metrical foot consisting of two syllables, both of which are stressed.** The words *true-blue* and *nineteen* are made of spondees. When Walt Whitman wrote "Beat! beat! drums," he used spondees. Spondaic feet are rarely used extensively because of their "thump-thump" sound. However, poets sometimes use spondees to provide a brief change from an iambic or trochaic beat or to provide emphasis.

See also *Foot, Meter, Trochee.*

STEREOTYPE **A fixed idea or conception of a character or an idea which does not allow for any individuality, often based on religious, social, or racial prejudices.** Some common stereotypes are the unsophisticated farmer, the socially inept honor student, the dumb athlete, and the lazy teenager. Stereotypes, also called **stock characters,** are often deliberately used in comedies and in melodramas, where they receive instant recognition from the audience and make fully fleshed characterization unnecessary. Dame Van Winkle and Rip are stereotypes (page 154), as are Walter and Mrs. Mitty (page 625).

See pages 166, 631.
See also *Character.*

STREAM OF CONSCIOUSNESS **A style of writing that portrays the inner (often chaotic) workings of a character's mind.** The stream-of-consciousness technique usually consists of a recording of the random flow of ideas, memories, associations, images, and emotions, as they arise spontaneously in a character's mind. William Faulkner, in his great novel *The Sound and the Fury,* used a stream-of-consciousness technique. Two of the other great writers that successfully used a stream-of-consciousness technique are the

Irish writer James Joyce and the English writer Virginia Woolf.

See pages 530, 703.

STYLE **The distinctive way in which a writer uses language.** Styles can be plain, ornate, metaphorical, spare, descriptive, and so on. Style is determined by such factors as sentence length and complexity, syntax, use of figurative language and imagery, and diction.

See pages 107, 1027.
See also *Plain Style, Stream of Consciousness.*

SURREALISM **A movement in art and literature that started in Europe during the 1920s. Surrealists wanted to replace conventional realism with the full expression of the unconscious mind, which they considered to be more real than the "real" world of appearances.** Surrealists, influenced by the psychoanalytic theories of Sigmund Freud, tried not to censor the images that came from their dreams or to impose logical connections on these images. This resulted in surprising combinations of "inner" and "outer" reality—a "suprareality." Surrealism affected writers as different as T. S. Eliot (page 661) and Donald Barthelme (page 955). Two famous Surrealist artists are Salvador Dali and Marc Chagall (see art on pages 982 and 989).

SUSPENSE **A feeling of uncertainty and curiosity about what will happen next in a story.** A key element in fiction and drama, suspense is one of the "hooks" a writer uses to keep the readers or audience interested.

SYMBOL **A person, place, thing, or event that has meaning in itself and that also stands for something more than itself.** We can distinguish between **public** and **personal symbols.** The dove, for example, is a public symbol of peace—that is, it is widely accepted the world over as such a symbol. Uncle Sam is a public symbol that stands for the United States; a picture of a skull and crossbones is a public symbol of death; two snakes coiled around a staff is a widely accepted symbol of the medical profession.

Most symbols used in literature are personal symbols; even though a symbol may be widely used, a writer will usually adapt it in some imaginative, personal way so that it can suggest not just one, but a myriad of meanings. One of the most commonly used symbols in literature, for example, is the journey, which can stand for a search for truth, for redemption from evil, or for discovery of the self and freedom. The journey of Huck Finn and Jim down the Mississippi River has been interpreted to symbolize all of these concepts, and more.

The writers known as the Dark Romantics—Poe, Hawthorne, and Melville—used symbolism heavily in their works, owing to the allegorical nature of much of what they wrote. One of American literature's most famous symbols is Melville's white whale, Moby-Dick (page 313).

See pages 280, 298.

SYMBOLISM **A literary movement that originated in late-nineteenth-century France, in which writers rearranged the world of appearances in order to reveal a more truthful version of reality.** The Symbolists believed that direct statements of feeling were inadequate; instead, they called for new and striking imaginative images to evoke complexities of meaning and mood. The French Symbolists were influenced by the poetry and critical writings of the American writer Edgar Allan Poe (page 260). The poetry of Ezra Pound (page 773), T. S. Eliot (page 661), and Wallace Stevens (page 783) is in the Symbolist tradition.

See pages 530, 771.

SYNECDOCHE **A figure of speech in which a part represents the whole.** The capital city of a nation, for example, is often spoken of as though it were the government: "Washington and Tehran are both claiming popular support for their positions." In "The Love Song of J. Alfred Prufrock" (page 663), T. S. Eliot writes, "And I have known the arms already. . . ." In that line, the word *arms* stands for the women he has known.

See also *Metonymy.*

SYNESTHESIA **The juxtaposition of one sensory image with another image that appeals to an unrelated sense.** In synesthesia, an image of sound might be conveyed in terms of an image of taste, as in "sweet laughter," or an image that appeals to the sense of touch might be combined with an image that appeals to the sense of sight, as in this example from Emily Dickinson: "golden touch."

See page 1091.

TALL TALE **An outrageously exaggerated, humorous story that is obviously unbelievable.** Tall tales are part of the folk literature of many countries, including America. Perhaps the most famous tall tale in American literature is Mark Twain's "The Celebrated Jumping Frog of Calaveras County."

THEME **The insight about human life that is revealed in a literary work.** Themes are rarely stated directly in literature. Most often, a reader has to infer the theme of a work after considerable thought. Theme is different from **subject.** A story's subject might be stated as "growing up," "love," "heroism," or "fear." The theme is the statement the writer wants to make about that subject: "For most young people, growing up is a process that involves the pain of achieving self-knowledge." Theme must be stated in at least one sentence; most themes are complex enough to require several sentences, or even an essay.

See page 634.

TONE The attitude a writer takes toward the subject of a work, the characters in it, or the audience. In speaking, we use voice inflections to show how we feel about what we are saying. Writers manipulate language in an attempt to achieve the same effect. For example, John Hersey takes an objective tone in telling about the nuclear explosion in *Hiroshima* (see "A Noiseless Flash," page 937). In contrast, the tone in Patrick Henry's speech to the Virginia Convention (page 102) is subjective, even impassioned. Tone is dependent on **diction** and **style,** and we cannot say we have understood any work of literature until we have sensed the writer's tone. Tone can be described in a single word: objective, solemn, playful, ironic, sarcastic, critical, reverent, irreverent, philosophical, cynical, and so on.

See pages 577, 764.
See also *Diction, Style.*

TRAGEDY In general, a story in which a heroic character either dies or comes to some other unhappy end. In most tragedies, the main character is in an enviable, even exalted position when the story begins (in classical tragedies and in Shakespeare, the tragic hero is of noble origin, often a king or queen, prince or princess). The character's downfall generally occurs because of some combination of fate, an error in judgment, or a personality failure known as a **tragic flaw** (Creon's stubbornness in *Antigone* or Hamlet's indecision, for example). The tragic character has usually gained wisdom at the end of the story, in spite of suffering defeat, or even death. Our feeling on reading or viewing a tragedy is usually exaltation—despite the unhappy ending—because we have witnessed the best that human beings are capable of.

See page 683.
See also *Comedy.*

TRANSCENDENTALISM A nineteenth-century movement in the Romantic tradition, which held that every individual can reach ultimate truths through spiritual intuition, which transcends reason and sensory experience. The Transcendental movement was centered in Concord, Massachusetts, the home of its leading exponents, Ralph Waldo Emerson (page 216) and Henry David Thoreau (page 230). The basic tenets of the Transcendentalists were (1) a belief that God is present in every aspect of Nature, including every human being; (2) the conviction that everyone is capable of apprehending God through the use of intuition; (3) the belief that all of Nature is symbolic of the spirit. A corollary of these beliefs was an optimistic view of the world as good and evil as nonexistent.

See pages 211, 212.

TROCHEE A metrical foot made up of an accented syllable followed by an unaccented syllable, as in the word *taxi.* A trochee is the opposite of an iamb and is sometimes used to vary the rhythm of an iambic poem.

See also *Foot, Meter, Spondee.*

UNDERSTATEMENT A statement that says less than what is meant. Understatement, paradoxically, can make us recognize the truth of something by saying that just the opposite is true. If you are sitting down to enjoy a ten-course meal and say, "Ah! A little snack before bedtime," you are using an understatement to emphasize the tremendous amount of food you are about to eat. Understatement is often used to make an ironic point; it can also be used for humor.

See pages 463, 1033.
See also *Hyperbole.*

VERNACULAR The language spoken by the people who live in a particular locality. Regionalist writers accurately record the vernacular speech of their area.

See page 398.
See also *Dialect.*

Workplace Writing

Your ability to write clear and effective business letters, memos, and résumés may mean the difference between success and failure in your career. As a student or graduate, you will write business letters to apply to colleges and universities for admission and to businesses for jobs. As an employee, you will write business letters, reports, and memos to communicate important information and decisions.

WRITING EFFECTIVE BUSINESS LETTERS

People who receive your business correspondence will develop a lasting impression of you or your employer based on the quality of the written documents they receive. If your readers are distracted from the content of your message by errors and inaccuracies or by an unprofessional appearance, they may assume that you, as well as your organization, are incompetent.

Types of Business Letters

Request or Order Letters You write a **request letter** to ask for information about a job, college, product, service, policy, or procedure. You write **order letters** to order merchandise by mail. When writing a request or order letter, state your request clearly, including all important details relating to time, location, size, style, cost, and so on. Make sure requests to an individual for extra assistance are reasonable, and let the person know that his or her help is important.

Complaint or Adjustment Letters You write a **complaint** or **adjustment letter** if you are dissatisfied with a person, product, or service. Your letter should explain exactly what is wrong and should request a satisfactory resolution of the problem, such as your receiving new merchandise or a refund. Keep the tone of your letter calm and courteous, and present all facts clearly, in order of occurrence.

Letters of Application A **letter of application** introduces you to a selection committee or a possible employer. The letter should provide the reader with enough information to determine whether you are a good candidate for a job or scholarship or whether you should be accepted by a college or university. Keep the following points in mind when writing a letter of application.

1. Identify the job or situation for which you are applying, and mention how you heard about it.
2. Depending on the situation, include
   - your grade in school and grade point average
   - your experience, activities, awards, and honors
   - personal qualities that make you a good choice
   - the dates or times you are available
3. Provide references—two or three responsible adults, other than relatives, who agree to recommend you. Include their addresses and telephone numbers.

Sample Letter of Application, Modified Block Style

Heading Your address and the date you write the letter	1632 Garden View Drive Allentown, PA 18103 May 23, 1996
Inside Address Name, title, and address of person you are writing	Personnel Director Superior Insurance Company 10 Central Avenue Allentown, PA 18102
Salutation Greeting, ended with a colon—*Dear Sir or Madam:* or *Dear (business title):* if you don't know person's name	Dear Personnel Director: Are you looking for someone who carries out assigned responsibilities and enjoys working with people? I have these qualities and good business skills to bring to the position of summer intern administrative assistant advertised in Sunday's Herald.

Body The main part of your letter, your message. If the body of your letter is longer than one paragraph, leave a blank line between paragraphs.	A 17-year-old junior at Jefferson High School, I have completed courses in typing, bookkeeping, computer skills, and business English. I can type 50 words per minute while transcribing from recordings. Last summer, as a fill-in receptionist at Quality Supply Company, I did filing and billing and performed other tasks in addition to my regular duties. I feel very at home in an office and enjoy responsibility. My résumé, which is enclosed, lists references who can tell you about my work and my personal characteristics. I believe that my background qualifies me for the summer intern position. Please call me at 555-7023 to set an interview appointment.
Closing *Yours truly, Sincerely,* etc., followed by a comma	Yours truly,
Signature Sign your name in ink below the closing; type or print your name two lines below the signature.	Veronica Zeno Veronica Zeno
Use "Enclosure" if you're including something with your letter.	Enclosure

WRITING A PERSONAL RÉSUMÉ

Your **résumé** summarizes who you are, what you have learned, and what you have accomplished. The information in your résumé should include skills, knowledge, and achievements that give a potential employer a positive overview of your qualifications. When you apply for a job, you usually include your résumé with your letter of application.

The structure, organization, and overall appearance of your résumé will give the reader an impression of you and your abilities. Type your résumé on white or ivory paper. Proofread your résumé carefully, making sure there are no factual or typographical errors, erasures, correction fluid, or stray marks. Remember, your goal is to get an interview: Try your best to make a good impression.

This model résumé is written in reverse chronological order; it lists the most recent work experience first.

VERONICA L. ZENO		1632 Garden View Drive Allentown, PA 18103 Telephone: (215) 555-7023
EDUCATION:	Junior, Jefferson High School Major studies: Business and foreign language courses Grade point average: 3.0 (B)	
WORK EXPERIENCE:	Summer 1995	Fill-in receptionist Quality Supply Company Allentown, PA
	Summer 1994	Volunteer office worker YWCA Allentown, PA

COMMUNICATIONS HANDBOOK

SKILLS:	Typing:	50 wpm
	Business machines:	Dictating, calculating, and copy machines; IBM-compatible personal computers
	Languages:	Can speak and translate Spanish fluently
EXTRACURRICULAR ACTIVITIES:	Vice president, Future Business Leaders of America Member, Spanish Club	
REFERENCES:	Dr. Walter A. Schmidt, Principal Jefferson High School Allentown, PA	(215) 555-1019
	Ms. Mary Frances Tate, Teacher Jefferson High School Allentown, PA	(215) 555-1019
	Mr. Glen Ramos, Owner Quality Supply Company Allentown, PA	(215) 555-4593

WRITING INTEROFFICE MEMOS AND REPORTS

Memos

Memos are standard forms of communication in many organizations. They are concise messages that do not include all the parts of a letter but still tell the reader *when, who, what, where, why,* and *how.* Memos contain guide words (*DATE, TO, FROM, SUBJECT*) that immediately identify the date, destination, origin, and purpose of a message. Memos generally cover only one topic. You can group most memos into one of the following categories.

- **Meeting Notices** Include the meeting date, time, place, purpose, and any additional information that relates to the meeting.
- **Meeting Summaries** Provide a brief, factual report of decisions and discussions. Include the names and titles of individuals involved.
- **Requests for Action or Information** Open by making the request, and then follow with details. If you have several requests, list them, phrasing each one similarly. Include a deadline stating when you need a response.

Technical and Business Reports

Technical and **business reports** are vital to the operation of a business. The reports vary in length, content, form, and formality, but they provide the information that people in organizations need in order to make plans and solve problems. You can group most reports into one of the following general categories.

Informational Reports Types of reports that present data include

- periodic operating or status reports such as weekly sales reports
- investigative reports that examine problems and supply facts
- compliance reports that show conformity to laws and regulations

Analytical Reports These technical reports present data, analyses, conclusions, and recommendations. They include

- justification/recommendation reports that analyze alternatives, interpret findings, and make recommendations
- project reports that are compiled at the end of a project to analyze results, what was learned, profitability, and benefits
- yardstick reports that establish criteria by which to measure alternatives
- feasibility reports that determine whether a project is practical and advisable

Research Studies These long technical reports thoroughly and scientifically examine problems, the attempts to solve these problems, and the results of such attempts.

Proposals These detailed business reports offer solutions to problems, investigate ideas, or sell products and services.

WRITING WITH COMPUTERS

Word Processing

Computers and software programs provide powerful tools that make the writing process easier and more efficient. You will find that all phases of the writing process are simplified when you use the computer.

Prewriting During the **prewriting** stage you can plan quickly, experiment with structure and phrasing, and expand the most promising ideas.

Writing a Draft You can write your first **draft** on the computer without stopping to correct errors or make changes, so you can concentrate on composing your thoughts.

Evaluating and Revising Word processing features make **evaluation** and **revision** of a work in progress much easier. You can save your document, make changes, and then undo the changes if you decide you don't like them. Once you make the revisions, you can print out a clean copy without having to repeat steps.

Proofreading Many word processing programs for the computer now include features that find and correct spelling, typographical, and grammatical errors. You can use search-and-replace functions to correct a specific type of error wherever it occurs in your document. You must do the final **proofreading** yourself because word processing programs do not correct misused words (for example, using the word "effect" where "affect" was called for).

Electronic Mail

Many business people use computers and **electronic mail (e-mail)** to send messages. E-mail uses computers, modems, and software to send messages over networks connected by telephone lines and satellites. You can send an electronic memo almost instantly to a computer at the next desk or around the world. E-mail messages usually are short and to the point, but they still require careful planning because they reflect on you, and privacy is not guaranteed.

RESEARCHING AND DOCUMENTING INFORMATION

When you write a research paper, you put together the ideas and views of others. You research what experts have said and written about your topic, and draw a new conclusion.

STEPS IN WRITING A RESEARCH PAPER

Writing a research paper involves a series of steps that will help you to organize your sources and notes.

Prewriting

1. Choose a topic that interests you, and be sure you can find enough sources and information.
2. Begin your research by posing questions that you want to answer. Make a source card for each resource you consult.
3. Take notes from your sources. Summarize main points in your own words, and record quotations you might use in your paper on note cards.
4. Write a thesis statement stating your topic and what you plan to say about it.
5. Develop a working outline that arranges your main ideas and quotations in a logical order.

Writing Your First Draft

1. The draft of your paper should have an introduction, body, and conclusion.
2. Use short quotations in your paper to add interest and authority.
3. Document the source of all original opinions or theories, facts and statistics, and quotations that you use. (See pages 1211–1213.)

Evaluating and Revising

1. Make sure you have included and supported your thesis statement, and check that you have information documented from three or more sources. Then prepare your Works Cited page. (See pages 1211–1213.)
2. Make sure that all the information is related to the topic, that your ideas are clear and easy to follow, and that your paper reads smoothly.

Proofreading and Publishing

1. Check your document for spelling, grammar, punctuation, and usage errors.
2. Make sure your documentation follows the recommended format. (See pages 1211–1213.)
3. Share your research by publishing your paper.

Model Research Paper

Burden of Sadness: Longfellow's "Divina Commedia I"

It is possible to understand a poem without knowing anything about the writer's life, but sometimes readers who do not know the biographical details miss a lot. To understand "Divina Commedia I" by Henry Wadsworth Longfellow, readers will find it helpful to know some details about Longfellow's life and about his poetry in general.

The details of Longfellow's life that relate to "Divina Commedia I" are tragic. After his wife's death in 1861, Longfellow used to begin each day translating some of Dante's epic poem, The Divine Comedy, into English (Wagenknecht 209). "Divina Commedia I" is the first of six sonnets that Longfellow wrote as prefaces to Dante's epic. Three years before this particular sonnet was written, Longfellow's wife burned to death in her home when some sealing wax fell on her dress and ignited it. Longfellow himself was badly burned when he tried to beat out the flames with his bare hands. The "burden" referred to in the sonnet (line 10) must refer to this burden of sadness the poet carries with him.

Knowing some of Longfellow's poetic techniques also helps to illuminate this sonnet. According to William Charvat, Longfellow's poems tend to teach austere lessons: "We are to work for work's sake. We are to accept life's labors, deprivals, and sorrows" (Charvat 432). The sonnet illustrates this belief. For Longfellow, the work of translation helped lessen life's sorrows. This stoic, almost puritanical belief seemed to have worked for Longfellow.

Another characteristic of Longfellow's poetry is revealed in this poem. According to Leonard Unger, Longfellow's lyric and meditative poems have a characteristic development. They move from "image to analogy to statement" (Unger 498). This is the pattern of "Divina Commedia I." The poem begins with the image of a laborer laying down his burden (probably his tools) and praying in a cathedral (lines 1–8). While he prays, the street noises retreat. With the words "So, as I enter. . ." (line 9), the speaker makes an analogy between the laborer's act and his own act. He too lays down his burden and kneels to pray. The speaker's burden is mental, not physical, but the prayer has the same effect on him that it has on the laborer. For the poet, prayer is a connection with eternity. The "disconsolate" present dies away, revealing the waiting ages of eternity.

Before I knew that the poet at the time was mourning the loss of his wife, I thought the poem was puzzling. Once I knew why Longfellow sought comfort in prayer, the poem became much more powerful and spoke to a feeling I could share.

INTRODUCTORY PARAGRAPH
Catches reader's interest

Thesis statement

BODY
Topic sentence
Supporting details
Secondary source citation

Primary source citation

Topic sentence

Supporting details

Secondary source citation

Topic sentence

Secondary source citation

Supporting details

Primary source citation

CONCLUSION
Summarizes topic

Works Cited

Charvat, William. "Henry Wadsworth Longfellow." Major Writers of America, Shorter Edition. Ed. Perry Miller, et al. New York: Harcourt, 1966. 431–40.

Unger, Leonard, ed. American Writers: A Collection of Literary Biographies. New York: Scribner's, 1979.

Wagenknecht, Edward. Henry Wadsworth Longfellow. New York: Oxford UP, 1966.

USING THE LIBRARY/ MEDIA CENTER

The library/media center is the most logical place to start gathering information for a research report. The **card catalog** contains alphabetized information about the books and audiovisuals in the library and can be searched by title or author. Nonfiction materials also have a subject card. The **on-line catalog** is a computerized card catalog. Some on-line systems can tell you where a book is located and whether it is currently available. The librarians will help you if you do not know how to use the card catalog or the on-line catalog.

Much information is available via computer with the use of a modem. The Internet provides access to materials from libraries, universities, museums, government agencies, and user groups all over the world that, in printed form, would be too expensive or not readily available. You can reach the Internet through either local service providers or such national on-line services as America Online®, CompuServe®, and Prodigy®.

Databases house information that can be accessed by computer. Many libraries and businesses now subscribe to a variety of electronic databases that are constantly updated. Computerized indexes of newspaper and magazine articles are available. InfoTrac®, for example, is updated monthly and provides an index of general interest magazines from 1985 to the present. Indexes will show a title, **abstract** (summary), or full text of an article. Many databases also are available on CD-ROM.

USING COMMUNITY RESOURCES

Community resources such as museums, historical societies, government offices, businesses, television and radio stations, associations, and video stores are valuable sources of information.

Contacting and Interviewing Sources

Some of the best information you get about a topic may come from individuals you interview. Look for someone who might be considered an expert on your topic. Sometimes organizations or local businesses can recommend a specialist in the field you are researching.

When you contact sources in your community to ask for information, be polite and professional. Whether you use the telephone or write a letter, remember that you are asking for someone's time. Be prepared to work around his or her schedule. Anticipate problems such as lack of transportation or schedule conflicts, and have solutions before you try to schedule the interview.

When you want to interview someone, prepare yourself by learning something about the person you are interviewing as well as background on the topic. The chart at the left lists the steps in the interviewing process.

PREPARING FOR THE INTERVIEW

- Make arrangements well in advance. Set up a time that is convenient for the other person. Tell the interviewee how much time you expect the interview to take.
- Make a list of questions to ask. Make sure the questions are arranged in a logical order and require more than yes or no answers.

PARTICIPATING IN THE INTERVIEW

- Arrive on time, and be polite and patient.
- Ask the other person's permission if you plan to use a tape recorder; be ready to take notes.
- Avoid argument. Be tactful and courteous. Remember, the interview was granted at your request.
- Listen carefully, and ask follow-up questions if you do not understand an answer or if you think you need more information.
- Conclude by asking if the interviewee has anything to add and by thanking the interviewee for his or her time.

FOLLOWING UP ON THE INTERVIEW

- Review your notes to refresh your memory, and then make a summary of the material you have gathered.
- Send a thank-you note to the interviewee.

EVALUATING SOURCES

Before you begin taking notes from any source—print, electronic, or interview—you should be sure that the source provides information that is up-to-date, accurate, and free of obvious bias. Use both primary and secondary sources. **Primary sources** include letters, autobiographies, works of literature, historical documents, and interviews. **Secondary sources** are derived from primary sources. They include encyclopedias, documentary films, biographies, literary criticism, and history books. To evaluate the usefulness of a source, use this **4R** test.

1. **Relevant** Does the information relate directly to your limited topic? For a book, check the table of contents and index. Skim magazine articles. Some nonprint sources include summaries and reviews.
2. **Reliable** Can you trust it? A respected scholar or a respected magazine such as *Smithsonian* usually is accurate. Look for authors who are quoted frequently or who appear in most bibliographies on your topic, and check with librarians or experts.
3. **Recent** Be sure you aren't using outdated information, especially for rapidly changing topics. For any topic, look for the most recent work about it. If the author is thorough, you'll learn which older sources of information still are being consulted.
4. **Representative** If you are working on a controversial topic, you'll need to show different points of view. Your task as a researcher is to study, balance, and interpret the views on all sides.

TAKING NOTES AND DOCUMENTING SOURCES

If you use another writer's words or ideas without indicating you are doing so, you are **plagiarizing.** Plagiarism is a serious offense; avoid it by documenting the source of each quotation, paraphrase, statistic, figure, and idea gained from research. Careful documentation starts with accurate source cards and notes.

Preparing Source Cards

As you gather information for your report, you can save time and ensure accurate documentation by preparing source cards in the format needed for the Works Cited list in your report. Put each source on a 3" × 5" card following the guidelines at the top of the next column.

GUIDELINES FOR SOURCE CARDS

1. **Assign each source a number.** Later, when you're taking notes, it will save time to write a number instead of the author and title.
2. **Record full publishing information.** Record everything you might need: subtitles, translators, and volume and edition numbers. Use a shortened form of the publisher's name, deleting articles (*a, an, the*) and business abbreviations (*Co., Corp., Inc., Ltd.*).
3. **Note the call number or location.** This information will help you relocate the source quickly if you need to.

Sample Source Card

5

Williams, Tennessee. Memoirs. Garden City, New York: Doubleday, 1975.

Oak Hill
Library

Taking Notes

After evaluating your sources and preparing source cards based on the research questions you want to answer, you are ready to read more carefully and take notes on the information you will use in your paper. Follow these guidelines to prepare useful note cards.

GUIDELINES FOR NOTE CARDS

1. Use a separate 4" × 6" note card or a half-sheet of paper for each source and item of information.
2. Write the number you have assigned to its source in the upper right-hand corner of each note card.
3. In the upper left-hand corner of the card, identify the main idea of your note card with a label, or heading. Note which of your research questions the information answers.
4. At the end of your note, write the page numbers from which the information comes. Reread the note to be sure you understand it.

Your notes will be direct quotations, summaries, and paraphrases. **Direct quotations** contain the author's exact words. For quotations, copy the statement word for word, including punctuation, capitalization, and spelling, and enclose it in quotation marks. Summaries and paraphrases record the author's ideas and facts in your own words. A **summary** condenses the original statement or paragraph, and a **paraphrase** has more detail than a summary. Use lists and phrases instead of complete sentences to summarize or paraphrase someone else's ideas efficiently.

Using Quotations

Good quotations add interest and authority to your research paper. They should be short and worked smoothly into your paper. The following chart identifies several ways to use quotations effectively.

GUIDELINES FOR USING QUOTATIONS

- **Quote a whole sentence, introducing it in your own words.**
  EXAMPLE Williams and Mead described the author's year at the University of Iowa as very productive: "Tom's preoccupation at Iowa must have been work, and huge amounts of it" (69).
- **Quote part of a sentence within a sentence of your own.**
  EXAMPLE According to his mother, Tennessee Williams changed his name because "Thomas Lanier Williams reminded him of bad poetry" (Williams and Mead 71).
- **Quote just one or a few words within a sentence of your own.**
  EXAMPLE Williams gathered material for dialogue, collecting "colorful idioms of speech" at beaches and hotels (Williams and Mead 71).
- **Use an ellipsis (three spaced periods) to indicate omissions from quotations.** Sometimes you need only a part of a quotation to make your point. Use an ellipsis to indicate words deleted from a quotation.
  EXAMPLE According to Patricia C. Click, Williams used "glass as an important symbol of impermanence . . . to imply that nothing lasts" (43).
- **Set off longer quotations as "blocks."** If a quotation will be more than four typed lines, start a new line, and indent the entire quotation ten spaces from the left. Double-space, and do not use quotation marks.

Documenting Sources

Parenthetical Citations A **parenthetical citation** gives source information in parentheses in the body of your research paper and contains just enough information to lead the reader to the entry in the Works Cited list. Most citations include the author's last name and a page number, with these exceptions:

- a nonprint source such as an interview
- a print source of only one page
- a sentence that includes the author's name (use page numbers only)

Guidelines for the placement of parenthetical citations follow. For more information on specific kinds of parenthetical citations, see the most recent edition of the *MLA Handbook for Writers of Research Papers.*

PLACEMENT OF CITATIONS

- Place the citation as close as possible to the material it documents—if possible, at the end of a sentence or at another point of punctuation. Try not to interrupt sentences.
- Place the citation *before* the punctuation mark of the sentence or phrase you are documenting.
  EXAMPLE Williams "uses glass as a symbol of impermanence" and "the illusion of reality" (Click 43).
- For a quotation that ends a sentence, put the citation *after* the quotation mark but *before* the end punctuation mark.
  EXAMPLE According to his mother, Tennessee Williams changed his name because "Thomas Lanier Williams reminded him of bad poetry" (Williams and Mead 71).
- For an indented quotation, put the citation *two spaces after* the final punctuation mark.

List of Works Cited The **Works Cited** list, which you should include at the end of your report, contains all the sources, print and nonprint, that you credit in your paper. To prepare the Works Cited list, center the words *Works Cited* on a new sheet of paper. Alphabetize the sources by the author's last name. If there is no author, alphabetize by title, ignoring *A, An,* and *The* as the first word of the title. Use shortened forms of publishers' names, and abbreviate *University* and *Press* as *U* and *P.* Begin each entry on a new line, even with the left margin. Indent other lines in the entry five spaces. Double-space all entries. The following chart lists sample citations in the Modern Language Association of America (MLA) style for different types of sources.

Instructional Support See **Bibliography Maker** in the ***Writer's Workshop 2*** software.

SAMPLE ENTRIES FOR THE LIST OF WORKS CITED	
STANDARD REFERENCE WORKS	
Encyclopedia	"Williams, Tennessee." The World Book Encyclopedia. 1992 ed.
Biographical Reference Book	Wealef, Gerald. "Williams, [Thomas Lanier] Tennessee." The Reader's Encyclopedia of World Drama. 1969 ed.
BOOKS	
Book with One Author	Miller, Arthur. Focus. New York: Reynal, 1945.
Book with Two or More Authors	Williams, Dakin, and Shepherd Mead. Tennessee Williams: An Intimate Biography. New York: Arbor, 1983.
Book with No Author Shown	American Statistics Index. Washington: Congressional Information Service, 1992.
Book with One Editor	Cooper, Charles W., ed. Preface to Drama. New York: Ronald, 1955.
Book with Two or More Editors	Block, Haskell, and Robert G. Shedd, eds. Masters of Modern Drama. New York: Random, 1962.
Translation	Williams, Tennessee. Pethe brau. Trans. Emyr Edwards. Llandysul, Wales: Gwasg, 1963. Trans. of The Glass Menagerie. New York: Random, 1945.
SELECTIONS WITHIN BOOKS	
Selection from Book of Works by One Author	Gould, Jean R. "Arthur Miller." Modern American Playwrights. New York: Dodd, 1966. 247–63.
Selection from Book of Works by Several Authors	Beaurline, Lester A. "The Director, the Script, and Author's Revisions: A Critical Problem." Papers in Dramatic Theory and Criticism. Ed. David M. Knauf. Iowa City: U of Iowa, 1969. 78–91.
Selection from Collection of Longer Works (Novels, Plays)	Williams, Tennessee. The Case of the Crushed Petunias: A Lyrical Fantasy. Ten Short Plays. Ed. Morton Jerome Weiss. New York: Dell, 1963. 31–53.
ARTICLES FROM MAGAZINES, NEWSPAPERS, AND JOURNALS	
Selection from Weekly Magazine Article	Chambers, Andrea. "In Winter, U.S. Writing Talent Pools on the Sensual, Timeless Port of Key West." People Weekly 23 Feb. 1981: 24–28.
Selection from Monthly or Quarterly Magazine Article	Berkvist, Robert. "The Big Daddy of Playwrights." After Dark Oct. 1981: 52–53.
Article with No Author Shown	"Tennessee Williams." Life Fall 1990: 78–79.
Daily Newspaper Article, with Byline	Blum, David J. "The Art and Anger of Tennessee Williams." Wall Street Journal 21 Nov. 1980: 29.
Daily Newspaper Article, No Byline	"Brandeis Presents Awards in the Arts." New York Times 29 Mar. 1965: 43.
Unsigned Daily Newspaper Editorial, No City in Title	"The Last Hurrah." Editorial. Star-Ledger [Newark, NJ] 29 Aug. 1991: 30.
Scholarly Journal	Click, Patricia C. "The Uncertain Universe of The Glass Menagerie: The Influence of the New Physics on Tennessee Williams." Journal of American Culture 12 (1989): 41–45.
Personal Interview	Williams, Tennessee. Personal interview. 5 Mar. 1981.
Telephone Interview	Miller, Arthur. Telephone interview. 8 Oct. 1966.
Published Interview	Williams, Tennessee. Interview. More Memoirs of an Aesthete. Ed. Harold Acton. London: Methuen, 1970.

Other Sources	
Radio or Television Interview	Morrison, Toni. Interview with Susan Stamberg. All Things Considered. Natl. Public Radio. WNYC, New York. 15 Jan. 1986.
Thesis or Dissertation	Fisher, Kerk. "The Front Porch in Modern American Drama: The Promise of Mobility in O'Neill, Williams, and Inge." Diss., U of Georgia, 1989.
Cartoon	Frascino, Edward. Cartoon. The New Yorker 2 Sept. 1991: 46.
Speech or Lecture	King, Rev. Martin Luther, Jr. "I Have A Dream." Lincoln Memorial. Washington, 28 Aug. 1963.
Recording	Robeson, Paul. "Going Home." Rec. 9 May 1958. Live at Carnegie Hall—1958. Vanguard, 1986.
Film, Filmstrip, or Videotape	A Streetcar Named Desire. Dir. John Erman. Perf. Ann-Margret, Treat Williams, Beverly D'Angelo, and Randy Quaid. Worldvision Enterprises, 1983.

Taking Essay Tests

Essay tests require you to think critically and express your understanding of selected material. Your answers to essay questions must be organized and complete with supporting details. A well-written answer must always be a complete response to the question asked and must contain sufficient information to demonstrate that you have thorough knowledge of the material.

Scan the questions on the test before you start writing. Determine how many questions you must answer, and decide which ones you can answer best. Plan the amount of time you have to spend on each question, and stay on this schedule. As you get ready to write, keep the following steps in mind.

1. Read each essay question carefully, and notice whether a question has several parts. Rewrite the question as a main idea for your answer.
2. Pay attention to the important terms in the question. Find the key verbs, and identify the tasks you must accomplish in your essay. Identify how much evidence is required for an adequate treatment.
3. Take a few minutes to use prewriting strategies. Make notes or a simple outline on scratch paper, organize your material logically, and write a thesis statement. Write one paragraph for each point you wish to make, and end with a paragraph that summarizes or restates your main points.
4. Evaluate and revise as you write. Keep your paper neat, and watch for spelling and grammatical errors. You will not have time to redraft the entire essay, but you can edit to strengthen specific parts.

Essay questions usually ask you to perform specific tasks expressed by the verb in the question. The following chart lists key verbs and the information called for in each task.

Essay Test Questions		
Key Verb	**Task**	**Sample Question**
analyze	Take something apart to see how it works.	Analyze the character of Captain Ahab in *Moby-Dick*.
argue	Take a stand on an issue, and give reasons supporting your opinion.	Argue whether your school should close its campus during lunch periods to keep students on campus.

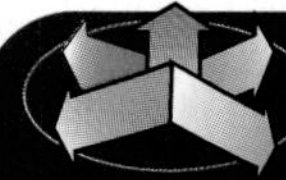

Program Manager

Instructional Support For instructional support and practice test items, see **Standardized Test Preparation,** pp. 281–312, in the ***Test Booklet.***

Key Verb	Task	Sample Question
compare/contrast	Discuss likenesses/differences.	Compare and contrast Hawkeye in Cooper's novel *The Last of the Mohicans* with Hawkeye in the movie of the same name.
define	Give specific details that make something unique.	Define the term *modernism* as it relates to literature.
demonstrate (also illustrate, present, and show)	Provide examples to support a point.	Demonstrate T. S. Eliot's use of symbolism to express feelings in his poetry.
describe	Give a picture in words.	Describe an incident in *Death of a Salesman* that features Linda Loman.
discuss	Examine in detail.	Discuss the elements of realism in Tennessee Williams's *The Glass Menagerie*.
explain	Give reasons.	Explain why Williams uses glass as a symbol in *The Glass Menagerie*.
identify	Discuss specific persons, places, things, or characteristics.	Identify the characteristics of realistic drama.
interpret	Give the meaning or significance of something.	Interpret the symbolism in *The Glass Menagerie*.
list (also outline, trace)	Give all steps in order or all details about a subject.	Outline the events that lead to the death of Willy Loman in *Death of a Salesman*.
summarize	Give a brief overview of the main points.	Summarize the plot of Amy Tan's *The Joy Luck Club*.

Giving Speeches and Debating with Others

PREPARING AND PRESENTING A SPEECH

Your first step in preparing a speech is to choose a topic, keeping in mind what you want to accomplish by giving the speech, the occasion, and the amount of time you will have to deliver it. The topic must be of interest to both you and your audience. Also consider what your audience already may know about your topic and what new information you can find.

Organizing Your Speech and Materials

Once you have determined your topic, you can begin to gather and organize information for your speech. Follow the same basic process as you would for writing a paper, organizing your information into an outline. Prepare your speech note cards according to the guidelines that follow.

GUIDELINES FOR SPEECH NOTE CARDS

1. Put only one key idea, possibly accompanied by a brief example or detail, on each card. Use key words and phrases rather than complete sentences.
2. Make a special note card for material that you plan to read word for word, such as a quotation, series of dates, or list of statistics.
3. Make a special note card to indicate when you should show a visual aid, such as a chart, diagram, graph, picture, or model.
4. Number your completed cards to keep them in order.

Practicing Your Speech

Practice your speech as often as you can before an audience of friends or family to make the setting more realistic and to get feedback. If you don't have an audience, practice in front of a mirror. Record your speech and use the playback to note areas that need improvement. If you plan to use any visual aids, prepare them in advance so that you can practice with them. Any point you are trying to emphasize with pictures, charts, maps, or diagrams will be lost if you fumble with your materials. Time your speech to be sure it falls within the time guidelines.

Using Body Language Using body language skillfully can reinforce your verbal message and emphasize points of your speech. Body language includes facial expressions, eye contact, gestures, posture, and movement. Practice using different expressions and gestures until they look and feel natural.

Using Your Voice Speak clearly and loudly enough for everyone in your audience to hear what you are saying. This sounds easy, but there are different aspects of speaking that affect how you sound to others: pitch, volume, stress, and rate.

- **Pitch** is the highness or lowness of a sound, the natural rise and fall of your voice. Use pitch to emphasize various ideas, and avoid a monotone.
- **Volume** is the loudness or intensity of sound. You need to be loud enough to be heard when you are speaking. You also can increase or decrease your volume for emphasis as you speak. Try to practice speaking louder by using the muscles in your lower chest and stomach area. This will keep you from becoming tired and hoarse as you speak.
- **Stress** is the emphasis you place on important words or phrases to convey a point to your audience.
- **Rate** is the speed at which you talk. Deliver your speech at a comfortable, relaxed pace, using changes in rate to communicate emotion and drama to your listeners.

Delivering Your Speech

Try not to allow nervousness to distract you or affect your speaking. The following suggestions will help you deliver your speech confidently and effectively.

- Be prepared. Organize carefully, and become familiar with your speech notes and visual aids.
- Focus on your purpose for speaking. Think about what you want your listeners to do, believe, know, or feel as a result of your speech.

DEBATING WITH OTHERS

Speaking to Persuade in a Traditional Debate

Traditional debate, sometimes called **team debate** or **policy debate,** is a formal speaking contest with two teams arguing opposing sides of an issue. Debaters argue for or against a **proposition** that recommends a specific policy or action. Propositions are worded in a special way:

> *Resolved,* That television cameras should be prohibited from all courtroom proceedings, including criminal trials.

The **affirmative** team argues in favor of the policy stated in the proposition; the **negative** team opposes it.

Choosing a Debatable Issue

A debate proposition deals with a serious issue, one that people disagree about. You've probably heard such issues discussed on television news shows or seen them argued in newspaper columns and editorials. Brainstorm possible issues. Then try stating each issue as a proposition, suggesting a specific action.

Preparing for the Debate

Plan your **argument,** or **case,** to appeal to the particular audience you're talking to. You'll need two or three **reasons** (statements why the proposition should or should not be enacted) and lots of **evidence.**

Logical Fallacies In a debate, you want your thinking and your reasons to be logical so that your opponents will have difficulty finding weaknesses in your argument. Be on the lookout for fallacies. **Fallacies** may look and sound like reasons, but they aren't reasons—they are illogical thinking. The following examples show five common types of fallacies.

1. **Begging the Question** Something is presented as true that really needs to be proven. For example: *Our local newspaper's bias against nuclear energy is responsible for public opposition to the proposed plant.* (This assumes both that the newspaper coverage is biased and that it is the only reason for public opposition.)
2. **Attacking the Person** or **Ad Hominem ("to the person")** This is name-calling. For example: *People who oppose setting a lower speed limit in this neighborhood don't care about the lives of their own and others' children.* (Opponents are attacked instead of the issue itself being faced.)

COMMUNICATIONS HANDBOOK

3. **Hasty Generalization** A conclusion has been based on insufficient evidence, or it ignores exceptions. For example: *Today's films are loaded with sex, violence, and foul language.* (This is not true of all of today's films.)
4. **Either-Or Reasoning** Only two extreme alternatives are presented for a question or course of action. For example: *If funding for the space program is cut, the United States will destroy its own future.* (Funding cuts may have a negative impact on research, but the future of the country does not depend upon only one program.)
5. **False Analogy** An illogical, trivial, or misleading comparison is made between two things. For example: *Failing to train students for real-life jobs is like condemning them to death row.* (Although untrained workers may have difficulties in the job market, they haven't been sentenced to death, and they can take steps to improve their situation.)

Follow these steps to plan your argument.

1. **Gather relevant evidence.** Use library resources (reference books, periodicals, newspapers, databases) and radio and TV news, documentary, and interview programs. Evidence includes facts, statistics, and examples; **anecdotes** (brief stories) about real people based on your reading or direct experience; **analogies** (comparisons) that help your audience understand a point; and quotations by experts. Keep only relevant evidence that directly supports the points you intend to make and/or **refutes** (disproves) your opponents' views.
2. **Select the evidence you will use.** Choose at least two reasons and the strongest evidence you have to support them.
3. **Organize the evidence.** Write a rough outline of your argument. If you save the strongest reason for last, your listeners will remember it.
4. **Anticipate your opponents' arguments.** Each team makes **constructive speeches** that set forth the team's argument and **rebuttal speeches** that refute opponents' arguments. Plan to spend almost as much time preparing your rebuttal speeches as you spend building your argument.

Conducting the Debate

The following rules and format have been simplified for classroom debate.

1. Each speaker speaks without interruption.
2. Speakers are courteous to each other.
3. Speakers may refer to notes or read a paper.
4. Speakers must stay within the time limits.

The following chart shows a standard format for debate that many school teams follow.

TRADITIONAL DEBATE FORMAT

Speaker	Time	Subject
1 AFF	4 min.	Prove (provide evidence): Proposition should be enacted.
1 NEG	5 min.	Refute 1 AFF argument. Prove (provide evidence): Proposition should not be enacted.
2 AFF	5 min.	Refute 1 NEG argument. Rebuild AFF case with additional evidence.
2 NEG	5 min.	Refute 2 AFF argument. Rebuild NEG case with additional evidence.
1 AFF	3 min.	Refute 2 NEG argument. Summarize main points of affirmative team's arguments.
1 NEG	2 min.	Summarize main points of negative team's arguments.

Evaluating the Debate

The following criteria apply to all types of debate.

CRITERIA FOR EVALUATING A DEBATE

1. Are the speakers' arguments clear and well organized?
2. Do the speakers present relevant evidence to prove their points?
3. Do the speakers present sufficient evidence?
4. Do the speakers speak clearly? Can they be understood easily?
5. Do the speakers convincingly refute their opponents' arguments?
6. Do the speakers convincingly defend their arguments from their opponents' attacks?

GUIDELINES FOR DEBATERS

- State your opinion clearly at the outset and at the end of your speech. Support your opinion with strong reasons and evidence.
- Give your listeners a "road map." Tell them, for example, that there are three reasons you favor the proposition; then use the words *first, second,* and *third* to introduce each reason as you get to it.
- Stick to the topic; don't wander.
- Express your ideas as clearly as you can. Don't use difficult words when simple ones will do.
- Make eye contact with your audience as you speak.
- Sound confident. Try not to fill pauses with *uh*'s and *um*'s.

STRATEGIES FOR READING AND RESPONDING

As you read, you can use strategies that allow you to search for connections between your prior knowledge and the information you are reading. These strategies will make you a more active reader and will help you understand and remember what you read.

PREREADING STRATEGIES

Previewing the Text **Preview** an assignment or a book to get an overview of the organization. Read the title, author, and date; look at the charts and diagrams; skim a few pages to check the difficulty of the vocabulary; and read the table of contents and the index. Then try to state the overall idea of the material in a sentence or two. Finally, think about what you already know about the topic of the text and what you would like to learn as you read.

Making Connections As you read, you should allow your mind to go back to your prior knowledge and experiences to make **connections** to new text. For example, while reading "Daughter of Invention," Julia Alvarez's short story about conflict between cultures and generations, you may remember reading a story with a similar theme, Amy Tan's "Two Kinds."

Making Predictions **Predictions** are based on your specific knowledge about a topic and your general knowledge. To start the prediction process, ask yourself: *What will happen next? What will the author talk about next?* For example, the introduction of "Daughter of Invention" discusses how important the idea of inventing something is to the mother. Based on that information and on the title, you might predict that the daughter will resent the time her mother spends on the inventions and that the story will revolve around that conflict.

ACTIVE READING STRATEGIES

Metacognition **Metacognition** is thinking about how you think, analyzing your own thought processes. The prereading strategies of previewing, making connections, and making predictions are examples of metacognition. To analyze your own thinking-reading process, begin with questions such as *What do I know that will help me with this? How should I get started? What do I want to learn?* As you are reading, ask yourself *Have I answered my questions? Did my predictions check out? What new questions or predictions should I think about?* And when you've finished reading, review and evaluate your thinking-reading process with such questions as *What did I learn that I can use again? What did I learn that I didn't know before? Was I disappointed in any of the results? What would I do differently?*

Noting Organization As you read, think about the way the author has organized and developed ideas. Make notes about important ideas or events as they unfold. When you re-read your notes, the order of ideas and events will become clearer to you. Ideas generally are organized into four major patterns.

- **Chronological Order** Actions or events are arranged according to the order in which they happened. Words such as *first, then, next, while,* and *finally* guide the reader. This type of organization is also called **sequential order.**
- **Spatial Order** This pattern tells you where one object is in relation to other objects—nearest to farthest, left to right, or any other reasonable arrangement.

- **Order of Importance** If one detail or piece of information is more important than another, the writer may arrange ideas by order of importance, either starting with the most important or ending with the most important.
- **Logical Order** Ideas or objects are grouped or arranged to show how they are related. Examples of logical order include presenting information in terms of a cause-and-effect relationship and comparing and contrasting things to show similarities and differences.

Noting Context Clues for Unfamiliar Words or Phrases The **context** of a word or phrase—the surrounding words and sentences—can help you figure out its meaning. Useful context clues depend on three things.

- **What is on the page** A word or phrase may sometimes be defined within the text itself, as in the following sentence: *The aluminum shreds melt in the furnace and then flow into molds to form* ingots, *or* bars of metal.
- **What you already know** The more information you already have about a subject, the more useful the context clues will be.
- **The connections you make** Make the most from context clues by asking yourself these questions: *What type of text am I reading? What topic might this word relate to? What kind of word would fit at this point in the sentence? Do the surrounding words and sentences give clues to what the unfamiliar word means?*

If you cannot determine the meaning of an unfamiliar word from context clues, look at the parts of the word itself. **Prefixes, suffixes,** and **root words** are the building blocks of the word. Use what you know about these word parts to figure out the meaning of a word. (For more on context clues and word parts, see pages 168, 475, and 1120.)

You also can follow clues provided by the author or editor of the text. If the word in the text has a superscript number beside it, that directs you to a footnote. Additional information, and sometimes definitions, are included in footnotes. The book also may contain a glossary you can consult.

Making Inferences An **inference** is an educated guess based on information in the text and your prior knowledge and experience. As you read, you are constantly having to make inferences, or draw conclusions, about ideas and details that writers don't tell you directly. For example, when you read a story, you may make inferences about the theme and about the motivations and traits of the characters. In "Daughter of Invention," you may infer that the mother was hurt by her family's lack of interest in her inventions.

Making and Confirming Predictions When you read actively, you make **predictions** about what is going to happen next or what you think an author is going to say. The predictions you make may not be accurate, but accuracy is not important at this point. As you read new information, you add it to your prior knowledge. You reject incorrect predictions and make new ones. You repeat this process over and over as you read.

RESPONDING TO LITERATURE

Whenever and whatever you read, you have a response. You may like or dislike a character, think the article is boring, or disagree with a point made by the writer. Sometimes, particularly in school, you are asked to explain your response, to provide support for it. In order to do that, you need to think critically about your response and look back in the text to identify the details and facts that led you to draw a conclusion or form an opinion.

Drawing Conclusions

You understand certain things as you read even if they are not stated directly. As you read, you pick up clues, connect them to other things you have read and experienced, and then draw **conclusions.** For example, the clues in a short story may help you conclude that the main character is very unhappy. Or, while reading a persuasive essay, you may make connections to a current situation in your town and draw conclusions about the author's biases.

Forming and Supporting Opinions

An **opinion** expresses a personal belief, attitude, or point of view. It cannot be proved right or wrong. Because opinions are based on personal experiences, it is easy to see how people can have different opinions about the same subject. Opinions fall into two categories: valid (justifiable) opinions and invalid opinions. Valid opinions express personal attitudes that are supported with facts, examples, quotations, and other kinds of evidence. Invalid opinions express personal attitudes that are not supported with specific details or facts. Invalid opinions often are based on emotions.

While you are reading, you constantly form and revise your opinions about what is happening in the text. When reading a story, novel, or play, you can find evidence to support these opinions in a character's actions, words, or thoughts; specific details and facts in the text; and your own prior knowledge and experience. For example, it may be your opinion after reading "Daughter of Invention" that the mother actually wants to become more "American" herself. You can base this opinion on details in the story that describe the mother's nightly reading of *The New York Times,* her quick adoption of the English language and its colorful sayings, her lack of desire to return to the Dominican Republic, and her subtle diversion of her husband's thoughts of returning.

Using a Reader's Log

Before, during, and after reading, a Reader's Log can be an invaluable tool in which you explore your responses to literature. You can use any and all active reading strategies in Reader's Log entries. There is no one right way to use a Reader's Log, but here are some strategies that you may find helpful.

Double-Entry or Dialectical Journal Make two columns on a page. In the left-hand column, take notes on the material you're reading, or simply jot down quotations from the text. The notes can be very focused (perhaps you are looking specifically for examples of conflict) or very free and loose (you're writing down passages that puzzle you or capture your attention in some way). In the right-hand column, you write your responses to the left-hand column in a kind of dialogue, reflecting on the text in any way that has meaning for you. You can also use the double-entry format to explore your speculations about causes and effects, comparisons and contrasts, problems and solutions, and differing interpretations.

Quickwrite Write quickly and without planning, perhaps responding to a prereading question in the text or a question your teacher has posed. A quickwrite can help you realize what you already know, make predictions about what you are about to read, or help you relate what you're about to read to your own experience.

Story Mapping Making a story map in your Reader's Log can help you get a better grasp of the plot. In a sequence of linked boxes, write the main events of the story in order.

Venn Diagram Use a Venn diagram—two overlapping circles—to indicate visually the similarities and differences between two characters, two settings, two stories, or any other two elements you're comparing.

KWL Chart Make a three-column chart. In the first column, write what you already know (K) about the work, the subject, or anything else in the selection. In the middle column, write what you want to know (W) while you're reading or after you've finished the selection. In the last column, record what you've learned (L) as an outcome of your reading.

Clustering You can explore your knowledge of a character, theme, plot, or any other aspect of a story or poem by using clustering. In the middle of a page, write and circle a subject—perhaps the name of a character. Then write words and ideas in balloons radiating out from the subject—perhaps key words and phrases to describe the character.

Brainstorming By yourself, or with a group, you can explore all your associations to a work of literature by writing down as many ideas as possible about the subject you are exploring—your thoughts about a character's possible motivations, for example, or your associations to particular imagery.

Discussing What You've Read

Explaining and Supporting Your Responses
You respond differently than other readers to what you read because you and your experiences are unique. Even so, when you are asked to respond to a selection you have read, you need to support that response with evidence.

Supporting your response helps you clarify your own thinking, helps your teacher understand the thinking behind your response, and may provide others with a new and fresh way of looking at the situation. Whether you are describing what you liked or didn't like about a selection, a conclusion that you drew, or an inference about a character's motivation, you should support your response with relevant evidence from the text or experiences from your own life.

Working in Groups In many of your classes, you work in groups with other students. Often the purpose of a group is to complete a task or solve a problem. Sometimes the purpose of a group is to discuss and share ideas on a particular topic. In such a group, you may share information you have gathered, your opinions about something you have read, or your questions and concerns. Being part of a student group requires that you do your part and come prepared for group meetings, whether you are the chairperson, the recorder, or another participant.

Deciding What to Share When you are participating in a discussion group, consider what you want to share. You may have certain personal issues related to the selection that you do not want to share with others. Don't feel pressured or obligated to talk about these issues. You can participate by discussing the task or topic on a nonpersonal basis. Respect for the privacy of each student is a key part of any good group experience.

PROGRAM MANAGER

- **Independent Practice or Reteaching** Use *Language and Writing Skills Worksheets,* pp. 11–24.
- **Practice** See *Language Workshop: Chapter 1: Parts of speech.*

1 The Parts of Speech

PART OF SPEECH	DEFINITION	EXAMPLES
NOUN	Names person, place, thing, or idea	poet, Sylvia Plath, city, Chicago, awards, Nobel Prize, *Of Mice and Men,* books, crew, herd, Harlem Renaissance, realism, stick-in-the-mud
PRONOUN	Takes place of one or more nouns	
Personal	Refers to one(s) speaking (first person), spoken to (second person), spoken about (third person)	I, me, my, mine, we, us, our, ours you, your, yours he, him, his, she, her, hers, it, its, they, them, their, theirs
Reflexive	Refers to subject and directs action of verb back to subject	myself, ourselves, yourself, yourselves, himself, herself, itself, themselves
Intensive	Refers to and emphasizes noun or another pronoun	(same as examples for Reflexive)
Demonstrative	Refers to specific one(s) of group	this, that, these, those
Interrogative	Introduces question	what, which, who, whom, whose
Relative	Introduces subordinate clause	that, which, who, whom, whose
Indefinite	Refers to one(s) not specifically named	all, any, anyone, both, each, either, everybody, many, none, nothing, someone
ADJECTIVE	Modifies noun or pronoun by telling *what kind, which one, how many,* or *how much*	**a large black** box, **an able-bodied** worker, **that** one, **the five Iroquois** nations, **enough** time, **less** money, **many** choices
VERB	Shows action or state of being	
Action	Expresses physical or mental activity	write, receive, run, think, imagine, understand
Linking	Connects subject with word identifying or describing it	appear, be, seem, become, feel, look, smell, sound, taste
Helping	Assists another verb to express time, voice, or mood	be, have, may, can, shall, will, would
ADVERB	Modifies verb, adjective, or adverb by telling *how, when, where,* or *to what extent*	speaks **clearly, quite** interesting, **rather** calmly, arrived **there late**
PREPOSITION	Relates noun or pronoun to another word	about, at, by, for, of, in, on, through, according to, in front of, out of

(continued)

PART OF SPEECH	DEFINITION	EXAMPLES
CONJUNCTION	Joins words or word groups	
Coordinating	Joins words or word groups used in same way	and, but, for, nor, or, so, yet
Correlative	Pair of conjunctions that join words or word groups used in same way	both . . . and, not only . . . but (also), either . . . or, neither . . . nor
Subordinating	Begins subordinate clause and connects it to independent clause	although, as if, because, since, so that, unless, when, where, while
INTERJECTION	Expresses emotion	hey, oh, ouch, wow, well, hooray

2 Agreement

AGREEMENT OF SUBJECT AND VERB

2a. A verb should agree in number with its subject. Singular subjects take singular verbs. Plural subjects take plural verbs.

SINGULAR The **character lives** on a farm in Yoknapatawpha County.
PLURAL **Both** of the stories **were written** by William Faulkner.

2b. The number of the subject is not changed by a phrase or a clause following the subject.

SINGULAR **Langston Hughes,** who wrote several books of poetry, **was** a major figure in the Harlem Renaissance.
PLURAL **The students,** as well as Ms. Ramos, **are** eager to use the new software.

2c. Indefinite pronouns may be singular, plural, or either.

(1) The following indefinite pronouns are singular: *anybody, anyone, anything, each, either, one, everybody, everyone, everything, neither, nobody, no one, nothing, somebody, someone,* and *something.*

EXAMPLE
Neither of the books **contains** that story.

(2) The following indefinite pronouns are plural: *both, few, many,* and *several.*

EXAMPLE
Both of the poems **were written** by Claude McKay.

(3) The indefinite pronouns *all, any, most, none,* and *some* are singular when they refer to singular words and are plural when they refer to plural words.

SINGULAR **Some** of her artwork **is** beautiful. [*Some* refers to *artwork.*]
PLURAL **Some** of her paintings **are** beautiful. [*Some* refers to *paintings.*]

2d. A *compound subject,* which is two or more subjects that have the same verb, may be singular, plural, or either.

(1) Subjects joined by *and* usually take a plural verb.

EXAMPLE
Hemingway, Steinbeck, and Morrison are Nobel Prize winners.

A compound subject that names only one person or thing takes a singular verb.

EXAMPLE
Roderick Usher's **sister and** sole **companion is** Madeline.

(2) Singular subjects joined by *or* or *nor* take a singular verb.

EXAMPLES
Either Amy or Eric plans to report on William Byrd.
Neither the **rain nor** the **wind has stopped.**

(3) When a singular subject and a plural subject are joined by *or* or *nor,* the verb agrees with the subject nearer the verb.

EXAMPLE
Neither the **performers nor** the **director was** eager to rehearse.

- **Independent Practice or Reteaching** Use *Language and Writing Skills Worksheets,* pp. 25–34.
- **Practice** See *Language Workshop: Chapter 2: Agreement.*

NOTE Whenever possible, revise the sentence to avoid this awkward construction.

EXAMPLE
The **director was** not eager to rehearse the scene again, and neither **were** the **performers.**

2e. **The verb agrees with its subject even when the verb precedes the subject, such as in sentences beginning with *here, there,* or *where*.**

EXAMPLES
Here **is** [*or* **here's**] a **copy** of the Declaration of Independence.
Here **are** [*not* here's] two **copies** of the Declaration of Independence.

2f. **A *collective noun* (such as *class, herd,* or *jury*) is singular in form but names a group of persons or things. A collective noun takes a singular verb when the noun refers to the group as a unit and takes a plural verb when the noun refers to the parts or members of the group.**

SINGULAR The **cast** of *A Raisin in the Sun* **is made** up entirely of juniors. [The cast as a unit is made up of juniors.]
PLURAL After the play, the **cast are joining** their families for a celebration. [The members of the cast are joining their families.]

2g. **An expression of an amount (a length of time, a statistic, or a fraction, for example) is singular when the amount is thought of as a unit or when it refers to a singular word. An amount is plural when it is thought of as many parts or when it refers to a plural word.**

SINGULAR **Twenty years was** a long time for Rip Van Winkle to sleep. [one unit]
PLURAL **Fifty percent** of the students **have** already **read** *Walden*. [The percentage refers to *students.*]

Expressions of measurement (length, weight, capacity, area) are usually singular.

EXAMPLES
Seventy-five degrees below zero was the air temperature the man in "To Build a Fire" suffered.
Four and a half miles was how far the man walked in an hour.

2h. **The title of a creative work (such as a book, song, film, or painting) or the name of an organization, a country, or a city (even if the name is plural in form) takes a singular verb.**

EXAMPLES
"Birches" was written by Robert Frost.
The **United States calls** its flag Old Glory.

2i. **A verb agrees with its subject, not with its predicate nominative.**

SINGULAR One **symptom** of flu **is** sore muscles.
PLURAL Sore **muscles are** one symptom of flu.

AGREEMENT OF PRONOUN AND ANTECEDENT

A pronoun usually refers to a noun or another pronoun. The word to which a pronoun refers is called its ***antecedent.***

2j. **A pronoun agrees with its antecedent in number and gender. Singular pronouns refer to singular antecedents. Plural pronouns refer to plural antecedents. A few singular pronouns indicate gender (neuter, feminine, masculine).**

EXAMPLES
Marianne Moore published **her** first book of poems in 1921. [singular, feminine]
Peyton Farquhar thinks **he** has escaped. [singular, masculine]
Benjamin Franklin wrote, "**Three** may keep a secret if two of **them** are dead." [plural]

2k. **Indefinite pronouns may be singular, plural, or either.**

(1) Singular pronouns are used to refer to the indefinite pronouns *anybody, anyone, anything, each, either, everybody, everyone, everything, neither, nobody, no one, nothing, one, somebody, someone,* and *something.* The gender of any of these pronouns is determined by a word in the phrase following the pronoun.

EXAMPLES
Each of the **girls** has already memorized **her** part.
One of the **boys** gave **his** interpretation of "Nothing Gold Can Stay."

If the antecedent may be either masculine or feminine, use both the masculine and feminine pronouns to refer to it.

EXAMPLE
Anyone who is qualified for the job may submit **his** or **her** application.

Whenever possible, revise the sentence to avoid this awkward construction.

EXAMPLE
Anyone who is qualified for the job may submit an application.

(2) Plural pronouns are used to refer to the indefinite pronouns *both, few, many,* and *several.*

EXAMPLE
Both of the finalists played **their** best.

(3) Singular or plural pronouns may be used to refer to the indefinite pronouns *all, any, most, none,* and *some.* These indefinite pronouns are singular when they refer to singular words and are plural when they refer to plural words.

SINGULAR **All** of our **planning** achieved **its** purpose.
PLURAL **All** of your **suggestions** had **their** good points.

2l. A plural pronoun is used to refer to two or more singular antecedents joined by *and.*

EXAMPLE
Jerry and Francesca read the sonnets **they** wrote about Olaudah Equiano.

2m. A singular pronoun is used to refer to two or more singular antecedents joined by *or* or *nor.*

EXAMPLE
Neither **Cindy nor Carla** thinks **she** is ready to write the final draft.

2n. When a singular and a plural antecedent are joined by *or* or *nor,* the pronoun agrees with the nearer antecedent.

EXAMPLE
Either **Jerry or** the **twins** will bring **their** stereo.

Revising Misleading Sentences

Sentences with antecedents joined by *or* or *nor* can be misleading when the antecedents are of different genders or numbers. Revise the sentences to avoid such constructions.

MISLEADING Either Christopher or Tiffany will give her report on Transcendentalism. [The sentence suggests that Christopher may give Tiffany's report.]
REVISED Either **Christopher** will give **his** report on Transcendentalism, or **Tiffany** will give **hers.**

2o. A collective noun (such as *audience, family,* or *team*) takes a singular pronoun when the noun refers to the group as a unit and takes a plural pronoun when the noun refers to the parts or members of the group.

SINGULAR The **debate club** elected **its** new officers.
PLURAL The **debate club** will practice **their** speeches in this week's workshop.

2p. The title of a creative work (such as a book, song, film, or painting) or the name of an organization, a country, or a city (even if it is plural in form) takes a singular pronoun.

EXAMPLES
The teacher read **"Mushrooms"** and then asked me to interpret **it.**
Anderson Outfitters advertises **itself** as "the first step in getting away from it all."

3 Using Verbs

REGULAR AND IRREGULAR VERBS

Every verb has four basic forms called the ***principal parts:*** the *base form,* the *present participle,* the *past,* and the *past participle.* A verb is classified as *regular* or *irregular* depending on the way it forms the past and past participle.

3a. A *regular verb* forms the past and past participle by adding *–d* or *–ed* to the base form. An *irregular verb* forms the past and the past participle in some other way.

The following examples include *is* and *have* in parentheses to show that helping verbs are used with the present participle and past participle forms.

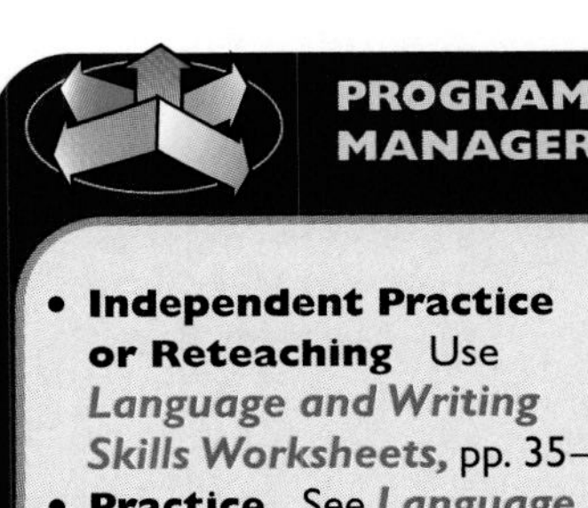

PROGRAM MANAGER

- **Independent Practice or Reteaching** Use *Language and Writing Skills Worksheets,* pp. 35–48.
- **Practice** See *Language Workshop:* Chapter 3: Using verbs correctly.

COMMON REGULAR AND IRREGULAR VERBS			
BASE FORM	PRESENT PARTICIPLE	PAST	PAST PARTICIPLE
REGULAR			
ask	(is) asking	asked	(have) asked
attack	(is) attacking	attacked	(have) attacked
drown	(is) drowning	drowned	(have) drowned
plan	(is) planning	planned	(have) planned
try	(is) trying	tried	(have) tried
use	(is) using	used	(have) used
IRREGULAR			
be	(is) being	was, were	(have) been
begin	(is) beginning	began	(have) begun
catch	(is) catching	caught	(have) caught
drink	(is) drinking	drank	(have) drunk
drive	(is) driving	drove	(have) driven
go	(is) going	went	(have) gone
lend	(is) lending	lent	(have) lent
shake	(is) shaking	shook	(have) shaken
swim	(is) swimming	swam	(have) swum
tear	(is) tearing	tore	(have) torn
throw	(is) throwing	threw	(have) thrown

Before adding the suffix *–ing* or *–ed* to form the present participle or the past or past participle of a verb, double the final consonant if the base form satisfies both of these conditions:
(1) It has only one syllable or has the accent on the last syllable.
(2) It ends in a single consonant preceded by a single vowel.

EXAMPLES
grin + -ing = grin**ning**
refer + -ed = refer**red**

See page 1250 for exceptions.

If you are not sure about the principal parts of a verb, look in a current dictionary. Entries for irregular verbs give the principal parts. If no principal parts are listed, the verb is a regular verb.

TENSES AND THEIR USES

3b. The *tense* of a verb indicates the time of the action or the state of being expressed by the verb.

(1) The ***present tense*** is used mainly to express an action or a state of being that is occurring now.

EXAMPLE
We **understand** now.

The present tense is also used

- to show a customary or habitual action or state of being
- to convey a general truth—something that is always true
- to make a historical event seem current (such use is called the ***historical present***)
- to summarize the plot or subject matter of a literary work or to refer to an author's relationship to his or her work (such use is called the ***literary present***)
- to express future time

EXAMPLES
For breakfast I **eat** cereal and **drink** orange juice. [customary action]
The earth **revolves** once around the sun each year. [general truth]
Several of the *Mayflower* passengers **die** before the ship **reaches** Plymouth. [historical present]
Moby-Dick **tells** the story of a man who **pursues** a white whale. [literary present]
The workshop **begins** tomorrow. [future time]

(2) The ***past tense*** is used to express an action or a state of being that occurred in the past but did not continue into the present.

EXAMPLES
Pepe **grabbed** his rifle and **crawled** into the brush.

(3) The ***future tense*** (*will* or *shall* + base form) is used to express an action or a state of being that will occur.

EXAMPLES
Elisa **will play** the part of Beneatha Younger.
I **will** [*or* **shall**] **serve** as her understudy.

(4) The ***present perfect tense*** (*have* or *has* + past participle) is used mainly to express an action or a state of being that occurred at some indefinite time in the past.

EXAMPLE
Have you **read** any stories by Sandra Cisneros?

The present perfect tense is also used to express an action or a state of being that began in the past and continues into the present.

EXAMPLE
My sister **has been** a Girl Scout for two years.

(5) The ***past perfect tense*** (*had* + past participle) is used to express an action or a state of being that was completed in the past before another action or state of being occurred.

EXAMPLE
Miss Emily returned the tax notice that she **had received.**

Use the past perfect tense in "if" clauses that express the earlier of two past actions.

EXAMPLE
If he **had taken** [*not* would have taken *or* took] more time, he would have won.

(6) The ***future perfect tense*** (*will have* or *shall have* + past participle) is used to express an action or a state of being that will be completed in the future before some other future occurrence.

EXAMPLE
By the time Rip Van Winkle returns to his village, the Revolutionary War **will have occurred.**

3c. Avoid unnecessary shifts in tense.

INCONSISTENT Shiftlet marries Lucynell and then abandoned her.
CONSISTENT Shiftlet **marries** Lucynell and then **abandons** her.
CONSISTENT Shiftlet **married** Lucynell and then **abandoned** her.

When describing events that occur at different times, use verbs in different tenses to show the order of events.

EXAMPLE
She now **works** for *The New York Times,* but she **worked** for *The Wall Street Journal* last year.

ACTIVE VOICE AND PASSIVE VOICE

3d. *Voice* is the form a verb takes to indicate whether the subject of the verb performs or receives the action.

A verb is in the ***active voice*** when its subject performs the action.

ACTIVE VOICE Julia Alvarez **wrote** "Daughter of Invention."

A verb is in the ***passive voice*** when its subject receives the action. A passive voice verb is always a verb phrase that includes a form of *be* and the past participle of an action verb.

PASSIVE VOICE "Daughter of Invention" **was written** by Julia Alvarez.

3e. Use the passive voice sparingly.

In general, the passive voice is less direct and less forceful than the active voice. In some cases, the passive voice may sound awkward.

AWKWARD PASSIVE A memorable speech was delivered by William Faulkner when the Nobel Prize was accepted by him in 1950.
ACTIVE William Faulkner delivered a memorable speech when he accepted the Nobel Prize in 1950.

The passive voice is useful

1. when you do not know the performer of the action
2. when you do not want to reveal the performer of the action
3. when you want to emphasize the receiver of the action.

EXAMPLES
Hemingway **was** severely **wounded** during the war.
Many careless errors **were made** in some of the essays about Amy Tan.
Madeline Usher **had been buried** alive!

4 Using Pronouns

CASE

Case is the form that a noun or a pronoun takes to indicate its use in a sentence. In English, there are three cases: *nominative, objective,* and *possessive.*

The form of a noun is the same for both the nominative case and the objective case. A noun changes form only in the possessive case. Unlike nouns, most personal pronouns have one form for each case. The form a pronoun takes depends on its function in a sentence.

PROGRAM MANAGER

- **Independent Practice or Reteaching** Use *Language and Writing Skills Worksheets,* pp. 49–60.
- **Practice** See ***Language Workshop:* Chapter 4: Using pronouns correctly.**

The Nominative Case

4a. **A subject of a verb is in the nominative case.**

EXAMPLES

They were happy that **he** was home from the war. [*They* is the subject of *were,* and *he* is the subject of *was.*]

4b. **A predicate nominative is in the nominative case.**

EXAMPLE

The one who jilts Granny Weatherall is **he.** [*He* follows *is* and identifies the subject *one.*]

The Objective Case

4c. **An object of a verb is in the objective case.**

EXAMPLES

My stepbrother and stepsister don't have driver's licenses yet, so I usually give **them** a ride to school. [*Them* is the direct object of the verb *give.*]

The Jazz Age collage earned **Donna and him** blue ribbons. [*Donna and him* is a compound indirect object of the verb *earned.*]

4d. **An object of a preposition is in the objective case.**

EXAMPLES

Did you send copies of *Blue Highways* to **her and him**? [*Her and him* is a compound object of the preposition *to.*]

The Possessive Case

4e. **A noun or a pronoun preceding a gerund is in the possessive case.**

EXAMPLE

Warren did not appreciate **Silas's** [*or* **his**] leaving during haying time. [*Silas's* (or *his*) modifies *leaving,* a gerund used as a direct object telling what Warren did not appreciate.]

SPECIAL PRONOUN PROBLEMS

4f. **An appositive is in the same case as the noun or pronoun to which it refers.**

EXAMPLES

The Ushers, **Madeline and he,** live in a gloomy mansion. [The appositive, *Madeline and he,* refers to the subject, *Ushers,* which is in the nominative case.]

Tom T. Shiftlet deceives both of them, **Mrs. Crater and her.** [The appositive, *Mrs. Crater and her,* refers to the object of the preposition, *them,* which is in the objective case.]

4g. **The pronoun *who* (*whoever*) is in the nominative case. The pronoun *whom* (*whomever*) is in the objective case.**

EXAMPLES

Who wrote *Dangling Man*? [*Who* is the subject of *wrote.*]

With **whom** did Moss Hart write the play? [*Whom* is the object of *with.*]

PERSONAL PRONOUNS			
SINGULAR			
	NOMINATIVE	OBJECTIVE	POSSESSIVE
FIRST PERSON	I	me	my, mine
SECOND PERSON	you	you	your, yours
THIRD PERSON	he, she, it	him, her, it	his, her, hers, its
PLURAL			
	NOMINATIVE	OBJECTIVE	POSSESSIVE
FIRST PERSON	we	us	our, ours
SECOND PERSON	you	you	your, yours
THIRD PERSON	they	them	their, theirs

NOTE Notice in the chart that *you* and *it* have the same forms for the nominative and the objective cases. All other personal pronouns have different forms for each case. Notice also that only third-person singular pronouns indicate gender.

For more information about possessive pronouns, see *its, it's* on page 1255, *their, there, they're* on page 1256, and *who's, whose* and *your, you're* on page 1257.

4h. **A pronoun ending in *–self* or *–selves* should not be used in place of a personal pronoun.**

EXAMPLE
Lupe and **I** [*not* myself] went to the ballet.

4i. **A pronoun following *than* or *as* in an elliptical construction is in the same case as it would be if the construction were completed.**

An ***elliptical construction*** is a clause from which words have been omitted. Notice how the meaning of each of the following sentences depends on the pronoun form in the elliptical construction.

NOMINATIVE CASE I have known Leigh longer **than she.** [I have known Leigh longer than she has known Leigh.]

OBJECTIVE CASE I have known Leigh longer **than her.** [I have known Leigh longer than I have known her.]

CLEAR PRONOUN REFERENCE

4j. **A pronoun should refer clearly to its antecedent. Avoid an ambiguous, a general, a weak, or an indefinite reference by (1) rephrasing the sentence, (2) replacing the pronoun with a noun, or (3) giving the pronoun a clear antecedent.**

AMBIGUOUS Jody talked to Billy Buck while he was working. [*He* refers to either antecedent, *Jody* or *Billy Buck.*]

CLEAR While Billy Buck was working, Jody talked to him.

CLEAR While Jody was working, he talked to Billy Buck.

GENERAL The wind rose, and dark clouds descended on the House of Usher. This seemed to bewilder Roderick. [*This* has no specific antecedent.]

CLEAR The wind rose, and dark clouds descended on the House of Usher. These ominous conditions seemed to bewilder Roderick.

CLEAR The rising wind and dark clouds that descended on the House of Usher seemed to bewilder Roderick.

WEAK He was superstitious. One of these was that walking under a ladder brings bad luck. [The antecedent of *these* is not expressed.]

CLEAR He was superstitious. One of his superstitions was that walking under a ladder brings bad luck.

CLEAR He believed in many superstitions, one of which was that walking under a ladder brings bad luck.

INDEFINITE In this history book, it refers to the American Civil War as the War Between the States. [*It* is unnecessary to the meaning of the sentence.]

CLEAR This history book refers to the American Civil War as the War Between the States.

LANGUAGE HANDBOOK

5 USING MODIFIERS

WHAT IS A MODIFIER?

A ***modifier*** is a word or group of words that limits the meaning of another word or group of words. The two kinds of modifiers are *adjectives* and *adverbs.*

COMPARISON OF MODIFIERS

5a. ***Comparison*** **refers to the change in the form of an adjective or an adverb to show increasing or decreasing degrees in the quality the modifier expresses.**

The three degrees of comparison are *positive, comparative,* and *superlative.*

(1) Most one-syllable modifiers form the comparative and superlative degrees by adding *–er* (*less*) and *–est* (*least*).

(2) Some two-syllable modifiers form the comparative and superlative degrees by adding *–er* and *–est;* others form the comparative and superlative degrees by using *more* and *most.* All two-syllable modifiers form decreasing comparisons by using *less* and *least.*

(3) Modifiers of more than two syllables form the comparative and superlative degrees by using *more* (*less*) and *most* (*least*).

PROGRAM MANAGER

- **Independent Practice or Reteaching** Use *Language and Writing Skills Worksheets,* pp. 61–70.
- **Practice** See *Language Workshop:* **Chapter 5: Using modifiers correctly.**

POSITIVE	COMPARATIVE	SUPERLATIVE
neat	neater	neatest
simple	less simple	least simple
calmly	more calmly	most calmly
optimistic	less optimistic	least optimistic

(4) Some modifiers form the comparative and superlative degrees in other ways.

POSITIVE	COMPARATIVE	SUPERLATIVE
bad	worse	worst
far	farther (further)	farthest (furthest)
good (well)	better	best
little	less	least
many (much)	more	most

5b. Use the comparative degree when comparing two things. Use the superlative degree when comparing more than two.

COMPARATIVE Although both puppies look cute, the **more active** one seems **healthier.**

SUPERLATIVE Of the four plays that we saw, I think *Death of a Salesman* was the **most moving.**

5c. Avoid a double comparison or a double negative. A *double comparison* is the use of two comparative forms (usually *–er* and *more*) or two superlative forms (usually *–est* and *most*) to modify the same word. A *double negative* is the use of two negative words when one is enough.

EXAMPLES

Samuel Clemens is **better** [*not* more better] known as Mark Twain.

She did**n't** say **anything** [*not* nothing]

5d. Include the word *other* or *else* when comparing one member of a group with the rest of the group.

EXAMPLE

Esteban is taller than anyone **else** on the team.

5e. Avoid comparing items that cannot logically be compared.

ILLOGICAL Hemingway's style is perhaps more imitated than any other American **writer.** [illogical comparison between a style and a writer]

LOGICAL Hemingway's style is perhaps more imitated than any other American **writer's (style).** [logical comparison of styles]

PLACEMENT OF MODIFIERS

5f. Avoid using a *misplaced modifier*—a modifying word, phrase, or clause that sounds awkward because it modifies the wrong word or group of words.

To correct a misplaced modifier, place the word, phrase, or clause as close as possible to the word or words you intend it to modify.

MISPLACED Thoreau listened intently to the song of a distant robin **looking at the glittering pond.** [Was the robin or Thoreau looking at the pond?]

CLEAR **Looking at the glittering pond,** Thoreau listened intently to the song of a distant robin.

For information about phrases, see Part 6: Phrases. For more on clauses, see Part 7: Clauses.

5g. Avoid using a *dangling modifier*—a modifying word, phrase, or clause that does not sensibly modify any word or words in a sentence.

You may correct a dangling modifier by

- adding a word or words that the dangling word, phrase, or clause can sensibly refer to
- adding a word or words to the dangling word, phrase, or clause
- rewording the sentence

DANGLING Alone, the mountain is virtually impossible to climb. [Who or what is alone?]

CLEAR **For a person alone,** the mountain is virtually impossible to climb.

CLEAR The mountain is virtually impossible **for a person** to climb **alone.**

DANGLING After winning the Pulitzer Prize, the novel *Maud Martha* was written. [Who won the Pulitzer Prize?]

CLEAR After winning the Pulitzer Prize, **Gwendolyn Brooks wrote** the novel *Maud Martha.*

CLEAR After **Gwendolyn Brooks won** the Pulitzer Prize, **she wrote** the novel *Maud Martha.*

6 Phrases

6a. **A *phrase* is a group of related words that is used as a single part of speech and that does not contain a verb and its subject.**

EXAMPLES

At two o'clock [adverb phrase], **the event of the year** [adjective phrase], **the company picnic** [noun phrase], **will commence** [verb phrase].

THE PREPOSITIONAL PHRASE

6b. **A *prepositional phrase* begins with a preposition and ends with the *object of the preposition,* a word or word group that functions as a noun.**

EXAMPLES

On the pillow was a strand **of gray hair.** [The noun *pillow* is the object of the preposition *on.* The noun *hair* is the object of the preposition *of.*]

Brian's Song is an inspiring story **about friendship and courage.** [Both *friendship* and *courage* are objects of the preposition *about.*]

(1) An ***adjective phrase*** is a prepositional phrase that modifies a noun or a pronoun. An adjective phrase follows the word it modifies. That word may be the object of another preposition.

EXAMPLES

Cassie Soldierwolf made a batch **of fry bread,** using a recipe very similar to that **of her ancestors.** [*Of fry bread* modifies the noun *batch. Of her ancestors* modifies the pronoun *that.*]

Sarah Kemble Knight kept a journal **of her trip to New York.** [*Of her trip* modifies the noun *journal. To New York* modifies *trip,* which serves as the object of the preposition *of.*]

More than one adjective phrase may modify the same word.

EXAMPLE

Sarah Kemble Knight's journey **on horseback from Boston to New York** was long and difficult. [*On horseback, from Boston,* and *to New York* modify the noun *journey.*]

(2) An ***adverb phrase*** is a prepositional phrase that modifies a verb, an adjective, or an adverb. An adverb phrase tells *how, when, where, why,* or *to what extent* (*how long* or *how far*).

More than one adverb phrase can modify the same word. Also, an adverb phrase, unlike an adjective phrase, can precede the word it modifies.

EXAMPLES

During the Civil War, Louisa May Alcott worked **in a hospital as a nurse for six weeks.** [Each phrase modifies the verb *worked. During the Civil War* tells *when, in a hospital* tells *where, as a nurse* tells *how,* and *for six weeks* tells *how long.*]

VERBALS AND VERBAL PHRASES

A ***verbal*** is a form of a verb used as a noun, an adjective, or an adverb. A ***verbal phrase*** consists of a verbal and its modifiers and complements.

Participles and Participial Phrases

6c. **A *participle* is a verb form that is used as an adjective. A *participial phrase* consists of a participle and all words related to the participle.**

There are two kinds of participles—the *present participle* and the *past participle.*

(1) **Present participles** end in *–ing.*

EXAMPLES

The explorer could hear something **moving in the brush.** [The participial phrase modifies the pronoun *something. In the brush* is an adverb phrase modifying the present participle *moving.*]

A mountain lion stood there **watching him.** [The participial phrase modifies the noun *mountain lion.* The pronoun *him* is the direct object of the present participle *watching.*]

(2) Most **past participles** end in *–d* or *–ed.* Others are irregularly formed.

EXAMPLES

Obsessed with revenge, Captain Ahab pursued the white whale. [The participial phrase modifies the noun *Captain Ahab.* The adverb phrase *with revenge* modifies the past participle *obsessed.*]

Samuel Clemens, **better known as Mark Twain,** was born in Florida, Missouri, in 1835. [The participial phrase modifies the noun *Samuel Clemens.* The adverb *better* and the adverb phrase *as Mark Twain* modify the past participle *known.*]

PROGRAM MANAGER

- **Independent Practice or Reteaching** Use *Language and Writing Skills Worksheets,* pp. 71–78.
- **Practice** See *Language Workshop:* Lessons 23–25: Prepositional phrases, Verbal phrases, and Appositive phrases.

Do not confuse a participle used as an adjective with a participle used as part of a verb phrase.

ADJECTIVE The Vietnam Veterans Memorial, **designed** by Maya Ying Lin, is made of black granite.

VERB PHRASE The Vietnam Veterans Memorial, which **was designed** by Maya Ying Lin, is made of black granite.

For information about misplaced participial phrases, see page 1228.

Gerunds and Gerund Phrases

6d. A *gerund* is a verb form ending in *–ing* that is used as a noun. A *gerund phrase* consists of a gerund and all words related to the gerund.

EXAMPLES

Exercising regularly is important for maintaining good health. [The gerund phrase is the subject of the verb *is.* The adverb *regularly* modifies the gerund *exercising.*]

Dexter enjoyed **working at the golf club.** [The gerund phrase is the direct object of the verb *enjoyed.* The adverb phrase *at the golf club* modifies the gerund *working.*]

Walter Mitty daydreamed of **being a pilot.** [The gerund phrase is the object of the preposition *of.* The noun *pilot* is a predicate nominative completing the meaning of the gerund *being.*]

One way to build your vocabulary is **reading good literature.** [The gerund phrase is a predicate nominative explaining the subject *way. Literature* is the direct object of the gerund *reading.*]

Do not confuse a gerund with a present participle used as an adjective or as part of a verb phrase.

GERUND I enjoy **reading** at night. [direct object of the verb *enjoy*]

PRESENT PARTICIPLE I sometimes fall asleep **reading** at night. [adjective modifying the pronoun *I*]

PRESENT PARTICIPLE Sometimes, I listen to classical music while I am **reading** at night. [part of the verb phrase *am reading*]

A noun or pronoun directly before a gerund takes the possessive case.

EXAMPLES

Grandad's cooking tastes great.

The bandleader said that he was pleased with **our** marching.

Infinitives and Infinitive Phrases

6e. An *infinitive* is a verb form that can be used as a noun, an adjective, or an adverb. An infinitive usually begins with *to.* An *infinitive phrase* consists of an infinitive and all words related to the infinitive.

NOUNS

To find Moby-Dick was Ahab's burning ambition. [The infinitive phrase is the subject of *was. Moby-Dick* is the direct object of the infinitive *to find.*]

Ahab's burning ambition was **to find Moby-Dick.** [The infinitive phrase is a predicate nominative identifying the subject *ambition.*]

ADJECTIVES

Napoleon's plan **to conquer the world** failed. [The infinitive phrase modifies the noun *plan. World* is the direct object of the infinitive *to conquer.*]

The one **to ask** is your guidance counselor. [The infinitive modifies the pronoun *one.*]

ADVERBS

With his dog Wolf, Rip Van Winkle went into the woods **to hunt squirrels.** [The infinitive phrase modifies *went. Squirrels* is the direct object of the infinitive *to hunt.*]

Nearly everyone was reluctant **to speak to her.** [The infinitive phrase modifies *reluctant.* The adverb phrase *to her* modifies the infinitive *to speak.*]

The word *to,* the sign of the infinitive, is sometimes omitted.

EXAMPLE

Will you help [to] dry the dishes?

Do not confuse an infinitive with a prepositional phrase that begins with *to.*

INFINITIVES **To have** a friend, you need **to be** a friend.

PREPOSITIONAL PHRASES Give one sample **to each** of the customers, and return the rest **to Rhonda.**

The Infinitive Clause

6f. Unlike other verbals, an infinitive may have a subject. Such a construction is called an *infinitive clause.*

EXAMPLE

Our teacher asked **us to read "Thanatopsis."** [*Us* is the subject of the infinitive *to read.* The entire infinitive clause is the direct object of *asked.*]

APPOSITIVES AND APPOSITIVE PHRASES

6g. An *appositive* is a noun or a pronoun placed beside (usually after) another noun or pronoun to identify or explain it. An *appositive phrase* consists of an appositive and its modifiers.

An appositive or appositive phrase usually follows the word it identifies or explains.

EXAMPLES

We went to the Navajo Gallery in Taos, New Mexico, to see R. C. Gorman's artwork ***Freeform Lady.*** [The appositive *Freeform Lady* identifies the noun *artwork.*]

Can you believe that I **myself** plan to become a writer? [The pronoun *myself* refers to the pronoun *I.*]

For emphasis, however, an appositive or appositive phrase may come at the beginning of a sentence.

EXAMPLE

A young painter, Jaune Quick-to-See Smith shows a deep awareness of her French, Shoshone, and Cree heritage.

Appositives are sometimes introduced by a colon or by the expressions *or, namely, such as, for example, i.e.,* or *e.g.*

EXAMPLES

The homeless shelter is accepting donations of the following items**:** canned **foods, blankets,** and winter **coats.**

Beneficial insects, such as **ladybugs** and **praying mantises,** can help control the population of harmful insects in a garden.

For information on how to punctuate appositives, see pages 1243–1244.

7 CLAUSES

7a. A *clause* is a group of words that contains a verb and its subject and that is used as part of a sentence. There are two kinds of clauses: the *independent clause* and the *subordinate clause.*

THE INDEPENDENT CLAUSE

7b. An *independent* (or *main*) *clause* expresses a complete thought and can stand by itself as a sentence.

EXAMPLE

SUBJECT VERB
Emily Dickinson wrote nearly eighteen hundred poems.

THE SUBORDINATE CLAUSE

7c. A *subordinate* (or *dependent*) *clause* does not express a complete thought and cannot stand alone as a sentence.

EXAMPLE

SUBJECT VERB
that **we** **read**

The thought expressed by a subordinate clause becomes complete when the clause is combined with an independent clause.

EXAMPLE

The last book **that we read** was *Blue Highways.*

The Adjective Clause

7d. An *adjective clause* is a subordinate clause that modifies a noun or a pronoun.

An adjective clause follows the word or words that it modifies. Usually, an adjective clause begins with a relative pronoun, which (1) relates the adjective clause to the word or words the clause modifies and (2) performs a function within the adjective clause.

EXAMPLE

Li recommends every poem **that Denise Levertov has written.** [The relative pronoun *that* relates the adjective clause to the noun *poem* and serves as the direct object of the verb *has written.*]

An adjective clause may begin with a relative adverb, such as *when* or *where.*

EXAMPLE

From 1914 to 1931, Isak Dinesen lived in Kenya, **where she operated a coffee plantation.**

PROGRAM MANAGER

- **Independent Practice or Reteaching** Use ***Language and Writing Skills Worksheets,*** pp. 79–84.
- **Practice** See ***Language Workshop:*** **Lessons 26–27: Clauses.**

Sometimes the relative pronoun or relative adverb is not expressed.

EXAMPLE
The book [that] **I am reading** is a biography.

The Noun Clause

7e. **A *noun clause* is a subordinate clause that may be used as a subject, a predicate nominative, a direct object, an indirect object, or an object of a preposition.**

Words commonly used to introduce noun clauses include *how, that, what, whether, who,* and *why.*

EXAMPLES
A catchy slogan is **what we will need for this campaign.** [predicate nominative]
Emerson liked **what Whitman wrote.** [direct object]
The director will give **whoever does best in this audition** the lead role. [indirect object]

The word that introduces a noun clause may or may not have another function in the clause.

EXAMPLES
Do any of you know **who wrote *Spoon River Anthology*?** [The word *who* introduces the noun clause and serves as subject of the verb *wrote.*]
She told Walter **that he was driving too fast and should slow down.** [The word *that* introduces the noun clause but does not have any function within the noun clause.]

The word that introduces a noun clause is not always expressed.

EXAMPLE
I think [that] **I've read all of Langston Hughes's poetry.**

The Adverb Clause

7f. **An *adverb clause* is a subordinate clause that modifies a verb, an adjective, or an adverb.**

An adverb clause, which may come before or after the word or words it modifies, tells *how, when, where, why, to what extent,* or *under what condition.* An adverb clause is introduced by a ***subordinating conjunction***—a word or word group that relates the adverb clause to the word or words the clause modifies.

EXAMPLES
William Cullen Bryant wrote the first version of "Thanatopsis" **when he was a teenager.** [The adverb clause modifies the verb *wrote,* telling *when* Bryant wrote the first version.]
Zoë can explain naturalism to you better **than I can.** [The adverb clause modifies the adverb *better,* telling *to what extent* Zoë can better explain naturalism.]

An adverb clause that begins a sentence is always set off by a comma.

The Elliptical Clause

7g. **Part of a clause may be left out when the meaning can be understood from the context of the sentence. Such a clause is called an *elliptical clause*.**

EXAMPLES
Roger knew the rules better **than Elgin [did].**
While [he was] living at Walden Pond, Thoreau wrote his first book.

For information about using pronouns in elliptical clauses, see page 1227.

8 Sentence Structure

SENTENCE OR FRAGMENT?

8a. **A *sentence* is a group of words that expresses a complete thought.**

EXAMPLE
Benjamin Franklin lived in London and in Paris.

Only a sentence should begin with a capital letter and end with either a period, a question mark, or an exclamation point. A group of words that looks like a sentence but does not make sense by itself is called a ***sentence fragment.***

FRAGMENT Collapses during a storm.
SENTENCE The House of Usher collapses during a storm.

For information about how to correct sentence fragments, see page 1236. For information about using end marks with sentences, see page 1242.

PROGRAM MANAGER

- **Independent Practice or Reteaching** Use *Language and Writing Skills Worksheets,* pp. 85–96.
- **Practice** See *Language Workshop:* Chapter 7: Sentences.

SUBJECT AND PREDICATE

8b. A sentence consists of two parts: a *subject* and a *predicate*. A *subject* tells *whom* or *what* the sentence is about. A *predicate* tells something about the subject.

In the following examples, all the words labeled *subject* make up the ***complete subject,*** and all the words labeled *predicate* make up the ***complete predicate.***

SUBJECT | PREDICATE
Walt Whitman | wrote *Leaves of Grass.*

PREDICATE | SUBJECT | PREDICATE
Why did | Phoenix | walk to town?

The Simple Subject

8c. A *simple subject* is the main word or group of words that tells *whom* or *what* the sentence is about.

EXAMPLE
Harold Krebs, the protagonist of the story, returns home from the war. [The complete subject is *Harold Krebs, the protagonist of the story.*]

The Simple Predicate

8d. A *simple predicate* is a verb or verb phrase that tells something about the subject.

EXAMPLE
Did Judy **marry** Dexter? [The complete predicate is *did marry Dexter.*]

The Compound Subject and the Compound Verb

8e. A *compound subject* consists of two or more subjects that are joined by a conjunction—usually *and* or *or*—and that have the same verb.

EXAMPLE
Reuben and **I** are preparing a report on "A Wagner Matinée."

8f. A *compound verb* consists of two or more verbs that are joined by a conjunction—usually *and, but,* or *or*—and that have the same subject.

EXAMPLE
Kendra **recognized** the song but **could** not **remember** its title.

How to Find the Subject of a Sentence

8g. To find the subject of a sentence, ask *Who?* or *What?* before the verb.

(1) The subject of a sentence is never within a prepositional phrase.

EXAMPLE
On the quarter-deck stood **Captain Ahab.** [Who stood? Captain Ahab stood. *Quarter-deck* is the object of the preposition *on.*]

(2) The subject of a sentence expressing a command or a request is always understood to be *you,* although *you* may not appear in the sentence.

COMMAND Identify two of the most striking characteristics of E. E. Cummings's poetry. [Who is being told to identify? *You* is understood.]

The subject of a command or a request is *you* even when a sentence contains a ***noun of direct address***—a word naming the one or ones spoken to.

REQUEST Jordan, [you] please read aloud Jimmy Santiago Baca's "Fall."

(3) The subject of a sentence expressing a question usually follows the verb or a part of the verb phrase. Turning the question into a statement will often help you find the subject.

QUESTION Was Pearl Buck awarded the Nobel Prize in literature in 1938? [Who was awarded?]
STATEMENT Pearl Buck was awarded the Nobel Prize in literature in 1938.

QUESTION Where is the dog's leash? [Where is what?]
STATEMENT The dog's leash is where.

(4) The word *there* or *here* is never the subject of a sentence.

EXAMPLE
Here are your **gloves.** [What are here? Gloves are.]

COMPLEMENTS

8h. A *complement* is a word or a group of words that completes the meaning of a verb. There are four main kinds of complements: *direct object, indirect object, objective complement,* and *subject complement.*

The Direct Object and the Indirect Object

8i. **A *direct object* is a word or word group that receives the action of a verb or that shows the result of the action. A direct object, which may be a noun, a pronoun, or a word group that functions as a noun, tells *whom* or *what* after a transitive verb.**

EXAMPLES

Kerry called **me** at noon. [called whom? me]

Captain Ahab sacrifices his **ship** and almost **all** of his crew. [sacrifices what? ship and all—compound direct object]

8j. **An *indirect object* is a word or word group that comes between a transitive verb and a direct object. An indirect object, which may be a noun, a pronoun, or a word group that functions as a noun, tells *to whom* or *to what* or *for whom* or *for what* the action of the verb is done.**

EXAMPLES

Emily Dickinson sent **Thomas Wentworth Higginson** four poems. [sent to whom? Thomas Wentworth Higginson]

Ms. Cruz showed **José** and **me** pictures of her trip to Walden Pond. [showed to whom? José and me—compound indirect object]

A sentence that has an indirect object must always have a direct object as well.

For more information about verbs, see Part 3: Using Verbs.

The Objective Complement

8k. **An *objective complement* is a word or word group that helps complete the meaning of a transitive verb by identifying or modifying the direct object. An objective complement, which may be a noun, a pronoun, an adjective, or a word group that functions as a noun or adjective, almost always follows the direct object.**

EXAMPLES

Everyone considered her **dependable.** [The adjective *dependable* modifies the direct object *her.*]

Many literary historians call Poe **the master of the macabre.** [The word group *the master of the macabre* modifies the direct object *Poe.*]

The Subject Complement

8l. **A *subject complement* is a word or word group that completes the meaning of a linking verb and identifies or modifies the subject. There are two kinds of subject complements: the *predicate nominative* and the *predicate adjective*.**

(1) A ***predicate nominative*** is the word or group of words that follows a linking verb and refers to the same person or thing as the subject of the verb.

A predicate nominative may be a noun, a pronoun, or a word group that functions as a noun.

EXAMPLES

Of the three applicants, Carlos is the most competent **one.** [The pronoun *one* refers to the subject *Carlos.*]

The main characters are **Aunt Georgiana** and **Clark.** [The nouns *Aunt Georgiana* and *Clark* refer to the subject *characters.*]

(2) A ***predicate adjective*** is an adjective that follows a linking verb and modifies the subject of the verb.

EXAMPLES

Eben Flood felt very **lonely.** [The adjective *lonely* modifies the subject *Eben Flood.*]

Shiftlet is **sly** and **scheming.** [The adjectives *sly* and *scheming* modify the subject *Shiftlet.*]

SENTENCES CLASSIFIED ACCORDING TO STRUCTURE

8m. **According to structure, sentences are classified as *simple, compound, complex,* and *compound-complex*.**

(1) A ***simple sentence*** has one independent clause and no subordinate clauses.

EXAMPLE

Thornton Wilder's *Our Town* is one of my favorite plays.

(2) A ***compound sentence*** has two or more independent clauses but no subordinate clauses.

EXAMPLE

Jack London was a prolific writer; he wrote nearly fifty books in less than twenty years. [two independent clauses joined by a semicolon]

Do not confuse a simple sentence that has a compound subject or a compound verb with a compound sentence.

(3) A ***complex sentence*** has one independent clause and at least one subordinate clause.

EXAMPLE
Before we read *The Great Gatsby,* let's talk about the Jazz Age. [The independent clause is *let's talk about the Jazz Age.* The subordinate clause is *before we read* The Great Gatsby.]

(4) A ***compound-complex*** sentence has two or more independent clauses and at least one subordinate clause.

EXAMPLE
The two eyewitnesses told the police officer what they saw, but their accounts of the accident were quite different. [The two independent clauses are *the two eyewitnesses told the police officer* and *their accounts of the accident were quite different.* The subordinate clause is *what they saw.*]

SENTENCES CLASSIFIED ACCORDING TO PURPOSE

8n. **Sentences may be classified according to purpose.**

(1) A ***declarative sentence*** makes a statement. It is followed by a period.

EXAMPLE
Swimming fast toward the ship was the white whale**.**

(2) An ***interrogative sentence*** asks a question. It is followed by a question mark.

EXAMPLE
Have you ever read *Blue Highways***?**

(3) An ***imperative sentence*** makes a request or gives a command. It is usually followed by a period. A strong command, however, is followed by an exclamation point.

EXAMPLES
Please give me the dates for the class meetings**.**
Read Act I of *A Raisin in the Sun* by tomorrow**.**
Help me**!**

(4) An ***exclamatory sentence*** expresses strong feeling or shows excitement. It is followed by an exclamation point.

EXAMPLE
What a noble leader he was**!**

9 SENTENCE STYLE

WAYS TO ACHIEVE CLARITY

Coordinating Ideas

9a. **To *coordinate* two or more ideas, or to give them equal emphasis, link them with a connecting word, an appropriate mark of punctuation, or both.**

EXAMPLE
Edgar Allan Poe wrote "The Raven"**;** Edgar Lee Masters wrote *Spoon River Anthology.*

Subordinating Ideas

9b. **To *subordinate* an idea, or to show that one idea is related to but less important than another, use an adverb clause or an adjective clause.**

An ***adverb clause*** begins with a subordinating conjunction, which shows how the adverb clause relates to the main clause. Usually, the relationship is *time, cause or reason, purpose or result,* or *condition.*

EXAMPLES
Whenever I think of Boston, I think of the Lowells. [time]
Janet got a lead role in *Our Town* **because she is one of the best actors in our school.** [cause]
Let's finish now, **so that we won't have to come back tomorrow.** [purpose]

An ***adjective clause*** usually begins with *who, whom, whose, which, that,* or *where.*

EXAMPLE
Tamisha is the one **whose essay won first prize.**

For more about adjective clauses and adverb clauses, see pages 1231–1232.

Using Parallel Structure

9c. **Use the same grammatical form (*parallel structure*) to express ideas of equal weight.**

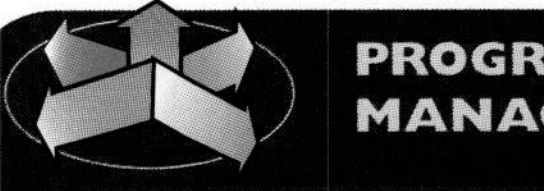

PROGRAM MANAGER

- **Independent Practice or Reteaching** Use *Language and Writing Skills Worksheets,* pp. 97–110.
- **Practice** See *Language Workshop:* Lessons 31–33 and 39–40: Obstacles to clarity, Ways to achieve clarity, Revising for variety, and Revising to reduce wordiness.

1. Use parallel structure when you link coordinate ideas.

EXAMPLE
The company guaranteed **that salaries would be increased and that working days would be shortened.** [noun clause paired with noun clause]

2. Use parallel structure when you compare or contrast ideas.

EXAMPLE
Thinking logically is as important as **calculating** accurately. [gerund compared with gerund]

3. Use parallel structure when you link ideas with correlative conjunctions (such as *both . . . and, either . . . or, neither . . . nor,* and *not only . . . but also*).

EXAMPLE
With *Ship of Fools,* Katherine Anne Porter proved she was talented not only **as a short-story writer** but also **as a novelist.** [Note that the correlative conjunctions come directly before the parallel terms.]

When you revise for parallel structure, you may need to repeat an article, a preposition, or a pronoun before each of the parallel terms.

UNCLEAR Through Kate Chopin's stories, we can learn almost as much about the author as the social condition of women in her era.

CLEAR Through Kate Chopin's stories, we can learn almost as much **about** the author as **about** the social condition of women in her era.

OBSTACLES TO CLARITY

Sentence Fragments

9d. **Avoid using a *sentence fragment*—a part of a sentence that has been punctuated as if it were a complete thought.**

Attach the fragment to the sentence that comes before or after it, or add words to the fragment to make it a complete sentence.

FRAGMENT Nina Otero was one of the first Mexican American women. To hold a major public post in New Mexico.

SENTENCE Nina Otero was one of the first Mexican American women **to hold a major public post in New Mexico.**

For more information about sentence fragments, see page 1232.

Run-on Sentences

9e. **Avoid using a *run-on sentence*—two or more complete thoughts that run together as if they were one complete thought.**

There are two kinds of run-on sentences.

- A ***fused sentence*** has no punctuation at all between the complete thoughts.
- A ***comma splice*** has just a comma between the complete thoughts.

FUSED SENTENCE Emerson praised Whitman's poetry most other poets sharply criticized it.

COMMA SPLICE Emerson praised Whitman's poetry, most other poets sharply criticized it.

You may correct a run-on sentence in one of the following ways. Depending on the relationship you want to show between ideas, facts, and other information, one method will often prove to be more effective than another.

1. Make two sentences.

EXAMPLE
Emerson praised Whitman's poetry**. M**ost other poets sharply criticized it.

2. Use a comma and a coordinating conjunction.

EXAMPLE
Emerson praised Whitman's poetry**, but** most other poets sharply criticized it.

3. Change one of the independent clauses to a subordinate clause.

EXAMPLE
Emerson praised Whitman's poetry, **while most other poets sharply criticized it.**

4. Use a semicolon.

EXAMPLE
Emerson praised Whitman's poetry**;** most other poets sharply criticized it.

5. Use a semicolon and a conjunctive adverb followed by a comma.

EXAMPLE
Emerson praised Whitman's poetry**; however,** most other poets sharply criticized it.

Unnecessary Shifts in Sentences

9f. Avoid making unnecessary shifts in subject, in verb tense, and in voice.

AWKWARD Athletes should be at the parking lot by 7:00 so that you can leave by 7:15. [shift in subject]
BETTER **Athletes** should be at the parking lot by 7:00 so that **they** can leave by 7:15.

AWKWARD She walked into the room, and she says, "The lights of the car outside are on." [shift in verb tense]
BETTER She **walked** into the room, and she **said,** "The lights of the car outside are on."

AWKWARD Russell Means starred as Chingachgook in *The Last of the Mohicans,* and an outstanding performance was delivered. [shift in voice]
BETTER Russell Means **starred** as Chingachgook in *The Last of the Mohicans* and **delivered** an outstanding performance.

REVISING FOR VARIETY

9g. Use a variety of sentence beginnings.

The following examples show how a writer can revise sentences to avoid beginning with the subject every time.

SUBJECT FIRST *Billy Budd* was published in 1924 and helped revive an interest in Melville's other works.
PARTICIPIAL PHRASE FIRST **Published in 1924,** *Billy Budd* helped revive an interest in Melville's other works.
PREPOSITIONAL PHRASE FIRST **In 1924,** *Billy Budd* was published and helped revive interest in Melville's other works.
ADVERB CLAUSE FIRST **When *Billy Budd* was published in 1924,** it helped revive interest in Melville's other works.

Varying Sentence Structure

9h. Use a mix of simple, compound, complex, and compound-complex sentences in your writing.

The following paragraph shows a mix of sentence structures.

San Francisco is famous for its scenic views. [simple] Because the city sprawls over forty-two hills, driving through San Francisco is like riding a roller coaster. [complex] Atop one of San Francisco's hills is Chinatown; atop another is Coit Tower. [compound] The most popular place to visit is the San Francisco Bay area, where the Golden Gate Bridge and Fisherman's Wharf attract a steady stream of tourists. [complex]

For information about the four types of sentence structure, see pages 1234–1235.

Revising to Reduce Wordiness

9i. Avoid using unnecessary words in your writing.

The following guidelines suggest some ways to revise wordy sentences.

1. Take out a whole group of unnecessary words.

WORDY After climbing down to the edge of the river, we boarded a small houseboat that was floating there on the surface of the water.
BETTER After climbing down to the edge of the river, we boarded a small houseboat.

2. Replace pretentious words and expressions with straightforward ones.

WORDY The young woman, who was at some indeterminate point in her teenage years, sported through her hair a streak of pink dye that could be considered extremely garish.
BETTER The **teenager** sported a streak of **shocking**-pink dye in her hair.

3. Reduce a clause to a phrase.

WORDY Emily Dickinson fell in love with Charles Wadsworth, who was a Presbyterian minister.
BETTER Emily Dickinson fell in love with Charles Wadsworth, **a Presbyterian minister.**

4. Reduce a phrase or a clause to one word.

WORDY One of the writers from the South was William Faulkner.
BETTER One of the **Southern** writers was William Faulkner.

PROGRAM MANAGER

- **Independent Practice or Reteaching** Use *Language and Writing Skills Worksheets,* pp. 111–118.
- **Practice** See *Language Workshop:* Lessons 37–38: Combining sentences by inserting words and phrases and Combining sentences by inserting clauses and coordinating ideas.

10 Sentence Combining

COMBINING SENTENCES FOR VARIETY

Combining by Inserting Words and Phrases

10a. Combine related sentences by taking a key word (or using another form of the word) from one sentence and inserting it into another.

ORIGINAL Jack London describes the man's attempt to build a fire. The description is vivid.

COMBINED Jack London **vividly** describes the man's attempt to build a fire. [The adjective *vivid* becomes the adverb *vividly.*]

10b. Combine related sentences by taking (or creating) a phrase from one sentence and inserting it into another.

ORIGINAL Our class is reading "Everyday Use." It is by Alice Walker.

COMBINED Our class is reading "Everyday Use" **by Alice Walker.** [prepositional phrase]

Combining by Coordinating Ideas

10c. Combine related sentences whose ideas are equally important by using coordinating conjunctions (*and, but, or, nor, for, yet*) or correlative conjunctions (*both . . . and, either . . . or, neither . . . nor, not only . . . but also*).

The relationship of the ideas determines which connective will work best. When joined, the coordinate ideas form compound elements.

ORIGINAL Robert Frost did not receive the Nobel Prize. Carl Sandburg never received it, either.

COMBINED **Neither Robert Frost nor Carl Sandburg** received the Nobel Prize.

You can also form a compound sentence by linking independent clauses with a semicolon and a conjunctive adverb or with just a semicolon.

EXAMPLE
We planned to go swimming**; however,** the weather did not oblige.

Combining by Subordinating Ideas

10d. Combine related sentences whose ideas are not equally important by placing the less important idea in a subordinate clause.

ORIGINAL The National Air and Space Museum is in Washington, D.C. It contains exhibits on the history of aeronautics.

COMBINED The National Air and Space Museum, **which contains exhibits on the history of aeronautics,** is in Washington, D.C. [adjective clause]

ORIGINAL Shiftlet married Lucynell. He wanted her mother's car.

COMBINED Shiftlet married Lucynell **because he wanted her mother's car.** [adverb clause]

ORIGINAL Judy Jones was married. Devlin told Dexter this.

COMBINED Devlin told Dexter **that Judy Jones was married.** [noun clause]

PROGRAM MANAGER

- **Independent Practice or Reteaching** Use *Language and Writing Skills Worksheets,* pp. 119–128.
- **Practice** See *Language Workshop:* Lessons 53–54: Conventional uses of capital letters and Rules of capitalization.

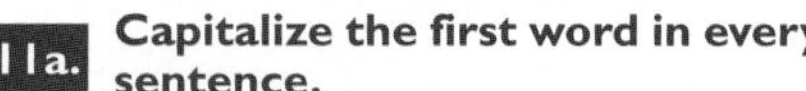

11 Capitalization

11a. Capitalize the first word in every sentence.

EXAMPLES
The author Leslie Marmon Silko was born in Albuquerque, New Mexico.
Stop!

(1) Capitalize the first word of a sentence following a colon.

EXAMPLE
The police commissioner issued a surprising statement: In light of new evidence, the investigation of the Brooks burglary will be reopened.

(2) Capitalize the first word of a direct quotation that is a complete sentence.

EXAMPLE
When he finally surrendered in 1877, Chief Joseph declared, "**F**rom where the sun now stands I will fight no more forever."

When quoting from another writer's work, capitalize the first word of the quotation only if the writer has capitalized it in the original work.

EXAMPLE
When he finally surrendered in 1877, Chief Joseph declared that he would "**f**ight no more forever."

For more information about using capital letters in quotations, see page 1246.

(3) Traditionally, the first word of a line of poetry is capitalized.

EXAMPLES
I placed a jar in Tennessee,
And round it was, upon a hill.
—Wallace Stevens, from "Anecdote of the Jar"

Some writers, for reasons of style, do not follow this rule. When you quote from a writer's work, always use capital letters exactly as the writer uses them.

11b. Capitalize the first word in the salutation and the closing of a letter.

EXAMPLES
Dear Maria, **D**ear Sir or Madam: **S**incerely,

11c. Capitalize proper nouns and proper adjectives.

A ***common noun*** is a general name for a person, place, thing, or idea. A ***proper noun*** is the specific name of a particular person, place, thing, or idea. A ***proper adjective*** is formed from a proper noun. Common nouns are capitalized only if they begin a sentence (also, in most cases, a line of poetry) or a direct quotation or are part of a title.

COMMON NOUNS	PROPER NOUNS	PROPER ADJECTIVES
poet	**H**omer	**H**omeric epithet
country	**R**ussia	**R**ussian diplomat
state	**H**awaii	**H**awaiian climate

In proper nouns made up of two or more words, do *not* capitalize articles (*a, an, the*), short prepositions (those with fewer than five letters, such as *at, of, for, to, with*), the mark of the infinitive (*to*), and coordinating conjunctions (*and, but, for, nor, or, so, yet*).

EXAMPLES
Army of the **P**otomac "**W**riting to **P**ersuade"

(1) Capitalize the names of persons and animals.

GIVEN NAMES	**J**ulia	**R**ichard
SURNAMES	**A**lvarez	**W**right
ANIMALS	**M**oby-**D**ick	**W**hite **F**ang

(2) Capitalize geographical names.

TYPE OF NAME	EXAMPLES	
Countries	**M**ozambique	**C**osta **R**ica
Continents	**N**orth **A**merica	**A**sia
Islands	**C**atalina **I**sland	**I**sle of **P**ines
Mountains	**B**lue **R**idge **M**ountains	**M**ount **M**cKinley
Other Land Forms and Features	**C**ape **C**od **M**ojave **D**esert	**I**sthmus of **P**anama **H**orse **C**ave
Bodies of Water	**G**reat **L**akes **A**mazon **R**iver	**S**trait of **H**ormuz **L**ake **H**uron
Parks	**M**ississippi **H**eadwaters **S**tate **F**orest **G**ates of the **A**rctic **N**ational **P**ark	
Roads, Highways, Streets	**R**oute 30 **I**nterstate 55 **P**ennsylvania **T**urnpike	**M**ichigan **A**venue **T**hirty-first **S**treet **M**orningside **D**rive

(*continued*)

NOTE The second word in a hyphenated number begins with a lowercase letter.

EXAMPLES
Forty-second **S**treet
Eighty-**n**inth **D**istrict

In addresses, abbreviations such as *St., Ave., Dr.,* and *Blvd.* are capitalized. For more about abbreviations, see pages 1242–1243.

TYPE OF NAME	EXAMPLES	
Towns, Cities	Boston South Bend	Rio de Janeiro St. Petersburg
Counties, Townships, Provinces	Yoknapatawpha County	Lawrence Township
States and Territories	Wisconsin Yukon Territory	Nuevo León The Virgin Islands
Regions	New England the Sunbelt	the West Coast the Southwest

Words such as *north* and *western* are not capitalized when they indicate direction.

EXAMPLES
east of the river   driving southeast

The abbreviations of names of states are always capitalized. For more about using and punctuating such abbreviations, see pages 1242–1243.

(3) Capitalize the names of organizations, teams, business firms, institutions, buildings and other structures, and government bodies.

TYPE OF NAME	EXAMPLES	
Organizations	National Science Foundation Guide Dog Foundation for the Blind	Future Farmers of America Disabled American Veterans
Teams	Detroit Pistons Harlem Globetrotters	Cedar Hill Bulldogs San Diego Padres
Business Firms	American Broadcasting Corporation University Square Mall	Hip-Hop Music, Inc. La Fiesta Restaurant
Institutions	University of California, Los Angeles the Library of Congress	Mayo Clinic Habitat for Humanity
Buildings and Other Structures	Meadowlawn Junior High School the Pyramid of Khufu	the Golden Gate Bridge Rialto Theater
Government Bodies	Atomic Energy Commission Federal Bureau of Investigation	United States Marine Corps House of Representatives

(4) Capitalize the names of historical events and periods, special events, holidays and other calendar items, and time zones.

TYPE OF NAME	EXAMPLES	
Historical Events and Periods	Boston Tea Party Battle of Saratoga Middle Ages	Roaring Twenties French Revolution Mesozoic Era
Special Events	Olympics Earth Summit	Ohio State Fair Sunshine Festival
Holidays and Other Calendar Items	Wednesday September	Fourth of July Hispanic Heritage Month
Time Zones	Mountain Standard Time (**MST**) Eastern Daylight Time (**EDT**)	

NOTE Do not capitalize the name of a season unless the season is being personified or unless it is used as part of a proper noun.

EXAMPLES
The winter was unusually warm.
Overnight, Winter crept in, trailing her snowy veil.
We plan to attend the school's Winter Carnival.

(5) Capitalize the brand names of business products.

EXAMPLES

Borden milk **C**olonial bread **Z**enith television

Notice in these examples that the noun that follows a brand name is not capitalized. Also, over time, some brand names become common nouns. To find out if a name is a brand name, consult a current dictionary.

(6) Capitalize the names of nationalities, races, and peoples.

EXAMPLES

Chinese **J**ewish **H**opi **C**aucasian

(7) Capitalize the names of ships, trains, aircraft, spacecraft, monuments, awards, planets, and any other particular places, things, or events.

TYPE OF NAME	EXAMPLES	
Ships	*Cunard Princess*	**U.S.S.** *Forrestal*
Trains	*Orient Express*	*North Coast Limited*
Aircraft	*Spirit of St. Louis*	*Air Force One*
Spacecraft	*Atlantis*	*Apollo 11*
Monuments	**L**incoln **M**emorial	**S**tatue of **L**iberty
Awards	**A**cademy **A**ward	**P**ulitzer **P**rize
Planets, Stars, Constellations	**J**upiter **U**rsa **M**inor	**O**rion the **M**ilky **W**ay
Other Particular Things, Places, and Events	**U**nderground **R**ailroad **S**ilk **R**oute **H**urricane **A**ndrew	**T**reaty **O**ak **V**alkyries **M**arshall **P**lan

NOTE Do not capitalize the words *sun* and *moon.* Do not capitalize the word *earth* unless it is used along with the names of other heavenly bodies that are capitalized.

EXAMPLES

This orchid grows wild in only one place on earth.

Venus is closer to the sun than **E**arth is.

11d. Do not capitalize the names of school subjects, except for names of languages and course names followed by a number.

EXAMPLES

Spanish chemistry **C**hemistry **II**

11e. Capitalize titles.

(1) Capitalize a title belonging to a particular person when it comes before the person's name. Also capitalize abbreviations such as *Jr., M.D.,* and *Ph.D.* after a name.

EXAMPLES

General Davis **M**s. Diaz **P**resident Kennedy
Rev. Martin Luther King, **J**r. **D**r. Kerry Jones, **M.D.**

In general, do not capitalize a title used alone or following a name. Some titles, however, are by tradition capitalized. If you are unsure of whether or not to capitalize a title, check in a dictionary.

EXAMPLE

Who is the **g**overnor of Kansas?

A title is usually capitalized when it is used alone in direct address.

EXAMPLE

Have you reached your decision, **G**overnor?

(2) Capitalize words showing family relationships except when preceded by a possessive.

EXAMPLES

Aunt Amy my **a**unt **M**other Bill's **m**other

(3) Capitalize the names of religions and their followers, holy days and celebrations, holy writings, and specific deities and venerated beings.

TYPE OF NAME	EXAMPLES	
Religions and Followers	**I**slam	**R**oman **C**atholic
Holy Days and Celebrations	**E**piphany	**R**osh **H**ashanah
Holy Writings	**B**ible	**U**panishads
Specific Deities and Venerated Beings	**G**od the **P**rophet (**M**ohammed)	

NOTE The words *god* and *goddess* are not capitalized when they refer to the deities of mythology. The names of specific mythological deities are capitalized, however.

EXAMPLES

The Greek **g**od of war was **A**res.

(4) Capitalize the first and last words and all important words in titles of books, periodicals, poems, stories, essays, speeches, plays, historical documents, movies, radio and television programs, works of art, musical compositions, and cartoons.

Unimportant words in a title include articles (*a, an, the*), short prepositions (those with fewer than five letters, such as *of, to, in, for, from, with*), and coordinating conjunctions (*and, but, for, nor, or, so, yet*).

TYPE OF NAME	EXAMPLES
Books	*The Call of the Wild*
Periodicals	*Car and Driver*
Poems	"Once by the Pacific"
Stories	"The Fall of the House of Usher"
Essays and Speeches	"The Lost Worlds of Ancient America" "I Have a Dream"
Plays	*A Raisin in the Sun*
Historical Documents	Declaration of Independence
Movies	*Raiders of the Lost Ark*
Radio and TV Programs	*Star Trek: The Next Generation*
Works of Art	*Double Dutch on the Golden Gate Bridge*
Musical Compositions	"Lift Every Voice and Sing"
Cartoons	*Where I'm Coming From*

NOTE The article *the* before a title is not capitalized unless it is part of the official title. The official title of a book is found on the title page. The official title of a newspaper or periodical is found on the masthead (usually on the editorial page).

EXAMPLES
the *Odyssey*
the *Philadelphia Inquirer*
The Wall Street Journal
The Man in the Iron Mask

For information about which titles should be italicized and which should be enclosed in quotation marks, see pages 1245 and 1247.

PROGRAM MANAGER

- **Independent Practice or Reteaching** Use *Language and Writing Skills Worksheets,* pp. 129–142.
- **Practice** See *Language Workshop:* Lessons 41–45: Punctuating sentences and Lesson 50: Other common uses of punctuation marks.

12 PUNCTUATION

END MARKS

For information about how sentences are classified according to purpose, see page 1235.

12a. A statement (or declarative sentence) is followed by a period.

EXAMPLE
Felipe asked whether Edgar Allan Poe was primarily a poet, an essayist, or a short-story writer**.**

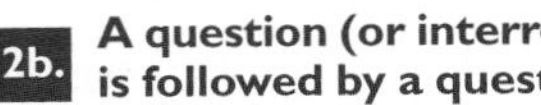

12b. A question (or interrogative sentence) is followed by a question mark.

EXAMPLE
Have you read any of Edgar Allan Poe's poetry**?**

12c. A request or command (or imperative sentence) is followed by either a period or an exclamation point.

EXAMPLES
Answer the phone, please**.**
Turn the music down now**!**

12d. An exclamation (or exclamatory sentence) is followed by an exclamation point.

EXAMPLE
What an imagination Edgar Allan Poe had**!**

NOTE An exclamation point may be used after a single word (especially an interjection) as well as after a sentence.

EXAMPLE
Hey**!** Wait for me**!**

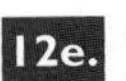

12e. An abbreviation is usually followed by a period.

(See the chart at the top of the next page for examples.)

Some common abbreviations, including many for units of measurement, are written without periods.

EXAMPLES
AM/FM, FBI, IOU, MTV, PC, ROTC, SOS, cc, db, ft, lb, kw, ml, psi, rpm [Use a period with the abbreviation *in.* (*inch*) to avoid confusion with the word *in*.]

TYPE OF ABBREVIATION	EXAMPLES
Personal Names	N. Scott Momaday E. A. Robinson
Organizations and Companies	Assn. Co. Corp. Ltd. Inc.
Titles Used with Names	Dr. Jr. Ms. Ph.D.
Times of Day	A.M. (*or* a.m.) P.M. (*or* p.m.)
Years	B.C. (*written after the date*) A.D. (*written before the date*)
Addresses	Ave. Blvd. Dr. St. P.O. Box
States	Ark. Fla. R. I. N. Mex.

NOTE If an abbreviation has a period, do not place a period after it at the end of a sentence.

NOTE Two-letter state abbreviations without periods are used only when the ZIP Code is included.

EXAMPLE
Springfield, **MA** 01101

COMMAS

12f. Use commas to separate items in a series.

EXAMPLE
The main characters are Huckleberry Finn**,** Tom Sawyer**,** and Jim.

If all the items in a series are linked by *and, or,* or *nor,* do not use commas to separate them.

EXAMPLE
Saul Bellow **and** Isaac Bashevis Singer **and** Toni Morrison won Nobel Prizes.

12g. Use a comma to separate two or more adjectives preceding a noun.

EXAMPLE
Whitman saw Lincoln as a noble**,** compassionate**,** wise leader.

12h. Use a comma before *and, but, or, nor, for, so,* and *yet* when they join independent clauses.

EXAMPLE
I read an excerpt from Amy Tan's *The Joy Luck Club***,** and now I want to read the entire book.

12i. Use commas to set off nonessential clauses and nonessential participial phrases.

A ***nonessential*** clause or phrase is one that can be left out without changing the meaning of the sentence.

NONESSENTIAL CLAUSE Eudora Welty**, who was born in Mississippi,** uses her home state as the setting in many stories.

NONESSENTIAL PHRASE Lee**, noticing my confusion,** rephrased her question.

An ***essential*** clause or phrase is one that can't be left out without changing the meaning of the sentence. Essential clauses and phrases are *not* set off by commas.

ESSENTIAL CLAUSE Material **that is quoted verbatim** should be placed in quotation marks.

ESSENTIAL PHRASE The only word **spoken by the raven** is *nevermore.*

12j. Use a comma after certain introductory elements.

(1) Use a comma after a one-word adverb such as *first, yes,* or *no* and after any mild exclamation such as *well* or *why* at the beginning of a sentence.

EXAMPLE
Yes, Hemingway is my favorite author.

(2) Use a comma after an introductory participial phrase or introductory adverb clause.

EXAMPLES
Standing on the quarter-deck, Captain Ahab spoke to his crew. [participial phrase]
After he had driven around the lake several times, he decided to go to the drive-in restaurant. [adverb clause]

(3) Use a comma after two or more introductory prepositional phrases.

EXAMPLE
At the end of the story, Walter Mitty imagines that he is facing a firing squad.

12k. Use commas to set off elements that interrupt a sentence.

(1) Appositives and appositive phrases are usually set off by commas.

EXAMPLE
My favorite book by Claude McKay**, *Banjo*,** was first published in 1929.

Sometimes an appositive is so closely related to the word or words it refers to that it should not be set off by commas.

EXAMPLE
The poet **Maya Angelou** recited some of her work on Inauguration Day.

(2) Words used in direct address are set off by commas.

EXAMPLE
Your essay**,** **Theo,** was well organized.

(3) Parenthetical expressions are set off by commas.

Parenthetical expressions are remarks that add incidental information or that relate ideas to each other.

EXAMPLE
Simón Bolívar liberated much of South America from Spanish rule; he went on**,** **moreover,** to become the most powerful person on the continent.

12l. Use a comma in certain conventional situations.

(1) Use a comma to separate items in dates and addresses.

EXAMPLES
On Friday**,** October 23**,** 1994**,** my niece Leslie was born.
Please address all further inquiries to 92 Keystone Crossings**,** Indianapolis**,** IN 46240. [Notice that a comma is not used between a state abbreviation and a ZIP Code.]

(2) Use a comma after the salutation of a friendly letter and after the closing of any letter.

EXAMPLES
Dear Rosa**,**   Sincerely yours**,**

(3) Use a comma to set off an abbreviation such as *Jr., Sr., RN, M.D., Ltd.,* or *Inc.*

EXAMPLE
Is Juan Fuentes**,** Jr.**,** your cousin?

SEMICOLONS

12m. Use a semicolon between independent clauses that are closely related in thought and are not joined by *and, but, for, nor, or, so,* or *yet.*

EXAMPLE
"Tart words make no friends**;** a spoonful of honey will catch more flies than a gallon of vinegar."
—Benjamin Franklin, *Poor Richard's Almanack*

12n. Use a semicolon between independent clauses joined by a conjunctive adverb or a transitional expression.

A ***conjunctive adverb*** (such as *consequently, however,* or *therefore*) or a ***transitional expression*** (such as *as a result, for example,* or *in other words*) indicates the relationship of the independent clauses that it joins. Notice in the following examples that a comma is placed after the conjunctive adverb or transitional expression.

EXAMPLE
Dexter knew that Judy was selfish and insensitive**;** **nevertheless,** he continued to adore her.

12o. Use a semicolon (rather than a comma) before a coordinating conjunction to join independent clauses that contain commas.

EXAMPLE
During the nineteenth century—the era of such distinguished poets as Longfellow**,** Whittier**,** and Holmes—most poetry was written in traditional metrical patterns**;** but one poet**,** Walt Whitman**,** rejected the conventional verse forms.

12p. Use a semicolon between items in a series if the items contain commas.

EXAMPLE
The summer reading list includes *Behind the Trail of Broken Treaties***,** by Vine Deloria, Jr.**;** *House Made of Dawn***,** by N. Scott Momaday**;** and *Blue Highways: A Journey into America***,** by William Least Heat-Moon.

COLONS

12q. Use a colon to mean "note what follows."

(1) Use a colon before a list of items, especially after expressions such as *as follows* and *the following.*

EXAMPLE
The magazine article profiles the following famous American authors of the nineteenth century**:** Edgar Allan Poe, Nathaniel Hawthorne, and Herman Melville.

Do not use a colon before a list that directly follows a verb or a preposition.

EXAMPLE
The anthology includes "The Raven," "Richard Cory," and "Thanatopsis." [The list directly follows the verb *includes.*]

(2) Use a colon before a quotation that lacks a speaker tag such as *he said* or *she remarked.*

EXAMPLE
Dad's orders were loud and clear**:** "Everybody up and at 'em."

(3) Use a colon before a long, formal statement or quotation.

EXAMPLE
Patrick Henry concluded his fiery speech before the Virginia House of Burgesses with these words**:** "Is life so dear, or peace so sweet, as to be purchased at the price of chains and slavery? Forbid it, Almighty God! I know not what course others may take; but as for me, give me liberty, or give me death!"

12r. Use a colon in certain conventional situations.

EXAMPLES
5**:**20 P.M. [between the hour and the minute]
Deuteronomy 5**:**6–21 [between chapter and verse in referring to passages from the Bible]
Dear Sir or Madam**:** [after the salutation of a business letter]
"Cold Kills**:** Hypothermia" [between a title and a subtitle]

LANGUAGE HANDBOOK

13 Punctuation

ITALICS

Italics are printed characters that slant to the right. To indicate italics in handwritten or typewritten work, use underlining.

PRINTED Who wrote *Black Boy*?
HANDWRITTEN Who wrote Black Boy?

13a. Use italics (underlining) for titles of books, plays, long poems, periodicals, newspapers, works of art, films, television series, long musical compositions, recordings, comic strips, computer software, court cases, trains, ships, aircraft, and spacecraft.

TYPE OF NAME	EXAMPLES	
Books	*The Scarlet Letter*	*Fifth Chinese Daughter*
Plays	*The Crucible*	*West Side Story*
Long Poems	*I Am Joaquín*	the *Epic of Gilgamesh*
Periodicals	*Reader's Digest*	*Newsweek*
Newspapers	*The Wall Street Journal*	the *Austin American-Statesman*
Works of Art	*The Kiss*	*The Starry Night*
Films	*Forrest Gump*	*Stand and Deliver*
TV Series	*Jeopardy!*	*Star Trek: The Next Generation*
Long Musical Compositions	*Liverpool Oratorio*	*Hiawatha's Wedding Feast*
Recordings	*Achtung Baby*	*Sketches of Spain*
Comic Strips	*Peanuts*	*Calvin and Hobbes*
Computer Software	*WordPerfect*	*Paintbrush*
Court Cases	*Plessy* v. *Ferguson*	*Bailey* v. *Alabama*
Trains, Ships	*Century Limited*	*Queen Mary*
Aircraft, Spacecraft	*Solar Challenger*	*Apollo 11*

NOTE The article *the* before the title of a book, periodical, or newspaper is not italicized or capitalized unless it is part of the official title. The official title of a book appears on the title page. The official title of a periodical or newspaper is the name given on the masthead, which usually appears on the editorial page.

EXAMPLES
The article appeared in both the *Philadelphia Inquirer* and *The New York Times.*

For examples of titles that are not italicized but that are enclosed in quotation marks, see page 1247.

PROGRAM MANAGER

- **Independent Practice or Reteaching** Use *Language and Writing Skills Worksheets,* pp. 143–156.
- **Practice** See *Language Workshop:* Lesson 43: Punctuating interrupters and Lessons 46–52: Punctuating possessives, contractions, and plurals, Punctuating titles and quotations, Conventional uses of punctuation, Hyphens, and Ellipsis points.

13b. **Use italics (underlining) for words, letters, numerals, and symbols referred to as such and for foreign words that have not been adopted into English.**

EXAMPLES

Should the use of *their* for *there* be considered a spelling error or a usage error?

The teacher couldn't tell whether I had written a script *S,* the number *5,* or an *&.*

All U.S. coins are stamped with the inscription *e pluribus unum.*

QUOTATION MARKS

13c. **Use quotation marks to enclose a *direct quotation*—a person's exact words.**

EXAMPLE

Chief Joseph said, "The earth is the mother of all people, and all people should have equal rights upon it."

Notice that a direct quotation begins with a capital letter. However, if the quotation is only part of a sentence, it does not begin with a capital letter.

EXAMPLE

Chief Joseph called the earth "the mother of all people."

(1) When the expression identifying the speaker divides a quoted sentence, the second part begins with a lowercase letter.

EXAMPLE

"I really have to leave now," said Gwen, "so that I will be on time." [Notice that each part of a divided quotation is enclosed in quotation marks.]

When the second part of a divided quotation is a new sentence, it begins with a capital letter.

EXAMPLE

"Teddy Roosevelt was the first U.S. President to express concern about the depletion of the nation's natural resources," explained Mr. Fuentes. "He established a conservation program that expanded the national park system."

(2) When used with quotation marks, other marks of punctuation are placed according to the following rules.

- Commas and periods are always placed inside the closing quotation marks.

EXAMPLES

"On the other hand," he said, "your decision may be correct."

- Semicolons and colons are always placed outside the closing quotation marks.

EXAMPLES

My neighbor said, "Sure I'll buy a subscription"; it was lucky that I asked her on payday.

Edna St. Vincent Millay uses these devices in her poem "Spring": alliteration, slant rhyme, and personification.

- Question marks and exclamation points are placed inside the closing quotation marks if the quotation itself is a question or an exclamation. Otherwise, they are placed outside.

EXAMPLES

Was it you who wrote the poem "Upon Turning Seventeen"?

"What a tortured soul Reverend Dimmesdale is!" said Mr. Klein.

(3) When quoting a passage that consists of more than one paragraph, put quotation marks at the beginning of each paragraph and the end of only the last paragraph.

EXAMPLE

"As he neared the house, each detail of the scene became vivid to him. He was aware of some bricks of the vanished chimney lying on the sod. There was a door which hung by one hinge.

"Rifle bullets called forth by the insistent skirmishers came from the far-off bank of foliage. They mingled with the shells and the pieces of shells until the air was torn in all directions by hootings, yells, howls. The sky was full of fiends who directed all their wild rage at his head."

—Stephen Crane, "A Mystery of Heroism"

(4) Use single quotation marks to enclose a quotation within a quotation.

EXAMPLES

The teacher requested, "Jorge, please explain what Emerson meant when he said, 'To be great is to be misunderstood.'"

"Have you read 'Rip Van Winkle'?" Jill asked.

(5) When writing ***dialogue*** (a conversation), begin a new paragraph every time the speaker changes, and enclose the speaker's words in quotation marks.

EXAMPLE

"How far is it to the Owl Creek bridge?" Farquhar asked.

"About thirty miles."

"Is there no force on this side the creek?"

"Only a picket post half a mile out, on the railroad, and a single sentinel at this end of the bridge."

—Ambrose Bierce, "An Occurrence at Owl Creek Bridge"

13d. Use quotation marks to enclose titles of short works, such as short stories, poems, essays, articles, songs, episodes of television series, and chapters and other parts of books.

TYPE OF NAME	EXAMPLES	
Short Stories	"Tamar"	"The Tell-Tale Heart"
Poems	"The Latin Deli"	"Thanatopsis"
Essays	"On the Mall"	"The Creative Process"
Articles	"Old Poetry and Modern Music"	
Songs	"On Top of Old Smoky"	
TV Episodes	"The Flight of the Condor"	
Chapters and Parts of Books	"The World Was New" "The Colonies' Struggle for Freedom"	

NOTE Neither italics nor quotation marks are used for titles of major religious works or titles of legal or historical documents.

EXAMPLES
Bible   Bill of Rights

For a list of titles that are italicized rather than placed in quotation marks, see page 1245.

ELLIPSIS POINTS

13e. Use three spaced periods called *ellipsis points* (. . .) to mark omissions from quoted material and pauses in a written passage.

ORIGINAL The second half of the program consisted of four numbers from the *Ring,* and closed with Siegfried's funeral march. My aunt wept quietly, but almost continuously, as a shallow vessel overflows in a rainstorm. From time to time her dim eyes looked up at the lights which studded the ceiling, burning softly under their dull glass globes; doubtless they were stars in truth to her. I was still perplexed as to what measure of musical comprehension was left to her, she who had heard nothing but the singing of gospel hymns at Methodist services in the square frame schoolhouse on Section Thirteen for so many years. I was wholly unable to gauge how much of it had been dissolved in soapsuds, or worked into bread, or milked into the bottom of a pail.

—Willa Cather, "A Wagner Matinée"

(1) If the quoted material that comes before the ellipsis points is not a complete sentence, use three ellipsis points with a space before the first point.

EXAMPLE
The narrator notes, "The second half of the program **. . .** closed with Siegfried's funeral march."

(2) If the quoted material that comes before or after the ellipsis points is a complete sentence, use an end mark before the ellipsis points.

EXAMPLE
The narrator observes, "My aunt wept quietly**. . . .** "

(3) If one sentence or more is omitted, ellipsis points follow the end mark that precedes the omitted material.

EXAMPLE
Recalling the experience, the narrator says, "My aunt wept quietly, but almost continuously, as a shallow vessel overflows in a rainstorm**. . . .** I was still perplexed as to what measure of musical comprehension was left to her, she who had heard nothing but the singing of gospel hymns at Methodist services in the square frame schoolhouse on Section Thirteen for so many years."

(4) To show that a full line or more of poetry has been omitted, use an entire line of spaced periods.

ORIGINAL
If you were coming in the Fall,
I'd brush the Summer by
With half a smile, and half a spurn,
As Housewives do, a Fly.
—Emily Dickinson, "If you were coming in the Fall"

WITH OMISSION
If you were coming in the Fall,
I'd brush the Summer by
. . . .
As Housewives do, a Fly.

APOSTROPHES

13f. Use an apostrophe in forming the possessive of nouns and indefinite pronouns.

(1) To form the possessive of a singular noun, add an apostrophe and an *s*.

EXAMPLES
the minister**'s** veil   Ross**'s** opinion

NOTE When forming the possessive of a singular noun ending in an *s* sound, add only an apostrophe if the addition of *'s* will make the noun awkward to pronounce. Otherwise, add *'s*.

EXAMPLES
Douglass**'s** autobiography   Texas**'** population

(2) To form the possessive of a plural noun ending in *s*, add only the apostrophe. If the plural noun does not end in *s*, add an apostrophe and an *s*.

EXAMPLES
the authors**'** styles   the Ushers**'** house
men**'s** fashions   children**'s** toys

(3) To form the possessive of an indefinite pronoun, add an apostrophe and an *s*.

EXAMPLES
each one**'s** time   everybody**'s** opinion

In such forms as *anyone else* and *somebody else*, the correct possessives are *anyone else's* and *somebody else's*.

(4) Form the possessive of only the last word in a compound word, in the name of an organization or business firm, or in a word group showing joint possession.

EXAMPLES
father-in-law**'s** gloves   Roz and Denise**'s** idea
Taylor, Sanders, and Weissman**'s** law office

(5) Form the possessive of each noun in a word group showing individual possession of similar items.

EXAMPLE
Baldwin**'s** and Ellison**'s** writings

When a possessive pronoun is part of a word group showing joint possession, each noun in the word group is also possessive.

EXAMPLE
Walter Mitty**'s** and **her** relationship

(6) When used in the possessive form, words that indicate time (such as *hour, week,* and *year*) and words that indicate amounts of money require apostrophes.

EXAMPLES
a week**'s** vacation   five dollars**'** worth

13g. Use an apostrophe to show where letters, words, or numbers have been omitted in a contraction.

EXAMPLES
they had . . . **they'd**   Kerry is . . . **Kerry's**
let us . . . **let's**   of the clock . . . **o'clock**
where is . . . **where's**   1997 . . . **'97**

The word *not* can be shortened to *–n't* and added to a verb, usually without any change in the spelling of the verb.

EXAMPLES
is not . . . **isn't**   has not . . . **hasn't**

EXCEPTION
will not . . . **won't**

13h. Use an apostrophe and an *s* to form the plurals of all lowercase letters, some uppercase letters, numerals, and some words referred to as words.

EXAMPLES
There are two ***r*'s** and two ***s*'s** in *embarrassed.*
Soon after Tom and Lucynell said their ***I do*'s,** he abandoned her.

You may add only an *s* to form the plurals of such items—except lowercase letters—if the plural forms will not cause misreading.

EXAMPLES
Compact discs (**CDs**) were introduced in the **1980s.**
On her report card were three **A's** and three **C's.**

HYPHENS

13i. Use a hyphen to divide a word at the end of a line.

When dividing a word at the end of a line, remember the following rules:

(1) Do not divide a one-syllable word.

EXAMPLE
Peyton Farquhar was captured, and he was finally **hanged** from the bridge.

(2) Divide a word only between syllables.

EXAMPLE
Ernest Hemingway's *A Farewell to Arms* was **pub-lished** in 1929.

(3) Divide an already hyphenated word at the hyphen.

EXAMPLE
Stephen Crane died in Germany at the age of **twenty-eight.**

(4) Do not divide a word so that one letter stands alone.

EXAMPLE
One fine autumn day, Rip Van Winkle fell fast **asleep** in the mountains.

13j. **Use a hyphen with compound numbers from twenty-one to ninety-nine and with fractions used as modifiers.**

EXAMPLES
six hundred **twenty-five**
a **three-fourths** quorum [*but* **three fourths** of the audience]

DASHES

13k. **Use dashes to set off abrupt breaks in thoughts.**

EXAMPLE
The poor condition of this road**—**it really needs to be paved**—**makes this route unpopular.

13l. **Use dashes to set off an appositive or a parenthetical expression that contains commas.**

EXAMPLE
Several of the nineteenth-century American poets**—**Poe, Dickinson, and Whitman, for example**—**led remarkable lives.

PARENTHESES

13m. **Use parentheses to enclose informative or explanatory material of minor importance.**

EXAMPLES
Harriet Tubman **(**c. 1820–1913**)** is remembered for her work in the Underground Railroad.
On our vacation we visited Natchitoches **(**it's pronounced nak'ə·täsh'**)**, Louisiana.
Thoreau lived at Walden Pond for two years. **(**See the map on page 350.**)**

BRACKETS

13n. **Use brackets to enclose an explanation within quoted or parenthetical material.**

EXAMPLE
I think that Hilda Doolittle (more commonly known as H. D. **[**1886–1961**]**) is best remembered for her Imagist poetry.

14 Spelling

UNDERSTANDING WORD STRUCTURE

Many English words are made up of roots and affixes (prefixes and suffixes).

Roots

14a. **The *root* of a word is the part that carries the word's core meaning.**

ROOTS	MEANINGS	EXAMPLES
–bio–	life	biology, symbiotic
–duc–, –duct–	lead	educate, conductor
–mit–, –miss–	send	remit, emissary
–port–	carry, bear	transport, portable

To find the meaning of a root or an affix, look in a dictionary. Most dictionaries have individual entries for word parts.

Prefixes

14b. **A *prefix* is one or more letters or syllables added to the beginning of a word to create a new word with a different meaning.**

PREFIXES	MEANINGS	EXAMPLES
a–	lacking, without	amorphous, apolitical
dia–	through, across, apart	diagonal, diameter, diagnose
inter–	between, among	intercede, international
mis–	badly, wrongly	misfire, misspell

PROGRAM MANAGER

- **Independent Practice or Reteaching** Use *Language and Writing Skills Worksheets,* pp. 157–164.
- **Practice** See *Language Workshop:* Lessons 55–57: Rules of spelling and Words often confused.

Suffixes

14c. A *suffix* is one or more letters or syllables added to the end of a word to create a new word with a different meaning.

SUFFIXES	MEANINGS	EXAMPLES
–ation, –ition	action, result	repetition, starvation
–er	doer, native of	baker, westerner
–ible	able, likely, fit	edible, possible, divisible
–or	doer, office, action	director, juror, error

SPELLING RULES

ie and *ei*

14d. Write *ie* when the sound is long *e*, except after *c*.

EXAMPLES
bel**ie**ve f**ie**ld c**ei**ling rec**ei**ve
EXCEPTIONS
either l**ei**sure w**ei**rd prot**ei**n

14e. Write *ei* when the sound is not long *e*.

EXAMPLES
eight n**ei**ghbor w**ei**gh for**ei**gn
EXCEPTIONS
anc**ie**nt v**ie**w fr**ie**nd effic**ie**nt

–cede, –ceed, and *–sede*

14f. The only English word ending in *–sede* is *supersede*. The only words ending in *–ceed* are *exceed, proceed,* and *succeed*. All other words with this sound end in *–cede*.

EXAMPLES
ac**cede** con**cede** inter**cede** re**cede**

Adding Prefixes

14g. When adding a prefix, do not change the spelling of the original word.

EXAMPLES
mis + spell = **mis**spell
inter + national = **inter**national

Adding Suffixes

14h. When adding the suffix *–ness* or *–ly*, do not change the spelling of the original word.

EXAMPLES
plain + ness = plain**ness** casual + ly = casual**ly**
EXCEPTIONS
For most words ending in *y*, change the *y* to *i* before adding *-ness* or *-ly*.
empty + ness = empt**iness** busy + ly = bus**ily**

One-syllable adjectives ending in *y* generally follow rule 14h.

EXAMPLES
dry + ness = dry**ness** shy + ly = shy**ly**

14i. Drop the final silent e before a suffix beginning with a vowel.

EXAMPLES
care + ing = car**ing** dose + age = dos**age**
EXCEPTIONS
Keep the final silent e
- in a word ending in *ce* or *ge* before a suffix beginning with *a* or *o*: peace**able**, courage**ous**
- in *dye* and in *singe* before *–ing*: dye**ing**, singe**ing**
- in *mile* before *–age*: mile**age**

When adding *–ing* to words that end in *ie*, drop the e and change the *i* to *y*.

EXAMPLES
die + ing = d**ying** lie + ing = l**ying**

14j. Keep the final silent e before a suffix beginning with a consonant.

EXAMPLES
hope + ful = hope**ful** love + ly = love**ly**
EXCEPTIONS
awe + ful = aw**ful** whole + ly = whol**ly**
nine + th = nin**th** argue + ment = argu**ment**

14k. For words ending in y preceded by a consonant, change the y to *i* before any suffix that does not begin with *i*.

EXAMPLES
thirsty + est = thirst**iest** plenty + ful = plent**iful**

14l. For words ending in y preceded by a vowel, keep the y when adding a suffix.

EXAMPLES
joy + ful = joy**ful** obey + ing = obey**ing**
EXCEPTIONS
day—da**ily** lay—la**id** pay—pa**id** say—sa**id**

14m. Double the final consonant before a suffix that begins with a vowel if the word both

(1) has only one syllable or has the accent on the last syllable

and

(2) ends in a single consonant preceded by a single vowel.

EXAMPLES
thin + est = thi**nnest** occur + ed = occu**rred**
EXCEPTIONS

- For words ending in *w* or *x*, do not double the final consonant.

  new + er = **newer** relax + ing = relax**ing**

- For words ending in *c*, add *k* before the suffix instead of doubling the *c*.

  picnic + k + ed = picnic**ked**

NOTE The final consonant of some words may or may not be doubled, such as *traveled*/*travelled.* If you are unsure about doubling a final consonant, consult a dictionary.

Forming the Plurals of Nouns

14n. Remembering the following rules will help you spell the plural forms of nouns.

(1) For most nouns, add –*s*.

EXAMPLES
player**s** island**s** Jefferson**s**

(2) For nouns ending in *s, x, z, ch,* or *sh,* add –*es*.

EXAMPLES
class**es** match**es** tax**es** Chávez**es**

(3) For nouns ending in *y* preceded by a vowel, add –*s*.

EXAMPLES
monkey**s** alloy**s** McKay**s**

In some names, diacritical marks (marks that show pronunciation) are as essential to correct spelling as the letters themselves. If you are not sure about the spelling of a name, check with the person whose name it is or consult a reference source.

EXAMPLES
Abolfat'h Hélène Bashō Da 'Shawn

(4) For nouns ending in *y* preceded by a consonant, change the *y* to *i* and add –*es*.

EXAMPLES
fl**ies** countr**ies** troph**ies**
EXCEPTIONS
For proper nouns, add –*s:* Kennedy**s**

(5) For some nouns ending in *f* or *fe,* add –*s*. For others, change the *f* or *fe* to *v* and add –*es*. For proper nouns, add –*s*.

EXAMPLES
gulf**s** roof**s** lea**ves** kni**ves** wol**ves**
Tallchief**s** Wolfe**s**

(6) For nouns ending in *o* preceded by a vowel, add –*s*.

EXAMPLES
studio**s** stereo**s** Ignacio**s**

(7) For nouns ending in *o* preceded by a consonant, add –*es*.

EXAMPLES
tomato**es** hero**es** veto**es**

For some common nouns ending in *o* preceded by a consonant, especially those referring to music, and for proper nouns, add only an –*s*.

EXAMPLES
taco**s** piano**s** alto**s** Suro**s**

NOTE For some nouns ending in *o* preceded by a consonant, either –*s* or –*es* may be added.

EXAMPLES
zero**s** *or* zero**es** mosquito**s** *or* mosquito**es**

(8) The plurals of a few nouns are formed in irregular ways.

EXAMPLES
t**ee**th wom**e**n m**ice** g**ee**se

(9) For a few nouns, the singular and the plural forms are the same.

EXAMPLES
sheep trout aircraft Japanese Sioux

(10) For most compound nouns, form the plural of only the last word of the compound.

EXAMPLES
bookshel**ves** baby sitter**s** ten-year-old**s**

(11) For compound nouns in which one of the words is modified by the other word or words, form the plural of the noun modified.

EXAMPLES
sister**s**-in-law runner**s**-up mountain goat**s**

(12) For some nouns borrowed from other languages, the plural is formed as in the original languages.

EXAMPLES
alga—alg**ae** hypothesis—hypothes**es**
ellipsis—ellips**es** phenomenon—phenomen**a**

(13) To form the plurals of figures, most uppercase letters, signs, and words used as words, add an –*s* or both an apostrophe and an –*s*.

EXAMPLES
1990—1990**s** *or* 1990**'s** *C*—*C***s** *or C***'s**
and—*and***s** *or and***'s** *&*—*&***s** *or &***'s**

To prevent confusion, add both an apostrophe and an –*s* to form the plural of all lowercase letters, certain uppercase letters, and some words used as words.

EXAMPLES
The word *Mississippi* contains four ***s*'s** and four ***i*'s.** [Without an apostrophe, the plural of *i* could be confused with *is.*]
Because I mistakenly thought Flannery O'Connor was a man, I used ***his*'s** instead of ***her*'s** in my paragraph. [Without an apostrophe, the plural of *his* would look like the word *hiss,* and the plural of *her* would look like the pronoun *hers.*]

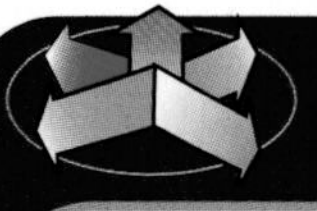

PROGRAM MANAGER

- **Independent Practice or Reteaching** Use *Language and Writing Skills Worksheets,* pp. 1–10.
- **Practice** See *Language Workshop:* Chapter 11: Usage.

15 Glossary of Usage

The **Glossary of Usage** is an alphabetical list of words and expressions with definitions, explanations, and examples. Some examples in this list are labeled *standard, nonstandard, formal,* or *informal.* The labels ***standard*** and ***formal*** identify usage that is appropriate in serious writing and speaking (such as in compositions and speeches). The label ***informal*** indicates standard English commonly used in conversation and in everyday writing such as personal letters. The label ***nonstandard*** identifies usage that does not follow the guidelines of standard English usage.

accept, except *Accept* is a verb meaning "to receive." *Except* may be either a verb meaning "to leave out" or a preposition meaning "excluding."

EXAMPLES
I will **accept** another yearbook assignment. [verb]
Should the military services **except** women from combat duty? [verb]
I have read all of Willa Cather's novels **except** *My Ántonia.* [preposition]

affect, effect *Affect* is a verb meaning "to influence." *Effect* may be either a verb meaning "to bring about or accomplish" or a noun meaning "the result [of an action]."

EXAMPLES
How did the House of Usher **affect** the narrator?
Renewed interest in *Moby-Dick* during the 1920s **effected** a change in Melville's reputation.
What **effect** did the war have on Paul Berlin?

all ready, already *All ready* means "all prepared." *Already* means "previously."

EXAMPLES
Are you **all ready** to give your report?
We have **already** read that story.

all the farther, all the faster Avoid using these expressions in formal situations. Use *as far as* or *as fast as.*

EXAMPLE
The first act was **as far as** [*not* all the farther] we had read in *A Raisin in the Sun.*

all together, altogether *All together* means "everyone or everything in the same place." *Altogether* means "entirely."

EXAMPLES
My family will be **all together** for the holidays this year.
The president is **altogether** opposed to the bill.

allusion, illusion An *allusion* is an indirect reference to something. An *illusion* is a mistaken idea or a misleading appearance.

EXAMPLES
In her stories, Flannery O'Connor makes numerous **allusions** to the Bible.
Illusions of success haunt Willy Loman.
Makeup can be used to create an **illusion.**

almost, most Avoid using *most* for *almost* in all writing other than dialogue.

EXAMPLE
Almost [*not* most] everyone in class was surprised by the outcome in Ambrose Bierce's story "An Occurrence at Owl Creek Bridge."

a lot Avoid this expression in formal situations by using *many* or *much.*

already See **all ready, already.**

altogether See **all together, altogether.**

among See **between, among.**

amount, number Use *amount* to refer to a singular word. Use *number* to refer to a plural word.

EXAMPLES

The library has a large **amount** of resource material about the Harlem Renaissance. [*Amount* refers to *material.*]

The library has a large **number** of books about the Harlem Renaissance. [*Number* refers to *books.*]

and, but In general, avoid beginning a sentence with *and* or *but* in formal writing.

and etc. *Etc.* stands for the Latin words *et cetera,* meaning "and others" or "and so forth." Always avoid using *and* before *etc.* In general, avoid using *etc.* in formal situations. Use one of its meanings instead.

EXAMPLE

We are studying twentieth-century American novelists: Ernest Hemingway, Margaret Walker, Jean Toomer, **and others** [*or* **etc.,** *but not* and etc.].

and/or Avoid using this confusing construction. Decide which alternative, *and* or *or,* expresses what you mean, and use it alone.

any more, anymore The expression *any more* specifies a quantity. *Anymore* means "now; nowadays."

EXAMPLES

Do you know **any more** Caddo folk tales?

Kam doesn't work at the record store **anymore.**

any one, anyone The expression *any one* specifies one member of a group. *Anyone* is a pronoun meaning "one person, no matter which."

EXAMPLES

Any one of you can play the part.

Anyone can try out for the part.

anyways, anywheres Omit the final *s* from these words and others like them (*everywheres, nowheres, somewheres*).

EXAMPLE

I can't go **anywhere** [*not* anywheres] until I finish.

as See **like, as.**

as if See **like, as if.**

at Avoid using *at* after a construction beginning with *where.*

EXAMPLE

Where was Chief Joseph [*not* where was Chief Joseph at] when he delivered his famous surrender speech?

a while, awhile *A while* means "a period of time." *Awhile* means "for a short time."

EXAMPLES

Let's wait here **awhile.**

Let's sit here for **a while** and listen to the band.

bad, badly *Bad* is an adjective. *Badly* is an adverb. In standard English, *bad* should follow a sense verb, such as *feel, look, sound, taste,* or *smell,* or other linking verb.

NONSTANDARD If the cole slaw smells badly, don't eat it.

STANDARD If the cole slaw smells **bad,** don't eat it.

because In formal situations, do not use the construction *reason . . . because.* Instead, use *reason . . . that.*

EXAMPLE

The **reason** for the eclipse is **that** [*not* because] the moon has come between the earth and the sun.

being as, being that Avoid using either of these expressions for *since* or *because.*

EXAMPLE

Because [*not* being as *or* being that] Ms. Ribas is a gemologist, she may know what these stones are.

beside, besides *Beside* is a preposition meaning "by the side of" or "next to." *Besides* may be either a preposition meaning "in addition to" or "other than" or an adverb meaning "moreover."

EXAMPLES

Rip Van Winkle laid his rifle **beside** him on the ground. [preposition]

No one **besides** Lurleen has read all of *Leaves of Grass.* [preposition]

I'm not in the mood to go shopping; **besides,** I have an English test tomorrow. [adverb]

between, among Use *between* to refer to only two items or to more than two when comparing each item individually to each of the others.

EXAMPLES

The money from the sale of the property was evenly divided **between** Sasha and Antonio.

Don't you know the difference **between** a simile, a metaphor, and an analogy? [Each figure of speech is compared individually to each of the others.]

Use *among* to refer to more than two items when you are not considering each item in relation to each other item individually.

EXAMPLE

The money from the sale of the property was evenly divided **among** the four relatives.

bring, take *Bring* means "to come carrying something." *Take* means "to go carrying something."

EXAMPLES
I'll **bring** my Wynton Marsalis tapes when I come over.
When he went hunting, Rip Van Winkle **took** his gun and dog.

but See **and, but.**

cannot (can't) help but Avoid using *but* followed by the infinitive form of a verb after the expression *cannot (can't) help.* Instead, use a gerund after the expression.

NONSTANDARD I can't help but tap my foot whenever I hear mariachi music.
STANDARD I can't help **tapping** my foot whenever I hear mariachi music.

compare, contrast Used with *to, compare* means "to look for similarities between." Used with *with, compare* means "to look for similarities and differences between." *Contrast* is always used to point out differences.

EXAMPLES
Write a simile **comparing** a manufactured product **to** something in nature.
How do the haiku of Taniguchi Buson **compare with** those of Matsuo Bashō?
The teacher **contrasted** the two writing styles of Walt Whitman and Emily Dickinson.

could of See **of.**

double subject Avoid using an unnecessary pronoun after the subject of a sentence.

EXAMPLE
Judy Jones [*not* Judy Jones she] fascinates Dexter Green.

due to Avoid using *due to* for "because of" or "owing to."

EXAMPLE
The game was postponed **because of** [*not* due to] rain.

each and every The expression *each and every* is redundant. Instead, use either *each* or *every* alone.

EXAMPLE
Every [*not* each and every] resident of Jefferson attended Miss Emily Grierson's funeral.

effect See **affect, effect.**

either, neither *Either* usually means "one or the other of two." *Neither* usually means "not one or the other of two." Avoid using *either* or *neither* when referring to more than two.

EXAMPLE
Consider writing about the Jazz Age, the Harlem Renaissance, or the Great Depression; **any one** [*not* either] of those topics would be interesting.

emigrate, immigrate *Emigrate* means "to leave a country or a region to settle elsewhere." *Immigrate* means "to come into a country or a region to settle there."

EXAMPLES
Claude McKay **emigrated** from Jamaica in 1912.
Claude McKay **immigrated** to the United States in 1912.

etc. See **and etc.**

every See **each and every.**

every day, everyday *Every day* means "each day." *Everyday* means "daily" or "usual."

EXAMPLES
Parson Hooper wore the black veil **every day.**
Walking the dog is one of my **everyday** chores.

every one, everyone *Every one* specifies every person or thing of those named. *Everyone* means "every person; everybody."

EXAMPLES
Every one of these poems was written by Anne Sexton.
Has **everyone** read "The Bells"?

except See **accept, except.**

farther, further Use *farther* to express physical distance. Use *further* to express abstract relationships of degree or quantity.

EXAMPLES
We swam **farther** than we usually do.
After discussing "The Road Not Taken" **further,** we agreed with Karl's interpretation of the poem.

fewer, less Use *fewer* to modify a plural noun and *less* to modify a singular noun.

EXAMPLES
Later in life, Emily Dickinson entertained even **fewer** guests.
Later in life, Emily Dickinson spent **less** time entertaining guests.

further See **farther, further.**

good, well Avoid using the adjective *good* to modify a verb. Instead, use the adverb *well,* meaning "capably" or "satisfactorily." As an adjective, *well* means "in good health" or "satisfactory in appearance or condition."

EXAMPLES
The school orchestra played **well** [adverb].
He says that he feels quite **well** [adjective].
It's midnight, and all is **well** [adjective].

had of See **of.**

had ought, hadn't ought Do not use *had* or *hadn't* with *ought.*

EXAMPLE
His scores **ought** [*not* had ought] to be back by now.

half Avoid using an indefinite article (*a* or *an*) both before and after *half.*

EXAMPLE
We've waited for **half an hour** [*or* **a half hour**].

if, whether Avoid using *if* for *whether* in indirect questions and in expressions of doubt.

EXAMPLE
Dickinson wanted to know **whether** [*not* if] her poems were "alive."

illusion See **allusion, illusion.**

immigrate See **emigrate, immigrate.**

imply, infer *Imply* means "to suggest indirectly." *Infer* means "to interpret" or "to draw a conclusion."

EXAMPLES
The speaker of "Thanatopsis" **implies** that nature can allay one's fear of death.
I **infer** from the poem that nature can cure many ills.

in, into *In* generally shows location. *Into* generally shows direction.

EXAMPLES
Randall Jarrell was born **in** Nashville, Tennessee.
When Rip walked **into** the village, everybody stared.

irregardless, regardless *Irregardless* is nonstandard. Use *regardless* instead.

EXAMPLE
Regardless [*not* irregardless] of the children's pleas, their father said they had to go to bed.

its, it's *Its* is the possessive form of *it. It's* is the contraction of *it is* or *it has.*

EXAMPLES
The crew prepares for **its** fight with Moby-Dick.
It's [it is] Captain Ahab's obsession.
It's [it has] been many years since Ahab lost his leg.

kind of, sort of In formal situations, avoid using these terms for the adverb *somewhat* or *rather.*

INFORMAL Roderick became kind of agitated.
FORMAL Roderick became **rather** agitated.

kind of a(n), sort of a(n) In formal situations, omit the *a*(*n*).

INFORMAL What kind of an essay is Baldwin's "The Creative Process"?
FORMAL What **kind of** essay is Baldwin's "The Creative Process"?

kind(s), sort(s), type(s) With the singular form of each of these nouns, use *this* or *that.* With the plural form, use *these* or *those.*

EXAMPLE
This kind of gas is safe, but **those kinds** aren't.

lay, lie See **lie, lay.**

learn, teach *Learn* means "to gain knowledge." *Teach* means "to provide with knowledge."

EXAMPLE
The more you **teach** someone else, the more you **learn** yourself.

less See **fewer, less.**

lie, lay The verb *lie* means "to rest" or "to stay, to recline, or to remain in a certain state or position." Its principal parts are *lie, lying, lay,* and *lain. Lie* never takes an object. The verb *lay* means "to put [something] in a place." Its principal parts are *lay, laying, laid,* and *laid. Lay* usually takes an object.

EXAMPLES
Their land **lay** in the shadow of Rainy Mountain. [no object]
Eduardo **laid** the strips of grilled meat on the tortilla. [*Strips* is the object of *laid.*]

like, as In formal situations, do not use *like* for the conjunction *as* to introduce a subordinate clause.

INFORMAL Plácido Domingo sings like Caruso once did.
FORMAL Plácido Domingo sings **as** Caruso once did.

like, as if In formal situations, avoid using the preposition *like* for the conjunction *as if* or *as though* to introduce a subordinate clause.

INFORMAL The singers sounded like they had not rehearsed.
FORMAL The singers sounded **as if** [*or* **as though**] they had not rehearsed.

might of, must of See **of.**

most See **almost, most.**

neither See **either, neither.**

nor See **or, nor.**

number See **amount, number.**

of *Of* is a preposition. Do not use *of* in place of *have* after verbs such as *could, should, would, might, must,* and *ought* [*to*]. Also, do not use *had of* for *had.*

EXAMPLES

You ought to **have** [*not* of] studied harder.

If he **had** [*not* had of] remembered the name of the author of "Mending Wall," he **would have** [*not* would of] made a perfect score.

Avoid using *of* after other prepositions such as *inside, off,* and *outside.*

EXAMPLE

Chian-Chu dived **off** [*not* off of] the side of the pool into the water.

on to, onto In the expression *on to, on* is an adverb and *to* is a preposition. *Onto* is a preposition.

EXAMPLES

Dexter held **on to** his winter dreams.

The cat leapt gracefully **onto** the windowsill.

or, nor Use *or* with *either;* use *nor* with *neither.*

EXAMPLES

On Tuesdays the school cafeteria offers a choice of **either** a taco salad **or** a pizza.

I wonder why **neither** Ralph Ellison **nor** Robert Frost was given the Nobel Prize in literature.

ought See **had ought, hadn't ought.**

ought to of See **of.**

reason . . . because See **because.**

regardless See **irregardless, regardless.**

rise, raise The verb *rise* means "to go up" or "to get up." Its principal parts are *rise, rising, rose,* and *risen. Rise* never takes an object. The verb *raise* means "to cause [something] to rise" or "to lift up." Its principal parts are *raise, raising, raised,* and *raised. Raise* usually takes an object.

EXAMPLES

The queen **rose** from her throne. [no object]

The movers **raised** the boxes onto their shoulders. [*Boxes* is the object of *raised.*]

should of See **of.**

sit, set The verb *sit* means "to rest in an upright, seated position." Its principal parts are *sit, sitting, sat,* and *sat. Sit* seldom takes an object. The verb *set* means "to put [something] in a place." Its principal parts are *set, setting, set,* and *set. Set* usually takes an object.

EXAMPLES

The raven **sat** on the bust of Pallas above the door. [no object]

Eben **set** the jug down. [*Jug* is the object of *set.*]

some, somewhat In formal situations, use *somewhat* instead of *some* to mean "to some extent."

EXAMPLE

My grades have improved **somewhat** [*not* some].

sort(s) See **kind(s), sort(s), type(s)** and **kind of a(n), sort of a(n).**

sort of See **kind of, sort of.**

take See **bring, take.**

teach See **learn, teach.**

than, then *Than* is a conjunction used in comparisons. *Then* is an adverb meaning "at that time" or "next."

EXAMPLES

Tyrone is more studious **than** I am.

First, mix the wet ingredients; **then,** add the flour and other dry ingredients.

that See **who, which, that.**

their, there, they're *Their* is a possessive form of *they.* As an adverb, *there* means "at that place." *There* can also be used to begin a sentence. *They're* is the contraction of *they are.*

EXAMPLES

The performers are studying **their** lines.

I will be **there** after rehearsal. [adverb]

There will be four acts in the play. [expletive]

They're performing a play by Lorraine Hansberry.

theirs, there's *Theirs* is a possessive form of the pronoun *they. There's* is the contraction for *there is* or *there has.*

EXAMPLES

These posters are ours; **theirs** are the ones on the opposite wall.

There's [there is] a biography of W.E.B. DuBois in the library.

There's [there has] been a change in plans.

them Do not use *them* as an adjective. Use *those.*

EXAMPLE
Those [*not* them] lines illustrate Poe's use of internal rhyme.

then See **than, then.**

this here, that there Avoid using *here* or *there* after *this* or *that.*

EXAMPLE
This [*not* this here] magazine has an article about Andrea Lee.

try and, try to Use *try to,* not *try and.*

EXAMPLE
I will **try to** [*not* try and] finish my report on John Updike.

type, type of Avoid using the noun *type* as an adjective. Add *of* after *type.*

EXAMPLE
I prefer this **type of** [*not* type] shirt.

type(s) See **kind(s), sort(s), type(s).**

ways Use *way,* not *ways,* when referring to distance.

EXAMPLE
My home in Wichita is a long **way** [*not* ways] from Tokyo, where my pen pal lives.

well See **good, well.**

when, where Avoid using *when* or *where* to begin a definition.

NONSTANDARD A predicament is where you are in an embarrassing situation.
STANDARD A predicament is **an embarrassing situation.**

where, when Avoid using *where* or *when* for *that.*

EXAMPLE
I read **that** [*not* where] the Smithsonian Institution has preserved a great many of William H. Johnson's paintings.

where . . . at See **at.**

whether See **if, whether.**

who, which, that *Who* refers to persons only. *Which* refers to things only. *That* may refer to either persons or things.

EXAMPLES
Wasn't Beethoven the composer **who** [*or* **that**] continued to write music after he lost his hearing?
First editions of Poe's first book, **which** is titled *Tamerlane and Other Poems,* are worth thousands of dollars.
Is this the only essay **that** James Baldwin wrote?
I've never met or even seen the person **that** delivers our newspaper each morning.

who's, whose *Who's* is the contraction of *who is* or *who has. Whose* is the possessive form of *who.*

EXAMPLES
Who's [who is] going to portray the Navajo detective in the play?
Who's [who has] been using my computer?
Whose artwork is this?

would of See **of.**

your, you're *Your* is a possessive form of *you. You're* is the contraction of *you are.*

EXAMPLES
Is this **your** book?
I hope **you're** able to come to my graduation.

GLOSSARY

The glossary that follows is an alphabetical list of words found in the selections in this book. Use this glossary just as you use a dictionary—to find out the meanings of unfamiliar words. (A few technical, foreign, or more obscure words in this book are not listed here but are defined instead in the footnotes that accompany each selection.) Many words in the English language have more than one meaning. This glossary gives the meanings that apply to the words as they are used in the selections in this book. Words closely related in form and meaning are usually listed together in one entry (*irk* and *irksome*), and the definition is given for the first form.

The following abbreviations are used:

adj.:	adjective	*n.:*	noun	*v.:*	verb
adv.:	adverb	*pl.:*	plural form		

Unless a word is very simple to pronounce, its pronunciation is given in parentheses. A guide to the pronunciation symbols appears at the bottom of each right-hand glossary page.

For more information about the words in this glossary, or about words not listed here, consult a dictionary.

abate (ə·bāt′) *v.:* to lessen.
abdicate (ab′di·kāt′) *v.:* to give up responsibility for.
abhor (ab·hôr′) *v.:* to scorn; hate; disdain.
abominable (ə·bäm′ə·nə·bəl) *adj.:* disgusting; loathsome.
abrasion (ə·brā′zhən) *n.:* scrape.
abstinence (ab′stə·nəns) *n.:* staying away.
acquiesce (ak′wē·es′) *v.:* to agree or accept quietly.
acrid (ak′rid) *adj.:* bitter; irritating.
acrimonious (ak′ri·mō′nē·əs) *adj.:* bitter; harsh. —**acrimoniously** *adv.*
acute (ə·kyo͞ot′) *adj.:* keen; sharp.
admonish (ad·män′ish) *v.:* to warn mildly. —**admonishing** *adj.*
adversary (ad′vər·ser′ē) *n.:* opponent.
affected (a·fekt′id) *adj.:* put on for show.
affliction (ə·flik′shən) *n.:* pain; hardship.
affluent (af′lo͞o·ənt) *adj.:* rich.
afford (ə·fôrd′) *v.:* to give; provide.
agitated (aj′i·tāt′id) *adj.:* anxious; frantic.
alacrity (ə·lak′rə·tē) *n.:* promptness in responding; eagerness.
allay (a·lā′) *v.:* to lessen; relieve.
alleviate (ə·lē′vē·āt′) *v.:* to relieve; reduce.
alliance (ə·lī′əns) *n.:* close association for a common objective.
ally (al′ī) *n.:* supporter; friend.
ambiguous (am·big′yo͞o·əs) *adj.:* unclear; not certain. —**ambiguousness** *n.*
amble (am′bəl) *n.:* leisurely pace.
amiable (ā′mē·ə·bəl) *adj.:* agreeable; likable.
anarchy (an′ər·kē) *n.:* complete disorder.
ancestral (an·ses′trəl) *adj.:* inherited.
anguish (aŋ′gwish) *n.:* pain and suffering; heartache.
anonymity (an′ə·nim′ə·tē) *n.:* being unnamed or not identified.
antagonist (an·tag′ə·nist) *n.:* adversary; opponent.
antipathy (an·tip′ə·thē) *n.:* strong dislike.
apocryphal (ə·päk′rə·fəl) *adj.:* of questionable authority; false.
appalling (ə·pôl′iŋ) *adj.:* dismaying.
apparition (ap′ə·rish′ən) *n.:* unexpected sight or ghostlike figure that appears suddenly.
appease (ə·pēz′) *v.:* to calm; satisfy.
appoint (ə·point′) *v.:* to assign.
appreciable (ə·prē′shə·bəl) *adj.:* measurable.
appropriate (ə·prō′prē·āt′) *v.:* to take over.
arbitrary (är′bə·trer′ē) *adj.:* based on whims or individual preferences.
archaic (är·kā′ik) *adj.:* old-fashioned.
ardent (ärd′′nt) *adj.:* intense; eager.
arduous (är′ jo͞o·əs) *adj.:* difficult.
arrogant (ar′ə·gənt) *adj.:* proud and overly confident.
ascetic (ə·set′ik) *adj.:* severe; stern.
ascribe (ə·skrīb′) *v.:* to attribute to a certain cause.
assailant (ə·sāl′ənt) *n.:* attacker.
assert (ə·surt′) *v.:* to declare; claim.
assess (ə·ses′) *v.:* to evaluate; judge the value of.
atrocity (ə·träs′ə·tē) *n.:* cruelty; brutality.
attribute (ə·trib′yo͞ot) *v.:* to believe to result from.
avarice (av′ə·ris) *n.:* greed.
aversion (ə·vur′zhən) *n.:* intense dislike.
avert (ə·vurt′) *v.:* to prevent; turn away.

bedlam (bed′ləm) *n.:* place or condition of noise and confusion.
benefactor (ben′ə·fak′tər) *n.:* person who helps others.
benevolence (bə·nev′ə·ləns) *n.:* kindness.
bewitch (bē·wich′) *v.:* to entice; fascinate.
blanch *v.:* to drain of color.
bland *adj.:* mild.
bleak (blēk) *adj.:* cheerless.
blithe (blīth) *adj.:* carefree.
brazen (brā′zən) *adj.:* bold. —**brazenness** *n.*
bustle (bus′əl) *v.:* to be busy or energetically active.

candid (kan′did) *adj.:* unbiased; fair.
cannonade (kan′ən·ād′) *v.:* to fire artillery.
caper (kā′pər) *n.:* foolish prank.
careen (kə·rēn′) *v.:* to lurch sideways.
celestial (sə·les′chəl) *adj.:* divine; perfect.
censor (sen′sər) *v.:* to cut or change to remove objectionable material.
censure (sen′shər) *n.:* strong, disapproving criticism.
ceremonial (ser′ə·mō′nē·əl) *adj.:* formal.

chafe (chāf) *v.:* to become impatient.
chronological (krän'ō • läj'i • kəl) *adj.:* arranged in order of occurrence.
circumvent (sur'kəm • vent') *v.:* to get the better of by craft or ingenuity.
clammy (klam'ē) *adj.:* cold and damp.
clamor (klam'ər) *n.:* loud noise; uproar.
cleft (kleft) *n.:* opening.
clientele (klī'ən • tel') *n.:* customers; clients.
coherent (kō • hir'ənt) *adj.:* connected logically.
coincide (kō'in • sīd') *v.:* to occur at the same time.
commence (kə • mens') *v.:* to start.
commodious (kə • mō'dē • əs) *adj.:* spacious.
communal (kə • myo͞on'əl) *adj.:* belonging to an entire group or community.
complacency (kəm • plā'sən • sē) *n.:* self-satisfaction.
comply (kəm • plī') *v.:* to obey a command; agree to a request.
comprise (kəm • prīz') *v.:* to include.
conceive (kən • sēv') *v.:* to think; imagine.
conception (kən • sep'shən) *n.:* idea.
concession (kən • sesh'ən) *n.:* act of giving in.
confederate (kən • fed'ər • it) *n.:* ally; person who shares a common purpose with another.
confiscation (kän'fis • kā'shən) *n.:* seizure of property by authority.
conflagration (kän'flə • grā'shən) *n.:* huge fire.
conscientious (kän'shē • en'shəs) *adj.:* careful and honest.
consequence (kän'si • kwens') *n.:* result of an action.
consolation (kän'sə • lā'shən) *n.:* comfort.
console (kän'sōl') *n.:* desklike control panel.
conspiracy (kən • spir'ə • sē) *n.:* secret plot with a harmful or illegal purpose.
constitution (kän'stə • to͞o'shən) *n.:* physical condition.
constrain (kən • strān') *v.:* to force.
consultation (kän'səl • tā'shən) *n.:* meeting to discuss or plan.
contemptuous (kən • temp'cho͞o • əs) *adj.:* scornful.
contrivance (kən • trī'vəns) *n.:* scheme; plan.
conundrum (kə • nun'drəm) *n.:* riddle.
convene (kən • vēn') *v.:* to assemble.
conviction (kən • vik'shən) *n.:* belief.
convivial (kən • viv'ē • əl) *adj.:* jovial; sociable.
copious (kō'pē • əs) *adj.:* great amounts of.
correspondence (kôr'ə • spän'dəns) *n.:* communication by letters.
countenance (koun'tə • nəns) *n.:* face.
craven (krā'vən) *adj.:* very fearful; cowardly.
crucial (kro͞o'shəl) *adj.:* difficult; decisive.
curry (kur'ē) *v.:* to groom.

debris (də • brē') *n.:* rubble; broken pieces.
decrepit (dē • krep'it) *adj.:* run-down; worn out by age or use.
deference (def'ər • əns) *n.:* respect.
defiant (dē • fī'ənt) *adj.:* openly disobedient.
dejection (dē • jek'shən) *n.:* discouragement.
deluge (del'yo͞oj') *n.:* rush; flood.
demeanor (di • mēn'ər) *n.:* behavior; conduct.
derision (di • rizh'ən) *n.:* ridicule; contempt.
discern (di • surn') *v.:* to notice; perceive.
disclaimer (dis • klām'ər) *n.:* refusal of responsibility.
disconsolate (dis • kän'sə • lit) *adj.:* unhappy.
discourse (dis'kôrs') *n.:* conversation.
discreet (di • skrēt') *adj.:* wisely cautious.
disdain (dis • dān') *v.:* to refuse; disapprove; scorn.
disembody (dis'im • bäd'ē) *v.:* to separate from the body.
disheveled (di • shev'əld) *adj.:* rumpled; messed up.
dispel (di • spel') *v.:* to drive away.
disperse (di • spurs') *v.:* to scatter.
dispirit (di • spir'it) *v.:* to discourage.
dispute (di • spyo͞ot') *v.:* to contest.
distraction (di • strak'shən) *n.:* mental disturbance or distress.
distraught (di • strôt') *adj.:* troubled.
divergence (dī • vur'jəns) *n.:* variance; difference.
docile (däs'əl) *adj.:* passive.
doddering (däd'ər • iŋ) *adj.:* shaky; trembling from old age.
dominant (däm'ə • nənt) *adj.:* prevailing; principal.
dominion (də • min'yən) *n.:* rule.
dowry (dou'rē) *n.:* money or goods the bride brings with her in a marriage.
drily (drī'lē) *adv.:* matter-of-factly; without emotion.
drone (drōn) *n.:* monotonous hum.
dwindle (dwin'dəl) *v.:* to diminish.

edible (ed'ə • bəl) *adj.:* capable of being eaten.
effectual (e • fek'cho͞o • əl) *adj.:* productive; efficient.
effete (e • fēt') *adj.:* sterile; unproductive.
elaborate (ē • lab'ə • rāt') *v.:* to develop with great care.
elapse (ē • laps') *v.:* to pass by; slip away.
elation (ē • lā'shən) *n.:* celebration.
eloquence (el'ə • kwəns) *n.:* well-articulated, persuasive speech.
elude (ē • lo͞od') *v.:* to escape.
emaciate (ē • mā'shē • āt') *v.:* to cause to be unusually thin.
eminent (em'ə • nənt) *adj.:* well known for excellence; important; outstanding.
encumbrance (en • kum'brəns) *n.:* burden; hindrance.
engagement (en • gāj'mənt) *n.:* battle.
enmity (en'mə • tē) *n.:* hatred.
ensue (en • so͞o') *v.:* to result.
enthrall (en • thrôl') *v.:* to fascinate.

fat, āpe, cär; ēven; is, bīte; gō, hôrn, look, to͞ol; yoo, cure; yo͞o, use; oil, out; up, fur; get; joy; yet; chin; she; thin; *th*en; zh, leisure; ŋ, ring; ə for *a* in *ago, e* in *agent, i* in *sanity, o* in *comply, u* in *focus;* ' as in *battle* (bat''l).

entreat (en·trēt′) *v.:* to ask sincerely; pray to.
epitaph (ep′ə·taf′) *n.:* memorable or descriptive phrase written on a tombstone or in memory of the dead.
equivocal (ē·kwiv′ə·kəl) *adj.:* having more than one meaning.
eradicate (i·rad′i·kāt′) *v.:* to eliminate.
erudite (er′yo͞o·dīt′) *adj.:* scholarly; well informed.
ethereal (ē·thir′ē·əl) *adj.:* not earthly; spiritual.
eulogy (yo͞o′lə·jē) *n.:* public speech of praise.
evident (ev′ə·dənt) *adj.:* clear; obvious.
exaggeration (eg·zaj′ər·ā′·shən) *n.:* overstatement.
exalt (eg·zôlt′) *v.:* to lift up.
excruciating (eks·kro͞o′shē·āt′iŋ) *adj.:* extreme; intense.
execration (ek′si·krā′shən) *n.:* angry word; curse.
exemplary (eg·zem′plə·rē) *adj.:* serving as a model.
expedient (ek·spē′dē·ənt) *n.:* convenience; means to an end.
expire (ek·spīr′) *v.:* to die.
explicit (eks·plis′it) *adj.:* clear; definite.
expunge (ek·spunj′) *v.:* to erase; remove.
extremity (ek·strem′ə·tē) *n.:* limb of the body, especially a hand or foot.
exuberant (eg·zo͞o′bər·ənt) *adj.:* intensely happy; visibly enthusiastic.
exult (eg·zult′) *v.:* to rejoice greatly.

facilitate (fə·sil′ə·tāt′) *v.:* to simplify.
fastidious (fas·tid′ē·əs) *adj.:* difficult to please; critical.
ferocity (fə·räs′ə·tē) *n.:* fierce cruelty.
fidelity (fə·del′ə·tē) *n.:* accuracy.
fitful (fit′fəl) *adj.:* restless.
flippancy (flip′ən·sē) *n.:* impertinence; glibness.
florid (flôr′id) *adj.:* showy.
flourish (flʉr′ish) *v.:* to do well; blossom.
fraternal (frə·tʉrn′əl) *adj.:* brotherly; friendly.
frenzy (fren′zē) *n.:* frantic behavior; wildness.
frippery (frip′ər·ē) *n.:* something showy, frivolous, or unnecessary.
frugal (fro͞o′gəl) *adj.:* thrifty; economical.
furrow (fʉr′ō) *n.:* groove in the land made by a plow.
furtive (fʉr′tiv) *adj.:* secret; stealthy.
futile (fyo͞ot′'l) *adj.:* useless; pointless.

gait (gāt) *n.:* way of walking; stride.
gall *v.:* to irritate; anger.
garnish (gär′nish) *v.:* to top.
gaudy (gôd′ē) *adj.:* cheap; showy.
gaunt (gônt) *adj.:* very thin.
gesticulate (jes·tik′yo͞o·lāt′) *v.:* to gesture, especially with the hands and arms, while speaking.
gregarious (grə·ger′ē·əs) *adj.:* sociable. —**gregariousness** *n.*
grope (grōp) *v.:* to search; fumble.
grotesque (grō·tesk′) *adj.:* strange; absurd.
guffaw (gu·fô′) *v.:* to burst out laughing.
guileless (gīl′lis) *adj.:* innocent or frank; without slyness.
gyration (jī·rā′shən) *n.:* circular movement; whirling.

habitual (hə·bich′o͞o·əl) *adj.:* usual.
haggard (hag′ərd) *adj.:* wasted or worn in appearance.
hail *v.:* to greet.
haughty (hôt′ē) *adj.:* proud; disdainful of something or someone.
hedonism (hē′dən·iz′əm) *n.:* self-indulgent pursuit of pleasure. —**hedonistic** *adj.*
hierarchy (hī′ər·är′kē) *n.:* class system of social ranking.
hinder (hin′dər) *v.:* to thwart; impede.
humor (hyo͞o′mər) *v.:* to indulge.
hysteria (hi·ster′ē·ə) *n.:* uncontrolled excitement.

idealist (ī·dē′əl·ist) *n.:* one who believes in noble, though often impractical, goals; dreamer.
illumine (i·lo͞o′mən) *v.:* to light up.
immune (im·myo͞on′) *adj.:* protected.
impart (im·pärt′) *v.:* to reveal.
imperative (im·per′ə·tiv) *adj.:* absolutely necessary; compulsory.
imperceptible (im′pər·sep′tə·bəl) *adj.:* not easily perceived.
impervious (im·pʉr′vē·əs) *adj.:* resistant; impenetrable.
impetuous (im·pech′o͞o·əs) *adj.:* impulsive.
impious (im′pē·əs) *adj.:* irreverent.
implore (im·plôr′) *v.:* to plead; entreat.
imprecation (im′pri·kā′shən) *n.:* curse.
improvident (im·präv′ə·dənt) *adj.:* careless; not providing for the future.
inanimate (in·an′ə·mit) *adj.:* lifeless.
inarticulate (in′är·tik′yo͞o·lit) *adj.:* not understandable.
incapacitate (in′kə·pas′ə·tāt′) *v.:* to disable.
incendiary (in·sen′dē·er′ē) *adj.:* designed to cause fires.
incessant (in·ses′ənt) *adj.:* never stopping.
incised (in·sīzd′) *adj.:* deeply marked.
inconceivable (in′kən·sēv′ə·bəl) *adj.:* unimaginable; beyond understanding.
indiscreet (in′di·skrēt′) *adj.:* lack of care in speech or action.
indolent (in′də·lənt) *adj.:* lazy.
indubitable (in·do͞o′bi·tə·bəl) *adj.:* that which cannot be doubted.
induce (in·do͞os′) *v.:* to persuade; force; cause.
indulge (in·dulj′) *v.:* to satisfy; please; humor.
inert (in·ʉrt′) *adj.:* dull; slow.
inevitable (in·ev′i·tə·bəl) *adj.:* not avoidable.
infallible (in·fal′ə·bəl) *adj.:* sure; never wrong.
infirm (in·fʉrm′) *adj.:* physically weak.
ingenious (in·jēn′yəs) *adj.:* clever; original.
inherent (in·hir′ənt) *adj.:* inborn.
iniquity (i·nik′wi·tē) *n.:* wickedness.
inordinate (in·ôr′də·nit) *adj.:* excessive.
inscrutable (in·skro͞ot′ə·bəl) *adj.:* mysterious.
insidious (in·sid′ē·əs) *adj.:* sly; sneaky.
insinuate (in·sin′yo͞o·āt′) *v.:* to suggest.
insipid (in·sip′id) *adj.:* bland; without flavor.
insolent (in′sə·lənt) *adj.:* arrogant.
insurrection (in′sə·rek′shən) *n.:* rebellion; revolt.
intangible (in·tan′jə·bəl) *adj.:* difficult to define; vague.

integrate (in′tə • grāt′) *v.:* to unify.
integrity (in • teg′rə • tē) *n.:* sound moral principles; honesty.
intent (in • tent′) *adj.:* purposeful.
interject (in′tər • jekt′) *v.:* to interrupt with; insert.
interloper (in′tər • lō′pər) *n.:* intruder or meddler.
interminable (in • tʉr′mi • nə • bəl) *adj.:* endless.
intermittent (in′tər • mit′′nt) *adj.:* pausing occasionally.
interpose (in′tər • pōz′) *v.:* to put forth in order to intervene.
intersperse (in′tər • spʉrs′) *v.:* to place at intervals.
intimate (in′tə • māt′) *v.:* to state indirectly; hint.
intricate (in′tri • kit) *adj.:* complicated.
intrigue (in′trēg′) *n.:* scheming.
intuitive (in • to͞o′i • tiv) *adj.:* known without conscious reasoning.
inviolate (in • vī′ə • lit) *adj.:* uncorrupted; safe.
irk (ʉrk) *v.:* to annoy; irritate. —**irksome** *adj.*
itinerant (ī • tin′ər • ənt) *adj.:* traveling.

jaunty (jônt′ē) *adj.:* fashionable.
jilt *v.:* to reject after previously accepting.
jocular (jäk′yo͞o • lər) *adj.:* joking; comical.
judicious (jo͞o • dish′əs) *adj.:* cautious; wise.

laborious (lə • bôr′ē • əs) *adj.:* difficult; involving much hard work.
labyrinth (lab′ə • rinth′) *n.:* puzzling path.
lamentable (lam′ən • tə • bəl) *adj.:* regrettable; distressing.
languid (laŋ′gwid) *adj.:* weak, as from exhaustion.
legacy (leg′ə • sē) *n.:* inheritance.
list *v.:* to tilt.
loiter (loit′ər) *v.:* to spend time; hang around.
lore (lôr) *n.:* traditional knowledge or teachings.
lucidity (lo͞o • sid′i • tē) *n.:* clarity; rationality.
ludicrous (lo͞o′di • krəs) *adj.:* laughable; absurd.
lurk (lʉrk) *v.:* to hide unnoticed.
luxuriant (lug • zhoor′ē • ənt) *adj.:* rich; abundant.

machination (mak′ə • nā′shən) *n.:* plot; crafty scheme.
magnanimity (mag′nə • nim′ə • tē) *n.:* nobility of spirit.
malicious (mə • lish′əs) *adj.:* intentionally hurtful.
malign (mə • līn′) *adj.:* harmful; evil.
malleable (mal′ē • ə • bəl) *adj.:* capable of being shaped.
malodorous (mal′ō′dər • əs) *adj.:* bad smelling.
manifest (man′ə • fest′) *adj.:* plain; clear.
manifold (man′ə • fōld′) *adj.:* many and different.
margin (mär′jən) *n.:* extra amount.
marshal (mär′shəl) *v.:* to lead; guide.
martial (mär′shəl) *adj.:* warlike.
meager (mē′gər) *adj.:* poor; inadequate.
meditative (med′ə • tāt′iv) *adj.:* deeply thoughtful.
medium (mē′dē • əm) *n.:* means of expressing art.

melancholy (mel′ən • käl′ē) *adj.:* sad; sorrowful.
mesmerize (mez′mər • īz′) *v.:* to hypnotize.
mincing (mins′iŋ) *adj.:* affectedly dainty.
mirth (mʉrth) *n.:* joyfulness.
misgiving (mis′giv′iŋ) *n.:* doubt; worry.
misnomer (mis • nō′mər) *n.:* wrong term or name.
moderate (mäd′ər • it) *adj.:* gentle.
monologue (män′ə • lôg′) *n.:* speech given by one person.
morbid (môr′bid) *adj.:* diseased; unhealthy.
morose (mə • rōs′) *adj.:* gloomy.
mortal (môr′təl) *adj.:* life-threatening; causing death.
mortar (môrt′ər) *n.:* cannon used to fire explosive shells.
municipal (myo͞o • nis′ə • pəl) *adj.:* belonging to a city or town.
mutual (myo͞o′cho͞o • əl) *adj.:* shared.
myriad (mir′ē • əd) *adj.:* countless.

nape (nāp) *n.:* back of the neck.
nauseate (nô′zhē • āt′) *v.:* to cause to feel sickness or discomfort in the stomach.
negotiate (ni • gō′shē • āt′) *v.:* to make a bargain; come to an agreement.
nether (ne*th*′ər) *adj.:* lower.
nimbus (nim′bəs) *n.:* aura; halo.
nomadic (nō • mad′ik) *adj.:* wandering.
nominal (näm′ə • nəl) *adj.:* very small.
nostalgia (näs • tal′jə) *n.:* longing.
nuptial (nup′shəl) *adj.:* related to weddings or marriage.

oblique (ō • blēk′) *adj.:* slanted.
obliterate (ə • blit′ər • āt′) *v.:* to destroy.
obscure (əb • skyoor′) *v.:* to conceal. —**obscurity** *n.*
obsequious (əb • sē′kwē • əs) *adj.:* obedient; submissive.
obsess (əb • ses′) *v.:* to preoccupy; haunt.
obstinate (äb′stə • nət) *adj.:* stubborn.
obstruction (əb • struk′shən) *n.:* blockage; hindrance.
occult (ə • kult′) *adj.:* hidden.
ominous (äm′ə • nəs) *adj.:* sinister; dangerous.
omnipotent (äm • nip′ə • tənt) *adj.:* all-powerful.
omniscient (äm • nish′ənt) *adj.:* all-knowing.
opaque (ō • pāk′) *adj.:* not transparent; not letting light pass through.
oppression (ə • presh′ən) *n.:* feeling of being tyrannized.
opulent (äp′yo͞o • lənt) *adj.:* abundant; plentiful.
oscillation (äs′ə • lā′shən) *n.:* regular back-and-forth movement.
ostentation (äs′tən • tā′shən) *n.:* conspicuous display.
overcast (ō′vər • kast′) *adj.:* cloudy; gloomy.
overture (ō′vər • chər) *n.:* approach; offer.

pallid (pal′id) *adj.:* pale.
palpable (pal′pə • bəl) *adj.:* obvious; perceivable.
pandemonium (pan′də • mō′nē • əm) *n.:* wild confusion.

---

fat, āpe, cär; ēven; is, bīte; gō, hôrn, look, to͞ol; yoo, cure; yo͞o, use; oil, out; up, fʉr; get; joy; yet; chin; she; thin; *th*en; zh, leisure; ŋ, ring; ə for *a* in *ago, e* in *agent, i* in *sanity, o* in *comply, u* in *focus;* ′ as in *battle* (bat′′l).

---

pauper (pô′pər) *n.:* extremely poor person.
pendulum (pen′dyo͞o • ləm) *n.:* freely swinging weight suspended from a fixed point to regulate a clock's movement.
penitent (pen′i • tənt) *adj.:* sorry for doing wrong.
pensive (pen′siv) *adj.:* thinking deeply or seriously.
perennial (pər • en′ē • əl) *adj.:* recurring yearly.
perilous (per′ə • ləs) *adj.:* dangerous.
permeate (pʉr′mē • āt′) *v.:* to spread through and affect every part of.
perpetual (pər • pech′o͞o • əl) *adj.:* constant; unchanging.
perpetuity (pʉr′pə • to͞o′ə • tē) *n.:* eternity.
perseverance (pʉr′sə • vir′əns) *n.:* persistence.
persistent (pər • sist′ənt) *adj.:* continuing.
pertinent (pʉr′tə • nənt) *adj.:* to the point; applying to the situation.
perturbation (pʉr′tər • bā′shən) *n.:* feeling of alarm or agitation.
pervade (pər • vād′) *v.:* to spread throughout.
pervert (pər • vʉrt′) *v.:* to misdirect; corrupt.
petulance (pech′ə • ləns) *n.:* irritability; impatience.
philanthropies (fə • lan′thrə • pēz) *n. pl.:* charitable gifts.
pious (pī′əs) *adj.:* devoted to one's religion.
pivotal (piv′ə • təl) *adj.:* central; something around which other things turn.
placid (plas′id) *adj.:* calm; quiet.
plague (plāg) *v.:* to annoy.
plaintive (plān′tiv) *adj.:* expressing sadness.
plausibility (plô′zə • bil′i • tē) *n.:* believability.
plunder (plun′dər) *n.:* goods seized, especially during wartime.
poignant (poin′yənt) *adj.:* emotionally moving.
populous (päp′yo͞o • ləs) *adj.:* crowded with people.
portend (pôr • tend′) *v.:* to signify.
posterity (päs • ter′ə • tē) *n.:* generations to come.
potency (pōt′′n • sē) *n.:* strength; power.
precedence (pres′ə • dəns) *n.:* order.
précis (prā • sē′) *n.:* summary.
predominate (prē • däm′ə • nāt′) *v.:* to have influence over.
preeminent (prē • em′ə • nənt) *adj.:* above all else.
preposterous (prē • päs′tər • əs) *adj.:* ridiculous.
prestigious (pres • tij′əs) *adj.:* impressive; having an excellent reputation.
pretense (prē • tens′) *n.:* false claim.
procure (prō • kyoor′) *v.:* to gain; obtain; acquire.
prodigal (präd′i • gəl) *adj.:* extremely abundant.
prodigious (prō • dij′əs) *adj.:* of great size and power.
prodigy (präd′ə • jē) *n.:* extremely gifted person.
profane (prō • fān′) *adj.:* irreverent.
profound (prō • found′) *adj.:* deep.
profundity (prō • fun′də • tē) *n.:* intellectual depth.
profuse (prō • fyo͞os′) *adj.:* abundant.
propagate (präp′ə • gāt′) *v.:* to transmit; spread.
proportionate (prō • pôr′shən • it) *adj.:* having a correct relationship between parts; balanced.
prostrate (präs′trāt′) *adj.:* lying flat on the ground.
protrude (prō • tro͞od′) *v.:* to stick out.
provisional (prō • vizh′ə • nəl) *adj.:* temporary; for the time being.
provoke (prō • vōk′) *v.:* to enrage; anger.
prudent (pro͞od′′nt) *adj.:* well thought out; cautious.
pulverize (pul′vər • īz′) *v.:* to crush; destroy.

radiation (rā′dē • ā′shən) *n.:* pattern; arrangement.
rakish (rāk′ish) *adj.:* dashing; jaunty.
rancor (raŋ′kər) *n.:* anger.
raucous (rô′kəs) *adj.:* loud; boisterous.
ravage (rav′ij) *n.:* act of violent destruction.
ravenous (rav′ə • nəs) *adj.:* very eager.
realm (relm) *n.:* kingdom.
recede (ri • sēd′) *v.:* to become more distant and indistinct.
recoil (ri • koil′) *v.:* to shrink away; draw back.
recollect (rek′ə • lekt′) *v.:* to remember.
reconcile (rek′ən • sīl′) *v.:* to make peace.
rectitude (rek′tə • to͞od′) *n.:* correctness.
reflective (ri • flek′tiv) *adj.:* thoughtful; contemplative.
reiterate (rē • it′ə • rāt′) *v.:* to repeat.
rejoinder (ri • join′dər) *n.:* answer.
relent (ri • lent′) *v.:* to soften; to diminish in intensity.
relinquish (ri • liŋ′kwish) *v.:* to give up.
render (ren′dər) *v.:* to make.
rendezvous (rän′dā • vo͞o′) *n.:* meeting place.
rend *v.:* to rip apart violently.
renounce (ri • nouns′) *v.:* to give up.
reprobate (rep′rə • bāt′) *n.:* person without any sense of duty or decency.
reprove (ri • pro͞ov′) *v.:* to reprimand.
reserve (ri • zʉrv′) *n.:* self-restraint.
resignation (rez′ig • nā′shən) *n.:* acquiescence; reluctant acceptance.
resolute (rez′ə • lo͞ot′) *adj.:* determined.
resolve (ri • zälv′) *v.:* to make a decision; determine.
retort (ri • tôrt′) *n.:* quick answer.
retraction (ri • trak′shən) *n.:* withdrawal.
revelation (rev′ə • lā′shən) *n.:* disclosure; something made known.
revel (rev′əl) *v.:* to take pleasure.
reverential (rev′ə • ren′shəl) *adj.:* deeply respectful.
reverie (rev′ər • ē) *n.:* daydream; fantasy.
rue (ro͞o) *v.:* to regret.
ruse (ro͞oz) *n.:* trick; deception.

sacrilege (sak′rə • lij) *n.:* violation of something sacred.
sagacious (sə • gā′shəs) *adj.:* wise; keenly perceptive.
sappy (sap′ē) *adj.:* foolish.
sarcastic (sär • kas′tik) *adj.:* scornful; mocking.
sate (sāt) *v.:* to satisfy.
saturated (sach′ə • rāt′id) *adj.:* completely soaked.
saucy (sô′sē) *adj.:* sassy; impertinent. —**saucily** *adv.*
savory (sā′vər • ē) *adj.:* appetizing; agreeable.
scrupulous (skro͞o′pyə • ləs) *adj.:* careful; painstaking.
scrutinize (skro͞ot′′n • īz′) *v.:* to carefully observe.

sedate (si • dāt′) *adj.:* calm and composed.
semblance (sem′bləns) *n.:* outward appearance.
seminary (sem′ə • ner′ē) *n.:* school for training ministers.
sensor (sen′sər) *n.:* detecting device.
sentinel (sen′ti • nəl) *n.:* guard; sentry.
serene (sə • rēn′) *adj.:* calm.
sibling (sib′liŋ) *n.:* brother or sister.
similitude (sə • mil′ə • to͞od′) *n.:* likeness.
simultaneous (sī′məl • tā′nē • əs) *adj.:* at the same time.
singular (siŋ′gyə • lər) *adj.:* remarkable.
slough (sluf) *n.:* outer layer of snake's skin, shed periodically.
sobriety (sə • brī′ə • tē) *n.:* state or quality of being sober.
sojourn (sō′jʉrn) *n.:* short stay.
solace (säl′is) *v.:* to comfort.
solemn (säl′əm) *adj.:* serious. —**solemnity** *n.*
solidity (sə • lid′ə • tē) *n.:* firmness; solidness.
somber (säm′bər) *adj.:* gloomy; dark.
specious (spē′shəs) *adj.:* seemingly sound, but not really so.
spurn (spʉrn) *v.:* to reject with contempt.
squeamish (skwēm′ish) *adj.:* easily offended.
stolid (stäl′id) *adj.:* showing no emotion.
striking (strī′kiŋ) *adj.:* impressive; attractive.
stupor (sto͞o′pər) *n.:* state of mental dullness; loss of the senses.
sublime (sə • blīm′) *adj.:* awe-inspiring.
subsequent (sub′si • kwənt) *adj.:* following.
subside (səb • sīd′) *v.:* to settle down.
subsist (səb • sist′) *v.:* to stay alive.
successive (sək • ses′iv) *adj.:* consecutive.
sultry (sul′trē) *adj.:* humid and still.
sundry (sun′drē) *adj.:* some.
superficial (so͞o′pər • fish′əl) *adj.:* obvious; shallow.
superfluous (sə • pʉr′flo͞o • əs) *adj.:* unnecessary.
supplication (sup′lə • kā′shən) *n.:* earnest plea.
suppress (sə • pres′) *v.:* to restrain; hold back.
surmise (sər • mīz′) *n.:* guess.
sustain (sə • stān′) *v.:* to prolong.
symmetrical (si • me′tri • kəl) *adj.:* equally balanced.

taboo (tə • bo͞o′) *n.:* something that is forbidden.
tacit (tas′it) *adj.:* implied but not expressed openly.
tactful (takt′fəl) *adj.:* skilled in saying the right thing.
tactile (tak′təl) *adj.:* able to be perceived by touch.
taut (tôt) *adj.:* tense; rigid.
tedious (tē′dē • əs) *adj.:* tiring; dreary.
temple (tem′pəl) *n.:* side of the forehead, just above and in front of each ear.
temporal (tem′pə • rəl) *adj.:* worldly.
tenuous (ten′yo͞o • əs) *adj.:* slight; insubstantial; not firm.
tepid (tep′id) *adj.:* lukewarm.
theologian (thē′ə • lō′jən) *n.:* scholar of religious doctrine.
torpor (tôr′pər) *n.:* inactive period.
tout (tout) *v.:* to praise highly.
traditional (trə • dish′ə • nel) *adj.:* established; customary.
tranquil (tran′kwil) *adj.:* calm; quiet.
transcendent (tran • sen′dənt) *adj.:* excelling; surpassing.
transcribe (tran • skrīb′) *v.:* to write down.
transient (tran′shənt) *adj.:* temporary; passing.
translucent (trans • lo͞o′sənt) *adj.:* so fine that light seems to pass through it.
tread (tred) *n.:* stepping.
trepidation (trep′ə • dā′shən) *n.:* anxious uncertainty.
tumultuous (to͞o • mul′cho͞o • əs) *adj.:* stormy; turbulent.
turbulence (tʉr′byo͞o • ləns) *n.:* irregular behavior.
tyranny (tir′ə • nē) *n.:* oppression.

ubiquitous (yo͞o • bik′wə • təs) *adj.:* everywhere at the same time.
ultimatum (ul′tə • māt′əm) *n.:* last offer; final proposition.
undulation (un′dyo͞o • lā′shən) *n.:* wavelike motion.
unobtrusive (un • əb • tro͞o′siv) *adj.:* inconspicuous; quiet.
unseemly (un • sēm′lē) *adj.:* improper.
upbraid (up • brād′) *v.:* to criticize severely.

valance (val′əns) *n.:* short decorative drapery.
valor (val′ər) *n.:* great courage.
vanity (van′ə • tē) *n.:* excessive pride.
vehement (vē′ə • mənt) *adj.:* emphatic.
venerable (ven′ər • ə • bəl) *adj.:* respected; esteemed for age or distinguished character.
vengeful (venj′fəl) *adj.:* intent on revenge.
venture (ven′chər) *v.:* to dare or risk going.
veritable (ver′i • tə • bəl) *adj.:* genuine; true.
vibrant (vī′brənt) *adj.:* full of energy.
vigilant (vij′ə • lənt) *adj.:* watchful.
vigor (vig′ər) *n.:* intense strength; vitality.
vindicate (vin′də • kāt′) *v.:* to prove correct.
virulent (vir′yo͞o • lənt) *adj.:* full of hate; venomous.
vista (vis′tə) *n.:* view.
vital (vīt′'l) *adj.:* filled with life.
vivacious (vī • vā′shəs) *adj.:* cheerful; lively.
void (void) *adj.:* empty.
volition (vō • lish′ən) *n.:* will.
volley (väl′ē) *n.:* firing of many shots at once.
vouch (vouch) *v.:* to guarantee.
vulnerability (vul′nər • ə • bil′ə • tē) *n.:* state of being open to attack.

wariness (wer′ē • nis) *n.:* caution; carefulness.
wearisome (wir′i • səm) *adj.:* fatiguing; exhausting.
wistfulness (wist′fəl • nes) *n.:* vague longing.
wither (with′ər) *v.:* to dry up; weaken.
wrought (rôt) *adj.:* created; made.

fat, āpe, cär; ēven; is, bīte; gō, hôrn, look, to͞ol; yoo, cure; yo͞o, use; oil, out; up, fʉr; get; joy; yet; chin; she; thin; *th*en; zh, leisure; ŋ, ring; ə for *a* in *ago, e* in *agent, i* in *sanity, o* in *comply, u* in *focus;* ′ as in *battle* (bat′'l).

ACKNOWLEDGMENTS

For permission to reprint copyrighted material, grateful acknowledgment is made to the following sources:

Agencia Literaria Carmen Balcells on behalf of Fundación Pablo Neruda: "Plenos Poderes" by Pablo Neruda. Copyright © 1958, 1959, 1961, 1962, 1964, 1967 by Pablo Neruda.

Edward Albee: From *Conversations with Edward Albee,* edited by Philip C. Kolin. Copyright © 1966 by Edward Albee.

The American Scholar: From "An American Childhood in the Dominican Republic" by Julia Alvarez from *The American Scholar,* vol. 56, no. 1, Winter 1987. Copyright © 1986 by Julia Alvarez.

Andrews & McMeel: "Coyote Finishes His Work" from *Giving Birth to Thunder, Sleeping with His Daughter* by Barry Holstun Lopez. Copyright © 1977 by Barry Holstun Lopez. All rights reserved.

Arte Público Press: "The Latin Deli: An Ars Poetica" by Judith Ortiz Cofer from *The Americas Review,* vol. 19, no. 1. Published by Arte Público Press–University of Houston, 1991. From *Silent Dancing* by Judith Ortiz Cofer. Copyright © 1990 by Judith Ortiz Cofer. Published by Arte Público Press–University of Houston, 1990. "Now and Then, America" from *Borders* by Pat Mora. Copyright © 1986 by Pat Mora. Published by Arte Público Press–University of Houston, 1986.

Elizabeth Barnett, Literary Executor: "Dirge Without Music," from "First Fig," and "Recuerdo" from *Collected Poems* by Edna St. Vincent Millay. Copyright © 1922, 1928, 1935, 1950 by Edna St. Vincent Millay and Norma Millay Ellis. Published by HarperCollins.

Beacon Press: "Autobiographical Notes" from *Notes of a Native Son* by James Baldwin. Copyright © 1955 and renewed © 1983 by James Baldwin.

Belles Lettres: Quote by Rita Dove from "Judith Pierce Rosenberg Interviews Our New Poet Laureate" from *Belles Lettres,* Winter 1993/94.

Susan Bergholz Literary Services, New York: "Daughter of Invention" from *How the Garcia Girls Lost Their Accents* by Julia Alvarez. Copyright © 1991 by Julia Alvarez. Published by Plume, an imprint of New American Library, a division of Penguin USA, New York; originally published in hardcover by Algonquin Books of Chapel Hill. "Straw into Gold" by Sandra Cisneros. Copyright © 1987 by Sandra Cisneros. First published in *The Texas Observer,* September 1987.

Brandt & Brandt Literary Agents: From "Qualified Homage to Thoreau" by Wallace Stegner from *Heaven Is Under Our Feet,* edited by Don Henley and Dave Marsh. Copyright © 1991 by The Isis Fund.

Gwendolyn Brooks: "Exhaust the little moment," "The Explorer," and "of De Witt Williams on his way to Lincoln Cemetery" from *Blacks* by Gwendolyn Brooks. Copyright © 1991 by Gwendolyn Brooks. Published by Third World Press, Chicago, 60619.

Lewis Buzbee: From "Interview with Raymond Carver" by Mona Simpson and Lewis Buzbee from *The Paris Review,* 1983.

Capra Press: "Everything Stuck to Him" from *Furious Seasons* by Raymond Carver. Copyright © 1977 by Raymond Carver.

Grace Cavalieri: From "Rita Dove: An Interview" by Grace Cavalieri from *American Poetry Review,* March/April 1995. Copyright © 1995 by Grace Cavalieri.

Joan Chatfield-Taylor: From "Cosmo Talks to Amy Tan" by Joan Chatfield-Taylor from *Cosmopolitan,* November 1989, pages 178–180. Copyright © 1989 by Joan Chatfield-Taylor.

Lucha Corpi and Catherine Rodríguez-Nieto: "Emily Dickinson" from *Palabras de Mediodía/Noon Words* by Lucha Corpi, translated by Catherine Rodríguez-Nieto. Copyright © 1980 by Lucha Corpi; translation © 1980 by Catherine Rodríguez-Nieto. Published by El Fuego de Aztlán Publications, Berkeley, Calif., 1980.

Victor Hernandez Cruz: "Don Arturo Says" by Victor Hernandez Cruz from *After Aztlan,* edited by Ray González. Copyright © 1992 by Victor Hernandez Cruz. Published by David R. Godine, Publisher, Inc., 1992.

Curbstone Press: "Who Understands Me but Me" from *What's Happening* by Jimmy Santiago Baca. Copyright © 1982 by Jimmy Santiago Baca.

Delacorte Press/Seymour Lawrence, a division of Bantam Doubleday Dell Publishing Group, Inc.: "Tamar" (and excerpts) from *Ellis Island & Other Stories* by Mark Helprin. Copyright © 1976, 1977, 1979, 1980, 1981 by Mark Helprin.

Doubleday, a division of Bantam Doubleday Dell Publishing Group, Inc.: From *The Power of Myth* by Joseph Campbell with Bill Moyers. Copyright © 1988 by Apostrophe S Productions, Inc., and Alfred van der Marck Editions. From *The Theatre of the Absurd* by Martin Esslin. Copyright © 1961 by Martin Esslin. From "Preface" from *The Open Boat: Poems from Asian America,* edited and with an Introduction by Garrett Hongo. Copyright © 1993 by Garrett Hongo. "Elegy for Jane" and "Open House" from *The Collected Poems of Theodore Roethke.* Copyright 1941, 1950 by Theodore Roethke.

Rita Dove: "The Satisfaction Coal Company" from *Selected Poems* by Rita Dove. Copyright © 1993 by Rita Dove. Quote by Rita Dove from *Washington Post,* April 17, 1987. Copyright © 1987 by Rita Dove.

Dutton Signet, a division of Penguin Books USA Inc.: "Borges and Myself" from *The Aleph and Other Stories* by Jorge Luis Borges, translated by Norman Thomas di Giovanni. Translation copyright © 1968, 1969, 1970 by Emece Editores, S.A., and Norman Thomas di Giovanni.

Faber and Faber Ltd.: From *The Criterion,* Vol. IX, by T. S. Eliot. Copyright © 1967 by Faber and Faber Ltd.

Far Corner Books: "Trying to Name What Doesn't Change" from *Words Under the Words: Selected Poems* by Naomi Shihab Nye. Copyright © 1995 by Naomi Shihab Nye. Published by Far Corner Books, Portland, OR.

Farrar, Straus & Giroux, Inc.: "The Fish" (and excerpts) from *The Complete Poems 1927–1979* by Elizabeth Bishop. Copyright © 1979, 1983 by Alice Helen Methfessel. From Introduction and "The Death of the Ball Turret Gunner" from *The Complete Poems* by Randall Jarrell. Copyright © 1969 by Mrs. Randall Jarrell. "For the Union Dead" (and excerpts) from *For the Union Dead* by Robert Lowell. Copyright © 1964 by Robert Lowell; copyright renewed © 1992 by Caroline Lowell, Harriet Lowell, and Sheridan Lowell. From "Memories of West Street and Lepke" from *Life Studies* by Robert Lowell. Copyright © 1956, 1959 by Robert Lowell; copyright renewed © 1987 by Caroline Lowell. "The Magic Barrel" from *The Magic Barrel* by Bernard Malamud. Copyright © 1950, 1958 and renewed © 1977, 1986 by Bernard Malamud. From *Passions and Impressions* by Pablo Neruda, translated by Margaret Sayers Peden. Translation copyright © 1983 by Farrar, Straus & Giroux, Inc. From *The Habit of Being* by Flannery O'Connor, edited by Sally Fitzgerald. Copyright © 1979 by Regina O'Connor. From "The Fiction Writer and His Country," from "The Grotesque in Southern Fiction," and from "Writing Short Stories" from *Mystery and Manners* by Flannery O'Connor, edited by Sally and Robert Fitzgerald. Copyright © 1969 by the Estate of Mary Flannery O'Connor. From *The Nobel Lecture* by Isaac Bashevis Singer. Copyright © 1978 by the Nobel Foundation. "Sea Canes" from *Sea Grapes* by Derek Walcott. Copyright © 1976 by Derek Walcott.

Gerard Flynn: From *Sor Juana Inés de la Cruz* by Gerard Flynn. Copyright © 1971 by Twayne Publishers, Inc. Published in *Twayne's World Authors Series,* edited by John P. Dyson.

Fondo de Cultura Económica: "World, in hounding me what do you gain?" by Sor Juana Inés de la Cruz from *Obras completas,* edited by Alfonso Méndez Plancarte. Copyright 1952 and © 1955 by Fondo de Cultura Económica.

Fulcrum Publishing: "The Sky Tree," retold by Joseph Bruchac from *Keepers of Life: Discovering Plants Through Native American Stories and Earth Activities for Children* by Michael J. Caduto and Joseph Bruchac.

Copyright © 1994 by Fulcrum Publishing, 350 Indiana St., #350, Golden, CO 80401.

GRM Associates, Inc., Agents for the Estate of Ida M. Cullen: "Incident" and "Tableau" (and excerpts) from *Color* by Countee Cullen. Copyright © 1925 by Harper & Brothers; copyright renewed © 1953 by Ida M. Cullen.

Gale Research, Inc.: Quote by James Merrill from *Contemporary Authors, New Revision Series,* Vol. 10, edited by Ann Evory and Linda Metzger. Copyright © 1983 by Gale Research Company. Quote by Judith Cofer from *Contemporary Authors, New Revision Series,* Vol. 32, edited by James G. Lesniak. Copyright © 1991 by Gale Research, Inc. Quote by Allen Ginsberg from *Contemporary Authors, New Revision Series,* Vol. 41, edited by Susan M. Trosky. Copyright © 1994 by Gale Research, Inc.

Peter A. Gilbert, Executor of the Robert Frost Estate: Quote by Robert Frost from "Robert Frost Relieves His Mind" interviewed by Rose C. Feld, from *The New York Times Book Review,* October 21, 1923. Copyright 1923 by Robert Frost.

Paul Gitlin, Administrator of the Estate of Thomas Wolfe: "His Father's Earth" from *The Web and the Rock* by Thomas Wolfe. Copyright 1937, 1938, 1939 by Maxwell Perkins as Executor; copyright renewed © 1967 by Paul Gitlin, C.T.A., Administrator of the Estate of Thomas Wolfe.

Donald J. Greiner: Quote by Donald J. Greiner from *Dictionary of Literary Biography, Volume 143: American Novelists Since World War II,* Third Series, edited by James R. Giles and Wanda H. Giles. Published by Gale Research, Inc., 1994.

Grosset & Dunlap: From "Knoxville: Summer 1915" from *A Death in the Family* by James Agee. Copyright 1938, © 1956, 1957 by the James Agee Trust; © renewed 1985 by Mia Agee.

Grove/Atlantic, Inc.: "Full Powers" from *A New Decade (Poems: 1958-1967)* by Pablo Neruda, translated by Alastair Reid. English translation copyright © 1969 by Alastair Reid. "The Journey" from *Dream Work* by Mary Oliver. Copyright © 1986 by Mary Oliver.

Harcourt Brace & Company: From *Cinco maestros: Cuentos modernos de Hispanoamerica,* edited by Alexander Coleman. Copyright © 1969 by Harcourt Brace & Company. "The Love Song of J. Alfred Prufrock" and excerpt from *Collected Poems, 1909–1962* by T. S. Eliot. Copyright 1930, 1940, 1941, 1942, 1943, © 1958, 1962, 1963 by T. S. Eliot; copyright 1954, © 1956, 1959, 1963 by Thomas Stearns Eliot; copyright 1934, 1936 by Harcourt Brace & Company; copyright © 1970 by Esme Valerie Eliot. From *Selected Prose of T. S. Eliot,* edited by Frank Kermode. Copyright © 1975 by Valerie Eliot. From "Washington Irving: 1783–1859" by William L. Hedges from *Major Writers of America.* Copyright © 1962 by Harcourt, Brace & World, Inc. "The Life You Save May Be Your Own" from *A Good Man Is Hard to Find and Other Stories* by Flannery O'Connor. Copyright 1953 by Flannery O'Connor; copyright renewed © 1981 by Regina O'Connor. "The Jilting of Granny Weatherall" and excerpt from *Flowering Judas and Other Stories* by Katherine Anne Porter. Copyright 1930 and renewed © 1958 by Katherine Anne Porter. From "In Search of Our Mothers' Gardens" from *In Search of Our Mothers' Gardens: Womanist Prose* by Alice Walker. Copyright © 1974 by Alice Walker. "Women" (as it appears in "In Search of Our Mothers' Gardens") from *Revolutionary Petunias & Other Poems* by Alice Walker. Copyright © 1970 by Alice Walker. "A Worn Path" from *A Curtain of Green and Other Stories* by Eudora Welty. Copyright 1941 and renewed © 1969 by Eudora Welty. From "A Memory" from *The Collected Stories of Eudora Welty.* Copyright 1936, 1937, 1938, 1939, 1941, 1942, 1943, 1947, 1948, 1949, 1951, 1952, 1954 © 1955, 1963, 1966, 1980 by Eudora Welty; copyright renewed © 1965, 1966, 1967, 1969, 1970, 1971, 1975, 1976, 1977, 1979, 1980 by Eudora Welty. "The Beautiful Changes" from *The Beautiful Changes and Other Poems* by Richard Wilbur. Copyright 1947 and renewed © 1975 by Richard Wilbur.

Joy Harjo: From "Three Generations of Native American Women's Birth Experience" by Joy Harjo from *Ms.,* vol. II, no. 1, July/August 1991. Copyright © 1991 by Joy Harjo.

HarperCollins Publishers, Inc.: "Homework" and from "Howl" from *Collected Poems 1947–1980* by Allen Ginsberg. Copyright © 1955, 1982 by Allen Ginsberg. From *Dust Tracks on a Road* by Zora Neale Hurston. Copyright 1942 by Zora Neale Hurston; copyright renewed © 1970 by John C. Hurston. "The Handsomest Drowned Man in the World" from *Leaf Storm and Other Stories* by Gabriel García Márquez. Copyright © 1971 by Gabriel García Márquez. From "The Rookers" from *Shiloh and Other Stories* by Bobbie Ann Mason. Copyright © 1982 by Bobbie Ann Mason. From "Foreword" by Robert Lowell from *Ariel* by Sylvia Plath. Copyright © 1961, 1962, 1963, 1964, 1965, 1966 by Ted Hughes. "Mirror" from *Crossing the Water* by Sylvia Plath. Copyright © 1963 by Ted Hughes. Originally appeared in *The New Yorker.* From *Black Boy* by Richard Wright. Copyright 1937, 1942, 1944, 1945 by Richard Wright; copyright renewed © 1973 by Ellen Wright. From *Walt Whitman: The Making of a Poet* by Paul Zweig. Copyright © 1984 Paul Zweig.

Harvard University Press: "Here follow Some Verses upon the Burning of Our House, July 10, 1666" and excerpts from *The Works of Anne Bradstreet,* edited by Jeannine Hensley. Copyright © 1967 by the President and Fellows of Harvard College. Published by The Belknap Press of Harvard University Press, Cambridge, Mass. "28: World, in hounding me, what do you gain?" by Juana Inés de la Cruz from *A Sor Juana Anthology,* translated by Alan S. Trueblood. Copyright © 1988 by the President and Fellows of Harvard College. Published by Harvard University Press, Cambridge, Mass. From *i: Six Nonlectures* by e. e. cummings. Copyright © 1953 by e. e. cummings. From *The Narrative of the Life of Frederick Douglass: An American Slave, Written by Himself,* edited by Benjamin Quarles. Copyright © 1960 by the President and Fellows of Harvard College. Published by The Belknap Press of Harvard University Press, Cambridge, Mass. From *Sor Juana: Or, The Traps of Faith* by Octavio Paz. Copyright © 1988 by the President and Fellows of Harvard College. Published by The Belknap Press of Harvard University Press, Cambridge, Mass.

Harvard University Press and the Trustees of Amherst College: "1624: Apparently with no surprise," "712: Because I could not stop for Death," "47: Heart! We will forget him!," "465: I heard a Fly buzz—when I died," "214: I taste a liquor never brewed," "288: I'm Nobody! Who are you?," and "1129: Tell all the Truth but tell it slant—" from *The Poems of Emily Dickinson,* edited by Thomas H. Johnson. Copyright © 1951, 1955, 1979, 1983 by the President and Fellows of Harvard College. Published by The Belknap Press of Harvard University Press, Cambridge, Mass. All rights reserved.

Heritage: "Imagination" by Shelby Pearl from *Heritage,* vol. 31, Spring 1991. Published by James Madison High School, Vienna, VA.

Hill and Wang, a division of Farrar, Straus & Giroux, Inc.: From "When the Negro Was in Vogue" from *The Big Sea* by Langston Hughes. Copyright © 1940 by Langston Hughes; copyright renewed © 1968 by Arna Bontemps and George Houston Bass.

Holocaust Museum & Library: Quote by Martin Niemöller from *Their Brothers' Keepers* by Philip Friedman. Copyright © by Holocaust Museum & Library.

Henry Holt and Company, Inc.: From *Interviews with Robert Frost,* edited by Edward Connery Lathem. Copyright © 1966 by Holt, Rinehart and Winston, Inc. "Design," "Neither Out Far Nor in Deep," "Nothing Gold Can Stay," and "Once by the Pacific" from *The Poetry of Robert Frost,* edited by Edward Connery Lathem. Copyright 1936, 1951, © 1956 by Robert Frost; copyright © 1964 by Lesley Frost Ballantine; copyright 1923, 1928, © 1969 by Henry Holt and Co., Inc. From "Take Something Like a Star" from *Robert Frost: Poetry and Prose,* edited by Edward Connery Lathem and Lawrence Thompson. Copyright 1949, © 1969 by Henry Holt and Co., Inc.; copyright © 1977 by Lesley Frost Ballantine. From *Tennessee Williams' Letters to Donald Windham 1940–1965,* edited by Donald Windham. Copyright © 1976, 1977, 1980 by Donald Windham.

Johns Hopkins University Press: Quote by Tim O'Brien from "Two Interviews: Talks with Tim O'Brien and Robert Stone" by Eric James Schroeder from *Modern Fiction Studies,* 30 Spring 1984. Copyright © 1984 by Eric James Schroeder.

Houghton Mifflin Company: From *Let Us Now Praise Famous Men* by James Agee and Walker Evans. Copyright 1939, 1940 by James Agee; copyright 1941 by James Agee and Walker Evans; copyright renewed © 1969 by Mia Fritsch Agee and Walker Evans. All rights reserved. From "The Congressional Library" from *What's O'Clock* by Amy Lowell. Copyright 1925 by Houghton Mifflin Company. All rights reserved. "Ars Poetica" from *Collected Poems 1917–1982* by Archibald MacLeish. Copyright © 1985 by The Estate of Archibald MacLeish. All rights reserved. "The Bells" from *To Bedlam and Part Way Back* by Anne Sexton. Copyright © 1960 by Anne Sexton; copyright renewed © 1988 by Linda G. Sexton. All rights reserved.
The Hudson Review, Inc.: From "Interview with Anne Sexton" by Patricia Marx from *The Hudson Review,* vol. XVIII, no. 4, Winter 1965–66. Copyright © 1966 by The Hudson Review, Inc.
Illinois State Historical Library, Springfield, IL: From letter by Sullivan Ballou, July 14, 1861, from the Adin Ballou Papers.
International Creative Management: From *Critical Essays on Arthur Miller* by James J. Martine. Copyright © 1960 by Arthur Miller. From "II: The State of the Theatre" by Arthur Miller, interviewed by Henry Brandom from *Harper's Magazine,* November 1960, vol. 221, no. 1326. Copyright © 1960 by Arthur Miller.
Jesse Jackson, Jr. on behalf of Jesse Jackson: From Reverend Jesse Jackson's speech to the Democratic Convention in 1988 from *Vital Speeches of the Day,* Vol. LIV, No. 21, August 15, 1988. Copyright © 1988 by Jesse Jackson.
Estate of Kirkland C. Jones: Quotes by Kirkland C. Jones from *Dictionary of Literary Biography ®, Volume One Hundred Twenty: American Poets Since World War II,* Third Series, edited by R. S. Gwynn. Published by Gale Research, Inc., 1992.
Alfred Kazin: From *Contemporaries* by Alfred Kazin. Copyright 1924, 1946, 1952, 1955, © 1956, 1957, 1958, 1959, 1960, 1961, 1962, 1982 by Alfred Kazin.
The Heirs to the Estate of Martin Luther King, Jr., c/o Joan Daves Agency as agent for the proprietor: From "I Have a Dream" by Martin Luther King, Jr., Copyright © 1963 by Martin Luther King, Jr.; copyright renewed © 1991 by Coretta Scott King. From "Letter from Birmingham City Jail" from *A Testament of Hope,* edited by James M. Washington. Copyright © 1963, 1964 by Martin Luther King, Jr.; copyright renewed © 1991, 1992 by Coretta Scott King.
Alfred A. Knopf, Inc.: "A Noiseless Flash" from *Hiroshima* by John Hersey. Copyright 1946 and renewed © 1974 by John Hersey. Originally appeared in *The New Yorker.* "Kubota" from *Volcano* by Garrett Hongo. Copyright © 1995 by Garrett Hongo. From "Let America Be America Again" from *Collected Poems* by Langston Hughes. Copyright © 1994 by the Estate of Langston Hughes. "Dream Deferred" from *The Panther and the Lash* by Langston Hughes. Copyright 1951 by Langston Hughes. "Harlem" from *Selected Poems* by Langston Hughes. Copyright 1951 by Langston Hughes. "I, Too" and "The Weary Blues" from *Selected Poems* by Langston Hughes. Copyright 1926 by Alfred A. Knopf, Inc.; copyright renewed 1954 by Langston Hughes. From "Ernest Hemingway" from *An American Procession* by Alfred Kazin. Copyright © 1984 by Alfred Kazin. "The Girl Who Wouldn't Talk" from *The Woman Warrior* by Maxine Hong Kingston. Copyright © 1975, 1976 by Maxine Hong Kingston. "The Fifteenth Summer" from *The Inner Room* by James Merrill. Copyright © 1988 by James Merrill. "Autobiographia Literaria" from *The Collected Poems of Frank O'Hara,* edited by Donald Allen. Copyright © 1967 by Maureen Granville-Smith, Administratrix of the Estate of Frank O'Hara. "Bells for John Whiteside's Daughter" from *Selected Poems* by John Crowe Ransom. Copyright 1924 by Alfred A. Knopf, Inc.; copyright renewed 1952 by John Crowe Ransom. "Anecdote of the Jar" from *Collected Poems* by Wallace Stevens. Copyright 1923 and renewed 1951 by Wallace Stevens. From "Of Modern Poetry" from *Collected Poems* by Wallace Stevens. Copyright 1942 by Wallace Stevens; copyright renewed © 1970 by Holly Stevens. From *Letters of Wallace Stevens,* selected and edited by Holly Stevens. Copyright © 1966 by Holly Stevens. From acceptance speech for the American Book Award for fiction, April 27, 1982, from *Hugging the Shore* by John Updike. Copyright © 1983 by John Updike. "Son" from *Problems and Other Stories* by John Updike. Copyright © 1979 by John Updike.
Kenneth Koch, c/o Maxine Groffsky Agency: "Permanently" from *Selected Poems, 1950–1982* by Kenneth Koch. Copyright © 1962, 1994 by Kenneth Koch.
Yusef Komunyakaa: Quote by Yusef Komunyakaa from "A Man of His Words" by Jeffrey Walker from *Los Angeles Times,* April 13, 1994. "Monsoon Season" from *Toys in a Field* by Yusef Komunyakaa. Copyright © 1986 by Yusef Komunyakaa.
Martin Levin: From "The Dogwood Tree: A Boyhood" from *Five Boyhoods* by John Updike, edited by Martin Levin. Copyright © 1951, 1956, 1957, 1958, 1959, 1960, 1961, 1962, 1963, 1964, 1965 by John Updike; copyright © 1962 by Martin Levin.
Estate of Vachel Lindsay: From letter from Vachel Lindsay to Langston Hughes.
Little, Brown and Company: From *Longfellow: His Life and Work* by Newton Arvin. Copyright © 1963 by Newton Arvin. From *Blue Highways* by William Least Heat-Moon. Copyright © 1982 by William Least Heat-Moon.
Liveright Publishing Corporation: From "Introduction" to *New Poems* from *Complete Poems: 1904–1962* by E. E. Cummings, edited by George J. Firmage. Copyright © 1938, 1966, 1991 by the Trustees for the E. E. Cummings Trust. "what if a much of a which of a wind" from *Complete Poems: 1904–1962* by E. E. Cummings, edited by George J. Firmage. Copyright © 1944, 1972, 1991 by the Trustees for the E. E. Cummings Trust.
Louisiana State University Press: "A Strange Beautiful Woman" from *Mama's Promises: Poems* by Marilyn Nelson Waniek. Copyright © 1985 by Marilyn Nelson Waniek.
Macmillan Reference USA, a Division of Simon & Schuster, Inc.: From *Webster's New World Dictionary,* Third College Edition. Copyright © 1988, 1991, 1994 by Simon & Schuster, Inc.
James Madison High School, Vienna, VA: From "An Interview with Rita Dove" by Moira Hanley and Catherine Nicholas from *Heritage,* vol. 34, Spring 1994.
Ellen C. Masters: From *Across Spoon River* by Edgar Lee Masters. Copyright 1936 by Edgar Lee Masters; copyright renewed © 1964 by Ellen Coyne Masters. Originally published by Farrar & Rinehart.
J. D. McClatchy: Quotes by Robert Lowell and James Dickey from *Anne Sexton: The Artist and Her Critics,* edited by J. D. McClatchy. Copyright © 1978 by J. D. McClatchy.
The Archives of Claude McKay, Carl Cowl, Administrator: "America" from *Selected Poems of Claude McKay.* Copyright 1953 by Bookman Associates, Inc.
Merlyn's Pen, Inc.: "The Mirror Girl—stares back at me—" from "Walt and Emily Revisited" by Brigid Spackman from *Merlyn's Pen,* February/March 1993. Copyright © 1993 by Merlyn's Pen Inc. First appeared in *Merlyn's Pen: The National Magazine of Student Writing.*
Merriam-Webster Inc.: Definition of "proud" from *Webster's Third New International Dictionary,* edited by Philip Babcock Grove, Ph.D. Copyright © 1993 by Merriam-Webster Inc.
William Morrow & Company, Inc.: From "Intimate and Untidy Stories" from *Kate Chopin* by Emily Toth. Copyright © 1990 by Emily Toth.
New Directions Publishing Corporation: "Fall" from *Black Mesa Poems* by Jimmy Santiago Baca. Copyright © 1989 by Jimmy Santiago Baca. "Oread" from *Collected Poems, 1912–1944* by H. D. Copyright © 1982 by The Estate of Hilda Doolittle. From "Early Success" from *The Crack-Up* by F. Scott Fitzgerald. Copyright © 1945 by New Directions Publishing Corporation. From "A Few Don'ts by an Imagiste" from *Literary Essays of Ezra Pound.* Copyright © by Faber and Faber Ltd. "A Pact," "In a Station of the Metro," and "The River-Merchant's Wife: A Letter" from *Personae: The Collected Poems of Ezra Pound.* Copyright © 1926 by Ezra Pound. From letter to Harriet Monroe from *Selected Letters of Ezra Pound.* Copyright © 1950 by Ezra Pound. From *Selected Prose 1909–1965* by Ezra Pound, edited

by William Cookson. Copyright © 1973 by New Directions Publishing Corporation. Quote by Ezra Pound from *Remembering Poets* by Donald Hall. Copyright © 1977, 1978 by Donald Hall. "Pine Tree Tops" from *Turtle Island* by Gary Snyder. Copyright © 1974 by Gary Snyder. From *The Autobiography of William Carlos Williams.* Copyright © 1951 by William Carlos Williams. "The Great Figure" and "The Red Wheelbarrow" from *Collected Poems: 1909–1939,* Volume I, by William Carlos Williams. Copyright © 1938 by New Directions Publishing Corporation.

The New York Review of Books: Quote by Thomas R. Edwards from *The New York Review of Books,* November 24, 1983. Copyright © 1983 by NYREV, Inc. From "Fitzgerald Revisited" by Jay McInerney from *The New York Review of Books,* August 15, 1991. Copyright © 1991 by NYREV, Inc.

The New York Times Company: Quote by Carl Sandburg from *The New York Times,* February 15, 1959. Copyright © 1959 by The New York Times Company. Quote by Sugar Ray Leonard from "Durán, Leonard Fit" from *The New York Times,* June 17, 1980. Copyright © 1980 by The New York Times Company. From "Black and Well-to-Do" by Andrea Lee from *The New York Times,* 1984. Copyright © 1984 by The New York Times Company. From "Mississippi Honors a 'Native Son' Who Fled" by Edwin McDowell from *The New York Times,* November 23, 1985. Copyright © 1985 by The New York Times Company. Quote by Tim O'Brien from "A Storyteller For the War That Won't End" by D.J.R. Bruckner from *The New York Times,* April 3, 1990. Copyright © 1990 by The New York Times Company. Quote by Toni Morrison from "Toni Morrison Is '93 Winner Of Nobel Prize in Literature" by William Grimes from *The New York Times,* October 8, 1993. Copyright © 1993 by The New York Times Company. "An American Story" by Anthony Lewis from *The New York Times,* November 26, 1993. Copyright © 1993 by The New York Times Company. "Poetry Emotion" by Anna Quindlen from *The New York Times,* April 16, 1994. Copyright © 1994 by The New York Times Company. Quote by Yusef Komunyakaa from "A Poet's Values: It's the Words Over the Man" by Bruce Weber from *The New York Times,* May 2, 1994. Copyright © 1994 by The New York Times Company. From "The New Measure of Man" by Vaclav Havel from *The New York Times,* July 8, 1994. Copyright © 1994 by The New York Times Company. Quote by Helen Vendler from a review of "James Merrill's *Braving the Elements*" as it appeared in *The New York Times Book Review,* September 24, 1972. Copyright © 1972 by The New York Times Company. From "Malamud's Dark Fable" by Alan Lelchuk from *The New York Times Book Review,* August 29, 1982. Copyright © 1982 by The New York Times Company. From "Pictures of Malamud" by Philip Roth from *The New York Times Book Review,* April 20, 1986. Copyright © 1986 by The New York Times Company. From "The Promiscuous Cool of Postmodernism" by Denis Donoghue from *The New York Times Book Review,* June 22, 1986. Copyright © 1986 by The New York Times Company. Quote by Raymond Carver from "Grace Has Come into My Life" by Stewart Kellerman from *The New York Times Book Review,* May 15, 1988. Copyright © 1988 by The New York Times Company. Quote by Roberto Márquez from *The New York Times Book Review,* September 24, 1989. Copyright © 1989 by The New York Times Company. From review of *Garcia Girls* by Julia Alvarez from *The New York Times Book Review,* October 6, 1991. Copyright © 1991 by The New York Times Company. From "A Poet's Safe Haven in Amherst" by Anne Bernays from *The New York Times Magazine, Part 2: The Sophisticated Traveler,* October 1, 1989. Copyright © 1989 by The New York Times Company.

The New Yorker: From "James Thurber" from *E. B. White: Writings from "The New Yorker," 1927–1976.* Copyright © 1961, 1989 by E. B. White. Originally appeared in *The New Yorker.* Published by HarperCollins.

The Nobel Foundation: Acceptance speeches by William Faulkner, Ernest Hemingway, and John Steinbeck from *Nobel Lectures in Literature: 1901–1967,* edited by Horst Frenz. Copyright 1949, 1954, and © 1962 by The Nobel Foundation.

Northern Illinois University Press: From *James Russell Lowell's The Biglow Papers: A Critical Edition* by Thomas Wortham. Copyright © 1977 by Northern Illinois University Press.

W. W. Norton & Company, Inc.: From "Foreword" from *Mother Love* by Rita Dove. Copyright © 1995 by Rita Dove. "Emily Dickinson" from *PM/AM: New and Selected Poems* by Linda Pastan. Copyright © 1982 by Linda Pastan. "Aunt Jennifer's Tigers" from *The Fact of a Doorframe: Poems Selected and New, 1950–1984* by Adrienne Rich. Copyright © 1975, 1978 by W. W. Norton & Company, Inc.; copyright © 1981, 1984 by Adrienne Rich. From "Still Just Writing" by Anne Tyler from *The Writer on Her Work,* Volume I, edited by Janet Sternburg. Copyright © 1980 by Janet Sternburg.

Harold Ober Associates Incorporated: From letter to George Freitag [August 27, 1938] from *Letters of Sherwood Anderson,* edited by H. M. Jones and Walter Rideout. Copyright 1953 by Eleanor Copenhaver Anderson. James Weldon Johnson Collection: Quotations from "Draft Ideas" December 3, 1964, by Langston Hughes, as they appear in *The Life of Langston Hughes, Vol. II: 1941–1967—I Dream a World.*

Tim O'Brien, c/o Janklow & Nesbit Associates: "Speaking of Courage" by Tim O'Brien from *The Massachusetts Review,* Summer 1976. Copyright © 1976 by Tim O'Brien. Slightly adapted.

Simon J. Ortiz: "Speaking" by Simon J. Ortiz. Copyright © 1989 by Simon J. Ortiz.

Pantheon Books, a division of Random House, Inc.: "House Taken Over" from *End of the Game and Other Stories* by Julio Cortázar, translated by Paul Blackburn. Copyright © 1967 by Random House, Inc.

The Paris Review: From "The Art of Fiction LXXXIII Julio Cortázar" from *The Paris Review,* vol. 26, no. 93, Fall 1984. Copyright © 1984 by The Paris Review, Inc.

Perspective: Quote by Andrew V. Ettin from *Perspective,* Spring 1967. Copyright © 1967 by Perspective.

Monica L. Porter: "rollerskating" by Monica Porter from *Stylus Literary Magazine,* vol. XV, June 1989. Copyright © 1989 by Monica L. Porter. Published by David Starr Jordan High School, Long Beach, CA.

Prentice Hall, a Division of Simon & Schuster: From *To Be Young, Gifted and Black: Lorraine Hansberry in Her Own Words,* adapted by Robert Nemiroff. Copyright © 1969 by Robert Nemiroff and Robert Nemiroff as Executor of the Estate of Lorraine Hansberry.

Gerard W. Purcell Associates: "My Guilt" from *Just Give Me a Cool Drink of Water 'fore I Diiie* by Maya Angelou. Copyright © 1969 by Hirt Music, Inc.

G. P. Putnam's Sons: From "Rules of the Game" from *The Joy Luck Club* by Amy Tan. Copyright © 1989 by Amy Tan.

Random House, Inc.: "The Unknown Citizen" from *W. H. Auden: Collected Poems.* Copyright © 1939 and copyright renewed © 1967 by W. H. Auden. From *Death Comes for the Archbishop* by Willa Cather. Copyright 1927 by Willa Cather; copyright renewed © 1955 by the Executors of the Estate of Willa Cather. Slightly adapted from *A Raisin in the Sun,* Expanded 25th Anniversary Edition, by Lorraine Hansberry. Copyright © 1958 by Robert Nemiroff as an unpublished work; copyright © 1959, 1966, 1984, 1987 by Robert Nemiroff. "A Rose for Emily" (and excerpts) from *Collected Stories of William Faulkner.* Copyright 1930 and renewed © 1958 by William Faulkner. "New African" from *Sarah Phillips* by Andrea Lee. Copyright © 1984 by Andrea Lee. From Appendix from *Hugging the Shore* by John Updike. Copyright © 1983 by John Updike. "Is Phoenix Jackson's Grandson Really Dead?" from *The Eye of the Story* by Eudora Welty. Copyright © 1978 by Eudora Welty.

St. James Press, an imprint of Gale Research, Inc.: From "James Merrill" by Paul Christensen, from "Rita Dove" by Julie Miller, and quote by Garrett Hongo from *Contemporary Poets,* Fifth Edition, edited by Tracy Chevalier. Copyright © 1991 by St. James Press.

The Saturday Evening Post Society: From "I Saw Lee Surrender" by Seth M. Flint from *The Saturday Evening Post,* vol. 248, no. 5, July/August 1976. Copyright © 1976 by The Saturday Evening Post Society.

Saturday Review: From "James Baldwin on the Sixties: Acts and Revelations" by Benjamin DeMott from the *Saturday Review,* May 27, 1972, pp. 63–64. Copyright © 1972 by SR Publications, Ltd.

Scribner, a Division of Simon & Schuster, Inc.: From *The Night Country* by Loren Eiseley. Copyright © 1971 by Loren Eiseley. From Letter to Scottie Fitzgerald, August 8, 1933, from *F. Scott Fitzgerald: A Life in Letters,* edited by Matthew J. Bruccoli. Copyright © 1994 by the Trustees Under Agreement Dated July 3, 1975, Created by Frances Scott Fitzgerald Smith. "Winter Dreams" from *The Short Stories of F. Scott Fitzgerald,* edited by Matthew J. Bruccoli. Copyright 1922 by Metropolitan Publications, Inc.; copyright renewed 1950 by Frances Scott Fitzgerald Lanahan. From "Absolution" from *The Short Stories of F. Scott Fitzgerald,* edited by Matthew J. Bruccoli. Copyright 1924 by American Mercury, Inc.; copyright renewed 1952 by Frances Scott Fitzgerald Lanahan. Copyright 1951 by Charles Scribner's Sons. "Soldier's Home" (and excerpts) from *In Our Time* by Ernest Hemingway. Copyright 1925 by Charles Scribner's Sons; copyright renewed 1953 by Ernest Hemingway. From "10. One True Sentence" from *Ernest Hemingway: A Life Story* by Carlos Baker. Copyright © 1969 by Carlos Baker; copyright © 1969 by Mary Hemingway.

Shades Valley Resource Learning Center: "The Sea" by Elizabeth Enloe from *Counterpane,* vol. 18, 1993. Published by Shades Valley Resource Learning Center, Birmingham, AL.

Margaret Shi: "The Skaters" by Maggie Shi from *Glyphs,* Vol. XXI, 1992. Published by Madison High School, Madison, NJ.

Simon & Schuster: From "All My Pretty Ones: Confession" from *Anne Sexton* by Caroline King Barnard Hall. Copyright © 1989 by G. K. Hall & Co. From *Catch-22* by Joseph Heller. Copyright © 1955, 1961 by Joseph Heller. "Poetry" (and excerpts) from *The Collected Poems of Marianne Moore.* Copyright 1935 by Marianne Moore; copyright renewed © 1963 by Marianne Moore and T. S. Eliot. From *The Cycle of American Literature: An Essay in Historical Criticism* by Robert E. Spiller. Copyright © 1955 by Macmillan Company.

Mona Simpson, c/o Eliza Girzwald: From "Interview with Raymond Carver" by Mona Simpson and Lewis Buzbee from *The Paris Review,* 1983.

Estate of William Stafford: "At the Bomb Testing Site" from *Stories That Could Be True* by William Stafford. Copyright © 1960, 1977 by William Stafford.

The Texas Folklore Society: Song lyrics from "Follow the Drinking Gourd" by H. B. Parks from *Follow de Drinkin' Gou'd,* Publications of the Texas Folklore Society, No. VII, edited by J. Frank Dobie. Copyright 1928 by the Texas Folklore Society.

Thunder's Mouth Press: From "Anchorage," from "Motion," and "Remember" from *She Had Some Horses* by Joy Harjo. Copyright © 1983 by Joy Harjo.

Rosemary A. Thurber: From "A Biographical Sketch of James Thurber" from *Collecting Himself* by James Thurber. Copyright © 1989 by Rosemary A. Thurber. Published by HarperCollins. "The Secret Life of Walter Mitty" from *My World—and Welcome to It* by James Thurber. Copyright © 1942 by James Thurber; copyright © 1970 by Helen Thurber and Rosemary A. Thurber. Published by Harcourt Brace & Company.

Time Inc.: From "Book of Changes: *The Woman Warrior* by Maxine Hong Kingston" by Paul Gray from *Time,* December 6, 1976. Copyright © 1976 by Time Inc.

Times Mirror Magazines: From "Winning the Cold War" by Paul G. Gill, Jr. from *Outdoor Life,* vol. 191, February 1993. Copyright © 1993 by Times Mirror Magazines.

Twayne Publishers, an imprint of Simon & Schuster Macmillan: From *Alice Walker* by Donna Haisty Winchell. Copyright © 1995 by Twayne Publishers, Inc.

University of Minnesota Press: "The Fall of the House of Usher" from *Fifty Poems Fifty* by Reed Whittemore. Copyright © 1970 by the University of Minnesota Press.

The University of New Mexico Press: From "Introduction" and from *The Way to Rainy Mountain* by N. Scott Momaday. Copyright © 1969 by The University of New Mexico Press. First published in *The Reporter,* January 26, 1967.

University of North Carolina Press: From *The Invasion of America* by Francis Jennings. Copyright © 1975 by the University of North Carolina Press.

University of Oklahoma Press: "For More Than a Hundred Winters Our Nation Was a Powerful, Happy, and United People" by Black Hawk and "I Will Fight No More Forever" by Chief Joseph from *Indian Oratory: Famous Speeches by Noted Indian Chieftains,* compiled by W. C. Vanderwerth. Copyright © 1971 by the University of Oklahoma Press.

University of Texas Press: "The Feather Pillow" from *The Decapitated Chicken and Other Stories* by Horacio Quiroga, translated by Margaret Sayers Peden. Copyright © 1976 by the University of Texas Press.

University Press of New England: "What For" from *Yellow Light* by Garrett Kaoru Hongo. Copyright © 1982 by Garrett Kaoru Hongo. Published by Wesleyan University Press. "We Never Knew" from *Dien Cai Dau* by Yusef Komunyakaa. Copyright © 1988 by Yusef Komunyakaa. "Changes; or, Reveries at a Window Overlooking a Country Road, with Two Women Talking Blues in the Kitchen" from *Neon Vernacular* by Yusef Komunyakaa. Copyright © 1993 by Yusef Komunyakaa. Published by Wesleyan University Press. "A Blessing" from *The Branch Will Not Break* by James Wright. Copyright © 1963 by James Wright. Published by Wesleyan University Press.

The University Press of Virginia: Quote by William Faulkner about "A Rose for Emily" from *Faulkner in the University: Class Conferences at the University of Virginia 1957–1958,* edited by Frederick L. Gwynn and Joseph L. Blotner. Copyright © 1959 by University of Virginia Press.

Pindar VanArman: "What About Glory" by Pindar VanArman from *Phoenix: The Gonzaga Fine Arts Magazine,* vol. XVI, No. 1, May 1992. Published by Gonzaga College High School, Washington, D.C.

Vanguard Press, Inc., a division of Random House, Inc.: From *Dangling Man* by Saul Bellow. Copyright © 1944 and renewed © 1972 by Saul Bellow.

Viking Penguin, a division of Penguin Books USA Inc.: From *Along This Way: The Autobiography of James Weldon Johnson.* Copyright © 1933 by James Weldon Johnson. "Go Down Death—A Funeral Sermon" and "Preface" from *God's Trombones* by James Weldon Johnson. Copyright 1927 by The Viking Press, Inc.; copyright renewed © 1955 by Grace Nail Johnson. "The Leader of the People" from *The Red Pony* by John Steinbeck. Copyright 1933, 1937, 1938, and renewed © 1961, 1965, 1966 by John Steinbeck.

Villard Books, a division of Random House, Inc.: From *All I Really Need to Know I Learned in Kindergarten* by Robert L. Fulghum. Copyright © 1986, 1988 by Robert L. Fulghum.

Walden Woods Project, An Activity of The Isis Fund: From "Preface" by Don Henley from *Heaven Is Under Our Feet,* edited by Don Henley and Dave Marsh. Copyright © 1991 by The Isis Fund.

The Washington Post Company: Quote by Juan Williams from *Washington Post,* December 2, 1987. Copyright © 1987 by The Washington Post.

Washington Post Book World Service/Washington Post Writers Group: From "Mah-Jongg and The Ladies of the Club" by Susan Dooley from *The Washington Post Book World,* March 5, 1989, p. 7. Copyright © 1989 by Washington Post Book World Service/Washington Post Writers Group. From William McPherson's review of Maxine Hong Kingston's *The Woman Warrior* from *Washington Post Book World,* October 10, 1976. Copyright © 1976 by Washington Post Book World Service/Washington Post Writers Group. From Jonathan Yardley's review of Raymond Carver's *Cathedral* from *Washington Post Book World,* September 20, 1983. Copyright © 1983 by Washington Post Book World Service/Washington Post Writers Group.

A. P. Watt, Ltd.: "The Face in the Mirror" from *Collected Poems* by Robert Graves. Copyright 1938, 1948, © 1955, 1959, 1961, 1965, 1966, 1975 by Robert Graves.

Rhoda Weyr Literary Agency, NY: From "The One Who Was Different" from *The Lost World* by Randall Jarrell. Copyright © 1965 by Randall Jarrell. Reprinted in *The Complete Poems of Randall Jarrell,* published by Farrar, Straus & Giroux, 1989.

Doretha Williams: "Africa" by Doretha Williams from *Calliope 1993.* Copyright © 1993 by Doretha Williams. Published by Topeka West High School, Topeka, KS.

The H. W. Wilson Company: From "Gabriel García Márquez" from *Spanish American Authors: The Twentieth Century* by Angel Flores. Copyright © 1992 by Angel Flores.

Wylie, Aitken & Stone, Inc.: "Game" from *Unspeakable Practices, Unnatural Acts* by Donald Barthelme. Copyright © 1964, 1965, 1966, 1967, 1968 by Donald Barthelme. From "Not-Knowing" by Donald Barthelme. Copyright © 1985 by Donald Barthelme.

Yale Collection of American Literature, Beinecke Rare Book and Manuscript Library, Yale University: James Weldon Johnson Collection: Quotations from "Draft Ideas," December 3, 1964, by Langston Hughes, as they appear in *The Life of Langston Hughes, Vol. II: 1941–1967—I Dream a World.*

Yale University Press: From *Selected Letters of Eugene O'Neill,* edited by Travis Bogard and Jackson R. Bryer. Copyright © 1988 by Yale University.

David Young: From "Introduction" from *Magical Realist Fiction,* edited by David Young and Keith Hollaman. Copyright © 1984 by David Young.

REFERENCE LIST

From "Revolutionary Charter" from *Inventing America: Jefferson's Declaration of Independence* by Garry Wills. Copyright © 1978 by Garry Wills. Published by Doubleday, a division of Bantam Doubleday Dell Publishing Group, Inc.

Quote by William Faulkner from "Preface" from *The Enigma of Thomas Wolfe,* edited by Richard Walser. Copyright 1953 by the President and Fellows of Harvard College. Published by Harvard University Press.

From "Empty Bamboo" by Leslie Li from *American Identities: Contemporary Multicultural Voices,* edited by Robert Pack and Jay Parini. Copyright © 1994 by the President and Fellows of Middlebury College. Published by University Press of New England.

From "The Phantom Dawn" from *The Spirit of Romance* by Ezra Pound. Copyright © 1968 by Ezra Pound. Published by New Directions Publishing Corporation.

From "Some Self-Analysis" from *On the Poet and His Craft: Selected Prose of Theodore Roethke,* edited by Ralph J. Mills, Jr. Copyright © 1965 by Beatrice Roethke as administratrix of the estate of Theodore Roethke. Published by University of Washington Press.

Quote by Eugene O'Neill from *O'Neill: Son and Artist* by Louis Sheaffer. Copyright © 1973 by Louis Sheaffer. Published by Little, Brown and Company.

Quote by Diarmuid Russell from *Author and Agent: Eudora Welty and Diarmuid Russell* by Michael Kreyling. Copyright © 1991 by Michael Kreyling. Published by Farrar, Straus & Giroux, Inc.

From "Notes Toward a Biography" by Lois Ames from *TriQuarterly,* no. 7, Fall 1966. Copyright © 1966 by Lois Ames. Published by TriQuarterly Books, Northwestern University.

PICTURE CREDITS

Table of Contents: Page: viii (T), David Muench Photography; viii (BL), Free Library of Philadelphia; viii (BR), *Puritan Deacon Samuel Chapin,* James Graham & Sons; ix, FPG International; x (T), *The Grand Canyon of the Yellowstone* by Thomas Moran, Loaned by the U.S. Department of the Interior. Office of the Secretary. National Museum of American Art, Washington, D.C./Courtesy Art Resource; x (B), Scott Camazine/Photo Researchers; xi (T), *A Philosopher's Camp in the Adirondacks* by William James Stillman, Concord Free Public Library, Concord, Massachusetts; xi (B), *Dover Plains, Dutchess County, New York* by Asher Brown Durand, National Museum of American Art, Washington, D.C./Courtesy Art Resource; xii (T), Frank Siteman/Photographic Resources; xii (B), Julie Habel/Woodfin Camp & Associates; xiii (T), *A Ride for Liberty—The Fugitive Slaves* by Eastman Johnson, The Brooklyn Museum, Gift of Miss Gwendolyn O.L. Conkling; xiii (B), *Memories* by William M. Chase, Munson-Williams-Proctor Institute Museum of Art, Utica, New York; xiv (T), *Evening Gun, Fort Sumter* (1864) by John Gadsby Chapman from sketch made by his son, Conrad Wise Chapman, Museum of the Confederacy Collection, Richmond, Virginia; xiv (B), *Frederick Douglass Series No. 10* by Jacob Lawrence, Hampton University Museum, Hampton, Virginia; xv (B), *Sixth Avenue Elevated at Third Street* by John Sloan, Photograph Copyright © 1997 Whitney Museum of American Art, New York. Photo by Geoffrey Clements; xvi (T), *Fall Plowing* by Grant Wood, From the Deere & Company Art Collection, Moline, Illinois. © 1997 Estate of Grant Wood/Licensed by VAGA, New York; xvi (B), Eudora Welty Collection, Mississippi Department of Archives and History; xvii (T), *The Sentimental Yearner* by Grant Wood, The Minneapolis Institute of Arts; Gift of Alan Goldstein, 1980. © 1997 Estate of Grant Wood/Licensed by VAGA, New York; xvii (B), *Portrait of Mother* by Nan Phelps, Collection of the Museum of American Folk Art, New York. Donated by Robert Phelps in loving memory of his wife, Nan Phelps; xviii, Tony Galindo/The Image Bank; xviii (B), *Jockey Club* by Archibald John Motley, Jr., Schomburg Center for Research in Black Culture. Art and Artifacts Division. The New York Public Library, Astor, Lenox and Tilden Foundations; xix (T), *The Figure 5 in Gold* by Charles Henry Demuth, The Metropolitan Museum of Art, Alfred Stieglitz Collection, 1949 (49.59.1); xix (B), *Chicago* by Louis Lozowick, Private Collection, Washington, D.C.; xx (T), Photofest; xx (B), Jake Rajs/Photonica; xxi (T), *Three Flags* by Jasper Johns, 50th Anniversary Gift of the Gilman Foundation, Inc., The Lauder Foundation, A. Alfred Taubman, an anonymous donor, and purchase. Collection of Whitney Museum of American Art, New York. Photo by Geoffrey Clements. © 1997 Jasper Johns/Licensed by VAGA, New York; xxi (B), Art by Sergio Bustamente/Photo by Clint Clemens; xxii, *Maudell Sleet's Magic Garden* by Romare Bearden, from the *Profile/Part I: The Twenties* series (Mecklenburg County). Courtesy Estate of Romare Bearden/ACA Galleries, New York; xxiii, *Drawing Hands* by M.C. Escher, © 1995 M.C. Escher/Cordon Art, Baarn, Holland. All rights reserved. **Collection 1:** Page: 2 (left), Michael S. Yamashita/Woodfin Camp & Associates; 2–3, Kathleen Campbell/Tony Stone Images; 5 (center) Kirchoff/Wohlberg; 6–13 & 16–18 (background), Kirchoff/Wohlberg; 9 (top left), John Carter Brown Library/Brown University, Providence, Rhode Island, (right) Courtesy American Antiquarian Society; 14, Tom Bross/Stock Boston; 14–15 (background), Library of Congress; 15 (left), William Johnson/Stock Boston, (right) Richard Pasley/Stock Boston; 19 (background), Marion Stirrup/Alaska Stock Images; 20–21, Theo Westenberger; 27 (background), John Coletti/Stock Boston; 28–33 (background), Kirchoff/Wohlberg; 35, Haffenreffer Museum of Anthropology/Brown University, Providence, Rhode Island. Photo by Cathy Carver; 42–43 (background), Fred M. Dole—f/Stop Pictures; 48–49, Gene Ahrens/Bruce Coleman, Inc; 52–53, Wendell Metzen/Bruce Coleman, Inc; 54, Haffenreffer Museum of Anthropology/Brown University, Providence, Rhode Island; 56–57, 65, (background), Marc & Evelyne Bernheim/Woodfin Camp & Associates. **Collection 2:** Page: 67, Superstock; 68–70 (background), Reproduced by kind permission of the vicar and church wardens of St. Botolph's Church, Boston, England; 72–73 (background), 73, FPG International; 90–91 (top background), Telegraph Colour Library/FPG International; 96, B. Timmons/The Image Bank. **Collection 3:** Page: 99 (upper left), Bruce Mathews/Photographic Resources, (lower right) Jim Madden/New England Stock Photo; 100–101 (center), John Henley/The Stock Market, (top background) Gene Moore/Phototake, (bottom background) Peter Cole/New England Stock Photography; 106–107 (background), 108 (background), 109 (inset left), 110 (inset top), 112 (background), North Wind Picture Archives; 109, 110,

Joe Viesti/Viesti Associates; 120–121, Charlie Ott/ Photo Researchers. **Collection 4:** Pages: 143, 190, 192, Culver Pictures; 146, Charles Scribner's Sons, 1925; 151, Robert Maier/Animals Animals; 153 (top), Frank Whitney/The Image Bank, (bottom) M. Antman/The Image Works; 154 (top), Neil Meyerhoff/Panoramic Images; 154 (bottom), 164, 165, Ronald F. Thomas/Bruce Coleman, Inc; 155, Courtesy Millport Conservancy, Lititz, Pennsylvania; 160, Robin Jane Solvang/Bruce Coleman, Inc.; 162, Gary Braasch/Tony Stone Images; 173, Hitchcock-Chase Collection of Grass Drawings/Hunt Institute for Botanical Documentation/Carnegie Mellon University, Pittsburgh, Pennsylvania; 179, By permission of the Houghton Library, Harvard University, Cambridge, Massachusetts; 187 (center), Courtesy *The Atlantic Monthly,* (bottom) Massachusetts Historical Society, Massachusetts; 188, Scott Camazine/Photo Researchers; 189, The Library of the New York Botanical Garden (Bronx, New York). **Collection 5:** Pages: 206–214 (background), Branson Reynolds/ ProFiles West; 207 (left), Massachusetts Historical Society, Boston; 208 (right), 208–209 (bottom), 210–211 (bottom), North Wind Picture Archives; 215, 218–221 (background), William D. Adams/Picture Perfect USA, Inc.; 215 (inset), David Julian/Phototake; 218–221 (background), Douglas Pulsinher/ The Stock Solution, Koji Yamashita/Panoramic Images; 226 (background), Phototone; 227, Kevin Alexander/ProFiles West; 245, Kevin Mazur/London Features International; 249, 251, 254, Robert Essel/The Stock Market. **Collection 6:** Pages: 263, 268, 287, Reprinted by permission of Warner Books, Inc., New York, New York, USA. From *The Illustrated Edgar Allan Poe* by Wilfred Satty and Edgar Allan Poe. Copyright © 1976. All rights reserved; 267, James Strachan/Tony Stone Images; 273, Curtis Martin/Photographic Resources; 274, Frederica Georgia/Photographic Resources; 276 (background), F. Nagele/FPG International; 278, Frank Siteman/ Photographic Resources; 279, Illustration by R. Hoffman; 282, 284–285, 286, Illustrations by Arvis Stewart for "The Raven"; 291, 293–295 (background), Charles A. Mauzy/Tony Stone Images; 297 (bottom), Penguin Books Ltd.; 298–299, 304, 307, Tom Hopkins Studio; 314–315, Marion Stirrup/Alaska Stock Images; 321, Lon Lauber/Alaska Stock Images; 326, J. Coolidge/The Image Bank. **Collection 7:** Pages: 340–341, 359, Julie Habel/Woodfin Camp & Associates; 342–346 (background), Maria Stenzel/National Geographic Society Image Collection; 343 (bottom), 345 (top left), Amherst College, Amherst, Massachusetts/Courtesy The Emily Dickinson Homestead; 345, The Bettmann Archive; 345 (right), Courtesy of the Amherst History Museum at the Strong House, Amherst, Massachusetts; 347, University of Virginia Library, Charlottesville, Courtesy NGS; 351, Karen Kasmauski/Woodfin Camp & Associates; 353, From the David T. Vernon Collection of Native American Indian Art, Colter Bay Indian Arts Museum, Grand Teton National Park, Wyoming. Photo by J. Oldenkamp; 360 (background), W. Cody/WestLight; 367, AP/Wide World Photos; 368–370 (background), Eastcott & Momatiuk/ Woodfin Camp & Associates. **Collection 8:** Page: 371, John Eastcott-Iva Momatiuk/Woodfin Camp & Associates; 377 (background), Stephen P. Parker/Photo Researchers; 384–385, Timothy Eaggan/Woodfin Camp & Associates; 391, Brown Brothers. **Collection 9:** Pages: 424–425 (background), Lyle Leduc/Index Stock Photography; 426 (background), Wallace Garrison/ Index Stock Photography; 440 (bottom), The Bettmann Archive; 448, University of Washington Libraries, Special Collections Division, Seattle, Washington. **Collection 10:** Page: 449, Gene Ahrens/ Bruce Coleman, Inc.; 452, 454, 460, 461, The Bettmann Archive; 467 (right), Garry Gay/The Image Bank; 467 (left), © Erika Klass; 468, Daniel Nichols/Gamma Liaison; 470, Allen Russell/ProFiles West; 473, Brett Baunton/Tony Stone Images; 496–497, Don Pitcher/Alaska Stock Images; 500, 500 (inset), Michael DeYoung/Alaska Stock Images; 503, Johnny Johnson/Alaska Stock Images; 503 (inset), 507, 508, Jeff Schultz/ Alaska Stock Images; 507 (inset), Christopher Arend/Alaska Stock Images; 509, Alaska Stock Images. **Collection 11:** Pages: 524–525 (top), Brown Brothers; 524–525 (bottom), UPI/Bettmann; 526 (right), 527 (top right), The Bettmann Archive, (top left) Archive Photos, (bottom left and bottom center) FPG International, (bottom right) Jeffrey D. Smith/Woodfin Camp & Associates; 528 (bottom), Liberty Collection/The Image Bank; 528–529, Kirchoff/Wohlberg; 532, Culver Pictures; 537, Ludovic Molin/Photonica; 539, Archive Photos; 540–541 (background), Kazuya Shimizu/Photonica; 540, Charles Shotwell/ Panoramic Images; 545 (bottom), Color Box/FPG International; 559 (background), Royce Blair/The Stock Solution; 562 (background), Bruce Heinemann/The Stock Market; 562 (inset), Michael P. Gadomski/ Photo Researchers; 563 (inset), Rick Schafer/The Stock Market; 564, 565, PhotoDisc; 566, Barry O'Rourke/The Stock Market; 567–568 (background), Ron Thomas/FPG International; 569–573, Don & Liysa King/The Image Bank; 575, C. Bradley Simmons/Bruce Coleman, Inc.; 579, Ron Sanford/ The Stock Market. **Collection 12:** Page: 583, Randy O'Rourke/The Stock Market; 586, 587, 594, 598–599, 600, 602, Liberty Collection/The Image Bank; 595, 606–607 (background), 616–617 (background), Culver Pictures; 616, Photofest; 624–625 (background), Kirchoff/Wohlberg; 634–635 (background), Marco Polo/Phototake. **Collection 13:** Page: 643, Susan Stang/Photo Researchers; 652, Kirchoff/Wohlberg; 656–657 (background), Phototone; 688, Robert Brenner/PhotoEdit. **Collection 14:** Page: 691, Nicholas Devore III/Photographers Aspen; 693, Frederic Stein/FPG International; 694–695 (background), 703–704 (top and bottom), 714–717, 722, 727, 729–731, Kirchoff/Wohlberg; 704 (left), FPG International; 732, R. A. Clevenger/ WestLight. **Collection 15:** Page: 733, Bonnot/The Image Bank; 734–735 (background), Phototone; 749, Stephen Marks/The Image Bank; 750, The Beinecke Rare Book and Manuscript Library, Yale University, New Haven, Connecticut. Estate of Carl Van Vechten, Joseph Solomon, Executor; 763 (top), Javier Romero Design/The Image Bank; 763 (bottom), Ayako Parks/Tony Stone Images. **Collection 16:** Page: 769, Richard Dunoff/The Stock Market; 769 (inset), Steven Gottlieb/FPG International; 770–772 (background), Picture Perfect USA; 782, Gordon R. Gainer/The Stock Market; 784–785, Esto Photographics; 789 (background), Henry Horenst/ Photonica; 790 (background), Larry West/FPG International; 794, Telegraph Colour Library/FPG International; 797, Erwin & Peggy Bauer/Bruce Coleman, Inc.; 798 (background), Rick Gayle/The Stock Market; 799, NASA/The Stock Solution. **Collection 17:** Pages: 812–813, Ron Chapple/FPG International; 813, 814 (top), Shubert Archives, New York; 814 (middle), New York Public Library; 814 (bottom), 818, 822, PLAYBILL® covers printed by permission of PLAYBILL Incorporated. PLAYBILL® is a registered Trademark of PLAYBILL Incorporated, New York, New York; 815, Kirchoff/Wohlberg; 816, © Debra P. Hershkowitz; 823, T. Charles Erickson for the Long Wharf Theatre; 824, Martha Swope © Time, Inc.; 825, Hulton Deutsch/Woodfin Camp & Associates; 827, Eli Reed/Magnum; 828 (left), 829, PhotoDisc; 851, John Van Hasselt/ Sygma; 872 (background), Marc & Evelyne Bernheim/Woodfin Camp & Associates; 895, Comstock. **Collection 18:** Pages: 902–903, Jake Rajs/Photonica; 904, Department of Energy/FPG International; 906 (left), UPI/Corbis/ Bettmann, (middle and right) UPI/Bettmann; 907 (top), Jean-Marc Giboux/Gamma-Liaison, (bottom left) Eric Bouvet/Gamma-Liaison, (bottom right) Chip Hires/ Gamma-Liaison; 908, Courtesy Art Resource; 908–909 (top background), FPG International, (bottom) NASA/FPG International; 909 (top), UPI/ Bettmann; 910 (bottom left), Claude Charlier/The Stock Market, (middle top), Phillip A. Harrington/The Stock Market, (middle bottom) Chris Rogers/The Stock Market; 910–911 (background), 917 (top), 918 (left), PhotoDisc; 911, Chris Jones/The Stock Market; 912, 915, © Lynn Saville; 913, Bruce Davidson/Magnum; 914 (left), Ira Wyman/Sygma, (top right) Archive Photos; 916, Patti McConville/The Image Bank; 918 (right), Robert Azzi/Woodfin Camp & Associates; 919, Joe McDonald/Photo Researchers, (background) Department of Energy/FPG International; 926–927 (top), Jewish Museum, New York, Courtesy Art Resource; 932–933, Lieb Image Archives; 951, Massachusetts Historical Society, Boston; 956, 958–960, Gary Buss/FPG International; 957, Bob Elsdale/The Image Bank; 966–967, John Gordon/Black Star; 975, Larry Burrows © 1967 Time, Inc. **Collection 19:** Page: 979, Don Landwehrle/The Image Bank; 1009, David Zaitz/Photonica; 1010, Joe Sohm/The Stock Market; 1012, The Beinecke Rare Book and Manuscript Library, Yale University, New Haven, Connecticut. Estate of Carl Van Vechten, Joseph Solomon, Executor; 1012–1013 (background), 1023, 1023 (background), Mississippi Valley Collection, University of Memphis Libraries; 1044–1045, Leon Sun Photography; 1050–1051, Dallas and John Heaton/The Stock Shop. **Collection 20:** Page: 1067, Terry Vine/Tony Stone Images; 1076–1077, 1079, 1080, 1086, 1123, PhotoDisc; 1088, 1089, 1091, 1093 (background), Kirchoff/Wohlberg; 1095, 1096, 1099, James Barnett/ The Stock Market; 1102–1103, © Richard Hamilton Smith; 1107 (top and bottom), Masao Ota/Photonica; 1109 (bottom), 1112, 1115 (inset), 1119, Pascal Perret/ The Image Bank; 1110–1111, John Banagan/ The Image Bank; 1123 (top left), Jeff Gnass/The Stock Market. **Collection 21:** Page: 1127, Akira Inoue/Photonica; 1128–1129, Jeff Isaac Greenberg/ Photo Researchers; 1130–1131, Ursula Markus/ Photo Researchers; 1135, Michael Schwarz/Gamma Liaison; 1142, Steve Schapiro/Black Star; 1143, Sygma; 1150, Michael McGovern/NonStock; 1156–1157, Philip Condit II/Tony Stone Images; 1159, © Brent Jones; 1166, 1167 (top), 1168, 1169, PhotoDisc; 1167 (bottom), Dennis Lisl/The Image Bank; 1173, Chuck Keeler/Tony Stone Images; 1174, Thomas Brase/Tony Stone Images; 1180, Michael Newman/ PhotoEdit. Borders for The American Language features and for Language Workshops and Writer's Workshops, Paul Kazmercyk. Macintosh window elements and icons © 1984 Apple Computer, Inc. All rights reserved. Used with the permission of Apple Computer, Inc.

INDEX OF SKILLS

LITERARY TERMS

The boldface page numbers indicate an extensive treatment of the topic.

READING AND CRITICAL THINKING

LANGUAGE

VOCABULARY AND SPELLING

WRITING

SPEAKING, LISTENING, AND VIEWING

RESEARCH AND STUDY SKILLS

CROSSING THE CURRICULUM

CRITICAL COMMENTS

CREATIVE PROBLEM SOLVING

INDEX OF ART

Fine Art

Illustrations

Cartoons

Maps

INDEX OF AUTHORS AND TITLES

Page numbers in italic type refer to the pages on which author biographies appear.

Index of Student Authors and Titles